D0819103

TIME Almanac 2006

with Information Please®

BORGNA BRUNNER
EDITOR IN CHIEF

Information Please®
www.infoplease.com
a Pearson Education Company

Information Please
www.infoplease.com
a Pearson Education Company

Editor in Chief Borgna Brunner

Editor Beth Rowen

Senior Contributing Editor
Christine Frantz

Contributing Editors Susan Hyde,
Shmuel Ross

Production Director
Susan Hyde

Production Editor Christine Frantz

Vice President George Kane

Proofreading and Fact-Checking
Kathryn Blatt, Elissa Giroux, Erin Martin,
Elizabeth Olson

Editorial Assistant Shmuel Ross

Graphics Sean M. Dessureau

Technical Support Karl DeBisschop

Time Inc.
HOME ENTERTAINMENT

Contributing Editor Kelly Knauer
Design Anthony Kosner
Pictures Patricia Cadley

Publisher Richard Fraiman

Executive Director, Marketing Services
Carol Pittard

Director, Retail & Special Sales Tom Mifsud

Marketing Director, Branded Businesses
Swati Rao

Director, New Product Development
Peter Harper

Assistant Financial Director
Steven Sandonato

Prepress Manager Emily Rabin

Book Production Manager Jonathan Polsky

Marketing Manager Kristin Walker

Associate Prepress Manager
Anne-Michelle Gallero

Special thanks to: Bozena Bannett, Alexandra Bliss, Glenn Buonocore, Bernadette Corbie, Suzanne Janso, Robert Marasco, Brooke McGuire, Chavaughn Raines, Ilene Schreider, Adriana Tierno, Britney Williams

The *TIME Almanac* welcomes comments and suggestions from readers. We prefer hearing from you through email (ipa@infoplease.com), if possible. Although the editors carefully consider each suggestion, because of the volume of correspondence we receive we cannot respond personally to each writer. The *TIME Almanac* does not rule on bets or wagers.

Editorial Office
Information Please
Pearson Education
20 Park Plaza
Boston, MA 02116
Email: ipa@infoplease.com

Customer Service
Attention: TIME Almanac
PO Box 11016
Des Moines, IA 50336-1016

ISBN: 1-932994-41-6 Paperback
ISBN: 1-932994-17-3 Hardcover
ISSN: 0073-7860

For updates to the almanac, *see* www.infoplease.com.

Keyword Index

Abbreviations of States......................442
Academy Awards........................247–251
AIDS......................................555–557
Animals...................................588–589
Architecture 443–451
Associations and Societies..............653–662
Astronomy...............................398–421
Aviation..................................435–439
Awards................................44, 225–263
Biographies 59–76, 282–317, 957–961
Books..............241–245, 254–257, 266–270
Buildings and Structures................443–451
Business and Economy 618–646
Cabinet, U.S..............................85–90
Calendars 346–359
Chemical Elements.......................572–575
Cities, U.S. 180–209
Colleges and Universities...............323–345
Computers and the Internet.............563–568
Congress, U.S. 46–49
Constitution, U.S. 109–118
Consumer Resources....................647–652
Copyrights, Trademarks, Patents 651–652
Countries of the World..................718–906
Crime Statistics.........................385–391
Crossword Puzzle Guide................460–472
Current Events 32–44, 505–518, 1030–1039
Deaths..................................1035–1039
Declaration of Independence 107–108
Disasters, Great 210–224
Drugs..560
Earthquakes 211–212, 490–492
Economic Figures.......................618–646
Education 318–345
Elections...................................45–49
Embassies and Ambassadors 910–916
Emmy Awards......................44, 259–260
Endangered Species 589
Entertainment and Culture.............264–281
Environment and Nature................584–594
Explorers 484–485
Firsts in America........................101–102
Flags of the World 519–522
Foreign Words and Phrases 478, 479–480
Gender Issues 371–375
Geography 484–504
Governors, U.S.....................49, 142–177
Grammar and Writing Guide 473–475
Grammy Awards 253–254
Health and Nutrition 552–562
History, U.S. 50–119
History, World..........................663–701
Holidays and Observances 346, 355–359
House of Representatives, U.S. 47–49
Hurricanes 32, 211, 214–215, 595–596
International Relations 907–916

Internet....................................564–567
Inventions and Discoveries..570–571, 578–583
Law Enforcement and Crime............385–391
Maps of the World 523–536
Mayors of 50 Largest U.S. Cities 180–203
Metric System 452, 455–458
Military Affairs.........................392–397
Mountains..........................492–493, 502
Movies 247–251, 281
Music 245, 253–254, 264–265, 275–278
Mythology 468–472
National Parks...........................590–594
Newspapers and Magazines.......257, 272–273
Nobel Prizes.............................225–234
Obituaries 1035–1039
Olympics 917–933
Passports 605
People 282–317, 957–961, 1030–1039
Pictures, Year in.........................505–518
Population, U.S. 120–124
Population, World 702–706
Postal Regulations.......................440–442
Presidents, U.S. 57, 59–76
Pulitzer Prizes............................234–247
Race and Ethnicity......................376–384
Religion....................................360–370
Science and Inventions 559–583
Senate, U.S. 46–47
Social Security 631–632
Societies and Associations..............653–662
Space Exploration 422–434
Sports....................................917–1023
States, U.S. 142–179
Super Bowl...............................941–943
Supreme Court 91–95
Taxes 1024–1028
Television 44, 251, 258, 259–260, 279–280
Temperatures......................605, 597–602
Terrorism 34, 211, 223–224, 715–717
Time People of the Year....................1029
Time Zones 523
Tony Awards 252
Travel and Transportation...............603–617
United Nations 907–910
U.S. Geography 500–504
U.S. Government and History 50–119
U.S. Statistics 120–141
Vice Presidents, U.S. 57–58
Volcanoes....................211–213, 488–489
Weather and Climate...................595–602
Websites......................................566
Weights and Measures 452–459
World Series 1006–1009, 1022
World Statistics..........................702–717
Writing and Language 473–483

Section Index

ASTRONOMY	**398**
AVIATION	**435**
AWARDS	**225**
BUSINESS AND ECONOMY	**618**
America's House Party	618
CALENDAR AND HOLIDAYS	**346**
COMPUTERS AND THE INTERNET	**563**
Who Is Playing Games—And Why	563
CONSUMER RESOURCES	**647**
COUNTRIES OF THE WORLD	**718**
CROSSWORD PUZZLE GUIDE	**460**
CURRENT EVENTS	**32**
The News of 2005: Nation	32
The News of 2005: World	33
What Happened in 2005: Month by Month	35
DEATHS	**1035**
EDUCATION	**318**
ENTERTAINMENT AND CULTURE	**264**
ENVIRONMENT AND NATURE	**584**
FLAGS	**519**
GENDER ISSUES	**371**
The Math and Science Gender Myth	371
GEOGRAPHY	**484**
GREAT DISASTERS	**210**
HEADLINE HISTORY	**663**
HEALTH AND NUTRITION	**552**
Thinking Outside the Pyramid	552
HAPPINESS—TIME SPECIAL	**537**
The New Science of Happiness	537
The Biology of Joy	542
How Full Is That Glass, Really?	544
Couch Potatoes Arise	545
The Real Truth About Money	546
How to Live to Be 100—Happily	548
Can Pets Make You Happy?	551
INDEX, COMPREHENSIVE	**5**
INTERNATIONAL RELATIONS	**907**
LAW ENFORCEMENT AND CRIME	**385**
Too Young to Die	385
MAPS	**523**
MILITARY AFFAIRS	**392**
Military Conflicts in U.S. History	392
PEOPLE	**282**
PEOPLE IN THE NEWS	**1030**
POSTAL REGULATIONS	**440**
RACE AND ETHNICITY	**376**
Famous Firsts by African Americans	376
RELIGION	**360**
SCIENCE AND INVENTIONS	**569**
The Revolution in Therapeutic Cloning	569
Roundup of Recent Discoveries	570
SPACE EXPLORATION	**422**
SPORTS	**917**
Auto Racing	998
Baseball	1003
Baseball, College World Series	1022
Baseball Hall of Fame	1003
Baseball, Little League	1002
Basketball, College	948
Basketball, Professional	952
Basketball, Women's Professional	956
Bicycling	1002
Bowling	966
Boxing	974
Extreme Sports	1023
Figure Skating	970
Football, College	934
Football Hall of Fame, College	937
Football Hall of Fame, Professional	946
Football, Professional	941
Golf	994
Harness Racing	992
Heisman Trophy	937
Hockey	962
Horse Racing	979
Marathons	1002
Olympic Games, Summer	917
Olympic Games, Winter	930
Personalities, Sports	957
Skiing	968
Soccer	1022
Speed Skating	969
Sullivan Award	961
Swimming	971
Tennis	987
Track and Field	983
World Series Records, Baseball	1006
STRUCTURES AND BUILDINGS	**443**
Eastward, Ho! Skyscrapers Migrate to Asia	443
TAXES	**1024**
TRAVEL AND TRANSPORTATION	**603**
U.S. CITIES	**180**
U.S. GOVERNMENT AND HISTORY	**45**
U.S. SOCIETIES AND ASSOCIATIONS	**653**
U.S. STATES	**142**
U.S. STATISTICS	**120**
WEATHER AND CLIMATE	**595**
WEIGHTS AND MEASURES	**452**
WORLD STATISTICS	**702**
WRITING AND LANGUAGE	**473**
YEAR IN PICTURES	**505**

Page numbers followed by "n" indicate information in footnotes.

A

AAA, 610, 653
Abacha, Sani, 836
Abbas, Mahmoud, 34, 35, 36, 282, 509, 798, 840, 841, 1030
Abbreviations:
  postal, 442
  state, 442
  of weights and measures, 454, 456
Abdullah II, King, 802–803
Abidjan, Côte d'Ivoire, 754
Abortion, 42, 559, 687, 688, 690, 692
Abscam, 100, 688
Absolute zero, 452, 455, 582
Absolute records. See Airplanes, Aviation.
Abu Dhabi, United Arab Emirates, 884
Abu Ghraib, 35, 36, 40, 701, 794
Abuja, Nigeria, 835
Academy Awards (Oscars), 247–251
Acadia, 671, 742
Acadia National Park, 590, 594
Accidents. See also Disasters
  aircraft, 211, 219–221
  deaths from, 210–224
  fires and explosions, 217–218
  first aircraft fatality, 435
  railroad, 211, 221–222
  shipwrecks, 218–219
  space, 221
Accra, Ghana, 779
Aceh peace accord, 33, 43, 791
Aconcagua Peak, 487, 493, 723
Acre (measure), 454, 456
Acropolis, 445, 664
Actium, Battle of, 665
Actors and actresses:
  awards for, 247–252
  biographical information, 282–317
Adams, John, 52, 57, 60, 96, 103, 107. See also Presidents, U.S.
Adams, John Quincy, 52, 55, 57, 61, 96. See also Presidents, U.S.
Addis Ababa, Ethiopia, 767
Adenauer, Konrad, 282, 778
Administration, Office of, 82
Admirals (U.S.), first, 101
Adoption, 133
Adrenaline, isolation of, 578
Adriatic Sea, 719, 799, 856
Advent (season), 346, 357
Advertising, 643
Aegean Sea, 879
Aerial combat, first, 436
Aerial photographers, first, 435
Aeschylus, 664
Affirmative action, 384, 699
Afghanistan, 39, 40, 688, 698, 851
AFL-CIO, 653, 684
Africa. See also Countries of world
  area and elevation of, 487
  exploration of, 484
  map of, 532
  Portuguese territory in, 847
  southernmost point of, 865
African Americans. See Blacks in U.S.
African Union, 910
Age:
  at first marriage, 128
  life expectancy by, 136
  population by, 121, 123, 124
Age limits, driving licenses, 608
Agencies, U.S., 82–85
Aggtelek Cavern, 497
Agincourt, Battle of, 668
Agnew, Spiro T., 58, 58n, 99, 687

Agriculture:
  ancient, 663
  farm index, 642
  number of farms by state, 642
  number of farms in U.S., 642
Agriculture, U.S. Dept. of (USDA):
  description, 82
  secretaries of, 82, 87–90
Ahmadinejad, Mahmoud, 40, 511, 791, 1030
Aid, foreign, 711
AIDS, 213, 555, 556, 557
Air (atmosphere), 402
Air Force, U.S. See also Armed forces, U.S.
  Secretary of, 83
Airlines:
  cargo carried by, 606
  first scheduled passenger service, 436
  passenger traffic, 606
Airmail:
  first, 101, 436
  international, 442
  rates, 442
Airplanes. See also Airlines; Aviation
  accidents, 211, 219–221
  exports and imports, 639
  invention of, 435
  passenger traffic, 606
Airports, world's busiest, 606
Airship, invention of, 578
Air transport company, first, 435
Akayev, Askar, 37, 38, 1030
Akkadian civilization, 663, 664
Alabama, 142
Alabama-Coosa River, 500
Al-Aksa intifada, 798, 840
Alamo, The, 96, 172, 199, 674
Åland Islands, 769
Alaska, 143
  discovery of, 671
  exploration of, 143, 484
  mountain peaks, 502
  national parks in, 143, 590–591
  purchase of, 104, 143, 675
Albania, 719–720
Albany, N.Y., 164, 178
Albany Medical Center Prize, 263
Alberta, Canada, 743
Albert Canal, 451
Albright, Madeleine, 90, 694
Albums, top-selling, 275
Albuquerque, N.M., 163, 178, 180
Alcohol, 561
  Alcoholics Anonymous, 653
  drunk driving, 608
Aldrin, Edwin E., Jr., 428, 686
Aleutian Islands, 672
Aleuts, 143
Alexander the Great, 282, 484, 665, 718, 764, 792
Alexandria, Egypt, 763
  Pharos of, 447
Alfred the Great, 666
Algeria, 720–721
  independence of, 683, 685, 770
Algiers, Algeria, 720
Alhambra, 446
Ali, Muhammad (Cassius Clay), 957, 974
Allawi, Iyad, 701, 795
Allende, Salvador, 747
All Saints' Day, 346, 356
All-Star Game (baseball), 1005–1006
Al-Manámah, Bahrain, 728
Alpha Centauri, 401

Alps, 726, 770, 872
  tunnels under, 451
Altamaha-Ocmulgee River, 500
Altamira Cave, 497
Altiplano, 734
Altitudes. See Elevations
Aluminum, chemical properties of, 574
Amazon River, 485, 495, 737, 750
Ambassadors, 914–916
Amendments to Constitution, 95, 97, 98, 99, 100, 114–118
  civil rights, 114
  right to bear arms, 114
  unreasonable search and seizure, 114
American Federation of Labor, 653, 684
American history. See United States history
American League. See Baseball; Football
American Library Association Awards, 255–257
American manual alphabet, 483
American Red Cross, 660
American Revolution. See Revolutionary War, American
American Samoa, 897
American Sign Language, 483
Amin, Idi, 882
Amman, Jordan, 802
Amperes, 455
Amsterdam, Netherlands, 831
Amsterdam-Rhine Canal, 451
Amtrak, 85
Amu Darya River, 495
Amur (Heilong) River, 495
Ancestry, U.S. population, 381
Anchorage, Alaska, 143, 178
Ancient empires, 663–665
Ancient history, events of, 663
Andaman Sea, 494
Andes, 493, 723, 746, 750, 844
Andorra, 721
Andorra la Vella, Andorra, 721
Andropov, Yuri V., 689, 851
Anesthetic, first use of, 578
Angel Falls, 496
Angkor Wat, 446
Angola, 721–722, 847
Angstrom, 456, 457n
Anguilla, 891
Animals:
  classification of, 572
  endangered species, 589
  gestation, incubation, and longevity of, 588
  group terminology, 589
  names of, 588
  speed of, 588
Ankara, Turkey, 879
Annan, Kofi, 43, 694, 907, 1030
Annapolis, Md., 155, 178
  Naval Academy, 155
Antananarivo, Madagascar, 817
Antarctica:
  area and elevation of, 487, 497
  exploration of, 485, 680
  Falkland Islands, 892
  first flight over, 437
  French Antarctica, 774
Antarctic Circle, 353, 485, 486
Antarctic icecap, 589
Anthem, National, 106
Anthony, Susan B., 374
Anthrax, 698
Antibiotics, 578

Anti-Comintern Treaty, 681, 778
Antietam, Battle of, 675
Antigua and Barbuda, 722
Antimony, 574
Antiparos Cavern, 497
Antiseptic, 578
Antoinette Perry (Tony) Awards, 252
Antwerp, Belgium, 730
Anzio beachhead, 681
Apalachicola-Chattahoochee River, 500
Apartheid, 691, 866
Apennine Mountains, 799, 856, 872
Apennine Tunnel, 451
Aphelion, 353, 398
Apia, Samoa, 855
Apollo space flights, 428
   Apollo/Soyuz Test Project, 428, 430, 687
Apostrophe (punctuation), 475
Apothecaries' fluid measure, 454
Apothecaries' weight, 455
Appalachian Regional Commission, 84
Appalachian Trail, 594
Appomattox surrender, 174, 675
Aqaba, Gulf of, 764
Aquino, Benigno, 689
Aquino, Corazon C., 690
Arab ancestry, U.S., 378
Arabia, explored, 484. See also specific Arab countries
Arabian Desert, 498
Arab-Israeli conflict, 684, 686, 687, 688, 763–765, 797–799, 802, 811, 857, 873, 879. See also Egypt; Israel; Jordan; Lebanon; Saudi Arabia; Syria
Arab League, 793, 808, 857, 884, 910
Arabs, 666
Arafat, Yasir, 698, 701, 798
Aral Lake, 494
Arbor Day, 358
Archaeozoic Eon, 576
Archery, 929
Architecture, 445–447. See also Structures
   ancient, 445–447
   tallest buildings, 444
Arctic Circle, 353, 486
   area and elevation of, 497
   exploration of, 485
   first flight over, 436
Arctic Ocean, 494, 497
Area:
   of cities of U.S., 180–204
   of continents, 487
   of countries, 705–706, 718–906
   of deserts, 498
   formulas for, 459
   of islands, 496
   largest countries, 703
   measures of, 456
   of oceans and seas, 494
   smallest countries, 703
   of states of U.S., 142–177, 178
   territorial expansion of U.S., 104, 105
   of territories of U.S., 895–898
   of U.S., 120
   of world, 487
Area codes, 207–208
Argentina, 684, 688, 722–723
Aristide, Jean-Bertrand, 693, 700, 785
Aristotle, 283, 665
Arithmetic. See Mathematics
Arizona, 143–144
Arkansas, 144
Arkansas River, 484, 495, 500
Arlington, Texas, 180
Arlington National Cemetery, 594n
Armada, Spanish, 670, 867, 885
Armed conflicts, worldwide, 714
Armed forces, U.S. See also Defense, U.S. Dept. of; Selective Service System; Veterans

active duty personnel, 395, 396
foreign countries, military personnel in, 395
gays in, 692
highest ranking officers, 394
Joint Chiefs of Staff, 83, 394
last living veterans, 397
Medal of Honor, 396
military spending, 394
prisoners of war, 393
ranks, 395
veterans, 393
war casualties, 393
wars, 392, 393
women in, 682
Armenia, 724
Armenian Massacre, 678
Armistice Day, 356
Armstrong, Lance, 957, 1002
Armstrong, Neil A., 428, 686
Army, U.S. Dept. of. See also Armed forces, U.S.
   Secretary of, 83
Arrests, 390. See also Crime; Law Enforcement
Arroyo, Gloria, 1030
Arsenic, 574
Arson, arrests for, 390
Artemis, Temple of, 447
Arthur (king of the Britons), 666
Arthur, Chester A., 53, 57, 58, 65, 97. See also Presidents, U.S.
Articles of Confederation, 95, 102
Art Ross Trophy, 964
Arts and the Humanities, National Foundation on, 84
Aruba, 832–833
Ascension Day, 356, 357n, 357
Ascension Island, 894
ASEAN, 910
Ashgabat, Turkmenistan, 880
Ashmore and Cartier Islands, 726
Ash Wednesday, 346, 355, 357
Asia. See also Countries of world
   area and elevation of, 487
   exploration of, 484–485
   map of, 534–535
Asian population, U.S., 379
Asmara, Eritrea, 766
Assad, Hafez, 872–873
Assal, Lake, 487
Assassinations and attempts, 119
Assault, 390
Assembly of the Eighth Day, 356, 357n
Associations, 653–662
Assyrian Empire, 664, 793
Astana, Kazakhstan, 803
Asteroids, 414–415
Astrological signs, 347
Astronauts, 427–429
   first women, 102
Astronomical unit (A.U.), 400
Astronomy, 398–421
   asteroids, 414–415
   atmosphere, 402
   auroras, 417
   Big Bang theory, 399
   comets, 415–416
   conjunctions, 398, 418–421
   constants, 400
   constellations, 401, 416–417
   earliest, 663
   Hubble Space Telescope, 691
   measures, 400
   meteors and meteorites, 406, 416
   Moon, 401
   Moon phases, 418–421
   phenomena, 418–421
   planets, 402–414, 418–421
   seasons, 353, 402
   stars, 399, 400–401
   Sun, 399, 400–401, 418–421
   terms, 398–399
   universal time, 421
   Zodiac, 417

Asunción, Paraguay, 843
Aswan Dam, 764
Atacama Desert, 498, 746
Athens, Greece, 664, 780
Athletes. See Sports personalities
Atlanta, Ga., 148, 178, 181, 675
Atlantic Charter, 681
Atlantic Ocean, 494
   islands of, 496
   U.S. coastline, 502
Atlas Mountains, 827
Atmosphere, 402
Atomic bomb, 681, 682, 801
Atomic numbers, 574–575
Atomic theory, 578
Atomic weights, 574–575
Atonement, Day of, 356, 357n
Attila the Hun, 283, 666
Attlee, Clement, 886
Attorneys General:
   state, 142–177
   U.S., 83, 85–90
Augusta, Maine, 154, 178
Augustus (Roman emperor), 283, 665
Auroras, 417
Auschwitz, 680
Austerlitz, Battle of, 673
Austin, Tex., 172, 178, 181
Australasia. See Oceania
Australia, 724–726
   area and elevation of, 487
   dependencies, 702
   desert, 498, 725
   exploration of, 485
   islands of, 496, 724–726
   map of, 536
Austria, 681, 726–727
Authors. See People
Autogyro flight, 436
Automobiles, 609–611. See also Drivers
   drunken driving arrests, 390
   exports and imports, 639
   invention of, 578
   most expensive, 610
   most popular colors, 609
   most stolen, 609
   polluting, most and least, 610
   registrations, 611
   seat belt use, 609
   speed limits, 608
   state laws, 608
   theft statistics, 390
   top-selling, 609
Auto racing, 998–1000
Avalanches, 211, 213
Average, mathematical, 453
Aviation, 435–439. See also Airlines; Airplanes
   accidents, 43, 211, 219–221
   air distances, 614–617
   airports, world's busiest, 606
   ballooning, 435–439, 439
   firsts in, 435–439
   helicopter records, 439
   inventions in, 435–439
   records, 439
   solar-powered, 438
   traffic (passengers and freight), 606
   women in, 435–439
   world records, 439
Avoirdupois weight, 452, 455, 457
Awards, 225–263
   Academy (Oscars), 247–251
   Albany Medical Center Prize, 263
   American Library Association, 255–257
   Baseball Hall of Fame, 165, 1003–1004
   Batchelder, 257
   Bollingen, 258
   broadcasting, 258–260
   Caldecott Medal, 256–257
   Carnegie, 257
   Coretta Scott King, 257
   Country Music, 254

Cy Young Award, 1016
Daytime Emmys, 260
Drama Desk Awards, 252
duPont–Columbia, 260
Eclipse, 982
Emmy, 44, 259–260
Fermi, 261
Fields Medal, 261
Golden Globe, 251
Grammy, 253–254
Hart Trophy, 963
Heisman Trophy, 937
Ingalls Wilder, 257
James E. Sullivan Memorial, 961
Kennedy Center Honors, 262–263
King, 257
MacArthur Foundation, 261
magazine, 257
Man Booker Prize, 255
Most Valuable Player (baseball), 1014
Most Valuable Player (basketball), 954
Most Valuable Player (hockey), 963
music, 245–246, 253–254, 258
NAACP Image, 258
National Book, 254
National Book Critics Circle, 254
National Magazine, 257
Newbery Medal, 255–256
Nobel Prizes, 225–234
Obie, 252
Peabody, 260
Presidential Medal of Freedom, 262
Printz, 257
Pulitzer Prizes, 234–247
Rookie of the Year (baseball), 1016
Sibert, 257
Spingarn Medal, 259
Tony (Antoinette Perry) Awards, 252
Truman Capote, 255
Tufts Poetry Prize, 258
Webby, 263
"Axis of evil", 698, 792, 794, 806
Axis Powers, 681
Azerbaijan, 727
Aziz, Fahd ibn Abdul, 1036
Azores, 847
Azov, Sea of, 494n
Aztecs, 668, 823

B

Babbage, Charles, 578, 674
Babylon, Hanging Gardens of, 447, 664
Babylonian Empire, 664, 793
Bach, Johann Sebastian, 283, 671
Bacteria, 578, 663
Baffin Bay, 484
Baffin Island, 496
Baghdad, 793
Bahamas, 727–728
Bahrain, 728
Baikal, Lake, 494
Baker Island, 898
Bakke case, 384, 688
Baku, Azerbaijan, 727
Balaton, Lake, 786
Balearic Islands, 867
Balfour Declaration, 678
Bali, 790, 791
Balkan crisis, 734–736, 756, 859
Balkan Wars, 678
Balloons:
  flights of, 435, 436, 438
  invention of, 435
  records, 439
Ball-point pen, 580
Baltic Sea, 494
Baltimore, Md., 155, 178, 182
Bamako, Mali, 820
Bancroft, Anne, 1035
Bandar Seri Begawan, Brunei, 737
Bangkok, Thailand, 876
Bangladesh, 728–729, 729, 789, 838

Bangui, Central African Republic, 745
Banjul, Gambia, 776
Bank of North America, 101
Bankruptcies, 643
Banks and banking:
  firsts in, 101
  largest, 644
Banks Island, 496
Barak, Ehud, 695, 798
Barbados, 729–730
Barbuda. See Antigua and Barbuda
Barometer, 578
Baseball, 1003–1022
  2004 season, 1018–1020
  All-Star Game, 1005–1006
  American League statistics, 1019
  batting statistics, 1010, 1010–1011, 1012, 1015, 1017, 1019
  club standings, 1009, 1018
  Cy Young Award, 1016
  Hall of Fame, 165, 1003–1004
  history of, 1003
  home run statistics, 1010–1011, 1012–1013, 1017
  Little League, 1002–1003
  Most Valuable Player, 1014
  National League statistics, 1019
  no-hit and perfect games, 1010
  pennant winners, 1020–1021
  pitching statistics, 1010–1011, 1015, 1019
  records, 1010–1011, 1017
  Rookie of the Year, 1016
  World Series, 1006–1009
Basketball, 948–956
  college, 948–951
  history of, 948
  Most Valuable Players, 954
  Olympic Games, 929
  professional, 952
  women's professional, 956
Basse-Terre, Guadeloupe, 773
Basseterre, St. Kitts, 854
Bastille Day, 672
Basutoland. See Lesotho
Bataan surrender, 681
Baton Rouge, La., 153, 178
Battlefields, National, 592
Battles. See names of specific battles
Bay of Pigs invasion, 99, 684, 757
Beatles, The, 275, 277, 686
Beaumont-Port Arthur Canal, 451
Bechuanaland. See Botswana
Beethoven, Ludwig van, 284, 672, 673
Begin, Menachem, 688, 764, 797
Beijing, China, 691, 747
Beirut, Lebanon, 797, 811
Belarus, 730
Belfast, Northern Ireland, 888
Belgian Congo. See Congo, Democratic Republic of
Belgium, 730–731
Belgrade, Yugoslavia, 859
Belize, 731–732
Bell, Alexander Graham, 284, 582, 676
Bellow, Saul, 517, 1035
Belmont Stakes, 981, 982
Belmopan, Belize, 731
Benedict XVI, Pope, 369, 512, 900, 901, 1030
Benelux, 816
Benin, 732–733
Bering, Vitus, 143
Bering Sea, 494
Bering Strait, 484
  migrations across, 663
Berlin, Congress of, 676
Berlin, Germany, 777
  airlift, 98, 682, 778
  East Berlin uprising, 683
  in World War II, 681
Berlin Wall, 684, 691
Berlusconi, Silvio, 859

Bermuda, 891
Bern, Switzerland, 872
Beslan hostage crisis, 701, 852
Bessarabia, 849, 851
Bhutan, 733
Bhutto, Benazir, 690
Biafra, 686, 836
Biathlon, 933
Bible:
  books of, 370
  English translation of, 668
  first printed, 668
  King James Version, 670
  New Testament, 361, 370
  Old Testament, 361, 370, 466–468, 664, 665
  Pentateuch, 665
Bicentennial, U.S., 687
Bicycles, 578. See also Cycling
Bifocal lens, 580
Big Bang theory, 399, 578
Bikini Atoll, 684, 821
Billings, Mont., 160, 178
Bill of Rights, 95, 114, 672
Bills (Congressional), procedures for, 81, 110
Bills (money), 453
Bin Laden, Osama, 75, 101, 698, 718, 719, 869
Biographies:
  of people, 282
  of U.S. presidents, 59–77
Bioko (formerly Fernando Po), 765
Birds, state, 142–177
Birdseye, Clarence, 583
Birendra (king of Nepal), 831
Birmingham, Ala., 142, 178
Birmingham, England, 884
Birth control, 678
Birth dates, of famous people, 282–317
Birth rates, world, 707
Births, U.S., 129–132
  by age of mother, 130
  cesarean births, 130, 131
  by race of mother, 130, 131
  rates, 129, 130
  sex ratios, 130
  by state, 129
  to teens, 132
  to unmarried women, 132
Birthstones, 359
Bisexuality, 373
Bishkek (Frunze), Kyrgyzstan, 808
Bismarck, N.D., 165, 178
Bismarck, Otto von, 285, 778
Bissau, Guinea-Bissau, 783
Black Death, 668, 885
Black Friday panic, 675
Black Hills, 171
Black Hole of Calcutta, 671
Black holes, 398
Blackout, Northeast (1965), 686
Black Sea, 849, 850
Blacks in U.S. See also Civil rights; Race and Ethnicity; Slavery
  births and birth rates, 130, 131
  civil rights timeline, 383–384
  firsts by, 101, 376–377
  life expectancy, 137
  population statistics, 121, 123, 124, 377, 378
Blair, Tony, 34, 39, 511, 699, 884, 887, 1030
Blanc, Mont, 770
  tunnel, 451
Blizzards, 215
Blogs, 565
Blood, circulation of, 578
Blood pressure, 562
Blood types, 562
Blue Grotto, 497
Blue Nile, 767
Bobsledding, 933
Body mass index, 553
Boers, 865

Boer War, 677, 865, 885
Bogotá (Santafé de Bogotá), Colombia, 750
Bohr, Niels, 227, 285, 581
Boiling points:
  of elements, 574–575
  of water, 452
Boise, Idaho, 149, 178
Bolivia, 37, 733–734
Bollingen Prize, 258
Bolsheviks, 679, 850
Bolt and screw sizes, metric conversion of, 458
Bolton, John, 37, 40, 43, 910, 1030
Bombay, India, 788
Bombing:
  of Afghanistan, 718
  embassy (1998), 695, 804, 876
  London (2005), 34, 41, 42, 510, 888, 1033
  Sept. 11, 2001, 211, 224, 698, 719, 858
  of Sudan, 869
Bonaire, 832
Bonaparte, Napoléon. See Napoleon Bonaparte
Bonds, Barry, 957, 1010, 1011, 1017
Booker Prize, 255
Books:
  awards for, 241–245, 254–257
  best of century, 268–269, 269–270
  best-selling adult, 267
  best-selling children's, 268
  reading statistics, 266, 267
Boone, Daniel, 153, 285
Booth, John Wilkes, 64, 97, 119, 285, 675
Borneo (island), 496, 790, 819
  Brunei, 737
Boron, 574
Boroughs of New York City, 195–196
Bosnia, 734–736. See also Balkan crisis
Boston, Mass., 156, 178, 182
  fire (1872), 217
Boston Massacre, 95, 671
Boston Tea Party, 95, 156, 671
Botanic garden, first, 101
Botanic Garden, U.S., 84
Botswana, 736
Bounty, H.M.S., 672, 894
Bourbon kings of France, 770, 771
Boutros-Ghali, Boutros, 907
Bowl games (football), 934–936
Bowling, 966–968
Boxer Rebellion, 677, 748
Boxing, 974–979
  bare-knuckle, 974
  heavyweight championship fights, 974–975
  history of, 974
  Olympic Games, 928
  professional, 974–979
  titleholders, 974–979
Boyne, Battle of the, 671
Boy Scouts of America, 655, 677
Brackets (punctuation), 475
Brady, Tom, 515
Brahmaputra River, 495, 729, 788
Braille, 483, 578
Braingate Neural Interface System, 570
Brandt, Willy, 286
Brasília, Brazil, 736
Bratislava, Slovakia, 862
Brazil, 485, 736–737
Brazos River, 500
Brazzaville, Congo, 753
Breitling Orbiter 3 (Cameron Balloons R-650), 439
Bremer, Paul, 699
Brest-Litovsk, Treaty of, 850
Bretton Woods Conference, 682
Brezhnev, Leonid, 286, 689, 851
Bribery, 710
Bridgeport, Conn., 146, 178

Bridges, 448–449
Bridgetown, Barbados, 729
British Columbia, Canada, 743
British Guiana. See Guyana
British Honduras. See Belize
British Indian Ocean Territory, 891
British New Guinea. See Papua New Guinea
British Open Champions, 997
British Solomon Islands. See Solomon Islands
British Virgin Islands, 892
Broadcasting awards, 258–260
Broadway, 516
Broadway theater, longest runs, 266
Bronx, 195–196
Brooklyn, 195–196
Brooklyn Bridge, 447, 676
Brown, John, 96, 286, 674
Brown, Michael, 32, 44, 1031
Brown v. Board of Education of Topeka, 93, 383, 683
Brunei Darussalam, 737–738
Brussels, Belgium, 730
Bryan, William Jennings, 53, 54, 87, 286, 677
Buchanan, James, 53, 55, 57, 63, 96. See also Presidents, U.S.
Bucharest, Romania, 848
Budapest, Hungary, 786
Buddha, 364–365, 664
Buddhism, 364–365
  founding of, 664
  introduced into China, 665
  in Japan, 666
Budget, federal, 633, 634, 635. See also Management and Budget, Office of
Buenos Aires, Argentina, 722
Buffalo, N.Y., 164
Buffalo Bill (William F. Cody), 286
Buildings, tallest, 444–445
Bujumbura, Burundi, 739
Bulganin, Nikolai A., 684
Bulgaria, 738–739
Bulge, Battle of the, 681
Bullet, 578
Bull Run, Battle of, 675
Bunche, Ralph J., 376
Burger, Warren E., 92
Burgesses, House of, 101
Burglary, 390
Burkina Faso, 739
Burlington, Vt., 173, 178
Burma. See Myanmar
Burr, Aaron, 52, 57, 286, 673
Burundi, 739–740
Bush, Barbara Pierce, 59, 72
Bush, George H. W., 35, 57, 58, 72–73, 100, 510, 690. See also Presidents, U.S.
Bush, George W., 32–33, 32, 33, 35, 36, 44, 45, 55–57, 74–76, 506, 696, 697, 698, 699, 700, 701, 793–795. See also Presidents, U.S.
Business and economy, 618–646. See also Foreign trade
  largest businesses, 644
Busing to achieve school integration, 686
Byrd, Richard E., 286, 437, 680
Byzantine architecture, 446
Byzantium, 664, 666, 668

C

Cabinets, U.S., 82–83, 85–90
  first black member of, 101
  first woman member of, 102
Caesar, Julius, 287, 665, 770
Cafta (Central American Free Trade Agreement, 33, 42
Cairo, Egypt, 763, 764
Cairo Conference, 681
Calcium, 574
Calcutta, India, 788

Caldecott Medal, 256–257
Calder Trophy, 964
Calendars, 663, 665, 666
  Chinese, 354, 358
  Egyptian, 350
  Gregorian, 350
  Hindu, 354, 358
  history of, 350–351
  Islamic, 354, 357
  Jain, 358
  Jewish, 354, 357
  Julian, 350
  lunar, 350
  names of days and months, 352
  perpetual, 1800–2063, 348–349
  Roman, 350
  Sikh, 358
  years 2005, 2006, 2007, 346–347
Calgary, Canada, 742
Calhoun, John C., 52, 287
California, 145
  Gold Rush in, 145, 674
  mountain peaks, 502
Californium, 574
Calvin, John, 287, 669
Cambodia, 685, 687, 688, 740–741
  Angkor Wat, 446
Cambrian Mountains, 885, 890
Cambrian Period, 576
Camera, 676
Cameroon, 741–742
Camp Fire Boys and Girls, 655
Canada, 742–744
  economy of, 742
  geography of, 742
  government of, 742
  history of, 742–744
  latitudes and longitudes of, 504
  map of, 528
  Nunavut, 742
  population of, 743
  provinces of, 743
  territories of, 743
Canadian River, 500
Canals, 451
Canary Islands, 867
Canberra, Australia, 724
Cancer:
  cancer rates, U.S., 557
  mortality, leading causes, 556
Cancer, Tropic of, 353
Candela, 455
Canoe racing, 929
Cape Canaveral, 689
Cape Horn, 485, 746
Cape of Good Hope, 484, 865
Capetian Dynasty, 666, 770, 771
Cape Town, South Africa, 865
Cape Verde, 744–745
Capitalization, rules for, 473
Capital punishment. See Executions
Capitals, foreign, 718–906
Capitals, of states, 142–177, 178
Capitals, of U.S.:
  early capitals, 102, 169
  Washington, DC, 203
Capone, Al, 680
Capote, Truman, literary award, 255
Capri, 497
Capriati, Jennifer, 958
Capricorn, Tropic of, 353
Caracas, Venezuela, 901
Carat (measure), 457
Carbon, 574
Carbon emissions, 584
Carboniferous Period, 576
Carbon monoxide, 586
Cardiff, Wales, 890
Caribbean area. See also specific countries
  islands of, 496
  map of, 525
Caribbean Sea, 494, 496
Carlsbad Caverns, 164, 497, 590
Carnegie, Andrew, 287
Carnival season, 355
Carolingian Dynasty, 770, 771

Carpathian Mountains, 846, 849
Carpooling, 606
Cars. *See* Automobiles
Carson, Johnny, 518, 1035
Carson, Kit, 161
Carson City, Nev., 161, 178
CART champions, 1001
Carter, Jimmy (James E., Jr.), 54, 57, 58, 71, 99. *See also* Presidents, U.S.
Carthage, 664, 665, 666
Cartoons, awards for, 235–236
Carver, George Washington, 142, 159
Casablanca, Morocco, 827
Casablanca Conference, 681
Caspian Sea, 487, 494n, 494
Cassini-Huygens mission, 410, 423
Castries, St. Lucia, 854
Castro, Fidel, 287, 684, 757
Casualties, in U.S. wars, 393
Caterpillar Club, 436
Cathedrals, 445–447
Catholic Church. *See* Roman Catholic Church
Caucasus, 850
Cavaliers, 670
Caves and caverns, 497
Cayenne, French Guiana, 772
Cayman Islands, 892
CDs, 275
Ceasefires, recent, 714
Celebes (Sulawesi), 790
Celluloid, discovery of, 581
Celsius (Centigrade) scale, 452, 455
Cemeteries, National, 594
  Arlington, 594n
Cenozoic Era, 577
Census:
  2000 census figures, 120–124
  national censuses, 124
Centigrade (Celsius) scale, 452, 455
Central African Republic, 745
Central America. *See also* specific countries
  Central America, map, 528
Central Intelligence Agency (CIA), 83, 98, 692
Central Powers, 678
Cermak, Anton J., 119, 680
Ceylon. *See* Sri Lanka
Chaco, 843
Chad, 745–746
Chad, Lake, 494, 746
Challenger (space shuttle), 100, 221, 422, 428, 431, 689
Chamberlain, Neville, 288, 681, 886
Channel Islands: Jersey and Guernsey, 892
Charitable contributions, 140
Charities, top U.S., 140
Charlemagne, 288, 666, 770, 771, 778
Charles (prince of Wales), 288, 513, 1031
Charles, Prince (of England), 39
Charles I (king of England), 155, 165, 170, 670, 885
Charleston, W. Va., 175, 176, 178
Charlotte, N.C., 165, 178, 183
Chavez, Hugo, 698, 699, 700, 701, 901, 902
Chechnya, 696, 852
Check Verification Companies, 648
Chemicals:
  export and import of, 639
  Producer Price Index, 637
Chemistry:
  discoveries and theories, 578–582
  elements, 572, 574–575
  Nobel Prizes for, 228–230
Cheney, Richard B., 55, 58, 75
Chernenko, Konstantin U., 689, 851
Chernobyl nuclear accident, 216, 690, 730, 851
Chertoff, Michael, 32, 36
Chesapeake Bay, 155
Chesapeake-Delaware Canal, 451
Cheyenne, Wyo., 177, 178
Chiang Kai-shek, 288, 681, 748, 874

Chicago, Ill., 150, 178, 183
  climate of, 601
  fire (1871), 217, 675
  St. Valentine's Day Massacre, 680
Chickens, 588, 640
Child abuse and neglect, 134
Children:
  abuse and neglect of, 134
  best-selling books for, 268
  birth rates, 707
  birth statistics, 129–132, 707
  book awards, 255–256, 256–257
  death rates, 707
  life expectancy of, 136, 137, 707
Children's Crusade, 667
Chile, 746–747
China, 37, 747–750. *See also* Headline history
  Boxer Rebellion, 677, 748
  Great Wall of, 446, 665, 747
  history of, 747–749
  and Japan, 676, 680, 681, 748, 801
  Ming Dynasty, 668, 748
  nuclear weapons testing by, 686
  People's Republic established, 683
  structures, 446
  and U.S., 748
  Yuan Dynasty, 668, 748
China (Taiwan). *See* Taiwan
"China seat" (UN), 686, 748, 874
Chinese:
  calendar, 354
  New Year, 358
Chinese civilization, ancient, 664
Chinese-Japanese War (1894–95), 748, 801
Chinese New Year, 355
Chirac, Jacques, 39, 698, 772
Chisholm Trail, 181, 187
Chisinau, Moldova, 824
Cholera, 213
Chou En-lai. *See* Zhou Enlai
Christ. *See* Jesus Christ
Christian holidays, 355–357
Christianity:
  development of, 665
  history of, 361–363
  in Roman Empire, 361, 665
  spread of, 666
Christmas, 346, 357
Christmas Island, 726, 862
Christo, 516, 1031
Chromium, 574
Chromosphere, 400
Chronology:
  civil rights, 383–384
  of disasters, 210–224
  of major Supreme Court cases, 93
  of staffed space flights, 429–434
  of U.S. history, 95–101
  of unstaffed space flights, 425–427
  of women's rights movement, 374–375
  of world history, 663–701
Chrysler Building, 444, 447
Churches (buildings):
  famous, 445–447
  in largest U.S. cities, 180–204
Churches (organizations). *See* Religion
Churchill, Sir Winston, 288, 681, 682, 886
Church of England, 669, 885
CIA. *See* Central Intelligence Agency
Cicero, 665
Cigarettes, 562
Cimarron River, 500
Cimmerian civilization, 664
Cincinnati, Ohio, 166
Circular measure, 455, 459
Circumference, formula for, 459
Citadel (Cairo), 446
Cities, Canadian:
  latitude and longitude of, 504
  time of day, 504
Cities, U.S., 180–209. *See also* specific cities
  bridges, 448–449

chambers of commerce, 180–204
climate of, 601–602
Consumer Price Index, 638
crime rates, 391
labor force, 180–204
largest, 180–204, 209
largest of each state, 178
latitudes and longitudes of, 504
mayors and managers of, 180–204
mileages between, 612–615
newspapers, 272
per capita income, 180–204
polluted, most, 586
population of, 142–177, 180–204, 205–207
ports, 643
tallest buildings, 444–445
temperatures, 180–204
time of day, 504
tunnels, 451
unemployment, 180–204
Cities, world, 704. *See also* specific cities
  air distances, 614–617
  bridge, 448–449
  capitals, 718–906
  largest, by country, 718–906
  latitudes and longitudes of, 499, 504
  population of, 718–906
  southernmost, 746
  subway systems, 606
  tallest buildings, 444–445
  temperatures, 605
  time of day in, 499
  tourism, 604
  tunnels, 451
City managers, U.S., 180–204
Civilian labor force:
  mothers in, 624
  women in, 624
Civil rights, 383–384
  Bill of Rights, 114
  Fourteenth Amendment, 116, 675
  gay rights organization, 101
  Montgomery boycott, 684
  other constitutional provisions about, 113, 114, 116, 118
  school desegregation, 683
  timeline, 383–384
  trial rights, 115
Civil Rights, U.S. Commission on, 83
Civil Rights Act, 99
Civil Service Commission, U.S., 676. *See also* Office of Personnel Management
Civil time, 351, 421
Civil War, American, 97, 392, 675
  casualties, 396
  chronology, 675
  Confederate States, 104
  Gettysburg Address, 119
Civil War, English, 885
Civil War, Russian, 679, 850
Civil War, Spanish, 681, 867
Clark, George Rogers, 671
Classification, scientific, 578
Clay, Cassius. *See* Ali, Muhammad
Clay, Henry, 52, 53, 61, 288, 674
Cleopatra, 665, 764
Cleveland, Grover, 53, 55, 56, 57, 65, 97. *See also* Presidents, U.S.
Cleveland, Ohio, 166, 183–184
Climate. *See* Weather and Climate
Clinton, Hillary Rodham, 46, 59, 73, 288, 696
Clinton, William Jefferson, 35, 55, 57, 73–74, 100, 288, 510, 697. *See also* Presidents, U.S.
  impeachment of, 91, 100, 695
  sex scandal, 695
Clocks, pendulum, 578
Cloning, 40, 43, 569
Clothing:
  Consumer Price Index, 638
  export and import of, 639
  Producer Price Index, 637
Cloture rule, 81

Clouds, 597
Coal:
  export and import of, **639**
Coastline of U.S., **502**
Cobalt, **574**
Cocaine, **560**
Cochise, **144**
Cochran, Johnnie, Jr., 517, 1035
Cocos (Keeling) Islands, **726**
Code of Hammurabi, **663**
Coffee:
  export and import of, **639**
  U.S. consumption of, **640**
Coins, U.S., **454**
Coldest weather, 597, 598
Cold war, 98, 692
Colleges and universities, 322,
  323–345
  costs, 321
  degrees granted, 319, 322
  endowments, 322
  enrollments, 320, 323–345
  firsts, 101
  in U.S., 323–345
Collins, Eileen, 422
Colombia, 750–751
Colombo, Sri Lanka, 868
Colon (punctuation), 475
Colonial population, **123**
Colonial Williamsburg, **174**
Colonies, **702**
Colorado, 145–146, 502
Colorado Desert, **498**
Colorado River (Colorado-Mexico),
  484, 495, 500
Colorado River (Texas), **500**
Colorado Springs, Colo., 145, 184
Colors, state, **142–177**
Colosseum (Rome), 445, 665
Colossus at Rhodes, 447
Columbia (space shuttle), 221, 422,
  428, 429, 430, 434, 699, 700
Columbia, S.C., 170, 178
Columbia River, 495, 500
  Grand Coulee Dam, 175
Columbus, Christopher, 288, 484,
  668, 761, 773, 800, 878
Columbus, Ohio, 166, 178, 184–185
Columbus Day, 346, 356
Colville River, **500**
Combustion, **578**
Comet Hale-Bopp, **694**
Comets, 42, 415–416, 424, 514, 571
Comet Tempel I, 571
Comintern, 679
Comma (punctuation), 474
Commandments, Ten, 94
Commerce. *See* Foreign trade
Commerce, U.S. Dept. of:
  description of, **83**
  secretaries of, 83, 87–90
Commission of Fine Arts, **84**
Committees:
  Congressional, **77**
  National, 51
Commodities:
  imports and exports of, **639**
  Producer Price Index, 637
Commodity Futures Trading
  Commission, **84**
Common Market, 684, 689. *See also*
  European Economic Community
Commonwealth, Puritan, **885**
Commonwealth of Independent
  States (CIS), 692, 850, 852, 910
Commonwealth of Nations, **910**
Commune, Revolutionary (French),
  672
Communism, 674, 678, 679
Communist Internationals, 676, 679
Communist Manifesto, 674
Communist Party, USSR, **684**
Commuting characteristics, 606
Como, Lake, 681
Comoros, 751–752
Composers, awards for, 245–246,
  253–254

Computers, 563–568
  blogs, 565
  games, 568
  game software, 568
  inventions, 579
  software, 568
  statistics, 717
  usage, 567
Comstock Lode, 161
Conakry, Guinea, 783
Concentration camps, 680
Concert tours, 275
Concord, N.H., 162, 178
Conditioned reflex, 579
Confederate Memorial Day, 358
Confederate States, 97, 104, 675
  secession and readmission dates of,
    104
Conflicts, armed, 714
Confucianism, 366
Confucius, 289, 366, 664, 747
Congo:
  Democratic Republic of, 752–753, 752
  Republic of (Brazzaville), 753–754
Congo River, 484, 495, 753
Congress, U.S. *See also* House of
  Representatives; Senate
  adjournment of, 110
  assembling time of, 110, 117
  committees, 77
  compensation and privileges of
    members of, 110
  composition of, 46, 79–80
  conventions, political, 51
  first black members of, 101
  first sessions, 102
  first women members of, 102
  legislative powers of, 81, 110, 115, 117
  members of, 46–49
  powers and duties of, 110
  salaries of members of, 80, 110, 118
Congresses, Continental, 102, 107, 671
Congressional Medal of Honor, 396
Congress of Industrial
  Organizations, 684
Congress of Vienna, 673, 726, 770
Conjunctions (planetary), 398
Connecticut, 146
Connecticut River, 146, 500
Conservation. *See* Environment
Constantine, Arch of, 445
Constantinople, 666, 668, 781, 880.
  See also Istanbul
Constantinople, Peace of, 669
Constellations, 401, 416–417
Constitution, U.S., 109–118, 169
  amendment procedure for, 114
  amendments to, 114–118
  drafting of, 95, 109
  ratification of, 102, 109, 114
  signing of, 672
  supremacy of, 114
Constitution, USS, 673
Constitutions, state:
  dates adopted, 142–177
  first, 102, 146
Consumer Price Index (CPI), 638
Consumer Product Safety
  Commission, 83
Consumers:
  credit, 628
  organizations, 649–650
  price indexes, 638
  recalls, 650
  resource guide, 647–652
Consumption of food items, 640
Continental Congresses, 95, 102,
  107, 671
Continental Divide, 160, 500
Continental drift, 402, 487
Continents. *See also* specific continents
  area and elevations of, 487
  exploration of, 484–485
Controllers of states, 142–177
Conventions, National, 50, 51
Conversion, weights and measures,
  452, 454, 456–458, 458

Cook, Frederick, 485n
Cook, James, 149, 168
Cook Islands, 833
Coolidge, Calvin, 54, 57, 67, 98. *See
  also* Presidents, U.S.
Cooper, Matthew, 41, 42, 1031
Copenhagen, Denmark, 759
Copernicus, Nicolaus, 669
Copper, 574
Coptic Christians, 362, 764, 767
Copyrights, 652
Coral Sea Islands, 726
Core (of Earth), 402
Coronado, Francisco Vásquez de,
  144, 152, 163, 167, 172
Corona of Sun, 400
Corporation for National Service, 83
Corporations:
  taxes on, 1025, 1028
Corpus Christi (holiday), 357n
Corregidor, 681
Corruption:
  leaders, 710
  prosecutions for, 387
  world, 710
Corruption index, countries, 709
Corsica, 770
Cortés, Hernando, 289, 484, 669, 823
Cosmetics, 579
Cosmonauts, 429
Costa Rica, 754
Côte d'Ivoire, 754–755
Cotton:
  export and import of, 639
Cotton Bowl, 936
Council of Economic Advisers, 82
Council of Nicaea, 361, 666
Council of Trent, 350, 669
Council on Environmental Quality, 82
Counterfeiting, 390
Counties, per state, 142–177
Countries of world, 718–906. *See
  also* Geography, world; History, world
  agriculture, 718–906
  areas of, 705–706, 718–906
  birth rates, 707, 718–906
  capitals of, 718–906
  cities, large, 718–906
  colonies, 702
  comparative statistics, 703
  computers, telephones, 717
  corruption, 709, 710
  death rates, 707
  economic conditions, 718–906
  economics, 703, 712–713
  environmental comparisons, 584
  exploration of selected areas,
    484–485
  exports, 718–906
  failed states, 715
  foreign aid, 711
  foreign trade, 718–906
  freedom, political, 708
  general statistics, 703
  governments of, 718–906
  gross domestic product, 712–713
  history of, 718–906
  holidays, 359
  imports, 718–906
  income inequality, 711
  income tax, 2003, 712
  industry, 718–906
  infant mortality rate, 703
  inflation, 712–713, 718–906
  labor force, 718–906
  languages of, 718–906
  life expectancy in, 707
  "livable," most and least, 710
  monetary units of, 718–906
  most populous, 704
  natural features of, 718–906
  political parties, 718–906
  poorest, 711
  population densities of, 718–906
  population of, 705–706
  premiers and prime ministers of,
    718–906

presidents of, **718–906**
race/ethnicity, **718–906**
refugees, **715**
rulers of, **718–906**
standard of living, **710, 711**
statistics, **702–717**
structures, **443–451**
taxes, **712**
telephones, computers, **717**
unemployment, **718–906**
UN members, **909**
in World Wars I and II, **678, 681**
Country Music Association Awards, **254**
Country Music Hall of Fame, **278**
Courts, federal, 113. *See also* Supreme Court, U.S.
"Coxey's Army", **676**
Crater Lake National Park, **590**
Craters, meteorite, **416**
Credit, consumer, **628**
Credit cards, **640**
Credit reporting bureaus, **648**
Creeds:
  Nicene, **361, 666**
Cretaceous Period, **576**
Crete, **663, 664, 666**
Crime, **385–391.** *See also* Law enforcement
  arrests, **390**
  assassinations and attempts, **119**
  by city, **391**
  corruption, prosecutions for, **387**
  hate crimes, **389**
  homicide rate, **388**
  index, **389**
  murder, **388, 390**
  rates, **390, 391**
  by states, **390**
  trial rights, **113**
  by weapon, **388**
Crimean War, **674, 880, 885**
Croatia, **755–756**
Crockett, Davy, **289, 674**
Cro-Magnon man, **663**
Cromwell, Oliver, **289, 670, 885**
Crossbow, invention of, **579**
Crossword puzzles:
  guide to, **460–472**
Crucifixion of Christ, **361, 665**
Crusades, **667**
Crust (of Earth), **402**
Cuba, **756–757**
  Bay of Pigs invasion, **99, 684, 757**
  island, **496**
Cuban missile crisis, **69, 99, 685, 757, 851**
Cubic measure, **452, 454, 456**
Cultural Revolution (China), **748**
Cumberland River, **500**
Cuneiform, **663**
Curaçao, **832**
Curie, Marie, **226, 229, 289, 677**
Curie, Pierre, **226, 289, 677**
Curling (sport), **933**
Currency. *See* Money
Currency, U.S., **453**
Current events, **32–44**
  international, **33–35**
  people in the news, **1030–1034**
  recent deaths, **1035**
  in U.S., **32–33**
Custer, George A., **97, 160, 290, 676**
Cycling, **929**
Cyclones, **214**
Cyclotron, **579, 680**
Cyprus, **757–758**
  Greek-Turkish crisis, **700, 757, 880**
Cy Young Award, **1016**
Czechoslovakia, **681, 692**
  separation of, **759**
  Warsaw Pact invasion of, **686**
Czech Republic, **758–759**

D

da Gama, Vasco, **290, 484, 668, 788**
Dahomey. *See* Benin
Dairy products, U.S. consumption of, **640**
Dakar, Senegal, **858**
Dalai Lama, **225, 290, 684**
Dallas, Tex., **172, 185**
  climate of, **601**
  Kennedy assassination in, **69, 119, 685**
Damascus, Syria, **872**
Damavend, Mount, **792**
Dams, **450**
Dance companies, U.S., **265**
Danish dependencies, **702**
Danube River, **495, 726, 738, 777, 786, 849, 859**
Dardanelles, **678, 879**
Dare, Virginia, **101, 165**
Dar es Salaam, Tanzania, **875**
Darfur, Sudan, **34, 35, 701, 869**
Darling River, **495**
Darrow, Clarence, **290, 679**
Darwin, Charles, **290, 674**
Dash (punctuation), **475**
Da Silva, Lula, **736, 737**
Date line, **352**
Davis, Jefferson, **290, 675**
  birthday, **358**
Davis, Ossie, **1035**
Davis Cup, **987**
Daylight saving time, **346, 352–353**
Days:
  names of, **352**
  sidereal and solar, **351, 400**
Daytime Emmy Awards, **260**
D-Day, **681**
Dead Sea, **797**
Death and dying, **134–138.** *See also* Infant mortality
  in disasters, **210–224**
  diseases, **137**
  of famous people, **282–317, 1035**
  by firearms, **135**
  leading causes of, **135, 137, 556**
  recent (2004), **1035**
  smoking-related, **561**
  suicide, **137, 138**
  U.S. death rates, **135**
Death penalty. *See* Executions
Death rates, world, **707**
Death Row, **386**
Death Valley, **145, 487, 500, 503**
Debs, Eugene V., **54, 290, 676**
Debt, national, **633, 634**
Decimals, fractions, **459**
Declaration of Independence, **107–108, 169**
Decoration Day. *See* Memorial Day
Deep Impact spacecraft, **42, 424, 514, 571**
"Deep Throat", **40, 1031**
Deerfield Massacre, **671**
Defense, U.S. Dept. of. *See also* Armed forces, U.S.
  description of, **83**
  secretaries of, **83, 88–90**
Defibrillator, **579**
Deficit, national, **33**
de Gaulle, Charles, **290, 684, 770**
Degrees, academic, first for women, **102**
Degrees granted, **319, 322**
Delaware, **147**
Delaware River, **500**
DeLay, Tom, **35, 39, 290, 1031**
Democratic Party:
  members of Congress, **46–49**
  National Committee chairmen, **51**
  national conventions, **51, 677, 689, 690**
  presidential candidates, **52–55**

Senate floor leaders, **78**
Denali National Park, **143, 590**
Deng Xiaoping, **687, 691, 747–749**
Denmark, **759–760**
Densities of population:
  in countries, **718–906**
  in U.S., **124**
Denver, Colo., **145, 178, 185–186**
  climate of, **601**
Dependent political entities, **702**
Depression (economics), **680**
Desegregation in schools, **683, 686**
Deserts, **498**
Des Moines, Iowa, **151, 152, 178**
De Soto, Hernando, **142, 144, 148, 154, 158, 159, 171**
Detroit, Mich., **156, 178, 186**
Deuterium, **579**
Devil's Hole, **497**
Devonian Period, **576**
Devon Island, **496**
Dhaka, Bangladesh, **728**
Diamond mine (Arkansas), **144**
Diamonds, **675, 865**
Diana (Princess of Wales), **694**
Diesel engine, **579, 676**
Dili, East Timor, **762**
Dionne quintuplets, **680**
Diphtheria, antitoxin, **578**
Diplomatic personnel, **914–916**
  first black, **101**
Director of National Intelligence (DNI), Office of, **84**
Directory, French, **673, 771**
Dirigibles, first flight of, **435**
Disasters, **210–224**
  aircraft accidents, **211, 219–221**
  avalanches, **211, 213**
  blizzards, **211, 215**
  drought, **211, 216**
  earthquakes, **211–213**
  epidemics, **211, 213**
  explosions, **211, 217–218, 223–224**
  fires, **211, 217–218**
  floods, **211, 213**
  hurricanes, **32, 33, 43, 44, 211, 214–215, 505, 596, 701, 742, 1031**
  nuclear and chemical accidents, **216**
  oil spills, **211, 222**
  railroad accidents, **211, 221–222**
  shipwrecks, **211, 218–219**
  space, **221**
  sports, **223**
  storms, **211, 214–215**
  terrorist attacks in U.S., **211, 223–224**
  tidal waves, **213**
  tornadoes, **211, 215–216**
  tsunamis, **210, 213**
  volcanic eruptions, **211–213**
Discoveries, **578–582**
  of chemical elements, **572, 574–575**
  recent scientific, **570–571**
Discovery (space shuttle), **42, 43, 422, 434, 514**
Diseases:
  deaths from, **137**
  medical discoveries, **578–582**
Disneyland, **145**
Disney World, **148**
Distance, airplane records, **439**
District of Columbia, 203. *See also* Washington, DC
Diving. *See* Swimming
"Divorce capitals", **161**
Divorce statistics, **128, 129**
Djibouti (city), Republic of Djibouti, **760**
Djibouti, Republic of, **760**
DNA, **230, 232, 579**
  crime exonerations, **386**
Dnieper River, **495**
Doctors, (physicians), first woman, **102**

Doha, Qatar, 848
Dollar, value of, 638
Dome of the Rock, 446
Dominica, 760–761
Dominican Republic, 761–762
Don River, 495
Dover, Del., 147, 178
Draft evaders, pardoning of, 687
Dram (measure), 455, 457
Drama, awards for, 246, 252
Drama Desk Awards, 252
Dred Scott v. *Sanford*, 93, 674
Dreyfus, Alfred, 291, 676
Drivers:
  arrests for drunkenness, 390
  fatalities, 607
  licenses, 608, 611
  most and least knowledgeable, 610
  number of, 611
  seat belt use, 609
  state laws, 608
Dropout rates (high school), 320
Drought, 211, 216
Drug Control Policy, Office of
  National, 82
Drug use and abuse, 560
  alcohol, 560
  cocaine, 560
  heroin, 560
  marijuana, 560
  tobacco, 560, 561
Drunk driving, 607
Drunkenness, arrests for, 390
Dry measures, 452, 455, 457
Duarte, José Napoleón, 765
Dublin, Ireland, 795, 796
Du Bois, W.E.B., 677
Dukakis, Michael S., 55, 690
Dumbarton Oaks Conference, 682
Dunkerque evacuation, 681
Duomo (Florence), 446
duPont–Columbia University
  Broadcast Awards, 260
Dushanbe, Tajikistan, 874
Dust bowl (1930s), 211, 216
Dutch dependencies, 702
Dutch East Indies. See Indonesia
Dutch Guiana. See Suriname
Duvalier, Jean-Claude, 690, 785
DVDs, 277, 278
Dynamite, 579, 675
Dynamo. See Generator, electric
Dzaoudzi, Mayotte, 775

E

Earhart, Amelia, 291, 437, 680, 681
Earnings:
  women, 375
Earnings, by educational level, 321
Earth (planet), 402–403, 407. See also
  Planets
  astronomical constants, 400
  atmosphere, 402
  continental drift, 402
  formation of, 663
  geological periods, 576–577
  life on, 576–577, 663
  origin of, 402
Earthquakes, 211–213, 677, 690, 692,
  693
  deaths from, 491, 492
  frequency worldwide, 491
  largest, worldwide, 490
  magnitude scales, 491
  major, 2005, 492
  Mercalli intensity scale, 491
  number, 491
  Richter magnitude, 490
  severity measured, 490
East China Sea, 494
Easter Island, 746
Eastern Europe, map, 531
Eastern Front (World War I), 678
Eastern Orthodoxy, 362
Easter Rebellion, 678, 796

Easter Sunday, 346, 356, 357
East Germany. See Germany
East India Company, 670, 788
East Timor, 698, 762, 790, 791
Ebbers, Bernard, 38, 1031
Ebert, Friedrich, 778
Eclipses, 421
Economic Advisers, Council of. See
  Council of Economic Advisors
Economic and Social Council, UN,
  907–908
Economic Community, 684
Economics, Nobel Prizes for, 233–
  234
Economics, world statistics, 712–713
Economic statistics, U.S., 643–646
Economy:
  outlook through 2010, 619–620
  U.S. business and, 643–646
  world, 702
Ecstasy, 560
Ecuador, 763
Ecumenical councils:
  Council of Nicaea, 361, 666
  Council of Trent, 669
  Vatican Council I, 363
  Vatican Council II, 363, 685, 689,
    901
Eden, Sir Anthony, 291, 684, 886
Edinburgh, Scotland, 884, 890
Edison, Thomas A., 291, 579, 580,
  676
Education, 318–345. See also
  Colleges and universities
  attainment, 319
  civil rights, 383–384
  college costs, 321, 323–345
  degrees awarded, 319, 322
  dropout rates, 320
  endowments, 322
  enrollments, 320, 323–345
  General educational development
    (GED), 320
  math and science scores, 318
  prayer in schools, 685
  pupil-teacher ratios, 320
  by race, 319
  by sex, 319
  software, 568
  Supreme Court school decisions,
    683, 685, 686, 688, 689
Education, U.S. Dept. of:
  description of, 83
  secretaries of, 83, 88–90
Education statistics, 120
Edward VIII (king of England), 681,
  886
Egypt, 41, 43
Egypt, Arab Republic of, 763–765.
  See also Arab-Israeli conflict
  Great Sphinx, 445
  and Israel, 684, 687, 763–765,
    797–799
  Pyramids, 447, 663
  Suez Canal, 451, 684, 764, 797
Egyptian Empire, 663, 664
  mythology, 472
  structures, 447
Eichmann, Adolf, 684
Eid al-Adha, 355
Eid al-Fitr, 346, 356, 357
Eiffel Tower, 446, 676
Einstein, Albert, 227, 292, 677, 681
  Theorem, 459, 579, 581
Eire. See Ireland, Republic of
Eisenhower, Dwight D., 54, 57, 58,
  68, 99, 153, 169, 172. See also
  Presidents, U.S.
Eisenhower Doctrine, 68, 684
Elbe River, 777
Elbert, Mount, 502
Elbrus, Russia, 487
Election, presidential (2004), 45
Election Day, 346, 356, 357
Elections:
  closest presidential, 56
  congressional, 46–49

  facts about, 56
  presidential, 45, 52–55, 701
  presidential, procedure for, 50, 112,
    115
  results (1789–2004), 45, 52–55, 701
  voter turnout, 56
  women voters, 373
Electoral College, 45, 50, 115, 116
  votes, 50, 52–56
Electricity:
  average prices, 641
  electric current, 455
  inventions and discoveries, 578–582
Electric lamp, invention of, 579
Electrocution, first, 101
Electrocution as death penalty, 387
Electromagnet, 579
Electron microscope, 580
Electrons, discovery of, 579
Elementary schools:
  enrollment, 320
  pupil-teacher ratios, 320
Elements, chemical, 572, 574–575
Elevations:
  of cities of U.S., 180–204
  of continents, 487
  of deserts, 498
  extremes of U.S., 500
  of mountain peaks, 493
  of states of U.S., 503
  of volcanoes, 488–489
Elizabeth I (queen of England), 669,
  885
Elizabeth II (queen of England), 683,
  885, 886
Elks (BPOE), 656
Ellesmere Island, 496
Ellice Islands. See Tuvalu
Ellington, Duke, 687
El Paso, Tex., 172, 186–187
El Salvador, 688, 689, 765
Email providers, 566
Embassies, foreign, 910–913
Embassy bombings (Kenya and
  Tanzania), 695
Embezzlement, arrests for, 390
Emmy Awards, 44, 259–260
Empire, Second (French), 674, 770,
  771
Empires, ancient, 663–665
Empire State Building, 444, 447
Employment, 619–624. See also
  Cities, U.S.; Labor force
  growth, 620
  labor force, 624
  median income, 621
  by occupation, 622
  projections, 619–620
  by race, 622
  by sex, 623
  taxes, 1024–1025
  unions, 625
  wage gap, 375
Endangered species, 589
Endowments, college and university,
  322
Energy:
  consumption of, 584
  oil and gas reserves, 585
  prices, increasing, 33
Energy, U.S. Dept. of:
  description of, 83
  secretaries of, 83, 89–90
Enewetak (Eniwetok) Atoll, 683, 821
Engels, Friedrich, 292, 674
Engines:
  diesel, 579
  internal combustion, 579
  steam, 582, 672
England:
  poets laureate, 274
  rulers of, 886
  structures, 446
England, Lynndie, 40
English Channel, tunnel under, 451
English language development, 481
Enlightenment, The, 671

Enrollment:
in colleges and universities, **320, 323–345**
in elementary schools, **320**
in secondary schools, **320**
Enron, 698
Entebbe, 687
Entente Cordiale, 677
Entertainment and culture:
best-selling books, **267–268**
dance companies, **265**
movie revenues, **281**
opera companies, **265**
symphonies, **264**
websites, **566**
Environment, 584–594
air pollutants, **586–587**
cities, most polluted, **586**
country comparisons, **584**
endangered species, **589**
National Park System, **590–594, 594**
oceans, debris in, **587**
polluting cars, most and least, **610**
rivers, endangered, **587**
sustainability, **584**
Environmental Protection Agency (EPA), 83
Environmental Quality, Council on, 82
Epidemics, 211, 213, 555
Epiphany, 346, 355
Episcopal Church, 363, 687
"E pluribus unum", 103
Equal Employment Opportunity Commission (EEOC), 83
Equal Rights Amendment (ERA), 374, 688
Equator, 486
Equatorial Guinea, 765–766
Equestrian events, 929
Equinoxes, 353, 403
Erie, Lake, 494
Battle of, **167, 673**
Erie Canal, **150, 164**
Erie Canal, 451
Eriksson, Leif, 484, 667, 742
Eritrea, 766
and Ethiopia, **767–768**
Eros (asteroid), 414–415
Eskimos, 143
Espionage, 689
Estonia, 682, 691, 766–767
Ether (anesthetic), 578, 674
Ethiopia, 680, 681, 767–768, 799
and Eritrea, **767–768**
Ethnicity, 376–384
Etruscans, 664
Euclid, 292, 579, 665
Euphrates River, 495, 793
Europe. See also Countries of world
area and elevation of, **487**
exploration of, **484**
map of, **530, 531**
European constitution, 39, 40, 511
European Economic Community, 684, 867, 886
European Union (EU), 910
Everest, Mount, 487, 492, 493, 683, 830
Everglades National Park, 148, 590
Evers, Medgar, 383
Evolution, human, 572, 663, 674, 679
Scopes trial, **679**
Exclamation point (punctuation), 474
Executions:
death row, **386**
exonerations, **386**
first state to abolish capital punishment, **102**
methods by state, **387**
statistics, **386, 706**
Executive departments and agencies, U.S., 82–85
Exercise, 545, 554
Exosphere, 402
Expectation of life, 136, 137, 707

Expenditures:
consumer, **127**
family, **127**
by federal government, **634, 635**
gross domestic product, **633**
personal consumption, **641**
Explorations, 484–485
Explorer (satellite), **684**
Explosions, 211, 217–218, 223–224
Explosives, inventions of, 579, 580
Export-Import Bank of the United States, 84
Exports:
from countries, **718–906**
from U.S., **638, 639**
Extradition between states, 113
Extreme sports, 1023
Exxon Valdez (oil tanker), **73, 100, 211, 223**
Eyre, Lake, 487

F

Fabre, Henri, 435
Fahrenheit scale, 452, 455
Failed states, 715
Falkland Islands, 688, 723, 886, 892
Falling bodies:
formulas for, **459**
law of, **579**
Families:
child abuse and neglect, **134**
credit card use by, **640**
income of, **627**
teen pregnancy, **132**
of U.S. presidents, **59**
Famous people, 282–317, 957–961, 1029. See also Awards; Headline history
Faraday, Michael, 292, 579, 580
Fargo, N.D., 166, 178
Farm Credit Administration, 83
Farm Index, 642
Faroe Islands, 759–760
Farragut, Adm. David G., 101, 675
Fascists, 679, 799
Fatalities:
driving, **607**
tornadoes, **597**
Father's Day, 346, 356
Fat intake, 554
Fat Tuesday. See Mardi Gras
Faubus, Orval, 383
FBI. See Federal Bureau of Investigation
Feasts, Jewish, 355–357
Federal budget:
distribution by state, **635**
outlays by agency, **633**
public debt, **633**
receipts and outlays, **634**
Federal Bureau of Investigation (FBI), 688
director of, **83**
founding, **97, 98**
Federal Communications Commission (FCC), 83
Federal courts, 113. See also
Supreme Court, U.S.
Federal Deposit Insurance Corporation (FDIC), 83
Federal Election Campaign Act, 687
Federal Election Commission (FEC), 83
Federal Emergency Management Agency (FEMA), 32, 84
Federal Energy Administration. See
Energy, U.S. Dept. of
Federal government. See United
States government
Federal Housing Finance Board, 84
Federalist Papers, **60**
Federalist Party, 52, 57n, 60
Federal Labor Relations Authority, 84
Federal Maritime Commission, 83

Federal Mediation and Conciliation Service (FMCS), 84
Federal Power Commission. See
Energy, U.S. Dept. of
Federal Reserve System (FRS), 678
Board of Governors of, **84**
Federal Trade Commission (FTC), 84, 678
Felt, W. Mark, 40, 513, 1031
Feminist movement, 374–375
Fencing, 929
Fermentation, 579
Fermi, Enrico, 227, 261, 292, 580, 682
Fermi Award, 261
Fernando Po, Equatorial Guinea. See
Bioko
Fertility rates, U.S., 129
Festival of Lights, 357, 357n
Fiction, awards for, 241–242, 254–257, 258
Fields Medal, 261
Fifth Republic (French), 684, 770, 771
Figure skating, 930, 933, 970–971
Fiji, 768–769
Filibusters, 33, 81
Fillmore, Millard, 53, 57, 63, 96. See
also Presidents, U.S.
Films. See Motion pictures
Fingal's Cave, 497
Finland, 709, 769
Firearms, 388, 390
deaths by, **135**
inventions, **580, 581**
Fireballs, 416
Fires:
arson arrests, **390**
disastrous, **211, 217–218**
forest fires, **218**
First Fruits, Feast of, 356, 357n
Firsts:
in aviation, **435–439**
in black history, **376–377**
in U.S. history, **101–102**
Fish:
export and import of, **639**
U.S. consumption of, **640**
Fitzgerald, Ella, 694
Five and dime store, first, 101
Flag Day, 346, 356
Flags:
adoption of first U.S., **95**
history of U.S., **103**
pledge of allegiance to, **103**
world, **519–522**
Fleming, Alexander, 231, 293, 578, 680
Flight Programs:
U.S. staffed, **427–429, 429–434**
Flights:
first, **435–439**
orbital, **851**
records, **439**
Floods, 211, 213
Johnstown, Pa. (1889), **211, 213, 676**
Floor leaders of Senate, 78
Florence, Italy, 446, 668
Florida, 147–148
exploration of, **484**
Spanish cession of, **671**
Flowers, state, 142–177
Food:
Consumer Price Index, **638**
export and import of, **639**
prices, historical, **639**
spending on, **127**
U.S. consumption of, **640**
Food insecurity, 631
Food pyramid, 39, 552
Food stamps, 631
Foot-and-mouth disease, 697
Football, 515, 934–948
American Conference Champions, **944–945**
American League Champions, **944**
bowl games, **934–936**
college, **934–941**

Hall of Fame (college), **937–941**
Hall of Fame (professional), **946–948**
Heisman Memorial Trophy, **937**
history of, **934**
National Conference champions, 943–944
National Football League, **941–948**
National League champions, **943**
professional, **941–948**
records (professional), **945–946**
Super Bowl, **515**, 941–942, 942
Forbidden City (Beijing), 446
Ford, Gerald R., 54, 57, 58, 70–71, 99.
See also Presidents, U.S.
assassination attempts on, 119, 687
Ford, Henry, 293, 677
Foreign aid, from U.S., 637
Foreign-born population, 382
Foreign embassies, 910–913
Foreign investment, 636–637
Foreign languages studied, U.S., 476
Foreign trade:
U.S., **639**
world, 718–906
Foreign travel, 603, 604, 605
Foreign words and phrases, 478, 479–481
Forests:
resources of countries, 718–906
Forgery, 390
Formosa. See Taiwan
Formulas, math and physics, 459
Fort-de-France, Martinique, 773
Fort Dodge, 152
Fort Sumter, Battle of, 170, 675
Fort Ticonderoga, 165, 174
Fort Worth, Tex., 172, 187
Fossett, Steve, 38, 439
Fossil hominids, earliest, 663
Fountain pen, 580
Four Freedoms, 682
Four Noble Truths, 365
Fourth of July, 356
Fox Quesada, Vicente, 697, 823–824
Fractions, decimals, 459
France, 511, 769–775
in NATO, 770
overseas departments and territories of, 773–774
rulers of, 771
structures, 446
Franco, Francisco, 293, 681
Franco-Prussian War, 675, 770
Frank, Anne, 682
Frankfort, Ky., 153, 178
Frankfurt, Germany, 777
Franklin, Benjamin, 84, 103, 107, 293, 580, 671
Fraternity, first, 101
Freedom, global trends, 708
"Freedom March", 142
Freedom of the press, 114, 671
Freedoms, Constitutional, 114
Freeman, Cathy, 922, 958
Freetown, Sierra Leone, 861
Frémont, John C., 145, 161
French and Indian Wars, 95, 150, 154, 157, 158, 166, 171, 174, 176, 671
French dependencies, 702
French Guiana, 772
French Polynesia, 773
French Revolution, 672, 770
French Somaliland. See Djibouti
French Southern and Antarctic Lands, 774
French Sudan. See Mali
French Territory of the Afars and Issas. See Djibouti
Fresno, Calif., 145, 187
Freud, Sigmund, 293, 581, 677, 679
Friedan, Betty, 374, 685
Friendly Islands, 877
Friends (Quakers), 363
Frobisher Bay, 484
Frost, Robert, 684

Fruit:
U.S. consumption of, **640**
U.S. export and import of, **639**
Fuel. See also specific fuels
average prices, **641**
export and import of, **639**
Producer Price Index, **637**
Fujimori, Alberto, 843–844
Funafuti, Tuvalu, 881
Fundamental Orders of Connecticut,
102, 146
Fur, export and import of, 639
Furniture:
export and import of, **639**
Producer Price Index, **637**

G

Gabon, 775–776
Gaborone, Botswana, 736
Gadsden Purchase, 96, 104, 105, 144, 163
Gagarin, Yuri A., 429, 684, 851
Galápagos Islands, 485, 763
Galaxy, 398
Galilee, Sea of, 797
Galileo (astronomer), 293, 399, 579, 582, 670
Galileo space program, 426
Gambia, The, 776
Gambia River, 484, 776
Gambier Island, 774
Gambling, 161, 163, 390, 825
Game software, 568
Gandhi, Indira, 293, 689, 789
Gandhi, Mohandas K., 293, 679, 682, 788
Ganges River, 495, 729, 788
Gang of 14, 33, 40, 1031
"Gang of Four", 687, 748
Garang, John, 34
Garfield, James A., 53, 55, 57, 64–65, 97. See also Presidents, U.S.
assassination of, 65, 97, 119, 676
Gas, natural, 639
Gas reserves, 585
Gates, Bill, 294
Gator Bowl, 936
Gautama, Buddha, 364
Gay rights organization, first, 101
Gays, 40, 44, 373, 701, 744
Gaza Strip, 34, 36, 42, 43, 509, 686, 700, 764, 797, 798, 841
GDPs per capita, world's highest and lowest, 703
Gemini space flights, 427
Gemstones, 359
Gender Issues, 371–375
General Assembly, UN, 907
General educational development (GED), 320
General Services Administration (GSA), 84
Generator, electric, 579
Genetic fingerprinting, 583
Genetics, 371–373
Genetics (heredity), 579, 675
Geneva, Lake, 872
Geneva, Switzerland, 679, 872
Geneva Conference (1954), 685
Genghis Khan, 294, 667, 718
Genocide, 680
Geographic centers:
of states, 142–177
of U.S., 500
Geographic Society, National, 657
Geography, 484–504
caves and caverns, 497
coastline of U.S., 502
Continental Divide, 500
continents, 487
of countries, 718–906
deserts, 498
elevations, 487
explorations, 484–485

glossary of terms, **485**
islands, **496**
map projections, **486**
mountain peaks, **493**
national parks, 590–594, 594
oceans and seas, **494**
rivers, 495, 500–501
volcanoes, 488–489
waterfalls, **496**
world, 702
Geological periods, 576–577
Geometric formulas, 459
Geometry, 579
Georgetown, Guyana, 784
Georgia (U.S. state), 148
Georgia, Republic of, 776–777
Germany, 777–779
history of, 777–779
Nazi regime, 679, 680, 778
reconstruction of, 682
reunification of, 691, 779
rulers of, 777
in World War I, 678, 778
in World War II, 681, 778
Geronimo, 144, 163, 294, 676
Gestation periods, animals, 588
Gettysburg, Battle of, 119, 169, 675
Gettysburg Address, 119
Ghana, 779–780
Ghent, Treaty of, 61, 673
Ghraib, Abu, 39
Gibbons v. *Ogden,* 93
Gideon v. *Wainwright ,* 93
Gift taxes, federal, 1025, 1027
Gilbert Islands, 805, 833. See also Kiribati
Ginsburg, Ruth Bader, 92, 692
Giotto probes, 426
Girl Scouts of U.S.A., 657
Giza, Great Pyramid, 746
Glacier National Park, 160, 590
Glasgow, Scotland, 884, 890
Glenn, John, 422
Glenn, John H., Jr., 99, 427, 428, 685
Globe, 486
"Glorious Revolution", 670
Gobi Desert, 498, 747
Gods and goddesses, 468–472
Godthaab, Greenland, 760
Golan Heights, 686, 764, 797, 873
Gold:
chemical properties of, 574
karat (measure of purity), 458
as monetary standard, 676
terminology, 458
Gold Coast. See Ghana
Golden Gate Bridge, 145, 447, 448
Golden Globe Awards, 251
Golden Temple (India), 689, 789
Gold Rush:
in Alaska, 143
in California, 145, 200, 674
in Idaho, 150
Golf, 995–998
British Open Champions, **997**
history of, **994**
L.P.G.A. tour winners, **998**
Masters Tournament winners, **995**
other tour winners, **998**
U.S. Amateur Champions, 996, 997
U.S. Open Champions, 995–996, 997
U.S. P.G.A. Champions, **996**
Gonzales, Alberto, 36, 294, 506, 1032
González, Elián, 696, 697
Good Friday, 346, 355, 357n
Good Friday Peace Accord, 695, 696, 697, 796, 887, 888, 889
Good Hope, Cape of, 484, 865
Gorbachev, Mikhail S., 225, 294, 689, 691, 851
Gore, Albert A., Jr., 55, 56, 58
Gospels, 361, 665
Göta Canal, 451
Gothic architecture, 446
Goths, 666

Gotland, Sweden, 871
Government Accountability Office (GAO), 84
Government Printing Office (GPO), 84
Governments:
  foreign heads of state, 718–906
  of U.S.. *See* United States government
  world, 718–906
Governors, 49
  first black, 101
  first woman, 102, 177, 679
  of Puerto Rico, 895
  of U.S. states, 142–177
  of U.S. territories, 895–898
Grain, U.S. export and import of, 639. *See also* specific grains
Grammar, 473–475
Grammy Awards, 253–254
Grams (measure), 456, 458
Grand Canal, 451
Grand Canyon, 144
Grand Canyon National Park, 590, 594
Grand Coulee Dam, 175
Grand Prix (auto racing), 1001
Grand Teton National Park, 590, 594
Grant, Ulysses S., 53, 57, 64, 97, 675. *See also* Presidents, U.S.
Gravitation, law of, 579
Great Arabian Desert, 498
Great Bear Lake, 494
Great Britain, 496
Great Lakes, 494
Great Salt Lake, 173, 494, 674
Great Seal of U.S., 103
Great Slave Lake, 494
Great Smoky Mountains National Park, 165, 172, 590, 594
Great Sphinx of Egypt, 445, 663
Great Wall of China, 446, 665, 747
Greece, 780–781
Greece, ancient, 663, 665, 781, 917
  mythology, 468–471
  Persian Wars, 665
  structures, 445
Greek word elements, 481–482
Greenback Party, 53
Greeneville (submarine), 697
Greenhouse gases, 585, 587
Greenland, 484, 496, 666, 760
Green Mountain Boys, 174
Green River (Ky.), 500
Green River (Wyo.-Utah), 500
Greensboro sit-in, 383
Greenwich time, 352
Gregorian calendar, 350
Grenada, 781
  U.S. military intervention in, 689, 782
Griswold v. *Connecticut*, 374
Gromyko, Andrei A., 295
Gross domestic product, 633, 718–906
  by country, 712
  world's highest and lowest, 703
Groundhog Day, 346, 355
Group of Eight, 41, 910
Guadalcanal, 864
Guadalupe Hidalgo, Treaty of, 96
Guadalupe Mountains National Park, 172
Guadeloupe, 772
Guam, 896
Guantánamo Bay, Cuba, 39, 701, 507
Guatemala, 782–783
Guatemala City, Guatemala, 782
Guernsey, 892
Guevara, Ché, 734, 757
Guiana, British. *See* Guyana
Guiana, Dutch. *See* Suriname
Guiana, French, 772
Guinea (Republic), 783
Guinea, Portuguese. *See* Guinea-Bissau
Guinea, Spanish. *See* Equatorial Guinea

Guinea-Bissau, 783–784
Gulf of Tonkin Resolution, 98, 685, 686
Gulf War, 100, 691, 693, 794, 808
Gunpowder, invention of, 579
Guns, 135, 388, 390
Gunter's chain (measure), 455
Gupta dynasty, 666
Gutenberg, Johann, 295, 581, 668
Guthrie, Woody, 684
Guyana, 784–785
Gyanendra (king of Nepal), 36, 1032
Gymnastics, 929
Gyrocompass, 579
Gyroscope, 579

H

Habibie, B. J., 791
Hague Conventions, 677
Haider, Jörg, 726
Haile Selassie I (emperor of Ethiopia), 295, 768
Hailstone, largest, 597
Haiti, 673, 692, 700, 785
  U.S. military intervention in, 785
Haleakala National Park, 590
Hale-Bopp comet, 694
Halicarnassus, Mausoleum at, 447
Halley's comet, 415, 690
Halliburton, 41
Hall of Fame:
  Baseball, 165, 1003–1004
  Country Music, 278
  Football (college), 937–941
  Football (professional), 167, 946–948
  Inventors, 583
  Rock and Roll, 167, 277
Halloween, 346, 356
Hallucinogens, 560
Hamas, 716
Hambletonian, 993
Hamburg, Germany, 777
Hamilton, Alexander, 60, 85, 295, 673
Hammarskjöld, Dag, 295, 683, 907
Hammurabi, Code of, 663
Han dynasty, 666
Hanging as death penalty, 387
Hanging Gardens of Babylon, 447, 664
Hannibal, 295, 665
Hanoi, Vietnam, 902
Hanover, House of, 885
Hanukkah, 346, 357
Happiness, 537–551
Hapsburg, House of, 726, 786
Harare, Zimbabwe, 906
Harding, Warren G., 54, 57, 66–67, 98. *See also* Presidents, U.S.
Hariri, Rafik, 34, 36, 43, 509, 812, 1036
Harness racing, 992–994
Harper's Ferry raid, 674
Harrisburg, Pa., 168, 178
Harrison, Benjamin, 53, 55, 57, 65, 97. *See also* Presidents, U.S.
Harrison, William Henry, 52–53, 57, 62, 96. *See also* Presidents, U.S.
Hartford, Conn., 146, 178
Hart Trophy, 963
Harvard University, 101, 322
Harvest, Feast of, 356, 357n
Hashemite Kingdom. *See* Jordan
Hastings, Battle of, 667, 885
Hate crime statistics, 389
Havana, Cuba, 756
Hawaii, 149
  discovery of, 672
  volcanoes in, 149
Hawaiians, 379
Hawaii Volcanoes National Park, 149, 590
Hayes, Rutherford B., 53, 55, 57, 64, 97. *See also* Presidents, U.S.
Haymarket Riots, 676
Headline history, 663–701

Health, 552–562
  AIDS, 555
  best hospitals, 562
  blood pressure, 562
  blood types, 562
  body mass index, 553
  cancer, 556
  drug use, 560
  exercise, 554
  expenditures, 558
  insurance, 558
  obesity, 553
  organ transplants, 559
  smoking, 561
Health, Education, and Welfare, U.S. Dept. of. *See also* Education, U.S. Dept. of; Health and Human Services, U.S. Dept. of
  secretaries of, 89
Health and Human Services, U.S. Dept. of:
  description of, 83
  secretaries of, 83, 89–90
Health insurance, 558
Heaney, Seamus, 693
Heard Island, 726
Hearst, Patricia, 687
Heart, human:
  first artificial, 685, 689
  transplants, 686
Heath, Edward, 886
Heaven's Gate cult, 694
Hebrew Pentecost, 356, 357n
Hebrides, 890
Hectares, 452, 456
Hegira (Hijra), 363, 666
Heisman Memorial Trophy, 937
Helena, Mont., 159, 178
Helicopters:
  first flights of, 437
  invention of, 437, 579
  records, 439
Helium:
  chemical properties of, 574
  discovered on sun, 579
  first use in balloon, 436
Helsinki, Finland, 769
Hemisphere, 486
Henry the Navigator (prince of Portugal), 668
Heredity, 579, 675
Heritage Areas, National, 594
Heritage Corridors, National, 594
Hermitage, The (Andrew Jackson's home), 172
Heroin, 560
Herschel Space Observatory, 424
Herto man, 570
Herzegovina, 734–736
Hezbollah, 716
Hides:
  export and import of, 639
  Producer Price Index, 637
Higher education, 321, 323–345
Highest points:
  U.S., 503
  world, 487
High school:
  dropout rates, 320
  enrollment, 320
  percentage graduated, 319
Hijackings, 687, 689
Hijra. *See* Hegira
Hillary, Sir Edmund, 297, 492, 683
Himalayas, 788, 789, 831
Hindenburg (zeppelin), 219
Hindenburg, Paul von, 297, 315, 778
Hinduism, 364
  calendar, 354
  festival dates, 358
Hindu Kush range, 718
Hippocrates, 665
Hirohito (emperor of Japan), 297, 690
Hiroshima, 681, 682, 801
Hispanics:
  births, 130, 131
  population, 378, 381

Hispaniola, 496, 761, 785
Hiss, Alger, 682
Historical parks and sites, U.S., 591, 592–593, 594
Historic Area, National, 594
Historic Trails, National, 594
History, Pulitzer Prizes for, 242–243
History, U.S. *See* United States history
History, world, 663–701
 by country, 718–906
 explorations, 484–485
 Seven Wonders, 447
Hitler, Adolf, 297, 679, 681, 778
Hittite civilization, 663, 664
HIV. *See* AIDS
Ho Chi Minh, 685, 903
Ho Chi Minh City, Vietnam, 902
Hockey, ice, 962–965
 history of, 962
 NHL trophy winners, 963–964
 Olympic Games, 932
 professional, 962–965
Hokkaido, Japan, 496, 801
Holidays, 355–357
 Christian and secular, 357
 Hindu, 358
 Islamic, 355–357
 Jain, 358
 Jewish, 357
 national, by country, 359
 Orthodox, 357
 religious and secular (2006), 355–357
 Sikh, 358
 state, 358
Holland. *See* Netherlands
Hollywood, 145
Holocaust, 680
Holocene Period, 577
Holy Roman Empire, 666, 669, 778
Holy Saturday, 357n
Homeland Security, U.S. Dept. of, 32, 42, 75
 description of, 83
 secretaries of, 83
Homeownership, 125, 126
Homer, 297, 664
Home run records, 1010–1011, 1012–1013, 1017
Home sales, 618, 619
Homestead Act, 97
Homestead Strike, 676
Homicide, 388. *See also* Murder
Hominids, 572
Homo erectus, 572
Homo sapiens sapiens, 572
Homosexuality, 373
 firsts in U.S., 101
 same-sex unions, 696
 societies and associations, 657
 in U.S. armed forces, 692
Honduras, 785–786
Honduras, British. *See* Belize
Hong Kong, 749
Honiara, Solomon Islands, 863
Honolulu, Hawaii, 149, 178, 187–188
Honshu, Japan, 496, 801
Hood, Mount, 168, 503
Hoover, Herbert, 54, 57, 58, 67, 98, 152. *See also* Presidents, U.S.
Hoover Dam, 144, 162, 450
 Lake Mead, 594
Horace, 665
Horn, Cape, 485, 746
Horse racing, 979–982
 Belmont Stakes, 981, 982
 Eclipse Awards, 982
 harness racing, 992–994
 history of, 979
 Kentucky Derby, 153, 676, 980, 982
 Preakness Stakes, 980, 982
 Triple Crown, 979, 982
Hospitals, highest rated, 562
Hostages, American, 688, 689, 690, 692
Hot-air balloons. *See* Balloons
Hot Springs National Park, 144, 590

Hottest weather, 597, 598
Households, 125
 income, 626
 by size, 1790–2003, **125**
 by type, 125, 126
House of Burgesses, 101
House of Representatives, U.S., 109, 112. *See also* Congress, U.S.
 apportionment of, 80, 109, 116
 committees of, 77
 eligibility for, 109
 first black member of, 101
 first woman member of, 102
 members, 47–49
 salaries of representatives, 80
 shooting on floor of, 683
 Speakers of, 78
Housing and Urban Development, U.S. Dept. of:
 description of, 83
 secretaries of, 83, 89–90
Housing prices, 618, 619
Houston, Tex., 172, 178, 188
Houston Canal, 451
Howland Island, 898
Hsi River (Si Kiang). *See* Xi Jiang
Huang He (Yellow River), , 495, 747
Hubble Space Telescope, 431, 433, 434, 691
Hudson, Henry, 147, 164
Hudson Bay, 484, 494, 742
Hudson River, 164, 196, 484
Hudson's Bay Company, 742
Huguenots, 669, 671
Hu Jintao, 38, 699, 749
Human ancestors, 572, 663, 674, 679
Human development index (U.N.), 710
Humphrey, Hubert H., 58
"Hundred Days", 673
Hundred Years' War, 770, 885
Hungary, 786–787
 1956 uprisings, 787
Hunger, 631
Huns. *See* Mongols
Hun Sen, 741
Huron, Lake, 157, 494, 742
Hurricanes, 44, 211, 214–215, 701
 costliest, 595
 deadliest, 595
 Katrina, 32, 33, 43, 101, 214, 505, 595, 596, 1031
 most intense, 596
 names, Atlantic, 595
 names, retired, 596
Hus, Jan, 668
Hussein (king of Jordan), 297, 802
Hussein, Saddam, 39, 297, 691, 700, 793–795, 808
Hyde Park, N.Y., 164
Hydrogen:
 chemical properties of, 574
 first use in balloon, 435
 heavy hydrogen, 579, 680
 hydrogen bomb, 683, 684, 851
Hyphen (punctuation), 475

I

i.e./e.g., 478
Ibn Batuta, 485
Ice hockey. *See* Hockey, ice
Iceland, 666, 787
 area of, 496
 exploration of, 484
Ice skating. *See* Skating
Idaho, 149–150
Ikhnaton, 664
Iliad (Homer), 664
Illinois, 150–151
Illinois River, 500
Immigration, 381, 382
Impeachment, 90, 110, 113
 of Andrew Johnson, 64, 90, 97
 of Bill Clinton, 74, 91, 100, 695
 of Richard Nixon, 70, 687

Imperial gallon, 457
Imports:
 of U.S., 638, 639
 of world, 718–906
Incas, 668, 669, 734, 746, 763, 844
Income. *See also* Cities, U.S.
 by education, 321
 family, 627
 gap between men and women, 375
 household, 628
 median income, U.S., 627, 628
 per capita, 626, 628
 per household, 626
 by race, 626
 by state, 628
 weekly, 621
Income inequality, world, 711
Income tax, by country, 712
Income tax, federal, 1024–1026
 brackets, 1026
 collection of, 1025, 1026, 1028
 established, 116, 675, 1024
 withholding for, 682
Incubation periods, animals, 588
Independence, Declaration of, 107–108
Independence Day, 346, 356
Independence Hall, 103, 169
India, 41, 729, 788–790, 838
 British control of, 671, 674, 885
 independence of, 682
 Sikh rebellion in, 689, 789
 structures, 446
 Taj Mahal, 670
Indiana, 151
Indianapolis, Ind., 151, 178, 188–189
Indianapolis "500", 515, 998–999
Indian Ocean, 494
 islands, 496
Indian Removal Act, 96
Indians (American):
 Aztecs, 668, 823
 Incas, 668, 734, 746, 763, 844
 languages, 381
 Mayans, 666
 population of, 379
 reservations, 144, 380
 tribes, 379
 wars, 392
Indochina. *See* Cambodia; Laos; Vietnam
Indonesia, 38, 790–791
 Aceh peace accord, 791
Indus River, 495, 788, 838
Industrial Revolution, 672
Indus Valley civilization, 663, 664
IndyCar champions, 1001
Indy Racing League, 1001
Infantile paralysis. *See* Poliomyelitis
Infant mortality, 138, 556
Infant mortality rates, 703, 707
Inflation:
 by country, 712–713
 world's highest and lowest, 703
Influenza, 211, 213, 679
"Information Please" quiz show, 101
Ingathering, Feast of, 356, 357n
"In God We Trust", 119
Inini, 772
Inquisition, 668, 670
Institute of Medicine, U.S., 85
Insulin, 229, 231, 580, 687
Insurance:
 health, 558
Intelligence testing, 580
Inter-American Foundation, 84
Interior, U.S. Dept. of:
 description of, 83
 secretaries of, 83, 86–90
Internal Revenue Service, 1024–1025. *See also* Taxes
International adoptions, 133
International Court of Justice, UN, 907
International Date Line, 352, 486
International Monetary Fund, 682
International Organizations, 910

U.S. contributions to, **637**
International Relations, 907–916
International Space Station, 428, 429, 433
International Trade Commission, U.S., 84
Internet:
access, **564, 565**
activities, **565**
advertisers, **567**
connection types, **564**
iPod playlists, **276**
music sales, **275**
search engines, **567**
shopping, **565**
sites, **566**
top websites, **566**
usage worldwide, **567**
use, **564**
Internment, Japanese Americans, 681, 682
Interplanetary probes, 425–427
Interracial couples, 383
Inuit, 143
Inventions, 578–582
Inventors, Hall of Fame, 583
Investment, U.S. abroad, 636–637
Iolani Palace, 149
Ionosphere, 402
Iowa, 151–152
Iran, 35, 37, 511, 791–793
hostage crisis, **99, 688, 792**
Khomeini, Ayatollah Ruhollah, **792**
shah of (Mohammad Reza Pahlavi), **792**
war with Iraq, **688, 792, 793**
Iran-Contra affair, 100, 690, 692
Iraq, 32, 39, 43, 688, 691, 793–795
2005 elections, **36, 508, 795**
constitution, **41, 43, 795**
National Assembly, **37, 38, 39, 43, 795, 1032**
U.S. air strikes on, **695**
war with Iran, **688, 792**
war with U.S. (2003), **793–795**
Iraq war (2003), 32, 35, 41, 44, 75, 101, 393, 508, 699, 700, 793–795
intelligence failures, **725, 794, 795, 888**
Ireland, Northern, 796, 885, 888–890
Ireland, Republic of, 496, 678, 795–796
Irian Jaya, 790–791
Irish Republican Army (IRA), 36, 38, 42, 688, 693, 698, 796, 888
Iron:
chemical properties of, **574**
export and import of, **639**
"Iron Curtain", 682
Irrawaddy River, 495, 828
Irtish River, 495
Islam, 363–364
calendar, **354**
holidays, **355–357**
largest Muslim countries, **364**
Sunni and Shi'ite, **364**
Islamabad, Pakistan, 838
Islands, 496
Isle of Man, 893
Isotopes of elements, 574–575, 580
Israel, 796–799
ancient, **664, 797**
Balfour Declaration, **678**
Entebbe rescue, **687**
Gaza withdrawal, **34, 43, 700, 798, 841**
independence of, **682, 797**
intifada, **798, 840**
invasion of Lebanon, **688, 811**
security barrier, **34, 701, 798**
settlements, **38**
wars with Arabs, **684, 686, 687, 688, 698, 763–765, 793, 797–799, 802, 811, 857, 873, 879**
Israel, ancient, 360
Israel, kings of, 467–468

Istanbul, Turkey, 879. *See also* Constantinople
Italicization, rules for, 474
Italy, 799–800. *See also* Roman Empire
structures, **445–446**
unification of, **674**
in World War I, **678**
in World War II, **681**
Ivan IV ("the Terrible"), 669
Ivory Coast. *See* Côte d'Ivoire

J

Jaafari, Ibrahim, 36, 793, 795, 1032
Jackson, Andrew, 52, 57, 61–62, 96, 170, 172. *See also* Presidents, U.S.
Jackson, Michael, 41, 513, 1032
Jackson, Miss., 158, 178
Jacksonville, Fla., 147, 178, 189
Jack the Ripper, 676
Jain festival dates, 358
Jakarta, Indonesia, 790
Jamaica, 800–801
James River, 500
Jamestown, 95
Jamestown, Va., 174, 484, 670
Jammu, 788
Japan, 44
and China, **676, 680, 681, 748, 801**
exploration of, **484**
islands of, **496, 801**
open to foreigners, **669, 674**
and Russia, **677, 801, 851**
space program, **424, 426**
structures, **446–447**
war trial, **682**
in World War I, **678, 801**
in World War II, **681**
World War II peace treaty of, **683**
Japan, Sea of, 494, 801
Japanese-American internment, 681, 682
Japurá River, 495
Jarvis Island, 898
Java, 496, 790. *See also* Indonesia
Java man, 572
Jeanne-Claude, 516, 1031
Jefferson, Thomas, 52, 56, 57, 60, 96, 103, 107, 672. *See also* Presidents, U.S.
birthday, **358**
Jefferson City, Mo., 159, 178
Jeffords, Jim, 697
Jennings, Peter, 1037
Jenolan Caves, 497
Jersey (island), 892
Jerusalem, 360, 664, 665, 666, 796, 802
Jesus Christ, 361, 665
Jet propulsion:
first use in aviation, **437**
invention of, **580**
Jewelry, birthstones, 359
Jewish holidays, 355–357
Jewish New Year, 356, 357n
Jews. *See* Judaism
Jiang Zemin, 699
Jin Mao Building (Shanghai), 444
Joan of Arc, 298, 668
John Paul II, Pope, 39, 512, 1037
Johnson, Andrew, 53, 57, 64, 90, 97. *See also* Presidents, U.S.
impeachment of, **64, 90, 97**
Johnson, Lyndon B., 54, 57, 58, 69, 99. *See also* Presidents, U.S.
Johnson, Philip, 518, 1037
Johnston Atoll, 898
Johnstown flood (1889), 211, 213, 676
Joint Chiefs of Staff, 83, 394
Joliet, Louis, 150, 152, 157, 171
Jones, Brian, 439
Jones, Marion, 922, 959
Jordan, 43, 802–803

and Israel, **802**
Jordan, Michael, 953, 954, 959
Jordan, Vernon E., Jr., 119
Journalism:
best American of century, **270–272**
Pulitzer Prizes for, **234–247**
Journalists, deadliest countries for, 280
Juan Fernández Islands, 746
Judah, kings of, 467–468
Judaism, 360
calendar, **354**
holidays, **355–357**
Judiciary, U.S., 113. *See also* Supreme Court, U.S.
Judiciary Act of 1789, 101
Judo, 929
Julian calendar, 350
Juneau, Alaska, 143, 178
Jupiter (planet), 401, 406–409. *See also* Planets
exploration of, **425–427**
Jura Mountains, 576, 872
Jurassic Period, 576
Jury trial, 113, 115, 689
Justice, U.S. Dept. of:
attorneys general, **83, 85–90**
description of, **83**
Justices. *See* Supreme Court, U.S.
Justinian Code, 666
Justinian I ("the Great"), 666
Jutland, Battle of, 678

K

Kabbah, Ahmad Tejan, 861
Kabila, Laurent, 697, 753
Kabul, Afghanistan, 718
Kampala, Uganda, 882
Kanawha-New River, 500
Kansas, 152–153
Kansas City, Mo., 159, 178, 189–190
climate of, **601**
Kansas-Nebraska Act, 674
Kansas River, 500
Karafuto. *See* Sakhalin
Kara Kum Desert, 498
Karat (measure), 458
Karzai, Hamid, 701, 718
Kashmir, 38, 789, 839
Kathmandu, Nepal, 830
Katrina, hurricane, 32, 33, 43, 44, 101, 154, 195, 214, 505, 595, 596, 1031
Kay, David, 700, 794
Keller, Helen, 142
Kellogg-Briand Pact, 680
Kelly, Grace, 517
Kelvin (scale), 455
Kennan, George, 1037
Kennedy, Edward M., 71, 77, 686
Kennedy, John F., 54, 55, 57, 58, 68–69, 99, 684. *See also* Presidents, U.S.
assassination of, **68, 99, 119, 685**
Warren Report, **686**
Kennedy, Robert F., 89, 686
assassination of, **99, 119**
Kennedy Center Honors, 262–263
Kennedy International Airport, 164
Kennedy Space Center, 148
Kent's Cavern, 497
Kent State University, 686, 688
Kentucky, 153
Kentucky Derby, 153, 676, 980, 982
Kenya, 804–805
Kepler, Johannes, 299, 399, 415, 581, 670
Kerry, John F., 45, 55, 700, 701
Key, Francis Scott, 96, 103, 106, 155, 182, 299
Khan, A. Q., 700
Khan, Abdul Qadeer, 839
Khartoum, Sudan, 676, 868
Khatami, Mohammad, 698, 792

Khmer Republic. *See* Cambodia
Khmer Rouge, 741
Khodorkovsky, Mikhail, 40, 1032
Khomeini, Ayatollah Ruhollah, 688, 690, 792
Khrushchev, Nikita, 69, 299, 684, 851
Kiel Canal, 451
Kiev (Kyiv), Ukraine, 883
Kigali, Rwanda, 853
Kilimanjaro, Mount, 487, 493
Killen, Edgar Ray, 384
Kilograms, 452, 455, 457, 458
Kilometers, 452, 456
Kim Jong II, 805–806
King, Coretta Scott, book awards, 257
King, Rev. Martin Luther, Jr., 181, 299, 383, 384, 684, 686
assassination of, 99, 119
King, Rodney, 692
Kingdoms, 710
King Jong II, 511
Kingman Reef, 898
Kings:
of England, **886**
of France, 771
of Judah and Israel, 467–468
of Russia, 851
Kingsley Tufts Poetry Prize, 258
Kingston, Jamaica, 800
Kingstown, St. Vincent and the Grenadines, 855
Kinshasa, Congo, 752
Kiribati, 805
Kissinger, Henry A., 89–90, 225, 299, 748, 903
Kitty Hawk, N.C., 165, 435, 677
Kiwanis International, 658
Kjölen Mountains, 871
Knights of Columbus, 658
Know-Nothing Party, 55n
Knox, John, 299, 669
Kohl, Helmut, 779
Kohoutek (comet), 415
Koizumi, Junichiro, 44, 801, 802
Koran (Qur'an), 363
Korea, North, 35, 36, 39, 42, 44, 76, 511, 700, 805–806. *See also* Korean War
Korea, South, 43, 511, 806–807. *See also* Korean War
Korean Airlines Incident (1983), 689
Korean War, 98, 683, 806
casualties, 396
Koror, Palau, 839
Kosciusko, Mount, 487, 725
Kosovo, 695, 860
Kosovo casualties, 393
Kostunica, Vojislav, 860
Kosygin, Aleksei N., 299, 851
Koyukuk River, 500
Kozlowski, L. Dennis, 699
Krakatau, 212
Kremlin (structure), 446
Kuala Lumpur, Malaysia, 818
tallest buildings, 444
Kublai Khan, 300, 668, 748, 826
Kuiper Belt Objects, 571
Ku Klux Klan, 679, 697
Kunlun Mountains, 747
Kuomintang, 748, 874
Kuril Islands, 801, 851
Kuskokwim River, 500
Kuwait, 39, 40, 808
Kuwait (city), Kuwait, 808
Kwanzaa, 357
Kyoto protocol, 37, 697, 698
Kyrgyzstan, 808–809
Kyushu, Japan, 801
Kyzyl Kum Desert, 498

L

Labor. *See also* Employment
civilian labor force in U.S. cities, 180–204
farm and non-farm, **622**
historical figures, **622**
leading unions, 625
National Labor Relations Board, 84
statistics, 619–624
strikes, 624
unions, 42
women, 624
Labor, U.S. Dept. of:
description of, 83
secretaries of, 83, 87–89
Labor Day, 346, 356, 357
Labor force:
civilian, 120
median age of, 625
persons in, 622
projections, 619–620
women in, 371–373, 375, 624
Labor organizations, 625
Labrador, 484, 742
Labrador, Canada, 743
Lady Byng Trophy, 964
Lagos, Nigeria, 835
Lakes. *See specific lakes*
Lakeshores, National, 593
"Lame Duck" Amendment, 98, 117
Lamps, electric incandescent, 579
Lancaster, House of, 885
Land area:
of countries, 705–706, 718–906
largest countries, 703
smallest countries, 703
of states, 142–177, 178
of U.S. cities, 180–204
of world, 487
Land rush, 167
Languages:
American Sign Language, 483
basic phrases in other languages, 478
Braille, 483
foreign spoken, in U.S., 381
foreign words and phrases, 479–481
most studied, U.S., 476
most widely spoken, 476
use by country, 718–906
Lansing, Mich., 156, 178
Laos, 809–810
Lao-tse, 300, 664, 747
La Paz, Bolivia, 733
Larceny, 390
La Salle, Robert Cavelier, Sieur de, 151, 152, 154, 157, 159, 166, 171, 172
Laser, invention of, 580
Lassen Peak, 145
Last names, most common in U.S., 140
Las Vegas, Nev., 161, 178, 190
Lateran Treaty, 680, 901
Latin America. *See specific countries*
Latinos, 378, 381
Latin word elements, 481–482
Latitude, 485
Latitudes of cities, 499, 504
Latvia, 682, 691, 810–811
Lausanne, Switzerland, 872
Lava, 488
Law:
codes of, 663, 666, 673
first unconstitutional, 93, 101
Law, Cardinal Bernard, 699
Law enforcement, 385–391. *See also* Arrests; Crime; Prisoners
corruption, prosecutions for, 387
officers killed or assaulted, 387
Laws. *See* Bills (Congressional)
Lawyers, first woman, 102
Lay, Kenneth L., 698
Lead, 574
Lead poisoning, 587

League of Nations, 679, 680, 681, 682, 778, 872, 873
Leaning Tower of Pisa, 446
Lebanon, 34, 36, 40, 509, 811–812
civil war in, 811
Israeli invasion of, 688, 811
terrorism in, 688
U.S. military action in, 684
Lee, Robert E., 97, 300, 675
birthday, 358
Leeward Islands. *See* British Virgin Islands; Montserrat
Lefkosia (Nicosia), Cyprus, 757
Lefkow, Joan Humphrey, 37, 1032
Legal holidays, 358
Legionnaire's disease, 687
Legislatures, state:
only unicameral, 161
Legislatures, world:
by country, 718–906
oldest, 787
Lena River, 495
Lend-Lease, 682
Length, units of, 454, 456
metric system, 452, 456
Lenin, Vladimir, 300, 678, 679, 850
Leningrad, 850. *See also* St. Petersburg, Russia
Lens, bifocal, 580
Lent, 355
Leonardo da Vinci, 301, 668
Leopold-Loeb case, 679
Lepanto, Battle of, 669
Lesotho, 812–813
Lethal injection as death penalty, 387
Letters:
postal rates since 1847, 442
postal regulations, 440–442
Lewis and Clark expedition, 150, 152, 160, 166, 168, 171, 175, 484, 673
Lexington-Concord, Battle of, 156, 671
Lexington-Fayette, Ky., 153, 178
Liberia, 813
Liberty, Statue of, 164, 676
Liberty Bell, 103, 169
Libraries:
first circulating, 101
major public, 274
presidential, 58
Libraries and Information Science, National Commission on, 84
Library of Congress, 84
Libreville, Gabon, 775
Libya, 689, 813–814
Licenses:
drivers, 608
Lidice, Czechoslovakia, 681
Lie, Trygve, 907
Liechtenstein, 814–815
Life expectancy, 136, 137
highest and lowest, 703
selected countries, 707
Life on Earth, 576–577
Light:
discoveries of, 580
velocity of, 400, 580
Lightning, 596
Lightning rods, 580
Light-years, 400
Lilongwe, Malawi, 818
Lima, Peru, 843
Lincoln, Abraham, 53, 55, 57, 63–64, 97, 150. *See also* Presidents, U.S.
assassination of, 64, 119, 675
Gettysburg Address, 119
home of, 150
Lincoln-Douglas debates, 674
Lincoln, Neb., 160, 178
Lincoln's Birthday, 346, 355
Lindbergh, Charles A., 98, 301, 436, 679, 680
Lindh, John Walker, 698
Linear measures, 454, 456
Linotype machines, 581
Lions Clubs International, 658

Liquid measures, 452, 454, 457
Liquor. See also Prohibition
  export and import of, 639
  law violations, 390
  taxes, 1025
Lisbon, Portugal, 847
  earthquake in (1755), 211, 671
Literature:
  authors. See People
  prizes for, 226, 241–245, 255, 258
Liters, 452, 456, 457, 458
Lithium, 575
Lithography, 581
Lithuania, 682, 691, 815–816
Little Big Horn, Battle of, 97, 160, 676
Little Brown Jug (harness racing), 993
Little League (baseball), 1002–1003
Little Missouri River, 501
Little Rock, Ark., 144, 178
"Little Rock Nine", 383
"Little White House", 148
Livestock, 639
Ljubljana, Slovenia, 863
Locarno Conferences, 679
Locke, John, 671
Locomotives, 580
Logan, Mount, 742
Logarithms, 578
Lomé, Togo, 877
London, England, 884
  bombings (2005), 34, 41, 42, 510, 888, 1033
  Great Fire of (1666), 217, 670
  Great Plague in, 670
  structures, 446
  subway system, 606
London, Tower of, 446
Long, Huey P., 301, 681
  assassination of, 119
Long Beach, Calif., 190–191
Longevity, 548–550
Longevity, of animals, 588
Long Island, Battle of, 671
Longitude, 485
Longitudes of cities, 499, 504
Looms, 580
Lord's Prayer, 685
Los Angeles, Calif., 145, 178, 191
  climate of, 601
Lots, Feast of, 355, 357n
Lott, Trent, 699
Louis, Joe, 959, 974
Louisiana, 153–154
  Hurricane Katrina, 154
Louisiana Purchase, 60, 96, 104, 105, 144, 146, 152, 157, 159, 160, 166, 167, 171, 177, 673
Louisville, Ky., 153
Louisville/Jefferson County, Ky., 191–192
Louis XIV (king of France), 770
Louis XVI (king of France), 672
Louvre, 446
Lowest points, U.S., 500, 503
Luanda, Angola, 721
"Lucy" (hominid), 572
Luge (sport), 933
Lumber and wood. See also Forests
  export and import of, 639
  Producer Price Index, 637
Lunar flights, 425–427
Lunar Orbiter program, 425
Lunar probes, 425–427
Lunation, 350
Luray Cavern, 497
Lusaka, Zambia, 905
Lusitania, 678
Luther, Martin, 301, 363, 669, 778
Lutherans, 363, 690
Luxembourg, 816
Luxembourg (city), Luxembourg, 816
Luzon, Philippines, 496, 845
Lydian civilization, 664

M

Maastricht Treaty, 692
Macao, 750
MacArthur, Douglas, 301, 680, 683, 801, 806
MacArthur, Ellen, 37
MacArthur Foundation Awards, 261
Maccabean revolt, 665
MacDonald, Ramsay, 301
Macedonia, Greece, 780
Macedonia, Republic of, 697, 698, 816–817
Machine guns, 580
Machinery:
  export and import of, 639
  inventions, 578–582
  Producer Price Index, 637
Machu Picchu (Peru), 447, 666
Mackenzie River, 484, 495, 742
Mackinac Straits Bridge, 157, 448
Macmillan, Harold, 302, 886
Madagascar, 496, 817–818
Madeira, Portugal, 847
Madeira River, 495
Madison, James, 52, 57, 60–61, 96.
  See also Presidents, U.S.
Madison, Wis., 176, 178
Madrid, Spain, 866
Magazines, 273
  awards for, 257
  circulation, 273
Magellan, Ferdinand, 302, 485, 669, 845
Magellan space project, 426
Maggiore, Lake, 872
Magna Carta, 667, 885
Magnesium, 575
Magnitude, earthquakes, 490–491
Mahabharata, 364
Mail:
  first airmail route, 101, 436
  postal regulations, 440–442
Maine, 154–155
Maine (battleship), 676, 756
Major, John, 887
Majorca, 867
Majuro, Marshall Islands, 821
Malabo, Equatorial Guinea, 765
Malagasy, 817
Malawi, 818
Malaya. See Malaysia
Malaysia, 818–819
Malcolm X, 119, 384, 686
Maldives, 819–820
Malé, Maldives, 819
Malenkov, Georgi M., 683
Mali, 820
Mali Empire, 668
Malta, 820–821
Mammals:
  Age of, 577
  endangered, 589
Mammoth Cave, 153, 497, 590
Man, Isle of, 893
Management and Budget, Office of, 82
Managua, Nicaragua, 833
Man Booker Prize, 255
Manchester, N.H., 162, 178
Manchu Dynasty, 670, 677, 748, 801
Manchukuo, 748, 801
Manchuria, 680, 748, 801
Mandela, Nelson, 691, 693, 866
Manganese, 575
Manhattan, 164, 195–196
Manhattan Project, 682
Manila, Philippines, 844
Manila Bay, Battle of, 676
Manitoba, Canada, 743
Manslaughter, 390n
Mantle (of Earth), 402

Manual Alphabet, American, 483
Manufacturing. See Business and economy
Mao Zedong (Tse-tung), 302, 683, 687, 747–749
Map projections, 486
Maps:
  of territorial expansion of U.S., 105
  time zones, 523
  world, 524–536
Maputo, Mozambique, 828
Marathon, Battle of, 665
Marathons, 1002
Marbury v. Madison, 93, 101
March on Washington, 384
Marconi, Guglielmo, 302, 677
Marcos, Ferdinand, 689, 690, 845
Mardi Gras, 195, 355, 357n
Marie Antoinette, 302, 672
Marijuana, 560
Marine Corps, U.S. See also Armed forces, U.S.
  actions, 678, 679, 684, 686, 689, 761, 834
  Commandant of, 83
Mariner space program, 425
Marne, Battles of the, 678
Marquesas Islands, 774
Marquette, Jacques, 150, 152, 157, 171
Marriage:
  median age at, 128
  mixed-race, 383
  percent never married, 128
  same-sex, 744
  statistics, U.S., 126, 128
Mars (planet), 401, 404–406, 407. See also Planets
  exploration of, 404–406, 423, 424
  rovers, 424
Mars Global Surveyor, 423
Marshall, John, 91, 302
Marshall, Thurgood, 376, 686
Marshall Islands, 821
Marshall Plan, 68, 98, 682
Mars Odyssey, 423
Martin, Paul, 744
Martinique, 773
Martin Luther King, Jr.'s Birthday, 346, 355
Marx, Karl, 302, 674, 675
Mary, Queen of Scots, 302, 670
Maryland, 155
Maseru, Lesotho, 812
Masoud, Ahmed Shah, 719
Mass:
  chemical elements, 574–575
  metric system, 455
Massachusetts, 156
Mass-energy theorem, 459, 579
Massive, Mount, 502
Masters Tournament (golf), 995
Mata-Utu, Wallis and Futuna Islands, 774
Mathematics:
  averages, 453
  awards for, 261
  decimals and fractions, 459
  formulas, 459
  mean and median, 453
  metric and U.S. equivalents, 452, 456–458
  prefixes and multiples, 459
  prime numbers, 453
Math scores, international comparisons, 318
Matisse, Henri, 677
Mauna Kea, 149, 503
Mauna Loa, 149
Maundy Thursday, 357n
Mauritania, 821–822
Mauritius, 822–823
Mawlid al-Nabi, 355, 357

Maximilian (emperor of Mexico), 303, 675, 823
Maxwell, James Clerk, 303, 580, 581
Mayaguez incident, 687
Mayans, 665, 666
Mayflower (ship), 670
Mayors, U.S., 180–204
Mayotte, 775
Mbabane, Swaziland, 870
McCarthy (Joseph) hearings, 99, 683
McDonald Islands, 726
McGwire, Mark, 959, 1017
McHenry, Fort, 106, 673
McKinley, Mount (Denali), 487, 500, 502, 503, 590
McKinley, William, 53, 57, 65, 97. *See also* Presidents, U.S.
  assassination of, 119, 677
McVeigh, Timothy, 224, 693, 694, 698
Mean and median, 453
Measures and weights, 452–459
  capacities and volumes, 454, 456, 456–458
  conversion factors, 452
  cooking, 458
Meat, 639, 640
Mecca, Saudi Arabia, 363, 666, 857
Medal of Freedom, 262
Medal of Honor, U.S., 396
Mede civilization, 664
Media:
  magazines, 273
  newspapers, 272
Media statistics, world, 717
Mediation and Conciliation Service (FMCS), Federal, 84
Mediation Board, National, 84
Medical care, Consumer Price Index, 638
Medicare program, 632, 686
Medicine, 552–562
  Albany Medical Center Prize, 263
  best hospitals, 562
  discoveries in, 578–582
  Nobel Prizes for, 231–233
Medina, Saudi Arabia, 363, 666, 857
Mediterranean Sea, 494, 665
Mein Kampf (Hitler), 679
Mekong River, 495, 902
Melting points, of elements, 574–575
Memorial Day, 346, 356
  Confederate, 358
Memorials, National, 593
Memphis, Tenn., 171, 178, 192
Mendelevium, 575
Mendelian Law, 579
Mensk (Minsk), Belarus, 730
Mercator projection, 486
Mercury (element), 575
Mercury (planet), 403, 407. *See also* Planets
  exploration of, 424
Mercury, Project, 427
Mercury-vapor lamp, 579
Meredith, James, 383, 685
Meridians, 485
Merrimac (ship), 675
Mesa, Ariz., 192–193
Mesa, Carlos, 40
Mesa Verde National Park, 146, 591
Mesopause, 402
Mesopotamia, 663, 664, 793
Mesosphere, 402
Mesozoic Era, 576
Messner, Reinhold, 492
Metals:
  as elements, 574–575
  export and import of, 639
  mineral wealth in countries, 718–906
  Producer Price Index, 637
Meteors and meteorites, 406, 416
  showers, 416
Meters (measure), 452, 456
Methodism and Methodists, 363, 672
Metric system, 455–458, 456–458
  conversion tables, 452, 456–458
Metropolitan Opera House, 676

Mexican Cession, 104, 105, 674, 823
Mexican War, 96, 144, 146, 160, 161, 163, 172, 173, 177, 674, 823
Mexico, 823–824
  ancient civilizations of, 665, 666
  conquest of, 484, 669, 823
  pre-Columbian cultures of, 664
  revolution in, 678, 823
  U.S. military actions in, 678, 823
Mexico, Gulf of, 494, 823
Mexico City, Mexico, 823
  subway system, 606
Miami, Fla., 147, 193
  climate of, 601
Michelangelo, 668
Michigan, 156–157
Michigan, Lake, 151, 157, 484, 494
Micronesia, 824
Microscope, compound, 580
Middle East, 687
  Arab-Israeli conflicts, 76, 684, 686, 688, 696, 697, 699, 700, 763–765, 793, 797–799, 798, 811, 857, 873, 879
  map of, 533
  peace talks, 797–799, 798
Midway Islands, 897–898
Mile records:
  runners, 985
Military, 392–397. *See* Armed forces, U.S.; National defense
Military budgets, world, 714
Military forces. *See* Armed forces, U.S.
Military Parks, National, 592
Military spending, 394
Milk, U.S. consumption of, 640
Milk River, 501
Milky Way, 398
Miller, Arthur, 518, 1038
Miller, Judith, 42, 1033
Million Man March, 693
Milosevic, Slobodan, 697, 698, 859, 860
Milton, John, 670
Milwaukee, Wis., 176, 178, 193–194
Mindanao, Philippines, 496, 845
Mindszenty, József Cardinal, 787
Mine disasters, 211, 217
Minerals. *See* Coal
Ming Dynasty, 670, 748
Minimum wage rates, 627
Minneapolis, Minn., 157, 178, 194
Minnesota, 157–158
Minoan culture, 663, 664
Minute Men, 156
Miquelon. *See* St. Pierre and Miquelon
Mir (space station), 429, 431
Miranda v. *Arizona*, 93
Mispronounced words, commonly, 476
Missile defense system, 36
Mississippi, 158–159
  civil rights workers slain in, 686
Mississippi-Missouri-Red Rock River, 495, 501
Mississippi River, 154, 158, 484, 495, 501
Missouri, 159
Missouri (battleship), 681
Missouri Compromise, 61, 96, 159, 673
Missouri-Red Rock River, 501
Missouri River, 495, 501
Mistletoe, 357
Mobile-Alabama-Coosa River, 501
Mogadishu, Somalia, 864
Mohammed, 666, 857. *See also* Muhammad
Mojave Desert, 498
Moldova, 824–825
Mole (measure), 455
Moluccas Islands, 790
Monaco, 825–826
Monarchies, 710
Mondale, Walter F., 55, 58

Money:
  coins, new U.S., 454
  of countries, 718–906
  designs of U.S. bills, 453
  and happiness, 546–547
  portraits on U.S. bills, 453
  value of dollar, 638
Mongolia, 484, 826
Mongols, 666, 668, 748, 850
Monitor (ship), 675
"Monkey Trial," 679
Monroe, James, 52, 57, 61, 96, 106. *See also* Presidents, U.S.
Monroe Doctrine, 61, 96, 106, 673
Monrovia, Liberia, 813
Montana, 159–160
Mont Blanc tunnel, 451
Monte Carlo, Monaco, 825
Montenegro, 859–860
Montevideo, Uruguay, 898
Montgomery, Ala., 142, 178
  bus boycott, 684
Months:
  birthstones, 359
  names of, 352
Monticello, Va., 60, 174
Montpelier, Vt., 173, 178
Montreal, Canada, 742
Montserrat, 893
"Monumental Mountain", 497
Monuments, National, 591
Moon:
  configurations (2006), 418–421
Moon (Earth's), 401
  Apollo space program, 428
  eclipses of, 421
  first staffed landing, 428, 686
  lunar probes, 425–427
Moons (satellites), 401, 406–413
  defined, 399
  orbits defined, 398
  phenomena (2006), 418–421
Moors, 668
Mormons, 173, 674
Moro, Aldo, 688
Morocco, 827
Moroni, Comoros, 751
Morrison, Toni, 692
Morse, Samuel F. B., 304, 582, 674
Mortality, 556. *See also* Death and dying
Mortality, infant, selected countries, 707
Moscow, Russia, 849
  subway system, 606
Moses, 664
Most Valuable Players:
  baseball, 1014
  basketball, 954
  hockey, 963
"Mother of Presidents", 174
Mother's Day, 346, 356
Mother Teresa, 694
Motion pictures:
  awards for, 247–251, 258
  best, 281
  inventions, 580
  top grosses, 281
Motorcycles, 580
Motor vehicles. *See also* Automobiles
  export and import of, 639
  theft of, 390
Mottoes:
  national, 119
  state, 142–177
Mountain climbing, 493
Mountains. *See also* names of mountains; Volcanoes
  "Seven Summits", 493
  in U.S., 502, 503
  world, 493
Mount Rainier National Park, 591
Mount Vernon, Va., 59, 174
Movies. *See* Motion pictures
Movie stars. *See* People
Mozambique, 827–828, 847
Mozart, Wolfgang Amadeus, 304, 672

Mubarak, Hosni, 43, 764
Mugabe, Robert, 906
Muhammad, 304, 363
Muharram, 354, 355, 357
Mulroney, Brian, 689, 743
Munich, Germany, 777
  Beer Hall Putsch (1923), 679
Munich Conference (1938), 681, 778
Murder, 388, 390
Murray River, 495
Muscat, Oman, 837
Museum, first science, 102
Museveni, Yoweri, 882
Musharraf, Pervez, 43, 838, 839
Music:
  awards for, 245–246, 253–254, 254, 258
  Country Music Hall of Fame, 278
  earliest written, 664
  Rock and Roll Hall of Fame, 277
  state songs, 142–177
  symphonies, 264
  top downloads, 275
  top-selling albums, 275
Musicians. See People
Muslim architecture, 446
Muslims. See Islam
Mussolini, Benito, 305, 679, 680, 681, 799
Myanmar, 828–829
Mythology:
  Egyptian, 472
  Greek and Roman, 468–471
  Norse, 471–472

N

NAACP, 659, 677
  Image Awards, 258
Nagasaki, 681, 682, 801
Nagin, Ray, 44, 1033
NAIA football championships, 937
Nairobi, Kenya, 804
Names:
  of days, 352
  of hurricanes, 595, 596
  of months, 352
  Old Testament, 466–468
  of states, origins of, 142–177
Names, most common in U.S., 139, 140
Namibia, 829–830
Nantes, Edict of, 669, 671
Napoléon Bonaparte, 285, 672, 673, 770
Napoleonic Code, 673
Napoleonic Wars, 673, 770, 850, 885
Narcotics:
  arrests for violations, 390
  use, 560
NASA, 514
NASCAR, 1000
NASDAQ, 646
Nashville-Davidson, Tenn., 171, 178, 194–195
Nassau, Bahamas, 727
Nasser, Gamal Abdel, 305, 764, 857
National Academy of Engineering, 85
National Academy of Sciences, 85
National Aeronautics and Space Administration (NASA). See also Space exploration
  address, 84
  administrator, 84
National Anthem, 106
National Archives and Records Administration (NARA), 84
National Association for the Advancement of Colored People (NAACP), 659, 677
National Basketball Association (NBA), 952–956
National Book Awards, 254
National Book Critics Circle Awards, 254
National Committees, 51

National Conventions, 50, 51
National Credit Union Administration, 84
National debt, 633
  constitutional validity of, 116
National Foundation on the Arts and the Humanities, 84
National Historical Parks, 591
National Historic Sites, 592
National Hockey League, 37, 962–965
National holidays (by country), 359
National Intelligence, 84
National Labor Relations Board (NLRB), 84
National League. See Baseball; Football
National Magazine Awards, 257
National Mediation Board, 84
National Missile Defense, 36
National Organization of Women, 374
National Park System, 590–594, 594
National Railroad Passenger Corporation (Amtrak), 85
National Republican Party, 52
National Research Council, 85
National Science Foundation (NSF), 84
National Security Adviser, 82
National Security Council, 82
National Service, Corporation for, 83
National Transportation Safety Board, 84
Native Americans. See Indians (American)
NATO, 910. See also North Atlantic Treaty Organization
Natural features, of countries, 718–906. See also Geography
Natural resources:
  of countries, 718–906
Nature, 588–594
Nautilus (submarine), 683
Naval Academy, U.S., 155
Navassa Island, 898
Navy, U.S.. See also Armed forces, U.S.
  first admiral of, 101
  secretaries of, 83, 88
Nazis, 679, 680, 682, 684, 777–779
NCAA basketball, 948–951
NCAA football championships, 937
N'Djamena, Chad, 745
Neanderthal man, 663
Neap tides, 402
Nebraska, 160–161
  Kansas-Nebraska Act, 674
Nebuchadnezzar, 447, 664
Negev Desert, 797
Negroponte, John, 39, 1033
Nehru, Jawaharlal, 305, 788
Nelson River, 495
Neosho River, 501
Nepal, 36, 830–831, 1032
Neptune (planet), 401, 407, 412–414. See also Planets
Neptunium, 575, 580
Netherlands, 511, 831–833
Netherlands Antilles, 832
Neutron, discovery of, 580
Neutron star, 398
Nevada, 161–162
Nevis, 854
New Amsterdam, 164, 670
Newark, N.J., 162, 178
Newbery Medal, 255–256
New Brunswick, Canada, 743
New Caledonia, 774
New Cornelia Tailings, 144
New Deal, 67, 680, 681
New Delhi, India, 788
Newfoundland, Canada, 496, 671, 743
New Freedom, 66
"New Frontier", 69
New Guinea, 496. See also Papua New Guinea; Irian Jaya

New Hampshire, 162
New Hebrides. See Vanuatu
New Jersey, 162–163
New Mexico, 163–164
New Orleans, La., 153, 178, 195
  Battle of, 673
  climate of, 601
  Hurricane Katrina, 32, 44, 195
News:
  deaths in 2005, 1035
  websites, 566
Newspapers, 272
  awards for, 234–241
  circulation, 272
  first black, 101
  first in U.S., 671
  firsts in, 101
Newton (measure), 455
Newton, Sir Isaac, 305, 579, 582, 670, 671
New Year:
  Chinese, 358
  Jewish, 356, 357n
New Year's Day, 346, 355
New York City, 164, 178, 195–196
  boroughs of, 195–196
  bridges, 448
  buildings and structures, 444–445, 447
  climate, 601
  Kennedy Airport, 164
  Sept. 11, 2001, attacks, 211, 224, 698, 719, 858
  Statue of Liberty, 164
  subway commuters, 606
  subway system, 606, 677
  tunnels, 451
  Tweed Ring, 675
  U.N. Headquarters, 165
  World's Fairs, 681
New York State, 164–165
New York Stock Exchange, 645
New Zealand, 833
  exploration of, 485
New Zealand dependencies, 702
Niagara Falls, 164
Niamey, Niger, 834
Nicaea, Council of, 361, 666
Nicaragua, 833–834
  U.S. military actions in, 834
Nicene Creed, 361, 666
Nickel (element), 575
Nicknames of states, 142–177
Niger, 834–835
Nigeria, 686, 835–836
Niger River, 495, 835
Nightingale, Florence, 674
Nile River, 495, 764, 869
  Aswan Dam, 764
Niobrara River, 501
Nirvana, 365
Nitrogen, 575
Nitrogen dioxide, 586
Nitroglycerin, 580
Niue Island, 833
Nixon, Richard M., 54, 55, 56, 57, 58, 69–70, 99. See also Presidents, U.S.
  resignation of, 70, 687
Noatak River, 501
Nobel, Alfred, 305, 579, 675, 677
Nobel Prizes, 225–234, 677
Nomenclature, binomial, 572
Nonfiction (general), awards for, 245, 254
Nonfiction, best of 20th century, 269–270
Nordic Combined, 933
Norfolk Island, 725
Normandy, House of, 885
Normandy Invasion, 681
Norris Trophy, 964
Norse mythology, 471–472
North, Oliver, Jr., 690
North America:
  area and elevation of, 487
  exploration of, 484

map of, **525**
North American Free Trade Agreement (NAFTA), **692**
North Atlantic Treaty Organization (NATO), 98, 100, 683, 700, 770, 880, 910
North Canadian River, **501**
North Carolina, 165
North Dakota, 165–166
Northeast Passage, 484
Northern Ireland, 796, 885, 888–890
Good Friday Peace Accord, 695, 696, 697, 796, 888, 889
"Northern lights", 417
Northern Mariana Islands, 897
Northern Rhodesia. *See* Zambia
North Island (New Zealand), 496, 833
North Korea, 35, 36, 39, 42, 44, 511, 699
North Platte River, 501
North Pole, 485, 497
flights over, 436, 438
reached, 677
North Sea, 494, 731, 831, 836, 885
Northwest Passage, 168, 484
Northwest Territories, Canada, 743
Norway, 836–837
Norwegian dependencies, 702
Notre-Dame de Paris, 446
Nouakchott, Mauritania, 822
Nouméa, New Caledonia, 774
Nova Scotia, Canada, 484, 743
Novelists. *See* People
Novels, best of 20th century, 268–269
Nuclear fission, 580
Nuclear physics:
discoveries and theories, 578–582
Nuclear power:
accidents, 216, 688, 690
Nuclear-proliferation agreement, 688, 691
Nuclear Regulatory Commission (NRC), 84
Nuclear weapons:
countries with, 714
India, 789
Iran, 35, 792
North Korea, 35, 806
Pakistan, 839
testing of, 683, 686
Nuku'alofa, Tonga, 877
Numbers:
cardinal, 453
decimals and fractions, 459
nominal, 453
ordinal, 453
prime, 453
Roman, 453
Nunavut, Canada, 742
Nuremberg laws, 680
Nuremberg war crimes trial, 680, 682
Nutrition:
obesity guidelines, 553
Nyasa, Lake, 494
Nyasaland. *See* Malawi
Nylon, invention of, 579

O

O.K. Corral, 144
Oakland, Calif., 145, 196
Oaths:
constitutional, 112, 114
presidential, 112
Obama, Barack, 376
Obesity, 553
Obie Awards, 252
Ob River, 495
Occupational Safety and Health Review Commission, 84
Occupations, 620, 621, 625
Oceania:
area and elevation of, 487
exploration of, 485
map of, 536

Ocean liners. *See* Steamships
Oceans, 494
O'Connor, Sandra Day, 42, 1033
Odd Fellows, Independent Order of, 660
Oder-Neisse Line, 779
Odyssey (Homer), 664
Office of Personnel Management (OPM), 84
Offices, Executive, 82–83
Ohio, 166–167
Ohio-Allegheny River, 495, 501
Ohio River, 501
Ohm's Law, 580
Oil (petroleum):
export and import of, 639
Exxon Valdez, 211, 223, 690, 692
first commercial well in U.S., 101
producers and consumers, top, 585
reserves by country, 585
spills, 211, 222–223
Okhotsk Sea, 494
Oklahoma, 167–168
Oklahoma City, Okla., 100, 167, 178, 196–197
bombing (1995), 224, 693, 694, 695
Öland, Sweden, 871
Old North Church, 156
Old Testament names, 466–468
Olmecs, 664
Olympia, Wash., 175, 178
Olympic Games, 917–934
2004 games, 781, 917–930
ancient, 664
Athens (2004), 701
first modern, 677
history and sites, 917
London (2012), 42
Munich Massacre, 687
Soviet withdrawal from (1984), 689
Summer Games, 701, 917–930
Winter Games, 930–934
Olympic National Park, 591, 594
Omaha, Nebr., 160, 178, 197
Oman, 837–838
Omo skulls, 570, 572
Ontario, Canada, 743
Ontario, Lake, 494
OPEC, 910
Opera companies, U.S., 265
Operas, frequently produced, 265
Operation Iraqi Freedom, 794
Opium War, 674
Orange Bowl, 935
Orange River, 495
Oranjestad, Aruba, 832
Orbits:
of comets, 398, 415–416
defined, 398
of Moon, 400, 401
of planets, 398
Oregon, 168
Oregon Treaty, 96
Organization of American States, 682
Organization of Petroleum Exporting Countries (OPEC), 857
Organizations, 653–662
consumers', 649–650
Organ transplants, 559
Orinoco River, 495, 750
Orkney Islands, 890
Orthodox:
churches, 667
Easter, 346, 356, 357
holidays, 357
Osage River, 501
Oscars (Academy Awards), 247–251
Oslo, Norway, 836
Ostrogothic Kingdom, 666
Oswald, Lee Harvey, 69, 119, 685
Ottawa, Canada, 742
Ottoman Turks, 873, 880
Ouachita River, 501
Ouagadougou, Burkina Faso, 739
Outer Mongolia. *See* Mongolia

Overweight, 553
Oxygen, 575
Ozone, 580
atmospheric, 586, 587
ozone-polluted cities, 586
Ozonosphere, 402

P

Pacific Islander, 379
Pacific Ocean, 494. *See also* Oceania
islands, 496, 895–898
sighted, 484
U.S. coastline, 502
Pagodas, 446
Painted Desert, 498
Painters. *See* People
Paintings, most expensive, 280
Pakistan, 682, 729, 788, 838–839
Palau, 839–840
Paleontology, 570, 572
Paleozoic Era, 576
Palestine, 797
Palestine, ancient, 664
Palestine Liberation Organization (PLO), 688, 803, 811
Achille Lauro hijacked, 689
Palestinian Authority, 698
Palestinian state (proposed), 701, 798, 840–841
Gaza withdrawal, 34, 509, 700, 798, 841
Palikir, Micronesia, 824
Palm Sunday, 346, 355, 357n
Palmyra Atoll, 898
Pamir Mountain Range, 493
Panama:
U.S. military intervention in, 691
Panama Canal, 97, 99, 451, 678, 842
treaties, 688, 842
Panama City, Panama, 841
Panay (gunboat), 681
Panmunjom, North Korea, 807
Pantheon (Rome), 445, 665, 666
Papal States, 900
Papeete, French Polynesia, 773
Paper:
Chinese development of, 665
export and import of, 639
invention of, 580
Producer Price Index, 637
Paper currency, 453
Papua New Guinea, 485, 496, 842
Parachutes, 580
Parachuting:
Caterpillar Club, 436
first jumps, 435, 436
Paraguay, 843
Paraguay River, 495, 737, 843
Parallels, 485
Paramaribo, Suriname, 870
Paraná River, 495, 737, 843
Parentheses, 475
Paris, France, 770
structures, 446
subway system, 606
in World War I, 678
in World War II, 681, 770
Paris, Peace of, 671
Paris, Treaty of:
in 1898, 676
in 1947, 682, 787
Parks:
city-owned, 180–204
most visited, 594
National Park System, 590–594, 594
state parks, 142–177
Parks, Rosa, 383
Parliament (Great Britain), 668, 670, 673, 680, 885
Parole Commission, U.S., 84
Parsec (measure), 400
Parthenon, 445, 665
Parties, political (world), 718–906
Passover, 346, 355, 357
Passports, 605

Pasteur, Louis, 306, 579, 581, 675
Patents, 651–652
Patrick, Danica, 515, 1033
Paul, Alice, 374
Paul, Les, 583
Peabody Awards for Broadcasting, 260
Peace Corps, 84
Peacekeeping Operations, UN, 908
Peace Prizes, Nobel, 225
Peace River, 495
Peak Cavern, 497
Pearl, Daniel, 698
Pearl Harbor attack, 149, 188, 681, 682, 801
Pearl River (Miss.-La.), 501
Pearl River (Zhu Jiang), China, 747
Peary, Robert E., 306, 484, 485, 677
Pecos River, 501
Pee Dee-Yadkin River, 501
Peking, China, 747. See also Beijing
Peloponnesian Wars, 665
PEN/Faulkner Award, 254
Pend Oreille-Clark Fork River, 501
Penicillin, 231, 578, 680
Penn, William, 147
Pennsylvania, 168–169
Pennyweight, 455, 457
Pension Benefit Guaranty Corporation, 84
Pentagon, 83
  bombing, 211, 224
Pentagon Papers, 685
Pentecost, 346, 356, 357
People, 282–317, 957–961, 1029, 1030–1034
People's Party (Populists), 53
Per capita income, 626
  by countries, 718–906
  by states, 628
Pérez de Cuéllar, Javier, 907
Performers. See People
Pericles, 665
Perihelion, 353, 398
Period (punctuation), 474
Periodic law, 580
Periodic table, 572
Periodic table, development of, 580
Permian Period, 576
Perón, Juan D., 307, 684, 723
Persia, ancient, 664
Persia, modern. See Iran
Persian Gulf States. See United Arab Emirates
Persian Gulf War, 100, 691, 693, 794, 808
Peru, 485, 843–844
Petition, right of, 114
Petrified Forest National Park, 591
Petronas Towers, 444
Pets:
  and happiness, 551
  names, 551
  ownership, U.S., 551
Pharos of Alexandria, 447
Philadelphia, Pa., 168, 178, 197–198, 672
  Continental Congresses in, 102
  Liberty Bell, 103, 169
Philippines, 689, 844–846
  as U.S. Territory, 97, 104
Philosophers. See People
Phnom Penh, Cambodia, 688, 740
Phoenician Empire, 664
Phoenix, Ariz., 143, 178, 198
  climate of, 602
Phoenix Islands, 805
Phonographs, invention of, 676
Photography:
  first aerial, 435
  inventions, 580, 676
  Pulitzer Prizes for, 236–237
Photosphere, 400
Phrases, foreign, 479–481
Phyrgian civilization, 664
Physical activity, 554

Physical Fitness and Sports, President's Council on, 84
Physicians, 559
Physics:
  inventions and discoveries, 578–582
  Nobel Prizes for, 226–228
Physiology:
  Nobel Prizes for, 231–233
Pi (measure), 459
Picasso, Pablo, 681
Piccard, Bertrand, 439
Pierce, Franklin, 53, 57, 63, 96. See also Presidents, U.S.
Pierre, S.D., 170, 171, 178
Pigs, 588, 589
Pikes Peak, 146, 184, 502
Pilcomayo River, 495
Pilgrims, 156, 182, 670
Pindus Mountains, 780
Pinochet, Augusto, 746–747
Pioneer space program, 425, 426
Pisa, Leaning Tower of, 446
Pitcairn Island, 672, 894
Pittsburgh, Pa., 168
Pizarro, Francisco, 307, 485, 669, 763, 844, 867
Plague, 666, 668, 670, 885
Planck, Max, 227, 307, 581
Planets, 402–414
  basic data, 407
  configurations (2006), 418–421
  conjunctions, 398
  defined, 398
  exploration of, 423–427
  extrasolar, 398
  minor planets (asteroids), 414–415
  moons of, 401, 406–413
  new, 398
  origin of, 399
  phenomena (2006), 418–421
  possible planets, 571
  Sedna, 414
  tenth planet, 414
  visibility, 421
Plantagenet, House of, 885
Plants:
  classification of, 578
  endangered species, 589
Plastics, invention of, 581
Plata River, 737, 898
Plate-tectonics theory, 487
Plato, 307, 665
Platte River, 501
Plays, longest Broadway runs, 266
Playwrights. See People; Theater
Pledge of allegiance to flag, 103
Pleistocene Period, 577
Plessy v. Ferguson, 93
Plow, invention of, 581
Pluto, 571
Pluto (planet), 401, 407, 414. See also Planets
Plutonium, 575, 581
Plymouth Colony, 156, 670
Plymouth Rock, 670
Pocahontas, 670
Pocket veto, 81
Poetry, awards for, 244–245, 258
Poets. See People
Poets laureate:
  of England, 274
  of U.S., 273
Point Four Program, 683
Poland, 678, 681, 846–847
  Kosciusko uprising (1794), 672
  partition of, 672
  Poznan uprising (1956), 684
  Solidarity Union, 846
  workers strikes in, 846
  in World War II, 681, 778
Polar flights, first, 436, 438
Polar regions, 497. See also Antarctica; Arctic Circle
Policemen, statistics, 387
Poliomyelitis, 213, 581, 683

Political parties:
  in U.S. See specific parties
  world, 718–906
Polk, James Knox, 53, 55, 57, 62–63, 96. See also Presidents, U.S.
Poll tax, 118
Pollution:
  automobile, 610
  carbon dioxide, 584
  cities, 586
  greenhouse gases, 585
Polo, Marco, 307, 484, 668
Pol Pot, 688, 741, 903
Polynesia, French, 773
Pompeii, 211
Pompidou, Georges, 771
Ponce de León, Juan, 147
Pontiffs, Roman Catholic, 367–369
Pony Express, 159
Popes, 367–369
  Benedict XVI, 39, 369, 512, 900, 901, 1030
  John Paul I, 369, 688, 901
  John Paul II, 39, 369, 512, 688, 901, 1037
  John XXIII, 369, 685, 901
  Paul VI, 369, 685, 688, 901
Popular vote, 45, 50, 53–55, 56
Population, U.S., 120–124, 142–177
  by age, 121, 123, 124
  age 65 and over, 142–177
  of American Indians, 379, 380
  and ancestry, 381, 382
  and Asians, U.S., 378, 379
  black, 121, 123, 124, 142–177, 377
  census required by Constitution, 109
  in census years, 124
  cities: largest of each state, 142–177, 178
  colonial estimates, 123
  densities (1790–2000), 124
  distribution, 124
  ethnicity, 378, 381–382
  foreign-born, 124, 382
  growth of, 122, 124
  Hispanic origin, 121, 123, 142–177, 378, 381
  immigrants, 382
  languages spoken, 381
  and Pacific islanders, 379
  persons below poverty level, 630
  persons living alone, 126
  by race, 121, 123, 142–177, 378
  ratio of males to females, 123
  by region, 123
  by sex, 121, 123
  of states, 122
  of territories, 122, 895–898
  total U.S., 120, 121, 122
  urban, 205–207
Population, U.S. cities:
  by age, 180–204
  black, 180–204
  cities, largest, 180–204, 209
  Hispanic origin, 180–204
  by race, 180–204
Population, world, 702, 704, 705–706, 718–906
  cities, 704
  cities, by countries, 718–906
  of countries, 705–706, 718–906
  densities, 718–906
  urban areas, 704
  world's highest and lowest densities, 703
Populists. See People's Party
Porcupine River, 501
Port-au-Français, French Southern and Antarctic Lands, 774
Port-au-Prince, Haiti, 785
Portland, Maine, 154, 178
Portland, Ore., 168, 178, 198–199
Port Louis, Mauritius, 822
Port Moresby, Papua New Guinea, 842
Port-of-Spain, Trinidad and Tobago, 878

Porto-Novo, Benin, 732
Ports, world sea, 643
Portsmouth, Treaty of, 162
Portugal, 847–848
Portuguese Guinea. *See*
    Guinea-Bissau
Portuguese West Africa. *See* Angola
Port Vila, Vanuatu, 900
Positron, 581
Post, Wiley, 307, 437
Postal regulations, 440–442
Postal Service, U.S., 84, 671
    rates, 440–442
Postmasters General, 84, 89
Post Office. *See* Postal Service, U.S.
Postojna Grotto, 497
Potomac River, 203, 501
Potsdam Conference, 681
Poultry, U.S. consumption of, 640
Poverty, 629–631
    level, 630
    people and families in, 629, 630
    population in, 630
    by state, 630
    thresholds, 630
    in U.S., 43, 629, 630
Poverty, worldwide, 711
Powder River, 501
Powell, Colin, 376, 691
Power failure of 1965 (Ontario), 686
Power looms, 580
Prague, Czech Republic, 758
Praia, Cape Verde, 744
Preakness Stakes, 980, 982
Precambrian, 576
Precipitation. *See* Rainfall
Prefix, 481
Pregnancy:
    cigarette smoking during, 131
    teen, 132
Premiers and prime ministers:
    of Canada, 743
    of countries, 718–906
    of Great Britain, 887
    of Soviet Union, 851
Presbyterian churches, 363, 669
Preserves, National, 592
Presidential Medal of Freedom, 262
Presidents, foreign, 718–906, 769–
    775
Presidents, U.S. *See also* Presidential
    candidates; Presidential elections
    assassinations and attempts on, 119
    biographies of, 59–77
    cabinets under, 85–90
    constitutional provisions about, 112
    of Continental Congresses, 102
    election (2004), 45
    election of, 45, 50, 52–55, 56
    election procedure for, 50, 112, 115
    families of, 59
    list of, 57
    minority (electoral), 55
    Mount Rushmore carvings, 171
    National Historic Sites, 592
    nomination of, 50
    oath of office of, 112
    powers and duties of, 112–113
    presidential libraries, 58
    qualifications of, 112
    religious affiliations of, 57
    salary of, 80, 112
    succession to, 82, 112, 117, 118
    tabulated data about, 57
    term of office of, 57, 112, 117
    vetoes, 81
    wives and children of, 59
President's Council on Physical
    Fitness and Sports, 84
Press, freedom of, 114, 671
Price indexes:
    consumer, 638
    farm, 642
    producer, 637
Prices, historical food, 639
Prices, homes, 618, 619
Prime meridian, 486

Prime numbers, 453
Prince Edward Island, Canada, 743
Prince of Wales Trophy, 963
Princeton University, 322
Príncipe, 856–857
Printing, 581
Printz, Michael L., book awards, 257
Prisoners:
    under sentence of death, 386
    statistics, 385
Prisoners of war, 393
Prizes. *See* Awards
Probes, lunar and deep space,
    425–427
Production indexes, U.S. industries,
    637. *See also specific industries and
    products*
Product recalls, 650
Professional Golfers Association
    (P.G.A.) Champions, 996
Profiles:
    of U.S., 120, 121
    of world, 702
Programming, computer, 578
Progressive Party:
    national conventions, 51
    presidential candidates, 54
Prohibition, 98, 116, 679, 680
Promontory Summit, 173
Propeller, screw, 581
Prostitution, arrests for, 390
Proterozoic Eon, 576
Protestant churches, U.S., 363
Protestantism, 363
    Reformation, 363, 778
Proton, discovery of, 581
Providence, R.I., 169, 178
Prudhoe Bay, Alaska, 143
Prussia, 778
Psychoanalysis, development of, 581
Public debt, 633
Publishing:
    best-selling books, 267
    magazines, 273
    newspapers, 272
Pueblo (ship), 686
Puerto Rico, 99, 895–896
    holidays in, 358
Pulitzer Prizes, 234–247
Pullman strike, 676
Pulsars, 398
Punctuation, rules for, 474–475
Punic Wars, 665
Punjab, 484, 838
Purim, 346, 355, 357
Puritan Commonwealth, 885
Puritans, 182
Purus River, 495
Putin, Vladimir, 696, 849, 851, 852
Pyongyang, North Korea, 683, 805
Pyramids of Egypt, 447, 663
Pythagoras, 664

Q

Qaddafi, Muammar, 746, 814
Qaeda, al-, 101, 224, 698, 699, 700,
    717, 719, 827
Qatar, 848
Quadriplegic, 570
Quakers. *See* Friends
Quantum theory, 581
Quart, 452, 454, 457, 458
Quarters, U.S., 454
Quasars, 398
Quayle, J. Danforth, 58
Quebec, Canada, 742–744
    city, 742
    province, 743
Queen Anne's War, 671
Queens (NYC), 195–196
Queensberry Rules, 974
Queens of England, 886
Question mark (punctuation), 474
Quisling, Maj. Vidkun, 837
Quito, Ecuador, 763

Quiz show, first panel, 101
Quotation marks (punctuation), 475
Qur'an. *See* Koran
Qurei, Amhed, 841

R

Rabat, Morocco, 827
Rabies, immunization, 581
Rabin, Yitzhak, 693
Race and ethnicity, 376–384
Racial statistics:
    arrests, 390
    educational attainment, 319, 320
    hate crimes, 389
    life expectancy, 137
    population, 121, 123, 378, 379, 380
Racing. *See* Auto racing; Canoe
    racing; Horse racing; Marathons;
    Track and field
Radar, 581
Radiation, neutron-induced, 580
Radio:
    awards for, 260
    first station licensed, 101
    inventions, 581
    most played songs, 275
    stations in U.S., 120, 180–204
Radioactivity, 581, 677
Radiocarbon dating, development of,
    581
Railroad Retirement Board, U.S., 84
Railroads:
    accidents and deaths, 211, 221–222
    first passenger service, 673
    firsts in, 97, 101, 673
    ridership, 611
Railroad tunnels, 451
Rainfall:
    extremes, 597
    greatest, 598
    lowest precipitation, 598
    in U.S. cities, 601–602
Rainier, Mount, 175, 502, 503
Rainier III (prince of Monaco), 517,
    1038
Raleigh, N.C., 165, 178
Ramadan, 346, 356, 357
Ramakrishna, 364
Ramayana, 364
Ranger space program, 425
Rangoon (Yangon), Myanmar, 828
Rape, 390
Ratzinger, Cardinal Joseph, 39, 369,
    512, 900, 901, 1030
Reactors, nuclear, 216
Reading statistics, 266, 267
Reagan, Nancy Davis, 59
Reagan, Ronald, 54, 56, 58, 71–72,
    100. *See also* Presidents, U.S.
    assassination attempt on, 72, 100,
    119, 688
Real estate, 618, 619
Reaper, invention of, 581
Reconstruction, 676
Reconstruction Finance Corporation
    (1932), 680
Recording Industry Association of
    America, 275
Records, 275
    aviation, 439
    sports. *See* under specific sports
Recreation Areas, National, 594
Red Cross, American, 85, 660
Red Guards, 748
Red River (Minn.-Manitoba), 501
Red River (N.M.-La.), 501
Red Rock River, 495, 501
Red Sea, 494
Redwood National Park, 591
Reformation, 361, 363, 669, 778
Refugees, 715
Rehnquist, William H., 33, 35, 44,
    91–92, 507, 690, 1038
Reichstag fire, 680
Reign of Terror (1793–94), 672

Relativity theories, 581, 677
Religion, 360–370. *See also specific religions and churches*
  churches in U.S., **180–204**, 362
  freedom of religion, 114
  history of world, 360–366
  holidays, 355–357
  largest religions, 360
  popes, 367–369
  practice by country, **718–906**
  in U.S., 361, 367
Religious affiliations:
  of presidents, 57
  of Supreme Court justices, **91–92**
Renaissance, 668, 669
  architecture, 446
Reparations (World War I), 679
Reporting:
  Pulitzer Prizes for, **237–240**
Representatives. *See* House of Representatives, U.S.
Reptiles, Age of, 576
Republic, oldest, 856
Republican Party:
  founding of, 674
  Gang of 14, 40
  members of Congress, **46–49**
  National Committee chairmen, 51
  national conventions, 51, 689, 690
  presidential candidates, **52–55**
  Senate floor leaders, 78
Republican River, 501
Reservations, American Indian, 144
Reservations, U.S. Indian, 380
Reserves, National, 592
Réunion, 773
Revels, Hiram, 376
Revenue:
  bills for raising of, 110
  national, 634
Revolutionary War, American, 95, 392, 672
Revolvers, 581
Reykjavik, Iceland, 787
Rhine River, 770, 777, 831, 872
Rhode Island, 169–170
Rhodes, Cecil, 308, 865, 905, 906
Rhodes, Colossus at, 447
Rhodesia, 686. *See also* Zambia; Zimbabwe
Rhône River, 770
Ribbon Falls, 496
Rice, Condoleezza, 36, 308, 376, 506, 1033
Rice, export and import of, 639
Richmond, Va., 174, 178
Richter scale, 490
Ride, Sally K., 102, 689
Riga, Latvia, 810
Rio de Janeiro, Brazil, 736
Rio de la Plata, 898
Rio Grande, 495, 501
Río Muni, 765
Rivers:
  U.S., **500–501**
  world, 495
Rivers, endangered, 587
Rivers, National, 593
Riyadh, Saudi Arabia, 857
Riyadh bombing (2003), 858
Road mileages, U.S. cities., 612–613
Roanoke Island, 165
Roanoke River, 165, 501
Robbery, 390
Roberts, John, 33, 42, 44, 1033
Robinson projection, 486
Rock and Roll Hall of Fame, 167, 277
Rockefeller, John D., 309
Rockefeller, Nelson A., 58, 99
Rocket engine flight, first, 437
Rocky Mountain National Park, 591, 594
Rocky Mountains, 146
Roentgen, Wilhelm Konrad, 226, 309, 581, 676
Roe v. Wade, 93, 375
Roller bearing, 581

Roman Catholic Church:
  Council of Nicaea, 361, 666
  Council of Trent, 350, 669
  description of, 362–363
  Great Schism, 668
  hierarchy, 362
  history of, 361–363
  Inquisition, 668, 670
  in Italy, 689
  membership in, 362
  popes, 362, 367–369, 901
  Vatican City, 446, 900
  Vatican Council I, 363
  Vatican Council II, 363, 685, 689, 901
Roman Empire, 664, 665
  mythology, 468–471
  structures, 445
Romanesque architecture, 446
Romania, 848–849
Roman numerals, 453
Rome, Italy, 799
  architecture, 445, 446
  founding of, 664
  in World War II, 681
Rookie of the Year (baseball), 1016
Roosevelt, Eleanor, 59, 67, 309
Roosevelt, Franklin D., 54, 57, 58, 67, 98, 148, 164, 165. *See also* Presidents, U.S.
  assassination attempt on, 119
  birthday, 358
Roosevelt, Theodore, 53, 57, 65–66, 97, 225. *See also* Presidents, U.S.
  assassination attempt on, 119
Roots, word, 481–482
Roseau, Dominica, 760
Rose Bowl, 934
Rosenberg, Julius and Ethel, 99, 683
Roses, Wars of the, 668, 885
Rosh Hashanah, 346, 356, 357
Ross, Betsy, 309
Ross Trophy, 964
Rota (island), 897
Rotary International, 661
Rough Riders, 65
Rove, Karl, 42, 1033
Rowing, 930
Rowley, Coleen, 698
Royalty, 710
Rubber, vulcanized, 581
Ruby, Jack, 69, 119, 685
Rudolph, Eric, 38
Rulers:
  monarchs, contemporary, 710
  most corrupt, 710
Rumania. *See* Romania
Rumsfeld, Donald, 310, 700
Running. *See* Track and field
Rupert's Land, 742
Rushmore, Mount, 171
Russia, 849–853
  Beslan, 852
  Chechen war, 852
  financial crisis (1998), 852
  history of, 850–853
  Kremlin (structure), 446
  Revolution, 678, 850
  rulers of, 851
  structures, 446
  in World War I, 678, 850
  in World War II, 681, 851
Russo-Finnish War, 681, 769, 850
Russo-Japanese War, 66, 162, 677, 801, 850
Russo-Turkish War, 676, 880
Rwanda, 693, 694, 853–854
Ryukyu Islands, 801

S

Sabah, Malaysia, 737, 819
Sabine River, 501
Sabin vaccine, 581
Sacco-Vanzetti case, 679
Sacramento, Calif., 145, 178, 199

Sacramento River, 501
Sadat, Anwar el-, 310, 688, 763–765, 797
Sahara, 484, 498, 720, 814, 879
Saigon, Vietnam. *See* Ho Chi Minh City
Sailing, 930
St. Bartholomew's Day Massacre, 669
St. Christopher-Nevis. *See* St. Kitts and Nevis
St. Croix, V.I., 896
Saint-Denis, Réunion, 773
Saint Francis River, 501
St. George's, Grenada, 781
St. Helena, 673, 894
St. Helens, Mount, 175
St. John, V.I., 896
St. John's, Antigua and Barbuda, 722
St. John the Divine, Cathedral of, 447
St. Kitts and Nevis, 854
St. Lawrence River, 484, 495, 742
St. Lawrence Seaway, 164, 451, 684
St. Louis, Mo., 159
St. Lucia, 854–855
St. Mark's Cathedral, 446
St. Mihiel, Battle of, 678
St. Patrick's Day, 346, 355
St. Paul, Minn., 157, 178
St. Peter, Basilica of, 446, 669
St. Petersburg, Russia, 849. *See also* Leningrad
St. Pierre and Miquelon, 774
St. Thomas, V.I., 896
St. Valentine's Day, 346, 355
St. Valentine's Day Massacre, 680
St. Vincent and the Grenadines, 855
Saipan, 897
Sakhalin, 496
Saladin, 667
Salamis, Battle of, 665
Salaries, 620, 621
  of government officials, 80
Salem, Ore., 168, 178
Salisbury, Zimbabwe. *See* Harare, Zimbabwe
Salk vaccine, 581, 683
Salmon River, 501
SALT. *See* Strategic Arms Limitation Talks
Salt Lake City, Utah, 173, 178
Salvador, El. *See* El Salvador
Salvation Army, 661
Salween River, 495
Same-sex marriage unions and marriage, 744
Same-sex unions and marriages, 40, 44, 696, 701, 744
Samoa, 855–856
Samoa, American, 897
Sanaá, Yemen, 904
San Antonio, Tex., 172, 199–200
San Diego, Calif., 145, 200
Sandinista guerrillas, 834
Sandwich Islands, 149
San Francisco, Calif., 145, 200–201
  climate, 602
  earthquakes, 97, 211, 212, 677
  Golden Gate Bridge, 447, 448
Sanger, Margaret, 374
San Jacinto, Battle of, 172, 674
San Joaquin River, 501
San Jose, Calif., 145, 201
San José, Costa Rica, 754
San Juan River, 501
San Marino, 856
San Salvador, El Salvador, 765
San Stefano, Treaty of, 676
Santa Claus, 357
Santa Fe, N.M., 163, 178
Santee-Wateree-Catawba River, 501
Santiago, Chile, 746
Santiago de Cuba, 756
Santo Domingo, Dominican Republic, 761
São Francisco River, 495

São Tomé and Príncipe, 856–857
Sappho of Lesbos, 664
Sarajevo, Bosnia, 734
Saratoga, Battle of, 671
Sarawak, Malaysia, 737, 819
Sardinia, 666, 799
Saskatchewan, Canada, 743
Saskatchewan River, 495
Satellites (moons), 401, 406–413
  defined, 399
  exploration of, 425–427
  orbits defined, 398
Satellites, scientific, 684
SAT scores, 321
"Saturday Night Massacre", 687
Saturn (planet), 401, 407, 409–411.
  See also Planets
  exploration of, 423, 426
Saud, Fahd bin Abdel Aziz (king of
  Saudi Arabia), 42
Saudi Arabia, 36, 857–858
Sault Ste. Marie Canal, 157, 451
Savimbi, Jonas, 722
Savings bank, first in U.S., 101
Saxe-Coburg, House of, 885
Scenic Trails, National, 594
Schiavo, Terri, 33, 37, 41, 507, 1034
Schism, Great, 668
Schmidt, Helmut, 779
Schools. See also Colleges and
  universities; Education
  first public, 101
  and Supreme Court, 683, 685, 686,
    688, 689
Schröder, Gerhard, 39, 41, 695, 779
Schuman Plan (1951), 683
Schwarzenegger, Arnold, 700
Science, 569–583. See also
  Chemistry; Mathematics; Medicine
  branches of, 577
  chemical elements, 574–575
  classification, 572
  Fermi Award, 261
  human ancestors, 572
  inventions and discoveries, 578–582
  metric system, 455, 456–458
  Nobel Prizes, 225–234
  transfermium elements, 574
  websites, 578
  weights and measures, 452–459
  and women, 371–373
Science and Technology, Office of,
  82
Science scores, international
  comparisons, 318
Scientific classification, 572
Scientific instruments, export and
  import of, 639
Scopes Monkey Trial, 98, 679
Scotland, 671, 885, 890
Scott, Dred, 93, 674
Screw propeller, 581
Scythian civilization, 664
Seaborg, Glenn, 583
Seal of U.S., Great, 103
Sea ports, 643
Sears Tower, 444, 447
Seas, 494
Seashores, National, 593
Seasons, 353, 402
Seat belts, 608, 609
SEATO. See Southeast Asia Treaty
  Organization
Seattle, Wash., 175, 178, 201–202
  climate of, 602
Secretaries-General, UN, 907
Securities and Exchange
  Commission (SEC), 84
Security Council, National, 82
Security Council, UN, 907
Sedna, 571
Seine River, 770
Selassie, Haile. See Haile Selassie I
Selective Service System (SSS), 84,
  682
Seljuk Turks, 667
Selma, Ala., 142

Semicolon (punctuation), 475
Senate, U.S., 46–47, 109, 112. See
  also Congress, U.S.
  birthdates of members, 46–47
  committees of, 77
  eligibility for, 109
  first black member, 101
  first woman member, 102
  floor leaders of, 78
  impeachment cases heard by, 110
  members, 46–47
Seneca Falls convention, 165, 374
Senegal, 858–859
Seoul, South Korea, 806
  subway system, 606
Sepoy Mutiny, 674, 788
Sept. 11, 2001, attacks, 38, 101, 211,
  224, 698, 719, 858
Sept. 11 commission, 36
Serbia and Montenegro, 859–860
Seven Cities of Gold, 144
Seven Deadly Sins, 370
Seven summits, 493
Seven Weeks' War, 675
Seven Wonders of the World, 447
Seven Years' War, 671, 742
Seward, William H., 86, 119, 143
"Seward's Folly", 143
Sexes, distribution by:
  educational attainment, 319, 320
  genetic differences, 371–373
  life expectancy, 136, 137
  marriage statistics, 128
  median age at first marriage, 128
  sex ratios at birth, 130
  wages, 375
Sex offenses, arrests for, 390
Sexual activity, U.S., 373
Sexual harassment, 693
Sexual partners, 373
Seychelles, 860–861
Sgrena, Giuliana, 37
Shah of Iran (Mohammad Reza
  Pahlavi), 688, 792
Shang Dynasty, 664
Shanghai, China, 747, 748
Shannon River, 795
Sharon, Ariel, 34, 36, 697, 699, 796,
  798
  Gaza withdrawal, 509, 700
Shasta, Mount, 502
Shatt-al-Arab, 793
Shavuot, 346, 356, 357
Shays's Rebellion, 95
Sheehan, Cindy, 1034
Shemini Atzeret, 356
Shenandoah (dirigible), 219
Shenandoah National Park, 174
Shepard, Alan B., Jr., 427, 428, 684
Sherman, William T., 148, 167
Sherman Antitrust Act, 676
Shetland Islands, 484, 890
Shi'ite, 364
Shikoku, Japan, 801
Shintoism, 366
Ship canals, 451
Shipping, commerce, 643
Ships. See Steamships
Shipwrecks, 211, 218–219
Shooting stars, 416
Shoreline of U.S., 502
Shrove Tuesday, 195, 355, 357n
Siam. See Thailand
Sicily, Italy, 666, 777, 799
Sidereal time, 351, 400
Sierra Leone, 484, 861
Sign language, 483
Sihanouk, Norodom, 740
Sikh festival dates, 358
Sikhism, 365
Sikh Rebellion (India), 689, 789
Sikkim, Kingdom of, 789
Silurian Period, 576
Silver, 575
Simchat Torah, 356, 357
Simplon Tunnels, 451
Simpson, O. J., 693

Sinai Peninsula, 684, 686, 763–765,
  797
Singapore, 681, 819, 861–862
Singers. See People
Singing Cave, 497
Sino-Japanese War (1894–95), 676,
  748
Sins, Seven Deadly, 370
Sioux Falls, S.D., 171, 178
Sirhan, Sirhan Bishara, 119, 686
Sistine Chapel, 446, 669
Six-Day War, 686, 797. See also
  Arab-Israeli conflict
Skating:
  figure, 930, 933, 970–971
  speed, 931, 933, 969–970
Skiing, 931, 968–969
Skopje, Macedonia, 816
Skylab, 428
Skyscrapers, 444–445
  first, 102
Slavery:
  abolished in British Empire, 674
  Dred Scott case, 674
  first slaves to America, 95, 102, 174,
    668
  first state to forbid, 174
  importation barred to U.S., 673
  Kansas-Nebraska Act, 674
  prohibited in U.S., 97, 115
Slovakia, 862–863
Slovenia, 863
Small Business Administration
  (SBA), 84
Smallpox, 672
Smallpox vaccination, 582
Smith, Bessie, 679
Smith, John, 155, 162
Smith, Joseph, 150, 174
Smithsonian Institution, 85
Smoking, 561, 562
Smoky Hill River, 501
Snake River, 501
Snowdon, Mount, 890
Snowfalls, greatest, 597
Snyder-Gray case, 679
Soccer, 1022–1023
  Major League, 1023
  World Cup, 1022–1023
Socialist parties, U.S., 54
Social Security, 33, 36, 39
Social security, 632
  benefits, 631
  Social Security Act, 632
Societies and associations, 653–662
Society Islands, 774
Socrates, 312, 665
Sofia, Bulgaria, 738
Software, top-selling, 568
Solar-powered aircraft, 438
Solar system, 400–414, 571, 581
Solar time, 351, 400
Solomon Islands, 863–864
Solon, 664
Solstices, 403
Somalia, 864–865
Somaliland, French. See Djibouti
Somme, Battle of the, 678
Somoza Debayle, Gen. Anastasio,
  688, 834
Songs:
  most downloaded, 275
  most played, 275
Songs, state, 142–177
Sonoran Desert, 498
"Sooners", 167
Sophocles, 312, 665
Sorority, first, 102
Sosa, Sammy, 960, 1017
Sound:
  first flight faster than, 437
  speed of, 459
South Africa, Republic of, 677,
  865–866
  Truth and Reconciliation
    Commission, 866

South America:
 area and elevation of, **487**
 exploration of, **485**
 map of, **529**
 southernmost point of, **746**
South Carolina, 170
South China Sea, 494
South Dakota, 170–171
Southeast Asia Treaty Organization (SEATO), 683
Southeast Asia War. *See* Vietnam War
Southern Cameroons. *See* Nigeria
"Southern lights", 417
Southern Ocean, 494
Southern Rhodesia. *See* Zimbabwe
South Georgia, 894
South Island (New Zealand), 496, 833
South Korea, 43, 511
South Platte River, 501
South Pole:
 exploration of, **485**
 first flight over, **437**
 geography of, **497**
 reached, **677**
South Sandwich Islands, 894
South West Africa. *See* Namibia
Soviet Union, 718
 Afghanistan invasion, **688**
 Germany, nonaggression pact with (1939), **681**
 hydrogen bomb, **683, 684**
 Korean Airlines incident, **689**
 nuclear weapons testing, **683**
 in World War II, **681**
Soybeans, export and import of, **639**
Soyuz space flights, 429, 430, 431, 433
Space. *See* Astronomy
Space accidents, 221
Space exploration, 422–434
 astronauts, **427–429**
 of Jupiter, **425–427**
 of Mars, **422, 423, 424**
 of Mercury, **424**
 Moon landings and explorations, **424, 425–427**
 of Saturn, **423, 426**
 Soviet space program, **429**
 space shuttles, **42, 43, 422, 428, 430, 689**
 staffed flights, **429–434**
 of the Moon, **422**
 of the Sun, **423, 425–427**
 U.S. staffed flight programs, **427–429**
 unstaffed flights, **425–427**
 women in space program, **427**
Space Needle (Seattle), 447
SpaceShipOne, 434
Spain, 700, 866–867
 Arabs in, **666**
 civil war in, **681, 867**
 Cuban rebellion from, **676**
 exploration by, **669**
 French occupation of, **673**
 loss of New World colonies, **671, 673**
 Phoenician colony in, **664**
 republic in, **680**
 revolution in, **675**
 Spanish Armada defeated, **670, 867, 885**
 structures, **446**
Spamalot, 516
Spanish-American War, 97, 676, 677
Spanish Armada, 670, 867, 885
Spanish Civil War, 681, 867
Spanish influenza, 211, 213
Spanish Succession, War of, 671
Sparta, 665
Spartacus, 665
Speakers of the House, 78
Speech, freedom of, 114
Speed:
 of animals, **588**
 of light, **400**
Speed limits, 608
Speed records:
 airplanes, **439**

 sports. *See under individual sports*
Speed skating, 931, 933, 969–970
Spelling bee, 476
Spermatozoa, 582
Sphinx, Great, 445, 663
Spingarn Medal, 259
Spinning, inventions, 582
Spiral nebula, 398
Spirit of St. Louis (plane), 436
Spitsbergen Islands, 485, 837
Sports, 917–1023. *See also individual sports*
 disasters, **223**
 Olympic Games, **917–934**
 personalities, **957–961**
Springfield, Ill., 150, 178
Spring tides, 401
Sputnik I (satellite), 684, 851
Sri Jayawardenepura Kotte, Sri Lanka, 868
Sri Lanka, 496, 868
Stalin, Joseph, 312, 679, 681, 682, 683, 850
Stalingrad, Battle of, 681
Stamp Act, 671
Stamps:
 postage, **101, 440–442**
Standard of living, world, 710
Standard Oil Trust, 676
Standard time, 351–352
Stanford University, 322
Stanley Cup, 962
Stanton, Elizabeth Cady, 97, 374
Stardust space mission, 423
Starr, Kenneth, 73–74
Stars, 399, 400–401
 birth and death of, **399**
 brightest, **401**
 configurations (2006), **418–421**
 constellations, **401, 416–417**
 defined, **399**
 neutron, **398**
 phenomena (2006), **418–421**
"Stars" of entertainment. *See* People
"Star-Spangled Banner", 96, 98, 103, 106, 182
START. *See* Strategic Arms Reduction Talks
Star Wars, 516
State, Secretaries of (U.S. states), 142–177
State, U.S. Dept. of:
 description of, **83**
 secretaries of, **83, 85–90, 102, 694**
Staten Island, 195–196
States, Confederate, 97, 104
States of U.S., 142–179
 births and birth rates, **129**
 capitals, **142–177, 178**
 cities: largest of each state, **142–177, 178**
 coastlines, **502**
 colleges and universities, **323–345**
 Congress members, **46–49**
 constitutional provisions about, **111, 113**
 crime index, **99**
 deaths and death rates, **134**
 execution methods, **387**
 first, **102, 104**
 governors of, **49, 142–177**
 health insurance, **558**
 holidays, **358**
 land and water area of, **178**
 minimum wages, **627**
 motor vehicle laws, **608**
 newspapers, **272**
 order of entry into Union, **104**
 per capita personal income, **628**
 populations of, **122, 142–177**
 poverty in, **630**
 presidential election results (2004), **45**
 procedure for admitting new states to, **113**
 Representatives, **47–49**
 Senators, **46–47**

 taxes. *See* Taxes
 taxes collected and spent, federal, **1028**
 temperature highs and lows, **599–600**
 thirteen original, **109**
 tourism, **603, 604**
States' rights, 111, 113, 115
States' Rights Democratic Party, 54
Statistics, U.S., 120–141
Statue of Liberty, 164, 592, 676
Steam engines, 582, 672
Steam heat, first, 102
Steamships, 582
 disasters, **211, 218–219**
Steel, export and import of, **639**
Steinem, Gloria, 374
Stem cells, 40, 569
Steroids, 38
Stewart, Martha, 513
Stikine River, 501
Stimulants (drugs), 560
Stock-car racing, 1000
Stockholm, Sweden, 871
Stock market:
 most active stocks, **645, 646**
 top stocks (by dollar value), **645**
 top stocks (by market value), **646**
Stolen identity, 647–648
Stonehenge, 663
Stone Mountain, 148
Storms, 214–215
Strategic Arms Limitation Talks (SALT), 688, 851
Strategic Arms Reduction Talks (START), 691, 692
Stratopause, 402
Stratosphere, 402
 first flight into, **437**
Strikes (labor), 624
 first in U.S., **102**
Structures, 447
 ancient, **445–447**
 bridges, **448–449**
 buildings, **444–445**
 canals, **451**
 dams, **450**
 famous, **445–447**
 museums, **446, 447**
 Seven Wonders, **447**
 towers, **445**
 tunnels, **451**
Stuart, House of, 885
Students, 318–345
 in educational institutions, **320**
Style guide (writing), 473–475
Submarines, 678
 disasters, **211, 218–219**
 first atomic powered, **683**
Subways:
 commuter use, **606**
 first in U.S., **102**
 world's largest, **606**
Sucre, Bolivia, 733
Sudan, 34, 35, 42, 484, 868–869
 Darfur, **34, 35, 701**
Suez Canal, 451, 674, 675, 684, 764, 797
Suffix, 481
Suffragists, 678
Sugar:
 export and import of, **639**
 U.S. consumption of, **640**
Sugar Bowl (football), 935
Suharto, 790
Suicide, 137, 138
Sukarno, 790
Sukkot, 356, 357
Sulawesi (Celebes), 496
Suleiman I ("the Magnificent"), 669
Sulfa drugs, 582
Sulfur dioxide, 586
Sumatra, 496, 790
Sumerian civilization, 664
Summers, Lawrence, 1034
Sun, 399, 400–401
 eclipses of, **421**

exploration of, **423, 425–427**
seasons, **353**
time based on, **351**
Sungari River, 495
Sunni, 364
Sunspots, 400
Sun Yat-sen, 313, 677, 748
Super Bowl, 515, 941, 942
Superior, Lake, 157, 494, 742
Supernovas, 399
Supersonic aircraft, 437, 438
Supreme Court, U.S., 91–95, 95, 701
constitutional provisions about, **113**
first black member, **101, 686**
first law declared unconstitutional, **93, 101**
first woman member, **100, 102, 688**
justices of, **91–92, 686, 688, 690, 692, 693**
major decisions, **383–384**
milestone cases, **93, 677, 683, 686**
notable decisions (2004–2005), **94–95**
salaries of justices, **80**
Surgery, first antiseptic, 675
Suriname, 870
Surveying measures, 455
Surveyor space program, 425
Susquehanna River, 501
Sutter's Mill, 96, 145
Suu Kyi, Aung San, 829
Suva, Fiji, 768
Sverdrup Islands, 743
Swaziland, 870–871
Sweden, 871–872
Swimming, 923–928, 930, 971–974
synchronized, **930**
Switzerland, 872
Sydney, Australia, 724
Symbols of chemical elements, 574–575
Symphonies, 264
Syndicated TV programs, 279
Synodic month, 400
Syphilis, 582
Syria, 34, 36, 38, 509, 812, 872–873
and Israel, **797, 812, 872–873**

T

T. rex, **570**
Tabernacles, Feast of, 356, 357n
Tabloid newspaper, first, 102
Taft, William Howard, 54, 57, 66, 92, 97. See also Presidents, U.S.
Tahiti, 774
Taipei, Taiwan, 873
Taiwan (Republic of China), 748, 873–874
Tajikistan, 874–875
Taj Mahal, 446, 670
Talabani, Jalal, 38, 793, 795
Taliban, 694, 698, 718–719
Tallahassee, Fla., 147, 178
Tallinn, Estonia, 767
Talmud, 360
Tamerlane, 313, 718
Tamil Tiger guerrillas, 868
Tanana River, 501
Tanganyika. See Tanzania
Tanganyika, Lake, 484, 494
T'ang Dynasty, 748
Tannenberg, Battle of, 678
Tanzania, 875–876
Taoism, 366, 664
Tarawa, Kiribati, 805
Tashkent, Uzbekistan, 899
Tasmania, 485, 496, 725
Tax cuts, 76
Taxes, 1024–1028
Bush tax cuts, **1024**
collection of, **1028**
constitutional provisions for, **110, 111, 116, 118**
corporation, **1025, 1028**
estate, **1025, 1027**

franchise, **1028**
gift, **1025, 1027**
income tax, federal, **1024–1026**
income tax, history of, **1024**
Internal Revenue Service, **1024–1025**
returns filed electronically, **1026**
state, **1027, 1028**
Taxonomy, 572
Taylor, Charles, 700, 813
Taylor, Zachary, 53, 55, 57, 63, 96.
See also Presidents, U.S.
Tbilisi, Georgia, 776
Teapot Dome scandal, 67, 98, 679
Technology. See Computers
Teen birth rates, 132
Teen pregnancy, 132
Tegucigalpa, Honduras, 785
Teheran, Iran, 791
Teheran Conference (1943), 681
Tektites, 416
Telegraph:
first transatlantic cable, **674**
invention of, **582, 674**
Telephones:
Bell System broken up, **689**
invention of, **582, 676**
Telephone statistics, world, 717
Telescopes, invention of, 582
Television, 279–280
awards for, **251, 258, 259, 260**
first color, **683**
inventions, **582, 679**
network programs, **279**
set ownership, **279**
specials, **279**
stations in U.S., **120, 180–204**
syndicated programs, **279**
viewing, **279**
Tempel 1 comet, 42, 424, 514
Temperatures:
record highs and lows, **597, 599–600**
scales, **452, 455**
in U.S. cities, **180–204, 601–602**
U.S. extremes, **597, 598**
wind chill factors, **602**
in world cities, **605**
world extremes, **597, 598**
Ten Commandments, 370, 664
Tennessee, 171–172
Tennessee-French River, 501
Tennessee River, 501
Tennessee Valley Authority (TVA), 84, 172
Tennis, 515, 987–992
Tenzing Norgay, 492
Teotihuacán, 445, 665
Territorial expansion of U.S., 104, 105
Territories, 702
Territories of U.S., 895–898
acquisition of, **104**
execution methods, **387**
governors of, **895–898**
land areas, **104, 895–898**
population, **122, 895–898**
Terrorism, 211, 223–224, 676, 687, 689, 690, 692, 698, 719, 804, 811, 869, 876, 888, 901
London bombings (2005), **34, 41, 42, 510, 888, 1033**
Sept. 11, 2001, attacks, **101, 211, 224, 698, 719, 858**
Terrorist organizations, 715–717
Texas, 172–173, 674
Textiles:
export and import of, **639**
Producer Price index, **637**
Thailand, 876–877
Thames River, 885
Thanksgiving Day, 346, 356, 357
Thant, U, 907
Thatcher, Margaret, 688, 689, 691, 886
Theater:
awards for, **246, 252**

first vaudeville, **102**
longest Broadway runs, **266**
Theft, 390
The Hague, The Netherlands, 831
Theories, scientific, 578–582
Thermodynamics, 582
Thermometer:
invention, **582**
scales, **582**
Thermopause, 402
Thermopylae, Battles of, 665
Thermosphere, 402
Thieu, Nguyen Van, 685, 903
Thimphu, Bhutan, 733
Third Estate, 672
Thirty Years' War, 670, 778, 871
Thomas, Norman, 54, 56
Thomas Aquinas, 668
Thompson, Hunter, 517
Thorshavn, Faroe Islands, 760
Threatened and endangered species, 589
Three Mile Island, 216, 688
Tibet, 484, 747
Tidal shoreline of U.S., 502
Tidal waves, 213
Tides, 401
Tien Shan Mountains, 747, 809
Tierra del Fuego, 746
Tigris River, 495, 793
Till, Emmett, 383
Time:
kinds of, **351**
time of day, cities, **504**
universal and civil, **351, 421**
in world cities, **499**
Timelines:
of civil rights, **383–384**
of staffed space flights, **429–434**
of U.S. history, **95–101**
of unstaffed space flights, **425–427**
of women's rights movement, **374–375**
of world history, **663–701**
TIME Man of the Year, 1029
Time zones, 351–352
Timor, East, 696, 790
Tin, 575
Tinian (island), 897
Tippecanoe, Battle of, 62, 151
Tirana, Albania, 719
Tires, pneumatic: invention of, 676
Titan (moon), 410
***Titanic* (ocean liner), 218, 678**
Titanium, 575
Titicaca, Lake, 494, 734
Title IX, 375
Tito (Josip Broz), 314, 682, 859
Titus, Arch of, 445
Tobacco:
taxes, **1025**
use of, **561**
Tobago. See Trinidad and Tobago
Tocantins River, 495
Togo, 36, 877, 1036
Tojo, Hideki, 682
Tokelau Island, 833
Tokyo, Japan, 670, 801
subway system, **606**
Toledo, Ohio, 166
Tombigbee River, 501
Ton:
gross or long, **452, 457**
metric, **452, 456, 457**
net or short, **452, 457**
Tonga, 877–878
Tony Awards, 252
Topeka, Kans., 152, 178
Torah, 356, 360
Tornadoes, 211, 215–216, 597
Toronto, Canada, 742
Toulouse, France, 770
Tourism, 603, 604, 605
Tower, Leaning, of Pisa, 446
Tower of London, 446
Towers, tallest, 445

Toxic air pollutants, 587
Toys and games, export and import of, 639
Track and field, 983–986
  history of mile run, 985
  mile records, 985
  Olympic Games, 917–923
  world and U.S. records, 983–985
Tractor, invented, 582
Trade. See Foreign trade
Trade Commission, Federal, 84
Trade Commission, U.S. International, 84
Trademarks, 652
Trade Representative, Office of U.S., 82
Trade unions, 625
Trafalgar, Battle of, 673
Traffic jams:
  major causes, 607
  worst highway bottlenecks, 607
Trail of Tears, 96
Trans-Alaska Pipeline, 143
Transarctic flight, first, 437
Transatlantic flights, 435–439
Transcontinental flights, 436, 438
Transistor, 582
Transpacific flights, 435–439
Transplants, organ, 559
Transportation. See also Aviation
  commuting, 606
  driving, 607, 608, 609
  inventions, 578–582
  railroads, 611
  subways, 606
Transportation, U.S. Dept. of:
  description of, 83
  secretaries of, 83, 89–90
Travel:
  current travel warnings, 604
  diplomatic personnel, 914–916
  foreign embassies, 910–913
  National parks, most visited, 594
  temperatures in tourist cities, 605
  top destinations, 603
  top states and cities visited, 603, 604
  tourism, 603, 604, 605
  U.S., to, 604
  U.S. tourists, 603
  warnings, 604
  websites, 566
  world travel statistics, 603
Treason, defined, 113
Treasurers, of states, 142–177
Treasury, U.S. Dept. of:
  description of, 83
  secretaries of, 83, 85–90
Trees, state, 142–177
Trent, Council of, 350, 669
Trenton, N.J., 162, 178
Triangle Shirtwaist Factory fire (1911), 217, 677
Triassic Period, 576
Tribes, Indian, 379
Trieste, 799
Trimble, David, 888, 889
Trinidad and Tobago, 878
Trinity River, 501
Trinity Sunday, 357n
Triple Alliance, 676
Triple Crown (horse racing), 979, 982
Tripoli, Libya, 814
Tristan da Cunha, 894
Trojan War, 664
Tropical year, 400
Tropic of Cancer, 353, 486
Tropic of Capricorn, 353, 486
Tropopause, 402
Troposphere, 402
Trotsky, Leon, 314, 678, 680, 682, 850
Trotting. See Harness racing
Troy, ancient, 664
Troy weight, 452, 455, 457
Trucial States. See United Arab Emirates
Trucks, best-selling, 609
Trudeau, Pierre E., 314, 743

Truman, Harry S., 54, 55, 57, 58, 67–68, 98, 159, 683. See also Presidents, U.S.
  assassination attempt on, 119
Truman Doctrine, 68, 682
Trusteeship Council, UN, 908
Trusteeships, UN, 908
Tsunami (2004), 33, 35, 210, 213, 510, 701
Tsunamis, 210, 213
Tuberculosis, 676
Tubman, Harriet, 674
Tucson, Ariz., 202
Tudor, House of, 885
Tufts Poetry Prize, 258
Tugela Falls, 496
Tulsa, Okla., 167, 202
Tungsten filament, invention of, 579
Tunis, Tunisia, 878
Tunisia, 878–879
Tunnels, 451
Turbojet, first flight, 437
Turkey, 879–880
Turkmenistan, 880–881
Turks and Caicos Islands, 894
Turner, Nat, 674
Tuskegee Institute, 142
Tutankhamen, 664
Tutu, Rev. Desmond, 225, 690
Tuvalu, 881–882
Tweed Ring, 675
Twelfth Night (holiday), 355
Tydings-McDuffie Act, 845
Tyler, John, 52–53, 57, 62, 96. See also Presidents, U.S.
Typhoons, 215
Tyrannosaurus rex, 570

U

U-2 incident (1960), 684
Uganda, 882
Ukraine, 701, 883–884
Ulaan Baatar, Mongolia, 826
Ulbricht, Walter, 779
Ulster, Northern Ireland, 888
Ulysses space mission, 423, 426
Uncertainty principle, 582
Underage drinking, 561
Unemployment. See also Cities, U.S.
  rate, 623, 624
Union Islands. See Tokelau Island
Union Labor Party, 53
Unions, labor, 42, 625
  labor organizations, 625
  membership by occupation, 625
  membership by state, 625n, 626
United Arab Emirates, 884
United Arab Republic, 684
United Kingdom, 884–894
  dependencies of, 702, 891
  formation of, 671
  London bombings (2005), 34, 41, 42, 510, 88, 1033
  prime ministers of, 887
  rulers of, 886
United Nations, 98, 907–910
  charter of, 907
  "China seat", 686, 748, 874
  established, 682
  events, 682, 686
  General Assembly, 907
  in Persian Gulf War, 794
  member nations of, 909
  oil-for-food program, 37, 38, 42, 43, 1030
  peacekeeping operations, 908
  in Persian Gulf War, 691
  representatives to, U.S., 910
  Secretariat, 907
  Security Council, 907
United Nations Development Index, 710
United States. See also Foreign trade; United States government; United States history

air distances, 614–615
area of, 104
armed forces of, 392–397
birth statistics, 129–132
bridges, 448–449
canals, 451
charities in, 140
church membership in, 362
cities, 180–204, 209
climate extremes, 598
coastline, 502
colleges and universities, 323–345
contributions to other countries, 637
crime statistics, 120
current events, 32–33
dams, 450
dance companies, 265
death statistics, 134–138
diplomatic personnel to and from, 914–916
direct investment in other countries, 636–637
disasters, 210–224
divorce statistics, 120, 128, 129
economic statistics, 643–646
education statistics, 120
epidemics, 211, 213
exports from, 639
extreme points of, 500
family statistics, 627
foreign-born population, 382
foreign embassies in, 910–913
geography, 120
great seal of, 103
growth of, 122, 123
health statistics, 552–562
highest points, 503
holidays, 355–357
immigration to, 382
imports of, 639
labor force, 120, 619–624
latitudes and longitudes, 504
libraries, 274
life expectancy in, 120, 136, 137
lowest points, 503
magazines, 273
map of, 526–527
marriage statistics, 128
motor vehicle laws, 608
national anthem, 106
National Park System, 590–594, 594
newspapers, 272
opera companies, 265
poets laureate, 273
population, 120–124
postal regulations, 440–442
race and ethnicity, 376–384
societies and associations, 653–662
state profiles, 142–177
state temperatures, 599–600
statistical profile of, 120
structures, 447
symphonies of, 264
tallest buildings, 444–445
territories of, 104, 895–898
travel and transportation, 603–615
tunnels, 451
weather and climate in, 598, 599–600, 601–602
United States dependencies, 702
United States government. See also individual agencies, offices, and subjects
  armed forces, 392–397
  budget of. See Federal budget
  cabinet, 85–90
  Congress, 46–49, 77–80
  Constitution (text), 109–118
  executive departments and agencies, 82–85
  expenditures and receipts of, 634–635
  foreign aid, 637
  foreign investment, 636–637
  House of Representatives, 47–49, 77, 80

independent agencies, 84–85
judicial powers, 113
National Park System, 590–594, 594
presidents of, 57, 59–77
receipts and outlays of, 634
salaries of U.S. officials, 80
Senate, 46–47, 77
Speakers of the House, 78
Supreme Court, 91–95, 113
vice presidents, 57–58
voting qualifications, 116, 118
United States history, 50–119
armed services, 392–397
Articles of Confederation, 95, 102
assassinations and attempts in, 119
Atlantic Charter, 681
cabinets, 85–90
chronology of, 671
civil rights, 383–384
Civil War, 675
colonization, 670
Continental Congresses, 95, 102, 671
Declaration of Independence, 95, 107–108
exploration, 484
firsts in, 101–102
Gettysburg Address, 119
immigration, 381
Indians, American, 379, 380
Monroe Doctrine, 106
national committee chairmen, 51
national political conventions, 51
presidential elections, 45, 52–55
presidents, 57, 59–77
Pulitzer Prizes for, 242–243
Revolutionary War period, 671
"Star-Spangled Banner", 106
territorial expansion, 104, 105
timeline of, 95–101
women's rights movement, 374–375
Universal time, 421
Universe, origin of, 399
Universities. See Colleges and universities
Unleavened Bread, Feast of, 355, 357n
Upanishads, 364
Upper Volta. See Burkina Faso
Ural River, 495
Uranium, chemical properties of, 575
Uranus (planet), 401, 407, 411–412. See also Planets
Urban populations, world's largest, 704
Urey, Harold, 315, 579, 680
Uruguay, 37, 898–899
Uruguay River, 737, 898
Utah, 173
Utrecht, Peace of, 671
Uzbekistan, 39, 899–900, 1032

V

VA. See Veterans' Affairs (VA), U.S. Dept. of
Vacations:
average length, 605
types, 603
Vaccinations:
polio, 581, 683
smallpox, 582, 672
Vacuum tube, 581
Vaduz, Liechtenstein, 814
Valdes Peninsula, Argentina, 487
Valentine's Day, 346, 355
Valletta, Malta, 820
Valley Forge, Pa., 169, 671
Valois, House of, 771
Van Allen Belt (layer), 417, 582
Van Buren, Martin, 52–53, 57, 62, 96. See also Presidents, U.S.
Vancouver, Canada, 742
Vandalism arrests, 390
Vandals, 666
Vanuatu, 900

Vatican, 446
Vatican City (Holy See), 900–901. See also Roman Catholic Church
Vatican Council I, 363
Vatican Council II, 363, 685, 689, 901
Vaudeville theater, first, 102
Vedas, 364
V-E Day (1945), 681
Vegetables and fruits:
export and import of, 639
U.S. consumption of, 640
Venera probes, 425–427
Venezuela, 701, 901–902
Venus (planet), 401, 403–404, 407. See also Planets
Venus de Milo, 665
Vermont, 173–174
Verrazano-Narrows Bridge, 448
Versailles, Palace of, 446, 670, 778
Versailles, Treaty of, 679, 680, 681, 778
Vesuvius, Mount, 211
Veterans:
March on Washington, 680
Veterans' Affairs (VA), U.S. Dept. of:
description of, 83
secretaries of, 83, 90
Veterans Day, 346, 356
Veterans from U.S. wars, 393, 397
Veteran statistics, 397
Veto power, 81, 110
Vezina Trophy, 963
Vice presidential candidates, 52–55
Vice presidents, U.S.:
as acting president, 118
election procedure for, 112, 115
first woman candidate for, 102
list of, 57–58
nomination of, 50
powers and duties of, 109
salary of, 80
succession to presidency, 82, 112, 117, 118
Vichy, France, 770, 771, 903
Vicksburg, Battle of, 675
Victoria (island), 496
Victoria (queen of England), 674, 676, 677, 885
Victoria, Lake, 494, 875, 882
Victoria, Seychelles, 860
Victoria Falls, 484
Videocassettes, 278
Video games, 563, 564
Vienna, Austria, 726
Vienna, Congress of, 673, 726, 770
Vientiane, Laos, 809
Viet Cong, 685, 903
Vietnam, 809, 902–903
Vietnam War, 98, 683, 685, 903. See also Cambodia; Laos; Thailand
Vikings, 759, 837
Viking space program, 425, 426
Vilnius, Lithuania, 815
Vinson Massif, 487
Violent crime, 385–391
Virgil, 665
Virginia, 174–175
Virginia Beach, Va., 174, 178, 203
Virgin Islands, British, 892
Virgin Islands, U.S., 678, 896
Vitamins, discoveries, 582
V-J Day (1945), 681
Vocabulary:
basic foreign words, 478
foreign expressions, 479
Latin and Greek word elements, 481–482
misused, 477–478
Volcanoes, 488–489
current eruptions, 488
eruptions, 211–213
"Ring of Fire", 488
volcanic eruptions, 489
Volga River, 495
Volume:
formulas for, 459
measure of, 454, 456

Volunteer work, 141
Voskhod flights, 429
Vostok flights, 429
Voting:
by 18-year-olds, 118, 686
in presidential elections, 45, 50, 52–55, 56
rights, 116, 118
voter turnout, 56
women's suffrage, 102, 117, 373, 679
Voting Rights Act, 99
Voyager space program, 423, 426, 689, 691

W

Wabash River, 501
Wage gap, 375
Wages and hours:
minimum wages, 627
by occupation, 621
Wake Island, 898
Waldheim, Kurt, 690, 726, 907
Wales, 885, 890
Wales, Prince of, 39, 288, 513, 1031
Walesa, Lech, 225, 691, 846
Walking. See Track and field
Wallace, George, 687
assassination attempt on, 119
Wallis and Futuna Islands, 774
Wall of China, Great, 446, 665, 747
Wannsee Conference, 680, 682
War, U.S. Dept. of:
secretaries of, 85–88
War casualties, 393
War crimes, 680, 682, 689
War of 1812, 96, 673
Warren, Earl, 92
Warren Report (1964), 686
Wars, 392. See also specific wars
Wars, current, 714
Warsaw, Poland, 846
Warsaw Ghetto, 680
Warsaw Pact, 684, 691
Warsaw Treaty Organization, 787, 846, 849, 851
Wars of the Roses, 668, 885
War veterans, 393
Washington (state), 175, 502
Washington, DC, 203–204
civil rights rally in (1963), 685
established, 673
march on, 384
Twenty-third Amendment, 118
U.S. capital moved to, 96
in War of 1812, 673
Washington Monument, 107
Washington, George, 52, 57, 59, 95, 671, 672. See also Presidents, U.S.
Washington, Mount, 503
Washington Monument, 107
Washington's Birthday, 346, 355
Washita River, 501
Water, boiling and freezing points, 452
Waterfalls, 496
Watergate scandal, 40, 70, 99, 513, 687, 1031
Waterloo, Battle of, 673, 778, 885
Water supply of the world, 589
Watt, James, 316, 582, 682
Watts riots (1965, 1966), 99, 686
Weapons, 388, 390
Weapons of mass destruction, 35, 39, 76, 700, 701, 794
Weather and climate, 595–602
blizzards, 215
clouds, 597
disastrous storms, 211, 214–215
floods, 213
hail and hailstones, 597
hurricanes, 214–215, 595–596
snowfalls, 597
tidal waves, 213
tornadoes, 211, 215–216, 597

tropical storms, **214–215**
of U.S. cities, **601–602**
U.S. extremes, **598**
of U.S. states, **599, 600**
world extremes, **597, 598**
Weaving, cloth, **580**
Webby Awards, **263**
Websites, **566**
science, **578**
Weights, atomic, **574–575**
Weights and measures, **452–459**
capacities and volumes, **454, 456, 456–458**
conversion tables, **456–458**
Weimar Republic, **778**
Weise, Jeff, **38**
Wellington, New Zealand, **833**
Western Sahara (proposed state), **827, 903–904**
Western Samoa. *See* Samoa
West Indies. *See also specific islands*
exploration of, **484**
Westminster Abbey, **446**
Westmoreland, William, **1039**
West Papua, **790**
West Point (U.S. Military Academy), **164**
West Virginia, **175–176**
Wheel, **582**
Whig Party (U.S.), **52, 53, 61, 63**
Whipple's theory (of comets), **415**
Whiskey Rebellion, **672**
White-collar crime, **387**
White House, **82**
White River, **501**
Whitney, Mount, **145, 502, 503**
Whitsunday, **356**
Wichita, Kans., **152, 178**
Willemstad, Netherlands Antilles, **832**
William II (kaiser of Germany), **778**
Williams, Serena, **961, 988, 990, 991**
Williams, Venus, **515, 961, 988, 990, 991**
Williamsburg, Va., **174**
William the Conqueror, **885**
Wilmington, Del., **147, 178**
Wilson, Harold, **317, 886**
Wilson, Woodrow, **54, 55, 57, 66, 97.**
See also Presidents, U.S.
Wimbledon champions, **515, 990–991**
Wind Cave National Park, **497**
Wind chill factors, **602**
Windhoek, Namibia, **829**
Windmill, **582**
Windward Islands. *See* St. Lucia; St. Vincent and the Grenadines
Winnie Mae (plane), **437**
Winnipeg, Lake, **494**
Wisconsin, **176–177**
Wisconsin River, **501**
Wives of presidents, **59**
Wolfowitz, Paul, **38**
Wollaston Islands, **746**
Women:
in armed forces, **682**
firsts by, **102**
firsts in aviation, **435–439**
income, **375**
in labor force, **624**
life expectancy of, **136, 137**
marriage statistics, **128**
math and science performance, **371**
mothers, **130, 131**
mothers employed, **624**
political firsts by, **102**
presidents' wives, **59**
suffrage for, **98, 102, 117, 679**
Title IX, **375**
voting, **373**
wage gap, **375**
women's rights convention, **96**
women's rights movement, **374–375**
Women, famous. *See* People
Women's National Basketball Association, **956**

Wonders of the World, Seven, **447**
Wood. *See* Lumber and wood
Wood pulp, **637, 639**
Woods, Tiger, **961, 995, 996, 998**
Word roots, **481**
Words:
crossword puzzle guide, **460–472**
easily confused, **477–478**
foreign, **478, 479–481**
Latin and Greek, **481–482**
mispronounced, **476**
Work stoppages, **624**
World. *See also* Earth (planet)
area, **487**
bridges, **448–449**
canals, **451**
caves and caverns, **497**
cities. *See* Cities, world
climate extremes, **597, 598**
comparative statistics, **703**
corrupt leaders, most, **710**
countries of, **718–906**
current events, **33–35**
deserts, **498**
disasters, **210–224**
elevations, **487**
energy, **585**
environment, **584**
explorations, **484–485**
famous structures, **445–447**
flags of, **519–522**
foreign aid, **711**
freedom, political, **708**
governments. *See* Governments, world
highest mountain peaks, **493**
history, **663–701.** *See also* History, world
islands, **496**
maps of, **523–536**
military expenditures, **714**
national holidays, **359**
profile of, **702**
rivers, **495**
Seven Wonders of, **447**
statistics, **702–717**
subway systems, **606**
tallest buildings, **444–445**
tallest towers, **445**
time zones, **351–352**
tourism destinations, **603**
tunnels, **451**
volcanoes, **488–489**
waterfalls, **496**
water supply, **589**
World Bank (IBRD), **682**
World Court, International Court of Justice, **690**
World Cup, Soccer, **1022–1023**
World history:
by country, **718–906**
World sea ports, **643**
World Series, **1006–1009**
records and standing, **1006–1009**
World's Fair, New York (1939–40), **681**
World statistics, **702–717**
World Trade Center (New York), **100, 101, 211, 224**
Sept. 11, 2001, bombing, **692, 694, 695, 698, 719, 858**
World War I, **97, 678**
World War II, **98.** *See also specific countries*
chronology, **681**
declarations of war, **681**
treaties, **681**
World Wide Web, **582**
Wrangell, Mount, **502**
Wrestling, **930**
Wright, Orville and Wilbur, **97, 317, 435, 436, 677**
Writers. *See* People
Writing and language, **473–483**
American Sign Language, **483**

ancient, **663**
capitalization, **473**
easily confused words, **477–478**
foreign languages studied, **476**
foreign words and phrases, **478, 479–481**
italicization, **474**
mispronounced words, **476**
most widely spoken, **476**
punctuation, **474–475**
Wyandotte Cave, **151, 497**
Wyoming, **177**

X

Xavier, St. Francis, **484**
Xenon, **575**
Xerography, **582**
Xi Jiang (Si Kiang), **495**
X-rays, **581, 676**

Y

Yale University, **322**
Yalta Conference, **681**
Yamoussoukro, Côte d'Ivoire, **754**
Yangon (Rangoon), Myanmar, **828**
Yangtze River (Chang Jiang), **495, 747**
Yaoundé, Cameroon, **741**
Yaren, Nauru, **830**
Yeager, Chuck, **437, 682**
Year, defined, **351**
Yeats, William Butler, **679**
Yellow fever, **213, 582**
Yellow River, **495, 747**
Yellowstone National Park, **160, 177, 590, 591, 594**
Yellowstone River, **501**
Yeltsin, Boris, **691, 694, 851**
Yemen, **904–905**
Yenisei River, **495**
Yerevan, Armenia, **724**
YMCA, **662**
Yom Kippur, **346, 356, 357**
York, House of, **885**
Yorktown, Battle of, **174, 671**
Yosemite National Park, **145, 591, 594**
Young, Andrew, **376**
Young, Brigham, **317, 674**
Young Women's Christian Association (YWCA), **662**
Yudhoyono, Susilo Bambang, **791**
Yugoslavia. *See* Serbia and Montenegro
Yukon River, **495, 501**
Yukon Territory, Canada, **743**
Yushchenko, Viktor, **35, 44, 701, 883, 884**

Z

Zagreb, Croatia, **755**
Zaire. *See* Congo, Democratic Republic of
Zaire River, **484, 495**
Zama, Battle of, **665**
Zambezi River, **484, 495**
Zambia, **905–906**
Zanzibar. *See* Tanzania
Zenger, John Peter, **671**
Zeppelin, first flight, **435**
Zero, **582**
Zeus, statue of, **447**
Zhou Enlai, **317, 748**
Zimbabwe, **38, 39, 41, 906**
Zinc, **575**
ZIP codes, **205–207, 441**
Zodiac, **417**
Zugspitze Mountains, **777**
Zwingli, Ulrich, **669**

The News of 2005: Nation

By Borgna Brunner (as of Sept. 20, 2005)

Hurricane Katrina

Disaster. Hurricane Katrina slammed into the U.S. Gulf Coast on Aug. 29, destroying towns in Mississippi and Louisiana, displacing a million people, and killing more than 1,000. When levees in New Orleans were breached, 80% of the city was submerged by the flooding. About 20% of its 500,000 citizens were trapped in the city without electricity, food, or drinking water. Rescue efforts were so delayed and haphazard that many were stranded for days on rooftops and in attics before help arrived. The city became a toxic pool of sewage, chemicals, and corpses, and in the ensuing chaos, mayhem and looting were rampant—about a third of the city's police force had simply walked off the job. The 20,000 people who made their way to the Superdome, the city's emergency shelter, found themselves crammed into sweltering and fetid conditions. At a second shelter, the convention center, evacuees were terrorized by roaming gangs and random gunfire. Relief workers, medical help, security forces, and essential supplies remained profoundly inadequate during the first critical days of the disaster.

As most of the city's citizens fled the city, those without cars or the financial means to relocate were left behind. The 100,000 who remained in the drowning city were largely poor and predominantly black, exposing the racial dimension of New Orleans's persistent poverty: 28% of New Orleanians are poor (twice the national average) and 84% of those are black. The elderly poor were also disproportionately affected by the disaster: 70% of the New Orleans area's 53 nursing homes were not evacuated before the hurricane struck.

Hurricane Katrina has been called the most anticipated disaster in modern American history. For years, the Federal Emergency Management Agency (FEMA) had ranked New Orleans and San Francisco as the two cities most vulnerable to catastrophic natural disaster, and a day before Katrina's landfall, the National Weather Service warned that the hurricane would cause "human suffering incredible by modern standards."

Aftermath. Americans were shaken not simply by the magnitude of the disaster but by how ill-prepared all levels of government were in its aftermath. Although New Orleans had performed a hurricane drill the previous year, the city and state governments had no transportation or crime prevention plans in place, and such negligence had devastating consequences. The Department of Homeland Security, the new cabinet agency created for the very purpose of increasing domestic security, had unveiled its National Response Plan in Jan. 2005, which promised "vastly improved coordination among federal, state, local, and tribal organizations . . . by increasing the speed, effectiveness, and efficiency of incident management." Yet Michael Chertoff, the department's secretary, waited until two days after the hurricane hit before putting the plan into effect by declaring it an "incident of national significance." Critics claimed Homeland Security's efforts had been focused on the prevention of terrorism at the expense of preparing for natural catastrophes. Seeming not to grasp the scale of the disaster, Chertoff and Michael Brown, FEMA's director, expressed surprise at the dangerous conditions in the convention center in New Orleans, days after its horrific images had saturated the airwaves, making them appear less informed than the average TV viewer. Brown was so inept in managing the crisis that he was quietly removed after two weeks. All three top jobs at FEMA had been filled by political appointees with no emergency management experience, and half of the agency's senior career professionals had been cut since 2000.

In sharp contrast to the leadership he displayed after the Sept. 11 terrorist attack, President Bush initially seemed off-key and out of touch, declaring that he didn't "think anybody anticipated the breach of the levees" and waiting four days before his first brief visit to the region. Trust in the president's ability to lead the country during a crisis had been a central factor in his reelection, but two-thirds of Americans considered his response to Katrina inadequate. To repair his image, Bush acknowledged the government's faltering response and pledged "one of the largest reconstruction efforts the world has ever seen."

Iraq

Election. Perhaps the most hopeful sign in Iraq since the fall of Saddam Hussein was the country's first free elections in 50 years. About 8.5 million people voted in January, representing about 58% of eligible Iraqis. A coalition of Shiites received 48% of the vote and the Kurdish parties received 26%. Sunni parties received just 2%—most Sunni leaders, feeling marginalized, had called for a boycott.

Insurgency. The elections, however, did not stem the insurgency, which grew increasingly sectarian during 2005 and predominantly involved Sunni insurgents targeting Shiite and Kurdish civilians in suicide bombings. According to a British-based antiwar group, the death toll for Iraqi civilians reached almost 25,000 since the start of the war (no official U.S. or Iraqi tally of civilian casualties exists). The lack of security has continued to frustrate reconstruction efforts. Despite investing $9 billion over the past two years, the U.S. has made only "limited progress" on rebuilding the country's infrastructure. According to the Government Accountability Office, Iraq's oil output and power generation have in fact diminished since the war began.

U.S. Strategy. By mid-September, about 1,900 U.S. soldiers had died and more than 14,000 had been wounded. The absence of a clear strategy for winning the war beyond "staying the course" caused Americans' support for Bush's handling of the war to plummet to an all-time low of 37%, according to a September *Wall Street Journal*/NBC News poll.

The U.S. and Iraqi governments agreed that no firm timetable for the withdrawal of U.S. troops should be set, maintaining that this would simply encourage the insurgency. Withdrawal would take place as Iraqi security forces grew strong enough to assume responsibility for the country's stability. "As Iraqis stand up, Americans will stand down," Bush stated. But the training of Iraqi security forces had been far below what was anticipated. A July 2005 Pentagon report acknowledged that only "a small number" of Iraqi security forces are capable of fighting the insurgency without American help.

Political Uncertainty. In Aug. 2005, after three months of fractious negotiations, Iraqi lawmakers completed a draft constitution that is to be voted on in a national referendum on Oct. 15. Shiites and Kurds supported a decentralized government with autonomous regions in the Kurdish north and the Shiite south; the minority Sunnis wanted strong centralization, fearing that they would otherwise be deprived of the oil wealth of the north and south. That issue, as well as the role of Islam—some Shiites have advocated a theocratic government and the reduction of women's rights—remained unresolved in the final draft. In the end, the Sunnis' objections were overridden, and they in turn vowed to defeat the constitution at the referendum stage. Given that the insurgency is largely fueled by Sunnis, their further disaffection from the political process is likely to bring more division and the possibility of civil war.

The Domestic Agenda

Economy and Legislation. Bush's priority in the first year of his second term was the overhaul of the Social Security system, but despite months of campaigning, the president failed to convince the electorate that the program was in need of a massive restructuring. Legislative accomplishments included the passage of the Central American Free Trade Agreement (CAFTA) and an energy bill, which did not, however, address what Americans consider the single most pressing economic issue: skyrocketing fuel prices. President Bush has firmly ruled out tax cuts to pay for the astronomical costs of the Iraq war ($5 billion a month) and hurricane recovery (estimated to exceed $200 billion) or to offset the federal budget deficit, which had reached $331 billion before Hurricane Katrina struck.

Senate Standoff. When Bush proposed several judicial nominations that Senate Democrats considered emphatically "out of the mainstream," they threatened to filibuster. Republicans, who controlled 55 votes (overruling a filibuster takes 60) vowed to set off the "nuclear option," which meant changing Senate rules to ban filibusters—in which case, Democrats warned, the work of the Senate would be brought to a standstill. A bipartisan "gang of 14" moderate senators ended the showdown through a compromise in May: Democrats would not block several of the controversial nominees from an "up-or-down vote" and would use filibusters only under "extraordinary circumstances"; Republicans would preserve the 200-year-old tradition of filibusters, considered an essential right of the minority party.

Congress and the Courts. Terri Schiavo, a brain-damaged Florida woman who had been kept alive by a feeding tube for 15 years, became the focus of an emotionally charged battle between those who felt removing her feeding tube was tantamount to murder and those who believed she had the right to die instead of remaining in a persistent vegetative state. In an unprecedented intervention, congressional Republicans stepped in to "affirm a culture of life," overriding a decade of legal battles in the Schiavo case involving 19 judges and six state courts, by passing emergency legislation to reopen the case before a federal court. The court upheld the earlier rulings. Schiavo died 13 days after her feeding tube was removed, and her autopsy revealed that her brain had deteriorated to half its normal size and that no treatment could have helped her. While Republican leaders railed against "activist judges," a majority of Americans (70% in an ABC poll) disapproved of Congress's intervention and sized up its motives as political opportunism (67%).

Supreme Court. Two Supreme Court vacancies opened up with the retirement of Sandra Day O'Connor and the death of Chief Justice William Rehnquist, offering the president the opportunity to make his mark on the court. He nominated John Roberts, widely seen as solidly conservative but nonideological, to replace Rehnquist.   □

The News of 2005: World

Indian Ocean Tsunami

On Dec. 26, 2004, a 9.0 magnitude earthquake—the largest earthquake in 40 years—ruptured the floor of the Indian Ocean off the coast of the Indonesian island of Sumatra. The earthquake triggered a tsunami so powerful that the waves caused casualties on the coast of Africa and were detected as far away as the East Coast of the United States. The death toll remains uncertain, but most estimates state that the final tally will exceed 225,000, making it by far the deadliest tsunami in history. Eleven countries bordering the Indian Ocean—all relatively poor and vulnerable—suffered devastation, and millions were left homeless. Hardest hit were Indonesia, Sri Lanka, India, Thailand, and the Maldives. The catastrophic damage included the destruction of entire cities, the contamination of farmland and forests, and the depletion of fishing stocks. Even countries with relatively low death tolls have suffered enormous damage—the Maldives, for example, had damage amounting to 62% of its GDP. Worldwide aid to the afflicted countries was swift and generous.

Aceh: Civil War Ends Amid Destruction

The Asian tsunami focused its worst destruction on the northern Indonesian province of Aceh, killing more than 130,000 people and leaving half a million homeless. But the disaster and relief efforts also led to renewed negotiations to end the three-decades-long civil war. On Aug. 15, the Indonesian government signed a peace deal with the Free Aceh Movement (GAM) that was meant to end Aceh's struggle to secede from Indonesia and create an independent

Islamic state. Indonesia's attempts to crush the movement had led to a brutal military occupation, and the war has claimed 15,000 lives, many of them civilians. As part of the accord, the GAM agreed to give up its demand for independence in exchange for the right to establish political parties and 70% of the revenues from its considerable oil and gas reserves. The last peace deal, signed just two years ago, unraveled within six months when the rebels failed to disarm and Indonesia failed to withdraw troops. Many peg the success of the 2005 peace treaty on what progress the Indonesian government makes in rebuilding a province devastated by war and natural disaster.

The London Terrorist Bombing

On July 7, 2005, London became the victim of a terrorist bombing, Britain's worst attack since World War II. Four bombs exploded in three subway stations and on one double-decker bus during the morning rush hour, killing 52 and wounding more than 700. A group calling itself the Secret Organization of al-Qaeda in Europe claimed responsibility. A week later, on July 21, terrorists attempted another attack on the transit system, but the bombs failed to explode. The following day, London police shot and killed a Brazilian electrician on a subway train in what they said was a case of mistaken identity. It was later revealed that the 27-year-old had exhibited none of the suspicious behavior attributed to him by the police.

A leaked document by a top British government official warned Prime Minister Blair more than a year before the bombings that Britain's engagement in Iraq was fueling Islamic extremism and the perception that the country was a "crusader state," but Blair has repeatedly denied such a link, contending that the bombings were the result of an "evil ideology" that had taken root before the Iraq war.

Blair, who was narrowly reelected to a third term as the country's prime minister in May, has proposed legislation that would toughen the country's antiterrorism measures. These include deporting individuals and banning organizations that "foment, justify, or glorify terrorist violence," and giving the police new powers to arrest terrorism suspects. British polls have shown strong support for the measures, despite the government's acknowledgment that such measures will curb civil liberties.

Withdrawal from Gaza

In mid-August, some 8,000 Israeli settlers were evacuated from the Gaza Strip, which had been occupied by Israel for the previous 38 years. The withdrawal involved 21 Gaza settlements as well as four of the more isolated settlements on the West Bank. The majority of Israelis supported Prime Minister Ariel Sharon's unilateral plan—which he pushed through the Knesset in Oct. 2004—viewing it as Israel's just and humane response toward the Palestinians as well as a significant step toward real security for Israelis. But tens of thousands on the right protested that Sharon, an architect of the settlement movement, had become the agent of Gaza's dismantlement. It was seen as an enormous betrayal.

While Sharon has been lauded for what has arguably been the most significant step in the Israeli-Palestinian peace process since the Oslo peace accord, the prime minister's unstated motives in con-ceding Gaza have been generally assumed to be the strengthening of Israel's hold on the West Bank. This assumption has been borne out by Sharon's approval of additional West Bank housing construction and in pressing ahead with the controversial West Bank security barrier—concrete "facts on the ground" complicating a viable Palestinian state in the West Bank. Whether for philosophical or pragmatic reasons, Sharon is unlikely to offer further gestures toward the Palestinians in the foreseeable future, given that former prime minister Benjamin Netanyahu, riding the crest of a right-wing backlash, is now vying with him for leadership of the Likud Party.

For Palestinians living in Gaza, the withdrawal meant a significant improvement in the quality of life. Gaza, which has the world's highest population density, has gained 25% more land and plans on replacing the settlers' single-family houses with apartment buildings to alleviate a severe housing shortage. A private group of American philanthropists purchased 800 acres of greenhouses from the departing settlers and donated them to the Palestinians, preserving an important source of jobs and revenue in an area with 40% unemployment. The next move toward peace is in Palestinian hands and hinges on whether President Mahmoud Abbas can effectively govern Gaza and stem the influence of militant groups.

War and Peace in Sudan

On Jan. 9, 2005, after three years of negotiations, a peace deal ended Sudan's two-decades-long civil war. The conflict between the Arab-Muslim government of the North and the black Christian and animist South had left a staggering 2 million dead. The protracted negotiations had largely stalled over oil reserves, 75% of which are located in the South. International pressure, especially from the U.S., had worn down the Khartoum government's intransigence. The peace agreement gave roughly half of Sudan's oil wealth to the south, as well as nearly complete autonomy and the right to secede after six years. John Garang, the charismatic leader of the largest rebel group, the SPLA, was sworn in as vice president in July as part of the power-sharing agreement. But the entire peace process was nearly upended just weeks later when Garang was killed in a helicopter crash. Violent rioting erupted in Khartoum, killing nearly 100. Garang's deputy, Salva Kiir, was quickly sworn in as the new vice-president, and both North and South vowed that the peace agreement, so long in the making, would hold.

No peace, however, appears in sight for the western region of Sudan, where the massacres in the Darfur region continued. The Janjaweed, pro-government Arabic militias, continued to slaughter black villagers and rebel groups with impunity. By the fall of 2005, between 200,000 and 400,000 Darfuris had been killed and more than 2 million displaced. International condemnation and a modest force of African Union peacekeepers slowed the violence in 2005, but according to the UN, Darfur remains the world's worst humanitarian disaster.

Lebanon's Revolution

On Feb. 14, 2005, Lebanon's former prime minister Rafik Hariri was killed in a car bombing. Hariri was largely responsible for the country's economic rebirth over the past decade and had been a vigorous critic of Syria's decades-long occupation of Lebanon. Suspected Syrian involvement in the assassination ignited a popular revolt in the country, which called for the resignation of Lebanon's pro-Syrian government and Syria's military withdrawal from the country. Weeks of protests by Sunni Muslim, Christian, and Druze parties were buttressed by widespread international pressure condemning Syria's continuing iron grip on its fragile neighbor. But the "cedar revolution" was challenged by massive pro-Syrian rallies, primarily made up of Shiites and sponsored by the militant group Hezbollah. As the political winds shifted back and forth in March and April, pro-Syrian prime minister Omar Karami resigned, was reappointed, and resigned a final time.

Bowing to pressure in mid-March, Syria withdrew 4,000 troops and redeployed the remaining 10,000 to Lebanon's Bekaa Valley, which borders Syria. On April 26, after 29 years of occupation, Syria withdrew entirely.

After May and June parliamentary elections, former finance minister Fouad Siniora, who was closely associated with Hariri, became prime minister. President Emile Lahoud, whose term was extended by three years in 2004 at Syria's insistence, remains the last significant vestige of Syrian control.

Nuclear Ambitions Ebb and Flow

In June 2005, Iran elected a new president—former Teheran mayor Mahmoud Ahmadinejad, a hard-liner and conservative—who staunchly supported the continuation of Iran's nuclear pursuits. In Aug. 2005, he rejected an EU disarmament plan, backed by the U.S., which had been negotiated over the past two years, and resumed uranium conversion.

In Sept. 2005, the fourth round of nuclear negotiations involving North Korea took place. Since 2003, all six-nation talks between the U.S., Russia, China, Japan, South Korea, and North Korea had ended in deadlock. This time, however, North Korea made a vague promise with an unspecified timetable agreeing to abandon its nuclear-weapons program and rejoin the Non-Proliferation Treaty. Given North Korea's characteristic unpredictability and reversals, the news has been greeted with a mixture of skepticism and hope.   □

What Happened in 2005: Month by Month

Below are highlights of key events of the year, organized month by month, in three categories for easy reference. For the year's major U.S. Supreme Court decisions, *see* p. 149. "Countries of the World," pp. 718–906, covers specific international events, country by country. *See also* "People in the News," pp. 1030–1034, and "2005 Deaths," pp. 1035–1039, for more current-events coverage. Go to www.infoplease.com/2005currentevents for additional events.

January

WORLD

Relief Pours into Asia (Jan. 2): Helicopters based on American aircraft carriers off the Indonesian coast begin dropping tons of supplies to survivors of the tsunami that devastated 11 Asian nations. International community has pledged more than $2 billion in aid. **(Jan. 19):** Number of victims in the disaster reaches more than 225,000. Indonesia hit the hardest by far, with about 150,000 victims.

Iraqi Violence Intensifies as Election Nears (Jan. 4): Ali al-Haidari, governor of Baghdad Province, assassinated by insurgents who seek to thwart upcoming elections. **(Jan. 10):** Deputy police chief of Baghdad and his son, a policeman, assassinated by insurgents in Baghdad. Militant group headed by Jordanian Abu Musab al-Zarqawi takes responsibility. **(Jan. 11):** Iraqi prime minister Ayad Allawi admits that some areas of Iraq are likely to be too dangerous to hold elections. **(Jan. 19):** Five car bombs explode in Baghdad and kill 26 people, including several Iraqi security troops. **(Jan. 30):** Rocket attack on the American Embassy in Baghdad kills two Americans. **(Jan. 30):** About 8.5 million Iraqis, 57% of the population, turn out to vote in first democratic elections in more than 50 years. Election-day violence kills more than 40, but vote was much smoother than anticipated. Iraqis vote to select a 275-seat National Assembly and 18 provincial assemblies.

Abbas Wins Election in a Landslide (Jan. 9): Mahmoud Abbas, chairman of the Palestine Liberation Organization, takes 62.3% of the vote in race for president of the Palestinian Authority. Abbas succeeds Yasir Arafat, who died in Nov. 2004.

Sudanese Government and Rebels Sign Peace Agreement (Jan. 9): Islamic government and Christian rebels from the south agree to end 20-year conflict that has claimed about two million people.

U.S. Ends Search for Weapons (Jan. 12): The White House announces that the search for weapons of mass destruction in Iraq, one of the main justifications for the war, is over and that no such weapons were found.

New Ukrainian President Sworn In (Jan. 23): Viktor Yushchenko, who defeated Viktor Yanukovich in third round of controversial election, takes oath of office in Kiev.

Dozens of Marines Die in Copter Crash (Jan. 26): On the deadliest day in Iraq in nearly two years, 31 U.S. soldiers are killed when their helicopter goes down near the Jordanian border.

UN Reports on Darfur (Jan. 31): Commission investigating violence finds war crimes and crimes against humanity have occurred in western Sudan, but genocide has not.

NATION

Former Presidents to Lead Aid Drive (Jan. 3): President Bush calls on George H. W. Bush and Bill Clinton to lead a nationwide charity campaign to raise funds for victims of Dec. 2004's devastating tsunami.

House Changes Ethics Rules (Jan. 3): At the request of House majority leader Tom DeLay, Republicans vote to rescind a rule enacted in Nov. 2004 that would allow leaders and committee members to retain positions if indicted. Rule was passed on behalf of DeLay, who was admonished three times in 2004 for ethical missteps. **(Jan. 4):** On the opening day of the 109th Congress, House votes, 220–195, to dismiss complaints if the ethics committee deadlocks.

Abu Ghraib Abuser Convicted (Jan. 13): U.S. Army reservist Charles Graner found guilty by a military jury of abusing prisoners at the Abu Ghraib prison in Iraq. **(Jan. 14):** Jury sentences Graner to serve 10 years in a military prison.

President Bush Begins Second Term (Jan. 20): George W. Bush is officially sworn in by Supreme Court chief justice William Rehnquist. Referring to the war in Iraq, Bush says, "All who live in tyranny and hopelessness can know: the United States will not ignore your oppression, or excuse your oppressors. When you stand for your liberty, we will stand with you."

Senate Confirms Rice (Jan. 26): Senate votes, 85–13, to confirm Condoleezza Rice as secretary of state. She's the first black woman to hold the position.

BUSINESS/SCIENCE/SOCIETY

Train Crash Kills Several in South Carolina (Jan. 6): Mistake involving a switching mechanism causes train in Graniteville to crash into parked railcars, killing nine people and releasing toxic chlorine gas.

Government Changes Dietary Guidelines (Jan. 12): Updated Dietary Guidelines for Americans say that people should exercise at least 30 minutes every day.

European Spacecraft Lands on Saturn Moon (Jan. 14): Photos of Titan sent back to Earth by craft *Huygens* reveal rocky surface and lakes of what astronomers think are frozen gases.

Largest Passenger Plane Launched (Jan. 18): The prototype of the Airbus A380 debuts in France. The plane is seven stories high and can seat 555 passengers.

Deficit Expected to Continue to Grow (Jan. 25): The bipartisan Congressional Budget Office estimates a 2005 deficit of $368 billion, excluding expenses incurred in Iraq. The White House releases its own estimate—$427 billion, including an additional $80 billion for Iraq.

February

WORLD

Nepalese King Fires Government (Feb. 1): King Gyanendra also declares a state of emergency. Many of the country's politicians are placed under house arrest, phone and Internet lines are cut, and the airports are closed. Gyanendra says the government was making no progress toward elections and had not pursued a peace process with Maoist rebels. **(Feb. 2):** King appoints a new 10-member cabinet.

IRA Withdraws from Peace Process (Feb. 2): Irish Republican Army says it will no longer participate in peace talks with British government and is canceling plans to disarm and end paramilitary actions.

Report Criticizes Conduct of Oil-for-Food Official (Feb. 3): Independent investigation into UN-run program in Iraq finds that Benon Sevan, who headed the program, breached UN charter by helping friends secure contracts to sell Iraqi oil. **(Feb. 4):** UN suspends Sevan and Joseph Stephanides, another program official.

Presidential Succession in Togo Condemned (Feb. 7): Faure Gnassingbe is appointed president of the West African country following the death of his father. **(Feb. 25):** Under pressure from neighboring African countries, Gnassingbe resigns.

Abbas and Sharon Declare a Truce (Feb. 8): In the highest-level summit in four years, Palestinian president and Israeli prime minister agree to end acts of violence against each other.

Saudis Vote for the First Time (Feb. 10): Kingdom holds municipal elections for local city or town officials. Voting is held in Riyadh. Women are not allowed to vote, and less than a third of eligible voters registered.

North Korea Admits to Having Nuclear Weapons (Feb. 10): First time country makes formal declaration. Also says it will not engage in disarmament talks.

Counting Complete in Iraqi Elections (Feb. 13): Alliance of Shiites, United Iraqi Alliance, wins 48% of the vote, giving it 140 out of 275 seats in the National Assembly. Alliance of Kurds takes 75 seats, while group headed by Prime Minister Ayad Allawi wins 40 seats.

Former Prime Minister of Lebanon Killed (Feb. 14): Rafik Hariri and 11 others die when a car bomb explodes near his motorcade in Beirut.

Suicide Bombers Kill Dozens in Baghdad (Feb. 18): Five attackers kill nearly 40 people at religious gatherings observing the holy day of Ashura.

Israeli Cabinet Approves Withdrawal from Gaza (Feb. 20): Votes, 17–5, in favor of Prime Minister Ariel Sharon's plan to withdraw troops and settlers from the Gaza Strip. Cabinet also approves new route for barrier that cuts into Palestinian-controlled areas in the West Bank.

Shiites Nominate Prime Minister (Feb. 22): The United Iraqi Alliance, the group of Shiite political parties that won the most votes in Iraq's Jan. 30 election, selects Ibrahim Jaafari to be the prime minister of Iraq.

British Soldiers Convicted in Iraqi Prisoner Abuse (Feb. 23): In what has been called Britain's Abu Ghraib scandal, two soldiers are found guilty by a military jury of abusing prisoners. Abuse occurred in May 2003 near the southern Iraqi city of Basra.

Syria Promises Withdrawal from Lebanon (Feb. 24): Faced with strong international pressure, Syria announces that it will withdraw the 15,000 troops it has stationed in Lebanon.

Bomb Kills Dozens in Iraq (Feb. 28): In the deadliest attack by insurgents, suicide bomber blows up a car in Hilla, killing about 115 people who were seeking employment with the Iraqi police.

Lebanese Government Resigns (Feb. 28): Prime Minister Omar Karami steps down and dissolves the Syrian-backed government. Move follows two weeks of protests against Syria's iron grip on the country and its suspected connection to the assassination of former Lebanese prime minister Rafik Hariri.

NATION

Bush Delivers State of the Union (Feb. 2): President discusses his proposed reform of the Social Security system as well as the fight against terrorism and his commitment to remaining in Iraq until a stable democracy has been established.

Senate Confirms New Attorney General (Feb. 3): In a tighter vote than anticipated, Senate approves, 60–36, Alberto Gonzales, former counsel to President Bush, as the country's first Hispanic attorney general.

Bush Releases Budget Proposal (Feb. 7): The plan, which would cost $2.57 trillion and aims to reduce budget deficit, would increase spending on national security and the military and reduce allocations to education, health care, agriculture, human services, and transportation.

Sept. 11 Report Critical of FAA (Feb. 9): Previously released report, which was kept classified, indicates that the Federal Aviation Administration had received warnings before the Sept. 11, 2001, terrorist attacks about plans by al-Qaeda and Osama bin Laden to hijack airplanes and conduct suicide bombings.

Cost of Medicare Drug Plan Rises (Feb. 9): Prescription drug benefit, initially estimated to cost $400 billion over 10 years, now projected to top $724 billion.

Senate Approves Limit on Class-Action Suits (Feb. 10): Votes, 72–26, in favor of measure that limits states from trying many types of class-action suits.

Bush Requests Additional Funds (Feb. 14): Asks Congress for $81.9 billion for current-year expenses, including operations in Iraq and Afghanistan, tsunami aid, and new benefits for families of troops killed in combat.

Missile Defense System Fails Again (Feb. 14): The latest test of the strategic missile defense system, or National Missile Defense (NMD), fails when the intercepting rocket does not fire due to a software malfunction.

Senate Confirms Homeland Security Secretary (Feb. 15): Michael Chertoff unanimously approved to succeed Tom Ridge.

Task Force Criticizes Education Law (Feb. 23): Report by bipartisan group of state legislators says No Child Left Behind Act is unconstitutional and its requirements thwart school-improvement programs under way in many states.

Federal Judge Rules Against Bush (Feb. 28): Henry F. Floyd says President Bush has overstepped his authority by detaining Jose Padilla for almost three years as an enemy combatant without charging him with a crime. Padilla was arrested in 2002 and accused of planning to detonate a "dirty bomb" on American soil.

Federal Judge's Family Members Killed (Feb. 28): Husband and mother of Joan Humphrey Lefkow shot in her Chicago home.

BUSINESS/SCIENCE/SOCIETY

Astronomers Find Hot Spot on Saturn (Feb. 4): Astronomers positioned on top of the Mauna Kea volcano in Honolulu, Hawaii, report they have caught a glimpse of what they believe to be a warm polar vortex on Saturn.

Woman Breaks Circumnavigation Record (Feb. 7): British sailor Ellen MacArthur completes a solo circumnavigation in 71 days, 14 hours, 18 minutes, and 33 seconds.

Kyoto Protocol Goes into Effect (Feb. 16): The international environmental treaty requires 35 industrialized nations to reduce heat-trapping gases such as carbon dioxide. Developing nations have promised to try to limit their emissions of such gases. The United States, which emits the largest amount of heat-trapping gases in the world, has refused to sign the treaty.

Professional Hockey Season Canceled (Feb. 16): As National Hockey League owners and players fail to reach a deal on salary cap for players, Commissioner Gary Bettman formally cancels the season.

Earthquake Kills Hundreds in Iran (Feb. 22): More than 500 people die and about 40 villages destroyed in central part of the country.

March

WORLD

Leftist Government Assumes Power in Uruguay (March 1): Tabaré Vázquez, a Socialist, sworn in as president. Inauguration marks the first time in the country's history the left is in control.

UN Troops Battle Congo Militia (March 1): More than 50 militiamen, who have terrorized northeastern Congo, and nine UN soldiers are killed in the fighting.

Syria Announces Pullback from Lebanon (March 5): President Bashar al-Assad tells Parliament that he will gradually order troops back toward Syrian border. Syrian officials later say troops would eventually be moved to Syrian territory. **(March 12):** Assad confirms withdrawal to within Syrian borders.

U.S. Troops Shoot Italian Journalist (March 5): Soldiers shoot at car carrying Giuliana Sgrena, who had been held hostage by Iraqi insurgents and just released from captivity. Sgrena is wounded and an Italian intelligence agent is killed.

Bolivian President Resigns (March 7): Amid protests over a tax on foreign oil and gas companies that opponents feel isn't sufficient, Carlos Mesa tells Congress he will step down. **(March 8):** Congress rejects Mesa's offer to resign and gives him a vote of confidence.

Chechnyan Separatist Leader Killed (March 8): Russian troops kill Aslan Maskhadov in a raid in a village near Grozny.

Thousands of Syrian Supporters March in Lebanon (March 8): Militant group Hezbollah organizes pro-Syria demonstration in Beirut. Crowd estimated at 500,000.

Lebanese Prime Minister Reelected (March 9): Omar Karami reelected by Lebanese Parliament. He stepped down in February.

Hong Kong Leader Resigns (March 10): Tung Chee-hwa steps down as chief executive after eight years in office. His deputy, Donald Tsang, will succeed him.

Fraud Alleged in Kyrgyzstan Elections (March 13): The opposition and international monitors declare the elections, which hand victory to parties that support President Askar Akayev, seriously flawed. **(March 24):** Akayev flees to Russia. Parliament elects opposition leader Ishenbai Kadyrbekov as interim president and prime minister.

China Passes Anti-Secession Law (March 14): Bill says the country can use force if Taiwan moves toward achieving independence.

Iraqi Assembly Meets (March 16): Diverse group of 275 newly elected leaders convene for the first time in a largely ceremonial meeting. Shiites and Kurds, who fared best in January elections, have not yet appointed leaders. **(March 29):** Assembly meets for the second time and fails again to agree on the composition of the new Iraqi government.

Palestinians Take Control of Jericho (March 16): Move is first stage in truce agreement between Israelis and Palestinians that will give Palestinians control of five towns in the West Bank.

Afghan Elections Postponed Again (March 20): Electoral commission reschedules parliamentary elections for September 18. They were originally set to be held in June 2004, then in May 2005.

Israel to Expand Settlement (March 21): Government announces plans to build 3,500 housing units in Maale Adumim, a West Bank settlement near Jerusalem. Palestinians call the move a violation of the peace plan.

U.S. to Sell Fighter Jets to Pakistan (March 25): President Bush announces the U.S. will sell Pakistan F-16 fighter jets.

Independent Panel Clears UN Chief (March 29): Committee investigating Iraq's oil-for-food program reports that Kofi Annan was not involved in wrongdoing when the UN awarded a contract to his son's employer. The panel, headed by Paul Volcker, did criticize Annan for not investigating the contract further once he was made aware of the potential conflict of interest.

Commission Criticizes U.S. Intelligence Agencies (March 31): Panel set up by President Bush calls assessment on Iraq's weapons capabilities "dead wrong" and finds that agencies exaggerated evidence and relied on shaky sources in making the case for war in Iraq.

NATION

Bush Nominates UN Ambassador (March 7): Selects John Bolton, state department official and critic of the United Nations, as American envoy to the organization.

EPA Introduces Rules to Cut Pollution (March 10): Clean Air Interstate Rule, announced by the Environmental Protection Agency, aims to reduce emissions of nitrogen oxides and sulfur dioxide in the eastern U.S. by 60% by 2015.

Suicide Victim Admits to Killing Judge's Family (March 10): In a suicide note, troubled electrician Bart Ross admits to killing Joan Humphrey Lefkow's mother and husband in February.

Suspect Kills Three in Georgia Court (March 11): Brian Nichols, on trial for rape, shoots and kills the presiding judge, a court stenographer, and a sheriff's deputy in Atlanta's Fulton County Courthouse. **(March 12):** Nichols surrenders after the hostage he captured called the police.

Report Finds Aviation System Still at Risk (March 13): Government study indicates that al-Qaeda and other terrorist groups could charter planes and helicopters to launch an attack against the U.S.

Congress Intervenes in Case of Brain-Damaged Woman (March 20): The House and Senate vote to allow a federal court to rule whether the feeding tube should be reinserted into the mouth of Terri Schiavo, a woman who has been in a persistent vegetative state for 15 years. **(March 22):** Federal judge James Whittemore refuses to order that the feeding tube be reinserted. **(March 23):** A federal appeals court upholds Whittemore's decision. **(March 24):** The U.S. Supreme Court declines the case. **(March 31):** Schiavo dies, 13 days after her feeding tube was removed.

Minnesota Student Goes on Shooting Rampage (March 21): Jeff Weise, 16, kills nine people, including his grandfather, before turning the gun on himself. Five students at Red Lake High School also killed. **(March 28):** Police arrest 16-year-old Louis Jourdain, the son of a tribal leader, in connection with the shootings.

Bush Hawk to Lead World Bank (March 31): Paul Wolfowitz, former deputy defense secretary and one of the chief advocates of the war in Iraq, unanimously confirmed by World Bank's executive board.

BUSINESS/SCIENCE/SOCIETY

Greenspan Urges Action on Deficit (March 2): Urges Congress to work toward reining in budget deficit, saying it is "unsustainable."

Man Makes Circumnavigation Record (March 3): Steve Fossett completes a 23,000-mile journey when his plane GlobalFlyer lands in Kansas. He's the first person to make the solo nonstop journey around the world.

WorldCom Chief Found Guilty (March 15): Bernard Ebbers convicted of securities fraud, conspiracy, and seven counts of filing false reports. Fraud cost the telecommunications giant about $11 billion.

Obesity Shortens Life Expectancy of Children (March 16): Report in the *New England Journal of Medicine* indicates that if childhood obesity continues, the current generation of children may be expected to live two to five fewer years than adults today.

Baseball Players Testify at Hearings (March 17): Ten players, including home-run kings Mark McGwire and Sammy Sosa, appear before the House Government Reform Committee to answer questions on steroid use in major league baseball.

Fed Raises Interest Rates (March 22): Increases short-term rates a quarter point, to 2.75%.

Indonesia Hit by Earthquake (March 29): Temblor, with a magnitude of 8.7, strikes the island of Nias. Residents, fearing another deadly tsunami, flee for higher ground. Hundreds are killed.

April

WORLD

Ruling Party Takes Elections in Zimbabwe (April 1): President Robert Mugabe's party, Zimbabwe African National Union-Patriotic Front (ZANU-PF), dominates parliamentary elections, taking 55 out of 120 seats. The opposition, led by Morgan Tsvangirai, wins 34 seats. Tsvangirai and international observers say the election was rigged and marred by fraud.

Iraqi Assembly Moves Toward Forming a Government (April 3): Members name Hajim al-Hassani, a Sunni, as speaker; and Hussain al-Shahristani, a Shiite, and Arif Taifour, a Kurd, as deputies. **(April 6):** Assembly selects Kurdish leader Jalal Talabani as president; Shiite Adel Abdul Mahdi as vice president; and Sheik Ghazi al-Yawar, the Sunni president of the interim government, as the second vice president. **(April 7):** National Assembly names Shiite Ibrahim Jaafari as prime minister. Interim prime minister Ayad Allawi resigns. **(April 28):** Assembly approves 32-member cabinet of 17 Shiite Arabs, 8 Kurds, 6 Sunni Arabs, and 1 Christian.

President of Kyrgyzstan Resigns (April 4): Askar Akayev signs resignation letter at the Kyrgyz Embassy in Moscow. The move clears the way for a new presidential election.

Sinn Fein Leader Calls on IRA to End Violence (April 6): Gerry Adams advises Irish Republican Army to use political means to achieve independence from Britain.

Bus Service Begins in Kashmir (April 7): Families divided for more than 50 years by Line of Control are reunited when buses transport passengers across Peace Bridge.

Bush Speaks Out Against Settlements (April 11): At a meeting at Bush's Texas ranch, president tells Israeli prime minister Ariel Sharon that he opposes the construction of any new settlements in the West Bank.

Lebanese Prime Minister Quits (April 13): Pro-Syrian prime minister Omar Karami announces his resignation, citing his failure to form a government. **(April 15):** President Emile Lahoud names Najib Mikati, a pro-Syrian member of Parliament, as interim prime minister.

Two Indicted in Connection with Oil-for-Food Scandal (April 14): Texan David Bay Chalmers, Jr., and his Houston company, Bayoil U.S.A., charged with paying Saddam Hussein millions in illegal kickbacks in exchange for oil contracts in Iraq. Separately, South Korean businessman Tongsun Park charged with making as much as $2 million as a liaison between Iraq and the United Nations.

Iraqi President Says Dozens of Bodies Found (April 20): Jalal Talabani says the bodies of about 50 kidnap victims were recovered from Tigris River. Other Iraqi officials, however, dispute the claim. Disclosure comes amid increased insurgent violence in Iraq. **(April 21):** Iraqi police say they have pulled bodies from the river over several days and are not sure if the victims were all killed at the same time.

Italian Prime Minister Resigns (April 20): Under pressure after a weak showing in regional elections, Silvio Berlusconi steps down and dissolves government. **(April 23):** Berlusconi reclaims his post by forming a new government.

Ecuador's Congress Ousts President (April 20): Lucio Gutierrez removed from office and takes refuge in Brazil. Vice President Alfredo Palacio assumes the presidency.

Civilian Helicopter Shot Down in Iraq (April 21): Eleven people, six of them Americans working for security company Blackwater U.S.A., die in attack.

Sept. 11 Suspect Pleads Guilty (April 22): Zacarias Moussaoui enters guilty plea but denies involvement in Sept. 11 terrorist attacks. Instead, he says he was part of a separate plan to fly a plane into the White House.

Syrian Military Exits Lebanon (April 26): Troops, which had been stationed in Lebanon for 29 years, complete withdrawal.

Iraqi Legislator Murdered (April 28): Sheikha Lameah Khaddouri al-Sakri, Shiite member of National Assembly, gunned down by three men in front of her Baghdad home.

Taiwanese Opposition Leader Travels to China (April 29): Lien Chan, head of Taiwan's Nationalist Party, and Chinese president Hu Jintao promise to collaborate to end Taiwan's drive for independence. Meeting is the first between a Taiwanese Nationalist and Chinese Communist since 1949.

Insurgent Attacks Kill Dozens in Iraq (April 29): More than 40 people die in a series of coordinated attacks in and around Baghdad.

U.S. Soldiers Cleared in Death of Italian Intelligence Agent (April 30): Italian prime minister Silvio Berlusconi outraged that troops are exonerated in death of Nicola Calipari.

NATION

Education Department Revises New Legislation (April 7): Secretary of Education Margaret Spellings announces increased flexibility to states in conforming to requirements under No Child Left Behind Act.

Three Indicted in Terror Plot (April 12): Federal grand jury in New York indicts three Britons for an alleged plan to attack financial institutions in New York, New Jersey, and Washington. They were arrested in 2004.

Olympic Bombing Suspect Pleads Guilty (April 13): Eric Rudolph pleads guilty to bombings at the Olympics in Atlanta in 1996, a gay club and a family-planning clinic in Atlanta in 1997, and an abortion clinic in Birmingham, Alabama, in 1998. He'll serve four consecutive life sentences rather than face the death penalty.

Amtrak Halts Acela Service (April 15): High-speed service between Boston, New York, and Washington shut down when inspectors find cracks in the brakes of hundreds of trains.

Senate Confirms Intelligence Director (April 21): Career diplomat John Negroponte wins resounding approval to become country's first director of national intelligence.

Army Officers Cleared in Abu Ghraib Scandal (April 22): Investigation exonerates top officers, including Lt. Gen. Ricardo Sanchez, of wrongdoing in abuse controversy. One officer, Army Reserve Brig. Gen. Janis Karpinski, found guilty of dereliction of duty.

House Reverses Ethics Rules (April 27): Votes, 406–20, to overturn rules changes enacted in January, which were widely believed to have passed to protect majority leader Tom DeLay.

Bush Outlines Social Security Plan (April 28): In prime-time press conference, president says benefit cuts will be necessary for future generations of retirees with highest incomes to keep funds solvent over the long term.

BUSINESS/SCIENCE/SOCIETY

Pope John Paul II Dies (April 2): John Paul, the first Polish pope and the first non-Italian pope since 1522, dies after a long struggle with Parkinson's disease. **(April 8):** John Paul II is buried at the Vatican. Leaders from more than 70 nations gather for the largest funeral for a pope in history. **(April 19):** Conclave of cardinals selects Cardinal Joseph Ratzinger of Germany as the new pope. He will call himself Benedict the 16th. **(April 24):** Benedict XVI is installed as pope at outdoor mass at St. Peter's Square.

Prince Charles Remarries (April 8): British prince marries longtime lover Camilla Parker Bowles.

Agriculture Department Releases New Food Pyramid (April 19): Government calls MyPyramid an "interactive food guidance system." There are 12 versions of the new pyramid, allowing people to choose one based on their age, sex, and level of physical activity.

Overweight People Face Lower Risk of Death Than Those of Normal Weight (April 20): Federal researchers also find that being very thin can increase one's risk of death. Study seems to contradict earlier reports.

Dozens Die in Train Accident (April 25): Derailment of speeding commuter train near Osaka, Japan, kills more than 100 people and injures about 400.

May

WORLD

Insurgents Continue Series of Attacks (May 1): At least 35 Iraqis die in bombings in Mosul and Baghdad. Insurgent attacks have intensified since formation of new government in late April. **(May 4):** At least 60 Kurds killed and more than 150 wounded when suicide bomber strikes in Kurdish capital of Erbil. Militant group Ansar al-Sunna claims responsibility. **(May 9):** In the biggest U.S. offensive in months, marines attack insurgents in western Iraq, killing about 100 of them. **(May 11):** Nearly 80 people are killed in attacks in three cities. **(May 31):** Violence during the month claims 80 Americans and about 800 Iraqis.

Leaked Memo Creates Stir in England (May 1): The *Sunday Times* reports that a top-secret memo from July 2002 indicated that eight months before the Iraq war was launched, British foreign secretary Jack Straw acknowledged that "the case [for war] was thin." Memo also says the U.S. wanted the war "justified by the conjunction of terrorism and WMD. But the intelligence and facts were being fixed around the policy."

Iran Says It Plans to Resume Nuclear Activity (May 3): Iranian official makes statement at conference on the Nuclear Nonproliferation Treaty. **(May 25):** Officials from Britain, France, and Germany persuade Iran to freeze nuclear activity.

Iraqi Cabinet Sworn In (May 3): Six cabinet positions remain unfilled as Shiite and Sunni leaders continue to negotiate. Sunni vice president Sheik Ghazi al-Yawar boycotts ceremony over impasse. **(May 7):** National Assembly approves final six cabinet members selected by Prime Minister Ibrahim Jaafar. One, however, Sunni Hashim al-Shibli, rejects the position of human rights minister. **(May 10):** National Assembly selects a 55-person committee to write a permanent constitution.

British Prime Minister Reelected (May 5): Tony Blair becomes first Labour Party prime minister to win three successive terms. The Labour Party, however, is severely hurt in the elections, winning just 36% of the national vote, the lowest percentage by a ruling party in British history. Labour's majority in the House of Commons is reduced from 161 to about 60 seats.

Anti-American Protests Turn Deadly (May 11): Four people killed in Jalalabad, Afghanistan, when police and troops open fire on student demonstrators, who were protesting the reported desecration of the Koran by American guards at the prison at Guantánamo Bay, Cuba. **(May 12):** Protests spread throughout Afghanistan and spill into Pakistan, killing at least 17 people. **(May 16):** Under intense pressure from the White House, *Newsweek*, which first reported the desecration incident, retracts the story. **(May 25):** FBI releases documents from 2002 and 2003 that include complaints by detainees at the Guantánamo Bay prison that interrogators abused the Koran. One complaint said guards flushed a Koran down a toilet.

North Korea Says It Has Harvested Fuel for Nuclear Weapons (May 11): Officials continue to taunt President Bush and other world leaders with claim that country has extracted thousands of spent fuel rods, enough to manufacture up to three weapons.

Violence Erupts in Uzbekistan (May 13): Gunmen, who charge prison in Andijon to protest allegedly rigged trial of 23 businessmen, release about 2,000 prisoners. Government troops use force to quell the uprising. Thousands of demonstrators unhappy with repressive government spill into the city square, and police fire into the crowds. More than 160 people are killed.

Women Win Right to Vote in Kuwait (May 16): Parliament votes, 35–23, with one abstention, to change the country's electoral laws to allow women to vote and run for office in local and parliamentary elections.

Iraq Admits to Being Aggressor in 1980s War (May 19): Government blames Saddam Hussein for 8-year war with Iran and says he must face trial for war crimes.

Iraqi Sunnis Form Coalition (May 21): About 2,000 Sunni Arabs gather and form an alliance to have a voice in Shiite-dominated government.

German Leader Calls for Early Elections (May 22): After his Social Democratic Party faced a stinging defeat in Germany's largest state, North Rhine–Westphalia, Chancellor Gerhard Schröder announces elections for the fall, a year earlier than planned.

Amnesty International Releases Withering Report (May 25): In its annual report, watchdog organization paints a bleak portrait of the world's attitude toward human rights and singles out the United States as setting a particularly bad example. Report compares Guantánamo Bay prison to a gulag.

French Reject European Constitution (May 29): French vote, 55%–45%, in a nationwide referendum against proposed constitution for European Union.

Zimbabwe Begins Destroying Slums (May 29): President Mugabe orders bulldozing of shacks, workshops, and market stalls throughout Zimbabwe's cities in a program he calls "Operation Restore Order."

French Prime Minister Resigns (May 31): Jean-Pierre Raffarin steps down days after France rejects referendum on new constitution for Europe. President Jacques Chirac appoints career diplomat Dominique de Villepin as prime minister.

Russian Oil Tycoon Convicted (May 31): Court sentences Mikhail Khodorkovsky, founder of Yukos oil company and once the country's wealthiest man, to nine years in prison after being found guilty of fraud, embezzlement, tax evasion, and other charges.

NATION

Army Reservist Pleads Guilty in Abu Ghraib Abuse Scandal (May 2): Pfc. Lynndie England, the woman shown in several photos with naked Iraqi prisoners, pleads guilty to seven criminal counts. **(May 4):** Judge declares a mistrial after former army specialist Charles Graner, who was convicted in the scandal and is the father of England's son, testifies that the maltreatment of the prisoners was permissible, thus implying that England did not realize she was committing a crime.

Federal Appeals Court Rules in Favor of Cheney (May 10): In unanimous decision, court says Vice President Cheney was not obligated to disclose details of his task-force meetings that helped the administration draft energy policies.

Senate Passes Military Funding Bill (May 10): Votes unanimously for $82 billion emergency spending bill, which includes $72 billion for armor, ammunition, and an increase in death benefits for soldiers killed in combat. Measure also includes changes to immigration law and new requirements to states in granting and renewing driver's licenses.

Off-Course Plane Strays Near White House (May 11): The White House and the Capitol are evacuated when a Cessna 152 accidentally enters restricted airspace.

Pentagon Recommends Extensive Base Closings (May 13): About 800 military bases, offices, and installations would be closed in vast restructuring. Job losses estimated at 26,000.

Senators Reach Deal to Avoid Filibuster Fight (May 23): A group of moderates agree to a compromise: Republicans say they will not move to change the filibuster rules, while Democrats agree to use filibuster of judicial nominees only in "extraordinary" circumstances. **(May 25):** Senate votes, 55–43, to confirm Priscilla Owen for a seat on the 5th U.S. Circuit Court of Appeals. Before the compromise was reached, Democrats were filibustering her nomination.

House Passes Bill to Expand Stem Cell Research (May 24): Votes, 238–194, to allow federal financing of embryos that have been frozen at fertility clinics. President Bush has said he will veto the legislation.

Senate Delays Vote on Bolton (May 26): Maneuver by Democrats postpones vote on John Bolton as ambassador to the UN. Democrats insist that the White House hand over documents related to Bolton's conduct before it will allow the vote.

"Deep Throat" Reveals Himself (May 31): In an interview to be published in *Vanity Fair,* W. Mark Felt, a former top FBI official, admits to being the anonymous source who leaked information to the *Washington Post* about the White House's involvement in the 1972 Watergate break-in.

BUSINESS/SCIENCE/SOCIETY

Fed Raises Interest Rates (May 3): Federal reserve increases short-term interest rate by a quarter point, to 3%. It is the eighth increase in less than one year.

Jobs Increase in April (May 6): Bureau of Labor Statistics reports that 274,000 new jobs were added to the economy.

South Koreans Report Success in Therapeutic Cloning (May 20): Researchers announce they have devised a new procedure to successfully produce human stem cell lines from a cloned human embryo.

June

WORLD

European Constitution in Jeopardy (June 1): Following France's lead, Dutch vote, 61.6%–38.4%, against proposed treaty in a nonbinding referendum. **(June 6):** Britain suspends a nationwide referendum on the constitution. **(June 16):** Leaders of the European Union abandon plans to ratify the constitution by 2006.

Prominent Opponents of Syria Killed in Lebanon (June 2): Samir Kassir, a respected columnist and critic of Syria's influence in Lebanon, dies when a bomb explodes in his car in Beirut. **(June 21):** George Hawi, former head of the Communist Party and a champion of the opposition candidates in parliamentary elections, killed by a car bomb.

Military Investigation Finds Abuse of Koran (June 3): Report details five cases in which interrogators or guards mishandled the Koran. Brig. Gen. Jay Hood says, however, that the inquiry failed to find evidence that it was flushed down the toilet.

Bolivian President Resigns (June 8): Carlos Mesa steps down as protesters, who want to nationalize the country's oil and gas companies, continue their blockade of La Paz. **(June 9):** Congress selects Eduardo Rodríguez, president of the Supreme Court, as president.

Kuwait Adds Woman to Government (June 12): Prime Minister Sheik Sabah al-Ahmed al-Sabah appoints political science professor Massouma al-Mubarak to two ministry posts. She's the country's first woman to ever hold a cabinet position.

Sunnis Agree to Help Write Iraq's Constitution (June 16): In compromise with Shiite-led committee, Sunni Arabs will seat 15 representatives on the 55-member panel, with 10 others serving as advisers.

Iran Faces Runoff Election (June 17): Because none of the seven candidates for president receive more than 50% of the vote, ultraconservative Teheran mayor Mahmoud Ahmadinejad and moderate former president Akbar Hashemi Rafsanjani will compete in runoff election. **(June 24):** Mahmoud Ahmadinejad wins runoff election in a landslide, taking 17.2 million votes to Akbar Hashemi Rafsanjani's 10 million.

Anti-Syrian Coalition Wins Parliamentary Majority in Lebanon (June 20): After four rounds of voting, alliance headed by Saad Hariri, son of the slain former prime minister, and Walid Jumblatt holds 72 of the 128 seats in Parliament.

General Says Insurgency Still Strong in Iraq (June 23): Contradicting recent statements by Vice President Dick Cheney that the insurgency is in its "last throes," General John Abizaid tells Congress that the strength of the insurgency is about the same as it was six months ago.

Italy Issues Arrest Warrants for CIA Employees (June 24): Thirteen people sought in connection to the 2003 kidnapping of Egyptian cleric, Chiara Nobili. He was allegedly seized in Milan and later sent to Egypt, where his family said he was interrogated and tortured. Government officials think Nobili, who is still missing, has ties to al-Qaeda.

Nations Approve Gay Marriage (June 28): Canadian House of Commons votes to extend right to entire country. **(June 30):** Spain legalizes gay marriage.

U.S. Helicopter Crashes in Afghanistan (June 28): Insurgents shoot down Chinook helicopter, killing eight Navy SEALs and eight other Special Operations troops who were on a mission to rescue four Navy Seals engaged in a firefight with members of the Taliban. Three of the SEALs were killed.

NATION

Controversial Governor's Race Decided (June 6): Washington judge dismisses lawsuit filed by Republicans that claimed fraudulent and illegal votes gave the election to Democrat Christine Gregoire. Republican candidate Dino Rossi says he will not appeal the decision.

Senate Confirms Controversial Nominee (June 8): Votes, 56–43, to confirm Janice Rogers Brown as a judge on the U.S. Court of Appeals.

Government Revises Award Sought in Tobacco Case (June 8): Justice Department asks tobacco companies to fund a $10 billion smoking cessation program rather than $130 billion as recommended.

Justice Department Report Faults FBI (June 9): Report written by department's inspector general says communication breakdown, obsolete computer system, and cumbersome bureaucracy allowed the FBI to miss five opportunities to catch two of the Sept. 11 hijackers in the months before the terrorist attacks.

Senate Apologizes for Failure to Enact Antilynching Law (June 13): Issues a formal apology for decades-long failure to pass law making lynching illegal. From 1882 to 1968, 4,742 people, 3,446 of them black, were killed by lynch mobs.

House Opposes Part of Patriot Act (June 15): Votes, 238–187, against provision that allows federal officials to seize records from libraries and bookstores for terrorism investigations.

Senate Democrats Block Bolton Vote (June 20): For the second time, Republicans are short of the 60 votes required to end the filibuster that has prevented John Bolton's nomination as ambassador to the UN.

Report on Halliburton Finds Questionable Costs (June 27): Audit by Democratic lawmakers reveals the Pentagon has disputed about $1 billion in bills and costs submitted by Halliburton for work performed in Iraq.

Bush Defends War in Iraq (June 28): In nationally televised speech on the first anniversary of the transfer of sovereignty to Iraqis, Bush says the mounting loss of American and Iraqi lives "is worth it, and it is vital to the future security of our country."

Senate Passes Energy Bill (June 28): Votes, 85–12, for legislation that calls for $14 billion in tax incentives for the production of renewable energy sources, energy conservation, and alternative transportation fuels. Also offers tax breaks to consumers who buy efficient appliances and hybrid cars.

Bush Calls for Overhaul of Intelligence Agencies (June 29): Following the recommendation of a presidential commission reviewing the new intelligence law that created the position of director of national intelligence, Bush creates a national security division at the FBI.

TIME to Hand Over Reporter's Notes (June 30): Magazine to surrender notes from interviews with confidential sources taken by reporter Matthew Cooper for a story about Valerie Plame, a covert CIA operative whose identity was revealed in 2003 by columnist Robert Novak.

BUSINESS/SCIENCE/SOCIETY

SEC Chief Announces Resignation (June 1): William Donaldson, chairman of the Security and Exchange Commission, steps down amid criticism that he was too tough in enforcing regulations. **(June 2):** President Bush nominates California congressman Christopher Cox to replace Donaldson.

Pop Singer Cleared of Molestation Charges (June 13): A California jury acquits Michael Jackson of 10 charges, including molesting a child, conspiracy, and providing alcohol to minors.

Schiavo Autopsy Results Released (June 15): Examination finds that Terri Schiavo's brain had deteriorated to half normal size and no treatment could have helped her. Autopsy also reveals no evidence of abuse.

Tyco Chief Convicted (June 17): L. Dennis Kozlowski, former chief executive of Tyco, and Mark Swartz, the company's former chief financial officer, found guilty of fraud, conspiracy, and grand larceny. They bilked the company out of $600 million in a stock-fraud scheme and used the money for personal purposes.

July

WORLD

Diplomats Kidnapped in Iraq (July 3): Ihab al-Sharif, who was to become Egypt's ambassador to Iraq, is seized by gunmen in Baghdad. **(July 7):** Militant group al-Qaeda in Iraq says it has killed Sharif. **(July 21):** Algeria's top diplomat, Ali Billaroussi, and envoy Azzedine Belakdi are kidnapped by gunmen in Baghdad.

Bombs Explode in London (July 7): Four coordinated terrorist attacks on the city's subway and bus systems during rush hour kill 52 people, including the attackers, and wound more than 700. Violence coincides with Group of Eight summit meeting of world's wealthiest nations. **(July 13):** British Home Secretary Charles Clarke says the bombings were carried out by British Muslims. **(July 18):** Pakistani officials say that three of the four bombers visited Pakistan in 2004. **(July 21):** Terrorists attempt another attack on London's transit system. Bombs on three subway trains and a bus fail to explode. Explosives discovered when detonators go off, causing loud cracking sounds. **(July 22):** London police shoot and kill a suspect on a subway train. **(July 23):** Officials say the victim, Brazilian electrician, Jean Charles de Menezes, was not involved in the failed bombings. **(July 27):** Police arrest Yasin Hassan Omar, a 24-year-old Somali man, who they think was involved in the July 21st attempted bombings. **(July 29):** London police arrest four other suspects in the July 21 bombing attempt. A fifth suspect is arrested in Rome, Italy.

World's Wealthy Nations Agree to Aid Africa (July 8): Group of Eight industrial nations ends summit meeting with pledge to double aid to Africa to $50 billion a year by 2010, cancel the debt of many poor countries, and open trade. Joint statement fails to set goals for reducing emissions of greenhouse gases.

Opposition Leader Takes Election in Kyrgyzstan (July 10): Kurmanbek Bakiyev, who served as interim president and prime minister since President Askar Akayev resigned in April, wins 88.7% of the vote.

Suicide Bomber Kills Group of Children (July 13): About 27 people, mostly children who were gathered around a U.S. military jeep, die in attack in Baghdad.

Three Trains Crash in Pakistan (July 13): At least 130 people killed when three commuter trains crash in southern Pakistan. Driver error is suspected.

Dozens Die in Suicide Attack in Iraq (July 17): Suicide bomber detonates bomb under a fuel tanker in Musayyib, killing at least 70 people and wounding more than 150. Four other suicide bombers hit Baghdad on the same day.

India and the U.S. in Accord on Nuclear Power (July 18): President Bush and Prime Minister Manmohan Singh reach an agreement that would allow India to seek outside help in developing its civilian nuclear energy program while maintaining its nuclear weapons. In addition, India would submit the civilian program, but not its weapon program, to inspections.

Sunnis Involved in Drafting Constitution Killed (July 19): Mejbil al-Sheik Isa and Damin al-Obeidi are shot in central Baghdad. **(July 20):** Sunnis say they will boycott drafting process until the government increases security for panel members. **(July 25):** Sunnis say their demand for better security has been met, and they will return to drafting process.

Report Concludes Iraqi Forces Are Weak (July 20): Pentagon assessment finds Iraq's police force is, at best, "partially capable" of fighting the country's insurgency.

German President Calls for Early Elections (July 21): Horst Köhler agrees to plan suggested by beleaguered chancellor Gerhard Schröder to dissolve Parliament and hold elections in Sept. 2005, a year early.

UN Condemns Zimbabwe (July 22): Report calls President Mugabe's program of destroying slums a "disastrous venture." The plan, called "Operation Restore Order," has left about 700,000 people homeless.

Explosions Kill Dozens in Egypt (July 23): At least 90 people die in a series of car bomb explosions at popular Red Sea resort Sharm el Sheik. Two militant groups claim responsibility.

Talks with North Korea Begin (July 25): U.S. and North Korean officials meet to discuss the eventual dismantling of North Korea's nuclear weapons program in exchange for energy and financial assistance. Bilateral talks are a departure from Bush administration policy. Talks precede six-nation negotiations.

IRA Renounces Violence (July 27): Irish Republican Army announces it is ending its armed campaign for a united Ireland and will instead pursue its goals politically.

NATION

Supreme Court Justice Retires (July 1): Sandra Day O'Connor, the first woman on the U.S. Supreme Court, announces her retirement. She served on the Court for 24 years.

Reporter Jailed for Refusing to Testify (July 6): Judith Miller of the *New York Times* is sent to a Washington, DC, prison when she fails to comply with a court order to answer questions before a grand jury about confidential sources she interviewed while researching the disclosure of a CIA operative's identity.

Court Rules Abortion Ban Is Unconstitutional (July 8): Federal appeals court upholds lower court decision that Partial-Birth Abortion Ban Act is unlawful because it fails to make an exception to the law for women whose health would be in jeopardy without the late-term procedure.

Bush Adviser Named as Secret Source (July 10): *Newsweek* magazine's website reports that in a 2003 background interview, Karl Rove strongly implied to *TIME* magazine reporter Matthew Cooper that Valerie Plame Wilson was a covert CIA operative. **(July 17):** Cooper writes in *TIME* magazine that Karl Rove told him that Plame Wilson worked at the "agency" on "wmd," meaning weapons of mass destruction. **(July 18):** In his first statement on the issue, Bush says, "If someone committed a crime, they will no longer work in my administration."

Head of Homeland Security Announces Reorganization (July 13): Michael Chertoff says sweeping changes will help to prevent terrorist attacks and better respond to those that occur. He is criticized for saying the priority should be on aviation rather than mass transit.

Senate Confirms FDA Chief (July 18): Votes, 78–16, to confirm Dr. Lester Crawford as commissioner of the Food and Drug Administration.

President Nominates Supreme Court Justice (July 19): Bush selects John G. Roberts, who has served on the U.S. Court of Appeals for the District of Columbia Circuit since 2003, to succeed Sandra Day O'Connor as an associate justice.

Labor Unions in Disarray (July 24): Leaders of the service employees union, the food and commercial workers union, the Teamsters, and Unite Here say they will not participate in the AFL-CIO convention because its leader, John Sweeney, has failed to reverse the decrease in union membership. **(July 25):** The Service Employees International Union and the Teamsters announce they are severing ties to the AFL-CIO. The unions have memberships of 1.8 million and 1.4 million, respectively.

House Approves Trade Bill (July 28): Votes, 217–215, in favor of Central American Free Trade Agreement, also called Cafta, which will remove trade barriers between the U.S. and Costa Rica, the Dominican Republic, El Salvador, Guatemala, Honduras, and Nicaragua.

Congress Passes Several Measures (July 29): In a flurry of activity before it adjourns for August recess, Senate passes, 65–31, bill that protects gun manufacturers from lawsuits. Also votes unanimously to make perma-

nent most provisions of the USA PATRIOT Act and approves, 74–26, energy measure that President Bush has been pursuing for five years. House passed similar energy legislation a day earlier. Both House and Senate vote, 412–8 and 91–4, respectively, in favor of a $286.4 billion highway bill.

BUSINESS/SCIENCE/SOCIETY

Musicians Urge World to Unite to End Poverty in Africa (July 2): Millions of people attend Live 8, free concerts in nine countries—South Africa and each of the Group of Eight nations—to promote increased aid to Africa.

Spacecraft Crashes into Comet (July 4): After a 6-month 83-million-mile journey, NASA's *Deep Impact* hits comet named Tempel 1. Scientists will examine pieces of the comet and photos of the collision.

London to Host 2012 Olympics (July 6): City chosen over Paris as the site of the summer games. It will be the third time London has hosted the Olympics.

China Revalues Currency (July 21): After months of pressure from the Bush administration, China announces it will no longer peg the yuan to the dollar.

Shuttle Problems Continue (July 26): *Discovery* launches from Cape Canaveral, Florida, for a 12½-day mission to the International Space Station. A piece of foam insulation breaks off from the shuttle's external fuel tank. **(July 27):** NASA announces it will ground the shuttle fleet.

Scientists Discover Potential Tenth Planet (July 29): Astronomers at the California Institute of Technology find rocky, icy planet that's larger than Pluto and about nine billion miles away from the Sun.

August

WORLD

Sudan Leader Killed in Crash (Aug. 1): Government confirms that John Garang, leader of the opposition Sudan People's Liberation Army (SPLA) who was recently named vice president, had been killed in a helicopter crash. Fragile peace agreement, signed in January, is jeopardized. Dozens die in street demonstrations that follow. Salva Kiir Mayardit assumes role as chairman of the SPLA. **(Aug. 5):** Ugandan president Yoweri Museveni suggests that the helicopter crash may not have been an accident.

Saudi King Dies (Aug. 1): King Fahd bin Abdel Aziz al-Saud, 82, dies after a bout with pneumonia. Prince Abdullah, 81, assumes the throne. Abdullah had been Saudi Arabia's leader since King Fahd suffered a stroke in 1995.

Europe Presents Nuclear Program Plan to Iran (Aug. 4): Britain, France, and Germany offer to allow Iran to acquire nuclear reactors and fuel if it promises to end conversion and enrichment of uranium. **(Aug. 6):** Iran says it will reject the proposal. **(Aug. 10):** Iran removes UN seals at a nuclear production site and begins uranium conversion. **(Aug. 11):** UN issues resolution calling on Iran to "reestablish full suspension of all enrichment activities."

Terror Suspects Charged in London (Aug. 6): Yassin Hassan Omar indicted on charges of attempted murder, conspiracy to commit murder, and possession of explosives. **(Aug. 7):** Ibrahim Muktar Said and Ramzi Mohamed indicted on the same charges.

Talks on North Korea Weapons Suspended (Aug. 7): Officials put on hold six-nation negotiations when they deadlock on North Korea's insistence on operating a light-water nuclear reactor.

Israeli Cabinet Approves Gaza Withdrawal (Aug. 7): Finance minister and former prime minister Benjamin Netanyahu quits in protest.

Crew of Russian Sub Rescued (Aug. 7): British and American rescuers save seven sailors who were trapped in a submarine more than 600 feet deep in the Pacific Ocean.

UN Aide Accused of Taking Bribes (Aug. 8): Panel investigating the UN's oil-for-food program in Iraq reports that Benon Sevan, the former director of the program, received kickbacks from oil sales. Another official, Aleksandr Yakovlev, pleads guilty to conspiracy, wire fraud, and money laundering in connection to the program.

Aceh Peace Accord Signed (Aug. 15): Indonesian government and the Free Aceh Movement (GAM) agree to end their nearly 30-year-long civil war.

Iraq Delays Final Draft of Constitution (Aug. 15): Parliament votes to extend deadline so Sunni, Shiite, and Kurdish delegates can compromise on disputed issues, such as the distribution of oil revenues, the rights of women, and the role of Islam in government. **(Aug. 22):** Iraqi leaders give National Assembly a partially complete constitution and promise to complete the document within days. **(Aug. 27):** Frustrated with demands by Sunni Arabs, Shiite and Kurdish leaders end negotiations with Sunnis. **(Aug. 28):** Iraqi National Assembly receives the new constitution, which will be voted on by Iraqi citizens on Oct. 15. Sunni negotiators denounce the document.

Settlement Withdrawal Begins (Aug. 15): Israeli police officers and soldiers start process of evacuating about 8,700 residents from the Gaza Strip and 675 from the West Bank. Palestinians will assume control of the areas. **(Aug. 17):** Soldiers begin removing those settlers who refuse to leave Gaza. **(Aug. 18):** Troops storm synagogues in the Kfar Darom and Neve Dekalim settlements to remove protesters. **(Aug. 22):** The last settlers leave the Gaza Strip. **(Aug. 23):** Israeli troops and police evacuate the remaining settlers in the four affected settlements in the West Bank.

Bombs Explode at Baghdad Bus Station (Aug. 17): Three car bombs kill about 45 people and injure dozens during morning rush hour.

U.S. Ships Attacked in Jordan (Aug. 19): Rockets fired at two U.S. Navy ships, the *Kearsarge* and the *Ashland,* docked in Aqaba. No U.S. casualties, but a Jordanian soldier is killed. **(Aug. 22):** Jordanian officials arrest Muhammad Hassan al-Sihli in connection with the bombing and acknowledge that Iraqi insurgents were involved in the attack.

Pakistan Says North Korea Received Nuclear Machines (Aug. 24): Pakistani president Pervez Musharraf admits that nuclear scientist A. Q. Khan sent North Korea centrifuge machines, which can be used to make fuel for a nuclear bomb.

Hundreds of Shiite Pilgrims Killed in Baghdad (Aug. 31): Nearly 1,000 people die and hundreds are wounded in a stampede on a bridge over the Tigris River. Rumors that a suicide bomber was in the crowd caused a panic.

NATION

President Appoints Bolton (Aug. 1): Bush installs controversial figure John Bolton as U.S. ambassador to the UN during congressional recess. Democratic senators had refused to put his confirmation to a vote.

Bush Signs Bills (Aug. 8): New energy law calls for increased domestic oil and gas production, as well as the construction of new nuclear power plants. It also encourages research into alternative sources of energy. Bill is criticized for failing to increase the fuel efficiency of vehicles. **(Aug. 10):** President signs $286.4 billion transportation legislation that includes 6,000 special projects.

Southwestern States Make Emergency Declarations (Aug. 12): Citing a lack of funds from the federal government to stem illegal immigration, drug smuggling, and violence along the border with Mexico, New Mexico governor Bill Richardson declares a state of emergency in four counties. **(Aug. 16):** Arizona governor Janet Napolitano makes similar declarations. Moves free up more than $1.5 million for additional policing.

Administration Releases Plan for Fuel Efficiency (Aug. 23): Proposal calls for increasing average mileage per

gallon of light trucks to 24 mpg from 21.2. Environmentalists say plan does not go far enough.

Panel Spares New England Naval Sites (Aug. 24): Base Closure and Realignment Commission agrees with Pentagon plan to close about 800 installations nationwide, but it overturns closure of the Naval Submarine Base in Groton, Conn., and the Portsmouth Naval Shipyard in Kittery, Maine. **(Aug. 26):** Group also votes to keep open the Ellsworth Air Force Base in South Dakota.

Hurricane Causes Catastrophic Damage (Aug. 29): Hurricane Katrina, a category 4 storm, pounds Gulf Coast. Harrison County, Miss., hit particularly hard. More than 80 people are killed and millions lose power. **(Aug. 30):** New Orleans, which was spared the full force of the hurricane when the storm moved east, suffers calamitous damage as levees break, submerging about 80% of the city. The Pentagon sends six U.S. Navy ships and eight rescue teams to the Gulf Coast to help in the relief effort. Looting is rampant. **(Aug. 31):** Death toll in New Orleans is feared to be in the thousands. Officials call the devastation the worst natural disaster in U.S. history.

Poverty Increased in 2004 (Aug. 30): Overall poverty rate in the United States rose to 12.7% from 12.5%, and 37 million people lived in poverty. Median income of full-time males dropped 2%, to $40,800. Women's median income decreased 1%, to $31,200.

Energy Department Releases Energy Reserves (Aug. 31): Announces it will release oil from the Strategic Petroleum Reserve. Crude oil prices immediately drop 49 cents a barrel, to $69.32; gas prices, however, increase. Hurricane Katrina had shut down most oil and natural gas refineries in the Gulf Coast.

BUSINESS/SCIENCE/SOCIETY

China Withdraws Bid for Oil Company (Aug. 2): The China National Oil Corporation rescinds $18.5 billion bid for Unocal.

South Korean Scientists Clone a Dog (Aug. 3): After a three-year effort and 1,095 eggs, researchers clone the first dog, a male Afghan hound.

Shuttle Lands Safely (Aug. 9): *Discovery* returns to Earth after a 14-day mission. Landing moved to Edwards Air Force Base in California because of bad weather in Florida. Mission included the first-ever spacewalk to remove a piece of material sticking out of the shuttle's skin.

Five Planes Crash During Month (Aug. 2): All passengers and crew of an Air France flight survive when a jetliner overruns the runway in Toronto, lands in a gully, and bursts into flames. **(Aug. 6):** Plane crashes off Sicily, killing 13 people. **(Aug. 14):** Everyone on board a Helios Airways dies when the Boeing 737 crashes into mountains north of Athens, Greece. **(Aug. 16):** West Caribbean Airways plane dives to the ground in Machiques, Venezuela, killing all 160 people on board. **(Aug. 23):** About 40 people die when plane crashes in Peru's northern jungle.

September

WORLD

Four Charged in Murder of Lebanese Prime Minister (Sept. 1): Commander of Lebanon's Republican Guard, former head of general security, former chief of Lebanon's police, and former military intelligence officer are indicted for the February assassination of Rafik Hariri.

Israel and Pakistan Officials Meet (Sept. 1): In what is called historic progress, foreign ministers of both countries meet. Meeting, brokered by Turkey, is a result of Israel's withdrawal from Gaza.

Report on UN Faults Annan (Sept. 6): Panel, headed by Paul Volcker, investigating Iraq's oil-for-food program criticizes Secretary-General Kofi Annan for not determining if his son's employment and other activities posed a potential conflict of interest. Annan is also cited for not stemming corruption and mismanagement at the UN.

Egypt Holds First Multicandidate Elections (Sept. 7): President Hosni Mubarak faces nine opponents in his bid for a fifth term. He overwhelmingly wins the race, but monitors say the election is marred by fraud. **(Sept. 9):** Mubarak is declared the winner of the election, taking 88.5% of the vote. Turnout is low, at 23%.

Ukrainian President Fires Cabinet (Sept. 8): Viktor Yushchenko also replaces Prime Minister Yulia Tymoshenko, citing internal struggles in his administration.

U.S. and Iraqi Troops Launch Offensive (Sept. 10): About 11,000 soldiers attack insurgents in the northern city of Tal Afar. **(Sept. 11):** Insurgents leave the city.

Ruling Party Dominates Elections in Japan (Sept. 11): Prime Minister Junichiro Koizumi's Liberal Democratic Party wins in a landslide in parliamentary elections. In the lower house, party takes 296 of the 480 seats in the lower house of parliament, up from 249 seats.

Talks on North Korea's Nuclear Weapons Program Resume (Sept. 13): Few expect six-nation negotiations to yield any progress as North Korea continues to insist on maintaining nuclear energy program once it dismantles its weapons program. **(Sept. 19):** North Korea promises to dismantle its nuclear weapons program in exchange for economic aid and diplomatic recognition. Agreement, brokered by China, will allow North Korea to have access to a light-water nuclear reactor for energy "at the appropriate time."

World Leaders Gather at UN Session (Sept. 14): President Bush endorses millennium development goals at meeting marking the 60th anniversary of the UN. Administration had previously backed away from such goals. Security Council passes a resolution that bans incitement of terrorism.

Suicide Bombers Wreak Havoc on Baghdad (Sept. 14): About 150 people die and 500 are wounded in a series of coordinated attacks. Al-Qaeda in Mesopotamia claims responsibility. **(Sept. 15):** Another 20 people—16 of them police officers—killed by suicide bomber.

Afghanistan Holds Elections (Sept. 18): Voters choose from about 5,800 candidates in the country's first democratic parliamentary elections in more than 25 years. Turnout low, at about 50%.

German Elections Inconclusive (Sept. 19): Chancellor Gerhard Schröder's Social Democratic Party, with 34.3% of the vote, falls to Angela Merkel's Free Democratic Party, which takes 35.2%. With neither party winning a clear majority, the future composition of the government is unclear.

NATION

New Orleans Descends into Chaos (Sept. 1): Lawlessness and anger prevail as millions are left homeless and displaced as a result of Hurricane Katrina and broken levees. Federal, state, and local officials are harshly criticized for failing to act quickly and decisively. Thousands of people are stranded for days without food or water at the city's Convention Center, while thousands of others arrive at Houston's Astrodome for temporary shelter. Damage estimated at well over $200 billion. **(Sept. 2):** Attempting to quell criticism of his administration's response to the crisis, President Bush visits New Orleans and other parts of the Gulf Coast. More than 220,000 refugees from the hurricane take refuge in Houston. **(Sept. 3):** President Bush signs $10.5 billion emergency aid package for the region. **(Sept. 5):** Officials restart pumps to begin removing water from New Orleans. **(Sept. 6):** New Orleans mayor Ray Nagin issues an evacuation order for the 5,000 to 10,000 people who have remained in the city. **(Sept. 7):** Congressional leaders order a joint inquiry into the government's response to the disaster. **(Sept. 9):** President Bush removes embattled FEMA director Michael Brown from relief effort in New Orleans. **(Sept. 12):** Michael Brown resigns and is replaced by David Paulison. **(Sept. 13):** President Bush takes responsibility for flaws in the federal government's response to Hurricane Katrina. **(Sept. 15):** In a nationally televised address, Bush promises to rebuild New Orleans and help victims with rebuilding, housing, and job training.

Chief Justice Rehnquist Dies (Sept. 3): William H. Rehnquist, who served on the U.S. Supreme Court for 33 years, 19 of them as chief justice, dies after battle with thyroid cancer. He was 80. Death leaves two vacancies on the Court. **(Sept. 5):** President Bush nominates John Roberts, who was selected to replace retiring justice Sandra Day O'Connor, for chief justice of the Court. **(Sept. 7):** More than 1,000 mourners attend Rehnquist's funeral.

California Legalizes Same-Sex Marriage (Sept. 6): State legislators approve law that defines marriage as a union of "two persons." **(Sept. 7):** Governor Arnold Schwarzenegger says he will veto the bill.

Roberts Confirmation Hearings Begin (Sept. 12): In his first appearance before the Senate Judiciary Committee Roberts, who was nominated to replace William Rehnquist as chief justice of the U.S. Supreme Court, says he will "confront every case with an open mind."

2005 Primetime Emmy Awards

Drama Series: Lost (ABC)
  Actor: James Spader, *Boston Legal*
  Actress: Patricia Arquette, *Medium*
  Supporting Actor: William Shatner, *Boston Legal*
  Supporting Actress: Blythe Danner, *Huff*
  Guest Actor: Ray Liotta, *ER*
  Guest Actress: Amanda Plummer, *Law & Order: Special Victims Unit*
  Directing: J. J. Abrams, *Lost*
  Writing: David Shore, *House*
Comedy Series: *Everybody Loves Raymond* (CBS)
  Actor: Tony Shalhoub, *Monk*
  Actress: Felicity Huffman, *Desperate Housewives*
  Supporting Actor: Brad Garrett, *Everybody Loves Raymond*
  Supporting Actress: Doris Roberts, *Everybody Loves Raymond*
  Guest Actor: Bobby Cannavale, *Will & Grace*
  Guest Actress: Kathryn Joosten, *Desperate Housewives*
  Directing: Charles McDougall, *Desperate Housewives*
  Writing: Mitchell Hurwitz and Jim Vallely, *Arrested Development*

Variety, Music, or Comedy Series: *The Daily Show with Jon Stewart* (Comedy Central)
Individual Performance: Hugh Jackman, *58th Annual Tony Awards (2004)*
Outstanding Miniseries: *The Lost Prince (Masterpiece Theatre)* (PBS)
Outstanding Made-for-Television Movie: *Warm Springs* (HBO)
Actor in a Miniseries or Movie: Geoffrey Rush, *The Life and Death of Peter Sellers*
Actress in a Miniseries or Movie: S. Epatha Merkerson, *Lackawanna Blues*
Supporting Actor in a Miniseries or Movie: Paul Newman, *Empire Falls*
Supporting Actress in a Miniseries or Movie: Jane Alexander, *Warm Springs*
Reality/Competition Program: *The Amazing Race* (CBS)
Reality Program: *Extreme Makeover: Home Edition* (ABC)
Children's Program (tie): *Classical Baby* (HBO) and *Nick News with Linda Ellerbee: Never Again? From the Holocaust to the Sudan* (Nickelodeon)

Presidential Election of 2004, Electoral and Popular Vote Summary

Principal Candidates for President and Vice President:
Republican—George W. Bush; Richard B. Cheney (winner)
Democratic—John F. Kerry; John Edwards

	George W. Bush		John F. Kerry		Electoral votes	
	Popular vote	%	Popular vote	%	R	D
Alabama	1,176,394	62.5%	693,933	36.8%	9	
Alaska	190,889	61.1	111,025	35.5	3	
Arizona	1,104,294	54.9	893,524	44.4	10	
Arkansas	572,898	54.4	469,953	44.5	6	
California	5,509,826	44.4	6,745,485	54.3		55
Colorado	1,101,255	51.7	1,001,732	47.0	9	
Connecticut	693,826	43.9	857,488	54.3		7
Delaware	171,660	45.8	200,152	53.3		3
District of Columbia	21,256	09.3	202,970	89.2		3
Florida	3,964,522	52.1	3,583,544	47.1	27	
Georgia	1,914,254	58.0	1,366,149	41.4	15	
Hawaii	194,191	45.3	231,708	54.0		4
Idaho	409,235	68.4	181,098	30.3	4	
Illinois	2,345,946	44.5	2,891,550	54.8		21
Indiana	1,479,438	59.9	969,011	39.3	11	
Iowa	751,957	49.9	741,898	49.3	7	
Kansas	736,456	62.0	434,993	36.6	6	
Kentucky	1,069,439	59.5	712,733	39.7	8	
Louisiana	1,102,169	56.7	820,299	42.2	9	
Maine	330,201	44.6	396,842	53.6		4
Maryland	1,024,703	43.0	1,334,493	56.0		10
Massachusetts	1,071,109	36.9	1,803,800	62.0		12
Michigan	2,313,746	47.8	2,479,183	51.2		17
Minnesota	1,346,695	48.0	1,445,014	51.5		9[1]
Mississippi	672,660	59.1	457,766	40.1	6	
Missouri	1,455,713	53.3	1,259,171	46.1	11	
Montana	266,063	59.1	173,710	38.6	3	
Nebraska	512,814	66.0	254,328	32.7	5	
Nevada	418,690	50.7	397,190	48.1	5	
New Hampshire	331,237	49.0	340,511	50.4		4
New Jersey	1,670,003	46.2	1,911,430	53.0		15
New Mexico	376,930	49.8	370,942	49.0	5	
New York	2,962,567	40.1	4,314,280	58.4		31
North Carolina	1,961,166	56.1	1,525,849	43.6	15	
North Dakota	196,651	62.9	111,052	35.5	3	
Ohio	2,859,764	50.8	2,741,165	48.7	20	
Oklahoma	959,792	65.6	503,966	34.4	7	
Oregon	866,831	47.4	943,163	51.6		7
Pennsylvania	2,793,847	48.5	2,938,095	51.0		21
Rhode Island	169,046	38.7	259,760	59.4		4
South Carolina	937,974	58.1	661,699	41.0	8	
South Dakota	232,584	59.9	149,244	38.4	3	
Tennessee	1,384,375	56.9	1,036,477	42.6	11	
Texas	4,526,917	61.1	2,832,704	38.2	34	
Utah	663,742	72.7	241,199	26.4	5	
Vermont	121,180	38.8	184,067	58.9		3
Virginia	1,716,959	53.8	1,454,742	45.6	13	
Washington	1,304,894	45.6	1,510,201	52.8		11
West Virginia	423,778	56.1	326,541	43.2	5	
Wisconsin	1,478,120	49.4	1,489,504	49.7		10
Wyoming	167,629	69.0	70,776	29.1	3	
Total	**62,028,285**	**50.7**	**59,028,109**	**48.3**	**286**	**251**

NOTE: Total electoral votes = 538. Total electoral votes needed to win = 270. Percentages may not add up to 100% due to rounding and other candidates. 1. One Minnesota electoral vote was cast for John Edwards. Source: Figures are from the Federal Election Commission, 2004 Official Presidential Election Results, Feb. 11, 2005.

Voting age population (United States Election Project for Nov. 2004): 221,256,931
Estimated number of voters in the 2004 election was 122,294,978.

The One Hundred Ninth Congress

Composition of the 108th and 109th Congresses

109th Congress	Rep.	Dem.	Ind.	Vacancies	108th Congress	Rep.	Dem.	Ind.	Vacancies
Senate	55	44	1	—	Senate	51	48	1	—
House	231	202	1	1	House	227	205	1	2

The Senate

Dates in left column indicate term in office; birth years are given in parentheses after party affiliation. All terms are for six years and expire in January. Senators listed in italics were elected or reelected in 2004.

Alabama
1987–2011 *Richard Shelby (R) (1934)*
1997–2009 Jeff Sessions (R) (1946)
Alaska
1969–2009 Ted Stevens (R) (1923)
2002–2011 *Lisa Murkowski (R) (1957)*
Arizona
1987–2011 *John McCain (R) (1936)*
1995–2007 Jon Kyl (R) (1942)
Arkansas
2003–2009 Mark Pryor (D) (1963)
1999–2011 *Blanche Lincoln (D) (1960)*
California
1993–2009 Dianne Feinstein (D) (1933)
1993–2011 *Barbara Boxer (D) (1940)*
Colorado
1997–2009 Wayne Allard (R) (1943)
2005–2011 *Ken Salazar (D) (1955)*
Connecticut
1981–2011 *Christopher J. Dodd (D) (1944)*
1989–2007 Joseph I. Lieberman (D) (1942)
Delaware
1973–2009 Joseph R. Biden, Jr. (D) (1942)
2001–2007 Thomas R. Carper (D) (1947)
Florida
2001–2007 Bill Nelson (D) (1942)
2005–2011 *Mel Martinez (R) (1946)*
Georgia
2003–2009 Saxby Chambliss (R) (1943)
2005–2011 *Johnny Isakson (R) (1944)*
Hawaii
1963–2011 *Daniel K. Inouye (D) (1924)*
1990–2007 Daniel K. Akaka (D) (1924)
Idaho
1991–2009 Larry E. Craig (R) (1945)
1999–2011 *Mike Crapo (R) (1951)*
Illinois
1997–2009 Richard J. Durbin (D) (1944)
2005–2011 *Barack Obama (D) (1961)*
Indiana
1977–2007 Richard G. Lugar (R) (1932)
1999–2011 *Evan Bayh (D) (1955)*
Iowa
1981–2011 *Charles E. Grassley (R) (1933)*
1985–2009 Tom Harkin (D) (1939)
Kansas
1997–2011 *Sam Brownback (R) (1956)*
1997–2009 Pat Roberts (R) (1936)
Kentucky
1985–2009 Mitch McConnell (R) (1942)
1999–2011 *Jim Bunning (R) (1931)*
Louisiana
1997–2009 Mary L. Landrieu (D) (1955)
2005–2011 *David Vitter (R) (1961)*
Maine
1995–2007 Olympia J. Snowe (R) (1947)
1997–2009 Susan M. Collins (R) (1952)

Maryland
1977–2007 Paul S. Sarbanes (D) (1933)
1987–2011 *Barbara A. Mikulski (D) (1936)*
Massachusetts
1963–2007 Edward M. Kennedy (D) (1932)
1985–2009 John F. Kerry (D) (1943)
Michigan
1979–2009 Carl Levin (D) (1934)
2001–2007 Debbie A. Stabenow (D) (1950)
Minnesota
2003–2009 Norm Coleman (R) (1949)
2001–2007 Mark Dayton (D) (1947)
Mississippi
1979–2009 Thad Cochran (R) (1937)
1989–2007 Trent Lott (R) (1941)
Missouri
1987–2011 *Christopher S. Bond (R) (1939)*
2003–2009 James M. Talent (R) (1956)
Montana
1978–2009 Max Baucus (D) (1941)
1989–2007 Conrad Burns (R) (1935)
Nebraska
1997–2009 Charles Hagel (R) (1946)
2001–2007 Ben Nelson (D) (1941)
Nevada
1987–2011 *Harry Reid (D) (1939)*
2001–2007 John Ensign (R) (1958)
New Hampshire
1993–2011 *Judd Gregg (R) (1947)*
2003–2009 John E. Sununu (R) (1964)
New Jersey
2001–2007 Jon Corzine (D) (1947)
2003–2009 Frank R. Lautenberg (D) (1924)
New Mexico
1973–2009 Pete V. Domenici (R) (1932)
1983–2007 Jeff Bingaman (D) (1943)
New York
1999–2011 *Charles E. Schumer (D) (1950)*
2001–2007 Hillary Rodham Clinton (D) (1947)
North Carolina
2003–2009 Elizabeth Dole (R) (1936)
2005–2011 *Richard Burr (R) (1955)*
North Dakota
1987–2007 Kent Conrad (D) (1948)
1993–2011 *Byron L. Dorgan (D) (1942)*
Ohio
1995–2007 Mike DeWine (R) (1947)
1999–2011 *George Voinovich (R) (1936)*
Oklahoma
1994–2009 James Inhofe (R) (1934)
2005–2011 *Tom Coburn (R) (1948)*
Oregon
1996–2011 *Ron Wyden (D) (1949)*
1997–2009 Gordon H. Smith (R) (1952)
Pennsylvania
1981–2011 *Arlen Specter (R) (1930)*
1995–2007 Rick Santorum (R) (1958)

Rhode Island
1997–2009 Jack Reed (D) (1949)
1999–2007 Lincoln Chafee (R) (1953)
South Carolina
2003–2009 Lindsey Graham (R) (1955)
2005–2011 Jim DeMint (R) (1951)
South Dakota
2005–2011 John R. Thune (R) (1961)
1997–2009 Tim Johnson (D) (1946)
Tennessee
1995–2007 William Frist (R) (1952)
2003–2009 Lamar Alexander (R) (1940)
Texas
1995–2007 Kay Bailey Hutchison (R) (1943)
2003–2009 John Cornyn (R) (1952)
Utah
1977–2007 Orrin G. Hatch (R) (1934)
1993–2011 Robert Bennett (R) (1933)

Vermont
1975–2011 Patrick J. Leahy (D) (1940)
1989–2007 James M. Jeffords (I) (1934)
Virginia
1979–2009 John Warner (R) (1927)
2001–2007 George Allen (R) (1952)
Washington
1993–2011 Patty Murray (D) (1950)
2001–2007 Maria Cantwell (D) (1958)
West Virginia
1959–2007 Robert C. Byrd (D) (1917)
1985–2009 John D. "Jay" Rockefeller IV (D) (1937)
Wisconsin
1989–2007 Herbert Kohl (D) (1935)
1993–2011 Russ Feingold (D) (1953)
Wyoming
1995–2007 Craig Thomas (R) (1933)
1997–2009 Michael B. Enzi (R) (1944)

The House of Representatives

In the following lists, the numeral indicates the congressional district represented; AL is for representatives at large. All terms run from Jan. 2005 to Jan. 2007.

Alabama
1. Jo Bonner (R)
2. Terry Everett (R)
3. Mike Rogers (R)
4. Robert B. Aderholt (R)
5. Robert E. "Bud" Cramer, Jr. (D)
6. Spencer Bachus (R)
7. Artur Davis (D)

Alaska
AL Don Young (R)

Arizona
1. Rick Renzi (R)
2. Trent Franks (R)
3. John Shadegg (R)
4. Ed Pastor (D)
5. J. D. Hayworth (R)
6. Jeff Flake (R)
7. Raul Grijalva (D)
8. Jim Kolbe (R)

Arkansas
1. Marion Berry (D)
2. Vic Snyder (D)
3. John Boozman (R)
4. Mike Ross (D)

California
1. Mike Thompson (D)
2. Wally Herger (R)
3. Dan Lungren (R)
4. John T. Doolittle (R)
5. Doris Matsui[1] (D)
6. Lynn C. Woolsey (D)
7. George Miller (D)
8. Nancy Pelosi (D)
9. Barbara Lee (D)
10. Ellen O. Tauscher (D)
11. Richard W. Pombo (R)
12. Tom Lantos (D)
13. Fortney Pete Stark (D)
14. Anna G. Eshoo (D)
15. Michael M. Honda (D)
16. Zoe Lofgren (D)
17. Sam Farr (D)
18. Dennis Cardoza (D)
19. George P. Radanovich (R)
20. Jim Costa (D)
21. Devin Nunes (R)
22. Bill Thomas (R)
23. Lois Capps (D)
24. Elton Gallegly (R)
25. Howard P. McKeon (R)
26. David Dreier (R)
27. Brad Sherman (D)
28. Howard L. Berman (D)
29. Adam B. Schiff (D)
30. Henry A. Waxman (D)
31. Xavier Becerra (D)
32. Hilda L. Solis (D)
33. Diane Watson (D)
34. Lucille Roybal-Allard (D)
35. Maxine Waters (D)
36. Jane Harman (D)
37. Juanita Millender-McDonald (D)
38. Grace F. Napolitano (D)
39. Linda T. Sanchez (D)
40. Ed Royce (R)
41. Jerry Lewis (R)
42. Gary G. Miller (R)
43. Joe Baca (D)
44. Ken Calvert (R)
45. Mary Bono (R)
46. Dana Rohrabacher (R)
47. Loretta Sanchez (D)
48. Vacant[2]
49. Darrell Issa (R)
50. Randy Cunningham (R)
51. Bob Filner (D)
52. Duncan Hunter (R)
53. Susan Davis (D)
1. A special election was held on March 8, 2005, to fill the seat of Robert Matsui, who died in January 2005.
2. Christopher Cox left to become chairman of the Securities and Exchange Commission.

Colorado
1. Diana DeGette (D)
2. Mark Udall (D)
3. John T. Salazar (D)
4. Marilyn Musgrave (R)
5. Joel Hefley (R)
6. Thomas G. Tancredo (R)
7. Bob Beauprez (R)

Connecticut
1. John B. Larson (D)
2. Robert R. Simmons (R)
3. Rosa L. DeLauro (D)
4. Christopher Shays (R)
5. Nancy L. Johnson (R)

Delaware
AL Michael N. Castle (R)

Florida
1. Jeff Miller (R)
2. Allen Boyd (D)
3. Corrine Brown (D)
4. Ander Crenshaw (R)
5. Virginia Brown-Waite (R)
6. Cliff Stearns (R)
7. John L. Mica (R)
8. Ric Keller (R)
9. Michael Bilirakis (R)
10. C. W. Bill Young (R)
11. Jim Davis (D)
12. Adam Putnam (R)
13. Katherine Harris (R)
14. Connie Mack (R)
15. Dave Weldon (R)
16. Mark Foley (R)
17. Kendrick Meek (D)
18. Ileana Ros-Lehtinen (R)
19. Robert Wexler (D)
20. Debbie Wasserman Schultz (D)
21. Lincoln Diaz-Balart (R)
22. E. Clay Shaw, Jr. (R)
23. Alcee L. Hastings (D)
24. Tom Feeney (R)
25. Mario Diaz-Balart (R)

Georgia
1. Jack Kingston (R)
2. Sanford D. Bishop, Jr. (D)
3. Jim Marshall (D)
4. Cynthia McKinney (D)
5. John Lewis (D)
6. Tom Price (R)
7. John Linder (R)
8. Lynn A. Westmoreland (R)
9. Charlie Norwood (R)
10. Nathan Deal (R)
11. Phil Gingrey (R)
12. John Barrow (D)
13. David Scott (D)

Hawaii
1. Neil Abercrombie (D)
2. Ed Case (D)

Idaho
1. C. L. Otter (R)
2. Mike Simpson (R)

Illinois
1. Bobby L. Rush (D)
2. Jesse L. Jackson, Jr. (D)
3. Dan Lipinski (D)
4. Luis V. Gutierrez (D)

5. Rahm Emanuel (D)
6. Henry J. Hyde (R)
7. Danny K. Davis (D)
8. Melissa L. Bean (D)
9. Janice Schakowsky (D)
10. Mark Steven Kirk (R)
11. Jerry Weller (R)
12. Jerry F. Costello (D)
13. Judy Biggert (R)
14. J. Dennis Hastert (R)
15. Timothy V. Johnson (R)
16. Donald Manzullo (R)
17. Lane Evans (D)
18. Ray LaHood (R)
19. John Shimkus (R)

Indiana
1. Peter J. Visclosky (D)
2. Chris Chocola (R)
3. Mark E. Souder (R)
4. Steve Buyer (R)
5. Dan Burton (R)
6. Mike Pence (R)
7. Julia Carson (D)
8. John Hostettler (R)
9. Mike Sodrel (R)

Iowa
1. Jim Nussle (R)
2. Jim Leach (R)
3. Leonard L. Boswell (D)
4. Tom Latham (R)
5. Steve King (R)

Kansas
1. Jerry Moran (R)
2. Jim Ryun (R)
3. Dennis Moore (D)
4. Todd Tiahrt (R)

Kentucky
1. Edward Whitfield (R)
2. Ron Lewis (R)
3. Anne M. Northup (R)
4. Geoff Davis (R)
5. Harold Rogers (R)
6. Ben Chandler (D)

Louisiana
1. Bobby Jindal (R)
2. William J. Jefferson (D)
3. Charlie Melancon (D)
4. Jim McCrery (R)
5. Rodney Alexander (R)
6. Richard H. Baker (R)
7. Charles Boustany, Jr.(R)

Maine
1. Thomas H. Allen (D)
2. Mike Michaud (D)

Maryland
1. Wayne T. Gilchrest (R)
2. C. A. "Dutch" Ruppersberger (D)
3. Benjamin L. Cardin (D)
4. Albert R. Wynn (D)
5. Steny H. Hoyer (D)
6. Roscoe G. Bartlett (R)
7. Elijah E. Cummings (D)
8. Chris Van Hollen (D)

Massachusetts
1. John W. Olver (D)
2. Richard E. Neal (D)
3. Jim McGovern (D)
4. Barney Frank (D)
5. Marty Meehan (D)
6. John F. Tierney (D)
7. Edward J. Markey (D)
8. Michael E. Capuano (D)
9. Stephen F. Lynch (D)
10. William Delahunt (D)

Michigan
1. Bart Stupak (D)
2. Peter Hoekstra (R)
3. Vernon J. Ehlers (R)
4. Dave Camp (R)
5. Dale Kildee (D)
6. Fred Upton (R)
7. Joe Schwarz (R)
8. Mike Rogers (R)
9. Joseph Knollenberg (R)
10. Candice Miller (R)
11. Thaddeus McCotter (R)
12. Sander M. Levin (D)
13. Carolyn C. Kilpatrick (D)
14. John Conyers, Jr. (D)
15. John D. Dingell (D)

Minnesota
1. Gil Gutknecht (R)
2. John Kline (R)
3. Jim Ramstad (R)
4. Betty McCollum (D)
5. Martin Olav Sabo (D)
6. Mark Kennedy (R)
7. Collin C. Peterson (D)
8. James L. Oberstar (D)

Mississippi
1. Roger Wicker (R)
2. Bennie Thompson (D)
3. Charles Pickering (R)
4. Gene Taylor (D)

Missouri
1. William Lacy Clay (D)
2. Todd Akin (R)
3. Russ Carnahan (D)
4. Ike Skelton (D)
5. Emanuel Cleaver (D)
6. Sam Graves (R)
7. Roy Blunt (R)
8. Jo Ann Emerson (R)
9. Kenny Hulshof (R)

Montana
AL Denny Rehberg (R)

Nebraska
1. Jeff Fortenberry (R)
2. Lee Terry (R)
3. Tom Osborne (R)

Nevada
1. Shelley Berkley (D)
2. James A. Gibbons (R)
3. Jon C. Porter (R)

New Hampshire
1. Jeb Bradley (R)
2. Charles Bass (R)

New Jersey
1. Robert E. Andrews (D)
2. Frank A. LoBiondo (R)
3. Jim Saxton (R)
4. Christopher H. Smith (R)
5. Scott Garrett (R)
6. Frank Pallone, Jr. (D)
7. Michael A. Ferguson (R)
8. Bill Pascrell, Jr. (D)
9. Steven R. Rothman (D)
10. Donald M. Payne (D)
11. Rodney Frelinghuysen (R)
12. Rush D. Holt (D)
13. Robert Menendez (D)

New Mexico
1. Heather Wilson (R)
2. Steve Pearce (R)
3. Tom Udall (D)

New York
1. Tim Bishop (D)
2. Steve J. Israel (D)
3. Peter King (R)
4. Carolyn McCarthy (D)
5. Gary L. Ackerman (D)
6. Gregory W. Meeks (D)
7. Joseph Crowley (D)
8. Jerrold Nadler (D)
9. Anthony D. Weiner (D)
10. Edolphus Towns (D)
11. Major R. Owens (D)
12. Nydia Velázquez (D)
13. Vito J. Fossella (R)
14. Carolyn Maloney (D)
15. Charles B. Rangel (D)
16. José E. Serrano (D)
17. Eliot L. Engel (D)
18. Nita M. Lowey (D)
19. Sue W. Kelly (R)
20. John E. Sweeney (R)
21. Michael R. McNulty (D)
22. Maurice Hinchey (D)
23. John McHugh (R)
24. Sherwood L. Boehlert (R)
25. James T. Walsh (R)
26. Thomas Reynolds (R)
27. Brian M. Higgins (D)
28. Louise McIntosh Slaughter (D)
29. John "Randy" Kuhl, Jr. (R)

North Carolina
1. G. K. Butterfield (D)
2. Bob Etheridge (D)
3. Walter Jones (R)
4. David E. Price (D)
5. Virginia Foxx (R)
6. Howard Coble (R)
7. Mike McIntyre (D)
8. Robin Hayes (R)
9. Sue Myrick (R)
10. Patrick McHenry (R)
11. Charles H. Taylor (R)
12. Melvin L. Watt (D)
13. Brad Miller (D)

North Dakota
AL Earl Pomeroy (D)

Ohio
1. Steve Chabot (R)
2. Jean Schmidt[3] (R)
3. Michael Turner (R)
4. Michael G. Oxley (R)
5. Paul E. Gillmor (R)
6. Ted Strickland (D)
7. David Hobson (R)
8. John A. Boehner (R)
9. Marcy Kaptur (D)
10. Dennis J. Kucinich (D)
11. Stephanie Tubbs Jones (D)
12. Patrick J. Tiberi (R)
13. Sherrod Brown (D)
14. Steven C. LaTourette (R)
15. Deborah Pryce (R)
16. Ralph Regula (R)
17. Tim Ryan (D)
18. Bob Ney (R)
3. Replaced Rob Portman, who became U.S. Trade Representative.

Oklahoma
1. John Sullivan (R)
2. Dan Boren (D)
3. Frank D. Lucas (R)
4. Tom Cole (R)
5. Ernest Istook (R)

Oregon
1. David Wu (D)
2. Greg Walden (R)
3. Earl Blumenauer (D)

4. Peter A. DeFazio (D)
5. Darlene Hooley (D)

Pennsylvania
1. Robert A. Brady (D)
2. Chaka Fattah (D)
3. Philip S. English (R)
4. Melissa A. Hart (R)
5. John E. Peterson (R)
6. Jim Gerlach (R)
7. Curt Weldon (R)
8. Mike Fitzpatrick (R)
9. Bill Shuster (R)
10. Don Sherwood (R)
11. Paul E. Kanjorski (D)
12. John P. Murtha (D)
13. Allyson Y. Schwartz (D)
14. Mike Doyle (D)
15. Charles W. Dent (R)
16. Joseph R. Pitts (R)
17. Tim Holden (D)
18. Timothy F. Murphy (R)
19. Todd R. Platts (R)

Rhode Island
1. Patrick J. Kennedy (D)
2. James R. Langevin (D)

South Carolina
1. Henry E. Brown, Jr. (R)
2. Joe Wilson (R)
3. J. Gresham Barrett (R)
4. Bob Inglis (R)
5. John M. Spratt (D)
6. James E. Clyburn (D)

South Dakota
AL Stephanie Herseth (D)

Tennessee
1. William L. Jenkins (R)
2. John J. Duncan (R)
3. Zach Wamp (R)
4. Lincoln Davis (D)

5. Jim Cooper (D)
6. Bart Gordon (D)
7. Marsha Blackburn (R)
8. John Tanner (D)
9. Harold E. Ford, Jr. (D)

Texas
1. Louie Gohmert (R)
2. Ted Poe (R)
3. Sam Johnson (R)
4. Ralph M. Hall (R)
5. Jeb Hensarling (R)
6. Joe Barton (R)
7. John A. Culberson (R)
8. Kevin P. Brady (R)
9. Al Green (D)
10. Michael McCaul (R)
11. Mike Conaway (R)
12. Kay Granger (R)
13. William Thornberry (R)
14. Ron E. Paul (R)
15. Rubén E. Hinojosa (D)
16. Silvestre Reyes (D)
17. Chet Edwards (D)
18. Sheila Jackson-Lee (D)
19. Randy Neugebauer (R)
20. Charles A. Gonzalez (D)
21. Lamar S. Smith (R)
22. Tom DeLay (R)
23. Henry Bonilla (R)
24. Kenny Marchant (R)
25. Lloyd Doggett (D)
26. Michael C. Burgess (R)
27. Solomon P. Ortiz (D)
28. Henry Cuellar (D)
29. Gene Green (D)
30. Eddie Bernice Johnson (D)
31. John R. Carter (R)
32. Pete Sessions (R)

Utah
1. Rob Bishop (R)
2. Jim Matheson (D)

3. Chris Cannon (R)

Vermont
AL Bernard Sanders (I)

Virginia
1. Jo Ann S. Davis (R)
2. Thelma D. Drake (R)
3. Bobby Scott (D)
4. Randy Forbes (R)
5. Virgil H. Goode, Jr. (R)
6. Bob Goodlatte (R)
7. Eric I. Cantor (R)
8. James P. Moran (D)
9. Rick Boucher (D)
10. Frank R. Wolf (R)
11. Thomas M. Davis (R)

Washington
1. Jay Inslee (D)
2. Rick Larsen (D)
3. Brian Baird (D)
4. Doc Hastings (R)
5. Cathy McMorris (R)
6. Norman D. Dicks (D)
7. Jim McDermott (D)
8. Dave Reichert (R)
9. Adam Smith (D)

West Virginia
1. Alan B. Mollohan (D)
2. Shelley Moore Capito (R)
3. Nick J. Rahall II (D)

Wisconsin
1. Paul D. Ryan (R)
2. Tammy Baldwin (D)
3. Ron J. Kind (D)
4. Gwen S. Moore (D)
5. F. James Sensenbrenner, Jr. (R)
6. Thomas E. Petri ((R)
7. David R. Obey (D)
8. Mark Green (R)

Wyoming
AL Barbara Cubin (R)

The Governors of the Fifty States

State	Governor	Current term[1]	State	Governor	Current term[1]
Ala.	Robert Riley (R)	2003–2007	*Mont.*	*Brian Schweitzer (D)*	*2005–2009*
Alaska	Frank H. Murkowski (R)	2002–2006[2]	Nebr.	David Heineman (R)[5]	2003–2007
Ariz.	Janet Napolitano (D)	2003–2007	Nev.	Kenny Guinn (R)	2003–2007
Ark.	Mike Huckabee (R)	2003–2007	*N.H.*	*John Lynch (D)*	*2005–2007*
Calif.	Arnold Schwarzenegger (R)[3]	2003–2007	N.J.	Richard Codey (D)[6]	2002–2006
Colo.	Bill Owens (R)	2003–2007	N.M.	Bill Richardson (D)	2003–2007
Conn.	M. Jodi Rell (R)[4]	2004–2007	N.Y.	George E. Pataki (R)	2003–2007
Del.	*Ruth Ann Minner (D)*	*2005–2009*	*N.C.*	*Mike F. Easley (D)*	*2005–2009*
Fla.	Jeb Bush (R)	2003–2007	N.D.	John Hoeven (R)	2004–2008[2]
Ga.	Sonny Perdue (R)	2003–2007	Ohio	Bob Taft (R)	2003–2007
Hawaii	Linda Lingle (R)	2002–2006[2]	Okla.	Brad Henry (D)	2003–2007
Idaho	Dirk Kempthorne (R)	2003–2007	Ore.	Ted Kulongoski (D)	2003–2007
Ill.	Rod R. Blagojevich (D)	2003–2007	Pa.	Ed Rendell (D)	2003–2007
Ind.	*Mitchell Daniels (R)*	*2005–2009*	R.I.	Don Carcieri (R)	2003–2007
Iowa	Tom Vilsack (D)	2003–2007	S.C.	Mark Sanford (R)	2003–2007
Kans.	Kathleen Sebelius (D)	2003–2007	S.D.	Mike Rounds (R)	2003–2007
Ky.	Ernie Fletcher (R)	2003–2007[2]	Tenn.	Phil Bredesen (D)	2003–2007
La.	Kathleen Blanco (D)	2004–2008	Tex.	Rick Perry (R)	2003–2007
Maine	John Baldacci (D)	2003–2007	*Utah*	*Jon Huntsman (R)*	*2005–2009*
Md.	Robert L. Ehrlich, Jr. (R)	2003–2007	*Vt.*	*James H. Douglas (R)*	*2005–2007*
Mass.	Mitt Romney (R)	2003–2007	Va.	Mark Warner (D)	2002–2006
Mich.	Jennifer Granholm (D)	2002–2007	*Wash.*	*Christine Gregoire (D)*	*2005–2009*
Minn.	Tim Pawlenty (R)	2003–2007	*W. Va.*	*Joe Manchin III (D)*	*2005–2009*
Miss.	Haley Barbour (R)	2004–2008	Wis.	Jim Doyle (D)	2003–2007
Mo.	*Matt Blunt (R)*	*2005–2009*	Wyo.	Dave Freudenthal (D)	2003–2007

NOTE: Governors listed in italics were elected or reelected in 2004. 1. Except where indicated, all terms begin and end in January. 2. Term begins and ends in December. 3. Gray Davis (D) was voted out of office in a recall election Oct. 7, 2003. 4. John Rowland resigned in June 2004 and in April 2005 went to prison on corruption charges. Rell was the lieutenant governor. 5. Mike Johanns left in Jan. 2005 to become Secretary of Agriculture. David Heineman was the lieutenant governor. 6. Jim McGreevey resigned Nov. 15, 2004. Senate president Richard Codey became acting governor.

How a President Is Nominated and Elected

The Conventions

The national conventions of both major parties are held during the summer of a presidential election year. Earlier, each party selects delegates by primaries, conventions, committees, etc.

At each convention, a temporary chairman is chosen. After a credentials committee seats the delegates, a permanent chairman is elected. The convention then votes on a platform, drawn up by the platform committee.

By the third or fourth day, presidential nominations begin. The chairman calls the roll of states alphabetically. A state may place a candidate in nomination or yield to another state.

Voting, again alphabetically by roll call of states, begins after all nominations have been made and seconded. A simple majority is required in each party, although this may require many ballots.

Finally, the vice-presidential candidate is selected. Although there is no law saying that the candidates *must* come from different states, it is, practically, necessary for this to be the case. Otherwise, according to the Constitution (*see* the 12th Amendment), electors from that state could vote for only one of the candidates and would have to cast their other vote for some person of another state. This could result in a presidential candidate's receiving a majority electoral vote and his or her running mate's failing to do so.

The Electoral College

The next step in the process is the nomination of electors in each state, according to its laws. These electors must not be federal office holders. In the November election, the voters cast their votes for electors, not for president. In some states, the ballots include only the names of the presidential and vice-presidential candidates; in others, they include only names of the electors. Nowadays, it is rare for electors to be split between parties. The last such occurrence was in North Carolina in 1968; the last before that, in Tennessee in 1948. On four occasions (1824, 1876, 1888, and 2000), the presidential candidate with the largest popular vote failed to obtain an electoral vote majority.

Each state has as many electors as it has senators and representatives. For the 2000 election, the total electors were 538, based on 100 senators and 435 representatives, plus 3 electoral votes from the District of Columbia as a result of the 23rd Amendment to the Constitution.

On the first Monday after the second Wednesday in December, the electors cast their votes in their respective state capitols. Constitutionally they may vote for someone other than the party candidate but usually they do not since they are pledged to one party and its candidate on the ballot. Should the presidential or vice-presidential candidate die between the November election and the December meetings, the electors pledged to vote for him or her could vote for whomever they pleased. However, it seems certain that the national committee would attempt to get an agreement among the state party leaders for a replacement candidate.

The votes of the electors, certified by the states, are sent to Congress, where the president of the Senate opens the certificates and has them counted in the presence of both houses on Jan. 6. The new president is inaugurated at noon on Jan. 20.

Should no candidate receive a majority of the electoral vote for president, the House of Representatives chooses a president from among the three highest candidates, voting, not as individuals, but as states, with a majority (now 26) needed to elect. Should no vice-presidential candidate obtain the majority, the Senate, voting as individuals, chooses from the highest two.

Electoral College Votes by State, 2004 Presidential Elections

(total electoral votes: 538; majority needed to elect: 270)

Alabama	9	Kentucky	8	North Dakota	3
Alaska	3	Louisiana	9	Ohio	20
Arizona	10	Maine	4	Oklahoma	7
Arkansas	6	Maryland	10	Oregon	7
California	55	Massachusetts	12	Pennsylvania	21
Colorado	9	Michigan	17	Rhode Island	4
Connecticut	7	Minnesota	10	South Carolina	8
Delaware	3	Mississippi	6	South Dakota	3
District of Columbia	3	Missouri	11	Tennessee	11
Florida	27	Montana	3	Texas	34
Georgia	15	Nebraska	5	Utah	5
Hawaii	4	Nevada	5	Vermont	3
Idaho	4	New Hampshire	4	Virginia	13
Illinois	21	New Jersey	15	Washington	11
Indiana	11	New Mexico	5	West Virginia	5
Iowa	7	New York	31	Wisconsin	10
Kansas	6	North Carolina	15	Wyoming	3

National Political Conventions Since 1856

Opening date	Party	Where held	Opening date	Party	Where held
June 17, 1856	Republican	Philadelphia	June 27, 1932	Democratic	Chicago
June 2, 1856	Democratic	Cincinnati	June 9, 1936	Republican	Cleveland
May 16, 1860	Republican	Chicago	June 23, 1936	Democratic	Philadelphia
April 23, 1860	Democratic	Charleston and Baltimore	June 24, 1940	Republican	Philadelphia
June 7, 1864	Republican[1]	Baltimore	July 15, 1940	Democratic	Chicago
Aug. 29, 1864	Democratic	Chicago	June 26, 1944	Republican	Chicago
May 20, 1868	Republican	Chicago	July 19, 1944	Democratic	Chicago
July 4, 1868	Democratic	New York City	June 21, 1948	Republican	Philadelphia
June 5, 1872	Republican	Philadelphia	July 12, 1948	Democratic	Philadelphia
June 9, 1872	Democratic	Baltimore	July 17, 1948	[3]	Birmingham
June 14, 1876	Republican	Cincinnati	July 22, 1948	Progressive	Philadelphia
June 28, 1876	Democratic	St. Louis	July 7, 1952	Republican	Chicago
June 2, 1880	Republican	Chicago	July 21, 1952	Democratic	Chicago
June 23, 1880	Democratic	Cincinnati	Aug. 20, 1956	Republican	San Francisco
June 3, 1884	Republican	Chicago	Aug. 13, 1956	Democratic	Chicago
July 11, 1884	Democratic	Chicago	July 25, 1960	Republican	Chicago
June 19, 1888	Republican	Chicago	July 11, 1960	Democratic	Los Angeles
June 6, 1888	Democratic	St. Louis	July 13, 1964	Republican	San Francisco
June 7, 1892	Republican	Minneapolis	Aug. 24, 1964	Democratic	Atlantic City
June 21, 1892	Democratic	Chicago	Aug. 5, 1968	Republican	Miami Beach
June 16, 1896	Republican	St. Louis	Aug. 26, 1968	Democratic	Chicago
July 7, 1896	Democratic	Chicago	July 10, 1972	Democratic	Miami Beach
June 19, 1900	Republican	Philadelphia	Aug. 21, 1972	Republican	Miami Beach
July 4, 1900	Democratic	Kansas City	July 12, 1976	Democratic	New York City
June 21, 1904	Republican	Chicago	Aug. 16, 1976	Republican	Kansas City, Mo.
July 6, 1904	Democratic	St. Louis	Aug. 11, 1980	Democratic	New York City
June 16, 1908	Republican	Chicago	July 14, 1980	Republican	Detroit
July 7, 1908	Democratic	Denver	Aug. 20, 1984	Republican	Dallas
June 18, 1912	Republican	Chicago	July 16, 1984	Democratic	San Francisco
June 25, 1912	Democratic	Baltimore	July 18, 1988	Democratic	Atlanta
June 7, 1916	Republican	Chicago	Aug. 15, 1988	Republican	New Orleans
June 14, 1916	Democratic	St. Louis	July 13, 1992	Democratic	New York City
June 8, 1920	Republican	Chicago	Aug. 17, 1992	Republican	Houston
June 28, 1920	Democratic	San Francisco	Aug. 10, 1996	Republican	San Diego
June 10, 1924	Republican	Cleveland	Aug. 26, 1996	Democratic	Chicago
June 24, 1924[2]	Democratic	New York City	July 29, 2000	Republican	Philadelphia
June 12, 1928	Republican	Kansas City	Aug. 14, 2000	Democratic	Los Angeles
June 26, 1928	Democratic	Houston	July 26, 2004	Democratic	Boston
June 14, 1932	Republican	Chicago	Aug. 30, 2004	Republican	New York City

1. The convention adopted name Union Party to attract War Democrats and others favoring prosecution of war. 2. In session until July 10, 1924. 3. States' Rights delegates from 13 southern states.

National Committee Chairs Since 1944

Chairman and (state)—Republican	Term	Chairman and (state)—Democratic	Term
Herbert Brownell, Jr. (N.Y.)	1944–1946	Robert E. Hannegan (Mo.)	1944–1947
Carroll Reece (Tenn.)	1946–1948	J. Howard McGrath (R.I.)	1947–1949
Hugh D. Scott, Jr. (Pa.)	1948–1949	William M. Boyle, Jr. (Mo.)	1949–1951
Guy G. Gabrielson (N.J.)	1949–1952	Frank E. McKinney (Ind.)	1951–1952
Arthur E. Summerfield (Mich.)	1952–1953	Stephen A. Mitchell (Ill.)	1952–1954
Wesley Roberts (Kan.)	1953	Paul M. Butler (Ind.)	1955–1960
Leonard W. Hall (N.Y.)	1953–1957	Henry M. Jackson (Wash.)	1960–1961
Meade Alcorn (Conn.)	1957–1959	John M. Bailey (Conn.)	1961–1968
Thruston B. Morton (Ky.)	1959–1961	Lawrence F. O'Brien (Mass.)	1968–1969
William E. Miller (N.Y.)	1961–1964	Fred R. Harris (Okla.)	1969–1970
Dean Burch (Ariz.)	1964–1965	Lawrence F. O'Brien (Mass.)	1970–1972
Ray C. Bliss (Ohio)	1965–1969	Jean Westwood (Utah)	1972
Rogers C. B. Morton (Md.)	1969–1971	Robert S. Strauss (Tex.)	1972–1977
Robert Dole (Kan.)	1971–1973	Kenneth M. Curtis (Me.)	1977
George H. Bush (Tex.)	1973–1974	John C. White (Tex.)	1977–1981
Mary Louise Smith (Iowa)	1974–1977	Charles T. Manatt (Calif.)	1981–1985
William E. Brock III (Tenn.)	1977–1981	Paul G. Kirk, Jr. (Mass.)	1985–1989
Richard Richards (Utah)	1981–1983	Ronald H. Brown (D.C.)	1989–1993
Frank J. Fahrenkopf, Jr. (Nevada)	1983–1989	David Wilhelm (Ill.)	1993–1994
Lee Atwater (S.C.)	1989–1991	Christopher J. Dodd (Conn.)	1995–1996
Clayton K. Yeutter (Neb.)	1991–1992	Steven Grossman (Mass.)	1996–1999
Richard Bond (N.Y.)	1992–1993	Joe Andrew (Ind.)	1999–2001
Haley Barbour (Miss.)	1993–1997	Terry McAuliffe (Va.)	2001–2005
Jim Nicholson (Colo.)	1997–2001	Howard Dean (Vt.)	2005–
Jim Gilmore (Va.)	2001–2002		
Marc Racicot (Mont.)	2002–2003		
Ed Gillespie (DC)	2003–2005		
Ken Mehlman (Md.)	2005–		

Republican National Committee: 310 First St., SE, Washington, DC 20003. *Democratic National Committee:* 430 South Capitol St., SE, Washington, DC 20003.

Presidential Elections, 1789–2004

For the original method of electing the president and the vice president (elections of 1789, 1792, 1796, and 1800), *see* Article II, Section 1, of the Constitution. The election of 1804 was the first one in which the electors voted for president and vice president on separate ballots. (See Amendment XII to the Constitution.)

Year	Presidential candidate	Party	Electoral votes	Year	Presidential candidate	Party	Electoral votes
1789[1]	George Washington	(no party)	69	1796	John Adams	Federalist	71
	John Adams	(no party)	34		Thomas Jefferson	Dem.-Rep.	68
	Scattering	(no party)	35		Thomas Pinckney	Federalist	59
	Votes not cast		8		Aaron Burr	Dem.-Rep.	30
					Scattering		48
1792	George Washington	Federalist	132				
	John Adams	Federalist	77	1800[2]	Thomas Jefferson	Dem.-Rep.	73
	George Clinton	Anti-Federalist	50		Aaron Burr	Dem.-Rep.	73
	Thomas Jefferson	Anti-Federalist	4		John Adams	Federalist	65
	Aaron Burr	Anti-Federalist	1		Charles C. Pinckney	Federalist	64
	Votes not cast		6		John Jay	Federalist	1

Year	Presidential candidate	Party	Electoral votes	Vice-presidential candidate	Party	Electoral votes
1804	Thomas Jefferson	Dem.-Rep.	162	George Clinton	Dem.-Rep.	162
	Charles C. Pinckney	Federalist	14	Rufus King	Federalist	14
1808	James Madison	Dem.-Rep.	122	George Clinton	Dem.-Rep.	113
	Charles C. Pinckney	Federalist	47	Rufus King	Federalist	47
	George Clinton	Dem.-Rep.	6	John Langdon	Ind. (no party)	9
	Votes not cast		1	James Madison	Dem.-Rep.	3
				James Monroe	Dem.-Rep.	3
				Votes not cast		1
1812	James Madison	Dem.-Rep.	128	Elbridge Gerry	Dem.-Rep.	131
	De Witt Clinton	Federalist	89	Jared Ingersoll	Federalist	86
	Votes not cast		1	Votes not cast		1
1816	James Monroe	Dem.-Rep.	183	Daniel D. Tompkins	Dem.-Rep.	183
	Rufus King	Federalist	34	John E. Howard	Federalist	22
	Votes not cast		4	James Ross	Ind (no party)	5
				John Marshall	Federalist	4
				Robert G. Harper	Ind. (no party)	3
				Votes not cast		4
1820	James Monroe	Dem-Rep	231	Daniel D. Tompkins	Dem.-Rep.	218
	John Quincy Adams	Ind. (no party)	1	Richard Stockton	Ind. (no party)	8
	Votes not cast		3	Daniel Rodney	Ind. (no party)	4
				Richard Rush	Ind. (no party)	1
				Robert G. Harper	Ind. (no party)	1
				Votes not cast		3
1824[3]	John Quincy Adams	(no party)	84	John C. Calhoun	(no party)	182
	Andrew Jackson	(no party)	99	Nathan Sanford	(no party)	30
	William H. Crawford	(no party)	41	Nathaniel Macon	(no party)	24
	Henry Clay	(no party)	37	Andrew Jackson	(no party)	13
				Martin Van Buren	(no party)	9
				Henry Clay	(no party)	2
				Votes not cast		1
1828	Andrew Jackson	Democratic	178	John C. Calhoun	Democratic	171
	John Quincy Adams	Natl. Rep.	83	Richard Rush	Natl. Rep.	83
				William Smith	Democratic	7
1832	Andrew Jackson	Democratic	219	Martin Van Buren	Democratic	189
	Henry Clay	Natl. Rep.	49	John Sergeant	Natl. Rep.	49
	John Floyd	Ind. (no party)	11	Henry Lee	Ind. (no party)	11
	William Wirt	Antimasonic[4]	7	Amos Ellmaker	Antimasonic	7
	Votes not cast		2	William Wilkins	Ind. (no party)	30
				Votes not cast		2
1836	Martin Van Buren	Democratic	170	Richard M. Johnson[5]	Democratic	147
	William H. Harrison	Whig	73	Francis Granger	Whig	77
	Hugh L. White	Whig	26	John Tyler	Whig	47
	Daniel Webster	Whig	14	William Smith	Ind. (no party)	23
	W. P. Mangum	Ind. (no party)	11			

Year	Presidential candidate	Party	Electoral votes	Vice-presidential candidate	Party	Electoral votes
1840	William H. Harrison[6]	Whig	234	John Tyler	Whig	234
	Martin Van Buren	Democratic	60	Richard M. Johnson	Democratic	48
				L. W. Tazewell	Ind. (no party)	11
				James K. Polk	Democratic	1
1844	James K. Polk	Democratic	170	George M. Dallas	Democratic	170
	Henry Clay	Whig	105	Theo. Frelinghuysen	Whig	105
1848	Zachary Taylor[7]	Whig	163	Millard Fillmore	Whig	163
	Lewis Cass	Democratic	127	William O. Butler	Democratic	127
1852	Franklin Pierce	Democratic	254	William R. King	Democratic	254
	Winfield Scott	Whig	42	William A. Graham	Whig	42
1856	James Buchanan	Democratic	174	John C. Breckinridge	Democratic	174
	John C. Fremont	Republican	114	William L. Dayton	Republican	114
	Millard Fillmore	American[8]	8	A. J. Donelson	American[8]	8
1860	Abraham Lincoln	Republican	180	Hannibal Hamlin	Republican	180
	John C. Breckinridge	Democratic	72	Joseph Lane	Democratic	72
	John Bell	Const. Union	39	Edward Everett	Const. Union	39
	Stephen A. Douglas	Democratic	12	H. V. Johnson	Democratic	12
1864	Abraham Lincoln[9]	Union[10]	212	Andrew Johnson	Union[10]	212
	George B. McClellan	Democratic	21	G. H. Pendleton	Democratic	21
1868	Ulysses S. Grant	Republican	214	Schuyler Colfax	Republican	214
	Horatio Seymour	Democratic	80	Francis P. Blair, Jr.	Democratic	80
	Votes not counted[11]		23	Votes not counted[11]		23

NOTE: The Constitution specifies that the president and vice president be chosen through the votes cast by electors chosen by the states, rather than by a direct popular vote. At first, some electors were chosen by state legislatures, but by 1836 all states but South Carolina chose electors through a statewide popular vote. (S.C. followed suit in 1860.) Today, all states but Maine and Nebraska have a winner-take-all system in which all of a given state's electors vote for the winner of that state's popular vote. While not legally significant, the number of popular votes given nationwide to each major presidential candidate are listed here for elections beginning in 1872.

Year	Presidential candidate	Party	Electoral votes	Popular votes	Vice-presidential candidate and party
1872	Ulysses S. Grant	Republican	286	3,597,132	Henry Wilson—R
	Horace Greeley	Dem., Liberal Rep.	[12]	2,834,125	B. Gratz Brown—D, LR—(47)
	Thomas A. Hendricks	Democratic	42		Scattering—(19)
	B. Gratz Brown	Dem., Liberal Rep.	18		Vote not counted—(14)
	Charles J. Jenkins	Democratic	2		
	David Davis	Democratic	1		
	Votes not counted		17		
1876[13]	Rutherford B. Hayes	Republican	185	4,033,768	William A. Wheeler—R
	Samuel J. Tilden	Democratic	184	4,285,992	Thomas A. Hendricks—D
	Peter Cooper	Greenback	0	81,737	Samuel F. Cary—G
1880	James A. Garfield[14]	Republican	214	4,449,053	Chester A. Arthur—R
	Winfield S. Hancock	Democratic	155	4,442,035	William H. English—D
	James B. Weaver	Greenback	0	308,578	B. J. Chambers—G
1884	Grover Cleveland	Democratic	219	4,911,017	Thomas A. Hendricks—D
	James G. Blaine	Republican	182	4,848,334	John A. Logan—R
	Benjamin F. Butler	Greenback	0	175,370	A. M. West—G
	John P. St. John	Prohibition	0	150,369	William Daniel—P
1888	Benjamin Harrison	Republican	233	5,440,216	Levi P. Morton—R
	Grover Cleveland	Democratic	168	5,538,233	A. G. Thurman—D
	Clinton B. Fisk	Prohibition	0	249,506	John A. Brooks—P
	Alson J. Streeter	Union Labor	0	146,935	Charles E. Cunningham—UL
1892	Grover Cleveland	Democratic	277	5,556,918	Adlai E. Stevenson—D
	Benjamin Harrison	Republican	145	5,176,108	Whitelaw Reid—R
	James B. Weaver	People's[15]	22	1,041,028	James G. Field—Peo
	John Bidwell	Prohibition	0	264,133	James B. Cranfill—P
1896	William McKinley	Republican	271	7,035,638	Garret A. Hobart—R
	William J. Bryan	Dem., People's[15]	176	6,467,946	Arthur Sewall—D—(149) Thomas E. Watson—Peo—(27)
	John M. Palmer	Natl. Dem.	0	133,148	Simon B. Buckner—ND
	Joshua Levering	Prohibition	0	132,007	Hale Johnson—P
1900	William McKinley[16]	Republican	292	7,219,530	Theodore Roosevelt—R
	William J. Bryan	Dem., People's[15]	155	6,358,071	Adlai E. Stevenson—D, Peo
	Eugene V. Debs	Social Democratic	0	94,768	Job Harriman—SD

Year	Presidential candidate	Party	Electoral votes	Popular votes	Vice-presidential candidate and party
1904	Theodore Roosevelt	Republican	336	7,628,834	Charles W. Fairbanks—R
	Alton B. Parker	Democratic	140	5,084,491	Henry G. Davis—D
	Eugene V. Debs	Socialist	0	402,400	Benjamin Hanford—S
1908	William H. Taft	Republican	321	7,679,006	James S. Sherman—R
	William J. Bryan	Democratic	162	6,409,106	John W. Kern—D
	Eugene V. Debs	Socialist	0	402,820	Benjamin Hanford—S
1912	Woodrow Wilson	Democratic	435	6,286,214	Thomas R. Marshall—D
	Theodore Roosevelt	Progressive	88	4,126,020	Hiram Johnson—Prog
	William H. Taft	Republican	8	3,483,922	Nicholas M. Butler—R[17]
	Eugene V. Debs	Socialist	0	897,011	Emil Seidel—S
1916	Woodrow Wilson	Democratic	277	9,129,606	Thomas R. Marshall—D
	Charles E. Hughes	Republican	254	8,538,221	Charles W. Fairbanks—R
	A. L. Benson	Socialist	0	585,113	G. R. Kirkpatrick—S
1920	Warren G. Harding[18]	Republican	404	16,152,200	Calvin Coolidge—R
	James M. Cox	Democratic	127	9,147,353	Franklin D. Roosevelt—D
	Eugene V. Debs	Socialist	0	917,799	Seymour Stedman—S
1924	Calvin Coolidge	Republican	382	15,725,016	Charles G. Dawes—R
	John W. Davis	Democratic	136	8,385,586	Charles W. Bryan—D
	Robert M. LaFollette	Progressive, Socialist	13	4,822,856	Burton K. Wheeler—Prog, S
1928	Herbert Hoover	Republican	444	21,392,190	Charles Curtis—R
	Alfred E. Smith	Democratic	87	15,016,443	Joseph T. Robinson—D
	Norman Thomas	Socialist	0	267,420	James H. Maurer—S
1932	Franklin D. Roosevelt	Democratic	472	22,821,857	John N. Garner—D
	Herbert Hoover	Republican	59	15,761,841	Charles Curtis—R
	Norman Thomas	Socialist	0	884,781	James H. Maurer—S
1936	Franklin D. Roosevelt	Democratic	523	27,751,597	John N. Garner—D
	Alfred M. Landon	Republican	8	16,679,583	Frank Knox—R
	Norman Thomas	Socialist	0	187,720	George Nelson—S
1940	Franklin D. Roosevelt	Democratic	449	27,244,160	Henry A. Wallace—D
	Wendell L. Willkie	Republican	82	22,305,198	Charles L. McNary—R
	Norman Thomas	Socialist	0	99,557	Maynard C. Krueger—S
1944	Franklin D. Roosevelt[19]	Democratic	432	25,602,504	Harry S. Truman—D
	Thomas E. Dewey	Republican	99	22,006,285	John W. Bricker—R
	Norman Thomas	Socialist	0	80,518	Darlington Hoopes—S
1948	Harry S. Truman	Democratic	303	24,179,345	Alben W. Barkley—D
	Thomas E. Dewey	Republican	189	21,991,291	Earl Warren—R
	J. Strom Thurmond	States' Rights Dem.	39	1,176,125	Fielding L. Wright—SR
	Henry A. Wallace	Progressive	0	1,157,326	Glen Taylor—Prog
	Norman Thomas	Socialist	0	139,572	Tucker P. Smith—S
1952	Dwight D. Eisenhower	Republican	442	33,936,234	Richard M. Nixon—R
	Adlai E. Stevenson	Democratic	89	27,314,992	John J. Sparkman—D
1956	Dwight D. Eisenhower	Republican	457	35,590,472	Richard M. Nixon—R
	Adlai E. Stevenson	Democratic	73[20]	26,022,752	Estes Kefauver—D
1960	John F. Kennedy[21]	Democratic	303	34,226,731	Lyndon B. Johnson—D
	Richard M. Nixon	Republican	219[22]	34,108,157	Henry Cabot Lodge—R
1964	Lyndon B. Johnson	Democratic	486	43,129,484	Hubert H. Humphrey—D
	Barry M. Goldwater	Republican	52	27,178,188	William E. Miller—R
1968	Richard M. Nixon	Republican	301	31,785,480	Spiro T. Agnew—R
	Hubert H. Humphrey	Democratic	191	31,275,166	Edmund S. Muskie—D
	George C. Wallace	American Independent	46	9,906,473	Curtis F. LeMay—AI
1972	Richard M. Nixon[23]	Republican	520[24]	47,169,911	Spiro T. Agnew—R
	George McGovern	Democratic	17	29,170,383	Sargent Shriver—D
	John G. Schmitz	American	0	1,099,482	Thomas J. Anderson—A
1976	Jimmy Carter	Democratic	297	40,830,763	Walter F. Mondale—D
	Gerald R. Ford	Republican	240[25]	39,147,973	Robert J. Dole—R
	Eugene J. McCarthy	Independent	0	756,631	None
1980	Ronald Reagan	Republican	489	43,899,248	George Bush—R
	Jimmy Carter	Democratic	49	36,481,435	Walter F. Mondale—D
	John B. Anderson	Independent	0	5,719,437	Patrick J. Lucey—I

Year	Presidential candidate	Party	Electoral votes	Popular votes	Vice-presidential candidate and party
1984	Ronald Reagan	Republican	525	54,455,075	George Bush—R
	Walter F. Mondale	Democratic	13	37,577,185	Geraldine A. Ferraro—D
1988	George H. Bush	Republican	426	48,886,097	J. Danforth Quayle—R
	Michael S. Dukakis	Democratic	111[26]	41,809,074	Lloyd Bentsen—D
1992	William J. Clinton	Democratic	370	44,909,889	Albert A. Gore, J.—D
	George H. Bush	Republican	168	39,104,545	J. Danforth Quayle—R
	H. Ross Perot	Independent	0	19,742,267	James B. Stockdale—I
1996	William J. Clinton	Democratic	379	47,402,357	Albert A. Gore, Jr.—D
	Robert J. Dole	Republican	159	39,198,755	Jack F. Kemp—R
	H. Ross Perot	Reform Party[27]	0	8,085,402	Pat Choate—RP[27]
2000	George W. Bush	Republican	271	50,456,002	Richard B. Cheney—R
	Albert A. Gore	Democratic	266[28]	50,999,897	Joseph I. Lieberman—D
	Ralph Nader	Green Party	0	2,882,955	Winona LaDuke—GP
2004	George W. Bush	Republican	286	62,028,285	Richard B. Cheney—R
	John F. Kerry	Democratic	251[29]	29,028,109	John Edwards—D

1. Only 10 states participated in the election. The New York legislature chose no electors, and North Carolina and Rhode Island had not yet ratified the Constitution. 2. As Jefferson and Burr were tied, the House of Representatives chose the president. In a vote by states, 10 votes were cast for Jefferson, 4 for Burr; 2 votes were not cast. 3. As no candidate had an electoral-vote majority, the House of Representatives chose the president from the first three. In a vote by states, 13 votes were cast for Adams, 7 for Jackson, and 4 for Crawford. 4. The Antimasonic Party on Sept. 26, 1831, was the first party to hold a nominating convention to choose candidates for president and vice president. 5. As Johnson did not have an electoral-vote majority, the Senate chose him 33–14 over Granger, the others being legally out of the race. 6. Harrison died April 4, 1841, and Tyler succeeded him April 6. 7. Taylor died July 9, 1850, and Fillmore succeeded him July 10. 8. Also known as the Know-Nothing Party. 9. Lincoln died April 15, 1865, and Johnson succeeded him the same day. 10. Name adopted by the Republican National Convention of 1864. Johnson was a War Democrat. 11. 23 Southern electoral votes were excluded. 12. Greeley died Nov. 29, 1872, before his 66 electors voted; 63 of Greeley's votes were scattered among four of the other candidates. 13. Hayes was chosen by a special electoral commission since initially neither candidate had the requisite 185 electoral votes. 14. Garfield died Sept. 19, 1881, and Arthur succeeded him Sept. 20. 15. Members of People's Party were called Populists. 16. McKinley died Sept. 14, 1901, and Roosevelt succeeded him the same day. 17. James S. Sherman, Republican candidate for vice president, died Oct. 30, 1912, and the Republican electoral votes were cast for Butler. 18. Harding died Aug. 2, 1923, and Coolidge succeeded him Aug. 3. 19. Roosevelt died April 12, 1945, and Truman succeeded him the same day. 20. One electoral vote from Alabama was cast for Walter B. Jones. 21. Kennedy died Nov. 22, 1963, and Johnson succeeded him the same day. 22. Sen. Harry F. Byrd received 15 electoral votes. 23. Nixon resigned Aug. 9, 1974, and Gerald R. Ford succeeded him the same day. 24. One electoral vote from Virginia was cast for John Hospers, Libertarian Party. 25. One electoral vote from Washington was cast for Ronald Reagan. 26. One electoral vote from West Virginia was cast for Lloyd Bentsen. 27. Perot helped establish the Reform Party following his defeat in the 1992 election. 28. One elector from the District of Columbia left her ballot blank to protest the city's lack of representation in Congress, leaving Gore with 266 electoral votes instead of 267. 29. One elector from Minnesota cast a vote for John Edwards.

Plurality and Majority

In order to win a plurality, a candidate must receive a greater number of votes than anyone running against him. If he receives 50 votes, for example, and two other candidates receive 49 and 2, he will have a plurality of one vote over his closest opponent.

However, a candidate does not have a majority unless he receives more than 50% of the total votes cast. In the example above, the candidate does not have a majority, because his 50 votes are 50% or less than the 101 votes cast.

Presidents Elected Without a Majority

Fifteen candidates (three of them twice) have become president of the United States with a popular vote less than 50% of the total cast. It should be noted, however, that in elections before 1872, presidential electors were not chosen by popular vote in all states. Adams's election in 1824 was by the House of Representatives, which chose him over Jackson, who had a plurality of both electoral and popular votes, but not a majority in the electoral college.

The "minority" presidents are listed below.

Year	President	Electoral percent	Popular percent	Year	President	Electoral percent	Popular percent
1824	John Q. Adams	31.8%	29.8%	1892	Grover Cleveland (D)	62.4%	46.0%
1844	James K. Polk (D)	61.8	49.3	1912	Woodrow Wilson (D)	81.9	41.8
1848	Zachary Taylor (W)	56.2	47.3	1916	Woodrow Wilson (D)	52.1	49.3
1856	James Buchanan (D)	58.7	45.3	1948	Harry S. Truman (D)	57.1	49.5
1860	Abraham Lincoln (R)	59.4	39.9	1960	John F. Kennedy (D)	56.4	49.7
1876	Rutherford B. Hayes (R)	50.1	47.9	1968	Richard M. Nixon (R)	56.1	43.4
1880	James A. Garfield (R)	57.9	48.3	1992	William J. Clinton (D)	68.8	43.0
1884	Grover Cleveland (D)	54.6	48.8	1996	William J. Clinton (D)	70.4	49.0
1888	Benjamin Harrison (R)	58.1	47.8	2000	George W. Bush (R)	50.3	47.8

The Closest Presidential Races

Although the 2000 presidential race was extremely close, there have been others that were also too close to call immediately after the election. Indeed, the results of the Nov. 7 election in 1876 were not known until March 2, 1877, just three days before the inauguration. More recently, John F. Kennedy's defeat of Richard M. Nixon in 1960 wasn't official until noon the following day.

President	Electoral votes	Popular votes	President	Electoral votes	Popular votes
1800[1]			**1916**		
Thomas Jefferson (Dem.-Rep.)	73	—	Woodrow Wilson (D)	277	9,129,606
Aaron Burr (Dem.-Rep.)	73	—	Charles E. Hughes (R)	254	8,538,221
John Adams (Federalist)	65	—	**1960**		
Charles C. Pinckney (Federalist)	64	—	John F. Kennedy (D)	303	34,226,731
John Jay (Federalist)	1	—	Richard M. Nixon (R)	219	34,108,157
1824[2]			**1968**		
John Quincy Adams (no party)	84	—	Richard M. Nixon (R)	301	31,785,480
Andrew Jackson (no party)	99	—	Hubert H. Humphrey (R)	191	31,275,166
William H. Crawford (no party)	41	—	George C. Wallace	46	9,906,473
Henry Clay (no party)	37	—	(American Independent)		
1876			**1976**		
Rutherford B. Hayes (R)	185	4,033,768	Jimmy Carter (D)	297	40,830,763
Samuel J. Tilden (D)	184	4,285,992	Gerald R. Ford (R)	240	39,147,973
1880			**2000**		
James A. Garfield (R)	214	4,449,053	George W. Bush (R)	271	50,455,156
Winfield S. Hancock (D)	155	4,442,035	Albert A. Gore (D)	266[3]	50,992,335

1. As Jefferson and Burr were tied, the House of Representatives chose the president. In a vote by states, 10 votes were cast for Jefferson, 4 for Burr; 2 votes were not cast. For the original method of electing the president and vice president (elections of 1789, 1792, 1796, and 1800), see Article II, Section 1, of the Constitution. 2. As no candidate had an electoral vote majority, the House of Representatives chose the president from the first three. In a vote by states, 13 votes were cast for Adams, 7 for Jackson, and 4 for Crawford. 3. One elector from the District of Columbia left her ballot blank to protest the city's lack of representation in Congress, leaving Gore with 266 electoral votes instead of 267.

National Voter Turnout in Federal Elections: 1964–2004

Year	Voting-age population	Voter registration	Voter turnout	Turnout of voting-age population (percent)
2004	**221,256,931**	**174,800,000**	**122,294,978**	**55.3%**
2002	215,473,000	150,990,598	79,830,119	37.0
2000	**205,815,000**	**156,421,311**	**105,586,274**	**51.3**
1998	200,929,000	141,850,558	73,117,022	36.4
1996	**196,511,000**	**146,211,960**	**96,456,345**	**49.1**
1994	193,650,000	130,292,822	75,105,860	38.8
1992	**189,529,000**	**133,821,178**	**104,405,155**	**55.1**
1990	185,812,000	121,105,630	67,859,189	36.5
1988	**182,778,000**	**126,379,628**	**91,594,693**	**50.1**
1986	178,566,000	118,399,984	64,991,128	36.4
1984	**174,466,000**	**124,150,614**	**92,652,680**	**53.1**
1982	169,938,000	110,671,225	67,615,576	39.8
1980	**164,597,000**	**113,043,734**	**86,515,221**	**52.6**
1978	158,373,000	103,291,265	58,917,938	37.2
1976	**152,309,190**	**105,037,986**	**81,555,789**	**53.6**
1974	146,336,000	96,199,020[1]	55,943,834	38.2
1972	**140,776,000**	**97,328,541**	**77,718,554**	**55.2**
1970	124,498,000	82,496,747[2]	58,014,338	46.6
1968	**120,328,186**	**81,658,180**	**73,211,875**	**60.8**
1966	116,132,000	76,288,283[3]	56,188,046	48.4
1964	**114,090,000**	**73,715,818**	**70,644,592**	**61.9**

n.a. = not available. NOTE: Presidential election years are in boldface. 1. Registrations from Iowa not included. 2. Registrations from Iowa and Mo. not included. 3. Registrations from Iowa, Kans., Miss., Mo., Nebr., and Wyo. not included. D.C. did not have independent status. *Source:* Federal Election Commission. Data drawn from Congressional Research Service reports, Election Data Services Inc., and State Election Offices.

Facts About Elections

Candidate with highest popular vote: Reagan (1984), 54,455,075.

Candidate with highest electoral vote: Reagan (1984), 525.

Candidate carrying most states: Nixon (1972) and Reagan (1984), 49.

Candidate running most times: Norman Thomas (Socialist Party), six (1928, 1932, 1936, 1940, 1944, 1948).

Candidate elected, defeated, then reelected: Cleveland (1884, 1888, 1892).

Presidents

	Name and (party)[1]	Term	State of birth	Born	Died	Religion[2]	Age at inaug.	Age at death
1.	Washington (F)[3]	1789–1797	Va.	2/22/1732	12/14/1799	Episcopalian	57	67
2.	J. Adams (F)	1797–1801	Mass.	10/30/1735	7/4/1826	Unitarian	61	90
3.	Jefferson (DR)	1801–1809	Va.	4/13/1743	7/4/1826	Deist	57	83
4.	Madison (DR)	1809–1817	Va.	3/16/1751	6/28/1836	Episcopalian	57	85
5.	Monroe (DR)	1817–1825	Va.	4/28/1758	7/4/1831	Episcopalian	58	73
6.	J. Q. Adams (DR)	1825–1829	Mass.	7/11/1767	2/23/1848	Unitarian	57	80
7.	Jackson (D)	1829–1837	S.C.	3/15/1767	6/8/1845	Presbyterian	61	78
8.	Van Buren (D)	1837–1841	N.Y.	12/5/1782	7/24/1862	Reformed Dutch	54	79
9.	W. H. Harrison (W)[4]	1841	Va.	2/9/1773	4/4/1841	Episcopalian	68	68
10.	Tyler (W)	1841–1845	Va.	3/29/1790	1/18/1862	Episcopalian	51	71
11.	Polk (D)	1845–1849	N.C.	11/2/1795	6/15/1849	Methodist	49	53
12.	Taylor (W)[4]	1849–1850	Va.	11/24/1784	7/9/1850	Episcopalian	64	65
13.	Fillmore (W)	1850–1853	N.Y.	1/7/1800	3/8/1874	Unitarian	50	74
14.	Pierce (D)	1853–1857	N.H.	11/23/1804	10/8/1869	Episcopalian	48	64
15.	Buchanan (D)	1857–1861	Pa.	4/23/1791	6/1/1868	Presbyterian	65	77
16.	Lincoln (R)[5]	1861–1865	Ky.	2/12/1809	4/15/1865	Liberal	52	56
17.	A. Johnson (U)[6]	1865–1869	N.C.	12/29/1808	7/31/1875	([7])	56	66
18.	Grant (R)	1869–1877	Ohio	4/27/1822	7/23/1885	Methodist	46	63
19.	Hayes (R)	1877–1881	Ohio	10/4/1822	1/17/1893	Methodist	54	70
20.	Garfield (R)[5]	1881	Ohio	11/19/1831	9/19/1881	Disciples of Christ	49	49
21.	Arthur (R)	1881–1885	Vt.	10/5/1829	11/18/1886	Episcopalian	50	56
22.	Cleveland (D)	1885–1889	N.J.	3/18/1837	6/24/1908	Presbyterian	47	71
23.	B. Harrison (R)	1889–1893	Ohio	8/20/1833	3/13/1901	Presbyterian	55	67
24.	Cleveland (D)[8]	1893–1897	N.J.	3/18/1837	6/24/1908	Presbyterian	55	71
25.	McKinley (R)[5]	1897–1901	Ohio	1/29/1843	9/14/1901	Methodist	54	58
26.	T. Roosevelt (R)	1901–1909	N.Y.	10/27/1858	1/6/1919	Reformed Dutch	42	60
27.	Taft (R)	1909–1913	Ohio	9/15/1857	3/8/1930	Unitarian	51	72
28.	Wilson (D)	1913–1921	Va.	12/28/1856	2/3/1924	Presbyterian	56	67
29.	Harding (R)[3]	1921–1923	Ohio	11/2/1865	8/2/1923	Baptist	55	57
30.	Coolidge (R)	1923–1929	Vt.	7/4/1872	1/5/1933	Congregationalist	51	60
31.	Hoover (R)	1929–1933	Iowa	8/10/1874	10/20/1964	Quaker	54	90
32.	F. D. Roosevelt (D)[4]	1933–1945	N.Y.	1/30/1882	4/12/1945	Episcopalian	51	63
33.	Truman (D)	1945–1953	Mo.	5/8/1884	12/26/1972	Baptist	60	88
34.	Eisenhower (R)	1953–1961	Tex.	10/14/1890	3/28/1969	Presbyterian	62	78
35.	Kennedy (D)[5]	1961–1963	Mass.	5/29/1917	11/22/1963	Roman Catholic	43	46
36.	L. B. Johnson (D)	1963–1969	Tex.	8/27/1908	1/22/1973	Disciples of Christ	55	64
37.	Nixon (R)[9]	1969–1974	Calif.	1/9/1913	4/22/1994	Quaker	56	81
38.	Ford (R)	1974–1977	Neb.	7/14/1913	—	Episcopalian	61	—
39.	Carter (D)	1977–1981	Ga.	10/1/1924	—	Southern Baptist	52	—
40.	Reagan (R)	1981–1989	Ill.	2/6/1911	6/5/2004	Disciples of Christ	69	93
41.	G.H.W. Bush (R)	1989–1993	Mass.	6/12/1924	—	Episcopalian	64	—
42.	Clinton (D)	1993–2001	Ark.	8/19/1946	—	Baptist	46	—
43.	G. W. Bush (R)	2001–	Conn.	7/6/46	—	Methodist	54	—

NOTE: 1. F—Federalist; DR—Democratic-Republican; D—Democratic; W—Whig; R—Republican; U—Union. 2. Religious affiliation at election. Several presidents changed religions during their lifetimes. 3. No party for first election. The party system in the U.S. made its appearance during Washington's first term. 4. Died in office. 5. Assassinated in office. 6. The Republican National Convention of 1864 adopted the name Union Party. It renominated Lincoln for president; for vice-president it nominated Johnson, a War Democrat. Although frequently listed as a Republican vice president and president, Johnson undoubtedly considered himself strictly a member of the Union Party. When that party broke apart after 1868, he returned to the Democratic Party. 7. Johnson was not a professed church member; however, he admired the Baptist principles of church government. 8. Second nonconsecutive term. 9. Resigned Aug. 9, 1974.

Vice Presidents

	Name and (party)[1]	Term	State of birth	Birth and death dates	President served under
1.	John Adams (F)[2]	1789–1797	Massachusetts	1735–1826	Washington
2.	Thomas Jefferson (DR)	1797–1801	Virginia	1743–1826	J. Adams
3.	Aaron Burr (DR)	1801–1805	New Jersey	1756–1836	Jefferson
4.	George Clinton (DR)[3]	1805–1812	New York	1739–1812	Jefferson and Madison
5.	Elbridge Gerry (DR)[3]	1813–1814	Massachusetts	1744–1814	Madison
6.	Daniel D. Tompkins (DR)	1817–1825	New York	1774–1825	Monroe
7.	John C. Calhoun[4]	1825–1832	South Carolina	1782–1850	J. Q. Adams and Jackson
8.	Martin Van Buren (D)	1833–1837	New York	1782–1862	Jackson
9.	Richard M. Johnson (D)	1837–1841	Kentucky	1780–1850	Van Buren
10.	John Tyler (W)[5]	1841	Virginia	1790–1862	W. H. Harrison
11.	George M. Dallas (D)	1845–1849	Pennsylvania	1792–1864	Polk
12.	Millard Fillmore (W)[5]	1849–1850	New York	1800–1874	Taylor
13.	William R. King (D)[3]	1853	North Carolina	1786–1853	Pierce

	Name and (party)[1]	Term	State of birth	Birth and death dates	President served under
14.	John C. Breckinridge (D)	1857–1861	Kentucky	1821–1875	Buchanan
15.	Hannibal Hamlin (R)	1861–1865	Maine	1809–1891	Lincoln
16.	Andrew Johnson (U)[5]	1865	North Carolina	1808–1875	Lincoln
17.	Schuyler Colfax (R)	1869–1873	New York	1823–1885	Grant
18.	Henry Wilson (R)[3]	1873–1875	New Hampshire	1812–1875	Grant
19.	William A. Wheeler (R)	1877–1881	New York	1819–1887	Hayes
20.	Chester A. Arthur (R)[5]	1881	Vermont	1829–1886	Garfield
21.	Thomas A. Hendricks (D)[3]	1885	Ohio	1819–1885	Cleveland
22.	Levi P. Morton (R)	1889–1893	Vermont	1824–1920	B. Harrison
23.	Adlai E. Stevenson (D)	1893–1897	Kentucky	1835–1914	Cleveland
24.	Garrett A. Hobart (R)[3]	1897–1899	New Jersey	1844–1899	McKinley
25.	Theodore Roosevelt (R)[5]	1901	New York	1858–1919	McKinley
26.	Charles W. Fairbanks (R)	1905–1909	Ohio	1852–1918	T. Roosevelt
27.	James S. Sherman (R)[3]	1909–1912	New York	1855–1912	Taft
28.	Thomas R. Marshall (D)	1913–1921	Indiana	1854–1925	Wilson
29.	Calvin Coolidge (R)[5]	1921–1923	Vermont	1872–1933	Harding
30.	Charles G. Dawes (R)	1925–1929	Ohio	1865–1951	Coolidge
31.	Charles Curtis (R)	1929–1933	Kansas	1860–1936	Hoover
32.	John N. Garner (D)	1933–1941	Texas	1868–1967	F. D. Roosevelt
33.	Henry A. Wallace (D)	1941–1945	Iowa	1888–1965	F. D. Roosevelt
34.	Harry S. Truman (D)[5]	1945	Missouri	1884–1972	F. D. Roosevelt
35.	Alben W. Barkley (D)	1949–1953	Kentucky	1877–1956	Truman
36.	Richard M. Nixon (R)	1953-1961	California	1913–1994	Eisenhower
37.	Lyndon B. Johnson (D)[5]	1961–1963	Texas	1908–1973	Kennedy
38.	Hubert H. Humphrey (D)	1965–1969	South Dakota	1911–1978	L. B. Johnson
39.	Spiro T. Agnew (R)[6]	1969–1973	Maryland	1918–1996	Nixon
40.	Gerald R. Ford (R)[7]	1973–1974	Nebraska	1913–	Nixon
41.	Nelson A. Rockefeller (R)[8]	1974–1977	Maine	1908–1979	Ford
42.	Walter F. Mondale (D)	1977–1981	Minnesota	1928–	Carter
43.	George Bush (R)	1981–1989	Massachusetts	1924–	Reagan
44.	J. Danforth Quayle (R)	1989–1993	Indiana	1947–	G.H.W. Bush
45.	Albert A. Gore, Jr. (D)	1993–2001	Washington, D.C.	1948–	Clinton
46.	Richard B. Cheney (R)	2001–	Nebraska	1941–	G. W. Bush

1. F—Federalist; DR—Democratic-Republican; D—Democratic; W—Whig; R—Republican; U—Union. 2. No party for first election. The party system in the U.S. made its appearance during Washington's first term as president. 3. Died in office. 4. Democratic-Republican with J. Q. Adams; Democratic with Jackson. Calhoun resigned in 1832 to become a U.S. senator. 5. Succeeded to presidency on death of president. Prior to the passage of the 25th Amendment (ratified Feb. 10, 1967), there were no provisions for filling a vacancy in the vice presidency. In the event of a vacancy, the president pro tempore took over most of the vice president's duties. 6. Resigned Oct. 10, 1973, after pleading no contest to federal income tax evasion charges. 7. Nominated by Nixon on Oct. 12, 1973, under provisions of 25th Amendment. Confirmed by Congress on Dec. 6, 1973, and was sworn in same day. He became president Aug. 9, 1974, upon Nixon's resignation. 8. Nominated by Ford Aug. 20, 1974; confirmed by Congress on Dec. 19, 1974, and was sworn in same day.

Presidential Libraries

These are not traditional libraries, but rather repositories for preserving and making available the papers, records, and other historical materials of the presidents since Herbert Hoover. The presidential library system formally began in 1939, when President Franklin Roosevelt donated his personal and presidential papers to the federal government.

Hoover Library
210 Parkside Drive
P.O. Box 488
West Branch, IA 52358-0488
http://hoover.archives.gov

Roosevelt Library
4079 Albany Post Road
Hyde Park, NY 12538-1999
http://www.fdrlibrary.marist.edu/

Truman Library
500 West U.S. Highway 24
Independence, MO 64050-1798
http://www.trumanlibrary.org

Eisenhower Library
200 SE 4th Street
Abilene, KS 67410-2900
http://www.eisenhower.utexas.edu

Kennedy Library
Columbia Point
Boston, MA 02125-3398
http://www.jfklibrary.org

Johnson Library
2313 Red River Street
Austin, TX 78705-5702
http://www.lbjlib.utexas.edu

The Nixon Project[1]
National Archives at College Park
8601 Adelphi Road
College Park, MD 20740-6001
http://www.nixon.archives.gov/

Ford Library
1000 Beal Avenue
Ann Arbor, MI 48109-2114
http://www.ford.utexas.edu

Carter Library
441 Freedom Parkway
Atlanta, GA 30307-1498
http://www.jimmycarterlibrary.org/

Reagan Library
40 Presidential Drive
Simi Valley, CA 93065-0666
http://www.reagan.utexas.edu

George H. W. Bush Library
1000 George Bush Drive West
College Station, TX 77845
http://bushlibrary.tamu.edu/

Clinton Library
1200 President Clinton Ave.
Little Rock, AK 72201
http://www.clintonpresidentialcenter.org

1. The Nixon Project is not affiliated with the Richard Nixon Library and Birthplace in Yorba Linda, Calif., a private institution that was established by Nixon in 1990. *Source:* National Archives and Records Administration. Web: www.archives.gov/.

Wives and Children of the Presidents

President	Wife's name	Year and place of wife's birth	Married	Wife died	Children[1] Sons	Daughters
Washington	Martha Dandridge Custis	1732, Va.	1759	1802	—	—
John Adams	Abigail Smith	1744, Mass.	1764	1818	3	2
Jefferson[2]	Martha Wayles Skelton	1748, Va.	1772	1782	1	5
Madison	Dorothy "Dolley" Payne Todd	1768, N.C.	1794	1849	—	—
Monroe	Elizabeth "Eliza" Kortright	1768, N.Y.	1786	1830	—	2
J. Q. Adams	Louisa Catherine Johnson	1775, England	1797	1852	3	1
Jackson	Rachel Donelson Robards	1767, Va.	1791	1828	—	—
Van Buren	Hannah Hoes	1788, N.Y.	1807	1819	4	—
W. H. Harrison	Anna Symmes	1775, N.J.	1795	1864	6	4
Tyler	Letitia Christian	1790, Va.	1813	1842	3	5
	Julia Gardiner	1820, N.Y.	1844	1889	5	2
Polk	Sarah Childress	1803, Tenn.	1824	1891	—	—
Taylor	Margaret Smith	1788, Md.	1810	1852	1	5
Fillmore	Abigail Powers	1798, N.Y.	1826	1853	1	1
	Caroline Carmichael McIntosh	1813, N.J.	1858	1881	—	—
Pierce	Jane Means Appleton	1806, N.H.	1834	1863	3	—
Buchanan	(Unmarried)	—	—	—	—	—
Lincoln	Mary Todd	1818, Ky.	1842	1882	4	—
A. Johnson	Eliza McCardle	1810, Tenn.	1827	1876	3	2
Grant	Julia Dent	1826, Mo.	1848	1902	3	1
Hayes	Lucy Ware Webb	1831, Ohio	1852	1889	7	1
Garfield	Lucretia Rudolph	1832, Ohio	1858	1918	5	2
Arthur	Ellen Lewis Herndon	1837, Va.	1859	1880	2	1
Cleveland	Frances Folsom	1864, N.Y.	1886	1947	2	3
B. Harrison	Caroline Lavinia Scott	1832, Ohio	1853	1892	1	1
	Mary Scott Lord Dimmick	1858, Pa.	1896	1948	—	1
McKinley	Ida Saxton	1847, Ohio	1871	1907	—	2
T. Roosevelt	Alice Hathaway Lee	1861, Mass.	1880	1884	—	1
	Edith Kermit Carow	1861, Conn.	1886	1948	4	1
Taft	Helen Herron	1861, Ohio	1886	1943	2	1
Wilson	Ellen Louise Axson	1860, Ga.	1885	1914	—	3
	Edith Bolling Galt	1872, Va.	1915	1961	—	—
Harding	Florence Kling DeWolfe	1860, Ohio	1891	1924	—	—
Coolidge	Grace Anna Goodhue	1879, Vt.	1905	1957	2	—
Hoover	Lou Henry	1875, Iowa	1899	1944	2	—
F. D. Roosevelt	(Anna) Eleanor Roosevelt	1884, N.Y.	1905	1962	5	1
Truman	Bess Wallace	1885, Mo.	1919	1982	—	1
Eisenhower	Mamie Geneva Doud	1896, Iowa	1916	1979	2	—
Kennedy	Jacqueline Lee Bouvier	1929, N.Y.	1953	1994	2	1
L. B. Johnson	Claudia Alta "Lady Bird" Taylor	1912, Tex.	1934	—	—	2
Nixon	Thelma Catherine "Pat" Ryan	1912, Nev.	1940	1993	—	2
Ford	Elizabeth "Betty" Bloomer Warren	1918, Ill.	1948	—	3	1
Carter	Rosalynn Smith	1928, Ga.	1946	—	3	1
Reagan	Jane Wyman	1914, Mo.	1940[3]	—	1[4]	1
	Nancy Davis	1921, N.Y.	1952	—	1	1
G.H.W. Bush	Barbara Pierce	1925, N.Y.	1945	—	4	2
Clinton	Hillary Rodham	1947, Ill.	1975	—	—	1
G. W. Bush	Laura Welch	1946, Tex.	1977	—	—	2

1. Includes children who died in infancy. 2. Number of children listed here reflects only children Jefferson had with Martha Wayles Skelton. Scientists and historians agree, based on DNA evidence, that Jefferson may have fathered at least one child with slave Sally Hemings. 3. Divorced in 1948. 4. Adopted.

Biographies of the Presidents

GEORGE WASHINGTON was born on Feb. 22, 1732 (Feb. 11, 1731/2, old style) in Westmoreland County, Va. While in his teens, he trained as a surveyor, and at the age of 20 he was appointed adjutant in the Va. militia. For the next three years, he fought in the wars against the French and Indians, serving as Gen. Edward Braddock's aide in the disastrous campaign against Ft. Duquesne. In 1759, he resigned from the militia, married Martha Dandridge Custis, a widow with children, and settled down as a gentleman farmer at Mount Vernon, Va.

As a militiaman, Washington had been exposed to the arrogance of the British officers, and his experience as a planter with British commercial restrictions increased his anti-British sentiment. He opposed the Stamp Act of 1765 and after 1770 became increasingly prominent in organizing resistance. A delegate to the Continental Congress, Washington was selected as commander in chief of the Continental Army and took command at Cambridge, Mass., on July 3, 1775.

Inadequately supported and sometimes covertly sabotaged by the Congress, in charge of troops who were inexperienced, badly equipped, and impatient of discipline, Washington conducted the war on the policy of avoiding major engagements with the British and wearing them down by harassing tactics. His able generalship, along with the French alliance and the growing weariness within Britain, brought the war to a conclusion with the surrender of Cornwallis at Yorktown, Va., on Oct. 19, 1781.

The chaotic years under the Articles of Confederation led Washington to return to public life in the hope of promoting the formation of a strong central government. He presided over the Constitutional Convention and yielded to the universal demand that he serve as first president. He was inaugurated on April 30, 1789, in New York, the first national capital. In office, he sought to unite the nation and establish the authority of the new government at home and abroad. Greatly distressed by the emergence of the Hamilton-Jefferson rivalry, Washington worked to maintain neutrality but actually sympathized more with Hamilton. Following his unanimous reelection in 1792, his second term was dominated by the Federalists. His Farewell Address on Sept. 17, 1796 (published but never delivered) rebuked party spirit and warned against "permanent alliances" with foreign powers.

He died at Mount Vernon on Dec. 14, 1799.

JOHN ADAMS born on Oct. 30 (Oct. 19, old style), 1735, at Braintree (now Quincy), Mass. A Harvard graduate, he considered teaching and the ministry but finally turned to law and was admitted to the bar in 1758. Six years later, he married Abigail Smith. He opposed the Stamp Act, served as lawyer for patriots indicted by the British, and by the time of the Continental Congresses, was in the vanguard of the movement for independence. In 1778, he went to France as commissioner. Subsequently he helped negotiate the peace treaty with Britain, and in 1785 became envoy to London. Resigning in 1788, he was elected vice president under Washington and was reelected in 1792.

Though a Federalist, Adams did not get along with Hamilton, who sought to prevent his election to the presidency in 1796 and thereafter intrigued against his administration. In 1798, Adams's independent policy averted a war with France but completed the break with Hamilton and the right-wing Federalists; at the same time, the enactment of the Alien and Sedition Acts, directed against foreigners and against critics of the government, exasperated the Jeffersonian opposition. The split between Adams and Hamilton resulted in Jefferson's becoming the next president. Adams retired to his home in Quincy. He and Jefferson died on the same day, July 4, 1826, the 50th anniversary of the adoption of the Declaration of Independence.

His *Defence of the Constitutions of Government of the United States* (1787) contains original and striking, if conservative, political ideas.

THOMAS JEFFERSON was born on April 13 (April 2, old style), 1743, at Shadwell in Goochland (now Albemarle) County, Va. A William and Mary graduate, he studied law, but from the start showed an interest in science and philosophy. His literary skills and political clarity brought him to the fore-front of the revolutionary movement in Virginia. As delegate to the Continental Congress, he drafted the Declaration of Independence. In 1776, he entered the Virginia House of Delegates and initiated a comprehensive reform program for the abolition of feudal survivals in land tenure and the separation of church and state.

In 1779, he became governor, but constitutional limitations on his power, combined with his own lack of executive energy, caused an unsatisfactory administration, culminating in Jefferson's virtual abdication when the British invaded Virginia in 1781. He retired to his beautiful home at Monticello, Va., to his family. His wife, Martha Wayles Skelton, whom he married in 1772, died in 1782.

Jefferson's *Notes on Virginia* (1784–85) illustrate his many-faceted interests, his limitless intellectual curiosity, his deep faith in agrarian democracy. Sent to Congress in 1783, he helped lay down the decimal system and drafted basic reports on the organization of the western lands. In 1785 he was appointed minister to France, where the Anglo-Saxon liberalism he had drawn from John Locke, the British philosopher, was stimulated by contact with the thought that would soon ferment in the French Revolution. In 1789, Washington appointed him secretary of state. While favoring the Constitution and a strengthened central government, Jefferson came to believe that Hamilton contemplated the establishment of a monarchy. Growing differences resulted in Jefferson's resignation on Dec. 31, 1793.

Elected vice president in 1796, Jefferson continued to serve as spiritual leader of the opposition to Federalism, particularly to the repressive Alien and Sedition Acts. He was elected president in 1801 by the House of Representatives as a result of Hamilton's decision to throw the Federalist votes to him rather than to Aaron Burr, who had tied him in electoral votes. He was the first president to be inaugurated in Washington, which he had helped to design.

The purchase of Louisiana from France in 1803, though in violation of Jefferson's earlier constitutional scruples, was the most notable act of his administration. Reelected in 1804, with the Federalist Charles C. Pinckney opposing him, Jefferson tried desperately to keep the United States out of the Napoleonic Wars in Europe, employing to this end the unpopular embargo policy.

After his retirement to Monticello in 1809, he developed his interest in education, founding the University of Virginia and watching its development with never-flagging interest. He died at Monticello on July 4, 1826. Jefferson had an enormous variety of interests and skills, ranging from education and science to architecture and music.

JAMES MADISON was born in Port Conway, Va., on March 16, 1751 (March 5, 1750/1, old style). A Princeton graduate, he joined the struggle for independence on his return to Virginia in 1771. In the 1770s and 1780s he was active in state politics, where he championed the Jefferson reform program, and in the Continental Congress. Madison was influential in the Constitutional Convention as leader of the group favoring a strong central government and as recorder of the debates; and he subsequently wrote, in collaboration with Alexander Hamilton and John Jay, the *Federalist* papers to aid the campaign for the adoption of the Constitution.

Serving in the new Congress, Madison soon emerged as the leader in the House of the men who opposed Hamilton's financial program and his pro-British leanings in foreign policy. Retiring from Congress in 1797, he continued to be active in Virginia and drafted the Virginia Resolution protesting the Alien and Sedition Acts. His intimacy with Jefferson made him the natural choice for secretary of state in 1801.

In 1809, Madison succeeded Jefferson as president, defeating Charles C. Pinckney. His wife, Dolley Payne Todd, whom he married in 1794, brought a new social sparkle to the executive mansion. In the meantime, increasing tension with Britain culminated in the War of 1812—a war for which the United States was unprepared and for which Madison lacked the executive talent to clear out incompetence and mobilize the nation's energies. Madison was reelected in 1812, running against the Federalist De Witt Clinton. In 1814, the British actually captured Washington and forced Madison to flee to Virginia.

Madison's domestic program capitulated to the Hamiltonian policies that he had resisted 20 years before and he now signed bills to establish a United States Bank and a higher tariff.

After his presidency, he remained in retirement in Virginia until his death on June 28, 1836.

JAMES MONROE was born on April 28, 1758, in Westmoreland County, Va. A William and Mary graduate, he served in the army during the first years of the Revolution and was wounded at Trenton. He then entered Virginia politics and later national politics under the sponsorship of Jefferson. In 1786, he married Elizabeth (Eliza) Kortright.

Fearing centralization, Monroe opposed the adoption of the Constitution and, as senator from Virginia, was highly critical of the Hamiltonian program. In 1794, he was appointed minister to France, where his ardent sympathies with the Revolution exceeded the wishes of the State Department. His troubled diplomatic career ended with his recall in 1796. From 1799 to 1802, he was governor of Virginia. In 1803, Jefferson sent him to France to help negotiate the Louisiana Purchase and for the next few years he was active in various negotiations on the Continent.

In 1808, Monroe flirted with the radical wing of the Republican Party, which opposed Madison's candidacy; but the presidential boom came to naught and, after a brief term as governor of Virginia in 1811, Monroe accepted Madison's offer to become secretary of state. During the War of 1812, he vainly sought a field command and instead served as secretary of war from September 1814 to March 1815.

Elected president in 1816 over the Federalist Rufus King, and reelected without opposition in 1820, Monroe, the last of the Virginia dynasty, pursued the course of systematic tranquilization that won for his administrations the name "the era of good feeling." He continued Madison's surrender to the Hamiltonian domestic program, signed the Missouri Compromise, acquired Florida, and with the able assistance of his secretary of state, John Quincy Adams, promulgated the Monroe Doctrine in 1823, declaring against foreign colonization or intervention in the Americas. He died in New York City on July 4, 1831, the third president to die on the anniversary of Independence.

JOHN QUINCY ADAMS was born on July 11, 1767, at Braintree (now Quincy), Mass., the son of John Adams, the second president. He spent his early years in Europe with his father, graduated from Harvard, and entered law practice. His anti-Paine newspaper articles won him political attention. In 1794, he became minister to the Netherlands, the first of several diplomatic posts that occupied him until his return to Boston in 1801. In 1797, he married Louisa Catherine Johnson.

In 1803, Adams was elected to the Senate, nominally as a Federalist, but his repeated displays of independence on such issues as the Louisiana Purchase and the embargo caused his party to demand his resignation and ostracize him socially. In 1809, Madison rewarded him for his support of Jefferson by appointing him minister to St. Petersburg. He helped negotiate the Treaty of Ghent in 1814, and in 1815 became minister to London. In 1817 Monroe appointed him secretary of state where he served with great distinction, gaining Florida from Spain without hostilities and playing an equal part with Monroe in formulating the Monroe Doctrine.

When no presidential candidate received a majority of electoral votes in 1824, Adams, with the support of Henry Clay, was elected by the House in 1825 over Andrew Jackson, who had the original plurality. Adams had ambitious plans of government activity to foster internal improvements and promote the arts and sciences, but congressional obstructionism, combined with his own unwillingness or inability to play the role of a politician, resulted in little being accomplished. After being defeated for reelection by Jackson in 1828, he successfully ran for the House of Representatives in 1830. There, though nominally a Whig, he pursued as ever an independent course. He led the fight to force Congress to receive antislavery petitions and fathered the Smithsonian Institution.

Adams had a stroke while on the floor of the House, and died two days later on Feb. 23, 1848. His long and detailed *Diary* gives a unique picture of the personalities and politics of the times.

ANDREW JACKSON was born on March 15, 1767, in what is now generally agreed to be Waxhaw, S.C. After a turbulent boyhood as an orphan and a British prisoner, he moved west to Tennessee, where he soon qualified for law practice but found time for such frontier pleasures as horse racing, cockfighting, and dueling. His marriage to Rachel Donelson Robards in 1791 was complicated by subsequent legal uncertainties about the status of her divorce. During the 1790s, Jackson served in the Tennessee Constitutional Convention, the United States House of Representatives and Senate, and on the Tennessee Supreme Court.

After some years as a country gentleman, living at the Hermitage near Nashville, Jackson in 1812 was given command of Tennessee troops sent against the Creeks. He defeated the Indians at Horseshoe Bend in 1814; subsequently he became a major general and won the Battle of New Orleans over veteran British troops, though after the treaty of peace had been signed at Ghent. In 1818, Jackson invaded Florida, captured Pensacola, and hanged two Englishmen named Arbuthnot and Ambrister, creating an international incident. A presidential boom began for him in 1821, and to foster it, he returned to the Senate (1823–25). Though he won a plurality of electoral votes in 1824, he lost in the House when Clay threw his strength to Adams. Four years later, he easily defeated Adams. Jackson, the first president to come from humble origins, built his reputation as a populist and a defender of the common man over the political elite.

As president, Jackson greatly expanded the power and prestige of the presidential office and carried through an unprecedented program of domestic reform, vetoing the bill to extend the United States Bank, moving toward a hard-money currency policy, and checking the program of federal internal improvements. He also vindicated federal authority against South Carolina with its doctrine of nullification and against France on the question of debts. The support given his policies by the workingmen of the East as well as by the farmers of the East, West, and South resulted in his triumphant reelection in 1832 over Clay.

After watching the inauguration of his handpicked successor, Martin Van Buren, Jackson retired to the Hermitage, where he maintained a lively interest in national affairs until his death on June 8, 1845.

MARTIN VAN BUREN was born on Dec. 5, 1782, at Kinderhook, N.Y. After graduating from the village school, he became a law clerk, entered practice in 1803, and soon became active in state politics as state senator and attorney general. In 1820, he was elected to the United States Senate. He threw the support of his efficient political organization, known as the Albany Regency, to William H. Crawford in 1824 and to Jackson in 1828. After leading the opposition to Adams's administration in the Senate, he served briefly as governor of New York (1828–1829) and resigned to become Jackson's secretary of state. He was soon on close personal terms with Jackson and played an important part in the Jacksonian program.

In 1832, Van Buren became vice president; in 1836, president. The Panic of 1837 overshadowed his term. He attributed it to the overexpansion of the credit and favored the establishment of an independent treasury as repository for the federal funds. In 1840, he established a 10-hour day on public works. Defeated by Harrison in 1840, he was the leading contender for the Democratic nomination in 1844 until he publicly opposed immediate annexation of Texas, and was subsequently beaten by the Southern delegations at the Baltimore convention. This incident increased his growing misgivings about the slave power.

After working behind the scenes among the anti-slavery Democrats, Van Buren joined in the movement that led to the Free-Soil Party and became its candidate for president in 1848. He subsequently returned to the Democratic Party while continuing to object to its pro-Southern policy. He died in Kinderhook on July 24, 1862. His *Autobiography* throws valuable sidelights on the political history of the times.

His wife, Hannah Hoes, whom he married in 1807, died in 1819.

WILLIAM HENRY HARRISON was born in Charles City County, Va., on Feb. 9, 1773. Joining the army in 1791, he was active in Indian fighting in the Northwest, became secretary of the Northwest Territory in 1798 and governor of Indiana in 1800. He married Anna Symmes in 1795. Growing discontent over white encroachments on Indian lands led to the formation of an Indian alliance under Tecumseh to resist further aggressions. In 1811, Harrison won a nominal victory over the Indians at Tippecanoe and in 1813 a more decisive one at the Battle of the Thames, where Tecumseh was killed.

After resigning from the army in 1814, Harrison had an obscure career in politics and diplomacy, ending up 20 years later as a county recorder in Ohio. Nominated for president in 1835 as a military hero whom the conservative politicians hoped to be able to control, he ran surprisingly well against Van Buren in 1836. Four years later, he defeated Van Buren but caught pneumonia and died in Washington on April 4, 1841, a month after his inauguration. Harrison was the first president to die in office.

JOHN TYLER was born in Charles City County, Va., on March 29, 1790. A William and Mary graduate, he entered law practice and politics, serving in the House of Representatives (1817–21), as governor of Virginia (1825–27), and as senator (1827–36). A strict constructionist, he supported Crawford in 1824 and Jackson in 1828, but broke with Jackson over his United States Bank policy and became a member of the Southern state-rights group that cooperated with the Whigs. In 1836, he resigned from the Senate rather than follow instructions from the Virginia legislature to vote for a resolution expunging censure of Jackson from the Senate record.

Elected vice president on the Whig ticket in 1840, Tyler succeeded to the presidency on Harrison's death. His strict-constructionist views soon caused a split with the Henry Clay wing of the Whig party and a stalemate on domestic questions. Tyler's more considerable achievements were his support of the Webster-Ashburton Treaty with Britain and his success in bringing about the annexation of Texas.

After his presidency he lived in retirement in Virginia until the outbreak of the Civil War, when he emerged briefly as chairman of a peace convention and then as delegate to the provisional Congress of the Confederacy. He died on Jan. 18, 1862. He married Letitia Christian in 1813 and, two years after her death in 1842, Julia Gardiner.

JAMES KNOX POLK was born in Mecklenburg County, N.C., on Nov. 2, 1795. A graduate of the University of North Carolina, he moved west to Tennessee, was admitted to the bar, and soon became prominent in state politics. In 1825, he was elected to the House of Representatives, where he opposed Adams and, after 1829, became Jackson's floor leader in the fight against the Bank. In 1835, he became Speaker of the House. Four years later, he was elected governor of Tennessee, but was beaten in tries for reelection in 1841 and 1843.

The supporters of Van Buren for the Democratic nomination in 1844 counted on Polk as his running mate, but when Van Buren's stand on Texas alienated Southern support, the convention swung to Polk on the ninth ballot. He was elected over Henry Clay, the Whig candidate. Rapidly disillusioning those who thought that he would not run his own administration, Polk proceeded steadily and precisely to achieve four major objectives—the acquisition of California, the settlement of the Oregon question, the reduction of the tariff, and the establishment of the independent treasury. He also enlarged the Monroe Doctrine to exclude all non-American intervention in American affairs, whether forcible or not, and he forced Mexico into a war that he waged to a successful conclusion.

His wife, Sarah Childress, whom he married in 1824, was a woman of charm and ability. Polk died in Nashville, Tenn., on June 15, 1849.

ZACHARY TAYLOR

ZACHARY TAYLOR was born at Montebello, Orange County, Va., on Nov. 24, 1784. Embarking on a military career in 1808, Taylor fought in the War of 1812, the Black Hawk War, and the Seminole War, meanwhile holding garrison jobs on the frontier or desk jobs in Washington. A brigadier general as a result of his victory over the Seminoles at Lake Okeechobee (1837), Taylor held a succession of Southwestern commands and in 1846 established a base on the Rio Grande, where his forces engaged in hostilities that precipitated the war with Mexico. He captured Monterrey in Sept. 1846 and, disregarding Polk's orders to stay on the defensive, defeated Santa Anna at Buena Vista in Feb. 1847, ending the war in the northern provinces.

Though Taylor had never cast a vote for president, his party affiliations were Whiggish and his availability was increased by his difficulties with Polk. He was elected president over the Democrat Lewis Cass. During the revival of the slavery controversy, which was to result in the Compromise of 1850, Taylor began to take an increasingly firm stand against appeasing the South; but he died in Washington on July 9, 1850, during the fight over the Compromise. He married Margaret Mackall Smith in 1810. His bluff and simple soldierly qualities won him the name Old Rough and Ready.

MILLARD FILLMORE

MILLARD FILLMORE was born at Locke, Cayuga County, N.Y., on Jan. 7, 1800. A lawyer, he entered politics with the Anti-Masonic Party under the sponsorship of Thurlow Weed, editor and party boss, and subsequently followed Weed into the Whig Party. He served in the House of Representatives (1833–35 and 1837–43) and played a leading role in writing the tariff of 1842. Defeated for governor of New York in 1844, he became state comptroller in 1848, was put on the Whig ticket with Taylor as a concession to the Clay wing of the party, and became president upon Taylor's death in 1850.

As president, Fillmore broke with Weed and William H. Seward and associated himself with the pro-Southern Whigs, supporting the Compromise of 1850. Defeated for the Whig nomination in 1852, he ran for president in 1856 as candidate of the American, or Know-Nothing, Party, which sought to unite the country against foreigners in the alleged hope of diverting it from the explosive slavery issue. Fillmore opposed Lincoln during the Civil War. He died in Buffalo on March 8, 1874.

He was married in 1826 to Abigail Powers, who died in 1853, and in 1858 to Caroline Carmichael McIntosh.

FRANKLIN PIERCE

FRANKLIN PIERCE was born at Hillsboro, N.H., on Nov. 23, 1804. A Bowdoin graduate, lawyer, and Jacksonian Democrat, he won rapid political advancement in the party, in part because of the prestige of his father, Gov. Benjamin Pierce. By 1831 he was Speaker of the New Hampshire House of Representatives; from 1833 to 1837, he served in the federal House and from 1837 to 1842 in the Senate. His wife, Jane Means Appleton, whom he married in 1834, disliked Washington and the somewhat dissipated life led by Pierce; in 1842 Pierce resigned from the Senate and began a successful law practice in Concord, N.H. During the Mexican War, he was a brigadier general.

Thereafter Pierce continued to oppose antislavery tendencies within the Democratic Party. As a result, he was the Southern choice to break the deadlock at the Democratic convention of 1852 and was nominated on the 49th ballot. In the election, Pierce overwhelmed Gen. Winfield Scott, the Whig candidate.

As president, Pierce followed a course of appeasing the South at home and of playing with schemes of territorial expansion abroad. The failure of his foreign and domestic policies prevented his renomination. He died in Concord on Oct. 8, 1869, in relative obscurity.

JAMES BUCHANAN

JAMES BUCHANAN was born near Mercersburg, Pa., on April 23, 1791. A Dickinson graduate and a lawyer, he entered Pennsylvania politics as a Federalist. With the disappearance of the Federalist Party, he became a Jacksonian Democrat. He served with ability in the House (1821–31), as minister to St. Petersburg (1832–33), and in the Senate (1834–45), and in 1845 became Polk's secretary of state. In 1853, Pierce appointed Buchanan minister to Britain, where he participated with other American diplomats in Europe in drafting the expansionist Ostend Manifesto.

He was elected president in 1856, defeating John C. Frémont, the Republican candidate, and former President Millard Fillmore of the American Party. The growing crisis over slavery presented Buchanan with problems he lacked the will to tackle. His appeasement of the South alienated the Stephen Douglas wing of the Democratic Party without reducing Southern militancy on slavery issues. While denying the right of secession, Buchanan also denied that the federal government could do anything about it. He supported the administration during the Civil War and died in Lancaster, Pa., on June 1, 1868.

The only president to remain a bachelor throughout his term, Buchanan used his charming niece, Harriet Lane, as White House hostess.

ABRAHAM LINCOLN

ABRAHAM LINCOLN was born in Hardin (now Larue) County, Ky., on Feb. 12, 1809. His family moved to Indiana and then to Illinois, and Lincoln gained what education he could along the way. While reading law, he worked in a store, managed a mill, surveyed, and split rails. In 1834, he went to the Illinois legislature as a Whig and became the party's floor leader. For the next 20 years, he practiced law in Springfield, except for a single term (1847–49) in Congress, where he denounced the Mexican War. In 1855, he was a candidate for senator and the next year he joined the new Republican Party.

A leading but unsuccessful candidate for the vice-presidential nomination with Frémont, Lincoln gained national attention in 1858 when, as Republican candidate for senator from Illinois, he engaged in a series of debates with Stephen A. Douglas, the Democratic candidate. He lost the election, but continued to prepare the way for the 1860 Republican convention and was rewarded with the presidential nomination on the third ballot. He won the election over three opponents.

From the start, Lincoln made clear that, unlike Buchanan, he believed the national government had the power to crush the rebellion. Not an abolitionist, he held the slavery issue subordinate to that of preserving the Union, but soon perceived that the war could not be brought to a successful conclusion without freeing the slaves. His administration was hampered by the incompetence of many Union generals, the inexperience of the troops, and the harassing political tactics both of the Republican Radicals, who favored a hard policy toward the South, and the Democratic Copperheads, who desired a negotiated peace. The Gettysburg Address of Nov. 19, 1863, marks the high point in the record of American eloquence. Lincoln's long search for a winning combination finally brought generals Ulysses S. Grant and William T. Sherman to the top; and their series of victories in 1864 dispelled the mutterings from both Radicals and Peace Democrats that at one time seemed to threaten Lincoln's reelection. He was reelected in 1864, defeating Gen. George B. McClellan, the Democratic candidate. His inaugural address urged leniency toward the South: "With malice toward none, with charity for all . . . let us strive on to finish the work we are in; to bind up the nation's wounds . . ." This policy aroused growing opposition on the part of the Republican Radicals, but before the matter could be put to the test, Lincoln was shot by the actor John Wilkes Booth at Ford's Theater, Washington, on April 14, 1865. He died the next morning.

Lincoln's marriage to Mary Todd in 1842 was often unhappy and turbulent, in part because of his wife's pronounced instability.

ANDREW JOHNSON was born at Raleigh, N.C., on Dec. 29, 1808. Self-educated, he became a tailor in Greeneville, Tenn., but soon went into politics, where he rose steadily. He served in the House of Representatives (1843–54), as governor of Tennessee (1853–57), and as a senator (1857–62). Politically he was a Jacksonian Democrat and his specialty was the fight for a more equitable land policy. Alone among the Southern Senators, he stood by the Union during the Civil War. In 1862 he became war governor of Tennessee and carried out a thankless and difficult job with great courage. Johnson became Lincoln's running mate in 1864 as a result of an attempt to give the ticket a nonpartisan and nonsectional character. Succeeding to the presidency on Lincoln's death, Johnson sought to carry out Lincoln's policy, but without his political skill. The result was a hopeless conflict with the Radical Republicans who dominated Congress, passed measures over Johnson's vetoes, and attempted to limit the power of the executive concerning appointments and removals. The conflict culminated with Johnson's impeachment for attempting to remove his disloyal secretary of war in defiance of the Tenure of Office Act, which required senatorial concurrence for such dismissals. The opposition failed by one vote to get the two thirds necessary for conviction.

After his presidency, Johnson maintained an interest in politics and in 1875 was again elected to the Senate. He died near Carter Station, Tenn., on July 31, 1875. He married Eliza McCardle in 1827.

ULYSSES SIMPSON GRANT was born (as Hiram Ulysses Grant) at Point Pleasant, Ohio, on April 27, 1822. He graduated from West Point in 1843 and served without particular distinction in the Mexican War. In 1848 he married Julia Dent. He resigned from the army in 1854, after warnings from his commanding officer about his drinking habits, and for the next six years held a wide variety of jobs in the Middle West. With the outbreak of the Civil War, he sought a command and soon, to his surprise, was made a brigadier general. His continuing successes in the western theaters, culminating in the capture of Vicksburg, Miss., in 1863, brought him national fame and soon the command of all the Union armies. Grant's dogged, implacable policy of concentrating on dividing and destroying the Confederate armies brought the war to an end in 1865. The next year, he was made full general.

In 1868, as Republican candidate for president, Grant was elected over the Democrat, Horatio Seymour. From the start, Grant showed his unfitness for the office. His cabinet was weak, his domestic policy was confused, and many of his intimate associates were corrupt. The notable achievement in foreign affairs was the settlement of controversies with Great Britain in the Treaty of London (1871), negotiated by his able secretary of state, Hamilton Fish.

Running for reelection in 1872, he defeated Horace Greeley, the Democratic and Liberal Republican candidate. The Panic of 1873 graft scandals close to the presidency created difficulties for his second term.

After retiring from office, Grant toured Europe for two years and returned in time to accede to a third-term boom, but was beaten in the convention of 1880. Illness and bad business judgment darkened his last years, but he worked steadily at the *Personal Memoirs,* which were to be successful when published after his death at Mount McGregor, near Saratoga, N.Y., on July 23, 1885.

RUTHERFORD BIRCHARD HAYES was born in Delaware, Ohio, on Oct. 4, 1822. A graduate of Kenyon College and the Harvard Law School, he practiced law in Lower Sandusky (now Fremont) and then in Cincinnati. In 1852 he married Lucy Webb. A Whig, he joined the Republican party in 1855. During the Civil War he rose to major general. He served in the House of Representatives from 1865 to 1867 and then confirmed a reputation for honesty and efficiency in two terms as governor of Ohio (1868–72). His election to a third term in 1875 made him the logical candidate for those Republicans who wished to stop James G. Blaine in 1876, and he was nominated.

The result of the election was in doubt for some time and hinged upon disputed returns from South Carolina, Louisiana, Florida, and Oregon. Samuel J. Tilden, the Democrat, had the larger popular vote but was adjudged by the strictly partisan decisions of the Electoral Commission to have one fewer electoral vote, 185 to 184. The national acceptance of this result was due in part to the general understanding that Hayes would pursue a conciliatory policy toward the South. He withdrew the troops from the South, took a conservative position on financial and labor issues, and urged civil service reform.

Hayes served only one term by his own wish and spent the rest of his life in various humanitarian endeavors. He died in Fremont on Jan. 17, 1893.

JAMES ABRAM GARFIELD, the last president to be born in a log cabin, was born in Cuyahoga County, Ohio, on Nov. 19, 1831. A Williams graduate, he taught school for a time and entered Republican politics in Ohio. In 1858, he married Lucretia Rudolph. During the Civil War, he had a promising career, rising to major general of volunteers; but he resigned in 1863, having been elected to the House of Representatives, where he served until 1880. His oratorical and parliamentary abilities soon made him the leading Republican in the House, though his record was marred by his unorthodox acceptance of a fee in the DeGolyer paving contract case and by suspicions of his complicity in the Crédit Mobilier scandal.

In 1880, Garfield was elected to the Senate, but instead became the presidential candidate on the 36th ballot as a result of a deadlock in the Republican convention. In the election, he defeated Gen. Winfield Scott Hancock, the Democratic candidate. Garfield's administration was barely under way when he was shot by Charles J. Guiteau, a disappointed office seeker, in Washington on July 2, 1881. He died in Elberton, N.J., on Sept. 19.

CHESTER ALAN ARTHUR was born at Fairfield, Vt., on Oct. 5, 1829. A graduate of Union College, he became a successful New York lawyer. In 1859, he married Ellen Herndon. During the Civil War, he held administrative jobs in the Republican state administration and in 1871 was appointed collector of the Port of New York by Grant. This post gave him control over considerable patronage. Though not personally corrupt, Arthur managed his power in the interests of the New York machine so openly that President Hayes in 1877 called for an investigation and the next year Arthur was suspended.

In 1880 Arthur was nominated for vice president in the hope of conciliating the followers of Grant and the powerful New York machine. As president upon Garfield's death, Arthur, stepping out of his familiar role as spoilsman, backed civil service reform, reorganized the cabinet, and prosecuted political associates accused of post office graft. Losing machine support and failing to gain the reformers, he was not nominated for a full term in 1884. He died in New York City on Nov. 18, 1886.

(STEPHEN) GROVER CLEVELAND was born at Caldwell, N.J., on March 18, 1837. He was admitted to the bar in Buffalo, N.Y., in 1859 and lived there as a lawyer, with occasional incursions into Democratic politics, for more than 20 years. He did not participate in the Civil War. As mayor of Buffalo in 1881, he carried through a reform program so ably that the Democrats ran him successfully for governor in 1882. In 1884 he won the Democratic nomination for president. The campaign contrasted Cleveland's spotless public career with the uncertain record of James G. Blaine, the Republican candidate, and Cleveland received enough Mugwump (independent Republican) support to win.

As president, Cleveland pushed civil service reform, opposed the pension grab and attacked the high tariff rates. While in the White House, he married Frances Folsom in 1886. Renominated in 1888, Cleveland was defeated by Benjamin Harrison, polling more popular but fewer electoral votes. In 1892, he was elected over Harrison. When the Panic of 1893 burst upon the country, Cleveland's attempts

to solve it by sound-money measures alienated the free-silver wing of the party, while his tariff policy alienated the protectionists. In 1894, he sent troops to break the Pullman strike. In foreign affairs, his firmness caused Great Britain to back down in the Venezuela border dispute.

In his last years Cleveland was an active and much-respected public figure. He died in Princeton, N.J., on June 24, 1908.

BENJAMIN HARRISON was born in North Bend, Ohio, on Aug. 20, 1833, the grandson of William Henry Harrison, the ninth president. A graduate of Miami University in Ohio, he took up the law in Indiana and became active in Republican politics. In 1853, he married Caroline Lavinia Scott. During the Civil War, he rose to brigadier general. A sound-money Republican, he was elected senator from Indiana in 1880. In 1888, he received the Republican nomination for president on the eighth ballot. Though behind on the popular vote, he won over Grover Cleveland in the electoral college by 233 to 168.

As president, Harrison failed to please either the bosses or the reform element in the party. In foreign affairs he backed Secretary of State Blaine, whose policy foreshadowed later American imperialism. Harrison was renominated in 1892 but lost to Cleveland. His wife died in the White House in 1892 and Harrison married her niece, Mary Scott (Lord) Dimmick, in 1896. After his presidency, he resumed law practice. He died in Indianapolis on March 13, 1901.

WILLIAM MCKINLEY was born in Niles, Ohio, on Jan. 29, 1843. He taught school, then served in the Civil War, rising from the ranks to become a major. Subsequently he opened a law office in Canton, Ohio, and in 1871 married Ida Saxton. Elected to Congress in 1876, he served there until 1891, except for 1883–85. His faithful advocacy of business interests culminated in the passage of the highly protective McKinley Tariff of 1890. With the support of Mark Hanna, a shrewd Cleveland businessman interested in safeguarding tariff protection, McKinley became governor of Ohio in 1892 and Republican presidential candidate in 1896. The business community, alarmed by the progressivism of William Jennings Bryan, the Democratic candidate, spent considerable money to assure McKinley's victory.

The chief event of McKinley's administration was the war with Spain, which resulted in the United States' acquisition of the Philippines and other islands. With imperialism an issue, McKinley defeated Bryan again in 1900. On Sept. 6, 1901, he was shot at Buffalo, N.Y., by Leon F. Czolgosz, an anarchist, and he died there eight days later.

THEODORE ROOSEVELT was born in New York City on Oct. 27, 1858. A Harvard graduate, he was early interested in ranching, in politics, and in writing picaresque historical narratives. He was a Republican member of the New York Assembly in 1882–84, an unsuccessful candidate for mayor of New York in 1886, a U.S. civil service commissioner under Benjamin Harrison, police commissioner of New York City in 1895, and assistant secretary of the Navy under McKinley in 1897. He resigned in 1898 to help organize a volunteer regiment, the Rough Riders, and take a more direct part in the war with Spain. He was elected governor of

New York in 1898 and vice president in 1900, in spite of lack of enthusiasm on the part of the bosses.

Assuming the presidency of the assassinated McKinley in 1901, Roosevelt embarked on a wide-ranging program of government reform and conservation of natural resources. He ordered antitrust suits against several large corporations, threatened to intervene in the anthracite coal strike of 1902, which prompted the operators to accept arbitration, and, in general, championed the rights of the "little man" and fought the "malefactors of great wealth." He was also responsible for such progressive legislation as the Elkins Act of 1903, which outlawed freight rebates by railroads; the bill establishing the Department of Commerce and Labor; the Hepburn Act, which gave the I.C.C. greater control over the railroads; the Meat Inspection Act; and the Pure Food and Drug Act.

In foreign affairs, Roosevelt pursued a strong policy, permitting the instigation of a revolt in Panama to dispose of Colombian objections to the Panama Canal and helping to maintain the balance of power in the East by bringing the Russo-Japanese War to an end, for which he won the Nobel Peace Prize, the first American to achieve a Nobel prize in any category. In 1904, he decisively defeated Alton B. Parker, his conservative Democratic opponent.

Roosevelt's increasing coldness toward his successor, William Howard Taft, led him to overlook his earlier disclaimer of third-term ambitions and to reenter politics. Defeated by the machine in the Republican convention of 1912, he organized the Progressive Party (Bull Moose) and polled more votes than Taft, though the split brought about the election of Woodrow Wilson. From 1915 on, Roosevelt strongly favored intervention in the European war. He became deeply embittered at Wilson's refusal to allow him to raise a volunteer division. He died in Oyster Bay, N.Y., on Jan. 6, 1919. He was married twice: in 1880 to Alice Hathaway Lee, who died in 1884, and in 1886 to Edith Kermit Carow.

WILLIAM HOWARD TAFT was born in Cincinnati on Sept. 15, 1857. A Yale graduate, he entered Ohio Republican politics in the 1880s. In 1886 he married Helen Herron. From 1887 to 1890, he served on the Ohio Superior Court; 1890–92, as solicitor general of the United States; 1892–1900, on the federal circuit court. In 1900 McKinley appointed him president of the Philippine Commission and in 1901 governor general. Taft had great success in pacifying the Filipinos, solving the problem of the church lands, improving economic conditions, and establishing limited self-government. His period as secretary of war (1904–08) further demonstrated his capacity as administrator and conciliator, and he was Roosevelt's hand-picked successor in 1908. In the election, he polled 321 electoral votes to 162 for William Jennings Bryan, who was running for the presidency for the third time.

Though he carried on many of Roosevelt's policies, Taft got into increasing trouble with the progressive wing of the party and displayed mounting irritability and indecision. After his defeat in 1912, he became professor of constitutional law at Yale. In 1921 he was appointed chief justice of the United States Supreme Court. He died in Washington, DC, on March 8, 1930.

(THOMAS) WOODROW WILSON was born in Staunton, Va., on Dec. 28, 1856. A Princeton graduate, he turned from law practice to post-graduate work in political science at Johns Hopkins University, receiving his Ph.D. in 1886. He taught at Bryn Mawr, Wesleyan, and Princeton, and in 1902 was made president of Princeton. After an unsuccessful attempt to democratize the social life of the university, he welcomed an invitation in 1910 to be the Democratic gubernatorial candidate in New Jersey, and was elected. His success in fighting the machine and putting through a reform program attracted national attention.

In 1912, at the Democratic convention in Baltimore, Wilson won the nomination on the 46th ballot and went on to defeat Roosevelt and Taft in the election. Wilson proceeded under the standard of the New Freedom to enact a program of domestic reform, including the Federal Reserve Act, the Clayton Antitrust Act, the establishment of the Federal Trade Commission, and other measures designed to restore competition in the face of the great monopolies. In foreign affairs, while privately sympathetic with the Allies, he strove to maintain neutrality in the European war and warned both sides against encroachments on American interests.

Reelected in 1916 as a peace candidate, he tried to mediate between the warring nations; but when the Germans resumed unrestricted submarine warfare in 1917, Wilson brought the United States into what he now believed was a war to make the world safe for democracy. He supplied the classic formulations of Allied war aims and the armistice of Nov. 11, 1918, was negotiated on the basis of Wilson's Fourteen Points. In 1919 he strove at Versailles to lay the foundations for enduring peace. He accepted the imperfections of the Versailles Treaty in the expectation that they could be remedied by action within the League of Nations. He probably could have secured ratification of the treaty by the Senate if he had adopted a more conciliatory attitude toward the mild reservationists; but his insistence on all or nothing eventually caused the diehard isolationists and diehard Wilsonites to unite in rejecting a compromise.

In Sept. 1919 Wilson suffered a paralytic stroke that limited his activity. After leaving the presidency he lived on in retirement in Washington, dying on Feb. 3, 1924. He was married twice—in 1885 to Ellen Louise Axson, who died in 1914, and in 1915 to Edith Bolling Galt.

WARREN GAMALIEL HARDING was born in Morrow County, Ohio, on Nov. 2, 1865. After attending Ohio Central College, Harding became interested in journalism and in 1884 bought the *Marion* (Ohio) *Star.* In 1891 he married a wealthy widow, Florence Kling De Wolfe. As his paper prospered, he entered Republican politics, serving as state senator (1899–1903) and as lieutenant governor (1904–06). In 1910, he was defeated for governor, but in 1914 was elected to the Senate. His reputation as an orator made him the keynoter at the 1916 Republican convention.

When the 1920 convention was deadlocked between Leonard Wood and Frank O. Lowden, Harding became the dark-horse nominee on his solemn affirmation that there was no reason in his past that he should not be. Straddling the League question, Harding was easily elected over James M. Cox, his

Democratic opponent. His cabinet contained some able men, but also some manifestly unfit for public office. Harding's own intimates were mediocre when they were not corrupt. The impending disclosure of the Teapot Dome scandal in the Interior Department and illegal practices in the Justice Department and Veterans' Bureau, as well as political setbacks, profoundly worried him. On his return from Alaska in 1923, he died unexpectedly in San Francisco on Aug. 2.

(JOHN) CALVIN COOLIDGE was born in Plymouth, Vt., on July 4, 1872. An Amherst graduate, he went into law practice at Northampton, Mass., in 1897. He married Grace Anna Goodhue in 1905. He entered Republican state politics, becoming successively mayor of Northampton, state senator, lieutenant governor and, in 1919, governor. His use of the state militia to end the Boston police strike in 1919 won him a somewhat undeserved reputation for decisive action and brought him the Republican vice-presidential nomination in 1920. After Harding's death Coolidge handled the Washington scandals with care and finally managed to save the Republican Party from public blame for the widespread corruption.

In 1924, Coolidge was elected without difficulty, defeating the Democrat, John W. Davis, and Robert M. La Follette running on the Progressive ticket. His second term, like his first, was characterized by a general satisfaction with the existing economic order. He stated that he did not choose to run in 1928.

After his presidency, Coolidge lived quietly in Northampton, writing an unilluminating autobiography and a syndicated column. He died there on Jan. 5, 1933.

HERBERT CLARK HOOVER was born at West Branch, Iowa, on Aug. 10, 1874, the first president to be born west of the Mississippi. A Stanford graduate, he worked from 1895 to 1913 as a mining engineer and consultant throughout the world. In 1899, he married Lou Henry. During World War I, he served with distinction as chairman of the American Relief Committee in London, as chairman of the Commission for Relief in Belgium, and as U.S. Food Administrator. His political affiliations were still too indeterminate for him to be mentioned as a possibility for either the Republican or Democratic nomination in 1920, but after the election he served Harding and Coolidge as secretary of commerce.

In the election of 1928, Hoover overwhelmed Gov. Alfred E. Smith of New York, the Democratic candidate and the first Roman Catholic to run for the presidency. He soon faced the worst depression in the nation's history, but his attacks upon it were hampered by his devotion to the theory that the forces that brought the crisis would soon bring the revival and then by his belief that there were too many areas in which the federal government had no power to act. In a succession of vetoes, he struck down measures proposing a national employment system or national relief, he reduced income tax rates, and only at the end of his term did he yield to popular pressure and set up agencies such as the Reconstruction Finance Corporation to make emergency loans to assist business.

After his 1932 defeat, Hoover returned to private business. In 1946, President Truman charged him with various world food missions; and from 1947 to 1949 and 1953 to 1955, he was head of the Commission on Organization of the Executive Branch of the Government. He died in New York City on Oct. 20, 1964.

FRANKLIN DELANO ROOSEVELT was born in Hyde Park, N.Y., on Jan. 30, 1882. A Harvard graduate, he attended Columbia Law School and was admitted to the New York bar. In 1910, he was elected to the New York State Senate as a Democrat. Reelected in 1912, he was appointed assistant secretary of the navy by Woodrow Wilson the next year. In 1920, his radiant personality and his war service resulted in his nomination for vice president as James M. Cox's running mate. After his defeat, he returned to law practice in New York. In Aug. 1921, Roosevelt was stricken with infantile paralysis while on vacation at Campobello, New Brunswick. After a long and gallant fight, he recovered partial use of his legs. In 1924 and 1928, he led the fight at the Democratic national conventions for the nomination of Gov. Alfred E. Smith of New York, and in 1928 Roosevelt was himself induced to run for governor of New York. He was elected, and was reelected in 1930.

In 1932, Roosevelt received the Democratic nomination for president and immediately launched a campaign that brought new spirit to a weary and discouraged nation. He defeated Hoover by a wide margin. His first term was characterized by an unfolding of the New Deal program, with greater benefits for labor, the farmers, and the unemployed, and the progressive estrangement of most of the business community.

At an early stage, Roosevelt became aware of the menace to world peace posed by totalitarian fascism, and from 1937 on he tried to focus public attention on the trend of events in Europe and Asia. As a result, he was widely denounced as a warmonger. He was reelected in 1936 over Gov. Alfred M. Landon of Kansas by the overwhelming electoral margin of 523 to 8, and the gathering international crisis prompted him to run for an unprecedented third term in 1940. He defeated Wendell L. Willkie.

Roosevelt's program to bring maximum aid to Britain and, after June 1941, to Russia was opposed, until the Japanese attack on Pearl Harbor restored national unity. During the war, Roosevelt shelved the New Deal in the interests of conciliating the business community, both in order to get full production during the war and to prepare the way for a united acceptance of the peace settlements after the war. A series of conferences with Winston Churchill and Joseph Stalin laid down the bases for the postwar world. In 1944 he was elected to a fourth term, running against Gov. Thomas E. Dewey of New York.

On April 12, 1945, Roosevelt died of a cerebral hemorrhage at Warm Springs, Ga., shortly after his return from the Yalta Conference. His wife, (Anna) Eleanor Roosevelt, whom he married in 1905, was a woman of great ability who made significant contributions to her husband's policies.

HARRY S. TRUMAN was born on a farm near Lamar, Mo., on May 8, 1884. During World War I, he served in France as a captain with the 129th Field Artillery. He married Bess Wallace in 1919. After engaging briefly and unsuccessfully in the haberdashery business in Kansas City, Mo., Truman entered local politics. Under the sponsorship of Thomas Pendergast, Democratic boss of Missouri, he held a number of local offices, preserving his personal honesty in the midst of a notoriously corrupt political machine. In 1934, he was elected to the Senate and was reelected in 1940. During his first term he was a loyal but quiet supporter of the New Deal, but in his second term, an appointment as head of a Senate committee to investigate war production brought out his special qualities of honesty, common sense, and hard work, and he won widespread respect.

Elected vice president in 1944, Truman became president upon Roosevelt's sudden death in April 1945 and was immediately faced with the problems of winding down the war against the Axis and preparing the nation for postwar adjustment. Germany surrendered on May 8, and in July Truman attended the Potsdam Conference to discuss the settlement plans for postwar Europe. To end the war with Japan, he authorized the dropping of atomic bombs on Hiroshima and Nagasaki on Aug. 6 and Aug. 9, 1945. Japan surrendered on Aug. 14. Although the action undoubtedly saved many American lives by bringing the war to an end, the morality of the decision is still debated.

The years 1947–48 were distinguished by civil-rights proposals, the Truman Doctrine to contain the spread of Communism, and the Marshall Plan to aid in the economic reconstruction of war-ravaged nations. Truman's general record, highlighted by a vigorous Fair Deal campaign, brought about his unexpected election in 1948 over the heavily favored Thomas E. Dewey.

Truman's second term was primarily concerned with the cold war with the Soviet Union, the implementing of the North Atlantic Pact, the United Nations police action in Korea, and the vast rearmament program with its accompanying problems of economic stabilization.

On March 29, 1952, Truman announced that he would not run again for the presidency. After leaving the White House, he returned to his home in Independence, Mo., to write his memoirs. He further busied himself with the Harry S. Truman Library there. He died in Kansas City, Mo., on Dec. 26, 1972.

DWIGHT·DAVID EISENHOWER was born in Denison, Tex., on Oct. 14, 1890. His ancestors lived in Germany and emigrated to America, settling in Pennsylvania, early in the 18th century. His father, David, had a general store in Hope, Kans., which failed. After a brief time in Texas, the family moved to Abilene, Kan.

After graduating from Abilene High School in 1909, Eisenhower did odd jobs for almost two years. He won an appointment to the Naval Academy at Annapolis, but was too old for admittance. Then he received an appointment in 1910 to West Point, from which he graduated as a second lieutenant in 1915.

He did not see service in World War I, having been stationed at Fort Sam Houston, Tex. There he met Mamie Geneva Doud, whom he married in Denver on July 1, 1916, and by whom he had two sons: Doud Dwight (died in infancy) and John Sheldon Doud.

Eisenhower served in the Philippines from 1935 to 1939 with Gen. Douglas MacArthur. Afterward, Gen. George C. Marshall, the army chief of staff, brought him into the War Department's General Staff and in 1942 placed him in command of the invasion of North Africa. In 1944, he was made Supreme Allied Commander for the invasion of Europe.

After the war, Eisenhower served as army chief of staff from Nov. 1945 until Feb. 1948, when he was appointed president of Columbia University.

In Dec. 1950, President Truman recalled Eisenhower to active duty to command the North Atlantic Treaty Organization forces in Europe. He held his post until the end of May 1952.

At the Republican convention of 1952 in Chicago, Eisenhower won the presidential nomination on the first ballot in a close race with Sen. Robert A. Taft of Ohio. In the election, he defeated Gov. Adlai E. Stevenson of Illinois.

Through two terms, Eisenhower hewed to moderate domestic policies. He sought peace through Free World strength in an era of new nationalisms, nuclear missiles, and space exploration. He fostered alliances pledging the United States to resist "Red" aggression in Europe, Asia, and Latin America. The Eisenhower Doctrine of 1957 extended commitments to the Middle East.

At home, the popular president lacked Republican congressional majorities after 1954, but he was reelected in 1956 by 457 electoral votes to 73 for Stevenson.

While retaining most Fair Deal programs, he stressed "fiscal responsibility" in domestic affairs. A moderate in civil rights, he sent troops to Little Rock, Ark., to enforce court-ordered school integration.

With his wartime rank restored by Congress, Eisenhower returned to private life and the role of elder statesman, with his vigor hardly impaired by a heart attack, an ileitis operation, and a mild stroke suffered while in office. He died in Washington, DC, on March 28, 1969.

JOHN FITZGERALD KENNEDY was born in Brookline, Mass., on May 29, 1917. His father, Joseph P. Kennedy, was ambassador to Great Britain from 1937 to 1940.

Kennedy was graduated from Harvard University in 1940 and joined the navy the next year. He became skipper of a PT boat that was sunk in the Pacific by a Japanese destroyer. Although given up for lost, he swam to a safe island, towing an injured enlisted man.

After recovering from a war-aggravated spinal injury, Kennedy entered politics in 1946 and was elected to Congress. In 1952, he ran against Sen. Henry Cabot Lodge, Jr., of Massachusetts, and won.

Kennedy was married on Sept. 12, 1953, to Jacqueline Lee Bouvier, by whom he had three children: Caroline, John Fitzgerald, Jr. (died in a 1999 plane crash), and Patrick Bouvier (died in infancy).

In 1957 Kennedy won the Pulitzer Prize for a book he had written earlier, *Profiles in Courage.*

After strenuous primary battles, Kennedy won the Democratic presidential nomination on the first ballot at the 1960 Los Angeles convention. With a plurality of only 118,574 votes, he carried the election over Vice President Richard M. Nixon and became the first Roman Catholic president.

Kennedy brought to the White House the dynamic idea of a "New Frontier" approach in dealing with problems at home, abroad, and in the dimensions of space. Out of his leadership in his first few months in office came the 10-year Alliance for Progress to aid Latin America, the Peace Corps, and accelerated programs that brought the first Americans into orbit in the race in space.

Failure of the U.S.-supported Cuban invasion in April 1961 led to the entrenchment of the Communist-backed Castro regime, only 90 mi from United States soil. When it became known that Soviet offensive missiles were being installed in Cuba in 1962, Kennedy ordered a naval "quarantine" of the island and moved troops into position to eliminate this threat to U.S. security. The world seemed on the brink of a nuclear war until Soviet premier Khrushchev ordered the removal of the missiles.

A sudden "thaw," or the appearance of one, in the cold war came with the agreement with the Soviet Union on a limited test-ban treaty signed in Moscow on Aug. 6, 1963.

In his domestic policies, Kennedy's proposals for medical care for the aged and aid to education were defeated, but on minimum wage, trade legislation, and other measures he won important victories.

Widespread racial disorders and demonstrations led to Kennedy's proposing sweeping civil rights legislation. As his third year in office drew to a close, he also recommended an $11-billion tax cut to bolster the economy. Both measures were pending in Congress when Kennedy, looking forward to a second term, journeyed to Texas for a series of speeches.

While riding in an automobile procession in Dallas on Nov. 22, 1963, he was shot to death by an assassin firing from an upper floor of a building. The alleged assassin, Lee Harvey Oswald, was killed two days later in the Dallas city jail by Jack Ruby, owner of a strip-tease club.

At 46 years of age, Kennedy became the fourth president to be assassinated and the eighth to die in office.

LYNDON BAINES JOHNSON was born in Stonewall, Tex., on Aug. 27, 1908. On both sides of his family he had a political heritage mingled with a Baptist background of preachers and teachers. Both his father and his paternal grandfather served in the Texas House of Representatives.

After his graduation from Southwest Texas State Teachers College, Johnson taught school for two years. He went to Washington in 1932 as secretary to Rep. Richard M. Kleberg. During this time, he married Claudia Alta Taylor, known as "Lady Bird." They had two children: Lynda Bird and Luci Baines.

In 1935, Johnson became Texas administrator for the National Youth Administration. Two years later, he was elected to Congress as an all-out supporter of Franklin D. Roosevelt, and served until 1949. He was the first member of Congress to enlist in the armed forces after the attack on Pearl Harbor. He served in the navy in the Pacific and won a Silver Star.

Johnson was elected to the Senate in 1948 after he had captured the Democratic nomination by only 87 votes. He was 40 years old. He became the Senate Democratic leader in 1953. A heart attack in 1955 threatened to end his political career, but he recovered fully and resumed his duties.

At the height of his power as Senate leader, Johnson sought the Democratic nomination for president in 1960. When he lost to John F. Kennedy, he surprised even some of his closest associates by accepting second place on the ticket.

Johnson was riding in another car in the motorcade when Kennedy was assassinated in Dallas on Nov. 22, 1963. He took the oath of office in the presidential jet on the Dallas airfield.

With Johnson's insistent backing, Congress finally adopted a far-reaching civil-rights bill, a voting-rights bill, a Medicare program for the aged, and measures to improve education and conservation. Congress also began what Johnson described as "an all-out war" on poverty.

Amassing a record-breaking majority of nearly 16 million votes, Johnson was elected president in his own right in 1964, defeating Sen. Barry Goldwater of Arizona.

The double tragedy of a war in Southeast Asia and urban riots at home marked Johnson's last two years in office. Faced with disunity in the nation and challenges within his own party, Johnson surprised the country on March 31, 1968, with the announcement that he would not be a candidate for reelection. He died of a heart attack suffered at his LBJ Ranch on Jan. 22, 1973.

RICHARD MILHOUS NIXON was born in Yorba Linda, Calif., on Jan. 9, 1913, to Midwestern-bred parents, Francis A. and Hannah Milhous Nixon, who raised their five sons as Quakers.

Nixon was a high school debater and was undergraduate president at Whittier College in California, where he was graduated in 1934. As a scholarship student at Duke University Law School in North Carolina, he graduated third in his class in 1937.

After five years as a lawyer, Nixon joined the navy in August 1942. He was an air transport officer in the South Pacific and a legal officer stateside before his discharge in 1946 as a lieutenant commander.

Running for Congress in California as a Republican in 1946, Nixon defeated Rep. Jerry Voorhis. As a member of the House Un-American Activities Committee, he made a name as an investigator of Alger Hiss, a former high State Department official, who was later jailed for perjury. In 1950, Nixon defeated Rep. Helen Gahagan Douglas, a Democrat, for the Senate. He was criticized for portraying her as a Communist dupe.

Nixon's anti-Communism ideals, his Western roots, and his youth figured into his selection in 1952 to run for vice president on the ticket headed by Dwight D. Eisenhower. Demands for Nixon's withdrawal followed disclosure that California businessmen had paid some of his Senate office expenses. His televised rebuttal, known as "the Checkers speech" (named for a cocker spaniel given to the Nixons), brought him support from the public and from Eisenhower. The ticket won easily in 1952 and again in 1956.

Eisenhower gave Nixon substantive assignments, including missions to 56 countries. In Moscow in 1959, Nixon won acclaim for his defense of U.S. interests in an impromptu "kitchen debate" with Soviet premier Nikita S. Khrushchev.

Nixon lost the 1960 race for the presidency to John F. Kennedy.

In 1962, Nixon failed in a bid for California's governorship and seemed to be finished as a national candidate. He became a Wall Street lawyer, but kept his old party ties and developed new ones through constant travels to speak for Republicans.

Nixon won the 1968 Republican presidential nomination after a shrewd primary campaign, then made Gov. Spiro T. Agnew of Maryland his surprise choice for vice president. In the election, they edged out the Democratic ticket headed by Vice President Hubert H. Humphrey by 510,314 votes out of 73,212,065 cast.

Committed to winding down the U.S. role in the Vietnamese War, Nixon pursued "Vietnamization"—training and equipping South Vietnamese to do their own fighting. American ground combat forces in Vietnam fell steadily from 540,000 when Nixon took office to none in 1973 when the military draft was ended. But there was heavy continuing use of U.S. air power.

Nixon improved relations with Moscow and reopened the long-closed door to mainland China with a good-will trip there in Feb. 1972. In May of that same year, he visited Moscow and signed agreements on arms limitation and trade expansion and approved plans for a joint U.S.–Soviet space mission in 1975.

Inflation was a campaign issue for Nixon, but he failed to master it as president. On Aug. 15, 1971, with unemployment edging up, Nixon abruptly announced a new economic policy: a 90-day wage-price freeze, stimulative tax cuts, a temporary 10% tariff, and spending cuts. A second phase, imposing guidelines on wage, price, and rent boosts, was announced Oct. 7.

The economy responded in time for the 1972 campaign, in which Nixon played up his foreign-policy achievements. Played down was the burglary on June 17, 1972, of Democratic national headquarters in the Watergate apartment complex in Washington. The Nixon–Agnew reelection campaign cost a record $60 million and swamped the Democratic ticket headed by Sen. George McGovern of South Dakota with a plurality of 17,999,528 out of 77,718,554 votes. Only Massachusetts, with 14 electoral votes, and the District of Columbia, with 3, went for McGovern.

In Jan. 1973, hints of a cover-up emerged at the trial of six men found guilty of the Watergate burglary. With a Senate investigation under way, Nixon announced on April 30 the resignations of his top aides, H. R. Haldeman and John D. Ehrlichman, and the dismissal of White House counsel John Dean III. Dean was the star witness at televised Senate hearings that exposed both a White House cover-up of Watergate and massive illegalities in Republican fund-raising in 1972.

The hearings also disclosed that Nixon had routinely tape-recorded his office meetings and telephone conversations.

On Oct. 10, 1973, Agnew resigned as vice president, then pleaded no-contest to a negotiated federal charge of evading income taxes on alleged bribes. Two days later, Nixon nominated the House minority leader, Rep. Gerald R. Ford of Michigan, as the new vice president. Congress confirmed Ford on Dec. 6, 1973.

In June 1974, Nixon visited Israel and four Arab nations. Then he met in Moscow with Soviet leader Leonid I. Brezhnev and reached preliminary nuclear arms limitation agreements.

But, in the month after his return, Watergate ended the Nixon regime. On July 24 the Supreme Court ordered Nixon to surrender subpoenaed tapes. On July 30, the Judiciary Committee referred three impeachment articles to the full membership. On Aug. 5, Nixon bowed to the Supreme Court and released tapes showing he halted an FBI probe of the Watergate burglary six days after it occurred. It was in effect an admission of obstruction of justice, and impeachment appeared inevitable.

Nixon resigned on Aug. 9, 1974, the first president ever to do so. A month later, President Ford issued an unconditional pardon for any offenses Nixon might have committed as president, thus forestalling possible prosecution.

In 1940, Nixon married Thelma Catherine (Pat) Ryan. They had two daughters, Patricia (Tricia) and Julie, who married Dwight David Eisenhower II, grandson of the former president.

He died on April 22, 1994, in New York City of a massive stroke.

GERALD RUDOLPH FORD was born Leslie King Jr. in Omaha, Neb., on July 14, 1913, the only child of Leslie and Dorothy Gardner King. His parents were divorced in 1915. His mother moved to Grand Rapids, Mich., and married Gerald R. Ford. The boy was renamed for his stepfather.

Ford captained his high school football team in Grand Rapids, and a football scholarship took him to the University of Michigan, where he starred as varsity center before his graduation in 1935. A job as assistant football coach at Yale gave him an opportunity to attend Yale Law School, from which he graduated in the top third of his class in 1941.

He returned to Grand Rapids to practice law, but entered the Navy in April 1942. He saw wartime service in the Pacific on the light aircraft carrier *Monterey* and was a lieutenant commander when he returned to Grand Rapids early in 1946 to resume law practice and dabble in politics.

Ford was elected to Congress in 1948 for the first of his 13 terms in the House. He was soon assigned to the influential Appropriations Committee and rose to become the ranking Republican on the subcommittee on Defense Department appropriations.

As a legislator, Ford described himself as "a moderate on domestic issues, a conservative in fiscal affairs, and a dyed-in-the-wool internationalist." He carried the ball for Pentagon appropriations, was a hawk on the war in Vietnam, and kept a low profile on civil-rights issues.

Ford was also dependable and hard-working and popular with his colleagues. In 1963, he was elected chairman of the House Republican Conference. He served in 1963–1964 as a member of the Warren Commission, which investigated the assassination of John F. Kennedy. A revolt by dissatisfied younger Republicans in 1965 made him minority leader.

On Oct. 12, 1973, Nixon nominated Ford to fill the vice presidency left vacant by Agnew's resignation under fire. It was the first use of the procedures for filling vacancies in the vice presidency laid down in the 25th Amendment to the Constitution, which Ford had helped enact. Once in office, he said he did not believe Nixon had been involved in the

Watergate scandals, but he criticized Nixon's stubborn court battle against releasing tape recordings of Watergate-related conversations for use as evidence. The scandals led to Nixon's unprecedented resignation on Aug. 9, 1974, and Ford was sworn in immediately as the 38th president, the first to enter the White House without winning a national election.

Ford assured the nation when he took office that "our long national nightmare is over" and pledged "openness and candor" in all his actions. He won a warm response from the Democratic 93rd Congress when he said he wanted "a good marriage" rather than a honeymoon with his former colleagues. In Dec. 1974 congressional majorities backed his choice of former New York governor Nelson A. Rockefeller as his vice president.

The cordiality was chilled by Ford's announcement on Sept. 8, 1974, that he had granted an unconditional pardon to Nixon for any crimes he might have committed as president. Although no formal charges were pending, Ford said he feared "ugly passions" would be aroused if Nixon were brought to trial. The pardon was widely criticized.

To fight inflation, the new president first proposed fiscal restraints and spending curbs and a 5% tax surcharge that got nowhere in the Senate and House. Congress again rebuffed Ford in the spring of 1975 when he appealed for emergency military aid to help the governments of South Vietnam and Cambodia resist massive Communist offensives.

Politically, Ford's fortunes improved steadily in the first half of 1975. Badly divided Democrats in Congress were unable to muster votes to override his vetoes of spending bills that exceeded his budget. He faced some right-wing opposition in his own party, but moved to preempt it with an early announcement—on July 8, 1975—of his intention to be a candidate in 1976. During the election campaign, Ford was regarded as a caretaker president lacking in strength and vision. He was defeated in November by Jimmy Carter.

In 1948, Ford married Elizabeth Anne (Betty) Bloomer. They had four children, Michael Gerald, John Gardner, Steven Meigs, and Susan Elizabeth.

JAMES EARL CARTER, JR., was born in the tiny village of Plains, Ga., Oct. 1, 1924, and grew up on the family farm at nearby Archery. Both parents were fifth-generation Georgians. His father, James Earl Carter, was known as a segregationist, but treated his black and white workers equally. Carter's mother, Lillian Gordy, was a matriarchal presence in home and community and opposed the then-prevailing code of racial inequality. The future president was baptized in 1935 in the conservative Southern Baptist Church and spoke often of being a "born again" Christian, although committed to the separation of church and state.

Carter married Rosalynn Smith, a neighbor, in 1946. Their first child, John William, was born a year later in Portsmouth, Va. Their other children are James Earl III, born in Honolulu in 1950; Donnel Jeffrey, born in New London, Conn., in 1952; and Amy Lynn, born in Plains in 1967.

In 1946 Carter was graduated from the U.S. Naval Academy at Annapolis and served in the nuclear-submarine program under Adm. Hyman G. Rickover. In 1954, after his father's death, he resigned from the Navy to take over the family's flourishing warehouse and cotton gin, with several thousand acres for growing seed peanuts.

Carter was elected to the Georgia Senate in 1962. In 1966 he lost the race for governor, but was elected in 1970. His term brought a state government reorganization, sharply reduced agencies, increased economy and efficiency, and new social programs, all with no general tax increase. In 1972 the peanut farmer–politician set his sights on the presidency and in 1974 built a base for himself as he criss-crossed the country as chairman of the Democratic Campaign Committee, appealing for revival and reform. In 1975 he won the support of most of the old Southern civil-rights coalition after endorsement by Rep. Andrew Young, black Democrat from Atlanta, who had been the closest aide to the Rev. Martin Luther King, Jr. Having won 19 out of 31 primaries with a broad appeal to conservatives and liberals, black and white, poor and well-to-do, he defeated Gerald R. Ford in Nov. 1976.

In his one term, Carter fought hard for his programs against resistance from an independent-minded Democratic Congress that frustrated many pet projects although it overrode only two vetoes. Public dissatisfaction with the "stagflation" economy, staff problems, friction with Congress, long gasoline lines, and the months-long Iranian crisis, including the abortive sally in April 1980 to free the hostages also proved problematic for the administration. Yet, assessments of his record have noted many positive elements. There was, for one thing, peace throughout his term, with no American combat deaths and with a brake on the advocates of force. Regarded as perhaps his greatest personal achievements were the Camp David accords between Israel and Egypt and the resulting treaty— the first between Israel and an Arab neighbor. The treaty with China and the Panama Canal treaties were also major achievements. Carter worked for nuclear-arms control. His concern for international human rights was credited with saving lives and reducing torture, and he supported the British policy that ended internecine warfare in Rhodesia, now Zimbabwe. Domestically, his environmental record was a major accomplishment. His judicial appointments won acclaim, with 265 choices for the federal bench that included minority members and women.

In 1980 Carter was renominated on the first ballot after vanquishing Sen. Edward M. Kennedy of Massachusetts in the primaries. In the election campaign, he attacked his rivals, Ronald Reagan and John B. Anderson, independent, with the warning that a Reagan Republican victory would heighten the risk of war and impede civil rights and economic opportunity. In November Carter lost to Reagan, who won 489 electoral college votes and 51% of the popular tally, to 49 electoral votes and 41% for Carter. He was awarded the 2002 Nobel Peace Prize.

RONALD WILSON REAGAN rode to the presidency in 1980 on a tide of resurgent right-wing sentiment among an electorate longing for a distant, simpler era. He left office in Jan. 1989 with two-thirds of the American people approving his performance during his two terms. It was the highest rating for any retiring president since World War II.

Reagan, an actor turned politician, a New Dealer turned conservative, came to films and politics from a thoroughly Middle-American background—middle class, Middle West, and small town. He was born in Tampico, Ill., Feb. 6, 1911, the second son of John Edward Reagan and Nelle Wilson Reagan; the family later moved to Dixon, Ill. His father was a shop clerk and merchant with Democratic sympathies. It was an impoverished family; young Ronald sold homemade popcorn at high school games and worked as a lifeguard to earn money for his college tuition. When his father got a New Deal WPA job, the future president became an ardent Roosevelt Democrat.

Reagan earned a BA degree in 1932 from Eureka (Ill.) College, where a photographic memory aided in his studies and in debating and college theatricals. During the Depression, he made $100 a week as a sports announcer for radio station WHO in Des Moines, Iowa. His career as a film and TV actor stretched from 1937 to 1966, and his salary climbed to $3,500 a week. As a World War II captain in army film studios, Reagan recoiled from what he saw as the laziness of civil service workers, and moved to the Right. As president of the Screen Actors Guild, he resisted what he considered a Communist plot to subvert the film industry. With advancing age, Reagan left leading-man roles and became a television spokesman for the General Electric Company.

With oratorical skill as his trademark, Reagan became an active Republican. In 1966, at the behest of a small group of conservative businessmen, he ran for governor of California with a pledge to cut spending; he was elected by almost a million votes over the political veteran, Democratic governor Edmund G. Brown. Reelected to a second term, he served as governor until 1975.

In the 1980 election battle against Jimmy Carter, Reagan broadened his appeal by espousing moderate policies, gaining much of his support from disaffected Democrats and blue-collar workers. The incoming administration immediately set out to "turn the government around" with a new economic program. Over strenuous congressional opposition, Reagan pushed through his "supply side" economic program to stimulate production and control inflation through tax cuts and sharp reductions in government spending. However, in 1982, as the economy declined into the worst recession in 40 years, the president's popularity slipped and support for supply-side economics faded.

Barely three months into his first term, Reagan was the target of an assassin's bullet; his courageous comeback won public admiration. The president also won high acclaim for his nomination of Sandra Day O'Connor as the first woman on the Supreme Court. His later nominations met increasing opposition and did much to tilt the Court's orientation to the Right.

Internationally, Reagan confronted numerous problems in his first term. In an effort to establish order on the Caribbean island of Grenada and eliminate the Cuban military presence there, Reagan ordered an invasion of the tiny nation on Oct. 25, 1983. The troops met strong resistance from Cuban military personnel on the island but soon occupied it. Another military effort, in Lebanon, ended in failure, however. U.S. Marines engaged as part of a multinational peacekeeping force in Beirut were forced to withdraw in 1984 after a disastrous terrorist attack left 241 marines dead.

With the economy improving and inflation under control, the popular president won reelection in a landslide in 1984. Domestically, a tax reform bill that Reagan backed became law. But the constantly growing budget deficit remained an irritant, with the president and Congress persistently at odds over priorities in spending for defense and domestic programs. Congress was also increasingly reluctant to increase spending for the Nicaraguan "Contras." But even severe critics praised Reagan's restrained but decisive handling of the crisis following the hijacking of an American plane in Beirut by Muslim extremists. The attack on Libya in April 1986 galvanized the nation, although it drew scathing disapproval from the NATO alliance.

Reagan's popularity with the public dipped sharply in 1986 when the Iran-Contra scandal broke, shortly after the Democrats gained control of the Senate. The weeks-long congressional hearings in the summer of 1987 heard an array of administration officials, present and former, reveal a web of deceit and undercover maneuvering in the White House. Yet the president's personal reputation remained untouched; on Aug. 12, 1987, he told the nation that he had not known of questionable activities but agreed that he was ultimately accountable.

Reagan's place in history will rest, perhaps, on the short- and intermediate-range missile treaty consummated on a cordial visit to the Soviet Union that he had once reviled as an "evil empire." Its provisions, including a ground-breaking agreement on verification inspection, were formulated in four days of summit talks in Moscow in May 1988 with the Soviet leader, Mikhail S. Gorbachev. Reagan could point to numerous domestic achievements as well: sharp cuts in income tax rates, creating economic growth without inflation, and reducing the unemployment rate, among others. He failed, however, to win the "Reagan Revolution" on such issues as abortion and school prayer.

Reagan married his wife, Nancy, four years after his divorce from the screen actress Jane Wyman. The children from his first marriage are Maureen, his daughter by Wyman, and Michael, an adopted son. He had two children by Nancy: Patricia and Ron. Reagan suffered from Alzheimer's disease, which he developed around 1994, and died in Los Angeles on June 5, 2004.

GEORGE HERBERT WALKER BUSH was born June 12, 1924, in Milton, Mass., to Prescott and Dorothy Bush. The family later moved to Connecticut. The youth studied at the elite Phillips Academy in Andover, Mass.

The future president joined the Navy after war broke out and at 18 became the Navy's youngest commissioned pilot, serving from 1942 to 1945, and was awarded the Distinguished Flying Cross. He fought the Japanese on 58 missions and was shot down once.

After the war, Bush earned an economics degree and a Phi Beta Kappa key in two and a half years at Yale University.

In 1945 Bush married Barbara Pierce of Rye, N.Y., daughter of a magazine publisher. With his bride, Bush moved to Texas instead of entering his father's investment banking business. There he founded his oil company and by 1980 reported an estimated wealth of $1.4 million.

Throughout his whole career, Bush had the backing of an established family, headed by his father, Prescott Bush, who was elected to the Senate from Connecticut in 1952. The family helped the young patrician become established in his early business ventures, a rich uncle raising most of the capital required for founding the oil company.

In the 1960s, Bush won two contests for a Texas Republican seat in the House of Representatives, but lost two bids for a Senate seat. After Bush's second race for the Senate, President Nixon appointed him U.S. delegate to the United Nations and he later became Republican National Committee chairman. He headed the U.S. liaison office in Beijing before becoming Director of Central Intelligence. In 1980 Bush became Reagan's running mate despite earlier criticism of Reagan "voodoo economics" and by the 1984 election had won acclaim for his devotion to Reagan's conservative agenda.

The vice president entered the 1988 presidential campaign and easily defeated Democrat Michael Dukakis. Bush's choice of Sen. Dan Quayle of Indiana as a running mate provoked criticism and ridicule that continued even after the administration was in office. Nonetheless Bush strongly defended his choice. George Herbert Walker Bush became president on Jan. 20, 1989, with his theme harmony and conciliation after the often-turbulent Reagan years.

Bush's early Cabinet choices reflected a pragmatic desire for an efficient, nonideological government. And with his usual cautious instinct, in 1990 he nominated to the Supreme Court the scholarly David H. Souter, with broadly conservative views.

In his first year, Bush was confronted with the Lebanese hostage crisis, the *Exxon Valdez* oil spill in Alaska, and the ongoing war against drug trafficking. His public approval soared following the invasion of Panama in late 1989. But a staggering budget deficit and the savings and loan crisis caused the president's popularity to dip sharply in his second year. This plunge followed Bush's recantation of his campaign "no new taxes" pledge as he sat down with congressional leaders to tame the budget deficit and deal with a faltering economy.

In 1991, the president emerged as the leader of an international coalition of Western democracies, Japan, and even some Arab states that came together to free Kuwait following an invasion of the country by Iraq in Aug. 1990. The coalition forces defeated Iraq in only a little more than a month after Operation Desert Storm was launched on Jan. 16–17, 1991, and a nation grateful at feeling the end of the "Vietnam syndrome" gave the president an 89% approval rating. However, the high rating fell as the year went on, as doubts persisted about the war's outcome—Iraqi president Saddam Hussein remained in power and persistently avoided complying with the terms of the peace treaty—and as concerns began to grow about the faltering U.S. economy and other domestic problems.

A major Bush accomplishment in 1991 was the Strategic Arms Reduction Treaty (START), signed in July with Soviet president Mikhail S. Gorbachev at their fourth summit conference, marking the end of the long weapons buildup.

In the 1992 presidential election, Bush was defeated by Gov. Bill Clinton of Arkansas.

The Bushes have four sons, George, Jeb, Neil, and Marvin, and a daughter, Dorothy. Another daughter, Robin, died at age three from leukemia. Son George served as governor of Texas from 1995 to 2000, when he was elected the 43rd U.S. president. Jeb Bush was elected governor of Florida in 1998.

WILLIAM JEFFERSON CLINTON was born William Jefferson Blythe IV in Hope, Ark., on Aug. 19, 1946. He was named for his father, who was killed in an automobile accident before Clinton's birth. Virginia Kelley, his mother, eventually married Roger Clinton, a car dealer, whose surname the future president later adopted.

In high school in Hot Springs, Ark., Clinton considered becoming a doctor, but politics beckoned after a meeting with President John F. Kennedy in Washington, DC, on a Boys' Nation trip. He earned a BS in international affairs in 1968 at Georgetown University, having spent his junior year working for Arkansas senator J. William Fulbright. He was a Rhodes scholar at Oxford between 1968 and 1970. He then attended Yale Law School, where he met his future wife, Hillary Rodham, a Wellesley graduate. The couple has one child, Chelsea.

Clinton taught at the University of Arkansas (1974–1976), was elected state attorney general (1976), and in 1979 became the nation's youngest governor. But he was defeated for reelection in 1980 by voters irate at a rise in the state's automobile license fees. In 1982 he was elected again. This time he reined in liberal tendencies to accommodate conservative bent of the voters.

Clinton became the 42nd U.S. president following a turbulent political campaign. He overcame vigorous personal attacks on his character and on his actions during the Vietnam War, which he actively opposed. The "character issue" stemmed from allegations of infidelity, which Clinton refuted in a television interview in which he and Hillary avowed their relationship was solid. Throughout his term in office, Clinton was dogged by allegations relating to the Whitewater real estate deal in which he and Hillary were involved prior to the 1992 election. Though the Clintons were never accused of any wrongdoing, partners in the venture were convicted of fraud and conspiracy in a trial in 1996.

The problems faced by the new president were as daunting as they were varied. In Jan. 1993 he became embroiled with the military leadership over his campaign pledge to allow homosexuals to serve openly in the armed services. He ultimately agreed to a compromise, dubbed the "don't ask, don't tell" policy. Clinton's first year also saw him wrangling with Congress over the federal budget and economic policy.

In his second year, Clinton was faced with acrimonious battles over health care, welfare reform, and crime prevention. A health care reform package crafted by his wife failed to gain sufficient support. Clinton had to reduce his objective from massive overhaul to incremental reform.

Clinton won major victories with the passage of the North American Free Trade Agreement (NAFTA), which took effect Jan. 1, 1994, and the Global Agreement on Tariffs and Trade (GATT), which led to the establishment in 1995 of the World Trade Organization (WTO). Congress also approved a deficit reduction bill, rules allowing abortion counseling in federally funded clinics, a waiting period for handgun purchases (the Brady Bill), and a national service program.

Foreign affairs became a proving ground for Clinton, since he has been elected primarily on a domestic economic agenda. He improved his international image when the Israel–Jordan peace agreement was signed at the White House in the summer of 1994 by Israeli prime minister Yitzhak Rabin and Jordan's King Hussein. In the fall of that year, the administration succeeded in restoring Haiti's ousted president, Jean-Bertrand Aristide, to power. Clinton scored again by bolstering Russian president Boris Yeltsin's popularity with promises of economic aid.

The problems in Eastern Europe were Clinton's next big challenge. Though he wanted desperately to end the brutal ethnic cleansing in Bosnia, he did not want to commit American ground troops to do so. A peace accord involving American peacekeeping troops was ultimately signed in Dayton, Ohio, in Nov. 1995.

The 1994 elections resulted in a Republican-controlled Congress, and 1995 was largely a tug-of-war between the White House and Capitol Hill over budget-balancing and other key points of the GOP's "Contract with America," crafted by Speaker of the House Newt Gingrich.

In 1996, aided by a booming economy, Clinton won reelection to a second term, becoming the first Democratic president since Franklin D. Roosevelt to do so. The country's general prosperity also made it possible in 1997 for Clinton and the Republicans to reach an agreement to balance the federal budget in three decades.

However, the character issues that had followed Clinton for years soon began to emerge once again. A series of investigations was begun to determine whether Clinton and Vice President Gore had participated in questionable fund-raising practices in their 1996 campaign.

As his tenure wore on, Clinton came under increasing pressure from Kenneth Starr, the independent counsel who in 1994 took over the investigation of the Clintons' involvement in the Whitewater land deal. Over time, Starr's brief was expanded to include other matters, such as the suicide of White House lawyer Vincent Foster, the handling of firings in the White House travel office, and allegations of sexual misconduct by Clinton.

In Jan. 1998, Clinton was called to testify in a long-pending sexual harassment suit brought against him by Paula Corbin Jones, a former Arkansas state employee. The hearing also addressed another scandalous relationship, and in his testimony, Clinton denied that he had had a sexual relationship with a young White House intern, Monica Lewinsky, and that he had attempted to cover it up. Although a federal judge in Arkansas threw out the Jones sexual harassment suit in April 1998, by this time the Lewinsky affair had become the focus of Kenneth Starr's investigation as well as a national obsession.

Finally, on Aug. 17, 1998, after relentless media attention, leaks, and news of Lewinsky's upcoming testimony, Clinton made history by becoming the first U.S. president to testify in front of a grand jury in an investigation of his own possibly criminal conduct. In an address to the nation that evening, he admitted to having had an "inappropriate relationship" with Lewinsky, but reaffirmed that he had not asked anyone to lie about or cover up the affair.

In spite of the scandalous outcome of events, Clinton's overall popularity among Americans remained high. The country seemed willing to ignore his weaknesses in character, much as they had in the 1992 elections, as long as the economy was good, his policies were popular, and the United States remained strong abroad.

On Sept. 9, Starr—a conservative Republican whose investigation was seen by Clinton supporters as a politically inspired vendetta—delivered his report to the House of Representatives. While the report outlined 11 possible grounds for impeachment, none stemmed from the initial subjects of the investigation, including the Whitewater real estate deal. The real focus of the accusations seemed to be Clinton's moral conduct, and the "Starr Report" graphically detailed his sexual affair.

Despite the American population's general disapproval of a trial, reflected in poll after poll, Congress moved forward with impeachment proceedings and on Dec. 19, Clinton became the second president in American history to be impeached. Two of the four articles of impeachment—Article I, grand jury perjury, and Article III, obstruction of justice—passed, the votes drawn along party lines. After a Senate trial in Jan.–Feb. 1999, Clinton was acquitted on both counts.

While the impeachment trial overshadowed all other activity in Washington for a good portion of 1998, Clinton was forced to respond to continued problems with Iraq at the end of the year. In December, Saddam Hussein blocked a weapons inspection by the United Nations. The UN responded with airstrikes that would continue on a nearly daily basis for the next three months, and then off and on through the spring and summer, as Iraq taunted the U.S. and its allies further by shooting at jets patrolling the no-fly zones set up after the Persian Gulf war.

In the spring of 1999, reports grew of continued ethnic cleansing in the Serbian province of Kosovo. Clinton and his British counterpart, Tony Blair, led the push for NATO intervention, which resulted in a 78-day bombing campaign against Serbia beginning in March. Although Clinton received some sharp criticism for holding back on the deployment of NATO ground troops, he was vindicated when Serbian president Slobodan Milosevic signed a peace treaty on June 9.

In his final year of office, the president maintained a relatively low profile but took several major trips overseas, to South Asia, Europe, and Africa. He also prepared for the 2000 elections, lending his support not only to presidential hopeful Al Gore, but also to his wife, Hillary Clinton, who successfully ran for U.S. senator from New York.

On Jan. 19, 2001, the day before he left office, Clinton agreed to a five-year suspension of his Arkansas law license and his paying of a $25,000 fine to the Arkansas Bar Association. In exchange, Kenneth Starr's successor, Robert Ray, agreed to close the Whitewater probe, ending the threat of criminal liability for Mr. Clinton after he left office.

GEORGE WALKER BUSH was born on July 6, 1946, in New Haven, Conn., the first child of future president George H. W. Bush. In 1948, the family moved to Odessa, Tex., where the senior Bush went to work in the oil business. George W. grew up mainly in Midland, Tex., and Houston, and later attended two of his father's alma maters, Phillips Academy in Andover, Mass., and Yale.

After graduating from Yale with a history degree in 1968, Bush joined the Texas Air National Guard, where he served as a part-time fighter pilot until 1973. After receiving an MBA from Harvard Business School in 1975, he returned to Texas, where he established his own oil and gas business. In 1977 he met and married his wife, Laura Welch, a librarian. The couple has twin daughters, Jenna and Barbara, born in 1981.

Coming from a prominent political family—his grandfather Prescott Bush had been a senator from Connecticut and his father a U.S. congressman and political appointee—George W. had been immersed in politics since childhood. In 1977 he entered the fray himself, unsuccessfully running for U.S. Congress from the West Texas district that included his hometown of Midland.

Following his defeat, Bush returned to the oil business. In 1985, however, oil prices fell sharply, and Bush's company verged on collapse until it was acquired by a Dallas firm. Bush then headed to Washington to become a paid adviser to his father's successful 1988 presidential campaign. After the election, Bush returned to Texas and assembled a group of investors to buy the Texas Rangers.

Bush again entered politics in 1993, running for the Texas governorship. Although he had a tough opponent in the immensely popular incumbent Ann Richards, he created a clear agenda focused on issues such as education and juvenile justice and won with 53% of the vote. He was reelected in 1998, not long before he announced plans to run for president.

During the 2000 campaign, Bush adhered closely to the traditional conservative line, favoring small government, tax cuts, a strong military, and opposing gun control and abortion. His choice of running mate, Dick Cheney, secretary of defense during his father's administration, provided his campaign with seasoned Washington political experience.

With the country in a state of general prosperity, the 2000 election between George W. Bush and Vice President Al Gore was perceived to be one of the least dynamic on issues. As it turned out, the race was one of the closest in the country's history. By early evening on election night, it was apparent that whoever won Florida would win the election. Bush's razor-thin margin of about 1,200 votes prompted an automatic recount. The case ultimately ended up in the U.S. Supreme Court. Bush officially became the president-elect on Dec. 13, after the Supreme Court reversed a decision by the Florida Supreme Court to allow manual recounts of ballots in some Florida counties, contending that such a partial recount violated the Constitution's equal protection and due process guarantees. With Florida in his column, Bush won the presidency with 271 electoral votes, just one more than he needed, although he lost the popular vote by half a million. The divided 5–4 Supreme Court decision generated enormous controversy, with critics asserting that the Supreme Court, and not the electorate, had effectively determined the outcome of the presidential election.

The top item on Bush's domestic agenda—a $1.35 trillion tax cut over 11 years—was swiftly enacted in June 2001. In his first year in office, President Bush also championed an antimissile defense system, meant to intercept long-range missiles lobbed at U.S. shores.

Opponents of the plan argued that it was technologically unfeasible and astronomically expensive. Bush's early foreign policy was defined by the rejection of a number of international treaties that the White House felt were detrimental to American interests, including the Kyoto treaty on global warming, the biological weapons convention banning germ warfare, and a treaty to establish an international war-crimes court. Bush also withdrew from the 1972 Antiballistic Missile Treaty, the basis for three decades of nuclear stability with the Soviet Union, but at the same time succeeded in persuading Russia to agree to a landmark treaty that would cut U.S. and Russian nuclear weapons stockpiles by two-thirds over the next decade.

The terrorist attacks on the World Trade Center and the Pentagon on Sept. 11, 2001, irrevocably altered the direction of the Bush presidency; his primary focus became the war on international terrorism. Bush shored up enormous support from the international community to fight terrorism worldwide. On Oct. 7, the U.S. and Britain began air strikes against Afghanistan, after the Taliban government repeatedly refused to surrender Osama bin Laden, the mastermind of the Sept. 11 attacks. The Taliban collapsed on Dec. 9, but despite this outstanding military success, bin Laden remained at large.

National security efforts included creating the Department of Homeland Security, a domestic security cabinet agency that consolidated 20 federal agencies in a massive government reorganization. More controversial was the passage of the USA PATRIOT Act, antiterrorism legislation that presented law enforcement officials with sweeping new powers to conduct searches without warrants, and to detain and deport individuals in secret.

President Bush's broad characterizations of the terrorist threat led him to expand the scope of his foreign policy from al-Qaeda and other terrorist organizations to other regimes hostile to the United States, regardless of their connection to the Sept. 11 attacks. Following the war in Afghanistan, Bush designated Iraq as the primary new threat to American security. He famously labeled Iraq, along with North Korea and Iran, as part of an "axis of evil." Over the course of 2002, President Bush announced that the U.S. foreign strategy of containment and deterrence was an outdated cold war policy. In an age of terrorism, he maintained, the United States could no longer wait by defensively until a potential threat to its security grew into an actual one—a preemptive strike was called for. In Sept. 2002, Bush addressed the UN, challenging the organization to swiftly enforce its own resolutions against Iraq, or else the U.S. would have no choice but to act on its own. Many world leaders expressed alarm at this shift in U.S. policy, which stressed unilateralism rather than international consensus. The alleged existence of weapons of mass destruction, Iraq's links to terrorism, and Saddam Hussein's despotism and human rights abuses were cited as the casus belli for "regime change." The UN Security Council unanimously approved a resolution imposing tough new arms inspections on Iraq, but after three months of inspections that resulted in only modest Iraqi cooperation, U.S. patience ran out: on March 19, President Bush declared war on Iraq and U.S. troops, along with their British allies, began bombing Baghdad. By April 9, Baghdad had fallen, and by May 1, combat was officially declared over.

The official phase of the war was swift, but the post-war reconstruction period proved far more difficult. The country was enveloped in violence and chaos and its infrastructure was in ruins, As American casualties grew and costs mounted (the Pentagon estimated $1 billion per week), the U.S.'s hasty go-it-alone policy began to haunt them: only about 10,000 foreign troops came to the aid of American and British soldiers in Iraq. While the Bush administration successfully turned over sovereignty to an interim Iraqi government in June 2004, by the fall of 2004, pockets of Iraq were essentially under the control of insurgents. Progress in rebuilding Iraq's shattered infrastructure was also dismal: by fall 2004, just 6% ($1 billion) of the funds approved by Congress in 2003 had in fact been used on reconstruction projects. President Bush assured the country that despite these difficulties, the United States would stay the course until Iraq emerged as a free and democratic country.

More than a year-and-a-half of searching for Iraq's weapons of mass destruction—one of the prime reasons the Bush and Blair administrations cited for launching the war—yielded no hard evidence, and the administration and its intelligence agencies came under fire. There were also mounting allegations that the existence of these weapons and their imminent threat to American security was exaggerated or distorted as a pretext to justify the war. The Senate Intelligence Committee's unanimous, bipartisan "Report on Pre-War Intelligence on Iraq," harshly criticized the CIA: "most of the major key judgments" on Iraq's weapons of mass destruction were "either overstated, or were not supported by, the underlying intelligence report." The report disputed the CIA's assertions that Iraq was reconstituting its nuclear program and that it had chemical and biological weapons, and also concluded that there was no "established formal relationship" between al-Qaeda and Saddam Hussein. With the justifications for the war evaporating, the Bush administration began emphasizing that the removal of dictator Saddam Hussein had been grounds enough for waging war, and that the United States was more secure as a result of it.

Critics of the administration's policy in Iraq described it as a distraction from the war on terror, preventing the United States from effectively battling the war on its genuine fronts. Osama bin Laden was still at large, and despite the U.S. intervention in Afghanistan, the country remained rife with warlords, Taliban, and al-Qaeda operatives. Since the start of the U.S. war in Iraq, the two remaining countries in the "axis of evil," North Korea and Iran, had grown into alarming nuclear threats. The Bush administration's diplomatic efforts made little headway against Iran and North Korea's defiance and evasion.

Early in his presidency, Bush disengaged the U.S. from the Palestinian-Israeli crisis. Following the war in Iraq, which had been fought in part to introduce democracy to the Middle East, Bush presented a "road map" for peace to Israel and the Palestinians in May 2003. But within months, the escalating violence on both sides made it clear that the road map was going nowhere.

On the domestic front, President Bush promoted an "ownership society" that would give Americans more control over health care, education, and retirement. In Jan. 2002, he passed the No Child Left Behind Act, a federal program dedicated to improving schools across the country. Several states have sued the government over its commitment to funding the law. In June 2003 he signed into law the largest expansion of Medicare since its creation. The law provided prescription drug coverage under Medicare for the first time.

In early 2003, President Bush unveiled a sweeping economic stimulus plan that characteristically centered around tax cuts. The plan, in its original form, would have cut taxes by $670 billion over ten years; Congress approved a $350 billion version. Although all workers were to benefit from the tax plan, it strongly favored two groups: two-parent households with several children and the wealthy—nearly half the proposed tax benefits were reserved for the richest 10% of American taxpayers. Critics of the plan, including fiscally conservative Republicans, argued that it was unsound to offer tax cuts while the country was involved in an expensive war and in the midst of a jobless recovery. The federal budget deficit, according to the nonpartisan Congressional Budget Office, reached a record $412 billion in 2004. The White House countered that the Bush tax cuts had in fact kept the recession remarkably shallow and brief.

The 2004 presidential campaign between the president and Democratic senator John Kerry was one of the most closely followed and heated races in recent history. Terrorism, the war in Iraq, tax cuts, health care, the economy, and the deficit were the major issues. Kerry accused the president of mismanaging the war on Iraq and the fight against terrorism and promised to roll back the Bush tax cuts for the wealthiest Americans. The president accused his opponent of being a "flip-flopper" on issues and of not having the leadership to fight the war on terror. On Nov. 3, President Bush won reelection with 286 electoral votes and 51% of the popular vote. Moral values and fighting terrorism were cited as the two main issues that won the president his second term.

In the first year of his second term, Bush's priority was the restructuring of Social Security, but despite months of campaigning, the president failed to convince the electorate that the program was in need of a major overhaul. Legislative accomplishments included the passage of the Central American Free Trade Agreement (CAFTA), an energy bill, which did not, however, address Americans' growing concern over high fuel prices.

Iraq's continued insurgency, lack of political stability, and the acknowledgment that only a small number of Iraqi forces were capable of replacing American troops stationed in the country led to increased domestic discontent. In the face of growing American casualties and the absence of a clear strategy for winning the protracted war beyond "staying the course," the president's approval ratings dipped to their lowest point—40% in Aug. 2005. In early September, the delayed and inept handling of Hurricane Katrina's emergency relief efforts led to widespread criticism of the Bush administration, even among its Republican base. To bolster his image as a strong leader in a crisis—one of the major factors responsible for his reelection—the president acknowledged mistakes in the government's response and promised a massive reconstruction effort.

Senate and House Standing Committees, 109th Congress

Committees of the Senate

Agriculture, Nutrition, and Forestry (20 members)
Chairman: Saxby Chambliss (Ga..)
Ranking Dem.: Tom Harkin (Iowa)

Appropriations (28 members)
Chairman: Thad Cochran (Miss.)
Ranking Dem.: Robert C. Byrd (W.Va.)

Armed Services (24 members)
Chairman: John Warner (Va.)
Ranking Dem.: Carl Levin (Mich.)

Banking, Housing, and Urban Affairs (20 members)
Chairman: Richard C. Shelby (Ala.)
Ranking Dem.: Paul S. Sarbanes (Md.)

Budget (22 members)
Chairman: Judd Gregg (N.H.)
Ranking Dem.: Kent Conrad (N.D.)

Commerce, Science, and Transportation (22 members)
Chairman: Ted Stevens (Alaska)
Ranking Dem.: Daniel K. Inouye (Hawaii)

Energy and Natural Resources (22 members)
Chairman: Pete V. Domenici (N.M.)
Ranking Dem.: Jeff Bingaman (N.M.)

Environment and Public Works (18 members)
Chairman: James M. Inhofe (Okla.)
Ranking Member: James Jeffords (Vt.)

Finance (20 members)
Chairman: Charles E. Grassley (Iowa)
Ranking Dem.: Max Baucus (Mont.)

Foreign Relations (18 members)
Chairman: Richard G. Lugar (Ind.)
Ranking Dem.: Joseph R. Biden, Jr. (Del.)

Health, Education, Labor, and Pensions (20 members)
Chairman: Mike Enzi (Wyo.)
Ranking Dem.: Edward M. Kennedy (Mass.)

Homeland Security and Governmental Affairs (16 members)
Chairman: Susan Collins (Maine)
Ranking Dem.: Joseph Lieberman (Conn.)

Judiciary (18 members)
Chairman: Arlen Specter (Pa.)
Ranking Dem.: Patrick J. Leahy (Vt.)

Rules and Administration (18 members)
Chairman: Trent Lott (Miss.)
Ranking Dem.: Christopher Dodd (Conn.)

Small Business (18 members)
Chairman: Olympia J. Snowe (Maine)
Ranking Dem.: John Kerry (Mass.)

Veterans' Affairs (14 members)
Chairman: Larry Craig (Idaho)
Ranking Dem.: Daniel Akaka (Hawaii)

Senate Special or Select Committees

Aging (19 members)
Chairman: Gordon Smith (Oregon)
Ranking Dem.: Herb Kohl (Wis.)

Ethics (6 members)
Chairman: George V. Voinovich (Ohio)
Ranking Dem.: Tim Johnson (South Dakota)

Indian Affairs (14 members)
Chairman: John McCain (Ariz.)
Ranking Dem.: Byron L. Dorgan (N.D.)

Intelligence (15 members)
Chairman: Pat Roberts (Kans.)
Ranking Dem.: John D. Rockefeller IV (W. Va.)

Committees of the House

Agriculture (46 members)
Chairman: Bob Goodlatte (Va.)
Ranking Dem.: Collin C. Peterson (Minn.)

Appropriations (66 members)
Chairman: Jerry Lewis (Calif.)
Ranking Dem.: David R. Obey (Wis.)

Armed Services (66 members)
Chairman: Duncan Hunter (Calif.)
Ranking Dem.: Ike Skelton (Mo.)

Budget (39 members)
Chairman: Jim Nussle (Iowa)
Ranking Dem.: John M. Spratt, Jr. (S.C.)

Education and the Workforce (49 members)
Chairman: John A. Boehner (Ohio)
Ranking Dem.: George Miller (Calif.)

Energy and Commerce (58 members)
Chairman: Joe Barton (Tex.)
Ranking Dem.: John D. Dingell (Mich.)

Financial Services (72 members)
Chairman: Michael G. Oxley (Ohio)
Ranking Dem.: Barney Frank (Mass.)

Government Reform (41 members)
Chairman: Tom Davis (Va.)
Ranking Dem.: Henry A. Waxman (Calif.)

Homeland Security (34 members)
Chairman: Peter King (N.Y.)
Ranking Dem.: Bennie G. Thompson (Miss.)

House Administration (9 members)
Chairman: Robert W. Ney (Ohio)
Ranking Dem.: Juanita Millender-McDonald (Calif.)

International Relations (49 members)
Chairman: Henry J. Hyde (Ill.)
Ranking Dem.: Tom Lantos (Calif.)

Judiciary (40 members)
Chairman: F. James Sensenbrenner, Jr. (Wis.)
Ranking Dem.: John Conyers, Jr. (Mich.)

Resources (52 members)
Chairman: Richard Pombo (Calif.)
Ranking Dem.: Nick J. Rahall II (W. Va.)

Rules (13 members)
Chairman: David Dreier (Calif.)
Ranking Dem.: Louise McIntosh Slaughter (N.Y.)

Science (44 members)
Chairman: Sherwood L. Boehlert (N.Y.)
Ranking Dem.: Bart Gordon (Tenn.)

Small Business (36 members)
Chairman: Donald A. Manzullo (Ill.)
Ranking Dem.: Nydia M. Velázquez (N.Y.)

Standards of Official Conduct (10 members)
Chairman: Doc Hastings (Wash.)
Ranking Dem.: Alan B. Mollohan (W. Va.)

Transportation and Infrastructure (75 members)
Chairman: Don Young (Alaska)
Ranking Dem.: James L. Oberstar (Minn.)

Veterans' Affairs (28 members)
Chairman: Steve Buyer (Ind.)
Ranking Dem.: Lane Evans (Ill.)

Ways and Means (41 members)
Chairman: William M. Thomas (Calif.)
Ranking Dem.: Charles B. Rangel (N.Y.)

Speakers of the House of Representatives

Dates served	Congress	Name and state	Dates served	Congress	Name and state
1789–1791	1	Frederick A. C. Muhlenberg (Pa.)	1869–1875	41–43	James G. Blaine (Maine)
1791–1793	2	Jonathan Trumbull (Conn.)	1875–1876	44	Michael C. Kerr (Ind.)[6]
1793–1795	3	Frederick A. C. Muhlenberg (Pa.)	1876–1881	44–46	Samuel J. Randall (Pa.)
1795–1799	4–5	Jonathan Dayton (N.J.)[1]	1881–1883	47	J. Warren Keifer (Ohio)
1799–1801	6	Theodore Sedgwick (Mass.)	1883–1889	48–50	John G. Carlisle (Ky.)
1801–1807	7–9	Nathaniel Macon (N.C.)	1889–1891	51	Thomas B. Reed (Maine)
1807–1811	10–11	Joseph B. Varnum (Mass.)	1891–1895	52–53	Charles F. Crisp (Ga.)
1811–1814	12–13	Henry Clay (Ky.)[2]	1895–1899	54–55	Thomas B. Reed (Maine)
1814–1815	13	Langdon Cheves (S.C.)	1899–1903	56–57	David B. Henderson (Iowa)
1815–1820	14–16	Henry Clay (Ky.)[3]	1903–1911	58–61	Joseph G. Cannon (Ill.)
1820–1821	16	John W. Taylor (N.Y.)	1911–1919	62–65	Champ Clark (Mo.)
1821–1823	17	Philip P. Barbour (Va.)	1919–1925	66–68	Frederick H. Gillett (Mass.)
1823–1825	18	Henry Clay (Ky.)	1925–1931	69–71	Nicholas Longworth (Ohio)
1825–1827	19	John W. Taylor (N.Y.)	1931–1933	72	John N. Garner (Tex.)
1827–1834	20–23	Andrew Stevenson (Va.)[4]	1933–1934	73	Henry T. Rainey (Ill.)[7]
1834–1835	23	John Bell (Tenn.)	1935–1936	74	Joseph W. Byrns (Tenn.)[8]
1835–1839	24–25	James K. Polk (Tenn.)	1936–1940	74–76	William B. Bankhead (Ala.)[9]
1839–1841	26	Robert M. T. Hunter (Va.)	1940–1947	76–79	Sam Rayburn (Tex.)
1841–1843	27	John White (Ky.)	1947–1949	80	Joseph W. Martin, Jr. (Mass.)
1843–1845	28	John W. Jones (Va.)	1949–1953	81–82	Sam Rayburn (Tex.)
1845–1847	29	John W. Davis (Ind.)	1953–1955	83	Joseph W. Martin, Jr. (Mass.)
1847–1849	30	Robert C. Winthrop (Mass.)	1955–1961	84–87	Sam Rayburn (Tex.)[10]
1849–1851	31	Howell Cobb (Ga.)	1963–1971	87–91	John W. McCormack (Mass.)[11]
1851–1855	32–33	Linn Boyd (Ky.)	1971–1977	92–94	Carl Albert (Okla.)[12]
1855–1857	34	Nathaniel P. Banks (Mass.)	1977–1987	95–99	Thomas P. O'Neill, Jr. (Mass.)[13]
1857–1859	35	James L. Orr (S.C.)	1987–1989	100–101	James C. Wright, Jr. (Tex.)[14]
1859–1861	36	Wm. Pennington (N.J.)	1989–1995	101–103	Thomas S. Foley (Wash.)
1861–1863	37	Galusha A. Grow (Pa.)	1995–1999	104–105	Newt Gingrich (Ga.)[15]
1863–1869	38–40	Schuyler Colfax (Ind.)	1999–	106–	Dennis Hastert (Ill.)
1869–1869	40	Theodore M. Pomeroy (N.Y.)[5]			

1. George Dent (Md.) was elected Speaker pro tempore for April 20 and May 28, 1798. 2. Resigned during second session of 13th Congress. 3. Resigned between first and second sessions of 16th Congress. 4. Resigned during first session of 23rd Congress. 5. Elected Speaker and served the day of adjournment. 6. Died between first and second sessions of 44th Congress. During first session, there were two Speakers pro tempore: Samuel S. Cox (N.Y.), appointed for Feb. 17, May 12, and June 19, 1876, and Milton Sayler (Ohio), appointed for June 4, 1876. 7. Died in 1934 after adjournment of second session of 73rd Congress. 8. Died during second session of 74th Congress. 9. Died during third session of 76th Congress. 10. Died between first and second sessions of 87th Congress. 11. Not a candidate in 1970 election. 12. Not a candidate in 1976 election. 13. Not a candidate in 1986 election. 14. Resigned during first session of 101st Congress. 15. Resigned Jan. 3, 1999, three days before the first session of the 106th Congress. *Source: Congressional Directory.*

Floor Leaders of the Senate

Democratic	Republican
Gilbert M. Hitchcock, Neb. (Min. 1919–20)	Charles Curtis, Kan. (Maj. 1925–29)
Oscar W. Underwood, Ala. (Min. 1920–23)	James E. Watson, Ind. (Maj. 1929–33)
Joseph T. Robinson, Ark. (Min. 1923–33, Maj. 1933–37)	Charles L. McNary, Ore. (Min. 1933–44)
Alben W. Barkley, Ky. (Maj. 1937–46, Min. 1947–48)	Wallace H. White, Jr., Maine (Min. 1944–47, Maj. 1947–48)
Scott W. Lucas, Ill. (Maj. 1949–50)	Kenneth S. Wherry, Neb. (Min. 1949–51)
Ernest W. McFarland, Ariz. (Maj. 1951–52)	Styles Bridges, N.H. (Min. 1951–52)
Lyndon B. Johnson, Tex. (Min. 1953–54, Maj. 1955–60)	Robert A. Taft, Ohio (Maj. 1953)
Mike Mansfield, Mont. (Maj. 1961–77)	William F. Knowland, Calif. (Maj. 1953–54, Min. 1955–58)
Robert C. Byrd, W. Va. (Maj. 1977–81, Min. 1981–86, Maj. 1987–88)	Everett M. Dirksen, Ill. (Min. 1959–69)
George John Mitchell, Maine (Maj. 1989–1994)	Hugh Scott, Pa. (Min. 1969–1977)
Thomas A. Daschle, S.D. (Min. 1995–2001, Maj. 2001–2002, Min. 2003–2004)	Howard H. Baker, Jr., Tenn. (Min. 1977–81, Maj. 1981–84)
Harry Reid, Nev. (Min. 2005–)	Robert J. Dole, Kan. (Maj. 1985–86, Min. 1987–94, Maj. 1995–96)
	Trent Lott, Miss. (Maj. 1996–2001, Min. 2001–2002)
	Bill Frist, Tenn. (Maj. 2003–)

NOTE: Min. = Minority Leader; Maj. = Majority Leader. *Source:* United States Senate, Secretary for the Majority.

Composition of Congress, by Political Party, 1855–2005

Congress	Years	Senate					House				
		Total	Dems	Reps	Others	Vacant	Total	Dems	Reps	Others	Vacant
34th	1855–1857	62	42	15	5	—	234	83	108	43	—
35th	1857–1859	64	39	20	5	—	237	131	92	14	—
36th	1859–1861	66	38	26	2	—	237	101	113	23	—
37th	1861–1863	50	11	31	7	1	178	42	106	28	2
38th	1863–1865	51	12	39	—	—	183	80	103	—	—
39th	1865–1867	52	10	42	—	—	191	46	145	—	—
40th	1867–1869	53	11	42	—	—	193	49	143	—	1
41st	1869–1871	74	11	61	—	2	243	73	170	—	—
42nd	1871–1873	74	17	57	—	—	243	104	139	—	—
43rd	1873–1875	74	19	54	—	1	293	88	203	—	2
44th	1875–1877	76	29	46	—	1	293	181	107	3	2
45th	1877–1879	76	36	39	1	—	293	156	137	—	—
46th	1879–1881	76	43	33	—	—	293	150	128	14	1
47th	1881–1883	76	37	37	2	—	293	130	152	11	—
48th	1883–1885	76	36	40	—	—	325	200	119	6	—
49th	1885–1887	76	34	41	—	1	325	182	140	2	1
50th	1887–1889	76	37	39	—	—	325	170	151	4	—
51st	1889–1891	84	37	47	—	—	330	156	173	1	—
52nd	1891–1893	88	39	47	2	—	333	231	88	14	—
53rd	1893–1895	88	44	38	3	3	356	220	126	10	—
54th	1895–1897	88	39	44	5	—	357	104	246	7	—
55th	1897–1899	90	34	46	10	—	357	134	206	16	1
56th	1899–1901	90	26	53	11	—	357	163	185	9	—
57th	1901–1903	90	29	56	3	2	357	153	198	5	1
58th	1903–1905	90	32	58	—	—	386	178	207	—	1
59th	1905–1907	90	32	58	—	—	386	136	250	—	—
60th	1907–1909	92	29	61	—	2	386	164	222	—	—
61st	1909–1911	92	32	59	—	1	391	172	219	—	—
62nd	1911–1913	92	42	49	—	1	391	228	162	1	—
63rd	1913–1915	96	51	44	1	—	435	290	127	18	—
64th	1915–1917	96	56	39	1	—	435	231	193	8	3
65th	1917–1919	96	53	42	1	—	435	210[1]	216	9	—
66th	1919–1921	96	47	48	1	—	435	191	237	7	—
67th	1921–1923	96	37	59	—	—	435	132	300	1	2
68th	1923–1925	96	43	51	2	—	435	207	225	3	—
69th	1925–1927	96	40	54	1	1	435	183	247	5	—
70th	1927–1929	96	47	48	1	—	435	195	237	3	—
71st	1929–1931	96	39	56	1	—	435	163	267	1	4
72nd	1931–1933	96	47	48	1	—	435	216[2]	218	1	—
73rd	1933–1935	96	59	36	1	—	435	313	117	5	—
74th	1935–1937	96	69	25	2	—	435	322	103	10	—
75th	1937–1939	96	75	17	4	—	435	333	89	13	—
76th	1939–1941	96	69	23	4	—	435	262	169	4	—
77th	1941–1943	96	66	28	2	—	435	267	162	6	—
78th	1943–1945	96	57	38	1	—	435	222	209	4	—
79th	1945–1947	96	57	38	1	—	435	243	190	2	—
80th	1947–1949	96	45	51	—	—	435	188	246	1	—
81st	1949–1951	96	54	42	—	—	435	263	171	1	—
82nd	1951–1953	96	48	47	1	—	435	234	199	2	—
83rd	1953–1955	96	46	48	2	—	435	213	221	1	—
84th	1955–1957	96	48	47	1	—	435	232	203	—	—
85th	1957–1959	96	49	47	—	—	435	234	201	—	—
86th	1959–1961	98	64	34	—	—	436[3]	283	153	—	—
87th	1961–1963	100	64	36	—	—	437[4]	262	175	—	—
88th	1963–1965	100	67	33	—	—	435	258	176	—	1
89th	1965–1967	100	68	32	—	—	435	295	140	—	—
90th	1967–1969	100	64	36	—	—	435	248	187	—	—
91st	1969–1971	100	58	42	—	—	435	243	192	—	—
92nd	1971–1973	100	54	44	2	—	435	255	180	—	—
93rd	1973–1975	100	56	42	2	—	435	242	192	1	—
94th	1975–1977	100	61	37	2	—	435	291	144	—	—
95th	1977–1979	100	61	38	1	—	435	292	143	—	—
96th	1979–1981	100	58	41	1	—	435	277	158	—	—
97th	1981–1983	100	46	53	1	—	435	242	192	1	—
98th	1983–1985	100	46	54	—	—	435	269	166	—	—
99th	1985–1987	100	47	53	—	—	435	253	182	—	—
100th	1987–1989	100	55	45	—	—	435	258	177	—	—
101st	1989–1991	100	55	45	—	—	435	260	175	—	—

Congress	Years	Senate					House				
		Total	Dems	Reps	Others	Vacant	Total	Dems	Reps	Others	Vacant
102nd	1991–1993	100	56	44	—	—	435	267	167	1	—
103rd	1993–1995	100	57	43	—	—	435	258	176	1	—
104th	1995–1997	100	48	52	—	—	435	204	230	1	—
105th	1997–1999	100	45	55	—	—	435	207	226	2	—
106th	1999–2001	100	45	55	—	—	435 *	211	223	1	—
107th	2001–2003	100	50	50	—	—	435	212	221	2	—
108th	2003–2005	100	48	51	1	—	435	205	229	1	—
109th	2005–	100	44	55	1	—	435	202	232	1	1

NOTE: All figures reflect immediate results of elections. 1. Democrats organized House with help of other parties. 2. Democrats organized House due to Republican deaths. 3. Proclamation declaring Alaska a state issued Jan 3., 1959. 4. Proclamation declaring Hawaii a state issued Aug. 21, 1959. *Source:* Office of the Clerk of the House of Representatives. Web: http://clerkweb.house.gov/histrecs/history.htm.

Salaries of the President, Vice President, and Other U.S. Officials, 2005

(per year)

Position	Salary	Position	Salary
President		Vice President	$208,100[2]
1789	$ 25,000	Senator	162,100
1873	50,000	Representative	162,100
1909	75,000	Majority and Minority Leaders	180,100
1949	100,000[1]	Speaker of the House	208,100
1969	200,000[1]	Chief Justice, U.S. Supreme Court	208,100
2001	400,000[1]	Assoc. Justice, U.S. Supreme Court	199,200

1. Plus $50,000 non-taxable expense allowance to assist in defraying expenses relating to or resulting from the discharge of his official duties. 2. Plus $10,000 taxable expense allowance. *Source:* Office of Personnel Management. Web: www.opm.gov/.

Congressional Apportionment, 2000

Source: U.S. Census Bureau

Apportionment is the process of dividing the 435 seats in the House of Representatives among the 50 states. The number of seats, or representatives, each state is entitled to is apportioned according to the new census figures that are compiled every 10 years. States with larger populations have more representatives than states with smaller populations. Each state must have at least one representative.

Once the number of seats is assigned to each state, it is up to the individual state legislatures to redraw new congressional districts. Each representative is elected by voters from a congressional district within their state.

Who Counts?

The population figure used to calculate the apportionment of House seats is based on the total resident population of the United States, including citizens and noncitizens, plus U.S. military personnel and federal civilian employees and their dependents living overseas. It excludes the populations of the District of Columbia, Puerto Rico, and other U.S. territories that do not have voting seats in the House of Representatives. The Census 2000 apportionment population was 281,424,177.

Congressional District Size

The number of representatives in the U.S. House of Representatives has remained constant at 435 since 1911, except for a temporary increase to 437 at the time of admission of Alaska and Hawaii as states in 1959. However, the apportionment based on the 1960 census, which took effect for the election of 1962, reverted to 435 seats.

The average size of a congressional district based on the Census 2000 apportionment population will be 646,952, more than triple the average district size of 193,167 based on the 1900 census apportionment, and about 74,486 more than the average size of 572,466 based on the 1990 census.

Congressional Seats Gained/Lost in the 108th Congress[1]

Seats gained		Seats lost	
+ 2 seats	+1 seat	–1 seat	–2 seats
Arizona (8)	California (53)	Connecticut (5)	New York (29)
Florida (25)	Colorado (7)	Illinois (19)	Pennsylvania (19)
Georgia (13)	Nevada (3)	Indiana (9)	
Texas (32)	North Carolina (13)	Michigan (15)	
		Mississippi (4)	
		Ohio (18)	
		Oklahoma (5)	
		Wisconsin (8)	

NOTE: The number of representatives based on Census 2000 is given in parentheses after each state. 1. Based on Census 2000. *Source:* U.S. Census Bureau, Census 2000. Web: www.census.gov.

How a Bill Becomes a Law

When a senator or a representative introduces a bill, he or she sends it to the clerk of his house, who gives it a number and title. This is the *first reading,* and the bill is referred to the proper committee.

The committee may decide the bill is unwise or unnecessary and *table* it, thus killing it at once. Or it may decide the bill is worthwhile and hold hearings to listen to facts and opinions presented by experts and other interested persons. After members of the committee have debated the bill and perhaps offered amendments, a vote is taken; and if the vote is favorable, the bill is sent back to the floor of the house.

The clerk reads the bill sentence by sentence to the house, and this is known as the *second reading.* Members may then debate the bill and offer amendments. In the House of Representatives, the time for debate is limited by a *cloture rule,* but there is no such restriction in the Senate for cloture, where 60 votes are required. This makes possible a *filibuster,* in which one or more opponents hold the floor to defeat the bill.

The *third reading* is by title only, and the bill is put to a vote, which may be by voice or roll call, depending on the circumstances and parliamentary rules. A member who must be absent at the time of a vote may contract (or "pair") with a member of the opposition to abstain, balancing each other out.

The bill then goes to the other house of Congress, where it may be defeated, or passed with or without amendments. If the bill is defeated, it dies. If it is passed with amendments, a joint congressional committee must be appointed by both houses to iron out the differences.

After its final passage by both houses, the bill is sent to the president. If he approves, he signs it, and the bill becomes a law. However, if he disapproves, he *vetoes* the bill by refusing to sign it and sending it back to the house of origin with his reasons for the veto. The objections are read and debated, and a roll-call vote is taken. If the bill receives less than a two-thirds vote, it is defeated and goes no further. But if it receives a two-thirds vote or greater, it is sent to the other house for a vote. If that house also passes it by a two-thirds vote, the president's veto is *overridden,* and the bill becomes a law.

Should the president desire neither to sign nor to veto the bill, he may retain it for ten days, Sundays excepted, after which time it automatically becomes a law without signature. However, if Congress has adjourned within those ten days, the bill is automatically killed, that process of indirect rejection being known as a *pocket veto.*

Presidential Vetoes, 1789–2005

President	Coincident Congresses	Regular vetoes	Pocket vetoes	Total vetoes	Vetoes overridden
Washington	1st–4th	2	—	2	—
Adams	5th–6th	—	—	—	—
Jefferson	7th–10th	—	—	—	—
Madison	11th–14th	5	2	7	—
Monroe	15th–18th	1	—	1	—
J. Q. Adams	19th–20th	—	—	—	—
Jackson	21st–24th	5	7	12	—
Van Buren	25th–26th	—	1	1	—
W. H. Harrison	27th	—	—	—	—
Tyler	27th–28th	6	4	10	1
Polk	29th–30th	2	1	3	—
Taylor	31st	—	—	—	—
Fillmore	31st–32nd	—	—	—	—
Pierce	33rd–34th	9	—	9	5
Buchanan	35th–36th	4	3	7	—
Lincoln	37th–39th	2	5	7	—
A. Johnson	39th–40th	21	8	29	15
Grant	41st–44th	45	48	93	4
Hayes	45th–46th	12	1	13	1
Garfield	47th	—	—	—	—
Arthur	47th–48th	4	8	12	1
Cleveland	49th–50th	304	110	414	2
B. Harrison	51st–52nd	19	25	44	1
Cleveland	53rd–54th	42	128	170	5
McKinley	55th–57th	6	36	42	—
T. Roosevelt	57th–60th	42	40	82	1
Taft	61st–62nd	30	9	39	1
Wilson	63rd–66th	33	11	44	6
Harding	67th	5	1	6	—
Coolidge	68th–70th	20	30	50	4
Hoover	71st–72nd	21	16	37	3
F. D. Roosevelt	73rd–79th	372	263	635	9
Truman	79th–82nd	180	70	250	12
Eisenhower	83rd–86th	73	108	181	2
Kennedy	87th–88th	12	9	21	—
L. B. Johnson	88th–90th	16	14	30	—
Nixon	91st–93rd	26	17	43	7

President	Coincident Congresses	Regular vetoes	Pocket vetoes	Total vetoes	Vetoes overridden
Ford	93rd–94th	48	18	66	12
Carter	95th–96th	13	18	31	2
Reagan	97th–100th	39	39	78	9
G.H.W. Bush[1]	101st–102nd	29	15	44	1
Clinton	103rd–106th	36	1	37	2
G. W. Bush	107th–108th	—	—	—	—
Total		**1,484**	**1,066**	**2,550**	**106**

1. President Bush attempted to pocket veto two bills during intrasession recess periods. Congress considered the two bills enacted into law because of the president's failure to return the legislation. The bills are not counted as pocket vetoes in this table. *Source:* Office of the Clerk of the House. Web: http://clerk.house.gov.

Order of Presidential Succession

According to the Presidential Succession Act of 1792, the Senate president pro tempore[1] was next in line after the vice president to succeed to the presidency, followed by the Speaker of the House.

In 1886, however, Congress changed the order of presidential succession, replacing the president pro tempore and the Speaker with the cabinet officers. Proponents of this change argued that the congressional leaders lacked executive experience, and none had served as president, while six former secretaries of state had later been elected to that office.

The Presidential Succession Act of 1947, signed by President Harry Truman, changed the order again to what it is today. The cabinet members are ordered in the line of succession according to the date their offices were established.

Prior to the ratification of the 25th Amendment in 1967, there was no provision for filling a vacancy in the vice presidency. When a president died in office, the vice president succeeded him, and the vice presidency then remained vacant. The first vice president to take office under the new procedure was Gerald Ford, who was nominated by Nixon on Oct. 12, 1973, and confirmed by Congress the following Dec. 6.

1. The Vice President
2. Speaker of the House
3. President pro tempore of the Senate[1]
4. Secretary of State
5. Secretary of the Treasury
6. Secretary of Defense
7. Attorney General
8. Secretary of the Interior
9. Secretary of Agriculture
10. Secretary of Commerce
11. Secretary of Labor
12. Secretary of Health and Human Services
13. Secretary of Housing and Urban Development
14. Secretary of Transportation
15. Secretary of Energy
16. Secretary of Education
17. Secretary of Veterans Affairs
18. Secretary of Homeland Security[2]

NOTE: An official cannot succeed to the Presidency unless that person meets the Constitutional requirements. 1. The president pro tempore presides over the Senate when the vice president is absent. By tradition the position is held by the senior member of the majority party. 2. In late July 2005, the Senate passed a bill moving the Homeland Security secretary to number 8 on the list. The bill is awaiting House approval.

Executive Departments and Agencies

Source: United States Government Manual, 2002–2003

Unless otherwise indicated, addresses shown are in Washington, DC. ZIP codes are in parentheses.

White House Offices and Agencies

Office of Administration
Eisenhower Executive Office Bldg., 725 17th St., NW (20503)
Established: Dec. 12, 1977
Director: John E. Straub
Office of National Drug Control Policy
Executive Office of the President (20503)
Established: Jan. 29, 1989
Director: John P. Walters
Council of Economic Advisers (CEA)
1800 G. St., NW (20502)
Members: 3
Established: Feb. 20, 1946
Chair: Dr. Ben Bernanke
Council on Environmental Quality
722 Jackson Place, NW (20503)
Established: 1969
Chair: James Connaughton
Office of Management and Budget
Executive Office of the President, 725 17th St., NW (20503)
Established: July 1, 1939

Director: Joshua B. Bolten
Office of Science and Technology Policy
Executive Office of the President, 725 17th St., NW, Room 5228 (20502)
Established: May 11, 1976
Director: John H. Marburger III
National Security Council (NSC)
Eisenhower Executive Office Bldg. (20504)
Members: 4
Established: July 26, 1947
Chair: The President
National Security Adviser: Stephen Hadley
Other members: Vice President; Secretary of State; Secretary of Defense
Office of the United States Trade Representative
600 17th St., NW (20508)
Established: Jan. 15, 1963
Trade Representative: Rob Portman

Executive Departments

Department of Agriculture
1400 Independence Ave., SW (20250)
Established: May 15, 1862. Administered by Commissioner of Agriculture until 1889, when it was made executive department.

Secretary: Mike Johanns
Department of Commerce
1401 Constitution Ave., NW (20230)
   Established: Department of Commerce and Labor was created Feb. 14, 1903. On March 4, 1913, all labor activities were transferred out of Department of Commerce and Labor and it was renamed Department of Commerce.
   Secretary: Carlos Gutierrez
Department of Defense
Office of the Secretary, The Pentagon (20301-1155)
   Established: July 26, 1947, as National Military Establishment; name changed to Department of Defense on Aug. 10, 1949. Subordinate to Secretary of Defense are Secretaries of Army, Navy, Air Force.
   Secretary: Donald H. Rumsfeld
   Deputy Secretary: Gordon R. England (acting)
   Secretary of Army: Dr. Francis J. Harvey
   Secretary of Navy: Gordon R. England
   Secretary of Air Force: Pete Geren (acting)
   Commandant of Marine Corps: Gen. Michael W. Hagee
   Joint Chiefs of Staff: Gen. Peter Pace, Marine Corps, Chairman; Adm. Edmund P. Giambastiani, Jr., Navy, Vice Chairman; Gen. Peter J. Schoomaker, Army; Adm. Vernon E. Clark, Navy; Gen. T. Michael Moseley, Air Force; Gen. Michael W. Hagee, Marine Corps.
Department of Education
400 Maryland Ave., SW (20202)
   Established: Oct. 17, 1979
   Secretary: Margaret Spellings
Department of Energy
1000 Independence Ave., SW (20585)
   Established: Oct. 1, 1977
   Secretary: Samuel Bodman
Department of Health and Human Services
200 Independence Ave., SW (20201)
   Established: Formed April 11, 1953, replacing Federal Security Agency created in 1939. On Oct. 17, 1979, the Department of Education became a separate department.
   Secretary: Mike Leavitt
   Surgeon General: Dr. Richard Carmona
Department of Homeland Security
Washington, DC 20528
   Established: The most significant transformation of the U.S. government since 1947 was formed in the aftermath of Sept. 11, 2001, when 22 separate agencies were combined to become the cabinet-level Department of Homeland Security. It became an official cabinet department Jan. 24, 2003
   Secretary: Michael Chertoff
Department of Housing and Urban Development
451 7th St., SW (20410)
   Established: Nov. 9, 1965, replacing Housing and Home Finance Agency created in 1947
   Secretary: Alphonso Jackson
Department of the Interior
1849 C St., NW (20240)
   Established: March 3, 1849
   Secretary: Gale A. Norton
Department of Justice
950 Pennsylvania Ave., NW (20530-0001)
   Established: Office of Attorney General was created Sept. 24, 1789. Although one of the original cabinet members, the attorney general was not an executive department head until June 22, 1870, when the Department of Justice was established.
   Attorney General: Alberto Gonzales
   Solicitor General: Paul D. Clement
   Director of FBI: Robert S. Mueller, III
Department of Labor
200 Constitution Ave., NW (20210)
   Established: Bureau of Labor was created in 1884 under Department of the Interior; later became independent department without executive rank. Returned to bureau status in Department of Commerce and Labor, but on

March 4, 1913, became independent executive department under its present name.
   Secretary: Elaine L. Chao
Department of State
2201 C St., NW (20520)
   Established: 1781 as Department of Foreign Affairs; reconstituted, 1789, following adoption of Constitution; name changed to Department of State Sept. 15, 1789.
   Secretary: Condoleezza Rice
   UN Ambassador: John R. Bolton
   Deputy UN Ambassador: Anne W. Patterson
Department of Transportation
400 7th St., SW (20590)
   Established: Oct. 15, 1966, as result of Department of Transportation Act, which became effective April 1, 1967.
   Secretary: Norman Y. Mineta
Department of the Treasury
1500 Pennsylvania Ave., NW (20220)
   Established: Sept. 2, 1789
   Secretary: John Snow
   Treasurer of the U.S.: Anna Escobedo Cabral
Department of Veterans Affairs
810 Vermont Ave., NW (20420)
   Established: March 15, 1989, replacing Veterans Administration created in 1930
   Secretary: Jim Nicholson

Major Independent Agencies

Central Intelligence Agency (CIA)
Office of Public Affairs (20505)
   Established: 1947
   Director of Central Intelligence: Porter J. Goss
U.S. Commission on Civil Rights
624 9th St., NW (20425)
   Established: 1957
   Staff Director: Kenneth L. Marcus
Consumer Product Safety Commission
Washington, DC 20207-0001
   Established: Oct. 27, 1972
   Chair: Harold D. Stratton
Corporation for National and Community Service
1201 New York Ave., NW (20525)
   Established: Sept. 1993
   CEO: David Eisner
Environmental Protection Agency (EPA)
1200 Pennsylvania Ave., NW (20460)
   Established: Dec. 2, 1970
   Administrator: Stephen Johnson
Equal Employment Opportunity Commission (EEOC)
P.O. Box 7033, Lawrence, KS 66044
   Members: 5
   Established: July 2, 1965
   Chair: Cari M. Dominguez
Farm Credit Administration (FCA)
1501 Farm Credit Dr., McLean, Va. 22102-5090
   Members: 13
   Established: March 27, 1933
   Chair: Nancy C. Pellett
Federal Communications Commission (FCC)
445 12th Street, SW (20554)
   Established: 1934
   Chair: Kevin J. Martin
Federal Deposit Insurance Corporation (FDIC)
550 17th St., NW (20429-9990)
   Established: June 16, 1933
   Chair: Donald E. Powell
Federal Election Commission (FEC)
999 E St., NW (20463)
   Members: 6
   Established: 1975
   Chair: Scott E. Thomas
Federal Maritime Commission
800 North Capitol St., NW (20573-0001)
   Members: 5

Established: Aug. 12, 1961
  Chair: Steven R. Blust
Federal Mediation and Conciliation Service (FMCS)
2100 K St., NW (20427)
  Established: 1947
  Director: Scot L. Beckenbaugh (acting)
Federal Reserve System (FRS), Board of Governors of
20th St. & Constitution Ave., NW (20551)
  Members: 7
  Established: Dec. 23, 1913
  Chair: Alan Greenspan
Federal Trade Commission (FTC)
600 Pennsylvania Ave., NW (20580)
  Members: 5
  Established: Sept. 26, 1914
  Chair: Deborah Platt Majoras
General Services Administration (GSA)
1800 F St., NW (20405)
  Established: July 1, 1949
  Administrator: Stephen A. Perry
U.S. International Trade Commission
500 E St., SW (20436)
  Members: 6
  Established: Sept. 8, 1916
  Chair: Stephen Koplan
National Aeronautics and Space Administration (NASA)
*Public Inquiries Business Center, NASA Headquarters,
Suite 1M32 (20546-0001)*
  Established: 1958
  Administrator: Michael Griffin
National Archives and Records Administration (NARA)
8601 Adelphi Road, College Park, Md. 20740-6001
  Established: Oct. 19, 1984. NARA is the successor
  agency to the National Archives Establishment, which
  was created in 1934 and later incorporated into the Gen-
  eral Services Administration as the National Archives and
  Records Service in 1949.
  Archivist of the U.S.: Allen Weinstein
National Foundation on the Arts and the Humanities
1100 Pennsylvania Ave., NW (20506)
  Established: 1965
  Chairs: National Endowment for the Arts, Chair, Dana
  Gioia; National Endowment for the Humanities, Chair,
  Bruce Cole
Director of National Intelligence (DNI), Office of
  Established: Dec. 2004
  Director: John D. Negroponte
  Deputy: Gen. Michael Hayden
National Labor Relations Board (NLRB)
1099 14th St., NW (20570-0001)
  Members: 5
  Established: July 5, 1935
  Chair: Robert J. Battista
National Mediation Board
1301 K St., NW, Suite 250 East (20005-7011)
  Established: June 21, 1934
  Chair: Read Van de Water
National Science Foundation (NSF)
4201 Wilson Blvd., Arlington, Va. 22230
  Established: 1950
  Director: Arden L. Bement
National Transportation Safety Board
490 L'Enfant Plaza, SW (20594)
  Members: 5
  Established: April 1, 1967, as an independent agency
  supported by the Dept. of Transportation. Ties with Dept.
  of Transportation officially ended in 1975.
  Chair: Mark V. Rosenker (acting)
Nuclear Regulatory Commission (NRC)
Washington, DC 20555
  Members: 5
  Established: Jan. 19, 1975
  Chair: Nils J. Diaz
Office of Personnel Management (OPM)

1900 E St., NW (20415-1000)
  Established: Jan. 1, 1979
  Director: Linda M. Springer
U.S. Postal Service
475 L'Enfant Plaza, SW (20260-0010)
  Established: In 1775 with the appointment of Benjamin
  Franklin as the first postmaster general under the Conti-
  nental Congress. In 1970 became independent agency
  headed by 11-member board of governors.
  Postmaster General: John E. Potter
Securities and Exchange Commission (SEC)
100 F St., NE (20549)
  Members: 5
  Established: July 2, 1934
  Chair: Christopher Cox
Selective Service System (SSS)
National Headquarters, Arlington, Va., 22209-2425
  Established: Sept. 16, 1940
  Director: William A. Chatfield
Small Business Administration (SBA)
409 3rd St., SW (20416)
  Established: July 30, 1953
  Administrator: Hector V. Barreto
Tennessee Valley Authority (TVA)
400 West Summit Hill Drive, Knoxville, Tenn. 37902-1499
  Members of Board of Directors: 3
  Established: May 18, 1933
  Chairman: Bill Baxter

Other Independent Agencies

Appalachian Regional Commission—1666 Connecticut
Ave., NW, Suite 700 (20009-1068)
Commission of Fine Arts—401 F St., NW, Ste. 312
(20001)
Commodity Futures Trading Commission—Three Lafay-
ette Centre, 1155 21st St., NW (20581)
Export-Import Bank of the United States—811 Vermont
Ave., NW (20571)
Federal Emergency Management Agency—500 C St.,
SW (20472)
Federal Housing Finance Board—1625 Eye St., NW (20006-
4001)
Federal Labor Relations Authority—1400 K St., NW
(20005)
Inter-American Foundation—901 N. Stuart St., 10th Floor,
Arlington, Va. 22203
**National Commission on Libraries and Information
Science**—1800 M St., NW, Suite 350 North Tower
(20036-5841)
National Credit Union Administration—1775 Duke St.,
Alexandria, Va. 22314-3428
Occupational Safety and Health Review Commission—
1120 20th St., NW (20036-3419)
U.S. Parole Commission—Dept. of Justice, 5550 Friend-
ship Blvd., Ste. 420, Chevy Chase, Md. 20815-7286
Peace Corps—1111 20th St., NW (20526)
Pension Benefit Guaranty Corporation—1200 K St., NW
(20005-4026)
President's Council on Physical Fitness and Sports—
Dept. W, 200 Independence Ave., SW, Room 738-H
(20201-0004)
Railroad Retirement Board (RRB)—844 N. Rush St.,
Ninth Floor, Chicago, Ill. 60611-2092; Office of Legislative
Affairs: 1310 G St., N.W, Ste. 500 (20005-3004).

Legislative Department

Architect of the Capitol—U.S. Capitol Building (20515)
Government Accountability Office (GAO)—441 G St., NW
(20548)
Government Printing Office (GPO)—732 North Capitol
St., NW (20401)
Library of Congress—101 Independence Ave., SE (20540)
United States Botanic Garden—245 1st St., SW (20024)

Quasi-Official Agencies

American Red Cross—2025 E St., NW (20006)
National Academy of Sciences, National Academy of Engineering, National Research Council, Institute of Medicine—500 Fifth St., NW (20001)

National Railroad Passenger Corporation (Amtrak)—60 Massachusetts Ave., NE (20002)

Smithsonian Institution—PO Box 37012 SI Bldg., Rm. 153, MRC 010 (20013-7012)

Government Officials
Cabinet Members with Dates of Appointment

Although the Constitution made no provision for a president's advisory group, the heads of the three executive departments (State, Treasury, and War) and the attorney general were organized by Washington into such a group; and by about 1793, the name "cabinet" was applied to it. With the exception of the attorney general up to 1870 and the postmaster general from 1829 to 1872, cabinet members have been heads of executive departments.

Cabinet members are appointed by the president, subject to the confirmation of the Senate; and as their terms are not fixed, they may be replaced at any time by the president. At a change in administration, it is customary for cabinet members to resign, but they remain in office until successors are appointed.

The table of cabinet members lists only those members who actually served after being duly commissioned. The dates shown are those of appointment. "Cont." indicates that the term continued from the previous administration for a substantial amount of time.

Washington

Secretary of State	Thomas Jefferson, 1789
	Edmund Randolph, 1794
	Timothy Pickering, 1795
Secretary of the Treasury	Alexander Hamilton, 1789
	Oliver Wolcott, Jr., 1795
Secretary of War	Henry Knox, 1789
	Timothy Pickering, 1795
	James McHenry, 1796
Attorney General	Edmund Randolph, 1789
	William Bradford, 1794
	Charles Lee, 1795

J. Adams

Secretary of State	Timothy Pickering (Cont.)
	John Marshall, 1800
Secretary of the Treasury	Oliver Wolcott, Jr. (Cont.)
	Samuel Dexter, 1801
Secretary of War	James McHenry (Cont.)
	Samuel Dexter, 1800
Attorney General	Charles Lee (Cont.)
Secretary of the Navy	Benjamin Stoddert, 1798

Jefferson

Secretary of State	James Madison, 1801
Secretary of the Treasury	Samuel Dexter (Cont.)
	Albert Gallatin, 1801
Secretary of War	Henry Dearborn, 1801
Attorney General	Levi Lincoln, 1801
	Robert Smith, 1805
	John Breckinridge, 1805
	Caesar A. Rodney, 1807
Secretary of the Navy	Benjamin Stoddert (Cont.)
	Robert Smith, 1801

Madison

Secretary of State	Robert Smith, 1809
	James Monroe, 1811
Secretary of the Treasury	Albert Gallatin (Cont.)
	George W. Campbell, 1814
	Alexander J. Dallas, 1814
	William H. Crawford, 1816
Secretary of War	William Eustis, 1809
	John Armstrong, 1813
	James Monroe, 1814
	William H. Crawford, 1815
Attorney General	Caesar A. Rodney (Cont.)
	William Pinckney, 1811
	Richard Rush, 1814
Secretary of the Navy	Paul Hamilton, 1809
	William Jones, 1813
	B. W. Crowninshield, 1814

Monroe

Secretary of State	John Quincy Adams, 1817
Secretary of the Treasury	William H. Crawford (Cont.)
Secretary of War	John C. Calhoun, 1817
Attorney General	Richard Rush (Cont.)
	William Wirt, 1817
Secretary of the Navy	B. W. Crowninshield (Cont.)
	Smith Thompson, 1818
	Samuel L. Southard, 1823

J. Q. Adams

Secretary of State	Henry Clay, 1825
Secretary of the Treasury	Richard Rush, 1825
Secretary of War	James Barbour, 1825
	Peter B. Porter, 1828
Attorney General	William Wirt (Cont.)
Secretary of the Navy	Samuel L. Southard (Cont.)

Jackson

Secretary of State	Martin Van Buren, 1829
	Edward Livingston, 1831
	Louis McLane, 1833
	John Forsyth, 1834
Secretary of the Treasury	Samuel D. Ingham, 1829
	Louis McLane, 1831
	William J. Duane, 1833
	Roger B. Taney[1], 1833
	Levi Woodbury, 1834
Secretary of War	John H. Eaton, 1829
	Lewis Cass, 1831
Attorney General	John M. Berrien, 1829
	Roger B. Taney, 1831
	Benjamin F. Butler, 1833
Postmaster General[2]	William T. Barry, 1829
	Amos Kendall, 1835
Secretary of the Navy	John Branch, 1829
	Levi Woodbury, 1831
	Mahlon Dickerson, 1834

1. Not confirmed by the Senate. 2. The postmaster general did not become a cabinet member until 1829. Earlier postmasters general were: Samuel Osgood (1789), Timothy Pickering (1791), Joseph Habersham (1795), Gideon Granger (1801), Return J. Meigs, Jr. (1814), and John McLean (1823).

Van Buren

Secretary of State	John Forsyth (Cont.)
Secretary of the Treasury	Levi Woodbury (Cont.)
Secretary of War	Joel R. Poinsett, 1837
Attorney General	Benjamin F. Butler (Cont.)
	Felix Grundy, 1838
	Henry D. Gilpin, 1840

Postmaster General	Amos Kendall (Cont.)
	John M. Niles, 1840
Secretary of the Navy	Mahlon Dickerson (Cont.)
	James K. Paulding, 1838

W. H. Harrison

Secretary of State	Daniel Webster, 1841
Secretary of the Treasury	Thomas Ewing, 1841
Secretary of War	John Bell, 1841
Attorney General	John J. Crittenden, 1841
Postmaster General	Francis Granger, 1841
Secretary of the Navy	George E. Badger, 1841

Tyler

Secretary of State	Daniel Webster (Cont.)
	Abel P. Upshur, 1843
	John C. Calhoun, 1844
Secretary of the Treasury	Thomas Ewing (Cont.)
	Walter Forward, 1841
	John C. Spencer[1], 1843
	George M. Bibb, 1844
Secretary of War	John Bell (Cont.)
	John C. Spencer, 1841
	James M. Porter[1], 1843
	William Wilkins, 1844
Attorney General	John J. Crittenden (Cont.)
	Hugh S. Legaré, 1841
	John Nelson, 1843
Postmaster General	Francis Granger (Cont.)
	Charles A. Wickliffe, 1841
Secretary of the Navy	George E. Badger (Cont.)
	Abel P. Upshur, 1841
	David Henshaw[1], 1843
	Thomas W. Gilmer, 1844
	John Y. Mason, 1844

1. Not confirmed by the Senate.

Polk

Secretary of State	James Buchanan, 1845
Secretary of the Treasury	Robert J. Walker, 1845
Secretary of War	William L. Marcy, 1845
Attorney General	John Y. Mason, 1845
	Nathan Clifford, 1846
	Isaac Toucey, 1848
Postmaster General	Cave Johnson, 1845
Secretary of the Navy	George Bancroft, 1845
	John Y. Mason, 1846

Taylor

Secretary of State	John M. Clayton, 1849
Secretary of the Treasury	William M. Meredith, 1849
Secretary of War	George W. Crawford, 1849
Attorney General	Reverdy Johnson, 1849
Postmaster General	Jacob Collamer, 1849
Secretary of the Navy	William B. Preston, 1849
Secretary of the Interior	Thomas Ewing, 1849

Fillmore

Secretary of State	Daniel Webster, 1850
	Edward Everett, 1852
Secretary of the Treasury	Thomas Corwin, 1850
Secretary of War	Charles M. Conrad, 1850
Attorney General	John J. Crittenden, 1850
Postmaster General	Nathan K. Hall, 1850
	Samuel D. Hubbard, 1852
Secretary of the Navy	William A. Graham, 1850
	John P. Kennedy, 1852
Secretary of the Interior	Thos. M. T. McKennan, 1850
	Alex. H. H. Stuart, 1850

Pierce

Secretary of State	William L. Marcy, 1853
Secretary of the Treasury	James Guthrie, 1853
Secretary of War	Jefferson Davis, 1853
Attorney General	Caleb Cushing, 1853
Postmaster General	James Campbell, 1853
Secretary of the Navy	James C. Dobbin, 1853
Secretary of the Interior	Robert McClelland, 1853

Buchanan

Secretary of State	Lewis Cass, 1857
	Jeremiah S. Black, 1860
Secretary of the Treasury	Howell Cobb, 1857
	Philip F. Thomas, 1860
	John A. Dix, 1861
Secretary of War	John B. Floyd, 1857
	Joseph Holt, 1861
Attorney General	Jeremiah S. Black, 1857
	Edwin M. Stanton, 1860
Postmaster General	Aaron V. Brown, 1857
	Joseph Holt, 1859
	Horatio King, 1861
Secretary of the Navy	Isaac Toucey, 1857
Secretary of the Interior	Jacob Thompson, 1857

Lincoln

Secretary of State	William H. Seward, 1861
Secretary of the Treasury	Salmon P. Chase, 1861
	William P. Fessenden, 1864
	Hugh McCulloch, 1865
Secretary of War	Simon Cameron, 1861
	Edwin M. Stanton, 1862
Attorney General	Edward Bates, 1861
	James Speed, 1864
Postmaster General	Montgomery Blair, 1861
	William Dennison, 1864
Secretary of the Navy	Gideon Welles, 1861
Secretary of the Interior	Caleb B. Smith, 1861
	John P. Usher, 1863

A. Johnson

Secretary of State	William H. Seward (Cont.)
Secretary of the Treasury	Hugh McCulloch (Cont.)
Secretary of War	Edwin M. Stanton (Cont.)
	John M. Schofield, 1868
Attorney General	James Speed (Cont.)
	Henry Stanbery, 1866
	William M. Evarts, 1868
Postmaster General	William Dennison (Cont.)
	Alexander W. Randall, 1866
Secretary of the Navy	Gideon Welles (Cont.)
Secretary of the Interior	John P. Usher (Cont.)
	James Harlan, 1865
	Orville H. Browning, 1866

Grant

Secretary of State	Elihu B. Washburne, 1869
	Hamilton Fish, 1869
Secretary of the Treasury	George S. Boutwell, 1869
	William A. Richardson, 1873
	Benjamin H. Bristow, 1874
	Lot M. Morrill, 1876
Secretary of War	John A. Rawlins, 1869
	William W. Belknap, 1869
	Alphonso Taft, 1876
	James D. Cameron, 1876
Attorney General	Ebenezer R. Hoar, 1869
	Amos T. Akerman, 1870
	George H. Williams, 1871
	Edwards Pierrepont, 1875
	Alphonso Taft, 1876
Postmaster General	John A. J. Creswell, 1869
	Marshall Jewell, 1874
	James N. Tyner, 1876
Secretary of the Navy	Adolph E. Borie, 1869
	George M. Robeson, 1869
Secretary of the Interior	Jacob D. Cox, 1869
	Columbus Delano, 1870
	Zachariah Chandler, 1875

Hayes

Secretary of State	William M. Evarts, 1877
Secretary of the Treasury	John Sherman, 1877
Secretary of War	George W. McCrary, 1877
	Alexander Ramsey, 1879
Attorney General	Charles Devens, 1877
Postmaster General	David M. Key, 1877
	Horace Maynard, 1880
	Richard W. Thompson, 1877
	Nathan Goff, Jr., 1881
Secretary of the Interior	Carl Schurz, 1877

Garfield

Secretary of State	James G. Blaine, 1881
Secretary of the Treasury	William Windom, 1881
Secretary of War	Robert T. Lincoln, 1881
Attorney General	Wayne MacVeagh, 1881
Postmaster General	Thomas L. James, 1881
Secretary of the Navy	William H. Hunt, 1881
Secretary of the Interior	Samuel J. Kirkwood, 1881

Arthur

Secretary of State	James G. Blaine (Cont.)
	F. T. Frelinghuysen, 1881
Secretary of the Treasury	William Windom (Cont.)
	Charles J. Folger, 1881
	Walter Q. Gresham, 1884
	Hugh McCulloch, 1884
Secretary of War	Robert T. Lincoln (Cont.)
Attorney General	Wayne MacVeagh (Cont.)
	Benjamin H. Brewster, 1881
Postmaster General	Thomas L. James (Cont.)
	Timothy O. Howe, 1881
	Walter Q. Gresham, 1883
	Frank Hatton, 1884
Secretary of the Navy	William.H. Hunt (Cont.)
	William E. Chandler, 1882
Secretary of the Interior	Samuel J. Kirkwood (Cont.)
	Henry M. Teller, 1882

Cleveland

Secretary of State	Thomas F. Bayard, 1885
Secretary of the Treasury	Daniel Manning, 1885
	Charles S. Fairchild, 1887
Secretary of War	William C. Endicott, 1885
Attorney General	Augustus H. Garland, 1885
Postmaster General	William F. Vilas, 1885
	Don M. Dickinson, 1888
Secretary of the Navy	William C. Whitney, 1885
Secretary of the Interior	Lucius Q. C. Lamar, 1885
	William F. Vilas, 1888
Secretary of Agriculture	Norman J. Colman, 1889

B. Harrison

Secretary of State	James G. Blaine, 1889
	John W. Foster, 1892
Secretary of the Treasury	William Windom, 1889
	Charles Foster, 1891
Secretary of War	Redfield Proctor, 1889
	Stephen B. Elkins, 1891
Attorney General	William H. H. Miller, 1889
Postmaster General	John Wanamaker, 1889
Secretary of the Navy	Benjamin F. Tracy, 1889
Secretary of the Interior	John W. Noble, 1889
Secretary of Agriculture	Jeremiah M. Rusk, 1889

Cleveland

Secretary of State	Walter Q. Gresham, 1893
	Richard Olney, 1895
Secretary of the Treasury	John G. Carlisle, 1893
Secretary of War	Daniel S. Lamont, 1893
Attorney General	Richard Olney, 1893
	Judson Harmon, 1895
Postmaster General	Wilson S. Bissell, 1893
	William L. Wilson, 1895
Secretary of the Navy	Hilary A. Herbert, 1893
Secretary of the Interior	Hoke Smith, 1893
	David R. Francis, 1896
Secretary of Agriculture	Julius Sterling Morton, 1893

McKinley

Secretary of State	John Sherman, 1897
	William R. Day, 1898
	John Hay, 1898
Secretary of the Treasury	Lyman J. Gage, 1897
Secretary of War	Russell A. Alger, 1897
	Elihu Root, 1899
Attorney General	Joseph McKenna, 1897
	John W. Griggs, 1898
	Philander C. Knox, 1901
Postmaster General	James A. Gary, 1897
	Charles E. Smith, 1898
Secretary of the Navy	John D. Long, 1897
Secretary of the Interior	Cornelius N. Bliss, 1897
	Ethan A. Hitchcock, 1898
Secretary of Agriculture	James Wilson, 1897

T. Roosevelt

Secretary of State	John Hay (Cont.)
	Elihu Root, 1905
	Robert Bacon, 1909
Secretary of the Treasury	Lyman J. Gage (Cont.)
	Leslie M. Shaw, 1902
	George B. Cortelyou, 1907
Secretary of War	Elihu Root (Cont.)
	William H. Taft, 1904
	Luke E. Wright, 1908
Attorney General	Philander C. Knox (Cont.)
	William H. Moody, 1904
	Charles J. Bonaparte, 1906
Postmaster General	Charles E. Smith (Cont.)
	Henry C. Payne, 1902
	Robert J. Wynne, 1904
	George B. Cortelyou, 1905
	George von L. Meyer, 1907
Secretary of the Navy	John D. Long (Cont.)
	William H. Moody, 1902
	Paul Morton, 1904
	Charles J. Bonaparte, 1905
	Victor H. Metcalf, 1906
	Truman H. Newberry, 1908
Secretary of the Interior	Ethan A. Hitchcock (Cont.)
	James R. Garfield, 1907
Secretary of Agriculture	James Wilson (Cont.)
Secretary of Commerce and Labor	George B. Cortelyou, 1903
	Victor H. Metcalf, 1904
	Oscar S. Straus, 1906

Taft

Secretary of State	Philander C. Knox, 1909
Secretary of the Treasury	Franklin MacVeagh, 1909
Secretary of War	Jacob M. Dickinson, 1909
	Henry L. Stimson, 1911
Attorney General	George W. Wickersham, 1909
Postmaster General	Frank H. Hitchcock, 1909
Secretary of the Navy	George von L. Meyer, 1909
Secretary of the Interior	Richard A. Ballinger, 1909
	Walter L. Fisher, 1911
Secretary of Agriculture	James Wilson (Cont.)
Secretary of Commerce and Labor	Charles Nagel, 1909

Wilson

Secretary of State	William J. Bryan, 1913
	Robert Lansing, 1915
	Bainbridge Colby, 1920
Secretary of the Treasury	William G. McAdoo, 1913
	Carter Glass, 1918
	David F. Houston, 1920
Secretary of War	Lindley M. Garrison, 1913
	Newton D. Baker, 1916

Attorney General	James C. McReynolds, 1913
	Thomas W. Gregory, 1914
	A. Mitchell Palmer, 1919
Postmaster General	Albert S. Burleson, 1913
Secretary of the Navy	Josephus Daniels, 1913
Secretary of the Interior	Franklin K. Lane, 1913
	John B. Payne, 1920
Secretary of Agriculture	David F. Houston, 1913
	Edwin T. Meredith, 1920
Secretary of Commerce	William C. Redfield, 1913
	Joshua W. Alexander, 1919
Secretary of Labor	William B. Wilson, 1913

Harding

Secretary of State	Charles E. Hughes, 1921
Secretary of the Treasury	Andrew W. Mellon, 1921
Secretary of War	John W. Weeks, 1921
Attorney General	Harry M. Daugherty, 1921
Postmaster General	Will H. Hays, 1921
	Hubert Work, 1922
	Harry S. New, 1923
Secretary of the Navy	Edwin Denby, 1921
Secretary of the Interior	Albert B. Fall, 1921
	Hubert Work, 1923
Secretary of Agriculture	Henry C. Wallace, 1921
Secretary of Commerce	Herbert Hoover, 1921
Secretary of Labor	James J. Davis, 1921

Coolidge

Secretary of State	Charles E. Hughes (Cont.)
	Frank B. Kellogg, 1925
Secretary of the Treasury	Andrew W. Mellon (Cont.)
Secretary of War	John W. Weeks (Cont.)
	Dwight F. Davis, 1925
Attorney General	Harry M. Daughtery (Cont.)
	Harlan F. Stone, 1924
	John G. Sargent, 1925
Postmaster General	Harry S. New (Cont.)
Secretary of the Navy	Edwin Denby (Cont.)
	Curtis D. Wilbur, 1924
Secretary of the Interior	Hubert Work (Cont.)
	Roy O. West, 1928
Secretary of Agriculture	Henry C. Wallace (Cont.)
	Howard M. Gore, 1924
	William M. Jardine, 1925
Secretary of Commerce	Herbert Hoover (Cont.)
	William F. Whiting, 1928
Secretary of Labor	James J. Davis (Cont.)

Hoover

Secretary of State	Frank B. Kellogg (Cont.)
	Henry L. Stimson, 1929
Secretary of the Treasury	Andrew W. Mellon (Cont.)
	Ogden L. Mills, 1932
Secretary of War	James W. Good, 1929
	Patrick J. Hurley, 1929
Attorney General	William D. Mitchell, 1929
Postmaster General	Walter F. Brown, 1929
Secretary of the Navy	Charles F. Adams, 1929
Secretary of the Interior	Ray Lyman Wilbur, 1929
Secretary of Agriculture	Arthur M. Hyde, 1929
Secretary of Commerce	Robert P. Lamont, 1929
	Roy D. Chapin, 1932
Secretary of Labor	James J. Davis (Cont.)
	William N. Doak, 1930

F. D. Roosevelt

Secretary of State	Cordell Hull, 1933
	E. R. Stettinius, Jr., 1944
Secretary of the Treasury	William H. Woodin, 1933
	Henry Morgenthau, Jr., 1934
Secretary of War	George H. Dern, 1933
	Harry H. Woodring, 1936
	Henry L. Stimson, 1940

Attorney General	Homer S. Cummings, 1933
	Frank Murphy, 1939
	Robert H. Jackson, 1940
	Francis Biddle, 1941
Postmaster General	James A. Farley, 1933
	Frank C. Walker, 1940
Secretary of the Navy	Claude A. Swanson, 1933
	Charles Edison, 1940
	Frank Knox, 1940
	James Forrestal, 1944
Secretary of the Interior	Harold L. Ickes, 1933
Secretary of Agriculture	Henry A. Wallace, 1933
	Claude R. Wickard, 1940
Secretary of Commerce	Daniel C. Roper, 1933
	Harry L. Hopkins, 1938
	Jesse H. Jones, 1940
	Henry A. Wallace, 1945
Secretary of Labor	Frances Perkins, 1933

Truman

Secretary of State	E. R. Stettinius, Jr. (Cont.)
	James F. Byrnes, 1945
	George C. Marshall, 1947
	Dean Acheson, 1949
Secretary of the Treasury	Henry Morgenthau, Jr. (Cont.)
	Frederick M. Vinson, 1945
	John W. Snyder, 1946
Secretary of Defense	James Forrestal, 1947
	Louis A. Johnson, 1949
	George C. Marshall, 1950
	Robert A. Lovett, 1951
Attorney General	Francis Biddle (Cont.)
	Tom C. Clark, 1945
	J. Howard McGrath, 1949
	James P. McGranery, 1952
Postmaster General	Frank C. Walker (Cont.)
	Robert E. Hannegan, 1945
	Jesse M. Donaldson, 1947
Secretary of the Interior	Harold L. Ickes (Cont.)
	Julius A. Krug, 1946
	Oscar L. Chapman, 1949
Secretary of Agriculture	Claude R. Wickard (Cont.)
	Clinton P. Anderson, 1945
	Charles F. Brannan, 1948
Secretary of Commerce	Henry A. Wallace (Cont.)
	W. Averell Harriman, 1946
	Charles Sawyer, 1948
Secretary of Labor	Frances Perkins (Cont.)
	Lewis B. Schwellenbach, 1945
	Maurice J. Tobin, 1948
Secretary of War[1]	Henry L. Stimson (Cont.)
	Robert P. Patterson, 1945
	Kenneth C. Royall, 1947
Secretary of the Navy[1]	James Forrestal (Cont.)

1. On July 26, 1947, the Departments of War and of the Navy were incorporated into the Department of Defense.

Eisenhower

Secretary of State	John Foster Dulles, 1953
	Christian A. Herter, 1959
Secretary of the Treasury	George M. Humphrey, 1953
	Robert B. Anderson, 1957
Secretary of Defense	Charles E. Wilson, 1953
	Neil H. McElroy, 1957
	Thomas S. Gates, Jr., 1959
Attorney General	Herbert Brownell, Jr., 1953
	William P. Rogers, 1958
Postmaster General	Arthur E. Summerfield, 1953
Secretary of the Interior	Douglas McKay, 1953
	Frederick A. Seaton, 1956
Secretary of Agriculture	Ezra Taft Benson, 1953
Secretary of Commerce	Sinclair Weeks, 1953
	Lewis L. Strauss[1], 1958
	Frederick H. Mueller, 1959

Secretary of Health, Education, and Welfare	Oveta Culp Hobby, 1953
	Marion B. Folsom, 1955
	Arthur S. Flemming, 1958
Secretary of Labor	Martin P. Durkin, 1953
	James P. Mitchell, 1953

1. Not confirmed by the Senate.

Kennedy

Secretary of State	Dean Rusk, 1961
Secretary of the Treasury	C. Douglas Dillon, 1961
Secretary of Defense	Robert S. McNamara, 1961
Attorney General	Robert F. Kennedy, 1961
Postmaster General	J. Edward Day, 1961
	John A. Gronouski, 1963
Secretary of the Interior	Stewart L. Udall, 1961
Secretary of Agriculture	Orville L. Freeman, 1961
Secretary of Commerce	Luther H. Hodges, 1961
Secretary of Labor	Arthur J. Goldberg, 1961
	W. Willard Wirtz, 1962
Secretary of Health, Education, and Welfare	Abraham A. Ribicoff, 1961
	Anthony J. Celebrezze, 1962

L. B. Johnson

Secretary of State	Dean Rusk (Cont.)
Secretary of the Treasury	C. Douglas Dillon (Cont.)
	Henry H. Fowler, 1965
	Joseph W. Barr[1], 1968
Secretary of Defense	Robert S. McNamara (Cont.)
	Clark M. Clifford, 1968
Attorney General	Robert F. Kennedy (Cont.)
	N. de B. Katzenbach, 1965
	Ramsey Clark, 1967
Postmaster General	John A. Gronouski (Cont.)
	Lawrence F. O'Brien, 1965
	W. Marvin Watson, 1968
Secretary of the Interior	Stewart L. Udall (Cont.)
Secretary of Agriculture	Orville L. Freeman (Cont.)
Secretary of Commerce	Luther H. Hodges (Cont.)
	John T. Connor, 1964
	A. B. Trowbridge, 1967
	C. R. Smith, 1968
Secretary of Labor	W. Willard Wirtz (Cont.)
Secretary of Health, Education, and Welfare	Anthony J. Celebrezze (Cont.)
	John W. Gardner, 1965
	Wilbur J. Cohen, 1968
Secretary of Housing and Urban Development	Robert C. Weaver, 1966
	Robert C. Wood[1], 1969
Secretary of Transportation	Alan S. Boyd, 1966

1. Recess appointment.

Nixon

Secretary of State	William P. Rogers, 1969
	Henry A. Kissinger, 1973
Secretary of the Treasury	David M. Kennedy, 1969
	John B. Connally, 1971
	George P. Shultz, 1972
	William E. Simon, 1974
Secretary of Defense	Melvin R. Laird, 1969
	Elliot L. Richardson, 1973
	James R. Schlesinger, 1973
Attorney General	John N. Mitchell, 1969
	Richard G. Kleindienst, 1972
	Elliot L. Richardson, 1973
	William B. Saxbe, 1974
Postmaster General[1]	William M. Blount, 1969
Secretary of the Interior	Walter J. Hickel, 1969
	Rogers C. B. Morton, 1971
Secretary of Agriculture	Clifford M. Hardin, 1969
	Earl L. Butz, 1971
Secretary of Commerce	Maurice H. Stans, 1969
	Peter G. Peterson, 1972
	Frederick B. Dent, 1973
Secretary of Labor	George P. Shultz, 1969
	James D. Hodgson, 1970
	Peter J. Brennan, 1973

Secretary of Health, Education, and Welfare	Robert H. Finch, 1969
	Elliot L. Richardson, 1970
	Caspar W. Weinberger, 1973
Secretary of Housing and Urban Development	George Romney, 1969
	James T. Lynn, 1973
Secretary of Transportation	John A. Volpe, 1969
	Claude S. Brinegar, 1973

1. The postmaster general is no longer a cabinet member.

Ford

Secretary of State	Henry A. Kissinger (Cont.)
Secretary of the Treasury	William E. Simon (Cont.)
Secretary of Defense	James R. Schlesinger (Cont.)
	Donald H. Rumsfeld, 1975
Attorney General	William B. Saxbe (Cont.)
	Edward H. Levi, 1975
Secretary of the Interior	Rogers C. B. Morton (Cont.)
	Stanley K. Hathaway, 1975
	Thomas S. Kleppe, 1975
Secretary of Agriculture	Earl L. Butz (Cont.)
	John Knebel, 1976
Secretary of Commerce	Frederick B. Dent (Cont.)
	Rogers C. B. Morton, 1975
	Elliot L. Richardson, 1976
Secretary of Labor	Peter J. Brennan (Cont.)
	John T. Dunlop, 1975
	William J. Usery, Jr., 1976
Secretary of Health, Education, and Welfare	Caspar W. Weinberger (Cont.)
	F. David Mathews, 1975
Secretary of Housing and Urban Development	James T. Lynn (Cont.)
	Carla A. Hills, 1975
Secretary of Transportation	Claude S. Brinegar (Cont.)
	William T. Coleman, Jr., 1975

Carter

Secretary of State	Cyrus R. Vance, 1977
	Edmund S. Muskie, 1980
Secretary of the Treasury	W. Michael Blumenthal, 1977
	G. William Miller, 1979
Secretary of Defense	Harold Brown, 1977
Attorney General	Griffin B. Bell, 1977
	Benjamin R. Civiletti, 1979
Secretary of the Interior	Cecil D. Andrus, 1977
Secretary of Agriculture	Bob S. Bergland, 1977
Secretary of Commerce	Juanita M. Kreps, 1977
	Philip M. Klutznick, 1979
Secretary of Labor	F. Ray Marshall, 1977
Secretary of Health and Human Services[1]	Joseph A. Califano, Jr., 1977
	Patricia Roberts Harris, 1979
Secretary of Housing and Urban Development	Patricia Roberts Harris, 1977
	Moon Landrieu, 1979
Secretary of Transportation	Brock Adams, 1977
	Neil E. Goldschmidt, 1979
Secretary of Energy	James R. Schlesinger, 1977
	Charles W. Duncan, Jr., 1979
Secretary of Education	Shirley Mount Hufstedler, 1979

1. Known as Department of Health, Education, and Welfare until May 1980.

Reagan

Secretary of State	Alexander M. Haig, Jr., 1981
	George P. Shultz, 1982
Secretary of the Treasury	Donald T. Regan, 1981
	James A. Baker 3rd, 1985
	Nicholas F. Brady, 1988
Secretary of Defense	Caspar W. Weinberger, 1981
	Frank C. Carlucci, 1987
Attorney General	William French Smith, 1981
	Edwin Meese 3rd, 1985
	Richard L. Thornburgh, 1988
Secretary of the Interior	James G. Watt, 1981
	William P. Clark, 1983
	Donald P. Hodel, 1985
Secretary of Agriculture	John R. Block, 1981
	Richard E. Lyng, 1986

Secretary of Commerce	Malcolm Baldrige, 1981
	C. William Verity, Jr., 1987
Secretary of Labor	Raymond J. Donovan, 1981
	William E. Brock, 1985
	Ann Dore McLaughlin, 1987
Secretary of Health and	Richard S. Schweiker, 1981
Human Services	Margaret M. Heckler, 1983
	Otis R. Bowen, 1985
Secretary of Housing and	Samuel R. Pierce, Jr., 1981
Urban Development	
Secretary of Transportation	Andrew L. Lewis, Jr., 1981
	Elizabeth H. Dole, 1983
	James H. Burnley 4th, 1987
Secretary of Energy	James B. Edwards, 1981
	Donald P. Hodel, 1983
	John S. Herrington, 1985
Secretary of Education	T. H. Bell, 1981
	William J. Bennett, 1985
	Lauro F. Cavazos, 1988

G. H. W. Bush

Secretary of State	James A. Baker 3d, 1989
	Lawrence S. Eagleburger, 1992
Secretary of the Treasury	Nicholas F. Brady (Cont.)
Secretary of Defense	Richard Cheney, 1989
Attorney General	Richard L. Thornburgh (Cont.)
	William P. Barr, 1992
Secretary of the Interior	Manuel Lujan Jr., 1989
Secretary of Agriculture	Clayton K. Yeutter, 1989
	Edward Madigan, 1991
Secretary of Commerce	Robert A. Mosbacher Sr., 1989
	Barbara H. Franklin, 1992
Secretary of Labor	Elizabeth H. Dole, 1989
	Lynn Martin, 1991
Secretary of Health and	Louis W. Sullivan, 1989
Human Services	
Secretary of Housing and	Jack F. Kemp, 1989
Urban Development	
Secretary of Transportation	Samuel K. Skinner, 1989
	Andrew Card, 1992
Secretary of Energy	James D. Watkins, 1989
Secretary of Education	Lauro F. Cavazos (Cont.)
	Lamar Alexander, 1991
Secretary of Veterans'	Edward J. Derwinski, 1989
Affairs	

Clinton

Secretary of State	Warren M. Christopher, 1993
	Madeleine Albright, 1996
Secretary of the Treasury	Lloyd Bentsen, 1993
	Robert E. Rubin, 1995–1999
	Lawrence H. Summers, 1999

Secretary of Defense	Les Aspin, 1993
	William J. Perry, 1994
	William S. Cohen, 1997
Attorney General	Janet Reno, 1993
Secretary of the Interior	Bruce Babbitt, 1993
Secretary of Agriculture	Mike Espy, 1993
	Dan Glickman, 1995
Secretary of Commerce	Ronald H. Brown, 1993
	Mickey Kantor, 1996
	William M. Daley, 1997
	Norman Y. Mineta, 2000
Secretary of Labor	Robert B. Reich, 1993
	Alexis Herman, 1997
Secretary of Health and	Donna E. Shalala, 1993
Human Services	
Secretary of Housing and	Henry G. Cisneros, 1993
Urban Development	Andrew M. Cuomo, 1997
Secretary of Transportation	Federico F. Pena, 1993
	Rodney Slater, 1997
Secretary of Energy	Hazel R. O'Leary, 1993
	Frederico F. Pena, 1997
	Bill Richardson, 1998
Secretary of Education	Richard W. Riley, 1993
Secretary of Veterans'	Jesse Brown, 1993
Affairs	Togo D. West, Jr., 1998

G. W. Bush

Secretary of State	Gen. Colin L. Powell, 2001–2005
	Condoleezza Rice, 2005
Secretary of the Treasury	Paul H. O'Neill, 2001–2002
	John Snow, 2003
Secretary of Defense	Donald H. Rumsfeld, 2001
Attorney General	John Ashcroft, 2001–2005
	Alberto Gonzales, 2005
Secretary of the Interior	Gale A. Norton, 2001
Secretary of Agriculture	Ann M. Veneman, 2001–2005
	Mike Johanns, 2005
Secretary of Commerce	Donald L. Evans, 2001–2005
	Carlos Gutierrez, 2005
Secretary of Labor	Elaine L. Chao, 2001
Secretary of Health and	Tommy G. Thompson, 2001–2005
Human Services	Mike Leavitt, 2005
Secretary of Homeland	Tom Ridge, 2003–2005
Security	Michael Chertoff, 2005
Secretary of Housing and	Melquiades R. Martinez, 2001
Urban Development	Alphonso Jackson, 2003
Secretary of Transportation	Norman Y. Mineta, 2001
Secretary of Energy	Spencer Abraham, 2001–2005
	Samuel Bodman, 2005
Secretary of Education	Roderick R. Paige, 2001–2005
	Margaret Spellings, 2005
Secretary of Veterans'	Anthony Principi, 2001–2005
Affairs	Jim Nicholson, 2005

Impeachments of Federal Officials

Source: Congressional Directory

The procedure for the impeachment of federal officials is detailed in Article I, Section 3, of the Constitution. The Senate has sat as a court of impeachment in the following cases:

William Blount, senator from Tennessee; charges dismissed for want of jurisdiction, Jan. 14, 1799.

John Pickering, judge of the U.S. District Court for New Hampshire; removed from office March 12, 1804.

Samuel Chase, associate justice of the Supreme Court; acquitted March 1, 1805.

James H. Peck, judge of the U.S. District Court for Missouri; acquitted Jan. 31, 1831.

West H. Humphreys, judge of the U.S. District Court for the middle, eastern, and western districts of Tennessee; removed from office June 26, 1862.

Andrew Johnson, president of the United States; acquitted May 26, 1868.

William W. Belknap, secretary of war; acquitted Aug. 1, 1876.

Charles Swayne, judge of the U.S. District Court for the northern district of Florida; acquitted Feb. 27, 1905.

Robert W. Archbald, associate judge, U.S. Commerce Court; removed Jan. 13, 1913.

George W. English, judge of the U.S. District Court for eastern district of Illinois; resigned Nov. 4, 1926; proceedings dismissed.

Harold Louderback, judge of the U.S. District Court for the northern district of California; acquitted May 24, 1933.

Halsted L. Ritter, judge of the U.S. District Court for the southern district of Florida; removed from office April 17, 1936.

Harry E. Claiborne, judge of the U.S. District Court for the district of Nevada; removed from office Oct. 9, 1986.

Alcee L. Hastings, judge of the U.S. District Court for the southern district of Florida; removed from office Oct. 20, 1988.

Walter L. Nixon, judge of the U.S. District Court for Mississippi; removed from office Nov. 3, 1989.

William J. Clinton, president of the United States; acquitted Feb. 12, 1999.

Members of the Supreme Court of the United States

Mailing address for the Supreme Court: U.S. Supreme Court Building, 1 First Street NE Washington, DC 20543

Name, state	Service Assoc. Justice	Service Chief Justice	Yrs	Birth Place	Date	Died	Religion
John Jay , N.Y.		1789–1795	5	N.Y.	1745	1829	Episcopal
James Wilson, Pa.	1789–1798		8	Scotland	1742	1798	Episcopal
John Rutledge, S.C.*	1790–1791	1795	1	S.C.	1739	1800	Church of England
William Cushing, Mass.	1790–1810		20	Mass.	1732	1810	Unitarian
John Blair, Va.	1790–1796		5	Va.	1732	1800	Presbyterian
James Iredell, N.C.	1790–1799		9	England	1751	1799	Episcopal
Thomas Johnson, Md.	1792–1793		0	Md.	1732	1819	Episcopal
William Paterson, N.J.	1793–1806		13	Ireland	1745	1806	Protestant
Oliver Ellsworth, Conn.		1796–1800	4	Conn.	1745	1807	Congregational
Samuel Chase, Md.	1796–1811		15	Md.	1741	1811	Episcopal
Bushrod Washington, Va.	1799–1829		30	Va.	1762	1829	Episcopal
Alfred Moore, N.C.	1800–1804		3	N.C.	1755	1810	Episcopal
John Marshall, Va.		1801–1835	34	Va.	1755	1835	Episcopal
William Johnson, S.C.	1804–1834		30	S.C.	1771	1834	Presbyterian
Brockholst Livingston, N.Y.	1807–1823		16	N.Y.	1757	1823	Presbyterian
Thomas Todd, Ky.	1807–1826		18	Va.	1765	1826	Presbyterian
Gabriel Duval, Md.	1811–1835		23	Md.	1752	1844	French Protestant
Joseph Story, Mass.	1812–1845		33	Mass.	1779	1845	Unitarian
Smith Thompson, N.Y.	1823–1843		20	N.Y.	1768	1843	Presbyterian
Robert Trimble, Ky.	1826–1828		2	Va.	1777	1828	Protestant
John McLean, Ohio	1830–1861		31	N.J.	1785	1861	Methodist-Epis.
Henry Baldwin, Pa.	1830–1844		14	Conn.	1780	1844	Trinity Church
James M. Wayne, Ga.	1835–1867		32	Ga.	1790	1867	Protestant
Philip P. Barbour, Va.	1836–1841		4	Va.	1783	1841	Episcopal
Roger B. Taney, Md.		1836–1864	28	Md.	1777	1864	Roman Catholic
John Catron, Tenn.	1837–1865		28	Pa.	1786	1865	Presbyterian
John McKinley, Ala.	1837–1852		14	Va.	1780	1852	Protestant
Peter V. Daniel, Va.	1841–1860		18	Va.	1784	1860	Episcopal
Samuel Nelson, N.Y.	1845–1872		27	N.Y.	1792	1873	Protestant
Levi Woodbury, N.H.	1845–1851		5	N.H.	1789	1851	Protestant
Robert C. Grier, Pa.	1846–1870		23	Pa.	1794	1870	Presbyterian
Benjamin R. Curtis, Mass.	1851–1857		5	Mass.	1809	1874	(2)
John A. Campbell, Ala.	1853–1861		8	Ga.	1811	1889	Episcopal
Nathan Clifford, Maine	1858–1881		23	N.H.	1803	1881	(1)
Noah H. Swayne, Ohio	1862–1881		18	Va.	1804	1884	Quaker
Samuel F. Miller, Iowa	1862–1890		28	Ky.	1816	1890	Unitarian
David Davis, Ill.	1862–1877		14	Md.	1815	1886	(4)
Stephen J. Field, Calif.	1863–1897		34	Conn.	1816	1899	Episcopal
Salmon P. Chase, Ohio		1864–1873	8	N.H.	1808	1873	Episcopal
William Strong, Pa.	1870–1880		10	Conn.	1808	1895	Presbyterian
Joseph P. Bradley, N.J.	1870–1892		21	N.Y.	1813	1892	Presbyterian
Ward Hunt, N.Y.	1872–1882		9	N.Y.	1810	1886	Episcopal
Morrison R. Waite, Ohio		1874–1888	14	Conn.	1816	1888	Episcopal
John M. Harlan, Ky.	1877–1911		33	Ky.	1833	1911	Presbyterian
William B. Woods, Ga.	1880–1887		6	Ohio	1824	1887	Protestant
Stanley Matthews, Ohio	1881–1889		7	Ohio	1824	1889	Presbyterian
Horace Gray, Mass.	1882–1902		20	Mass.	1828	1902	(3)
Samuel Blatchford, N.Y.	1882–1893		11	N.Y.	1820	1893	Presbyterian
Lucius Q. C. Lamar, Miss.	1888–1893		5	Ga.	1825	1893	Methodist

Name, state	Service Assoc. Justice	Chief Justice	Yrs	Birth Place	Date	Died	Religion
Melville W. Fuller, Ill.		1888–1910	21	Maine	1833	1910	Episcopal
David J. Brewer, Kan.	1889–1910		20	Asia Minor	1837	1910	Protestant
Henry B. Brown, Mich.	1890–1906		15	Mass.	1836	1913	Protestant
George Shiras, Jr., Pa.	1892–1903		10	Pa.	1832	1924	Presbyterian
Howell E. Jackson, Tenn.	1893–1895		2	Tenn.	1832	1895	Baptist
Edward D. White, La.*	1894–1910	1910–1921	26	La.	1845	1921	Roman Catholic
Rufus W. Peckham, N.Y.	1895–1909		13	N.Y.	1838	1909	Episcopal
Joseph McKenna, Calif.	1898–1925		26	Pa.	1843	1926	Roman Catholic
Oliver W. Holmes, Mass.	1902–1932		29	Mass.	1841	1935	Unitarian
William R. Day, Ohio	1903–1922		19	Ohio	1849	1923	Protestant
William H. Moody, Mass.	1906–1910		3	Mass.	1853	1917	Episcopal
Horace H. Lurton, Tenn.	1909–1914		4	Ky.	1844	1914	Episcopal
Charles E. Hughes, N.Y.*	1910–1916	1930–1941	16	N.Y.	1862	1948	Baptist
Willis Van Devanter, Wyo.	1910–1937		26	Ind.	1859	1941	Episcopal
Joseph R. Lamar, Ga.	1910–1916		4	Ga.	1857	1916	Ch. of Disciples
Mahlon Pitney, N.J.	1912–1922		10	N.J.	1858	1924	Presbyterian
James C. McReynolds, Tenn.	1914–1941		26	Ky.	1862	1946	Disciples of Christ
Louis D. Brandeis, Mass.	1916–1939		22	Ky.	1856	1941	Jewish
John H. Clarke, Ohio	1916–1922		5	Ohio	1857	1945	Protestant
William H. Taft, Conn.		1921–1930	8	Ohio	1857	1930	Unitarian
George Sutherland, Utah	1922–1938		15	England	1862	1942	Episcopal
Pierce Butler, Minn.	1923–1939		16	Minn.	1866	1939	Roman Catholic
Edward T. Sanford, Tenn.	1923–1930		7	Tenn.	1865	1930	Episcopal
Harlan F. Stone, N.Y.*	1925–1941	1941–1946	20	N.H.	1872	1946	Episcopal
Owen J. Roberts, Pa.	1930–1945		15	Pa.	1875	1955	Episcopal
Benjamin N. Cardozo, N.Y.	1932–1938		6	N.Y.	1870	1938	Jewish
Hugo L. Black, Ala.	1937–1971		34	Ala.	1886	1971	Baptist
Stanley F. Reed, Ky.	1938–1957		19	Ky.	1884	1980	Protestant
Felix Frankfurter, Mass.	1939–1962		23	Austria	1882	1965	Jewish
William O. Douglas, Conn.	1939–1975		36	Minn.	1898	1980	Presbyterian
Frank Murphy, Mich.	1940–1949		9	Mich.	1890	1949	Roman Catholic
James F. Byrnes, S.C.	1941–1942		1	S.C.	1879	1972	Episcopal
Robert H. Jackson, N.Y.	1941–1954		13	N.Y.	1892	1954	Episcopal
Wiley B. Rutledge, Iowa	1943–1949		6	Ky.	1894	1949	Unitarian
Harold H. Burton, Ohio	1945–1958		13	Mass.	1888	1964	Unitarian
Frederick M. Vinson, Ky.		1946–1953	7	Ky.	1890	1953	Methodist
Tom C. Clark, Tex.	1949–1967		17	Tex.	1899	1977	Presbyterian
Sherman Minton, Ind.	1949–1956		7	Ind.	1890	1965	Roman Catholic
Earl Warren, Calif.		1953–1969	15	Calif.	1891	1974	Protestant
John M. Harlan, N.Y.	1955–1971		16	Ill.	1899	1971	Presbyterian
William J. Brennan, Jr., N.J.	1956–1990		33	N.J.	1906	1997	Roman Catholic
Charles E. Whittaker, Mo.	1957–1962		5	Kan.	1901	1973	Methodist
Potter Stewart, Ohio	1958–1981		23	Mich.	1915	1985	Episcopal
Byron R. White, Colo.	1962–1993		31	Colo.	1917	2002	Episcopal
Arthur J. Goldberg, Ill.	1962–1965		2	Ill.	1908	1990	Jewish
Abe Fortas, Tenn.	1965–1969		3	Tenn.	1910	1982	Jewish
Thurgood Marshall, N.Y.	1967–1991		24	Md.	1908	1993	Episcopal
Warren E. Burger, Va.		1969–1986	17	Minn.	1907	1995	Presbyterian
Harry A. Blackmun, Minn.	1970–1994		24	Ill.	1908	1999	Methodist
Lewis F. Powell, Jr., Va.	1972–1987		15	Va.	1907	1998	Presbyterian
William H. Rehnquist, Ariz.*	1972–1986	1986–2005	33	Wis.	1924	2005	Lutheran
John Paul Stevens, Ill.	1975–		—	Ill.	1920	—	Protestant
Sandra Day O'Connor, Ariz.	1981–2005		24	Tex.	1930	—	Episcopal
Antonin Scalia, DC	1986–		—	N.J.	1936	—	Roman Catholic
Anthony M. Kennedy, Calif.	1988–		—	Calif.	1936	—	Roman Catholic
David H. Souter, N.H.	1990–		—	Mass.	1939	—	Episcopal
Clarence Thomas, DC	1991–		—	Ga.	1948	—	Roman Catholic
Ruth Bader Ginsburg, DC	1993–		—	N.Y.	1933	—	Jewish
Stephen G. Breyer, Mass.	1994–		—	Calif.	1938	—	Jewish

NOTE: **Bold=Chief Justice** *Served as both chief justice and associate justice. 1. Congregational; later Unitarian. 2. Unitarian; then Episcopal. 3. Unitarian or Congregational. 4. Not a member of any church.

Milestone Cases in Supreme Court History

1803 *Marbury* **v.** *Madison* was the first instance in which a law passed by Congress was declared unconstitutional. The decision greatly expanded the power of the Court by establishing its right to overturn acts of Congress, a power not explicitly granted by the Constitution. Initially the case involved Secretary of State James Madison, who refused to seat four judicial appointees although they had been confirmed by the Senate.

1824 *Gibbons* **v.** *Ogden* defined broadly Congress's right to regulate commerce. Aaron Ogden had filed suit in New York against Thomas Gibbons for operating a rival steamboat service between New York and New Jersey ports. Ogden had exclusive rights to operate steamboats in New York under a state law, while Gibbons held a federal license. Gibbons lost the case and appealed to the U.S. Supreme Court, which reversed the decision. The Court held that the New York law was unconstitutional, since the power to regulate interstate commerce, which extended to the regulation of navigation, belonged exclusively to Congress. In the 20th century, Chief Justice John Marshall's broad definition of commerce was used to uphold civil rights.

1857 *Dred Scott* **v.** *Sandford* was a highly controversial case that intensified the national debate over slavery. The case involved Dred Scott, a slave, who was taken from a slave state to a free territory. Scott filed a lawsuit claiming that because he had lived on free soil he was entitled to his freedom. Chief Justice Roger B. Taney disagreed, ruling that blacks were not citizens and therefore could not sue in federal court. Taney further inflamed antislavery forces by declaring that Congress had no right to ban slavery from U.S. territories.

1896 *Plessy* **v.** *Ferguson* was the infamous case that asserted that "equal but separate accommodations" for blacks on railroad cars did not violate the "equal protection under the laws" clause of the 14th Amendment. By defending the constitutionality of racial segregation, the Court paved the way for the repressive Jim Crow laws of the South. The lone dissenter on the Court, Justice John Marshall Harlan, protested, "The thin disguise of 'equal' accommodations . . . will not mislead anyone."

1954 *Brown* **v.** *Board of Education of Topeka* invalidated racial segregation in schools and led to the unraveling of de jure segregation in all areas of public life. In the unanimous decision spearheaded by Chief Justice Earl Warren, the Court invalidated the Plessy ruling, declaring "in the field of public education, the doctrine of 'separate but equal' has no place" and contending that "separate educational facilities are inherently unequal." Future Supreme Court justice Thurgood Marshall was one of the NAACP lawyers who successfully argued the case.

1963 *Gideon* **v.** *Wainwright* guaranteed a defendant's right to legal counsel. The Supreme Court overturned the Florida felony conviction of Clarence Earl Gideon, who had defended himself after having been denied a request for free counsel. The Court held that the state's failure to provide counsel for a defendant charged with a felony violated the Fourteenth Amendment's due process clause. Gideon was given another trial, and with a court-appointed lawyer defending him, he was acquitted.

1964 *New York Times* **v.** *Sullivan* extended the protection offered the press by the First Amendment. L.B. Sullivan, a police commissioner in Montgomery, Ala., had filed a libel suit against the *New York Times* for publishing inaccurate information about certain actions taken by the Montgomery police department. In overturning a lower court's decision, the Supreme Court held that debate on public issues would be inhibited if public officials could sue for inaccuracies that were made by mistake. The ruling made it more difficult for public officials to bring libel charges against the press, since the official had to prove that a harmful untruth was told maliciously and with reckless disregard for truth.

1966 *Miranda* **v.** *Arizona* was another case that helped define the due process clause of the 14th Amendment. At the center of the case was Ernesto Miranda, who had confessed to a crime during police questioning without knowing he had a right to have an attorney present. Based on his confession, Miranda was convicted. The Supreme Court overturned the conviction, ruling that criminal suspects must be warned of their rights before they are questioned by police. These rights are: the right to remain silent, to have an attorney present, and, if the suspect cannot afford an attorney, to have one appointed by the state. The police must also warn suspects that any statements they make can be used against them in court. Miranda was retried without the confession and convicted.

1973 *Roe* **v.** *Wade* legalized abortion and is at the center of the current controversy between "pro-life" and "pro-choice" advocates. The Court ruled that a woman has the right to an abortion without interference from the government in the first trimester of pregnancy, contending that it is part of her "right to privacy." The Court maintained that right to privacy is not absolute, however, and granted states the right to intervene in the second and third trimesters of pregnancy.

1978 *Regents of the University of California* **v.** *Bakke* imposed limitations on affirmative action to ensure that providing greater opportunities for minorities did not come at the expense of the rights of the majority. In other words, affirmative action was unfair if it lead to reverse discrimination. The case involved the University of Calif., Davis, Medical School and Allan Bakke, a white applicant who was rejected twice even though there were minority applicants admitted with significantly lower scores than his. A closely divided Court ruled that while race was a legitimate factor in school admissions, the use of rigid quotas was not permissible.

2003 *Grutter* v. *Bollinger* upheld the University of Michigan Law School's consideration of race and ethnicity in admissions. In her majority opinion, Justice O'Connor said that the law school used a "highly individualized, holistic review of each applicant's file." Race, she said, was not used in a "mechanical way." Therefore, the university's program was consistent with the requirement of "individualized consideration" set in 1978's *Bakke* case. "In order to cultivate a set of leaders with legiti-

macy in the eyes of the citizenry, it is necessary that the path to leadership be visibly open to talented and qualified individuals of every race and ethnicity," O'Connor said. However, the court ruled that the University of Michigan's undergraduate admissions system, which awarded 20 points to black, Hispanic, and American-Indian applicants, was "nonindividualized, mechanical," and thus unconstitutional.

Notable Decisions of the U.S. Supreme Court, 2004–2005 Term

Court Declares Sentencing Guidelines Unconstitutional (Jan. 12, 2005): In the first part of a two-part ruling in *United States v. Booker,* Court rules, 5–4, that federal sentencing guidelines in criminal cases violate the Sixth Amendment's right to a trial by jury because the guidelines allow judges to make factual findings that could increase a sentence beyond the maximum permitted by a jury. In the second part of the ruling, the Court resolves the issue, ruling, 5–4, that a defendant's rights would be protected by making the guidelines discretionary instead of mandatory.

Court Rules Against Execution of Juveniles (March 1, 2005): In *Roper v. Simmons,* Court decides, 5–4, that executing people who commit crimes before they turn 18 constitutes cruel and unusual punishment, a violation of the Eighth Amendment. Writing the majority opinion, Justice Kennedy points out that since the United States is the only country in the world that officially allows the execution of juveniles, it should be considered unusual punishment.

Justices Expand Protection under Title IX (March 29, 2005): Voting 5–4 in *Jackson v. Birmingham Board of Education,* the Court rules that the federal law, known as Title IX, that forbids sex discrimination in schools and colleges also protects third-party "whistleblowers" who file such complaints. "The statute is broadly worded: it does not require that the victim of the retaliation must also be the victim of the discrimination that is the subject of the original complaint," writes Justice O'Connor.

Ruling Broadens Criteria for Age Discrimination Suits (March 30, 2005): Court rules, 5–3, in *Smith v. City of Jackson,* that employees who sue for age discrimination do not have to prove that the discrimination was intentional, only that it negatively affected older workers.

Court Ends Ban on Wine Shipments (May 16, 2005): Votes, 5–4, to allow wineries to ship wine directly to out-of-state customers if state law allows in-state wineries to do so. Ruling in *Granholm v. Heald* invalidates state laws in New York and Michigan that the majority says violate the Commerce Clause of the Constitution.

Justices Overturn Verdict in Enron Scandal (May 31, 2005): Justices unanimously reject criminal conviction of auditing firm Arthur Andersen, saying the jury received improper instructions from the judge in the case. The company was convicted of shredding documents related to the Enron scandal. Chief Justice Rehnquist writes in the Court's opinion in *Arthur Andersen v. United States* that the jury was not instructed to prove that the company's auditors knew such acts were wrong.

Court Rules in Favor of Religion in Prisons (May 31, 2005): In a unanimous decision in *Cutter v. Wilkinson,* the justices say the Religious Land Use and Institutionalized Persons Act, a federal law that requires prison officials to accommodate inmates' religious

requirements, does not violate the Establishment Clause of the First Amendment.

Congress Can Ban Use of Medical Marijuana (June 6, 2005): In a 6–3 decision in *Gonzales v. Raich,* the Court upholds the right of Congress to prohibit the use of medical marijuana and to prosecute those who violate the law even in the 11 states that have passed initiatives legalizing it for medical purposes.

Disabilities Act Applies to Cruise Ships (June 6, 2005): Court rules, 6–3, that passengers of cruise ships that are operated by foreign companies but stop at American ports are protected by the Americans with Disabilities Act. The decision in *Spector v. Norwegian Cruise Line Ltd.,* however, says that the ships are not required to make structural changes if they can't accommodate the disabled.

Justices Reverse Murder Conviction (June 13, 2005): Court, 6–3, invalidates 1986 conviction of Thomas Miller-El, a black man from Texas, ruling that the jury selection in his trial was racially biased because the prosecution used peremptory strikes to exclude 10 out of 11 potential black jurors. The decision in *Miller-El v. Dretke* is the Court's second in Miller-El's favor.

Court Overturns Death Sentence (June 20, 2005): Justices vote, 5–4, in *Rompilla v. Beard,* to overturn the death sentence of Ronald Rompilla, a Pennsylvania man convicted of murder, saying that his lawyers failed to provide him with a defense that met minimum constitutional standards.

Justices Uphold Government's Use of Eminent Domain (June 23, 2005): In one of the most controversial cases of the session, the Court rules, 5–4, in *Kelo v. City of New London,* that a government can take possession of private property against the owner's will and transfer it to private developers when the result will promote economic development. The Fifth Amendment allows the government to take private property for public use. In writing the majority opinion, Justice John Paul Stevens says "public use" also means "public purpose." "Promoting economic development is a traditional and long accepted function of government," he says. "Clearly, there is no basis for exempting economic development from our traditionally broad understanding of public purpose."

Court Hands Down Divergent Rulings on Displays of Religious Symbols (June 27, 2005): In *Van Orden v. Perry,* Court rules, 5–4, that taken in historical context, the 6-foot-tall monument of the Ten Commandments on display on the grounds of the Texas Capitol in Austin does not violate the Establishment Clause. The monument, which has been up for about 40 years without causing controversy, is one of 17 in the 22-acre park. "Simply having religious content or promoting a message consistent with a religious doctrine does not run afoul of the Establishment Clause," says Chief Justice Rehnquist. In the second decision, *McCreary County v. American Civil Liberties Union,* however, the justices, 5–4, find that the framed copies of the Ten Commandments on display inside two county courthouses in Kentucky are unconstitutional because officials in the counties sought to promote religion. The framed copies were originally displayed by themselves, but officials hung historical documents beside them once litigation began in an attempt to put them in historical context. Justice Souter calls the counties' claims that they were secular displays "an apparent sham." He also writes, "Reasonable observers have reasonable memories."

Justices Reinstate Copyright-Infringement Suit (June 27, 2005): Court unanimously rules that companies that produce file-sharing services and software that allow—and encourage—users to illegally download music should be liable for copyright infringement. The companies "acted with a purpose to cause copyright violations by use of software suitable for illegal use," says Justice Souter. The decision, *Metro-Goldwyn-Mayer Studios v. Grokster, Ltd.*, sends the case back to a lower court.

U.S. History Timeline

NOTES: o.s. = old style (according to the Julian calendar). *See also*, States by Order of Entry into the Union; Presidential Elections 1789–2000; the Confederate States of America; National Censuses; Milestone Cases in Supreme Court History; World History; and Current Events.

c. 12,000 B.C.   North American Indian cultures flourish.

A.D. 1000   Norse seaman Leif Ericsson lands in Newfoundland, which he calls Vinland.

1492   Christopher Columbus, financed by Spain, makes the first of four voyages to the New World. He lands in the Bahamas (**Oct. 12**).

1513   Spanish explorer Juan Ponce de León lands on the coast of Florida.

1565   Saint Augustine, Florida, settled by the Spanish, becomes the first permanent European colony in North America.

1607   Jamestown, the first permanent English settlement in America, is established by the London Company in southeast Virginia (**May 14 o.s.**).

1619   The House of Burgesses, the first representative assembly in America, meets for the first time in Virginia (**July 30 o.s.**). The first African slaves are brought to Jamestown (**summer**).

1620   The Plymouth Colony in Massachusetts is established by Pilgrims from England (**Dec. 11 o.s.**). Before disembarking from their ship, the *Mayflower*, 41 male passengers sign the Mayflower Compact, an agreement that forms the basis of the colony's government.

1650   Colonial population is estimated at 50,400.

1752   Britain and the British colonies switch from the Julian to the Gregorian calendar (**Sept. 2**).

1754–1763   French and Indian War: Final conflict in the ongoing struggle between the British and French for control of eastern North America. The British win a decisive victory over the French on the Plains of Abraham outside Quebec (**Sept. 13, 1759**) and, by the Treaty of Paris (signed **Feb. 10, 1763**), formally gain control of Canada and all the French possessions east of the Mississippi.

1770   Boston Massacre: British troops fire into a mob, killing five men and leading to intense public protests (**March 5**).

1773   Boston Tea Party: Group of colonial patriots disguised as Mohawk Indians board three ships in Boston harbor and dump more than 300 crates of tea overboard as a protest against the British tea tax (**Dec. 16**).

1774   First Continental Congress meets in Philadelphia, with 56 delegates representing every colony except Georgia. Delegates include Patrick Henry, George Washington, and Samuel Adams (**Sept. 5–Oct. 26**).

1775–1783   American Revolution: War of independence fought between Great Britain and the 13 British colonies on the eastern seaboard of North America. Battles of Lexington and Concord, Mass., between the British Army and colonial minutemen, mark the beginning of the war (**April 19, 1775**). Battle-weary and destitute Continental army spends brutally cold winter and following spring at Valley Forge, Pa. (**Dec. 19, 1777–June 19, 1778**). British general Charles Cornwallis surrenders to Gen. George Washington at Yorktown, Va. (**Oct. 19, 1781**). Great Britain formally acknowledges American independence in the Treaty of Paris, which officially brings the war to a close (**Sept. 3, 1783**).

1776   Continental Congress adopts the Declaration of Independence in Philadelphia (**July 4**).

1777   Continental Congress approves the first official flag of the United States (**June 14**). Continental Congress adopts the Articles of Confederation, the first U.S. constitution (**Nov. 15**).

1786   Shays's Rebellion erupts (**Aug.**); farmers from New Hampshire to South Carolina take up arms to protest high state taxes and stiff penalties for failure to pay.

1787   Constitutional Convention, made up of delegates from 12 of the original 13 colonies, meets in Philadelphia to draft the U.S. Constitution (**May–Sept.**).

1789   George Washington is unanimously elected president of the United States in a vote by state electors (**Feb. 4**). U.S. Constitution goes into effect, having been ratified by nine states (**March 4**). U.S. Congress meets for the first time at Federal Hall in New York City (**March 4**). Washington is inaugurated as president at Federal Hall in New York City (**April 30**).

1790   U.S. Supreme Court meets for the first time at the Merchants Exchange Building in New York City (**Feb. 2**). The court, made up of one chief justice and five associate justices, hears its first case in 1792. The nation's first census shows that the population has climbed to nearly 4 million.

1791   First ten amendments to the Constitution, known as the Bill of Rights, are ratified (**Dec. 15**).

1793   Washington's second inauguration is held in Philadelphia (**March 4**). Eli Whitney's invention of the cotton gin greatly increases the demand for slave labor.

1797 John Adams is inaugurated as the second president in Philadelphia (**March 4**).

1800 The U.S. capital is moved from Philadelphia to Washington, DC (**June 15**). U.S. Congress meets in Washington, DC, for the first time (**Nov. 17**).

1801 Thomas Jefferson is inaugurated as the third president in Washington, DC (**March 4**).

1803 Louisiana Purchase: United States agrees to pay France $15 million for the Louisiana Territory, which extends west from the Mississippi River to the Rocky Mountains and comprises about 830,000 sq mi (treaty signed **May 2**). As a result, the U.S. nearly doubles in size.

1804 Lewis and Clark set out from St. Louis, Mo., on expedition to explore the West and find a route to the Pacific Ocean. (**May 14**).

1805 Jefferson's second inauguration (**March 4**). Lewis and Clark reach the Pacific Ocean (**Nov. 15**).

1809 James Madison is inaugurated as the fourth president (**March 4**).

1812–1814 War of 1812: U.S. declares war on Britain over British interference with American maritime shipping and westward expansion (**June 18, 1812**). Madison's second inauguration (**March 4, 1813**). British capture Washington, DC, and set fire to White House and Capitol (**Aug. 1814**). Francis Scott Key writes *Star-Spangled Banner* as he watches British attack on Fort McHenry at Baltimore (**Sept. 13–14, 1814**). Treaty of Ghent is signed, officially ending the war (**Dec. 24, 1814**).

1817 James Monroe is inaugurated as the fifth president (**March 4**).

1819 Spain agrees to cede Florida to the United States (**Feb. 22**).

1820 Missouri Compromise: In an effort to maintain the balance between free and slave states, Maine (formerly part of Massachusetts) is admitted as a free state so that Missouri can be admitted as a slave state; except for Missouri, slavery is prohibited in the Louisiana Purchase lands north of latitude 36°30′ (**March 3**).

1821 Monroe's second inauguration (**March 5**).

1823 Monroe Doctrine: In his annual address to Congress, President Monroe declares that the American continents are henceforth off-limits for further colonization by European powers (**Dec. 2**).

1825 John Quincy Adams is inaugurated as the sixth president (**March 4**). Erie Canal, linking the Hudson River to Lake Erie, is opened for traffic (**Oct. 26**).

1828 Construction is begun on the Baltimore and Ohio Railroad, the first public railroad in the U.S. (**July 4**).

1829 Andrew Jackson is inaugurated as seventh president (**March 4**).

1830 President Jackson signs the Indian Removal Act, which authorizes the forced removal of Native Americans living in the eastern part of the country to lands west of the Mississippi River (**May 28**). By the late 1830s the Jackson administration has relocated nearly 50,000 Native Americans.

1833 Jackson's second inauguration (**March 4**).

1836 Texas declares its independence from Mexico (**March 1**). Texan defenders of the Alamo are all killed during siege by the Mexican Army (**Feb. 24–March 6**). Texans defeat Mexicans at San Jacinto (**April 21**).

1837 Martin Van Buren is inaugurated as the eighth president (**March 4**).

1838 More than 15,000 Cherokee Indians are forced to march from Georgia to Indian Territory in present-day Oklahoma. Approximately 4,000 die from starvation and disease along the "Trail of Tears."

1841 William Henry Harrison is inaugurated as the ninth president (**March 4**). He dies one month later (**April 4**) and is succeeded in office by his vice president, John Tyler.

1845 U.S. annexes Texas by joint resolution of Congress (**March 1**). James Polk is inaugurated as the 11th president (**March 4**). The term "manifest destiny" appears for the first time in a magazine article by John L. O'Sullivan (**July–August**). It expresses the belief held by many white Americans that the United States is destined to expand across the continent.

1846 Oregon Treaty fixes U.S.-Canadian border at 49th parallel; U.S. acquires Oregon territory (**June 15**). The Wilmot Proviso attempts to ban slavery in territory gained in the Mexican War The proviso is blocked by Southerners, but continues to enflame the debate over slavery.

1846–1848 Mexican War: U.S. declares war on Mexico in effort to gain California and other territory in Southwest (**May 13, 1846**). War concludes with signing of Treaty of Guadalupe Hidalgo (**Feb. 2, 1848**). Mexico recognizes Rio Grande as new boundary with Texas and, for $15 million, agrees to cede territory comprising present-day California, Nevada, Utah, most of New Mexico and Arizona, and parts of Colorado and Wyoming.

1848 Gold is discovered at Sutter's Mill in California (**Jan. 24**); gold rush reaches its height the following year. Women's rights convention is held at Seneca Falls, N.Y. (**July 19–20**).

1849 Zachary Taylor is inaugurated as the 12th president (**March 5**).

1850 President Taylor dies (**July 9**) and is succeeded by his vice president, Millard Fillmore. The continuing debate whether territory gained in the Mexican War should be open to slavery is decided in the Compromise of 1850.

1853 Franklin Pierce is inaugurated as the 14th president (**March 4**). Gadsden Purchase treaty is signed; U.S. acquires border territory from Mexico for $10 million (**Dec. 30**).

1854 Congress passes the Kansas-Nebraska Act, establishing the territories of Kansas and Nebraska (**May 30**). The legislation repeals the Missouri Compromise of 1820 and renews tensions between anti- and proslavery factions.

1857 James Buchanan is inaugurated as the 15th president (**March 4**).

1858 Abraham Lincoln comes to national attention in a series of seven debates with Sen. Stephen A. Douglas during Illinois state election campaign (**Aug.–Oct.**).

1859 Abolitionist John Brown and 21 followers capture federal arsenal at Harpers Ferry, Va. (now W. Va.), in an attempt to spark a slave revolt (**Oct. 16**).

1860 Abraham Lincoln is elected president (**Nov. 6**). South Carolina secedes from the Union (**Dec. 20**).

1861 Mississippi, Florida, Alabama, Georgia, and Louisiana secede **(Jan.)**. Confederate States of America is established **(Feb. 8)**. Jefferson Davis is elected president of the Confederacy **(Feb. 9)**. Texas secedes **(March 2)**. Abraham Lincoln is inaugurated as the 16th president **(March 4)**.

1861–1865 Civil War: Conflict between the North (the Union) and the South (the Confederacy) over the expansion of slavery into western states. Confederates attack Ft. Sumter in Charleston, S.C., marking the start of the war **(April 12, 1861)**. Virginia, Arkansas, North Carolina, and Tennessee secede **(April–June)**. Emancipation Proclamation is issued, freeing slaves in the Confederate states **(Jan. 1, 1863)**. Gen. William T. Sherman captures Atlanta **(Sept. 2, 1864)**. Lincoln's second inauguration **(March 4, 1865)**. Gen. Ulysses S. Grant captures Richmond, Va., the capital of the Confederacy **(April 3)**. Confederate general Robert E. Lee surrenders to Ulysses S. Grant at Appomattox Courthouse, Va., **(April 9)**.

1863 Homestead Act becomes law, allowing settlers to claim land (160 acres) after they have lived on it for five years **(Jan. 1)**.

1865 Lincoln is assassinated **(April 14)** by John Wilkes Booth in Washington, DC, and is succeeded by his vice president, Andrew Johnson. Thirteenth Amendment to the Constitution is ratified, prohibiting slavery **(Dec. 6)**.

1867 U.S. acquires Alaska from Russia for the sum of $7.2 million (treaty concluded **March 30**).

1868 President Johnson is impeached by the House of Representatives **(Feb. 24)**, but he is acquitted at his trial in the Senate **(May 26)**. Fourteenth Amendment to the Constitution is ratified, defining citizenship **(July 9)**.

1869 Ulysses S. Grant is inaugurated as the 18th president **(March 4)**. Central Pacific and Union Pacific railroads are joined at Promontory, Utah, creating first transcontinental railroad **(May 10)**.

1870 Fifteenth Amendment to the Constitution is ratified, giving blacks the right to vote **(Feb. 3)**.

1871 Chicago fire kills 300 and leaves 90,000 people homeless **(Oct. 8–9)**.

1872 Crédit Mobilier scandal breaks, involving several members of Congress **(Sept.)**.

1873 Grant's second inauguration **(March 4)**.

1876 Lt. Col. George A. Custer's regiment is wiped out by Sioux Indians under Sitting Bull at the Little Big Horn River, Mont. **(June 25)**.

1877 Rutherford B. Hayes is inaugurated as the 19th president **(March 5)**. The first telephone line is built from Boston to Somerville, Mass.; the following year, President Hayes has the first telephone installed in the White House.

1881 James A. Garfield is inaugurated as the 20th president **(March 4)**. He is shot **(July 2)** by Charles Guiteau in Washington, DC, and later dies from complications of his wounds in Elberon, N.J. **(Sept. 19)**. Garfield's vice president, Chester Alan Arthur, succeeds him in office.

1882 U.S. adopts standard time **(Nov. 18)**.

1885 Grover Cleveland is inaugurated as the 22nd president **(March 4)**.

1886 Statue of Liberty is dedicated **(Oct. 28)**. American Federation of Labor is organized **(Dec.)**.

1889 Benjamin Harrison is inaugurated as the 23rd president **(March 4)**. Oklahoma is opened to settlers **(April 22)**.

1890 National American Woman Suffrage Association (NAWSA) is founded, with Elizabeth Cady Stanton as president. Sherman Antitrust Act is signed into law, prohibiting commercial monopolies **(July 2)**. Last major battle of the Indian Wars occurs at Wounded Knee, S.D. **(Dec. 29)**. In reporting the results of the 1890 census, the Census Bureau announces that the West has been settled and the frontier is closed.

1892 Ellis Island becomes chief immigration station of the U.S. **(Jan. 1)**.

1893 Grover Cleveland is inaugurated a second time, as the 24th president **(March 4)**. He is the only president to serve two nonconsecutive terms.

1897 William McKinley is inaugurated as the 25th president **(March 4)**.

1898 Spanish-American War: USS *Maine* is blown up in Havana harbor **(Feb. 15)**, prompting U.S. to declare war on Spain **(April 25)**. Treaty of Paris is signed, ending the Spanish-American War **(Dec. 10)**; Spain gives up control of Cuba, which becomes an independent republic, and cedes Puerto Rico, Guam, and (for $20 million) the Philippines to the U.S.

1898 U.S. annexes Hawaii by an act of Congress **(July 7)**.

1899 U.S. acquires American Samoa by treaty with Great Britain and Germany **(Dec. 2)**.

1900 Galveston hurricane leaves an estimated 6,000 to 8,000 dead **(Sept. 8)**. According to the census, the nation's population numbers nearly 76 million.

1901 McKinley's second inauguration **(March 4)**. He is shot **(Sept. 6)** by anarchist Leon Czolgosz in Buffalo, N.Y., and later dies from his wounds **(Sept. 14)**. He is succeeded by his vice president, Theodore Roosevelt.

1903 U.S. acquires Panama Canal Zone (treaty signed **Nov. 17**). Wright brothers make the first controlled, sustained flight in heavier-than-air aircraft at Kitty Hawk, N.C. **(Dec. 17)**.

1905 Theodore Roosevelt's second inauguration **(March 4)**.

1906 San Francisco earthquake leaves 500 dead or missing and destroys about 4 sq mi of the city **(April 18)**.

1908 Bureau of Investigation, forerunner of the FBI, is established **(July 26)**.

1909 William Howard Taft is inaugurated as the 27th president **(March 4)**.

1913 Woodrow Wilson is inaugurated as the 28th president **(March 4)**. Seventeenth Amendment to the Constitution is ratified, providing for the direct election of U.S. senators by popular vote rather than by the state legislatures **(April 8)**.

1914–1918 World War I: U.S. enters World War I, declaring war on Germany **(April 6, 1917)** and Austria-Hungary **(Dec. 7, 1917)** three years after conflict began in 1914. Armistice ending World War I is signed **(Nov. 11, 1918)**.

1914 Panama Canal opens to traffic **(Aug. 15)**.

1915 First long distance telephone service, between New York and San Francisco, is demonstrated **(Jan. 25)**.

1916 U.S. agrees to purchase Danish West Indies (Virgin Islands) for $25 million (treaty signed **Aug. 14**). Jeannette Rankin of Montana is the first woman elected to the U.S. House of Representatives **(Nov. 7).**

1917   Wilson's second inauguration **(March 5).** First regular airmail service begins between Washington, DC, and New York **(May 15).**

1918   Worldwide influenza epidemic strikes; by 1920, nearly 20 million are dead. In U.S., 500,000 perish.

1919   League of Nations meets for the first time; U.S. is not represented **(Jan. 13).** Eighteenth Amendment to the Constitution is ratified, prohibiting the manufacture, sale, and transportation of liquor **(Jan. 16).** It is later repealed by the Twenty-First Amendment in 1933. Nineteenth Amendment to the Constitution is ratified, granting women the right to vote **(Aug. 18).** President Wilson suffers a stroke **(Sept. 26).** Treaty of Versailles, outlining terms for peace at the end of World War I, is rejected by the Senate **(Nov. 19).**

1921   Warren G. Harding is inaugurated as the 29th president **(March 4).** He signs resolution declaring peace with Austria and Germany **(July 2).**

1923   President Harding dies suddenly **(Aug. 2).** He is succeeded by his vice president, Calvin Coolidge. Teapot Dome scandal breaks, as Senate launches an investigation into improper leasing of naval oil reserves during Harding administration **(Oct.)**

1925   Coolidge's second inauguration **(March 4).** Tennessee passes a law against the teaching of evolution in public schools **(March 23),** setting the stage for the Scopes Monkey Trial **(July 10–25).**

1927   Charles Lindbergh makes the first solo nonstop transatlantic flight in his plane *The Spirit of St. Louis* **(May 20–21).**

1929   Herbert Hoover is inaugurated as the 31st president **(March 4).** Stock market crash precipitates the Great Depression **(Oct. 29).**

1931   *The Star-Spangled Banner* is adopted as the national anthem **(March 3).**

1932   Hattie Wyatt Caraway of Arkansas is the first woman elected to the U.S. Senate, to fill a vacancy caused by the death of her husband **(Jan. 12).** She is reelected in 1932 and 1938. Amelia Earhart completes first solo nonstop transatlantic flight by a woman **(May 21).**

1933   Twentieth Amendment to the Constitution, sometimes called the "Lame Duck Amendment," is ratified, moving the president's inauguration date from March 4 to Jan. 20 **(Jan. 23).** Franklin Roosevelt is inaugurated as the 32nd president **(March 4).** New Deal recovery measures are enacted by Congress **(March 9–June 16).** Twenty-First Amendment to the Constitution is ratified, repealing Prohibition **(Dec. 5).**

1935   Works Progress Administration is established **(April 8).** Social Security Act is passed **(Aug. 14).** Bureau of Investigation (established 1908) becomes the Federal Bureau of Investigation under J. Edgar Hoover.

1937   F. Roosevelt's second inauguration **(Jan. 20).**

1938   Fair Labor Standards Act is passed, setting the first minimum wage in the U.S. at 25 cents per hour **(June 25).**

1939–1945   World War II: U.S. declares its neutrality in European conflict **(Sept. 5, 1939).** F. Roosevelt's third inauguration **(Jan. 20, 1941).** He is the first and only president elected to a third term. Japan attacks Hawaii, Guam, and the Philippines **(Dec. 7, 1941).** U.S. declares war on Japan **(Dec. 8).** Germany and Italy declare war on the United States; U.S. reciprocates by declaring war on both countries **(Dec. 11).** Allies invade North Africa **(Oct.–Dec. 1942)** and Italy **(Sept.–Dec. 1943).** Allies invade France on D-Day **(June 6, 1944).** F. Roosevelt's fourth inauguration **(Jan. 20, 1945).** President Roosevelt, Churchill, and Stalin meet at Yalta in the USSR to discuss postwar occupation of Germany **(Feb. 4–11).** President Roosevelt dies of a stroke **(April 12)** and is succeeded by his vice president, Harry Truman. Germany surrenders unconditionally **(May 7).** First atomic bomb is detonated at Alamogordo, N.M. **(July 16).** President Truman, Churchill, and Stalin meet at Potsdam, near Berlin, Germany, to demand Japan's unconditional surrender and to discuss plans for postwar Europe **(July 17–Aug. 2).** U.S. drops atomic bomb on Hiroshima, Japan **(Aug. 6).** U.S. drops atomic bomb on Nagasaki, Japan **(Aug. 9).** Japan agrees to unconditional surrender **(Aug. 14).** Japanese envoys sign surrender terms aboard the USS *Missouri* in Tokyo harbor **(Sept. 2).**

1945   United Nations is established **(Oct. 24).**

1946   The Philippines, which had been ceded to the U.S. by Spain at the end of the Spanish-American War, becomes an independent republic **(July 4).**

1947   Central Intelligence Agency is established.

1948   Congress passes foreign aid bill including the Marshall Plan, which provides for European postwar recovery **(April 2).** Soviets begin blockade of Berlin in the first major crisis of the cold war **(June 24).** In response, U.S. and Great Britain begin airlift of food and fuel to West Berlin **(June 26).**

1949   Truman's second inauguration **(Jan. 20).** North Atlantic Treaty Organization (NATO) is established **(April 4).** Soviets end blockade of Berlin **(May 12),** but airlift continues until Sept. 30.

1950–1953   Korean War: Cold war conflict between Communist and non-Communist forces on Korean Peninsula. North Korean communists invade South Korea **(June 25, 1950).** President Truman, without the approval of Congress, commits American troops to battle **(June 27).** Armistice agreement is signed **(July 27, 1953).**

1950–1975   Vietnam War: Prolonged conflict between Communist forces of North Vietnam, backed by China and the USSR, and non-Communist forces of South Vietnam, backed by the United States. President Truman authorizes $15 million in economic and military aid to the French, who are fighting to retain control of French Indochina, including Vietnam. As part of the aid package, Truman also sends 35 military advisers **(May 1950).** North Vietnamese torpedo boats allegedly attack U.S. destroyer in Gulf of Tonkin off the coast of North Vietnam **(Aug. 2, 1964).** Congress approves Gulf of Tonkin resolution, authorizing President Johnson to take any measures necessary to defend U.S. forces and prevent further aggression **(Aug. 7).** U.S. planes begin bombing raids of North Vietnam **(Feb. 1965).** First U.S. combat troops arrive in South Vietnam **(March 8–9).** North Vietnamese army and Viet Cong launch Tet

Offensive, attacking Saigon and other key cities in South Vietnam (**Jan.–Feb. 1968**). American soldiers kill 300 Vietnamese villagers in My Lai massacre (**March 16**). U.S. troops invade Cambodia (**May 1, 1970**). Representatives of North and South Vietnam, the Viet Cong, and the U.S. sign a cease-fire agreement in Paris (**Jan. 27, 1973**). Last U.S. troops leave Vietnam (**March 29**). South Vietnamese government surrenders to North Vietnam; U.S. embassy Marine guards and last U.S. civilians are evacuated (**April 30, 1975**).

1951 Twenty-Second Amendment to the Constitution is ratified, limiting the president to two terms (**Feb. 27**). President Truman speaks in first coast-to-coast live television broadcast (**Sept. 4**).

1952 Puerto Rico becomes a U.S. commonwealth (**July 25**). First hydrogen bomb is detonated by the U.S. on Eniwetok, an atoll in the Marshall Islands (**Nov. 1**).

1953 Dwight Eisenhower is inaugurated as the 34th president (**Jan. 20**). Julius and Ethel Rosenberg are executed for passing secret information about U.S. atomic weaponry to the Soviets (**June 19**).

1954 Sen. Joseph R. McCarthy accuses army officials, members of the media, and other public figures of being Communists during highly publicized hearings (**April 22–June 17**).

1957 Eisenhower's second inauguration (**Jan. 21**). President sends federal troops to Central High School in Little Rock, Ark., to enforce integration of black students (**Sept. 24**).

1958 *Explorer I*, first American satellite, is launched (**Jan. 31**).

1959 Alaska becomes the 49th state (**Jan. 3**) and Hawaii becomes the 50th (**Aug. 21**).

1961 U.S. severs diplomatic relations with Cuba (**Jan. 3**). John F. Kennedy is inaugurated as the 35th president (**Jan. 20**). Bay of Pigs invasion of Cuba fails (**April 17–20**). A mixed-race group of volunteers sponsored by the Committee on Racial Equality—the so-called Freedom Riders—travel on buses through the South in order to protest racially segregated interstate bus facilities (**May**).

1962 Lt. Col. John Glenn becomes first U.S. astronaut to orbit Earth (**Feb. 20**). Cuban Missile Crisis: President Kennedy denounces Soviet Union for secretly installing missile bases on Cuba and initiates a naval blockade of the island (**Oct. 22–Nov. 20**).

1963 Rev. Martin Luther King, Jr., delivers his "I Have a Dream" speech before a crowd of 200,000 during the civil rights march on Washington, DC (**Aug. 28**). President Kennedy is assassinated in Dallas, Tex. (**Nov. 22**). He is succeeded in office by his vice president, Lyndon B. Johnson.

1964 President Johnson signs the Civil Rights Act (**July 2**).

1965 In his annual state of the Union address, President Johnson proposes his Great Society program (**Jan. 4**). L. Johnson's second inauguration (**Jan. 20**). State troopers attack peaceful demonstrators led by Rev. Martin Luther King, Jr., as they try to cross bridge in Selma, Ala. (**March 7**). President Johnson signs the Voting Rights Act, which prohibits discriminatory voting practices (**Aug. 6**). In six days of rioting in Watts, a black section of Los Angeles, 35 people are killed and 883 injured (**Aug. 11–16**).

1967 Twenty-Fifth Amendment to the Constitution is ratified, outlining the procedures for filling vacancies in the presidency and vice presidency (**Feb. 10**).

1968 Rev. Martin Luther King, Jr., is assassinated in Memphis, Tenn. (**April 4**). Sen. Robert F. Kennedy is assassinated in Los Angeles, Calif. (**June 5–6**).

1969 Richard Nixon is inaugurated as the 37th president (**Jan. 20**). Astronauts Neil Armstrong and Edwin Aldrin, Jr., become the first men to land on the Moon (**July 20**).

1970 Four students are shot to death by National Guardsmen during an antiwar protest at Kent State University (**May 1**).

1971 The Twenty-Sixth Amendment to the Constitution is ratified, lowering the voting age from 21 to 18 (**July 1**).

1972 Nixon makes historic visit to Communist China (**Feb. 21–27**). U.S. and Soviet Union sign strategic arms control agreement known as SALT I (**May 26**). Five men, all employees of Nixon's reelection campaign, are caught breaking into rival Democratic headquarters at the Watergate complex in Washington, DC (**June 17**).

1973 Nixon's second inauguration (**Jan. 20**). Senate Select Committee begins televised hearings to investigate Watergate cover-up (**May 17–Aug. 7**). Vice President Spiro T. Agnew resigns over charges of corruption and income tax evasion (**Oct. 10**). President Nixon nominates Gerald R. Ford as vice president (**Oct. 12**). Ford is confirmed by Congress and sworn in (**Dec. 6**).

1974 House Judiciary Committee recommends to full House that Nixon be impeached on grounds of obstruction of justice, abuse of power, and contempt of Congress (**July 27–30**). Nixon resigns; he is succeeded in office by his vice president, Gerald Ford (**Aug. 9**). Nixon is granted an unconditional pardon by President Ford (**Sept. 8**). Five former Nixon aides go on trial for their involvement in the Watergate cover-up (**Oct. 15**); H. R. Haldeman, John D. Ehrlichman, and John Mitchell eventually serve time in prison. Nelson Rockefeller is confirmed and sworn in as vice president (**Dec. 19**).

1977 Jimmy Carter is inaugurated as the 39th president (**Jan. 20**). President Carter signs treaty (**Sept. 7**) agreeing to turn control of Panama Canal over to Panama on Dec. 31, 1999.

1978 President Carter meets with Egyptian president Anwar Sadat and Israeli prime minister Menachem Begin at Camp David (**Sept. 6**); Sadat and Begin sign Camp David Accord, ending 30-year conflict between Egypt and Israel (**Sept. 17**).

1979 U.S. establishes diplomatic ties with mainland China for the first time since Communist takeover in 1949 (**Jan. 1**). Malfunction at Three Mile Island nuclear reactor in Pennsylvania causes near meltdown (**March 28**). Panama takes control of the Canal Zone, formerly administered by U.S. (**Oct. 1**). Iranian students storm U.S. embassy in Teheran and hold 66 people hostage (**Nov. 4**); 13 of the hostages are released (**Nov. 19–20**).

1980 President Carter announces that U.S. athletes will not attend Summer Olympics in Moscow unless Soviet Union withdraws from Afghanistan (**Jan. 20**). FBI's undercover bribery investigation, code named Abscam, implicates a U.S. senator, seven members of the House, and 31 other public officials (**Feb. 2**). U.S. mission to rescue hostages in Iran is aborted after a helicopter and cargo plane collide at the staging site in a remote part of Iran and 8 servicemen are killed (**April 25**).

1981 Ronald Reagan is inaugurated as the 40th president (**Jan. 20**). U.S. hostages held in Iran are released after 444 days in captivity (**Jan. 20**). President Reagan is shot in the chest by John Hinckley, Jr. (**March 30**). Sandra Day O'Connor is sworn in as the first woman Supreme Court justice (**Sept. 25**).

1982 Deadline for ratification of the Equal Rights Amendment to the Constitution passes without the necessary votes (**June 30**).

1983 U.S. invades Caribbean island of Grenada after a coup by Marxist faction in the government (**Oct. 25**).

1985 Reagan's second inauguration (**Jan. 21**).

1986 Space shuttle *Challenger* explodes 73 seconds after liftoff, killing all seven crew members (**Jan. 28**). It is the worst accident in the history of the U.S. space program. U.S. bombs military bases in Libya in effort to deter terrorist strikes on American targets (**April 14**). Iran-Contra scandal breaks when White House is forced to reveal secret arms-for-hostages deals (**Nov.**).

1987 Congress holds public hearings in Iran-Contra investigation (**May 5–Aug. 3**). In a speech in Berlin, President Reagan challenges Soviet leader Mikhail Gorbachev to "tear down this wall" and open Eastern Europe to political and economic reform (**June 12**). Reagan and Gorbachev sign INF treaty, the first arms-control agreement to reduce the superpowers' nuclear weapons (**Dec. 8**).

1989 George H. W. Bush is inaugurated as the 41st president (**Jan. 20**). Oil tanker *Exxon Valdez* runs aground in Prince William Sound, spilling more than 10 million gallons of oil (**March 24**). It is the largest oil spill in U.S. history. President Bush signs legislation to provide for federal bailout of nearly 800 insolvent savings and loan institutions (**Aug. 9**). U.S. forces invade Panama in an attempt to capture Gen. Manuel Noriega, who previously had been indicted in the U.S. on drug trafficking charges (**Dec. 20**).

1991 Persian Gulf War: U.S. leads international coalition in military operation (code named "Desert Storm") to drive Iraqis out of Kuwait (**Jan. 16–Feb. 28**). Iraq accepts terms of UN ceasefire, marking an end of the war (**April 6**).

1991 U.S. and Soviet Union sign START I treaty, agreeing to further reduce strategic nuclear arms (**July 31**). Senate Judiciary Committee conducts televised hearings to investigate allegations of past sexual harassment brought against Supreme Court nominee Clarence Thomas by Anita Hill, a law professor at the University of Oklahoma (**Oct. 11–13**).

1992 Following the breakup of the Soviet Union in Dec. 1991, President Bush and Russian president Boris Yeltsin meet at Camp David and formally declare an end to the cold war (**Feb. 1**). The acquittal of four white police officers charged in the 1991 beating of black motorist Rodney King in Los Angeles sets off several days of rioting, leading to more than 50 deaths, thousands of injuries and arrests, and $1 billion in property damage (**April 29**). President Bush authorizes sending U.S. troops to Somalia as part of UN relief effort (**Dec. 4**). President Bush grants pardons to six officials convicted or indicted in the Iran-Contra scandal, leading some to suspect a cover-up (**Dec. 24**).

1993 Bill Clinton is inaugurated as the 42nd president (**Jan. 20**). Bomb explodes in basement garage of World Trade Center, killing 6, injuring 1,000, and causing more than $500 million in damage (**Feb. 26**). After 51-day standoff with federal agents, Branch Davidian compound in Waco, Tex., burns to the ground, killing 80 cult members (**April 19**). President Clinton orders missile attack against Iraq in retaliation for alleged plot to assassinate former President Bush (**June 26**). Eighteen U.S. soldiers are killed in ambush by Somali militiamen in Mogadishu (**Oct. 3–4**). President Clinton signs North American Free Trade Agreement into law (**Dec. 8**).

1994 Paula Jones, a former Arkansas state employee, files a federal lawsuit against President Clinton for sexual harassment (**May 6**).

1995 Bombing of federal office building in Oklahoma City kills 168 people (**April 19**). U.S. establishes full diplomatic relations with Vietnam (**July 11**). President Clinton sends first 8,000 of 20,000 U.S. troops to Bosnia for 12-month peacekeeping mission (**Dec.**). Budget standoff between President Clinton and Congress results in partial shutdown of U.S. government (**Dec. 16–Jan. 6**).

1997 Clinton's second inauguration (**Jan. 20**).

1998 President Clinton denies having had a sexual relationship with a White House intern named Monica Lewinsky (**Jan. 17**). President Clinton releases 1999 federal budget plan; it is the first balanced budget since 1969 (**Feb. 2**). In televised address, President Clinton admits having had a sexual relationship with Monica Lewinsky (**Aug. 17**). U.S. launches missile attacks on targets in Sudan and Afghanistan following terrorist attacks on U.S. embassies in Kenya and Tanzania (**Aug. 20**). U.S. and Britain launch air strikes against weapons sites in Iraq (**Dec. 16**). House of Representatives votes to impeach President Clinton on charges of perjury and obstruction of justice (**Dec. 19**).

1999 Senate acquits Clinton of impeachment charges (**Feb. 12**). NATO wages air campaign against Yugoslavia over killing and deportation of ethnic Albanians in Kosovo (**March 24–June 10**). School shooting at Columbine High School in Littleton, Colo., leaves 14 students (including the 2 shooters) and 1 teacher dead and 23 others wounded (**April 20**).

2000 According to the census, the nation's population numbers more than 280 million (**April 1**). No clear winner is declared in the close presidential election contest between Vice President Al Gore and Texas governor George W. Bush (**Nov. 7**). More than a month after the presidential election, the U.S. Supreme Court rules against a manual recount of ballots in certain Florida counties, which it contends would violate the Constitution's equal protection and due process guarantees. The decision provokes enormous controversy, with critics maintaining that the court has in effect determined the outcome of the election (**Dec. 12**). Bush formally accepts the presidency, having won a slim majority in the electoral college but not a majority of the popular vote (**Dec. 13**).

2001 George W. Bush is inaugurated as the 43rd president (**Jan. 20**). Two hijacked jetliners ram twin towers of World Trade Center in worst terrorist attack against U.S.; a third hijacked plane flies into the Pentagon, and a fourth crashes in rural Pennsylvania. More than 3,000 people die in the attacks (**Sept. 11**). U.S. and Britain launch air attacks against targets in Afghanistan after Taliban government fails to hand over Saudi terrorist Osama bin Laden, the suspected mastermind behind the Sept. 11 attacks (**Oct. 7**). Following air campaign and ground assault by Afghani opposition troops, the Taliban regime topples (**Dec. 9**); however, the hunt for bin Laden and other members of al-Qaeda terrorist organization continues.

2002 In his first State of the Union address, President Bush labels Iran, Iraq, and North Korea an "axis of evil" and declares that U.S. will wage war against states that develop weapons of mass destruction (**Jan. 29**). President Bush signs legislation creating a new cabinet department of Homeland Security. (**Nov. 25**).

2003 Space shuttle *Columbia* explodes upon reentry into Earth's atmosphere, killing all seven astronauts on board (**Feb. 1**). War waged by the U.S. and Britain against Iraq begins (**March 19**). President Bush signs $350 billion tax-cut bill (**May 28**).

2004 The U.S. returns sovereignty to an interim government in Iraq, but maintains roughly 135,000 troops in the country to fight a growing insurgency (**June 28**).

2005 The U.S. engagement in Iraq continues amid that country's escalating violence and fragile political stability. Hurricane Katrina wreaks catastrophic damage on Mississippi and Louisiana; 80% of New Orleans is flooded (**Aug. 29–30**). All levels of government are criticized for the delayed and inadequate response to the disaster.

See also Current Events, pp. 32–44.

Firsts in America

This selection is based on our editorial judgment. Other sources may list different firsts.

Admiral in U.S. Navy: David Glasgow Farragut, 1866.

Airmail route, first transcontinental: Between New York City and San Francisco, 1920.

Assembly, representative: House of Burgesses, founded in Virginia, 1619.

Bank established: Bank of North America, Philadelphia, 1781.

Birth in America to English parents: Virginia Dare, born Roanoke Island, N.C., 1587.

Black newspaper: *Freedom's Journal,* 1827, edited by John B. Russworm.

Black U.S. diplomat: Ebenezer D. Bassett, 1869, minister-resident to Haiti.

Black elected governor of a state: L. Douglas Wilder, Virginia, 1990.

Black elected to U.S. Senate: Hiram Revels, 1870, Mississippi.

Black elected to U.S. House of Representatives: Jefferson Long, Georgia, 1870.

Black associate justice of U.S. Supreme Court: Thurgood Marshall, Oct. 2, 1967.

Black secretary of state: Gen. Colin Powell, appointed Dec. 2000.

Black U.S. cabinet minister: Robert C. Weaver, 1966, Secretary of the Department of Housing and Urban Development.

Botanic garden: Established by John Bartram in Philadelphia, 1728, and is still in existence in its original location.

College: Harvard, founded 1636.

College to establish coeducation: Oberlin College (Ohio), 1833.

Electrocution of a criminal: William Kemmler in Auburn Prison, Auburn, N.Y., Aug. 6, 1890.

Five and Dime store: Founded by Frank Woolworth, Utica, N.Y., 1879 (moved to Lancaster, Pa., same year).

Fraternity, Greek-letter: Phi Beta Kappa; founded Dec. 5, 1776, at College of William and Mary.

Gay and lesbian civil rights advocacy organization, national: National Gay and Lesbian Task Force, founded in New York City, 1973.

Lesbian, acknowledged, elected to high local office: Kathy Kozachenko, 1974, Ann Arbor City Council.

Gay man, acknowledged, elected to high local office: Harvey Milk, 1977, San Francisco Board of Supervisors.

Law to be declared unconstitutional by U.S. Supreme Court: Judiciary Act of 1789. Case: *Marbury* v. *Madison,* 1803.

Library, circulating: Philadelphia, 1731.

Newspaper, illustrated daily: *New York Daily Graphic,* 1873.

Newspaper published daily: *Pennsylvania Packet and General Advertiser,* Philadelphia, Sept. 1784.

Newspaper published over a continuous period: *The Boston News-Letter,* April 1704.

Oil well, commercial: Titusville, Pa., 1859.

Panel quiz show on radio: *Information Please,* May 17, 1938.

Postage stamps issued: 1847.

Public school: Boston Latin School, Boston, 1635.

Radio station licensed: KDKA, Pittsburgh, Pa., Oct. 27, 1920.

Railroad, transcontinental: Central Pacific and Union Pacific railroads, joined at Promontory, Utah, May 10, 1869.

Savings bank: The Provident Institute for Savings, Boston, 1816.

Science museum: Founded by Charleston (S.C.) Library Society, 1773.

Skyscraper: Home Insurance Co., Chicago, 1885 (10 floors, 2 added later).

Slaves brought into America: At Jamestown, Va., 1619, from a Dutch ship.

Sorority: Alpha Delta Pi, at Wesleyan Female College, 1851.

State to abolish capital punishment: Michigan, 1847.

State to enter Union after original 13: Vermont, 1791.

Steam-heated building: Eastern Hotel, Boston, 1845.

Steam railroad (carried passengers and freight): Baltimore & Ohio, 1830.

Strike on record by union: Journeymen Printers, New York City, 1776.

Subway: Opened in Boston, 1897.

"Tabloid" picture newspaper: *The Illustrated Daily News* (now the *Daily News*), New York City, 1919.

Vaudeville theater: Gaiety Museum, Boston, 1883.

Woman astronaut appointed shuttle commander: Lt. Col. Eileen Collins, *Columbia*, launched July 1999.

Woman astronaut to ride in space: Dr. Sally K. Ride, 1983.

Woman astronaut to walk in space: Dr. Kathryn D. Sullivan, 1984.

Woman cabinet member: Frances Perkins, Secretary of Labor, 1933.

Woman candidate for president: Victoria Claflin Woodhull, nominated by National Woman's Suffrage Assn. on ticket of Nation Radical Reformers, 1872.

Woman candidate for vice president: Geraldine A. Ferraro, nominated on a major party ticket, Democratic Party, 1984.

Woman doctor of medicine: Elizabeth Blackwell, M.D. from Geneva Medical College of Western New York, 1849.

Woman elected governor of a state: Nellie Tayloe Ross, Wyoming, 1925.

Woman elected to U.S. Senate: Hattie Caraway, Arkansas; elected Nov. 1932.

Woman graduate of law school: Ada H. Kepley, Union College of Law, Chicago, 1870.

Woman member of U.S. House of Representatives: Jeannette Rankin (Mont.); elected Nov. 1916.

Woman member of U.S. Senate: Rebecca Latimer Felton (Ga.); appointed Oct. 3, 1922.

Woman member of U.S. Supreme Court: Sandra Day O'Connor; appointed July 1981.

Woman secretary of state: Madeleine Albright, appointed Dec. 1996.

Woman suffrage granted: Wyoming Territory, 1869.

Written constitution: *Fundamental Orders of Connecticut,* 1639.

The Early Congresses

At the urging of Massachusetts and Virginia, the First Continental Congress met in Philadelphia on Sept. 5, 1774, and was attended by representatives of all the colonies except Georgia. Patrick Henry of Virginia declared: "The distinctions between Pennsylvanians, New Yorkers, and New Englanders are no more. I am not a Virginian but an American." This Congress, which adjourned Oct. 26, 1774, passed intercolonial resolutions calling for extensive boycott by the colonies against British trade.

The following year, most of the delegates from the colonies were chosen by popular election to attend the Second Continental Congress, which assembled in Philadelphia on May 10. As war had already begun between the colonies and England, the chief problems before the Congress were the procuring of military supplies, the establishment of an army and proper defenses, the issuing of continental bills of credit, etc. On June 15, 1775, George Washington was elected to command the Continental army. Congress adjourned Dec. 12, 1776.

Other Continental Congresses were held in Baltimore (1776–1777), Philadelphia (1777), Lancaster, Pa. (1777), York, Pa. (1777–1778), and Philadelphia (1778–1781).

In 1781, the Articles of Confederation, although establishing a league of the thirteen states rather than a strong central government, provided for the continuance of Congress. Known thereafter as the Congress of the Confederation, it held sessions in Philadelphia (1781–1783), Princeton, N.J. (1783), Annapolis, Md. (1783–1784), and Trenton, N.J. (1784). Five sessions were held in New York City between the years 1785 and 1789.

The Congress of the United States, established by the ratification of the Constitution, held its first meeting on March 4, 1789, in New York City. Several sessions of Congress were held in Philadelphia, and the first meeting in Washington, DC, was on Nov. 17, 1800.

Presidents of the Continental Congresses

Name	Elected	Birth and death dates	Name	Elected	Birth and death dates
Peyton Randolph, Va.	9/5/1774	c.1721–1775	John Hanson, Md.	11/5/1781	1715–1783
Henry Middleton, S.C.	10/22/1774	1717–1784	Elias Boudinot, N.J.	11/4/1782	1740–1821
Peyton Randolph, Va.	5/10/1775	c.1721–1775	Thomas Mifflin, Pa.	11/3/1783	1744–1800
John Hancock, Mass.	5/24/1775	1737–1793	Richard Henry Lee, Va.	11/30/1784	1732–1794
Henry Laurens, S.C.	11/1/1777	1724–1792	John Hancock, Mass.[1]	11/23/1785	1737–1793
John Jay, N.Y.	12/10/1778	1745–1829	Nathaniel Gorham, Mass.	6/6/1786	1738–1796
Samuel Huntington, Conn.	9/28/1779	1731–1796	Arthur St. Clair, Pa.	2/2/1787	1734–1818
Thomas McKean, Del.	7/10/1781	1734–1817	Cyrus Griffin, Va.	1/22/1788	1748–1810

1. Resigned May 29, 1786, never having served, because of continued illness.

History of the American Flag

According to popular legend, the first American flag was made by Betsy Ross, a Philadelphia seamstress who was acquainted with George Washington, leader of the Continental Army, and other influential Philadelphians. In May 1776, so the story goes, General Washington and two representatives from the Continental Congress visited Ross at her upholstery shop and showed her a rough design of the flag. Although Washington initially favored using a star with six points, Ross advocated for a five-pointed star, which could be cut with just one quick snip of the scissors, and the gentlemen were won over.

Unfortunately, historians have never been able to verify this charming version of events, although it is known that Ross made flags for the navy of Pennsylvania. The story of Washington's visit to the flagmaker became popular about the time of the country's first centennial, after William Canby, a grandson of Ross, told about her role in shaping U.S. history in a speech given at the Philadelphia Historical Society in March 1870.

What is known is that the first unofficial national flag, called the Grand Union Flag or the Continental Colours, was raised at the behest of General Washington near his headquarters outside Boston, Mass.,

on Jan. 1, 1776. The flag had 13 alternating red and white horizontal stripes and the British Union Flag (a predecessor of the Union Jack) in the canton. Another early flag had a rattlesnake and the motto "Don't Tread on Me."

The first official national flag, also known as the Stars and Stripes, was approved by the Continental Congress on June 14, 1777. The blue canton contained 13 stars, representing the original 13 colonies, but the layout varied. Although nobody knows for sure who designed the flag, it may have been Continental Congress member Francis Hopkinson.

After Vermont and Kentucky were admitted to the Union in 1791 and 1792, respectively, two more stars and two more stripes were added in 1795. This 15-star, 15-stripe flag was the "star-spangled banner" that inspired lawyer Francis Scott Key to write the poem that later became the U.S. national anthem.

In 1818, after five more states had gained admittance, Congress passed legislation fixing the number of stripes at 13 and requiring that the number of stars equal the number of states. The last new star, bringing the total to 50, was added on July 4, 1960, after Hawaii became a state.

The Pledge of Allegiance to the Flag[1]

I pledge allegiance to the Flag of the United States of America, and to the Republic for which it stands, one Nation under God,[2] indivisible, with liberty and justice for all.

1. The original pledge was published in the Sept. 8, 1892, issue of *The Youth's Companion* in Boston. For years, the authorship was in dispute between James B. Upham and Francis Bellamy of the magazine's staff. In 1939, after a study of the controversy, the United States Flag Association decided that authorship be credited to Bellamy.
2. The phrase "under God" was added to the pledge on June 14, 1954.

The Great Seal of the U.S.

On July 4, 1776, the Continental Congress appointed a committee consisting of Benjamin Franklin, John Adams, and Thomas Jefferson "to bring in a device for a seal of the United States of America." After many delays, a verbal description of a design by William Barton was finally approved by Congress on June 20, 1782. The seal shows an American bald eagle with a ribbon in its mouth bearing the device *E pluribus unum* (One out of many). In its talons are the arrows of war and an olive branch of peace. On the reverse side it shows an unfinished pyramid with an eye (the eye of Providence) above it. Although this description was adopted in 1782, the first drawing was not made until four years later, and no die has ever been cut.

The Liberty Bell

The Liberty Bell was cast in England in 1752 for the Pennsylvania Statehouse (now named Independence Hall) in Philadelphia. It was recast in Philadelphia in 1753. It is inscribed with the words, "Proclaim liberty throughout all the land unto all the inhabitants thereof" (Lev. 25:10). The bell was rung on July 8, 1776, for the first public reading of the

Declaration of Independence. Hidden in Allentown during the British occupation of Philadelphia, it was re-placed in Independence Hall in 1778. The bell cracked on July 8, 1835, while tolling the death of Chief Justice John Marshall. In 1976 the Liberty Bell was moved to a special exhibition building near Independence Hall.

States by Order of Entry into Union

State	Entered Union	Year settled	State	Entered Union	Year settled
1. Delaware	Dec. 7, 1787	1638	26. Michigan	Jan. 26, 1837	1668
2. Pennsylvania	Dec. 12, 1787	1682	27. Florida	Mar. 3, 1845	1565
3. New Jersey	Dec. 18, 1787	1660	28. Texas	Dec. 29, 1845	1682
4. Georgia	Jan. 2, 1788	1733	29. Iowa	Dec. 28, 1846	1788
5. Connecticut	Jan. 9, 1788	1634	30. Wisconsin	May 29, 1848	1766
6. Massachusetts	Feb. 6, 1788	1620	31. California	Sept. 9, 1850	1769
7. Maryland	Apr. 28, 1788	1634	32. Minnesota	May 11, 1858	1805
8. South Carolina	May 23, 1788	1670	33. Oregon	Feb. 14, 1859	1811
9. New Hampshire	June 21, 1788	1623	34. Kansas	Jan. 29, 1861	1727
10. Virginia	June 25, 1788	1607	35. West Virginia	June 20, 1863	1727
11. New York	July 26, 1788	1614	36. Nevada	Oct. 31, 1864	1849
12. North Carolina	Nov. 21, 1789	1660	37. Nebraska	Mar. 1, 1867	1823
13. Rhode Island	May 29, 1790	1636	38. Colorado	Aug. 1, 1876	1858
14. Vermont	Mar. 4, 1791	1724	39. North Dakota	Nov. 2, 1889	1812
15. Kentucky	June 1, 1792	1774	40. South Dakota	Nov. 2, 1889	1859
16. Tennessee	June 1, 1796	1769	41. Montana	Nov. 8, 1889	1809
17. Ohio	Mar. 1, 1803	1788	42. Washington	Nov. 11, 1889	1811
18. Louisiana	Apr. 30, 1812	1699	43. Idaho	July 3, 1890	1842
19. Indiana	Dec. 11, 1816	1733	44. Wyoming	July 10, 1890	1834
20. Mississippi	Dec. 10, 1817	1699	45. Utah	Jan. 4, 1896	1847
21. Illinois	Dec. 3, 1818	1720	46. Oklahoma	Nov. 16, 1907	1889
22. Alabama	Dec. 14, 1819	1702	47. New Mexico	Jan. 6, 1912	1610
23. Maine	Mar. 15, 1820	1624	48. Arizona	Feb. 14, 1912	1776
24. Missouri	Aug. 10, 1821.	1735	49. Alaska	Jan. 3, 1959	1784
25. Arkansas	June 15, 1836	1686	50. Hawaii	Aug. 21, 1959	1820

Source: Compiled from various sources by the editors.

The Confederate States of America

State	Seceded from Union	Readmitted to Union[1]	State	Seceded from Union	Readmitted to Union[1]
1. South Carolina	Dec. 20, 1860	July 9, 1868	7. Texas	March 2, 1861	March 30, 1870
2. Mississippi	Jan. 9, 1861	Feb. 23, 1870	8. Virginia	April 17, 1861	Jan. 26, 1870
3. Florida	Jan. 10, 1861	June 25, 1868	9. Arkansas	May 6, 1861	June 22, 1868
4. Alabama	Jan. 11, 1861	July 13, 1868	10. North Carolina	May 20, 1861	July 4, 1868
5. Georgia	Jan. 19, 1861	July 15, 1870[2]	11. Tennessee	June 8, 1861	July 24, 1866
6. Louisiana	Jan. 26, 1861	July 9, 1868			

NOTE: Four other slave states—Delaware, Maryland, Kentucky, and Missouri—remained in the Union. The latter two were actually represented on the Confederate flag, which, like the Stars and Stripes, featured a star for every state. 1. Date of readmission to representation in U.S. House of Representatives. 2. Second readmission date. First date was July 21, 1868, but the representatives were unseated March 5, 1869.

Territorial Expansion

Accession	Date	Area[1]	Accession	Date	Area[1]
United States	—	3,717,796	Other territory		
Territory in 1790	—	891,364	Philippines[2]	1898	115,600
Louisiana Purchase	1803	831,321	Puerto Rico	1899	3,508
Florida	1819	69,866	Guam	1899	217
Texas	1845	384,958	American Samoa	1900	90
Oregon	1846	283,439	Canal Zone[3]	1904	553
Mexican Cession	1848	530,706	Virgin Islands of U.S.	1917	171
Gadsden Purchase	1853	29,640	Trust Territory of Pacific Islands[4]	1947	241
Alaska	1867	591,004	Northern Mariana Islands	1986	189
Hawaii	1898	6,471	All other	—	16
			Total, 1990	—	**3,722,228**

1. Total area (land and water), in square miles. 2. Became independent in 1946. 3. Reverted to Panama in 1979. 4. Palau, the last remaining trust territory, became a sovereign state in 1994. *Source:* U.S. Bureau of the Census, Web: www.census.gov.

The EXPANSION of the UNITED STATES

The Star-Spangled Banner
Francis Scott Key, 1814

O say, can you see, by the dawn's early light,
What so proudly we hail'd at the twilight's last gleaming?
Whose broad stripes and bright stars, thro' the perilous fight,
O'er the ramparts we watch'd, were so gallantly streaming?
And the rockets' red glare, the bombs bursting in air,
Gave proof thro' the night that our flag was still there.
O say, does that star-spangled banner yet wave
O'er the land of the free and the home of the brave?

On the shore dimly seen thro' the mists of the deep,
Where the foe's haughty host in dread silence reposes,
What is that which the breeze, o'er the towering steep,
As it fitfully blows, half conceals, half discloses?
Now it catches the gleam of the morning's first beam,
In full glory reflected, now shines on the stream:
'Tis the star-spangled banner: O, long may it wave
O'er the land of the free and the home of the brave!

And where is that band who so vauntingly swore
That the havoc of war and the battle's confusion,
A home and a country should leave us no more?
Their blood has wash'd out their foul footsteps' pollution.
No refuge could save the hireling and slave
From the terror of flight or the gloom of the grave:
And the star-spangled banner in triumph doth wave
O'er the land of the free and the home of the brave.

O thus be it ever when free-men shall stand
Between their lov'd home and the war's desolation;
Blest with vict'ry and peace, may the heav'n-rescued land
Praise the Pow'r that hath made and preserv'd us a nation!
Then conquer we must, when our cause it is just,
And this be our motto: "In God is our trust!"
And the star-spangled banner in triumph shall wave
O'er the land of the free and the home of the brave!

On Sept. 13, 1814, Francis Scott Key visited the British fleet in Chesapeake Bay to secure the release of Dr. William Beanes, who had been captured after the burning of Washington, DC. The release was secured, but Key was detained on ship overnight during the shelling of Fort McHenry, one of the forts defending Baltimore. In the morning, he was so delighted to see the American flag still flying over the fort that he began a poem to commemorate the occasion. First published under the title "Defense of Fort M'Henry," the poem soon attained wide popularity as sung to the tune "To Anacreon in Heaven." The origin of this tune is obscure, but it may have been written by John Stafford Smith, a British composer born in 1750. "The Star-Spangled Banner" was officially made the national anthem by Congress in 1931, although it already had been adopted as such by the army and the navy.

The Monroe Doctrine

The Monroe Doctrine was announced in President James Monroe's message to Congress, during his second term on Dec. 2, 1823, in part as follows:

"In the discussions to which this interest has given rise, and in the arrangements by which they may terminate, the occasion has been deemed proper for asserting as a principle in which rights and interests of the United States are involved, that the American continents, by the free and independent condition which they have assumed and maintain, are henceforth not to be considered as subjects for future colonization by any European power. . . . We owe it, therefore, to candor and to the amicable relations existing between the United States and those powers to declare that we should consider any attempt on their part to extend their system to any portion of this hemisphere as dangerous to our peace and safety. With the existing colonies or dependencies of any European power we have not interfered and shall not interfere. But with the governments who have declared their independence and maintain it, and whose independence we have, on great consideration and on just principles, acknowledged, we could not view any interposition for the purpose of oppressing them or controlling in any other manner their destiny by any European power in any other light than as the manifestation of an unfriendly disposition toward the United States."

Washington Monument

Construction of this magnificent Washington, DC, monument took nearly a century of planning, building, and controversy. Provision for a large equestrian statue of George Washington was made in the original city plan, but the project was soon dropped. After Washington's death it was taken up again, and a number of false starts and changes of design were made. Finally, in 1848, work was begun on the monument that stands today. The design, by architect Robert Mills, then featured an ornate base. In 1854, however, political squabbling and a lack of money brought construction to a halt. Work was resumed in 1880, and the monument was completed in 1884 and opened to the public in 1888. The tapered shaft, faced with white marble and rising from walls 15 ft (4.6 m) thick at the base, was modeled after the obelisks of ancient Egypt. The monument, one of the tallest masonry constructions in the world, stands just over 555 ft (169 m). Memorial stones from the 50 states, foreign countries, and organizations line the interior walls. The top, reached only by elevator, commands a panoramic view of the city.

The Declaration of Independence

On April 12, 1776, the legislature of North Carolina authorized its delegates to the Continental Congress to join with others in a declaration of separation from Great Britain; the first colony to instruct its delegates to take the actual initiative was Virginia on May 15. On June 7, 1776, Richard Henry Lee of Virginia offered a resolution to the Congress to the effect "that these United Colonies are, and of right ought to be, free and independent States. . . ." A committee consisting of Thomas Jefferson, John Adams, Benjamin Franklin, Robert R. Livingston, and Roger Sherman was organized to "prepare a declaration to the effect of the said first resolution." The Declaration of Independence was adopted on July 4, 1776. Most delegates signed the Declaration August 2, but George Wythe (Va.) signed August 27; Richard Henry Lee (Va.), Elbridge Gerry (Mass.), and Oliver Wolcott (Conn.) in September; Matthew Thornton (N.H.), not a delegate until September, in November; and Thomas McKean (Del.), although present on July 4, not until 1781 by special permission, having served in the army in the interim.

In Congress, July 4, 1776
The unanimous Declaration of the thirteen United States of America

When in the Course of human events it becomes necessary for one people to dissolve the political bands which have connected them with another, and to assume among the powers of the earth, the separate and equal station to which the Laws of Nature and of Nature's God entitle them, a decent respect to the opinions of mankind requires that they should declare the causes which impel them to the separation.

We hold these truths to be self-evident, that all men are created equal, that they are endowed by their Creator with certain unalienable Rights, that among these are Life, Liberty and the pursuit of Happiness.—That to secure these rights, Governments are instituted among Men, deriving their just powers from the consent of the governed.—That whenever any Form of Government becomes destructive of these ends, it is the Right of the People to alter or to abolish it, and to institute new Government, laying its foundation on such principles and organizing its powers in such form, as to them shall seem most likely to effect their Safety and Happiness. Prudence, indeed, will dictate that Governments long established should not be changed for light and transient causes; and accordingly all experience hath shewn that mankind are more disposed to suffer, while evils are sufferable, than to right themselves by abolishing the forms to which they are accustomed. But when a long train of abuses and usurpations, pursuing invariably the same Object evinces a design to reduce them under absolute Despotism, it is their right, it is their duty, to throw off such Government, and to provide new Guards for their future security.—Such has been the patient sufferance of these Colonies; and such is now the necessity which constrains them to alter their former Systems of Government. The history of the present King of Great Britain is a history of repeated injuries and usurpations, all having in direct object the establishment of an absolute Tyranny over these States. To prove this, let Facts be submitted to a candid world.

He has refused his Assent to Laws, the most wholesome and necessary for the public good.

He has forbidden his Governors to pass Laws of immediate and pressing importance, unless suspended in their operation till his Assent should be obtained; and when so suspended, he has utterly neglected to attend to them.

He has refused to pass other Laws for the accommodation of large districts of people, unless those people would relinquish the right of Representation in the Legislature, a right inestimable to them and formidable to tyrants only.

He has called together legislative bodies at places unusual, uncomfortable, and distant from the depository of their Public Records, for the sole purpose of fatiguing them into compliance with his measures.

He has dissolved Representative Houses repeatedly, for opposing with manly firmness his invasions on the rights of the people.

He has refused for a long time, after such dissolutions, to cause others to be elected; whereby the Legislative Powers, incapable of Annihilation, have returned to the People at large for their exercise; the State remaining in the mean time exposed to all the dangers of invasion from without, and convulsions within.

He has endeavoured to prevent the population of these States; for that purpose obstructing the Laws for Naturalization of Foreigners; refusing to pass others to encourage their migrations hither, and raising the conditions of new Appropriations of Lands.

He has obstructed the Administration of Justice, by refusing his Assent to Laws for establishing Judiciary Powers.

He has made Judges dependent on his Will alone, for the tenure of their offices, and the amount and payment of their salaries.

He has erected a multitude of New Offices, and sent hither swarms of Officers to harass our people, and eat out their substance.

He has kept among us, in times of peace, Standing Armies without the Consent of our legislatures.

He has affected to render the Military independent of and superior to the Civil Power.

He has combined with others to subject us to a jurisdiction foreign to our constitution, and unacknowledged by our laws; giving his Assent to their Acts of pretended Legislation:

For quartering large bodies of armed troops among us:

For protecting them, by a mock Trial, from punishment for any Murders which they should commit on the Inhabitants of these States:

For cutting off our Trade with all parts of the world:

For imposing Taxes on us without our Consent:

For depriving us in many cases, of the benefits of Trial by Jury:

For transporting us beyond Seas to be tried for pretended offences:

For abolishing the free System of English Laws in a neighbouring Province, establishing therein an Arbitrary government, and enlarging its Boundaries so as to render it at once an example and fit instrument for introducing the same absolute rule into these Colonies:

For taking away our Charters, abolishing our most valuable Laws and altering fundamentally the Forms of our Governments:

For suspending our own Legislatures, and declaring themselves invested with power to legislate for us in all cases whatsoever.

He has abdicated Government here, by declaring us out of his Protection and waging War against us.

He has plundered our seas, ravaged our Coasts, burnt our towns, and destroyed the lives of our people.

He is at this time transporting large Armies of foreign Mercenaries to compleat the works of death, desolation, and tyranny, already begun with circumstances of Cruelty & Perfidy scarcely paralleled in the most barbarous ages, and totally unworthy the Head of a civilized nation.

He has constrained our fellow Citizens taken Captive on the high Seas to bear Arms against their Country, to become the executioners of their friends and Brethren, or to fall themselves by their Hands.

He has excited domestic insurrections amongst us, and has endeavoured to bring on the inhabitants of our frontiers, the merciless Indian Savages, whose known rule of warfare, is an undistinguished destruction of all ages, sexes and conditions.

In every stage of these Oppressions We have Petitioned for Redress in the most humble terms: Our repeated Petitions have been answered only by repeated injury. A Prince, whose character is thus marked by every act which may define a Tyrant, is unfit to be the ruler of a free people.

Nor have We been wanting in attentions to our British brethren. We have warned them from time to time of attempts by their legislature to extend an unwarrantable jurisdiction over us. We have reminded them of the circumstances of our emigration and settlement here. We have appealed to their native justice and magnanimity, and we have conjured them by the ties of our common kindred to disavow these usurpations, which would inevitably interrupt our connections and correspondence. They too have been deaf to the voice of justice and of consanguinity. We must, therefore, acquiesce in the necessity, which denounces our Separation, and hold them, as we hold the rest of mankind, Enemies in War, in Peace Friends.

We, therefore, the Representatives of the United States of America, in General Congress, Assembled, appealing to the Supreme Judge of the world for the rectitude of our intentions, do, in the Name, and by Authority of the good People of these Colonies, solemnly publish and declare, That these United Colonies are, and of Right ought to be Free and Independent States; that they are Absolved from all Allegiance to the British Crown, and that all political connection between them and the State of Great Britain, is and ought to be totally dissolved; and that as Free and Independent States, they have full Power to levy War, conclude Peace, contract Alliances, establish Commerce, and to do all other Acts and Things which Independent States may of right do.—And for the support of this Declaration, with a firm reliance on the protection of Divine Providence, we mutually pledge to each other our Lives, our Fortunes and our sacred Honor.

—John Hancock

New Hampshire
Josiah Bartlett
Wm. Whipple
Matthew Thornton

Rhode Island
Step. Hopkins
William Ellery

Connecticut
Roger Sherman
Sam'el Huntington
Wm. Williams
Oliver Wolcott

New York
Wm. Floyd
Phil. Livingston
Frans. Lewis
Lewis Morris

New Jersey
Richd. Stockton
Jno. Witherspoon
Fras. Hopkinson
John Hart
Abra. Clark

Pennsylvania
Robt. Morris
Benjamin Rush
Benj. Franklin
John Morton
Geo. Clymer
Jas. Smith
Geo. Taylor
James Wilson
Geo. Ross

Massachusetts-Bay
Saml. Adams
John Adams
Robt. Treat Paine
Elbridge Gerry

Delaware
Caesar Rodney
Geo. Read
Tho. M'Kean

Maryland
Samuel Chase
Wm. Paca
Thos. Stone
Charles Carroll of
  Carrollton

Virginia
George Wythe
Richard Henry Lee
Th. Jefferson
Benj. Harrison
Ths. Nelson, Jr.
Francis Lightfoot Lee
Carter Braxton

North Carolina
Wm. Hooper
Joseph Hewes
John Penn

South Carolina
Edward Rutledge
Thos. Heyward, Junr.
Thomas Lynch, Junr.
Arthur Middleton

Georgia
Button Gwinnett
Lyman Hall
Geo. Walton

Constitution of the United States of America

(Historical text has been edited to conform to contemporary American usage. The bracketed words are designations for your convenience; they are not part of the Constitution.)

The oldest federal constitution in existence was framed by a convention of delegates from twelve of the thirteen original states in Philadelphia in May 1787, Rhode Island failing to send a delegate. George Washington presided over the session, which lasted until September 17, 1787. The draft (originally a preamble and seven Articles) was submitted to all thirteen states and was to become effective when ratified by nine states. It went into effect on the first Wednesday in March 1789, having been ratified by New Hampshire, the ninth state to approve, on June 21, 1788. The states ratified the Constitution in the following order:

Delaware	December 7, 1787	South Carolina	May 23, 1788
Pennsylvania	December 12, 1787	New Hampshire	June 21, 1788
New Jersey	December 18, 1787	Virginia	June 25, 1788
Georgia	January 2, 1788	New York	July 26, 1788
Connecticut	January 9, 1788	North Carolina	November 21, 1789
Massachusetts	February 6, 1788	Rhode Island	May 29, 1790
Maryland	April 28, 1788		

[Preamble]

We the people of the United States, in order to form a more perfect Union, establish justice, insure domestic tranquility, provide for the common defence, promote the general welfare, and secure the blessings of liberty to ourselves and our posterity, do ordain and establish this Constitution for the United States of America.

Article I

Section 1

[Legislative powers vested in Congress.] All legislative powers herein granted shall be vested in a Congress of the United States, which shall consist of a Senate and House of Representatives.

Section 2

[Composition of the House of Representatives.—1.] The House of Representatives shall be composed of members chosen every second year by the people of the several States, and the electors in each State shall have the qualifications requisite for electors of the most numerous branch of the State Legislature.

[Qualifications of Representatives.—2.] No Person shall be a Representative who shall not have attained to the age of twenty-five years, and been seven years a citizen of the United States, and who shall not, when elected, be an inhabitant of that State in which he shall be chosen.

[Apportionment of Representatives and direct taxes—census.[1]—3.] (Representatives and direct taxes shall be apportioned among the several States which may be included within this Union, according to their respective numbers, which shall be determined by adding to the whole number of free persons, including those bound to service for a term of years, and excluding Indians not taxed, three fifths of all other persons.) The actual enumeration shall be made within three years after the first meeting of the Congress of the United States, and within every subsequent term of ten years, in such manner as they shall by law direct. The number of Representatives shall not exceed one for every thirty thousand, but each State shall have at least one Representative; and until such enumeration shall be made, the State of New Hampshire shall be entitled to choose three, Massachusetts eight, Rhode-Island and Providence Plantations one, Connecticut five, New York six, New Jersey four, Pennsylvania eight, Delaware one, Maryland six, Virginia ten, North Carolina five, South Carolina five, and Georgia three.

[Filling of vacancies in representation.—4.] When vacancies happen in the representation from any State, the Executive Authority thereof shall issue writs of election to fill such vacancies.

[Selection of officers; power of impeachment.—5.] The House of Representatives shall choose their Speaker and other officers; and shall have the sole power of impeachment.

Section 3[2]

[The Senate.—1.] The Senate of the United States shall be composed of two Senators from each State, chosen by the Legislature thereof, for six years; and each Senator shall have one vote.

[Classification of Senators; filling of vacancies.—2.] Immediately after they shall be assembled in consequence of the first election, they shall be divided as equally as may be into three classes. The seats of the Senators of the first class shall be vacated at the expiration of the second year, of the second class at the expiration of the fourth year, and of the third class at the expiration of the sixth year, so that one-third may be chosen every second year; and if vacancies happen by resignation, or otherwise, during the recess of the Legislature of any State, the Executive thereof may make temporary appointments (until the next meeting of the Legislature, which shall then fill such vacancies).

[Qualification of Senators.—3.] No person shall be a Senator who shall not have attained to the age of thirty years, and been nine years a citizen of the United States, and who shall not, when elected, be an inhabitant of that State for which he shall be chosen.

[Vice President to be President of Senate.—4.] The Vice President of the United States shall be President of the Senate, but shall have no vote, unless they be equally divided.

[Selection of Senate officers; President pro tempore.—5.] The Senate shall choose their other

---

1. The clause included in parentheses is amended by the 14th Amendment, Section 2. 2. The first paragraph of this section and the part of the second paragraph included in parentheses are amended by the 17th Amendment.

officers, and also a President pro tempore, in the absence of the Vice President, or when he shall exercise the office of President of the United States.

[**Senate to try impeachments.—6.**] The Senate shall have the sole power to try all impeachments. When sitting for that purpose, they shall be on oath or affirmation. When the President of the United States is tried, the Chief Justice shall preside: and no person shall be convicted without the concurrence of two thirds of the members present.

[**Judgment in cases of Impeachment.—7.**] Judgment in cases of impeachment shall not extend further than to removal from office, and disqualification to hold and enjoy any office of honor, trust, or profit under the United States: but the party convicted shall nevertheless be liable and subject to indictment, trial, judgment and punishment, according to Law.

Section 4

[**Control of congressional elections.—1.**] The times, places, and manner of holding elections for Senators and Representatives, shall be prescribed in each State by the Legislature thereof; but the Congress may at any time by law make or alter such regulations, except as to the places of choosing Senators.

[**Time for assembling of Congress[3]—2.**] The Congress shall assemble at least once in every year, and such meeting shall be on the first Monday in December, unless they shall by law appoint a different day.

Section 5

[**Each house to be the judge of the election and qualifications of its members; regulations as to quorum.—1.**] Each House shall be the judge of the elections, returns, and qualifications of its own members, and a majority of each shall constitute a quorum to do business; but a smaller number may adjourn from day to day, and may be authorized to compel the attendance of absent members, in such manner, and under such penalties as each House may provide.

[**Each house to determine its own rules.—2.**] Each House may determine the rules of its proceedings, punish its members for disorderly behavior, and, with the concurrence of two thirds, expel a member.

[**Journals and yeas and nays.—3.**] Each House shall keep a journal of its proceedings, and from time to time publish the same, excepting such parts as may in their judgment require secrecy; and the yeas and nays of the members of either House on any question shall, at the desire of one fifth of those present, be entered on the journal.

[**Adjournment.—4.**] Neither House, during the session of Congress, shall, without the consent of the other, adjourn for more than three days, nor to any other place than that in which the two Houses shall be sitting.

Section 6

[**Compensation and privileges of members of Congress.—1.**] The Senators and Representatives shall receive a compensation for their services, to be ascertained by law, and paid out of the Treasury of the United States. They shall in all cases, except

treason, felony, and breach of the peace, be privileged from arrest during their attendance at the session of their respective Houses, and in going to and returning from the same; and for any speech or debate in either House, they shall not be questioned in any other place.

[**Incompatible offices; exclusions.—2.**] No Senator or Representative shall, during the time for which he was elected, be appointed to any civil office under the authority of the United States, which shall have been created, or the emoluments whereof shall have been increased during such time; and no person holding any office under the United States shall be a member of either House during his continuance in office.

Section 7

[**Revenue bills to originate in House.—1.**] All bills for raising revenue shall originate in the House of Representatives; but the Senate may propose or concur with amendments as on other bills.

[**Manner of passing bills; veto power of President.—2.**] Every bill which shall have passed the House of Representatives and the Senate, shall, before it becomes a law, be presented to the President of the United States; if he approve he shall sign it, but if not he shall return it, with his objections to that House in which it shall have originated, who shall enter the objections at large on their journal, and proceed to reconsider it. If after such reconsideration two thirds of that House shall agree to pass the bill, it shall be sent, together with the objections, to the other House, by which it shall likewise be reconsidered, and if approved by two thirds of that House, it shall become a law. But in all such cases the votes of both Houses shall be determined by yeas and nays, and the names of the persons voting for and against the bill shall be entered on the journal of each house, respectively. If any bill shall not be returned by the President within ten days (Sundays excepted) after it shall have been presented to him, the same shall be a law, in like manner as if he had signed it, unless the Congress by their adjournment prevent its return, in which case it shall not be a law.

[**Concurrent orders or resolutions, to be passed by President.—3.**] Every order, resolution, or vote to which the concurrence of the Senate and House of Representatives may be necessary (except on a question of adjournment) shall be presented to the President of the United States; and before the same shall take effect, shall be approved by him, or being disapproved by him, shall be repassed by two thirds of the Senate and House of Representatives, according to the rules and limitations prescribed in the case of a bill.

Section 8

[**General powers of Congress.[4]**]
[**Taxes, duties, imposts, and excises.—1.**] The Congress shall have power to lay and collect taxes, duties, imposts and excises, to pay the debts and provide for the common defense and general welfare of the United States; but all duties, imposts and excises shall be uniform throughout the United States;

---

3. Amended by the 20th Amendment, Section 2.   4. By the 16th Amendment, Congress is given the power to lay and collect taxes on income.

[**Borrowing of money.—2.**] To borrow money on the credit of the United States;

[**Regulation of commerce.—3.**] To regulate commerce with foreign nations, and among the several States, and with the Indian tribes;

[**Naturalization and bankruptcy.—4.**] To establish a uniform rule of naturalization, and uniform laws on the subject of bankruptcies throughout the United States;

[**Money, weights and measures.—5.**] To coin money, regulate the value thereof, and of foreign coin, and fix the standard of weights and measures;

[**Counterfeiting.—6.**] To provide for the punishment of counterfeiting the securities and current coin of the United States;

[**Post offices.—7.**] To establish post offices and post roads;

[**Patents and copyrights.—8.**] To promote the progress of science and useful arts, by securing for limited times to authors and inventors the exclusive right to their respective writings and discoveries;

[**Inferior courts.—9.**] To constitute tribunals inferior to the Supreme Court;

[**Piracies and felonies.—10.**] To define and punish piracies and felonies committed on the high seas, and offences against the law of nations;

[**War; marque and reprisal.—11.**] To declare war, grant letters of marque and reprisal, and make rules concerning captures on land and water;

[**Armies.—12.**] To raise and support armies, but no appropriation of money to that use shall be for a longer term than two years;

[**Navy.—13.**] To provide and maintain a navy;

[**Land and naval forces.—14.**] To make rules for the government and regulation of the land and naval forces;

[**Calling out militia.—15.**] To provide for calling forth the militia to execute the laws of the Union, suppress insurrections, and repel invasions;

[**Organizing, arming, and disciplining militia. —16.**] To provide for organizing, arming, and disciplining, the militia, and for governing such part of them as may be employed in the service of the United States, reserving to the States, respectively, the appointment of the officers, and the authority of training the militia according to the discipline prescribed by Congress;

[**Exclusive legislation over District of Columbia.—17.**] To exercise exclusive legislation in all cases whatsoever, over such district (not exceeding ten miles square) as may, by cession of particular States, and the acceptance of Congress, become the seat of the Government of the United States, and to exercise like authority over all places purchased by the consent of the Legislature of the State in which the same shall be, for the erection of forts, magazines, arsenals, dock-yards, and other needful buildings;—And

[**To enact laws necessary to enforce Constitution.—18.**] To make all laws which shall be necessary and proper for carrying into execution the foregoing powers, and all other powers vested by this Constitution in the Government of the United States, or in any department or officer thereof.

Section 9

[**Migration or importation of certain persons not to be prohibited before 1808.—1.**] The migration or importation of such persons as any of the States now existing shall think proper to admit, shall not be prohibited by the Congress prior to the year one thousand eight hundred and eight, but a tax or duty may be imposed on such importation, not exceeding ten dollars for each person.

[**Writ of habeas corpus not to be suspended; exception.—2.**] The privilege of the writ of habeas corpus shall not be suspended, unless when in cases of rebellion or invasion the public safety may require it.

[**Bills of attainder and ex post facto laws prohibited.—3.**] No bill of attainder or ex post facto law shall be passed.

[**Capitation and other direct taxes.—4.**] No capitation, or other direct, tax shall be laid, unless in proportion to the census or enumeration herein before directed to be taken.[5]

[**Exports not to be taxed.—5.**] No tax or duty shall be laid on articles exported from any State.

[**No preference to be given to ports of any States; interstate shipping.—6.**] No preference shall be given by any regulation of commerce or revenue to the ports of one State over those of another: nor shall vessels bound to, or from, one State, be obliged to enter, clear, or pay duties in another.

[**Money, how drawn from treasury; financial statements to be published.—7.**] No money shall be drawn from the Treasury, but in consequence of appropriations made by law; and a regular statement and account of the receipts and expenditures of all public money shall be published from time to time.

[**Titles of nobility not to be granted; acceptance by government officers of favors from foreign powers.—8.**] No title of nobility shall be granted by the United States: and no person holding any office of profit or trust under them, shall, without the consent of the Congress, accept of any present, emolument, office, or title, of any kind whatever, from any king, prince, or foreign state.

Section 10

[**Limitations of the powers of the several States.—1.**] No State shall enter into any treaty, alliance, or confederation; grant letters of marque and reprisal; coin money; emit bills of credit; make any thing but gold and silver coin a tender in payment of debts; pass any bill of attainder, ex post facto law, or law impairing the obligation of contracts, or grant any title of nobility.

[**State imposts and duties.—2.**] No State shall, without the consent of the Congress, lay any imposts or duties on imports or exports, except what may be absolutely necessary for executing its inspection laws; and the net produce of all duties and imposts, laid by any State on imports or exports, shall be for the use of the Treasury of the United States; and all such laws shall be subject to the revision and control of the Congress.

[**Further restrictions on powers of States.—3.**] No State shall, without the consent of Congress, lay any duty of tonnage, keep troops, or ships of war in time of peace, enter into any agreement or compact

---

5. *See* the 16th Amendment.

with another state, or with a foreign power, or engage in war, unless actually invaded, or in such imminent danger as will not admit of delay.

Article II

Section 1

[**The president; the executive power.—1.**] The executive power shall be vested in a President of the United States of America. He shall hold his office during the term of four years, and, together with the Vice President, chosen for the same term, be elected, as follows

[**Appointment and qualifications of presidential electors.—2.**] Each State shall appoint, in such manner as the Legislature thereof may direct, a number of electors, equal to the whole number of Senators and Representatives to which the State may be entitled in the Congress: but no Senator or Representative, or person holding an office of trust or profit under the United States, shall be appointed an elector.

[**Original method of electing the president and vice president.[6]**] (The electors shall meet in their respective States, and vote by ballot for two persons, of whom one at least shall not be an inhabitant of the same State with themselves. And they shall make a list of all the persons voted for, and of the number of votes for each; which list they shall sign and certify, and transmit sealed to the seat of the Government of the United States, directed to the President of the Senate. The President of the Senate shall, in the presence of the Senate and House of Representatives, open all the certificates, and the votes shall then be counted. The person having the greatest number of votes shall be the President, if such number be a majority of the whole number of electors appointed; and if there be more than one who have such majority, and have an equal number of votes, then the House of Representatives shall immediately choose by ballot one of them for President; and if no person have a majority, then from the five highest on the list the said House shall in like manner choose the President. But in choosing the President, the votes shall be taken by States, the representation from each State having one vote; A quorum for this purpose shall consist of a member or members from two thirds of the States, and a majority of all the states shall be necessary to a choice. In every case, after the choice of the President, the person having the greatest number of votes of the electors shall be the Vice President. But if there should remain two or more who have equal votes, the Senate should choose from them by ballot the Vice President.)

[**Congress may determine time of choosing electors and day for casting their votes.—3.**] The Congress may determine the time of choosing the electors, and the day on which they shall give their votes; which day shall be the same throughout the United States.

[**Qualifications for the office of president.[7]—4.**] No person except a natural born citizen, or a citizen of the United States, at the time of the adoption of this Constitution, shall be eligible to the office of President; neither shall any person be eligible to that office who shall not have attained to the age of thirty-five years, and been fourteen years a resident within the United States.

[**Filling vacancy in the office of president.[8]—5.**] In case of the removal of the President from office, or of his death, resignation, or inability to discharge the powers and duties of the said office, the same shall devolve on the Vice President, and the Congress may by law provide for the case of removal, death, resignation or inability, both of the President and Vice President, declaring what officer shall then act as President, and such officer shall act accordingly, until the disability be removed, or a President shall be elected.

[**Compensation of the president.—6.**] The President shall, at stated times, receive for his services, a compensation, which shall neither be increased nor diminished during the period for which he shall have been elected, and he shall not receive within that period any other emolument from the United States, or any of them.

[**Oath to be taken by the president.—7.**] Before he enter on the execution of his office, he shall take the following oath or affirmation:—"I do solemnly swear (or affirm) that I will faithfully execute the office of President of the United States, and will to the best of my ability, preserve, protect, and defend the Constitution of the United States."

Section 2

[**The president to be commander in chief of army and navy and head of executive departments; may grant reprieves and pardons.—1.**] The President shall be Commander in Chief of the Army and Navy of the United States, and of the militia of the several States, when called into the actual service of the United States; he may require the opinion, in writing, of the principal officer in each of the executive departments, upon any subject relating to the duties of their respective offices, and he shall have power to grant reprieves and pardons for offences against the United States, except in cases of impeachment.

[**President may, with concurrence of Senate, make treaties, appoint ambassadors, etc.; appointment of inferior officers, authority of Congress over.—2.**] He shall have power, by and with the advice and consent of the Senate, to make treaties, provided two thirds of the Senators present concur; and he shall nominate, and by and with the advice and consent of the Senate, shall appoint ambassadors, other public ministers and consuls, judges of the Supreme Court, and all other officers of the United States, whose appointments are not herein otherwise provided for, and which shall be established by law: but the Congress may by law vest the appointment of such inferior officers, as they think proper, in the President alone, in the courts of law, or in the heads of departments.

[**President may fill vacancies in office during recess of Senate.—3.**] The President shall have power to fill up all vacancies that may happen during the recess of the Senate, by granting commissions which shall expire at the end of their session.

---

6. This clause has been superseded by the 12th Amendment. 7. For qualifications of the vice president, *see* the 12th Amendment. 8. Amended by the 20th Amendment, Sections 3 and 4.

Section 3

[**President to give advice to Congress; may convene or adjourn it on certain occasions; to receive ambassadors, etc.; have laws executed and commission all officers.**] He shall from time to time give to the Congress information of the state of the Union, and recommend to their consideration such measures as he shall judge necessary and expedient; he may, on extraordinary occasions, convene both Houses, or either of them, and in case of disagreement between them, with respect to the time of adjournment, he may adjourn them to such time as he shall think proper; he shall receive ambassadors and other public ministers: he shall take care that the laws be faithfully executed, and shall commission all the officers of the United States.

Section 4

[**All civil officers removable by impeachment.**] The President, Vice President, and all civil officers of the United States shall be removed from office on impeachment for, and conviction of, treason, bribery, or other high crimes and misdemeanors.

Article III

Section 1

[**Judicial powers; how vested; term of office and compensation of judges.**] The judicial Power of the United States, shall be vested in one Supreme Court, and in such inferior courts as the Congress may from time to time ordain and establish. The judges, both of the supreme and inferior courts, shall hold their offices during good behavior, and shall, at stated times, receive for their services, a compensation, which shall not be diminished during their continuance in office.

Section 2

[**Jurisdiction of federal courts[9]—1.**] The judicial power shall extend to all cases, in law and equity, arising under this Constitution, the laws of the United States, and treaties made, or which shall be made, under their authority; to all cases affecting ambassadors, other public ministers and consuls; to all cases of admiralty and maritime jurisdiction; to controversies to which the United States, shall be a party; to controversies between two or more States; between a State and citizens of another State; between citizens of different States; between citizens of the same State claiming lands under grants of different states, and between a State, or the citizens thereof, and foreign states, citizens, or subjects.

[**Original and appellate jurisdiction of Supreme Court.—2.**] In all cases affecting ambassadors, other public ministers and consuls, and those in which a State shall be party, the Supreme Court shall have original jurisdiction. In all the other cases before mentioned, the Supreme Court shall have appellate jurisdiction, both as to law and fact, with such exceptions, and under such regulations, as the Congress shall make.

[**Trial of all crimes, except impeachment, to be by jury.—3.**] The trial of all crimes, except in cases of impeachment, shall be by jury; and such trial shall be held in the State where the said crimes shall have been committed; but when not committed within any State, the trial shall be at such place or places as the Congress may by law have directed.

Section 3

[**Treason defined; conviction of.—1.**] Treason against the United States, shall consist only in levying war against them, or, in adhering to their enemies, giving them aid and comfort. No person shall be convicted of treason unless on the testimony of two witnesses to the same overt act, or on confession in open court.

[**Congress to declare punishment for treason; proviso.—2.**] The Congress shall have power to declare the punishment of treason, but no attainder of treason shall work corruption of blood, or forfeiture except during the life of the person attained.

Article IV

Section 1

[**Each state to give full faith and credit to the public acts and records of other states.**] Full faith and credit shall be given in each State to the public acts, records, and judicial proceedings of every other State. And the Congress may by general laws prescribe the manner in which such acts, records, and proceedings shall be proved, and the effect thereof.

Section 2

[**Privileges of citizens.—1.**] The citizens of each State shall be entitled to all privileges and immunities of citizens in the several States.

[**Extradition between the several states.—2.**] A person charged in any State with treason, felony, or other crime, who shall flee from justice, and be found in another State, shall on demand of the Executive authority of the State from which he fled, be delivered up, to be removed to the State having jurisdiction of the crime.

[**Persons held to labor or service in one state, fleeing to another, to be returned.—3.**] No person held to service or labor in one State, under the laws thereof, escaping into another, shall, in consequence of any law or regulation therein, be discharged from such service or labor, but shall be delivered up on claim of the party to whom such service or labor may be due.

Section 3

[**New states.—1.**] New States may be admitted by the Congress into this Union; but no new State shall be formed or erected within the jurisdiction of any other State; nor any State be formed by the junction of two or more States, or parts of States, without the consent of the Legislatures of the States concerned as well as of the Congress.

[**Regulations concerning territory.—2.**] The Congress shall have power to dispose of and make all needful rules and regulations respecting the territory or other property belonging to the United States; and nothing in this Constitution shall be so construed as to prejudice any claims of the United States, or of any particular State.

Section 4

[**Republican form of government and protection guaranteed the several states.**] The United States shall guarantee to every State in this Union a Republican form of government, and shall protect each of them against invasion; and on application of the Legislature, or of the Executive (when the Legislature cannot be convened) against domestic violence.

---

9. This section is abridged by the 11th Amendment.

Article V

[Ways in which the Constitution can be amended.] The Congress, whenever two thirds of both Houses shall deem it necessary, shall propose amendments to this Constitution, or, on the application of the Legislatures of two thirds of the several States shall call a convention for proposing amendments, which, in either case, shall be valid to all intents and purposes, as part of this Constitution, when ratified by the Legislatures of three fourths of the several States, or by conventions in three fourths thereof, as the one or the other mode of ratification may be proposed by the Congress; provided that no amendment which may be made prior to the year one thousand eight hundred and eight shall in any manner affect the first and fourth clauses in the ninth Section of the first Article; and that no State, without its consent, shall be deprived of its equal suffrage in the Senate.

Article VI

[Debts contracted under the confederation secured.—1.] All debts contracted and engagements entered into, before the adoption of this Constitution, shall be as valid against the United States under this Constitution, as under the Confederation.

[Constitution, laws, and treaties of the United States to be supreme.—2.] This Constitution, and the laws of the United States which shall be made in pursuance thereof; and all treaties made, or which shall be made, under the authority of the United States, shall be the supreme law of the land; and the judges in every State shall be bound thereby; any thing in the Constitution or laws of any State to the contrary notwithstanding.

[Who shall take constitutional oath; no religious test as to official qualification.—3.] The Senators and Representatives before mentioned, and the members of the several State Legislatures, and all executive and judicial officers, both of the United States and of the several States, shall be bound by oath or affirmation, to support this Constitution; but no religious test shall ever be required as a qualification to any office or public trust under the United States.

Article VII

[Constitution to be considered adopted when ratified by nine states.] The ratification of the conventions of nine States shall be sufficient for the establishment of this Constitution between the States so ratifying the same.

Done in convention by the unanimous consent of the States present the seventeenth day of September in the year of our Lord one thousand seven hundred and eighty seven and of the independence of the United States of America the Twelfth. In witness whereof we have hereunto subscribed our names.

George Washington
President and Deputy from Virginia

New Hampshire John Langdon Nicholas Gilman	David Brearley Jona. Dayton	John Dickinson Richard Bassett Jaco. Broom	**South Carolina** J. Rutledge Charles Cotesworth Pinckney
Massachusetts Nathaniel Gorham Rufus King	**Pennsylvania** B. Franklin Thomas Mifflin	**Maryland** James McHenry Dan. of St. Thos. Jenifer Danl. Carroll	Charles Pinckney Pierce Butler
Connecticut Wm. Saml. Johnson Roger Sherman	Robt. Morris Geo. Clymer Thos. FitzSimons Jared Ingersoll	**Virginia** John Blair	**Georgia** William Few Abr. Baldwin
New York Alexander Hamilton	James Wilson Gouv. Morris	James Madison, Jr.	Attest: William Jackson, Secretary
New Jersey Wil. Livingston Wm. Paterson	**Delaware** Geo. Read Gunning Bedford Jun.	**North Carolina** Wm. Blount Richd Dobbs Spaight Hu. Williamson	

Amendments to the Constitution of the United States

(Amendments I to X inclusive, popularly known as the Bill of Rights, were proposed and sent to the states by the first session of the First Congress. They were ratified Dec. 15, 1791.)

Amendment I

[Freedom of religion, speech, of the press, and right of petition.] Congress shall make no law respecting an establishment of religion, or prohibiting the free exercise thereof; or abridging the freedom of speech, or of the press; or the right of the people peaceably to assemble, and to petition the Government for a redress of grievances.

Amendment II

[Right of people to bear arms not to be infringed.] A well regulated militia, being necessary to the security of a free State, the right of the people to keep and bear arms, shall not be infringed.

Amendment III

[Quartering of troops.] No soldier shall, in time of peace be quartered in any house, without the consent of the owner, nor in time of war, but in a manner to be prescribed by law.

Amendment IV

[Persons and houses to be secure from unreasonable searches and seizures.] The right of the people to be secure in their persons, houses, papers, and effects, against unreasonable searches and seizures, shall not be violated, and no warrants shall issue, but upon probable cause, supported by oath or affirmation, and particularly describing the place to be searched, and the persons or things to be seized.

Amendment V

[Trials for crimes; just compensation for private property taken for public use.] No person shall be held to answer for a capital, or otherwise infamous crime, unless on a presentment or indictment of a Grand Jury, except in cases arising in the land or naval forces, or in the militia, when in actual service in time of war or public danger; nor shall any person be subject for the same offence to be twice put in jeopardy of life or limb; nor shall be compelled in any criminal case to be a witness, against himself, nor be deprived of life, liberty, or property, without due process of law; nor shall private property be taken for public use, without just compensation.

Amendment VI

[Civil rights in trials for crimes enumerated.] In all criminal prosecutions, the accused shall enjoy the right to a speedy and public trial, by an impartial jury of the State and district wherein the crime shall have been committed, which district shall have been previously ascertained by law, and to be informed of the nature and cause of the accusation; to be confronted with the witnesses against him; to have compulsory process for obtaining witnesses in his favor, and to have the assistance of counsel for his defense.

Amendment VII

[Civil rights in civil suits.] In suits at common law, where the value in controversy shall exceed twenty dollars, the right of trial by jury shall be preserved, and no fact tried by a jury, shall be otherwise re-examined in any court of the United States, than according to the rules of the common law.

Amendment VIII

[Excessive bail, fines, and punishments prohibited.] Excessive bail shall not be required, nor excessive fines imposed, nor cruel and unusual punishments inflicted.

Amendment IX

[Reserved rights of people.] The enumeration in the Constitution, of certain rights, shall not be construed to deny or disparage others retained by the people.

Amendment X

[Powers not delegated, reserved to states and people respectively.] The powers not delegated to the United States by the Constitution, nor prohibited by it to the States, are reserved to the States, respectively, or to the people.

Amendment XI

(The proposed amendment was sent to the states Mar. 5, 1794, by the Third Congress. It was ratified Feb. 7, 1795.)
[Judicial power of United States not to extend to suits against a state.] The judicial power of the United States shall not be construed to extend to any suit in law or equity, commenced or prosecuted against one of the United States by citizens of another State, or by citizens or subjects of any foreign state.

Amendment XII

(The proposed amendment was sent to the states Dec. 12, 1803, by the Eighth Congress. It was ratified July 27, 1804.)
[Present mode of electing president and vice president by electors.[1]]
The electors shall meet in their respective states, and vote by ballot for President and Vice President, one of whom, at least, shall not be an inhabitant of the same state with themselves; they shall name in their ballots the person voted for as President, and in distinct ballots the person voted for as Vice President, and they shall make distinct lists of all persons voted for as President, and of all persons voted for as Vice President, and of the number of votes for each, which lists they shall sign and certify, and transmit sealed to the seat of the government of the United States, directed to the President of the Senate; the President of the Senate shall, in the presence of the Senate and House of Representatives, open all the certificates and the votes shall then be counted; the person having the greatest number of votes for President, shall be the President, if such number be a majority of the whole number of electors appointed; and if no person have such majority, then from the persons having the highest numbers not exceeding three on the list of those voted for as President, the House of Representatives shall choose immediately, by ballot, the President. But in choosing the President, the votes shall be taken by states, the representation from each State having one vote; a quorum for this purpose shall consist of a member or members from two thirds of the states, and a majority of all the states shall be necessary to a choice. And if the House of Representatives shall not choose a President whenever the right of choice shall devolve upon them, before the fourth day of March next following, then the Vice President shall act as President, as in the case of the death or other constitutional disability of the President. The person having the greatest number of votes as Vice President, shall be the Vice President, if such number be a majority of the whole number of electors appointed, and if no person have a majority, then from the two highest numbers on the list, the Senate shall choose the Vice President; a quorum for the purpose shall consist of two thirds of the whole number of Senators, and a majority of the whole number shall be necessary to a choice. But no person constitutionally ineligible to the office of President shall be eligible to that of Vice President of the United States.

Amendment XIII

(The proposed amendment was sent to the states Feb. 1, 1865, by the Thirty-eighth Congress. It was ratified Dec. 6, 1865.)

Section 1
[Slavery prohibited.] Neither slavery nor involuntary servitude, except as a punishment for crime whereof the party shall have been duly convicted, shall exist within the United States, or any place subject to their jurisdiction.

Section 2
[Congress given power to enforce this article.] Congress shall have power to enforce this article by appropriate legislation.

1. Amended by the 20th Amendment, Sections 3 and 4.

Amendment XIV

(The proposed amendment was sent to the states June 16, 1866, by the Thirty-ninth Congress. It was ratified July 9, 1868.)

Section 1

[Citizenship defined; privileges of citizens.] All persons born or naturalized in the United States, and subject to the jurisdiction thereof, are citizens of the United States and of the State wherein they reside. No State shall make or enforce any law which shall abridge the privileges or immunities of citizens of the United States; nor shall any State deprive any person of life, liberty, or property, without due process of law; nor deny to any person within its jurisdiction the equal protection of the laws.

Section 2

[Apportionment of Representatives.] Representatives shall be apportioned among the several States according to their respective numbers, counting the whole number of persons in each State, excluding Indians not taxed. But when the right to vote at any election for the choice of electors for President and Vice President of the United States, Representatives in Congress, the executive and judicial officers of a State, or the members of the Legislature thereof, is denied to any of the male inhabitants of such State, being twenty-one years of age, and citizens of the United States, or in any way abridged, except for participation in rebellion, or other crime, the basis of representation therein shall be reduced in the proportion which the number of such male citizens shall bear to the whole number of male citizens twenty-one years of age in such State.

Section 3

[Disqualification for office; removal of disability.] No person shall be a Senator or Representative in Congress, or elector of President and Vice President, or hold any office, civil or military, under the United States, or under any State, who, having previously taken an oath, as a member of Congress, or as an officer of the United States, or as a member of any State Legislature, or as an executive or judicial officer of any State, to support the Constitution of the United States, shall have engaged in insurrection or rebellion against the same, or given aid or comfort to the enemies thereof. But Congress may, by a vote of two thirds of each House, remove such disability.

Section 4

[Public debt not to be questioned; payment of debts and claims incurred in aid of rebellion forbidden.] The validity of the public debt of the United States, authorized by law, including debts incurred for payment of pensions and bounties for services in suppressing insurrection or rebellion, shall not be questioned. But neither the United States nor any State shall assume or pay any debt or obligation incurred in aid of insurrection or rebellion against the United States, or any claim for the loss or emancipation of any slave; but all such debts, obligations, and claims shall be held illegal and void.

Section 5

[Congress given power to enforce this article.] The Congress shall have power to enforce, by appropriate legislation, the provisions of this article.

Amendment XV

(The proposed amendment was sent to the states Feb. 27, 1869, by the Fortieth Congress. It was ratified Feb. 3, 1870.)

Section 1

[Right of certain citizens to vote established.] The right of citizens of the United States to vote shall not be denied or abridged by the United States or by any State on account of race, color, or previous condition of servitude.

Section 2

[Congress given power to enforce this article.] The Congress shall have power to enforce this article by appropriate legislation.

Amendment XVI

(The proposed amendment was sent to the states July 12, 1909, by the Sixty-first Congress. It was ratified Feb. 3, 1913.)

[Taxes on income; Congress given power to lay and collect.] The Congress shall have power to lay and collect taxes on incomes, from whatever source derived, without apportionment among the several States, and without regard to any census or enumeration.

Amendment XVII

(The proposed amendment was sent to the states May 16, 1912, by the Sixty-second Congress. It was ratified April 8, 1913.)

[Election of U.S. senators; filling of vacancies; qualifications of electors.] The Senate of the United States shall be composed of two Senators from each State, elected by the people thereof, for six years; and each Senator shall have one vote. The electors in each State shall have the qualifications requisite for electors of the most numerous branch of the State Legislatures.

When vacancies happen in the representation of any State in the Senate, the executive authority of such State shall issue writs of election to fill such vacancies: Provided, that the legislature of any State may empower the executive thereof to make temporary appointment until the people fill the vacancies by election as the legislature may direct.

This amendment shall not be so construed as to affect the election or term of any Senator chosen before it becomes valid as part of the Constitution.

Amendment XVIII[2]

(The proposed amendment was sent to the states Dec. 18, 1917, by the Sixty-fifth Congress. It was ratified by three quarters of the states by Jan. 16, 1919, and became effective Jan. 16, 1920.)

Section 1

[Manufacture, sale, or transportation of intoxicating liquors, for beverage purposes, prohibited.] After one year from the ratification of this

2. Repealed by the 21st Amendment.

article the manufacture, sale, or transportation of intoxicating liquors within, the importation thereof into, or the exportation thereof from the United States and all territory subject to the jurisdiction thereof for beverage purposes is hereby prohibited.

Section 2

[Congress and the several states given concurrent power to pass appropriate legislation to enforce this article.] The Congress and the several States shall have concurrent power to enforce this article by appropriate legislation.

Section 3

[Provisions of article to become operative, when adopted by three fourths of the states.] This article shall be inoperative unless it shall have been ratified as an amendment to the Constitution by the legislatures of the several States, as provided in the Constitution, within seven years from the date of submission hereof to the States by Congress.

Amendment XIX

(The proposed amendment was sent to the states June 4, 1919, by the Sixty-sixth Congress. It was ratified Aug. 18, 1920.)

[The right of citizens to vote shall not be denied because of sex.] The right of citizens of the United States to vote shall not be denied or abridged by the United States or by any State on account of sex.

[Congress given power to enforce this article.] Congress shall have power to enforce this article by appropriate legislation.

Amendment XX

(The proposed amendment, sometimes called the "Lame Duck Amendment," was sent to the states Mar. 3, 1932, by the Seventy-second Congress. It was ratified Jan. 23, 1933; but, in accordance with Section 5, Sections 1 and 2, did not go into effect until Oct. 15, 1933.)

Section 1

[Terms of president, vice president, senators, and representatives.] The terms of the President and Vice President shall end at noon on the twentieth day of January, and the terms of Senators and Representatives at noon on the third day of January, of the years in which such terms would have ended if this article had not been ratified; and the terms of their successors shall then begin.

Section 2

[Time of assembling Congress.] The Congress shall assemble at least once in every year, and such meeting shall begin at noon on the third day of January, unless they shall by law appoint a different day.

Section 3

[Filling vacancy in office of president.] If, at the time fixed for the beginning of the term of the President, the President-elect shall have died, the Vice President-elect shall become President. If a President shall not have been chosen before the time fixed for the beginning of his term, or if the President-elect shall have failed to qualify, then the Vice President shall have qualified; and the Congress may by law provide for the case wherein neither a President-elect nor a Vice President-elect shall have qualified, declaring who shall then act as President, or the manner in which one who is to act shall be selected, and such person shall act accordingly until a President or Vice President shall have qualified.

Section 4

[Power of Congress in presidential succession.] The Congress may by law provide for the case of the death of any of the persons from whom the House of Representatives may choose a President whenever the right of choice shall have devolved upon them, and for the case of the death of any of the persons from whom the Senate may choose a Vice President whenever the right of choice shall have devolved upon them.

Section 5

[Time of taking effect.] Sections 1 and 2 shall take effect on the 15th day of October following the ratification of this article.

Section 6

[Ratification.] This article shall be inoperative unless it shall have been ratified as an amendment to the Constitution by the legislatures of three fourths of the several States within seven years from the date of its submission.

Amendment XXI

(The proposed amendment was sent to the states Feb. 20, 1933, by the Seventy-second Congress. It was ratified Dec. 5, 1933.)

Section 1

[Repeal of Prohibition Amendment.] The eighteenth article of amendment to the Constitution of the United States is hereby repealed.

Section 2

[Transportation of intoxicating liquors.] The transportation or importation into any State, territory, or possession of the United States for delivery or use therein of intoxicating liquors, in violation of the laws thereof, is hereby prohibited.

Section 3

[Ratification.] This article shall be inoperative unless it shall have been ratified as an amendment to the Constitution by convention in the several States, as provided in the Constitution, within seven years from the date of the submission thereof to the States by the Congress.

Amendment XXII

(The proposed amendment was sent to the states Mar. 21, 1947, by the Eightieth Congress. It was ratified Feb. 27, 1951.)

Section 1

[Limit to number of terms a president may serve.] No person shall be elected to the office of the President more than twice, and no person who has held the office of President, or acted as President, for more than two years of a term to which some other person was elected President shall be elected to the office of the President more than once. But this article shall not apply to any person holding the office of President when this article was proposed by the Congress, and shall not prevent any person who may be holding the office of President, or acting as President, during the term within which this article becomes operative from holding the office of President or acting as President during the remainder of such term.

Section 2

[Ratification.] This article shall be inoperative unless it shall have been ratified as an amendment to the Constitution by the legislatures of three fourths of the several States within seven years from the date of its submission to the States by the Congress.

Amendment XXIII

(The proposed amendment was sent to the states June 16, 1960, by the Eighty-sixth Congress. It was ratified March 29, 1961.)

Section 1

[Electors for the District of Columbia.] The District constituting the seat of Government of the United States shall appoint in such manner as the Congress may direct: A number of electors of President and Vice President equal to the whole number of Senators and Representatives in Congress to which the District would be entitled if it were a State, but in no event more than the least populous State; they shall be in addition to those appointed by the States, but they shall be considered, for the purposes of the election of President and Vice President, to be electors appointed by a State; and they shall meet in the District and perform such duties as provided by the twelfth article of amendment.

Section 2

[Congress given power to enforce this article.] The Congress shall have the power to enforce this article by appropriate legislation.

Amendment XXIV

(The proposed amendment was sent to the states Aug. 27, 1962, by the Eighty-seventh Congress. It was ratified Jan. 23, 1964.)

Section 1

[Payment of poll tax or other taxes not to be prerequisite for voting in federal elections.] The right of citizens of the United States to vote in any primary or other election for President or Vice President, for electors for President or Vice President, or for Senator or Representative in Congress, shall not be denied or abridged by the United States or any State by reasons of failure to pay any poll tax or other tax.

Section 2

[Congress given power to enforce this article.] The Congress shall have the power to enforce this article by appropriate legislation.

Amendment XXV

(The proposed amendment was sent to the states July 6, 1965, by the Eighty-ninth Congress. It was ratified Feb. 10, 1967.)

Section 1

[Succession of vice president to presidency.] In case of the removal of the President from office or of his death or resignation, the Vice President shall become President.

Section 2

[Vacancy in office of vice president.] Whenever there is a vacancy in the office of the Vice President, the President shall nominate a Vice President who shall take office upon confirmation by a majority vote of both Houses of Congress.

Section 3

[Vice president as acting president.] Whenever the President transmits to the President pro tempore of the Senate and the Speaker of the House of Representatives his written declaration that he is unable to discharge the powers and duties of his office, and until he transmits to them a written declaration to the contrary, such powers and duties shall be discharged by the Vice President as Acting President.

Section 4

[Vice president as acting president.] Whenever the Vice President and a majority of either the principal officers of the executive departments or of such other body as Congress may by law provide, transmit to the President pro tempore of the Senate and the Speaker of the House of Representatives their written declaration that the President is unable to discharge the powers and duties of his office, the Vice President shall immediately assume the powers and duties of the office as Acting President.

Thereafter, when the President transmits to the President pro tempore of the Senate and the Speaker of the House of Representatives his written declaration that no inability exists, he shall resume the powers and duties of his office unless the Vice President and a majority of either the principal officers of the executive department or of such other body as Congress may by law provide, transmit within four days to the President pro tempore of the Senate and the Speaker of the House of Representatives their written declaration that the President is unable to discharge the powers and duties of his office. Thereupon Congress shall decide the issue, assembling within forty-eight hours for that purpose if not in session. If the Congress, within twenty-one days after receipt of the latter written declaration, or, if Congress is not in session, within twenty-one days after Congress is required to assemble, determines by two thirds vote of both Houses that the President is unable to discharge the powers and duties of his office, the Vice President shall continue to discharge the same as Acting President; otherwise, the President shall resume the powers and duties of his office.

Amendment XXVI

(The proposed amendment was sent to the states Mar. 23, 1971, by the Ninety-second Congress. It was ratified July 1, 1971.)

Section 1

[Voting for 18-year-olds.] The right of citizens of the United States, who are 18 years of age or older, to vote shall not be denied or abridged by the United States or by any state on account of age.

Section 2

[Congress given power to enforce this article.] The Congress shall have power to enforce this article by appropriate legislation.

Amendment XXVII

(Ratified May 7, 1992.)

[Congressional raises.] No law, varying the compensation for the services of the Senators and Representatives, shall take effect, until an election of Representatives shall have intervened.

Lincoln's Gettysburg Address

The Battle of Gettysburg, one of the most noted battles of the Civil War, was fought on July 1–3, 1863. On Nov. 19, 1863, the field was dedicated as a national cemetery by President Lincoln in a two-minute speech that was to become immortal. At the time of its delivery the speech was relegated to the inside pages of the papers, while a two-hour address by Edward Everett, the leading orator of the time, caught the headlines.

> Four score and seven years ago our fathers brought forth on this continent a new nation conceived in liberty and dedicated to the proposition that all men are created equal. Now we are engaged in a great civil war testing whether that nation, or any nation so conceived and so dedicated, can long endure. We are met on a great battlefield of that war. We have come to dedicate a portion of that field as a final resting-place for those who here gave their lives that that nation might live. It is altogether fitting and proper that we should do this. But, in a larger sense, we cannot dedicate, we cannot consecrate, we cannot hallow this ground. The brave men, living and dead, who struggled here have consecrated it far above our poor power to add or detract. The world will little note nor long remember what we say here, but it can never forget what they did here. It is for us the living rather to be dedicated here to the unfinished work which they who fought here have thus far so nobly advanced. It is rather for us to be here dedicated to the great task remaining before us—that from these honored dead we take increased devotion to that cause for which they gave the last full measure of devotion—that we here highly resolve that these dead shall not have died in vain, that this nation under God shall have a new birth of freedom, and that government of the people, by the people, for the people shall not perish from the earth.

Assassinations and Attempts in U.S. Since 1865

Lincoln, Abraham (president of U.S.): Shot April 14, 1865, in Washington, DC, by John Wilkes Booth; died April 15.

Seward, William H. (secretary of state): Escaped assassination (though injured) April 14, 1865, in Washington, DC, by Lewis Powell (or Paine), accomplice of John Wilkes Booth.

Garfield, James A. (president of U.S.): Shot July 2, 1881, in Washington, DC, by Charles J. Guiteau; died Sept. 19.

McKinley, William (president of U.S.): Shot Sept. 6, 1901, in Buffalo by Leon Czolgosz; died Sept. 14.

Roosevelt, Theodore (ex-president of U.S.): Escaped assassination (though shot) Oct. 14, 1912, in Milwaukee while campaigning for president.

Cermak, Anton J. (mayor of Chicago): Shot Feb. 15, 1933, in Miami by Giuseppe Zangara, who attempted to assassinate Franklin D. Roosevelt; Cermak died March 6.

Roosevelt, Franklin D. (president-elect of U.S.): Escaped assassination unhurt Feb. 15, 1933, in Miami.

Long, Huey P. (U.S. senator from Louisiana): Shot Sept. 8, 1935, in Baton Rouge by Dr. Carl A. Weiss; died Sept. 10.

Truman, Harry S. (president of U.S.): Escaped assassination unhurt Nov. 1, 1950, in Washington, DC, as 2 Puerto Rican nationalists attempted to shoot their way into Blair House.

Kennedy, John F. (president of U.S.): Shot Nov. 22, 1963, in Dallas, Tex., allegedly by Lee Harvey Oswald; died same day. Injured was Gov. John B. Connally of Texas. Oswald was shot and killed two days later by Jack Ruby.

Malcolm X, also known as El-Hajj Malik El-Shabazz (black activist): Shot and killed in a New York City auditorium, Feb. 21, 1965; his killer(s) were never positively identified.

King, Martin Luther, Jr. (civil rights leader): Shot April 4, 1968, in Memphis by James Earl Ray; died same day.

Kennedy, Robert F. (U.S. senator from New York): Shot June 5, 1968, in Los Angeles by Sirhan Bishara Sirhan; died June 6.

Wallace, George C. (governor of Alabama): Shot and critically wounded in assassination attempt May 15, 1972, at Laurel, Md., by Arthur Herman Bremer. Wallace paralyzed from waist down.

Ford, Gerald R. (president of U.S.): Escaped assassination attempt Sept. 5, 1975, in Sacramento, Calif., by Lynette Alice (Squeaky) Fromme, who pointed but did not fire .45-caliber pistol. Escaped assassination attempt in San Francisco, Calif., Sept. 22, 1975, by Sara Jane Moore, who fired one shot from a .38-caliber pistol that was deflected.

Jordan, Vernon E., Jr. (civil rights leader): Shot and critically wounded in assassination attempt May 29, 1980, in Fort Wayne, Ind.

Reagan, Ronald (president of U.S.): Shot in left lung in Washington by John W. Hinckley, Jr., on March 30, 1981; three others also wounded.

"In God We Trust"

"In God We Trust" first appeared on U.S. coins after April 22, 1864, when Congress passed an act authorizing the coinage of a 2-cent piece bearing this motto. Thereafter, Congress extended its use to other coins. On July 30, 1956, it became the national motto.

Profile of the United States

This profile was created by the editors of the almanac from many data sources. Most figures are approximate. For additional details about the U.S., please refer to the appropriate sections of the almanac.

Geography

Number of states: 50
Territories: 15
Area (2000): total: 3,794,083 sq mi (9,826,675 sq km), land only: 3,537,438 sq mi (9,161,964 sq km), water: 256,645 sq mi (664,711 sq km). Share of world land area (1990): 6.2%
Northernmost point: Point Barrow, Alaska
Easternmost point: West Quoddy Head, Maine
Southernmost point: Ka Lae (South Cape), Hawaii
Westernmost point: Cape Wrangell, Alaska[1]
Geographic center (50 states): in Butte County, S.D. (44′ 58′ N. lat., 103′ 46′ W. long.)
Highest point: Mt. McKinley, Alaska (20,320 ft)
Lowest point: Death Valley, Calif. (282 ft below sea level)

1. The extreme points are measured from the geographic center of the United States (incl. Alaska and Hawaii), west of Castle Rock, S.D., 44° 58′ N. lat., 103° 46′ W. long. If measured from the prime meridian in Greenwich, England, Cape Wrangell, Alaska, would be the easternmost point.

Population

(Based on Census 2000 data unless otherwise noted.)

Total Resident Pop. (July 2005 est.)[1]: 296,496,649
Population density: 79.6 people per sq mi
Mean center of population: 3 mi east of Edgar Springs in Phelps County, Mo.
Males: 138,053,563 (49.1% of pop.)
Females: 143,368,343 (50.9% of pop.)
White: 211,460,626 (75.1% of pop.)
Black: 34,658,190 (12.3% of pop.)
Asian: 10,242,998 (3.6% of pop.)
American Indian and Alaska Native: 2,475,956 (0.9% of pop.)
Hispanic/Latino[2]: 35,305,818 (12.5% of pop.)
Native Hawaiian and Other Pacific Islander: 398,835 (0.1% of pop.)
Median age: 35.3
Metropolitan population: 225,981,679
Nonmetropolitan population: 55,440,227
Families: 71,787,347
Average family size: 3.14
Homeownership (2004): 69.0% of pop.
Married couples (2003): 57,320,000
Never married: 48,200,000
Divorced: 19,800,000
Widowed: 13,700,000

1. Excludes the U.S. Armed Forces overseas. 2. People of Hispanic or Latino origin may be of any race.

Vital Statistics

Births (2003): 4,091,063 (14.1 per 1,000 pop.)
Deaths (2003): 2,423,000 (8.3 per 1,000 pop.)
Marriages (2004): 2,181,000 (7.4 per 1,000 pop.)
Divorces (2004): 3.7 per 1,000 pop.[1]
Infant mortality rate (2002): 7.0 per 1,000 live births
Legal abortions (2000): 857,475
Life expectancy (2002): Total U.S., both sexes, 77.3; total men, 74.5; total women, 79.9; white men, 75.1; white women, 80.3; black men, 68.8; black women, 75.6

1. U.S. totals no longer available.

Civilian Labor Force

All (2004): 147,401,000 (5.5% unemployed)
Men (2004): 78,980,000 (5.6% unemployed)
Women (2004): 68,422,000 (5.4% unemployed)
Work at home (2001 est.): 19.8 million
Farms (2004): 2,113,470; total acres (2004): 936,600,000
Avg. weekly earnings of workers (2004): $638
Avg. weekly hours of workers (2000): 34.5

Income and Credit

GDP (2004): $11,735.0 billion
Fed. Budget (2004): total receipts, $1,880.1 billion; total outlays, $2,292.2 billion; (2005 est.): total receipts, $2,052.8 billion; total outlays, $2,479.4 billion
Personal income per capita (2004): $32,937
Median four-person family income (2003): $65,093
Consumer credit outstanding (2004): $2,140.4 billion
Number below poverty level (2003): total, 35,861,000; white, 24,272,000; black, 8,781,000; Hispanic, 9,051,000; Asian, 1,401,000

Education

Public elementary school pupils, pre-K–grade 8 (2002):[1] 33,942,000
Public secondary school pupils, grades 9–12 (2002):[1] 13,976,000
Private elementary school pupils, K–grade 8 (2002):[1] 4,885,000
Private secondary school pupils, grades 9–12 (2002):[1] 1,356,000
High school dropout rate, ages 16–24 (2001): 10.7%
Total 2- and 4-year colleges and universities (2002): 4,168
Total higher education enrollment (2002): 15,927,987
   Undergraduate (2002): 13,715,610
   Graduate (2002): 1,903,730
   Professional (2002): 308,647

1. Estimated.

Conveniences

Radio stations (March 2005): AM, 4,761; FM, 9,053
Television stations (March 2005): 1,745
Registered automobiles (2003): 135,669,897
Daily newspaper circulation (2002): 55,186,157
Total TV households (2003): 106,700,000
Percent households with a TV set (2003): 98%
Avg. number TV sets per household (2000): 2.4
Cable TV households (2003): 70%
Avg. number TV households with VCRs (2003): 92%
Percent households with a computer (2001): 56.5%
Percent households with Internet access (2001): 50.5%
Number of books sold (2000): 2,500,000,000

Crime

Total arrests (2003): 9.5 million
State, federal, and local prison inmates (2004): 2,131,180
Prisoners under sentence of death (2002): 3,557
Persons executed under civil authority (2004): 59
Law enforcement officers killed (2002): 132
Total murder victims (2003): 14,408
Violent crimes per 100,000 people (2003): 475.0
Property crimes per 100,000 people (2003): 3,588.4
Homicides per 100,000 people (2003): 5.7
Hate crime victims (2003): 9,100

Profile of General Demographic Characteristics, Census 2000

Subject	Number	Percent
Total population	**281,421,906**	**100.0%**
Sex and age		
Male	138,053,563	49.1
Female	143,368,343	50.9
Under 5 years	19,175,798	6.8
5 to 9 years	20,549,505	7.3
10 to 14 years	20,528,072	7.3
15 to 19 years	20,219,890	7.2
20 to 24 years	18,964,001	6.7
25 to 34 years	39,891,724	14.2
35 to 44 years	45,148,527	16.0
45 to 54 years	37,677,952	13.4
55 to 59 years	13,469,237	4.8
60 to 64 years	10,805,447	3.8
65 to 74 years	18,390,986	6.5
75 to 84 years	12,361,180	4.4
85 years and over	4,239,587	1.5
Median age (years)	35.3	n.a.
18 years and over	209,128,094	74.3
Male	100,994,367	35.9
Female	108,133,727	38.4
21 years and over	196,899,193	70.0
62 years and over	41,256,029	14.7
65 years and over	34,991,753	12.4
Male	14,409,625	5.1
Female	20,582,128	7.3
Race		
One race	274,595,678	97.6
White	211,460,626	75.1
Black or African American	34,658,190	12.3
American Indian and Alaska Native	2,475,956	0.9
Asian	10,242,998	3.6
Asian Indian	1,678,765	0.6
Chinese	2,432,585	0.9
Filipino	1,850,314	0.7
Japanese	796,700	0.3
Korean	1,076,872	0.4
Vietnamese	1,122,528	0.4
Other Asian[1]	1,285,234	0.5
Native Hawaiian and Other Pacific Islander	398,835	0.1
Native Hawaiian	140,652	—
Guamanian or Chamorro	58,240	—
Samoan	91,029	—
Other Pacific Islander[2]	108,914	—
Some other race	15,359,073	5.5
Two or more races	6,826,228	2.4
Race alone or in combination with one or more other races:[3]		
White	216,930,975	77.1
Black or African American	36,419,434	12.9
American Indian and Alaska Native	4,119,301	1.5
Asian	11,898,828	4.2
Native Hawaiian and Other Pacific Islander	874,414	0.3
Some other race	18,521,486	6.6

Subject	Number	Percent
Hispanic or Latino and race		
Total population	**281,421,906**	**100.0%**
Hispanic or Latino (of any race)	35,305,818	12.5
Mexican	20,640,711	7.3
Puerto Rican	3,406,178	1.2
Cuban	1,241,685	0.4
Other Hispanic or Latino	10,017,244	3.6
Not Hispanic or Latino	246,116,088	87.5
White alone	194,552,774	69.1
Relationship		
Total population	**281,421,906**	**100.0%**
In households	273,643,273	97.2
Householder	105,480,101	37.5
Spouse	54,493,232	19.4
Child	83,393,392	29.6
Own child under 18	64,494,637	22.9
Other relatives	15,684,318	5.6
Under 18	6,042,435	2.1
Nonrelatives	14,592,230	5.2
Unmarried partner	5,475,768	1.9
In group quarters	7,778,633	2.8
Institutionalized pop.	4,059,039	1.4
Noninstitutionalized pop.	3,719,594	1.3
Household by type		
Total households	**105,480,101**	**100.0**
Family households (families)	71,787,347	68.1
With own children under 18	34,588,368	32.8
Married-couple family	54,493,232	51.7
With own children under 18	24,835,505	23.5
Female householder, no husband present	12,900,103	12.2
With own children under 18	7,561,874	7.2
Nonfamily households	33,692,754	31.9
Householder living alone	27,230,075	25.8
Householder 65 and over	9,722,857	9.2
Households with individuals under 18	38,022,115	36.0
Households with individuals 65 and over	24,672,708	23.4
Average household size	2.59	n.a.
Average family size	3.14	n.a.
Housing occupancy		
Total housing units	**115,904,641**	**100.0**
Occupied housing units	105,480,101	91.0
Vacant housing units	10,424,540	9.0
For seasonal, recreational, or occasional use	3,578,718	3.1
Homeowner vacancy rate (%)	1.7	n.a.
Rental vacancy rate (%)	6.8	n.a.
Housing tenure		
Occupied housing units	**105,480,101**	**100.0**
Owner-occupied housing units	69,815,753	66.2
Renter-occupied housing units	35,664,348	33.8
Average household size of owner-occupied units	2.69	n.a.
Average household size of renter-occupied units	2.40	n.a.

NOTES: (—) represents zero or rounds to zero; n.a. = not applicable. 1. Other Asian alone, or two or more Asian categories. 2. Other Pacific Islander alone, or two or more Native Hawaiian and Other Pacific Islander categories. 3. In combination with one or more of the other races listed. The six numbers may add to more than the total population and the six percentages may add to more than 100% because individuals may report more than one race. *Source:* U.S. Census Bureau, Census 2000. Web: www.census.gov.

Population by State

State	July 2004 pop.	2000	1990	1950	1900	1790
Alabama	4,530,182	4,447,100	4,040,587	3,061,743	1,828,697	—
Alaska	655,435	626,932	550,043	128,643	63,592	—
Arizona	5,743,834	5,130,632	3,665,228	749,587	122,931	—
Arkansas	2,752,629	2,673,400	2,350,725	1,909,511	1,311,564	—
California	35,893,799	33,871,648	29,760,021	10,586,223	1,485,053	—
Colorado	4,601,403	4,301,261	3,294,394	1,325,089	539,700	—
Connecticut	3,503,604	3,405,565	3,287,116	2,007,280	908,420	237,946
Delaware	830,364	783,600	666,168	318,085	184,735	59,096
DC	553,523	572,059	606,900	802,178	278,718	—
Florida	17,397,161	15,982,378	12,937,926	2,771,305	528,542	—
Georgia	8,829,383	8,186,453	6,478,216	3,444,578	2,216,331	82,548
Hawaii	1,262,840	1,211,537	1,108,229	499,794	154,001	—
Idaho	1,393,262	1,293,953	1,006,749	588,637	161,772	—
Illinois	12,713,634	12,419,293	11,430,602	8,712,176	4,821,550	—
Indiana	6,237,569	6,080,485	5,544,159	3,934,224	2,516,462	—
Iowa	2,954,451	2,926,324	2,776,755	2,621,073	2,231,853	—
Kansas	2,735,502	2,688,418	2,477,574	1,905,299	1,470,495	—
Kentucky	4,145,922	4,041,769	3,685,296	2,944,806	2,147,174	73,677
Louisiana	4,515,770	4,468,976	4,219,973	2,683,516	1,381,625	—
Maine	1,317,253	1,274,923	1,227,928	913,774	694,466	96,540
Maryland	5,558,058	5,296,486	4,781,468	2,343,001	1,188,044	319,728
Massachusetts	6,416,505	6,349,097	6,016,425	4,690,514	2,805,346	378,787
Michigan	10,112,620	9,938,444	9,295,297	6,371,766	2,420,982	—
Minnesota	5,100,958	4,919,479	4,375,099	2,982,483	1,751,394	—
Mississippi	2,902,966	2,844,658	2,573,216	2,178,914	1,551,270	—
Missouri	5,754,618	5,595,211	5,117,073	3,954,653	3,106,665	—
Montana	926,865	902,195	799,065	591,024	243,329	—
Nebraska	1,747,214	1,711,263	1,578,385	1,325,510	1,066,300	—
Nevada	2,334,771	1,998,257	1,201,833	160,083	42,335	—
New Hampshire	1,299,500	1,235,786	1,109,252	533,242	411,588	141,885
New Jersey	8,698,879	8,414,350	7,730,188	4,835,329	1,883,669	184,139
New Mexico	1,903,289	1,819,046	1,515,069	681,187	195,310	—
New York	19,227,088	18,976,457	17,990,455	14,830,192	7,268,894	340,120
North Carolina	8,541,221	8,049,313	6,628,637	4,061,929	1,893,810	393,751
North Dakota	634,366	642,200	638,800	619,636	319,146	—
Ohio	11,459,011	11,353,140	10,847,115	7,946,627	4,157,545	—
Oklahoma	3,523,553	3,450,654	3,145,585	2,233,351	790,391[1]	—
Oregon	3,594,586	3,421,399	2,842,321	1,521,341	413,536	—
Pennsylvania	12,406,292	12,281,054	11,881,643	10,498,012	6,302,115	434,373
Rhode Island	1,080,632	1,048,319	1,003,464	791,896	428,556	68,825
South Carolina	4,198,068	4,012,012	3,486,703	2,117,027	1,340,316	249,073
South Dakota	770,883	754,844	696,004	652,740	401,570	—
Tennessee	5,900,962	5,689,283	4,877,185	3,291,718	2,020,616	35,691
Texas	22,490,022	20,851,820	16,986,510	7,711,194	3,048,710	—
Utah	2,389,039	2,233,169	1,722,850	688,862	276,749	—
Vermont	621,394	608,827	562,758	377,747	343,641	85,425
Virginia	7,459,827	7,078,515	6,187,358	3,318,680	1,854,184	747,610[2]
Washington	6,203,788	5,894,121	4,866,692	2,378,963	518,103	—
West Virginia	1,815,354	1,808,344	1,793,477	2,005,552	958,800	—
Wisconsin	5,509,026	5,363,675	4,891,769	3,434,575	2,069,042	—
Wyoming	506,529	493,782	453,588	290,529	92,531	—
Total U.S.	**293,655,404**	**281,421,906**	**248,709,873**	**151,325,798**	**76,212,168**	**3,929,214**

1. Includes population of Indian Territory, 1900: 392,960. 2. Until 1863, Virginia included what is now West Virginia. *Source:* U.S. Bureau of the Census. Web: www.census.gov.

Total U.S. Population

Area	2000	1990	1980	Area	2000	1990	1980
50 states[1]	281,421,906	248,709,873	226,545,805	N. Mariana Is.[3]	69,221	43,345	[4]
48 coterminous[1]	279,583,437	247,051,601	225,179,263	Puerto Rico	3,808,610	3,522,037	3,196,520
Alaska	626,932	550,043	401,851	Trust Ter. of Pac. Is.	[7]	15,122[6]	132,929[5]
Hawaii	1,211,537	1,108,229	964,691	Virgin Is. of U.S.	108,612	101,809	96,569
American Samoa	57,291	46,773	32,297	Wake Island	[2]	[2]	302
Guam	154,805	133,152	105,979	Population abroad	576,367[8]	922,819	995,546
Johnston Atoll	[2]	[2]	327	Armed forces	n.a.	910,611	515,408
Midway	[2]	[2]	453	**Total**	**286,196,812**	**253,451,585**	**231,106,727**

NOTE: n.a. = not available. 1. Includes the District of Columbia. 2. No indigenous population. 3. The Commonwealth of the Northern Mariana Islands (CNMI) became part of the United States in 1986. 4. Included under the territory of the Pacific Islands. 5. Includes Northern Mariana Islands. 6. Palau only trust territory remaining. 7. Palau, the last remaining trust territory, became an independent country in 1994. 8. Includes overseas U.S. military and federal civilian employees and their dependents living with them. *Source:* U.S. Bureau of the Census. Web: www.census.gov.

Colonial Population Estimates
(in round numbers)

Year	Population	Year	Population	Year	Population	Year	Population
1610	350	1660	75,100	1710	331,700	1760	1,593,600
1620	2,300	1670	111,900	1720	466,200	1770	2,148,100
1630	4,600	1680	151,500	1730	629,400	1780	2,780,400
1640	26,600	1690	210,400	1740	905,600		
1650	50,400	1700	250,900	1750	1,170,800		

Covers years before the establishment of the U.S. Census in 1790.

U.S. Population by Region, 1990–2004

Area	Population			Change, 1990–2000	
	April 1, 1990	April 1, 2000	July 1, 2004	Number	Percent
United States	**248,709,873**	**281,421,906**	**293,655,404**	**32,712,033**	**13.2%**
Region[1]					
Northeast	50,809,229	53,594,378	54,571,147	2,785,149	5.5
Midwest	59,668,632	64,392,776	65,729,852	4,724,144	7.9
South	85,445,930	100,236,820	105,944,965	14,790,890	17.3
West	52,786,082	63,197,932	67,409,440	10,411,850	19.7

1. The Northeast region includes Conn., Maine, Mass., N.H., N.J., N.Y., Pa., R.I., and Vt. The Midwest includes Ill., Ind., Iowa, Kans., Mich., Minn., Mo., Neb., N.D., Ohio, S.D., and Wis. The South includes Ala., Ark., Del., D.C., Fla., Ga., Ky., La., Md., Miss., N.C., Okla., S.C., Tenn., Tex., Va., and W.Va.. The West includes Alaska, Ariz., Calif., Colo., Hawaii, Idaho, Mont., Nev., N.M., Ore., Utah, Wash., and Wyo. *Source:* U.S. Census Bureau, Census 2000; 1990 Census. Web: www.census.gov.

Resident Population—Selected Characteristics, 1790–2004
(in thousands)

Date	Male	Female	White	Black	Total	Other			
						American Indian, Eskimo, Aleut	Asian and Pacific Islanders	Two or more races	Hispanic origin[1]
1790 (Aug. 2)	n.a.	n.a.	3,172	757	n.a.	n.a.	n.a.	n.a.	n.a.
1800 (Aug. 4)	n.a.	n.a.	4,306	1,002	n.a.	n.a.	n.a.	n.a.	n.a.
1850 (June 1)	11,838	11,354	19,553	3,639	n.a.	n.a.	n.a.	n.a.	n.a.
1900 (June 1)	38,816	37,178	66,809	8,834	351	n.a.	n.a.	n.a.	n.a.
1910 (Apr. 15)	47,332	44,640	81,732	9,828	413	n.a.	n.a.	n.a.	n.a.
1920 (Jan. 1)	53,900	51,810	94,821	10,463	427	n.a.	n.a.	n.a.	n.a.
1930 (Apr. 1)	62,137	60,638	110,287	11,891	597	n.a.	n.a.	n.a.	n.a.
1940 (Apr. 1)	66,062	65,608	118,215	12,866	589	n.a.	n.a.	n.a.	n.a.
1950 (Apr. 1)[2]	74,833	75,864	134,942	15,042	713	n.a.	n.a.	n.a.	n.a.
1950 (Apr. 1)	75,187	76,139	135,150	15,045	1,131	n.a.	n.a.	n.a.	n.a.
1960 (Apr. 1)	88,331	90,992	158,832	18,872	1,620	n.a.	n.a.	n.a.	n.a.
1970 (Apr. 1)	98,926	104,309	178,098	22,581	2,557	n.a.	n.a.	n.a.	n.a.
1980 (Apr. 1)	110,053	116,493	194,713	26,683	5,150	1,420	3,729	n.a.	14,609
1990 (Apr. 1)	121,271	127,494	208,727	30,511	9,527	2,065	7,462	n.a.	22,372
2000 (Apr. 1)[3]	138,054	143,368	228,104	35,704	17,613	2,664	11,052	3,898	35,306
2004 (July 1)[4]	144,529	149,094	235,991	37,521	20,110	2,825	12,843	4,443	41,330

NOTES: n.a. = not available. 1. Persons of Hispanic origin may be of any race. 2. Excludes Alaska and Hawaii. 3. Total population count has been revised, as have the sex, race, and Hispanic origin numbers. 4. Estimated. *Source: U.S. Census Bureau.* Web: www.census.gov.

Ratio of Males to Females, by Age Group, 1950–2004
(number of males per 100 females, total resident population)

Age	1950	1960	1970	1980	1990[1]	2000	2004[2]
All ages	**98.6**	**97.1**	**94.8**	**94.5**	**95.1**	**96.3**	**96.9**
Under 14 years	103.7	103.4	103.9	104.6	104.9	104.9	104.7
14 to 24 years	98.2	98.7	98.7	101.9	104.6	105.1	105.8
25 to 44 years	96.4	95.7	95.5	97.4	98.9	100.2	101.4
45 to 64 years	100.1	95.7	91.6	90.7	92.5	94.8	95.0
65 years and over	89.6	82.8	72.1	67.6	67.2	70.8	71.7

NOTES: As of April 1 for all years except 2004. 1. The April 1, 1990, census count (248,765,170) includes count resolution corrections processed through August 1997, and does not include adjustments for census coverage errors except for adjustments estimated for the 1995 Census Test in Oakland, Calif.; Paterson, N.J.; and six Louisiana parishes. These adjustments amounted to a total of 55,297 persons. 2. As of July 1; estimated. *Source:* U.S. Census Bureau, *Current Population Reports,* P25-1095 and P25-1130; and unpublished data. From *Statistical Abstract of the United States 1999.* 2000 data are from Census 2000; 2003 data are from NC-EST2003-02.

National Censuses, 1790–2000[1]

Year	Resident population[2]	Land area, sq mi	Pop. per sq mi	Year	Resident population[2]	Land area, sq mi	Pop. per sq mi
1790	3,929,214	864,746	4.5	1900	75,994,575	2,969,834	25.6
1800	5,308,483	864,746	6.1	1910	91,972,266	2,969,565	31.0
1810	7,239,881	1,681,828	4.3	1920	105,710,620	2,969,451	35.6
1820	9,638,453	1,749,462	5.5	1930	122,775,046	2,977,128	41.2
1830	12,866,020	1,749,462	7.4	1940	131,669,275	2,977,128	44.2
1840	17,069,453	1,749,462	9.8	1950	150,697,361	2,974,726	50.7
1850	23,191,876	2,940,042	7.9	1960	179,323,175	3,540,911	50.6
1860	31,443,321	2,969,640	10.6	1970	203,302,031	3,540,023	57.4
1870	39,818,449	2,969,640	13.4	1980	226,545,805	3,539,289	64.0
1880	50,155,783	2,969,640	16.9	1990	248,709,873	3,536,278	* 70.3
1890	62,947,714	2,969,640	21.2	2000	281,421,906	3,537,441	79.6

1. Beginning with 1960, figures include Alaska and Hawaii. 2. Excludes armed forces overseas. *Source:* U.S. Bureau of the Census. Web: www.census.gov.

Population Distribution by Age, Race, Nativity, and Sex Ratio, 1860–2004

| | | | Age | | | | Race and nativity | | | | |
| | | | | | | | White[1] | | | | |
Year	Total	Under 5	5–19	20–44	45–64	65 and over	Total	Native born	Foreign born	Black	Other races[1]
Percent distribution											
1860[2]	100.0%	15.4%	35.8%	35.7%	10.4%	2.7%	85.6%	72.6%	13.0%	14.1%	0.3%
1870[2]	100.0	14.3	35.4	35.4	11.9	3.0	87.1	72.9	14.2	12.7	0.2
1880[2]	100.0	13.8	34.3	35.9	12.6	3.4	86.5	73.4	13.1	13.1	0.3
1890[3]	100.0	12.2	33.9	36.9	13.1	3.9	87.5	73.0	14.5	11.9	0.3
1900	100.0	12.1	32.3	37.7	13.7	4.1	87.9	74.5	13.4	11.6	0.5
1910	100.0	11.6	30.4	39.0	14.6	4.3	88.9	74.4	14.5	10.7	0.4
1920	100.0	10.9	29.8	38.4	16.1	4.7	89.7	76.7	13.0	9.9	0.4
1930	100.0	9.3	29.5	38.3	17.4	5.4	89.8	78.4	11.4	9.7	0.5
1940	100.0	8.0	26.4	38.9	19.8	6.8	89.8	81.1	8.7	9.8	0.4
1950	100.0	10.7	23.2	37.6	20.3	8.1	89.5	82.8	6.7	10.0	0.5
1960	100.0	11.3	27.1	32.2	20.1	9.2	88.6	83.4	5.2	10.5	0.9
1970[2]	100.0	8.4	29.5	31.7	20.6	9.8	87.6	83.4	4.3	11.1	1.4
1980	100.0	7.2	24.8	37.1	19.6	11.3	83.1	—	—	11.7	5.2
1990	100.0	7.6	21.3	40.1	18.6	12.5	83.9	—	—	12.3	3.8
2000	100.0	6.8	21.8	37.0	22.0	12.4	75.1[4]	—	—	12.3[4]	10.1[5]
2004[6]	100.0	6.8	20.9	35.8	24.1	12.3	80.4	—	—	12.8[4]	6.8[5]
Males per 100 females											
1860[2]	104.7	102.4	101.2	107.9	111.5	98.3	105.3	103.7	115.1	99.6	260.8
1870[2]	102.2	102.9	101.2	99.2	114.5	100.5	102.8	100.6	115.3	96.2	400.7
1880[2]	103.6	103.0	101.3	104.0	110.2	101.4	104.0	102.1	115.9	97.8	362.2
1890[3]	105.0	103.6	101.4	107.3	108.3	104.2	105.4	102.9	118.7	99.5	165.2
1900	104.4	102.1	100.9	105.8	110.7	102.0	104.9	102.8	117.4	98.6	185.2
1910	106.0	102.5	101.3	108.1	114.4	101.1	106.6	102.7	129.2	98.9	185.6
1920	104.0	102.5	100.8	102.8	115.2	101.3	104.4	101.7	121.7	99.2	156.6
1930	102.5	103.0	101.4	100.5	109.1	100.5	102.9	101.1	115.8	97.0	150.6
1940	100.7	103.2	102.0	98.1	105.2	95.5	101.2	100.1	111.1	95.0	140.5
1950	98.6	103.9	102.5	96.2	100.1	89.6	99.0	98.8	102.0	93.7	129.7
1960	97.1	103.4	102.7	95.6	95.7	82.8	97.4	97.6	94.2	93.3	109.7
1970[2]	94.8	104.0	103.3	95.1	91.6	72.1	95.3	95.9	83.8	90.8	100.2
1980	94.5	104.7	104.0	98.1	90.7	67.6	94.8	—	—	89.6	100.3
1990	95.1	104.8	105.0	99.8	92.5	67.2	95.9	—	—	89.8	96.5
2000	96.3	104.8	105.3	101.0	94.8	70.0	96.4[4]	—	—	90.5[4]	102.5[5]
2004[6]	96.9	104.6	105.1	102.4	95.0	71.7	98.0	—	—	91.1[4]	95.8[5]

NOTES: Data exclude armed forces overseas. (—) Data not available. 1. The racial census data for 1980 and all years following are not directly comparable to those of other years because of changes in the way some persons reported their race, as well as changes in procedures relating to racial classification. 2. Excludes persons for whom age is not available. 3. Excludes persons enumerated in the Indian Territory and on Indian reservations. 4. Includes only those claiming one race only. 5. Includes American Indian and Alaska Native, Asian, Native Hawaiian and other Pacific Islander, and those claiming more than one race. 6. Estimated. *Source:* U.S. Bureau of the Census. Web: www.census.gov.

Household and Family Statistics

Households by Size, 1790–2003

		Percent distribution of number of households							
Year	Number of households (in thousands)	1 person	2 persons	3 persons	4 persons	5 persons	6 persons	7 or more persons	Avg. pop. per household
1790 (Mar.)	558	3.7%	7.8%	11.7%	13.8%	13.9%	13.2%	35.8%	—
1890 (June)	12,690	3.6	13.2	16.7	16.8	15.1	11.6	23.0	4.93
1900 (Mar.)	15,964	5.1	15.0	17.6	16.9	14.2	10.9	20.4	—
1930 (Apr.)	29,905	7.9	23.4	20.8	17.5	12.0	7.6	10.9	4.11
1940 (Apr.)	34,949	7.1	24.8	22.4	18.1	11.5	6.8	9.3	3.67
1950 (Apr.)[1]	43,468	10.9	28.8	22.6	17.8	10.0	5.1	4.9	3.37
1955 (Mar.)	47,788	10.9	28.5	20.4	18.9	11.1	5.4	4.9	3.33
1960 (Mar.)	52,610	13.1	27.8	18.9	17.6	11.5	5.7	5.4	3.35
1965 (Mar.)	57,251	15.0	28.1	17.9	16.1	11.0	5.8	6.1	3.32
1970 (Mar.)	62,874	17.0	28.8	17.3	15.8	10.4	5.6	5.1	3.14
1975 (Mar.)	71,120	19.6	30.6	17.4	15.6	9.0	4.3	3.5	2.94
1980 (Mar.)	80,776	22.7	31.3	17.5	15.7	7.5	3.1	2.2	2.76
1985 (Mar.)	86,789	23.7	31.6	17.8	15.7	7.0	2.6	1.5	2.69
1990 (Mar.)	93,347	24.6	32.2	17.2	15.5	6.7	2.3	1.4	2.63
1995 (Mar.)	98,990	25.0	32.1	17.0	15.5	6.7	2.3	1.4	2.65
2000 (Mar.)	104,705	25.5	33.1	16.4	14.6	6.7	2.3	1.4	2.62
2003 (Mar.)[2]	111,278	26.4	33.3	16.1	14.3	6.3	2.3	1.2	2.57

1. Covers related persons only; therefore, not strictly comparable with other years. 2. Based on Census 2000 and an expanded sample of households. Source: U.S. Census Bureau. Web: www.census.gov.

Households by Type, 1980–2003

	Households					
	Number				Percent distribution	
Type of household	1980	1990	2000	2003	1990	2000
Total households	**80,776,000**	**93,347,000**	**104,705,000**	**111,278,000**	**100%**	**100%**
Family households	**59,550,000**	**66,090,000**	**72,025,000**	**75,596,000**	**71**	**69**
Married couple family	49,112,000	52,317,000	55,311,000	57,320,000	56	53
Male householder, no spouse present	1,733,000	2,884,000	4,028,000	4,656,000	3	4
Female householder, no spouse present	8,705,000	10,890,000	12,687,000	13,620,000	12	12
Nonfamily households	**21,226,000**	**27,257,000**	**32,680,000**	**35,682,000**	**29**	**31**
Living alone	18,296,000	22,999,000	26,724,000	29,431,000	25	26
Male householder	8,807,000	11,606,000	14,641,000	16,020,000	12	14
Living alone	6,966,000	9,049,000	11,181,000	12,511,000	10	11
Female householder	12,419,000	15,651,000	18,039,000	19,662,000	17	17
Living alone	11,330,000	13,950,000	15,543,000	16,919,000	15	15

Source: U.S. Census Bureau, Current Population Reports. From Statistical Abstract of the United States, 2002.

Homeownership Rates by Race and Ethnicity of Householder

	1996	1997	1998	1999	2000	2001	2002	2003	2004
U.S. total	**65.4**	**65.7**	**66.3**	**66.8**	**67.4**	**67.8**	**67.9**	**68.3**	**69.0**
White, total	69.1	69.3	70.0	70.5	71.1	71.6	71.8	72.1	72.8
White, non-Hispanic	71.7	72.0	72.6	73.2	73.8	74.3	74.5	75.4	76.0
Black, total	44.1	44.8	45.6	46.3	47.2	47.4	47.3	48.1	49.1
Other race	51.0	52.5	53.0	53.7	53.5	54.2	54.7	56.0	58.6
American Indian, Aleut, Eskimo	51.6	51.7	54.3	54.5	56.2	55.4	54.6	54.3	55.6
Asian or Pacific Islander	50.8	52.8	52.6	53.1	52.8	53.9	54.7	56.3	59.8
Hispanic	42.8	43.3	44.7	45.5	46.3	47.3	48.2	46.7	48.1
Non-Hispanic	67.4	67.8	68.3	68.9	69.5	69.9	70.0	70.8	71.5

Source: U.S. Census Bureau. Web: www.census.gov.

Homeownership by State, 1990 and 2004

State	Homeownership rate (%) 1990	2004	State	Homeownership rate (%) 1990	2004	State	Homeownership rate (%) 1990	2004
U.S. total	63.9%	69.0%	Kentucky	65.8%	73.3	Ohio	68.7%	73.1
Alabama	68.4	78.0	Louisiana	67.8	70.6	Oklahoma	70.3	71.1
Alaska	58.4	67.2	Maine	74.2	74.7	Oregon	64.4	69.0
Arizona	64.5	68.7	Maryland	64.9	72.1	Pennsylvania	73.8	74.9
Arkansas	67.8	69.1	Massachusetts	58.6	63.8	Rhode Island	58.5	61.5
California	53.8	59.7	Michigan	72.3	77.1	South Carolina	71.4	76.2
Colorado	59.0	71.1	Minnesota	68.0	76.4	South Dakota	66.2	68.5
Connecticut	67.9	71.7	Mississippi	69.4	74.0	Tennessee	68.3	71.6
Delaware	67.7	77.3	Missouri	64.0	72.4	Texas	59.7	65.5
DC	36.4	45.6	Montana	69.1	72.4	Utah	70.1	74.9
Florida	65.1	72.2	Nebraska	67.3	71.2	Vermont	72.6	72.0
Georgia	64.3	70.9	Nevada	55.8	65.7	Virginia	69.8	73.4
Hawaii	55.5	60.6	New Hampshire	65.0	73.3	Washington	61.8	66.0
Idaho	69.4	73.7	New Jersey	65.0	68.8	West Virginia	72.0	80.3
Illinois	63.0	72.7	New Mexico	68.6	71.5	Wisconsin	68.3	73.3
Indiana	67.0	75.8	New York	53.3	54.8	Wyoming	68.9	72.8
Iowa	70.7	73.2	North Carolina	69.0	69.8			
Kansas	69.0	69.9	North Dakota	67.2	70.0			

Source: U.S. Census Bureau. Web: www.census.gov.

Persons Living Alone, by Sex and Age
(in thousands)

	1990 Number	%	2000 Number	%	2003 Number	%
Both sexes	**22,999**	**100**	**26,724**	**100**	**29,431**	**100**
15 to 24 years old	1,210	5	1,144	4	1,540	5
25 to 34 years old	3,972	17	3,848	14	3,809	13
35 to 44 years old	3,138	14	4,109	15	4,210	14
45 to 64 years old	5,502	24	7,842	29	9,324	32
65 to 74 years old	4,350	19	4,091	15	4,201	14
75 years old and over	4,825	21	5,692	21	6,347	22
Male	**9,049**	**39**	**11,181**	**42**	**12,511**	**43**
15 to 24 years old	674	3	556	2	722	2
25 to 34 years old	2,395	10	2,279	9	2,212	8
35 to 44 years old	1,836	8	2,569	10	2,573	9
45 to 64 years old	2,203	10	3,422	13	4,280	15
65 to 74 years old	1,042	5	1,108	4	1,291	4
75 years old and over	901	4	1,247	5	1,434	5
Female	**13,950**	**61**	**15,543**	**58**	**16,919**	**57**
15 to 24 years old	536	2	588	2	818	3
25 to 34 years old	1,578	7	1,568	6	1,597	5
35 to 44 years old	1,303	6	1,540	6	1,638	6
45 to 64 years old	3,300	14	4,420	17	5,044	17
65 to 74 years old	3,309	14	2,983	11	2,911	10
75 years old and over	3,924	17	4,444	17	4,913	17

Source: U.S. Census Bureau, *Current Population Reports,* P20-547, and earlier reports; and unpublished data.

Married-Couple and Unmarried-Partner Households for the U.S. and Regions, 2000

Area	Total number of coupled households[1]	Coupled households (% of all households)	Married couples (% of coupled households)	Unmarried partners (% of coupled households)	Opposite sex unmarried partners (% of coupled households)	Same-sex unmarried partners (% of coupled households)
United States	**59,969,000**	**56.9%**	**90.9%**	**9.1%**	**8.1%**	**1.0%**
Region						
Northeast	11,205,641	55.2	90.4	9.6	8.6	1.1
Midwest	14,222,533	57.5	91.1	8.9	8.1	0.7
South	21,549,582	56.7	91.6	8.4	7.4	1.0
West	12,991,244	57.9	89.8	10.2	9.0	1.2

NOTE: Totals may not add up due to rounding. 1. Coupled households represent total of married-couple and unmarried-partner households. *Source:* U.S. Census Bureau, Census 2000 Summary File 1.

Weekly Household Food Spending per Person, 2003

Category	Number of households[1]	Per person	Category	Number of households[1]	Per person
All households	104,924	$38.00	Women living alone	15,273	$50.00
Household composition:			Men living alone	11,785	55.00
With children < 18	38,287	31.25	With elderly	23,466	37.50
At least one child < 6	17,328	28.00	Elderly, living alone	9,410	40.00
Married-couple families	26,191	32.00	Race/ethnicity of households:		
Female head, no spouse	9,063	28.00	White non-Hispanic	76,000	40.00
Male head, no spouse	2,344	30.00	Black non-Hispanic	12,059	33.33
Other household with child[2]	689	30.00	Hispanic[3]	11,357	31.25
With no children < 18	66,637	45.00	Other non-Hispanic	5,507	37.50
More than one adult	39,579	40.00			

1. Totals exclude households that did not answer questions about spending on food. These represented 6.0% of all households. 2. Households with children in complex living arrangements, e.g., children of other relatives or unrelated roommate or border. 3. Hispanics may be of any race. *Source:* Economic Research Service, U.S. Department of Agriculture, *Household Food Security in the United States, 2003.* Web: www.ers.usda.gov

Estimated Annual Expenditures on a Child by Husband-Wife Families, Overall United States, 2004

Family income and age of child	Total	Housing	Food	Transportation	Clothing	Health care	Child care and education	Miscellaneous[1]
Before-tax income: Less than $41,700 (Average = $26,100)								
0–2	$ 7,040	$ 2,680	$ 980	$ 820	$ 350	$ 530	$ 1,020	$ 660
3–5	7,210	2,650	1,090	800	340	500	1,150	680
6–8	7,250	2,560	1,400	930	380	580	680	720
9–11	7,220	2,310	1,680	1,010	420	630	410	760
12–14	8,070	2,580	1,770	1,130	710	640	290	950
15–17	8,000	2,080	1,910	1,530	630	680	480	690
Total	$134,370	$ 44,580	$26,490	$18,660	$ 8,490	$10,680	$12,090	$13,380
Before-tax income: $41,700 to $70,200 (Average = $55,500)								
0–2	$ 9,840	$ 3,630	$ 1,170	$ 1,230	$ 410	$ 690	$ 1,680	$ 1,030
3–5	10,120	3,600	1,350	1,200	400	660	1,860	1,050
6–8	10,030	3,510	1,720	1,330	440	750	1,190	1,090
9–11	9,910	3,260	2,030	1,410	490	820	780	1,120
12–14	10,640	3,520	2,050	1,540	830	820	570	1,310
15–17	10,900	3,030	2,270	1,950	740	870	980	1,060
Total	$184,320	$ 61,650	$31,770	$25,980	$ 9,930	$13,830	$21,180	$19,980
Before-tax income: More than $70,200 (Average = $105,100)								
0–2	$ 14,620	$ 5,770	$ 1,550	$ 1,720	$ 540	$ 790	$ 2,530	$ 1,720
3–5	14,960	5,730	1,760	1,690	530	760	2,750	1,740
6–8	14,710	5,640	2,120	1,820	580	870	1,900	1,780
9–11	14,470	5,400	2,460	1,900	630	940	1,320	1,820
12–14	15,270	5,660	2,580	2,030	1,040	940	1,010	2,010
15–17	15,810	5,160	2,720	2,460	950	990	1,780	1,750
Total	$269,520	$100,080	$39,570	$34,860	$12,810	$15,870	$33,870	$32,460

1. Expenses include personal care items, entertainment, and reading materials. *Source:* Dept. of Agriculture, Center for Nutrition Policy and Promotion, *Expenditures on Children by Families, 2004 Annual Report.*

Percent Distribution of Total Annual Expenditures by Major Category, Consumer Expenditure Survey, 1999–2002

Item	1999	2000	2001	2002	Item	1999	2000	2001	2002
Average annual expenditures	100.0%	100.0%	100.0%	100.0%	Other transportation	7.2%	7.1%	7.0%	7.0%
Food	13.6	13.6	13.5	13.2	Health care	5.3	5.4	5.5	5.8
Food at home	7.9	7.9	7.8	7.6	Entertainment	5.1	4.9	4.9	5.1
Food away from home	5.7	5.6	5.7	5.6	Personal insurance and pensions	9.3	8.8	9.5	9.6
Housing	32.6	32.4	32.9	32.7	Life and other personal insurance	1.1	1.0	1.0	1.0
Apparel and services	4.7	4.9	4.4	4.3	Pensions and Social Security	8.2	7.8	8.4	8.6
Transportation	19.0	19.5	19.3	19.1	Other expenditures[1]	10.5	10.5	10.0	10.3
Vehicles	8.9	9.0	9.1	9.0					
Gasoline and motor oil	2.9	3.4	3.2	3.0					

1. Includes expenditures for alcoholic beverages, personal care products and services, reading, education, and tobacco products and supplies, as well as cash contributions and miscellaneous expenditures. *Source:* U.S. Department of Labor, Bureau of Labor Statistics, *Consumer Expenditures in 2002.*

Marital Status

Marriages and Divorces, 1900–2004

Year	Marriage Number	Marriage Rate[2]	Divorce[1] Number	Divorce[1] Rate[2]	Year	Marriage Number	Marriage Rate[2]	Divorce[1] Number	Divorce[1] Rate[2]
1900	709,000	9.3	55,751	0.7	1960	1,523,000	8.5	393,000	2.2
1910	948,166	10.3	83,045	0.9	1970	2,158,802	10.6	708,000	3.5
1920	1,274,476	12.0	170,505	1.6	1980	2,406,708	10.6	1,182,000	5.2
1930	1,126,856	9.2	195,961	1.6	1990	2,448,000	9.8	1,175,000	4.7
1940	1,595,879	12.1	264,000	2.0	2000	2,329,000	8.5	—	4.1
1950	1,667,231	11.1	385,144	2.6	2004	2,181,000	7.4	—	3.7

NOTE: (—) Data not available. Marriage and divorce figures for most years include some estimated data. Alaska is included beginning 1959, Hawaii beginning 1960. 1. Includes annulments. 2. Per 1,000 population. *Source:* U.S. Dept. of Health and Human Services, National Center for Health Statistics. Web: www.cdc.gov/nchs/.

Median Age at First Marriage

Year	Males	Females	Year	Males	Females	Year	Males	Females
1890	26.1	22.0	1940	24.3	21.5	1990	26.1	23.9
1900	25.9	21.9	1950	22.8	20.3	1995	26.9	24.5
1910	25.1	21.6	1960	22.8	20.3	2000	26.8	25.1
1920	24.6	21.2	1970	23.2	20.8	2001	26.9	25.1
1930	24.3	21.3	1980	24.7	22.0	2003	27.1	25.3

Source: U.S. Bureau of the Census; Web: www.census.gov.

Percent Never Married

Age	1970	1999	2000	2002	2003	Age	1970	1999	2000	2002	2003
Male:						**Female:**					
20 to 24 years	35.8%	83.2%	83.7%	85.4%	86.0%	20 to 24 years	54.7%	72.3%	72.8%	74.0%	75.4%
25 to 29 years	10.5	52.1	51.7	53.7	54.6	25 to 29 years	19.1	38.9	38.9	40.4	40.3
30 to 34 years	6.2	30.7	30.0	34.0	33.1	30 to 34 years	9.4	22.1	21.9	23.0	22.7
35 to 39 years	5.4	21.1	20.3	21.1	21.8	35 to 39 years	7.2	15.2	14.3	14.7	14.3
40 to 44 years	4.9	15.8	15.7	16.7	17.4	40 to 44 years	6.3	10.9	11.8	11.5	12.2

NOTE: Data apply to the U.S. *Source:* U.S. Bureau of the Census. From *Statistical Abstract of the United States 2004.*

Marital Status of the Population by Sex, 1900–2003

(numbers are in thousands)

	Males Total	Males Never married	Males Married	Males Widowed	Males Divorced	Females Total	Females Never married	Females Married	Females Widowed	Females Divorced
1900	25,493.0	10,262.0	13,919.0	1,173.0	84.0	24,176.0	7,549.0	13,781.0	2,706.0	114.0
1910	32,311.0	12,521.0	18,065.0	1,467.0	156.0	29,993.0	8,918.0	17,664.0	3,167.0	185.0
1920	36,828.0	12,940.0	21,820.0	1,754.0	234.0	35,122.0	9,601.0	21,295.0	3,909.0	273.0
1930	43,829.0	14,938.0	26,311.0	2,023.0	489.0	42,795.0	11,294.0	26,156.0	4,728.0	572.0
1940	49,336.0	16,377.0	30,191.0	2,144.0	624.0	49,362.0	12,752.0	30,087.0	5,700.0	823.0
1950	53,511.0	13,319.0	36,859.0	2,262.0	1,070.0	56,055.0	10,379.0	37,570.0	6,734.0	1,373.0
1960	59,913.0	13,919.0	42,623.0	2,072.0	1,299.0	63,616.0	10,990.0	42,891.0	7,880.0	1,855.0
1970	69,349.0	18,315.0	46,981.0	2,128.0	1,925.0	75,861.0	15,604.0	47,644.0	9,610.0	3,002.0
1980	83,836.0	25,132.0	52,009.0	2,156.0	4,539.0	91,420.0	21,027.0	52,497.0	11,318.0	6,577.0
1990	93,817.0	28,805.0	55,678.0	2,378.0	6,957.0	101,325.0	23,755.0	55,821.0	12,122.0	9,627.0
2000	107,027.0	32,381.0	62,692.0	2,699.0	9,255.0	114,121.0	27,532.0	62,309.0	11,975.0	12,305.0
2003	102,313.0	28,577.0	62,087.0	2,692.0	8,957.0	110,115.0	23,333.0	62,834.0	11,288.0	12,660.0
Percent distribution										
1900	100.0%	40.3%	54.6%	4.6%	0.3%	100.0%	31.2%	57.0%	11.2%	0.5%
1910	100.0	38.8	55.9	4.5	0.5	100.0	29.7	58.9	10.6	0.6
1920	100.0	35.1	59.2	4.8	0.6	100.0	27.3	60.6	11.1	0.8
1930	100.0	34.1	60.0	4.6	1.1	100.0	26.4	61.1	11.0	1.3
1940	100.0	33.2	61.2	4.3	1.3	100.0	25.8	61.0	11.5	1.7
1950	100.0	24.9	68.9	4.2	2.0	100.0	18.5	67.0	12.0	2.4
1960	100.0	23.2	71.1	3.5	2.2	100.0	17.3	67.4	12.4	2.9
1970	100.0	26.4	67.7	3.1	2.8	100.0	20.6	62.8	12.7	4.0
1980	100.0	30.0	62.0	2.6	5.4	100.0	23.0	57.4	12.4	7.2
1990	100.0	30.7	59.3	2.5	7.4	100.0	23.4	55.1	12.0	9.5
2000	100.0	30.3	58.6	2.5	8.6	100.0	24.1	54.6	10.5	10.8
2003	100.0	27.9	60.7	2.6	8.8	100.0	21.2	57.1	10.3	11.5

Source: Statistical Abstract of the United States 2004.

Divorce Rates by State, 1990–2001

	Rates per 1,000 population[1,2]				Rates per 1,000 population[1,2]		
	1990	1995	2001		1990	1995	2001
U.S.[3]	4.7	4.4	4.0	Missouri	5.1	5.0	4.3
Alabama	6.1	6.1	5.3	Montana	5.1	4.8	2.6
Alaska	5.5	5.0	4.1	Nebraska	4.0	3.8	3.7
Arizona	6.9	6.6	4.2	Nevada	11.4	8.1	6.8
Arkansas	6.9	6.5	6.6	New Hampshire	4.7	4.2	5.0
California	4.3	n.a.	n.a.	New Jersey	3.0	3.1	3.5
Colorado	5.5	n.a.	n.a.	New Mexico	4.9	6.7	5.1
Connecticut	3.2	2.9	2.9	New York	3.2	3.1	3.0
Delaware	4.4	5.1	4.0	North Carolina	5.1	5.1	4.5
Dist. of Columbia	4.5	3.4	2.3	North Dakota	3.6	3.4	2.7
Florida	6.3	5.6	5.4	Ohio	4.7	4.4	4.0
Georgia	5.5	5.2	3.8	Oklahoma	7.7	6.7	3.4
Hawaii	4.6	4.6	3.8	Oregon	5.5	4.8	4.9
Idaho	6.5	5.8	5.6	Pennsylvania	3.3	3.3	3.2
Illinois	3.8	3.3	3.2	Rhode Island	3.7	3.7	3.3
Indiana	n.a.	n.a.	n.a.	South Carolina	4.5	4.0	3.5
Iowa	3.9	3.7	3.2	South Dakota	3.7	4.0	3.4
Kansas	5.0	4.2	3.2	Tennessee	6.5	6.3	5.2
Kentucky	5.8	5.9	5.5	Texas	5.5	5.3	4.1
Louisiana	n.a.	n.a.	n.a.	Utah	5.1	4.6	4.4
Maine	4.3	4.4	3.9	Vermont	4.5	4.8	4.0
Maryland	3.4	3.0	3.0	Virginia	4.4	4.4	4.3
Massachusetts	2.8	2.2	2.4	Washington	5.9	5.5	4.5
Michigan	4.3	4.2	3.9	West Virginia	5.3	5.1	5.2
Minnesota	3.5	3.4	3.3	Wisconsin	3.6	3.4	3.2
Mississippi	5.5	4.8	5.4	Wyoming	6.6	6.7	6.1

n.a. = not available 1. Based on total population residing in area; population enumerated as of April 1 for 1990; estimated as of July 1 for all other years. 2. Includes annulments. 3. U.S. totals for the number of divorces is an estimate which includes states not reporting (California, Colorado, Indiana, and Louisiana). Source: U.S. Census Bureau, Statistical Abstract of the United States: 2003.

Births

Births, Birth Rates, and Fertility Rates by State, 2003

State	Number of births	Birth rate[1]	Fertility rate[2]	State	Number of births	Birth rate[1]	Fertility rate[2]
United States[3]	4,091,063	14.1	66.1	Nevada	33,644	15.0	72.2
Alabama	59,621	13.2	62.6	New Hampshire	14,393	11.2	52.7
Alaska	10,122	15.6	72.7	New Jersey	116,269	13.5	64.5
Arizona	91,005	16.3	79.3	New Mexico	27,845	14.9	71.5
Arkansas	38,159	14.0	68.1	New York	254,187	13.2	61.1
California	540,995	15.2	69.9	North Carolina	118,308	14.1	65.8
Colorado	69,363	15.2	69.5	North Dakota	7,975	12.6	61.6
Connecticut	42,848	12.3	59.6	Ohio	151,983	13.3	63.7
Delaware	11,264	13.8	64.3	Oklahoma	50,484	14.4	69.2
District of Columbia	7,606	13.5	53.8	Oregon	45,975	12.9	62.5
Florida	212,286	12.5	63.4	Pennsylvania	140,660	11.4	56.0
Georgia	136,012	15.7	69.3	Rhode Island	13,192	12.3	56.5
Hawaii	18,114	14.4	72.3	South Carolina	55,658	13.4	63.0
Idaho	21,802	16.0	76.0	South Dakota	11,035	14.4	70.8
Illinois	182,590	14.4	67.0	Tennessee	78,901	13.5	63.1
Indiana	86,600	14.0	66.5	Texas	381,239	17.2	78.3
Iowa	38,182	13.0	63.3	Utah	49,870	21.2	92.2
Kansas	39,493	14.5	69.5	Vermont	6,591	10.6	51.1
Kentucky	55,281	13.4	63.2	Virginia	101,226	13.7	63.3
Louisiana	65,298	14.5	66.4	Washington	80,474	13.1	61.2
Maine	13,861	10.6	52.1	West Virginia	20,908	11.5	58.1
Maryland	74,856	13.6	62.3	Wisconsin	70,053	12.8	60.7
Massachusetts	80,250	12.5	57.2	Wyoming	6,708	13.4	65.7
Michigan	130,937	13.0	61.6				
Minnesota	70,157	13.9	64.2	Puerto Rico	49,427	n.a.	n.a.
Mississippi	42,362	14.7	67.9	Virgin Islands	997	n.a.	n.a.
Missouri	77,079	13.5	64.1	Guam	3,286	n.a.	n.a.
Montana	11,416	12.4	62.6	American Samoa	1,015	n.a.	n.a.
Nebraska	25,924	14.9	71.4	Northern Marianas	1,344	n.a.	n.a.

NOTE: Data by place of residence. n.a. = data not available. 1. Birth rates are live births per 1,000 estimated population in each area. 2. Fertility rates are live births per 1,000 women aged 15–44 years estimated in each area. 3. Excludes data for Puerto Rico, Virgin Islands, Guam, American Samoa, and Northern Marianas. Source: National Center for Health Statistics, National Vital Statistics Reports, vol. 53, no. 9, Nov. 23, 2004. Web: www.cdc.gov/nchs.

Live Births by Age and Race of Mother, 1940–2003

		Age of mother							
Year[1]/race	Total	Under 15	15–19	20–24	25–29	30–34	35–39	40–44	45–49[2]
1940	2,558,647	3,865	332,667	799,537	693,268	431,468	222,015	68,269	7,558
1945	2,858,449	4,028	298,868	832,746	785,299	554,906	296,852	78,853	6,897
1950	3,631,512	5,413	432,911	1,155,167	1,041,360	610,816	302,780	77,743	5,322
1955	4,014,112	6,181	493,770	1,290,939	1,133,155	732,540	352,320	89,777	5,430
1960	4,257,850	6,780	586,966	1,426,912	1,092,816	687,722	359,908	91,564	5,182
1965	3,760,358	7,768	590,894	1,337,350	925,732	529,376	282,908	81,716	4,614
1970	3,731,386	11,752	644,708	1,418,874	994,904	427,806	180,244	49,952	3,146
1975	3,144,198	12,642	582,238	1,093,676	936,786	375,500	115,409	26,319	1,628
1980	3,612,258	10,169	552,161	1,226,200	1,108,291	550,354	140,793	23,090	1,200
1985	3,760,561	10,220	467,485	1,141,320	1,201,350	696,354	214,336	28,334	1,162
1990	4,158,212	11,657	521,826	1,093,730	1,277,108	886,063	317,583	48,607	1,638
1995	3,899,589	12,242	499,873	965,547	1,063,539	904,666	383,745	67,250	2,727
2000	4,058,814	8,519[3]	468,990	1,017,806	1,087,547	929,278	452,057	90,013	4,604[2]
2003	4,091,063	6,665	414,961	1,032,337	1,086,898	975,964	467,520	100,873	5,845[2]
White	3,227,755	3,682	298,821	971,106	872,288	796,520	379,703	80,929	4,706[2]
Black	599,414	2,722	100,855	106,112	139,853	97,526	49,810	11,880	645[2]
American Indian[4]	42,647	156	7,617	14,480	10,421	6,372	2,900	660	43[2]
Asian or Pacific Islander	221,247	105	7,658	30,639	64,336	75,546	35,107	7,405	451[2]
Hispanic origin[5]	912,256	2,349	128,472	273,258	246,388	169,056	75,812	16,169	753[2]

NOTE: Data refer only to births occurring within the U.S. 1. Data for 1940–1955 are adjusted for under-registration. Beginning 1960, only registered births are shown. Data for 1960–1970 based on a 50% sample of births. For 1972–1984, based on 100% of births in selected states and on 50% sample in all other states. Beginning 1989, births are tabulated by race of mother; previously based on race of child. 2. Beginning 1998, ages 45–54. 3. Ages 10–14. 4. Includes births to Aleuts and Eskimos. 5. Persons of Hispanic origin may be any race. *Source:* National Center for Health Statistics, *National Vital Statistics Reports*, vol. 53, no. 9, Nov. 23, 2004. Web: www.cdc.gov/nchs.

Live Births by Sex and Sex Ratio

	Total[1, 2]			White			Black		
Year	Male	Female	Males per 1,000 females	Male	Female	Males per 1,000 females	Male	Female	Males per 1,000 females
1985	1,927,983	1,832,578	1,052	1,536,646	1,454,727	1,056	308,575	299,618	1,030
1986	1,924,868	1,831,679	1,051	1,523,914	1,446,525	1,053	315,788	305,433	1,034
1987	1,951,153	1,858,241	1,050	1,535,517	1,456,971	1,054	325,259	316,308	1,028
1988	2,002,424	1,907,086	1,050	1,562,675	1,483,487	1,053	341,441	330,535	1,033
1989	2,069,490	1,971,468	1,050	1,606,757	1,525,234	1,053	360,131	349,264	1,031
1990	2,129,495	2,028,717	1,050	1,654,928	1,570,415	1,054	367,455	357,121	1,029
1991	2,101,518	2,009,389	1,046	1,659,077	1,582,196	1,049	346,455	336,147	1,031
1992	2,082,097	1,982,917	1,050	1,641,811	1,559,867	1,053	342,726	330,907	1,036
1993	2,048,861	1,951,379	1,050	1,616,332	1,533,501	1,054	333,984	324,891	1,028
1994	2,022,589	1,930,178	1,048	1,599,803	1,521,401	1,051	322,554	313,837	1,028
1995	1,996,355	1,930,234	1,049	1,588,427	1,510,458	1,052	308,115	297,024	1,031
1996	1,990,480	1,901,014	1,047	—	—	1,050	—	—	1,028
1997	1,985,596	1,895,298	1,048	—	—	1,052	—	—	1,031
1998	2,016,205	1,925,348	1,047	—	—	1,052	—	—	1,034
1999	2,026,854	1,932,563	1,049	—	—	1,052	—	—	1,031
2000	2,076,969	1,981,845	1,048	—	—	1,050	—	—	1,031
2001	2,057,922	1,968,011	1,046	—	—	1,047	—	—	1,032
2002	2,057,979	1,963,747	1,048	—	—	1,054	—	—	1,032

NOTE: (—) Data not available. 1. Excludes births to nonresidents of U.S. 2. Includes races other than white and black. *Source:* National Center for Health Statistics, *National Vital Statistics Reports*, vol. 52, no. 10, Dec. 17, 2003. Web: www.cdc.gov/nchs.

Live Births by Method of Delivery and Rates of Cesarean Delivery, 1989–2003

	All births	Vaginal	Cesarean	Cesarean rate		All births	Vaginal	Cesarean	Cesarean rate
1989	3,798,734	2,793,463	826,955	22.8	2000	4,058,814	3,108,188	923,991	22.9
1990	4,110,563	3,111,421	914,096	22.7	2002	4,021,726	2,958,423	1,043,846	26.1
1995	3,899,589	3,063,724	806,722	20.8	2003[1]	4,091,063	2,961,930	1,129,133	27.6

1. Preliminary data. *Source:* National Center for Health Statistics, *National Vital Statistics Reports*, vol. 52, no. 10, Dec. 17, 2003. Web: www.cdc.gov/nchs.

Births: Other Data for 2003

The source for the data on U.S. births, birth rates, and fertility rates in this section is the *National Vital Statistics Reports* series published by the National Center for Health Statistics, a part of the Centers for Disease Control and Prevention. The report issued on Nov. 23, 2004, showing final birth data for 2003 also highlighted these findings:

Births in the United States increased 2% in 2003, to 4,091,063 from 4,021,726 in 2002. This marks the first increase after two consecutive declines in the number of births. Births to non-Hispanic white mothers and American Indian mothers rose 1% from 2002 to 2003; births to Hispanic and Asian or Pacific Islander (API) women rose 4% and 5%, respectively. In contrast, the number of births to non-Hispanic black mothers, the only group that did not experience an increase, fell in 2003 by less than 1%. The **birth rate** rose to 14.1 births per 1,000 people in 2003, an increase of 1% from 13.9 in 2002. This is the first increase in the rate since 2000. The rate has generally trended downward; the rate for 2003 was 16% lower than the recent high point for the rate, 16.7, in 1990. The **fertility rate** rose to 66.1 in 2003, a 2% increase from the rate for 2002.

The **mean or average age at first birth** was 26.7 years, an all-time high for the nation. This average has risen from 21.4 years since 1970.

Unmarried childbearing increased 4% in 2003, to a preliminary total of 1,415,804, compared with 1,365,966 in 2002. The steep rise from 2002 to 2003 is due mainly to an increase in the birth rate for unmarried women and—to a lesser extent—to an increase in the unmarried population of reproductive age. The birth rate increased 3%, from 43.7 to 44.9 per 1,000 unmarried women aged 15–44 years, while the population grew about 1%.

Cigarette smoking during pregnancy decreased in 2003 to 11.0%, compared with 11.4% in 2002. This continues a steady decline from 19.5 percent in 1989. Infant health can be seriously compromised by prenatal smoking.

The **cesarean delivery rate** increased 6% to 27.6% of all births from 2002 to 2003, the highest rate ever reported in the United States. The cesarean rate fell between 1989 and 1996 but has risen 33% since 1996. The escalation in the total cesarean rate is fueled by both the rise in the primary cesarean rate and the steep decline in the rate of vaginal birth after cesarean (VBAC) delivery. The primary rate rose 7% in 2003, from 18.0% to 19.1%, while the rate of VBAC dropped from 12.6% to 10.6%, a 16% decline. The primary rate has climbed 31% and the VBAC rate has plunged 63% since only 1996.

The **preterm birth rate,** or percentage of infants born after less than 37 completed weeks of gestation, increased again in 2003 to 12.3% of all births. The low birthweight rate (percent of infants born at less than 2,500 grams) rose from 7.8% to 7.9%. Preterm and low birthweight levels rose slowly in recent years, up 16% and 13% respectively, since 1990. The rise in preterm and low birthweight rates is related in part to the growth in the multiple birth rate; multiple births are much more likely to be delivered preterm and/or low birthweight. Preterm and low birthweight rates also increased among singleton deliveries. Preterm delivery is a leading cause of neonatal mortality and birth-related morbidity.

Selected Demographic and Health Characteristics of Births by Race of Mother, 2003

Characteristic	All races	White (non-Hispanic)	Black (non-Hispanic)	Hispanic origin[1]	American Indian[2]	Asian or Pacific Islander
No. of births	4,091,063	2,320,778	576,347	912,256	42,647	221,247
Prenatal care beginning in first trimester	84.1	89.0	76.0	77.4	70.9	85.4
Prenatal care beginning in third trimester or no care[3]	3.5	2.1	6.0	5.3	7.6	3.1
Smoker[4]	11.0	14.5	8.5	2.8	18.3	2.3
Preterm infant[5]	12.3	11.3	17.8	11.9	13.5	10.6
Low birthweight infant[6]	7.9	7.0	13.5	6.7	7.4	7.8
Very low birthweight infant[6]	1.4	1.2	3.1	1.2	1.3	1.1

1. Hispanic origin may be of any race. 2. Includes births to Aleuts and Eskimos. 3. Excludes data for Pa. and Wash. 4. Excludes data for Calif. 5. Percent of births less than 37 completed weeks of gestation. 6. Low birthweight is birthweight of less than 2,500 grams (5 lb 8 oz). Very low birthweight is birthweight of less than 1,500 grams (3 lb 4 oz). *Source:* National Center for Health Statistics, *National Vital Statistics Reports*, vol. 53, no. 9, Nov. 23, 2004. Web: www.cdc.gov/nchs.

Live Births and Birth Rates, 1910–2003

Year	Births[1] (thousands)	Birth rate per 1,000 population[1]	Year	Births[1] (thousands)	Birth rate per 1,000 population[1]
1910	2,777	30.1	1980	3,612	15.9
1920	2,950	27.7	1990	4,158	16.7
1930	2,618	21.3	1995	3,900	14.6
1940	2,559	19.4	2000	4,059	14.4
1950	3,632	24.1	2001	4,026	14.1
1960	4,258	23.7	2002	4,021	13.9
1970	3,731	18.4	2003	4,091	14.1

NOTE: n.a. = not available. 1. Prior to 1960 data adjusted for under registration. *Source:* 1900-1970, U.S. Public Health Service, *Vital Statistics of the United States,* annual, Vol. I and Vol II; 1971-2001, U.S. National Center for Health Statistics, *Vital Statistics of the United States,* annual; *National Vital Statistics Report* (NVSR) (formerly *Monthly Vital Statistics Report*); and unpublished data. From *Statistical Abstract of the United States: 2003.*

Teen Birth Rates Continue to Decline

Source: Centers for Disease Control, National Center for Health Statistics, *National Vital Statistics Reports,* vol. 53, no. 9, Nov. 23, 2004.

Teenage childbearing has been on a long-term decline in the United States since the late 1950s, except for a brief, but steep, upward climb in the late 1980s through 1991. The 2003 rate (41.7 births per 1,000 for teens ages 15–19) is 3% lower than in 2002 and 33% lower than the most recent peak in 1991 (61.8). The declining teenage birth rate has had an impressive impact on the number of babies born to teenagers. If the birth rates by age had remained at 1991 levels throughout the 1990s instead of declining as they did, there would have been an additional 546,000 births to teenagers over the decade. Possible factors accounting for the decline include decreased sexual activity reflecting changing attitudes toward premarital sex, an increase in condom use, and the adoption of newly available hormonal contraception, implants, and injectables.

Despite the rates' reaching record lows in 2003, U.S. teenage birth rates remain substantially higher than rates for other developed countries. □

Teen Birth Rates in the U.S., Selected Years
(rates per 1,000 females in specified group)

Age	1980	1985	1990	1991	1993	1995	1998	2000	2001	2002	2003
All races											
10–14 years	1.1	1.2	1.4	1.4	1.4	1.3	1.0	0.9	0.8	0.7	0.6
15–19 years	53.0	51.0	59.9	62.1	59.6	56.8	51.1	47.7	45.8	43.0	41.7
White, total											
10–14 years	—	—	0.7	0.8	0.8	0.8	0.6	0.6	0.5	0.5	0.5
15–19 years	—	—	50.8	52.8	51.1	50.1	45.4	43.2	41.2	39.4	38.3
White, non-Hispanic											
10–14 years	0.4	—	0.5	0.5	0.5	0.4	0.3	0.3	0.3	0.2	0.2
15–19 years	41.2	—	42.5	43.4	40.7	39.3	35.2	32.6	30.3	—	27.5
Black											
10–14 years	4.3	4.5	4.9	4.8	4.6	4.2	2.9	2.3	2.0	1.8	1.6
15–19 years	97.8	95.4	112.8	115.5	108.6	96.1	85.4	77.4	71.8	66.6	63.7
American Indian[1]											
10–14 years	1.9	1.7	1.6	1.6	1.4	1.8	1.6	1.1	1.0	0.9	1.0
15–19 years	82.2	79.2	81.1	85.0	83.1	78.0	72.1	58.3	56.3	53.8	52.6
Asian/Pacific Islander											
10–14 years	0.3	0.4	0.7	0.8	0.6	0.7	0.4	0.3	0.2	0.3	0.2
15–19 years	26.2	23.8	26.4	27.4	27.0	26.1	23.1	20.5	19.8	18.3	17.6
Hispanic[2]											
10–14 years	1.7	—	2.4	2.4	2.7	2.7	2.1	1.7	1.6	1.4	1.3
15–19 years	82.2	—	100.3	106.7	106.8	106.7	93.6	87.3	86.4	83.4	82.2

NOTE: (—) = Data not available. 1. Includes births to Aleuts and Eskimos. 2. Persons of Hispanic origin may be of any race.
Source: Centers for Disease Control, National Center for Health Statistics, *National Vital Statistics Reports,* vol. 53, no. 9, Nov. 23, 2004.

Births to Teenagers and to Unmarried Women, 1940–2003

	Teen childbearing		Nonmarital childbearing		
Year	Total number of births to women 15–19 years	Birth rate per 1,000 women 15–19 years	Total number of births to unmarried women	Birth rate per 1,000 unmarried women 15–44 years	Percent of all births to unmarried women
1940	300,747	54.1	89,500	7.1	3.8%
1950	419,535	81.6	141,600	14.1	4.0
1960	586,966	89.1	224,300	21.6	5.3
1970	644,708	68.3	398,700	26.4	10.7
1980	552,161	53.0	665,747	29.4	18.4
1990	521,826	59.9	1,165,384	43.8	28.0
2000	468,990	48.5	1,347,043	45.2	33.2
2002	425,493	43.0	1,365,966	n.a.	34.0
2003[1]	414,961	41.7	1,415,804	n.a.	34.6

1. Preliminary data. *Source:* U.S. National Center for Health Statistics, *Nonmarital Childbearing in the United States, 1940-99, National Vital Statistics Reports,* vol. 48, no. 16; *Births to Teenagers in the United States, 1940–2000, National Vital Statistics Reports,* vol. 49, no. 10; and *Births: Final Data for 2003, National Vital Statistics Reports,* vol. 53, no. 9. From U.S. Census Bureau, *Statistical Abstract of the United States: 2003.*

Adoption Trends

Background

Although adoption is mentioned in the legal codes and writings of many ancient peoples, including the Romans and Hebrews, no such laws existed in England or her colonies prior to the middle of the 19th century. Instead, indigent children were generally sent to public institutions known as almshouses until the age of six or seven, when they could be "put out" as indentured servants or apprentices. Families also sometimes took in children informally, especially in rural areas to help on the farm.

In the United States, these practices worked well enough until the early 19th century, when changes in economic conditions and the size of the population produced numbers of children the system couldn't cope with. At the same time, largely through the efforts of certain social reformers, society's attitude toward adoption began to change. Private agencies were established to place children in homes where they would be treated as members of the family rather than servants. And families who took in children increasingly petitioned state legislatures for private adoption acts to ensure the legal status and inheritance rights of adopted children.

Finally, as a result of pressure from individual families and to provide better care for destitute children, the state legislatures were prompted to take action. Between 1851 and 1873, 17 states enacted adoption legislation, and by 1929 all states had such laws. (England did not enact general adoption laws until 1926.) Under these new statutes, adoptions had to be approved by a judge, after which the adopted child assumed the same rights accorded any natural, legitimate child of the petitioners.

Adoption in the 20th Century

Despite the legislation, foundling homes continued to exist, and legal adoption was still relatively infrequent. Many people feared that poor, abandoned, or illegitimate children were doomed to grow into troubled adults. Infants in particular were undesirable because of high mortality rates and the lack of readily available breast milk.

Following World War I, however, the demand for babies began to grow. This was partly a response to the sharp drop in population caused by the war and the influenza epidemic of 1918 and partly also due to the development of a successful feeding formula. The number of adoptions exploded, and "closed" adoptions became the norm. In closed adoptions, the identities of the birth parents and adoptive parents were kept a secret because, it was thought, this helped the child bond to his or her new family and avoid the stigma of illegitimacy.

By the mid-1950s the demand for healthy infants began to exceed the number available. Agencies started screening prospective parents more selectively, and by 1975 many had stopped accepting applications for nondisabled white children altogether. Other agencies were obliged to put prospective parents on waiting lists, usually for an average of three to five years. Factors contributing to the decline in available infants included the increased availability of effective contraception, a rise in the abortion rate following *Roe* v. *Wade* in 1973, and an increase in the number of unmarried women keeping their babies rather than giving them up for adoption.

It was also during the 1970s that "open" adoption, in which adoptive and birth parents were known to each other, became more accepted. A growing number of prospective parents adopted through private placement, contacting a birth mother directly through an advertisement or through the services of a lawyer or other professional specializing in adoption.

More Recent Trends

Since the end of the 20th century, infertile couples and single people have increasingly turned to transracial and international adoptions, as well as new medical techniques for treating infertility and providing alternative methods of reproduction. Meanwhile, the number of older special-needs children awaiting adoption has skyrocketed. These children often come from backgrounds of abuse and neglect, and finding appropriate placements for them is one of the most pressing concerns in child welfare today.

Source: Columbia Encyclopedia, 6th Edition. Web: www.infoplease.com. Sokoloff, Burton Z., "Antecedents of American Adoption" in *The Future of Children: Adoption*, vol. 3, no. 1. (David and Lucile Packard Foundation: Los Altos, Calif.) Spring 1993. Web: www.futureofchildren.org.

Top Countries of Origin for U.S. International Adoptions

Rank	Fiscal Year 2004 Country of origin	Number[1]	Fiscal Year 2003 Country of origin	Number[1]	Rank	Fiscal Year 2004 Country of origin	Number[1]	Fiscal Year 2003 Country of origin	Number[1]
1.	China	7,044	China	6,859	12.	Philippines	196	Romania	200
2.	Russia	5,865	Russia	5,209	13.	Bulgaria	110	Bulgaria	198
3.	Guatemala	3,264	Guatemala	2,328	14.	Poland	102	Belarus	191
4.	South Korea	1,716	South Korea	1,790	15.	Mexico	89	Ethiopia	135
5.	Kazakhstan	826	Kazakhstan	825	16.	Liberia	86	Cambodia	124
6.	Ukraine	723	Ukraine	702	17.	Nepal	73	Poland	97
7.	India	406	India	472	18.	Nigeria	71	Thailand	72
8.	Haiti	356	Vietnam	382	19.	Thailand	69	Azerbaijan	62
9.	Ethiopia	289	Colombia	272		Brazil	69		
10.	Columbia	287	Haiti	250	20.	Romania	57	Mexico	61
11.	Belarus	202	Philippines	214		Total[2]	22,884	Total[2]	21,616

1. Figures based on number of immigrant visas issued to orphans. 2. Includes countries not listed here. *Source:* U.S. State Department. Web: www.travel.state.gov/family/adoption_resources_02.html.

Child Abuse and Neglect

Item	1990 Number	Percent	1995 Number	Percent	2000 Number	Percent	2002 Number	Percent
Types of substantiated maltreatment								
Victims, total[1]	690,658	—	970,285	—	864,837	—	897,168	—
Neglect	338,770	49.1%	507,015	52.3%	517,118	59.8%	525,131	58.5%
Physical abuse	186,801	27.0	237,840	24.5	167,713	19.4	167,168	18.6
Sexual abuse	119,506	17.3	122,964	12.7	87,770	10.2	88,688	9.9
Emotional maltreatment	45,621	6.6	42,051	4.3	66,965	7.7	58,029	6.5
Medical neglect	n.a.	n.a.	28,541	2.9	25,498	3.0	18,128	2.0
Sex of victim								
Victims, total	742,519	100.0	809,634	100.0	864,837	100.0	897,168	100.0
Male	323,339	43.5	381,075	47.1	413,744	47.8	429,637	47.9
Female	369,919	49.8	425,193	52.5	446,230	51.6	463,675	51.7
Age of victim								
Victims, total	731,282	100.0	808,575	100.0	864,837	100.0	897,168	100.0
1 year and younger	97,101	13.3	103,335	12.8	133,094	15.4	142,189	15.9
2 to 5 years old	172,791	23.6	215,303	26.6	205,790	23.8	218,000	24.3
6 to 9 years old	157,681	21.6	195,400	24.2	212,186	24.5	207,862	23.2
10 to 13 years old	135,130	18.5	154,682	19.1	176,071	20.4	188,492	21.0
14 to 17 years old	103,383	14.1	121,548	15.0	126,207	14.6	135,070	15.0
18 years and over	4,880	0.7	7,506	0.9	992	0.1	994	0.1

NOTE: n.a. = not available. (—) = not applicable. 1. More than one type of maltreatment may be substantiated per child. Therefore, totals for this category will add up to more than 100 percent. Victim totals and maltreatment types are based on subset of states that reported both the number of child victims and maltreatment incidences by type for that year. *Source: Statistical Abstract of the United States, 2004–2005.*

Mortality

Deaths, by State

(number in thousands; rates per 1,000 population in each area)

Area	2002 number	Rate	Area	2002 number	Rate	Area	2002 number	Rate
United States[1]	2,448	8.5	Maine	13	9.8	Rhode Island	10	9.6
Alabama	46	10.3	Maryland	44	8.1	South Carolina	38	9.2
Alaska	3	4.7	Massachusetts	57	8.9	South Dakota	7	9.1
Arizona	43	7.8	Michigan	88	8.7	Tennessee	57	9.8
Arkansas	29	10.5	Minnesota	39	7.7	Texas	159	7.3
California	235	6.7	Mississippi	29	10.0	Utah	13	5.7
Colorado	29	6.5	Missouri	56	9.9	Vermont	5	8.2
Connecticut	30	8.7	Montana	9	9.4	Virginia	57	7.8
Delaware	7	8.5	Nebraska	16	9.1	Washington	45	7.5
District of Columbia	6	10.2	Nevada	17	7.8	West Virginia	21	11.7
Florida	168	10.0	New Hampshire	10	7.7	Wisconsin	47	8.6
Georgia	65	7.6	New Jersey	74	8.6	Wyoming	4	8.4
Hawaii	9	7.1	New Mexico	14	7.7			
Idaho	10	7.4	New York	158	8.3	Puerto Rico	28	7.2
Illinois	n.a.	n.a.	North Carolina	72	8.7	Virgin Islands	1	5.7
Indiana	55	9.0	North Dakota	6	9.3	Guam	1	4.0
Iowa	28	9.5	Ohio	110	9.6	American Samoa	n.a.	5.1
Kansas	25	9.2	Oklahoma	36	10.2	Northern Marianas	n.a.	2.2
Kentucky	41	10.1	Oregon	31	8.8			
Louisiana	42	9.4	Pennsylvania	130	10.6			

1. Excludes data for Puerto Rico, Virgin Islands, Guam, American Samoa, and Northern Marianas. *Source:* U.S. National Center for Health Statistics, *National Vital Statistics Report.* From *Statistical Abstract of the United States, 2004–2005.*

Deaths, 1900–2003

Year	Total number of deaths (thousands)	Total deaths per 1,000 population	Year	Total number of deaths (thousands)	Total deaths per 1,000 population
1900	343	17.2	1960	1,712	9.5
1910	697	14.7	1970	1,921	9.5
1920	1,118	13.0	1980	1,990	8.8
1930	1,327	11.3	1990	2,148	8.6
1940	1,417	10.8	2000	2,403	8.7
1950	1,452	9.6	2003	2,423	8.3

Source: U.S. National Center for Health Statistics, *Vital Statistics of the United States,* annual; *National Vital Statistics Reports NVSR)* (formerly *Monthly Vital Statistics Report).*

U.S. Annual Death Rates per 1,000 Population

Year	Rate	Year	Rate	Year	Rate	Year	Rate	Year	Rate	Year	Rate	Year	Rate
1900	17.2	1942	10.3	1952	9.6	1963	9.6	1973	9.3	1983	8.6	1993	8.8
1905	15.9	1943	10.9	1953	9.6	1964	9.4	1974	9.1	1984	8.6	1994	8.8
1910	14.7	1944	10.6	1954	9.2	1965	9.4	1975	8.8	1985	8.7	1995	8.8
1915	13.2	1945	10.6	1955	9.3	1966	9.5	1976	8.8	1986	8.7	1996	8.8
1920	13.0	1946	10.0	1956	9.4	1967	9.4	1977	8.6	1987	8.7	1997	8.6
1925	11.7	1947	10.1	1957	9.6	1968	9.7	1978	8.7	1988	8.8	1998	8.6
1930	11.3	1948	9.9	1958	9.5	1969	9.5	1979	8.5	1989	8.7	1999	8.8
1935	10.9	1949	9.7	1959	9.4	1970[1]	9.5	1980	8.7	1990	8.6	2000	8.7
1940	10.8	1950	9.6	1960	9.5	1971	9.3	1981	8.6	1991	8.5	2001	8.5
1941	10.5	1951	9.7	1962	9.5	1972	9.4	1982	8.5	1992	8.5	2003	8.3

NOTES: Includes only deaths occurring within the registration states. Beginning with 1933, area includes entire U.S.; with 1959 includes Alaska, and with 1960 includes Hawaii. Excludes fetal deaths. Rates as of April 1 for 1940, 1950, 1960, 1970, and 1980, and estimated as of July 1 for all other years. 1. First year for which deaths of nonresidents are excluded. *Sources:* Department of Health and Human Services, National Center for Health Statistics; *National Vital Statistics Reports,* vol. 52, no. 3, Sept. 18, 2003. Web: www.dhhs.gov.

Deaths by Major Causes, 1960–2002

(age-adjusted death rates per 100,000 population)

Year	Heart disease	Cancer	Cerebro-vascular diseases	Chronic lower respiratory diseases	Accidents	Diabetes mellitus	Influenza and pneumonia	Suicide	Chronic liver disease and cirrhosis	Homicide
1960	559.0	193.9	177.9	12.5	63.1	22.5	53.7	12.5	13.3	5.2
1965	542.5	195.6	166.4	18.3	65.8	22.9	46.8	13.0	14.9	6.1
1970	492.7	198.6	147.7	21.3	62.2	24.3	41.7	13.1	17.8	9.0
1975	431.2	200.1	123.5	23.7	50.8	20.3	34.9	13.6	16.7	10.2
1980	412.1	207.9	96.4	28.3	46.4	18.1	31.4	12.2	15.1	10.5
1985	375.0	211.3	76.6	34.5	38.5	17.4	34.5	12.5	12.3	8.0
1990	321.8	216.0	65.5	37.2	36.3	20.7	36.8	12.5	11.1	9.5
1995	296.3	211.7	63.9	40.5	34.9	23.4	33.8	12.0	10.0	8.6
2000	257.6	199.6	60.9	44.2	34.9	25.0	23.7	10.4	9.5	5.9
2002	240.4	194.0	56.3	43.7	35.3	25.4	22.7	10.6	9.3	5.9

Source: U.S. National Center for Health Statistics, *Vital Statistics of the United States,* annual. From *Statistical Abstract of the United States: 2004–2005.*

Deaths by Firearms, 1980–2002

(per 100,000 population in specified group)

Year	All races[1] Number of deaths	Death rate[2]	White Number of deaths	Death rate[2]	Black Number of deaths	Death rate[2]
1980	33,780	14.9	24,849	12.8	8,505	31.9
1981	34,050	14.8	25,237	12.8	8,324	30.7
1982	32,957	14.2	25,071	12.7	7,415	27.0
1983	31,099	13.3	24,038	12.1	6,589	23.6
1984	31,331	13.3	24,419	12.2	6,449	22.9
1985	31,566	13.3	24,507	12.1	6,565	23.0
1986	33,373	13.9	25,339	12.5	7,494	25.9
1987	32,895	13.6	24,789	12.1	7,586	25.9
1988	33,989	13.9	24,892	12.1	8,475	28.5
1989	34,776	14.1	25,023	12.1	9,077	30.1
1990	37,155	14.9	26,299	12.6	10,175	33.4
1991	38,317	15.2	26,455	12.5	11,025	35.4
1992	37,776	14.8	26,120	12.3	10,906	34.5
1993	39,595	15.4	26,948	12.5	11,763	36.6
1994	38,505	14.8	26,403	12.2	11,223	34.4
1995	35,957	13.7	25,438	11.7	9,643	29.1
1996	34,040	12.8	24,114	11.0	9,175	27.4
1997	32,436	12.1	23,270	10.5	8,389	24.7
1998	30,708	11.4	22,480	10.1	7,503	21.8
1999	28,874	10.6	21,143	9.4	7,017	20.1
2000	28,663	10.4	20,945	9.3	7,054	20.0
2001	29,573	10.4	21,760	9.4	7,184	19.3
2002	30,242	10.5	21,902	9.3	7,623	20.2

1. Includes races other than black or white. 2. On an annual basis, per 100,000 population in specified group. *Source:* Centers for Disease Control and Prevention, *National Vital Statistics Reports,* vol. 53, no. 5, Oct. 12, 2004.

Life Expectancy by Age, 1850–2003

The expectation of life at a specified age is the average number of years that members of a hypothetical group of people of the same age would continue to live if they were subject throughout the remainder of their lives to the same mortality rate.

Calendar period	Age								
	0	10	20	30	40	50	60	70	80
White males									
1850[1]	38.3	48.0	40.1	34.0	27.9	21.6	15.6	10.2	5.9
1890[1]	42.50	48.45	40.66	34.05	27.37	20.72	14.73	9.35	5.40
1900–1902[2]	48.23	50.59	42.19	34.88	27.74	20.76	14.35	9.03	5.10
1909–1911[2]	50.23	51.32	42.71	34.87	27.43	20.39	13.98	8.83	5.09
1919–1921[3]	56.34	54.15	45.60	37.65	29.86	22.22	15.25	9.51	5.47
1929–1931	59.12	54.96	46.02	37.54	29.22	21.51	14.72	9.20	5.26
1939–1941	62.81	57.03	47.76	38.80	30.03	21.96	15.05	9.42	5.38
1949–1951	66.31	58.98	49.52	40.29	31.17	22.83	15.76	10.07	5.88
1959–1961[5]	67.55	59.78	50.25	40.98	31.73	23.22	16.01	10.29	5.89
1969–1971[6]	67.94	59.69	50.22	41.07	31.87	23.34	16.07	10.38	6.18
1979–1981	70.82	61.98	52.45	43.31	34.04	25.26	17.56	11.35	6.76
1990	72.7	63.5	54.0	44.7	35.6	26.7	18.7	12.1	7.1
2000	74.8	65.4	55.7	46.4	37.1	28.2	20.0	13.0	7.6
2003	75.4	66.0	56.3	47.0	37.6	28.8	20.6	13.5	8.0
White females									
1850[1]	40.5	47.2	40.2	35.4	29.8	23.5	17.0	11.3	6.4
1890[1]	44.46	49.62	42.03	35.36	28.76	22.09	15.70	10.15	5.75
1900–1902[2]	51.08	52.15	43.77	36.42	29.17	21.89	15.23	9.59	5.50
1909–1911[2]	53.62	53.57	44.88	36.96	29.26	21.74	14.92	9.38	5.35
1919–1921[3]	58.53	55.17	46.46	38.72	30.94	23.12	15.93	9.94	5.70
1929–1931	62.67	57.65	48.52	39.99	31.52	23.41	16.05	9.98	5.63
1939–1941	67.29	60.85	51.38	42.21	33.25	24.72	17.00	10.50	5.88
1949–1951	72.03	64.26	54.56	45.00	35.64	26.76	18.64	11.68	6.59
1959–1961[5]	74.19	66.05	56.29	46.63	37.13	28.08	19.69	12.38	6.67
1969–1971[6]	75.49	66.97	57.24	47.60	38.12	29.11	20.79	13.37	7.59
1979–1981	78.22	69.21	59.44	49.76	40.16	30.96	22.45	14.89	8.65
1990	79.4	70.1	60.3	50.6	41.0	31.6	23.0	15.4	9.0
2000	80.0	70.5	60.7	50.9	41.3	32.0	23.2	15.5	9.1
2003	80.5	71.1	61.2	51.5	41.9	32.6	23.8	16.0	9.6
All other males[4]									
1900–1902[2]	32.54	41.90	35.11	29.25	23.12	17.34	12.62	8.33	5.12
1909–1911[2]	34.05	40.65	33.46	27.33	21.57	16.21	11.67	8.00	5.53
1919–1921[3]	47.14	45.99	38.36	32.51	26.53	20.47	14.74	9.58	5.83
1929–1931	47.55	44.27	35.95	29.45	23.36	17.92	13.15	8.78	5.42
1939–1941	52.33	48.54	39.74	32.25	25.23	19.18	14.38	10.06	6.46
1949–1951	58.91	52.96	43.73	35.31	27.29	20.25	14.91	10.74	7.07
1959–1961[5]	61.48	55.19	45.78	37.05	28.72	21.28	15.29	10.81	6.87
1969–1971[6]	60.98	53.67	44.37	36.20	28.29	21.24	15.35	10.68	7.57
1979–1981	65.63	57.40	47.87	39.13	30.64	22.92	16.54	11.36	7.22
1990	67.0	58.5	49.0	40.3	31.9	23.9	17.0	11.4	7.0
2000	68.3	59.6	50.0	41.1	32.3	24.3	17.5	11.8	7.4
2003	69.2	60.5	50.9	41.9	33.1	24.9	18.0	12.2	8.0
All other females[4]									
1900–1902[2]	35.04	43.02	36.89	30.70	24.37	18.67	13.60	9.62	6.48
1909–1911[2]	37.67	42.84	36.14	29.61	23.34	17.65	12.78	9.22	6.05
1919–1921[3]	46.92	44.54	37.15	31.48	25.60	19.76	14.69	10.25	6.58
1929–1931	49.51	45.33	37.22	30.67	24.30	18.60	14.22	10.38	6.90
1939–1941	55.51	50.83	42.14	34.52	27.31	21.04	16.14	11.81	8.00
1949–1951	62.70	56.17	46.77	38.02	29.82	22.67	16.95	12.29	8.15
1959–1961[5]	66.47	59.72	50.07	40.83	32.16	24.31	17.83	12.46	7.66
1969–1971[6]	69.05	61.49	51.85	42.61	33.87	25.97	19.02	13.30	9.01
1979–1981	74.00	65.64	55.88	46.39	37.16	28.59	20.49	14.44	9.17
1990	75.2	66.6	56.8	47.3	38.1	29.2	21.3	14.5	8.8
2000	75.0	66.2	56.4	46.8	37.6	29.0	21.0	14.1	8.7
2003	76.1	67.3	57.4	47.9	38.6	30.0	22.1	15.3	9.8

1. Massachusetts only; white and nonwhite combined, the latter being about 1% of the total. *Source:* U.S. Dept. of Commerce, Bureau of the Census, *Historical Statistics of the United States.* 2. Original Death Registration States. 3. Death Registration States of 1920. 4. Data for periods 1900–1902, 1929–1931, and 2000–2003 relate to blacks only. 5. Alaska and Hawaii included beginning in 1959. 6. Deaths of nonresidents of the United States excluded starting in 1970. *Sources:* Department of Health and Human Services, National Center for Health Statistics; *National Vital Statistics Reports,* vol 53., no. 6, Nov. 10, 2004. Web: www.dhhs.gov.

Life Expectancy at Birth by Race and Sex, 1940–2002

Year	All races Both sexes	All races Male	All races Female	White Both sexes	White Male	White Female	Black Both sexes	Black Male	Black Female
2002	77.3	74.5	79.9	77.7	75.1	80.3	72.3	68.8	75.6
2001	77.2	74.4	79.8	77.7	75.0	80.2	72.2	68.6	75.5
2000[1]	77.0	74.3	79.7	77.6	74.9	80.1	71.9	68.3	75.2
1995	75.8	72.5	78.9	76.5	73.4	79.6	69.6	65.2	73.9
1990	75.4	71.8	78.8	76.1	72.7	79.4	69.1	64.5	73.6
1985	74.7	71.1	78.2	75.3	71.8	78.7	69.3	65.0	73.4
1980	73.7	70.0	77.4	74.4	70.7	78.1	68.1	63.8	72.5
1975	72.6	68.8	76.6	73.4	69.5	77.3	66.8	62.4	71.3
1970	70.8	67.1	74.7	71.7	68.0	75.6	64.1	60.0	68.3
1960	69.7	66.6	73.1	70.6	67.4	74.1	—	—	—
1950	68.2	65.6	71.1	69.1	66.5	72.2	—	—	—
1940	62.9	60.8	65.2	64.2	62.1	66.6	—	—	—

(—) Data not available. 1. Figures are revised. *Source:* National Center for Health Statistics, *National Vital Statistics Reports,* vol. 52, no. 3, Sept. 18, 2003. Web: www.cdc.gov/nchs.

10 Leading Causes of Death in the U.S., 2002

Leading causes of death differ somewhat by age, sex, and race. In 2002, as in previous years, accidents were the leading cause of death for those under 34 years, while in older age groups chronic diseases such as cancer and heart disease were the leading causes.

Rank[1]	Causes of death	All persons	Causes of death	Male	Causes of death	Female
	All causes	2,443,387	All causes	1,199,264	All causes	1,244,123
1.	Diseases of heart	696,947	Diseases of heart	340,933	Diseases of heart	356,014
2.	Malignant neoplasms (cancer)	557,271	Malignant neoplasms (cancer)	288,768	Malignant neoplasms (cancer)	268,503
3.	Cerebrovascular diseases	162,672	Unintentional injuries	69,257	Cerebrovascular diseases	100,050
4.	Chronic lower respiratory diseases	124,816	Cerebrovascular diseases	62,622	Chronic lower respiratory diseases	64,103
5.	Unintentional injuries	106,742	Chronic lower respiratory diseases	60,713	Alzheimer's disease	41,877
6.	Diabetes mellitus	73,249	Diabetes mellitus	34,301	Diabetes mellitus	38,948
7.	Influenza and pneumonia	65,681	Influenza and pneumonia	28,918	Unintentional injuries	37,485
8.	Alzheimer's disease	58,866	Suicide	25,409	Influenza and pneumonia	36,763
9.	Nephritis, nephrotic syndrome, and nephrosis	40,974	Nephritis, nephrotic syndrome, and nephrosis	19,695	Nephritis, nephrotic syndrome, and nephrosis	21,279
10.	Septicemia	33,865	Chronic liver disease and cirrhosis	17,401	Septicemia	18,918

Source: U.S. National Center for Health Statistics, *Health, United States, 2004.*

Death Rates by Cause of Death, 1900–2002

(per 100,000 population)

Year	Tuberculosis, all forms	Malignant neoplasms (cancer)	Major cardiovascular diseases	Influenza and pneumonia	Motor vehicle accidents
1900	194.4	64.0	345.2	202.2	n.a.
1910	153.8	76.2	371.9	155.9	1.8
1920	113.1	83.4	364.9	207.3	10.3
1930	71.1	97.4	414.4	102.5	26.7
1940	45.9	120.3	485.7	70.3	26.2
1950	22.5	139.8	510.8	31.3	23.1
1960	6.1	149.2	521.8	37.3	21.3
1970	2.6	162.8	496.0	30.9	26.9
1980	0.9	183.9	436.4	24.1	23.5
1990	0.7	203.2	368.3	32.0	18.8
2000	0.3	200.5	340.4	24.3	15.2
2001	0.3	194.4	323.9	21.8	15.4
2002	0.3	193.8	318.3	22.9	15.5

Source: 1900-1970, U.S. Public Health Service, *Vital Statistics of the United States,* annual, Vol. I and Vol II; 1971-2001, U.S. National Center for Health Statistics, *Vital Statistics of the United States,* annual; *National Vital Statistics Report (NVSR)* (formerly *Monthly Vital Statistics Report);* and unpublished data. From *Statistical Abstract of the United States: 2004-2005.*

Infant Mortality Rates, 1950–2002

		Deaths per 1,000 live births				
		Neonatal			Fetal	Late fetal
Year	Infant	Under 28 days	Under 7 days	Postneonatal	mortality rate[1]	mortality rate[2]
All races						
1950[3]	29.2	20.5	17.8	8.7	18.4	14.9
1960[3]	26.0	18.7	16.7	7.3	15.8	12.1
1970	20.0	15.1	13.6	4.9	14.0	9.5
1980	12.6	8.5	7.1	4.1	9.1	6.2
1985	10.6	7.0	5.8	3.7	7.8	4.9
1990	9.2	5.8	4.8	3.4	7.5	4.3
1995	7.6	4.9	4.0	2.7	7.0	3.6
2000	6.9	4.6	3.7	2.3	6.6	3.3
2001	6.8	4.5	3.6	2.3	6.5	3.3
2002	7.0	4.7	3.7	2.3	6.4	3.2
Race of child: white						
1950	26.8	19.4	17.1	7.4	16.6	13.3
1960	22.9	17.2	15.6	5.7	13.9	10.8
1970	17.8	13.8	12.5	4.0	12.3	8.6
1980	11.0	7.5	6.2	3.5	8.1	5.7
Race of mother: white						
1980	10.9	7.4	6.1	3.5	8.1	5.7
1985	9.2	6.0	5.0	3.2	6.9	4.5
1990	7.6	4.8	3.9	2.8	6.4	3.8
1995	6.3	4.1	3.3	2.2	5.9	3.3
2000	5.7	3.8	3.0	1.9	5.6	2.9
2001	5.7	3.8	3.0	1.9	5.5	2.9
2002	5.8	3.9	3.1	1.9	5.5	2.8
Race of child: black						
1950	43.9	27.8	23.0	16.1	32.1	—
1960	44.3	27.8	23.7	16.5	—	—
1970	32.6	22.8	20.3	9.9	23.2	—
1980	21.4	14.1	11.9	7.3	14.4	8.9
Race of mother: black						
1980	22.2	14.6	12.3	7.6	14.7	9.1
1985	19.0	12.6	10.8	6.4	12.8	7.2
1990	18.0	11.6	9.7	6.4	13.3	6.7
1995	15.1	9.8	8.2	5.3	12.7	5.7
2000	14.1	9.4	7.6	4.7	12.4	5.4
2001	14.0	9.2	7.6	4.8	12.1	5.3
2002	14.4	9.5	7.8	4.8	11.9	5.2

NOTES: "Infant" is defined as under 1 year of age; "neonatal" is under 28 days; "postneonatal" is 28 days–11 months. 1. Number of fetal deaths of 20 weeks or more gestation per 1,000 live births plus fetal deaths. 2. Number of fetal deaths of 28 weeks or more gestation per 1,000 live births plus late fetal deaths. 3. Includes birth and deaths of persons who were not residents of the 50 states and the District of Columbia. *Sources:* Centers for Disease Control and Prevention, National Center for Health Statistics. From *Health, United States, 2004.*

Death Rates for Suicide, 1950–2002

(deaths per 100,000 resident population)

	1950	1960	1970	1980	1990	1995	2000	2001	2002
All ages, age adjusted	13.2	13.2	13.2	13.2	12.5	11.8	10.4	10.7	10.9
5–14 years	0.2	0.3	0.3	0.4	0.8	0.9	0.7	0.7	0.6
15–24 years	4.5	5.2	8.8	12.3	13.2	13.0	10.2	9.9	9.9
25–44 years	11.6	12.2	15.4	15.6	15.2	15.1	13.4	13.8	14.0
45–64 years	23.5	22.0	20.6	15.9	15.3	13.9	13.5	14.4	14.9
65 years and over	30.0	24.5	20.8	17.6	20.5	17.9	15.2	15.3	15.6
85 years and over	28.8	26.0	19.0	19.2	22.2	21.3	19.6	17.5	18.0
Male, all ages, age adjusted	21.2	20.0	19.8	19.9	21.5	20.3	17.7	18.2	18.4
Female, all ages	5.6	5.6	7.4	5.7	4.8	4.3	4.0	4.0	4.2

Sources: Centers for Disease Control and Prevention, National Center for Health Statistics. From *Health, United States, 2004.*

Miscellaneous

Personal Consumption Expenditures for Recreation: 1990–2002

(dollars in billions)

Type of product or service	1990	1995	2000	2002
Books and maps	$ 16.2	$ 23.2	$ 33.7	$ 35.8
Magazines, newspapers, and sheet music	21.6	27.5	35.0	34.2
Nondurable toys and sport supplies	32.8	44.4	56.6	59.7
Video and audio products, computer equipment, and musical instruments	53.0	81.5	116.6	120.8
Video and audio goods, including musical instruments	44.1	57.2	72.8	76.7
Computers, peripherals, and software	8.9	24.3	43.8	44.2
Radio and television repair	3.2	3.6	4.2	4.0
Flowers, seeds, and potted plants	10.9	14.0	18.0	18.2
Admissions to specified spectator amusements	15.1	21.1	30.4	35.3
Motion picture theaters	5.1	5.6	8.6	9.6
Legitimate theaters and opera, and entertainments of nonprofit institutions[1]	5.2	8.1	10.3	12.1
Spectator sports[2]	4.8	7.4	11.5	13.6
Clubs and fraternal organizations except insurance[3]	13.5	17.4	19.0	22.4
Commercial participant amusements[4]	25.2	48.8	75.8	83.7
Pari-mutuel net receipts	3.5	3.7	5.0	5.3
Other[5]	65.4	93.4	133.9	152.6
Total recreation expenditures	**$290.2**	**$418.1**	**$585.7**	**$633.9**
Percent of total personal consumption	7.6%	8.4%	8.7%	8.6%

1. Except athletic. 2. Consists of admissions to professional and amateur athletic events and to racetracks, including horse, dog, and auto. 3. Consists of dues and fees excluding insurance premiums. 4. Consists of billiard parlors; bowling alleys; dancing, riding, shooting, skating, and swimming places; amusement devices and parks; golf courses; sightseeing buses and guides; private flying operations; casino gambling; and other commercial participant amusements. 5. Consists of net receipts of lotteries and expenditures for purchases of pets and pet care services, cable TV, film processing, photographic studios, sporting and recreation camps, video cassette rentals, and recreational services, elsewhere classified. *Source:* U.S. Department of Commerce, Bureau of Economic Analysis, *Survey of Current Business,* January 2004. *See also* www.bea.gov/bea/dn/nipaweb/selecttable.asp?selected=N (released as of 16 December, 2003). From *Statistical Abstracts of the United States, 2004–2005.*

Most Popular Given Names, 1880–2004

Boys

1880: John, William, Charles, George, James, Joseph, Frank, Henry, Thomas, Harry

1890: John, William, James, George, Charles, Joseph, Frank, Harry, Henry, Edward

1900: John, William, James, George, Charles, Joseph, Frank, Henry, Robert, Harry

1910: John, William, James, Robert, Joseph, Charles/George (tie), Edward, Frank, Henry

1920: John, William, James, Robert, Joseph, Charles, George, Edward, Thomas, Frank

1930: Robert, James, John, William, Richard, Charles, Donald, George, Joseph, Edward

1940: James, Robert, John, William, Richard, Charles, David, Thomas, Donald, Ronald

1950: John, James, Robert, William, Michael, David, Richard, Thomas, Charles, Gary

1960: David, Michael, John, James, Robert, Mark, William, Richard, Thomas, Steven

1970: Michael, David, John, James, Robert, Christopher, William, Mark, Richard, Brian

1980: Michael, Jason, Christopher, David, James, Matthew, John, Joshua, Robert, Daniel

1990: Michael, Christopher, Joshua, Matthew, David, Daniel, Andrew, Joseph, Justin, James

2000: Jacob, Michael, Matthew, Joshua, Christopher, Nicholas, Andrew, Joseph, Daniel, Tyler

2002: Jacob, Michael, Joshua, Matthew, Ethan, Joseph, Andrew, Christopher, Daniel, Nicholas

2003: Jacob, Michael, Joshua, Matthew, Andrew, Joseph, Ethan, Daniel, Christopher, Anthony

2004: Jacob, Michael, Joshua, Matthew, Ethan, Andrew, Daniel, William, Joseph, Christopher

Girls

1880: Mary, Anna, Elizabeth, Margaret, Minnie, Emma, Martha, Alice, Marie, Annie/Sarah (tie)

1890: Mary, Anna, Elizabeth, Emma, Margaret, Rose, Ethel, Florence, Ida, Bertha/Helen (tie)

1900: Mary, Helen, Anna, Margaret, Ruth, Elizabeth, Marie, Rose, Florence, Bertha

1910: Mary, Helen, Margaret, Dorothy, Ruth, Anna, Mildred, Elizabeth, Alice, Ethel

1920: Mary, Dorothy, Helen, Margaret, Ruth, Virginia, Elizabeth, Anna, Mildred, Betty

1930: Mary, Betty, Dorothy, Helen, Barbara, Margaret, Maria, Patricia, Doris, Joan/Ruth (tie)

1940: Mary, Barbara, Patricia, Carol, Judith, Betty, Nancy, Maria, Margaret, Linda

1950: Linda, Mary, Patricia, Barbara, Susan, Maria, Sandra, Nancy, Deborah, Kathleen

1960: Mary, Susan, Maria, Karen, Lisa, Linda, Donna, Patricia, Debra, Deborah

1970: Jennifer, Lisa, Kimberly, Michelle, Angela, Maria, Amy, Melissa, Mary, Tracy

1980: Jennifer, Jessica, Amanda, Melissa, Sarah, Nicole, Heather, Amy, Michelle, Elizabeth

1990: Jessica, Ashley, Brittany, Amanda, Stephanie, Jennifer, Samantha, Sarah, Megan, Lauren

2000: Emily, Hannah, Madison, Ashley, Sarah, Alexis, Samantha, Jessica, Taylor, Elizabeth

2002: Emily, Madison, Hannah, Emma, Alexis, Ashley, Abigail, Sarah, Samantha, Olivia

2003: Emily, Emma, Madison, Hannah, Olivia, Abigail, Alexis, Ashley, Elizabeth, Samantha

2004: Emily, Emma, Madison, Olivia, Hannah, Abigail, Isabella, Ashley, Samantha, Elizabeth

NOTE: Represents the most frequently used given names for births, based on a sampling of Social Security card applications. *Source:* Social Security Administration. Web: www.ssa.gov/OACT/babynames.

Most Common Last Names in the U.S.

Rank	Name	Frequency[1]	Rank	Name	Frequency[1]	Rank	Name	Frequency[1]
1.	Smith	1.01%	11.	Anderson	0.31%	21.	Clark	0.23%
2.	Johnson	0.81	12.	Thomas	0.31	22.	Rodriguez	0.23
3.	Williams	0.70	13.	Jackson	0.31	23.	Lewis	0.23
4.	Jones	0.62	14.	White	0.28	24.	Lee	0.22
5.	Brown	0.62	15.	Harris	0.28	25.	Walker	0.22
6.	Davis	0.48	16.	Martin	0.27	26.	Hall	0.20
7.	Miller	0.42	17.	Thompson	0.27	27.	Allen	0.20
8.	Wilson	0.34	18.	Garcia	0.25	28.	Young	0.19
9.	Moore	0.31	19.	Martinez	0.23	29.	Hernandez	0.19
10.	Taylor	0.31	20.	Robinson	0.23	30.	King	0.19

NOTE: Based on 1990 Census data. Numbers are rounded. 1. Percent of U.S. population sample. *Source:* U.S. Census Bureau. Web: www.census.gov/genealogy/names/dist.all.last.

2004 Charitable Contributions by Type of Recipient Organization
(in billions)

Type of organization	Amount contributed	Percent	Type of organization	Amount contributed	Percent
Total	$248.52	100.0%	Human services	$19.17	7.7%
Religion	88.30	35.5	Arts, culture, and		
Education	33.84	13.6	humanities	13.99	5.6
Unallocated giving	21.36	8.6	Public-society benefit	12.96	5.2
Foundations[1]	24.00	9.7	Environment/animals	7.61	3.1
Health	21.95	8.8	International affairs	5.34	2.1

NOTE: All figures are rounded. Total may not be 100%. 1. Estimate. *Source:* AAFRC Trust for Philanthropy/*Giving USA 2004*.

U.S. Charities Receiving Highest Donations in 2004

Rank	Organization	Private support	Total income	Total expenses
1.	Salvation Army (Alexandria, Va.)	$1,324,089,000	$3,039,922,000	$2,546,935,000
2.	American Cancer Society (Atlanta)	794,000,000	836,295,000	859,007,000
3.	Gifts in Kind International (Alexandria, Va.)	787,192,199	790,561,819	794,456,126
4.	YMCA (Chicago)	756,649,000	4,656,520,000	4,320,054,000
5.	Lutheran Services in America (Baltimore)	723,253,495	8,030,780,248	6,959,844,547
6.	AmeriCares Foundation (Stamford, Conn.)	695,571,993	697,947,679	655,869,559
7.	Fidelity Charitable Gift Fund (Boston)	618,772,978	530,400,945	597,063,694
8.	American National Red Cross (Washington)	587,492,458	3,018,783,874	3,354,661,690
9.	Feed the Children (Oklahoma City)	564,592,423	568,360,522	565,557,617
10.	Harvard University (Cambridge, Mass.)	557,600,000	3,318,575,528	2,464,425,797
11.	Catholic Charities USA (Alexandria, Va.)	532,024,010	2,858,623,665	2,861,694,876
12.	Boys & Girls Clubs of America (Atlanta)	501,101,244	1,150,991,444	1,076,823,902
13.	Stanford University (Calif.)	486,075,131	2,506,694,254	2,419,490,048
14.	World Vision (Federal Way, Wash.)	481,720,000	679,215,000	648,730,000
15.	Nature Conservancy (Arlington, Va.)	480,250,395	761,698,221	569,529,901
16.	America's Second Harvest (Chicago)	465,277,321	467,948,807	469,568,879
17.	King Benevolent Fund (Bristol, Va.)	432,848,505	432,402,687	327,041,757
18.	Habitat for Humanity International (Americus, Ga.)	418,033,000	760,147,000	661,611,000
19.	Food for the Poor (Deerfield Beach, Fla.)	405,264,136	465,206,402	461,192,199
20.	University of Pennsylvania (Philadelphia)	399,641,000	n.a.	n.a.
21.	American Heart Association (Dallas)	384,415,612	503,037,949	510,169,083
22.	University of Arkansas at Fayetteville	365,307,446	439,760,368	421,756,293
23.	Campus Crusade for Christ International (Orlando, Fla.)	364,877,000	404,686,000	n.a.
24.	Goodwill Industries International (Bethesda, Md.)	359,663,000	2,214,825,000	2,124,451,000
25.	United Jewish Communities (New York)	344,869,000	422,916,000	414,453,000
26.	The Johns Hopkins University (Baltimore)	319,546,969	2,498,651,000	2,485,896,000
27.	University of California at Los Angeles	319,463,000	n.a.	n.a.
28.	Cornell University (Ithaca, N.Y.)	317,043,000	n.a.	n.a.
29.	University of Washington (Seattle)	311,251,000	n.a.	n.a.
30.	University of Texas at Austin	309,484,000	n.a.	n.a.

Source: The Chronicle of Philanthropy, 2004. Reprinted with permission.

Volunteers by Selected Characteristics, 2004

Age, sex, race, and Hispanic origin	Percent of population volunteering	Median annual hours	Educational attainment and employment status	Percent of population volunteering	Median annual hours
Total	28.8%	52	**Educational attainment**		
			Less than high school graduate	9.6%	40
Total, 16 years and over	28.8	52	High school graduate	21.6	50
16–24 years	24.2	36	Some college	34.2	52
25–34 years	25.8	40	4-year college degree	45.7	60
35–44 years	34.2	51			
45–54 years	32.8	52	**Employment status**		
55–64 years	30.1	60	Civilian labor force	30.9	48
65 years and over	24.6	96	Employed	31.2	48
			Full time	29.6	48
Male	25.0	52	Part time	38.5	50
Female	32.4	50	Unemployed	25.6	46
			Not in labor force	24.7	64
White	30.5	52			
Black	20.8	56			
Hispanic[1]	14.5	48			

Type of activity	Percent of population involved in activity	Type of activity	Percent of population involved in activity
Civic, political, professional, or international	7.0%	Public safety	1.5%
		Religious	34.4
Educational or youth service	27.0	Social or community service	12.4
Environmental or animal care	1.7	Sport, hobby, cultural, or arts	3.6
Hospital or other health	7.5	Other	3.3

1. Hispanic persons may be of any race. NOTE: Covers persons 21 years and over. Volunteers are persons who worked in some way to help others for no monetary pay during the previous year. Based on a sample survey conducted during the spring of the following year and subject to sampling variability. *Source: Bureau of Labor Statistics.*

Generosity Index, 2004

The "Generosity Index" was created by the Catalogue for Philanthropy. It has long been generally agreed that philanthropic generosity is not just how much one gives, but how much one gives in relation to how much one has. For example, Mississippi is ranked first on the Generosity Index. The Average Adjusted Gross Income is $33,754 and the average charitable contribution is $4,484. New Hampshire, on the other hand, is ranked last in generosity. Its Average Adjusted Gross Income is $49,720 and the average charitable contribution is $2,312.

State	Generosity index[1]	"Having" rank[2]	"Giving" rank[3]	Rank relation[4]	State	Generosity index[1]	"Having" rank[2]	"Giving" rank[3]	Rank relation[4]
Mississippi	1	50	5	45	New York	26	5	9	−4
Arkansas	2	47	6	41	Iowa	27	36	44	−8
Oklahoma	3	43	8	35	Ohio	28	32	42	−10
Louisiana	4	42	10	32	California	29	6	17	−11
Alabama	5	38	7	31	Maryland	30	4	16	−12
Tennessee	6	34	3	31	Illinois	31	10	22	−12
South Dakota	7	44	14	30	Maine	32	37	50	−13
Utah	8	31	2	29	Delaware	33	13	27	−14
South Carolina	9	40	12	28	Washington	34	11	25	−14
Idaho	10	41	20	21	Vermont	35	33	47	−14
Wyoming	11	21	1	20	Oregon	36	26	41	−15
Texas	12	23	4	19	Hawaii	37	30	45	−15
West Virginia	13	48	31	17	Virginia	38	7	23	−16
Nebraska	14	35	19	16	Arizona	39	22	38	−16
North Dakota	15	46	30	16	Nevada	40	14	32	−18
North Carolina	16	27	15	12	Pennsylvania	41	18	36	−18
Kansas	17	25	18	7	Michigan	42	16	35	−19
Florida	18	20	13	7	Colorado	43	8	28	−20
Georgia	19	17	11	6	Connecticut	44	1	26	−25
Kentucky	20	39	33	6	Minnesota	45	12	37	−25
Montana	21	49	43	6	Wisconsin	46	19	46	−27
Missouri	22	29	24	5	New Jersey	47	2	34	−32
New Mexico	23	45	40	5	Rhode Island	48	15	49	−34
Alaska	24	24	21	3	Massachusetts	49	3	39	−36
Indiana	25	28	29	−1	New Hampshire	50	9	48	−39

Average Adjusted Gross Income figures are from 2002. 1. **Generosity Index:** The index is created by comparing the rank of each state's average adjusted gross income to the rank of each state's average itemized charitable deductions (AICD). The arithmetical differences between these two rankings are then themselves ranked, resulting in the Generosity Index rank. 2. **"Having" Rank:** a ranking of the Average Adjusted Gross Income by state. 3. **"Giving" Rank:** a ranking of the average donations by state. 4. **Rank Relation:** Having Rank minus the Giving Rank. Source: Catalogue for Philanthropy www.catalogueforphilanthropy.org/.

States

Data for state populations are the latest available from the U.S. Census Bureau. NOTE: Persons of Hispanic origin can be of any race. "American Indian" includes American Indians, Eskimos, and Aleuts. "Asian" includes Asian Indians, Chinese, Filipino, Japanese, Korean, and Vietnamese. Largest cities include incorporated places only, as defined by the U.S. Census Bureau. They do not include adjacent or suburban areas. Population data for U.S. cities are also the latest available from the U.S. Census Bureau.

For secession and readmission dates of the former Confederate states, *see* U.S. Government & History: The Confederate States of America. For a separate list of governors, and lists of senators and representatives elected to terms beginning in 2004, *see* U.S. Government & History: The Governors of the Fifty States, The Senate, and The House of Representatives. For U.S. Territories, *see* Countries of the World: United States.

Alabama

Capital: Montgomery
Governor: Bob Riley, R (to Jan. 2007)
Lieut. Governor: Lucy Baxley, D (to Jan. 2007)
Senators: Jeff Sessions, R (to Jan. 2009); Richard C. Shelby, R (to Jan. 2011)
U.S. Representatives: 7
Secy. of State: Nancy Worley, D (to Jan. 2007)
Treasurer: Kay Ivey, R (to Jan. 2007)
Atty. General: Troy King, R (to Jan. 2007)
Organized as territory: March 3, 1817
Entered Union (rank): Dec. 14, 1819 (22)
Present constitution adopted: 1901
Motto: *Audemus jura nostra defendere* (We dare defend our rights)
State symbols: flower, camellia (1959); **bird,** yellowhammer (1927); **song,** "Alabama" (1931); **tree,** Southern longleaf pine (1949, 1997); **salt water fish,** fighting tarpon (1955); **fresh water fish,** largemouth bass (1975); **horse,** racking horse (1975); **mineral,** hematite (1967); **rock,** marble (1969); **game bird,** wild turkey (1980); **dance,** square dance (1981); **nut,** pecan (1982); **fossil,** species *Basilosaurus Cetoides* (1984); **official mascot and butterfly,** eastern tiger swallowtail (1989); **insect,** monarch butterfly (1989); **reptile,** Alabama red-bellied turtle (1990); **gemstone,** star blue quartz (1990); **shell,** *scaphella junonia johnstoneae* (1990)
Nickname: Yellowhammer State
Origin of name: May come from Choctaw meaning "thicket-clearers" or "vegetation-gatherers"
10 largest cities (2003 est.): Birmingham, 236,620; Montgomery, 200,123; Mobile, 193,464; Huntsville, 164,237; Tuscaloosa, 79,294; Hoover, 65,070; Dothan, 60,036; Decatur, 54,239; Auburn, 46,923; Gadsden, 37,619
Land area: 50,744 sq mi. (131,427 sq km)
Geographic center: In Chilton Co., 12 mi. SW of Clanton
Number of counties: 67
Largest county by population and area: Jefferson, 658,495 (2004); Baldwin, 1,596 sq mi.
State parks: 22 (45,614 ac.)
Residents: Alabamian, Alabama
2004 resident population est.: 4,530,182
2000 resident census population (rank): 4,447,100 (23). **Male:** 2,146,504 (48.3%); **Female:** 2,300,596 (51.7%). **White:** 3,162,808 (71.1%); **Black:** 1,155,930 (26.0%); **American Indian:** 22,430 (0.5%); **Asian:** 31,346 (0.7%); **Other race:** 28,998 (0.7%); **Two or more races:** 44,179 (1.0%); **Hispanic/Latino:** 75,830 (1.7%). **2000 percent population 18 and over:** 74.7; **65 and over:** 13.0; **median age:** 35.8.

Spanish explorers are believed to have arrived at Mobile Bay in 1519, and the territory was visited in 1540 by the explorer Hernando de Soto. The first permanent European settlement in Alabama was founded by the French at Fort Louis de la Mobile in 1702. The British gained control of the area in 1763 by the Treaty of Paris but had to cede almost all the Alabama region to the U.S. and Spain after the American Revolution. The Confederacy was founded at Montgomery in Feb. 1861, and, for a time, the city was the Confederate capital.

During the later 19th century, the economy of the state slowly improved with industrialization. At Tuskegee Institute, founded in 1881 by Booker T. Washington, Dr. George Washington Carver carried out his famous agricultural research.

In the 1950s and '60s, Alabama was the site of such landmark civil-rights actions as the bus boycott in Montgomery (1955–56) and the "Freedom March" from Selma to Montgomery (1965).

Today paper, chemicals, rubber and plastics, apparel and textiles, primary metals, and automobile manufacturing constitute the leading industries of Alabama. Continuing as a major manufacturer of coal, iron, and steel, Birmingham is also noted for its world-renowned medical center. The state ranks high in the production of poultry, soybeans, milk, vegetables, livestock, wheat, cattle, cotton, peanuts, fruits, hogs, and corn.

Points of interest include the Helen Keller birthplace at Tuscumbia, the Space and Rocket Center at Huntsville, the White House of the Confederacy, the restored state Capitol, the Civil Rights Memorial, the Rosa Parks Museum & Library, and the Shakespeare Festival Theater Complex in Montgomery; the Civil Rights Institute and the McWane Center in Birmingham; the Russell Cave near Bridgeport; the Bellingrath Gardens at Theodore; the USS *Alabama* at Mobile; Mound State Monument near Tuscaloosa; and the Gulf Coast area.

Selected famous natives and residents: Hank Aaron, baseball player; Ralph Abernathy, civil rights activist; Tallulah Bankhead, actress; Hugo L. Black, jurist; George Washington Carver, educator, agricultural chemist; Nat "King" Cole, entertainer; Lionel Hampton, jazz musician; W. C. Handy, composer; Courtney Cox-Arquette, actress; Helen Keller, author and educator; Coretta Scott King, civil rights leader; Harper Lee, writer; Joe Louis, boxer; Willie Mays, baseball player; Jim Nabors, actor; Jesse Owens, athlete; Rosa Parks, civil rights activist; Wayne Rogers, actor; Tascaluza, Choctaw chief; George Wallace, governor; William Weatherford (Red Eagle), Creek leader; Heather Whitestone, Miss America (1995). Hank Williams, singer and songwriter.

Alaska

Capital: Juneau
Governor: Frank H. Murkowski, R (to Dec. 2006)
Lieut. Governor: Loren Leman, R (to Dec. 2006)
Senators: Lisa Murkowski, R (to Jan. 2011); Ted Stevens, R (to Jan. 2009)
U.S. Representatives: 1
Atty. General: Scott J. Nordstrand, R (acting, apptd. by gov.)
Organized as territory: 1912
Entered Union (rank): Jan. 3, 1959 (49)
Constitution ratified: April 24, 1956
Motto: North to the Future
State symbols: flower, forget-me-not (1949); **tree,** sitka spruce (1962); **bird,** willow ptarmigan (1955); **fish,** king salmon (1962); **song,** "Alaska's Flag" (1955); **gem,** jade (1968); **marine mammal,** bowhead whale (1983); **fossil,** woolly mammoth (1986); **mineral,** gold (1968); **sport,** dog mushing (1972)
Nickname: The state is commonly called "The Last Frontier" or "Land of the Midnight Sun"
Origin of name: Corruption of Aleut word meaning "great land" or "that which the sea breaks against"
10 largest cities (2003 est.): Anchorage, 270,951; Juneau, 31,187; Fairbanks, 30,970; Sitka, 8,876; Ketchikan, 7,453; Kenai, 7,347; Wasilla, 7,084; Kodiak, 6,302; Bethel, 5,983; Palmer, 5,742
Land area: 571,951 sq mi. (1,4 81,353 sq km)
Geographic center: 60 mi. NW of Mt. McKinley
Number of boroughs (counties): 27
Largest borough by population and area: Anchorage, 272,687 (2004); Yukon-Koyukuk, 157,121 sq mi.
State parks: more than 100 (3.5 million acres)
Residents: Alaskan
2004 resident population est.: 655,435
2000 resident census population (rank): 626,932 (48). **Male:** 324,112 (51.7%); **Female:** 302,820 (48.3%). **White:** 434,534 (69.3%); **Black:** 21,787 (3.5%); **American Indian and Alaska Native:** 98,043 (15.6%); **Asian:** 25,116 (4.0%); **Other race:** 9,997 (1.6%); **Two or more races:** 34,146 (5.4%); **Hispanic/Latino:** 25,852 (4.1%). **2000 percent population 18 and over:** 69.6; **65 and over:** 5.7; **median age:** 32.4.

Vitus Bering, a Dane working for the Russians, and Alexei Chirikov discovered the Alaskan mainland and the Aleutian Islands in 1741. The tremendous land mass of Alaska—equal to one-fifth of the continental U.S.—was unexplored in 1867 when Secretary of State William Seward arranged for its purchase from the Russians for $7,200,000. The transfer of the territory took place on Oct. 18, 1867. Despite a price of about two cents an acre, the purchase was widely ridiculed as "Seward's Folly." The first official census (1880) reported a total of 33,426 Alaskans, all but 430 being of aboriginal stock. The Gold Rush of 1898 resulted in a mass influx of more than 30,000 people. Since then, Alaska has contributed billions of dollars' worth of products to the U.S. economy.

In 1968, a large oil and gas reservoir near Prudhoe Bay on the Arctic Coast was found. The Prudhoe Bay reservoir, with an estimated recoverable 10 billion barrels of oil and 27 trillion cubic feet of gas, is twice as large as any other oil field in North America. The Trans-Alaska pipeline was completed in 1977 at a cost of $7.7 billion. Oil flows through the 800-mile-long pipeline from Prudhoe Bay to the port of Valdez.

Other important industries are fisheries, wood and wood products, furs, and tourism.

Denali National Park and Mendenhall Glacier in North Tongass National Forest are of interest, as is the large totem pole collection at Sitka National Historical Park. The Katmai National Park includes the "Valley of Ten Thousand Smokes," an area of active volcanoes.

The Alaska Native population includes Eskimos, Indians, and Aleuts. About half of all Alaska Natives are Eskimos. (*Eskimo* is used for Alaska Natives; *Inuit* is used for Eskimos living in Canada.) The two main Eskimo groups, Inupiat and Yupik, are distinguished by their language and geography. The former live in the north and northwest parts of Alaska and speak Inupiaq, while the latter live in the south and southwest and speak Yupik.

About a third of Alaska Natives are American Indians. The major tribes are the Alaskan Athabaskan in the central part of the state, and the Tlingit, Tsimshian, and Haida in the southeast.

The Aleuts, native to the Aleutian Islands, Kodiak Island, the lower Alaska and Kenai Peninsulas, and Prince William Sound, are physically and culturally related to the Eskimos. About 15% of Alaska Natives are Aleuts.

Selected famous natives and residents: Clarence L. Andrews, author; Aleksandr Baranov, first governor of Russian America; Margaret Elizabeth Bell, author; Benny Benson, designed state flag at age 13; Vitus Bering, explorer; Charles E. Bunnell, educator; Susan Butcher, sled-dog racer; William A. Egan, first state governor; Carl Ben Eielson, pioneer pilot; Henry E. Gruennig, political leader; B. Frank Heintzleman, territorial governor; Walter J. Hickel, governor; Sheldon Jackson, educator and missionary; Joe Juneau, prospector; Austin Lathrop, industrialist; Sydney Lawrence, painter; Ray Mala, actor; Virgil F. Partch, cartoonist; Joe Redington, Sr., sled-dog musher and promoter; Peter Trinble Rowe, first Episcopal bishop; Ivan Popov-Veniaminov (St. Innocent), Russian Orthodox missionary; Ferdinand Wrangel, educator; Samuel Hall Young, founder of first American church.

Arizona

Capital: Phoenix
Governor: Janet Napolitano, D (to Jan. 2007)
Senators: Jon Kyl, R (to Jan. 2007); John McCain, R (to Jan. 2011)
U.S. Representatives: 8
Secy. of State: Jan Brewer, R (to Jan. 2007)
Atty. General: Terry Goddard, D (to Jan. 2007)
Treasurer: David Petersen, R (to Jan. 2007)
Organized as territory: Feb. 24, 1863
Entered Union (rank): Feb. 14, 1912 (48)
Present constitution adopted: 1911
Motto: *Ditat Deus* (God enriches)
State symbols: flower, flower of saguaro cactus (1931); **bird,** cactus wren (1931); **colors,** blue and old gold (1915); **song,** "Arizona" (1919); **tree,** palo verde (1954); **neckwear,** bola tie (1971); **fossil,** petrified wood (1988); **gemstone,** turquoise (1974); **mammal,** ringtail (1986); **reptile,** Arizona ridgenose rattlesnake (1986); **fish,** Arizona trout (1986); **amphibian,** Arizona tree frog (1986); **butterfly,** two-tailed swallowtail (2001)
Nickname: Grand Canyon State
Origin of name: From the Indian "Arizonac," meaning "little spring" or "young spring"
10 largest cities (2003 est.): Phoenix, 1,388,416; Tucson, 507,658; Mesa, 432,376; Glendale, 232,838; Scottsdale, 217,989; Chandler, 211,299; Tempe, 158,880; Gilbert, 145,250; Peoria, 127,580; Yuma, 81,605
Land area: 113,635 sq mi. (294,315 sq km)
Geographic center: In Yavapai Co., 55 mi. ESE of Prescott
Number of counties: 15
Largest county by population and area: Maricopa, 3,501,001 (2004); Coconino, 18,562 sq mi.
State parks: 28

Residents: Arizonan, Arizonian
2004 resident population est.: 5,743,834
2000 resident census population (rank): 5,130,632 (20). **Male:** 2,561,057 (49.9%); **Female:** 2,569,575 (50.1%). **White:** 3,873,611 (75.5%); **Black:** 158,873 (3.1%); **American Indian:** 255,879 (5.0%); **Asian:** 92,236 (1.8%); **Other race:** 596,774 (11.6%); **Two or more races:** 146,526 (2.9%); **Hispanic/Latino:** 1,295,617 (25.3%). **2000 percent population 18 and over:** 73.4; **65 and over:** 13.0; **median age:** 34.2.

Marcos de Niza, a Spanish Franciscan friar, was the first European to explore Arizona. He entered the area in 1539 in search of the mythical Seven Cities of Gold. Although he was followed a year later by another gold seeker, Francisco Vásquez de Coronado, most of the early settlement was for missionary purposes. In 1775 the Spanish established Fort Tucson. In 1848, after the Mexican War, most of the Arizona territory became part of the U.S., and the southern portion of the territory was added by the Gadsden Purchase in 1853.

Arizona history is rich in legends of America's Old West. It was here that the great Indian chiefs Geronimo and Cochise led their people against the frontiersmen. Tombstone, Ariz., was the site of the West's most famous shoot-out—the gunfight at the O.K. Corral. Today, Arizona has one of the largest U.S. Indian populations; more than 14 tribes are represented on 20 reservations.

Manufacturing has become Arizona's most important industry. Principal products include electrical, communications, and aeronautical items. The state produces over half of the country's copper. Agriculture is also important to the state's economy. Top commodities are cattle and calves, dairy products, and cotton. In 1973 one of the world's most massive dams, the New Cornelia Tailings, was completed near Ajo.

State attractions include the Grand Canyon, the Petrified Forest, the Painted Desert, Hoover Dam, Lake Mead, Fort Apache, and the reconstructed London Bridge at Lake Havasu City.

Selected famous natives and residents: Apache Kid, Indian outlaw; Erma Bombeck, humorist and writer; Glen Campbell, singer; Lynda Carter, actress; Cesar Chavez, labor leader; Cochise, Apache chief; Alice Cooper, singer and songwriter; Wyatt Earp, marshall; Max Ernst, painter; Geronimo (Goyathlay), Apache chief; Barry Goldwater, politician; Zane Grey, novelist; Carl Trumbull Hayden, politician; George W. P. Hunt, first state governor; Bill Keane, cartoonist; Eusebio Kino, missionary; Percival Lowell, astronomer; Frank Luke, Jr., WWI fighter ace; Charles Mingus, jazz musician and composer; Carlos Montezuma, doctor and Indian spokesman; Stevie Nicks, singer; Sandra Day O'Connor, jurist; William O'Neill, frontier sheriff; Alexander M. Patch, general; William H. Pickering, astronomer; Linda Ronstadt, singer; Paolo Soleri, architect; Clyde W. Tombaugh, astronomer; Tanya Tucker, singer; Stewart Udall, secretary of the Interior; Frank Lloyd Wright, architect.

Arkansas

Capital: Little Rock
Governor: Mike Huckabee, R (to Jan. 2007)
Lieut. Governor: Winthrop Rockefeller, R (to Jan. 2007)
Senators: Mark Pryor, D (to Jan. 2009);
Blanche Lambert Lincoln, D (to Jan. 2011)
U.S. Representatives: 4
Secy. of State: Charlie Daniels, D (to Jan. 2007)
Atty. General: Mike Beebe, D (to Jan. 2007)
Treasurer: Gus Wingfield, D
(to Jan. 2007)
Organized as territory: March 2, 1819

Entered Union (rank): June 15, 1836 (25)
Present constitution adopted: 1874
Motto: *Regnat populus* (The people rule)
State symbols: flower, apple blossom (1901); **tree,** pine (1939); **bird,** mockingbird (1929); **insect,** honeybee (1973); **song,** "Arkansas" (1963)
Nickname: The Natural State
Origin of name: From the Quapaw Indians
10 largest cities (2003 est.): Little Rock, 184,053; Fort Smith, 81,562; Fayetteville, 62,078; North Little Rock, 59,687; Jonesboro, 57,435; Pine Bluff, 53,905; Springdale, 52,471; Conway, 47,840; Rogers, 42,795; Hot Springs, 36,770
Land area: 52,068 sq mi. (134,856 sq km)
Geographic center: In Pulaski Co., 12 mi. SW of Little Rock
Number of counties: 75
Largest county by population and area: Pulaski, 365,913 (2004); Union, 1,039 sq mi.
State parks: 51
Residents: Arkansan
2004 resident population est.: 2,752,629
2000 resident census population (rank): 2,673,400 (33). **Male:** 1,304,693 (48.8%); **Female:** 1,368,707 (51.2%). **White:** 2,138,598 (80.0%); **Black:** 418,950 (15.7%); **American Indian:** 17,808 (0.7%); **Asian:** 20,220 (0.8%); **Other race:** 40,412 (1.5%); **Two or more races:** 35,744 (1.3%); **Hispanic/Latino:** 86,866 (3.2%). **2000 percent population 18 and over:** 74.6; **65 and over:** 14.0; **median age:** 36.0.

Spaniard Hernando de Soto was among the early European explorers to visit the territory in the mid-16th century, but it was a Frenchman, Henri de Tonti, who in 1686 founded the first permanent white settlement—the Arkansas Post. In 1803 the area was acquired by the U.S. as part of the Louisiana Purchase.

Part of the Territory of Missouri from 1812, the area became a separate entity in 1819 after the first large wave of settlers arrived. The next several decades were marked by the development of the cotton industry and the spread of the Southern plantation system west into Arkansas. Arkansas joined the Confederacy in 1861, but from 1863 the northern part of the state was occupied by Union troops.

Food products are the state's largest employing sector, with lumber and wood products a close second. Arkansas is also a leader in the production of cotton, rice, and soybeans. It also has the country's only active diamond mine; located near Murfreesboro, it is operated as a tourist attraction.

Hot Springs National Park and Buffalo National River in the Ozarks are major state attractions. Blanchard Springs Caverns, the Historic Arkansas Museum at Little Rock, the William J. Clinton Birthplace in Hope, and the Arkansas Folk Center in Mountain View are also of interest.

Selected famous natives and residents: Maya Angelou, author and poet; Daisy Bates, social reformer; Dee Brown, author; Helen Gurley Brown, editor; Dale Bumpers, governor and senator; Glen Campbell, singer; Hattie Caraway, first elected woman senator; Johnny Cash, singer; Eldridge Cleaver, social activist; William Jefferson Clinton, former president; William Darby, founder of the Darby Rangers Dizzy Dean, baseball player; Orval Faubus, governor; John Gould Fletcher, poet; J. William Fulbright, former senator; John Grisham, author; Tess Harper, actress; John H. Johnson, publisher; E. Fay Jones, architect; Scott Joplin, composer; Douglas MacArthur, general; Patsy Montana, singer; Isaac C. Parker, judge; Albert Pike, pioneer teacher and lawyer; Mary Steenburgen, actress; Billy Bob Thornton, actor; Sam Walton, founder of Wal-Mart; William C. Warfield, concert singer and actor.

California

Capital: Sacramento
Governor: Arnold Schwarzenegger,[1] R (to Jan. 2007)
Lieut. Governor: Cruz M. Bustamante, D (to Jan. 2007)
Senators: Barbara Boxer, D (to Jan. 2011);
  Dianne Feinstein, D (to Jan. 2007)
U.S. Representatives: 53
Secy. of State: Bruce McPherson, R (to Jan. 2007)
Atty. General: Bill Lockyer, D (to Jan. 2007)
Treasurer: Phil Angelides, D (to Jan. 2007)
Entered Union (rank): Sept. 9, 1850 (31)
Present constitution adopted: 1879
Motto: *Eureka* (I have found it)
State symbols: flower, golden poppy (1903); **tree,**
  California redwoods (*Sequoia sempervirens &*
  Sequoiadendron giganteum) (1937, 1953); **bird,**
  California valley quail (1931); **animal,** California grizzly
  bear (1953); **fish,** California golden trout (1947);
  colors, blue and gold (1951); **song,** "I Love You,
  California" (1951)
Nickname: Golden State
Origin of name: From a book, *Las Sergas de Espland-*
  ián, by Garcia Ordóñez de Montalvo, c. 1500
10 largest cities (2003 est.): Los Angeles, 3,819,951;
  San Diego, 1,266,753; San Jose, 898,349; San
  Francisco, 751,682; Long Beach, 475,460; Fresno,
  451,455; Sacramento, 445,335; Oakland, 398,844;
  Santa Ana, 342,510; Anaheim, 332,361
Land area: 155,959 sq mi. (403,934 sq km)
Geographic center: In Madera Co., 38 mi. E of Madera
Number of counties: 58
Largest county by population and area: Los Angeles,
  9,937,739 (2004); San Bernardino, 20,062 sq mi.
National forests: 18
State parks and beaches: 278 (1.5 million ac.)
Residents: Californian
2004 resident population est.: 35,893,799
2000 resident census population (rank): 33,871,648
  (1). **Male:** 16,874,892 (49.8%); **Female:** 16,996,756
  (50.2%). **White:** 20,170,059 (59.5%). **Black:**
  2,263,882 (6.7%). **American Indian:** 333,346 (1.0%);
  Asian: 3,697,513 (10.9%); **Other race:** 5,682,241
  (16.8%); **Two or more races:** 1,607,646 (4.7%);
  Hispanic/Latino: 10,966,556 (32.4%). **2000 percent**
  population 18 and over: 72.7; **65 and over:** 10.6;
  median age: 33.3.

1. Gray Davis (D) was voted out of office in a recall election Oct. 7, 2003.

Although California was sighted by Spanish navigator Juan Rodríguez Cabrillo in 1542, its first Spanish mission (at San Diego) was not established until 1769. California became a U.S. territory in 1847 when Mexico surrendered it to John C. Frémont. On Jan. 24, 1848, James W. Marshall discovered gold at Sutter's Mill, starting the California Gold Rush and bringing settlers to the state in large numbers. By 1964, California had surpassed New York to become the most populous state. One reason for this may be that more immigrants settle in California than any other state—more than one-third of the nation's total in 1994. Asians and Pacific Islanders led the influx.

Leading industries include agriculture, manufacturing (transportation equipment, machinery, and electronic equipment), biotechnology, aerospace-defense, and tourism. Principal natural resources include timber, petroleum, cement, and natural gas.

Death Valley, in the southeast, is 282 ft below sea level, the lowest point in the nation. Mt. Whitney (14,491 ft) is the highest point in the contiguous 48 states. Lassen Peak is one of two active U.S. volca-

noes outside of Alaska and Hawaii; its last eruptions were recorded in 1917.

Other points of interest include Yosemite National Park, Disneyland, Hollywood, the Golden Gate Bridge, Sequoia National Park, San Simeon State Park, and Point Reyes National Seashore.

Selected famous natives and residents: Gertrude Atherton, author; David Belasco, playwright and producer; Shirley Temple Black, actress, ambassador; Dave Brubeck, musician; Luther Burbank, horticulturalist; Julia Child, chef; Joe DiMaggio, baseball player; James H. Doolittle, air force general; Isadora Duncan, dancer; John Frémont, explorer; Robert Frost, poet; Henry George, economist; George E. Hale, astronomer; Bret Harte, writer; William Randolph Hearst, publisher; Helen Hunt Jackson, writer; Robinson Jeffers, poet; Anthony M. Kennedy, jurist; Jack London, author; James W. Marshall, first discovered gold; Aimee Semple McPherson, evangelist; Marilyn Monroe, actress; John Muir, naturalist; Richard M. Nixon, president; Isamu Noguchi, sculptor; Kathleen Norris, novelist; George S. Patton, Jr., general; Robert Redford, actor; Sally K. Ride, astronaut; William Saroyan, author; Junípero Serra, missionary; Upton Sinclair, novelist; Leland Stanford, railroad magnate; Lincoln Steffens, journalist, author; John Steinbeck, author; Adlai Stevenson, statesman; Johann Sutter, pioneer; Michael Tilson Thomas, conductor; Earl Warren, jurist.

Colorado

Capital: Denver
Governor: Bill Owens, R (to Jan. 2007)
Lieut. Governor: Jane Norton, R (to Jan. 2007)
Senators: Wayne A. Allard, R (to Jan. 2009);
  Ken Salazar, D (to Jan. 2011)
U.S. Representatives: 7
Secy. of State: Donetta Davidson, R (to Jan. 2007)
Treasurer: Mike Coffman, R (to Jan. 2007)
Atty. General: John W. Suthers, R (to Jan. 2007)
Organized as territory: Feb. 28, 1861
Entered Union (rank): Aug. 1, 1876 (38)
Present constitution adopted: 1876
Motto: *Nil sine Numine* (Nothing without Providence)
State symbols: flower, Rocky Mountain columbine
  (1899); **tree,** Colorado blue spruce (1939); **bird,** lark
  bunting (1931); **animal,** Rocky Mountain bighorn
  sheep (1961); **gemstone,** aquamarine (1971); **colors,**
  blue and white (1911); **song,** "Where the Columbines
  Grow" (1915); **fossil,** stegosaurus (1991)
Nickname: Centennial State
Origin of name: From the Spanish, "ruddy" or "red"
10 largest cities (2003 est.): Denver, 557,478; Colorado
  Springs, 370,448; Aurora, 290,418; Lakewood,
  142,474; Fort Collins, 125,740; Pueblo, 103,648;
  Westminster, 103,391; Arvada, 101,972; Centennial,
  98,586; Thornton, 96,584
Land area: 103,717 sq mi. (268,627 sq km)
Geographic center: In Park Co., 30 mi. NW of
  Pikes Peak
Number of counties: 64
Largest county by population and area: Denver,
  556,835 (2004); Las Animas, 4,773 sq mi.
State parks: 44 (160,000 ac.)
Residents: Coloradan, Coloradoan
2004 resident population est.: 4,601,403
2000 resident census population (rank): 4,301,261
  (24). **Male:** 2,165,983 (50.4%); **Female:** 2,135,278
  (49.6%). **White:** 3,560,005 (82.8%); **Black:** 165,063
  (3.8%); **American Indian:** 44,241 (1.0%); **Asian:**
  95,213 (2.2%); **Other race:** 309,931 (7.2%); **Two or**
  more races: 122,187 (2.8%); **Hispanic/Latino:**
  735,601 (17.1%). **2000 percent population 18 and**
  over: 74.4; **65 and over:** 9.7; **median age:** 34.3.

First visited by Spanish explorers in the 1500s, the territory was claimed for Spain by Juan de Ulibarri in 1706. The U.S. obtained eastern Colorado as part of the Louisiana Purchase in 1803, the central portion in 1845 with the admission of Texas as a state, and the western part in 1848 as a result of the Mexican War.

Colorado has the highest mean elevation of any state, with more than 1,000 Rocky Mountain peaks over 10,000 ft high and 54 towering above 14,000 ft. Pikes Peak, the most famous of these mountains, was discovered by U.S. Army lieutenant Zebulon M. Pike in 1806.

Once primarily a mining and agricultural state, Colorado's economy is now driven by the service industries, including medical providers and other business and professional services. Colorado's economy also has a strong manufacturing base. The primary manufactures are food products, printing and publishing, machinery, and electrical instruments. The state is also a communications and transportation hub for the Rocky Mountain region.

The farm industry, which is primarily concentrated in livestock, is also an important element of the state's economy. The primary crops in Colorado are corn, hay, and wheat.

Breathtaking scenery and world-class skiing make Colorado a prime tourist destination. The main tourist attractions in the state include Rocky Mountain National Park, Mesa Verde National Park, the Great Sand Dunes and Dinosaur National Monuments, Colorado National Monument, and the Black Canyon of the Gunnison National Monument.

Selected famous natives and residents: Tim Allen, actor and comedian; William Bent, fur trader and pioneer; Charles F. Brannan, lawyer and public official; M. Scott Carpenter, astronaut; Lon Chaney, actor; Mary Coyle Chase, playwright; Jack Dempsey, boxer; John Evans, physician, educator; Douglas Fairbanks, actor; Eugene Fodor, violinist; Gene Fowler, writer; Erick Hawkins, choreographer; Helen Hunt Jackson, novelist and Indian rights activist; Ted Mack, TV host; Ouray, Ute Indian chief; Anne Parrish, writer; Barbara Rush, actress; Horace A. Tabor, silver king and lieut. governor; Lowell Thomas, commentator and author; Dalton Trumbo, screenwriter, novelist; Amy Van Dyken, athlete; Byron R. White, jurist; Paul Whiteman, conductor; Don Wilson, announcer.

Connecticut

Capital: Hartford
Governor: M. Jodi Rell,[1] R (to Jan. 2007)
Lieut. Governor: Kevin Sullivan,[2] D (to Jan. 2007)
Senators: Christopher J. Dodd, D (to Jan. 2011); Joseph I. Lieberman, D (to Jan. 2007)
U.S. Representatives: 5
Secy. of the State: Susan Bysiewicz, D (to Jan. 2007)
Treasurer: Denise Nappier, D (to Jan. 2007)
Atty. General: Richard Blumenthal, D (to Jan. 2007)
Entered Union (rank): Jan. 9, 1788 (5)
Present constitution adopted: Dec. 30, 1965
Motto: Qui transtulit sustinet (He who transplanted still sustains)
State symbols: flower, mountain laurel (1907); **tree,** white oak (1947); **animal,** sperm whale (1975); **bird,** American robin (1943); **hero,** Nathan Hale (1985); **heroine,** Prudence Crandall (1995); **insect,** praying mantis (1977); **mineral,** garnet (1977); **song,** "Yankee Doodle" (1978); **ship,** USS Nautilus (1983); **shellfish,** eastern oyster (1989); **fossil,** Eubrontes Giganteus (1991); **composer,** Charles Edward Ives (1991)
Nickname: Constitution State (official, 1959); Nutmeg State
Origin of name: From an Indian word (Quinnehtukqut) meaning "beside the long tidal river"
10 largest cities (2003 est.): Bridgeport, 139,664; New Haven, 124,512; Hartford, 124,387; Stamford,

120,107; Waterbury, 108,130; Norwalk, 84,170; Danbury, 77,353; New Britain, 71,572; Greenwich, 61,972; West Hartford, 61,424
Land area: 4,844 sq mi. (12,545 sq km)
Geographic center: In Hartford Co., at East Berlin
Number of counties: 8
Largest county by population and area: Fairfield, 903,291 (2004); Litchfield, 920 sq mi.
State parks: 93 (32,960 ac.)
Residents: Connecticuter; Nutmegger
2004 resident population est.: 3,503,604
2000 resident census population (rank): 3,405,565 (29). **Male:** 1,649,319 (48.4%); **Female:** 1,756,246 (51.6%). **White:** 2,780,355 (81.6%); **Black:** 309,843 (9.1%); **American Indian:** 9,639 (0.3%); **Asian:** 82,313 (2.4%); **Other race:** 147,201 (4.3%); **Two or more races:** 74,848 (2.2%); **Hispanic/Latino:** 320,323 (9.4%). **2000 percent population 18 and over:** 75.3; **65 and over:** 13.8; **median age:** 37.4.

1. John Rowland resigned in June 2004 and in April 2005 went to prison on corruption charges. Rell was the lieutenant governor. 2. Sullivan was the Connecticut Senate president.

The Dutch navigator, Adriaen Block, was the first European of record to explore the area, sailing up the Connecticut River in 1614. In 1633, Dutch colonists built a fort and trading post near present-day Hartford but soon lost control to English Puritans from the Massachusetts Bay Colony. English settlements established in the 1630s at Windsor, Wethersfield, and Hartford united in 1639 to form the Connecticut Colony under the Fundamental Orders, the first modern constitution.

Connecticut played a prominent role in the Revolutionary War, serving as the Continental Army's major supplier. Sometimes called the "Arsenal of the Nation," the state became one of the most industrialized in the nation.

Today, Connecticut factories produce weapons, sewing machines, jet engines, helicopters, motors, hardware and tools, cutlery, clocks, locks, silverware, and submarines. Hartford has the oldest U.S. newspaper still being published—the Hartford Courant, established 1764—and is the insurance capital of the nation.

Connecticut leads New England in the production of eggs, pears, peaches, and mushrooms, and its oyster crop is the nation's second largest. Poultry and dairy products also account for a large portion of farm income.

Connecticut is a popular resort area with its 250-mile Long Island Sound shoreline and many inland lakes. Among the major points of interest are Yale University's Gallery of Fine Arts and Peabody Museum. Other famous museums include the P. T. Barnum, Winchester Gun, and American Clock and Watch. The town of Mystic features a re-created 19th-century New England seaport and the Mystic Marinelife Aquarium.

Selected famous natives and residents: Dean Acheson, statesman; Ethan Allan, American Revolutionary soldier; Benedict Arnold, American Revolutionary general; P. T. Barnum, showman; John Brown, abolitionist; Prudence Crandell, educator and reformer; Charles Goodyear, inventor; Nathan Hale, American Revolutionary officer; Dorothy Hamill, ice skater; Katharine Hepburn, actress; Charles Ives, composer; John Pierpont Morgan, financier; Frederick Law Olmsted, landscape designer; Rosa Ponselle, soprano; Adam Clayton Powell, Jr., congressman; Benjamin Spock, pediatrician; Harriet Beecher Stowe, author; Noah Webster, lexicographer.

Delaware

Capital: Dover
Governor: Ruth Ann Minner, D (to Jan. 2009)
Lieut. Governor: John C. Carney, Jr., D (to Jan. 2009)
Senators: Joseph R. Biden, Jr., D (to Jan. 2009); Thomas R. Carper, D (to Jan. 2007)
U.S. Representatives: 1
Secy. of State: Harriet Smith Windsor, D (to Jan. 2007)
Treasurer: Jack Markell, D (to Jan. 2007)
Atty. General: Jane Brady, R (to Jan. 2007)
Entered Union (rank): Dec. 7, 1787 (1)
Present constitution adopted: 1897
Motto: Liberty and independence
State symbols: colors, colonial blue and buff; **flower,** peach blossom (1895); **tree,** American holly (1939); **bird,** blue hen chicken (1939); **insect,** ladybug (1974); **butterfly,** tiger swallowtail (1999); **fish,** weakfish, *cynoscion regalis* (1981); **song,** "Our Delaware"; **beverage,** milk; **fossil,** belemnite
Nicknames: Diamond State; First State; Small Wonder
Origin of name: From Delaware River and Bay; named in turn for Sir Thomas West, Baron De La Warr
10 largest cities (2003 est.): Wilmington, 72,051; Dover, 32,808; Newark, 29,821; Milford, 6,991; Seaford, 6,948; Middletown, 6,496; Smyrna, 6,207; Elsmere, 5,764; Georgetown, 4,811; New Castle, 4,787
Land area: 1,954 sq mi. (5,161 sq km)
Geographic center: In Kent Co., 11 mi. S of Dover
Number of counties: 3
Largest county by population and area: New Castle, 519,396 (2004); Sussex, 938 sq mi.
State parks: 14 (over 20,000 ac.)
Residents: Delawarean
2004 resident population est.: 830,364
2000 resident census population (rank): 783,600 (45). **Male:** 380,541 (48.6%); **Female:** 403,059 (51.4%). **White:** 584,773 (74.6%); **Black:** 150,666 (19.2%); **American Indian:** 2,731 (0.3%); **Asian:** 16,259 (2.1%); **Other race:** 15,855 (2.0%); **Two or more races:** 13,033 (1.7%); **Hispanic/Latino:** 37,277 (4.8%). **2000 percent population 18 and over:** 75.2; **65 and over:** 13.0; **median age:** 36.0.

Henry Hudson, sailing under the Dutch flag, is credited with Delaware's discovery in 1609. The following year, Capt. Samuel Argall of Virginia named Delaware for his colony's governor, Thomas West, Baron De La Warr. An attempted Dutch settlement failed in 1631. Swedish colonization began at Fort Christina (now Wilmington) in 1638, but New Sweden fell to Dutch forces led by New Netherlands' governor Peter Stuyvesant in 1655.

England took over the area in 1664, and it was transferred to William Penn as the lower Three Counties in 1682. Semiautonomous after 1704, Delaware fought as a separate state in the American Revolution and became the first state to ratify the Constitution in 1787.

During the Civil War, although a slave state, Delaware did not secede from the Union.

In 1802, Éleuthère Irénée du Pont established a gunpowder mill near Wilmington that laid the foundation for Delaware's huge chemical industry. Delaware's manufactured products now also include vulcanized fiber, textiles, paper, medical supplies, metal products, machinery, machine tools, and automobiles.

Delaware also grows a great variety of fruits and vegetables and is a U.S. pioneer in the food-canning industry. Corn, soybeans, potatoes, and hay are important crops. Delaware's broiler-chicken farms supply the big Eastern markets, and fishing and dairy products are other important industries.

Points of interest include the Fort Christina Monument, Hagley Museum, Holy Trinity Church (erected in 1698, the oldest Protestant church in the United States still in use), and Winterthur Museum, in and near Wilmington; central New Castle, an almost unchanged late 18th-century capital; and the Delaware Museum of Natural History.

Popular recreation areas include Cape Henlopen, Delaware Seashore, Trap Pond State Park, and Rehoboth Beach.

Selected famous natives and residents: Richard Allen, founder of the African Methodist Episcopal Church; Henry S. Canby, editor and author; Annie Jump Cannon, astronomer; Elizabeth Margaret Chandler, author; Felix Darley, artist; John Dickinson, statesman; E. I. du Pont, industrialist; Thomas Garrett, abolitionist; Henry Heimlich, surgeon, inventor; William Julius "Judy" Johnson, baseball player; J. P. Marquand, novelist; Howard Pyle, artist and author; George Read, jurist, signer of Declaration of Independence; Caesar Rodney, patriot, signer of Declaration of Independence; Estelle Taylor, actress; George Alfred Townsend, journalist and author.

District of Columbia

See Washington, DC, listing in U.S. Cities.

Florida

Capital: Tallahassee
Governor: Jeb Bush, R (to Jan. 2007)
Lieut. Governor: Toni Jennings, R (to Jan. 2007)
Senators: Mel Martinez, R (to Jan. 2011); Bill Nelson, D (to Jan. 2007)
U.S. Representatives: 25
Secy. of State: Glenda Hood, R (to Jan. 2007)
Atty. General: Charlie Crist, R (to Jan. 2007)
Chief Financial Officer: Tom Gallagher, R (to Jan. 2007)
Organized as territory: March 30, 1821
Entered Union (rank): March 3, 1845 (27)
Present constitution adopted: 1969
Motto: In God we trust (1868)
State symbols: flower, orange blossom (1909); **bird,** mockingbird (1927); **song,** "Suwannee River" (1935)
Nickname: Sunshine State (1970)
Origin of name: From the Spanish *Pascua Florida,* meaning "feast of flowers" (Easter)
10 largest cities (2003 est.): Jacksonville, 773,781; Miami, 376,815; Tampa, 317,647; St. Petersburg, 247,610; Hialeah, 226,401; Orlando, 199,336; Fort Lauderdale, 162,917; Tallahassee, 153,938; Pembroke Pines, 148,927; Hollywood, 143,408
Land area: 53,927 sq mi. (139,671 sq km)
Geographic center: In Hernando Co., 12 mi. NNW of Brooksville
Number of counties: 67
Largest county by population and area: Miami-Dade, 2,363,600 (2004); Palm Beach, 2,034 sq mi.
State parks: 158 (over 700,000 ac.)
Residents: Floridian, Floridan
2004 resident population est.: 17,397,161
2000 resident census population (rank): 15,982,378 (4). **Male:** 7,797,715 (48.8%); **Female:** 8,184,663 (51.2%). **White:** 12,465,029 (78.0%); **Black:** 2,335,505 (14.6%); **American Indian:** 53,541 (0.3%); **Asian:** 266,256 (1.7%); **Other race:** 477,107 (3.0%); **Two or more races:** 376,315 (2.4%); **Hispanic/Latino:** 2,682,715 (16.8%). **2000 percent population 18 and over:** 77.2; **65 and over:** 17.6; **median age:** 38.7.

In 1513, Ponce de León, seeking the mythical "Fountain of Youth," discovered and named Florida, claiming it for Spain. Later, Florida would be held at different times by Spain and England until Spain finally sold it to the United States in 1819. (Incidentally, France established a colony named Fort Caroline in 1564 in the state that was to become Florida.)

Florida's history in the early 19th century was marked by wars with the Seminole Indians, which did not end until 1842.

Florida's economy rests on a solid base of tourism, manufacturing, and agriculture. Leading the manufacturing sector are electrical equipment and electronics, printing and publishing, transportation equipment, food processing, and machinery. Oranges, grapefruit, and other citrus fruits lead Florida's agricultural products list, followed by potatoes, melons, strawberries, sugar cane, peanuts, dairy products, and cattle.

Major tourist attractions are Miami Beach, Palm Beach, St. Augustine (founded in 1565, thus the oldest permanent city in the U.S.), Daytona Beach, and Fort Lauderdale on the East Coast; Sarasota, Tampa, and St. Petersburg on the West Coast; and Key West off the southern tip of Florida. The Orlando area, where Disney World is located on a 27,000-acre site, is Florida's most popular tourist destination. Also drawing many visitors are the NASA Kennedy Space Center's Spaceport USA, Everglades National Park, and the Epcot Center.

Selected famous natives and residents: Julian "Cannonball" Adderley, jazz saxophonist; Pat Boone, singer; Fernando Bujones, ballet dancer; Steve Carlton, baseball player; Faye Dunaway, actress; Stepin Fetchit (Lincoln Theodore Perry), comedian; Lue Gim Gong, horticulturist; Dwight Gooden, baseball player; Zora Neale Hurston, writer; Daniel James, air force general; James Weldon Johnson, author and educator; Frances Langford, singer; Butterfly McQueen, actress; Jim Morrison, singer; Osceola, Seminole Indian leader; Sidney Poitier, actor; A. Philip Randolph, labor leader; Marjorie Kinnan Rawlings, author; Burt Reynolds, actor; Charles and John Ringling, circus entrepreneurs; Joseph W. Stilwell, army general; Norman E. Thagard, astronaut; Clarence Thomas, jurist; Ben Vereen, actor.

Georgia

Capital: Atlanta
Governor: Sonny Perdue, R (to Jan. 2007)
Lieut. Governor: Mark Taylor, D (to Jan. 2007)
Senators: Saxby Chambliss, R (to Jan. 2009); Johnny Isakson, R (to Jan. 2011)
U.S. Representatives: 13
Secy. of State: Cathy Cox, D (to Jan. 2007)
Atty. General: Thurbert Baker, D (to Jan. 2007)
Entered Union (rank): Jan. 2, 1788 (4)
Present constitution adopted: 1983
Motto: Wisdom, justice, and moderation
State symbols: flower, Cherokee rose (1916); **tree,** live oak (1937); **bird,** brown thrasher (1935); **song,** "Georgia on My Mind" (1922)
Nicknames: Peach State, Empire State of the South
Origin of name: In honor of George II of England
10 largest cities (2003 est.): Atlanta, 423,019; Augusta-Richmond County,[1] 193,316; Columbus,[1] 185,702; Savannah, 127,573; Athens-Clarke County,[1] 102,498; Macon, 95,267; Roswell, 78,229; Albany, 76,202; Marietta, 61,282; Warner Robins, 54,264
Land area: 57,906 sq mi. (149,977 sq km)
Geographic center: In Twiggs Co., 18 mi. SE of Macon
Number of counties: 159
Largest county by population and area: Fulton, 814,438 (2004); Ware, 903 sq mi.
State parks: 63 (72,835 ac.)
Residents: Georgian
2004 resident population est.: 8,829,383

2000 resident census population (rank): 8,186,453 (10). **Male:** 4,027,113 (49.2%); **Female:** 4,159,340 (50.8%). **White:** 5,327,281 (65.1%); **Black:** 2,349,542 (28.7%); **American Indian:** 21,737 (0.3%); **Asian:** 173,170 (2.1%); **Other race:** 196,289 (2.4%); **Two or more races:** 114,188 (1.4%); **Hispanic/Latino:** 435,227 (5.3%). **2000 percent population 18 and over:** 73.5; **65 and over:** 9.6; **median age:** 33.4.

1. The city is part of a consolidated city-county government; the city and county are coextensive.

Hernando de Soto, the Spanish explorer, first traveled parts of Georgia in 1540. British claims later conflicted with those of Spain. After obtaining a royal charter, Gen. James Oglethorpe established the first permanent settlement in Georgia in 1733 as a refuge for English debtors. In 1742, Oglethorpe defeated Spanish invaders in the Battle of Bloody Marsh.

A Confederate stronghold, Georgia was the scene of extensive military action during the Civil War. Union general William T. Sherman burned Atlanta and destroyed a 60-mile-wide path to the coast, where he captured Savannah in 1864.

The largest state in the southeast, Georgia is typical of the changing South with an ever-increasing industrial development. Atlanta, largest city in the state, is the communications and transportation center for the Southeast and the area's chief distributor of goods.

Georgia leads the nation in the production of paper and board, tufted textile products, and processed chicken. Other major manufactured products are transportation equipment, food products, apparel, and chemicals.

Important agricultural products are corn, cotton, tobacco, soybeans, eggs, and peaches. Georgia produces twice as many peanuts as the next leading state. From its vast stands of pine come more than half of the world's resins and turpentine and 74.4 percent of the U.S. supply. Georgia is a leader in the production of marble, kaolin, barite, and bauxite.

Principal tourist attractions in Georgia include the Okefenokee National Wildlife Refuge, Andersonville Prison Park and National Cemetery, Chickamauga and Chattanooga National Military Park, the Little White House at Warm Springs where Pres. Franklin D. Roosevelt died in 1945, Sea Island, the enormous Confederate Memorial at Stone Mountain, Kennesaw Mountain National Battlefield Park, and Cumberland Island National Seashore.

Selected famous natives and residents: Conrad Aiken, poet; James Bowie, soldier; James Brown, singer; Jim Brown, actor and athlete; Erskine Caldwell, writer; James E. Carter, former president; Ray Charles, singer; Lucius D. Clay, banker and general; Ty Cobb, baseball player; Ossie Davis, actor and writer; James Dickey, poet; Melvyn Douglas, actor; Rebecca Latimer Felton, first appointed woman U.S. senator; Roosevelt Grier, entertainer and former athlete; Oliver Hardy, comedian; Joel Chandler Harris, journalist and author; Larry Holmes, boxer; Miriam Hopkins, actress; Alan Jackson, singer; Harry James, trumpeter; Jasper Johns, painter and sculptor; Bobby Jones, golfer; Stacy Keach, actor; DeForest Kelley, actor; Martin Luther King, Jr., civil rights leader; Gladys Knight, singer; Joseph R. Lamar, jurist; Little Richard, singer; Juliette Gordon Low, U.S. Girl Scouts founder; Carson McCullers, novelist; Johnny Mercer, songwriter; Margaret Mitchell, novelist; Elijah Muhammad, religious leader; Jessye Norman, soprano; Otis Redding, singer; Burt Reynolds, actor; Jackie Robinson, baseball player; Dean Rusk, former secretary of state; Nipsey Russell, comedian; Travis Tritt, singer; Alice Walker, author; Joanne Woodward, actress; Trisha Yearwood, singer.

Hawaii

Capital: Honolulu (on Oahu)
Governor: Linda Lingle, R (to Dec. 2006)
Lieut. Governor: James "Duke" Aiona, R (to Dec. 2006)
Senators: Daniel K. Akaka, D (to Jan. 2007); Daniel K. Inouye, D (to Jan. 2011)
U.S. Representatives: 2
Atty. General: Mark J. Bennett, R (to Dec. 2006)
Organized as territory: 1900
Entered Union (rank): Aug. 21, 1959 (50)
Motto: Ua Mau Ke Ea O Ka Aina I Ka Pono (The life of the land is perpetuated in righteousness)
State symbols: flower, hibiscus (yellow) (1988); **song,** "Hawaii Ponoi" (1967); **bird,** nene (Hawaiian goose) (1957); **tree,** kukui (candlenut) (1959)
Nickname: Aloha State (1959)
Origin of name: Uncertain. The islands may have been named by Hawaii Loa, their traditional discoverer. Or they may have been named after Hawaii or Hawaiki, the traditional home of the Polynesians.
10 largest cities[1] (2000): Honolulu, 371,657; Hilo, 40,759; Kailua, 36,513; Kaneohe, 34,970; Waipahu, 33,108; Pearl City, 30,976; Waimalu, 29,371; Mililani Town, 28,608; Kahului, 20,146; Kihei, 16,749
Land area: 6,423 sq mi. (16,637 sq km)
Geographic center: Between islands of Hawaii and Maui
Number of counties: 5 (Kalawao non-functioning)
Largest county by population and area: Honolulu, 899,593 (2004); Hawaii, 4,028 sq mi.
State park: 52 (25,000 ac.)
Residents: Hawaiian, also kamaaina (native-born nonethnic Hawaiian), malihini (newcomer)
2004 resident population est.: 1,262,840
2000 resident census population (rank): 1,211,537 (42). **Male:** 608,671 (50.2%); **Female:** 602,866 (49.8%). **White:** 294,102 (24.3%); **Black:** 22,003 (1.8%); **American Indian:** 3,535 (0.3%); **Asian:** 503,868 (41.6%); **Native Hawaiian and Other Pacific Islander:** 113,539 (9.4%); **Other race:** 15,147 (1.3%); **Two or more races:** 259,343 (21.4%); **Hispanic/Latino:** 87,699 (7.2%). **2000 percent population 18 and over:** 75.6; **65 and over:** 13.3; **median age:** 36.2.

1. Census Designated Places.

First settled by Polynesians sailing from other Pacific islands between A.D. 300 and 600, Hawaii was visited in 1778 by British captain James Cook, who called the group the Sandwich Islands.

Hawaii was a native kingdom throughout most of the 19th century, when the expansion of the sugar industry (pineapple came after 1898) meant increasing U.S. business and political involvement. In 1893, Queen Liliuokalani was deposed, and a year later the Republic of Hawaii was established with Sanford B. Dole as president. Following annexation (1898), Hawaii became a U.S. territory in 1900.

The Japanese attack on the naval base at Pearl Harbor on Dec. 7, 1941, was directly responsible for U.S. entry into World War II.

Hawaii, 2,397 mi west-southwest of San Francisco, is a 1,523-mile chain of islets and eight main islands—Hawaii, Kahoolawe, Maui, Lanai, Molokai, Oahu, Kauai, and Niihau. The Northwestern Hawaiian Islands, other than Midway, are administratively part of Hawaii.

The temperature is mild, and cane sugar, pineapple, and flowers and nursery products are the chief products. Hawaii also grows coffee beans, bananas, and macadamia nuts. The tourist business is Hawaii's largest source of outside income.

Hawaii's highest peak is Mauna Kea (13,796 ft). Mauna Loa (13,679 ft) is the largest volcanic mountain in the world by volume.

Among the major points of interest are Hawaii Volcanoes National Park (Hawaii), Haleakala National Park (Maui), Puuhonua o Honaunau National Historical Park (Hawaii), Polynesian Cultural Center (Oahu), the USS *Arizona* and USS *Missouri* Memorial at Pearl Harbor, The National Memorial Cemetery of the Pacific (Oahu), and Iolani Palace (the only royal palace in the U.S.), Bishop Museum, and Waikiki Beach (all in Honolulu).

Selected famous natives and residents: Salevaa Atisanoe (Konishiki), sumo wrestler; George Ariyoshi, first Japanese-American elected governor; Angela Perez Baraquio, Miss America (2001); Tia Carrere, singer, actress; Steve Case, business executive; Father Damien, priest; Hiram L. Fong, first Chinese-American senator; Don Ho, entertainer; Kaahumanu, Hawaiian queen; Duke Paoa Kahanamoku, Olympic swimming champion; Kamehameha I, first Hawaiian king; Kamehameha V, last of the dynasty; Liliuokalani, queen, last Hawaiian monarch; Bette Midler, singer; Ellison Onizuka, astronaut; Chad Rowan (Akebono), sumo wrestler; Carolyn Suzanne Sapp, Miss America (1991); John Waihee, first Hawaiian elected governor.

Idaho

Capital: Boise
Governor: Dirk Kempthorne, R (to Jan. 2007)
Lieut. Governor: Jim Risch, R (to Jan. 2007)
Senators: Larry E. Craig, R (to Jan. 2009); Mike Crapo, R (to Jan. 2011)
U.S. Representatives: 2
Secy. of State: Ben Ysursa, R (to Jan. 2007)
Atty. General: Lawrence Wasden, R (to Jan. 2007)
Treasurer: Ron G. Crane, R (to Jan. 2007)
Organized as territory: March 3, 1863
Entered Union (rank): July 3, 1890 (43)
Present constitution adopted: 1890
Motto: Esto perpetua (It is forever)
State symbols: flower, syringa (1931); **tree,** white pine (1935); **bird,** mountain bluebird (1931); **horse,** Appaloosa (1975); **gem,** star garnet (1967); **song,** "Here We Have Idaho"; **folk dance,** square dance; **fish,** cutthroat trout (1990); **fossil,** Hagerman horse fossil (1988)
Nickname: Gem State
Origin of name: Though popularly believed to be an Indian word, it is an invented name whose meaning is unknown.
10 largest cities (2003 est.): Boise, 190,117; Nampa, 64,269; Idaho Falls, 51,507; Pocatello, 51,009; Meridian, 41,127; Coeur d'Alene, 37,262; Twin Falls, 36,742; Caldwell, 31,041; Lewiston, 30,937; Rexburg, 21,862
Land area: 82,747 sq mi. (214,315 sq km)
Geographic center: In Custer Co., at Custer, SW of Challis
Number of counties: 44, plus small part of Yellowstone National Park
Largest county by population and area: Ada, 332,523 (2004); Idaho, 8,485 sq mi.
State parks: 27 (43,000+ ac.)
Residents: Idahoan
2004 resident population est.: 1,393,262
2000 resident census population (rank): 1,293,953 (39). **Male:** 648,660 (50.1%); **Female:** 645,293 (49.9%). **White:** 1,177,304 (91.0%); **Black:** 5,456 (0.4%); **American Indian:** 17,645 (1.4%); **Asian:** 11,889 (0.9%); **Other race:** 54,742 (4.2%); **Two or more races:** 25,609 (2.0%); **Hispanic/Latino:** 101,690 (7.9%). **2000 percent population 18 and over:** 71.5; **65 and over:** 11.3; **median age:** 33.2.

The region was explored by Meriwether Lewis and William Clark in 1805–1806. It was then a part of the Oregon country, held jointly by the United States and Great Britain. Boundary disputes with Great Britain were settled by the Oregon Treaty in 1846, and the first permanent U.S. settlement in Idaho was established by the Mormons at Franklin in 1860.

After gold was discovered at Orofino Creek in 1860, prospectors swarmed into the territory, but they left little more than a number of ghost towns.

In the 1870s, growing white occupation of Indian lands led to a series of battles between U.S. forces and the Nez Percé, Bannock, and Sheepeater tribes.

Mining and lumbering have been important for years. Idaho ranks high among the states in silver, antimony, lead, cobalt, garnet, phosphate rock, vanadium, zinc, and mercury.

Agriculture is a major industry: The state produces about one fourth of the nation's potato crop, as well as wheat, apples, corn, barley, sugar beets, and hops.

The 1990s saw a remarkable growth in the high technology industries, concentrated in the metropolitan Boise area.

With the growth of winter sports, tourism now outranks other industries in revenue. Idaho's many streams and lakes provide fishing, camping, and boating sites. The nation's largest elk herds draw hunters from all over the world, and the famed Sun Valley resort attracts thousands of visitors to its swimming, golfing, and skiing facilities.

Points of interest are the Craters of the Moon National Monument; Nez Percé National Historic Park, which includes many sites visited by Lewis and Clark; and the State Historical Museum in Boise. Other attractions are the Snake River Birds of Prey National Conservation Area south of Boise, Hells Canyon on the Idaho-Oregon border, and the Sawtooth National Recreation Area in south-central Idaho.

Selected famous natives and residents: Joe Albertson, grocery chain founder; Cecil Andrus, governor; T. H. Bell, educator; Ezra Taft Benson, secretary of Agriculture, pres. LDS church, marketing specialist; William E. Borah, senator; Gutzon Borglum, Mt. Rushmore sculptor; Carol R. Brink, author; Frank F. Church, senator; Fred Dubois, senator; Vardis Fisher, novelist; Lawrence H. Gipson, historian; Ernest Hemingway, author; Mariel Hemingway, actress; Chief Joseph, Nez Percé chief; Harmon Killebrew, baseball player; Jerry Kramer, football player, author; Ezra Pound, poet; Sacagawea, Shoshonean guide; J. R. Simplot, industrialist; Robert E. Smylie, political leader; Henry Spalding, missionary; Frank Steunenberg, governor; Picabo Street, skier; David Tompson, founded first trading post; Lana Turner, actress.

Illinois

Capital: Springfield
Governor: Rod R. Blagojevich, D (to Jan. 2007)
Lieut. Governor: Patrick Quinn, D (to Jan. 2007)
Senators: Richard J. Durbin, D (to Jan. 2009); Barack Obama, D (to Jan. 2011)
U.S. Representatives: 19
Atty. General: Lisa Madigan, D (to Jan. 2007)
Secy. of State: Jesse White, D (to Jan. 2007)
Treasurer: Judith Baar Topinka, R (to Jan. 2007)
Organized as territory: Feb. 3, 1809
Entered Union (rank): Dec. 3, 1818 (21)
Present constitution adopted: 1970
Motto: State sovereignty, national union
State symbols: flower, violet (1908); **tree,** white oak (1973); **bird,** cardinal (1929); **animal,** white-tailed deer (1982); **fish,** bluegill (1987); **insect,** monarch butterfly (1975); **song,** "Illinois" (1925); **mineral,** fluorite (1965)
Nickname: Prairie State
Origin of name: Algonquin for "tribe of superior men"
10 largest cities (2003 est.): Chicago, 2,869,121; Aurora, 162,184; Rockford, 151,725; Naperville, 137,894; Joliet, 123,570; Springfield, 113,586; Peoria, 112,907; Elgin, 97,117; Waukegan, 91,452; Cicero, 83,029
Land area: 55,584 sq mi. (143,963 sq km)
Geographic center: In Logan Co., 28 mi. NE of Springfield
Number of counties: 102
Largest county by population and area: Cook, 5,327,777 (2004); McLean, 1,184 sq mi.
Public use areas: 186 (275,000 ac.), incl. state parks, memorials, forests and conservation areas
Residents: Illinoisan
2004 resident population est.: 12,713,634
2000 resident census population (rank): 12,419,293 (5). **Male:** 6,080,336 (49.0%); **Female:** 6,338,957 (51.0%). **White:** 9,125,471 (73.5%); **Black:** 1,876,875 (15.1%); **American Indian:** 31,006 (0.2%); **Asian:** 423,603 (3.4%); **Other race:** 722,712 (5.8%); **Two or more races:** 235,016 (1.9%); **Hispanic/Latino:** 1,530,262 (12.3%). **2000 percent population 18 and over:** 73.9; **65 and over:** 12.1; **median age:** 34.7.

French explorers Jacques Marquette and Louis Joliet, in 1673, were the first Europeans of record to visit the region. In 1699 French settlers established the first permanent settlement at Cahokia, near present-day East St. Louis. Great Britain obtained the region at the end of the French and Indian Wars in 1763. The area figured prominently in frontier struggles during the Revolutionary War and in Indian wars during the early 19th century.

Significant episodes in the state's early history include the influx of settlers following the opening of the Erie Canal in 1825; the Black Hawk War, which virtually ended the Indian troubles in the area; and the rise of Abraham Lincoln from farm laborer to president.

Today, Illinois stands high in manufacturing, coal mining, agriculture, and oil production. The state's manufactures include food and agricultural products, transportation equipment, chemicals, industrial machinery, and computer equipment. The sprawling Chicago district (including a slice of Indiana) is a great iron and steel producer, meat packer, grain exchange, and railroad center. Chicago is also famous as a Great Lakes port.

Illinois is a leading producer of soybeans, corn, and hogs. Other agricultural commodities include cattle, wheat, oats, sorghum, and hay.

Central Illinois is noted for shrines and memorials associated with the life of Abraham Lincoln. In Springfield are the Lincoln Home, the Lincoln Tomb, and the restored Old State Capitol. Other points of interest are the home of Mormon leader Joseph Smith in Nauvoo and, in Chicago: the Art Institute, Field Museum, Museum of Science and Industry, Shedd Aquarium, Adler Planetarium, Merchandise Mart, and Chicago Portage National Historic Site.

Selected famous natives and residents: Franklin Pierce Adams, author; Jane Addams, social worker; Mary Astor, actress; Jack Benny, comedian; Black Hawk, Sauk Indian chief; Harry A. Blackmun, jurist; Ray Bradbury, author; William Jennings Bryan, orator and politician; Edgar Rice Burroughs, novelist; Gower Champion, choreographer; John Chancellor, TV commentator; Raymond Chandler, writer; Jimmy Connors, tennis champion; James Gould Cozzens, novelist; Richard J. Daley, mayor of Chicago; Miles Davis, musician; Peter

DeVries, novelist; Everett Dirksen, senator; Walt Disney, film animator and producer; John Dos Passos, author; James T. Farrell, novelist; Dan Fogelberg, singer and songwriter; Betty Friedan, feminist; Benny Goodman, musician; John Gunther, author; Ernest Hemingway, author; Charlton Heston, actor; Wild Bill Hickok, scout; William Holden, actor; Rock Hudson, actor; Burl Ives, singer; James Jones, novelist; John Jones, civil rights leader; Archibald MacLeish, poet; David Mamet, playwright; Robert A. Millikan, physicist; Sherrill Milnes, baritone; Bill Murray, actor; Bob Newhart, actor and comedian; William S. Paley, broadcasting executive; Drew Pearson, columnist; Richard Pryor, comedian and actor; Ronald Reagan, former president and actor; Carl Sandburg, poet; Sam Shepard, playwright; William L. Shirer, author and historian; John Paul Stevens, jurist; Archibald MacLeish... Gloria Swanson, actress; Carl Van Doren, writer and educator; Melvin Van Peebles, playwright; Irving Wallace, novelist; Alfred Wallenstein, conductor; Raquel Welch, actress; Oprah Winfrey, television talk show host and actress; Florenz Ziegfield, theatrical producer.

Indiana

Capital: Indianapolis
Governor: Mitchell Daniels, R (to Jan. 2009)
Lieut. Governor: Becky Skillman, R (to Jan. 2009)
Senators: Evan Bayh, D (to Jan. 2011); Richard G. Lugar, R (to Jan. 2007)
U.S. Representatives: 9
Secy. of State: Todd Rokita, R (to Dec. 2006)
Treasurer: Tim Berry, R (to Feb. 2007)
Atty. General: Stephen Carter, R (to Jan. 2009)
Organized as territory: May 7, 1800
Entered Union (rank): Dec. 11, 1816 (19)
Present constitution adopted: 1851
Motto: The Crossroads of America
State symbols: flower, peony (1957); **tree,** tulip tree (1931); **bird,** cardinal (1933); **song,** "On the Banks of the Wabash, Far Away" (1913); **river,** Wabash; **stone,** limestone
Nickname: Hoosier State
Origin of name: Meaning "land of Indians"
Official language: English
10 largest cities (2003 est.): Indianapolis, 783,438; Fort Wayne, 219,495; Evansville, 117,881; South Bend, 105,540; Gary, 99,961; Hammond, 80,547; Bloomington, 70,642; Muncie, 66,521; Lafayette, 61,229; Anderson, 58,394
Land area: 35,867 sq mi. (92,896 sq km)
Geographic center: In Boone Co., 14 mi. NNW of Indianapolis
Number of counties: 92
Largest county by population and area: Marion, 863,596 (2004); Allen, 657 sq mi.
State parks: 23 (56,409 ac.)
State historic sites: 17 (2,007 ac.)
Residents: Indianan, Indianian, Hoosier
2004 resident population est.: 6,237,569
2000 resident census population (rank): 6,080,485 (14). **Male:** 2,982,474 (49.0%); **Female:** 3,098,011 (51.0%); **White:** 5,320,022 (87.5%); **Black:** 510,034 (8.4%); **American Indian:** 15,815 (0.3%); **Asian:** 59,126 (1.0%); **Other race:** 97,811 (1.6%); **Two or more races:** 75,672 (1.2%); **Hispanic/Latino:** 214,536 (3.5%). **2000 percent population 18 and over:** 74.1%; **65 and over:** 12.4; **median age:** 35.2.

First explored for France by Robert Cavelier, Sieur de la Salle, in 1679–1680, the region figured importantly in the Franco-British struggle for North America that culminated with British victory in 1763. George Rogers Clark led American forces against the British in the area during the Revolutionary War, and prior to becoming a state, Indiana was the scene of frequent Indian uprisings until the victories of Gen. Anthony Wayne at Fallen Timbers in 1794 and Gen. William Henry Harrison at Tippecanoe in 1811.

During the 19th century, Indiana was the site of several experimental communities, including those established by George Rapp and Robert Owen at New Harmony.

Indiana's 41-mile Lake Michigan waterfront—one of the world's great industrial centers—turns out iron, steel, and oil products. Products include automobile parts and accessories, mobile homes and recreational vehicles, truck and bus bodies, aircraft engines, farm machinery, and fabricated structural steel. Wood office furniture and pharmaceuticals are also manufactured.

The state is a leader in agriculture with corn the principal crop. Hogs, soybeans, wheat, oats, rye, tomatoes, onions, and poultry also contribute heavily to Indiana's agricultural output.

Much of the building limestone used in the U.S. is quarried in Indiana, which is also a large producer of coal. Other mineral commodities include crushed stone, cement, and sand and gravel.

Wyandotte Cave, one of the largest in the U.S., is located in Crawford County in southern Indiana, and West Baden and French Lick are well known for their mineral springs. Other attractions include Indiana Dunes National Lakeshore, Indianapolis Motor Speedway, Lincoln Boyhood National Memorial, and the George Rogers Clark National Historical Park.

Selected famous natives and residents: George Ade, humorist; Leon Ames, actor; Anne Baxter, actress; Albert J. Beveridge, political leader; Larry Bird, basketball player; Bill Blass, fashion designer; Frank Borman, astronaut; Hoagy Carmichael, songwriter; James Dean, actor; Eugene V. Debs, Socialist leader; Theodore Dreiser, writer; Bernard F. Gimbel, merchant; Virgil Grissom, astronaut; Phil Harris, actor and band leader; John Milton Hay, statesman; James R. Hoffa, labor leader; Michael Jackson, singer; Buck Jones, actor; Alfred C. Kinsey, zoologist; David Letterman, TV host and comedian; Carole Lombard, actress; Shelley Long, actress; Marjorie Main, actress; James McCracken, tenor; Joaquin Miller, poet; Paul Osborn, playwright; Cole Porter, songwriter; Gene Stratton Porter, naturalist and author; Ernest Taylor Pyle, journalist; J. Danforth Quayle, former vice president; James Whitcomb Riley, poet; Knute Rockne, football coach; Ned Rorem, composer; Red Skelton, comedian; Rex Stout, mystery writer; Booth Tarkington, author; Twyla Tharp, dancer and choreographer; Forrest Tucker, actor; Harold C. Urey, physicist; Kurt Vonnegut, Jr., author; Robert Wise, director; Jessamyn West, novelist; Wendell Willkie, lawyer; Wilbur Wright, inventor.

Iowa

Capital: Des Moines
Governor: Tom Vilsack, D (to Jan. 2007)
Lieut. Governor: Sally Pederson, D (to Jan. 2007)
Senators: Chuck Grassley, R (to Jan. 2011); Tom Harkin, D (to Jan. 2009)
U.S. Representatives: 5
Secy. of State: Chet Culver, D (to Jan. 2007)
Treasurer: Michael L. Fitzgerald, D (to Jan. 2007)
Atty. General: Tom Miller, D (to Jan. 2007)
Organized as territory: June 12, 1838
Entered Union (rank): Dec. 28, 1846 (29)
Present constitution adopted: 1857
Motto: Our liberties we prize and our rights we will maintain
State symbols: flower, wild rose (1897); **bird,** eastern goldfinch (1933); **colors,** red, white, and blue (in state flag); **song,** "Song of Iowa"
Nickname: Hawkeye State
Origin of name: Probably from an Indian word meaning "this is the place" or "the Beautiful Land"

10 largest cities (2003 est.): Des Moines, 196,093;
Cedar Rapids, 122,542; Davenport, 97,512; Sioux City,
83,876; Waterloo, 67,054; Iowa City, 63,807; Council
Bluffs, 58,656; Dubuque, 57,204; Ames, 53,284; West
Des Moines, 51,699
Land area: 55,869 sq mi. (144,701 sq km)
Geographic center: In Story Co., 5 mi. NE of Ames
Number of counties: 99
Largest county by population and area: Polk, 393,184
(2004); Kossuth, 973 sq mi.
State parks: 83 (53,000 ac.)
Residents: Iowan
2004 resident population est.: 2,954,451
2000 resident census population (rank): 2,926,324 (30).
Male: 1,435,515 (49.1%); **Female:** 1,490,809 (50.9%).
White: 2,748,640 (93.9%); **Black:** 61,853 (2.1%);
American Indian: 8,989 (0.3%); **Asian:** 36,635 (1.3%);
Other race: 37,420 (1.3%); **Two or more races:** 31,778
(1.1%); **Hispanic/Latino:** 82,473 (2.8%). **2000 percent
population 18 and over:** 74.9; **65 and over:** 14.9;
median age: 36.6.

The first Europeans to visit the area were the
French explorers Jacques Marquette and Louis Joliet
in 1673. The U.S. obtained control of the area in
1803 as part of the Louisiana Purchase, and during
the first half of the 19th century, there was heavy
fighting between white settlers and Indians. Lands
were taken from the Indians after the Black Hawk
War in 1832 and again in 1836 and 1837.

When Iowa became a state in 1846, its capital was
Iowa City; the more centrally located Des Moines
became the new capital in 1857. At that time, the
state's present boundaries were also drawn.

Although Iowa produces a tenth of the nation's
food supply, the value of Iowa's manufactured products is twice that of its agriculture. Major industries
are food and associated products, non-electrical
machinery, electrical equipment, printing and publishing, and fabricated products.

Iowa stands in a class by itself as an agricultural
state. Its farms sell over $10 billion worth of crops
and livestock annually. Iowa leads the nation in all
corn, soybean, and hog marketings, and comes in
third in total livestock sales. Iowa's forests produce
hardwood lumber, particularly walnut, and its mineral products include cement, limestone, sand,
gravel, gypsum, and coal.

Tourist attractions include the Herbert Hoover
birthplace and library near West Branch; the Amana
Colonies; Fort Dodge Historical Museum, Fort, and
Stockade; the Iowa State Fair at Des Moines in
August; and the Effigy Mounds National Monument,
a prehistoric Indian burial site at Marquette.

Selected famous natives and residents: Bix Beiderbecke,
jazz musician; Norman Borlaug, plant pathologist, geneticist,
and Nobel Peace Prize winner; William "Buffalo Bill" F. Cody,
scout; Johnny Carson, TV entertainer; Gardner Cowles, Jr.,
publisher; Simon Estes, bass-baritone; William Frawley,
actor; George H. Gallup, poll taker; Susan Glaspell, writer;
Herbert Hoover, president; MacKinlay Kantor, novelist;
Charles A. Kettering, inventor; Ann Landers, columnist;
Cloris Leachman, actress; John L. Lewis, labor leader;
Glenn L. Martin, aviator and manufacturer; Elsa Maxwell,
writer; Frederick L. Maytag, inventor and manufacturer;
Glenn Miller, bandleader; Kate Mulgrew, actress; Harriet
Nelson, actress; Nathan M. Pusey, educator; David Rabe,
playwright; Harry Reasoner, TV commentator; Donna Reed,
actress; Lillian Russell, soprano; Robert Schuller, evangelist;
Wallace Stegner, novelist and critic; Billy Sunday, evangelist;
James A. Van Allen, space physicist; Abigail Van Buren,
columnist; Henry A. Wallace, statesman and vice president;
John Wayne, actor; Andy Williams, singer; Meredith Willson,
composer; Grant Wood, painter.

Kansas

Capital: Topeka
Governor: Kathleen Sebelius, D (to Jan. 2007)
Lieut. Governor: John E. Moore, D (to Jan. 2007)
Senators: Sam Brownback, R (to Jan. 2011);
Pat Roberts, R (to Jan. 2009)
U.S. Representatives: 4
Secy. of State: Ron Thornburgh, R (to Jan. 2007)
Treasurer: Lynn Jenkins, R (to Jan. 2007)
Atty. General: Phill Kline, R (to Jan. 2007)
Organized as territory: May 30, 1854
Entered Union (rank): Jan. 29, 1861 (34)
Present constitution adopted: 1859
Motto: *Ad astra per aspera* (To the stars through
difficulties)
State symbols: flower, sunflower (1903); **tree,**
cottonwood (1937); **bird,** western meadowlark (1937);
animal, buffalo (1955); **song,** "Home on the Range"
(1947)
Nicknames: Sunflower State; Jayhawk State
Origin of name: From a Sioux word meaning "people of
the south wind"
10 largest cities (2003 est.): Wichita, 354,617;
Overland Park, 160,368; Kansas City, 145,757;
Topeka, 122,008; Olathe, 105,274; Lawrence, 82,120;
Shawnee, 54,093; Salina, 45,833; Manhattan, 44,733;
Lenexa, 41,995
Land area: 81,815 sq mi. (211,901 sq km)
Geographic center: In Barton Co., 15 mi. NE of
Great Bend
Number of counties: 105
Largest county by population and area: Johnson,
496,691 (2004); Butler, 1,428 sq mi.
State parks: 24
Residents: Kansan
2004 resident population est.: 2,735,502
2000 resident census population (rank): 2,688,418
(32). **Male:** 1,328,474 (49.4%); **Female:** 1,359,944
(50.6%). **White:** 2,313,944 (86.1%); **Black:** 154,198
(5.7%); **American Indian:** 24,936 (0.9%); **Asian:**
46,806 (1.7%); **Other race:** 90,725 (3.4%); **Two or
more races:** 56,496 (2.1%); **Hispanic/Latino:**
188,252 (7.0%). **2000 percent population 18 and
over:** 73.5; **65 and over:** 13.3; **median age:** 35.2.

Spanish explorer Francisco de Coronado, in 1541,
is considered the first European to have traveled this
region. Sieur de la Salle's extensive land claims for
France (1682) included present-day Kansas. Ceded
to Spain by France in 1763, the territory reverted to
France in 1800 and was sold to the U.S. as part of
the Louisiana Purchase in 1803.

Lewis and Clark, Zebulon Pike, and Stephen H.
Long explored the region between 1803 and 1819.
The first permanent white settlements in Kansas
were outposts—Fort Leavenworth (1827), Fort Scott
(1842), and Fort Riley (1853)—established to protect travelers along the Santa Fe and Oregon Trails.

Just before the Civil War, the conflict between the
pro- and anti-slavery forces earned the region the
grim title of Bleeding Kansas.

Today, wheat fields, oil-well derricks, herds of
cattle, and grain-storage elevators are chief features
of the Kansas landscape. A leading wheat-growing
state, Kansas also raises corn, sorghum, oats, barley,
soybeans, and potatoes. Kansas stands high in petroleum production and mines zinc, coal, salt, and lead.
It is also the nation's leading producer of helium.

Wichita is one of the nation's leading aircraft-
manufacturing centers, ranking first in production of
private aircraft. Kansas City is an important transportation, milling, and meat-packing center.

Points of interest include the Kansas History Center at Topeka, the Eisenhower boyhood home and the Eisenhower Memorial Museum and Presidential Library at Abilene, John Brown's cabin at Osawatomie, re-created Front Street in Dodge City, Fort Larned (an important military post on the Santa Fe Trail), Fort Leavenworth, and Fort Riley.

Selected famous natives and residents: Roscoe "Fatty" Arbuckle, actor; Clarence D. Batchelor, political cartoonist; Gwendolyn Brooks, poet; Walter P. Chrysler, auto manufacturer; Clark M. Clifford, secretary of defense; John Steuart Curry, painter; Charles Curtis, vice president; Robert Dole, senator; Amelia Earhart, aviator; Dwight D. Eisenhower, general and president; Milton S. Eisenhower, educator; Gary Hart, politician; William Inge, playwright; Walter Johnson, baseball pitcher; Osa L. Johnson, documentary film producer; Buster Keaton, comedian; Emmett Kelly, clown; Stan Kenton, jazz musician; James Lehrer, broadcast journalist; Edgar Lee Masters, poet; Hattie McDaniel, actress; Karl Menninger, psychiatrist; Carry A. Nation, temperance leader; Gordon Parks, film director; ZaSu Pitts, actress; Samuel Ramey, opera singer; Charles Robinson, statesman and first governor; Charles (Buddy) Rogers, actor; Damon Runyon, journalist; Gale Sayers, football player; Eugene W. Smith, photojournalist; Milburn Stone, actor; John Cameron Swayze, news commentator; William Allen White, journalist; Charles E. Whittaker, jurist; Jess Willard, boxer.

Kentucky

Capital: Frankfort
Governor: Ernie Fletcher, R (to Dec. 2007)
Lieut. Governor: Stephen B. Pence, R (to Dec. 2007)
Senators: Jim Bunning, R (to Jan. 2011);
  Mitch McConnell, R (to Jan. 2009)
U.S. Representatives: 6
Secy. of State: C.M. "Trey" Grayson, R (to Dec. 2007)
Treasurer: Jonathan Miller, D (to Dec. 2007)
Atty. General: Gregory D. Stumbo, D (to Dec. 2007)
Entered Union (rank): June 1, 1792 (15)
Present constitution adopted: 1891
Motto: United we stand, divided we fall
State symbols: tree, tulip poplar (1994); **flower,**
  goldenrod; **bird,** Kentucky cardinal; **song,** "My Old Kentucky Home"
Nickname: Bluegrass State
Origin of name: From an Iroquoian word "Ken-tah-ten" meaning "land of tomorrow"
10 largest cities (2003 est.): Lexington-Fayette,[1] 266,798; Louisville, 248,762; Owensboro, 54,312; Bowling Green, 50,663; Covington, 42,687; Richmond, 29,080; Hopkinsville, 28,678; Henderson, 27,468; Frankfort, 27,408; Jeffersontown, 26,331
Land area: 39,728 sq mi. (102,896 sq km)
Geographic center: In Marion Co., 3 mi. NNW of Lebanon
Number of counties: 120
Largest county by population and area: Jefferson, 700,030 (2004); Pike, 787 sq mi.
State parks: 49
Residents: Kentuckian
2004 resident population est.: 4,145,922
2000 resident census population (rank): 4,041,769 (25). **Male:** 1,975,368 (48.9%); **Female:** 2,066,401 (51.1%). **White:** 3,640,889 (90.1%); **Black:** 295,994 (7.3%); **American Indian:** 8,616 (0.2%); **Asian:** 29,744 (0.7%); **Other race:** 22,623 (0.6%); **Two or more races:** 42,443 (1.1%); **Hispanic/Latino:** 59,939 (1.5%). **2000 percent population 18 and over:** 75.4; **65 and over:** 12.5; **median age:** 35.9.

1. Coextensive with Fayette County.

Kentucky was the first region west of the Allegheny Mountains to be settled by American pioneers. James Harrod established the first permanent settlement at Harrodsburg in 1774; the following year

Daniel Boone, who had explored the area in 1767, blazed the Wilderness Trail through the Cumberland Gap and founded Boonesboro.

Politically, the Kentucky region was originally part of Virginia, but statehood was gained in 1792. Gen. Anthony Wayne's victory in 1794 at Fallen Timbers in Ohio marked the end of Native American resistance in the area and secured the Kentucky frontier.

As a slaveholding state with a considerable abolitionist population, Kentucky was caught in the middle during the Civil War, supplying both Union and Confederate forces with thousands of troops.

Kentucky prides itself on producing some of the nation's best tobacco, horses, and whiskey. Corn, soybeans, wheat, fruit, hogs, cattle, and dairy products are among the agricultural items produced.

Among the manufactured items produced in the state are motor vehicles, furniture, aluminum ware, brooms, apparel, lumber products, machinery, textiles, and iron and steel products. Kentucky also produces significant amounts of petroleum, natural gas, fluorspar, clay, and stone. However, coal accounts for 85% of the total mineral income.

Louisville is famous for the Kentucky Derby at Churchill Downs, and the Bluegrass country around Lexington is the home of some of the world's finest race horses. Other attractions are Mammoth Cave, the George S. Patton, Jr., Military Museum at Fort Knox, and Old Fort Harrod State Park.

Selected famous natives and residents: John Adair, pioneer and political leader; Muhammad Ali, boxer; Alben W. Barkley, vice president; Louis D. Brandeis, jurist; John Mason Brown, critic; Kit Carson, scout; Champ Clark, politician; George Clooney, actor; Rosemary Clooney, singer; Irvin S. Cobb, humorist; Jefferson Davis, president of the Confederacy; Johnny Depp, actor; Irene Dunne, actress; Crystal Gayle, singer; David W. Griffith, film producer; John M. Harlan, jurist; Elizabeth Hardwick, writer; Casey Jones, locomotive engineer; Ashley Judd, actress; Naomi Judd, singer; Wynona Judd, singer; Barbara Kingsolver, writer; Abraham Lincoln, president; Loretta Lynn, singer; Bill Monroe, bluegrass musician; Carry A. Nation, temperance leader; Patricia Neal, actress; George Reeves, actor; Wiley B. Rutledge, jurist; Diane Sawyer, broadcast journalist; Phil Simms, football player; Adlai Stevenson, vice president; Allen Tate, poet and critic; Hunter Thompson, writer; Frederick M. Vinson, jurist; Robert Penn Warren, novelist.

Louisiana

Capital: Baton Rouge
Governor: Kathleen Blanco, D (to Jan. 2008)
Lieut. Governor: Mitch Landrieu, D (to Jan. 2008)
Senators: David Vitter, R (to Jan. 2011);
  Mary Landrieu, D (to Jan. 2009)
U.S. Representatives: 7
Secy. of State: W. Fox McKeithen, R (to Jan. 2008)
Treasurer: John Neely Kennedy, D (to Jan. 2008)
Atty. General: Charles C. Foti, Jr., D (to Jan. 2008)
Organized as territory: March 26, 1804
Entered Union (rank): April 30, 1812 (18)
Present constitution adopted: 1974
Motto: Union, justice, and confidence
State symbols: flower, magnolia (1900); **tree,** bald cypress (1963); **bird,** eastern brown pelican (1958); **songs,** "Give Me Louisiana" and "You Are My Sunshine"
Nickname: Pelican State
Origin of name: In honor of Louis XIV of France
10 largest cities (2003 est.): New Orleans, 469,032; Baton Rouge, 225,090; Shreveport, 198,364; Lafayette, 111,667; Lake Charles, 70,735; Kenner, 70,202; Bossier City, 58,111; Monroe, 52,163; Alexandria, 45,649; New Iberia, 32,502

Land area: 43,562 sq mi. (112,826 sq km)
Geographic center: In Avoyelles Parish, 3 mi. SE of Marksville
Number of parishes (counties): 64
Largest parish by population and area: Orleans, 462,269 (2004); Vernon, 1,328 sq mi.
State parks: 35
Residents: Louisianan, Louisianian
2004 resident population est.: 4,515,770
2000 resident census population (rank): 4,468,976 (22). **Male:** 2,162,903 (48.4%); **Female:** 2,306,073 (51.6%). **White:** 2,856,161 (63.9%); **Black:** 1,451,944 (32.5%); **American Indian:** 25,477 (0.6%); **Asian:** 54,758 (1.2%); **Other race:** 31,131 (0.7%); **Two or more races:** 48,265 (1.1%); **Hispanic/Latino:** 107,738 (2.4%). **2000 percent population 18 and over:** 72.7; **65 and over:** 11.6; **median age:** 34.0.

Louisiana has a rich, colorful historical background. Early Spanish explorers were Alvárez Piñeda, 1519; Álvar Núñez Cabeza de Vaca, 1528; and Hernando de Soto in 1541. Sieur de la Salle reached the mouth of the Mississippi and claimed all the land drained by it and its tributaries for Louis XIV of France in 1682.

Louisiana became a French crown colony in 1731 but was ceded to Spain in 1763 after the French and Indian Wars. (The portion east of the Mississippi came under British control in 1764.) Louisiana reverted to France in 1800 and was sold by Napoleon to the U.S. in 1803. The southern part, known as the territory of Orleans, became the state of Louisiana in 1812.

During the Civil War, Louisiana joined the Confederacy, but New Orleans was captured by Union Adm. David Farragut in April 1862. The state's economy suffered during Reconstruction; however, the situation improved at the turn of the 20th century, with the discovery of oil and natural gas and the growth of industry.

Louisiana is a leader in natural gas, salt, petroleum, and sulfur production. Much of the oil and sulfur comes from offshore deposits. The state also produces large crops of sweet potatoes, rice, sugar cane, pecans, soybeans, corn, and cotton. Leading manufactured items include chemicals, processed food, petroleum and coal products, paper, lumber and wood products, transportation equipment, and apparel.

The state has become a popular tourist destination. New Orleans is the major draw, known particularly for its picturesque French Quarter and the annual Mardi Gras celebration, held since 1838.

Other major points of interest include the Superdome in New Orleans, historic plantation homes near Natchitoches and New Iberia, Cajun country in the Mississippi Delta Region, Chalmette National Historic Park, and the state capital at Baton Rouge.

On Aug. 29, 2005, Louisiana was hit by Hurricane Katrina, devastating New Orleans, and killing hundreds elsewhere in the state, particularly in the parishes of Jefferson and St. Bernard.

Selected famous natives and residents: Louis Armstrong, musician; Geoffrey Beene, fashion designer; Truman Capote, writer; Kitty Carlisle, singer and actress; Van Cliburn, concert pianist; Michael De Bakey, heart surgeon; Fats Domino, musician; Louis Moreau Gottschalk, pianist and composer; Bryant Gumbel, TV newscaster; Lillian Hellman, playwright; Al Hirt, trumpeter; Mahalia Jackson, gospel singer; Jean Laffite, privateer; Dorothy Lamour, actress; John A. Lejeune, Marine Corps general; Elmore Leonard, author; Jerry Lee Lewis, singer; Huey P. Long, politician; Wynton Marsalis, musician; Jelly Roll Morton, jazz musician and composer; Huey Newton, black activist; Paul Prudhomme, chef; Howard K. Smith, TV commentator; Ben Turpin, comedian; Ray Walston, actor; Edward Douglas White, jurist.

Maine

Capital: Augusta
Governor: John Baldacci, D (to Jan. 2007)
Lt. Governor/Senate President: Beth Edmonds, D (to Jan. 2007)
Senators: Susan Collins, R (to Jan. 2009); Olympia J. Snowe, R (to Jan. 2007)
U.S. Representatives: 2
Secy. of State: Matthew Dunlap, D (to Jan. 2007)
Treasurer: David Lemoine, D (to Jan. 2007)
Atty. General: G. Steven Rowe, D (to Jan. 2007)
Entered Union (rank): March 15, 1820 (23)
Present constitution adopted: 1820
Motto: *Dirigo* (I lead)
State symbols: flower, white pine cone and tassel (1895); **tree,** white pine tree (1945); **bird,** chickadee (1927); **fish,** landlocked salmon (1969); **mineral,** tourmaline (1971); **song,** "State of Maine Song" (1937); **animal,** moose (1979); **cat,** Maine coon cat (1985); **fossil,** *pertica quadrifaria* (1985); **insect,** honeybee (1975)
Nickname: Pine Tree State
Origin of name: First used to distinguish the mainland from the offshore islands. It has been considered a compliment to Henrietta Maria, queen of Charles I of England. She was said to have owned the province of Mayne in France.
10 largest cities (2003 est.): Portland, 63,635; Lewiston, 35,922; Bangor, 31,550; South Portland, 23,553; Auburn, 23,313; Biddeford, 21,685; Sanford, 21,666; Brunswick, 21,529; Augusta, 18,618; Scarborough, 18,459
Land area: 30,862 sq mi. (79,933 sq km)
Geographic center: In Piscataquis Co., 18 mi. N of Dover-Foxcroft
Number of counties: 16
Largest county by population and area: Cumberland, 273,505 (2004); Aroostook, 6,672 sq mi.
State parks: 30+
State historic sites: 18 (403 ac.)
Residents: Mainer
2004 resident population est.: 1,317,253
2000 resident census population (rank): 1,274,923 (40). **Male:** 620,309 (48.7%); **Female:** 654,614 (51.3%). **White:** 1,236,014 (96.9%); **Black:** 6,760 (0.5%); **American Indian:** 7,098 (0.6%); **Asian:** 9,111 (0.7%); **Other race:** 2,911 (0.2%); **Two or more races:** 12,647 (1.0%); **Hispanic/Latino:** 9,360 (0.7%); **2000 percent population 18 and over:** 76.4; **65 and over:** 14.4; **median age:** 38.6.

John Cabot and his son, Sebastian, are believed to have visited the Maine coast in 1498. However, the first permanent English settlements were not established until more than a century later, in 1623.

The first naval action of the Revolutionary War occurred in 1775 when colonials captured the British sloop *Margaretta* off Machias on the Maine coast. In that same year, the British burned Falmouth (now Portland).

Long governed by Massachusetts, Maine became the 23rd state as part of the Missouri Compromise in 1820.

Maine produces 98% of the nation's low-bush blueberries. Farm income is also derived from apples, potatoes, dairy products, and vegetables, with poultry and eggs the largest selling items.

The state is one of the world's largest pulp-paper producers. With almost 89% of its area forested,

Maine turns out wood products from boats to tooth-picks. Maine also leads the world in the production of the familiar flat tins of sardines, producing more than 75 million of them annually. In 2001, Maine lobstermen landed nearly 48 million pounds of lob-ster, compared with an estimated 53 million pounds in 2000.

A scenic seacoast, beaches, lakes, mountains, and resorts make Maine a popular vacationland. There are more than 2,500 lakes and 5,000 streams, plus 26 state parks to attract hunters, fishermen, skiers, and campers.

Major points of interest are Bar Harbor, Acadia National Park, Allagash National Wilderness Water-way, the Wadsworth-Longfellow House in Portland, Roosevelt Campobello International Park, and the St. Croix Island National Monument.

Selected famous natives and residents: F. Lee Bailey, defense attorney; Charles F. Browne (Artemus Ward), humorist; Cyrus Curtis, publisher; Dorothea Dix, civil rights reformer; John Ford, film director; Melville Fuller, jurist; Marsden Hartley, painter; Henry Wadsworth Longfellow, poet; Sarah Orne Jewett, author; Stephen King, writer; Linda Lavin, actress; Edna St. Vincent Millay, poet; Marston Morse, mathematician; Frank Munsey, publisher; Walter Piston, composer; George Putnam, publisher; Kenneth Roberts, historical novelist; Edwin Arlington Robinson, poet; Margaret Chase Smith, politician; Samantha Smith, peacemaker and actress; John Hay Whitney, publisher.

Maryland

Capital: Annapolis
Governor: Robert L. Ehrlich, Jr., R (to Jan. 2007)
Lieut. Gov.: Michael Steele, R (to Jan. 2007)
Senators: Barbara A. Mikulski, D (to Jan. 2011);
Paul S. Sarbanes, D (to Jan. 2007)
U.S. Representatives: 8
Secy. of State: R. Karl Aumann, R (to Jan. 2007)
Treasurer: Nancy K. Kopp, D
Atty. General: J. Joseph Curran, Jr., D (to Jan. 2007)
Entered Union (rank): April 28, 1788 (7)
Present constitution adopted: 1867
Motto: *Fatti maschii, parole femine* (Manly deeds, womanly words)
State symbols: bird, Baltimore oriole (1947); **boat,** skipjack (1985); **crustacean,** Maryland blue crab (1989); **dinosaur,** Astrodon johnstoni (1998); **dog,** Chesapeake Bay retriever (1964); **beverage,** milk (1998); **flower,** black-eyed susan (1918); **fish,** rockfish (1965); **folk dance,** square dance (1994); **fossil shell,** *ecphora gardnerae gardnerae* (Wilson) (1994); **insect,** Baltimore checkerspot butterfly (1973); **reptile,** Diamondback terrapin (1994); **song,** "Maryland! My Maryland!" (1939); **sport,** jousting (1962); **team sport,** lacrosse (2004); **tree,** white oak (1941)
Nicknames: Free State; Old Line State
Origin of name: In honor of Henrietta Maria (queen of Charles I of England)
10 largest cities (2003 est.): Baltimore, 628,670; Gaithersburg, 57,365; Frederick, 56,128; Rockville, 55,213; Bowie, 53,660; Hagerstown, 36,953; Annapolis, 36,178; College Park, 25,329; Salisbury, 25,247; Greenbelt, 22,096
Land area: 9,774 sq mi. (25,315 sq km)
Geographic center: In Prince Georges Co., 4½ mi. NW of Davidsonville
Number of counties: 23, and 1 independent city
Largest county by population and area: Montgomery, 921,690 (2004); Frederick, 663 sq mi.
State parks: 40 (90,239 ac.)
Residents: Marylander
2004 resident population est.: 5,558,058
2000 resident census population (rank): 5,296,486 (19). **Male:** 2,557,794 (48.3%); **Female:** 2,738,692

(51.7%). **White:** 3,391,308 (64.0%); **Black:** 1,477,411 (27.9%); **American Indian:** 15,423 (0.3%); **Asian:** 210,929 (4.0%); **Other race:** 95,525 (1.8%); **Two or more races:** 103,587 (2.0%); **Hispanic/Latino:** 227,916 (4.3%). **2000 percent population 18 and over:** 74.4; **65 and over:** 11.3; **median age:** 36.0.

In 1608, Capt. John Smith explored Chesapeake Bay. Charles I granted a royal charter for Maryland to Cecil Calvert, Lord Baltimore, in 1632, and English settlers, many of whom were Roman Catho-lic, landed on St. Clement's (now Blakistone) Island in 1634. Religious freedom, granted all Christians in the Toleration Act passed by the Maryland assembly in 1649, was ended by a Puritan revolt, 1654–1658.

From 1763 to 1767, Charles Mason and Jeremiah Dixon surveyed Maryland's northern boundary line with Pennsylvania. In 1791, Maryland ceded land to form the District of Columbia.

In 1814, during the British attempt to capture Bal-timore, the bombardment of Fort McHenry inspired Francis Scott Key to write the words to "The Star-Spangled Banner." During the Civil War, Maryland was a slave state but remained in the Union. Conse-quently, Marylanders fought on both sides and many families were divided.

Maryland's Eastern Shore and Western Shore embrace the Chesapeake Bay, and the many estuar-ies and rivers create one of the longest waterfronts of any state. The Bay produces more seafood—oysters, crabs, clams, fin fish—than any comparable body of water. Important agricultural products are green-house and nursery products, chickens, dairy prod-ucts, eggs, and soybeans. Stone, coal, sand, gravel, cement, and clay are the chief mineral products.

Manufacturing industries include food products, chemicals, computer and electronic products, trans-portation equipment, and primary metals. Baltimore, home of the Johns Hopkins University and Hospital, ranks as the nation's second port in foreign tonnage. The capital, Annapolis, is the site of the U.S. Naval Academy.

Among the popular attractions in Maryland are the Fort McHenry National Monument; Harpers Ferry and Chesapeake and Ohio Canal National His-toric Parks; Antietam National Battlefield; National Aquarium, USS *Constellation,* and Maryland Sci-ence Center at Baltimore's Inner Harbor; Historic St. Mary's City; Jefferson Patterson Historical Park and Museum at St. Leonard; U.S. Naval Academy in Annapolis; Goddard Space Flight Center at Green-belt; Assateague Island National Park Seashore; Ocean City beach resort; and Catoctin Mountain, Fort Frederick, and Piscataway parks.

Selected famous natives and residents: Benjamin Banneker, mathematician and astronomer; John Barth, writer; Eubie Blake, musician; John Wilkes Booth, actor and Lincoln assassin; Francis X. Bushman, actor; James M. Cain, writer; Samuel Chase, jurist; Frederick Douglass, abolitionist; John Fletcher Hurst, Methodist bishop and educator; Christopher Gist, frontiersman; Philip Glass, composer; John Hanson, president of Continental Congress; Matthew Henson, polar explorer; Billie Holiday, jazz-blues singer; Johns Hopkins, financier; Reverdy Johnson, lawyer and statesman; Thomas Johnson, political leader; Francis Scott Key, lawyer and poet; Thurgood Marshall, jurist; H. L. Mencken, writer; Hezekiah Niles, journalist; Charles Willson Peale, painter; Frank Perdue, farmer, businessman; James R. Randall, journalist and writer of the state song; Babe Ruth, baseball player; Upton Sinclair, novelist; Roger B. Taney, jurist; George Alfred Townsend (Gath), journalist; Harriet Tubman, abolitionist; Leon Uris, novelist; Frank Zappa, singer.

Massachusetts

Capital: Boston
Governor: Mitt Romney, R (to Jan. 2007)
Lieut. Governor: Kerry Healey, R (to Jan. 2007)
Senators: Edward M. Kennedy, D (to Jan. 2007);
   John F. Kerry, D (to Jan. 2009)
U.S. Representatives: 10
Secy. of the Commonwealth: William F. Galvin, D
   (to Jan. 2007)
Treasurer: Timothy P. Cahill, D (to Jan. 2007)
Atty. General: Thomas F. Reilly, D (to Jan. 2007)
Present constitution drafted: 1780 (oldest U.S. state
   constitution in effect today)
Entered Union (rank): Feb. 6, 1788 (6)
Motto: *Ense petit placidam sub libertate quietem*
   (By the sword we seek peace, but peace only
   under liberty)
State symbols: flower, mayflower (1918); **tree,**
   American elm (1941); **bird,** chickadee (1941); **song,**
   "All Hail to Massachusetts" (1966); **beverage,**
   cranberry juice (1970); **insect,** ladybug (1974);
   cookie, chocolate chip (1997); **muffin,** corn muffin
   (1986); **dessert,** Boston cream pie (1996)
Nicknames: Bay State; Old Colony State
Origin of name: From Massachusett tribe of Native
   Americans, meaning "at or about the great hill"
10 largest cities (2003 est.): Boston, 581,616;
   Worcester, 175,706; Springfield, 152,157; Lowell,
   104,351; Cambridge, 101,587; Brockton, 95,090; New
   Bedford, 94,112; Fall River, 92,760; Lynn, 89,571;
   Quincy, 89,059
Land area: 7,840 sq mi. (20,306 sq km)
Geographic center: In the town of Rutland in Worcester
   Co.
Number of counties: 14
Largest county by population and area: Middlesex,
   1,464,628 (2004); Worcester, 1,513 sq mi.
State forests and parks: 450,000 ac.
Residents: Bay Stater
2004 resident population est.: 6,416,505
2000 resident census population (rank): 6,349,097
   (13). **Male:** 3,058,816 (48.2%); **Female:** 3,290,281
   (51.8%). **White:** 5,367,286 (84.5%); **Black:** 343,454
   (5.4%); **American Indian:** 15,015 (0.2%); **Asian:**
   238,124 (3.8%); **Other race:** 236,724 (3.7%); **Two or
   more races:** 146,005 (2.3%); **Hispanic/Latino:**
   428,729 (6.8%). **2000 percent population 18 and
   over:** 76.4; **65 and over:** 13.5; **median age:** 36.5.

Massachusetts has played a significant role in
American history since the Pilgrims, seeking religious freedom, founded Plymouth Colony in 1620.
As one of the most important of the 13 colonies,
Massachusetts became a leader in resisting British
oppression. In 1773, the Boston Tea Party protested
unjust taxation. The Minute Men started the American Revolution by battling British troops at Lexington and Concord on April 19, 1775.

During the 19th century, Massachusetts was
famous for the intellectual activity of its writers and
educators and for its expanding commercial fishing,
shipping, and manufacturing interests. Massachusetts pioneered the manufacture of textiles and
shoes. Today, these industries have been replaced in
importance by the electronics and communications
equipment fields.

The state's cranberry crop is the nation's second-
largest (after Wisconsin). Also important are dairy
and poultry products, nursery and greenhouse produce, vegetables, and fruit.

Tourism has become an important factor in the
economy of the state because of its numerous recreational areas and historical landmarks. Cape Cod
has beaches, summer theaters, and an artists' colony
at Provincetown. The Berkshires, in the western part
of the state, is the site of Tanglewood, the summer
home of the Boston Symphony; art museums,
including Mass MoCA and the Clark Institute; and
Jacob's Pillow, a world renowned dance center.

Among the many other points of interest are Old
Sturbridge Village in Sturbridge, Minute Man
National Historical Park between Lexington and
Concord, and Plimoth Plantation in Plymouth. In
Boston there are many places of historical interest,
including Old North Church, Old State House,
Faneuil Hall, the USS *Constitution*, and the John F.
Kennedy Library and Museum.

Selected famous natives and residents: John Adams,
president; John Quincy Adams, president; Samuel Adams,
patriot; Bronson Alcott, educator and social reformer; Louisa
May Alcott, writer; Horatio Alger, novelist; Susan B.
Anthony, woman suffragist; Clara Barton, American Red
Cross founder; Leonard Bernstein, conductor; George H. W.
Bush, president; William Cullen Bryant, poet and editor;
Luther Burbank, horticulturalist; John Cheever, novelist;
John Singleton Copley, painter; E. E. Cummings, poet;
Jacques d'Amboise, ballet dancer; Bette Davis, actress;
Cecil B. DeMille, film director; Emily Dickinson, poet; Ralph
Waldo Emerson, philosopher and poet; Geraldine Farrar,
soprano, actress; Benjamin Franklin, statesman and
scientist; Buckminster Fuller, architect and educator; Robert
Goddard, father of modern rocketry; John Hancock,
statesman; Nathaniel Hawthorne, novelist; Oliver Wendell
Holmes, jurist; Winslow Homer, painter; Elias Howe,
inventor; John F. Kennedy, president; Amy Lowell, poet;
James Russell Lowell, poet; Robert Lowell, poet; Horace
Mann, educator; Cotton Mather, clergyman; Herman
Melville, writer; Samuel F. B. Morse, painter and inventor;
Edgar Allan Poe, writer; Paul Revere, silversmith and
Revolutionary War figure; Norman Rockwell, artist; Dr.
Seuss (Theodore Geisel), author and illustrator; David
Souter, jurist; Lucy Stone, woman suffragist; Louis Henry
Sullivan, architect; Henry David Thoreau, author; Barbara
Walters, TV commentator; James McNeill Whistler, painter;
Eli Whitney, inventor; John Greenleaf Whittier, poet.

Michigan

Capital: Lansing
Governor: Jennifer Granholm, D (to Jan. 2007)
Lieut. Governor: John D. Cherry, D (to Jan. 2007)
Senators: Carl Levin, D (to Jan. 2009);
   Debbie A. Stabenow, D (to Jan. 2007)
U.S. Representatives: 15
Secy. of State: Terri Lynn Land, R (to Jan. 2007)
Atty. General: Mike Cox, R (to Jan. 2007)
Treasurer: Jay B. Rising (apptd. by governor)
Organized as territory: Jan. 11, 1805
Entered Union (rank): Jan. 26, 1837 (26)
Present constitution adopted: April 1, 1963, (effective
   Jan. 1, 1964)
Motto: *Si quaeris peninsulam amoenam circumspice*
   (If you seek a pleasant peninsula, look around you)
State symbols: flower, apple blossom (1897); **bird,**
   robin (1931); **mammal,** white-tailed deer (1997);
   fishes, trout (1965), brook trout (1988); **gem,** isle
   royal greenstone (chlorastrolite) (1972); **stone,**
   petoskey stone (1965); **tree,** white pine (1955); **soil,**
   kalkaska soil series (1990); **reptile,** painted turtle
   (1995); **flag,** "Blue charged with the arms of the state"
   (1911); **wildflower,** Dwarf Lake iris (1998)
Nickname: Wolverine State
Origin of name: From Indian word "Michigana" meaning
   "great or large lake"
10 largest cities (2003 est.): Detroit, 911,402; Grand
   Rapids, 195,601; Warren, 136,016; Sterling Heights,
   126,182; Flint, 120,292; Lansing, 118,379; Ann Arbor,
   114,498; Livonia, 99,487; Dearborn, 96,670; Westland,
   85,707

Land area: 56,804 sq mi. (147,122 sq km)
Geographic center: In Wexford Co., 5 mi. NNW of Cadillac
Number of counties: 83
Largest county by population and area: Wayne, 2,016,202 (2004); Marquette, 1,821 sq mi.
State parks and recreation areas: 97
Residents: Michigander, Michiganian, Michiganite
2004 resident population est.: 10,112,620
2000 resident census population (rank): 9,938,444 (8). **Male:** 4,873,095 (49.0%); **Female:** 5,065,349 (51.0%). **White:** 7,966,053 (80.2%); **Black:** 1,412,742 (14.2%); **American Indian:** 58,479 (0.6%); **Asian:** 176,510 (1.8%); **Other race:** 129,552 (1.3%); **Two or more races:** 192,416 (1.9%); **Hispanic/Latino:** 323,877 (3.3%). **2000 percent population 18 and over:** 73.9; **65 and over:** 12.3; **median age:** 35.5.

Indian tribes were living in the Michigan region when the first European, Etienne Brulé of France, arrived in 1618. Other French explorers, including Jacques Marquette, Louis Joliet, and Sieur de la Salle, followed, and the first permanent settlement was established in 1668 at Sault Ste. Marie. France was ousted from the territory by Great Britain in 1763, following the French and Indian Wars.

After the Revolutionary War, the U.S. acquired most of the region, which remained the scene of constant conflict between the British and U.S. forces and their respective Indian allies through the War of 1812.

Bordering on four of the five Great Lakes, Michigan is divided into Upper and Lower peninsulas by the Straits of Mackinac, which link lakes Michigan and Huron. The two parts of the state are connected by the Mackinac Bridge, one of the world's longest suspension bridges. To the north, connecting lakes Superior and Huron, are the busy Sault Ste. Marie Canals.

While Michigan ranks first among the states in production of motor vehicles and parts, it is also a leader in many other manufacturing and processing lines, including prepared cereals, machine tools, airplane parts, refrigerators, hardware, and furniture.

The state produces important amounts of iron, copper, iodine, gypsum, bromine, salt, lime, gravel, and cement. Michigan's farms grow apples, cherries, beans, pears, grapes, potatoes, and sugar beets. Michigan's forests contribute significantly to the state's economy, supporting thousands of jobs in the wood-product, tourism, and recreation industries. With 10,083 inland lakes and 3,288 mi of Great Lakes shoreline, Michigan is a prime area for both commercial and sport fishing.

Points of interest are the automobile plants in Dearborn, Detroit, Flint, Lansing, and Pontiac; Mackinac Island; Pictured Rocks and Sleeping Bear Dunes National Lakeshores; Greenfield Village in Dearborn; and the many summer resorts along both the inland lakes and Great Lakes.

Selected famous natives and residents: Nelson Algren, novelist; Tim Allen, actor and comedian; Anita Baker, singer; William Boeing, Sr., airplane manufacturer; Ralph J. Bunche, statesman; Ellen Burstyn, actress; Bruce Catton, historian; Roger Chaffee, astronaut; Francis Ford Coppola, film director; Thomas E. Dewey, politician; Edna Ferber, novelist; Gerald Ford, former president; Henry Ford, industrialist; Ali Haji-Sheikh, football player; Julie Harris, actress; Earvin "Magic" Johnson, basketball player; Casey Kasem, radio personality; John Harvey Kellogg, surgeon and health reformer; Ring Lardner, writer; Charles A. Lindbergh, aviator; Madonna, singer; Dick Martin, comedian; Terry McMillan, author; John N. Mitchell, attorney general; Ted Nugent, singer; Chief Pontiac, Ottawa chief; Iggy Pop, musician; Gilda Radner, comedienne; Della Reese, singer; Jason Robards, Sr., actor; Diana Ross, singer; Steven Seagal, actor; Bob Seger, singer; Tom Selleck, actor; Thomas Schippers, conductor; Potter Stewart, jurist; Lily Tomlin, actress; Danny Thomas, entertainer; William E. Upjohn, pharmaceuticals manufacturer; Margaret Whiting, singer; Robin Williams, comedian and actor; Stevie Wonder, singer.

Minnesota

Capital: St. Paul
Governor: Tim Pawlenty, R (to Jan. 2007)
Lieut. Governor: Carol Molnau, R (to Jan. 2007)
Senators: Norm Coleman, R (to Jan. 2009)
   Mark Dayton, D (to Jan. 2007)
U.S. Representatives: 8
Secy. of State: Mary Kiffmeyer, R (to Jan. 2007)
Atty. General: Mike Hatch, D (to Jan. 2007)
Commissioner of Finance: Peggy Ingison (to Jan. 2007)
Organized as territory: March 3, 1849
Entered Union (rank): May 11, 1858 (32)
Present constitution adopted: 1858
Motto: L'Étoile du Nord (The North Star)
State symbols: flower, lady slipper (1902); **tree,** red (or Norway) pine (1953); **bird,** common loon (also called great northern diver) (1961); **song,** "Hail Minnesota" (1945); **fish,** walleye (1965); **mushroom,** morel (1984)
Nicknames: North Star State; Gopher State; Land of 10,000 Lakes
Origin of name: From a Dakota Indian word meaning "sky-tinted water"
10 largest cities (2003 est.): Minneapolis, 373,188; St. Paul, 280,404; Rochester, 92,507; Duluth, 85,734; Bloomington, 83,080; Plymouth, 69,164; Brooklyn Park, 67,781; Eagan, 64,006; Coon Rapids, 62,310; Burnsville, 59,805
Land area: 79,610 sq mi. (206,190 sq km)
Geographic center: In Crow Wing Co., 10 mi. SW of Brainerd
Number of counties: 87
Largest county by population and area: Hennepin, 1,120,897 (2004); St. Louis, 6,226 sq mi.
State parks: 66 (226,000 ac.)
Residents: Minnesotan
2004 resident population est.: 5,100,958
2000 resident census population (rank): 4,919,479 (21). **Male:** 2,435,631 (49.5%); **Female:** 2,483,848 (50.5%). **White:** 4,400,282 (89.4%); **Black:** 171,731 (3.5%); **American Indian:** 54,967 (1.1%); **Asian:** 141,968 (2.9%); **Other race:** 65,810 (1.3%); **Two or more races:** 82,742 (1.7%); **Hispanic/Latino:** 143,382 (2.9%). **2000 percent population 18 and over:** 73.8; **65 and over:** 12.1; **median age:** 35.4.

Following the visits of several French explorers, fur traders, and missionaries, including Jacques Marquette, Louis Joliet, and Robert Cavelier, Sieur de la Salle, the region was claimed for Louis XIV by Daniel Greysolon, Sieur Duluth, in 1679.

The U.S. acquired eastern Minnesota from Great Britain after the Revolutionary War and 20 years later bought the western part from France in the Louisiana Purchase of 1803. Much of the region was explored by U.S. Army lieutenant Zebulon M. Pike before the northern strip of Minnesota bordering Canada was ceded by Britain in 1818.

The state is rich in natural resources. A few square miles of land in the north in the Mesabi, Cuyuna, and Vermilion ranges produce more than 75% of the nation's iron ore. The state's farms rank high in yields of corn, wheat, rye, alfalfa, and sugar beets. Other leading farm products include butter, eggs, milk, potatoes, green peas, barley, soybeans, oats, and livestock.

Minnesota's factories produce nonelectrical machinery, fabricated metals, flour-mill products, plastics, electronic computers, scientific instruments, and processed foods. The state is also a leader in the printing and paper-products industries.

Minneapolis is the trade center of the Midwest, and the headquarters of the world's largest super-computer and grain distributor. St. Paul is the nation's biggest publisher of calendars and law books. These "twin cities" are the nation's third-largest trucking center. Duluth has the nation's largest inland harbor and now handles a significant amount of foreign trade. Rochester is home to the Mayo Clinic, a world-famous medical center.

Tourism is a major revenue producer in Minnesota, with arts, fishing, hunting, water sports, and winter sports bringing in millions of visitors each year.

Among the most popular attractions are the St. Paul Winter Carnival; the Tyrone Guthrie Theatre, the Institute of Arts, Walker Art Center, and Minnehaha Park, in Minneapolis; Boundary Waters Canoe Area; Voyageurs National Park; North Shore Drive; the Minnesota Zoological Gardens; and the state's more than 10,000 lakes.

Selected famous natives and residents: LaVerne, Maxene, and Patti Andrews, singers; Warren E. Burger, jurist; William E. Colby, CIA director; William Demarest, actor; William O. Douglas, jurist; Bob Dylan, singer and composer; F. Scott Fitzgerald, novelist; Judy Garland, singer and actress; J. Paul Getty, oil executive; Cass Gilbert, architect; Duane Hanson, sculptor; Hubert H. Humphrey, senator and vice president; Jessica Lange, actress; Sinclair Lewis, novelist; Cornell MacNeil, baritone; Roger Maris, baseball player; E. G. Marshall, actor; Charles H. Mayo, surgeon; William J. Mayo, surgeon; Eugene J. McCarthy, former senator; Kate Millett, feminist; Walter F. Mondale, former vice president; Gen. Lauris Norstad, NATO commander; Westbrook Pegler, columnist; John Sargent Pillsbury, businessman; Marion Ross, actress; Jane Russell, actress; Harrison E. Salisbury, journalist; Charles M. Schulz, cartoonist; Max Shulman, novelist; Maurice H. Stans, secretary of commerce; Harold E. Stassen, government official; Michael Todd, producer; Frederick Weyerhaeuser, businessman; Gig Young, actor.

Mississippi

Capital: Jackson
Governor: Haley Barbour, R (to Jan. 2008)
Lieut. Governor: Amy Tuck, R (to Jan. 2008)
Senators: Thad Cochran, R (to Jan. 2009);
Trent Lott, R (to Jan. 2007)
U.S. Representatives: 4
Secy. of State: Eric Clark, D (to Jan. 2008)
Treasurer: Tate Reeves R (to Jan. 2008)
Atty. General: Jim Hood, D (to Jan. 2008)
Organized as territory: April 7, 1798
Entered Union (rank): Dec. 10, 1817 (20)
Present constitution adopted: 1890
Motto: *Virtute et armis* (By valor and arms)
State symbols: flower, flower or bloom of the magnolia or evergreen magnolia (1952); **wildflower,** coreopsis (1991); **tree,** magnolia (1938); **bird,** mockingbird (1944); **song,** "Go, Mississippi" (1962); **stone,** petrified wood (1976); **fish,** largemouth or black bass (1974); **insect,** honeybee (1980); **shell,** oyster shell (1974); **water mammal,** bottlenosed dolphin or porpoise (1974); **fossil,** prehistoric whale (1981); **land mammal,** white-tailed deer (1974), red fox (1997); **waterfowl,** wood duck (1974); **beverage,** milk (1984); **butterfly,** spicebush swallowtail (1991); **dance,** square dance (1995)

Nickname: Magnolia State
Origin of name: From an Indian word meaning "Father of Waters"
10 largest cities (2003 est.): Jackson, 179,599; Gulfport, 71,810; Biloxi, 48,972; Hattiesburg, 46,664; Meridian, 39,559; Greenville, 39,521; Tupelo, 35,297; Southhaven, 34,760; Vicksburg, 26,005; Pascagoula, 25,865
Land area: 46,907 sq mi. (121,489 sq km)
Geographic center: In Leake Co., 9 mi. WNW of Carthage
Number of counties: 82
Largest county by population and area: Hinds, 249,987 (2004); Yazoo, 920 sq mi.
State parks: 28
Residents: Mississippian
2004 resident population est.: 2,902,966
2000 resident census population (rank): 2,844,658 (31). **Male:** 1,373,554 (48.3%); **Female:** 1,471,104 (51.7%). **White:** 1,746,099 (61.4%); **Black:** 1,033,809 (36.3%); **American Indian:** 11,652 (0.4%); **Asian:** 18,626 (0.7%); **Other race:** 13,784 (0.5%); **Two or more races:** 20,021 (0.7%); **Hispanic/Latino:** 39,569 (1.4%). **2000 percent population 18 and over:** 72.7; **65 and over:** 12.1; **median age:** 33.8.

First explored for Spain by Hernando de Soto, who discovered the Mississippi River in 1540, the region was later claimed by France. In 1699, a French group under Sieur d'Iberville established the first permanent settlement near present-day Ocean Springs.

Great Britain took over the area in 1763 after the French and Indian Wars, ceding it to the U.S. in 1783 after the Revolution. Spain did not relinquish its claims until 1798, and in 1810 the U.S. annexed West Florida from Spain, including what is now southern Mississippi.

For a little more than one hundred years, from shortly after the state's founding through the Great Depression, cotton was the undisputed king of Mississippi's largely agrarian economy. Over the last half-century, however, Mississippi has diversified its economy by balancing agricultural output with increased industrial activity.

Today, agriculture continues as a major segment of the state's economy. For almost four decades soybeans occupied the most acreage, while cotton remained the largest cash crop. In 2001, however, more acres of cotton were planted than soybeans, and Mississippi jumped to second in the nation in cotton production (exceeded only by Texas). The state's farmlands also yield important harvests of corn, peanuts, pecans, rice, sugar cane, and sweet potatoes as well as poultry, eggs, meat animals, dairy products, feed crops, and horticultural crops. Mississippi remains the world's leading producer of pond-raised catfish.

The state abounds in historical landmarks and is the home of the Vicksburg National Military Park. Other National Park Service areas are Brices Cross Roads National Battlefield Site, Tupelo National Battlefield, and part of Natchez Trace National Parkway. Pre–Civil War mansions are the special pride of Natchez, Oxford, Columbus, Vicksburg, and Jackson.

On Aug. 29, 2005, Mississippi was hit by Hurricane Katrina, killing hundreds, mostly in Harrison County.

Selected famous natives and residents: Red Barber, sportscaster; Jimmy Buffett, singer and songwriter; Craig Claiborne, columnist and restaurant critic; Bo Diddley, guitarist; Charles Evers, civil rights leader; Medgar Evers, civil rights leader; William Faulkner, novelist; Brett Favre, football player; Shelby Foote, historian; Richard Ford, novelist; John Grisham, novelist; Barry Hannah, novelist; Beth Henley, playwright and actress; Jim Henson, puppeteer; James Earl Jones, actor; B. B. King, guitarist; Steve McNair, football player; Mary Ann Mobley, actress; Willie Morris, writer; Elvis Presley, singer and actor; Leontyne Price, soprano; William Raspberry, columnist; Jerry Rice, football player; Jimmie Rodgers, singer; Sela Ward, actress; Muddy Waters, singer and guitarist; Eudora Welty, novelist; Tennessee Williams, playwright; Oprah Winfrey, talk-show host and actress; Richard Wright, novelist; Tammy Wynette, singer.

Missouri

Capital: Jefferson City
Governor: Matt Blunt, R (to Jan. 2009)
Lieut. Governor: Peter Kinder, R (to Jan. 2009)
Senators: Christopher S. Bond, R (to Jan. 2011); James M. Talent, R (to Jan. 2009)
U.S. Representatives: 9
Secy. of State: Robin Carnahan, D (to Jan. 2009)
Treasurer: Sarah Steelman, R (to Jan. 2009)
Atty. General: Jeremiah "Jay" W. Nixon, D (to Jan. 2009)
Organized as territory: June 4, 1812
Entered Union (rank): Aug. 10, 1821 (24)
Present constitution adopted: 1945
Motto: *Salus populi suprema lex esto* (The welfare of the people shall be the supreme law)
State symbols: flower, hawthorn (1923); **bird,** bluebird (1927); **aquatic animal,** paddlefish (1997); **fish,** channel catfish (1997); **song,** "Missouri Waltz" (1949); **fossil,** crinoid (1989); **musical instrument,** fiddle (1987); **rock,** mozarkite (1967); **mineral,** galena (1967); **insect,** honeybee (1985); **tree,** flowering dogwood (1955); **tree nut,** eastern black walnut (1990); **animal,** mule (1995); **dance,** square dance (1995); **Missouri Day,** third Wednesday in October (1969)
Nickname: Show-me State
Origin of name: Named after the Missouri Indian tribe. "Missouri" means "town of the large canoes."
10 largest cities (2003 est.): Kansas City, 442,768; St. Louis, 332,223; Springfield, 150,867; Independence, 112,079; Columbia, 88,534; Lee's Summit, 77,052; St. Joseph, 72,663; O'Fallon, 63,677; St. Charles, 61,253; St. Peter's, 53,397
Land area: 68,886 sq mi. (178,415 sq km)
Geographic center: In Miller Co., 20 mi. SW of Jefferson City
Number of counties: 114, plus 1 independent city
Largest county by population and area: St. Louis, 1,009,235 (2004); Texas, 1,179 sq mi.
State parks and historic sites: 81
Residents: Missourian
2004 resident population est.: 5,754,618
2000 resident census population (rank): 5,595,211 (17). **Male:** 2,720,177 (48.6%); **Female:** 2,875,034 (51.4%). **White:** 4,748,083 (84.9%); **Black:** 629,391 (11.2%); **American Indian:** 25,076 (0.4%); **Asian:** 61,595 (1.1%); **Other race:** 45,827 (0.8%); **Two or more races:** 82,061 (1.5%); **Hispanic/Latino:** 118,592 (2.1%). **2000 percent population 18 and over:** 74.5; **65 and over:** 13.5; **median age:** 36.1.

Hernando de Soto visited the Missouri area in 1541. France's claim to the entire region was based on Sieur de la Salle's travels in 1682. French fur traders established Ste. Genevieve in 1735, and St. Louis was first settled in 1764.

The U.S. gained Missouri from France as part of the Louisiana Purchase in 1803, and the territory was admitted as a state following the Missouri Compromise of 1820. Throughout the pre–Civil War period and during the war, Missourians were sharply divided in their opinions about slavery and in their allegiances, supplying both Union and Confederate forces with troops. However, the state itself remained in the Union.

Historically, Missouri played a leading role as a gateway to the West, St. Joseph being the eastern starting point of the Pony Express, while the much-traveled Santa Fe and Oregon trails began in Independence.

Missouri's economy is highly diversified. Service industries provide more income and jobs than any other segment, and include a growing tourism and travel sector. Wholesale and retail trade, manufacturing, and agriculture also play significant roles in the state's economy.

Missouri is a leading producer of transportation equipment (including automobile manufacturing and auto parts), beer and beverages, and defense and aerospace technology. Food processing is the state's fastest-growing industry.

Missouri mines produce 90% of the nation's principal (non-recycled) lead supply. Other natural resources include iron ore, zinc, barite, limestone, and timber.

The state's top agricultural products include grain, sorghum, hay, corn, soybeans, and rice. Missouri also ranks high among the states in cattle and calves, hogs, and turkeys and broilers. A vibrant wine industry also contributes to the economy.

Tourism draws hundreds of thousands of visitors to a number of Missouri points of interest: the country-music shows of Branson; Bass Pro Shops national headquarters (Springfield); the Gateway Arch at the Jefferson National Expansion (St. Louis); Mark Twain's boyhood home (Hannibal); the Harry S Truman home and library (Independence); the scenic beauty of the Ozark National Scenic Riverways; and the Pony Express and Jesse James museums (St. Joseph). The state's different lake regions also attract fishermen and sun-seekers from throughout the Midwest.

Selected famous natives and residents: Robert Altman, film director; Burt Bacharach, songwriter; Josephine Baker, singer and dancer; Wallace Beery, actor; Robert Russell Bennett, composer; Yogi Berra, baseball player; Thomas Hart Benton, painter; Bill Bradley, basketball player and N.J. senator; Omar N. Bradley, general; Grace Bumbry, soprano; William Burroughs, writer; Sarah Caldwell, opera director and conductor; Martha Jane Canary (Calamity Jane), frontierswoman; George Washington Carver, scientist; Don Cheadle, actor; Walter Cronkite, TV newscaster; Robert Cummings, actor; Jane Darwell, actress; Walt Disney, artist; T. S. Eliot, poet; Redd Foxx, actor and comedian; Betty Grable, actress; Dick Gregory, comic and activist; Jean Harlow, actress; Coleman Hawkins, jazz musician; George Hearn, actor; Edwin Hubble, astronomer; Langston Hughes, poet; John Huston, film director; Jesse James, outlaw; Scott Joplin, composer; Marianne Moore, poet; Geraldine Page, actress; James C. Penney, merchant; John Joseph Pershing, general; Vincent Price, actor; Joseph Pulitzer, journalist; Ginger Rogers, dancer and actress; Casey Stengel, baseball player; Gladys Swarthout, soprano; Sara Teasdale, poet; Virgil Thomson, composer; Harry S. Truman, president; Mark Twain, author; Dick Van Dyke, actor; Ruth Warrick, actress; Dennis Weaver, actor; Mary Wickes, actress; Laura Ingalls Wilder, author; Roy Wilkins, civil rights leader.

Montana

Capital: Helena
Governor: Brian Schweitzer, D (to Jan. 2009)
Lieut. Governor: John C. Bohlinger, D (to Jan. 2009)
Senators: Max Baucus, D (to Jan. 2009); Conrad R. Burns, R (to Jan. 2007)
U.S. Representatives: 1

Secy. of State: Brad Johnson R (to Jan. 2009)
Auditor: John Morrison, D (to Jan. 2009)
Atty. General: Mike McGrath, D (to Jan. 2009)
Organized as territory: May 26, 1864
Entered Union (rank): Nov. 8, 1889 (41)
Present constitution adopted: 1972
Motto: *Oro y plata* (Gold and silver)
State symbols: flower, bitterroot (1895); **tree,** ponderosa pine (1949); **stones,** sapphire and agate (1969); **bird,** Western meadowlark (1981); **song,** "Montana" (1945)
Nickname: Treasure State
Origin of name: Chosen from Latin dictionary by J. M. Ashley. It is a Latinized Spanish word meaning "mountainous."
10 largest cities (2003): Billings, 95,220; Missoula, 60,722; Great Falls, 56,155; Butte-Silver Bow,[1] 32,519; Bozeman, 30,753; Helena, 26,718; Kalispell, 16,391; Havre, 9,448; Anaconda–Deer Lodge County, 8,953; Miles City, 8,242
Land area: 145,552 sq mi. (376,980 sq km)
Geographic center: In Fergus Co., 11 mi. W of Lewistown
Number of counties: 56
Largest county by population and area: Yellowstone, 134,717 (2004); Beaverhead, 5,543 sq mi.
State parks: 42
Residents: Montanan
2004 resident population est.: 926,865
2000 resident census population (rank): 902,195 (44). **Male:** 449,480 (49.8%); **Female:** 452,715 (50.2%). **White:** 817,229 (90.6%); **Black:** 2,692 (0.3%); **American Indian:** 56,068 (6.2%); **Asian:** 4,691 (0.5%); **Other race:** 5,315 (0.6%); **Two or more races:** 15,730 (1.7%); **Hispanic/Latino:** 18,081 (2.0%). **2000 percent population 18 and over:** 74.5; **65 and over:** 13.4; **median age:** 37.5.

1. The city is part of a consolidated city-county government and is coextensive with Silver Bow County.

First explored for France by François and Louis-Joseph Verendrye in the early 1740s, much of the region was acquired by the U.S. from France as part of the Louisiana Purchase in 1803. Before western Montana was obtained from Great Britain in the Oregon Treaty of 1846, American trading posts and forts had been established in the territory.

The major Indian Wars (1867–1877) included the famous 1876 Battle of the Little Big Horn, better known as "Custer's Last Stand," in which Cheyenne and Sioux defeated George A. Custer and more than 200 of his men in southeast Montana.

Much of Montana's early history was concerned with mining, with copper, lead, zinc, silver, coal, and oil as principal products. Butte is the center of the area that once supplied half of the U.S. copper.

Fields of grain cover much of Montana's plains. It ranks high among the states in wheat and barley, with rye, oats, flaxseed, sugar beets, and potatoes as other important crops. Sheep and cattle raising make significant contributions to the economy.

Tourist attractions include hunting, fishing, skiing, and dude ranching. Glacier National Park, on the Continental Divide, has 60 glaciers, 200 lakes, and many streams with good trout fishing. Other major points of interest include the Little Bighorn Battlefield National Monument, Virginia City, Yellowstone National Park, Fort Union Trading Post and Grant-Kohr's Ranch National Historic Sites, and the Museum of the Plains Indians at Browning.

Selected famous natives and residents: Dorothy Baker, author; Dirk Benedict, actor; W. A. (Tony) Boyle, labor union official; Gary Cooper, actor; John Cowan, prospector and founder of Last Chance Gulch (now Helena); Alfred Bertram Guthrie, Pulitzer Prize–winning author; Chet Huntley, TV newscaster; Will James, writer and artist; Dorothy Johnson, author; Evel Knievel, daredevil motorcyclist; Myrna Loy, actress; David Lynch, filmmaker; Mike Mansfield, senator; George Montgomery, actor; Jeannette Rankin, first woman elected to Congress; Martha Raye, actress; Charles M. Russell, painter; Michael Smuin, choreographer; Lester C. Thurow, economist and educator.

Nebraska

Capital: Lincoln
Governor: David Heineman, R (to Jan. 2007)[1]
Lieut. Governor: Rick Sheehy, R (to Jan. 2007)
Senators: Charles Hagel, R (to Jan. 2009); Ben Nelson, D (to Jan. 2007)
U.S. Representatives: 3
Secy. of State: John Gale, R (to Jan. 2007)
Atty. General: Jon Bruning, R (to Jan. 2007)
Treasurer: Ron Ross, R (to Jan. 2007)
Organized as territory: May 30, 1854
Entered Union (rank): March 1, 1867 (37)
Present constitution adopted: Oct. 12, 1875 (extensively amended 1919–20)
Motto: Equality before the law
State symbols: flower, goldenrod (1895); **fish,** channel catfish (1997); **American folk dance,** square dance (1997); **ballad,** "A Place Like Nebraska" (1997); **tree,** cottonwood (1972); **bird,** Western meadowlark (1929); **insect,** honeybee (1975); **gemstone,** blue agate (1967); **rock,** prairie agate (1967); **fossil,** mammoth (1967); **song,** "Beautiful Nebraska" (1967); **soil,** typic argiustolls, holdreges series (1979); **mammal,** whitetail deer (1981); **grass,** little bluestem (1969); **beverage,** milk (1998)
Nicknames: Cornhusker State (1945); Beef State
Origin of name: From an Oto Indian word meaning "flat water"
10 largest cities (2003 est.): Omaha, 404,267; Lincoln, 235,594; Bellevue, 46,734; Grand Island, 43,771; Kearney, 28,211; Fremont, 25,198; Norfolk, 24,061; North Platte, 23,924; Hastings, 23,536; Columbus, 20,880
Land area: 76,872 sq mi. (199,098 sq km)
Geographic center: In Custer Co., 10 mi. NW of Broken Bow
Number of counties: 93
Largest county by population and area: Douglas, 482,112 (2004); Cherry, 5,961 sq mi.
State parks: 87
Residents: Nebraskan
2004 resident population est.: 1,747,214
2000 resident census population (rank): 1,711,263 (38). **Male:** 843,351 (49.3%); **Female:** 867,912 (50.7%). **White:** 1,533,261 (89.6%); **Black:** 68,541 (4.0%); **American Indian:** 14,896 (0.9%); **Asian:** 21,931 (1.3%); **Other race:** 47,845 (2.8%); **Two or more races:** 23,953 (1.4%); **Hispanic/Latino:** 94,425 (5.5%). **2000 percent population 18 and over:** 73.7; **65 and over:** 13.6; **median age:** 35.3.

1. Mike Johanns left in Jan. 2005 to become Secretary of Agriculture. Lieutenant governor David Heineman became governor and appointed former Hastings mayor Rick Sheehy as the new lieutenant governor.

French fur traders first visited Nebraska in the late 1600s. Part of the Louisiana Purchase in 1803, eastern Nebraska was explored by Lewis and Clark in 1804–1806. A few years later, Robert Stuart pioneered the Oregon Trail across Nebraska in 1812–1813, and the first permanent white settlement was established at Bellevue in 1823.

Western Nebraska was acquired by treaty following the Mexican War in 1848. The Union Pacific began its transcontinental railroad at Omaha in 1865. In 1937, Nebraska became the only-state in the Union to have a unicameral (one-house) legislature. Members are elected to it without party designation.

Nebraska is a leading grain-producer with bumper crops of sorghum, corn, and wheat. More varieties of grass, valuable for forage, grow in this state than in any other in the nation. The state's sizable cattle and hog industries make Dakota City and Lexington among the nation's largest meat-packing centers.

Manufacturing has become diversified: Firms making electronic components, auto accessories, pharmaceuticals, and mobile homes have joined such older industries as clothing, farm machinery, chemicals, and transportation equipment. Oil was discovered in 1939 and natural gas in 1949.

Among the principal attractions are Agate Fossil Beds, Homestead, and Scotts Bluff National Monuments; Chimney Rock National Historic Site; a recreated pioneer village at Minden; Boys Town; the Sheldon Memorial Art Gallery and the Lied Center for the Performing Arts at the University of Nebraska in Lincoln; the State Capitol in Lincoln; the Joslyn Art Museum in Omaha; the Henry Doorly Zoo in Omaha; Museum of Nebraska Art in Kearney; Museum of Nebraska History in Lincoln; and the University of Nebraska State Museum in Lincoln.

Selected famous natives and residents: Grace Abbott, social worker; Bess Streeter Aldrich, author; Grover Cleveland Alexander, baseball pitcher; Fred Astaire, dancer and actor; Max Baer, boxer; Bil Baird, puppeteer; George Beadle, geneticist; Marlon Brando, actor; William Jennings Bryan, political leader; Warren Buffett, investor; Johnny Carson, TV host; Willa Cather, author; Dick Cavett, TV entertainer; Richard B. Cheney, vice president; Montgomery Clift, actor; James Coburn, actor; William "Buffalo Bill" Cody, showman; Sandy Dennis, actress; Mignon Eberhart, author; Harold "Doc" Edgerton, inventor; Ruth Etting, singer and actress; Fr. Edward J. Flanagan, founder of Boys Town; Henry Fonda, actor; Gerald Ford, former president; Bob Gibson, baseball player; Howard Hanson, conductor; Leland Hayward, producer; Marlon Henri, painter; David Janssen, actor; Francis La Flesche, ethnologist; Melvin Laird, politician; Frank W. Leahy, football coach; Harold Lloyd, actor; Malcolm X, civil rights advocate; Dorothy McGuire, actress; Julius Sterling Morton, politician and journalist; John G. Neihardt, epic poet; Nick Nolte, actor; George W. Norris, senator; John J. Pershing, army general; Nathan Roscoe Pound, educator and botanist; Red Cloud, Indian rights advocate; Mari Sandoz, author; Standing Bear, Indian rights advocate; Robert Taylor, actor; Susette La Flesche Tibbles, Omaha Indian activist; Paul Williams, singer, composer, and actor; Julie Wilson, singer and actress; Darryl F. Zanuck, film producer.

Nevada

Capital: Carson City
Governor: Kenny Guinn, R (to Jan. 2007)
Lieut. Governor: Lorraine Hunt, R (to Jan. 2007)
Senators: Harry Reid, D (to Jan. 2011); John Ensign, R (to Jan. 2007)
U.S. Representatives: 3
Secy. of State: Dean Heller, R (to Jan. 2007)
Treasurer: Brian Krolicki, R (to Jan. 2007)
Atty. General: Brian Sandoval, R (to Jan. 2007)
Organized as territory: March 2, 1861
Entered Union (rank): Oct. 31, 1864 (36)
Present constitution adopted: 1864
Motto: All for Our Country
State symbols: flower, sagebrush (1959); **trees,** single-leaf pinon (1953) and bristlecone pine (1987); **bird,** mountain bluebird (1967); **animal,** desert bighorn sheep (1973); **colors,** silver and blue (1983); **song,** "Home Means Nevada" (1933); **rock,** sandstone

(1987); **precious gemstone,** virgin valley black fire opal (1987); **semiprecious gemstone,** Nevada turquoise (1987); **grass,** Indian ricegrass (1977); **metal,** silver (1977); **fossil,** ichthyosaur (1977); **fish,** lahontan cutthroat trout (1981); **reptile,** desert tortoise (1989); **state artifact,** tule duck decoy (1995)
Nicknames: Sagebrush State; Silver State; Battle Born State
Origin of name: Spanish: "snowcapped"
10 largest cities (2003 est.): Las Vegas, 517,017; Henderson, 214,852; Reno, 193,882; North Las Vegas, 144,502; Sparks, 77,295; Carson City, 55,311; Elko, 16,075; Boulder City, 15,314; Mesquite, 11,780; Fernley, 10,047
Land area: 109,826 sq mi. (284,449 sq km)
Geographic center: In Lander Co., 26 mi. SE of Austin
Number of counties: 16, plus 1 independent city
Largest county by population and area: Clark, 1,650,671 (2004); Nye, 18,147 sq mi.
State parks: 24
Residents: Nevadan, Nevadian
2004 resident population est.: 2,334,771
2000 resident census population (rank): 1,998,257 (35). **Male:** 1,018,051 (50.9%); **Female:** 980,206 (49.1%). **White:** 1,501,886 (75.2%); **Black:** 135,477 (6.8%); **American Indian:** 26,420 (1.3%); **Asian:** 90,266 (4.5%); **Other race:** 159,354 (8.0%); **Two or more races:** 76,428 (3.8%); **Hispanic/Latino:** 393,970 (19.7%). **2000 percent population 18 and over:** 74.4; **65 and over:** 11.0; **median age:** 35.0.

Trappers and traders, including Jedediah Smith and Peter Skene Ogden, entered the Nevada area in the 1820s. In 1843–1845, John C. Frémont and Kit Carson explored the Great Basin and Sierra Nevada. The U.S. obtained the region in 1848 following the Mexican War, and the first permanent settlement was a Mormon trading post near present-day Genoa.

The driest state in the nation, with an average annual rainfall of only about 7 in., much of Nevada is uninhabited, sagebrush-covered desert. The wettest part of the state receives about 40 in. of precipitation per year, while the driest spot has less than 4 in. per year.

Nevada was made famous by the discovery of the Comstock Lode, the richest known U.S. silver deposit, in 1859, and its mines have produced large quantities of gold, silver, copper, lead, zinc, mercury, barite, and tungsten. Oil was discovered in 1954. Gold now far exceeds all other minerals in value of production.

In 1931, the state created two industries, divorce and gambling. For many years, Reno and Las Vegas were the "divorce capitals of the nation." More liberal divorce laws in many states have ended this distinction, but Nevada is still the gambling capital of the U.S. and a leading entertainment center. State gambling taxes account for 34.1% of general fund tax revenues.

The state's leading agricultural industry is cattle and calves. Agricultural crops consist mainly of hay, alfalfa seed, barley, wheat, and potatoes.

Nevada manufactures gaming equipment; lawn and garden irrigation devices; titanium products; seismic and machinery monitoring devices; and specialty printing.

Lake Tahoe, Reno, and Las Vegas are major resorts. Recreation areas include Pyramid Lake, Lake Tahoe, and Lake Mead and Lake Mohave, both in

Lake Mead National Recreation Area. Other attractions are Hoover Dam, Virginia City, and Great Basin National Park (includes Lehman Caves).

Selected famous natives and residents: Eva Adams, director of U.S. Mint; Andre Agassi, tennis player; Raymond T. Baker, director of U.S. Mint; Helen Delich Bentley, government official and newspaperwoman; Robert Caples, painter; Walter Van Tilburg Clark, writer; Henry Comstock, prospector; Abby Dalton; actress; Michele Greene, actress; Sarah Winnemucca Hopkins, author and Paiute interpreter and peacemaker; Jack Kramer, tennis player; Paul Laxalt, politician; Robert Laxalt, writer; William Lear, aviation inventor; Robert C. Lynch, surgeon; John W. Mackay, benefactor, one of Big Four of Comstock Lode; Emma Nevada, opera singer; Thelma "Pat" Nixon, first lady; James W. Nye, territory governor and senator; Lute Pease, cartoonist and Pulitzer Prize winner; Edna Purviance, actress; Patty Sheehan, golfer; Jack Wilson, Paiute Indian prophet; George Wingfield, mining millionaire.

New Hampshire

Capital: Concord
Governor: John Lynch, D (to Jan. 2007)
Senators: Judd Gregg, R (to Jan. 2011); John E. Sununu, R (to Jan. 2009)
U.S. Representatives: 2
Treasurer: Michael Ablowich, R (to Dec. 2008)
Secy. of State: William M. Gardner, D (to Dec. 2008)
Atty. General: Kelly Ayotte, R (to March 2009)
Entered Union (rank): June 21, 1788 (9)
Present constitution adopted: 1784
Motto: Live free or die
State symbols: flower, purple lilac (1919); **tree,** white birch (1947); **animal,** white-tailed deer (1983); **insect,** ladybug (1977); **saltwater fish,** striped bass (1994); **freshwater fish,** brook trout (1995); **amphibian,** spotted newt (1985); **butterfly,** karner blue (1992); **bird,** purple finch (1957); **songs,** "Old New Hampshire" (1949) and "New Hampshire, My New Hampshire" (1963)
Nickname: Granite State
Origin of name: From the English county of Hampshire
10 largest cities (2003 est.): Manchester, 108,871; Nashua, 87,285; Concord, 41,823; Derry, 34,471; Rochester, 29,654; Salem, 29,115; Dover, 28,216; Merrimack, 26,394; Londonderry, 24,201; Hudson, 23,839
Land area: 8,968 sq mi. (23,227 sq km)
Geographic center: In Belknap Co., 3 mi. E of Ashland
Number of counties: 10
Largest county by population and area: Hillsborough, 398,574 (2004); Coos, 1,801 sq mi.
State parks: 65 (50,000+ ac.)
Residents: New Hampshirite
2004 resident population est.: 1,299,500
2000 resident census population (rank): 1,235,786 (41). **Male:** 607,687 (49.2%); **Female:** 628,099 (50.8%). **White:** 1,186,851 (96.0%); **Black:** 9,035 (0.7%); **American Indian:** 2,964 (0.2%); **Asian:** 15,931 (1.3%); **Other race:** 7,420 (0.6%); **Two or more races:** 13,214 (1.1%); **Hispanic/Latino:** 20,489 (1.7%). **2000 percent population 18 and over:** 75.0; **65 and over:** 12.0; **median age:** 37.1.

Under an English land grant, Capt. John Smith sent settlers to establish a fishing colony at the mouth of the Piscataqua River, near present-day Rye and Dover, in 1623. Capt. John Mason, who participated in the founding of Portsmouth in 1630, gave New Hampshire its name.

After a 38-year period of union with Massachusetts, New Hampshire was made a separate royal colony in 1679. As leaders in the revolutionary cause, New Hampshire delegates received the honor of being the first to vote for the Declaration of Independence on July 4, 1776. New Hampshire gained a measure of international attention in 1905 when Portsmouth Naval Base played host to the signing of the treaty ending the Russo-Japanese War, known as the Treaty of Portsmouth.

Abundant water power turned New Hampshire into an industrial state early on, and manufacturing is the principal source of income. The most important industrial products are electrical and other machinery, textiles, pulp and paper products, and stone and clay products. Dairy and poultry, and growing fruit, truck vegetables, corn, potatoes, and hay are the major agricultural pursuits.

Because of New Hampshire's scenic and recreational resources, tourism now brings over $3.5 billion into the state annually.

Vacation attractions include Lake Winnipesaukee, largest of 1,300 lakes and ponds; the 724,000-acre White Mountain National Forest; Daniel Webster's birthplace near Franklin; and Strawbery Banke, restored buildings of the original settlement at Portsmouth. In 2003, the famous "Old Man of the Mountain" granite head profile, the state's official emblem, fell from its perch in Franconia.

Selected famous natives and residents: Sherman Adams, former governor and presidential advisor; Salmon P. Chase, jurist; Charles Anderson Dana, editor; Mary Baker Eddy, founder of the Christian Science Church; Dustin Farnum, actor; Thomas Green Fessenden, journalist and satirical poet; Daniel Chester French, sculptor; Robert Frost, poet; Horace Greeley, journalist and politician; Sarah J. Hale, editor; John Irving, writer; Benjamin F. Keith, theater entrepreneur; Jackson Hall Kelly, promoter of Oregon settlement; John Langdon, political leader; Sharon Christa McAuliffe, teacher and astronaut; Franklin Pierce, former president; Augustus Saint-Gaudens, sculptor; Alan Shepard, astronaut; Harlan F. Stone, jurist; Daniel Webster, statesman; Henry Wilson, politician and former vice president; Noah Worcester, clergyman and pacifist.

New Jersey

Capital: Trenton
Acting Governor: Richard Codey,[1] D (to Jan. 2006)
Senators: Frank R. Lautenberg, D (to Jan. 2009); Jon Corzine, D (to Jan. 2007)
U.S. Representatives: 13
Secy. of State: Regena L. Thomas (to Jan. 2006)
Treasurer: John E. McCormac
Atty. General: Peter C. Harvey, I (to Jan. 2006)
Entered Union (rank): Dec. 18, 1787 (3)
Present constitution adopted: 1947
Motto: Liberty and prosperity
State symbols: flower, purple violet (1913); **bird,** eastern goldfinch (1935); **insect,** honeybee (1974); **tree,** red oak (1950); **animal,** horse (1977); **colors,** buff and blue (1965); **folk dance,** square dance; **dinosaur,** hadrosaurus foulkii; **fish,** brook trout; **shell,** knobbed whelk; **fruit,** blueberry (2004)
Nickname: Garden State
Origin of name: From the Channel Isle of Jersey
10 largest cities (2003 est.): Newark, 277,911; Jersey City, 239,097; Paterson, 150,782; Elizabeth, 123,215; Woodbridge, 100,866; Edison, 100,138; Dover, 93,671; Hamilton, 89,632; Trenton, 85,314; Camden, 80,089
Land area: 7,417 sq mi. (19,210 sq km)
Geographic center: In Mercer Co., 5 mi. SE of Trenton
Number of counties: 21
Largest county by population and area: Bergen, 902,998 (2004); Burlington, 805 sq mi.
State parks: 39
Residents: New Jerseyite, New Jerseyan

2004 resident population est.: 8,698,879
2000 resident census population (rank): 8,414,350 (9). **Male:** 4,082,813 (48.5%); **Female:** 4,331,537 (51.5%). **White:** 6,104,705 (72.6%); **Black:** 1,141,821 (13.6%); **American Indian:** 19,492 (0.2%); **Asian:** 480,276 (5.7%); **Other race:** 450,972 (5.4%); **Two or more races:** 213,755 (2.5%); **Hispanic/Latino:** 1,117,191 (13.3%). **2000 percent population 18 and over:** 75.2; **65 and over:** 13.2; **median age:** 36.7.

1. Jim McGreevey resigned in Aug. 2004, effective Nov. 15. Richard Codey, president of the Senate, became acting governor.

New Jersey's early colonial history was involved with that of New York (New Netherlands), of which it was a part. One year after the Dutch surrender to England in 1664, New Jersey was organized as an English colony under Gov. Philip Carteret.

In 1676 the colony was divided between Carteret and a company of English Quakers who had obtained the rights belonging to John, Lord Berkeley. New Jersey became a united crown colony in 1702, administered by the royal governor of New York. Finally, in 1738, New Jersey was separated from New York under its own royal governor, Lewis Morris. Because of its key location between New York City and Philadelphia, New Jersey saw much fighting during the American Revolution.

Today, New Jersey, an area of wide industrial diversification, is known as the Crossroads of the East. Products from over 15,000 factories can be delivered overnight to almost 60 million people, representing 12 states and the District of Columbia. The greatest single industry is chemicals; New Jersey is one of the foremost research centers in the world. Many large oil refineries are located in northern New Jersey. Other important manufactured items are pharmaceuticals, instruments, machinery, electrical goods, and apparel.

Productive farmland covers nearly one million acres, about 20% of New Jersey's land area. The state ranks high in the production of almost all garden vegetables, as well as cranberries, blueberries, and peaches. Poultry, dairy products, and seafood are also top commodities.

Tourism is the second-largest industry in New Jersey. The state has numerous resort areas on 127 mi of Atlantic coastline. In 1977, New Jersey voters approved legislation allowing legalized casino gambling in Atlantic City. Points of interest include the Delaware Water Gap, the Edison National Historic Site in West Orange, Princeton University, Liberty State Park, Jersey City, and the N.J. State Aquarium in Camden.

Selected famous natives and residents: Bud Abbott, comedian; Charles Addams, cartoonist; Edwin Aldrin, astronaut; Count Basie, band leader; Joan Bennett, actress; Jon Bon Jovi, musician; Zach Braff, actor, director; William J. Brennan, jurist; Aaron Burr, political leader; James Fenimore Cooper, novelist; Lou Costello, comedian; Stephen Crane, writer; Helen Gahagan Douglas, representative; Allen Ginsberg, poet; William Frederick Halsey, Jr., admiral; Alfred Joyce Kilmer, poet; Ernie Kovacs, comedian; Jerry Lewis, comedian and film director; Anne Morrow Lindbergh, author; Norman Mailer, novelist; Patricia McBride, ballerina; Richard Nixon, president; Dorothy Parker, author; Joe Piscopo, comedian and actor; Paul Robeson, singer and actor; Philip Roth, novelist; Ruth St. Denis, dancer and choreographer; Antonin Scalia, jurist; H. Norman Schwarzkopf, general; Frank Sinatra, singer and actor; Bruce Springsteen, musician; Alfred Stieglitz, photographer; Albert Payson Terhune, journalist and novelist; Sarah Vaughan, singer; William Carlos Williams, physician and poet; Bruce Willis, actor; Edmund Wilson, literary critic and author.

New Mexico

Capital: Santa Fe
Governor: Bill Richardson, D (to Jan. 2007)
Lieut. Governor: Diane Denish, D (to Jan. 2007)
Senators: Jeff Bingaman, D (to Jan. 2007);
Pete V. Domenici, R (to Jan. 2009)
U.S. Representatives: 3
Secy. of State: Rebecca Vigil-Giron, D (to Jan. 2007)
Atty. General: Patricia A. Madrid, D (to Jan. 2007)
State Treasurer: Robert E. Vigil, D (to Jan. 2007)
Organized as territory: Sept. 9, 1850
Entered Union (rank): Jan. 6, 1912 (47)
Present constitution adopted: 1911
Motto: *Crescit eundo* (It grows as it goes)
State symbols: flower, yucca (1927); **tree,** pinon (1949); **animal,** black bear (1963); **bird,** roadrunner (1949); **fish,** cutthroat trout (1955); **vegetables,** chili and frijol (1965); **gem,** turquoise (1967); **song,** "O Fair New Mexico" (1917); **Spanish-language song,** "Asi Es Nuevo Méjico" (1971); **poem,** "A Nuevo México" (1991); **grass,** blue gramma (1973); **fossil,** coelophysis (1981); **cookie,** bizcochito (1989); **insect,** tarantula hawk wasp (1989); **ballad,** "Land of Enchantment" (1989); **bilingual song,** "New Mexico—Mi Lindo Nuevo Mexico", (1995); **question,** "Red or Green?" (1999)
Nickname: Land of Enchantment (1999)
Origin of name: From Mexico, "place of Mexitli," an Aztec god or leader
10 largest cities (2003 est.): Albuquerque, 471,856; Las Cruces, 76,990; Santa Fe, 66,476; Rio Rancho, 58,981; Roswell, 44,228; Farmington, 41,420; Alamogordo, 35,551; Clovis, 32,815; Hobbs, 28,311; Carlsbad, 25,303
Land area: 121,356 sq mi. (314,312 sq km)
Geographic center: In Torrance Co., 12 mi. SSW of Willard
Number of counties: 33
Largest county by population and area: Bernalillo, 593,765 (2004); Catron, 6,928 sq mi.
State parks: 32
Residents: New Mexican
2004 resident population est.: 1,903,289
2000 resident census population (rank): 1,819,046 (36). **Male:** 894,317 (49.2%); **Female:** 924,729 (50.8%). **White:** 1,214,253 (66.8%); **Black:** 34,343 (1.9%); **American Indian:** 173,483 (9.5%); **Asian:** 19,255 (1.1%); **Other race:** 309,882 (17.0%); **Two or more races:** 66,327 (3.6%); **Hispanic/Latino:** 765,386 (42.1%). **2000 percent population 18 and over:** 72.0; **65 and over:** 11.7; **median age:** 34.6.

Francisco Vásquez de Coronado, a Spanish explorer searching for gold, traveled the region that became New Mexico in 1540–1542. In 1598 the first Spanish settlement was established on the Rio Grande River by Juan de Onate; in 1610 Santa Fe was founded and made the capital of New Mexico.

The U.S. acquired most of New Mexico in 1848, as a result of the Mexican War, and the remainder in the 1853 Gadsden Purchase. Union troops captured the territory from the Confederates during the Civil War. With the surrender of Geronimo in 1886, the Apache Wars and most of the Indian conflicts in the area were ended.

Since 1945, New Mexico has been a leader in energy research and development with extensive experiments conducted at Los Alamos Scientific Laboratory and Sandia Laboratories in the nuclear, solar, and geothermal areas.

Minerals are the state's richest natural resource, and New Mexico is one of the U.S. leaders in output of uranium and potassium salts. Petroleum, natural gas, copper, gold, silver, zinc, lead, and molybdenum also contribute heavily to the state's income.

The principal manufacturing industries include food products, chemicals, transportation equipment, lumber, electrical machinery, and stone-clay-glass products. More than two-thirds of New Mexico's farm income comes from livestock products, especially sheep. Cotton, pecans, and sorghum are the most important field crops. Corn, peanuts, beans, onions, chilies, and lettuce are also grown.

Tourist attractions include the Carlsbad Caverns National Park, Inscription Rock at El Morro National Monument, the ruins at Fort Union, Billy the Kid mementos at Lincoln, the White Sands and Gila Cliff Dwellings National Monuments, Bandelier National Monument, and the Chaco Culture National Historical Park.

Selected famous natives and residents: Kathy Baker, actress; Notah Begay III, golfer; Judy Blume, author; Ernest L. Blumenshein, artist; William "Billy the Kid" Bonney, outlaw; Richard Bradford, author; Ralph Bunche, Nobel Peace Prize winner; Bruce Cabot, actor; Glen Campbell, singer; Kit Carson, army scout and trapper; Dennis Chavez, former senator; John Chisum, cattle king; Mangus Coloradas, Apache leader; Edward Condon, physicist; Bill Daily, actor; John Denver, singer; Bo Diddley, blues guitarist; Patrick Garrett, lawman; Greer Garson, actress; Sid Gutierrez, astronaut; William Hanna, animator; Neil Patrick Harris, actor; Carl Hatch, senator; Tony Hillerman, author; Conrad Hilton, hotel executive; Dennis Hopper, actor; Peter Hurd, artist; Preston Jones, playwright and actor; Ralph Kiner, baseball player and sportscaster; Nancy Lopez, golfer; Maria Martínez, San Ildefonso Pueblo potter; Demi Moore, actress; Jim Morrison, singer and songwriter; Bill Mauldin, political cartoonist; Popé, San Juan Pueblo medicine man and leader; Georgia O'Keeffe, painter; Harrison Schmitt, astronaut and representative; Kim Stanley, actress; Slim Summerville, actor; Clyde Tombaugh, astronomer; Al Unser, Bobby Unser, auto racers; Victorio, Apache chief; Linda Wertheimer, NPR correspondent; Kathy Whitworth, golfer.

New York

Capital: Albany
Governor: George E. Pataki, R (to Jan. 2007)
Lieut. Governor: Mary Donohue, R (to Jan. 2007)
Senators: Charles E. Schumer, D (to Jan. 2011); Hillary Rodham Clinton, D (to Jan. 2007)
U.S. Representatives: 29
Secy. of State: Randy A. Daniels, R (apptd. by governor)
Comptroller: Alan G. Hevesi, D (to Jan. 2007)
Atty. General: Eliot Spitzer, D (to Jan. 2007)
Entered Union (rank): July 26, 1788 (11)
Present constitution adopted: 1777 (last revised 1938)
Motto: *Excelsior* (Ever upward)
State symbols: animal, beaver (1975); **fish,** brook trout (1975); **gem,** garnet (1969); **flower,** rose (1955); **tree,** sugar maple (1956); **bird,** bluebird (1970); **insect,** ladybug (1989); **song,** "I Love New York" (1980)
Nickname: Empire State
Origin of name: In honor of the Duke of York
10 largest cities (2003 est.): New York, 8,085,742; Buffalo, 285,018; Rochester, 215,093; Yonkers, 197,388; Syracuse, 144,001; Albany, 93,919; New Rochelle, 72,582; Mount Vernon, 68,404; Schenectady, 61,016; Utica, 59,485
Land area: 47,214 sq mi. (122,284 sq km)
Geographic center: In Madison Co., 12 mi. S of Oneida and 26 mi. SW of Utica
Number of counties: 62
Largest county by population and area: Kings, 2,475,290 (2004); St. Lawrence, 2,686 sq mi.
State parks: 168
Residents: New Yorker

2004 resident population est.: 19,227,088
2000 resident census population (rank): 18,976,457 (3). **Male:** 9,146,748 (48.2%); **Female:** 9,829,709 (51.8%). **White:** 12,893,689 (67.9%); **Black:** 3,014,385 (15.9%); **American Indian:** 82,461 (0.4%); **Asian:** 1,044,976 (5.5%); **Other race:** 1,341,946 (7.1%); **Two or more races:** 590,182 (3.1%); **Hispanic/Latino:** 2,867,583 (15.1%). **2000 percent population 18 and over:** 75.3; **65 and over:** 12.9; **median age:** 35.9.

Giovanni da Verrazano, an Italian-born navigator sailing for France, discovered New York Bay in 1524. Henry Hudson, an Englishman employed by the Dutch, reached the bay and sailed up the river now bearing his name in 1609, the same year that northern New York was explored and claimed for France by Samuel de Champlain.

In 1624 the first permanent Dutch settlement was established at Fort Orange (now Albany). One year later Peter Minuit purchased Manhattan Island from the Indians for trinkets worth about 60 Dutch guilders and founded the Dutch colony of New Amsterdam (now New York City), which was surrendered to the English in 1664.

New York's extremely rapid commercial growth may be partly attributed to Gov. De Witt Clinton, who pushed through the construction of the Erie Canal (Buffalo to Albany), which was opened in 1825. Today, the 641-mile Gov. Thomas E. Dewey Thruway connects New York City with Buffalo and with Connecticut, Massachusetts, and Pennsylvania express highways. Two toll-free superhighways, the Adirondack Northway (linking Albany with the Canadian border) and the North-South Expressway (crossing central New York from the Pennsylvania border to the Thousand Islands), have been opened.

The great metropolis of New York City is the nerve center of the nation. It is a leader in manufacturing, foreign trade, commerce and banking, book and magazine publishing, and theatrical production. A leading seaport, its John F. Kennedy International Airport is one of the busiest airports in the world. New York is also home to the New York Stock Exchange, the largest in the world. The printing and publishing industry is the city's largest manufacturing employer, with the apparel industry second.

Nearly all the rest of the state's manufacturing is done on Long Island, along the Hudson River north to Albany, and through the Mohawk Valley, Central New York, and Southern Tier regions to Buffalo. The St. Lawrence seaway and power projects have opened the North Country to industrial expansion and have given the state a second seacoast.

The state ranks seventh in the nation in manufacturing, with 805,200 employees in 2002. The principal industries are printing and publishing, industrial machinery and equipment, electronic equipment, and instruments. The convention and tourist business is also an important source of income.

New York farms produce cattle and calves, corn and poultry, and vegetables and fruits. The state is a leading wine producer.

Major points of interest are Castle Clinton, Fort Stanwix, and Statue of Liberty National Monuments; Niagara Falls; U.S. Military Academy at West Point; National Historic Sites that include homes of Franklin D. Roosevelt at Hyde Park and Theodore Roosevelt in Oyster Bay and New York City; the Women's Rights National Historical Park in Seneca Falls; National Memorials, including Grant's Tomb and Federal Hall in New York City; Fort Ticonderoga; the Baseball Hall of Fame in Cooperstown; and the United Nations, skyscrapers, museums, theaters, and parks in New York City.

Selected famous natives and residents: Kareem Abdul-Jabbar, basketball player; Lucille Ball, actress; Humphrey Bogart, actor; James Cagney, actor; Maria Callas, opera singer; Benjamin N. Cardozo, jurist; Paddy Chayefsky, playwright; Peter Cooper, industrialist and philanthropist; Aaron Copland, composer; Tom Cruise, actor; Sammy Davis, Jr., actor and singer; Agnes de Mille, choreographer; Eamon De Valera, president of Ireland; George Eastman, inventor; Millard Fillmore, president; Lou Gehrig, baseball player; George Gershwin, composer; Learned Hand, jurist; Edward Hopper, painter; Julia Ward Howe, poet and reformer; Charles Evans Hughes, jurist; Washington Irving, author; Henry James, novelist; John Jay, jurist; Michael Jordan, basketball player; Jerome Kern, composer; Rockwell Kent, painter; Vince Lombardi, football coach; Chico, Groucho, Harpo, and Zeppo Marx, comedians; Herman Melville, author; Ethel Merman, singer and actress; Ogden Nash, poet; Rosie O'Donnell, comedian; Eugene O'Neill, playwright; Red Jacket, Seneca chief; John D. Rockefeller, industrialist; Norman Rockwell, painter and illustrator; Mickey Rooney, actor; Anna Eleanor Roosevelt, reformer and humanitarian; Franklin D. Roosevelt, president; Theodore Roosevelt, president; Jonas Salk, polio researcher; Margaret Sanger, birth control advocate; Beverly Sills, opera singer; Barbara Stanwyck, actress; Risë Stevens, opera singer; Joe Torre, baseball player and manager; Richard Tucker, tenor; Martin Van Buren, president; Mae West, actress; Walt Whitman, poet; Edith Wharton, novelist.

North Carolina

Capital: Raleigh
Governor: Mike Easley, D (to Jan. 2009)
Lieut. Governor: Beverly Perdue, D (to Jan. 2009)
Senators: Richard Burr, R (to Jan. 2011);
   Elizabeth Dole, R (to Jan. 2009)
U.S. Representatives: 13
Secy. of State: Elaine F. Marshall, D (to Jan. 2009)
Treasurer: Richard H. Moore, D (to Jan. 2009)
Atty. General: Roy Cooper, D (to Jan. 2009)
Entered Union (rank): Nov. 21, 1789 (12)
Present constitution adopted: 1971
Motto: *Esse quam videri* (To be rather than to seem)
State symbols: flower, dogwood (1941); **tree,** pine (1963); **bird,** cardinal (1943); **mammal,** gray squirrel (1969); **insect,** honeybee (1973); **reptile,** eastern box turtle (1979); **gemstone,** emerald (1973); **shell,** scotch bonnet (1965); **historic boat,** shad boat (1987); **beverage,** milk (1987); **rock,** granite (1979); **dog,** plott hound (1989); **song,** "The Old North State" (1927); **colors,** red and blue (1945); **fruit,** scuppernong grape (2001)
Nickname: Tar Heel State
Origin of name: In honor of Charles I of England
10 largest cities (2003 est.): Charlotte, 584,658; Raleigh, 316,802; Greensboro, 229,110; Durham, 198,376; Winston-Salem, 190,299; Fayetteville, 124,372; Cary, 99,824; High Point, 91,543; Wilmington, 91,137; Asheville, 69,045
Land area: 48,711 sq mi. (126,161 sq km)
Geographic center: In Chatham Co., 10 mi. NW of Sanford
Number of counties: 100
Largest county by population and area: Mecklenburg, 771,617 (2004); Robeson, 949 sq mi.
State parks: 29
Residents: North Carolinian
2004 resident population est.: 8,541,221
2000 resident census population (rank): 8,049,313 (11). **Male:** 3,942,695 (49.0%); **Female:** 4,106,618 (51.0%). **White:** 5,804,656 (72.1%); **Black:** 1,737,545 (21.6%); **American Indian:** 99,551 (1.2%); **Asian:**

113,689 (1.4%); **Other race:** 186,629 (2.3%); **Two or more races:** 103,260 (1.3%); **Hispanic/Latino:** 378,963 (4.7%). **2000 percent population 18 and over:** 75.6; **65 and over:** 12.0; **median age:** 35.3.

English colonists, sent by Sir Walter Raleigh, unsuccessfully attempted to settle Roanoke Island in 1585 and 1587. Virginia Dare, born there in 1587, was the first child of English parentage born in America.

In 1653 the first permanent settlements were established by English colonists from Virginia near the Roanoke and Chowan rivers. The region was established as an English proprietary colony in 1663–1665 and in its early history was the scene of Culpeper's Rebellion (1677), the Quaker-led Cary Rebellion (1708), the Tuscarora Indian War (1711–1713), and many pirate raids.

During the American Revolution, there was relatively little fighting within the state, but many North Carolinians saw action elsewhere. Despite considerable pro-Union, antislavery sentiment, North Carolina joined the Confederacy during the Civil War.

North Carolina is the nation's largest furniture, tobacco, brick, and textile producer. Metalworking, chemicals, and paper are also important industries. The major agricultural products are tobacco, corn, cotton, hay, peanuts, and vegetable crops. The state is the country's leading producer of mica and lithium.

Tourism is also important, with visitors spending more than $1 billion annually. Sports include year-round golfing, skiing at mountain resorts, both fresh- and salt-water fishing, and hunting.

Among the major attractions are the Great Smoky Mountains, the Blue Ridge National Parkway, the Cape Hatteras and Cape Lookout National Seashores, the Wright Brothers National Memorial at Kitty Hawk, Guilford Courthouse and Moores Creek National Military Parks, Carl Sandburg's home near Hendersonville, and the Old Salem Restoration in Winston-Salem.

Selected famous natives and residents: David Brinkley, TV newscaster; Howard Cosell, sportscaster; Virginia Dare, first person born in America to English parents; Elizabeth Dole, government official; James B. Duke, industrialist; Donna Fargo, singer; Roberta Flack, singer; Ava Gardner, actress; Richard Gatling, inventor; Billy Graham, evangelist; Kathryn Grayson, singer and actress; Andy Griffith, actor; Jesse Helms, politician; O. Henry, writer; Barbara Howar, broadcaster and writer; Andrew Johnson, president; Charles Kuralt, TV journalist; Sugar Ray Leonard, boxer; Dolley Madison, first lady; Ronnie Milsap, singer; Thelonious Monk, pianist; Alfred Moore, jurist; Edward R. Murrow, commentator and government official; Walter Hines Page, journalist and ambassador; Floyd Patterson, boxer; Richard Petty, auto racer; James K. Polk, president; Soupy Sales, comedian; Earl Scruggs, bluegrass musician; Randy Travis, musician; John Scott Trotter, orchestra leader; Thomas Wolfe, novelist.

North Dakota

Capital: Bismarck
Governor: John Hoeven, R (to Dec. 15, 2008)
Lieut. Governor: Jack Dalrymple, R (to Dec. 15, 2008)
Senators: Kent Conrad, D (to Jan. 2007);
   Byron L. Dorgan, D (to Jan. 2011)
U.S. Representatives: 1
Secy. of State: Alvin A. Jaeger, R (to Dec. 31, 2008)
Treasurer: Kelly Schmidt, R (to Dec. 31, 2008)
Atty. General: Wayne Stenehjem, R (to Dec. 31, 2008)
Organized as territory: March 2, 1861
Entered Union (rank): Nov. 2, 1889 (39)

Present constitution adopted: 1889
Motto: Liberty and union, now and forever: one and inseparable
State symbols: tree, American elm (1947); **bird,** western meadowlark (1947); **song,** "North Dakota Hymn" (1947); **fish,** northern pike (1969); **grass,** western wheatgrass (1977); **fossil,** teredo petrified wood (1967); **beverage,** milk (1983); **state march,** Spirit of the Land (1975); **flower,** wild prairie rose (1907); **equine,** Nokota horse (1993); **dance,** square dance (1995)
Nickname: Sioux State; Flickertail State; Peace Garden State; Rough Rider State
Origin of name: From the Sioux tribe, meaning "allies"
10 largest cities (2003 est.): Fargo, 91,484; Bismarck, 56,344; Grand Forks, 48,618; Minot, 35,424; Mandan, 16,781; West Fargo, 16,431; Dickinson, 15,683; Jamestown, 15,158; Williston, 12,224; Wahpeton, 8,443
Land area: 68,976 sq mi. (178,648 sq km)
Geographic center: In Sheridan Co., 5 mi. SW of McClusky
Number of counties: 53
Largest county by population and area: Cass, 128,615 (2004); McKenzie, 2,742 sq mi.
State parks: 17
Residents: North Dakotan
2004 resident population est.: 634,366
2000 resident census population (rank): 642,200 (47). **Male:** 320,524 (49.9%); **Female:** 321,676 (50.1%). **White:** 593,181 (92.4%); **Black:** 3,916 (0.6%); **American Indian:** 31,329 (4.9%); **Asian:** 3,606 (0.6%); **Other race:** 2,540 (0.4%); **Two or more races:** 7,398 (1.2%); **Hispanic/Latino:** 7,786 (1.2%). **2000 percent population 18 and over:** 75.0; **65 and over:** 14.7; **median age:** 36.2.

North Dakota was explored in 1738–1740 by French Canadians led by Sieur de la Verendrye. In 1803, the U.S. acquired most of North Dakota from France in the Louisiana Purchase. Lewis and Clark explored the region in 1804–1806, and the first settlements were made at Pembina in 1812 by Scottish and Irish families while this area was still in dispute between the U.S. and Great Britain. In 1818, the U.S. obtained the northeast part of North Dakota by treaty with Great Britain and took possession of Pembina in 1823. However, the region remained largely unsettled until the construction of the railroad in the 1870s and 1880s.

North Dakota is the most rural of all the states, with farms covering more than 90% of the land. North Dakota ranks first in the nation's production of spring and durum wheat; other agricultural products include barley, rye, sunflowers, dry edible beans, honey, oats, flaxseed, sugar beets, hay, beef cattle, sheep, and hogs.

Recently, manufacturing industries have grown, especially food processing and farm equipment. The state's coal and oil reserves are plentiful, and it also produces natural gas, lignite, clay, sand, and gravel.

The Garrison Dam on the Missouri River provides extensive irrigation and produces 400,000 kilowatts of electricity for the Missouri Basin areas.

Known for its waterfowl, grouse, pheasant, and deer hunting and bass, trout, and pike fishing, North Dakota has 20 state parks and recreation areas. Points of interest include the International Peace Garden near Dunseith, Fort Union Trading Post National Historic Site near Williston, Knife River Indian Villages National Historic Site in Stanton, the State Capitol at Bismarck, the Badlands, Theodore Roosevelt National Park, and Fort Abraham Lincoln State Park.

Selected famous natives and residents: Lynn Anderson, singer; Maxwell Anderson, playwright; Elizabeth Bodine, humanitarian; Dr. Anne Carlsen, educator; Warren Christopher, statesman; Ronald N. Davies, jurist; Angie Dickinson, actress; Ivan Dmitre, artist; Carl Ben Eielson, aviator; Phyllis Frelich, actress; Bertin C. Gamble, founder of Gamble-Skogmo; William H. Gass, writer and philosopher; Brynhild Haugland, state legislator; Phil D. Jackson, basketball player and coach; Dr. Leon O. Jacobson, researcher and educator; Harold K. Johnson, general; David C. Jones, general; Louis L'Amour, author; Peggy Lee, singer; William Lemke, representative; Roger Maris, baseball player; Marquis de Mores, cattleman who established Medora; Gerald P. Nye, senator; Casper Oimoen, skier; William A. Owens, admiral; Arthur Peterson, radio and TV actor; Cliff (Fido) Purpur, hockey player and coach; James Rosenquist, painter; Harold Schafer, founder of Gold Seal Co.; Eric Sevareid, TV commentator; Ann Sothern, actress; Dorothy Stickney, actress; Edward K. Thompson, editor; Era Bell Thompson, editor; Tommy Tucker, band leader; Lawrence Welk, band leader; Larry Woiwode, writer.

Ohio

Capital: Columbus
Governor: Bob Taft II, R (to Jan. 2007)
Lieut. Governor: Bruce Johnson (to Jan. 2007)
Senators: Mike DeWine, R (to Jan. 2007); George V. Voinovich, R (to Jan. 2011)
U.S. Representatives: 18
Secy. of State: J. Kenneth Blackwell, R (to Jan. 2007)
Treasurer: Jennette B. Bradley, R (apptd. 2005)
Atty. General: Jim Petro, R (to Jan. 2007)
Entered Union (rank): March 1, 1803 (17)
Present constitution adopted: 1851
Motto: With God all things are possible
State symbols: flower, scarlet carnation (1904); **tree,** buckeye (1953); **bird,** cardinal (1933); **insect,** ladybug (1975); **gemstone,** flint (1965); **song,** "Beautiful Ohio" (1969); **beverage,** tomato juice (1965); **fossil,** trilobite (1985); **animal,** white-tailed deer (1988); **wildflower,** large white trillium (1987)
Nickname: Buckeye State
Origin of name: From an Iroquoian word meaning "great river"
10 largest cities (2003 est.): Columbus, 728,432; Cleveland, 461,324; Cincinnati, 317,361; Toledo, 308,973; Akron, 212,215; Dayton, 161,696; Parma, 83,861; Youngstown, 79,271; Canton, 79,255; Lorain, 67,955
Land area: 40,948 sq mi. (106,055 sq km)
Geographic center: In Delaware Co., 25 mi. NNE of Columbus
Number of counties: 88
Largest county by population and area: Cuyahoga, 1,351,009 (2004); Ashtabula, 703 sq mi.
State parks: 73 (more than 204,000 ac.)
Residents: Ohioan
2004 resident population est.: 11,459,011
2000 resident census population (rank): 11,353,140 (7). **Male:** 5,512,262 (48.6%); **Female:** 5,840,878 (51.4%). **White:** 9,645,453 (85.0%); **Black:** 1,301,307 (11.5%); **American Indian:** 24,486 (0.2%); **Asian:** 132,633 (1.2%); **Other race:** 88,627 (0.8%); **Two or more races:** 157,885 (1.4%); **Hispanic/Latino:** 217,123 (1.9%). **2000 percent population 18 and over:** 74.6; **65 and over:** 13.3; **median age:** 36.2.

First explored for France by Robert Cavelier, Sieur de la Salle, in 1669, the Ohio region became British property after the French and Indian Wars. Ohio was acquired by the U.S. after the Revolutionary War in 1783. In 1788, the first permanent settlement was established at Marietta, capital of the Northwest Territory.

The 1790s saw severe fighting with the Indians in Ohio; a major battle was won by Maj. Gen. Anthony

Wayne at Fallen Timbers in 1794. In the War of 1812, Commodore Oliver H. Perry defeated the British in the Battle of Lake Erie on Sept. 10, 1813.

Ohio is one of the nation's industrial leaders, ranking third in manufacturing employment nationwide. Important manufacturing centers are located in or near Ohio's major cities. Akron is known for rubber; Canton for roller bearings; Cincinnati for jet engines and machine tools; Cleveland for auto assembly, auto parts, and steel; Dayton for office machines, refrigeration, and heating and auto equipment; Youngstown and Steubenville for steel; and Toledo for glass and auto parts.

The state's fertile soil produces soybeans, corn, oats, greenhouse and nursery products, wheat, hay, and fruit, including apples, peaches, strawberries, and grapes. More than half of Ohio's farm receipts come from dairy farming and sheep and hog raising. Ohio ranks fourth among the states in lime production and also ranks high in sand and gravel and crushed stone production.

Tourism is a valuable revenue producer, bringing in $25.7 billion in 2000. Attractions include the Rock and Roll Hall of Fame, Indian burial grounds at Mound City Group National Monument, Perry's Victory International Peace Memorial, the Pro Football Hall of Fame at Canton, and the homes of presidents Grant, Taft, Hayes, Harding, and Garfield.

Selected famous natives and residents: Neil Armstrong, astronaut; Kathleen Battle, soprano; George Bellows, painter and lithographer; Ambrose Bierce, journalist; Erma Bombeck, columnist; Bill Boyd (Hopalong Cassidy), actor; Milton Caniff, cartoonist; Hart Crane, poet; George Armstrong Custer, army officer; Dorothy Dandridge, actress; Doris Day, singer and actress; Clarence Darrow, lawyer; Ruby Dee, actress; Rita Dove, poet; Hugh Downs, TV broadcaster; Thomas A. Edison, inventor; Clark Gable, actor; James A. Garfield, president; Lillian Gish, actress; John Glenn, astronaut and senator; Ulysses S. Grant, president; Warren G. Harding, president; Rutherford Hayes, president; Benjamin Harrison, president; William Dean Howells, novelist and critic; Zane Grey, author; Robert Henri, painter; Kenisaw Mountain Landis, first baseball commissioner; Dean Martin, singer and actor; William McKinley, president; Paul Newman, actor; Jack Nicklaus, golfer; Annie Oakley, markswoman; Norman Vincent Peale, clergyman; Tyrone Power, actor; Judith Resnik, astronaut; Eddie Rickenbacker, aviator; Roy Rogers, actor and singer; Arthur M. Schlesinger, Jr., historian; William Tecumseh Sherman, army general; Gloria Steinem, feminist; William H. Taft, president; Tecumseh, Shawnee Indian chief; Lowell Thomas, explorer and commentator; James Thurber, author and cartoonist; Orville Wright, inventor; Cy Young, baseball player.

Oklahoma

Capital: Oklahoma City
Governor: Brad Henry, D (to Jan. 2007)
Lieut. Governor: Mary Fallin, R (to Jan. 2007)
Senators: Tom Coburn, R (to Jan. 2011);
 James Inhofe, R (to Jan. 2009)
U.S. Representatives: 5
Secy. of State: M. Susan Savage, D (to Jan. 2007)
Treasurer: Robert Butkin, D (to Jan. 2007)
Atty. General: W. A. Drew Edmondson, D (to Jan. 2007)
Organized as territory: May 2, 1890
Entered Union (rank): Nov. 16, 1907 (46)
Present constitution adopted: 1907
Motto: *Labor omnia vincit* (Labor conquers all things)
State symbols: flower, mistletoe (1893); **tree,** redbud (1937); **bird,** scissor-tailed flycatcher (1951); **animal,** bison (1972); **reptile,** mountain boomer lizard (1969); **stone,** rose rock (barite rose) (1968); **colors,** green and white (1915); **song,** "Oklahoma" (1953);

beverage, milk; **butterfly,** black swallowtail; **fish,** white or sand bass; **folk dance,** square dance; **furbearer,** raccoon; **game animal,** white-tailed deer; **grass,** Indiangrass; **insect,** honeybee; **musical instrument,** fiddle; **poem,** "Howdy Folks," David Randolph Milsten; **waltz,** "Oklahoma Wind"; **wildflower,** Indian blanket
Nickname: Sooner State
Origin of name: From two Choctaw Indian words meaning "red people"
10 largest cities (2003 est.): Oklahoma City, 523,303; Tulsa, 387,807; Norman, 99,197; Lawton, 91,730; Broken Arrow, 83,607; Edmond, 71,643; Midwest City, 54,662; Enid, 46,436; Moore, 44,987; Stillwater, 41,320
Land area: 68,667 sq mi. (177,848 sq km)
Geographic center: In Oklahoma Co., 8 mi. N of Oklahoma City
Number of counties: 77
Largest county by population and area: Oklahoma, 680,815 (2004); Osage, 2,251 sq mi.
State parks: 51 (72,000 ac.)
Residents: Oklahoman
2004 resident population est.: 3,523,553
2000 resident census population (rank): 3,450,654 (27). **Male:** 1,696,895 (49.1%); **Female:** 1,754,759 (50.9%). **White:** 2,628,434 (76.2%); **Black:** 260,968 (7.6%); **American Indian:** 273,230 (7.9%); **Asian:** 46,767 (1.4%); **Other race:** 82,898 (2.4%); **Two or more races:** 155,985 (4.5%); **Hispanic/Latino:** 179,304 (5.2%). **2000 percent population 18 and over:** 74.1; **65 and over:** 13.2; **median age:** 35.5.

Francisco Vásquez de Coronado first explored the region for Spain in 1541. The U.S. acquired most of Oklahoma in 1803 in the Louisiana Purchase from France; the Western Panhandle region became U.S. territory with the annexation of Texas in 1845.

Set aside as Indian Territory in 1834, the region was divided into Indian Territory and Oklahoma Territory on May 2, 1890. The two were combined to make a new state, Oklahoma, on Nov. 16, 1907.

On April 22, 1889, the first day homesteading was permitted, 50,000 people swarmed into the area. Those who tried to beat the noon starting gun were called "Sooners," hence the state's nickname.

Oil made Oklahoma a rich state, but natural-gas production has now surpassed it. Oil refining, meat packing, food processing, and machinery manufacturing (especially construction and oil equipment) are important industries. Minerals produced in Oklahoma include helium, gypsum, zinc, cement, coal, copper, and silver.

Oklahoma's rich plains produce bumper yields of wheat, as well as large crops of sorghum, hay, cotton, and peanuts. More than half of Oklahoma's annual farm receipts are contributed by livestock products, including cattle, dairy products, swine, and broilers.

Tourist attractions include the National Cowboy Hall of Fame in Oklahoma City, the Will Rogers Memorial in Claremore, the Cherokee Cultural Center with a restored Cherokee village, the restored Fort Gibson Stockade near Muskogee, the Lake Texoma recreation area, pari-mutuel horse racing at Remington Park in Oklahoma City, and Blue Ribbon Downs in Sallisaw.

Selected famous natives and residents: Johnny Bench, baseball player; John Berryman, poet; Garth Brooks, singer; Iron Eyes Cody, Cherokee actor; L. Gordon Cooper, astronaut; Ralph Ellison, writer; James Garner, actor; Owen K. Garriott, astronaut; Vince Gill, singer; Chester Gould, cartoonist; Woody Guthrie, singer and composer; Roy Harris, composer; Paul Harvey, broadcaster; Van Heflin, actor; Ron Howard, actor and director; Ben Johnson, actor; Jennifer Jones, actress; Jeane Kirkpatrick, educator and public-affairs spokesperson; Shannon Lucid, astronaut; Wilma P. Mankiller, principal chief of the Cherokee Nation of Oklahoma; Mickey Mantle, baseball player; Reba McEntire, singer; Shannon Miller, Olympic gymnast; Bill Moyers, journalist; Daniel Patrick Moynihan, N.Y. senator; Patti Page, singer; Mary Kay Place, actress and writer; Tony Randall, actor; Oral Roberts, evangelist; Dale Robertson, actor; Will Rogers, humorist; Dan Rowan, comedian; Thomas P. Stafford, astronaut; Maria Tallchief, ballerina; Jim Thorpe, athlete; Alfre Woodard, actress.

Oregon

Capital: Salem
Governor: Ted Kulongoski, D (to Jan. 2007)
Senators: Gordon Smith, R (to Jan. 2009);
  Ron Wyden, D (to Jan. 2011)
U.S. Representatives: 5
Secy. of State: Bill Bradbury, D
Treasurer: Randall Edwards, D
Atty. General: Hardy Myers, D
Organized as territory: Aug. 14, 1848
Entered Union (rank): Feb. 14, 1859 (33)
Present constitution adopted: 1859
Motto: *Alis volat Propriis* (She flies with her own wings) (1987)
State symbols: flower, Oregon grape (1899); **tree,** douglas fir (1939); **animal,** beaver (1969); **bird,** western meadowlark (1927); **fish,** chinook salmon (1961); **rock,** thunderegg (1965); **colors,** navy blue and gold (1959); **song,** "Oregon, My Oregon" (1927); **insect,** swallowtail butterfly (1979); **dance,** square dance (1977); **nut,** hazelnut (1989); **gemstone,** sunstone (1987); **seashell,** Oregon hairy triton (1991); **beverage,** milk (1997); **mushroom,** Pacific golden chanterelle (1999)
Nickname: Beaver State
Origin of name: Unknown. However, it is generally accepted that the name, first used by Jonathan Carver in 1778, was taken from the writings of Maj. Robert Rogers, an English army officer.
10 largest cities (2003 est.): Portland, 538,544; Salem, 142,914; Eugene, 142,185; Gresham, 95,816; Beaverton, 80,520; Hillsboro, 77,709; Medford, 66,638; Bend, 59,779; Springfield, 54,773; Corvallis, 50,126
Land area: 95,997 sq mi. (248,632 sq km)
Geographic center: In Crook Co., 25 mi. SSE of Prineville
Number of counties: 36
Largest county by population and area: Multnomah, 672,161 (2004); Harney, 10,135 sq mi.
State parks: 231 (95,462 ac.)
Residents: Oregonian
2004 resident population est.: 3,594,586
2000 resident census population (rank): 3,421,399 (28). **Male:** 1,696,550 (49.6%); **Female:** 1,724,849 (50.4%). **White:** 2,961,623 (86.6%); **Black:** 55,662 (1.6%); **American Indian:** 45,211 (1.3%); **Asian:** 101,350 (3.0%); **Other race:** 144,832 (4.2%); **Two or more races:** 104,745 (3.1%); **Hispanic/Latino:** 275,314 (8.0%). **2000 percent population 18 and over:** 75.3; **65 and over:** 12.8; **median age:** 36.3.

Spanish and English sailors are believed to have sighted the Oregon coast in the 1500s and 1600s. Capt. James Cook, seeking the Northwest Passage, charted some of the coastline in 1778. In 1792, Capt. Robert Gray, in the *Columbia,* discovered the river named after his ship and claimed the area for the U.S.

In 1805 the Lewis and Clark expedition explored the area. John Jacob Astor's fur depot, Astoria, was founded in 1811. Disputes for control of Oregon between American settlers and the Hudson Bay Company were finally resolved in the 1846 Oregon Treaty, in which Great Britain gave up claims to the region.

Oregon has a $3.3 billion lumber and wood products industry, and an $859 million paper and allied manufacturing industry. Its salmon-fishing industry is one of the world's largest.

In agriculture, the state leads in growing peppermint, cover seed crops, blackberries, boysenberries, loganberries, black raspberries, and hazelnuts. It is second in raising hops, red raspberries, prunes, snap beans, and onions.

With the low-cost electric power provided by dams, Oregon has developed steadily as a manufacturing state. Leading manufactured items are lumber and plywood, metalwork, machinery, aluminum, chemicals, paper, food packing, and electronic equipment.

Crater Lake National Park, Mount Hood, and Bonneville Dam on the Columbia are major tourist attractions. Other points of interest include the Oregon Dunes National Recreation Area, Oregon Caves National Monument, Cape Perpetua in Siuslaw National Forest, Columbia River Gorge between The Dalles and Troutdale, Hells Canyon, Newberry Volcanic National Monument, and John Day Fossil Beds National Monument.

Selected famous natives and residents: James Beard, food expert; Raymond Carver, writer and poet; Homer C. Davenport, political cartoonist; David Douglas, botanist; Abigail Scott Duniway, women's suffrage advocate; Robert Gray, sea captain and discoverer of Columbia River; Matt Groening, cartoonist; Mark Hatfield, senator; Donald P. Hodel, secretary of the Interior; Chief Joseph, Nez Percé chief; Dave Kingman, baseball player; Ursula LeGuin, writer; Edwin Markham, poet; Phyllis McGinley, author; Linus Pauling, chemist; Jane Powell, actress and singer; John Reed, poet and author; Harvey W. Scott, editor; Doc Severinsen, band leader; Norton Simon, business executive; Paul M. Simon, Illinois senator; William E. Stafford, poet; Sally Struthers, actress.

Pennsylvania

Capital: Harrisburg
Governor: Ed Rendell, D (to Jan. 2007)
Lieut. Governor: Catherine Baker Knoll, D (to Jan. 2007)
Senators: Rick Santorum, R (to Jan. 2007);
  Arlen Specter, R (to Jan. 2011)
U.S. Representatives: 19
Secy. of the Commonwealth: Pedro Cortes, D (at the pleasure of the governor)
Treasurer: Robert Casey, Jr., D (to Jan. 2009)
Atty. General: Tom Corbett, R (to Jan. 2009)
Entered Union (rank): Dec. 12, 1787 (2)
Present constitution adopted: 1968
Motto: Virtue, liberty, and independence
State symbols: flower, mountain laurel (1933); **tree,** hemlock (1931); **bird,** ruffed grouse (1931); **dog,** Great Dane (1965); **colors,** blue and gold (1907); **song,** "Pennsylvania" (1990)
Nickname: Keystone State
Origin of name: In honor of Adm. Sir William Penn, father of William Penn. It means "Penn's Woodland."
10 largest cities (2003 est.): Philadelphia, 1,479,339; Pittsburgh, 325,337; Allentown, 105,958; Erie, 101,373; Upper Darby, 80,556; Reading, 80,305; Scranton, 74,320; Lower Merion, 58,802; Bensalem, 58,639; Abington, 56,064
Land area: 44,817 sq mi. (116,076 sq km)

Geographic center: In Centre Co., 2½ mi. SW of Bellefonte
Number of counties: 67
Largest county by population and area: Philadelphia, 1,470,151 (2004); Lycoming, 1,235 sq mi.
State parks: 116
Residents: Pennsylvanian
2004 resident population est.: 12,406,292
2000 resident census population (rank): 12,281,054 (6). **Male:** 5,929,663 (48.3%); **Female:** 6,351,391 (51.7%). **White:** 10,484,203 (85.4%); **Black:** 1,224,612 (10.0%); **American Indian:** 18,348 (0.1%); **Asian:** 219,813 (1.8%); **Other race:** 188,437 (1.5%); **Two or more races:** 142,224 (1.2%); **Hispanic/Latino:** 394,088 (3.2%). **2000 percent population 18 and over:** 76.2; **65 and over:** 15.6; **median age:** 38.0.

Rich in historic lore, Pennsylvania territory was disputed in the early 1600s among the Dutch, the Swedes, and the English. England acquired the region in 1664 with the capture of New York, and in 1681 Pennsylvania was granted to William Penn, a Quaker, by King Charles II.

Philadelphia was the seat of the federal government almost continuously from 1776 to 1800; there the Declaration of Independence was signed in 1776 and the U.S. Constitution drawn up in 1787. Valley Forge, of Revolutionary War fame, and Gettysburg, site of the pivotal battle of the Civil War, are both in Pennsylvania. The Liberty Bell is located in a glass pavilion across from Independence Hall in Philadelphia.

The nation's first oil well was dug at Titusville in 1859, and the mining of iron ore and coal led to the development of the state's steel industry. More recently Pennsylvania's industry has diversified, although the state still leads the country in the production of specialty steel. The service, retail trade, and manufacturing sectors provide the most jobs; Pennsylvania is a leader in the production of chemicals and pharmaceuticals, food products, and electronic equipment.

Pennsylvania's 59,000 farms (occupying nearly 8 million acres) are the backbone of the state's economy, producing a wide variety of crops. Leading commodities are dairy products, cattle and calves, mushrooms, greenhouse and nursery products, poultry and eggs, a variety of fruits, sweet corn, potatoes, maple syrup, and Christmas trees.

Pennsylvania's rich heritage draws billions of tourist dollars annually. Among the chief attractions are the Gettysburg National Military Park, Valley Forge National Historical Park, Independence National Historical Park in Philadelphia, the Pennsylvania Dutch region, the Eisenhower farm near Gettysburg, and the Delaware Water Gap National Recreation Area.

Selected famous natives and residents: Louisa May Alcott, novelist; Marian Anderson, contralto; Maxwell Anderson, dramatist; Samuel Barber, composer; John Barrymore, actor; Donald Barthelme, author; Stephen Vincent Benét, poet and story writer; Daniel Boone, frontiersman; Ed Bradley, TV anchorman; James Buchanan, former president; Alexander Calder, sculptor; Rachel Carson, biologist and author; Mary Cassatt, painter; Henry Steele Commager, historian; Bill Cosby, actor; Stuart Davis, painter; Jimmy and Tommy Dorsey, band leaders; W. C. Fields, comedian; Stephen Foster, composer; Robert Fulton, inventor; Grace, Princess of Monaco; Martha Graham, choreographer; Alexander Haig, secretary of state; Marilyn Horne, mezzo-soprano; Lee Iacocca, auto executive; Reggie Jackson, baseball player; Gene Kelly, dancer and actor; Gelsey Kirkland, ballerina; S. S. Kresge, merchant; Mario Lanza, actor and singer; George C.

Marshall, general; George McClellan, general; Margaret Mead, anthropologist; Andrew Mellon, financier; Tom Mix, actor; Arnold Palmer, golfer; Robert E. Peary, explorer; Man Ray, painter; Mary Roberts Rinehart, novelist; Betsy Ross, flagmaker; B. F. Skinner, psychologist; John Sloan, painter; Gertrude Stein, author; James Stewart, actor; John Updike, novelist; Honus Wagner, baseball player; Fred Waring, band leader; Ethel Waters, singer and actress; Anthony Wayne, military officer; August Wilson, poet, writer, and playwright; Wallis Warfield, Duchess of Windsor; Andrew Wyeth, painter.

Rhode Island

Capital: Providence
Governor: Don Carcieri, R (to Jan. 2007)
Lieut. Governor: Charles J. Fogarty, D (to Jan. 2007)
Senators: Jack Reed, D (to Jan. 2009); Lincoln Chafee, R (to Jan. 2007)
U.S. Representatives: 2
Secy. of State: Matt Brown, D (to Jan. 2007)
Atty. General: Patrick Lynch, D (to Jan. 2007)
General Treasurer: Paul J. Tavares, D (to Jan. 2007)
Entered Union (rank): May 29, 1790 (13)
Present constitution adopted: 1843
Motto: Hope
State symbols: flower, violet (unofficial) (1968); **tree,** red maple (official) (1964); **bird,** Rhode Island red hen (official) (1954); **shell,** quahog (official); **mineral,** bowenite (1966); **stone,** cumberlandite (1966); **colors,** blue, white, and gold (in state flag); **song,** "Rhode Island, It's for Me" (1996);
Official name: The State of Rhode Island and Providence Plantations
Nickname: The Ocean State
Origin of name: From the Greek Island of Rhodes
10 largest cities (2003 est.): Providence, 176,365; Warwick, 87,365; Cranston, 81,679; Pawtucket, 74,330; East Providence, 49,906; Woonsocket, 44,654; Coventry, 34,910; Cumberland, 33,683; North Providence, 33,403; West Warwick, 29,996
Land area: 1,045 sq mi. (2,706 sq km)
Geographic center: In Kent Co., 1 mi. SSW of Crompton
Number of counties: 5
Largest county by population and area: Providence, 641,883 (2004); Providence, 413 sq mi.
State parks: 14
Residents: Rhode Islander
2004 resident population est.: 1,080,632
2000 resident census population (rank): 1,048,319 (43). **Male:** 503,635 (48.0%); **Female:** 544,684 (52.0%). **White:** 891,191 (85.0%); **Black:** 46,908 (4.5%); **American Indian:** 5,121 (0.5%); **Asian:** 23,665 (2.3%); **Other race:** 52,616 (5.0%); **Two or more races:** 28,251 (2.7%); **Hispanic/Latino:** 90,820 (8.7%). **2000 percent population 18 and over:** 76.4; **65 and over:** 14.5; **median age:** 36.7.

From its beginnings, Rhode Island has been distinguished by its support for freedom of conscience and action: Clergyman Roger Williams founded the present state capital, Providence, after being exiled by the Massachusetts Bay Colony Puritans in 1636. Williams was followed by other religious exiles who founded Pocasset, now Portsmouth, in 1638 and Newport in 1639.

Rhode Island's rebellious, authority-defying nature was further demonstrated by the burnings of the British revenue cutters *Liberty* and *Gaspee* prior to the Revolution; by its early declaration of independence from Great Britain in May 1776; by its refusal to participate actively in the War of 1812; and by Dorr's Rebellion of 1842, which protested property requirements for voting.

Rhode Island, smallest of the 50 states, is densely populated and highly industrialized. It is a major center for jewelry manufacturing. Electronics, metal, plastic products, and boat and ship construction are other important industries. Non-manufacturing employment includes research in health, medicine, and the ocean environment. Providence is a wholesale distribution center for New England.

Fishing ports are at Galilee and Newport. Rural areas of the state support small-scale farming, including grapes for local wineries, turf grass, and nursery stock. Tourism generates over a billion dollars a year in revenue.

Newport became famous as the summer capital of high society in the mid-19th century. Touro Synagogue (1763) is the oldest in the U.S. Other points of interest include the Roger Williams National Memorial in Providence, Samuel Slater's Mill in Pawtucket, the General Nathanael Greene Homestead in Coventry, and Block Island.

Selected famous natives and residents: Harry Anderson, actor; George M. Cohan, actor and dramatist; Eddie Dowling, actor and stage producer; Nelson Eddy, baritone and actor; Ann Smith Franklin, printer and almanac publisher; Charles Gorham, silversmith; Spalding Gray, writer, performance artist; Bobby Hackett, trumpeter; David Hartman, TV newscaster; Ruth Hussey, actress; Anne Hutchinson, religious leader; Thomas H. Ince, film producer; Wilbur John, Quaker leader; Van Johnson, actor; Clarence King, first director of the U.S. Geological Survey; Galway Kinnell, poet; Oliver La Farge, writer; Irving R. Levine, news correspondent; H. P. Lovecraft, author; Ida Lewis, lighthouse keeper; John McLaughlin, political commentator, broadcaster; Dana C. Munro, educator and historian; Matthew C. Perry, naval officer; Oliver Hazard Perry, naval officer; King Philip (Metacomet), Indian leader; Anthony Quinn, actor; Gilbert Stuart, painter; Sarah Helen (Power) Whitman, poet; Jemima Wilkinson, religious leader; Roger Williams, clergyman and founder of Rhode Island; Leonard Woodcock, labor union official; James Woods, actor.

South Carolina

Capital: Columbia
Governor: Mark Sanford, R (to Jan. 2007)
Lieut. Governor: R. Andre Bauer, R (to Jan. 2007)
Senators: Jim DeMint, R (to Jan. 2011);
  Lindsey Graham, R (to Jan. 2009)
U.S. Representatives: 6
Secy. of State: Mark Hammond, R (to Jan. 2007)
Treasurer: Grady L. Patterson, Jr. , D (to Jan. 2007)
Atty. General: Henry McMaster, R (to Jan. 2007)
Entered Union (rank): May 23, 1788 (8)
Present constitution adopted: 1895
Mottoes: *Animis opibusque parati* (Prepared in mind and resources) and *Dum spiro spero* (While I breathe, I hope)
State symbols: flower, Carolina yellow jessamine (1924); **tree,** palmetto tree (1939); **bird,** Carolina wren (1948); **song,** "Carolina" (1911)
Nickname: Palmetto State
Origin of name: In honor of Charles I of England
10 largest cities (2003 est.): Columbia, 117,357; Charleston, 101,024; North Charleston, 81,577; Rock Hill, 56,114; Greenville, 55,926; Mount Pleasant, 54,788; Sumter, 39,790; Spartanburg, 38,718; Hilton Head Island, 34,407; Summerville, 31,734
Land area: 30,109 sq mi. (77,982 sq km)
Geographic center: In Richland Co., 13 mi. SE of Columbia
Number of counties: 46
Largest county by population and area: Greenville, 401,174 (2004); Horry, 1,134 sq mi.
State forests: 4
State parks: 47 (80,000+ ac.)

Residents: South Carolinian
2004 resident population est.: 4,198,068
2000 resident census population (rank): 4,012,012 (26). **Male:** 1,948,929 (48.6%); **Female:** 2,063,083 (51.4%). **White:** 2,695,560 (67.2%); **Black:** 1,185,216 (29.5%); **American Indian:** 13,718 (0.3%); **Asian:** 36,014 (0.9%); **Other race:** 39,926 (1.0%); **Two or more races:** 39,950 (1.0%); **Hispanic/Latino:** 95,076 (2.4%). **2000 percent population 18 and over:** 74.8; **65 and over:** 12.1; **median age:** 35.4.

Following exploration of the coast in 1521 by Francisco de Gordillo, the Spanish tried unsuccessfully to establish a colony near present-day Georgetown in 1526, and the French also failed to colonize Parris Island near Fort Royal in 1562. The first English settlement was made in 1670 at Albemarle Point on the Ashley River, but poor conditions drove the settlers to the site of Charleston (originally called Charles Town).

South Carolina, officially separated from North Carolina in 1729, was the scene of extensive military action during the Revolution and again during the Civil War. The Civil War began in 1861 as South Carolina troops fired on federal Fort Sumter in Charleston Harbor, and the state was the first to secede from the Union.

Once primarily agricultural, South Carolina today has many large textile and other mills that produce several times the output of its farms in cash value. Charleston makes asbestos, wood, pulp, steel products, chemicals, machinery, and apparel.

Farms have become fewer but larger in recent years. South Carolina ranks third in peach production; it ranks fourth in overall tobacco production. Other top agricultural commodities include nursery and greenhouse products, watermelons, peanuts, broilers and turkeys, and cattle and calves. The only commercial tea plantation in America is 20 mi south of Charleston on Wadmalaw Island.

Points of interest include Fort Sumter National Monument, Fort Moultrie, Fort Johnson, and aircraft carrier USS *Yorktown* in Charleston Harbor; the Middleton, Magnolia, and Cypress Gardens in Charleston; Cowpens National Battlefield; the Hilton Head resorts; and the Riverbanks Zoo and Botanical Garden in Columbia.

Selected famous natives and residents: Bernard Baruch, statesman; Mary McLeod Bethune, educator; James F. Byrnes, senator, jurist and secretary of state; John C. Calhoun, statesman; Mark Clark, general; Joe Frazier, prize fighter; Althea Gibson, tennis champion; Dizzy Gillespie, jazz trumpeter; DuBose Heyward, poet, playwright, and novelist; Andrew Jackson, president; Jesse Jackson, civil rights leader; Eartha Kitt, singer; Francis Marion ("Swamp Fox"), Revolutionary general; Ronald McNair, astronaut; John Rutledge, jurist; Strom Thurmond, politician; Charles Townes, physicist; William Westmoreland, general; Vanna White, TV personality.

South Dakota

Capital: Pierre
Governor: Mike Rounds, R (to Jan. 2007)
Lieut. Governor: Dennis Daugaard, R (to Jan. 2007)
Senators: John R. Thune, R (to Jan. 2011);
  Tim Johnson, D (to Jan. 2009)
U.S. Representatives: 1
Atty. General: Larry Long, R (to Jan. 2007)
Secy. of State: Chris Nelson, R (to Jan. 2007)
Treasurer: Vernon L. Larson, R (to Jan. 2007)
Organized as territory: March 2, 1861
Entered Union (rank): Nov. 2, 1889 (40)

Present constitution adopted: 1889
Motto: Under God the people rule
State symbols: flower, American pasqueflower (1903);
grass, Western wheat grass (1970); **soil,** houdek
(1990); **tree,** black hills spruce (1947); **bird,**
ring-necked pheasant (1943); **insect,** honeybee
(1978); **animal,** coyote (1949); **mineral stone,** rose
quartz (1966); **gemstone,** fairburn agate (1966);
colors, blue and gold (in state flag); **song,** "Hail!
South Dakota" (1943); **fish,** walleye (1982); **musical
instrument,** fiddle (1989); **dessert,** kuchen (2000)
Nicknames: Mount Rushmore State; Coyote State
Origin of name: From the Sioux tribe, meaning "allies"
10 largest cities (2003 est.): Sioux Falls, 133,834;
Rapid City, 60,876; Aberdeen, 24,086; Watertown,
20,191; Brookings, 18,464; Mitchell, 14,677; Pierre,
13,939; Yankton, 13,440; Huron, 11,377; Vermillion,
10,070
Land area: 75,885 sq mi. (196,542 sq km)
Geographic center: In Hughes Co., 8 mi. NE of Pierre
Number of counties: 66 (64 county governments)
Largest county by population and area: Minnehaha,
157,366 (2004); Meade, 3,471 sq mi.
State parks: 12 plus 39 recreational areas (87,269 ac.)[1]
Residents: South Dakotan
2004 resident population est.: 770,883
2000 resident census population (rank): 754,844 (46).
Male: 374,558 (49.6%); **Female:** 380,286 (50.4%).
White: 669,404 (88.7%); **Black:** 4,685 (0.6%); **American Indian:** 62,283 (8.3%); **Asian:** 4,378 (0.6%);
Other race: 3,677 (0.5%); **Two or more races:**
10,156 (1.3%); **Hispanic/Latino:** 10,903 (1.4%). **2000
percent population 18 and over:** 73.2; **65 and over:**
14.3; **median age:** 35.6.

1. Acreage includes 39 recreation areas and 80 roadside parks, in addition to 12 state parks.

Exploration of this area began in 1743 when
Louis-Joseph and François Verendrye came from
France in search of a route to the Pacific.

The U.S. acquired the region as part of the Louisiana Purchase in 1803, and it was explored by
Lewis and Clark in 1804–1806. Fort Pierre, the first
permanent settlement, was established in 1817.

Settlement of South Dakota did not begin in earnest until the arrival of the railroad in 1873 and the
discovery of gold in the Black Hills in 1874.

Agriculture is a cultural and economic mainstay,
but it no longer leads the state in employment or
share of gross state product. Durable-goods manufacturing and private services have evolved as the
drivers of the economy. Tourism is also a booming
industry in the state, generating over a billion dollars' worth of economic activity each year.

South Dakota is the second-largest producer of
flaxseed and sunflower seed in the nation. It is the
third-largest producer of hay and rye.

The Black Hills are the highest mountains east of
the Rockies. Mt. Rushmore, in this group, is famous
for the likenesses of Washington, Jefferson, Lincoln,
and Theodore Roosevelt, which were carved in
granite by Gutzon Borglum. A memorial to Crazy
Horse is also being carved in granite near Custer.

Other tourist attractions include the Badlands; the
World's Only Corn Palace, in Mitchell; and the city
of Deadwood, where Wild Bill Hickok was killed in
1876 and where gambling was recently legalized.

Selected famous natives and residents: Sparky Anderson,
baseball manager; Gertrude Bonnin (Zitkala-Sa), Sioux
writer and pan-Indian activist; Tom Brokaw, TV newscaster;
Robert Casey, writer; Myron Floren, accordionist; Joseph J.
Foss, WW II Marine fighter ace; Mary Hart, TV host; Crazy
Horse, Oglala chief; Oscar Howe, Sioux artist; Hubert H.
Humphrey, vice president; Cheryl Ladd, actress; Ernest
Orlando Lawrence, physicist; Russell Means, American
Indian activist; George McGovern, politician; Arthur C.
Mellette, first governor; Dorothy Provine, actress;
Rain-in-the-Face, Hunkpapa Sioux chief; Red Cloud, chief
of the Oglala Sioux; Ben Reifel, Brulé Sioux congressman;
Ole Edvart Rølvaag, writer; Sitting Bull, chief of Hunkpappa
Sioux; Norm Van Brocklin, football player; Mamie Van
Doren, actress.

Tennessee

Capital: Nashville
Governor: Phil Bredesen, D (to Jan. 2007)
Lieut. Governor: John S. Wilder, D (to Jan. 2007)
Senators: Lamar Alexander, R (to Jan. 2009);
William Frist, R (to Jan. 2007)
U.S. Representatives: 9
Secy. of State: Riley C. Darnell, D (to Jan. 2007)
Atty. General: Paul G. Summers, D (to Feb. 2007)
Treasurer: Dale Sims, D (to Jan. 2007)
Comptroller: John G. Morgan, D (to Jan. 2006)
Entered Union (rank): June 1, 1796 (16)
Present constitution adopted: 1870; amended 1953,
1960, 1966, 1972, 1978
Motto: Agriculture and Commerce (1987)
Slogan: Tennessee—America at its best! (1965)
State symbols: flower, iris (1933); **tree,** tulip poplar
(1947); **bird,** mockingbird (1933); **horse,** Tennessee
walking horse; **animal,** raccoon (1971); **wild flower,**
passion flower (1973); **songs,** "My Homeland,
Tennessee" (1925); "When It's Iris Time in Tennessee"
(1935); "My Tennessee" (1955); "Tennessee Waltz"
(1965); "Rocky Top" (1982); "Tennessee" (1992); "The
Pride of Tennessee" (1996)
Nickname: Volunteer State
Origin of name: Of Cherokee origin; the exact meaning
is unknown
10 largest cities (2003 est.): Memphis, 645,978;
Nashville-Davidson,[1] 544,765; Knoxville, 173,278;
Chattanooga, 154,887; Clarksville, 107,953;
Murfreesboro, 78,074; Jackson, 61,110; Johnson City,
57,394; Franklin, 46,528; Kingsport, 44,231
Land area: 41,217 sq mi. (106,752 sq km)
Geographic center: In Rutherford Co., 5 mi. NE
of Murfreesboro
Number of counties: 95
Largest county by population and area: Shelby,
908,175 (2004); Shelby, 755 sq mi.
State parks: 54
Residents: Tennessean, Tennesseean
2004 resident population est.: 5,900,962
2000 resident census population (rank): 5,689,283
(16). **Male:** 2,770,275 (48.7%); **Female:** 2,919,008
(51.3%). **White:** 4,563,310 (80.2%); **Black:** 932,809
(16.4%); **American Indian:** 15,152 (0.3%); **Asian:**
56,662 (1.0%); **Other race:** 56,036 (1.0%); **Two or
more races:** 63,109 (1.1%); **Hispanic/Latino:**
123,838 (2.2%). **2000 percent population 18 and
over:** 75.4; **65 and over:** 12.4; **median age:** 35.9.

1. The city is part of a consolidated city-county government and is coextensive with Davidson County.

First visited by the Spanish explorer Hernando de
Soto in 1540, the Tennessee area would later be
claimed by both France and England as a result of
the 1670s and 1680s explorations of Jacques Marquette and Louis Joliet, Sieur de la Salle, and James
Needham and Gabriel Arthur. Great Britain obtained
the area after the French and Indian Wars in 1763.

During 1784–1787, the settlers formed the "state"
of Franklin, which was disbanded when the region
was allowed to send representatives to the North
Carolina legislature. In 1790 Congress organized the
territory south of the Ohio River, and Tennessee
joined the Union in 1796.

Although Tennessee joined the Confederacy during the Civil War, there was much pro-Union sentiment in the state, which was the scene of extensive military action.

The state is now predominantly industrial; the majority of its population lives in urban areas. Among the most important products are chemicals, textiles, apparel, electrical machinery, furniture, and leather goods. Other lines include food processing, lumber, primary metals, and metal products. The state ranks high in the production of marble, zinc, pyrite, and ball clay.

Tennessee is a leading tobacco-producing state. Other farming income is derived from livestock and dairy products, as well as greenhouse and nursery products and cotton.

With six other states, Tennessee shares the extensive federal reservoir developments on the Tennessee and Cumberland River systems. The Tennessee Valley Authority operates a number of dams and reservoirs in the state.

Among the major points of interest are the Andrew Johnson National Historic Site at Greeneville, the American Museum of Atomic Energy at Oak Ridge, Great Smoky Mountains National Park, the Hermitage (home of Andrew Jackson near Nashville), Rock City Gardens near Chattanooga, and three National Military Parks.

Selected famous natives and residents: James Agee, writer; Eddy Arnold, singer; Chet Atkins, guitarist; Julian Bond, Georgia legislator; Davy Crockett, frontiersman; David G. Farragut, first American admiral; Lester Flatt, bluegrass musician; Tennessee Ernie Ford, singer; Abe Fortas, jurist; Aretha Franklin, singer; Nikki Giovanni, poet; Al Gore, Jr., vice president; Red Grooms, artist; Isaac Hayes, composer; Benjamin L. Hooks, civil rights activist; Cordell Hull, secretary of state; Andrew Jackson, president; Andrew Johnson, president; Estes Kefauver, legislator; Anita Kerr, singer; Grace Moore, soprano; Dolly Parton, singer; Minnie Pearl, singer and comedienne; James K. Polk, president; Grantland Rice, sportswriter; Carl Rowan, journalist; Wilma Rudolph, sprinter; Sequoyah, Cherokee scholar and educator; Cybil Shepherd, actress; Dinah Shore, actress and singer; Tina Turner, singer; Alvin York, World War I hero.

Texas

Capital: Austin
Governor: Rick Perry, R (to Jan. 2007)
Lieut. Governor: David Dewhurst, R (to Jan. 2007)
Senators: John Cornyn, R (to Jan. 2009);
  Kay Bailey Hutchison, R (to Jan. 2007)
U.S. Representatives: 32
Secy. of State: Roger Williams (apptd. by gov.)
Comptroller: Carole Keeton Strayhorn, R (to Jan. 2007)
Atty. General: Greg Abbott, R (to Jan. 2007)
Entered Union (rank): Dec. 29, 1845 (28)
Present constitution adopted: 1876
Motto: Friendship
State symbols: flower, bluebonnet (1901); **tree,** pecan (1919); **bird,** mockingbird (1927); **song,** "Texas, Our Texas" (1929); **fish,** guadalupe bass (1989); **seashell,** lightning whelk (1987); **dish,** chili (1977); **folk dance,** square dance (1991); **fruit,** Texas red grapefruit (1993); **gem,** Texas blue topaz (1969); **gemstone cut,** Lone Star cut (1977); **grass,** sideoats grass (1971); **reptile,** horned lizard (1993); **stone,** petrified palmwood (1969); **plant,** prickly pear cactus; **insect,** monarch butterfly; **pepper,** jalapeño pepper; **mammal,** longhorn; **small mammal,** armadillo; **flying mammal,** Mexican free-tailed bat
Nickname: Lone Star State
Origin of name: From an Indian word meaning "friends"

10 largest cities (2003 est.): Houston, 2,009,690; San Antonio, 1,214,725; Dallas, 1,208,318; Austin, 672,011; Fort Worth, 585,122; El Paso, 584,113; Arlington, 355,007; Corpus Christi, 279,208; Plano, 241,991; Garland, 218,027
Land area: 261,797 sq mi. (678,054 sq km)
Geographic center: In McCulloch Co., 15 mi. NE of Brady
Number of counties: 254
Largest county by population and area: Harris, 3,644,285 (2004); Brewster, 6,193 sq mi.
State parks: 120 (600,000+ ac.)
Residents: Texan
2004 resident population est.: 22,490,022
2000 resident census population (rank): 20,851,820 (2). **Male:** 10,352,910 (49.6%); **Female:** 10,498,910 (50.4%). **White:** 14,799,505 (71.0%); **Black:** 2,404,566 (11.5%); **American Indian:** 118,362 (0.6%); **Asian:** 562,319 (2.7%); **Other race:** 2,438,001 (11.7%); **Two or more races:** 514,633 (2.5%); **Hispanic/Latino:** 6,669,666 (32.0%). **2000 percent population 18 and over:** 71.8; **65 and over:** 9.9; **median age:** 32.3.

Spanish explorers, including Álvar Núñez Cabeza de Vaca and Francisco Vásquez de Coronado, were the first to visit the region in the 16th and 17th centuries, settling at Ysleta near El Paso in 1682. In 1685, Robert Cavelier, Sieur de la Salle, established a short-lived French colony at Matagorda Bay.

Americans, led by Stephen F. Austin, began to settle along the Brazos River in 1821 when Texas was controlled by Mexico, recently independent from Spain. In 1836, following a brief war between the American settlers in Texas and the Mexican government, the Independent Republic of Texas was proclaimed with Sam Houston as president. This war was famous for the battles of the Alamo and San Jacinto. After Texas became a state in 1845, border disputes led to the Mexican War of 1846–1848.

Possessing enormous natural resources, Texas is a major agricultural state and an industrial giant. Second only to Alaska in land area, it leads all other states in such categories as oil, cattle, sheep, and cotton. Texas ranches and farms also produce poultry and eggs, dairy products, greenhouse and nursery products, wheat, hay, rice, sugar cane, and peanuts, and a variety of fruits and vegetables.

Sulfur, salt, helium, asphalt, graphite, bromine, natural gas, cement, and clays are among the state's valuable resources. Chemicals, oil refining, food processing, machinery, and transportation equipment are among the major Texas manufacturing industries.

Millions of tourists spend well over $20.6 billion annually visiting more than 100 state parks, recreation areas, and points of interest such as the Gulf Coast resort area, the Lyndon B. Johnson Space Center in Houston, the Alamo in San Antonio, the state capital in Austin, and the Big Bend and Guadalupe Mountains National Park.

Selected famous natives and residents: Alvin Ailey, choreographer; Mary Kay Ash, cosmetics entrepreneur; Stephen Fuller Austin, founding father of Texas; Gene Autry, singer and actor; Carol Burnett, comedienne; George W. Bush, president and governor; Cyd Charisse, actress and dancer; Denton A. Cooley, heart surgeon; Joan Crawford, actress; Dwight David Eisenhower, president and general; A. J. Foyt, auto racer; Ben Hogan, golfer; Sam Houston, general and statesman; Howard Hughes, industrialist and film producer; Jack Johnson, boxer; Lyndon B. Johnson, president; George Jones, singer; Tommy Lee Jones, actor; Janis Joplin, singer; Scott Joplin, composer; Trini Lopez, singer; Mary Martin, singer and actress; Spanky McFarland, actor; Audie Murphy, actor and war hero; Chester Nimitz, admiral; Sandra Day O'Connor, jurist; Buck Owens, singer;

Selena Pérez, singer; Lou Diamond Phillips, actor; Katherine Anne Porter, novelist; Wiley Post, aviator; Dan Rather, TV newscaster; Robert Rauschenberg, painter; Tex Ritter, singer; Rip Torn, actor and director; Tommy Tune, dancer and choreographer; Stevie Ray Vaughan, guitarist and singer; Lupe Velez, actress; Dooley Wilson, actor and musician; Babe Didrikson Zaharias, athlete and golfer.

Utah

Capital: Salt Lake City
Governor: Jon Huntsman, Jr., R (to Jan. 2009)
Lieut. Governor: Gary Herbert, R (to Jan. 2009)
Senators: Robert F. Bennett, R (to Jan. 2011); Orrin G. Hatch, R (to Jan. 2007)
U.S. Representatives: 3
Treasurer: Edward T. Alter, R (Jan. 2009)
Atty. General: Mark Shurtleff, R (to Jan. 2009)
Organized as territory: Sept. 9, 1850
Entered Union (rank): Jan. 4, 1896 (45)
Present constitution adopted: 1896
Motto: Industry
State symbols: flower, sego lily (1911); **tree,** blue spruce (1933); **bird,** California gull (1955); **emblem,** beehive (1959); **song,** "Utah, We Love Thee" (1953); **gem,** topaz; **animal,** Rocky Mountain elk (1971); **insect,** honeybee (1983); **grass,** Indian rice grass (1990); **fossil,** allosaurus (1988); **cooking pot,** dutch oven (1997); **fish,** Bonneville cutthroat trout (1997); **fruit,** cherry (1997); **mineral,** copper; **rock,** coal (1991)
Nickname: Beehive State
Origin of name: From the Ute tribe, meaning "people of the mountains"
10 largest cities (2003 est.): Salt Lake City, 179,894; West Valley City, 111,687; Provo, 105,410; Sandy, 89,319; Orem, 87,599; West Jordan, 84,701; Ogden, 78,293; Layton, 60,769; Taylorsville, 58,701; St. George, 56,382
Land area: 82,144 sq mi. (212,753 sq km)
Geographic center: In Sanpete Co., 3 mi. N. of Manti
Number of counties: 29
Largest county by population and area: Salt Lake, 935,295 (2004); San Juan, 7,821 sq mi.
National parks: 5
National monuments: 6
State parks/forests: 45 (64,097 ac.)
Residents: Utahan, Utahn
2004 resident population est.: 2,389,039
2000 resident census population (rank): 2,233,169 (34). **Male:** 1,119,031 (50.1%); **Female:** 1,114,138 (49.9%). **White:** 1,992,975 (89.2%); **Black:** 17,657 (0.8%); **American Indian:** 29,684 (1.3%); **Asian:** 37,108 (1.7%); **Other race:** 93,405 (4.2%); **Two or more races:** 47,195 (2.1%); **Hispanic/Latino:** 201,559 (9.0%). **2000 percent population 18 and over:** 67.8; **65 and over:** 8.5; **median age:** 27.1.

The region was first explored for Spain by Franciscan friars Escalante and Dominguez in 1776. In 1824 the famous American frontiersman Jim Bridger discovered the Great Salt Lake.

Fleeing religious persecution in the East and Midwest, the Mormons arrived in 1847 and began to build Salt Lake City. The U.S. acquired the Utah region in the treaty ending the Mexican War in 1848, and the first transcontinental railroad was completed with the driving of a golden spike at Promontory Summit in 1869.

Mormon difficulties with the federal government about polygamy did not end until the Mormon Church renounced the practice in 1890, six years before Utah became a state.

Rich in natural resources, Utah has long been a leading producer of copper, gold, silver, lead, zinc, and molybdenum. Oil has also become a major product. Utah shares rich oil shale deposits with Colorado and Wyoming. Utah also has large deposits of low sulphur coal.

The state's top agricultural commodities include cattle and calves, dairy products, hay, greenhouse and nursery products, and hogs.

Utah's traditional industries of agriculture and mining are complemented by increased tourism and growing aerospace, biomedical, and computer-related businesses.

Utah is a great vacationland with 11,000 mi of fishing streams and 147,000 acres of lakes and reservoirs. Among the many tourist attractions are Arches, Bryce Canyon, Canyonlands, Capitol Reef, and Zion National Parks; Cedar Breaks, Dinosaur, Hovenweep, Natural Bridges, Rainbow Bridge, Timpanogos Cave, and Grand Staircase (Escalante) National Monuments; the Mormon Tabernacle in Salt Lake City; and Monument Valley. Salt Lake City hosted the 2002 Winter Olympics.

Selected famous natives and residents: Maude Adams, actress; Roseanne, actress; Frank Borzage, film director and producer; John M. Browning, inventor; Butch Cassidy, outlaw; Laraine Day, actress; Bernard De Voto, writer; Avard Fairbanks, sculptor; Philo Farnsworth, television pioneer; Jake Garn, senator; John Gilbert, actor; J. Willard Marriott, restaurant and hotel chain founder; Peter Skene Ogden, fur trader and trapper; Merlin Olsen, football player; Donny Osmond, Marie Osmond, singers; Ivy Baker Priest, U.S. treasurer; Lee Greene Richards, painter; Leroy Robertson, composer; Brent Scowcroft, business executive and consultant; Reed Smoot, first Mormon elected to U.S. Senate; Mack Swain, actor; Everett Thorpe, painter; Robert Walker, actor; James Woods, actor; Brigham Young, territory governor and religious leader; Loretta Young, actress.

Vermont

Capital: Montpelier
Governor: Jim Douglas, R (to Jan. 2007)
Lieut. Governor: Brian Dubie, R (to Jan. 2007)
Senators: James M. Jeffords, I (to Jan. 2007); Patrick Leahy, D (to Jan. 2011)
U.S. Representatives: 1
Secy. of State: Deborah L. Markowitz, D (to Jan. 2007)
Treasurer: Jeb Spaulding, D (to Jan. 2007)
Atty. General: William Sorrell, D (to Jan. 2007)
Entered Union (rank): March 4, 1791 (14)
Present constitution adopted: 1793
Motto: Vermont, Freedom and Unity
State symbols: flower, red clover (1894); **tree,** sugar maple (1949); **bird,** hermit thrush (1941); **animal,** Morgan horse (1961); **insect,** honeybee (1978); **song,** "These Green Mountains" (2000)
Nickname: Green Mountain State
Origin of name: From the French "vert mont," meaning "green mountain"
10 largest cities (2003 est.): Burlington, 39,148; Essex, 18,933; Colchester, 17,175; Rutland, 17,103; South Burlington, 16,285; Bennington, 15,637; Brattleboro, 11,996; Hartford, 10,610; Milton, 9,924; Barre, 9,166
Land area: 9,250 sq mi. (23,958 sq km)
Geographic center: In Washington Co., 3 mi. E of Roxbury
Number of counties: 14
Largest county by population and area: Chittenden, 149,286 (2004); Windsor, 971 sq mi.
State parks: 52
Residents: Vermonter
2004 resident population est.: 621,394
2000 resident census population (rank): 608,827 (49). **Male:** 298,337 (49.0%); **Female:** 310,490 (51.0%).

White: 589,208 (96.8%); **Black:** 3,063 (0.5%); **American Indian:** 2,420 (0.4%); **Asian:** 5,217 (0.9%); **Other race:** 1,443 (0.2%); **Two or more races:** 7,335 (1.2%); **Hispanic/Latino:** 5,504 (0.9%). **2000 percent population 18 and over:** 75.8; **65 and over:** 12.7; **median age:** 37.7.

The Vermont region was explored and claimed for France by Samuel de Champlain in 1609, and the first French settlement was established at Fort Ste. Anne in 1666. The first English settlers moved into the area in 1724 and built Fort Dummer on the site of present-day Brattleboro. England gained control of the area in 1763 after the French and Indian Wars.

First organized to drive settlers from New York out of Vermont, the Green Mountain Boys, led by Ethan Allen, won fame by capturing Fort Ticonderoga from the British on May 10, 1775, in the early days of the Revolutionary War. In 1777 Vermont adopted its first constitution, abolishing slavery and providing for universal male suffrage without property qualifications.

Vermont leads the nation in the production of monument granite, marble, and maple syrup. It is also a leader in the production of talc. Vermont's rugged, rocky terrain discourages extensive agricultural farming, but is well suited to raising fruit trees and to dairy farming.

Principal industrial products include electrical equipment, fabricated metal products, printing and publishing, and paper and allied products.

Tourism is a major industry in Vermont. Vermont's many famous ski areas include Stowe, Killington, Mt. Snow, Okemo, Jay Peak, and Sugarbush. Hunting and fishing also attract many visitors to Vermont each year. Among the many points of interest are the Green Mountain National Forest, Bennington Battle Monument, the Calvin Coolidge Homestead at Plymouth, and the Marble Exhibit in Proctor.

Selected famous natives and residents: Chester A. Arthur, president; Orson Bean, actor; Calvin Coolidge, president; George Dewey, admiral; John Dewey, philosopher and educator; Stephen A. Douglas, politician; James Fisk, financial speculator; Willbur Fisk, clergyman and educator; Richard Morris Hunt, architect; William Morris Hunt, painter; Elisha Otis, inventor; Moses Pendleton, choreographer; Joseph Smith, religious leader; Ernest Thompson, actor and writer; Rudy Vallee, singer and band leader; Henry Wells, pioneer entrepreneur (Wells Fargo & Co.); Brigham Young, religious leader.

Virginia

Capital: Richmond
Governor: Mark Warner, D (to Jan. 2006)
Lieut. Governor: Tim Kaine, D (to Jan. 2006)
Senators: John Warner, R (to Jan. 2009);
  George Allen, R (to Jan. 2007)
U.S. Representatives: 11
Secy. of the Commonwealth: Anita Rimler, D (apptd. by gov.)
Treasurer: Jody M. Wagner, R (to Jan. 2006)
Atty. General: Judith Jagdmann, R (to Jan. 2006)
Entered Union (rank): June 25, 1788 (10)
Present constitution adopted: 1970
Motto: *Sic semper tyrannis* (Thus always to tyrants)
State symbols: flower, American dogwood (1918); **bird,** cardinal (1950); **dog,** American foxhound (1966); **shell,** oyster shell (1974); **tree,** dogwood (1956)
Nicknames: The Old Dominion; Mother of Presidents
Origin of name: In honor of Elizabeth "Virgin Queen" of England
10 largest cities (2003 est.): Virginia Beach, 439,467; Norfolk, 241,727; Chesapeake, 210,834; Richmond,

194,729; Newport News, 181,647; Hampton, 146,878; Alexandria, 128,923; Portsmouth, 99,617; Roanoke, 92,863; Suffolk, 73,515
Land area: 39,594 sq mi. (102,558 sq km)
Geographic center: In Buckingham Co., 5 mi. SW of Buckingham
Number of counties: 95, plus 39 independent cities
Largest county by population and area: Fairfax, 1,003,157 (2004); Augusta, 972 sq mi.
State parks/natural areas: 44
Residents: Virginian
2004 resident population est.: 7,459,827
2000 resident census population (rank): 7,078,515 (12). **Male:** 3,471,895 (49.0%); **Female:** 3,606,620 (51.0%). **White:** 5,120,110 (72.3%); **Black:** 1,390,293 (19.6%); **American Indian:** 21,172 (0.3%); **Asian:** 261,025 (3.7%); **Other race:** 138,900 (2.0%); **Two or more races:** 143,069 (2.0%); **Hispanic/Latino:** 329,540 (4.7%). **2000 percent population 18 and over:** 75.4; **65 and over:** 11.2; **median age:** 35.7.

The history of America is closely tied to that of Virginia, particularly during the Colonial period. Jamestown, founded in 1607, was the first permanent English settlement in North America and slavery was introduced there in 1619. The surrenders ending both the American Revolution (Yorktown) and the Civil War (Appomattox) occurred in Virginia. The state is called the "Mother of Presidents" because eight U.S. presidents were born there.

Today, the service sector provides one-third of all jobs in Virginia, generating as much income as the manufacturing and retail industries combined in 1999 and accounting for 23% of gross state product. (The largest component of the service sector is business services, which includes computer and data processing services.)

Virginia has a large number of manufacturing industries, including transportation equipment, food processing, electronic and other electrical equipment, chemicals, textiles and apparel, lumber and wood products, and furniture.

Agriculture remains an important sector, and the state ranks among the top ten in a variety of agricultural products, including tomatoes, tobacco, peanuts, apples, summer potatoes, sweet potatoes, snap beans, and turkeys and broilers. Virginia also has a large dairy industry.

Virginia is one of the top ten coal producers in the U.S. Coal accounts for roughly 70% of Virginia's mineral value; crushed stone, sand and gravel, lime, and kyanite are also mined.

Points of interest include Mt. Vernon, home of George Washington; Monticello, home of Thomas Jefferson; Stratford, home of the Lees; Richmond, capital of the Confederacy and of Virginia; and Williamsburg, the restored Colonial capital.

Other attractions are the Shenandoah National Park, Colonial National Historical Park, Fredericksburg and Spotsylvania National Military Park, the Booker T. Washington birthplace near Roanoke, Arlington House (the Robert E. Lee Memorial), Luray Caverns, the Skyline Drive, and the Blue Ridge National Parkway.

Selected famous natives and residents: Richard Arlen, actor; Arthur Ashe, tennis player; Pearl Bailey, singer; Russell Baker, columnist; Warren Beatty, actor; George Bingham, painter; Richard E. Byrd, polar explorer; Willa Cather, novelist; Roy Clark, country music artist; William Clark, explorer; Henry Clay, statesman; Joseph Cotten, actor; Ella Fitzgerald, singer; William H. Harrison, president; Patrick Henry, statesman; Sam Houston, political leader;

Thomas Jefferson, president; Robert E. Lee, Confederate general; Meriwether Lewis, explorer; Shirley MacLaine, actress; James Madison, president; Moses Malone, basketball player; John Marshall, jurist; Cyrus McCormick, inventor; James Monroe, president; Opechancanough, Powhatan leader; John Payne, actor; Walter Reed, army surgeon; Matthew Ridgway, general; Bill "Bojangles" Robinson, dancer; George C. Scott, actor; Sam Snead, golfer; James "Jeb" Stuart, Confederate army officer; Thomas Sumter, general; Zachary Taylor, president; Nat Turner, leader of slave uprising; John Tyler, president; Booker T. Washington, educator; George Washington, first president; James E. West,, inventor; Woodrow Wilson, president; Tom Wolfe, journalist.

Washington

Capital: Olympia
Governor: Christine Gregoire, D (to Jan. 2009)
Lieut. Governor: Brad Owen, D (to Jan. 2009)
Senators: Patty Murray, D (to Jan. 2011);
    Maria Cantwell, D (to Jan. 2007)
U.S. Representatives: 9
Secy. of State: Sam Reed, R (to Jan. 2009)
Treasurer: Michael J. Murphy, D (to Jan. 2009)
Atty. General: Rob McKenna, R (to Jan. 2009)
Auditor: Brian Sonntag, D (to Jan. 2009)
Organized as territory: March 2, 1853
Entered Union (rank): Nov. 11, 1889 (42)
Present constitution adopted: 1889
Motto: *Al-Ki* (Indian word meaning "by and by")
State symbols: flower, coast rhododendron (1892); **tree,** western hemlock (1947); **bird,** willow goldfinch (1951); **fish,** steelhead trout (1969); **gem,** petrified wood (1975); **colors,** green and gold (1925); **song,** "Washington, My Home" (1959); **folk song,** "Roll On Columbia, Roll On" (1987); **dance,** square dance (1979); **grass,** bluebunch wheatgrass (1989); **insect,** blue darner dragonfly (1997); **fossil,** Columbian mammoth (1998); **fruit,** apple (1989)
Nicknames: Evergreen State
Origin of name: In honor of George Washington
10 largest cities (2003 est.): Seattle, 569,101; Tacoma, 196,790; Spokane, 196,624; Vancouver, 151,654; Bellevue, 112,344; Everett, 96,643; Federal Way, 81,711; Kent, 81,567; Yakima, 80,223; Bellingham, 71,289
Land area: 66,544 sq mi. (172,349 sq km)
Geographic center: In Chelan Co., 10 mi. WSW of Wenatchee
Number of counties: 39
Largest county by population and area: King, 1,777,143 (2004); Okanogan, 5,268 sq mi.
State parks: 215 (260,000 ac.)[1]
Residents: Washingtonian
2004 resident population est.: 6,203,788
2000 resident census population (rank): 5,894,121 (15). **Male:** 2,934,300 (49.8%); **Female:** 2,959,821 (50.2%). **White:** 4,821,823 (81.8%); **Black:** 190,267 (3.2%); **American Indian:** 93,301 (1.6%); **Asian:** 322,335 (5.5%); **Other race:** 228,923 (3.9%); **Two or more races:** 213,519 (3.6%); **Hispanic/Latino:** 441,509 (7.5%). **2000 percent population 18 and over:** 74.3; **65 and over:** 11.2; **median age:** 35.3.

1. Parks and undeveloped areas administered by State Parks and Recreation Commission. Dept. of Wildlife administers wildlife and recreation areas totaling 428,989.5 acres.

As part of the vast Oregon Country, Washington territory was visited by Spanish, American, and British explorers—Bruno Heceta for Spain in 1775, the American Capt. Robert Gray in 1792, and Capt. George Vancouver for Britain in 1792–1794. Lewis and Clark explored the Columbia River region and coastal areas for the U.S. in 1805–1806.

Rival American and British settlers and conflicting territorial claims threatened war in the early 1840s. However, in 1846 the Oregon Treaty set the boundary at the 49th parallel and war was averted.

Washington is a leading lumber producer. Its rugged surface is rich in stands of Douglas fir, hemlock, ponderosa and white pine, spruce, larch, and cedar. The state holds first place in apples, lentils, dry edible peas, hops, pears, red raspberries, spearmint oil, and sweet cherries, and ranks high in apricots, asparagus, grapes, peppermint oil, and potatoes. Livestock and livestock products make important contributions to total farm revenue and the commercial fishing catch of salmon, halibut, and bottomfish makes a significant contribution to the state's economy.

Manufacturing industries in Washington include aircraft and missiles, shipbuilding and other transportation equipment, lumber, food processing, metals and metal products, chemicals, and machinery.

Washington has over 1,000 dams, including the Grand Coulee, built for a variety of purposes including irrigation, power, flood control, and water storage.

Among the major points of interest: Mt. Rainier, Olympic, and North Cascades National Parks. Mount St. Helens, a peak in the Cascade Range, erupted in May 1980. Also of interest are Whitman Mission and Fort Vancouver National Historic Sites; and the Pacific Science Center and the Space Needle, in Seattle.

Selected famous natives and residents: Earl Anthony, professional bowler; Mildred Bailey, singer; Bob Barker, TV host; Dyan Cannon, actress; Raymond Carver, writer; Carol Channing, actress; Ray Charles, singer and musician; Kurt Cobain, rock musician; Judy Collins, singer; Chris Cornell, rock musician; Fred Couples, professional golfer; Bing Crosby, singer and actor; Bob Crosby, musician; Merce Cunningham, choreographer; Howard Duff, actor; Frances Farmer, actress; Kenny G., saxophonist; Bill Gates, software executive; Jimi Hendrix, guitarist; Frank Herbert, writer; Robert Joffrey, choreographer; Chuck Jones, animator; Quincy Jones, music producer; Hank Ketcham, cartoonist; Gary Larson, cartoonist; Gypsy Rose Lee, entertainer; Kenny Loggins, rock musician; Mary McCarthy, novelist; Guthrie McClintic, theatrical producer and director; John McIntire, actor; Steve Miller, rock musician; Robert Motherwell, artist; Patrice Munsel, soprano; Craig T. Nelson, actor; Ella Raines, actress; Ahmad Rashad, football player; Ann Reinking, dancer and actress; Tom Robbins, novelist; Ann Rule, writer; Francis Scobee, astronaut; Seattle, Suquamish chief; Smohalla, Indian prophet and chief; Hillary Swank, actress; Julia Sweeney, actress; Adam West, actor; Audrey Wurdemann, poet.

West Virginia

Capital: Charleston
Governor: Joe Manchin III, D (to Jan. 2009)
Lt. Governor/Senate President: Earl Ray Tomblin, D (to Jan. 2009)
Senators: Robert C. Byrd, D (to Jan. 2007);
    John D. "Jay" Rockefeller IV, D (to Jan. 2009)
U.S. Representatives: 3
Secy. of State: Betty Ireland (to Jan. 2009)
Treasurer: John D. Perdue, D (to Jan. 2009)
Atty. General: Darrell V. McGraw, Jr., D (to Jan. 2009)
Entered Union (rank): June 20, 1863 (35)
Present constitution adopted: 1872
Motto: *Montani semper liberi* (Mountaineers are always free)
State symbols: flower, rhododendron (1903); **tree,** sugar maple (1949); **bird,** cardinal (1949); **animal,** black bear (1973); **colors,** blue and gold (official) (1863); **songs,** "West Virginia, My Home Sweet Home," "The West Virginia Hills," and "This Is My

West Virginia" (adopted by Legislature in 1947, 1961, and 1963 as official state songs);
Nickname: Mountain State
Origin of name: In honor of Elizabeth, "Virgin Queen" of England
10 largest cities (2003 est.): Charleston, 51,394; Huntington, 49,533; Parkersburg, 32,100; Wheeling, 30,096; Morgantown, 27,969; Weirton, 19,838; Fairmont, 18,984; Beckley, 16,994; Clarksburg, 16,425; Martinsburg, 15,309
Land area: 24,077 sq mi. (62,359 sq km)
Geographic center: In Braxton Co., 4 mi. E of Sutton
Number of counties: 55
Largest county by population and area: Kanawha, 195,218 (2004); Randolph, 1,040 sq mi.
State parks: 37 (74,508 ac.)
Residents: West Virginian
2004 resident population est.: 1,815,354
2000 resident census population (rank): 1,808,344 (37). **Male:** 879,170 (48.6%); **Female:** 929,174 (51.4%). **White:** 1,718,777 (95.0%); **Black:** 57,232 (3.2%); **American Indian:** 3,606 (0.2%); **Asian:** 9,434 (0.5%); **Other race:** 3,107 (0.2%); **Two or more races:** 15,788 (0.9%); **Hispanic/Latino:** 12,279 (0.7%). **2000 percent population 18 and over:** 77.7; **65 and over:** 15.3; **median age:** 38.9.

West Virginia's early history from 1609 until 1863 is largely shared with Virginia, of which it was a part until Virginia seceded from the Union in 1861. The delegates of the 40 western counties who opposed secession formed their own government, which was granted statehood in 1863.

In 1731 Morgan Morgan established the first permanent white settlement on Mill Creek in present-day Berkeley County. Coal, a mineral asset that would figure significantly in West Virginia's history, was discovered in 1742. Other important natural resources are oil, natural gas, and hardwood forests, which cover about 75% of the state's area.

The state's rapid industrial expansion began in the 1870s, drawing thousands of European immigrants and African Americans into the region. Miners' strikes between 1912 and 1921 required the intervention of state and federal troops to quell the violence.

Today, the state ranks second in total coal production, with about 15% of the U.S. total. It is also a leader in steel, glass, aluminum, and chemical manufactures. Major agricultural commodities are poultry and eggs, dairy products, and apples.

Tourism is increasingly popular in mountainous West Virginia. More than a million acres have been set aside in 37 state parks and recreation areas and in 9 state forests and 2 national forests. Major points of interest include Harpers Ferry and New River Gorge National River, The Greenbrier and Berkeley Springs resorts, the scenic railroad at Cass, and the historic homes in the Eastern Panhandle.

Selected famous natives and residents: George Brett, baseball player; Pearl S. Buck, author; Phyllis Curtin, soprano; Martin R. Delany, first black army major; Billy Dixon, frontiersman and scout; Joanne Dru, actress; Thomas "Stonewall" Jackson, Confederate general; John S. Knight, publisher; Don Knotts, actor; Peter Marshall, TV host; Kathy Mattea, singer; Whitney D. Morrow, banker and diplomat; Mary Lou Retton, gymnast; Walter Reuther, labor leader; Eleanor Steber, soprano; Lewis L. Strauss, naval officer and scientist; Cyrus Vance, government official; Jerry West, basketball player; William Lyne Wilson, legislator and university president; Chuck Yeager, test pilot and Air Force general.

Wisconsin

Capital: Madison
Governor: Jim Doyle, D (to Jan. 2007)
Lieut. Governor: Barbara Lawton, D (to Jan. 2007)
Senators: Russell D. Feingold, D (to Jan. 2011); Herbert Kohl, D (to Jan. 2007)
U.S. Representatives: 8
Secy. of State: Douglas J. La Follette, D (to Jan. 2007)
State Treasurer: Jack C. Voight, R (to Jan. 2007)
Atty. General: Peg Lautenschlager, D (to Jan. 2007)
Superintendent of Public Instruction: Elizabeth Burmaster, Nonpartisan (to July 2005)
Organized as territory: July 4, 1836
Entered Union (rank): May 29, 1848 (30)
Present constitution adopted: 1848
Motto: Forward
State symbols: flower, wood violet (1949); **tree,** sugar maple (1949); **grain,** corn (1990); **bird,** robin (1949); **animal,** badger; **wild life animal,** white-tailed deer (1957); **domestic animal,** dairy cow (1971); **insect,** honeybee (1977); **fish,** musky (muskellunge) (1955); **song,** "On Wisconsin"; **mineral,** galena (1971); **rock,** red granite (1971); **symbol of peace,** mourning dove (1971); **soil,** antigo silt loam (1983); **fossil,** trilobite (1985); **dog,** American Water Spaniel (1986); **beverage,** milk (1988); **dance,** polka (1994); **waltz,** "The Wisconsin Waltz" (2001); **ballad,** "Oh Wisconsin, Land of My Dreams" (2001)
Nickname: Badger State
Origin of name: French corruption of an Indian word whose meaning is disputed
10 largest cities (2003 est.): Milwaukee, 586,941; Madison, 218,432; Green Bay, 101,467; Kenosha, 92,871; Racine, 80,266; Appleton, 70,354; Waukesha, 66,840; Oshkosh, 63,237; Eau Claire, 62,496; Janesville, 61,145
Land area: 54,310 sq mi. (140,673 sq km)
Geographic center: In Wood Co., 9 mi. SE of Marshfield
Number of counties: 72
Largest county by population and area: Milwaukee, 928,018 (2004); Marathon, 1,545 sq mi.
State parks, forests, and recreation areas: 93
Residents: Wisconsinite
2004 resident population est.: 5,509,026
2000 resident census population (rank): 5,363,675 (18). **Male:** 2,649,041 (49.4%); **Female:** 2,714,634 (50.6%). **White:** 4,769,857 (88.9%); **Black:** 304,460 (5.7%); **American Indian:** 47,228 (0.9%); **Asian:** 88,763 (1.7%); **Other race:** 84,842 (1.6%); **Two or more races:** 66,895 (1.2%); **Hispanic/Latino:** 192,921 (3.6%). **2000 percent population 18 and over:** 74.5; **65 and over:** 13.1; **median age:** 36.0.

The Wisconsin region was first explored for France by Jean Nicolet, who landed at Green Bay in 1634. In 1660 a French trading post and Roman Catholic mission were established near present-day Ashland.

Great Britain obtained the region in settlement of the French and Indian Wars in 1763; the U.S. acquired it in 1783 after the Revolutionary War. However, Great Britain retained actual control until after the War of 1812. The region was successively governed as part of the territories of Indiana, Illinois, and Michigan between 1800 and 1836, when it became a separate territory.

Wisconsin is a leading state in milk and cheese production. Other important farm products are peas, beans, beets, corn, potatoes, oats, hay, and cranberries.

The chief industrial products of the state are automobiles, machinery, furniture, paper, beer, and processed foods. Wisconsin ranks second among the 47 paper-producing states. The state's mines produce copper, iron ore, lead, and zinc.

Wisconsin is a pioneer in social legislation, providing pensions for the blind (1907), aid to dependent children (1913), and old-age assistance (1925). In labor legislation, the state was the first to enact an unemployment compensation law (1932) and the first in which a workman's compensation law actually took effect. In 1984, Wisconsin became the first state to adopt the Uniform Marital Property Act.

The state has over 14,000 lakes, of which Winnebago is the largest. Water sports, ice-boating, and fishing are popular, as are skiing and hunting. Public parks and forests take up one-seventh of the land, with 43 state parks, 12 state forests, 14 state trails, 3 recreational areas, and 2 national forests.

Among the many points of interest are the Apostle Islands National Lakeshore; Ice Age National Scientific Reserve; the Circus World Museum at Baraboo; the Wolf, St. Croix, and Lower St. Croix national scenic riverways; and the Wisconsin Dells.

Selected famous natives and residents: Don Ameche, actor; Roy Chapman Andrews, naturalist and explorer; Walter Annenberg, media tycoon and philanthropist; Carrie Catt, woman suffragist; John R. Commons, economist; Tyne Daly, actress; August Derleth, author; Jeanne Dixon, seer; Zona Gale, novelist; Eric Heiden, skater; Woody Herman, band leader; Hildegarde, singer; Harry Houdini, magician; Hans V. Kaltenborne, journalist; Pee Wee King, singer; George F. Kennan, diplomat; Robert La Follette, politician; William D. Leahy, admiral; Liberace, pianist; Charles Litel, actor; Allen Ludden, TV host; Alfred Lunt, actor; Frederic March, actor; Jackie Mason, comedian; John Ringling North, circus director; Pat O'Brien, actor; Georgia O'Keeffe, painter; Charlotte Rae, actress; William H. Rehnquist, jurist; Gena Rowlands, actress; Tom Snyder, newscaster; Spencer Tracy, actor; Thorstein Veblen, economist; Orson Welles, actor and producer; Thornton Wilder, author; Charles Winninger, actor; Frank Lloyd Wright, architect.

Wyoming

Capital: Cheyenne
Governor: Dave Freudenthal, D (to Jan. 2007)
Senators: Michael B. Enzi, R (to Jan. 2009); Craig Thomas, R (to Jan. 2007)
U.S. Representatives: 1
Secy. of State: Joe Meyer, R (to Jan. 2007)
Treasurer: Cynthia M. Lummis, R (to Jan. 2007)
Atty. General: Patrick Crank, D (to Jan. 2007)
Organized as territory: May 19, 1869
Entered Union (rank): July 10, 1890 (44)
Present constitution adopted: 1890
Motto: Equal rights (1955)
State symbols: flower, Indian paintbrush (1917); **tree,** cottonwood (1947); **bird,** western meadowlark (1927); **dinosaur,** *Triceratops* (1994); **fish,** cutthroat trout (1987); **fossil,** *Knightia* (1987); **gemstone,** jade (1967); **insignia,** bucking horse (unofficial); **mammal,** bison (1985); **reptile,** horned toad (1993); **soil,** Forkwood series (unofficial); **song,** "Wyoming" (1955)
Nickname: Equality State
Origin of name: From the Delaware Indian word, meaning "mountains and valleys alternating"; the same as the Wyoming Valley in Pennsylvania
10 largest cities (2003): Cheyenne, 54,374; Casper, 50,632; Laramie, 26,956; Gillette, 21,840; Rock Springs, 18,400; Sheridan, 16,016; Green River, 11,541; Evanston, 11,375; Riverton, 9,314; Cody, 8,973
Land area: 97,100 sq mi. (251,501 sq km)

Geographic center: In Fremont Co., 58 mi. ENE of Lander
Number of counties: 23, plus Yellowstone National Park
Largest county by population and area: Laramie, 85,296 (2004); Sweetwater, 10,426 sq mi.
State parks and historic sites: 23 (58,498 ac.)
Residents: Wyomingite
2004 resident population est.: 506,529
2000 resident census population (rank): 493,782 (50). **Male:** 248,374 (50.3%); **Female:** 245,408 (49.7%). **White:** 454,670 (92.1%); **Black:** 3,722 (0.8%); **American Indian:** 11,133 (2.3%); **Asian:** 2,771 (0.6%); **Other race:** 12,301 (2.5%); **Two or more races:** 8,883 (1.8%); **Hispanic/Latino:** 31,669 (6.4%). **2000 percent population 18 and over:** 73.9; **65 and over:** 11.7; **median age:** 36.2.

The U.S. acquired the land comprising Wyoming from France as part of the Louisiana Purchase in 1803. John Colter, a fur-trapper, is the first white man known to have entered the region. In 1807 he explored the Yellowstone area and brought back news of its geysers and hot springs.

Robert Stuart pioneered the Oregon Trail across Wyoming in 1812–1813 and, in 1834, Fort Laramie, the first permanent trading post in Wyoming, was built. Western Wyoming was obtained by the U.S. in the 1846 Oregon Treaty with Great Britain and as a result of the treaty ending the Mexican War in 1848.

When the Wyoming Territory was organized in 1869, Wyoming women became the first in the nation to obtain the right to vote. In 1925 Mrs. Nellie Tayloe Ross became the first woman governor in the United States.

Wyoming's towering mountains and vast plains provide spectacular scenery, grazing lands for sheep and cattle, and rich mineral deposits.

Mining, particularly oil and natural gas, is the most important industry. Wyoming has the world's largest sodium carbonate (natrona) deposits and has the nation's second largest uranium deposits.

In 2000 Wyoming ranked second among the states in wool production (exceeded only by Texas) and third in sheep and lambs (exceeded only by Texas and California); it also had 1,580,000 cattle. Principal crops include wheat, oats, sugar beets, corn, barley, and alfalfa.

Second in mean elevation to Colorado, Wyoming has many attractions for the tourist trade, notably Yellowstone National Park. Hikers, campers and skiers are attracted to Grand Teton National Park and Jackson Hole National Monument in the Teton Range of the Rockies. Cheyenne is famous for its annual "Frontier Days" celebration. Flaming Gorge, the Fort Laramie National Historic Site, and Devils Tower and Fossil Butte National Monuments are other points of interest.

Selected famous natives and residents: James Bridger, trapper, guide, and storyteller; Dick Cheney, vice president; Buffalo Bill Cody, scout; John Colter, trader and first white man to enter Wyoming; June E. Downey, educator; Thomas Fitzpatrick, mountain man and guide; Curt Gowdy, sportscaster; Tom Horn, detective; Isabel Jewell, actress; Velma Linford, writer; Esther Morris, first woman judge; Ted Olson, writer; John "Portugee" Phillips, frontiersman; Jackson Pollock, painter; Nellie Tayloe Ross, first woman elected governor of a state; Alan K. Simpson, senator; Jedediah S. Smith, mountain man and first American to reach California from the East; Alan Swallow, publisher and author; Willis Van Devanter, jurist; Francis E. Warren, first state governor; Chief Washakie, chief of the Shoshone; James G. Watt, secretary of the Interior.

Land and Water Area of States, 2000

(in square miles)

State	Rank (total area)	Land[1] area	Water[2] area	Total area	State	Rank (total area)	Land[1] area	Water[2] area	Total area
Alabama	30	50,744.00	1,675.01	52,419.02	Montana	4	145,552.43	1,489.96	147,042.40
Alaska	1	571,951.26	91,316.00	663,267.26	Nebraska	16	76,872.41	481.31	77,353.73
Arizona	6	113,634.57	363.73	113,998.30	Nevada	7	109,825.99	734.71	110,560.71
Arkansas	29	52,068.17	1,110.45	53,178.62	New				
California	3	155,959.34	7,736.23	163,695.57	Hampshire	46	8,968.10	381.84	9,349.94
Colorado	8	103,717.53	376.00	104,093.57	New Jersey	47	7,417.34	1,303.96	8,721.30
Connecticut	48	4,844.80	698.53	5,543.33	New Mexico	5	121,355.53	233.96	121,589.48
Delaware	49	1,953.56	535.71	2,489.27	New York	27	47,213.79	7,342.22	54,556.00
Dist. of					North Carolina	28	48,710.88	5,107.63	53,818.51
Columbia	—	61.4	6.94	68.34	North Dakota	19	68,975.93	1,723.86	70,699.79
Florida	22	53,926.82	11,827.77	65,754.59	Ohio	34	40,948.38	3,876.53	44,824.90
Georgia	24	57,906.14	1,518.63	59,424.77	Oklahoma	20	68,667.06	1,231.13	69,898.19
Hawaii	43	6,422.62	4,508.36	10,930.98	Oregon	9	95,996.79	2,383.85	98,380.64
Idaho	14	82,747.21	822.87	83,570.08	Pennsylvania	33	44,816.61	1,238.63	46,055.24
Illinois	25	55,583.58	2,330.79	57,914.38	Rhode Island	50	1,044.93	500.12	1,545.05
Indiana	38	35,866.90	550.83	36,417.73	South Carolina	40	30,109.47	1,910.73	32,020.20
Iowa	26	55,869.36	402.2	56,271.55	South Dakota	17	75,884.64	1,231.85	77,116.49
Kansas	15	81,814.88	461.96	82,276.84	Tennessee	36	41,217.12	926.15	42,143.27
Kentucky	37	39,728.18	680.85	40,409.02	Texas	2	261,797.12	6,783.70	268,580.82
Louisiana	31	43,561.85	8,277.85	51,839.70	Utah	13	82,143.65	2,755.18	84,898.83
Maine	39	30,861.55	4,523.10	35,384.65	Vermont	45	9,249.56	364.7	9,614.26
Maryland	42	9,773.82	2,632.86	12,406.68	Virginia	35	39,594.07	3,180.13	42,774.20
Massachusetts	44	7,840.02	2,714.55	10,554.57	Washington	18	66,544.06	4,755.58	71,299.64
Michigan	11	56,803.82	39,912.28	96,716.11	West Virginia	41	24,077.73	152.03	24,229.76
Minnesota	12	79,610.08	7,328.79	86,938.87	Wisconsin	23	54,310.10	11,187.72	65,497.82
Mississippi	32	46,906.96	1,523.24	48,430.19	Wyoming	10	97,100.40	713.16	97,813.56
Missouri	21	68,885.93	818.39	69,704.31	**U.S. total**		**3,537,438.44**	**256,644.62**	**3,794,083.06**

1. Dry land and land temporarily or partially covered by water, such as marshland, swamps, etc.; streams and canals under one-eighth statute mile wide; and lakes, reservoirs, and ponds under 40 acres. 2. Permanent inland water surface, such as lakes, reservoirs, and ponds having an area of 40 acres or more; streams, sloughs, estuaries, and canals one-eighth statute mile or more in width; deeply indented embayments and sounds, and other coastal waters behind or sheltered by headlands or islands separated by less than 1 nautical mile of water, and islands under 40 acres in area. Excludes areas of oceans, bays, sounds, etc. lying within U.S. jurisdiction but not defined as inland water. *Source:* Department of Commerce, Bureau of the Census.

State Capitals and Largest Cities

State	Capital	Largest city	State	Capital	Largest city
Alabama	Montgomery	Birmingham	**Montana**	Helena	Billings
Alaska	Juneau	Anchorage	**Nebraska**	Lincoln	Omaha
Arizona	Phoenix	Phoenix	**Nevada**	Carson City	Las Vegas
Arkansas	Little Rock	Little Rock	**New Hampshire**	Concord	Manchester
California	Sacramento	Los Angeles	**New Jersey**	Trenton	Newark
Colorado	Denver	Denver	**New Mexico**	Santa Fe	Albuquerque
Connecticut	Hartford	Bridgeport	**New York**	Albany	New York City
Delaware	Dover	Wilmington	**North Carolina**	Raleigh	Charlotte
Florida	Tallahassee	Jacksonville	**North Dakota**	Bismarck	Fargo
Georgia	Atlanta	Atlanta	**Ohio**	Columbus	Columbus
Hawaii	Honolulu	Honolulu	**Oklahoma**	Oklahoma City	Oklahoma City
Idaho	Boise	Boise	**Oregon**	Salem	Portland
Illinois	Springfield	Chicago	**Pennsylvania**	Harrisburg	Philadelphia
Indiana	Indianapolis	Indianapolis	**Rhode Island**	Providence	Providence
Iowa	Des Moines	Des Moines	**South Carolina**	Columbia	Columbia
Kansas	Topeka	Wichita	**South Dakota**	Pierre	Sioux Falls
Kentucky	Frankfort	Lexington	**Tennessee**	Nashville	Memphis
Louisiana	Baton Rouge	New Orleans	**Texas**	Austin	Houston
Maine	Augusta	Portland	**Utah**	Salt Lake City	Salt Lake City
Maryland	Annapolis	Baltimore	**Vermont**	Montpelier	Burlington
Massachusetts	Boston	Boston	**Virginia**	Richmond	Virginia Beach
Michigan	Lansing	Detroit	**Washington**	Olympia	Seattle
Minnesota	St. Paul	Minneapolis	**West Virginia**	Charleston	Charleston
Mississippi	Jackson	Jackson	**Wisconsin**	Madison	Milwaukee
Missouri	Jefferson City	Kansas City	**Wyoming**	Cheyenne	Cheyenne

Source: U.S. Bureau of the Census, 2000 figures.

Most Livable States, 2005

2005 rank	State	2004 rank	2005 rank	State	2004 rank	2005 rank	State	2004 rank
1.	New Hampshire	1.	18.	Idaho	17.	35.	California	36.
2.	Minnesota	2.	19.	Utah	19.	36.	Arizona	38.
3.	Vermont	3.	20.	Kansas	11.	37.	Florida	37.
4.	Wyoming	6.	21.	Indiana	20.	38.	Georgia	35.
5.	Virginia	7.	22.	Missouri	20.	39.	Alabama	47.
6.	Iowa	4.	23.	Rhode Island	24.	40.	North Carolina	45.
7.	Massachusetts	16.	24.	Montana	27.	41.	Kentucky	42.
8.	New Jersey	5.	25.	Washington	25.	42.	New Mexico	41.
9.	South Dakota	10.	26.	Hawaii	32.	43.	Oklahoma	40.
10.	Nebraska	8.	27.	Alaska	31.	44.	South Carolina	48.
11.	North Dakota	15.	28.	Michigan	34.	45.	Texas	39.
12.	Maryland	14.	29.	Nevada	30.	46.	West Virginia	43.
13.	Wisconsin	13.	30.	New York	33.	47.	Tennessee	46.
14.	Connecticut	9.	31.	Illinois	26.	48.	Arkansas	44.
15.	Maine	12.	32.	Ohio	29.	49.	Louisiana	49.
16.	Colorado	23.	33.	Pennsylvania	22.	50.	Mississippi	50.
17.	Delaware	18.	34.	Oregon	27.			

Methodology: To determine a state's livability rating, each state's rankings in 44 categories were averaged. Some of the positive factors included household income, homeownership, job growth, and educational attainment. The negative factors included crime rate, poverty rate, infant mortality rate, and unemployment rate. *Source:* Morgan Quitno Press. Web: www.morganquitno.com.

Healthiest States, 2005

2005 rank	State	2004 rank	2005 rank	State	2004 rank	2005 rank	State	2004 rank
1.	Vermont	2.	18.	California	14.	35.	Delaware	44.
2.	New Hampshire	1.	19.	Oregon	15.	36.	Missouri	37.
3.	Massachusetts	8.	20.	Idaho	20.	37.	Alaska	35.
4.	Minnesota	5.	21.	Pennsylvania	26.	38.	Tennessee	36.
5.	Maine	9.	22.	South Dakota	19.	39.	Arizona	40.
6.	Iowa	4.	23.	Michigan	25.	40.	Arkansas	38.
7.	Utah	6.	24.	Indiana	28.	41.	Alabama	47.
8	Hawaii	3.	25..	Montana	23.	42.	Georgia	42.
9.	Nebraska	7.	26.	Ohio	24.	43.	South Carolina	46.
10.	Connecticut	10.	27.	Colorado	27.	44.	Florida	41.
11.	North Dakota	12.	28.	West Virginia	34.	45.	Texas	42.
12.	Rhode Island	18.	29.	Maryland	32.	46.	Oklahoma	39.
13.	Washington	13.	30.	Wyoming	16.	47.	Nevada	45.
14.	Wisconsin	21.	31.	New York	33.	48.	New Mexico	49.
15.	Kansas	17.	32.	Kentucky	29.	49.	Mississippi	50.
16.	New Jersey	11.	33.	North Carolina	30.	50.	Louisiana	48.
17.	Virginia	22.	34.	Illinois	31.			

Methodology: The Healthiest State designation is awarded on the basis of 21 factors selected from the 2005 edition of Morgan Quitno's annual reference book, *Health Care State Rankings*. These factors reflect access to health care providers, affordability of health care, and the general health of a state's population. *Source:* Morgan Quitno Press. Web: www.morganquitno.com.

Most Dangerous States, 2005

2005 rank	State	2004 rank	2005 rank	State	2004 rank	2005 rank	State	2004 rank
1.	Nevada	1.	18.	North Carolina	15.	35.	Nebraska	34.
2.	Louisiana	2.	19.	Alabama	18.	36.	Minnesota	35.
3.	Arizona	3.	20.	Washington	21.	37.	Kentucky	36.
4.	Maryland	4.	21.	Missouri	19.	38.	Virginia	37.
5.	South Carolina	5.	22.	Arkansas	25.	39.	Connecticut	39.
6.	Florida	7.	23.	Ohio	22.	40.	Montana	44.
7.	Tennessee	8.	24.	Colorado	24.	41.	Idaho	40.
8.	Alaska	12.	25.	Hawaii	23.	42.	Wisconsin	41.
9.	New Mexico	6.	26.	Kansas	31.	43.	Iowa	42.
10.	California	10.	27.	Indiana	26.	44.	West Virginia	45.
11.	Texas	9.	28.	Oregon	32.	45.	Wyoming	43.
12.	Michigan	11.	29.	Massachusetts	27.	46.	South Dakota	46.
13.	Georgia	17.	30.	Pennsylvania	30.	47.	New Hampshire	47.
14.	Oklahoma	16.	31.	New York	28.	48.	Maine	48.
15.	Delaware	20.	32.	New Jersey	33.	49.	Vermont	50.
16.	Illinois	13.	33.	Rhode Island	29.	50.	North Dakota	49.
17.	Mississippi	14.	34.	Utah	38.			

Methodology: To determine the most dangerous states, rates for six crime categories—murder, rape, robbery, aggravated assault, burglary, and motor vehicle theft—are compared to the national average for a given crime category. *Source:* Morgan Quitno Press. Web: www.morganquitno.com.

50 Largest Cities of the United States

Data supplied by U.S. Census Bureau and by the cities in response to questionnaires. Per capita personal income data are given for the Metropolitan Statistical Area (MSA), the Primary Metropolitan Statistical Area (PMSA), the New England County Metropolitan Area (NECMA), or the Consolidated Metropolitan Statistical Area (CMSA), as noted. NOTE: Persons of Hispanic origin may be of any race.

Albuquerque, N.M.

Mayor: Martin Chavez (to Nov. 2005)
2000 census population (rank): 448,607 (35); **% change:** 16.6; **Male:** 217,887 (48.6%); **Female:** 230,720 (51.4%); **White:** 321,179 (71.6%); **Black:** 13,854 (3.1%); **American Indian and Alaska Native:** 17,444 (3.9%); **Asian:** 10,068 (2.2%); **Other race:** 66,292 (14.8%); **Two or more races:** 19,318 (4.3%); **Hispanic/Latino:** 179,075 (39.9%). **2000 percent population 18 and over:** 75.5%; **65 and over:** 12.0%; **Median age:** 34.9.
2004 population estimate (rank): 484,246 (33)
Land area: 181 sq mi. (469 sq km); **Alt.:** 4,958 ft.
Avg. daily temp.: Jan., 34.2° F; July, 78.5° F
Churches: 211; **City-owned parks:** 189; **Radio stations:** 43 (AM, 17; FM, 26); **Television stations:** 11
Civilian Labor Force (MSA) March 2005: 402,900; **Unemployed:** 21,400, **Percent:** 5.3; **Per capita personal income (MSA) 2003:** $28,519
Chamber of Commerce: Greater Albuquerque Chamber of Commerce, PO Box 25100, Albuquerque, N.M. 87125. Albuquerque Hispano Chamber of Commerce, 1309 Fourth St. S.W., Albuquerque, NM 87102

Albuquerque is the largest city in New Mexico and the seat of Bernalillo County. It is situated in west-central New Mexico on the upper Rio Grande.

Spanish settlers arrived in the mid-1600s, but they retreated from the area in 1680 after the Pueblo revolt. The old town was founded in 1706 by Don Francisco Cuervo y Valdés, the governor of New Mexico, and named after the Duke of Alburquerque, the viceroy of New Spain.

The opening of the Santa Fe Trail in the early 19th century brought an influx of settlers, and an army post was established following U.S. occupation in 1846. Albuquerque remained loyal to the Union during the Civil War, although it was briefly occupied by Confederate forces in 1862. The new town was laid out in 1880 after the Santa Fe Railroad was built one mile east of the original plaza. The Spanish old town and the mission church of San Felipe de Neri (1706) were soon enveloped by the new construction but survive today.

The city is noted as a center for health and medical services in the region, and government agencies, nuclear research, banking, and tourism are important to the economy. There is a growing high-tech center in Albuquerque, and Intel Corp.'s largest manufacturing facility is located there.

Albuquerque is the seat of the University of New Mexico (1889). Its numerous attractions include the Albuquerque Biological Park, the Indian Pueblo Cultural Center, the National Atomic Museum, Petroglyph National Monument, and the Sandia Mountain Wilderness.

Selected famous natives and residents: Annabeth Gish, actress; Fred Haney, baseball player; Ernie Pyle, war correspondent; Al and Bobby Unser, auto racers.

Arlington, Texas

Mayor: Dr. Robert N. Cluck (to May 2007)
2000 census population (rank): 332,969 (54); **% change:** 27.2; **Male:** 166,465 (50%); **Female:** 166,504 (50%); **White:** 225,379 (67.7%); **Black:** 45,727 (13.7%); **American Indian and Alaska Native:** 1,817 (0.5%); **Asian:** 20,015 (6%); **Other race:** 29,763 (8.9%); **Two or more races:** 9,793 (2.9%); **Hispanic/Latino:** 60,817 (18.3%). **2000 percent population 18 and over:** 71.7%; **65 and over:** 6.1%; **Median age:** 30.7.
2004 population estimate (rank): 359,467 (50)
Land area: 99.5 sq mi. (257.7 sq km); **Avg. alt.:** 616 ft.
Avg. daily temp.: Jan., 43.5° F; Jul., 84.5° F
City-owned parks: 88 (4,500+ ac.); **Radio stations:** AM, 13; FM,20[1]; **Television stations:** 25[1]
Civilian Labor Force (MSA) April 2005: 990,000[2]; **Unemployed:** 49,800[2], **Percent:** 5.0[2]; **Per capita personal income (MSA) 2003:** $30,163[2]
Chamber of Commerce: Arlington Chamber of Commerce, 505 E. Border St., Arlington, TX 76010

1. Arlington-Fort Worth-Dallas area. 2. Fort Worth-Arlington, TX.

Arlington, the seventh-largest city in Texas, is located in Tarrant County, between Dallas and Fort Worth. It was named for Arlington, Va., home of General Robert E. Lee.

In 1875, the Texas and Pacific Railroad chose a site for a new station, which opened as Arlington Station in 1876. The surrounding city of Arlington was incorporated in 1884. Arlington College opened in 1895; it would, in 1966, become the University of Texas at Arlington.

Arlington is one of the nation's fastest-growing cities, more than doubling in population between 1980 and 2000. Its General Motors plant employs 3,000, producing automobiles and parts. The city also produces medical, electronic, and oil-field equipment, plus rubber and plastic products.

Arlington is perhaps best known for its recreational and sports attractions. In 1961, the Six Flags Over Texas amusement park opened its doors. In 1972, the Washington Senators baseball team moved to their new home at Turnpike Stadium (now Ameriquest Field), becoming the Texas Rangers. A new $650 million football stadium for the Dallas Cowboys was approved by Arlington voters in 2004 and is slated for completion in 2009. Located just five miles from the Dallas/Fort Worth International Airport, Arlington continues to serve as a transportational hub for the area.

Selected famous natives and residents: Sandra Brown, author; Kalpana Chawla, astronaut; Tommy Franks, general; Ben Grieve, baseball player; Lou Diamond Phillips, actor; B. J. Thomas, singer; Verne Troyer, actor.

Atlanta, Ga.

Mayor: Shirley Franklin (to Jan. 2006)
2000 census population (rank): 416,474 (39);
% change: 5.7; **Male:** 206,725 (49.6%); **Female:**
209,749 (50.4%); **White:** 138,352 (33.2%); **Black:**
255,689 (61.4%); **American Indian and Alaska
Native:** 765 (0.2%); **Asian:** 8,046 (1.9%);
Other race: 8,272 (2.0%); **Two or more races:** 5,177
(1.2%); **Hispanic/Latino:** 18,720 (4.5%). **2000 percent population 18 and over:** 77.7%; **65 and over:**
9.7%; **Median age:** 31.9.
2004 population estimate (rank): 419,122 (42)
Land area: 132 sq mi. (341 sq km); **Alt.:** Highest, 1,050
ft.; lowest, 940 ft.
Avg. daily temp.: Jan., 41.0° F; July, 78.8° F
Churches: 1,500; **City-owned parks:** 277 (3,178 ac.);
Radio stations: AM, 7; FM, 20; **Television stations:**
8 commercial; 2 PBS
Civilian Labor Force (MSA) March 2005: 2,526,100[1];
Unemployed: 123,500[1], **Percent:** 4.9[1]; **Per capita
personal income (MSA) 2003:** $33,308[1]
Chamber of Commerce: Metro Atlanta Chamber of
Commerce, 235 Andrew Young International Blvd.,
Atlanta, GA 30303

1. Atlanta-Sandy Springs–Marietta, Ga.

Atlanta, the largest city and capital of Georgia, is
the seat of Fulton County. It is situated in the northwest part of the state at the base of the Blue Ridge
Mountains near the Chattahoochee River. The first
European settler was Hardy Ivy, who built a cabin
there in 1833.

Founded as Terminus in 1837, the town served as
the end of the Georgia railroad line (Western and
Atlantic Railroad) and later became incorporated as
Marthasville in 1843 in honor of ex-governor Lump-
kin's daughter Martha. It was renamed Atlanta in
1845 and incorporated as a city in 1847. The name
was suggested by the railroad's chief engineer, J.
Edgar Thomson, and was derived from its location at
the end of the Georgia and Atlantic railroad line. The
city became the capital of Georgia in 1868.

During the Civil War, the city was burned and
almost completely destroyed while occupied by
Gen. William T. Sherman's troops in Nov. 1864. It
was rebuilt after the war and grew rapidly due to the
expansion of the railroads in the southwest.

Today, Atlanta is the major commercial and transportation hub of the southeast United States, and its
international airport is one of the busiest in the
world. The city's economy is led by the service,
communications, retail trade, manufacturing,
finance, and insurance industries. The convention
business is also important, and Atlanta is home to
many major corporations, including Coca-Cola,
which was founded there in 1892.

Atlanta is also a major educational center, with
many prestigious universities and colleges, including Emory University (1836), Georgia Institute of
Technology (1885), and Georgia State University
(1913). Morehouse College (1867), Spelman College (1881), and Clark Atlanta University (1865;
1869) are important historically black colleges.

Major attractions include Martin Luther King, Jr.,
National Historic Site, Grant Park, and the Carter
Presidential Center. The 1996 Summer Olympics
were held in Atlanta.

Selected famous natives and residents: Hank Aaron,
baseball player; Arrested Development, recording artists;
Jimmy Carter, former president; Ray Charles, singer;
James Dickey, poet; Mattiwilda Dobbs, soprano; Walt
Frazier, basketball player; Oliver Hardy, comedian;
Evander Holyfield, boxer; Alan Jackson, singer; Bobby
Jones, golfer; DeForest Kelley, actor; Martin Luther King,
Jr., civil rights leader and Nobel Peace Prize winner;
Gladys Knight, singer; Kriss Kross, recording artists;
Margaret Mitchell, novelist; Bert Parks, entertainer; Eric
Roberts, actor; Julia Roberts, actress; Doug Stone, singer;
Gwen Torrence, Olympic athlete; Lee Tracy, actor; Travis
Tritt, singer; Ted Turner, TBS and CNN founder; Jane
Withers, actress; Joanne Woodward, actress; Andrew
Young, civil rights activist.

Austin, Tex.

Mayor: Will Wynn (to June 2006)
2000 census population (rank): 656,562 (16);
% change: 41.0; **Male:** 337,569 (51.4%); **Female:**
318,993 (48.6%); **White:** 429,100 (65.4%); **Black:**
65,956 (10.0%); **American Indian and Alaska Native:**
3,889 (0.6%); **Asian:** 30,960 (4.7%); **Other race:**
106,538 (16.2%); **Two or more races:** 19,650 (3.0%);
Hispanic/Latino: 200,579 (30.5%). **2000 percent
population 18 and over:** 77.5%; **65 and over:** 6.7%;
Median age: 29.6.
2004 population estimate (rank): 681,804 (16)
Land area: 252 sq mi. (653 sq km); **Alt.:** From 425 ft. to
over 1000 ft.
Avg. daily temp.: Jan., 48.8° F; July, 84.5° F
Churches: 353 churches, representing 45 denominations; **City-owned parks and playgrounds:** 205
(16,076 ac.); **Radio stations:** AM, 12; FM, 27;
Television stations: 7 commercial; 1 PBS;
1 independent
Civilian Labor Force (MSA) March 2005: 783,800[1];
Unemployed: 35,700[1], **Percent:** 4.6[1]; **Per capita per-
sonal income (MSA) 2003:** $31,135[1]
Chamber of Commerce: Greater Austin Chamber of
Commerce, 210 Barton Springs Rd., Ste. 400, Aus-
tin, TX 78704

1. Austin–Round Rock, Tex.

Austin, the state capital of Texas and seat of
Travis County, is the fourth-largest city in Texas. It
is situated in the south-central part of the state on
the Colorado River.

The site was called Waterloo in 1838, and in 1839
it was incorporated as a city and chosen as the capital of the independent Republic of Texas. Waterloo
was renamed Austin in honor of Stephen F. Austin,
the founder of the Texas Republic. It became the
permanent capital of the state of Texas in 1870.

Austin's growth was spurred by several developments after the Civil War—the railroads reached the
city in the 1870s; it was crossed by the important
Chisholm cattle trail; and it became the seat of the
state university in 1883.

Austin has a growing commercial and diversified
manufacturing sector. Civilian government employment is 20% of the labor force and is important to
the economy. As home to the University of Texas,
Austin is a major center for research and development and is nationally recognized as a high-
technology center.

Austin's visitor attractions include the Austin
Museum of Art, the Lyndon B. Johnson Library and
Museum, the Lady Bird Johnson Wildflower Center,
and the Austin Zoo.

Selected famous natives and residents: Don Baylor,
baseball player and manager; Earl Campbell, football
player; Liz Carpenter, author; Dabney Coleman, actor; Ben
Crenshaw, golfer; Michael Dell, founder Dell Computer
Corp.; Tobe Hooper, film director; Lady Bird Johnson,
former first lady; Tom Kite, golfer; James Michener, author;
Willie Nelson, musician; Amado Pena, artist; Darrell Royal,
football coach; Zachary Scott, actor; Jerry Jeff Walker,
musician; Dalhart Windberg, artist.

Baltimore, Md.

Mayor: Martin O'Malley (to Dec. 2008)
2000 census population (rank): 651,154 (17);
% change: −11.5; **Male:** 303,687 (46.6%); **Female:**
347,467 (53.4%); **White:** 205,982 (31.6%); **Black:**
418,951 (64.3%); **American Indian and Alaska**
Native: 2,097 (0.3%); **Asian:** 9,985 (1.5%); **Other**
race: 4,363 (0.7%); **Two or more races:** 9,554
(1.5%); **Hispanic/Latino:** 11,061 (1.7%). **2000 per-**
cent population 18 and over: 75.2%; **65 and over:**
13.2%; **Median age:** 35.0.
2004 population estimate (rank): 636,251 (18)
Land area: 81 sq mi. (210 sq km); **Alt.:** Highest,
490 ft.; lowest, sea level
Avg. daily temp.: Jan., 31.8° F; July, 77.0° F
Churches: Roman Catholic, 72; Jewish, 50; Protestant
and others, 344; **City-owned parks:** 347 park areas
and tracts (6,314 ac.); **Radio stations:** AM, 10; FM,
11; **Television stations:** 7
Civilian Labor Force (PMSA) March 2005: 1,340,500[1];
Unemployed: 63,800[1], **Percent:** 4.8[1]; **Per capita per-**
sonal income (MSA) 2003: $336,733[1]
Chamber of Commerce: Baltimore City Chamber of
Commerce, 312 N. Martin Luther King, Jr. Blvd., Baltimore, MD 21201

1. Baltimore–Towson, Md.

Baltimore, the largest city in Maryland, is situated in the northern part of the state on the Patap-
sco River estuary, an arm of Chesapeake Bay. The
city is independent and does not fall within any
county.

The site was settled in the early 17th century and
founded as a town in 1729. The town was named
after Lord Baltimore, the founder of Maryland, and
was incorporated as a city in 1797. It has an excellent harbor and has been a principal port since the
18th century. Baltimore was a pioneer shipbuilding
center, and the Baltimore clipper was used extensively in world trade.

The city has been greatly affected by the nation's
wars. During the War of 1812, the British bombarded nearby Fort McHenry, inspiring Francis
Scott Key to write the *Star-Spangled Banner*. And
although Maryland never seceded from the Union,
Baltimore was occupied by Union troops throughout the Civil War. The city was also an important
shipbuilding and supply center during the World
Wars.

Baltimore's economy is very diverse, with strong
financial, legal, and nonprofit service industries. The
city also leads in scientific research and development through two highly acclaimed medical institutions, Johns Hopkins Hospital and University of
Maryland Hospital. There is also a significant tourist sector. Major attractions include the the National
Aquarium, Harborplace, the Maryland Science Center, the Babe Ruth Museum, Fort McHenry National
Monument, and Pimlico Race Course, site of the
Preakness.

Selected famous natives and residents: Larry Adler,
musician; John Astin, actor; Eubie Blake, pianist; Francis X.
Bushman, actor; Charlie Chase, actor; Hans Conried, actor;
Mildred Dunnock, actress; "Mama" Cass Elliot, singer; Barry
Farber, broadcaster; Paul Ford, actor; Philip Glass,
composer; Billie Holiday, singer; Barry Levinson, director;
H. L. Mencken, writer; Babe Ruth, baseball player; Upton
Sinclair, novelist; Leon Uris, novelist; John Waters, film
director, writer, and actor; Frank Zappa, musician.

Boston, Mass.

Mayor: Thomas Menino (to Jan. 2006)
2000 census population (rank): 589,141 (20);
% change: 2.6; **Male:** 283,588 (48.1%); **Female,**
305,553 (51.9%); **White:** 320,944 (54.5%); **Black:**
149,202 (25.3%); **American Indian and Alaska**
Native: 2,365 (0.4%); **Asian:** 44,284 (7.5%); **Other**
race: 46,102 (7.8%); **Two or more races:** 25,878
(4.4%); **Hispanic/Latino:** 85,089 (14.4%). **2000 per-**
cent population 18 and over: 80.2%; **65 and over:**
10.4%; **Median age:** 31.1.
2004 population estimate (rank): 569,165 (24)
Land area: 48 sq mi. (124 sq km); **Alt.:** Highest, 330 ft.;
lowest, sea level
Avg. daily temp.: Jan., 28.6° F; July, 73.5° F
Churches: Protestant, 187; Roman Catholic, 70; Jewish,
13; others, 100; **City-owned parks, playgrounds,**
etc.: 2,260 ac.; **Radio stations:**[1] AM, 24; FM, 22;
Television stations:[1] 27
Civilian Labor Force (PMSA) March 2005: 1,466,500[2];
Unemployed: 67,300[2], **Percent:** 4.6[2]; **Per capita per-**
sonal income (MSA) 2003: $43,135[2]
Chamber of Commerce: Greater Boston Chamber of
Commerce, 75 State St., 2nd Fl., Boston, MA 02109

1. Metropolitan area. 2. Boston–Cambridge–Quincy, Mass.

Boston is the state capital, the seat of Suffolk
County, and the largest city in Massachusetts. It is
located in the eastern part of the state on Massachusetts Bay. It was incorporated as a city in 1822. No
city in the U.S. is richer in historical associations
than Boston, and no city has retained more of its
original buildings as memorials to America's past.

The first European settler was Rev. William
Blackstone, who arrived in 1623, just three years
after the Pilgrims had landed at Plymouth in 1620.
He was joined by Puritans from England in 1630.
They named their new town Boston, after the former
home of many of them in Lincolnshire, England.
Fourteen years later, the pioneer Bostonians set
aside the first public park in the U.S.—the Boston
Common. The following year, 1635, they opened
the first free public school in America. Today, the
Boston area is home to 68 colleges and universities.

Boston is a major industrial, financial, and educational hub and has one of the finest ports in the
world. The city's banking and financial services,
insurance, and real estate sectors continue to drive
Boston's economy. Boston is also a leading city in
health care, with 25 inpatient hospitals and numerous community health centers. The city's unique
cultural and historic heritage makes it a center of
tourism, and its hotel industry ranks among the
highest in the nation in occupancy. Boston's other
businesses are in high technology, biotechnology,
software, and electronics.

The city's tourist attractions include Faneuil Hall
Marketplace, the JFK Library and Museum, the
Museum of Fine Arts, the New England Aquarium,
the USS *Constitution*, and many historic buildings
and neighborhoods.

Selected famous natives and residents: Samuel Adams,
patriot; Louisa May Alcott, author; John Singleton Copley,
painter; Ralph Waldo Emerson, philosopher and poet;
Arthur Fiedler, conductor; Benjamin Franklin, statesman
and scientist; Edward Everett Hale, clergyman and author;
Oliver Wendell Holmes, Supreme Court justice; Winslow
Homer, painter; Joseph P. Kennedy, financier; Jack
Lemmon, actor; Robert Lowell, poet; Edgar Allan Poe,
writer; Paul Revere, patriot and silversmith; John L.
Sullivan, boxer; Barbara Walters, TV journalist.

Charlotte, N.C.

Mayor: Pat McCrory (to Nov. 2005)
2000 census population (rank): 540,828 (26);
% change: 36.6; **Male:** 264,978 (49.0%); **Female:**
275,850 (51.0%); **White:** 315,061 (58.3%); **Black:**
176,964 (32.7%); **American Indian and Alaska
Native:** 1,863 (0.3%); **Asian:** 18,418 (3.4%); **Other
race:** 19,242 (3.6%); **Two or more races:** 8,997
(1.7%); **Hispanic/Latino:** 39,800 (7.4%). **2000 percent population 18 and over:** 75.3%; **65 and over:**
8.8%; **Median age:** 32.7.
2004 population estimate (rank): 594,359 (20)
Land area: 242 sq mi. (627 sq km); **Alt.:** 765 ft.
Avg. daily temp.: Jan., 39.3° F; July, 79.3° F
Churches: Protestant, over 500; Roman Catholic, 13;
Jewish, 3; Greek Orthodox, 1; **City-owned parks
and parkways:** 150+; **Radio stations:** AM, 10; FM,
19; **Television stations:** 6 commercial; 1 PBS
Civilian Labor Force (MSA) March 2005: 780,300;
Unemployed: 39,700, **Percent:** 5.1; **Per capita per-
sonal income (MSA) 2003:** $33,251[1]
Chamber of Commerce: Charlotte Chamber of Com-
merce, 330 S. Tryon St., P.O. Box 32785, Charlotte,
NC, 28232

1. Charlotte–Gastonia–Concord, N.C.–S.C.

Charlotte, North Carolina's largest city and the
seat of Mecklenburg County, is located in the southern part of the state near the South Carolina border.
It was named for King George III of England's wife,
Charlotte Sophia of Mecklenburg-Strelitz.

Settled about 1750, Charlotte was incorporated as
a city in 1768 and made the county seat in 1774.
From 1800 to 1848, Charlotte was the center of U.S.
gold production. A branch of the U.S. mint operated
there from 1837 to 1913. Charlotte was a leading
Confederate city during the Civil War and was the
last meeting place of the full Confederate cabinet.

Charlotte is the second-largest banking center in
the United States, and two of the nation's top banks,
Wachovia and Bank of America, are headquartered
there. Other major employers are the education,
health care, government, technology, and communications sectors. The city is a hub for US Airways.

Charlotte is the home of the University of North
Carolina at Charlotte (1946) as well as the Carolina
Panthers (football) and Lowe's Motor Speedway.

Selected famous natives and residents: Romare Bearden,
artist; Billy Graham, evangelist; Charles Gwathmey, architect;
Hamilton Jordan, government official; Randolph Scott, actor.

Chicago, Ill.

Mayor: Richard M. Daley (to April 2007)
2000 census population (rank): 2,896,016 (3);
% change: 4.0; **Male:** 1,405,107 (48.5%); **Female:**
1,490,909 (51.5%); **White:** 1,215,315 (42.0%); **Black:**
1,065,009 (36.8%); **American Indian and Alaska
Native:** 10,290 (0.4%); **Asian:** 125,974 (4.3%); **Other
race:** 393,203 (13.6%); **Two or more races:** 84,437
(2.9%); **Hispanic/Latino:** 753,644 (26.0%). **2000 percent population 18 and over:** 73.8%; **65 and over:**
10.3%; **Median age:** 31.5.
2004 population estimate (rank): 2,862,244 (3)
Land area: 227 sq mi. (588 sq km); **Alt.:** Highest, 672
ft.; lowest, 578.5 ft.
Avg. daily temp.: Jan., 22.4° F; July, 75.1° F
Churches: Protestant, 850; Roman Catholic, 252; Jewish, 51; **City-owned parks:** 552 (7,300 ac.); **Radio
stations:** AM, 21; FM, 37; **Television stations:** 31
Civilian Labor Force (PMSA) April 2005: 4,005,100[1];
Unemployed: 248,800[1], **Percent:** 6.2[1]; **Per capita
personal income (MSA) 2003:** $35,464[1]

Chamber of Commerce: Chicagoland Chamber of
Commerce, One IBM Plaza, 330 N. Wabash, Suite
2800, Chicago, IL 60611

1. Chicago–Naperville–Joliet, Ill.

Chicago is the largest city in Illinois and the seat
of Cook County. It stretches for 22 mi along the
southwest shore of Lake Michigan in the northeast
part of the state.

The first white men known to have visited the
region were Louis Joliet and Jacques Marquette in
1673. The first permanent white settler was John
Kinzie, who is sometimes called the Father of Chicago. He took over a trading post in 1796 that had
been established in 1791 by Jean-Baptiste Point du
Sable, a black fur trapper. Fort Dearborn, a block-
house and stockade, was built in 1804 but was
evacuated in 1812, at which time more than half of
its garrison was massacred by Potawatomi and
Ottawa Indians loyal to the British.

The name Chicago is thought to come from an
Algonquian word meaning "onion" or "skunk."

Laid out in 1830, Chicago was incorporated as a
village in 1833 and as a city in 1837. In the Great
Chicago Fire of 1871, an area of the city about 4 mi
long and nearly a mile wide—more than two thousand acres—was totally destroyed. However, much
of the city, including the railroads and stockyards,
survived intact, and from the ashes of the old
wooden structures there arose more modern constructions in steel and stone.

Today, Chicago is a major Great Lakes port and
the commercial, financial, industrial, and cultural
center of the Midwest. The manufacturing industries
dominate the wholesale and retail trade, and trade in
agricultural commodities is important to the
economy. The Chicago Board of Trade is the largest
agricultural futures market in the world.

Among Chicago's many attractions are the Art
Institute of Chicago, the Field Museum of Natural
History, the Jane Addams–Hull House Museum,
Navy Pier, and numerous architectural landmarks
such as the Sears Tower and Frank Lloyd Wright's
Robie House.

Selected famous natives and residents: Jack Benny,
comedian; Edgar Rice Burroughs, author; Raymond
Chandler, author; Hillary Rodham Clinton, U.S. senator,
lawyer, and former first lady; Michael Crichton, author; Walt
Disney, filmmaker; John Dos Passos, author; Bobby Fischer,
chess player; Bob Fosse, choreographer and director; Benny
Goodman, clarinetist; Dorothy Hamill, figure skater; Quincy
Jones, composer; Gene Krupa, drummer; David Mamet,
playwright; Bob Newhart, comedian; Kim Novak, actress;
Donald O'Connor, actor; William L. Shirer, journalist and
historian; Gloria Swanson, actress; Melvin Van Peebles,
playwright; Alfred Wallenstein, conductor; Robin Williams,
comedian and actor; Robert Young, actor.

Cleveland, Ohio

Mayor: Jane Campbell (to Jan. 2006)
2000 census population (rank): 478,403 (33);
% change: −5.4; **Male:** 226,550 (47.4%); **Female:**
251,853 (52.6%); **White:** 198,510 (41.5%); **Black:**
243,939 (51.0%); **American Indian and Alaska
Native:** 1,458 (0.3%); **Asian:** 6,444 (1.3%); **Other
race:** 17,173 (3.6%); **Two or more races:** 10,701
(2.2%); **Hispanic/Latino:** 34,728 (7.3%). **2000 percent population 18 and over:** 71.5%; **65 and over:**
12.5%; **Median age:** 33.0.
2004 population estimate (rank): 458,684 (36)
Land area: 78 sq mi. (202 sq km); **Alt.:** Highest, 1048
ft.; lowest, 573 ft.
Avg. daily temp.: Jan., 24.8° F; July, 71.9° F

Churches:[1] Protestant, 980; Roman Catholic, 187; Jewish, 31; Eastern Orthodox, 22; **City-owned parks:** 41 (1,930 ac.); **Radio stations:** AM, 9; FM, 19; **Television stations:** 22
Civilian Labor Force (PMSA) April 2005: 1,095,800[1]; **Unemployed:** 60,300[1], **Percent:** 5.5[1]; **Per capita personal income (MSA) 2003:** $33,196[1]
Chamber of Commerce: Greater Cleveland Partnership, 50 Public Sq., Ste. 200, Cleveland, OH 44113

1. Cleveland–Elyria–Mentor, Ohio.

Cleveland is the second-largest city in Ohio and the seat of Cuyahoga County. It is located in the northeast part of the state on Lake Erie.

In the colonial era, the Cleveland area was known as the Connecticut Western Reserve, part of a land grant made to Connecticut by King Charles II in 1662. The city was founded in 1796 by Gen. Moses Cleaveland, who was the head surveyor of the Connecticut Land Company. This company had bought 3 million acres in what is now northern Ohio. A permanent settlement was founded in 1799, named after the general, and the spelling was shortened to Cleveland. The city was incorporated in 1836.

Cleveland's industrial growth was stimulated by the opening of the Ohio and Erie canals in 1832 and, later, by the advent of the Civil War, with the increasing demand for machinery, railroad equipment, ships, and other items. Today, the port of Cleveland is the largest overseas general cargo port on Lake Erie.

Greater Cleveland has long been famous as a durable goods manufacturing area. Following the national trend, however, Cleveland has been shifting to a more services-based economy. Greater Cleveland is a world corporate center for leading national and multinational companies in industries ranging from transportation, insurance, retailing, and utilities, to commercial banking and finance.

The city's cultural attractions include the Cleveland Museum of Art and the Cleveland Orchestra, one of the country's most highly acclaimed symphony orchestras. Jacobs Field, a major league ballpark, and the Rock & Roll Hall of Fame also draw thousands of visitors to the city.

Selected famous natives and residents: Jim Backus, actor; Drew Carey, actor and comedian; Dorothy Dandridge, actress; Ruby Dee, actress; Phil Donahue, talk-show host; Joel Grey, actor; Arsenio Hall, talk-show host; Margaret Hamilton, actress; Philip Johnson, architect; Henry Mancini, composer; Burgess Meredith, actor; Paul Newman, actor; Carl Stokes, jurist.

Colorado Springs, Colo.

Mayor: Lionel Rivera (to April 2007)
2000 census population (rank): 360,890 (48);
% change: 28.4; **Male:** 178,469 (49.5%); **Female:** 182,421 (50.5%); **White:** 291,095 (80.7%); **Black:** 23,677 (6.6%); **American Indian and Alaska Native:** 3,175 (0.9%); **Asian:** 10,179 (2.8%); **Other race:** 18,091 (5.0%); **Two or more races:** 13,909 (3.9%); **Hispanic/Latino:** 43,330 (12.0%). **2000 percent population 18 and over:** 73.5%; **65 and over:** 9.6%; **Median age:** 33.6.
2004 population estimate (rank): 369,363 (49)
Land area: 186 sq mi. (482 sq km); **Alt.:** 6,035 ft.
Avg. daily temp.: Jan., 28.8° F; July, 70.8° F
Churches: Protestant, 400+; Roman Catholic, 20; Jewish, 3; **City parks and playgrounds:** 156 (12,000+ ac.); **Radio stations:** AM, 7; FM, 17; **Television stations:** 7

Civilian Labor Force (MSA) March 2005: 290,300; **Unemployed:** 17,100, **Percent:** 5.9; **Per capita personal income (MSA) 2003:** $30,736
Chamber of Commerce: Colorado Springs Chamber of Commerce, 2 N. Cascade Ave., Suite 110, Colorado Springs, CO 80903

Colorado Springs is the second-largest city in Colorado, after Denver. It is the seat of El Paso County, making up about three-quarters of the county's population. It is located on the edge of the Rocky Mountains, with Pikes Peak (14,110 ft) towering beside it to the west. To the east begin the Great Plains.

The city was founded in 1871. Gen. William Jackson Palmer, a Pennsylvania-born Civil War veteran, came across the scenic spot in his railroad travels and was inspired to begin a new resort community there. The subsequent development of Colorado Springs was influenced in part by an influx of English tourists later in the 1870s and by the discovery of gold in nearby Cripple Creek in the 1890s. Millionaire businessmen and philanthropists, such as Spencer Penrose, Charles Tutt, and Winfield Scott Stratton, helped to establish the city's infrastructure and shape its popularity as a tourist destination.

During World War II, Colorado Springs sold a large amount of land just south of the city to the military. The U.S. Army established Fort Carson as a training facility. The military presence in Colorado Springs continued to grow with the establishment of the U.S. Air Force Academy there in the 1950s and, later, the construction of Peterson Air Force Base, Falcon Air Force Base, and Cheyenne Mountain Air Force Base. The bases are all home to space command centers (with Cheyenne Mountain housing the headquarters for the North American Aerospace Defense Command [NORAD]) and have collectively earned Colorado Springs its national reputation as the leading center for military space operations.

The city's economy is still based heavily on tourism, although in more recent years, Colorado Springs has gained a strong foothold in the electronics, high-technology, and manufacturing industries. The city is the headquarters of the U.S. Olympic Committee and Olympic Training Center facility.

Selected famous natives and residents: Bert Andrews, journalist; Kelly Bishop, actress; Spring Byington, actress; Lon Chaney, actor; Marjorie Daw, actress; Marceline Day, actress; Rich "Goose" Gossage, baseball player; Helen Hunt Jackson, writer and poet; Chase Masterson, actress; Sherry Stringfield, actress.

Columbus, Ohio

Mayor: Michael B. Coleman (to Nov. 2007)
2000 census population (rank): 711,470 (15);
% change: 12.4; **Male:** 345,878 (48.6%); **Female:** 365,592 (51.4%); **White:** 483,332 (67.9%); **Black:** 174,065 (24.5%); **American Indian and Alaska Native:** 2,090 (0.3%); **Asian:** 24,495 (3.4%); **Other race:** 8,292 (1.2%); **Two or more races:** 18,829 (2.6%); **Hispanic/Latino:** 17,471 (2.5%). **2000 percent population 18 and over:** 75.8%; **65 and over:** 8.9%; **Median age:** 30.6.
2004 population estimate (rank): 730,008 (15)
Land area: 210 sq mi. (544 sq km); **Alt.:** Highest, 902 ft.; lowest, 702 ft.
Avg. daily temp.: Jan., 26.4° F; July, 73.2° F
Churches: Protestant, 436; Roman Catholic, 62; Jewish,

5; Other, 8; **City-owned parks:** 203 (12,891 ac.);
Radio stations: AM, 10; FM, 16; **Television stations:** 9 commercial; 3 PBS
Civilian Labor Force (MSA) March 2005: 911,700;
Unemployed: 53,300, **Percent:** 5.8; **Per capita personal income (MSA) 2002:** $32,930
Chamber of Commerce: Columbus Area Chamber of Commerce, 37 N. High St., Columbus, OH 43215

Columbus, the largest city in Ohio, is the state capital and the seat of Franklin County. It is located in central Ohio on the Scioto River.

The first structures near the site of downtown Columbus were earthen mounds constructed by Indian tribes known as Mound Builders. Native Americans lived undisturbed in Central Ohio until the 1700s, when the first white explorers entered the Midwest. The first permanent white settlement in the area was founded by a surveyor from Kentucky, Lucas Sullivant, in 1797 and was named Franklinton. The state capital was laid out nearby in 1812 and named after Christopher Columbus. It became the capital in 1816. Columbus was chartered as a city in 1834 and annexed Franklinton in 1870. The city's growth was stimulated by the development of transportation facilities—a feeder to the Ohio Canal completed in 1832, the National Road in 1833, and the arrival of the railroad in 1850.

Columbus is a port of entry and a major commercial, distribution, and cultural center. It is the seat of Ohio State University (1870). The city has enjoyed steady growth over the years due to its economic diversity, and no single activity dominates the economy.

Selected famous natives and residents: Warner Baxter, actor; George Bellows, painter; Michael Feinstein, singer and pianist; Eileen Heckart, actress; Jack Nicklaus, golfer; Tom Poston, actor; Eddie Rickenbacker, aviator; Arthur M. Schlesinger, historian; James Thurber, writer and cartoonist; Nancy Wilson, singer.

Dallas, Tex.

Mayor: Laura Miller (to May 2007)
City Manager: Mary Suhm
2000 census population (rank): 1,188,580 (8);
% change: 18.0; **Male:** 598,991 (50.4%); **Female:** 589,589 (49.6%); **White:** 604,209 (50.8%); **Black:** 307,957 (25.9%); **American Indian and Alaska Native:** 6,472 (0.5%); **Asian:** 32,118 (2.7%); **Other race:** 204,883 (17.2%); **Two or more races:** 32,351 (2.7%); **Hispanic/Latino:** 422,587 (35.6%). **2000 percent population 18 and over:** 73.4%; **65 and over:** 8.6%; **Median age:** 30.5.
2004 population estimate (rank): 1,210,393 (9)
Land area: 343 sq mi. (888 sq km); **Alt.:** Highest, 750 ft.; lowest, 375 ft.
Avg. daily temp.: Jan., 44.6° F; July, 85.9° F
Churches: 1,974 (in Dallas Co.); **City-owned parks:** 406 (21,000+ ac.); **Radio stations:** AM, 19; FM, 30; **Television stations:** 10 commercial; 1 PBS
Civilian Labor Force (PMSA) March 2005: 2,958,800[1];
Unemployed: 160,100[1], **Percent:** 5.4[1]; **Per capita personal income (MSA) 2003:** $33,790[1]
Chamber of Commerce: Greater Dallas Chamber of Commerce, 700 N. Pearl St., Ste. 1200, Dallas, TX 75201

1. Dallas–Fort Worth–Arlington, Tex.

Dallas is the second-largest city in Texas and the seat of Dallas County. It is situated 185 mi northeast of Austin on the Trinity River near the junction of its three forks.

Dallas was first settled by Tennessee lawyer John Neely Bryan as a trading post on the Trinity River in 1841. Many historians believe that Bryan named the city after George Mifflin Dallas, vice president under James K. Polk, but there is no official agreement on this. It was incorporated as a town in 1856 and as a city in 1871. Located in the chief cotton-producing region of Texas, the city developed as a cotton market in the 1870s.

The economy is highly diversified, and the city is the leading commercial, marketing, and industrial center of the southwest. The insurance business is important, and the service sector has experienced rapid growth. Dallas is also a popular tourist and convention city.

Selected famous natives and residents: Tex Avery, animator and director; Robby Benson, actor; Ernie Banks, baseball player; Bebe Daniels, actress; Linda Darnell, actress; Lee Elder, golfer; Morgan Fairchild, actress; Trini Lopez, singer; Aaron Spelling, producer; Stephen Stills, singer; Sharon Tate, actress; Lee Trevino, golfer.

Denver, Colo.

Mayor: John Hickenlooper (to June 2007)
2000 census population (rank): 554,636 (25);
% change: 18.6; **Male:** 280,207 (50.5%); **Female:** 274,429 (49.5%); **White:** 362,180 (65.3%); **Black:** 61,649 (11.1%); **American Indian and Alaska Native:** 7,290 (1.3%); **Asian:** 15,611 (2.8%); **Other race:** 86,464 (15.6%); **Two or more races:** 20,794 (3.7%); **Hispanic/Latino:** 175,704 (31.7%). **2000 percent population 18 and over:** 78.0%; **65 and over:** 11.3%; **Median age:** 33.1.
2004 population estimate (rank): 556,835 (25)
Land area: 155 sq mi. (401 sq km); **Alt.:** Highest, 5,672 ft.; lowest, 5,140 ft.
Avg. daily temp.: Jan., 29.7° F; July, 73.5° F
Churches: [1] Protestant, 859; Roman Catholic, 60; Jewish, 13; **City-owned parks:** 301 (5,100 ac.); **City-owned mountain parks:** 40 (13,600 ac.); **Radio stations:** [1] AM, 23; FM, 20; **Television stations:** [1] 10
Civilian Labor Force (PMSA) March 2005 1,270,000[2];
Unemployed: 73,000[2], **Percent:** 5.7[2]; **Per capita personal income (MSA) 2003:** $39,203[2]
Chamber of Commerce: Denver Metro Chamber of Commerce, 1445 Market Street, Denver, CO 80202

1. Metropolitan area. 2. Denver–Aurora, Colo.

Denver is the largest city in Colorado, the state capital, and the seat of Denver County. It lies at the foot of the Rocky Mountains at the junction of the South Platte River and Cherry Creek.

The city was born in 1858, when gold was discovered in the sands of Cherry Creek, at first just a tough village of cabins, shacks, and tents. It was incorporated as a city in 1861 and became the territorial capital in 1867. The city is named for James W. Denver, governor of the Kansas Territory, which included part of Colorado. The city prospered following the opening of the famous gold and silver mines of the 1870s and 1880s.

Today, Denver is an important communications, transportation, manufacturing, and agribusiness hub. Telecommunications and biomedical technology are two of the largest industries; construction, real estate, and retail trade are among the fastest-growing industries. The city is also home to many environmental organizations, including federal government agencies such as the Environmental Protection Agency and the National Oceanic and Atmospheric Administration.

Denver International Airport opened to passenger traffic in 1995. At 53 sq mi, it is the largest airport in North America.

The city's tourist attractions include the Denver Zoo, the Six Flags Elitch Gardens amusement park, the Red Rocks Amphitheatre, the Coors Brewery, and nearby Rocky Mountain National Park.

Selected famous natives and residents: Tim Allen, comedian and actor; Ward Bond, actor; Douglas Fairbanks, Sr., actor; John Hart, newsman; Pat Hingle, actor; Ted Mack, TV host; Barbara Rush, actress; Alan K. Simpson, U.S. senator; Paul Whiteman, bandleader; Don Wilson, announcer.

Detroit, Mich.

Mayor: Kwame Kilpatrick (to Jan. 2006)
2000 census population (rank): 951,270 (10);
% change: −7.5; **Male:** 448,319 (47.1%); **Female:** 502,951 (52.9%); **White:** 116,599 (12.3%); **Black:** 775,772 (81.6%); **American Indian and Alaska Native:** 3,140 (0.3%); **Asian:** 9,268 (1.0%); **Other race:** 24,199 (2.5%); **Two or more races:** 22,041 (2.3%); **Hispanic/Latino:** 47,167 (5.0%). **2000 percent population 18 and over:** 68.9%; **65 and over:** 10.4%; **Median age:** 30.9.
2004 population estimate (rank): 900,198 (11)
Land area: 139 sq mi. (360 sq km); **Alt.:** Highest, 685 ft.; lowest, 574 ft.
Avg. daily temp.: Jan., 24.7° F; July, 74.2° F
Churches[1]: Protestant, 1,165; Roman Catholic, 89; Jewish, 2; **City-owned parks:** 56 parks (3,843 ac.); 393 sites (5,838 ac.); **Radio stations:** AM, 27; FM, 30 (includes 3 in Windsor, Ont.); **Television stations:** 8[2] (includes 1 in Windsor, Ont.)
Civilian Labor Force (PMSA) March 2005: 920,400[3]; **Unemployed:** 84,600[3], **Percent:** 9.2[3]; **Per capita personal income (MSA) 2003:** $35,972[4]
Chamber of Commerce: Detroit Regional Chamber of Commerce, One Woodward Avenue, P.O. Box 33840, Detroit MI 48232-0840

1. Six-county metropolitan area. 2. Within four counties of Metro Detroit. 3. Detroit–Livonia–Dearborn, Mich. 4. Detroit–Warren–Livonia, Mich.

Detroit, the largest city in Michigan, is situated in the southeast part of the state on the Detroit River. The seat of Wayne County, Detroit was incorporated as a city in 1815 and reincorporated in 1824.

Detroit is the oldest city of any size west of the seaboard colonies, having been founded by Antoine de la Mothe Cadillac on July 24, 1701, more than a century before Chicago was founded. The French were the first settlers, and they gave the city its name from their word meaning "strait," referring to the 27-mile-long Detroit River, which connects Lake Erie and Lake St. Clair. The river forms part of the international boundary, and marks the only point where Canada lies directly south of U.S. territory.

Because of its strategic location, Detroit was fought over by the French, the British, and the Indians during the French and Indian Wars. It was the headquarters for the British forces in the Northwest Territory during the American Revolutionary War.

The first steam vessel, the *Walk-in-the-Water*, made its appearance on the Great Lakes in 1818, and Detroit was the western terminus for most of its voyages from Buffalo. Its link to all the important cities on the Great Lakes made it a major exporting center.

Detroit is one of the largest manufacturing cities in the U.S. and is the center of the automobile manufacturing industry, which has experienced a decline due to foreign competition in the past decade. The health and medical care sector is important to the economy, and employment in the finance, insurance, and real-estate industries has inched up in the Detroit metropolitan area since the early 1990s.

Selected famous natives and residents: Anita Baker, singer; Sonny Bono, congressman and singer; Ralph Bunche, statesman; Ellen Burstyn, actress; Francis Ford Coppola, director; Aretha Franklin, singer; Casey Kasem, radio personality; Charles Lindbergh, aviator; Madonna, singer and actress; John Mitchell, former U.S. attorney general; Harry Morgan, actor; Rosa Parks, activist; George Peppard, actor; Gilda Radner, comedian; Della Reese, singer; Smokey Robinson, singer; Sugar Ray Robinson, boxer; Diana Ross, singer; George C. Scott, actor; Tom Selleck, actor; Lily Tomlin, comedian and actress; Margaret Whiting, singer.

El Paso, Tex.

Mayor: Joe Wardy (to May 2007)
2000 census population (rank): 563,662 (23);
% change: 9.4; **Male:** 267,651 (47.5%); **Female:** 296,011 (52.5%); **White:** 413,061 (73.3%); **Black:** 17,586 (3.1%); **American Indian and Alaska Native:** 4,601 (0.8%); **Asian:** 6,321 (1.1%); **Other race:** 102,320 (18.2%); **Two or more races:** 19,190 (3.4%); **Hispanic/Latino:** 431,875 (76.6%). **2000 percent population 18 and over:** 69.0%; **65 and over:** 10.7%; **Median age:** 31.1
2004 population estimate (rank): 592,099 (21)
Land area: 249 sq mi. (645 sq km); **Alt.:** 4,000 ft.
Avg. daily temp.: Jan., 42.8° F; July, 82.3° F
Churches: Protestant, 320; Roman Catholic, 39; Jewish, 3; others, 20; **City-owned parks:** 145 (2,150 ac.);[1] **Radio Stations:** AM, 18; FM, 17; **Television stations:** 6
Civilian Labor Force (MSA) March 2005: 291,400; **Unemployed:** 22,400, **Percent:** 7.7; **Per capita personal income (MSA) 2003:** $20,875
Chamber of Commerce: Greater El Paso Chamber of Commerce, 10 Civic Center Plaza, El Paso, TX 79944; Hispanic Chamber of Commerce, 201 E. Main, Ste. 100, Austin, TX 79901

1. Includes 129 developed and 16 undeveloped parks.

El Paso, the sixth-largest city in Texas and the seat of El Paso County, is located in the far western part of the state on the north bank of the Rio Grande, opposite the Mexican city of Ciudad Juárez on the south bank.

On April 30, 1598, Juan de Oñate took formal possession of the area for King Philip II of Spain. Subsequently he crossed the Rio Grande near a site west of present downtown El Paso, which he called "El Paso del Rio del Norte," meaning the crossing of the river—the first use of the name "El Paso." In 1659, the mission of Nuestra Señora de Guadalupe was founded on a site that is present-day downtown Ciudad Juárez; the mission is still in use today. In 1682, Spanish colonists from Mexico founded the settlement of Ysleta on the site of the present-day city. However, it wasn't until 1827 that the first permanent settlement at El Paso was established by Juan María Ponce de León. The city's real growth started with the arrival of the Southern Pacific Railroad in 1881. El Paso was incorporated as a city in 1873.

In 1888, Mexico changed the name of Paso del Norte to Ciudad Juárez in honor of Benito Juárez. Later, in 1967, the U.S. agreed to cede a long-disputed part of El Paso to Mexico due to changes in the course of the Rio Grande, which forms the international boundary between the two countries. El Paso and its sister city of Ciudad Juárez across the U.S./Mexico border are inexorably joined by culture and economy. El Paso and Juárez make up the largest international metroplex in the world.

El Paso is an important port of entry to the U.S. from Mexico. The high technology, medical device manufacturing, plastics, refining, automotive, food processing, and defense-related industries are important to the economy. El Paso's service sector has experienced healthy growth since the 1980s. El Paso is also a major tourist resort.

Selected famous natives and residents: Manuel Acosta, artist; Don Bluth, animation director; Vicki Carr, singer; Jose Cisneros, artist; Sam Donaldson, newsman; Albert Fall, government official; Judith Ivey, actress; Guy Kibbee, actor; Sandra Day O'Connor, Supreme Court justice; Debbie Reynolds, actress; Irene Ryan, actress.

Fort Worth, Tex.

Mayor: Mike Moncrief (to May 2007)
City Manager: Charles Boswell
2000 census population (rank): 534,694 (27);
  % change: 19.5; **Male:** 263,720 (49.3%); **Female:** 270,974 (50.7%); **White:** 319,159 (59.7%); **Black:** 108,310 (20.3%); **American Indian and Alaska Native:** 3,144 (0.6%); **Asian:** 14,105 (2.6%); **Other race:** 75,100 (14.0%); **Two or more races:** 14,535 (2.7%); **Hispanic/Latino:** 159,368 (29.8%). **2000 percent population 18 and over:** 71.7%; **65 and over:** 9.6%; **Median age:** 30.9.
2004 population estimate (rank): 603,337 (19)
Land area: 293 sq mi. (759 sq km); **Alt.:** Highest, 780 ft.; lowest, 520 ft.
Avg. daily temp.: Jan., 43.4° F; July, 85.3° F
Churches: 1,032, representing 72 denominations; **City-owned parks:** 222 (10,380 ac.); **Radio stations:**[1] AM, 29; FM, 48; **Television stations:** 13
Civilian Labor Force (PMSA) March 2005: 986,600;[2] **Unemployed:** 51,500,[2] **Percent:** 5.2;[2] **Per capita personal income (MSA) 2003:** $33,790[3]
Chamber of Commerce: Fort Worth Chamber of Commerce, 777 Taylor Street, Suite 900, Fort Worth, TX 76102

1. Dallas–Fort Worth area. 2. Fort Worth–Arlington, Tex. 3. Dallas–Fort Worth–Arlington, Tex.

Fort Worth, seat of Tarrant County, is situated in the north-central part of Texas on the Trinity River.

The city was founded by Maj. Ripley Arnold in 1849 as a military outpost on the Trinity River to protect settlers moving westward from frequent Indian attacks. It was named after Gen. William J. Worth, the commander of the Texas army. Fort Worth was incorporated in 1873. Its growth was stimulated in the 1870s by its proximity to the Chisholm cattle trail. It prospered as a meat-packing and shipping center when the Texas and Pacific Railway arrived in 1876 and later experienced a new boom when oil was discovered nearby in 1917. The establishment of military installations in the area during both world wars also spurred the economy.

Fort Worth has traditionally been a diverse center of manufacturing and is not dependent on the oil or financial sectors. The city's industries range from clothing and food products to jet fighters, helicopters, computers, pharmaceuticals, and plastics. Fort Worth is a national leader in aviation products, electronic equipment, and refrigeration equipment. It is home to a multitude of major corporate headquarters, offices, and distribution centers.

Selected famous natives and residents: Robert Bass, financier; Mark Brooks, golfer; Betty Buckley, singer and actress; Kate Capshaw, actress; Ornette Coleman,

composer; Sandra Haynie, golfer; Patricia Highsmith, writer; Spanky McFarland, actor; R. Bruce Merrifield, Nobelist in chemistry; Roger Miller, singer; Fess Parker, actor; Bill Paxton, actor; Rex Reed, critic; Johnny Rutherford, auto racer; Liz Smith, columnist.

Fresno, Calif.

Mayor: Alan Autry (to March 2008)
City Manager: Andrew T. Souza
2000 census population (rank): 427,652 (37);
  % change: 20.7; **Male:** 210,107 (49.1%); **Female:** 217,545 (50.9%); **White:** 214,556 (50.2%); **Black:** 35,763 (8.4%); **American Indian and Alaska Native:** 6,763 (1.6%); **Asian:** 48,028 (11.2%); **Other race:** 99,898 (23.4%); **Two or more races:** 22,061 (5.2%); **Hispanic/Latino:** 170,520 (39.9%). **2000 percent population 18 and over:** 67.1%; **65 and over:** 9.3%; **Median age:** 28.5.
2004 population estimate (rank): 457,719 (37)
Land area: 104 sq mi. (269 sq km); **Alt.:** 328 ft.
Avg. daily temp.: Jan., 45.7° F; July, 81.9° F
Churches: 450 (approximate); **City-owned parks:** 38 (690 ac.); **Radio stations:** AM, 11[1]; FM, 13[1]; Bilingual 1; **Television stations:** 8[1]
Civilian Labor Force (MSA) March 2005: 393,700; **Unemployed:** 42,200, **Percent:** 10.7; **Per capita personal income (MSA) 2003:** $24,277
Chamber of Commerce: Fresno Chamber of Commerce, 2331 Fresno St., Fresno, CA 93721

1. Metropolitan area.

Fresno is located in central California, 184 mi southeast of San Francisco and 222 mi northwest of Los Angeles. It is the seat of Fresno County. Fresno was incorporated as a city in 1885.

Fresno began as a station for the Central Pacific Railroad in 1872 and was made the seat of Fresno County in 1874. The city's name is Spanish for the ash trees that the early explorers found in the area.

Fresno is a leading agribusiness hub, with 250 different crops produced by 7,500 farmers on 1.9 million irrigated acres, worth $3 billion a year. Fresno County's top agricultural products are grapes, cotton, tomatoes, cattle and calves, and turkeys.

The city is also a distribution and manufacturing center. Its diverse industries include agricultural chemicals, farm equipment, canned fruit and vegetables, clothing, computer software, electric wire, pumps, glass, and plastic products.

Selected famous natives and residents: Mike Connors, actor; Maynard Dixon, painter; Bruce Furniss, swimmer; Jon Hall, actor; Daryle Lamonica, football player; Sam Peckinpah, director; William Saroyan, novelist; Tom Seaver, baseball player.

Honolulu, Hawaii

Mayor: Mufi Hannemann (to Jan. 2009)
2000 census population (rank):[1] 371,657 (46);
  % change: 1.7; **Male:** 182,628 (49.1%); **Female:** 189,029 (50.9%); **White:** 73,093 (19.7%); **Black:** 6,038 (1.6%); **American Indian and Alaska Native:** 689 (0.2%); **Asian:** 207,588 (55.9%); **Native Hawaiian and Other Pacific Islander:** 25,457 (6.8%); **Other race:** 3,318 (0.9%); **Two or more races:** 55,474 (14.9%); **Hispanic/Latino:** 16,229 (4.4%). **2000 percent population 18 and over:** 80.8%; **65 and over:** 17.8%; **Median age:** 39.7
2004 population estimate (rank): 377,260 (47)
Land area: 85.7 sq mi. (221.9 sq km)[1]; **Alt.:** Highest, 2,013 ft.[1]; lowest, sea level
Avg. daily temp.: Jan., 71.4° F; July, 78.9° F
Churches: Roman Catholic, 39; Buddhist, 51; Jewish, 2;

Protestant and others, 402; **City-owned parks**[1]: 6,108 ac.; **Radio stations**[1]: AM, 17; FM, 11; **Television stations**[1]: 12

Civilian Labor Force (MSA) March 2005: 439,800[2]; **Unemployed:** 11,400[2]; **Percent:** 2.6[2]; **Per capita personal income (MSA) 2003:** $32,463[2]

Chamber of Commerce: Chamber of Commerce of Hawaii, 1132 Bishop St., Suite 402, Honolulu, HI 96813

1. Census Designated Place, approximately Salt Lake to Hawaii Kai. 2. City and county.

Honolulu is the capital and largest city of Hawaii, on the southeast coast of the island of Oahu. The city is legally coextensive with the county of Honolulu, which includes the entire island of Oahu and most of the Northwest Hawaiian Islands, from Nihoa to Kure Atoll, except Midway. The population of Oahu makes up 73% of the state's total population. It is situated in the central Pacific Ocean 2,397 mi west-southwest of San Francisco. Honolulu's name derives from the native words *hono,* meaning "a bay," and *lulu,* meaning "sheltered."

Honolulu's early history was one of turbulence and conflict. One of the last areas on the globe to be explored and exploited by Europeans (it was first visited by British captain James Cook in 1778), Hawaii was subject to strong pressures from many forces, including American missionaries, who arrived in 1820, and opportunistic whalers. These whalers were among those who built Honolulu originally, bringing trade, commerce, and prosperity that led to expansion into the sugar and pineapple industries.

As early as 1814, Russia tried to move in, and Russian soldiers built a bastion at the harbor's edge. The British flag was raised in 1843 and French forces occupied Honolulu in 1849. Each time control was returned to the independent native kingdom without bloodshed. In 1898, a group of Americans completed a project attempted at intervals during the previous 65 years—annexation to the United States. Honolulu was incorporated as a city in 1907.

The Honolulu area was bombed by Japan in a surprise attack on the unprepared U.S. naval base at Pearl Harbor on Dec. 7, 1941. This action forced the United States to enter World War II. "Remember Pearl Harbor" became a famous American wartime slogan.

Hawaiian statehood in 1959 and the viability of commercial air travel to the island brought boom times to Honolulu. Tourism is the city's principal industry, followed by federal defense expenditures and agricultural exports (chiefly pineapples).

Selected famous natives and residents: Hiram Bingham, explorer; Jean Erdman, dancer and choreographer; Hiram Fong, senator; Daniel Inouye, senator; Duke Kahanamoku, surfer and Olympian swimmer; Bette Midler, actress and singer; Kelly Preston, actress; Louise Morgan Sill, author; Don Stroud, actor; Merlin D. Tuttle, biologist and wildlife photographer.

Houston, Tex.

Mayor: Bill White (to Dec. 2005)
2000 census population (rank): 1,953,631 (4); **% change:** 19.8; **Male:** 975,551 (49.9%); **Female:** 978,080 (50.1%); **White:** 962,610 (49.3%); **Black:** 494,496 (25.3%); **American Indian and Alaska Native:** 8,568 (0.4%); **Asian:** 103,694 (5.3%); **Other race:** 321,603 (16.5%); **Two or more races:** 61,478 (3.1%); **Hispanic/Latino:** 730,865 (37.4%). **2000 percent population 18 and over:** 72.5%; **65 and over:** 8.4%; **Median age:** 30.9.

2004 population estimate (rank): 2,012,626 (4)
Land area: 579 sq mi. (1,500 sq km); **Alt.:** Highest, 120 ft.; lowest, sea level
Avg. daily temp.: Jan., 52.2° F; July, 83.5° F
Churches[1]: 1,750; **City-owned parks:** 293 (32,733 ac.); **Radio stations**[1]: AM, 23; FM, 32; **Television stations:** 15 commercial; 1 PBS
Civilian Labor Force (PMSA) March 2005: 2,639,100[2]; **Unemployed:** 144,900[2]; **Percent:** 5.5[2]; **Per capita personal income (MSA) 2003:** $34,578[2]
Chamber of Commerce: Greater Houston Partnership, 1200 Smith, Suite 700, Houston, TX 77002-4400

1. Harris County. 2. Houston–Baytown–Sugar Land, Tex.

Houston, the largest city in Texas and seat of Harris County, is located in the southeast part of the state near the Gulf of Mexico.

Sam Houston was the commander-in-chief of the Texas troops who fought a successful war of rebellion against Mexico, which had been in possession of Texas. On April 21, 1836, Houston's men won a decisive victory in which the Mexican dictator, Gen. Santa Anna, was taken prisoner and forced to sign the treaty that launched the Republic of Texas. In September, a constitution was ratified, and Houston was elected president. The Texas Republic was recognized by the U.S. and by the major European powers. The present city of Houston was incorporated in 1837 and named after Sam Houston; it was the Republic's first capital.

The port of Houston ranks high among U.S. ports in foreign tonnage handled. The city is a major business, financial, science, and technology center. Houston is outstanding in oil and natural-gas production and is the energy capital of the world. It is the home of one of the largest medical facilities in the world—the Texas Medical Center—and the focus of the aerospace industry. The Lyndon B. Johnson Space Center is the nation's headquarters for staffed spaceflight.

Among the city's many visitor attractions are Space Center Houston, the Houston Arboretum and Nature Center, Six Flags AstroWorld, George Ranch Historical Park, the Astrodome baseball stadium, and nearby San Jacinto Battlefield.

Selected famous natives and residents: Debbie Allen, choreographer; Lance Alworth, football player; Denton Cooley, heart surgeon; Jim Demaret, golfer; Allen Drury, novelist; Shelly Duvall, actress; A. J. Foyt, auto racer; Howard Hughes, industrialist and film producer; Barbara C. Jordan, educator, lawyer, and politician; Barbara Mandrell, singer; Annette O'Toole, actress; Dennis and Randy Quaid, actors; Kenny Rogers, singer; Patrick Swayze, actor and dancer.

Indianapolis, Ind.

Mayor: Bart Peterson (to Dec. 2007)
2000 census population (rank): 781,870 (12); **% change:** 6.7; **Male:** 378,310 (48.4%); **Female:** 403,560 (51.6%); **White:** 540,212 (69.1%); **Black:** 199,412 (25.5%); **American Indian and Alaska Native:** 1,985 (0.3%); **Asian:** 11,161 (1.4%); **Other race:** 15,921 (2.0%); **Two or more races:** 12,857 (1.6%); **Hispanic/Latino:** 30,636 (3.9%). **2000 percent population 18 and over:** 74.3%; **65 and over:** 11.0%; **Median age:** 33.5.
2004 population estimate (rank): 784,242 (12)
Land area: 366 sq mi. (948 sq km); **Alt.:** Highest, 840 ft.; lowest, 700 ft.
Avg. daily temp.: Jan., 25.5° F; July, 75.4° F
Churches[1]: 1,191; **City-owned parks:** 172 (10,174 ac.); **Radio stations**[2]: AM, 8; FM, 17; **Television stations**[1]: 7

Civilian Labor Force (MSA) March 2005: 820,700;
Unemployed: 47,000, Percent: 5.7; Per capita personal income (MSA) 2003: $33,618
Chamber of Commerce: Greater Indianapolis Chamber of Commerce, 111 Monument Circle, Ste. 1950, Indianapolis, IN 46204

1. Marion County. 2. Metropolitan area.

Indianapolis, the largest city in Indiana and seat of Marion County, is located in the central part of the state on the West Fork of the White River. Its name derives from combining "Indiana" with "polis," the Greek word for city.

Indianapolis was settled in 1820, and five years later it was chosen as the state capital. It was incorporated as a city in 1832 and reincorporated in 1838. The city's growth began when the railroad reached it in 1847. Toward the end of the 19th century, the discovery of nearby natural gas and the start of the automobile industry hastened its industrial expansion. In 1970, Indianapolis merged with surrounding Marion County.

Indianapolis is at the center of a rich agricultural region and is a major grain and livestock market. It is also a focal point of commerce, transportation, and manufacturing for the region. Some leading industries are electronics, pharmaceuticals, and food processing. The financial sector and service and insurance industries are growing rapidly.

Indianapolis is the site of the world-famous 500-mile automobile race and the Indiana State Fair.

Selected famous natives and residents: Monte Blue, actor; David Letterman, TV host; Steve McQueen, actor; Jane Pauley, TV newscaster; Booth Tarkington, author; Kurt Vonnegut, Jr., author; Harry Von Zell, announcer; Clifton Webb, actor.

Jacksonville, Fla.

Mayor: John Peyton (to June 2007)
2000 census population (rank): 735,617 (14);
% change: 15.8; Male: 356,284 (48.4%); Female: 379,333 (51.6%); White: 474,307 (64.5%); Black: 213,514 (29.0%); American Indian and Alaska Native: 2,474 (0.3%); Asian: 20,427 (2.8%); Other race: 9,816 (1.3%); Two or more races: 14,631 (2.0%); Hispanic/Latino: 30,594 (4.2%). 2000 percent population 18 and over: 73.3%; 65 and over: 10.3%; Median age: 33.8.
2004 population estimate (rank): 777,704 (13)
Land area: 758 sq mi. (1,963 sq km), Alt.: Highest, 71 ft.; lowest, sea level
Avg. daily temp.: Jan., 52.4° F; July, 81.6° F
Churches: Protestant, 794; Roman Catholic, 21; Jewish, 5; others, 22; City-owned parks and playgrounds: 337 (8,000+ ac.); Radio stations: AM, 14; FM, 16; Television stations: 6 commercial; 1 PBS; 1 religious
Civilian Labor Force (MSA) March 2005: 618,000; Unemployed: 26,200, Percent: 4.2; Per capita personal income (MSA) 2003: $30,525
Chamber of Commerce: Jacksonville Area Chamber of Commerce, 3 Independent Dr., Jacksonville, FL 32202

Jacksonville, Florida's largest city, is located in Duval County in the northeast corner of Florida, on the banks of the St. Johns River and adjacent to the Atlantic Ocean. It is the largest metropolitan area in northeast Florida and southeast Georgia.

Starting in the 16th century, French, Spanish, and English explorers and colonists were attracted to the region by the St. Johns River. The site was settled by Lewis Hogans in 1816. Jacksonville was laid out in 1822 and was named after Gen. Andrew Jackson,

the first military governor of Florida. It was incorporated as a city in 1832.

During the Civil War, much of the city was destroyed by Union forces, who occupied Jacksonville four times. The city was rebuilt and, following the development of its harbor and the railroads, quickly became the transportation hub and leading industrial city in Florida by the 1880s. In 1968, the city and county governments consolidated.

Jacksonville is the leading transportation and distribution hub in the state. However, the strength of the city's economy lies in its broad diversification. The area's economy is balanced among distribution, financial services, biomedical technology, consumer goods, information services, manufacturing, and other industries. Jacksonville has the largest deepwater port in the South Atlantic and is a leading port in the U.S. for automobile imports.

Selected famous natives and residents: Pat Boone, singer; Judy Canova, comedian; Harold Carmichael, football player; Billy Daniels, vocalist; Storm Davis, athlete; Bob Hayes, athlete; Wanda Hendrix, actress; James Weldon Johnson, author and educator; John Rosamond Johnson, musician and composer; Mark McCumber, pro golfer; Ray Mercer, boxer; Charles "Hoss" Singleton, songwriter; Bill Terry, baseball player and manager; Donnie Van Zant, rock musician; Ronnie Van Zant, rock musician; Leeroy Yarbrough, auto racer.

Kansas City, Mo.

Mayor: Kay Barnes (to April 2007)
City Manager: Wayne Cauthen (apptd. April 2003)
2000 census population (rank): 441,545 (36);
% change: 1.5; Male: 213,141 (48.3%); Female: 228,404 (51.7%); White: 267,931 (60.7%); Black: 137,879 (31.2%); American Indian and Alaska Native: 2,122 (0.5%); Asian: 8,182 (1.9%); Other race: 14,158 (3.2%); Two or more races: 10,780 (2.4%); Hispanic/Latino: 30,604 (6.9%). 2000 percent population 18 and over: 74.6%; 65 and over: 11.7%; Median age: 34.0.
2004 population estimate (rank): 444,387 (39)
Land area: 314 sq mi. (813 sq km), Alt.: Highest, 1,014 ft.; lowest, 722 ft.
Avg. daily temp.: Jan., 25.7° F; July, 78.5° F
Churches: 1,100 churches of all denominations;[1] City-owned parks and playgrounds: 211 (9,685 ac.); Radio stations[1]: AM, 14; FM, 19; Television stations[1]: 7
Civilian Labor Force (MSA) March 2005: 1,153,300;[2] Unemployed: 63,100[2], Percent: 5.5[2];[1] Per capita personal income (MSA) 2003: $33,335[2]
Chamber of Commerce: Greater Kansas City Chamber of Commerce, 911 Main St., Kansas City, MO 64105

1. Metropolitan area. 2. Kansas City, Mo.–Kans.

Kansas City is the largest city in Missouri. It is located in the western part of the state, at the junction of the Missouri and Kansas rivers. Kansas City is located in Jackson, Clay, Platte, and Cass counties.

In 1821, the year Missouri entered the Union, French trader François Chouteau came from St. Louis to establish a trading post on the site of the present city to take advantage of the growing fur trade with the Kansa, Osage, Wyandotte, and other tribes. In 1833, a settlement called Westport Landing was laid out by John Calvin McCoy and developed. The community became the Town of Kansas and was incorporated as a city in 1850 and renamed Kansas City in 1889. The city's name reflects its Native American heritage—its site was within the territory of the Kansa, or Kaw, Indians.

The city grew rapidly in the mid-1880s as the starting point for gold prospectors and settlers heading westward. The coming of the Missouri-Pacific Railroad in 1865 and the spanning of the Missouri River by the Hannibal Bridge in 1869 also contributed to the city's growth. It also prospered as a center for the nation's cattle business.

The Kansas City metropolitan area, once known primarily for agriculture and manufacturing, has expanded its economic base to include strong growth in areas of telecommunications, banking and finance, and the service industry. A transportation hub since the 1800s, the area enjoys a national and regional prominence as a distribution and manufacturing center. Kansas City ranks nationally as first in greeting-card publishing (Hallmark Cards is located there), frozen food storage and distribution, and hard winter-wheat marketing; second in wheat flour production; and third in auto and truck assembly. The area is one of ten federal regional centers, and the federal, state, and local governments are among the top employers. The city is also a regional center for health care.

Selected famous natives and residents: Robert Altman, director; Edward Asner, actor; Burt Bacharach, composer; Noah and Wallace Beery, actors; Robert Russell Bennett, composer; Jeanne Eagels, actress; Jean Harlow, actress; Ted Shawn, dancer and choreographer; Casey Stengel, baseball player; Virgil Thompson, composer; Tom Watson, golfer.

Las Vegas, Nev.

Mayor: Oscar Goodman (to May 2007)
2000 census population (rank): 478,434 (32);
  % change: 85.2; **Male:** 243,077 (50.8%); **Female:** 235,357 (49.2%); **White:** 334,230 (69.9%); **Black:** 49,570 (10.4%); **American Indian and Alaska Native:** 3,570 (0.7%); **Asian:** 22,879 (4.8%); **Other race:** 46,643 (9.7%); **Two or more races:** 19,397 (4.1%); **Hispanic/Latino:** 112,962 (23.6%). **2000 percent population 18 and over:** 74.1%; **65 and over:** 11.6%; **Median age:** 34.5.
2004 population estimate (rank): 534,847 (29)
Land area: 113 sq mi. (293 sq km); **Alt.:** 2,174 ft.
Avg. daily temp.: Jan., 45.5° F; July, 91.1° F
Churches: over 500 churches and synagogues; **Parks:** 50 (799 ac.) **Radio stations:** AM, 4; FM, 8; **Television stations:** 7
Civilian Labor Force (MSA) March 2005: 838,400[1];
  Unemployed: 33,000[1], **Percent:** 3.9[1]; **Per capita personal income (MSA) 2003:** $30,961[1]
Chamber of Commerce: Las Vegas Chamber of Commerce, 3720 Howard Hughes Parkway, Las Vegas, NV 89109

1. Las Vegas–Paradise, Nev.

Las Vegas, seat of Clark County in southeast Nevada, is the largest city in the state and one of the fastest-growing cities in the United States. Between April 1990 and April 2000, the Las Vegas metropolitan area population increased by 83%, growing from 852,737 to 1,563,282.

The area was discovered by Spanish explorers in 1829. The site of Las Vegas ("The Meadows" in Spanish) was originally a watering place for travelers on their way to southern California. It was first settled by Mormons in 1855, who were attracted by its artesian springs. They abandoned their settlement two years later in 1857, and the U.S. Army established Fort Baker there in 1864. In 1867, Las Vegas was detached from the Arizona Territory and joined with Nevada.

The town was established and started to grow with the arrival of the railroad in 1905. However, its growth did not really take off until shortly after 1931, when the Nevada legislature legalized gambling in an effort to lift the state from the Great Depression. The construction of nearby Hoover Dam aided the area economically as well.

The Las Vegas that we know today basically began after World War II, when the idea of large hotels along the brand new "strip" was developed. Las Vegas is the "marriage capital" of America; there are 50 wedding chapels in the city. Tourism and the convention industry are the city's major sources of income. In addition, manufacturing, government, warehousing, and trucking are major sources of employment. Many high-technology companies are also located in Las Vegas.

Las Vegas has a favorable business climate: taxes are relatively low, and there are neither city nor state income taxes. This is because gambling and sales taxes, paid by tourists, have allowed the city and state governments to avoid personal and corporate income taxes.

Popular nearby tourist attractions are Hoover Dam and Lake Mead (the largest man-made lake in the U.S.), Lake Mojave, the Mt. Charleston Recreation Area, Red Rock Canyon, and the Death Valley National Monument.

Selected famous natives and residents: Andre Agassi, tennis player; Clara Bow, actress; Jack Kramer, tennis player; Phyllis McGuire, singer; Benjamin Siegel, hotel-casino promoter; Orson Welles, actor and producer; Joe Williams, jazz singer.

Long Beach, Calif.

Mayor: Beverly O'Neill (to June 2006)
City Manager: Gerald Miller
2000 census population (rank): 461,522 (34);
  % change: 7.5; **Male:** 226,718 (49.1%); **Female:** 234,804 (50.9%); 1996 est. population breakdown:
  White: 208,410 (45.2%); **Black:** 68,618 (14.9%); **American Indian and Alaska Native:** 3,881 (0.8%); **Asian:** 55,591 (12.0%); **Other race:** 95,107 (20.6%); **Two or more races:** 24,310 (5.3%); **Hispanic/Latino:** 165,092 (35.8%). **2000 percent population 18 and over:** 70.8%; **65 and over:** 9.1%; **Median age:** 30.8.
2004 population estimate (rank): 476,564 (34)
Land area: 50 sq mi. (130 sq km); **Alt.:** Highest, 170 ft.; lowest, sea level
Avg. daily temp.: Jan., 55.9° F; July, 73.1° F
Churches: 236; **City-owned parks:** 92 (plus 5 golf courses); **Radio stations:** AM, 2; FM, 2; **Television stations:** 8 (metro area)
Civilian Labor Force (PMSA) April 2005: 4,894,600[1];
  Unemployed: 265,800[1], **Percent:** 5.4[1]; **Per capita personal income (MSA) 2003:** $33,347[2]
Chamber of Commerce: Long Beach Area Chamber of Commerce, One World Trade Center, Suite 206, Long Beach, CA 90831-0350

1. Los Angeles–Long Beach–Glendale, Calif. 2. Los Angeles–Long Beach–Santa Ana, Calif.

Long Beach is the fifth-largest city in California and is situated on San Pedro Bay, south of Los Angeles, in Los Angeles County.

The town was laid out and settled in 1881 by developer W. E. Willmore, who sold lots on the site as a seaside resort community called Willmore City. It was renamed Long Beach for its 8½-mile beach in 1884. The city was incorporated in 1888 and reincorporated in 1897.

Long Beach is a major industrial port, ranked second-busiest in the U.S. and tenth-busiest in the world. In addition to international trade through the port, high technology has also been an important economic engine for the Long Beach area. Major technology and aerospace corporations such Gulf-stream and Raytheon have large facilities in Long Beach, and Boeing continues to be the top employer, with over 17,000 employees.

Tourism is also important to the economy. Major attractions are the RMS *Queen Mary,* the Aquarium of the Pacific, whale watching tours, and water sports.

Selected famous natives and residents: Jack Anderson, journalist; Jennifer Bartlett, artist; Barbara Britton, actress; Nicholas Cage, actor; Spike Jones, orchestra leader; Sally Kellerman, actress; Billie Jean King, tennis player; Martha Rae Watson, track star; Heather Watts, dancer.

Los Angeles, Calif.

Mayor: Antonio Villaraigosa (to June 2009)
2000 census population (rank): 3,694,820 (2);
% change: 6.0; **Male:** 1,841,805 (49.8%); **Female:** 1,853,015 (50.2%); **White:** 1,734,036 (46.9%); **Black:** 415,195 (11.2%); **American Indian and Alaska Native:** 29,412 (0.8%); **Asian:** 369,254 (10.0%); **Other race:** 949,720 (25.7%); **Two or more races:** 191,288 (5.2%); **Hispanic/Latino:** 1,719,073 (46.5%). **2000 percent population 18 and over:** 73.4%; **65 and over:** 9.7%; **Median age:** 31.6.
2004 population estimate (rank): 3,845,541 (2)
Land area: 469 sq mi. (1,215 sq km); **Alt.:** Highest, 5,081 ft.; lowest, sea level
Avg. daily temp.: Jan., 58.3° F; July, 74.3° F
Churches: 2,000 of all denominations; **City-owned parks:** 387 (15,600 ac.); **Radio stations:** AM, 35; FM, 53; **Television stations:** 19
Civilian Labor Force (PMSA) April 2005: 4,894,600[1]; **Unemployed:** 265,800[1], **Percent:** 5.4[1]; **Per capita personal income (MSA) 2003:** $33,347[2]
Chamber of Commerce: Los Angeles Chamber of Commerce, 350 S. Bixel St., Los Angeles, CA 90017

1. Los Angeles–Long Beach–Glendale, Calif. 2. Los Angeles–Long Beach–Santa Ana, Calif.

Los Angeles is the largest city in California and the second-largest urban area in the nation. It is located in the southern part of the state on the Pacific Ocean. It is the seat of Los Angeles County. Geographically, it extends more than 40 mi from the mountains to the sea.

The Spanish explorer Gaspar de Portolá visited the site in 1769. On Sept. 4, 1781, the Mexican provincial governor, Filipe de Neve, founded "El Pueblo de Nuestra Señora la Reina de Los Angeles," meaning "The Village of Our Lady, the Queen of the Angels." The pueblo became the capital of the Mexican province, Alta California, and it was the last place to surrender to the United States at the time of the American occupation in 1847. By the Treaty of Guadalupe Hidalgo in 1848, Mexico ceded California to the United States, and Los Angeles was incorporated as a city in 1850.

The city's phenomenal growth was brought about by its equable climate, which attracted people and industry from all parts of the nation; the development of its citrus-fruit industry; the discovery of oil in the area during the early 1890s; the development of its man-made harbor—its port is one of the busiest in the United States; and the growth of the motion picture industry in the early 20th century. Today, Hollywood is a suburb of Los Angeles.

Los Angeles is a major hub of shipping, manufacturing, industry, and finance, and is world-renowned in the entertainment and communications fields. It is a favorite vacation destination and attracts millions of tourists to the area each year from all over the world. Apart from the movie studios and other landmarks associated with the movie industry, points of interest include the J. Paul Getty Museum, the Los Angeles County Museum of Art, the La Brea Tar Pits (famous for Ice Age fossils), Disneyland (Anaheim), and the Santa Anita and Hollywood racetracks.

Los Angeles County is the nation's largest manufacturing center, and the ports of Los Angeles and Long Beach are second only to New York as the largest customs district in the United States. Major employers in the Los Angeles Five-County area are in the business and management sector. Growth in the key wholesale industries—apparel and textiles, furniture, jewelry, and toys—and the boom in industrial trade were the trend for the region in the 1990s. Other important sectors are health services and international trade and investment. After some lean years, the aerospace industry is making a modest comeback as a result of increased federal defense spending.

Selected famous natives and residents: Busby Berkeley, choreographer and director; Marge Champion, dancer and choreographer; Jackie Coogan, actor; Jackie Cooper, actor; Linda Fratianne, figure skater; Jodie Foster, actress and director; John Gavin, actor and diplomat; Pancho Gonzalez, tennis player; Cynthia Gregory, ballerina; Jerome Hines, basso; Dustin Hoffman, actor; Theodore Harold Maiman, laser inventor; Marilyn Monroe, actress; Isamu Noguchi, sculptor; Leonard Slotkin, conductor; Duke Snider, baseball player; Adlai E. Stevenson, statesman; Madeleine Stowe, actress; Darryl Strawberry, baseball player.

Louisville/Jefferson County, Ky.

Mayor: Jerry E. Abramson (to Jan. 2007)
2000 census population (rank)[1]: 256,231 (67);
% change: –4.8%; **Male:** 121,153 (47.3%); **Female:** 135,078 (52.7%); **White:** 161,261 (62.9%); **Black:** 84,586 (33.0%); **American Indian and Alaska Native:** 578 (0.2%); **Asian:** 3,705 (1.4%);
Other race: 1,709 (0.7%); **Two or more races:** 4,281 (1.7%); **Hispanic/Latino:** 4,755 (1.9%). **2000 percent population 18 and over:** 76.3%; **65 and over:** 14.6%; **Median age:** 35.8.
2004 population estimate (rank): 556,332 (26)
Land area: 385 sq mi. (997.15 sq km); **Avg. alt.:** 482 ft.
Avg. daily temp.: Jan., 33° F; July, 78.4° F
Churches: 908; **City-owned parks:** 122 (14,000+ ac.); **Radio stations:** AM, 20; FM, 41; **Television stations:** 4 commercial; 1 PBS; 1 city
Civilian Labor Force (MSA) April 2005: 606,900[2]; **Unemployed:** 32,700[2], **Percent:** 5.4[2]; **Per capita personal income (MSA) 2003:** $32,485[2]
Chamber of Commerce: Greater Louisville, Inc., 614 West Main St., Suite 6000, Louisville, KY 40202

1. Louisville consolidated with Jefferson County in Jan. 2003. Figures prior to 2003 are for Louisville city only. 2. Louisville, KY-IN.

Louisville, which merged with Jefferson County in 2003, is the largest city in Kentucky. It is situated at the Falls of the Ohio, at the Kentucky-Indiana border.

In 1778, Lt. Col. George Rogers Clark and his troops established Fort Nelson within the current boundaries of Louisville. The following year, the town was named for France's King Louis XVI, who supported the colonists in the Revolutionary War. Its location at the Ohio River's falls gave the city both military and economic importance. By the early

19th century, it had become a major river port. The completion of the Portland Canal around the falls in 1830 further stimulated its economic growth and cultural development.

Between 1956 and 1984, Jefferson County voters rejected three proposals to create a consolidated local government for the entire county. Finally, in 2000, they approved a merger between Jefferson County and the City of Louisville, until then the county seat. The new Louisville-Jefferson County Metro Government was formed on January 6, 2003.

The city is well-known for horse racing (the Kentucky Derby has been held there since 1875), and is a leading producer of gin, whiskey, tobacco, and Louisville Slugger baseball bats. Other major exports include chemicals, rubber, paint, and electrical appliances. It is home to the American Printing House for the Blind, the world's largest publisher of books in Braille, and the Kentucky School for the Blind. The University of Louisville was the first city-owned university in the U.S., founded in 1798, and the Louisville Free Public Library was one of the first public systems in the country.

Selected famous natives and residents: Muhammad Ali, boxer; Ned Beatty, actor; Louis D. Brandeis, Supreme Court justice; John Mason Brown, critic; Tod Browning, director; Julia Carson, U.S. representative; A. B. "Happy" Chandler, baseball player; William Conrad, actor; Michael Dorris, author; Irene Dunne, actress; Sue Grafton, author; Lionel Hampton, vibraharpist; Paul Hornung, football player; Henry Hull, actor; Victor Mature, actor; Marsha Norman, playwright; Hunter S. Thompson, author; Mary Travers, folksinger; Gus Van Sant, director.

Memphis, Tenn.

Mayor: W. W. Herenton (to Dec. 2007)
2000 census population (rank): 650,100 (18);
% change: 6.5; **Male:** 307,643 (47.3%); **Female:** 342,457 (52.7%); **White:** 223,728 (34.4%); **Black:** 399,208 (61.4%); **American Indian and Alaska Native:** 1,217 (0.2%); **Asian:** 9,482 (1.5%); **Other race:** 9,438 (1.5%); **Two or more races:** 6,788 (1.0%); **Hispanic/Latino:** 19,317 (3.0%). **2000 percent population 18 and over:** 72.1%; **65 and over:** 10.9%; **Median age:** 31.9.
2004 population estimate (rank): 671,929 (17)
Land area: 279 sq mi. (723 sq km); **Alt.:** Highest, 417 ft.
Avg. daily temp.: Jan., 39.7° F; July, 82.6° F
Churches: 2000+; **Parks and playgrounds:** 187 (5,387 ac.); **Radio stations:** AM, 17; FM, 25; **Television stations:** 6
Civilian Labor Force (MSA) March 2005: 589,300[1];
Unemployed: 39,000[1], **Percent:** 6.6[1]; **Per capita personal income (MSA)** 2003: $31,677[1]
Chamber of Commerce: Memphis Regional Chamber of Commerce, 22 N. Front St., Memphis, TN 38103

1. Memphis, Tenn.–Miss.–Ark.

Memphis, the largest city in Tennessee and the seat of Shelby County, is located in the southwest corner of the state, on the Mississippi River near the borders of Arkansas and Mississippi.

The first settlers of Memphis were the Chickasaw Indians, who had a village named Chisca there on the bluffs overlooking the Mississippi River. Hernando de Soto, in 1541, is said to have had his first glimpse of the Mississippi from the site of Memphis; in the next century, Louis Joliet and Jacques Marquette stopped there to trade with the Indians. The French explorer Robert Cavelier, Sieur de La Salle, tried to claim the region for France in 1682 and built Fort Prudhomme on the site.

The area was ceded to the United States by the Chickasaw Indians in 1818. Memphis was officially established in 1819 by three enterprising businessmen from Nashville, James Winchester, John Overton, and future president Andrew Jackson. Jackson named it after the ancient Egyptian city because of its site on the Nile-like Mississippi River. Memphis was incorporated as a city in 1826 and became an important Mississippi River port.

During the Civil War, Memphis was a Confederate military center. In 1862, federal forces won a gunboat battle on the river at Memphis, and General Sherman was able to take the city. After the war, Memphis's population was devastated by several yellow-fever epidemics during the 1870s. As a result, the city fell into decline and went bankrupt, losing its charter in 1879. However, owing to its superior location, the city was able to recover economically, and a new city charter was granted in 1893.

Memphis is known as "America's Distribution Center," serving the northeast, southeast, and southwest regions of the country. The city has one of the country's largest inland ports and is the national headquarters for the Fed Ex air-courier company. Health care and related activities such as medical education and biomedical research are Memphis's largest industries, bringing over $5 billion a year to the local economy.

Many of the city's tourist attractions are landmarks associated with the great Memphis music legends, such as Graceland, Elvis Presley's home.

Selected famous natives and residents: Kathy Bates, actress; Dixie Carter, actress; Rosalind Cash, singer; Abe Fortas, jurist; Aretha Franklin, singer; Morgan Freeman, actor; Al Green, singer; George Hamilton, actor; Anfernee "Penny" Hardaway, basketball player; Isaac Hayes, singer; Hal Holbrook, actor; Benjamin Hooks, organization official; Elvis Presley, singer and actor; Charlie Rich, singer; Cybill Shepherd, actress; Robert Siodmak, director; Fred Smith, business executive; Rufus Thomas, singer; Kemmons Wilson, business executive.

Mesa, Ariz.

Mayor: Keno Hawker (to June 2008)
City Manager: Mike Hutchinson
2000 census population (rank): 396,375 (42);
% change: 37.6; **Male:** 196,378 (49.5%); **Female:** 199,997 (50.5%); **White:** 323,655 (81.7%); **Black:** 9,977 (2.5%); **American Indian and Alaska Native:** 6,572 (1.7%); **Asian:** 5,917 (1.5%); **Other race:** 38,271 (9.7%); **Two or more races:** 11,051 (2.8%); **Hispanic/Latino:** 78,281 (19.7%). **2000 percent population 18 and over:** 72.7%; **65 and over:** 13.3%; **Median age:** 32.0
2004 population estimate (rank): 437,454 (41)
Land area: 125 sq mi. (324 sq km); **Alt.:** 1,241 ft.
Avg. daily temp.: Jan., 52.9° F; July, 91.2° F
City-owned parks: 55; **Radio stations:** AM, 23; FM, 12; **Television stations:** 7
Civilian Labor Force (MSA) March 2005: 1,861,500[1];
Unemployed: 78,400[1], **Percent:** 4.2[1]; **Per capita personal income (MSA)** 2003: $29,590[1]
Chamber of Commerce: Mesa Chamber of Commerce, 120 N. Center St., P.O. Box 5820, Mesa, AZ 85201

1. Phoenix–Mesa–Scottsdale, Ariz.

Mesa is the third-largest city in Arizona and is located in the south-central portion of the state in Maricopa County. Sitting atop a plateau overlooking the Valley of the Sun, the city gets its name from the Spanish word for "tabletop."

Prior to the arrival of Europeans, the area had been inhabited for centuries by native peoples, including the Hohokam and later the Pima. The Hohokam culture developed an extensive system of irrigation canals, some of which are still used today.

Controlled by Spain and then by Mexico, the area was ceded to the U.S. following the Mexican War (1846–1848). Mormon settlers arrived on the site in 1878 and used the old irrigation canals for farming in the Salt River valley. Mesa was incorporated as a town in 1883 and as a city in 1930.

Falcon Field Airport and Williams Air Force Base were built in 1941 to train fighter pilots during World War II. After the war, the city grew rapidly, as many military families decided to settle in Mesa permanently, and tourism also became a major force. Williams AFB closed in the early 1990s, but Falcon Field has become one of the ten largest U.S. airports in terms of based aircraft and supports more than 30 aviation-related businesses.

Currently Mesa is one of the fastest-growing cities in the United States, due to its excellent climate and strong local economy, which boasts some of the country's top manufacturers. Electronics, automotive testing, propulsion equipment, aerospace, and heavy machinery firms are among the most significant in the region.

With 313 days of sunshine a year, Mesa has been an ideal choice for several major-league baseball spring training camps.

Selected famous natives and residents: Danielle Fishel, actress; Liz Reney, actress; John J. Rhodes, politician; Keri Russell, actress.

Miami, Fla.

Mayor: Manuel A. Diaz (to Nov. 2005)
City Manager: Joe Arriola
2000 census population (rank): 362,470 (47); **% change:** 1.1; **Male:** 180,194 (49.7%); **Female:** 182,276 (50.3%); **White:** 241,470 (66.6%); **Black:** 80,858 (22.3%); **American Indian and Alaska Native:**, 810 (0.2%); **Asian:** 2,376 (0.7%); **Other race:** 19,644 (5.4%); **Two or more races:** 17,182 (4.7%); **Hispanic/Latino:** 238,351 (65.8%). **2000 percent population 18 and over:** 78.3%; **65 and over:** 17.0%; **Median age:** 37.7.
2004 population estimate (rank): 379,724 (46)
Land area: 36 sq mi. (93 sq km); **Water area:** 19.5 sq mi.; **Avg. alt.:** 12 ft.
Avg. daily temp.: Jan., 67.2° F; July, 82.6° F
Churches:[1] Protestant, 850; Roman Catholic, 61; Jewish, 64; **City-owned parks:** 109; **Radio stations:**[1] 29; **Television stations:**[1] 9 TV; 1 Cable
Civilian Labor Force (PMSA) April 2005: 1,130,700[2]; **Unemployed:** 50,600[2], **Percent:** 4.5[2]; **Per capita personal income (MSA) 2003:** $33,094[3]
Chamber of Commerce: Greater Miami Chamber of Commerce, 1601 Biscayne Blvd., Miami, FL 33132

1. Dade County. 2. Miami–Miami Beach–Kendall, Fla. 3. Miami–Fort Lauderdale–Miami Beach, Fla.

Miami, the second-largest city in Florida and seat of Miami-Dade County, is located in the southeast part of the state, on Biscayne Bay.

The area was once the home of the Tequesta Indians until they were nearly wiped out by European diseases and warfare brought on by two centuries of Spanish control of Florida. Miami was founded in 1870 near the site of Ft. Dallas, built in 1835 during the Seminole Indian wars. The city's name is probably derived from "Mayaimi," an Indian word for "big water."

Miami is the only U.S. city to have been planned by a woman. Julia Tuttle, a Clevelander, arrived there in 1891 and bought several hundred acres on the bank of the Miami River. She convinced New York financier Henry M. Flagler of the area's vast potential and persuaded him to extend his Florida East Coast Railroad to Miami in 1896, the year the city was incorporated. Flagler dredged Miami Harbor, built the renowned Royal Palm Hotel, and promoted the area as a winter playground. Tourists flocked there, and by 1910 the city was a thriving recreational area. Miami survived the collapse of a land speculation boom in the 1920s and severe hurricanes in 1926 and 1935 and continued to grow. It experienced a monumental population boost during the 1960s, when about 260,000 Cuban refugees arrived on its shore. They made a great impact on Miami, which is now a bilingual metropolis.

Miami is an international banking and finance center and has the greatest concentration of international and Edge Act banks (banks making only foreign loans and deposits) in North America; these constitute a major employment base. Greater Miami has a highly diversified economy with numerous multinational and Fortune 500 companies. It is a national leader in biomedical technology, and the health care sector is a major industry. Greater Miami is also part of an area known as the Computer Coast of Florida, and its growing technologies include computers, electrical engineering, and plastics manufacturing.

Miami is one of the world's leading year-round resort centers. The city is a major transportation hub, and the port of Miami is the world's largest cruise port and a major seaport for cargo. The famous island resort of Miami Beach, incorporated in 1915, is connected to Miami by four causeways.

Selected famous natives and residents: Fernando Bujones, dancer; Steve Carlton, baseball player; Debbie Harry, singer; Dick Howser, baseball player and manager; Sidney Poitier, actor; Janet Reno, former attorney general of the U.S.; Ben Vereen, actor; Ellen Zwilich, composer.

Milwaukee, Wis.

Mayor: Tom Barrett (to April 2008)
2000 census population (rank): 596,974 (19); **% change:** –5.0; **Male:** 285,363 (47.8%); **Female:** 311,611 (52.2%); **White:** 298,379 (50.0%); **Black:** 222,933 (37.3%); **American Indian and Alaska Native:** 5,212 (0.9%); **Asian:** 17,571 (2.9%); **Other race:** 36,428 (6.1%); **Two or more races:** 16,150 (2.7%); **Hispanic/Latino:** 71,646 (12.0%). **2000 percent population 18 and over:** 71.4%; **65 and over:** 10.9%; **Median age:** 30.6.
2004 population estimate (rank): 583,624 (22)
Land area: 96 sq mi. (249 sq km); **Alt.:** 580.60 ft.
Avg. daily temp.: Jan., 19.9° F; July, 73.6° F
Churches: 411; **County-owned parks:** 140 (15,000+ ac.); **Radio stations:** AM, 6; FM, 13; **Television stations:** 11
Civilian Labor Force (PMSA) March 2005: 795,000;[1] **Unemployed:** 42,100[1], **Percent:** 5.3[1]; **Per capita personal income (MSA) 2003:** $35,133[1]
Chamber of Commerce: Metropolitan Milwaukee Association of Commerce, 756 N. Milwaukee St., Milwaukee, WI 53202; Milwaukee Minority Chamber of Commerce, P.O. Box 1662, Milwaukee, WI 53201; Hispanic Chamber of Commerce, 816 W. National Ave., Milwaukee, WI 53204

1. Milwaukee–Waukesha–West Allis, Wis.

Milwaukee, the largest city in Wisconsin and seat of Milwaukee County, is located in the southeast part of the state on Lake Michigan.

French missionaries visited the site of Milwaukee in the 17th century, but it was not until 1795 that Jacques Vieau established a fur-trading post there. The first permanent white settler, Vieau's son-in-law, Solomon Juneau, an agent of the American Fur Company, made his home there in 1818. The settlement merged with several neighboring villages in 1838 to form Milwaukee, and the city was incorporated in 1846. A large wave of German immigrants arrived after 1848 and contributed greatly to the city's political, economic, and cultural development.

The origins of the word "Milwaukee" are disputed; it may come from the Potawatomi "Mahn-ah-wauk," meaning council grounds of the Potawatomi; "Mah-an-wauk-seepe," meaning gathering place of rivers; or the Algonquian "Milo-aki," meaning beautiful land.

Milwaukee is one of the great industrial centers in the country and one of the largest Great Lakes ports. Manufacturing remains strong, and Milwaukee manufacturers are national leaders in lithographic commercial printing and the production of medical diagnostic instruments, small gasoline engines, malt beverages, iron and steel forgings, mining machinery, and robotics. Milwaukee's high-tech manufacturing community is one of the largest among the nation's major metropolitan areas.

Though Milwaukee was once known as a "beer town," only a small percentage of its workforce is now involved in beer production. However, beer still plays an important role, and almost 11% of the nation's malt beverage is produced there.

Selected famous natives and residents: Donald Gramm, bass-baritone; Woody Herman, band leader; Al Jarreau, singer; Kristen Johnston, actress; George F. Kennan, diplomat; Alfred Lunt, actor; Douglas MacArthur, army general; Pat O'Brien, actor; Tom Snyder, TV personality; Speech, member of the rap group Arrested Development; Spencer Tracy, actor; Gene Wilder, actor; Jerry and David Zucker, film producers.

Minneapolis, Minn.

Mayor: R. T. Rybak (to Jan. 2006)
2000 census population (rank): 382,618 (45);
  % change: 3.9; **Male:** 192,232 (50.2%); **Female:** 190,386 (49.8%); **White:** 249,186 (65.1%); **Black:** 68,818 (18.0%); **American Indian and Alaska Native:** 8,378 (2.2%); **Asian:** 23,455 (6.1%); **Other race:** 15,798 (4.1%); **Two or more races:** 16,694 (4.4%); **Hispanic/Latino:** 29,175 (7.6%). **2000 percent population 18 and over:** 78.0%; **65 and over:** 9.1%; **Median age:** 31.2
2004 population estimate (rank): 373,943 (48)
Land area: 55 sq mi. (142 sq km); **Alt.:** Highest, 945 ft.; lowest, 695 ft.
Avg. daily temp.: Jan., 11.8° F; July, 73.6° F
Churches: 419; **City-owned parks:** 170+ (6,400 ac.); **Radio stations**[1]**:** AM, 17; FM, 15; **Television stations**[1]**:** 6
Civilian Labor Force (MSA) March 2005: 1,841,000[2]; **Unemployed:** 82,900[2], **Percent:** 4.5[2]; **Per capita personal income (MSA) 2003:** $38,601[2]
Chamber of Commerce: Minneapolis Regional Chamber of Commerce, 81 S. Ninth St., Suite 200, Minneapolis, MN 55402-3223

1. Metropolitan area. 2. Minneapolis–St. Paul–Bloomington, Minn.–Wis.

Minneapolis, the largest city in Minnesota and the seat of Hennepin County, is located in the southeast central part of the state on the Mississippi River. It is adjacent to its "twin city" of St. Paul.

In 1680, Father Louis Hennepin visited the future site of Minneapolis and gave the Falls of St. Anthony their name. Lt. Zebulon Pike made a treaty with the Sioux Indians in 1805–1806, by which they ceded to the whites much land, including the Falls of St. Anthony and the site of Minneapolis. Fort Snelling was built in 1819–1820, and in 1823 the government built a lumber and flour mill. Flour milling became the major industry of early Minneapolis and made the city the milling capital of the world. The town of St. Anthony was established on the east bank of the Mississippi in 1848, and the town of Minneapolis grew up on the opposite bank of the river. The name Minneapolis is a combination of the Dakota Sioux word "minna," for water, and the Greek word "polis," for city. Minneapolis was incorporated as a city in 1867, and in 1872 the city of St. Anthony (chartered in 1860) was annexed to it. After the spread of the railroads in the 1870s, Minneapolis became the gateway to the Northern Great Plains.

Minneapolis is a center of industry and commerce serving a large agricultural region. During the 20th century, manufacturing, food processing, milling, computers, health services, and graphic arts developed as Minneapolis's major industries. Fifteen Fortune 500 companies are headquartered in the Minneapolis–St. Paul metropolitan area. The city is the headquarters of the Ninth Federal Reserve Bank.

The Twin Cities are known for their wide array of cultural attractions, and Minneapolis is home to many fine museums, including the Minneapolis Institute of Arts, the Walker Center, and the Frederick R. Weisman Art Museum at the University of Minnesota's Minneapolis campus.

Selected famous natives and residents: La Verne, Maxene, and Patti Andrews, singers; James Arness, actor; Lew Ayres, actor; Patty Berg, golfer; Virginia Bruce, actress; J. Paul Getty, oil executive; Peter Graves, actor; George Roy Hill, director; Cornell MacNeil, baritone; Ralph Meeker, actor; Westbrook Pegler, columnist; Prince, singer; Harrison Salisbury, journalist; Charles Schulz, cartoonist; Anne Tyler, writer; Bud Wilkinson, football coach; David Winfield, baseball player.

Nashville-Davidson, Tenn.

Mayor: Bill Purcell (to Oct. 2007)
2000 census population (rank):[1] 545,524 (22);
  % change: 11.6; **Male:** 264,095 (48.4%); **Female:** 281,429 (51.6%); **White:** 359,581 (65.9%); **Black:** 146,235 (26.8%); **American Indian and Alaska Native:** 1,639 (0.3%); **Asian:** 12,992 (2.4%); **Other race:** 13,677 (2.5%); **Two or more races:** 11,000 (2.0%); **Hispanic/Latino:** 25,774 (4.7%). **2000 percent population 18 and over:** 77.9%; **65 and over:** 11.0%; **Median age:** 33.9.
2004 population estimate (rank): 546,719 (28)
Land area: 502 sq mi. (1,300 sq km); **Altitude:** Highest, 1,100 ft.; lowest, approx. 400 ft.
Avg. daily temp.: Jan., 36.2° F; July, 79.3° F
Churches: Protestant, 781; Roman Catholic, 18; Jewish, 3; **City-owned parks:** 100 (10,200 ac.); **Radio stations:** AM, 15; FM, 19; **Television stations:** 11
Civilian Labor Force (MSA) March 2005: 727,000[2]; **Unemployed:** 35,300[2], **Percent:** 4.9[2]; **Per capita personal income (MSA) 2003:** $33,368[2]
Chamber of Commerce: Nashville Area Chamber of Commerce, 211 Commerce Street, Suite 100, Nashville, TN 37201

1. Nashville-Davidson city is consolidated with Davidson County. 2. Nashville–Davidson–Murfreesboro, Tenn.

Nashville-Davidson is the state capital and second-largest city in Tennessee and is located in the north-central part of the state on the Cumberland River. It is coextensive with Davidson County.

During the winter of 1779–1780, James Robertson and John Donelson founded a settlement at Big Salt Lick by the Cumberland River at the present site of the city. They built forts on both sides of the river, naming one of them Fort Nashborough in honor of Francis Nash, a Revolutionary War general. In 1784, the town was named Nashville, and it was incorporated as a city in 1806.

Nashville became the capital of Tennessee in 1843 and was the seat of Davidson County until 1963, when it merged with the county to become Nashville-Davidson.

The city is a port of entry and an important industrial and commercial center serving the Upper South. Its economy is based on a number of industries, including automobiles, apparel, publishing, insurance, and banking. Health care services are the largest sector, but Nashville is best known for its music industry. It is a major recording center, especially for country music and is home to the Grand Ole Opry.

Nashville is home to several religious organizations and is a major tourist attraction and convention center. Its many institutions of higher education include Vanderbilt University, Fisk University, and the Tennessee State University.

Selected famous natives and residents: Roy Acuff, singer; Gregg Allman, singer; Pat Boone, singer; Rita Coolidge, singer; Jeff Gordon, race car driver; Al Gore, former vice president; Red Grooms, artist; Alex Haley, author; Barbara Howar, hostess and writer; Brenda Lee, singer; Minnie Pearl, comedienne; Annie Potts, actress; Paula Robeson, flutist; Wilma Rudolph, athlete; Dinah Shore, actress and singer; Tina Turner, singer; Oprah Winfrey, entertainer.

New Orleans, La.

Mayor: C. Ray Nagin (to May 2006)
2000 census population (rank): 484,674 (31);
% change: –2.5; **Male:** 227,094 (46.9%); **Female:** 257,580 (53.1%); **White:** 135,956 (28.1%); **Black:** 325,947 (67.3%); **American Indian and Alaska Native:** 991 (0.2%); **Asian:** 10,972 (2.3%); **Other race:** 4,498 (0.9%); **Two or more races:** 6,201 (1.3%); **Hispanic/Latino:** 14,826 (3.1%). **2000 percent population 18 and over:** 73.3%; **65 and over:** 11.7%; **Median age:** 33.1.
2004 population estimate (rank): 462,269 (35)
Land area: 181 sq mi. (469 sq km); **Alt.:** Highest, 15 ft.; lowest, –4 ft.
Avg. daily temp.: Jan., 51.3° F; July, 81.9° F
Churches: 712; **City-owned parks:** 165; **Radio stations:** AM, 12; FM, 14; **Television stations:** 7
Civilian Labor Force (MSA) April 2005: 616,400[1]; **Unemployed:** 25,000[1], **Percent:** 4.0[1]; **Per capita personal income (MSA) 2003:** $30,092[1]
Chamber of Commerce: Greater New Orleans, Inc., 601 Poydras St., Suite 1700, New Orleans, LA 70130

1. New Orleans–Metairie–Kenner, La.

New Orleans, the largest city in Louisiana, is located in the southeast part of the state, between the Mississippi River and Lake Ponchartrain. It is coextensive with Orleans Parish.

One of the few cities of the nation that has been under three flags, New Orleans has belonged to Spain, France, and the United States. The French founded it in 1718 and named it in honor of the Duke of Orleans. In 1762, France ceded the city and the territory to Spain. In 1800, the territory was returned to France, but government authorities did not take over until 1803, just 20 days before the region became part of the United States in the Louisiana Purchase.

New Orleans is famous for its French Quarter, with its mixture of French, Spanish, and native architectural styles. The Mardi Gras—a week of carnival held in New Orleans before the beginning of Lent—is the most spectacular festival in the U.S. and is a popular tourist attraction.

New Orleans has one of the world's greatest international ports and it is a major focus of the city's economy. New Orleans is home to the corporate offices of oil companies with major offshore operations in the Gulf of Mexico, as well as the distribution and service centers of offshore equipment suppliers and fabricators.

The manufacturing industry is a significant part of the economy, with petroleum, petrochemical, shipbuilding, and aerospace industries all playing a role. The New Orleans region also functions as a mining, processing, and transportation center for other minerals, principally sulfur. Service industries are playing a larger role, with health care and telecommunications leading the way.

(As this edition went to press, New Orleans was devastated by Hurricane Katrina. *See* www.infoplease.com for updated information.)

Selected famous natives and residents: Louis Armstrong, musician; Truman Capote, author; Fats Domino, musician; Louis Gottschalk, pianist and composer; Bryant Gumbel, TV personality; Lillian Hellman, playwright and author; Al Hirt, musician; Mahalia Jackson, singer; Dorothy Lamour, actress; Wynton Marsalis, musician; Huey Newton, activist; Marguerite Piazza, soprano; Rusty Staub, baseball player; Ben Turpin, comedian; Shirley Verrett, mezzo-soprano; Carl Weathers, actor; Del Williams, football player.

New York, N.Y.

Mayor: Michael R. Bloomberg (to Dec. 2005)
Borough Presidents: Bronx, Adolfo Carrion; Brooklyn, Marty Markowitz; Manhattan, C. Virginia Fields; Queens, Helen M. Marshall; Staten Island, James P. Molinaro
2000 census population (rank): 8,008,278 (1);
% change: 9.4; **Male:** 3,794,204 (47.4%); **Female:** 4,214,074 (52.6%); **White:** 3,576,385 (44.7%); **Black:** 2,129,762 (26.6%); **American Indian and Alaska Native:** 41,289 (0.5%); **Asian:** 787,047 (9.8%); **Other race:** 1,074,406 (13.4%); **Two or more races:** 393,959 (4.9%); **Hispanic/Latino:** 2,160,554 (27.0%). **2000 percent population 18 and over:** 75.8%; **65 and over:** 11.7%; **Median age:** 34.2.
2004 population estimate (rank): 8,104,079 (1)
Land area: 303 sq mi (785 sq km) (Queens, 109 sq mi; Brooklyn, 71 sq mi; Staten Island, 58 sq mi; Bronx, 42 sq mi; Manhattan, 23 sq mi); **Alt.:** Highest, 426 ft.; lowest, sea level
Avg. daily temp.: Jan., 31.5° F; July, 76.8° F
Churches: Protestant, 1,766; Jewish, 1,256; Roman Catholic, 437; Orthodox, 66; **City-owned parks:** 1,701 (28,312 ac.); **Radio stations:** AM, 13; FM, 18; **Television stations:** 6 commercial; 1 public
Civilian Labor Force (PMSA) March 2005: 5,455,700[1]; **Unemployed:** 271,100[1], **Percent:** 5.0[1]; **Per capita personal income (MSA) 2003:** $40,899[2]
Chamber of Commerce: Greater New York Chamber of Commerce and Industry, 172 Madison Ave., New York, NY 10016

1. New York–Wayne–White Plains, N.Y.–N.J. 2. New York–Northern N.J.–Long Island, N.Y.–N.J.–Pa.

New York City is the largest city in the United States. It is located in the southern part of New York State, at the mouth of the Hudson River (also known as North River as it passes Manhattan Island).

In 1609, Henry Hudson sailed up the river that now bears his name and went as far as Albany. Five years later, a permanent settlement was established at what is now New York, but it was originally called New Amsterdam by the Dutch governors. One of them, Peter Minuit, was said to have bought Manhattan Island from the Indians in exchange for beads, buttons, and trinkets. In 1664, Great Britain's Duke of York sent a fleet that quietly seized the settlement from the Dutch without bloodshed and rechristened the colony in honor of the duke.

Control of New York passed to the young U.S. at the end of the Revolutionary War, and George Washington was inaugurated president in New York's old City Hall. Congress met in New York from 1785 to 1790.

In 1898, when Greater New York was chartered, the city expanded to include the following five boroughs, which are also counties in New York State: Manhattan (New York County); Brooklyn (Kings County); Bronx (Bronx County); Queens (Queens County); and Staten Island (Richmond County).

"The Big Apple" is a major world capital and a world leader in finance, the arts, and communications. The port of New York is one of the finest in the world and ranks as the largest port complex on the East Coast. The city is the home of the United Nations and is headquarters for some of the world's largest corporations. The city is also the center of advertising, fashion, publishing, and radio broadcasting in the United States.

In Sept. 2001, terrorist hijackers crashed two commercial jets into the World Trade Center in lower Manhattan, causing the complete destruction of the twin towers and major loss of life.

Selected famous natives and residents: Kareem Abdul-Jabbar, basketball player; Woody Allen, actor and director; Lauren Bacall, actress; James Baldwin, novelist; Harry Belafonte, singer and actor; Humphrey Bogart, actor; James Cagney, actor; Maria Callas, soprano; Aaron Copland, composer; Sammy Davis, Jr., singer and actor; Agnes de Mille, choreographer; Robert De Niro, actor; Eamon De Valera, former president of Ireland; Gertrude Elion, Nobel Prize winner in medicine; Lou Gehrig, baseball player; George Gershwin, composer; Ira Gershwin, lyricist; Rita Hayworth, actress; Lena Horne, singer; Julia Ward Howe, poet and reformer; Washington Irving, author; Henry James, novelist; Michael Jordan, basketball player; Sandy Koufax, baseball player; Roy Lichtenstein, painter; Vince Lombardi, football player and coach; Chico, Groucho, Harpo, and Zeppo Marx, comedians; Herman Melville, novelist; Yehudi Menuhin, violinist; Arthur Miller, playwright; Eugene O'Neill, playwright; J. Robert Oppenheimer, nuclear physicist; Al Pacino, actor; Jerome Robbins, choreographer; Eleanor Roosevelt, reformer and humanitarian; Theodore Roosevelt, former president; Jonas Salk, polio researcher; Beverly Sills, soprano; Neil Simon, playwright; Barbra Streisand, singer and actress; Mae West, actress; Edith Wharton, novelist.

Oakland, Calif.

Mayor: Jerry Brown (to March 2006)
2000 census population (rank): 399,484 (41); **% change:** 7.3; **Male:** 192,757 (48.3%); **Female:** 206,727 (51.7%); **White:** 125,013 (31.3%); **Black:** 142,460 (35.7%); **American Indian and Alaska Native:** 2,655 (0.7%); **Asian:** 60,851 (15.2%); **Other race:** 46,592 (11.7%); **Two or more races:** 19,911 (5.0%); **Hispanic/Latino:** 87,467 (21.9%). **2000 per-**cent population 18 and over: 75.0%; **65 and over:** 10.5%; **Median age:** 33.3.
2004 population estimate (rank): 397,976 (44)
Land area: 56 sq mi. (145 sq km); **Alt.:** Highest, 1,700 ft.; lowest, sea level
Avg. daily temp.: Jan., 49.9° F; July, 62.1° F
Churches: 374, representing over 78 denominations in the city; over 500 churches in Alameda County; **City-owned parks:** 2,196 ac.; **Radio stations:** AM, 1; **Television stations:** 1 commercial; 1 government access; 2 education access; 1 local
Civilian Labor Force (PMSA) March 2005: 1,261,200[1]; **Unemployed:** 64,300[1], **Percent:** 5.1[1]; **Per capita personal income (MSA) 2003:** $46,958[2]
Chamber of Commerce: Oakland Chamber of Commerce, 475 Fourteenth St., Oakland, CA 94612

1. Oakland–Fremont–Hayward, Calif. 2. San Francisco–Oakland–Fremont, Calif.

Oakland is located in the west-central part of California on the east side of San Francisco Bay. It is the seat of Alameda County.

Don Luis Peralta first settled the site of Oakland in 1820 when he established the Rancho San Antonio. The gold rush of 1849 attracted more people to the area, and the city's population continued to grow after a ferry service to San Francisco was started in 1851. Oakland was incorporated as a town in 1852 and as a city in 1854. It was named after the numerous oak trees found in the area. Oakland became the western terminus of the Central Pacific Railroad in 1869 and the seat of Alameda County in 1873.

In the latter part of the 19th century and also in 1910, additional territory was annexed to Oakland and the city assumed its present size. In 1906, thousands of people fled to Oakland in the aftermath of the San Francisco earthquake and settled there permanently, furthering the city's growth. Oakland's economic development continued to rise with the opening of the San Francisco–Oakland Bay Bridge in 1936.

Oakland is a major center of culture and commerce. It is an important container shipping port and the terminus of three transcontinental railroads. Oakland's industries include food processing, transportation, software, telecommunications, pharmaceuticals, and electrical and high technology manufacturing. The city is the headquarters of many national and international corporations.

Selected famous natives and residents: Buster Crabbe, actor; Frederick Cottrell, inventor; Clint Eastwood, actor and director; Dennis Eckersley, athlete; Mark Hamill, singer, dancer, and songwriter; Hammer, actor; Tom Hanks, actor; Rod McKuen, singer and composer; Russ Meyer, producer and director; Eddie (Anderson) Rochester, actor; George Stevens, director; Amy Tan, writer; Jo Van Fleet, actress.

Oklahoma City, Okla.

Mayor: Mick Cornett (to April 2008)
City Manager: James D. Couch
2000 census population (rank): 506,132 (29); **% change:** 13.8; **Male:** 247,313 (48.9%); **Female:** 258,819 (51.1%); **White:** 346,226 (68.4%); **Black:** 77,810 (15.4%); **American Indian and Alaska Native:** 17,743 (3.5%); **Asian:** 17,595 (3.5%); **Other race:** 26,705 (5.3%); **Two or more races:** 19,693 (3.9%); **Hispanic/Latino:** 51,368 (10.1%). **2000 percent population 18 and over:** 74.5%; **65 and over:** 11.5%; **Median age:** 34.0.
2004 population estimate (rank): 528,042 (31)
Land area: 607 sq mi. (1,572 sq km); **Alt.:** Highest, 1,320 ft.; lowest, 1,140 ft.
Avg. daily temp.: Jan., 35.9° F; July, 82.0° F

Churches: Roman Catholic, 25; Jewish, 4; Protestant and others, 741; **City-owned parks:** 144 (5,225 ac.); **Radio stations:** AM, 10; FM, 14; **Television stations:** 8
Civilian Labor Force (MSA) March 2005: 584,600; **Unemployed:** 26,500, **Percent:** 4.5; **Per capita personal income (MSA) 2003:** $28,958
Chamber of Commerce: Greater Oklahoma City Chamber of Commerce, 123 Park Ave., Oklahoma City, OK 73102

Oklahoma City, the state capital and seat of Oklahoma County, is the largest city in Oklahoma. It is located in the central part of the state on the North Canadian River.

Oklahoma City sprang into being almost overnight. On April 22, 1889, the U.S. government opened the territory for settlement, and there was a rush across the border line to stake claims. A sprawling tent city sprang up near the Santa Fe railroad tracks, and within a short time Oklahoma City was a bustling town of 10,000. The city was incorporated in 1890 and replaced Guthrie as the state capital in 1910. Oil was discovered in the city in 1928, and petroleum production became a mainstay of the city's economy.

Oklahoma City is the wholesale and distributing center for the state, and the city's stockyards are the largest stocker and feeder cattle market in the world. Following the decline of the energy sector, Oklahoma City is fostering a private entrepreneurial environment and a more diversified economy. Within the service sector, health services are projected to grow, followed by retail trade and business services. Nearby Tinker Air Force Base, one of the world's largest air depots, is a major city employer.

In 1995 the city was the scene of a devastating terrorist bombing, which destroyed a federal office building and killed 168 people.

Selected famous natives and residents: Johnny Bench, baseball player; Lon Chaney, Jr., actor; Ralph Ellison, writer; Kay Francis, actress; Vince Gill, country singer; Dale Robertson, actor; Ted Shackleford, actor; Pamela Tiffin, actress.

Omaha, Nebr.

Mayor: Michael Fahey (to June 2009)
2000 census population (rank): 390,007 (44); **% change:** 16.1; **Male:** 190,032 (48.7%); **Female:** 199,975 (51.3%); **White:** 305,745 (78.4%); **Black:** 51,917 (13.3%); **American Indian and Alaska Native:** 2,616 (0.7%); **Asian:** 6,773 (1.7%); **Other race:** 7,478 (1.9%); **Two or more races:** 7,478 (1.9%); **Hispanic/Latino:** 29,397 (7.5%). **2000 percent population 18 and over:** 74.4%; **65 and over:** 11.8%; **Median age:** 33.5.
2004 population estimate (rank): 409,416 (43)
Land area: 116 sq mi. (300 sq km); **Alt.:** Highest, 1,270 ft.
Avg. daily temp.: Jan., 21.1° F; July, 76.9° F
Churches: Protestant, 192; Roman Catholic, 44; Jewish, 4; **City-owned parks:** 200+ (over 8,000 ac.); **Radio stations:** AM, 7; FM, 13; **Television stations:** 4
Civilian Labor Force (MSA) March 2005: 448,700[1]; **Unemployed:** 22,000[1], **Percent:** 4.9[1]; **Per capita personal income (MSA) 2003:** $33,537[1]
Chamber of Commerce: Omaha Chamber of Commerce, 1301 Harney St., Omaha, NE 68102

1. Omaha–Council Bluffs, Nebr.–Iowa.

Omaha, the largest city in Nebraska and the seat of Douglas County, is located in the eastern part of the state on the west bank of the Missouri River, opposite Council Bluffs, Iowa.

The Lewis and Clark expedition visited the area in 1804, and the U.S. Army built Ft. Atkinson nearby in 1819. Pierre Cabanne established a fur-trading post at the site in 1825. The first Mormon migrants wintered there in 1846–1847 on their way to Utah. The city grew rapidly as the most northerly supply point for overland wagons to the Far West.

The city was officially founded in 1854 after the Nebraska Territory was opened for settlement. It was named for the Omaha Indians living nearby. Omaha was incorporated as a city in 1857 and was the capital of the Nebraska Territory from 1855 to 1867. The city continued to thrive as a point of entry and a major transportation center when the Union Pacific transcontinental railroad arrived in 1869.

Omaha is a major market for grain and livestock, food processing, telecommunications, and insurance. Other important industries include electrical equipment and finance as well as printing and publishing. It continues to be a major railroad hub.

Selected famous natives and residents: Fred Astaire, dancer and actor; Max Baer, boxer; Robert Boozer, basketball player; Marlon Brando, actor; Montgomery Clift, actor; Gerald Ford, former president; Bob Gibson, baseball player; Swoosie Kurtz, actress; Melvin Laird, former secretary of defense; Dorothy McGuire, actress; Nick Nolte, actor; Gale Sayers, football player; Malcolm X, political activist; Paul Williams, singer and composer.

Philadelphia, Pa.

Mayor: John F. Street (to Jan. 2008)
2000 census population (rank): 1,517,550 (5); **% change:** –4.3; **Male:** 705,107 (46.5%); **Female:** 812,443 (53.5%); **White:** 683,267 (45.0%); **Black:** 655,824 (43.2%); **American Indian and Alaska Native:** 4,073 (0.3%); **Asian:** 67,654 (4.5%); **Other race:** 72,429 (4.8%); **Two or more races:** 33,574 (2.2%); **Hispanic/Latino:** 128,928 (8.5%). **2000 percent population 18 and over:** 74.7%; **65 and over:** 14.1%; **Median age:** 34.2.
2004 population estimate (rank): 1,470,151 (5)
Land area: 135 sq mi. (350 sq km); **Alt.:** Highest, 440 ft.; lowest, sea level
Avg. daily temp.: Jan., 30.4° F; July, 76.7° F
Churches: Roman Catholic, 133; Jewish, 55; Protestant and others, 830; **City-owned parks:** 630 (10,252 ac.); **Radio stations:**[1] AM, 40; FM, 43; **Television stations:** 14
Civilian Labor Force (PMSA) March 2005: 1,930,900; **Unemployed:** 108,500, **Percent:** 5.6; **Per capita personal income (MSA) 2003:** $37,059[2]
Chamber of Commerce: Philadelphia Chamber of Commerce, 200 South Broad St., Suite 700, Philadelphia, PA 19102

1. Metropolitan area. 2. Philadelphia–Camden–Wilmington, Pa–N.J.–Del.–Md.

Philadelphia, the largest city in Pennsylvania, is located in the southeast part of the state at the junction of the Schuylkill and Delaware Rivers. It is coextensive with Philadelphia County.

Philadelphia, the City of Brotherly Love, was settled in 1681 by Capt. William Markham, who, with a small band of colonists, had been sent out by his cousin, William Penn. Penn arrived the following year with the intention of creating a refuge for the Quakers.

In the period before the American Revolution, the city outstripped all others in the colonies in education, arts, science, industry, and commerce. In 1774–1776, the First and Second Continental Congresses met in Philadelphia, and, from 1781–1783, the city was the capital of the United States under the

Articles of Confederation. In 1790, it became the nation's capital under the Constitution and remained so until the seat of the federal government moved to Washington in 1800.

Within a half-century of the founding of the nation at Independence Hall, Philadelphia had emerged as a leader in America's Industrial Revolution. Today the steam locomotives and hat factories of the 19th century have been replaced by diverse manufacturing specialties such as chemicals (including pharmaceuticals), medical devices, transportation equipment, and printing and publishing. In the services sector, Philadelphia leads in subsectors such as health services, insurance carriers, legal services, and architecture and engineering services. Philadelphia is also home to branches of the U.S. Mint, the Federal Reserve System, and the Internal Revenue Service.

The city's harbor, one of the largest freshwater ports in the world, is the centerpiece of the Ameri-Port facility in south Philadelphia, a major shipping center with rail links to the Midwest and Canada.

The city abounds in landmarks of early American history, including Independence Hall, where the Declaration of Independence was signed, and the Liberty Bell. Other significant tourist attractions are the Philadelphia Museum of Art, the Franklin Institute Science Museum, and the Philadelphia Zoological Gardens.

Selected famous natives and residents: Marian Anderson, contralto; Frankie Avalon, singer and actor; John, Lionel, and Ethel Barrymore, actors; Kevin Bacon, actor; Boyz II Men, R&B group; Mary Cassatt, artist; Wilt Chamberlain, basketball player; Chubby Checker, singer; Bill Cosby, actor; Stuart Davis, painter; Thomas Eakins, painter and sculptor; W. C. Fields, comedian; Benjamin Franklin, inventor and statesman; Grace (Kelly), actress and princess of Monaco; Walt Kelly, cartoonist; Patti LaBelle, singer; Mario Lanza, singer and actor; George McClellan, general; Margaret Mead, anthropologist; Edgar Allen Poe, author; Anna Quindlen, writer and Pulitzer Prize winner; Man Ray, painter; Betsy Ross, flagmaker; Will Smith, actor; Jacqueline Susann, novelist; Robert Venturi, architect.

Phoenix, Ariz.

Mayor: Phil Gordon (to Oct. 2007)
2000 census population (rank): 1,321,045 (6);
% change: 34.3; **Male:** 671,760 (50.9%); **Female:** 649,285 (49.1%); **White:** 938,853 (71.1%); **Black:** 67,416 (5.1%); **American Indian and Alaska Native:** 26,696 (2.0%); **Asian:** 26,449 (2.0%); **Other race:** 216,589 (16.4%); **Two or more races:** 43,276 (3.3%); **Hispanic/Latino:** 449,972 (34.1%). **2000 percent population 18 and over:** 71.1%; **65 and over:** 8.1%; **Median age:** 30.7.
2004 population estimate (rank): 1,418,041 (6)
Land area: 475 sq mi. (1,230 sq km); **Alt.:** Highest, 2,740 ft.; lowest, 1,017 ft.
Avg. daily temp.: Jan., 53.6° F; July, 93.5° F
City-owned parks: 200+ (25,235 ac.); **Radio stations:** AM, 20; FM, 20; **Television stations:** 9 commercial; 1 PBS
Civilian Labor Force (MSA) March 2005: 1,861,500[1];
Unemployed: 78,400[1], **Percent:** 4.2[1]; **Per capita personal income (MSA) 2003** $29,590[1]
Chamber of Commerce: Phoenix Chamber of Commerce, 201 N. Central, Phoenix, AZ 85073

1. Phoenix–Mesa–Scottsdale, Ariz.

Phoenix, the capital of Arizona and seat of Maricopa County, is the largest city in the state. It is located in the center of Arizona, on the Salt River.

The prehistoric Hohokam Indians first settled the area about 300 B.C. and dug a system of extensive irrigation canals for farming. The Indian culture mysteriously broke up in the 1400s.

The site was permanently resettled by Jack Swilling and "Lord Darrell" Duppa about 1867. Because the city was founded on the ruins of the ancient civilization, it was named Phoenix after the legendary bird that could regenerate itself. The irrigation canals were restored for farming, and ranching and prospecting began in the surrounding area. The city quickly grew as an important trading center. Phoenix was incorporated as a city in 1881 and was made the territorial capital in 1889. It became the state capital when Arizona was admitted to the Union in 1912.

Partly owing to its warm, dry climate, the city developed rapidly in the decades after World War II. Between 1950 and 1990 the population increased from 100,000 to 980,000. And Phoenix continues to be one of the fastest growing cities in the U.S.; between 1990 and 2000, its population increased another 34%, to 1.3 million.

Phoenix is a commercial and manufacturing center in an agricultural region. Major industries include government, agricultural products, aerospace technology, electronics, air-conditioning, leather goods, and Indian arts and crafts. Mining, timbering, and tourism also contribute to the economy.

Selected famous natives and residents: Lynda Carter, actress; Alice Cooper, musician; Arthur A. Fletcher, government official; Barry Goldwater, politician; Stevie Nicks, musician; Charles S. Robb, politician; Mare Winningham, actress.

Portland, Ore.

Mayor: Tom Potter (to Dec. 2008)
2000 census population (rank): 529,121 (28);
% change: 21.0; **Male:** 261,565 (49.4%); **Female:** 267,556 (50.6%); **White:** 412,241 (77.9%); **Black:** 35,115 (6.6%); **American Indian and Alaska Native:** 5,587 (1.1%); **Asian:** 33,470 (6.3%); **Other race:** 18,760 (3.5%); **Two or more races:** 21,955 (4.1%); **Hispanic/Latino:** 36,058 (6.8%). **2000 percent population 18 and over:** 78.9%; **65 and over:** 11.6%; **Median age:** 35.2.
2004 population estimate (rank): 533,492 (30)
Land area: 134 sq mi. (347 sq km); **Alt.:** Highest, 1073 ft.; lowest, sea level
Avg. daily temp.: Jan., 39.6° F; July, 68.2° F
Churches: Protestant, 450; Roman Catholic, 48; Jewish, 9; Buddhist, 6; other, 190; **City-owned parks:** 200 (over 10,000 ac.); **Radio stations:** AM: 14, FM: 14; **Television stations:** 5 commercial; 1 public
Civilian Labor Force (PMSA) March 2005: 1,100,600[1]; **Unemployed:** 70,300[1], **Percent:** 6.4[1]; **Per capita personal income (MSA) 2003** $32,152[1]
Chamber of Commerce: Portland Business Alliance, 520 S.W. Yamhill St., Ste. 1000, Portland, OR 97204

1. Portland–Vancouver–Beaverton, Ore.–Wash.

Portland, the largest city in Oregon and seat of Multnomah County, is located in the northwest part of the state on the Willamette River.

Lewis and Clark camped at the site of Portland in 1805 on their expedition across the continent. Portland was founded in 1845 and was almost called Boston after the city in Massachusetts. Founders Amos Lovejoy from Massachusetts and Francis Pettygrove from Maine flipped a coin to decide the name of the new town. Pettygrove won the toss and named the place Portland after his hometown. Portland was incorporated as a city in 1851.

In the 1850s Portland served as a supply base for the California gold rush, and it grew with the development of its salmon and lumber industries and the arrival of the railroad in 1883. The city continued to grow from 1879 to 1900 as a supply point for the Alaska gold rush and as the site of the Lewis and Clark Centennial Exposition in 1905.

The port of Portland leads the West in grain exports and is among the top five auto-import centers in the United States.

Portland has a diverse economy with a broad base of manufacturing, distribution, wholesale and retail trade, regional government, and business services. Major manufacturing industries include machinery, electronics, metals, transportation equipment, and lumber and wood products. Technology is a thriving part of Portland's economy, with over 1,700 high-tech companies located in the metropolitan area. Tourism is also important to Portland's economy, drawing more than 7 million visitors annually.

Selected famous natives and residents: James Beard, food expert; Pietro Belluschi, architect; Richard Fosbury, high jumper; Matt Groening, cartoonist; Margaux Hemingway, actress; Phil Knight, founder of Nike; Terrance Knox, actor; Jeff Lorber, jazz musician; Linus Pauling, chemist; Jane Powell, singer and actress; Ahmad Rashad, football player and sportscaster; Susan Ruttan, actress; Doc Severinson, band leader; Norton Simon, business executive; Sally Ann Struthers, actress; Gus Van Sant, film director; Lindsay Wagner, actress; Mitch Williams, baseball pitcher.

Sacramento, Calif.

Mayor: Heather Fargo (to March 2008)
City Manager: Robert P. Thomas
2000 census population (rank): 407,018 (40);
  % change: 10.2; **Male:** 197,784 (48.6%); **Female:** 209,234 (51.4%); **White:** 196,549 (48.3%); **Black:** 62,968 (15.5%); **American Indian and Alaska Native:** 5,300 (1.3%); **Asian:** 67,635 (16.6%); **Other race:** 44,627 (11.0%); **Two or more races:** 26,078 (6.4%); **Hispanic/Latino:** 87,974 (21.6%). **2000 percent population 18 and over:** 72.7%; **65 and over:** 11.4%; **Median age:** 32.8.
2004 population estimate (rank): 454,330 (38)
Land area: 97 sq mi. (251 sq km). **Alt.:** 25 ft
Avg. daily temp.: Jan., 45.2° F; July, 75.7° F
City park & recreational facilities: 160+ (2,000+ ac.);
  Television stations: 7
Civilian Labor Force (PMSA) March 2005: 1,012,300[1];
  Unemployed: 49,600[1], **Percent:** 4.9[1]; **Per capita personal income (MSA) 2003** $31,425[1]
Chamber of Commerce: Sacramento Chamber of Commerce, 917 7th St., Sacramento, CA 95814

1. Sacramento–Arden–Arcade–Roseville, Calif.

Sacramento is the capital of California and the seat of Sacramento County. It is located in the north-central part of the state at the confluence of the Sacramento and American rivers.

In 1839, German-born Swiss citizen John Augustus Sutter obtained a grant from the Mexican governor to establish a colony for fellow Swiss emigrants on a large tract of land that he named New Helvetia (New Switzerland). He established Fort Sutter there as a trading post.

After gold was discovered on Sutter's property in 1848, the settlement rapidly expanded as the prominent supply point for gold prospectors coming from the East. Sacramento was laid out in 1848 and named after California's principal river, which ran beside it. The river's name in Spanish honors the Holy Sacrament. It became incorporated as a city in 1849 and

was made the state capital in 1854. Sacramento was the terminus of the first railroad in 1856 and the western terminus of the Pony Express in 1860.

The city has always been a hub of river transportation and is a major deep-water port connected to the Pacific Ocean. Sacramento's economy is highly diversified and, along with state government and military installations, its industries include aerospace, high technology, furniture, chemicals, pharmaceuticals, meat packing, and food processing of crops from the Central Valley.

Selected famous natives and residents: Joan Didion, author; Mark Goodson, TV producer; Tom Hanks, actor; Henry Hathaway, director; Anthony M. Kennedy, Supreme Court justice; Molly Ringwald, actress.

San Antonio, Tex.

Mayor: Phil Hardberger (to May 2007)
City Manager: J. Rolando Bono
2000 census population (rank): 1,144,646 (9);
  % change: 22.3; **Male:** 553,245 (48.3%); **Female:** 591,401 (51.7%); **White:** 774,708 (67.7%); **Black:** 78,120 (6.8%); **American Indian and Alaska Native:** 9,584 (0.8%); **Asian:** 17,934 (1.6%); **Other race:** 221,362 (19.3%); **Two or more races:** 41,871 (3.7%); **Hispanic/Latino:** 671,394 (58.7%). **2000 percent population 18 and over:** 71.5%; **65 and over:** 10.4%; **Median age:** 31.7.
2004 population estimate (rank): 1,236,249 (8)
Land area: 408 sq mi. (1,057 sq km); **Alt.:** 700 ft.
Avg. daily temp.: Jan., 49.3° F; July, 85.0° F
City-owned parks: 193 (15,546 ac.); **Radio stations:** AM, 20; FM, 22; **Television stations:** 9
Civilian Labor Force (MSA) March 2005: 893,000;
  Unemployed: 45,800, **Percent:** 5.1; **Per capita personal income (MSA) 2003** $27,81
Chamber of Commerce: Greater San Antonio Chamber of Commerce, 602 E. Commerce, San Antonio, TX 78205

San Antonio, the third-largest city in Texas and the seat of Bexar County, is located in the south-central part of the state, on the San Antonio River.

The site of San Antonio was first visited in 1691 by a Franciscan friar on the feast day of St. Anthony and was named San Antonio de Padua in his honor. San Antonio was permanently settled on May 1, 1718, when the Spanish governor of Coahuila and Texas, Martin de Alarcón, founded the presidio (a fort) of San Antonio de Bejar (Bexar) and the mission of San Antonio de Valero (later called the Alamo) on the site of a Coahuiltecan Indian village. San Antonio remained almost continuously under Spanish rule until 1812, when Mexico won its independence from Spain.

During the outbreak of the Texas revolution (1835) against the tyranny of Mexican dictator General Santa Anna, San Antonio was captured by a small band of rebels who occupied the fortified mission of the Alamo in Dec. 1835. The historic battle of the Alamo was fought there (Feb. 24 to March 6, 1836), and its 183 besieged defenders were massacred by Santa Anna's troops. Their heroism aroused the anger and fighting spirit of Texans and led them to shout their famous battle cry "Remember the Alamo!" and defeat the Mexicans six weeks later (April 21, 1836) at the battle of San Jacinto. Texas became an independent republic in 1836, and San Antonio was incorporated as a city on Jan. 5, 1837.

After the Civil War, with the arrival of the railroad in 1877, San Antonio prospered as a major shipping point for cattle. The city has been an important military center since World War II and is the home to five of the largest military installations in the nation, including Fort Sam Houston, constructed in 1876. San Antonio is a leading livestock center and one of the largest produce exchange markets. The city's industries are highly diversified, and tourism is also important to the economy.

Selected famous natives and residents: Carol Burnett, comedienne; George W. Bush, U.S. president; Cody Carlson, football player; Henry G. Cisneros, secretary of HUD; Joan Crawford, actress; Cito Gaston, baseball manager; Ann Harding, actress; Jesse James Leija, boxer; Emilio Navaira, Tejano music singer; Oliver North, military officer and government official; Suzy Parker, model and actress; Paula Prentiss, actress; Kyle Rote, football player; David R. Scott, astronaut; Patsy Torres, Tejano music singer; Edward H. White, astronaut.

San Diego, Calif.

Interim Mayor: Toni Atkins[1]
City Manager: P. Lamont Ewell (apptd. March 2004)
2000 census population (rank): 1,223,400 (7);
% change: 10.2; Male: 616,884 (50.4%); Female: 606,516 (49.6%); White: 736,207 (60.2%); Black: 96,216 (7.9%); American Indian and Alaska Native: 7,543 (0.6%); Asian: 166,968 (13.6%); Other race: 151,532 (12.4%); Two or more races: 59,081 (4.8%); Hispanic/Latino: 310,752 (25.4%). 2000 percent population 18 and over: 76.0%; 65 and over: 10.5%; Median age: 32.5.
2004 population estimate (rank): 1,263,756 (7)
Land area: 324 sq miles (839 sq km), Alt.: Highest, 1,591 ft.; lowest, sea level
Avg. daily temp.: Jan., 57.4° F; July, 71.0° F
Churches: Roman Catholic, 39; Jewish, 9; Protestant, 334; Eastern Orthodox, 8; other, 18; City park and recreation facilities: 337 (36,300 ac.); Radio stations: AM, 14; FM, 25; Television stations: 9
Civilian Labor Force (MSA) March 2005: 1,507,900[2]; Unemployed: 64,100[2], Percent: 4.3[2]; Per capita personal income (MSA) 2002 $35,841[2]
Chamber of Commerce: San Diego Chamber of Commerce, 402 West Broadway, Suite 1000, San Diego, CA 92101

1. Dick Murphy, elected mayor in Nov. 2004, resigned in July 2005 after scandals rocked his administration. The council member who took his place was suspended for accepting bribes. A July 26 election led to a November runoff. 2. San Diego–Carlsbad–San Marcos, Calif.

San Diego is the second-largest city in California. It is located in the southwest part of the state, on San Diego Bay.

Portuguese navigator Juan Rodríguez Cabrillo claimed the bay for Spain in 1542. The site was named San Miguel by Cabrillo. On Nov. 12, 1602, Don Sebastian de Viscaíno came ashore with his party on the day of St. Didacus (San Diego in Spanish) and celebrated a mass in the saint's honor. By coincidence, Viscaíno's flagship was named *San Diego*. He renamed the place San Diego after the 15th-century saint.

In 1769, Franciscan father Junípero Serra established the first California mission there—San Diego del Alcala. In 1822, Mexico won control of the town after declaring its independence from Spain. In 1846, during the Mexican War, San Diego was seized by the U.S., and it was incorporated as a city in 1850, just after California joined the Union.

Today, San Diego's excellent natural harbor is a busy commercial port and a hub of U.S. naval operations (although the naval training center at San Diego has closed due to defense cutbacks). Other leading industries are electronics, aerospace and missiles, medical and scientific research, oceanography, and agriculture. Its magnificent climate and proximity to Mexico have made tourism a significant part of the city's economy.

Selected famous natives and residents: Billy Casper, golfer; Florence Chadwick, swimmer; Dennis Conner, yacht racer; Ted Danson, actor; Robert Duvall, actor; Nanette Fabray, actress; Margaret O'Brien, actress; Carol Vaness, soprano; Ted Williams, baseball player; Mickey Wright, golfer.

San Francisco, Calif.

Mayor: Gavin Newsom (to Jan. 2008)
2000 census population (rank): 776,733 (13);
% change: 7.3; Male: 394,828 (50.8%); Female: 381,905 (49.2%); White: 385,728 (49.7%); Black: 60,515 (7.8%); American Indian and Alaska Native: 3,458 (0.4%); Asian: 239,565 (30.8%); Other race: 50,368 (6.5%); Two or more races: 33,255 (4.3%); Hispanic/Latino: 109,504 (14.1%). 2000 percent population 18 and over: 85.5%; 65 and over: 13.7%; Median age: 36.5.
2004 population estimate (rank): 744,230 (14)
Land area: 47 sq mi. (122 sq km), Alt.: Highest, 925 ft.; lowest, sea level
Avg. daily temp.: Jan., 51.1° F; July, 59.1° F
Churches: 540 of all denominations; City-owned parks and squares: 200+; Radio stations: 29; Television stations: 10
Civilian Labor Force (PMSA) March 2005: 923,500[1]; Unemployed: 43,000[1], Percent: 4.7[1]; Per capita personal income (MSA) 2002: $46,958[2]
Chamber of Commerce: San Francisco Chamber of Commerce, 235 Montgomery St., San Francisco, CA 94104

1. San Francisco–San Mateo–Redwood City, Calif. 2. San Francisco–Oakland–Fremont, Calif.

San Francisco, the fourth-largest city in California, is coextensive with San Francisco County. It is located in the northern part of the state between the Pacific Ocean and San Francisco Bay on a narrow arm of land that embraces San Francisco Bay, the largest land-locked harbor in the world.

A Franciscan father who was sailing with Sebastián Rodríguez Cermeño named the bay San Francisco on Nov. 7, 1595. In 1776, the Spaniards established a presidio, or military post, and a Franciscan mission on the end of the beautiful peninsula. In the following year, a little town was founded around the mission. It was called Yerba Buena, Spanish for "Good Herb," because mint grew in abundance there. In 1846, during the Mexican War, Yerba Buena was taken over by the United States. It was renamed San Francisco in 1847 and became incorporated as a city in 1850.

When gold was discovered in California in 1848, the city's population jumped to 10,000, and it experienced turbulent years until order was established by Vigilance Committees, first in 1851, and again in 1856. Then followed a period of more orderly growth, and the foundations of the great commerce and industry of today were laid.

In 1906, San Francisco experienced the nation's most destructive earthquake, which, together with the fire that followed, practically destroyed the city. The city was quickly rebuilt and grew rapidly as a leading transportation, industrial, and cultural center. In the 19th century, the American explorer and soldier John C. Frémont, known as The Pathfinder, named the entrance to the bay the Golden Gate, and the famous bright orange Golden Gate Bridge was dedicated in May 1937.

A vital part of the economic and cultural fabric of northern California, the port of San Francisco covers 7½ mi of waterfront. The port is home to a broad range of commercial, maritime, and public activities. Its major shipping terminals serve shipping lines from around the world. Fisherman's Wharf, Alcatraz, Hyde St. Pier, and Pier 39 all make the port of San Francisco one of the world's leading visitor destinations.

The electronics and biotechnology industries are well represented throughout the Bay Area. With nearly 30% of the worldwide biotechnology labor force and 360 biotech firms, the Bay Area has been appropriately called "Bionic Bay."

Tourism is one of San Francisco's largest industries and the largest employer of city residents. In 2000, more than 17 million people visited San Francisco, and visitor spending was $7.6 billion, providing 82,000 jobs.

San Francisco is also the banking and financial center of the West and is home to a Federal Reserve Bank and a United States Mint. More than 60 foreign banks maintain offices there.

Selected famous natives and residents: Gracie Allen, comedienne; Luis Walter Alvarez, Nobel Prize winner in physics; David Belasco, dramatist and producer; Mel Blanc, actor and voice specialist; Rosemary Casals, tennis player; Isadora Duncan, dancer; Clint Eastwood, actor; Robert Frost, poet; Rube Goldberg, cartoonist; William Randolph Hearst, publisher; Bruce Lee, actor; Mervyn LeRoy, director; Jack London, novelist; Johnny Mathis, singer; Lloyd Nolan, actor; O. J. Simpson, football player; Robert G. Sproul, educator; Irving Stone, novelist; Natalie Wood, actress.

San Jose, Calif.

Mayor: Ron Gonzales (to Nov. 2006)
City Manager: Del D. Borgsdorf
2000 census population (rank): 894,943 (11);
% change: 14.4; **Male:** 454,798 (50.8%); **Female:** 440,145 (49.2%); **White:** 425,017 (47.5%); **Black:** 31,349 (3.5%); **American Indian and Alaska Native:** 6,865 (0.8%); **Asian:** 240,375 (26.9%); **Other race:** 142,691 (15.9%); **Two or more races:** 45,062 (5.0%); **Hispanic/Latino:** 269,989 (30.2%). **2000 percent population 18 and over:** 73.6%; **65 and over:** 8.3%; **Median age:** 32.6.
2004 population estimate (rank): 904,522 (10)
Land area: 175 sq mi. (453 sq km); **Alt.:** Highest, 4,372 ft.; lowest, sea level
Avg. daily temp.: Jan., 49.4° F; July, 69.5° F
Churches: 403; **City-owned parks and playgrounds:** 152 (3,136 ac.); **Radio stations:** 14; **Television stations:** 4
Civilian Labor Force (PMSA) March 2005: 844,400[1]; **Unemployed:** 48,900[1], **Percent:** 5.8[1]; **Per capita personal income (MSA) 2003:** $46,072[1]
Chamber of Commerce: San Jose Chamber of Commerce, 310 S. First St., San Jose, CA 95113

1. San Jose–Sunnyvale–Santa Clara, Calif.

San Jose, the third-largest city in California and seat of Santa Clara County, is located in the northern part of the state in the Santa Clara Valley, 50 mi south of downtown San Francisco.

San Jose was founded on Nov. 29, 1777, by Spanish colonizers who named the settlement Pueblo de San José de Guadalupe in honor of Saint Joseph and after the Guadalupe River on which the pueblo (town) was situated. San Jose was the first city to be established in California.

After California became a U.S. territory in 1847, San Jose was the state capital from 1849 to 1852 and was incorporated as a city in 1850. It developed commercially as a supply base for gold prospectors and, when the railroad connected it with San Francisco in 1864, it became the distribution point for agricultural products from the Santa Clara Valley.

Today, the city continues to be the distribution and food-processing center for the surrounding rich agricultural region, which produces seasonal fruits and grapes. More than 50 wineries grace the valley.

San Jose is the capital of Silicon (Santa Clara) Valley, where many high-tech companies are located. The area is also one of the world's leading centers for medical treatment and research. Heart transplants, gene splicing, and transportable baby incubators were developed there.

San Jose has healthy retail, transportation, and tourism industries and is the primary center for real estate and industrial development in the area. In 2001, it ranked second in the U.S. based on the median household income of $71,000.

Selected famous natives and residents: "Fatty" Arbuckle, actor; Cesar Chavez, labor leader; Peggy Fleming, figure skater; Farley Granger, actor; Edmund Lowe, actor; Jim Plunkett, football player.

Seattle, Wash.

Mayor: Greg Nickels (to Dec. 31, 2005)
2000 census population (rank): 563,374 (24);
% change: 9.1; **Male:** 280,973 (49.9%); **Female:** 282,401 (50.1%); **White:** 394,889 (70.1%); **Black:** 47,541 (8.4%); **American Indian and Alaska Native:** 5,659 (1.0%); **Asian:** 73,910 (13.1%); **Other race:** 13,423 (2.4%); **Two or more races:** 25,148 (4.5%); **Hispanic/Latino:** 29,719 (5.3%). **2000 percent population 18 and over:** 84.4%; **65 and over:** 12.0%; **Median age:** 35.4.
2004 population estimate (rank): 571,480 (23)
Land area: 84 sq mi. (218 sq km); **Alt.:** Highest, 521 ft.; lowest, sea level
Avg. daily temp.: Jan., 40.1° F; July, 65.2° F
Churches: Roman Catholic, 35; Jewish, 12; Protestant, 447; others, 42; **City-owned parks, playgrounds, etc.:** 400 (6,200 ac.); **Radio stations:** AM, 15; FM, 22; **Television stations:** 6
Civilian Labor Force (PMSA) April 2005: 1,332,300[1]; **Unemployed:** 57,500[1], **Percent:** 4.3[1]; **Per capita personal income (MSA) 2003:** $39,008[2]
Chamber of Commerce: Greater Seattle Chamber of Commerce, 1301 5th Ave., Suite 2400, Seattle, WA 98101-2603

1. Seattle–Bellevue–Everett, Wash. 2. Seattle–Tacoma–Bellevue, Wash.

Seattle is the largest city in Washington and the seat of King County. A city of steep hills, Seattle lies in western Washington between two bodies of water—Puget Sound on the west and Lake Washington on the east. Its fine landlocked harbor has made Seattle one of the major ports in the United States.

Seattle was first settled by five pioneer families from Illinois at Alki Point at the south end of Elliott Bay in 1851. They moved in 1852 to the eastern shore of the bay and laid out a town in 1853. It was named Seattle after a friendly Suquamish Indian chief (Seattle is only an approximation of his name).

Seattle successfully withstood an Indian attack in 1856 and was incorporated as a city in 1869. A disastrous fire almost destroyed the entire business district in 1889. When the Great Northern Railway arrived in 1893, the city became a major rail terminus and it grew rapidly. It was a boom town during the Alaska gold rush of 1897 and continued to prosper as a major Pacific port of entry with the opening of the Panama Canal in 1914.

Seattle is the region's commercial and transportation hub and the center of manufacturing, trade, and finance. Its important diversified industries include aircraft, lumber and forest products, fishing, high technology, food processing, boat building, machinery, fabricated metals, chemicals, pharmaceuticals, and apparel.

Selected famous natives and residents: Chester Carlson, Xerox inventor; Carol Channing, actress; Judy Collins, singer; Fred Couples, golfer; Gail Devers, athlete; Frances Farmer, actress; William Gates, Microsoft founder; June Havoc, actress; Jimi Hendrix, guitarist; Robert Joffrey, choreographer; Gypsy Rose Lee, entertainer; Mary Livingstone, comedienne; Kevin McCarthy, actor; Mary McCarthy, novelist; Jeff Smith, food expert; Martha Wright, singer.

Tucson, Ariz.

Mayor: Bob Walkup (to Dec. 2007)
2000 census population (rank): 486,699 (30);
  % change: 20.1; **Male:** 238,408 (49.0%); **Female:** 248,291 (51.0%); **White:** 341,424 (70.2%); **Black:** 21,057 (4.3%); **American Indian and Alaska Native:** 11,038 (2.3%); **Asian:** 11,959 (2.5%); **Other race:** 81,988 (16.8%); **Two or more races:** 18,437 (3.8%); **Hispanic/Latino:** 173,868 (35.7%). **2000 percent population 18 and over:** 75.4%; **65 and over:** 11.9%; **Median age:** 32.1.
2004 population estimate (rank): 512,023 (32)
Land area: 195 sq mi. (505 sq km); **Alt.:** 2,400 ft.
Avg. daily temp.: Jan., 51.3° F; July, 86.6° F
Churches: Protestant, 340; Roman Catholic, 42; other, 150; **City-owned parks and parkways:** (25,349 ac.); **Radio stations:** AM, 15; FM, 17; **Television stations:** 3 commercial; 1 educational; 3 other
Civilian Labor Force (MSA) March 2005: 448,400; **Unemployed:** 19,500, **Percent:** 4.3; **Per capita personal income (MSA) 2003:** $25,906
Chamber of Commerce: Tucson Metropolitan Chamber of Commerce, 465 W. St. Mary's Rd., Tucson, AZ 85701

Tucson is the second-largest city in Arizona and the seat of Pima County. It is located in the southeast part of the state on the Santa Cruz River.

The site was originally settled by the prehistoric Hohokam Indians (300 B.C.–A.D.1400s). The first Europeans to visit the area were Spanish missionaries in the 17th century. In 1700, the Jesuit missionary explorer Father Eusebio Francisco Kino founded the mission of San Xavier del Bac close by the Papago Indian village of Stjukshon (later called Tucson). Stjukshon is an Indian word meaning "village of the dark spring at the foot of the mountain." The Papago Indians are descendants of the ancient Hohokam peoples.

In 1776, Spanish colonists from Mexico constructed a presidio (fort) at Tucson as protection against the hostile Apache Indians and also established the mission of San Jose de Tucson nearby. Tucson remained a military outpost under Spanish and later Mexican control until the area was sold to the United States as part of the Gadsden Purchase in 1853. Tucson was the capital of the Arizona Territory from 1867 to 1877. It was incorporated as a city in 1877. The town grew rapidly when the Southern Pacific Railroad arrived in 1880 and silver and copper deposits were discovered nearby.

Tucson is a popular vacation and health resort due to its sunny, mild, dry climate and unique desert location. Tourism is important to the city's economy. Major industries include aerospace and missile production, high technology, optics, biotechnology, environmental technology, software, and electronics. Tucson is also the commercial center for the surrounding area's agricultural and mining industries. The city is the home of the University of Arizona.

Selected famous natives and residents: Rose E. Bird, jurist; Dennis De Concini, senator; Barbara Eden, actress; Linda Ronstadt, singer.

Tulsa, Okla.

Mayor: Bill LaFortune (to April 2006)
2000 census population (rank): 393,049 (43);
  % change: 7.0; **Male:** 189,937 (48.3%); **Female:** 203,112 (51.7%); **White:** 275,468 (70.1%); **Black:** 60,794 (15.5%); **American Indian and Alaska Native:** 18,551 (4.7%); **Asian:** 7,150 (1.8%); **Other race:** 13,564 (3.5%); **Two or more races:** 17,300 (4.4%); **Hispanic/Latino:** 28,111 (7.2%). **2000 percent population 18 and over:** 75.2%; **65 and over:** 12.9%; **Median age:** 34.5.
2004 population estimate (rank): 383,764 (45)
Land area: 183 sq mi. (474 sq km); **Alt.:** 674 ft.
Avg. daily temp.: Jan., 35.2° F; July, 83.3° F
Churches: Protestant, 290; Roman Catholic, 40; Jewish, 3; others, 4; **City parks and playgrounds:** 128 (5,987 ac.); **Radio stations:** AM, 10; FM, 16; **Television stations:** 7 commercial; 1 PBS; 123 cable
Civilian Labor Force (MSA) March 2005: 445,100; **Unemployed:** 19,700, **Percent:** 4.4; **Per capita personal income (MSA) 2003:** $30,908
Chamber of Commerce: Metropolitan Tulsa Chamber of Commerce, 2 West Second St., Ste. 150, Tulsa, OK 74103

Tulsa, the second-largest city in Oklahoma and seat of Tulsa County, is located in the northeast part of the state on the Arkansas River.

Tulsa was settled in the 1830s by Creek Indians from Alabama who were forcibly sent to the area (then part of Indian Territory) under the Indian Removal Act of 1830. Creek medicine men planted ashes from their old home at the new site, and the Creeks named their new village "Tulsy," meaning old town, in memory of their former home in Tallassee, Ala. In time, the village became the town of Tulsa.

The coming of the first railroad in 1882 attracted white settlers to Tulsa, and the town developed into a cattle-shipping center. When enormous oil deposits were discovered at nearby Red Fork in 1901 and at Glenn Pool in 1905, the city experienced rapid growth as a center of a booming petroleum industry. Tulsa was incorporated as a city in 1898 and chartered in 1908.

Tulsa is the center of the state's petroleum and telecommunications industries and has a diversified economy. Other important industries include aerospace, chemicals, computer parts, automobile glass, fabricated metals, and industrial machinery. The city became a major inland port when the Tulsa port of Catoosa opened in 1971.

Selected famous natives and residents: Garth Brooks, singer; Blake Edwards, director; Paul Harvey, commentator; Jennifer Jones, actress; Henry R. Kravis, investment banker; Daniel Patrick Moynihan, senator; Tony Randall, actor; Alfre Woodard, actress; Judy Woodruff, journalist.

Virginia Beach, Va.

Mayor: Meyera E. Oberndorf (to June 2008)
2000 census population (rank): 425,257 (38);
% change: 8.2; **Male:** 210,524 (49.5%); **Female:**
214,733 (50.5%); **White:** 303,681 (71.4%); **Black:**
80,593 (19.0%); **American Indian and Alaska Native:**
1,619 (0.4%); **Asian:** 20,869 (4.9%); **Other race:**
6,402 (1.5%); **Two or more races:** 11,677 (2.7%);
Hispanic/Latino: 17,770 (4.2%). **2000 percent population 18 and over:** 72.5%; **65 and over:** 8.4%;
Median age: 32.7.
2004 population estimate (rank): 440,098 (40)
Land area: 248 sq mi. (642 sq km); **Alt.:** 12 ft.
Avg. daily temp.: Jan., 39.1° F; July, 78.2° F
Churches: Protestant, 235; Catholic, 13; Jewish, 5;
City-owned parks: 208 (4,000+ ac.); **Radio stations:**
AM 13; FM 31; **Television stations:** 8 commercial; 1
PBS; 1 cable
Civilian Labor Force (MSA) March 2005: 806,200[1];
Unemployed: 31,100[1], **Percent:** 3.9[1]; **Per capita personal income (MSA) 2002:** $29,337[1]
Chamber of Commerce: Hampton Roads Chamber of
Commerce, P.O. Box 327, Norfolk, VA 23501

1. Virginia Beach–Norfolk–Newport News, Va.–N.C.

Virginia Beach, the most populous city in Virginia, is located in the southeast part of the state on the Atlantic coastline. It is independent and is not part of any county.

The first English settlers to set foot in America landed at Cape Henry at the tip of Virginia Beach on April 29, 1607. They were led by John Smith on his way to establishing Jamestown. The first permanent settlement within the city limits was made at Lynnhaven Bay in 1621. Cape Henry became an important port for British merchant ships calling on America, and it was here that the French fleet led by Admiral Comte de Grasse blockaded the British fleet during the American Revolution.

Virginia Beach gained its reputation as a famous vacation resort in the 19th century, following the building of a railroad connecting its oceanfront with Norfolk and the construction of its first hotel in 1883. Virginia Beach was incorporated as a town in 1906 and as a city in 1952.

Tourism is a mainstay of the economy; more than 3 million people visit Virginia Beach each year. Virginia Beach's economy is also supported by four military bases and diverse industries, including agriculture, computer software, engineering, and technical services.

Selected famous natives and residents: V. C. Andrews, novelist; D. J. Dozier, football and baseball player; George Eastman, inventor; Juice Newton, singer; Kenneth S. Reightler, Jr., astronaut; Pat Robertson, evangelist; Henry Walke, naval officer; Pernell "Sweet Pea" Whitaker, boxer; Skip Wilkins, wheelchair athlete.

Washington, DC

Created municipal corporation: Feb. 21, 1871

Mayor: Anthony Williams (to Jan. 2007)
Motto: *Justitia omnibus* (Justice to all)
Flower: American beauty rose; **Tree:** Scarlet oak
2000 census population (rank): 572,059 (21);
% change: –5.7; **Male:** 269,366 (47.1%); **Female:**
302,693 (52.9%); **White:** 176,101 (30.8%); **Black:**
343,312 (60.0%); **American Indian and Alaska
Native:** 1,713 (0.3%); **Asian:** 15,189 (2.7%); **Other
race:** 21,950 (3.8%); **Two or more races:** 13,446
(2.4%); **Hispanic/Latino:** 44,953 (7.9%). **2000 percent population 18 and over:** 79.9%; **65 and over:**
12.2%; **Median age:** 34.6.

2004 population estimate (rank): 553,523 (27)
Land area: 61 sq mi. (158 sq km); **Alt.:** Highest, 420 ft.;
lowest, sea level
Avg. daily temp.: Jan., 34.6° F; July, 80.0° F
Churches: Protestant, 610; Roman Catholic, 132; Jewish, 9; **City parks:** 300 (800 ac.); **Radio stations:**
AM, 9; FM, 38; **Television stations:** 19
Civilian Labor Force (MSA) April 2005: 303,400;
Unemployed: 23,500, **Percent:** 7.7; **Per capita personal income (MSA) 2002:** $44,056[1]
Board of Trade: Greater Washington Board of Trade,
1129 20th Street N.W., Washington, DC 20036
Chamber of Commerce: DC Chamber of Commerce,
1213 K St. NW, Washington, DC 20005

1. Washington–Arlington–Alexandria, DC–Va.–Md.–W.Va.

The District of Columbia—identical with the city of Washington—is the capital of the United States. It is located between Virginia and Maryland on the Potomac River. The district is named after Columbus.

DC history began in 1790 when Congress directed selection of a new capital site, 100 sq mi, along the Potomac. When the site was determined, it included 30.75 sq mi on the Virginia side of the river. In 1846, however, Congress returned that area to Virginia, leaving the 68.25 sq mi ceded by Maryland in 1788. The seat of government was transferred from Philadelphia to Washington on Dec. 1, 1800, and President John Adams became the first resident in the White House.

The city was planned and partly laid out by Maj. Pierre Charles L'Enfant, a French engineer. This work was perfected and completed by Maj. Andrew Ellicott and Benjamin Banneker, a freeborn black man who was an astronomer and mathematician. In 1814, during the War of 1812, a British force burned the capital including the White House.

Until Nov. 3, 1967, the District of Columbia was administered by three commissioners appointed by the president. On that day, a government consisting of a mayor-commissioner and a 9-member council, all appointed by the president with the approval of the Senate, took office. On May 7, 1974, the citizens of the District of Columbia approved a Home Rule Charter, giving them an elected mayor and 13-member council—their first elected municipal government in more than a century. The district also has one nonvoting member in the House of Representatives and an elected Board of Education.

On Aug. 22, 1978, Congress passed a proposed constitutional amendment to give Washington, DC, voting representation in the Congress. The amendment had to be ratified by at least 38 state legislatures within seven years to become effective. It died in 1985. A petition asking for the district's admission to the Union as the 51st state was filed in Congress on Sept. 9, 1983, and new statehood bills were introduced in 1993. The district is continuing this drive for statehood.

The federal government and tourism are the mainstays of the city's economy, and many unions, business, professional, and nonprofit organizations are headquartered there. Among the city's many educational institutions are the Catholic University of America, Georgetown University, Howard University, and Gallaudet University. Cultural attractions include the National Gallery of Art, the Smithsonian Institution, the John F. Kennedy Center for the Performing Arts, and the Folger Shakespeare Library.

Selected famous natives and residents: Edward Albee, playwright; Billie Burke, comedienne; Ina Claire, actress; John Foster Dulles, statesman; Duke Ellington, musician; Jane Greer, actress; Goldie Hawn, actress; Helen Hayes, actress; J. Edgar Hoover, former director of the F.B.I.; William Hurt, actor; Noor al-Hussein, queen of Jordan; Michael Learned, actress; Roger Mudd, newscaster; Eleanor Holmes Norton, government official; Chita Rivera, dancer and actress; Leonard Rose, cellist; John Philip Sousa, composer; Frances Sternhagen, actress.

Population of the 15 Largest U.S. Cities, 1900–2004

Rank	1900 Place	Population	1920 Place	Population	1940 Place	Population
1.	New York, N.Y.	3,437,202	New York, N.Y.	5,620,048	New York, N.Y.	7,454,995
2.	Chicago, Ill.	1,698,575	Chicago, Ill.	2,701,705	Chicago, Ill.	3,396,808
3.	Philadelphia, Pa.	1,293,697	Philadelphia, Pa.	1,823,779	Philadelphia, Pa.	1,931,334
4.	St. Louis, Mo.	575,238	Detroit, Mich.	993,078	Detroit, Mich.	1,623,452
5.	Boston, Mass.	560,892	Cleveland, Ohio	796,841	Los Angeles, Calif.	1,504,277
6.	Baltimore, Md.	508,957	St. Louis, Mo.	772,897	Cleveland, Ohio	878,336
7.	Cleveland, Ohio	381,768	Boston, Mass.	748,060	Baltimore, Md.	859,100
8.	Buffalo, N.Y.	352,387	Baltimore, Md.	733,826	St. Louis, Mo.	816,048
9.	San Francisco, Calif.	342,782	Pittsburgh, Pa.	588,343	Boston, Mass.	770,816
10.	Cincinnati, Ohio	325,902	Los Angeles, Calif.	576,673	Pittsburgh, Pa.	671,659
11.	Pittsburgh, Pa.	321,616	Buffalo, N.Y.	506,775	Washington, DC	663,091
12.	New Orleans, La.	287,104	San Francisco, Calif.	506,676	San Francisco, Calif.	634,536
13.	Detroit, Mich.	285,704	Milwaukee, Wis.	457,147	Milwaukee, Wis.	587,472
14.	Milwaukee, Wis.	285,315	Washington, DC	437,571	Buffalo, N.Y.	575,901
15.	Washington, DC	278,718	Newark, N.J.	414,524	New Orleans, La.	494,537

Rank	1960 Place	Population	1980 Place	Population	2004[1] Place	Population
1.	New York, N.Y.	7,781,984	New York, N.Y.	7,071,639	New York, N.Y.	8,104,079
2.	Chicago, Ill.	3,550,404	Chicago, Ill.	3,005,072	Los Angeles, Calif.	3,845,541
3.	Los Angeles, Calif.	2,479,015	Los Angeles, Calif.	2,966,850	Chicago, Ill.	2,862,244
4.	Philadelphia, Pa.	2,002,512	Philadelphia, Pa.	1,688,210	Houston, Tex.	2,012,626
5.	Detroit, Mich.	1,670,144	Houston, Tex.	1,595,138	Philadelphia, Pa.	1,470,151
6.	Baltimore, Md.	939,024	Detroit, Mich.	1,203,339	Phoenix, Ariz.	1,418,041
7.	Houston, Tex.	938,219	Dallas, Tex.	904,078	San Diego, Calif.	1,263,756
8.	Cleveland, Ohio	876,050	San Diego, Calif.	875,538	San Antonio, Tex.	1,236,249
9.	Washington, DC	763,956	Phoenix, Ariz.	789,704	Dallas, Tex.	1,210,393
10.	St. Louis, Mo.	750,026	Baltimore, Md.	786,775	San Jose, Calif.	904,522
11.	Milwaukee, Wis.	741,324	San Antonio, Tex.	785,880	Detroit, Mich.	900,198
12.	San Francisco, Calif.	740,316	Indianapolis, Ind.	700,807	Indianapolis, Ind.	784,242
13.	Boston, Mass.	697,197	San Francisco, Calif.	678,974	Jacksonville, Fla.	777,704
14.	Dallas, Tex.	679,684	Memphis, Tenn.	646,356	San Francisco, Calif.	744,230
15.	New Orleans, La.	627,525	Washington, DC	638,333	Columbus, Ohio	730,008

1. Populations for 1900–1980 are Census figures. 2004 figures are population estimates. *Source:* U.S. Census Bureau. For 2000 Census figures, see Top 50 Cities in the U.S. by Population and Rank, 1990, 2000, and 2004 p. 209.

Safest and Most Dangerous U.S. Cities, 2003

(Population 75,000 and over)

	Safest				Most dangerous		
Rank	City	Rank	City	Rank	City	Rank	City
1.	Newton, Mass.	14.	Parma, Ohio	1.	Camden N.J.	14.	Jackson, Miss.
2.	Brick Township, N.J.	15.	Hamilton Township, N.J.	2.	Detroit, Mich.	15.	Tampa, Fla.
3.	Amherst, N.Y.	16.	Danbury, Conn.	3.	Atlanta, Ga.	16.	San Bernardino, Calif.
4.	Mission Viejo, Calif.	17.	Simi Valley, Calif.	4.	St. Louis, Mo.	17.	Compton, Calif.
5.	Clarkstown, N.Y.	18.	Sunnyvale, Calif.	5.	Gary, Ind.	18.	Springfield, Mass.
6.	Lake Forest, Calif.	19.	Sterling Heights, Mich.	6.	Washington, DC	19.	Miami, Fla.
7.	Thousand Oaks, Calif.	20.	Livonia, Mich.	7.	Hartford, Conn.	20.	Cleveland, Ohio
8.	Colonie, N.Y.	21.	Lee's Summit, Mo.	8.	New Orleans, La.	21.	Dayton, Ohio
9.	Cary, N.C.	22.	Farmington Hills, Mich.	9.	Richmond, Va.	22.	North Charleston, S.C.
10.	Dover Township, N.J.	23.	Orem, Utah	10.	Birmingham, Ala.	23.	Little Rock, Ark.
11.	Irvine, Calif.	24.	Fargo, N.D.	11.	Baltimore, Md.	24.	Oakland, Calif.
12.	Troy, Mich.	25.	Stamford, Conn.	12.	Richmond, Calif.	25.	Cincinnati, Ohio
13.	Greece, N.Y.			13.	Memphis, Tenn.		

NOTE: The rankings are based on a city's rate for six crime categories: murder, rape, robbery, aggravated assault, burglary, and motor vehicle theft. *Source:* Morgan Quitno Corporation. Web: www.morganquitno.com.

U.S. Cities with Population over 100,000

ZIP codes provided below indicate the primary ZIP code for each city. Consult a ZIP code directory to find the appropriate ZIP code for a particular address, or try the U.S. Postal Service's online "ZIP Code Lookup," www.usps.gov/zip4/.

	July 2004 est. pop	2004 rank	ZIP code
Alabama			
Birmingham	233,149	76	35203
Huntsville	164,146	132	35813
Mobile	192,759	108	36601
Montgomery	200,983	97	36119
Alaska			
Anchorage	272,687	68	99599
Arizona			
Chandler	223,991	81	85225
Gilbert town	156,917	140	85296
Glendale	235,591	75	85302
Mesa	437,454	41	85201
Peoria	132,487	172	85381
Phoenix	1,418,041	6	85026
Scottsdale	221,792	82	85251
Tempe	160,676	135	85282
Tucson	512,023	32	85726
Arkansas			
Little Rock	184,081	114	72202
California			
Anaheim	333,776	54	92803
Antioch	100,923	246	94509
Bakersfield	283,936	62	93380
Berkeley	101,517	241	94704
Burbank	104,114	229	91505
Chula Vista	204,879	92	91910
Concord	124,328	189	94520
Corona	145,398	154	91718
Costa Mesa	110,411	214	92628
Daly City	100,620	251	94015
Downey	110,318	215	90241
El Monte	122,123	191	91734
Elk Grove	100,760	250	95624
Escondido	135,462	169	92025
Fairfield	103,949	232	94533
Fontana	158,715	139	92335
Fremont	202,373	94	94537
Fresno	457,719	37	93706
Fullerton	133,439	171	92834
Garden Grove	167,347	127	92842
Glendale	201,326	96	91205
Hayward	140,795	163	94544
Huntington Beach	195,305	104	92647
Inglewood	115,313	205	90301
Irvine	178,317	121	92619
Lancaster	128,928	177	93534
Long Beach	476,564	34	90802
Los Angeles	3,845,541	2	90052
Modesto	206,769	90	95350
Moreno Valley	166,290	129	92553
Norwalk	106,683	224	90650
Oakland	397,976	44	94612
Oceanside	167,438	126	92054
Ontario	170,057	125	91761
Orange	133,819	170	92863
Oxnard	183,587	115	93030
Palmdale	131,153	173	93550
Pasadena	144,068	158	91103
Pomona	155,448	142	91769
Rancho Cucamonga	159,346	137	91729
Richmond	102,318	239	94801
Riverside	288,384	61	92507
Roseville	103,609	236	95661
Sacramento	454,330	38	95813
Salinas	148,183	151	93907
San Bernardino	198,406	99	92401
San Buenaventura (Ventura)	104,068	230	93001
San Diego	1,263,756	7	92199
San Francisco	744,230	14	94188
San Jose	904,522	10	95101
Santa Ana	342,715	53	92711
Santa Clara	104,001	231	95050
Santa Clarita	164,800	130	91355
Santa Rosa	153,636	145	95402
Simi Valley	118,893	196	93065
Stockton	279,888	66	95208
Sunnyvale	128,012	180	94086
Thousand Oaks	125,054	185	91362
Torrance	142,841	160	90503
Vallejo	118,349	198	94590
Visalia	104,655	228	93277
West Covina	108,668	219	91793
Colorado			
Arvada	102,562	238	80004
Aurora	291,843	60	80017
Colorado Springs	369,363	49	80903
Denver	556,835	25	80202
Fort Collins	126,967	183	80525
Lakewood	141,301	162	80202
Pueblo	103,621	235	81003
Thornton	102,072	240	80221
Westminster	104,759	227	80030
Connecticut			
Bridgeport	139,910	166	06602
Hartford	124,848	186	06101
New Haven	124,829	187	06511
Stamford	120,226	194	06904
Waterbury	108,429	221	06702
District of Columbia			
Washington[1]	553,523	27	20090
Florida			
Cape Coral	127,985	181	33909
Clearwater	108,606	220	33990
Coral Springs	128,355	178	33075
Fort Lauderdale	164,578	131	33310
Gainesville	108,856	218	32601
Hialeah	224,522	79	33010
Hollywood	144,535	156	33022
Jacksonville	777,704	13	32203
Miami	379,724	46	33152
Miami Gardens	100,887	248	33015
Miramar	101,486	242	33023
Orlando	205,648	91	32802
Pembroke Pines	150,104	150	33024
Port St. Lucie	118,396	197	34952
St. Petersburg	249,090	70	33730
Tallahassee	156,612	141	32301
Tampa	321,772	57	33630
Georgia			
Athens-Clarke County[2]	102,744	237	30608
Atlanta	419,122	42	30304
Augusta-Richmond County[3]	191,326	111	30901
Columbus	182,850	116	31908
Savannah	129,808	174	31402
Hawaii			
Honolulu CDP[4]	377,260	47	96820
Idaho			
Boise City	190,122	112	83708
Illinois			
Aurora	166,614	128	60505
Chicago	2,862,244	3	60607
Joliet	129,519	176	60436
Naperville	140,106	165	60540
Peoria	112,720	209	61601
Rockford	152,452	146	61125
Springfield	114,738	207	62703

	July 2004 est. pop	2004 rank	ZIP code
Indiana			
Evansville	117,156	201	47708
Fort Wayne	219,351	84	46802
Indianapolis	784,242	12	46206
South Bend	105,494	225	46624
Iowa			
Cedar Rapids	122,206	190	52401
Des Moines	194,311	107	50318
Kansas			
Kansas City	145,004	155	66106
Olathe	108,390	222	66051
Overland Park	162,728	133	66204
Topeka	121,809	192	66603
Wichita	353,823	51	67276
Kentucky			
Lexington-Fayette	266,358	69	40511
Louisville-Jefferson County[5]	556,332	26	40231
Louisiana			
Baton Rouge	224,097	80	70826
Lafayette	111,966	212	70509
New Orleans	462,269	35	70113
Shreveport	198,675	98	71102
Maryland			
Baltimore	636,251	18	21202
Massachusetts			
Boston	569,165	24	02205
Cambridge	100,771	249	02139
Lowell	103,655	234	01853
Springfield	152,091	147	01101
Worcester	175,966	124	01613
Michigan			
Ann Arbor	113,567	208	48104
Detroit	900,198	11	48233
Flint	119,716	195	48502
Grand Rapids	195,115	105	49501
Lansing	116,941	202	48924
Sterling Heights	127,476	182	48311
Warren	136,118	168	48090
Minnesota			
Minneapolis	373,943	48	55401
St. Paul	276,963	67	55109
Mississippi			
Jackson	179,298	119	39205
Missouri			
Independence	111,023	213	64052
Kansas City	444,387	39	64108
Springfield	150,704	149	65801
St. Louis	343,279	52	63155
Nebraska			
Lincoln	236,146	74	68501
Omaha	409,416	43	68108
Nevada			
Henderson	224,829	78	89015
Las Vegas	534,847	29	89199
North Las Vegas	158,748	138	89030
Reno	197,963	100	89510
New Hampshire			
Manchester	109,310	216	03103
New Jersey			
Elizabeth	124,724	188	07208
Jersey City	239,079	72	07302
Newark	280,451	65	07102
Paterson	150,869	148	07510
New Mexico			
Albuquerque	484,246	33	87101
New York			
Buffalo	282,864	63	14240
New York	8,104,079	1	10199
Rochester	212,481	87	14692
Syracuse	143,101	159	13220
Yonkers	197,126	101	10701
North Carolina			
Cary	101,265	243	27511
Charlotte	594,359	20	28228
Durham	201,726	95	27701
Fayetteville	125,241	184	28302
Greensboro	231,543	77	27420
Raleigh	326,653	55	27613
Winston-Salem	191,523	110	27102
Ohio			
Akron	212,179	88	44309
Cincinnati	314,154	58	45225
Cleveland	458,684	36	44101
Columbus	730,008	15	43216
Dayton	160,293	136	45401
Toledo	304,973	59	43601
Oklahoma			
Norman	100,923	246	73019
Oklahoma City	528,042	31	73125
Tulsa	383,764	45	74107
Oregon			
Eugene	142,681	161	97401
Portland	533,492	30	97208
Salem	146,120	152	97309
Pennsylvania			
Allentown	106,732	223	18101
Erie	103,925	233	16515
Philadelphia	1,470,151	5	19104
Pittsburgh	322,450	56	15290
Rhode Island			
Providence	178,126	122	02904
South Carolina			
Charleston	104,883	226	29401
Columbia	116,331	204	29201
South Dakota			
Sioux Falls	136,695	167	57104
Tennessee			
Chattanooga	154,853	144	37421
Clarksville	108,972	217	37043
Knoxville	178,118	123	37950
Memphis	671,929	17	38101
Nashville-Davidson[6]	546,719	28	37230
Texas			
Abilene	114,807	206	79604
Amarillo	180,791	118	79120
Arlington	359,467	50	76004
Austin	681,804	16	78710
Beaumont	112,294	211	77707
Brownsville	161,225	134	78520
Carrollton	117,823	200	75006
Corpus Christi	281,196	64	78469
Dallas	1,210,393	9	75260
El Paso	592,099	21	79910
Fort Worth	603,337	19	76161
Garland	217,176	85	75040
Grand Prairie	140,320	164	75051
Houston	2,012,626	4	77201
Irving	194,547	106	75061
Laredo	203,212	93	78041
Lubbock	207,852	89	79402
McAllen	120,743	193	78501
Mesquite	129,710	175	75149
Pasadena	144,174	157	77501
Plano	245,411	71	75074
San Antonio	1,236,249	8	78284
Waco	118,093	199	76702
Wichita Falls	100,929	245	76307
Utah			
Salt Lake City	178,605	120	84199
West Valley City	112,678	210	84199
Virginia			
Alexandria	128,206	179	22314

	July 2004 est. pop	2004 rank	ZIP code		July 2004 est. pop	2004 rank	ZIP code
Arlington CDP	186,117	113	23320	Seattle	571,480	23	98108
Chesapeake	214,725·	86	23670	Spokane	196,721	102	99201
Hampton	145,951	153	23607	Tacoma	196,094	103	98413
Newport News	181,913	117	23501	Vancouver	155,053	143	98668
Norfolk	237,835	73	23707	**Wisconsin**			
Richmond	192,494	109	23232	Green Bay	101,100	244	54303
Virginia Beach	440,098	40	23450	Madison	220,332	83	53714
Washington				Milwaukee	583,624	22	53203
Bellevue	116,914	203	98009				

1. Washington city is coextensive with the District of Columbia. 2. Clarke County and the incorporated place of Athens-Clarke County are coextensive. 3. Richmond County and the incorporated place of Augusta-Richmond County are coextensive. 4. Honolulu Census Designated Place; data are not given separately for the city of Honolulu, which is coextensive with Honolulu County. 5. Louisville, Ky. city merged with Jefferson County in Jan. 2003. 6. Nashville-Davidson city is consolidated with Davidson County. *Source:* U.S. Census Bureau. Web: www.census.gov.

Area Codes: United States, Canada, Caribbean

Area codes	Selected cities
UNITED STATES	
Alabama	
205	Birmingham, Tuscaloosa
251	Jackson, Mobile
256	Huntsville, Florence
334	Montgomery, Dothan, Selma
Alaska	
907	Entire state
Arizona	
480	Chandler, Scottsdale
520	Tucson
602	Phoenix
623	Sun City, Peoria
928	Flagstaff, Yuma
Arkansas	
479	Fayetteville, Fort Smith
501	Hot Springs, Little Rock
870	Jonesboro, Texarkana
California	
209	Stockton, Modesto
213, 323	Los Angeles
310	Santa Monica, Beverly Hills, Torrance
408	San Jose
415	San Francisco, San Rafael
510	Oakland, Berkeley
530	Redding, Davis
559	Fresno
562	Long Beach, Whittier
619	San Diego
626	Pasadena, Azusa
650	Palo Alto, San Mateo
661	Bakersfield
707	Vallejo, Eureka, Santa Rosa
714	Orange, Anaheim, Huntington Beach
760	Barstow, Palm Springs
805	San Luis Obispo, Santa Barbara, Simi Valley
818	San Fernando, Burbank
831	Santa Cruz, Salinas
858	Poway
909	Pomona, San Bernardino
916	Sacramento
925	Concord, Walnut Creek
949	Irvine, Newport Beach
951	Riverside, San Jacinto
Colorado	
303, 720	Denver, Boulder
719	Colorado Springs, Pueblo
970	Aspen, Fort Collins

Area codes	Selected cities
Connecticut	
203	Bridgeport, New Haven, Danbury
860	Hartford, Norwich, New London
Delaware	
302	Entire state
District of Columbia	
202	Entire district
Florida	
239	Fort Myers, Naples
305	Miami, Key West
321	Orlando, Cape Canaveral
352	Gainesville, Ocala
386	Daytona Beach
407	Kissimmee, Orlando
561	West Palm Beach, Boca Raton
727	Clearwater, St. Petersburg
772	Fort Pierce, Port St. Lucie
786	Miami, Homestead
813	Tampa
850	Tallahassee, Pensacola
863	Lakeland, Winter Haven
904	Jacksonville
941	Port Charlotte, Sarasota
954, 754	Ft. Lauderdale
Georgia	
229	Albany, Valdosta
404	Atlanta
478	Macon
678, 770	Atlanta, Smyrna, Marietta
706	Athens, Augusta
912	Savannah
Hawaii	
808	Entire state
Idaho	
208	Entire state
Illinois	
217	Springfield, Champaign
224	Evanston, Schaumburg
309	Peoria, Bloomington
312, 773	Chicago
618	Carbondale, East St. Louis
630	Aurora, Naperville
708	Chicago Heights, Cicero
815	Rockford, Joliet
847	Waukegan, Skokie
Indiana	
219	Gary
260	Fort Wayne
317	Indianapolis
574	South Bend, La Porte

Area codes	Selected cities
765	Lafayette, Muncie, Kokomo
812	Bloomington, Terre Haute
Iowa	
319	Cedar Rapids, Burlington
515	Des Moines, Ames
563	Dubuque, Davenport
641	Mason City, Ottumwa
712	Sioux City, Council Bluffs
Kansas	
316	Wichita
620	Dodge City, Emporia
785	Topeka, Lawrence
913	Kansas City, Leavenworth
Kentucky	
270	Owensboro, Bowling Green
502	Frankfort, Louisville
606	Ashland
859	Lexington, Covington
Louisiana	
225	Baton Rouge
318	Shreveport
337	Lafayette, Lake Charles
504	New Orleans, Metairie
985	Houma, Slidell
Maine	
207	Entire state
Maryland	
240, 301	Frederick, Hagerstown, Bethesda
410, 443	Baltimore, Salisbury, Annapolis
Massachusetts	
413	Springfield, Northampton
508, 774	Worcester, New Bedford
617, 857	Boston, Cambridge
781, 339	Waltham, Lynn
978, 351	Lowell, Gloucester
Michigan	
231	Muskegon, Shelby
248, 947	Troy, Pontiac
269	Kalamazoo, Battle Creek
313	Detroit, Dearborn
517	Lansing, Jackson
586	Warren, St. Clair Shores
616	Grand Rapids, Holland
734	Ann Arbor, Monroe, Ypsilanti
810	Flint, Port Huron
906	Sault Ste. Marie
989	Saginaw, Midland
Minnesota	
218	Duluth, Moorhead
320	St.Cloud

Area codes	Selected cities
507	Rochester, Mankato
612	Minneapolis
651	St. Paul
763	Maple Grove, Coon Rapids
952	Bloomington, Edina
Mississippi	
228	Gulfport, Biloxi
601, 769	Jackson, Vicksburg
662	Tupelo, Greenville
Missouri	
314	St. Louis, Webster Groves
417	Springfield, Joplin
573	Jefferson City, Columbia
636	Chesterfield, St. Charles
660	Sedalia
816	Kansas City, Independence
Montana	
406	Entire state
Nebraska	
308	Grand Island, Kearney
402	Lincoln, Omaha
Nevada	
702	Las Vegas, Henderson
775	Carson City, Reno
New Hampshire	
603	Entire state
New Jersey	
201, 551	Jersey City, Hackensack
609	Trenton, Atlantic City
732, 848	New Brunswick, Long Branch
856	Cherry Hill, Vineland, Camden
908	Elizabeth, Summit
973, 862	Newark, Paterson
New Mexico	
505	Entire state
New York	
212, 646	Manhattan
315	Syracuse, Utica
347, 718	Bronx, Brooklyn, Queens, Staten Island
516	Mineola, Hicksville
518	Albany, Troy
585	Rochester
607	Binghamton, Elmira
631	Riverhead, Islip
716	Buffalo, Niagara Falls
845	Poughkeepsie, Kingston
914	White Plains, Yonkers
917	Manhattan, Bronx, Queens, Staten Island, Brooklyn
North Carolina	
252	Greenville, Rocky Mount
336	Winston-Salem, Greensboro
704, 980	Charlotte, Gastonia
828	Asheville, Hickory
910	Fayetteville, Wilmington
919	Raleigh, Chapel Hill
North Dakota	
701	Entire state
Ohio	
216	Cleveland, Shaker Heights
234, 330	Akron, Youngstown
419, 567	Toledo, Sandusky
440	Ashtabula, Lorain
513	Cincinnati
614	Columbus
740	Chillicothe, Zanesville
937	Dayton, Xenia

Area codes	Selected cities
Oklahoma	
405	Oklahoma City, Shawnee
580	Enid, Lawton
918	Tulsa, Muskogee
Oregon	
503, 971	Salem, Portland
541	Eugene, Corvallis
Pennsylvania	
215, 267	Philadelphia, Levittown
412, 878	Pittsburgh, McKeesport
484, 610	Allentown, Reading
570	Scranton, Williamsport
717	Harrisburg, Lancaster
724, 878	Uniontown, New Castle
814	Erie, State College
Rhode Island	
401	Entire state
South Carolina	
803	Columbia, Aiken
843	Charleston, Myrtle Beach
864	Greenville, Spartanburg
South Dakota	
605	Entire state
Tennessee	
423	Chattanooga, Johnson City
615	Nashville, Gallatin
731	Jackson
865	Knoxville, Oak Ridge
901	Memphis
931	Columbia, Clarksville
Texas	
210	San Antonio
214,	
469, 972	Dallas, Plano
254	Waco, Killeen
281,	
713, 832	Houston
325	Abilene
361	Corpus Christi, Victoria
409	Galveston, Port Arthur
432	Midland, Odessa
512	Austin
682, 817	Fort Worth, Arlington
806	Lubbock, Amarillo
830	Uvalde, Seguin
903, 430	Tyler, Texarkana, Paris
915	El Paso
936	Huntsville, Nacogdoches
940	Wichita Falls, Denton
956	Laredo, Brownsville
979	Bryan, College Station
Utah	
435	Moab, St. George
801	Salt Lake City, Provo
Vermont	
802	Entire state
Virginia	
276	Abingdon, Wytheville
434	Danville, Lynchburg, Charlottesville
540	Roanoke, Harrisonburg
571, 703	Alexandria, Mount Vernon
757	Norfolk, Virginia Beach
804	Richmond, Hopewell
Washington	
206	Seattle, Bainbridge Island
253	Tacoma, Auburn
360	Olympia, Bellingham
425	Bellevue, Redmond
509	Spokane, Yakima

Area codes	Selected cities
West Virginia	
304	Entire state
Wisconsin	
262	Racine, Kenosha
414	Milwaukee, Wauwatosa
608	Madison, Beloit
715	Eau Claire, Wausau
920	Green Bay, Oshkosh
Wyoming	
307	Entire state
U.S. TERRITORIES	
684	American Samoa
671	Guam
670	Marianas Islands
787, 939	Puerto Rico
340	U.S. Virgin Islands
CANADA	
Alberta	
403	Calgary
780	Edmonton
British Columbia	
250	Victoria
604, 778	Vancouver
Manitoba	
204	Entire province
New Brunswick	
506	Entire province
Newfoundland	
709	Entire province
Nova Scotia	
902	Nova Scotia, Prince Edward Island
Ontario	
289, 905	Hamilton
416, 647	Toronto
519	Windsor
613	Ottawa
705	Sudbury
807	Thunder Bay
Quebec	
418	Quebec
450	Laval
514	Montreal
819	Trois-Rivieres
Saskatchewan	
306	Entire province
Yukon, Northwest Territories, & Nunavut	
867	All provinces
CARIBBEAN AND ATLANTIC ISLANDS	
264	Anguilla
268	Antigua and Barbuda
242	Bahamas
246	Barbados
441	Bermuda
284	British Virgin Islands
345	Cayman Islands
809, 829	Dominican Republic
767	Dominica
473	Grenada
876	Jamaica
664	Montserrat
869	St. Kitts & Nevis
758	St. Lucia
784	St. Vincent & the Grenadines
868	Trinidad & Tobago
649	Turks & Caicos

Source: North American Numbering Plan Administration. Web: www.nanpa.com.

Top 50 Cities in the U.S. by Population and Rank, 1990, 2000, and 2004

	7/1/2004 population estimate	4/1/2000 census population	4/1/1990 census population	Size rank 1990	Size rank 2000	Size rank 2004
New York, N.Y.	8,104,079	8,008,278	7,322,564	1	1	1
Los Angeles, Calif.	3,845,541	3,694,820	3,485,398	2	2	2
Chicago, Ill.	2,862,244	2,896,016	2,783,726	3	3	3
Houston, Tex.	2,012,626	1,953,631	1,630,553	4	4	4
Philadelphia, Pa.	1,470,151	1,517,550	1,585,577	5	5	5
Phoenix, Ariz.	1,418,041	1,321,045	983,403	10	6	6
San Diego, Calif.	1,263,756	1,223,400	1,110,549	6	7	7
San Antonio, Tex.	1,236,249	1,144,646	935,933	9	9	8
Dallas, Tex.	1,210,393	1,188,580	1,006,877	8	8	9
San Jose, Calif.	904,522	894,943	782,248	11	11	10
Detroit, Mich.	900,198	951,270	1,027,974	7	10	11
Indianapolis, Ind.	784,242	781,870	741,952	13	12	12
Jacksonville, Fla.	777,704	735,617	635,230	15	14	13
San Francisco, Calif.	744,230	776,733	723,959	14	13	14
Columbus, Ohio	730,008	711,470	632,910	16	15	15
Austin, Tex.	681,804	656,562	465,622	25	16	16
Memphis, Tenn.	671,929	650,100	610,337	18	18	17
Baltimore, Md.	636,251	651,154	736,014	12	17	18
Fort Worth, Tex.	603,337	534,694	447,619	29	27	19
Charlotte, N.C.	594,359	540,828	395,934	33	26	20
El Paso, Tex.	592,099	563,662	515,342	22	23	21
Milwaukee, Wis.	583,624	596,974	628,088	17	19	22
Seattle, Wash.	571,480	563,374	516,259	21	24	23
Boston, Mass.	569,165	589,141	574,283	20	20	24
Denver, Colo.	556,835	554,636	467,610	28	25	25
Louisville-Jefferson County, Ky.[1]	556,332	256,231	269,063	58	67	26
Washington, DC	553,523	572,059	606,900	19	21	27
Nashville-Davidson, Tenn.[2]	546,719	545,524	510,784	26	22	28
Las Vegas, Nev.	534,847	478,434	258,295	63	32	29
Portland, Ore.	533,492	529,121	437,319	27	28	30
Oklahoma City, Okla.	528,042	506,132	444,719	30	29	31
Tucson, Ariz.	512,023	486,699	405,390	34	30	32
Albuquerque, N.M.	484,246	448,607	384,736	40	35	33
Long Beach, Calif.	476,564	461,522	429,433	32	34	34
New Orleans, La.	462,269	484,674	496,938	24	31	35
Cleveland, Ohio	458,684	478,403	505,616	23	33	36
Fresno, Calif.	457,719	427,652	354,202	48	37	37
Sacramento, Calif.	454,330	407,018	369,365	37	40	38
Kansas City, Mo.	444,387	441,545	435,146	31	36	39
Virginia Beach, Va.	440,098	425,257	393,069	39	38	40
Mesa, Ariz.	437,454	396,375	288,091	53	42	41
Atlanta, Ga.	419,122	416,474	394,017	38	39	42
Omaha, Nebr.	409,416	390,007	335,795	47	44	43
Oakland, Calif.	397,976	399,484	372,242	35	41	44
Tulsa, Okla.	383,764	393,049	367,302	44	43	45
Miami, Fla.	379,724	362,470	358,548	46	47	46
Honolulu CDP,[3] Hawaii	377,260	371,657	365,272	41	46	47
Minneapolis, Minn.	373,943	382,618	368,383	43	45	48
Colorado Springs, Colo.	369,363	360,890	281,140	54	48	49
Arlington, Tex.	359,467	332,969	261,721	62	54	50

1. Louisville and Jefferson County merged in Jan. 2003. Figures prior to 2003 are for Louisville city only. 2. Nashville-Davidson city is consolidated with Davidson County. 3. Honolulu Census Designated Place; by agreement with the State of Hawaii, the Census Bureau does not show data separately for the city of Honolulu, which is coextensive with Honolulu County. *Source:* U.S. Census Bureau. Web: www.census.gov. For 2003 population estimates, see Population of the 15 Largest U.S. Cities, 1900–2004, p. 204.

Tsunami FAQs

Source: The International Tsunami Information Center

What is a tsunami?

The phenomenon we call tsunami is a series of large waves of extremely long length and occurring at distant intervals, usually generated by a violent, impulsive undersea disturbance or activity near the coast or in the ocean. When a sudden displacement of a large volume of water occurs or if the sea floor is suddenly raised or dropped by an earthquake, big tsunami waves can be formed by forces of gravity. The waves travel out of the area of origin and can be extremely dangerous and damaging when they reach the shore. The word *tsunami* (pronounced tsoo-nah'-mee) is composed of the Japanese words *tsu* (which means "harbor") and *nami* (which means "wave"). Often the term *seismic* or *tidal sea wave* is used to describe the same phenomenon. These terms are misleading, however, because tsunami waves can be generated by other, nonseismic disturbances such as volcanic eruptions or underwater landslides, and they have physical characteristics different from tidal waves.

How do earthquakes and volcanic eruptions create tsunamis?

By far, the most destructive tsunamis are generated from large, shallow earthquakes with an epicenter or fault line near or on the ocean floor. These usually occur in regions of the earth characterized by tectonic subduction along tectonic plate boundaries. The high seismicity of such regions is caused by the collision of tectonic plates. When these plates move past each other, they cause earthquakes, which tilt, offset, or displace large areas of the ocean floor from a few kilometers to as much as 1,000 km or more. The sudden vertical displacements disturb the ocean's surface, displace water, and generate destructive tsunami waves. The waves can travel great distances from the source region, spreading destruction along their path. The deadliest tsunami of all time was the Dec. 26, 2004, Indian Ocean tsunami, triggered by a 9.0 magnitude earthquake of the coast of Sumatra, Indonesia.

Although relatively infrequent, tsunami waves may be caused by the sudden displacement of water caused by a volcanic explosion, by a volcano's slope failure, or more likely by a phreatomagmatic explosion and collapse/engulfment of the volcanic magmatic chambers. One of the largest and most destructive tsunamis ever recorded struck on August 26, 1883, after the explosion and collapse of the volcano of Krakatoa (Krakatau), in Indonesia. This explosion created waves that reached 135 feet and destroyed coastal towns and villages along the Sunda Strait in both the islands of Java and Sumatra, killing 36,500 people.

What types of damage do tsunamis cause?

Tsunamis directly destroy through inundation, wave impact on structures, and erosion. Strong, tsunami-induced currents lead to the erosion of foundations and the collapse of bridges and seawalls. Flotation and drag forces move houses and overturn railroad cars. Additional damage is caused by free-floating cars, boats, and other debris, which become dangerous projectiles; these may crash into buildings, break power lines, and start fires. Fires from damaged ships in ports or from ruptured coastal oil storage tanks and refinery facilities can cause damage greater than that inflicted directly by the tsunami.

Why aren't tsunamis seen at sea or from the air?

In the deep ocean, tsunami wave amplitude is usually less than 1 m (3.3 ft). The crests of tsunami waves may be more than a hundred kilometers or more away from each other. Therefore, passengers on boats at sea, far away from shore where the water is deep, will not feel nor see the tsunami waves as they pass by underneath at high speeds. The tsunami may be perceived as nothing more than a gentle rise and fall of the sea surface. The Great Sanriku tsunami, which struck Honshu, Japan, on June 15, 1896, was completely undetected by fishermen twenty miles out to sea. The deep-water height of this tsunami was only about 40 centimeters when it passed them and yet, when it arrived on the shore, it had transformed into huge waves that killed over 26,000 people and destroyed the port of Sanriku and villages along 275 km of coastline. For the same reason (low amplitude and very long periods in the deep ocean), tsunami waves cannot be seen nor detected from the air.

Deadliest Tsunamis in History

Fatalities	Year	Magnitude	Principal areas	Fatalities	Year	Magnitude	Principal areas
225,000+	2004	9.0	Indian Ocean	30,000	1707	8.4	Tokaido-Nankaido, Japan
100,000	1645? B.C.		Crete-Santorini, Ancient Greece	26,360	1896	7.6	Sanriku, Japan
60,000	1755	8.5	Portugal, Morocco	25,674	1868	8.5	Northern Chile
40,000	1782	7.0	South China Sea	15,030	1792	6.4	Kyushu Island, Japan
36,500	1883		Krakatau, Indonesia	13,486	1771	7.4	Ryukyu Trench, Japan

Source: National Geophysical Data Center, National Oceanic and Atmospheric Administration.

The following lists are not all-inclusive due to space limitations. Only disasters involving great loss of life and/or property, historical interest, or unusual circumstances are listed. Data as of Aug. 2005. For other disasters *see* Current Events: What Happened in 2005, pp. 32–44. For updated information, *see* www.infoplease.com/greatdisasters.

WORST U. S. DISASTERS

AIRCRAFT

1979 May 25, Chicago: American Airlines DC-10 crashed seconds after takeoff, killing all 272 people aboard and 3 on the ground.

AVALANCHE

1910 March 1, Wellington, Wash.: 2 trains snowbound in Stevens Pass in Cascade Range swept off tracks into canyon 150 ft below, killing 96.

DROUGHT

1930s Many states: longest drought of 20th century. Peak periods were 1930, 1934, 1936, 1939, and 1940. During 1934, dry regions stretched solidly from N.Y. and Pa. across the Great Plains to the Calif. coast. A great "dust bowl" covered 50 million acres in the south-central plains during the winter of 1935–1936.

EARTHQUAKE

1906 April 18, San Francisco: earthquake accompanied by fire razed more than 4 sq mi; over 500 dead or missing.

EPIDEMIC

1918 Nationwide: Spanish influenza killed over 500,000 Americans.

EXPLOSION

1947 April 16–18, Texas City, Tex.: a fire and subsequent explosion on the French freighter *Grandcamp* destroyed most of the city; 516 killed.

FIRE

1871 Oct. 8, Peshtigo, Wis.: over 1,500 lives lost and 3.8 million acres burned in forest fire.

FLOOD

1889 May 31, Johnstown, Pa.: collapse of South Fork Dam left more than 2,200 dead.

HURRICANE

1900 Sept. 8, Galveston, Tex.: an estimated 6,000–8,000 dead, mostly from devastation due to tidal surge.

MARINE

1865 April 27, Mississippi River, nr. Memphis, Tenn.: explosion on steamboat *Sultana* killed 1,547.

MINE

1907 Dec. 6, Monongah, W. Va.: coal mine explosion killed 362.

OIL SPILL

1989 March 24, Prince William Sound, Alaska: tanker *Exxon Valdez* hit an undersea reef and released 10 million-plus gallons of oil into the water.

RAILROAD

1918 July 9, Nashville, Tenn.: 101 killed in a two-train collision near Nashville.

SUBMARINE

1963 April 10, North Atlantic: atomic-powered submarine *Thresher* sank; 129 dead.

TERRORIST ATTACK

2001 Sept. 11, New York City, Arlington, Va., and Shanksville, Pa.: hijackers crashed 2 commercial jets into twin towers of World Trade Center; 2 more hijacked jets were crashed into the Pentagon and a field in rural Pa. Total dead numbered 2,992, including the 19 hijackers. Islamic al-Qaeda terrorist group blamed.

TORNADO

1925 March 18, Mo., Ill., and Ind.: great "Tri-State Tornado"; 689 dead; over 2,000 injured. Property damage estimated at $16.5 million.

WINTER STORM

1888 March 11–14, East Coast: the "Blizzard of 1888." 400 people died; accumulation of up to 5 ft of snow. Damage estimated at $20 million.

EARTHQUAKES AND VOLCANIC ERUPTIONS

A.D. 79 Aug. 24, Italy: eruption of Mt. Vesuvius buried cities of Pompeii and Herculaneum, killing thousands.

856 Dec. 22, Damghan, Iran: earthquake killed 200,000.

893 March 23, Ardabil, Iran: earthquake killed about 150,000 people.

1138 Aug. 9, Aleppo, Syria: deadly earthquake claimed lives of 230,000 people.

1290 Sept., Chihli, China: earthquake killed about 100,000 people.

1556 Jan. 23, Shaanxi (Shensi) province, China: most deadly earthquake in history; 830,000 killed.

1667 Nov., Shemakha, Caucasia: earthquake killed about 80,000 people.

1693 Jan. 11, Sicily, Italy: earthquake killed about 60,000 people.

1707 Oct. 28, Japan: tsunami caused by an earthquake drowned 30,000.

1727 Nov. 18, Tabriz, Iran: about 77,000 victims killed in deadly earthquake.

1755 Nov. 1, Portugal: earthquake, fires, and Atlantic tsunami leveled Lisbon; 70,000 killed.

1782 South Sea, China: tsunami killed 40,000.

1783 Feb. 4, Calabria, Italy: series of 6 earthquakes over two-month period caused massive destruction, killing 50,000.

June 8, Iceland: eruption of Laki volcano lasted until Feb. 1784. Haze from eruption resulted in loss of island's livestock and widespread crop failure; 9,350 deaths, mostly due to starvation.

1792 May 21, Kyushu Island, Japan: collapse of old lava dome during eruption of Unzen volcano caused avalanche and tsunami that killed an estimated 14,300 people. (Most were killed by the tsunami.) Japan's greatest volcano disaster.

1811 Dec. 16, Mississippi Valley, nr. New Madrid, Mo.: earthquake reversed the course of the Mississippi River. Fatalities unknown due to sparse population in area. Aftershocks and tremors continued into 1812. It is the largest series of earthquakes known to have occurred in North America.

1815 April 5, 10–11, Netherlands Indies (Sumbawa, Indonesia): eruption of Tambora largest in historic times. An estimated 92,000 people were killed, about 10,000 directly as a result of explosions and ash fall and about 82,000 indirectly from starvation and disease.

1877 **June 26, north-central Ecuador:** eruption of Mt. Cotopaxi caused severe mudflows that wiped out surrounding cities and valleys; 1,000 deaths.

1883 **Aug. 26–28, Netherlands Indies (Krakatau, Indonesia):** eruption of Krakatau; violent explosions destroyed two-thirds of island and caused a tsunami on Java and Sumatra, killing more than 36,000. It was felt as far away as Cape Horn and possibly England.

1886 **Aug. 31, Charleston, S.C.:** magnitude 7.3 quake, killed 60 people and caused extensive damage.

1896 **June 15, Sanriku, Japan:** earthquake and tidal wave killed 27,000.

1902 **May 8, Martinique, West Indies:** Mt. Pelée erupted and wiped out city of St. Pierre; 40,000 dead.

1906 **April 18, San Francisco:** earthquake accompanied by fire razed more than 4 sq mi; more than 500 dead or missing.

1908 **Dec. 28, Messina, Sicily:** city totally destroyed by earthquake. Death toll, from quake and tsunami, 70,000–100,000 in Sicily and southern Italy.

1915 **Jan. 13, Avezzano, Italy:** earthquake left 29,980 dead.

1920 **Dec. 16, Gansu province, China:** magnitude 8.6 earthquake killed 200,000 in northwest China.

1923 **Sept. 1, Japan:** magnitude 8.3 earthquake destroyed one-third of Tokyo and most of Yokohama. More than 140,000 killed.

1927 **May 22, nr. Xining, China:** magnitude 8.3 earthquake claimed approximately 200,000 victims.

1932 **Dec. 25, Gansu, China:** magnitude 7.6 earthquake killed approximately 70,000.

1935 **May 30, Pakistan:** earthquake at Quetta killed 30,000–60,000.

1939 **Jan. 24, Chile:** earthquake razed 50,000 sq mi; about 30,000 killed.

  Dec. 27, northern Turkey: severe quakes destroyed city of Erzingan; about 100,000 casualties.

1948 **Oct. 5, Ashgabat, Turkmenistan:** magnitude 7.3 earthquake destroyed the city, killing 110,000.

1950 **Aug. 15, India:** earthquake affected 30,000 sq mi in Assam; 20,000–30,000 believed killed.

1960 **Feb. 29, Agadir, Morocco:** 10,000–12,000 dead as earthquake set off tidal wave and fire, destroying most of city.

  May 22, Chile: strongest earthquake ever recorded (9.5 magnitude) struck near the coast, causing a tsunami that traveled as far as Hawaii, Japan, and New Zealand, killing more than 2,000, wounding 3,000.

1964 **March 28, Alaska** (03:36:14 UT; March 27, 5:36 P.M. local time)**:** strongest earthquake ever to strike North America (9.2 magnitude) hit 80 mi east of Anchorage; followed by seismic wave (tsunami) 50 ft high that traveled 8,445 mi at 450 mph; 117 killed..

1970 **Jan. 5, Yunnan province, China:** magnitude 7.7 quake killed 15,621.

  May 31, Peru: earthquake left more than 66,000 dead.

1972 **Dec. 22, Managua, Nicaragua:** earthquake devastated city, leaving up to 6,000 dead.

1976 **Feb. 4, Guatemala:** quake left over 23,000 dead.

  July 28, Tangshan, China: worst earthquake to hit China in 20th century; devastated 20 sq mi of city, leaving 255,000 dead.

  Aug. 17, Mindanao, Philippines: earthquake and tidal wave left up to 8,000 dead or missing.

1978 **Sept. 16, Tabas, Iran:** earthquake destroyed city in eastern Iran, leaving 25,000 dead.

1985 **Sept. 19–20, Mexico:** magnitude 8.1 earthquake devastated part of Mexico City and three coastal states; estimated 25,000 killed.

  Nov. 14–16, Colombia: eruption of Nevada del Ruiz, 85 mi northwest of Bogotá. Mudslides buried most of the town of Armero and devastated Chinchiná; 21,800 killed.

1988 **Dec. 7, Armenia:** earthquake measuring 6.9 in magnitude killed nearly 25,000.

1989 **Oct. 17, San Francisco Bay area:** earthquake measuring 7.1 in magnitude killed 67. Over 100,000 buildings damaged or destroyed.

1990 **June 21, northwest Iran:** magnitude 7.7 earthquake destroyed cities and villages in Caspian Sea area. At least 40,000 dead, over 60,000 injured, and 400,000 homeless.

  July 16, northern Philippines: magnitude 7.7 quake killed nearly 2,000.

1991 **July 15, Luzon Island, Philippines:** eruption of Mt. Pinatubo buried over 300 sq mi under volcanic ash and resulted in more than 800 deaths.

1993 **Sept. 29, India:** earthquake measuring 6.2 killed 9,748.

1994 **Jan. 17, San Fernando Valley, Calif.:** earthquake measuring 6.6 in magnitude killed 61 and injured over 8,000. Damage estimated at $13–20 billion.

1995 **Jan. 17, Osaka, Kyoto, and Kobe, Japan:** 5,200 killed and 26,800 injured; estimated damage $100 billion. Magnitude: 6.9.

1997 **May 12, northeast Iran:** severe earthquake measuring 7.3 in magnitude left more than 1,500 people dead and at least 4,460 injured.

  June–Sept., southern Montserrat: ongoing eruption of Soufrière Hills volcano since July 1995; killed 20 people in major eruption on June 25, 1997, rendered southern two-thirds of Montserrat uninhabitable, and forced some 8,000 of the island's 12,000 residents to abandon the island.

1998 **May 30, northern Afghanistan:** magnitude 6.6 earthquake and aftershocks killed at least 4,000. A quake on Feb. 4 in same area killed about 2,300.

  July 17, Papua New Guinea: three tsunamis, possibly spurred by an undersea landslide following an earthquake, wiped out entire villages. At least 2,100 killed.

1999 **Jan. 25, Armenia, Colombia:** 1,185 dead and more than 4,000 injured in magnitude 6.2 earthquake. Over 200,000 left homeless.

  Aug. 17, northwest Turkey: magnitude 7.6 quake centered near Izmit killed over 17,000 and injured about 44,000.

  Sept. 21, central Taiwan: severe 7.7 earthquake and aftershocks killed 2,295 and injured 8,729.

2001 **Jan. 13, El Salvador:** earthquake set off some 185 landslides across El Salvador; at least 850 died and nearly 100,000 houses were destroyed.

  Jan. 26, Bhuj, India: magnitude 7.7 earthquake rocked western Indian state of Gujarat, killing more than 20,000 people and leaving 600,000 homeless.

2003 **May 21, Northern Algeria:** magnitude 6.8 earthquake caused the collapse of numerous buildings, killing 2,266 people.

  Dec. 26, Bam, Iran: magnitude 6.6 earthquake devastated the ancient historic city of Bam in southeast Iran, killing 26,200 people.

2004 Dec. 26, Sumatra, Indonesia: magnitude 9.0 earthquake, off the west coast of Sumatra, caused a tremendously powerful tsunami in the Indian Ocean that hit 12 Asian countries, killing more than 225,000 and leaving millions homeless. It was the deadliest tsunami in history.

2005 Mar. 28, Sumatra, Indonesia: magnitude 8.7 earthquake, off the west coast of Sumatra, killed 1,313.

MAJOR U.S. EPIDEMICS

1793 Philadelphia: more than 4,000 residents died from yellow fever.

1832 July–Aug., New York City: over 3,000 people killed in a cholera epidemic.

Oct., New Orleans: cholera took the lives of 4,340 people.

1848 New York City: more than 5,000 deaths caused by cholera.

1853 New Orleans: yellow fever killed 7,790.

1867 New Orleans: 3,093 perished from yellow fever.

1878 Southern states: over 13,000 people died from yellow fever in lower Mississippi Valley.

1916 Nationwide: over 7,000 deaths occurred and 27,363 cases were reported of polio (infantile paralysis) in America's worst polio epidemic.

1918 March–Nov., nationwide: outbreak of Spanish influenza killed over 500,000 people in the worst single U.S. epidemic.

1949 Nationwide: 2,720 deaths occurred from polio, and 42,173 cases were reported.

1952 Nationwide: polio killed 3,300; 57,628 cases reported.

1981–Dec. 2003: total estimated U.S. AIDS cases: 929,985; total estimated AIDS deaths: 524,060 (Centers for Disease Control); 2003 total world AIDS cases: 38 million; total world AIDS deaths: 20 million.

FLOODS, AVALANCHES, AND TIDAL WAVES

1228 Holland: 100,000 people reputedly drowned by sea flood in Friesland.

1642 China: rebels destroyed Kaifeng seawall; 300,000 drowned.

1889 May 31, Johnstown, Pa.: more than 2,200 died in flood after South Fork Dam collapsed.

1910 March 1, Wellington, Wash.: avalanche in Cascade Range swept 2 trains into canyon, killing 96. Worst U.S. avalanche.

1928 March 12, Santa Paula, Calif.: collapse of St. Francis Dam left 450 dead.

1931 July–Aug., China: flood along Yangtze River left 3.7 million people dead from disease, starvation, or drowning.

1953 Jan. 31–Feb. 5, northwest Europe: storm followed by floods devastated North Sea coastal areas. Netherlands hit hardest; 1,794 dead.

1954 Aug., Teheran, Iran: flood rains resulted in some 10,000 deaths.

1959 Dec. 2, Fréjus, France: flood caused by collapse of Malpasset Dam left 412 dead.

1962 Jan. 10, Peru: avalanche down extinct Huascaran volcano killed more than 3,000.

1963 Oct. 9, Italy: landslide into the Vaiont Dam; flood killed about 2,000.

1966 Oct. 21, Aberfan, Wales: avalanche of coal, waste, mud, and rocks killed 144 people, including 116 children in school.

1969 Jan. 18–26, southern Calif.: floods and mudslides from heavy rains caused widespread property damage; at least 100 dead.

1970 Nov. 13, East Pakistan: 200,000 killed by cyclone-driven tidal wave from Bay of Bengal.

1971 Aug., Hanoi, North Vietnam: heavy rains flooded the Red River Delta, killing 100,000.

1972 Feb. 26, Man, W. Va.: a slag-pile dam collapsed under pressure of torrential rains, flooding 17-mi valley, killing more than 118.

June 9–10, Rapid City, S.D.: flash flood caused 237 deaths.

1975 Aug. 5, Yangtze River, China: 63 dams failed, killing an estimated 80,000 to 200,000 people from floods and subsequent famine. The Chinese government never acknowledged the event.

1976 Aug. 1, Loveland, Colo.: flash flood along Route 34 in Big Thompson Canyon left 139 dead.

1988 Aug.–Sept., Bangladesh: heaviest monsoon in 70 years inundated three-fourths of country, killing more than 1,300 and leaving 30 million homeless.

1993 June–Aug., Ill., Iowa, Kan., Ky., Minn., Mo., Neb., N.D., S.D., Wis.: two months of heavy rain caused Mississippi River and tributaries to flood; 50 deaths and about $12 billion in damage. Almost 70,000 left homeless.

1997 March, Ohio and Mississippi Valleys: flooding and tornadoes plagued Ark., Mo., Miss., Tenn., Ill., Ind., Ky., Ohio, and W.Va. 67 were killed.

1999 Oct., southwest Mexico: over a week of heavy rains killed at least 360 people in mudslides and flood waters.

Dec. 15–16, northern Venezuela: heavy rains caused catastrophic flooding and mudslides, killing an estimated 5,000 to 20,000 people. Country's worst modern-day natural disaster.

2000 Feb., southeast Africa: weeks of rain resulted in deadly floods in Mozambique and Zimbabwe, killing more than 700 people and leaving 280,000 homeless.

2002 Sept. 20, Karmadon Gorge, North Ossetia, Russia: an avalanche caused by a 500-ft chunk of glacier left 150 people dead.

Aug., Europe: record flooding across central and eastern Europe killed 108 people and caused billions of dollars of extensive infrastructure damage and deforestation.

2004 May 18–26, Dominican Republic and Haiti: torrential rains overflowed the Soliel River, causing floods and mudslides, destroying villages, and killing more than 2,000.

2005 July 26, Mumbai, India: a record 37 in of rain in a 24-hour period and a week of monsoon rains left 1,000 dead in western India.

MAJOR STORMS

Cyclones, hurricanes, and typhoons are the same kind of tropical storm but are called by different names in different areas of the world.

CYCLONES

1864 Oct. 5, Calcutta, India: 70,000 killed.

1942 Oct. 16, Bengal, India: about 40,000 lives lost.

1960 Oct. 10, East Pakistan: cyclone and tidal wave killed about 6,000.

1963 May 28–29, East Pakistan: cyclone killed about 22,000 along coast.

1965 May 11–12 and June 1–2, East Pakistan: cyclones killed about 47,000.

Dec. 15, Karachi, Pakistan: about 10,000 killed.

1970 Nov. 12–13, East Pakistan: cyclone and tidal waves killed 200,000 and another 100,000 were reported missing.

1971 Sept. 29, Orissa state, India: cyclone and tidal wave killed as many as 10,000.

1974 Dec. 25, Darwin, Australia: cyclone destroyed nearly the entire city; 50 reported dead.

1977 Nov. 19, Andhra Pradesh, India: cyclone and tidal wave claimed lives of 20,000.

1991 April 30, southeast Bangladesh: cyclone killed over 131,000 and left up to 9 million homeless.

1999 Oct. 29, Orissa state, India: supercyclone swept in from Bay of Bengal, killing at least 9,573 and leaving over 10 million homeless.

U.S. HURRICANES

(U.S. deaths only, except where noted. Damages are actual cost in U.S. dollars, followed in parentheses by dollar figures adjusted to the year 2000.)

1776 Sept. 2–9, N.C. to Nova Scotia: called the "Hurricane of Independence," it is believed that 4,170 in the U.S. and Canada died in the storm.

1856 Aug. 11, Last Island, La.: 400 died.

1893 Aug. 28, Savannah, Ga., Charleston, S.C., Sea Islands, S.C.: at least 1,000 died.

1900 Sept. 8, Galveston, Tex.: an estimated 6,000–8,000 died in hurricane and tidal surge. The "Galveston Hurricane" is considered the deadliest in U.S. history.

1909 Sept. 10–21, La. and Miss.: 350 deaths.

1915 Aug. 5–23, Galveston, Tex., and New Orleans, La.: 275 killed.

1919 Sept. 2–15, Fla. Keys, La., and southern Tex.: more than 600 killed, mostly lost on ships at sea.

1926 Sept. 11–22, southeast Fla. and Ala.: 243 deaths.

1928 Sept. 6–20, Lake Okeechobee, southeast Fla.: 1,836 deaths. Second-deadliest U.S. hurricane on record.

1935 Aug. 29–Sept. 10, Fla. Keys: "Labor Day Hurricane"; 408 deaths.

1938 Sept. 10–22, Long Island, N.Y., and southern New England: "New England Hurricane"; 600 deaths.

1944 Sept. 9–16, N.C. to New England: 390 deaths, 344 of which were at sea.

1954 Aug. 25–31, N.C. to New England: "Carol" killed 60 in Long Island–New England area.

Oct. 5–18, S.C. to N.Y.: "Hazel" killed 95 in U.S.; about 400–1,000 in Haiti; 78 in Canada.

1955 Aug. 7–21, N.C. to New England: "Diane" took 184 lives and cost $8.3 million ($5.5 billion).

1957 June 25–28, southwest La. and northern Tex.: "Audrey" wiped out Cameron, La., causing 390 deaths.

1960 Aug. 29–Sept. 13, Fla. to New England: "Donna" killed 50 in the U.S.; 115 deaths in Antilles.

1961 Sept. 3–15, Tex. coast: "Carla" devastated Tex. gulf cities, taking 46 lives.

1965 Aug. 27–Sept. 12, southern Fla. and La.: "Betsy" killed 75 and cost more than $1.4 ($8.5) billion.

1969 Aug. 14–22, Miss., La., Ala., Va., and W. Va.: 256 killed as a result of "Camille." Damages estimated at $1.4 ($6.9) billion.

1972 June 14–23, northwest Fla. to N.Y.: "Agnes" caused widespread flash floods killing 117 (50 in Pa). Damages estimated at over $2.1 ($8.6) billion. Still the worst natural disaster ever in Pa.

1979 Aug. 29–Sept. 15, Ala. and Miss.: "Frederic" devastated Mobile, Ala., and caused $2.3 ($4.9) billion in damage overall.

1985 Oct. 6–Nov. 1: "Juan" struck La. and the Southeast. Though only a Category 1 hurricane, it caused severe flooding and $1.5 ($2.4) billion in damages; 63 lives were lost.

1989 Sept. 10–22, Caribbean Sea, S.C., and N.C.: "Hugo" claimed 86 lives (57 U.S. mainland) and damages estimated over $7 ($9.7) billion.

1992 Aug. 22–26, Bahamas, southern Fla., and La.: Hurricane "Andrew" left 26 dead and more than 100,000 homes destroyed or damaged. Total U.S. damages estimated at $26.5 ($34.9) billion.

1994 Nov. 8–21, Caribbean and southern Fla.: "Gordon" led to an estimated 1,122 deaths in Haiti. Eight died in Fla.

1995 Nov. 29, Fla. Panhandle and Ala.: storm surge during "Opal" caused extensive damage; nine U.S. deaths and damages of $3 ($3.5) billion.

1996 Sept. 5, N.C. and Va.: "Fran" took 37 lives and caused more than $3.2 ($3.6) billion in damage.

1999 Sept. 14–18, Bahamas to New England: "Floyd" and associated flooding caused at least 57 deaths. Damage estimated at $4.5 ($4.6) billion.

2001 June 8–15, Gulf Coast to southern New England: tropical storm "Allison" caused severe flooding, damage estimated at $5 billion (actual cost); 41 deaths.

2003 Sept. 18, N.C. and Va.: "Isabel" took 50 lives and caused more than $3.7 billion in damage.

2004 Aug. 13–Sept. 26, Fla., Ala., and southern U.S.: Four major hurricanes hit Fla. in 6 weeks. "Charley," on Aug. 13, a Category 4 hurricane, killed 34; "Frances," on Sept. 5, killed 38. "Ivan" swept from Grenada to Ala. and Fla. on Sept. 16, killing 52 in the U.S., 66 in the Caribbean. "Jeanne," on Sept. 26, flooded Fla. again, killing 28.

2005 Aug. 25–Aug. 30, Fla., Miss. and La.: "Katrina" hit southern Fla. and on Aug. 29th slammed the Gulf Coast with 145 mph winds and major storm surges, destroying hundreds of homes and businesses, and causing massive flooding in Miss., Ala., and New Orleans where the levees failed. While the number of fatalities and amount of damage are still unknown, "Katrina" is among the most devastating and deadly of U.S. hurricanes.

OTHER HURRICANES

1780 Oct. 10–16, Barbados, West Indies: "The Great Hurricane of 1780" killed 20,000–22,000 people and completely flattened the islands of Barbados, Martinique, and St. Eustatius; it is the deadliest Western Hemisphere hurricane on record.

1926 Oct. 20, Cuba: powerful hurricane killed 650.

1930 Sept. 3, Dominican Republic: hurricane killed about 8,000 people.

1955 Sept. 19, Mexico: "Hilda" took 200 lives.

Sept. 22–28, Caribbean: "Janet" killed 200 in Honduras and 300 in Mexico.

1961 Oct. 31, British Honduras: "Hattie" devastated capital of Belize, killing at least 400.

1963 Oct. 2–7, Caribbean: "Flora" killed about 7,200 in Haiti and Cuba.

1966 Sept. 24–30, Caribbean area: "Inez" killed 293.

1974 Sept. 14–19, Honduras: "Fifi" struck northern part of country, leaving 8,000 dead and 100,000 homeless.

1988 Sept. 12–17, Caribbean Sea and Gulf of Mexico: "Gilbert" took at least 260 lives and caused some 39 tornadoes in Tex.

1997 Oct. 8–10, southern Mexico: "Pauline" devastated resort city of Acapulco, leaving 217 dead and 20,000 homeless.

1998 Sept. 20–29, Caribbean, Fla. Keys, and Gulf Coast: "Georges" killed about 600 people, mostly in Dominican Republic.

Oct. 26–Nov. 4, Honduras, Nicaragua, Guatemala: "Mitch" killed more than 14,500 people, becoming the deadliest Atlantic storm in 200 years. Two to three million people were left homeless; damages were more than $5 billion.

2004 Sept. 18, Haiti: Floods from tropical storm "Jeanne" killed more than 2,400 in Haiti and left 300,000 homeless.

TYPHOONS

1906 Sept. 18, Hong Kong: typhoon with tsunami killed an estimated 10,000 people.

1934 Sept. 21, Japan: typhoon killed more than 4,000 on Honshu.

1949 Dec. 5, off Korea: typhoon struck fishing fleet; several thousand men reported dead.

1958 Sept. 27, Honshu, Japan: "Vera" left nearly 5,000 dead and 1.5 million homeless.

1959 Aug. 20, Fukien province, China: "Iris" killed 2,334.

1960 June 9, Fukien province, China: "Mary" caused at least 1,600 deaths.

1984 Sept. 2–3, Philippines: "Ike" hit seven major islands, leaving 1,300 dead.

1991 Nov. 5, central Philippines: flash floods from tropical storm "Thelma" killed about 3,000 people.

BLIZZARDS

1888 Jan. 12, Dakota and Montana territories, Minn., Nebr., Kans., and Tex.: "Schoolchildren's Blizzard" resulted in 235 deaths, many of which were children on their way home from school.

March 11–14, East Coast: "Blizzard of 1888" resulted in 400 deaths and as much as 5 ft of snow. Damage was estimated at $20 million.

1949 Jan. 2–4, Nebr., Wyo., S.D., Utah, Colo., and Nev.: Although only 1 ft to 30 in. of snow fell, fierce winds of up to 72 mph created drifts as high as 30 ft. Tens of thousands of cattle and sheep perished.

1950 Nov. 25–27, eastern U.S.: "Storm of the Century" generated heavy snow and hurricane-force winds across 22 states and claimed 383 lives. Damages estimated at $70 million.

1978 Feb. 6–8, eastern U.S.: "Blizzard of 1978" battered the East Coast; claimed 54 lives and caused $1 billion in damage. Snowfall ranged from 2–4 ft in New England, plus nearly 2 ft of snow from an earlier storm.

1993 March 12–14, eastern U.S.: "Superstorm" paralyzed the eastern seaboard, causing the deaths of some 270 people. Record snowfalls (with rates of 2–3 in. per hour) and high winds caused $3 billion to $6 billion in damage.

1996 Jan. 6–8, eastern U.S.: heavy snow paralyzed the Appalachians, the mid-Atlantic, and the Northeast; 187 were killed in the blizzard and in the floods that resulted after a sudden warm-up. Damages reached $3 billion.

U.S. TORNADOES

1840 May 6, Natchez, Miss.: tornado struck heart of the city, killing 317 and injuring over 1,000.

1880 April 18, Marshfield, Mo.: series of 24 tornadoes demolished city, killing 99 people.

1884 Feb. 19, Miss., Ala., N.C., S.C., Tenn., Ky., Ind.: series of 60 tornadoes caused estimated 800 deaths.

1896 May 27, eastern Mo. and southern Ill.: series of 18 tornadoes; 1 tornado destroyed large section of St. Louis, Mo., killing 255.

1899 June 12, New Richmond, Wis.: tornado struck while circus was in town, causing 117 deaths.

1902 May 18, Goliad, Tex.: tornado killed 114.

1903 June 1, Gainesville, Holland, Ga.: twister caused 98 deaths.

1905 May 10, Snyder, Okla.: tornado killed 97.

1908 April 24–25, La., Miss., Ala., Ga.: 18 tornadoes resulted in 310 deaths (143 of these caused by 1 tornado that moved from Amite, La. to Purvis, Miss.).

April 24, Natchez, Miss.: twister struck, causing 91 deaths.

1913 March 23, eastern Nebr. and western Iowa: Easter Sunday: 8 tornadoes resulted in 181 deaths (94 in Omaha, Nebr.).

1917 May 26, Mattoon, Ill.: tornado smashed area, causing 101 deaths.

1925 March 18, Mo., Ill., Ind.: the "Tri-State Tornado" was the most violent single twister in U.S. history. It caused the deaths of 689 people and injured over 2,000. Property damage was estimated at $16.5 million.

1927 May 9, Poplar Bluff, Mo.: twister killed 98.

Sept. 29, St. Louis, Mo.: a five-minute tornado ripped through the city and caused 79 deaths.

1932 March 21–22, Ala., Miss., Ga., Tenn.: outbreak of 33 tornadoes killed 334 (268 in Ala.).

1936 April 5–6, Deep South: series of 17 tornadoes; 216 killed in Tupelo, Miss., and 203 killed in Gainesville, Ga.

1944 June 23, W. Va., Pa., Md.: 4 tornadoes caused 153 deaths.

1947 April 9, Woodward, Okla.: tornado demolished town, killing 181.

1952 **March 21–22, Ark. and Tenn.:** 28 tornadoes caused 204 deaths.

1953 **May 11, Waco, Tex.:** a single tornado killed 114.

June 8, Flint, Mich.: tornado killed 116.

June 9, Worcester, Mass.: tornado hit town, killing 90.

1955 **May 25, Udall, Kans.:** tornado killed 80.

1965 **April 11–12, Midwest–Great Lakes region:** tornadoes in Iowa, Ill., Ind., Ohio, Mich., and Wis. caused 256 deaths.

1967 **April 21, northern Ill., also Mo., Iowa, lower Mich.:** series of 52 tornadoes caused 58 deaths.

1971 **Feb. 21, Miss., La., Ark., Tenn.:** series of 10 tornadoes resulted in 121 deaths.

1974 **April 3–4:** a series of 148 twisters within 16 hours comprised the deadly "Super Tornado Outbreak" that struck 13 states in the East, South, and Midwest. Before it was over, 330 died and 5,484 were injured in a damage path covering more than 2,500 mi.

1979 **April 10, northern Tex. and southern Okla.:** 11 tornadoes caused 59 deaths.

1985 **May 31, Pa. and Ohio:** 27 tornadoes resulted in 756 deaths.

1994 **March 27, Ala., Ga., and N.C.:** Palm Sunday tornado outbreak resulted in 42 deaths, 320 injuries. Twenty people died and 90 were injured when a tornado caused the roof of a church near Piedmont, Ala., to collapse.

1999 **May 3, Okla. and Kans.:** unusually large twister, thought to have been a mile wide at times, killed 44 people and injured at least 748 others in Okla.

2002 **Nov. 9–11, central and southeast U.S.:** series of more than 70 tornadoes across 9 states from Miss. to Pa. killed 36 people.

2003 **May 1–10, southern and midwestern U.S.:** a record-breaking number of more than 400 tornadoes in 10 days killed 42.

DROUGHTS AND HEAT WAVES

1930s **Many states:** longest drought of the 20th century. Peak periods were 1930, 1934, 1936, 1939, and 1940. A great "dust bowl" covered some 50 million acres in the south-central plains during the winter of 1935–1936.

1955 **Aug. 31–Sept. 7, Los Angeles:** 8-day run of 100°-plus heat left 946 people dead.

1972 **July 14–26, New York City:** 891 people died in 14-day heat wave.

1980 **June–Sept., central and eastern U.S.:** an estimated 10,000 people were killed during the summer in a long heat wave and drought. Damages totaled about $20 billion.

1982–1983 **worldwide:** El Niño caused wildly unusual weather in the U.S. and elsewhere throughout 1983. Drought in the western Pacific region led to disastrous forest fires in Indonesia and Australia. Overall loss to world economy was over $8 billion. Similar event in 1997–1998 resulted in estimated loss of $25–$33 billion.

1988 **Summer, central and eastern U.S.:** a severe drought and heat wave killed an estimated 5,000–10,000 people. Damages reached $40 billion.

1995 **July 12–17, Chicago:** 739 people died in record heat wave.

1998 **Summer, southern U.S.:** severe heat and drought spread across Tex. and Okla., all the way to N.C. and S.C, killing at least 200. Estimated damages of $6–$9 billion.

1999 **Summer, eastern U.S.:** rainfall shortages resulted in worst drought on record for Md., Del., N.J., and R.I. The state of W.Va. was declared a disaster area. 3.81 million acres were consumed by fire as of mid-Aug. Record heat throughout the country resulted in 502 deaths nationwide.

2000 **Spring–summer, southern U.S.:** severe drought and heat killed an estimated 140 people. Damages were estimated at $4 billion.

2003 **May–June, southern India:** a monthlong intense heat wave claimed more than 1,500 lives.

Aug., Europe: drought conditions and a heat wave, one of the worst in 150 years, covered Europe, broke temperature records from London to Portugal, fueled deadly forest fires, ruined crops, and caused thousands of deaths. (French fatalities estimated at more than 14,000.)

NUCLEAR AND CHEMICAL ACCIDENTS

1952 **Dec. 12, Chalk River, nr. Ottawa, Canada:** a partial meltdown of the reactor's uranium fuel core resulted after the accidental removal of four control rods. There were no injuries.

1953 **Love Canal, nr. Niagara Falls, N.Y.:** was destroyed by waste from chemical plants. By the 1990s, the town had been cleaned up enough for families to begin moving back to the area.

1957 **Oct. 7, Windscale Pile No. 1, north of Liverpool, England:** fire in a graphite-cooled reactor spewed radiation over the countryside, contaminating a 200-square-mile area.

South Ural Mountains: explosion of radioactive wastes at Soviet nuclear weapons factory 12 mi from city of Kyshtym forced the evacuation of over 10,000 people from a contaminated area. No casualties were reported by Soviet officials.

1979 **March 28, Three Mile Island, nr. Harrisburg, Pa.:** one of two reactors lost its coolant, which caused overheating and partial meltdown of its uranium core. Some radioactive water and gases were released. This was the worst accident in U.S. nuclear-reactor history.

1984 **Dec. 3, Bhopal, India:** toxic gas, methyl isocyanate, seeped from Union Carbide insecticide plant, killing more than 2,000 and injuring about 150,000.

1986 **April 26, Chernobyl, nr. Kiev, Ukraine:** explosion and fire in the graphite core of one of four reactors released radioactive material that spread over part of the Soviet Union, eastern Europe, Scandinavia, and later western Europe. 31 claimed dead. Total casualties are unknown. Worst such accident to date.

1987 **Sept. 18, Goiânia, Brazil:** 244 people contaminated with cesium-137 from a cancer-therapy machine that had been sold as scrap. Four people died in worst radiation disaster in Western Hemisphere.

2004 **Aug. 9, Mihama, Japan:** nonradioactive steam leaked from a nuclear power plant, killing four workers and severely burning seven others.

FIRES AND EXPLOSIONS

1666 **Sept. 2, England:** "Great Fire of London" destroyed much of the city, including St. Paul's Cathedral. Damage £10 million.

1835 **Dec. 16, New York City:** 530 buildings destroyed by fire.

1871 **Oct. 8, Chicago:** the "Chicago Fire" burned 17,450 buildings and killed 250 people; $196 million in damage.

1872 **Nov. 9, Boston:** fire destroyed 800 buildings; $75 million in damage.

1876 **Dec. 5, New York City:** fire in Brooklyn Theater killed more than 300.

1881 **Dec. 8, Vienna:** at least 620 died in fire at Ring Theatre.

1900 **June 30, Hoboken, N.J.:** piers of North German Lloyd Steamship line burned; 326 dead.

1903 **Dec. 30, Chicago:** Iroquois Theatre fire killed 602.

1904 **Feb. 7, Baltimore, Md.:** blaze spread through downtown Baltimore. More than 1,500 buildings were destroyed

1906 **March 10, France:** explosion in coal mine in Courrières killed 1,060.

1907 **Dec. 6, Monongah, W. Va.:** coal mine explosion killed 362.

Dec. 19, Jacobs Creek, Pa.: explosion in coal mine left 239 dead.

1908 **Jan. 13, Boyertown, Pa.:** fire in Rhoads Opera House killed 170 people.

March 4, Collinwood, Ohio: fire in Collinwood school killed 176. Led to revision of fire codes for schools.

1909 **Nov. 13, Cherry, Ill.:** explosion in coal mine killed 259.

1911 **March 25, New York City:** fire in Triangle Shirtwaist Factory fatal to 145.

1913 **Oct. 22, Dawson, N.M.:** coal mine explosion left 263 dead.

1917 **Dec. 6, Halifax Harbor, Nova Scotia:** Belgian steamer collided with ammunition ship *Mont Blanc*, which was carrying over 2,500 tons of explosives. Explosion leveled part of Halifax and left about 1,600 people dead.

1921 **Sept. 21, Oppau, Germany:** ammonium nitrate exploded destroying the BASF plant and nearby houses, killing 430 people.

1930 **April 21, Columbus, Ohio:** fire in Ohio State Penitentiary killed 320 convicts.

1937 **March 18, New London, Tex.:** explosion destroyed schoolhouse; 294 killed.

1942 **April 26, Manchuria:** explosion in Honkeiko Colliery killed 1,549.

Nov. 28, Boston, Mass.: Coconut Grove nightclub fire killed 491.

1944 **July 6, Hartford, Conn.:** fire and ensuing stampede in main tent of Ringling Brothers Circus killed 168 and injured 487.

July 17, Port Chicago, Calif.: 322 killed when ammunition ships exploded.

Oct. 20, Cleveland: spilled liquid natural gas exploded, killing 130.

1946 **Dec. 7, Atlanta:** fire in Winecoff Hotel killed 119.

1947 **April 16–18, Texas City, Tex.:** most of the city destroyed by a fire and subsequent explosion on the French freighter *Grandcamp*, which was carrying a cargo of ammonium nitrate. At least 516 were killed and over 3,000 injured.

1949 **Sept. 2, China:** fire on Chongqing (Chungking) waterfront killed 1,700.

1954 **May 26, off Quonset Point, R.I.:** explosion and fire aboard aircraft carrier *Bennington* killed 103 crewmen.

1956 **Aug. 7, Colombia:** seven army ammunition trucks exploded at Cali, killing about 1,100.

Aug. 8, Belgium: 262 died in coal mine fire at Marcinelle.

1960 **Jan. 21, Coalbrook, South Africa:** coal mine explosion killed 437.

Nov. 13, Syria: 152 children killed in moviehouse fire.

1961 **Dec. 17, Niteroi, Brazil:** circus fire fatal to 323.

1962 **Feb. 7, Saarland, West Germany:** coal mine gas explosion killed 298.

1963 **Nov. 9, Japan:** explosion in coal mine at Omuta killed 447.

1965 **May 28, India:** coal mine fire in state of Bihar killed 375.

June 1, nr. Fukuoka, Japan: coal mine explosion killed 236.

1967 **May 22, Brussels, Belgium:** fire in L'Innovation department store left 322 dead.

July 29, off North Vietnam: fire on U.S. carrier *Forrestal* killed 134.

1972 **June 6, Wankie, Rhodesia:** explosion in coal mine killed 427.

1973 **Nov. 29, Kumamoto, Japan:** fire in Taiyo department store killed 101.

1975 **Dec. 27, Dhanbad, India:** explosion in coal mine followed by flooding from nearby reservoir left 372 dead.

1977 **May 28, Southgate, Ky.:** fire in Beverly Hills Supper Club; 167 dead.

1978 **Aug. 20, Abadan, Iran:** nearly 400 killed when arsonists set fire to crowded theater.

1986 **Dec. 31, San Juan, P.R.:** fire in Dupont Plaza Hotel set by three employees, killing 96 people.

1989 **June 3, Ural Mountains:** gas leaking from a pipeline exploded and destroyed 2 passing passenger trains, killing 575.

Oct. 23, Pasadena, Tex.: a huge explosion and a raging fire at a Phillips Petroleum Co. plastics manufacturing plant killed 23 and injured 132 people. A large leak of ethylene was presumed to be the cause.

1990 **March 25, New York City:** arson fire in the illegal Happy Land Social Club killed 87 people.

1993 **May 10, nr. Bangkok, Thailand:** fire in doll factory killed at least 187 people and injured 500 others. World's deadliest factory fire.

1999 **March 24, Chamonix, France:** fire in Belgian truck in the Mont Blanc tunnel trapped dozens of cars. Death toll was at least 42.

2000 **Nov. 11, nr. Kaprun, Austria:** cable car transporting skiers broke into flames in a mountain tunnel, killing 156. It was Austria's worst Alpine disaster.

Dec. 25, Luoyang, China: at least 309 people were killed in fire at shopping center.

2002 **Jan. 27, Lagos, Nigeria:** explosions at military depot triggered a stampede from the surrounding neighborhoods. More than 1,000 killed.

2003 **Feb. 18, Daegu, South Korea:** subway fire raced through two trains, killing 189 people and injuring more than 140.

Feb. 20, West Warwick, R.I.: fire, caused by a pyrotechnics display, engulfed a nightclub, killing 100 and injuring more than 150.

2004   **July 16, southern India:** thatched roof of a private elementary school caught fire, killing 94 children.

        Aug. 1, Asunción, Paraguay: fire, caused by a gas leak, swept through a supermarket, killing at least 400 people.

        Dec. 30, Buenos Aires, Argentina: a lit flare started a fire at an overcrowded nightclub, killing 175 people.

2005   **Feb. 14, Liaoning province, China:** A gas explosion killed 209 miners at the Sujiawan mine.

WORST U.S. FOREST FIRES

1871   **Oct. 8–14, Peshtigo, Wis:** over 1,500 lives lost and 3.8 million acres burned in nation's worst forest fire.

1889   **June 6, Seattle, Wash.:** fire destroyed 64 acres of the city and killed 2 people. Damage was estimated at $15 million.

1894   **Sept. 1, Minn.:** forest fires ravaged over 160,000 acres and destroyed 6 towns; 600 killed, including 413 in town of Hinckley.

1902   **Sept., Wash. and Ore.:** Yacoult fire destroyed 1 million acres and left 38 dead.

1910   **Aug. 10, Idaho and Mont.:** fires burned 3 million acres of woods and killed 85 people.

1918   **Oct. 13–15, Minn. and Wis.:** forest fire struck towns in both states; 1,000 died, including 400 in town of Cloquet, Minn. About $1 million in losses.

1947   **Oct. 25–27, Maine:** forest fire destroyed part of Bar Harbor and damaged Acadia National Park. In all, 205,678 acres burned and 16 lives were lost.

1949   **Aug. 5, Mann Gulch, Mont.:** 12 smokejumpers—firefighters who parachuted near the fire—and 1 forest ranger died after being overtaken by a 200-ft wall of fire at the top of a gulch near Helena, Mont. Three smokejumpers survived.

1970   **Sept. 26, Laguna, Calif.:** large-scale brush fire burned 175,425 acres and 382 structures.

1988   **Aug.–Sept., western U.S.:** fires destroyed over 1.2 million acres in Yellowstone National Park and damaged Alaska woodlands.

1990   **June, Santa Barbara, Calif.:** Painted Cave fire consumed 4,900 acres and destroyed 641 structures.

1991   **Oct. 20–23, Oakland–Berkeley, Calif.:** brush fire in drought-stricken area destroyed over 3,000 homes and apartments. At least 24 people died; damage estimated at $1.5 billion.

1994   **July 2–11, South Canyon, Colo.:** relatively small fire (2,000 acres) resulted in deaths of 14 firefighters.

2000   **April–May, northern N.M.:** prescribed fire started by National Park Service raged out of control, destroying 235 structures and forcing evacuation of more than 20,000 people.

        Spring–Summer, western U.S.: dry conditions led to one of the most destructive forest fire seasons in U.S. history. About 7.2 million acres burned nationwide, nearly double the 10-year average. States hardest hit included Alaska, Idaho, Mont., N.M., Nev., and Ore.

2002   **June–early July, mainly western U.S.:** Hayman fire in Pike National Forest destroyed 137,760 acres and 600 structures, making it the worst wildfire in Colorado history. In central Ariz., the Rodeo fire, the worst in Arizona's history, merged with the Chediski fire to form an inferno that destroyed 468,638 acres and more than 400 structures.

2003   **Oct. 25–29, southern Calif.:** 15 devastating forest fires burned for two weeks, forcing more than 80,000 people to evacuate their homes and burning 800,000 acres. More than 15,500 firefighters battled the blazes that killed 24 people and destroyed 3,640 homes. The Cedar Fire in San Diego, which burned through 200,000 acres, was the largest fire in California's history.

2004   **July–Aug., Alaska:** wildfires in Alaska burned more than 5 million acres, the worst year for Alaska fires.

SHIPWRECKS

1833   **May 11, *Lady of the Lake:*** bound from England to Quebec, struck iceberg; 215 perished.

1853   **Sept. 29, *Annie Jane:*** emigrant vessel wrecked off coast of Scotland; 348 died.

1865   **April 27, *Sultana:*** boiler explosion on Mississippi River steamboat, near Memphis; 1,547 killed. Most of the dead were Union POWs finally heading home at the end of the Civil War.

1898   **Feb. 15, *Maine:*** U.S. battleship destroyed in Havana harbor by an explosion that killed 260 men. The incident led to the outbreak of the Spanish-American War in April 1898.

        Nov. 26, *City of Portland:* 157 died nr. Cape Cod.

1904   **June 15, *General Slocum:*** excursion steamer burned in East River, N.Y.; 1,021 perished.

1912   **March 5, *Principe de Asturias:*** Spanish steamer struck rock off Sebastien Point; 500 drowned.

        April 15, *Titanic:* supposedly unsinkable British ocean liner went down on maiden voyage after colliding with an iceberg. More than 1,500 people died.

1914   **May 29, *Empress of Ireland:*** sank after collision in St. Lawrence River; 1,024 perished.

1915   **July 24, *Eastland:*** Great Lakes excursion steamer overturned in Chicago River; 812 died.

1934   **Sept. 8, *Morro Castle:*** 134 killed in fire off Asbury Park, N.J.

1945   **Jan. 30, *Wilhelm Gustloff:*** cruise ship carrying German refugees and soldiers sunk by Soviet submarine in Baltic. It is thought that as many as 10,000 people were aboard, of which only about 900 survived.

1949   **Sept. 17, *Noronic:*** Canadian Great Lakes cruise ship burned at Toronto dock; about 130 died.

1952   **April 26, *Hobson:*** minesweeper collided with aircraft carrier *Wasp* and sank during night maneuvers in mid-Atlantic; 176 people lost.

1953   **Jan. 9, *Chang Tyong-Ho:*** South Korean ferry foundered off Pusan; 249 reported dead.

1954   **Sept. 26, *Toya Maru:*** more than 1,000 killed when commercial ferry sank in Tsugaru Strait, Japan.

1956   **July 25, *Andrea Doria:*** Italian liner collided with Swedish liner *Stockholm* off Nantucket Island, Mass., and sank the next day. 51 people died.

1962   **April 8, *Dara:*** British liner exploded and sank in Persian Gulf; 236 dead. Caused by time bomb.

1963   **April 10, *Thresher:*** atomic-powered U.S. submarine sank in North Atlantic; 129 dead.

1968   **Late May, *Scorpion:*** U.S. nuclear submarine sank in Atlantic 400 mi southwest of Azores; 99 dead.

1975 **Nov. 10, *Edmund Fitzgerald:*** cargo vessel carrying 26,000 long tons of iron ore pellets sank in eastern Lake Superior; all 29 crew lost.

1983 **May 25, *10th of Ramadan:*** Nile steamer caught fire and sank in Lake Nasser, near Aswan, Egypt; 272 dead and 75 missing.

1987 **March 6, *Herald of Free Enterprise:*** British ferry capsized after leaving Belgian port of Zeebrugge with 500 aboard; 134 drowned.

Dec. 20, *Dona Paz:* over 4,000 killed when passenger ferry collided with oil tanker *Victor* off Mindoro Is., south of Manila, Philippines.

1990 **April 7, *Scandinavian Star:*** suspected arson aboard Danish-owned North Sea ferry killed at least 110 passengers in Skagerrak Strait off Norway.

1991 **Dec. 15, *Salem Express:*** ferry carrying 569 passengers sank in Red Sea off coast of Safaga, Egypt, after hitting a coral reef. Over 460 people believed drowned.

1993 **Feb. 17, *Neptune:*** triple-deck ferry capsized off southern peninsula of Haiti during a squall. Over 1,000 passengers believed drowned. About 300 survived the sinking.

1994 **Sept. 28, *Estonia:*** passenger ferry capsized off coast of southwest Finland and sank in a stormy Baltic Sea. Only about 140 of the estimated 1,040 passengers aboard survived.

1996 **Jan. 21, *Gurita:*** overloaded ferry sank off the coast of northern Sumatra, killing 340.

1999 **Feb., *Harta Rimba:*** ship sank in the South China Sea, killing about 325 people. The ship had not been licensed for passenger use.

2000 **June 29, *Cahaya Bahari:*** ferry carrying refugees sank off Sulawesi, killing the 492 people aboard.

Aug. 12, *Kursk:* Russian nuclear submarine sank to bottom of Barents Sea following an explosion; 118 dead.

2001 **Feb. 9, *Ehime Maru:*** U.S. submarine *Greeneville* collided with Japanese fishing boat near Pearl Harbor, Hawaii. 26 people aboard the *Ehime Maru* were rescued; 9 others were presumed dead.

2002 **Sept. 26, *Joola:*** overloaded Senegalese ferry capsized off the coast of Gambia, drowning 1,863 people. Only 64 passengers were rescued.

MYSTERIOUS DISAPPEARANCES

1872 ***Mary Celeste:*** the brigantine set sail from New York harbor for Genoa, Italy, on Nov. 5. A British brigantine, the *DeGratia,* discovered the ship derelict on Dec. 5 and boarded her. Everyone aboard the *Mary Celeste* had vanished—her captain, his family, and its 14-man crew. The ship was in perfect order with ample supplies and there was no sign of violence or trouble. The fate of the crew remains unknown.

1918 **USS *Cyclops:*** the navy coal ship, used to deliver fuel and other supplies to U.S. battlefleet during World War I, disappeared while en route from Brazil to Baltimore. The ship docked briefly at Barbados on March 3–4. When it failed to arrive in Baltimore on March 13, a search was made, but neither her wreck nor any of the 309 people aboard were ever found, and the cause of her loss remains unknown.

1928 ***Köbenhavn:*** five-masted Danish steel barque, a sail-training ship with a crew of 75 including 45 boy cadets, sailed from the River Plate for Melbourne, Australia, on Dec. 14. The last radio contact with the ship was made on Dec. 22 and all was well. The *Köbenhavn* and its crew disappeared without a trace and no one knows what happened to it.

AIRCRAFT CRASHES

(150 deaths or more, with exceptions. *See also* Terrorist Attacks, pp. 223–224.)

1921 **Aug. 24, England:** British dirigible *AR-2* broke in two on trial trip near Hull; 62 died.

1925 **Sept. 3, Caldwell, Ohio:** U.S. dirigible *Shenandoah* broke apart; 14 dead.

1930 **Oct. 5, Beauvais, France:** British dirigible *R 101* crashed, killing 47.

1933 **April 4, N.J.:** U.S. dirigible *Akron* crashed; 73 died.

1937 **May 6, Lakehurst, N.J.:** German zeppelin *Hindenburg* destroyed by fire at tower mooring; 36 killed.

1945 **July 28, New York City:** U.S. Army bomber B-25 crashed into Empire State Building; 13 dead.

1960 **Dec. 16, New York City:** United DC-8 and Trans World Super Constellation collided and then crashed in two boroughs, killing 134 in air and on ground.

1961 **Feb. 15, nr. Brussels, Belgium:** 72 on board and farmer on ground killed in crash of Sabena plane; U.S. figure skating team wiped out.

1966 **Dec. 24, Binh Thai, South Vietnam:** crash of military-chartered CL-44 into village killed 129.

1971 **July 30, Morioka, Japan:** Japanese Boeing 727 and F-86 fighter collided in midair; 162 died.

1972 **Aug. 14, East Berlin, East Germany:** Soviet-built East German Ilyushin Il-62 plane crashed, killing 156.

Oct. 13, Moscow, Russia: Aeroflot Ilyushin IL-14 crashed during landing due to pilot fatigue and 176 people perish.

1973 **Jan. 22, Kano, Nigeria:** 171 Nigerian Muslims returning from Mecca and 5 crewmen died in crash.

Feb. 21, Sinai: civilian Libyan Arab Airlines Boeing 727 shot down by Israeli fighters after it had strayed off course; 108 died, 5 survived. Officials claimed that the pilot had ignored fighters' warnings to land.

1974 **March 3, Paris:** Turkish DC-10 jumbo jet crashed in forest shortly after takeoff; all 346 passengers and crew killed:

Dec. 4, Colombo, Sri Lanka: Dutch DC-8 carrying Muslims to Mecca crashed on landing approach, killing all 191 people aboard.

1975 **April 4, nr. Saigon, Vietnam:** Air Force Galaxy C-5A crashed after takeoff, killing 172, mostly Vietnamese children.

Aug. 3, Agadir, Morocco: chartered Boeing 707, returning Moroccan workers home after vacation in France, plunged into mountainside; all 188 aboard killed.

1976 **Sept. 10, Zagreb, Yugoslavia:** midair collision between British Airways Trident and Yugoslav charter DC-9 fatal to all 176 people aboard.

1977 **March 27, Santa Cruz de Tenerife, Canary Islands:** Pan American and KLM Boeing 747s collided on runway. All 249 on KLM plane and 333 of 394 aboard Pan Am jet killed. Total of 582 is highest for any type of aviation disaster.

1978   Jan. 1, Bombay: Air India 747 with 213 aboard exploded and plunged into sea minutes after takeoff.

Nov. 15, Colombo, Sri Lanka: chartered Icelandic Airlines DC-8, carrying 249 Muslim pilgrims from Mecca, crashed in thunderstorm during landing approach; 183 killed.

1979   May 25, Chicago: American Airlines DC-10 lost left engine upon takeoff and crashed seconds later, killing all 272 people aboard and 3 on the ground in worst U.S. air disaster.

Nov. 26, Jeddah, Saudi Arabia: Pakistan International Airlines 707 carrying pilgrims returning from Mecca crashed on takeoff; all 156 aboard killed.

Nov. 28, Mt. Erebus, Antarctica: Air New Zealand DC-10 crashed on sightseeing flight; 257 killed.

1980   Aug. 19, Riyadh, Saudi Arabia: all 301 aboard Saudi Arabian jet killed when burning plane made safe landing but passengers were unable to escape.

1981   Dec. 1, Ajaccio, Corsica: Yugoslav DC-9 Super 80 carrying tourists crashed into mountain on landing approach, killing all 178 aboard.

1983   Aug. 30, nr. island of Sakhalin off Siberia: Korean Air Lines Boeing 747 shot down by Soviet fighter after it strayed off course into Soviet airspace. All 269 aboard killed.

Nov. 27, Madrid: Colombian Avianca Boeing 747 crashed near Mejorada del Campó Airport, killing 181 people aboard. Eleven people survived.

1985   June 23, Atlantic Ocean: Air India 747 exploded over the ocean killing 329. The probable cause was a Sikh terrorist bomb.

Aug. 12, Japan: Japan Air Lines Boeing 747 crashed into a mountain, killing 520 of the 524 aboard. Highest death toll in a single-plane crash in aviation history.

Dec. 12, Gander, Newfoundland: a chartered Arrow Air DC-8 bringing American soldiers home crashed on takeoff. All 256 aboard died.

1987   May 9, Poland: Polish airliner Ilyushin 62M, on charter flight to N.Y., crashed after takeoff from Warsaw, killing 183.

Aug. 16, Romulus, Mich.: Northwest Airlines McDonnell Douglas MD-80 crashed into a highway shortly after takeoff from Detroit Metropolitan Airport, killing 156 (including 2 on the ground). Girl, 4, only survivor.

Nov. 29, Burma: Korean Air Boeing 747 jetliner exploded from bomb planted by North Korean agents and crashed into sea, killing all 115 aboard.

1988   July 3, Persian Gulf: U.S. Navy cruiser *Vincennes* shot down Iran Air Airbus A-300 after mistaking it for an attacking jet fighter; 290 killed.

Aug. 28, Ramstein Air Force Base, West Germany: 3 jets from Italian Air Force acrobatic team collided in midair during air show and crashed, killing 70 people, including the pilots and spectators on the ground.

Dec. 21, Lockerbie, Scotland: N.Y.-bound Pan-Am Boeing 747 exploded in flight from a terrorist bomb and crashed into Scottish village, killing all 259 aboard and 11 on the ground. *See* Terrorist Attacks, pp. 223–224.

1989   June 7, Paramaribo, Suriname: a Surinam Airways DC-8 carrying 174 passengers crashed into the jungle while making a third attempt to land in a thick fog, killing 168 aboard.

1991   May 26, nr. Bangkok, Thailand: Austrian Lauda Air Boeing 767, en route to Vienna, crashed into jungle hilltop shortly after takeoff from Bangkok airport, killing all 223 aboard. Thailand's worst air disaster.

July 11, Jeddah, Saudi Arabia: Canadian-chartered DC-8 carrying pilgrims returning to Nigeria crashed after takeoff, killing 261 people.

1994   April 26, Nagoya, Japan: China Airlines Airbus A-300 from Taiwan crash-landed and exploded on the tarmac. Only 7 of the 271 passengers aboard survived.

June 6, Xian, China: China Northwest Airlines Tupolev-154 crashed 10 minutes after takeoff, killing all 160 aboard.

Sept. 8, nr. Aliquippa, Pa.: USAir Boeing 737 crashed into a ravine shortly before it was supposed to land at Pittsburgh International Airport. All 132 aboard were killed.

1995   Dec. 20, nr. Cali, Colombia: 160 people killed when American Airlines Boeing 757 crashed in Andean Mountains.

1996   Jan. 8, Kinshasa, Zaire: Russian-built Antonov-32 cargo plane crashed after takeoff from Kinshasa into the center of the city, killing over 350 people.

Feb. 6, off coast of Puerto Plata, Dominican Republic: Dominican Alas Nacionales Boeing 737 crashed into Atlantic Ocean after takeoff, killing 189.

July 17, off coast of Long Island, N.Y.: TWA Boeing 747-100, Flight 800, bound for Paris from N.Y., exploded over L.I. and crashed into Atlantic Ocean, killing all 230 aboard.

Nov. 12, nr. New Delhi, India: shortly after takeoff, Saudi Arabian Airlines Boeing 747 collided in midair with Kazak Airlines Ilyushin 76 approaching the New Delhi airport. All 349 passengers and crew were killed; the world's worst midair collision.

1997   Aug. 6, Guam: Korean Air Boeing 747-300 from Seoul crashed into jungle near Agana International Airport, killing 228 people; 26 survived.

Sept. 26, nr. northern Indonesia: Indonesian Garuda Airlines A-300 Airbus jetliner crashed while approaching Medan Airport, Sumatra, killing all 234 people aboard.

1998   Feb. 16, Taipei, Taiwan: China Airlines Airbus A-300 jumbo jet crashed while trying to land in fog at Chiang Kai-shek International Airport, killing all 196 aboard and at least 6 people on the ground.

Sept. 2, off Nova Scotia, Canada: Swissair flight from N.Y. to Geneva crashed off Canadian coast, killing all 229 aboard. 136 Americans were on the McDonnell Douglas MD-11.

1999   Oct. 31, southeast of Nantucket Island: Egypt Air Boeing 767-300 on flight from N.Y. to Cairo crashed into the Atlantic Ocean, killing all 217 aboard.

2000   Jan. 30, off the Ivory Coast: Kenya Airways Airbus A-310, carrying 179 passengers and crew, crashed into the Atlantic Ocean after takeoff from Abidjan. Ten people survived.

July 25, Gonesse, France: Air France Concorde jet en route to N.Y. crashed into a hotel after taking off from Charles de Gaulle airport near Paris; all 109 aboard and 4 on the ground were killed; first Concorde jet to crash since the plane went into commercial service in 1976.

2001 **Sept. 11, New York City, Arlington, Va., and Shanksville, Pa.:** For the attacks on the World Trade Center and the Pentagon, *see* p. 224.

Nov. 12, Queens, N.Y.: American Airlines Airbus A-300, bound for the Dominican Republic, crashed minutes after taking off from JFK International Airport. All 260 people aboard and 5 on the ground were killed.

2002 **May 25, nr. Pescadores off western Taiwan:** China Airlines Boeing 747, bound for Hong Kong with 225 people aboard, broke apart in midair and plunged into sea 20 minutes after takeoff from Taipei. There were no survivors.

July 27, nr. Lviv, Ukraine: Russian-built Sukhoi-27 fighter jet crashed while performing an acrobatic maneuver during an air show. 83 people were killed. It is the worst air show disaster in history.

2003 **Feb. 19, nr. Shahdad, Iran:** Iranian military airplane, Ilyushin Il-76MD, carrying members of Iran's Revolutionary Guards, crashed in the Sirach Mountains, killing all 276 on board.

2004 **Aug. 24, Moscow, Russia:** two Russian planes, both departing from Moscow's airport, crashed within minutes of each other, killing a total of 89 people. Explosives were found on both flights.

2005 **Feb. 3, Kabul, Afghanistan:** Afghan Kam Air, Boeing 737, bound to Kabul crashed, killing 104.

Aug. 14, Athens, Greece: a Helios Airways, Boeing 737, en route from Cyprus to Athens lost cabin pressure and crashed when it ran out of fuel, killing all 121 on board.

Aug. 16, western Venezuela: a chartered West Caribbean Airways, MD-82, en route from Panama to Martinique, crashed in remote western Venezuela, killing all 160 on board.

SPACE ACCIDENTS

1967 **Jan. 27, *Apollo 1*:** a fire aboard the space capsule on the ground at Cape Kennedy, Fla., killed astronauts Virgil I. Grissom, Edward H. White, and Roger Chaffee.

April 23–24, *Soyuz 1*: Vladimir M. Komarov was killed when his craft crashed after its parachute lines, released at 23,000 ft for reentry, became snarled.

1971 **June 6–30, *Soyuz 11*:** 3 cosmonauts, Georgi T. Dolrovolsky, Vladislav N. Volkov, and Viktor I. Patsayev, found dead in the craft after its automatic landing. Apparent cause of death was loss of pressurization in the space craft during reentry into Earth's atmosphere.

1980 **March 18, USSR:** a Vostok rocket exploded on its launch pad while being refueled, killing 50 at the Plesetsk Space Center.

1986 **Jan. 28, *Challenger* Space Shuttle:** exploded 73 seconds after liftoff, killing all 7 crew members. They were: Francis R. Scobee, Michael J. Smith, Judith A. Resnik, Ronald E. McNair, Ellison S. Onizuka, Gregory B. Jarvis, and schoolteacher Christa McAuliffe. A booster leak ignited the fuel, causing the explosion.

2003 **Feb. 1, *Columbia* Space Shuttle:** broke up on reentering Earth's atmosphere, killing all 7 crew members. They were: Rick D. Husband, William C. McCool, Michael P. Anderson, David M. Brown, Kalpana Chawla, Laurel Clark, and the first Israeli astronaut, Ilan Ramon. Foam insulation fell from the shuttle during launch, damaging the left wing. On reentry, hot gases entered the wing, leading to the disintegration of the shuttle.

RAILROAD ACCIDENTS

NOTE: Very few passengers were killed in a single U.S. train wreck up until 1853. The early trains ran slowly and made short trips, night travel was rare, and there were not many of them in operation.

1831 **June 17, nr. Charleston, S.C.:** boiler exploded on America's first passenger locomotive, *The Best Friend of Charleston*, injuring the fireman and the engineer.

1833 **Nov. 8, nr. Heightstown, N.J.:** world's first train wreck and first passenger fatalities recorded. A 24-passenger Camden & Amboy train derailed due to a broken axle, killing 2 passengers and injuring all others. Former president John Quincy Adams and Cornelius Vanderbilt, who later made a fortune in railroads, were aboard.

1853 **May 6, Norwalk, Conn.:** New Haven Railroad train ran through an open drawbridge and plunged into the Norwalk River. 46 passengers were crushed to death or drowned. This was the first major drawbridge accident.

1856 **July 17, Camp Hill, nr. Ft. Washington, Pa.:** 2 Northern Penn trains crashed head-on. Approximately 50–60 people died, mostly children on their way to a Sunday school picnic.

1876 **Dec. 29, Ashtabula, Ohio:** Lake Shore train fell into the Ashtabula River when the bridge it was crossing collapsed; 92 people were killed.

1887 **Aug. 10, nr. Chatsworth, Ill.:** a burning railroad trestle collapsed while a Toledo, Peoria & Western train was crossing, killing 81 and injuring 372.

1904 **Aug. 7, Eden, Colo.:** train derailed on bridge during flash flood; 96 killed.

1910 **March 1, Wellington, Wash.:** 2 trains swept into canyon by avalanche; 96 dead.

1915 **May 22, Quintinshill, Scotland:** 2 passenger trains and troop train collided; 227 killed.

1917 **Dec. 12, Modane, France:** nearly 550 killed in derailment of troop train near mouth of Mt. Cenis tunnel.

1918 **July 9, Nashville, Tenn.:** 101 killed in a 2-train collision near Nashville.

Nov. 1, New York City: derailment of subway train in Malbone St. tunnel in Brooklyn left 92 dead.

1926 **March 14, Virilla River Canyon, Costa Rica:** an overcrowded train carrying pilgrims derailed while crossing the Colima Bridge, killing over 300 people and injuring hundreds more.

1939 **Dec. 22, nr. Magdeburg, Germany:** more than 125 killed in collision; 99 killed in another wreck near Friedrichshafen.

1943 **Dec. 16, nr. Rennert, N.C.:** 72 killed in derailment and collision of 2 Atlantic Coast Line trains.

1944 **March 2, nr. Salerno, Italy:** 521 suffocated when Italian train stalled in tunnel.

1949 **Oct. 22, nr. Nowy Dwor, Poland:** more than 200 reported killed in derailment of Danzig-Warsaw express.

1950 **Nov. 22, Richmond Hill, N.Y.:** 79 died when one Long Island Railroad commuter train crashed into rear of another.

1951 **Feb. 6, Woodbridge, N.J.:** 85 died when Pennsylvania Railroad commuter train plunged through temporary overpass.

1952 **Oct. 8, Harrow-Wealdstone, England:** 2 express trains crashed into commuter train; 112 dead.

1957 **Sept. 1, nr. Kendal, Jamaica:** about 175 killed when train plunged into ravine.

Sept. 29, nr. Montgomery, West Pakistan: express train crashed into standing oil train; nearly 300 killed.

Dec. 4, St. John's, England: 92 killed and 187 injured as one commuter train crashed into another in fog.

1960 **Nov. 14, Pardubice, Czechoslovakia:** 2 trains collided; 110 dead, 106 injured.

1962 **May 3, nr. Tokyo:** 163 killed and 400 injured when train crashed into wreckage of collision between inbound freight train and outbound commuter train.

1963 **Nov. 9, nr. Yokohama, Japan:** 2 passenger trains crashed into derailed freight train, killing 162.

1964 **July 26, Custoias, Portugal:** passenger train derailed; 94 dead.

1970 **Feb. 4, nr. Buenos Aires:** 236 killed when express train crashed into standing commuter train.

1972 **Oct. 6, nr. Saltillo, Mexico:** train carrying religious pilgrims derailed and caught fire, killing 204 and injuring over 1,000.

Oct. 30, Chicago: 2 Illinois Central commuter trains collided during morning rush hour; 45 dead and over 200 injured.

1974 **Aug. 30, Zagreb, Yugoslavia:** train entering station derailed, killing 153 and injuring over 60.

1981 **June 6, nr. Mansi, India:** driver of train carrying over 500 passengers braked to avoid hitting a cow, causing train to plunge off a bridge into the Baghmati River; 268 passengers were reported killed, but at least 300 more were missing.

1982 **July 11, Tepic, Mexico:** Nogales-Guadalajara train plunged down mountain gorge, killing 120.

1989 **Jan. 15, Maizdi Khan, Bangladesh:** train carrying Muslim pilgrims crashed head-on with a mail train, killing at least 110 people and injuring as many as 1,000.

June 3, Ural Mountains: gas exploded beneath 2 trains, killing 575.

Aug. 10, nr. Los Mochis, Mexico: a passenger train traveling from Mazatlán to Mexicali plunged off a bridge at Puente del Rio Bamoa, killing an estimated 85 people and injuring 107.

1990 **Jan. 4, Sangi village, Sindh province, Pakistan:** overcrowded 16-car passenger train rammed into a standing freight train. At least 210 people were killed and 700 were believed injured in what is said to be Pakistan's worst train disaster.

1993 **Sept. 22, nr. Mobile, Ala.:** Amtrak's *Sunset Limited*, en route to Miami, jumped rails on weakened bridge and plunged into Big Bayou Canot, killing 47 people.

1995 **Aug. 20, Firozabad, northern India:** a speeding passenger train rammed another train that was stalled, killing 358.

1997 **March 3, Punjab province, Pakistan:** passenger train crashed due to failed brakes, killing 119 and injuring at least 80 people.

1998 **June 3, nr. Eschede, Germany:** Inter City Express passenger train traveling at 125 mph crashed into support pier of overpass, killing 98. It is nation's worst postwar train accident.

1999 **Aug. 2, Calcutta, India:** 2 trains collided north of Calcutta, killing at least 285.

Oct. 5, London: outbound Thames commuter train passed a red signal near Paddington Station and collided with London-bound Great Western express, killing 31 people and injuring 245.

2002 **Feb. 20, nr. Ayyat, Egypt:** 361 killed in fire after gas cylinder used for cooking exploded aboard crowded passenger train. Egypt's worst train disaster.

May 25, Muamba, Mozambique: 192 died and dozens more injured when passenger cars rolled for several miles at top speed into freight cars.

June 24, nr. Msagali, central Tanzania: runaway passenger train collided with freight train on same track, leaving 200 dead.

2004 **Feb. 18, Neishabour, Iran:** runaway rail cars, loaded with fertilizer, petrol, and sulfur products, exploded, killing more than 320 and devastating 5 villages.

April 22, Ryongchon, North Korea: 2 trains carrying flammable liquids collided, causing a huge explosion near the Chinese border, killing at least 161 and injuring more than 1,300.

2005 **Apr. 25, Osaka, Japan:** commuter train derailed and hit an apartment building near Osaka, killing at least 107 and injuring 460. It's the worst Japanese train accident since 1963.

July 13, Ghotki, Pakistan: 3 trains collide near Ghotki. At least 133 are killed.

OIL SPILLS AND DISASTERS

1967 **March 18, Cornwall, Eng.:** *Torrey Canyon* ran aground, spilling 38 million gallons of crude oil off the Scilly Islands.

1976 **Dec. 15, Buzzards Bay, Mass.:** *Argo Merchant* ran aground southeast of Nantucket Island, spilling 7.7 million gallons of fuel oil.

1977 **April, North Sea:** blowout of well in Ekofisk oil field leaked 81 million gallons.

1978 **March 16, off Portsall, France:** wrecked supertanker *Amoco Cadiz* spilled 68 million gallons, causing widespread environmental damage over 100 mi of Brittany coast.

1979 **June 3, Gulf of Mexico:** exploratory oil well Ixtoc 1 blew out, spilling an estimated 140 million gallons of crude oil into the open sea.

Although it is one of the largest known oil spills, it had a low environmental impact.

July 19, Tobago: the *Atlantic Empress* and the *Aegean Captain* collided, spilling 46 million gallons of crude. While being towed, the *Atlantic Empress* spilled an additional 41 million gallons off Barbados on Aug. 2.

1980 **March 30, Stavanger, Norway:** floating hotel in North Sea collapsed, killing 123 oil workers.

1983 **Feb. 4, Persian Gulf, Iran:** Nowruz Field platform spilled 80 million gallons of oil.

Aug. 6, Cape Town, South Africa: the Spanish tanker *Castillo de Bellver* caught fire, spilling 78 million gallons of oil off the coast.

1988 **July 6, North Sea off Scotland:** 166 workers killed in explosion and fire on Occidental Petroleum's *Piper Alpha* rig in North Sea; 64 survivors. It is the world's worst offshore oil disaster.

Nov. 10, Saint John's, Newfoundland : *Odyssey* spilled 43 million gallons of oil.

1989 **March 24, Prince William Sound, Alaska:** tanker *Exxon Valdez* hit an undersea reef and spilled 10 million–plus gallons of oil into the water, causing the worst oil spill in U.S. history.

1991 **Jan. 23–27, southern Kuwait:** during the Persian Gulf War, Iraq deliberately released 240–460 million gallons of crude oil into the Persian Gulf.

1992 **March 2, Fergana Valley, Uzbekistan:** 88 million gallons of oil spilled from an oil well.

SPORTS DISASTERS

1955 **June 11, Le Mans, France:** racing car in Grand Prix hurtled into grandstand, killing 82 spectators.

1964 **May 24, Lima, Peru:** more than 300 soccer fans killed and over 500 injured during riot and panic following unpopular ruling by referee in Peru vs. Argentina soccer game. It is worst soccer disaster on record.

1971 **Jan. 2, Glasgow, Scotland:** 66 killed in crush at Glasgow Rangers home stadium when soccer fans trying to leave encountered fans trying to return to stadium after hearing that a late goal had been scored.

1972 **Sept. 5, Munich, Germany:** Arab terrorists invaded the Olympic village killing 2 Israeli athletes and taking 9 hostage. In shootout, 9 athletes, 5 guerrillas, and 1 policeman killed.

1980 **Jan. 20, Sincelejo, Colombia:** bleachers at a bull-ring collapsed, leaving 222 dead.

1982 **Oct. 20, Moscow:** according to *Sovietsky Sport*, as many as 340 died at Lenin Stadium when exiting soccer fans collided with returning fans after final goal was scored. All the fans had been crowded into one section of stadium by police.

1985 **May 11, Bradford, England:** 56 burned to death and over 200 injured when fire engulfed main grandstand at Bradford's soccer stadium.

May 29, Brussels, Belgium: when British Liverpool club fans attacked rival Italian supporters of Juventus team at the Heysel Stadium before the European Champion's Cup final, a concrete retaining wall collapsed and 39 people were trampled to death. More than 400 people were injured.

1988 **March 12, Katmandu, Nepal:** some 80 soccer fans seeking cover during a violent hail storm at the national stadium were trampled to death in a stampede because the stadium doors were locked.

1989 **April 15, Sheffield, England:** 96 people were killed at Hillsborough stadium during a semifinal match between Liverpool and Nottingham Forest. It is Britain's worst soccer disaster.

1996 **Oct. 16, Guatemala City:** at least 84 killed and 147 injured by stampeding soccer fans before a 1998 World Cup qualifying match between Guatemala and Costa Rica held at Mateo Flores National Stadium.

2001 **May 9, Accra, Ghana:** at least 120 people were killed in a stampede at a soccer match. It was Africa's worst soccer-related disaster.

TERRORIST ATTACKS

(within the United States or against Americans abroad)

1920 **Sept. 16, New York City:** TNT bomb planted in unattended horse-drawn wagon exploded on Wall Street opposite House of Morgan, killing 35 people and injuring hundreds more. Bolshevist or anarchist terrorists believed responsible, but crime never solved.

1975 **Jan. 24, New York City:** bomb set off in historic Fraunces Tavern killed 4 and injured more than 50 people. Puerto Rican nationalist group (FALN) claimed responsibility, and police tied 13 other bombings to the group.

1979 **Nov. 4, Tehran, Iran:** Iranian radical students seized the U.S. embassy, taking 66 hostages. 14 were later released. The remaining 52 were freed after 444 days.

1983 **April 18, Beirut, Lebanon:** U.S. embassy destroyed in suicide car-bomb attack; 63 dead, including 17 Americans.

Oct. 23, Beirut, Lebanon: Shiite suicide bombers exploded truck near U.S. military barracks at Beirut airport, killing 241 Marines. Minutes later a second bomb killed 58 French paratroopers in their barracks in West Beirut.

Dec. 12, Kuwait City, Kuwait: Shiite truck bombers attacked the U.S. embassy and other targets, killing 5 and injuring 80.

1984 **Sept. 20, east Beirut, Lebanon:** truck bomb exploded outside the U.S. embassy annex, killing 24, including 2 U.S. military.

Dec. 3, Beirut, Lebanon: Kuwait Airways Flight 221, from Kuwait to Pakistan, hijacked and diverted to Tehran. 2 Americans killed.

1985 **June 14, Beirut, Lebanon:** TWA Flight 847 en route from Athens to Rome hijacked to Beirut by Hezbollah terrorists and held for 17 days. A U.S. Navy diver executed.

Oct. 7, Mediterranean Sea: gunmen attack Italian cruise ship, *Achille Lauro*. One U.S. tourist killed. Hijacking linked to Libya.

Dec. 18, Rome, Italy, and Vienna, Austria: airports in Rome and Vienna were bombed, killing 20 people, 5 of whom were Americans. Bombing linked to Libya.

1988 **Dec. 21, Lockerbie, Scotland:** N.Y.-bound Pan-Am Boeing 747 exploded in flight from a terrorist bomb and crashed into Scottish village, killing all 259 aboard and 11 on the ground. Passengers included 35 Syracuse University students and many U.S. military personnel. Libya formally admitted responsibility 15 years later (Aug. 2003) and offered $2.7 billion compensation to victims' families.

1993 **Feb. 26, New York City:** bomb exploded in basement garage of World Trade Center, killing 6 and injuring at least 1,040 others. In 1995, militant Islamist Sheik Omar Abdel Rahman and 9 others were convicted of conspiracy charges, and in 1998, Ramzi Yousef, believed to have been the mastermind, was convicted of the bombing. Al-Qaeda involvement is suspected.

1995 April 19, Oklahoma City: car bomb exploded outside federal office building, collapsing wall and floors. 168 people were killed, including 19 children. Over 220 buildings sustained damage. Timothy McVeigh and Terry Nichols later convicted in the antigovernment plot to avenge the Branch Davidian standoff in Waco, Tex., exactly 2 years earlier.

Nov. 13, Riyadh, Saudi Arabia: car bomb exploded at U.S. military headquarters, killing 5 U.S. military servicemen.

1996 June 25, Dhahran, Saudi Arabia: truck bomb exploded outside Khobar Towers military complex, killing 19 American servicemen and injuring hundreds of others.

1998 Aug. 7, Nairobi, Kenya, and Dar es Salaam, Tanzania: truck bombs exploded almost simultaneously near 2 U.S. embassies, killing 224 (213 in Kenya and 11 in Tanzania) and injuring about 4,500. 4 men connected with al-Qaeda were convicted of the killings.

2000 Oct. 12, Aden, Yemen: U.S. Navy destroyer USS *Cole* heavily damaged when a small boat loaded with explosives blew up alongside it. 17 sailors killed. Linked to al-Qaeda terrorist network.

2001 Sept. 11, New York City, Arlington, Va., and Shanksville, Pa.: hijackers crashed 2 commercial jets into twin towers of World Trade Center; 2 more hijacked jets were crashed into the Pentagon and a field in rural Pa. Total dead and missing numbered 2,992: 2,749 in New York City, 184 at the Pentagon, 40 in Pa., and 19 hijackers. Islamic al-Qaeda terrorist group blamed.

2002 June 14, Karachi, Pakistan: bomb exploded outside American consulate in Karachi, Pakistan, killing 12. Linked to al-Qaeda.

2003 May 12, Riyadh, Saudi Arabia: suicide bombers killed 34, including 8 Americans, at housing compounds for Westerners. Al-Qaeda suspected.

2004 Dec. 6, Jeddah, Saudi Arabia: terrorists storm the U.S. consulate killing 5 consulate employees. 4 terrorists were killed by Saudi security.

Suspected al-Qaeda Terrorist Acts

1993 (Feb.): Bombing of World Trade Center (WTC); 6 killed.

1993 (Oct.): Killing of U.S. soldiers in Somalia.

1996 (June): Truck bombing at Khobar Towers barracks in Dhahran, Saudi Arabia, killed 19 Americans.

1998 (Aug.): Bombing of U.S. embassies in Kenya and Tanzania; 224 killed, including 12 Americans.

1999 (Dec.): Plot to bomb millennium celebrations in Seattle foiled when customs agents arrest an Algerian smuggling explosives into the U.S.

2000 (Oct.): Bombing of the USS *Cole* in port in Yemen; 17 U.S. sailors killed.

2001 (Sept.): Destruction of WTC; attack on Pentagon. Total dead 2,992.

2002 (April): Explosion at historic synagogue in Tunisia left 21 dead, including 14 German tourists.

2002 (May): Car exploded outside hotel in Karachi, Pakistan, killing 14.

2002 (June): Bomb exploded outside American consulate in Karachi, Pakistan, killing 12.

2002 (Oct.): Boat crashed into oil tanker off Yemen coast, killing 1.

2002 (Oct.): Nightclub bombings in Bali, Indonesia, killed 202, mostly Australian citizens.

2002 (Nov.): Suicide attack on a hotel in Mombasa, Kenya, killed 16.

2003 (May): Suicide bombers killed 34, including 8 Americans, at housing compounds for Westerners in Riyadh, Saudi Arabia.

2003 (May): 4 bombs killed 33 people in Casablanca, Morocco.

2003 (Aug.): Suicide car-bomb killed 12, injured 150 at Marriott Hotel in Jakarta, Indonesia.

2003 (Nov.): Explosions rocked a Riyadh, Saudi Arabia housing compound, killing 17.

2003 (Nov.): Suicide car-bombers simultaneously attacked 2 synagogues in Istanbul, Turkey, killing 25 and injuring hundreds.

2003 (Nov.): Truck bombs detonated at London bank and British consulate in Istanbul, Turkey, killing 26.

2004 (March): 10 bombs on 4 trains exploded almost simultaneously during the morning rush hour in Madrid, Spain, killing 202 and injuring more than 1,400.

2004 (May): Terrorists attacked Saudi oil company offices in Khobar, Saudi Arabia, killing 22.

2004 (Sept.): Car bomb outside the Australian embassy in Jakarta, Indonesia, killed 9.

2004 (Dec.): Terrorists entered the U.S. Consulate in Jeddah, Saudi Arabia, killing 9 (including 4 attackers).

2005 (July): Bombs exploded on 3 trains and a bus in London, England, killing 52.

MISCELLANEOUS DISASTERS

1981 July 18, Kansas City, Mo.: suspended walkway in Hyatt Regency Hotel collapsed; 113 dead, 186 injured.

1990 July 2, Mecca, Saudi Arabia: a stampede in a 1,800-foot-long pedestrian tunnel resulted in the deaths of 1,426 pilgrims.

1995 June 29, Seoul, Korea: five-story wing of Sampoong Department Store collapsed, killing at least 206 people, injuring 910 others.

2005 Aug. 31, Baghdad, Iraq: rumor of a bomber led to a stampede of Shiite pilgrims on a bridge over the Tigris, killing more than 950.

Nobel Prizes

(For years not listed, no award was made. For 2005 prizes, *see* www.infoplease.com/nobelprizes.)

PEACE

1901 Henri Dunant (Switzerland); Frederick Passy (France)
1902 Elie Ducommun and Albert Gobat (Switzerland)
1903 Sir William R. Cremer (UK)
1904 Institut de Droit International (Belgium)
1905 Bertha von Suttner (Austria)
1906 Theodore Roosevelt (U.S.)
1907 Ernesto T. Moneta (Italy) and Louis Renault (France)
1908 Klas P. Arnoldson (Sweden) and Frederik Bajer (Denmark)
1909 Auguste M. F. Beernaert (Belgium) and Baron Paul H.B.B. d'Estournelles de Constant de Rebecque (France)
1910 Bureau International Permanent de la Paix (Switzerland)
1911 Tobias M. C. Asser (Holland) and Alfred H. Fried (Austria)
1912 Elihu Root (U.S.)
1913 Henri La Fontaine (Belgium)
1917 International Red Cross
1919 Woodrow Wilson (U.S.)
1920 Léon Bourgeois (France)
1921 Karl H. Branting (Sweden) and Christian L. Lange (Norway)
1922 Fridtjof Nansen (Norway)
1925 Sir Austen Chamberlain (UK) and Charles G. Dawes (U.S.)
1926 Aristide Briand (France) and Gustav Stresemann (Germany)
1927 Ferdinand Buisson (France) and Ludwig Quidde (Germany)
1929 Frank B. Kellogg (U.S.)
1930 Lars O. J. Söderblom (Sweden)
1931 Jane Addams and Nicholas M. Butler (U.S.)
1933 Sir Norman Angell (UK)
1934 Arthur Henderson (UK)
1935 Karl von Ossietzky (Germany)
1936 Carlos de S. Lamas (Argentina)
1937 Lord Cecil of Chelwood (UK)
1938 Office International Nansen pour les Réfugiés (Switzerland)
1944 International Red Cross
1945 Cordell Hull (U.S.)
1946 Emily G. Balch and John R. Mott (U.S.)
1947 American Friends Service Committee (U.S.) and British Society of Friends' Service Council (UK)
1949 Lord John Boyd Orr (Scotland)
1950 Ralph J. Bunche (U.S.)
1951 Léon Jouhaux (France)
1952 Albert Schweitzer (French Equatorial Africa)
1953 George C. Marshall (U.S.)
1954 Office of the UN High Commissioner for Refugees
1957 Lester B. Pearson (Canada)
1958 Rev. Dominique Georges Henri Pire (Belgium)
1959 Philip John Noel-Baker (UK)
1960 Albert John Luthuli (South Africa)
1961 Dag Hammarskjöld (Sweden)
1962 Linus Pauling (U.S.)
1963 Intl. Comm. of Red Cross; League of Red Cross Societies (both Switzerland)
1964 Rev. Dr. Martin Luther King, Jr. (U.S.)
1965 UNICEF (United Nations Children's Fund)
1968 René Cassin (France)
1969 International Labour Organization
1970 Norman E. Borlaug (U.S.)
1971 Willy Brandt (West Germany)
1973 Henry A. Kissinger (U.S.); Le Duc Tho (North Vietnam)[1]
1974 Eisaku Sato (Japan); Sean MacBride (Ireland)
1975 Andrei D. Sakharov (USSR)
1976 Mairead Corrigan and Betty Williams (both Northern Ireland)
1977 Amnesty International
1978 Menachem Begin (Israel) and Anwar el-Sadat (Egypt)
1979 Mother Teresa of Calcutta (India)
1980 Adolfo Pérez Esquivel (Argentina)
1981 Office of the UN High Commissioner for Refugees
1982 Alva Myrdal (Sweden) and Alfonso García Robles (Mexico)
1983 Lech Walesa (Poland)
1984 Bishop Desmond Tutu (South Africa)
1985 International Physicians for the Prevention of Nuclear War
1986 Elie Wiesel (U.S.)
1987 Oscar Arias Sánchez (Costa Rica)
1988 UN Peacekeeping Forces
1989 Dalai Lama (Tibet)
1990 Mikhail S. Gorbachev (USSR)
1991 Daw Aung San Suu Kyi (Burma)
1992 Rigoberta Menchú (Guatemala)
1993 F. W. de Klerk and Nelson Mandela (both South Africa)
1994 Yasir Arafat (Palestine), Shimon Peres, and Yitzhak Rabin (both Israel)
1995 Joseph Rotblat and Pugwash Conference on Science and World Affairs (UK)
1996 Carlos Filipe Ximenes Belo and José Ramos-Horta (East Timor)
1997 International Campaign to Ban Landmines, and Jody Williams (U.S.)
1998 John Hume and David Trimble (both Northern Ireland)
1999 Doctors Without Borders (France)
2000 Kim Dae Jung (South Korea)
2001 United Nations and Kofi Annan
2002 Jimmy Carter (U.S.)
2003 Shirin Ebadi (Iran)
2004 Wangari Maathai (Kenya)

1. Le Duc Tho refused prize, charging that peace had not yet really been established in South Vietnam.

LITERATURE

1901 René F. A. Sully Prudhomme (France)
1902 Theodor Mommsen (Germany)
1903 Björnstjerne Björnson (Norway)
1904 Frédéric Mistral (France) and José Echegaray (Spain)
1905 Henryk Sienkiewicz (Poland)
1906 Giosuè Carducci (Italy)
1907 Rudyard Kipling (UK)
1908 Rudolf Eucken (Germany)
1909 Selma Lagerlöf (Sweden)
1910 Paul von Heyse (Germany)
1911 Maurice Maeterlinck (Belgium)
1912 Gerhart Hauptmann (Germany)
1913 Rabindranath Tagore (India)
1915 Romain Rolland (France)
1916 Verner von Heidenstam (Sweden)
1917 Karl Gjellerup and Henrik Pontoppidan (both Denmark)
1919 Carl Spitteler (Switzerland)
1920 Knut Hamsun (Norway)
1921 Anatole France (France)
1922 Jacinto Benavente (Spain)
1923 William B. Yeats (Ireland)
1924 Wladyslaw Reymont (Poland)
1925 George Bernard Shaw (Ireland)
1926 Grazia Deledda (Italy)
1927 Henri Bergson (France)
1928 Sigrid Undset (Norway)
1929 Thomas Mann (Germany)
1930 Sinclair Lewis (U.S.)
1931 Erik A. Karlfeldt (Sweden)
1932 John Galsworthy (UK)
1933 Ivan G. Bunin (Russia)
1934 Luigi Pirandello (Italy)
1936 Eugene O'Neill (U.S.)
1937 Roger Martin du Gard (France)
1938 Pearl S. Buck (U.S.)
1939 Frans Eemil Sillanpää (Finland)
1944 Johannes V. Jensen (Denmark)
1945 Gabriela Mistral (Chile)
1946 Hermann Hesse (Switzerland)
1947 André Gide (France)
1948 Thomas Stearns Eliot (UK)
1949 William Faulkner (U.S.)
1950 Bertrand Russell (UK)
1951 Pär Lagerkvist (Sweden)
1952 François Mauriac (France)
1953 Sir Winston Churchill (UK)
1954 Ernest Hemingway (U.S.)
1955 Halldór Kiljan Laxness (Iceland)
1956 Juan Ramón Jiménez (Spain)
1957 Albert Camus (France)
1958 Boris Pasternak (USSR) (declined)
1959 Salvatore Quasimodo (Italy)
1960 St. John Perse (Alexis Léger) (France)
1961 Ivo Andric (Yugoslavia)
1962 John Steinbeck (U.S.)
1963 Giorgios Seferis (Seferiades) (Greece)
1964 Jean-Paul Sartre (France) (declined)
1965 Mikhail Sholokhov (USSR)
1966 Shmuel Yosef Agnon (Israel) and Nelly Sachs (Sweden)
1967 Miguel Angel Asturias (Guatemala)
1968 Yasunari Kawabata (Japan)
1969 Samuel Beckett (Ireland)
1970 Aleksandr Solzhenitsyn (USSR)
1971 Pablo Neruda (Chile)
1972 Heinrich Böll (West Germany)
1973 Patrick White (Australia)
1974 Eyvind Johnson and Harry Martinson (both Sweden)
1975 Eugenio Montale (Italy)
1976 Saul Bellow (U.S.)
1977 Vicente Aleixandre (Spain)
1978 Isaac Bashevis Singer (U.S.)
1979 Odysseus Elytis (Greece)
1980 Czeslaw Milosz (U.S.)
1981 Elias Canetti (Bulgaria)
1982 Gabriel García Márquez (Colombia)
1983 William Golding (UK)
1984 Jaroslav Seifert (Czechoslovakia)
1985 Claude Simon (France)
1986 Wole Soyinka (Nigeria)
1987 Joseph Brodsky (U.S.)
1988 Naguib Mahfouz (Egypt)
1989 Camilo José Cela (Spain)
1990 Octavio Paz (Mexico)
1991 Nadine Gordimer (South Africa)
1992 Derek Walcott (St. Lucia)
1993 Toni Morrison (U.S.)
1994 Kenzaburo Oe (Japan)
1995 Seamus Heaney (Ireland)
1996 Wislawa Szymborska (Poland)
1997 Dario Fo (Italy)
1998 José Saramago (Portugal)
1999 Günter Grass (Germany)
2000 Gao Xingjian (China)
2001 V. S. Naipaul (UK)
2002 Imre Kertész (Hungary)
2003 J. M. Coetzee (South Africa)
2004 Elfriede Jelinek (Austria)

PHYSICS

1901 Wilhelm K. Roentgen (Germany), for discovery of Roentgen rays
1902 Hendrik A. Lorentz and Pieter Zeeman (Netherlands), for work on influence of magnetism upon radiation
1903 A. Henri Becquerel (France), for work on spontaneous radioactivity; and Pierre and Marie Curie (France), for study of radiation
1904 John Strutt (Lord Rayleigh) (UK), for discovery of argon in investigating gas density
1905 Philipp Lenard (Germany), for work with cathode rays
1906 Sir Joseph Thomson (UK), for investigations on passage of electricity through gases
1907 Albert A. Michelson (U.S.), for spectroscopic and metrologic investigations
1908 Gabriel Lippmann (France), for method of reproducing colors by photography
1909 Guglielmo Marconi (Italy) and Ferdinand Braun (Germany), for development of wireless
1910 Johannes D. van der Waals (Netherlands), for work with the equation of state for gases and liquids
1911 Wilhelm Wien (Germany), for his laws governing the radiation of heat
1912 Gustaf Dalén (Sweden), for discovery of automatic regulators used in lighting lighthouses and light buoys
1913 Heike Kamerlingh-Onnes (Netherlands), for work leading to production of liquid helium
1914 Max von Laue (Germany), for discovery of diffraction of Roentgen rays passing through crystals
1915 Sir William Bragg and William L. Bragg (both UK), for analysis of crystal structure by X-rays

1917 Charles G. Barkla (UK), for discovery of Roentgen radiation of the elements

1918 Max Planck (Germany), for discoveries in connection with quantum theory

1919 Johannes Stark (Germany), for discovery of Doppler effect in Canal rays and decomposition of spectrum lines by electric fields

1920 Charles E. Guillaume (Switzerland), for discoveries of anomalies in nickel-steel alloys

1921 Albert Einstein (Germany), for discovery of the law of photoelectric effect

1922 Niels Bohr (Denmark), for investigation of structure of atoms and radiations emanating from them

1923 Robert A. Millikan (U.S.), for work on elementary charge of electricity and photoelectric phenomena

1924 Karl M. G. Siegbahn (Sweden), for investigations in X-ray spectroscopy

1925 James Franck and Gustav Hertz (Germany), for discovery of laws governing impact of electrons upon atoms

1926 Jean B. Perrin (France), for work on discontinuous structure of matter and discovery of the equilibrium of sedimentation

1927 Arthur H. Compton (U.S.), for discovery of Compton phenomenon; and Charles T. R. Wilson (UK), for method of perceiving paths taken by electrically charged particles

1928 In 1929, the 1928 prize was awarded to Sir Owen Richardson (UK), for work on the phenomenon of thermionics and discovery of the Richardson Law

1929 Prince Louis Victor de Broglie (France), for discovery of the wave character of electrons

1930 Sir Chandrasekhara Raman (India), for work on diffusion of light and discovery of the Raman effect

1932 In 1933, the prize for 1932 was awarded to Werner Heisenberg (Germany), for creation of quantum mechanics

1933 Erwin Schrödinger (Austria) and Paul A. M. Dirac (UK), for discovery of new fertile forms of the atomic theory

1935 James Chadwick (UK), for discovery of the neutron

1936 Victor F. Hess (Austria), for discovery of cosmic radiation; and Carl D. Anderson (U.S.), for discovery of the positron

1937 Clinton J. Davisson (U.S.) and George P. Thomson (UK), for discovery of diffraction of electrons by crystals

1938 Enrico Fermi (Italy), for identification of new radioactive elements and discovery of nuclear reactions effected by slow neutrons

1939 Ernest Orlando Lawrence (U.S.), for development of the cyclotron

1943 Otto Stern (U.S.), for detection of magnetic momentum of protons

1944 Isidor Isaac Rabi (U.S.), for work on magnetic movements of atomic particles

1945 Wolfgang Pauli (Austria), for work on atomic fissions

1946 Percy Williams Bridgman (U.S.), for studies and inventions in high-pressure physics

1947 Sir Edward Appleton (UK), for discovery of layer that reflects radio short waves in the ionosphere

1948 Patrick M. S. Blackett (UK), for improvement on Wilson chamber and discoveries in cosmic radiation

1949 Hideki Yukawa (Japan), for mathematical prediction, in 1935, of the meson

1950 Cecil Frank Powell (UK), for method of photographic study of atom nucleus, and for discoveries about mesons

1951 Sir John Douglas Cockcroft (UK) and Ernest T. S. Walton (Ireland), for work in 1932 on transmutation of atomic nuclei

1952 Edward Mills Purcell and Felix Bloch (U.S.), for work in measurement of magnetic fields in atomic nuclei

1953 Fritz Zernike (Netherlands), for development of "phase contrast" microscope

1954 Max Born (UK), for work in quantum mechanics; Walther Bothe (West Germany), for work in cosmic radiation

1955 Polykarp Kusch and Willis E. Lamb, Jr. (both U.S.), for atomic measurements

1956 William Shockley, Walter H. Brattain, and John Bardeen (all U.S.), for developing electronic transistor

1957 Tsung Dao Lee and Chen Ning Yang (both China), for disproving principle of conservation of parity

1958 Pavel A. Cherenkov, Ilya M. Frank, and Igor E. Tamm (all USSR), for work resulting in development of cosmic-ray counter

1959 Emilio Segre and Owen Chamberlain (both U.S.), for demonstrating the existence of the anti-proton

1960 Donald A. Glaser (U.S.), for invention of "bubble chamber" to study subatomic particles

1961 Robert Hofstadter (U.S.), for determination of shape and size of atomic nucleus; Rudolf Mössbauer (West Germany), for method of producing and measuring recoil-free gamma rays

1962 Lev D. Landau (USSR), for his theories about condensed matter

1963 Eugene Paul Wigner, Maria Goeppert Mayer (both U.S.), and J. Hans D. Jensen (West Germany), for research on structure of atom and its nucleus

1964 Charles Hard Townes (U.S.), Nikolai G. Basov, and Aleksandr M. Prochorov (both USSR), for developing maser and laser principle of producing high-intensity radiation

1965 Richard P. Feynman, Julian S. Schwinger (both U.S.), and Shinichiro Tomonaga (Japan), for research in quantum electrodynamics

1966 Alfred Kastler (France), for work on energy levels inside atom

1967 Hans A. Bethe (U.S.), for work on energy production of stars

1968 Luis Walter Alvarez (U.S.), for study of subatomic particles

1969 Murray Gell-Mann (U.S.), for study of subatomic particles

1970 Hannes Alfvén (Sweden), for theories in plasma physics; Louis Néel (France), for discoveries in antiferromagnetism and ferromagnetism

1971 Dennis Gabor (UK), for invention of holographic method of three-dimensional imagery

1972 John Bardeen, Leon N. Cooper, and John Robert Schrieffer (all U.S.), for theory of superconductivity, where electrical resistance in certain metals vanishes above absolute zero temperature

1973 Ivar Giaever (U.S.), Leo Esaki (Japan), and Brian D. Josephson (UK), for theories that have advanced and expanded the field of miniature electronics

1974 Antony Hewish (UK), for discovery of pulsars; Martin Ryle (UK), for using radiotelescopes to probe outer space with precision

1975 James Rainwater (U.S.), Ben Mottelson, and Aage N. Bohr (both Denmark), for showing that the atomic nucleus is asymmetrical

1976 Burton Richter and Samuel C. C. Ting (both U.S.), for discovery of subatomic particles known as J and psi

1977 Philip W. Anderson, John H. Van Vleck (both U.S.), and Nevill F. Mott (UK), for work underlying computer memories and electronic devices

1978 Arno A. Penzias and Robert W. Wilson (both U.S.), for work in cosmic microwave radiation; Piotr L. Kapitsa (USSR), for basic inventions and discoveries in low-temperature physics

1979 Steven Weinberg, Sheldon L. Glashow (both U.S.), and Abdus Salam (Pakistan), for developing theory that electromagnetism and the "weak" force, which causes radioactive decay in some atomic nuclei, are facets of the same phenomenon

1980 James W. Cronin and Val L. Fitch (both U.S.), for work concerning the asymmetry of subatomic particles

1981 Nicolaas Bloembergen, Arthur L. Schawlow (both U.S.), and Kai M. Siegbahn (Sweden), for developing technologies with lasers and other devices to probe the secrets of complex forms of matter

1982 Kenneth G. Wilson (U.S.), for analysis of changes in matter under pressure and temperature

1983 Subrahmanyam Chandrasekhar and William A. Fowler (both U.S.), for complementary research on processes involved in the evolution of stars

1984 Carlo Rubbia (Italy) and Simon van der Meer (Netherlands), for their role in discovering three subatomic particles, a step toward developing a single theory to account for all natural forces

1985 Klaus von Klitzing (West Germany), for developing an exact way of measuring electrical conductivity

1986 Ernst Ruska, Gerd Binnig (both West Germany), and Heinrich Rohrer (Switzerland), for work on microscopes

1987 K. Alex Müller (Switzerland) and J. Georg Bednorz (West Germany), for their discovery of high-temperature superconductors

1988 Leon M. Lederman, Melvin Schwartz, and Jack Steinberger (all U.S.), for research that improved the understanding of elementary particles and forces

1989 Norman F. Ramsey (U.S.), for work leading to development of the atomic clock; Hans G. Dehmelt (U.S.) and Wolfgang Paul (West Germany), for developing methods to isolate atoms and subatomic particles

1990 Richard E. Taylor (Canada), Jerome I. Friedman, and Dr. Henry W. Kendall (both U.S.), for their "breakthrough in our understanding of matter" that confirmed the reality of quarks

1991 Pierre-Gilles de Gennes (France), for his discoveries about the ordering of molecules in substances ranging from "super" glue to an exotic form of liquid helium

1992 George Charpak (France), for his inventions of particle detectors

1993 Joseph H. Taylor and Russell A. Hulse (both U.S.), for their discovery of a binary pulsar

1994 Clifford G. Shull (U.S.) and Bertram N. Brockhouse (Canada), for adapting beams of neutrons as probes to explore the atomic structure of matter

1995 Martin L. Perl and Frederick Reines (both U.S.), for their discoveries of "two of nature's most remarkable subatomic particles"—the tau and the neutrino

1996 David M. Lee, Robert C. Richardson, and Douglas D. Osheroff (all U.S.), for their discovery of superfluity in helium-3

1997 Steven Chu, William D. Phillips (both U.S.), and Claude Cohen-Tannoudji (France), for developing a method to cool and trap atoms using light from lasers

1998 Robert B. Laughlin (U.S.), Horst L. Störmer (Germany), and Daniel C. Tsui (U.S.), for their discovery of a new form of quantum fluid with fractionally charged excitations

1999 Gerardus 't Hooft (Netherlands) and Martinus J. G. Veltman (Netherlands), for their theory concerning the production of the Sun's energy

2000 Zhores I. Alferov (Russia), Herbert Kroemer, and Jack S. Kilby (both U.S.), for work in the development of transistors and microchip technology

2001 Wolfgang Ketterle (Germany), Eric A. Cornell, and Carl E. Wieman (both U.S.), for discovering Bose-Einstein condensate, a new state of matter

2002 Raymond Davis, Jr. (U.S.), and Masatoshi Koshiba (Japan), for the detection of cosmic neutrinos; Riccardo Giacconi (U.S.), for contributions to astrophysics, which have led to the discovery of cosmic X-ray sources

2003 Alexei A. Abrikosov (Russia, U.S.), Anthony J. Leggett (UK, U.S.), and Vitaly L. Ginzburg (Russia), for theories about superconductivity

2004 David J. Gross, H. David Politzer, and Frank Wilczek (all U.S.), "for the discovery of asymptotic freedom in the theory of the strong interaction"

CHEMISTRY

1901 Jacobus H. van't Hoff (Netherlands), for laws of chemical dynamics and osmotic pressure in solutions

1902 Emil Fischer (Germany), for experiments in sugar and purin groups of substances

1903 Svante A. Arrhenius (Sweden), for his electrolytic theory of dissociation

1904 Sir William Ramsay (UK), for discovery and determination of place of inert gaseous elements in air

1905 Adolf von Baeyer (Germany), for work on organic dyes and hydroaromatic combinations

1906 Henri Moissan (France), for isolation of fluorine and introduction of electric furnace

1907 Eduard Buchner (Germany), discovery of cell-less fermentation and investigations in biological chemistry

1908 Sir Ernest Rutherford (UK), for investigations into disintegration of elements

1909 Wilhelm Ostwald (Germany), for work on catalysis and investigations into chemical equilibrium and reaction rates

1910 Otto Wallach (Germany), for work in the field of alicyclic compounds

1911 Marie Curie (France), for discovery of the elements radium and polonium

1912 Victor Grignard (France), for reagent discovered by him; Paul Sabatier (France), for methods of hydrogenating organic compounds

1913 Alfred Werner (Switzerland), for linking up atoms within the molecule

1914 Theodore W. Richards (U.S.), for determining atomic weight of many chemical elements

1915 Richard Willstätter (Germany), for research into coloring matter of plants, especially chlorophyll

1918 Fritz Haber (Germany), for synthetic production of ammonia

1920 Walther Nernst (Germany), for work in thermochemistry

1921 Frederick Soddy (UK), for investigations into origin and nature of isotopes

1922 Francis W. Aston (UK), for discovery of isotopes in nonradioactive elements and for discovery of the whole-number rule

1923 Fritz Pregl (Austria), for method of microanalysis of organic substances discovered by him

1925 In 1926, the 1925 prize was awarded to Richard Zsigmondy (Germany), for work on the heterogeneous nature of colloid solutions

1926 Theodor Svedberg (Sweden), for work on disperse systems

1927 In 1928, the 1927 prize was awarded to Heinrich Wieland (Germany), for investigations of bile acids and kindred substances

1928 Adolf Windaus (Germany), for investigations on constitution of the sterols and their connection with vitamins

1929 Sir Arthur Harden (UK) and Hans K.A.S. von Euler-Chelpin (Sweden), for research on fermentation of sugars

1930 Hans Fischer (Germany), for work on coloring matter of blood and leaves and for his synthesis of hemin

1931 Karl Bosch and Friedrich Bergius (both Germany), for invention and development of chemical high-pressure methods

1932 Irving Langmuir (U.S.), for work in realm of surface chemistry

1934 Harold C. Urey (U.S.), for discovery of heavy hydrogen

1935 Frédéric and Irène Joliot-Curie (both France), for synthesis of new radioactive elements

1936 Peter J. W. Debye (Netherlands), for investigations on dipole moments and diffraction of X-rays and electrons in gases

1937 Walter N. Haworth (UK), for research on carbohydrates and vitamin C; Paul Karrer (Switzerland), for work on carotenoids, flavins, and vitamins A and B

1938 Richard Kuhn (Germany), for carotenoid study and vitamin research (declined)

1939 Adolf Butenandt (Germany), for work on sexual hormones (declined prize); Leopold Ruzicka (Switzerland), for work with polymethylenes

1943 Georg Hevesy De Heves (Hungary), for work on use of isotopes as indicators

1944 Otto Hahn (Germany), for work on atomic fission

1945 Artturi Illmari Virtanen (Finland), for research in the field of conservation of fodder

1946 James B. Sumner (U.S.), for crystallizing enzymes; John H. Northrop and Wendell M. Stanley (both U.S.), for preparing enzymes and virus proteins in pure form

1947 Sir Robert Robinson (UK), for research in plant substances

1948 Arne Tiselius (Sweden), for biochemical discoveries and isolation of mouse paralysis virus

1949 William Francis Giauque (U.S.), for research in thermodynamics, especially effects of low temperature

1950 Otto Diels and Kurt Alder (both West Germany), for discovery of diene synthesis, enabling scientists to study structure of organic matter

1951 Glenn T. Seaborg and Edwin H. McMillan (both U.S.), for discovery of plutonium

1952 Archer John Porter Martin and Richard Laurence Millington Synge (both UK), for development of partition chromatography

1953 Hermann Staudinger (West Germany), for research in giant molecules

1954 Linus C. Pauling (U.S.), for study of forces holding together protein and other molecules

1955 Vincent du Vigneaud (U.S.), for work on pituitary hormones

1956 Sir Cyril Hinshelwood (UK) and Nikolai N. Semenov (USSR), for parallel research on chemical reaction kinetics

1957 Sir Alexander Todd (UK), for research with chemical compounds that are factors in heredity

1958 Frederick Sanger (UK), for determining molecular structure of insulin

1959 Jaroslav Heyrovsky (Czechoslovakia), for development of polarography, an electrochemical method of analysis

1960 Willard F. Libby (U.S.), for "atomic time clock" to measure age of objects by measuring their radioactivity

1961 Melvin Calvin (U.S.), for establishing chemical steps during photosynthesis

1962 Max F. Perutz and John C. Kendrew (both UK), for mapping protein molecules with X-rays

1963 Karl Ziegler (West Germany) and Giulio Natta (Italy), for work in uniting simple hydrocarbons into large molecular substances

1964 Dorothy Mary Crowfoot Hodgkin (UK), for determining structure of compounds needed in combatting pernicious anemia

1965 Robert B. Woodward (U.S.), for work in synthesizing complicated organic compounds

1966 Robert Sanderson Mulliken (U.S.), for research on bond holding atoms together in molecule

1967 Manfred Eigen (West Germany), Ronald G. W. Norrish, and George Porter (both UK), for work in high-speed chemical reactions

1968 Lars Onsager (U.S.), for development of system of equations in thermodynamics

1969 Derek H. R. Barton (UK) and Odd Hassel (Norway), for study of organic molecules

1970 Luis F. Leloir (Argentina), for discovery of sugar nucleotides and their role in biosynthesis of carbohydrates

1971 Gerhard Herzberg (Canada), for contributions to knowledge of electronic structure and geometry of molecules, particularly free radicals

1972 Christian Boehmer Anfinsen, Stanford Moore, and William Howard Stein (all U.S.), for pioneering studies in enzymes

1973 Ernst Otto Fischer (West Germany) and Geoffrey Wilkinson (UK), for work that could solve problem of automobile exhaust pollution

1974 Paul J. Flory (U.S.), for developing analytic methods to study properties and molecular structure of long-chain molecules

1975 John W. Cornforth (Australia) and Vladimir Prelog (Switzerland), for research on structure of biological molecules such as antibiotics and cholesterol

1976 William N. Lipscomb, Jr. (U.S.), for work on the structure and bonding mechanisms of boranes

1977 Ilya Prigogine (Belgium), for contributions to nonequilibrium thermodynamics, particularly the theory of dissipative structures

1978 Peter Mitchell (UK), for contributions to the understanding of biological energy transfer

1979 Herbert C. Brown (U.S.) and Georg Wittig (West Germany), for developing a group of substances that facilitate very difficult chemical reactions

1980 Paul Berg, Walter Gilbert (both U.S.), and Frederick Sanger (UK), for developing methods to map the structure and function of DNA, the substance that controls the activity of the cell

1981 Roald Hoffmann (U.S.) and Kenichi Fukui (Japan), for applying quantum-mechanics theories to predict the course of chemical reactions

1982 Aaron Klug (UK), for research in the detailed structures of viruses and components of life

1983 Henry Taube (U.S.), for research on how electrons transfer between molecules in chemical reactions

1984 R. Bruce Merrifield (U.S.), for research that revolutionized the study of proteins

1985 Herbert A. Hauptman and Jerome Karle (both U.S.), for their outstanding achievements in the development of direct methods for the determination of crystal structures

1986 Dudley R. Herschback, Yuan T. Lee (both U.S.), and John C. Polanyi (Canada), for their work on "reaction dynamics"

1987 Donald J. Cram, Charles J. Pedersen (both U.S.), and Jean-Marie Lehn (France), for wide-ranging research that has included the creation of artificial molecules that can mimic vital chemical reactions of the processes of life

1988 Johann Deisenhofer, Robert Huber, and Hartmut Michel (all West Germany), for unraveling the structure of proteins that play a crucial role in photosynthesis

1989 Thomas R. Cech and Sidney Altman (both U.S.), for their discovery, independently, that RNA could actively aid chemical reactions in the cells

1990 Elias James Corey (U.S.), for developing new ways to synthesize complex molecules ordinarily found in nature

1991 Richard R. Ernst (Switzerland), for refinements he developed in nuclear magnetic-resonance spectroscopy

1992 Rudolph A. Marcus (U.S.), for his mathematical analysis of how the overall energy in a system of interacting molecules changes and induces an electron to jump from one molecule to another

1993 Kary B. Mullis (U.S.) and Michael Smith (Canada), for their contributions to the science of genetics

1994 George A. Olah (U.S.), for research that opened new ways to break apart and rebuild compounds of carbon and hydrogen

1995 F. Sherwood Rowland, Mario Molina (both U.S.), and Paul Crutzen (Netherlands), for their pioneering work in explaining the chemical processes that deplete the Earth's ozone shield

1996 Richard E. Smalley, Robert F. Curl, Jr. (both U.S.), and Harold W. Kroto (UK), for discovery of a new class of carbon molecule

1997 Paul D. Boyer (U.S.), Jens C. Skou (Denmark), and John E. Walker (UK), for discoveries about a molecule that allows the human body to store and transfer energy between cells

1998 Walter Kohn (U.S.) and John A. Pople (UK), for their developments in the study of the properties of molecules and the chemical processes in which they are involved

1999 Ahmed H. Zewail (Egypt and U.S.), for creating the world's fastest camera, which captures atoms in motion

2000 Alan J. Heeger, Alan G. MacDiarmid (both U.S.), and Hideki Shirakawa (Japan), for the discovery and development of conductive polymers

2001 William S. Knowles (U.S.) and Ryoji Noyori (Japan), for their work on chirally catalyzed hydrogenation reactions, and K. Barry Sharpless (U.S.), for his work on chirally catalyzed oxidation reactions

2002 John B. Fenn (U.S.) and Koichi Tanaka (Japan), for development of methods for analyses of biological macromolecules; Kurt Wüthrich (Switzerland), for determining the three-dimensional structure of biological macromolecules in solution

2003 Peter Agre and Roderick MacKinnon (both U.S.), for studies of channels in cell walls

2004 Aaron Ciechanover (Israel), Avram Hershko (Israel), and Irwin Rose (U.S.), "for the discovery of ubiquitin-mediated protein degradation"

PHYSIOLOGY OR MEDICINE

1901 Emil A. von Behring (Germany), for work on serum therapy against diphtheria

1902 Sir Ronald Ross (UK), for work on malaria

1903 Niels R. Finsen (Denmark), for his treatment of lupus vulgaris with concentrated light rays

1904 Ivan P. Pavlov (USSR), for work on the physiology of digestion

1905 Robert Koch (Germany), for work on tuberculosis

1906 Camillo Golgi (Italy) and Santiago Ramón y Cajal (Spain), for study of structure of the nervous system

1907 Charles L. A. Laveran (France), for work with protozoa in the generation of disease

1908 Paul Ehrlich (Germany) and Elie Metchnikoff (USSR), for work on immunity

1909 Theodor Kocher (Switzerland), for work on the thyroid gland

1910 Albrecht Kossel (Germany), for achievements in the chemistry of the cell

1911 Allvar Gullstrand (Sweden), for work on the dioptrics of the eye

1912 Alexis Carrel (France), for work on vascular ligature and grafting of blood vessels and organs

1913 Charles Richet (France), for work on anaphylaxy

1914 Robert Bárány (Austria), for work on physiology and pathology of the vestibular system

1919 Jules Bordet (Belgium), for discoveries in connection with immunity

1920 August Krogh (Denmark), for discovery of regulation of capillaries' motor mechanism

1922 In 1923, the 1922 prize was shared by Archibald V. Hill (UK), for discovery relating to heat-production in muscles, and Otto Meyerhof (Germany), for correlation between consumption of oxygen and production of lactic acid in muscles

1923 Sir Frederick Banting (Canada) and John J. R. Macleod (Scotland), for discovery of insulin

1924 Willem Einthoven (Netherlands), for discovery of the mechanism of the electrocardiogram

1926 Johannes Fibiger (Denmark), for discovery of the Spiroptera carcinoma

1927 Julius Wagner-Jauregg (Austria), for use of malaria inoculation in treatment of dementia paralytica

1928 Charles Nicolle (France), for work on typhus exanthematicus

1929 Christiaan Eijkman (Netherlands), for discovery of the antineuritic vitamins; Sir Frederick Hopkins (UK), for discovery of growth-promoting vitamins

1930 Karl Landsteiner (U.S.), for discovery of human blood groups

1931 Otto H. Warburg (Germany), for discovery of the character and mode of action of the respiratory ferment

1932 Sir Charles Sherrington (UK) and Edgar D. Adrian (U.S.), for discoveries of the function of the neuron

1933 Thomas H. Morgan (U.S.), for discoveries on hereditary function of the chromosomes

1934 George H. Whipple, George R. Minot, and William P. Murphy (all U.S.), for discovery of liver therapy against anemias

1935 Hans Spemann (Germany), for discovery of the organizer effect in embryonic development

1936 Sir Henry Dale (UK) and Otto Loewi (Germany), for discoveries on chemical transmission of nerve impulses

1937 Albert Szent-Györgyi von Nagyrapolt (Hungary), for discoveries on biological combustion

1938 Corneille Heymans (Belgium), for determining importance of sinus and aorta mechanisms in the regulation of respiration

1939 Gerhard Domagk (Germany), for antibacterial effect of prontocilate

1943 Henrik Dam (Denmark) and Edward A. Doisy (U.S.), for analysis of vitamin K

1944 Joseph Erlanger and Herbert Spencer Gasser (both U.S.), for work on functions of the nerve threads

1945 Sir Alexander Fleming, Ernst Boris Chain, and Sir Howard Florey (all UK), for discovery of penicillin

1946 Herman J. Muller (U.S.), for hereditary effects of X-rays on genes

1947 Carl F. and Gerty T. Cori (U.S.), for work on animal starch metabolism; Bernardo A. Houssay (Argentina), for study of the pituitary lobe

1948 Paul Mueller (Switzerland), for discovery of insect-killing properties of DDT

1949 Walter Rudolf Hess (Switzerland), for research on brain control of body; Antonio Caetano de Abreu Freire Egas Moniz (Portugal), for development of brain operation

1950 Philip S. Hench, Edward C. Kendall (both U.S.), and Tadeus Reichstein (Switzerland), for discoveries about hormones of adrenal cortex

1951 Max Theiler (South Africa), for development of vaccine against yellow fever

1952 Selman A. Waksman (U.S.), for discovery of streptomycin

1953 Fritz A. Lipmann (Germany, U.S.) and Hans Adolph Krebs (Germany, UK), for studies of living cells

1954 John F. Enders, Thomas H. Weller, and Frederick C. Robbins (all U.S.), for work with cultivation of polio virus

1955 Hugo Theorell (Sweden), for work on oxidation enzymes

1956 Dickinson W. Richards, Jr., André F. Cournand (both U.S.), and Werner Forssmann (West Germany), for new techniques in treating heart disease

1957 Daniel Bovet (Italy), for development of drugs to relieve allergies and relax muscles during surgery

1958 Joshua Lederberg (U.S.), for work with genetic mechanisms; George W. Beadle and Edward L. Tatum (both U.S.), for discovering how genes transmit hereditary characteristics

1959 Severo Ochoa and Arthur Kornberg (both U.S.), for discoveries related to compounds within chromosomes that play a vital role in heredity

1960 Sir Macfarlane Burnet (Australia) and Peter Brian Medawar (UK), for discovery of acquired immunological tolerance

1961 Georg von Bekesy (U.S.), for discoveries about physical mechanisms of stimulation within cochlea

1962 James D. Watson (U.S.), Maurice H. F. Wilkins, and Francis H. C. Crick (both UK), for determining structure of deoxyribonucleic acid (DNA)

1963 Alan Lloyd Hodgkin, Andrew Fielding Huxley (both UK), and Sir John Carew Eccles (Australia), for research on nerve cells

1964 Konrad E. Bloch (U.S.) and Feodor Lynen (West Germany), for research on mechanism and regulation of cholesterol and fatty-acid metabolism

1965 François Jacob, André Lwoff, and Jacques Monod (all France), for study of regulatory activities in body cells

1966 Charles Brenton Huggins (U.S.), for studies in hormone treatment of cancer of prostate; Francis Peyton Rous (U.S.), for discovery of tumor-producing viruses

1967 Haldan K. Hartline, George Wald (both U.S.), and Ragnar Granit (Sweden), for work on human eye

1968 Robert W. Holley, Har Gobind Khorana, and Marshall W. Nirenberg (all U.S.), for studies of genetic code

1969 Max Delbruck, Alfred D. Hershey, and Salvador E. Luria (all U.S.), for study of mechanism of virus infection in living cells

1970 Julius Axelrod (U.S.), Ulf S. von Euler (Sweden), and Sir Bernard Katz (UK), for studies of how nerve impulses are transmitted within the body

1971 Earl W. Sutherland, Jr. (U.S.), for research on how hormones work

1972 Gerald M. Edelman (U.S.) and Rodney R. Porter (UK), for research on the chemical structure and nature of antibodies

1973 Karl von Frisch, Konrad Lorenz (both Austria), and Nikolaas Tinbergen (Netherlands), for their studies of individual and social behavior patterns

1974 George E. Palade, Christian de Duve (both U.S.), and Albert Claude (Belgium), for contributions to understanding inner workings of living cells

1975 David Baltimore, Howard M. Temin, and Renato Dulbecco (all U.S.), for work in interaction between tumor viruses and genetic material of the cell

1976 Baruch S. Blumberg and D. Carleton Gajdusek (both U.S.), for discoveries concerning new mechanisms for the origin and dissemination of infectious diseases

1977 Rosalyn S. Yalow, Roger C. L. Guillemin, and Andrew V. Schally (all U.S.), for research in role of hormones in chemistry of the body

1978 Daniel Nathans, Hamilton Smith (both U.S.), and Werner Arber (Switzerland), for discovery of restriction enzymes and their application to problems of molecular genetics

1979 Allan McLeod Cormack (U.S.) and Godfrey Newbold Hounsfield (UK), for developing computed axial tomography (CAT scan) X-ray technique

1980 Baruj Benacerraf, George D. Snell (both U.S.), and Jean Dausset (France), for discoveries that explain how the structure of cells relates to organ transplants and diseases

1981 Roger W. Sperry, David H. Hubel (both U.S.), and Torsten N. Wiesel (Sweden), for studies vital to understanding the organization and functioning of the brain

1982 Sune Bergstrom, Bengt Samuelsson (both Sweden), and John R. Vane (UK), for research in prostaglandins, hormonelike substances involved in a wide range of illnesses

1983 Barbara McClintock (U.S.), for her discovery of mobile genes in the chromosomes of a plant that change the future generations of plants they produce

1984 Cesar Milstein (UK/Argentina), Georges J. F. Kohler (West Germany), and Niels K. Jerne (UK/Denmark), for their work in immunology

1985 Michael S. Brown and Joseph L. Goldstein (both U.S.), for their work, which has drastically widened our understanding of the cholesterol metabolism and increased our possibilities to prevent and treat atherosclerosis and heart attacks

1986 Rita Levi-Montalcini (dual U.S., Italy) and Stanley Cohen (U.S.), for their contributions to the understanding of substances that influence cell growth

1987 Susumu Tonegawa (Japan), for his discoveries of how the body can suddenly marshal its immunological defenses against millions of different disease agents that it has never encountered before

1988 Gertrude B. Elion, George H. Hitchings (both U.S.), and Sir James Black (UK), for their discoveries of important principles for drug treatment

1989 J. Michael Bishop and Harold E. Varmus (both U.S.), for their unifying theory of cancer development

1990 Joseph E. Murray and E. Donnall Thomas (both U.S.), for their pioneering work in transplants

1991 Erwin Neher and Bert Sakmann (both Germany), for their research, particularly for the development of a technique called patch clamp

1992 Edmond H. Fischer and Edwin G. Krebs (both U.S.), for their discovery of a regulatory mechanism affecting almost all cells

1993 Phillip A. Sharp (U.S.) and Richard J. Roberts (UK), for their independent discovery in 1977 of "split genes"

1994 Alfred G. Gilman and Martin Rodbell (both U.S.), for discovery of G-proteins that help cells respond to outside signals

1995 Edward B. Lewis, Eric F. Wieschaus (both U.S.), and Christiane Nüsslein-Volhard (Germany), for studies of the fruit fly that will help explain congenital malformations in humans

1996 Peter C. Doherty (Australia) and Rolf M. Zinkernagel (Switzerland), for discoveries about how the immune system recognizes virus-infected cells

1997 Stanley B. Prusiner (U.S.), for discovery of a new type of germ, called prions, that causes degenerative brain disorders

1998 Robert F. Furchgott, Louis J. Ignarro, and Ferid Murad (all U.S.), for discovering that nitric oxide acts as a signal in the cardiovascular system

1999 Günter Blobel (U.S.), for discovering that proteins have intrinsic signals that govern their transport and localization in the cell

2000 Arvid Carlsson (Sweden), Paul Greengard, and Eric R. Kandel (both U.S.), for discoveries concerning signal transduction in the nervous system

2001 Leland H. Hartwell (U.S.), R. Timothy Hunt, and Paul M. Nurse (both UK), for discoveries concerning control of the cell cycle, which may make new cancer treatments possible

2002 Sydney Brenner (UK), H. Robert Horvitz (U.S.), and John E. Sulston (UK), for discoveries concerning genetic regulation of organ development and programmed cell death

2003 Paul C. Lauterbur (U.S.) and Sir Peter Mansfield (UK) for discoveries leading to magnetic resonance imaging (MRI)

2004 Richard Axel and Linda Buck (both U.S.), "for their discoveries of odorant receptors and the organization of the olfactory system"

ECONOMIC SCIENCES

1969 Ragnar Frisch (Norway) and Jan Tinbergen (Netherlands), for work in econometrics (application of mathematics and statistical methods to economic theories and problems)

1970 Paul A. Samuelson (U.S.), for efforts to raise the level of scientific analysis in economic theory

1971 Simon Kuznets (U.S.), for developing concept of using a country's gross national product to determine its economic growth

1972 Kenneth J. Arrow (U.S.) and Sir John R. Hicks (UK), for theories that help to assess business risk and government economic and welfare policies

1973 Wassily Leontief (U.S.), for devising the input-output technique to determine how different sectors of an economy interact

1974 Gunnar Myrdal (Sweden) and Friedrich A. von Hayek (UK) for pioneering analysis of the interdependence of economic, social, and institutional phenomena

1975 Leonid V. Kantorovich (USSR) and Tjalling C. Koopmans (U.S.), for work on the theory of optimum allocation of resources

1976 Milton Friedman (U.S.), for work in consumption analysis and monetary history and theory, and for demonstration of complexity of stabilization policy

1977 Bertil Ohlin (Sweden) and James E. Meade (UK), for contributions to theory of international trade and international capital movements

1978 Herbert A. Simon (U.S.), for research into the decision-making process within economic organizations

1979 Sir Arthur Lewis (UK) and Theodore Schultz (U.S.), for work on economic problems of developing nations

1980 Lawrence R. Klein (U.S.), for developing models for forecasting economic trends and shaping policies to deal with them

1981 James Tobin (U.S.), for analyses of financial markets and their influence on spending and saving by families and businesses

1982 George J. Stigler (U.S.), for work on government regulation in the economy and the functioning of industry

1983 Gerard Debreu (U.S.), in recognition of his work on the basic economic problem of how prices operate to balance what producers supply with what buyers want

1984 Sir Richard Stone (UK), for his work to develop the systems widely used to measure the performance of national economics

1985 Franco Modigliani (U.S.), for his pioneering work in analyzing the behavior of household savers and the functioning of financial markets

1986 James M. Buchanan (U.S.), for his development of new methods for analyzing economic and political decision-making

1987 Robert M. Solow (U.S.), for seminal contributions to the theory of economic growth

1988 Maurice Allais (France), for his pioneering development of theories to better understand market behavior and the efficient use of resources

1989 Trygve Haavelmo (Norway), for his pioneering work in methods for testing economic theories

1990 Harry M. Markowitz, William F. Sharpe, and Merton H. Miller (all U.S.), whose work provided new tools for weighing the risks and rewards of different investments and for valuing corporate stocks and bonds

1991 Ronald Coase (U.S.), for his pioneering work in how property rights and the cost of doing business affect the economy

1992 Gary S. Becker (U.S.), for "having extended the domain of economic theory to aspects of human behavior which had previously been dealt with—if at all—by other social science disciplines"

1993 Robert W. Fogel and Douglass C. North (both U.S.), for their work in economic history

1994 John F. Nash, John C. Harsanyi (both U.S.), and Reinhard Selten (Germany), for their pioneering work in game theory

1995 Robert E. Lucas, Jr. (U.S.), for having had the greatest influence on macroeconomic research since 1970

1996 James A. Mirrlees (UK) and William Vickrey (U.S.), for their fundamental contributions to the economic theory of incentives

1997 Robert C. Merton and Myron S. Scholes (both U.S.), for developing a formula that determines the value of stock options and other derivatives

1998 Amartya Sen (India), for his contributions to welfare economics

1999 Robert A. Mundell (Canada), for his work on monetary dynamics and optimum currency areas

2000 James J. Heckman and Daniel L. McFadden (both U.S.), for developing methods used in statistical analysis of individual and household behavior

2001 George A. Akerlof, A. Michael Spence, and Joseph E. Stiglitz (all U.S.), for market analyses with asymmetric information

2002 Daniel Kahneman (U.S.), for having integrated insights from psychological research into economic science; Vernon L. Smith (U.S.), for having established laboratory experiments as a tool in empirical economic analysis

2003 Robert F. Engle (U.S.) and Clive W. J. Granger (UK), for developing statistical tools to improve analysis of stock prices and other data

2004 Finn E. Kydland (Norway) and Edward C. Prescott (U.S.), "for their contributions to dynamic macroeconomics: the time consistency of economic policy and the driving forces behind business cycles"

Pulitzer Prizes

(For years not listed, no award was made.)

PULITZER PRIZES IN JOURNALISM

Meritorious Public Service

1918 *New York Times;* also special award to Minna Lewinson and Henry Beetle Hough
1919 *Milwaukee Journal*
1921 *Boston Post*
1922 *New York World*
1923 *Memphis Commercial Appeal*
1924 *New York World*
1926 *Columbus* (Ga.) *Enquirer Sun*
1927 *Canton* (Ohio) *Daily News*
1928 *Indianapolis Times*
1929 *New York Evening World*
1931 *Atlanta Constitution*
1932 *Indianapolis News*
1933 *New York World-Telegram*
1934 *Medford* (Ore.) *Mail Tribune*
1935 *Sacramento Bee*
1936 *Cedar Rapids* (Iowa) *Gazette*
1937 *St. Louis Post-Dispatch*
1938 *Bismarck* (N.D.) *Tribune*
1939 *Miami Daily News*
1940 *Waterbury* (Conn.) *Republican and American*
1941 *St. Louis Post-Dispatch*
1942 *Los Angeles Times*
1943 *Omaha World-Herald*
1944 *New York Times*
1945 *Detroit Free Press*
1946 *Scranton* (Pa.) *Times*
1947 *Baltimore Sun*
1948 *St. Louis Post-Dispatch*
1949 (Lincoln) *Nebraska State Journal*
1950 *Chicago Daily News* and *St. Louis Post-Dispatch*
1951 *Miami Herald* and *Brooklyn Eagle*
1952 *St. Louis Post-Dispatch*
1953 *Whiteville* (N.C.) *News Reporter* and *Tabor City* (N.C.) *Tribune*
1954 *Newsday* (Garden City, N.Y.)
1955 *Columbus* (Ga.) *Ledger* and *Sunday Ledger-Enquirer*
1956 *Watsonville* (Calif.) *Register-Pajaronian*
1957 *Chicago Daily News*
1958 (Little Rock) *Arkansas Gazette*
1959 *Utica* (N.Y.) *Observer Dispatch* and *Utica Daily Press*
1960 *Los Angeles Times*
1961 *Amarillo* (Tex.) *Globe-Times*
1962 *Panama City* (Fla.) *News-Herald*
1963 *Chicago Daily News*
1964 *St. Petersburg* (Fla.) *Times*
1965 *Hutchinson* (Kans.) *News*
1966 *Boston Globe*
1967 *Louisville Courier-Journal* and *Milwaukee Journal*
1968 *Riverside* (Calif.) *Press-Enterprise*
1969 *Los Angeles Times*
1970 *Newsday* (Garden City, N.Y.)
1971 *Winston-Salem* (N.C.) *Journal and Sentinel*

1972 *New York Times*
1973 *Washington Post*
1974 *Newsday* (Garden City, N.Y.)
1975 *Boston Globe*
1976 *Anchorage* (Alaska) *Daily News*
1977 *Lufkin* (Tex.) *News*
1978 *Philadelphia Inquirer*
1979 *Point Reyes* (Calif.) *Light*
1980 *Gannett News Service*
1981 *Charlotte* (N.C.) *Observer*
1982 *Detroit News*
1983 *Jackson* (Miss.) *Clarion-Ledger*
1984 *Los Angeles Times*
1985 *Fort Worth Star-Telegram*
1986 *Denver Post*
1987 *Pittsburgh Press,* for reporting by Andrew Schneider and Matthew Brelis
1988 *Charlotte* (N.C.) *Observer*
1989 *Anchorage Daily News*
1990 *Philadelphia Inquirer* and *Washington* (N.C.) *Daily News*
1991 *Des Moines Register,* for reporting by Jane Schorer
1992 *Sacramento Bee* for "The Sierra in Peril" series by Tom Knudson
1993 *Miami Herald*
1994 *Akron* (Ohio) *Beacon Journal*
1995 *Virgin Islands Daily News*
1996 *News and Observer* (Raleigh, N.C.)
1997 *Times-Picayune* (New Orleans, La.)
1998 *Grand Forks* (N.D.) *Herald*
1999 *Washington Post*
2000 *Washington Post*
2001 *Oregonian*
2002 *New York Times*
2003 *Boston Globe*
2004 *New York Times*
2005 *Los Angeles Times*

Editorial

1917 *New York Tribune*
1918 *Louisville Courier-Journal*
1920 Harvey E. Newbranch *(Omaha Evening World-Herald)*
1922 Frank M. O'Brien *(New York Herald)*
1923 William Allen White *(Emporia* [Kan.] *Gazette)*
1924 *Boston Herald;* special prize: Frank I. Cobb *(New York World)*
1925 *Charleston* (S.C.) *News and Courier*
1926 Edward M. Kingsbury *(New York Times)*
1927 F. Lauriston Bullard *(Boston Herald)*
1928 Grover Cleveland Hall *(Montgomery* [Ala.] *Advertiser)*
1929 Louis Isaac Jaffe *(Norfolk Virginian-Pilot)*
1931 Charles S. Ryckman *(Fremont* [Neb.] *Tribune)*
1933 *Kansas City* (Mo.) *Star*
1934 E. P. Chase *(Atlantic* [Iowa] *News Telegraph)*
1936 Felix Morley *(Washington Post);* George B. Parker (Scripps-Howard Newspapers)
1937 John W. Owens *(Baltimore Sun)*

1938 W. W. Waymack (Des Moines Register and Tribune)
1939 Ronald G. Callvert (Portland Oregonian)
1940 Bart Howard (St. Louis Post-Dispatch)
1941 Reuben Maury (New York Daily News)
1942 Geoffrey Parsons (New York Herald Tribune)
1943 Forrest W. Seymour (Des Moines Register and Tribune)
1944 Henry J. Haskell (Kansas City [Mo.] Star)
1945 George W. Potter (Providence [R.I.] Journal-Bulletin)
1946 Hodding Carter (Delta Democrat-Times [Greenville, Miss.])
1947 William H. Grimes (Wall Street Journal)
1948 Virginius Dabney (Richmond Times-Dispatch)
1949 John H. Crider (Boston Herald); Herbert Elliston (Washington Post)
1950 Carl M. Saunders (Jackson [Mich.] Citizen Patriot)
1951 William H. Fitzpatrick (New Orleans States)
1952 Louis LaCoss (St. Louis Globe-Democrat)
1953 Vermont C. Royster (Wall Street Journal)
1954 Don Murray (Boston Herald)
1955 Royce Howes (Detroit Free Press)
1956 Lauren K. Soth (Des Moines Register and Tribune)
1957 Buford Boone (Tuscaloosa [Ala.] News)
1958 Harry S. Ashmore (Arkansas Gazette)
1959 Ralph McGill (Atlanta Constitution)
1960 Lenoir Chambers (Virginian-Pilot)
1961 William J. Dorvillier (San Juan [P.R.] Star)
1962 Thomas M. Storke (Santa Barbara [Calif.] News-Press)
1963 Ira B. Harkey, Jr. (Pascagoula [Miss.] Chronicle)
1964 Hazel Brannon Smith (Lexington [Miss.] Advertiser)
1965 John R. Harrison (Gainesville [Fla.] Daily Sun)
1966 Robert Lasch (St. Louis Post-Dispatch)
1967 Eugene Patterson (Atlanta Constitution)
1968 John S. Knight (Knight Newspapers)
1969 Paul Greenberg (Pine Bluff [Ark.] Commercial)
1970 Phillip L. Geyelin (Washington Post)
1971 Horance G. Davis, Jr. (Gainesville [Fla.] Sun)
1972 John Strohmeyer (Bethlehem [Pa.] Globe Times)
1973 Roger Bourne Linscott (Berkshire Eagle [Pittsfield, Mass.])
1974 F. Gilman Spencer (Trenton [N.J.] Trentonian)
1975 John Daniell Maurice (Charleston [W. Va.] Daily Mail)
1976 Philip P. Kerby (Los Angeles Times)
1977 Warren L. Lerude, Foster Church, and Norman F. Cardoza (Reno [Nev.] Gazette and Nevada State Journal)
1978 Meg Greenfield (Washington Post)
1979 Edwin M. Yoder, Jr. (Washington Star)
1980 Robert L. Bartley (Wall Street Journal)
1982 Jack Rosenthal (New York Times)
1983 Editorial Board, Miami Herald
1984 Albert Scardino (Georgia Gazette)
1985 Richard Aregood (Philadelphia Daily News)
1986 Jack Fuller (Chicago Tribune)
1987 Jonathan Freedman (San Diego Tribune)
1988 Jane E. Healy (Orlando Sentinel)
1989 Lois Wille (Chicago Tribune)
1990 Thomas J. Hylton (Pottstown [Pa.] Mercury)
1991 Ron Casey, Harold Jackson, and Joey Kennedy (Birmingham [Ala.] News)

1992 Maria Henson (Lexington [Ky.] Herald-Leader)
1994 R. Bruce Dold (Chicago Tribune)
1995 Jeffrey Good (St. Petersburg [Fla.] Times)
1996 Robert B. Semple, Jr. (New York Times)
1997 Michael Gartner (Daily Tribune [Ames, Iowa])
1998 Bernard L. Stein (The Riverdale Press [Bronx, N.Y.])
1999 Editorial Board (Daily News [New York, N.Y.])
2000 John C. Bersia (The Orlando Sentinel [Orlando, Fla.])
2001 David Moats (Rutland Herald [Rutland, Vt.])
2002 Alex Raksin and Bob Sipchen (Los Angeles Times)
2003 Cornelia Grumman (Chicago Tribune)
2004 William Stall (Los Angeles Times)
2005 Tom Philp (The Sacramento Bee)

Correspondence
1929 Paul Scott Mowrer (Chicago Daily News)
1930 Leland Stowe (New York Herald Tribune)
1931 H. R. Knickerbocker (Philadelphia Public Ledger and New York Evening Post)
1932 Walter Duranty (New York Times); Charles G. Ross (St. Louis Post-Dispatch)
1933 Edgar Ansel Mowrer (Chicago Daily News)
1934 Frederick T. Birchall (New York Times)
1935 Arthur Krock (New York Times)
1936 Wilfred C. Barber (Chicago Tribune)
1937 Anne O'Hare McCormick (New York Times)
1938 Arthur Krock (New York Times)
1939 Louis P. Lochner (Associated Press)
1940 Otto D. Tolischus (New York Times)
1941 Group award[1]
1942 Carlos P. Romulo (Philippines Herald)
1943 Hanson W. Baldwin (New York Times)
1944 Ernie Pyle (Scripps-Howard Newspaper Alliance)
1945 Harold V. (Hal) Boyle (Associated Press)
1946 Arnaldo Cortesi (New York Times)
1947 Brooks Atkinson (New York Times)

1. For the public services and the individual achievements of American news reporters in the war zones.

Editorial Cartooning
1922 Rollin Kirby (New York World)
1924 Jay Norwood Darling (New York Tribune)
1925 Rollin Kirby (New York World)
1926 D. R. Fitzpatrick (St. Louis Post-Dispatch)
1927 Nelson Harding (Brooklyn Eagle)
1928 Nelson Harding (Brooklyn Eagle)
1929 Rollin Kirby (New York World)
1930 Charles R. Macauley (Brooklyn Eagle)
1931 Edmund Duffy (Baltimore Sun)
1932 John T. McCutcheon (Chicago Tribune)
1933 H. M. Talburt (Washington Daily News)
1934 Edmund Duffy (Baltimore Sun)
1935 Ross A. Lewis (Milwaukee Journal)
1937 C. D. Batchelor (New York Daily News)
1938 Vaughn Shoemaker (Chicago Daily News)
1939 Charles G. Werner (Daily Oklahoman [Oklahoma City])
1940 Edmund Duffy (Baltimore Sun)
1941 Jacob Burck (Chicago Times)
1942 Herbert L. Block (NEA Service)
1943 Jay Norwood Darling (New York Herald Tribune)
1944 Clifford K. Berryman (Washington Evening Star)
1945 Bill Mauldin (United Features Syndicate)
1946 Bruce Alexander Russell (Los Angeles Times)
1947 Vaughn Shoemaker (Chicago Daily News)

1948 Reuben L. Goldberg *(New York Sun)*
1949 Lute Pease *(Newark Evening News)*
1950 James T. Berryman *(Washington Evening Star)*
1951 Reg (Reginald W.) Manning *(Arizona Republic* [Phoenix]*)*
1952 Fred L. Packer *(New York Mirror)*
1953 Edward D. Kuekes *(Cleveland Plain Dealer)*
1954 Herbert L. Block *(Washington Post* and *Times-Herald)*
1955 Daniel R. Fitzpatrick *(St. Louis Post-Dispatch)*
1956 Robert York *(Louisville Times)*
1957 Tom Little *(Nashville Tennessean)*
1958 Bruce M. Shanks *(Buffalo Evening News)*
1959 Bill Mauldin *(St. Louis Post-Dispatch)*
1961 Carey Orr *(Chicago Tribune)*
1962 Edmund S. Valtman *(Hartford Times)*
1963 Frank Miller *(Des Moines Register)*
1964 Paul Conrad (formerly of *Denver Post,* later of *Los Angeles Times*)
1966 Don Wright *(Miami News)*
1967 Patrick B. Oliphant *(Denver Post)*
1968 Eugene Gray Payne *(Charlotte* [N.C.] *Observer)*
1969 John Fischetti *(Chicago Daily News)*
1970 Thomas F. Darcy *(Newsday* [Garden City, N.Y.]*)*
1971 Paul Conrad *(Los Angeles Times)*
1972 Jeffrey K. MacNelly *(Richmond* [Va.] *News Leader)*
1974 Paul Szep *(Boston Globe)*
1975 Garry Trudeau (Universal Press Syndicate)
1976 Tony Auth *(Philadelphia Inquirer)*
1977 Paul Szep *(Boston Globe)*
1978 Jeffrey K. MacNelly *(Richmond* [Va.] *News Leader)*
1979 Herbert L. Block *(Washington Post)*
1980 Don Wright *(Miami News)*
1981 Mike Peters *(Dayton* [Ohio] *Daily News)*
1982 Ben Sargent *(Austin* [Tex.] *American-Statesman)*
1983 Richard Locher *(Chicago Tribune)*
1984 Paul Conrad *(Los Angeles Times)*
1985 Jeff MacNelly *(Chicago Tribune)*
1986 Jules Feiffer *(Village Voice)*
1987 Berke Breathed *(Washington Post* Writers Group)
1988 Doug Marlette *(Atlanta Constitution* and *Charlotte* [N.C.] *Observer)*
1989 Jack Higgins *(Chicago Sun-Times)*
1990 Tom Toles *(Buffalo News)*
1991 Jim Borgman *(Cincinnati Inquirer)*
1992 Signe Wilkinson *(Philadelphia Daily News)*
1993 Stephen R. Benson *(Arizona Republic)*
1994 Michael P. Ramirez *(Commercial Appeal,* Memphis)
1995 Mike Luckovich *(Atlanta Constitution)*
1996 Jim Morin *(Miami Herald)*
1997 Walt Handelsman *(Times-Picayune)*
1998 Stephen P. Breen *(Asbury Park* [N.J.] *Press)*
1999 David Horsey *(Seattle Post-Intelligencer)*
2000 Joel Pett *(Lexington* [Ky.] *Herald-Leader)*
2001 Ann Telnaes *(Los Angeles Times* Syndicate)
2002 Clay Bennett *(Christian Science Monitor)*
2003 David Horsey *(Seattle Post-Intelligencer)*
2004 Matt Davies *(The Journal News* [White Plains, N.Y.]*)*
2005 Nick Anderson (*The Courier-Journal,* [Louisville, Ky.]*)*

News Photography

1942 Milton Brooks *(Detroit News)*
1943 Frank Noel (Associated Press)
1944 Frank Filan (Associated Press); Earle L. Bunker *(Omaha World-Herald)*
1945 Joe Rosenthal (Associated Press)
1947 Arnold Hardy
1948 Frank Cushing *(Boston Traveler)*
1949 Nat Fein *(New York Herald Tribune)*
1950 Bill Crouch *(Oakland Tribune)*
1951 Max Desfor (Associated Press)
1952 John Robinson and Don Ultang *(Des Moines Register and Tribune)*
1953 William M. Gallagher *(Flint* [Mich.] *Journal)*
1954 Mrs. Walter M. Schau
1955 John L. Gaunt, Jr. *(Los Angeles Times)*
1956 *New York Daily News*
1957 Harry A. Trask *(Boston Traveler)*
1958 William C. Beall *(Washington Daily News)*
1959 William Seaman *(Minneapolis Star)*
1960 Andrew Lopez (United Press International)
1961 Yasushi Nagao (Mainichi Newspapers, Tokyo)
1962 Paul Vathis (Harrisburg [Pa.] bureau of Associated Press)
1963 Hector Rondon (*La Republica,* Caracas, Venezuela)
1964 Robert H. Jackson *(Dallas Times Herald)*
1965 Horst Faas (Associated Press)
1966 Kyoichi Sawada (United Press International)
1967 Jack R. Thornell (Associated Press)
1968 News: Rocco Morabito *(Jacksonville* [Fla.] *Journal);* features: Toshio Sakai (United Press International)
1969 Spot news: Edward T. Adams (Associated Press); features: Moneta Sleet, Jr.
1970 Spot news: Steve Starr (Associated Press); features: Dallas Kinney *(Palm Beach Post)*
1971 Spot news: John Paul Filo (*Valley Daily News* and *Daily Dispatch* [Tarentum and New Kensington, Pa.]); features: Jack Dykinga *(Chicago Sun-Times)*
1972 Spot news: Horst Faas and Michel Laurent (Associated Press); features: Dave Kennerly (United Press International)
1973 Spot news: Huynh Cong Ut *(Associated Press);* features: Brian Lanker *(Topeka Capital-Journal)*
1974 Spot news: Anthony K. Roberts (Associated Press); features: Slava Veder (Associated Press)
1975 Spot news: Gerald H. Gay *(Seattle Times);* features: Matthew Lewis *(Washington Post)*
1976 Spot news: Stanley J. Forman *(Boston Herald-American);* features: staff of *Louisville Courier-Journal* and *Times*
1977 Spot news: Neal Ulevich (Associated Press) and Stanley J. Forman *(Boston Herald-American);* features: Robin Hood *(Chattanooga News-Free Press)*
1978 Spot news: John Blair, freelance, Evansville, Ind.; features: J. Ross Baughman (Associated Press)
1979 Spot news: Thomas J. Kelly, 3rd *(Pottstown* [Pa.] *Mercury);* features: staff of *Boston Herald-American*
1980 Features: Erwin H. Hagler *(Dallas Times Herald)*
1981 Spot news: Larry C. Price *(Fort Worth Star-Telegram);* features: Taro M. Yamasaki *(Detroit Free Press)*

1982 Spot news: Ron Edmonds (Associated Press); features: John H. White (Chicago Sun-Times)
1983 Spot news: Bill Foley (Associated Press); features: James B. Dickman (Dallas Times Herald)
1984 Spot news: Stan Grossfeld (Boston Globe); features: Anthony Suau (Denver Post)
1985 Spot news: staff of Register, Santa Ana, Calif.; features: Stan Grossfeld (Boston Globe)
1986 Spot news: Michel duCille and Carol Guzy (Miami Herald); features: Tom Gralish (Philadelphia Inquirer)
1987 Spot news: Kim Komenich (San Francisco Examiner); features: David Peterson (Des Moines Register)
1988 Spot news: Scott Shaw (Odessa [Texas] American); features: Michel duCille (Miami Herald)
1989 Spot news: Ron Olshwanger (St. Louis Post-Dispatch); features: Manny Crisostomo (Detroit Free Press)
1990 Spot news: Oakland Tribune; features: David C. Turnley (Detroit Free Press)
1991 Spot news: Greg Marinovich (Associated Press); features: William Snyder (Dallas Morning News)
1992 Spot news: Associated Press staff; features: John Kaplan (Herald [Monterey, Calif.] and Pittsburgh Post-Gazette)
1993 Spot news: William Snyder and Ken Geiger (Dallas Morning News); features: Associated Press
1994 Spot news: Paul Watson (Toronto Star); features: Kevin Carter, freelancer for New York Times
1995 Spot news: Carol Guzy (Washington Post); features: Associated Press staff
1996 Spot news: Charles Porter IV, freelancer for Associated Press; features: Stephanie Walsh, freelancer for Newhouse News Service
1997 Spot news: Annie Wells (Press Democrat [Santa Rosa, Calif.]); features: Alexander Zemlianichenko (Associated Press)
1998 Spot news: Martha Rial (Pittsburgh Post-Gazette); features: Clarence Williams (Los Angeles Times)
1999 Spot news: Associated Press photo staff; features: Associated Press photo staff
2000 Breaking news: photographic staff of Denver Rocky Mountain News; features: Carol Guzy, Michael Williamson, and Lucian Perkins (Washington Post)
2001 Breaking news: Alan Diaz (Associated Press); features: Matt Rainey (Star-Ledger [Newark, N.J.])
2002 Breaking news: New York Times staff; features: New York Times staff
2003 Breaking news: Rocky Mountain News staff; features: Don Bartletti (Los Angeles Times)
2004 Breaking news: David Leeson and Cheryl Diaz Meyer (Dallas Morning News); features: Carolyn Cole (Los Angeles Times)
2005 Breaking news: Associated Press staff; features: Deanne Fitzmaurice (San Francisco Chronicle)

National Telegraphic Reporting
1942 Louis Stark (New York Times)
1944 Dewey L. Fleming (Baltimore Sun)

1945 James Reston (New York Times)
1946 Edward A. Harris (St. Louis Post-Dispatch)
1947 Edward T. Folliard (Washington Post)

National Reporting
1948 Bert Andrews (New York Herald Tribune); Nat S. Finney (Minneapolis Tribune)
1949 C. P. Trussell (New York Times)
1950 Edwin O. Guthman (Seattle Times)
1952 Anthony Leviero (New York Times)
1953 Don Whitehead (Associated Press)
1954 Richard Wilson (Cowles Newspapers)
1955 Anthony Lewis (Washington Daily News)
1956 Charles L. Bartlett (Chattanooga Times)
1957 James Reston (New York Times)
1958 Relman Morin (Associated Press) and Clark Mollenhoff (Des Moines Register and Tribune)
1959 Howard Van Smith (Miami News)
1960 Vance Trimble (Scripps-Howard Newspaper Alliance)
1961 Edward R. Cony (Wall Street Journal)
1962 Nathan G. Caldwell and Gene S. Graham (Nashville Tennessean)
1963 Anthony Lewis (New York Times)
1964 Merriman Smith (United Press International)
1965 Louis M. Kohlmeier (Wall Street Journal)
1966 Haynes Johnson (Washington Evening Star)
1967 Stanley Penn and Monroe Karmin (Wall Street Journal)
1968 Howard James (Christian Science Monitor); Nathan K. (Nick) Kotz (Des Moines Register and Minneapolis Tribune)
1969 Robert Cahn (Christian Science Monitor)
1970 William J. Eaton (Chicago Daily News)
1971 Lucinda Franks and Thomas Powers (United Press International)
1972 Jack Anderson (United Feature Syndicate)
1973 Robert Boyd and Clark Hoyt (Knight Newspapers)
1974 Jack White (Providence [R.I.] Journal-Bulletin); James R. Polk (Washington Star-News)
1975 Donald L. Barlett and James B. Steele (Philadelphia Inquirer)
1976 James Risser (Des Moines Register)
1977 Walter Mears (Associated Press)
1978 Gaylord D. Shaw (Los Angeles Times)
1979 James Risser (Des Moines Register)
1980 Bette Swenson Orsini and Charles Stafford (St. Petersburg Times)
1981 John M. Crewdson (New York Times)
1982 Rick Atkinson (Kansas City [Mo.] Times)
1983 Boston Globe
1984 John N. Wilford (New York Times)
1985 Thomas J. Knudson (Des Moines Register)
1986 Craig Flournoy and George Rodrigue (Dallas Morning News) and Arthur Howe (Philadelphia Inquirer)
1987 Miami Herald staff; New York Times staff
1988 Tim Weiner (Philadelphia Inquirer)
1989 Donald L. Barlett and James B. Steele (Philadelphia Inquirer)
1990 Ross Anderson, Bill Dietrich, Mary Ann Gwinn, and Eric Nalder (Seattle Times)
1991 Marjie Lundstrom and Rochelle Sharpe (Gannett News Service)
1992 Jeff Taylor and Mike McGraw (Kansas City Star)
1993 David Maraniss (Washington Post)
1994 Eileen Welsome (Albuquerque [N.M.] Tribune)

1995 Tony Horwitz *(Wall Street Journal)*
1996 Alix M. Freedman *(Wall Street Journal)*
1997 *Wall Street Journal* staff
1998 Russell Carollo and Jeff Nesmith *(Dayton [Ohio] Daily News)*
1999 *New York Times* staff
2000 *Wall Street Journal* staff
2001 *New York Times* staff
2002 *Washington Post* staff
2003 Alan Miller and Kevin Sack *(Los Angeles Times)*
2004 *Los Angeles Times* staff
2005 Walt Bogdanich *(New York Times)*

International Telegraphic Reporting

1942 Laurence Edmund Allen (Associated Press)
1943 Ira Wolfert (North American Newspaper Alliance, Inc.)
1944 Daniel De Luce (Associated Press)
1945 Mark S. Watson *(Baltimore Sun)*
1946 Homer W. Bigart *(New York Herald Tribune)*
1947 Eddy Gilmore (Associated Press)

International Reporting

1948 Paul W. Ward *(Baltimore Sun)*
1949 Price Day *(Baltimore Sun)*
1950 Edmund Stevens *(Christian Science Monitor)*
1951 Keyes Beech and Fred Sparks *(Chicago Daily News);* Homer Bigart and Marguerite Higgins *(New York Herald Tribune);* Relman Morin and Don Whitehead (Associated Press)
1952 John M. Hightower (Associated Press)
1953 Austin C. Wehrwein *(Milwaukee Journal)*
1954 Jim G. Lucas (Scripps-Howard Newspapers)
1955 Harrison E. Salisbury *(New York Times)*
1956 William Randolph Hearst, Jr., and Frank Conniff (Hearst Newspapers); Kingsbury Smith (INS)
1957 Russell Jones (United Press)
1958 *New York Times*
1959 Joseph Martin and Philip Santora *(New York Daily News)*
1960 A. M. Rosenthal *(New York Times)*
1961 Lynn Heinzerling (Associated Press)
1962 Walter Lippmann *(New York Herald Tribune Syndicate)*
1963 Hal Hendrix *(Miami News)*
1964 Malcolm W. Browne (Associated Press); David Halberstam *(New York Times)*
1965 J. A. Livingston *(Philadelphia Bulletin)*
1966 Peter Arnett (Associated Press)
1967 R. John Hughes *(Christian Science Monitor)*
1968 Alfred Friendly *(Washington Post)*
1969 William Tuohy *(Los Angeles Times)*
1970 Seymour M. Hersh (Dispatch News Service)
1971 Jimmie Lee Hoagland *(Washington Post)*
1972 Peter R. Kann *(Wall Street Journal)*
1973 Max Frankel *(New York Times)*
1974 Hedrick Smith *(New York Times)*
1975 William Mullen and Ovie Carter *(Chicago Tribune)*
1976 Sydney H. Schanberg *(New York Times)*
1978 Henry Kamm *(New York Times)*
1979 Richard Ben Cramer *(Philadelphia Inquirer)*
1980 Joel Brinkley and Jay Mather *(Louisville Courier-Journal)*
1981 Shirley Christian *(Miami Herald)*
1982 John Darnton *(New York Times)*
1983 Thomas L. Friedman *(New York Times)*
1984 Karen E. House *(Wall Street Journal)*

1985 Josh Friedman, Dennis Bell, and Ozier Muhammad *(Newsday)*
1986 Lewis M. Simons, Pete Carey, and Katherine Ellison *(San Jose Mercury News)*
1987 Michael Parks *(Los Angeles Times)*
1988 Thomas L. Friedman *(New York Times)*
1989 Bill Keller *(New York Times);* Glenn Frankel *(Washington Post)*
1990 Nicholas D. Kristof and Sheryl WuDunn *(New York Times)*
1991 Caryle Murphy *(Washington Post);* Serge Schmemann *(New York Times)*
1992 Patrick J. Sloyan *(Newsday)*
1993 John F. Burns *(New York Times);* Roy Gutman *(Newsday)*
1994 *Dallas Morning News* team
1995 Mark Fritz (Associated Press)
1996 David Rohde *(Christian Science Monitor)*
1997 John F. Burns *(New York Times)*
1998 *New York Times* staff
1999 *Wall Street Journal* staff
2000 Mark Schoofs *(Village Voice)*
2001 Ian Johnson *(Wall Street Journal)* and Paul Salopek *(Chicago Tribune)*
2002 Barry Bearak *(New York Times)*
2003 Kevin Sullivan and Mary Jordan *(Washington Post)*
2004 Anthony Shadid *(Washington Post)*
2005 Kim Murphy *(Los Angeles Times)* and Dele Olojede *(Newsday* [Long Island, N.Y.])

Reporting

1917 Herbert B. Swope *(New York World)*
1918 Harold A. Littledale *(New York Evening Post)*
1920 John J. Leary, Jr. *(New York World)*
1921 Louis Seibold *(New York World)*
1922 Kirke L. Simpson (Associated Press)
1923 Alva Johnston *(New York Times)*
1924 Magner White *(San Diego Sun)*
1925 James W. Mulroy and Alvin H. Goldstein *(Chicago Daily News)*
1926 William Burke Miller *(Louisville Courier-Journal)*
1927 John T. Rogers *(St. Louis Post-Dispatch)*
1929 Paul Y. Anderson *(St. Louis Post-Dispatch)*
1930 Russell D. Owen *(New York Times);* special award: W. O. Dapping *(Auburn* [N.Y.] *Citizen)*
1931 A. B. MacDonald *(Kansas City* [Mo.] *Star)*
1932 W. C. Richards, D. D. Martin, J. S. Pooler, F. D. Webb, and J. N. W. Sloan *(Detroit Free Press)*
1933 Francis A. Jamieson (Associated Press)
1934 Royce Brier *(San Francisco Chronicle)*
1935 William H. Taylor *(New York Herald Tribune)*
1936 Lauren D. Lyman *(New York Times)*
1937 John J. O'Neill *(New York Herald Tribune);* William Leonard Laurence *(New York Times);* Howard W. Blakeslee (Associated Press); Gobind Behari Lal (Universal Service); David Dietz (Scripps-Howard Newspapers)
1938 Raymond Sprigle *(Pittsburg Post-Gazette)*
1939 Thomas L. Stokes *(New York World-Telegram)*
1940 S. Burton Heath *(New York World-Telegram)*
1941 Westbrook Pegler *(New York World-Telegram)*
1942 Stanton Delaplane *(San Francisco Chronicle)*
1943 George Weller *(Chicago Daily News)*
1944 Paul Schoenstein and associates *(New York Journal-American)*

1945 Jack S. McDowell *(San Francisco Call-Bulletin)*
1946 William Leonard Laurence *(New York Times)*
1947 Frederick Woltman *(New York World-Telegram)*
1948 George E. Goodwin *(Atlanta Journal)*
1949 Malcolm Johnson *(New York Sun)*
1950 Meyer Berger *(New York Times)*
1951 Edward S. Montgomery *(San Francisco Examiner)*
1952 George de Carvalho *(San Francisco Chronicle)*
1953 Editorial staff *(Providence Journal and Evening Bulletin);*[1] Edward J. Mowery *(New York World-Telegram and Sun)*[2]
1954 Editorial staff *Vicksburg* (Miss.) *Sunday Post-Herald;*[1] Alvin Scott McCoy *(Kansas City* [Mo.] *Star)*[2]
1955 Mrs. Caro Brown *(Alice* [Tex.] *Daily Echo);*[1] Roland Kenneth Towery *(Cuero* [Tex.] *Record)*[2]
1956 Lee Hills *(Detroit Free Press);*[1] Arthur Daley *(New York Times)*[2]
1957 *Salt Lake Tribune;*[1] Wallace Turner and William Lambert *(Portland Oregonian)*[2]
1958 Editorial staff *Fargo* [N.D.] *Forum;*[1] George Beveridge *(Washington* [D.C.] *Evening Star)*[2]
1959 Mary Lou Werner *(Washington* [D.C.] *Evening Star);*[1] John Harold Brislin *(Scranton* [Pa.] *Tribune & Scrantonian)*[2]
1960 Jack Nelson *(Atlanta Constitution);*[1] Miriam Ottenberg *(Washington* [D.C.] *Evening Star)*[2]
1961 Sanche de Gramont *(New York Herald Tribune);*[1] Edgar May *(Buffalo Evening News)*[2]
1962 Robert D. Mullins *(Deseret News* [Salt Lake City]);*[1] George Bliss *(Chicago Tribune)*[2]
1963 Sylvan Fox, Anthony Shannon, and William Longgood *(New York World-Telegram and Sun);*[1] Oscar Griffin, Jr. (former editor of *Pecos* [Tex.] *Independent and Enterprise,* now on staff of *Houston Chronicle)*[2]

1. Reporting under pressure of edition deadlines.
2. Reporting not under pressure of edition deadlines.

General Local Reporting
1964 Norman C. Miller *(Wall Street Journal)*
1965 Melvin H. Ruder *(Hungry Horse News* [Columbia Falls, Mont.])
1966 *Los Angeles Times* staff
1967 Robert V. Cox *(Chambersburg* [Pa.] *Public Opinion)*
1968 *Detroit Free Press* staff
1969 John Fetterman *(Louisville Times and Courier-Journal)*
1970 Thomas Fitzpatrick *(Chicago Sun-Times)*
1971 *Akron* (Ohio) *Beacon* staff
1972 Richard Cooper and John Machacek *(Rochester* [N.Y.] *Times-Union)*
1973 *Chicago Tribune* staff
1974 Arthur M. Petacque and Hugh F. Hough *(Chicago Sun-Times)*
1975 *Xenia* (Ohio) *Daily Gazette* staff
1976 Gene Miller *(Miami Herald)*
1977 Margo Huston *(Milwaukee Journal)*
1978 Richard Whitt *(Louisville Courier-Journal)*
1979 *San Diego* (Calif.) *Evening Tribune* staff
1980 *Philadelphia Inquirer* staff
1981 *Longview* (Wash.) *Daily News* staff

1982 Staff of *Kansas City* (Mo.) *Star* and *Kansas City* (Mo.) *Times*
1983 *Fort Wayne* (Ind.) *News-Sentinel* staff
1984 *Newsday* staff

General News Reporting
1985 Thomas Turcol *(Virginian-Pilot and Ledger-Star)*
1986 Edna Buchanan *(Miami Herald)*
1987 *Akron Beacon Journal* staff
1988 *Alabama Journal* (Montgomery) staff; *Lawrence* (Mass.) *Eagle-Tribune* staff
1989 *Louisville Courier-Journal* staff
1990 *San Jose* (Calif.) *Mercury News* staff

Spot News Reporting
1991 *Miami Herald* staff
1992 *New York Newsday* staff
1993 *Los Angeles Times* staff
1994 *New York Times* staff
1995 *Los Angeles Times* staff
1996 Robert D. McFadden *(New York Times)*
1997 *Newsday* staff (Long Island, N.Y.)

Breaking News Reporting
1998 *Los Angeles Times* staff
1999 *Hartford Courant* staff
2000 *Denver Post* staff
2001 *The Miami Herald* staff
2002 *Wall Street Journal* staff
2003 *Eagle-Tribune* staff (Lawrence, Mass.)
2004 *Los Angeles Times* staff
2005 *The Star-Ledger* staff (Newark, N.J.)

Special Local Reporting
1964 James V. Magee, Albert V. Gaudiosi, and Frederick A. Meyer *(Philadelphia Bulletin)*
1965 Gene Goltz *(Houston Post)*
1966 John A. Frasca *(Tampa Tribune)*
1967 Gene Miller *(Miami Herald)*
1968 J. Anthony Lukas *(New York Times)*
1969 Albert L. Delugach and Denny Walsh *(St. Louis Globe-Democrat)*
1970 Harold Eugene Martin *(Montgomery Advertiser)*
1971 William Hugh Jones *(Chicago Tribune)*
1972 Timothy Leland, Gerard N. O'Neill, Stephen A. Kurkjian, and Ann DeSantis *(Boston Globe)*
1973 Sun Newspapers of Omaha, Neb.
1974 William Sherman *(New York Daily News)*
1975 *Indianapolis Star* staff
1976 *Chicago Tribune* staff
1977 Acel Moore and Wendell Rawls, Jr. *(Philadelphia Inquirer)*
1978 Anthony R. Dolan *(Stamford* [Conn.] *Advocate)*
1979 Gilbert M. Gaul and Elliot G. Jaspin *(Pottsville* [Pa.] *Republican)*
1980 Nils J. Bruzelius, Alexander B. Hawes, Jr., Stephen A. Kurkjian, Robert M. Porterfield, and Joan Vennochi *(Boston Globe)*
1981 Clark Hallas and Robert B. Lowe *(Arizona Daily Star,* Tucson)
1982 Paul Henderson *(Seattle Times)*
1983 Loretta Tofani *(Washington Post)*
1984 Kenneth Cooper, Joan FitzGerald, Jonathan Kaufman, Norman Lockman, Gary McMillan, Kirk Scharfenberg, and David Wessel *(Boston Globe)*

Investigative Reporting

1985 Lucy Morgan, Jack Reed *(St. Petersburg* [Fla.] *Times),* and William K. Marimow *(Philadelphia Inquirer)*
1986 Jeffrey A. Marx and Michael M. York *(Lexington* [Ky.] *Herald Leader)*
1987 Daniel R. Biddle, H. G. Bissinger, and Fredric N. Tulsky *(Philadelphia Inquirer)*
1988 Dean Baquet, William C. Gaines, and Ann Marie Lipinski *(Chicago Tribune)*
1989 Bill Dedman *(Atlanta Journal and Constitution)*
1990 Lou Kilzer and Chris Ison *(Minneapolis-St. Paul Star Tribune)*
1991 Joseph T. Hallinan and Susan M. Headden *(Indianapolis Star)*
1992 Lorraine Adams and Dan Malone *(Dallas Morning News)*
1993 Jeff Brazil and Steve Berry *(Orlando* [Fla.] *Sentinel)*
1994 *Providence* (R.I.) *Journal-Bulletin* staff
1995 Stephanie Saul and Brian Donovan *(Newsday)*
1996 *Orange County Register* staff (Santa Ana, Calif.)
1997 Eric Nalder, Deborah Nelson, and Alex Tizon *(Seattle Times)*
1998 Gary Cohn and Will Englund *(Baltimore Sun)*
1999 *Miami Herald* staff
2000 Sang-Hun Choe, Charles J. Hanley, and Martha Mendoza (Associated Press)
2001 David Willman *(Los Angeles Times)*
2002 Sari Horwitz, Scott Higham, and Sarah Cohen *(Washington Post)*
2003 Clifford J. Levy *(New York Times)*
2004 Michael D. Sallah, Mitch Weiss, and Joe Mahr *(The Blade* [Toledo, Ohio])
2005 Nigel Jaquiss *(Willamette Week* [Portland, Ore.])

Feature Writing

1979 Jon D. Franklin *(Baltimore Evening Sun)*
1980 Madeleine Blais *(Miami Herald)*
1981 Teresa Carpenter *(Village Voice)*
1982 Saul Pett (Associated Press)
1983 Nan Robertson *(New York Times)*
1984 Peter M. Rinearson *(Seattle Times)*
1985 Alice Steinbach *(Baltimore Sun)*
1986 John Camp *(St. Paul Pioneer Press Dispatch)*
1987 Steve Twomey *(Philadelphia Inquirer)*
1988 Jacqui Banaszynski *(St. Paul Pioneer Press Dispatch)*
1989 David Zucchino *(Philadelphia Inquirer)*
1990 Dave Curtin *(Colorado Springs Gazette Telegraph)*
1991 Sheryl James *(St. Petersburg* [Fla.] *Times)*
1992 Howell Raines *(New York Times)*
1993 George Lardner, Jr. *(Washington Post)*
1994 Isabel Wilkerson *(New York Times)*
1995 Ron Suskind *(Wall Street Journal)*
1996 Rick Bragg *(New York Times)*
1997 Lisa Pollak *(Baltimore Sun)*
1998 Thomas French *(St. Petersburg* [Fla.] *Times)*
1999 Angelo B. Henderson *(Wall Street Journal)*
2000 J. R. Moehringer *(Los Angeles Times)*
2001 Tom Hallman, Jr. *(Oregonian)*
2002 Barry Siegel *(Los Angeles Times)*
2003 Sonia Nazario *(Los Angeles Times)*
2004 No award
2005 Julia Keller *(Chicago Tribune)*

Commentary

1970 Marquis W. Childs *(St. Louis Post-Dispatch)*
1971 William A. Caldwell *(Record* [Hackensack, N.J.])
1972 Mike Royko *(Chicago Daily News)*
1973 David S. Broder *(Washington Post)*
1974 Edwin A. Roberts, Jr. *(National Observer)*
1975 Mary McGrory *(Washington Star)*
1976 Walter W. (Red) Smith *(New York Times)*
1977 George F. Will *(Washington Post* Writers Group)
1978 William Safire *(New York Times)*
1979 Russell Baker *(New York Times)*
1980 Ellen H. Goodman *(Boston Globe)*
1981 Dave Anderson *(New York Times)*
1982 Art Buchwald *(Los Angeles Times* Syndicate)
1983 Claude Sitton *(Raleigh* [N.C.] *News and Observer)*
1984 Vermont Royster *(Wall Street Journal)*
1985 Murray Kempton *(Newsday)*
1986 Jimmy Breslin *(New York Daily News)*
1987 Charles Krauthammer *(Washington Post* Writers Group)
1988 Dave Barry *(Miami Herald)*
1989 Clarence Page *(Chicago Tribune)*
1990 Jim Murray *(Los Angeles Times)*
1991 Jim Hoagland *(Washington Post)*
1992 Anna Quindlen *(New York Times)*
1993 Liz Balmaseda *(Miami Herald)*
1994 William Raspberry *(Washington Post)*
1995 Jim Dwyer *(New York Newsday)*
1996 E. R. Shipp *(New York Daily News)*
1997 Eileen McNamara *(Boston Globe)*
1998 Mike McAlary *(New York Daily News)*
1999 Maureen Dowd *(New York Times)*
2000 Paul A. Gigot *(Wall Street Journal)*
2001 Dorothy Rabinowitz *(Wall Street Journal)*
2002 Thomas Friedman *(New York Times)*
2003 Colbert King *(Washington Post)*
2004 Leonard Pitts, Jr. *(Miami Herald)*
2005 Connie Schultz *(The Plain Dealer* [Cleveland, Ohio])

Criticism

1970 Ada Louise Huxtable *(New York Times)*
1971 Harold C. Schonberg *(New York Times)*
1972 Frank Peters, Jr. *(St. Louis Post-Dispatch)*
1973 Ronald Powers *(Chicago Sun-Times)*
1974 Emily Genauer *(Newsday* Syndicate)
1975 Roger Ebert *(Chicago Sun-Times)*
1976 Alan M. Kriegsman *(Washington Post)*
1977 William McPherson *(Washington Post)*
1978 Walter Kerr *(New York Times)*
1979 Paul Gapp *(Chicago Tribune)*
1980 William A. Henry III *(Boston Globe)*
1981 Jonathan Yardley *(Washington Star)*
1982 Martin Bernheimer *(Los Angeles Times)*
1983 Manuela Hoelterhoff *(Wall Street Journal)*
1984 Paul Goldberger *(New York Times)*
1985 Howard Rosenberg *(Los Angeles Times)*
1986 Donal Henahan *(New York Times)*
1987 Richard Eder *(Los Angeles Times)*
1988 Tom Shales *(Washington Post)*
1989 Michael Skube *(News and Observer* [Raleigh, N.C.])
1990 Allan Temko *(San Francisco Chronicle)*
1991 David Shaw *(Los Angeles Times)*
1993 Michael Dirda *(Washington Post)*
1994 Lloyd Schwartz *(Boston Phoenix)*
1995 Margo Jefferson *(New York Times)*
1996 Robert Campbell *(Boston Globe)*
1997 Tim Page *(Washington Post)*

1998 Michiko Kakutani *(New York Times)*
1999 Blair Kamin *(Chicago Tribune)*
2000 Henry Allen *(Washington Post)*
2001 Gail Caldwell *(Boston Globe)*
2002 Justin Davidson *(Newsday* [Long Island, N.Y.]*)*
2003 Stephen Hunter *(Washington Post)*
2004 Dan Neil *(Los Angeles Times)*
2005 Joe Morgenstern *(Wall Street Journal)*

Explanatory Reporting

1985 Jon Franklin *(Baltimore Evening Sun)*
1986 *New York Times* staff
1987 Jeff Lyon and Peter Gorner *(Chicago Tribune)*
1988 Daniel Hertzberg and James B. Stewart *(Wall Street Journal)*
1989 David Hanners, William Snyder, and Karen Blessen *(Dallas Morning News)*
1990 David A. Vise and Steve Coll *(Washington Post)*
1991 Susan C. Faludi *(Wall Street Journal)*
1992 Robert S. Capers and Eric Lipton *(Hartford Courant)*
1993 Mike Toner *(Atlanta Journal-Constitution)*
1994 Ronald Kotulak *(Chicago Tribune)*
1995 Leon Dash and Lucian Perkins *(Washington Post)*
1996 Laurie Garrett *(Newsday* [Long Island, N.Y.]*)*
1997 Michael Vitez, Ron Cortes, and April Saul *(Philadelphia Inquirer)*
1998 Paul Salopek *(Chicago Tribune)*
1999 Richard Read *(Oregonian)*
2000 Eric Newhouse *(Great Falls* [Mont.] *Tribune)*
2001 *Chicago Tribune* staff
2002 *New York Times* staff
2003 *Wall Street Journal* staff
2004 Kevin Helliker and Thomas M. Burton *(Wall Street Journal)*
2005 Gareth Cook *(Boston Globe)*

Specialized Reporting

1985 Randall Savage and Jackie Crosby *(Macon* [Ga.] *Telegraph and News)*
1986 Andrew Schneider and Mary Pat Flaherty *(Pittsburgh Press)*
1987 Alex S. Jones *(New York Times)*
1988 Walt Bogdanich *(Wall Street Journal)*
1989 Edward Humes *(Orange County Register)*
1990 Tamar Stieber *(Albuquerque* (N.M.) *Journal)*

Beat Reporting

1991 Natalie Angier *(New York Times)*
1992 Deborah Blum *(Sacramento Bee)*
1993 Paul Ingrassia and Joseph B. White *(Wall Street Journal)*
1994 Eric Freedman and Jim Mitzelfeld *(Detroit News)*
1995 David M. Shribman *(Boston Globe)*
1996 Bob Keeler *(Newsday* [Long Island, N.Y.]*)*
1997 Byron Acohido *(Seattle Times)*
1998 Linda Greenhouse *(New York Times)*
1999 Chuck Philips and Michael A. Hiltzik *(Los Angeles Times)*
2000 George Dohrmann *(St. Paul Pioneer Press)*
2001 David Cay Johnston *(New York Times)*
2002 Gretchen Morgenson *(New York Times)*
2003 Diana K. Sugg *(Baltimore Sun)*
2004 Daniel Golden *(Wall Street Journal)*
2005 Amy Dockser Marcus *(Wall Street Journal)*

PULITZER PRIZES IN LETTERS

Fiction[1]

1918 *His Family,* Ernest Poole
1919 *The Magnificent Ambersons,* Booth Tarkington
1921 *The Age of Innocence,* Edith Wharton
1922 *Alice Adams,* Booth Tarkington
1923 *One of Ours,* Willa Cather
1924 *The Able McLaughlins,* Margaret Wilson
1925 *So Big,* Edna Ferber
1926 *Arrowsmith,* Sinclair Lewis
1927 *Early Autumn,* Louis Bromfield
1928 *The Bridge of San Luis Rey,* Thornton Wilder
1929 *Scarlet Sister Mary,* Julia Peterkin
1930 *Laughing Boy,* Oliver La Farge
1931 *Years of Grace,* Margaret Ayer Barnes
1932 *The Good Earth,* Pearl S. Buck
1933 *The Store,* T. S. Stribling
1934 *Lamb in His Bosom,* Caroline Miller
1935 *Now in November,* Josephine Winslow Johnson
1936 *Honey in the Horn,* Harold L. Davis
1937 *Gone with the Wind,* Margaret Mitchell
1938 *The Late George Apley,* John Phillips Marquand
1939 *The Yearling,* Marjorie Kinnan Rawlings
1940 *The Grapes of Wrath,* John Steinbeck
1942 *In This Our Life,* Ellen Glasgow
1943 *Dragon's Teeth,* Upton Sinclair
1944 *Journey in the Dark,* Martin Flavin
1945 *A Bell for Adano,* John Hersey
1947 *All the King's Men,* Robert Penn Warren
1948 *Tales of the South Pacific,* James A. Michener
1949 *Guard of Honor,* James Gould Cozzens
1950 *The Way West,* A. B. Guthrie, Jr.
1951 *The Town,* Conrad Richter
1952 *The Caine Mutiny,* Herman Wouk
1953 *The Old Man and the Sea,* Ernest Hemingway
1955 *A Fable,* William Faulkner
1956 *Andersonville,* MacKinlay Kantor
1958 *A Death in the Family,* James Agee
1959 *The Travels of Jaimie McPheeters,* Robert Lewis Taylor
1960 *Advise and Consent,* Allen Drury
1961 *To Kill a Mockingbird,* Harper Lee
1962 *The Edge of Sadness,* Edwin O'Connor
1963 *The Reivers,* William Faulkner
1965 *The Keepers of the House,* Shirley Ann Grau
1966 *Collected Stories of Katherine Anne Porter,* Katherine Anne Porter
1967 *The Fixer,* Bernard Malamud
1968 *The Confessions of Nat Turner,* William Styron
1969 *House Made of Dawn,* N. Scott Momaday
1970 *Collected Stories,* Jean Stafford
1972 *Angle of Repose,* Wallace Stegner
1973 *The Optimist's Daughter,* Eudora Welty
1975 *The Killer Angels,* Michael Shaara
1976 *Humboldt's Gift,* Saul Bellow
1978 *Elbow Room,* James Alan McPherson
1979 *The Stories of John Cheever,* John Cheever
1980 *The Executioner's Song,* Norman Mailer
1981 *A Confederacy of Dunces,* John Kennedy Toole
1982 *Rabbit Is Rich,* John Updike
1983 *The Color Purple,* Alice Walker
1984 *Ironweed,* William Kennedy
1985 *Foreign Affairs,* Alison Lurie
1986 *Lonesome Dove,* Larry McMurtry
1987 *A Summons to Memphis,* Peter Taylor
1988 *Beloved,* Toni Morrison
1989 *Breathing Lessons,* Anne Tyler

1990 *The Mambo Kings Play Songs of Love*, Oscar Hijuelos
1991 *Rabbit at Rest*, John Updike
1992 *A Thousand Acres*, Jane Smiley
1993 *A Good Scent from a Strange Mountain*, Robert Olen Butler
1994 *The Shipping News*, E. Annie Proulx
1995 *The Stone Diaries*, Carol Shields
1996 *Independence Day*, Richard Ford
1997 *Martin Dressler: The Tale of an American Dreamer*, Steven Millhauser
1998 *American Pastoral*, Philip Roth
1999 *The Hours*, Michael Cunningham
2000 *Interpreter of Maladies*, Jhumpa Lahiri
2001 *The Amazing Adventures of Kavalier & Clay*, Michael Chabon
2002 *Empire Falls*, Richard Russo
2003 *Middlesex*, Jeffrey Eugenides
2004 *The Known World*, Edward P. Jones
2005 *Gilead*, Marilynne Robinson
1. Before 1948, award was for novels only.

History

1917 *With Americans of Past and Present Days*, J. J. Jusserand
1918 *A History of the Civil War, 1861–1865*, James Ford Rhodes
1920 *The War with Mexico*, Justin H. Smith
1921 *The Victory at Sea*, William Sowden Sims, in collaboration with Burton J. Hendrick
1922 *The Founding of New England*, James Truslow Adams
1923 *The Supreme Court in United States History*, Charles Warren
1924 *The American Revolution—A Constitutional Interpretation*, Charles Howard McIlwain
1925 *A History of the American Frontier*, Frederic L. Paxson
1926 *The History of the United States*, Edward Channing
1927 *Pinckney's Treaty*, Samuel Flagg Bemis
1928 *Main Currents in American Thought*, Vernon Louis Parrington
1929 *The Organization and Administration of the Union Army, 1861–1865*, Fred Albert Shannon
1930 *The War of Independence*, Claude H. Van Tyne
1931 *The Coming of the War: 1914*, Bernadotte E. Schmitt
1932 *My Experiences in the World War*, John J. Pershing
1933 *The Significance of Sections in American History*, Frederick J. Turner
1934 *The People's Choice*, Herbert Agar
1935 *The Colonial Period of American History*, Charles McLean Andrews
1936 *The Constitutional History of the United States*, Andrew C. McLaughlin
1937 *The Flowering of New England*, Van Wyck Brooks
1938 *The Road to Reunion, 1865–1900*, Paul Herman Buck
1939 *A History of American Magazines*, Frank Luther Mott
1940 *Abraham Lincoln: The War Years*, Carl Sandburg
1941 *The Atlantic Migration, 1607–1860*, Marcus Lee Hansen
1942 *Reveille in Washington*, Margaret Leech

1943 *Paul Revere and the World He Lived In*, Esther Forbes
1944 *The Growth of American Thought*, Merle Curti
1945 *Unfinished Business*, Stephen Bonsal
1946 *The Age of Jackson*, Arthur M. Schlesinger, Jr.
1947 *Scientists Against Time*, James Phinney Baxter III
1948 *Across the Wide Missouri*, Bernard DeVoto
1949 *The Disruption of American Democracy*, Roy Franklin Nichols
1950 *Art and Life in America*, Oliver W. Larkin
1951 *The Old Northwest, Pioneer Period 1815–1840*, R. Carlyle Buley
1952 *The Uprooted*, Oscar Handlin
1953 *The Era of Good Feelings*, George Dangerfield
1954 *A Stillness at Appomattox*, Bruce Catton
1955 *Great River: The Rio Grande in North American History*, Paul Horgan
1956 *The Age of Reform*, Richard Hofstadter
1957 *Russia Leaves the War: Soviet-American Relations, 1917–1920*, George F. Kennan
1958 *Banks and Politics in America: From the Revolution to the Civil War*, Bray Hammond
1959 *The Republican Era: 1869–1901*, Leonard D. White, assisted by Jean Schneider
1960 *In the Days of McKinley*, Margaret Leech
1961 *Between War and Peace: The Potsdam Conference*, Herbert Feis
1962 *The Triumphant Empire: Thunder-Clouds Gather in the West*, Lawrence H. Gipson
1963 *Washington, Village and Capital, 1800–1878*, Constance McLaughlin Green
1964 *Puritan Village: The Formation of a New England Town*, Sumner Chilton Powell
1965 *The Greenback Era*, Irwin Unger
1966 *Life of the Mind in America*, Perry Miller
1967 *Exploration and Empire: The Explorer and Scientist in the Winning of the American West*, William H. Goetzmann
1968 *The Ideological Origins of the American Revolution*, Bernard Bailyn
1969 *Origins of the Fifth Amendment*, Leonard W. Levy
1970 *Present at the Creation: My Years in the State Department*, Dean Acheson
1971 *Roosevelt: The Soldier of Freedom*, James McGregor Burns
1972 *Neither Black nor White: Slavery and Race Relations in Brazil and the United States*, Carl N. Degler
1973 *People of Paradox: An Inquiry Concerning the Origin of American Civilization*, Michael Kammen
1974 *The Americans: The Democratic Experience, Vol. 3*, Daniel J. Boorstin
1975 *Jefferson and His Time*, Dumas Malone
1976 *Lamy of Santa Fe*, Paul Horgan
1977 *The Impending Crisis: 1841–1861*, David M. Potter
1978 *The Invisible Hand: The Managerial Revolution in American Business*, Alfred D. Chandler, Jr.
1979 *The Dred Scott Case: Its Significance in Law and Politics*, Don E. Fehrenbacher
1980 *Been in the Storm So Long*, Leon F. Litwack
1981 *American Education: The National Experience; 1783–1876*, Lawrence A. Cremin
1982 *Mary Chesnut's Civil War*, C. Vann Woodward, editor

1983 *The Transformation of Virginia, 1740–1790,* Rhys L. Isaac

1985 *The Prophets of Regulation,* Thomas K. McCraw

1986 *The Heavens and the Earth: A Political History of the Space Age,* Walter A. McDougall

1987 *Voyagers to the West: A Passage in the Peopling of America on the Eve of the Revolution,* Bernard Bailyn

1988 *The Launching of Modern American Science 1846–1876,* Robert V. Bruce

1989 *Parting the Waters,* Taylor Branch; *Battle Cry of Freedom,* James M. McPherson

1990 *In Our Image: America's Empire in the Philippines,* Stanley Karnow

1991 *A Midwife's Tale: The Life of Martha Ballard, Based on Her Diary 1785–1812,* Laurel Thatcher Ulrich

1992 *The Fate of Liberty: Abraham Lincoln and Civil Liberties,* Mark E. Neely, Jr.

1993 *The Radicalism of the American Revolution,* Gordon S. Wood

1995 *No Ordinary Time: Franklin and Eleanor Roosevelt: The Home Front in World War II,* Doris Kearns Goodwin

1996 *William Cooper's Town: Power and Persuasion on the Frontier of the Early American Republic,* Alan Taylor

1997 *Original Meanings: Politics and Ideas in the Making of the Constitution,* Jack N. Rakove

1998 *Summer for the Gods: The Scopes Trial and America's Continuing Debate over Science and Religion,* Edward J. Larson

1999 *Gotham: A History of New York City to 1898,* Edwin G. Burrows and Mike Wallace

2000 *Freedom from Fear: The American People in Depression and War, 1929–1945,* David M. Kennedy

2001 *Founding Brothers: The Revolutionary Generation,* Joseph J. Ellis

2002 *The Metaphysical Club: A Story of Ideas in America,* Louis Menand

2003 *An Army at Dawn: The War in North Africa, 1942–1943,* Rick Atkinson

2004 *A Nation Under Our Feet,* Steven Hahn

2005 *Washington's Crossing,* David Hackett Fischer

Biography or Autobiography

1917 *Julia Ward Howe,* Laura E. Richards and Maude Howe Elliott, assisted by Florence Howe Hall

1918 *Benjamin Franklin, Self-Revealed,* William Cabell Bruce

1919 *The Education of Henry Adams,* Henry Adams

1920 *The Life of John Marshall,* Albert J. Beveridge

1921 *The Americanization of Edward Bok,* Edward Bok

1922 *A Daughter of the Middle Border,* Hamlin Garland

1923 *The Life and Letters of Walter H. Page,* Burton J. Hendrick

1924 *From Immigrant to Inventor,* Michael Idvorsky Pupin

1925 *Barrett Wendell and His Letters,* M. A. DeWolfe Howe

1926 *The Life of Sir William Osler,* Harvey Cushing

1927 *Whitman,* Emory Holloway

1928 *The American Orchestra and Theodore Thomas,* Charles Edward Russell

1929 *The Training of an American: The Earlier Life and Letters of Walter H. Page,* Burton J. Hendrick

1930 *The Raven,* Marquis James

1931 *Charles W. Eliot,* Henry James

1932 *Theodore Roosevelt,* Henry F. Pringle

1933 *Grover Cleveland,* Allan Nevins

1934 *John Hay,* Tyler Dennett

1935 *R. E. Lee,* Douglas S. Freeman

1936 *The Thought and Character of William James,* Ralph Barton Perry

1937 *Hamilton Fish,* Allan Nevins

1938 *Pedlar's Progress,* Odell Shepard; *Andrew Jackson,* Marquis James

1939 *Benjamin Franklin,* Carl Van Doren

1940 *Woodrow Wilson: Life and Letters,* Vols. VII and VIII, Ray Stannard Baker

1941 *Jonathan Edwards,* Ola E. Winslow

1942 *Crusader in Crinoline,* Forrest Wilson

1943 *Admiral of the Ocean Sea,* Samuel Eliot Morison

1944 *The American Leonardo: The Life of Samuel F. B. Morse,* Carleton Mabee

1945 *George Bancroft: Brahmin Rebel,* Russel Blaine Nye

1946 *Son of the Wilderness,* Linnie Marsh Wolfe

1947 *The Autobiography of William Allen White*

1948 *Forgotten First Citizen: John Bigelow,* Margaret Clapp

1949 *Roosevelt and Hopkins,* Robert E. Sherwood

1950 *John Quincy Adams and the Foundations of American Foreign Policy,* Samuel Flagg Bemis

1951 *John C. Calhoun: American Portrait,* Margaret Louise Coit

1952 *Charles Evans Hughes,* Merlo J. Pusey

1953 *Edmund Pendleton, 1721–1803,* David J. Mays

1954 *The Spirit of St. Louis,* Charles A. Lindbergh

1955 *The Taft Story,* William S. White

1956 *Benjamin Henry Latrobe,* Talbot F. Hamlin

1957 *Profiles in Courage,* John F. Kennedy

1958 *George Washington,* Douglas Southall Freeman (Vols. I–VI), and John Alexander Carroll and Mary Wells Ashworth (Vol VII)

1959 *Woodrow Wilson, American Prophet,* Arthur Walworth

1960 *John Paul Jones,* Samuel Eliot Morison

1961 *Charles Sumner and the Coming of the Civil War,* David Donald

1963 *Henry James: Vol. II, The Conquest of London, 1870–1881; Vol. III, The Middle Years, 1881–1895,* Leon Edel

1964 *John Keats,* Walter Jackson Bate

1965 *Henry Adams* (3 Vols.), Ernest Samuels

1966 *A Thousand Days,* Arthur M. Schlesinger, Jr.

1967 *Mr. Clemens and Mark Twain,* Justin Kaplan

1968 *Memoirs, 1925–1950,* George F. Kennan

1969 *The Man from New York,* B. L. Reid

1970 *Huey Long,* T. Harry Williams

1971 *Robert Frost: The Years of Triumph, 1915–1938,* Lawrence Thompson

1972 *Eleanor and Franklin: The Story of Their Relationship Based on Eleanor Roosevelt's Private Papers,* Joseph P. Lash

1973 *Luce and His Empire,* W. A. Swanberg

1974 *O'Neill, Son and Artist,* Louis Sheaffer

1975 *The Power Broker: Robert Moses and the Fall of New York,* Robert A. Caro

1976 *Edith Wharton: A Biography,* Richard W. B. Lewis

1977   *A Prince of Our Disorder*, John E. Mack
1978   *Samuel Johnson*, Walter Jackson Bate
1979   *Days of Sorrow and Pain: Leo Baeck and the Berlin Jews*, Leonard Baker
1980   *The Rise of Theodore Roosevelt*, Edmund Morris
1981   *Peter the Great*, Robert K. Massie
1982   *Grant: A Biography*, William S. McFeely
1983   *Growing Up*, Russell Baker
1984   *Booker T. Washington*, Louis R. Harlan
1985   *The Life and Times of Cotton Mather*, Kenneth Silverman
1986   *Louise Bogan: A Portrait*, Elizabeth Frank
1987   *Bearing the Cross: Martin Luther King, Jr., and the Southern Christian Leadership Conference*, David J. Garrow
1988   *Look Homeward: A Life of Thomas Wolfe*, David Herbert Donald
1989   *Oscar Wilde*, Richard Ellmann
1990   *Machiavelli in Hell*, Sebastian de Grazia
1991   *Jackson Pollock: An American Saga*, Steven Naifeh and Gregory White Smith
1992   *Fortunate Son: The Healing of a Vietnam Vet*, Lewis B. Puller, Jr.
1993   *Truman*, David McCullough
1994   *W. E. B. Du Bois: Biography of a Race, 1868–1919*, David Levering Lewis
1995   *Harriet Beecher Stowe: A Life*, Joan D. Hedrick
1996   *God: A Biography*, Jack Miles
1997   *Angela's Ashes: A Memoir*, Frank McCourt
1998   *Personal History*, Katharine Graham
1999   *Lindbergh*, A. Scott Berg
2000   *Vera (Mrs. Vladimir Nabokov)*, Stacy Schiff
2001   *W. E. B. DuBois: The Fight for Equality and the American Century, 1919–1963*, David Levering Lewis
2002   *John Adams*, David McCullough
2003   *Master of the Senate*, Robert A. Caro
2004   *Krushchev: The Man and His Era*, William Taubman
2005   *de Kooning: An American Master*, Mark Stevens and Annalyn Swan

Poetry[1]
1918   *Love Songs*, Sara Teasdale
1919   *Old Road to Paradise*, Margaret Widdemer; *Corn Huskers*, Carl Sandburg
1922   *Collected Poems*, Edwin Arlington Robinson
1923   *The Ballad of the Harp-Weaver; A Few Figs from Thistles;* eight sonnets in *American Poetry, 1922, A Miscellany*, Edna St. Vincent Millay
1924   *New Hampshire: A Poem with Notes and Grace Notes*, Robert Frost
1925   *The Man Who Died Twice*, Edwin Arlington Robinson
1926   *What's O'Clock*, Amy Lowell
1927   *Fiddler's Farewell*, Leonora Speyer
1928   *Tristram*, Edwin Arlington Robinson
1929   *John Brown's Body*, Stephen Vincent Benét
1930   *Selected Poems*, Conrad Aiken
1931   *Collected Poems*, Robert Frost
1932   *The Flowering Stone*, George Dillon
1933   *Conquistador*, Archibald MacLeish
1934   *Collected Verse*, Robert Hillyer
1935   *Bright Ambush*, Audrey Wurdemann
1936   *Strange Holiness*, Robert P. T. Coffin
1937   *A Further Range*, Robert Frost
1938   *Cold Morning Sky*, Marya Zaturenska
1939   *Selected Poems*, John Gould Fletcher

1940   *Collected Poems*, Mark Van Doren
1941   *Sunderland Capture*, Leonard Bacon
1942   *The Dust Which Is God*, William Rose Benét
1943   *A Witness Tree*, Robert Frost
1944   *Western Star*, Stephen Vincent Benét
1945   *V-Letter and Other Poems*, Karl Shapiro
1947   *Lord Weary's Castle*, Robert Lowell
1948   *The Age of Anxiety*, W. H. Auden
1949   *Terror and Decorum*, Peter Viereck
1950   *Annie Allen*, Gwendolyn Brooks
1951   *Complete Poems*, Carl Sandburg
1952   *Collected Poems*, Marianne Moore
1953   *Collected Poems, 1917–1952*, Archibald MacLeish
1954   *The Waking*, Theodore Roethke
1955   *Collected Poems*, Wallace Stevens
1956   *Poems—North & South*, Elizabeth Bishop
1957   *Things of This World*, Richard Wilbur
1958   *Promises: Poems, 1954–1956*, Robert Penn Warren
1959   *Selected Poems, 1928–1958*, Stanley Kunitz
1960   *Heart's Needle*, William Snodgrass
1961   *Times Three: Selected Verse from Three Decades*, Phyllis McGinley
1962   *Poems*, Alan Dugan
1963   *Pictures from Breughel*, William Carlos Williams
1964   *At the End of the Open Road*, Louis Simpson
1965   *77 Dream Songs*, John Berryman
1966   *Selected Poems*, Richard Eberhart
1967   *Live or Die*, Anne Sexton
1968   *The Hard Hours*, Anthony Hecht
1969   *Of Being Numerous*, George Oppen
1970   *Untitled Subjects*, Richard Howard
1971   *The Carrier of Ladders*, William S. Merwin
1972   *Collected Poems*, James Wright
1973   *Up Country*, Maxine Winokur Kumin
1974   *The Dolphin*, Robert Lowell
1975   *Turtle Island*, Gary Snyder
1976   *Self-Portrait in a Convex Mirror*, John Ashbery
1977   *Divine Comedies*, James Merrill
1978   *Collected Poems*, Howard Nemerov
1979   *Now and Then: Poems, 1976–1978*, Robert Penn Warren
1980   *Selected Poems*, Donald Rodney Justice
1981   *The Morning of the Poem*, James Schuyler
1982   *The Collected Poems*, Sylvia Plath
1983   *Selected Poems*, Galway Kinnell
1984   *American Primitive*, Mary Oliver
1985   *Yin*, Carolyn Kizer
1986   *The Flying Change*, Henry Taylor
1987   *Thomas and Beulah*, Rita Dove
1988   *Partial Accounts: New and Selected Poems*, William Meredith
1989   *New and Collected Poems*, Richard Wilbur
1990   *The World Doesn't End*, Charles Simic
1991   *Near Changes*, Mona Van Duyn
1992   *Selected Poems*, James Tate
1993   *The Wild Iris*, Louise Gluck
1994   *Neon Vernacular*, Yusef Komunyakaa
1995   *Simple Truth*, Philip Levine
1996   *The Dream of the Unified Field*, Jorie Graham
1997   *Alive Together: New and Selected Poems*, Lisel Mueller
1998   *Black Zodiac*, Charles Wright
1999   *Blizzard of One*, Mark Strand
2000   *Repair*, C. K. Williams
2001   *Different Hours*, Stephen Dunn
2002   *Practical Gods*, Carl Dennis

2003   *Moy Sand and Gravel,* Paul Muldoon
2004   *Walking to Martha's Vineyard,* Franz Wright
2005   *Delights & Shadows,* Ted Kooser

1. The poetry prize was established in 1922. The 1918 and 1919 awards were made from gifts provided by the Poetry Society.

General Nonfiction

1962   *The Making of the President, 1960,* Theodore H. White
1963   *The Guns of August,* Barbara W. Tuchman
1964   *Anti-Intellectualism in American Life,* Richard Hofstadter
1965   *O Strange New World,* Howard Mumford Jones
1966   *Wandering Through Winter,* Edwin Way Teale
1967   *The Problem of Slavery in Western Culture,* David Brion Davis
1968   *Rousseau and Revolution,* Will and Ariel Durant
1969   *So Human an Animal,* Rene Jules Dubos; *The Armies of the Night,* Norman Mailer
1970   *Gandhi's Truth,* Erik H. Erikson
1971   *The Rising Sun,* John Toland
1972   *Stilwell and the American Experience in China, 1911–1945,* Barbara W. Tuchman
1973   *Fire in the Lake: The Vietnamese and the Americans in Vietnam,* Frances FitzGerald; *Children of Crisis* (Vols. 1 and 2), Robert M. Coles
1974   *The Denial of Death,* Ernest Becker
1975   *Pilgrim at Tinker Creek,* Annie Dillard
1976   *Why Survive? Being Old in America,* Robert N. Butler
1977   *Beautiful Swimmers: Watermen, Crabs and the Chesapeake Bay,* William W. Warner
1978   *The Dragons of Eden,* Carl Sagan
1979   *On Human Nature,* Edward O. Wilson
1980   *Gödel, Escher, Bach: An Eternal Golden Braid,* Douglas R. Hofstadter
1981   *Fin-de-Siècle Vienna: Politics and Culture,* Carl E. Schorske
1982   *The Soul of a New Machine,* Tracy Kidder
1983   *Is There No Place on Earth for Me?,* Susan Sheehan
1984   *Social Transformation of American Medicine,* Paul Starr
1985   *The Good War: An Oral History of World War II,* Studs Terkel
1986   *Move Your Shadow: South Africa, Black and White,* Joseph Lelyveld; *Common Ground: A Turbulent Decade in the Lives of Three American Families,* J. Anthony Lukas
1987   *Arab and Jew: Wounded Spirits in a Promised Land,* David K. Shipler
1988   *The Making of the Atomic Bomb,* Richard Rhodes
1989   *A Bright Shining Lie,* Neil Sheehan
1990   *And Their Children After Them,* Dale Maharidge and Michael Williamson
1991   *The Ants,* Bert Holldobler and Edward O. Wilson
1992   *The Prize: The Epic Quest for Oil, Money and Power,* Daniel Yergin
1993   *Lincoln at Gettysburg: The Words That Remade America,* Garry Wills
1994   *Lenin's Tomb: The Last Days of the Soviet Empire,* David Remick
1995   *The Beak of the Finch: A Story of Evolution in Our Time,* Jonathan Weiner
1996   *The Haunted Land: Facing Europe's Ghosts After Communism,* Tina Rosenberg
1997   *Ashes to Ashes: America's Hundred-Year Cigarette War, the Public Health, and the Unabashed Triumph of Philip Morris,* Richard Kluger
1998   *Guns, Germs, and Steel: The Fates of Human Societies,* Jared Diamond
1999   *Annals of the Former World,* John McPhee
2000   *Embracing Defeat: Japan in the Wake of World War II,* John W. Dower
2001   *Hirohito and the Making of Modern Japan,* Herbert P. Bix
2002   *Carry Me Home: Birmingham, Alabama, the Climactic Battle of the Civil Rights Revolution,* Diane McWhorter
2003   *"A Problem from Hell": America and the Age of Genocide,* Samantha Power
2004   *Gulag: A History,* Anne Applebaum
2005   *Ghost Wars,* Steve Coll

PULITZER PRIZES IN MUSIC

1943   *Secular Cantata No. 2, A Free Song,* William Schuman
1944   *Symphony No. 4* (Op. 34), Howard Hanson
1945   *Appalachian Spring,* Aaron Copland
1946   *The Canticle of the Sun,* Leo Sowerby
1947   *Symphony No. 3,* Charles Ives
1948   *Symphony No. 3,* Walter Piston
1949   *Louisiana Story* music, Virgil Thomson
1950   *The Consul,* Gian Carlo Menotti
1951   Music for opera *Giants in the Earth,* Douglas Stuart Moore
1952   *Symphony Concertante,* Gail Kubik
1954   *Concerto for Two Pianos and Orchestra,* Quincy Porter
1955   *The Saint of Bleecker Street,* Gian Carlo Menotti
1956   *Symphony No. 3,* Ernst Toch
1957   *Meditations on Ecclesiastes,* Norman Dello Joio
1958   *Vanessa,* Samuel Barber
1959   *Concerto for Piano and Orchestra,* John La Montaine
1960   *Second String Quartet,* Elliott Carter
1961   *Symphony No. 7,* Walter Piston
1962   *The Crucible,* Robert Ward
1963   *Piano Concerto No. 1,* Samuel Barber
1966   *Variations for Orchestra,* Leslie Bassett
1967   *Quartet No. 3,* Leon Kirchner
1968   *Echoes of Time and the River,* George Crumb
1969   *String Quartet No. 3,* Karel Husa
1970   *Time's Encomium,* Charles Wuorinen
1971   *Synchronisms No. 6 for Piano and Electronic Sound,* Mario Davidowsky
1972   *Windows,* Jacob Druckman
1973   *String Quartet No. 3,* Elliott Carter
1974   *Notturno,* Donald Martino
1975   *From the Diary of Virginia Woolf,* Dominick Argento
1976   *Air Music,* Ned Rorem
1977   *Visions of Terror and Wonder,* Richard Wernick
1978   *Déjà Vu for Percussion Quartet and Orchestra,* Michael Colgrass
1979   *Aftertones of Infinity,* Joseph Schwantner
1980   *In Memory of a Summer Day,* David Del Tredici
1982   *Concerto for Orchestra,* Roger Sessions
1983   *Three Movements for Orchestra,* Ellen T. Zwilich

1984   *Canti del Sole*, Bernard Rands
1985   *Symphony RiverRun*, Stephen Albert
1986   *Wind Quintet IV*, George Perle
1987   *The Flight into Egypt*, John Harbison
1988   *12 New Etudes for Piano*, William Bolcom
1989   *Whispers out of Time*, Roger Reynolds
1990   *Duplicates: A Concerto for Two Pianos and Orchestra*, Mel Powell
1991   *Symphony*, Shulamit Ran
1992   *The Face of the Night, The Heart of the Dark*, Wayne Peterson
1993   *Trombone Concerto*, Christopher Rouse
1994   *Of Reminiscences and Reflections*, Gunther Schuller
1995   *Stringmusic*, Morton Gould
1996   *Lilacs*, George Walker
1997   *Blood on the Field*, Wynton Marsalis
1998   *String Quartet No. 2, Musica Instrumentalis*, Aaron Jay Kernis
1999   *Concerto for Flute, Strings and Percussion*, Melinda Wagner
2000   *Life Is a Dream, Opera in Three Acts: Act II, Concert Version*, Lewis Spratlan
2001   *Symphony No. 2 for String Orchestra*, John Corigliano
2002   *Ice Field*, Henry Brant
2003   *On the Transmigration of Souls*, John Adams
2004   *Tempest Fantasy*, Paul Moravec
2005   *Second Concerto for Orchestra*, Steven Stucky

PULITZER PRIZES IN DRAMA

1918   *Why Marry?*, Jesse Lynch Williams
1920   *Beyond the Horizon*, Eugene O'Neill
1921   *Miss Lulu Bett*, Zona Gale
1922   *Anna Christie*, Eugene O'Neill
1923   *Icebound*, Owen Davis
1924   *Hell-Bent fer Heaven*, Hatcher Hughes
1925   *They Knew What They Wanted*, Sidney Howard
1926   *Craig's Wife*, George Kelly
1927   *In Abraham's Bosom*, Paul Green
1928   *Strange Interlude*, Eugene O'Neill
1929   *Street Scene*, Elmer L. Rice
1930   *The Green Pastures*, Marc Connelly
1931   *Alison's House*, Susan Glaspell
1932   *Of Thee I Sing*, George S. Kaufman, Morrie Ryskind, and Ira Gershwin
1933   *Both Your Houses*, Maxwell Anderson
1934   *Men in White*, Sidney Kingsley
1935   *The Old Maid*, Zöe Akins
1936   *Idiot's Delight*, Robert E. Sherwood
1937   *You Can't Take It with You*, Moss Hart and George S. Kaufman
1938   *Our Town*, Thornton Wilder
1939   *Abe Lincoln in Illinois*, Robert E. Sherwood
1940   *The Time of Your Life*, William Saroyan
1941   *There Shall Be No Night*, Robert E. Sherwood
1943   *The Skin of Our Teeth*, Thornton Wilder
1945   *Harvey*, Mary Chase
1946   *State of the Union*, Russel Crouse and Howard Lindsay
1948   *A Streetcar Named Desire*, Tennessee Williams
1949   *Death of a Salesman*, Arthur Miller
1950   *South Pacific*, Richard Rodgers, Oscar Hammerstein II, and Joshua Logan
1952   *The Shrike*, Joseph Kramm
1953   *Picnic*, William Inge

1954   *The Teahouse of the August Moon*, John Patrick
1955   *Cat on a Hot Tin Roof*, Tennessee Williams
1956   *The Diary of Anne Frank*, Frances Goodrich and Albert Hackett
1957   *Long Day's Journey into Night*, Eugene O'Neill
1958   *Look Homeward, Angel*, Ketti Frings
1959   *J. B.*, Archibald MacLeish
1960   *Fiorello!*, George Abbott, Jerome Weidman, Jerry Bock, and Sheldon Harnick
1961   *All the Way Home*, Tad Mosel
1962   *How to Succeed in Business Without Really Trying*, Frank Loesser and Abe Burrows
1965   *The Subject Was Roses*, Frank D. Gilroy
1967   *A Delicate Balance*, Edward Albee
1969   *The Great White Hope*, Howard Sackler
1970   *No Place to Be Somebody*, Charles Gordone
1971   *The Effect of Gamma Rays on Man-in-the-Moon Marigolds*, Paul Zindel
1973   *That Championship Season*, Jason Miller
1975   *Seascape*, Edward Albee
1976   *A Chorus Line*, conceived by Michael Bennett
1977   *The Shadow Box*, Michael Cristofer
1978   *The Gin Game*, Donald L. Coburn
1979   *Buried Child*, Sam Shepard
1980   *Talley's Folly*, Lanford Wilson
1981   *Crimes of the Heart*, Beth Henley
1982   *A Soldier's Play*, Charles Fuller
1983   *'Night, Mother*, Marsha Norman
1984   *Glengarry Glen Ross*, David Mamet
1985   *Sunday in the Park with George*, Stephen Sondheim and James Lapine
1987   *Fences*, August Wilson
1988   *Driving Miss Daisy*, Alfred Uhry
1989   *The Heidi Chronicles*, Wendy Wasserstein
1990   *The Piano Lesson*, August Wilson
1991   *Lost in Yonkers*, Neil Simon
1992   *The Kentucky Cycle*, Robert Schenkkan
1993   *Angels in America: Millennium Approaches*, Tony Kushner
1994   *Three Tall Women*, Edward Albee
1995   *The Young Man from Atlanta*, Horton Foote
1996   *Rent*, Jonathan Larson
1998   *How I Learned to Drive*, Paula Vogel
1999   *W;t*, Margaret Edson
2000   *Dinner with Friends*, Donald Margulies
2001   *Proof*, David Auburn
2002   *Topdog/Underdog*, Suzan-Lori Parks
2003   *Anna in the Tropics*, Nilo Cruz
2004   *I Am My Own Wife*, Doug Wright
2005   *Doubt, a parable*, John Patrick Shanley

SPECIAL CITATIONS

1938   *Edmonton [Alberta] Journal*, special bronze plaque for editorial leadership in defense of freedom of the press in province of Alberta
1941   *New York Times*, for the public educational value of its foreign news report
1944   Byron Price, director of the Office of Censorship, for the creation and administration of the newspaper and radio codes; Mrs. William Allen White, for her husband's interest and services during the past seven years as a member of the Advisory Board of the Graduate School of Journalism, Columbia University; Richard Rodgers and Oscar Hammerstein II, for their musical *Oklahoma!*
1945   The cartographers of the American press, for their war maps

1947 Columbia University and the Graduate School of Journalism, for their efforts to maintain and advance the high standards governing the Pulitzer Prize awards; the *St. Louis Post-Dispatch,* for its unswerving adherence to the public and professional ideals of its founder and its leadership in American journalism
1948 Dr. Frank D. Fackenthal, for his interest and service
1951 Cyrus L. Sulzberger *(New York Times),* for his exclusive interview with Archbishop Stepinac in a Yugoslav prison
1952 *Kansas City Star,* for coverage of 1951 floods; Max Kase *(New York Journal-American),* for exposures of bribery in basketball
1953 *New York Times,* for its 17-year publication of "Review of the Week," and Lester Markel, its founder
1957 Kenneth Roberts, for his historical novels
1958 Walter Lippmann *(New York Herald Tribune),* for his "wisdom, perception and high sense of responsibility" in his commentary on national and international affairs
1960 Garrett Mattingly, for *The Armada*
1961 *American Heritage Picture History of the Civil War,* as a distinguished example of American book publishing
1964 Gannett Newspapers, Rochester, N.Y.
1973 James Thomas Flexner, for his biography *George Washington*

1974 Roger Sessions, for his "life's work in music"
1976 John Hohenberg, for "services for 22 years as Administrator of the Pulitzer Prizes"; Scott Joplin, for his contributions to American music
1977 Alex Haley, for his novel *Roots*
1978 E. B. White of *New Yorker* magazine and Richard L. Strout of *Christian Science Monitor*
1982 Milton Babbitt, "for his life's work as a distinguished and seminal American composer"
1984 Theodor Seuss Geisel (Dr. Seuss), for "books full of playful rhymes, nonsense words and strange illustrations"
1985 William Schuman, for "more than half a century of contribution to American music as a composer and educational leader"
1987 Joseph Pulitzer, Jr., "for extraordinary services to American journalism and letters during his 31 years as chairman of the Pulitzer Prize Board and for his accomplishments as an editor and publisher"
1992 *Maus,* Art Spiegelman
1996 Herb Caen *(San Francisco Chronicle),* "for his extraordinary and continuing contribution as a voice and conscience of his city"
1998 George Gershwin
1999 Edward Kennedy "Duke" Ellington, who "made an indelible contribution to art and culture"

Academy Awards (Oscars)

1928
Picture: *Wings,* Paramount
Director: Frank Borzage, *Seventh Heaven;* Lewis Milestone, *Two Arabian Nights*
Actress: Janet Gaynor, *Seventh Heaven, Street Angel, Sunrise*
Actor: Emil Jannings, *The Way of All Flesh, The Last Command*

1929
Picture: *The Broadway Melody,* MGM
Director: Frank Lloyd, *The Divine Lady*
Actress: Mary Pickford, *Coquette*
Actor: Warner Baxter, *In Old Arizona*

1930
Picture: *All Quiet on the Western Front,* Universal
Director: Lewis Milestone, *All Quiet on the Western Front*
Actress: Norma Shearer, *The Divorcee*
Actor: George Arliss, *Disraeli*

1931
Picture: *Cimarron,* RKO Radio
Director: Norman Taurog, *Skippy*
Actress: Marie Dressler, *Min and Bill*
Actor: Lionel Barrymore, *A Free Soul*

1932
Picture: *Grand Hotel,* MGM
Director: Frank Borzage, *Bad Girl*
Actress: Helen Hayes, *The Sin of Madelon Claudet*
Actor: Fredric March, *Dr. Jekyll and Mr. Hyde;* Wallace Beery, *The Champ*

1933
Picture: *Cavalcade,* Fox
Director: Frank Lloyd, *Cavalcade*
Actress: Katharine Hepburn, *Morning Glory*
Actor: Charles Laughton, *The Private Life of Henry VIII*

1934
Picture: *It Happened One Night,* Columbia
Director: Frank Capra, *It Happened One Night*
Actress: Claudette Colbert, *It Happened One Night*
Actor: Clark Gable, *It Happened One Night*

1935
Picture: *Mutiny on the Bounty,* MGM
Director: John Ford, *The Informer*
Actress: Bette Davis, *Dangerous*
Actor: Victor McLaglen, *The Informer*

1936
Picture: *The Great Ziegfeld,* MGM
Director: Frank Capra, *Mr. Deeds Goes to Town*
Actress: Luise Rainer, *The Great Ziegfeld*
Actor: Paul Muni, *The Story of Louis Pasteur*
Supporting Actress: Gale Sondergaard, *Anthony Adverse*
Supporting Actor: Walter Brennan, *Come and Get It*

1937
Picture: *The Life of Emile Zola,* Warner Bros.
Director: Leo McCarey, *The Awful Truth*
Actress: Luise Rainer, *The Good Earth*
Actor: Spencer Tracy, *Captains Courageous*
Supporting Actress: Alice Brady, *In Old Chicago*
Supporting Actor: Joseph Schildkraut, *The Life of Emile Zola*

1938
Picture: *You Can't Take It with You,* Columbia
Director: Frank Capra, *You Can't Take It with You*
Actress: Bette Davis, *Jezebel*
Actor: Spencer Tracy, *Boys Town*
Supporting Actress: Fay Bainter, *Jezebel*
Supporting Actor: Walter Brennan, *Kentucky*

1939
Picture: *Gone with the Wind,* Selznick MGM
Director: Victor Fleming, *Gone with the Wind*
Actress: Vivien Leigh, *Gone with the Wind*
Actor: Robert Donat, *Goodbye, Mr. Chips*
Supporting Actress: Hattie McDaniel, *Gone with the Wind*
Supporting Actor: Thomas Mitchell, *Stagecoach*

1940
Picture: *Rebecca,* Selznick-United Artists
Director: John Ford, *The Grapes of Wrath*
Actress: Ginger Rogers, *Kitty Foyle*
Actor: James Stewart, *The Philadelphia Story*
Supporting Actress: Jane Darwell, *The Grapes of Wrath*
Supporting Actor: Walter Brennan, *The Westerner*

1941
Picture: *How Green Was My Valley,* 20th Century–Fox
Director: John Ford, *How Green Was My Valley*
Actress: Joan Fontaine, *Suspicion*
Actor: Gary Cooper, *Sergeant York*
Supporting Actress: Mary Astor, *The Great Lie*
Supporting Actor: Donald Crisp, *How Green Was My Valley*

1942
Picture: *Mrs. Miniver,* MGM
Director: William Wyler, *Mrs. Miniver*
Actress: Greer Garson, *Mrs. Miniver*
Actor: James Cagney, *Yankee Doodle Dandy*
Supporting Actress: Teresa Wright, *Mrs. Miniver*
Supporting Actor: Van Heflin, *Johnny Eager*

1943
Picture: *Casablanca,* Warner Bros.
Director: Michael Curtiz, *Casablanca*
Actress: Jennifer Jones, *The Song of Bernadette*
Actor: Paul Lukas, *Watch on the Rhine*
Supporting Actress: Katina Paxinou, *For Whom the Bell Tolls*
Supporting Actor: Charles Coburn, *The More the Merrier*

1944
Picture: *Going My Way,* Paramount
Director: Leo McCarey, *Going My Way*
Actress: Ingrid Bergman, *Gaslight*
Actor: Bing Crosby, *Going My Way*
Supporting Actress: Ethel Barrymore, *None but the Lonely Heart*
Supporting Actor: Barry Fitzgerald, *Going My Way*

1945
Picture: *The Lost Weekend,* Paramount
Director: Billy Wilder, *The Lost Weekend*
Actress: Joan Crawford, *Mildred Pierce*
Actor: Ray Milland, *The Lost Weekend*
Supporting Actress: Anne Revere, *National Velvet*
Supporting Actor: James Dunn, *A Tree Grows in Brooklyn*

1946
Picture: *The Best Years of Our Lives,* Goldwyn-RKO Radio
Director: William Wyler, *The Best Years of Our Lives*
Actress: Olivia de Havilland, *To Each His Own*
Actor: Fredric March, *The Best Years of Our Lives*
Supporting Actress: Anne Baxter, *The Razor's Edge*
Supporting Actor: Harold Russell, *The Best Years of Our Lives*

1947
Picture: *Gentleman's Agreement,* 20th Century–Fox
Director: Elia Kazan, *Gentleman's Agreement*
Actress: Loretta Young, *The Farmer's Daughter*
Actor: Ronald Colman, *A Double Life*
Supporting Actress: Celeste Holm, *Gentleman's Agreement*
Supporting Actor: Edmund Gwenn, *Miracle on 34th Street*

1948
Picture: *Hamlet,* Rank–Two Cities–UI
Director: John Huston, *Treasure of Sierra Madre*
Actress: Jane Wyman, *Johnny Belinda*
Actor: Laurence Olivier, *Hamlet*

Supporting Actress: Claire Trevor, *Key Largo*
Supporting Actor: Walter Huston, *Treasure of Sierra Madre*

1949
Picture: *All the King's Men,* Rossen-Columbia
Director: Joseph L. Mankiewicz, *A Letter to Three Wives*
Actress: Olivia de Havilland, *The Heiress*
Actor: Broderick Crawford, *All the King's Men*
Supporting Actress: Mercedes McCambridge, *All the King's Men*
Supporting Actor: Dean Jagger, *Twelve O'Clock High*

1950
Picture: *All About Eve,* 20th Century–Fox
Director: Joseph L. Mankiewicz, *All About Eve*
Actress: Judy Holliday, *Born Yesterday*
Actor: José Ferrer, *Cyrano de Bergerac*
Supporting Actress: Josephine Hull, *Harvey*
Supporting Actor: George Sanders, *All About Eve*

1951
Picture: *An American in Paris,* MGM
Director: George Stevens, *A Place in the Sun*
Actress: Vivien Leigh, *A Streetcar Named Desire*
Actor: Humphrey Bogart, *The African Queen*
Supporting Actress: Kim Hunter, *A Streetcar Named Desire*
Supporting Actor: Karl Malden, *A Streetcar Named Desire*

1952
Picture: *The Greatest Show on Earth,* DeMille-Paramount
Director: John Ford, *The Quiet Man*
Actress: Shirley Booth, *Come Back, Little Sheba*
Actor: Gary Cooper, *High Noon*
Supporting Actress: Gloria Grahame, *The Bad and the Beautiful*
Supporting Actor: Anthony Quinn, *Viva Zapata!*

1953
Picture: *From Here to Eternity,* Columbia
Director: Fred Zinnemann, *From Here to Eternity*
Actress: Audrey Hepburn, *Roman Holiday*
Actor: William Holden, *Stalag 17*
Supporting Actress: Donna Reed, *From Here to Eternity*
Supporting Actor: Frank Sinatra, *From Here to Eternity*

1954
Picture: *On the Waterfront,* Horizon-American Corp., Columbia
Director: Elia Kazan, *On the Waterfront*
Actress: Grace Kelly, *The Country Girl*
Actor: Marlon Brando, *On the Waterfront*
Supporting Actress: Eva Marie Saint, *On the Waterfront*
Supporting Actor: Edmond O'Brien, *The Barefoot Contessa*

1955
Picture: *Marty,* Hecht and Lancaster, United Artists
Director: Delbert Mann, *Marty*
Actress: Anna Magnani, *The Rose Tattoo*
Actor: Ernest Borgnine, *Marty*
Supporting Actress: Jo Van Fleet, *East of Eden*
Supporting Actor: Jack Lemmon, *Mister Roberts*

1956
Picture: *Around the World in 80 Days,* Michael Todd Co., Inc.–United Artists
Director: George Stevens, *Giant*
Actress: Ingrid Bergman, *Anastasia*
Actor: Yul Brynner, *The King and I*
Supporting Actress: Dorothy Malone, *Written on the Wind*
Supporting Actor: Anthony Quinn, *Lust for Life*

1957
Picture: *The Bridge on the River Kwai,* Horizon Films, Columbia
Director: David Lean, *The Bridge on the River Kwai*
Actress: Joanne Woodward, *The Three Faces of Eve*
Actor: Alec Guinness, *The Bridge on the River Kwai*
Supporting Actress: Miyoshi Umeki, *Sayonara*
Supporting Actor: Red Buttons, *Sayonara*

1958
Picture: *Gigi,* Arthur Freed Productions, Inc., MGM
Director: Vincente Minnelli, *Gigi*
Actress: Susan Hayward, *I Want to Live!*
Actor: David Niven, *Separate Tables*
Supporting Actress: Wendy Hiller, *Separate Tables*
Supporting Actor: Burl Ives, *The Big Country*

1959
Picture: *Ben-Hur,* MGM
Director: William Wyler, *Ben-Hur*
Actress: Simone Signoret, *Room at the Top*
Actor: Charlton Heston, *Ben-Hur*
Supporting Actress: Shelley Winters, *The Diary of Anne Frank*
Supporting Actor: Hugh Griffith, *Ben-Hur*

1960
Picture: *The Apartment,* Mirisch Co., Inc., United Artists
Director: Billy Wilder, *The Apartment*
Actress: Elizabeth Taylor, *Butterfield 8*
Actor: Burt Lancaster, *Elmer Gantry*
Supporting Actress: Shirley Jones, *Elmer Gantry*
Supporting Actor: Peter Ustinov, *Spartacus*

1961
Picture: *West Side Story,* Mirisch Pictures, Inc., and B and P Enterprises, Inc., United Artists
Director: Robert Wise and Jerome Robbins, *West Side Story*
Actress: Sophia Loren, *Two Women*
Actor: Maximillian Schell, *Judgment at Nuremberg*
Supporting Actress: Rita Moreno, *West Side Story*
Supporting Actor: George Chakiris, *West Side Story*

1962
Picture: *Lawrence of Arabia,* Horizon Pictures, Ltd.– Columbia
Director: David Lean, *Lawrence of Arabia*
Actress: Anne Bancroft, *The Miracle Worker*
Actor: Gregory Peck, *To Kill a Mockingbird*
Supporting Actress: Patty Duke, *The Miracle Worker*
Supporting Actor: Ed Begley, *Sweet Bird of Youth*

1963
Picture: *Tom Jones,* A Woodfall Production, United Artists–Lopert Pictures
Director: Tony Richardson, *Tom Jones*
Actress: Patricia Neal, *Hud*
Actor: Sidney Poitier, *Lilies of the Field*
Supporting Actress: Margaret Rutherford, *The V.I.P.s*
Supporting Actor: Melvyn Douglas, *Hud*

1964
Picture: *My Fair Lady,* Warner Bros.
Director: George Cukor, *My Fair Lady*
Actress: Julie Andrews, *Mary Poppins*
Actor: Rex Harrison, *My Fair Lady*
Supporting Actress: Lila Kedrova, *Zorba the Greek*
Supporting Actor: Peter Ustinov, *Topkapi*

1965
Picture: *The Sound of Music,* Argyle Enterprises Production, 20th Century–Fox
Director: Robert Wise, *The Sound of Music*
Actress: Julie Christie, *Darling*
Actor: Lee Marvin, *Cat Ballou*
Supporting Actress: Shelley Winters, *A Patch of Blue*
Supporting Actor: Martin Balsam, *A Thousand Clowns*

1966
Picture: *A Man for All Seasons,* Highland Films, Ltd., Production, Columbia
Director: Fred Zinnemann, *A Man for All Seasons*
Actress: Elizabeth Taylor, *Who's Afraid of Virginia Woolf?*
Actor: Paul Scofield, *A Man for All Seasons*
Supporting Actress: Sandy Dennis, *Who's Afraid of Virginia Woolf?*
Supporting Actor: Walter Matthau, *The Fortune Cookie*

1967
Picture: *In the Heat of the Night,* Mirisch Corp. Productions, United Artists
Director: Mike Nichols, *The Graduate*
Actress: Katharine Hepburn, *Guess Who's Coming to Dinner*
Actor: Rod Steiger, *In the Heat of the Night*
Supporting Actress: Estelle Parsons, *Bonnie and Clyde*
Supporting Actor: George Kennedy, *Cool Hand Luke*

1968
Picture: *Oliver!,* Columbia Pictures
Director: Sir Carol Reed, *Oliver!*
Actress: Katharine Hepburn, *The Lion in Winter* and Barbra Streisand, *Funny Girl*
Actor: Cliff Robertson, *Charly*
Supporting Actress: Ruth Gordon, *Rosemary's Baby*
Supporting Actor: Jack Albertson, *The Subject Was Roses*

1969
Picture: *Midnight Cowboy,* Jerome Hellman–John Schlesinger Production, United Artists
Director: John Schlesinger, *Midnight Cowboy*
Actress: Maggie Smith, *The Prime of Miss Jean Brodie*
Actor: John Wayne, *True Grit*
Supporting Actress: Goldie Hawn, *Cactus Flower*
Supporting Actor: Gig Young, *They Shoot Horses, Don't They?*

1970
Picture: *Patton,* Frank McCarthy–Franklin J. Schaffner Production, 20th Century–Fox
Director: Franklin J. Schaffner, *Patton*
Actress: Glenda Jackson, *Women in Love*
Actor: George C. Scott, *Patton*
Supporting Actress: Helen Hayes, *Airport*
Supporting Actor: John Mills, *Ryan's Daughter*

1971
Picture: *The French Connection,* D'Antoni Productions, 20th Century–Fox
Director: William Friedkin, *The French Connection*
Actress: Jane Fonda, *Klute*
Actor: Gene Hackman, *The French Connection*
Supporting Actress: Cloris Leachman, *The Last Picture Show*
Supporting Actor: Ben Johnson, *The Last Picture Show*

1972
Picture: *The Godfather,* Albert S. Ruddy Production, Paramount
Director: Bob Fosse, *Cabaret*
Actress: Liza Minnelli, *Cabaret*
Actor: Marlon Brando, *The Godfather*
Supporting Actress: Eileen Heckart, *Butterflies Are Free*
Supporting Actor: Joel Gray, *Cabaret*

1973
Picture: *The Sting,* Universal–Bill Phillips–George Roy Hill Production, Universal
Director: George Roy Hill, *The Sting*
Actress: Glenda Jackson, *A Touch of Class*
Actor: Jack Lemmon, *Save the Tiger*
Supporting Actress: Tatum O'Neal, *Paper Moon*
Supporting Actor: John Houseman, *The Paper Chase*

1974
Picture: *The Godfather, Part II,* Coppola Co. Production, Paramount
Director: Francis Ford Coppola, *The Godfather, Part II*
Actress: Ellen Burstyn, *Alice Doesn't Live Here Anymore*
Actor: Art Carney, *Harry and Tonto*
Supporting Actress: Ingrid Bergman, *Murder on the Orient Express*
Supporting Actor: Robert De Niro, *The Godfather, Part II*

1975
Picture: *One Flew over the Cuckoo's Nest,* Fantasy Films Production, United Artists
Director: Milos Forman, *One Flew over the Cuckoo's Nest*
Actress: Louise Fletcher, *One Flew over the Cuckoo's Nest*
Actor: Jack Nicholson, *One Flew over the Cuckoo's Nest*

Supporting Actress: Lee Grant, *Shampoo*
Supporting Actor: George Burns, *The Sunshine Boys*

1976

Picture: *Rocky,* Robert Chartoff–Irwin Winkler Production, United Artists
Director: John G. Avildsen, *Rocky*
Actress: Faye Dunaway, *Network*
Actor: Peter Finch, *Network*
Supporting Actress: Beatrice Straight, *Network*
Supporting Actor: Jason Robards, *All the President's Men*

1977

Picture: *Annie Hall,* Jack Rollins–Charles H. Joffe Production, United Artists
Director: Woody Allen, *Annie Hall*
Actress: Diane Keaton, *Annie Hall*
Actor: Richard Dreyfuss, *The Goodbye Girl*
Supporting Actress: Vanessa Redgrave, *Julia*
Supporting Actor: Jason Robards, *Julia*

1978

Picture: *The Deer Hunter,* Michael Cimino Film Production, Universal
Director: Michael Cimino, *The Deer Hunter*
Actress: Jane Fonda, *Coming Home*
Actor: Jon Voight, *Coming Home*
Supporting Actress: Maggie Smith, *California Suite*
Supporting Actor: Christopher Walken, *The Deer Hunter*

1979

Picture: *Kramer vs. Kramer,* Stanley Jaffe Production, Columbia Pictures
Director: Robert Benton, *Kramer vs. Kramer*
Actress: Sally Field, *Norma Rae*
Actor: Dustin Hoffman, *Kramer vs. Kramer*
Supporting Actress: Meryl Streep, *Kramer vs. Kramer*
Supporting Actor: Melvyn Douglas, *Being There*

1980

Picture: *Ordinary People,* Wildwood Enterprises Production, Paramount
Director: Robert Redford, *Ordinary People*
Actress: Sissy Spacek, *Coal Miner's Daughter*
Actor: Robert De Niro, *Raging Bull*
Supporting Actress: Mary Steenburgen, *Melvin and Howard*
Supporting Actor: Timothy Hutton, *Ordinary People*

1981

Picture: *Chariots of Fire,* Enigma Productions, Ladd Company/Warner Bros.
Director: Warren Beatty, *Reds*
Actress: Katharine Hepburn, *On Golden Pond*
Actor: Henry Fonda, *On Golden Pond*
Supporting Actress: Maureen Stapleton, *Reds*
Supporting Actor: John Gielgud, *Arthur*

1982

Picture: *Gandhi,* Indo-British Films Production/Columbia
Director: Richard Attenborough, *Gandhi*
Actress: Meryl Streep, *Sophie's Choice*
Actor: Ben Kingsley, *Gandhi*
Supporting Actress: Jessica Lange, *Tootsie*
Supporting Actor: Louis Gossett, Jr., *An Officer and a Gentleman*

1983

Picture: *Terms of Endearment,* Paramount
Director: James L. Brooks, *Terms of Endearment*
Actress: Shirley MacLaine, *Terms of Endearment*
Actor: Robert Duvall, *Tender Mercies*
Supporting Actress: Linda Hunt, *The Year of Living Dangerously*
Supporting Actor: Jack Nicholson, *Terms of Endearment*

1984

Picture: *Amadeus,* Orion
Director: Milos Forman, *Amadeus*
Actress: Sally Field, *Places in the Heart*
Actor: F. Murray Abraham, *Amadeus*

Supporting Actress: Dame Peggy Ashcroft, *A Passage to India*
Supporting Actor: Haing S. Ngor, *The Killing Fields*

1985

Picture: *Out of Africa,* Universal
Director: Sydney Pollack, *Out of Africa*
Actress: Geraldine Page, *The Trip to Bountiful*
Actor: William Hurt, *Kiss of the Spider Woman*
Supporting Actress: Anjelica Huston, *Prizzi's Honor*
Supporting Actor: Don Ameche, *Cocoon*

1986

Picture: *Platoon,* Orion
Director: Oliver Stone, *Platoon*
Actress: Marlee Matlin, *Children of a Lesser God*
Actor: Paul Newman, *The Color of Money*
Supporting Actress: Dianne Wiest, *Hannah and Her Sisters*
Supporting Actor: Michael Caine, *Hannah and Her Sisters*

1987

Picture: *The Last Emperor,* Columbia Pictures
Director: Bernardo Bertolucci, *The Last Emperor*
Actress: Cher, *Moonstruck*
Actor: Michael Douglas, *Wall Street*
Supporting Actress: Olympia Dukakis, *Moonstruck*
Supporting Actor: Sean Connery, *The Untouchables*

1988

Picture: *Rain Man,* United Artists
Director: Barry Levinson, *Rain Man*
Actress: Jodie Foster, *The Accused*
Actor: Dustin Hoffman, *Rain Man*
Supporting Actress: Geena Davis, *The Accidental Tourist*
Supporting Actor: Kevin Kline, *A Fish Called Wanda*

1989

Picture: *Driving Miss Daisy,* Warner Bros.
Director: Oliver Stone, *Born on the Fourth of July*
Actress: Jessica Tandy, *Driving Miss Daisy*
Actor: Daniel Day-Lewis, *My Left Foot*
Supporting Actress: Brenda Fricker, *My Left Foot*
Supporting Actor: Denzel Washington, *Glory*

1990

Picture: *Dances with Wolves,* Orion
Director: Kevin Costner, *Dances with Wolves*
Actress: Kathy Bates, *Misery*
Actor: Jeremy Irons, *Reversal of Fortune*
Supporting Actress: Whoopi Goldberg, *Ghost*
Supporting Actor: Joe Pesci, *Goodfellas*

1991

Picture: *The Silence of the Lambs,* Orion
Director: Jonathan Demme, *The Silence of the Lambs*
Actress: Jodie Foster, *The Silence of the Lambs*
Actor: Anthony Hopkins, *The Silence of the Lambs*
Supporting Actress: Mercedes Ruehl, *The Fisher King*
Supporting Actor: Jack Palance, *City Slickers*

1992

Picture: *Unforgiven,* Warner Bros.
Director: Clint Eastwood, *Unforgiven*
Actress: Emma Thompson, *Howards End*
Actor: Al Pacino, *Scent of a Woman*
Supporting Actress: Marisa Tomei, *My Cousin Vinny*
Supporting Actor: Gene Hackman, *Unforgiven*

1993

Picture: *Schindler's List,* Universal
Director: Steven Spielberg, *Schindler's List*
Actress: Holly Hunter, *The Piano*
Actor: Tom Hanks, *Philadelphia*
Supporting Actress: Anna Paquin, *The Piano*
Supporting Actor: Tommy Lee Jones, *The Fugitive*

1994

Picture: *Forrest Gump,* Paramount
Director: Robert Zemeckis, *Forrest Gump*
Actress: Jessica Lange, *Blue Sky*
Actor: Tom Hanks, *Forrest Gump*

Supporting Actress: Dianne Wiest, *Bullets over Broadway*
Supporting Actor: Martin Landau, *Ed Wood*

1995
Picture: *Braveheart*, Paramount
Director: Mel Gibson, *Braveheart*
Actress: Susan Sarandon, *Dead Man Walking*
Actor: Nicolas Cage, *Leaving Las Vegas*
Supporting Actress: Mira Sorvino, *Mighty Aphrodite*
Supporting Actor: Kevin Spacey, *The Usual Suspects*

1996
Picture: *The English Patient*, Miramax
Director: Anthony Minghella, *The English Patient*
Actress: Frances McDormand, *Fargo*
Actor: Geoffrey Rush, *Shine*
Supporting Actress: Juliette Binoche, *The English Patient*
Supporting Actor: Cuba Gooding, Jr., *Jerry Maguire*

1997
Picture: *Titanic*, 20th Century–Fox and Paramount
Director: James Cameron, *Titanic*
Actress: Helen Hunt, *As Good As It Gets*
Actor: Jack Nicholson, *As Good As It Gets*
Supporting Actress: Kim Basinger, *L.A. Confidential*
Supporting Actor: Robin Williams, *Good Will Hunting*

1998
Picture: *Shakespeare in Love*, Miramax
Director: Steven Spielberg, *Saving Private Ryan*
Actress: Gwyneth Paltrow, *Shakespeare in Love*
Actor: Roberto Benigni, *Life Is Beautiful*
Supporting Actress: Judi Dench, *Shakespeare in Love*
Supporting Actor: James Coburn, *Affliction*

1999
Picture: *American Beauty*, DreamWorks SKG
Director: Sam Mendes, *American Beauty*
Actress: Hilary Swank, *Boys Don't Cry*
Actor: Kevin Spacey, *American Beauty*
Supporting Actress: Angelina Jolie, *Girl, Interrupted*
Supporting Actor: Michael Caine, *The Cider House Rules*

2000
Picture: *Gladiator*, DreamWorks and Universal
Director: Steven Soderbergh, *Traffic*
Actress: Julia Roberts, *Erin Brockovich*
Actor: Russell Crowe, *Gladiator*
Supporting Actress: Marcia Gay Harden, *Pollock*
Supporting Actor: Benicio Del Toro, *Traffic*

2001
Picture: *A Beautiful Mind*, Universal and DreamWorks
Director: Ron Howard, *A Beautiful Mind*
Actress: Halle Berry, *Monster's Ball*
Actor: Denzel Washington, *Training Day*
Supporting Actress: Jennifer Connelly, *A Beautiful Mind*
Supporting Actor: Jim Broadbent, *Iris*

2002
Picture: *Chicago*, Miramax
Director: Roman Polanski, *The Pianist*
Actress: Nicole Kidman, *The Hours*
Actor: Adrien Brody, *The Pianist*
Supporting Actress: Catherine Zeta-Jones, *Chicago*
Supporting Actor: Chris Cooper, *Adaptation*

2003
Picture: *The Lord of the Rings: The Return of the King*, New Line
Director: Peter Jackson, *The Lord of the Rings: The Return of the King*
Actress: Charlize Theron, *Monster*
Actor: Sean Penn, *Mystic River*
Supporting Actress: Renée Zellweger, *Cold Mountain*
Supporting Actor: Tim Robbins, *Mystic River*

2004
Picture: *Million Dollar Baby*, Warner Bros.
Director: Clint Eastwood, *Million Dollar Baby*
Actress: Hilary Swank, *Million Dollar Baby*
Actor: Jamie Foxx, *Ray*
Supporting Actress: Cate Blanchett, *The Aviator*
Supporting Actor: Morgan Freeman, *Million Dollar Baby*

Other Academy Awards for 2004

Art Direction: Dante Ferretti, art direction; Francesca Lo Schiavo, set decoration, *The Aviator*
Cinematography: Robert Richardson, *The Aviator*
Costume Design: Sandy Powell, *The Aviator*
Documentary (feature): *Born into Brothels* (Ross Kauffman and Zana Briski)
Editing: Thelma Schoonmaker, *The Aviator*
Foreign-Language Film: *The Sea Inside* (Spain)
Makeup: Valli O'Reilly and Bill Corso, *Lemony Snicket's A Series of Unfortunate Events*
Music (original score): Jan A. P. Kaczmarek, *Finding Neverland*
Best Original Song: Jorge Drexler, "Al Otro Lado del Río," *The Motorcycle Diaries*

Animated Film: *The Incredibles* (Pixar/Walt Disney)
Adapted Screenplay: Alexander Payne and Jim Taylor, *Sideways*
Original Screenplay: Charlie Kaufman, *Eternal Sunshine of the Spotless Mind*
Short Subject (live action): *Wasp* (Andrea Arnold)
Sound: Scott Millan, Greg Orloff, Bob Beemer, and Steve Cantamessa, *Ray*
Sound Editing: Michael Silvers and Randy Thom, *The Incredibles*
Visual Effects: John Dykstra, Scott Stokdyk, Anthony LaMolinara, and John Frazier, *Spider-Man 2*
Honorary Award: Sidney Lumet

2005 Golden Globe Awards

Film Awards

Best Motion Picture—Drama: *The Aviator*
Best Actor in a Drama: Leonardo DiCaprio, *The Aviator*
Best Actress in a Drama: Hilary Swank, *Million Dollar Baby*
Best Motion Picture—Musical or Comedy: *Sideways*
Best Actor in a Musical or Comedy: Jamie Foxx, *Ray*
Best Actress in a Musical or Comedy: Annette Bening, *Being Julia*
Best Supporting Actor: Clive Owen, *Closer*
Best Supporting Actress: Natalie Portman, *Closer*
Best Director: Clint Eastwood, *Million Dollar Baby*
Best Screenplay: Alexander Payne and Jim Taylor, *Sideways*
Best Original Score: Howard Shore, *The Aviator*

Best Original Song: "Old Habits Die Hard," Mick Jagger and David A. Stewart, *Alfie*
Best Foreign Film: *The Sea Inside* (Spain)
Cecil B. DeMille Award: Robin Williams

Television Awards
Best Series—Drama: *Nip/Tuck* (FX)
Best Actor in a Drama: Ian McShane, *Deadwood*
Best Actress in a Drama: Mariska Hargitay, *Law & Order: Special Victims Unit*
Best Series—Musical or Comedy: *Desperate Housewives* (ABC)
Best Actor in a Musical or Comedy Series: Jason Bateman, *Arrested Development*
Best Actress in a Musical or Comedy Series: Teri Hatcher, *Desperate Housewives*
Best Miniseries or Movie Made for Television: *The Life*

and Death of Peter Sellers (HBO)
Best Actor in a Miniseries or Movie Made for Television: Geoffrey Rush, The Life and Death of Peter Sellers
Best Actress in a Miniseries or Movie Made for Television: Glenn Close, The Lion in Winter

Best Supporting Actor in a Series, Miniseries, or Movie Made for Television: William Shatner, Boston Legal
Best Supporting Actress in a Series, Miniseries, or Movie Made for Television: Anjelica Huston, Iron Jawed Angels

2005 Tony (Antoinette Perry) Awards

Play: Doubt
Musical: Monty Python's Spamalot
Revival—Play: Glengarry Glen Ross
Revival—Musical: La Cage aux Folles
Actor—Play: Bill Irwin, Who's Afraid of Virginia Woolf?
Actress—Play: Cherry Jones, Doubt
Actor—Musical: Norbert Leo Butz, Dirty Rotten Scoundrels
Actress—Musical: Victoria Clark, The Light in the Piazza
Featured Actor—Play: Liev Schreiber, Glengarry Glen Ross
Featured Actress—Play: Adriane Lenox, Doubt
Featured Actor—Musical: Dan Fogler, The 25th Annual Putnam County Spelling Bee
Featured Actress—Musical: Sara Ramirez, Monty Python's Spamalot
Director—Play: Doug Hughes, Doubt
Director—Musical: Mike Nichols, Monty Python's Spamalot
Book—Musical: Rachel Sheinkin, The 25th Annual

Putnam County Spelling Bee
Score—Musical: Adam Guettel, The Light in the Piazza
Orchestration: Ted Sperling, Adam Guettel, and Bruce Coughlin, The Light in the Piazza
Scenic Designer—Play: Scott Pask, The Pillowman
Scenic Designer—Musical: Michael Yeargan, The Light in the Piazza
Costume Designer—Play: Jess Goldstein, The Rivals
Costume Designer—Musical: Catherine Zuber, The Light in the Piazza
Choreographer: Jerry Mitchell, La Cage aux Folles
Lighting Designer—Play: Brian MacDevitt, The Pillowman
Lighting Designer—Musical: Christopher Akerlind, The Light in the Piazza
Regional Theater: Theatre de la Jeune Lune, Minneapolis, Minn.
Special Award: Edward Albee, for lifetime achievement
Special Theatrical Event: Billy Crystal, 700 Sundays

2004–2005 Drama Desk Awards

Outstanding Play: Doubt
Outstanding Musical: Monty Python's Spamalot
Outstanding Musical Revival: La Cage aux Folles
Outstanding Play Revival: Twelve Angry Men
Best Actor in a Play: Brian F. O'Byrne, Doubt
Best Actress in a Play: Cherry Jones, Doubt
Best Featured Actor in a Play: Michael Stuhlbarg, The Pillowman
Best Featured Actress in a Play: Adriane Lenox, Doubt
Best Actor in a Musical: Norbert Leo Butz, Dirty Rotten Scoundrels
Best Actress in a Musical: Victoria Clark, The Light in the Piazza
Best Featured Actor in a Musical: Denis O'Hare, Sweet Charity
Best Featured Actress in a Musical: Jan Maxwell, Chitty Chitty Bang Bang
Best Director of a Play: Doug Hughes, Doubt
Best Director of a Musical: James Lapine, The 25th Annual Putnam County Spelling Bee
Best Choreography: Jerry Mitchell, La Cage aux Folles
Best Book of a Musical: Rachel Sheinkin, The 25th

Annual Putnam County Spelling Bee
Best Music: Adam Guettel, The Light in the Piazza
Best Lyrics: Eric Idle, Monty Python's Spamalot
Outstanding Orchestration: Ted Sperling, Adam Guettel, Bruce Coughlin, The Light in the Piazza
Outstanding Set Design of a Play: Santo Loquasto, Glengarry Glen Ross
Outstanding Set Design of a Musical: Michael Yeargan, The Light in the Piazza
Outstanding Costume Design: Tim Hatley, Monty Python's Spamalot
Outstanding Lighting Design: Christopher Akerlind, The Light in the Piazza
Outstanding Sound Design: Paul Arditti, The Pillowman
Outstanding Solo Performance: Billy Crystal, 700 Sundays
Unique Theatrical Experience: Slava's Snowshow
Outstanding Ensemble Performances: Cast of Glengarry Glen Ross and cast of The 25th Annual Putnam County Spelling Bee
Career Achievement: Julie Harris
Special Awards: Keen Company and The Public Theater

2004–2005 Obie Awards

The Obie Awards, presented by The Village Voice, honor superior off-Broadway theater.

Direction: Dan Wackerman, Counsellor-At-Law; Ivo van Hove, Hedda Gabler; Doug Hughes for sustained excellence of direction
Performance: Jeremy Shamos, Engaged; Elizabeth Marvel, Hedda Gabler; Jason Butler Harner, Hedda Gabler; Rosemary Allen, Good Samaritans; Cherry Jones, Doubt; Larry Bryggman, Romance; Kieran Culkin, After Ashley; Mercedes Ruehl, Woman Before a Glass; LaChanze, Dessa Rose; Deidre O'Connell for her sustained excellence of performance; Vivienne Benesch, Going to St. Ives; L. Scott Caldwell, Going to St. Ives
Design: John Lee Beatty, set design, Engaged; Rui Rita, lighting design, Engaged; Aural Fixation Sound & Music, sound design, Engaged; Catherine Zuber, costume design, Engaged; Thomas Lynch, set design, Woman Before a Glass; Phil Monat, lighting design, Woman

Before a Glass; David Van Tieghem, sound design, Woman Before a Glass; Willa Kim, costume design, Woman Before a Glass; Jan Versweyveld, set design, Hedda Gabler
Playwriting: Christopher Shinn, Where Do We Live; John Patrick Shanley, Doubt; Caryl Churchill, A Number; Lynn Nottage, Fabulation
Special Citations: The Imagine Festival of Arts, Issues & Ideas; Hell Meets Henry Halfway; Sin: A Cardinal Deposed
Sustained Achievement: John Guare
Grants: 13P, Epic Theatre Company, Little Theater at Tonic, Gina Gionfriddo for Distinguished Emerging Playwright, Margo Skinner Memorial Acting Scholarship
Ross Wetzsteon Award: New Dramatists

Major Grammy Awards for Recordings in 2004

Record: "Here We Go Again," Ray Charles & Norah Jones
Album: *Genius Loves Company,* Ray Charles & Various Artists
Song: "Daughters," John Mayer, songwriter (John Mayer)
New Artist: Maroon 5
Female Pop Vocal: "Sunrise," Norah Jones
Male Pop Vocal: "Daughters," John Mayer
Pop Duo or Group with Vocals: "Heaven," Los Lonely Boys
Pop Collaboration with Vocals: "Here We Go Again," Ray Charles & Norah Jones
Pop Instrumental: "11th Commandment," Ben Harper
Pop Instrumental Album: *Henry Mancini: Pink Guitar,* Various Artists
Pop Vocal Album: *Genius Loves Company,* Ray Charles & Various Artists
Dance Recording: "Toxic," Britney Spears
Electronic/Dance Recording: "Kish Kash," Basement Jaxx
Traditional Pop Vocal Album: *Stardust . . . The Great American Songbook: Volume III,* Rod Stewart
Solo Rock Vocal: "Code of Silence," Bruce Springsteen
Rock Duo or Group with Vocals: "Vertigo," U2
Hard Rock: "Slither," Velvet Revolver
Metal: "Whiplash," Motörhead
Rock Instrumental: "Mrs. O'Leary's Cow," Brian Wilson
Rock Song: "Vertigo," Bono, Adam Clayton, The Edge & Larry Mullen, songwriters (U2)
Rock Album: *American Idiot,* Green Day
Alternative Music Album: *A Ghost Is Born,* Wilco
Female R&B Vocal: "If I Ain't Got You," Alicia Keys
Male R&B Vocal: "Call My Name," Prince
R&B Duo or Group with Vocals: "My Boo," Usher & Alicia Keys
Traditional R&B Vocal: "Musicology," Prince
Urban/Alternative Vocal: "Cross My Mind," Jill Scott
R&B Song: "You Don't Know My Name," Alicia Keys, Harold Lilly & Kanye West, songwriters (Alicia Keys)
R&B Album: *The Diary of Alicia Keys,* Alicia Keys
Contemporary R&B Album: *Confessions,* Usher
Rap Solo: "99 Problems," Jay-Z
Rap Duo or Group: "Let's Get It Started," The Black Eyed Peas
Rap Sung/Collaboration: "Yeah!," Usher featuring Lil Jon & Ludacris
Rap Song: "Jesus Walks," Miri Ben Ari, C. Smith, & Kanye West, songwriters (Kanye West)
Rap Album: *The College Dropout,* Kanye West
Female Country Vocal: "Redneck Woman," Gretchen Wilson
Male Country Vocal: "Live Like You Were Dying," Tim McGraw
Country Duo or Group with Vocals: "Top of the World," Dixie Chicks
Country Collaboration with Vocals: "Portland Oregon," Loretta Lynn & Jack White
Country Instrumental: "Earl's Breakdown," Nitty Gritty Dirt Band Featuring Earl Scruggs, Randy Scruggs, Vassar Clements, & Jerry Douglas
Country Song: "Live Like You Were Dying," Tim Nichols & Craig Wiseman, songwriters (Tim McGraw)
Country Album: *Van Lear Rose,* Loretta Lynn
Bluegrass Album: *Brand New Strings,* Ricky Skaggs & Kentucky Thunder
New Age Album: *Returning,* Will Ackerman
Contemporary Jazz Album: *Unspeakable,* Bill Frisell
Jazz Vocal Album: *R.S.V.P. (Rare Songs, Very Personal),* Nancy Wilson
Jazz Instrumental, Solo: "Speak Like a Child," Herbie Hancock
Jazz Instrumental Album: *Illuminations,* McCoy Tyner with Gary Bartz, Terence Blanchard, Christian McBride, & Lewis Nash
Large Jazz Ensemble Album: *Concert in the Garden,* Maria Schneider Orchestra
Latin Jazz Album: *Land of the Sun,* Charlie Haden
Gospel Performance: "Heaven Help Us All," Ray Charles & Gladys Knight
Rock Gospel Album: *Wire,* Third Day
Pop/Contemporary Gospel Album: *All Things New,* Steven Curtis Chapman
Southern, Country, or Bluegrass Gospel Album: *Worship & Faith,* Randy Travis
Traditional Soul Gospel Album: *There Will Be a Light,* Ben Harper & The Blind Boys of Alabama
Contemporary Soul Gospel Album: *Nothing Without You,* Smokie Norful
Gospel Album by a Choir or Chorus: *Live . . . This Is Your House,* Carol Cymbala, choir director; The Brooklyn Tabernacle Choir
Latin Pop Album: *Amar Sin Mentiras,* Marc Anthony
Latin Rock/Alternative Album: *Street Signs,* Ozomatli
Tropical Latin Album: *¡Ahora Sí!,* Israel López "Cachao"
Salsa/Merengue Album: *Across 110th Street,* Spanish Harlem Orchestra featuring Ruben Blades
Mexican/Mexican-American Album: *Intimamente,* Intocable
Tejano Album: *Polkas, Gritos y Acordeónes,* David Lee Garza, Joel Guzman, & Sunny Sauceda
Traditional Blues Album: *Blues to the Bone,* Etta James
Contemporary Blues Album: *Keep It Simple,* Keb' Mo'
Traditional Folk Album: *Beautiful Dreamer—The Songs of Stephen Foster,* Various Artists
Contemporary Folk Album: *The Revolution Starts . . . Now,* Steve Earle
Native American Music Album: *Cedar Dream Songs,* Bill Miller
Hawaiian Music Album: *Slack Key Guitar: Volume 2,* Various Artists
Reggae Album: *True Love,* Toots & The Maytals
Traditional World Music Album: *Raise Your Spirit Higher,* Ladysmith Black Mambazo
Contemporary World Music Album: *Egypt,* Youssou N'Dour
Polka Album: *Let's Kiss: 25th Anniversary Album,* Brave Combo
Musical Album for Children: *cELLAbration! A Tribute to Ella Jenkins,* Various Artists
Spoken Word Album for Children: *The Train They Call the City of New Orleans,* Tom Chapin
Spoken Word Album: *My Life,* Bill Clinton
Comedy Album: *The Daily Show with Jon Stewart Presents . . . America: A Citizen's Guide to Democracy Inaction,* Jon Stewart and the cast of *The Daily Show*
Musical Show Album: *Wicked,* Stephen Schwartz, producer/composer/lyricist
Best Compilation Soundtrack Album for a Motion Picture, Television, or Other Visual Media: *Garden State,* Various Artists
Best Score Soundtrack Album for a Motion Picture, Television, or Other Visual Media: *The Lord of the Rings: The Return of the King,* Howard Shore, composer
Song Written for a Motion Picture, Television, or Other Visual Media: "Into the West " (from *The Lord of the Rings: The Return of the King*), Annie Lennox, Howard Shore, & Fran Walsh, songwriters
Instrumental Composition: "Merengue," Paquito D'Rivera, composer (Yo-Yo Ma)
Instrumental Arrangement: "Past Present & Future," Slide Hampton, arranger (The Vanguard Jazz Orchestra)
Instrumental Arrangement with Accompanying Vocals: "Over the Rainbow," Victor Vanacore, arranger (Ray Charles & Johnny Mathis)
Historical Album: *Night Train to Nashville: Music City Rhythm & Blues, 1945–1970*
Producer, Nonclassical: John Shanks
Classical Producer: David Frost
Classical Album: *Adams: On the Transmigration of Souls,*

Lorin Maazel, conductor; John Adams & Lawrence Rock, producers

Orchestral Performance: *Adams: On the Transmigration of Souls,* Lorin Maazel, conductor (Brooklyn Youth Chorus & New York Choral Artists; New York Philharmonic)

Opera Recording: *Mozart: Le Nozze di Figaro,* René Jacobs, conductor

Choral Performance: *Berlioz: Requiem,* Robert Spano, conductor

Instrumental Soloist with Orchestra: *Previn: Violin Concerto "Anne-Sophie"/Bernstein: Serenade,* André Previn, conductor; Anne-Sophie Mutter, violin (Boston Symphony Orchestra & London Symphony Orchestra)

Instrumental Soloist Without Orchestra: *Aire Latino (Morel, Villa-Lobos, Ponce, etc.),* David Russell, guitar

Chamber Music: *Prokofiev (Arr. Pletnev): Cinderella— Suite for Two Pianos/Ravel: Ma Mère L'Oye,* Martha Argerich, piano & Mikhail Pletnev, piano

Small Ensemble Performance (with or Without Conductor): *Carlos Chávez: Complete Chamber Music, Vol. 2,*

Jeff von der Schmidt, conductor; Southwest Chamber Music

Classical Vocal: *Ives: Songs (The Things Our Fathers Loved; The Housatonic at Stockbridge, Etc.),* Susan Graham, mezzo soprano (Pierre-Laurent Aimard, piano)

Classical Contemporary Composition: *Adams: On the Transmigration of Souls,* John Adams

Classical Crossover Album: *LAGQ's Guitar Heroes,* Los Angeles Guitar Quartet

Music Video, Short Form: "Vertigo" (U2), Alex & Martin, video director

Music Video, Long Form: *Concert for George* (Various Artists), David Leland, video director

Lifetime Achievement Awards: Eddy Arnold, Art Blakey, the Carter Family, Morton Gould, Janis Joplin, Led Zeppelin, Jerry Lee Lewis, Jelly Roll Morton, Pinetop Perkins, and the Staple Singers

Trustees Awards: Hoagy Carmichael, Don Cornelius, Alfred Lion, and Dr. Billy Taylor

2004 Country Music Association Awards

Entertainer of the Year: Kenny Chesney
Male Vocalist of the Year: Keith Urban
Female Vocalist of the Year: Martina McBride
Horizon Award: Gretchen Wilson
Vocal Group of the Year: Rascal Flatts
Vocal Duo of the Year: Brooks & Dunn
Single of the Year: "Live Like You Were Dying," Tim McGraw
Album of the Year: *When the Sun Goes Down,* Kenny Chesney

Song of the Year: "Live Like You Were Dying," Tim Nichols and Craig Wiseman
Vocal Event of the Year: "Whiskey Lullaby," Brad Paisley featuring Alison Krauss
Musician of the Year: Dann Huff
Music Video of the Year: "Whiskey Lullaby," Brad Paisley and Alison Krauss

2004 National Book Awards

Fiction: *The News from Paraguay,* Lily Tuck (HarperCollins Publishers)
Nonfiction: *Arc of Justice: A Saga of Race, Civil Rights, and Murder in the Jazz Age,* Kevin Boyle (Henry Holt & Company, LLC)
Poetry: *Door in the Mountain: New and Collected Poems,*

1965–2003, Jean Valentine (Wesleyan University Press)
Young People's Literature: *Godless,* Pete Hautman (Simon & Schuster Books for Young Readers)
Medal for Distinguished Contribution to American Literature: Judy Blume

2004 National Book Critics Circle Awards

Fiction: *Gilead,* Marilynne Robinson (Farrar, Straus and Giroux)
General Nonfiction: *The Reformation: A History,* Diarmaid MacCulloch (Viking)
Biography or Autobiography: *de Kooning: An American Master,* Mark Stevens and Annalyn Swan (Knopf)
Poetry: *The School Among the Ruins,* Adrienne Rich (Norton)

Criticism: *Where You're At: Notes from the Frontline of a Hip-Hop Planet,* Patrick Neate (Riverhead)
Ivan Sandrof Lifetime Achievement Award: Louis D. Rubin, Jr., founder of Algonquin Press and the author and editor of over 50 books
Nona Balakian Citation for Excellence in Reviewing: David Orr, *New York Times Book Review* and *Poetry* magazine

PEN/Faulkner Award

The PEN/Faulkner award is the largest annual juried prize for fiction in the United States. The winner receives $15,000.

1981	Walter Abish, *How German Is It?*		1994	Philip Roth, *Operation Shylock*
1982	David Bradley, *The Chaneysville Incident*		1995	David Guterson, *Snow Falling on Cedars*
1983	Toby Olson, *Seaview*		1996	Richard Ford, *Independence Day*
1984	John Edgar Wideman, *Sent for You Yesterday*		1997	Gina Berriault, *Women in Their Beds*
1985	Tobias Wolff, *The Barracks Thief*		1998	Rafi Zabor, *The Bear Comes Home*
1986	Peter Taylor, *The Old Forest*		1999	Michael Cunningham, *The Hours*
1987	Richard Wiley, *Soldiers in Hiding*		2000	Ha Jin, *Waiting*
1988	T. Coraghessan Boyle, *World's End*		2001	Philip Roth, *The Human Stain*
1989	James Salter, *Dusk*		2002	Ann Patchett, *Bel Canto*
1990	E. L. Doctorow, *Billy Bathgate*		2003	Sabina Murray, *The Caprices*
1991	John Edgar Wideman, *Philadelphia Fire*		2004	John Updike, *The Early Stories*
1992	Don Delillo, *Mao II*		2005	Ha Jin, *War Trash*
1993	E. Annie Proulx, *Postcards*			

Man Booker Prize

Britain's most prestigious literary award, formerly called the Booker Prize, honors the best full-length novel written in English by a citizen of a current or former British Commonwealth country.

1969	*Something to Answer For*, P. H. Newby	1987	*Moon Tiger*, Penelope Lively
1970	*The Elected Member*, Bernice Rubens	1988	*Oscar and Lucinda*, Peter Carey
1971	*In a Free State*, V. S. Naipaul	1989	*The Remains of the Day*, Kazuo Ishiguro
1972	*G.: A Novel*, John Berger	1990	*Possession: A Romance*, A. S. Byatt
1973	*The Siege of Krishnapur*, J. G. Farrell	1991	*The Famished Road*, Ben Okri
1974	(tie) *The Conservationist*, Nadine Gordimer; *Holiday*, Stanley Middleton	1992	(tie) *The English Patient*, Michael Ondaatje; *Sacred Hunger*, Barry Unsworth
1975	*Heat and Dust*, Ruth Prawer Jhabvala	1993	*Paddy Clarke, Ha Ha Ha*, Roddy Doyle
1976	*Saville*, David Storey	1994	*How Late It Was, How Late*, James Kelman
1977	*Staying On*, Paul Scott	1995	*The Ghost Road*, Pat Barker
1978	*The Sea, the Sea*, Iris Murdoch	1996	*Last Orders*, Graham Swift
1979	*Offshore*, Penelope Fitzgerald	1997	*The God of Small Things*, Arundhati Roy
1980	*Rites of Passage*, William Golding	1998	*Amsterdam*, Ian McEwan
1981	*Midnight's Children*, Salman Rushdie	1999	*Disgrace*, J. M. Coetzee
1982	*Schindler's List*, Thomas Keneally	2000	*The Blind Assassin*, Margaret Atwood
1983	*Life & Times of Michael K*, J. M. Coetzee	2001	*True History of the Kelly Gang*, Peter Carey
1984	*Hotel du Lac*, Anita Brookner	2002	*Life of Pi*, Yann Martel
1985	*The Bone People*, Keri Hulme	2003	*Vernon God Little*, DBC Pierre
1986	*The Old Devils*, Kingsley Amis	2004	*The Line of Beauty*, Alan Hollinghurst

Truman Capote Award for Literary Criticism

The award is administered for the Truman Capote estate by the University of Iowa Writers' Workshop. The $50,000 award is the largest cash prize for literary criticism in the English language.

1996	Helen Vendler, *The Given and the Made*	2002	Declan Kiberd, *Irish Classics*
1997	John Felstiner, *Paul Celan: Poet, Survivor, Jew*	2003	Seamus Heaney, *Finders Keepers: Selected Prose 1971–2001*
1998	John Kerrigan, *Revenge Tragedy*		
1999	Charles Rosen, *Romantic Poets, Critics, and Other Madmen*	2004	Susan Stewart, *Poetry and the Fate of the Senses*
2000	Elaine Scarry, *Dreaming by the Book*; Philip Fisher, *Still the New World*	2005	Angus Fletcher, *A New Theory for American Poetry: Democracy, the Environment, and the Future of Imagination*
2001	Malcolm Bowie, *Proust Among the Stars*		

Newbery Medal

The Newbery Medal is awarded annually by the American Library Association for the most distinguished contribution to American literature for children.

2005 Newbery Medal and Honor Books

Newbery Medal for Best Book: *Kira-Kira*, Cynthia Kadohata (Atheneum Books for Young Readers/Simon & Schuster)

Newbery Honor Books: *Al Capone Does My Shirts*, Gennifer Choldenko (G. P. Putnam's Sons/Penguin Young Readers Group); *The Voice that Challenged a Nation: Marian Anderson and the Struggle for Equal Rights*, Russell Freedman (Clarion Books/Houghton Mifflin); *Lizzie Bright and the Buckminster Boy*, Gary D. Schmidt (Clarion Books/Houghton Mifflin)

1922–2004

1922	*The Story of Mankind*, Hendrick Willem Van Loon
1923	*The Voyages of Dr. Doolittle*, Hugh A. Lofting
1924	*The Dark Frigate*, Charles Boardman Hawes
1925	*Tales from Silver Lands*, Charles Joseph Finger
1926	*Shen of the Sea*, Arthur Bowie Chrisman
1927	*Smoky, the Cow Horse*, Will James
1928	*Gay-Neck, the Story of a Pigeon*, Dhan Gopal Mukerji
1929	*The Trumpeter of Krakow*, Eric P. Kelly
1930	*Hitty, Her First Hundred Years*, Rachel Field
1931	*The Cat Who Went to Heaven*, Elizabeth Jane Coatsworth
1932	*Waterless Mountain*, Laura Adams Armer
1933	*Young Fu of the Upper Yangtze*, Elizabeth Foreman Lewis
1934	*Invincible Louisa*, Cornelia Meigs
1935	*Dobry*, Monica Shannon
1936	*Caddie Woodlawn*, Carol Ryrie Brink
1937	*Roller Skates*, Ruth Sawyer
1938	*The White Stag*, Kate Seredy
1939	*Thimble Summer*, Elizabeth Enright
1940	*Daniel Boone*, James Henry Daugherty
1941	*Call It Courage*, Armstrong Sperry
1942	*The Matchlock Gun*, Walter Dumax Edmonds
1943	*Adam of the Road*, Elizabeth Janet Gray
1944	*Johnny Tremain*, Esther Forbes
1945	*Rabbit Hill*, Robert Lawson
1946	*Strawberry Girl*, Lois Lenski
1947	*Miss Hickory*, Carolyn Sherwin Bailey
1948	*The Twenty-One Balloons*, William Pène du Bois
1949	*King of the Wind*, Marguerite Henry
1950	*The Door in the Wall*, Marguerite de Angeli
1951	*Amos Fortune, Free Man*, Elizabeth Yates
1952	*Ginger Pye*, Eleanor Estes
1953	*Secret of the Andes*, Ann Nolan Clark
1954	*. . . And Now Miguel*, Joseph Krumgold
1955	*The Wheel on the School*, Meindert DeJong
1956	*Carry On, Mr. Bowditch*, Jean Lee Latham
1957	*Miracles on Maple Hill*, Virginia Eggertsen Sorensen
1958	*Rifles for Watie*, Harold Keith

1959 *The Witch of Blackbird Pond*, Elizabeth George Speare	1981 *Jacob Have I Loved*, Katherine Paterson
1960 *Onion John*, Joseph Krumgold	1982 *A Visit to William Blake's Inn: Poems for Innocent and Experienced Travelers*, Nancy Willard
1961 *Island of the Blue Dolphins*, Scott O'Dell	1983 *Dicey's Song*, Cynthia Voigt
1962 *The Bronze Bow*, Elizabeth George Speare	1984 *Dear Mr. Henshaw*, Beverly Cleary
1963 *A Wrinkle in Time*, Madeleine L'Engle	1985 *The Hero and the Crown*, Robin McKinley
1964 *It's Like This, Cat*, Emily Cheney Neville	1986 *Sarah, Plain and Tall*, Patricia MacLachlan
1965 *Shadow of a Bull*, Maia Wojciechowska	1987 *The Whipping Boy*, Sid Fleischman
1966 *I, Juan de Pareja*, Elizabeth Borton de Treviño	1988 *Lincoln: A Photobiography*, Russell Freedman
1967 *Up a Road Slowly*, Irene Hunt	1989 *Joyful Noise: Poems for Two Voices*, Paul Fleischman
1968 *From the Mixed-Up Files of Mrs. Basil E. Frankweiler*, E. L. Konigsburg	1990 *Number the Stars*, Lois Lowry
1969 *The High King*, Lloyd Alexander	1991 *Maniac Magee: a Novel*, Jerry Spinelli
1970 *Sounder*, William H. Armstrong	1992 *Shiloh*, Phyllis Reynolds Naylor
1971 *Summer of the Swans*, Betsy Byars	1993 *Missing May*, Cynthia Rylant
1972 *Mrs. Frisby and the Rats of NIMH*, Robert C. O'Brien	1994 *The Giver*, Lois Lowry
1973 *Julie of the Wolves*, Jean Craighead George	1995 *Walk Two Moons*, Sharon Creech
1974 *The Slave Dancer*, Paula Fox	1996 *The Midwife's Apprentice*, Karen Cushman
1975 *M. C. Higgins, the Great*, Virginia Hamilton	1997 *The View from Saturday*, E. L. Konigsburg
1976 *The Grey King*, Susan Cooper	1998 *Out of the Dust*, Karen Hesse
1977 *Roll of Thunder, Hear My Cry*, Mildred D. Taylor	1999 *Holes*, Louis Sachar
1978 *Bridge to Terabithia*, Katherine Paterson	2000 *Bud, Not Buddy*, Christopher Paul Curtis
1979 *The Westing Game*, Ellen Raskin	2001 *A Year Down Yonder*, Richard Peck
1980 *A Gathering of Days: A New England Girl's Journal, 1830–32*, Joan W. Blos	2002 *A Single Shard*, Linda Sue Park
	2003 *Crispin: The Cross of Lead*, Avi
	2004 *The Tale of Despereaux*, Kate DiCamillo

Caldecott Medal

The Caldecott Medal is awarded annually by the American Library Association for the most distinguished American picture book for children.

2005 Caldecott Medal and Honor Books

Caldecott Medal for Best Picture Book: *Kitten's First Full Moon*, illustrated and written by Kevin Henkes (Greenwillow Books/HarperCollins Publishers)

Caldecott Honor Books: *The Red Book*, illustrated and written by Barbara Lehman (Houghton Mifflin Company); *Coming on Home Soon*, illustrated by E. B. Lewis and written by Jacqueline Woodson (G. P. Putnam's Sons/Penguin Young Readers Group); *Knuffle Bunny: A Cautionary Tale*, illustrated and written by Mo Willems (Hyperion Books for Children)

1938–2003

1938 *Animals of the Bible, a Picture Book*, text selected by Helen Dean Fish, illustrated by Dorothy P. Lathrop

1939 *Mei Li*, written and illustrated by Thomas Handforth

1940 *Abraham Lincoln*, written and illustrated by Ingri and Edgar Parin D'Aulaire

1941 *They Were Strong and Good*, written and illustrated by Robert Lawson

1942 *Make Way for Ducklings*, written and illustrated by Robert McCloskey

1943 *The Little House*, written and illustrated by Virginia Lee Burton

1944 *Many Moons*, written by James Thurber, illustrated by Louis Slobodkin

1945 *Prayer for a Child*, written by Elizabeth Orton Jones

1946 *The Rooster Crows*, written and illustrated by Maud and Miska Petersham

1947 *The Little Island*, written by Golden MacDonald, illustrated by Leonard Weisgard

1948 *White Snow, Bright Snow*, written by Alvin Tresselt, illustrated by Roger Duvoisin

1949 *The Big Snow*, written and illustrated by Berta and Elmer Hader

1950 *Song of the Swallows*, written and illustrated by Leo Politi

1951 *The Egg Tree*, written and illustrated by Katherine Milhous

1952 *Finders Keepers*, written by William Lipkind, illustrated by Nicolas Mordivinoff

1953 *The Biggest Bear*, written and illustrated by Lynd Ward

1954 *Madeline's Rescue*, written and illustrated by Ludwig Bemelmans

1955 *Cinderella, or, The Little Glass Slipper*, translated and illustrated by Marcia Brown

1956 *Frog Went A-Courtin'*, retold by John Langstaff, illustrated by Feodor Rojankovsky

1957 *A Tree Is Nice*, written by Janice May Udry, illustrated by Marc Simont

1958 *Time of Wonder*, written and illustrated by Robert McCloskey

1959 *Chanticleer and the Fox*, adapted and illustrated by Barbara Cooney

1960 *Nine Days to Christmas*, written by Marie Hall Ets and Aurora Labastida, illustrated by Marie Hall Ets

1961 *Baboushka and the Three Kings*, written by Ruth Robbins, illustrated by Nicolas Sidjakov

1962 *Once a Mouse*, retold and illustrated by Marcia Brown

1963 *The Snowy Day*, written and illustrated by Ezra Jack Keats

1964 *Where the Wild Things Are*, written and illustrated by Maurice Sendak

1965 *May I Bring a Friend?*, written by Beatrice Schenk de Regniers, illustrated by Beni Montresor

1966 *Always Room for One More*, written by Sorche Nic Leodhas, illustrated by Nonny Hogrogian

1967 *Sam, Bangs and Moonshine*, written and illustrated by Evaline Ness

1968 *Drummer Hoff*, written by Barbara Emberley, illustrated by Ed Emberley

1969 *The Fool of the World and the Flying Ship,* retold by Arthur Ransome, illustrated by Uri Shulevitz

1970 *Sylvester and the Magic Pebble,* written and illustrated by William Steig

1971 *A Story, a Story: An African Tale,* retold and illustrated by Gail E. Haley

1972 *One Fine Day,* written and illustrated by Nonny Hogrogian

1973 *The Funny Little Woman,* retold by Arlene Mosel, illustrated by Blair Lent

1974 *Duffy and the Devil,* retold by Harve Zemach, illustrated by Margot Zemach

1975 *Arrow to the Sun: A Pueblo Indian Tale,* adapted and illustrated by Gerald H. McDermott

1976 *Why Mosquitos Buzz in People's Ears (An African Tale),* retold by Verna Aardema, illustrated by Leo and Diane Dillon

1977 *Ashanti to Zulu: African Traditions,* written by Margaret Musgrove, illustrated by Leo and Diane Dillon

1978 *Noah's Ark,* written by Jacob Revius, illustrated by Peter Spier

1979 *The Girl Who Loved Wild Horses,* written and illustrated by Paul Goble

1980 *Ox-Cart Man,* written by Donald Hall, illustrated by Barbara Cooney

1981 *Fables,* written and illustrated by Arnold Lobel

1982 *Jumanji,* written and illustrated by Chris Van Allsburg

1983 *Shadow,* translated and illustrated by Marcia Brown

1984 *The Glorious Flight: Across the Channel with Louis Blériot,* written and illustrated by Alice and Martin Provensen

1985 *St. George and the Dragon,* retold by Margaret Hodges, illustrated by Trina Schart Hyman

1986 *The Polar Express,* written and illustrated by Chris Van Allsburg

1987 *Hey, Al,* written by Arthur Yorinks, illustrated by Richard Egielski

1988 *Owl Moon,* written by Jane Yolen, illustrated by John Schoenherr

1989 *Song and Dance Man,* written by Karen Ackerman, illustrated by Stephen Gammell

1990 *Lon Po Po: A Red-Riding Hood Story from China,* by Ed Young

1991 *Black & White,* written and illustrated by David Macaulay

1992 *Tuesday,* written and illustrated by David Wiesner

1993 *Mirette on the High Wire,* written and illustrated by Emily Arnold McCully

1994 *Grandfather's Journey,* written and illustrated by Allen Say

1995 *Smoky Night,* written by Eve Bunting, illustrated by David Diaz

1996 *Officer Buckle and Gloria,* written and illustrated by Peggy Rathmann

1997 *Golem,* written and illustrated by David Wisniewski

1998 *Rapunzel,* illustrated and retold by Paul O. Zelinsky

1999 *Snowflake Bentley,* written by Jacqueline Briggs Martin, illustrated by Mary Azarian

2000 *Joseph Had a Little Overcoat,* illustrated by Simms Taback

2001 *So You Want to Be President?,* by Judith St. George, illustrated by David Small

2002 *The Three Little Pigs,* written and illustrated by David Wiesner

2003 *My Friend Rabbit,* written and illustrated by Eric Rohmann

2004 *The Man Who Walked Between the Towers,* illustrated and written by Mordicai Gerstein

Other American Library Association Awards for Children's Books, 2005

Coretta Scott King Award, honoring black authors and illustrators: *Remember: The Journey to School Integration,* Toni Morrison (Houghton Mifflin); **(illustrator):** *Ellington Was Not a Street,* Kadir Nelson (Simon & Schuster); **(Coretta Scott King/John Steptoe New Talent Author):** *Missy Violet and Me,* Barbara Hathaway (Houghton Mifflin); **(Coretta Scott King/John Steptoe New Talent Illustrator):** *Jazzy Miz Mozetta,* Frank Morrison (Farrar, Straus, and Giroux)

Michael L. Printz Award for excellence in young adult literature: *how i live now,* Meg Rosoff (Random House)

Robert F. Sibert Award for informational book: *The Voice that Challenged a Nation: Marian Anderson and the Struggle for Equal Rights,* Russell Freedman (Clarion Books/Houghton Mifflin)

Mildred L. Batchelder Award, for best book originally published in a foreign language in a foreign country: *The Shadows of Ghadames,* written by Joëlle Stolz in French and translated by Catherine Temerson (Delacorte Press/Random House)

May Hill Arbuthnot Honor Lecture Award: Russell Freedman

Andrew Carnegie Medal for best children's video: *The Dot,* based on the book written by Peter H. Reynolds, produced by Paul R. Gagne and Melissa Reilly of Weston Woods Studios

Laura Ingalls Wilder Award for lasting contributions to children's literature: Laurence Yep

2005 National Magazine Awards

General Excellence:
Print (circulation less than 100,000)
Dwell (circulation 100,000 to 250,000)
Martha Stewart Weddings (circulation 250,000 to 500,000)
Wired (circulation 500,000 to 1,000,000)
The New Yorker (circulation 1,000,000 to 2,000,000)
Glamour (circulation more than 2,000,000)
Personal Service: *BabyTalk*
Leisure Interests: *Sports Illustrated*
Reporting: *The New Yorker*
Public Interest: *The New Yorker*

Feature Writing: *Esquire*
Profiles: *The New Yorker*
Essays: *National Geographic*
Columns and Commentary: *National Journal*
Reviews and Criticism: *The New Yorker*
Magazine Section: *Popular Science*
Single-topic Issue: *Newsweek*
Design: *Kids: Fun Stuff to Do Together*
Photo Portfolio/Photo Essay: *TIME*
Photography: *Gourmet*
Fiction: *The Atlantic Monthly*
General Excellence Online: *Style.com*

Bollingen Prize in Poetry

The Bollingen Prize in Poetry is administered by the Yale University Library.

1949 Ezra Pound
1950 Wallace Stevens
1951 John Crowe Ransom
1952 Marianne Moore
1953 Archibald MacLeish and William Carlos
Williams
1954 W. H. Auden
1955 Léonie Adams and Louise Bogan
1956 Conrad Aiken
1957 Allen Tate
1958 e. e. cummings
1959 Theodore Roethke
1960 Delmore Schwartz
1961 Yvor Winters
1962 John Hall Wheelock and Richard Eberhart
1963 Robert Frost
1965 Horace Gregory
1967 Robert Penn Warren
1969 John Berryman and Karl Shapiro

1971 Richard Wilbur and Mona Van Duyn
1973 James Merrill
1975 Archie Randolph Ammons
1977 David Ignatow
1979 W. S. Merwin
1981 Howard Nemerov and May Swenson
1983 Anthony Hecht and John Hollander
1985 John Ashbery and Fred Chappell
1987 Stanley Kunitz
1989 Edgar Bowers
1991 Laura Riding Jackson and Donald Justice
1993 Mark Strand
1995 Kenneth Koch
1997 Gary Snyder
1999 Robert Creeley
2001 Louise Glück
2003 Adrienne Rich
2005 Jay Wright

Kingsley Tufts Poetry Prize

1993 Susan Mitchell, *Rapture*
1994 Yusef Komunyakaa, *Neon Vernacular*
1995 Thomas Lux, *Split Horizon*
1996 Deborah Digges, *Rough Music*
1997 Campbell McGrath, *Spring Comes to Chicago*
1998 John Koethe, *Falling Water*
1999 B. H. Fairchild, *The Art of the Lathe*

2000 Robert Wrigley, *Reign of Snakes*
2001 Alan Shapiro, *The Dead Alive and Busy*
2002 Carl Phillips, *The Tether*
2003 Linda Gregerson, *Waterborne*
2004 Henri Cole, *Middle Earth*
2005 Michael Ryan, *New and Selected Poems*

2005 NAACP Image Awards

MOTION PICTURE

Outstanding Motion Picture: *Ray*
Outstanding Actress in a Motion Picture: Kerry Washington, *Ray*
Outstanding Actor in a Motion Picture: Jamie Foxx, *Ray*
Outstanding Supporting Actress in a Motion Picture: Regina King, *Ray*
Outstanding Supporting Actor in a Motion Picture: Morgan Freeman, *Million Dollar Baby*
Outstanding Independent or Foreign Film: *Woman Thou Art Loosed*

TELEVISION

Outstanding Comedy Series: *The Bernie Mac Show*
Outstanding Actress in a Comedy Series: Mo'Nique, *The Parkers*
Outstanding Actor in a Comedy Series: Bernie Mac, *The Bernie Mac Show*
Outstanding Supporting Actress in a Comedy Series: Camille Winbush, *The Bernie Mac Show*
Outstanding Supporting Actor in a Comedy Series: Reggie Hayes, *Girlfriends*
Outstanding Drama Series: *Law & Order*
Outstanding Actress in a Drama Series: Nia Long, *Third Watch*
Outstanding Actor in a Drama Series: Taye Diggs, *Kevin Hill*
Outstanding Supporting Actress in a Drama Series: Khandi Alexander, *CSI: Miami*
Outstanding Supporting Actor in a Drama Series: Mekhi Phifer, *ER*
Outstanding Television Movie, Miniseries, or Dramatic Special: *Something the Lord Made*

Outstanding Actress in a Television Movie, Miniseries, or Dramatic Special: Lynn Whitfield, *Redemption*
Outstanding Actor in a Television Movie, Miniseries, or Dramatic Special: Jamie Foxx, *Redemption*
Outstanding Actress in a Daytime Drama Series: Victoria Rowell, *The Young and the Restless*
Outstanding Actor in a Daytime Drama Series: Shemar Moore, *The Young and the Restless*
Outstanding Variety Series or Special: *Genius: A Night for Ray Charles*
Outstanding News, Talk, or Information Series or Special: *Tavis Smiley*
Outstanding Performance in a Youth or Children's Series or Special: Raven Symoné, *That's So Raven*

RECORDING

Outstanding New Artist: Kanye West
Outstanding Female Artist: Fantasia
Outstanding Male Artist: Usher
Outstanding Duo or Group: Destiny's Child
Outstanding Jazz Artist: Nancy Wilson
Outstanding Gospel Artist: Ben Harper & The Blind Boys of Alabama
Outstanding Music Video: Alicia Keys, "If I Ain't Got You"
Outstanding Song: Alicia Keys, "If I Ain't Got You"
Outstanding Album: Prince, *Musicology*

LITERATURE

Outstanding Literary Work, Fiction: *Woman, Thou Art Loosed! The Novel,* Bishop T. D. Jakes
Outstanding Literary Work, Nonfiction: *Hallelujah! The Welcome Table,* Maya Angelou
Outstanding Literary Work, Children's: *The 1963 Civil Rights March,* Scott Ingram

The Spingarn Medal

The Spingarn Medal is awarded annually by the National Association for the Advancement of Colored People for outstanding achievement by a black American.

1915 Ernest E. Just	1946 Thurgood Marshall	1976 Alvin Ailey
1916 Charles Young	1947 Percy Julian	1977 Alex Haley
1917 Harry T. Burleigh	1948 Channing H. Tobias	1978 Andrew Young
1918 William Stanley Braithwaite	1949 Ralph J. Bunche	1979 Rosa L. Parks
1919 Archibald H. Grimke	1950 Charles Hamilton Houston	1980 Rayford W. Logan
1920 W.E.B. Du Bois	1951 Mabel Keaton Staupers	1981 Coleman Young
1921 Charles S. Gilpin	1952 Harry T. Moore	1982 Benjamin E. Mays
1922 Mary B. Talbert	1953 Paul R. Williams	1983 Lena Horne
1923 George Washington Carver	1954 Theodore K. Lawless	1984 Tom Bradley
1924 Roland Hayes	1955 Carl Murphy	1985 Bill Cosby
1925 James Weldon Johnson	1956 Jackie Robinson	1986 Benjamin L. Hooks
1926 Carter G. Woodson	1957 Martin Luther King, Jr.	1987 Percy Ellis Sutton
1927 Anthony Overton	1958 Daisy Bates and the Little Rock Nine	1988 Frederick Douglass Patterson
1928 Charles W. Chesnutt	1959 Edward Kennedy (Duke) Ellington	1989 Jesse Jackson
1929 Mordecai Wyatt Johnson	1960 Langston Hughes	1990 L. Douglas Wilder
1930 Henry A. Hunt	1961 Kenneth B. Clark	1991 Colin T. Powell
1931 Richard Berry Harrison	1962 Robert C. Weaver	1992 Barbara Jordan
1932 Robert Russa Moton	1963 Medgar Evers	1993 Dorothy Irene Height
1933 Max Yergan	1964 Roy Wilkins	1994 Maya Angelou
1934 William T. B. Williams	1965 Leontyne Price	1995 John Hope Franklin
1935 Mary McLeod Bethune	1966 John H. Johnson	1996 A. Leon Higginbotham, Jr.
1936 John Hope	1967 Edward W. Brooke III	1997 Carl Rowan
1937 Walter White	1968 Sammy Davis, Jr.	1998 Myrlie Evers-Williams
1938 No award	1969 Clarence M. Mitchell, Jr.	1999 Earl G. Graves, Sr.
1939 Marian Anderson	1970 Jacob Lawrence	2000 Oprah Winfrey
1940 Louis T. Wright	1971 Leon Howard Sullivan	2001 Vernon E. Jordan, Jr.
1941 Richard Wright	1972 Gordon Parks	2002 John Lewis
1942 A. Philip Randolph	1973 Wilson C. Riles	2003 Constance Baker Motley
1943 William H. Hastie	1974 Damon Keith	2004 Robert L. Carter
1944 Charles Drew	1975 Hank Aaron	2005 Oliver W. Hill
1945 Paul Robeson		

2004 Major Emmy Awards

See page 44 for 2005 winners.

Drama Series: *The Sopranos* (HBO)
  Actress: Allison Janney, *The West Wing*
  Actor: James Spader, *The Practice*
  Supporting Actress: Drea De Matteo, *The Sopranos*
  Supporting Actor: Michael Imperioli, *The Sopranos*
  Guest Actor: William Shatner, *The Practice*
  Guest Actress: Sharon Stone, *The Practice*
  Directing: Walter Hill, *Deadwood:* "Pilot"
  Writing: Terence Winter, *The Sopranos:* "Long Term Parking"
Comedy Series: *Arrested Development* (Fox)
  Actress: Sarah Jessica Parker, *Sex and the City*
  Actor: Kelsey Grammer, *Frasier*
  Supporting Actress: Cynthia Nixon, *Sex and the City*
  Supporting Actor: David Hyde Pierce, *Frasier*
  Guest Actress: Laura Linney, *Frasier*
  Guest Actor: John Turturro, *Monk*
  Directing: Joe Russo and Anthony Russo, *Arrested Development:* "Pilot"
  Writing: Michael Hurwitz, *Arrested Development:* "Pilot"
Variety, Music, or Comedy Series: *The Daily Show with Jon Stewart* (Comedy Central)
Variety, Music, or Comedy Special: *Elaine Stritch: At Liberty* (HBO)
Individual Performance, Variety, or Music Program: Elaine Stritch, *Elaine Stritch: At Liberty*
Directing in a Variety, Music, or Comedy Program: Louis J. Horvitz, *The 76th Annual Academy Awards*
Writing in a Variety, Music, or Comedy Program: *The Daily Show with Jon Stewart*

Miniseries or Special: *Angels in America* (HBO)
  Actress: Meryl Streep, *Angels in America*
  Actor: Al Pacino, *Angels in America*
  Supporting Actress: Mary-Louise Parker, *Angels in America*
  Supporting Actor: Jeffrey Wright, *Angels in America*
  Directing: Mike Nichols, *Angels in America*
  Writing: Tony Kushner, *Angels in America*
Made-for-Television Movie: *Something the Lord Made* (HBO)
Outstanding Nonfiction Series: *American Masters:* (PBS)
Outstanding Nonfiction Special: *The Forgetting: A Portrait of Alzeimher's* (PBS)
Outstanding Writing for Nonfiction Programming: Susan Lacy and Stephen Stept, *American Masters* "Judy Garland: By Myself" (PBS)
Outstanding Reality/Competition Program: *The Amazing Race* (CBS)
Outstanding Reality Program: *Queer Eye for the Straight Guy* (Bravo)
Outstanding Children's Program: *Happy to Be Nappy and Other Stories of Me* (HBO)
Outstanding Animated Program (one hour or less): *Samurai Jack:* "The Birth of Evil"
Outstanding Special Class Program: *Live from Lincoln Center:* "New York City Ballet—Lincoln Center Celebrates Balanchine at 100" (PBS)
Outstanding Commercial: *Outfit* (Citibank Identity Theft Card Protection), Thomas Thomas Films, Production Company Fallon, Ad Agency

2004–2005 Daytime Emmy Awards

Outstanding Drama Series: *General Hospital* (ABC)
Lead Actor in a Drama Series: Christian Jules LeBlanc, *The Young and the Restless* (CBS)
Lead Actress in a Drama Series: Erika Slezak, *One Life to Live* (ABC)
Supporting Actor in a Drama Series: Greg Rikaart, *The Young and the Restless* (CBS)
Supporting Actress in a Drama Series: Natalia Livingston, *General Hospital* (ABC)
Younger Actor in a Drama Series: David Lago, *The Young and the Restless* (CBS)
Younger Actress in a Drama Series: Eden Riegel, *All My Children* (ABC)
Outstanding Pre-School Children's Series: *Sesame Street* (PBS)
Outstanding Children/Youth/Family Special: *Mighty Times: The Legacy of Rosa Parks* (HBO)
Outstanding Children's Animated Program: *Peep and the Big Wide World* (The Learning Channel)
Outstanding Special Class Children's Animated Program: *Rolie Polie Olie* (Disney)
Outstanding Performer in a Children's Series: Kevin Clash, *Sesame Street* (PBS)
Outstanding Performer in a Children/Youth/Family Special: Stockard Channing, *Jack* (Showtime)
Outstanding Performer in an Animated Program: Henry Winkler, *Clifford's Puppy Days* (PBS)
Outstanding Children's Series: *Reading Rainbow* (PBS)
Outstanding Special Class Series: *Starting Over* (syndicated)
Outstanding Special Class Special: *9/11 Memorial from Ground Zero* (syndicated)
Outstanding Game/Audience Participation Show: *Jeopardy!* (syndicated)
Outstanding Game-Show Host: Meredith Vieira, *Who Wants to Be a Millionaire* (syndicated)
Outstanding Talk Show: *The Ellen DeGeneres Show* (syndicated)
Outstanding Talk-Show Host: Ellen DeGeneres, *The Ellen DeGeneres Show* (syndicated)
Outstanding Service Show: *Martha Stewart Living* (syndicated)
Outstanding Service-Show Host: Bobby Flay, *Boy Meets Grill* (Food Network)

2005 Alfred I. duPont–Columbia University Awards in Television and Radio

SILVER BATONS

ABC News and PJ Productions for *Jesus and Paul: The Word and the Witness*
ABC News and Primetime Thursday for the Nuclear Smuggling Project
David Appleby and the University of Memphis for *Hoxie: The First Stand* on PBS
Frontline and WGBH-TV for *Ghosts of Rwanda* on PBS
Frontline and WGBH-TV for *Truth, War, and Consequences* on PBS
HBO/Cinemax Reel Life, Victoria Bruce, and Karin Hayes for *The Kidnapping of Ingrid Betancourt*

Louisiana Public Broadcasting for *Louisiana: Currents of Change*
MSNBC and National Geographic Ultimate Explorer for *Liberia: American Dream?*
NBC News and Dateline for *A Pattern of Suspicion*
NPR and Radio Diaries for *Mandela: An Audio History*
WBAP-AM, Dallas, for *JFK 40*
WCNC-TV, Charlotte, for Medicaid Dental Centers Investigation
WFAA-TV, Dallas, for *State of Denial*

2005 George Foster Peabody Awards for Broadcasting

On the Media: WNYC Radio, New York, National Public Radio
Studio 360 American Icons: Melville's Moby Dick: WNYC Radio, New York, Public Radio International
The War in Iraq: National Public Radio, Washington
Leonard Bernstein: An American Life: CultureWorks, presented on WNYC, New York, and the WFMT Radio Network, Chicago
Let the Good Times Roll: The Rhythm and Blues Foundation, Washington, Public Radio International
To the Best of Our Knowledge: Wisconsin Public Radio, Public Radio International
The Darfur Crisis: BBC Television News, London
Mosaic: World News from the Middle East: Link TV, San Francisco
State of Denial: WFAA-TV, Dallas, Tex.
Friends in High Places: WTVF-TV, Nashville, Tenn.
Chesapeake Bay Pollution Investigation: WBAL-TV, Baltimore, Md.
60 Minutes II: Abuse at Abu Ghraib: CBS News
Black Sky: The Race for Space: Discovery Channel and Vulcan Productions in association with Gemini Productions and Antenna Films
Bus 174: Zendo Entertainment in association with Cinemax Reel Life
Balseros: Televiso de Catalunya, Bausan Films in association with Cinemax Reel Life
Beah: A Black Woman Speaks: Clinica Estetico and LisaGay Inc. in association with HBO
Something the Lord Made: a Cort/Madden Production in association with HBO Films
Deadwood: Red Board Productions and Paramount Television in association with HBO Entertainment
The N-Word: Trio and Post Consumer Media
American Experience: Tupperware!: Filmmakers Collaborative, Blueberry Hill Productions for American Experience, WGBH-TV, Boston
Rwanda: Do Scars Ever Fade?: Bill Brummel Productions for The History Channel
The Age of Wal-Mart: Inside America's Most Powerful Company: CNBC
The Daily Show with Jon Stewart: Indecision 2004: Comedy Central
Human Cargo: Howe Sound Films and Force Four Entertainment in association with the Canadian Broadcasting Corp.
State of Play: Endor Production in association with BBC, BBC America
The Kumars at No. 42: Hat Trick Productions, BBC America
Nursery Tap, Hip to Toe: Nursery Tap, LLC
The Suffering of Sudan: Channel One Network
Takalani Sesame Presents "talk to me . . . ": Sesame Workshop (USA) and Kwasukasukela (South Africa)
The Bully Project: WITI-TV, Milwaukee, Wis.
Univision Communications, Salud es Vida . . . Enterate! (Lead a Healthy Life . . . Get the Facts!): Univision, Miami, Fla.
Grant Tinker: former head of MTM Enterprises and NBC chairman in the 1980s

2004 MacArthur Foundation Awards

The MacArthur Foundation awards $500,000 over five years to each MacArthur Fellow.

Angela Belcher, 37, nanotechnologist; Cambridge, Mass.
Gretchen Berland, 40, physician, filmmaker; New Haven, Conn.
James Carpenter, 55, glass technologist; New York, N.Y.
Joseph DeRisi, 35, molecular biologist; San Francisco, Calif.
Katherine Gottlieb, 52, Alaskan health-care leader; Anchorage, Alaska
David Green, 48, technology transfer innovator; Berkeley, Calif.
Aleksandar Hemon, 40, short story writer; Chicago, Ill.
Heather Hurst, 29, archaeological illustrator; New Haven, Conn.
Edward P. Jones, 53, novelist; Arlington, Va.
John Kamm, 53, businessman, human-rights strategist; San Francisco, Calif.

Daphne Koller, 36, computer scientist; Stanford, Calif.
Naomi Ehrich Leonard, 40, marine roboticist; Princeton, N.J.
Tommie Lindsey, 53, high school debating coach; Union City, Calif.
Rueben Martinez, 64, bookseller; Santa Ana; Calif.
Maria Mavroudi, 37, philologist; Berkeley, Calif.
Vamsi Mootha, 33, physician, researcher; Boston, Mass.
Judy Pfaff, 58, sculptor; Annandale-on-Hudson, N.Y.
Aminah Robinson, 64, folk artist; Columbus, Ohio
Reginald R. Robinson, 31, ragtime pianist and composer; Chicago, Ill.
Cheryl Rogowski, 43, farmer; Pine Island, N.Y.
Amy Smith, 41, inventor, instructor; Cambridge, Mass.
Julie Theriot, 36, microbiologist; Stanford, Calif.
C. D. Wright, 55, poet, professor; Providence, R.I.

Enrico Fermi Award

The $100,000 award is given in recognition of scientific and technical achievement in atomic energy. Awarded by the president, it is the U.S. government's oldest science and technology award.

1954	Enrico Fermi
1956	John von Neumann
1957	Ernest O. Lawrence
1958	Eugene P. Wigner
1959	Glenn T. Seaborg
1961	Hans A. Bethe
1962	Edward Teller
1963	J. Robert Oppenheimer
1964	Hyman G. Rickover
1966	Otto Hahn, Lise Meitner, and Fritz Strassman
1968	John A. Wheeler
1969	Walter H. Zinn
1970	Norris E. Bradbury
1971	Shields Warren and Stafford L. Warren
1972	Manson Benedict
1976	William L. Russell
1978	Harold M. Agnew and Wolfgang K. H. Panofsky
1980	Alvin M. Weinberg and Rudolf E. Peirls
1981	W. Bennett Lewis
1982	Herbert Anderson and Seth Neddermeyer
1983	Alexander Hollaender and John Lawrence
1984	Robert R. Wilson and Georges Vendryès
1985	Norman C. Rasmussen and Marshall N. Rosenblath
1986	Ernest D. Courant and M. Stanley Livingston
1987	Luis W. Alvarez and Gerald F. Tape
1988	Richard B. Setlow and Victor F. Weisskopf
1990	George A. Cowan and Robley D. Evans
1992	Leon M. Lederman, Harold Brown, and John S. Foster, Jr.
1993	Freeman J. Dyson and Liane B. Russell
1995	Ugo Fano and Martin Kamen
1996	Richard Garwin, Mortimer Elkind, and H. Rodney Withers
1998	Maurice Goldhaber and Michael E. Phelps
2000	Sidney Drell, Sheldon Datz, and Herbert York
2003	John N. Bahcall, Raymond Davis, Jr., and Seymour Sack

Fields Medal Winners

The Fields Medal has been awarded quadrennially since 1936 by the International Congress of Mathematicians in Toronto to recognize outstanding mathematics achievement.

1936 Lars Valerian Ahlfors (Harvard University) and Jesse Douglas (Massachusetts Institute of Technology)
(Fields Medals were not awarded during World War II)
1950 Laurent Schwarts (University of Nancy) and Atle Selberg (Institute for Advanced Study, Princeton)
1954 Kunihiko Kodaira (Princeton University) and Jean-Pierre Serre (University of Paris)
1958 Klaus Friedrich Roth (University of London) and René Thom (University of Strasbourgh)
1962 Lars V. Hörmander (University of Stockholm) and John Willard Milnor (Princeton University)
1966 Michael Francis Atiyah (Oxford University), Paul Joseph Cohen (Stanford University), Alexander Grothendieck (University of Paris), and Stephen Smale (University of California, Berkeley)
1970 Alan Baker (Cambridge University), Heisuke Hironaka (Harvard University), Serge P. Novikov (Moscow University), and John Griggs Thompson (Cambridge University)
1974 Enrico Bombieri (University of Pisa) and David Bryant Mumford (Harvard University)
1978 Pierre René Deligne (Institut des Hautes Études Scientifiques), Charles Louis Fefferman (Princeton University), Gregori Alexandrovitch Margulis (Moscow University), and Daniel G. Quillen (Massachusetts Institute of Technology)

1982 Alain Connes (Institut des Hautes Études Scientifiques), William P. Thurston (Princeton University), and Shing-Tung Yau (Institute for Advanced Study, Princeton)
1986 Simon Donaldson (Oxford University), Gerd Faltings (Princeton University), and Michael Freedman (University of California, San Diego)
1990 Vladimir Drinfeld (Phys. Inst. Kharkov), Vaughan Jones (University of California, Berkeley), Shigefumi Mori (University of Kyoto), and Edward Witten (Institute for Advanced Study, Princeton)
1994 Pierre-Louis Lions (University of Paris–Dauphine), Jean-Christophe Yoccoz (University of Paris–Sud), Jean Bourgain (Institute for Advanced Study, Princeton), and Efim Zelmanov (University of Wisconsin)
1998 Richard E. Borcherds (Cambridge University), William T. Gowers (Cambridge University), Maxim Kontsevich (Institut des Hautes Études Scientifiques and Rutgers University), and Curtis T. McMullen (Harvard University)
2002 Laurent Lafforgue (Institut des Hautes Études Scientifiques) and Vladimir Voevodsky (Institute for Advanced Study, Princeton)

Presidential Medal of Freedom

The Presidential Medal of Freedom, the nation's highest civilian award, recognizes exceptional meritorious service. (These are the medals awarded during President Bush's administrations.)

2002 Hank Aaron (baseball player), Bill Cosby (comedian and actor), Plácido Domingo (tenor), Peter Drucker (management theorist), Katharine Graham* (newspaper publisher), Dr. D. A. Henderson (leader in eradication of smallpox), Irving Kristol (author and editor), Nelson Mandela (former president of South Africa), Gordon Moore (Intel cofounder), Nancy Reagan (former first lady), Fred Rogers (children's television host), A. M. Rosenthal (editor and columnist)

2003 Jacques Barzun (writer and historian), Julia Child (chef), Roberto W. Clemente* (baseball player), Van Cliburn (pianist), Vaclav Havel (playwright and former president of Czech Republic), Charlton Heston (actor), Lord Robertson (secretary general of NATO), Edward Teller (physicist), R. David Thomas*

(Wendy's founder and adoption advocate), Byron R. White* (Supreme Court justice), James Q. Wilson (professor), John R. Wooden (basketball coach)

2004 Robert L. Bartley (editor), L. Paul Bremer (diplomat), Edward Brooke III (politician), Doris Day (actress), Tommy Franks (U.S. Army general), Vartan Gregorian (historian), Gilbert Melville Grosvenor (president of the National Geographic Society), Gordon B. Hinckley (president of the Mormon Church), John Paul II (pope), Estee Lauder (founder of cosmetics company), Rita Moreno (dancer and actress), Arnold Palmer (golfer), Arnall Patz (ophthalmology researcher), Norman Podhoretz (journalist), George Tenet (former CIA director), Walter Wriston (economist and banker)

NOTE: An asterisk following a name denotes a posthumous award.

Recipients of Kennedy Center Honors

The Kennedy Center Honors recognize the lifetime achievements of selected American performing artists.

1978 Marian Anderson (contralto), Fred Astaire (dancer-actor), Richard Rodgers (Broadway composer), Arthur Rubinstein (pianist), George Balanchine (choreographer)

1979 Ella Fitzgerald (jazz singer), Henry Fonda (actor), Martha Graham (choreographer), Tennessee Williams (playwright), Aaron Copland (composer)

1980 James Cagney (actor), Leonard Bernstein (composer-conductor), Agnes de Mille (choreographer), Lynn Fontanne (actress), Leontyne Price (soprano)

1981 Count Basie (jazz composer–pianist), Cary Grant (actor), Helen Hayes (actress), Jerome Robbins (choreographer), Rudolf Serkin (pianist)

1982 George Abbott (Broadway producer), Lillian Gish (actress), Benny Goodman (jazz clarinetist), Gene Kelly (dancer-actor), Eugene Ormandy (conductor)

1983 Katherine Dunham (dancer-choreographer), Elia Kazan (director-author), James Stewart (actor), Virgil Thomson (music critic–composer), Frank Sinatra (singer)

1984 Lena Horne (singer), Danny Kaye (comedian-actor), Gian Carlo Menotti (composer), Arthur Miller (playwright), Isaac Stern (violinist)

1985 Merce Cunningham (dancer-choreographer), Irene Dunne (actress), Bob Hope (comedian), Alan Jay Lerner (lyricist-playwright), Frederick Loewe (composer), Beverly Sills (soprano)

1986 Lucille Ball (comedienne), Ray Charles (musician), Yehudi Menuhin (violinist), Antony Tudor (choreographer), Hume Cronyn and Jessica Tandy (husband-and-wife acting team)

1987 Perry Como (singer), Bette Davis (actress), Sammy Davis, Jr. (entertainer), Nathan Milstein (violinist), Alwin Nikolais (choreographer)

1988 Alvin Ailey (choreographer), George Burns (comedian-actor), Myrna Loy (actress), Alexander Schneider (violinist), Roger L.

Stevens (theatrical producer and the Kennedy Center's founding chairman)

1989 Harry Belafonte (singer-actor), Claudette Colbert (actress), Alexandra Danilova (ballerina), Mary Martin (actress), William Schuman (composer)

1990 Dizzy Gillespie (jazz trumpeter), Katharine Hepburn (actress), Risë Stevens (mezzo soprano), Jule Styne (composer), Billy Wilder (director)

1991 Roy Acuff (country singer–songwriter), Betty Comden and Adolph Green (co-authors of books and lyrics of musicals), the brothers Fayard and Harold Nicholas (dancers), Gregory Peck (actor), Robert Shaw (choral director)

1992 Lionel Hampton (jazz musician), Paul Newman (actor), Joanne Woodward (actress), Ginger Rogers (dancer-actress), Mstislav Rostropovich (cellist-conductor), Paul Taylor (choreographer)

1993 Johnny Carson (talk-show host), Arthur Mitchell (dancer-choreographer), Georg Solti (conductor), Stephen Sondheim (composer-lyricist), Marion Williams (gospel singer)

1994 Kirk Douglas (actor), Aretha Franklin (singer), Morton Gould (composer), Harold Prince (producer-director), Pete Seeger (folk singer)

1995 Jacques d'Amboise (choreographer), Marilyn Horne (mezzo soprano), B. B. King (blues singer), Sidney Poitier (actor), Neil Simon (playwright)

1996 Edward Albee (playwright), Benny Carter (jazz musician), Johnny Cash (musician), Jack Lemmon (actor), Maria Tallchief (ballerina)

1997 Lauren Bacall (actress), Bob Dylan (singer-songwriter), Charlton Heston (actor), Jessye Norman (soprano), Edward Villella (ballet dancer–director)

1998 Bill Cosby (actor-comedian), John Kander and Fred Ebb (Broadway composer-and-lyricist team), Willie Nelson

(singer-songwriter), André Previn (composer-conductor), Shirley Temple Black (actress)
1999 Victor Borge (comedian-pianist), Sean Connery (actor), Judith Jamison (dancer-teacher), Jason Robards (actor), Stevie Wonder (singer-songwriter)
2000 Mikhail Baryshnikov (dancer), Plácido Domingo (tenor), Angela Lansbury (actress), Chuck Berry (rock 'n' roll musician), Clint Eastwood (actor-director-producer)
2001 Julie Andrews (actress), Van Cliburn (pianist), Quincy Jones (music producer–composer), Jack Nicholson (actor), Luciano Pavarotti (singer)
2002 James Earl Jones (actor), James Levine (conductor), Chita Rivera (dancer-actress), Paul Simon (singer), Elizabeth Taylor (actress)
2003 James Brown (soul singer), Carol Burnett (comedian-actress), Loretta Lynn (country singer), Mike Nichols (film and theater director), Itzhak Perlman (violinist)
2004 Warren Beatty (actor), Ossie Davis (actor), Ruby Dee (actress), Elton John (singer), Joan Sutherland (soprano), John Williams (composer)
2005 Tony Bennett (singer), Suzanne Farrell (ballerina), Julie Harris (actress), Robert Redford (actor), Tina Turner (singer)

2005 Webby Awards

Activism: World Citizen's Guide: www.worldcitizenguide.com
Arts: Graffiti Archaeology: http://grafarc.org
Associations: New York Academy of Sciences: www.nyas.org
Automotive: Mercedes-Benz USA SLK: www.mbusa.com/microsite/slk/index.jsp
Banking/Bill Paying: E*TRADE FINANCIAL: www.etrade.com/bank
Beauty and Cosmetics: Come Clean: www.comeclean.com
Best Copy/Writing: McSweeney's Internet Tendency: www.mcsweeneys.net
Best Home/Welcome Page: Words at Play: www.wordsatplay.com
Best Navigation/Structure: 10x10: http://tenbyten.org
Best Practices: Google: www.google.com
Best Use of Animation or Moving Images: SK Telecom Mobile Museum: www.momu.co.kr
Best Use of Sound or Music: spacesounds.com: http://spacesounds.com
Blog: Boing Boing: www.boingboing.net
Broadband: Elevator Moods: www.elevatormoods.com
Celebrity/Fan: Jamie Oliver website: www.jamieoliver.com
Charitable Organizations Nonprofit: The Meatrix: www.themeatrix.com
Community: Dogster: www.dogster.com
Consumer Electronics: Sony Location Free TV: www.sony.com/locationfreetv
Cultural Institutions: Lakota Winter Counts: An Online Exhibit: http://wintercounts.si.edu
Education: Knowing Poe: http://knowingpoe.thinkport.org
Employment: Central Intelligence Agency: http://cia.gov/employment/index.html
Events: Voices of Civil Rights Bus Tour: www.voicesofcivilrights.org/bustour/
Family/Parenting: KidsHealth: http://KidsHealth.org
Fashion: Alexander McQueen website: www.alexandermcqueen.com
Financial Services: Fortune: www.fortune.com
Food and Beverage: Emerald of California: www.emeraldnuts.com
Games: Metaphorical.net: www.metaphorical.net
Games-Related: i love bees (Halo 2 Promotion): www.ilovebees.com
Government: National Cancer Institute website: www.cancer.gov

Guides/Ratings/Reviews: ConsumerReports.org: http://consumerreports.org
Health: The Merck Manual—Second Home Edition Online: www.merckhomeedition.com
Humor: Rathergood: www.rathergood.com
Insurance: GEICO Redesign: www.geico.com
Investor Relations: The Kellogg Company: http://kelloggcompany.com
IT Hardware/Software: Download.com: www.download.com
Law: FindLaw: www.findlaw.com
Lifestyle: Epicurious.com: www.epicurious.com
Magazine: AlterNet.org: www.alternet.org
Movie and Film: The Uninvited: www.postvisual.com/theuninvited/
Music: BBC OneMusic: www.bbc.co.uk/radio1/onemusic/index.shtml?hp_lhn
News: BBC News: http://news.bbc.co.uk
Newspaper: Guardian Unlimited: www.guardian.co.uk
Personal Website: Rtm86.com: www.rtm86.com
Pharmaceuticals: ParkinsonsHealth.com: http://parkinsonshealth.com
Politics: Weapons of Misdirection: www.weaponsofmisdirection.com
Professional Services: Muzak.com: www.muzak.com
Radio: Virgin Radio: www.virginradio.co.uk
Real Estate: Rows at SoMa: www.rowsatsoma.com
Religion and Spirituality: Speaking of Faith: http://speakingoffaith.publicradio.org/
Restaurant: Chipotle: www.chipotle.com
Retail: CafePress.com: www.cafepress.com
School: School of Visual Arts website: www.schoolofvisualarts.edu
Science: Hands on CERN: http://hands-on-cern.physto.se
Services: Singingfish.com—The Destination for Audio/Video Search on the Web: www.singingfish.com
Social Networking: 43 Things: http://43things.com
Sports: WhatIfSports: www.whatifsports.com
Students: The Paly Voice: http://voice.paly.net
Telecommunications: Skype: www.skype.com
Television: Comedy Central's Indecision 2004: www.comedycentral.com/tv_shows/indecision2004/
Tourism: newzealand.com: www.newzealand.com/travel
Travel: Flightmaker: www.flightmaker.com
Weird: Rathergood: www.rathergood.com
Youth: ChannelOne.com: http://ChannelOne.com

2005 Albany Medical Center Prize in Medicine and Biomedical Research

Each year the Albany Medical Center honors a physician, scientist, or group whose work has led to significant advances in the fields of health care and biomedical research.

Robert Langer, professor of chemical and biomedical engineering at the Massachusetts Institute of Technology, for developing an implantable, biodegradable polymer that delivers chemotherapy directly to a tumor.

U.S. Symphony Orchestras and Their Music Directors

Akron Symphony Orchestra: Ya-Hui Wang
Alabama Symphony Orchestra: Christopher Confessore[1]
American Composers Orchestra: Steven Sloane
American Symphony Orchestra: Leon Botstein
Arkansas Symphony Orchestra: David Itkin
Aspen Chamber Symphony: David Zinman
Atlanta Symphony Orchestra: Robert Spano
Austin Symphony Orchestra: Peter Bay
Baltimore Symphony Orchestra: Yuri Temirkanov
Baton Rouge Symphony: Timothy Muffitt
Boston Philharmonic: Benjamin Zander
Boston Pops: Keith Lockhart
Boston Symphony Orchestra: James Levine
Boulder Philharmonic Orchestra: Theodore Kuchar
Brooklyn Philharmonic: Robert Spano
Buffalo Philharmonic Orchestra: JoAnn Falletta
Cedar Rapids Symphony: Christian Tiemeyer
Charleston Symphony Orchestra: David Stahl
Charlotte Symphony: Christof Perick
Chattanooga Symphony & Opera: Robert Bernhardt
Chicago Sinfonietta: Paul Freeman
Chicago Symphony Orchestra: Daniel Barenboim
Cincinnati Symphony Orchestra: Paavo Järvi
Cleveland Orchestra: Franz Welser-Möst
Columbus Symphony Orchestra: Alessandro Siciliani
Dallas Symphony Orchestra: Andrew Litton
Dayton Philharmonic Orchestra: Neal Gittleman
Delaware Symphony Orchestra: David Amado
Des Moines Symphony: Joseph Giunta
Detroit Symphony Orchestra: Neeme Järvi
Elgin Symphony Orchestra: Robert Hanson
El Paso Symphony Orchestra: Gürer Aykal
Erie Philharmonic: Hugh Keelan
Evansville Philharmonic Orchestra: Alfred Savia
Florida Orchestra: Stefan Sanderling
Florida West Coast Symphony: Leif Bjaland[1, 2]
Fort Wayne Philharmonic: Edvard Tchivzhel
Fort Worth Symphony Orchestra: Miguel Harth-Bedoya
Fresno Philharmonic Orchestra: Theodore Kuchar
Grand Rapids Symphony: David Lockington
Grant Park Orchestra (Chicago): Carlos Kalmar[1]
Greensboro Symphony Orchestra: Dmitry Sitkovetsky
Greenville Symphony Orchestra: Edvard Tchivzhel
Handel & Haydn Society (Boston): Grant Llewellyn
Harrisburg Symphony Orchestra: Stuart Malina
Hartford Symphony Orchestra: Edward Cumming
Honolulu Symphony Orchestra: Samuel Wong
Houston Symphony: Hans Graf
Indianapolis Symphony: Mario Venzago
Jacksonville Symphony Orchestra: Fabio Mechetti
Kalamazoo Symphony Orchestra: Raymond Harvey
Kansas City Symphony: Timothy Hankewich[1]
Kennedy Center Opera House Orchestra: Heinz Fricke
Knoxville Symphony Orchestra: Lucas Richman
Little Orchestra Society of New York: Dino Anagnost
Long Beach Symphony Orchestra: Enrique Arturo Diemecke
Long Island Philharmonic: David Wiley
Los Angeles Chamber Orchestra: Jeffrey Kahane
Los Angeles Philharmonic: Esa-Pekka Salonen

Louisiana Philharmonic Orchestra: Klauspeter Seibel
Louisville Orchestra: Uriel Segal
Madison Symphony Orchestra: John DeMain
Memphis Symphony Orchestra: David Loebel
Milwaukee Symphony Orchestra: Andreas Delfs
Minnesota Orchestra: Osmo Vänskä
Mississippi Symphony Orchestra: Crafton Beck
Monterey Symphony: Max Bragado-Darman
Music of the Baroque (Chicago): Jane Glover
Naples Philharmonic Orchestra: Jorge Mester
Nashville Symphony: Kenneth Schermerhorn
National Symphony (DC): Leonard Slatkin
New Haven Symphony Orchestra: Jung-Ho Pak
New Jersey Symphony Orchestra: Neeme Järvi
New Mexico Symphony Orchestra: Guillermo Figueroa
New West Symphony: Boris Brott
New World Symphony (Fla.): Michael Tilson Thomas[2]
New York Philharmonic: Lorin Maazel
New York Pops: Skitch Henderson
North Carolina Symphony: Grant Llewellyn
Northeastern Pennsylvania Philharmonic: Clyde Mitchell
Oklahoma City Philharmonic: Joel Levine
Omaha Symphony: Victor Yampolsky
Omaha Symphony Chamber Orchestra: Victor Yampolsky
Oregon Symphony: Carlos Kalmar
Pacific Symphony Orchestra (Calif.): Carl St. Clair
Palm Beach Pops: Bob Lappin
Philadelphia Orchestra: Christoph Eschenbach
Philharmonia Baroque Orchestra: Nicholas McGegan
Phoenix Symphony: Hermann Michael
Pittsburgh Symphony: Mariss Jansons
Portland Symphony Orchestra: Toshiyuki Shimada
Quad City Symphony Orchestra: Donald Schleicher
Rhode Island Philharmonic: Larry Rachleff
Richmond Symphony: Mark Russell Smith
River City Brass Band: Denis Colwell
Rochester Philharmonic Orchestra: Christopher Seaman
St. Louis Symphony Orchestra: David Robertson
St. Paul Chamber Orchestra: Andreas Delfs
San Antonio Symphony: Larry Rachleff
San Francisco Symphony: Michael Tilson Thomas
Santa Barbara Symphony Orchestra: Gisèle Ben-Dor
Santa Rosa Symphony: Jeffrey Kahane
Seattle Symphony: Gerard Schwarz
Shreveport Symphony: Kermit Poling
Spokane Symphony: Eckart Preu
Springfield Symphony (Mass.): Kevin Rhodes
Stamford Symphony Orchestra: Roger Nierenberg
Syracuse Symphony Orchestra: Daniel Hege
Toledo Symphony: Stefan Sanderling[1]
Tucson Symphony Orchestra: George Hanson
Utah Symphony: Keith Lockhart
Virginia Symphony: JoAnn Falletta
Westchester Philharmonic: Paul Lustig Dunkel
West Virginia Symphony Orchestra: Grant Cooper[1, 2]
Wichita Symphony: Andrew Sewell
Winston-Salem Symphony: Robert Moody
Youngstown Symphony Orchestra: Isaiah Jackson

1. Principal Conductor. 2. Artistic Director.

U.S. Dance Companies

Alvin Ailey American Dance Theatre (1958): Judith Jamison, art. dir.
American Ballet Theatre (1940): Kevin McKenzie, art. dir.
Atlanta Ballet Company (1929): John McFall, art. dir.
Ballet Florida (1986): Marie Hale, art. dir.
BalletMet Columbus (1978): Gerard Charles, art. dir.
Ballet San Jose of Silicon Valley (1986): Dennis Nahat, art. dir.
Ballet West (1963): Jonas Kåge, art. dir.
Bill T. Jones/Arnie Zane Dance Company (1982): Bill T. Jones, art. dir.
Boston Ballet (1963): Mikko Nissinen, art. dir.
Cincinnati Ballet (1958): Victoria Morgan, art. dir.
Colorado Ballet (1961): Martin Fredmann, art. dir. and CEO
Dance Theater of Harlem (1969): Arthur Mitchell, art. dir.
Houston Ballet (1969): Stanton Welch, art. dir.

Joffrey Ballet of Chicago (1956): Gerald Arpino, art. dir.
José Limón Dance Company (1946): Carla Maxwell, art. dir.
Miami City Ballet (1986): Edward Villella, art. dir. and CEO
Milwaukee Ballet (1970): Michael Pink, art. dir.
Mark Morris Dance Group (1980): Mark Morris, art. dir.
Martha Graham Dance Company (1926): Terese Capucilli and Christine Dakin, art. dir.
Merce Cunningham Dance Company (1953): Merce Cunningham, art. dir.
New York City Ballet (1948): Peter Martins, ballet-master-in-chief
Pacific Northwest Ballet (1972): Kent Stowell and Francia Russell, art. dirs.
Paul Taylor Dance Company (1954): Paul Taylor, art. dir.
Pittsburgh Ballet Theater (1970): Terrence S. Orr, art. dir.
San Francisco Ballet (1933): Helgi Tomasson, art. dir.
Texas Ballet Theatre (1961): Ben Stevenson, art. dir.
Washington Ballet (1976): Septime Webre, art. dir.

NOTE: Year founded appears in parentheses after name.

U.S. Opera Companies

American Musical Theatre of San Jose: Stewart Slater, pres.
Arizona Opera Company: Joel Revzen, art. dir.
Aspen Opera Theater Center: Ed Berkeley, gen. dir.
Atlanta Opera: William Fred Scott, art. dir.
Austin Lyric Opera: Richard Buckley, art. dir.
Baltimore Opera Company: Michael Harrison, gen. dir.
Boston Lyric Opera Company: Janice Mancini Del Sesto, gen. dir.
Central City Opera: Pelham G. Pearce, gen. dir.
Cincinnati Opera Association: Nicholas Muni, art. dir.
Civic Light Opera: Jim Mercer, admin. dir.
Cleveland Opera: David Bamberger, gen. dir.
Dallas Opera: Karen Stone, gen. dir.
Florentine Opera Company: Dennis Hanthorn, gen. dir.
Florida Grand Opera: Robert M. Heuer, gen. dir.
Glimmerglass Opera: Joanne Cossa, gen. dir.
Goodspeed Musicals: Michael Price, exec. dir.
Hawaii Opera Theatre: Henry G. Akina, gen. and art. dir.
Houston Grand Opera: David Gockley, gen. dir.
Kentucky Opera: Deborah Sandler, gen. dir.
Los Angeles Opera: Plácido Domingo, gen. dir.
Lyric Opera of Chicago: William Mason, gen. dir.
Lyric Opera of Kansas City: Evan R. Luskin, gen. dir.
Metro Lyric Opera: Era M. Tognoli, art. dir.

Metropolitan Opera: James Levine, art. dir.
Michigan Opera Theatre: David DiChiera, gen. dir.
Minnesota Opera: Dale Johnson, art. dir.
New York City Opera: Paul Kellogg, gen. dir. and art. dir.
Ohio Light Opera: Steven Daigle, art. dir.
Opera Colorado: Peter Russell, gen. dir.
Opera Company of Philadelphia: Robert B. Driver, producing art. dir.
Opera Pacific: John DeMain, art. dir.
Opera Theatre of St. Louis: Charles MacKay, gen. dir.
Orlando Opera Company: Robert Swedberg, gen. dir.
Palm Beach Opera: Joseph Barnette, gen. dir.
Pittsburgh Opera: Mark Weinstein, gen. dir.
Portland Opera: Christopher Mattaliano, gen. dir.
San Diego Civic Light Opera Association: Brian Wells, prod. art. dir.
San Diego Opera: Ian D. Campbell, gen. dir.
San Francisco Opera: Pamela Rosenberg, gen. dir.
San Francisco Opera Center: Sheri Greenawald, gen. dir.
Santa Fe Opera: Richard Gaddes, gen. dir.
Sarasota Opera Association: Victor DeRenzi, art. dir.
Seattle Opera Association: Speight Jenkins, gen. dir.
Utah Opera Company: Anne Ewers, gen. dir.
Virginia Opera: Peter Mark, art. dir.
Washington (DC) Opera: Plácido Domingo, gen. dir.

Most Frequently Produced Operas in North America

Over the Past Ten Seasons, 1995–1996 through 2004–2005		Most-Produced Works of the 2004–2005 Season	
Opera (composer)	No. of productions	Opera (composer)	No. of productions
Madama Butterfly (Puccini)	172	Madama Butterfly (Puccini)	21
La bohème (Puccini)	168	Don Giovanni (Mozart)	14
La traviata (Verdi)	157	La bohème (Puccini)	13
Carmen (Bizet)	142	Carmen (Bizet)	13
The Barber of Seville (Rossini)	131	The Marriage of Figaro (Mozart)	12
The Marriage of Figaro (Mozart)	131	Tosca (Puccini)	12
Don Giovanni (Mozart)	130	Rigoletto (Verdi)	10
Tosca (Puccini)	122	Aida (Verdi)	9
Rigoletto (Verdi)	117	The Mikado (Sullivan)	9
The Magic Flute (Mozart)	116	La traviata (Verdi)	9

Source: Opera America. Web: www.operaamerica.org.

Longest Broadway Runs

Show	Dates	Performances[1]	Show	Dates	Performances[1]
1. *Cats*	10/82–9/2000	7,485	12. *Fiddler on the Roof*	9/64–7/72	3,242
2. *The Phantom of the Opera*	1/88–present	7,221	13. *Life with Father*	11/39–7/47	3,224
3. *Les Misérables*	3/87–5/2003	6,680	14. *Tobacco Road*	12/33–5/41	3,182
4. *A Chorus Line*	7/75–4/90	6,137	15. *The Lion King*	11/97–present	3,139
5. *Oh! Calcutta!* (revival)	9/76–8/89	5,959	16. *Hello, Dolly!*	1/64–12/70	2,844
6. *Beauty and the Beast*	4/94–present	4,548	17. *My Fair Lady*	3/56–9/62	2,717
7. *Miss Saigon*	4/91–1/2001	4,092	18. *Annie*	4/77–1/83	2,377
8. *Rent*	4/96–present	3,776	19. *Cabaret* (revival)	3/98–1/04	2,377
9. *Chicago* (revival)	11/96–present	3,547	20. *Man of La Mancha*	11/65–6/71	2,328
10. *42nd Street*	8/80–1/89	3,486	21. *Abie's Irish Rose*	5/22–10/27	2,327
11. *Grease*	2/72–4/80	3,388	22. *Oklahoma!*	3/43–5/48	2,212
			23. *Smokey Joe's Cafe*	3/95–1/2000	2,036
			24. *Pippin*	10/72–6/77	1,944
			25. *South Pacific*	4/49–1/54	1,925

1. As of 5/25/05. *Source:* League of American Theatres and Producers, Inc.

Trends in Book and Literary Reading

The percentage of adult Americans reading literature has dropped dramatically over the past 20 years. "Literature" includes novels, short stories, plays, and poetry but not works of nonfiction.

	U.S. adult population			Rate of decline 1992–2002
	1982	1992	2002	
Number of literary readers (in millions)	**96**	**100**	**96**	
Percentage reading literature	56.9 %	54.0%	46.7%	–14%
Percentage reading any book	n.a.	60.9	56.6	–7

Source: National Endowment for the Arts, *Reading at Risk: A Survey of Literary Reading in America,* June 2004.

Demographic Characteristics of U.S. Adults Reading Literature[1]

(12-month period ending Aug. 2002)

Demographic characteristics	Percent reading literature	Number reading literature (in millions)	Demographic characteristics	Percent reading literature	Number reading literature (in millions)
Overall population	**46.7%**	**96**	**Education**		
Gender			Grade school	14.0%	2
Female	55.1	59	Some high school	23.4	5
Male	37.6	37	High school graduate	37.7	24
Ethnicity and race			Some college	52.9	30
Hispanic	26.5	6	College graduate	63.1	23
White	51.4	77	Graduate school	74.3	13
African American	37.1	9	**Family income**		
Other	43.7	4	$9,999 or less	32.1	5
Age			$10,000 to $19,999	37.5	8
18 to 24	42.8	11	$20,000 to $29,999	37.5	9
25 to 34	47.7	18	$30,000 to $39,999	44.1	11
35 to 44	46.6	21	$40,000 to $49,999	47.9	8
45 to 54	51.6	20	$50,000 to $74,999	52.3	18
55 to 64	48.9	13	$75,000 or more	60.8	28
65 to 74	45.3	8	Income not reported	39.8	9
75 or older	36.7	6			

1. "Literature" includes novels, short stories, plays, and poetry but not works of nonfiction. *Source:* National Endowment for the Arts, *Reading at Risk: A Survey of Literary Reading in America,* June 2004.

Family Reading, 1993–2001

Percentage of children ages 3–5 who were read to every day in the last week by a family member

	1993	1995	1996	1999	2001
Percentage of U.S. children	53%	58%	57%	54%	58%

Source: U.S. Department of Education, National Center for Education Statistics, National Household Education Survey.

U.S. Adult Participation in Literary Activities

(12-month period ending Aug. 2002)

	Percent of population	Millions of people		Percent of population	Millions of people
Read any book	56.6%	117	**Did personal creative writing**	7.0%	14
Read literature[1]	46.7	96	Published	1.0	2
Read a novel or short story	45.1	93	Unpublished	6.1	13
Read poetry	12.1	25	**Took creative writing classes**		
Read a play	3.6	7	**or lessons**		
Listened to live or recorded			In past year	1.0	2
readings of novels			Ever	13.3	27
or books	9.3	19	**Used Internet to learn about,**		
Read or listened to poetry	14.3	30	**read, or discuss topics**		
Read poetry	12.1	25	**related to literature**	9.2	19
Listened to live or recorded					
readings of poetry	5.9	12			

1. "Literature" includes novels, short stories, plays, and poetry but not works of nonfiction. *Source:* National Endowment for the Arts, *Reading at Risk: A Survey of Literary Reading in America*, June 2004.

Best-Selling Books, 2004

Source: Publishers Weekly.

Hardcover Fiction

1. *The Da Vinci Code,* Dan Brown
2. *The Five People You Meet in Heaven,* Mitch Albom
3. *The Last Juror,* John Grisham
4. *Glorious Appearing,* Tim LaHaye and Jerry B. Jenkins
5. *Angels and Demons,* Dan Brown
6. *State of Fear,* Michael Crichton
7. *London Bridges,* James Patterson
8. *Trace,* Patricia Cornwell
9. *The Rule of Four,* Ian Caldwell and Dustin Thomason
10. *The Da Vinci Code: Special Illustrated Collector's Edition,* Dan Brown
11. *I Am Charlotte Simmons,* Tom Wolfe
12. *Night Fall,* Nelson De Mille
13. *A Salty Piece of Land,* Jimmy Buffett
14. *Ten Big Ones,* Janet Evanovich
15. *Black Wind,* Clive Cussler and Dirk Cussler

Trade Paperback

1. *The South Beach Diet Good Fats/Good Carbs Guide,* Arthur Agatston, M.D.
2. *The 9/11 Commission Report,* The 9/11 Commission
3. *The Secret Life of Bees,* Sue Monk Kidd
4. *The Lovely Bones,* Alice Sebold
5. *The Wedding,* Nicholas Sparks
6. *Anna Karenina,* Leo Tolstoy
7. *Reading Lolita in Tehran,* Azar Nafisi
8. *1,000 Places to See Before You Die,* Patricia Schultz
9. *One Hundred Years of Solitude,* Gabriel García Márquez
10. *The Curious Incident of the Dog in the Night-Time,* Mark Haddon
11. *The Kite Runner,* Khaled Hosseini
12. *Atkins for Life,* Robert C. Atkins, M.D.
13. *The Good Earth,* Pearl S. Buck
14. *The Heart Is a Lonely Hunter,* Carson McCullers
15. *The Devil in the White City,* Erik Larson

Hardcover Nonfiction

1. *The Purpose-Driven Life,* Rick Warren
2. *The South Beach Diet,* Arthur Agatston, M.D.
3. *My Life,* Bill Clinton
4. *America (The Book),* Jon Stewart and the *Daily Show* writers
5. *The South Beach Diet Cookbook,* Arthur Agatston, M.D.
6. *Family First,* Dr. Phil McGraw
7. *He's Just Not That into You,* Greg Behrendt and Liz Tuccillo
8. *Eats, Shoots & Leaves,* Lynne Truss
9. *Your Best Life Now,* Joel Osteen
10. *Guinness World Records 2005,* Guinness World Records
11. *Unfit for Command,* John O'Neill and Jerome R. Corsi
12. *The Automatic Millionaire,* David Bach
13. *The Proper Care and Feeding of Husbands,* Dr. Laura Schlessinger
14. *The Family,* Kitty Kelley
15. *Plan of Attack,* Bob Woodward

Mass Market Paperback

1. *Angels & Demons,* Dan Brown
2. *Bleachers,* John Grisham
3. *The Last Juror,* John Grisham
4. *Deception Point,* Dan Brown
5. *Skipping Christmas,* John Grisham
6. *Safe Harbour,* Danielle Steel
7. *Blue Dahlia,* Nora Roberts
8. *Digital Fortress,* Dan Brown
9. *Dr. Atkins' New Diet Revolution,* Robert C. Atkins, M.D.
10. *The Notebook,* Nicholas Sparks
11. *The Guardian,* Nicholas Sparks
12. *Prey,* Michael Crichton
13. *Birthright,* Nora Roberts
14. *Blow Fly,* Patricia Cornwell
15. *The Big Bad Wolf,* James Patterson

Best-Selling Children's Books, 2004

Hardcover

1. *The Grim Grotto (A Series of Unfortunate Events #11),* Lemony Snicket; illustrated by Brett Helquist
2. *santaKid,* James Patterson; illustrated by Michael Garland
3. *Mister Seahorse,* Eric Carle
4. *Summer of the Serpent (Magic Tree House #31),* Mary Pope Osborne; illustrated by Sal Murdocca
5. *A Series of Unfortunate Events: The Bad Beginning* (movie tie-in), Lemony Snicket; illustrated by Brett Helquist
6. *It's Hard to Be Five,* Jamie Lee Curtis; illustrated by Laura Cornell
7. *I Already Know I Love You,* Billy Crystal; illustrated by Elizabeth Sayles
8. *The O'Reilly Factor for Kids,* Bill O'Reilly and Charles Flowers
9. *Peter and the Starcatchers,* Ridley Pearson and Dave Barry
10. *Dragon Rider,* Cornelia Funke

Paperback

1. *Harry Potter and the Order of the Phoenix,* J. K. Rowling
2. *Disney/Pixar's The Incredibles* (movie novelization), Irene Trimble
3. *Spider Man 2: Spider-Man Versus Doc Ock,* Acton Figueroa; illustrated by Jesus Redondo
4. *Shark Tale: The Movie Novel,* Louise Gikow
5. *My Little Pony: Pony Party,* Kate Egan; illustrated by Carlo LoRaso
6. *Spider-Man 2: Everyday Hero,* Acton Figueroa; illustrated by Ivan Vasquez
7. *Spider-Man 2: Doc around the Clock,* Jacob Ben Gunter
8. *The Sisterhood of the Traveling Pants* (trade paper and mass market), Ann Brashares
9. *The Polar Express the Movie: The Journey Begins,* Kitty Richards
10. *The Polar Express the Movie: The Magic Journey,* Tracy West

All-Time Best-Selling Children's Books

Source: Publishers Weekly.
From the date of publication (in parentheses) through the end of 2000.

Hardcover

1. *The Poky Little Puppy,* Janette Sebring Lowrey (1942)
2. *The Tale of Peter Rabbit,* Beatrix Potter (1902)
3. *Tootle,* Gertrude Crampton (1945)
4. *Green Eggs and Ham,* Dr. Seuss (1960)
5. *Harry Potter and the Goblet of Fire,* J. K. Rowling (2000)
6. *Pat the Bunny,* Dorothy Kunhardt (1940)
7. *Saggy Baggy Elephant,* Kathryn and Byron Jackson (1947)
8. *Scuffy the Tugboat,* Gertrude Crampton (1955)
9. *The Cat in the Hat,* Dr. Seuss (1957)
10. *Harry Potter and the Chamber of Secrets,* J. K. Rowling (1999)

Paperback

1. *Charlotte's Web,* E. B. White; illustrated by Garth Williams (1974)
2. *The Outsiders,* S. E. Hinton (1968)
3. *Tales of a Fourth Grade Nothing,* Judy Blume (1976)
4. *Love You Forever,* Robert Munsch; illustrated by Sheila McGraw (1986)
5. *Where the Red Fern Grows,* Wilson Rawls (1973)
6. *Island of the Blue Dolphins,* Scott O'Dell (1971)
7. *Harry Potter and the Sorcerer's Stone,* J. K. Rowling (1999)
8. *Are You There, God? It's Me, Margaret,* Judy Blume (1972)
9. *Shane,* Jack Schaeffer (1972)
10. *The Indian in the Cupboard,* Lynne Reid Banks (1982)

The 100 Best English-Language Novels of the 20th Century

The Board of the Modern Library, a division of Random House, published its selections in July 1998.

1. *Ulysses,* James Joyce (1922)
2. *The Great Gatsby,* F. Scott Fitzgerald (1925)
3. *A Portrait of the Artist as a Young Man,* James Joyce (1916)
4. *Lolita,* Vladimir Nabokov (1958)
5. *Brave New World,* Aldous Huxley (1932)
6. *The Sound and the Fury,* William Faulkner (1929)
7. *Catch-22,* Joseph Heller (1961)
8. *Darkness at Noon,* Arthur Koestler (1941)
9. *Sons and Lovers,* D. H. Lawrence (1913)
10. *The Grapes of Wrath,* John Steinbeck (1939)
11. *Under the Volcano,* Malcolm Lowry (1947)
12. *The Way of All Flesh,* Samuel Butler (1903)
13. *1984,* George Orwell (1949)
14. *I, Claudius,* Robert Graves (1934)
15. *To the Lighthouse,* Virginia Woolf (1927)
16. *An American Tragedy,* Theodore Dreiser (1925)
17. *The Heart Is a Lonely Hunter,* Carson McCullers (1940)
18. *Slaughterhouse-Five,* Kurt Vonnegut (1969)
19. *Invisible Man,* Ralph Ellison (1952)
20. *Native Son,* Richard Wright (1940)
21. *Henderson the Rain King,* Saul Bellow (1959)
22. *Appointment in Samarra,* John O'Hara (1934)
23. *U.S.A.* (trilogy), John Dos Passos (1937— trilogy completed)
24. *Winesburg, Ohio,* Sherwood Anderson (1919)
25. *A Passage to India,* E. M. Forster (1924)
26. *The Wings of the Dove,* Henry James (1902)
27. *The Ambassadors,* Henry James (1903)
28. *Tender Is the Night,* F. Scott Fitzgerald (1934)
29. *The Studs Lonigan Trilogy,* James T. Farrell (1935)
30. *The Good Soldier,* Ford Madox Ford (1915)
31. *Animal Farm,* George Orwell (1946)
32. *The Golden Bowl,* Henry James (1904)
33. *Sister Carrie,* Theodore Dreiser (1900)
34. *A Handful of Dust,* Evelyn Waugh (1934)

35. *As I Lay Dying*, William Faulkner (1930)
36. *All the King's Men*, Robert Penn Warren (1946)
37. *The Bridge of San Luis Rey*, Thornton Wilder (1927)
38. *Howards End*, E. M. Forster (1910)
39. *Go Tell It on the Mountain*, James Baldwin (1953)
40. *The Heart of the Matter*, Graham Greene (1948)
41. *Lord of the Flies*, William Golding (1954)
42. *Deliverance*, James Dickey (1969)
43. *A Dance to the Music of Time* (series), Anthony Powell (1975—series completed)
44. *Point Counter Point*, Aldous Huxley (1928)
45. *The Sun Also Rises*, Ernest Hemingway (1926)
46. *The Secret Agent*, Joseph Conrad (1907)
47. *Nostromo*, Joseph Conrad (1904)
48. *The Rainbow*, D. H. Lawrence (1915)
49. *Women in Love*, D. H. Lawrence (1921)
50. *Tropic of Cancer*, Henry Miller (1934)
51. *The Naked and the Dead*, Norman Mailer (1948)
52. *Portnoy's Complaint*, Philip Roth (1969)
53. *Pale Fire*, Vladimir Nabokov (1962)
54. *Light in August*, William Faulkner (1932)
55. *On the Road*, Jack Kerouac (1957)
56. *The Maltese Falcon*, Dashiell Hammett (1930)
57. *Parade's End*, Ford Madox Ford (1950)
58. *The Age of Innocence*, Edith Wharton (1920)
59. *Zuleika Dobson*, Max Beerbohm (1911)
60. *The Moviegoer*, Walker Percy (1961)
61. *Death Comes for the Archbishop*, Willa Cather (1927)
62. *From Here to Eternity*, James Jones (1951)
63. *The Wapshot Chronicles*, John Cheever (1957)
64. *The Catcher in the Rye*, J. D. Salinger (1951)
65. *A Clockwork Orange*, Anthony Burgess (1962)
66. *Of Human Bondage*, W. Somerset Maugham (1915)
67. *Heart of Darkness*, Joseph Conrad (1902)

68. *Main Street*, Sinclair Lewis (1920)
69. *The House of Mirth*, Edith Wharton (1905)
70. *The Alexandria Quartet*, Lawrence Durrell (1960—series completed)
71. *A High Wind in Jamaica*, Richard Hughes (1929)
72. *A House for Mr. Biswas*, V. S. Naipaul (1961)
73. *The Day of the Locust*, Nathanael West (1939)
74. *A Farewell to Arms*, Ernest Hemingway (1929)
75. *Scoop*, Evelyn Waugh (1938)
76. *The Prime of Miss Jean Brodie*, Muriel Spark (1961)
77. *Finnegans Wake*, James Joyce (1939)
78. *Kim*, Rudyard Kipling (1901)
79. *A Room with a View*, E. M. Forster (1908)
80. *Brideshead Revisited*, Evelyn Waugh (1945)
81. *The Adventures of Augie March*, Saul Bellow (1953)
82. *Angle of Repose*, Wallace Stegner (1971)
83. *A Bend in the River*, V. S. Naipaul (1979)
84. *The Death of the Heart*, Elizabeth Bowen (1938)
85. *Lord Jim*, Joseph Conrad (1900)
86. *Ragtime*, E. L. Doctorow (1975)
87. *The Old Wives' Tale*, Arnold Bennett (1908)
88. *The Call of the Wild*, Jack London (1903)
89. *Loving*, Henry Green (1945)
90. *Midnight's Children*, Salman Rushdie (1981)
91. *Tobacco Road*, Erskine Caldwell (1933)
92. *Ironweed*, William Kennedy (1983)
93. *The Magus*, John Fowles (1966)
94. *Wide Sargasso Sea*, Jean Rhys (1966)
95. *Under the Net*, Iris Murdoch (1954)
96. *Sophie's Choice*, William Styron (1979)
97. *The Sheltering Sky*, Paul Bowles (1949)
98. *The Postman Always Rings Twice*, James M. Cain (1934)
99. *The Ginger Man*, J. P. Donleavy (1955)
100. *The Magnificent Ambersons*, Booth Tarkington (1918)

The 100 Best English-Language Nonfiction Books of the 20th Century

The Board of the Modern Library, a division of Random House, published its selections in April 1999.

1. *The Education of Henry Adams*, Henry Adams (1906)
2. *The Varieties of Religious Experience*, William James (1902)
3. *Up from Slavery*, Booker T. Washington (1901)
4. *A Room of One's Own*, Virginia Woolf (1929)
5. *Silent Spring*, Rachel Carson (1962)
6. *Selected Essays, 1917–1932*, T. S. Eliot (1932)
7. *The Double Helix*, James D. Watson (1968)
8. *Speak, Memory*, Vladimir Nabokov (1967)
9. *The American Language*, H. L. Mencken (1919)
10. *The General Theory of Employment, Interest, and Money*, John Maynard Keynes (1935–1936)
11. *The Lives of a Cell*, Lewis Thomas (1974)
12. *The Frontier in American History*, Frederick Jackson Turner (1920)
13. *Black Boy*, Richard Wright (1945)
14. *Aspects of the Novel*, E. M. Forster (1927)
15. *The Civil War*, Shelby Foote (1958–1974)
16. *The Guns of August*, Barbara Tuchman (1962)
17. *The Proper Study of Mankind*, Isaiah Berlin (1997)
18. *The Nature and Destiny of Man*, Reinhold Niebuhr (1941–1943)
19. *Notes of a Native Son*, James Baldwin (1955)
20. *The Autobiography of Alice B. Toklas*, Gertrude Stein (1933)

21. *The Elements of Style*, William Strunk and E. B. White (1959)
22. *An American Dilemma*, Gunnar Myrdal (1944)
23. *Principia Mathematica*, Alfred North Whitehead and Bertrand Russell (1910–1913)
24. *The Mismeasure of Man*, Stephen Jay Gould (1981)
25. *The Mirror and the Lamp*, Meyer Howard Abrams (1953)
26. *The Art of the Soluble*, Peter B. Medawar (1967)
27. *The Ants*, Bert Hoelldobler and Edward O. Wilson (1990)
28. *A Theory of Justice*, John Rawls (1971)
29. *Art and Illusion*, Ernest H. Gombrich (1961)
30. *The Making of the English Working Class*, E. P. Thompson (1963)
31. *The Souls of Black Folk*, W.E.B. Du Bois (1903)
32. *Principia Ethica*, G. E. Moore (1903)
33. *Philosophy and Civilization*, John Dewey (1927)
34. *On Growth and Form*, D'Arcy Thompson (1917)
35. *Ideas and Opinions*, Albert Einstein (1954)
36. *The Age of Jackson*, Arthur Schlesinger, Jr. (1945)
37. *The Making of the Atomic Bomb*, Richard Rhodes (1986)
38. *Black Lamb and Grey Falcon*, Rebecca West (1942)
39. *Autobiographies*, W. B. Yeats (1926)

40. *Science and Civilization in China,*
    Joseph Needham (1954–)
41. *Goodbye to All That,* Robert Graves (1929)
42. *Homage to Catalonia,* George Orwell (1938)
43. *The Autobiography of Mark Twain,*
    Mark Twain (1924)
44. *Children of Crisis,* Robert Coles (1967)
45. *A Study of History,* Arnold J. Toynbee
    (1934–1961)
46. *The Affluent Society,* John Kenneth Galbraith
    (1958)
47. *Present at the Creation,* Dean Acheson (1969)
48. *The Great Bridge,* David McCullough (1972)
49. *Patriotic Gore,* Edmund Wilson (1962)
50. *Samuel Johnson,* Walter Jackson Bate (1977)
51. *The Autobiography of Malcolm X,*
    Alex Haley and Malcolm X (1965)
52. *The Right Stuff,* Tom Wolfe (1979)
53. *Eminent Victorians,* Lytton Strachey (1918)
54. *Working,* Studs Terkel (1974)
55. *Darkness Visible,* William Styron (1990)
56. *The Liberal Imagination,* Lionel Trilling (1950)
57. *The Second World War,* Winston Churchill
    (1948–1953)
58. *Out of Africa,* Isak Dinesen (1937)
59. *Jefferson and His Time,* Dumas Malone
    (1948–1981)
60. *In the American Grain,* William Carlos Williams
    (1925)
61. *Cadillac Desert,* Marc Reisner (1986)
62. *The House of Morgan,* Ron Chernow (1990)
63. *The Sweet Science,* A. J. Liebling (1956)
64. *The Open Society and Its Enemies,* Karl Popper
    (1945)
65. *The Art of Memory,* Frances A. Yates (1966)
66. *Religion and the Rise of Capitalism,* R. H.
    Tawney (1926)
67. *A Preface to Morals,* Walter Lippmann (1929)
68. *The Gate of Heavenly Peace,*
    Jonathan D. Spence (1981)
69. *The Structure of Scientific Revolutions,*
    Thomas S. Kuhn (1962)

70. *The Strange Career of Jim Crow,*
    C. Vann Woodward (1955)
71. *The Rise of the West,* William H. McNeill (1963)
72. *The Gnostic Gospels,* Elaine Pagels (1979)
73. *James Joyce,* Richard Ellmann (1959)
74. *Florence Nightingale,* Cecil Woodham-Smith
    (1950)
75. *The Great War and Modern Memory,*
    Paul Fussell (1975)
76. *The City in History,* Lewis Mumford (1961)
77. *Battle Cry of Freedom,* James M. McPherson
    (1988)
78. *Why We Can't Wait,* Martin Luther King, Jr. (1964)
79. *The Rise of Theodore Roosevelt,*
    Edmund Morris (1979)
80. *Studies in Iconology,* Erwin Panofsky (1939)
81. *The Face of Battle,* John Keegan (1976)
82. *The Strange Death of Liberal England,*
    George Dangerfield (1935)
83. *Vermeer,* Lawrence Gowing (1952)
84. *A Bright Shining Lie,* Neil Sheehan (1988)
85. *West with the Night,* Beryl Markham (1942)
86. *This Boy's Life,* Tobias Wolff (1989)
87. *A Mathematician's Apology,* G. H. Hardy (1940)
88. *Six Easy Pieces,* Richard P. Feynman (1963)
89. *Pilgrim at Tinker Creek,* Annie Dillard (1974)
90. *The Golden Bough,* James George Frazer
    (1922) (1 vol. ed.)
91. *Shadow and Act,* Ralph Ellison (1964)
92. *The Power Broker,* Robert A. Caro (1974)
93. *The American Political Tradition,*
    Richard Hofstadter (1948)
94. *The Contours of American History,*
    William Appleman Williams (1966)
95. *The Promise of American Life,*
    Herbert Croly (1909)
96. *In Cold Blood,* Truman Capote (1965)
97. *The Journalist and the Murderer,*
    Janet Malcolm (1990)
98. *The Taming of Chance,* Ian Hacking (1990)
99. *Operating Instructions,* Anne Lamott (1994)
100. *Melbourne,* Lord David Cecil (1939 & 1954)

Best American Journalism of the 20th Century

The following works were chosen as the 20th century's best American journalism by a panel of experts assembled by New York University's journalism department.

1. **John Hersey:** "Hiroshima," *The New Yorker,* 1946
2. **Rachel Carson:** *Silent Spring,* book, 1962
3. **Bob Woodward and Carl Bernstein:**
   Investigation of the Watergate break-in, *The
   Washington Post,* 1972
4. **Edward R. Murrow:** *Battle of Britain,* CBS
   radio, 1940
5. **Ida Tarbell:** "The History of the Standard Oil
   Company," *McClure's,* 1902–1904
6. **Lincoln Steffens:** "The Shame of the Cities,"
   McClure's, 1902–1904
7. **John Reed:** *Ten Days That Shook the World,*
   book, 1919
8. **H. L. Mencken:** Scopes "Monkey" trial, *The
   Sun* of Baltimore, 1925
9. **Ernie Pyle:** Reports from Europe and the
   Pacific during World War II, Scripps-Howard
   newspapers, 1940–1945
10. **Edward R. Murrow and Fred Friendly:**
    Investigation of Sen. Joseph McCarthy,
    CBS, 1954
11. **Edward R. Murrow, David Lowe, and Fred
    Friendly:** "Harvest of Shame," documentary,
    CBS television, 1960

12. **Seymour Hersh:** Investigation of massacre by
    American soldiers at My Lai in Vietnam,
    Dispatch News Service, 1969
13. **The New York Times:** Publication of the
    Pentagon Papers, 1971
14. **James Agee and Walker Evans:** *Let Us Now
    Praise Famous Men,* book, 1941
15. **W.E.B. Du Bois:** *The Souls of Black Folk,*
    collected articles, 1903
16. **I. F. Stone:** *I. F. Stone's Weekly,* 1953–1967
17. **Henry Hampton:** "Eyes on the Prize,"
    documentary, 1987
18. **Tom Wolfe:** *The Electric Kool-Aid Acid Test,*
    book, 1968
19. **Norman Mailer:** *The Armies of the Night,*
    book, 1968
20. **Hannah Arendt:** *Eichmann in Jerusalem: A
    Report on the Banality of Evil,* collected
    articles, 1963
21. **William Shirer:** *Berlin Diary: The Journal of a
    Foreign Correspondent, 1939–1941,* collected
    articles, 1941
22. **Truman Capote:** *In Cold Blood,* book, 1965

23. **Joan Didion:** *Slouching Towards Bethlehem,* collected articles, 1968
24. **Tom Wolfe:** *The Kandy-Kolored Tangerine-Flake Streamline Baby,* collected articles, 1965
25. **Michael Herr:** *Dispatches,* book, 1977
26. **Theodore White:** *The Making of the President: 1960,* book, 1961
27. **Robert Capa:** Ten photographs from D-Day, 1944
28. **J. Anthony Lukas:** *Common Ground: A Turbulent Decade in the Lives of Three American Families,* book, 1985
29. **Richard Harding Davis:** Coverage of German march into Belgium, Wheeler Syndicate and magazines, 1914
30. **Dorothy Thompson:** Reports on the rise of Hitler, *Cosmopolitan* and *Saturday Evening Post,* 1931–1934
31. **John Steinbeck:** Reports on Okie migrant camp life, *The San Francisco News,* 1936
32. **A. J. Liebling:** *The Road Back to Paris,* collected articles, 1944
33. **Ernest Hemingway:** Reports on the Spanish Civil War, *The New Republic,* 1937–1938
34. **Martha Gellhorn:** *The Face of War,* collected articles, 1959
35. **James Baldwin:** *The Fire Next Time,* book, 1963
36. **Joseph Mitchell:** *Up in the Old Hotel and Other Stories,* collection of much older articles, 1992
37. **Betty Friedan:** *The Feminine Mystique,* book, 1963
38. **Ralph Nader:** *Unsafe at Any Speed: The Designed-In Dangers of the American Automobile,* book, 1965
39. **Herblock (Herbert Block):** Cartoons on McCarthyism, *The Washington Post,* 1950
40. **James Baldwin:** "Letter from the South: Nobody Knows My Name," *The Partisan Review,* 1959
41. **Nick Ut:** Photograph of a burning girl running from a napalm attack, The Associated Press, 1972
42. **Pauline Kael:** "Trash, Art, and the Movies," *Harper's,* 1969
43. **Gay Talese:** *Fame and Obscurity: Portraits by Gay Talese,* collected articles, 1970
44. **Randy Shilts:** Reports on AIDS, *The San Francisco Chronicle,* 1981–1985
45. **Janet Flanner (Genet):** *Paris Journals* chronicling Paris's emergence from the Occupation, *The New Yorker,* 1944–1945
46. **Neil Sheehan:** *A Bright Shining Lie: John Paul Vann and America in Vietnam,* book, 1988
47. **A. J. Liebling:** *The Wayward Pressman,* collected articles, 1947
48. **Tom Wolfe:** *The Right Stuff,* book, 1979
49. **Murray Kempton:** *America Comes of Middle Age: Columns 1950–1962,* collected articles, 1963
50. **Murray Kempton:** *Part of Our Time: Some Ruins and Monuments of the Thirties,* book, 1955
51. **Donald L. Barlett and James B. Steele:** "America: What Went Wrong?," *The Philadelphia Inquirer,* 1991
52. **Taylor Branch:** *Parting the Waters: America in the King Years, 1954–1963,* book, 1988
53. **Harrison Salisbury:** Reporting from the Soviet Union, *The New York Times,* 1949–1954
54. **John McPhee:** *The John McPhee Reader,* collected articles, 1976
55. **ABC:** Live television broadcast of Army-McCarthy hearings, 1954
56. **Frederick Wiseman:** *Titicut Follies,* documentary, 1967
57. **David Remnick:** *Lenin's Tomb: The Last Days of the Soviet Empire,* book, 1993
58. **Richard Ben Cramer:** *What It Takes: The Way to the White House,* book, 1992
59. **Jonathan Schell:** *The Fate of the Earth,* book, 1982
60. **Russell Baker:** "Francs and Beans," *The New York Times,* 1975
61. **Homer Bigart:** Account of being over Japan in a bomber when World War II came to an end, The New York *Herald-Tribune,* 1945
62. **Ben Hecht:** *1,001 Afternoons in Chicago,* collected articles, 1922
63. **Walter Cronkite:** Documentary on Vietnam, CBS television, 1968
64. **Walter Lippmann:** Early essays, *The New Republic,* 1914
65. **Margaret Bourke-White:** Photographs following the defeat of Germany, *Life* magazine, 1945
66. **Lillian Ross:** *Reporting,* collected articles, 1964
67. **Nicholas Lemann:** *The Promised Land: The Great Black Migration and How It Changed America,* book, 1991
68. **Joe Rosenthal:** Photograph of Marines raising an American flag on Mount Suribachi on the island of Iwo Jima, The Associated Press, 1945
69. **Hodding Carter Jr.:** "Go for Broke," editorial, Carter's *Delta Democrat-Times* (Greenville, Miss.), 1945
70. **The New Yorker:** *The New Yorker Book of War Pieces,* collected articles, 1947
71. **Meyer Berger:** Report on the murderer Howard Unruh, *The New York Times,* 1949
72. **Norman Mailer:** *The Executioner's Song,* book, 1979
73. **Robert Capa:** Spanish Civil War photos, *Life* magazine, 1936
74. **Susan Sontag:** "Notes on 'Camp,'" *The Partisan Review,* 1964
75. **Bob Woodward and Carl Bernstein:** *All the President's Men,* book, 1974
76. **John Hersey:** *Here to Stay,* collected articles, 1963
77. **A. J. Liebling:** *The Earl of Louisiana,* book, 1961
78. **Mike Davis:** *City of Quartz: Excavating the Future in Los Angeles,* book, 1990
79. **Melissa Fay Greene:** *Praying for Sheetrock,* book, 1991
80. **J. Anthony Lukas:** "The Two Worlds of Linda Fitzpatrick," *The New York Times,* 1967
81. **Herbert Bayard Swope:** "Klan Exposed," *The New York World,* 1921
82. **William Allen White:** "To an Anxious Friend," *The Emporia* (Kan.) *Gazette,* 1922
83. **Edward R. Murrow:** Report of the liberation of Buchenwald, CBS radio, 1945
84. **Joseph Mitchell:** *McSorley's Wonderful Saloon,* collected articles, 1943
85. **Lillian Ross:** *Picture,* book, 1952
86. **Earl Brown:** Series of articles on race, *Harper's* and *Life* magazines, 1942–1944
87. **Greil Marcus:** *Mystery Train: Images of America in Rock 'n' Roll Music,* book, 1975
88. **Morley Safer:** Atrocities committed by American soldiers on the hamlet of Cam Ne in Vietnam, CBS television, 1965
89. **Ted Poston:** Coverage of the "Little Scottsboro" trial, *The New York Post,* 1949

90. **Leon Dash:** "Rosa Lee's Story," *The Washington Post,* 1994
91. **Jane Kramer:** *Europeans,* collected articles, 1988
92. **Eddie Adams and Vo Suu:** Associated Press photograph and NBC television footage of a Saigon execution, 1968
93. **Grantland Rice:** "Notre Dame's 'Four Horsemen,'" The New York *Herald-Tribune,* 1924
94. **Jane Kramer:** *The Politics of Memory: Looking for Germany in the New Germany,* collected articles, 1996

95. **Frank McCourt:** *Angela's Ashes,* book, 1996
96. **Vincent Sheean:** *Personal History,* book, 1935
97. **W.E.B. Du Bois:** Columns on race during his tenure as editor of *The Crisis,* 1910–1934
98. **Damon Runyon:** Crime reporting, *The New York American,* 1926
99. **Joe McGinniss:** *The Selling of the President 1968,* book, 1969
100. **Hunter S. Thompson:** *Fear and Loathing on the Campaign Trail,* book, 1973

Top 100 Daily Newspapers in the United States

Rank	Newspaper	Circulation	Rank	Newspaper	Circulation
1.	*USA Today* (Arlington, Va.)	2,154,539	51.	*Oklahoman* (Oklahoma City)	207,538
2.	*Wall Street Journal* (New York, N.Y.)	2,091,062	52.	*Virginian-Pilot* (Norfolk, Va.)	201,141
3.	*Times* (New York, N.Y.)	1,118,565	53.	*World-Herald* (Omaha, Neb.)	192,075
4.	*Times* (Los Angeles)	914,584	54.	*Pioneer Press* (St. Paul, Minn.)	190,392
5.	*Post* (Washington, DC)	732,872	55.	*Times-Dispatch* (Richmond, Va.)	188,540
6.	*Daily News* (New York, N.Y.)	729,124	56.	*Courant* (Hartford, Conn.)	185,570
7.	*Tribune* (Chicago)	680,879	57.	*Press-Enterprise* (Riverside, Calif.)	183,974
8.	*Post* (New York, N.Y.)	652,426	58.	*Democrat-Gazette* (Little Rock, Ark.)	183,343
9.	*Newsday* (Long Island, N.Y.)	580,069	59.	*American-Statesman* (Austin, Tex.)	183,312
10.	*Chronicle* (Houston)	553,018	60.	*Contra Costa Times* (Walnut Creek, Calif.)	182,541
11.	*Chronicle* (San Francisco)	512,640	61.	*Enquirer* (Cincinnati)	182,176
12.	*Morning News* (Dallas)	510,133	62.	*Record* (Bergen County, N.J.)	179,270
13.	*Sun-Times* (Chicago)	481,798	63.	*Daily News* (Los Angeles)	178,360
14	*Globe* (Boston)	450,538	64.	*Democrat and Chronicle* (Rochester, N.Y.)	173,900
15.	*Arizona Republic* (Phoenix)	432,284	65.	*Tennessean* (Nashville)	172,149
16.	*Star-Ledger* (Newark, N.J.)	408,672	66.	*Post* (W. Palm Beach, Fla.)	168,147
17.	*Star Tribune* (Minneapolis)	380,354	67.	*Times-Union* (Jacksonville, Fla.)	167,851
18.	*Inquirer* (Philadelphia)	376,493	68.	*Journal* (Providence, R.I.)	167,609
19.	*Journal-Constitution* (Atlanta)	371,853	69.	*Asbury Park Press* (Neptune, N.J.)	167,284
20.	*Plain Dealer* (Cleveland)	365,288	70.	*News & Observer* (Raleigh, N.C.)	163,769
21.	*Free Press* (Detroit)	352,714	71.	*Review-Journal* (Las Vegas)	160,391
22.	*Oregonian* (Portland)	334,783	72.	*Bee* (Fresno, Calif.)	158,651
23.	*Times* (St. Petersburg, Fla.)	334,742	73.	*Commercial Appeal* (Memphis)	157,820
24.	*Union-Tribune* (San Diego)	328,531	74.	*Register* (Des Moines, Iowa)	152,885
25.	*Herald* (Miami)	315,850	75.	*Post-Intelligencer* (Seattle)	150,851
26.	*Register* (Orange County, Calif.)	302,864	76.	*Daily Herald* (Chicago)	150,364
27.	*Sun* (Baltimore)	301,186	77.	*News* (Birmingham, Ala.)	148,938
28.	*Bee* (Sacramento, Calif.)	289,905	78.	*Daily News* (Philadelphia)	143,631
29.	*Post* (Denver)	288,937	79.	*Journal News* (Westchester Co., N.Y.)	142,873
30.	*Rocky Mountain News* (Denver)	288,889	80.	*Advertiser* (Honolulu)	142,025
31.	*Post-Dispatch* (St. Louis)	285,869	81.	*Blade* (Toledo, Ohio)	139,520
32.	*Mercury News* (San Jose, Calif.)	271,997	82.	*World* (Tulsa, Okla.)	139,383
33.	*Star* (Kansas City, Mo.)	267,273	83.	*Press* (Grand Rapids, Mich.)	138,620
34.	*Sentinel* (Orlando, Fla.)	257,222	84.	*Tribune* (Salt Lake City)	134,985
35.	*Times-Picayune* (New Orleans)	253,610	85.	*Beacon Journal* (Akron, Ohio)	134,401
36.	*Dispatch* (Columbus, Ohio)	252,564	86.	*News Tribune* (Tacoma, Wash.)	128,511
37.	*Star* (Indianapolis)	249,891	87.	*Daily News* (Dayton, Ohio)	126,642
38.	*Journal Sentinel* (Milwaukee)	244,288	88.	*La Opinion* (Los Angeles, Calif.)	124,692
39.	*Post-Gazette* (Pittsburgh, Pa.)	242,546	89.	*Post-Standard* (Syracuse, N.Y.)	120,701
40.	*Herald* (Boston)	241,457	90.	*Tribune-Review* (Greensburg, Pa.)	119,646
41.	*Sun-Sentinel* (Fort Lauderdale, Fla.)	233,634	91.	*News Journal* (Wilmington, Del.)	116,398
42.	*Times* (Seattle)	231,505	92.	*News-Sentinel* (Knoxville, Tenn.)	114,593
43.	*News* (Detroit)	227,392	93.	*State* (Columbia, S.C.)	114,442
44.	*Observer* (Charlotte, N.C.)	226,849	94.	*Morning Call* (Allentown, Pa.)	111,594
45.	*Tribune* (Tampa, Fla.)	224,220	95.	*Journal* (Albuquerque)	109,693
46.	*Express-News* (San Antonio, Tex.)	222,536	96.	*Herald-Leader* (Lexington, Ky.)	106,941
47.	*Investors Business Daily* (Los Angeles)	215,788	97.	*Herald-Tribune* (Sarasota, Fla.)	105,636
48.	*Star-Telegram* (Fort Worth, Tex.)	215,452	98.	*News-Journal* (Daytona Beach, Fla.)	104,664
49.	*Courier-Journal* (Louisville, Ky.)	213,176	99.	*Telegram & Gazette* (Worcester, Mass.)	102,592
50.	*News* (Buffalo, N.Y.)	207,989	100.	*Times* (Washington, DC)	102,255

NOTES: By circulation, as of Sept. 30, 2003. Most circulations are based on partial-week averages; therefore, above circulations do not reflect full-week circulations. *Source: Editor & Publisher International Year Book 2004.* Web: www.editorandpublisher.com.

Top 100 Consumer Magazines, 2004

Rank	Magazine	Total paid circulation	Rank	Magazine	Total paid circulation
1.	AARP the Magazine	22,668,583	52.	First for Women	1,555,765
2.	AARP Bulletin	22,103,758	53.	Fitness	1,541,371
3.	Reader's Digest	10,155,054	54.	Teen People	1,536,394
4.	TV Guide	9,015,866	55.	Field & Stream	1,518,942
5.	Better Homes & Gardens	7,627,256	56.	Health	1,470,716
6.	National Geographic	5,471,803	57.	Popular Science	1,468,374
7.	Good Housekeeping	4,631,527	58.	National Enquirer	1,466,489
8.	Family Circle	4,252,730	59.	Sunset	1,456,418
9.	Woman's Day	4,130,507	60.	Golf Magazine	1,417,751
10.	Ladies' Home Journal	4,114,353	61.	US Weekly	1,413,087
11.	TIME—The Weekly Newsmagazine	4,034,272	62.	Cosmo Girl!	1,373,028
12.	People	3,690,387	63.	Car and Driver	1,363,611
13.	AAA Westways	3,608,349	64.	Self	1,360,308
14.	Home & Away	3,343,759	65.	American Rifleman	1,346,743
15.	Prevention	3,334,404	66.	Bon Appetit	1,318,109
16.	Sports Illustrated	3,319,300	67.	Stuff	1,280,644
17.	Newsweek	3,135,476	68.	Vogue	1,268,623
18.	Playboy	3,113,780	69.	Rolling Stone	1,267,110
19.	Cosmopolitan	2,989,301	70.	Country Home	1,266,266
20.	Southern Living	2,718,108	71.	Star Magazine	1,240,058
21.	Via Magazine	2,686,173	72.	Popular Mechanics	1,236,494
22.	O, the Oprah Magazine	2,685,755	73.	Boys' Life	1,224,106
23.	Guideposts	2,646,622	74.	FHM (For Him Magazine)	1,219,665
24.	American Legion Magazine	2,567,988	75.	Scholastic Parent & Child	1,211,570
25.	Maxim	2,524,447	76.	Vanity Fair	1,150,072
26.	Redbook	2,384,102	77.	Weight Watchers	1,144,337
27.	Glamour	2,379,573	78.	Family Handyman	1,139,639
28.	AAA Going Places	2,366,198	79.	Motor Trend	1,127,739
29.	Seventeen	2,129,622	80.	Elle	1,060,578
30.	Smithsonian	2,046,499	81.	Essence	1,060,500
31.	Parenting	2,027,818	82.	Scouting	1,038,660
32.	Parents	2,022,932	83.	Michigan Living	1,026,777
33.	U.S. News & World Report	2,018,403	84.	Allure	1,023,866
34.	Money	1,945,917	85.	Kiplinger's Personal Finance	1,011,785
35.	Martha Stewart Living	1,907,231	86.	New Yorker	1,011,084
36.	Game Informer Magazine	1,846,631	87.	PC World	1,008,069
37.	YM	1,828,157	88.	Home	1,007,744
38.	Entertainment Weekly	1,810,562	89.	Lucky	1,003,584
39.	ESPN the Magazine	1,791,219	90.	American Hunter	997,459
40.	Real Simple	1,765,432	91.	More	992,757
41.	In Style	1,754,475	92.	BusinessWeek	982,790
42.	FamilyFun	1,737,920	93.	Traditional Home	975,024
43.	Country Living	1,731,490	94.	Travel + Leisure	972,259
44.	VFW Magazine	1,700,463	95.	Gourmet	971,676
45.	Men's Health	1,692,282	96.	This Old House	969,456
46.	Ebony	1,681,183	97.	Marie Claire	948,726
47.	Cooking Light	1,671,852	98.	Outdoor Life	943,666
48.	Endless Vacation	1,654,639	99.	Food & Wine	935,414
49.	Shape	1,618,060	100.	Jet	927,402
50.	Woman's World	1,584,244	**Top 100**		**247,496,691**
51.	Golf Digest	1,577,524			

Source: Audit Bureau of Circulations, tabulated by Magazine Publishers of America.

Poets Laureate of the United States

Robert Penn Warren	1986–1987	Robert Hass	1995–1997
Richard Wilbur	1987–1988	Robert Pinsky	1997–2000
Howard Nemerov	1988–1990	Stanley Kunitz	2000–2001
Mark Strand	1990–1991	Billy Collins	2001–2003
Joseph Brodsky	1991–1992	Louise Glück	2003–2004
Mona Van Duyn	1992–1993	Ted Kooser	2004–
Rita Dove	1993–1995		

NOTE: The post was established in 1985. Appointment is for a one-year term, but is renewable.

Poets Laureate of England

Edmund Spenser	1591–1599	Laurence Eusden	1718–1730	Alfred Austin	1896–1913
Samuel Daniel	1599–1619	Colley Cibber	1730–1757	Robert Bridges	1913–1930
Ben Jonson	1619–1637	William Whitehead	1757–1785	John Masefield	1930–1967
William Davenant	1638–1668	Thomas Warton	1785–1790	Cecil Day-Lewis	1967–1972
John Dryden[1]	1668–1689	Henry James Pye	1790–1813	Sir John Betjeman	1972–1984
Thomas Shadwell	1689–1692	Robert Southey	1813–1843	Ted Hughes	1984–1998
Nahum Tate	1692–1715	William Wordsworth	1843–1850	Andrew Motion	1999–
Nicholas Rowe	1715–1718	Alfred Lord Tennyson	1850–1892		

1. First to bear the title officially.

The Largest Libraries in the U.S.

Rank	Institution	Volumes held	Rank	Institution	Volumes held
1.	Library of Congress	28,689,159	51.	University of Southern California	3,666,034
2.	Harvard University	14,685,926	52.	Arizona State University Libraries	3,614,279
3.	Boston Public Library	14,612,532	53.	Buffalo & Erie County Public Library	3,492,039
4.	Chicago Public Library	10,943,765	54.	Washington University–St. Louis	3,486,079
5.	Yale University	10,707,270	55.	Johns Hopkins University	3,451,227
6.	The Public Library of Cincinnati & Hamilton County	9,829,015	56.	St. Louis Public Library	3,398,110
7.	University of Illinois–Urbana-Champaign	9,647,652	57.	Hawaii State Public Library System	3,356,529
			58.	University of South Carolina	3,283,749
8.	University of California–Berkeley	9,280,266	59.	Cuyahoga County Public Library	3,256,906
9.	Queens Borough Public Library	9,151,020	60.	State University of New York–Buffalo	3,256,131
10.	County of Los Angeles Public Library	8,796,269	61.	University of California–Davis	3,250,545
11.	University of Texas–Austin	8,074,630	62.	San Diego Public Library	3,199,014
12.	University of California–Los Angeles	7,653,382	63.	University of Hawaii	3,180,383
13.	Stanford University	7,488,125	64.	Wayne State University	3,158,539
14.	University of Michigan	7,484,343	65.	Louisiana State University	3,133,626
15.	Columbia University	7,400,416	66.	Brown University	3,131,454
16.	Detroit Public Library	7,314,712	67.	University of Rochester	3,111,632
17.	Cornell University	6,797,144	68.	North Carolina State University	3,061,005
18.	University of Chicago	6,693,321	69.	University of Missouri–Columbia	3,060,509
19.	New York Public Library	6,647,603	70.	University of Massachusetts	3,048,106
20.	Indiana University	6,385,603	71.	University of Connecticut	3,043,706
21.	The Free Library of Philadelphia	6,219,231	72.	Mid-Continent Public Library	3,027,430
22.	University of Washington	6,158,797	73.	University of Colorado	3,014,969
23.	University of Wisconsin–Madison	6,143,455	74.	Milwaukee Public Library	2,953,733
24.	Brooklyn Public Library	6,049,372	75.	University of Kentucky	2,936,426
25.	Princeton University	5,989,601	76.	Columbus Metropolitan Library	2,928,785
26.	University of Minnesota	5,979,843	77.	University of Utah	2,909,643
27.	Dallas Public Library	5,844,333	78.	University of Maryland	2,897,466
28.	Los Angeles Public Library	5,765,741	79.	University of Notre Dame	2,891,460
29.	Ohio State University	5,491,498	80.	University of California–San Diego	2,890,650
30.	University of North Carolina–Chapel Hill	5,234,540	81.	Texas A&M University Libraries	2,844,379
			82.	Syracuse University	2,831,492
31.	Duke University	5,149,772	83.	Montgomery County Dept. of Public Libraries	2,826,392
32.	University of Pennsylvania	5,027,301			
33.	University of Arizona	4,825,657	84.	University of Cincinnati Libraries	2,801,910
34.	University of Virginia	4,779,269	85.	Toledo-Lucas County Public Library	2,793,320
35.	Houston Public Library	4,713,879	86.	Enoch Pratt Free Library	2,786,000
36.	Pennsylvania State University Libraries	4,614,949	87.	University of Tennessee–Knoxville	2,771,642
			88.	Southern Illinois University–Carbondale	2,717,653
37.	Michigan State University	4,420,208	89.	Vanderbilt University	2,689,580
38.	University of Pittsburgh	4,299,579	90.	University of California–Santa Barbara	2,674,331
39.	University of Oklahoma	4,234,695			
40.	University of Iowa	4,210,463	91.	District of Columbia Public Library	2,672,488
41.	King County Library System	4,197,403	92.	University of Nebraska–Lincoln	2,668,833
42.	Northwestern University Library	4,150,148	93.	Emory University	2,653,346
43.	New York University	4,044,704	94.	Fairfax County Public Library	2,639,432
44.	Cleveland Public Library	3,998,473	95.	Auburn University	2,628,411
45.	Rutgers University	3,918,930	96.	Massachusetts Institute of Technology	2,623,154
46.	University of Florida	3,854,264			
47.	University of Kansas	3,829,530	97.	Temple University	2,596,923
48.	Miami-Dade Public Library System	3,811,881	98.	Brigham Young University	2,591,801
49.	University of Georgia	3,789,228	99.	Kent State University Libraries	2,530,468
50.	Minneapolis Public Library	3,706,928	100.	St. Louis County Library District	2,512,804

Source: American Library Association, www.ala.org/ala/alalibrary/libraryfactsheet/alalibraryfactsheet22.htm, Aug. 2003.

Most Played Songs on the Radio, 2004

Rank	Title	Artist (Label)	Rank	Title	Artist (Label)
1.	"Yeah"	Usher featuring Ludacris and Lil Jon (Laface/Zomba)	6.	"My Immortal"	Evanescence (Wind-Up)
2.	"The Reason"	Hoobastank (Island)	7.	"If I Ain't Got You"	Alicia Keys (J Records)
3.	"This Love"	Maroon 5 (Octone/J Records)	8.	"Tipsy"	J-Kwon (So So Def/Zomba)
4.	"Burn"	Usher (Laface/Zomba)	9.	"I Don't Wanna Know"	Mario Winans featuring P. Diddy (Bad Boy/UMRG)
5.	"Someday"	Nickelback (Roadrunner)	10.	"Here Without You"	3 Doors Down (Universal)

Source: Nielsen Media Research. © 2005, Nielsen Media Research.

2004 Top 15 Concert Tours

Rank	Gross in millions	Artist	Average ticket price	No. of cities/ shows	Rank	Gross in millions	Artist	Average ticket price	No. of cities/ shows
1.	$87.4	Prince	$ 61.04	69/96	9.	$43.7	Toby Keith	$ 47.83	74/75
2.	80.4	Celine Dion	136.33	1/154	10.	43.3	Elton John	158.22	11/60
3.	79.5	Madonna	143.59	14/39	11.	42.5	Rod Stewart	74.78	79/81
4.	60.5	Metallica	57.39	76/83	12.	41.2	Dave Matthews Band	43.32	34/47
5.	59.4	Bette Midler	99.12	61/66	13.	40.1	Tim McGraw	52.48	60/64
6.	54.3	Van Halen	76.44	72/79	14.	34.6	Jimmy Buffett	59.57	26/30
7.	50.8	Kenny Chesney	44.40	75/77	15.	34.5	Shania Twain	65.55	40/42
8.	50.1	Sting	66.84	73/83					

NOTE: All figures are for North American dates only. *Source:* Pollstar.

CD Sales, 1995, 2000, and 2004

(in millions)

CDs	1995	2000	2004
Units shipped	722.9	942.5	766.9
Dollar value[1]	$9,377.4	$13,214.5	$11,446.5

1. Dollar value reflects suggested retail price. *Source:* The Recording Industry Association of America.

Internet Music Sales, 2002–2004

(in millions)

	2002	2003	2004
Internet album sales (units sold)	18.1	21.7	22.2
Digital single sales (units sold)	n.a.	19.2	140.9

Source: Nielsen Media Research. © 2004, Nielsen Media Research.

Top 10 Selling Albums, 2004

Rank	Title, Artist	Units sold
1.	*Confessions,* Usher	7,978,594
2.	*Feels Like Home,* Norah Jones	3,842,920
3.	*Encore,* Eminem	3,517,097
4.	*When the Sun Goes . . . ,* Kenny Chesney	3,072,224
5.	*Here for the Party,* Gretchen Wilson	2,931,097
6.	*Live Like You Were Dying,* Tim McGraw	2,786,840
7.	*Songs About Jane,* Maroon 5	2,708,415
8.	*Fallen,* Evanescence	2,614,226
9.	*Autobiography,* Ashlee Simpson	2,576,945
10.	*Now That's What I Call Music 16,* Various Artists	2,560,316

From Jan. 5, 2004–Jan 2, 2005. *Source:* Nielsen Media Research. © 2005, Nielsen Media Research.

Top 10 Music Downloads, 2004

Rank	Title	Number
1.	"The Reason," Hoobastank	379,839
2.	"This Love," Maroon 5	346,922
3.	"Let's Get it Started," Black Eyed Peas	328,239
4.	"Hey Ya! (Radio Mix)," Outkast	324,848
5.	"Yeah," Usher	314,009
6.	"She Will Be Loved," Maroon 5	306,550
7.	"1985," Bowling for Soup	260,962
8.	"Toxic," Britney Spears	243,873
9.	"Drop It Like It's Hot," Snoop Dogg	234,046
10.	"Lose My Breath," Destiny's Child	225,204

Source: Nielsen Media Research. © 2005, Nielsen Media Research.

The Recording Industry Association of America's Top-Selling Albums of All Time[*]

28 Million
Eagles: Their Greatest Hits, 1971–1975, Eagles (Elektra)

26 Million
Thriller, Michael Jackson (Epic)

23 Million
The Wall, Pink Floyd (Columbia)

22 Million
Led Zeppelin IV, Led Zeppelin (Swan Song)

21 Million
Greatest Hits, Volumes I & II, Billy Joel (Columbia)

19 Million
Rumours, Fleetwood Mac (Warner Bros.)
Back in Black, AC/DC (Elektra)
The Beatles, The Beatles (Capitol)
Come On Over, Shania Twain (Mercury Nashville)

17 Million
Boston, Boston (Epic)
The Bodyguard (soundtrack), Whitney Houston (Arista)

16 Million
Cracked Rear View, Hootie & the Blowfish (Atlantic)
Greatest Hits, Elton John (Island/Mercury)
Jagged Little Pill, Alanis Morissette (Maverick)
The Beatles: 1967–1970, The Beatles (Capitol)
No Fences, Garth Brooks (Capitol Nashville)
Hotel California, Eagles (Elektra)

15 Million
Double Live, Garth Brooks (Capitol Nashville)
The Beatles: 1962–1966, The Beatles (Capitol)

Saturday Night Fever (soundtrack), Bee Gees (Polydor/Atlas)
Dark Side of the Moon, Pink Floyd (Capitol)
Physical Graffiti, Led Zeppelin (Swan Song)
Appetite for Destruction, Guns 'N Roses (Geffen)
Supernatural, Santana (Arista)
Born in the U.S.A., Bruce Springsteen (Columbia)

14 Million

Simon & Garfunkel's Greatest Hits, Simon & Garfunkel (Columbia)
Bat out of Hell, Meat Loaf (Epic)
Metallica, Metallica (Elektra)
Ropin' the Wind, Garth Brooks (Capitol Nashville)
Backstreet Boys, Backstreet Boys (Jive)

13 Million

Millennium, Backstreet Boys (Jive)
Greatest Hits: 1974–1978, Steve Miller Band (Capitol)
Whitney Houston, Whitney Houston (Arista)
Purple Rain (soundtrack), Prince and the Revolution (Warner Bros.)
Bruce Springsteen & the E Street Band Live: 1975–1985 (box set), Bruce Springsteen & the E Street Band (Columbia)
. . . Baby One More Time, Britney Spears (Jive)

12 Million

Forrest Gump (soundtrack) (Epic)
Kenny Rogers's Greatest Hits, Kenny Rogers (Capitol Nashville)

Hot Rocks, The Rolling Stones (abkco)
The Woman in Me, Shania Twain (Mercury Nashville)
Breathless, Kenny G (Arista)
Led Zeppelin II, Led Zeppelin (Atlantic)
Ten, Pearl Jam (Epic)
Yourself or Someone Like You, Matchbox Twenty (Atlantic)
Abbey Road, The Beatles (Capitol)
II, Boyz II Men (Motown)
Slippery When Wet, Bon Jovi (Mercury)
Wide Open Spaces, Dixie Chicks (Monument)
No Jacket Required, Phil Collins (Atlantic)
Hysteria, Def Leppard (Mercury)

11 Million

Human Clay, Creed (Wind-Up Records)
Falling into You, Celine Dion (Epic)
Eagles Greatest Hits, Vol. II, Eagles (Elektra)
Sgt. Pepper's Lonely Hearts Club Band, The Beatles (Capitol)
No Strings Attached, 'N Sync (Jive)
Houses of the Holy, Led Zeppelin (Atlantic)
Devil Without a Cause, Kid Rock (Lava)
Candle in the Wind, 1997/Something About the Way You Look Tonight (Single), Elton John (Rocket)
Pieces of You, Jewel (Atlantic)
CrazySexyCool, TLC (LaFace)
Dirty Dancing (soundtrack) (RCA)
Titanic (soundtrack) (Sony Classical)
James Taylor's Greatest Hits, James Taylor (Warner Bros.)

*Through 5/16/2005.

iPod Celebrity Playlists

Macintosh computers and Apple's many sleek gadgets have long been at the forefront of technology, setting trends and high standards. But the company's customer base has constituted only a small percentage of computer users—until the 2001 debut of the iPod. The portable digital audio player is the must-have accessory for students, professionals, and even President Bush. Here's a sample of what some celebrities have loaded on their iPods.

President Bush
"Centerfield," John Fogerty
"New Biography," Van Morrison
"Brown-Eyed Girl," Van Morrison
"Castanets, " Alejandro Escovedo
"(You're So Square) Baby, I Don't Care," Joni Mitchell
"El Paso," The Gourds
"Swinging from the Chains of Love," Blackie and the Rodeo Kings
"The House Is Rockin'," Stevie Ray Vaughan
"Valley Road," James McMurty
"My Sharona," The Knack

Andrew Lloyd Webber
"David," Nellie McKay
"Señorita," Justin Timberlake
"Lose Yourself," Eminem
"Tosca, Act II, Vissi d'arte," Maria Callas
"Jailhouse Rock," Elvis Presley
"In Dreams," Roy Orbison
"No Matter What," Boyzone
"Let's Dance," David Bowie
"Sk8er Boi," Avril Lavigne
"Love Is Strange," The Everly Brothers

Dale Earnhardt, Jr.
"A Horse with No Name," America
"Seven Spanish Angels," Ray Charles, Willie Nelson (Ray Charles & Friends)
"You Got Lucky," Tom Petty & The Heartbreakers
"Right Now," Korn
"Strange Days," The Matthew Good Band
"Rebel Sodville," Marcy Playground
"Amanda," Boston
"Away from the Sun," 3 Doors Down
"The Back of Your Hand," Dwight Yoakam
"Caught Up in You," .38 Special

"Blown Wide Open," Big Wreck
"Seeing Things," The Black Crowes
"Chain," The Fire Theft
"Sara," Fleetwood Mac
"I Can Still Make Cheyenne," George Strait
"Sundown," Gordon Lightfoot
"Mr. Moon," O.A.R.
"King of Pain," The Police

Michael Moore
"Chimes of Freedom," Bruce Springsteen
"With God on Our Side," Bob Dylan
"We Want It All," Zack de la Rocha
"Boom!," System of a Down
"Masters of War," Pearl Jam
"Fortunate Son," John Fogerty
"Know Your Rights," The Clash
"The Revolution Starts . . . ," Steve Earle
"Now Where Is the Love?," Black Eyed Peas & Justin Timberlake
"Good Night, New York," Nanci Griffith
"Hallelujah," Jeff Buckley
"American Tune," Paul Simon

Patti Smith
"Lorca," Tim Buckley
"Visite du Vigile," Miles Davis
"The WASP (Texas Radio and the Big Beat)," The Doors
"Two Soldiers," Bob Dylan
"If I Were a Carpenter," Tim Hardin
"Bold as Love," The Jimi Hendrix Experience
"Little Girl Blue," Janis Joplin
"Somebody to Love," Jefferson Airplane
"Cupid Come," My Bloody Valentine
"Blue Eyes Crying in the Rain," Willie Nelson
"Orange Crush," R.E.M.
"Hurt," Timi Yuro

Source: iTunes, 2005, and *The New York Times*.

Rock and Roll Hall of Fame

1986
Chuck Berry
James Brown
Ray Charles
Sam Cooke
Fats Domino
The Everly Brothers
Buddy Holly
Jerry Lee Lewis
Elvis Presley
Little Richard
Nonperformers
Alan Freed
Sam Phillips
Early Influences
Robert Johnson
Jimmie Rodgers
Jimmy Yancey
**Lifetime
   Achievement**
John Hammond

1987
The Coasters
Eddie Cochran
Bo Diddley
Aretha Franklin
Marvin Gaye
Bill Haley
B. B. King
Clyde McPhatter
Ricky Nelson
Roy Orbison
Carl Perkins
Smokey Robinson
Joe Turner
Muddy Waters
Jackie Wilson
Nonperformers
Leonard Chess
Ahmet Ertegun
Jerry Leiber and Mike
   Stoller
Jerry Wexler
Early Influences
Louis Jordan
T-Bone Walker
Hank Williams

1988
The Beach Boys
The Beatles
The Drifters
Bob Dylan
The Supremes
Nonperformer
Berry Gordy, Jr.
Early Influences
Woody Guthrie
Leadbelly
Les Paul

1989
Dion
Otis Redding
The Rolling Stones
The Temptations
Stevie Wonder
Nonperformer
Phil Spector
Early Influences
The Ink Spots
Bessie Smith
The Soul Stirrers

1990
Hank Ballard
Bobby Darin
The Four Seasons
The Four Tops
The Kinks
The Platters
Simon and Garfunkel
The Who
Nonperformers
Gerry Goffin and
   Carole King
Brian Holland, Eddie
   Holland, and
   Lamont Dozier
Early Influences
Louis Armstrong
Charlie Christian
Ma Rainey

1991
LaVern Baker
The Byrds
John Lee Hooker
The Impressions
Wilson Pickett
Jimmy Reed
Ike and Tina Turner
Nonperformers
Dave Bartholomew
Ralph Bass
Early Influence
Howlin' Wolf
**Lifetime
   Achievement**
Nesuhi Ertegun

1992
Bobby "Blue" Bland
Booker T. and
   the MG's
Johnny Cash
Jimi Hendrix
   Experience
Isley Brothers
Sam and Dave
The Yardbirds
Nonperformers
Leo Fender

Bill Graham
Doc Pomus
Early Influences
Elmore James
Professor Longhair

1993
Ruth Brown
Cream
Creedence
   Clearwater Revival
The Doors
Etta James
Frankie Lymon and
   the Teenagers
Van Morrison
Sly and the
   Family Stone
Nonperformers
Dick Clark
Milt Gabler
Early Influence
Dinah Washington

1994
The Animals
The Band
Duane Eddy
The Grateful Dead
Elton John
John Lennon
Bob Marley
Rod Stewart
Nonperformer
Johnny Otis
Early Influence
Willie Dixon

1995
The Allman Brothers
   Band
Al Green
Janis Joplin
Led Zeppelin
Martha and the
   Vandellas
Neil Young
Frank Zappa
Nonperformer
Paul Ackerman
Early Influence
The Orioles

1996
David Bowie
Jefferson Airplane
Little Willie John
Gladys Knight and the
   Pips
Pink Floyd
The Shirelles
The Velvet
   Underground

Nonperformer
Tom Donahue
Early Influence
Pete Seeger

1997
The Bee Gees
Buffalo Springfield
Crosby, Stills
   and Nash
The Jackson Five
Joni Mitchell
Parliament-Funkadelic
The (Young) Rascals
Nonperformer
Syd Nathan
Early Influences
Mahalia Jackson
Bill Monroe

1998
The Eagles
Fleetwood Mac
Mamas and Papas
Lloyd Price
Santana
Gene Vincent
Nonperformer
Allen Toussaint
Early Influence
"Jelly Roll" Morton

1999
Billy Joel
Curtis Mayfield
Paul McCartney
Del Shannon
Dusty Springfield
Bruce Springsteen
The Staple Singers
Nonperformer
George Martin
Early Influences
Charles Brown
Bob Wills and His
   Texas Playboys

2000
Eric Clapton
Earth, Wind, and Fire
Lovin' Spoonful
The Moonglows
Bonnie Raitt
James Taylor
Nonperformer
Clive Davis
Early Influences
Nat King Cole
Billie Holiday
Side-Men
Hal Blaine
King Curtis
James Jamerson

Scotty Moore
Earl Palmer

2001
Aerosmith
Solomon Burke
The Flamingos
Michael Jackson
Queen
Paul Simon
Steely Dan
Ritchie Valens
Nonperformer
Chris Blackwell
Side-Men
James Burton
Johnnie Johnson

2002
Isaac Hayes
Brenda Lee
Tom Petty and the
   Heartbreakers
Gene Pitney
Ramones
Talking Heads
Nonperformer
Jim Stewart
Side-Men
Chet Atkins

2003
AC/DC
The Clash
Elvis Costello and the
   Attractions
The Police
The Righteous
   Brothers
Nonperformer
Mo Ostin
Side-Men
Benny Benjamin
Floyd Cramer
Steve Douglas

2004
Jackson Browne
The Dells
George Harrison
Prince
Bob Seger
Traffic
ZZ Top

2005
Buddy Guy
The O'Jays
The Pretenders
Percy Sledge
U2
Nonperformers
Frank Barsalona
Seymour Stein

Top 10 DVD Sales, 2004

1. *Shrek 2* (DreamWorks/Universal)
2. *The Lord of the Rings: The Return of the King*
   (New Line/Warner)
3. *Star Wars Trilogy* (Fox)
4. *The Passion of the Christ* (Fox)
5. *Harry Potter and the Prisoner of Azkaban* (Warner)

6. *Spider-Man 2* (Sony)
7. *The Matrix Revolutions* (Warner)
8. *Elf* (Warner)
9. *The Lion King 1½* (Buena Vista)
10. *Brother Bear* (Buena Vista)

Source: Rentrak Home Video Essentials.

Country Music Hall of Fame

1961
Jimmie Rodgers
Fred Rose
Hank Williams

1962
Roy Acuff

1963
No candidate received
enough votes for induction.

1964
Tex Ritter

1965
Ernest Tubb

1966
Eddy Arnold
James R. Denny
George D. Hay
Uncle Dave Macon

1967
Red Foley
J. L. Frank
Jim Reeves
Stephen H. Sholes

1968
Bob Wills

1969
Gene Autry

1970
Bill Monroe
Original Carter Family

1971
Arthur Edward Satherley

1972
Jimmie H. Davis

1973
Chet Atkins
Patsy Cline

1974
Owen Bradley
Frank "Pee Wee" King

1975
Minnie Pearl

1976
Paul Cohen
Kitty Wells

1977
Merle Travis

1978
Grandpa Jones

1979
Hubert Long
Hank Snow

1980
Johnny Cash
Connie B. Gay
Original Sons of the Pioneers

1981
Vernon Dalhart
Grant Turner

1982
Lefty Frizzell
Roy Horton
Marty Robbins

1983
Little Jimmy Dickens

1984
Ralph Sylvester Peer
Floyd Tillman

1985
Lester Flatt and Earl Scruggs

1986
Whitey Ford
Wesley H. Rose

1987
Rod Brasfield

1988
Loretta Lynn
Roy Rogers

1989
Jack Stapp
Cliffie Stone
Hank Thompson

1990
Tennessee Ernie Ford

1991
Boudleaux and Felice Bryant

1992
George Jones
Frances Williams Preston

1993
Willie Nelson

1994
Merle Haggard

1995
Roger Miller
Jo Walker-Meador

1996
Patsy Montana
Buck Owens
Ray Price

1997
Harlan Howard
Brenda Lee
Cindy Walker

1998
George Morgan
Elvis Presley
E. W. "Bud" Wendell
Tammy Wynette

1999
Johnny Bond
Dolly Parton
Conway Twitty

2000
Charley Pride
Faron Young

2001
Bill Anderson
The Delmore Brothers
The Everly Brothers
Don Gibson
Homer & Jethro
Waylon Jennings
The Jordanaires
Don Law
The Louvin Brothers
Ken Nelson
Sam Phillips
Webb Pierce

2002
Bill Carlisle
Porter Wagoner

2003
Floyd Cramer
Carl Smith

2004
Jim Foglesong
Kris Kristofferson

Top 10 DVD Rentals, 2004

1. *The Day After Tomorrow* (Fox)
2. *Man on Fire* (Fox)
3. *Mystic River* (Warner)
4. *50 First Dates* (Sony)
5. *The Butterfly Effect* (New Line/Warner)
6. *Along Came Polly* (Universal)
7. *The Last Samurai* (Warner)
8. *Secret Window* (Sony)
9. *Cold Mountain* (Buena Vista)
10. *Radio* (Sony)

Source: Rentrak Home Video Essentials.

Top 10 VHS Sales, 2004

1. *The Passion of the Christ* (Fox)
2. *Brother Bear* (Buena Vista)
3. *The Lion King 1½* (Buena Vista)
4. *Shrek 2* (DreamWorks/Universal)
5. *The Lord of the Rings: The Return of the King* (New Line/Warner)
6. *The Cat in the Hat* (DreamWorks/Universal)
7. *Cheaper by the Dozen* (Fox)
8. *Harry Potter and the Prisoner of Azkaban* (Warner)
9. *Open Range* (Buena Vista)
10. *Haunted Mansion* (Buena Vista)

Source: Video Business Research.

Top 10 VHS Rentals, 2004

1. *Open Range* (Buena Vista)
2. *Out of Time* (MGM)
3. *Radio* (Sony)
4. *Cheaper by the Dozen* (Fox)
5. *Something's Gotta Give* (Sony)
6. *Mystic River* (Warner)
7. *American Wedding* (Universal)
8. *Secondhand Lions* (New Line/Warner)
9. *School of Rock* (Paramount)
10. *The Day After Tomorrow* (Fox)

Source: Rentrak Home Video Essentials.

Weekly TV Viewing by Age
(in hours and minutes)

	Time per week				Time per week		
	Oct. 2004	Oct. 2003	Nov. 2002		Oct. 2004	Oct. 2003	Nov. 2002
Women 18–24	23 hr 41 min	23 hr 11 min	23 hr 52 min	Male teens 12–17	20 hr 14 min	20 hr 28 min	22 hr 20 min
Women 25–54	34 hr 56 min	33 hr 46 min	33 hr 56 min	Children 2–5	24 hr 22 min	23 hr 35 min	24 hr 32 min
Women 55+	44 hr 01 min	42 hr 50 min	44 hr 52 min	Children 6–11	19 hr 49 min	19 hr 19 min	20 hr 10 min
Men 18–24	21 hr 10 min	21 hr 20 min	23 hr 31 min				
Men 25–54	19 hr 49 min	30 hr 25 min	31 hr 05 min				
Men 55+	20 hr 14 min	38 hr 18 min	40 hr 29 min				
Female teens 12–17	19 hr 49 min	18 hr 08 min	21 hr 30 min				

Source: Nielsen Media Research. © 2005, Nielsen Media Research.

Television Set Ownership in the U.S.
Estimated total number of TV households: 109,600,000[1]

	1950	1955	1960	1965	1970	1975	1980	1985	1990	1995	2000	2001	2002	2003
% of total households:														
TV households	10%	67%	87%	94%	96%	97%	98%	98%	98%	98%	98%	98%	98%	98%
% of TV households:														
Multiset	—	4	12	22	35	43	50	57	65	71	76	74	75	79
Color	—	—	—	7	41	74	83	91	98	99	99	100	100	99
VCR	—	—	—	—	—	—	14	66	79	86	91	92	90	
Remote control	—	—	—	—	—	—	—	29	77	91	95	95	95	95
Wired pay cable	—	—	—	—	—	—	—	26	29	28	32	40	48	32
Wired cable and/or ADS[2]	—	—	—	—	—	—	—	—	—	—	—	—	—	85

1. As of January 2005. 2. ADS (alternative delivery systems) includes satellite. Source: Nielsen Media Research. © 2005, Nielsen Media Research.

Top 10 Television Specials, 2004–2005[1]

Rank	Program name (network)	Rating (% of TV households)	Rank	Program name (network)	Rating (% of TV households)
1.	Academy Awards (ABC)	25.4%	7.	American Idol Special (Fox)	13.5%
2.	Oscar Countdown 2005 (ABC)	17.4	7.	CSI—Thanksgiving (CBS)	13.5
3.	ABC Premiere Event (ABC)	15.9	9.	American Idol Special (Fox)	13.3
4.	Numb3rs Preview (CBS)	15.7	10.	Happy Days 30th Anniversary Reunion (ABC)	12.5
5.	Raymond: Last Laugh (CBS)	15.3			
6.	American Idol Special (Fox)	14.0	10.	Law & Order (NBC)	12.5

NOTES: Each rating point represents 1,096,000 households using television. Does not include sports telecasts. 1. Sept. 20, 2004–May 25, 2005. Source: Nielsen Media Research. © 2005, Nielsen Media Research.

Top 10 Syndicated TV Programs, 2004–2005[1]

Rank	Program name	Rating (% of TV households)	Rank	Program name	Rating (% of TV households)
1.	Wheel of Fortune	9.0%	7.	Seinfeld (weekend) (AT)	5.5%
2.	Jeopardy	7.8	7.	Friends (AT)	5.5
3.	Oprah Winfrey Show (AT)	7.5	9.	CSI–Syndicated (AT)	5.4
4.	Everybody Loves Raymond (AT)	6.8	9.	ESPN NFL Regular Season 2	5.4
5.	ESPN NFL Regular Season	6.6	9.	Dr. Phil Show	5.4
6.	Seinfeld (AT)	5.9			

NOTES: Each rating point represents 1,096,000 households using television. (AT) = Additional Telecasts. 1. Aug. 30, 2004–May 22, 2005. Source: Nielsen Media Research. © 2005, Nielsen Media Research.

Top 10 Regularly Scheduled Network Programs, 2004–2005[1]

Rank	Program name (network)	Rating (% of TV households)	Rank	Program name (network)	Rating (% of TV households)
1.	CSI (CBS)	16.5%	6.	Without a Trace (CBS)	12.3%
2.	American Idol—Tuesday (Fox)	15.7	7.	Survivor: Palau (CBS)	12.2
3.	American Idol—Wednesday (Fox)	15.3	8.	Survivor: Vanuatu (CBS)	11.7
4.	Desperate Housewives (ABC)	14.5	9.	Grey's Anatomy (ABC)	11.6
5.	CSI: Miami (CBS)	12.4	10.	Everybody Loves Raymond (CBS)	11.2

NOTE: Each rating point represents 1,096,000 households using television. 1. Sept. 20, 2004–May 25, 2005. Source: Nielsen Media Research. © 2005, Nielsen Media Research.

Top-Rated Series Finales

Rank	Date	Program	Rating	Number of homes	Number of persons
1.	2/28/83	*M*A*S*H* (CBS)	60.2	50,150,000	105,466,950
2.	8/29/67	*The Fugitive* (ABC)	45.9	25,700,000	n.a.
3.	5/20/93	*Cheers* (NBC)	45.5	42,361,000	80,401,000
4.	5/14/98	*Seinfeld* (NBC)	41.3	40,509,000	76,260,000
5.	5/1/88	*CBS Sunday Movie: Magnum P.I.—Finale* (CBS)	32.0	28,350,000	50,660,000
6.	5/6/04	*Friends* (NBC)	29.8	32,303,000	52,458,000
7.	4/30/92	*The Cosby Show* (NBC)	28.0	25,788,000	44,384,000
8.	4/8/79	*All in the Family* (CBS)	26.6	19,820,000	40,214,780
9.	3/19/77	*Mary Tyler Moore* (CBS)	25.5	18,160,000	n.a.
10.	5/3/91	*Dallas* (CBS)	22.0	20,480,000	33,259,520

Source: Nielsen Media Research. © 2004, Nielsen Media Research.

Deadliest Countries for Journalists

Each year, the Committee to Protect Journalists (CPJ) publishes a list of journalists killed while on assignment. The following list does not include those who were killed in accidents, such as car or plane crashes, unless the accident was caused by hostile action. The following statistics indicate where the most deaths occurred between 1995 and 2004.

Country	Number of deaths, 1995–2004	Country	Number of deaths, 1995–2004	Country	Number of deaths, 1995–2004
Iraq	36	Philippines	22	Afghanistan	10
Algeria	33	India	16	Bangladesh	10
Colombia	30	Sierra Leone	15	Mexico	9
Russia	29	Brazil	12		

Daily Entertainment and Cultural Activities

Did yesterday	Jan. 1994 (percent)	April 1998 (percent)	April 2000 (percent)	April 2002 (percent)	April 2004 (percent)
Watched TV news	72%	59%	56%	55%	60%
Read newspaper	49	48	47	41	42
Listened to radio news	47	49	43	41	40
Any news yesterday[1]	90	85	83	80	82
Went online from home	—	17	23[5]	34	38
Went online from work[2]	—	12	13[5]	20	20
Total online yesterday[2]	4[3]	25	30[5]	43	47
Online news yesterday	—	—	—	—	24
Watched non-news TV	69	64[4]	57	59	63
Read a magazine	33	29	26	23	25
Read a book	31	35[4]	35[6]	34	35
Watched movie at home	—	—	—	23	24
Made personal phone call	63	67	—	63	66
Emailed friend/relative	—	—	—	27	28
Ate family meal together	64	67	—	63	65
Prayed	56	—	—	66	66
Exercised/ran/sports	26	36	—	39	38
Shopped	23	30	—	27	28

1. For trending purposes, this measure includes only TV, newspaper, and radio news. 2. Based on weekdays. 3. From June 1995. 4. From November 1997. 5. From Pew Internet & American Life Project, April 2000. 6. From September 1999. *Source:* Pew Research Center for the People & the Press.

The 10 Most Expensive Paintings Ever Sold

1. $104 million for *Boy with a Pipe* by Pablo Picasso (2004)
2. $82.5 million for *Portrait du Dr. Gachet* by Vincent van Gogh (1990)
3. $78.1 million for *Au Moulin de la Galette* by Pierre-Auguste Renoir (1990)
4. $76.7 million for *The Massacre of the Innocents* by Paul Rubens (2002)
5. $71.5 million for *Portrait de L'Artiste sans Barbe* by Vincent van Gogh (1998)
6. $60.5 million for *Rideau, Cruchon et Compotier* by Paul Cézanne (1999)
7. $55 million for *Femme aux Bras Croises* by Pablo Picasso (2000)
8. $53.9 million for *Irises* by Vincent van Gogh (1987)
9. $51.7 million for *Les Noces de Pierrette* by Pablo Picasso (1989)
10. $49.5 million for *Femme Assise dans Un Jardin* by Pablo Picasso (1999)

All-*TIME* 100 Movies

TIME magazine's film critics Richard Corliss and Richard Schickel compiled a list of what they think are the best movies ever made.

Aguirre: The Wrath of God (1972)
The Apu Trilogy (1955, 1956, 1959)
The Awful Truth (1937)
Baby Face (1933)
Bande à part (1964)
Barry Lyndon (1975)
Berlin Alexanderplatz (1980)
Blade Runner (1982)
Bonnie and Clyde (1967)
Brazil (1985)
Bride of Frankenstein (1935)
Camille (1936)
Casablanca (1942)
Charade (1963)
Children of Paradise (1945)
Chinatown (1974)
Chungking Express (1994)
Citizen Kane (1941)
City Lights (1931)
City of God (2002)
Closely Watched Trains (1966)
The Crime of Monsieur Lange (1936)
The Crowd (1928)
Day for Night (1973)
The Decalogue (1989)
Detour (1945)
The Discreet Charm of the
  Bourgeoisie (1972)
Dodsworth (1936)
Double Indemnity (1944)
Dr. Strangelove: Or How I Learned to
  Stop Worrying and Love the Bomb
  (1964)
Drunken Master II (1994)
E.T. The Extra-Terrestrial (1982)

8½ (1963)
The 400 Blows (1959)
Farewell My Concubine (1993)
Finding Nemo (2003)
The Fly (1986)
The Godfather, Parts I and II (1972,
  1974)
The Good, the Bad and the Ugly
  (1966)
Goodfellas (1990)
A Hard Day's Night (1964)
His Girl Friday (1940)
Ikiru (1952)
In a Lonely Place (1950)
Invasion of the Body Snatchers (1956)
It's a Gift (1934)
It's a Wonderful Life (1946)
Kandahar (2001)
Kind Hearts and Coronets (1949)
King Kong (1933)
The Lady Eve (1941)
The Last Command (1928)
Lawrence of Arabia (1962)
Léolo (1992)
The Lord of the Rings (2001–03)
The Man with a Camera (1929)
The Manchurian Candidate (1962)
Meet Me in St. Louis (1944)
Metropolis (1927)
Miller's Crossing (1990)
Mon Oncle d'Amérique (1980)
Mouchette (1967)
Nayakan (1987)
Ninotchka (1939)
Notorious (1946)

Olympia, Parts 1 and 2 (1938)
On the Waterfront (1954)
Once upon a Time in the West (1968)
Out of the Past (1947)
Persona (1966)
Pinocchio (1940)
Psycho (1960)
Pulp Fiction (1994)
The Purple Rose of Cairo (1985)
Pyaasa (1957)
Raging Bull (1980)
Schindler's List (1993)
The Searchers (1956)
Sherlock, Jr. (1924)
The Shop Around the Corner (1940)
Singin' in the Rain (1952)
The Singing Detective (1986)
Smiles of a Summer Night (1955)
Some Like It Hot (1959)
Star Wars (1977)
A Streetcar Named Desire (1951)
Sunrise (1927)
Sweet Smell of Success (1957)
Swing Time (1936)
Talk to Her (2002)
Taxi Driver (1976)
Tokyo Story (1953)
A Touch of Zen (1971)
Ugetsu (1953)
Ulysses' Gaze (1995)
Umberto D (1952)
Unforgiven (1992)
White Heat (1949)
Wings of Desire (1987)
Yojimbo (1961)

Movie Revenues

All-Time Box Office Grosses[1]		
1.	Titanic (1997)	$600,788,188
2.	Star Wars (1977)[2]	460,998,007
3.	Shrek 2 (2004)	436,471,036
4.	E.T. The Extra-Terrestrial (1982)[2]	434,949,459
5.	Star Wars: Episode One—The Phantom Menace (1999)	431,088,295
6.	Spider-Man (2002)	403,706,375
7.	The Lord of the Rings: The Return of the King (2003)	377,019,252
8.	Spider-Man 2 (2004)	373,377,893
9.	The Passion of the Christ (2004)	370,270,943
10.	Jurassic Park (1993)	357,067,947
11.	Lord of the Rings: The Two Towers (2002)	341,748,130
12.	Finding Nemo (2003)	339,714,978
13.	Forrest Gump (1994)[2]	329,694,499
14.	The Lion King (1994)[2]	328,539,505
15.	Harry Potter and the Sorcerer's Stone (2001)	317,575,550
16.	The Lord of the Rings: The Fellowship of the Ring (2001)	314,776,170
17.	Star Wars: Episode II—Attack of the Clones (2002)	310,676,740
18.	Return of the Jedi (1983)[2]	309,205,079
19.	Independence Day (1996)	306,169,255
20.	Pirates of the Caribbean: The Curse of the Black Pearl (2003)	305,411,224
21.	The Sixth Sense (1999)	293,506,292
22.	The Empire Strikes Back (1980)[2]	290,271,960
23.	Home Alone (1990)	285,761,243
24.	The Matrix Reloaded (2003)	281,519,061
25.	Meet the Fockers (2004)	278,487,890[3]

Top 25 Movies of 2004[1]		
1.	Shrek 2 (DreamWorks)	436,471,036
2.	Spider-Man 2 (Sony)	373,377,893
3.	The Passion of the Christ (New Market)	370,270,943
4.	Meet the Fockers (Universal)	278,487,890[3]
5.	The Incredibles (Buena Vista/Pixar)	261,437,578[3]
6.	Harry Potter and the Prisoner of Azkaban (Warner Bros.)	249,367,187
7.	The Day After Tomorrow (Fox)	186,740,799
8.	The Bourne Supremacy (Universal)	176,049,130
9.	National Treasure (Buena Vista)	171,896,717[3]
10.	Shark Tale (DreamWorks)	160,762,022
11.	The Polar Express (Warner Bros.)	155,112,441
12.	I, Robot (Fox)	144,801,023
13.	Troy (Warner Bros.)	133,259,341
14.	Ocean's Twelve (Warner Bros.)	125,531,634
15.	50 First Dates (Sony)	120,776,832
16.	Van Helsing (Universal)	120,073,130
17.	Fahrenheit 9/11 (Lions Gate)	119,078,393
18.	Lemony Snicket's A Series of Unfortunate Events (Paramount)	118,575,406[3]
19.	Dodgeball: A True Underdog Story (Fox)	114,326,736
20.	The Village (Buena Vista)	114,195,633
21.	The Grudge (Sony)	110,175,871
22.	The Aviator (Miramax)	101,912,229[3]
23.	Collateral (DreamWorks)	100,003,492
24.	Million Dollar Baby (Warner Bros.)	97,825,712[3]
25.	The Princess Diaries 2: Royal Engagement (Buena Vista)	95,149,435

1. As of April 10, 2005. 2. Including reissues. 3. Still tracking. *Source:* Exhibitor Relations Co. Inc.

Many public figures not listed here may be found elsewhere in the almanac.

U.S. Presidents
U.S. Vice Presidents
Families of U.S. Presidents
U.S. Governors
U.S. Congress
U.S. Supreme Court Justices
U.S. Government Officials

British Prime Ministers
Rulers of England
Rulers of France
Rulers of Judah and Israel
Rulers of Prussia
Rulers of Russia
Sports Personalities

Names in parentheses indicate a person's original name or nickname. Locations in parentheses are the present-day name of the birthplace. Dates of birth appear as month/day/year. **Boldface** years in parentheses are dates of **(birth–death).**

Information has been gathered from many sources, including the individuals themselves. However, the almanac cannot guarantee the accuracy of every item.

A

Aalto, Alvar (architect); Kuortane, Finland **(1898–1976)**
Abbado, Claudio (orchestra conductor); Milan, Italy, 6/26/33
Abbas, Mahmoud (Abu Mazen) (president of Palestinian National Authority); Safed, British Palestine, 1935
Abbott, Bud (William Abbott) (comedian); Asbury Park, N.J. **(1898–1974)**
Abbott, George (stage producer); Forestville, N.Y. **(1887–1995)**
Abelard, Peter (theologian); nr. Nantes, France **(1079–1142)**
Abernathy, Ralph (civil rights leader); Linden, Ala. **(1926–1990)**
Abraham, F(ahrid) Murray (actor); Pittsburgh, 10/24/39
Abraham, Spencer (ex-secretary of Energy); East Lansing, Mich., 6/12/52
Achebe, Chinua (writer); Ogidi, Nigeria, 11/16/30
Acheson, Dean (statesman); Middletown, Conn. **(1893–1971)**
Acuff, Roy Claxton (musician); nr. Maynardsville, Tenn. **(1903–1992)**
Adams, Abigail (First Lady, writer); Weymouth, Mass. **(1744–1818)**
Adams, Bryan (singer, songwriter); Kingston, Ont., Canada, 11/5/59
Adams, Charles Francis (diplomat); Boston **(1807–1886)**
Adams, Don (actor); New York City, 4/19/26
Adams, Edie (Edie Enke) (actress); Kingston, Pa., 4/16/29
Adams, Franklin Pierce (columnist, author); Chicago **(1881–1960)**
Adams, Gerry (political leader); West Belfast, Northern Ireland, 10/6/48
Adams, Henry Brooks (historian); Boston **(1838–1918)**
Adams, Joey (comedian); New York City **(1911–1999)**
Adams, John (2nd U.S. president); Braintree (Quincy), Mass. **(1735–1826)**
Adams, John Quincy (6th U.S. president); Braintree (Quincy), Mass. **(1767–1848)**
Adams, Mason (actor); New York City **(1919–2005)**
Adams, Maude (Maude Kiskadden) (actress); Salt Lake City **(1872–1953)**
Adams, Samuel (American Revolutionary patriot); Boston **(1722–1803)**
Adams, Scott (cartoonist); Catskill, N.Y., 6/8/57
Adamson, Joy (naturalist, writer); Troppau, Silesia **(1910–1980)**
Addams, Charles (cartoonist); Westfield, N.J. **(1912–1988)**
Addams, Jane (social worker, Nobel laureate); Cedarville, Ill. **(1860–1935)**
Adderley, Julian "Cannonball" (jazz saxophonist); Tampa, Fla. **(1928–1975)**
Ade, George (humorist); Kentland, Ind. **(1866–1944)**
Adenauer, Konrad (statesman); Cologne, Germany **(1876–1967)**
Adler, Alfred (psychoanalyst); Vienna **(1870–1937)**
Adler, Larry (musician); Baltimore **(1914–2001)**
Adler, Richard (songwriter); New York City, 8/3/21
Aeschylus (dramatist); Eleusis, Greece **(525–456 B.C.)**
Aesop (fabulist); Samos?, Greece, fl. c. 500 B.C.
Affleck, Ben (actor); Berkeley, Calif., 8/15/72
Agnew, Spiro (political figure); Baltimore **(1918–1996)**
Aiello, Danny (actor); New York City, 6/20/33
Aiken, Conrad (poet); Savannah, Ga. **(1889–1973)**
Ailey, Alvin (choreographer); Rogers, Tex. **(1931–1989)**
Akhmatova, Anna (poet); Odessa, Ukraine **(1889–1966)**
Akihito, Tsugunomiya (Emperor of Japan); Tokyo, 12/23/33
Albanese, Licia (operatic soprano); Bari, Italy, 7/22/13
Albee, Edward (playwright); Washington, D.C., 3/12/28
Albers, Josef (painter); Bottrop, Germany **(1888–1976)**

Albert, Eddie (Edward Albert Heimberger) (actor); Rock Island, Ill., 4/22/08
Albert, Edward (actor); Los Angeles **(1951–2005)**
Albertson, Jack (actor); Malden, Mass. **(1907–1981)**
Albright, Madeleine (diplomat, ex-secretary of State); Prague, Czechoslovakia, 5/15/37
Alcott, Louisa May (novelist); Germantown, Pa. **(1832–1888)**
Alda, Alan (actor); New York City, 1/28/36
Alden, John (American Pilgrim); England **(c. 1599–1687)**
Alexander, Jane (Quigley) (actress); Boston, 10/28/39
Alexander, Jason (Jay Scott Greenspan) (actor); Newark, N.J., 9/23/59
Alexander the Great (monarch, conqueror); Pella, Macedonia, Greece **(356–323 B.C.)**
Alger, Horatio (author); Revere, Mass. **(1834–1899)**
Algren, Nelson (novelist); Detroit **(1909–1981)**
Allen, Debbie (dancer-choreographer, actress); Houston, 1/16/50
Allen, Ethan (American Revolutionary soldier); Litchfield, Conn. **(1738–1789)**
Allen, Fred (John Florence Sullivan) (comedian); Cambridge, Mass. **(1894–1956)**
Allen, Gracie (Grace Ethel Cecile Rosalie Allen) (comedienne); San Francisco **(1906–1964)**
Allen, Joan (actress); Rochelle, Ill., 8/20/56
Allen, Mel (Melvin Israel) (sportscaster); Birmingham, Ala. **(1913–1996)**
Allen, Peter (actor, songwriter); Tenterfield, Australia **(1944–1992)**
Allen, Steve (TV entertainer); New York City **(1921–2000)**
Allen, Woody (Allen Stewart Konigsberg) (actor, writer, director); Brooklyn, N.Y., 12/1/35
Allende, Isabel (novelist); Lima, Peru, 8/2/42
Alley, Kirstie (actress); Wichita, Kans., 1/12/55
Allison, Fran (actress); LaPorte City, Iowa **(1908?–1989)**
Allman, Gregg (singer); Nashville, Tenn., 12/8/47
Allyson, June (Ella Geisman) (actress); New York City, 10/7/17
Alonso, Alicia (ballet dancer); Havana, 12/21/21?
Alpert, Herb (band leader); Los Angeles, 3/31/35?
Alsop, Joseph W., Jr. (journalist); Avon, Conn. **(1910–1989)**
Alsop, Stewart (journalist); Avon, Conn. **(1914–1974)**
Alt, Carol (model); Flushing, New York, 12/1/60
Altman, Robert (director); Kansas City, Mo., 2/20/25
Amanpour, Christiane (broadcast journalist); London, 1958
Amati, Nicola (violin maker); Cremona, Italy **(1596–1684)**
Ambler, Eric (suspense writer); London **(1909–1998)**
Ambrose, Stephen (author, historian); Whitewater, Wis. **(1936–2002)**
Ameche, Don (Dominic Amici) (actor); Kenosha, Wis. **(1908–1993)**
Amis, Kingsley (novelist); London **(1922–1995)**
Amis, Martin (novelist); Oxford, England, 8/25/49
Amory, Cleveland (conservationist); Nahant, Mass. **(1917–1998)**
Amos (Freeman F. Gosden) (radio comedian); Richmond, Va. **(1899–1982)**
Amos, John (actor); Newark, N.J., 12/27/41
Amos, Tori (singer); Newton, N.C., 8/22/63
Amsterdam, Morey (actor); Chicago **(1908–1996)**
Andersen, Hans Christian (author of fairy tales); Odense, Denmark **(1805–1875)**
Anderson, Eddie (Rochester) (actor); Oakland, Calif. **(1905–1977)**
Anderson, Gillian (actress); Chicago, 8/9/68
Anderson, Harry (actor); Newport, R.I., 10/14/52
Anderson, Ib (ballet dancer); Copenhagen, 12/14/54

Anderson, Jack (journalist); Long Beach, Calif., 10/19/22

Anderson, Dame Judith (actress); Adelaide, Australia (1898–1992)

Anderson, Lindsay (Gordon) (director); Bangalore, India (1923–1994)

Anderson, Loni (actress); St. Paul, Minn., 8/5/45

Anderson, Lynn (singer); Grand Forks, N.D., 9/26/47

Anderson, Marian (contralto); Philadelphia (1897–1993)

Anderson, Maxwell (dramatist); Atlantic, Pa. (1888–1959)

Anderson, Pamela (Pamela Anderson) (model, actress); Ladysmith, B.C., Canada, 7/1/67

Anderson, Richard Dean (actor); Minneapolis, Minn., 1/23/50

Anderson, Robert (playwright); New York City, 4/28/17

Anderson, Sherwood (novelist); Camden, Ohio (1876–1941)

Andress, Ursula (actress); Bern, Switzerland, 3/19/36

Andrews, Julie (Julia Wells) (actress, singer); Walton-on-Thames, England, 10/1/35

Andrews, La Verne (singer); Minneapolis (1911–1967)

Andrews, Maxene (singer); Minneapolis (1916–1995)

Andrews, Patti (singer); Minneapolis, 2/16/20

Andropov, Yuri Vladimirovich (Communist Party secretary); Nagutskoye, Russia? (1914–1984)

Andy (Charles J. Correll) (radio comedian); Peoria, Ill. (1890–1972)

Angelico, Fra (Guido di Pietro; Giovanni de Fiesole) (painter); nr. Florence (c. 1400–1455)

Angelou, Maya (Marguerite Johnson) (poet, novelist); St. Louis, 4/4/28

Aniston, Jennifer (Jennifer Anistonapoulos) (actress); Sherman Oaks, Calif., 2/11/69

Anka, Paul (singer, composer); Ottawa, Ont., Canada, 7/30/41

Annan, Kofi (diplomat, UN secretary general); Kumasi, Ghana, 4/8/38

Ann-Margret (Ann-Margaret Olsson) (actress); Valsjobyn, Sweden, 4/28/41

Anouilh, Jean (playwright); Bordeaux, France (1910–1987)

Anthony, Susan Brownell (woman suffragist); Adams, Mass. (1820–1906)

Antonioni, Michelangelo (director); Ferrara, Italy, 9/29/12

Antony, Mark (Marcus Antonius) (statesman); Rome (c. 83–30 B.C.)

Anuszkiewicz, Richard (painter); Erie, Pa., 5/23/30

Apple, Fiona (singer); New York City, 4/8/68

Applegate, Christina (actress); Los Angeles, Calif., 11/25/71

Aquinas, St. Thomas (philosopher); nr. Aquino, Italy (1225–1274)

Aquino, Corazón (Maria Corazón "Cory" Aquino) (president of the Philippines); Tarlac province, Philippines, 1/25/33

Arafat, Yasir (Mohammed Abdel-Raouf Arafat al Qudwa al Husseini) (chairman of the Palestine Liberation Organization); Cairo, Egypt (1929–2004)

Arbuckle, Roscoe "Fatty" (actor, director); Smith Center, Kans. (1887–1933)

Archimedes (physicist, mathematician); Syracuse, Sicily (287–212 B.C.)

Archipenko, Alexandre (sculptor); Kiev, Ukraine (1887–1964)

Arden, Elizabeth (Florence Nightingale Graham) (cosmetics executive); Woodbridge, Canada (1878–1966)

Arden, Eve (Eunice Quedens) (actress); Mill Valley, Calif. (1912–1990)

Arendt, Hannah (historian); Hanover, Germany (1906–1975)

Aristophanes (dramatist); Athens (c. 448–c. 385 B.C.)

Aristotle (philosopher); Stagirus, Macedonia (384–322 B.C.)

Arkin, Adam (actor); New York City, 8/19/57

Arkin, Alan (actor, director); New York City, 3/26/34

Arledge, Roone (TV executive); Forest Hills, N.Y. (1931–2002)

Arlen, Harold (Hyman Arluck) (composer); Buffalo, N.Y. (1905–1986)

Armani, Georgio (fashion designer); Piacenza, Italy, 7/11/34

Armstrong, Louis ("Satchmo") (musician); New Orleans (1901–1971)

Arnaz, Desi (Desiderio Alberto Araz y de Acha III) (actor, producer); Santiago, Cuba (1917–1986)

Arness, James (James Aurness) (actor); Minneapolis, 5/26/23

Arno, Peter (cartoonist); New York City (1904–1968)

Arnold, Benedict (American Revolutionary War general, charged with treason); Norwich, Conn. (1741–1801)

Arnold, Matthew (poet, critic); Laleham, England (1822–1888)

Arp, Jean (sculptor, painter); Strasbourg, France (1887–1966)

Arquette, Cliff (actor); Toledo, Ohio (1905–1974)

Arquette, Patricia (actress); Chicago, 4/8/68

Arquette, Rosanna (actress); New York City, 8/10/59

Arrau, Claudio (pianist); Chillán, Chile (1903–1991)

Arroyo, Martina (soprano); New York City, 2/2/40

Arthur, Bea (Bernice Frankel) (actress); New York City, 5/13/23

Arthur, Chester Alan (21st U.S. president); Fairfield, Vt. (1829–1886)

Ashcroft, John (U.S. attorney general); Chicago, Ill., 5/9/42

Ashcroft, Dame Peggy (actress); Croydon, England (1907–1991)

Ashkenazy, Vladimir (concert pianist); Gorki, U.S.S.R., 7/6/37

Ashley, Elizabeth (actress); Ocala, Fla., 8/30/39

Ashton, Sir Frederick William Mallandaine (choreographer); Guayaquil, Ecuador (1904–1988)

Asimov, Isaac (author); Petrovichi, Russia (1920–1992)

Asner, Edward (actor); Kansas City, Mo., 11/15/29

Assante, Armand (actor); New York City, 10/4/49

Astaire, Fred (Frederick Austerlitz) (dancer, actor); Omaha, Neb. (1899–1987)

Astin, John (actor, director); Baltimore, 3/30/30

Astor, Brooke (socialite, philanthropist); Portsmouth, N.H., 3/30/1902

Astor, John Jacob (financier); Waldorf, Germany (1763–1848)

Astor, Mary (Lucile Langhanke) (actress); Quincy, Ill. (1906–1987)

Ataturk, Kemal (Mustafa Kemal) (Turkish soldier, statesman); Salonika, Greece (1881–1938)

Atkins, Chet (guitarist); nr. Luttrell, Tenn. (1924–2001)

Atkins, Robert (nutritionist); Columbus, Ohio (1930–2003)

Atkinson, Rowan (actor); Newcastle-Upon-Tyne, England, 1/6/55

Attenborough, Richard (actor, director); Cambridge, England, 8/29/23

Attila (King of Huns); (406?–453)

Attucks, Crispus (American Revolutionary patriot); Boston (c. 1723–1770)

Auberjonois, Rene (actor); New York City, 6/1/40

Auchincloss, Louis (author); Lawrence, N.Y., 9/27/17

Auden, W(ystan) H(ugh) (poet); York, England (1907–1973)

Audubon, John James (naturalist, painter); Haiti (1785–1851)

Auer, Leopold (violinist, teacher); Veszprém, Hungary (1845–1930)

Augustine, Saint (Aurelius Augustinus) (theologian); Tagaste, Numidia, Algeria (354–430)

Augustus (Gaius Octavius) (Roman emperor); Rome (63 B.C.– A.D. 14)

Aung San Suu Kyi (human rights activist); Rangoon, Burma, 6/19/45

Austen, Jane (novelist); Steventon, England (1775–1817)

Autry, Gene (singer, actor); Tioga, Tex. (1907–1998)

Avalon, Frankie (singer); Philadelphia, 9/18/39

Avedon, Richard (photographer); New York City (1923–2004)

Avery, Milton (painter); Altmar, N.Y. (1893–1965)

Ax, Emanuel (pianist); Lvov, Ukraine, 6/8/49

Axelrod, George (playwright); New York City (1922–2003)

Ayckbourn, Alan (playwright); London, 4/12/39

Ayckroyd, Dan (actor); Ottawa, Ont., Canada, 7/1/52

Ayres, Lew (actor); Minneapolis (1908–1996)

B

Bacall, Lauren (Betty Joan Perske) (actress); New York City, 9/16/24

Bach, Carl Phillipp Emanuel (composer); Weimar, Germany (1714–1788)

Bach, Johann Sebastian (composer); Eisenach, Germany (1685–1750)

Bacharach, Burt (songwriter); Kansas City, Mo., 5/12/29

Backus, Jim (actor); Cleveland (1913–1989)

Bacon, Francis (philosopher, essayist); London (1561–1626)

Bacon, Francis (painter); Dublin (1910–1992)

Bacon, Kevin (actor); Philadelphia, 7/8/58

Bacon, Roger (philosopher, scientist); Ilchester, England (c. 1214–1294?)

Badu, Erykah (Erykah Wright) (singer); Dallas, 2/26/71

Baez, Joan (folk singer); Staten Island, N.Y., 1/9/41

Bailey, F. Lee (lawyer); Waltham, Mass., 6/10/33

Bailey, Pearl (singer); Newport News, Va. (1918–1990)

Bain, Conrad (actor); Lethbridge, Alba., Canada, 2/4/23

Baio, Scott (actor); Brooklyn, N.Y., 9/22/61

Baird, Bil (William B. Baird) (puppeteer); Grand Island, Neb. (1904–1987)

Baker, Anita (singer); Toledo, Ohio, 1958?

Baker, Carroll (actress); Johnstown, Pa., 5/28/31

Baker, Josephine (singer, dancer); St. Louis (1906–1975)

Baker, Russell (columnist); Loudoun County, Va., 8/14/25

Balanchine, George (choreographer); St. Petersburg, Russia (1904–1983)

Balboa, Vasco Nuñez de (explorer); Jerez de los Caballeros, Spain (1475–1517)

Baldwin, Alec (actor); Massapequa, N.Y., 4/3/58

Baldwin, James (novelist); New York City (1924–1987)

Bale, Christian (actor); Pembrokeshire, Wales, 1/30/74

Balenciaga, Cristóbal (fashion designer); Guetaria, Spain **(1895– 1972)**

Ball, Lucille (Lucille Désirée Ball) (actress, producer); Celoron (nr. Jamestown), N.Y. **(1911–1989)**

Balsam, Martin (actor); Bronx, New York **(1919–1996)**

Balzac, Honoré de (novelist); Tours, France **(1799–1850)**

Bancroft, Anne (Annemarie Italiano) (actress); New York City **(1931–2005)**

Banderas, Antonio (José Antonio Dominguez Banderas) (actor, model); Málaga, Spain, 8/10/60

Bankhead, Tallulah (actress); Huntsville, Ala. **(1902–1968)**

Banks, Tyra (model); Los Angeles, 12/4/73

Bara, Theda (Theodosia Goodman) (actress); Cincinnati **(1890– 1955)**

Barak, Ehud (former Israeli prime minister); Kibbutz Mishmar Hasharon, Israel, 2/12/42

Barbera, Joseph (animator, producer); New York City, 3/24/11

Baranski, Christine (actress); Buffalo, N.Y., 5/2/52

Barber, Red (Walter Lanier) (sportscaster); Columbus, Miss. **(1908–1992)**

Barber, Samuel (composer); West Chester, Pa. **(1910–1981)**

Barbie, Klaus (Nazi, "The Butcher of Lyon"); Bad Godesberg, Germany **(1913–1991)**

Bardem, Javier (actor); Gran Canaria, Spain, 3/1/69

Bardot, Brigitte (Camille Javal) (actress); Paris, 9/28/34

Barenboim, Daniel (concert pianist, conductor); Buenos Aires, 11/15/42

Barker, Bob (game-show host); Darrington, Wash., 12/12/23

Barkin, Ellen (actress); Bronx, N.Y., 4/16/54

Barnard, Christiaan N. (heart surgeon); Beauford West, South Africa **(1922–2001)**

Barnum, Phineas Taylor (showman); Bethel, Conn. **(1810–1891)**

Barrie, Sir James Matthew (author); Kirriemuir, Scotland **(1860– 1937)**

Barry, John (naval officer); County Wexford, Ireland **(1745–1803)**

Barrymore, Diana (actress); New York City **(1921–1960)**

Barrymore, Drew (actress); Los Angeles, 2/22/75

Barrymore, Ethel (Ethel Blythe) (actress); Philadelphia **(1879– 1959)**

Barrymore, Georgiana Drew (actress); Philadelphia **(1856–1893)**

Barrymore, John (John Blythe) (actor); Philadelphia **(1882–1942)**

Barrymore, Lionel (Lionel Blythe) (actor); Philadelphia **(1878–1954)**

Barrymore, Maurice (Herbert Blythe) (actor, playwright); Agra, India **(1847–1905)**

Barth, John (novelist); Cambridge, Md., 5/27/30

Barthelme, Donald (novelist); Philadelphia **(1931–1989)**

Bartók, Béla (composer); Nagyszentmiklo, Hungary **(1881–1945)**

Barton, Clara (founder of American Red Cross); Oxford, Mass. **(1821–1912)**

Baruch, Bernard Mannes (statesman); Camden, S.C. **(1870–1965)**

Baryshnikov, Mikhail Nikolayevich (ballet dancer, artistic director); Riga, Latvia, 1/27/48

Basie, Count (William Basie) (band leader); Red Bank, N.J. **(1904– 1984)**

Basinger, Kim (actress); Athens, Ga., 12/8/53

Bassett, Angela (actress); New York City, 8/16/58

Batchelor, Clarence Daniel (political cartoonist); Osage City, Kans. **(1888–1977)**

Bateman, Jason (actor); Rye, N.Y., 1/14/69

Bateman, Justine (actress); Rye, N.Y., 2/19/66

Bates, Alan (actor); Allestree, England **(1934–2003)**

Bates, Kathy (Kathleen Doyle Bates) (actress); Memphis, Tenn., 6/28/48

Battle, Kathleen (soprano); Portsmouth, Ohio, 8/13/48

Baudelaire, Charles Pierre (poet); Paris **(1821–1867)**

Baxter, Anne (actress); Michigan City, Ind. **(1923–1985)**

Baxter, Meredith (actress); Los Angeles, 6/21/47

Beardsley, Aubrey Vincent (illustrator); Brighton, England **(1872– 1898)**

Beaton, Cecil (photographer, designer); London **(1904–1980)**

Beatty, Clyde (animal trainer); Bainbridge, Ohio **(1903–1965)**

Beatty, Warren (Henry Warren Beaty) (actor, producer); Richmond, Va., 3/30/37

Beaumont, Francis (dramatist); Grace-Dieu, England **(1584–1616)**

Beck (Beck Hansen) (musician); Los Angeles, Calif., 7/8/70

Becket, Thomas à (archbishop of Canterbury); London **(1118?– 1170)**

Beckett, Samuel (playwright); Dublin **(1906–1989)**

Beckmann, Max (painter); Leipzig, Germany **(1884–1950)**

Bede, Saint ("The Venerable Bede") (scholar); Monkwearmouth, England **(673–735)**

Beecham, Sir Thomas (conductor); St. Helens, England **(1879– 1961)**

Beecher, Henry Ward (clergyman); Litchfield, Conn. **(1813–1887)**

Beerbohm, Sir Max (author); London **(1872–1956)**

Beery, Noah (actor); Kansas City, Mo. **(1884–1946)**

Beery, Noah, Jr. (actor); New York City **(1913–1994)**

Beery, Wallace (actor); Kansas City, Mo. **(1886–1949)**

Beethoven, Ludwig van (composer); Bonn, Germany **(1770–1827)**

Begin, Menachem (Israeli prime minister); Brest-Litovsk, Belarus **(1913–1992)**

Begley, Ed (actor); Hartford, Conn. **(1901–1970)**

Beiderbecke, Bix (jazz musician); Davenport, Iowa **(1903–1931)**

Beineix, Jean-Jacques (director, producer, screenwriter) 10/8/46

Belafonte, Harry (singer, actor); New York City, 3/1/27

Belafonte-Harper, Shari (actress); New York City, 9/22/54

Belasco, David (dramatist, producer); San Francisco **(1854–1931)**

Bell, Alexander Graham (inventor); Edinburgh, Scotland **(1847– 1922)**

Bell, Quentin (author, artist); England **(1910–1996)**

Bellamy, Edward (author); Chicopee Falls, Mass. **(1850–1898)**

Bellamy, Ralph (actor); Chicago **(1904–1991)**

Bellini, Giovanni (painter); Venice **(c. 1430–1516)**

Bello, Maria (actress); Norristown, Penn., 4/18/67

Bellow, Saul (novelist); Lachine, Que., Canada **(1915–2005)**

Bellows, George Wesley (painter, lithographer); Columbus, Ohio **(1882–1925)**

Belushi, Jim (actor); Chicago, 6/15/54

Belushi, John (comedian, actor); Chicago **(1949–1982)**

Benchley, Peter Bradford (novelist); New York City, 5/8/40

Benchley, Robert Charles (humorist); Worcester, Mass. **(1889– 1945)**

Bendix, William (actor); New York City **(1906–1964)**

Benedict, Ruth Fulton (anthropologist); New York City **(1887–1948)**

Benedict XVI (Joseph Alois Ratzinger) (pope); Bavaria, Germany, 4/16/27

Benes, Eduard (statesman); Kozlany, former Czechoslovakia **(1884–1948)**

Benét, Stephen Vincent (poet, story writer); Bethlehem, Pa. **(1898– 1943)**

Benét, William Rose (poet, novelist); Ft. Hamilton, Brooklyn, N.Y. **(1886–1950)**

Ben-Gurion, David (David Green) (statesman); Plónsk, Poland **(1886–1973)**

Benigni, Roberto (actor, director, screenwriter); Misericordia, Arezzo, Italy, 10/27/52

Bening, Annette (actress); Topeka, Kans., 5/29/58

Bennett, Enoch Arnold (novelist, dramatist); Hanley, England **(1867–1931)**

Bennett, James Gordon (editor); Keith, Scotland **(1795–1872)**

Bennett, Joan (actress); Palisades, N.J. **(1910–1990)**

Bennett, Robert Russell (composer); Kansas City, Mo. **(1894– 1981)**

Bennett, Tony (Anthony Benedetto) (singer); Astoria, Queens, N.Y., 8/3/26

Benny, Jack (Benjamin Kubelsky) (comedian); Chicago **(1894– 1974)**

Benson, Robby (Robert Segal) (actor); Dallas, 1/21/56

Bentham, Jeremy Heinrich (economist); London **(1748–1832)**

Benton, Thomas Hart (painter); Neosho, Mo. **(1889–1975)**

Berendt, John (writer); Syracuse, N.Y., 12/5/39

Berenger, Tom (actor); Chicago, 5/31/50

Berg, Alban (composer); Vienna **(1885–1935)**

Berg, Gertrude (writer, actress); New York City **(1899–1966)**

Bergen, Candice (actress); Beverly Hills, Calif., 5/9/46

Bergen, Edgar (ventriloquist); Chicago **(1903–1978)**

Bergen, Polly (Nellie Paulina Burgin) (actress, singer); Knoxville, Tenn., 7/14/30

Bergerac, Cyrano de (poet); Paris **(1619–1655)**

Bergman, Ingmar (film director); Uppsala, Sweden, 7/14/18

Bergman, Ingrid (actress); Stockholm **(1915–1982)**

Bergson, Henri (philosopher); Paris **(1859–1941)**

Berkeley, Busby (William Berkeley Enos) (choreographer, director); Los Angeles **(1895–1976)**

Berle, Milton (Milton Berlinger) (comedian); New York City **(1908– 2002)**

Berlin, Irving (Israel Baline) (songwriter); Temum, Russia **(1888– 1989)**

Berlioz, Louis Hector (composer); La Côte-Saint-André, France **(1803–1869)**

Berman, Lazar (concert pianist); Leningrad (St. Petersburg), Russia **(1930–2005)**

Bernardin, Joseph Cardinal (prelate); Columbia, S.C. **(1928–1996)**

Berners-Lee, Tim (Internet pioneer); London, 6/8/55

Bernhard, Sandra (actress, comedian); Flint, Mich., 6/6/55
Bernhardt, Sarah (Rosine Bernard) (actress); Paris **(1844–1923)**
Bernini, Gian Lorenzo (sculptor, painter); Naples, Italy **(1598–1680)**
Bernoulli, Jacques (scientist); Basel, Switzerland **(1654–1705)**
Bernsen, Corbin (actor); North Hollywood, Calif., 9/7/54
Bernstein, Leonard (conductor); Lawrence, Mass. **(1918–1990)**
Berry, Chuck (Charles Edward Berry) (singer, guitarist); St. Louis, Mo., 10/19/26
Berry, Halle (actress, model); Cleveland, Ohio, 8/14/68
Berry, Ken (actor); Moline, Ill., 11/3/30
Berry, Richard (songwriter); Extension, S.C. **(1935–1997)**
Berryman, John (poet); McAlester, Okla. **(1914–1972)**
Bertinelli, Valerie (actress); Wilmington, Del., 4/23/60
Bertolucci, Bernardo (actor); Parma, Italy, 3/16/40
Bethune, Mary McLeod (educator); Mayesville, S.C. **(1875–1955)**
Betjeman, Sir John (poet laureate); London **(1906–1984)**
Bettelheim, Bruno (psychoanalyst); Vienna **(1903–1990)**
Beyoncé (Beyoncé Giselle Knowles) (singer); Houston, Tex., 9/4/81
Bezos, Jeff (entrepreneur); Albuquerque, N.M., 1/12/64
Bierce, Ambrose Gwinnett (journalist); Meigs County, Ohio **(1842–1914?)**
Bikel, Theodore (actor, folk singer); Vienna, 5/2/24
Bill W. (William Griffith Wilson) (founder of Alcoholics Anonymous); East Dorset, Vermont **(1895–1971)**
Bing, Sir Rudolf (opera manager); Vienna **(1902–1997)**
Bingham, George Caleb (painter); Augusta Co., Va. **(1811–1879)**
Binoche, Juliette (actress); Paris, 3/9/64
Bishop, Joey (Joseph Gottlieb) (comedian); New York City, 2/3/18
Bismarck-Schönhausen, Prince Otto Eduard Leopold von (statesman); Schönhausen, Germany **(1815–1898)**
Bisset, Jacqueline (actress); Weybridge, England, 9/13/44
Bixby, Bill (actor); San Francisco **(1934–1993)**
Bizet, Georges (Alexandre César Léopold Bizet) (composer); Paris **(1838–1875)**
Bjoerling, Jussi (tenor); Stora Tuna, Sweden **(1911–1960)**
Björk (Björk Gudmundsdottir) (pop musician, singer); Reykjavik, Iceland, 11/21/65
Black, Clint (singer, songwriter); Long Branch, N.J., 2/4/62
Black, Karen (Karen Ziegler) (actress); Park Ridge, Ill., 7/1/42
Black, Shirley Temple (child actress, former ambassador); Santa Monica, Calif., 4/23/28
Blackstone, Sir William (jurist); London **(1723–1780)**
Blackwell, Elizabeth (physician, educator); England **(1821–1910)**
Blades, Ruben (actor, musician, composer); Panama City, Panama, 7/16/48
Blair, Tony (British prime minister); Edinburgh, Scotland, 5/6/53
Blake, Amanda (Beverly Louise Neill) (actress); Buffalo, N.Y. **(1929–1989)**
Blake, Eubie (James Hubert) (pianist); Baltimore **(1883–1983)**
Blake, Robert (Michael Gubitosi) (actor); Nutley, N.J., 9/18/33
Blake, William (poet, artist); London **(1757–1827)**
Blanc, Mel (Melvin Jerome) (actor, voice specialist); San Francisco **(1908–1989)**
Blanchett, Cate (actress); Melbourne, Australia, 5/14/69
Blass, Bill (fashion designer); Fort Wayne, Ind. **(1922–2002)**
Bleeth, Yasmine (model, actress); New York City, 6/14/68
Blige, Mary J. (hip-hop singer); Bronx, N.Y., 1/11/71
Bloch, Ernest (composer); Geneva **(1880–1959)**
Bloom, Claire (actress); London, 2/15/31
Bloom, Orlando (actor); Kent, England, 1/13/77
Bloomberg, Michael (mayor of New York City); Melrose, Mass., 2/14/42
Bloomgarden, Kermit (producer); Brooklyn, N.Y. **(1904–1976)**
Blume, Judy (Judy Sussman) (young adult novelist); Elizabeth, N.J., 2/12/38
Bly, Nellie (pseud. for Elizabeth Seaman) (journalist); Cochrane Mills, Pa. **(1867–1922)**
Bly, Robert (poet, critic); Madison, Minn., 12/23/26
Boccaccio, Giovanni (author); Paris **(1313–1375)**
Boccherini, Luigi (Rodolfo) (composer); Lucca, Italy **(1743–1805)**
Boccioni, Umberto (painter, sculptor); Reggio di Calabria, Italy **(1882–1916)**
Bochco, Steven (TV producer, writer); New York City, 12/16/43
Bock, Jerry (composer); New Haven, Conn., 11/23/28
Bodman, Samuel (secretary of Energy); Chicago, Ill., 11/26/38
Bogarde, Dirk (Derek Van den Bogaerde) (film actor, director); London **(1921–1999)**
Bogart, Humphrey DeForest (actor); New York City **(1899–1957)**
Bogdanovich, Peter (producer, director); Kingston, N.Y., 7/30/39
Bogosian, Eric (playwright, screenwriter, actor, monologuist); Woburn, Mass., 4/24/53
Bohr, Niels (atomic physicist); Copenhagen **(1885–1962)**
Bok, Sissela (Sissela Ann Myrdal) (scholar); Stockholm, 12/2/34

Bolger, Ray (dancer, actor); Dorchester, Mass **(1904–1987)**
Bolivar, Simón (South American liberator); Caracas, Venezuela **(1783–1830)**
Bologna, Giovanni da (sculptor); Douai, France **(1529–1608)**
Bombeck, Erma (author, columnist); Dayton, Ohio **(1927–1996)**
Bonaparte, Napoléon (Emperor of the French); Ajaccio, Corsica, France **(1769–1821)**
Bond, Julian (Georgia legislator); Nashville, Tenn., 1/14/40
Bonet, Lisa (actress); San Francisco, 11/16/67
Bonham Carter, Helena (actress); London, 5/23/66
Bon Jovi, Jon (musician, songwriter); Sayreville, N.J., 3/2/62
Bonnard, Pierre (painter); Fontenayaux-Roses, France **(1867–1947)**
Bono (Paul Hewson) (singer, songwriter); Dublin, Ireland, 5/10/60
Bono, Sonny (Salvatore Bono) (singer, politician); Detroit **(1935–1998)**
Boone, Daniel (frontiersman); nr. Reading, Pa. **(1734–1820)**
Boone, Pat (Charles Boone) (singer); Jacksonville, Fla., 6/1/34
Boone, Richard (actor); Los Angeles **(1917–1981)**
Boorstin, Daniel (historian); Atlanta **(1914–2004)**
Booth, Edwin Thomas (actor); Bel Air, Md. **(1833–1893)**
Booth, Evangeline Cory (religious leader); London **(1865–1950)**
Booth, John Wilkes (actor; assassin of Lincoln); Harford County, Md. **(1838–1865)**
Booth, Shirley (Thelma Booth Ford) (actress); New York City **(1907–1992)**
Borden, Lizzie (Elizabeth Andrew Borden) (accused murderer); Fall River, Mass. **(1860–1927)**
Borge, Victor (pianist, comedian); Copenhagen **(1909–2000)**
Borgia, Cesare (nobleman, soldier); Rome **(1476–1507)**
Borgia, Lucrezia (Duchess of Ferrara); Rome **(1480–1519)**
Borgnine, Ernest (actor); Hamden, Conn., 1/24/17
Borromini, Francesco (architect); Bissone, Italy **(1599–1667)**
Bosch, Hieronymus (Hieronymus van Aeken) (painter); Hertogenbosch, Netherlands **(c. 1450–1516)**
Bosley, Tom (actor); Chicago, 10/1/27
Bostwick, Barry (actor); San Mateo, Calif., 2/24/45
Boswell, James (diarist, biographer); Edinburgh, Scotland **(1740–1795)**
Botticelli, Sandro (Alessandro di Mariano dei Filipepi) (painter); Florence, Italy **(1444–1510)**
Bottoms, Timothy (actor); Santa Barbara, Calif., 8/30/50
Boulez, Pierre (conductor); Montbrison, France, 3/26/25
Bourke-White, Margaret (photographer); New York City **(1906–1971)**
Boutros-Ghali, Boutros (ex-secretary general of the UN); Cairo, Egypt, 11/14/22
Bow, Clara (actress); Brooklyn, N.Y. **(1905–1965)**
Bowen, Catherine Drinker (biographer); Haverford, Pa. **(1897–1973)**
Bowie, David (David Robert Jones) (actor, musician); London, 1/8/47
Bowie, James (soldier); Burke County, Ga. **(1799–1836)**
Bowles, Camilla Parker (Duchess of Cornwall); London, England, 7/17/47
Bowles, Chester (diplomat); Springfield, Mass. **(1901–1986)**
Boxleitner, Bruce (actor); Elgin, Ill., 5/12/50
Boyce, William (composer); London? **(1710–1779)**
Boyd, Bill ("Hopalong Cassidy") (actor); Cambridge, Ohio **(1895–1972)**
Boyd, Stephen (Stephen Millar) (actor); Belfast, Northern Ireland **(1928–1977)**
Boyer, Charles (actor); Figeac, France **(1897–1978)**
Boy George (George Alan O'Dowd) (singer); London, 6/14/61
Boyle, Peter (actor); Philadelphia, 10/18/33
Boyle, Robert (scientist); Lismore Castle, Munster, Ireland **(1627–1691)**
Bracken, Eddie (actor); Astoria, Queens, N.Y. **(1915–2002)**
Bradbury, Ray Douglas (science-fiction writer); Waukegan, Ill., 8/22/20
Bradlee, Benjamin C. (editor); Boston, 8/26/21
Bradley, Ed (broadcast journalist); Philadelphia, 6/22/41
Bradley, Omar N. (5-star general); Clark, Mo. **(1893–1981)**
Bradley, Thomas (mayor of Los Angeles); Calvert, Tex. **(1917–1998)**
Brady, Mathew (early photographer); Warren Co., N.Y. **(c. 1823–1896)**
Braff, Zach (actor); South Orange, N.J., 4/6/75
Bragg, Billy (singer, songwriter); Barking, England, 12/20/57
Brahe, Tycho (astronomer); Knudstrup, Denmark **(1546–1601)**
Brahms, Johannes (composer); Hamburg, Germany **(1833–1897)**
Braille, Louis (teacher of blind); Coupvray, France **(1809–1852)**

Bramante, Donato D'Agnolo (architect); Monte Asdrualdo (now Fermignano), Italy **(1444–1514)**

Branagh, Kenneth (actor, director, writer, producer); Belfast, Northern Ireland, 12/10/60

Brancusi, Constantin (sculptor); Pestisansi, Romania **(1876–1957)**

Brandauer, Klaus Maria (Klaus Maria Steng) (actor); Bad Aussee, Steiermark, Austria , 6/22/44

Brando, Marlon (actor); Omaha, Neb. **(1924–2004)**

Brandt, Willy (Herbert Frahm) (ex-chancellor); Lúbeck, Germany **(1913– 1992)**

Brandy (Brandy Norwood) (actress, singer); McComb, Miss., 2/11/79

Braque, Georges (painter); Argenteuil, France **(1882–1963)**

Bratt, Benjamin (actor); San Francisco, 12/16/63

Braugher, André (actor); Chicago, 7/1/62

Braxton, Toni (R&B singer); Severn, Maryland, 10/7/67

Brazelton, T(homas) Berry II (pediatrician, writer); Waco, Tex., 5/10/18

Brecht, Bertolt (dramatist, poet); Augsburg, Bavaria **(1898–1956)**

Brel, Jacques (singer, composer); Brussels **(1929–1978)**

Brennan, Walter (actor); Lynn, Mass. **(1894–1974)**

Brennan, William J., Jr. (Supreme Court justice); Newark, N.J. **(1906–1997)**

Breslin, Jimmy (journalist); Jamaica, Queens, N.Y., 10/17/30

Breton, André (writer); Tinchebray, France **(1896–1966)**

Breuer, Marcel (architect, designer); Pécs, Hungary **(1902–1981)**

Brewster, Kingman, Jr. (ex-president of Yale); Longmeadow, Mass. **(1919–1988)**

Brezhnev, Leonid I. (Communist Party secretary); Dneprodzerzhinsk, Ukraine **(1906–1982)**

Brice, Fanny (Fannie Borach) (comedienne); New York City **(1892–1951)**

Bridges, Beau (actor); Los Angeles, 12/9/41

Bridges, Jeff (actor); Los Angeles, 12/4/49

Bridges, Lloyd (actor); San Leandro, Calif. **(1913–1998)**

Brin, Sergey (Google co-founder); Moscow, Russia, 8/21/73

Brinkley, Christie (model, actress); Malibu, Calif., 2/2/54

Brinkley, David (TV newscaster); Wilmington, N.C. **(1920–2003)**

Britten, Benjamin (composer); Lowestoft, England **(1913–1976)**

Broderick, Matthew (actor); New York City, 3/21/62

Brodsky, Joseph Alexandrovitch (poet); St. Petersburg, Russia **(1940–1996)**

Brody, Jane (journalist); Brooklyn, N.Y., 5/19/41

Brokaw, Tom (TV newscaster); Webster, S.D., 2/6/40

Brolin, James (actor); Los Angeles, 7/18/40

Bromfield, Louis (novelist); Mansfield, Ohio **(1896–1956)**

Bronson, Charles (Charles Buchinsky) (actor); Ehrenfield, Pa. **(1921–2003)**

Brontë, Charlotte (novelist); Thornton, England **(1816–1855)**

Brontë, Emily Jane (novelist); Thornton, England **(1818–1848)**

Bronzino, Agnolo (painter); Monticelli, Italy **(1503–1572)**

Brook, Peter (director); London, 3/21/25

Brooke, Edward William III (senator); Washington, D.C., 10/26/19

Brooke, Rupert (poet); Rugby, England **(1887–1915)**

Brooks, Albert (Albert Einstein) (actor, writer, director); Beverly Hills, Calif., 7/22/47

Brooks, Avery (actor) 4/18/49

Brooks, Gwendolyn (poet); Topeka, Kans. **(1917–2000)**

Brooks, James L. (film and television producer); New York City, 5/9/40

Brooks, Mel (Melvin Kaminsky) (writer, film director); Brooklyn, N.Y., 6/28/26

Brosnan, Pierce (actor); County Meath, Ireland, 5/16/52

Brothers, Joyce (Bauer) (psychologist, author, radio-TV personality); New York City, 9/20/28

Broun, Matthew Heywood Campbell (journalist); Brooklyn, N.Y. **(1888–1939)**

Brown, Charles Brockden (novelist); Philadelphia **(1771–1810)**

Brown, Gordon (James Gordon Brown) (British politician); Glasgow, Scotland, 2/20/5†

Brown, Helen Gurley (editor, author); Green Forest, Ark., 2/18/22

Brown, James (singer); Augusta, Ga., 5/3/34

Brown, Joe E. (comedian); Holgate, Ohio **(1892–1973)**

Brown, John (abolitionist); Torrington, Conn. **(1800–1859)**

Brown, Les (band leader); Reinerton, Pa. **(1912–2000)**

Brown, Margaret Wise (children's author); Brooklyn, N.Y. **(1910–1952)**

Brown, Trisha (choreographer); Aberdeen, Wash., 11/25/36

Browne, Jackson (singer, guitarist); Heidelberg, Germany, 10/9/48

Browning, Elizabeth Barrett (poet); Durham, England **(1806–1861)**

Browning, Robert (poet); London **(1812–1889)**

Brubeck, Dave (musician); Concord, Calif., 12/6/20

Bruce, Lenny (comedian); Long Island, N.Y. **(1926–1966)**

Bruce, Nigel (actor); Ensenada, Mexico **(1895–1953)**

Brueghel, Pieter (painter); nr. Breda, Flanders, Netherlands **(c. 1520–1569)**

Bruhn, Erik (Belton Evers) (ballet dancer); Copenhagen **(1928–1986)**

Brunelleschi, Filippo (architect); Florence, Italy **(1377–1446)**

Bruno, Giordano (philosopher); Nola, Italy **(1548–1600)**

Brutus, Marcus Junius (Roman politician) **(85–42 B.C.)**

Bryan, William Jennings (orator, politician); Salem, Ill. **(1860–1925)**

Bryant, Anita (singer); Barnsdall, Okla., 3/25/40

Bryant, William Cullen (poet, editor); Cummington, Mass. **(1794–1878)**

Brynner, Yul (Taidje Khan) (actor); Sakhalin Island, Russia **(1920–1985)**

Brzezinski, Zbigniew (ex-presidential adviser); Warsaw, 3/28/28

Buber, Martin (philosopher, theologian); Vienna **(1878–1965)**

Buchanan, James (15th U.S. president); near Mercersburg, Pa. **(1791–1868)**

Buchanan, Pat (politician); Washington, D.C., 11/2/38

Buchholz, Horst (actor); Berlin, 12/4/33

Büchner, Georg (dramatist); Goddelau, Germany **(1813–1837)**

Buchwald, Art (Arthur Buchwald) (columnist); Mount Vernon, N.Y., 10/20/25

Buck, Pearl S(ydenstricker) (author); Hillsboro, W. Va. **(1892–1973)**

Buckley, Christopher (writer); New York City, 1952

Buckley, Jeff (singer, songwriter); Orange County, Calif. **(1966–1997)**

Buckley, William F., Jr. (journalist); New York City, 11/24/25

Buffalo Bill (William Frederick Cody) (scout); Scott County, Iowa **(1846–1917)**

Buffett, Jimmy (singer, writer); Pascogoula, Miss., 12/25/46

Buffett, Warren (investment expert); Omaha, Neb., 8/30/30

Bujold, Genevieve (actress); Montreal, 7/1/42

Bujones, Fernando (ballet dancer); Miami, Fla., 3/9/55

Bulgakov, Mikhail (novelist); Kiev, Ukraine **(1891–1940)**

Bullins, Ed (playwright); Philadelphia, 7/2/35

Bullock, Sandra (actress); Washington D.C., 7/26/64

Bunche, Ralph J. (statesman); Detroit **(1904–1971)**

Bündchen, Gisele (model); Rio Grande do Sul, Brazil, 7/20/80

Bundy, McGeorge (educator); Boston **(1919–1996)**

Bundy, William Putnam (editor); Washington, D.C. **(1917–2000)**

Buñuel, Luis (film director); Calanda, Spain **(1900–1983)**

Bunyan, John (preacher, author); Elstow, England **(1628–1688)**

Burbank, Luther (horticulturist); Lancaster, Mass. **(1849–1926)**

Burke, Adm. Arleigh A. (ex-chief of Naval Operations); Boulder, Colo. **(1901–1996)**

Burke, Billie (Mary William Ethelbert Appleton Burke) (comedienne); Washington, D.C. **(1885–1970)**

Burke, Delta (actress); Orlando, Fla., 7/30/56

Burke, Edmund (statesman); Dublin **(1729–1797)**

Burne-Jones, Edward Coley (painter); Birmingham, England **(1833–1898)**

Burnett, Carol (comedienne); San Antonio, 4/26/33

Burney, Fanny (Frances) (writer); King's Lynn, England **(1752–1840)**

Burns, Edward (actor, film director, screenwriter, producer); Long Island, N.Y., 1/29/68

Burns, George (Nathan Birnbaum) (comedian); New York City **(1896–1996)**

Burns, Ken (documentary filmmaker); Brooklyn, N.Y., 7/29/53

Burns, Robert (poet); Alloway, Scotland **(1759–1796)**

Burr, Aaron (political leader); Newark, N.J. **(1756–1836)**

Burr, Raymond (William Stacey Burr) (actor); New Westminster, B.C., Canada **(1917–1993)**

Burroughs, Edgar Rice (novelist); Chicago **(1875–1950)**

Burroughs, William S. (writer); St. Louis **(1914–1997)**

Burrows, Abe (playwright, director); New York City **(1910–1985)**

Burstyn, Ellen (Edna Rae Gillooly) (actress); Detroit, 12/7/32

Burton, LeVar (actor, director); Landsthul, Germany, 2/16/57

Burton, Richard (Richard Jenkins) (actor); Pontrhydfen, Wales **(1925–1984)**

Burton, Tim (filmmaker); Burbank, Calif., 8/25/58

Buscemi, Steve (actor); Brooklyn, N.Y., 12/13/57

Bush, George Herbert Walker (41st U.S. president); Milton, Mass., 6/12/24

Bush, George Walker (43rd U.S. president); New Haven, Conn., 7/6/46

Butkus, Dick (NFL linebacker, actor); Chicago, 12/9/42

Butler, Samuel (author); Langar, England **(1835–1902)**

Buttons, Red (Aaron Chwatt) (actor); New York City, 2/5/19

Buzzi, Ruth (comedienne); Westerly, R.I., 7/24/36

Bynes, Amanda (actress); Thousand Oaks, Calif., 4/3/86

Byrd, Richard Evelyn (polar explorer); Winchester, Va. **(1888–1957)**

Byrne, David (composer, musician, director, actor); Dumbarton, Scotland, 5/14/52

Byrne, Gabriel (actor); Dublin, 5/12/50

Byron, George Gordon (6th Baron Byron) (poet); London **(1788–1824)**

C

Caan, James (actor); Queens, N.Y.,·3/26/39

Caballé, Montserrat (soprano); Barcelona, Spain, 4/12/33

Cabot, John (Giovanni Caboto) (navigator); Genoa **(1450–1498)**

Cabot, Sebastian (navigator); Venice **(c. 1476–1557)**

Cadmus, Paul (painter, etcher); New York City **(1904–1999)**

Caesar, Irving (lyricist); New York City **(1895–1996)**

Caesar, Gaius Julius (statesman); Rome **(100–44 B.C.)**

Caesar, Sid (comedian); Yonkers, N.Y., 9/8/22

Cage, Nicolas (Nicolas Coppola) (actor); Long Beach, Calif., 1/7/64

Cagney, James (actor); New York City **(1899–1986)**

Cahn, Sammy (songwriter); New York City **(1913–1993)**

Caine, Michael (Maurice J. Micklewhite) (actor); London, 3/14/33

Calder, Alexander (sculptor); Lawnton, Pa. **(1898–1976)**

Calderón del al Barca, Pedro (dramatist); Madrid **(1600–1681)**

Caldwell, Erskine (novelist); White Oak, Ga. **(1903–1987)**

Caldwell, Sarah (opera director, conductor); Maryville, Mo., 3/6/24

Caldwell, Taylor (novelist); Manchester, England **(1900–1985)**

Caldwell, Zoe (actress); Hawthorn, Australia, 9/14/33

Calhoun, John Caldwell (statesman); nr. Calhoun Mills, S.C. **(1782–1850)**

Caligula Gaius Caesar (Roman emperor); Antium, Latium **(12–41)**

Calisher, Hortense (novelist); New York City, 12/20/11

Callas, Maria (Maria Calogeropoulos) (operatic soprano); New York City **(1923–1977)**

Calloway, Cab (Cabell Calloway) (band leader); Rochester, N.Y. **(1907–1994)**

Calvin, John (Jean Chauvin) (religious reformer); Noyon, Picardy, France **(1509–1564)**

Calvin, Melvin (chemist, Nobel laureate); St. Paul, Minn. **(1911–1997)**

Cambridge, Godfrey (comedian); New York City **(1933–1976)**

Cameron, James (director); Kapuskasing, Ont., Canada, 8/16/54

Cameron, Rod (Rod Cox) (actor); Calgary, Alba., Canada **(1912–1983)**

Campbell, Glen (singer); nr. Delight, Ark., 4/22/38

Campbell, Naomi (model); London, England, 5/22/70

Campbell, Neve (actress); Guelph, Ont., Canada, 10/3/73

Campion, Jane (director, screenwriter); Waikanae, New Zealand, 1954

Camus, Albert (author); Mondovi, Algeria **(1913–1960)**

Canaletto (Giovanni Antonio Canale) (painter); Venice **(1697–1768)**

Candy, John (actor, comedian); Toronto **(1950–1994)**

Caniff, Milton (cartoonist); Hillsboro, Ohio **(1907–1988)**

Cannon, Dyan (Samille Diane Friesen) (actress); Tacoma, Wash., 1/4/37

Cantinflas (Mario Moreno-Reyes) (comedian); Mexico City **(1911–1993)**

Cantor, Eddie (Edward Iskowitz) (actor); New York City **(1892–1964)**

Capone, Al(fonse) (gangster); Brooklyn, N.Y. **(1899–1947)**

Capote, Truman (Truman Streckfus Persons) (novelist); New Orleans **(1924–1984)**

Capp, Al (Alfred Gerald Caplin) (cartoonist); New Haven, Conn. **(1909–1979)**

Capra, Frank (film producer, director); Palermo, Italy **(1897–1991)**

Caputo, Phil (Philip Joseph Caputo) (author, journalist); Chicago, 6/10/41

Caravaggio, Michelangelo Merisi da (painter); Caravaggio, Italy **(1573–1610)**

Cardin, Pierre (fashion designer); nr. Venice, 7/7/22

Cardinale, Claudia (actress); Tunis, Tunisia, 4/15/39

Carey, Drew (actor, producer); Cleveland, 5/23/58

Carey, Harry (actor); New York City **(1878–1947)**

Carey, Macdonald (actor); Sioux City, Iowa **(1913–1994)**

Carlin, George (comedian); Bronx, N.Y., 5/12/37

Carlisle, Kitty (singer, actress); New Orleans, 9/3/15

Carlyle, Robert (actor); Glasgow, Scotland, 4/14/61

Carlyle, Thomas (essayist, historian); Ecclefechan, Scotland **(1795–1881)**

Carmichael, Hoagy (Hoagland Howard) (songwriter); Bloomington, Ind. **(1899–1981)**

Carne, Judy (Joyce Botterill) (singer, actress); Northampton, England, 4/27/39

Carnegie, Andrew (industrialist); Dunfermline, Scotland **(1835–1919)**

Carney, Art (actor); Mt. Vernon, N.Y. **(1918–2003)**

Caron, Leslie (actress); Paris, 7/1/31

Carpenter, Mary Chapin (singer, songwriter); Princeton, N.J., 2/21/58

Carr, Vikki (Florencia Bisenta de Casillas Martinez Cardona) (singer); El Paso, Tex., 7/19/41

Carracci, Annibale (painter); Bologna, Italy **(1560–1609)**

Carracci, Lodovico (painter); Bologna, Italy **(1555–1619)**

Carradine, David (actor); Hollywood, Calif., 12/8/36

Carradine, John (actor); New York City **(1906–1988)**

Carradine, Keith (actor); San Mateo, Calif., 8/8/49

Carreras, José (tenor); Barcelona, Spain, 12/5/46

Carroll, Diahann (Carol Diahann Johnson) (singer, actress); Bronx, N.Y., 7/17/35

Carroll, Leo G. (actor); Weedon, England **(1892–1972)**

Carroll, Lewis (Charles Lutwidge Dodgson) (author, mathematician); Daresbury, England **(1832–1898)**

Carson, Johnny (TV entertainer); Corning, Iowa **(1925–2005)**

Carson, Kit (Christopher Carson) (scout); Madison County, Ky. **(1809–1868)**

Carson, Rachel (biologist, author); Springdale, Pa. **(1907–1964)**

Carter, Betty (jazz singer, composer); Flint, Mich. **(1930–1998)**

Carter, Chris (television and film writer, director, producer); Bellflower, Calif., 10/13/57

Carter, Dixie (actress); McLemoresville, Tenn., 5/25/39

Carter, Jack (comedian); New York City, 6/24/23

Carter, James Earl, Jr. (39th U.S. president); Plains, Ga., 10/1/24

Carter, Lynda (actress); Phoenix, Ariz., 7/24/51

Cartier, Jacques (explorer); Saint-Malo, Brittany, France **(1491–1557)**

Cartier-Bresson, Henri (photographer); Chanteloup, France **(1908–2004)**

Cartland, Barbara (author); England **(1901–2000)**

Caruso, Enrico (Errico Caruso) (tenor); Naples, Italy **(1873–1921)**

Carver, George Washington (botanist); Diamond Grove, Mo. **(1864–1943)**

Cary, Arthur Joyce Lunel (novelist); Londonderry, Ireland **(1888–1957)**

Casals, Pablo (cellist); Vendrell, Spain **(1876–1973)**

Casanova de Seingalt, Giovanni Jacopo (adventurer); Venice **(1725–1798)**

Case, Steve (business executive); Honolulu, 8/21/58

Cash, Johnny (singer); nr. Kingsland, Ark. **(1932–2003)**

Cass, Peggy (Mary Margaret Cass) (comedienne); Boston **(1924–1999)**

Cassatt, Mary (painter); Allegheny, Pa. **(1844–1926)**

Cassavetes, John (director); New York City **(1929–1989)**

Cassidy, David (singer); New York City, 4/12/50

Cassidy, Jack (actor); Richmond Hill, Queens, N.Y. **(1927–1976)**

Cassidy, Shaun (actor, television producer, singer); Los Angeles, 9/27/58

Cassini, Oleg (Oleg Lolewski-Cassini) (fashion designer); Paris, 4/11/13

Castagno, Andrea del (painter); San Martino a Corella, Italy **(c. 1421–1457)**

Castaneda, Carlos (cultural anthropologist, author); São Paulo, Brazil **(1931–1998)**

Castle, Irene (Irene Foote) (actress, dancer); New Rochelle, N.Y. **(1893–1969)**

Castle, Vernon Blythe (dancer, aviator); Norwich, England **(1887–1918)**

Castro Ruz, Fidel (premier); Mayari, Oriente, Cuba, 8/13/26

Cather, Willa Sibert (novelist); Winchester, Va. **(1873?–1947)**

Cato, Marcus Porcius (called Cato the Elder) (statesman); Tusculum, Italy **(234–149 B.C.)**

Catt, Carrie Lane Chapman (woman suffragist); Ripon, Wis. **(1859–1947)**

Catton, Bruce (historian); Petoskey, Mich. **(1899–1978)**

Catullus, Gaius Valerius (poet); Verona **(c. 84–c. 54 B.C.)**

Cavallaro, Carmen (band leader); New York City **(1913–1989)**

Cavett, Dick (Richard Cavett) (TV entertainer); Gibbon, Neb., 11/19/36

Ceausescu, Nicolae (head of state); Scorniscesti, Romania **(1918–1989)**

Céline, Louis Ferdinand (pseud. of Louis Fuch Destouches) (novelist); Paris **(1894–1961)**

Cellini, Benvenuto (goldsmith, sculptor); Florence, Italy **(1500–1571)**

Cervantes Saavedra, Miguel de (novelist); Alcalá de Henares, Spain **(1547–1616)**

Cézanne, Paul (painter); Aix-en-Provence, France **(1839–1906)**

Chagall, Marc (painter); Vitebsk, Russia **(1887–1985)**

Chaliapin, Feodor Ivanovitch (operatic basso); Kazan, Russia **(1873–1938)**

Chamberlain, Arthur Neville (statesman); Edgbaston, England **(1869–1940)**

Chamberlain, Richard (actor, producer); Los Angeles, 3/31/35

Champion, Gower (choreographer); Geneva, Ill. **(1921–1980)**

Champion, Marge (Marjorie Celeste Belcher) (actress, dancer); Los Angeles, 9/2/23

Champlain, Samuel de (explorer); nr. Rochefort, France **(1567–1635)**

Chan, Jackie (Chan Kwong Sang) (actor); Hong Kong, 4/7/54

Chancellor, John (TV commentator); Chicago **(1927–1996)**

Chandler, Jeff (Ira Grossel) (actor); Brooklyn, N.Y. **(1918–1961)**

Chandler, Raymond (writer); Chicago **(1883–1959)**

Chanel, "Coco" (Gabriel Bonheur) (fashion designer); Issoire, France **(1883–1971)**

Chaney, Lon (actor); Colorado Springs, Colo. **(1883–1930)**

Channing, Carol (actress); Seattle, 1/31/23

Channing, Stockard (Susan Stockard) (actress); New York City, 2/13/44

Chao, Elaine (secretary of Labor); Taiwan, 3/26/53

Chapin, Harry (singer, songwriter, activist); New York City **(1942–1981)**

Chaplin, Geraldine (actress); Santa Monica, Calif., 7/31/44

Chaplin, Sir Charles (actor); London **(1889–1977)**

Charisse, Cyd (Tula Finklea) (dancer, actress); Amarillo, Tex., 3/8/21

Charlemagne (Holy Roman Emperor); birthplace unknown **(742–814)**

Charles, Prince of Wales (Charles Philip Arthur George Windsor) (heir to the throne of Great Britain); Buckingham Palace, 11/14/48

Charles, Ray (Ray Charles Robinson) (pianist, singer, songwriter); Albany, Ga. **(1930–2004)**

Charo (Maria Rosario Pilar Martinez) (actress); Murcia, Spain, 1/15/51

Chase, Chevy (Cornelius Crane Chase) (comedian); New York City, 10/8/43

Chase, Lucia (founder Ballet Theatre [now American Ballet Theatre]); Waterbury, Conn. **(1907–1986)**

Chateaubriand, François René de (writer, statesman); St. Malo, France **(1768–1848)**

Chaucer, Geoffrey (poet); London **(c. 1340–1400)**

Chuan, Leekpai (prime minister of Thailand); Muang District, Thailand, 7/28/38

Chávez, Carlos (composer); nr. Mexico City **(1899–1978)**

Chavez, Cesar (labor leader); nr. Yuma, Ariz. **(1927–1993)**

Chayefsky, Paddy (Sidney Chayefsky) (playwright); New York City **(1923–1981)**

Cheadle, Don (actor); Kansas City, Mo., 11/29/64

Checker, Chubby (Ernest Evans) (performer); Philadelphia, 10/3/41

Cheever, John (novelist); Quincy, Mass. **(1912–1982)**

Chekhov, Anton Pavlovich (dramatist, short-story writer); Taganrog, Russia **(1860–1904)**

Chen Shui-bian (president of Taiwan); Taiwan, 2/18/51

Cher (Cherilyn Sarkisian La Piere) (actress, singer); El Centro, Calif., 5/20/46

Chertoff, Michael (secretary of Homeland Security); Elizabeth, N.J., 11/28/53

Cherubini, Luigi (composer); Florence **(1760–1842)**

Chesterton, Gilbert Keith (author); Kensington, England **(1874–1936)**

Chesnutt, Charles Waddell (author); Cleveland **(1858–1932)**

Chevalier, Maurice (entertainer); Paris **(1888–1972)**

Chiang Kai-shek (chief of state); Feng-hwa, China **(1887–1975)**

Child, Julia (food expert); Pasadena, Calif. **(1912–2004)**

Chippendale, Thomas (cabinet-maker); Otley, England **(1718–1779)**

Chirac, Jacques (president of France); Paris, 11/29/32

Chirico, Giorgio de (painter); Vólos, Greece **(1888–1978)**

Chisholm, Shirley Anita St. Hill (U.S. representative); Brooklyn, N.Y. **(1924–2005)**

Chlumsky, Anna (actress); Chicago, 12/3/80

Chomsky, (Avram) Noam (linguist, educator, activist); Philadelphia, 12/7/28

Chopin, Frédéric François (composer); nr. Warsaw **(1810–1849)**

Chopin, Kate O'Flaherty (author); St. Louis **(1851–1904)**

Chow, Yun-Fat (actor); Hong Kong, 5/18/55

Chrétien, Jean Joseph-Jacques (former prime minister of Canada); Shawinigan, Que., Canada, 1/11/34

Christie, Agatha (mystery writer); Torquay, England **(1890–1976)**

Christie, Julie (actress); Chukua, India, 4/14/41

Chung, Connie (broadcast journalist); Washington, D.C., 8/20/46

Church, Thomas Haden (actor); El Paso, Tex., 6/17/61

Churchill, Sir Winston Leonard Spencer (statesman); Blenheim Palace, Oxfordshire, England **(1874–1965)**

Cicero, Marcus Tullius (orator, statesman); Arpinum, Italy **(106–43 b.c.)**

Cid, El (Rodrigo [or Ruy] Diez de Bivar) (Spanish national hero); nr. Burgos, Spain **(c. 1043–1099)**

Cilento, Diane (actress); Queensland, Australia, 10/5/33

Cimabue, Giovanni (painter); Florence, Italy **(c. 1240–c. 1302)**

Cimino, Michael (director, writer, producer); New York City, 11/16/43

Claire, Ina (Ina Fagan) (actress); Washington, D.C. **(1895–1985)**

Clancy, Tom (novelist); Baltimore, 4/12/47

Clapton, Eric (singer, guitarist); Ripley, England, 3/30/45

Clark, Dick (TV personality); Mt. Vernon, N.Y., 11/30/29

Clark, Mary Higgins (writer); New York City, 12/24/31

Clark, Petula (singer); Epsom, England, 11/15/32

Clark, Roy (country music artist); Meherrin, Va., 4/15/33

Clark, William (explorer); Caroline County, Va. **(1770–1838)**

Clarke, Arthur C. (science fiction writer); Minehead, England, 12/16/17

Clarkson, Kelly (singer); Fort Worth, Tex., 4/24/82

Claude Lorrain (Claude Gellée) (painter); Champagne, France **(1600–1682)**

Clausewitz, Karl von (military strategist); Burg, Germany **(1780–1831)**

Clay, Henry (statesman); Hanover County, Va. **(1777–1852)**

Clay, Lucius D. (banker, ex-general); Marietta, Ga. **(1897–1978)**

Clayburgh, Jill (actress); New York City, 4/30/44

Cleary, Beverly (Beverly Atlee Bunn) (children's author); McMinnville, Ore., 1916

Cleaver, Eldridge (Leroy) (author, activist); Wabbaseka, Ark. **(1935–1998)**

Cleese, John (writer, actor); Weston-super-Mare, England, 10/27/39

Clemenceau, Georges (statesman); Mouilleron-en-Pareds, Vondée, France **(1841–1929)**

Cleopatra (queen of Egypt); Alexandria, Egypt **(69–30 b.c.)**

Cleveland, Stephen Grover (22nd & 24th U.S. president); Caldwell, N.J. **(1837–1908)**

Cliburn, Van (Harvey Lavan Cliburn, Jr.) (concert pianist); Shreveport, La., 7/12/34

Clift, Montgomery (actor); Omaha, Neb. **(1920–1966)**

Cline, Patsy (singer); Winchester, Va. **(1932–1963)**

Clinton, Hillary Rodham (ex-first lady, U.S. senator); Park Ridge, Ill., 10/26/47

Clinton, William Jefferson (42nd U.S. president); Hope, Ark., 8/19/46

Clooney, George (actor); Lexington, Ky., 5/6/61

Clooney, Rosemary (singer); Maysville, Ky. **(1928–2002)**

Close, Glenn (actress); Greenwich, Conn., 3/19/47

Cobain, Kurt (musician); Hoquiam, Wash. **(1967–1994)**

Cobb, Irvin Shrewsbury (humorist); Paducah, Ky. **(1876–1944)**

Cobb, Lee J. (Leo Jacob Cobb) (actor); New York City **(1911–1976)**

Coburn, Charles Douville (actor); Savannah, Ga. **(1877–1961)**

Coburn, James (actor); Laurel, Neb. **(1928–2002)**

Coca, Imogene (comedienne); Philadelphia **(1908–2001)**

Cocker, Jarvis (singer, songwriter); Sheffield, England, 9/19/63

Cocker, Joe (John Robert Cocker) (singer); Sheffield, England, 5/20/44

Coco, James (actor); New York City **(1929–1987)**

Cocteau, Jean (author); Maison-Lafitte, France **(1889–1963)**

Cohan, George Michael (actor, dramatist); Providence, R.I. **(1878–1942)**

Cohen, Leonard (composer); Montreal, Que., Canada, 9/21/34

Colbert, Claudette (Lily Chauchoin) (actress); Paris **(1903–1996)**

Cole, Nat "King" (singer); Montgomery, Ala. **(1919–1965)**

Cole, Natalie (singer); Los Angeles, 2/6/50

Cole, Thomas (painter); Lancashire, England **(1801–1848)**

Coleman, Dabney (actor); Austin, Tex., 1/3/32

Coleridge, Samuel Taylor (poet); Ottery St. Mary, England **(1772–1834)**

Colette (Sidonie-Gabrielle Colette) (novelist); St.-Sauveur, France **(1873–1954)**

Collingwood, Charles (TV commentator); Three Rivers, Mich. **(1917–1985)**

Collins, Joan (actress); London, 5/23/33

Collins, Judy (singer); Seattle, 5/1/39

Colman, Ronald (actor); Richmond, England **(1891–1958)**

Colonna, Jerry (comedian); Boston **(1905–1986)**

Coltrane, John (jazz musician); Hamlet, N.C. **(1926–1967)**

Columbus, Chris (director, screenwriter); Spangler, Pa., 9/10/58

Columbus, Christopher (Cristoforo Colombo) (explorer); Genoa, Italy **(1451–1506)**

Colvin, Shawn (folk singer); Vermillion, S.D., 1/10/58

Combs, Sean "Puffy" (singer, record producer); New York City, 11/9/69

Comden, Betty (writer); New York City, 5/3/19

Comenius, Johann Amos (educational reformer); Nivnice, Moravia, Czech Republic **(1592–1670)**

Commager, Henry Steele (historian); Pittsburgh **(1902–1998)**

Como, Perry (Pierino Como) (singer); Canonsburg, Pa. **(1912–2001)**

Compton, Karl Taylor (physicist); Wooster, Ohio **(1887–1954)**

Comte, Auguste (philosopher); Montpellier, France **(1798–1857)**

Conant, James B. (educator, statesman); Dorchester, Mass. **(1893–1978)**

Condon, Eddie (jazz musician); Goodland, Ind. **(1905–1973)**

Confucius (K'ung Fu-tzu) (philosopher); Shantung province, China **(c. 551– 479 B.C.)**

Congreve, William (dramatist); nr. Leeds, England **(1670–1729)**

Connelly, Marc (playwright); McKeesport, Pa. **(1890–1980)**

Connery, Sean (actor); Edinburgh, Scotland, 8/25/30

Connick, Jr., Harry (musician, actor); New Orleans, La., 9/11/67

Conniff, Ray (band leader); Attleboro, Mass. **(1916–2002)**

Connors, Chuck (actor); Brooklyn, N.Y. **(1921–1992)**

Connors, Mike (Krekor Ohanian) (actor); Fresno, Calif., 8/15/25

Conrad, Joseph (Teodor Jozef Konrad Korzeniowski) (novelist); Berdichev, Ukraine **(1857–1924)**

Conrad, Robert (Conrad Robert Falk) (actor); Chicago, 3/1/35

Conrad, William (actor); Louisville, Ky. **(1920–1994)**

Conried, Hans Georg, Jr. (actor); Baltimore **(1917–1982)**

Conroy, Pat (author); Atlanta, 10/26/45

Constable, John (painter); East Bergholt, Suffolk, England **(1776–1837)**

Constantine II (ex-king of Greece); Athens, 6/2/40

Constantine, Michael (actor); Reading, Pa., 5/22/27

Conte, Richard (actor); New York City **(1910–1975)**

Conti, Tom (actor); Paisley, Scotland, 11/22/41

Convy, Bert (actor, host); St. Louis **(1933–1991)**

Conway, Tim (comedian); Chagrin Falls, Ohio, 12/15/33

Coogan, Jackie (actor); Los Angeles **(1914–1984)**

Cook, Peter (actor, writer); Torquay, England **(1937–1995)**

Cooke, Alistair (Alfred Alistair) (TV narrator, journalist); Manchester, England **(1908–2004)**

Cooke, Jack Kent (business executive); Hamilton, Ont., Canada **(1912–1997)**

Cooley, Denton A(rthur) (heart surgeon); Houston, 8/22/20

Coolidge, (John) Calvin (30th U.S. president); Plymouth, Vt. **(1872–1933)**

Coolidge, Rita (singer); Nashville, Tenn., 5/1/45

Coolio (Artis Ivey, Jr.) (rap artist); Los Angeles, Calif., 8/1/63

Cooper, Alice (Vincent Furnier) (rock musician); Detroit, 2/4/48

Cooper, Gary (Frank James Cooper) (actor); Helena, Mont. **(1901–1961)**

Cooper, Dame Gladys (actress); Lewisham, England **(1888–1971)**

Cooper, Jackie (actor, director); Los Angeles, 9/15/22

Cooper, James Fenimore (novelist); Burlington, N.J. **(1789–1851)**

Cooper, Peter (industrialist, philanthropist); New York City **(1791–1883)**

Copernicus, Nicolaus (Mikolaj Kopernik) (astronomer); Thorn, Poland **(1473–1543)**

Copland, Aaron (composer); Brooklyn, N.Y. **(1900–1990)**

Copley, John Singleton (painter); Boston **(1738–1815)**

Copperfield, David (David Kotkin) (illusionist); Metuchen, N.J., 9/16/56

Coppola, Francis Ford (film director); Detroit, 4/7/39

Corelli, Arcangelo (composer); Fusignano, Italy **(1653–1713)**

Corelli, Franco (operatic tenor); Ancona, Italy **(1923–2003)**

Corgan, Billy (musician); Elk Grove, Ill., 3/17/67

Corneille, Pierre (dramatist); Rouen, France **(1606–1684)**

Cornell, Katharine (actress); Berlin **(1893–1974)**

Corot, Jean Baptiste Camille (painter); Paris **(1796–1875)**

Corella, Angel (ballet dancer); Madrid, Spain, 11/8/75

Correggio, Antonio Allegri da (painter); Correggio, Italy **(1494–1534)**

Corsaro, Frank (opera director); New York harbor, 12/22/24

Cortés (or Cortez), Hernando (explorer); Medellín, Spain **(1485–1547)**

Cosby, Bill (actor); Philadelphia, 7/12/37

Cosell, Howard (Howard Cohen) (sportscaster); Winston-Salem, N.C. **(1918–1995)**

Costello, Elvis (Declan Patrick McManus) (singer, musician, songwriter); London, 1954

Costello, Lou (Louis Cristillo) (comedian); Paterson, N.J. **(1906–1959)**

Costner, Kevin (actor); Los Angeles, 1/18/55

Cotten, Joseph (actor); Petersburg, Va. **(1905–1994)**

Coulter, Ann (writer, critic); New Canaan, Conn., 12/8/61

Couperin, François (composer); Paris **(1668–1733)**

Courbet, Gustave (painter); Ornans, France **(1819–1877)**

Couric, Katie (TV host); Arlington, Va., 1/7/57

Courtenay, Tom (actor); Hull, England, 2/25/37

Cousins, Norman (publisher); Union Hill, N.J. **(1915–1990)**

Cousteau, Jacques-Yves (marine explorer); St. André-de-Cubzac, France **(1910–1997)**

Covey, Stephen R. (author); Salt Lake City, 10/24/32

Coward, Sir Noel (playwright, actor); Teddington, England **(1899–1973)**

Cowles, Gardner, Jr. (newspaper publisher); Algona, Iowa **(1903–1985)**

Cowper, William (poet); Great Berkhamstead, England **(1731–1800)**

Cox, Archibald (Watergate prosecutor); Plainfield, N.J. **(1912–2004)**

Cox, Courteney (actress); Birmingham, Ala., 6/15/64

Coyote, Peter (actor); New York City, 10/10/41

Cozzens, James Gould (novelist); Chicago **(1903–1978)**

Crabbe, Buster (Clarence Crabbe) (actor); Oakland, Calif. **(1908–1983)**

Cranach, Lucas, the elder (painter); Kronach, Germany **(1472–1553)**

Crane, Hart (poet); Garrettsville, Ohio **(1899–1932)**

Crane, Stephen (novelist, poet); Newark, N.J. **(1871–1900)**

Cranmer, Thomas (churchman); Aslacton, England **(1489–1556)**

Craven, Wes (director, producer, screenwriter); Cleveland, 8/2/39

Crawford, Broderick (actor); Philadelphia **(1911–1986)**

Crawford, Cheryl (stage producer); Akron, Ohio **(1902–1986)**

Crawford, Cindy (model, actress); De Kalb, Ill., 2/20/66

Crawford, Joan (Lucille LeSueur) (actress, business executive); San Antonio **(1908–1977)**

Crazy Horse (Lakota Indian leader); nr. Bear Butte, S.D. **(1840?–1877)**

Crenna, Richard (actor); Los Angeles **(1927–2003)**

Crichton, (John) Michael (novelist, film producer); Chicago, 10/23/42

Crick, Francis Harry Compton (scientist, Nobel laureate); Northampton, England **(1916–2004)**

Crisp, Donald (actor); London **(1880–1974)**

Croce, Benedetto (philosopher); Peseasseroli, Aquila, Italy **(1866–1952)**

Croce, Jim (singer); Philadelphia **(1942–1973)**

Crockett, Davy (David) (frontiersman); Greene County, Tenn. **(1786–1836)**

Cromwell, Oliver (statesman); Huntingdon, England **(1599–1658)**

Cronenberg, David (film director); Toronto, Canada, 3/15/43

Cronin, A. J. (Archibald J. Cronin) (novelist); Cardross, Scotland **(1896–1981)**

Cronkite, Walter (TV newscaster); St. Joseph, Mo., 11/4/16

Cronyn, Hume (actor); London, Ont., Canada **(1911–2003)**

Crosby, Bing (Harry Lillis) (singer, actor); Tacoma, Wash. **(1904–1977)**

Crosby, Bob (musician); Spokane, Wash. **(1913–1993)**

Crosby, Cathy Lee (actress); Los Angeles, 12/2/48

Crosby, Norm (comedian); Boston, 9/15/27

Cross, Milton (opera commentator); New York City **(1897–1975)**

Crouse, Russell (playwright); Findlay, Ohio **(1893–1966)**

Crow, Sheryl (musician, record producer); Kennett, Mo., 2/11/62

Crowe, Russell (actor, musician); Auckland, New Zealand, 4/7/64

Crudup, Billy (actor); Manhasset, N.Y., 7/8/68

Cruise, Tom (Thomas Mapother IV) (actor, producer); Syracuse, N.Y., 7/3/62

Cruz, Penelope (Penélope Cruz Sánchez) (actress); Madrid, Spain, 4/28/74

Crystal, Billy (comedian, actor); Long Beach, N.Y., 3/14/47

Cugat, Xavier (band leader); Barcelona, Spain **(1900–1990)**

Cukor, George (film director); New York City **(1899–1983)**

Culkin, Macaulay (actor); New York City, 8/26/80

Cullen, Bill (William Lawrence Cullen) (radio and TV entertainer); Pittsburgh **(1920–1990)**

Cullen, Countee (poet); New York City **(1903–1946)**

Culp, Robert (actor); Berkeley, Calif., 8/16/30

Cummings, E. E. (Edward Estlin Cummings) (poet); Cambridge, Mass. **(1894–1962)**

Cummings, Robert (actor); Joplin, Mo. **(1908–1990)**

Cunningham, Merce (choreographer); Centralia, Wash., 4/16/19

Curie, Marie (Marja Sklodowska) (physical chemist, Nobel laureate); Warsaw **(1867–1934)**

Curie, Pierre (physicist); Paris **(1859–1906)**

Curtin, Jane (actress); Cambridge, Mass., 9/6/47

Curtin, Phyllis (soprano); Clarksburg, W. Va., 12/3/27

Curtis, Jamie Lee (actress); Los Angeles, 11/22/58

Curtis, Tony (Bernard Schwartz) (actor); Bronx, N.Y., 6/3/25
Curzon, Clifford (concert pianist); London **(1907–1982)**
Cusack, Joan (actress); New York City, 10/11/62
Cusack, John (actor); Chicago, 6/28/66
Custer, George Armstrong (army officer); New Rumley, Ohio **(1839–1876)**

D

Dafoe, Willem (William Dafoe, Jr.) (actor); Appleton, Wis., 7/22/55
da Gama, Vasco (explorer); Sines, Portugal **(1460–1524)**
Daguerre, Louis (photographic pioneer); nr. Paris **(1787–1851)**
Dahl, Arlene (actress); Minneapolis, 8/11/28
Dahl, Roald (writer); Llandaff, Wales **(1916–1990)**
Dalai Lama (Tenzin Gyatso) (spiritual and temporal head of Tibet); Taktser, China, 1935
Daley, Richard J. (mayor of Chicago); Chicago **(1902–1976)**
Dali, Salvador (painter); Figueras, Spain **(1904–1989)**
Dalton, John (chemist); nr. Cockermouth, England **(1766–1844)**
Dalton, Timothy (actor); Colwyn Bay, Wales, U.K., 3/21/46
Daly, Tyne (actress); Madison, Wis., 2/21/46
d'Amboise, Jacques (ballet dancer); Dedham, Mass., 7/28/34
Damon, Matt (actor); Cambridge, Mass., 10/8/70
Damrosch, Walter Johannes (orchestra conductor); Breslau, Poland **(1862–1950)**
Dana, Charles Anderson (editor); Hinsdale, N.H. **(1819–1897)**
Dandridge, Dorothy (actress); Cleveland **(1923–1965)**
Danes, Claire (actress); New York City, 4/12/79
Dangerfield, Rodney (Jacob Cohen) (actor, comedian); Babylon, N.Y. **(1922–2004)**
Daniels, Jeff (actor); Athens, Ga., 2/19/55
Daniels, William (actor); Brooklyn, N.Y., 3/31/27
Danilova, Alexandra (ballet dancer); Peterhof, Russia **(1904–1997)**
Dannay, Frederic (novelist, pseudonym Ellery Queen); Brooklyn, N.Y. **(1905–1982)**
Danner, Blythe (actress); Philadelphia, 2/3/43
D'Annunzio, Gabriele (soldier, author); Francaville at Mare, Pescara, Italy **(1863–1938)**
Danson, Ted (actor); San Diego, Calif., 12/29/47
Dante (or Durante) Alighieri (poet); Florence, Italy **(1265–1321)**
Danton, Georges Jacques (French Revolutionary leader); Arcis-sur-Aube, France **(1759–1794)**
Danza, Tony (actor); Brooklyn, N.Y., 4/21/51
Darren, James (actor); Philadelphia, 6/8/36
Darrow, Clarence Seward (lawyer); Kinsman, Ohio **(1857–1938)**
Darwin, Charles Robert (naturalist); Shrewsbury, England **(1809–1882)**
Dassin, Jules (film director); Middletown, Conn., 12/18/11
Daumier, Honoré (caricaturist); Marseilles, France **(1808–1879)**
David, Jacques-Louis (painter); Paris **(1748–1825)**
David (king of Israel and Judah); died c. 973 B.C.
Davidson, John (singer, actor); Pittsburgh, 12/13/41
Davies, Marion (Marion Douras) (actress); New York City **(1897–1961)**
Davies, (William) Robertson (writer); Thamesville, Ont., Canada **(1913–1996)**
Davis, Angela (social activist); Birmingham, Ala., 1/26/44
Davis, Ann B. (actress); Schenectady, N.Y., 5/5/26
Davis, Lt. Gen. Benjamin O., Jr. (Air Force general); Washington, D.C. **(1912–2002)**
Davis, Brig. Gen. Benjamin O., Sr. (U.S. Army general); Washington, D.C. **(1877–1970)**
Davis, Bette (actress); Lowell, Mass. **(1908–1989)**
Davis, Geena (Virginia Davis) (actress); Wareham, Mass., 1/21/57
Davis, Jefferson (president of the Confederacy); Christian (now Todd) County, Ky. **(1808–1889)**
Davis, Judy (actress); Perth, Australia, 1955
Davis, Mac (singer); Lubbock, Tex., 1/21/42
Davis, Miles (jazz trumpeter); Alton, Ill. **(1926–1991)**
Davis, Ossie (actor, writer); Cogdell, Ga. **(1917–2005)**
Davis, Sammy, Jr. (actor, singer); New York City **(1925–1990)**
Davis, Stuart (painter); Philadelphia **(1894–1964)**
Dawson, Richard (actor, host); Gosport, Hampshire, England, 11/20/32
Day, Doris (Doris Kappelhoff) (singer, actress); Cincinnati, 4/3/24
Dayan, Moshe (ex-defense minister of Israel); Dagania, Palestine **(1915–1981)**
Day-Lewis, Daniel (actor); London, 4/29/58
Dean, James (actor); Marion, Ind. **(1931–1955)**
Dean, Jimmy (singer); Seth Ward, nr. Plainview, Tex., 8/10/28
De Bakey, Michael E. (heart surgeon); Lake Charles, La., 9/7/08
de Beauvoir, Simone (novelist, philosopher); Paris **(1908–1986)**

Debs, Eugene Victor (Socialist leader); Terre Haute, Ind. **(1855–1926)**
Debussy, Claude Achille (composer); St. Germain-en-Laye, France **(1862–1918)**
De Carlo, Yvonne (Peggy Yvonne Middleton) (actress); Vancouver, B.C., Canada, 9/1/22
Dee, Ruby (Ruby Ann Wallace) (actress); Cleveland, 10/27/24
Dee, Sandra (Alexandra Zuck) (actress); Bayonne, N.J. **(1942–2005)**
Degas, Hilaire Germain Edgar (painter); Paris **(1834–1917)**
De Gasperi, Alcide (statesman); Pieve Tesino, Italy **(1881–1954)**
de Gaulle, Charles André Joseph Marie (soldier, statesman); Lille, France **(1890–1970)**
de Havilland, Olivia (actress); Tokyo, 7/1/16
de Klerk, Frederik Willem (ex-president of South Africa); Johannesburg, 3/18/1936
de Kooning, Willem (artist); Rotterdam **(1904–1997)**
Delacroix, Eugène (painter); Charenton-St. Maurice, France **(1798–1863)**
Delany, Dana (actress); New York City, 3/15/56
de la Renta, Oscar (fashion designer); Santo Domingo, Dominican Republic, 7/22/32
Delaunay, Robert (painter); Paris **(1885–1941)**
De Laurentiis, Dino (film producer); Torre Annunziata, Bay of Naples, Italy, 8/8/18
DeLay, Tom (House majority leader); Laredo, Tex., 4/8/47
della Robbia, Andrea (sculptor); Florence **(1435–1525)**
della Robbia, Luca (sculptor); Florence **(1400–1482)**
Delpy, Julie (actress); Paris, France, 12/21/69
Del Toro, Benicio (actor); Santurce, Puerto Rico, 2/19/67
DeLuise, Dom (actor, comedian); Brooklyn, N.Y., 8/1/33
Demarest, William (actor); St. Paul, Minn. **(1892–1983)**
de Mille, Agnes (choreographer); New York City **(1905–1993)**
De Mille, Cecil Blount (film director); Ashfield, Mass. **(1881–1959)**
Demme, Jonathan (director, producer, screenwriter); Baldwin, N.Y., 2/22/44
Demosthenes (orator); Athens **(384?–322 B.C.)**
Dench, Dame Judi (film and stage actress); York, England, 12/9/34
Deneuve, Catherine (actress); Paris, 10/22/43
Deng Xiaoping (Chinese leader); Sichuan province, China **(1904–1997)**
De Niro, Robert (actor, director); New York City, 8/17/43
Dennehy, Brian (actor); Bridgeport, Conn., 7/9/39
Dennis, Sandy (actress); Hastings, Neb. **(1937–1992)**
Denny, Reginald (actor); Richmond, England **(1891–1967)**
Denver, John (Henry John Deutschendorf, Jr.) (singer, actor); Roswell, N.M. **(1943–1997)**
De Palma, Brian (film director); Newark, N.J., 9/11/40
Depp, Johnny (actor); Owensboro, Ky., 6/9/63
Derain, André (painter); Chatou, Seine-et-Oise, France **(1880–1954)**
Derek, John (Derek Harris) (actor, director); Los Angeles **(1926–1998)**
Dern, Bruce (actor); Winnetka, Ill., 6/4/36
Dern, Laura (actress); Los Angeles, 2/10/67
Dershowitz, Alan (lawyer); Brooklyn, N.Y., 9/1/38
Derrida, Jacques (philosopher); El-Biar, Algeria **(1930–2004)**
Descartes, René (philosopher, mathematician); La Haye, France **(1596–1650)**
De Seversky, Alexander P. (aviator); Tiflis (Tbilisi), Georgia **(1894–1974)**
De Sica, Vittorio (film director); Sora, Italy **(1901–1974)**
Desmond, Johnny (singer, composer); Detroit **(1921–1985)**
De Soto, Hernando (explorer); Barcarrota, Spain **(c. 1500–1542)**
De Valera, Eamon (ex-president of Ireland); New York City **(1882–1975)**
Devane, William (actor); Albany, N.Y., 9/5/39
Devine, Andy (actor); Flagstaff, Ariz. **(1905–1977)**
DeVito, Danny (Daniel Michael DeVito) (actor, director, producer); Neptune, N.J., 11/17/44
De Vries, Peter (novelist); Chicago **(1910–1993)**
de Waart, Edo (conductor); Amsterdam, the Netherlands, 6/1/41
Dewey, George (admiral); Montpelier, Vt. **(1837–1917)**
Dewey, John (philosopher, educator); Burlington, Vt. **(1859–1952)**
Dewey, Thomas E. (political figure); Owosso, Mich. **(1902–1971)**
Dewhurst, Colleen (actress); Montreal **(1926–1991)**
Diaghilev, Sergei (ballet impressario); Novgorod, Russia **(1872–1929)**
Diamond, Neil (singer); Brooklyn, N.Y., 1/24/41
Diaz, Cameron (actress, model); San Diego, Calif., 8/30/72
DiCaprio, Leonardo (actor); Los Angeles, 11/11/74
Dickens, Charles John Huffam (novelist); Portsea, England **(1812–1870)**

Dickey, James (writer); Atlanta **(1923–1997)**

Dickinson, Angie (Angeline Brown) (actress); Kulm, N.D., 9/30/31

Dickinson, Emily Elizabeth (poet); Amherst, Mass. **(1830–1886)**

Diddley, Bo (Elias McDaniel) (guitarist); McComb, Miss., 12/30/28

Diderot, Denis (encyclopedist); Langres, France **(1713–1784)**

Dietrich, Marlene (Maria Magdalena von Losch) (actress); Berlin **(1901–1992)**

DiFranco, Ani (singer, songwriter); Buffalo, N.Y., 9/23/70

Diller, Phyllis (Phyllis Driver) (comedienne); Lima, Ohio, 7/17/17

Dillon, Matt (actor); New Rochelle, N.Y., 2/18/64

Dine, Jim (painter); Cincinnati, 6/16/35

Dinesen, Isak (Karen Blixen) (author); Rungsted, Denmark **(1885–1962)**

Dinkins, David (ex-mayor of New York City); Trenton, N.J., 7/10/27

Diogenes (philosopher); Sinope, Turkey **(c. 412–323 b.c.)**

Dion (Dion DiMucci) (singer); Bronx, N.Y., 7/18/39

Dion, Celine (musician); Charlemagne, Que., Canada, 3/30/68

Dior, Christian (fashion designer); Granville, France **(1905–1957)**

Disney, Walt(er) Elias (film animator, producer); Chicago **(1901–1966)**

Disraeli, Benjamin (Earl of Beaconsfield) (statesman); London **(1804–1881)**

Dix, Dorothea (civil rights reformer); Hampden, Maine **(1802–1887)**

Dixon, Jeane (Jeane Pinckert) (seer); Medford, Wis. **(1918–1997)**

Dobbs, Mattiwilda (soprano); Atlanta, 7/11/25

Doctorow, E(dgar) L(aurence) (novelist); New York City, 1/6/31

Dole, Elizabeth Hanford (public official); Salisbury, N.C., 7/29/36

Dole, Robert (political figure); Russell, Kans., 7/22/23

Dolin, Anton (dancer); Slinfold, England **(1904–1983)**

Domingo, Placido (tenor); Madrid, 1/21/41

Domino, Fats (Antoine) (musician); New Orleans, 2/26/28

Donahue, Phil (TV host); Cleveland, 12/21/35

Donahue, Troy (Merle Johnson) (actor); New York City **(1936–2001)**

Donaldson, Sam (broadcast journalist); El Paso, Tex., 3/11/34

Donat, Robert (actor); Withington, England **(1905–1958)**

Donatello (Donato Niccolò di Betto Bardi) (sculptor); Florence **(c. 1386–1466)**

Donlevy, Brian (actor); Portadown, Ireland **(1899–1972)**

Donne, John (poet); London **(1573–1631)**

Donner, Richard (director, producer); New York City, 1939

D'Onofrio, Vincent (actor); Brooklyn, N.Y., 6/30/59

Donovan (Donovan Leitch) (singer, songwriter); Glasgow, Scotland, 2/10/46

Doolittle, James H. (ex-Air Force general); Alameda, Calif. **(1896–1993)**

Doohan, James (actor); Vancouver, B.C. **(1920–2005)**

Dorati, Antal (orchestra conductor); Budapest **(1906–1988)**

Dorn, Michael (actor); Luling, Tex., 12/9/52

Dorris, Michael (anthropologist, writer); Louisville, Ky. **(1945–1997)**

Dorsey, Jimmy (band leader); Shenandoah, Pa. **(1904–1957)**

Dorsey, Thomas Andrew (father of gospel music); Villa Rice, Ga. **(1899–1993)**

Dorsey, Tommy (band leader); Mahanoy Plane, Pa. **(1905–1956)**

Dos Passos, John (author); Chicago **(1896–1970)**

Dostoevski, Fyodor Mikhailovich (novelist); Moscow **(1821–1881)**

Dotrice, Roy (actor); Guernsey, Channel Islands, England, 5/26/23

Douglas, Aaron (painter); Topeka, Kans. **(1900–1979)**

Douglas, Helen Gahagan (ex-representative); Boonton, N.J. **(1900–1980)**

Douglas, Kirk (Issur Danielovitch) (actor); Amsterdam, N.Y., 12/9/16

Douglas, Melvyn (Melvyn Hesselberg) (actor); Macon, Ga. **(1901–1981)**

Douglas, Michael (actor, producer); New Brunswick, N.J., 9/25/44

Douglas, Mike (Michael D. Dowd, Jr.) (TV host); Chicago, 8/11/25

Douglas, Stephen Arnold (politician); Brandon, Vt. **(1813–1861)**

Douglass, Frederick (abolitionist, author, orator); Tuckahoe, Md. **(1817–1895)**

Dow, Charles (financier); Sterling, Conn. **(1851–1902)**

Down, Lesley-Ann (actress); London, 3/17/54

Downey, Robert, Jr. (actor, director); New York City, 4/4/65

Downs, Hugh (broadcast journalist); Akron, Ohio, 2/14/21

Doyle, Sir Arthur Conan (novelist, spiritualist); Edinburgh, Scotland **(1859–1930)**

Doyle, David (actor); Lincoln, Neb. **(1929–1997)**

Drake, Sir Francis (navigator); Tavistock, England **(1540–1596)**

Dr. Dre (Andre Young) (rap singer); Los Angeles, 2/18/65

Dreiser, Theodore (writer); Terre Haute, Ind. **(1871–1945)**

Drescher, Fran (television and film actress); New York City, 9/30/57

Dreyfus, Alfred (French army officer); Mulhouse, France **(1859–1935)**

Dreyfuss, Richard (actor); Brooklyn, N.Y., 10/29/47

Drury, Allen (novelist); Houston **(1918–1998)**

Dryden, John (poet); Northamptonshire, England **(1631–1700)**

Dryer, Fred (ex-NFL player, actor); Hawthorne, Calif., 7/6/46

Dubček, Alexander (ex-president of Czechoslovakia); Uhrovek, Slovakia **(1921–1992)**

Dubinsky, David (David Dobnievski) (labor leader); Brest-Litovsk, Belarus **(1892–1982)**

Du Bois, W(illiam) E(dward) B(urghardt) (scholar, civil rights activist); Great Barrington, Mass. **(1868–1963)**

Dubus, Andre (writer); Lake Charles, La. **(1936–1999)**

Dubus, Andre III (writer); Oceanside, Calif., 1959

Duchamp, Marcel (painter); Blainville, France **(1887–1968)**

Duchin, Eddy (pianist, bandleader); Cambridge, Mass. **(1909–1951)**

Duchin, Peter (pianist, band leader); New York City, 7/28/37

Duchovny, David (actor); New York City, 8/7/60

Dufay, Guillaume (composer); Cambrai, France **(c. 1400–1474)**

Duff, Hilary (actress, singer); Houston, Texas, 9/28/87

Duffy, Julia (actress); Minneapolis, Minn., 6/27/51

Dufy, Raoul (painter); Le Havre, France **(1877–1953)**

Dukakis, Olympia (actress); Lowell, Mass., 6/20/31

Duke, James B. (industrialist); nr. Durham, N.C. **(1856–1925)**

Duke, Patty (Anna Marie Duke) (actress); New York City, 12/14/46

Dulles, Allen Welsh (ex-director of CIA); Watertown, N.Y. **(1893–1969)**

Dulles, John Foster (political figure); Washington, D.C. **(1888–1959)**

Dumas, Alexandre (called Dumas fils) (novelist); Paris **(1824–1895)**

Dumas, Alexandre (called Dumas père) (novelist); Villers-Cotterets, France **(1802–1870)**

du Maurier, Daphne (novelist); London **(1907–1989)**

du Maurier, George Louis Palmella Busson (novelist); Paris **(1834–1896)**

Dumont, Margaret (actress); Brooklyn, N.Y. **(1889–1965)**

Dunaway, Faye (actress); Bascom, Fla., 1/14/41

Dunbar, Paul Laurence (poet, novelist); Dayton, Ohio **(1872–1906)**

Duncan, Isadora (dancer); San Francisco **(1878–1927)**

Duncan, Michael Clarke (actor); Chicago, 12/10/57

Duncan, Sandy (actress); Henderson, Tex., 2/20/46

Dunham, Katherine (dancer, choreographer); Chicago, 6/22/09

Dunne, Irene (actress); Louisville, Ky. **(1898–1990)**

Duns Scotus, John (theologian); Duns, Scotland **(1265–1303)**

Dunst, Kirsten (actress); Point Pleasant, N.J., 4/30/82

Du Pont, Pierre S. (economist); Paris **(1739–1817)**

Durante, Jimmy (comedian); New York City **(1893–1980)**

Duras, Marguerite (Donnadieu) (novelist, dramatist); Gia Dinh, Vietnam **(1914–1996)**

Durbin, Deanna (Edna Mae) (actress); Winnipeg, Canada, 12/4/21

Dürer, Albrecht (painter, engraver); Nürnberg, Germany **(1471–1528)**

Durning, Charles (actor); Highland Falls, N.Y., 2/28/23

Durrell, Lawrence George (novelist); Julundur, India **(1912–1990)**

Duse, Eleonora (actress); Chioggia, Italy **(1859–1924)**

Dussault, Nancy (actress); Pensacola, Fla., 6/30/36

Duvall, Robert (actor, director, producer); San Diego, Calif., 1/5/31

Duvall, Shelley (actress); Houston, 7/7/49

Dvořák, Antonin (composer); Nelahozeves, Czechoslovakia **(1841–1904)**

Dylan, Bob (Robert Zimmerman) (singer, songwriter, guitarist); Duluth, Minn., 5/24/41

Dysart, Richard (actor); Brighton, Mass., 3/30/29

E

Eakins, Thomas (painter, sculptor); Philadelphia **(1844–1916)**

Earhart, Amelia (aviator); Atchison, Kans. **(1897–1937)**

Earp, Wyatt (Berry Stapp) (sheriff, gunfighter); Monmouth, Ill. **(1848–1929)**

Eastman, George (camera inventor); Waterville, N.Y. **(1854–1932)**

Eastwood, Clint (actor, director, producer); San Francisco, 5/31/30

Ebert, Roger (film critic); Urbana, Ill., 6/18/42

Ebsen, Buddy (Christian Ebsen, Jr.) (actor); Belleville, Ill. **(1908–2003)**

Eckstine, Billy (singer); Pittsburgh **(1914–1993)**

Eddy, Mary Baker (founder of Christian Science Church); Bow, N.H. **(1821–1910)**

Eddy, Nelson (baritone, actor); Providence, R.I. **(1901–1967)**

Edel, Leon (author); Pittsburgh **(1907–1997)**

Edelman, Marian Wright (social activist); Bennettsville, S.C., 6/6/39

Eden, Sir Anthony (Earl of Avon) (ex-prime minister); Durham, England **(1897–1977)**

Eden, Barbara (Barbara Huffman) (actress); Tucson, Ariz., 8/23/34

Edison, Thomas Alva (inventor); Milan, Ohio **(1847–1931)**

Edwards, Anthony (actor); Santa Barbara, Calif., 7/19/62

Edwards, Blake (film writer, producer); Tulsa, Okla., 7/26/22

Edwards, Jonathan (theologian); East Windsor, Conn. **(1703–1758)**

Edwards, Ralph (TV and radio producer); Merino, Colo., 6/13/13

Edwards, Vincent (Vincent Edward Zoino) (actor); Brooklyn, N.Y. **(1928–1996)**

Eggers, Dave (writer, editor); Boston, 3/12/70

Eglevsky, André (ballet dancer); Moscow **(1917–1977)**

Egoyan, Atom (film director, writer, editor); Cairo, 7/19/60

Ehrlich, Paul (bacteriologist); Strzelin, Poland **(1854–1915)**

Eichmann, (Karl) Adolf (Nazi, mass murderer); Solingen, Germany **(1906–1962)**

Eikenberry, Jill (actress); New Haven, Conn., 1/21/47

Einstein, Albert (physicist); Ulm, Germany **(1879–1955)**

Eisner, Michael (entertainment executive); Mt. Kisco, N.Y., 3/7/42

Eisenhower, Dwight David (34th U.S. president); Denison, Tex. **(1890–1969)**

Eisenhower, Milton S. (educator); Abilene, Kans. **(1899–1985)**

Eisenstaedt, Alfred (photographer, photojournalist); Dirschau (Prussia, now Tczew), Poland **(1898–1995)**

Ekland, Britt (Britt-Marie) (actress); Stockholm, 10/6/42

Electra, Carmen (Tara Patrick) (model, actress); Cincinnati, Ohio, 4/20/73

Elfman, Jenna (Jennifer Mary Butala) (actress); Los Angeles, 9/30/71

Elgar, Sir Edward (composer); Worcester, England **(1857–1934)**

Elgart, Larry (band leader); New London, Conn., 3/20/22

El Greco (Domenicos Theotocopoulos) (painter); Candia, Crete, Greece **(c. 1541–1614)**

Elion, Gertrude B. (chemist, Nobel laureate); New York City **(1918–1999)**

Eliot, George (Mary Ann Evans) (novelist); Chilvers Coton, England **(1819–1880)**

Eliot, Thomas Stearns (poet); St. Louis **(1888–1965)**

Elizabeth I (queen of England); Greenwich, England **(1533–1603)**

Elizabeth II (queen of England); London, 4/21/26

Elizondo, Hector (actor); New York City, 12/22/36

Ellington, Duke (Edward Kennedy) (jazz musician); Washington, D.C. **(1899–1974)**

Elliot, "Mama" Cass (Ellen Naomi Cohen) (singer); Baltimore **(1941–1974)**

Elliott, Sam (actor); Sacramento, Calif., 8/9/44

Ellison, Lawrence J. (computer industry executive); New York City, 1944

Ellison, Ralph (novelist); Oklahoma City, Okla. **(1914–1994)**

Ellsberg, Daniel (activist); Chicago, 4/7/31

Elman, Mischa (violinist); Stalnoye, Ukraine **(1891–1967)**

Emerson, Ralph Waldo (philosopher, poet); Boston **(1803–1882)**

Enesco, Georges (composer); Dorohoi, Romania **(1881–1955)**

Englund, Robert (actor); Glendale, Calif., 6/6/49

Entremont, Philippe (concert pianist); Rheims, France, 6/7/34

Ephron, Nora (writer, director); New York City, 5/19/41

Epicurus (philosopher); Samos, Greece **(341–270 B.C.)**

Epstein, Sir Jacob (sculptor); New York City **(1880–1959)**

Erasmus, Desiderius (Gerhard Gerhards) (scholar); Rotterdam **(1469–1536)**

Erdrich, (Karen) Louise (writer); Little Falls, Minn., 7/6/54

Erickson, Leif (actor); Alameda, Calif. **(1911–1986)**

Ericsson, Leif (navigator) c. 10th century A.D.

Erikson, Erik H. (psychoanalyst); Frankfurt, Germany **(1902–1994)**

Ernst, Max (painter); Bruhl, Germany **(1891–1976)**

Erté (Romain de Tirtoff) (artist, designer); St. Petersburg, Russia **(1892–1990)**

Estevez, Emilio (actor, director, screenwriter); New York City, 5/12/62

Eszterhas, Joe (screenwriter); Csakanydoroslo, Hungary, 11/23/44

Euclid (mathematician); Megara, Greece, fl. 300 B.C.

Euler, Leonhard (mathematician); Basel, Switzerland **(1707–1783)**

Euripides (dramatist); Salamis, Greece **(c. 484–407 B.C.)**

Evangelista, Linda (model); St. Catharines, Ont., Canada, 5/10/65

Evans, Dale (born Lucille Wood Smith but raised as Frances Octavia Smith) (actress, singer); Uvalde, Tex. **(1912–2001)**

Evans, Dame Edith (actress); London **(1888–1976)**

Evans, Donald L. (ex-secretary of Commerce); Houston, Tex., 7/27/46

Evans, Linda (actress); Hartford, Conn., 11/18/42

Evans, Maurice (actor); Dorchester, England **(1901–1989)**

Everett, Chad (Raymond Lee Cramton) (actor); South Bend, Ind., 6/11/36

Everett, Rupert (actor, model, musician); Norfolk, England, 5/29/59

Everhart, Angie (model, actress); Akron, Ohio, 9/7/69

Evers, Charles (civil rights leader); Decatur, Miss., 9/14/22

Evers, Medgar (civil rights leader); Decatur, Miss. **(1925–1963)**

Evers-Williams, Myrlie (civil rights leader); Vicksburg, Miss., 3/17/33

F

Fabares, Shelley (actress); Santa Monica, Calif., 1/19/44

Fabian (Fabian Anthony Forte) (singer); Philadelphia, 2/6/43

Fabray, Nanette (Nanette Fabarés) (actress); San Diego, Calif., 10/27/22

Fahrenheit, Gabriel (German physicist); Danzig, Poland **(1686–1736)**

King Faisal (Faisal ibn Abd al-Aziz ibn Saud) (king of Saudi Arabia); Riyadh **(1905–1975)**

Fairbanks, Douglas (Douglas Ulman) (actor); Denver **(1883–1939)**

Fairbanks, Douglas, Jr. (actor); New York City **(1909–2000)**

Fairchild, Morgan (Patsy Ann McClenny) (actress); Dallas, 2/3/50

Faith, Percy (conductor); Toronto **(1908–1976)**

Falk, Peter (actor); New York City, 9/16/27

Falla, Manuel de (composer); Cadiz, Spain **(1876–1946)**

Fallon, Jimmy (actor); Brooklyn, N.Y., 9/19/74

Faludi, Susan (journalist, writer); New York City, 4/18/59

Falwell, Jerry (fundamentalist preacher); Lynchburg, Va., 8/11/33

Faraday, Michael (physicist); Newington, England **(1791–1867)**

Farentino, James (actor); Brooklyn, N.Y., 2/24/38

Farley, Chris (actor, comedian); Madison, Wis. **(1964–1997)**

Farmer, James (civil rights leader); Marshall, Tex. **(1920–1999)**

Farnsworth, Philo (inventor); Beaver, Utah **(1906–1971)**

Farnsworth, Richard (actor); Los Angeles **(1920–2000)**

Farr, Jamie (Jameel Joseph Farah) (actor); Toledo, Ohio, 7/1/34

Farrar, Geraldine (soprano, actress); Melrose, Mass. **(1882–1967)**

Farrell, Colin (actor); Castleknock, Ireland, 5/31/76

Farrell, Eileen (operatic soprano); Willimantic, Conn. **(1920–2002)**

Farrell, James T. (novelist); Chicago **(1904–1979)**

Farrell, Mike (actor); St. Paul, Minn., 2/6/39

Farrell, Perry (Perry Bernstein) (lead singer); Queens, N.Y., 3/29/59

Farrell, Suzanne (Roberta Sue Ficker) (ballet dancer); Cincinnati, 8/16/45

Farrelly, Bobby (writer/director); Cumberland, R.I., 6/17/58

Farrelly, Peter (writer/director); Phoenixville, Pa., 12/17/56

Farrow, Mia (actress); Los Angeles, 2/9/45

Fasanella, Ralph (painter); New York City **(1914–1997)**

Fassbinder, Rainer Werner (film, stage director); Bad Wörishofen, Germany **(1946–1982)**

Fast, Howard (novelist); New York City **(1914–2003)**

Faubus, Orval E(ugene) (governor of Arkansas); Combs, Ark. **(1910–1994)**

Faulkner, William (novelist); New Albany, Miss. **(1897–1962)**

Fauré, Gabriel Urbain (composer); Pamiers, France **(1845–1924)**

Fawcett, Farrah (Mary Farrah Leni Fawcett) (actress); Corpus Christi, Tex., 2/2/47

Faye, Alice (Ann Leppert) (actress); New York City **(1912–1998)**

Feiffer, Jules (cartoonist); New York City, 1/26/29

Feininger, Lyonel (painter); New York City **(1871–1956)**

Feldman, Marty (actor, screenwriter, director); London **(1938–1982)**

Feldon, Barbara (actress); Pittsburgh, 3/12/41

Feliciano, José (singer); Larez, Puerto Rico, 9/10/45

Felker, Clay S. (editor, publisher); St. Louis, 10/2/25

Fell, Norman (actor); Philadelphia **(1923–1998)**

Fellini, Federico (film director); Rimini, Italy **(1920–1993)**

Fender, Freddie (Baldemar Huerta) (singer); San Benito, Tex., 6/4/37

Ferber, Edna (novelist); Kalamazoo, Mich. **(1885–1968)**

Ferguson, Maynard (jazz trumpeter); Verdun, Que., Canada, 5/4/28

Ferlinghetti, Lawrence (poet, writer, translator); Yonkers, N.Y., 3/24/19

Fermi, Enrico (atomic physicist); Rome **(1901–1954)**

Fernandel (Fernand Joseph Desire Contandin) (actor); Marseilles, France **(1903–1971)**

Ferraro, Geraldine Anne (political figure); New York City, 8/26/35

Ferrer, José (actor, director); Santurce, Puerto Rico **(1912–1992)**

Ferrer, Mel (actor); Elberon, N.J., 8/25/17

Fiedler, Arthur (conductor); Boston **(1894–1979)**

Field, Eugene (poet); St. Louis **(1850–1895)**

Field, Marshall (merchant); nr. Conway, Mass. **(1834–1906)**

Field, Sally (actress); Pasadena, Calif., 11/6/46

Fielding, Henry (novelist); nr. Glastonbury, England **(1707–1754)**

Fields, W. C. (William Claude Dukenfield) (comedian); Philadelphia **(1880–1946)**

Fiennes, Joseph (actor); Salisbury, England, 5/27/70

Fiennes, Ralph (actor); Suffolk, England, 12/22/62

Fierstein, Harvey (Forbes) (playwright, actor); Brooklyn, 6/6/54

50 Cent (Curtis Jackson) (rapper); Queens, N.Y., 7/6/76

Figgis, Mike (director, screenwriter, composer, actor); Carlisle, England, 2/28/48

Filene, Edward A. (merchant); Salem, Mass. **(1860–1937)**

Fillmore, Millard (13th U.S. president); Locke, Cayuga County, N.Y. **(1800–1874)**

Finch, Peter (actor); Kensington, England **(1916–1977)**

Finney, Albert (actor); Salford, England, 5/9/36

Fiorentino, Linda (Clorinda Fiorentino) (actress); Philadelphia, 3/9/60

Firkusny, Rudolf (pianist); Napajedia, former Czechoslovakia **(1912–1994)**

Firth, Colin (actor); Grayshot, England, 9/10/60

Fischer-Dieskau, Dietrich (baritone); Berlin, 5/28/25

Fishburne, Laurence (actor); Augusta, Ga., 7/30/61

Fisher, Carrie (actress); Los Angeles, 10/21/56

Fisher, Eddie (Edwin) (singer); Philadelphia, 8/10/28

Fitzgerald, Barry (William Joseph Shields) (actor); Dublin **(1888–1961)**

Fitzgerald, Ella (singer); Newport News, Va. **(1917–1996)**

Fitzgerald, F. Scott (Francis Scott Key Fitzgerald) (novelist); St. Paul, Minn. **(1896–1940)**

Fitzgerald, Geraldine (actress); Dublin **(1914–2005)**

Fitzgerald, Pegeen (radio broadcaster); Norcatur, Kans. **(1910–1989)**

Flack, Roberta (singer); Black Mountain, N.C., 2/10/40

Flagstad, Kirsten (Wagnerian soprano); Hamar, Norway **(1895–1962)**

Flatt, Lester Raymond (bluegrass musician); Overton County, Tenn. **(1914–1979)**

Flaubert, Gustave (novelist); Rouen, France **(1821–1880)**

Fleming, Sir Alexander (bacteriologist); Lochfield, Scotland **(1881–1955)**

Fletcher, John (dramatist); Rye, Sussex, England **(1579–1625)**

Flockhart, Calista (actress); Freeport, Ill., 11/11/64

Flynn, Errol (actor); Hobart, Tasmania **(1909–1959)**

Fodor, Eugene (violinist); Turkey Creek, Colo., 3/5/50

Fokine, Michel (dancer, choreographer); St. Petersburg, Russia **(1880–1942)**

Fonda, Bridget (actress); Los Angeles, 1/27/64

Fonda, Henry (actor); Grand Island, Neb. **(1905–1982)**

Fonda, Jane (actress); New York City, 12/21/37

Fonda, Peter (actor); New York City, 2/23/39

Fontaine, Frank (singer, comedian); Cambridge, Mass. **(1920–1979)**

Fontaine, Joan (Joan de Havilland) (actress); Tokyo, 10/22/17

Fontanne, Lynn (actress); London **(1887–1983)**

Fonteyn, Dame Margot (Margaret Hookham) (ballet dancer); Reigate, England **(1919–1991)**

Foote, Shelby (historian); Greenville, Miss. **(1916–2005)**

Forbes, Malcolm S(tevenson) (publisher, sportsman); Brooklyn, N.Y. **(1919–1990)**

Ford, Gerald Rudolph (38th U.S. president); Omaha, Neb., 7/14/13

Ford, Glenn (Gwyllyn Ford) (actor); Ste.-Christine, Que., Canada, 5/1/16

Ford, Harrison (actor); Chicago, 7/13/42

Ford, Henry (industrialist); Greenfield, Mich. **(1863–1947)**

Ford, John (film director); Cape Elizabeth, Maine **(1895–1973)**

Ford, Tennessee Ernie (Ernie Jennings Ford) (singer); Bristol, Tenn. **(1919–1991)**

Foreman, George (boxer, actor); Marshall, Tex., 1/10/49

Forrester, Maureen (contralto); Montreal, 7/25/30

Forsythe, John (John Lincoln Freund) (actor); Penn's Grove, N.J., 1/29/18

Fosdick, Harry Emerson (clergyman); Buffalo, N.Y. **(1878–1968)**

Fosse, Bob (Robert Louis Fosse) (choreographer, director); Chicago **(1927–1987)**

Foster, Jodie (Alicia Christian Foster) (actress, director, producer); Los Angeles, 11/19/62

Foster, Stephen Collins (composer); nr. Pittsburgh **(1826–1864)**

Fountain, Pete (jazz musician); New Orleans, 7/3/30

Fox, Matthew (actor); Crowheart, Wyo., 7/14/66

Fox, Michael J. (actor, producer); Edmonton, Alta., Canada, 6/9/61

Foxx, Jamie (Eric Morlon Bishop) (comedian, actor); Terrell, Tex., 12/13/67

Foxx, Redd (John Elroy Sanford) (actor, comedian); St. Louis **(1922–1991)**

Foy, Eddie, Jr. (dancer, actor); New Rochelle, N.Y. **(1905–1983)**

Fracci, Carla (ballet dancer); Milan, Italy, 8/20/36

Fragonard, Jean Honoré (painter); Grasse, France **(1732–1806)**

Frakes, Jonathan (actor); Bethlehem, Pa., 8/19/52

Frampton, Peter (rock musician); Beckenham, England, 4/20/50

France, Anatole (Jacques Anatole François Thibault) (author); Paris **(1844–1924)**

Francescatti, Zino (violinist); Marseilles, France **(1902–1991)**

Franciosa, Anthony (Anthony Papaleo) (actor); New York City, 10/25/28

Francis, Anne (actress); Ossining, N.Y., 7/16/30

Francis, Connie (Concetta Franconero) (singer); Newark, N.J., 12/12/38

Francis, Genie (actress); Englewood, N.J., 5/26/62

Francis of Assisi, Saint (Giovanni Francesco Barnardone) (founder of Franciscans); Assisi, Italy **(1182–1226)**

Franck, César Auguste (composer); Liège, Belgium **(1822–1890)**

Franco Bahamonde, Francisco (chief of state); El Ferrol, Spain **(1892–1975)**

Frank, Anne (diarist); Frankfurt **(1929–1945)**

Frankenheimer, John (movie director, producer); New York City, 1930

Frankenthaler, Helen (artist); New York City, 12/12/28

Frankl, Victor E. (psychiatrist); Vienna **(1905–1997)**

Franklin, Aretha (singer); Memphis, Tenn., 3/25/42

Franklin, Benjamin (statesman, scientist); Boston **(1706–1790)**

Franklin, Bonnie (actress); Santa Monica, Calif., 1/6/44

Franklin, John Hope (historian); Rentiesville, Okla., 1/2/15

Frann, Mary (actress); St. Louis **(1943–1998)**

Franz, Dennis (Dennis Schlachta) (actor); Chicago, 10/28/44

Fraser, Brendan (actor); Indianapolis, Ind., 12/3/67

Frazer, Sir James George (anthropologist); Glasgow, Scotland **(1854–1941)**

Freeman, Morgan (actor); Memphis, Tenn., 6/1/37

Freud, Sigmund (psychoanalyst); Moravia, Czech Repubic **(1856–1939)**

Frey, Glenn (musician); Detroit, 11/6/48

Frick, Henry Clay (industrialist); Westmoreland Co., Pa. **(1849–1919)**

Friedan, Betty (Betty Naomi Goldstein) (feminist, writer); Peoria, Ill., 2/4/21

Frist, Bill (Senate majority leader, surgeon); Nashville, Tenn., 2/22/52

Fromm, Erich (psychoanalyst); Frankfurt-am-Main, Germany **(1900–1980)**

Frost, David (TV entertainer); Tenterden, England, 4/7/39

Frost, Robert Lee (poet); San Francisco **(1874–1963)**

Fry, Christopher (playwright); Bristol, England, 12/18/07

Fugard, Athol (playwright); Middleburg, South Africa, 6/11/32

Fulbright, J. William (politician); Sumner, Mo. **(1905–1995)**

Fuller, Charles (playwright); Philadelphia, 3/5/39

Fuller, R(ichard) Buckminster (Jr.) (architect, educator); Milton, Mass. **(1895–1983)**

Fulton, Robert (inventor); Lancaster County, Pa. **(1765–1815)**

Funicello, Annette (actress); Utica, N.Y., 10/22/42

Funt, Allen (TV producer); Brooklyn, N.Y. **(1914–1999)**

G

Gabin, Jean (actor); Paris **(1904–1976)**

Gable, (William) Clark (actor); Cadiz, Ohio **(1901–1960)**

Gabo, Naum (sculptor); Briansk, Russia **(1890–1977)**

Gabor, Eva (actress); Budapest **(1920–1995)**

Gabor, Zsa Zsa (Sari) (actress); Budapest, 2/6/17

Gabriel, Peter (musician); Cobham, England, 2/13/50

Gabrielli, Giovanni (composer); Venice **(c. 1557–1612)**

Gaddis, William (novelist); New York City **(1922–1998)**

Gainsborough, Thomas (painter); Sudbury, Suffolk, England **(1727–1788)**

Galbraith, John Kenneth (economist); Iona Station, Ont., Canada, 10/15/08

Galilei, Galileo (astronomer, physicist); Pisa, Italy **(1564–1642)**

Gallico, Paul (novelist); New York City **(1897–1976)**

Gallup, George H. (poll taker); Jefferson, Iowa **(1901–1984)**

Galsworthy, John (novelist, dramatist); Coombe, England **(1867–1933)**

Galway, James (flutist); Belfast, Northern Ireland, 12/8/39

Gambling, John A. (radio broadcaster); New York City, 1930

Gandhi, Indira (Indira Nehru) (former prime minister); Allahabad, India **(1917–1984)**

Gandhi, Mohandas Karamchand (called Mahatma Gandhi) (Hindu leader); Porbandar, India **(1869–1948)**

Gannett, Frank E. (editor, publisher) **(1876–1957)**

Garagiola, Joe (Joseph Henry Garagiola) (sportscaster); St. Louis, 2/12/26

Garbo, Greta (Greta Gustafsson) (actress); Stockholm **(1905–1990)**

Garcia, Andy (Andres Arturo Garcia-Menendez) (actor); Havana, Cuba, 4/12/56

Garcia, Jerry (rock musician); San Francisco **(1942–1995)**

Garcia Lorca, Frederico (poet, dramatist); Fuente Vaqueros, Spain **(1898–1936)**

Garden, Mary (soprano); Aberdeen, Scotland **(1874–1967)**

Gardenia, Vincent (Vincente Scognamiglio) (actor); Naples, Italy **(1922–1992)**

Gardner, Ava (actress); Smithfield, N.C. **(1922–1990)**

Gardner, Erle Stanley (novelist); Malden, Mass. **(1889–1970)**

Garfield, James Abram (20th U.S. president); Cuyahoga County, Ohio **(1831–1881)**

Garfunkel, Art (Arthur) (singer); Newark, N.J., 11/5/41

Garibaldi, Giuseppe (Italian nationalist leader); Nice, France **(1807–1882)**

Garland, Judy (Frances Gumm) (actress, singer); Grand Rapids, Minn. **(1922–1969)**

Garner, Erroll (jazz pianist); Pittsburgh **(1921–1977)**

Garner, James (James Bumgarner) (actor); Norman, Okla., 4/7/28

Garner, Jennifer (actress); Houston, Tex., 4/17/72

Garofalo, Janeane (actress, comedienne); Newton, N.J., 9/28/64

Garr, Teri (actress); Lakewood, Ohio, 12/11/49

Garrison, William Lloyd (abolitionist); Newburyport, Mass. **(1805–1879)**

Garroway, Dave (TV host); Schenectady, N.Y. **(1913–1982)**

Garson, Greer (actress); County Down, Northern Ireland **(1903–1996)**

Garth, Jennie (actress); Urbana, Ill., 4/3/72

Garvey, Marcus Moziah (black nationalist leader); Jamaica **(1887–1940)**

Gassman, Vittorio (film actor, director); Genoa, Italy **(1922–2000)**

Gates, Bill (William Henry Gates III) (software pioneer); Seattle, 10/28/55

Gates, Henry Louis, Jr. (scholar); Keyser, W. Va., 9/16/50

Gaudí, Antonio (architect); Reus, Spain **(1852–1926)**

Gauguin, (Eugène Henri) Paul (painter); Paris **(1848–1903)**

Gautama Buddha (Prince Siddhartha) (philosopher); Lumbini, Nepal **(c. 563–c. 483 B.C.)**

Gavin, John (actor, diplomat); Los Angeles, 4/8/35

Gavras, Konstantinos (Costa-Gavras) (film director); Loutra-Iraias, Greece, 2/13/33

Gaye, Marvin (singer); Washington, D.C. **(1939–1984)**

Gayle, Crystal (Brenda Gayle Webb) (singer); Paintsville, Ky., 1/9/51

Gaynor, Janet (actress); Philadelphia **(1906–1984)**

Gaynor, Mitzi (Francesca Mitzi Marlene de Czanyi von Gerber) (actress); Chicago, 9/4/31

Gazzara, Ben (Biagio Anthony Gazzara) (actor); New York City, 8/28/30

Gedda, Nicolai (tenor); Stockholm, 7/11/25

Gellar, Sarah Michelle (actress); New York City, 4/14/77

Genet, Jean (playwright); Paris **(1910–1986)**

Genghis Khan (Temujin) (conqueror); nr. Lake Baikal, Russia **(1162–1227)**

Gentry, Bobbie (Roberta Streeter) (singer); Chickasaw Co., Miss., 7/27/44

George, David Lloyd (statesman); Manchester, England **(1863–1945)**

George, Henry (economist, reformer); Philadelphia **(1839–1897)**

Gere, Richard (actor); Philadelphia, 8/31/49

Géricault, Jean Louis (painter); Rouen, France **(1791–1824)**

Geronimo (Goyathlay) (Apache chieftain); Arizona **(1829–1909)**

Gershwin, George (composer); Brooklyn, N.Y. **(1898–1937)**

Gershwin, Ira (lyricist); New York City **(1896–1983)**

Getty, J. Paul (oil executive); Minneapolis **(1892–1976)**

Getz, Stan (saxophonist); Philadelphia **(1927–1991)**

Ghiberti, Lorenzo (goldsmith, sculptor); Florence **(1378–1455)**

Ghostley, Alice (actress); Eve, Mo., 8/14/26

Giacometti, Alberto (sculptor); Switzerland **(1901–1966)**

Giannini, Giancarlo (actor); La Spezia, Italy, 8/1/42

Gibbon, Edward (historian); Putney, England **(1737–1794)**

Gibson, Charles Dana (illustrator); Roxbury, Mass. **(1867–1944)**

Gibson, Mel (actor, director, producer); Peekskill, N.Y., 1/3/56

Gide, André (author); Paris **(1869–1951)**

Gielgud, Sir John (actor); London **(1904–2000)**

Gifford, Kathie Lee (Kathie Lee Epstein) (talk show host); Paris, 8/16/53

Gilbert, Melissa (actress); Los Angeles, 5/8/64

Gilbert, Walter (chemist, Nobel laureate); Boston, 3/21/32

Gilbert, Sir William Schwenck (librettist); London **(1836–1911)**

Gilels, Emil (concert pianist); Odessa, Ukraine **(1916–1985)**

Gillespie, Dizzy (John Birks Gillespie) (jazz trumpeter); Cheraw, S.C. **(1917–1993)**

Gilligan, Carol (Friedman) (psychologist); New York City, 11/28/36

Gimbel, Bernard F. (merchant); Vincennes, Ind. **(1885–1966)**

Gingrich, Newt (politician); Harrisburg, Pa., 6/17/43

Ginsberg, Allen (poet); Newark, N.J. **(1926–1997)**

Giordano, Luca (painter); Naples, Italy **(1632–1705)**

Giorgione (painter); Castelfranco, Italy **(c. 1477–1510)**

Giotto di Bondone (painter); Vespignamo, Italy **(c. 1266–1337)**

Giovanni, Nikki (poet); Knoxville, Tenn., 6/7/43

Giroud, Françoise (French government official); Geneva **(1916–2003)**

Gish, Dorothy (actress); Massillon, Ohio **(1898–1968)**

Gish, Lillian (Lillian de Guiche) (actress); Springfield, Ohio **(1893–1993)**

Giuliani, Rudolph (public official); Brooklyn, N.Y., 5/28/44

Givenchy, Hubert (fashion designer); Beauvais, France, 2/21/27

Gladstone, William Ewart (statesman); Liverpool, England **(1809–1898)**

Glaser, Paul Michael (actor, director); Cambridge, Mass., 3/25/43

Glass, Philip (composer); Baltimore, 1/31/37

Gleason, Jackie (comedian); Brooklyn, N.Y. **(1916–1987)**

Glenn, John (legislator, astronaut); Cambridge, Ohio, 7/18/21

Gless, Sharon (actress); Los Angeles, 5/31/43

Glover, Danny (actor); San Francisco, 7/22/47

Gluck, Christoph Willibald (composer); Erasbach, Germany **(1714–1787)**

Gobel, George (comedian); Chicago **(1920–1991)**

Godard, Jean Luc (film director); Paris, 12/3/30

Goddard, Paulette (Marion Levy) (actress); Great Neck, N.Y. **(1911–1990)**

Goddard, Robert Hutchings (father of modern rocketry); Worcester, Mass. **(1882–1945)**

Gödel, Kurt (mathematician); Brünn (now Brno, Czech Republic) **(1906–1978)**

Godfrey, Arthur (entertainer); New York City **(1903–1983)**

Goebbels, Joseph Paul (Nazi leader); Rheydt, Germany **(1897–1945)**

Goering, Hermann (Nazi leader); Rosenheim, Germany **(1893–1946)**

Goethals, George Washington (engineer); Brooklyn, N.Y. **(1858–1928)**

Goethe, Johann Wolfgang von (poet, playwright, novelist); Frankfurt-am-Main, Germany **(1749–1832)**

Gogol, Nikolai Vasilievich (novelist); nr. Mirgorod, Ukraine **(1809–1852)**

Goldberg, Rube (cartoonist); San Francisco **(1883–1970)**

Goldberg, Whoopi (Caryn Johnson) (actress); New York City, 11/13/49

Goldblum, Jeff (actor); Pittsburgh, 10/22/52

Golden, Harry (Harry Goldhurst) (author); New York City **(1902–1981)**

Goldman, Emma (anarchist); Kovno, Lithuania **(1869–1940)**

Goldsmith, Oliver (dramatist, poet); County Longford, Ireland **(1728–1774)**

Goldwyn, Samuel (Schmuel Gelbfisz) (film producer); Warsaw **(1879–1974)**

Gompers, Samuel (labor leader); London **(1850–1924)**

Gonzales, Alberto (attorney general); San Antonio, Tex., 8/4/55

Goodall, Jane (Baroness van Lawick-Goodall) (ethologist); London, 4/3/34

Gooding, Jr., Cuba (actor); Bronx, New York, 1/2/68

Goodman, Benny (clarinetist); Chicago **(1909–1986)**

Goodman, John (actor); St. Louis, 6/20/52

Goodwin, Doris (Helen) Kearns (historian); Rockville Center, N.Y., 1/4/43

Goodyear, Charles (inventor); New Haven, Conn. **(1800–1860)**

Gorbachev, Mikhail Sergeyevich (former Soviet leader); Privolnoye, Russia, 3/2/31

Gordimer, Nadine (novelist, short-story writer); Springs, South Africa, 12/20/23

Gordon, Dexter (jazz musician); Los Angeles **(1923–1990)**

Gordon, Ruth (actress); Wollaston, Mass. **(1896–1985)**

Gore, Albert, Jr. (ex-vice president of the U.S.); Washington, D.C., 3/31/48

Gordy, Berry, Jr. (record company executive); Detroit, 11/28/29

Gorey, Edward (St. John) (illustrator, author); Chicago **(1925–2000)**

Gorki, Maxim (Alexei Maximovich Peshkov) (author); Nizhni Novgorod, Russia **(1868–1936)**

Gorky, Arshile (painter); Armenia **(1904–1948)**

Gormé, Eydie (singer); Bronx, N.Y., 8/16/32

Gorshin, Frank (actor); Pittsburgh **(1934–2005)**

Gossett, Louis, Jr. (actor); Brooklyn, N.Y., 5/27/36

Gottschalk, Louis Moreau (pianist, composer); New Orleans **(1829–1869)**

Gould, Chester (cartoonist); Pawnee, Okla. **(1900–1985)**

Gould, Elliott (Elliott Goldstein) (actor); Brooklyn, N.Y., 8/29/38

Gould, Glenn (concert pianist); Toronto **(1932–1982)**

Gould, Morton (composer); Richmond Hill, Queens, N.Y. **(1913–1996)**

Gould, Stephen Jay (paleontologist, science writer); New York City **(1941–2002)**

Goulet, Robert (singer); Lawrence, Mass., 11/26/33

Gounod, Charles François (composer); Paris **(1818–1893)**

Goya y Lucientes, Francisco José de (painter); Fuendetodos, Spain **(1746–1828)**

Grable, Betty (actress); St. Louis **(1916–1973)**

Grace, Princess of Monaco (Grace Kelly) (ex-actress); Philadelphia **(1929–1982)**

Grace, Topher (actor); New York City, 7/12/78

Graham, Bill (Wolfgang Grajonca) (rock impresario); Berlin **(1930–1991)**

Graham, Billy (William F. Graham) (evangelist); Charlotte, N.C., 11/7/18

Graham, Katharine Meyer (newspaper publisher); New York City **(1917–2001)**

Graham, Martha (choreographer); Pittsburgh **(1894–1991)**

Grainger, Percy Aldridge (pianist, composer); Melbourne, Australia **(1882–1961)**

Gramm, Donald (Grambach) (bass-baritone); Milwaukee **(1927–1983)**

Grammer, Kelsey (actor); St. Thomas, V.I., 2/21/55

Granger, Stewart (James Stewart) (actor); London **(1913–1993)**

Grant, Cary (Alexander Archibald Leach) (actor); Bristol, England **(1904–1986)**

Grant, Hugh (actor); London, England, 9/9/60

Grant, Lee (Lyova Haskell Rosenthal) (actress); New York City, 10/31/30

Grant, Ulysses Simpson (18th U.S. president); Point Pleasant, Ohio **(1822–1885)**

Grass, Günter (novelist); Danzig, Poland, 10/16/27

Graves, Nancy (Stevenson) (artist); Pittsfield, Mass. **(1940–1996)**

Graves, Peter (Peter Aurness) (actor); Minneapolis, 3/18/26

Graves, Robert (writer); London **(1895–1985)**

Gray, Thomas (poet); London **(1716–1771)**

Greco, José (dancer); Montorio nei Frentani, Italy **(1918–2000)**

Greeley, Horace (journalist, politician); Amherst, N.H. **(1811–1872)**

Green, Adolph (actor, lyricist); New York City **(1915–2002)**

Green, Al (singer); Forrest City, Ark., 4/13/46

Greene, Graham (novelist); Berkhamsted, England **(1904–1991)**

Greene, Lorne (actor); Ottawa, Ont., Canada **(1915–1987)**

Greene, Shecky (comedian, actor); Chicago, 4/8/25

Greenstreet, Sydney (actor); Sandwich, England **(1879–1954)**

Greenspan, Alan (chairman of the Federal Reserve); New York City, 3/6/26

Greer, Germaine (feminist, writer); Melbourne, Australia, 1/29/39

Gregory, Dick (comedian); St. Louis, 10/12/32

Gregory, Frederick D. (astronaut); Washington, D.C., 1/7/41

Gregory, Lady (Isabella) Augusta (playwright); Roxborough, Ireland **(1852–1932)**

Greuze, Jean-Baptiste (painter); Tournus, France **(1725–1805)**

Grey, Joel (Joel Katz) (actor, dancer); Cleveland, 4/11/32

Grey, Zane (author); Zanesville, Ohio **(1875–1939)**

Grieg, Edvard Hagerup (composer); Bergen, Norway **(1843–1907)**

Grier, Pam (actress); Winston-Salem, N.C., 5/26/49

Griffin, Merv (TV host, producer); San Mateo, Calif., 7/6/25

Griffith, Andy (actor); Mount Airy, N.C., 6/1/26

Griffith, David Lewelyn Wark (film producer); La Grange, Ky. **(1875–1948)**

Griffith, Melanie (actress); New York City, 8/9/57

Grigorovich, Yuri (choreographer); Leningrad (St. Petersburg), Russia, 1/1/27

Grimes, Tammy (actress); Lynn, Mass., 1/30/34

Grimm, Jacob (author of fairy tales); Hanau, Germany **(1785–1863)**

Grimm, Wilhelm (author of fairy tales); Hanau, Germany **(1786–1859)**

Grint, Rupert (actor); Hertfordshire, England, 8/24/88

Gris, Juan (José Victoriano González) (painter); Madrid **(1887–1927)**

Grisham, John (attorney, author); Jonesboro, Ark., 2/8/55

Grodin, Charles (actor); Pittsburgh, 4/21/35

Groening, Matt (animator, producer); Portland, Ore., 2/14/54

Gromyko, Andrei A. (diplomat); Starye Gromyki, Russia **(1909–1989)**

Gropius, Walter (architect); Berlin **(1883–1969)**

Gropper, William (painter, illustrator); New York City **(1897–1977)**

Gross, Michael (actor); Chicago, 6/21/47

Grosz, George (painter); Germany **(1893–1959)**

Grove, Andrew (Andras Grof) (computer industry executive); Budapest, Hungary, 9/2/36

Grünewald, Matthias (Mathis Gothart Neithart) (painter); Würzburg, Germany **(c. 1470–1528)**

Guest, Christopher (Christopher Haden-Guest) (actor, writer, director); New York City, 2/5/48

Guevara, Ernesto "Che" (revolutionary, political leader); Argentina **(1928–1967)**

Guggenheim, Meyer (capitalist); Langnau, Switzerland **(1828–1905)**

Guillaume, Robert (Robert Williams) (actor); St. Louis, 11/30/27

Guinness, Sir Alec (actor); London **(1914–2000)**

Guitry, Sacha (Alexandre Guitry) (actor, film director); St. Petersburg, Russia **(1885–1957)**

Gumbel, Bryant Charles (TV newscaster); New Orleans, 9/29/48

Gunther, John (author); Chicago **(1901–1970)**

Gutenberg, Johann (printer); Mainz, Germany **(c. 1397–1468)**

Guthrie, Arlo (singer); New York City, 7/10/47

Guthrie, Woody (folk singer, composer); Okemah, Okla. **(1912–1967)**

Gutierrez, Carlos (secretary of Commerce); Havana, Cuba, 11/4/53

Gwenn, Edmund (actor); London **(1875–1959)**

Gwynne, Fred (actor); New York City **(1926–1993)**

Gyllenhaal, Jake (actor); Los Angeles, Calif., 12/19/80

Gyllenhaal, Maggie (actress); Los Angeles, Calif., 11/16/77

H

Habibie, Bacharuddin, Jusuf (president of Indonesia); Pare-Pare, Indonesia, 6/25/36

Hackett, Bobby (trumpeter); Providence, R.I. **(1915–1976)**

Hackett, Buddy (Leonard Hacker) (comedian, actor); Brooklyn, N.Y. **(1924–2003)**

Hackman, Gene (actor); San Bernardino, Calif., 1/30/31

Hagen, Uta (actress); Göttingen, Germany **(1919–2004)**

Haggard, Merle (songwriter, singer); Bakersfield, Calif., 4/6/37

Hagman, Larry (Larry Hageman) (actor); Weatherford, Tex., 9/21/31

Haig, Alexander Meigs, Jr. (ex-secretary of state, ex-general); Bala-Cynwyd, Pa., 12/2/24

Haile Selassie (Ras Tafari Makonnen) (ex-emperor); Ethiopia **(1892–1975)**

Hailey, Arthur (novelist); Luton, England, 4/5/20

Halberstam, David (journalist); New York City, 4/10/34

Hale, Alan (actor, director); Washington, D.C. **(1892–1950)**

Hale, Barbara (actress); DeKalb, Ill., 4/18/21

Hale, Edward Everett (clergyman, author); Boston **(1822–1909)**

Hale, Nathan (American Revolutionary officer); Coventry, Conn. **(1755–1776)**

Halevi, Judah (Jewish poet); Toledo, Spain **(1085–1140)**

Haley, Alex (writer); Ithaca, N.Y. **(1921–1992)**

Haley, Jack (actor); Boston **(1899–1979)**

Hall, Anthony Michael (Michael Anthony Thomas Charles Hall) (actor, singer); Boston, 4/14/68

Hall, Arsenio (comedian, talk-show host); Cleveland, 2/12/58

Hall, Donald (Andrew, Jr.) (poet); New Haven, Conn., 9/20/28

Hall, Huntz (actor); New York City **(1919–1999)**

Hall, Jerry (model, actress); Mesquite, Tex., 7/2/56

Hall, Monty (TV personality); Winnipeg, Canada, 8/25/23

Halley, Edmund (astronomer); London **(1656–1742)**

Hals, Frans (painter); Antwerp, Netherlands **(c. 1580–1666)**

Halsey, William Frederick, Jr. (naval officer); Elizabeth, N.J. **(1882–1959)**

Hamel, Veronica (actress); Philadelphia, 11/20/43

Hamill, Mark (actor); Oakland, 9/25/52

Hamilton, Alexander (statesman); Nevis, British West Indies **(1755–1804)**

Hamilton, Alice (physician, reformer); New York City **(1869–1970)**

Hamilton, Edith (scholar); Dresden, Germany **(1867–1963)**

Hamilton, George (actor); Memphis, Tenn., 8/12/39

Hamlin, Harry (actor); Pasadena, Calif., 10/30/51

Hamlisch, Marvin (composer, pianist); New York City, 6/2/44

Hammarskjöld, Dag (UN secretary-general); Jönköping, Sweden **(1905–1961)**

Hammerstein, Oscar, II (librettist, stage producer); New York City **(1895–1960)**

Hampton, Lionel (vibraharpist, band leader); Louisville, Ky. **(1913–2002)**

Hamsun, Knut (Knut Pedersen) (novelist); Lom, Norway **(1859–1952)**

Hancock, Herbie (jazz musician); Chicago, 4/12/40

Hancock, John (statesman); Braintree, Mass. **(1737–1793)**

Hand, Learned (jurist); Albany, N.Y. **(1872–1961)**

Handel, George Frideric (Georg Friedrich Händel) (composer); Halle, Germany **(1685–1759)**

Handy, William Christopher (blues composer); Florence, Ala. **(1873–1958)**

Hanks, Tom (actor, director, writer); Concord, Calif., 7/9/56

Hannah, Daryl (actress); Chicago, 12/3/60

Hannibal (Carthaginian general); North Africa **(247–182 B.C.)**

Hansberry, Lorraine (playwright); Chicago **(1930–1965)**
Hanson, Howard (conductor); Wahoo, Neb. **(1896–1981)**
Harburg, E. Y. "Yip" (songwriter); New York City **(1896–1981)**
Harden, Marcia Gay (actress); La Jolla, Calif., 8/14/59
Harding, Warren Gamaliel (29th U.S. president); Morrow County, Ohio **(1865–1923)**
Hardwicke, Sir Cedric (actor); Stourbridge, England **(1893–1964)**
Hardy, Oliver (comedian); Harlem, Ga. **(1892–1957)**
Hardy, Thomas (novelist); Dorsetshire, England **(1840–1928)**
Harkness, Edward S. (business executive); Cleveland **(1874–1940)**
Harlow, Jean (Harlean Carpenter) (actress); Kansas City, Mo. **(1911–1937)**
Harlow, Shalom (model, TV personality); Oshawa, Ontario, Canada, 12/5/73
Harmon, Mark (actor); Burbank, Calif., 9/2/51
Harnick, Sheldon (lyricist); Chicago, 4/30/24
Harper, Valerie (actress); Suffern, N.Y., 8/22/40
Harrell, Lynn (cellist); New York City, 1/30/44
Harrelson, Woody (actor); Midland, Tex., 7/23/61
Harriman, Pamela (ambassador); Farnborough, England **(1920–1997)**
Harriman, W. (William) Averell (ex-governor of New York); New York City **(1891–1986)**
Harrington, Pat, Jr. (actor, comedian); New York City, 8/13/29
Harris, Barbara (Sandra Markowitz) (actress); Evanston, Ill., 7/25/35
Harris, Ed (actor); Englewood, N.J., 11/28/50
Harris, Emmylou (singer); Birmingham, Ala., 4/2/47
Harris, Julie (actress); Grosse Pointe Park, Mich., 12/2/25
Harris, Patricia Roberts (cabinet member); Maroon, Ill. **(1924–1985)**
Harris, Phil (actor, band leader); Linton, Ind. **(1906–1995)**
Harris, Richard (actor); Limerick, Ireland **(1930–2002)**
Harris, Rosemary (actress); Ashby, England, 9/19/30
Harris, Roy (composer); Lincoln County, Okla. **(1898–1979)**
Harrison, Benjamin (23rd U.S. president); North Bend, Ohio **(1833–1901)**
Harrison, George (singer, songwriter); Liverpool, England **(1943–2001)**
Harrison, Gregory (actor); Avalon, Catalina Island, Calif., 5/31/50
Harrison, Sir Rex (Reginald Carey) (actor); Huyton, England **(1908–1990)**
Harrison, William Henry (9th U.S. president); Charles City County, Va. **(1773–1841)**
Harry, Deborah (Blondie) (musician); Miami, Fla., 7/1/45
Hart, Lorenz (lyricist); New York City **(1895–1943)**
Hart, Mary (Mary Johanna Harum) (host); Sioux Falls, S.D., 11/8/50
Hart, Moss (playwright); New York City **(1904–1961)**
Harte, Bret (Francis Brett Harte) (author); Albany, N.Y. **(1836–1902)**
Hartford, Huntington (George Huntington Hartford II) (A.&P. heir); New York City, 4/18/11
Hartford, John (singer, banjoist); New York City **(1937–2001)**
Hartley, Mariette (actress); New York City, 6/21/40
Hartman, David Downs (TV newscaster); Pawtucket, R.I., 5/19/35
Hartman, Phil (actor, comedian); Brantford, Ont., Canada **(1948–1998)**
Hartman Black, Lisa (actress); Houston, 6/1/56
Harvey, Laurence (Larushka Skikne) (actor); Joniskis, Lithuania **(1928–1973)**
Harvey, Polly Jean (PJ Harvey) (singer, songwriter); Yeovil, England, 10/9/69
Harvey, William (physician); Folkestone, England **(1578–1657)**
Hasselhoff, David (actor, producer); Baltimore, 7/17/52
Hastert, Dennis (speaker of the House); Aurora, Ill., 1/2/42
Hatcher, Teri (actress); Sunnyvale, Calif., 12/8/64
Havel, Vaclav (political leader, dramatist, poet); Prague, 10/5/36
Havens, Richie (musician); Brooklyn, N.Y., 1/21/41
Hawke, Ethan (actor); Austin, Tex., 11/6/70
Hawking, Stephen (physicist, astronomer); Oxford, England, 1/8/42
Hawkins, Coleman (jazz musician); St. Joseph, Mo. **(1904–1969)**
Hawkins, Jack (actor); London **(1910–1973)**
Hawn, Goldie (actress, producer); Washington, D.C., 11/21/45
Haworth, Jill (actress); Sussex, England, 8/15/45
Hawthorne, Nathaniel (novelist); Salem, Mass. **(1804–1864)**
Hay, John Milton (statesman); Salem, Ind. **(1838–1905)**
Hayakawa, Sessue (actor); Honshu, Japan **(1890–1973)**
Hayden, Melissa (ballet dancer); Toronto, 4/25/23
Hayden, Sterling (Sterling Relyea Walter) (actor, writer); Montclair, N.J. **(1916–1986)**
Haydn, Franz Joseph (composer); Rohrau, Austria **(1732–1809)**
Hayek, Salma (actress); Coatzacoalcos, Mexico, 9/2/66
Hayes, Helen (Helen Hayes Brown) (actress); Washington, D.C. **(1900–1993)**
Hayes, Isaac (composer); Covington, Tenn., 8/20/42

Hayes, Peter Lind (comedian, singer); San Francisco **(1915–1998)**
Hayes, Rutherford Birchard (19th U.S. president); Delaware, Ohio **(1822–1893)**
Hayward, Leland (producer); Nebraska City, Neb. **(1902–1971)**
Hayward, Susan (Edythe Marrener) (actress); Brooklyn, N.Y. **(1918–1975)**
Hayworth, Rita (Margarita Cansino) (actress); New York City **(1918–1987)**
Head, Edith (costume designer); Los Angeles **(1907–1981)**
Heaney, Seamus (poet); Londonderry, Northern Ireland, 4/13/39
Hearst, Patricia (Campbell) (heiress); San Francisco, 2/20/54
Hearst, William Randolph (publisher); San Francisco **(1863–1951)**
Hearst, William Randolph, Jr. (publisher); New York City **(1908–1993)**
Heatherton, Joey (actress); Rockville Centre, N.Y., 9/14/44
Heche, Anne (actress); Aurora, Ohio, 5/25/69
Hecht, Ben (author); New York City **(1894–1964)**
Heckart, Eileen (actress); Columbus, Ohio **(1919–2001)**
Heflin, Van (Emmet Evan Heflin) (actor); Walters, Okla. **(1910–1971)**
Hefner, Hugh (publisher); Chicago, 4/9/26
Hegel, Georg Wilhelm Friedrich (philosopher); Stuttgart, Germany **(1770–1831)**
Heidegger, Martin (existentialist philosopher); Messkirch, Germany **(1889–1976)**
Heifetz, Jascha (concert violinist); Vilna, Russia **(1901–1987)**
Heine, Heinrich (Harry) (poet); Düsseldorf, Germany **(1797–1856)**
Heinemann, Gustav (ex-president of Germany); Schweim, Germany **(1899–1976)**
Heisenberg, Werner Karl (physicist); Würzburg, Germany **(1901–1976)**
Heller, Joseph (novelist); Brooklyn, N.Y. **(1923–1999)**
Hellman, Lillian (playwright); New Orleans **(1905–1984)**
Helmond, Katherine (actress); Galveston, Tex., 7/5/34
Helms, Jesse (politician); Monroe, N.C., 10/18/21
Helmsley, Harry Brakmann (business executive); New York City **(1909–1997)**
Hemingway, Ernest Miller (novelist); Oak Park, Ill. **(1899–1961)**
Hemingway, Margaux (actress); Portland, Ore. **(1955–1996)**
Hemmings, David (actor); Guilford, England **(1941–2003)**
Henderson, Florence (actress); Dale, Ind., 2/14/34
Henderson, Skitch (Lyle Russell Cedric) (conductor, pianist); Birmingham, England?, 1/27/18
Hendrix, Jimi (James Marshall Hendrix) (guitarist); Seattle **(1942–1970)**
Henley, Don (musician); Linden, Tex., 7/22/47
Henner, Marilu (actress); Chicago, 4/6/52
Henning, Doug (magician, actor); Winnipeg, Canada **(1947–2000)**
Henri, Robert (painter); Cincinnati **(1865–1926)**
Henriksen, Lance (actor, screenwriter); New York City, 5/4/40
Henry VIII (king of England); Greenwich, England **(1491–1547)**
Henry, O. (William Sydney Porter) (story writer); Greensboro, N.C. **(1862–1910)**
Henry, Patrick (statesman); Hanover County, Va. **(1736–1799)**
Henson, Jim (puppeteer); Greenville, Miss. **(1936–1990)**
Hepburn, Audrey (actress); Brussels **(1929–1993)**
Hepburn, Katharine (actress); Hartford, Conn. **(1907–2003)**
Hepplewhite, George (furniture designer); England **(?–1786)**
Hepworth, Barbara (sculptor); Wakefield, England **(1903–1975)**
Herbert, George (poet); Montgomery Castle, Wales **(1593–1633)**
Herbert, Victor (composer); Dublin **(1859–1924)**
Herblock (Herbert L. Block) (political cartoonist); Chicago **(1909–2001)**
Herman, Pee-wee (Paul Rubenfeld) (comedian); Peekskill, N.Y., 8/27/52
Herman, Woody (Woodrow Charles Herman) (band leader); Milwaukee **(1913–1987)**
Herod (called Herod the Great) (king of Judea) **(73–4 B.C.)**
Herodotus (historian); Halicarnassus, Asia Minor (Turkey) **(c. 484–425 B.C.)**
Herrick, Robert (poet); London **(1591–1674)**
Herschbach, Dudley Robert (chemist, Nobel laureate); San Jose, Calif., 6/18/32
Herschel, William (Frederich Wilhelm Herschel) (astronomer); Hannover, Germany **(1738–1822)**
Hershey, Barbara (Barbara Herzstein) (actress); Hollywood, Calif., 2/5/48
Herzog, Chaim (Israeli statesman); Belfast, Northern Ireland **(1918–1997)**
Hesburgh, Theodore M. (educator); Syracuse, N.Y., 5/25/17
Heston, Charlton (actor); Evanston, Ill., 10/4/24
Heyerdahl, Thor (ethnologist, explorer); Larvik, Norway **(1914–2002)**

Hildegarde (Hildegarde Loretta Sell) (singer); Adell, Wis. **(1906–2005)**

Hill, Anita (lawyer, professor); Lone Tree, Okla., 7/30/56

Hill, Benny (comedian); Southampton, England **(1925–1992)**

Hill, Lauryn (actress, musician); South Orange, N.J., 5/25/75

Hillary, Sir Edmund (mountain climber); New Zealand, 7/20/19

Hiller, Wendy (actress); Bramhall, England **(1912–2003)**

Hillerman, John (actor); Denison, Tex., 12/20/32

Hilton, Conrad (hotelier); San Antonio, N.M. **(1887–1979)**

Hilton, Paris (celebrity); New York City, 2/17/81

Hindemith, Paul (composer); Hanau, Germany **(1895–1963)**

Hindenburg, Paul von (Paul Ludwig Hans Anton von Hindenburg und Beneckendorff) (German field marshal, president); Poznan, Poland **(1847– 1934)**

Hines, Earl "Fatha" (jazz pianist); Duquesne, Pa. **(1903–1983)**

Hines, Gregory (dancer, actor); New York City **(1946–2003)**

Hines, Jerome (Jerome Heinz) (basso); Los Angeles **(1921–2003)**

Hippocrates (physician); Cos, Greece **(c. 460–c. 377 B.C.)**

Hirohito (Emperor of Japan); Tokyo **(1901–1989)**

Hiroshige, Ando (painter); Edo, Tokyo **(1797–1858)**

Hirsch, Judd (actor); New York City, 3/15/35

Hirschfeld, Al (Albert) (cartoonist); St. Louis **(1903–2003)**

Hirschhorn, Joseph Herman (financier, speculator, art collector); Mitau, Latvia **(1899–1981)**

Hirt, Al (trumpeter); New Orleans **(1922–1999)**

Hiss, Alger (public official); Baltimore **(1904–1996)**

Hitchcock, Alfred J. (film director); London **(1899–1980)**

Hitler, Adolf (German dictator); Braunau, Austria **(1889–1945)**

Hobbes, Thomas (philosopher); Westport, England **(1588–1679)**

Hobson, Laura Z. (Laura K. Zametkin) (novelist); New York City **(1900–1986)**

Ho Chi Minh (Nguyen That Tranh) (Vietnamese nationalist leader); Kim Lien, Vietnam **(1890–1969)**

Hockney, David (artist); Bradford, England, 7/9/37

Hodgkin, Dorothy Mary Crowfoot (chemist, Nobel laureate); Cairo, Egypt **(1910–1994)**

Hoffa, "Jimmy" James R(iddle) (labor leader); Brazil, Ind. **(1913–1975?; presumed murdered.)**

Hoffman, Dustin (actor, director); Los Angeles, 8/8/37

Hoffman, Phillip Seymour (actor); Fairport, N.Y., 1968

Hofmann, Hans (painter); Germany **(1880–1966)**

Hoffmann, Roald (chemist, Nobel laureate); Zloczow, Poland, 7/18/37

Hofstadter, Richard (historian); Buffalo, N.Y. **(1916–1970)**

Hogan, Paul (actor); Lightning Ridge, N.S.W., Australia, 10/8/39

Hogarth, William (painter, engraver); London **(1697–1764)**

Hokusai, Katsushika (artist); Yedo, Japan **(1760–1849)**

Holbein, Hans (the Elder) (painter); Augsburg, Germany **(c. 1465–1524)**

Holbein, Hans (the Younger) (painter); Augsburg, Germany **(c. 1497–1543)**

Holbrook, Hal (actor); Cleveland, 2/17/25

Holden, William (William Franklin Beedle, Jr.) (actor); O'Fallon, Ill. **(1918–1981)**

Holder, Geoffrey (dancer); Port-of-Spain, Trinidad, 8/1/30

Holiday, Billie (Eleanora Fagan) (jazz-blues singer); Baltimore **(1915–1959)**

Holliman, Earl (Henry Earl Holliman) (actor); Delhi, La., 9/11/28

Holly, Buddy (singer); Lubbock, Tex. **(1936–1959)**

Holly, Lauren (actress); Geneva, N.Y., 10/28/63

Holm, Celeste (actress); New York City, 4/29/19

Holmes, Katie (actress); Toledo, Ohio, 12/18/78

Holmes, Oliver Wendell (jurist); Boston **(1841–1935)**

Home, Lord (Alexander Frederick Douglas-Home) (diplomat); London **(7/2/1903–10/9/1995)**

Homer, Winslow (painter); Boston **(1836–1910)**

Homer (Greek poet) fl. 850 B.C.

Honegger, Arthur (composer); Le Havre, France **(1892–1955)**

Hook, Sidney (philosopher); New York City **(1902–1989)**

Hooker, John Lee (blues guitarist, singer, songwriter); Clarksdale, Miss. **(1917–2001)**

Hoover, Herbert Clark (31st U.S. president); West Branch, Iowa **(1874–1964)**

Hoover, J. Edgar (FBI director); Washington, D.C. **(1895–1972)**

Hope, Bob (Leslie Townes Hope) (comedian); London **(1903–2003)**

Hopkins, Sir Anthony (actor); Port Talbot, Wales, 12/31/37

Hopkins, Gerald Manley (poet); Stratford, England **(1844–1899)**

Hopkins, Johns (financier); Anne Arundel County, Md. **(1795–1873)**

Hopper, Dennis (actor); Dodge City, Kans., 5/17/36

Hopper, Edward (painter); Nyack, N.Y. **(1882–1967)**

Horace (Quintus Horatius Flaccus) (poet); Venosa, Italy **(65–8 B.C.)**

Hornby, Nick (writer); Maidenhead, England, 4/17/57

Horne, Lena (singer); Brooklyn, N.Y., 6/30/17

Horne, Marilyn (mezzo-soprano); Bradford, Pa., 1/16/34

Horowitz, Vladimir (pianist); Kiev, Ukraine **(1903–1989)**

Horsley, Lee (actor); Muleshoe, Tex., 5/15/55

Horton, Edward Everett (comedian); Brooklyn, N.Y. **(1887–1970)**

Hoskins, Bob (actor); Bury St. Edmunds, England, 10/26/42

Houdini, Harry (Ehrich Weiss) (magician); Budapest, Hungary **(1874–1926)**

Houseman, John (Jacques Haussmann) (producer, director, actor); Bucharest **(1902–1988)**

Housman, A(lfred) E(dward) (poet); Fockburg, England **(1859–1936)**

Houston, Charles Hamilton (civil rights lawyer); Washington, D.C. **(1895–1950)**

Houston, Samuel (political leader); Rockbridge County, Va. **(1793–1863)**

Houston, Whitney (singer); Newark, N.J., 8/9/63

Howard, John (prime minister of Australia); Sydney, Australia, 7/26/39

Howard, Ken (actor); El Centro, Calif., 3/28/44

Howard, Leslie (Leslie Stainer) (actor); London **(1893–1943)**

Howard, Ron (actor, producer, director); Duncan, Okla., 3/1/54

Howard, Trevor (actor); Kent, England **(1916–1988)**

Howe, Elias (inventor); Spencer, Mass. **(1819–1867)**

Howe, Irving (literary critic); New York City **(1920–1993)**

Howe, Julia Ward (poet, reformer); New York City **(1819–1910)**

Hubble, Edwin Powell (astronomer); Marshfield, Mo. **(1889–1953)**

Hudson, Henry (English navigator) **(fl. 1607–1611)**

Hudson, Rock (born Roy Scherer, Jr.; took Roy Fitzgerald as legal name) (actor); Winnetka, Ill. **(1925–1985)**

Huggins, Nathan Irvin (historian); Chicago **(1927–1989)**

Hughes, Charles Evans (jurist); Glens Falls, N.Y. **(1862–1948)**

Hughes, Howard (industrialist, film producer); Houston **(1905–1976)**

Hughes, Langston (poet); Joplin, Mo. **(1902–1967)**

Hughes, Ted (poet); Mytholmroyd, England **(1930–1998)**

Hugo, Victor Marie (author); Besançon, France **(1802–1885)**

Hulce, Tom (actor); Detroit, 12/6/53

Hume, David (philosopher); Edinburgh, Scotland **(1711–1776)**

Humperdinck, Engelbert (composer); Siegburg, Germany **(1854–1921)**

Humperdinck, Engelbert (Arnold Dorsey) (singer); Madras, India, 5/2/36

Hunt, Helen (actress); Los Angeles, 6/15/63

Hunt, Linda (actress); Morristown, N.J., 4/2/45

Hunter, Holly (actress); Atlanta, 3/20/58

Hunter, Kim (Janet Cole) (actress); Detroit **(1922–2002)**

Hunter, Tab (Arthur Andrew Gelien) (actor); New York City, 7/11/31

Hunter-Gault, Charlayne (activist, broadcast journalist); Due West, S.C., 2/27/42

Huntley, Chet (TV newscaster); Cardwell, Mont. **(1911–1974)**

Hurley, Elizabeth (actress, model); Backingstoke, England, 6/10/65

Hurok, Sol (Solomon Hurok) (impresario); Pogar, Russia **(1884–1974)**

Hurst, Fannie (novelist); Hamilton, Ohio **(1889–1968)**

Hurston, Zora Neale (author); Eatonville, Fla. **(1901–1960)**

Hurt, John (actor); Shirebrook, England, 1/22/40

Hurt, William (actor); Washington, D.C., 3/20/50

Hus, Jan (Bohemian religious reformer); Husinetz, nr. Budweis, Czech Republic **(c. 1369–1415)**

Husing, Ted (sportscaster); New York City **(1901–1962)**

Hussein I (king); Jordan **(1935–1999)**

Hussein, Saddam (al-Tikriti) (Iraqi president); Tikrit, Iraq, 4/28/37

Hussey, Ruth (Ruth Carol O'Rourke) (actress); Providence, R.I. **(1914–2005)**

Huston, Anjelica (actress); Los Angeles, 7/8/51

Huston, John (actor, director, writer); Nevada, Mo. **(1906–1987)**

Huston, Walter (Walter Houghston) (actor); Toronto **(1884–1950)**

Hutchins, Robert M. (educator); Brooklyn, N.Y. **(1899–1977)**

Hutton, Betty (Betty Thornburg) (actress); Battle Creek, Mich., 2/26/21

Hutton, Lauren (actress, model); Charleston, S.C., 11/17/43

Hutton, Timothy (actor); Los Angeles, 8/16/60

Huxley, Aldous (author); Godalming, England **(1894–1963)**

Huxley, Sir Julian S. (biologist, author); London **(1887–1975)**

Huxley, Thomas Henry (biologist); Ealing, England **(1825–1895)**

Hynde, Chrissie (singer); Akron, Ohio, 9/7/51

I

Iacocca, Lee (Lido Anthony) (business executive); Allentown, Pa., 10/15/24

Ian, Janis (singer); New York City, 5/7/51

Ibsen, Henrik (dramatist); Skien, Norway **(1828–1906)**

Ice Cube (O'Shea Jackson) (musician, actor); Los Angeles, 6/15/69
Ice-T (Tracy Morrow) (rap musician, actor); Newark, N.J., 2/16/68
Inge, William (playwright); Independence, Kans. **(1913–1973)**
Ingres, Jean Auguste Dominique (painter); Montauban, France **(1780–1867)**
Inness, George (painter); nr. Newburgh, N.Y. **(1825–1894)**
Ionesco, Eugene (playwright); Slatina, Romania **(1909–1994)**
Ireland, Jill (actress); London **(1936–1990)**
Ireland, Kathy (model, actress); Glendale, Calif., 3/8/63
Ireland, Patricia (feminist, social activist); Oak Park, Ill., 10/19/45
Irons, Jeremy (actor); Cowes, Isle of Wight, England, 9/19/48
Irving, Amy (actress); Palo Alto, Calif., 9/10/53
Irving, John (Winslow) (writer); Exeter, N.H., 3/2/42
Irving, Washington (author); New York City **(1783–1859)**
Isaak, Chris (musician, actor); Stockton, Calif., 6/26/56
Isherwood, Christopher (novelist, playwright); nr. Dilsey and High Lane, England **(1904–1986)**
Iturbi, José (concert pianist); Valencia, Spain **(1895–1980)**
Ives, Burl (Icle Ivanhoe) (singer); Hunt, Ill. **(1909–1995)**
Ives, Charles E(dward) (composer); Danbury, Conn. **(1874–1954)**
Ivins, Molly (journalist); Monterey, Calif., 8/30/44
Ivory, James (director, producer); Berkeley, Calif., 6/7/28

J

Jackson, Alphonso (secretary of Housing and Development); Marshall, Tex., 9/9/45
Jackson, Andrew (7th U.S. president); Waxhaw, S.C. **(1767–1845)**
Jackson, Anne (actress); Millvale, Pa., 9/3/26
Jackson, Glenda (actress); Cheshire, England, 5/9/36
Jackson, Janet (singer); Gary, Ind., 5/16/66
Jackson, Rev. Jesse (civil rights leader); Greenville, S.C., 10/8/41
Jackson, Kate (actress); Birmingham, Ala., 10/29/49
Jackson, Mahalia (gospel singer); New Orleans **(1911–1972)**
Jackson, Maynard (mayor of Atlanta); Dallas **(1938–2003)**
Jackson, Michael (singer); Gary, Ind., 8/29/58
Jackson, Peter (director); Wellington, New Zealand, 10/31/61
Jackson, Samuel L. (actor); Washington, D.C., 12/21/48
Jackson, Thomas Jonathan ("Stonewall") (general); Clarksburg, Va. (now W. Va.) **(1824–1863)**
Jacobi, Derek (actor); Leytonstone, England, 10/22/38
Jacobs, Jane (urbanologist); Scranton, Pa., 5/1/16
Jagger, Mick (Michael Phillip Jagger) (singer); Dartford, England, 7/26/43
James, Harry (trumpeter); Albany, Ga. **(1916–1983)**
James, Henry (novelist); New York City **(1843–1916)**
James, Jesse Woodson (outlaw); Clay County, Mo. **(1847–1882)**
James, William (psychologist); New York City **(1842–1910)**
Jameson, (Margaret) Storm (novelist); Whitby, England **(1897–1986)**
Janis, Byron (pianist); McKeesport, Pa., 3/24/28
Janis, Conrad (actor, musician); New York City, 2/11/28
Janssen, David (David Meyer) (actor); Naponee, Nebr. **(1930–1980)**
Jaworski, Leon (Watergate special prosecutor); Waco, Tex. **(1905–1982)**
Jay, John (statesman, jurist); New York City **(1745–1829)**
Jay-Z (Shawn Corey Carter) (rapper); Brooklyn, N.Y., 12/4/69?
Jeanmaire, Renée (dancer); Paris, 4/29/24
Jefferson, Thomas (3rd U.S. president); Shadwell, Va. **(1743–1826)**
Jemison, Mae C. (astronaut, physician); Decatur, Ala., 10/17/56
Jenner, Edward (physician); Berkeley, England **(1749–1823)**
Jennings, Peter (news anchor); Toronto **(1938–2005)**
Jennings, Waylon (singer); Littlefield, Tex. **(1937–2002)**
Jessel, George (entertainer); New York City **(1898–1981)**
Jessup, Philip C. (diplomat); New York City **(1897–1986)**
Jillian, Ann (Ann Jura Nauseda) (actress); Cambridge, Mass., 1/29/51
Joan of Arc (Jeanne d'Arc) (saint, patriot); Domremy-la-Pucelle, France **(1412–1431)**
Jobs, Steven Paul (computer industry pioneer); San Francisco, 1955
Joel, Billy (singer); New York City, 5/9/49
Joffrey, Robert (Abdullah Jaffa Bey Khan) (choreographer); Seattle **(1930–1988)**
Johanns, Mike (secretary of Agriculture); Osage, Iowa, 6/18/50
John, Elton (Reginald Kenneth Dwight) (singer, pianist); Pinner, England, 3/25/47
John Paul II (Karol Józef Wojtya) (pope); Wadowice, Poland **(1920–2005)**
John XXIII (Angelo Giuseppe Roncalli) (pope); Sotto il Monte, Italy **(1881–1963)**

Johns, Jasper (painter, sculptor); Augusta, Ga., 5/15/30
Johnson, Andrew (17th U.S. president); Raleigh, N.C. **(1808–1875)**
Johnson, Don (actor); Flatt Creek, Mo., 12/15/49
Johnson, James Weldon (author, educator); Jacksonville, Fla. **(1871–1938)**
Johnson, Lyndon Baines (36th U.S. president); Stonewall, Tex. **(1908–1973)**
Johnson, Philip Cortelyou (architect); Cleveland **(1906–2005)**
Johnson, Samuel (lexicographer, author); Lichfield, England **(1709–1784)**
Johnson, Van (actor); Newport, R.I., 8/20/16
Johnson, Virginia (human sexuality expert); Springfield, Mo., 2/11/25
Jolie, Angelina (actress); Los Angeles, 6/4/75
Joliot-Curie, Frédéric (chemist, Nobel laureate); Paris **(1900–1958)**
Joliot-Curie, Irène (Irène Curie) (chemist, Nobel laureate); France **(1897–1956)**
Jolliet, Louis (Louis Joliet) (explorer); Beaupré, Canada **(1645–1700)**
Jolson, Al (Asa Yoelson) (actor, singer); St. Petersburg, Russia **(1886–1950)**
Jones, Dean (actor); Morgan County, Ala., 1/25/35
Jones, George (singer); Saratoga, Tex., 9/12/31
Jones, Inigo (architect); London **(1573–1652)**
Jones, James (novelist); Robinson, Ill. **(1921–1977)**
Jones, James Earl (actor); Arkabutla, Miss., 1/17/31
Jones, Jennifer (Phylis Isley) (actress); Tulsa, Okla., 3/2/19
Jones, John Paul (John Paul) (naval officer); Scotland **(1747–1792)**
Jones, Quincy (composer); Chicago, 3/14/33
Jones, Shirley (singer, actress); Smithtown, Pa., 3/31/34
Jones, Spike (host, orchestra leader); Long Beach, Calif. **(1911–1965)**
Jones, Tom (Thomas Jones Woodward) (singer); Pontypridd, Wales, 6/7/40
Jones, Tommy Lee (actor); San Saba, Tex., 9/15/46
Jong, Erica (writer); New York City, 3/26/42
Jonson, Ben (Benjamin Jonson) (poet, dramatist); Westminster, England **(1572–1637)**
Joplin, Janis (singer); Port Arthur, Tex. **(1943–1970)**
Joplin, Scott (ragtime pianist, composer); Texarkansas, Tex. **(1868–1917)**
Jordan, Barbara (U.S. representative); Houston **(1936–1996)**
Jordan, Neil (film director, screenwriter); Sligo, Ireland, 2/25/50
Joseph (Chief Joseph) (Nez Perce Indian leader); eastern Ore. **(1841–1904)**
Josquin des Prés (usually known as Josquin) (composer); Conde-sur-L'Escaut?, Hainaut, Belgium **(c. 1445–1521)**
Jovovich, Milla (actress, model, singer); Kiev, Ukraine, 12/17/75
Joyce, James (novelist); Dublin **(1882–1941)**
Juárez, Benito Pablo (statesman); Guelatao, Mexico **(1806–1872)**
Judd, Ashley (actress); Los Angeles, 4/19/68
Julia, Raul (Raúl Rafael Carlos Julia y Arcelay) (actor); San Juan, P.R. **(1940–1994)**
Jung, Carl Gustav (psychoanalyst); Basel, Switzerland **(1875–1961)**
Jurado, Katy (Maria Christina Jurado Garcia) (actress); Guadalajara, Mexico **(1924–2002)**

K

Kabalevsky, Dmitri (composer); St. Petersburg, Russia **(1904–1987)**
Kafka, Franz (author); Prague **(1883–1924)**
Kádár, János (Communist Party leader); Hungary **(1912–1989)**
Kahn, Gus (songwriter); Coblenz, Germany **(1886–1941)**
Kahn, Louis I. (architect); Oesel Island, Estonia **(1901–1974)**
Kahn, Madeline (actress); Boston **(1942–1999)**
Kandinsky, Wassily (painter); Moscow **(1866–1944)**
Kanin, Garson (playwright); Rochester, N.Y. **(1912–1999)**
Kant, Immanuel (philosopher); Königsberg (Kaliningrad), Russia **(1724–1804)**
Kantor, MacKinlay (novelist); Webster City, Iowa **(1904–1977)**
Kaplan, Justin (writer, editor); New York City, 9/5/25
Karan, Donna (fashion designer); Forest Hills, N.Y., 10/2/48
Karloff, Boris (William Henry Pratt) (actor); London **(1887–1969)**
Kasdan, Lawrence (film director, writer, actor, producer); Miami, 1/14/49
Kasem, Casey (disc jockey); Detroit, 4/27/32
Kaufman, Andy (actor, comedian); New York City **(1949–1984)**
Kaufman, George S. (playwright); Pittsburgh **(1889–1961)**
Kavner, Julie (actress); Los Angeles, 9/7/51
Kaye, Danny (David Daniel Kominski) (comedian); Brooklyn, N.Y. **(1913–1987)**
Kaye, Sammy (band leader); Cleveland **(1910–1987)**

Kazan, Elia (director); Constantinople, Turkey **(1909–2003)**

Kazan, Lainie (Levine) (singer); New York City, 5/15/40

Kazantzakis, Nikos (writer); Herakleion, Crete **(1883–1957)**

Keach, Stacy (actor); Savannah, Ga., 6/2/41

Keaton, Buster (Joseph Frank Keaton) (comedian); Piqua, Kans. **(1896–1966)**

Keaton, Diane (actress); Los Angeles, 1/5/46

Keaton, Michael (Michael Douglas) (actor); Robinson Township, Pa., 9/9/51

Keats, John (poet); London **(1795–1821)**

Keel, Howard (Harold Clifford Leek) (singer, actor); Gillespie, Ill., 4/13/19

Keeler, Ruby (Ethel Hilde Keeler) (actress, dancer); Halifax, N.S., Canada **(1910–1993)**

Keener, Catherine (actress); Miami, Fla., 3/26/60

Kefauver, Estes (legislator); Madisonville, Tenn **(1903–1963)**

Keitel, Harvey (actor); Brooklyn, N.Y., 5/13/39

Keith, Brian (Robert Brian Keith, Jr.) (actor); Bayonne, N.J. **(1921–1997)**

Keller, Helen Adams (author, educator); Tuscumbia, Ala. **(1880–1968)**

Kelley, DeForest (actor); Atlanta **(1920–1999)**

Kelly, Emmett (clown); Sedan, Kans. **(1898–1979)**

Kelly, Gene (dancer, actor); Pittsburgh **(1912–1996)**

Kelly, Grace (actress, Princess of Monaco); Philadelphia **(1929–1982)**

Kelly, R. (Robert Kelly) (singer, record producer, actor); Chicago, 1969

Kempis, Thomas à (mystic); Kempis, Prussia (Germany) **(1380–1471)**

Kendall, Henry W. (physicist, Nobel laureate); Boston **(1926–1999)**

Kennan, George F. (diplomat); Milwaukee **(1904–2005)**

Kennedy, Anthony (jurist); Sacramento, Calif., 7/23/36

Kennedy, Carolyn Bessette (socialite); White Plains, N.Y. **(1966–1999)**

Kennedy, George (actor); New York City, 2/18/25

Kennedy, John Fitzgerald (35th U.S. president); Brookline, Mass. **(1917–1963)**

Kennedy, John F., Jr. (publisher); Washington, D.C. **(1960–1999)**

Kennedy, Joseph P. (financier); Boston **(1888–1969)**

Kennedy, Robert Francis (legislator); Brookline, Mass. **(1925–1968)**

Kennedy, Rose Fitzgerald (president's mother); Boston **(1890–1995)**

Kent, Allegra (ballet dancer); Santa Monica, Calif., 8/11/38

Kent, Rockwell (painter); Tarrytown Heights, N.Y. **(1882–1971)**

Kenton, Stan (Stanley Newcomb) (jazz musician); Wichita, Kans. **(1911–1979)**

Kepler, Johannes (astronomer); Weil, Germany **(1571–1630)**

Kercheval, Ken (actor); Wolcottville, Ind., 7/15/35

Kerensky, Alexander Fedorovich (statesman); Simbirsk, Russia **(1881–1970)**

Kern, Jerome David (composer); New York City **(1885–1945)**

Kerns, Joanna (actress); San Francisco, 2/12/53

Kerouac, Jack (Jean-Louis Kerouac) (writer); Lowell, Mass. **(1922–1969)**

Kerr, Deborah (actress); Helensburgh, Scotland, 9/30/21

Kerry, John (U.S. senator); Denver, Colo., 12/11/43

Kettering, Charles F. (engineer, inventor); nr. Loudonville, Ohio **(1876–1958)**

Kevorkian, Jack (medical pathologist); Pontiac, Mich., 3/26/28

Key, Francis Scott (lawyer, author of national anthem); Frederick (Carroll) County, Md. **(1779–1843)**

Keyes, Frances Parkinson (novelist); Charlottesville, Va. **(1885–1970)**

Keynes, John Maynard (1st Baron of Tilton) (economist); Cambridge, England **(1883–1946)**

Keys, Alicia (Alicia Augello-Cook) (singer, songwriter); New York City, 1/25/81

Khachaturian, Aram (composer); Tiflis, Russia **(1903–1978)**

Khomeini, Ayatollah Ruhollah (Islamic religious leader); Iran **(1900–1989)**

Khrushchev, Nikita S. (Soviet leader); Kalinovka, nr. Kursk, Ukraine **(1894–1971)**

Kidd, Michael (Milton Greenwald) (choreographer); Brooklyn, N.Y., 8/12/19

Kidd, William (called Captain Kidd) (pirate); Greenock, Scotland **(c. 1645–1701)**

Kidder, Margot (actress); Yellowknife, N.W.T., Canada, 10/17/48

Kidman, Nicole (actress); Honolulu, 6/20/67

Kiepura, Jan (tenor); Sosnowiec, Poland **(1902–1966)**

Kieran, John (writer); New York City **(1892–1981)**

Kierkegaard, Sören Aalys (philosopher); Copenhagen **(1813–1855)**

Kiesinger, Kurt Georg (diplomat); Ebingen, Germany **(1904–1988)**

Kiley, Richard (actor, singer); Chicago **(1922–1999)**

Kilmer, Alfred Joyce (poet); New Brunswick, N.J. **(1886–1918)**

Kilmer, Val (actor); Los Angeles, 12/31/59

Kimmel, Jimmy (TV host); Brooklyn, 11/13/67

King, Alan (Irwin Alan Kniberg) (entertainer); Brooklyn, N.Y. **(1927–2004)**

King, B. B. (Riley King) (guitarist); Itta Bena, Miss., 9/16/25

King, Carole (singer, songwriter); Brooklyn, N.Y., 2/9/41

King, Coretta Scott (civil rights leader); Marion, Ala., 4/27/27

King, Larry (Lawrence Harvey Zeigler) (TV host); New York City, 11/19/33

King, Martin Luther, Jr. (civil rights leader); Atlanta **(1929–1968)**

King, Stephen (writer); Portland, Maine, 9/21/47

Kingsley, Ben (Krishna Bhanji) (actor); Snainton, England, 12/31/43

Kingsley, Sidney (Sidney Kirschner) (playwright); New York City **(1906–1995)**

Kingsolver, Barbara (writer); Annapolis, Md., 4/8/55

Kingston, Maxine Hong (novelist); Stockton, Calif., 10/27/40

Kinsey, Alfred Charles (human sexuality expert); Hoboken, N.J. **(1894–1956)**

Kinski, Nastassja (Nastassja Nakszynski) (actress); West Berlin, 1/24/61

Kipling, Rudyard (author); Bombay (Mumbai) **(1865–1936)**

Kipnis, Alexander (basso); Ukraine **(1891–1978)**

Kirby, George (comedian); Chicago **(1923–1995)**

Kirchner, Ernst Ludwig (painter); Aschaffenburg, Germany **(1880–1938)**

Kirk, Grayson (educator); Jeffersonville, Ohio **(1903–1997)**

Kirkland, Gelsey (ballet dancer); Bethlehem, Pa., 12/29/52

Kirkpatrick, Jeane Jordan (educator-public affairs); Duncan, Okla., 11/19/26

Kirkpatrick, Ralph (harpsichordist); Leominster, Mass. **(1911–1984)**

Kirstein, Lincoln (dance, theater executive); Rochester, N.Y. **(1907–1996)**

Kirsten, Dorothy (soprano); Montclair, N.J. **(1910–1992)**

Kissinger, Henry (Heinz Alfred Kissinger) (ex-U.S. secretary of state); Furth, Germany, 5/27/23

Kitt, Eartha (singer); North, S.C., 1/26/28

Klee, Paul (painter); Münchenbuchsee, nr. Bern, Switzerland **(1879–1940)**

Klein, Calvin (fashion designer); Bronx, N.Y., 11/19/42

Klein, Robert (comedian); New York City, 2/8/42

Kleist, Henrich von (poet); Frankfurt an der Oder, Germany **(1777–1811)**

Klemperer, Otto (conductor); Breslau, Poland **(1885–1973)**

Klemperer, Werner (actor); Cologne, Germany **(1920–2000)**

Klimt, Gustav (painter); Vienna **(1862–1918)**

Kline, Kevin (actor); St. Louis, 10/24/47

Klugman, Jack (actor); Philadelphia, 4/27/22

Knight, Gladys (singer); Atlanta, 5/28/44

Knight, John S. (publisher); Bluefield, W. Va. **(1894–1981)**

Knight, Ted (Tadeus Wladyslaw Konopka) (actor); Terryville, Conn. **(1923–1986)**

Knight, Wayne (actor); Cartersville, Ga., 8/7/55

Knopf, Alfred A. (publisher); New York City **(1892–1984)**

Knopfler, Mark (musician); Glasgow, Scotland, 8/12/49

Knotts, Don (actor); Morgantown, W. Va., 7/21/24

Knox, John (religious reformer); Haddington, East Lothian, Scotland **(1505–1572)**

Koch, Robert (physician); Klausthal, Germany **(1843–1910)**

Koenig, Walter (actor); Chicago, 9/14/36

Koestler, Arthur (novelist); Budapest **(1905–1983)**

Kokoschka, Oskar (painter); Pöchlarn, Austria **(1886–1980)**

Kollwitz, Käthe (graphic artist, sculptor); Königsberg, Russia **(1867–1945)**

Koop, C. Everett (ex-surgeon general); Brooklyn, N.Y., 10/14/16

Kooper, Al (singer, pianist); Brooklyn, N.Y., 2/5/44

Kopell, Bernie (actor); New York City, 6/21/33

Koppel, Ted (broadcast journalist); Lancashire, England, 2/8/40

Korman, Harvey (actor); Chicago, 2/15/27

Kosciusko, Thaddeus (Tadeusz Andrzej Bonawentura Kosciuszko) (military officer and statesman) **(1746–1817)**

Kossuth, Lajos (patriot); Monok, Hungary **(1802–1894)**

Kostelanetz, André (orchestra conductor); St. Petersburg, Russia **(1901–1980)**

Kostunica, Vojislav (president of Yugoslavia); Belgrade, 3/24/44

Kosygin, Aleksei N. (premier); St. Petersburg, Russia **(1904–1980)**

Kotto, Yaphet (actor); New York City, 11/15/37

Koussevitzky, Serge (Sergei) Alexandrovitch (orchestra conductor); Vishni Volochek, Tver, Russia **(1874–1951)**

Kramer, Stanley E. (film producer, director); New York City **(1913–2001)**

Kraus, Lili (pianist); Budapest **(1905–1986)**
Krause, Peter (actor); Alexandria, Minn., 8/12/65
Kravitz, Lenny (musician); New York City, 5/26/64
Kreisler, Fritz (violinist, composer); Vienna **(1875–1962)**
Kresge, S. S. (merchant); Bald Mount, Pa. **(1867–1966)**
Krips, Josef (orchestra conductor); Vienna **(1902–1974)**
Kristofferson, Kris (singer); Brownsville, Tex., 6/22/36
Kroc, Ray (restaurateur); Chicago **(1902–1984)**
Krupa, Gene (drummer); Chicago **(1909–1973)**
Krupp, Alfred (munitions magnate); Essen, Germany **(1812–1887)**
Kubelik, Rafael (conductor); Bychory, former Czechoslovakia **(1914–1996)**
Kublai Khan (Mongol conqueror) **(1216–1294)**
Kubrick, Stanley (film director, producer); New York City **(1928–1999)**
Kudrow, Lisa (actress); Encino, Calif., 7/30/63
Kuralt, Charles (TV journalist); Wilmington, N.C. **(1934–1997)**
Kurosawa, Akira (film director); Tokyo **(1910–1998)**
Kurtz, Efrem (conductor); St. Petersburg, Russia **(1900–1995)**
Kurtz, Swoosie (actress); Omaha, Nebr., 9/6/44
Kutcher, Ashton (actor); Cedar Rapids, Iowa, 2/7/78

L

LaBelle, Patti (singer, actress); Philadelphia, 5/24/44
LaBute, Neil (director, screenwriter); Detroit, Mich., 3/19/63
Ladd, Cheryl (Cheryl Stoppelmoor) (actress); Huron, S.D., 7/12/51
Ladd, Diane (actress); Meridian, Miss., 11/29/42
Laden, Osama bin (terrorist); Riyadh, Saudi Arabia, c. 1957
Lafayette, Marquis de (Marie Joseph Paul Yves Roch Gilbert du Motier) (military officer); Auvergne, France **(1757–1834)**
Lafitte, Jean (pirate); Bayonne?, France **(1780–1826)**
La Follette, Robert Marin (politician); Primrose, Wis. **(1855–1925)**
La Fontaine, Jean de (poet); Château-Thierry, France **(1621–1695)**
Lagasse, Emeril (chef); Fall River, Mass., 10/15/59
La Guardia, Fiorello Henry (mayor of New York); New York City **(1882–1947)**
Lahti, Christine (actress, director); Birmingham, Mich., 4/4/50
Laine, Frankie (Frank Paul LoVecchio) (singer); Chicago, 3/30/13
Laird, Melvin (ex-secretary of defense); Omaha, Neb., 9/1/22
Lamarck, Chevalier de (Jean Baptiste Pierre Antoine de Monet) (naturalist); Bazantin, France **(1744–1829)**
Lamas, Lorenzo (actor); Los Angeles, 1/20/58
Lamb, Charles (Elia) (essayist); London **(1775–1834)**
L'Amour, Louis (author); Jamestown, N.D. **(1908–1988)**
Lancaster, Burt (actor); New York City **(1913–1994)**
Landau, Martin (actor); Brooklyn, N.Y., 6/20/31
Landers, Ann (Esther Pauline Friedman) (columnist); Sioux City, Iowa **(1918–2002)**
Landon, Michael (Eugene Maurice Orowitz) (actor, director, producer); Forest Hills, Queens, N.Y. **(1936–1991)**
Lane, Abbe (Abigail Francine Lassman) (singer); New York City, 1933
Lane, Burton (songwriter); New York City **(1912–1997)**
Lane, Nathan (Joseph Lane) (actor, singer); Jersey City, N.J., 2/3/56
Lang, Fritz (film director); Vienna **(1890–1976)**
Lange, Hope (actress); Redding Ridge, Conn. **(1933–2003)**
Lange, Jessica (actress); Cloquet, Minn., 4/20/49
Langella, Frank (actor); Bayonne, N.J., 1/1/40
Langmuir, Irving (chemist); Brooklyn, N.Y. **(1881–1957)**
Langtry, Lillie (Emily Le Breton) (actress); Island of Jersey **(1852–1929)**
Lansbury, Angela (actress, producer); London, 10/16/25
Lansing, Robert (Robert Howell Brown) (actor); San Diego, Calif. **(1928–1994)**
Lanza, Mario (Alfred Arnold Cocozza) (singer, actor); Philadelphia **(1921–1959)**
Lao-tse (Li Erh) (philosopher); Honan Province, China **(c. 604–531 B.C.)**
Lardner, Ring (Ringgold Wilmar Lardner) (story writer); Niles, Mich. **(1885–1933)**
La Rouchefoucauld, Francois duc de (author); Paris **(1613–1680)**
Larroquette, John (actor); New Orleans, 11/25/47
Larson, Gary (cartoonist); Tacoma, Wash., 8/14/50
La Salle, Sieur de (Robert Cavelier) (explorer); Rouen, France **(1643–1687)**
Lasch, Christopher (historian, social critic); Omaha, Nebr. **(1932–1994)**
La Tour, Georges de (painter); Vic-sur-Seille, France **(1593–1652)**
Lauder, Estée Josephine Esther Mentzer (beautician, business executive) **(1910–2004)**
Lauer, Matt (TV host); New York City, 12/20/57
Laughton, Charles (actor); Scarborough, England **(1899–1962)**

Lauper, Cyndi (singer); New York City, 6/20/53
Laurel, Stan (Arthur Jefferson) (comedian); Ulverston, England **(1890–1965)**
Laurents, Arthur (playwright); New York City, 7/14/18
Laurie, Piper (Rosetta Jacobs) (actress); Detroit, 1/22/32
Lavigne, Avril (singer, songwriter); Belleville, Ontario, 9/27/84
Lavin, Linda (actress); Portland, Maine, 10/15/37
Lavoisier, Antoine-Laurent (chemist); Paris **(1743–1794)**
Law, Jude (actor); London, England, 12/29/72
Lawford, Peter (actor); London **(1923–1984)**
Lawrence, David Herbert (novelist); Nottingham, England **(1885–1930)**
Lawrence, Jacob (painter); Atantic City, N.J. **(1917–2000)**
Lawrence, Martin (actor); Frankfurt, Germany, 4/16/65
Lawrence, Sharon (actress); Charlotte, N.C., 6/29/62
Lawrence, Steve (Sidney Leibowitz) (singer); Brooklyn, N.Y., 7/8/35
Lawrence of Arabia (Thomas Edward Lawrence, later changed to Shaw) (author, soldier); Tremadoc, Wales **(1888–1935)**
Lawrence, Vicki (actress); Inglewood, Calif., 3/26/49
Leach, Penelope (Balchin) (child psychologist, writer); London, 11/19/37
Leach, Robin (host, producer); London, 8/29/41
Leachman, Cloris (actress); Des Moines, Iowa, 4/30/26
Leadbelly (Huddie Ledbetter) (blues singer, guitarist); Mooringsport, La. **(1885–1949)**
Leakey, Louis Seymour Bazett (anthropologist); Kabete, Kenya **(1903–1972)**
Leakey, Mary (anthropologist); London **(1913–1996)**
Leakey, Richard (paleoanthropologist, wildlife conservationist); Kenya, 12/19/44
Lean, David (film director); Croydon, England **(1908–1991)**
Lear, Edward (nonsense poet); London **(1812–1888)**
Lear, Evelyn (Shulman) (soprano); Brooklyn, N.Y., 1/8/26
Lear, Norman (TV producer); New Haven, Conn., 7/27/22
Learned, Michael (actress); Washington, D.C., 4/9/39
Leary, Denis (actor, screenwriter, film director); Worcester, Mass., 8/18/57
Leary, Timothy (psychologist, LSD advocate); Springfield, Mass. **(1920–1996)**
Leavitt, Mike (secretary of Health and Human Services); Cedar City, Utah, 2/11/51
Le Blanc, Matt (actor); Newton, Mass., 7/25/67
le Carré, John (David John Moore Cornwell) (novelist); Poole, England, 10/19/31
Le Corbusier (Charles Edouard Jeanneret) (architect); La Chaux-de-Fonds, Switzerland **(1887–1965)**
Lee, Ang (film director); Pingtung, Taiwan, 10/23/54
Lee, Bruce (actor); San Francisco **(1940–1973)**
Lee, Christopher (actor); London, 5/27/22
Lee, Manfred B. (pseudonym Ellery Queen) (novelist); Brooklyn, N.Y. **(1905–1971)**
Lee, Peggy (Norma Engstrom) (singer); Jamestown, N.D. **(1920–2002)**
Lee, Robert E(dward) (Confederate general); Stratford Estate, Va. **(1807–1870)**
Lee, Spike (Shelton Jackson Lee) (actor, director, writer, producer); Atlanta, 3/20/57
Leeuwenhoek, Anton van (zoologist); Delft, Netherlands **(1632–1723)**
Lehár, Franz (composer); Komárom, Hungary **(1870–1948)**
Lehman, Herbert H. (governor, senator); New York City **(1878–1963)**
Lehmann, Lotte (soprano); Perleberg, Germany **(1888–1976)**
Lehrer, Jim (TV newscaster); Wichita, Kans., 5/19/34
Leibniz, Gottfried W. von (scientist); Leipzig, Germany **(1646–1716)**
Leibovitz, Annie (photographer); Westbury, Conn., 10/2/49
Leigh, Janet (Jeanette Helen Morrison) (actress); Merced, Calif. **(1927–2004)**
Leigh, Jennifer Jason (Jennifer Morrow) (actress); Los Angeles, 2/5/62
Leigh, Mike (film director, screenwriter); Manchester, England, 2/20/43
Leigh, Vivien (Vivian Mary Hartley) (actress); Darjeeling, India **(1913–1967)**
Leinsdorf, Erich (conductor); Vienna **(1912–1993)**
Lemmon, Jack (actor); Boston **(1925–2001)**
Lenin, Vladimir (Vladimir Ilich Ulyanov) (Soviet leader); Simbirsk, Russia **(1870–1924)**
Lennon, John (singer, songwriter); Liverpool, England **(1940–1980)**
Leno, Jay (comedian, TV host); New Rochelle, N.Y., 4/28/50
Leonard, Sheldon (Sheldon Leonard Bershad) (actor, producer); New York City **(1907–1997)**

Leonardo da Vinci, (painter, scientist); Vinci, Tuscany, Italy **(1452–1519)**

Leoni, Téa (actress); New York City, 2/25/66

Lerner, Alan Jay (lyricist); New York City **(1918–1986)**

Lerner, Max (columnist); Minsk, Russia **(1902–1992)**

Lessing, Doris (novelist); Kermanshah, Iran, 10/22/19

Leto, Jared (actor); Bossier City, La., 12/26/71

Letterman, David (TV host, producer); Indianapolis, 4/12/47

Levant, Oscar (pianist); Pittsburgh **(1906–1972)**

Levenson, Sam (humorist); New York City **(1911–1980)**

Levi, Carlo (novelist); Turin, Italy **(1902–1975)**

Levine, James (artistic director, Metropolitan Opera); Cincinnati, 6/23/43

Levine, Joseph E. (film producer); Boston **(1905–1987)**

Levinson, Barry (screenwriter, director, producer, actor); Baltimore, 4/6/42

Levitt, William (suburbia pioneer); New York City **(1907–1994)**

Lewis, C(live) S(taples) (author); Belfast, Northern Ireland **(1898–1963)**

Lewis, Gilbert Newton (chemist, Nobel laureate); Weymouth, Mass. **(1875–1946)**

Lewis, Jerry (Joseph Levitch) (comedian, film director); Newark, N.J., 3/16/26

Lewis, Jerry Lee (singer); Ferriday, La., 9/29/35

Lewis, John Llewellyn (labor leader); Lucas, Iowa **(1880–1969)**

Lewis, Juliette (actress); Los Angeles, 12/21/73

Lewis, Meriwether (explorer); Albemarle Co., Va. **(1774–1809)**

Lewis, (Percy) Wyndham (artist, writer); Bay of Fundy, Maine (at sea) **(1884–1957)**

Lewis, Shari (Shari Hurwitz) (puppeteer); New York City **(1934–1998)**

Lewis, Sinclair (novelist); Sauk Centre, Minn. **(1885–1951)**

Ley, Willy (science writer); Berlin **(1906–1969)**

Liberace (Wladziu Liberace) (pianist); West Allis, Wis. **(1919–1987)**

Lichtenstein, Roy (painter); New York City **(1923–1997)**

Lie, Trygve Halvdan (first U.N. secretary-general); Oslo **(1896–1968)**

Light, Judith (actress); Trenton, N.J., 2/9/49

Lightfoot, Gordon (singer, songwriter); Orillia, Ont., Canada, 11/17/38

Limbaugh, Rush (political commentator); Cape Girardeau, Mo., 1/12/51

Lin, Maya (architect, sculptor); Athens, Ohio, 10/5/59

Lin Yutang (author); Changchow, China **(1895–1976)**

Lincoln, Abraham (16th U.S. president); Hardin (Larue) County, Ky. **(1809–1865)**

Lind, Jenny (Johanna Maria Lind) (soprano); Stockholm **(1820–1887)**

Lindbergh, Anne Morrow (author); Englewood, N.J. **(1906–2001)**

Lindbergh, Charles A. (aviator); Detroit **(1902–1974)**

Linden, Hal (Harold Lipshitz) (actor); New York City, 3/20/31

Lindsay, Howard (playwright); Waterford, N.Y. **(1889–1968)**

Linkletter, Art (radio-TV personality); Moose Jaw, Sask., Canada, 7/17/12

Linnaeus, Carolus (Carl von Linné) (botanist); Råshult, Sweden **(1707–1778)**

Linney, Laura (actress); New York City, 2/5/64

Liotta, Ray (actor); Union, N.J., 12/18/55

Lipchitz, Jacques (sculptor); Druskieniki, Latvia **(1891–1973)**

Lippi, Fra Filippo (painter); Florence **(1406–1469)**

Lippmann, Walter (columnist, author, political analyst); New York City **(1889–1974)**

Lister, Joseph (1st Baron of Lyme Regis) (surgeon); Upton, England **(1827–1912)**

Liszt, Franz (composer, pianist); Raiding, Hungary **(1811–1886)**

Lithgow, John (actor); Rochester, N.Y., 6/6/45

Little, Rich (impressionist); Ottawa, Ont., Canada, 11/26/38

Livingstone, David (missionary, explorer); Lanarkshire, Scotland **(1813–1873)**

L. L. Cool J (James Todd Smith) (rap artist); New York City, 1/14/68

Llewellyn, Richard (novelist); St. David's, Wales **(1906–1983)**

Lloyd, Jake (actor); Fort Collins, Colo., 3/5/89

Lloyd George, David (Earl of Dwyfor) (statesman); Manchester, England **(1863–1945)**

Lloyd Webber, Andrew (composer); London, 3/22/48

Locke, Alain L. (philosopher); Philadelphia **(1886–1954)**

Locke, John (philosopher); Somersetshire, England **(1632–1704)**

Lockhart, June (actress); New York City, 6/25/25

Locklear, Heather (actress); Los Angeles, 9/25/61

Lodge, Henry Cabot (legislator); Boston **(1850–1924)**

Lodge, Henry Cabot, Jr. (diplomat); Nahant, Mass. **(1902–1985)**

Loesser, Frank (composer); New York City **(1910–1969)**

Loewe, Frederick (composer); Vienna **(1901–1988)**

Logan, Joshua (director, producer); Texarkana, Tex. **(1908–1988)**

Lohan, Lindsay (actress, singer); New York City, 7/2/86

Lollobrigida, Gina (Luigina Lollobrigida) (actress); Subiaco, Italy, 7/4/27

Lombard, Carole (Jane Alice Peters) (actress); Ft. Wayne, Ind. **(1908–1942)**

Lombardo, Guy (band leader); London, Ont., Canada **(1902–1977)**

London, George (baritone); Montreal **(1920–1985)**

London, Jack (John Griffith London) (novelist); San Francisco **(1876–1916)**

Long, Huey Pierce (politician); Winnfield, La. **(1893–1935)**

Longfellow, Henry Wadsworth (poet); Portland, Maine **(1807–1882)**

Longworth, Alice Roosevelt (social figure); New York City **(1884–1980)**

Loos, Anita (novelist); Sissons, Calif. **(1888–1981)**

Lopez, Jennifer (actress, singer); Bronx, N.Y., 7/24/70

Lopez, Trini (singer); Dallas, 5/15/37

Lopez, Vincent (band leader); Brooklyn, N.Y. **(1895–1975)**

Lord, Jack (John Joseph Ryan) (actor); New York City **(1920–1998)**

Loren, Sophia (Sofia Scicolone) (actress); Rome, 9/20/34

Lorenz, Konrad (ethologist); Vienna **(1903–1989)**

Lorre, Peter (Laszlo Löewenstein) (actor); Rosenberg, former Czechoslovakia **(1904–1964)**

Loudon, Dorothy (actress, singer); Boston, 9/17/33

Louis-Dreyfus, Julia (actress); New York City, 1/13/61

Louis XIV (King of France); St.-Germain-en-Laye, France **(1638–1715)**

Louise, Tina (actress); New York City, 2/11/37

Love, Susan (surgeon, oncologist, activist); Long Branch, N.J., 2/9/48

Lovecraft, Howard Phillips (author); Providence, R.I. **(1890–1937)**

Lovett, Lyle (country singer, songwriter); Klein, Tex., 11/1/57

Lowe, Rob (actor); Charlottesville, Va., 3/17/64

Lowell, Amy (poet); Brookline, Mass. **(1874–1925)**

Lowell, James Russell (poet); Cambridge, Mass. **(1819–1891)**

Lowell, Robert (poet); Boston **(1917–1977)**

Loy, Myrna (Myrna Williams) (actress); nr. Helena, Mont. **(1905–1993)**

Loyola, St. Ignatius of (Iñigo de Oñez y Loyola) (founder of Jesuits); Gúipuzcoa Province, Spain **(1491– 1556)**

Lubitsch, Ernst (film director); Berlin **(1892–1947)**

Lucas, George (film director); Modesto, Calif., 5/14/44

Lucci, Susan (actress); Scarsdale, N.Y., 12/23/46

Luce, Clare Boothe (playwright, former ambassador); New York City **(1903–1987)**

Luce, Henry Robinson (editor, publisher); Tengchow, China **(1898–1967)**

Luciano, Charles "Lucky" (Salvatore Lucania) (mobster); Sicily, Italy **(1897–1962)**

Ludlum, Robert (author); New York City **(1927–2001)**

Lugosi, Béla (Béla Blasko) (actor); Lugos, Hungary **(1888–1956)**

Lukas, J. Anthony (author); New York City **(1933–1997)**

Lukas, Paul (actor); Budapest **(1895–1971)**

Lully, Jean Baptiste (French composer); Florence **(1632–1687)**

Lumet, Sidney (director); Philadelphia, 6/25/24

Lunden, Joan (TV host); Fair Oaks, Calif., 9/19/50

Lunt, Alfred (actor); Milwaukee **(1892–1977)**

Lupino, Ida (actress, director); London **(1918–1995)**

LuPone, Patti (actress, singer); Northport, N.Y., 4/21/49

Luther, Martin (religious reformer); Eisleben, East Germany **(1483–1546)**

Lynch, David (film director); Missoula, Mont., 1/20/46

Lynn, Loretta (singer); Butcher's Hollow, Ky., 4/14/35

M

Ma, Yo-Yo (cellist); Paris, 10/7/55

Maazel, Lorin (conductor); Neuilly, France, 3/5/30

MacArthur, Charles (playwright); Scranton, Pa. **(1895–1956)**

MacArthur, Douglas (five-star general); Little Rock Barracks, Ark. **(1880–1964)**

MacArthur, James (actor); Los Angeles, 12/8/37

Macaulay, Thomas Babington (author); Rothley Temple, England **(1800–1859)**

MacDermot, Galt (composer); Montreal, 12/19/28

MacDonald, James Ramsay (statesman); Lossiemouth, Scotland **(1866–1937)**

MacDonald, Jeanette (actress, soprano); Philadelphia **(1907–1965)**

Macdonald, Ross (Kenneth Millar) (mystery writer); Los Gatos, Calif. **(1915–1983)**

MacDowell, Edward Alexander (composer); New York City **(1861–1908)**

MacDowell, Andie (Rosalie Anderson MacDowell) (actress); Gaffney, S.C., 4/21/58
MacFadden, Bernarr (physical culturist); nr. Mill Spring, Mo. **(1868–1955)**
Machaut, Guillaume de (composer); Marchault, France **(1300–1377)**
Machiavelli, Niccolò (political philosopher); Florence, Italy **(1469–1527)**
Mackie, Bob (designer); Monterey Park, Calif., 3/24/40
MacLaine, Shirley (Shirley MacLean Beaty) (actress); Richmond, Va., 4/24/34
MacLeish, Archibald (poet); Glencoe, Ill. **(1892–1982)**
Macmillan, Harold (ex-prime minister); London **(1894–1986)**
MacMurray, Fred (actor); Kankakee, Ill. **(1908–1991)**
MacNeil, Cornell (baritone); Minneapolis, 9/24/22
MacNeil, Robert (TV newscaster); Montreal, 1/19/31
MacNicol, Peter (actor); Dallas, 4/10/54
Macpherson, Elle (Eleanor Gow) (model, actress); Sydney, Australia, 3/29/64
MacRae, Gordon (singer, actor); East Orange, N.J. **(1921–1986)**
MacRae, Sheila (comedienne); London, 9/24/24
Madison, James (4th U.S. president); Port Conway, Va. **(1751–1836)**
Madonna (Madonna Louise Ciccone) (singer, actress); Bay City, Mich., 8/16/58
Maeterlinck, Count Maurice (author); Ghent, Belgium **(1862–1949)**
Magellan, Ferdinand (Fernando de Magalhaes) (navigator); Sabrosa, Portugal **(c. 1480–1521)**
Magliozzi, Ray ("Car Talk" host); Cambridge, Mass., 3/30/49
Magliozzi, Tom ("Car Talk" host); Cambridge, Mass., 6/28/37
Magritte, René (painter); Belgium **(1898–1967)**
Magsaysay, Ramón (statesman); Iba, Luzon, Philippines **(1907–1957)**
Maguire, Tobey (actor); Santa Monica, Calif., 6/27/75
Mahan, Alfred Thayer (naval historian); West Point, N.Y. **(1840–1914)**
Maher, Bill (TV host); New York City, 1/20/56
Mahler, Gustav (composer, conductor); Kalischt, Czechoslovakia **(1860–1911)**
Mahoney, John (actor); Manchester, England, 6/20/40
Mailer, Norman (novelist); Long Branch, N.J., 1/31/23
Maillol, Aristide (sculptor); Banyuls-sur-Mer, Rousillion, France **(1861–1944)**
Maimonides, Moses (Jewish philosopher); Cordoba, Spain **(1135–1204)**
Mainbocher (Main Rousseau Bocher) (fashion designer); Chicago **(1891–1976)**
Majors, Lee (Harvey Lee Yeary) (actor); Wyandotte, Mich., 4/23/40
Makarova, Natalia (ballet dancer); Leningrad (St. Petersburg), Russia, 11/21/40
Makeba, Miriam (singer); Johannesburg, South Africa, 3/4/32
Malamud, Bernard (novelist); Brooklyn, N.Y. **(1914–1986)**
Malcolm X (Malcolm Little; el Hajj Malik el-Shabazz) (Black nationalist, religious leader); Omaha, Neb. **(1925–1965)**
Malden, Karl (Karl Mladen Sekulovich) (actor); Chicago, 3/22/13
Malkovich, John (actor); Christopher, Ill., 12/9/53
Mallarmé, Stephane (poet, essayist); Paris **(1842–1898)**
Malle, Louis (director); Thumeries, France **(1932–1995)**
Malraux, André (author); Paris **(1901–1976)**
Malthus, Thomas Robert (economist); nr. Dorking, England **(1766–1834)**
Maltin, Leonard (film critic and historian); New York City, 12/18/50
Mamet, David (playwright); Chicago, 11/30/47
Manchester, Melissa (singer); Bronx, N.Y., 2/15/51
Manchester, William (writer); Attleboro, Mass. **(1922–2004)**
Mancini, Henry (composer, conductor); Cleveland **(1924–1994)**
Mandela, Nelson (Rolihlahla) (former president of South Africa); Umtata, Transkei, 7/18/18
Mandela, Winnie (Nomzamo) (South African political activist); Pondoland district, of the Transkei, 1936?
Mandrell, Barbara (singer); Houston, 12/25/48
Manet, Edouard (painter); Paris **(1832–1883)**
Mangione, Chuck (hornist, pianist, composer); Rochester, N.Y., 11/29/40
Manheim, Camryn (actress); New York City, 3/8/61
Manilow, Barry (singer); Brooklyn, N.Y., 6/17/46
Mankiewicz, Frank F. (columnist); New York City, 5/16/24
Mankiewicz, Joseph L. (film writer, director); Wilkes-Barre, Pa. **(1909–1993)**
Mann, Horace (educator); Franklin, Mass. **(1796–1859)**
Mann, Thomas (novelist); Lübeck, Germany **(1875–1955)**
Mannes, Marya (writer); New York City **(1904–1990)**

Mansfield, Jayne (Jayne Palmer) (actress); Bryn Mawr, Pa. **(1933–1967)**
Mansfield, Katherine (story writer); Wellington, New Zealand **(1888–1923)**
Manson, Marilyn (Brian Warner) (rock musician); Canton, Ohio, 1/5/69
Mantegna, Andrea (painter); Isola di Carturo, Italy **(1431–1506)**
Mantegna, Joe (actor); Chicago, 11/13/47
Mantovani, Annunzio (conductor); Venice **(1905–1980)**
Mao Zedong (Tse-tung) (Chinese leader); Shao Shan, China **(1893– 1976)**
Mapplethorpe, Robert (photographer); Floral Park, Queens, N.Y. **(1946–1989)**
Marat, Jean Paul (French revolutionist); Boudry, Neuchâtel, Switzerland **(1743–1793)**
Marceau, Marcel (mime); Strasbourg, France, 3/22/23
Marceau, Sophie (actress); Paris, 11/17/66
March, Fredric (Frederick Bickel) (actor); Racine, Wis. **(1897–1975)**
Marchand, Nancy (actress); Buffalo, N.Y. **(1928–2000)**
Marconi, Guglielmo (inventor); Bologna, Italy **(1874–1937)**
Marcus Aurelius (Marcus Annius Verus) (Roman emperor); Rome **(121–180)**
Marcus, Rudolph Arthur (chemist, Nobel laureate); Montreal, 7/21/23
Marcuse, Herbert (philosopher); Berlin **(1898–1979)**
Margaret Rose (princess of England); Glamis Castle, Angus, Scotland, 8/21/30
Margrethe II (queen of Denmark); Copenhagen, 4/16/40
Margulies, Julianna (actress); Spring Valley, N.Y., 6/8/65
Marie Antoinette (Josephe Jeanne Marie Antoinette) (queen of France); Vienna **(1755 –1793)**
Marisol (Escobar) (Venezuelan-American sculptor); Paris, 1930
Markham, Edwin (poet); Oregon City, Ore. **(1852–1940)**
Markova, Dame Alicia (Lilian Alice Marks) (ballet dancer); London **(1910–2004)**
Marley, Bob (singer, songwriter); Kingston, Jamaica **(1945–1981)**
Marlowe, Christopher (dramatist); Canterbury, England **(1564–1593)**
Marquand, J(ohn) P(hillips) (novelist); Wilmington, Del. **(1893–1960)**
Marquette, Jacques (missionary, explorer); Laon, France **(1637–1675)**
Marriner, Neville (conductor); Lincoln, England, 4/15/24
Marsalis, Wynton (musician); New Orleans, 10/18/61
Marshall, E. G. (actor); Owatonna, Minn. **(1910–1998)**
Marshall, Garry (director, producer, screenwriter, actor); New York City, 11/13/34
Marshall, George Catlett (general); Uniontown, Pa. **(1880–1959)**
Marshall, Herbert (actor); London **(1890–1968)**
Marshall, John (jurist); nr. Germantown, Va. **(1755–1835)**
Marshall, Penny (Penny Marscharelli) (actress, director, producer); Bronx, N.Y., 10/15/42
Marshall, Thurgood (U.S. Supreme Court justice); Baltimore **(1908–1993)**
Martin, Dean (Dino Crocetti) (singer, actor); Steubenville, Ohio **(1917–1995)**
Martin, Mary (singer, actress); Weatherford, Tex. **(1913–1990)**
Martin, Steve (actor, writer, producer); Waco, Tex., 8/14/45
Martin, Tony (Alvin Morris) (singer); San Francisco, 12/25/12
Martinelli, Giovanni (tenor); Montagnana, Italy **(1885–1969)**
Martinez, Melquiades R. (ex-secretary of Housing and Development); Sagua La Grande, Cuba, 10/23/46
Martins, Peter (dancer, choreographer); Copenhagen, 10/27/45
Marvell, Andrew (poet); Winestead, England **(1621–1678)**
Marvin, Lee (actor); New York City **(1924–1987)**
Marx, Chico (Leonard) (comedian); New York City **(1887–1961)**
Marx, Groucho (Julius) (comedian); New York City **(1890–1977)**
Marx, Harpo (Arthur) (comedian); New York City **(1888–1964)**
Marx, Karl (Socialist writer); Treves, Germany **(1818–1883)**
Marx, Zeppo (Herbert) (comedian); New York City **(1901–1979)**
Mary Stuart (Mary, Queen of Scots) (queen of Scotland); Linlithgow, Scotland **(1542–1587)**
Masaccio, (Tommaso di Giovanni di Simone Cassai) (painter); San Giovanni Valdarno, Tuscany **(1401–c. 1428)**
Masaryk, Jan Garrigue (statesman); Prague **(1886–1948)**
Masaryk, Thomas Garrigue (statesman); Hodonin, Czech Republic **(1850–1937)**
Masefield, John (poet); Ledbury, England **(1878–1967)**
Masekela, Hugh (trumpeter); Wilbank, South Africa, 4/4/39
Mason, Jackie (Jacob Moshe Maza) (comedian); Sheboygan, Wis., 6/9/31
Mason, James (actor); Huddersfield, England **(1909–1984)**
Mason, Marsha (actress); St. Louis, 4/3/42

Massenet, Jules Emile Frédéric (composer); Montaud, France **(1842–1912)**

Massine, Léonide (choreographer); Moscow **(1896–1979)**

Masters, Edgar Lee (poet); Garnett, Kans. **(1869–1950)**

Masters, William (human sexuality expert); Cleveland **(1915–2001)**

Masterson, Mary Stuart (actress, writer, director); New York City, 6/28/66

Mastroianni, Marcello (actor); Fontana Liri, Italy **(1924–1996)**

Mather, Cotton (clergyman); Boston **(1663–1728)**

Mathis, Johnny (singer); Gilmer, Texas, 9/30/35

Matisse, Henri (painter); Le Cateau, France **(1869–1954)**

Matthau, Walter (Walter Matuschanskayasky) (actor); New York City **(1920–2000)**

Matthews, Dave (singer, guitarist); Johannesburg, South Africa, 1/9/67

Mature, Victor (actor); Louisville, Ky. **(1915–1999)**

Maugham, W(illiam) Somerset (author); Paris **(1874–1965)**

Mauldin, Bill (political cartoonist); Mountain Park, N.M. **(1921–2003)**

Maupassant, Henri René Albert Guy de (story writer); Normandy, France **(1850–1893)**

Maurois, André (Emile Herzog) (author); Elbauf, France **(1885–1967)**

Maximilian (Ferdinand Maximilian Joseph) (emperor of Mexico); Vienna (**1832–1867)**

Maxwell, James Clerk (physicist); Edinburgh, Scotland **(1831–1879)**

Maxwell, (Ian) Robert (publisher); Selo Slatina, Czechoslavakia **(1923–1991)**

May, Elaine (Elaine Berlin) (entertainer, writer); Philadelphia, 4/21/32

May, Rollo (psychologist); Ada, Ohio **(1909–1994)**

Mayer, Louis B. (movie executive); Minsk, Russia **(1885–1957)**

Mayo, Charles H. (surgeon); Rochester, Minn. **(1865–1939)**

Mayo, Charles W. (surgeon); Rochester, Minn. **(1898–1968)**

Mayo, Virginia (Jones) (actress); St. Louis **(1920–2005)**

Mayo, William J. (surgeon); Le Sueur, Minn. **(1861–1939)**

Mayron, Melanie (actress); Philadelphia, 10/20/52

Mazzini, Giuseppe (patriot); Genoa **(1805–1872)**

McBride, Patricia (ballet dancer); Teaneck, N.J., 8/23/42

McCallum, David (actor); Glasgow, Scotland, 9/19/33

McCambridge, Mercedes (actress); Joliet, Ill. **(1918–2004)**

McCarthy, Eugene J. (ex-senator); Watkins, Minn., 3/29/16

McCarthy, Joseph Raymond (senator); Grand Chute, Wis. **(1908–1957)**

McCarthy, Mary (novelist); Seattle **(1912–1989)**

McCartney, Linda (photographer, singer); New York City **(1941–1998)**

McCartney, Paul (singer, songwriter); Liverpool, England, 6/18/42

McClanahan, Rue (actress); Healdton, Okla., 2/21/35

McClellan, George Brinton (general); Philadelphia **(1826–1885)**

McClintock, Barbara (geneticist, Nobel laureate) **(1902–1992)**

McCloy, John J. (lawyer, banker); Philadelphia **(1895–1989)**

McCormack, John (tenor); Athlone, Ireland **(1884–1945)**

McCormack, John W. (ex-Speaker of House); Boston **(1891–1980)**

McCormick, Cyrus Hall (inventor); Rockbridge County, Va. **(1809–1884)**

McCourt, Frank (writer); Brooklyn, N.Y., 8/19/30

McCracken, James (dramatic tenor); Gary, Ind. **(1926–1988)**

McCrea, Joel (actor); Los Angeles **(1905–1990)**

McCullers, Carson (novelist); Columbus, Ga. **(1917–1967)**

McCullough, David (author, historian); Pittsburgh, 7/7/33

McDermott, Dylan (actor); Waterbury, Conn., 10/26/62

McDormand, Frances (actress); Illinois, 6/23/57

McDowall, Roddy (actor); London **(1928–1998)**

McDowell, Malcolm (actor); Leeds, England, 6/15/43

McEwan, Ian (writer); Aldershot, England, 5/21/48

McFadden, James A. (actress); Cuyahoga Falls, Ohio, 3/2/49

McGavin, Darren (actor); San Joaquin, Calif., 5/7/22

McGillis, Kelly (actress); Newport Beach, Calif., 7/9/57

McGinley, Phyllis (poet, writer); Ontario, Ore. **(1905–1978)**

McGoohan, Patrick (actor); Astoria, Queens, N.Y., 3/19/28

McGovern, Elizabeth (actress); Evanston, Ill., 7/18/61

McGovern, Maureen (singer); Youngstown, Ohio, 7/27/49

McGregor, Ewan (actor); Crieff, Scotland, 3/31/71

McKellen, Ian (actor); Burnley, England, 5/25/39

McKinley, William (25th U.S. president); Niles, Ohio **(1843–1901)**

McKuen, Rod (singer, composer); Oakland, Calif., 4/29/33

McLachlan, Sarah (singer, songwriter); Halifax, N.S., 1/28/68

McLaughlin, John (guitarist); Yorkshire, England, 1/4/42

McLean, Don (singer, songwriter); New Rochelle, N.Y., 10/2/45

McLuhan, Marshall (Herbert Marshall) (communications writer); Edmonton, Alta., Canada **(1911–1980)**

McMahon, Ed (TV personality); Detroit, 3/6/23

McMurtry, Larry (novelist); Wichita Falls, Tex., 6/3/36

McQueen, Butterfly (Thelma) (actress); Tampa, Fla. **(1911–1995)**

McQueen, Steve (Terence Stephen McQueen) (actor); Beech Grove, Indiana **(1930–1980)**

McRaney, Gerald (actor); Collins, Miss., 8/19/47

McTeer, Janet (actress); York, England, 1962

Mead, Margaret (anthropologist); Philadelphia **(1901–1978)**

Meadows, Audrey (actress); Wu Chang, China **(1924–1996)**

Meadows, Jayne (actress); Wu Chang, China, 9/27/26

Meaney, Colm (actor); Dublin, 5/30/53

Meany, George (labor leader); New York City **(1894–1980)**

Meara, Anne (actress); New York City, 9/20/29

Medici, Lorenzo de' (called Lorenzo the Magnificent) (Florentine ruler); Florence, Italy **(1449–1492)**

Mehta, Zubin (conductor); Bombay (Mumbai), 4/29/36

Meir, Golda (Golda Myerson, nee Mabovitz) (ex-premier of Israel); Kiev, Ukraine **(1898–1978)**

Melba, Dame Nellie (Helen Porter Mitchell) (soprano); nr. Melbourne, Australia **(1861–1931)**

Melchior, Lauritz (Lebrecht Hommel) (heroic tenor); Copenhagen **(1890–1973)**

Mellon, Andrew William (financier); Pittsburgh **(1855–1937)**

Melville, Herman (novelist); New York City **(1819–1891)**

Mencken, Henry Louis (writer); Baltimore **(1880–1956)**

Mendel, Gregor Johann (geneticist); Heinzendorf, Austrian Silesia **(1822–1884)**

Mendeleyev, Dmitri Ivanovich (chemist); Tobolsk, Russia **(1834–1907)**

Mendelssohn-Bartholdy, Jakob Ludwig Felix (composer); Hamburg **(1809–1847)**

Mendès-France, Pierre (ex-Premier); Paris **(1905–1982)**

Mengele, Josef (Nazi, "Angel of Death"); Günzberg, Germany **(1911–1979)**

Mennin, Peter (Peter Mennini) (composer); Erie, Pa. **(1923–1983)**

Menninger, William C. (psychiatrist); Topeka, Kans. **(1899–1966)**

Menotti, Gian Carlo (composer); Cadegliano, Italy, 7/7/11

Menuhin, Yehudi (violinist, conductor); New York City **(1916–1999)**

Menzies, Robert Gordon (ex-prime minister); Jeparit, Australia **(1894–1978)**

Mercer, Johnny (songwriter); Savannah, Ga. **(1909–1976)**

Mercer, Mabel (singer); Burton-on-Trent, England **(1900–1984)**

Merchant, Ismail (Ismail Noormohamed Abdul Rehman) (film producer); Bombay (Mumbai) **(1936–2005)**

Merchant, Natalie (singer, songwriter); Jamestown, N.Y., 10/26/63

Mercury, Freddie (Farookh Bulsara) (musician, singer); Zanzibar **(1946–1991)**

Meredith, Burgess (actor); Cleveland **(1908–1997)**

Meredith, James (author, civil-rights leader); Kosciusko, Miss., 6/26/23

Merman, Ethel (Ethel Zimmerman) (singer, actress); Astoria, Queens, N.Y. **(1909–1984)**

Merrick, David (David Margulois) (stage producer); St. Louis **(1911–2000)**

Merton, Thomas (clergyman, writer); France **(1915–1968)**

Mesmer, Franz Anton (physician); Itzmang, nr. Constance, Germany **(1733–1815)**

Mesta, Perle (social figure); Sturgis, Mich. **(1889–1975)**

Metacom, (King Philip) (Wampanoag Indian sachem); southeastern Mass. **(1640–1676)**

Metternich, Prince Klemens Wenzel Nepomuk Lothar von (statesman); Coblenz, Germany **(1773–1859)**

Mfume, Kweisi (Frizzell Gray) (politician, NAACP leader); Baltimore, 10/24/48

Michaels, Lorne (producer); Toronto, 11/17/44

Michelangelo Buonarroti (painter, sculptor, architect); Caprese, Italy **(1475–1564)**

Michener, James A. (novelist); New York City **(1907–1997)**

Mickiewicz, Adam (Polish poet); Zozie, Belorussia (Belarus) **(1798–1855)**

Midler, Bette (singer, actress, producer); Honolulu, 12/1/45

Mielziner, Jo (stage designer); Paris **(1901–1976)**

Mifune, Toshiro (actor, film producer); Tsingtao, China **(1920–1997)**

Mies van der Rohe, Ludwig (architect, designer); Aachen, Germany **(1886–1969)**

Mikoyan, Anastas I. (diplomat); Sanain, Armenia **(1895–1978)**

Milano, Alyssa (actress); Brooklyn, New York, 12/19/72

Milhaud, Darius (composer); Aix-en-Provence, France **(1892–1974)**

Milk, Harvey (activist); Long Island, N.Y. **(1931–1978)**

Mill, John Stuart (philosopher); London **(1806–1873)**

Milland, Ray (Reginald Truscott-Jones) (actor); Neath, Wales **(1907–1986)**

Millay, Edna St. Vincent (poet); Rockland, Maine **(1892–1950)**

Miller, Ann (Lucille Ann Collier) (dancer, actress); Cherino, Tex. **(1923–2004)**

Miller, Arthur (playwright); New York City **(1915–2005)**

Miller, Glenn (band leader); Clarinda, Iowa **(1904–1944)**

Miller, Henry (novelist); New York City **(1891–1980)**

Miller, Jason (John Miller) (playwright, actor); New York City **(1939–2001)**

Miller, Mitch (Mitchell) (musician); Rochester, N.Y., 7/4/11

Miller, Roger (singer); Fort Worth **(1936–1992)**

Millet, Jean François (painter); Gruchy, France **(1814–1875)**

Millett, Kate (feminist, writer); St. Paul, Minn., 9/14/34

Millikan, Robert A. (physicist); Morrison, Ill. **(1869–1953)**

Mills, Donna (actress); Chicago, 12/11/41

Mills, Hayley (actress); London, 4/18/46

Mills, John (actor); Felixstowe, England **(1908–2005)**

Mills, Juliet (actress); London, 11/21/41

Milne, A(lan) A(lexander) (author); London **(1882–1956)**

Milner, Martin (actor); Detroit, 12/28/31

Milnes, Sherrill (baritone); Downers Grove, Ill., 1/10/35

Milosevic, Slobodan (Yugoslav President); Pozarevac, Serbia, 8/29/41

Milstein, Nathan (concert violinist); Odessa, Ukraine **(1904–1992)**

Milton, John (poet); London **(1608–1674)**

Mineta, Norman Y. (secretary of Transportation); San Jose, Calif., 11/12/31

Mingus, Charles (jazz composer); Nogales, Ariz. **(1922–1979)**

Minnelli, Liza (singer, actress); Hollywood, Calif., 3/12/46

Minnelli, Vincente (film director); Chicago **(1913–1986)**

Minuit, Peter (Governor of New Amsterdam); Wesel, Germany **(1580–1638)**

Miranda, Carmen (Maria do Carmo da Cunha) (singer, dancer); Lisbon **(1909–1955)**

Miró, Joan (painter); Barcelona **(1893–1983)**

Mirren, Helen (Ilynea Lydia Mironoff) (actress); London, 7/26/45

Mitchell, John N. (former Attorney General); Detroit **(1913–1988)**

Mitchell, Joni (Roberta Joan Anderson) (singer, songwriter); Ft. Macleod, Alb., Canada, 11/7/43

Mitchell, Margaret (novelist); Atlanta **(1900–1949)**

Mitchell, Maria (astronomer); Nantucket, Mass. **(1818–1889)**

Mitchum, Robert (actor); Bridgeport, Conn. **(1917–1997)**

Mitropoulos, Dimitri (orchestra conductor); Athens **(1896–1960)**

Mitterand, François (Maurice) (ex-prime minister of France); Jarnac, France **(1916–1996)**

Mix, Tom (actor); Mix Run, Pa. **(1880–1940)**

Miyazaki, Hayao (director, animator); Tokyo, Japan, 1/5/41

Mobutu Sese Seko (Zairean dictator); Lisala, Congo **(1930–1997)**

Moby (Richard Melville Hall) (musician); Darien, Conn., 9/11/65

Modigliani, Amedeo (painter); Leghorn, Italy **(1884–1920)**

Moffo, Anna (soprano); Wayne, Pa., 6/27/34

Mohammed (prophet); Mecca, Saudi Arabia **(570–632)**

Molière (Jean Baptiste Poquelin) (dramatist); Paris **(1622–1673)**

Molina, Mario (chemist, Nobel laureate); Mexico City, 3/19/43

Moll, Richard (actor); Pasadena, Calif., 1/13/43?

Molnar, Ferenc (dramatist); Budapest **(1878–1952)**

Molotov, Vyacheslav M. (V. M. Skryabin) (diplomat); Kukarka, Russia **(1890–1986)**

Mondrian, Piet (painter); Amersfoort, Netherlands **(1872–1944)**

Monet, Claude (painter); Paris **(1840–1926)**

Monica Monica Arnold (singer); Atlanta, Ga., 10/24/80

Monk, Meredith (choreographer, composer, performing artist); Lima, Peru, 11/20/42

Monk, Thelonious (pianist); Rocky Mount, N.C. **(1918–1982)**

Monroe, James (5th U.S. president); Westmoreland County, Va. **(1758–1831)**

Monroe, Marilyn (Norma Jean Mortenson or Baker) (actress); Los Angeles **(1926–1962)**

Monsarrat, Nicholas (novelist); Liverpool, England **(1910–1979)**

Montaigne, Michel Eyquem de (essayist); nr. Bordeaux, France **(1533–1592)**

Montalban, Ricardo (actor); Mexico City, 11/25/20

Montand, Yves (Ivo Livi) (actor, singer); Florence, Italy **(1921–1991)**

Montesquieu, Charles-Louis de Secondat, baron de La Brède and de (philosopher); nr. Bordeaux, France **(1689–1755)**

Montessori, Maria (physician, educator); Chiaravalle, Italy **(1870–1952)**

Monteux, Pierre (conductor); Paris **(1875–1964)**

Monteverdi, Claudio (composer); Cremona Italy **(1567–1643)**

Montezuma II (Aztec emperor); Mexico **(1466–1520)**

Montgomery, Elizabeth (actress); Hollywood, Calif. **(1933–1995)**

Montgomery, Robert (Henry, Jr.) (actor); Beacon, N.Y. **(1904–1981)**

Montgomery of Alamein, 1st Viscount of Hindhead (Sir Bernard Law Montgomery) (military leader); London **(1887–1976)**

Montoya, Carlos (guitarist); Madrid **(1903–1993)**

Moore, Clayton (Jack Moore) (actor); Chicago **(1914–1999)**

Moore, Clement Clarke (author); New York City **(1779–1863)**

Moore, Demi (Demi Guynes) (actress); Roswell, N.M., 11/11/62

Moore, Dudley (actor, writer, musician); Dagenham, England **(1935–2002)**

Moore, Grace (soprano); Jellico, Tenn. **(1901–1947)**

Moore, Henry (sculptor); Castleford, England **(1898–1986)**

Moore, Julianne (actress); Fayetteville, N.C., 12/3/60

Moore, Marianne (poet); Kirkwood, Mo. **(1887–1972)**

Moore, Mary Tyler (actress); Brooklyn, N.Y., 12/29/36

Moore, Melba (Beatrice) (singer, actress); New York City, 10/27/45

Moore, Michael (director, writer, activist); Davison, Mich., 4/23/54

Moore, Roger (actor); London, 10/14/27

Moore, Thomas (poet); Dublin **(1779–1852)**

Moorehead, Agnes (actress); Clinton, Mass. **(1906–1974)**

Moranis, Rick (actor); Toronto, 4/18/53

More, Henry (philosopher); Grantham, England **(1614–1687)**

More, Sir Thomas (statesman, author); London **(1478–1535)**

Moreno, Rita (Rosita Dolores Alverio) (actress); Humacao, P.R., 12/11/31

Morgan, Harry (Harry Bratsburg) (actor); Detroit, 4/10/15

Morgan, John Pierpont (financier); Hartford, Conn. **(1837–1913)**

Moriarty, Michael (actor); Detroit, 4/5/41

Morini, Erica (concert violinist); Vienna **(1904–1995)**

Morison, Samuel Eliot (historian); Boston **(1887–1976)**

Morissette, Alanis (singer, songwriter); Ottawa, Ontario, 6/1/74

Morita, Pat (Noriyuki Morita) (actor); Berkeley, Calif., 8/28/32

Morley, Christopher Darlington (novelist); Haverford, Pa. **(1890–1957)**

Morley, Robert (actor); Semley, England **(1908–1992)**

Morris, Mark (choreographer); Seattle, 8/29/56

Morris, William (poet, craftsman); Walthamstow, England **(1834–1896)**

Morrison, Jim (James Douglas Morrison) (singer, songwriter); Melbourne, Fla. **(1943–1971)**

Morrison, Toni (Chloe Anthony Wofford) (novelist); Lorain, Ohio, 2/18/31

Morrison, Van (singer); Belfast, Northern Ireland, 8/31/45

Morse, Marston (mathematician); Waterville, Maine **(1892–1977)**

Morse, Samuel Finley Breese (painter, inventor); Charlestown, Mass. **(1791–1872)**

Morton, Jelly Roll (Ferdinand Joseph La Menthe) (jazz composer); New Orleans **(1890–1941)**

Mos Def (Dante Smith) (rapper, actor); Brooklyn, N.Y., 12/11/73

Moseley-Braun, Carol (U.S. Senator); Chicago, 8/16/47

Moses, Grandma (Mrs. Anna Mary Robertson Moses) (painter); Greenwich, N.Y. **(1860–1961)**

Moses, Robert (urban planner); New Haven, Conn. **(1888–1981)**

Moss, Kate (model); London, England, 1/16/74

Mostel, Zero (Samuel Joel Mostel) (actor); Brooklyn, N.Y. **(1915–1977)**

Mother Teresa (Gonxha Agnes Bojaxhiu) (nun); Skopje, Macedonia **(1910–1997)**

Motherwell, Robert (artist, "action" painter); Aberdeen, Wash. **(1915–1991)**

Mott, Lucretia (Coffin) (feminist, reformer, abolitionist); Nantucket, Mass. **(1793–1880)**

Moussorgsky, Modest Petrovich (composer); Karev, Russia **(1839–1881)**

Moyers, Bill D. (Billy Don) (journalist); Hugo, Okla., 6/5/34

Moynihan, Daniel Patrick (New York senator); Tulsa, Okla. **(1927–2003)**

Mozart, Wolfgang Amadeus (Johannes Chrysostomus Wolfgangus Theophilus Mozart) (composer); Salzburg, Austria **(1756–1791)**

Mudd, Roger (TV newscaster); Washington, D.C., 2/9/28

Muggeridge, Malcolm (Thomas) (writer); Croydon, England **(1903–1990)**

Muhammad (founder of Islam); Mecca, Saudi Arabia **(c. 570–632)**

Muhammad, Elijah (Elijah Poole) (religious leader); Sandersville, Ga. **(1897–1975)**

Mulgrew, Kate (actress); Dubuque, Iowa, 4/29/55

Mulhare, Edward (actor); Ireland **(1923–1997)**

Mulliken, Robert Sanderson (chemist, Nobel laureate); Newburyport, Mass. **(1896–1986)**

Mulroney, Dermot (actor, musician, producer); Alexandria, Va., 10/31/63

Mumford, Lewis (cultural historian, city planner); Flushing, Queens, N.Y. **(1895–1990)**

Munch, Edvard (painter); Löten, Norway **(1863–1944)**

Munchhausen, Karl Friedrich Hieronymus, baron von (anecdotist); Hannover, Germany **(1720–1797)**

Muni, Paul (Muni Weisenfreund) (actor); Lemburg, Austria **(1895–1967)**

Muniz, Frankie (actor); Ridgewood, N.J., 12/5/85
Muñoz Marin, Luis (ex-governor of Puerto Rico); San Juan, P.R. **(1898–1980)**
Munsel, Patrice (soprano); Spokane, Wash., 5/14/25
Murdoch, Iris (novelist); Dublin **(1919–1999)**
Murdoch, Rupert (publisher); Melbourne, Australia, 3/11/31
Murillo, Bartolomé Esteban (painter); Seville, Spain **(1617–1682)**
Murphy, Audie (actor, war hero); Kingston, Tex. **(1924–1971)**
Murphy, Eddie (actor, comedian); Brooklyn, N.Y., 4/3/61
Murphy, George (actor, dancer, ex-senator); New Haven, Conn. **(1902–1992)**
Murray, Arthur (dance teacher); New York City **(1895–1991)**
Murray, Bill (actor, comedian); Wilmette, Ill., 9/21/50
Murray, Kathryn (dance teacher); Jersey City, N.J. **(1906–1999)**
Murrow, Edward R. (commentator, government official); Greensboro, N.C. **(1908–1965)**
Musil, Robert (novelist); Klagenfurt, Austria **(1880–1942)**
Muskie, Edmund (political figure); Rumford, Maine **(1914–1996)**
Mussolini, Benito (Italian dictator); Dovia, Forli, Italy **(1883–1945)**
Muti, Riccardo (orchestra conductor); Naples, Italy, 7/28/41
Mutter, Anne-Sophie (violinist); Rheinfelden, Germany, 6/29/63
Myers, Mike (actor, writer, comedian); Scarborough, Ont., Canada, 5/25/63
Myerson, Bess (consumer advocate); Bronx, N.Y., 7/16/24
Myrdal, Gunnar (sociologist, economist); Gustaf Parish, Sweden **(1898–1987)**

N

Nabokov, Vladimir (novelist); St. Petersburg, Russia **(1899–1977)**
Nabors, Jim (actor, singer); Sylacauga, Ala., 6/12/32
Nader, Ralph (consumer advocate); Winsted, Conn., 2/27/34
Nair, Mira (director, screenwriter); Bhubaneswar, India, 10/15/57
Nash, Graham (singer); Blackpool, England, 1942
Nash, Ogden (poet); Rye, N.Y. **(1902–1971)**
Nasser, Gamal Abdel (statesman); Beni Mor, Egypt **(1918–1970)**
Nast, Thomas (cartoonist); Landau, Germany **(1840–1902)**
Nation, Carry Amelia (temperance leader); Garrard County, Ky. **(1846–1911)**
Natta, Giulio (chemist, Nobel laureate); Imperia, Italy **(1903–1979)**
Natwick, Mildred (actress); Baltimore **(1905–1994)**
Neagle, Anna (Marjorie Robertson) (actress); London **(1908–1986)**
Neal, Patricia (actress); Packard, Ky., 1/20/26
Neeson, Liam (William John) (actor); Ballymena, Northern Ireland, 6/7/52
Negri, Pola (Apolina Mathias-Chalupec) (actress); Bromberg, Poland **(1899–1987)**
Nehru, Jawaharlal (first prime minister of India); Allahabad, India **(1889–1964)**
Neill, Sam (Nigel Neill) (actor); Omagh, Northern Ireland, 9/14/47
Nelligan, Kate (actress); London, Ont., Canada, 3/16/51
Nelson, Barry (Robert Haakon Nielsen) (actor); San Francisco, 4/16/20
Nelson, David (actor); New York City, 10/24/36
Nelson, Harriet Hilliard (Peggy Lou Snyder) (actress); Des Moines, Iowa **(1909–1994)**
Nelson, Ozzie (Oswald) (actor); Jersey City, N.J. **(1906–1975)**
Nelson, Ricky (Eric) (singer, actor); Teaneck, N.J. **(1940–1985)**
Nelson, Viscount Horatio (naval officer); Burnham Thorpe, England **(1758–1805)**
Nelson, Willie (singer); Waco, Tex., 4/30/33
Nenni, Pietro (Socialist leader); Faenza, Italy **(1891–1980)**
Nero (Nero Claudius Caesar Drusus Germanicus) (Roman emperor); Antium, Italy **(A.D. 37–68)**
Nero, Peter (pianist); New York City, 5/22/34
Netanyahu, Benjamin (Binyamin) (former Israeli prime minister); Tel Aviv, Israel, 10/21/49
Neuwirth, Bebe (Beatrice Neuwirth) (actress); Newark, N.J., 12/31/58
Nevelson, Louise (sculptor); Kiev, Russia **(1899–1988)**
Neville, Aaron (singer); New Orleans, 1/24/41
Newhart, Bob (actor); Chicago, 9/5/29
Newhouse, Samuel I. (publisher); New York City **(1895–1979)**
Newley, Anthony (actor, songwriter); London **(1931–1999)**
Newman, Edwin (news commentator); New York City, 1/25/19
Newman, John Henry (prelate); London **(1801–1890)**
Newman, Paul (actor, director); Cleveland, 1/26/25
Newman, Randy (singer); Los Angeles, 11/28/43
Newton, Huey (black activist); New Orleans **(1942–1989)**
Newton, Sir Isaac (mathematician, scientist); nr. Grantham, England **(1642–1727)**
Newton, Wayne (singer); Norfolk, Va., 4/3/42
Newton-John, Olivia (singer); Cambridge, England, 9/26/48

Nichols, Mike (Michael Peschkowsky) (stage and film director, actor); Berlin, 11/6/31
Nichols, Nichelle (actress); Robbins, Ill., 12/28/33
Nicholson, Jack (actor, director, writer); Neptune, N.J., 4/22/37
Nicholson, Jim (secretary of Veterans Affairs); Struble, Iowa, 2/4/38
Nicks, Stevie (Stephanie Lynn Nicks) (singer, songwriter); Phoenix, Ariz., 5/26/48
Nielsen, Leslie (actor); Regina, Sask., Canada, 2/11/26
Nietzsche, Friedrich Wilhelm (philosopher); nr. Lützen, Saxony, Germany **(1844–1900)**
Nightingale, Florence (nurse); Florence, Italy **(1820–1910)**
Nijinsky, Vaslav (ballet dancer); Warsaw **(1890–1950)**
Nilsson, Birgit (soprano); West Karup, Sweden, 5/17/23
Nilsson, Harry (singer, songwriter); Brooklyn, N.Y. **(1941–1994)**
Nimitz, Chester W. (naval officer); Fredericksburg, Tex. **(1885–1966)**
Nimoy, Leonard (actor, director, writer, producer); Boston, 3/26/31
Nin, Anais (author, diarist); Neuilly, France **(1903–1977)**
Niven, David (actor); Kirriemuir, Scotland **(1910–1983)**
Nixon, Richard Milhous (37th U.S. president); Yorba Linda, Calif. **(1913–1994)**
Nizer, Louis (lawyer, author); London **(1902–1994)**
Nobel, Alfred Bernhard (industrialist); Stockholm **(1833–1896)**
Noguchi, Isamu (sculptor); Los Angeles **(1904–1988)**
Nolan, Lloyd (actor); San Francisco **(1902–1985)**
Nolte, Nick (actor); Omaha, Neb., 2/8/40
Norell, Norman (Norman Levinson) (fashion designer); Noblesville, Ind. **(1900–1972)**
Norgay, Tenzing (mountaineer); Solo Khumbu, Nepal **(1914–1986)**
Norman, Jessye (soprano); Augusta, Ga., 9/15/45
Norman, Marsha (Marsha Williams) (playwright); Louisville, Ky., 9/21/47
Normand, Mabel (actress); Boston **(1894–1930)**
Norris, Chuck (Carlos Ray Norris) (actor, athlete); Ryan, Oklahoma, 3/10/40
Norstad, Gen. Lauris (ex-commander of NATO forces); Minneapolis **(1907–1988)**
North, John Ringling (circus director); Baraboo, Wis. **(1903–1985)**
North, Oliver (ex-military officer); San Antonio, 10/7/43
North, Sheree (actress); Los Angeles, 1/17/33
Norton, Edward (actor); Columbia, Md., 8/18/69
Norton, Eleanor Holmes (New York City government official, lawyer); Washington, D.C., 6/13/37
Norton, Gail (secretary of the Interior); Wichita, Kans., 3/11/54
Nostradamus (Michel de Notredame) (astrologer); St. Rémy, France **(1503–1566)**
Novaes, Guiomar (pianist); São João de Boa Vista, Brazil **(1895–1979)**
Novak, Kim (Marilyn Novak) (actress); Chicago, 2/13/33
Novarro, Ramon (Ramon Samaniegoes) (actor); Durango, Mexico **(1899–1968)**
Novello, Ivor (actor, playwright, composer); Cardiff, Wales **(1893–1951)**
Nugent, Elliott (actor, director); Dover, Ohio **(1899–1980)**
Nureyev, Rudolf (ballet dancer); Siberia **(1938–1993)**
Nyro, Laura (singer, songwriter); Bronx, N.Y. **(1947–1997)**

O

Oakie, Jack (actor); Sedalia, Mo. **(1903–1978)**
Oakley, Annie (Phoebe Anne Oakley Mozee) (markswoman); Darke County, Ohio **(1860–1926)**
Oates, Joyce Carol (novelist); Lockport, N.Y., 6/16/38
Obama, Barack (senator); Honolulu, Hawaii, 8/4/61
Oberon, Merle (Estelle Merle O'Brien Thompson) (actress); Bombay, India **(1911–1979)**
Oberth, Hermann (rocketry and space flight pioneer); Nagyszeben, Austria-Hungary (Sibiu, Romania) **(1894–1989)**
O'Brian, Hugh (Hugh J. Krampe) (actor); Rochester, N.Y., 4/19/25
O'Brien, Conan (TV personality); Brookline, Mass., 4/18/63
O'Brien, Edmond (actor); New York City **(1915–1985)**
O'Brien, Margaret (Angela Maxine O'Brien) (actress); San Diego, Calif., 1/15/37
O'Brien, Pat (William Joseph O'Brien, Jr.) (actor); Milwaukee **(1899–1983)**
O'Brien, Tim (novelist); Austin, Minn., 10/1/46
Obuchi, Keizo (former prime minister of Japan); Nakanojo, Japan **(1937–2000)**
O'Casey, Sean (playwright); Dublin **(1881–1964)**
Ochs, Adolph Simon (publisher); Cincinnati **(1858–1935)**
O'Connor, Carroll (actor); New York City **(1924–2001)**
Odets, Clifford (playwright); Philadelphia **(1906–1963)**

Odetta (Odetta Holmes) (folk singer, actress); Birmingham, Ala., 12/31/30

O'Donnell, Chris (actor); Winnetka, Ill., 6/26/70

O'Donnell, Rosie (actress, talk show host); Commack, N.Y., 3/21/62

Offenbach, Jacques (composer); Cologne, Germany (1819–1880)

O'Hara, John (novelist); Pottsville, Pa. (1905–1970)

O'Hara, Maureen (Maureen FitzSimons) (actress); Dublin, 8/17/20

Ohlsson, Garrick (pianist); Bronxville, N.Y., 4/3/48

Oistrakh, David (concert violinist); Odessa, Russia (1908–1974)

O'Keeffe, Georgia (painter); Sun Prairie, Wis. (1887–1986)

Oland, Warner (actor); Umea, Sweden (1880–1938)

Oldenburg, Claes (painter); Stockholm, 1/28/29

Oldman, Gary (actor, director); London, 3/21/58

Olin, Lena (actress); Stockholm, 3/22/55

Oliphant, Patrick B. (editorial cartoonist); Adelaide, Australia, 7/24/35

Olivier, Sir Laurence (actor); Dorking, England (1907–1989)

Olmos, Edward James (actor); East Los Angeles, 2/24/47

Olmsted, Frederick Law (landscape architect); Hartford, Conn. (1822–1903)

Olsen, Ashley (actress); Sherman Oaks, Calif., 6/13/86

Olsen, Mary-Kate (actress); Sherman Oaks, Calif., 6/13/86

Olsen, Ole (John Sigvard Olsen) (comedian); Peru, Ind. (1892–1963)

Omar Khayyam (poet, astronomer); Nishapur, Iran (died c. 1123)

Onassis, Aristotle (shipping executive); Smyrna, Turkey (1906–1975)

Onassis, Christina (shipping executive); New York City (1950–1988)

Onassis, Jacqueline Kennedy (Jacqueline Bouvier) (first lady); Southampton, N.Y. (1929–1994)

O'Neal, Ryan (Patrick) (actor); Los Angeles, 4/20/41

O'Neal, Tatum (actress); Los Angeles, 11/5/63

O'Neill, Eugene Gladstone (playwright); New York City (1888–1953)

O'Neill, Jennifer (actress); Rio de Janeiro, 2/20/49

Oppenheimer, J. Robert (nuclear physicist); New York City (1904–1967)

Orbach, Jerry (actor); New York City (1935–2004)

Orff, Carl (composer); Munich, Germany (1895–1982)

Orlando, Tony (Michael Anthony Orlando Cassavitis) (singer); New York City, 4/3/44

Ormandy, Eugene (conductor); Budapest (1899–1985)

Ormond, Julia (actress); Epsom, Surrey, England, 1/4/65

Orozco, José Clemente (painter); Zapotlán, Jalisco, Mexico (1883–1949)

Orwell, George (Eric Arthur Blair) (British author); Motihari, India (1903–1950)

Osborn, Paul (playwright); Evansville, Ind. (1901–1988)

Osborne, John (playwright); London (1929–1994)

Osbourne, Ozzy (John Osbourne) (singer); Birmingham, England, 12/3/48

Osler, Sir William (physician); Bondhead, Ont., Canada (1849–1919)

Osmond, Donny (singer, actor); Ogden, Utah, 12/9/57

Osmond, Marie (Olive Marie) (singer, actress); Ogden, Utah, 10/13/59

O'Sullivan, Maureen (actress); County Roscommon, Ireland (1911–1998)

Oswald, Lee Harvey (presumed assassin); New Orleans (1939–1963)

Otis, Elisha (inventor); Halifax, Vt. (1811–1861)

O'Toole, Peter (actor); Connemara, Ireland, 8/2/32

Ovid (Publius Ovidius Naso) (poet); Sulmona, Italy (43 B.C.–A.D. 17)

Ovitz, Michael (entertainment executive); Chicago, 12/14/46

Owens, Buck (Alvis Edgar Owens) (singer); Sherman, Tex., 8/12/29

Ozawa, Seiji (orchestra conductor); Fentian (Shenyan), Manchuria, 9/1/35

P

Paar, Jack (TV personality); Canton, Ohio (1918–2004)

Pacino, Al (Alfred) (actor); New York City, 4/25/40

Packard, Vance (author); Granville Summit, Pa. (1914–1996)

Paderewski, Ignace Jan (pianist, statesman); Kurylowka, Russian Podolia (1860–1941)

Paganini, Nicolò (violinist); Genoa, Italy (1782–1840)

Page, Geraldine (actress); Kirksville, Mo. (1924–1987)

Page, Jimmy (musician); Heston, Ireland, 1/9/44

Page, Larry (Google co-founder); East Lansing, Mich., 3/26/73

Page, Patti (Clara Ann Fowler) (singer, entertainer); Claremore, Okla., 11/8/27

Pagels, Elaine Hiesey (religious scholar); Palo Alto, Calif., 2/13/43

Paglia, Camille (writer, social critic); Endicott, N.Y., 4/2/47

Paige, Roderick R. (ex-secretary of Education); Monticello, Miss., 6/17/33

Paine, Thomas (political philosopher); Thetford, England (1737–1809)

Pakula, Alan J. (film director); New York City (1928–1998)

Palance, Jack (Walter Palanuik) (actor); Lattimer, Pa., 2/18/19

Palestrina, Giovanni Pierluigi da (composer); Palestrina, Italy (1526–1594)

Paley, William S. (broadcasting executive); Chicago (1901–1990)

Palladio, Andrea (architect); Padua or Vicenza, Italy (1508–1580)

Palmer, Robert (rock musician); Batley, England (1949–2003)

Palmerston, Henry John Templeton (3rd Viscount) (statesman); Broadlands, England (1784–1865)

Palminteri, Chazz (Calogero Lorenzo Palminteri) (actor, writer); Bronx, New York, 5/15/51

Paltrow, Gwyneth (actress); Los Angeles, 9/27/72

Pankhurst, Emmeline Goulden (suffragist); Manchester, England (1858–1928)

Papanicolaou, George N. (physician); Coumi, Greece (1883–1962)

Papas, Irene (Lelekou) (actress); Chiliomodian, Greece, 3/9/26

Papp, Joseph (Joseph Papirofsky) (stage producer, director); Brooklyn, N.Y. (1921–1991)

Paracelsus, Philippus (Aureolus Theophrastus Bombastus von Hohenheim) (physican); Einsiedeln, Switzerland (1493–1541)

Park, Chung Hee (ex-president of South Korea); Sangmo-ri, Korea (1917–1979)

Parker, Alan (director); London, 2/14/44

Parker, Charlie "Bird" (jazz musician); Kansas City, Kans. (1920–1955)

Parker, Dorothy (Dorothy Rothschild) (author); West End, N.J. (1893–1967)

Parker, Fess (actor); Fort Worth, Tex., 8/16/25

Parker, Sarah Jessica (actress); Nelsonville, Ohio, 3/25/65

Parker, Suzy (model, actress); San Antonio (1933–2003)

Parkinson, C(yril) Northcote (historian); Durham, England (1909–1993)

Parkman, Francis (historian); Boston (1823–1893)

Parks, Bert (Bert Jacobson) (entertainer); Atlanta (1914–1992)

Parks, Gordon (film director); Ft. Scott, Kans., 11/30/12

Parks, Rosa (civil rights activist); Tuskegee, Ala., 2/4/13

Parnell, Charles Stewart (statesman); Avondale, Ireland (1846–1891)

Parnis, Mollie (Mollie Parnis Livingston) (fashion designer); New York City (1905?–1992)

Parsons, Estelle (actress); Marblehead, Mass., 11/20/27

Parton, Dolly (singer); Locust Ridge, Tenn., 1/19/46

Pascal, Blaise (philosopher); Clermont, France (1623–1662)

Pasternak, Boris Leonidovich (author); Moscow (1890–1960)

Pasternak, Joseph (film producer); Szilagy-Somlyo, Hungary (1901–1991)

Pasteur, Louis (chemist); Dôle, France (1822–1895)

Pastor, Tony (Antony) (actor, theater manager); New York City (1837–1908)

Pater, Walter (Horatio) (writer); London (1839–1894)

Patinkin, Mandy (Mandel) (actor, singer); Chicago, 11/30/52

Paton, Alan (author); Pietermaritzburg, South Africa (1903–1988)

Patric, Jason (actor); Queens, N.Y., 6/17/66

Patti, Adelina (soprano); Madrid (1843–1919)

Patton, George Smith, Jr. (general); San Gabriel, Calif. (1885–1945)

Paul, Alice (feminist, woman suffragist); Moorestown, N.J. (1885–1977)

Paul, Les (Lester William Polfus) (guitarist); Waukesha, Wis., 6/9/15

Paul VI (Giovanni Battista Montini) (Pope); Concesio, nr. Brescia, Italy (1897–1978)

Pauley, Jane (Margaret Jane Pauley) (TV newscaster); Indianapolis, 10/31/50

Pauling, Linus Carl (chemist, Nobel laureate); Portland, Ore. (1901–1994)

Pavarotti, Luciano (tenor); Modena, Italy, 10/12/35

Pavlov, Ivan Petrovich (physiologist); Ryazan district, Russia (1849–1936)

Pavlova, Anna (ballet dancer); St. Petersburg, Russia (1881–1931)

Paxton, Bill (actor); Fort Worth, Texas, 5/17/55

Payne, Alexander (director, screenwriter); Omaha, Nebr., 2/10/61

Peale, Norman Vincent (clergyman); Bowersville, Ohio (1898–1993)

Pearl, Minnie (Sarah Ophelia Colley Cannon) (comedienne, singer); Centerville, Tenn. (1912–1996)

Pears, Peter (tenor); Farnham, England (1910–1986)

Pearson, Drew (Andrew Russel Pearson) (columnist); Evanston, Ill. (1897–1969)

Pearson, Lester B. (statesman); Toronto (1897–1972)

Peary, Robert Edwin (explorer); Cresson, Pa. (1856–1920)

Peck, Gregory (Eldred Gregory Peck) (actor); La Jolla, Calif. (1916–2003)

Peckinpah, Sam (film director); Fresno, Calif. (1925–1984)

Peerce, Jan (tenor); New York City (1904–1984)

Pegler, (James) Westbrook (columnist); Minneapolis (1894–1969)

Pei, I(eoh) M(ing) (architect); Canton, China, 4/26/17

Penn, Arthur (director); Philadelphia, 9/27/22

Penn, Sean (actor, filmmaker); Los Angeles, 8/17/60

Penn, William (American colonist); London (1644–1718)

Penney, James C. (merchant); Hamilton, Mo. (1875–1971)

Peppard, George (actor); Detroit (1928–1994)

Pepys, Samuel (diarist); Bampton, England (1633–1703)

Perelman, S(idney) J(oseph) (writer); Brooklyn, N.Y. (1904–1979)

Perez, Rosie (actress, dancer, choreographer); Brooklyn, New York, 9/6/64

Pergolesi, Giovanni Battista (composer); Jesi, Italy (1710–1736)

Pericles (statesman); Athens died 429 B.C.

Perkins, Anthony (actor); New York City (1932–1992)

Perkins, Frances (social reformer); Boston (1882–1965)

Perlman, Itzhak (violinist); Tel Aviv, Israel, 8/31/45

Perlman, Rhea (actress); Brooklyn, N.Y., 3/31/48

Perón, Isabel (María Estela Martínez Cartas) (former chief of state); La Rioja, Argentina, 2/4/31

Perón, Juan D. (statesman); nr. Lobos, Argentina (1895–1974)

Perón, Maria Eva Duarte de (political leader); Los Toldos, Argentina (1919–1952)

Perot, H. Ross (business executive); Texarkana, Tex., 6/27/30

Perrine, Valerie (actress, dancer); Galveston, Tex., 9/3/43

Perry, Luke (Coy Luther Perry III) (actor); Fredericktown, Ohio, 10/11/66

Perry, Matthew (actor); Williamstown, Mass., 8/19/69

Pershing, John Joseph (general); Linn County, Mo. (1860–1948)

Pestalozzi, Johann (educator); Zurich, Switzerland (1746–1827)

Peters, Bernadette (Bernadette Lazzara) (actress); New York City, 2/28/48

Peters, Brock (actor, singer); New York City (1927–2005)

Peters, Jean (actress); Canton, Ohio (1926–2000)

Peters, Roberta (Roberta Peterman) (soprano); New York City, 5/4/30

Petit, Roland (choreographer, dancer); Villemombe, France, 1924

Petrarch (Francesco Petrarca) (poet); Arezzo, Italy (1304–1374)

Petty, Tom (folk/rock musician); Gainesville, Fla., 10/20/50

Pfeiffer, Michelle (actress); Santa Ana, Calif., 4/29/58

Phair, Liz (singer, songwriter); New Haven, Conn., 4/17/67

Philbin, Regis (talk show host); New York City, 8/25/33

Philip (Philip Mountbatten) (Duke of Edinburgh); Corfu, Greece, 6/10/21

Phillippe, Ryan (actor); New Castle, Del., 9/10/74

Phoenix, Joaquin (actor); San Juan, Puerto Rico, 10/28/74

Phoenix, River (actor); Madras, Ore. (1970–1993)

Piaf, Edith (Edith Gassion) (singer); Paris (1915–1963)

Piaget, Jean (psychologist); Neuchâtel, Switzerland (1896–1980)

Piatigorsky, Gregor (cellist); Ekaterinoslav, Russia (1903–1976)

Piazza, Marguerite (soprano); New Orleans, 5/6/26

Picasso, Pablo (painter, sculptor); Málaga, Spain (1881–1973)

Pickett, Wilson (singer); Prattville, Ala., 3/18/41

Pickford, Mary (Gladys Mary Smith) (actress); Toronto (1892–1979)

Picon, Molly (actress); New York City (1898–1992)

Pidgeon, Walter (actor); East St. John, N.B., Canada (1898–1984)

Pierce, David Hyde (actor); Saratoga Springs, N.Y., 4/3/59

Pierce, Franklin (14th U.S. president); Hillsboro, N.H. (1804–1869)

Pileggi, Mitch (actor); Portland, Ore., 4/5/52

Pinkett-Smith, Jada (actress); Baltimore, 9/18/71

Pinsky, Robert (ex-poet laureate of the U.S.); Long Branch, N.J., 10/20/40

Pinochet (Ugarte), Augusto (former leader of Chile's military government); Valparaiso, Chile, 11/25/15

Pinter, Harold (playwright); London, 10/10/30

Pinza, Ezio (basso); Rome (1892–1957)

Pirandello, Luigi (dramatist, novelist); nr. Girgenti, Italy (1867–1936)

Piranesi, Giambattista (artist); Mestre, Italy (1720–1778)

Pissaro, Camille Jacob (painter); St. Thomas, U.S. Virgin Islands (1830–1903)

Piston, Walter (composer); Rockland, Maine (1894–1976)

Pitman, Sir [Isaac] James (educator, publisher); Bath, England (1813–1897)

Pitt, Brad (actor); Shawnee, Okla., 12/18/63

Pitt, William ("Younger Pitt") (statesman); nr. Bromley, England (1759–1806)

Pitts, ZaSu (actress); Parsons, Kans. (1898–1963)

Pius XII (Eugenio Pacelli) (Pope); Rome (1876–1958)

Pizarro, Francisco (explorer); Trujillo, Spain (c. 1476–1541)

Planck, Max (physicist); Kiel, Germany (1858–1947)

Plant, Robert (musician, singer, song writer); West Bromwich, Staffordshire, England, 8/20/48

Plath, Sylvia (poet); Boston (1932–1963)

Plato (Aristocles) (philosopher); Athens (c. 427–347 B.C.)

Pleasence, Donald (actor); Worksop, England (1919–1995)

Pleshette, Suzanne (actress); New York City, 1/31/37

Plimpton, George (author); New York City (1927–2003)

Plimpton, Martha (actress); New York City, 11/16/70

Plisetskaya, Maya (ballet dancer); Moscow, 11/20/25

Plowright, Joan (actress); Brigg, England, 10/28/29

Plummer, Christopher (actor); Toronto, 12/13/29 or 27

Plutarch (biographer); Chaeronea, Greece (c. 46–c. 120)

Pocahontas (Matoaka) (American Indian princess); Virginia (c. 1595–1617)

Podhoretz, Norman (author); Brooklyn, N.Y., 1/16/30

Poe, Edgar Allan (poet, story writer); Boston (1809–1849)

Poitier, Sidney (actor, director); Miami, Fla., 2/20/24

Polanski, Roman (director); Paris, 8/18/33

Polk, James Knox (11th U.S. president); Mecklenburg County, N.C. (1795–1849)

Pollack, Sydney (film director, producer, actor); Lafayette, Ind., 7/1/34

Pollard, Michael J. (actor); Passaic, N.J., 5/30/39

Pollock, Jackson (painter); Cody, Wyo. (1912–1956)

Polo, Marco (traveler); Venice (c. 1254–1324)

Pol Pot (Cambodian dictator); Kompong Thom, Cambodia (1925–1998)

Pompadour, Mme. de (Jeanne Antoinette Poisson) (courtesan); Versailles (1721–1764)

Pompey (Gnaeus Pompeius Magnus) (general); Rome (106–48 B.C.)

Ponce de León, Juan (explorer); Servas, Spain (c. 1460–1521)

Pons, Lily (coloratura soprano); Cannes, France (1904–1976)

Ponselle, Rosa (soprano); Meriden, Conn. (1897–1981)

Ponti, Carlo (director); Milan, Italy, 12/11/13

Pontormo, Jacopo da (painter); Pontormo, Italy (1492–1557)

Pope, Alexander (poet); London (1688–1744)

Porter, Cole (songwriter); Peru, Ind. (1891–1964)

Porter, Katherine Anne (novelist); Indian Creek, Tex. (1891–1980)

Portman, Natalie (actress); Jerusalem, 6/9/81

Posey, Parker (actress); Baltimore, 11/8/68

Post, Wiley (aviator); Grand Plain, Tex. (1900–1935)

Poston, Tom (actor); Columbus, Ohio, 10/17/27

Potëmkin, Grigori Aleksandrovich, Prince (statesman); Khizovo (Khizov), Belarus (1739–1791)

Potok, Chaim (author); New York City (1929–2002)

Potter, (Helen) Beatrix (author, illustrator); South Kensington, Middlesex, England (1866–1943)

Potts, Annie (actress); Nashville, Tenn., 10/28/52

Poulenc, Francis (composer); Paris (1899–1963)

Pound, Ezra (poet); Hailey, Idaho (1885–1972)

Poussin, Nicolas (painter); Villers, France (1594–1665)

Powell, Adam Clayton, Jr. (congressman); New Haven, Conn. (1908–1972)

Powell, Colin L. (ex-secretary of State); New York City, 4/5/37

Powell, Dick (actor); Mt. View, Ark. (1904–1963)

Powell, Eleanor (actress, tap dancer); Springfield, Mass. (1912–1982)

Powell, Jane (Suzanne Burce) (actress, singer); Portland, Ore., 4/1/29

Powell, William (actor); Pittsburgh (1892–1984)

Power, Tyrone (actor); Cincinnati, Ohio (1914–1958)

Powers, Stefanie (Stefania Zofia Federkiewicz) (actress); Hollywood, Calif., 11/12/42

Praxiteles (sculptor); Athens (c. 370–c. 330 B.C.)

Preminger, Otto (director, producer); Vienna (1906–1986)

Prentiss, Paula (Paula Ragusa) (actress); San Antonio, 3/4/39

Presley, Elvis (singer, actor); Tupelo, Miss. (1935–1977)

Presley, Priscilla (actress); Brooklyn, N.Y., 5/24/45

Preston, Robert (Robert Preston Meservey) (actor); Newton Highlands, Mass. (1918–1987)

Previn, André (conductor); Berlin, 4/6/29

Price, Leontyne (Mary) (soprano); Laurel, Miss., 2/10/27

Price, Ray (country music artist); Perryville, Tex., 1/12/26

Price, Vincent (actor); St. Louis (1911–1993)

Pride, Charley (singer); Sledge, Miss., 3/18/38?

Priestley, Jason (actor, producer); Vancouver, B.C., Canada, 8/28/69

Priestley, J. B. (John B.) (author); Bradford, England (1894–1984)

Priestley, Joseph (chemist); nr. Leeds, England (1733–1804)

Primakov, Yevgeny (Russian political leader); Kiev, Ukraine, 10/29/29

Primrose, William (violist); Glasgow, Scotland (1904–1982)

Prince (Prince Rogers Nelson) (singer); Minneapolis, 6/7/58

Prince, Harold (stage producer); New York City, 1/30/28

Principal, Victoria (actress); Fukuoka, Japan, 1/3/46
Principi, Anthony (ex-secretary of Veterans Affairs); New York City, 4/16/44
Prinze, Freddie (actor); New York City **(1954–1977)**
Prinze, Freddie, Jr. (actor); Los Angeles, 3/8/76
Pritchett, V(ictor) S(awdon) (literary critic); Ipswich, England **(1900–1997)**
Procter, William (scientist); Cincinnati **(1872–1951)**
Prokofiev, Sergei Sergeevich (composer); St. Petersburg, Russia **(1891–1953)**
Proulx, E. Annie (novelist); Norwich, Conn., 8/22/35
Proust, Marcel (novelist); Paris **(1871–1922)**
Provine, Dorothy (actress); Deadwood, S.D., 1/20/37
Prowse, Juliet (actress, dancer); Bombay (Mumbai) **(1936–1996)**
Pryce, Jonathan (actor); Holywell, Wales, 6/1/47
Pryor, Richard (comedian); Peoria, Ill., 12/1/40
Ptolemy (Claudius Ptolemaeus) (astronomer, geographer); Ptolemais Hermii, Egypt, fl. 2nd cent.
Pucci, Emilio (Marchese di Barsento) (fashion designer); Naples, Italy **(1914–1992)**
Puccini, Giacomo (composer); Lucca, Italy **(1858–1924)**
Puente, Tito (band leader); New York City **(1923–2000)**
Pulaski, Casimir (military officer); Podolia, Poland **(1748–1779)**
Pulitzer, Joseph (publisher); Makó, Hungary **(1847–1911)**
Pullman, Bill (actor); Delphi, N.Y., 12/17/53
Pullman, George (inventor); Brockton, N.Y. **(1831–1897)**
Purcell, Henry (composer); London **(1658–1695)**
Pusey, Nathan M. (educator); Council Bluffs, Iowa **(1907–2001)**
Pushkin, Alexander Sergeevich (poet, dramatist); Moscow **(1799–1837)**
Putin, Vladimir (president of Russia); Leningrad, 1952
Puzo, Mario (novelist); New York City **(1920–1999)**
Pyle, Ernest Taylor (journalist); Dana, Ind. **(1900–1945)**
Pythagoras (mathematician, philosopher); Samos, Greece **(c. 582–c. 507A.D.)**

Q

Qaddafi, Muammar al- (Libyan leader); Libya, 1942
Quaid, Dennis (actor); Houston, 4/9/54
Quaid, Randy, (actor); Houston, 10/1/50
Quayle, Anthony (actor); Ainsdale, England **(1913–1989)**
Queen, Ellery: pen name of Frederic Dannay and Manfred B. Lee
Queen Latifah (Dana Owens) (rap musician, actress); Newark, New Jersey, 3/18/70
Queler, Eve (conductor); New York City, 1/1/36
Quennell, Sir Peter Courtney (biographer); Bromley, England **(1905–1993)**
Quindlen, Anna (writer); Philadelphia, 7/8/53
Quinn, Aidan (actor); Chicago, 3/8/59
Quinn, Anthony (Antonio Quiñones) (actor); Chihuahua, Mexico **(1915–2001)**

R

Rabe, David (playwright); Dubuque, Iowa, 3/10/40
Rabelais, François (satirist); nr. Chinon, France **(c. 1490–1553)**
Rabi, I(sidor) I(saac) (physicist); Rymanow, Poland **(1898–1988)**
Rabin, Yitzhak (former Israeli prime minister); Jerusalem **(1922–1995)**
Rachmaninoff, Sergei Wassilievitch (pianist, composer); Oneg Estate, Novgorod, Russia **(1873–1943)**
Racine, Jean Baptiste (dramatist); La Ferté-Milon, France **(1639–1699)**
Radcliffe, Daniel (actor); London, England, 7/23/89
Radner, Gilda (comedienne); Detroit **(1946–1989)**
Raft, George (actor); New York City **(1895–1980)**
Rainier III (Prince); Monaco **(1923–2005)**
Rains, Claude (actor); London **(1889–1967)**
Raitt, Bonnie (singer); Burbank, Calif., 11/8/49
Raitt, John (actor, singer); Santa Ana, Calif. **(1917–2005)**
Raleigh, Sir Walter (courtier, navigator); London **(1552?–1618)**
Rambeau, Marjorie (actress); San Francisco **(1889–1970)**
Rameau, Jean-Philippe (composer); Dijon, France **(1683–1764)**
Rampal, Jean-Pierre (Louis) (flutist); Marseilles, France **(1922–2000)**
Rand, Ayn (novelist, philosopher); St. Petersburg, Russia **(1905–1982)**
Randall, Tony (Leonard Rosenberg) (actor); Tulsa, Okla. **(1920–2004)**
Randolph, A(sa) Philip (labor leader); Crescent City, Fla. **(1889–1979)**
Rankin, Jeannette (politician, pacifist); Missoula, Mont. **(1880–1973)**

Raphael (Raffaello Santi) (painter, architect); Urbino, Italy **(1483–1520)**
Rasputin, Grigori Efimovich (monk); Tobolsk Province, Russia **(1872–1916)**
Rathbone, Basil (Philip St. John Basil Rathbone) (actor); Johannesburg, South Africa **(1892–1967)**
Rather, Dan (TV newscaster); Wharton, Tex., 10/31/31
Rattigan, Terence (playwright); London **(1911–1977)**
Ratzenberger, John (actor); Bridgeport, Conn., 4/6/47
Rauschenberg, Robert (painter); Port Arthur, Tex., 10/22/25
Ravel, Maurice Joseph (composer); Ciboure, France **(1875–1937)**
Ray, Aldo (DaRe) (actor); Pen Argyl, Pa. **(1926–1991)**
Ray, Gene Anthony (actor, dancer); Harlem, N.Y., 5/24/63
Ray, Man (painter); Philadelphia **(1890–1976)**
Ray, Satyajit (film director); Calcutta **(1921–1992)**
Raye, Martha (Margie Yvonne Reed) (comedienne, actress); Butte, Mont. **(1916–1994)**
Rea, Stephen (actor); Belfast, Ireland, 10/31/43
Reagan, Ronald Wilson (40th U.S. president, actor); Tampico, Ill. **(1911–2004)**
Reasoner, Harry (TV commentator); Dakota City, Iowa **(1923–1991)**
Redding, Otis (singer); Dawson, Ga. **(1941–1967)**
Reddy, Helen (singer); Melbourne, Australia, 10/25/41
Redford, Robert (Charles Robert Redford, Jr.) (actor); Santa Monica, Calif., 8/18/37
Redgrave, Lynn (actress); London, 3/8/43
Redgrave, Sir Michael (actor); Bristol, England **(1908–1985)**
Redgrave, Vanessa (actress); London, 1/30/37
Redon, Odilon (artist); Bordeaux, France **(1840–1916)**
Reed, Donna (Donna Belle Mullenger) (actress); Denison, Iowa **(1921–1986)**
Reed, Lou (Lewis Allen Reed) (musician, guitarist, singer, song writer); Freeport, N.Y., 3/ 2/42
Reed, Rex (critic); Ft. Worth, 10/2/40
Reed, Walter (army surgeon); Belroi, Va. **(1851–1902)**
Reese, Della (Deloreese Patricia Early) (singer, actress); Detroit, 7/6/32
Reeve, Christopher (actor, activist); New York City **(1952–2004)**
Reeves, Jim (singer); Panola County, Tex. **(1923–1964)**
Reeves, Keanu (actor, musician); Beirut, Lebanon, 9/2/64
Reich, Robert (Clinton cabinet member); Scranton, Pa., 6/24/46
Reich, Steve (composer); New York City, 10/3/36
Reid, Harry (Senate minority leader); Searchlight, Nev., 12/2/39
Reid, Wallace (actor); St. Louis **(1891–1923)**
Reiner, Carl (actor); New York City, 3/20/22
Reiner, Fritz (conductor); Budapest **(1888–1963)**
Reiner, Robert (actor, director, writer, producer); Bronx, N.Y., 3/6/45
Reinhardt, Max (Max Goldmann) (theater producer); nr. Vienna **(1873–1943)**
Reiser, Paul (actor, producer); New York City, 3/30/57
Remarque, Erich Maria (novelist); Osnabrük, Germany **(1898–1970)**
Rembrandt (Rembrandt Harmensz van Rijn) (painter); Leyden, Netherlands **(1605–1669)**
Remick, Lee (Ann) (actress); Boston **(1935–1991)**
Remnick, David (writer, editor); Hackensack, N.J., 10/29/58
Renfro, Brad (actor); Knoxville, Tenn., 7/25/82
Rennert, Günther (opera director, producer); Essen, Germany, 4/1/11
Rennie, Michael (actor); Bradford, England **(1909–1971)**
Reno, Janet (ex-U.S. attorney general); Miami, Fla., 7/21/38
Renoir, Jean (film director, writer); Paris **(1894–1979)**
Renoir, Pierre Auguste (painter); Limoges, France **(1841–1919)**
Resnais, Alain (film director); Vannes, France, 6/3/22
Resnik, Regina (mezzo-soprano); New York City, 8/30/22
Respighi, Ottorino (composer); Bologna, Italy **(1879–1936)**
Reston, James (journalist); Clydebank, Scotland **(1909–1995)**
Reuther, Walter (labor leader); Wheeling, W. Va. **(1907–1970)**
Revere, Paul (silversmith, hero of famous ride); Boston **(1735–1818)**
Revson, Charles (business executive); Boston **(1906–1975)**
Reynolds, Burt (actor, director, producer); Waycross, Ga., 2/11/36
Reynolds, Debbie (Marie Frances Reynolds) (actress); El Paso, Tex., 4/1/32
Reynolds, Sir Joshua (painter); nr. Plymouth, England **(1723–1792)**
Reynolds, Marjorie (Marjorie Goodspeed) (actress); Buhl, Idaho **(1921–1997)**
Reznor, Trent (musician); Mercer, Pa., 5/17/65
Rhodes, Cecil John (South African statesman); Bishop Stortford, England **(1853–1902)**
Ricci, Christina (actress); Santa Monica, Calif., 2/12/80
Rice, Anne (novelist); New Orleans, 10/14/41
Rice, Condoleezza (secretary of state); Birmingham, Ala., 11/14/54
Rice, Elmer (Elmer Leopold Reizenstein) (playwright); New York City **(1892–1967)**

Rice, Grantland (sports writer); Murfreesboro, Tenn. (1880–1954)
Rich, Buddy (Bernard) (drummer); Brooklyn, N.Y. (1917–1987)
Rich, Charlie (singer); Colt, Ark. (1932–1995)
Richard I the Lion-hearted (king of England); Oxford, England (1157–1199)
Richards, Ann (Dorothy Ann Willis) (ex-governor of Texas); Lakeview, Tex., 9/1/33
Richards, Keith (rock singer); Dartford, England, 12/18/43
Richards, Michael (actor); California, 7/21/48
Richardson, Elliot L. (ex-cabinet member); Boston (1920–1999)
Richardson, Sir Ralph (actor); Cheltenham, England (1902–1983)
Richardson, Tony (director); Shipley, England (1928–1991)
Richelieu, Duc de (Armand Jean du Plessis) (cardinal); Paris (1585–1642)
Richie, Lionel (singer, songwriter); Tuskegee, Ala., 6/20/49
Richter, Charles Francis (seismologist); Hamilton, Ohio (1900–1985)
Richter, Sviatoslav (pianist); Zhitomir, Ukraine (1914–1997)
Rickenbacker, Eddie (Edward V.) (aviator); Columbus, Ohio (1890–1973)
Rickles, Don (comedian); New York City, 5/8/26
Rickman, Alan (actor); London, England, 2/21/46
Rickover, Vice Admiral Hyman G. (atomic energy expert); Russia (1900–1986)
Riddle, Nelson (composer); Hackensack, N.J. (1921–1985)
Ride, Sally K(risten) (astronaut, astrophysicist); Encino, Calif., 5/26/51
Ridge, Tom (ex-secretary of Homeland Security); Munhall, Pa., 8/26/45
Ridgway, General Matthew B. (ex-Army chief of staff); Ft. Monroe, Va. (1895–1993)
Riemenschneider, Tilman (sculptor); Osterode, Germany (c. 1460–1531)
Rigg, Diana (actress); Doncaster, England, 7/20/38
Riley, James Whitcomb (poet); Greenfield, Ind. (1849–1916)
Rilke, Rainer Maria (poet); Prague (1875–1926)
Rimbaud, (Jean Nicolas) Arthur (poet); Charleville, France (1854–1891)
Rimes, LeAnn (singer); Jackson, Miss., 8/28/82
Rimsky-Korsakov, Nikolai Andreevich (composer); Tikhvin, Russia (1844–1908)
Rinehart, Mary (née Roberts) (novelist); Pittsburgh (1876–1958)
Ringwald, Molly (actress); Sacramento, Calif., 2/18/68
Ritchard, Cyril (actor, director); Sydney, Australia (1898–1977)
Ritter, John (Jonathan) (actor); Burbank, Calif. (1948–2003)
Ritter, Tex (Woodward Maurice Ritter) (singer); Panola County, Tex. (1905–1973)
Ritter, Thelma (actress); Brooklyn, N.Y. (1905–1969)
Rivera, Chita (Dolores Conchita Figuero del Rivero) (dancer, actress, singer); Washington, D.C., 1/23/33
Rivera, Diego (painter); Guanajuato, Mexico (1886–1957)
Rivera, Geraldo (Miguel Rivera) (TV host); New York City, 7/4/43
Rivers, Joan (comedienne); Brooklyn, N.Y., 6/8/33
Rivers, Larry (Yitzroch Loiza Grossberg) (painter); New York City (1923–2002)
Roach, Hal (film producer); Elmira, N.Y. (1892–1992)
Robards, Jason, Jr. (actor); Chicago (1922–2000)
Robards, Jason, Sr. (actor); Hillsdale, Mich. (1892–1963)
Robbins, Harold (Harold Rubin) (novelist); New York City (1916–1997)
Robbins, Jerome (Jerome Rabinowitz) (choreographer); New York City (1918–1998)
Robbins, Marty (singer); Glendale, Ariz. (1925–1982)
Robbins, Tim (Timothy Francis) (actor, director); West Covina, Calif., 10/16/58
Roberts, Cokie (Mary Martha Corinne Morrison Claiborne Boggs) (broadcast journalist); New Orleans, 12/27/43
Roberts, Eric (actor); Biloxi, Miss., 4/18/56
Roberts, Julia (actress); Smyrna, Ga., 10/28/67
Roberts, Oral (Granville) (evangelist, publisher); nr. Ada, Okla., 1/24/18
Robertson, Cliff (Clifford Parker Robertson III) (actor); La Jolla, Calif., 9/9/25
Robertson, Dale (Dayle) (actor); Oklahoma City, 7/14/23
Robeson, Paul (singer, actor); Princeton, N.J. (1898–1976)
Robespierre, Maximilien François Marie Isidore de (French Revolutionist); Arras, France (1758–1794)
Robinson, Bill "Bojangles" (Luther) (dancer); Richmond, Va. (1878–1949)
Robinson, Edward G. (Emanuel Goldenberg) (actor); Bucharest (1893–1973)
Robinson, Edwin Arlington (poet); Head Tide, Maine (1869–1935)
Robinson Peete, Holly (Holly Robinson) (actress); Philadelphia, 9/18/64

Robinson, Robert (chemist, Nobel laureate); Chesterfield, Derbyshire, England (1885–1975)
Robinson, Smokey (singer, songwriter); Detroit, 2/19/40
Rock, Chris (comedian, actor); Brooklyn, New York, 2/7/66
Rockefeller, David (banker); New York City, 6/12/15
Rockefeller, John Davison (business executive); Richford, N.Y. (1839–1937)
Rockefeller, John Davison, Jr. (industrialist); Cleveland (1874–1960)
Rockefeller, John D., 3rd (philanthropist); New York City (1906–1978)
Rockefeller, Laurance S. (conservationist); New York City (1910–2004)
Rockwell, Norman (painter, illustrator); New York City (1894–1978)
Roddenberry, Gene (creator of Star Trek); El Paso, Tex. (1921–1991)
Rodgers, Jimmie (singer); Meridian, Miss. (1897–1933)
Rodgers, Richard (composer); New York City (1902–1979)
Rodin, François Auguste René (sculptor); Paris (1840–1917)
Rodzinski, Artur (conductor); Spalato, Dalmatia (1894–1958)
Roeg, Nicolas (film director); London, 8/15/28
Roentgen, Wilhelm Konrad (physicist); Lennep, Prussia (1845–1923)
Roethke, Theodore (poet); Saginaw, Mich. (1908–1963)
Rogers, Buddy (Charles Rogers) (actor); Olathe, Kans. (1904–1999)
Rogers, Carl (psychologist); Oak Park, Ill. (1902–1987)
Rogers, Fred (TV producer, host); Latrobe, Pa. (1928–2003)
Rogers, Ginger (Virginia McMath) (dancer, actress); Independence, Mo. (1911–1995)
Rogers, Kenny (singer); Houston, 8/21/38
Rogers, Mimi (actress); Coral Gables, Fla., 1/27/56
Rogers, Roy (Leonard Frank Slye) (actor, singer); Cincinnati (1911–1998)
Rogers, Wayne (actor); Birmingham, Ala., 4/7/33
Rogers, Will (William Penn Adair Rogers) (humorist); Oologah, Okla. (1879–1935)
Rogers, William P. (ex-secretary of state); Norfolk, N.Y. (1913–2001)
Roland, Gilbert (Luis Antonio Damaso de Alonso) (actor); Juarez, Mexico (1905–1994)
Rolland, Romain (author); Clamecy, France (1866–1944)
Rollins, Sonny (saxophonist); New York, 9/7/30
Romano, Ray (actor); Queens, N.Y., 12/21/57
Romberg, Sigmund (composer); Szeged, Hungary (1887–1951)
Rome, Harold (composer); Hartford, Conn. (1908–1993)
Romero, Cesar (actor); New York City (1907–1994)
Romney, George W. (automobile executive, governor); Chihuahua, Mexico (1907–1995)
Romulo, Carlos P. (diplomat, educator); Manila (1899–1985)
Ronsard, Pierre de (poet); La Possonnière nr. Couture, France (1524–1585)
Ronstadt, Linda (singer); Tucson, Ariz., 7/15/46
Rooney, Andy (TV personality); Albany, N.Y., 1/14/19
Rooney, Mickey (Joe Yule, Jr.) (actor); Brooklyn, N.Y., 9/23/20
Roosevelt, (Anna) Eleanor (reformer, humanitarian); New York City (1884–1962)
Roosevelt, Franklin Delano (32nd U.S. president); Hyde Park, N.Y. (1882–1945)
Roosevelt, Theodore (26th U.S. president); New York City (1858–1919)
Rorem, Ned (composer); Richmond, Ind., 10/23/23
Rose, Billy (showman); New York City (1899–1966)
Rose, Leonard (concert cellist); Washington, D.C. (1918–1984)
Roseanne (Roseanne Barr) (actress); Salt Lake City, 11/3/52
Rosenberg, Ethel (spy); New York City (1915–1953)
Rosenberg, Julius (spy); New York City (1918–1953)
Ross, Betsy (Betsey Griscom) (flagmaker); Philadelphia (1752–1836)
Ross, Diana (singer); Detroit, 3/26/44
Ross, Katharine (actress); Hollywood, Calif., 1/29/42
Rossellini, Isabella (model, actress); Rome, Italy, 6/18/52
Rossellini, Roberto (film director); Rome (1906–1977)
Rossetti, Christina Georgina (poet); London (1830–1894)
Rossetti, Dante Gabriel (painter, poet); London (1828–1882)
Rossini, Gioacchino Antonio (composer); Pesaro, Italy (1792–1868)
Rosten, Leo (writer); Lódz, Poland (1908–1997)
Rostand, Edmond (dramatist); Marseilles, France (1868–1918)
Rostow, Walt Whitman (economist); New York City (1916–2003)
Rostropovich, Mstislav (cellist, conductor); Baku, Azerbaijan, 3/27/27
Roth, Henry (writer); Tysmenica, Ukraine (1906–1995)
Roth, Philip (novelist); Newark, N.J., 3/19/33
Roth, Tim (actor); London, 5/14/61
Rothko, Mark (Marcus Rothkovich) (painter); Russia (1903–1970)

Rouault, Georges (painter); Paris **(1871–1958)**
Roundtree, Richard (actor); New Rochelle, N.Y., 9/7/42
Rousseau, Henri (painter); Laval, France **(1844–1910)**
Rousseau, Jean Jacques (philosopher); Geneva **(1712–1778)**
Rovere, Richard H. (journalist); Jersey City, N.J., 5/5/15
Rowan, Carl Thomas (journalist); Ravenscroft, Tenn. **(1925–2000)**
Rowan, Dan (comedian); Beggs, Okla. **(1922–1987)**
Rowlands, Gena (actress); Cambria, Wis., 6/19/30
Rowling, J(oanne) K(athleen) (novelist); Chipping Sodbury, England, 7/31/65
Royko, Mike (columnist); Chicago **(1932–1997)**
Rubens, Sir Peter Paul (painter); Siegen, Germany **(1577–1640)**
Rubinstein, Arthur (concert pianist); Lódz, Poland **(1887–1982)**
Rubinstein, Helena (cosmetics executive); Kraków, Poland **(1870–1965)**
Rubinstein, John (actor, composer); Los Angeles, 12/8/46
Rucker, Darius (musician, singer, songwriter); Charleston, S.C., 5/13/66
Rudel, Julius (conductor); Vienna, 3/6/21
Ruffalo, Mark (actor); Kenosha, Wis., 11/22/67
Ruffo, Titta (baritone); Italy **(1878–1953)**
Rumsfeld, Donald (sec. of defense); Chicago, 7/9/32
Runyon, (Alfred) Damon (journalist); Manhattan, Kans. **(1884–1945)**
Rush, Geoffrey (actor); Toowoomba, Australia, 7/6/51
Rushdie, (Ahmed) Salman (novelist); Bombay (Mumbai), 6/19/47
Rusk, Dean (ex-sec. of state); Cherokee County, Ga. **(1909–1994)**
Ruskin, John (art critic); London **(1819–1900)**
Russell, Keri (actress); Fountain Valley, Calif., 3/23/76
Russell, Lord Bertrand (Arthur William) (mathematician, philosopher); Trelleck, Wales **(1872–1970)**
Russell, Jane (actress); Bemidji, Minn., 6/21/21
Russell, Ken (film director); Southhampton, England, 7/3/27
Russell, Kurt (actor); Springfield, Mass., 3/17/51
Russell, Leon (pianist, singer); Lawton, Okla., 4/2/41
Russell, Lillian (Helen Louise Leonard) (soprano); Clinton, Iowa **(1861–1922)**
Russell, Mark (satirist); Buffalo, N.Y., 8/23/32
Russell, Nipsy (comedian); Atlanta, 10/13/24
Russell, Rosalind (actress); Waterbury, Conn. **(1912–1976)**
Russo, Rene (actress); Burbank, Calif., 2/17/54
Russo, Richard (writer); Johnstown, NY, 7/15/49
Rustin, Bayard (civil rights leader); West Chester, Pa. **(1910–1987)**
Rutherford, Dame Margaret (actress); London **(1892–1972)**
Ryan, Meg (Margaret Mary Emily Anne Hyra) (actress); Fairfield, Conn., 11/19/61
Ryan, Robert (actor); Chicago **(1909–1973)**
Rydell, Bobby (Robert Ridarelli) (singer); Philadelphia, 4/26/42
Ryder, Winona (Winona Laura Horowitz) (actress); Winona, Minn., 10/29/71
Rysanek, Leonie (dramatic soprano); Vienna **(1926–1998)**

S

Saarinen, Eero (architect); Finland **(1910–1961)**
Sabin, Albert B. (polio researcher); Bialystok, Poland **(1906–1993)**
Sabu (Dastagir) (actor); Karapur, India **(1924–1963)**
Sacagawea (Shoshone Indian guide); Lemhi River valley (Idaho) **(c. 1786–1812)**
Sachs, Jeffrey D. (economist, educator); Michigan, 1954
Sadat, Anwar (former president); Egypt **(1918–1981)**
Sade, Marquis de (Donatien Alphonse François, Comte de Sade) (libertine, writer); Paris **(1740–1814)**
Safer, Morley (TV newscaster); Toronto, 11/8/31
Sagan, Carl (Edward) (astronomer, science writer); New York City **(1934–1996)**
Sagan, Françoise (novelist); Cajarc, France **(1935–2004)**
Sahl, Mort (Morton Lyon Sahl) (comedian); Montreal, 5/11/27
Saint, Eva Marie (actress); Newark, N.J., 7/4/24
St. Denis, Ruth (dancer, choreographer); Newark, N.J. **(1878–1968)**
St. James, Susan (Susan Miller) (actress); Los Angeles, 8/14/46
St. John, Jill (actress); Los Angeles, 8/19/40
St. Johns, Adela Rogers (journalist, author); Los Angeles **(1894–1988)**
Sainte-Marie, Buffy (Beverly) (folk singer); Craven, Sask., Canada, 2/20/41
Saint-Gaudens, Augustus (sculptor); Dublin **(1848–1907)**
Saint-Laurent, Yves (Henri Donat Mathieu) (fashion designer); Orán, Algeria, 8/1/36
Saint-Saens, Charles Camille (composer); Paris **(1835–1921)**
Sakharov, Andrei Dmitriyevich (nuclear physicist, peace activist); Russia **(1921–1989)**

Sales, Soupy (Milton Supman) (television entertainer); Franklinton, N.C., 1/6/26
Salinger, J(erome) D(avid) (novelist); New York City, 1/1/19
Salisbury, Harrison E. (journalist); Minneapolis **(1908–1993)**
Salk, Jonas (polio researcher); New York City **(1914–1995)**
Salk, Lee (psychologist); New York City **(1926–1992)**
Salomon, Haym (American Revolution financier); Leszno, Poland **(1740–1785)**
Sand, George (Amandine Lucille Aurore Dudevant, née Dupin) (novelist); Paris **(1804–1876)**
Sandburg, Carl (poet, biographer); Galesburg, Ill. **(1878–1967)**
Sanders, George (actor); St. Petersburg, Russia **(1906–1972)**
Sandler, Adam (comedian, musician, actor, screenwriter, singer); Brooklyn, N.Y., 9/9/66
Sands, Tommy (singer); Chicago, 8/27/37
Sanger, Margaret (birth-control advocate); Corning, N.Y. **(1879–1966)**
San Giacomo, Laura (actress); Hoboken, N.J., 11/14/62
San Martín, José de (revolutionary); Yapeyú, now in Argentina **(1778–1850)**
Santayana, George (philosopher); Madrid **(1863–1952)**
Sappho (poet); Lesbos, Greece **(610 B.C.–580 B.C.)**
Sarandon, Susan (Susan Tomalin) (actress); New York City, 10/4/46
Sargent, John Singer (painter); Florence, Italy **(1856–1925)**
Sarnoff, David (radio executive); Minsk, Belarus **(1891–1971)**
Saroyan, William (novelist); Fresno, Calif. **(1908–1981)**
Sarsgaard, Peter (actor); Bellville, Ill., 3/7/71
Sarto, Andrea del (Andrea Domenico d'Agnolo di Francesco) (painter); Florence, Italy **(1486–1531)**
Sartre, Jean-Paul (existentialist writer); Paris **(1905–1980)**
Sassoon, Vidal (hair stylist); London, 1/17/28
Satie, Erik (Alfred Leslie) (composer); Paris **(1866–1925)**
Saul (king of Israel) fl. 11th cent. B.C.
Savage, Fred (actor); Highland Park, Ill., 7/9/76
Savalas, Telly (Aristoteles) (actor); Garden City, N.Y. **(1924–1994)**
Savonarola, Girolamo (religious reformer); Ferrara, Italy **(1452–1498)**
Sawyer, Diane (broadcast journalist); Glasgow, Ky., 12/22/45
Sayão, Bidú (soprano); Rio de Janeiro **(1904–1999)**
Sayles, John (director, screenwriter, actor); Schenectady, N.Y., 9/28/50
Scarlatti, Alessandro (composer); Palermo, Italy **(1659–1725)**
Scarlatti, Domenico (composer); Naples, Italy **(1685–1757)**
Scavullo, Francesco (photographer); Staten Island, N.Y. **(1929–2004)**
Schama, Simon (historian); London, 2/13/45
Schapiro, Meyer (Meir) (art historian); Siauliai, Lithuania **(1904–1996)**
Schary, Dore (producer, writer); Newark, N.J. **(1905–1980)**
Schell, Maria (actress); Vienna **(1926–2005)**
Schell, Maximilian (actor); Vienna, 12/8/30
Schiaparelli, Elsa (fashion designer); Rome **(1890–1973)**
Schiff, Dorothy (newspaper publisher); New York City **(1903–1989)**
Schiffer, Claudia (model, actress); Rheinberg/Dusseldorf, Germany, 8/25/70
Schiller, Johann Christoph Friedrich von (dramatist, poet); Marbach, Germany **(1759–1805)**
Schipa, Tito (tenor); Lecce, Italy **(1890–1965)**
Schippers, Thomas (conductor); Kalamazoo, Mich. **(1930–1977)**
Schlegel, Friedrich von (philosopher); Hanover, Germany **(1772–1829)**
Schlesinger, Arthur M., Jr. (historian); Columbus, Ohio, 10/15/17
Schnabel, Artur (pianist, composer); Lipnik, Austria **(1882–1951)**
Schneider, Romy (Rose-Marie Albach-Retty) (actress); Vienna **(1938–1982)**
Schoenberg, Arnold (composer); Vienna **(1874–1951)**
Schomberg, Arthur (bibliophile, antiquarian); San Juan, P.R. **(1874–1938)**
Schopenhauer, Arthur (philosopher); Danzig, Poland **(1788–1860)**
Schröder, Gerhard (chancellor of Germany); Mossenberg, Germany, 4/7/44
Schubert, Franz Peter (composer); Vienna **(1797–1828)**
Schulberg, Budd (novelist); New York City, 3/27/14
Schulz, Charles M. (cartoonist); Minneapolis **(1922–2000)**
Schumacher, Joel (film director, producer, screenwriter); New York City, 8/29/39
Schuman, Robert (statesman); Luxembourg **(1886–1963)**
Schuman, William (composer); New York City **(1910–1992)**
Schumann, Robert Alexander (composer); Zwickau, Germany **(1810–1856)**
Schwartz, Arthur (songwriter); Brooklyn, N.Y. **(1900–1984)**

PEOPLE
311

Schwarzenegger, Arnold (bodybuilder, actor, governor of Calif.); Graz, Austria, 7/30/47
Schwarzkopf, Elisabeth (soprano); Poznán, Poland, 12/9/15
Schwarzkopf, H. Norman (retired general); Trenton, N.J., 8/22/34
Schweitzer, Albert (humanitarian, Nobel laureate); Kaysersburg, Upper Alsace (1875–1965)
Schwimmer, David (actor); New York City, 11/12/66
Scofield, Paul (actor); Hurstpierpoint, England, 1/21/22
Scorsese, Martin (actor, writer, director, producer); Flushing, N.Y., 11/17/42
Scott, George C. (actor); Wise, Va. (1927–1999)
Scott, Hazel (singer, pianist); Port of Spain, Trinidad (1920–1981)
Scott, Lizabeth (Emma Matzo) (actress); Scranton, Pa., 9/29/23
Scott, Randolph (Randolph Crane) (actor); Orange County, Va. (1898–1987)
Scott, Robert Falcon (explorer); Devonport, England (1868–1912)
Scott, Sir Walter (novelist); Edinburgh, Scotland (1771–1832)
Scott, Zachary (actor); Austin, Tex. (1914–1965)
Scotto, Renata (operatic soprano); Savona, Italy, 2/24/36
Scruggs, Earl Eugene (bluegrass musician); Cleveland County, N.C., 1/6/24
Seaborg, Glenn Theodore (chemist, Nobel laureate); Ishpeming, Mich. (1912–1999)
Seagal, Steven (actor); Lansing, Mich., 4/10/52
Seal (Sealhenry Olumide Samuel) (singer, songwriter); London, England, 2/19/63
Seattle (Chief Seattle) (Suquamish Indian leader); Blake Island (Wash.) (c. 1786–1866)
Sebastian, John (composer, singer); New York City, 3/17/44
Seberg, Jean (actress); Marshalltown, Iowa (1938–1979)
Sedaka, Neil (singer); Brooklyn, N.Y., 3/13/39
Sedgwick, Kyra (actress); New York City, 8/19/65
Seeger, Pete (folk singer); New York City, 5/3/19
Segal, Erich (novelist); Brooklyn, N.Y., 6/16/37
Segal, George (actor); New York City, 2/13/36
Segovia, Andrés (guitarist); Linares, Spain (1893–1987)
Seinfeld, Jerry (comedian); Brooklyn, N.Y., 4/29/54
Selena (Selena Quintanilla Perez) (singer); Lake Jackson, Tex. (1971–1995)
Selleck, Tom (actor); Detroit, 1/29/45
Sellars, Peter (theater director); Pittsburgh, 1958?
Sellers, Peter (actor); Southsea, England (1925–1980)
Selznick, David O. (producer); Pittsburgh (1902–1965)
Sendak, Maurice (Bernard) (children's book author, illustrator); Brooklyn, N.Y., 6/10/28
Sennett, Mack (Michael Sinnott) (film producer); Richmond, Que., Canada (1880–1960)
Sequoyah (Cherokee linguist); Taskigi, Tenn. (c. 1770–1843)
Serkin, Peter (pianist); New York City, 7/24/47
Serkin, Rudolf (pianist); Eger, Czech Republic (1903–1991)
Serling, Rod (writer, TV host); Syracuse, N.Y. (1924–1975)
Sessions, Roger (composer); Brooklyn, N.Y. (1896–1985)
Seurat, Georges (painter); Paris (1859–1891)
Seuss, Dr. (Theodor Seuss Geisel) (author, illustrator); Springfield, Mass. (1904–1991)
Sevareid, Eric (TV commentator); Velva, N.D. (1912–1991)
Severinsen, Doc (Carl) (band leader); Arlington, Ore., 7/7/27
Sevigny, Chlöe (actress); Darien, Conn., 11/18/74
Sewell, Rufus (actor, musician); London, 10/29/67
Sexton, Anne (poet); Newton, Mass. (1928–1974)
Seymour, Jane (Joyce Penelope Wilhelmina Frankenburg) (actress); Wimbledon, England, 2/15/51
Shabazz, Betty (Betty Sanders) (civil rights activist); Detroit (1936–1997)
Shaffer, Peter (playwright); Liverpool, England, 5/15/26
Shaham, Gil (violinist); Urbana, Ill., 1971
Shahn, Ben(jamin) (painter); Kaunas, Lithuania (1898–1969)
Shakespeare, William (dramatist); Stratford on Avon, England (1564–1616)
Shakur, Tupac (Amaru Shakur) (singer, actor); Brooklyn, N.Y. (1971–1996)
Shandling, Garry (comedian, actor, producer); Chicago, 11/29/49
Shange, Ntozake (Paulette Williams) (poet, playwright); Trenton, N.J., 10/18/48
Shankar, Ravi (sitar player); Benares, India, 4/7/20
Sharif, Omar (Michael Shalhoub) (actor); Alexandria, Egypt, 4/10/32
Shatner, William (actor); Montreal, 3/22/31
Shaw, Artie (Arthur Arshawsky) (band leader); New York City (1910–2004)
Shaw, George Bernard (dramatist); Dublin (1856–1950)
Shaw, Irwin (novelist); Brooklyn, N.Y. (1913–1984)
Shaw, Robert (actor); Lancashire, England (1927–1978)

Shaw, Robert (chorale conductor); Red Bluff, Calif. (1916–1999)
Shawn, Ted (Edwin Myers Shawn) (dancer, choreographer); Kansas City, Mo. (1891–1972)
Shawn, Wallace (actor); New York City, 11/12/43
Shearer, Moira (ballet dancer); Dunfermline, Scotland, 1/17/26
Shearer, Norma (actress); Montreal (1900–1983)
Shearing, George (pianist); London, 8/13/20
Sheedy, Ally (Alexandra Sheedy) (actress, writer); New York City, 6/13/62
Sheen, Charlie (actor); Los Angeles, 9/3/65
Sheen, Fulton J. (Peter Sheen) (Roman Catholic bishop); El Paso, Ill. (1895–1979)
Sheen, Martin (Ramon Estevez) (actor); Dayton, Ohio, 8/3/40
Shelley, Mary Wollstonecraft Godwin (writer); London (1797–1851)
Shelley, Percy Bysshe (poet); nr. Horsham, England (1792–1822)
Shelton, Henry (chairman of the Joint Chiefs of Staff); Tarboro, N.C., 1/2/42
Shepard, Sam (Samuel Shepard Rogers) (playwright); Ft. Sheridan, Ill., 11/5/43
Shepherd, Cybill (actress); Memphis, Tenn., 2/18/50
Sheraton, Thomas (furniture designer); Stockton-on-Tees, England (1751–1806)
Sheridan, Ann (Clara Lou Sheridan) (actress); Denton, Tex. (1915–1967)
Sheridan, Philip (army officer); Albany, N.Y. (1831–1888)
Sheridan, Richard Brinsley (dramatist); Dublin (1751–1816)
Sherman, William Tecumseh (army officer); Lancaster, Ohio (1820–1891)
Sherwood, Robert Emmet (playwright); New Rochelle, N.Y. (1896–1955)
Shevardnadze, Eduard Amvrosiyevich (State Council chairman, Georgia); Mamati, Georgia, 1/25/28
Shields, Brooke (actress); New York City, 5/31/65
Shire, Talia (Coppola) (actress); Lake Success, N.Y., 4/25/46
Shirer, William L. (journalist, historian); Chicago (1904–1993)
Sholokhov, Mikhail (novelist); Veshenskaya, Russia (1905–1984)
Shore, Dinah (Frances Rose Shore) (singer); Winchester,Tenn. (1917–1994)
Short, Bobby (Robert Waltrip Short) (singer, pianist); Danville, Ill. (1924–2005)
Short, Martin (actor); Hamilton, Ont., Canada, 3/26/50
Shostakovich, Dmitri (composer); St. Petersburg, Russia (1906–1975)
Shriner, Herb (humorist, host); Toledo, Ohio (1918–1970)
Shriver, Maria (TV co-host); Chicago, 11/6/55
Shriver, Sargent (Robert Sargent Shriver, Jr.) (business executive); Westminster, Md., 11/9/15
Shue, Andrew (actor, soccer player); South Orange, N.J., 2/20/67
Shue, Elisabeth (actress); Wilmington, Del., 6/10/63
Shulman, Max (novelist); St. Paul, Minn. (1919–1988)
Sibelius, Jean (Johann Julius Christian Sibelius) (composer); Tavastehus, Finland (1865–1957)
Sidney, Sir Philip (poet); Penshurst, England (1554–1586)
Sidney, Sylvia (Sophia Kosow) (actress); New York City (1910–1999)
Siegfried and Roy (illusionists) Siegfried Fischbacher; Rosenheim, Bavaria, Germany, 1939 Roy Uwe Ludwig Horn; Nordenham, nr. Bremen, Germany, 1944
Siepi, Cesare (basso); Milan, Italy, 2/10/23
Signoret, Simone (Simone Kaminker) (actress); Wiesbaden, Germany (1921–1985)
Sihanouk, Norodom (king of Cambodia); Cambodia, 10/31/22
Sikorsky, Igor I. (inventor); Kiev, Ukraine (1889–1972)
Sills, Beverly (Belle Silverman) (soprano, opera director); Brooklyn, N.Y., 5/25/29
Sills, Milton (actor); Chicago (1882–1930)
Silone, Ignazio (Secondo Tranquilli) (novelist); Pescina del Marsi, Italy (1900–1978)
Silver, Ron (Ron Zimelman) (actor); New York City, 7/2/46
Silverheels, Jay (Harold J. Smith) (actor); Brantford, Ont., Canada (1919–1980)
Silverman, Fred (broadcasting executive); New York City, 9/13/37
Silvers, Phil (Philip Silversmith) (comedian); Brooklyn, N.Y. (1912–1985)
Silverstein, Shel (writer, poet); Chicago (1932–1999)
Silverstone, Alicia (actress); San Francisco, 10/4/76
Simenon, Georges (Georges Sim) (mystery writer); Liège, Belgium (1903–1989)
Simmons, Jean (actress); Crouch Hill, London, 1/31/29
Simon, Carly (singer, songwriter); New York City, 6/25/45
Simon, Neil (playwright); Bronx, N.Y., 7/4/27
Simon, Norton (business executive); Portland, Ore. (1907–1993)
Simon, Paul (singer, songwriter); Newark, N.J., 10/13/1941

Simone, Nina (Eunice Kathleen Waymoa) (singer, pianist); Tryon, N.C. (1933–2003)

Simpson, Jessica (singer); Abilene, Tex., 7/10/80

Sinatra, Frank (Francis Albert Sinatra) (singer, actor); Hoboken, N.J. (1915–1998)

Sinbad (David Adkins) (actor, comedian); Benton Harbor, Mich., 11/10/56

Sinclair, Upton Beall (novelist); Baltimore (1878–1968)

Singer, Isaac Bashevis (novelist); Radzymin, Poland (1904–1991)

Singh, Manmohan (prime minister of India); Gah, Punjab (now in Pakistan), 9/26/32

Singleton, John (writer, director); Los Angeles, 1/6/68

Sinise, Gary (actor, director); Chicago, 3/17/55

Siqueiros, David (painter); Chihuahua, Mexico (1896–1974)

Sirica, John J. (judge); Waterbury, Conn. (1904–1992)

Sirtis, Marina (actress); London, 3/29/59

Siskel, Gene (film critic); Chicago (1946–1999)

Sisley, Alfred (painter); Paris (1839–1899)

Sitting Bull (Prairie Sioux Indian chief); on Grand River, S.D. (c. 1831–1890)

Skelton, Red (Richard) (comedian); Vincennes, Ind. (1913–1997)

Skerritt, Tom (actor); Detroit, 8/25/43

Skinner, B(urrhus) F(rederic) (psychologist); Susquehanna, Pa. (1904–1990)

Skinner, Otis (actor); Cambridge, Mass. (1858–1942)

Slater, Christian (Christopher Hawkins) (actor); New York City, 8/18/69

Slatkin, Leonard (conductor); Los Angeles, 9/1/44

Sloan, Alfred P., Jr. (industrialist); New Haven, Conn. (1875–1965)

Sloan, John (painter); Lock Haven, Pa. (1871–1951)

Smalley, Richard E. (chemist, Nobel laureate); Akron, Ohio, 6/6/43

Smetana, Bedrich (composer); Litomysl, Czech Republic (1824–1884)

Smith, Adam (economist); Kirkaldy, Scotland (1723–1790)

Smith, Alexis (actress); Penticton, Canada (1921–1993)

Smith, Alfred Emanuel (politician); New York City (1873–1944)

Smith, Bessie (blues singer); Chattanooga, Tenn. (1894–1937)

Smith, Sir C. Aubrey (actor); London (1863–1948)

Smith, David (sculptor); Decatur, Ind. (1906–1965)

Smith, Harry (TV co-anchor); Hammond, Ind., 8/21/51

Smith, Howard K. (TV commentator); Ferriday, La. (1914–2002)

Smith, Jaclyn (actress); Houston, 10/26/47

Smith, John (American colonist); Willoughby, Lincolnshire, England (1580–1631)

Smith, Joseph (religious leader); Sharon, Vt. (1805–1844)

Smith, Kate (Kathryn) (singer); Greenville, Va. (1909–1986)

Smith, Kevin (director, screenwriter); Red Bank, N.J., 8/2/70

Smith, Dame Maggie (actress); Ilford, England, 12/28/34

Smith, Patti Lee (singer, songwriter); Chicago, 12/30/46

Smith, Red (Walter) (sports columnist); Green Bay, Wis. (1905–1982)

Smith, Will (actor, rap singer); Philadelphia, 9/25/68

Smits, Jimmy (actor); New York City, 7/9/55

Smollett, Tobias (novelist); Dalquhurn, Scotland (1721–1771)

Smothers, Dick (Richard) (comedian); New York City, 11/20/39

Smothers, Tom (Thomas) (comedian); New York City, 2/2/37

Snipes, Wesley (actor); Orlando, Fla., 7/31/62

Snoop Dogg (Calvin Broadus) (musician); Long Beach, Calif., 10/20/72

Snow, John (secretary of the Treasury); Toledo, Ohio, 8/2/39

Snow, Lord (Charles Percy) (author); Leicester, England (1905–1980)

Snowdon, Earl of (Anthony Armstrong-Jones) (photographer); London, 3/7/30

Snyder, Tom (TV personality); Milwaukee, 5/12/36

Socrates (philosopher); Athens (469–399 B.C.)

Soderbergh, Steven (film director, screenwriter); Atlanta, Ga., 1/14/63

Solana, Javier (diplomat); Madrid, Spain, 7/14/42

Solomon (king of Israel); Jerusalem, fl. 950 B.C.

Solon (lawgiver); Salamis, Greece (c. 630–559 B.C.)

Solti, Sir Georg (conductor); Budapest (1912–1997)

Solzhenitsyn, Aleksandr (novelist); Kislovodsk, Russia, 12/11/18

Somers, Suzanne (Suzanne Mahoney) (actress); San Bruno, Calif., 10/16/46

Somes, Michael (ballet dancer); Horsley, England (1917–1994)

Sommer, Elke (Elke Schletz) (actress); Berlin, 11/5/42

Sondheim, Stephen (composer); New York City, 3/22/30

Sonnenfeld, Barry (cinematographer, film director); New York City, 4/1/53

Sontag, Susan (author, film director); New York City (1933–2004)

Sophocles (dramatist); nr. Athens (c. 496–406 B.C.)

Sorbo, Kevin (actor); Mound, Minn., 9/24/58

Sorvino, Mira (actress); Tenafly, N.J., 9/28/67

Sorvino, Paul (actor); Brooklyn, N.Y., 4/13/39

Sothern, Ann (Harriette Lake) (actress); Valley City, N.D. (1909–2001)

Soul, David (David Solberg) (actor); Chicago, 8/28/43

Sousa, John Philip (composer); Washington, D.C. (1854–1932)

Soyer, Raphael (painter); Borisoglebsk, Russia (1899–1987)

Spaak, Paul-Henri (statesman); Brussels (1899–1972)

Spacek, Sissy (Mary Elizabeth Spacek) (actress); Quitman, Tex., 12/25/49

Spacey, Kevin (actor); South Orange, N.J., 7/26/59

Spade, David (actor, comedian); Birmingham, Mich., 7/22/65

Spader, James (actor); Boston, 2/7/60

Spark, Muriel (novelist); Edinburgh, Scotland, 2/1/18

Spears, Britney (pop singer); Kentwood, La., 12/2/81

Spector, Phil (rock producer); Bronx, N.Y., 12/25/40

Spelling, Aaron (producer); Dallas, 4/22/28

Spelling, Tori (Victoria) (actress); Los Angeles, 5/16/73

Spellings, Margaret (secretary of Education); Mich., 11/30/57

Spencer, Herbert (philosopher); Derby, England (1820–1903)

Spender, Stephen (poet); nr. London (1909–1995)

Spengler, Oswald (philosopher); Blankenburg, Germany (1880–1936)

Spenser, Edmund (poet); London (1552?–1599)

Spewack, Bella (playwright); Hungary (1899–1990)

Spiegel, Sam (producer); Jaroslaw, Poland (1901–1985)

Spielberg, Steven (director, producer, writer, actor); Cincinnati, 12/18/47

Spillane, Mickey (Frank Spillane) (mystery writer); Brooklyn, N.Y., 3/9/18

Spiner, Brent (actor); Houston, 2/2/49

Spinoza, Baruch (philosopher); Amsterdam, Netherlands (1632–1677)

Spitalny, Phil (orchestra leader) (1890–1970)

Spitzer, Eliot (attorney general of New York); Bronx, N.Y., 6/10/59

Spivak, Lawrence (TV producer); Brooklyn, N.Y. (1900–1994)

Spock, Benjamin (pediatrician, writer); New Haven, Conn. (1903–1998)

Springsteen, Bruce (singer, songwriter); Freehold, N.J., 9/23/49

Sproul, Robert G. (educator); San Francisco (1891–1975)

Squanto (Wampanoag Indian emissary); Patuxet (Plymouth Bay, Mass.) (c. 1590–1622)

Stack, Robert (Robert Modini) (actor); Los Angeles (1919–2003)

Stafford, Jo (singer); Coalinga, Calif., 11/12/18

Stahl, Lesley (broadcast journalist); Swampscott, Mass., 12/16/41

Stalin, Joseph Vissarionovich (Iosif V. Dzhugashvili) (Soviet leader); nr. Tiflis (Tbilisi), Georgia (1879–1953)

Stallone, Sylvester (actor, writer, director); New York City, 7/6/46

Stamp, Terence (actor); London, 1938

Stander, Lionel (actor); New York City (1908–1994)

Stanislavski (Konstantin Sergeevich Alekseev) (stage producer); Moscow (1863–1938)

Stanley, Sir Henry Morton (John Rowlands) (explorer); Denbigh, Wales (1841–1904)

Stanley, Kim (Patricia Reid) (actress); Tularosa, N.M. (1925–2001)

Stans, Maurice H. (ex-secretary of commerce); Shakope, Minn. (1908–1998)

Stanton, Elizabeth Cady (woman suffragist); Johnstown, N.Y. (1815–1902)

Stanton, Frank (broadcasting executive); Muskegon, Mich., 3/20/08

Stanwyck, Barbara (Ruby Stevens) (actress); Brooklyn, N.Y. (1907–1990)

Stapleton, Jean (Jeanne Murray) (actress); New York City, 1/19/23

Stapleton, Maureen (actress); Troy, N.Y., 6/21/25

Starker, Janós (cellist); Budapest, 7/5/24

Starr, Kenneth (independent counsel for Whitewater investigation); Vernon, Tex., 7/21/46

Starr, Ringo (Richard Starkey) (singer, songwriter); Liverpool, England, 7/7/40

Stassen, Harold E. (ex-government official); West St. Paul, Minn. (1907–2001)

Staudinger, Hermann (chemist, Nobel laureate); Worms, Germany (1881–1965)

Steegmuller, Francis (biographer); New Haven, Conn. (1906–1994)

Steel, Danielle (Danielle Fernande Schuelein-Steel) (novelist); New York City, 8/14/47

Steele, Tommy (singer); London, 12/17/36

Stefani, Gwen (singer); Orange County, Calif., 10/3/69

Stegner, Wallace (Earle) (novelist, critic); Lake Mills, Iowa (1909–1993)

Steichen, Edward Jean (photographer, artist); Luxembourg (1879–1973)

Steiger, Rod (Rodney) (actor); Westhampton, N.Y. (1925–2002)

Stein, Gertrude (author); Allegheny, Pa. **(1874–1946)**

Steinbeck, John Ernst (novelist); Salinas, Calif. **(1902–1968)**

Steinberg, David (comedian); Winnipeg, Man., Canada, 8/19/42

Steinberg, William (conductor); Cologne, Germany **(1899–1978)**

Steinem, Gloria (feminist, publisher); Toledo, Ohio, 3/25/34

Steinmetz, Charles (electrical engineer); Breslau, Poland **(1865–1923)**

Steenburgen, Mary (actress); Newport, Ark., 2/8/53

Stendhal (Marie Henri Beyle) (novelist); Grenoble, France **(1783–1842)**

Stern, Howard (radio personality); New York City, 1/2/54

Stern, Isaac (concert violinist); Kreminlecz, Russia **(1920–2001)**

Sterne, Laurence (novelist); Clonmel, Ireland **(1713–1768)**

Stevens, Cat (Steven Georgiou) (singer, songwriter); London, 7/21/47

Stevens, Connie (Concetta Ingolia) (singer); Brooklyn, N.Y., 8/8/38

Stevens, George (film director); Oakland, Calif. **(1904–1975)**

Stevens, Risë (mezzo-soprano); New York City, 6/11/13

Stevens, Wallace (poet); Reading, Pa. **(1879–1955)**

Stevenson, Adlai Ewing (statesman); Los Angeles **(1900–1965)**

Stevenson, McLean (actor); Bloomington, Ill. **(1929–1996)**

Stevenson, Parker (actor); Philadelphia, 6/4/52

Stevenson, Robert Louis Balfour (novelist, poet); Edinburgh, Scotland **(1850–1894)**

Stewart, James (actor); Indiana, Pa. **(1908–1997)**

Stewart, Jon (Jonathan Stewart Leibowitz) (comedian, TV host); New York City, 11/28/62

Stewart, Martha (entrepreneurial home stylist); Nutley, N.J., 8/3/41

Stewart, Patrick (actor); Mirfield, England, 7/13/40

Stewart, Rod (Roderick David) (singer); London, 1/10/45

Stieglitz, Alfred (photographer); Hoboken, N.J. **(1864–1946)**

Stiers, David Ogden (actor); Peoria, Ill., 10/31/42

Stiller, Ben (actor, director, comic); New York City, 11/30/65

Stiller, Jerry (actor); Brooklyn, N.Y., 6/8/29

Stills, Stephen (singer, songwriter); Dallas, 1/3/45

Stine, R. L. (Robert Lawrence Stine) (writer); Columbus, Ohio, 10/8/43

Sting (Gordon Matthew Sumner) (singer, composer); Wallsend, England, 10/2/51

Stipe, Michael (singer); Decatur, Ga., 1/4/60

Stockwell, Dean (actor); North Hollywood, Calif., 3/5/36

Stoker, Bram (novelist); Dublin **(1847–1912)**

Stokes, Carl (TV newscaster); Cleveland **(1927–1996)**

Stokowski, Leopold (conductor); London **(1882–1977)**

Stoltz, Eric (actor); Whittier, Calif., 9/30/61

Stone, Edward Durell (architect); Fayetteville, Ark. **(1902–1978)**

Stone, I(sidor) F(einstein) (journalist); Philadelphia **(1907–1989)**

Stone, Irving (Irving Tennenbaum) (novelist); San Francisco **(1903–1989)**

Stone, Lucy (woman suffragist); nr. West Brookfield, Mass. **(1818–1893)**

Stone, Oliver (director, writer, producer); New York City, 9/15/46

Stone, Robert (novelist); Brooklyn, N.Y., 8/21/37

Stone, Sharon (actress); Meadville, Pa., 3/10/58

Stone, Sly (Sylvester Stone) (rock musician) 1944

Stooges, The Three (comedy team) **Moe Howard** (Moses Horwitz); Brooklyn, N.Y. **(1897–1975) Shemp Howard** (Samuel Horwitz); Brooklyn, N.Y. **(1900–1955) Larry Fine** (Laurence Feinburg); Philadelphia **(1911–1974) Curly Howard** (Jerome Horwitz); Brooklyn, N.Y. **(1906 –1952)**

Stoppard, Tom (Thomas Straussler) (playwright); Zlin, Slovakia, 7/3/37

Stout, Rex (mystery writer); Noblesville, Ind. **(1886–1975)**

Stowe, Harriet Elizabeth Beecher (novelist); Litchfield, Conn. **(1811–1896)**

Stowe, Madeleine (actress); Eagle Rock, Calif., 8/18/58

Strachey, (Giles) Lytton (biographer); London **(1880–1932)**

Stradivari, Antonio (violinmaker); Cremona, Italy **(1644–1737)**

Straight, Beatrice (actress); Old Westbury, N.Y. **(1918–2001)**

Strasberg, Lee (stage director); Budanov, Austria **(1901–1982)**

Strasberg, Susan (actress); New York City **(1938–1999)**

Stratas, Teresa (soprano); Toronto, 5/26/38

Straus, Oskar (composer); Vienna **(1870–1954)**

Strauss, Johann (composer); Vienna **(1825–1899)**

Strauss, Lewis L. (naval officer, scientist); Charleston, W. Va. **(1896–1974)**

Strauss, Peter (actor); New York City, 2/20/47

Strauss, Richard (composer); Munich, Germany **(1864–1949)**

Stravinsky, Igor (composer); Orlenbaum, Russia **(1882–1971)**

Streep, Meryl (Mary Louise) (actress); Summit, N.J., 6/22/49

Streisand, Barbra (singer, actress, director, producer, writer); Brooklyn, N.Y., 4/24/42

Strindberg, (Johan) August (dramatist); Stockholm **(1849–1912)**

Stritch, Elaine (actress); Detroit, 2/2/25

Stuart, Gilbert Charles (painter); Rhode Island **(1755–1828)**

Stuart, Gloria (film actress); Santa Monica, Calif., 7/4/10

Stuart, James Ewell Brown (known as Jeb) (Confederate army officer); Patrick County, Va. **(1833–1864)**

Sturges, Preston (Edmond P. Biden) (director, screenwriter, playwright); Chicago **(1898–1959)**

Stuyvesant, Peter (Governor of New Amsterdam); West Friesland, Netherlands **(1592–1672)**

Styne, Jule (Julius Kerwin Stein) (songwriter); London **(1905–1994)**

Styron, William (William Clark Styron, Jr.) (novelist); Newport News, Va., 6/11/25

Suharto (ex-president of Indonesia); Sedaju-Godean, Java, 2/20/21

Sukarno (Indonesian leader); Surabaja, Java **(1901–1970)**

Sullavan, Margaret Brooke (actress); Norfolk, Va. **(1911–1960)**

Sullivan, Sir Arthur Seymour (composer); London **(1842–1900)**

Sullivan, Ed (columnist, TV personality); New York City **(1901–1974)**

Sullivan, Frank (Francis John) (humorist); Saratoga Springs, N.Y. **(1892–1976)**

Sullivan, Louis Henry (architect); Boston **(1856–1924)**

Sulzberger, Arthur Ochs (newspaper publisher); New York City, 2/5/26

Sumac, Yma (singer); Ichocan, Peru, 9/10/27

Summer, Donna (La Donna Andrea Gaines) (singer); Boston, 12/31/48

Sun Ra (Herman "Sunny" Blount) (jazz composer); Birmingham, Ala. **(1914?–1993)**

Sun Tzu (writer, military strategist); China **(fl. c. 500–320 B.C.)**

Sun Yat-sen (statesman); nr. Macao **(1866–1925)**

Susann, Jacqueline (novelist); Philadelphia **(1918–1974)**

Susskind, David (TV producer); New York City **(1920–1987)**

Sutherland, Donald (actor); St. John, N.B., Canada, 7/17/34

Sutherland, Joan (soprano); Sydney, Australia, 11/7/26

Sutherland, Kiefer (actor); London, 12/18/66

Suzuki, Pat (actress); Cressey, Calif., 1931

Swados, Elizabeth (composer, playwright); Buffalo, N.Y., 2/5/51

Swank, Hilary (actress); Lincoln, Nebr., 7/30/74

Swanson, Gloria (Gloria May Josephine Svensson) (actress); Chicago **(1899–1983)**

Swarthout, Gladys (soprano); Deepwater, Mo. **(1904–1969)**

Swayze, John Cameron (news commentator); Wichita, Kans. **(1906–1995)**

Swayze, Patrick (actor, dancer); Houston, 8/18/54

Swedenborg, Emanuel (scientist, philosopher, mystic); Stockholm **(1688–1772)**

Swift, Jonathan (satirist); Dublin **(1667–1745)**

Swinburne, Algernon Charles (poet); London **(1837–1909)**

Swit, Loretta (actress); Passaic, N.J., 11/4/37

Swope, Herbert Bayard (journalist); St. Louis **(1882–1958)**

Sydow, Max von (Carl Adolf von Sydow) (actor); Lund, Sweden, 4/10/29

Symons, Arthur (poet, critic); Milford Haven, Wales **(1865–1945)**

Synge, John Millington (dramatist); nr. Dublin **(1871–1909)**

Szilard, Leo (physicist); Budapest **(1898–1964)**

T

Taft, Robert Alphonso (legislator); Cincinnati **(1889–1953)**

Taft, William Howard (27th U.S. president); Cincinnati **(1857–1930)**

Tagore, Sir Rabindranath (poet); Calcutta **(1861–1941)**

Talichief, Maria (ballet dancer); Fairfax, Okla., 1/24/25

Talleyrand-Pèrigord, Charles Maurice de (statesman); Paris **(1754–1838)**

Talmadge, Norma (actress); Niagara Falls, N.Y. **(1897–1957)**

Tamerlane (Timur) (Mongol conqueror); nr. Samarkand, Turkestan **(c. 1336–1405)**

Tamiroff, Akim (actor); Baku, Azerbaijan **(1899–1972)**

Tan, Amy (novelist); Oakland, Calif., 2/19/52

Tanaka, Tomoyuki (film producer); Osaka, Japan **(1910–1997)**

Tandy, Jessica (actress); London **(1909–1994)**

Tarbell, Ida Minerva (author; muckraker); Erie Co., Pa. **(1857–1944)**

Tarkington, (Newton) Booth (novelist); Indianapolis **(1869–1946)**

Tartikoff, Brandon (television executive); Freeport, N.Y. **(1949–1997)**

Tate, Allen (John Orley) (poet, critic); Winchester, Ky. **(1899–1979)**

Tate, Sharon (actress); Dallas **(1943–1969)**

Taylor, Deems (composer); New York City **(1885–1966)**

Taylor, Elizabeth (actress); London, 2/27/32

Taylor, Harold (educator); Toronto, 9/28/14

Taylor, James (singer, songwriter); Boston, 3/12/48

Taylor, Laurette (Laurette Cooney) (actress); New York City **(1884–1946)**

Taylor, Lili (actress); Glenco, Ill., 2/20/67
Taylor, Gen. Maxwell D. (former Army chief of staff); Keytesville, Mo. **(1901–1987)**
Taylor, Niki (model); Pembroke Pines, Fla., 3/5/75
Taylor, Paul (choreographer); Wilkinsburg, Pa., 7/29/30
Taylor, Rod (actor); Sydney, Australia, 1/11/30
Taylor, Zachary (12th U.S. president); Montebello, Orange County, Va. **(1784–1850)**
Tchaikovsky, Peter (Pëtr) Ilich (composer); Votkinsk, Russia **(1840–1893)**
Teasdale, Sara (poet); St. Louis **(1884–1933)**
Tebaldi, Renata (lyric soprano); Pesaro, Italy **(1922–2004)**
Tecumseh (Shawnee Indian chief); nr. Springfield, Ohio **(1768–1813)**
Te Kanawa, Kiri (soprano); Gisborne, New Zealand, 3/6/44
Telemann, Georg Philipp (composer); Magdeburg, Germany **(1681–1767)**
Teller, Edward (atomic physicist); Budapest **(1908–2003)**
Templeton, Alec Andrew (pianist, composer); Cardiff, Wales **(1910–1963)**
Tennille, Toni (singer); Montgomery, Ala., 5/8/43
Tennyson, Alfred (1st Baron Tennyson) (poet); Somersby, England **(1809–1892)**
Tenskwatawa (Shawnee prophet); Old Piqua, Ohio **(c. 1770–c. 1835)**
Terhune, Albert Payson (novelist, journalist); Newark, N.J. **(1872–1942)**
Terkel, Studs (writer, interviewer); New York City, 5/16/12
Terry, Ellen Alicia (actress); Coventry, England **(1848–1928)**
Terry-Thomas (Thomas Terry Hoar Stevens) (actor); London **(1911–1990)**
Tesla, Nikola (electrical engineer, inventor); Smiljan, Lika, Croatia **(1856–1943)**
Thackeray, William Makepeace (novelist); Calcutta **(1811–1863)**
Thalberg, Irving G. (producer); Brooklyn, N.Y. **(1899–1936)**
Thant, U (U.N. statesman); Pantanaw, Burma **(1909–1974)**
Tharp, Twyla (dancer, choreographer); Portland, Ind., 7/1/42
Thatcher, Margaret (former prime minister); Grantham, England, 10/13/25
Theodorakis, Mikis (composer); Chios, Greece, 7/29/25
Thicke, Alan (actor, composer); Kirland Lake, Ont., Canada, 3/1/47
Thieu, Nguyen Van (ex-president of South Vietnam); Trithuy, Vietnam, 4/5/23
Thomas, Danny (Amos Jacobs) (entertainer, TV producer); Deerfield, Mich. **(1912–1991)**
Thomas, Dylan Marlais (poet); Carmarthenshire, Wales **(1914–1953)**
Thomas, JonathanTaylor (actor); Bethlehem, Pa., 9/8/81
Thomas, Kristen Scott (actress); Redruth, Cornwall, England, 1960
Thomas, Lowell (explorer, commentator); Woodington, Ohio **(1892–1981)**
Thomas, Marlo (actress); Detroit, 11/21/43
Thomas, Michael Tilson (conductor); Hollywood, Calif., 12/21/44
Thomas, Norman Mattoon (Socialist leader); Marion, Ohio **(1884–1968)**
Thomas, Philip Michael (actor); Columbus, Ohio, 5/26/49
Thomas, Richard (actor); New York City, 6/13/51
Thomas, Rob (singer, songwriter); Landstuhl, Germany, 2/14/72
Thompson, Dorothy (writer); Lancaster, N.Y. **(1894–1961)**
Thompson, Emma (actress); London, 4/15/59
Thompson, Hunter (Stockton) (writer); Louisville, Ky. **(1939–2005)**
Thompson, Lea (actress); Rochester, Minn., 5/31/61
Thompson, Tommy G. (ex-secretary of Health and Human Services); Elroy, Wis., 11/19/41
Thomson, Virgil (Garnett) (composer); Kansas City, Mo. **(1896–1989)**
Thoreau, Henry David (naturalist, author); Concord, Mass. **(1817–1862)**
Thorndike, Dame Sybil (actress); Gainsborough, England **(1882–1976)**
Thorne-Smith, Courtney (actress); San Francisco, 11/8/67
Thornton, Billy Bob (actor, screenwriter); Hot Springs, Ark., 8/4/55
Thurber, James Grover (author, cartoonist); Columbus, Ohio **(1894–1961)**
Thurman, Robert A. F. (scholar, Indo-Tibetan Buddhist studies); New York City, 8/6/40
Thurman, Uma (actress); Boston, 4/29/70
Thurmond, (James) Strom (U.S. senator); Edgefield, S.C. **(1902–2003)**
Tibbett, Lawrence (baritone); Bakersfield, Calif. **(1896–1960)**
Tiberius Caesar Augustus (Roman emperor); Capri **(42 B.C.–A.D. 37)**
Tiegs, Cheryl (model, actress); Minnesota, 9/25/47
Tierney, Gene (actress); Brooklyn, N.Y. **(1920–1991)**

Tillich, Paul (philosopher, theologian); Starzeddel, Germany **(1886–1965)**
Tilly, Meg (Margaret Tilly) (actress); Texada Island, B.C., Canada, 2/14/60
Tintoretto, Il (Jacopo Robusti) (painter); Venice **(1518–1594)**
Tiny Tim (Herbert Khaury) (entertainer); New York City **(1932–1996)**
Tiomkin, Dmitri (composer); St. Petersburg, Russia **(1894–1979)**
Titian (Tiziano Vecelli) (painter); Pieve di Cadore, Italy **(1477–1576)**
Tito (Josip Broz or Brozovich) (president of Yugoslavia); Croatia (former Yugoslavia) **(1892–1980)**
Tocqueville, Alexis de (writer); Verneuil, France **(1805–1859)**
Todd, Michael (producer); Minneapolis **(1907–1958)**
Tolkien, J(ohn) R(onald) R(euel) (fantasy writer); Bloemfontein, South Africa **(1892–1973)**
Tolstoy, Count Leo (Lev) Nikolaevich (novelist); Tula Province, Russia **(1828–1910)**
Tomei, Marisa (actress); Brooklyn, N.Y., 12/4/64
Tomlin, Lily (actress, comedienne); Detroit, 9/1/36
Tone, Franchot (actor); Niagara Falls, N.Y. **(1905–1968)**
Tormé, Mel (Melvin) (singer); Chicago **(1925–1999)**
Torn, Rip (Elmore Torn, Jr.) (actor, director); Temple, Tex., 2/6/31
Torquamada, Tomásde (Spanish Inquisitor); Valladolid, Spain **(1420–1498)**
Toscanini, Arturo (orchestra conductor); Parma, Italy **(1867–1957)**
Totenberg, Nina (broadcast journalist); New York City, 1/14/44
Toulouse-Lautrec (Henri Marie Raymond de Toulouse-Lautrec Monfa) (painter); Albi, France **(1864–1901)**
Toynbee, Arnold J. (historian); London **(1889–1975)**
Tracy, Spencer (actor); Milwaukee **(1900–1967)**
Traubel, Helen (Wagnerian soprano); St. Louis **(1903–1972)**
Travanti, Daniel J. (actor); Kenosha, Wis., 3/7/40
Travolta, John (actor); Englewood, N.J., 2/18/54
Treacher, Arthur (actor); Brighton, England **(1894–1975)**
Tree, Sir Herbert Beerbohm (actor, manager); London **(1853–1917)**
Trevor, Claire (Wemlinger) (actress); New York City **(1909–2000)**
Trigère, Pauline (fashion designer); Paris **(1912–2002)**
Trilling, Diana (writer); New York City **(1905–1996)**
Trilling, Lionel (author, educator); New York City **(1905–1975)**
Trollope, Anthony (novelist); London **(1815–1882)**
Trotsky, Leon (Lev Davidovich Bronstein) (statesman); Elisavetgrad, Russia **(1879–1940)**
Trudeau, Garry (cartoonist); New York City, 1948
Trudeau, Pierre Elliott (former prime minister); Montreal **(1919–2000)**
Truffaut, François (film director); Paris **(1932–1984)**
Trujillo y Molina, Rafael Leonidas (dictator); San Cristóbal, Dominican Republic **(1891–1961)**
Truman, Harry S. (33rd U.S. president); near Lamar, Mo. **(1884–1972)**
Truman, Margaret (author); Independence, Mo., 2/17/24
Trump, Donald (business executive); New York City, 6/14/46
Truth, Sojourner (Isabella) (preacher, abolitionist); Ulster Co., N.Y. **(c. 1797–1883)**
Tryon, Thomas (actor, novelist); Hartford, Conn. **(1926–1991)**
Tsiolkovsky, Konstantin E. (father of cosmonautics); Izhevskoye, Russia **(1857–1935)**
Tsongas, Paul E. (politician); Lowell, Mass. **(1941–1997)**
Tubman, Harriet (Araminta) (abolitionist); Dorchester Co., Md. **(c. 1820–1913)**
Tuchman, Barbara (Wertheim) (historian, author); New York City **(1912–1989)**
Tucker, Forrest (actor); Plainfield, Ind. **(1919–1986)**
Tucker, Richard (tenor); New York City **(1913–1975)**
Tucker, Sophie (Sophia Kalish) (singer); Russia **(1884–1966)**
Tudor, Antony (choreographer); London **(1909–1987)**
Tune, Tommy (dancer, choreographer); Wichita Falls, Tex., 2/28/39
Turgenev, Ivan Sergeevich (novelist); Orel, Russia **(1818–1883)**
Turlington, Christy (model); San Francisco, 1/2/69
Turner, Frederick J. (historian); Portage, Wis. **(1861–1932)**
Turner, Ike (singer); Clarksdale, Miss., 11/5/31
Turner, Joseph M.W. (painter); London **(1775–1851)**
Turner, Kathleen (actress); Springfield, Mo., 6/19/54
Turner, Lana (Julia Jean Mildred Frances Turner) (actress); Wallace, Idaho **(1920–1995)**
Turner, Nat (civil rights leader); Southampton County, Va. **(1800–1831)**
Turner, Ted (business executive); Cincinnati, 11/19/38
Turner, Tina (Annie Mae Bullock) (singer); Nut Bush, Tenn., 11/26/39
Turpin, Ben (comedian); New Orleans **(1874–1940)**
Turturro, John (actor); Brooklyn, N.Y., 2/28/57
Twain, Mark (Samuel Langhorne Clemens) (author); Florida, Mo. **(1835–1910)**

Twain, Shania (Eileen Regina Twain) (country singer); Windsor, Ont., Canada, 8/28/65

Tweed, William Marcy (politician); New York City **(1823–1878)**

Twiggy (Leslie Hornby) (model); London, 9/19/49

Twining, Gen. Nathan F. (former Air Force chief of staff); Monroe, Wis. **(1897–1982)**

Twitty, Conway (Harold Lloyd Jenkins) (singer, guitarist); Friars Point, Miss. **(1933–1993)**

Tyler, John (10th U.S. president); Charles City County, Va. **(1790–1862)**

Tyler, Liv (actress, model); Portland, Maine, 7/1/77

Tyler, Steven (singer); New York City, 3/26/48

Tyson, Cicely (actress); New York City, 12/19/33

U

Uccello, Paolo (painter); Florence **(1397–1475)**

Udall, Stewart L. (ex-secretary of the interior); St. Johns, Ariz., 1/31/20

Uggams, Leslie (singer, actress); New York City, 5/25/43

Ulanova, Galina (ballet dancer); St. Petersburg, Russia **(1910–1998)**

Ullman, Tracey (actress, singer); Slough, England, 12/30/59

Ullmann, Liv (actress); Tokyo, 12/16/39

Ulrich, Skeet (actor, model); North Carolina, 1/20/70

Untermeyer, Louis (anthologist, poet); New York City **(1885–1977)**

Updike, John (novelist); Shillington, Pa., 3/18/32

Urey, Harold C. (chemist, Nobel laureate); Walkerton, Ind. **(1893–1981)**

Uris, Leon (novelist); Baltimore **(1924–2003)**

Ustinov, Peter (actor, producer); London **(1921–2004)**

Utrillo, Maurice (painter); Paris **(1883–1955)**

V

Vaccaro, Brenda (actress); Brooklyn, N.Y., 11/18/39

Vadim, Roger (Roger Vadim Plemiannikov) (film director); Paris **(1928–2000)**

Valentine, Karen (actress); Sabastopol, Calif., 5/25/47

Valentino, Rudolph (Rodolpho d'Antonguolla) (actor); Castellaneta, Italy **(1895–1926)**

Valentino (Valentino Garavani) (fashion designer); nr. Milan, Italy, 5/11/32

Valéry, Paul (Ambroise Toussaint Jules) (poet, critic); Sète, France **(1871–1945)**

Vallee, Rudy (Hubert Prior Rudy Vallée) (band leader, singer); Island Pond, Vt. **(1901–1986)**

Valli, Frankie (Frank Castellaccio) (singer); Newark, N.J., 5/3/37

Van Allen, James Alfred (space physicist); Mt. Pleasant, Iowa, 9/7/14

Van Buren, Abigail (Pauline Esther Friedman) (columnist); Sioux City, Iowa, 7/4/18

Van Buren, Martin (8th U.S. president); Kinderhook, N.Y. **(1782–1862)**

Vance, Vivian (Vivian Jones) (actress); Cherryvale, Kans. **(1909–1979)**

Van Der Beek, James (actor); Cheshire, Conn., 3/8/77

Vanderbilt, Alfred G. (sportsman); London **(1912–1999)**

Vanderbilt, Cornelius (financier); Port Richmond, N.Y. **(1794–1877)**

Vanderbilt, Gloria (fashion designer); New York City, 2/20/24

Van Doren, Carl (writer, educator); Hope, Ill. **(1885–1950)**

Van Doren, Mamie (actress); Rowena, S.D., 2/6/33

Vandross, Luther (R&B singer); New York City **(1951–2005)**

Van Dyke, Dick (actor); West Plains, Mo., 12/13/25

Vandyke (or Van Dyck), Sir Anthony (painter); Antwerp, Belgium **(1599–1641)**

Van Eyck, Jan (painter); Maeseyck, Belgium **(c. 1390–1441)**

Van Fleet, Jo (actress); Oakland, Calif. **(1915–1996)**

van Gogh, Vincent (painter); Groot Zundert, Brabant, The Netherlands **(1853–1890)**

van Hamel, Martine (ballet dancer); Brussels, 11/16/45

Van Heusen, Jimmy (Edward Chester Babcock) (songwriter); Syracuse, N.Y. **(1913–1990)**

Van Patten, Dick (actor); Richmond Hill, N.Y., 12/9/28

Van Peebles, Melvin (playwright); Chicago, 8/21/32

Vasari, Giorgio (art historian); Arezzo, Italy **(1511–1574)**

Vaughan, Sarah (singer); Newark, N.J. **(1924–1990)**

Vaughan Williams, Ralph (composer); Down Ampney, England **(1872–1958)**

Vaughn, Robert (actor); New York City, 11/22/32

Vaughn, Vince (actor); Minneapolis, 3/28/70

Veblen, Thorstein (economist, social critic); Cato Township, Wis. **(1857–1929)**

Veidt, Conrad (actor); Potsdam, Germany **(1893–1943)**

Velázquez, Diego Rodriguez de Silva y (painter); Seville, Spain **(1599–1660)**

Veneman, Ann (UNICEF executive director); Modesto, Calif., 6/29/49

Venturi, Robert (Charles) (architect); Philadelphia, 6/25/25

Verdi, Giuseppe (composer); Roncole, Italy **(1813–1901)**

Verdon, Gwen (actress); Culver City, Calif. **(1925–2000)**

Vereen, Ben (actor, singer); Miami, Fla., 10/10/46

Verlaine, Paul (poet); Metz, France **(1844–1896)**

Vermeer, Jan (or Jan van der Meer van Delft) (painter); Delft, Netherlands **(1632–1675)**

Verne, Jules (author); Nantes, France **(1828–1905)**

Veronese, Paolo (Paolo Cagliari) (painter); Verona, Italy **(1528–1588)**

Verrazano, Giovanni da (navigator); Florence, Italy **(c. 1485–1528)**

Verrett, Shirley (mezzo-soprano); New Orleans, 5/31/33

Versace, Gianni (fashion designer); Reggio di Calabria, Italy **(1946–1997)**

Vesalius, Andreas (anatomist); Brussels **(1515–1564)**

Vespucci, Amerigo (navigator); Florence, Italy **(1454–1512)**

Vico, Giovanni Battista (philosopher); Naples, Italy **(1668–1744)**

Victoria (queen of England); London **(1819–1901)**

Vidal, Gore (novelist); West Point, N.Y., 10/3/25

Vidor, King (film director, producer); Galveston, Tex. **(1895–1982)**

Vigoda, Abe (actor); New York City, 2/24/21

Villa, Pancho (Doroteo Arango) (revolutionary); Hacienda de Rio Grande, San Juan del Rio, Mexico **(1877–1923)**

Villella, Edward (ballet dancer); Bayside, Queens, N.Y., 10/1/36

Villon, François (François de Montcorbier) (poet); Paris **(1431–1463)**

Vinton, Bobby (singer); Canonsburg, Pa., 4/16/35

Virgil (or Vergil) (Publius Vergilius Maro) (poet); nr. Mantua, Italy **(70–19 b.c.)**

Vishnevskaya, Galina (soprano); St. Petersburg, Russia, 10/25/26

Vivaldi, Antonio (composer); Venice **(1678–1741)**

Vlaminck, Maurice de (painter); Paris **(1876–1958)**

Voight, Jon (actor); Yonkers, N.Y., 12/29/38

Volta, Alessandro (scientist); Como, Italy **(1745–1827)**

Voltaire (François Marie Arouet) (author); Paris **(1694–1778)**

von Braun, Wernher (rocket scientist); Wirsitz, Germany **(1912–1977)**

von Furstenberg, Betsy (Elizabeth Caroline Maria Agatha Felicitas Therese von Furstenberg-Hedringen) (actress); Nelheim-Heusen, Germany, 8/16/35

von Fürstenberg, Diane (Diane Simone Michelle Halfin) (fashion designer); Brussels, 12/31/46

von Hindenburg, Paul (statesman); Posen, Poland **(1847–1934)**

von Karajan, Herbert (conductor); Salzburg, Austria **(1908–1989)**

Vonnegut, Kurt, Jr. (novelist); Indianapolis, 11/11/22

Von Stade, Frederica (mezzo-soprano); Somerville, N.J., 6/1/45

Von Stroheim, Erich Oswald Hans Carl Maria von Nordenwall (actor, director); Vienna **(1885–1957)**

Von Zell, Harry (announcer); Indianapolis **(1906–1981)**

Vreeland, Diana (Diana Da Iziel) (fashion journalist, museum consultant); Paris **(1903?–1989)**

W

Wagner, Lindsay (actress); Los Angeles, 6/22/49

Wagner, Robert (actor); Detroit, 2/10/30

Wagner, Robert F. (ex-mayor of New York City); New York City **(1910–1991)**

Wagner, Wilhelm Richard (composer); Leipzig, Germany **(1813–1883)**

Wahlberg, Mark (actor, model, musician); Dorchester, Mass., 6/5/71

Waits, Tom (blues singer); Pomona, Calif., 12/7/49

Waldheim, Kurt (ex-UN secretary-general); St. Andrae-Wörden, Austria, 12/21/18

Walesa, Lech (Polish labor leader and ex-president); Popowo, Poland, 9/29/43

Walken, Christopher (actor); Queens, N.Y., 3/31/43

Walker, Alice (novelist, poet); Eatonon, Ga., 2/9/44

Walker, Nancy (Ann Myrtle Swoyer) (actress, comedienne); Philadelphia **(1922–1992)**

Walker, Robert (actor); Salt Lake City **(1918–1951)**

Walker, T-Bone (blues singer); Linden, Tex. **(1910–1975)**

Wallace, DeWitt (publisher); St. Paul, Minn. **(1889–1981)**

Wallace, George C. (ex-governor); Clio, Ala. **(1919–1998)**

Wallace, Irving (novelist); Chicago **(1916–1990)**

Wallace, Mike (Myron Wallace) (TV interviewer, commentator); Brookline, Mass., 5/9/18

Wallach, Eli (actor); Brooklyn, N.Y., 12/7/15

Wallenberg, Raoul (diplomat, humanitarian); Stockholm (1912–1947)
Wallenstein, Alfred (conductor); Chicago (1898–1983)
Waller, Thomas "Fats" (pianist); New York City (1904–1943)
Wallis, Hal (film producer); Chicago (1899–1986)
Walpole, Horace (statesman, novelist); London (1717–1797)
Walsh, J. T. (actor); San Francisco, Calif. (1944–1998)
Waltari, Mika (novelist); Helsinki (1903–1979)
Walter, Bruno (Bruno Walter Schlesinger) (orchestra conductor); Berlin (1876–1962)
Walters, Barbara (TV commentator); Boston, 9/25/31
Walton, Izaak (author); Stafford, England (1593–1683)
Walton, Sam (retailer); Kingfisher, Okla. (1918–1992)
Wambaugh, Joseph (author, screenwriter); East Pittsburgh, 1/22/37
Wanamaker, John (merchant); Philadelphia (1838–1922)
Wanamaker, Sam (actor, director); Chicago (1919–1993)
Ward, Barbara (economist); York, England (1914–1981)
Ward, Rachel (actress); Cornwell Manor, England, 9/12/57
Warhol, Andy (Warhola) (artist); McKeesport, Pa. (1928–1987)
Waring, Fred (band leader); Tyrone, Pa. (1900–1984)
Warner, H. B. (Henry Bryan Warner Lickford) (actor); London (1876–1958)
Warren, Lesley Ann (actress); New York City, 8/16/46
Warren, Robert Penn (novelist); Guthrie, Ky. (1905–1989)
Warrick, Ruth (actress); St. Joseph, Mo. (1915–2005)
Warwick, Dionne (singer); East Orange, N.J., 12/12/41
Washington, Booker T(aliaferro) (educator); Franklin County, Va. (1856–1915)
Washington, Denzel (actor); Mt. Vernon, N.Y., 12/28/54
Washington, George (1st U.S. president); Westmoreland County, Va. (1732–1799)
Washington, Harold (ex-mayor of Chicago); Chicago (1922–1987)
Waters, Ethel (actress, singer); Chester, Pa. (1896–1977)
Waters, Muddy (McKinley Morganfield) (singer, guitarist); Rolling Fork, Miss. (1915–1983)
Waterston, Sam (actor); Cambridge, Mass., 11/15/40
Watson, Emma (actress); Oxfordshire, England, 4/15/90
Watson, James Dewey (scientist, Nobel laureate); Chicago, 4/6/28
Watson, Thomas John (industrialist); Campbell, N.Y. (1874–1956)
Watt, James (inventor); Greenock, Scotland (1736–1819)
Watteau, Jean-Antoine (painter); Valanciennes, France (1684–1721)
Wattleton, Faye (family planning advocate); St. Louis, 7/8/43
Watts, André (concert pianist); Nuremberg, Germany, 6/20/46
Watts, Naomi (actress); Shoreham, England, 9/28/68
Waugh, Alec (Alexander Raban Waugh) (novelist); London (1898–1981)
Waugh, Evelyn (novelist); London (1903–1966)
Wayans, Damon (actor, comedian, writer, producer); New York City, 9/4/60
Wayans, Keenan Ivory (actor, comedian, writer, director); New York City, 6/8/58
Wayne, Anthony (military officer); Waynesboro (family farm), nr. Paoli, Pa. (1745–1796)
Wayne, David (David McMeekan) (actor); Traverse City, Mich. (1914–1995)
Wayne, John (Marion Michael Morrison) (actor); Winterset, Iowa (1907–1979)
Weaver, Dennis (actor); Joplin, Mo., 6/4/25
Weaver, Fritz (actor); Pittsburgh, 1/19/26
Weaver, Sigourney (actress); New York City, 10/8/49
Webb, Clifton (Webb Parmelee Hollenbeck) (actor); Indianapolis (1893–1966)
Webb, Jack (actor, producer); Santa Monica, Calif. (1920–1982)
Weber, Karl Maria Friedrich Ernst von (composer); nr. Lübeck, Germany (1786–1826)
Webster, Daniel (statesman); Salisbury, N.H. (1782–1852)
Webster, Margaret (producer, director, actress); New York City (1905–1973)
Webster, Noah (lexicographer); West Hartford, Conn. (1758–1843)
Weill, Kurt (composer); Dessau, Germany (1900–1950)
Weir, Peter (director); Sydney, Australia, 8/21/44
Weissmuller, Johnny (Peter John Weissmuller) (actor, swimmer); Freidorf, Romania (1904–1984)
Weizmann, Chaim (statesman); Grodno Province, Russia (1874–1952)
Welch, Raquel (Raquel Tejada) (actress); Chicago, 9/5/40
Weld, Tuesday (Susan Ker Weld) (actress); New York City, 8/27/43
Welk, Lawrence (band leader); Strasburg, N.D. (1903–1992)
Welles, Orson (actor, director, producer); Kenosha, Wis. (1915–1985)
Wellington, Duke of (Arthur Wellesley) (statesman); Ireland (1769–1852)
Wells, H(erbert) G(eorge) (author); Bromley, England (1866–1946)
Wells-Barnett, Ida B. (journalist); Holly Springs, Miss. (1862–1931)
Welty, Eudora (novelist); Jackson, Miss. (1909–2001)

Wenner, Jann (publisher); New York City, 1/7/46
Werfel, Franz (novelist); Prague (1890–1945)
Werner, Oskar (Josef Schliessmayer) (actor, director); Vienna (1922–1984)
Wertheimer, Linda (radio journalist); Carlsbad, N.M., 3/19/43
Wertmueller, Lina (Arcanguela Felice Assunta W. von Elgg) (director); Rome, 8/14/28
Wesley, John (religious leader); Epworth Rectory, Lincolnshire, England (1703–1791)
West, Benjamin (painter); Springfield, Pa. (1738–1820)
West, Dame Rebecca (Cicily Fairfield) (novelist); County Kerry, Ireland (1892–1983)
West, Jessamyn (novelist); nr. North Vernon, Ind. (1902–1984)
West, Mae (actress); Brooklyn, N.Y. (1893–1980)
West, Nathanael (Nathan Weinstein) (novelist); New York City (1902–1940)
Westheimer, Dr. Ruth (Karola Ruth Siegel) (human sexuality expert); Frankfurt, Germany, 1928
Westinghouse, George (inventor); Central Bridge, N.Y. (1846–1914)
Westmoreland, William Childs (ex-Army chief of staff); Saxon, S.C. (1914–2005)
Weyden, Roger van der (painter); Tournai, Belgium (c. 1400–1464)
Wharton, Edith Newbold (née Jones) (novelist); New York City (1862–1937)
Wheatley, Phillis (poet); Senegal (c. 1753–1784)
Whedon, Joss (screenwriter, director) 6/23/64
Wheeler, Bert (Albert Jerome Wheeler) (comedian); Paterson, N.J. (1895–1968)
Whistler, James Abbott McNeill (painter, etcher); Lowell, Mass. (1834–1903)
Whitaker, Forest (actor); Longview, Tex., 7/15/61
White, Betty (actress); Oak Park, Ill., 1/17/22
White, Edmund (writer); Cincinnati, Ohio, 1/13/40
White, E(lwyn) B(rooks) (author); Mt. Vernon, N.Y. (1899–1985)
White, Pearl (actress); Green Ridge, Mo. (1889–1938)
White, Stanford (architect); New York City (1853–1906)
White, Theodore H. (historian); Boston (1915–1986)
White, Vanna (TV personality); Conway, S.C., 2/18/57
White, William Allen (journalist); Emporia, Kans. (1868–1944)
Whitehead, Alfred North (mathematician, philosopher); Isle of Thanet, England (1861–1947)
Whiteman, Paul (band leader); Denver (1891–1967)
Whiting, Margaret (singer, actress); Detroit, 7/22/24
Whitman, Walt (Walter) (poet); West Hills, N.Y. (1819–1892)
Whitmore, James (actor); White Plains, N.Y., 10/1/21
Whitney, Cornelius Vanderbilt (sportsman); New York City (1899–1992)
Whitney, Eli (inventor); Westboro, Mass. (1765–1825)
Whitney, John Hay (publisher); Ellsworth, Maine (1904–1982)
Whittier, John Greenleaf (poet); Haverhill, Mass. (1807–1892)
Wideman, John Edgar (writer); Washington, D.C., 6/14/41
Widmark, Richard (actor); Sunrise, Minn., 12/26/14
Wiesel, Elie (Eliezer) (author); Signet, Romania, 9/30/28
Wiesenthal, Simon (Nazi hunter); Buchach, Ukraine, 12/31/08
Wilde, Cornel (film actor, producer); New York City (1915–1989)
Wilde, Oscar Fingal O'Flahertie Wills (author); Dublin (1854–1900)
Wilder, Billy (Samuel Wilder) (film producer, director); Vienna (1906–2002)
Wilder, Gene (Jerome Silberman) (actor, writer, director, producer); Milwaukee, 6/11/35
Wilder, Thornton (author); Madison, Wis. (1897–1975)
Wilkins, Roy (civil rights leader); St. Louis (1901–1981)
William, Prince (heir to British throne); London, 6/21/82
Williams, Andy (singer); Wall Lake, Iowa, 12/3/30
Williams, Anson (actor, director); Los Angeles, 9/25/49
Williams, Billy Dee (actor); New York City, 4/6/37
Williams, Cindy (actress); Van Nuys, Calif., 8/22/47
Williams, Edward Bennett (lawyer); Hartford, Conn. (1920–1988)
Williams, Emlyn (actor, playwright); Mostyn, Wales (1905–1987)
Williams, Esther (actress, swimmer); Los Angeles, 8/8/23
Williams, Gluyas (cartoonist); San Francisco (1888–1982)
Williams, Hank, Sr. (Hiram King Williams) (singer); Georgiana, Ala. (1923–1953)
Williams, Joe (singer); Cordele, Ga. (1918–1999)
Williams, John T. (composer, conductor); Queens, N.Y., 2/8/32
Williams, Lucinda (singer, songwriter); Lake Charles, La., 1/26/53
Williams, Paul (singer, composer, actor); Omaha, Neb., 9/19/40
Williams, Robin (actor, producer); Chicago, 7/21/52
Williams, Roger (clergyman); London (1603?–1683)
Williams, Tennessee (Thomas L. Williams) (playwright); Columbus, Miss. (1911–1983)
Williams, Treat (Richard Williams) (actor); Rowayton, Conn., 12/1/51

Williams, Vanessa (actress, singer); Milwood, N.Y., 3/18/63
Williams, William Carlos (physician, poet); Rutherford, N.J. **(1883–1963)**
Williamson, Nicol (actor); Hamilton, Scotland, 9/14/38
Willkie, Wendell Lewis (lawyer); Elwood, Ind. **(1892–1944)**
Willis, Bruce (actor); Germany, 3/19/55
Willson, Meredith (composer); Mason City, Iowa **(1902–1984)**
Wilson, August (poet, writer, playwright); Pittsburgh, 4/27/45
Wilson, Brian (musician); Inglewood, Calif., 6/20/42
Wilson, Don (radio and TV announcer); Lincoln, Neb. **(1900–1982)**
Wilson, Dooley (actor, musician); Tyler, Tex. **(1894–1953)**
Wilson, Edmund (literary critic, author); Red Bank, N.J. **(1895–1972)**
Wilson, Flip (Clerow Wilson) (comedian); Jersey City, N.J. **(1933–1998)**
Wilson, Harold (ex-prime minister); Huddersfield, England **(1916–1995)**
Wilson, Nancy (singer); Chillicothe, Ohio, 2/20/37
Wilson, Sloan (novelist); Norwalk, Conn. **(1920–2003)**
Wilson, (Thomas) Woodrow (28th U.S. president); Staunton, Va. **(1856–1924)**
Winchell, Walter (columnist); New York City **(1897–1972)**
Windsor, Duchess of (Bessie Wallis Warfield) Blue Ridge Summit, Pa. **(1896–1986)**
Windsor, Duke of (formerly King Edward VIII of England); Richmond Park, England **(1894–1972)**
Winfrey, Oprah (TV host, producer); Kosciusko, Miss., 1/29/54
Winger, Debra (Mary Debra) (actress); Cleveland, 5/17/55
Winkler, Henry (actor, director, producer); New York City, 10/30/45
Winningham, Mare (actress); Phoenix, Ariz., 5/16/59
Winslet, Kate (actress); Berkshire, England, 10/5/75
Winter, Johnny (guitarist); Leland, Miss., 2/23/44
Winters, Jonathan (comedian); Dayton, Ohio, 11/11/25
Winters, Shelley (Shirley Schrift) (actress); East St. Louis, Ill., 8/18/22
Winthrop, John (first governor, Massachusetts Bay Colony); Suffolk, England **(1588–1649)**
Wise, Stephen Samuel (rabbi); Budapest **(1874–1949)**
Withers, Jane (actress); Atlanta, 4/12/26
Witherspoon, Reese (actress); Nashville, 3/22/76
Wittig, Georg F. K. (chemist, Nobel laureate); Berlin, Germany **(1897–1987)**
Wittgenstein, Ludwig (Josef Johann) (philosopher); Vienna **(1889–1951)**
Wodehouse, P(elham) G(renville) (novelist); Guildford, England **(1881–1975)**
Wolf, Scott (actor); Boston, 6/4/68
Wolfe, Thomas Clayton (novelist); Asheville, N.C. **(1900–1938)**
Wolfe, Tom (journalist); Richmond, Va., 3/2/31
Wolff, Tobias (author); Birmingham, Ala., 6/19/45
Wolsey, Thomas (prelate, statesman); Ipswich, England **(c. 1475–1530)**
Wonder, Stevie (Steveland Judkins, later Steveland Morris) (singer, songwriter); Saginaw, Mich., 5/13/50
Wong, Anna May (Lu Tsong Wong) (actress); Los Angeles **(1907–1961)**
Woo, John (actor, film director, screenwriter); Guangzhou, Canton, China, 5/1/46
Wood, Elijah (actor); Cedar Rapids, Iowa, 1/28/81
Wood, Grant (painter); Anamosa, Iowa **(1892–1942)**
Wood, Natalie (Natasha Viparaeff) (actress); San Francisco **(1938–1981)**
Woods, James (actor); Vernal, Utah, 4/18/47
Woodhouse, Barbara (Blackburn) (dog trainer, author, TV personality); Rathfarnham, Ireland **(1910–1988)**
Woodruff, Judy (broadcast journalist); Tulsa, Okla., 11/20/46
Woodson, Carter G. (historian); New Canton, Va. **(1875–1950)**
Woodward, Edward (actor); Croydon, England, 6/1/30
Woodward, Joanne (actress); Thomasville, Ga., 2/27/30
Woodward, Robert Burns (chemist, Nobel laureate); Boston **(1917–1979)**
Woolf, (Adeline) Virginia (née Stephens) (novelist); London **(1882–1941)**
Woollcott, Alexander (author, critic); Phalanx, N.J. **(1887–1943)**
Woolley, Monty (Edgar Montillion Woolley) (actor); New York City **(1888–1963)**
Woolworth, Frank (merchant); Rodman, N.Y. **(1852–1919)**
Wopat, Tom (actor); Lodi, Wis., 9/9/50
Wordsworth, William (poet); Cockermouth, England **(1770–1850)**
Wouk, Herman (novelist); New York City, 5/27/15
Wovoka (Jack Wilson) (Paiute Indian religious leader); (western Nev.) **(c. 1858–1932)**

Wray, Fay (actress); nr. Cardston, Alb., Canada **(19/07–2004)**
Wren, Sir Christopher (architect); East Knoyle, England **(1632–1723)**
Wright, Frank Lloyd (architect); Richland Center, Wis. **(1869–1959)**
Wright, Martha (singer); Seattle, 3/23/26
Wright, Orville (inventor); Dayton, Ohio **(1871–1948)**
Wright, Richard (novelist); nr. Natchez, Miss. **(1908–1960)**
Wright, Teresa (actress); New York City **(1918–2005)**
Wright, Wilbur (inventor); Millville, Ind. **(1867–1912)**
Wyatt, Jane (actress); Campgaw, N.J., 8/12/12
Wycliffe, John (church reformer); Hipswell, England **(1320–1384)**
Wyeth, Andrew (painter); Chadds Ford, Pa., 7/12/17
Wyle, Noah (actor); Hollywood, Calif., 6/4/71
Wyler, William (director); Mulhouse, France **(1902–1981)**
Wyman, Jane (Sarah Jane Fulks) (actress); St. Joseph, Mo., 1/4/14
Wynette, Tammy (Virginia Wynette Pugh) (singer); Tupelo, Miss. **(1942–1998)**
Wynn, Ed (Isaiah Edwin Leopold) (comedian); Philadelphia **(1886–1966)**
Wynn, Keenan (actor); New York City **(1916–1986)**

X

Xavier, St. Francis (Jesuit missionary); Pamplona, Navarre, Spain **(1506–1552)**
Xenophon (soldier, historian, essayist); Athens **(c. 435–c. 355 B.C.)**
Xerxes, the Great (king); Persian Empire **(c. 519–465 B.C.)**

Y

Yeats, William Butler (poet); nr. Dublin **(1865–1939)**
Yeltsin, Boris (Russian president); Yekaterinburg (then Sverdlovsk), Russia, 2/1/31
Yevtushenko, Yevgeny (poet); Zima, Russia, 7/18/33
York, Michael (actor); Fulmer, England, 3/27/42
York, Susannah (Fletcher) (actress); London, 1/9/42
Yorty, Samuel W. (ex-mayor of Los Angeles); Lincoln, Nebr **(1909–1998)**
Yothers, Tina (actress); Whittier, Calif., 5/5/73
Young, Alan (actor); North Shield, England, 11/19/19
Young, Andrew (civil rights leader); New Orleans, 3/12/32
Young, Brigham (religious leader); Whitingham, Vt. **(1801–1877)**
Young, Gig (Byron Barr) (actor); St. Cloud, Minn. **(1913–1978)**
Young, Loretta (Gretchen Young) (actress); Salt Lake City **(1913–2000)**
Young, Neil (singer, songwriter); Toronto, 11/12/45
Young, Robert (actor); Chicago **(1907–1998)**
Youngman, Henny (comedian); Whitechapel, London **(1906–1998)**
Yushchenko, Victor (president of Ukraine); Khoruzhivka, Sumy Oblast, Ukraine, 2/23/54

Z

Zane, Billy (William George Zane, Jr.) (actor); Chicago, 2/24/66
Zanuck, Darryl F. (producer); Wahoo, Neb. **(1902–1979)**
Zappa, Frank (Francis Vincent Zappa, Jr.) (singer, songwriter); Baltimore **(1940–1993)**
Zeffirelli, Franco (director); Florence, Italy, 2/12/23
Zellweger, Renee (actress); Katy, Tex., 4/25/69
Zemeckis, Robert (filmmaker); Chicago, 1952
Zeta-Jones, Catherine (actress); West Glamorgan, Wales, 9/25/69
Zhou Enlai (premier); Hualyin, China **(1898–1976)**
Ziegfeld, Florenz (theatrical producer); Chicago **(1867–1932)**
Ziegler, Karl (chemist, Nobel laureate); Helsa, Germany **(1898–1973)**
Zimbalist, Efrem (violinist); Rostov-on-Don, Russia **(1889–1985)**
Zimbalist, Efrem, Jr. (actor); New York City, 11/30/23
Zimbalist, Stephanie (actress); New York City, 10/8/56
Zinnemann, Fred (director); Vienna **(1907–1997)**
Zola, Emile (novelist); Paris **(1840–1902)**
Zoroaster (religious leader); Persian Empire **(c. 628–c. 551 B.C.)**
Zucker, Jerry (film producer, director); Milwaukee, 3/11/50
Zukerman, Pinchas (violinist); Tel Aviv, Israel, 7/16/48
Zukor, Adolph (movie executive); Ricse, Hungary **(1873–1976)**
Zurbarán, Francisco de (painter); Fuentes de Cantos, Spain **(1598–1664)**
Zweig, Stefan (author); Vienna **(1881–1942)**
Zwingli, Huldrych (humanist); Wildaus, Switzerland **(1484–1531)**

Average Math and Science Scores of Fourth-Grade and Eighth-Grade Students by Country

Average Mathematics Scale Scores, 2003

	Fourth grade				Eighth grade		
Country	Average score	Country	Average score	Country	Average score	Country	Average score
International average	495	Cyprus	510	International average	466	Slovak Republic	508
Singapore	594	Moldova, Republic of	504	Singapore	605	Australia	505
Hong Kong SAR[1,2]	575	Italy	503	Korea, Republic of	589	(United States)	504
Japan	565	Australia[2]	499	Hong Kong SAR[1,2]	586	Lithuania[3]	502
Chinese Taipei	564	New Zealand	493	Chinese Taipei	585	Sweden	499
Belgium-Flemish	551	Scotland[2]	490	Japan	570	Scotland[1]	498
Netherlands[2]	540	Slovenia	479	Belgium-Flemish	537	(Israel)	496
Latvia	536	Armenia	456	Netherlands[1]	536	New Zealand	494
Lithuania[3]	534	Norway	451	Estonia	531	Slovenia	493
Russian Federation	532	Iran, Islamic Republic of	389	Hungary	529	Italy	484
England[2]	531	Philippines	358	Malaysia	508	Armenia	478
Hungary	529	Morocco	347	Latvia	508	Serbia[3]	477
United States[2]	518	Tunisia	339	Russian Federation	508	Bulgaria	476

NOTE: Countries are ordered by 2003 average score. The test for significance between the United States and the international average was adjusted to account for the U.S. contribution to the international average. Countries were required to sample students in the upper of the two grades that contained the largest number of 9- and 13-year-olds. In the United States and most countries, this corresponds to grade 4 and grade 8. Parentheses indicate countries that did not meet international sampling or other guidelines in 2003. 1. Hong Kong is a Special Administrative Region (SAR) of the People's Republic of China. 2. Met international guidelines for participation rates in 2003 only after replacement schools were included. 3. National desired population does not cover all of the international desired population. *Source:* International Association for the Evaluation of Educational Achievement (IEA), *Trends in International Mathematics and Science Study (TIMSS), 2003.*

Average Science Scale Scores, 2003

	Fourth grade				Eighth grade		
Country	Average score	Country	Average score	Country	Average score	Country	Average score
International average	489	Belgium-Flemish	518	International average	473	New Zealand	520
Singapore	565	Italy	516	Singapore	578	Lithuania[3]	519
Chinese Taipei	551	Lithuania[3]	512	Chinese Taipei	571	Slovak Republic	517
Japan	543	Scotland[2]	502	Korea, Republic of	558	Belgium-Flemish	516
Hong Kong SAR[1,2]	542	Moldova, Republic of	496	Hong Kong SAR[1,2]	556	Russian Federation	514
England[2]	540	Slovenia	490	Estonia	552	Latvia	512
United States[2]	536	Cyprus	480	Japan	552	Scotland[2]	512
Latvia	532	Norway	466	Hungary	543	Malaysia	510
Hungary	530	Armenia	437	Netherlands[2]	536	Norway	494
Russian Federation	526	Iran, Islamic Republic of	414	(United States)	527	Italy	491
Netherlands[2]	525	Philippines	332	Australia	527	(Israel)	488
Australia[2]	521	Tunisia	314	Sweden	524	Bulgaria	479
New Zealand	520	Morocco	304	Slovenia	520	Jordan	475

NOTE: Countries are ordered by 2003 average score. The test for significance between the United States and the international average was adjusted to account for the U.S. contribution to the international average. Countries were required to sample students in the upper of the two grades that contained the largest number of 9- and 13-year-olds. In the United States and most countries, this corresponds to grade 4 and grade 8. Parentheses indicate countries that did not meet international sampling or other guidelines in 2003. 1. Hong Kong is a Special Administrative Region (SAR) of the People's Republic of China. 2. Met international guidelines for participation rates in 2003 only after replacement schools were included. 3. National desired population does not cover all of the international desired population. *Source:* International Association for the Evaluation of Educational Achievement (IEA), *Trends in International Mathematics and Science Study (TIMSS), 2003.*

Highest Level of Educational Attainment of U.S. Population, 2004

Some high school	8.6%	Some college	17.0%	Bachelor's degree	18.1%	Doctoral degree	1.3%
High school graduate	32.0%	Associate's degree	8.4%	Master's degree	6.7%	Professional degree	1.6%

NOTE: Persons 25 years and older (187 million). *Source:* U.S. Census Bureau, *Current Population Survey,* March 2005.

Educational Attainment by Race and Hispanic Origin, 1940–2004

(percent of population ages 25 and older, by years of school completed)

	White[1]			Black[1]			Hispanic		
Age and year	Less than 5 years of elementary school	High school completion or higher[2]	4 or more years of college[3]	Less than 5 years of elementary school	High school completion or higher[2]	4 or more years of college[3]	Less than 5 years of elementary school	High school completion or higher[2]	4 or more years of college[3]
April 1940	10.9%	26.1%	4.9%	41.8%	7.7%	1.3%	—	—	—
April 1950	8.9	36.4	6.6	32.6	13.7	2.2	—	—	—
April 1960	6.7	43.2	8.1	23.5	21.7	3.5	—	—	—
March 1970	4.2	57.4	11.6	14.7	36.1	6.1	—	—	—
March 1980	1.9	71.9	18.4	9.1	51.4	7.9	15.8%	44.5%	7.6%
March 1985	1.4	77.5	20.8	6.1	59.9	11.1	13.5	47.9	8.5
March 1990	1.1	81.4	23.1	5.1	66.2	11.3	12.3	50.8	9.2
March 1995	0.7	85.9	23.4	2.5	73.8	13.3	10.6	53.4	9.3
March 1998	0.6	87.1	26.6	1.7	76.4	14.8	9.3	55.5	11.0
March 1999	0.6	87.7	27.7	1.8	77.4	15.5	9.0	56.1	10.9
March 2000	0.5	88.4	28.1	1.6	78.9	16.6	8.7	57.0	10.6
March 2001	0.5	88.7	28.6	1.3	79.5	16.1	9.3	56.5	11.2
March 2002	0.5	88.7	29.4	1.6	79.2	17.2	8.7	57.0	11.1
March 2004	0.4	90.0	30.6	1.4	80.6	17.6	8.1	58.4	12.1

NOTE: (—) = not available. 1. Includes persons of Hispanic origin for years prior to 1980. 2. Data for years prior to 1993 include all persons with at least 4 years of high school. 3. Data for 1993 and later years are for persons with a bachelor's or higher degree. *Source:* U.S. Department of Commerce, Bureau of the Census, U.S. Census of Population, 1960, Vol. 1, part 1; *Current Population Reports,* Series P-20 and unpublished data; and *1960 Census Monograph,* "Education of the American Population," by John K. Folger and Charles B. Nam. From U.S. Dept. of Education, National Center for Education Statistics, *Digest of Education Statistics 2003,* and U.S. Census Bureau, *Current Population Survey,* March 2005.

Educational Attainment by Sex, 1910–2004

(percent of population ages 25 and older)

	Both sexes			Male			Female		
Year	Less than 5 years of elementary school	High school completion or higher[1]	4 or more years of college[2]	Less than 5 years of elementary school	High school completion or higher[1]	4 or more years of college[2]	Less than 5 years of elementary school	High school completion or higher[1]	4 or more years of college[2]
1910[3]	23.8%	13.5%	2.7%	—	—	—	—	—	—
1920[3]	22.0	16.4	3.3	—	—	—	—	—	—
1930[3]	17.5	19.1	3.9	—	—	—	—	—	—
April 1940	13.7	24.5	4.6	15.1%	22.7%	5.5%	12.4%	26.3%	3.8%
April 1950	11.1	34.3	6.2	12.2	32.6	7.3	10.0	36.0	5.2
April 1960	8.3	41.1	7.7	9.4	39.5	9.7	7.4	42.5	5.8
March 1970	5.3	55.2	11.0	5.9	55.0	14.1	4.7	55.4	8.2
March 1980	3.4	68.6	17.0	3.6	69.2	20.9	3.2	68.1	13.6
March 1990	2.5	77.6	21.3	2.7	77.7	24.4	2.2	77.5	18.4
March 1995	1.9	81.7	23.0	2.0	81.7	26.0	1.7	81.6	20.2
March 1998	1.7	82.8	24.4	1.7	82.8	26.5	1.6	82.9	22.4
March 1999	1.6	83.4	25.2	1.6	83.5	27.5	1.6	83.4	23.1
March 2000	1.6	84.1	25.6	1.6	84.2	27.8	1.5	84.0	23.6
March 2001	1.6	84.3	26.1	1.6	84.4	28.0	1.5	84.2	24.3
March 2002	1.6	84.1	26.7	1.7	83.8	28.5	1.5	84.4	25.1
March 2004	1.5	85.2	27.7	1.7	84.8	29.4	1.4	85.4	26.1

NOTE: (—) = not available. 1. Data for years prior to 1993 include all persons with at least 4 years of high school. 2. Data for 1993 and later years are for persons with a bachelor's degree or higher. 3. Estimates based on Bureau of the Census retrojection of 1940 Census data on education by age. *Source:* Based on data from the U.S. Department of Commerce, Bureau of the Census, *U.S Census of Population, 1960,* Vol. 1, part 1; *Current Population Reports,* Series P-20 and unpublished data; and *1960 Census Monograph,* "Education of the American Population," by John K. Folger and Charles B. Nam. From U.S. Dept. of Education, National Center for Education Statistics, *Digest of Education Statistics 2003,* and U.S. Census Bureau, *Current Population Survey,* March 2005.

Enrollment in Educational Institutions, 1949–2004

(in thousands)

Year	Public elementary and secondary schools			Private elementary and secondary schools[1]			Degree-granting institutions[2]		
	Total	Pre-K through grade 8	Grades 9 through 12	Total	Pre-K through grade 8	Grades 9 through 12	Total	Public	Private
1949–50	25,111	19,387	5,725	3,380	2,708	672	2,659	1,355	1,304
Fall 1959	35,182	26,911	8,271	5,675	4,640	1,035	3,640	2,181	1,459
Fall 1970	45,894	32,558	13,336	5,363	4,052	1,311	8,581	6,428	2,153
Fall 1980	40,877	27,647	13,231	5,331	3,992	1,339	12,097	9,457	2,640
Fall 1990	41,217	29,878	11,338	5,234	4,084	1,150	13,819	10,845	2,974
Fall 2000	47,204	33,688	13,515	6,162[3]	4,875[3]	1,287[3]	15,312	11,753	3,560
Fall 2002[3]	47,918	33,942	13,976	6,241	4,885	1,356	16,102	12,354	3,749
Fall 2004[3]	48,175	33,669	14,506	6,279	4,871	1,408	16,468	12,627	3,841

NOTE: Elementary and secondary enrollment excludes home-schooled children. Based on the National Household Education Survey, there were approximately 850,000 home-schooled children in spring 1999. 1. Beginning in fall 1980, data include estimates for an expanded universe of private schools. Direct comparisons with earlier years should be avoided. 2. Two- and four-year institutions eligible to participate in Title IV federal financial aid programs. 3. Projected. *Source:* U.S. Department of Education, National Center for Education Statistics, *Digest of Education Statistics 2003.*

Public and Private Elementary and Secondary Pupil-Teacher Ratios, 1955–2002

Year	Total	Public	Private	Year	Total	Public	Private
1955	27.4	26.9	31.7[1]	1985	17.6	17.9	16.2
1960	26.4	25.8	30.7[1]	1990	16.9	17.2	14.7[1]
1965	25.1	24.7	28.3	1995	17.0	17.3	14.9
1970	22.4	22.3	23.0	2000	16.0	16.0	15.8[1]
1980	18.6	18.7	17.7	2002[2]	16.1	16.1	16.2

1. Estimated. 2. Projected. *Source:* U.S. Department of Education, National Center for Education Statistics; NCES Common Core of Data (CCD); Projections of Educational Statistics to 2013. From *Digest of Education Statistics 2003.*

High School Dropout Rates by Sex, 1960–2001

Year	Total	Male	Female
1960	27.2%	27.8%	26.7%
1970	15.0	14.2	15.7
1980	14.1	15.1	13.1
1985	12.6	13.4	11.8
1990	12.1	12.3	11.8
1995	12.0	12.2	11.7
1996	11.1	11.4	10.9
1997	11.0	11.9	10.1
1998	11.8	13.3	10.3
1999	11.2	11.9	10.5
2000	10.9	12.0	9.9
2001	10.7	12.2	9.3

High School Dropout Rates by Race/Ethnicity, 1960–2001

Year	White	Black	Hispanic
1960	—	—	—
1970	13.2%	27.9%	—
1980	11.4	19.1	35.2%
1985	10.4	15.2	27.6
1990	9.0	13.2	32.4
1995	8.6	12.1	30.0
1996	7.3	13.0	29.4
1997	7.6	13.4	25.3
1998	7.7	13.8	29.5
1999	7.3	12.6	28.6
2000	6.9	13.1	27.8
2001	7.3	10.9	27.0

NOTE: (—) = not available. Data apply to persons ages 16–24. Because of changes in data collection procedures, data for 1992–2000 may not be comparable with figures for earlier years. *Source:* U.S. Dept. of Education, National Center for Education Statistics, *Digest of Education Statistics 2002.*

General Educational Development (GED) Credentials Issued, 1971–2001

(in thousands)

Year	Number of credentials issued	Year	Number of credentials issued	Year	Number of credentials issued	Year	Number of credentials issued	Year	Number of credentials issued	Year	Number of credentials issued
1971	227	1976	333	1981	489	1986	428	1991	462	1997	460
1972	245	1977	332	1982	486	1987	444	1992	457	1998	481
1973	249	1978	381	1983	465	1988	410	1993	469	1999	498
1974	294	1979	426	1984	427	1989	357	1994	491	2000	487
1975	340	1980	479	1985	413	1990	410	1995	504	2001	648

Source: American Council on Education, General Educational Development Testing Service, *Who took the GED? Statistical Report,* various years.

Cost of Higher Education, 1986–2002[1]

Year	All institutions	4-year institutions	2-year institutions	Year	All institutions	4-year institutions	2-year institutions
Public institutions				**Private institutions**			
1986–1987	$3,805	$4,138	$2,989	1986–1987	$ 9,676	$10,039	$ 6,384
1991–1992	5,138	5,693	3,623	1991–1992	13,892	14,258	9,632
1996–1997	6,530	7,334	4,404	1996–1997	18,039	18,442	11,954
1997–1998	6,813	7,673	4,509	1997–1998	18,516	19,070	12,921
1998–1999	7,107	8,027	4,604	1998–1999	19,368	19,929	13,319
1999–2000	7,310	8,275	4,720	1999–2000	20,186	20,706	13,965
2000–2001	7,586	8,653	4,839	2000–2001	21,368	21,856	14,788
2001–2002	8,022	9,196	5,137	2001–2002	22,413	22,896	15,825
2002–2003[2]	8,556	9,828	5,596	2002–2003[2]	23,503	23,940	17,760

1. Average undergraduate tuition, fees, and room and board. 2. Preliminary data based on fall 2001 enrollment weights. *Source:* U.S. Department of Education, National Center for Education Statistics, *Digest of Education Statistics 2003.*

Median Annual Income, by Level of Education, 1990–2001

Sex and year	Elementary/secondary			College						
	Less than 9th grade	9th to 12th grade, no completion[1]	High school completion (includes equivalency)[2]	Some college, no degree[3]	Associate degree[4]	Bachelor's[5]	Master's[4]		Profes-sional[4]	Doc-torate[4]
Men										
1990	$17,394	$20,902	$26,653	$31,734	—	$39,328	—		—	—
1992	17,294	21,274	27,280	32,103	$33,433	41,355	$49,973	$	76,220	$57,418
1994	17,532	22,048	28,037	32,279	35,794	43,663	53,500		75,000	61,921
1996	17,962	22,717	30,709	34,845	37,131	45,846	60,508		85,963	71,227
1998	19,380	23,958	31,477	36,934	40,274	51,405	62,244		94,737	75,078
1999	20,429	25,035	33,184	39,221	41,638	52,985	66,243		100,000	81,687
2000	20,789	25,095	34,303	40,337	41,952	56,334	68,322		99,411	80,250
2001	21,361	26,209	34,723	41,045	42,776	55,929	70,899		100,000	86,965
Women										
1990	$12,251	$14,429	$18,319	$22,227	—	$28,017	—		—	—
1992	12,958	14,559	19,427	23,157	$25,624	30,326	$36,037	$	46,257	$45,790
1994	12,430	15,133	20,373	23,514	25,940	31,741	39,457		50,615	51,119
1996	14,414	16,953	21,175	25,167	28,083	33,525	41,901		57,624	56,267
1998	14,467	16,482	22,780	27,420	29,924	36,559	45,283		57,565	57,796
1999	15,098	17,015	23,061	27,757	30,919	37,993	48,097		59,904	60,079
2000	15,978	17,919	24,970	28,697	31,071	40,415	50,139		58,957	57,081
2001	16,691	19,156	25,303	30,418	32,153	40,994	50,669		61,748	62,123

NOTE: Year-round, full-time workers 25 years and older. (—) = not available. 1. Includes 1 to 3 years high school for 1990. 2. Includes 4 years of high school for 1990, and equivalency certificates for the other years. 3. Includes 1 to 3 years of college and associate degrees for 1990. 4. Not reported separately for 1990. 5. Includes 4 years of college for 1990. *Source:* U.S. Dept. of Commerce, Bureau of the Census, Current Population Reports, Series P-60, "Money Income of Households, Families, and Persons in the United States," "Income, Poverty, and Valuation of Noncash Benefits," various years; and Series P-60, "Money Income in the United States," various years. From *Digest of Education Statistics 2003.*

Average SAT I Scores, 1972–2004

Year	Verbal Score			Mathematical Score		
	Total	Male	Female	Total	Male	Female
1972	531	529	530	527	489	509
1976	511	508	509	520	475	497
1980	506	498	502	515	473	492
1984	511	498	504	518	478	497
1988	512	499	505	521	483	501
1990	505	496	500	521	483	501
1992	504	496	500	521	484	501
1994	501	497	499	523	487	504
1996	507	503	505	527	492	508
1998	509	502	505	531	496	512
2000	507	504	505	533	498	514
2002	507	502	504	534	500	516
2004	512	504	508	537	501	518

Average SAT I Scores by Race/Ethnicity, 2004

Self-identified as	Verbal	Math
American Indian or Alaskan Native	483	488
Asian, Asian-American, or Pacific Islander	507	577
Black or African-American	430	427
Hispanic or Latino Background:		
Mexican or Mexican-American	451	458
Puerto Rican	457	452
Latin American, South American, Central American, or Other Hispanic or Latino	461	465
White	528	531
Other	494	508
No Response	522	535

NOTE: The SAT I is the test formerly known as the SAT, the Scholastic Assessment Test, and the Scholastic Aptitude Test. Minimum score 200; maximum score 800. Scores prior to 2000 have been converted to the recentered scale. *Source:* College Entrance Examination Board, *2004 College-Bound Seniors.*

Number of U.S. Colleges and Universities and Degrees Awarded

	Number[1]	Enrollment[2]		Number		Number
Public 4-year institutions	631	6,236,455	**Degrees awarded:[3]**			
Private 4-year institutions	1,835	3,440,953	Associate	595,133	Doctorate	44,160
Public 2-year institutions	1,081	5,996,701	Bachelor's	1,291,900	Professional	80,698
Private 2-year institutions	621	253,878	Master's	482,118		
Total	**4,168**	**15,927,987**				
Undergraduate		13,715,610	**Enrollment highlights:[2]**			
Graduate		1,903,730	Women	56.3%	Minority	28.8%
Professional		308,647	Full-time	59.3%	Foreign	3.5%

1. 2002–03 figures. 2. Fall 2001 figures. 3. 2001–02 figures. *Source: Chronicle of Higher Education.*

College and University Endowments, 2004

Rank	Institution	Endowment[1]	Rank	Institution	Endowment[1]
1.	Harvard University (Cambridge, Mass.)	$22,587,305,000	27.	Univ. of Minnesota (Minneapolis, Minn.)	$1,774,436,617
2.	Yale University (New Haven, Conn.)	12,740,896,000	28.	Brown University (Providence, R.I.)	1,672,827,000
3.	Princeton University (Princeton, N.J.)	9,928,200,000	29.	Univ. of California, Los Angeles (Los Angeles, Calif.)	1,527,525,000
4.	Leland Stanford Junior University (Stanford, Calif.)	9,922,041,000	30.	New York University (New York, N.Y.)	1,472,012,509
5.	Univ. of Texas System Administration (Austin, Tex.)	9,360,113,745	31.	Case Western Reserve University (Cleveland, Ohio)	1,470,000,000
6.	Massachusetts Institute of Technology (Cambridge, Mass.)	5,869,800,000	32.	Rockefeller University (New York, N.Y.)	1,409,735,600
7.	Columbia University (New York, N.Y.)	4,493,085,000	33.	Williams College (Williamstown, Mass.)	1,389,266,399
8.	Univ. of Michigan (Ann Arbor, Mich.)	4,243,352,775	34.	Univ. of Pittsburgh (Pittsburgh, Pa.)	1,370,498,000
9.	Emory University (Atlanta, Ga.)	4,086,000,000	35.	California Institute of Technology (Pasadena, Calif.)	1,307,413,000
10.	Washington University (St. Louis, Mo.)	4,083,958,000	36.	Grinnell College (Grinnell, Iowa)	1,291,781,000
11.	Univ. of Pennsylvania (Philadelphia, Pa.)	4,019,000,000	37.	Univ. of Rochester (Rochester, N.Y.)	1,257,146,000
12.	Northwestern University (Evanston, Ill.)	3,884,629,679	38.	Univ. of North Carolina at Chapel Hill (Chapel Hill, N.C.)	1,232,118,534
13.	Univ. of Chicago (Chicago, Ill.)	3,620,728,000	39.	Boston College (Chestnut Hill, Mass.)	1,224,889,000
14.	Cornell University (Ithaca, N.Y.)	3,314,228,858	40.	Univ. of Washington (Seattle, Wash.)	1,215,571,905
15.	William Marsh Rice University (Houston, Tex.)	3,302,000,000	41.	Purdue University (West Lafayette, Ind.)	1,207,131,043
16.	Texas A&M University (College Station, Tex.)	3,240,693,652	42.	Wellesley College (Wellesley, Mass.)	1,180,405,000
17.	Univ. of Notre Dame (Notre Dame, Ind.)	3,123,454,523	43.	Pomona College (Claremont, Calif.)	1,149,720,000
18.	Duke University (Durham, N.C.)	2,832,921,999	44.	Ohio State University (Columbus, Ohio)	1,139,292,045
19.	Dartmouth College (Hanover, N.H.)	2,454,294,000	45.	Georgia Institute of Technology (Atlanta, Ga.)	1,129,819,594
20.	Univ. of Southern California (Los Angeles, Calif.)	2,399,960,000	46.	Pennsylvania State University (University Park, Pa.)	1,106,800,000
21.	Vanderbilt University (Nashville, Tenn.)	2,264,845,000	47.	Univ. of Richmond (Richmond, Va.)	1,103,390,000
22.	Univ. of Texas at Austin (Austin, Tex.)	2,038,938,294	48.	Baylor College of Medicine (Houston, Tex.)	1,092,840,531
23.	Univ. of California, Berkeley (Berkeley, Calif.)	2,037,297,000	49.	Swarthmore College (Swarthmore, Pa.)	1,080,026,000
24.	Univ. of Virginia (Charlottesville, Va.)	1,981,274,000	50.	Michigan State University (East Lansing, Mich.)	1,049,411,455
25.	Mayo Foundation (Rochester, Minn.)	1,968,200,000			
26.	Johns Hopkins University (Baltimore, Md.)	1,909,337,000			

NOTES: List includes only institutions that participated in the 2004 Voluntary Support of Education Survey. State systems that submitted combined endowments above the current cutoff are not included. 1. Endowment is market value at fiscal year-end 2004. *Source:* Council for Aid to Education, a subsidiary of RAND. Web: www.cae.org.

Accredited U.S. Senior Colleges and Universities

Criteria for inclusion: accredited four-year institutions offering at least a bachelor's degree. Because of space limitations, only schools with at least 800 students are included (a complete list, including smaller schools, can be found online at www.infoplease.com). "Total enrolled students" refers to the overall student body, which includes, where applicable, both undergraduate and graduate, full-time and part-time students. "Percent women" refers to the percentage of women who are full-time undergraduates. "Percentage students accepted" refers to the percentage of first-time, first-year, undergraduate applicants who are accepted as full-time undergraduates. Schools are listed alphabetically within each state.

(Pr) = private; (Pu) = public.

Source: Peterson's Database, copyright 2005. Peterson's, a part of the Thomson Corporation. Web: http://petersons.com/.

Institution name; city (Public/Private)	Total enrolled students	Percent Women	Students accepted	Tuition and fees In-state	Tuition and fees Out-of-state	Room and board
ALABAMA						
Alabama Agricultural and Mechanical University; Huntsville (Pu)	6,323	52%	45%	$ 4,420	$ 8,320	$3,498
Alabama State University; Montgomery (Pu)	5,653	59	51	4,008	8,016	3,700
American College of Computer & Information Sciences; Birmingham (Pr)	15,722	—	—	—	—	—
Auburn University; Auburn University (Pu)	22,928	49	84	4,828	14,048	6,686
Auburn University Montgomery; Montgomery (Pu)	5,123	63	98	4,460	12,920	5,780
Birmingham-Southern College; Birmingham (Pr)	1,453	58	83	21,055	21,055	7,080
Columbia Southern University; Orange Beach (Pr)	2,200	—	—	—	—	—
Concordia College; Selma (Pr)	902	61	80	6,174	6,174	3,600
Faulkner University; Montgomery (Pr)	2,583	63	60	10,425	10,425	5,200
Jacksonville State University; Jacksonville (Pu)	8,930	58	88	4,040	8,080	3,312
Miles College; Birmingham (Pr)	1,716	55	54	5,660	5,660	5,074
Oakwood College; Huntsville (Pr)	1,778	57	55	11,298	11,298	6,374
Samford University; Birmingham (Pr)	4,416	64	88	13,944	13,944	5,506
Spring Hill College; Mobile (Pr)	1,427	61	80	19,950	19,950	7,192
Stillman College; Tuscaloosa (Pr)	1,458	—	50	8,718	8,718	4,200
Troy University Dothan; Dothan (Pu)	1,894	69	66	4,162	8,012	—
Troy University Montgomery; Montgomery (Pu)	4,313	70	97	3,920	7,770	—
Troy University; Troy (Pu)	8,847	59	66	4,162	8,012	4,812
Tuskegee University; Tuskegee (Pr)	2,870	57	81	11,590	11,590	5,940
University of Alabama at Birmingham; Birmingham (Pu)	16,694	61	86	4,662	10,422	3,060
University of Alabama in Huntsville; Huntsville (Pu)	7,036	49	89	4,516	9,518	5,200
University of Alabama; Tuscaloosa (Pu)	20,929	53	77	4,630	12,664	4,734
University of Mobile; Mobile (Pr)	1,864	62	89	10,505	10,505	5,200
University of Montevallo; Montevallo (Pu)	3,061	68	80	5,474	10,664	3,850
University of North Alabama; Florence (Pu)	5,961	58	80	4,096	7,623	4,140
University of South Alabama; Mobile (Pu)	13,340	59	93	4,290	8,100	4,222
University of West Alabama; Livingston (Pu)	2,667	53	74	4,196	7,922	3,119
Virginia College at Birmingham; Birmingham (Pr)	2,407	66	86	8,820	8,820	—
ALASKA						
University of Alaska Anchorage; Anchorage (Pu)	16,261	58	81	3,465	9,561	7,810
University of Alaska Fairbanks; Fairbanks (Pu)	8,693	52	91	4,762	12,382	5,580
University of Alaska Southeast; Juneau (Pu)	3,379	57	63	3,342	9,438	5,370
ARIZONA						
Arizona State University East; Mesa (Pu)	3,983	48	76	4,015	12,869	5,155
Arizona State University; Tempe (Pu)	49,171	52	86	4,064	12,919	6,574
Arizona State University West; Phoenix (Pu)	7,348	68	87	4,064	12,919	4,455
Art Institute of Phoenix; Phoenix (Pr)	1,297	38	—	16,752	16,752	6,620
Collins College: A School of Design and Technology; Tempe (Pr)	2,142	33	65	—	—	—
Embry-Riddle Aeronautical University; Prescott (Pr)	1,668	18	87	23,490	23,490	6,516
Grand Canyon University; Phoenix (Pr)	4,113	66	69	14,500	14,500	7,130
Northcentral University; Prescott (Pr)	1,401	70	—	9,000	9,000	—
Northern Arizona University; Flagstaff (Pu)	19,147	59	85	4,073	12,593	5,785
Prescott College; Prescott (Pr)	1,036	59	84	17,450	17,450	—
University of Advancing Technology; Tempe (Pr)	1,004	9	93	14,600	14,600	—
University of Arizona; Tucson (Pu)	36,932	53	83	4,093	13,073	7,108
University of Phoenix Online Campus; Phoenix (Pr)	115,796	59	—	13,200	13,200	—
University of Phoenix–Phoenix Campus; Phoenix (Pr)	9,699	56	97	9,090	9,090	—
University of Phoenix–Southern Arizona Campus; Tucson (Pr)	3,660	57	—	8,910	8,910	—
Western International University; Phoenix (Pr)	3,751	56	—	9,760	9,760	—
ARKANSAS						
Arkansas State University; State University (Pu)	10,508	59	64	5,155	11,515	4,000
Arkansas Tech University; Russellville (Pu)	6,483	53	53	4,468	8,626	3,841
Harding University; Searcy (Pr)	5,348	54	59	10,780	10,780	5,182
Henderson State University; Arkadelphia (Pu)	3,461	56	61	4,110	7,750	3,738
Hendrix College; Conway (Pr)	1,049	57	85	21,636	21,636	6,010
John Brown University; Siloam Springs (Pr)	1,928	49	77	14,434	14,434	5,324

Institution name; city (Public/Private)	Total enrolled students	Percent Women	Percent Students accepted	Tuition and fees In-state	Tuition and fees Out-of-state	Room and board
Ouachita Baptist University; Arkadelphia (Pr)	1,511	54%	66%	$15,920	$15,920	$ 5,000
Philander Smith College; Little Rock (Pr)	949	66	100	7,766	7,766	5,090
Southern Arkansas University–Magnolia; Magnolia (Pu)	3,057	54	81	3,858	5,678	3,600
University of Arkansas at Fort Smith; Fort Smith (Pu)	6,623	63	100	2,430	7,380	—
University of Arkansas at Little Rock; Little Rock (Pu)	11,757	61	99	4,955	11,435	2,850
University of Arkansas at Monticello; Monticello (Pu)	2,875	57	73	3,765	7,335	3,150
University of Arkansas at Pine Bluff; Pine Bluff (Pu)	3,303	57	89	4,044	8,019	5,436
University of Arkansas; Fayetteville (Pu)	17,269	50	78	5,135	12,425	5,927
University of Central Arkansas; Conway (Pu)	10,071	60	68	5,053	8,609	3,920
CALIFORNIA						
Academy of Art University; San Francisco (Pr)	6,706	38	—	13,280	13,280	12,000
Alliant International University; San Diego (Pr)	3,556	50	88	19,360	19,360	7,430
American InterContinental University; Los Angeles (Pr)	1,405	47	38	16,190	16,190	5,500
Art Center College of Design; Pasadena (Pr)	1,519	40	77	25,044	25,044	—
Art Institute of California–Los Angeles; Santa Monica (Pr)	2,106	34	—	18,336	18,336	8,379
Art Institute of California–Orange County; Santa Ana (Pr)	1,833	—	68	—	—	9,920
Art Institute of California–San Diego; San Diego (Pr)	1,708	44	—	18,936	18,936	9,200
Art Institute of California–San Francisco; San Francisco (Pr)	1,347	—	—	18,486	18,486	—
Azusa Pacific University; Azusa (Pr)	8,162	65	73	20,666	20,666	6,132
Biola University; La Mirada (Pr)	5,370	62	78	22,702	22,702	7,100
Brooks Institute of Photography; Santa Barbara (Pr)	1,507	48	—	20,250	20,250	—
California Baptist University; Riverside (Pr)	2,905	65	72	15,940	15,940	6,310
California College of the Arts; San Francisco (Pr)	1,587	60	81	24,640	24,640	8,230
California Institute of Technology; Pasadena (Pr)	2,172	33	17	25,551	25,551	8,013
California Institute of the Arts; Valencia (Pr)	1,325	45	33	27,260	27,260	7,697
California Lutheran University; Thousand Oaks (Pr)	3,019	56	73	22,285	22,285	7,570
California Polytechnic State University, San Luis Obispo; San Luis Obispo (Pu)	17,582	43	38	3,972	16,080	8,146
California State Polytechnic University, Pomona; Pomona (Pu)	19,002	44	17	2,832	13,002	7,212
California State University, Bakersfield; Bakersfield (Pu)	7,924	—	63	2,959	9,739	5,946
California State University, Chico; Chico (Pu)	15,734	54	80	3,154	15,658	7,493
California State University, Dominguez Hills; Carson (Pu)	12,613	67	15	2,478	10,938	5,022
California State University, East Bay; Hayward (Pu)	13,061	—	47	2,706	12,876	3,705
California State University, Fresno; Fresno (Pu)	19,781	59	95	2,704	13,868	7,073
California State University, Fullerton; Fullerton (Pu)	32,744	59	63	2,804	12,974	4,356
California State University, Long Beach; Long Beach (Pu)	33,479	61	39	2,864	13,034	6,530
California State University, Los Angeles; Los Angeles (Pu)	20,637	63	54	3,034	13,204	3,338
California State University, Monterey Bay; Seaside (Pu)	3,020	58	83	2,947	13,795	6,900
California State University, Northridge; Northridge (Pu)	31,448	59	83	2,778	13,626	8,216
California State University, Sacramento; Sacramento (Pu)	27,972	58	51	3,010	15,700	6,574
California State University, San Bernardino; San Bernardino (Pu)	16,195	66	34	3,398	11,534	5,886
California State University, San Marcos; San Marcos (Pu)	6,728	61	38	2,786	10,922	7,470
California State University, Stanislaus; Turlock (Pu)	7,858	65	84	2,807	12,977	6,522
Chapman University; Orange (Pr)	5,565	58	58	26,150	26,150	10,000
Claremont McKenna College; Claremont (Pr)	1,066	47	22	29,210	29,210	9,780
Concordia University; Irvine (Pr)	1,834	64	67	19,930	19,930	7,050
Dominican University of California; San Rafael (Pr)	1,910	77	51	24,454	24,454	10,270
Fresno Pacific University; Fresno (Pr)	2,255	68	64	18,728	18,728	5,600
Golden Gate University; San Francisco (Pr)	4,069	54	—	10,320	10,320	—
Holy Names University; Oakland (Pr)	973	71	75	21,640	21,640	7,800
Hope International University; Fullerton (Pr)	1,275	63	79	16,400	16,400	5,400
Humboldt State University; Arcata (Pu)	7,550	55	58	2,866	13,868	7,281
John F. Kennedy University; Pleasant Hill (Pr)	1,653	65	—	14,436	14,436	—
La Sierra University; Riverside (Pr)	1,924	58	52	19,083	19,083	5,244
Loyola Marymount University; Los Angeles (Pr)	8,855	61	60	25,756	25,756	9,456
Master's College and Seminary; Santa Clarita (Pr)	1,523	54	48	18,170	18,170	6,370
Mills College; Oakland (Pr)	1,256	100	83	27,085	27,085	9,400
Mount St. Mary's College; Los Angeles (Pr)	2,257	96	86	21,782	21,782	8,635
Mt. Sierra College; Monrovia (Pr)	1,100	30	73	16,200	16,200	—
National University; La Jolla (Pr)	25,684	61	—	9,500	9,500	—
New College of California; San Francisco (Pr)	1,133	49	—	12,223	12,223	—
Notre Dame de Namur University; Belmont (Pr)	1,652	63	97	22,770	22,770	10,070
Occidental College; Los Angeles (Pr)	1,887	58	45	31,314	31,314	8,672
Otis College of Art and Design; Los Angeles (Pr)	1,043	66	58	25,100	25,100	—
Pacific Union College; Angwin (Pr)	1,547	54	44	18,054	18,054	5,136
Pepperdine University; Malibu (Pr)	7,919	58	29	28,720	28,720	8,640
Pitzer College; Claremont (Pr)	927	58	47	31,438	31,438	8,222
Point Loma Nazarene University; San Diego (Pr)	3,209	61	65	20,730	20,730	7,150
Pomona College; Claremont (Pr)	1,562	50	20	28,370	28,370	10,380
Saint Mary's College of California; Moraga (Pr)	4,536	61	83	25,150	25,150	9,530
Samuel Merritt College; Oakland (Pr)	1,008	93	56	23,928	23,928	10,055
San Diego State University; San Diego (Pu)	32,936	58	47	2,936	13,106	9,391
San Francisco State University; San Francisco (Pu)	28,804	60	55	3,066	15,756	8,870

Institution name; city (Public/Private)	Total enrolled students	Percent		Tuition and fees		Room and board
		Women	Students accepted	In-state	Out-of-state	
San Jose State University; San Jose (Pu)	29,044	50%	66%	—	—	—
Santa Clara University; Santa Clara (Pr)	7,908	56	57	$27,135	$27,135	$ 9,693
Scripps College; Claremont (Pr)	839	100	49	29,000	29,000	9,000
Simpson University; Redding (Pr)	1,134	65	59	17,000	17,000	5,900
Sonoma State University; Rohnert Park (Pu)	7,977	63	70	3,408	13,584	8,805
Stanford University; Stanford (Pr)	18,836	48	13	29,847	29,847	9,500
Touro University International; Cypress (Pr)	2,165	34	73	8,000	8,000	—
University of California, Berkeley; Berkeley (Pu)	32,814	54	25	6,730	23,686	11,630
University of California, Davis; Davis (Pu)	30,229	56	55	6,936	22,791	10,234
University of California, Irvine; Irvine (Pu)	24,307	50	53	6,313	24,590	9,176
University of California, Riverside; Riverside (Pu)	17,104	54	79	6,685	23,161	9,800
University of California, San Diego; La Jolla (Pu)	24,105	52	41	6,224	22,700	8,996
University of California, Santa Barbara; Santa Barbara (Pu)	21,026	56	53	6,495	22,971	9,897
University of California, Santa Cruz; Santa Cruz (Pu)	15,036	54	70	7,023	26,979	10,947
University of La Verne; La Verne (Pr)	4,021	64	59	22,800	22,800	9,110
University of Phoenix–Central Valley Campus; Fresno (Pr)	989	64	93	11,400	11,400	—
University of Phoenix–Northern California Campus; Pleasanton (Pr)	5,707	62	—	12,630	12,630	—
University of Phoenix–Sacramento Campus; Sacramento (Pr)	4,365	62	—	11,850	11,850	—
University of Phoenix–San Diego Campus; San Diego (Pr)	4,761	53	97	11,370	11,370	—
University of Phoenix–Southern California Campus; Costa Mesa (Pr)	15,913	61	—	12,360	12,360	—
University of Redlands; Redlands (Pr)	2,451	59	75	25,524	25,524	8,696
University of San Diego; San Diego (Pr)	7,486	61	66	26,856	26,856	10,190
University of San Francisco; San Francisco (Pr)	8,271	64	74	26,840	26,840	10,240
University of Southern California; Los Angeles (Pr)	32,160	51	27	30,512	30,512	8,988
University of the Pacific; Stockton (Pr)	6,268	57	64	24,750	24,750	7,858
Vanguard University of Southern California; Costa Mesa (Pr)	2,195	65	—	20,330	20,330	6,756
Westmont College; Santa Barbara (Pr)	1,376	63	73	26,240	26,240	8,610
Whittier College; Whittier (Pr)	1,307	56	78	26,138	26,138	7,928
Woodbury University; Burbank (Pr)	1,446	58	71	21,314	21,314	7,702
COLORADO						
Adams State College; Alamosa (Pu)	6,111	53	63	2,603	8,295	9,240
Art Institute of Colorado; Denver (Pr)	2,226	45	—	23,040	23,040	5,985
Colorado Christian University; Lakewood (Pr)	1,583	63	76	16,060	16,060	6,500
Colorado College; Colorado Springs (Pr)	2,044	53	44	28,644	28,644	7,216
Colorado School of Mines; Golden (Pu)	3,666	23	85	7,224	20,384	6,600
Colorado State University; Fort Collins (Pu)	26,801	51	83	3,790	14,377	5,766
Colorado State University-Pueblo; Pueblo (Pu)	5,835	56	94	3,220	14,239	5,912
Colorado Technical University; Colorado Springs (Pr)	1,684	21	93	9,438	9,438	
Fort Lewis College; Durango (Pu)	4,190	48	74	3,060	12,652	5,894
Johnson & Wales University; Denver (Pr)	1,512	—	77	20,100	20,100	8,490
Jones International University; Centennial (Pr)	1,146	—	100	9,407	9,407	—
Mesa State College; Grand Junction (Pu)	6,235	56	81	2,724	9,010	6,501
Metropolitan State College of Denver; Denver (Pu)	20,761	55	85	2,859	9,942	—
Naropa University; Boulder (Pr)	1,219	61	95	16,548	16,548	7,236
Regis University; Denver (Pr)	16,335	62	25	22,400	22,400	7,870
United States Air Force Academy; USAF Academy (Pu)	4,157	17	12	0	0	—
University of Colorado at Boulder; Boulder (Pu)	31,943	48	85	4,341	21,453	7,564
University of Colorado at Colorado Springs; Colorado Springs (Pu)	7,629	61	69	4,106	16,084	6,729
University of Colorado at Denver and Health Sciences Center - Downtown Denver Campus; Denver (Pu)	15,596	55	70	4,457	16,427	—
University of Denver; Denver (Pr)	9,808	52	87	26,610	26,610	8,363
University of Northern Colorado; Greeley (Pu)	13,204	61	81	3,370	12,260	5,954
University of Phoenix–Colorado Campus; Lone Tree (Pr)	3,364	57	—	9,000	9,000	—
University of Phoenix–Southern Colorado Campus; Colorado Springs (Pr)	1,410	50	—	9,000	9,000	—
Western State College of Colorado; Gunnison (Pu)	2,270	40	85	2,761	10,747	6,705
CONNECTICUT						
Albertus Magnus College; New Haven (Pr)	2,361	69	85	16,858	16,858	7,550
Central Connecticut State University; New Britain (Pu)	12,320	51	61	5,902	13,419	7,036
Charter Oak State College; New Britain (Pu)	1,495	—	—	—	—	—
Connecticut College; New London (Pr)	1,905	60	34	39,975	39,975	—
Eastern Connecticut State University; Willimantic (Pu)	5,156	56	68	6,472	13,258	7,580
Fairfield University; Fairfield (Pr)	5,060	57	64	28,415	28,415	9,270
Post University; Waterbury (Pr)	1,198	55	65	18,800	18,800	7,950
Quinnipiac University; Hamden (Pr)	7,220	61	55	24,340	24,340	10,300
Sacred Heart University; Fairfield (Pr)	5,454	59	71	21,990	21,990	9,280
Saint Joseph College; West Hartford (Pr)	1,792	100	70	21,970	21,970	9,225
Southern Connecticut State University; New Haven (Pu)	12,177	62	49	5,814	12,600	7,698
Trinity College; Hartford (Pr)	2,371	50	36	31,940	31,940	8,260
United States Coast Guard Academy; New London (Pu)	994	29	22	0	0	—
University of Bridgeport; Bridgeport (Pr)	3,274	58	76	19,525	19,525	8,400

Institution name; city (Public/Private)	Total enrolled students	Percent		Tuition and fees		Room and board
		Women	Students accepted	In-state	Out-of-state	
University of Connecticut; Storrs (Pu)	22,694	53%	50%	$ 7,912	$20,416	$ 7,848
University of Hartford; West Hartford (Pr)	7,246	50	60	23,480	23,480	8,996
University of New Haven; West Haven (Pr)	4,173	48	72	22,982	22,982	9,550
Wesleyan University; Middletown (Pr)	3,217	52	28	31,670	31,670	8,474
Western Connecticut State University; Danbury (Pu)	5,884	55	52	5,661	12,395	6,582
Yale University; New Haven (Pr)	11,441	50	10	29,820	29,820	9,030
DELAWARE						
Delaware State University; Dover (Pu)	3,178	59	50	4,976	10,633	6,816
Goldey-Beacom College; Wilmington (Pr)	1,324	55	78	13,736	13,736	4,240
University of Delaware; Newark (Pu)	20,713	58	45	6,954	16,640	6,458
Wesley College; Dover (Pr)	2,037	56	60	15,379	15,379	6,960
Wilmington College; New Castle (Pr)	7,156	65	100	7,340	7,340	—
DISTRICT OF COLUMBIA						
American University; Washington (Pr)	11,185	62	53	26,307	26,307	10,260
Catholic University of America; Washington (Pr)	5,981	55	82	26,000	26,000	9,838
Gallaudet University; Washington (Pr)	1,834	53	75	11,255	11,255	8,420
Georgetown University; Washington (Pr)	13,233	54	22	30,163	30,163	10,554
George Washington University; Washington (Pr)	23,092	57	38	34,030	34,030	10,210
Howard University; Washington (Pr)	10,623	67	47	11,645	11,645	5,870
Southeastern University; Washington (Pr)	935	64	66	9,705	9,705	—
Strayer University; Washington (Pr)	20,138	51	—	10,368	10,368	—
Trinity University; Washington (Pr)	1,672	99	86	17,360	17,360	7,574
University of the District of Columbia; Washington (Pu)	5,165	58	79	2,070	4,710	—
FLORIDA						
American InterContinental University; Weston (Pr)	1,939	49	—	58,500	58,500	—
Art Institute of Fort Lauderdale; Fort Lauderdale (Pr)	3,500	—	—	16,425	16,425	4,785
Barry University; Miami Shores (Pr)	9,207	69	70	22,430	22,430	7,620
Bethune-Cookman College; Daytona Beach (Pr)	2,895	60	59	10,610	10,610	6,374
Carlos Albizu University, Miami Campus; Miami (Pr)	1,007	81	64	9,369	9,369	—
Eckerd College; St. Petersburg (Pr)	1,688	56	74	24,362	24,362	6,326
Embry-Riddle Aeronautical University; Daytona Beach (Pr)	4,788	17	84	23,500	23,500	6,936
Embry-Riddle Aeronautical University, Extended Campus; Daytona Beach (Pr)	11,004	12	—	4,224	4,224	—
Flagler College; St. Augustine (Pr)	2,106	62	30	8,600	8,600	5,190
Florida Agricultural and Mechanical University; Tallahassee (Pu)	13,064	57	71	3,318	16,662	5,766
Florida Atlantic University; Boca Raton (Pu)	25,383	58	66	3,092	15,599	7,100
Florida Gulf Coast University; Fort Myers (Pu)	5,955	63	73	3,151	15,247	8,500
Florida Institute of Technology; Melbourne (Pr)	4,683	32	82	23,730	23,730	6,220
Florida International University; Miami (Pu)	34,865	57	49	3,158	15,664	8,860
Florida Memorial College; Miami-Dade (Pr)	2,161	—	—	11,110	11,110	4,842
Florida Metropolitan University–Brandon Campus; Tampa (Pr)	1,332	77	77	13,200	13,200	—
Florida Metropolitan University–Jacksonville Campus; Jacksonville (Pr)	954	—	—	8,640	8,640	—
Florida Metropolitan University–Melbourne Campus; Melbourne (Pr)	880	62	68	8,640	8,640	—
Florida Metropolitan University–North Orlando Campus; Orlando (Pr)	1,498	72	53	9,900	9,900	—
Florida Metropolitan University–Pinellas Campus; Clearwater (Pr)	1,201	73	70	11,430	11,430	—
Florida Metropolitan University–Pompano Beach Campus; Pompano Beach (Pr)	1,612	69	—	9,150	9,150	—
Florida Metropolitan University–South Orlando Campus; Orlando (Pr)	1,964	75	45	8,640	8,640	—
Florida Metropolitan University–Tampa Campus; Tampa (Pr)	1,390	59	53	9,900	9,900	—
Florida Southern College; Lakeland (Pr)	1,990	60	75	18,240	18,240	6,410
Florida State University; Tallahassee (Pu)	38,431	57	65	3,038	15,544	7,208
International Academy of Design & Technology; Tampa (Pr)	2,405	63	46	17,820	17,820	6,609
International College; Naples (Pr)	1,544	69	—	9,020	9,020	—
Jacksonville University; Jacksonville (Pr)	2,948	49	72	19,970	19,970	6,460
Johnson & Wales University; North Miami (Pr)	2,389	—	74	20,100	20,100	9,327
Jones College; Miami (Pr)	837	—	—	6,090	6,090	—
Lynn University; Boca Raton (Pr)	2,510	48	79	25,850	25,850	9,100
Miami International University of Art & Design; Miami (Pr)	1,406	64	51	17,952	17,952	4,880
Northwood University, Florida Campus; West Palm Beach (Pr)	956	43	62	15,183	15,183	7,257
Nova Southeastern University; Fort Lauderdale (Pr)	25,430	74	61	15,820	15,820	8,126
Palm Beach Atlantic University; West Palm Beach (Pr)	3,066	62	47	17,342	17,342	6,306
Ringling School of Art and Design; Sarasota (Pr)	1,008	46	72	20,195	20,195	8,811
Rollins College; Winter Park (Pr)	2,571	60	59	27,700	27,700	8,570
Saint Leo University; Saint Leo (Pr)	1,825	55	51	14,080	14,080	7,260
Southeastern College of the Assemblies of God; Lakeland (Pr)	1,964	55	86	10,140	10,140	5,470
Stetson University; DeLand (Pr)	3,577	58	74	24,135	24,135	7,060

Institution name; city (Public/Private)	Total enrolled students	Percent Women	Percent Students accepted	Tuition and fees In-state	Tuition and fees Out-of-state	Room and board
St. Thomas University; Miami Gardens (Pr)	2,630	59%	28%	$17,010	$17,010	$10,720
Universidad FLET; Miami (Pr)	866	35	100	—	—	—
University of Central Florida; Orlando (Pu)	42,568	55	55	3,180	15,686	7,232
University of Florida; Gainesville (Pu)	47,858	54	52	2,955	15,827	6,040
University of Miami; Coral Gables (Pr)	15,250	58	42	27,840	27,840	8,602
University of North Florida; Jacksonville (Pu)	14,534	58	69	3,101	14,851	6,278
University of Phoenix–Fort Lauderdale Campus; Fort Lauderdale (Pr)	2,586	69	—	10,170	10,170	—
University of Phoenix–Jacksonville Campus; Jacksonville (Pr)	2,122	55	—	10,170	10,170	—
University of Phoenix–Orlando Campus; Maitland (Pr)	2,142	59	—	10,170	10,170	—
University of Phoenix–Tampa Campus; Tampa (Pr)	2,570	57	—	10,170	10,170	—
University of South Florida; Tampa (Pu)	42,238	59	51	3,164	16,034	6,730
University of Tampa; Tampa (Pr)	4,879	62	53	18,172	18,172	6,666
University of West Florida; Pensacola (Pu)	9,518	59	66	3,039	15,546	6,294
Warner Southern College; Lake Wales (Pr)	1,024	59	30	11,990	11,990	5,160
GEORGIA						
Agnes Scott College; Decatur (Pr)	1,002	100	59	22,210	22,210	8,200
Albany State University; Albany (Pu)	3,668	65	91	2,896	9,864	3,690
American InterContinental University; Atlanta (Pr)	1,150	53	80	17,945	17,945	—
American InterContinental University; Atlanta (Pr)	1,732	65	93	15,525	15,525	4,500
Armstrong Atlantic State University; Savannah (Pu)	6,653	66	65	2,734	9,662	4,500
Art Institute of Atlanta; Atlanta (Pr)	2,651	47	—	17,040	17,040	7,311
Augusta State University; Augusta (Pu)	6,353	63	67	2,702	9,670	—
Berry College; Mount Berry (Pr)	2,008	65	76	16,240	16,240	6,450
Brewton-Parker College; Mt. Vernon (Pr)	1,136	62	99	12,600	12,600	5,200
Clark Atlanta University; Atlanta (Pr)	4,598	71	60	13,486	13,486	6,816
Clayton State University; Morrow (Pu)	5,954	68	—	2,802	9,770	—
Columbus State University; Columbus (Pu)	7,224	63	68	2,808	9,776	5,550
Covenant College; Lookout Mountain (Pr)	974	61	66	19,210	19,210	5,720
Dalton State College; Dalton (Pu)	4,252	62	70	1,592	5,996	—
Emory University; Atlanta (Pr)	11,781	57	39	29,322	29,322	9,650
Fort Valley State University; Fort Valley (Pu)	2,558	54	44	3,510	10,478	4,386
Georgia College & State University; Milledgeville (Pu)	5,531	60	44	3,862	13,318	6,482
Georgia Institute of Technology; Atlanta (Pu)	16,841	28	70	4,278	17,558	6,526
Georgia Southern University; Statesboro (Pu)	16,100	49	54	3,062	10,120	6,000
Georgia Southwestern State University; Americus (Pu)	2,323	63	75	2,892	9,860	4,506
Georgia State University; Atlanta (Pu)	27,267	60	56	4,464	15,378	7,368
Kennesaw State University; Kennesaw (Pu)	17,955	60	61	2,758	9,726	5,376
LaGrange College; LaGrange (Pr)	1,044	64	55	15,206	15,206	6,318
Life University; Marietta (Pr)	1,233	48	60	5,496	5,496	—
Luther Rice Bible College and Seminary; Lithonia (Pr)	1,600	38	100	3,964	3,964	—
Macon State College; Macon (Pu)	5,733	63	—	1,784	6,188	—
Mercer University; Macon (Pr)	7,180	67	85	22,050	22,050	7,060
Morehouse College; Atlanta (Pr)	2,891	0	67	15,740	15,740	8,748
North Georgia College & State University; Dahlonega (Pu)	4,552	58	60	2,944	9,912	4,408
Oglethorpe University; Atlanta (Pr)	1,053	65	64	22,300	22,300	8,000
Paine College; Augusta (Pr)	882	71	25	9,626	9,626	4,460
Piedmont College; Demorest (Pr)	2,222	64	62	13,500	13,500	4,700
Reinhardt College; Waleska (Pr)	1,096	57	52	12,200	12,200	5,762
Savannah College of Art and Design; Savannah (Pr)	6,776	51	72	22,100	22,100	8,700
Savannah State University; Savannah (Pu)	2,800	56	32	2,940	9,908	4,498
Shorter College; Rome (Pr)	896	56	87	12,770	12,770	5,900
Southern Polytechnic State University; Marietta (Pu)	3,801	17	62	2,892	10,174	4,946
South University; Savannah (Pr)	801	69	—	11,085	11,085	—
Spelman College; Atlanta (Pr)	2,186	100	47	15,945	15,945	8,455
Toccoa Falls College; Toccoa Falls (Pr)	829	55	75	12,050	12,050	4,600
University of Georgia; Athens (Pu)	33,405	57	62	4,272	15,588	6,006
University of Phoenix–Atlanta Campus; Atlanta (Pr)	2,031	63	—	10,830	10,830	—
University of West Georgia; Carrollton (Pu)	10,216	59	61	2,906	9,874	4,550
Valdosta State University; Valdosta (Pu)	10,400	59	66	2,992	9,960	5,208
GUAM						
University of Guam; Mangilao (Pu)	2,923	62	100	4,084	11,260	6,918
HAWAII						
Brigham Young University–Hawaii; Laie (Pr)	2,486	56	12	2,660	2,660	4,800
Chaminade University of Honolulu; Honolulu (Pr)	1,783	69	97	14,330	14,330	8,870
Hawai'i Pacific University; Honolulu (Pr)	7,800	63	80	11,002	11,002	9,020
University of Hawaii at Hilo; Hilo (Pu)	3,288	—	66	2,604	8,172	5,374
University of Hawaii at Manoa; Honolulu (Pu)	20,549	56	65	3,504	9,984	5,942
University of Phoenix–Hawaii Campus; Honolulu (Pr)	1,480	67	100	10,650	10,650	—
IDAHO						
Albertson College of Idaho; Caldwell (Pr)	807	55	82	15,890	15,890	6,475
Boise State University; Boise (Pu)	18,332	53	91	3,520	10,567	5,384
Idaho State University; Pocatello (Pu)	13,802	54	71	3,700	10,780	4,850
Lewis-Clark State College; Lewiston (Pu)	3,325	57	71	3,392	6,240	3,995

Institution name; city (Public/Private)	Total enrolled students	Percent Women	Students accepted	Tuition and fees In-state	Out-of-state	Room and board
Northwest Nazarene University; Nampa (Pr)	1,578	59%	68%	$17,730	$17,730	$ 4,860
University of Idaho; Moscow (Pu)	12,824	45	81	3,632	11,652	5,034
ILLINOIS						
Augustana College; Rock Island (Pr)	2,309	58	68	22,131	22,131	6,042
Aurora University; Aurora (Pr)	3,326	66	50	15,600	15,600	6,840
Benedictine University; Lisle (Pr)	3,232	59	80	18,310	18,310	6,290
Bradley University; Peoria (Pr)	6,069	54	84	17,730	17,730	6,150
Chicago State University; Chicago (Pu)	6,835	71	47	6,143	10,973	6,032
Columbia College Chicago; Chicago (Pr)	10,354	51	62	15,998	15,998	9,300
Concordia University; River Forest (Pr)	2,056	65	53	19,000	19,000	5,900
DePaul University; Chicago (Pr)	23,531	58	69	19,765	19,765	9,307
DeVry University; Addison (Pr)	1,853	—	—	11,580	11,580	—
DeVry University; Chicago (Pr)	2,477	—	—	11,580	11,580	—
Dominican University; River Forest (Pr)	3,188	70	83	19,000	19,000	5,890
Eastern Illinois University; Charleston (Pu)	11,651	57	76	5,782	14,047	7,150
East-West University; Chicago (Pr)	1,040	65	90	10,840	10,840	—
Elmhurst College; Elmhurst (Pr)	2,670	63	76	20,090	20,090	6,304
Greenville College; Greenville (Pr)	1,305	52	69	16,824	16,824	5,760
Harrington College of Design; Chicago (Pr)	1,555	90	66	17,050	17,050	5,000
Illinois College; Jacksonville (Pr)	1,037	54	89	14,600	14,600	6,200
Illinois Institute of Art; Chicago (Pr)	2,400	60	—	18,540	18,540	7,434
Illinois Institute of Art-Schaumburg; Schaumburg (Pr)	1,187	45	74	16,605	16,605	—
Illinois Institute of Technology; Chicago (Pr)	6,378	25	65	22,982	22,982	—
Illinois State University; Normal (Pu)	20,757	57	75	6,328	11,548	5,576
Illinois Wesleyan University; Bloomington (Pr)	2,118	56	49	27,624	27,624	6,426
International Academy of Design & Technology; Chicago (Pr)	2,905	68	60	20,000	20,000	—
Judson College; Elgin (Pr)	1,222	55	73	17,150	17,150	6,200
Knox College; Galesburg (Pr)	1,205	55	72	25,236	25,236	6,102
Lake Forest College; Lake Forest (Pr)	1,407	59	63	25,828	25,828	6,222
Lewis University; Romeoville (Pr)	4,826	58	68	17,990	17,990	7,500
Loyola University Chicago; Chicago (Pr)	13,909	66	83	23,836	23,836	9,060
McKendree College; Lebanon (Pr)	2,257	54	69	16,600	16,600	6,360
Millikin University; Decatur (Pr)	2,672	57	74	20,300	20,300	6,510
Monmouth College; Monmouth (Pr)	1,253	53	72	19,350	19,350	5,450
Moody Bible Institute; Chicago (Pr)	2,687	43	40	1,400	1,400	12,480
National-Louis University; Chicago (Pr)	7,665	70	—	16,320	16,320	6,213
North Central College; Naperville (Pr)	2,377	60	69	20,400	20,400	6,747
Northeastern Illinois University; Chicago (Pu)	12,164	62	75	4,235	7,955	—
Northern Illinois University; De Kalb (Pu)	24,818	53	56	5,760	10,620	5,740
North Park University; Chicago (Pr)	2,181	60	74	20,410	20,410	6,980
Northwestern University; Evanston (Pr)	16,663	53	30	31,789	31,789	9,873
Olivet Nazarene University; Bourbonnais (Pr)	4,364	60	65	16,490	16,490	6,100
Quincy University; Quincy (Pr)	1,294	57	92	17,650	17,650	5,725
Robert Morris College; Chicago (Pr)	5,520	66	82	14,250	14,250	6,390
Rockford College; Rockford (Pr)	1,280	60	59	22,460	22,460	7,221
Roosevelt University; Chicago (Pr)	7,385	65	51	16,330	16,330	8,400
Saint Xavier University; Chicago (Pr)	5,722	70	70	17,330	17,330	6,724
School of the Art Institute of Chicago; Chicago (Pr)	2,660	67	83	27,150	27,150	8,200
Southern Illinois University Carbondale; Carbondale (Pu)	21,589	43	76	6,341	13,721	5,200
Southern Illinois University Edwardsville; Edwardsville (Pu)	13,493	56	81	5,179	11,659	5,819
St. Augustine College; Chicago (Pr)	1,582	79	78	7,128	7,128	—
Trinity Christian College; Palos Heights (Pr)	1,234	63	94	16,400	16,400	6,044
Trinity International University; Deerfield (Pr)	2,815	58	78	18,150	18,150	6,080
University of Chicago; Chicago (Pr)	13,885	50	40	30,729	30,729	9,623
University of Illinois at Chicago; Chicago (Pu)	24,810	54	62	8,502	20,892	7,160
University of Illinois at Springfield; Springfield (Pu)	4,396	59	43	4,962	12,417	2,878
University of Illinois at Urbana–Champaign; Champaign (Pu)	40,694	47	68	8,553	22,639	6,710
University of Phoenix–Chicago Campus; Schaumburg (Pr)	1,399	55	99	10,350	10,350	—
University of St. Francis; Joliet (Pr)	2,110	67	46	17,670	17,670	6,180
Western Illinois University; Macomb (Pu)	13,558	48	70	6,183	10,721	5,768
Wheaton College; Wheaton (Pr)	2,898	52	50	20,000	20,000	6,466
INDIANA						
Anderson University; Anderson (Pr)	2,677	58	79	18,900	18,900	6,150
Ball State University; Muncie (Pu)	20,544	53	76	6,260	15,436	6,228
Bethel College; Mishawaka (Pr)	1,847	60	88	15,360	15,360	4,880
Butler University; Indianapolis (Pr)	4,415	63	72	22,484	22,484	7,780
Calumet College of Saint Joseph; Whiting (Pr)	1,327	61	63	9,450	9,450	—
DePauw University; Greencastle (Pr)	2,391	55	69	25,500	25,500	7,300
Earlham College; Richmond (Pr)	1,275	58	72	26,042	26,042	5,740
Franklin College; Franklin (Pr)	994	52	75	18,275	18,275	5,500
Goshen College; Goshen (Pr)	908	57	77	19,300	19,300	6,450
Grace College; Winona Lake (Pr)	1,258	49	72	15,030	15,030	6,150
Hanover College; Hanover (Pr)	1,062	54	75	20,600	20,600	6,200

Institution name; city (Public/Private)	Total enrolled students	Percent Women	Percent Students accepted	Tuition and fees In-state	Tuition and fees Out-of-state	Room and board
Huntington University; Huntington (Pr)	975	56%	90%	$18,490	$18,490	$6,340
Indiana Institute of Technology; Fort Wayne (Pr)	3,425	52	92	17,600	17,600	6,750
Indiana State University; Terre Haute (Pu)	11,200	50	83	5,640	12,368	5,615
Indiana University Bloomington; Bloomington (Pu)	37,821	52	83	6,777	18,590	6,006
Indiana University East; Richmond (Pu)	2,516	70	91	4,601	10,991	—
Indiana University Kokomo; Kokomo (Pu)	2,903	71	79	4,632	11,022	—
Indiana University Northwest; Gary (Pu)	5,138	69	79	4,707	11,097	—
Indiana University–Purdue University Fort Wayne; Fort Wayne (Pu)	11,810	56	96	5,312	12,250	—
Indiana University–Purdue University Indianapolis; Indianapolis (Pu)	29,953	59	73	5,930	15,767	2,656
Indiana University South Bend; South Bend (Pu)	7,501	63	87	4,755	11,826	—
Indiana University Southeast; New Albany (Pu)	6,238	63	86	4,673	11,063	—
Indiana Wesleyan University; Marion (Pr)	11,020	64	54	16,184	16,184	5,890
Manchester College; North Manchester (Pr)	1,068	55	71	19,360	19,360	6,910
Marian College; Indianapolis (Pr)	1,685	71	73	19,060	19,060	6,400
Oakland City University; Oakland City (Pr)	1,928	53	59	13,560	13,560	5,030
Purdue University Calumet; Hammond (Pu)	9,222	55	82	4,662	10,442	3,990
Purdue University North Central; Westville (Pu)	3,467	55	83	4,712	10,871	—
Purdue University; West Lafayette (Pu)	38,653	40	80	6,335	19,822	7,406
Rose-Hulman Institute of Technology; Terre Haute (Pr)	1,904	19	70	26,136	26,136	7,065
Saint Joseph's College; Rensselaer (Pr)	1,010	55	79	19,160	19,160	6,300
Saint Mary-of-the-Woods College; Saint Mary-of-the-Woods (Pr)	1,703	100	75	17,860	17,860	6,560
Saint Mary's College; Notre Dame (Pr)	1,418	100	76	24,358	24,358	8,180
Taylor University; Upland (Pr)	1,866	54	82	20,746	20,746	5,630
Tri-State University; Angola (Pr)	1,232	32	76	20,200	20,200	6,000
University of Evansville; Evansville (Pr)	2,687	61	88	20,515	20,515	6,010
University of Indianapolis; Indianapolis (Pr)	4,188	64	74	17,200	17,200	6,150
University of Notre Dame; Notre Dame (Pr)	11,479	47	30	29,512	29,512	7,418
University of Saint Francis; Fort Wayne (Pr)	1,883	67	67	16,460	16,460	5,450
University of Southern Indiana; Evansville (Pu)	10,050	59	92	4,077	9,642	5,480
Valparaiso University; Valparaiso (Pr)	3,969	52	81	21,700	21,700	5,840
Wabash College; Crawfordsville (Pr)	857	0	49	22,274	22,274	7,050
IOWA						
Briar Cliff University; Sioux City (Pr)	1,116	57	73	16,995	16,995	5,433
Buena Vista University; Storm Lake (Pr)	1,316	53	81	20,854	20,854	5,822
Central College; Pella (Pr)	1,750	56	83	18,892	18,892	6,486
Clarke College; Dubuque (Pr)	1,180	74	57	17,960	17,960	6,289
Coe College; Cedar Rapids (Pr)	1,354	55	72	22,650	22,650	5,950
Cornell College; Mount Vernon (Pr)	1,155	57	64	22,650	22,650	6,240
Dordt College; Sioux Center (Pr)	1,346	53	94	16,670	16,670	4,650
Drake University; Des Moines (Pr)	5,221	58	84	20,550	20,550	5,920
Graceland University; Lamoni (Pr)	2,351	55	55	16,150	16,150	5,400
Grand View College; Des Moines (Pr)	1,759	69	99	15,392	15,392	5,436
Grinnell College; Grinnell (Pr)	1,556	55	51	25,820	25,820	6,870
Iowa State University of Science and Technology; Ames (Pu)	26,380	44	90	5,426	15,128	5,958
Loras College; Dubuque (Pr)	1,743	50	94	19,678	19,678	5,845
Luther College; Decorah (Pr)	2,573	60	71	23,070	23,070	4,170
Morningside College; Sioux City (Pr)	1,204	55	78	17,170	17,170	5,400
Mount Mercy College; Cedar Rapids (Pr)	1,486	72	86	18,840	18,840	5,680
Northwestern College; Orange City (Pr)	1,284	62	85	16,360	16,360	4,656
Palmer College of Chiropractic; Davenport (Pr)	1,669	65	—	5,895	5,895	—
Simpson College; Indianola (Pr)	1,964	59	76	19,635	19,635	5,561
St. Ambrose University; Davenport (Pr)	3,534	58	86	17,565	17,565	6,635
University of Dubuque; Dubuque (Pr)	1,380	35	80	16,845	16,845	5,700
University of Iowa; Iowa City (Pu)	28,442	54	83	5,612	16,998	6,560
University of Northern Iowa; Cedar Falls (Pu)	12,927	57	80	5,387	12,705	5,261
Upper Iowa University; Fayette (Pr)	887	40	56	18,056	18,056	5,540
Wartburg College; Waverly (Pr)	1,804	55	84	19,700	19,700	5,515
William Penn University; Oskaloosa (Pr)	1,499	47	65	14,604	14,604	4,746
KANSAS						
Baker University; Baldwin City (Pr)	856	53	81	15,550	15,550	5,450
Benedictine College; Atchison (Pr)	1,441	49	99	15,126	15,126	6,128
Emporia State University; Emporia (Pu)	6,194	62	72	3,036	9,756	4,474
Fort Hays State University; Hays (Pu)	7,373	53	94	3,217	9,341	5,061
Friends University; Wichita (Pr)	3,190	—	93	14,600	14,600	—
Haskell Indian Nations University; Lawrence (Pu)	1,028	47	—	420	420	—
Kansas State University; Manhattan (Pu)	23,151	48	48	4,665	13,425	5,738
Kansas Wesleyan University; Salina (Pr)	805	57	53	15,000	15,000	5,400
MidAmerica Nazarene University; Olathe (Pr)	1,985	52	37	14,780	14,780	5,790
Newman University; Wichita (Pr)	2,179	63	—	16,002	16,002	6,586
Pittsburg State University; Pittsburg (Pu)	6,537	49	91	3,294	9,652	4,234
Southwestern College; Winfield (Pr)	1,410	54	69	16,118	16,118	2,334

Institution name; city (Public/Private)	Total enrolled students	Percent Women	Percent Students accepted	Tuition and fees In-state	Tuition and fees Out-of-state	Room and board
University of Kansas; Lawrence (Pu)	28,905	51%	69%	$ 4,737	$12,691	$5,216
University of Saint Mary; Leavenworth (Pr)	824	51	75	14,590	14,590	5,540
Washburn University; Topeka (Pu)	7,002	60	100	4,562	10,232	4,972
Wichita State University; Wichita (Pu)	14,297	56	82	3,909	12,121	4,900
KENTUCKY						
Asbury College; Wilmore (Pr)	1,278	59	74	17,808	17,808	4,498
Bellarmine University; Louisville (Pr)	3,134	66	82	21,530	21,530	6,380
Berea College; Berea (Pr)	1,556	59	27	516	516	4,748
Campbellsville University; Campbellsville (Pr)	2,187	51	73	13,952	13,952	5,440
Centre College; Danville (Pr)	1,069	52	69	21,800	21,800	7,300
Eastern Kentucky University; Richmond (Pu)	16,183	60	94	3,792	10,464	4,658
Georgetown College; Georgetown (Pr)	1,845	55	94	19,170	19,170	5,780
Kentucky State University; Frankfort (Pu)	2,335	55	—	3,780	9,537	5,658
Lindsey Wilson College; Columbia (Pr)	1,846	65	78	13,814	13,814	5,926
Mid-Continent University; Mayfield (Pr)	814	54	67	9,350	9,350	5,485
Midway College; Midway (Pr)	1,271	92	79	12,750	12,750	5,800
Morehead State University; Morehead (Pu)	9,293	57	66	3,840	10,200	4,410
Murray State University; Murray (Pu)	10,120	57	65	3,984	6,164	4,510
Northern Kentucky University; Highland Heights (Pu)	13,908	59	81	4,368	9,096	4,660
Pikeville College; Pikeville (Pr)	1,066	57	100	10,500	10,500	5,000
Spalding University; Louisville (Pr)	1,679	78	64	14,100	14,100	4,572
Sullivan University; Louisville (Pr)	4,928	—	—	12,655	12,655	3,690
Thomas More College; Crestview Hills (Pr)	1,465	49	63	18,320	18,320	6,100
Transylvania University; Lexington (Pr)	1,114	59	88	19,650	19,650	6,590
Union College; Barbourville (Pr)	1,047	47	72	13,750	13,750	4,400
University of Kentucky; Lexington (Pu)	25,686	52	79	5,165	11,945	4,735
University of Louisville; Louisville (Pu)	20,731	53	81	5,532	15,092	6,036
University of the Cumberlands; Williamsburg (Pr)	1,744	51	74	12,658	12,658	5,526
Western Kentucky University; Bowling Green (Pu)	18,485	57	93	5,391	13,167	4,778
LOUISIANA						
Centenary College of Louisiana; Shreveport (Pr)	1,040	64	70	17,360	17,360	6,070
Dillard University; New Orleans (Pr)	2,155	78	47	11,550	11,550	6,840
Grambling State University; Grambling (Pu)	5,039	59	65	3,506	8,856	4,034
Grantham University; Slidell (Pu)	6,000	—	—	—	—	—
Louisiana College; Pineville (Pr)	1,085	56	73	10,300	10,300	3,886
Louisiana State University and Agricultural and Mechanical College; Baton Rouge (Pu)	32,241	52	78	4,226	11,026	5,882
Louisiana State University Health Sciences Center; New Orleans (Pu)	2,240	87	—	4,392	7,517	2,916
Louisiana State University in Shreveport; Shreveport (Pu)	4,401	63	68	3,815	8,145	2,196
Louisiana Tech University; Ruston (Pu)	11,691	47	86	4,375	9,280	4,035
Loyola University New Orleans; New Orleans (Pr)	5,423	60	68	25,246	25,246	8,312
McNeese State University; Lake Charles (Pu)	8,785	58	89	3,159	9,225	4,637
New Orleans Baptist Theological Seminary; New Orleans (Pr)	2,712	17	82	3,770	3,770	—
Nicholls State University; Thibodaux (Pu)	7,473	61	99	3,240	9,793	3,534
Northwestern State University of Louisiana; Natchitoches (Pu)	10,546	62	91	3,241	9,319	3,426
Our Lady of Holy Cross College; New Orleans (Pr)	1,446	78	97	6,140	6,140	—
Our Lady of the Lake College; Baton Rouge (Pr)	1,990	—	91	7,280	7,280	—
Southeastern Louisiana University; Hammond (Pu)	15,472	60	94	3,191	8,519	4,290
Southern University and Agricultural and Mechanical College; Baton Rouge (Pu)	9,400	61	52	3,440	9,232	4,310
Southern University at New Orleans; New Orleans (Pu)	5,000	—	100	2,990	6,728	—
Tulane University; New Orleans (Pr)	12,691	51	45	31,210	31,210	7,925
University of Louisiana at Lafayette; Lafayette (Pu)	16,563	57	85	3,228	9,408	3,386
University of Louisiana at Monroe; Monroe (Pu)	8,831	63	90	3,076	9,028	3,290
University of New Orleans; New Orleans (Pu)	17,350	55	63	3,492	10,536	4,122
University of Phoenix–Louisiana Campus; Metairie (Pr)	2,585	65	—	9,330	9,330	—
Xavier University of Louisiana; New Orleans (Pr)	4,121	75	83	12,200	12,200	7,100
MAINE						
Bates College; Lewiston (Pr)	1,743	51	30	39,900	39,900	—
Bowdoin College; Brunswick (Pr)	1,677	49	24	31,626	31,626	8,054
Colby College; Waterville (Pr)	1,821	53	37	39,800	39,800	—
Husson College; Bangor (Pr)	2,039	57	97	11,050	11,050	5,850
Maine Maritime Academy; Castine (Pu)	861	17	65	7,045	12,785	6,400
Saint Joseph's College of Maine; Standish (Pr)	986	63	76	19,615	19,615	8,160
Thomas College; Waterville (Pr)	870	45	72	15,520	15,520	6,760
University of Maine at Augusta; Augusta (Pu)	5,538	69	—	4,695	10,335	—
University of Maine at Farmington; Farmington (Pu)	2,349	65	72	5,240	11,930	5,700
University of Maine at Fort Kent; Fort Kent (Pu)	1,076	59	81	4,514	10,154	5,600
University of Maine at Machias; Machias (Pu)	1,191	65	85	4,515	6,495	5,408
University of Maine at Presque Isle; Presque Isle (Pu)	1,652	63	87	4,460	10,400	5,114
University of Maine; Orono (Pu)	11,358	49	79	6,328	15,658	6,412
University of New England; Biddeford (Pr)	3,327	77	91	20,915	20,915	8,155

Institution name; city (Public/Private)	Total enrolled students	Percent		Tuition and fees		Room and board
		Women	Students accepted	In-state	Out-of-state	
University of Southern Maine; Portland (Pu)	11,089	59%	75%	$ 5,510	$13,670	$ 6,908
MARYLAND						
Bowie State University; Bowie (Pu)	5,415	63	53	6,846	14,838	8,674
Capitol College; Laurel (Pr)	801	24	90	17,688	17,688	3,869
College of Notre Dame of Maryland; Baltimore (Pr)	3,307	100	72	21,600	21,600	8,000
Columbia Union College; Takoma Park (Pr)	1,115	62	48	16,433	16,433	5,560
Coppin State University; Baltimore (Pu)	4,003	—	47	4,879	11,400	6,239
Frostburg State University; Frostburg (Pu)	5,327	49	72	6,230	14,480	6,148
Goucher College; Baltimore (Pr)	2,349	67	68	26,150	26,150	8,575
Hood College; Frederick (Pr)	1,948	83	55	22,335	22,335	7,750
Johns Hopkins University; Baltimore (Pr)	5,898	44	30	30,140	30,140	9,516
Loyola College in Maryland; Baltimore (Pr)	6,156	59	71	28,170	28,170	8,959
Maryland Institute College of Art; Baltimore (Pr)	1,608	62	44	25,204	25,204	7,080
McDaniel College; Westminster (Pr)	3,304	58	76	24,800	24,800	5,600
Morgan State University; Baltimore (Pu)	6,621	58	34	5,718	12,958	6,780
Mount St. Mary's University; Emmitsburg (Pr)	2,125	57	85	22,900	22,900	8,030
Salisbury University; Salisbury (Pu)	6,942	56	58	5,976	13,554	7,050
Sojourner-Douglass College; Baltimore (Pr)	1,124	85	—	6,190	6,190	—
St. Mary's College of Maryland; St. Mary's City (Pu)	1,935	59	57	9,680	17,160	7,400
Towson University; Towson (Pu)	17,667	62	67	6,672	15,352	6,468
United States Naval Academy; Annapolis (Pu)	4,349	17	10	0	0	—
University of Maryland, Baltimore County; Baltimore (Pu)	11,852	46	70	8,020	15,620	7,620
University of Maryland, College Park; College Park (Pu)	35,262	50	43	7,410	18,710	7,931
University of Maryland Eastern Shore; Princess Anne (Pu)	3,762	60	58	5,558	11,421	5,880
University of Maryland University College; Adelphi (Pu)	28,374	62	100	5,424	9,888	—
University of Phoenix–Maryland Campus; Columbia (Pr)	2,132	56	—	10,800	10,800	—
Villa Julie College; Stevenson (Pr)	2,740	71	71	14,653	14,653	6,600
Washington College; Chestertown (Pr)	1,426	61	59	26,550	26,550	6,000
MASSACHUSETTS						
American International College; Springfield (Pr)	1,625	53	85	18,000	18,000	8,500
Amherst College; Amherst (Pr)	1,638	48	21	31,364	31,364	8,160
Anna Maria College; Paxton (Pr)	1,108	64	91	20,135	20,135	7,415
Art Institute of Boston at Lesley University; Boston (Pr)	6,521	80	78	19,600	19,600	9,950
Assumption College; Worcester (Pr)	2,452	60	69	22,655	22,655	5,395
Babson College; Babson Park (Pr)	3,288	40	37	28,832	28,832	10,376
Bay Path College; Longmeadow (Pr)	1,417	100	69	19,440	19,440	8,260
Becker College; Worcester (Pr)	1,660	75	65	17,590	17,590	8,000
Bentley College; Waltham (Pr)	5,601	41	45	27,244	27,244	9,860
Berklee College of Music; Boston (Pr)	3,882	25	79	26,307	26,307	11,690
Boston Architectural Center; Boston (Pr)	910	37	91	8,630	8,630	—
Boston College; Chestnut Hill (Pr)	13,814	53	32	29,396	29,396	9,620
Boston University; Boston (Pr)	29,596	60	67	30,402	30,402	9,680
Brandeis University; Waltham (Pr)	5,072	56	40	31,072	31,072	8,656
Bridgewater State College; Bridgewater (Pu)	9,626	61	72	5,296	11,436	6,512
Cambridge College; Cambridge (Pr)	3,795	66	78	10,050	10,050	—
Clark University; Worcester (Pr)	3,115	61	62	28,265	28,265	5,400
College of the Holy Cross; Worcester (Pr)	2,745	54	44	29,686	29,686	8,860
Curry College; Milton (Pr)	2,877	54	74	21,670	21,670	8,180
Eastern Nazarene College; Quincy (Pr)	1,212	61	62	17,434	17,434	5,920
Elms College; Chicopee (Pr)	932	78	88	20,265	20,265	7,750
Emerson College; Boston (Pr)	4,398	58	48	—	—	—
Emmanuel College; Boston (Pr)	2,165	73	64	20,500	20,500	9,000
Endicott College; Beverly (Pr)	3,285	59	44	19,432	19,432	9,300
Fitchburg State College; Fitchburg (Pu)	5,201	56	68	4,588	10,668	5,882
Framingham State College; Framingham (Pu)	6,015	68	62	4,740	10,820	5,539
Gordon College; Wenham (Pr)	1,672	65	81	21,448	21,448	6,092
Hampshire College; Amherst (Pr)	1,352	58	59	30,978	30,978	8,113
Harvard University; Cambridge (Pr)	20,130	47	10	30,620	30,620	9,260
Lasell College; Newton (Pr)	1,181	71	65	19,700	19,700	8,800
Lesley University; Cambridge (Pr)	6,526	80	78	22,750	22,750	9,950
Massachusetts College of Art; Boston (Pu)	2,049	63	56	6,400	17,700	9,737
Massachusetts College of Liberal Arts; North Adams (Pu)	1,811	59	71	5,397	14,342	5,620
Massachusetts College of Pharmacy and Health Sciences; Boston (Pr)	2,587	70	72	20,220	20,220	10,570
Massachusetts Institute of Technology; Cambridge (Pr)	10,320	43	16	30,800	30,800	9,100
Massachusetts Maritime Academy; Buzzards Bay (Pu)	948	12	60	4,963	15,443	6,157
Merrimack College; North Andover (Pr)	2,326	53	64	22,100	22,100	9,200
Mount Holyoke College; South Hadley (Pr)	2,073	100	56	30,938	30,938	9,060
Mount Ida College; Newton (Pr)	1,297	69	79	19,096	19,096	9,830
Newbury College; Brookline (Pr)	1,161	57	80	16,100	16,100	8,250
New England Institute of Art; Brookline (Pr)	1,235	—	61	17,225	17,225	9,450
Nichols College; Dudley (Pr)	1,792	35	84	20,810	20,810	8,052
Northeastern University; Boston (Pr)	18,979	51	42	27,080	27,080	10,180
Regis College; Weston (Pr)	1,271	100	81	20,500	20,500	9,360

Institution name; city (Public/Private)	Total enrolled students	Percent		Tuition and fees		Room and board
		Women	Students accepted	In-state	Out-of-state	
Salem State College; Salem (Pu)	9,347	62%	85%	$ 5,284	$11,424	$ 7,350
Simmons College; Boston (Pr)	4,549	100	67	25,440	25,440	10,200
Smith College; Northampton (Pr)	3,159	100	52	29,156	29,156	9,730
Springfield College; Springfield (Pr)	3,119	48	74	21,360	21,360	7,350
Stonehill College; Easton (Pr)	2,490	58	57	23,008	23,008	10,206
Suffolk University; Boston (Pr)	8,188	57	85	19,870	19,870	11,411
Tufts University; Medford (Pr)	9,693	53	27	31,248	31,248	9,030
University of Massachusetts Amherst; Amherst (Pu)	24,646	50	81	9,008	17,231	6,189
University of Massachusetts Boston; Boston (Pu)	11,682	58	53	8,034	18,767	—
University of Massachusetts Dartmouth; North Dartmouth (Pu)	8,299	50	68	7,802	17,302	7,471
University of Massachusetts Lowell; Lowell (Pu)	11,089	42	66	7,891	15,004	6,011
Wellesley College; Wellesley (Pr)	2,289	100	38	29,796	29,796	9,202
Wentworth Institute of Technology; Boston (Pr)	3,597	20	63	18,500	18,500	9,000
Western New England College; Springfield (Pr)	4,025	41	79	21,986	21,986	8,524
Westfield State College; Westfield (Pu)	4,906	55	66	4,857	10,937	5,742
Wheaton College; Norton (Pr)	1,538	63	45	30,580	30,580	7,580
Wheelock College; Boston (Pr)	1,021	95	79	23,625	23,625	9,450
Williams College; Williamstown (Pr)	2,050	51	19	29,990	29,990	8,110
Worcester Polytechnic Institute; Worcester (Pr)	3,817	24	75	30,130	30,130	9,164
Worcester State College; Worcester (Pu)	5,404	58	57	4,579	10,659	6,896
MICHIGAN						
Adrian College; Adrian (Pr)	1,013	53	84	17,600	17,600	5,770
Albion College; Albion (Pr)	1,867	55	86	22,918	22,918	6,536
Alma College; Alma (Pr)	1,268	59	84	19,986	19,986	7,032
Andrews University; Berrien Springs (Pr)	3,017	55	43	16,506	16,506	5,280
Aquinas College; Grand Rapids (Pr)	2,235	65	82	16,992	16,992	5,600
Baker College of Allen Park; Allen Park (Pr)	1,033	76	100	6,120	6,120	—
Baker College of Auburn Hills; Auburn Hills (Pr)	3,488	73	100	6,120	6,120	—
Baker College of Cadillac; Cadillac (Pr)	1,546	75	100	6,120	6,120	—
Baker College of Clinton Township; Clinton Township (Pr)	4,823	78	100	6,120	6,120	—
Baker College of Flint; Flint (Pr)	6,034	70	100	6,120	6,120	2,600
Baker College of Jackson; Jackson (Pr)	1,603	76	100	6,120	6,120	—
Baker College of Muskegon; Muskegon (Pr)	4,433	70	100	6,120	6,120	2,400
Baker College of Owosso; Owosso (Pr)	2,716	69	100	6,120	6,120	2,400
Baker College of Port Huron; Port Huron (Pr)	1,505	77	100	6,120	6,120	—
Calvin College; Grand Rapids (Pr)	4,180	55	98	17,770	17,770	6,185
Central Michigan University; Mount Pleasant (Pu)	27,683	58	74	5,365	12,467	6,160
Cleary University; Ann Arbor (Pr)	895	61	93	11,760	11,760	—
College for Creative Studies; Detroit (Pr)	1,265	40	80	23,116	23,116	3,900
Cornerstone University; Grand Rapids (Pr)	2,414	63	77	14,700	14,700	5,520
Eastern Michigan University; Ypsilanti (Pu)	23,593	60	78	5,762	15,769	6,082
Ferris State University; Big Rapids (Pu)	11,803	45	49	6,332	12,522	6,522
Grand Valley State University; Allendale (Pu)	22,063	60	70	5,782	12,510	6,160
Hillsdale College; Hillsdale (Pr)	1,273	52	82	16,900	16,900	6,600
Hope College; Holland (Pr)	3,112	62	79	20,420	20,420	6,318
Kalamazoo College; Kalamazoo (Pr)	1,234	58	61	24,351	24,351	6,609
Kettering University; Flint (Pr)	2,992	16	70	23,360	23,360	—
Lake Superior State University; Sault Sainte Marie (Pu)	2,889	49	85	6,372	11,790	6,165
Lawrence Technological University; Southfield (Pr)	4,148	24	69	17,210	17,210	7,035
Madonna University; Livonia (Pr)	4,349	74	86	9,800	9,800	5,612
Marygrove College; Detroit (Pr)	4,610	76	40	12,440	12,440	6,000
Michigan State University; East Lansing (Pu)	44,836	53	79	7,000	17,845	5,458
Michigan Technological University; Houghton (Pu)	6,540	23	94	7,610	18,782	6,096
Northern Michigan University; Marquette (Pu)	9,846	55	83	5,434	8,842	6,182
Northwood University; Midland (Pr)	3,748	42	85	15,183	15,183	6,696
Oakland University; Rochester (Pu)	16,901	63	81	5,354	11,954	5,820
Olivet College; Olivet (Pr)	1,069	42	54	16,464	16,464	5,480
Rochester College; Rochester Hills (Pr)	1,011	59	81	11,456	11,456	6,316
Saginaw Valley State University; University Center (Pu)	9,448	60	90	4,913	11,019	5,850
Siena Heights University; Adrian (Pr)	2,153	—	64	15,520	15,520	5,460
Spring Arbor University; Spring Arbor (Pr)	3,511	66	83	16,096	16,096	5,610
University of Detroit Mercy; Detroit (Pr)	5,521	62	68	22,470	22,470	7,328
University of Michigan; Ann Arbor (Pu)	39,533	51	62	8,201	26,027	7,030
University of Michigan–Dearborn; Dearborn (Pu)	8,631	52	69	6,112	13,383	—
University of Michigan–Flint; Flint (Pu)	6,188	63	87	6,018	10,878	—
University of Phoenix–Metro Detroit Campus; Troy (Pr)	3,948	67	—	11,790	11,790	—
University of Phoenix–West Michigan Campus; Grand Rapids (Pr)	1,167	58	—	11,520	11,520	—
Wayne State University; Detroit (Pu)	33,314	59	63	5,399	11,567	6,700
Western Michigan University; Kalamazoo (Pu)	27,829	50	85	5,668	13,823	6,496
MINNESOTA						
Argosy University/Twin Cities; Eagan (Pr)	1,580	88	86	12,220	12,220	—
Art Institutes International Minnesota; Minneapolis (Pr)	1,391	52	78	16,944	16,944	6,864
Augsburg College; Minneapolis (Pr)	3,375	56	79	20,758	20,758	6,080

Institution name; city (Public/Private)	Total enrolled students	Percent Women	Students accepted	Tuition and fees In-state	Out-of-state	Room and board
Bemidji State University; Bemidji (Pu)	4,971	51%	73%	$ 6,404	$13,172	$5,012
Bethel University; St. Paul (Pr)	3,605	60	86	21,300	21,300	6,800
Carleton College; Northfield (Pr)	1,951	52	29	30,666	30,666	6,309
College of Saint Benedict; Saint Joseph (Pr)	2,033	100	85	22,148	22,148	6,208
College of St. Catherine–Minneapolis; Minneapolis (Pr)	4,807	99	77	14,270	14,270	5,808
College of St. Catherine; St. Paul (Pr)	4,809	99	78	18,550	18,550	5,460
College of St. Scholastica; Duluth (Pr)	3,012	71	89	20,760	20,760	5,916
Concordia College; Moorhead (Pr)	2,814	63	86	17,920	17,920	4,690
Concordia University, St. Paul; St. Paul (Pr)	2,217	59	63	21,312	21,312	6,464
Crown College; St. Bonifacius (Pr)	1,106	57	43	15,646	15,646	6,572
Gustavus Adolphus College; St. Peter (Pr)	2,577	57	77	22,955	22,955	5,810
Hamline University; St. Paul (Pr)	4,490	62	78	22,070	22,070	6,536
Macalester College; St. Paul (Pr)	1,900	56	39	28,810	28,810	7,858
Martin Luther College; New Ulm (Pr)	945	50	97	8,925	8,925	3,465
Metropolitan State University; St. Paul (Pu)	6,516	59	74	4,392	8,532	—
Minnesota State University Mankato; Mankato (Pu)	14,153	53	90	5,088	9,998	4,716
Minnesota State University Moorhead; Moorhead (Pu)	7,642	60	82	4,894	4,894	4,530
North Central University; Minneapolis (Pr)	1,241	57	86	11,284	11,284	4,350
Northwestern College; St. Paul (Pr)	2,734	62	97	18,370	18,370	6,020
Saint John's University; Collegeville (Pr)	2,015	0	86	22,148	22,148	6,118
Saint Mary's University of Minnesota; Winona (Pr)	4,861	55	77	17,925	17,925	5,450
Southwest Minnesota State University; Marshall (Pu)	5,636	56	—	5,294	5,294	4,806
St. Cloud State University; St. Cloud (Pu)	15,608	54	74	5,176	10,534	4,088
St. Olaf College; Northfield (Pr)	3,046	59	64	26,500	26,500	6,300
University of Minnesota, Crookston; Crookston (Pu)	2,088	45	92	7,608	7,608	4,800
University of Minnesota, Duluth; Duluth (Pu)	10,366	52	78	8,291	19,398	5,282
University of Minnesota, Morris; Morris (Pu)	1,836	60	78	9,056	9,056	5,250
University of Minnesota, Twin Cities Campus; Minneapolis (Pu)	50,954	53	74	8,030	19,660	6,458
University of St. Thomas; St. Paul (Pr)	10,474	50	81	21,828	21,828	6,542
Winona State University; Winona (Pu)	8,236	63	79	6,420	10,960	4,960
MISSISSIPPI						
Alcorn State University; Alcorn State (Pu)	3,443	61	35	4,465	9,196	4,012
Belhaven College; Jackson (Pr)	2,505	68	58	14,050	14,050	5,430
Delta State University; Cleveland (Pu)	3,853	59	50	4,072	9,012	3,734
Jackson State University; Jackson (Pu)	8,351	61	40	3,842	8,572	4,974
Millsaps College; Jackson (Pr)	1,146	52	85	20,690	20,690	7,566
Mississippi College; Clinton (Pr)	3,588	59	54	12,058	12,058	5,694
Mississippi State University; Mississippi State (Pu)	15,934	47	68	4,106	9,306	5,994
Mississippi University for Women; Columbus (Pu)	2,328	87	65	3,495	8,442	3,778
Mississippi Valley State University; Itta Bena (Pu)	3,621	69	25	3,832	8,840	3,506
Rust College; Holly Springs (Pr)	1,001	65	—	6,060	6,060	2,600
Tougaloo College; Tougaloo (Pr)	940	69	99	8,700	8,700	5,080
University of Mississippi; University (Pu)	14,497	52	81	4,110	9,264	5,610
University of Southern Mississippi; Hattiesburg (Pu)	15,253	60	57	4,106	9,276	5,010
William Carey College; Hattiesburg (Pr)	2,758	72	71	8,415	8,415	3,465
MISSOURI						
Avila University; Kansas City (Pr)	2,104	62	42	15,870	15,870	5,400
Central Bible College; Springfield (Pr)	817	41	71	8,722	8,722	4,560
Central Missouri State University; Warrensburg (Pu)	10,051	54	86	5,970	11,100	5,180
College of the Ozarks; Point Lookout (Pr)	1,723	56	13	280	280	3,850
Columbia College; Columbia (Pr)	1,108	62	63	11,995	11,995	5,011
Culver-Stockton College; Canton (Pr)	855	57	94	13,390	13,390	5,775
Drury University; Springfield (Pr)	1,894	56	78	14,669	14,669	5,280
Evangel University; Springfield (Pr)	1,801	60	96	12,750	12,750	4,620
Fontbonne University; St. Louis (Pr)	2,827	75	80	15,420	15,420	6,988
Global University of the Assemblies of God; Springfield (Pr)	6,735	29	—	2,160	2,160	—
Hannibal-LaGrange College; Hannibal (Pr)	1,067	64	96	10,876	10,876	4,050
Harris-Stowe State College; St. Louis (Pu)	1,605	64	33	4,255	8,227	—
Lincoln University; Jefferson City (Pu)	3,275	56	—	4,952	8,492	3,790
Lindenwood University; St. Charles (Pr)	8,615	56	47	11,720	11,720	5,600
Maryville University of Saint Louis; St. Louis (Pr)	3,140	75	73	16,300	16,300	7,000
Missouri Baptist University; St. Louis (Pr)	4,058	55	61	13,030	13,030	5,800
Missouri Southern State University; Joplin (Pu)	5,256	58	99	3,976	7,786	4,770
Missouri State University; Springfield (Pu)	19,114	56	77	5,128	9,748	4,660
Missouri Valley College; Marshall (Pr)	1,623	43	67	13,500	13,500	5,200
Missouri Western State College; St. Joseph (Pu)	5,065	59	100	4,778	8,408	4,396
Northwest Missouri State University; Maryville (Pu)	6,230	56	50	5,505	9,360	5,080
Park University; Parkville (Pr)	12,548	60	—	6,048	6,048	5,180
Rockhurst University; Kansas City (Pr)	2,764	51	72	18,560	18,560	5,500
Saint Louis University; St. Louis (Pr)	11,422	56	80	23,558	23,558	7,780
Southeast Missouri State University; Cape Girardeau (Pu)	9,618	—	91	4,875	8,460	5,317
Southwest Baptist University; Bolivar (Pr)	3,445	61	91	13,250	13,250	3,950
St. Louis College of Pharmacy; St. Louis (Pr)	991	—	35	18,150	18,150	7,133

Institution name; city (Public/Private)	Total enrolled students	Percent		Tuition and fees		Room and board
		Women	Students accepted	In-state	Out-of-state	
Truman State University; Kirksville (Pu)	5,862	59%	84%	$ 5,482	$ 9,582	$ 5,175
University of Missouri–Columbia; Columbia (Pu)	28,257	51	89	7,100	16,547	6,220
University of Missouri–Kansas City; Kansas City (Pu)	14,256	60	69	7,250	17,027	7,505
University of Missouri–Rolla; Rolla (Pu)	5,407	22	90	7,299	16,746	3,436
University of Missouri–St. Louis; St. Louis (Pu)	15,512	60	39	7,378	16,825	6,194
University of Phoenix–Kansas City Campus; Kansas City (Pr)	1,016	56	—	10,350	10,350	—
University of Phoenix–St. Louis Campus; St. Louis (Pr)	892	55	—	12,060	12,060	—
Washington University in St. Louis; St. Louis (Pr)	13,380	51	22	32,042	32,042	10,064
Webster University; St. Louis (Pr)	· 7,424	62	56	16,250	16,250	6,610
Westminster College; Fulton (Pr)	867	42	70	14,170	14,170	5,870
William Jewell College; Liberty (Pr)	1,310	59	73	17,500	17,500	5,100
William Woods University; Fulton (Pr)	2,191	76	84	14,720	14,720	5,700
MONTANA						
Carroll College; Helena (Pr)	1,461	59	80	16,978	16,978	6,246
Montana State University–Billings; Billings (Pu)	4,702	63	93	4,550	12,831	4,500
Montana State University; Bozeman (Pu)	12,003	45	77	4,577	14,177	5,500
Montana State University–Northern; Havre (Pu)	1,589	48	82	4,519	13,095	5,190
Montana Tech of The University of Montana; Butte (Pu)	2,188	42	99	—	—	5,128
Rocky Mountain College; Billings (Pr)	988	55	81	14,715	14,715	5,480
University of Montana–Missoula; Missoula (Pu)	13,558	53	93	4,699	13,415	5,646
University of Montana–Western; Dillon (Pu)	1,146	51	99	3,530	11,880	4,740
NEBRASKA						
Bellevue University; Bellevue (Pr)	5,524	48	92	4,740	4,740	—
Chadron State College; Chadron (Pu)	2,569	56	—	3,495	6,345	3,986
College of Saint Mary; Omaha (Pr)	994	100	44	17,000	17,000	5,700
Concordia University; Seward (Pr)	1,317	56	89	16,880	16,880	4,580
Creighton University; Omaha (Pr)	6,723	60	86	21,118	21,118	7,200
Doane College; Crete (Pr)	2,429	55	80	15,970	15,970	4,720
Hastings College; Hastings (Pr)	1,153	49	80	16,290	16,290	4,760
Midland Lutheran College; Fremont (Pr)	955	60	83	17,210	17,210	4,560
Nebraska Wesleyan University; Lincoln (Pr)	1,953	56	85	17,390	17,390	4,630
Peru State College; Peru (Pu)	1,683	56	62	3,534	6,384	4,486
Union College; Lincoln (Pr)	936	58	51	14,410	14,410	3,950
University of Nebraska at Kearney; Kearney (Pu)	6,382	55	85	4,260	7,913	4,990
University of Nebraska at Omaha; Omaha (Pu)	13,824	54	87	4,533	12,197	5,960
University of Nebraska–Lincoln; Lincoln (Pu)	21,792	47	74	5,268	13,758	6,008
Wayne State College; Wayne (Pu)	3,398	55	100	3,672	6,522	4,120
NEVADA						
Art Institute of Las Vegas; Henderson (Pr)	911	47	—	16,464	16,464	—
University of Nevada, Las Vegas; Las Vegas (Pu)	27,344	56	81	3,532	12,999 ·	8,326
University of Nevada, Reno; Reno (Pu)	15,950	55	87	3,010	11,684	7,385
University of Phoenix–Nevada Campus; Las Vegas (Pr)	4,125	60	—	9,300	9,300	—
NEW HAMPSHIRE						
Colby-Sawyer College; New London (Pr)	964	65	82	24,700	24,700	9,490
Daniel Webster College; Nashua (Pr)	1,109	25	79	21,630	21,630	8,170
Dartmouth College; Hanover (Pr)	5,704	50	19	30,575	30,575	9,124
Franklin Pierce College; Rindge (Pr)	1,608	50	77	23,710	23,710	7,990
Granite State College; Concord (Pu)	1,827	—	—	4,563	5,043	—
Keene State College; Keene (Pu)	4,937	58	71	6,900	13,340	5,966
New England College; Henniker (Pr)	1,329	50	83	23,010	23,010	8,456
Plymouth State University; Plymouth (Pu)	5,151	51	77	6,618	13,058	6,322
Rivier College; Nashua (Pr)	2,289	78	69	19,875	19,875	7,273
Saint Anselm College; Manchester (Pr)	1,987	58	66	24,660	24,660	9,070
Southern New Hampshire University; Manchester (Pr)	3,887	55	74	19,314	19,314	7,866
University of New Hampshire at Manchester; Manchester (Pu)	1,215	57	71	6,593	16,373	—
University of New Hampshire; Durham (Pu) ·	14,405	57	68	9,226	20,256	6,612
NEW JERSEY						
Bloomfield College; Bloomfield (Pr)	2,166	68	53	15,100	15,100	7,400
Caldwell College; Caldwell (Pr)	2,175	64	79	18,950	18,950	7,500
Centenary College; Hackettstown (Pr)	2,600	67	97	19,360	19,360	7,500
College of New Jersey; Ewing (Pu)	6,812	59	48	8,988	13,929	8,093
College of Saint Elizabeth; Morristown (Pr)	1,976	98	78	18,437	18,437	8,618
DeVry University; North Brunswick (Pr)	1,886	—	—	11,580	11,580	—
Drew University; Madison (Pr)	2,675	59	70	29,546	29,546	8,018
Fairleigh Dickinson University, College at Florham; Madison (Pr)	3,684	52	72	23,386	23,386	8,608
Fairleigh Dickinson University, Metropolitan Campus; Teaneck (Pr)	7,634	58	62	21,734	21,734	9,056
Felician College; Lodi (Pr)	1,665	75	76	17,100	17,100	7,500
Georgian Court University; Lakewood (Pr)	3,065	94	79	17,924	17,924	7,200
Kean University; Union (Pu)	12,897	62	65	7,151	9,656	8,093
Monmouth University; West Long Branch (Pr)	6,329	57	66	19,704	19,704	7,911
Montclair State University; Upper Montclair (Pu)	15,637	61	50	7,026	10,694	8,212

Institution name; city (Public/Private)	Total enrolled students	Percent Women	Percent Students accepted	Tuition and fees In-state	Tuition and fees Out-of-state	Room and board
New Jersey City University; Jersey City (Pu)	8,799	62%	51%	$ 6,550	$11,230	$ 6,958
New Jersey Institute of Technology; Newark (Pu)	8,249	20	58	9,180	14,978	8,242
Princeton University; Princeton (Pr)	6,836	47	13	29,910	29,910	8,387
Ramapo College of New Jersey; Mahwah (Pu)	5,617	60	40	8,081	12,633	8,208
Richard Stockton College of New Jersey; Pomona (Pu)	7,004	57	51	7,203	10,368	7,252
Rider University; Lawrenceville (Pr)	5,502	58	85	23,470	23,470	8,840
Rowan University; Glassboro (Pu)	9,688	54	52	7,970	13,798	7,642
Rutgers, The State University of New Jersey, Camden; Camden (Pu)	5,563	58	56	8,389	15,424	7,862
Rutgers, The State University of New Jersey, Newark; Newark (Pu)	10,293	58	51	8,209	15,244	8,570
Rutgers, The State University of New Jersey, New Brunswick/Piscataway; New Brunswick (Pu)	34,696	52	61	8,564	15,599	8,357
Saint Peter's College; Jersey City (Pr)	3,282	—	67	19,750	19,750	8,430
Seton Hall University; South Orange (Pr)	9,824	52	87	23,460	23,460	10,162
Stevens Institute of Technology; Hoboken (Pr)	4,634	24	53	29,760	29,760	8,926
Thomas Edison State College; Trenton (Pu)	11,000	—	—	—	—	—
William Paterson University of New Jersey; Wayne (Pu)	11,409	58	66	7,952	12,690	8,340
NEW MEXICO						
College of Santa Fe; Santa Fe (Pr)	1,769	56	90	20,840	20,840	6,250
Eastern New Mexico University; Portales (Pu)	3,939	54	67	2,616	8,172	4,340
New Mexico Highlands University; Las Vegas (Pu)	3,671	54	75	2,300	9,644	4,274
New Mexico Institute of Mining and Technology; Socorro (Pu)	1,806	23	80	3,280	9,911	4,670
New Mexico State University; Las Cruces (Pu)	16,428	54	82	3,666	12,210	5,046
University of New Mexico; Albuquerque (Pu)	25,686	57	76	4,364	13,127	6,180
University of Phoenix–New Mexico Campus; Albuquerque (Pr)	4,812	60	—	8,940	8,940	—
Western New Mexico University; Silver City (Pu)	3,074	—	—	2,451	9,003	4,280
NEW YORK						
Adelphi University; Garden City (Pr)	7,592	70	70	18,700	18,700	8,500
Albany College of Pharmacy of Union University; Albany (Pr)	886	62	64	17,900	17,900	6,000
Alfred University; Alfred (Pr)	2,355	50	73	20,060	20,060	9,374
Bard College; Annandale-on-Hudson (Pr)	1,726	55	36	30,742	30,742	9,418
Barnard College; New York (Pr)	2,287	100	27	28,340	28,340	10,800
Bernard M. Baruch College of the City University of New York; New York (Pu)	15,537	54	36	4,300	8,940	—
Boricua College; New York (Pr)	1,520	—	47	7,300	7,300	—
Briarcliffe College; Bethpage (Pr)	3,227	50	85	15,008	15,008	7,350
Brooklyn College of the City University of New York; Brooklyn (Pu)	15,384	59	33	4,353	8,993	—
Buffalo State College, State University of New York; Buffalo (Pu)	11,072	61	51	5,137	11,397	6,200
Canisius College; Buffalo (Pr)	5,018	56	82	21,811	21,811	8,395
Cazenovia College; Cazenovia (Pr)	1,180	77	85	18,940	18,940	7,590
Central Yeshiva Tomchei Tmimim-Lubavitch; Brooklyn (Pr)	1,000	—	—	4,800	4,800	—
City College of the City University of New York; New York (Pu)	12,108	48	49	4,339	8,899	—
Clarkson University; Potsdam (Pr)	3,123	23	86	25,585	25,585	9,345
Colgate University; Hamilton (Pr)	2,830	52	33	31,440	31,440	7,620
College of Mount Saint Vincent; Riverdale (Pr)	1,685	74	71	19,900	19,900	8,250
College of New Rochelle; New Rochelle (Pr)	2,564	97	45	20,596	20,596	7,880
College of Saint Rose; Albany (Pr)	4,971	74	71	16,780	16,780	7,472
College of Staten Island of the City University of New York; Staten Island (Pu)	12,442	56	100	4,308	8,948	—
Columbia College; New York (Pr)	4,115	50	11	31,472	31,472	9,066
Columbia University, School of General Studies; New York (Pr)	1,571	47	50	30,900	30,900	—
Columbia University, The Fu Foundation School of Engineering and Applied Science; New York (Pr)	1,387	26	28	31,472	31,472	9,066
Cooper Union for the Advancement of Science and Art; New York (Pr)	955	35	12	1,400	1,400	13,000
Cornell University; Ithaca (Pr)	19,518	50	29	30,167	30,167	9,882
Culinary Institute of America; Hyde Park (Pr)	2,409	36	70	18,795	18,795	6,510
Daemen College; Amherst (Pr)	2,186	76	73	16,020	16,020	7,370
Dominican College; Orangeburg (Pr)	1,639	60	85	17,250	17,250	8,470
Dowling College; Oakdale (Pr)	6,092	60	99	16,050	16,050	5,512
D'Youville College; Buffalo (Pr)	2,729	75	72	14,890	14,890	7,340
Elmira College; Elmira (Pr)	1,853	71	67	27,030	27,030	8,330
Excelsior College; Albany (Pr)	26,395	—	—	—	—	—
Farmingdale State University of New York; Farmingdale (Pu)	6,250	36	58	5,211	11,161	7,680
Fashion Institute of Technology; New York (Pu)	10,513	85	49	4,720	10,670	7,066
Five Towns College; Dix Hills (Pr)	1,162	40	—	14,100	14,100	10,250

Institution name; city (Public/Private)	Total enrolled students	Percent		Tuition and fees		Room and board
		Women	Students accepted	In-state	Out-of-state	
Fordham University; New York (Pr)	14,861	59%	50%	$27,047	$27,047	$10,248
Globe Institute of Technology; New York (Pr)	1,229	62	81	9,086	9,086	3,500
Hamilton College; Clinton (Pr)	1,792	50	34	31,700	31,700	7,825
Hartwick College; Oneonta (Pr)	1,479	57	89	26,480	26,480	7,480
Hilbert College; Hamburg (Pr)	1,108	58	93	14,300	14,300	5,380
Hobart and William Smith Colleges; Geneva (Pr)	1,847	55	63	30,643	30,643	7,987
Hofstra University; Hempstead (Pr)	12,999	54	67	20,012	20,012	9,000
Houghton College; Houghton (Pr)	1,480	67	76	18,660	18,660	6,320
Hunter College of the City University of New York; New York (Pu)	20,243	70	30	4,329	—	2,600
Iona College; New Rochelle (Pr)	4,329	54	60	19,530	19,530	9,698
Ithaca College; Ithaca (Pr)	6,337	57	67	23,690	23,690	9,704
John Jay College of Criminal Justice of the City of New York; New York (Pu)	12,984	61	44	4,259	8,899	—
Juilliard School; New York (Pr)	833	50	7	23,450	23,450	9,030
Keuka College; Keuka Park (Pr)	1,154	70	85	17,080	17,080	7,790
Lehman College of the City University of New York; Bronx (Pu)	10,281	71	27	4,270	8,910	—
Le Moyne College; Syracuse (Pr)	3,487	61	74	20,150	20,150	7,890
Long Island University, Brooklyn Campus; Brooklyn (Pr)	8,003	71	67	21,922	21,922	7,350
Long Island University, C.W. Post Campus; Brookville (Pr)	8,421	62	75	21,960	21,960	8,240
Manhattan College; Riverdale (Pr)	3,301	50	53	20,600	20,600	9,025
Manhattan School of Music; New York (Pr)	875	47	40	28,285	28,285	12,500
Manhattanville College; Purchase (Pr)	2,608	70	56	24,570	24,570	10,130
Marist College; Poughkeepsie (Pr)	5,646	57	49	21,015	21,015	9,218
Marymount College of Fordham University; Tarrytown (Pr)	1,036	98	78	19,702	19,702	9,760
Marymount Manhattan College; New York (Pr)	2,077	76	80	17,352	17,352	12,366
Medaille College; Buffalo (Pr)	2,526	63	94	14,320	14,320	6,800
Medgar Evers College of the City University of New York; Brooklyn (Pu)	5,098	74	100	4,230	8,870	—
Mercy College; Dobbs Ferry (Pr)	10,395	31	—	11,374	11,374	8,426
Metropolitan College of New York; New York (Pr)	1,591	79	92	14,124	14,124	—
Molloy College; Rockville Centre (Pr)	3,352	75	70	15,850	15,850	—
Mount Saint Mary College; Newburgh (Pr)	2,621	74	79	15,690	15,690	7,640
Nazareth College of Rochester; Rochester (Pr)	3,140	76	81	18,776	18,776	7,840
New York Institute of Technology; Old Westbury (Pr)	9,387	39	67	18,190	18,190	7,780
New York University; New York (Pr)	39,408	61	35	30,094	30,094	11,390
Niagara University; Niagara University (Pr)	3,807	62	80	18,420	18,420	8,050
Nyack College; Nyack (Pr)	2,908	60	—	15,550	15,550	7,600
Pace University; New York (Pr)	13,670	62	70	22,712	22,712	8,400
Parsons School of Design, New School University; New York (Pr)	2,958	76	42	25,925	25,925	10,810
Paul Smith's College of Arts and Sciences; Paul Smiths (Pr)	816	31	81	17,110	17,110	7,060
Polytechnic University, Brooklyn Campus; Brooklyn (Pr)	2,819	19	69	27,170	27,170	8,000
Pratt Institute; Brooklyn (Pr)	4,540	57	50	27,580	27,580	8,576
Purchase College, State University of New York; Purchase (Pu)	3,832	55	29	5,823	12,083	7,212
Queens College of the City University of New York; Flushing (Pu)	17,395	60	42	4,361	9,001	—
Rensselaer Polytechnic Institute; Troy (Pr)	7,521	25	75	29,786	29,786	9,083
Roberts Wesleyan College; Rochester (Pr)	1,926	67	82	19,324	19,324	5,028
Rochester Institute of Technology; Rochester (Pr)	14,552	29	67	22,413	22,413	8,136
Russell Sage College; Troy (Pr)	837	100	83	22,270	22,270	7,050
Sage College of Albany; Albany (Pr)	1,051	68	58	16,020	16,020	7,150
Sarah Lawrence College; Bronxville (Pr)	1,574	72	44	32,416	32,416	11,438
School of Visual Arts; New York (Pr)	3,442	52	68	19,620	19,620	11,250
Siena College; Loudonville (Pr)	3,338	57	60	19,130	19,130	7,575
Skidmore College; Saratoga Springs (Pr)	2,691	58	48	31,108	31,108	8,710
State University of New York at Binghamton; Binghamton (Pu)	13,860	49	44	5,756	12,016	7,710
State University of New York at New Paltz; New Paltz (Pu)	7,603	66	40	5,220	11,170	6,860
State University of New York at Oswego; Oswego (Pu)	8,289	54	57	5,238	11,048	7,890
State University of New York at Plattsburgh; Plattsburgh (Pu)	5,909	57	59	5,268	11,528	6,712
State University of New York College at Brockport; Brockport (Pu)	8,595	56	50	5,263	11,213	7,226
State University of New York College at Cortland; Cortland (Pu)	7,331	58	47	5,300	11,250	7,290
State University of New York College at Geneseo; Geneseo (Pu)	5,573	61	44	5,435	11,695	6,820
State University of New York College at Old Westbury; Old Westbury (Pu)	3,359	59	52	5,072	11,332	7,914
State University of New York College at Oneonta; Oneonta (Pu)	5,806	58	45	—	—	7,230

Institution name; city (Public/Private)	Total enrolled students	Percent		Tuition and fees		Room and board
		Women	Students accepted	In-state	Out-of-state	
State University of New York College at Potsdam; Potsdam (Pu)	4,311	59%	72%	$ 5,250	$11,510	$ 7,270
State University of New York College of Agriculture and Technology at Cobleskill; Cobleskill (Pu)	2,510	45	92	5,345	11,605	7,270
State University of New York College of Environmental Science and Forestry; Syracuse (Pu)	2,046	37	64	4,991	11,251	9,790
State University of New York Empire State College; Saratoga Springs (Pu)	9,750	68	43	4,555	10,505	—
State University of New York, Fredonia; Fredonia (Pu)	5,359	58	56	5,391	11,341	6,940
State University of New York Institute of Technology; Utica (Pu)	2,432	38	22	5,244	11,504	7,160
State University of New York Maritime College; Throggs Neck (Pu)	1,128	11	87	5,850	11,800	7,046
St. Bonaventure University; St. Bonaventure (Pr)	2,806	51	87	19,485	19,485	6,910
St. Francis College; Brooklyn Heights (Pr)	2,326	53	88	11,785	11,785	8,000
St. John Fisher College; Rochester (Pr)	3,376	57	70	18,450	18,450	7,900
St. John's University; Jamaica (Pr)	19,813	58	62	23,280	23,280	11,000
St. Joseph's College, New York; Brooklyn (Pr)	1,313	78	71	11,430	11,430	—
St. Joseph's College, Suffolk Campus; Patchogue (Pr)	4,005	75	80	11,954	11,954	—
St. Lawrence University; Canton (Pr)	2,277	52	61	30,480	30,480	7,755
Stony Brook University, State University of New York; Stony Brook (Pu)	21,685	49	49	5,389	11,649	7,730
St. Thomas Aquinas College; Sparkill (Pr)	2,336	56	82	16,600	16,600	8,850
Syracuse University; Syracuse (Pr)	16,753	56	59	26,734	26,734	9,970
Touro College; New York (Pr)	11,447	70	—	10,400	10,400	5,000
Union College; Schenectady (Pr)	2,192	45	49	38,703	38,703	—
United States Merchant Marine Academy; Kings Point (Pu)	1,007	14	16	0	0	—
United States Military Academy; West Point (Pu)	4,183	15	10	0	0	—
United Talmudical Seminary; Brooklyn (Pr)	1,670	—	—	6,000	6,000	—
University at Albany, State University of New York; Albany (Pu)	16,293	50	56	5,810	12,070	7,540
University at Buffalo, The State University of New York; Buffalo (Pu)	27,276	46	56	5,966	12,226	7,226
University of Rochester; Rochester (Pr)	8,365	47	48	28,982	28,982	9,565
Utica College; Utica (Pr)	2,652	56	80	21,270	21,270	8,600
Vassar College; Poughkeepsie (Pr)	2,475	60	29	31,350	31,350	7,680
Vaughn College of Aeronautics and Technology; Flushing (Pr)	1,244	12	—	13,780	13,780	—
Wagner College; Staten Island (Pr)	2,259	60	67	23,900	23,900	7,500
Yeshiva University; New York (Pr)	5,998	44	78	23,650	23,650	7,330
York College of the City University of New York; Jamaica (Pu)	5,743	67	32	4,242	8,882	—
NORTH CAROLINA						
Appalachian State University; Boone (Pu)	14,653	49	68	3,351	12,718	5,270
Barton College; Wilson (Pr)	1,231	70	74	16,670	16,670	5,800
Belmont Abbey College; Belmont (Pr)	800	59	69	16,724	16,724	8,586
Campbell University; Buies Creek (Pr)	4,256	55	56	14,386	14,386	5,100
Catawba College; Salisbury (Pr)	1,395	53	63	17,600	17,600	5,900
Davidson College; Davidson (Pr)	1,714	51	27	27,171	27,171	7,732
Duke University; Durham (Pr)	12,770	49	23	30,720	30,720	8,520
East Carolina University; Greenville (Pu)	22,767	59	78	3,454	13,668	6,640
Elizabeth City State University; Elizabeth City (Pu)	2,470	58	77	3,223	11,562	4,608
Elon University; Elon (Pr)	4,796	61	41	17,555	17,555	6,010
Fayetteville State University; Fayetteville (Pu)	5,441	64	84	2,832	12,568	4,120
Gardner-Webb University; Boiling Springs (Pr)	3,724	64	57	15,150	15,150	5,340
Greensboro College; Greensboro (Pr)	1,226	50	72	16,820	16,820	6,460
Guilford College; Greensboro (Pr)	2,511	60	71	21,640	21,640	6,530
High Point University; High Point (Pr)	2,842	62	77	16,760	16,760	6,950
Johnson C. Smith University; Charlotte (Pr)	1,415	59	53	13,712	13,712	5,298
Lenoir-Rhyne University; Hickory (Pr)	1,579	62	85	18,920	18,920	6,680
Livingstone College; Salisbury (Pr)	1,016	50	50	13,527	13,527	5,919
Mars Hill College; Mars Hill (Pr)	1,378	57	85	16,598	16,598	6,136
Meredith College; Raleigh (Pr)	2,168	100	91	19,950	19,950	5,600
Methodist College; Fayetteville (Pr)	2,257	43	77	17,850	17,850	6,770
Montreat College; Montreat (Pr)	1,035	62	78	15,560	15,560	5,008
Mount Olive College; Mount Olive (Pr)	2,582	60	80	11,800	11,800	4,800
North Carolina Agricultural and Technical State University; Greensboro (Pu)	9,115	52	81	3,066	12,508	5,070
North Carolina Central University; Durham (Pu)	7,727	65	83	3,042	12,486	4,311
North Carolina School of the Arts; Winston-Salem (Pu)	817	41	46	4,306	15,586	5,700
North Carolina State University; Raleigh (Pu)	29,957	42	59	4,667	16,565	6,851
North Carolina Wesleyan College; Rocky Mount (Pr)	1,776	45	72	14,814	14,814	6,555
Pfeiffer University; Misenheimer (Pr)	2,027	57	72	14,570	14,570	5,830
Queens University of Charlotte; Charlotte (Pr)	2,107	74	74	18,028	18,028	6,500
Saint Augustine's College; Raleigh (Pr)	1,395	48	55	10,388	10,388	5,312

Institution name; city (Public/Private)	Total enrolled students	Percent		Tuition and fees		Room and board
		Women	Students accepted	In-state	Out-of-state	
Salem College; Winston-Salem (Pr)	1,114	99%	66%	$16,490	$16,490	$8,870
Shaw University; Raleigh (Pr)	2,709	64	56	9,438	9,438	6,050
Southeastern Baptist Theological Seminary; Wake Forest (Pr)	1,979	27	—	—	—	—
University of North Carolina at Asheville; Asheville (Pu)	3,607	58	73	3,392	12,592	5,212
University of North Carolina at Chapel Hill; Chapel Hill (Pu)	26,878	58	36	4,451	17,549	6,245
University of North Carolina at Charlotte; Charlotte (Pu)	19,846	53	72	3,473	13,585	5,304
University of North Carolina at Greensboro; Greensboro (Pu)	14,328	68	47	3,435	14,403	5,000
University of North Carolina at Pembroke; Pembroke (Pu)	5,027	60	89	2,832	12,264	4,560
University of North Carolina at Wilmington; Wilmington (Pu)	11,327	59	60	3,626	13,336	5,800
Wake Forest University; Winston-Salem (Pr)	6,504	51	47	30,210	30,210	8,500
Warren Wilson College; Asheville (Pr)	865	60	80	19,160	19,160	5,460
Western Carolina University; Cullowhee (Pu)	8,396	50	76	3,449	12,885	4,028
Wingate University; Wingate (Pr)	1,560	53	83	16,000	16,000	6,200
Winston-Salem State University; Winston-Salem (Pu)	4,805	69	96	2,734	11,227	5,135
NORTH DAKOTA						
Dickinson State University; Dickinson (Pu)	2,479	55	99	4,559	9,636	—
Jamestown College; Jamestown (Pr)	1,064	57	96	10,000	10,000	4,130
Mayville State University; Mayville (Pu)	897	52	98	4,483	9,516	3,508
Minot State University; Minot (Pu)	3,851	62	79	3,712	8,437	3,592
North Dakota State University; Fargo (Pu)	12,026	44	98	4,775	11,423	4,727
University of Mary; Bismarck (Pr)	2,757	61	87	10,817	10,817	4,110
University of North Dakota; Grand Forks (Pu)	13,187	46	69	4,828	11,522	4,455
Valley City State University; Valley City (Pu)	1,033	48	91	3,130	8,357	4,074
OHIO						
Ashland University; Ashland (Pr)	6,922	57	85	19,778	19,778	7,314
Baldwin-Wallace College; Berea (Pr)	4,600	59	83	19,494	19,494	6,418
Bluffton University; Bluffton (Pr)	1,191	56	76	18,350	18,350	6,304
Bowling Green State University; Bowling Green (Pu)	18,989	56	90	8,072	15,380	6,588
Capital University; Columbus (Pr)	3,894	62	83	22,540	22,540	6,160
Case Western Reserve University; Cleveland (Pr)	9,095	40	71	27,062	27,062	8,202
Cedarville University; Cedarville (Pr)	3,070	55	85	16,032	16,032	5,010
Central State University; Wilberforce (Pu)	1,621	54	49	4,710	10,200	6,432
Cincinnati Christian University; Cincinnati (Pr)	922	45	99	9,690	9,690	5,390
Cleveland State University; Cleveland (Pu)	15,673	55	73	6,792	9,216	6,610
College of Mount St. Joseph; Cincinnati (Pr)	2,158	64	72	18,790	18,790	6,070
College of Wooster; Wooster (Pr)	1,827	53	72	26,560	26,560	6,640
Columbus College of Art & Design; Columbus (Pr)	1,562	51	75	19,330	19,330	6,400
David N. Myers University; Cleveland (Pr)	1,177	77	65	11,170	11,170	—
Defiance College; Defiance (Pr)	1,035	51	73	18,230	18,230	5,590
Denison University; Granville (Pr)	2,229	56	44	27,310	27,310	7,670
Franciscan University of Steubenville; Steubenville (Pr)	2,374	60	86	15,700	15,700	5,350
Franklin University; Columbus (Pr)	6,823	59	100	6,990	6,990	—
Heidelberg College; Tiffin (Pr)	1,398	50	93	14,900	14,900	6,710
Hiram College; Hiram (Pr)	1,125	55	86	22,595	22,595	7,505
John Carroll University; University Heights (Pr)	4,101	54	89	23,630	23,630	7,526
Kent State University; Kent (Pu)	24,347	60	92	7,504	14,516	6,410
Kenyon College; Gambier (Pr)	1,634	53	38	32,170	32,170	5,270
Lake Erie College; Painesville (Pr)	914	75	78	18,590	18,590	6,014
Lourdes College; Sylvania (Pr)	1,460	85	72	12,270	12,270	—
Malone College; Canton (Pr)	2,250	61	81	15,880	15,880	6,120
Marietta College; Marietta (Pr)	1,480	50	75	21,730	21,730	6,186
Miami University; Oxford (Pu)	17,151	54	71	9,642	19,642	7,010
Mount Union College; Alliance (Pr)	2,333	52	75	18,810	18,810	5,630
Mount Vernon Nazarene University; Mount Vernon (Pr)	2,455	58	87	14,976	14,976	4,734
Muskingum College; New Concord (Pr)	2,142	49	80	15,630	15,630	6,200
Notre Dame College; South Euclid (Pr)	1,299	59	64	18,350	18,350	6,460
Oberlin College; Oberlin (Pr)	2,827	55	40	31,163	31,163	7,643
Ohio Dominican University; Columbus (Pr)	2,844	63	85	18,050	18,050	6,200
Ohio Northern University; Ada (Pr)	3,495	47	78	25,815	25,815	6,360
Ohio State University at Lima; Lima (Pu)	1,281	57	97	4,977	15,564	6,012
Ohio State University at Marion; Marion (Pu)	1,521	58	98	4,977	15,564	6,012
Ohio State University; Columbus (Pu)	50,995	47	76	7,479	18,066	6,909
Ohio State University–Mansfield Campus; Mansfield (Pu)	1,634	61	98	4,977	15,564	6,012
Ohio State University–Newark Campus; Newark (Pu)	2,143	57	98	4,977	15,564	6,012
Ohio University; Athens (Pu)	20,096	53	86	7,770	16,734	7,539
Ohio University–Chillicothe; Chillicothe (Pu)	2,000	—	52	4,008	10,146	—
Ohio University–Eastern; St. Clairsville (Pu)	1,118	65	—	4,008	10,146	—
Ohio University–Lancaster; Lancaster (Pu)	1,744	63	100	4,008	10,146	—
Ohio University–Southern Campus; Ironton (Pu)	1,746	61	100	4,026	5,676	—
Ohio University–Zanesville; Zanesville (Pu)	1,877	—	100	4,263	8,511	—
Ohio Wesleyan University; Delaware (Pr)	1,944	53	74	26,820	26,820	7,330
Otterbein College; Westerville (Pr)	3,090	64	79	21,342	21,342	6,189
Shawnee State University; Portsmouth (Pu)	3,798	60	100	5,202	8,802	6,510

Institution name; city (Public/Private)	Total enrolled students	Percent Women	Percent Students accepted	Tuition and fees In-state	Tuition and fees Out-of-state	Room and board
Tiffin University; Tiffin (Pr)	1,407	52%	91%	$14,280	$14,280	$6,150
Union Institute & University; Cincinnati (Pr)	2,910	76	—	8,116	8,116	—
University of Akron; Akron (Pu)	23,282	53	87	7,510	15,740	6,660
University of Cincinnati; Cincinnati (Pu)	27,178	47	88	8,379	21,351	8,004
University of Dayton; Dayton (Pr)	10,495	50	80	20,250	20,250	6,300
University of Findlay; Findlay (Pr)	4,654	58	69	20,914	20,914	7,274
University of Phoenix–Cleveland Campus; Independence (Pr)	824	66	98	10,740	10,740	—
University of Rio Grande; Rio Grande (Pr)	2,522	58	100	12,555	13,575	6,024
University of Toledo; Toledo (Pu)	19,480	50	99	7,054	15,865	7,488
Urbana University; Urbana (Pr)	1,531	50	56	14,220	14,220	5,680
Ursuline College; Pepper Pike (Pr)	1,462	93	91	18,150	18,150	5,896
Walsh University; North Canton (Pr)	1,951	58	80	15,610	15,610	7,700
Wilberforce University; Wilberforce (Pr)	998	61	22	10,780	10,780	5,320
Wilmington College; Wilmington (Pr)	1,755	55	71	18,728	18,728	6,718
Wittenberg University; Springfield (Pr)	2,190	56	81	26,196	26,196	6,686
Wright State University; Dayton (Pu)	15,985	57	90	6,477	12,492	6,328
Xavier University; Cincinnati (Pr)	6,668	55	74	20,400	20,400	8,250
Youngstown State University; Youngstown (Pu)	13,092	55	100	5,884	11,092	6,100
OKLAHOMA						
Bacone College; Muskogee (Pr)	914	43	58	8,867	8,867	5,781
Cameron University; Lawton (Pu)	5,933	57	99	3,000	7,260	3,126
East Central University; Ada (Pu)	4,691	59	—	3,952	8,125	2,910
Langston University; Langston (Pu)	3,008	56	50	2,787	6,399	4,380
Northeastern State University; Tahlequah (Pu)	9,562	59	86	3,000	7,350	3,080
Northwestern Oklahoma State University; Alva (Pu)	2,129	52	100	3,000	7,410	2,920
Oklahoma Baptist University; Shawnee (Pr)	1,883	61	85	13,162	13,162	3,800
Oklahoma Christian University; Oklahoma City (Pr)	1,947	50	42	13,749	13,749	5,000
Oklahoma City University; Oklahoma City (Pr)	3,695	59	79	16,040	16,040	5,950
Oklahoma Panhandle State University; Goodwell (Pu)	1,237	48	60	2,720	3,440	2,810
Oklahoma State University; Stillwater (Pu)	23,626	50	89	4,071	11,361	5,602
Oklahoma Wesleyan University; Bartlesville (Pr)	887	54	77	13,750	13,750	5,200
Oral Roberts University; Tulsa (Pr)	3,828	58	70	15,880	15,880	6,530
Rogers State University; Claremore (Pu)	3,300	61	89	2,430	5,790	5,985
Southeastern Oklahoma State University; Durant (Pu)	4,203	52	80	3,123	7,452	3,470
Southern Nazarene University; Bethany (Pr)	2,177	51	56	13,638	13,638	5,266
Southwestern Oklahoma State University; Weatherford (Pu)	4,841	54	94	3,000	7,200	3,090
University of Central Oklahoma; Edmond (Pu)	15,584	57	94	3,012	7,587	4,206
University of Oklahoma; Norman (Pu)	24,551	50	82	4,140	11,658	5,814
University of Phoenix–Oklahoma City Campus; Oklahoma City (Pr)	1,049	60	—	8,910	8,910	—
University of Phoenix–Tulsa Campus; Tulsa (Pr)	1,202	56	—	8,910	8,910	—
University of Science and Arts of Oklahoma; Chickasha (Pu)	1,414	63	91	3,180	7,500	3,990
University of Tulsa; Tulsa (Pr)	4,174	49	74	17,630	17,630	5,926
OREGON						
Art Institute of Portland; Portland (Pr)	1,543	51	50	16,610	16,610	5,355
Concordia University; Portland (Pr)	1,404	64	68	18,390	18,390	5,780
Eastern Oregon University; La Grande (Pu)	3,338	57	75	5,517	5,517	6,099
George Fox University; Newberg (Pr)	2,981	61	84	20,590	20,590	6,550
Lewis & Clark College; Portland (Pr)	3,259	61	65	26,154	26,154	7,330
Linfield College; McMinnville (Pr)	1,656	54	78	22,022	22,022	6,370
Marylhurst University; Marylhurst (Pr)	1,245	73	57	14,220	14,220	—
Oregon Institute of Technology; Klamath Falls (Pu)	3,373	44	90	4,974	15,075	5,935
Oregon State University; Corvallis (Pu)	19,162	46	90	5,319	17,667	6,786
Pacific University; Forest Grove (Pr)	2,521	60	84	20,664	20,664	5,764
Portland State University; Portland (Pu)	23,444	54	92	4,311	13,707	8,310
Reed College; Portland (Pr)	1,341	55	47	30,900	30,900	8,070
Southern Oregon University; Ashland (Pu)	5,162	56	85	4,863	15,690	7,560
University of Oregon; Eugene (Pu)	20,295	53	91	5,550	16,980	7,331
University of Phoenix–Oregon Campus; Portland (Pr)	2,130	47	—	9,960	9,960	—
University of Portland; Portland (Pr)	3,343	61	71	23,520	23,520	7,050
Western Oregon University; Monmouth (Pu)	4,772	59	93	4,332	12,777	6,276
Willamette University; Salem (Pr)	2,663	56	83	26,852	26,852	6,800
PENNSYLVANIA						
Albright College; Reading (Pr)	2,243	59	70	24,580	24,580	7,510
Allegheny College; Meadville (Pr)	1,955	52	74	26,950	26,950	6,550
Alvernia College; Reading (Pr)	2,380	65	80	17,675	17,675	7,330
Arcadia University; Glenside (Pr)	3,391	73	72	24,270	24,270	9,300
Art Institute of Pittsburgh; Pittsburgh (Pr)	4,872	44	46	21,965	21,965	6,900
Baptist Bible College of Pennsylvania; Clarks Summit (Pr)	837	56	87	11,700	11,700	4,982
Bloomsburg University of Pennsylvania; Bloomsburg (Pu)	8,304	60	63	6,089	13,305	5,200
Bryn Mawr College; Bryn Mawr (Pr)	1,772	98	47	28,630	28,630	9,700
Bucknell University; Lewisburg (Pr)	3,609	50	36	32,788	32,788	6,872
Cabrini College; Radnor (Pr)	2,176	65	82	22,250	22,250	8,980
California University of Pennsylvania; California (Pu)	6,640	51	74	6,251	8,657	7,280

Institution name; city (Public/Private)	Total enrolled students	Percent Women	Percent Students accepted	Tuition and fees In-state	Tuition and fees Out-of-state	Room and board
Carlow University; Pittsburgh (Pr)	2,088	94%	59%	$16,460	$16,460	$ 6,538
Carnegie Mellon University; Pittsburgh (Pr)	9,803	39	42	31,036	31,036	8,244
Cedar Crest College; Allentown (Pr)	1,856	98	71	23,012	23,012	7,953
Central Pennsylvania College; Summerdale (Pr)	866	62	56	11,010	11,010	6,150
Chatham University; Pittsburgh (Pr)	1,249	100	62	21,996	21,996	7,050
Chestnut Hill College; Philadelphia (Pr)	1,679	74	72	20,380	20,380	7,500
Cheyney University of Pennsylvania; Cheyney (Pu)	1,545	52	58	5,565	12,781	5,524
Clarion University of Pennsylvania; Clarion (Pu)	6,497	60	78	4,810	9,620	4,816
College Misericordia; Dallas (Pr)	2,271	73	78	18,800	18,800	7,850
Delaware Valley College; Doylestown (Pr)	1,965	52	89	20,888	20,888	7,742
DeSales University; Center Valley (Pr)	2,927	55	75	19,390	19,390	7,590
Dickinson College; Carlisle (Pr)	2,321	55	49	32,120	32,120	8,050
Drexel University; Philadelphia (Pr)	17,656	39	73	22,020	22,020	10,050
Duquesne University; Pittsburgh (Pr)	9,722	59	85	20,360	20,360	7,820
Eastern University; St. Davids (Pr)	3,253	66	78	18,830	18,830	7,840
East Stroudsburg University of Pennsylvania; East Stroudsburg (Pu)	6,553	59	70	6,224	13,440	4,506
Edinboro University of Pennsylvania; Edinboro (Pu)	7,773	57	76	6,089	10,899	5,338
Elizabethtown College; Elizabethtown (Pr)	2,136	65	64	23,710	23,710	6,600
Franklin and Marshall College; Lancaster (Pr)	1,972	46	49	30,440	30,440	7,540
Gannon University; Erie (Pr)	3,441	59	82	17,500	17,500	6,990
Geneva College; Beaver Falls (Pr)	2,141	57	68	16,590	16,590	6,600
Gettysburg College; Gettysburg (Pr)	2,471	49	46	30,240	30,240	7,354
Grove City College; Grove City (Pr)	2,318	49	47	10,107	10,107	5,092
Gwynedd-Mercy College; Gwynedd Valley (Pr)	2,751	75	55	17,400	17,400	7,500
Haverford College; Haverford (Pr)	1,172	53	29	30,270	30,270	9,420
Holy Family University; Philadelphia (Pr)	2,670	75	77	16,490	16,490	—
Immaculata University; Immaculata (Pr)	3,811	95	89	19,625	19,625	8,850
Indiana University of Pennsylvania; Indiana (Pu)	13,998	56	55	6,085	13,301	4,868
Juniata College; Huntingdon (Pr)	1,427	54	74	25,890	25,890	7,240
King's College; Wilkes-Barre (Pr)	2,223	46	79	20,110	20,110	8,250
Kutztown University of Pennsylvania; Kutztown (Pu)	9,584	58	66	6,256	13,472	5,274
Lafayette College; Easton (Pr)	2,303	48	39	29,982	29,982	9,285
Lancaster Bible College; Lancaster (Pr)	973	52	54	12,360	12,360	5,520
La Roche College; Pittsburgh (Pr)	1,681	61	69	16,582	16,582	6,862
La Salle University; Philadelphia (Pr)	6,217	56	70	26,190	26,190	9,410
Lebanon Valley College; Annville (Pr)	1,882	56	—	23,600	23,600	6,590
Lehigh University; Bethlehem (Pr)	6,641	41	38	29,340	29,340	8,230
Lincoln University; Lincoln University (Pu)	2,012	59	39	7,268	10,820	6,560
Lock Haven University of Pennsylvania; Lock Haven (Pu)	5,126	58	81	6,100	11,316	5,516
Lycoming College; Williamsport (Pr)	1,536	55	76	22,886	22,886	6,242
Mansfield University of Pennsylvania; Mansfield (Pu)	3,556	60	73	6,230	13,446	5,456
Marywood University; Scranton (Pr)	3,127	74	76	21,640	21,640	9,100
Mercyhurst College; Erie (Pr)	4,035	59	78	19,113	19,113	7,074
Messiah College; Grantham (Pr)	2,917	63	83	20,790	20,790	6,560
Millersville University of Pennsylvania; Millersville (Pu)	7,998	57	60	6,081	13,297	5,642
Moravian College; Bethlehem (Pr)	2,078	62	63	23,574	23,574	7,310
Mount Aloysius College; Cresson (Pr)	1,500	71	75	14,530	14,530	5,960
Muhlenberg College; Allentown (Pr)	2,446	59	45	26,800	26,800	7,025
Neumann College; Aston (Pr)	2,682	66	94	17,190	17,190	7,740
Peirce College; Philadelphia (Pr)	1,892	71	79	12,310	12,310	—
Pennsylvania College of Technology; Williamsport (Pu)	6,358	30	93	9,480	11,940	5,132
Pennsylvania State University Abington College; Abington (Pu)	3,143	47	76	9,614	14,474	—
Pennsylvania State University Altoona College; Altoona (Pu)	3,766	48	76	10,026	15,140	6,230
Pennsylvania State University at Erie, The Behrend College; Erie (Pu)	3,593	33	81	10,026	15,910	6,230
Pennsylvania State University Berks Campus of the Berks–Lehigh Valley College; Reading (Pu)	2,416	39	82	10,026	15,140	6,810
Pennsylvania State University Harrisburg Campus of the Capital College; Middletown (Pu)	3,729	45	44	10,016	15,900	7,650
Pennsylvania State University Schuylkill Campus of the Capital College; Schuylkill Haven (Pu)	969	52	87	9,604	14,464	3,996
Pennsylvania State University University Park Campus; University Park (Pu)	41,289	47	58	10,856	20,784	6,230
Philadelphia Biblical University; Langhorne (Pr)	1,372	56	74	14,500	14,500	6,100
Philadelphia University; Philadelphia (Pr)	3,212	69	68	21,010	21,010	7,782
Point Park University; Pittsburgh (Pr)	3,292	61	80	15,960	15,960	7,000
Robert Morris University; Moon Township (Pr)	4,971	45	84	14,226	14,226	7,286
Rosemont College; Rosemont (Pr)	1,083	100	69	19,365	19,365	8,400
Saint Francis University; Loretto (Pr)	1,846	60	89	20,440	20,440	7,420
Saint Joseph's University; Philadelphia (Pr)	7,730	51	48	25,905	25,905	9,610
Saint Vincent College; Latrobe (Pr)	1,490	53	83	20,822	20,822	6,424
Seton Hill University; Greensburg (Pr)	1,706	68	77	20,630	20,630	6,420

Institution name; city (Public/Private)	Total enrolled students	Percent		Tuition and fees		Room and board
		Women	Students accepted	In-state	Out-of-state	
Shippensburg University of Pennsylvania; Shippensburg (Pu)	7,653	52%	64%	$ 5,986	$13,202	$5,274
Slippery Rock University of Pennsylvania; Slippery Rock (Pu)	7,928	55	79	6,096	8,502	4,714
Susquehanna University; Selinsgrove (Pr)	2,071	55	70	24,810	24,810	6,840
Swarthmore College; Swarthmore (Pr)	1,474	52	25	30,094	30,094	9,314
Temple University; Philadelphia (Pu)	33,552	57	63	9,102	16,268	7,522
Thiel College; Greenville (Pr)	1,245	48	79	16,390	16,390	6,584
Thomas Jefferson University; Philadelphia (Pr)	2,457	84	50	20,914	20,914	7,983
University of Pennsylvania; Philadelphia (Pr)	18,642	50	21	30,716	30,716	8,918
University of Phoenix–Philadelphia Campus; Wayne (Pr)	1,704	56	—	12,000	12,000	—
University of Pittsburgh at Bradford; Bradford (Pu)	1,460	54	96	9,980	19,850	6,344
University of Pittsburgh at Greensburg; Greensburg (Pu)	1,860	52	69	9,960	19,830	6,960
University of Pittsburgh at Johnstown; Johnstown (Pu)	3,209	49	95	9,972	19,842	5,930
University of Pittsburgh; Pittsburgh (Pu)	26,731	51	49	10,830	20,200	7,090
University of Scranton; Scranton (Pr)	4,795	57	75	22,474	22,474	9,524
University of the Arts; Philadelphia (Pr)	2,142	56	51	23,010	23,010	5,800
University of the Sciences in Philadelphia; Philadelphia (Pr)	2,824	63	65	22,648	22,648	8,932
Ursinus College; Collegeville (Pr)	1,499	53	73	31,450	31,450	7,350
Valley Forge Christian College; Phoenixville (Pr)	856	53	72	10,982	10,982	5,460
Villanova University; Villanova (Pr)	10,626	51	58	27,850	27,850	9,067
Washington & Jefferson College; Washington (Pr)	1,355	49	39	24,620	24,620	6,710
Waynesburg College; Waynesburg (Pr)	2,102	55	77	14,540	14,540	5,800
West Chester University of Pennsylvania; West Chester (Pu)	12,822	62	51	6,006	13,222	5,782
Westminster College; New Wilmington (Pr)	1,626	62	75	22,680	22,680	6,700
Widener University; Chester (Pr)	5,940	50	80	23,000	23,000	8,100
Wilkes University; Wilkes-Barre (Pr)	4,364	52	79	20,408	20,408	8,924
York College of Pennsylvania; York (Pr)	5,687	58	73	9,184	9,184	6,250
PUERTO RICO						
American University of Puerto Rico; Bayamón (Pr)	3,691	—	100	4,590	4,590	—
Bayamón Central University; Bayamón (Pr)	3,311	71	57	4,440	4,440	—
Caribbean University; Bayamón (Pr)	3,352	—	82	—	—	—
Inter American University of Puerto Rico, Aguadilla Campus; Aguadilla (Pr)	4,266	59	—	3,784	3,784	—
Inter American University of Puerto Rico, Arecibo Campus; Arecibo (Pr)	3,926	67	—	3,240	3,240	—
Inter American University of Puerto Rico, Barranquitas Campus; Barranquitas (Pr)	2,271	66	100	4,310	4,310	—
Inter American University of Puerto Rico, Bayamón Campus; Bayamón (Pr)	5,245	44	40	3,760	3,760	—
Inter American University of Puerto Rico, Fajardo Campus; Fajardo (Pr)	1,710	—	37	3,296	3,296	—
Inter American University of Puerto Rico, Guayama Campus; Guayama (Pr)	1,246	—	—	1,682	1,682	—
Inter American University of Puerto Rico, Metropolitan Campus; San Juan (Pr)	10,675	57	36	3,536	3,536	—
Inter American University of Puerto Rico, Ponce Campus; Mercedita (Pr)	5,265	63	42	4,296	4,296	—
Inter American University of Puerto Rico, San Germán Campus; San Germán (Pr)	6,217	54	—	4,616	4,616	2,400
Polytechnic University of Puerto Rico; Hato Rey (Pr)	5,674	25	93	5,550	5,550	—
Pontifical Catholic University of Puerto Rico; Ponce (Pr)	7,548	66	75	4,778	4,778	3,140
Universidad Adventista de las Antillas; Mayagüez (Pr)	836	63	75	7,920	7,920	2,600
Universidad del Este; Carolina (Pr)	7,077	66	54	4,498	4,498	—
Universidad del Turabo; Gurabo (Pr)	8,065	57	66	4,498	4,498	—
Universidad Metropolitana; Río Piedras (Pr)	5,857	65	57	4,498	4,498	—
University of Phoenix–Puerto Rico Campus; Guaynabo (Pr)	2,326	57	—	5,910	5,910	—
University of Puerto Rico, Aguadilla University College; Aguadilla (Pu)	3,312	—	42	—	—	—
University of Puerto Rico at Arecibo; Arecibo (Pu)	4,617	71	31	—	—	—
University of Puerto Rico at Bayamón; Bayamón (Pu)	5,826	57	78	—	—	—
University of Puerto Rico at Humacao; Humacao (Pu)	4,507	70	48	1,090	—	—
University of Puerto Rico at Ponce; Ponce (Pu)	3,837	66	54	—	—	—
University of Puerto Rico at Utuado; Utuado (Pu)	1,766	60	80	—	—	—
University of Puerto Rico, Cayey University College; Cayey (Pu)	3,987	71	22	1,245	—	—
University of Puerto Rico, Mayagüez Campus; Mayagüez (Pu)	12,108	50	62	—	—	—
University of Puerto Rico, Río Piedras; San Juan (Pu)	21,666	67	66	790	2,470	4,940
University of the Sacred Heart; San Juan (Pr)	5,206	66	74	4,810	4,810	2,000
RHODE ISLAND						
Brown University; Providence (Pr)	8,004	54	17	31,573	31,573	8,474
Bryant University; Smithfield (Pr)	3,518	40	63	24,762	24,762	9,568
Johnson & Wales University; Providence (Pr)	9,982	—	76	20,100	20,100	7,545

Institution name; city (Public/Private)	Total enrolled students	Percent		Tuition and fees		Room and board
		Women	Students accepted	In-state	Out-of-state	
Providence College; Providence (Pr)	5,366	56%	54%	$25,310	$25,310	$ 9,270
Rhode Island College; Providence (Pu)	8,881	67	72	4,676	11,988	7,010
Rhode Island School of Design; Providence (Pr)	2,282	66	34	27,975	27,975	7,722
Roger Williams University; Bristol (Pr)	5,070	51	78	22,866	22,866	10,237
Salve Regina University; Newport (Pr)	2,479	70	56	22,200	22,200	9,000
University of Rhode Island; Kingston (Pu)	14,749	55	70	6,752	18,338	7,810
SOUTH CAROLINA						
Anderson College; Anderson (Pr)	1,666	64	81	15,200	15,200	6,050
Benedict College; Columbia (Pr)	3,005	50	71	11,586	11,586	5,434
Charleston Southern University; Charleston (Pr)	2,875	61	72	15,332	15,332	5,878
Citadel, The Military College of South Carolina; Charleston (Pu)	3,351	6	79	6,828	15,446	4,684
Claflin University; Orangeburg (Pr)	1,814	66	46	12,584	12,584	5,908
Clemson University; Clemson (Pu)	17,110	45	69	8,074	16,638	5,292
Coastal Carolina University; Conway (Pu)	7,021	51	73	6,100	14,200	5,970
College of Charleston; Charleston (Pu)	11,607	65	65	6,202	14,140	6,506
Columbia College; Columbia (Pr)	1,453	99	85	18,040	18,040	5,620
Columbia International University; Columbia (Pr)	1,016	58	69	12,845	12,845	5,380
Converse College; Spartanburg (Pr)	1,419	100	76	19,960	19,960	6,110
Erskine College; Due West (Pr)	962	57	67	18,128	18,128	6,026
Francis Marion University; Florence (Pu)	3,698	62	76	5,540	10,945	4,656
Furman University; Greenville (Pr)	3,359	56	58	24,408	24,408	6,272
Lander University; Greenwood (Pu)	2,918	66	85	6,016	12,184	5,176
Morris College; Sumter (Pr)	897	62	86	7,985	7,985	3,724
North Greenville College; Tigerville (Pr)	1,766	53	81	10,350	10,350	5,950
Presbyterian College; Clinton (Pr)	1,187	52	78	21,622	21,622	6,326
South Carolina State University; Orangeburg (Pu)	4,294	57	53	6,355	13,163	5,776
Southern Wesleyan University; Central (Pr)	2,632	64	70	14,750	14,750	5,200
University of South Carolina Aiken; Aiken (Pu)	3,382	67	74	5,642	11,284	4,250
University of South Carolina Beaufort; Beaufort (Pu)	1,277	66	92	4,790	11,180	—
University of South Carolina; Columbia (Pu)	25,597	55	67	5,778	15,116	5,590
University of South Carolina Upstate; Spartanburg (Pu)	4,376	66	39	6,186	12,430	5,140
Voorhees College; Denmark (Pr)	847	66	41	7,276	7,276	4,572
Winthrop University; Rock Hill (Pu)	6,447	69	68	7,836	14,430	4,992
Wofford College; Spartanburg (Pr)	1,161	49	66	22,300	22,300	6,440
SOUTH DAKOTA						
Augustana College; Sioux Falls (Pr)	1,799	62	72	18,860	18,860	5,334
Black Hills State University; Spearfish (Pu)	3,846	62	49	4,820	9,986	3,449
Colorado Technical University Sioux Falls Campus; Sioux Falls (Pr)	1,036	61	—	12,840	12,840	—
Dakota State University; Madison (Pu)	2,282	44	96	4,614	9,657	3,193
Mount Marty College; Yankton (Pr)	1,163	76	80	14,936	14,936	4,764
Northern State University; Aberdeen (Pu)	2,346	58	95	4,448	9,291	3,733
Oglala Lakota College; Kyle (Pu)	1,000	—	—	1,796	1,796	—
Sinte Gleska University; Rosebud (Pr)	1,200	—	100	2,970	2,970	—
South Dakota School of Mines and Technology; Rapid City (Pu)	2,353	26	96	4,534	9,391	3,684
South Dakota State University; Brookings (Pu)	10,884	50	92	4,732	9,719	4,769
University of Sioux Falls; Sioux Falls (Pr)	1,586	54	95	14,900	14,900	4,350
University of South Dakota; Vermillion (Pu)	8,120	57	83	4,749	9,915	3,741
TENNESSEE						
Aquinas College; Nashville (Pr)	870	78	59	10,768	10,768	—
Austin Peay State University; Clarksville (Pu)	8,650	63	92	4,224	12,712	4,296
Baptist College of Health Sciences; Memphis (Pr)	823	—	—	—	—	—
Belmont University; Nashville (Pr)	3,941	61	77	16,220	16,220	6,156
Bethel College; McKenzie (Pr)	1,297	53	59	9,630	9,630	5,384
Carson-Newman College; Jefferson City (Pr)	2,053	54	82	14,420	14,420	4,930
Christian Brothers University; Memphis (Pr)	1,907	52	79	18,230	18,230	5,300
Crichton College; Memphis (Pr)	969	65	60	12,115	12,115	3,800
Cumberland University; Lebanon (Pr)	1,475	56	38	13,744	13,744	4,820
East Tennessee State University; Johnson City (Pu)	11,869	58	83	4,059	12,547	4,858
Fisk University; Nashville (Pr)	880	69	66	12,450	12,450	6,230
Freed-Hardeman University; Henderson (Pr)	1,942	54	100	12,440	12,440	6,200
Johnson Bible College; Knoxville (Pr)	889	49	62	6,490	6,490	4,090
King College; Bristol (Pr)	812	63	95	17,680	17,680	5,720
Lambuth University; Jackson (Pr)	806	50	62	12,490	12,490	5,436
Lane College; Jackson (Pr)	1,045	47	28	7,176	7,176	4,534
Lee University; Cleveland (Pr)	3,849	58	64	9,075	9,075	4,560
LeMoyne-Owen College; Memphis (Pr)	852	72	39	14,085	14,085	4,620
Lincoln Memorial University; Harrogate (Pr)	2,442	71	85	12,600	12,600	4,910
Lipscomb University; Nashville (Pr)	2,537	—	77	13,486	13,486	6,090
Maryville College; Maryville (Pr)	1,080	57	77	21,065	21,065	6,500
Middle Tennessee State University; Murfreesboro (Pu)	22,322	53	84	4,230	12,718	4,814
Milligan College; Milligan College (Pr)	914	61	72	16,360	16,360	4,600
Rhodes College; Memphis (Pr)	1,633	58	54	25,956	25,956	6,904

Institution name; city (Public/Private)	Total enrolled students	Percent Women	Percent Students accepted	Tuition and fees In-state	Tuition and fees Out-of-state	Room and board
Southern Adventist University; Collegedale (Pr)	2,391	—	81%	14,020	14,020	4,480
Tennessee State University; Nashville (Pu)	9,100	63%	53	4,038	12,526	4,270
Tennessee Technological University; Cookeville (Pu)	9,217	45	78	3,998	12,486	5,270
Tennessee Wesleyan College; Athens (Pr)	815	67	84	13,550	13,550	5,100
Trevecca Nazarene University; Nashville (Pr)	2,089	56	70	12,792	12,792	5,868
Tusculum College; Greeneville (Pr)	2,305	53	81	15,110	15,110	5,950
Union University; Jackson (Pr)	2,843	61	84	15,370	15,370	4,970
University of Memphis; Memphis (Pu)	20,668	60	70	4,480	13,204	4,920
University of Phoenix–Nashville Campus; Nashville (Pr)	1,106	54	—	10,410	10,410	—
University of Tennessee at Chattanooga; Chattanooga (Pu)	8,844	58	71	4,928	13,150	5,808
University of Tennessee at Martin; Martin (Pu)	6,104	55	76	4,134	12,388	4,100
University of Tennessee; Knoxville (Pu)	27,764	51	44	5,376	10,442	5,398
University of the South; Sewanee (Pr)	1,492	52	64	25,580	25,580	7,120
Vanderbilt University; Nashville (Pr)	11,294	52	38	29,990	29,990	9,736
TEXAS						
Abilene Christian University; Abilene (Pr)	4,761	55	54	14,200	14,200	5,270
Angelo State University; San Angelo (Pu)	6,137	55	99	3,126	9,318	4,696
Art Institute of Dallas; Dallas (Pr)	1,418	51	—	16,855	16,855	—
Art Institute of Houston; Houston (Pr)	1,647	46	98	16,740	16,740	4,545
Austin College; Sherman (Pr)	1,323	55	69	20,495	20,495	7,376
Baylor University; Waco (Pr)	13,799	59	73	21,070	21,070	6,485
College of Biblical Studies–Houston; Houston (Pr)	1,492	44	—	4,180	4,180	—
Concordia University at Austin; Austin (Pr)	1,155	53	76	16,160	16,160	6,570
Dallas Baptist University; Dallas (Pr)	4,714	57	65	11,610	11,610	4,644
East Texas Baptist University; Marshall (Pr)	1,412	52	96	12,000	12,000	3,873
Hardin-Simmons University; Abilene (Pr)	2,392	55	39	13,376	13,376	3,922
Houston Baptist University; Houston (Pr)	2,227	67	63	12,915	12,915	4,566
Howard Payne University; Brownwood (Pr)	1,319	51	78	12,000	12,000	4,242
Lamar University; Beaumont (Pu)	10,804	58	96	3,156	10,404	5,706
LeTourneau University; Longview (Pr)	3,758	31	96	15,890	15,890	6,286
Lubbock Christian University; Lubbock (Pr)	1,974	56	77	11,994	11,994	4,130
McMurry University; Abilene (Pr)	1,386	50	64	14,350	14,350	5,500
Midwestern State University; Wichita Falls (Pu)	6,348	57	87	3,740	11,480	4,844
Northwood University, Texas Campus; Cedar Hill (Pr)	1,139	57	64	15,183	15,183	6,849
Our Lady of the Lake University of San Antonio; San Antonio (Pr)	3,025	78	49	16,430	16,430	5,230
Paul Quinn College; Dallas (Pr)	871	50	27	5,250	5,250	3,800
Prairie View A&M University; Prairie View (Pu)	8,350	54	98	4,202	11,942	6,068
Rice University; Houston (Pr)	4,973	49	22	21,206	21,206	8,380
Sam Houston State University; Huntsville (Pu)	14,371	58	79	4,260	12,000	4,336
Schreiner University; Kerrville (Pr)	842	59	50	14,443	14,443	6,880
Southern Methodist University; Dallas (Pr)	10,901	54	64	26,880	26,880	9,208
Southwestern Adventist University; Keene (Pr)	1,191	56	64	11,858	11,858	5,534
Southwestern Assemblies of God University; Waxahachie (Pr)	1,676	—	34	8,430	8,430	4,470
Southwestern University; Georgetown (Pr)	1,276	59	66	20,220	20,220	6,359
St. Edward's University; Austin (Pr)	4,651	57	69	17,320	17,320	—
Stephen F. Austin State University; Nacogdoches (Pu)	11,287	59	75	4,298	12,038	5,012
St. Mary's University of San Antonio; San Antonio (Pr)	4,110	59	80	17,756	17,756	6,498
Sul Ross State University; Alpine (Pu)	1,954	47	73	3,870	11,610	4,050
Tarleton State University; Stephenville (Pu)	8,985	56	68	3,835	11,575	5,900
Texas A&M International University; Laredo (Pu)	4,078	63	52	3,813	11,553	5,240
Texas A&M University at Galveston; Galveston (Pu)	1,615	43	80	4,682	12,422	4,870
Texas A&M University; College Station (Pu)	44,435	50	72	5,955	13,695	6,887
Texas A&M University–Commerce; Commerce (Pu)	6,317	61	62	4,178	10,718	5,246
Texas A&M University–Corpus Christi; Corpus Christi (Pu)	8,227	61	85	4,279	12,019	5,355
Texas A&M University–Kingsville; Kingsville (Pu)	7,126	48	98	3,906	10,926	4,214
Texas Christian University; Fort Worth (Pr)	8,632	60	64	19,740	19,740	5,880
Texas Lutheran University; Seguin (Pr)	1,414	55	78	16,600	16,600	5,030
Texas Southern University; Houston (Pu)	11,635	58	33	3,732	9,924	5,824
Texas State University-San Marcos; San Marcos (Pu)	26,783	55	80	4,680	12,420	5,456
Texas Tech University; Lubbock (Pu)	28,325	46	67	5,848	13,588	6,421
Texas Wesleyan University; Fort Worth (Pr)	2,742	60	61	13,000	13,000	5,400
Texas Woman's University; Denton (Pu)	10,750	94	70	3,395	9,587	5,094
Trinity University; San Antonio (Pr)	2,718	54	60	20,010	20,010	8,205
University of Dallas; Irving (Pr)	3,005	54	87	20,411	20,411	7,026
University of Houston-Downtown; Houston (Pu)	11,408	59	99	3,934	10,126	—
University of Houston; Houston (Pu)	35,180	52	81	4,973	12,713	6,030
University of Mary Hardin-Baylor; Belton (Pr)	2,713	63	76	12,380	12,380	4,000
University of North Texas; Denton (Pu)	31,155	56	71	5,561	13,301	5,124
University of Phoenix–Dallas Campus; Dallas (Pr)	2,546	60	99	11,010	11,010	—
University of Phoenix–Houston Campus; Houston (Pr)	4,297	67	—	11,010	11,010	—
University of St. Thomas; Houston (Pr)	3,648	64	87	16,312	16,312	7,300
University of Texas at Arlington; Arlington (Pu)	25,297	53	72	5,300	14,360	5,212
University of Texas at Austin; Austin (Pu)	50,377	52	51	5,735	14,435	6,184

Institution name; city (Public/Private)	Total enrolled students	Percent Women	Percent Students accepted	Tuition and fees In-state	Tuition and fees Out-of-state	Room and board
University of Texas at Dallas; Richardson (Pu)	14,092	46%	53%	$ 6,363	$14,103	$6,244
University of Texas at El Paso; El Paso (Pu)	18,918	54	99	5,064	13,344	4,095
University of Texas at San Antonio; San Antonio (Pu)	26,175	53	55	5,272	13,012	5,306
University of Texas at Tyler; Tyler (Pu)	5,303	58	79	4,046	10,238	5,373
University of Texas of the Permian Basin; Odessa (Pu)	2,695	64	88	3,900	10,980	4,176
University of Texas–Pan American; Edinburg (Pu)	17,030	57	—	3,152	10,892	4,233
University of the Incarnate Word; San Antonio (Pr)	4,800	67	76	17,072	17,072	6,234
Wayland Baptist University; Plainview (Pr)	1,067	54	95	9,250	9,250	3,420
West Texas A&M University; Canyon (Pu)	7,299	58	70	3,472	11,212	4,592
UTAH						
Brigham Young University; Provo (Pr)	34,609	50	76	4,920	4,920	5,570
California College for Health Sciences; Salt Lake City (Pr)	5,458	—	—	13,975	13,975	—
Southern Utah University; Cedar City (Pu)	6,672	54	91	3,054	9,008	5,400
University of Phoenix–Utah Campus; Salt Lake City (Pr)	4,057	41	98	9,540	9,540	—
University of Utah; Salt Lake City (Pu)	28,933	44	86	4,000	12,410	5,726
Utah State University; Logan (Pu)	16,130	49	92	3,374	9,702	4,230
Utah Valley State College; Orem (Pu)	24,149	39	100	2,788	8,718	—
Weber State University; Ogden (Pu)	18,517	48	95	2,876	8,736	6,400
Western Governors University; Salt Lake City (Pr)	2,821	71	—	5,245	5,245	—
Westminster College; Salt Lake City (Pr)	2,417	61	87	18,476	18,476	5,636
VERMONT						
Bennington College; Bennington (Pr)	820	67	73	31,070	31,070	7,710
Castleton State College; Castleton (Pu)	1,971	57	83	6,484	13,804	6,674
Champlain College; Burlington (Pr)	2,555	48	68	14,910	14,910	9,695
Johnson State College; Johnson (Pu)	1,759	55	87	6,580	13,520	6,454
Lyndon State College; Lyndonville (Pu)	1,349	50	94	6,146	13,086	6,454
Middlebury College; Middlebury (Pr)	2,357	52	26	40,400	40,400	—
Norwich University; Northfield (Pr)	2,707	—	91	19,650	19,650	7,090
Saint Michael's College; Colchester (Pr)	2,424	55	70	25,535	25,535	6,250
University of Vermont; Burlington (Pu)	10,940	55	76	10,226	23,866	7,016
Vermont Technical College; Randolph Center (Pu)	1,332	36	64	7,502	13,986	6,454
VIRGINIA						
Averett University; Danville (Pr)	2,719	53	86	18,430	18,430	6,330
Bluefield College; Bluefield (Pr)	814	56	57	11,430	11,430	5,800
Bridgewater College; Bridgewater (Pr)	1,532	57	85	18,990	18,990	8,800
Christopher Newport University; Newport News (Pu)	4,681	54	71	5,314	12,626	7,200
College of William and Mary; Williamsburg (Pu)	7,575	55	35	7,096	21,796	6,066
Eastern Mennonite University; Harrisonburg (Pr)	1,297	60	53	19,500	19,500	5,950
Emory & Henry College; Emory (Pr)	1,028	52	76	16,690	16,690	6,250
Ferrum College; Ferrum (Pr)	941	44	74	16,870	16,870	5,700
George Mason University; Fairfax (Pu)	28,874	54	69	5,448	15,816	6,240
Hampden-Sydney College; Hampden-Sydney (Pr)	1,082	0	69	22,946	22,946	7,370
Hampton University; Hampton (Pr)	6,156	65	54	14,996	14,996	6,424
Hollins University; Roanoke (Pr)	1,057	100	87	21,675	21,675	7,700
James Madison University; Harrisonburg (Pu)	16,108	61	63	5,476	14,420	6,116
Liberty University; Lynchburg (Pr)	13,464	53	91	14,550	14,550	5,400
Longwood University; Farmville (Pu)	4,289	67	76	6,441	12,901	5,424
Lynchburg College; Lynchburg (Pr)	2,248	59	74	22,885	22,885	5,000
Mary Baldwin College; Staunton (Pr)	1,718	97	75	19,991	19,991	5,689
Marymount University; Arlington (Pr)	3,717	74	82	17,090	17,090	7,520
Norfolk State University; Norfolk (Pu)	6,846	62	71	4,295	14,255	6,236
Old Dominion University; Norfolk (Pu)	20,595	57	72	5,268	14,688	5,802
Radford University; Radford (Pu)	9,329	59	76	4,762	11,762	5,886
Randolph-Macon College; Ashland (Pr)	1,127	53	77	22,625	22,625	6,510
Regent University; Virginia Beach (Pr)	3,447	69	—	11,362	11,362	—
Roanoke College; Salem (Pr)	1,850	58	69	22,109	22,109	6,912
Shenandoah University; Winchester (Pr)	3,000	58	92	19,240	19,240	7,090
University of Mary Washington; Fredericksburg (Pu)	4,792	67	60	5,128	13,534	5,744
University of Phoenix–Northern Virginia Campus; Reston (Pr)	1,266	49	—	10,800	10,800	—
University of Richmond; University of Richmond (Pr)	3,637	52	40	27,850	27,850	5,660
University of Virginia; Charlottesville (Pu)	23,341	53	39	6,790	22,831	5,960
University of Virginia's College at Wise; Wise (Pu)	1,836	50	79	5,081	15,159	6,200
Virginia Commonwealth University; Richmond (Pu)	28,462	60	74	5,385	18,148	7,042
Virginia Intermont College; Bristol (Pr)	1,152	71	66	15,200	15,200	5,650
Virginia Military Institute; Lexington (Pu)	1,362	6	50	6,529	19,991	5,474
Virginia Polytechnic Institute and State University; Blacksburg (Pu)	25,619	41	71	5,836	16,530	4,288
Virginia State University; Petersburg (Pu)	4,859	59	64	4,602	11,462	6,260
Virginia Union University; Richmond (Pu)	1,777	60	71	12,260	12,260	5,436
Virginia Wesleyan College; Norfolk (Pr)	1,442	63	79	20,448	20,448	6,600
Washington and Lee University; Lexington (Pr)	2,166	49	30	25,760	25,760	6,790
VIRGIN ISLANDS						
University of the Virgin Islands; Saint Thomas (Pu)	2,565	75	72	3,796	9,796	7,740

Institution name; city (Public/Private)	Total enrolled students	Percent Women	Percent Students accepted	Tuition and fees In-state	Tuition and fees Out-of-state	Room and board
WASHINGTON						
Art Institute of Seattle; Seattle (Pr)	2,492	48%	67%	$16,020	$16,020	$8,355
Central Washington University; Ellensburg (Pu)	9,985	52	83	4,647	12,168	6,402
City University; Bellevue (Pr)	4,254	59	100	9,440	9,440	—
Eastern Washington University; Cheney (Pu)	10,707	57	77	4,056	13,533	5,460
Evergreen State College; Olympia (Pu)	4,410	54	95	4,056	14,670	5,784
Gonzaga University; Spokane (Pr)	6,016	54	80	22,118	22,118	6,650
Heritage University; Toppenish (Pr)	1,355	71	60	7,120	7,120	—
Northwest University; Kirkland (Pr)	1,180	63	85	15,944	15,944	6,450
Pacific Lutheran University; Tacoma (Pr)	3,643	65	76	20,790	20,790	6,410
Saint Martin's College; Lacey (Pr)	1,512	56	79	19,980	19,980	6,200
Seattle Pacific University; Seattle (Pr)	3,779	66	93	20,466	20,466	7,368
Seattle University; Seattle (Pr)	6,810	61	74	21,285	21,285	7,038
University of Phoenix–Washington Campus; Seattle (Pr)	2,197	55	—	10,290	10,290	—
University of Puget Sound; Tacoma (Pr)	2,892	58	70	26,880	26,880	6,730
University of Washington; Seattle (Pu)	39,246	52	68	5,286	17,916	7,017
Walla Walla College; College Place (Pr)	1,968	49	63	17,829	17,829	3,684
Washington State University; Pullman (Pu)	23,240	51	75	5,358	13,776	6,450
Western Washington University; Bellingham (Pu)	14,190	56	75	4,452	13,839	6,242
Whitman College; Walla Walla (Pr)	1,481	55	50	27,106	27,106	7,180
Whitworth College; Spokane (Pr)	2,373	58	71	22,678	22,678	6,760
WEST VIRGINIA						
American Public University System; Charles Town (Pr)	9,716	25	75	6,000	6,000	—
Bethany College; Bethany (Pr)	900	51	73	15,440	15,440	7,200
Bluefield State College; Bluefield (Pu)	3,506	62	98	3,114	6,894	—
Concord University; Athens (Pu)	2,937	56	60	3,588	8,008	5,600
Fairmont State University; Fairmont (Pu)	7,519	55	64	4,112	8,702	6,052
Glenville State College; Glenville (Pu)	1,319	51	100	3,276	7,854	5,060
Marshall University; Huntington (Pu)	13,920	56	84	4,296	10,606	6,060
Mountain State University; Beckley (Pr)	4,107	62	100	5,400	5,400	5,440
Shepherd University; Shepherdstown (Pu)	5,206	56	91	3,654	9,234	5,574
University of Charleston; Charleston (Pr)	941	61	60	20,200	20,200	7,400
West Liberty State College; West Liberty (Pu)	2,374	54	98	3,380	8,354	5,006
West Virginia State University; Institute (Pu)	3,344	58	—	3,222	7,400	4,720
West Virginia University Institute of Technology; Montgomery (Pu)	2,468	37	74	3,786	9,486	4,970
West Virginia University; Morgantown (Pu)	25,255	46	89	3,938	12,060	6,084
West Virginia Wesleyan College; Buckhannon (Pr)	1,522	53	77	21,250	21,250	5,500
Wheeling Jesuit University; Wheeling (Pr)	1,699	60	75	21,350	21,350	6,450
WISCONSIN						
Alverno College; Milwaukee (Pr)	2,241	100	55	14,410	14,410	5,400
Beloit College; Beloit (Pr)	1,389	60	70	25,736	25,736	5,696
Cardinal Stritch University; Milwaukee (Pr)	6,785	67	93	15,660	15,660	5,280
Carroll College; Waukesha (Pr)	3,014	67	78	19,050	19,050	5,810
Carthage College; Kenosha (Pr)	2,679	56	74	22,500	22,500	6,500
Concordia University Wisconsin; Mequon (Pr)	5,395	62	80	16,430	16,430	6,230
Edgewood College; Madison (Pr)	2,454	73	79	16,050	16,050	5,691
Lakeland College; Sheboygan (Pr)	4,013	54	76	15,770	15,770	5,635
Lawrence University; Appleton (Pr)	1,380	55	66	27,924	27,924	5,900
Maranatha Baptist Bible College; Watertown (Pr)	904	54	68	8,120	8,120	4,700
Marian College of Fond du Lac; Fond du Lac (Pr)	2,918	72	83	15,825	15,825	5,240
Marquette University; Milwaukee (Pr)	11,510	55	67	21,932	21,932	7,890
Milwaukee School of Engineering; Milwaukee (Pr)	2,363	19	63	23,955	23,955	5,892
Mount Mary College; Milwaukee (Pr)	1,632	98	84	16,155	16,155	5,350
Ripon College; Ripon (Pr)	927	53	82	20,730	20,730	5,360
Silver Lake College; Manitowoc (Pr)	1,034	82	91	16,000	16,000	4,250
St. Norbert College; De Pere (Pr)	2,103	57	84	21,510	21,510	5,980
University of Phoenix–Wisconsin Campus; Brookfield (Pr)	1,296	57	—	10,020	10,020	—
University of Wisconsin–Eau Claire; Eau Claire (Pu)	10,540	59	66	4,864	14,910	4,310
University of Wisconsin–Green Bay; Green Bay (Pu)	5,706	65	70	5,154	15,200	4,716
University of Wisconsin–La Crosse; La Crosse (Pu)	8,511	60	60	4,895	14,941	4,570
University of Wisconsin–Madison; Madison (Pu)	41,169	53	66	5,860	19,860	6,250
University of Wisconsin–Milwaukee; Milwaukee (Pu)	26,832	54	79	5,835	18,587	4,505
University of Wisconsin–Oshkosh; Oshkosh (Pu)	11,039	59	48	4,616	14,662	4,630
University of Wisconsin–Parkside; Kenosha (Pu)	5,072	58	95	4,652	14,698	5,415
University of Wisconsin–Platteville; Platteville (Pu)	6,158	37	85	4,812	14,858	4,412
University of Wisconsin–River Falls; River Falls (Pu)	5,950	61	76	4,968	15,014	—
University of Wisconsin–Stevens Point; Stevens Point (Pu)	9,023	55	75	4,704	14,750	4,094
University of Wisconsin–Stout; Menomonie (Pu)	7,547	50	80	6,262	16,587	4,334
University of Wisconsin–Superior; Superior (Pu)	2,804	57	77	4,808	14,854	4,342
University of Wisconsin–Whitewater; Whitewater (Pu)	10,938	52	71	5,080	15,675	4,210
Viterbo University; La Crosse (Pr)	2,690	72	85	16,660	16,660	5,430
WYOMING						
University of Wyoming; Laramie (Pu)	13,207	49	95	3,243	9,273	5,953

2006

January
S	M	T	W	T	F	S
1	2	3	4	5	6	7
8	9	10	11	12	13	14
15	16	17	18	19	20	21
22	23	24	25	26	27	28
29	30	31				

February
S	M	T	W	T	F	S
			1	2	3	4
5	6	7	8	9	10	11
12	13	14	15	16	17	18
19	20	21	22	23	24	25
26	27	28				

March
S	M	T	W	T	F	S
			1	2	3	4
5	6	7	8	9	10	11
12	13	14	15	16	17	18
19	20	21	22	23	24	25
26	27	28	29	30	31	

April
S	M	T	W	T	F	S
						1
2	3	4	5	6	7	8
9	10	11	12	13	14	15
16	17	18	19	20	21	22
23	24	25	26	27	28	29
30						

January
- 1—New Year's Day
- 6—Epiphany
- 10—(Eid) al-Adha*
- 16—Martin Luther King, Jr.'s birthday observed
- 29—Chinese New Year
- 31—1st Day of Muharram*

February
- 2—Groundhog Day
- 12—Lincoln's Birthday
- 14—St. Valentine's Day
- 20—Washington's Birthday (or Presidents' Day) observed
- 22—Washington's Birthday
- 28—Shrove Tuesday (Mardi Gras)

March
- 1—Ash Wednesday
- 14—Purim*
- 17—St. Patrick's Day
- 20—Spring begins (EST)**

April
- 2—Daylight Saving Time begins
- 9—Palm Sunday
- 11—Mawlid an-Nabi*
- 13—1st Day of Passover*
- 14—Good Friday
- 16—Easter
- 23—Orthodox Easter

May
S	M	T	W	T	F	S
	1	2	3	4	5	6
7	8	9	10	11	12	13
14	15	16	17	18	19	20
21	22	23	24	25	26	27
28	29	30	31			

June
S	M	T	W	T	F	S
				1	2	3
4	5	6	7	8	9	10
11	12	13	14	15	16	17
18	19	20	21	22	23	24
25	26	27	28	29	30	

July
S	M	T	W	T	F	S
						1
2	3	4	5	6	7	8
9	10	11	12	13	14	15
16	17	18	19	20	21	22
23	24	25	26	27	28	29
30	31					

August
S	M	T	W	T	F	S
		1	2	3	4	5
6	7	8	9	10	11	12
13	14	15	16	17	18	19
20	21	22	23	24	25	26
27	28	29	30	31		

May
- 14—Mother's Day
- 25—Ascension Day
- 29—Memorial Day

June
- 2—1st Day of Shavuot*
- 4—Pentecost
- 14—Flag Day
- 18—Father's Day
- 21—Summer begins (EDT)**

July
- 1—Canada Day
- 4—Independence Day

September
S	M	T	W	T	F	S
					1	2
3	4	5	6	7	8	9
10	11	12	13	14	15	16
17	18	19	20	21	22	23
24	25	26	27	28	29	30

October
S	M	T	W	T	F	S
1	2	3	4	5	6	7
8	9	10	11	12	13	14
15	16	17	18	19	20	21
22	23	24	25	26	27	28
29	30	31				

November
S	M	T	W	T	F	S
			1	2	3	4
5	6	7	8	9	10	11
12	13	14	15	16	17	18
19	20	21	22	23	24	25
26	27	28	29	30		

December
S	M	T	W	T	F	S
					1	2
3	4	5	6	7	8	9
10	11	12	13	14	15	16
17	18	19	20	21	22	23
24	25	26	27	28	29	30
31						

September
- 4—Labor Day
- 22—Autumn begins (EDT)**
- 23—1st Day of Rosh Hashanah*
- 24—Ramadan begins*

October
- 2—Yom Kippur*
- 7—1st Day of Sukkot*
- 9—Columbus Day observed
- 9—Thanksgiving Day (Canada)
- 14—Shemini Atzeret*
- 24—Ramadan ends (Eid al-Fitr)*
- 29—Daylight Saving Time ends
- 31—Halloween

November
- 1—All Saints' Day
- 7—Election Day
- 11—Veterans Day
- 23—Thanksgiving Day (U.S.)

December
- 3—1st Sunday of Advent
- 16—1st Day of Hanukkah*
- 21—Winter begins (EST)**
- 25—Christmas Day
- 26—1st Day of Kwanzaa
- 31—(Eid) al Adha*

*All Jewish and Islamic holidays begin at sundown the day before they are listed here. The Islamic calendar is based on lunar observation; thus, given dates of holidays may vary by one or two days.
**See p. 353 for 2006 solstices and equinoxes.

2005

	January					
S	M	T	W	T	F	S
						1
2	3	4	5	6	7	8
9	10	11	12	13	14	15
16	17	18	19	20	21	22
23	24	25	26	27	28	29
30	31					

	February					
S	M	T	W	T	F	S
		1	2	3	4	5
6	7	8	9	10	11	12
13	14	15	16	17	18	19
20	21	22	23	24	25	26
27	28					

	March					
S	M	T	W	T	F	S
		1	2	3	4	5
6	7	8	9	10	11	12
13	14	15	16	17	18	19
20	21	22	23	24	25	26
27	28	29	30	31		

	April					
S	M	T	W	T	F	S
					1	2
3	4	5	6	7	8	9
10	11	12	13	14	15	16
17	18	19	20	21	22	23
24	25	26	27	28	29	30

	May					
S	M	T	W	T	F	S
1	2	3	4	5	6	7
8	9	10	11	12	13	14
15	16	17	18	19	20	21
22	23	24	25	26	27	28
29	30	31				

	June					
S	M	T	W	T	F	S
			1	2	3	4
5	6	7	8	9	10	11
12	13	14	15	16	17	18
19	20	21	22	23	24	25
26	27	28	29	30		

	July					
S	M	T	W	T	F	S
					1	2
3	4	5	6	7	8	9
10	11	12	13	14	15	16
17	18	19	20	21	22	23
24	25	26	27	28	29	30
31						

	August					
S	M	T	W	T	F	S
	1	2	3	4	5	6
7	8	9	10	11	12	13
14	15	16	17	18	19	20
21	22	23	24	25	26	27
28	29	30	31			

	September					
S	M	T	W	T	F	S
				1	2	3
4	5	6	7	8	9	10
11	12	13	14	15	16	17
18	19	20	21	22	23	24
25	26	27	28	29	30	

	October					
S	M	T	W	T	F	S
						1
2	3	4	5	6	7	8
9	10	11	12	13	14	15
16	17	18	19	20	21	22
23	24	25	26	27	28	29
30	31					

	November					
S	M	T	W	T	F	S
		1	2	3	4	5
6	7	8	9	10	11	12
13	14	15	16	17	18	19
20	21	22	23	24	25	26
27	28	29	30			

	December					
S	M	T	W	T	F	S
				1	2	3
4	5	6	7	8	9	10
11	12	13	14	15	16	17
18	19	20	21	22	23	24
25	26	27	28	29	30	31

2007

	January					
S	M	T	W	T	F	S
	1	2	3	4	5	6
7	8	9	10	11	12	13
14	15	16	17	18	19	20
21	22	23	24	25	26	27
28	29	30	31			

	February					
S	M	T	W	T	F	S
				1	2	3
4	5	6	7	8	9	10
11	12	13	14	15	16	17
18	19	20	21	22	23	24
25	26	27	28			

	March					
S	M	T	W	T	F	S
				1	2	3
4	5	6	7	8	9	10
11	12	13	14	15	16	17
18	19	20	21	22	23	24
25	26	27	28	29	30	31

	April					
S	M	T	W	T	F	S
1	2	3	4	5	6	7
8	9	10	11	12	13	14
15	16	17	18	19	20	21
22	23	24	25	26	27	28
29	30					

	May					
S	M	T	W	T	F	S
		1	2	3	4	5
6	7	8	9	10	11	12
13	14	15	16	17	18	19
20	21	22	23	24	25	26
27	28	29	30	31		

	June					
S	M	T	W	T	F	S
					1	2
3	4	5	6	7	8	9
10	11	12	13	14	15	16
17	18	19	20	21	22	23
24	25	26	27	28	29	30

	July					
S	M	T	W	T	F	S
1	2	3	4	5	6	7
8	9	10	11	12	13	14
15	16	17	18	19	20	21
22	23	24	25	26	27	28
29	30	31				

	August					
S	M	T	W	T	F	S
			1	2	3	4
5	6	7	8	9	10	11
12	13	14	15	16	17	18
19	20	21	22	23	24	25
26	27	28	29	30	31	

	September					
S	M	T	W	T	F	S
						1
2	3	4	5	6	7	8
9	10	11	12	13	14	15
16	17	18	19	20	21	22
23	24	25	26	27	28	29
30						

	October					
S	M	T	W	T	F	S
	1	2	3	4	5	6
7	8	9	10	11	12	13
14	15	16	17	18	19	20
21	22	23	24	25	26	27
28	29	30	31			

	November					
S	M	T	W	T	F	S
				1	2	3
4	5	6	7	8	9	10
11	12	13	14	15	16	17
18	19	20	21	22	23	24
25	26	27	28	29	30	

	December					
S	M	T	W	T	F	S
						1
2	3	4	5	6	7	8
9	10	11	12	13	14	15
16	17	18	19	20	21	22
23	24	25	26	27	28	29
30	31					

Astrological Signs

♈ **Aries (Ram):** March 21–April 19

♉ **Taurus (Bull):** April 20–May 20

♊ **Gemini (Twins):** May 21–June 20

♋ **Cancer (Crab):** June 21–July 22

♌ **Leo (Lion):** July 23–Aug. 22

♍ **Virgo (Virgin):** Aug. 23–Sept. 22

♎ **Libra (Scales):** Sept. 23–Oct. 22

♏ **Scorpio (Scorpion):** Oct. 23–Nov. 21

♐ **Sagittarius (Archer):** Nov. 22–Dec. 21

♑ **Capricorn (Goat):** Dec. 22–Jan. 19

♒ **Aquarius (Water Bearer):** Jan. 20–Feb. 18

♓ **Pisces (Fish):** Feb. 19–March 20

PERPETUAL CALENDAR

1800...4	1844...9	1888...8	1932.13	1976.12	2020.11
1801...5	1845...4	1889...3	1933...1	1977...7	2021...6
1802...6	1846...5	1890...4	1934...2	1978...1	2022...7
1803...7	1847...6	1891...5	1935...3	1979...2	2023...1
1804...8	1848.14	1892.13	1936.11	1980.10	2024...9
1805...3	1849...2	1893...1	1937...6	1981...5	2025...4
1806...4	1850...3	1894...2	1938...7	1982...6	2026...5
1807...5	1851...4	1895...3	1939...1	1983...7	2027...6
1808.13	1852.12	1896.11	1940...9	1984...8	2028.14
1809...1	1853...7	1897...6	1941...4	1985...3	2029...2
1810...2	1854...1	1898...7	1942...5	1986...4	2030...3
1811...3	1855...2	1899...1	1943...6	1987...5	2031...4
1812.11	1856.10	1900...2	1944.14	1988.13	2032.12
1813...6	1857...5	1901...3	1945...2	1989...1	2033...7
1814...7	1858...6	1902...4	1946...3	1990...2	2034...1
1815...1	1859...7	1903...5	1947...4	1991...3	2035...2
1816...9	1860...8	1904.13	1948.12	1992.11	2036.10
1817...4	1861...3	1905...1	1949...7	1993...6	2037...5
1818...5	1862...4	1906...2	1950...1	1994...7	2038...6
1819...6	1863...5	1907...3	1951...2	1995...1	2039...7
1820.14	1864.13	1908.11	1952.10	1996...9	2040...8
1821...2	1865...1	1909...6	1953...5	1997...4	2041...3
1822...3	1866...2	1910...7	1954...6	1998...5	2042...4
1823...4	1867...3	1911...1	1955...7	1999...6	2043...5
1824.12	1868.11	1912.12	1956...8	2000.14	2044.13
1825...7	1869...6	1913...4	1957...3	2001...2	2045...1
1826...1	1870...7	1914...5	1958...4	2002...3	2046...2
1827...2	1871...1	1915...6	1959...5	2003...4	2047...3
1828.10	1872...9	1916.14	1960.13	2004.12	2048.11
1829...5	1873...4	1917...2	1961...1	2005...7	2049...6
1830...6	1874...5	1918...3	1962...2	2006...1	2050...7
1831...7	1875...6	1919...4	1963...3	2007...2	2051...1
1832...8	1876.14	1920.12	1964.11	2008.10	2052...9
1833...3	1877...2	1921...7	1965...6	2009...5	2053...4
1834...4	1878...3	1922...1	1966...7	2010...6	2054...5
1835...5	1879...4	1923...2	1967...1	2011...7	2055...6
1836.13	1880.12	1924.10	1968...9	2012...8	2056.14
1837...1	1881...7	1925...5	1969...4	2013...3	2057...2
1838...2	1882...1	1926...6	1970...5	2014...4	2058...3
1839...3	1883...2	1927...7	1971...6	2015...5	2059...4
1840.11	1884.10	1928...8	1972.14	2016.13	2060.12
1841...6	1885...5	1929...3	1973...2	2017...1	2061...7
1842...7	1886...6	1930...4	1974...3	2018...2	2062...1
1843...1	1887...7	1931...5	1975...4	2019...3	2063...2

DIRECTIONS: The number given with each year in the key above is the number of the calendar to use for that year.

7

JANUARY
S	M	T	W	T	F	S
						1
2	3	4	5	6	7	8
9	10	11	12	13	14	15
16	17	18	19	20	21	22
23	24	25	26	27	28	29
30	31					

FEBRUARY
S	M	T	W	T	F	S
		1	2	3	4	5
6	7	8	9	10	11	12
13	14	15	16	17	18	19
20	21	22	23	24	25	26
27	28					

MARCH
S	M	T	W	T	F	S
		1	2	3	4	5
6	7	8	9	10	11	12
13	14	15	16	17	18	19
20	21	22	23	24	25	26
27	28	29	30	31		

APRIL
S	M	T	W	T	F	S
					1	2
3	4	5	6	7	8	9
10	11	12	13	14	15	16
17	18	19	20	21	22	23
24	25	26	27	28	29	30

MAY
S	M	T	W	T	F	S
1	2	3	4	5	6	7
8	9	10	11	12	13	14
15	16	17	18	19	20	21
22	23	24	25	26	27	28
29	30	31				

JUNE
S	M	T	W	T	F	S
			1	2	3	4
5	6	7	8	9	10	11
12	13	14	15	16	17	18
19	20	21	22	23	24	25
26	27	28	29	30		

JULY
S	M	T	W	T	F	S
					1	2
3	4	5	6	7	8	9
10	11	12	13	14	15	16
17	18	19	20	21	22	23
24	25	26	27	28	29	30
31						

AUGUST
S	M	T	W	T	F	S
	1	2	3	4	5	6
7	8	9	10	11	12	13
14	15	16	17	18	19	20
21	22	23	24	25	26	27
28	29	30	31			

SEPTEMBER
S	M	T	W	T	F	S
				1	2	3
4	5	6	7	8	9	10
11	12	13	14	15	16	17
18	19	20	21	22	23	24
25	26	27	28	29	30	

OCTOBER
S	M	T	W	T	F	S
						1
2	3	4	5	6	7	8
9	10	11	12	13	14	15
16	17	18	19	20	21	22
23	24	25	26	27	28	29
30	31					

NOVEMBER
S	M	T	W	T	F	S
		1	2	3	4	5
6	7	8	9	10	11	12
13	14	15	16	17	18	19
20	21	22	23	24	25	26
27	28	29	30			

DECEMBER
S	M	T	W	T	F	S
				1	2	3
4	5	6	7	8	9	10
11	12	13	14	15	16	17
18	19	20	21	22	23	24
25	26	27	28	29	30	31

8

Perpetual calendar grid (JANUARY–DECEMBER), leap year beginning on Sunday.

9

Perpetual calendar grid (JANUARY–DECEMBER).

10

Perpetual calendar grid (JANUARY–DECEMBER).

11

Perpetual calendar grid (JANUARY–DECEMBER).

12

Perpetual calendar grid (JANUARY–DECEMBER).

13

Perpetual calendar grid (JANUARY–DECEMBER).

14

Perpetual calendar grid (JANUARY–DECEMBER).

History of the Calendar

The purpose of the calendar is to reckon past or future time, to show how many days until a certain event takes place—the harvest or a religious festival—or how long since something important happened. The earliest calendars must have been strongly influenced by the geographical location of the people who made them. In colder countries, the concept of the year was determined by the seasons, specifically by the end of winter. But in warmer countries, where the seasons are less pronounced, the Moon became the basic unit for time reckoning; an old Jewish book says that "the Moon was created for the counting of the days."

Most of the oldest calendars were lunar calendars, based on the time interval from one new moon to the next—a so-called lunation. But even in a warm climate there are annual events that pay no attention to the phases of the Moon. In some areas it was a rainy season; in Egypt it was the annual flooding of the Nile River. The calendar had to account for these yearly events as well.

The Egyptian Calendar

The ancient Egyptians used a calendar with 12 months of 30 days each, for a total of 360 days per year. About 4000 B.C. they added five extra days at the end of every year to bring it more into line with the solar year.[1] These five days became a festival because it was thought to be unlucky to work during that time.

The Egyptians had calculated that the solar year was actually closer to 365¼ days, but instead of having a single leap day every four years to account for the fractional day (the way we do now), they let the one-quarter day accumulate. After 1,460 solar years, or four periods of 365 years, 1,461 Egyptian years had passed. This means that as the years passed, the Egyptian months fell out of sync with the seasons, so that the summer months eventually fell during winter. Only once every 1,460 years did their calendar year coincide precisely with the solar year.

In addition to the civic calendar, the Egyptians also had a religious calendar that was based on the 29½-day lunar cycle and was more closely linked with agricultural cycles and the movements of the stars.

Lunar Calendars

During antiquity the lunar calendar that best approximated a solar-year calendar was based on a 19-year period, with 7 of these 19 years having 13 months. In all, the period contained 235 months. Still using the lunation value of 29½ days, this made a total of 6,932½ days, while 19 solar years added up to 6,939.7 days, a difference of just one week per period and about five weeks per century.

Even the 19-year period required adjustment, but it became the basis of the calendars of the ancient Chinese, Babylonians, Greeks, and Jews. This same calendar was also used by the Arabs, but Muhammad later forbade shifting from 12 months to 13 months, so that the Islamic calendar, even today, has a lunar year of 354 days. As a result, the months of the Islamic calendar, as well as the Islamic religious festivals, migrate through all the seasons of the year.

The Roman Calendar

When Rome emerged as a world power, the difficulties of making a calendar were well known, but the Romans complicated their lives because of their superstition that even numbers were unlucky. Hence their months were 29 or 31 days long, with the exception of February, which had 28 days. However, four months of 31 days, seven months of 29 days, and one month of 28 days added up to only 355 days. Therefore the Romans invented an extra month called Mercedonius of 22 or 23 days. It was added every second year.

Even with Mercedonius, the Roman calendar eventually became so far off that **Julius Caesar,** advised by the astronomer Sosigenes, ordered a sweeping reform in 45 B.C. One year, made 445 days long by imperial decree, brought the calendar back in step with the seasons. Then the solar year (with the value of 365 days and 6 hours) was made the basis of the calendar. The months were 30 or 31 days in length, and to take care of the 6 hours, every fourth year was made a 366-day year. Moreover, Caesar decreed the year began with the first of January, not with the vernal equinox in late March.

This calendar was named the **Julian calendar,** after Julius Caesar, and it continues to be the calendar of the Eastern Orthodox churches to this day. However, despite the correction, the Julian calendar is still 11½ minutes longer than the actual solar year, and after a number of centuries, even 11½ minutes adds up.

The Gregorian Reform

By the 15th century the Julian calendar had drifted behind the solar calendar by about a week, so that the vernal equinox was falling around March 12 instead of around March 20. Pope Sixtus IV (who reigned from 1471 to 1484) decided that another reform was needed and called the German astronomer Regiomontanus to Rome to advise him. Regiomontanus arrived in 1475, but unfortunately he died shortly afterward, and the pope's plans for reform died with him.

Then in 1545, the Council of Trent authorized Pope Paul III to reform the calendar once more. Most of the mathematical and astronomical work was done by Father Christopher Clavius, S.J. The immediate correction, advised by Father Clavius and ordered by Pope Gregory XIII, was that Thursday, Oct. 4, 1582, was to be the last day of the Julian calendar. The next day would be Friday, Oct. 15. For long-range accuracy, a formula suggested by the Vatican librarian Aloysius Giglio was adopted: every fourth year is a leap year *unless* it is a century year like 1700 or 1800. Century years can be leap years *only* when they are divisible by 400 (e.g., 1600 and 2000). This rule eliminates three leap years in four centuries, making the calendar sufficiently accurate.

In spite of the revised leap year rule, an average calendar year is still about 26 seconds longer than the Earth's orbital period. But this discrepancy will need 3,323 years to build up to a single day.

---

1. The correct figures are lunation: 29 d, 12 h, 44 min, 2.8 sec (29.530585 d); solar year: 365 d, 5 h, 48 min, 46 sec (365.242216 d); 12 lunations: 354 d, 8 h, 48 min, 34 sec (354.3671 d).

Adoption of the Gregorian Calendar

Year	Country	Year	Country	Year	Country
1582	Catholic states of Italy, Portugal, Spain, Belgium, Holland, and Poland	1700	German, Swiss, and Dutch Protestant States, Denmark, and Norway	1873	Japan
				1875	Egypt
1584	German and Swiss Catholic states	1752	Great Britain and its possessions (including the American colonies)	1918	Russia
				1924	Greece
1587	Hungary			1926	Turkey
				1949	China

Reform Adopted Gradually

The Gregorian reform was not adopted throughout the West immediately. Most Catholic countries quickly changed to the Pope's new calendar in 1582. But Europe's Protestant princes chose to ignore the papal bull and continued with the Julian calendar. It was not until 1700 that the Protestant rulers of Germany and the Netherlands changed to the new calendar. In Great Britain (and its colonies) the shift did not take place until 1752, and in Russia a revolution was needed to introduce the Gregorian calendar in 1918. In Turkey, the Islamic calendar was used until 1926.

A Better Calendar?

Despite its widespread use, the Gregorian calendar has a number of weaknesses. It cannot be divided into equal halves or quarters; the number of days per month is haphazard; and months and years may begin on any day of the week. Holidays pegged to specific dates may also fall on any day of the week, and few Americans can predict when Thanksgiving will occur next year. Since Gregory XIII, many other proposals for calendar reform have been made, but none has been permanently adopted. In the meantime, the Gregorian calendar keeps the calendar dates in reasonable unison with astronomical events. □

Time Measurement, Time Zones, and the International Date Line

The two natural cycles on which time measurements are based are the year and the day. The year is defined as the time required for Earth to complete one revolution around the Sun, while the day is the time required for Earth to complete one turn upon its axis. Earth needs 365 days plus about 6 hours to go around the Sun once, so a year does not consist of a round number of days; the fractional day has to be taken care of by an extra day every fourth year.

But because Earth, while turning upon its axis, also moves around the Sun, there are two kinds of days. A day may be defined as the interval between the highest point of the Sun in the sky on two successive days. This, averaged out over the year, produces the customary 24-hour day. But one might also define a day as the time interval between the moments when a certain point in the sky, say a conveniently located star, is directly overhead. This is called:

Sidereal time. A sidereal day is the time that it takes the Earth to complete one rotation on its axis so that a particular star can be observed twice at the meridian that runs directly overhead. Because the Earth is moving around the Sun as it rotates on its axis, the sidereal day is about 4 minutes shorter than the solar day, being equivalent to 23 hours, 56 minutes, and 4 seconds in mean solar time. As a result, a star will appear to rise about 4 minutes earlier every night, and different stars will be visible at different times of the year. Astronomers use a point that they call the "vernal equinox" to determine local sidereal time.

Apparent solar time is the time based directly on the Sun's position in the sky. In ordinary life the day runs from midnight to midnight. It begins when the Sun is invisible by being 12 hours from its zenith.

Mean solar time, rather than apparent solar time, is the basis for local civil and standard time. The mean solar time is based on the position of a fictitious "mean sun." The reason why this fictitious sun has to be introduced is the following: Earth turns on its axis regularly; it needs the same number of seconds regardless of the season. But the movement of Earth around the Sun is not regular because Earth's orbit is an ellipse. This has the result (as explained in the section on the seasons, p. 351) that Earth moves faster in January and slower in July. Though it is Earth that changes velocity, it looks to us as if the Sun does. In January, when Earth moves faster, the *apparent* movement of the Sun looks faster. The mean sun of time measurements, then, is a sun that moves regularly all year round; the real Sun will be either ahead of or behind the mean sun. The difference between the real Sun and the fictitious mean sun is called the *equation of time*.

Time zones. But if all clocks were actually set by mean solar time we would be plagued by a welter of time differences that would be "correct" but a major nuisance. A clock on Long Island, correctly showing mean solar time for its location (this would be *local civil time*), would be slightly ahead of a clock in Newark, N.J. The Newark clock would be slightly ahead of a clock in Trenton, N.J., which, in turn, would be ahead of a clock in Philadelphia. This condition prevailed until 1884, when a system of standard time was adopted by the International Meridian Conference. Earth's surface was divided into 24 zones. The standard time of each zone is the mean astronomical time of one of 24 meridians, 15 degrees apart, beginning at the Greenwich, England, meridian and extending east and west around the globe to the International Date Line. (This system was actually put into use a year earlier by the railroad companies of the U.S. and Canada, who, until then, had to contend with some 100 conflicting local sun times observed in terminals across the land.)

For practical purposes, this convention is sometimes altered. For example, Alaska, for a time, consisted of four of the eight U.S. time zones: the Pacific standard time zone (east of Juneau) and the 6th (Juneau), 7th (Anchorage), and 8th (Nome) zones, encompassing the 135°, 150°, and 165° meridians, respectively. In 1983, by act of Congress, the entire state (except the westernmost Aleutians) was united into the 6th zone, Alaska standard time.

The eight U.S. standard time zones are: Atlantic (includes Puerto Rico and the Virgin Islands), eastern, central, mountain, Pacific, Alaska, Hawaii-Aleutian (includes all of Hawaii and those Aleutians west of the Fox Islands), and Samoa standard time.

The Date Line. While the time zones are based on the natural event of the Sun crossing a meridian, the date must be an arbitrary decision. The meridians are traditionally counted from the meridian of the observatory of Greenwich, in England, which is called the zero meridian. The logical place for changing the date is 12 hours, or 180°, from Greenwich. Fortunately, the 180th meridian runs mostly through the open Pacific. The Date Line makes a zigzag in the north to incorporate the eastern tip of Siberia into the Siberian time system and then another one to incorporate a number of islands into the Hawaii-Aleutian time zone. In the south there is a similar zigzag for the purpose of tying a number of British-owned islands to the New Zealand time system. Otherwise, the Date Line is the same as 180° from Greenwich. At points to the east of the Date Line the calendar is one day earlier than at points to the west of it. A traveler going eastward across the Date Line from one island to another would not have to reset his watch because he would stay inside the time zone, but it would be the same time of the *previous* day.

For world and U.S. time zone map, *see* p. 523.

The Names of the Months

January: named after Janus, the god of doors and gates
February: named after Februalia, a time period when sacrifices were made to atone for sins
March: named after Mars, the god of war
April: from *aperire*, Latin for "to open" (buds)
May: named after Maia, the goddess of growth of plants
June: from *junius*, Latin for the goddess Juno

July: named after Julius Caesar in 44 B.C.
August: named after Augustus Caesar in 8 B.C.
September: from *septem*, Latin for "seven"
October: from *octo*, Latin for "eight"
November: from *novem*, Latin for "nine"
December: from *decem*, Latin for "ten"

NOTE: The earliest Latin calendar was a 10-month one, beginning with March; thus, September was the seventh month, October, the eighth, etc. July was originally called Quintilis, meaning fifth; August was originally called Sextilis, meaning sixth.

The Names of the Days of the Week

Latin	Old English	English	German	French	Italian	Spanish
Dies Solis	Sunnandaeg	Sunday	Sonntag	dimanche	domenica	domingo
Dies Lunae	Monandaeg	Monday	Montag	lundi	lunedì	lunes
Dies Martis	Tiwesdaeg	Tuesday	Dienstag	mardi	martedì	martes
Dies Mercurii	Wodnesdaeg	Wednesday	Mittwoch	mercredi	mercoledì	miércoles
Dies Jovis	Thunresdaeg	Thursday	Donnerstag	jeudi	giovedì	jueves
Dies Veneris	Frigedaeg	Friday	Freitag	vendredi	venerdì	viernes
Dies Saturni	Saeternesdaeg	Saturday	Samstag	samedi	sabato	sábado

NOTE: The seven-day week originated in ancient Mesopotamia and became part of the Roman calendar in A.D. 321. The names of the days are based on the seven celestial bodies (the Sun, the Moon, Mars, Mercury, Jupiter, Venus, and Saturn), believed at that time to revolve around Earth and influence its events. Most of Western Europe adopted the Roman nomenclature. The Germanic languages substituted Germanic equivalents for the names of four of the Roman gods: Tiw, the god of war, replaced Mars; Woden, the god of wisdom, replaced Mercury; Thor, the god of thunder, replaced Jupiter; and Frigg, the goddess of love, replaced Venus.

Daylight Saving Time

The United States. Daylight saving time, also called "summer time," is the practice of advancing clocks forward by one hour in the spring to gain additional daylight during the early evening. In the fall, clocks are again turned back an hour. The U.S. federal law that established "daylight time" in this country does not require its observance. Arizona, Hawaii, and the territories of Puerto Rico, Virgin Islands, and American Samoa do not use DST. These areas receive so much sun throughout the year that gaining another hour of sunlight in the summertime is not seen as a benefit.

DST Dawns in Indiana. Until April 2005, when Indiana passed a law agreeing to observe daylight saving time, the Hoosier state had its own unique and complex time system. Not only is the state split between two time zones, but until recently, only some parts of the state observed daylight saving time while the majority did not. Under the old system, 77 of the state's 92 counties were in the Eastern time zone but did not change to daylight time in April. Instead they remained on standard time all year. That is, except for two counties near Cincinnati, Ohio, and Louisville, Ky., which *did* use daylight time. But the counties in the northwest corner of the state (near Chicago) and the southwestern tip (near Evansville), which are in the central time zone, used both standard and daylight time.

The battle between the old system and DST was contentious and hard-won. Bills proposing DST had failed more than two dozen times before it squeaked through the state legislature in April 2005. In April 2006, Indiana joins 47 other states in observing DST for the first time.

New Federal Law Introduced: Springing Forward in March, Back in November. Just months after Indiana got in step with the rest of the country, the federal government announced a major change in Daylight Saving Time. In Aug. 2005, Congress passed an energy bill that included extending Daylight Saving Time by a month. Beginning in 2007, DST will start the second Sunday of March and end on the first Sunday of November.

Around the World. About 70 countries around the world observe daylight saving time in some form. Here are some interesting facts:

• Most of Canada uses DST. Some exceptions include the majority of Saskatchewan and parts of northeastern British Columbia.

• It wasn't until 1996 that Mexico adopted DST. Now all three Mexican time zones are on the same schedule as the United States.

• Also in 1996, members of the European Union agreed to observe a "summertime period" from the last Sunday in March to the last Sunday in October.

• In the winter months, Russia, which spans over 11 time zones, is always one hour ahead of standard time. In the summer, Russians turn their clocks ahead one more hour.

• Most countries near the equator don't deviate from standard time.

• In the Southern Hemisphere, where summer arrives in what we in the Northern Hemisphere consider the winter months, DST is observed from late October to late March.

• Three large regions in Australia do not participate in DST. Western Australia, the Northern Territory, and Queensland stay on standard time all year. The remaining south-central and southeastern sections of the continent (which is where Sydney and Melbourne are found) make the switch. This results in both vertical and horizontal time zones Down Under during the summer months.

• China, which spans five time zones, uses only one. The entire country is always eight hours ahead of Universal Time and it does not observe DST.

• In Japan, DST was implemented after World War II by the U.S. occupation. In 1952 it was abandoned because of strong opposition by Japanese farmers.

U.S. Daylight Saving Time Schedule

The year 2006 will be the last year in which clocks are set forward one hour on the first Sunday in April at 2:00 a.m. local time and set back one hour the last Sunday in October, also at 2:00 a.m. Starting in 2007, DST will be observed from the second Sunday in March to the first Sunday in November, adding a month to daylight saving time.

2006	April 2	October 29
2007	March 11	November 4
2008	March 9	November 2
2009	March 8	November 1
2010	March 14	November 7
2011	March 13	November 6

The Seasons

The seasons are caused by the tilt of Earth's axis (23.4°) and not by the fact that Earth's orbit around the Sun is an ellipse. The average distance of Earth from the Sun is 93 million miles; the difference between aphelion (farthest away from the Sun) and perihelion (closest to the Sun) is 3 million miles, so that perihelion is about 91.4 million miles from the Sun. Earth goes through the perihelion point a few days after New Year's Day, just when the Northern Hemisphere has winter. Aphelion is passed during the first days of July. This by itself shows that the distance from the Sun is not important within these limits. What is important is that when Earth passes through perihelion, the northern end of Earth's axis happens to tilt away from the Sun, so that the areas beyond the Tropic of Cancer receive only slanting rays from a Sun low in the sky.

The tilt of Earth's axis is responsible for four lines you find on every globe. When, say, the North Pole is tilted away from the Sun as much as possible, the farthest points in the North that can still be reached by the Sun's rays are 23.5° from the pole. This is the Arctic Circle. The Antarctic Circle is the corresponding limit 23.4° from the South Pole; the Sun's rays cannot reach beyond this point when we have midsummer in the North.

When the Sun is vertically above the equator, the day is of equal length all over Earth. This happens twice a year, and these are the "equinoxes" in March and in September. After having been over the equator in March, the Sun will seem to move northward. The northernmost point where the Sun can be straight overhead is 23.4° north of the equator. This is the Tropic of Cancer; the Sun can never be vertically overhead to the north of this line. Similarly the Sun cannot be vertically overhead to the south of a line 23.4° south of the equator—the Tropic of Capricorn.

This explains the climatic zones. In the belt (the Greek word *zone* means "belt") between the Tropic of Cancer and the Tropic of Capricorn, the Sun can be straight overhead; this is the tropical zone. The two zones where the Sun cannot be overhead but will be above the horizon every day of the year are the two temperate zones; the two areas where the Sun will not rise at all for varying lengths of time are the two polar areas, Arctic and Antarctic.   □

Seasons for the Northern Hemisphere, 2006

Vernal Equinox: Mar. 20, 1:26 p.m. EST (18:26 UT*), Sun enters sign of Aries; spring begins.

Summer Solstice: June 21, 7:26 a.m. EDT (12:26 UT*), Sun enters sign of Cancer; summer begins.

Autumnal Equinox: Sept. 22, 11:03 p.m. EDT (Sept. 23, 04:03 UT*), Sun enters sign of Libra; fall begins.

Winter Solstice: Dec. 21, 7:22 p.m. EST (Dec. 22, 00:22 UT*), Sun enters sign of Capricorn; winter begins.

*Universal time (UT), also known as Greenwich mean time (GMT). *See* p. 421 for a conversion table of universal time.

The Islamic (Hijri) Calendar

The Islamic calendar is based on the lunar year of 354 days. The number of days each month is adjusted according to the lunar cycle, beginning about two days after the new moon. The months drift backward over the seasons, beginning again on the same day every 32½ years. The Islamic year begins on the first day of Muharram, and is counted from the year of the Hegira (*anno Hegirae*)—the year in which Muhammad emigrated from Mecca to Medina (A.D. 622). The year 2006 translates to A.H. 1426–1427.

Month	Number of days	Month	Number of days	Month	Number of days	Month	Number of days
Muharram	29 or 30	Rabi II	29 or 30	Rajab	29 or 30	Shawwal	29 or 30
Safar	29 or 30	Jumada I	29 or 30	Sha'ban	29 or 30	Dhu'l-Qa'dah	29 or 30
Rabi I	29 or 30	Jumada II	29 or 30	Ramadan	29 or 30	Dhu'l-Hijjah	29 or 30

The Jewish Calendar

The Jewish calendar is based on both solar and lunar years. The average lunar year of 354 days is adjusted to the solar year by the addition of a leap year and an intercalary month. Nisan is considered the first month, although the new year begins with Rosh Hashanah, on the first of Tishri, which is in fact the seventh month—the calendar has different starting points for different purposes. The year 2006 translates to the Jewish year 5766–5767.

Month	Number of days	Month	Number of days	Month	Number of days
Nisan (March–April)*	30	Tishri (Sept.–Oct.)	30	Shevat (Jan.–Feb.)	30
Iyar (April–May)	29	Heshvan (Oct.–Nov.)	29	Adar (Feb.–March)	29
Sivan (May–June)	30	in some years	30	in some years	30
Tammuz (June–July)	29	Kislev (Nov.–Dec.)	29	Adar Sheni	29
Av (July–Aug.)	30	in some years	30	(intercalary month	
Elul (Aug.–Sept.)	29	Tevet (Dec.–Jan.)	29	in leap year only)	

*The months correspond approximately to those of the Gregorian calendar.

The Hindu (Indian National) Calendar

The Indian National Calendar, often called the "Hindu Calendar," is based on both lunar and solar years. This calendar was introduced in 1957 in a government push for all of India to use the same calendar, but various traditional calendars are also used. The start of the Indian National Calendar year coincides with March 22, except in a leap year, when it coincides with March 21. The year is counted from the first year of the Saka era, in A.D. 78. The year 2006 translates to Saka era 1927–1928.

Month	Number of days	Month	Number of days	Month	Number of days	Month	Number of days
Caitra	30*	Asadha	31	Asvina	30	Pausa	30
Vaisakha	31	Sravana	31	Kartika	30	Magha	30
Jyaistha	31	Bhadra	31	Agrahayana	30	Phalguna	30

* In a leap year Caitra has 31 days.

The Chinese Calendar

The Chinese lunar year is divided into 12 months of 29 or 30 days. The calendar is adjusted to the length of the solar year by the addition of extra months at regular intervals. The years are arranged in major cycles of 60 years. Each successive year is named after one of 12 animals. These 12-year cycles are continuously repeated. The Chinese New Year is celebrated at the second new moon after the winter solstice and falls between January 21 and February 19 on the Gregorian calendar. The year 2006 translates to the Chinese year 4703–4704.

Rat	Ox	Tiger	Rabbit	Dragon	Snake	Horse	Sheep (Goat)	Monkey	Rooster	Dog	Pig
1900	1901	1902	1903	1904	1905	1906	1907	1908	1909	1910	1911
1912	1913	1914	1915	1916	1917	1918	1919	1920	1921	1922	1923
1924	1925	1926	1927	1928	1929	1930	1931	1932	1933	1934	1935
1936	1937	1938	1939	1940	1941	1942	1943	1944	1945	1946	1947
1948	1949	1950	1951	1952	1953	1954	1955	1956	1957	1958	1959
1960	1961	1962	1963	1964	1965	1966	1967	1968	1969	1970	1971
1972	1973	1974	1975	1976	1977	1978	1979	1980	1981	1982	1983
1984	1985	1986	1987	1988	1989	1990	1991	1992	1993	1994	1995
1996	1997	1998	1999	2000	2001	2002	2003	2004	2005	2006	2007
2008	2009	2010	2011	2012	2013	2014	2015	2016	2017	2018	2019

Holidays

Religious and Secular, 2006

In the United States, there are ten federal holidays set by law. Four are set by date (New Year's Day, Independence Day, Veterans Day, and Christmas Day). The other six are set by a day of the week and month: Martin Luther King, Jr.'s Birthday, Washington's Birthday, Memorial Day, Labor Day, Columbus Day, and Thanksgiving. All but the last are celebrated on Mondays to create three-day weekends for federal employees. All Jewish and Islamic holidays begin at sundown the day before they are listed here.

New Year's Day, Sun., Jan. 1. A federal holiday in the United States, New Year's Day has its origin in Roman times, when sacrifices were offered to Janus, the two-faced Roman deity who looked back on the past and forward to the future.

Epiphany (from Greek *epiphaneia,* "manifestation"), Fri., Jan. 6. Falls on the 12th day after Christmas and commemorates the manifestation of Jesus Christ to the Gentiles, as represented by the Magi, the baptism of Jesus, and the miracle of the wine at the marriage feast at Cana. One of the three major Christian festivals, along with Christmas and Easter. Epiphany originally marked the beginning of the carnival season preceding Lent, and the evening preceding it is known as Twelfth Night.

Eid al-Adha, Tues., Jan. 10; Sun., Dec. 31. Eid al-Adha, or the Feast of Sacrifice, commemorates Abraham's willingness to obey God by sacrificing his son. Lasting for three days, it concludes the annual Hajj, or pilgrimage to Mecca. Muslims worldwide sacrifice a lamb or other animal and distribute the meat to relatives or the needy.

Martin Luther King, Jr.'s Birthday, Mon., Jan. 16. (The actual date of his birthday is Jan. 15.) A federal holiday observed on the third Monday in January that honors the late civil rights leader. It became a federal holiday in 1986.

Chinese New Year, Sun., Jan. 29, is the most important celebration in the Chinese calendar. Chinese months are reckoned by the lunar calendar, with each month beginning on the darkest day. New Year festivities traditionally start on the first day of the month and continue until the fifteenth, when the moon is brightest. In China, the New Year is a time for family reunions. In the United States, however, many early Chinese immigrants arrived without their families, and found a sense of community by celebrating the holiday through neighborhood associations.

Muharram, Tues., Jan. 31. The month of Muharram marks the beginning of the Islamic liturgical year. On the tenth day of the month, many Muslims may observe a day of fasting, known as Ashurah.

Groundhog Day, Thurs., Feb. 2. Legend has it that if the groundhog sees his shadow, he'll return to his hole, and winter will last another six weeks.

Lincoln's Birthday, Sun., Feb. 12. A holiday in many states, this day was first formally observed in Washington, DC, in 1866, when both houses of Congress gathered for a memorial address in tribute to the assassinated president.

St. Valentine's Day, Tues., Feb. 14. The holiday's roots are in an ancient Roman fertility festival. Circa 496, Pope Gelasius I recast this pagan festival as a Christian feast day in honor of St. Valentine, but there are at least three different early saints by that name. How the day became associated with romance remains obscure, and is further clouded by various fanciful legends.

Washington's Birthday or Presidents' Day, Mon., Feb. 20. (The actual date of his birthday is Feb. 22.) A federal holiday observed the third Monday in February. It is a common misperception that the federal holiday was changed to "Presidents' Day" and now celebrates both Washington and Lincoln. Only Washington is commemorated by the federal holiday; 12 states, however, officially celebrate "Presidents' Day."

Shrove Tuesday (Mardi Gras), Feb. 28. Falls the day before Ash Wednesday and marks the end of the carnival season, which once began on Epiphany but is now usually celebrated the last three days before Lent. In France, the day is known as Mardi Gras (Fat Tuesday), and celebrations are held in several American cities, particularly New Orleans.

Ash Wednesday, March 1. The seventh Wednesday before Easter and the first day of Lent, which lasts 40 days. Having its origin sometime before A.D. 1000, it is a day of public penance and is marked in the Roman Catholic Church by the burning of the palms blessed on the previous year's Palm Sunday. With the ashes from the palms the priest then marks a cross with his thumb upon the forehead of each worshiper. The Anglican Church and a few Protestant groups in the United States also observe the day, but generally without the use of ashes.

Purim (Feast of Lots), Tues., March 14. A day of joy and feasting celebrating the deliverance of the Jews from a massacre planned by the Persian minister Haman. The holiday is marked by the reading of the Book of Esther (the Megillah), by the exchange of gifts, and by donations to the poor.

St. Patrick's Day, Fri., March 17. St. Patrick, patron saint of Ireland, has been honored in America since the first days of the nation. Perhaps the most notable part of the observance is the annual St. Patrick's Day parade in New York City.

Palm Sunday, April 9. Observed the Sunday before Easter to commemorate the entry of Jesus into Jerusalem.

Mawlid an-Nabi, Tues., April 11. This holiday celebrates the birthday of Muhammad, the founder of Islam. It is fixed as the 12th day of the month of Rabi I in the Islamic calendar.

Passover (Pesach), Thurs., April 13. The Feast of the Passover, also called the Feast of Unleavened Bread, commemorates the escape of the Jews from Egypt. As the Jews fled, they ate unleavened bread, and from that time the Jews have allowed no leavening in their houses during Passover, bread being replaced by matzoh.

Good Friday, April 14. The Friday before Easter, it commemorates the Crucifixion, which is retold during services from the Gospel according to St. John. A feature in Roman Catholic churches is the Liturgy of the Passion; there is no Consecration, the Host having been consecrated the previous day. The eating of hot-cross buns on this day is said to have started in England.

Easter Sunday, April 16. Observed in all Western Christian churches, Easter commemorates the Resurrection of Jesus. It is celebrated on the first Sunday after the full moon that occurs on or next after the vernal equinox (fixed at March 21) and is therefore celebrated between March 22 and April 25 inclusive. This date was fixed by the Council of Nicaea in A.D. 325.

Orthodox Easter (Pascha), Sun., April 23. The Orthodox church uses the same formula to calculate Easter as the Western church, but bases it on the traditional Julian calendar instead of the more contemporary Gregorian calendar. For this reason Orthodox Easter generally falls on a different date than the Western Christian Easter.

Mother's Day, Sun., May 14. Observed the second Sunday in May, as proposed by Anna Jarvis of Philadelphia in 1907. West Virginia was the first state to recognize the holiday in 1910, and President Woodrow Wilson officially proclaimed Mother's Day a national holiday in 1914.

Ascension Day, Thurs., May 25. The Ascension of Jesus took place in the presence of his apostles 40 days after the Resurrection. It is traditionally thought to have occurred on Mount Olivet in Bethany.

Memorial Day, Mon., May 29. Memorial Day became a federal holiday in 1971 and is observed on the last Monday in May. It originated in 1868, when Union General John A. Logan designated a day in which the graves of Civil War soldiers would be decorated. Originally known as Decoration Day, the holiday was changed to Memorial Day within twenty years, becoming a holiday dedicated to the memory of all war dead.

Shavuot (Hebrew Pentecost), Fri., June 2. This festival, sometimes called the Feast of Weeks, or of Harvest, or of the First Fruits, falls 50 days after Passover and originally celebrated the end of the seven-week grain-harvesting season. In later tradition, it also celebrated the giving of the Law to Moses on Mount Sinai.

Pentecost (Whitsunday), June 4. This day commemorates the descent of the Holy Ghost upon the apostles 50 days after the Resurrection. "Whitsunday" is believed to have come from "white Sunday," when, among the English, white robes were worn by those baptized on the day.

Flag Day, Weds., June 14. This day commemorates the adoption by the Continental Congress on June 14, 1777, of the Stars and Stripes as the U.S. flag.

Father's Day, Sun., June 18. Observed the third Sunday in June. The exact origin of the holiday is not clear, but it was first celebrated June 19, 1910, in Spokane, Wash. In 1966 President Lyndon Johnson signed a proclamation making Father's Day official.

Independence Day, Tues., July 4. The day of the adoption of the Declaration of Independence in 1776, celebrated in all states and territories. The observance began the next year in Philadelphia.

Labor Day, Mon., Sept. 4. A federal holiday observed the first Monday in September. Labor Day was first celebrated in New York in 1882 under the sponsorship of the Central Labor Union, following the suggestion of Peter J. McGuire, of the Knights of Labor, that the day be set aside in honor of labor.

Rosh Hashanah (Jewish New Year), Sat., Sept. 23. This day marks the beginning of the Jewish year 5766 and opens the Ten Days of Penitence, which close with Yom Kippur.

First Day of Ramadan, Sun., Sept. 24. This day marks the beginning of a month-long fast that all Muslims must keep during the daylight hours. It commemorates the first revelation of the Qur'an. Following the last day of Ramadan, **Eid al-Fitr** is celebrated on Tues., Oct. 24.

Yom Kippur (Day of Atonement), Mon., Oct. 2. This day marks the end of the Ten Days of Penitence that began with Rosh Hashanah. It is described in Leviticus as a "Sabbath of rest," and synagogue services begin the preceding sundown, resume the following morning, and continue to sundown.

Sukkot (Feast of Tabernacles), Sat., Oct. 7. This festival, also known as the Feast of the Ingathering, is both a harvest festival and a commemoration of the forty years of wandering after the Jews were freed from Egypt. The name refers to the small huts Jews live in during the festival, symbolic of the shelters used during their wandering. Some say that they also represent the huts used by workers during the annual fruit harvest.

Columbus Day, Mon., Oct. 9. A federal holiday observed the second Monday in October, it commemorates Christopher Columbus's landing in the New World in 1492. Quite likely the first celebration of Columbus Day was that organized in 1792 by the Society of St. Tammany, or the Columbian Order, widely known as Tammany Hall.

Shemini Atzeret (Assembly of the Eighth Day), Sat., Oct. 14. This joyous holiday, encompassing Simchat Torah (Rejoicing in the Torah), falls immediately after the seven days of Sukkot. It marks the end of the year's weekly readings of the Torah (Five Books of Moses) in the synagogue, and the beginning of the new cycle of reading.

Halloween, Tues., Oct. 31. Eve of All Saints' Day, formerly called All Hallows and Hallowmass. Halloween is traditionally associated in some countries with customs such as bonfires, masquerading, and the telling of ghost stories. These are old Celtic practices marking the beginning of winter.

All Saints' Day, Weds., Nov. 1. A Roman Catholic and Anglican holiday celebrating all saints, known and unknown.

Election Day (legal holiday in certain states), Tues., Nov. 7. Since 1845, by act of Congress, the first Tuesday after the first Monday in November is the date for choosing presidential electors. State elections are also generally held on this day.

Veterans Day, Sat., Nov. 11. Armistice Day, a federal holiday, was established in 1926 to commemorate the signing in 1918 of the armistice ending World War I. On June 1, 1954, the name was changed to Veterans Day to honor all men and women who have served America in its armed forces.

Thanksgiving, Thurs., Nov. 23. A federal holiday observed the fourth Thursday in November by act of Congress (1941), it was the first such national proclamation issued by President Lincoln in 1863, on the urging of Mrs. Sarah J. Hale, editor of *Godey's*

Lady's Book. Most Americans believe that the holiday dates back to the day of thanks ordered by Governor Bradford of Plymouth Colony in New England in 1621, but scholars point out that days of thanks stem from ancient times.

Hanukkah (Festival of Lights), Sat., Dec. 16. This festival was instituted by Judas Maccabaeus in 165 B.C. to celebrate the purification of the Temple of Jerusalem, which had been desecrated three years earlier by Antiochus Epiphanes, who set up a pagan altar and offered sacrifices to Zeus Olympius. In Jewish homes, a lamp or candle is lighted on each night of the eight-day festival.

Christmas (Feast of the Nativity), Mon., Dec. 25. The most widely celebrated holiday of the Christian year, Christmas is observed as the anniversary of the birth of Jesus. Christmas customs are centuries old. The mistletoe, for example, comes from the Druids, who, in hanging the mistletoe, hoped for peace and good fortune. Comparatively recent is the Christmas tree, first set up in Germany in the 17th century. Colonial Manhattan Islanders introduced the name Santa Claus, a corruption of the Dutch name St. Nicholas, who lived in fourth-century Asia Minor.

Kwanzaa, Tues., Dec. 26. This secular seven-day holiday was created by Black Studies professor Dr. Maulana Karenga in 1966 in the U.S., to reaffirm African values and serve as a communal celebration among African peoples in the diaspora. Modeled on first-fruits celebrations, it reflects seven principles, the *Nguzo Saba:* unity, self-determination, collective work and responsibility, cooperative economics, purpose, creativity, and faith.

Christian and Secular Holidays, 2005–2008

Year	Ash Wednesday	Easter	Pentecost	Labor Day	Election Day	Thanksgiving	1st Sun. Advent
2005	Feb. 9	March 27	May 15	Sept. 5	Nov. 8	Nov. 24	Nov. 27
2006	March 1	April 16	June 4	Sept. 4	Nov. 7	Nov. 23	Dec. 3
2007	Feb. 21	April 8	May 27	Sept. 3	Nov. 1	Nov. 22	Dec. 2
2008	Feb. 6	March 23	May 11	Sept. 1	Nov. 4	Nov. 27	Nov. 30

Shrove Tuesday: 1 day before Ash Wednesday. Palm Sunday: 7 days before Easter. Maundy Thursday: 3 days before Easter. Good Friday: 2 days before Easter. Holy Saturday: 1 day before Easter. Ascension Day: 10 days before Pentecost. Trinity Sunday: 7 days after Pentecost. Corpus Christi: 11 days after Pentecost.

Orthodox Holidays, 2005–2008

Year	Great Lent Begins	Pascha (Easter)	Ascension	Pentecost	Year	Great Lent Begins	Pascha (Easter)	Ascension	Pentecost
2005	March 14	May 1	June 9	June 19	2007	Feb. 19	April 8	May 17	May 27
2006	March 6	April 23	June 1	June 11	2008	March 10	April 27	June 5	June 15

Jewish Holidays, 2005–2008

Year	Purim[1]	1st day Passover[2]	1st day Shavuot[3]	1st day Rosh Hashanah[4]	Yom Kippur[5]	1st day Sukkot[6]	Shemini Atzeret[7]	1st day Hanukkah[8]
2005	March 25	April 24	June 13	Oct. 4	Oct. 13	Oct. 18	Oct. 25	Dec. 26
2006	March 14	April 13	June 2	Sept. 23	Oct. 2	Oct. 7	Oct. 14	Dec. 16
2007	March 4	April 3	May 23	Sept. 13	Sept. 22	Sept. 27	Oct. 4	Dec. 5
2008	March 21	April 20	June 9	Sept. 30	Oct. 9	Oct. 14	Oct. 21	Dec. 22

1. Feast of Lots. 2. Feast of Unleavened Bread. 3. Hebrew Pentecost; or Feast of Weeks, or of Harvest, or of First Fruits. 4. Jewish New Year. 5. Day of Atonement. 6. Feast of Tabernacles, or the Ingathering. 7. Assembly of the Eighth Day. 8. Festival of Lights.
NOTE: All holidays begin at sundown on the evening before the date given. Length of Jewish holidays: **Orthodox and Conservative:** *In Israel:* Purim: 1 day. Passover: 7 days; first and last are holy. Shavuot: 1 day. Rosh Hashanah: 2 days. Yom Kippur: 1 day. Sukkot: 7 days; first is holy. Shemini Atzeret: 1 day. Hanukkah: 8 days.   *Outside Israel:* Purim: 1 day. Passover: 8 days; first 2 and last 2 are holy. Shavuot: 2 days. Rosh Hashanah: 2 days. Yom Kippur: 1 day. Sukkot: 7 days; first 2 are holy. Shemini Atzeret: 2 days (2nd called Simchat Torah). Hanukkah: 8 days. **Reform:** Purim: 1 day. Passover: 7 days; first and last are holy. Shavuot: 1 day. Rosh Hashanah: 1 day. Yom Kippur: 1 day. Sukkot: 7 days; first is holy. Shemini Atzeret: 1 day. Hanukkah: 8 days.

Islamic Holidays, 2005–2008 (A.H. 1425–1429)

In the Year of the Hegira	Muharram (Islamic New Year)	Mawlid al-Nabi (Muhammad's Birthday)	Ramadan begins	Eid al-Fitr (Ramadan ends)	Eid al-Adha (Festival of Sacrifice)
A.H. 1426	Feb. 10, 2005	April 21, 2005	Oct. 5, 2005	Nov. 4, 2005	Jan. 10, 2006
A.H. 1427	Jan. 31, 2006	April 11, 2006	Sept. 24, 2006	Oct. 24, 2006	Dec. 31, 2006
A.H. 1428	Jan. 20, 2007	March 31, 2007	Sept. 13, 2007	Oct. 13, 2007	Dec. 20, 2007
A.H. 1429	Jan. 10, 2008	March 20, 2008	Sept. 2, 2008	Oct. 2, 2008	Dec. 9, 2008

NOTE: All holidays begin at sundown on the evening before the date given. The Islamic calendar is based on lunar observation; thus, the above dates may vary by one or two days. Dates apply to North America.

Hindu Festival Dates, 2006

Source: Indian Calendars for the 21st Century, by Pal Singh Purewal.

Jan. 14	Makar Sankranti	Aug. 9	Raksha Bandhan
Feb. 2	Vasant Panchami	Aug. 15	Sri Krishna Jayanti
Feb. 26	Maha Shivaratri Vrat (fast)	Aug. 27	Ganesh Chaturathi
March 14	Holi (last day)	Sept. 7	Saradhas begin
March 30	Bikarami Samvat (2063 begins)	Sept. 23	Asuj Navratras begin
March 30	Chetra Navratras begin	Oct. 2	Dassehra
April 6	Rama Navmi	Oct. 10	Karva Chauth Vrat (fast)
April 14	Vaisakhi (solar new year)	Oct. 21	Diwali (Festival of Lights)

Sikh Festival Dates, 2006

Source: Indian Calendars for the 21st Century, by Pal Singh Purewal.

Jan. 5	Birthday of Guru Gobind Singh Sahib	Sept. 1	First Parkash Guru Granth Sahib
Jan. 13	Maghi	Oct. 20	Installation of Holy Scriptures as Guru Granth
March 14	New Year's Day (Nanakshahi Era 538 begins)		Sahib
March 15	Hola Mohalla	Oct. 21	Bandi Chhor Divas (Diwali)
April 14	Vaisakhi (birth anniversary of Khalsa)	Nov. 5	Birthday of Guru Nanak Dev Sahib
June 16	Martyrdom of Guru Arjan Dev Sahib	Nov. 24	Martyrdom of Guru Tegh Bahadur Sahib

NOTE: Dates for Sikh holidays are determined according to the date of their observance in India.

Jain Festival Dates, 2006

Source: Indian Calendars for the 21st Century, by Pal Singh Purewal.

April 11	Sri Mahavir Jyanti	Oct. 7	Oli ends
April 30	Akshya Tritiya	Oct. 27	Jnana Panchami
Aug. 28	Samvatatsari	Nov. 5	Rathayatra
Sept. 30	Oli begins		

Chinese New Year

2003	Feb. 1	**2006**	Jan. 29	**2009**	Jan. 26	**2012**	Jan. 23
2004	Jan. 22	**2007**	Feb. 18	**2010**	Feb. 14	**2013**	Feb. 10
2005	Feb. 9	**2008**	Feb. 7	**2011**	Feb. 3	**2014**	Jan. 31

State Holidays

Jan. 6, Three Kings' Day: P.R.
Jan. 8, Battle of New Orleans Day: La.
Jan. 11, De Hostos's Birthday: P.R.
Jan. 19, Robert E. Lee's Birthday: Ark., Fla., Ky., La., S.C.; **(third Mon.):** Ala., Miss.
Jan. 19, Confederate Heroes Day: Tex.
Jan. (third Mon.), Lee-Jackson-King Day: Va.
Jan. 30, F. D. Roosevelt's Birthday: Ky.
Feb. 15, Susan B. Anthony's Birthday: Fla., Minn.
March (first Tues.), Town Meeting Day: Vt.
March 2, Texas Independence Day: Tex.
March (first Mon.), Casimir Pulaski's Birthday: Ill.
March 17, Evacuation Day: Mass. (in Suffolk County)
March 20 (first day of spring), Youth Day: Okla.
March 22, Abolition Day: P.R.
March 25, Maryland Day: Md.
March 26, Prince Jonah Kuhio Kalanianaole Day: Hawaii
March (last Mon.), Seward's Day: Alaska
April 2, Pascua Florida Day: Fla.
April 13, Thomas Jefferson's Birthday: Ala., Okla.
April 16, De Diego's Birthday: P.R.
April (third Mon.), Patriots' Day: Maine, Mass.
April 21, San Jacinto Day: Tex.
April 22, Arbor Day: Nebr.
April 22, Oklahoma Day: Okla.
April 26, Confederate Memorial Day: Fla., Ga.
April (fourth Mon.), Fast Day: N.H.
April (last Mon.), Confederate Memorial Day: Ala., Miss.
May 1, Bird Day: Okla.
May 8, Truman Day: Mo.
May 11, Minnesota Day: Minn.
May 20, Mecklenburg Independence Day: N.C.

June (first Mon.), Jefferson Davis's Birthday: Ala., Miss.
June 3, Jefferson Davis's Birthday: Fla., S.C.
June 3, Confederate Memorial Day: Ky., La.
June 9, Senior Citizens Day: Okla.
June 11, King Kamehameha I Day: Hawaii
June 15, Separation Day: Del.
June 17, Bunker Hill Day: Mass. (in Suffolk County)
June 19, Emancipation Day: Tex.
June 20, West Virginia Day: W.Va.
July 17, Muñoz Rivera's Birthday: P.R.
July 24, Pioneer Day: Utah
July 25, Constitution Day: P.R.
July 27, Barbosa's Birthday: P.R.
Aug. (first Sun.), American Family Day: Ariz.
Aug. (first Mon.), Colorado Day: Colo.
Aug. (second Mon.), Victory Day: R.I.
Aug. 16, Bennington Battle Day: Vt.
Aug. (third Friday), Admission Day: Hawaii
Aug. 27, Lyndon B. Johnson's Birthday: Tex.
Aug. 30, Huey P. Long Day: La.
Sept. 9, Admission Day: Calif.
Sept. 12, Defenders' Day: Md.
Sept. 16, Cherokee Strip Day: Okla.
Sept. (first Sat. after full moon), Indian Day: Okla.
Oct. 10, Leif Eriksson Day: Minn.
Oct. 10, Oklahoma Historical Day: Okla.
Oct. 18, Alaska Day: Alaska
Oct. 31, Nevada Day: Nev.
Nov. 4, Will Rogers Day: Okla.
Nov. (week of the 16th), Oklahoma Heritage Week: Okla.
Nov. 19, Discovery Day: P.R.
Dec. 7, Delaware Day: Del.

Birthstones

Month	Stone	Month	Stone	Month	Stone
January	Garnet	June	Pearl, Alexandrite, or	October	Opal or Tourmaline
February	Amethyst		Moonstone	November	Topaz or Citrine
March	Aquamarine or Bloodstone	July	Ruby or Star Ruby	December	Turquoise, Lapis Lazuli,
April	Diamond	August	Peridot or Sardonyx		Blue Zircon, or Blue
May	Emerald	September	Sapphire or Star Sapphire		Topaz

Source: Jewelry Industry Council.

Traditional Wedding Anniversary Gift List

Anniv.	Gift	Anniv.	Gift	Anniv.	Gift	Anniv.	Gift
1st	Paper	7th	Copper, wool	13th	Lace	35th	Coral
2nd	Cotton	8th	Bronze, pottery	14th	Ivory	40th	Ruby
3rd	Leather	9th	Pottery, willow	15th	Crystal	45th	Sapphire
4th	Fruit, flowers	10th	Tin	20th	China	50th	Gold
5th	Wood	11th	Steel	25th	Silver	55th	Emerald
6th	Sugar	12th	Silk, linen	30th	Pearl	60th	Diamond

National Holidays Around the World

Afghanistan, Aug. 19
Albania, Nov. 28
Algeria, Nov. 1
Andorra, Sept. 8
Angola, Nov. 11
Antigua and Barbuda, Nov. 1
Argentina, May 25
Armenia, Sept. 21
Australia, Jan. 26
Austria, Oct. 26
Azerbaijan, May 28
Bahamas, July 10
Bahrain, Dec. 16
Bangladesh, March 26
Barbados, Nov. 30
Belarus, July 3
Belgium, July 21
Belize, Sept. 21
Benin, Aug. 1
Bhutan, Dec. 17
Bolivia, Aug. 6
Bosnia and Herzegovina, Nov. 25
Botswana, Sept. 30
Brazil, Sept. 7
Brunei, Feb. 23
Bulgaria, March 3
Burkina Faso, Dec. 11
Burundi, July 1
Cambodia, Nov. 9
Cameroon, May 20
Canada, July 1
Cape Verde, July 5
Central African Rep., Dec. 1
Chad, Aug. 11
Chile, Sept. 18
China, People's Rep. of, Oct. 1
Colombia, July 20
Comoros, July 6
Congo, Aug. 15
Congo, Dem. Rep. of, June 30
Costa Rica, Sept. 15
Côte d'Ivoire, Aug. 7
Croatia, Oct. 8
Cuba, Dec. 10
Cyprus, Oct. 1
Czech Rep., Oct. 28
Denmark, June 5

Djibouti, June 27
Dominica, Nov. 3
Dominican Rep., Feb. 27
East Timor, Nov. 28
Ecuador, Aug. 10
Egypt, July 23
El Salvador, Sept. 15
Equatorial Guinea, Oct. 12
Eritrea, May 24
Estonia, Feb. 24
Ethiopia, May 28
Fiji, 2nd Mon. of Oct.
Finland, Dec. 6
France, July 14
Gabon, March 12
Gambia, The, Feb. 18
Georgia, May 26
Germany, Oct. 3
Ghana, March 6
Greece, March 25
Grenada, Feb. 7
Guatemala, Sept. 15
Guinea, Oct. 2
Guinea-Bissau, Sept. 24
Guyana, Feb. 23
Haiti, Jan. 1
Honduras, Sept. 15
Hungary, Aug. 20
Iceland, June 17
India, Jan. 26
Indonesia, Aug. 17
Iran, April 1
Ireland, March 17
Israel, April or May[1]
Italy, June 2
Jamaica, Aug. 6
Japan, Dec. 23
Jordan, May 25
Kazakhstan, Dec. 16
Kenya, Dec. 12
Kiribati, July 12
Korea (North), Sept. 9
Korea (South), Aug. 15
Kuwait, Feb. 25
Kyrgyzstan, Aug. 31
Laos, Dec. 2
Latvia, Nov. 18
Lebanon, Nov. 22
Lesotho, Oct. 4
Liberia, July 26

Libya, Sept. 1
Liechtenstein, Aug. 15
Lithuania, Feb. 16
Luxembourg, June 23
Macedonia, Aug. 2
Madagascar, June 26
Malawi, July 6
Malaysia, Aug. 31
Maldives, July 26
Mali, Sept. 22
Malta, Sept. 21
Marshall Islands, May 1
Mauritania, Nov. 28
Mauritius, March 12
Mexico, Sept. 16
Micronesia, Federated States of, May 10
Moldova, Aug. 27
Monaco, Nov. 19
Mongolia, July 11
Morocco, July 30
Mozambique, June 25
Myanmar (Burma), Jan. 4
Namibia, March 21
Nauru, Jan. 31
Nepal, July 7
Netherlands, April 30
New Zealand, Feb. 6
Nicaragua, Sept. 15
Niger, Dec. 18
Nigeria, Oct. 1
Norway, May 17
Oman, Nov. 18
Pakistan, March 23
Palau, July 9
Panama, Nov. 3
Papua New Guinea, Sept. 16
Paraguay, May 14–15
Peru, July 28
Philippines, June 12
Poland, May 3
Portugal, June 10
Qatar, Sept. 3
Romania, Dec. 1
Russia, June 12
Rwanda, July 1
St. Kitts and Nevis, Sept. 19
St. Lucia, Feb. 22
St. Vincent and the Grenadines, Oct. 27

Samoa, June 1
San Marino, Sept. 3
São Tomé and Príncipe, July 12
Saudi Arabia, Sept. 23
Senegal, April 4
Serbia and Montenegro, April 27
Seychelles, June 18
Sierra Leone, April 27
Singapore, Aug. 9
Slovakia, Sept. 1
Slovenia, June 25
Solomon Islands, July 7
Somalia, July 1
South Africa, April 27
Spain, Oct. 12
Sri Lanka, Feb. 4
Sudan, Jan. 1
Suriname, Nov. 25
Swaziland, Sept. 6
Sweden, June 6
Switzerland, Aug. 1
Syria, April 17
Taiwan, Oct. 10
Tajikistan, Sept. 9
Tanzania, April 26
Thailand, Dec. 5
Togo, April 27
Tonga, June 4
Trinidad and Tobago, Aug. 31
Tunisia, March 20
Turkey, Oct. 29
Turkmenistan, Oct. 27
Tuvalu, Oct. 1
Uganda, Oct. 9
Ukraine, Aug. 24
United Arab Emirates, Dec. 2
United States, July 4
Uruguay, Aug. 25
Uzbekistan, Sept. 1
Vanuatu, July 30
Vatican, April 24
Venezuela, July 5
Vietnam, Sept. 2
Yemen, May 22
Zambia, Oct. 24
Zimbabwe, April 18

1. Variable holiday, falling on a different date each year. *Source:* CIA World Factbook.

Major Religions of the World

There are twelve classical world religions—those religions most often included in history of world religion surveys and studied in world religions classes: Baha'i, Buddhism, Christianity, Confucianism, Hinduism, Islam, Jainism, Judaism, Shinto, Sikhism, Taoism, and Zoroastrianism. Here are overviews of nine of these classical religions.

Judaism

Judaism is the oldest of the monotheistic faiths. It affirms the existence of one God, Yahweh, who entered into covenant with the descendants of Abraham, God's chosen people. Judaism's holy writings reveal how God has been present with them throughout their history. These writings are known as the Torah, specifically the five books of Moses, but most broadly conceived as the Hebrew Scriptures (traditionally called the Old Testament by Christians) and the compilation of oral tradition known as the Talmud (which includes the Mishnah, the oral law).

According to Scripture, the Hebrew patriarch Abraham (20th century? B.C.) founded the faith that would become known as Judaism. He obeyed the call of God to depart northern Mesopotamia and travel to Canaan. God promised to bless his descendants if they remained faithful in worship. Abraham's line descended through Isaac, then Jacob (also called Israel; his descendants came to be called Israelites). According to Scripture, 12 families that descended from Jacob migrated to Egypt, where they were enslaved. They were led out of bondage (13th century? B.C.) by Moses, who united them in the worship of Yahweh. The Hebrews returned to Canaan after a 40-year sojourn in the desert, conquering from the local peoples the "promised land" that God had provided for them.

The 12 tribes of Israel lived in a covenant association during the period of the judges (1200?–1000? B.C.), leaders known for wisdom and heroism. Saul first established a monarchy (r. 1025?–1005? B.C.); his successor, David (r. 1005?–965? B.C.), unified the land of Israel and made Jerusalem its religious and political center. Under his son, Solomon (r. 968?–928? B.C.), a golden era culminated in the building of a temple, replacing the portable sanctuary in use until that time. Following Solomon's death, the kingdom was split into Israel in the north and Judah in the south. Political conflicts resulted in the conquest of Israel by Assyria (721 B.C.) and the

defeat of Judah by Babylon (586 B.C.). Jerusalem and its temple were destroyed, and many Judeans were exiled to Babylon.

During the era of the kings, the prophets were active in Israel and Judah. Their writings emphasize faith in Yahweh as God of Israel and of the entire universe, and they warn of the dangers of worshiping other gods. They also cry out for social justice.

The Judeans were permitted to return in 539 B.C. to Judea, where they were ruled as a Persian province. Though temple and cult were restored in Jerusalem, during the exile a new class of religious leaders had emerged—the scribes. They became rivals to the temple hierarchy and would eventually evolve into the party known as the Pharisees.

Persian rule ended when Alexander the Great conquered Palestine in 332 B.C. After his death, rule of Judea alternated between Egypt and Syria. When the Syrian ruler Antiochus IV Epiphanes tried to prevent the practice of Judaism, a revolt was led by the Maccabees (a Jewish family), winning Jewish independence in 128 B.C. The Romans conquered Jerusalem in 63 B.C.

During this period the Sadducees (temple priests) and the Pharisees (teachers of the law in the synagogues) offered different interpretations of Judaism. Smaller groups that emerged were the Essenes, a religious order; the Apocalyptists, who expected divine deliverance led by the Messiah; and the Zealots, who were prepared to fight for national independence. Hellenism also influenced Judaism at this time.

When the Zealots revolted, the Roman armies destroyed Jerusalem and its temple (A.D. 70). The Jews were scattered in the Diaspora (dispersion) and experienced much persecution. Rabbinic Judaism, developed according to Pharisaic practice and centered on Torah and synagogue, became the primary expression of faith. The Scriptures became codified, and the Talmud took shape. In the 12th century Maimonides formulated the influential 13 Articles of Faith, including belief in God, God's oneness and lack of physical or other form, the changelessness of

Top Ten Organized Religions of the World

Statistics of the world's religions are only very rough approximations. Aside from Christianity, few religions, if any, attempt to keep statistical records; and even Protestants and Catholics employ different methods of counting members.

Religion	Members	Percentage	Religion	Members	Percentage
Christianity	2.1 billion	33.0%	Judaism	15 million	0.2%
Islam	1.3 billion	20.1	Baha'ism	7.5 million	0.1
Hinduism	851 million	13.3	Confucianism	6.4 million	0.1
Buddhism	375 million	5.9	Jainism	4.5 million	0.1
Sikhism	25 million	0.4	Shintoism	2.8 million	0.0

NOTES: As of mid-2004. This list includes only organized religions and excludes more loosely defined groups such as Chinese or African traditional religions. Source: Encyclopedia Britannica.

Torah, restoration of the monarchy under the Messiah, and resurrection of the dead.

Two branches of European Judaism developed during the Middle Ages: the Sephardic, based in Spain and with an affinity to Babylonian Jews; and the Ashkenazic, based in Franco-German lands and affiliated with Rome and Palestine. Two forms of Jewish mysticism also arose at this time: medieval Hasidism and attention to the Kabbalah (a mystical interpretation of Scripture).

After a respite during the 18th-century Enlightenment, anti-Semitism again plagued European Jews in the 19th century, sparking the Zionist movement that culminated in the founding of the state of Israel in 1948. The Holocaust of World War II took the lives of more than 6 million Jews.

Jews today continue synagogue worship, which includes readings from the Law and the Prophets and prayers, such as the Shema (Hear, O Israel) and the Amidah (the 18 Benedictions). Religious life is guided by the commandments of the Torah, which include the practice of circumcision and Sabbath observance.

Present-day Judaism has three main expressions: Orthodox, Conservative, and Reform. Reform movements, resulting from the Haskala (Jewish Enlightenment) of the 18th century, began in western Europe but took root in North America. Reform Jews do not hold the oral law (Talmud) to be a divine revelation, and they emphasize ethical and moral teachings. Orthodox Jews follow the traditional faith and practice with great seriousness. They follow a strict kosher diet and keep the Sabbath with care. Conservative Judaism, which developed in the mid-18th century, holds the Talmud to be authoritative and follows most traditional practices, yet tries to make Judaism relevant for each generation, believing that change and tradition can complement each other. Because the Torah assumes belief in God but does not require it, a strong secular movement also exists within Judaism, including atheist and agnostic elements.

In general, Jews do not proselytize, but they do welcome newcomers to their faith.

Christianity

Christianity is a monotheistic religion founded by the followers of Jesus of Nazareth. Jesus, a Jew, was born in about 7 B.C. and assumed his public life, probably after his 30th year, in Galilee. The New Testament Gospels describe Jesus as a teacher and miracle worker. He proclaimed the kingdom of God, a future reality that is at the same time already present. Jesus set the requirements for participation in the kingdom of God as a change of heart and repentance for sins, love of God and neighbor, and concern for justice. Circa A.D. 30 he was executed on a cross in Jerusalem, a brutal form of punishment for those considered a political threat to the Roman Empire.

After his death his followers came to believe in him as the Christ, the Messiah. The Gospels report his resurrection and how the risen Jesus was witnessed by many of his followers. The apostle Paul helped spread the new faith in his missionary travels. Historically, Christianity arose out of Judaism and claims that Jesus fulfilled many of the promises of the Hebrew Scripture (often referred to as the Old Testament).

The new religion spread rapidly throughout the Roman Empire. In its first two centuries, Christianity began to take shape as an organization, developing distinctive doctrine, liturgy, and ministry. By the fourth century the Christian church had taken root in countries stretching from Spain in the West to Persia and India in the East. Christians had been subject to persecution by the Roman state, but gained tolerance under Constantine the Great (A.D. 313). The church became favored under his successors, and in 380 the emperor Theodosius proclaimed Christianity the state religion. Other religions were suppressed.

Because differences in doctrine threatened to divide the church, a standard Christian creed was formulated by bishops at successive ecumenical councils, the first of which was held in A.D. 325 (Nicaea). Important doctrines were defined concerning the Trinity—in other words, that there is one God in three persons: Father, Son, and Holy Spirit (Constantinople, A.D. 381), and the nature of Christ as both divine and human (Chalcedon, A.D. 541). Christians came to accept both Hebrew Scripture and the New Testament as authoritative. The New Testament comprises four Gospels (narratives of Jesus' life), 21 Epistles, The Acts of the Apostles, and Revelation.

Because of differences between Christians of the East and West, the unity of the church was broken in 1054. The religious center for the Eastern Orthodox Church was Constantinople, and the Roman Catholic Church defined doctrine and practice for Christians in the West. In 1517 the Reformation began, which ultimately caused a schism in the Western church. Reformers wished to correct certain practices within the Roman church, but they also came to view the Christian faith in a distinctly new way. The major Protestant denominations (Lutheran, Presbyterian, Reformed, and Anglican [Episcopalian]) thus came into being. Over the centuries, numerous denominations have broken with these major traditions, resulting in a spectrum of Christian expression.

In the 21st century, many Christians hope to regain a sense of unity through dialogue and cooperation among different traditions. The ecumenical movement led to the formation of the World Council of Churches in 1948 (Amsterdam), which has since been joined by many denominations.

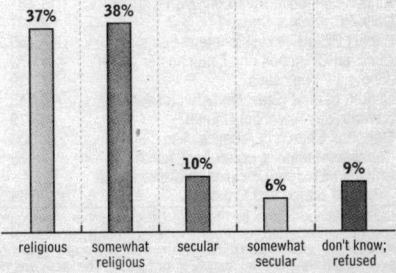

Outlook of U.S. Adult Population: Religious or Secular

"When it comes to your outlook, do you regard yourself as..."

religious	somewhat religious	secular	somewhat secular	don't know; refused
37%	38%	10%	6%	9%

Source: Barry A. Kosmin, Egon Mayer, & Ariela Keysar
Copyright © American Religious Identification Survey, 2001

Through its missionary activity Christianity has spread to most parts of the globe.

Eastern Orthodoxy

Eastern Orthodoxy comprises the faith and practices stemming from ancient churches in the eastern part of the Roman Empire. It encompasses Orthodox churches in communion with the see of Constantinople.

The Orthodox, Catholic, Apostolic Church is the direct descendant of the Byzantine state church and consists of independent national churches that are united by doctrine, liturgy, and hierarchical organization (church leaders include deacons and priests, who may either, be married or be monks before ordination, and bishops, who must be celibates). The heads of these churches are called patriarchs or metropolitans. Rivalry between the pope of Rome and the patriarch of Constantinople, as well as differences that existed for centuries between the eastern and western parts of the empire, led to a schism in 1054. The mutual excommunication pronounced in that year was lifted in 1965, however, and a climate of better understanding has ensued. Orthodox churches belong to the World Council of Churches.

Largest U.S. Churches, 2004

Denomination name	Members (thousands)
The Roman Catholic Church	66,407
Southern Baptist Convention	16,248
United Methodist Church, The	8,251
Church of God in Christ, The	5,500
Church of Jesus Christ of Latter-day Saints, The	5,411
Evangelical Lutheran Church in America	5,038
National Baptist Convention, USA, Inc	5,000
National Baptist Convention of America, Inc	3,500
Presbyterian Church (USA)	3,407
Assemblies of God	2,687
Lutheran Church—Missouri Synod (LCMS), The	2,513
African Methodist Episcopal Church	2,500
National Missionary Baptist Convention of America	2,500
Progressive National Baptist Convention, Inc	2,500
Episcopal Church	2,334
Churches of Christ	1,500
Greek Orthodox Archdiocese of America	1,500
Pentecostal Assemblies of the World, Inc	1,500
American Baptist Churches in the USA	1,484
African Methodist Episcopal Zion Church	1,431
United Church of Christ	1,331
Baptist Bible Fellowship International	1,200
Christian Churches and Churches of Christ	1,072
Jehovah's Witnesses	1,022
Church of God (Cleveland, Tennessee)	945
Seventh-day Adventist Church	919
Orthodox Church in America, The	900
Christian Methodist Episcopal Church	850
Christian Church (Disciples of Christ) in the United States and Canada	786

NOTE: Includes the self-reported membership of religious bodies with 650,000 or more as reported to the Yearbook of American and Canadian Churches. Groups may be excluded if they do not supply information. The data are not standardized so comparisons between groups are difficult. The definition of "church member" is determined by the religious body. *Source: 2004 Yearbook of American and Canadian Churches.*

The Eastern Orthodox churches recognize only the canons of the seven ecumenical councils (325–787) as binding for faith, and they reject doctrines that have been added in the West.

The central worship service is called the Liturgy, which is understood as representing God's acts of salvation. Its center is the celebration of the Eucharist, or Lord's Supper. Icons (sacred pictures) have a special place in Orthodox worship. The mother of Christ, angels, and saints are venerated. The Orthodox Church and the Western Catholic Church recognize the same number of sacraments.

Orthodox churches are found in Greece, Turkey, Russia, the Balkans, and other parts of the former Soviet Union. In this century Orthodox faith has spread to western Europe and other parts of the world, particularly North America.

Eastern Rite Churches

These include the Uniate Churches that recognize the authority of the pope but keep their own traditional liturgies and those churches dating back to the fifth century that emancipated themselves from the Byzantine state church. They include the Melchites, Syrian Catholics, Maronites (Arab Christians in Lebanon), Catholic Copts and Ethiopians, the autonomous Nestorian Church, and others.

Roman Catholicism

Roman Catholicism comprises the beliefs and practices of the Roman Catholic Church. It stands under the authority of the bishop of Rome, the pope, and is led by him and bishops who are held to be, through ordination, successors of Peter and the apostles. Doctrine and sacraments are administered by the hierarchy of archbishops, bishops, priests, and deacons. As successor to Peter, the pope is considered the Vicar of Christ. Roman Catholics believe their church to be the one, holy, catholic, and apostolic church, possessing all the properties of the one, true church of Christ.

The faith of the church is understood to be identical with that taught by Christ and his apostles and contained in the Bible and tradition. New definitions of doctrines, such as the Immaculate Conception of Mary (1854) and the bodily

Roman Catholic Church Hierarchy

The Catholic clergy is organized in a strict, sometimes overlapping hierarchy:

Pope: Head of the church, he is based at the Vatican.

Cardinal: Appointed by the pope, there are 178 cardinals worldwide.

Archbishop: An archbishop is a bishop of a main or metropolitan diocese, also called an archdiocese.

Bishop: A bishop, like a priest, is ordained to this station.

Priest: An ordained minister who can administer most of the sacraments.

Deacon: A transitional deacon is a seminarian studying for the priesthood. A permanent deacon can be married and assists a priest by performing some of the sacraments.

Source: Time Magazine.

Assumption of Mary (1950), have been declared by popes, however. At Vatican Council I (1870) the pope was proclaimed "endowed with infallibility, *ex cathedra*, in other words, when exercising the office of pastor and teacher of all Christians."

The center of Roman Catholic worship is the celebration of the Mass, the Eucharist, which is the commemoration of Christ's sacrificial death and resurrection. Other sacraments are baptism, confirmation, penance, matrimony, anointing of the sick (formerly known as extreme unction), and holy orders. The Virgin Mary and the other saints, and their relics, are venerated, and prayers are made to them to intercede with God, in whose presence they are believed to dwell.

The Roman Catholic Church is the largest Christian organization in the world, found in most countries.

Vatican Council II (1962–1965) sought to "update" the church, bringing about changes in practice and more deeply involving the laity. The immensely popular Pope John Paul II (1978–2005) took a more conservative course and reached out to Catholics worldwide through his extensive travels.

Protestantism

Protestantism encompasses the Christian churches that separated from Rome during the Reformation in the 16th century. This movement was initiated by an Augustinian monk, Martin Luther. The term *Protestant* was originally applied to followers of Luther, who protested at the Diet of Spires (1529) against the decree that prohibited all further ecclesiastical reforms. Other influential reformers included John Calvin, Ulrich Zwingli, and John Knox. Protestantism rejected attempts to tie God's revelation to earthly institutions and strictly adhered to the Word of God as sole authority in matters of faith and practice *(sola scriptura)*. Central in the reformers' understanding of the biblical message is the justification of the sinner by faith alone. The church is understood as a fellowship, and the priesthood of all believers is stressed.

The Augsburg Confession (1530) was the principal statement of Lutheran faith and practice. It became a model for other Protestant confessions of faith. Major Protestant denominations include the Lutheran, Reformed (Calvinist), Presbyterian, and Anglican (Episcopalian). Innumerable sects and denominations sprang from these roots, including Quakers, Baptists, Pentecostals, Congregationalists, Methodists, and nondenominational assemblies.

Since the latter part of the 19th century, national councils of churches have been established in many countries, for example, the Federal Council of Churches of Christ in America in 1908. Churches of a particular denomination have joined in federations and world alliances, beginning with the Anglican Lambeth Conference in 1867.

Protestant missionary activity, particularly strong in the 19th century, resulted in the founding of many churches in Asia and Africa. The ecumenical movement, which originated with Protestant missions, aims at unity among Christians and churches.

Islam

Islam, one of the three major monotheistic faiths, was founded in Arabia by Muhammad between 610 and 632. There are an estimated 5.1 million Muslims in North America and 1.3 billion Muslims worldwide.

Muhammad was born in A.D. 570 at Mecca and belonged to the Quraysh tribe, which was active in the caravan trade. At the age of 25 he joined the trade from Mecca to Syria in the employment of a rich widow, Khadija, whom he later married. Critical of the lax moral standards and polytheistic practices of the inhabitants of Mecca, he began to lead a contemplative life in the desert. In a dramatic religious vision, the angel Gabriel announced to Muhammad that he was to be a prophet. Encouraged by Khadija, he devoted himself to the reform of religion and society. Polytheism was to be abandoned. But leaders of the Quraysh generally rejected his teaching, and Muhammad gained only a small following and suffered persecution. He eventually fled Mecca.

The Hegira *(Hijra,* meaning "emigration") of Muhammad from Mecca, where he was not honored, to Medina, where he was well received, occurred in 622 and marks the beginning of the Muslim era. After a number of military conflicts with Mecca, in 630 he marched on Mecca and conquered it. Muhammad died at Medina in 632. His grave there has since been a place of pilgrimage.

Muhammad's followers, called Muslims, revered him as the prophet of Allah (God), the only God. Muslims consider Muhammad to be the last in the line of prophets that included Abraham and Jesus. Islam spread quickly, stretching from Spain in the west to India in the east within a century after the prophet's death. Sources of the Islamic faith are the Qur'an (Koran), regarded as the uncreated, eternal Word of God, and tradition *(hadith)* regarding sayings and deeds of the prophet.

Islam means "surrender to the will of Allah," the all-powerful, who determines humanity's fate. Good deeds will be rewarded at the Last Judgment in paradise, and evil deeds will be punished in hell.

The Five Pillars, or primary duties, of Islam are profession of faith; prayer, to be performed five times a day; almsgiving to the poor and the mosque (house of worship); fasting during daylight hours in the month of Ramadan; and pilgrimage to Mecca (the *hajj*) at least once in a Muslim's lifetime, if it is physically and financially possible. The pilgrimage includes homage to the ancient shrine of the Ka'aba, the most sacred site in Islam.

U.S. Protestant Groups

According to the Hartford Institute for Religion Research, U.S. Protestant groups are commonly divided into four broad categories:

Liberal Protestant: Episcopal, Presbyterian, Unitarian Universalist, United Church of Christ

Moderate Protestant: American Baptist, Disciples of Christ, Evangelical Lutheran, Mennonite, Reformed Church in America, United Methodist

Evangelical Protestant: Assemblies of God, Christian Reformed, Nazarene, Churches of Christ, Independent Christian Churches (Instrumental), Seventh-day Adventist, Southern Baptist

Historically Black Protestant: Various denominations

Countries with the Largest Muslim Populations	
1. Indonesia	6. Iran
2. Pakistan	7. Egypt
3. India	8. Nigeria
4. Bangladesh	9. Algeria
5. Turkey	10. Morocco

Muslims gather for corporate worship on Fridays. Prayers and a sermon take place at the mosque, which is also a center for teaching of the Qur'an. The community leader, the *imam*, is considered a teacher and prayer leader.

Islam succeeded in uniting an Arab world of separate tribes and castes, but disagreements concerning the succession of the prophet caused a division in Islam between two groups, Sunnis and Shi'ites. The Shi'ites rejected the first three successors to Muhammad as usurpers, claiming the fourth, Muhammad's son-in-law Ali, as the rightful leader. The Sunnis (from the word *tradition*), the largest division of Islam (today more than 80%), believe in the legitimacy of the first three successors. Among these, other sects arose (such as the conservative Wahhabi of Saudi Arabia), as well as different schools of theology. Another development within Islam, beginning in the eighth and ninth centuries, was Sufism, a form of mysticism. This movement was influential for many centuries and was instrumental in the spread of Islam in Asia and Africa.

Islam has expanded greatly under Muhammad's successors. It is the principal religion of the Middle East, Asia, and the northern half of Africa.

Hinduism

Hinduism is the major religion of India, practiced by more than 80% of the population. In contrast to other religions, it has no founder. Considered the oldest religion in the world, it dates back, perhaps, to prehistoric times.

No single creed or doctrine binds Hindus together. Intellectually there is complete freedom of belief, and one can be monotheist, polytheist, or atheist. Hinduism is a syncretic religion, welcoming and incorporating a variety of outside influences.

The most ancient sacred texts of the Hindu religion are written in Sanskrit and called the *Vedas* (*vedah* means "knowledge"). There are four Vedic books, of which the Rig-Veda is the oldest. It discusses multiple gods, the universe, and creation. The dates of these works are unknown (1000 B.C.?). Present-day Hindus rarely refer to these texts but do venerate them.

The Upanishads (dated 1000–300 B.C.), commentaries on the Vedic texts, speculate on the origin of the universe and the nature of deity, and *atman* (the individual soul) and its relationship to *Brahman* (the universal soul). They introduce the doctrine of *karma* and recommend meditation and the practice of yoga.

Further important sacred writings include the Epics, which contain legendary stories about gods and humans. They are the Mahabharata (composed between 200 B.C. and A.D. 200) and the Ramayana. The former includes the Bhagavad-Gita (Song of the Lord), an influential text that describes the three paths to salvation. The Puranas (stories in verse, probably written between the 6th and 13th centuries) detail myths of Hindu gods and heroes and also comment on religious practice and cosmology.

According to Hindu beliefs, Brahman is the principle and source of the universe. This divine intelligence pervades all beings, including the individual soul. Thus the many Hindu deities are manifestations of the one Brahman. Hinduism is based on the concept of reincarnation, in which all living beings, from plants on earth to gods above, are caught in a cosmic cycle of becoming and perishing.

Life is determined by the law of karma—one is reborn to a higher level of existence based on moral behavior in a previous phase of existence. Life on earth is regarded as transient and a burden. The goal of existence is liberation from the cycle of rebirth and death and entrance into the indescribable state of *moksha* (liberation).

The practice of Hinduism consists of rites and ceremonies centering on birth, marriage, and death. There are many Hindu temples, which are considered to be dwelling places of the deities and to which people bring offerings. Places of pilgrimage include Benares on the Ganges, the most sacred river in India. Of the many Hindu deities, the most popular are the cults of Vishnu, Shiva, and Shakti, and their various incarnations. Also important is Brahma, the creator god. Hindus also venerate human saints.

Orthodox Hindu society in India was divided into four major hereditary classes: (1) the Brahmin (priestly and learned class); (2) the Kshatriya (military, professional, ruling, and governing occupations); (3) the Vaishya (landowners, merchants, and business occupations); and (4) the Sudra (artisans, laborers, and peasants). Below the Sudra was a fifth group, the Untouchables (lowest menial occupations and no social standing). The Indian government banned discrimination against the Untouchables in the constitution of India in 1950. Observance of class and caste distinctions varies throughout India.

In modern times work has been done to reform and revive Hinduism. One of the outstanding reformers was Ramakrishna (1836–1886), who inspired many followers, one of whom founded the Ramakrishna mission. The mission is active both in India and in other countries and is known for its scholarly and humanitarian works.

Buddhism

Buddhism was founded in the fourth or fifth century B.C. in northern India by a man known traditionally as Siddhartha (meaning "he who has reached the goal") Gautama, the son of a warrior prince. Some scholars believe that he lived from 563 to 483 B.C., though his exact life span is uncertain. Troubled by the inevitability of suffering in human life, he left home and a pampered life at the age of 29 to wander as an ascetic, seeking religious insight and a solution to the struggles of human existence. He passed through many trials and practiced extreme self-denial. Finally, while meditating under the bodhi tree ("tree of perfect knowledge"), he reached enlightenment and taught his followers about his new spiritual understanding.

Gautama's teachings differed from the Hindu faith prevalent in India at the time. Whereas in Hinduism the Brahmin caste alone performed religious functions and attained the highest spiritual understanding,

Gautama's beliefs were more egalitarian, accessible to all who wished to be enlightened. At the core of his understanding were the Four Noble Truths: (1) all living beings suffer; (2) the origin of this suffering is desire—for material possessions, power, and so on; (3) desire can be overcome; and (4) there is a path that leads to release from desire. This way is called the Noble Eightfold Path: right views, right intention, right speech, right action, right livelihood, right effort, right concentration, and right ecstasy.

Gautama promoted the concept of *anatman* (that a person has no actual self) and the idea that existence is characterized by impermanence. This realization helps one let go of desire for transient things. Still, Gautama did not recommend extreme self-denial but rather a disciplined life called the Middle Way. Like the Hindus, he believed that existence consisted of reincarnation, a cycle of birth and death. He held that it could be broken only by reaching complete detachment from worldly cares. Then the soul could be released into *nirvana* (literally "blowing out")—an indescribable state of total transcendence. Gautama traveled to preach the *dharma* (sacred truth) and was recognized as the Buddha (enlightened one). After his death his followers continued to develop doctrine and practice, which came to center on the Three Jewels: the *dharma* (the sacred teachings of Buddhism), the *sangha* (the community of followers, which now includes nuns, monks, and laity), and the Buddha. Under the patronage of the Mauryan emperor Ashoka (third century B.C.), Buddhism spread throughout India and to other parts of Asia. Monasteries were established, as well as temples dedicated to Buddha; at shrines his relics were venerated. Though by the fourth century A.D. Buddhist presence in India had dwindled, it flourished in other parts of Asia.

Numerous Buddhist sects have emerged. The oldest, called the Theravada (Way of the Elders) tradition, interprets Buddha as a great sage but not a deity. It emphasizes meditation and ritual practices that help the individual become an *arhat*, an enlightened being. Its followers emphasize the authority of the earliest Buddhist scriptures, the Tripitaka (Three Baskets), a compilation of sermons, rules for celibates, and doctrine. This sect is prevalent in Southeast Asia and Sri Lanka. It is sometimes called the Hinayana (Lesser Vehicle) tradition (once considered a pejorative term).

Between the second century B.C. and the second century A.D., the Mahayana (Greater Vehicle) tradition refocused Buddhism to concentrate less on individual attainment of enlightenment and more on concern for humanity. It promotes the ideal of the *bodhisattva* (enlightened being), who shuns entering nirvana until all sentient beings can do so as well, willingly remaining in the painful cycle of birth and death to perform works of compassion. Members of this tradition conceive of Buddha as an eternal being to whom prayers can be made; other Buddhas are revered as well, adding a polytheistic dimension to the religion. Numerous sects have developed from the Mahayana tradition, which has been influential in China, Korea, and Japan.

A third broad tradition, variously called Vajrayana (Diamond Vehicle), Mantrayana (Vehicle of the Mantra), or Tantric Buddhism, offers a quicker, more demanding way to achieve nirvana. Because of its level of challenge—enabling one to reach enlightenment in one lifetime—it requires the guidance of a spiritual leader. It is most prominent in Tibet and Mongolia.

Zen Buddhism encourages individuals to seek the Buddha nature within themselves and to practice a disciplined form of sitting meditation in order to reach *satori*—spiritual enlightenment.

Sikhism

A major religion of India and the fifth-largest faith in the world, Sikhism emerged in the Punjab under the guidance of the guru Nanak (1469–1539?). This region had been influenced by the Hindu *bhakti* movement, which promoted both the idea that God comprises one reality alone as well as the practice of devotional singing and prayer. The Muslim mystical tradition of Sufism, with its emphasis on meditation, also had some prominence there. Drawing on these resources, Nanak forged a new spiritual path.

In his youth, Nanak began to compose hymns. At the age of 29, he had a mystical experience that led him to proclaim "There is no Hindu; there is no Muslim." A strict monotheist, he rejected Hindu polytheism but accepted the Hindu concept of life as a cycle of birth, death, and rebirth; *moksha,* release from this cycle into unity with God, could be achieved only with the help of a guru, or spiritual teacher. Nanak believed that communion with God could be gained through devotional repetition of the divine name, singing of hymns and praises, and adherence to a demanding ethical code. He rejected idols and the Hindu caste system; it became a custom for Sikhs of all social ranks to take meals together. These beliefs are still central to modern Sikhism.

Nanak was first in a line of ten gurus who shaped and inspired Sikhism. The fifth, Arjun (1563–1606), compiled hymns and other writings by earlier Sikh gurus, as well as medieval Hindu and Muslim saints, in the *Adi Granth* (First Book), or *Guru Granth Sahib* (the Granth Personified). This book became the sacred scripture of Sikhism. In addition to his spiritual leadership, Arjun wielded considerable secular power as he grappled with leaders of the Mughal Empire.

The tenth guru, Gobind Singh (1666–1708), was both a scholar and a military hero. He established the Khalsa (community of pure ones), an order that combined spiritual devotion, personal discipline, and ideals of military valor. Baptism initiates new members into the Khalsa. The *Adi Granth* took its final form under the supervision of Gobind Singh, as did the *Dasam Granth* (Tenth Book), a collection of prayers, poetry, and narrative. After the deaths of his four sons, Gobind Singh declared the line of gurus at an end. The *Adi Granth* would instead be reverenced in houses of worship, taking the place of a living guru.

Today, Sikhs worship at *gurdwaras* (temples), where the *Adi Granth* is the object of devotion. This book is consulted regarding questions of faith and practice. On certain occasions, it is recited in its entirety (requiring more than a day) or carried in procession; offerings may be placed before it. Worshipful singing, meditation, and focus on the divine name remain essential to spiritual life. Some Sikhs undertake pilgrimages to historical *gurdwaras,* such as the Golden Temple of Amritsar, that are associated with the gurus. Some become disciples of living saints. There is no established Sikh priesthood.

Confucianism

Confucius (K'ung Fu-tzu), born in the state of Lu (northern China), lived from 551 to 479 B.C. He was a brilliant teacher, viewing education not merely as the accumulation of knowledge but as a means of self-transformation. His legacy was a system of thought emphasizing education, proper behavior, and loyalty. His effect on Chinese culture was immense.

The teachings of Confucius are contained in the *Analects*, a collection of his sayings as remembered by his students. They were further developed by philosophers such as Mencius (Meng Tse, fl. 400 B.C.). Confucianism is little concerned with metaphysical discussion of religion or with spiritual attainments. It instead emphasizes moral conduct and right relationships in the human sphere.

Cultivation of virtue is a central tenet of Confucianism. Two important virtues are *jen*, a benevolent and humanitarian attitude, and *li*, maintaining proper relationships and rituals that enhance the life of the individual, the family, and the state. The "five relations," between king and subject, father and son, man and wife, older and younger brother, and friend and friend, are of utmost importance. These relationships are reinforced by participation in rituals, including the formal procedures of court life and religious rituals such as ancestor worship.

Confucius revolutionized educational thought in China. He believed that learning was not to be focused only on attaining the skills for a particular profession, but for growth in moral judgment and self-realization. Confucius's standards for the proper conduct of government shaped the statecraft of China for centuries. Hundreds of temples in honor of Confucius testify to his stature as sage and teacher.

Confucianism was far less dominant in 20th-century China, at least on an official level. The state cult of Confucius was ended in 1911. Still, Confucian traditions and moral standards are part of the cultural essence of China and other East Asian countries.

Shinto

Shinto comprises the religious ideas and practices indigenous to Japan. Ancient Shinto focused on the worship of the *kami*, a host of supernatural beings that could be known through forms (objects of nature, remarkable people, abstract concepts such as justice) but were ultimately mysterious. Shinto has no formal dogma and no holy writ, though early collections of Japanese religious thought and practice (*Kojiki*, "Records of Ancient Matters," A.D. 712, and *Nihon shoki*, "Chronicles of Japan," A.D. 720) are highly regarded.

Shinto has been influenced by Confucianism and by Buddhism, which was introduced in Japan in the 6th century. Syncretic schools (such as Ryobu Shinto) emerged, as did other sects that rejected Buddhism (such as Ise Shinto).

Under the reign of the emperor Meiji (1868–1912), Shinto became the official state religion. State Shinto, the national cult, emphasized the divinity of the emperor, whose succession was traced back to the first emperor, Jimmu (660 B.C.), and beyond him to the sun goddess Amaterasu-o-mi-kami. State Shinto was disestablished after World War II.

Sect Shinto, deriving from sects that developed during the 19th and 20th centuries, continues to thrive in Japan. Shrines dedicated to particular *kami* are visited by parishioners for prayer and traditional ceremonies, such as presenting a newborn child to the *kami*. Traditional festivals celebrated at the shrines include purification rites, presentation of food offerings, prayer, sacred music and dance, and a feast.

No particular day of the week is set aside for prayer. A person may visit a shrine at will, entering through the *torii* (gateway). It is believed that the *kami* can respond to prayer and can offer protection and guidance.

A variety of Shinto sects and practices exist today. Ten-rikyo emphasizes faith healing. Folk Shinto is characterized by veneration of roadside shrines and rites related to agriculture. Buddhist priests serve at many Shinto shrines, and many families keep a small shrine, or god-shelf, at home. Veneration of ancestors and pilgrimage are also common practices.

Taoism

Taoism, one of the major religions of China, is based on ancient philosophical works, primarily the Tao Te Ching, "Classic of Tao and Its Virtue." Traditionally, this book was thought to be the work of Lao-tzu, a quasi-historical philosopher of the 6th century B.C.; scholars now believe that the book dates from about the 3rd century B.C. The philosopher Chuang Tzu (4th–3rd centuries B.C.) also contributed to the seminal ideas of Taoism.

Tao, "the Way," is the ultimate reality of the universe, according to Taoism. It is a creative process, and humans can live in harmony with it by clearing the self of obstacles. By cultivating *wu-wei*, a type of inaction characterized by humility and prudence, a person can participate in the simplicity and spontaneity of Tao. Striving to attain virtue or achievement is counterproductive and unnecessary. Taoism values mystical contemplation and balance. The human being is viewed as a microcosm of the universe, and the Chinese principle of *yin-yang*, complementary duality, is a model of harmony.

The religious practices of Taoism emerged from these ancient philosophies and from Chinese shamanistic tradition; by the 2nd century A.D., it constituted an organized religion. Longevity and immortality were sought through regulating the energies of the body through breathing exercises, meditation, and use of medicinal plants, talismans, and magical formulas. A cult of immortals, including the divinized Lao-tzu, also developed. Influenced by Buddhism, Taoists organized monastic orders. Temple worship and forms of divination, including the *I ching*, were practiced.

Since its beginnings, many sects have arisen within Taoism. All subscribe to the philosophical origins of the religion; some have emphasized faith healing, exorcism, the worship of the immortals, meditation, or alchemy. Buddhism and Confucianism influenced some sects; some operated as secret societies.

Though the present Chinese government has tried to suppress it, Taoism is still practiced in mainland China, Taiwan, and Hong Kong. It profoundly influenced Chinese art and literature, and Taoist ideas have become popular in the West.

Self-Described Religious Identification Among American Adults

Religious group	2001 Total (in thousands)	Percent of population	Religious group	2001 Total (in thousands)	Percent of population
Total Christian	**159,506**	**76.7%**	Fundamentalist	61	*
Catholic	50,873	24.5	Salvation Army	25	*
Baptist	33,830	16.3	Independent		
Protestant[1]	4,647	2.2	Christian Church	71	*
Methodist/Wesleyan	14,150	6.8	**Total other religions**	**7,740**	**3.7%**
Lutheran	9,580	4.6	Jewish[3]	2,831	1.4
Christian[1]	14,150	6.8	Muslim/Islamic	1,104	0.5
Presbyterian	5,596	2.7	Buddhist	1,082	0.5
Pentecostal/Charismatic	4,407	2.1	Unitarian/Universalist	629	0.3
Episcopalian/Anglican	3,451	1.7	Hindu	766	0.4
Mormon/Latter-day			Native American	103	*
Saints	2,787	1.3	Scientologist	55	*
Churches of Christ	2,593	1.2	Baha'i	84	*
Jehovah's Witness	1,331	0.6	Taoist	40	*
Seventh-Day Adventist	724	0.3	New Age	68	*
Assemblies of God	1,106	0.5	Eckankar	26	*
Holiness/Holy	569	0.3	Rastafarian	11	*
Congregational/United			Sikh	57	*
Church of Christ	1,378	0.7	Wiccan	134	0.1
Church of the Nazarene	544	0.3	Deity	49	*
Church of God	944	0.5	Druid	33	*
Orthodox (Eastern)	645	0.3	Santeria	22	*
Evangelical[2]	1,032	0.5	Pagan	140	0.1
Mennonite	346	0.2	Spiritualist	116	0.1
Christian Science	194	0.1	Ethical Culture	4	*
Church of the Brethren	358	0.2	Other unclassified	386	0.2
Born Again[2]	56	0.0	**No religion specified,**		
Nondenominational[2]	2,489	1.2	**total**	**29,481**	**14.2**
Disciples of Christ	492	0.2	Atheist	902	0.4
Reformed/Dutch Reform	289	0.1	Agnostic	991	0.5
Apostolic/New Apostolic	254	0.1	Humanist	49	*
Quaker	217	0.1	Secular	53	*
Full Gospel	168	0.1	No religion	27,486	13.2
Christian Reform	79	*	**Refused to reply**		
Foursquare Gospel	70	*	**to question**	**11,246**	**5.4**

NOTES: * Less than 0.05%. 1. No denomination supplied. 2. These categories are the most unstable as they do not refer to clearly identifiable denominations as much as underlying feelings about religion. Thus they may be the most subject to fluctuation over time. 3. Refers to Jews by religion only. The American Religious Identification Survey (ARIS) 2001 was based on a random telephone survey of 50,281 American residential households in the continental U.S.A. (48 states). Respondents were asked to describe themselves in terms of religion with an open-ended question. The self-description of respondents was not based on whether established religious bodies considered them to be members; rather, the survey sought to determine whether the respondents themselves regarded themselves as adherents of a religious community. These figures thus represent subjective, rather than objective, standards of religious identification. Source: Barry A. Kosmin and Ariela Keysar, American Religious Identification Survey, 2001 (copyright). From the forthcoming book *Religion in a Free Market* (Paramount Market Publishing, 2005).

Roman Catholic Pontiffs

Name	Birthplace	Reigned From	To	Name	Birthplace	Reigned From	To
St. Peter	Bethsaida	42?	67?	St. Callistus I	Rome	217	222
St. Linus	Tuscia	c. 67	76	St. Urban I	Rome	222	230
St. Anacletus (Cletus)	Rome	76	88	St. Pontian	Rome	230	235
				St. Anterus	Greece	235	236
St. Clement	Rome	88	97	St. Fabian	Rome	236	250
St. Evaristus	Greece	97	105	St. Cornelius	Rome	251	253
St. Alexander I	Rome	105	115	St. Lucius I	Rome	253	254
St. Sixtus I	Rome	115	125	St. Stephen I	Rome	254	257
St. Telesphorus	Greece	125	136	St. Sixtus II	Greece	257	258
St. Hyginus	Greece	136	140	St. Dionysius	Unknown	259	268
St. Pius I	Aquileia	140	155	St. Felix I	Rome	269	274
St. Anicetus	Syria	155	166	St. Eutychian	Luni	275	283
St. Soter	Campania	166	175	St. Caius	Dalmatia	283	296
St. Eleutherius	Epirus	175	189	St. Marcellinus	Rome	296	304
St. Victor I	Africa	189	199	St. Marcellus I	Rome	308	309
St. Zephyrinus	Rome	199	217				

Name	Birthplace	Reigned From	Reigned To	Name	Birthplace	Reigned From	Reigned To
St. Eusebius	Greece	309[1]	309[1]	Stephen III (IV)	Sicily	768	772
St. Meltiades	Africa	311	314	Adrian I	Rome	772	795
St. Sylvester I	Rome	314	335	St. Leo III	Rome	795	816
St. Marcus	Rome	336	336	Stephen IV (V)	Rome	816	817
St. Julius I	Rome	337	352	St. Paschal I	Rome	817	824
Liberius	Rome	352	366	Eugene II	Rome	824	827
St. Damasus I	Spain	366	384	Valentine	Rome	827	827
St. Siricius	Rome	384	399	Gregory IV	Rome	827	844
St. Anastasius I	Rome	399	401	Sergius II	Rome	844	847
St. Innocent I	Albano	401	417	St. Leo IV	Rome	847	855
St. Zozimus	Greece	417	418	Benedict III	Rome	855	858
St. Boniface I	Rome	418	422	St. Nicholas I	Rome	858	867
St. Celestine I	Campania	422	432	(the Great)			
St. Sixtus III	Rome	432	440	Adrian II	Rome	867	872
St. Leo I	Tuscany	440	461	John VIII	Rome	872	882
(the Great)				Marinus I	Gallese	882	884
St. Hilary	Sardinia	461	468	St. Adrian III	Rome	884	885
St. Simplicius	Tivoli	468	483	Stephen V (VI)	Rome	885	891
St. Felix III (II)[2]	Rome	483	492	Formosus	Portus	891	896
St. Gelasius I	Africa	492	496	Boniface VI	Rome	896	896
Anastasius II	Rome	496	498	Stephen VI (VII)	Rome	896	897
St. Symmachus	Sardinia	498	514	Romanus	Gallese	897	897
St. Hormisdas	Frosinone	514	523	Theodore II	Rome	897	897
St. John I	Tuscany	523	526	John IX	Tivoli	898	900
St. Felix IV (III)	Samnium	526	530	Benedict IV	Rome	900	903
Boniface II	Rome	530	532	Leo V	Ardea	903	903
John II	Rome	533	535	Sergius III	Rome	904	911
St. Agapitus I	Rome	535	536	Anastasius III	Rome	911	913
St. Silverius	Campania	536	537	Landus	Sabina	913	914
Vigilius	Rome	537	555	John X	Tossignano	914	928
Pelagius I	Rome	556	561	Leo VI	Rome	928	928
John III	Rome	561	574	Stephen VII (VIII)	Rome	928	931
Benedict I	Rome	575	579	John XI	Rome	931	935
Pelagius II	Rome	579	590	Leo VII	Rome	936	939
St. Gregory I	Rome	590	604	Stephen VIII (IX)	Rome	939	942
(the Great)				Marinus II	Rome	942	946
Sabinianus	Tuscany	604	606	Agapitus II	Rome	946	955
Boniface III	Rome	607	607	John XII	Tusculum	955	964
St. Boniface IV	Marsi	608	615	Leo VIII[5]	Rome	963	965
St. Deusdedit	Rome	615	618	Benedict V[5]	Rome	964	966
(Adeodatus I)				John XIII	Rome	965	972
Boniface V	Naples	619	625	Benedict VI	Rome	973	974
Honorius I	Campania	625	638	Benedict VII	Rome	974	983
Severinus	Rome	640	640	John XIV	Pavia	983	984
John IV	Dalmatia	640	642	John XV	Rome	985	996
Theodore I	Greece	642	649	Gregory V	Saxony	996	999
St. Martin I	Todi	649	655	Sylvester II	Auvergne	999	1003
St. Eugene I[3]	Rome	654	657	John XVII	Rome	1003	1003
St. Vitalian	Segni	657	672	John XVIII	Rome	1004	1009
Adeodatus II	Rome	672	676	Sergius IV	Rome	1009	1012
Donus	Rome	676	678	Benedict VIII	Tusculum	1012	1024
St. Agatho	Sicily	678	681	John XIX	Tusculum	1024	1032
St. Leo II	Sicily	682	683	Benedict IX[6]	Tusculum	1032	1044
St. Benedict II	Rome	684	685	Sylvester III	Rome	1045	1045
John V	Syria	685	686	Benedict IX	Tusculum	1045	1045
Conon	Unknown	686	687	(2nd time)			
St. Sergius I	Syria	687	701	Gregory VI	Rome	1045	1046
John VI	Greece	701	705	Clement II	Saxony	1046	1047
John VII	Greece	705	707	Benedict IX	Tusculum	1047	1048
Sisinnius	Syria	708	708	(3rd time)			
Constantine	Syria	708	715	Damasus II	Bavaria	1048	1048
St. Gregory II	Rome	715	731	St. Leo IX	Alsace	1049	1054
St. Gregory III	Syria	731	741	Victor II	Germany	1055	1057
St. Zachary	Greece	741	752	Stephen IX (X)	Lorraine	1057	1058
Stephen II (III)[4]	Rome	752	757	Nicholas II	Burgundy	1059	1061
St. Paul I	Rome	757	767	Alexander II	Milan	1061	1073

Name	Birthplace	Reigned From	Reigned To	Name	Birthplace	Reigned From	Reigned To
St. Gregory VII	Tuscany	1073	1085	Sixtus IV	Savona	1471	1484
Bl. Victor III	Benevento	1086	1087	Innocent VIII	Genoa	1484	1492
Bl. Urban II	France	1088	1099	Alexander VI	Jativa	1492	1503
Paschal II	Ravenna	1099	1118	Pius III	Siena	1503	1503
Gelasius II	Gaeta	1118	1119	Julius II	Savona	1503	1513
Callistus II	Burgundy	1119	1124	Leo X	Florence	1513	1521
Honorius II	Flagnano	1124	1130	Adrian VI	Utrecht	1522	1523
Innocent II	Rome	1130	1143	Clement VII	Florence	1523	1534
Celestine II	Città di Castello	1143	1144	Paul III	Rome	1534	1549
Lucius II	Bologna	1144	1145	Julius III	Rome	1550	1555
Bl. Eugene III	Pisa	1145	1153	Marcellus II	Montepulciano	1555	1555
Anastasius IV	Rome	1153	1154	Paul IV	Naples	1555	1559
Adrian IV	England	1154	1159	Pius IV	Milan	1559	1565
Alexander III	Siena	1159	1181	St. Pius V	Bosco	1566	1572
Lucius III	Lucca	1181	1185	Gregory XIII	Bologna	1572	1585
Urban III	Milan	1185	1187	Sixtus V	Grottammare	1585	1590
Gregory VIII	Benevento	1187	1187	Urban VII	Rome	1590	1590
Clement III	Rome	1187	1191	Gregory XIV	Cremona	1590	1591
Celestine III	Rome	1191	1198	Innocent IX	Bologna	1591	1591
Innocent III	Anagni	1198	1216	Clement VIII	Florence	1592	1605
Honorius III	Rome	1216	1227	Leo XI	Florence	1605	1605
Gregory IX	Anagni	1227	1241	Paul V	Rome	1605	1621
Celestine IV	Milan	1241	1241	Gregory XV	Bologna	1621	1623
Innocent IV	Genoa	1243	1254	Urban VIII	Florence	1623	1644
Alexander IV	Anagni	1254	1261	Innocent X	Rome	1644	1655
Urban IV	Troyes	1261	1264	Alexander VII	Siena	1655	1667
Clement IV	France	1265	1268	Clement IX	Pistoia	1667	1669
Bl. Gregory X	Piacenza	1271	1276	Clement X	Rome	1670	1676
Bl. Innocent V	Savoy	1276	1276	Bl. Innocent XI	Como	1676	1689
Adrian V	Genoa	1276	1276	Alexander VIII	Venice	1689	1691
John XXI[7]	Portugal	1276	1277	Innocent XII	Spinazzola	1691	1700
Nicholas III	Rome	1277	1280	Clement XI	Urbino	1700	1721
Martin IV[8]	France	1281	1285	Innocent XIII	Rome	1721	1724
Honorius IV	Rome	1285	1287	Benedict XIII	Gravina	1724	1730
Nicholas IV	Ascoli	1288	1292	Clement XII	Florence	1730	1740
St. Celestine V	Isernia	1294	1294	Benedict XIV	Bologna	1740	1758
Boniface VIII	Anagni	1294	1303	Clement XIII	Venice	1758	1769
Bl. Benedict XI	Treviso	1303	1304	Clement XIV	Rimini	1769	1774
Clement V	France	1305	1314	Pius VI	Cesena	1775	1799
John XXII	Cahors	1316	1334	Pius VII	Cesena	1800	1823
Benedict XII	France	1334	1342	Leo XII	Genga	1823	1829
Clement VI	France	1342	1352	Pius VIII	Cingoli	1829	1830
Innocent VI	France	1352	1362	Gregory XVI	Belluno	1831	1846
Bl. Urban V	France	1362	1370	Pius IX	Senegallia	1846	1878
Gregory XI	France	1370	1378	Leo XIII	Carpineto	1878	1903
Urban VI	Naples	1378	1389	St. Pius X	Riese	1903	1914
Boniface IX	Naples	1389	1404	Benedict XV	Genoa	1914	1922
Innocent VII	Sulmona	1404	1406	Pius XI	Desio	1922	1939
Gregory XII	Venice	1406	1415	Pius XII	Rome	1939	1958
Martin V	Rome	1417	1431	John XXIII	Sotto il Monte	1958	1963
Eugene IV	Venice	1431	1447	Paul VI	Concesio	1963	1978
Nicholas V	Sarzana	1447	1455	John Paul I	Forno di Canale	1978	1978
Callistus III	Jativa	1455	1458	John Paul II	Wadowice, Poland	1978	2005
Pius II	Siena	1458	1464	Benedict XVI	Marktl Am Inn, Germany	2005	
Paul II	Venice	1464	1471				

1. Or 310. 2. He should be called Felix II, and his successors of the same name should be numbered accordingly. The discrepancy was caused by the erroneous insertion in some lists of the name of St. Felix of Rome, Martyr. 3. He was elected during the exile of St. Martin I, who endorsed him as pope. 4. After St. Zachary died, a Roman priest named Stephen was elected but died before his consecration as bishop of Rome. His name is not included in all lists for this reason. In view of this historical confusion, the *National Catholic Almanac* lists the true Stephen II as Stephen II (III), the true Stephen III as Stephen III (IV), etc. 5. Confusion exists concerning the legitimacy of claims. If the deposition of John was invalid, Leo was an antipope until after the end of Benedict's reign. If the deposition of John was valid, Leo was the legitimate pope and Benedict an antipope. 6. If the triple removal of Benedict IX was not valid, Sylvester III, Gregory VI, and Clement II were antipopes. 7. Elimination was made of the name of John XX in an effort to rectify the numerical designation of popes named John. The error dates back to the time of John XV. 8. The names of Marinus I and Marinus II were construed as Martin. In view of these two pontificates and the earlier reign of St. Martin I, this pontiff was called Martin IV. *Source: National Catholic Almanac*, from *Annuarto Pontificio*.

The Books of the Bible

Below is the Protestant canon of the Bible (New Revised Standard Version). The Roman Catholic canon also includes the Deuterocanonical books as part of the Old Testament (these are considered apocryphal by most Protestants). The Hebrew Bible recognizes the books referred to as the Old Testament in the Protestant Bible, but not the Apocryphal/Deuterocanonical books or the New Testament.

The Old Testament with the Apocryphal/Deuterocanonical Books

The Hebrew Scriptures

Genesis
Exodus
Leviticus
Numbers
Deuteronomy
Joshua
Judges
Ruth
1 Samuel
2 Samuel
1 Kings
2 Kings
1 Chronicles
2 Chronicles
Ezra
Nehemiah
Esther
Job
Psalms

Proverbs
Ecclesiastes
Song of Solomon
Isaiah
Jeremiah
Lamentations
Ezekiel
Daniel
Hosea
Joel
Amos
Obadiah
Jonah
Micah
Nahum
Habakkuk
Zephaniah
Haggai
Zechariah
Malachi

The Apocryphal/Deuterocanonical Books

Tobit
Judith

Additions to the Book of Esther
Wisdom of Solomon
Ecclesiasticus, or the Wisdom of Jesus Son of Sirach
Baruch
The Letter of Jeremiah
The Prayer of Azariah and the Song of the Three Jews
Susanna
Bel and the Dragon
1 Maccabees
2 Maccabees
1 Esdras
Prayer of Manasseh
Psalm 151
3 Maccabees
2 Esdras
4 Maccabees

The New Testament

Matthew
Mark
Luke
John
Acts of the Apostles
Romans
1 Corinthians
2 Corinthians
Galatians
Ephesians
Philippians
Colossians
1 Thessalonians
2 Thessalonians
1 Timothy
2 Timothy
Titus
Philemon
Hebrews
James
1 Peter
2 Peter
1 John
2 John
3 John
Jude
Revelation

The Ten Commandments

The Ten Commandments, also called the Decalogue (Greek, "ten words"), were divine laws revealed to Moses by God on Mt. Sinai. Appearing in both Exodus (Ex. 20: 2–17) and Deuteronomy (Deut. 5:6–21), the commandments are numbered differently depending on whether they appear in a Catholic, Protestant, or Hebrew Bible. The following is the version given in the Revised Standard Version of the Bible.

You shall have no other gods before me.

You shall not make for yourself a graven image, or any likeness of anything that is in heaven above, or that is in the earth beneath, or that is in the water under the earth; you shall not bow down to them or serve them; for I the Lord your God am a jealous God, visiting the iniquity of the fathers upon the children to the third and the fourth generation of those who hate me, but showing steadfast love to thousands of those who love me and keep my commandments.

You shall not take the name of the Lord your God in vain; for the Lord will not hold him guiltless who takes his name in vain.

Remember the Sabbath day, to keep it holy. Six days you shall labor, and do all your work; but the seventh day is a Sabbath to the Lord your God; in it you shall not do any work, you, or your son, or your daughter, your manservant, or your maidservant, or your cattle, or the sojourner who is within your gates; for in six days the Lord made heaven and earth, the sea, and all that is in them, and rested the seventh day; therefore the Lord blessed the Sabbath day and hallowed it.

Honor your father and your mother, that your days may be long in the land which the Lord your God gives you.

You shall not kill.

You shall not commit adultery.

You shall not steal.

You shall not bear false witness against your neighbor.

You shall not covet your neighbor's wife, or his manservant, or his maidservant, or his ox, or his ass, or anything that is your neighbor's.

Source: Revised Standard Version of the Bible (Ex. 20: 2–17).

The Seven Deadly Sins

In Christianity, the seven deadly sins are considered "deadly" because it is believed they can do terrible damage to the soul. The now-famous list does not appear in the Bible and may have been formulated by Gregory the Great (540–604). The deadly sins are sometimes known as "capital" or "cardinal" sins: pride, greed, lust, envy, gluttony, anger, and sloth.

See Calendar and Holidays for listings of religious holidays.

The Math and Science Gender Myth

Yes, men's and women's brains are different. But new research upends the old myths about who's good at what

By AMANDA RIPLEY TIME

What is the latest science on the differences between men's and women's aptitudes, anyway? Is it true, even a little bit, that men are better equipped for scientific genius? Or is it ridiculous—even pernicious—to ask such a question today? Thanks to new brain-imaging technology, we know there are indeed real differences between the male and the female brain, more differences than we would have imagined a decade ago. "The brain is a sex organ," says Sandra Witelson, a neuroscientist who became famous in the 1990s for her study of Albert Einstein's brain. "In the last dozen years, there has been an exponential increase in the number of studies that have found differences in the brain. It's very exciting."

But that's just the beginning of the conversation. It turns out that many of those differences don't seem to change our behavior. Others do—in ways we might not expect. Some of the most dramatic differences are not just in our brains but also in our eyes, noses, and ears—which feed informa-

tion to our brains. Still, almost none of those differences are static. The brain is constantly changing in response to hormones, encouragement, practice, diet, and drugs. Brain patterns fluctuate within the same person, in fact, depending on age and time of day. So it's absurd to conclude that the difference is primarily because of biology—or environment. The two interact from the time of conception, which only makes life more interesting. Any simplistic theory is "doomed to fail," says Yu Xie, a sociology professor at the University of Michigan. "I don't exclude biology as an explanation," he says. "But I know biological factors would not play a role unless they interacted with social conditions."

Now that scientists are finally starting to map the brain with some accuracy, the challenge is figuring out what to do with that knowledge. The possibilities for applying it to the classroom, workplace, and doctor's office are tantalizing. "If something is genetic, it means it must be biological. If we can figure out the biology, then we should be able to

Science Is Still a Man's World

The great majority of scientists and engineers in the U.S. are men, but that has less to do with differences in the brain than with academic history. The balance is changing, slowly, as more women pursue advanced degrees.

AT THE TOP OF THE IVORY TOWER

Women occupy 29% of science and engineering positions at U.S. educational institutions. But they fill only 15% of those positions at the top 50 research universities in these fields:

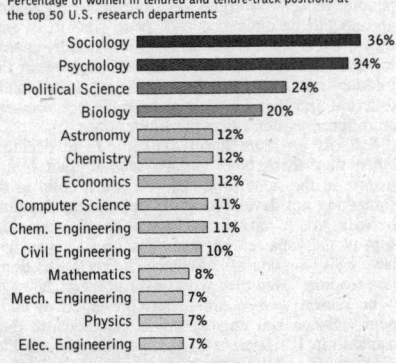

Percentage of women in tenured and tenure-track positions at the top 50 U.S. research departments

Field	Percentage
Sociology	36%
Psychology	34%
Political Science	24%
Biology	20%
Astronomy	12%
Chemistry	12%
Economics	12%
Computer Science	11%
Chem. Engineering	11%
Civil Engineering	10%
Mathematics	8%
Mech. Engineering	7%
Physics	7%
Elec. Engineering	7%

Source: Nelson Diversity Survey.

LIFE OUTSIDE ACADEMIA

In government and the private sector, women occupy just one-quarter of science and engineering jobs. As in the academic world, men dominate jobs in the physical sciences and engineering.

Employed doctoral scientists

Men 77% / Women 23%

Percentage of women by field

Field	Percentage
Health sciences	49%
Psychology	46%
Social Sciences	29%
Biology	27%
Mathematics	14%
Computer Science	13%
Physical sciences	13%
Engineering	7%

Source: National Science Foundation.

tweak the biology," says Richard Haier, a psychology professor who studies intelligence at the University of California at Irvine.

Lesson 1:
Function over Form

Scientists have been looking for sex differences in the brain since they have been looking at the brain. Many bold decrees have been issued. In the 19th century, the corpus callosum, a bundle of nerve fibers that connects the two hemispheres of the brain, was considered key to intellectual development. Accordingly, it was said to have a greater surface area in men. Then, in the 1980s, we were told that no, it is larger in women—and that explains why the emotional right side of women's brains is more in touch with the analytical left side. Aha. That theory has since been discredited, and scientists remain at odds over who has the biggest and what it might mean. Stay tuned for more breaking news.

But most studies agree that men's brains are about 10% bigger than women's brains overall. Even when the comparison is adjusted for the fact that men are, on average, 8% taller than women, men's brains are still slightly bigger. But size does not predict intellectual performance, as was once thought. Men and women perform similarly on IQ tests. And most scientists still cannot tell male and female brains apart just by looking at them.

Recently, scientists have begun to move away from the obsession with size. Thanks to new brain-imaging technology, researchers can get a good look at the living brain as it functions and grows. Earlier studies relied on autopsies or X-rays—and no one wanted to expose children or women, who might be pregnant, to regular doses of radiation.

The deeper you probe, the more interesting the differences. Women appear to have more connections between the two brain hemispheres. In certain regions, their brain is more densely packed with neurons. And women tend to use more parts of their brain to accomplish certain tasks. That might explain why they often recover better from a stroke, since the healthy parts of their mind compensate for the injured regions. Men do their thinking in more focused regions of the brain, whether they are solving a math problem, reading a book, or feeling a wave of anger or sadness.

Indeed, men and women seem to handle emotions quite differently. While both sexes use a part of the brain called the amygdala, which is located deep within the organ, women seem to have stronger connections between the amygdala and regions of the brain that handle language and other higher-level functions. That may explain why women are, on average, more likely to talk about their emotions and men tend to compartmentalize their worries and carry on. Or, of course, it may not.

"Men and women have different brain architectures, and we don't know what they mean," says Haier. By administering IQ tests to a group of college students and then analyzing scans of their brain structure, Haier's team recently discovered that the parts of the brain that are related to intelligence are different in men and women. "That is in some ways a major observation, because one of the assumptions of psychology has been that all human brains pretty much work the same way," he says. Now that we know they don't, we can try to understand why some brains react differently to, say, Alzheimer's, many medications, and even teaching techniques, Haier says.

Lesson 2:
The Segregation of the Senses

So how do we explain why, in study after study, boys and men are still on average better at rotating 3-D objects in their minds? As for girls and women, how do we explain why they tend to have better verbal skills and social sensitivities?

The most surprising differences may be outside the brain. "If you have a man and a woman looking at the same landscape, they see totally different things," asserts Leonard Sax, a physician, psychologist, and author of Why Gender Matters. "Women can see colors and textures that men cannot see. They hear things men cannot hear, and they smell things men cannot smell."

These differences may help explain why boys prefer to play with moving toys while girls favor richly textured dolls and tend to draw with a wider range of colors, Sax says. Likewise, baby girls hear certain ranges of sound better, and the divergence gets even bigger in adults. As for smell, a study published in the journal Nature Neuroscience in 2002 showed that women of childbearing age were many times more sensitive than men to several smells upon repeated exposure. (Another study has found that heterosexual women have the most sensitive smell and homosexual men have the least.) Rest assured, Sax says: none of that means women are, overall, better than men at perception. It just means the species is internally diverse, making it more likely to survive. "The female will remember the color and texture of a particular plant and be able to warn people if it's poisonous. A man looking at the same thing will be more alert to what is moving in the periphery," he says. "Which is better? You need both."

Lesson 3:
Never Underestimate the Brain

Until recently, there have been two groups of people: those who argue sex differences are innate and should be embraced and those who insist that they are learned and should be eliminated by changing the environment. Sax is one of the few in the middle—convinced that boys and girls are innately different and that we must change the environment so differences don't become limitations.

Schools do more harm than good, he decided, when they teach boys and girls as if their brains mature at the same time. "If you ask a child to do something not developmentally appropriate for him, he will, No. 1, fail. No. 2, he will develop an aversion to the subject," he says. "By age 12, you will have girls who don't like science and boys who don't like reading." And they won't ever go back, he says. "The reason women are underrepresented in computer science and engineering is not because they can't do it. It's because of the way they're taught."

Of course, we already manipulate the brain through drugs—many of which, doctors now realize, have dramatically different effects on different brains. Drugs for improving intelligence are in the works, says Haier, in the quest to find medication for Alzheimer's. "We're going to get a lot better at manipulating genetic biology. We may even be better at manipulating genetic biology than manipulating the environment."

Until then, one solution to overcoming biological tendencies is to consciously override them, to say to yourself, "O.K., I may have a hard time with this task, but I'm going to will myself to conquer it." Some experiments show that baby girls, when faced with failure, tend to give up and cry relatively quickly, while baby boys get angry and persist, says Witelson at Ontario's Michael G. DeGroote School of Medicine at McMaster University. "What we don't know is whether that pattern persists into adulthood," she says. But in her experience in academia, she says she knows of at least a couple of brilliant women who never realized their potential in science because they stopped trying when they didn't get grants or encountered some other obstacle. "It's much better," she says, "for people to understand what the differences are, act on their advantages, and be prepared for their disadvantages."

Lesson 4:
Expectations Matter

We have a tendency to make too much of test-score differences between the sexes (which are actually very small compared with the differences between, say, poor and affluent students). And regardless of what happens in school, personality and discipline can better predict success when it comes to highly competitive jobs.

One thing we know about the brain is that it is vulnerable to the power of suggestion. There is plenty of evidence that when young women are motivated and encouraged, they excel at science. For most of the 1800s, for example, physics, astronomy, chemistry, and botany were considered gender-appropriate subjects for middle- and upper-class American girls. By the 1890s, girls outnumbered boys in public high school science courses across the country, according to *The Science Education of American Girls*, a 2003 book by Kim Tolley. Records from top schools in Boston show that girls outperformed boys in physics in the mid-19th century. Latin and Greek, meanwhile, were considered the province of gentlemen—until the 20th century, when lucrative opportunities began to open up in the sciences.

Today, in Iceland and Sweden, girls consistently outperform boys in math and physics. In Sweden the gap is widest in the remote regions in the north. That may be because women want to move to the big cities farther south, where they would need to compete in high-tech economies, while men are focused on local hunting, fishing, and forestry opportunities, says Niels Egelund, a professor of educational psychology at the Danish University of Education. The phenomenon even has a name, the Jokkmokk effect, a reference to an isolated town in Swedish Lapland.

Back in the States, the achievement gap in the sciences is closing, albeit slowly. Female professors have been catching up with male professors in their publishing output. Today half of chemistry and almost 60% of biology bachelor of science degrees go to females. □

Gender of Sexual Partners in the United States
(sexually active only)

	Same gender		Both genders		Opposite gender	
	Men	Women	Men	Women	Men	Women
1988	2.3%	0.2%	0.3%	0.0%	97.4%	99.8%
1989	1.4	1.2	0.3	0.4	98.3	98.4
1990	1.1	0.5	0.9	0.0	98.0	99.5
1991	2.0	0.3	0.7	0.1	97.3	99.6
1993	1.8	1.8	0.3	0.4	97.9	97.8
1994	2.1	2.1	0.5	0.4	97.5	97.5
1996	3.5	2.1	0.6	0.9	96.0	97.0

Source: General Social Survey (GSS), National Opinion Research Center, University of Chicago, 1996.

International Women's Suffrage Timeline

1893 New Zealand	1920 United States	1950 India	1972 Bangladesh
1902 Australia[1]	1921 Sweden	1954 Colombia	1974 Jordan
1906 Finland	1928 Britain, Ireland	1957 Malaysia, Zimbabwe	1976 Portugal
1913 Norway	1931 Spain	1962 Algeria	1989 Namibia
1915 Denmark	1944 France	1963 Iran, Morocco	1990 Western Samoa
1917 Canada[2]	1945 Italy	1964 Libya	1993 Kazakhstan, Moldova
1918 Austria, Germany, Poland, Russia	1947 Argentina, Japan, Mexico, Pakistan	1967 Ecuador	1994 South Africa
1919 Netherlands	1949 China	1971 Switzerland	2005 Kuwait

NOTE: Two countries do not allow their people, male or female, to vote: Brunei and the United Arab Emirates. Saudi Arabia is the only country with suffrage that does not allow its women to vote. 1. Australian women, with the exception of aboriginal women, won the vote in 1902. Aboriginals, male and female, did not have the right to vote until 1962. 2. Canadian women, with the exception of Canadian Indian women, won the vote in 1917. Canadian Indians, male and female, did not win the vote until 1960. *Source: The New York Times*, May 22, 2005.

Key Events in the Women's Rights Movement

1848 The first women's rights convention is held in Seneca Falls, N.Y. A Declaration of Sentiments, which outlines grievances and sets the agenda for the women's rights movement, is signed by 68 women and 32 men.

1850 The first National Women's Rights Convention takes place in Worcester, Mass., attracting more than 1,000 participants. National conventions are held yearly (except for 1857) through 1860.

1869 In May, Susan B. Anthony and Elizabeth Cady Stanton form the National Woman Suffrage Association. Its primary goal is to achieve voting rights for women by means of a congressional amendment to the Constitution.

In November, Lucy Stone, Henry Blackwell, and others form the American Woman Suffrage Association, which focuses exclusively on gaining voting rights for women through amendments to individual state constitutions.

In December, the territory of Wyoming passes the first women's suffrage law. In 1870, women begin serving on juries in the territory.

1890 The National Woman Suffrage Association and the American Woman Suffrage Association merge to form the National American Woman Suffrage Association (NAWSA). As the movement's mainstream organization, NAWSA wages state-by-state campaigns to obtain voting rights for women.

1893 Colorado is the first state to adopt an amendment granting women the right to vote. Utah and Idaho follow suit in 1896; Washington State in 1910; California in 1911; Oregon, Kansas, and Arizona in 1912; Alaska and Illinois in 1913; Montana and Nevada in 1914; New York in 1917; Michigan, South Dakota, and Oklahoma in 1918.

1896 The National Association of Colored Women is formed, bringing together more than 100 black women's clubs. Leaders in the black women's club movement include Josephine St. Pierre Ruffin, Mary Church Terrell, and Anna Julia Cooper.

1913 Alice Paul and Lucy Burns form the Congressional Union to work toward the passage of a federal amendment to give women the vote. The group is later renamed the National Women's Party. Members picket the White House and practice other forms of civil disobedience.

1919 The federal woman suffrage amendment, originally written by Susan B. Anthony and introduced in Congress in 1878, is passed by the House of Representatives and the Senate. It is then sent to the states for ratification.

1920 On Aug. 26, the 19th Amendment to the Constitution, granting women the right to vote, is signed into law.

1921 Margaret Sanger founds the American Birth Control League, which evolves into the Planned Parenthood Federation of America in 1942.

1936 The federal law prohibiting the dissemination of contraceptive information through the mail is modified, and birth control information is no longer classified as obscene. Throughout the 1940s and 1950s, birth control advocates are engaged in numerous legal suits.

1961 President John F. Kennedy establishes the President's Commission on the Status of Women and appoints Eleanor Roosevelt as chairwoman. The report issued by the commission in 1963 documents substantial discrimination against women in the workplace and urges reform, including fair hiring practices, paid maternity leave, and affordable child care.

1963 Betty Friedan publishes her highly influential book *The Feminine Mystique,* which becomes a best-seller and galvanizes the modern women's rights movement.

In June, Congress passes the Equal Pay Act, making it illegal for employers to pay a woman less than what a man would receive for the same job.

1964 Title VII of the Civil Rights Act bars discrimination in employment on the basis of race and sex. At the same time it establishes the Equal Employment Opportunity Commission (EEOC) to investigate complaints and impose penalties.

1965 In *Griswold* v. *Connecticut,* the Supreme Court strikes down the one remaining state law prohibiting the use of contraceptives by married couples.

1966 The National Organization for Women (NOW) is founded. The largest women's rights group in the United States, NOW seeks to end sexual discrimination by means of legislative lobbying, litigation, and public demonstrations.

1967 Executive Order 11375 expands President Lyndon Johnson's affirmative action policy of 1965 to cover discrimination based on gender.

1968 The EEOC rules that sex-segregated help wanted ads in newspapers are illegal. This ruling is upheld in 1973 by the Supreme Court, opening the way for women to apply for higher-paying jobs hitherto open only to men.

1969 California becomes the first state to adopt a "no fault" divorce law, which allows couples to divorce by mutual consent. By 1985 every state has adopted a similar law. Laws are also passed regarding the equal division of common property.

1971 *Ms.* magazine is first published as a sample insert in *New York* magazine; 300,000 copies are sold out in 8 days. The first regular issue is published in July 1972. The magazine becomes the major forum for feminist voices and turns cofounder and editor Gloria Steinem into an icon of the modern feminist movement.

In *Eisenstadt* v. *Baird* the Supreme Court rules that the right to privacy includes an unmarried person's right to use contraceptives.

1972 The Equal Rights Amendment (ERA) is passed by Congress and sent to the states for ratification. Originally drafted by Alice Paul in 1923, the amendment reads: "Equality of rights under the law shall not be denied or abridged by the United States or by any State on account of sex." The amendment dies in 1982 when it fails to achieve ratification by a minimum of 38 states.

Title IX of the Education Amendments bans sex discrimination in schools. As a result, the enrollment of women in athletics programs and professional schools increases dramatically.

1973 As a result of *Roe* v. *Wade,* the Supreme Court establishes a woman's legal right to abortion, overriding the antiabortion laws of many states.

1978 The Pregnancy Discrimination Act bans employment discrimination against pregnant women.

1984 EMILY's List (Early Money Is Like Yeast) is established as a financial network for pro-choice Democratic women running for national political office. The organization makes a significant impact on the increasing number of women elected to Congress.

1994 The Violence Against Women Act tightens federal penalties for sex offenders, funds services for victims of rape and domestic violence, and provides for special training of police officers.

The Wage Gap

Source: National Women's Law Center.

The wage gap is a statistical indicator often used as an index of the status of women's earnings relative to men's. It is also used to compare the earnings of other races and ethnicities to those of white males, a group generally not subject to race- or sex-based discrimination. The wage gap is expressed as a percentage (e.g., in 2003, women earned 76% as much as men) and is calculated by dividing the median annual earnings for women by the median annual earnings for men.

The Equal Pay Act was signed in 1963, making it illegal for employers to pay unequal wages to men and women who hold the same job and do the same work. At the time of the EPA's passage, women earned just 58 cents for every dollar earned by men. By 2003, 40 years later, that rate had only increased to 76 cents, an improvement of less than half a penny a year. Minority women fare the worst. African-American women earn just 65 cents to every dollar earned by white men, and for Hispanic women that figure drops to merely 54 cents per dollar.

The wage gap between women and men cuts across a wide spectrum of occupations. The Bureau of Labor Statistics reported in 1999 that female physicians earned 62.5% of the median weekly wages of male physicians, and women in sales occupations earned just 59.9% of men's wages in equivalent positions.

If working women earned the same as men (those who work the same number of hours; have the same education, age, and union status; and live in the same region of the country), their annual family incomes would rise by $4,000 and poverty rates would be cut in half.

2003 Median Annual Earnings by Race and Sex

Race/gender	Earnings	Wage ratio	Race/gender	Earnings	Wage ratio
White men	$41,211	100.0%	All men	$40,668	
Black men	$32,241	78.2	All women	$30,724	
White women	$31,169	75.6	Wage gap		75.5%
Black women	$26,965	65.4			
Hispanic men	$26,083	63.3			
Hispanic women	$22,363	54.3			

NOTE: Includes full-time, year-round workers ages 15 and above. "White" and "Black" exclude those who reported more than one race category. "Hispanic" includes all those who so identified themselves, regardless of race. *Source:* U.S. Census Bureau, Current Population Survey, 2004 Annual Social and Economic Supplement.

Women's Earnings as a Percentage of Men's, 1951–2003

(for year-round, full-time work)

Year	Percent	Year	Percent	Year	Percent	Year	Percent	Year	Percent
1951	63.9%	1962	59.3%	1973	56.6%	1984	63.7%	1995	71.4%
1952	63.9	1963	58.9	1974	58.8	1985	64.6	1996	73.8
1953	63.9	1964	59.1	1975	58.8	1986	64.3	1997	74.2
1954	63.9	1965	59.9	1976	60.2	1987	65.2	1998	73.2
1955	63.9	1966	57.6	1977	58.9	1988	66.0	1999	72.2
1956	63.3	1967	57.8	1978	59.4	1989	68.7	2000	73.3
1957	63.8	1968	58.2	1979	59.7	1990	71.6	2001	76.3
1958	63.0	1969	58.9	1980	60.2	1991	69.9	2002	76.6
1959	61.3	1970	59.4	1981	59.2	1992	70.8	2003	75.5
1960	60.7	1971	59.5	1982	61.7	1993	71.5		
1961	59.2	1972	57.9	1983	63.6	1994	72.0		

Source: U.S. Women's Bureau and the National Committee on Pay Equity.

Famous Firsts by African Americans

The first black billionaire, combat pilot, Oscar winner, and poet laureate

Government

- **Local elected official:** John Mercer Langston, 1855, town clerk of Brownhelm Township, Ohio.
- **State elected official:** Alexander Lucius Twilight, 1836, the Vermont legislature.
- **Mayor of major city:** Carl Stokes, Cleveland, Ohio, 1967–1971. The first black woman to serve as a mayor of a major U.S. city was Sharon Pratt Dixon Kelly, Washington, DC, 1991–1995.
- **Governor (appointed):** P.B.S. Pinchback served as governor of Louisiana from Dec. 9, 1872–Jan. 13, 1873, during impeachment proceedings against the elected governor.
- **Governor (elected):** L. Douglas Wilder, Virginia, 1990–1994.
- **U.S. Representative:** Joseph Rainey became a Congressman from South Carolina in 1870 and was reelected four more times. The first black female U.S. Representative was Shirley Chisholm, Congresswoman from New York, 1969–1983.
- **U.S. Senator:** Hiram Revels became Senator from Mississippi from Feb. 25, 1870, to March 4, 1871, during Reconstruction. Edward Brooke (R-Mass.) became the first African-American Senator since Reconstruction, 1966–1979. Carol Mosely Braun became the first black woman Senator serving from 1992–1998 for the state of Illinois. (There have only been a total of five black senators in U.S. history: the remaining two are Blanche K. Bruce [1875–1881] and Barack Obama [2005–]).
- **U.S. cabinet member:** Robert C. Weaver, 1966–1968, Secretary of the Department of Housing and Urban Development under Lyndon Johnson; the first black female cabinet minister was Patricia Harris, 1977, Secretary of the Department of Housing and Urban Development under Jimmy Carter.
- **U.S. Secretary of State:** Gen. Colin Powell, 2001–2004. The first black female Secretary of State was Condoleezza Rice, 2005–.

Law

- **Editor, Harvard Law Review:** Charles Hamilton Houston, 1919. Barack Obama became the first President of the Harvard Law Review.
- **Federal Judge:** William Henry Hastie, 1946; Constance Baker Motely became the first black woman federal judge, 1966.
- **U.S. Supreme Court Justice:** Thurgood Marshall, 1967–1991. Clarence Thomas became the second African American to serve on the Court in 1991.

Diplomacy

- **U.S. diplomat:** Ebenezer D. Bassett, 1869, became minister-resident to Haiti; Patricia Harris became the first black female ambassador (1965; Luxembourg).
- **U.S. Representative to the UN:** Andrew Young (1977–1979).
- **Nobel Peace Prize winner:** Ralph J. Bunche received the prize in 1950 for mediating the Arab-Israeli truce. Martin Luther King, Jr., became the second African-American Peace Prize winner in 1964.

Military

- **Combat pilot:** Georgia-born Eugene Jacques Ballard, 1917, denied entry into the U.S. Army Air Corps because of his race, served throughout World War I in the French Flying Corps. He received the Legion of Honor, France's highest honor, among many other decorations.
- **First Congressional Medal of Honor winner:** Sgt. William H. Carney for bravery during the Civil War. He received his Congressional Medal of Honor in 1900.
- **General:** Benjamin O. Davis, Sr., 1940–1948.
- **Chairman of the Joint Chiefs of Staff:** Colin Powell, 1989–1993.

Science and Medicine

- **First patent holder:** Thomas L. Jennings, 1821, for a dry-cleaning process. Sarah E. Goode, 1885, became the first African-American woman to receive a patent, for a bed that folded up into a cabinet.
- **M.D. degree:** James McCune Smith, 1837, University of Glasgow; Rebecca Lee Crumpler became the first black woman to receive an M.D. degree. She graduated from the New England Female Medical College in 1864.
- **Inventor of the blood bank:** Dr. Charles Drew, 1940.
- **Successful open heart surgery:** Daniel Hale Williams, 1893.
- **First astronaut:** Robert H. Lawrence, Jr., 1967, was the first black astronaut, but he died in a plane crash during a training flight and never made it into space. Guion Bluford, 1983, became the first black astronaut to travel in space; Mae Jemison, 1992, became the first black female astronaut. Frederick D. Gregory, 1998, was the first African-American shuttle commander.

Scholarship

- **College graduate (B.A.):** Alexander Lucius Twilight, 1823, Middlebury College; first black woman to receive a B.A. degree: Mary Jane Patterson, 1862, Oberlin College.
- **Ph.D.:** Edward A. Bouchet, 1876, received a Ph.D. from Yale University. In 1921, three individuals became the first U.S. black women to earn Ph.D.s: Georgiana Simpson, University of Chicago; Sadie Tanner Mossell Alexander, University of Pennsylvania; and Eva Beatrice Dykes, Radcliffe College.
- **Rhodes Scholar:** Alain L. Locke, 1907.
- **College president:** Daniel A. Payne, 1856, Wilberforce University, Ohio.
- **Ivy League president:** Ruth Simmons, 2001, Brown University.

Literature

- **Novelist:** Harriet Wilson, *Our Nig* (1859).

- **Poet:** Lucy Terry, 1746, "Bar's Fight." It is her only surviving poem.
- **Poet (published):** Phillis Wheatley, 1773, *Poems on Various Subjects, Religious and Moral.* Considered the founder of African-American literature.
- **Pulitzer Prize winner:** Gwendolyn Brooks, 1950, won the Pulitzer Prize in poetry.
- **Nobel Prize for Literature winner:** Toni Morrison, 1993.
- **Poet Laureate:** Rita Dove, 1993–1995.

Music and Dance

- **Member of the New York City Opera:** Todd Duncan, 1945.
- **Member of the Metropolitan Opera Company:** Marian Anderson, 1955.
- **Principal dancer in a major dance company:** Arthur Mitchell, 1959, New York City Ballet.

Film

- **First Oscar:** Hattie McDaniel, 1940, supporting actress, *Gone with the Wind.*
- **Oscar, Best Actor/Actress:** Sidney Poitier, 1963, *Lilies of the Field;* Halle Berry, 2001, *Monster's Ball.*
- **Film director:** Oscar Micheaux, 1919, wrote, directed, and produced *The Homesteader,* a feature film.
- **Hollywood director:** Gordon Parks directed and wrote *The Learning Tree* for Warner Brothers in 1969.

Television

- **Network television show host:** Nat King Cole, 1956, *The Nat King Cole Show*; Oprah Winfrey became the first black woman television host in 1986, *The Oprah Winfrey Show.*
- **Star of a network television show:** Bill Cosby, 1965, *I Spy.*

Sports

- **Major league baseball player:** Jackie Robinson, 1947, Brooklyn Dodgers.
- **NFL quarterback:** Willie Thrower, 1953.
- **NFL football coach:** Fritz Pollard, 1922–1937.
- **Golf champion:** Tiger Woods, 1997, won the Masters golf tournament.

- **NHL hockey player:** Willie O'Ree, 1958, Boston Bruins.
- **Tennis champion:** Althea Gibson became the first black person to play in and win Wimbledon and the United States national tennis championship. She won both tournaments twice, in 1957 and 1958. In all, Gibson won 56 tournaments, including five Grand Slam singles events. The first black male champion was Arthur Ashe who won the 1968 U.S. Open, the 1970 Australian Open, and the 1975 Wimbledon championship.
- **Heavyweight boxing champion:** Jack Johnson, 1908.
- **Olympic gold medalist (Summer games):** John Baxter "Doc" Taylor won a gold medal as part of the 4×400 meter relay team.
- **Olympic gold medalist (Summer games; individual):** DeHart Hubbard, 1924, for the long jump; the first woman was Alice Coachman, who won the high jump in 1948.
- **Olympic gold medalist (Winter games):** Vonetta Flowers, 2002, bobsled.

Other African-American Firsts

- **Millionaire:** Madame C. J. Walker.
- **Billionaire:** Robert Johnson, 2001, owner of Black Entertainment Television; Oprah Winfrey, 2003.
- **Portrayal on a postage stamp:** Booker T. Washington, 1940 (and also 1956).
- **Miss America:** Vanessa Williams, 1984, representing New York. When controversial photos surfaced and Williams resigned, Suzette Charles, the runner-up and also an African American, assumed the title. She represented New Jersey. Three additional African Americans have been Miss Americas: Debbye Turner (1990), Marjorie Vincent (1991), and Kimberly Aiken (1994).
- **Explorer, North Pole:** Matthew A. Henson, 1909, accompanied Robert E. Peary on the first successful U.S. expedition to the North Pole.
- **Explorer, South Pole:** George Gibbs, 1939–1941 accompanied Richard Byrd.

African-American Population

In 1790, when the first census was taken, African Americans numbered about 760,000—about 19% of the population. In 1860, at the start of the Civil War, the African-American population increased to 4.4 million, but the percentage rate dropped to 14% of the overall population of the country. The vast majority were slaves, with only 488,000 counted as "freemen." By 1900, the black population had doubled and reached 8.8 million. In 1910, about 90% of African Americans lived in the South, but large numbers began migrating north looking for better job opportunities and living conditions, and to escape Jim Crow and racial violence. The Great Migration, as it was called, spanned the 1890s to the 1970s. From 1916 through the 1960s, more than 6 million black people moved north. But in the 1970s and 1980s, that trend reversed, with more African Americans moving south to the Sunbelt than leaving it. By 1990, the African-American population reached about 30 million and represented 12% of the population, roughly the same proportion as in 1900.

Year	Population (millions)	Percent of population	Year	Population (millions)	Percent of population
1790	0.8	19.3%	1940	12.9	9.8
1800	1.0	18.9	1950	15.0	10.0
1850	3.6	15.7	1960	18.9	10.5
1900	8.8	11.6	1970	22.6	11.1
1910	9.8	10.7	1980	26.5	11.7
1920	10.5	9.9	1990	30.0	12.1
1930	11.9	9.7	2000	34.6	12.3

Source: Statistical Abstract of the United States: 2003, and We, The American Blacks, U.S. Census Bureau, 1993.

Population of the United States by Race and Hispanic/Latino Origin, Census 2000 and July 1, 2004

Race and Hispanic/Latino origin	July 1, 2004, population[1]	Percent of population	Census 2000, population	Percent of population
Total Population	**293,622,764**	**100.0%**	**281,421,906**	**100.0%**
Single race				
White	235,990,895	80.4	211,460,626	75.1
Black or African American	37,521,497	12.8	34,658,190	12.3
American Indian and Alaska Native	2,824,505	1.0	2,475,956	0.9
Asian	12,337,650	4.2	10,242,998	3.6
Native Hawaiian and other Pacific Islander	505,394	0.2	398,835	0.1
Two or more races	4,442,823	1.5	6,826,228	2.4
Some other race	n.a.[2]	n.a.	15,359,073	5.5
Hispanic or Latino	41,329,556	14.1	35,305,818	12.5

NOTE: Percentages do not add up to 100% due to rounding, and because Hispanics may be of any race and are therefore counted under more than one category. 1. June 14, 2004 estimate. 2. Those answering "other" have been allocated to one of the recognized race categories. *Source:* U.S. Census Bureau, Census 2000 Brief, March 2001, and National Population Estimates.

Black or African-American Population for the United States by Region, 2002

Area	Percent of black population	Percent of total population	Area	Percent of black population	Percent of total population
United States	**100.0%**	**12.7%**	Midwest	18.1%	10.2%
Region			South	55.3	19.8
Northeast	18.1	12.2	West	8.6	4.8

Source: U.S. Census Bureau, *Current Population Survey,* March 2002.

U.S. Hispanic/Latino Population, Census 2000

National origin	Population	Percent	National origin	Population	Percent
Total	**35,305,818**	**100.0%**	Other Central American	103,721	0.3%
Mexican	**20,640,711**	**58.5**	**South American**	**1,353,562**	**3.8**
Puerto Rican	**3,406,178**	**9.6**	Argentinean	100,864	0.3
Cuban	**1,241,685**	**3.5**	Bolivian	42,068	0.1
Dominican (Dominican Republic)	**764,945**	**2.2**	Chilean	68,849	0.2
Central American (excludes Mexican)	**1,686,937**	**4.8**	Colombian	470,684	1.3
			Ecuadorian	260,559	0.7
Costa Rican	68,588	0.2	Paraguayan	8,769	([1])
Guatemalan	372,487	1.1	Peruvian	233,926	0.7
Honduran	217,569	0.6	Uruguayan	18,804	0.1
Nicaraguan	177,684	0.5	Venezuelan	91,507	0.3
Panamanian	91,723	0.3	Other South American	57,532	0.2
Salvadoran	655,165	1.9	**All other Hispanic or Latino**	**6,211,800**	**17.6**

NOTE: Hispanics may be of any race. 1. Less than 0.1%. *Source:* U.S. Census Bureau, Census 2000.

U.S. Population with Arab Ancestry, Census 2000

National origin	Arab ancestry alone		Arab ancestry alone or in combination with another ancestry	
	Number	Percent of U.S. population	Number	Percent of U.S. population
Total	850,027[1]	0.30%	1,189,731[2]	0.42%
Lebanese	244,525	0.09	440,279	0.16
Egyptian	123,489	0.04	142,832	0.05
Syrian	75,517	0.03	142,897	0.05
Palestinian	61,691	0.02	72,112	0.03
Jordanian	36,104	0.01	39,734	0.01
Moroccan	30,352	0.01	38,923	0.01
Iraqi	29,429	0.01	37,714	0.01
"Arab" or "Arabic"	167,166	0.06	205,822	0.07
Other Arab	81,754[3]	0.03	82,337[4]	0.03

1. Includes people who reported Arab ancestry only, regardless of whether they reported one or two Arab ancestries. 2. Includes people who reported one or two Arab ancestries and people who reported both an Arab and non-Arab ancestry. 3. Includes 68,614 people who reported one Arab ancestry not listed above and 13,140 people who reported two Arab ancestries, excluding the ancestries listed above. 4. Represents the number of people who reported one or two Arab ancestries, excluding the ancestries listed above. *Source:* U.S. Census Bureau, Census 2000 special tabulation.

U.S. Asian Population, Census 2000

National origin	Population[1]	Percent	National origin	Population[1]	Percent
Total[2]	**11,898,828**	**100.0%**	Korean	1,228,427	10.3%
Asian Indian	1,899,599	16.0	Laotian	198,203	1.7
Bangladeshi	57,412	0.5	Malaysian	18,566	0.2
Bhutanese	212	(3)	Maldivian	51	(3)
Burmese	16,720	0.1	Nepalese	9,399	0.1
Cambodian	206,052	1.7	Okinawan	10,599	0.1
Chinese, except Taiwanese	2,734,841	23.0	Pakistani	204,309	1.7
Filipino	2,364,815	19.9	Singaporean	2,394	(3)
Hmong	186,310	1.6	Sri Lankan	24,587	0.2
Indo-Chinese	199	(3)	Taiwanese	144,795	1.2
Indonesian	63,073	0.5	Thai	150,283	1.3
Iwo Jiman	78	(3)	Vietnamese	1,223,736	10.3
Japanese	1,148,932	9.7	Other Asian, not specified	369,430	3.1

1. The numbers by national origin do not add up to the total population figure because respondents may have put down more than one country. Respondents reporting several countries are counted several times. 2. Total includes Asians alone or in combination with one or more other races or other Asian groups. The Asian population alone in 2000 was 10,242,998. 3. Less than 0.1%. *Source:* U.S. Census Bureau, Census 2000.

Native Hawaiian and Other U.S. Pacific Islander Population, Census 2000

National origin	Population[1]	Percent	National origin	Population[1]	Percent
Total[2]	**874,414**	**100.0%**	Kosraean	226	(3)
Polynesian			Pohnpeian	700	0.1%
Native Hawaiian	401,162	45.9	Chuukese	654	0.1
Samoan	133,281	15.2	Yapese	368	(3)
Tongan	36,840	4.2	Marshallese	6,650	0.8
Tahitian	3,313	0.4	I-Kiribati	175	(3)
Tokelauan	574	0.1	Micronesian, not specified	9,940	1.1
Polynesian, not specified	8,796	1.0	**Melanesian**		
Micronesian			Fijian	13,581	1.6
Guamanian or Chamorro	92,611	10.6	Papua New Guinean	224	(3)
Mariana Islander	141	(3)	Solomon Islander	25	(3)
Saipanese	475	0.1	Ni-Vanuatu	18	(3)
Palauan	3,469	0.4	Melanesian, not specified	315	(3)
Carolinian	173	(3)	**Other Pacific Islander**	174,912	20.0

1. The numbers by national origin do not add up to the total population figure because respondents may have put down more than one country. Respondents reporting several countries are counted several times. 2. Total includes Native Hawaiian and other Pacific Islanders alone or in combination with other races or groups. Native Hawaiian and Pacific Islander population alone in 2000 was 398,835. 3. Less than 0.1%. *Source:* U.S. Census Bureau, Census 2000.

American Indian and Alaska Native Population by Selected Tribes, Census 2000

Tribe	Population[1]	Tribe	Population[1]
Total[2]	**4,119,301**	Pima	11,493
Apache	96,833	Potawatomi	25,595
Blackfeet	85,750	Pueblo	74,085
Cherokee	729,533	Puget Sound Salish	14,631
Cheyenne	18,204	Seminole	27,431
Chickasaw	38,351	Shoshone	12,026
Chippewa	149,669	Sioux	153,360
Choctaw	158,774	Tohono O'odham	20,087
Colville	9,393	Ute	10,385
Comanche	19,376	Yakama	10,851
Cree	7,734	Yaqui	22,412
Creek	71,310	Yuman	8,976
Crow	13,394	Other specified American	
Delaware	16,341	Indian tribes	357,658
Houma	8,713	American Indian tribe, not specified	195,902
Iroquois	80,822	Alaska Athabascan	18,838
Kiowa	12,242	Aleut	16,978
Latin American Indian	180,940	Eskimo	54,761
Lumbee	57,868	Tlingit-Haida	22,365
Menominee	9,840	Other specified Alaska Native tribes	3,973
Navajo	298,197	Alaska Native tribe, not specified	8,702
Osage	15,897	American Indian or Alaska Native	
Ottawa	10,677	tribe, not specified	1,056,457
Paiute	13,532		

1. The numbers by American Indian and Alaska Native tribe do not add up to the total population figure because respondents may have put down more than one tribe. Respondents reporting several tribes are counted several times. 2. Total includes American Indian and Alaska Natives alone or in combination with other tribal groups or races. Indian and Alaskan Native population alone in 2000 was 2,475,956. *Source:* U.S. Census Bureau, Census 2000.

Most Populous Indian Reservations, 2000

Reservation	Population[1]
Navajo Nation (Ariz.-N.M.-Utah)	175,228
Cherokee (Okla.)	104,482
Creek (Okla.)	77,253
Lumbee (N.C.)	62,327
Choctaw (Okla.)	39,984
Cook Inlet (Alaska)	35,972
Chickasaw (Okla.)	32,372
Calista (Alaska)	20,353
United Houma Nation (La.)	15,305
Sealaska (Alaska)	15,059
Pine Ridge (S.D.-Neb.)	14,484
Doyon (Alaska)	14,128
Kiowa-Comanche-Apache-Fort Sill Apache (Okla.)	13,045
Fort Apache (Ariz.)	11,854
Citizen Band Potawatomi Nation–Absentee Shawnee (Okla.)	10,617
Gila River (Ariz.)	10,578
Cheyenne/Arapaho (Okla.)	10,310
Tohono O'odham (Ariz.)	9,794
Osage (Okla.)	9,209
Rosebud (S.D.)	9,165
San Carlos (Ariz.)	9,065
Blackfeet (Mont.)	8,684
Yakama (Wash.)	8,193
Turtle Mountain (N.D.)	8,043
Flathead (Mont.)	7,883

1. Population listed includes only the American Indian and Alaska Native population alone or in combination with one or more races. Total population of reservation, which includes non-Indians, is not given. A reservation's total population is sometimes significantly larger than Indian population. *Source:* U.S. Census Bureau, 2000 Census of Population and Housing, Profiles of General Demographic Characteristics.

U.S. Federal and State Indian Reservations

Ancestry of U.S. Population by Rank

2000 Rank	Ancestry group	Percent	2000 Rank	Ancestry group	Percent	2000 Rank	Ancestry group	Percent
1.	German	15.2%	30.	Korean	0.4%	59.	Iranian	0.1%
2.	Irish	10.8	31.	African[1]	0.4	60.	Hawaiian	0.1
3.	African American[1]	8.8	32.	Portuguese	0.4	61.	Yugoslavian	0.1
4.	English	8.7	33.	Greek	0.4	62.	Ecuadorian	0.1
5.	American[1]	7.2	34.	Japanese	0.4	63.	Spaniard	0.1
6.	Mexican	6.5	35.	Cuban	0.4	64.	Taiwanese	0.1
7.	Italian	5.6	36.	British	0.4	65.	Peruvian	0.1
8.	Polish	3.2	37.	Vietnamese	0.4	66.	Honduran	0.1
9.	French	3.0	38.	Swiss	0.3	67.	Pennsylvania German	0.1
10.	American Indian[1]	2.8	39.	Dominican	0.3	68.	Pakistani	0.1
11.	Scottish	1.7	40.	Ukrainian	0.3	69.	Latin American[1]	0.1
12.	Dutch	1.6	41.	Salvadoran	0.3	70.	Asian[1]	0.1
13.	Norwegian	1.6	42.	Slovak	0.3	71.	Nicaraguan	0.1
14.	Scotch-Irish	1.5	43.	Jamaican	0.3	72.	Arab[1]	0.1
15.	Swedish	1.4	44.	Austrian	0.3	73.	Cambodian	0.1
16.	White[1]	1.4	45.	Lithuanian	0.2	74.	Brazilian	0.1
17.	Puerto Rican	0.9	46.	Canadian	0.2	75.	Laotian	0.1
18.	Russian	0.9	47.	Finnish	0.2	76.	Slovene	0.1
19.	Hispanic[1]	0.9	48.	Colombian	0.2	77.	Trinidadian and Tobagonian	0.1
20.	French Canadian	0.8	49.	Haitian	0.2	78.	Nigerian	0.1
21.	Chinese	0.8	50.	Guatemalan	0.2	79.	Northern European[1]	0.1
22.	Spanish	0.8	51.	Czechoslovakian	0.2	80.	Guyanese	0.1
23.	Filipino	0.8	52.	Lebanese	0.2	81.	West Indian[1]	0.1
24.	European[1]	0.7	53.	Scandinavian	0.2	82.	Thai	0.1
25.	Welsh	0.6	54.	United States[1]	0.1	83.	Syrian	0.1
26.	Asian Indian	0.5	55.	Armenian	0.1	84.	Egyptian	0.1
27.	Danish	0.5	56.	Croatian	0.1			
28.	Hungarian	0.5	57.	Romanian	0.1			
29.	Czech	0.4	58.	Belgian	0.1			

NOTES: Ancestry is a broad concept that can mean different things to different people. The ancestry groups listed on this table were self-identified. The Census Bureau defines ancestry as a person's ethnic origin, heritage, descent, or "roots," which may reflect their place of birth, place of birth of parents or ancestors, and ethnic identities that have evolved within the United States. Many respondents listed more than one area of ancestry; the sum of the persons reporting the ancestry is greater than the total. Ancestries making up at least 0.1% of the population are included in the table. Overall, about 500 different ancestries were reported during Census 2000. 1. Group may encompass several ancestries not listed separately. Source: U.S. Census Bureau, Ancestry: 2000, *issued June 2004.*

Persons Speaking a Language Other than English at Home, 2000

Language	Persons 5 years old and over who speak language	Language	Persons 5 years old and over who speak language
Population, 5 years and over	**262,375,152**	Persian	312,085
Speak only English	**215,423,557**	Gujarathi	235,988
Speak other language	**46,951,595**	Hindi	317,057
Spanish or Spanish Creole	**28,101,052**	Urdu	262,900
Other Indo-European languages	**10,017,989**	Other Indic languages	439,289
French (incl. Patois, Cajun)	1,643,838	Other Indo-European languages	327,946
French Creole	453,368	**Asian and Pacific Island languages**	**6,960,065**
Italian	1,008,370	Chinese	2,022,143
Portuguese or Portuguese Creole	564,630	Japanese	477,997
German	1,383,442	Korean	894,063
Yiddish	178,945	Mon-Khmer, Cambodian	181,889
Other West Germanic languages	251,135	Miao, Hmong	168,063
Scandinavian languages	162,252	Thai	120,464
Greek	365,436	Laotian	149,303
Russian	706,242	Vietnamese	1,009,627
Polish	667,414	Other Asian languages	398,434
Serbo-Croatian	233,865	Tagalog	1,224,241
Other Slavic languages	301,079	Other Pacific Island languages	313,841
Armenian	202,708	**Other languages**	**1,872,489**

Source: U.S. Census Bureau, Census 2000, Summary File 3, Table PCT 10, released Feb. 25, 2003.

Immigrants Admitted by Region and Top 20 Countries of Birth, 2003

Region and country of birth	Number	Percent	Region and country of birth	Number	Percent
Africa	48,738	6.9%	7. Vietnam	22,133	3.1%
Asia	244,759	34.7	8. Colombia	14,777	2.1
Europe	100,769	14.3	9. Guatemala	14,415	2.0
North America	250,726	35.5	10. Russia	13,951	2.0
Caribbean	68,815	9.7	11. Jamaica	13,384	1.9
Central America	54,565	7.7	12. Korea	12,512	1.8
Other North America	127,346	18.0	13. Haiti	12,314	1.7
Oceania	4,377	0.6	14. Ukraine	11,666	1.7
South America	55,247	7.8	15. Canada	11,446	1.6
Unknown	1,211	0.2	16. Poland	10,526	1.5
Specific countries			17. United Kingdom	9,601	1.4
1. Mexico	115,864	16.4%	18. Pakistan	9,444	1.3
2. India	50,372	7.1	19. Peru	9,444	1.3
3. Philippines	45,397	6.4	20. Cuba	9,304	1.3
4. China, People's Republic	40,659	5.8	Other	224,117	31.8
5. El Salvador	28,296	4.0	All countries	705,827	100.0
6. Dominican Republic	26,205	3.7			

Source: 2003 Yearbook of Immigration Statistics, U.S. Citizenship and Immigration Services.

Countries of Birth of the Foreign-Born Population, 1850–2000

(resident population)

Ten leading countries by rank[1]	1850	1880	1900	1930	1960
1.	Ireland 962,000	Germany 1,967,000	Germany 2,663,000	Italy 1,790,000	Italy 1,257,000
2.	Germany 584,000	Ireland 1,855,000	Ireland 1,615,000	Germany 1,609,000	Germany 990,000
3.	Great Britain 379,000	Great Britain 918,000	Canada 1,180,000	United Kingdom 1,403,000	Canada 953,000
4.	Canada 148,000	Canada 717,000	Great Britain 1,168,000	Canada 1,310,000	United Kingdom 833,000
5.	France 54,000	Sweden 194,000	Sweden 582,000	Poland 1,269,000	Poland 748,000
6.	Switzerland 13,000	Norway 182,000	Italy 484,000	Soviet Union 1,154,000	Soviet Union 691,000
7.	Mexico 13,000	France 107,000	Russia 424,000	Ireland 745,000	Mexico 576,000
8.	Norway 13,000	China 104,000	Poland 383,000	Mexico 641,000	Ireland 339,000
9.	Holland 10,000	Switzerland 89,000	Norway 336,000	Sweden 595,000	Austria 305,000
10.	Italy 4,000	Bohemia 85,000	Austria 276,000	Czechoslovakia 492,000	Hungary 245,000

Ten leading countries by rank[1]	1970	1980	1990	2000
1.	Italy 1,009,000	Mexico 2,199,000	Mexico 4,298,000	Mexico 7,841,000
2.	Germany 833,000	Germany 849,000	China 921,000	China 1,391,000
3.	Canada 812,000	Canada 843,000	Philippines 913,000	Philippines 1,222,000
4.	Mexico 760,000	Italy 832,000	Canada 745,000	India 1,007,000
5.	United Kingdom 686,000	United Kingdom 669,000	Cuba 737,000	Cuba 952,000
6.	Poland 548,000	Cuba 608,000	Germany 712,000	Vietnam 863,000
7.	Soviet Union 463,000	Philippines 501,000	United Kingdom 640,000	El Salvador 765,000
8.	Cuba 439,000	Poland 418,000	Italy 581,000	Korea 701,000
9.	Ireland 251,000	Soviet Union 406,000	Korea 568,000	Dominican Republic 692,000
10.	Austria 214,000	Korea 290,000	Vietnam 543,000	Canada 678,000

1. In general, countries as reported at each census. Data are not totally comparable over time due to changes in boundaries for some countries. Great Britain excludes Ireland. United Kingdom includes Northern Ireland. China in 1990 includes Hong Kong and Taiwan. Source: Profile of the Foreign-Born Population in the United States: 2000, U.S. Census Bureau, 2001.

Interracial Married Couples, 1980–2003
(in thousands)

Race and origin of spouses	1980	1990	1995	2000	2003
Married couples, total[1]	49,714	53,256	54,937	56,497	58,586
Interracial married couples, total[2]	651	964	1,392	1,464	2,094
Black/White	167	211	328	363	416
Black husband/White wife	122	150	206	268	275
White husband/Black wife	45	61	122	95	141
White/other race[3]	450	720	988	1,051	1,546
Black/other race[3]	34	33	76	50	132
Hispanic/other origin (not Hispanic)	891	1,193	1,434	1,743	1,888

1. Includes other married couples not shown separately. 2. Interracial married couples with at least one spouse of white or black race. 3. "Other race" is any race other than white or black, such as American Indian, Japanese, Chinese, etc. This total excludes combinations of other races. *Source:* U.S. Census Bureau, *Statistical Abstract of the United States: 2004–2005.*

Civil Rights Timeline

Milestones in the modern civil rights movement

May 17, 1954: The Supreme Court rules on the landmark case *Brown* v. *Board of Education of Topeka, Kans.,* unanimously agreeing that segregation in public schools is unconstitutional. The ruling paves the way for large-scale desegregation. The decision overturns the 1896 *Plessy* v. *Ferguson* ruling that sanctioned "separate but equal" segregation of the races, ruling that "separate educational facilities are inherently unequal." It is a victory for NAACP attorney Thurgood Marshall, who will later return to the Supreme Court as the nation's first black justice.

Aug. 1955: Fourteen-year-old black Chicagoan Emmett Till is visiting family in Mississippi when he is kidnapped, brutally beaten, shot, and dumped in the Tallahatchie River for allegedly whistling at a white woman. Two white men, J. W. Milam and Roy Bryant, are arrested for the murder and acquitted by an all-white jury. They later boast about committing the murder in a *Look* magazine interview. The case becomes a cause célèbre of the civil rights movement.

Dec. 1, 1955: In Montgomery, Ala., NAACP member Rosa Parks refuses to give up her seat at the front of the "colored section" of a bus to a white passenger, defying a southern custom of the time. In response to her arrest, the Montgomery black community launches a bus boycott, which will last for more than a year, until the buses are desegregated on Dec. 21, 1956. As newly elected president of the Montgomery Improvement Association (MIA), Reverend Martin Luther King, Jr., is instrumental in leading the boycott.

Jan.–Feb. 1957: Martin Luther King, Charles K. Steele, and Fred L. Shuttlesworth establish the Southern Christian Leadership Conference, of which King is made the first president. The SCLC becomes a major force in organizing the civil rights movement and bases its principles on nonviolence and civil disobedience. According to King, it is essential that the civil rights movement not sink to the level of the racists and hatemongers who oppose them: "We must forever conduct our struggle on the high plane of dignity and discipline," he urges.

Sept. 1957: In all-white Central High School in Little Rock, Ark., nine black students are blocked from entering the school on the orders of Governor Orval Faubus. President Eisenhower sends federal troops and the National Guard to intervene on behalf of the students, who become known as the "Little Rock Nine."

Feb. 1, 1960: Four black students from North Carolina Agricultural and Technical College in Greensboro, N.C., begin a sit-in at a segregated Woolworth's lunch counter. Although they are refused service, they are allowed to stay at the counter. In the following days, more black students join them. The event triggers many similar nonviolent protests throughout the South. Six months later the original four protesters are served lunch at the same Woolworth's counter. Student sit-ins would be effective throughout the Deep South in integrating parks, swimming pools, theaters, libraries, and other public facilities.

April 1960: The Student Nonviolent Coordinating Committee (SNCC) is founded at Shaw University in Raleigh, N.C., providing young blacks with a place in the civil rights movement. The SNCC later grows into a more radical organization, especially under the leadership of Stokely Carmichael (1966–1967).

May 4, 1961: The Congress of Racial Equality (CORE) begins sending student volunteers on bus trips to test the implementation of new laws prohibiting segregation in interstate travel facilities. One of the first two groups of "freedom riders," as they are called, encounters its first problem two weeks later, when a mob in Alabama sets the riders' bus on fire. The program continues, and by the end of the summer 1,000 volunteers, black and white, have participated.

Oct. 1, 1962: James Meredith becomes the first black student to enroll at the University of Mississippi. Violence and riots surrounding the incident cause President Kennedy to send 5,000 federal troops.

April 16, 1963: Martin Luther King is arrested and jailed during anti-segregation protests in Birmingham, Ala.; he writes his seminal "Letter From Birmingham City Jail," arguing that individuals have the moral duty to disobey unjust laws.

May 1963: During civil rights protests in Birmingham, Ala., Commissioner of Public Safety Eugene "Bull" Connor uses fire hoses and police dogs on black demonstrators. These images of brutality, which are televised and published widely, are instrumental in gaining sympathy for the civil rights movement around the world.

June 12, 1963: Mississippi's NAACP field secretary, 37-year-old Medgar Evers, is murdered outside his home in Jackson. Byron De La Beckwith is tried twice in 1964, both trials resulting in hung juries. Thirty years later he is convicted for murdering Evers.

Aug. 28, 1963: About 200,000 people join the March on Washington. Congregating at the Lincoln Memorial, in Washington, DC, participants listen as Martin Luther King delivers his famous "I Have a Dream" speech.

Sept. 15, 1963: Four young girls attending Sunday school in Birmingham, Ala., are killed when a bomb explodes at the Sixteenth Street Baptist Church, a popular location for civil rights meetings. Riots erupt in Birmingham, leading to the deaths of two more black youths.

Jan. 23, 1964: The 24th Amendment abolishes the poll tax, which originally had been instituted in 11 southern states after Reconstruction to make it difficult for poor blacks to vote.

Summer 1964: The Council of Federated Organizations (COFO), a network of civil rights groups that includes CORE and SNCC, launches a massive effort to register black voters during what becomes known as the Freedom Summer. It also sends delegates to the Democratic National Convention to protest—and attempt to unseat—the official all-white Mississippi contingent.

July 2, 1964: President Johnson signs the Civil Rights Act of 1964. The most sweeping civil rights legislation since Reconstruction, the Civil Rights Act prohibits discrimination of all kinds based on race, color, religion, or national origin. The law also provides the federal government with the powers to enforce desegregation.

Aug. 4, 1964: The bodies of three civil rights workers—two white, one black—are found in an earthen dam, six weeks into a federal investigation backed by President Johnson. James E. Chaney, 21; Andrew Goodman, 21; and Michael Schwerner, 24, had been working to register black voters in Mississippi, and, on June 21, had gone to investigate the burning of a black church. They were arrested by the police on speeding charges, incarcerated for several hours, and then released after dark into the hands of the Ku Klux Klan, who murdered them.

Feb. 21, 1965: Malcolm X, black nationalist and founder of the Organization of Afro-American Unity, is shot to death in Harlem. It is believed the assailants are members of the Black Muslim faith, which Malcolm had recently abandoned in favor of orthodox Islam.

March 7, 1965: Blacks begin a march from Selma, Ala., to Montgomery, Ala., in support of voting rights, but are stopped at the Pettus Bridge by a police blockade. Fifty marchers are hospitalized after police use tear gas, whips, and clubs against them. The incident is dubbed "Bloody Sunday" by the media.

Aug. 10, 1965: Congress passes the Voting Rights Act of 1965, making it easier for Southern blacks to register to vote. Literacy tests and other such requirements that were used to restrict black voting are made illegal.

Aug. 11–17, 1965: Race riots erupt in Watts, a black section of Los Angeles.

Sept. 24, 1965: Asserting that civil rights laws alone are not enough to remedy discrimination, President Johnson issues Executive Order 11246, which enforces affirmative action for the first time. It requires government contractors to "take affirmative action" toward prospective minority employees in all aspects of hiring and employment.

1966: The militant Black Panthers are founded in Oakland, Calif., by Huey Newton and Bobby Seale.

April 19, 1967: Stokely Carmichael, a leader of the Student Nonviolent Coordinating Committee (SNCC), coins the phrase "black power" in a speech in Seattle. He defines it as an assertion of black pride and "the coming together of black people to fight for their liberation by any means necessary." The term's radicalism alarms many who believe the civil rights movement's effectiveness and moral authority crucially depend on nonviolent civil disobedience.

June 12, 1967: In *Loving* v. *Virginia*, the Supreme Court rules that prohibiting interracial marriages is unconstitutional. Sixteen states that banned interracial marriage at the time are forced to revise their laws.

Summer 1967: Major race riots take place in Newark (July 12–16) and Detroit (July 23–30).

April 4, 1968: Martin Luther King, 39, is shot as he stands on the balcony outside his hotel room in Memphis, Tenn. Escaped convict and committed racist James Earl Ray is convicted of the crime.

April 11, 1968: President Johnson signs the Civil Rights Act of 1968, prohibiting discrimination in the sale, rental, and financing of housing.

April 20, 1971: The Supreme Court, in *Swann* v. *Charlotte-Mecklenburg Board of Education*, upholds busing as a legitimate means for achieving integration of public schools. Although largely unwelcome (and sometimes violently opposed) in local school districts, court-ordered busing plans in cities such as Charlotte, Boston, and Denver continue until the late 1990s.

June 28, 1978: In *Regents of the University of California* v. *Bakke,* the Supreme Court case imposed limitations on affirmative action, ruling that while race was a legitimate factor in school admissions, the use of inflexible quotas was not.

March 22, 1988: Overriding President Reagan's veto, Congress passes the Civil Rights Restoration Act, which expands the reach of nondiscrimination laws within private institutions receiving federal funds.

Nov. 22, 1991: After two years of debates, vetoes, and threatened vetoes, President Bush reverses himself and signs the Civil Rights Act of 1991, strengthening existing civil rights laws and providing for damages in cases of intentional employment discrimination.

April 29, 1992: The first large-scale race riots in decades erupt in south-central Los Angeles after a jury acquits four white police officers for the video-taped beating of African American Rodney King.

June 23, 2003: In the most important affirmative action decision since the 1978 *Bakke* case, the Supreme Court (5–4) upholds affirmative action in higher education, ruling that race can be one of many factors considered by colleges when selecting their students because it furthers "a compelling interest in obtaining the educational benefits that flow from a diverse student body."

June 21, 2005: The ringleader of the Mississippi civil rights murders (*see* Aug. 4, 1964), Edgar Ray Killen, is convicted of manslaughter on the 41st anniversary of the crimes.

Too Young to Die

The Supreme Court nixes the juvenile death penalty. What that says about the Justices' thinking—and ours

By CLAUDIA WALLIS TIME

In his Norman, Okla., law office, attorney Steven Presson stores two unusual keepsakes. One is a leather pouch that holds the ashes of Sean Sellers, the only person executed for a crime committed as a 16-year-old since the death penalty was reinstated in the U.S. in 1976. Sellers—who murdered his mother, his stepfather, and a store clerk—was dispatched by lethal injection in 1999, when he was 29. Presson's other memento is a plastic box containing the ashes of Scott Hain, who, it now seems fair to say, was the last juvenile offender to be executed in the U.S. Hain, sent to his death in 2003 at the age of 32, was 17 when he and a friend committed a grisly double murder.

Presson, who represented both boys, found it "very bittersweet" when the U.S. Supreme Court ruled in March 2005 that it was cruel and unusual to sentence anyone to death for crimes committed before the age of 18. "I'm happy for those on death row, but it came six years too late for Sean and two years too late for Scott," says Presson. "We've been arguing for decades that kids don't have the same moral culpability that adults have, and finally, finally, they listened."

It took 16 years for the high court to come around to Presson's point of view, by a narrow 5–4 vote. In 1989 the court ruled 5–4 the other way. Justice Antonin Scalia, who wrote the 1989 decision, argued that there was neither a "historical nor a modern societal consensus" forbidding capital punishment for 16- or 17-year-olds (though the court had found such a consensus for those under 16 a year earlier). In March 2005, however, Scalia was on the short side of the decision.

Judged Cruel and Unusual

What changed? The views of Justice Anthony Kennedy, for one thing. While Kennedy voted with Scalia in 1989, he wrote a very different majority opinion this time around. Why did Kennedy change his mind? Legal tradition invites him to do so. Since 1958 the Court has applied a flexible standard to interpreting the Eighth Amendment's ban on "cruel and unusual punishments." What we mean by the phrase, wrote then Chief Justice Earl Warren in *Trop* v. *Dulles*, depends on "the evolving standards of decency that mark the progress of a maturing society."

How do you know that society no longer believes in sentencing a 17-year-old killer to death? Kennedy's argument mirrors his reasoning in a 2002 decision that outlawed death sentences for the mentally retarded. He notes that since 1989 five states have banned capital punishment for juveniles, making the practice illegal in 30 states, including the 12 with an outright ban on executions. Second, Kennedy cites scientific literature showing that, like the retarded, adolescents lack mature judgment and a full appreciation of the consequences of their actions. They are also more vulnerable than adults to peer pressure. Third, Kennedy points out that only seven other countries have executed juvenile offenders since 1990, and all seven have repudiated the practice: "The United States now stands alone in a world that has turned its face against the juvenile death penalty."

International Practices

"This reference to international practices is a very big deal," says Cass Sunstein, a constitutional scholar at the University of Chicago Law School, and is part of a surprising new trend in Supreme Court thinking. Overseas legal practices were also cited by the court in the 2002 ruling on the mentally retarded and in a 2003 decision overturning a Texas law banning gay sex. For his part, Scalia blasted his brethren for suggesting that "American law should conform to the laws of the rest of the world" and pointed out that the U.S. has unique legal traditions.

In the 12 states where juvenile offenders have been languishing, death sentences will be lifted for 72 offenders. That brought dismay to many victims' families. Martin Soto-Fong was 17 in 1992 when he and two accomplices robbed the El Grande Market in Tucson, Ariz., for $300 and shot three workers. Richard Gee, who lost a brother and an uncle that day, is not happy to see the murderer exit death row. "We had him at the gates of hell," he says, "and he got kicked back." ☐

Prisoners in the United States, 1990–2004

Year	Total inmates	Federal prisoners	State prisoners	Local jails
1990	1,148,702	58,838	684,544	405,320
1995	1,585,586	89,538	989,004	507,044
2000	1,935,919[1]	133,921	1,176,269	621,149
2004	2,131,180[1]	169,370	1,241,034	713,990

1. Total counts include federal inmates in non-secure privately operated facilities (6,143 in 2000 and 6,786 in June 2004).
Source: Prison and Jail Inmates at Midyear 2004, U.S. Bureau of Justice Statistics.

Number of Persons Executed[1] by Jurisdiction, 1930–2004

State	Number executed since 1930	Number executed since 1976[2]	State	Number executed since 1930	Number executed since 1976[2]	State	Number executed since 1930	Number executed since 1976[2]
Texas	633	336	Oklahoma	135	75	Delaware	25	13
Georgia	402	36	Kentucky	105	2	Oregon	21	2
New York	329	0	Illinois	102	12	Connecticut	21	0
California	302	10	Tennessee	94	1	Utah	19	6
North Carolina	297	34	New Jersey	74	0	Iowa	18	0
Florida	229	59	Maryland	72	4	Kansas	15	0
South Carolina	194	32	Arizona	60	22	New Mexico	9	1
Virginia	186	94	Washington	51	4	Montana	8	2
Ohio	187	15	Indiana	52	11	Wyoming	8	1
Alabama	165	30	Colorado	48	1	Nebraska	7	3
Louisiana	160	27	District of Columbia	40	0	Idaho	4	1
Mississippi	160	6	West Virginia	40	0	Vermont	4	0
Pennsylvania	155	3	Nevada	41	11	New Hampshire	1	0
Arkansas	144	26	Federal system	36	3	South Dakota	1	0
Missouri	123	61	Massachusetts	27	0	U.S. total	4,803	944

NOTE: 59 people were executed in 2004. 1. Executed under civil authority; military authorities carried out an additional 160 executions, 1930–1997. 2. In 1972 the Supreme Court ruled that capital punishment, as it was then administered, was "cruel and unusual" and therefore unconstitutional. On July 1, 1976, however, the Court overturned the ruling by a 7–2 decision, and capital punishment was reinstated. *Source:* U.S. Bureau of Justice Statistics, and Death Penalty Information Center. Web: www.deathpenaltyinfo.org.

Characteristics of Prisoners Under Sentence of Death

Characteristic	1980	1990	2002	Characteristic	1980	1990	2002
Race and age				**Marital status**			
White	418	1,368	1,931	Never married	268	998	1,746
Black and other	270	978	1,626	Married	229	632	709
Under 20 years	11	8	4	Divorced[1]	217	726	1,102
20 to 24 years	173	168	153	**Time elapsed since sentencing**			
25 to 34 years	334	1,110	1,058	Less than 12 months	185	231	147
35 to 54 years	186	1,006	2,069	12 to 47 months	389	753	609
55 years and over	10	64	273	48 to 71 months	102	438	468
Years of schooling completed				72 months and over	38	934	2,333
7 years or less	68	178	215	**Legal status at arrest**			
8 years	74	186	234	Not under sentence	384	1,345	2,165
9 to 11 years	204	775	1,130	Parole or probation[2]	115	578	909
12 years	162	729	1,173	Prison or escaped	45	128	141
More than 12 years	43	209	294	Unknown	170	305	342
Unknown	163	279	511	**Total**	688	2,346	3,557

NOTE: Excludes prisoners under sentence of death confined in local correctional systems pending appeal or who have not been committed to prison. 1. Includes persons married but separated, widows, widowers, and unknown. 2. Includes prisoners on mandatory conditional release, work release, leave, AWOL, or bail. *Source:* U.S. Bureau of Justice Statistics, *Capital Punishment,* annual, from *Statistical Abstract of the United States, 2004–2005.*

Death Row Exonerations, 1973–2005

Between 1973 and March 2005, 119 inmates on death row have been exonerated and freed. The most common reasons for wrongful convictions are mistaken eyewitness testimony, the false testimony of informants and "incentivized witnesses," incompetent lawyers, defective or fraudulent scientific evidence, prosecutorial and police misconduct, and false confessions. In recent years, DNA played a role in overturning 12 of these wrongful death row convictions.

State	Number	State	Number	State	Number	State	Number
Florida	21	Georgia	5	Missouri	3	Nebraska	1
Illinois	18	North Carolina	5	Indiana	2	Nevada	1
Louisiana	8	Ohio	5	South Carolina	2	Virginia	1
Texas	8	Pennsylvania	5	Idaho	1	Washington	1
Arizona	7	New Mexico	4	Kentucky	1	**Total**	**119**
Oklahoma	7	California	3	Maryland	1		
Alabama	5	Massachusetts	3	Mississippi	1		

Source: The Death Penalty Information Center. Web: www.deathpenaltyinfo.org.

Methods of Execution Used in Capital Punishment

State	Method	State	Method
Alabama	Lethal injection or electrocution	Montana	Lethal injection
Alaska	No death penalty	Nebraska	Electrocution
Arizona[1]	Lethal injection or gas	Nevada	Lethal injection
Arkansas[2]	Lethal injection or electrocution	New Hampshire[5]	Lethal injection or hanging
California	Lethal injection or gas	New Jersey	Lethal injection
Colorado	Lethal injection	New Mexico	Lethal injection
Connecticut	Lethal injection	New York	Lethal injection
Delaware[3]	Lethal injection or hanging	North Carolina	Lethal injection
District of	No death penalty	North Dakota	No death penalty
Columbia		Ohio	Lethal injection
Florida	Lethal injection or electrocution	Oklahoma[6]	Lethal injection, electrocution,
Georgia	Lethal injection		or firing squad
Hawaii	No death penalty	Oregon	Lethal injection
Idaho	Lethal injection or firing squad	Pennsylvania	Lethal injection
Illinois	Lethal injection	Rhode Island	No death penalty
Indiana	Lethal injection	South Carolina	Lethal injection or electrocution
Iowa	No death penalty	South Dakota	Lethal injection
Kansas	Lethal injection	Tennessee[7]	Lethal injection or electrocution
Kentucky[4]	Lethal injection or electrocution	Texas	Lethal injection
Louisiana	Lethal injection	Utah	Lethal injection or firing squad
Maine	No death penalty	Vermont	No death penalty
Maryland	Lethal injection	Virginia	Lethal injection or electrocution
Massachusetts	No death penalty	Washington	Lethal injection or hanging
Michigan	No death penalty	West Virginia	No death penalty
Minnesota	No death penalty	Wisconsin	No death penalty
Mississippi	Lethal injection	Wyoming[8]	Lethal injection or gas
Missouri	Lethal injection or gas	Federal system[9]	Lethal injection

NOTE: As of March 1, 2005, the Supreme Court ruled that the Constitution bars capital punishment for crimes committed before the age of 18. 1. For those sentenced after 11/15/92, only lethal injection is authorized. 2. For those whose capital offense occurred on or after 7/4/83, only lethal injection is authorized. 3. For those whose capital offense occurred after 6/13/86, only lethal injection is authorized. 4. For those sentenced on or after 3/31/98, only lethal injection is authorized. 5. Hanging is authorized only if lethal injection cannot be given. 6. Electrocution is authorized if lethal injection is ever held to be unconstitutional, and firing squad if both lethal injection and electrocution are held unconstitutional. 7. For those whose capital offense occurred after 12/31/98, only lethal injection is authorized. 8. Lethal gas is authorized if lethal injection is ever held to be unconstitutional. 9. For offenses under the Violent Crime Control and Law Enforcement Act of 1994, the method is that of the state in which the conviction took place. *Source: Capital Punishment, 2003,* U.S. Bureau of Justice Statistics, and the Death Penalty Information Center.

Federal Prosecutions of Public Corruption

Prosecution status	2002	2001	2000	1999	1997	1996	1995	1990	1985	1980
Total: Indicted	1,136	1,087	1,000	1,134	1,057	984	1,051	1,176	1,157	727
Convicted	1,011	920	938	1,065	853	902	878	1,084	997	602
Federal officials: Indicted	478	502	441	480	459	456	527	615	563	123
Convicted	429	414	422	460	392	459	438	583	470	131
State officials: Indicted	110	95	92	115	51	109	61	96	79	72
Convicted	132	61	91	80	49	83	61	79	66	51
Local officials: Indicted	299	224	211	237	255	219	236	257	248	247
Convicted	262	184	183	219	169	190	191	225	221	168

NOTE: Figures are latest available. *Source:* U.S. Department of Justice, *Federal Prosecutions of Corrupt Public Officials, 1970–1980,* and *Report to Congress on the Activities and Operations of the Public Integrity Section,* annual. From *Statistical Abstract of the United States, 2004–2005.*

Law Enforcement Officers Killed or Assaulted[1]

	2002	2001	2000	1999	1997	1996	1995	1994	1990	1985	1980
Total officers killed	132	218	134	107	133	113	133	141	132	145	164
Officers assaulted											
Firearm	1,889	1,841	1,749	1,772	2,110	1,878	2,354	3,174	3,651	2,793	3,295
Knife or cutting instrument	1,056	1,168	1,015	999	971	871	1,356	1,510	1,647	1,715	1,653
Other dangerous weapon	8,326	8,233	8,132	7,560	5,800	5,069	6,414	7,197	7,423	5,263	5,415
Hands, fists, feet, etc.	46,795	46,221	47,502	45,640	43,268	38,790	47,638	53,086	59,370	51,953	47,484
Total assaulted	58,066	57,463	58,398	55,971	52,149	46,608	57,762	64,967	72,091	61,724	57,847

NOTE: Figures are latest available. 1. Covers officers killed feloniously and accidentally in line of duty; includes federal officers. *Source:* U.S. Federal Bureau of Investigation, *Law Enforcement Officers Killed and Assaulted,* annual. From *Statistical Abstract of the United States, 2004–2005.*

Homicide Rate (per 100,000), 1950–2003

Year	Homicide rate	Year	Homicide rate	Year	Homicide rate	Year	Homicide rate	Year	Homicide rate
1950	4.6	1961	4.8	1972	9.0	1983	8.3	1994	9.0
1951	4.4	1962	4.6	1973	9.4	1984	7.9	1995	8.2
1952	4.6	1963	4.6	1974	9.8	1985	7.9	1996	7.4
1953	4.5	1964	4.9	1975	9.6	1986	8.6	1997	6.8
1954	4.2	1965	5.1	1976	8.8	1987	8.3	1998	6.3
1955	4.1	1966	5.6	1977	8.8	1988	8.4	1999	5.7
1956	4.1	1967	6.2	1978	9.0	1989	8.7	2000	5.5
1957	4.0	1968	6.9	1979	9.7	1990	9.4	2001	5.6
1958	4.8	1969	7.3	1980	10.2	1991	9.8	2002	5.6
1959	4.9	1970	7.9	1981	9.8	1992	9.3	2003	5.7
1960	5.1	1971	8.6	1982	9.1	1993	9.5		

Source: Crime in the United States, 2003, FBI, Uniform Crime Reports.

Murder Victims: by Race and Sex, 2003

Race and sex	Total no. victims	Percent distribution[1]	Race and sex	Total no. victims	Percent distribution[1]
Race			**Sex**		
White	6,913	48.0%	Male	11,167	77.5%
Black	6,887	47.8	Female	3,215	22.3
Other	408	2.8	Unknown	26	0.2
Unknown	200	1.4	**Total**	**14,408**	**100.0**

1. Because of rounding, percentages may not add up to 100. Source: Crime in the United States, 2003, FBI, Uniform Crime Reports.

Murder Victims: Types of Weapon Used, 2003

Type of weapon	Total no. victims	Percent distribution[1]	Type of weapon	Total no. victims	Percent distribution[1]
Firearms	9,638	66.9%	Explosives	4	([3])
Knives or cutting instruments	1,816	12.6	Fire	163	1.1%
Blunt objects (clubs, hammers, etc.)	651	4.5	Narcotics	41	0.3
			Strangulation	184	1.3
Personal weapons (hands, fists, feet, etc.)[2]	946	6.6	Asphyxiation	128	0.9
Poison	9	0.1	Other weapon or not stated[4]	828	5.7
			Total	**14,408**	**100.0**

1. Because of rounding, percentages may not add up to 100. 2. Pushed is included in personal weapons. 3. Less than one-tenth of 1%. 4. Includes drowning. Source: Crime in the United States, 2003, FBI, Uniform Crime Reports.

Murderers, by Sex and Race, 2003

Race and sex	Total no. murders	Percent distribution[1]	Race and sex	Total no. murders	Percent distribution[1]
Race			**Sex**		
White	5,132	32.0%	Male	10,218	63.7%
Black	5,729	35.7	Female	1,123	7.0
Other	308	1.9	Unknown	4,702	29.3
Unknown	4,874	30.4	**Total**	**16,043**	**100.0**

1. Because of rounding, percentages may not add up to 100. Source: Crime in the United States, 2003, FBI, Uniform Crime Reports.

Number of School-Associated Violent Deaths Occurring At and Away from School, 1992–2002

School year	Total student, staff, and nonstudent school-associated violent deaths	Homicides of youths ages 5–19	
		Homicides at school	Homicides away from school
Total 1992–2000	**390**	**234**	**24,406**
1995–1996	53	32	3,303
1996–1997	48	28	2,950
1997–1998	57	34	2,728
1998–1999	47	33	2,366
1999–2000	32[1]	16[1]	2,124
2000–2001	27[1]	10[1]	2,045
2001–2002	31[1]	14[1]	n.a.

NOTE: At school includes on school property, on the way to or from school, and while attending or traveling to or from a school sponsored event. n.a. = not available. 1. Preliminary data. Source: Statistical Abstract of the United States: 2004–2005.

Summary of Hate Crime Statistics, 2003

	Number of incidents	Number of offenses	Number of victims	Number of known offenders
Race	3,844	4,574	4,754	3,866
Anti-white	830	969	1,006	1,019
Anti-black	2,548	3,032	3,150	2,456
Anti-American Indian/Alaskan native	76	83	85	80
Anti-Asian/Pacific Islander	231	277	289	196
Anti-multi-racial group	159	213	224	135
Religion	1,343	1,426	1,489	574
Anti-Jewish	927	987	1,025	332
Anti-Catholic	76	78	80	32
Anti-Protestant	49	50	54	20
Anti-Islamic	149	155	171	94
Anti-other religious group	109	118	120	69
Anti-multi-religious group	24	25	26	17
Anti-atheism/agnosticism/etc.	9	13	13	10
Sexual orientation	1,239	1,430	1,479	1,313
Anti-male homosexual	783	881	910	863
Anti-female homosexual	187	220	230	167
Anti-homosexual	247	305	314	257
Anti-heterosexual	14	15	15	10
Anti-bisexual	8	9	10	16
Disability	33	40	43	35
Anti-physical	24	30	32	24
Anti-mental	9	10	11	11
Multiple-bias incidents[1]	4	9	9	7
Total	7,489	8,715	9,100	6,934

1. A *multiple-bias incident* is a hate crime in which two or more offense types were committed as a result of two or more bias motivations. *Source: Crime in the United States, 2003,* FBI, Uniform Crime Reports.

Index of Crime, United States, 1979–2003

(rate per 100,000 inhabitants)

Year	Crime index total	Violent crime[1]	Property crime[2]	Murder and non-negligent man-slaughter	Forcible rape	Robbery	Aggra-vated assault	Burglary	Larceny-theft	Motor vehicle theft
1979	5,565.5	548.9	5,016.6	9.7	34.7	218.4	286.0	1,511.9	2,999.1	505.6
1980	5,950.0	596.6	5,353.3	10.2	36.8	251.1	298.5	1,684.1	3,167.0	502.2
1981	5,858.2	594.3	5,263.9	9.8	36.0	258.7	289.7	1,649.5	3,139.7	474.7
1982	5,603.6	571.1	5,032.5	9.1	34.0	238.9	289.2	1,488.8	3,084.8	458.8
1983	5,175.0	537.7	4,637.4	8.3	33.7	216.5	279.2	1,337.7	2,868.9	430.8
1984	5,031.3	539.2	4,492.1	7.9	35.7	205.4	290.2	1,263.7	2,791.3	437.1
1985	5,207.1	556.6	4,650.5	8.0	37.1	208.5	302.9	1,287.3	2,901.2	462.0
1986	5,480.4	617.7	4,862.6	8.6	37.9	225.1	346.1	1,344.6	3,010.3	507.8
1987	5,550.0	609.7	4,940.3	8.3	37.4	212.7	351.3	1,329.6	3,081.3	529.4
1988	5,664.2	637.2	5,027.1	8.4	37.6	220.9	370.2	1,309.2	3,134.9	582.9
1989	5,741.0	663.1	5,077.9	8.7	38.1	233.0	383.4	1,276.3	3,171.3	630.4
1990	5,820.3	731.8	5,088.5	9.4	41.2	257.0	424.1	1,235.9	3,194.8	657.8
1991	5,897.8	758.1	5,139.7	9.8	42.3	272.7	433.3	1,252.0	3,228.8	659.0
1992	5,660.2	757.5	4,902.7	9.3	42.8	263.6	441.8	1,168.2	3,103.0	631.5
1993	5,484.4	746.8	4,737.6	9.5	41.1	255.9	440.3	1,099.2	3,032.4	606.1
1994	5,373.5	713.6	4,660.0	9.0	39.3	237.7	427.6	1,042.0	3,026.7	591.3
1995	5,275.9	684.6	4,591.3	8.2	37.1	220.9	418.3	987.1	3,043.8	560.4
1996	5,086.6	636.5	4,450.1	7.4	36.3	201.9	390.9	944.8	2,797.7	525.6
1997	4,930.0	611.3	4,318.7	6.8	35.9	186.3	382.3	919.4	2,893.4	506.0
1998	4,619.3	567.5	4,051.8	6.3	34.5	165.4	361.3	863.0	2,729.0	459.8
1999	4,266.8	524.7	3,742.1	5.7	32.7	150.2	336.1	770.0	2,551.4	420.7
2000	4,124.0	506.1	3,617.9	5.5	32.0	144.9	323.6	728.4	2,475.3	414.2
2001	4,160.5	504.4	3,656.1	5.6	31.8	148.5	318.5	740.8	2,484.6	430.6
2002	4,118.8	494.6	3,624.1	5.6	33.0	145.9	310.1	746.2	2,445.8	432.1
2003	(3)	475.0	3,588.4	5.7	32.1	142.2	295.0	740.5	2,414.5	433.4

1. Violent crimes are offenses of murder, forcible rape, robbery, and aggravated assault. 2. Property crimes are offenses of burglary, larceny-theft, and motor vehicle theft. Data are not included for the property crime of arson. 3. The FBI has suspended use of the crime index, first used in the U.S. in 1960, because it "has not been a true indicator of the degree of criminality." *Source: Crime in the United States, 2003,* FBI, Uniform Crime Reports.

Arrests by Race, 2003

Offense charged	White	Black	American Indian or Alaskan Native	Asian or Pacific Islander
Total number	6,723,093	2,570,770	125,438	110,168
Total percent	70.6%	27.0%	1.3%	1.2%
Murder[2]	49.1	48.5	1.1	1.2
Forcible rape	64.1	33.3	1.3	1.3
Robbery	43.9	54.4	0.6	1.1
Aggravated assault	64.7	33.0	1.1	1.2
Burglary	70.5	27.5	1.0	1.0
Larceny-theft	68.5	28.8	1.3	1.5
Motor vehicle theft	61.3	35.9	1.0	1.8
Arson	77.5	20.9	0.9	0.7
Other assaults	65.7	31.8	1.3	1.2
Forgery and counterfeiting	69.3	28.9	0.6	1.2
Fraud	68.8	29.9	0.6	0.7
Embezzlement	68.3	29.8	0.5	1.4
Stolen property—buying, receiving, possessing	60.6	37.6	0.7	1.0
Vandalism	76.2	21.2	1.4	1.2
Weapons possession	62.1	36.1	0.7	1.1
Prostitution	58.0	39.3	0.5	2.2
Sex offenses, except forcible rape and prostitution	73.7%	23.9%	1.0%	1.4%
Drug abuse violation	66.0	32.6	0.6	0.8
Gambling	26.6	69.7	0.2	3.5
Offenses against family and children	67.2	30.4	1.3	1.2
Driving under the influence	88.0	9.6	1.4	1.0
Liquor laws	87.3	8.9	2.8	1.0
Drunkenness	84.1	12.8	2.6	0.6
Disorderly conduct	67.5	30.2	1.5	0.8
Vagrancy	55.9	41.6	1.8	0.7
All other offenses except traffic	66.9	30.4	1.4	1.3
Suspicion	64.5	34.0	0.6	0.8
Curfew and loitering law violations	67.9	30.0	0.8	1.3
Runaways	73.4	20.2	1.7	4.7

NOTE: For arrests 18 years and older. Total number of estimated arrests for all ages: 13.7 million. 1. Because of rounding, the percentages may not add up to total. 2. Includes nonnegligent manslaughter. *Source: Crime in the United States, 2003,* FBI, Uniform Crime Reports.

Crime Rate by State, 2003

(rate per 100,000 inhabitants)

State	Violent crime (total)[1]	Murder[2]	Forcible rape	Robbery	Property crime (total)[3]
Ala.	429.5	6.6	36.8	134.2	4,049.1
Alaska	593.4	6.0	92.5	68.4	3,742.2
Ariz.	513.2	7.9	33.3	136.5	5,632.4
Ark.	456.1	6.4	33.1	81.7	3,621.4
Calif.	579.3	6.8	28.2	179.7	3,424.3
Colo.	345.1	3.9	41.6	82.1	3,940.9
Conn.	308.2	3.0	18.7	119.0	2,606.7
Del.	658.0	2.9	43.2	169.9	3,384.4
DC	1,608.1	44.2	48.6	699.5	5,800.3
Fla.	730.2	5.4	39.5	185.2	4,452.0
Ga.	453.9	7.6	25.7	161.8	4,254.6
Hawaii	270.4	1.7	29.2	92.9	5,237.5
Idaho	242.7	1.8	37.2	17.9	2,908.7
Ill.[4]	556.8	7.1	32.9	188.2	3,284.4
Ind.	352.8	5.5	27.8	103.3	3,357.7
Iowa	272.4	1.6	25.9	38.1	2,961.1
Kans.	395.5	4.5	38.3	82.5	3,994.0
Ky.[4]	261.7	4.6	25.6	77.6	2,681.5
La.	646.3	13.0	41.1	157.2	4,349.5
Maine	108.9	1.2	27.1	22.1	2,456.7
Md.	703.9	9.5	24.7	241.5	3,801.4
Mass.	469.4	2.2	27.9	124.1	2,549.5
Mich.	511.2	6.1	54.1	111.7	3,277.3
Minn.	262.6	2.5	41.2	77.2	3,116.8
Miss.	325.5	9.3	37.4	104.8	3,720.4
Mo.	472.8	5.0	24.4	108.7	4,014.5
Mont.	365.2	3.3	26.8	32.5	3,098.0
Nebr.	289.0	3.2	28.5	66.8	3,711.4
Nev.	614.2	8.8	39.0	230.3	4,288.4
N.H.	148.8	1.4	33.2	37.1	2,053.9
N.J.	365.4	4.7	15.3	154.7	2,544.4
N.M.	665.2	6.0	50.0	104.0	4,123.6
N.Y.	465.2	4.9	19.7	186.3	2,248.3
N.C.	454.9	6.1	25.4	145.5	4,278.0
N.D.	77.8	1.9	23.8	8.0	2,096.1
Ohio	333.2	4.6	40.1	147.7	3,640.5
Okla.	505.7	5.9	42.7	91.8	4,306.0
Ore.	295.5	1.9	34.2	80.1	4,782.3
Pa.	398.0	5.3	28.8	145.4	2,431.3
P.R.	306.4	20.1	5.3	199.5	1,802.1
R.I.	285.6	2.3	46.9	77.1	2,995.0
S.C.	793.5	7.2	44.4	136.7	4,477.1
S.D.	173.4	1.3	46.3	13.6	2,001.7
Tenn.	687.8	6.8	35.7	160.4	4,379.4
Tex.	552.5	6.4	36.2	167.4	4,595.3
Utah	248.6	2.5	37.9	53.4	4,225.5
Vt.	110.2	2.3	19.5	9.7	2,200.1
Va.	275.8	5.6	24.0	90.3	2,704.1
Wash.	347.0	3.0	46.7	93.3	4,754.9
W. Va.	257.5	3.5	16.4	40.3	2,359.4
Wis.	221.0	3.3	21.9	80.1	2,882.6
Wyo.	262.1	2.8	27.1	16.8	3,321.3

NOTE: Violent crimes are murder, forcible rape, robbery, and aggravated assault. Property crimes are burglary, larceny-theft, and motor vehicle theft. Data are not included for the property crime of arson. 1. "Violent crime total" includes murder, forcible rape, robbery, and aggravated assault. 2. Includes nonnegligent manslaughter. 3. "Property crime total" includes burglary, larceny-theft, and motor vehicle theft. Data are not included for the property crime of arson. 4. Limited data for 2003 were available for the states of Illinois and Kentucky; therefore, it was necessary that their crime counts be estimated. *Source: Crime in the United States, 2003,* FBI, Uniform Crime Reports.

Crime Rates for Selected Large Cities, 2002
(offenses known to the police per 100,000 inhabitants)

City ranked by population size, 2002[1]	Crime index, total	Violent crime				Property crime		
		Murder	Forcible rape	Robbery	Aggravated assault	Burglary	Larceny-theft	Motor vehicle theft
New York, N.Y.	3,100.1	7.3	20.9	336.8	424.7	372.3	1,603.7	334.4
Los Angeles, Calif.	4,986.0	17.1	36.9	448.9	846.6	662.4	2,083.6	890.5
Chicago, Ill.	(2)	22.1	(2)	630.7	845.5	869.6	3,280.1	859.2
Houston, Tex.	7,313.9	12.5	43.7	549.5	617.4	1,318.5	3,599.2	1,173.1
Philadelphia, Pa.	5,471.1	18.9	67.9	581.9	647.2	737.7	2,544.8	872.7
Phoenix, Ariz.	7,823.5	12.6	29.2	290.0	395.8	1,199.7	4,072.4	1,823.9
San Diego, Calif.	3,951.9	3.7	26.0	128.3	409.1	602.3	1,937.7	844.8
Dallas, Tex.	9,024.7	15.8	52.8	647.7	654.5	1,639.3	4,535.4	1,479.3
San Antonio, Tex.	7,873.3	8.4	38.8	176.8	593.1	1,118.1	5,457.6	480.4
Las Vegas, Nev.[3]	4,924.8	11.9	42.8	327.3	396.5	965.4	2,098.2	1,082.7
Detroit, Mich.	8,839.5	41.8	73.6	653.6	1,303.8	1,496.8	2,790.0	2,480.0
San Jose, Calif.	2,601.7	2.8	40.8	89.1	312.8	326.1	1,470.3	359.7
Honolulu, Hawaii	6,360.4	2.0	33.8	119.1	134.0	992.0	4,136.9	942.7
Indianapolis, Ind.[3]	6,032.5	13.9	54.8	365.3	501.0	1,201.7	3,087.1	808.7
San Francisco, Calif.	5,299.0	8.4	26.1	398.4	319.5	738.5	3,038.5	769.6
Jacksonville, Fla.	6,632.5	11.7	36.0	262.1	605.8	1,192.5	3,820.7	703.8
Columbus, Ohio	9,257.7	11.3	94.0	489.4	313.2	2,244.7	5,038.6	1,066.5
Austin, Tex.	7,267.1	3.6	37.3	171.2	254.9	1,008.5	4,334.5	457.1
Baltimore, Md.	8,318.6	37.7	26.5	702.5	1,288.2	1,305.3	3,981.4	977.0
Memphis, Tenn.	9,947.2	22.5	78.0	640.7	831.2	2,469.7	4,513.5	1,391.7
Charlotte-Mecklenburg, N.C.	7,512.7	10.4	44.7	447.2	670.0	1,625.7	3,997.7	717.0
Milwaukee, Wis.	7,647.8	18.3	53.8	527.9	354.7	1,143.0	4,363.3	1,186.8
Boston, Mass.	5,986.5	10.1	61.9	424.7	669.6	642.1	2,988.4	1,189.7
El Paso, Tex.	4,585.6	2.4	37.5	97.7	523.5	377.2	3,208.0	339.4
Seattle, Wash.	8,004.3	4.5	26.2	271.7	403.0	1,256.7	4,610.0	1,432.2
Washington, DC	7,767.9	45.9	45.9	653.5	850.2	905.1	3,661.4	1,605.9
Denver, Colo.	5,511.1	8.8	55.2	205.0	265.2	1,049.6	2,646.7	1,280.7
Nashville, Tenn.	8,209.5	11.2	71.9	371.0	1,094.9	1,332.2	4,474.5	853.7
Fort Worth, Tex.	8,021.0	9.5	57.5	295.1	397.7	1,743.3	4,813.1	704.9
Portland, Ore.	7,955.7	3.7	65.0	237.6	522.2	1,047.0	5,129.0	951.1
Oklahoma City, Okla.	9,743.2	7.4	86.8	228.1	500.0	1,622.4	6,573.5	725.0
Tucson, Ariz.	9,692.9	9.1	65.3	260.8	574.6	1,297.7	6,286.4	1,199.0
New Orleans, La.	6,418.9	53.1	33.3	410.2	440.6	978.9	2,946.6	1,556.3
Cleveland, Ohio	6,900.2	16.6	128.6	678.0	499.1	1,682.2	2,753.1	1,142.6
Long Beach, Calif.	4,034.3	14.0	30.1	314.5	399.2	711.6	1,782.7	782.1
Albuquerque, N.M.	7,817.0	11.1	64.0	283.1	710.4	1,191.7	4,671.4	885.3
Kansas City, Mo.	10,039.5	18.5	67.0	449.2	817.6	1,782.2	5,397.3	1,507.7
Fresno, Calif.	7,648.1	9.5	35.6	333.6	473.9	1,009.6	4,167.7	1,618.3
Virginia Beach, Va.	3,671.4	0.7	31.5	101.1	85.8	522.6	2,736.6	193.1
Atlanta, Ga.	11,355.2	34.9	63.4	957.1	1,233.8	1,964.2	5,443.5	1,658.3
Sacramento, Calif.	7,294.3	11.1	43.8	410.9	374.7	1,189.4	3,684.6	1,579.7
Mesa, Ariz.	7,907.8	5.2	30.6	140.0	509.1	1,175.9	4,840.5	1,206.5
Oakland, Calif.	7,213.4	26.1	60.1	592.0	688.6	1,026.7	3,308.6	1,511.2
Tulsa, Okla.	7,568.5	6.5	61.1	226.4	792.3	1,586.4	4,000.0	895.8
Omaha, Nebr.	7,303.2	6.6	43.9	253.2	414.1	817.1	4,691.8	1,076.4
Minneapolis, Minn.	6,820.9	12.0	92.7	459.5	491.8	1,135.5	3,750.1	879.3
Miami, Fla.	8,957.3	17.1	25.3	713.9	1,150.5	1,572.9	4,191.1	1,286.4
Colorado Springs, Colo.	5,407.1	6.6	60.8	121.7	318.7	1,028.3	3,444.7	426.3
St. Louis, Mo.	14,285.7	31.4	38.5	798.3	1,256.1	1,999.7	7,375.6	2,786.1
Wichita, Kans.	6,930.4	5.8	59.8	228.9	386.4	1,282.1	4,463.2	504.3
Santa Ana, Calif.	3,435.6	6.6	18.8	248.6	276.8	349.6	1,850.8	684.4
Pittsburgh, Pa.	5,762.1	13.7	43.2	471.8	578.9	962.8	2,951.0	740.7
Arlington, Tex.	6,784.0	4.0	43.7	228.3	357.1	1,046.0	4,527.5	577.4
Anaheim, Calif.	3,587.0	5.0	23.5	136.7	243.2	586.7	2,042.3	549.6
Cincinnati, Ohio	8,506.8	21.0	105.0	718.0	431.2	1,929.6	4,240.4	1,061.6
Toledo, Ohio	8,468.1	8.9	58.6	436.8	504.6	1,841.8	4,599.0	1,018.4
Tampa, Fla.	11,194.6	11.7	64.3	735.5	1,170.4	1,980.0	5,069.9	2,117.7
Buffalo, N.Y.	6,436.8	14.6	62.6	550.7	643.8	1,305.5	3,085.2	774.4
St. Paul, Minn.	6,076.1	4.4	65.5	332.1	403.1	1,103.1	3,426.9	741.0
Aurora, Colo.	6,222.4	5.5	83.6	188.5	353.3	749.4	3,632.8	1,209.3
Corpus Christi, Tex.	7,238.1	6.6	83.9	176.3	445.1	1,235.7	4,881.6	499.0
Raleigh, N.C.	6,248.8	6.7	37.1	244.2	400.9	1,344.2	3,746.5	469.2
Newark, N.J.	6,378.8	23.3	31.5	561.1	527.4	806.7	2,160.3	2,268.4
Anchorage, Alaska	5,114.5	6.7	95.0	142.9	399.2	569.1	3,462.7	438.9

1. Resident population estimated by the U.S. Census Bureau. 2. The rates for forcible rape and crime index are not shown because the forcible rape figures were not in accordance with national Uniform Crime Reporting guidelines. 3. Due to reporting changes or annexations, figures are not comparable to previous years. *Source:* U.S. FBI, *Crime in the United States,* annual. From *Statistical Abstract of the United States, 2004–2005.*

Military Conflicts in U.S. History

American Revolution (1775–1783) Great Britain forced its 13 American colonies to pay taxes but did not give them representation in the British Parliament. This and other injustices led the colonies to declare independence on July 4, 1776. Independence was achieved in 1783, when the Treaty of Paris was signed with Britain.

War of 1812 (1812–1815) British interference with American trade, impressment of American seamen, and "war hawks" in Congress calling for western expansion into British territory led to war. At the war's conclusion, trade issues remained unresolved, but Britain gave up some of its territorial claims on the continent.

Mexican War (1846–1848) The U.S. annexation of Texas, and its stated desire to acquire California and other Mexican territory, precipitated this war. Mexico was forced to give up two-fifths of its territory. This land eventually became the states of California, Nevada, Arizona, New Mexico, and Utah.

Civil War (1861–1865) Economic and political rivalry between an agrarian South and an industrial North grew into a civil war fought over slavery and states' rights. Eleven states seceded from the Union to form the Confederate States of America. The Union victory led to the reunification of the country and ended slavery.

Indian Wars (colonial era to 1890) U.S. expansionism led to numerous military conflicts with the indigenous inhabitants of North America, forcing them to give up their land. The massacre at Wounded Knee, S.D., in 1890 is generally considered the last of these conflicts.

Spanish American War (1898) The U.S. supported Cuba's desire for independence from Spanish rule, and seized the opportunity to expand U.S. powers in other parts of the world. At the end of the brief conflict, Cuba gained its independence, and the U.S. gained several former Spanish territories: Puerto Rico, Guam, and the Philippines.

World War I (1914–1918) Rivalries over power, territory, and wealth led to the "Great War." In 1917, the U.S. joined the Allies (Britain, France, Russia, Italy, and Japan), who were at war with the Central Powers (Germany, Austria-Hungary, Bulgaria, and Turkey), after German submarines began sinking unarmed ships.

World War II (1939–1945) The Axis powers—Germany, Italy, and Japan—attempted to dominate the world. The Allies (U.S., Britain, France, USSR, and others) fought to stop them. The United States entered the war in 1941, after Japan's attack on Pearl Harbor. Germany surrendered in 1945, and Japan surrendered later that same year, after the U.S. dropped the atomic bomb on the cities of Hiroshima and Nagasaki.

Korean War (1950–1953) Communist North Korea, supported by China, invaded non-communist South Korea. UN forces, principally made up of U.S. troops, fought successfully to protect South Korea. The Korean War was the first armed conflict in the global struggle between democracy and communism, called the cold war.

Bay of Pigs (1961) The U.S. orchestrated the invasion, an unsuccessful attempt by Cuban exiles to overthrow Fidel Castro's communist regime in Cuba.

Vietnam War (1961–1973) In 1955, communist North Vietnam invaded non-communist South Vietnam in an attempt to unify the country and impose communist rule. The United States joined the war on the side of South Vietnam in 1961, but withdrew combat troops in 1973. In 1975 North Vietnam succeeded in taking control of South Vietnam.

Dominican Republic (1965) President Lyndon Johnson sent marines and troops to quash a leftist uprising in the Dominican Republic, fearing the island nation would follow in the footsteps of Cuba and turn communist.

Lebanon (1982–1984) U.S. troops formed part of a multinational peacekeeping force to help the fragile Lebanese government maintain power.

Grenada (1983) President Reagan invaded the Caribbean nation of Grenada to overthrow its socialist government, which had close ties with Cuba.

Panama (1989) President George H.W. Bush invaded Panama and overthrew Panamanian dictator and drug-smuggler Manuel Noriega.

Gulf War (1991) Iraq invaded Kuwait, and a U.S.-led multinational force came to Kuwait's aid and expelled Iraqi dictator Saddam Hussein's forces.

Somalia (1993) A U.S.-led multinational force attempted to restore order to war-torn Somalia so that food could be delivered and distributed within the famine-stricken country.

Bosnia (1994–1995) During the Bosnian civil war, which began shortly after the country declared independence in 1992, the U.S. launched air strikes on Bosnia to prevent "ethnic cleansing," primarily by Serbs against Bosnians. The U.S. became a part of NATO's peacekeeping force in the region.

Kosovo (1999) Yugoslavia's province of Kosovo erupted into violence in the spring of 1999. A U.S.-led NATO force intervened with air strikes after Slobodan Milosevic's Serbian forces uprooted the population and embarked on the ethnic cleansing of Kosovo's ethnic Albanian population.

Afghanistan (2001) The Taliban government harbored Osama bin Laden and the al-Qaeda terrorist group, responsible for the Sept. 11, 2001, attacks on the United States. After Afghanistan refused to turn over Bin Laden, the U.S. and UN coalition forces invaded. The Taliban government was ousted and many terrorist camps in Afghanistan were destroyed. U.S. and NATO troops remain in Afghanistan to support its fragile new government.

Iraq War (2003–) The U.S. and Great Britain invaded and toppled the government of dictator Saddam Hussein. Troops remain in Iraq to combat the insurgency that formed after Hussein's defeat.

America's Wars: U.S. Casualties and Veterans

American Revolution (1775–1783)

Total servicemembers	217,000
Battle deaths	4,435
Nonmortal woundings	6,188

War of 1812 (1812–1815)

Total servicemembers	286,730
Battle deaths	2,260
Nonmortal woundings	4,505

Indian Wars (approx. 1817–1898)

Total servicemembers	106,000[1]
Battle deaths	1,000[1]

Mexican War (1846–1848)

Total servicemembers	78,718
Battle deaths	1,733
Other deaths in service (nontheater)	11,550
Nonmortal woundings	4,152

Civil War (1861–1865)

Total servicemembers (Union)	2,213,363
Battle deaths (Union)	140,414
Other deaths in service (nontheater) (Union)	224,097
Nonmortal woundings (Union)	281,881
Total servicemembers (Conf.)	1,050,000
Battle deaths (Conf.)	74,524
Other deaths in service (nontheater) (Conf.)	59,297[2]
Nonmortal woundings (Conf.)	unknown

Spanish-American War (1898–1902)

Total servicemembers	306,760
Battle deaths	385
Other deaths in service (nontheater)	2,061
Nonmortal woundings	1,662

World War I (1917–1918)[3]

Total servicemembers	4,734,991
Battle deaths	53,402
Other deaths in service (nontheater)	63,114
Nonmortal woundings	204,002
Living veterans	fewer than 500

World War II (1940–1945)[3]

Total servicemembers	16,112,566
Battle deaths	291,557
Other deaths in service (nontheater)	113,842
Nonmortal woundings	671,846
Living veterans	4,762,000[1]

Korean War (1950–1953)

Total servicemembers	5,720,000
Serving in-theater	1,789,000
Battle deaths	33,741
Other deaths in service (theater)	2,827
Other deaths in service (nontheater)	17,730
Nonmortal woundings	103,284
Living veterans	3,734,000[1]

Vietnam War (1964–1975)

Total servicemembers	8,744,000
Serving in-theater	3,403,000
Battle deaths	47,410
Other deaths in service (theater)	10,789
Other deaths in service (nontheater)	32,000
Nonmortal woundings	153,303
Living veterans	8,295,000[1]

Gulf War (1990–1991)

Total servicemembers	2,225,000
Serving in-theater	665,476
Battle deaths	147
Other deaths in service (theater)	382
Other deaths in service (nontheater)	1,565
Nonmortal woundings	467
Living veterans	1,852,000[1]

America's Wars Total

Military service during war	42,348,460
Battle deaths	651,008
Other deaths in service (theater)	13,998
Other deaths in service (nontheater)	525,256
Nonmortal woundings	1,431,290
Living war veterans	17,578,500[4]
Living veterans	25,038,459

1. Veterans Administration estimate as of Sept. 30, 2002. 2. Estimated figure. Does not include 26,000–31,000 who died in Union prisons. 3. Years of U.S. involvement in war. 4. Approximately 1,065,000 veterans had service in multiple conflicts. They are counted under each conflict, but only once in the total. *Source:* Department of Defense and Veterans Administration.

Post-Vietnam Combat Casualties[1]

Place	Dates	Casualties	Place	Dates	Casualties
Lebanon	Aug. 1982–Feb. 1984	254	Haiti	Sept. 1994–April 1996	4
Grenada	Oct.–Nov. 1983	18	Former Yugoslavia	1992–2001	9
Libya	April 10–16, 1986	2			
Panama	Dec. 1989–Jan. 1990	23	Kosovo	March–June 1999	2
Persian Gulf	Jan. 16–April 6, 1991	147	Afghanistan	Oct. 2001–[2]	102
Somalia	Dec. 1992–May 1993	29	Iraq	March 20, 2003–[3]	1,455

1. Defined as battle deaths. Does not include deaths from accidents. 2. A total of 219 Americans have been killed, including 117 noncombat deaths (July 25, 2005). 537 have been wounded (Aug. 6, 2005)."Operation Enduring Freedom" deaths cover other Asian regions as well as Afghanistan. 3. A total of 1,871 Americans have been killed, including 416 non-combat deaths. (Aug. 22, 2005). 13,877 were wounded (Aug 6, 2006). Coalition deaths: Britain, 93; Italy, 26; Ukraine, 18; Poland, 17; Bulgaria, 13; Spain, 11; Slovakia, 3; Thailand, 2; Estonia, 2; The Netherlands, 2; Denmark, El Salvador, Hungary, Kazakhstan, and Latvia, 1 each (Aug. 22, 2005). *Source:* U.S. Dept. of Defense, AP, *Washington Post.*

American Prisoners of War

Congress defines a prisoner of war as a person who, while serving on active military, naval, or air service, is forcibly detained or interned in the line of duty by an enemy government or a hostile force.

	Total	WWI	WWII	Korea	Vietnam	Persian Gulf	Somalia	Iraq
Captured and interned	142,233	4,120	130,201	7,140	745	23	1	8
Returned to U.S. military control	125,208	3,973	116,129	4,418	661	23	1	8
Died while POW	17,004	147	14,072	2,701	84	0	0	0

NOTES: n.a. = not applicable. Not included are the more than 92,000 military personnel considered missing in action: WWI, 3,350; WWII, 78,773; Korea, 8,100; Vietnam, 1,912 (as of June 2002); and the Persian Gulf, 1. *Source:* U.S. Department of Veterans Affairs.

Highest-Ranking Officers in U.S. History

General and Commander-in-Chief[1]

George Washington (1732–1799), b. Westmoreland County, Va., unanimously voted by Congress on June 15, 1775, to the rank of general and commander-in-chief (of the Continental army).

General of the Armies[2]

John Joseph Pershing (1860–1948), b. Linn County, Mo., made permanent general of the armies, 1919.

General of the Army, General of the Air Force (Five-Stars)

George Catlett Marshall (1880–1959), b. Uniontown, Pa., promoted Dec. 1944.

Douglas MacArthur (1880–1964), b. Little Rock, Ark., promoted Dec. 1944.

Dwight David Eisenhower (1890–1969), b. Denison, Tex., promoted Dec. 1944.

Henry Harley Arnold (1886–1950), b. Gladwyne, Pa. Arnold had the unique distinction of being a five-star gen-

eral twice—in 1944 as general of the army, and in June 1949 as general of the air force. He is the only air force general to have held the five-star rank.

Omar Nelson Bradley (1893–1981), b. Clark, Mo., promoted Sept. 1950.

Admiral of the Navy

George Dewey (1837–1917), b. Montpelier, Vt., promoted March 1899.

Fleet Admiral (Five-Stars)

William Daniel Leahy (1875–1959), b. Hampton, Iowa, promoted Dec. 1944.

Ernest Joseph King (1878–1956), b. Lorain, Ohio, promoted Dec. 1944.

Chester William Nimitz (1885–1966), b. Fredericksburg, Tex., promoted Dec. 1944.

William Frederick Halsey (1882–1959), b. Elizabeth, N.J., promoted Dec. 1945.

1. On March 15, 1978, George Washington was promoted posthumously to the rank of General of the Armies of the United States—which had been created in 1919—to make it clear that Washington was the army's senior general. 2. General Pershing was given the option of five stars but he declined. *Source:* Department of Defense and U.S. Army Historian, Research and Analysis Center.

The Joint Chiefs of Staff (JCS)

The Joint Chiefs of Staff is composed of the highest-ranking member of each branch of the military. It consists of the chairman, the vice chairman, the chief of staff of the army, the chief of naval operations, the chief of staff of the air force, and the commandant of the Marine Corps.

The chairman is the principal military adviser to the president, the secretary of defense, and the National Security Council (NSC). The Joint Chiefs of Staff has no executive authority to commit combatant forces.

Joint Chiefs of Staff, 2005

Chairman of the Joint Chiefs of Staff, General Peter Pace, U.S. Marine Corps; vice chairman of the Joint Chiefs of Staff, Admiral Edmund P. Giambastiani, Jr., U.S. Navy; General Peter J. Schoomaker, chief of staff of the U.S. Army; Admiral Vern Clark, chief of naval operations; General T. Michael Moseley, chief of staff of the U.S. Air Force; and General Michael W. Hagee, commandant of the Marine Corps.

Past Chairmen of the JCS

General of the Army, Omar N. Bradley, 1949–1953
Adm. Arthur W. Radford, U.S. Navy, 1953–1957
Gen. Nathan F. Twining, U.S. Air Force, 1957–1960
Gen. Lyman L. Lemnitzer, U.S. Army, 1960–1962
Gen. Maxwell D. Taylor, U.S. Army, 1962–1964
Gen. Earle G. Wheeler, U.S. Army, 1964–1970
Adm. Thomas H. Moorer, U.S. Navy, 1970–1974
Gen. George S. Brown, U.S. Air Force, 1974–1978
Gen. David C. Jones, U.S. Air Force, 1978–1982
Gen. John W. Vessey, Jr., U.S. Army, 1982–1985
Adm. William J. Crowe, U.S. Navy, 1985–1989
Gen. Colin L. Powell, U.S. Army, 1989–1993
Gen. John M. Shalikashvili, U.S. Army, 1993–1997
Gen. Henry H. Shelton, U.S. Army, 1997–2001
Gen. Richard B. Myers, U.S. Air Force, 2001–2005

U.S. Military Spending, 1946–2006

(billions of 2002 dollars)

Year	Spending	Year	Spending	Year	Spending	Year	Spending	Year	Spending	Year	Spending
1946	$556.9	1956	$356.2	1966	$356.2	1976	$283.8	1986	$426.6	1996	$307.4
1947	52.4	1957	360.9	1967	412.0	1977	286.2	1987	427.9	1997	305.3
1948	103.9	1958	352.9	1968	449.3	1978	286.5	1988	426.4	1998	296.7
1949	144.2	1959	352.5	1969	438.1	1979	295.6	1989	427.7	1999	298.4
1950	141.2	1960	344.3	1970	406.3	1980	303.4	1990	409.7	2000	311.7
1951	224.3	1961	344.0	1971	370.6	1981	317.4	1991	358.1	2001	307.8
1952	402.1	1962	363.4	1972	343.8	1982	339.4	1992	379.5	2002	328.7
1953	442.3	1963	368.0	1973	313.3	1983	366.7	1993	358.6	2003	379.3[1]
1954	420.9	1964	364.4	1974	299.7	1984	381.7	1994	338.6	2004	379.9[1,2]
1955	376.9	1965	333.1	1975	293.3	1985	405.4	1995	321.6	2005	400.1[1,2]
										2006	419.3[1,2]

1. Figures based on requested defense budget, not actual spending. 2. Figures do not include expenses for the Iraq and Afghanistan wars. *Source:* Center for Defense Information.

U.S. Military Ranks

Source: U.S. Department of Defense.

Pay Grade	Army and Marine Corps	Navy and Coast Guard[1]	Air Force	Total number[2]
Commissioned Officers				
O-1	Second Lieutenant	Ensign	Second Lieutenant	24,183
O-2	First Lieutenant	Lieutenant Junior Grade	First Lieutenant	30,143
O-3	Captain	Lieutenant	Captain	70,172
O-4	Major	Lieutenant Commander	Major	44,052
O-5	Lieutenant Colonel	Commander	Lieutenant Colonel	28,383
O-6	Colonel	Captain	Colonel	11,558
O-7	Brigadier General	Rear Admiral	Brigadier General	435
O-8	Major General	Rear Admiral	Major General	271
O-9	Lieutenant General	Vice Admiral	Lieutenant General	128
O-10	General	Admiral	General	36
Special Grades[3]				
(5 stars)	General of the Army	Fleet Admiral	General of the Air Force	
Warrant Officers				
W-1	Warrant Officer	—	—	2,501
W-2–W-5	Chief Warrant Officer	Chief Warrant Officer[4]	—	13,511
TOTAL OFFICERS				**225,373**
Enlisted Personnel				
E-1	Private	Seaman Recruit	Recruit	39,734
E-2	Army Private/ Marine Private First Class	Seaman Apprentice	Airman	76,626
E-3	Army Private First Class/ Marine Lance Corporal	Seaman	Airman First Class	217,009
E-4	Corporal	Petty Officer, Third Class	Senior Airman	259,984
E-5	Sergeant	Petty Officer, Second Class	Staff Sergeant	251,040
E-6	Staff Sergeant	Petty Officer, First Class	Technical Sergeant	173,728
E-7	Army Sergeant First Class Marine Gunnery Sergeant	Chief Petty Officer	Master Sergeant	99,246
E-8	Master Sergeant	Senior Chief Petty Officer	Senior Master Sergeant	27,224
E-9	Sergeant Major	Master Chief Petty Officer	Chief Master Sergeant	10,596
Special Grades[5]				
	Sergeant Major	Master Chief Petty Officer	Chief Master Sergeant	
TOTAL ENLISTED				**1,155,187**
GRAND TOTAL				**1,142,813**

1. The United States Coast Guard operates within the Department of Homeland Security rather than the Department of Defense. 2. As of April 30, 2005. Excludes Coast Guard. 3. There are no living five-star commissioned officers. 4. Applies only to the Navy, not the Coast Guard. 5. Senior enlisted advisers. There is only one for each branch of service (Air Force, Army, Marine Corps, Navy). *Source:* Dept. of Defense and Center for Defense Information.

U.S. Military Personnel on Active Duty in Selected Regions/Countries[1]

Region/Country	Personnel[2]	Region/Country	Personnel[2]	Region/Country	Personnel[2]
United States and Territories	1,130,835[3]	Russia	81	Egypt	351
		Serbia (includes Kosovo)	1,773	Iraq	202,100
Continental U.S.	913,259	Spain*	1,835	Israel	35
Alaska	17,395	Turkey*	1,722	Qatar	272
Hawaii	34,658	United Kingdom*	11,341	Saudi Arabia	228
Guam	3,237	Afloat	2,431	United Arab Emirates	117
Puerto Rico	282	**East Asia and Pacific**	86,730[3]	Afloat	603
Transients	47,391	Australia	193	**Sub-Saharan Africa**	584[3]
Afloat	114,584	China (includes Hong Kong)	62	Djibouti	327
Europe	112,823[3]	Japan	36,036	**Western Hemisphere**	1,861[3]
Belgium*	1,451	Korea, Rep. of	36,050	The Bahamas	43
Bosnia and Herzegovina	894	Philippines	99	Brazil	37
France*	76	Singapore	164	Canada	155
Germany*	74,745	Thailand	115	Colombia	55
Greece*	444	Afloat	13,931	Cuba (Guantanamo)	753
Greenland*	122	**North Africa, Near East, and South Asia**	215,779[3]	Honduras	446
Iceland*	1,408	Afghanistan	19,200	**Undistributed**	73,842
Italy*	12,493	Bahrain	1,770	**Total foreign countries**	501,752
Macedonia	42	Diego Garcia	895	NATO Countries	107,384
Netherlands*	688			**Total worldwide**	1,632,587[3]
Norway*	80				
Portugal*	1,016				

NOTES: *NATO countries. 1. As of Dec. 31, 2004, unless otherwise noted. 2. Only countries with 35 or more U.S. military personnel are listed. 3. Includes all regions/countries, not simply those listed. *Source:* U.S. Department of Defense, *Selected Manpower Statistics, Annual.*

Active Duty Military Personnel, 1940–2005[1]

Year	Army	Air Force	Navy	Marine Corps	Total
1940	269,023		160,997	28,345	458,365
1945	8,266,373		3,319,586	469,925	12,055,884
1950	593,167	411,277	380,739	74,279	1,459,462
1955	1,109,296	959,946	660,695	205,170	2,935,107
1960	873,078	814,752	616,987	170,621	2,475,438
1965	969,066	824,662	669,985	190,213	2,653,926
1970	1,322,548	791,349	691,126	259,737	3,064,760
1975	784,333	612,751	535,085	195,951	2,128,120
1980	777,036	557,969	527,153	188,469	2,050,627
1985	780,787	601,515	570,705	198,025	2,151,032
1990	732,403	535,233	579,417	196,652	2,043,705
1991	710,821	510,432	570,262	194,040	1,985,555
1992	610,450	470,315	541,886	184,529	1,807,117
1993	572,423	444,351	509,950	178,379	1,705,103
1994	541,343	426,327	468,662	174,158	1,610,490
1995	508,559	400,409	434,617	174,639	1,518,224
1996	491,103	389,001	416,735	174,883	1,471,722
1997	491,707	377,385	395,564	173,906	1,438,562
1998	483,880	367,470	382,338	173,142	1,406,830
1999	479,426	360,590	373,046	172,641	1,385,703
2000	482,170	355,654	373,193	173,321	1,384,338
2001	480,801	353,571	377,810	172,934	1,385,116
2002	486,542	368,251	385,051	173,733	1,413,577
2003	490,174	376,402	379,742	177,030	1,423,348
2004	494,112	369,523	370,445	177,207	1,411,287
2005 (April)	490,472	360,578	364,504	177,380	1,392,934

NOTE: Figures for 1998 through 2005 include cadets/midshipmen. 1. Military personnel on extended or continuous active duty. Excludes reserves on active duty for training. *Source:* Department of Defense.

The Medal of Honor

Often called the Congressional Medal of Honor, it is the nation's highest military award for "uncommon valor" by men and women in the armed forces. It is given for actions that are above and beyond the call of duty in combat against an armed enemy. The first medal was awarded on March 25, 1863. More than 3,450 men have been awarded the medal, as well as one woman, Dr. Mary Walker, a surgeon in the Civil War. Recipients of the medal are awarded $400 per month for life, a right to burial at Arlington National Cemetery, admission for them or their children to a service academy (if they qualify and quotas permit), and free travel on government aircraft. In 2005, there were 124 Medal of Honor recipients living.

Medal of Honor Recipients

	Total[1]	Army	Navy	Marines	Coast Guard	Air Force	Civilian
Civil War	1,522	1,196	305	17	—	—	4
Noncombat, 1865–1870	13	1	12	—	—	—	—
Indian Wars (1861–1898)	426	422	—	—	—	—	4
Korea (1871)	15	—	9	6	—	—	—
Noncombat, 1871–1899	106	—	104	2	—	—	—
Spanish-American War	110	31	64	15	—	—	—
Samoa	4	—	1	3	—	—	—
Philippines	80	69	5	6	—	—	—
China	59	4	22	33	—	—	—
Noncombat, 1901–1910	49	1	46	2	—	—	—
Philippines (1911)	6	1	5	—	—	—	—
Mexican Campaign (1914)	56	1	46	9	—	—	—
Haiti (1915)	6	—	—	6	—	—	—
Noncombat, 1915–1916	8	—	8	—	—	—	—
Dominican Republic	3	—	—	3	—	—	—
World War I	119	90	21	8	—	—	—
Haiti (1919–1920)	2	—	—	2	—	—	—
Nicaragua (1927–1933)	2	—	—	2	—	—	—
Noncombat, 1920–1940	17	1	15	1	—	—	—
World War II	464	324	57	82	1	—	—
Korean War	131	82	7	42	—	—	—
Vietnam War	245	159	16	57	—	13	—
Somalia (1993)	2	2	—	—	—	—	—
Iraq (2003–)	1	1	—	—	—	—	—
Unknown Soldiers	9	9	—	—	—	—	8
Total	**3,455**	**2,394**	**743**	**296**	**1**	**13**	**8**

1. These totals reflect the total number of Medals of Honor awarded through April 2005. Nineteen men received a second award, and 5 of these double awardees received both the Army and Navy Medals of Honor for the same action. *Sources:* The Congressional Medal of Honor Society, Mt. Pleasant, S.C. Web: www.cmohs.org and Home of Heroes. Web: www.homeofheroes.com/moh/history/history_statistics.html.

The U.S. Veteran Population, 2000 Census

Period of service	Number in 2000	Percentage of all veterans	Median age	Percentage women	Percentage employed	Percentage in poverty in 1999	Percentage disabled
All veterans, 18 years and over	**26,403,703**	**100.0%**	**57.4%**	**6.0%**	**54.7%**	**5.6%**	**29.1%**
Aug. 1990 or later (including Gulf War)	3,024,503	11.5	33.3	15.7	81.4	6.2	16.3
Sept. 1980 to July 1990	3,806,602	14.4	38.8	13.0	82.7	5.5	18.2
May 1975 to Aug. 1980	2,775,492	10.5	45.5	9.9	78.0	5.6	22.7
Vietnam era (Aug. 1964 to April 1975)	8,380,356	31.7	53.2	3.2	75.4	5.1	24.8
Feb. 1955 to July 1964	4,355,323	16.5	62.8	2.4	51.4	4.9	29.4
Korean War (June 1950 to Jan. 1955)	4,045,521	15.3	70.1	2.2	24.6	4.5	33.6
World War II (Sept. 1940 to July 1947)	5,719,898	21.7	76.7	4.2	11.6	4.8	45.2
Some other time	323,785	1.2	74.3	4.5	16.1	6.6	46.4

NOTE: The figures do not add up to 100 percent because veterans may have served in more than one time period. *Source:* The U.S. Census Bureau, Census 2000 Summary File 3 and special tabulations.

Last Living Veterans of America's Wars

American Revolution (1775–1783)
- Last veteran, Daniel F. Bakeman, died 4/5/1869, age 109
- Last widow, Catherine S. Damon, died 11/11/1906, age 92
- Last dependent, Phoebe M. Palmeter, died 4/25/1911, age 90

War of 1812 (1812–1815)
- Last veteran, Hiram Cronk, died 5/13/1905, age 105
- Last widow, Carolina King, died 6/28/1936, age unknown
- Last dependent, Esther A. H. Morgan, died 3/12/1946, age 89

Indian Wars (c. 1861–1898)
- Last veteran, Fredrak Fraske, died 6/18/1973, age 101

Mexican War (1846–1848)
- Last veteran, Owen Thomas Edgar, died 9/3/1929, age 98
- Last widow, Lena James Theobald, died 6/20/1963, age 89
- Last dependent, Jesse G. Bivens, died 11/1/1962, age 94

Civil War (1861–1865)
- Last Union veteran, Albert Woolson, died 8/2/1956, age 109
- Last Confederate veteran, John Salling*, died 3/16/1958, age 112

Spanish-American War (1898)
- Last veteran, Nathan E. Cook, died 9/10/1992, age 106

*Disputed. *Source:* Department of Veterans Affairs and Department of Defense. Web: www.va.gov/pressrel/amwars01.htm.

Weapons that Changed Warfare

Invented by the Greeks in 400 B.C., **catapults** were used in ancient and medieval times to hurl stones, spears, and other objects at fortifications.

The **crossbow** was invented in China but developed into a significant weapon in medieval Europe. With a mechanism for holding the drawn bow until it was ready to release, it propelled arrows with tremendous force as far as 350–400 yards. The crossbow allowed soldiers to fire from great distances and avoid close contact with the enemy. Swords, which had to be used at close range, were no match.

The discovery of gunpowder led to the development of **cannons** in the 1300s. Cannons could demolish castle walls and blast through wooden ships.

Machine guns allowed for rapid, continuous fire, thereby eliminating frequent reloading. The first was the Gatling gun, used in the American Civil War.

The **tank,** an armored combat vehicle equipped with a cannon and machine guns, replaced the use of rifles in war. It put an end to trench warfare, since tanks, with their caterpillar traction, could easily bulldoze over trenches. Tanks were first used at the end of World War I, and they emerged as a symbol of modern warfare.

Combat aircraft, both **bombers** and **fighter planes,** changed the nature of war during World War II. Air superiority became critical to victory. The British Spitfire, American Mustang, and German Messerschmitt were among the most famous fighter planes of the war.

Nuclear weapons, first developed in 1945, allow for massive destruction. Atom and hydrogen bombs are examples of nuclear weapons. Because these weapons are so perilous to human existence, treaties limit their development.

Smart bombs (or **precision-guided munitions**) are highly accurate bombs that are guided to their targets by computers. Smart bombs hit their targets much more frequently than **dumb bombs** (which are unguided) and cause both fewer casualties and less damage to civilian areas.

For international military affairs, *see* p. 714.

Astronomical Terms

Aphelion: see **Orbit.**

Apogee: see **Orbit.**

Black hole: the theoretical end-product of the total gravitational collapse of a massive star or group of stars. Crushed even smaller than the incredibly dense neutron star, the black hole may become so dense that not even light can escape its gravitational field. In 1996, astronomers found strong evidence for a massive black hole at the center of the Milky Way. Recent evidence suggests that black holes are so common that they probably exist at the core of nearly all galaxies.

Conjunction: the alignment of two celestial objects at the same celestial longitude. Conjunction of the Moon and planets is often determined with reference to the Sun. For example, Saturn is said to be in conjunction with the Sun when Saturn and Earth are aligned on opposite sides of the Sun.

Mercury and Venus, the two planets with orbits within Earth's orbit, have two positions of conjunction. Mercury, for example, is said to be in *inferior conjunction* when the Sun and Earth are aligned on opposite sides of Mercury. Mercury is in *superior conjunction* when Mercury and Earth are aligned on opposite sides of the Sun.

Elongation: the angular distance between two points in the sky as measured from a third point. The elongation of Mercury, for example, is the angular distance between Mercury and the Sun as measured from Earth. Planets whose orbits are outside Earth's can have elongations between 0° and 180°. (When a planet's elongation is 0°, it is at conjunction; when it is 180°, it is at opposition.) Because Mercury and Venus are within Earth's orbit, their greatest elongations measured from Earth are 28° and 47°, respectively.

Galaxy: gas and millions of stars held together by gravity. All that you can see in the sky (with a very few exceptions) belongs to our galaxy—a system of roughly 200 billion stars. The exceptions you can see are other galaxies. Our own galaxy, the rim of which we see as the "Milky Way," is about 100,000 light-years in diameter and about 10,000 light-years in thickness. Its shape is roughly that of a thick lens; more precisely, it is a *spiral nebula*. Astronomers have estimated that the universe could contain 40 to 50 billion galaxies. In 2002, a galaxy discovered by a team of astronomers led by Esther Hu of the University of Hawaii was determined to be the most distant object ever observed—13.6 billion light-years away.

Neutron star: an extremely dense star with a powerful gravitational pull. Some neutron stars pulse radio waves into space as they spin; these are known as pulsars.

Occultation: the eclipse of one celestial object by another. For example, a star is occulted when the Moon passes between it and Earth.

Opposition: the alignment of two celestial objects when their longitude differs by 180°. Opposition of the Moon and planets is often determined with reference to the Sun. For example, Saturn is said to be at opposition when Saturn and the Sun are aligned on opposite sides of Earth. Only the planets whose orbits lie outside Earth's can be in opposition to the Sun.

Orbit: the path traveled by an object in space. Theoretically, there are four mathematical figures, or models, of possible orbits: two are open (hyperbola and parabola) and two are closed (ellipse and circle), but in reality all closed orbits are ellipses. Ellipses can be nearly circular, as are the orbits of most planets, or very elongated, as are the orbits of most comets, but the orbit revolves around a fixed, or *focal,* point. In our solar system, the Sun's gravitational pull keeps the planets in their elliptical orbits; the planets hold their moons in place similarly. For planets, the point of the orbit closest to the Sun is the *perihelion,* and the point farthest from the Sun is the *aphelion.* For orbits around Earth, the point of closest proximity is the *perigee;* the farthest point is the *apogee.* See also **Retrograde.**

Perigee: see **Orbit.**

Perihelion: see **Orbit.**

Planet: there is no set scientific definition for planet (from the Greek *planetes,* "wanderers"), but as a rule of thumb, a planet: 1) must directly orbit a star or an object that has nuclear fusion; 2) must be small enough that it has not undergone internal nuclear fusion (i.e., it is not a star or starlike object); and 3) must be large enough that its self-gravity gives it the general shape of a sphere.

In 1994, Dr. Alexander Wolszcan, an astronomer at Pennsylvania State University, presented convincing evidence of the first known planets to exist outside our solar system. They circle a pulsar, or exploded star, in the constellation *Virgo.*

In 1995, several of these *extrasolar planets* were discovered orbiting stars similar to our Sun. Swiss astronomers found the first extrasolar planet (HD 209458b, nicknamed "Osiris") to circle a normal Sun-like star. As of Feb. 2005, 136 such planets have been discovered.

In Aug. 2004, NASA and the National Science Foundation announced the discovery of two new planets, the smallest yet found, about the size of Neptune.

In April 2005, a team of American and European astronomers reported that the first image of an extrasolar planet had been made. The planet is orbiting a brown dwarf near the constellation Hydra, 230 million light-years from Earth. *See* pp. 414 and 571 for discussion of a possible tenth planet.

Pulsar: a celestial object, believed to be a rapidly spinning neutron star, that emits intense bursts of radio waves at regular intervals.

Quasar: "quasi-stellar" object. Originally thought to be peculiar stars in our own galaxy, quasars are now believed to be the most remote objects in the universe.

Quasars emit tremendous amounts of light and microwave radiation. Although they are not much bigger than Earth's solar system, quasars pour out 100 to 1,000 times as much light as an entire galaxy containing a hundred billion stars. It is believed that quasars are powered by massive black holes that suck up billions of stars.

The Milky Way, the galaxy containing our solar system, is about 100,000 light-years in diameter and about 10,000 light-years thick.

Retrograde: describes the clockwise orbit or rotation of a planet or other celestial object, which is in the direction opposite to Earth and most celestial bodies. As viewed from a position in space north of the solar system (from some great distance above Earth's North Pole), all the planets revolve counterclockwise around the Sun, and all but Venus, Uranus, and Pluto rotate counterclockwise on their own axes. These three planets have retrograde motion.

Sometimes *retrograde* is also used to describe apparent backward motion as viewed from Earth. This motion happens when two objects rotate at different speeds around another fixed object. For example, the planet Mars appears to be retrograde when Earth overtakes and passes by it as they both move around the Sun.

Satellite (or **moon**): an object in orbit around a planet. Until the discovery of Jupiter's four main moons by Galileo Galilei, celestial objects in orbit around a planet were called *moons*. However, upon Galilei's discovery, Johannes Kepler (in a letter to Galileo) suggested *satellite* (from the Latin *satelles*, which means "attendant") as a general term for such objects. The word *satellite* is used interchangeably with *moon*, and astronomers speak and write about the moons of Neptune, Saturn, etc. The term *satellite* is also used to describe man-made devices of any size that are launched into orbit.

Star: a celestial object consisting of intensely hot gases held together by gravity. Stars derive their energy from nuclear reactions going on in their interiors, generating heat and light. Stars are very large. Our Sun has a diameter of 865,400 mi—a comparatively small star.

A dwarf star is a small star that is of relatively low mass and average or below-average luminosity. The Sun is a *yellow dwarf*, which is in its main sequence, or prime of life. This means that nuclear reactions of hydrogen maintain its size and temperature. By contrast, a *white dwarf* is a star at the end of its life, with low luminosity, small size, and very high density.

A *red giant* is a star nearing the end of its life. When a star begins to lose hydrogen and burn helium instead, it gradually collapses, and its outer region begins to expand and cool. The light we see from these stars is red because of their cooler temperature.

Supernova: a celestial phenomenon in which a star explodes, releasing a great burst of light. There are two basic types of supernova. Type Ia happens when a white dwarf star draws large amounts of matter from a nearby star until it can no longer support itself and collapses. The second more well-known kind of supernova, type IIa, is the result of the collapse of a massive star. (Massive is a classification for a star that is at least eight times the size of our Sun.) Once the star's nuclear fuel is exhausted, if its core is heavy enough, the star will collapse in on itself, releasing a huge amount of energy (the supernova), which may be brighter than the star's host galaxy.

The Big Bang: Origin of the Universe

Before the universe as we now know it existed, there was no space or time. The Big Bang and its associated theories try to explain or describe the moment of change from nothingness and no time to the existence of the universe filled with space and marked by time. Many physicists describe this event as an explosion, or flash, hence the name *Big Bang*. The Big Bang is a process of expansion in our universe that is still active today.

The universe flashed into existence (according to the Big Bang theory) from a very small agglomeration of matter of extremely high density and temperatures. As a dense, hot globule of gas, containing nothing but hydrogen and a small amount of helium, it began expanding rapidly outward. There were no stars or planets. The first stars probably formed when the universe was about 200 million years old. Our Sun was formed 4.5 billion years ago, and through telescopes we can now see stars forming out of compressed pockets of hydrogen in outer space.

A 2003 study pinpointed the universe's age at 13.7 billion years, with just a 1% margin of error.

Birth and Death of a Star

Astronomers think that a star begins to form as a dense cloud of gas in the arms of spiral galaxies. Individual hydrogen atoms fall with increasing speed and energy toward the center of the cloud under the force of the star's gravity. The increase in energy heats the gas. When this process has continued for some millions of years, the temperature reaches about 20 million degrees Fahrenheit. At this temperature, the hydrogen within the star ignites and burns in a continuing series of nuclear reactions. The onset of these reactions marks the birth of a star.

When a star begins to exhaust its hydrogen supply, its life nears an end. The first sign of a star's old age is a swelling and reddening of its outer regions. Such an aging, swollen star is called a *red giant*. The Sun, a middle-aged star, will probably swell to a red giant in 5 billion years, vaporizing Earth and any creatures that may be on its surface. When all its fuel has been exhausted, a star cannot generate sufficient pressure at its center to balance the crushing force of gravity. The star collapses under the force of its own weight; if it is a small star, it collapses gently and remains collapsed. Such a collapsed star, at its life's end, is called a *white dwarf*. The Sun will probably end its life in this way. A different fate awaits a large star. Its final collapse generates a violent explosion, blowing the innards of

Astronomical Constants

Light-year (distance traveled by light in one year)	5,880,000,000,000 mi
Parsec (parallax of one second, or stellar distances)	3.259 light-years
Velocity of light	c. 186,282.4 mi/sec
Astronomical unit (A.U.), or mean distance Earth to Sun	ca. 93,000,000 mi[1]
Mean distance, Earth to Moon	238,860 mi
General precession	$50'.26$
Obliquity of the ecliptic	$23° 27'8'.26-0'.4684(t-1900)^2$
Equatorial radius of Earth	3963.34 statute mi
Polar radius of Earth	3949.99 statute mi
Earth's mean radius	3958.89 statute mi
Oblateness of Earth	1/297
Equatorial horizontal parallax of the moon	$57'2'.70$
Earth's mean velocity in orbit	18.5 mi/sec
Sidereal year	365d.2564
Tropical year	365d.2422
Sidereal month	27d.3217
Synodic month	29d.5306
Mean sidereal day	23h56m4s.091 of mean solar time
Mean solar day	24h3m56s.555 of sidereal time

1. Actual mean distance derived from radar bounces: 92,935,700 mi. The value of 92,897,400 mi (based on parallax of 8".80) is used in calculations. 2. *t* refers to the year in question, for example, 2003.

the star out into space. There, the materials of the exploded star mix with the primeval hydrogen of the universe. Later in the history of the galaxy, other stars are formed out of this mixture. The Sun is one of these stars. It contains the debris of countless other stars that exploded before the Sun was born.

Formation of the Solar System

Our solar system consists of one star (the Sun), nine planets and all their moons, several thousand minor planets called "asteroids" or "planetoids," and an equally large number of comets. The Sun's age was calculated in 1989 to be 4.5 billion years old, less than the 4.7 billion years previously believed. It was formed from a cloud of hydrogen mixed with small amounts of other substances that had been produced in the bodies of other stars before the Sun was born. This was the parent cloud of the solar system. The dense, hot gas at the center of the cloud gave rise to the Sun; the outer regions of the cloud—cooler and less dense—gave birth to the planets.

The Sun

All the stars, including our Sun, are gigantic balls of superheated gas, kept hot by atomic reactions in their centers. In our Sun, this atomic reaction is hydrogen fusion: four hydrogen atoms are combined to form one helium atom. The temperature at the core of our Sun is thought to be 36,000,000°F, or about 20,000,000°C, and the surface temperature averages 11,000°F, or about 6,000°C. The diameter of the Sun is 865,400 mi, and its surface area is approximately 12,000 times that of Earth. Compared with other stars, our Sun is just a bit below average in size and temperature, and is a yellow dwarf star. It is 4.5 billion years old, and its fuel supply (hydrogen) is estimated to be sufficient for another 5 billion years.

Our Sun is not motionless in space; in fact, it has two kinds of motion. One is a seemingly straight-line motion in the direction of the constellation Hercules at the rate of about 12 miles per second. But since the Sun is a part of the Milky Way system and since the whole system rotates slowly around its own center, the Sun also moves at the rate of 175 miles per second as part of the rotating Milky Way system.

In addition to this motion, the Sun rotates on its axis. Observations of the motion of sunspots (darkish areas that look like enormous whirling storms) and solar flares, which are usually associated with sunspots, have shown that the rotational period of the Sun is just short of 25 days. But this figure is valid for the Sun's equator only; the sections near the Sun's poles seem to have a rotational period of 34 days. Since the Sun generates its own heat and light, there is no temperature difference between poles and equator.

What we call the Sun's "surface" is scientifically known as the *photosphere*. Since the whole Sun is a ball of expanding hot gas, there is really no such thing as a surface; it is a question of visual impression. The layer outside the photosphere is known as the *chromosphere*, which extends several thousand miles beyond the photosphere. It is in steady motion, and often enormous prominences can be seen to burst from it, extending as much as 100,000 mi into space. Outside the chromosphere is the *corona*. The corona consists of very tenuous gases (essentially hydrogen) and makes a magnificent sight when the Sun is eclipsed.

In addition to heat and light, the Sun also generates solar wind, a stream of ionized particles that radiates outward through the solar system at high speeds. One of the effects of solar wind is that it forces the tails of comets to point away from the Sun. The solar wind also interacts with Earth's magnetic field, causing the auroras and other phenomena. Solar flares—eruptions of hydrogen gas on the surface of the Sun—can also cause disturbances in Earth's magnetic field.

As the Sun ages, it gradually expands and heats. It is estimated that the Sun's brilliancy will increase by 10% over the next 1.1 billion years or more, and, in about 6.5 billion years, our aging star will have doubled its present luminosity. The extreme heat generated will be catastrophic for Earth: the oceans will boil away and life as we know it will end. Eight

A Star's Magnitude

Magnitude is the degree of brightness of a star. In 1856, British astronomer Norman Pogson proposed a quantitative scale of stellar magnitudes, which was adopted by the astronomical community. He noted that we receive 100 times more light from a first magnitude star as from a sixth; thus with a difference of five magnitudes, there is a 100:1 ratio of incoming light energy, which is called *luminous flux.*

Because of the nature of human perception, equal intervals of brightness are actually equal ratios of luminous flux. Pogson's proposal was that one increment in magnitude be the fifth root of 100. This means that each increment in magnitude corresponds to an increase in the amount of energy by 2.512, approximately. A fifth magnitude star is 2.512 times as bright as a sixth, and a fourth magnitude star is 6.310 times as bright as a sixth, and so on. The naked eye, upon optimum conditions, can see down to around the sixth magnitude, that is, +6. Under Pogson's system, a few of the brighter stars now have negative magnitudes. For example, Sirius is –1.5. The lower the magnitude number, the brighter the object. The full Moon has a magnitude of about –12.5, and the Sun is a bright –26.51!

The Brightest Stars

Star	Constellation	Mag.	Dist (l.-y.)	Star	Constellation	Mag.	Dist (l.-y.)
Sirius	Canis Major	-1.5	8	Antares	Scorpius	1.2	170
Canopus	Carina	-0.9	650	Fomalhaut	Piscis Austrinus	1.3	27
Alpha Centauri	Centaurus	+0.1	4	Deneb	Cygnus	1.3	465
Vega	Lyra	0.1	23	Regulus	Leo	1.3	70
Capella	Auriga	0.2	42	Beta Crucis	Crux	1.5	465
Arcturus	Boötes	0.2	32	Eta Carinae	Carina	1–7	—
Rigel	Orion	0.3	545	Alpha-one Crucis	Crux	1.6	150
Procyon	Canis Minor	0.5	10	Castor	Gemini	1.6	44
Achernar	Eridanus	0.6	70	Gamma Crucis	Crux	1.6	—
Beta Centauri	Centaurus	0.9	130	Epsilon Canis Majoris	Canis Major	1.6	325
Altair	Aquila	0.9	18	Epsilon Ursae Majoris	Ursa Major	1.7	50
Betelgeuse	Orion	0.9	600	Bellatrix	Orion	1.7	215
Aldebaran	Taurus	1.1	54	Lambda Scorpii	Scorpius	1.7	205
Spica	Virgo	1.2	190	Epsilon Carinae	Carina	1.7	325
Pollux	Gemini	1.2	31	Mira	Cetus	2–10	250

billion years from now, the Sun's radius will extend beyond the present orbit of Venus, causing the total destruction of Earth.

The Moon

Mercury and Venus do not have any moons. The planet that comes after Earth, Mars, has two very small moons. Jupiter has 4 major moons and at least 59 minor ones. Saturn, the ringed planet, has 47 known moons, of which 1 (Titan) is larger than the planet Mercury. Uranus has at least 27 moons (4 of them large) as well as rings, while Neptune has 1 large and 12 small moons. Pluto has one moon, discovered in 1978. Some astronomers still consider Pluto to be a "runaway moon" of Neptune.

Our Moon, with a diameter of 2,160 mi, is one of the larger moons in our solar system and is especially large when compared with the planet that it orbits. In fact, the common center of gravity of the Earth-Moon system is only about 1,000 mi below Earth's surface. The closest the Moon can come to us (its perigee) is 221,463 mi; the farthest it can go away (its apogee) is 252,710 mi. The period of rotation of the Moon is equal to its period of revolution around Earth, so from Earth we can see only one hemisphere of the Moon. Both periods are 27 days, 7 hours, 43 minutes, and 11.47 seconds. But while the rotation of the Moon is constant, its velocity in its orbit is not, since it moves more slowly in apogee than in perigee. Consequently, some portions near the rim of the Moon that are not normally visible will appear briefly. This phenom-

enon is called *libration,* and by taking advantage of the librations, astronomers have succeeded in mapping approximately 59% of the lunar surface. The other 41% can never be seen from Earth but has been mapped by American and Russian Moon-orbiting spacecraft.

Though the Moon goes around Earth in the time mentioned, the interval from new moon to new moon is 29 days, 12 hours, 44 minutes, and 2.78 seconds. This delay of nearly two days is due to the fact that Earth is moving around the Sun, so that the Moon needs two extra days to reach a spot in its orbit where no part is illuminated by the Sun, as seen from Earth.

If the plane of Earth's orbit around the Sun (the ecliptic) and the plane of the Moon's orbit around Earth were the same, the Moon would be eclipsed by Earth every time it is full, and the Sun would be eclipsed by the Moon every time the Moon is "new" (it would be better to call it the "black moon" when it is in this position). But because the two orbits do not coincide, the Moon's shadow normally misses Earth and Earth's shadow misses the Moon. The inclination of the two orbital planes to each other is 5°.

The tides are caused by the Moon with the help of the Sun, but in the open ocean they are surprisingly low, amounting to about one yard. The very high tides that can be observed near the shore in some places are due to funneling effects of the shorelines. At new moon and full moon the tides raised by the Moon are reinforced by the Sun; these are the *spring tides.* If the Sun's tidal power acts at right angles to that of the Moon (quarter moons), we get the low *neap tides.*

The low-budget 1998 Lunar Prospector mission tentatively announced the presence of water ice on the Moon's polar caps, but a controlled crash of the spacecraft turned up no physical evidence of water.

Earth

Earth, circling the Sun at an average distance of 93 million miles, is the fifth-largest planet and the third from the Sun. It orbits the Sun at a speed of 67,000 mph, making one revolution in 365 days, 5 hours, 48 minutes, and 45.51 seconds. Earth completes one rotation on its axis every 23 hours, 56 minutes, and 4.09 seconds. Actually a bit pear-shaped rather than a true sphere, Earth has a diameter of 7,927 mi at the equator and a few miles less at the poles. It has an estimated mass of about 6.6 sextillion tons, with an average density of 5.52 grams per cubic centimeter. Earth's surface area encompasses 196,949,970 sq mi of which about three-fourths is water.

Origin of Earth

Earth, along with the other planets, is believed to have been born 4.5 billion years ago as a solidified cloud of dust and gases left over from the creation of the Sun. For perhaps 500 million years, the interior of Earth stayed solid and relatively cool, perhaps 2,000°F. The main ingredients, according to the best available evidence, were iron and silicates, with small amounts of other elements, some of them radioactive. As millions of years passed, energy released by radioactive decay—mostly of uranium, thorium, and potassium—gradually heated Earth, melting some of its constituents. The iron melted before the silicates, and, being heavier, sank toward the center. This forced up the silicates that it found there. After many years, the iron reached the center, almost 4,000 mi deep, and began to accumulate. No eyes were around at that time to view the turmoil that must have taken place on the face of Earth—gigantic heaves and bubblings on the surface, exploding volcanoes, and flowing lava covering everything in sight. Finally, the iron in the center accumulated as the core. Around it, a thin but fairly stable crust of solid rock formed as Earth cooled. Depressions in the crust were natural basins in which water, rising from the interior of the planet through volcanoes and fissures, collected to form the oceans. Slowly, Earth acquired its present appearance.

Earth Today

As a result of radioactive heating over millions of years, Earth's molten *core* is probably fairly hot today, around 11,000°F. By comparison, lead melts at around 800°F. Most of Earth's 2,100-mile-thick core is liquid, but the center of the core is mostly solid iron. The liquid outer portion, about 95% of the core, is constantly in motion. The interaction between the solid inner core and the fluid outer core creates a hydromagnetic dynamo that generates the magnetic field around Earth. The magnetic field protects Earth from harmful cosmic radiation and makes navigation by compass possible. Scientists have observed a 10% decline in the dipolar magnetic field over the last 150 years. There is a point off the coast of Brazil where the field is 30% weaker, causing glitches in satellites and spacecraft flying through it. This weakening of the magnetic field has scientists speculating that it may eventually

collapse in about 1,500–2,000 years and lead to a reversal of the South and North Poles. Polar reversals are a periodic occurrence.

Within the last decade, scientists have made some important discoveries about Earth's solid-iron core. In 1996, geophysicists discovered that the core rotates slightly faster than the rest of the planet and gains a quarter-turn every century. X-ray images of the inside of Earth show that the core is not a perfect sphere—there are vast mountains 6 to 7 mi high and deep valleys. These features are in an inverse, or upside-down, relationship to similar features on Earth's surface.

Outside the core is Earth's *mantle,* 1,800 mi thick and extending nearly to the surface. The mantle is composed of heavy silicate rock, similar to that brought up by volcanic eruptions. It is somewhere between liquid and solid, slightly yielding, and therefore contributing to an active, moving Earth. Most of Earth's radioactive material is in the thin *crust* that covers the mantle, but some is in the mantle and continues to give off heat. The crust's thickness ranges from 5 to 25 mi.

Continental Drift

A great deal of evidence confirms the theory that the continents of Earth, made mostly of relatively light granite, float in the slightly yielding mantle, like logs in a pond. For many years it had been noticed that if North and South America could be pushed toward western and southern Europe and western Africa, they would fit like pieces in a jigsaw puzzle. Today, there is little question—the continents have drifted widely and continue to do so.

In 10 million years, the world as we know it may be unrecognizable, with California drifting out to sea, Florida joining South America, and Africa moving farther away from Europe and Asia.

Earth's Atmosphere

The thin blanket of atmosphere that envelops Earth extends several hundred miles into space. From sea level—the very bottom of the ocean of air—to a height of about 60 mi, the air in the atmosphere is made up of the same gases in the same ratio: about 78% nitrogen, 21% oxygen, and the remaining 1% a mixture of argon, carbon dioxide, and tiny amounts of neon, helium, krypton, xenon, and other gases. The atmosphere becomes less dense with increasing altitude: more than three-fourths of Earth's huge envelope is concentrated in the first 5 to 10 mi above the surface. At sea level, a cubic foot of atmosphere weighs about an ounce and a quarter. The entire atmosphere weighs 5,700 trillion tons, and the force with which gravity holds it in place causes it to exert a pressure of nearly 15 psi. Going out from Earth's surface, the atmosphere is divided into five regions. The regions, and the heights to which they extend, are: *troposphere,* 0 to 7 mi (at middle latitudes); *stratosphere,* 7 to 30 mi; *mesosphere,* 30 to 50 mi; *thermosphere,* 50 to 400 mi; and *exosphere,* above 400 mi. The boundaries between each of the regions are known respectively as the *tropopause, stratopause, mesopause,* and *thermopause.* Alternative terms often used for the layers above the troposphere are *ozonosphere* (for stratosphere) and *ionosphere* for the remaining upper layers.

The Seasons

Seasons are caused by the 23.4° tilt of Earth's axis, which alternately turns the North and South

Poles toward the Sun. Times when the Sun's apparent path crosses the equator are known as *equinoxes*. Times when the Sun's apparent path is at the greatest distance from the equator are known as *solstices*. The lengths of the days are most extreme at each solstice. If Earth's axis were perpendicular to the plane of Earth's orbit around the Sun, there would be no seasons, and the days always would be equal in length. Since Earth's axis is at an angle, the Sun strikes Earth directly at the equator only twice a year: in March (vernal equinox) and September (autumnal equinox). In the Northern Hemisphere, spring begins at the vernal equinox, summer at the summer solstice, fall at the autumnal equinox, and winter at the winter solstice. The situation is reversed in the Southern Hemisphere.

Mercury

Mercury is the planet nearest the Sun. Appropriately named for the wing-footed Roman messenger of the gods, Mercury whizzes around the Sun at a speed of 30 miles per second, completing one circuit in 88 days. The days and nights are long on Mercury. It takes 59 Earth days for Mercury to make a single rotation. It spins at a rate of about 6 mph (about 10 km/h), measured at the equator, as compared to Earth's spin of about 1,000 mph (about 1,600 km/h) at the equator.

The photographs *Mariner 10* (1974–1975) radioed back to Earth revealed an ancient, heavily cratered surface on Mercury, closely resembling our own Moon. The pictures showed huge cliffs, or scarps, crisscrossing the planet. These apparently were created when Mercury's interior cooled and shrank, compressing the planet's crust. The cliffs are as high as 1.2 mi (2 km) and as long as 932 mi (1,500 km). Another unique feature is the Caloris Basin, a large impact crater about 808 mi (1,300 km) in diameter.

Mercury, like Earth, appears to have a crust of light silicate rock. Scientists believe it has a heavy iron-rich core that makes up about half of its volume.

Instruments on board *Mariner 10* discovered that the planet has a weak magnetic field and a trace of atmosphere—a trillionth the density of Earth's and composed chiefly of argon, neon, and helium. The spacecraft reported temperatures ranging from 950°F (510°C) on Mercury's sunlit side to –346°F (–210°C) on the dark side. Mercury literally bakes in daylight and freezes at night.

Until the *Mariner 10* probe, little was known about the planet. Even the best telescopic views from Earth showed Mercury as an indistinct object lacking any surface detail. The planet is so close to the Sun that it is usually lost in the Sun's glare.

Radar images taken by astronomers at Jet Propulsion Laboratories and California Institute of Technology during the summer of 1991 suggest that the polar regions of Mercury may be covered with patches of water ice. Although this seems impossible due to the planet's sizzling heat, the polar regions receive very little sunlight and may get as cold as –235°F (–148°C). The radar images showed bright patterns at the poles that are characteristic of ice reflecting radar signals. Other explanations may be offered for this unexpected discovery.

NASA's *Messenger*, the first Mercury mission in more than 30 years, was successfully launched on Aug. 3, 2004, and is scheduled to go into orbit in March 2011. Mercury will be almost completely mapped in color and images taken of areas missed by *Mariner*. *Messenger* will also measure the composition of the surface, atmosphere, and magnetosphere.

Mercury is visible to the naked eye at morning or evening twilight when it is at its greatest elongation.

Venus

Although Venus is Earth's closest neighbor, very little is known about the planet because it is permanently covered by thick clouds. In 1962, Soviet and American space probes, coupled with Earth-based radar and infrared spectroscopy, began slowly unraveling some of the mystery surrounding Venus. Twenty-eight years later, the *Magellan* spacecraft, sent by the United States, arrived at Venus in Aug. 1990 and began radar-mapping the planet's surface in greater detail.

According to the latest results, Venus's atmosphere exerts a pressure at the surface 94.5 times greater than Earth's. Walking on Venus would be as difficult as walking a half-mile beneath the ocean. Because of a thick blanket of carbon dioxide, a "greenhouse effect" exists on Venus. Venus intercepts twice as much of the Sun's light as does Earth. The light enters freely through the carbon dioxide gas and is changed to heat radiation in molecular collisions. But carbon dioxide prevents the heat from escaping. Consequently, the temperature of the surface of Venus is over 800°F (427°C), hot enough to melt lead.

The atmospheric composition of Venus is about 96% carbon dioxide, 4% nitrogen, and minor amounts of water, oxygen, and sulfur compounds. There are at least four distinct cloud and haze layers that exist at different altitudes above the planet's surface. The haze layers contain small aerosol particles, possibly droplets of sulfuric acid. A concentration of sulfur dioxide above the cloud tops has been observed to be decreasing since 1978. The source of sulfur dioxide at this altitude is unknown; it may be injected by volcanic explosions or atmospheric overturning.

Measurements of the Venusian atmosphere and its cloud patterns reveal nearly constant high-speed zonal winds, about 220 mph (100 meters per second) at the equator. The winds decrease toward the poles so that the atmosphere at cloud-top level rotates almost like a solid body. The wind speeds at the equator correspond to Venus's rotation period of four to five days at most latitudes. The circulation is always in the same direction—east to west—as Venus's slow retrograde motion. Earth's winds blow from west to east, the same direction as its rotation.

Venus is round, very different from the other planets and from the Moon. Venus has neither polar flattening nor an equatorial bulge. The diameter of Venus is 7,519 mi (12,100 km). Venus has a retrograde axial rotation period of 243.1 Earth days. The surface atmospheric pressure is 1,396 psi (95 Earth atmospheres). The planet's mean distance from the Sun is 67.2 million miles (108.2 million kilometers). The period of its revolution around the Sun is 224.7 days.

The highest point on Venus is the summit of Maxwell Montes, 6.71 mi (10.8 km) above the mean level, more than a mile higher than Mount Everest. There is some evidence that this huge mountain is an active volcano. The lowest point is in the rift valley, Diana Chasma, 1.8 mi (2.9 km) below the mean level.

Longest Channel in the Solar System. *Magellan* took the above image of a channel on Venus. At 4,200 mi (6,800 km) long and an average of 1.1 mi (1.8 km) wide, it is longer than the Nile River, making it the longest known channel in the solar system. Parts of the channel were originally mapped by the Soviet *Venera 15* and *16* spacecraft orbiters, but the *Magellan* mission determined its length. *Source:* NASA.

This point is about one-fifth the greatest depth on Earth, in the Marianas Trench.

Venus has an extreme lowland basin, Atalanta Planitia, which is about the size of Earth's North Atlantic Ocean basin. The smooth surface of the Atalanta Planitia resembles the mare basins of the Moon.

There are only two highland, or continental, masses on Venus: Ishtar Terra and Aphrodite Terra. Ishtar Terra is 6.8 mi (11 km) at its highest points (the highest peaks on Venus) and those of Aphrodite Terra rise to about 3.10 mi (5 km) above the planet. Ishtar Terra is about the size of the continental United States and Aphrodite Terra is about the size of Africa.

The unmanned NASA spacecraft *Magellan* was launched on May 4, 1989, from the shuttle *Atlantis* and arrived at Venus Aug. 10, 1990, to map most of the planet. Despite some problems with its radio transmissions, the results of the radar mapping delighted scientists and provided them with the sharpest images ever taken of the planet's surface. Images taken from *Magellan* show ten times more detail than ever seen before.

The radar images provided scientists with compelling evidence that the planet has been dominated by volcanism on a global scale. The photos also showed that the planet's second-highest mountain, Maat Mons, rising 5 mi (8 km) above the Venusian plains, appears to be covered with fresh lava and is possibly an active volcano.

Magellan discovered the longest known channel in the solar system on Venus. It is 4,200 mi (6,800 km) long and averages slightly over a mile (1.8 km) wide. Its origin is puzzling to scientists because high-temperature lava is unlikely to have caused such a long-distance flow on the surface, and there are no

known substances that could remain liquid long enough under the planet's atmospheric pressure and temperature to have carved out this snakelike feature. The channel is slightly longer than the Nile River, the longest river on Earth.

Magellan ended its radar and emissions mapping in Sept. 1992 after covering 98% of the planet's surface. The spacecraft continued to gather data until Oct. 1994, when it was intentionally crashed into the planet's surface. The European Space Agency (ESA) has scheduled an Oct. 2005 launch of the Venus Express to study the atmosphere and subsurface.

Venus is the brightest of all the planets and is often visible in the morning or evening, when it is frequently referred to as the Morning Star or Evening Star. At its brightest, it can sometimes be seen in full daylight with the naked eye, if one knows where to look.

A rare transit of Venus took place on June 8, 2004. This is when Venus crosses in front of the Sun and can be seen from Earth. Transits occur in pairs eight years apart (June 6, 2012, is the date of the second transit in the current pair), and then the next duo of transits happens either 105½ or 121½ years later. The next pair of transits will begin on Dec. 11, 2117.

Mars

Mars, on the other side of Earth from Venus, is Venus's direct opposite in terms of physical properties. Its atmosphere is cold, thin, and transparent, and readily permits observation of the planet's features. We know more about Mars than any other planet except Earth. Mars is a forbidding, rugged planet with huge volcanoes and deep chasms. The largest volcano, Olympus Mons (Olympic Mountain), rises 78,000 ft above the surface, higher than Mount Everest. The plains of Mars are pockmarked by the hits of thousands of meteors over the years.

Until the arrival of *Mars Pathfinder* and *Mars Global Surveyor* in 1997, most of our information about Mars came from the *Mariner* and *Viking* spacecrafts. *Mariner 9* orbited the planet in 1971 and photographed 100% of the planet, uncovering spectacular geological formations, including a Martian "Grand Canyon" that dwarfs the one on Earth. Called Valles Marineris (Mariner Valley), it stretches more than 3,000 mi along the equatorial region of Mars and is over 2.5 mi (4 km) deep in places and 50 to 62 mi (80 to 100 km) wide. The spacecraft's cameras also recorded what appeared to be dried riverbeds, suggesting the one-time presence of water on the planet. The latter idea gave encouragement to scientists looking for life on Mars, for where there is water, there may be life. However, to date, no evidence of life has been found. Temperatures range from 80°F at the equator during the day to –199°F at the poles at night.

Mars rotates upon its axis in nearly the same period as Earth—24 hours, 37 minutes—so that a Mars day is almost identical to an Earth day. Mars takes 687 days to make one trip around the Sun. Because of its eccentric orbit, Mars's distance from the Sun can vary by about 36 million miles. Its distance from Earth can vary by as much as 200 million miles. The atmosphere of Mars is much thinner than Earth's; atmospheric pressure is about 1% that of our planet. Its gravity is one-third of Earth's. Major constituents are carbon dioxide and nitrogen. Water vapor and oxygen are minor constituents. Mars's polar caps, composed mostly of frozen carbon dioxide (dry ice), recede and advance according to the Martian seasons.

Mars has four seasons like Earth, but they are much longer. For example, in the northern hemisphere, the Martian spring is 198 days, and the winter season lasts 158 days.

The *Mars Pathfinder* lander and its rover, *Sojourner*, set down on the edge of a boulder-strewn outflow channel known as *Ares Vallis* on July 4, 1997, and provided scientists with a wealth of information on the rocks, soils, and atmosphere of Mars. The lander sent back the first live pictures of the planet's topography, and its tiny rover explored a variety of rocks and analyzed their mineral composition with its cameras and onboard X-ray spectrometer.

In its three months of operation, the mission returned more than 16,000 images of the Martian landscape from the lander's camera and 550 images from the rover.

Scientists have inferred from the variety of rocks and sediments found in the *Ares* basin that the spacecraft landed in a channel that was once awash with torrential floods greater than any known on Earth.

The *Sojourner* rover traveled a total of about 328 ft (100 m), performed more than 16 chemical analyses of rocks and soil, and explored 820 sq ft (250 sq m) of the planet's surface. Communications were lost with the lander on Sept. 27, 1997, after 83 days of relaying data.

NASA launched the *Mars Global Surveyor* spacecraft on Nov. 7, 1996, to provide detailed maps of the planet's surface, to track its distribution of minerals, and to monitor its weather. The spacecraft entered Mars's orbit on Sept. 11, 1997, and began mapping operations in mid-March 1999.

Surveyor discovered the first clear evidence of an ancient hydrothermal system near the equator. This implies that water was stable at or near the surface and that a thicker atmosphere existed in Mars's early history.

Surveyor's three-dimensional views of the planet's northern polar ice cap showed often striking canyons and spiral troughs in the water and carbon dioxide ice that can reach depths as great as 3,600 ft below the surface. Its data also showed that large areas of the ice cap were extremely smooth, with elevations varying only a few feet over many miles.

NASA's Mars exploration program suffered a setback with the loss of the *Climate Orbiter* as it entered the Martian atmosphere in Sept. 1999. The following December scientists also failed to establish contact with the *Polar Lander* after it reached Mars.

In 2000, NASA announced that the *Mars Global Surveyor* had observed features that looked like gullies carved out by flowing water and deposits of soil and rocks that were transported by the flow. Because gullies had never been seen before on Mars, the *Surveyor* images suggested that there might be current sources of liquid water at or near the surface.

In the spring of 2002, NASA released exciting news that large quantities of water ice had been found just below the surface of Mars. The discovery was made by NASA's *Mars Odyssey* spacecraft, which was launched in April 2001 and has been collecting data since late 2001.

On June 10, 2003, NASA launched *Spirit*, the first of two Mars Exploration Rovers (MER), followed on July 7 by the takeoff of the second rover, *Opportunity*. *Spirit* landed on Mars in the Gusev Crater on Jan. 3, 2004, and within hours was transmitting the first panoramic images to Earth. *Opportunity* landed successfully on Jan. 25 in the Meridiani Planum region on the opposite side of the planet.

The main instruments on board the rovers are: a panoramic camera, a miniature thermal emission spectrometer for identifying rocks and soils and taking the temperature of the atmosphere, a Mossbauer spectrometer for studying the mineralogy of rocks and soil, an alpha particle X-ray spectrometer for chemical analysis of rocks and soil, magnets for collecting magnetic dust particles, a microscopic imager, and a rock abrasion tool to scrape rocks for a fresh surface to study.

Opportunity uncovered water evidence in the Meridiana Planum region in early March 2004. The rover discovered salts usually found in rocks either formed in water or subjected to long exposure to water. The physical characteristics of the rocks bolstered the water evidence with surfaces that appeared to have been pocked from salt deposits; round, BB-sized particles formed from mineral accumulation inside a porous, water-soaked rock; and a pattern or layering usually associated with the action of water. A few days later on the other side of Mars, *Spirit* found water evidence in a rock that appeared to have minerals crystallized out of water.

The rovers were designed for a 90-day mission but performed so well, NASA decided to extend their duties for as long as they keep working. As of the middle of June 2005, *Spirit* had travelled 2.73

PLANET SIZES. Shown from left to right: Mercury, Venus, Earth, Mars, Jupiter, Saturn, Uranus, Neptune, and Pluto. *Copyright 1990 Hansen Planetarium, Salt Lake City, Utah. Reproduced with permission.*

mi (4,395.5 m) and *Opportunity* had travelled 3.32 mi (5,346 m).

Mars was named for the Roman god of war, because when seen from Earth its distinct red color reminded the ancient people of blood. We know now that the reddish hue reflects the oxidized (rusted) iron in the surface material.

The Martian Moons

Mars has two very small elliptical-shaped moons, Deimos and Phobos—the Greek names for the companions of the god Mars: Deimos (terror) and Phobos (fear). They were discovered in Aug. 1877 by the American astronomer Asaph Hall (1829–1907) of the U.S. Naval Observatory in Washington, DC.

The inner satellite, Phobos, is 16.78 mi (27 km) long, and it revolves around the planet in 7.6 hours. The short orbital period of Phobos means that the satellite travels around Mars three times in a Martian day. The outer moon, Deimos, is 9.32 mi (15 km) long, and it circles the planet in 30.35 hours.

Phobos orbits Mars at a distance of only 5,627 mi (9,378 km) and is closer to its planet than any other moon in the solar system. Observation of Phobos has revealed that the moon's orbit is actually decreasing downward; in about 40 million years it will crash into the planet's surface or break up into a ring.

Meteorites from Mars

Thirty-four meteorites, almost certainly from Mars, have been discovered as of March 2005. They are known as SNCs[1] (named for the towns where the original 12 meteorites were found: Shergotty, India, in 1865; Nakhla, Egypt, in 1911; and Chassigny, France, in 1815). This hypothesis was based largely on the composition of noble gases (particularly argon and xenon) trapped in the meteorites, and the shergottites in particular, which resemble measurements of the Martian atmosphere made by the *Viking* spacecraft. Major element compositions of the SNCs are also similar to Martian soil analyses made by *Viking*.

---

1. Pronounced "snick."

The relatively young isotopic ages of the SNC meteorites (1.3 billion years or less) suggest that Mars has been volcanically active during its recent past.

A 40-pound meteorite that crashed to Earth in Nigeria in 1962 has been classified as coming from Mars. It was named Zagami for the region in which it was found. It is the largest single Martian meteorite ever found.

A 4-pound, 7-ounce (1.9-kilogram) meteorite, ALH 84001, found in the Allen Hills of Antarctica in 1984, was reclassified in 1993 as coming from the Red Planet, making it the tenth meteorite known to have originated from Mars. In 1996, NASA announced that meteorite ALH 84001 contained fossils of ancient Martian microbial life-forms.

Two rock specimens weighing 8.6 oz (245.4 g) and 16 oz (452.6 g) that were found in the Mojave Desert about 20 years ago were classified in Feb. 2000 as the fourteenth Mars meteorite. The rocks are known as the Los Angeles meteorites.

The most recent finds from 2001–2004 were discovered in Antarctica and the deserts of northern Africa, which have become the favored hunting grounds for meteorite collectors, since there is little or no ground cover to hide the rocks.

In April 2004, the Mars Exploration Rover *Opportunity* analyzed "Bounce Rock," a rock it hit during its January landing. Bounce Rock's composition resembled the original Shergotty meteorite and matched even more closely a meteorite found in 1979 in Antarctica.

Jupiter

Jupiter is the largest planet in the solar system—a gaseous world as large as 1,300 Earths. Its equatorial diameter is 88,736 mi (142,800 km), while from pole to pole, Jupiter measures only 84,201 mi (133,500 km). For comparison, the diameter of Earth is 7,926.2 mi (12,756 km). The massive planet rotates at a dizzying speed—once every 9 hours and 55 minutes. It takes Jupiter almost 12 Earth years to complete a journey around the Sun.

The giant planet appears as a banded disk of turbulent clouds with all of its stripes running parallel

Basic Planetary Data

	Mercury	Venus	Earth	Mars	Jupiter
Mean distance from Sun (millions of kilometers)	57.9	108.2	149.6	227.9	778.3
Mean distance from Sun (millions of miles)	36.0	67.24	92.9	141.71	483.88
Period of revolution	88 days	224.7 days	365.2 days	687 days	11.86 yrs
Rotation period	59 days	243 days retrograde	23 hr 56 min 4 sec	24 hr 37 min	9 hr 55 min 30 sec
Inclination of axis	Near 0°	3°	23°27'	25° 12'	3° 5'
Inclination of orbit to ecliptic	7°	3.4°	0°	1.9°	1.3°
Eccentricity of orbit	.206	.007	.017	.093	.048
Equatorial diameter (kilometers)	4,880	12,100	12,756	6,794	142,800
(miles)	3,032.4	7,519	7,926.2	4,194	88,736
Atmosphere (main components)	Virtually none	Carbon dioxide	Nitrogen oxygen	Carbon dioxide	Hydrogen helium
Satellites	0	0	1	2	63[1]
Rings	0	0	0	0	3

	Saturn	Uranus	Neptune	Pluto
Mean distance from Sun (millions of kilometers)	1,427	2,870	4,497	5,900
Mean distance from Sun (millions of miles)	887.14	1,783.98	2,796.46	3,666
Period of revolution	29.46 yrs	84 yrs	165 yrs	248 yrs
Rotation period	10 hr 40 min 24 sec	16.8 hr (?) retrograde	16 hr 11 min (?)	6 days 9 hr 18 mins retrograde
Inclination of axis	26°44'	97°55'	28°48'	60° (?)
Inclination of orbit to ecliptic	2.5°	0.8°	1.8°	17.2°
Eccentricity of orbit	.056	.047	.009	.254
Equatorial diameter (kilometers)	120,660	51,810	49,528	2,290 (?)
(miles)	74,958	32,193	30,775	1,423 (?)
Atmosphere (main components)	Hydrogen helium	Helium hydrogen methane	Hydrogen helium methane	None detected
Satellites	47[2]	27[3]	13[4]	1
Rings	1,000 (?)	11	4	?

1. Forty-five of these moons were discovered only recently, from 2000–2003. 2. Twelve new moons discovered in Dec. 2004 were announced in May 2005: S/2004 S07 through S/2004 S18. 3. S/2001 U2 and S/2003 U3 were announced in Fall 2003. 4. S/2003 N1 was announced in Fall 2003. *Source:* Basic NASA data and other sources.

to its bulging equator. Large dusky gray regions surround each pole. Darker gray or brown stripes called belts intermingle with lighter, yellow-white stripes called zones. The belts are regions of descending air masses and the zones are rising cloudy air masses. The strongest winds—up to 250 mph (400 km)—are found at boundaries between the belts and zones.

This uniquely colorful atmosphere is mainly 89% molecular hydrogen and 11% helium. It contains small amounts of methane, ammonia, ethane, and water.

Cloud-type lightning bolts similar to those on Earth have been found in the Jovian atmosphere. At the polar regions, auroras have been observed. A very thin ring of material less than 0.6 mi (1 km) in thickness and about 4,000 mi (6,000 km) in radial extent has been observed circling the planet about 35,000 mi (55,000 km) above the cloud tops.

The most prominent feature on Jupiter is its "Great Red Spot," an oval larger than the planet Earth. It is a tremendous atmospheric storm that rotates counterclockwise with one revolution every six days at the outer edge, while at the center almost no motion can be seen. The spot is about 16,000 mi (25,000 km) on its long axis, and would cover three Earths. Along

the outer rim the winds blow at speeds reaching 225 mph (360 km/h).

Jupiter is circled by faint rings. They are very tenuous and contain many microscopic-sized particles. The rings are formed by dust kicked up as interplanetary meteoroids smash into the planet's four small inner moons.

Jupiter emits 67% more heat than it absorbs from the Sun. This heat is thought to have been accumulated during the planet's formation several billion years ago.

Twenty-one fragments of comet Shoemaker-Levy 9 bombarded the cloud-covered surface of Jupiter, July 16–22, 1994. It was the most violent event in the recorded history of our solar system. The impact of the comet fragments caused towering plumes of debris and hot gas to rise from the planet's surface.

On Dec. 7, 1995, the *Galileo* spacecraft released a probe into Jupiter's atmosphere to study the planet's physical and chemical properties. The probe lasted 57 minutes and early results indicated a lower abundance of water than was expected. *Galileo* data has shown that Jupiter has both wet and dry regions, just as Earth has tropics and deserts. This could explain why the probe found less water than anticipated. These dry spots cover less than 1% of the Jovian atmosphere. The *Galileo* mission ended on Sept. 21, 2003, when the probe made a scheduled crash into the gas giant.

Jovian Moons

Jupiter has a total of 63 known satellites. The four great moons of Jupiter were discovered by Galileo Galilei (1564–1642) in Jan. 1610, and are called the Galilean satellites after their discoverer. Their names are Io, Europa, Ganymede, and Callisto. Like our Moon, the satellites always keep the same face turned toward the planet they circle. Jupiter's four largest moons all have thin atmospheres. A carbon dioxide atmosphere envelops Callisto; Europa and Ganymede each have thin oxygen atmospheres; and Io's contains sulfur dioxide.

Ganymede

Ganymede, 3,275 mi (5,270 km) in diameter, is Jupiter's largest moon, and it is also the largest satellite in the solar system. Ganymede is about one and one-half times the size of our Moon. It is heavily cratered and probably has the greatest variety of geologic process recorded on its surface. Ganymede is half water and half rock, resulting in a density about two-thirds that of Europa, an ice-coated satellite.

The first close-up photos of Ganymede, taken by the *Galileo* spacecraft during its June 1996 flyby, revealed a surface pockmarked with ancient craters and a landscape wrinkled and torn by the same forces that make mountains and move continents on Earth. *Galileo*'s findings also indicated that Ganymede is enveloped in its own magnetic field, possibly created by a molten iron core or even a thin layer of electricity-conducting salty water underneath its icy crust.

Ganymede is the first known moon with its own magnetosphere.

Europa

Europa, the brightest of Jupiter's satellites, is about 1,950 mi (3,160 km) in diameter or about the size of Earth's Moon. Its density is about three times that of water. The moon is covered with a thin ice crust and is crisscrossed with an amazingly complex network of ridges. Some of the fractures on its crust are more than 1,850 mi (3,000 km) long. Very few impact craters are visible on the surface. In fact, Europa is the smoothest object in the solar system. Its mostly flat surface doesn't exceed 0.62 mi (1 km) in height.

Galileo spacecraft photos taken at its closest flyby on Feb. 20, 1997, at a distance of 363 mi (586 km), showed the existence of ice flows on the surface that strongly suggest that the moon has a hidden subsurface ocean of water or ice-slush. The photos revealed chunky ice rafts that appear to be floating, comparable to icebergs on Earth. The presence of water and enough heat to keep water in a liquid state on Europa enhances the possibility that it could provide an environment for some form of extraterrestrial ocean life.

New evidence that a liquid ocean lies beneath Europa's crust was found when *Galileo* visited the moon in Jan. 2000. The spacecraft detected changes in Europa's magnetic field that are best explained by an electrically conducting (salty) body of water.

Callisto

Callisto, 2,400 mi (4,800 km) in diameter, is the outermost and, apparently, the least geologically active of Jupiter's four major satellites. Its density is less than twice that of water. Callisto has the oldest body and most cratered face of any body yet observed in the solar system. Like Ganymede, it seems to have a rocky core surrounded by ice. Unlike Ganymede, the surface of Callisto is completely covered with scars left by tens of thousands of meteoric impacts. Scientists estimate that it would take several billion years to accumulate the number of craters found there. So Callisto is believed to be inactive for at least that long. Although it is the darkest of the Galilean satellites, it is twice as bright as Earth's Moon.

Data from the *Galileo* spacecraft in 1998 suggest that Callisto has a salty ocean beneath its crust, similar to Europa's.

Io

Io, 2,262 mi (3,640 km) in diameter, is the most spectacular of the Galilean moons. Its brilliant colors of red, orange, and yellow set it apart from any other moon or planet. Active volcanoes have been detected on Io, with some plumes extending up to 200 mi (320 km) above the surface. The relative smoothness of Io's surface and its volcanic activity suggest that it has the youngest surface of Jupiter's moons. Its surface is composed of large amounts of sulfur and sulfur-dioxide frost, which account for the primarily yellow-orange surface color.

The volcanoes seem to eject a sufficient amount of sulfur dioxide to form a doughnut-shaped ring (torus) of ionized sulfur and oxygen atoms around Jupiter near Io's orbit. Close-up views taken in 1999 and 2000 showed that Io had more than 100 erupting volcanoes, gigantic lava flows and lava lakes, and towering, collapsing mountains. The eruptions of Loki, the most powerful volcano in the solar system, can be seen by Earth telescopes.

Observations by *Galileo* during 1998 revealed dozens of volcanic vents on Io where lava is hotter than any surface temperatures recorded on any planetary body in our solar system. At one such volcanic vent, known as Pillan Patera, two of the spacecraft's instruments indicated that the lava temperature may have been 3,140°F.

In 1996, the *Galileo* spacecraft detected a huge iron core within Io that occupies half the moon's diameter. *Galileo* also discovered evidence that Io has its own magnetic field.

Amalthea

Amalthea, Jupiter's innermost satellite, was discovered in 1892. It is so small—165 mi (265 km) long and 90 mi (150 km) wide—that it is extremely difficult to observe from Earth. Amalthea is an elongated, irregularly shaped satellite of reddish color. It orbits the planet every 12 hours and is in synchronous rotation, with its long axis always oriented toward Jupiter.

Originally thought to be heavily cratered, late 2002 data from the *Galileo* mission indicated that Amalthea may be a loosely-packed pile of rubble. It was discovered that the satellite had an unexpected low density, close to the density of ice. Amalthea may originally have been one piece that was bombarded and broken into chunks now held together by

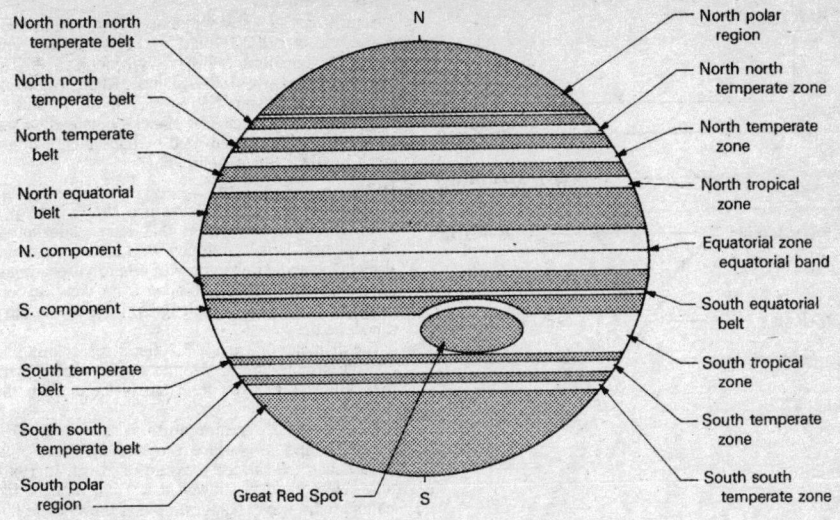

North north north
temperate belt

North north
temperate belt

North temperate
belt

North equatorial
belt

N. component

S. component

South temperate
belt

South south
temperate belt

South polar
region

N

Great Red Spot   S

North polar
region

North north
temperate zone

North temperate
zone

North tropical
zone

Equatorial zone
equatorial band

South equatorial
belt

South tropical
zone

South temperate
zone

South south
temperate zone

Schematic diagram of Jupiter's major features. *Source:* NASA.

the gravity of the pieces. The gaps between the boulderlike pieces may make up more of the moon's volume than the actual rocks. Amalthea may be mostly rock with some ice, rather than the rock and iron it was previously held to be.

Jupiter's other named moons are Adrasta, Metis, Thebe, Leda, Himalia, Lysithea, Elara, Ananke, Carne, Pasiphae, Sinope; those discovered in 1999 and 2000 are Themisto, Iocaste, Harpalyke, Praxidike, Taygete, Chaldene, Kalyke, Callirrhoe, Megaclite, Isonoe, and Erinome. The 2001 moons are Euporie, Orthosie, Euanthe, Thyone, Hermippa, Pasithee, Kale, Aitne, Eurydome, Autonoe, and Sponde. The names come from members of Jupiter's (or Zeus's) entourage. The 2003 Jovian moons were named after daughters of Zeus: Hegemone, Mneme, Aoede, Thelxinoe, Arche, Kallichore, Helike, Carpo, Eukelade, and Cyllene.

Between 2000 and 2003, 45 moons were found, bringing Jupiter's satellite total to 63, the greatest in the solar system. The new moons were generally small with distant retrograde orbits (orbital movement opposite to the planet's spin). Most of the new moons were sighted using Hawaii's 'Mauna Kea telescopes. Some astronomers believe that Jupiter's moon count could reach 100.

The Magnetosphere of Jupiter

Perhaps the largest structure in the solar system is the magnetosphere of Jupiter. This is the region of space that is filled with Jupiter's magnetic field and is bounded by the interaction of that magnetic field with the solar wind, which is the Sun's outward flow of charged particles. The plasma of electrically charged particles that exists in the magnetosphere is flattened into a large disk more than 3 million miles (4.8 million kilometers) in diameter, is coupled to the magnetic field, and rotates around Jupiter. The Galilean satellites are located in the inner regions of

the magnetosphere and are subjected to intense radiation bombardment.

The intense radiation field that surrounds Jupiter is fatal to humans. If astronauts were able to approach the planet as close as the *Voyager 1* spacecraft did, they would receive a dose of 400,000 rads, or roughly 1,000 times the lethal dose for humans.

Even when nearest Earth, Jupiter is still almost 400 million miles away. However, because of its size, it may rival Venus in brilliance when near. Jupiter's four large moons may be seen through field glasses moving rapidly around Jupiter and changing their positions from night to night.

Saturn

Saturn, the second-largest planet in the solar system, is the least dense. Its mass is 95 times the mass of Earth and its density is 0.70 gram per cubic centimeter, so that it would float in an ocean if there were one big enough to hold it.

Saturn radiates about 80% more energy than it receives from the Sun. However, the excess thermal energy cannot be primarily attributed to Saturn's primordial heat loss, as is speculated for Jupiter.

Saturn's diameter is 74,978 mi (120,660 km) but 10% less at the poles, a consequence of its rapid rotation. Its axis of rotation is tilted by 27° and the length of its day is 10 hours, 39 minutes, and 24 seconds.

Saturn is composed primarily of liquid metallic hydrogen (about 80%) and the second most common element is believed to be helium.

Saturn's atmospheric appearance is very similar to Jupiter's with dark and light cloud markings and swirls, eddies, and curling ribbons; the belts and zones are more numerous and a thick haze mutes the markings. Temperatures recorded by *Voyager II* ranged from 82°K (−312°F) to 143°K (−202°F).

A-Ring Gap

F-Ring
A-Ring

Cassini Division

"Spoke"

B-Ring

C-Ring

NASA illustration of the main divisions in Saturn's ring system.

Winds blow at extremely high speeds on Saturn. Near the equator, the *Voyagers* measured winds of about 1,100 mph (500 meters per second). The winds blow primarily in an eastward direction.

Saturn's Rings

Saturn's spectacular ring system is unique in the solar system, with uncountable billions of tiny particles of water ice (with traces of other material) in orbit around the planet. The ring particles range in size from smaller than grains of sugar to as large as a house. The main rings stretch out from about 4,350 mi (7,000 km) to above the atmosphere of the planet out to the F ring, a total span of 45,984 mi (74,000 km). Saturn's rings can be likened to a phonograph, rings within rings numbering in the hundreds, with spokes in the B rings, and shepherding satellites controlling the F ring.

The main rings are called the A, B, and C rings, moving from outside to inside. The gap between the A and B rings is called Cassini's Division and is named for the Italian-French astronomer Gian Domenico Cassini, who discovered four of Saturn's major moons and the dark, narrow gap, Cassini's Division, splitting the planet's rings. In Sept. 2004, the Cassini-Huygens mission discovered a new ring located between the A and F rings. Designated S/2004 1R, the ring is estimated to be about 190 mi (300 km) wide, but it has not yet been verified if the ring entirely circles the planet.

Saturn's magnetic field has well-defined north and south magnetic poles, and is aligned with Saturn's axis of rotation to within one degree.

Saturn's Moons

Saturn has 47 known moons, 12 of which were discovered in late 2004 and are known by the temporary designations S/2004 S7 through S18. The five largest moons—Tethys, Dione, Rhea, Titan, and Iapetus—range from 650 to 3,200 mi (1,060 to 5,150 km) in diameter. The planet's outstanding satellite is Titan, first discovered by the Dutch astronomer Christiaan Huygens in 1656.

Titan

Titan is remarkable because it is the only known moon in the solar system that has a substantial atmosphere—largely nitrogen with a minor amount of methane and a rich variety of other hydrocarbons. Its surface is completely hidden from view (except at infrared and radio wavelengths) by a dense, hazy atmosphere.

The diameter of Titan is 3,200 mi (5,150 km), and it is the second-largest satellite in the solar system after Jupiter's Ganymede. Titan is larger than the planet Mercury.

Titan's surface temperature is about –280°F (–175°C), and its surface pressure is about 50% greater than the surface pressure of Earth. In 1990, radio telescope data showed that Titan reflects and scatters radio waves, suggesting that the satellite has a solid surface, possibly with small hydrocarbon lakes or ponds.

Infrared images of Titan taken in late 1999 by the W. M. Keck II telescope in Hawaii also revealed features that could be frozen land masses separated by frigid hydrocarbon seas and lakes. Other features might be highlands, and one dark area appeared to be a large impact crater or basin.

Cassini-Huygens

The Cassini-Huygens mission, launched in 1997 as a joint endeavor of NASA, the European Space Agency (ESA), and the Italian space agency, went into orbit around Saturn on June 30, 2004, and began sending images of Saturn's rings back to Earth the next day. Cassini will orbit Saturn 74 times and will make 44 flybys of Titan and 8 flybys of other satellites in its 4-year orbiting schedule. In Jan. 2005, the Huygens probe descended through Titan's atmosphere, sending back 2 hours and 27 minutes of descent data and 1 hour and 12 minutes of surface data after the crash landing.

Other Notable Saturnian Moons

The other four largest moons of Saturn are Tethys, Dione, Rhea, and Iapetus.

Tethys is 650 mi (1,060 km) in diameter. Its surface is heavily cratered, and it has a huge, globe-girdling canyon, Ithaca Chasma. Part of the canyon stretches over three-quarters of the satellite's surface. Ithaca Chasma is about 1,550 mi (2,500 km) long. It has an average width of about 62 mi (100 km) and a depth of 1.8 to 3.1 mi (3 to 5 km).

Tethys also has a huge impact crater named Odysseus that is 244 mi (4,400 km) in diameter, or more than one-third of the moon's diameter.

Dione is slightly larger than Tethys, 696 mi (1,120 km) in diameter, and is more than half composed of water ice. It has bright, wispy markings resembling thin veils covering its features.

Rhea, the largest of the inner satellites, is 951 mi (1,530 km) in diameter. It is composed mainly of water ice, causing its reflective surface to present an almost uniform white appearance.

Iapetus is the outermost of Saturn's icy satellites. Its appearance is unique because it has one dark and one bright hemisphere. The origin of the black coating of its dark face is unknown. Iapetus has a diameter of 907 mi (1,460 km).

Other notable moons of Saturn are Mimas, Enceladus, Hyperion, Phoebe, and Pan.

Mimas is small, only 244 mi (329 km) in diameter. It has a huge impact crater, Herschel, nearly one-third of its diameter. The crater is about 81 mi (130 km) wide and its icy peak rises almost 6.2 mi (10 km) above the floor.

Mimas is believed to be composed mainly of water and ice and to contain between 20% and 50% rock.

Enceladus is remarkable in that its surface shows signs of extensive and recent geological activity. There may be active water volcanism. The surface is extremely bright, reflecting more than 90% of incident sunlight. This suggests that its surface is composed of extremely pure ice without dust or rocks to contaminate it. Enceladus has a diameter of 310 mi (500 km).

Hyperion orbits between Iapetus and Titan. It is irregular in shape, measuring about 248 by 155 by 124 mi (400 by 250 by 200 km). It may be a remnant of a much larger object that was shattered by impact with another space body. It appears that Hyperion is composed primarily of water ice.

Hyperion orbits Saturn with an irregular motion ("chaotic tumbling").

Phoebe travels in a retrograde orbit at a distance of over 6.2 million miles (10 million kilometers) away from the planet. It is the darkest moon of Saturn and is the planet's only known satellite that does not keep the same face always turned to Saturn. It has been speculated that it is an asteroid that was captured by the planet. Phoebe rotates in about nine hours and orbits Saturn in 406 days. It has a diameter of 124 mi (200 km).

Pan was discovered in 1990 from *Voyager 2* photos taken in 1981. The satellite is estimated to be about 12.43 mi (20 km) in diameter, and it orbits within the Encke Gap, a 202-mile (325-kilometer) division in Saturn's A ring. It was identified by Johann Franz Encke (1791–1865) in 1837.

Twenty-eight more moons of Saturn have been discovered since 2000, including 12 found in Dec. 2004 using Hawaii's Mauna Kea telescope. These 28 satellites range in size from 1.8 to 30 mi (3 to 48 km) in diameter.

Saturn is the last of the planets visible to the naked eye. Saturn is never an object of overwhelming brilliance, but it looks like a bright star. The rings can be seen with a small telescope.

Uranus

Uranus, the first planet discovered in modern times by Sir William Herschel in 1781, is the seventh planet from the Sun, twice as far out as Saturn. Its mean distance from the Sun is 1,783 million miles (2,869 million kilometers). Uranus's equatorial diameter is 32,200 mi (51,810 km). The axis of Uranus is tilted at 97°, so it goes around the Sun nearly lying on its side.

Due to Uranus's unusual inclination, the polar regions receive more sunlight than its equatorial region during a Uranus year (equivalent to 84 Earth years). Scientists had thought that the temperature of its poles would be warmer than that at its equator, but *Voyager 2* discovered that the equatorial temperatures were similar to the temperatures at the poles, −344°F (−209°C), implying that some redistribution of heat toward the equatorial region must occur within the atmosphere. The wind patterns on Uranus are much like Saturn's, flowing parallel to the equator in the direction of the planet's rotation.

Ninety-eight percent of the upper atmosphere is composed of hydrogen and helium; the remaining 2% is methane. Scientists speculate that the bulk of the lower atmosphere is composed of water (perhaps as much as 50%), methane, and ammonia. Methane is responsible for Uranus's blue-green color because it selectively absorbs red sunlight and condenses to form clouds of ice crystals in the cooler, higher regions of Uranus's atmosphere.

It was also discovered that the planet's magnetic field is 60° tilted from the planet's axis of rotation and offset from the planet's center by one-third of Uranus's radius. It may be generated at a depth where water is under sufficient pressure to be electrically conductive.

Uranus can—on rare occasions—become bright enough to be seen with the naked eye, if one knows exactly where to look; normally, a good set of field glasses or a small portable telescope is required.

The Uranian Rings

Voyager 2 also expanded the body of information pertaining to the rings and moons of Uranus. *Voyager*'s cameras obtained the first images of 9 previously known narrow rings and discovered at least 2 new rings, one narrow and one broadly diffused, bringing the total known rings to 11. It was found that a highly structured distribution of fine dust exists throughout the ring system.

The outermost (epsilon) ring contains nothing smaller than fist-sized particles. It is flanked by two small moons discovered interior to the orbit of the Uranian moon Miranda. The moons exert a shepherding influence on the epsilon ring and on the outer edges of the gamma and delta rings.

All of the rings lie within one planetary radius[1] of Uranus's cloud tops. Most of Uranus's rings are narrow, ranging in width from 0.6 to 58 mi (1 to 93 km), and are only a few kilometers thick. The Uranian rings are colorless and extremely dark. The dark material may be either irradiated methane ice or organic-rich minerals mixed with water-impregnated, silicon-based compounds. There is evidence that incomplete rings, or "ring arcs," exist at Uranus.

The Uranian Moons

There are 27 known moons of Uranus. In order of decreasing distance from the planet, the moons are Setebos (1999 U1), Prospero (1999 U3), Sycorax, Stephano (1999 U2), Caliban, Oberon, Titania, Umbriel, Ariel, Miranda, Puck, 1986 U10, Belinda, Rosalind, Portia, Juliet, Desdemona, Cressida, Bianca, Ophelia, and Cordelia. Ten of the moons range in size from 16 to 67 mi (26 to 108 km) in diameter and, being closer to the planet, have faster periods of revolution (8–15 hours) than their more distant relatives.

---

1. The equatorial radius of Uranus is 15,880 mi (25,560 km) at a pressure of 1 bar.

Oberon and Titania

The two largest moons, Oberon, 942 mi (1,516 km) in diameter, and Titania, 982 mi (1,580 km) in diameter, are less than half the diameter of Earth's Moon. Titania, the reddest of Uranus's moons, may have endured global tectonics as evidenced by complex valleys and fault lines etched into its surface. Smooth sections indicate that volcanic resurfacing has taken place.

Umbriel and Ariel

Umbriel and Ariel are roughly three-fourths the size of Oberon and Titania. Umbriel is the darkest of the large moons, with huge craters peppering its surface. Umbriel has a paucity of what are known as bright ray craters, which are formed on an older, darker surface when bright, submerged ice is excavated and sprayed by meteoroid impacts.

In contrast, the surface of Ariel, the brightest of the Uranian moons, is relatively free of pockmarks due to volcanism that periodically erases the damage done by foreign projectiles. However, there are several extremely deep cuts on Ariel's surface.

Miranda

The smallest of Uranus's large moons, Miranda, 293 mi (472 km) in diameter, has been described as "the most bizarre body in the solar system," with the most geologically complex surface. Miranda's remarkable terrain consists of rolling, heavily cratered plains (the oldest known in the Uranian system) adjoined by three huge, 120- to 180-mile (200- to 300-kilometer) oval-to-trapezoidal regions known as coronae, which are characterized by networks of concentric canyons.

Puck

Puck was the first new moon discovered by *Voyager*. It is 96 mi (154 km) in diameter and makes a trip around Uranus every 18 hours. Puck is shaped somewhat like a potato, with a huge impact crater marring roughly one-fourth of its surface.

Caliban and Sycorax

In 1997, two new moons, the first with irregular, noncircular orbits, were discovered around Uranus. Caliban has a diameter of 37 mi (60 km) and orbits Uranus at an average distance of 4.5 million miles (7.2 million kilometers). Sycorax has a diameter of 74.5 mi (120 km) and a much more elliptical orbit than Caliban, bringing it as close as 3.7 million miles (6 million km) to the planet.

New Uranian Moons Discovered

In Sept. 1999, Cornell University astronomers announced the discovery of three more satellites. The moons have been named Setebos, Stephano, and Prospero. The satellites are about 12 mi (20 km) in diameter and orbit in distant, elliptical paths. The moon Trinculo was announced in 2001. With the discovery of two new moons in 2003, the Uranian moon count is up to 27.

Neptune

Little was known about Neptune until Aug. 1989, when NASA's *Voyager 2* became the first spacecraft to observe the planet. Passing about 3,000 mi (4,950 km) above Neptune's north pole, *Voyager 2* made its closest approach to any planet since leaving Earth 12 years prior. The spacecraft passed about 25,000 mi (40,000 km) from Neptune's largest moon, Triton, the last solid body that *Voyager 2* studied before continuing on to the outer boundary of the solar system.

Nearly 3 billion miles (4.5 billion kilometers) from the Sun, Neptune orbits the Sun once in 165 years, and therefore has made not quite a full circle around the Sun since it was discovered.[1]

With an equatorial diameter of 30,775 mi (49,528 km), Neptune is the smallest of our solar system's four gas giants, which also include Jupiter, Saturn, and Uranus.[2] Even so, its volume could hold nearly 60 Earths. Neptune is also denser than the other gas giants and about 64% heavier than if it were composed entirely of water.

Neptune has a blue color as a result of methane in its atmosphere. Methane preferentially absorbs the longer wavelengths of sunlight (those near the red end of the spectrum). What are left to be reflected are colors at the blue end of the spectrum. The atmosphere of Neptune is mainly composed of hydrogen, with helium and traces of methane and ammonia.

Neptune is a dynamic planet even though it receives only 3% as much sunlight as Jupiter does. *Voyager 2* discovered several large, dark spots that were prominent features on the planet. The largest spot was about the size of Earth and was designated the "Great Dark Spot" by its discoverers. It appeared to be an anticyclone similar to Jupiter's Great Red Spot. While Neptune's Great Dark Spot is comparable in size, relative to the planet, and at the same latitude (22°S latitude) as Jupiter's Great Red Spot, it was far more variable in size and shape than its Jovian counterpart. Bright, wispy "cirrus-type" clouds overlaid the Great Dark Spot at its southern and northeast boundaries.

At about 42°S latitude, a bright, irregularly shaped eastward-moving cloud circled much faster than did the Great Dark Spot, "scooting" around Neptune in about 16 hours. This "scooter" may have been a cloud plume rising between cloud decks.

Another spot, designated "D2," was located far to the south of the Great Dark Spot, at 55°S latitude. It is almond-shaped, with a bright central core, and moves eastward around the planet in about 16 hours.

In 1995, images taken by the Hubble Space Telescope showed that the Great Dark Spot has vanished. The great storm center has either dissipated or is obscured by other atmospheric conditions.

The atmosphere above Neptune's clouds is hotter near the equator, cooler in the mid-latitudes, and warm again at the south pole. Temperatures in the stratosphere were measured to be 750°K (900°F), while at the 100-millibar pressure level they were measured to be 55°K (−360°F).

Long, bright clouds, reminiscent of cirrus clouds on Earth, were seen high in Neptune's atmosphere.

---

1. Astronomers have studied Neptune since Sept. 23, 1846, when Johann Gottfried Galle, of the Berlin Observatory, and Louis d'Arrest, an astronomy student, discovered the eighth planet on the basis of mathematical predictions by Urbain Jean Joseph Le Verrier. Similar predictions were made independently by John Couch Adams. Galileo Galilei had seen Neptune during several nights of observing Jupiter, in Jan. 1613, but didn't realize he was seeing a new planet.
2. These four planets are about 4 to 12 times greater in diameter than Earth. They have no solid surfaces, but possess massive atmospheres that contain substantial amounts of hydrogen and helium with traces of other gases.

They appear to form above most of the methane, and consequently are not blue.

At northern low latitudes (27°N), *Voyager* captured images of cloud streaks casting their shadows on cloud decks estimated to be about 30 to 60 mi (50 to 100 km) below. The widths of these cloud streaks range from 30 to 125 mi (50 to 200 km). Cloud streaks were also seen in the southern polar regions (71°S) where the cloud heights were about 30 mi (50 km).

Most of the winds on Neptune blow in a westward direction, which is retrograde, or opposite to the rotation of the planet.

In Jan. 2000, astronomers announced taking the best Earth-based infrared images of Neptune, captured by the W. M. Keck II telescope in Hawaii. The images revealed giant 600-mph (966-km/hr) storms born of heat generated from the planet's still-contracting core. Storm features are pulled across the face of Neptune as it whirls through its 16-hour day.

The Magnetic Field of Neptune

Neptune's magnetic field is tilted 47° from the planet's rotation axis and is offset at least 0.55 radii, about 8,500 mi (13,500 km) from the physical center. The dynamo electric currents produced within the planet, therefore, must be relatively closer to the surface than for Earth, Jupiter, or Saturn. Because of its unusual orientation, and the tilt of the planet's rotation axis, Neptune's magnetic field goes through dramatic changes as the planet rotates in the solar wind.

Voyager's planetary radio astronomy instrument measured the periodic radio waves generated by the magnetic field and determined that the rotation rate of the interior of Neptune is 16 hours and 7 minutes.

Voyager also detected auroras, similar to the northern and southern lights on Earth, in Neptune's atmosphere. Unlike those on Earth, due to Neptune's complex magnetic field, the auroras are extremely complicated processes that occur over wide regions of the planet, not just near the planet's magnetic poles.

Neptune's Moons

Triton

The largest of Neptune's 13 known satellites, Triton was discovered in 1846 by British astronomer William Lassell. Triton circles Neptune in a tilted, circular, retrograde orbit, completing an orbit in 5.875 days at an average distance of 205,000 mi (330,000 km) above the planet's cloud tops.

Triton shows evidence of a remarkable geologic history, and *Voyager 2* images show active geyser-like eruptions spewing invisible nitrogen gas and dark dust particles 1 to 5 mi (2 to 8 km) into space.

Triton is about three-quarters the size of Earth's Moon and has a diameter of about 1,680 mi (2,705 km) and a mean density of about 2.066 grams per cubic centimeter. (The density of water is 1.0 grams per cubic centimeter.) This means that Triton contains more rock in its interior than the icy satellites of Saturn and Uranus.

The relatively high density and the retrograde orbit offer strong evidence that Triton did not originate near Neptune, but is a captured object.

An extremely thin atmosphere extends as much as 500 mi (800 km) above the satellite's surface. Tiny nitrogen ice particles may form thin clouds a few kilometers above the surface. Triton is very bright, reflecting 60% to 95% of the sunlight that strikes it. (By comparison, Earth's Moon reflects only 11%.)

The atmospheric pressure at Triton's surface is about 14 microbars, a mere 1/70,000th the surface pressure on Earth. Temperature at the surface is about 38°K (–391°F), making it the coldest surface of any body yet visited in the solar system.

Nereid

Nereid was discovered in 1949 through Earth-based telescopes. Little is known about Nereid, which is slightly smaller than Proteus, having a diameter of 211 mi (340 km). The satellite's surface reflects about 14% of the sunlight that strikes it. Nereid's orbit is the most eccentric in the solar system, ranging from about 841,100 mi (1,353,600 km) to 5,980,200 mi (9,623,700 km).

The Smaller Satellites

In addition to the previously known moons, Triton and Nereid, *Voyager 2* found 6 satellites in 1989. In 2003, astronomers announced that 5 new moons had been discovered, bringing the total to 13.

Proteus

Proteus is one of the darkest objects in the solar system—"as dark as soot" is a good description. It reflects only 6% of the sunlight that strikes it. Proteus is an ellipsoid about 258 mi (416 km) in diameter, larger than Nereid. It circles Neptune at a distance of about 57,700 mi (92,800 km) above the cloud tops, and completes one orbit in 26 hours and 54 minutes. Scientists say that it is about as large as a satellite can be without being pulled into a spherical shape by its own gravity.

Proteus and its tiny companions are cratered and irregularly shaped—they are not round—and show no signs of any geologic modifications. All circle the planet in the same direction as Neptune rotates and remain close to Neptune's equatorial plane.

Larissa

This object is only about 30,300 mi (48,800 km) from Neptune and circles the planet in 13 hours and 18 minutes. Its diameter is 120 mi (190 km).

Despina

The satellite is 17,200 mi (27,700 km) from Neptune's clouds and makes one orbit every 8 hours. Its diameter is about 90 mi (150 km).

Galatea

It lies 23,100 mi (37,200 km) from Neptune. Its diameter is 110 mi (180 km), and it completes an orbit in 10 hours and 18 minutes.

Thalassa

Thalassa appears to be about 50 mi (80 km) in diameter. It orbits Neptune in 7 hours and 30 minutes some 15,700 mi (25,200 km) above the cloud tops.

Naiad

Naiad is about 37 mi (60 km) in diameter and orbits Neptune about 14,400 mi (23,200 km) above the clouds in 7 hours and 6 minutes.

New Neptunian Moons

In Jan. 2003, astronomers from the Harvard-Smithsonian Center for Astrophysics and the National Research Council of Canada announced that three new moons had been discovered orbiting Neptune. Two more moons were announced later in 2003, bringing the total to 13.

The First Ten Minor Planets (Asteroids)

Name	Year of discovery	Mean distance from Sun (millions of mi)	Orbital period (years)	Diameter (mi)	Magnitude
1. Ceres	1801	257.0	4.60	485	7.4
2. Pallas	1802	257.4	4.61	304	8.0
3. Juno	1804	247.8	4.36	118	8.7
4. Vesta	1807	219.3	3.63	243	6.5
5. Astraea	1845	239.3	4.14	50	9.9
6. Hebe	1847	225.2	3.78	121	8.5
7. Iris	1847	221.4	3.68	121	8.4
8. Flora	1847	204.4	3.27	56	8.9
9. Metis	1848	221.7	3.69	78	8.9
10. Hygeia	1849	222.6	5.59	40(?)	9.5

Neptune's Rings

Voyager found four rings and evidence of ring *arcs* or incomplete rings. The "Main Ring" orbits Neptune at about 23,812.5 mi (38,100 km) above the cloud tops. The "Inner Ring" is about 17,750 mi (28,400 km) from Neptune's cloud tops. An "Inside Diffuse Ring"—a complete ring—is located about 10,687.5 mi (17,100 km) from the planet's cloud tops. Some scientists suspect that this ring may extend all the way down to Neptune's cloud tops. An area called "the Plateau" is a broad, diffuse sheet of fine material just outside the so-called Inner Ring. The fine material is approximately the size of smoke particles. All other rings contain a greater proportion of larger material.

Pluto

Pluto, the outermost and smallest planet in the solar system, is the only planet not visited by an exploring spacecraft. So little is known about it that it is difficult to classify. Its distance is so great that the Hubble Space Telescope cannot reveal its surface features. Appropriately named for the Roman god of the underworld, it must be frozen, dark, and dead. Pluto's mean distance from the Sun is 3,687.5 million miles (5,900 million kilometers).

In 1978, light-curve studies gave evidence of a moon revolving around Pluto within the same period as Pluto's rotation; therefore, it stays over the same point on Pluto's surface. In addition, it keeps the same face toward the planet. The satellite was later named Charon and is estimated to be about 789 mi (1,262.4 km) in diameter. Recent estimates indicate Pluto's diameter is about 1,441.6 mi (2,306.56 km), making the pair more like a double planet than any other in the solar system. Previously, the Earth–Moon system held this distinction. The density of Pluto is slightly greater than that of water.

There is evidence that Pluto has an atmosphere containing methane and polar ice caps that increase and decrease in size with the planet's seasons. It is not known to have water. The Hubble Space Telescope's faint-object camera revealed light and dark regions on Pluto indicating an ice cap at the planet's north pole. It is not known if there is an ice cap at Pluto's south pole.

Pluto was predicted by calculation when Percival Lowell (1855–1916) noticed irregularities in the orbits of Uranus and Neptune. Clyde Tombaugh (1906–1997) discovered the planet in 1930, precisely where Lowell predicted it would be. The name Pluto was chosen because the first two letters represent the initials of Percival Lowell.

Pluto's eccentric orbit brings it at times closer to the Sun than Neptune. Pluto approached the perihelion of its orbit on Sept. 5, 1989, and until Feb. 1999 was closer to the Sun than Neptune. Even then, it could be seen only with a large telescope.

The *New Horizons* mission, scheduled to launch in 2006 and reach Pluto in 2015, would be the first to study Pluto, Charon, and the Kuiper Belt, a region beyond Neptune's orbit containing comets and what is believed to be detritus from the formation of the solar system.

Beyond Pluto

In July 2005, a possible tenth planet, temporarily called 2003 UB313, was announced by a team from the California Institute of Technology. This most distant object in our solar system, thought to be 1.5 times the size of Pluto, takes 560 years to make a very skewed orbit of the Sun. Most planets circle the Sun very near the same plane as Earth's orbit, but the new object's orbit is off this elliptic plane by about 44 degrees. *See also* p. 571.

A few of the other large objects found beyond Pluto are Varuna (2000), Ixion (2001), Quaoar (2002), and Sedna (2004).

The Asteroids

Between the orbits of Mars and Jupiter are an estimated 30,000 pieces of rocky debris, known collectively as the asteroids, or planetoids. The first and, incidentally, the largest (Ceres) was discovered Jan. 1, 1801, by the Italian astronomer Father Piazzi (1746–1826), and its orbit was calculated by the German mathematician Karl Friedrich Gauss (1777–1855). Gauss invented a new method of calculating orbits on that occasion. A few asteroids do not move in orbits beyond the orbit of Mars, but in orbits that cross the orbit of Mars. The first of them was named Eros because of this peculiar orbit. It had become the rule to bestow female names on the asteroids, but when it was found that Eros crossed the orbit of a major planet, it received a male name. These orbit-crossing asteroids are often referred to as the "male asteroids." A few of them—Albert, Adonis, Apollo, Amor, and Icarus—cross the orbit of Earth, and two of them may come closer than our Moon; but the crossing is like a bridge crossing a highway, not like two highways intersecting. Hence there is very little danger of collision from these bodies. They are all small, 3 to 5 mi (4.8 to 8.0 km) in diameter, and therefore very difficult objects to identify, even when quite close. Some scientists believe the asteroids represent the remains of an exploded planet.

On Oct. 29, 1991, the *Galileo* spacecraft took a historic photograph of asteroid 951 Gaspra from a distance of 10,000 mi (16,000 km) away. It was the first close-up photo ever taken of an asteroid in space. Gaspra is an irregular, potato-shaped object about 12.5 mi (20 km) by 7.5 mi (12 km) by 7 mi (11.2 km) in size. Its surface is covered with a layer of loose rubble and its terrain is marked by several dozen small craters.

NASA's *Near-Earth Asteroid Rendezvous* spacecraft was launched on Feb. 17, 1996. (Near-Earth asteroids come within 121 million miles [195 million kilometers] of the Sun. Their orbits come close enough that one could eventually hit Earth.) It flew within 750 mi (1,200 km) of minor planet 253 Mathilde on June 27, 1997, and took spectacular images of the dark, crater-battered world. The asteroid's mean diameter was found to be 33 mi (52.8 km). The *NEAR* spacecraft discovered that the carbon-rich Mathilde is one of the darkest objects in the solar system, only reflecting about 3% of the Sun's light, making it twice as dark as a chunk of charcoal. The asteroid is almost completely cratered, and at least five of its craters just on the lit side are larger than 12 mi (19.2 km).

On Feb. 14, 2000, *NEAR* successfully entered into orbit around Eros and remained in orbit for one year, taking photographs of the asteroid and gathering information about its composition, structure, size, and shape. The spacecraft landed safely on the surface of Eros in a controlled crash on Feb. 12, 2001, relaying information for another two weeks before being shut down. *NEAR* measured Eros to be 21 mi (33.6 km) long by 8 mi (12.8 km) wide and 8 mi (12.8 km) deep. It rotates once every 5.27 hours and has no visible moons. *NEAR* data also showed that the asteroid's ancient surface is covered with craters, ridges, boulders, and other complex features.

NEAR was the first spacecraft to orbit an asteroid and the first craft to operate on solar power so far from the Sun. The spacecraft was renamed *NEAR-Shoemaker* in honor of geologist Dr. Eugene M. Shoemaker (1928–1997), who researched the influence of asteroids and comets in shaping planets.

In March 2004, a 90-foot (30-meter) diameter asteroid made the closest-ever asteroid flyby of Earth, coming within 26,500 mi (43,000 km) of our planet. Scientists believed that had the asteroid (named 2004 FH) entered Earth's atmosphere, it would have broken up with no damage to the planet.

Comets

Comets, according to the noted astronomer Fred L. Whipple (1906–2004), are enormous "snowballs" of frozen gases (mostly carbon dioxide, methane, and water vapor) and contain very little solid material. The whole behavior of comets can then be explained as that of frozen gas being heated by the Sun. When the comet Kohoutek made its first appearance to human observers in 1973, its behavior seemed to confirm this theory, and later the international study by five spacecraft that encountered Halley's comet in March 1986 confirmed Whipple's idea of the makeup of comets.

Up until the middle of the 16th century, comets were believed to be phenomena of the upper atmosphere; they were usually explained as "burning vapors" that had risen from "distant swamps." That nobody had ever actually seen burning vapors rise from a swamp did not matter.

But a large comet that appeared in 1577 was carefully observed by Tycho Brahe (1546–1601), a Danish astronomer who insisted on precise measurements for everything. It was Tycho Brahe's accumulation of literally thousands of precise measurements that later enabled his younger collaborator, Johannes Kepler (1571–1630), to discover the laws of planetary motion. Measuring the motion of the comet of 1577, Brahe could show that it had been far beyond the atmosphere, even though he could not give figures for the distance. Brahe's work proved that comets were astronomical and not meteorological phenomena.

In 1682, the second Astronomer Royal of Great Britain, Dr. Edmond Halley (1656–1742), checked the orbit of a bright comet that was in the sky and then compared it with earlier comet orbits that were known in part. Halley found that the comet of 1682 was the third to move through what appeared to be the same orbit, and that the three appearances were roughly 76 years apart. Halley concluded that this was the same comet, moving around the Sun in a closed orbit, like the planets. He predicted that it would reappear in 1758 or 1759. Halley himself died in 1742, but a large comet appeared 16 years after his death as predicted and was immediately referred to as "Halley's comet."

Halley's comet appeared again in 1986, sparking a worldwide effort to study it up close. Five satellites in all took readings from the comet at various distances. Two Soviet craft, *Vega 1* and *Vega 2*, provided detailed pictures of the comet, including the first of the comet's core. The European Space Agency's craft, *Giotto,* entered the comet itself, coming to within 450 mi of the comet's center and successfully passing through its tail. In addition, two Japanese craft, the *Suisei* and the *Sakigake,* passed at a farther distance and analyzed the cloud and tail of the comet and the effect of solar radiation upon it.

Astronomers refer to comets as *periodic* or *non-periodic,* but the latter term does not mean that these comets have no period; it merely means that their period is not known. The actual periods of comets run from 3.3 years (the shortest known) to many thousands of years. Their orbits are elliptical, like those of the planets, but they are very eccentric, long, and narrow ellipses. Only comet Schwassmann-Wachmann has an orbit that has such a low eccentricity (for a cometary orbit) that it could be the orbit of a minor planet.

When a comet coming from deep space approaches the Sun, it is at first indistinguishable from a minor planet. Somewhere between the orbits of Mars and Jupiter, its outline becomes fuzzy; it is said to develop a *coma* (the word used here is the Latin word *coma,* which means "hair," not the phonetically identical Greek word that means "deep sleep"). Then, near the orbit of Mars, the comet develops its tail, which at first trails behind. This grows steadily as the comet comes closer and closer to the Sun. As it rounds the Sun (as first noticed by Girolamo Fracastoro, 1483–1553), the tail always points away from the Sun so that the comet, when moving away from the Sun, points its tail ahead like the landing lights of an airplane.

The reason for this behavior is that the tail is pushed in these directions by the radiation pressure of the Sun. It sometimes happens that a comet loses its tail at perihelion; it then grows another one. Although the tail is clearly visible against the black of the sky, it is very tenuous. It has been said that if the tail of Halley's comet could be compressed to the density of iron, it would fit into a small suitcase.

Although very low in mass, comets are among the largest members of the solar system. The nucleus of a comet may be up to 10,000 mi in diameter; its coma between 10,000 and 50,000 mi in diameter; and its tail as long as 28 million miles.

Comet Shoemaker-Levy 9 broke up into 21 fragments in July 1992 and crashed into the surface of Jupiter, July 16–22, 1994, in the most violent event in the recorded history of the solar system.

In 1951, Dutch astronomer Gerard Kuiper first suggested the existence of a disk-shaped swarm of short-period comets that begin beyond the orbit of Neptune and extend past Pluto. In 1995, the Hubble Space Telescope detected the long-sought Kuiper Belt and an estimated 200 million comets were discovered orbiting it.

On July 4, 2005, NASA's Deep Impact spacecraft traveled 268 million miles over a period of six months to blast a hole into Comet Tempel 1. The crash emitted the energy of 4.5 tons of TNT, releasing a tremendous plume of dust and gases. Comets are believed to have been formed out of the remaining dust and gases after our solar system formed 4.6 billion years ago. By blasting a crater into the surface of Tempel 1 and exposing its pristine interior, scientists hope to examine the primordial remnants of our solar system to gain insight into its formation.

Meteors and Meteorites

The term *meteor* for what is usually called a *shooting star* bears an unfortunate resemblance to the term *meteorology,* the science of weather and weather forecasting. This resemblance is due to an ancient misunderstanding that wrongly considered meteors an atmospheric phenomenon. Actually, the streak of light in the sky that scientists call a meteor is essentially an astronomical phenomenon: the entry of a small piece of cosmic matter into our atmosphere.

The distinction between *meteors* and *fireballs* (formerly also called *bolides*) is merely one of convenience; a fireball is an unusually bright meteor. Incidentally, it also means that a fireball is larger than a faint meteor.

Objects that enter our atmosphere become visible when they are about 60 mi above the ground. The fact that they grow hot enough to emit light is not due to the "friction" of the atmosphere, as one often reads. The phenomenon responsible for the heating is one of compression. Unconfined air cannot move faster than the speed of sound. Since the entering meteorite moves with 30 to 60 times the speed of sound, the air simply cannot get out of the way. Therefore, it is compressed like the air in the cylinder of a diesel engine and is heated by compression. This heat—or part of it—is transferred to the moving object. The details of this process are now fairly well understood as a result of reentry tests with ballistic-missile nose cones.

The average weight of an object producing a faint *shooting star* is only a small fraction of an ounce. Even a bright fireball may not weigh more than 2 or 3 lb. Naturally, the smaller objects are worn to dust by the passage through the atmosphere; only rather

large ones reach the ground. Those that are found are called meteorites. (The *meteor,* to repeat, is the term for the light streak in the sky.) Thousands of meteorites fall to Earth each year.

The largest meteorite known is still embedded in the ground near Grootfontein in southwest Africa and is estimated to weigh 70 tons. The second-largest known is the 34-ton Anighito (on exhibit in the Hayden Planetarium, New York), which was found by Admiral Peary in 1892 at Cape York in Greenland. The largest meteorite found in the United States is the Willamette meteorite (found in Oregon, weight ca. 15 tons), but large portions of this meteorite weathered away before it was found. Its weight as it struck the ground may have been 20 tons.

All these are iron meteorites (an iron meteorite normally contains about 7% nickel), which form one class of meteorites. The other class consists of the stony meteorites, and between them there are the so-called stony irons. Tektites consist of silica-rich glass similar to our volcanic glass obsidian, and because of the similarity, there is doubt in a number of cases whether the glass is of terrestrial or of extraterrestrial origin.

Though no meteorite larger than the Grootfontein is actually known, we do know that Earth has, on occasion, been struck by much larger bodies. Evidence for such hits are the meteorite craters, of which an especially good example is located near the Cañon Diablo in Arizona. Another meteor crater in the United States is a rather old crater near Odessa, Tex. Some scientists theorize that the mass extermination of dinosaurs from the face of Earth 65 million years ago was due to a large meteor that struck our planet at that time.

Meteor showers are caused by multitudes of very small bodies traveling in swarms. Earth travels in its orbit through these swarms like a car driving through falling snow. The point from which the meteors seem to emanate is called the *radiant* and is named for the constellation in that area. The Perseid meteor shower in August is the most spectacular of the year, boasting, at peak, roughly 60 meteors per hour under good atmospheric conditions.

The Constellations

Constellations are groupings of stars that form easily recognized and remembered patterns, such as Orion and the Big Dipper. The Big Dipper is actually an asterism, not a constellation, because it is only part of the constellation Ursa Major (the Big Bear). Actually, the stars in the majority of all constellations do not "belong together." Usually they are at greatly varying distances from Earth and just happen to lie more or less in the same line of sight as seen from our solar system. But in a few cases, the stars of a constellation are actually associated; most of the bright stars of the Big Dipper travel together and form what astronomers call an *open cluster*.

If you observe a planet, say Mars, for one complete revolution, you will see that it passes successively through 12 constellations. All planets (except Pluto at certain times) can be observed only in these 12 constellations, which form the so-called zodiac, and the Sun also moves through the zodiacal signs, though the Sun's apparent movement is actually caused by the movement of Earth.

Although the constellations are due mainly to the optical accident of line of sight and have no real

The 88 Recognized Constellations

In astronomical works, the Latin names of the constellations are used. The letter N or S following the Latin name indicates whether the constellation is located to the north or south of the Zodiac. The letter Z indicates that the constellation is within the Zodiac.

Latin name	Letter	English version	Latin name	Letter	English version	Latin name	Letter	English version
Andromeda	N	Andromeda	Delphinus	N	Dolphin	Pegasus	N	Pegasus
Antlia	S	Airpump	Dorado	S	Swordfish (Gold-	Perseus	N	Perseus
Apus	S	Bird of Paradise			fish)	Phoenix	S	Phoenix
Aquarius	Z	Water Bearer	Draco	N	Dragon	Pictor	S	Painter (or his
Aquila	N	Eagle	Equuleus	N	Filly			Easel)
Ara	S	Altar	Eridanus	S	Eridanus (river)	Pisces	Z	Fishes
Aries	Z	Ram	Fornax	S	Furnace	Piscis Austrinus	S	Southern Fish
Auriga	N	Charioteer	Gemini	Z	Twins	Puppis	S	Poop (of Argo)[1]
Boötes	N	Herdsmen	Grus	S	Crane	Pyxis	S	Mariner's Com-
Caelum	S	Sculptor's Tool	Hercules	N	Hercules			pass
Camelopardalis	N	Giraffe	Horologium	S	Clock	Reticulum	S	Net
Cancer	Z	Crab	Hydra	N	Sea Serpent	Sagitta	N	Arrow
Canes Venatici	N	Hunting Dogs	Hydrus	S	Water Snake	Sagittarius	Z	Archer
Canis Major	S	Great Dog	Indus	S	Indian	Scorpius	Z	Scorpion
Canis Minor	S	Little Dog	Lacerta	N	Lizard	Sculptor	S	Sculptor
Capricornus	Z	Goat (or Sea-	Leo	Z	Lion	Scutum	S	Shield
		Goat)	Leo Minor	N	Little Lion	Serpens	N	Serpent
Carina	S	Keel (of Argo)[1]	Lepus	S	Hare	Sextans	N	Sextant
Cassiopeia	N	Cassiopeia	Libra	Z	Scales	Taurus	Z	Bull
Centaurus	S	Centaur	Lupus	S	Wolf	Telescopium	S	Telescope
Cepheus	N	Cepheus	Lynx	N	Lynx	Triangulum	N	Triangle
Cetus	S	Whale	Lyra	N	Lyre (Harp)	Triangulum Aus-	S	Southern Triangle
Chameleon	S	Chameleon	Mensa	S	Table (mountain)	trale		
Circinus	S	Compasses	Microscopium	S	Microscope	Tucana	S	Toucan
Columba	S	Dove	Monoceros	S	Unicorn	Ursa Major	N	Big Dipper[2]
Coma Berenices	N	Berenice's Hair	Musca	S	Southern Fly	Ursa Minor	N	Little Dipper[3]
Corona Australis	S	Southern Crown	Norma	S	Rule (straight-	Vela	S	Sail (of Argo)[1]
Corona Borealis	N	Northern Crown			edge)	Virgo	Z	Virgin
Corvus	S	Crow (Raven)	Octans	S	Octant	Volans	S	Flying Fish
Crater	S	Cup	Ophiuchus	N	Serpent-Bearer	Vulpecula	N	Fox
Crux	S	Southern Cross	Orion	S	Orion			
Cygnus	N	Swan	Pavo	S	Peacock			

1. The original constellation Argo Navis (the Ship Argo) has been divided into Carina, Puppis, and Vela. Normally the brightest star in each constellation is designated by alpha, the first letter of the Greek alphabet, the second brightest by beta, the second letter of the Greek alphabet, and so forth. But the Greek letters run through Carina, Puppis, and Vela as if it were still one constellation. 2. The Big Dipper is only a part of the constellation Ursa Major (Great Bear) and is not a constellation by itself. 3. The Little Dipper is called Ursa Minor (Little Bear).

significance, astronomers have retained them as reference areas. It is much easier to speak of a star in Orion than to give its geometrical position in the sky. During the Astronomical Congress of 1928, it was decided to recognize 88 constellations. A description of their agreed-upon boundaries was published in Cambridge, England, in 1930, under the title *Atlas Céleste*.

The Auroras

The "northern lights" (*Aurora borealis*) as well as the "southern lights" (*Aurora australis*) are upperatmosphere phenomena of astronomical origin. The auroras center around the magnetic (not the geographical) poles of Earth, which explains why, in the Western Hemisphere, they have been seen as far to the south as New Orleans and Florida, while the equivalent latitude in the Eastern Hemisphere never sees an aurora. The northern magnetic pole happens to be in the Western Hemisphere.

The lower limit of an aurora is at about 50 mi (80 km). Upper limits have been estimated to be as high as 400 mi (640 km). Since about 1880, a connection between the auroras on Earth and sunspots has been suspected and has gradually come to be accepted. It was said that the sunspots probably eject "particles" (later the word *electrons* was substituted), which on striking Earth's atmosphere cause the auroras. But

this explanation suffered from certain difficulties. Sometimes a very large sunspot group on the Sun, with individual spots bigger than Earth itself, would not cause an aurora. Moreover, even if a sunspot caused an aurora, the time that passed between the appearance of the one and the occurrence of the other was highly unpredictable.

This problem of the time lag is, in all probability, solved by the discovery of the Van Allen belt[1], a double layer of charged subatomic particles around Earth. The inner layer, with its center some 1,500 mi (2,400 km) from the ground, reaches from about 40°N to about 40°S and does not touch the atmosphere. The outer layer, much larger and with its center several thousand miles from the ground, does touch the atmosphere in the vicinity of the magnetic poles.

It seems probable that the "leakage" of electrons from the outer Van Allen layer causes the auroras. A new burst of electrons from the Sun seems to be caught in the outer layer first. Under the assumption that all electrons are first caught in the outer layer, the time lag can be understood. There has to be an "overflow" from the outer layer to produce an aurora.

---

1. Named after the American physicist, James Alfred Van Allen (1914–), who discovered the broad bands of intense radiation surrounding Earth in 1958.

Phenomena, 2006

Configurations of Sun, Moon, and Planets

NOTE: The hour listings are in Universal Time. For conversion to U.S. time zones, *see* Conversion of Universal Time to Civil Time, p. 421. Terms in boldface can be found on pp. 398–399.

JANUARY

Day	Phenomenon	Hour
1	Venus is 7° north of the Moon.	1000
1	The Moon is at **perigee**.	2300
2	Neptune is 4° north of the Moon.	1200
4	Uranus is 2° north of the Moon.	0000
4	Earth is at **perihelion**.	1500
5	Vesta, the third largest asteroid, is at **opposition**.	2300
6	FIRST QUARTER	1900
8	Mars is 1° 3′ south of the Moon.	2000
14	Venus is in inferior **conjunction**.	0000
14	FULL MOON	1000
15	Saturn is 4° south of the Moon.	1300
16	The asteroid Juno appears to be motionless in the sky as it goes from **retrograde** to direct motion.	2000
17	The moon is at **apogee**.	1900
21	Spica, the brightest star in the constellation Virgo, is 0° 6′ south of the Moon. **Occultation** of Spica by the Moon.	2200
22	LAST QUARTER	1500
23	Jupiter is 5° north of the Moon.	2000
25	Antares, the brightest star in the constellation Scorpius, is 0° 02′ south of the Moon. **Occultation** of Antares by the Moon.	1200
26	Mercury is in superior **conjunction**.	2200
27	Saturn is at **opposition**.	2300
28	Venus is 12° north of the Moon.	0000
29	NEW MOON	1400
30	Moon is at **perigee**.	0800
31	Uranus is 1° 7′ north of the Moon.	1200

FEBRUARY

Day	Phenomenon	Hour
3	Venus appears to be motionless in the sky as it moves toward its greatest **elongation** west of the Sun from a position east of the Sun as viewed from Earth.	0700
5	FIRST QUARTER	0600
5	Mars is 2° south of the Moon.	2200
6	Neptune is in **conjunction** with the Sun.	0600
11	Saturn is 4° south of the Moon.	1500
13	FULL MOON	0500
14	Moon is at **apogee**.	0100
14	Mercury is 0° 03′ north of Uranus.	1600
17	Venus is at its greatest illuminated extent.	2000
18	Spica, the brightest star in the constellation Virgo, is 0° 4′ south of the Moon. **Occultation** of Spica by the Moon.	0500
20	Jupiter is 5° north of the Moon.	0800
21	LAST QUARTER	0700
21	Antares, the brightest star in the constellation Scorpius, is 0° 2′ north of the Moon. **Occultation** of Antares by the Moon.	2100
23	Vesta, the third-largest asteroid, appears to be motionless in the sky as it goes from **retrograde** to direct motion.	0800
24	Mercury is at its greatest **elongation**, at 18° east of the Sun.	0500
24	Venus is 10° north of the Moon.	2100
25	Ceres, the largest asteroid, is 0° 8′ north of the Moon. **Occultation** of Ceres by the Moon.	1000
26	Neptune is 4° north of the Moon.	1300
27	Moon is at **perigee**.	2000
28	NEW MOON	0100

MARCH

Day	Phenomenon	Hour
1	Mercury is 4° north of the Moon.	0200
1	Uranus is in **conjunction** with the Sun.	1100
2	Mercury appears to be motionless in the sky as it moves from its greatest **elongation** east of the Sun back toward a position west of the Sun as viewed from Earth.	0700
5	Jupiter appears to be motionless in the sky as it goes from direct motion to **retrograde** motion.	0000
6	Mars is 3° south of the Moon.	0700
6	FIRST QUARTER	2000
10	Saturn is 4° south of the Moon.	1800
11	Mars is 7° north of Aldebaran, the brightest star in the constellation Taurus.	0000
12	Mercury is in inferior **conjunction**.	0300
13	Moon is at **apogee**.	0200
15	FULL MOON. Penumbral eclipse of the Moon.	0000
17	Spica, the brightest star in the constellation Virgo, is 0° 3′ south of the Moon. **Occultation** of Spica by the Moon.	1100
19	Jupiter is 5° north of the Moon.	1400
20	Equinox	1800
21	Antares, the brightest star in the constellation Scorpius, is 0° 3′ north of the Moon. **Occultation** of Antares by the Moon.	0300
22	LAST QUARTER	1900
24	Mercury appears to be motionless in the sky as it moves toward its greatest **elongation** west of the Sun from a position east of the Sun as viewed from Earth.	1200
25	Venus is at its greatest **elongation**, at 47° west of the Sun.	0700
25	Ceres, the largest asteroid, is 0° 8′ south of the Moon. **Occultation** of Ceres by the Moon.	1200
25	Venus is 6° north of the Moon.	2300
26	Neptune is 4° north of the Moon.	0100
26	Venus is 1° 9′ north of Neptune.	2100
27	Uranus is 1° 4′ north of the Moon. **Occultation** of Uranus by the Moon.	1500
27	Mercury is 2° north of the Moon.	1700
28	Moon is at **perigee**.	0700
29	NEW MOON. Total eclipse of the Sun.	1000
29	Pluto appears to be motionless in the sky as it goes from direct motion to **retrograde** motion.	1500

APRIL

Day	Phenomenon	Hour
3	Mars is 4° south of the Moon.	2000
5	FIRST QUARTER	1200
5	Saturn appears to be motionless in the sky as it goes from **retrograde** motion to direct motion.	1200
6	Saturn is 4° south of the Moon.	2300
8	Mercury is at its greatest **elongation**, at 28° west of the Sun.	1900
9	The Moon is at **apogee**.	1300
13	FULL MOON	1700
13	Spica, the brightest star in the constellation Virgo, is 0° 3′ south of the Moon. **Occultation** of Spica by the Moon.	1700
15	Jupiter is 5° north of the Moon.	1500
17	Antares, the brightest star in the constellation Scorpius, is 0° 2′ north of the Moon. **Occultation** of Antares by the Moon.	0900

Day	Phenomenon	Hour
18	Venus is 0° 3′ north of Uranus.	1200
21	LAST QUARTER	0300
22	Neptune is 4° north of the Moon.	0900
24	Uranus is 1° 2′ north of the Moon. **Occultation** of Uranus by the Moon.	0200
24	Venus is 0° 5′ north of the Moon. **Occultation** of Venus by the Moon.	1400
25	The Moon is at **perigee**.	1100
26	Mercury is 4° south of the Moon.	0800
27	NEW MOON	2000

MAY

Day	Phenomenon	Hour
2	Mars is 4° south of the Moon.	1100
3	Pallas, the second-largest asteroid, appears to be motionless in the sky as it goes from direct motion to **retrograde** motion.	0300
4	Saturn is 4° south of the Moon.	0900
4	Jupiter is at **opposition**.	1500
5	FIRST QUARTER	0500
7	The Moon is at **apogee**.	0700
11	Spica, the brightest star in the constellation Virgo, is 0° 3′ south of the Moon. **Occultation** of Spica by the Moon.	0000
12	Jupiter is 5° north of the Moon.	1600
13	FULL MOON	0700
14	Antares, the brightest star in the constellation Scorpius, is 0° 1′ north of the Moon. **Occultation** of Antares by the Moon.	1500
18	Mercury is in superior **conjunction**.	2000
19	Neptune is 4° north of the Moon.	1500
20	LAST QUARTER	0900
21	Uranus is 1° 0′ north of the Moon. **Occultation** of Uranus by the Moon.	1000
22	The Moon is at **perigee**.	1500
22	Neptune appears to be motionless in the sky as it goes from direct motion to **retrograde** motion.	1700
24	Venus is 4° south of the Moon.	0800
25	Mars is 5° south of Pollux, the brightest star in the constellation Gemini.	0500
27	NEW MOON	0500
31	Mars is 3° south of the Moon.	0300
31	Vesta, the third-largest asteroid, is 0° 9′ south of the Moon. **Occultation** of Vesta by the Moon.	1200
31	Saturn is 4° south of the Moon.	2100

JUNE

Day	Phenomenon	Hour
3	FIRST QUARTER	2300
4	The Moon is at **apogee**.	0200
7	Spica, the brightest star in the constellation Virgo, is 0° 1′ south of the Moon. **Occultation** of Spica by the Moon.	0900
8	Jupiter is 5° north of the Moon.	1900
10	Antares, the brightest star in the constellation Scorpius, is 0° 1′ north of the Moon. **Occultation** of Antares by the Moon.	2300
11	FULL MOON	1800
15	Neptune is 3° north of the Moon.	2100
16	The Moon is at **perigee**.	1700
16	Pluto is at **opposition**.	1700
17	Uranus is 0° 6′ north of the Moon. **Occultation** of Uranus by the Moon.	1700
17	Mars is 0° 6′ north of Saturn.	2300
18	LAST QUARTER	1400
19	Uranus appears to be motionless in the sky as it goes from direct motion to **retrograde** motion.	1600
20	Mercury is at its greatest **elongation**, at 25° east of the Sun.	2000
20	Mercury is 6° south of Pollux.	2300
21	Solstice	1200

Day	Phenomenon	Hour
23	Venus is 6° south of the Moon.	0300
25	NEW MOON	1600
26	Ceres, the largest asteroid, appears to be motionless in the sky as it goes from direct motion to **retrograde** motion.	1200
27	Mercury is 5° south of the Moon.	1400
28	Saturn is 3° south of the Moon.	1100
28	Vesta, the third-largest asteroid, is 0° 2′ north of the Moon. **Occultation** of Vesta by the Moon.	1900
28	Mars is 2° south of the Moon.	2100

JULY

Day	Phenomenon	Hour
1	The Moon is at **apogee**.	2000
1	Pallas, the second-largest asteroid, is at **opposition**.	2000
2	Venus is 4° north of Aldebaran, the brightest star in the constellation Taurus.	2000
3	FIRST QUARTER	1700
3	Earth is at **aphelion**.	2300
4	Mercury appears to be motionless in the sky as it moves from its greatest **elongation** east of the Sun back toward a position west of the Sun as viewed from Earth.	0200
4	Spica, the brightest star in the constellation Virgo, is 0° 1′ north of the Moon. **Occultation** of Spica by the Moon.	1700
6	Jupiter is 5° north of the Moon.	0200
6	Jupiter appears to be motionless in the sky as it goes from **retrograde** to direct motion.	1900
8	Antares, the brightest star in the constellation Scorpius, is 0° 2′ north of the Moon. **Occultation** of Antares by the Moon.	0800
11	FULL MOON	0300
13	Neptune is 3° north of the Moon.	0400
13	The Moon is at **perigee**.	1800
14	Uranus is 0° 4′ north of the Moon. **Occultation** of Uranus by the Moon.	2300
17	LAST QUARTER	1900
18	Mercury is in inferior **conjunction**.	0700
22	Mars is 0° 7′ north of Regulus, the brightest star in the constellation Leo.	0600
23	Venus is 6° south of the Moon.	0000
25	NEW MOON	0500
27	Mars is 1° 1′ south of the Moon. **Occultation** of Mars by the Moon.	1700
28	Mercury appears to be motionless in the sky as it moves toward its greatest **elongation** west of the Sun from a position east of the Sun as viewed from Earth.	1700
29	The Moon is at **apogee.**	1300

AUGUST

Day	Phenomenon	Hour
1	Spica, the brightest star in the constellation Virgo, is 0° 4′ north of the Moon. **Occultation** of Spica by the Moon.	0100
2	FIRST QUARTER	0900
2	Jupiter is 5° north of the Moon.	1200
4	Antares, the brightest star in the constellation Scorpius, is 0° 4′ north of the Moon. **Occultation** of Antares by the Moon.	1800
6	Mercury is 9° south of Pollux, the brightest star in the constellation Gemini.	1200
7	Mercury is at its greatest **elongation**, at 19° west of the Sun.	0100
7	Saturn is in **conjunction** with the Sun.	1200
8	Venus is 7° south of Pollux, the brightest star in the constellation Gemini.	0800
9	FULL MOON	1100

Day	Phenomenon	Hour
9	Neptune is 3° north of the Moon.	1200
10	The Moon is at **perigee.**	1800
11	Neptune is at **opposition.**	0500
11	Uranus is 0° 6′ north of the Moon. **Occultation** of Uranus by the Moon.	0600
12	Ceres, the largest asteroid, is at **opposition.**	1500
16	LAST QUARTER	0200
20	Mercury is 0° 5′ north of Saturn.	2300
22	Venus is 3° south of the Moon.	0300
23	NEW MOON	1900
24	Pallas, the second-largest asteroid, appears to be motionless in the sky as it goes from **retrograde** to direct motion.	1000
25	Mars is 0° 6′ north of the Moon. **Occultation** of Mars by the Moon.	1400
26	The Moon is at **apogee.**	0100
26	Venus is 0° 07′ north of Saturn.	2300
28	Spica, the brightest star in the constellation Virgo, is 0° 5′ north of the Moon. **Occultation** of Spica by the Moon.	0800
30	Jupiter is 5° north of the Moon.	0100
31	FIRST QUARTER	2300

SEPTEMBER

Day	Phenomenon	Hour
1	Antares, the brightest star in the constellation Scorpius, is 0° 5′ north of the Moon. **Occultation** of Antares by the Moon.	0200
1	Mercury is in superior **conjunction.**	0500
2	The asteroid Juno is in **conjunction** with the Sun.	0600
5	Pluto appears to be motionless in the sky as it goes from **retrograde** to direct motion.	1100
5	Uranus is at **opposition.**	1100
5	Neptune is 3° north of the Moon.	2200
5	Venus is 0° 8′ north of Regulus, the brightest star in the constellation Leo.	2300
7	Uranus is 0° 4′ north of the Moon. **Occultation** of Uranus by the Moon.	1500
7	FULL MOON. Partial eclipse of the Moon.	1900
8	The Moon is at **perigee.**	0300
11	Vesta, the third largest asteroid, is in **conjunction** with the Sun.	0100
14	LAST QUARTER	1100
15	Mercury is 0° 2′ south of Mars.	2100
19	Saturn is 2° south of the Moon.	0300
22	The Moon is at **apogee.**	0500
22	NEW MOON. Annular eclipse of the Sun.	1200
23	Equinox	0400
24	Mercury is 1° 8′ north of the Moon.	0400
24	Spica, the brightest star in the constellation Virgo, is 0° 5′ north of the Moon. **Occultation** of Spica by the Moon.	1400
26	Jupiter is 5° north of the Moon.	1600
27	Mercury is 1° 3′ north Spica, the brightest star in the constellation Virgo.	1500
28	Antares, the brightest star in the constellation Scorpius, is 0° 5′ north of the Moon. **Occultation** of Antares by the Moon.	0800
30	FIRST QUARTER	1100

OCTOBER

Day	Phenomenon	Hour
3	Neptune is 3° north of the Moon.	0700
5	Uranus is 0° 5′ north of the Moon. **Occultation** of Uranus by the Moon.	0000
5	Ceres, the largest asteroid, appears to be motionless in the sky as it goes from **retrograde** to direct motion.	2000
6	The Moon is at **perigee.**	1400

Day	Phenomenon	Hour
7	FULL MOON	0300
14	LAST QUARTER	0000
16	Saturn is 2° south of the Moon.	1400
17	Mercury is at its greatest **elongation,** at 25° east of the Sun.	0400
19	The Moon is at **apogee.**	1000
19	The asteroid Juno is 0° 3′ north of the Moon. **Occultation** of Juno by the Moon.	1800
22	NEW MOON	0500
23	Mars is in **conjunction** with the Sun.	0700
24	Jupiter is 5° north of the Moon.	0800
24	Mercury is 1° 4′ north of the Moon.	0800
25	Antares, the brightest star in the constellation Scorpius, is 0° 4′ north of the Moon. **Occultation** of Antares by the Moon.	1400
25	Mercury is 4° south of Jupiter.	2200
27	Venus is in superior **conjunction.**	1800
28	Mercury is 4° south of Jupiter.	1400
29	Mercury appears to be motionless in the sky as it moves from its greatest **elongation** east of the Sun back toward a position west of the Sun as viewed from Earth.	0000
29	Neptune appears to be motionless in the sky as it goes from **retrograde** to direct motion.	0700
29	FIRST QUARTER	2100
30	Neptune is 3° north of the Moon.	1400

NOVEMBER

Day	Phenomenon	Hour
1	Uranus is 0° 5′ north of the Moon. **Occultation** of Uranus by the Moon.	0800
4	The Moon is at **perigee.**	0000
5	FULL MOON	1300
8	Mercury is in inferior **conjunction,** transit over the Sun.	2200
13	LAST QUARTER	1800
13	Saturn is 1° 6′ south of the Moon.	0100
15	The Moon is at **apogee.**	2300
17	Mercury appears to be motionless in the sky as it moves toward its greatest **elongation** west of the Sun from a position east of the Sun as viewed from Earth.	1900
18	Spica, the brightest star in the constellation Virgo, is 0° 6′ north of the Moon. **Occultation** of Spica by the Moon.	0300
19	Mercury is 6° north of the Moon.	1300
20	Uranus appears to be motionless in the sky as it goes from **retrograde** to direct motion.	1400
20	NEW MOON	2200
21	Jupiter is in **conjunction** with the Sun.	2300
25	Mercury is at its greatest **elongation,** at 20° west of the Sun.	1300
26	Neptune is 3° north of the Moon.	2100
28	FIRST QUARTER	0600
28	Uranus is 0° 3′ north of the Moon. **Occultation** of Uranus by the Moon.	1500

DECEMBER

Day	Phenomenon	Hour
2	The Moon is at **perigee.**	0000
5	FULL MOON	0000
6	Saturn appears to be motionless in the sky as it goes from direct motion to **retrograde** motion.	2000
9	Mercury is 1° 0′ north of Mars.	2000
10	Saturn is 1° 2′ south of the Moon. **Occultation** of Saturn by the Moon.	1100
10	Mercury is 0° 1′ north of Jupiter.	1600
12	Mars is 0° 8′ south of Jupiter.	0000
12	LAST QUARTER	1500
13	The Moon is at **apogee.**	1900

Day	Phenomenon	Hour	Day	Phenomenon	Hour
14	Mercury is 5° north of Antares, the brightest star in the constellation Scorpius.	0800	19	Mars is 5° north of the Moon.	0400
			20	NEW MOON	1400
			22	Solstice	0000
15	Spica, the brightest star in the constellation Virgo, is 0° 8′ north of the Moon. **Occultation** of Spica by the Moon.	1100	24	Neptune is 3° north of the Moon.	0300
			25	Uranus is 0° 08′ south of the Moon. Occultation of Uranus by the Moon.	2100
18	Pluto is in **conjunction** with the Sun.	1500	27	FIRST QUARTER	1500
18	Jupiter is 6° north of the Moon.	2100	28	The Moon is at **perigee**.	0200
19	Mars is 4° north of Antares, the brightest star in the constellation Scorpius.	0300			
19	Antares, the brightest star in the constellation Scorpius, is 0° 4′ north of the Moon. **Occultation** of Antares by the Moon.	0400			

Conversion of Universal Time (UT) to Civil Time

UT	EDT[1]	EST[2]	CST[3]	MST[4]	PST[5]
00	*8P	*7P	*6P	*5P	*4P
01	*9P	*8P	*7P	*6P	*5P
02	*10P	*9P	*8P	*7P	*6P
03	*11P	*10P	*9P	*8P	*7P
04	M	*11P	*10P	*9P	*8P
05	1A	M	*11P	*10P	*9P
06	2A	1A	M	*11P	*10P
07	3A	2A	1A	M	*11P
08	4A	3A	2A	1A	M
09	5A	4A	3A	2A	1A
10	6A	5A	4A	3A	2A
11	7A	6A	5A	4A	3A
12	8A	7A	6A	5A	4A
13	9A	8A	7A	6A	5A
14	10A	9A	8A	7A	6A
15	11A	10A	9A	8A	7A
16	N	11A	10A	9A	8A
17	1P	N	11A	10A	9A
18	2P	1P	N	11A	10A
19	3P	2P	1P	N	11A
20	4P	3P	2P	1P	N
21	5P	4P	3P	2P	1P
22	6P	5P	4P	3P	2P
23	7P	6P	5P	4P	3P

NOTES: * denotes previous day. N = noon. M = midnight. 1. Eastern Daylight Time. 2. Eastern Standard Time, same as Central Daylight Time. 3. Central Standard Time, same as Mountain Daylight Time. 4. Mountain Standard Time, same as Pacific Daylight Time. 5. Pacific Standard Time.

Eclipses of the Sun and Moon, 2006

Note: The day of an eclipse is given in Universal Time (UT) and may start a day earlier or later depending on your time zone. (*See* Phenomena, 2006, pp. 418–421, to find time of eclipse.)

March 15. Penumbral eclipse of the Moon.

March 29. Total eclipse of the Sun. Visible in Brazil, Ghana, Togo, Benin, Nigeria, Niger, northwest Chad, Libya, the northwest tip of Egypt, Turkey, northwest Georgia, southwest Russia, Kazakstan, the southern tip of Russia, and ends in the northern tip of Mongolia.

Sept. 7. Partial eclipse of the Moon. Visible from parts of Antarctica, Australasia, Asia, Africa, and Europe including the British Isles.

Sept. 22. Annular eclipse of the Sun. Visible in Guyana, Suriname, French Guiana, the South Atlantic Ocean, and ends southwest of the Kerguelen Islands

Visibility of Planets in Morning and Evening Twilight, 2006

Morning

Venus	January 19–September 19
Mars	December 10–December 31
Jupiter	January 1–May 4
	December 5–December 31
Saturn	January 1–January 7
	August 26–December 31

Evening

Venus	January 1–January 8
	December 8–December 31
Mars	January 1–September 7
Jupiter	May 4–November 9
Saturn	January 27–July 30

Space Shuttle Timeline

Overview of two decades of the U.S. shuttle program

April 12, 1981 John Young and Robert Crippin pilot the space shuttle *Columbia* on the maiden flight of the Space Transport System (STS-1).

Nov. 11, 1982 Space shuttle *Challenger* is launched.

June 18–24, 1983 Sally Ride becomes the first American woman astronaut on the STS-7 flight of *Challenger*.

Aug. 30, 1983 The STS-8 *Challenger* flight introduces Guion S. Bluford, the first African-American astronaut to travel in space.

Feb. 7, 1984 Astronauts Bruce McCandless and Robert Stewart make the first untethered space walks (with jet backpacks) on this *Challenger* flight.

Aug. 30, 1984 First flight of space shuttle *Discovery*.

Aug. 8, 1985 First flight of space shuttle *Atlantis*.

Oct. 3–7, 1985 *Atlantis* deploys a classified satellite for the Department of Defense.

Jan. 28, 1986 *Challenger* explodes 73 seconds into the flight.

Sept. 29–Oct. 3, 1988 The first shuttle flight after the *Challenger* disaster. *Discovery* launches a satellite.

May 4, 1989 The *Magellan* Venus probe is launched from *Atlantis*, the first U.S. planetary mission in 11 years and the first launched from a shuttle.

Oct. 18, 1989 *Atlantis* launches the Jupiter-bound *Galileo* spacecraft.

April 24–29, 1990 *Discovery* mission launches the Hubble Space Telescope.

May 2–16, 1992 *Endeavour's* maiden flight and the first 3-person spacewalk.

Dec. 2–13, 1993 This *Endeavour* flight successfully repairs the optics on the ailing Hubble Space Telescope.

Feb. 3–11, 1994 Sergei Krikalev becomes the first Russian cosmonaut on a U.S. shuttle mission.

Feb. 3–11, 1995 Eileen Collins becomes the first woman pilot, flying *Discovery* past the Russian space station *Mir*.

June 27–July 7, 1995 Space shuttle *Atlantis* docks with the Russian *Mir* space station.

March 22–31, 1996 U.S. astronaut Shannon Lucid is dropped off by *Atlantis* for a 181-day mission on the *Mir*, setting a record for a woman in space.

Oct. 29–Nov. 7, 1998 The first American to orbit the Earth, John Glenn, returns to space aboard the *Discovery*.

Dec. 4–12, 1998 *Endeavour* makes the first human flight to the International Space Station. The construction mission connects the Zarya and Unity modules.

July 22–27, 1999 Col. Eileen Collins becomes the first woman to command a shuttle mission. *Columbia* launches the Chandra X-Ray Observatory.

March 8–21, 2001 In the eighth shuttle mission to the International Space Station, *Discovery* picks up the Expedition One crew (delivered to the station in October by a Russian flight) and drops off Expedition Two.

March 1–12, 2002 *Columbia* makes the fourth Hubble Space Telescope maintenance/repair/upgrade visit.

Feb. 1, 2003 Fifteen minutes before completing its 28th mission, *Columbia* breaks up. All seven crew members are lost.

July 26, 2005 Eileen Collins commands *Discovery* on the first shuttle flight since the *Columbia* disaster. Despite the safety measures, in an incident similar to that which caused the *Columbia* disaster, some foam insulation breaks off the external tank after takeoff. *Discovery* continues its mission and successfully returns to Earth Aug. 9, but NASA grounds any further shuttle flights indefinitely.

To the Moon and Mars

In January 2004, President George W. Bush announced the ambitious goal of putting humans on Mars. The first stage involves returning to the Moon by the year 2020 and establishing a base there. Two staffed lunar missions per year would have crews conducting long-term research on the effects of extraterrestrial living on the human body as well as training astronauts for the grueling Mars missions. NASA director Michael D. Griffin is a gung-ho supporter of the program, although he is critical of the cost, estimated at $217 billion through 2025.

With the problem-plagued space shuttle program slated to be retired in 2010, a new system is being developed. Two rockets are planned for the Moon trips: one for cargo and one for the human crew. A booster rocket using some beefed-up shuttle technology would take off with the new Earth Departure Stage and the Crew Exploration Vehicle (CEV). The Earth Departure Stage would hurtle the CEV and a lunar lander into orbit around the Moon. The CEV

would stay in orbit while the lander descended to the surface carrying four astronauts. The base would have living quarters, a power plant, and communications systems; crews would explore in vehicles akin to dune buggies and airlocks would permit moonwalks.

After chalking up a few years of lunar living experience, next stop is the Red Planet, possibly by 2030. Prior to the six-person crew landing on Mars, NASA plans to send the base's structures on ahead and land them by remote control. The astronauts' trip to Mars would take about six months; the team would then spend 500 days on the planet itself before another six-month journey home.

The United States isn't the only country planning to visit Mars. The European Space Agency (ESA) has the Aurora mission to put humans on Mars, also by 2030. In July 2005, the Russian space agency announced they were looking for six volunteers to lock themselves in a mock space capsule for 15 months in preparation for a Mars mission in 2015.

Major Space Explorations

Ongoing Missions

Voyager (U.S.)
Destination: Jupiter and Saturn. **Launched:** Aug. 20 (*Voyager 2*) and Sept. 5 (*Voyager 1*), 1977. **Mission:** To explore Jupiter and the other outer planets. Launched in 1977, *Voyager 1* and *Voyager 2* passed Jupiter in 1979 and sent back surprising color TV images of that planet and its moons. *Voyager 1* passed Saturn in Nov. 1980. *Voyager 2* passed Saturn in Aug. 1981 and Uranus in Jan. 1986. *Voyager 2* encountered Neptune in 1989 and discovered four rings around the planet, six new moons, a giant spot, and evidence of volcanic-like activity on its largest moon, Triton. *Voyager 2* remains the only spacecraft ever to have visited the worlds of Neptune and Uranus.

Voyager 1, at 9 billion miles from the Sun, is currently the most distant human-made object in the universe, and *Voyager 2* is 7 billion miles from the Sun. Both spacecraft currently constitute the Voyager Interstellar Mission (VIM) and continue to relay news of their surroundings through the Deep Space Network (DSN). The craft and mission could last until 2020.

Ulysses (U.S. and European Space Agency)
Destination: The Sun. **Launched:** Oct. 6, 1990. **Mission:** To study the Sun and map the interstellar space above and below its poles. The spacecraft was put into orbit at right angles to the solar system's ecliptic plane. This special orbit enabled *Ulysses* to examine for the first time the Sun's north and south polar regions. Besides investigating the Sun, the spacecraft is also studying phenomena from the Milky Way and beyond. The spacecraft completed its first full orbit around the Sun on April 17, 1998, and continues to orbit the Sun. *Ulysses* made its closest approach to Jupiter in Feb. 2004.

Mars Global Surveyor (MGS) (U.S.)
Destination: Mars. **Launched:** Nov. 7, 1996. **Arrival:** Sept. 11, 1997. **Mission:** To provide detailed maps of the planet's surface and distribution of minerals, and to monitor the Martian weather. Six instruments on the orbiting spacecraft are studying Martian surface, atmosphere, and gravitational and magnetic fields. *Surveyor*'s cameras are able to distinguish features as small as 10 ft across.

The primary mapping mission was delayed until March 1999, due to problems with the craft's solar panels. MGS completed its primary mission in Jan. 2001, and is currently in an extended mission phase. Having studied the planet's entire surface, atmosphere, and interior, MGS has returned more Mars data than all other Martian missions combined. Its most significant results include photographs of gullies and debris flow that suggest the presence of water at or near the planet's surface. MGS is collecting and transmitting data from the Mars Exploration Rovers.

Cassini-Huygens (U.S., the European Space Agency, and the Italian Space Agency)
Destination: Saturn. **Launched:** Oct. 15, 1997. **Arrival:** July 1, 2004. **Mission:** To orbit Saturn for four years. The Cassini-Huygens mission is named for the Italian-French astronomer Jean Dominique Cassini, who discovered four of Saturn's major moons, and the Dutch scientist Christiaan Huygens, the first to find Saturn's rings and its largest moon, Titan. *Cassini-Huygens* encountered Jupiter on Dec. 30, 2000, and flew down the giant planet's magnetotail (the elongated tail of a planet's magnetic field facing away from the Sun), performing studies complementing the *Galileo* mission until March 31, 2001. On July 1, 2004, *Cassini* reached Saturn's rings and went into the first of 74 orbits of the planet and began sending back images of the rings and the moons. On Dec. 24, 2004, the *Huygens* probe separated from the *Cassini* spacecraft and in Jan. 2005 descended to Titan, transmitting information for its 2½ hour descent and then for more than 90 minutes on the moon's surface. The *Cassini* craft is slated to continue its mission until July 1, 2008.

Stardust (U.S.)
Destination: Comet Wild 2. **Launched:** Feb. 7, 1999. **Mission:** To fly through the coma of Comet Wild 2, capture particles spewing out of the comet, take pictures of the comet, and return comet dust samples to Earth. *Stardust* will be the first mission to return with comet samples. Additionally, the *Stardust* spacecraft will bring back samples of interstellar dust, which is believed to include remnants from the formation of the solar system. On April 18, 2002, *Stardust* reached the farthest distance from the Sun ever traveled by a solar-powered spacecraft, 2.72 AU (253 million miles or 407 million kilometers). In Jan. 2004, *Stardust* reached the comet, sent back the best images of a comet ever taken, and collected comet particles destined to return to Earth Jan. 16, 2006.

2001 Mars Odyssey (U.S.)
Destination: Mars. **Launched:** April 7, 2001. **Arrival:** Oct. 24, 2001. **Mission:** To conduct mineralogical mapping of the planet and study the radiation risk to humans over the course of three years. A goal of the program is to determine if Mars's atmosphere could support life.

Mars Odyssey's primary mission of mapping the amount and distribution of chemical elements and minerals that form the Martian surface and searching for evidence of hydrogen in the subsurface was completed in Aug. 2004. *Mars Odyssey* also provides support to the Mars Exploration Rovers program (MER), serving as the communications relay for MER's rovers. About 85% of MER's rovers' pictures have been relayed to Earth via *Odyssey*.

Wilkinson Microwave Anisotropy Probe (WMAP) (U.S.)
Destination: Solar orbit. **Launched:** June 30, 2001. **Arrival:** Oct. 1, 2001. **Mission:** To reveal conditions as they existed in the early universe by measuring the properties of cosmic microwave background radiation (CMB), the radiant heat left over from the Big Bang, over the full sky. Each sky scan takes approximately six months, and in April 2002, *WMAP* completed its first. The full sky map will be updated as more data is received and analyzed. Data from *WMAP*'s first full sky scan was released in Feb. 2003, revealing a map of the oldest

light in the universe, 13.7 billion years old. The mission is slated to continue mapping until 2006.

Mars Express (European Space Agency)
Destination: Mars. **Launched:** June 2, 2003. **Arrival:** Dec. 26, 2003. **Mission:** To search for subsurface water from orbit and drop a lander on the Martian surface. Instruments on the orbiting spacecraft study the atmosphere and the planet's structure and geology. The lander, *Beagle 2* (named after the ship on which Charles Darwin sailed), was scheduled to take photographs, gather soil samples, and examine rocks and soil microscopically—all in the search for signs of past life on Mars. *Beagle 2* separated from the orbiter on Dec. 19, 2003, but contact was lost. The orbiter continues its mission, imaging the planet's entire surface, mapping the composition of the surface and atmosphere, determining the structure of the subsurface, and studying the atmosphere.

Mars Exploration Rovers (MER) (U.S.)
Destination: Mars. **Launched:** June 10, 2003 (*Spirit*) and July 7 (*Opportunity*). **Arrival:** Jan. 2004. **Mission:** To deploy, in two different locations, *Spirit* and *Opportunity*, two identical long-range rovers (larger than *Pathfinder*'s *Sojourner*) that can trek up to 300 yards (100 m) across the surface in a Martian day. The rovers' sophisticated instruments enable them to act as mobile field geologists, taking color pictures, analyzing soil and rocks, and searching for past and present evidence of water. The rovers were designed to operate for 90 days but were performing so well the mission was extended. *Spirit* made a successful landing on Jan. 3, 2004, and started beaming 3-D images of the planet the next day. On Jan. 6, *Spirit* began to send sharp color pictures of the planet back to Earth. *Opportunity* landed on Jan. 24, 2004, on the opposite side of Mars from *Spirit* and began sending images the next day. Both rovers, on opposite sides of the planet, found evidence that water was present, and even flowed, in the planet's past. As of July 21, 2005, *Spirit* had racked up 2.91 mi (4,685 m) on its odometer and *Opportunity* has traveled 3.45 mi (5,555 m).

MESSENGER (MErcury Surface, Space ENvironment, GEochemistry, and Ranging mission) (U.S.)
Destination: Mercury. **Launched:** Aug. 3, 2004. **Arrival:** 2011. **Mission:** To study Mercury from orbit for the first time. *MESSENGER* is intended to spend at least a year in orbit photographing the planet, studying its makeup, and charting Mercury's magnetic field.

Deep Impact (U.S.)
Destination: Comet Tempel 1. **Launched:** Jan. 12, 2005. **Arrival:** July 4, 2005. **Mission:** To look beneath the surface of a comet at material relatively unchanged from the solar system's formation. With a fiery flash on July 4, 2005, the mission's probe smashed into the comet at nearly 23,000 miles per hour. The flyby spacecraft took pictures of the impact, collected data from the probe, and flew through the comet's tail. The project will end in April 2006.

Mars Reconnaisance Orbiter (MRO) (U.S.)
Destination: Mars orbit. **Launched:** Aug. 12, 2005. **Arrival:** March 2006. **Mission:** To study the history of water on Mars. From its Mars orbit, the mission will take pictures, analyze minerals, study the weather and atmosphere, probe the surface for water

ice, and assist spacecraft navigation and communications. MRO is expected to collect more data than all previous Mars missions combined. The primary mission is slated to end in 2010.

Future Missions
(Note: Dates are tentative.)

SELENE (SELenological and ENgineering Explorer) (Japan)
Destination: The Moon. **Launch:** 2006. **Mission:** To study the origin and evolution of the Moon, orbiting it for one year. It will map the entire surface and gather data on chemical and mineralogical composition, magnetic fields, and interior structure. After a year, the propulsion module of the orbiter will separate from the spacecraft and softland on the lunar surface to continue the mission for two more months.

Space Technology 5 (U.S.)
Destination: Earth's magnetosphere. **Launch:** 2006. **Mission:** To test new technology and aid scientists in understanding Earth's magnetosphere. It is the fourth deep-space mission of NASA's New Millennium program. The Nanosat Constellation Trailblazer, known as Space Technology 5 or ST5, will test methods for operating three miniature spacecraft as a single system. Each of the spacecraft is about 17 in. (42 cm) across by 8 in. (20 cm) high and weighs about 47 lb.

AIM (U.S.)
Destination: Earth orbit. **Launch:** 2006. **Mission:** To use the Aeronomy of Ice in the Mesosphere (AIM) mission to help scientists investigate the causes of the recent rise in noctilucent (glow-in-the-dark) clouds, wispy swirls that form about 50 mi (80 km) above the surface of the earth. The presence of the clouds over the polar regions has increased markedly in recent decades, and is thought by many scientists to be related to higher concentrations of greenhouse gases in Earth's atmosphere.

New Horizons (U.S.)
Destination: Pluto-Kuiper Belt. **Launch:** Jan. 2006. **Arrival:** Summer 2015. **Mission:** To study the worlds at the edge of our solar system. *New Horizons* will be the first mission specifically designed to study Pluto and its moon Charon. This mission plans to map Pluto's and Charon's surface appearances, study surface compositions, and probe their atmospheres. *New Horizons* then will go to the Kuiper Belt, located beyond Neptune's orbit, and examine Kuiper Belt objects, thought to be similar to the composition of the cores of the giant planets.

Herschel Space Observatory (European Space Agency)
Destination: Earth's magnetosphere. **Launch:** 2007. **Mission:** To study how the first stars and galaxies were formed and to search for water in space. Formerly called the Far Infrared and Submillimetre Telescope (FIRST), Herschel will be equipped with an infrared telescope, a high-resolution spectrograph, and two infrared cameras. Construction of the observatory began in the spring of 2002.

U.S. Unstaffed Planetary and Lunar Programs

Lunar Orbiter. Series of spacecraft designed to orbit the Moon, taking pictures and obtaining data in support of the subsequent staffed *Apollo* landings. The U.S. launched five *Lunar Orbiter*s between Aug. 10, 1966, and Aug. 2, 1967.

Mariner. Designation for a series of spacecraft designed to fly past or orbit the planets, particularly Mercury, Venus, and Mars. *Mariner*s provided the early information on Venus and Mars. *Mariner 9,* orbiting Mars in 1971, returned the most revealing photographs of that planet and helped pave the way for a *Viking* landing in 1976. *Mariner 10* explored Venus and Mercury in 1973 and was the first probe to use a planet's gravity to propel it toward another.

Pioneer. Designation for the United States' first series of sophisticated interplanetary spacecraft. *Pioneer*s *10* and *11* reached Jupiter in 1973 and 1974 and continued on to explore Saturn and the other outer planets. *Pioneer 11,* renamed *Pioneer Saturn,* examined the Saturn system in Sept. 1979. Significant discoveries were the finding of a small new moon and a narrow new ring. In 1986, *Pioneer 10* was the first man-made object to escape the solar system. *Pioneer Venus 1* and *2* reached Venus in 1978 and provided detailed information about that planet's surface and atmosphere.

Ranger. NASA's earliest Moon-exploration program. Spacecraft were designed for a crash landing on the Moon, taking pictures and returning scientific data up to the moment of impact. Provided the first close-up views of the lunar surface. The *Ranger*s provided more than 17,000 close-up pictures, giving us more information about the Moon in a few years than in all the time that had gone before.

Surveyor. Series of unstaffed spacecraft designed to land gently on the Moon and provide information on the surface in preparation for the staffed lunar landings. *Surveyor*'s legs were instrumented to return data on the surface hardness of the Moon. *Surveyor* dispelled the fear that *Apollo* spacecraft might sink several feet or more into the lunar dust.

Viking. Designation for two spacecraft designed to conduct detailed scientific examination of the planet Mars, including a search for life. *Viking 1* landed on July 20, 1976; *Viking 2,* Sept. 3, 1976. More was learned about the red planet in a few short months than in all previous missions, but the question of whether there is life on Mars remains unresolved.

Notable Unstaffed Lunar and Interplanetary Probes

Spacecraft	Launch date	Destination	Remarks
Pioneer 3 (U.S.)	Dec. 6, 1958	Moon	Max. alt.: 66,654 mi. Discovered outer Van Allen layer.
Luna 2 (USSR)	Sept. 12, 1959	Moon	Impacted on Sept. 14. First space vehicle to reach Moon.
Luna 3 (USSR)	Oct. 4, 1959	Moon	Flew around Moon and transmitted first pictures of lunar far side, Oct. 7.
Mariner 2 (U.S.)	Aug. 27, 1962	Venus	Venus probe. Successful mid-course correction. Passed 21,648 mi from Venus Dec. 14, 1962. Reported 800°F surface temp. Contact lost Jan. 3, 1963, at 54 million mi.
Ranger 7 (U.S.)	July 28, 1964	Moon	Impacted near Crater Guericke 68.5 hr after launch. Sent 4,316 pictures during last 15 min of flight as close as 1,000 ft above lunar surface.
Mariner 4 (U.S.)	Nov. 28, 1964	Mars	Transmitted first close-up pictures on June 14, 1965, from altitude of 6,000 mi.
Luna 9 (USSR)	Jan. 31, 1966	Moon	220 lb instrument capsule soft-landed Feb. 3, 1966. Sent back about 30 pictures.
Surveyor 1 (U.S.)	May 30, 1966	Moon	Landed June 2, 1966. Sent almost 10,400 pictures, a number after surviving the 14-day lunar night.
Lunar Orbiter 1 (U.S.)	Aug. 10, 1966	Moon	Orbited Moon Aug. 14. 21 pictures sent.
Surveyor 3 (U.S.)	April 17, 1967	Moon	Soft-landed on Oceanus Procellarum 65 hr after launch. Scooped and tested lunar soil.
Venera 4 (USSR)	June 12, 1967	Venus	Arrived Oct. 17. Instrument capsule sent temperature and chemical data.
Surveyor 5 (U.S.)	Sept. 8, 1967	Moon	Landed near lunar equator Sept. 10. Radiological analysis of lunar soil. Mechanical claw for digging soil.
Surveyor 7 (U.S.)	Jan. 6, 1968	Moon	Landed near Crater Tycho Jan. 10. Soil analysis. Sent 3,343 pictures.
Pioneer 9 (U.S.)	Nov. 8, 1968	Sun	Achieved orbit. Six experiments returned solar radiation data.
Venera 5 (USSR)	Jan. 5, 1969	Venus	Landed May 16, 1969. Returned atmospheric data.
Mariner 6 (U.S.)	Feb. 24, 1969	Mars	Came within 2,000 mi of Mars July 31, 1969. Sent back data and TV pictures.
Luna 16 (USSR)	Sept. 12, 1970	Moon	Soft-landed Sept. 20, scooped up rock, returned to Earth Sept. 24.
Luna 17 (USSR)	Nov. 10, 1970	Moon	Soft-landed on Sea of Rains Nov. 17. Lunokhod 1, self-propelled vehicle, used for first time. Sent TV photos, made soil analysis, etc.
Mariner 9 (U.S.)	May 30, 1971	Mars	First craft to orbit Mars, Nov. 13. 7,300 pictures, 1st close-ups of one of Mars's moons. Transmission ended Oct. 27, 1972.
Luna 20 (USSR)	Feb. 14, 1972	Moon	Soft-landed Feb. 21 in Sea of Fertility. Returned Feb. 25 with rock samples.
Pioneer 10 (U.S.)	March 3, 1972	Jupiter	620-million-mi flight path through asteroid belt past Jupiter Dec. 3, 1973, to give man first close-up of planet. In 1986, it became first man-made object to escape solar system.

Spacecraft	Launch date	Destination	Remarks
Luna 21 (USSR)	Jan. 8, 1973	Moon	Soft-landed Jan. 16. Lunokhod 2 (moon-car) scooped up soil samples, returned them to Earth Jan. 27.
Mariner 10 (U.S.)	Nov. 3, 1973	Venus, Mercury	Passed Venus Feb. 5, 1974. Arrived Mercury March 29, 1974, for man's first close-up look at planet. First time gravity of one planet (Venus) used to propel spacecraft toward another (Mercury).
Viking 1 (U.S.)	Aug. 20, 1975	Mars	Carrying life-detection labs. Landed July 20, 1976, for detailed scientific research, including pictures. Designed to work for only 90 days, it operated for almost 6½ years before it went silent in Nov. 1982.
Viking 2 (U.S.)	Sept. 9, 1975	Mars	Like Viking 1. Landed Sept. 3, 1976. Functioned 3½ years.
Luna 24 (USSR)	Aug. 9, 1976	Moon	Soft-landed Aug. 18, 1976. Returned soil samples Aug. 22, 1976.
Voyager 2 (U.S.)	Aug. 20, 1977	Jupiter, Saturn, Uranus	Launched before Voyager 1. Encountered Jupiter in July 1979; flew by Saturn Aug. 1981; passed Uranus Jan. 1986; and passed Neptune in Aug. 1989.
Voyager 1 (U.S.)	Sept. 5, 1977	Jupiter, Saturn	Flyby mission. Reached Jupiter in March 1979; passed Saturn Nov. 1980; passed Uranus 1986.
Pioneer Venus 1 (U.S.)	May 20, 1978	Venus	Arrived Dec. 4 and orbited Venus, photographing surface and atmosphere. Crashed into planet's surface mid-Oct. 1992 after circling Venus for 14 years.
Pioneer Venus 2 (U.S.)	Aug. 8, 1978	Venus	Four-part multiprobe, landed Dec. 9.
Venera 13 (USSR)	Oct. 30, 1981	Venus	Landed March 1, 1982. Took first X-ray fluorescence analysis of the planet's surface. Transmitted data 2 hours, 7 minutes.
VEGA 1 (USSR)	Deployed on Venus, June 10, 1985	Halley's Comet	In flyby over Venus while en route to encounter Halley's Comet, VEGA 1 and 2 dropped scientific capsules onto Venus to study atmosphere and surface material. Encountered Halley's Comet on March 6 and March 9, 1986. Took TV pictures and studied comet's dust particles.
VEGA 2 (USSR)	Deployed on Venus, June 14, 1985	Halley's Comet	See VEGA 1 above.
Suisei (Japan)	Aug. 18, 1985	Halley's Comet	Spacecraft made flyby of comet and studied atmosphere with ultraviolet camera; observed rotation nucleus (March 8, 1986).
Sakigake (Japan)	Jan. 8, 1985	Halley's Comet	Spacecraft made flyby to study solar wind and magnetic fields; detected plasma waves (March 11, 1986).
Giotto (E.S.A.)	July 2, 1985	Halley's Comet	European Space Agency spacecraft made closest approach to comet (March 13, 1986). Studied atmosphere and magnetic fields. Sent back best pictures of nucleus. Flew by comet Grigg-Skjellerup July 10, 1992. Unable to send pictures.
Phobos Mission (USSR)	July 7 and July 12, 1988	Mars and Phobos	Two spacecraft to probe Martian moon Phobos starting April 1989. Were to study orbit and soil chemistry, and send TV pictures and data of planet. Contact was lost with Phobos 1 in Aug. 1988 and with Phobos 2 in March 1989 after it reached the Martian moon.
Magellan (U.S.)	May 4, 1989	Venus	Arrived at Venus on Aug. 10, 1990, and made a geologic map of planet with a powerful radar. Crashed into Venus Oct. 12, 1994.
Galileo (U.S.)	Oct. 18, 1989	Jupiter	To study Jupiter's atmosphere and its moons during 22-month mission.
Ulysses (U.S., E.S.A.)	Oct. 6, 1990	Sun	To study the poles of the Sun and interstellar space above and below the poles. First solar encounter was in 1994, second encounter in 1995.
Gamma-Ray Observatory (U.S.)	April 7, 1991	Earth orbit	To make first survey of gamma-ray sources across the whole sky, studying explosive energy sources such as supernovae, quasars, neutron stars, pulsars, and black holes. Mission ended, it was deorbited and crashed into Pacific Ocean, June 4, 2000.
Clementine (U.S.)	Jan. 25, 1994	Moon and asteroid 1620 Geographos	Entered lunar orbit Feb. 21 and took close-up photos of lunar surface for two months. Computer malfunction prevented planned rendezvous with Geographos.
Near-Earth Asteroid Rendezvous (NEAR) (U.S.)	Feb. 17, 1996	Asteroid 433 Eros	Photographed asteroid 253 Mathilde June 27, 1997. Entered into orbit around Eros Feb. 14, 2000, and landed on surface in controlled crash Feb. 12, 2001. Took detailed measurements and generated about 160,000 images of Eros. Renamed NEAR-Shoemaker in honor of geologist Eugene M. Shoemaker. First craft to orbit an asteroid.
Mars Pathfinder (U.S.)	Dec. 5, 1996	Ares Vallis, Mars	Landed July 4, 1997. The spacecraft lander and its rover, Sojourner, provided a wealth of information on the Martian rocks, soil, and atmosphere. Sent back the first live pictures. All Pathfinder's objectives were fulfilled and communications failed on Sept. 27, 1997.

Spacecraft	Launch date	Destination	Remarks
Lunar Prospector (U.S.)	Jan. 6, 1998	Moon	Orbited Moon for one year, mapped chemical composition of lunar surface. Found frozen water at north and south poles. At end of its mission on July 31, 1999, it was intentionally crashed into south polar crater in hope of detecting plume of water ice, but no cloud of molecular water vapor was observed by powerful Earth telescopes.
Deep Space 1 (U.S.)	Oct. 24, 1998	Deep space	The first launch of NASA's New Millennium Program, a series of missions to test new technologies. Famous for its July 1999 photos of the near-Earth Braille asteroid and the first-ever photos of a comet nucleus when it staged a risky flyby of the comet Borelly in Sept. 2001. The second phase of New Millennium, Deep Space 2, was launched in 1999, but NASA lost contact with it in Dec. 1999.
Space Infrared Telescope Facility (SIRTF) (U.S.)	Aug. 25, 2003	Earth-trailing solar orbit	Final mission in NASA's Great Observatories Program which has four observatories studying the universe in different kinds of light—visible (Hubble Space Telescope), gamma rays (Compton Gamma-Ray Observatory), x-rays (Chandra X-Ray Observatory), and infrared (SIRTF).
Mars Exploration Rovers (U.S.)	June 10, 2003 (Spirit); July 7, 2003 (Opportunity)	Mars	Both rovers landed safely on Mars in Jan. 2004 and sent images back to Earth. Evidence of water was found by both rovers.
Deep Impact (U.S.)	Jan. 12, 2005	Comet Tempel 1	Probe smashed into comet while the flyby craft took pictures and collected data. The first look beneath the surface of a comet.

U.S. Staffed Space Flight Programs

Mercury. *Project Mercury,* initiated in 1958 and completed in 1963, was the United States' first human-in-space program. It was designed to further knowledge about humanity's capabilities in space.

In April 1959, seven military-jet test pilots were introduced to the public as America's first astronauts. They were: Lt. M. Scott Carpenter, USN; Capt. L. Gordon Cooper, Jr., USAF; Lt. Col. John H. Glenn, Jr., USMC; Cap. Virgil I. Grissom, USAF; Lt. Cdr. Walter M. Schirra, Jr., USN; Lt. Cdr. Alan B. Shepard, Jr., USN; and Capt. Donald K. Slayton, USAF. Six of the original seven would make a Mercury flight. Slayton was grounded for medical reasons but remained a director of NASA's astronaut office. He returned to flight status in 1975 as Docking Module Pilot on the *Apollo-Soyuz* flight.

Flight Summary

Each astronaut named his capsule and added the numeral 7 to denote the teamwork of the original astronauts.

May 5, 1961. Alan B. Shepard, Jr., made a suborbital flight in *Freedom 7* and became the first American in space. Time: 15 minutes, 22 seconds.

July 21, 1961. Virgil I. Grissom made the second successful suborbital flight in *Liberty Bell 7*, but spacecraft sank shortly after splashdown. Time: 15 minutes, 37 seconds. Grissom was later killed in *Apollo 1* fire, Jan. 27, 1967.

Feb. 20, 1962. John H. Glenn, Jr., made a three-orbit flight in *Friendship 7* and became the first American in orbit. Time: 4 hours, 55 minutes.

May 24, 1962. M. Scott Carpenter duplicated Glenn's flight in *Aurora 7*. Time: 4 hours, 56 minutes.

Oct. 3, 1962. Walter M. Schirra, Jr., made a six-orbit engineering test flight in *Sigma 7*. Time: 9 hours, 13 minutes.

May 15–16, 1963. L. Gordon Cooper, Jr., performed the last *Mercury* mission and completed 22 orbits in *Faith 7* to evaluate effects of one day in space. Time: 34 hours, 19 minutes.

The Women in Space Program

In 1960, NASA also tested the first female trainees for astronaut duty in the *Mercury* program. Thirteen out of America's 25 top female civilian pilots (women weren't allowed to be military pilots then) passed the same rigorous testing that male candidates underwent in the *Mercury 7* space program. Although all the pilots proved fit to become *Mercury* astronauts, NASA suddenly canceled its testing of qualified women in July 1961, claiming that they required jet test-pilot training at Edwards Air Force Base. Unfortunately, instruction at Edwards was closed to women. This new requirement ended America's chance to put the first women in space.

It is ironic that unlike her skilled American counterparts, Valentina Tereshkova, the first woman to fly in space, was a textile factory worker when she entered the Soviet space program. She had no experience as a pilot and her only qualification was that of an amateur parachute jumper before being trained as a cosmonaut in 1962.

These outstanding "Mercury 13" candidates deserve much credit for preparing the way for American women in space. They were: Jerrie Cobb, Rhea Allison, Jane Hart, Mary Wallace Funk, Jean Hixson, Myrtle Cagle, Irene Leverton, Sarah Gorelick, twins Jan and Marion Dietrich, Gene Stumbough, Bernice Steadman, and Gerry Sloan Truhill.

Gemini. *Gemini* was an extension of *Project Mercury,* to determine the effects of prolonged space flight on humans for two weeks or longer—the time it would take to reach the Moon and return. "Walks in space" provided invaluable information for astronauts' later walks on the Moon. The *Gemini* spacecraft, twice as large as the *Mercury* capsule, accommodated two astronauts. Its crew named the project *Gemini* for the third constellation of the Zodiac and its twin stars, Castor and Pollux. The capsule differed from the *Mercury* spacecrafts in that it had hatches above the capsules so that the astronauts could leave the spacecraft and perform spacewalks or extra-vehicular activities (EVAs).

There were 10 staffed flights in the *Gemini* program, starting with *Gemini 3* on March 23, 1965, and ending with the *Gemini 12* mission on Nov. 15, 1966. *Gemini 1* and *2* were unstaffed test flights of the equipment.

Apollo. *Apollo* was the designation for the United States' effort to land a person on the Moon and return him safely to Earth. Tragedy struck Jan. 27, 1967, on the launch pad during æ preflight test of what would have become *Apollo 1,* the first staffed mission. Astronauts Lt. Col. Virgil "Gus" Grissom, Lt. Col. Edward H. White, and Lt. Cdr. Roger Chafee lost their lives when a fire swept through the command module.

The moon landing was successfully accomplished with *Apollo 11* on July 20, 1969, culminating eight years of rehearsal and centuries of dreaming. Astronauts Neil A. Armstrong and Col. Edwin E. Aldrin, Jr., scooped up and brought back the first lunar rocks ever seen on Earth—about 47 pounds. Six *Apollo* flights followed, ending with *Apollo 17* in December 1972. The last three *Apollo*s carried mechanized vehicles called lunar rovers for wide-ranging surface exploration of the Moon by astronauts. The rendezvous and docking of an *Apollo* spacecraft with a Russian *Soyuz* craft in Earth orbit on July 18, 1975, closed out the *Apollo* program.

During the Apollo project, the following 12 astronauts explored the lunar terrain: Col. Edwin E. "Buzz" Aldrin, Jr., and Neil A. Armstrong, *Apollo 11;* Cdr. Alan L. Bean and Cdr. Charles "Pete" Conrad, Jr., *Apollo 12;* Edgar D. Mitchell and Alan B. Shepard, *Apollo 14;* Lt. Col. James B. Irwin and Col. David R. Scott, *Apollo 15;* Col. Charles M. Duke, Jr., and Capt. John W. Young, *Apollo 16;* and Capt. Eugene A. Cernan and Dr. Harrison H. Schmitt, *Apollo 17.*

Apollo was a three-part spacecraft: the command module (CM), the crew's quarters and flight control section; the service modules (SM) for the propulsion and spacecraft support systems (when together, the two modules were called CSM); and the lunar module (LM) that took two of the crew to the lunar surface, supported them on the Moon, and returned them to the CSM in orbit.

The third lunar attempt, *Apollo 13,* April 11–17, 1970, 5 days, 22.9 hours, was aborted after the service module oxygen tank ruptured. The *Apollo 13* crew members were James A. Lovell, Jr., John L. Swigert, Jr., and Fred W. Haise, Jr. The mission was classified as a "successful failure" because the crew was rescued.

Skylab. America's first Earth-orbiting space station was launched May 14, 1973. *Project Skylab* was designed to demonstrate that men could work and live in space for prolonged periods without ill effects. Originally the spent third stage of a *Saturn 5* Moon rocket, *Skylab* measured 118 ft from stem to stern, and carried the most varied assortment of experimental equipment ever assembled in a single spacecraft. Three three-man crews visited the space stations, spending more than 740 hours observing the Sun and bringing home more than 175,000 solar pictures. These were the first recordings of solar activity above Earth's obscuring atmosphere. *Skylab*

also evaluated systems designed to gather information on Earth's resources and environmental conditions. *Skylab*'s biomedical findings indicated that humans adapt well to space for at least a period of three months, provided they have a proper diet and adequately programmed exercise, sleep, work, and recreation periods. *Skylab* orbited Earth at a distance of about 300 mi. Five years after the last *Skylab* mission, the 77-ton space station's orbit began to deteriorate faster than expected, owing to unexpectedly high sunspot activity. On July 11, 1979, the parts of *Skylab* that did not burn up in the atmosphere came crashing down on parts of Australia and the Indian Ocean. No one was hurt.

Space Shuttle. The space shuttle *Columbia* was successfully launched on April 12, 1981. The second shuttle, *Challenger,* made its maiden flight on April 4, 1983. The third shuttle, *Discovery,* made its first flight on Aug. 30, 1984. The fourth space shuttle, *Atlantis,* made its maiden flight on Oct. 3, 1985.

A tragedy occurred on Jan. 28, 1986, when the shuttle *Challenger* exploded, killing the crew of seven 73 seconds after takeoff.

The crew members who were killed were: Francis R. Scobee, shuttle commander; Cdr. Michael J. Smith, pilot; mission specialists Judith A. Resnik, Lt. Col. Ellison S. Onizuka, and Ronald E. McNair; and payload specialists Gregory B. Jarvis and Christa McAuliffe (who was to be the first civilian schoolteacher in space).

The cause of the explosion was a rupture in a seal on one of the booster rockets, which let a jet of flame escape, igniting the fuel. The weakness in the seal was caused by the cold air temperature when the shuttle was launched.

The fifth orbiter, *Endeavour,* was built as a replacement for *Challenger.* It was named after the 16th-century British explorer James Cook's first ship. *Endeavour* was launched on its maiden voyage on May 7, 1992, with a crew of seven astronauts. During the mission, Dr. Kathryn Thornton became the second American woman to walk in space (Kathy Sullivan was the first in 1984).

The crew of the 50th shuttle mission, aboard the *Endeavour,* launched Sept. 12, 1992, included the first black woman astronaut, Dr. Mae C. Jemison, and the first married couple to fly together in space, Air Force Lt. Col. Mark C. Lee and Dr. N. Jan Davis.

Lt. Col. Eileen M. Collins became the first woman to pilot a shuttle, *Discovery,* during the spacecraft's historic rendezvous with the Russian space station *Mir* on Feb. 6, 1995. The shuttle *Atlantis* made the first link-up with the *Mir* on June 29, 1995.

The shuttle *Columbia* spent a record 17 days, 15 hours in space, Nov. 19–Dec. 7, 1996.

Lt. Col. Collins became the first woman to command a space shuttle when *Columbia* was launched in July 1999 on a mission to deploy the Chandra X-ray Observatory (formerly called AXAF).

Senator John Glenn, 76, the first American to orbit the Earth, flew as a payload specialist on the Oct. 1998 *Discovery* mission. He studied the effects of aging and microgravity on the human body.

In recent years, many of NASA's human spaceflight expeditions have involved improvement of the International Space Station. On May 27, 1999, the space shuttle *Discovery* began Flight STS-96, the first shuttle docking to the International Space Station.

Crewmembers brought new equipment to better operations between the Unity and Zarya modules, including nearly 1,360 kg of equipment for use by future ISS astronauts. In 2000, work on the ISS continued; two successive *Atlantis* missions spent several days making improvements. On Nov. 2, 2001, the ISS celebrated its first full year of continuous international human presence in space. On June 19, 2002, Capt. Daniel Bursch and Col. Carl Walz broke the U.S. record for space flight endurance, having spent 196 days aboard the International Space Station.

The shuttle program's second tragedy occurred on Feb. 1, 2003, when the shuttle *Columbia* broke up upon reentry into the Earth's atmosphere.

All crew members were killed: Rick Husband, shuttle commander; William McCool, pilot; payload commander Michael Anderson; payload specialist Ilan Ramon, also the first Israeli astronaut; mission specialists David M. Brown, Laurel Blair Salton Clark, and Kalpana Chawla, the first Indian-American woman in space.

The shuttle was returning after a 16-day scientific mission and was only minutes away from landing. The Columbia Accident Investigation Board subsequently ascertained that a chunk of fuel-tank foam insulation slammed into the wing edge during liftoff, creating a hole that allowed hot gases to enter the shuttle on reentry into the atmosphere.

After two delays, the space shuttle *Discovery*, commanded by Eileen Collins, launched on July 26, 2005, marking the craft's first flight since the Columbia disaster. The shuttle boasted new safety features, including a redesigned external tank, new sensors, and a boom attached to the shuttle's robotic arm that allowed astronauts to check for external damage. Despite the safety measures, in an incident similar to that which caused the Columbia disaster, some foam insulation broke off the external tank after takeoff. NASA grounded the shuttle fleet indefinitely, including an Atlantis flight scheduled for September 2005. *Discovery's* mission continued, delivering equipment and supplies to the International Space Station before landing Aug. 9.

Soviet Staffed Space Flight Programs

Vostok. The Soviets's first staffed capsule, roughly spherical, used to place the first six cosmonauts in Earth orbit (1961–1965).

Voskhod. Adaptation of the *Vostok* capsule to accommodate two and three cosmonauts. *Voskhod 1* orbited three persons, and *Voskhod 2* orbited two persons, performing the world's first staffed extravehicular activity.

Soyuz. Late-model staffed spacecraft with provisions for three cosmonauts and a "working compartment" accessible through a hatch. Soyuz is the Russian word for "union." The *Soyuz* spacecraft routinely brought cosmonauts and their foreign "guests" to the *Mir* space station. *Soyuz 19*, launched July 15, 1975, docked with the American *Apollo* spacecraft.

Salyut. Earth-orbiting space stations intended for prolonged occupancy and revisitation by cosmonauts. They were usually launched by Soviet Proton rockets. *Salyut 1* was launched April 19, 1971. *Salyut 2*, launched April 3, 1973, malfunctioned in orbit and was never occupied. *Salyut 3* was launched June 25, 1974. *Salyut 4* was launched Dec. 26, 1974. *Salyut 5* was launched June 22, 1976. *Salyut 6* was launched on Sept. 29, 1977. *Salyut 7* was launched on April 19, 1982. A record-breaking Russian endurance flight was set (Feb. 8, 1984–Oct. 2, 1985) when Soviet astronauts spent 237 days in orbit aboard *Salyut 7*. *Salyut 7* reentered the atmosphere and crashed into the Atlantic Ocean on Feb. 6, 1991.

Mir. Soviet space station, launched into orbit on Feb. 20, 1986. The Russian government had planned to deorbit the abandoned *Mir* in early 2000 due to lack of funds, but the space station got a new lease on life when private investors provided the cash to keep the craft in orbit. The new Russian partners, MirCorp, a Netherlands-based company, funded cosmonauts Sergei Zaloytin and Alexander Kaleri's return mission to reopen and repair the *Mir*, April 4 to June 15, 2000. However, *Mir* was deorbited on March 23, 2001.

Since the deorbiting of *Mir*, Russia's space program has revolved around projects at the International Space Station. Financial problems continue to curb cosmonaut capabilities, forcing the Russian Space Agency to seek funds elsewhere: in 2001, American businessman Dennis Tito paid a reported $20 million to become the world's first space tourist aboard a Russian spacecraft.

Notable Staffed Space Flights

Designation and country	Date	Astronauts	Flight time	Remarks
Vostok 1 (USSR)	April 12, 1961	Yuri A. Gagarin	1hr, 48 min	First person in space.
MR III (U.S.)	May 5, 1961	Alan B. Shepard, Jr.	15 min	Range 486 km (302 mi), peak 187 km (116.5 mi); capsule recovered. First American in space.
Vostok 2 (USSR)	Aug. 6–7, 1961	Gherman S. Titov	25 hr, 18 min	First long-duration flight.
MA VI (U.S.)	Feb. 20, 1962	John H. Glenn, Jr.	4 hr, 55 min	First American in orbit.
MA IX (U.S.)	May 15–16, 1963	L. Gordon Cooper, Jr.	34 hr, 20 min	Longest *Mercury* flight.
Vostok 6 (USSR)	June 16–19, 1963	Valentina V. Tereshkova	2 days, 22 hr, 50 min	First woman in space.
Voskhod 1 (USSR)	Oct. 12, 1964	Vladimir M. Komarov, Konstantin P. Feoktistov, Boris G. Yegorov	24 hr, 17 min	First 3-person orbital flight; also first flight without space suits.
Voskhod 2 (USSR)	March 18, 1965	Alexei A. Leonov, Pavel I. Belyayev	26 hr, 2 min	First "space walk" (by Leonov), 10 min.
GT III (U.S.)	March 23, 1965	Virgil I. Grissom, John W. Young	4hr, 53 min	First American 2-person crew.
GT IV (U.S.)	June 3–7, 1965	James A. McDivitt, Edward H. White, II	4 days, 1 hr, 48 min	First American "space walk" (by White), lasting slightly over 20 min.

Designation and country	Date	Astronauts	Flight time	Remarks
GT VIII (U.S.)	March 16–17, 1966	Neil A. Armstrong, David R. Scott	10 hr, 42 min	First docking between staffed spacecraft and an unstaffed space vehicle (an orbiting *Agena* rocket).
Apollo 7 (U.S.)	Oct. 11–22, 1968	Walter M. Schirra, Jr., Donn F. Eisele, R. Walter Cunningham	10 days, 19 hr, 9 min	First staffed test of *Apollo* command module; first live TV transmissions from orbit.
Soyuz 3 (USSR)	Oct. 26–30, 1968	Georgi T. Bergeovoi	3 days, 22 hr, 51 min	First spacecraft rendezvous and possible docking by Soviet cosmonaut.
Apollo 8 (U.S.)	Dec. 21–27, 1968	Frank Borman, James A. Lovell, Jr., William A. Anders	6 days, 3 hr	First spacecraft in circumlunar orbit; TV transmissions from this orbit. The three astronauts were also the first astronauts to view the whole Earth.
Apollo 9 (U.S.)	Mar. 3–13, 1969	James A. McDivitt, David R. Scott, Russell L. Schweikart	10 days, 1 hr, 1 min	First staffed flight of Lunar Module.
Apollo 10 (U.S.)	May 18–26, 1969	Thomas P. Stafford, Eugene A. Cernan, John W. Young	8 days, 3 min	First descent to within nine miles of Moon's surface by staffed craft.
Apollo 11 (U.S.)	July 16–24, 1969	Neil A. Armstrong, Edwin E. Aldrin, Jr., Michael Collins	8 days, 3 hr, 18 min	First staffed landing and EVA on Moon; soil and rock samples collected; experiments left on lunar surface.
Soyuz 6 (USSR)	Oct. 11–16, 1969	Gorgiy Shonin, Valriy Kabasov	4 days, 22 hr, 42 min	Three spacecraft and seven men put into Earth's orbit simultaneously for first time.
Apollo 12 (U.S.)	Nov. 14–24, 1969	Charles Conrad, Jr., Richard F. Gordon, Jr., Alan Bean	10 days, 4 hr, 36 min	Staffed lunar landing mission; investigated *Surveyor 3* spacecraft; collected lunar samples. EVA time: 15 hr, 30 min.
Apollo 13 (U.S.)	April 11–17, 1970	James A. Lovell, Jr., Fred W. Haise, Jr., John L. Swigert, Jr.	5 days, 22 hr, 54 min	Third staffed lunar landing attempt; aborted due to pressure loss in liquid oxygen in service module and failure of fuel cells.
Apollo 14 (U.S.)	Jan. 31–Feb. 9, 1971	Alan B. Shepard, Stuart A. Roosa, Edgar D. Mitchell	9 days, 42 min	Third staffed lunar landing: returned largest amount of lunar material.
Soyuz 11 (USSR)	June 6–30, 1971	Georgiy Tomofeyevich Dobrovolskiy, Vladislav Nikolayevich Volkov, Viktor Ivanovich Patsyev	23 days, 17 hrs, 40 min	Longest stay in space. Linked up with first space station, *Salyut 1*. Astronauts died just before reentry due to loss of pressurization in spacecraft.
Apollo 15 (U.S.)	July 26–Aug. 7, 1971	David R. Scott, James B. Irwin, Alfred M. Worden	12 days, 7 hr, 12 min	Fourth staffed lunar landing; first use of lunar rover propelled by Scott and Irwin; first live pictures of LM lift-off from Moon; exploration time: 18 hr.
Apollo 16 (U.S.)	April 16–27, 1972	John W. Young, Thomas K. Mattingly, Charles M. Duke, Jr.	11 days, 1 hr, 51 min	Fifth staffed lunar landing; second use of lunar rover vehicle, propelled by Young and Duke. Exploration time: 20 hr, 14 min. Mattingly's in-flight "walk in space" was 1 hr, 23 min. Approximately 213 lb of lunar rock returned.
Apollo 17 (U.S.)	Dec. 7–19, 1972	Eugene A. Cernan, Ronald E. Evans, Harrison H. Schmitt	12 days, 13 hr, 51 min	Sixth and last staffed lunar landing; third to carry lunar rover. Exploration time: 22 hr, 05 min, 3 sec. 250 lbs of lunar samples returned to Earth.
Skylab SL-2 (U.S.)	May 25–June 22, 1973	Charles Conrad, Jr., Joseph P. Kerwin, Paul J. Weitz	28 days, 50 min	First staffed *Skylab* launch. Established *Skylab* Orbital Assembly and conducted scientific and medical experiments.
Skylab SL-3 (U.S.)	July 28–Sept. 25, 1973	Alan L. Bean, Jr., Jack R. Lousma, Owen K. Garriott	59 days, 11 hr, 9 min	Second staffed *Skylab* launch. New crew remained in space for 59 days, continuing scientific and medical experiments and Earth observations from orbit.
Skylab SL-4 (U.S.)	Nov. 16, 1973– Feb. 8, 1974	Gerald Carr, Edward Gibson, William Pogue	84 days, 1 hr, 16 min	Third staffed *Skylab* launch; obtained medical data on crew for use in extending the duration of staffed space flight; crews "walked in space" 4 times, totaling 44 hr, 40 min. Splashdown in Pacific, Feb. 9, 1974.
Apollo/Soyuz Test Project (U.S. and USSR)	July 15–24, 1975 (U.S.)	U.S.: Brig. Gen. Thomas P. Stafford, Vance D. Brand, Donald K. Slayton	9 days, 5 min	World's first international staffed rendezvous and docking in space; aimed at developing a space rescue capability.
Apollo/Soyuz Test Project (U.S. and USSR)	July 15–21, 1975 (USSR)	USSR: Col. A. A. Leonov, V. N. Kubasov	9 days, 7 hr, 35 min	*Apollo* and *Soyuz* docked and crewmen exchanged visits on July 17, 1975. Mission duration for *Soyuz*: 142 hr, 31 min. For *Apollo*: 217 hr, 28 min.
Columbia (U.S.)	April 12–14, 1981	Capt. Robert L. Crippen, John W. Young	2 days, 5 hr, 20 min	Maiden voyage of space shuttle.

Designation and country	Date	Astronauts	Flight time	Remarks
Challenger (U.S.)	Jan. 28, 1986	Francis R. Scobee, Gregory Jarvis, Christa McAuliffe, Ronald McNair, Ellison Onizuka, Judith Resnik, Michael Smith	73 sec	Exploded upon takeoff from Kennedy Space Center, killing all 7 crew members. A booster lock ignited the fuel, causing the explosion.
Mir (USSR)	Dec. 21, 1987– Dec. 21, 1988	Col. Vladimir Titov, Musa Manarov	366 days	Set current record for Soviet team endurance flight in orbiting space station.
Endeavour (U.S.)	May 7–16, 1992	Richard J. Hieb, Maj. Thomas D. Akers, Cdr. Pierre J. Thugt	8 days, 23 hr, 17 min	The three mission specialists remained free of the *Endeavour* for 8 hr, 20 min on May 13 during the repair of communications satellite, setting an absolute record for extravehicular duration in space. First capture of a satellite using hands only.
Endeavour (U.S.)	Dec. 2–13, 1993	Col. Richard O. Covey, Cdr. Kenneth D. Bowersox, Lt. Col. Tom Akers, Dr. Jeffrey A. Hoffman, Dr. Story Musgrave, Claude Nicollier, Dr. Kathryn C. Thornton	10 days, 19 hr, 59 min	Repaired Hubble Space Telescope. Replaced gyroscopes, solar arrays, camera, electronics, and hardware. Installed COSTAR corrective optics to compensate for flaw in Hubble's primary mirror. Record five space walks in a single mission.
Mir-17 (Russia)	Jan. 8, 1994– Mar. 22, 1995	Dr. Valery Polyakov	439[1] days	Record single endurance flight in orbiting space station. Returned to Earth with crewmates, cosmonaut Helena Kondakova and commander Alexander Viktorenko, who spent 169 days each in *Mir*.
Discovery (U.S.)	Feb. 3–11, 1995	Cdr. James D. Wetherbee, Lt. Col. Eileen M. Collins, Dr. Janice Voss, Dr. Bernard A. Harris, Jr., Dr. C. Michael Foale, Russian cosmonaut Co. Vladimir G. Titov	8 days, 6 hr, 29 min	First rendezvous of U.S. spacecraft with a Russian space station *(Mir),* Feb. 6. Lt. Col. Collins was first female shuttle pilot. Deployed and retrieved solar observatory satellite. Extravehicular activity to test new space suit modifications and practice space station assembly techniques. EVA time: 4 hr, 35 min.
Soyuz TM-21 (Russia)	March 14–22, 1995	Russian cosmonauts Lt. Col. Vladimir N. Dezhurov and Gennady M. Strekalov, and U.S. astronaut Dr. Norman E. Thagard		Dr. Thagard became the first American astronaut to fly aboard a *Soyuz* spacecraft with a Russian crew launched from Baikonur Space Center in Kazakhstan. He also became the first American to enter the *Mir* space station on March 16.
Atlantis (U.S.)	June 27–July 7, 1995	Lt. Col. Charles J. Prescourt, Capt. Robert L. (Hoot) Gibson, Dr. Eileen S. Baker, Gregory J. Harbaugh, Dr. Bonnie Dunbar; Russian cosmonauts: *Mir-19* commander Anatoly Y. Solovyev, Nikolai M. Budarin	10 days	Marked 100th human mission in U.S. space program and first shuttle link-up with *Mir:* docked June 29, undocked July 4. Joined spacecraft held a record 10 people: 6 Americans and 4 Russians. Three *Mir* crew (*Mir-18* commander Lt. Col. Vladimir N. Dezhurov, cosmonaut Grennady M. Strekalov, and U.S. astronaut Dr. Norman E. Thagard) returned to Earth aboard the *Atlantis.* Cosmonauts Solovyev and Budarin remained aboard *Mir*.
Atlantis (U.S.)	Nov. 12–20, 1995	Col. Kenneth D. Cameron, Lt. Col. James D. Halsell, Jr., Col. Jerry L. Ross, Lt. Col. William S. McArthur, Jr., Canadian Major Chris A. Hadfield, who operated the robot arm	8 days, 4 hr, 31 min	Second docking with *Mir.* Carried 15-foot-long, Russian-made docking module and attached it to *Mir.* Brought 2 new solar-powered panels for *Mir* and also supplies and scientific equipment. U.S. and Russian astronauts spent 3 days together on *Mir* conducting experiments.
Endeavour (U.S.)	Jan. 11–20, 1996	Col. Brian Duffy, Brent Jett, Dr. Leroy Chiao, Capt. Winston E. Scott, Dr. Daniel T. Berry, and Japanese astronaut Koichi Wakata, who operated robot arm	8 days, 22 hr, 1 min	Deployed and retrieved NASA satellite, retrieved Japanese satellite. Two spacewalks performed to test spacesuit components and practice space station construction, tools, and techniques. Total EVA time: 13 hr.

Designation and country	Date	Astronauts	Flight time	Remarks
Atlantis (U.S.)	March 22–31, 1996	Col. Kevin P. Chilton, Lt. Col. Richard A. Searfoss, Dr. Ronald M. Sega, Dr. Linda M. Goodwin, Lt. Col. Michael R. Clifford, Shannon W. Lucid	9 days, 5 hr, 15 min	Third link-up with Mir (March 22–27). Clifford and Goodwin conducted 6-hour spacewalk in shuttle cargo bay while docked with Mir. Lucid remained on board Mir for scheduled 140-day tour to conduct biomedical and material science experiments. Booster problems delayed her return until mid-September. Lucid was first American woman to live on Mir. On July 15, 1996, she broke the previous record for the longest U.S. manned space flight.
Endeavour (U.S.)	May 19–29, 1996	Col. John H. Casper, Lt. Col. Curtis L. Brown, Jr., Cdr. Daniel W. Bursch, Mario Runco, Jr., Dr. Andrew S. W. Thomas, Canadian astronaut Dr. Marc Garneau	10 days, 0 hr, 40 min	Made record of four satellite rendezvous, including three with small PAMS satellite to test the concept of a self-stabilizing satellite in orbit. Deployed and retrieved a Spartan satellite that carried an experimental inflatable antenna.
Columbia (U.S.)	June 20–July 7, 1996	Col. Terence T. Henricks, Kevin R. Kregel, Lt. Col. Susan J. Helms, Richard M. Linnehan, Cdr. Charles E. Brady, Jr., Dr. Jean-Jacques Favier (France), Dr. Robert Brent Thirsk (Canada)	16 days, 21 hr, 48 min	Studied the effects of weightlessness on people, plants, and animals, and material manufacturing in near-zero gravity.
Atlantis (U.S.)	Sept. 16–26, 1996	William F. Readdy, Terrence W. Wilcutt, Thomas D. Akers, John E. Blaha, Jerome Apt, Carl E. Walz. Download: Shannon W. Lucid	10 days, 3hr, 19 min	Fourth Mir docking. Carried a Spacelab module. Transferred supplies and equipment to Mir. After breaking all American and women's space endurance records (188 days, 5 hr, 0 min), Lucid returned with Atlantis crew. John E. Blaha remained on Mir for a four-month stay.
Columbia (U.S.)	Nov. 19–Dec. 7, 1996	Kenneth D. Cockrell, Cdr. Kent V. Rominger, Tamara E. Jernigan, Thomas D. Jones, Dr. F. Story Musgrave	17 days, 15 hr, 53 min	Deployed and recovered two free-flying satellites: an ultraviolet telescope and Wake Shield (semiconductor processing) Facility. Dr. Musgrave, 61, became first person to fly on all five space shuttles.
Atlantis (U.S.)	Jan. 12–22, 1997	Capt. Michael A. Baker, Cdr. Brent W. Jett, Jr., John M. Grunsfeld, Marsha S. Ivins, Peter J.K. Wiscoff, Dr. Jerry L. Linenger. Download: John E. Blaha	10 days, 4 hr, 6 min	Fifth Mir docking (Jan.14–19). Carried Spacehab double module. Transferred supplies to Mir. Conducted experiments in Spacehab and Mir. John E. Blaha returned with Atlantis crew after 128 days in space, 118 aboard Mir. Jerry Linenger remained aboard Mir for 4.5-month stay.
Discovery (U.S.)	Feb. 11–21, 1997	Cdr. Kenneth Bowersox, Lt. Col. Scott J. Horowitz, Col. Mark C. Lee, Steven A. Hawley, Gregory J. Harbaugh, Steven L. Smith, Joseph R. Tanner	9 days, 23 hr, 38 min	Second space telescope servicing mission. Installed new imaging spectrograph and infrared camera. Also patched torn telescope insulating cover. Deployed telescope at higher altitude: 335 x 321 nautical mile orbit. Mission required five spacewalks totaling 33 hr, 11 min.
Atlantis (U.S.)	May 15–24, 1997	Col. Charles J. Precourt, Lt. Col. Eileen M. Collins, Edward T. Lu, Maj. Carlos I. Noriega, Jean-François Clervoy (France), Elena V. Kondakova (Russia), C. Michael Foale. Download: Dr. Jerry M. Linenger	9 days, 5 hr, 20 min	Sixth Mir docking (May 16–21). Carried a Spacehab double module. Transferred supplies and equipment. Jerry M. Linenger returned with Atlantis after 132 days in space. Michael Foale remained on Mir for a 4.5-month stay.
Atlantis (U.S.)	Sept. 25–Oct. 6, 1997	James T. Wetherbee, Michael J. Boomfield, Col. Vladimir G Titov, Scott E. Parazynski, Jean-Loup J. M. Chretien (France), Wendy B. Lawrence. Up: Dr. David Wolf. Down: C. Michael Foale	10 days, 19 hr, 22 min	Seventh Mir docking (Sept. 27–Oct. 3). 5-hr spacewalks (Oct.1) retrieved U.S. experimental packages from Mir for return to Earth. Transferred supplies. Tested emergency jet packs for space station workers. Dr. David Wolf replaced Michael Foale on Mir for 4-month stay.

Designation and country	Date	Astronauts	Flight time	Remarks
Endeavour (U.S.)	Jan. 22–31, 1998	Lt. Col. Terrence W. Wilcutt, Joe F. Edwards, Bonnie J. Dunbar, Maj. Michael P. Anderson, James F. Reilly, II, Salizhan S. Sharipov (Kyrgyzstan). Up: Andrew S. W. Thomas. Down: Dr. David Wol	8 days, 19 hr, 48 min	Eighth *Mir* docking (Jan. 24–29). Thomas replaced David Wolf after 128 days in orbit. Thomas is the seventh and last American to live aboard *Mir*.
Discovery (U.S.)	June 2–12, 1998	Col. Charles J. Precourt, Cmdr. Dominic L. Gorie, Cmdr. Wendy B. Lawrence, Franklin R. Chang-Diaz, Janet Kavandi, Valeriy Ruymin (Russia). Down: Andrew S. W. Thomas	9 days, 19 hr, 54 min	Ninth and final *Mir* docking mission concluded the joint U.S.–Russian program as a precursor to the International Space Station partnership. Thomas returned to Earth after a 4.5-month stay.
Discovery (U.S.)	Oct. 29–Nov.7, 1998	Lt. Col. Curtis L. Brown, Maj. Steven W. Lindsey, Stephen K. Robinson, Dr. Scott E. Parazynski, Pedro Duque (Spain), Dr. Chiaki Mukai (Japan), Sen. John H. Glenn, Jr.	8 days, 21 hr, 56 min	Deployed and retrieved *Spartan* solar observing satellite. Did research with Hubble Telescope Optical Systems Test Platform (HOST). Studied the effects of aging and microgravity in space.
Endeavour (U.S.)	Dec. 4–15, 1998	Col. Robert D. Cabana, Capt. Frederick W. Sturckow, Lt. Col. Nancy Currie, Col. Jerry L. Ross, James H. Newman, Sergei K. Krikalev (Russia)	11 days, 19 hr, 18 min	International Space Station assembly mission. Connected Node 1, "Unity," to Functional Cargo Block, "Zarya." Ross and Newman made three spacewalks, total EVA: 21 hr, 22 min.
Discovery (U.S.)	May 27–June 6, 1999	Cmdr. Ken V. Rominger, Rick D. Husband, Ellen Ochoa, Tamara E. Jernigan, Daniel T. Barry, Julie Payette (Canada), Valery Tokarev (Russia)	9 days, 19 hr, 13 min	Docked 5 days, 18 hr with uninhabited International Space Station. Readied it for arrival of first resident crew. Jernigan and Barry conducted space walks (7 hr, 55 min) for assembly work.
Columbia (U.S.)	July 22–27, 1999	Lt. Col. Eileen M. Collins, Capt. Jeffrey S. Ashby, Steven A. Hawley, Lt. Col. Catherine G. Coleman, Col. Michel Tognini (France)	4 days, 22 hr, 50 min	Deployed Chandra X-ray Observatory (formerly AXAF). Eileen Collins became the first female shuttle commander.
Discovery (U.S.)	Dec. 19–27, 1999	Col. Curtis L. Brown Jr., Lt. Cmdr. Scott J. Kelly, Steven L. Smith, C. Michael Foale, John M. Grunsfeld, Claude Nicollier (Switzerland), Jean-François Clervoy (France)	7 days, 23 hr, 10 min	Third Hubble Space Telescope servicing mission. Three EVAs totaled 24 hr, 33 min: Dec. 22, Smith and Grunsfeld, 8 hr, 15 min; Dec. 23, Foale and Nicollier, 8 hr, 10 min; Dec. 24, Smith and Grunsfeld, 8 hr, 8 min.
Endeavour (U.S.)	Feb.11–22, 2000	Cmdr. Dominic L. Pudwill Gorie, Janet Lynn Kavandi, Janet Voss, Kevin R. Kregel, Mamoru Mohri (Japan), Gerhard P. J. Thiele (Germany)	11 days, 5 hr, 38 min	Radar mapping obtained most detailed topographical map of Earth to date.
Atlantis (U.S.)	Sept. 8–18, 2000	Lt. Col. Terance Wilcutt, Lt. Cmdr. Scott Altman, Edward Tsang Lu, Richard Mastracchio, Lt. Cmdr. Dan Burbank, Col. Yuri I. Malenchenko (Russia), Boris Morukov (Russia)	10 days, 18 hr, 41 min	Prepared International Space Station for arrival of first resident crew. Outfitted *Zvezda* module.
Discovery (U.S.)	Oct. 11–22, 2000	Col. Brian Duffy, Lt. Col. Pamela A. Melroy, Koichi Wakata (Japan), Peter J. K. Wisoff, Cmdr. Michael E. Lopez-Alegria, Col. William S. McArthur, Jr.	10 days, 19 hr, 28 min	Assembled Integrated Truss Structure on space station to allow solar arrays to be installed. 100th space shuttle flight.
Soyuz (Russia)	Oct. 31, 2000– March 18, 2001	William M. Shepherd, Yuri Gidzenko (Russia), Sergei Krikalev (Russia)	138 days, 18 hr, 39 min	Expedition One, first crew aboard International Space Station.

Designation and country	Date	Astronauts	Flight time	Remarks
Discovery (U.S.)	March 8–21, 2001	Capt. James D. Wetherbee, Lt. Col. James M. Kelly, Andrew S. W. Thomas, Paul W. Richards, Yury Usachev (Russia), Jim Voss, Susan Helms	12 days, 19 hr, 49 min	Delivered Expedition Two crew (Usachev, Voss, Helms) to space station and returned Expedition One crew (Shepherd, Krikalev, Gidzenko) to Earth.
Discovery (U.S.)	Aug. 10–Aug. 22, 2001	Col. Scott J. Horowitz, Lt. Col. Frederick W. Sturckow, Col. Patrick G. Forrester, Daniel T. Barry, Frank Culbertson, Lt. Col. Vladimir Dezhurov (Russia), Mikhail Tyurin (Russia)	11 days, 21 hr, 13 min	Delivered Expedition Three crew (Culbertson, Dezhurov, Tyurin) to space station and returned Expedition Two crew (Usachev, Voss, Helms) to Earth.
Endeavour (U.S.)	Dec. 5–17, 2001	Capt. Dominic Gorie, Lt. Cmdr. Mark E. Kelly, Linda M. Godwin, Daniel M. Tani, Col. Yuri Onufrienko (Russia), Col. Carl E. Walz, Capt. Daniel W. Bursch	11 days, 19 hr, 36 min	Delivered Expedition Four crew (Onufrienko, Walz, Bursch) to space station and returned Expedition Three crew (Culbertson, Tyurin, Dezhurov) to Earth.
Columbia (U.S.)	March 1–12, 2002	Cmdr. Scott Altman, Lt. Col. Duane Carey, Nancy Currie, John Grunsfeld, Richard Linnehan, Michael Massimino, James Newman	10 days, 22 hr, 10 min	Fourth Hubble Space Telescope servicing mission. The latest upgrades leave Hubble with a new power unit, camera, and solar arrays. Five EVAs lasted a total of 35 hr 55 min.
Atlantis (U.S.)	April 8–19, 2002	Lt. Col. Michael Bloomfield, Stephen Frick, Rex Walheim, Ellen Ochoa, Lee Morin, Jerry Ross, Steven Smith.	10 days, 19 hr, 42 min	Installed S0 (S-Zero) Truss, the backbone for future expansion, onto International Space Station. Prepared Mobile Transporter, first railroad in space. Jerry Ross made two space walks, retaining U.S. record for most space walks (nine) and total space-walking time (58 hr, 18 min).
Endeavour (U.S.)	June 5–19, 2002	Kenneth D. Cockrell, Lt. Col. Paul Lockhart, Philippe Perrin (France), Franklin Chang-Diaz, Col. Valery Korzun (Russia), Peggy Whitson, Sergei Treschev (Russia).	13 days, 20 hr, 35 min	Delivered Expedition Five crew (Korzun, Whitson, Treschev) to space station and returned Expedition Four crew (Onufrienko, Walz, Bursch) to Earth. On June 19, Walz and Bursch broke the U.S. space flight endurance record (previously held by Shannon Lucid, who spent 188 days in space in 1996). The two spent a total of 196 days in space.
Columbia (U.S.)	Jan. 16–Feb. 1, 2003	Rick Husband, William McCool, Michael Anderson, Kalpana Chawla, David Brown, Laurel B. Clark, Ilan Ramon	16 days	Exploded upon reentry into Earth's atmosphere, killing all 7 crew members.
Soyuz TMA-2 (Russia)	Apr. 26–Oct. 28, 2003	Yuri Malenchenko (Russia), Ed Lu, Ken Bowersox, Don Pettit, Nikolai Budarin (Russia)	185 days	With shuttle flights grounded, *Soyuz TMA-2* delivered Expedition Seven crew (Malenchenko, Lu) to space station. Expedition Six crew (Bowersox, Pettit, Budarin) returned to Earth via *Soyuz TMA-1*, docked at space station since Dec. 1, 2002[2]. On Aug. 10, Malenchenko became the first man to get married from space.
Shenzhou V (China)	Oct. 15–16, 2003	Lt. Col. Yang Liwei	21 hr	With the launch of *Shenzhou V,* China became the third country, after the former Soviet Union and the United States, to have a space program.
SpaceShipOne (U.S., private)	June 21, 2004	Mike Melvill	4.5 hr	The first private staffed ship to leave the atmosphere. It achieved an altitude of 328,491 ft.
Discovery (U.S.)	July 26–Aug. 7, 2005	Eileen Collins, James Kelly, Charles Camarda, Wendy Lawrence, Soichi Noguchi, Steve Robinson, Andy Thomas	14 days	First shuttle flight since *Columbia* disaster. Mission was to test new safety features and deliver equipment to the International Space Station.

NOTES: EVA = Extravehicular Activity. The letters MR stand for Mercury (capsule) and Redstone (rocket); MA, for Mercury and Atlas (rocket); GT, for Gemini (capsule) and Titan-II (rocket). The first astronaut listed in the Gemini and Apollo flights is the command pilot. The Mercury capsules had names: MR-III was *Freedom 7*, MR-IV was *Liberty Bell 7*, MA-VI was *Friendship 7*, MA-VII was *Aurora 7*, MA-VIII was *Sigma 7*, and MA-IX was *Faith 7*. The figure 7 referred to the fact that the first group of U.S. astronauts numbered seven men. Only one Gemini capsule had a name: GT-III was called *Molly Brown* (after the Broadway musical *The Unsinkable Molly Brown*); thereafter the practice of naming the capsules was discontinued. 1. From launch to landing. 2. *Soyuz TMA-1* returned May 3, 2003.

Famous Firsts in Aviation

1783 **First balloon flight.** Jacques and Joseph Mont-golfier of Annonay, France, sent up a small smoke-filled balloon about mid-November.

First hydrogen-filled balloon flight. Jacques A. C. Charles, Paris physicist, supervised construction by A. J. and M. N. Robert of a 13-foot-diameter balloon that was filled with hydrogen. It got up to about 3,000 ft and traveled about 16 mi in a 45-minute flight (Aug. 27).

First human balloon flights. A Frenchman, Jean Pilâtre de Rozier, made the first captive-balloon ascension (Oct. 15). With the Marquis d'Arlandes, Pilâtre de Rozier made the first free flight, reaching a peak altitude of about 500 ft, and traveling about 5½ mi in 20 min. (Nov. 21).

1784 **First powered balloon.** Gen. Jean Baptiste Marie Meusnier developed the first propeller-driven and elliptically shaped balloon—the crew cranking three propellers on a common shaft to give the craft a speed of about 3 mph.

First balloon flight by a woman. Mme. Thible, a French opera singer (June 4).

1793 **First balloon flight in America.** Jean Pierre Blanchard, a French pilot, made it from Philadelphia to near Woodbury, N.J., in just over 45 min. (Jan. 9).

1794 **First military use of the balloon.** Jean Marie Coutelle, using a balloon built for the French Army, made two 4-hour observation ascents. The military purpose of the ascents seems to have been to damage the enemy's morale.

1797 **First parachute jump.** André-Jacques Garnerin dropped from about 6,500 ft over Monceau Park in Paris in a 23-foot-diameter parachute made of white canvas with a basket attached (Oct. 22).

1843 **First air transport company.** In London, William S. Henson and John Stringfellow filed articles of incorporation for the Aerial Transit Company (March 24). It failed.

1852 **First dirigible.** Henri Giffard, a French engineer, flew in a controllable (more or less) steam-engine-powered balloon, 144 ft long and 39 ft in diameter, inflated with 88,000 cu ft of coal gas. It reached 6.7 mph on a flight from Paris to Trappe (Sept. 24).

1860 **First aerial photographers.** Samuel Archer King and William Black made two photos of Boston, which are still in existence.

1872 **First gas-engine-powered dirigible.** Paul Haenlein, a German engineer, flew in a semi-rigid-frame dirigible, powered by a 4-cylinder internal-combustion engine running on coal gas drawn from the supporting bag.

1873 **First transatlantic attempt.** *The New York Daily Graphic* sponsored the attempt with a 400,000-cubic-foot balloon carrying a lifeboat. A rip in the bag during inflation brought the collapse of the balloon and the project.

1897 **First successful metal dirigible.** An all-metal dirigible, designed by David Schwarz, a Hungarian, took off from Berlin's Tempelhof Field and, powered by a 16-horsepower Daimler engine, got several miles before leaking gas caused it to crash (Nov. 13).

1900 **First zeppelin flight.** Germany's Count Ferdinand von Zeppelin flew the first of his long series of rigid-frame airships. It attained a speed of 18 mph and got 3½ mi before its steering gear failed (July 2).

1903 **First successful heavier-than-air machine flight.** Aviation was really born on the sand dunes at Kitty Hawk, N.C., when Orville Wright crawled to his prone position between the wings of the biplane he and his brother Wilbur had built, opened the throttle of their homemade 12-horsepower engine, and took to the air. He covered 120 ft in 12 sec. Later that day, in one of four flights, Wilbur stayed up 59 sec. and covered 852 ft (Dec. 17).

Wilbur and Orville Wright with their second powered machine. Source: Library of Congress.

1904 **First airplane maneuvers.** Orville Wright made the first turn with an airplane (Sept. 15); five days later his brother Wilbur made the first complete circle.

1905 **First airplane flight over half an hour.** Orville Wright kept his craft up 33 min., 17 sec. (Oct. 4).

1906 **First European airplane flight.** Alberto Santos-Dumont, a Brazilian, flew a heavier-than-air machine at Bagatelle Field, Paris (Sept. 13).

1908 **First airplane fatality.** Lt. Thomas E. Selfridge, U.S. Army Signal Corps, was in a group evaluating the Wright plane at Fort Myer, Va. He was up 75 ft with Orville Wright when the propeller hit a bracing wire and was broken, throwing the plane out of control, killing Selfridge and seriously injuring Wright (Sept. 17).

1909 **First cross-Channel flight.** Louis Blériot flew in a 25-horsepower Blériot VI monoplane from Les Baraques near Calais, France, to Dover Castle, England, in a 26.61-mi (38-kilometer) 37-min. flight across the English Channel (July 25).

First International Aviation Competition Meeting. American Glenn Curtiss narrowly beat France's Louis Blériot in the main event and won the Gordon Bennett Cup. Meet held at Rheims, France (Aug. 22–28).

1910 **First licensed woman pilot.** Baroness Raymonde de la Roche of France, who learned to fly in 1909, received ticket No. 36 on March 8.

First flight from shipboard. Lt. Eugene Ely, USN, took a Curtiss plane off from the deck of the cruiser *Birmingham* at Hampton Roads, Va., and flew to Norfolk (Nov. 14). The following January he reversed the process, flying from Camp Selfridge to the deck of the armored cruiser *Pennsylvania* in San Francisco Bay (Jan. 18).

First aircraft to take off from water. Henri Fabre in a Gnome-powered floatplane, at Martigues, France (March 28).

1911 **First U.S. woman pilot.** Harriet Quimby, a magazine writer, got ticket No. 37, making her the first licensed American female pilot.

1912 **First woman's cross-Channel flight.** Harriet Quimby flew from Dover, England, across the English Channel and landed at Hardelot, France, in a Blériot monoplane loaned to her by Louis Blériot (April 16). She was later killed in a flying accident over Dorchester Bay during a Harvard-Boston aviation meet on July 1, 1912.

    First parachute jump from a powered airplane. Albert Berry jumped in a test over Jefferson Barracks military post, St. Louis (March 1). Some sources credit Grant Morton as making first jump in 1911.

1913 **First multi-engined aircraft.** Built and flown by Igor Ivan Sikorsky while still in his native Russia.

1914 **First aerial combat.** In Aug., Allied and German pilots and observers started shooting at each other with pistols and rifles—with negligible results.

1915 **First air raids on England.** German zeppelins dropped bombs on four English communities (Jan. 19).

1917 **World's first black combat pilot.** Georgia-born Eugene Jacques Bullard, denied entry into the U.S. Army Air Corps because of his race, served throughout World War I in the French Flying Corps. He received the Legion of Honor, France's highest honor, among many other decorations.

1918 **First U.S. air squadron.** The U.S. Army Air Corps made its first independent raids over enemy lines, in DH-4 planes (British-designed) powered with 400-hp American-designed Liberty engines (April 8).

    First regular airmail service. Operated for the Post Office Department by the Army, the first regular service was inaugurated with one round trip a day (except Sunday) between Washington, DC, and New York City (May 15).

1919 **First transatlantic flight.** The NC-4, one of four Curtiss flying boats commanded by Lt. Comdr. Albert C. Read, reached Lisbon, Portugal (May 27), after hops from Trepassy Bay, Newfoundland, to Horta, Azores (May 16–17), to Ponta Delgada (May 20). The Liberty-powered craft was piloted by Walter Hinton.

    First nonstop transatlantic flight. Capt. John Alcock and Lt. Arthur Whitten Brown, British World War I flyers, made the 1,900-mile trip from St. John's, Newfoundland, to Clifden, Ireland, in 16 hr., 12 min. in a Vickers-Vimy bomber with two 350-horsepower Rolls-Royce engines (June 15–16).

    First lighter-than-air transatlantic flight. The British dirigible R-34, commanded by Maj. George H. Scott, left Firth of Forth, Scotland (July 2), and touched down at Mineola, L.I., 108 hr. later. The eastbound trip was made in 75 hr. (completed July 13).

    First scheduled London–Paris passenger service (using airplanes). Aircraft Travel and Transport inaugurated London–Paris service (Aug. 25). Later the company started the first trans-Channel mail service on the same route (Nov. 10).

    First free-fall parachute jump. Leslie Irvin jumped over McCook Field, Dayton, Ohio, to prove that one wouldn't lose consciousness during a delayed free-fall using a manually operated parachute (April 28).

1921 **First U.S. black female pilot.** Bessie Coleman received license June 15. Was killed April 30, 1926, in flying accident.

    First naval vessel sunk by aircraft. Two battleships being scrapped by treaty were sunk by bombs dropped from Army planes in demonstration put on by Brig. Gen. William S. Mitchell (July 21).

    First helium balloon. The C-7, nonrigid Navy dirigible was first to use noninflammable helium as lifting gas, making a flight from Hampton Roads, Va., to Washington, D.C. (Dec. 1).

1922 **First member of Caterpillar Club.** Lt. (later Maj. Gen.) Harold Harris bailed out of a crippled plane he was testing at McCook Field, Dayton, Ohio (Oct. 20), and became the first man to join the Caterpillar Club—those whose lives have been saved by parachutes.

1923 **First nonstop transcontinental flight.** Lts. John A. Macready and Oakley Kelly flew a single-engine Fokker T-2 nonstop from New York to San Diego, a distance of just over 2,500 mi in 26 hr., 50 min. (May 2–3).

    First autogyro flight. Juan de la Cierva, a brilliant Spanish mathematician, made the first successful flight in a rotary wing aircraft in Madrid (June 9).

1924 **First round-the-world flight.** Four Douglas Cruiser biplanes of the U.S. Army Air Corps took off from Seattle under command of Maj. Frederick Martin (April 6). 175 days later, two of the planes (Lt. Lowell Smith's and Lt. Erik Nelson's) landed in Seattle after a circuitous route—one source saying 26,345 mi, another saying 27,553 mi.

1926 **First polar flight.** Then–Lt. Cmdr. Richard E. Byrd, acting as navigator, and Floyd Bennett as pilot, flew a Trimotor Fokker from Kings Bay, Spitsbergen, over the North Pole and back in 15½ hr. (May 8–9).

1927 **First solo nonstop transatlantic flight.** Charles Augustus Lindbergh lifted his Wright-powered Ryan monoplane, *Spirit of St. Louis*, from Roosevelt Field, N.Y., to stay aloft 33 hr. 39 min. and travel 3,600 mi to Le Bourget Field outside Paris (May 20–21). Although 91 persons in 13 separate flights crossed the Atlantic before him, he flew directly between two great world cities and did it alone.

    First transatlantic passenger. Charles A. Levine was piloted by Clarence D. Chamberlin from Roosevelt Field, N.Y., to Eisleben, Germany, in a Wright-powered Bellanca (June 4–5).

1928 **First east–west transatlantic crossing.** Baron Guenther von Huenefeld, piloted by German Capt. Hermann Koehl and Irish Capt. James Fitzmaurice, left Dublin for New York City

Orville Wright, Major John F. Curry, and Colonel Charles Lindbergh in 1927. *Source:* Library of Congress.

(April 12) in a single-engine all-metal Junkers-monoplane. Some 37 hr. later, they crashed on Greely Island, Labrador. Rescued.

First transarctic flight. Sir Hubert Wilkins, an Australian explorer, and Carl Ben Eielson, who served as pilot, flew from Point Barrow, Alaska, to Spitsbergen (mid-April).

First U.S.–Australia flight. Sir Charles Kingsford-Smith and Capt. Charles T. P. Ulm, Australians, and two American navigators, Harry W. Lyon and James Warner, crossed the Pacific from Oakland to Brisbane. They went via Hawaii and the Fiji Islands in a trimotor Fokker (May 31–June 8).

1929 First of the endurance records. With Air Corps Maj. Carl Spaatz in command and Capt. Ira Eaker as chief pilot, an Army Fokker, aided by refueling in the air, remained aloft 150 hr. 40 min. at Los Angeles (Jan. 1–7).

First round-the-world airship flight. The LZ-127, known as the *Graf Zeppelin,* flew 21,300 mi in 20 days and 4 hr. Also set distance record (Aug.).

First blind flight. James H. Doolittle proved the feasibility of instrument-guided flying when he took off and landed entirely on instruments (Sept. 24).

First rocket-engine flight. Fritz von Opel, a German auto maker, stayed aloft in his small rocket-powered craft for 75 sec., covering nearly 2 mi (Sept. 30).

First South Pole flight. Comdr. Richard E. Byrd, with Bernt Balchen as pilot, Harold I. June, radio operator, and Capt. A. C. McKinley, photographer, flew a trimotor Fokker from the Bay of Whales, Little America, over the South Pole and back (Nov. 28–29).

1930 First Paris–New York nonstop flight. Dieudonné Costes and Maurice Bellonte, French pilots, flew a Hispano-powered Breguet biplane from Le Bourget Field to Valley Stream, L.I., in 37 hr., 18 min. (Sept. 2–3).

1931 First flight into the stratosphere. Auguste Piccard, a Swiss physicist, and Charles Knipfer ascended in a balloon from Augsburg, Germany, and reached a height of 51,793 ft in a 17-hr. flight that terminated on a glacier near Innsbruck, Austria (May 27).

First nonstop transpacific flight. Hugh Herndon and Clyde Pangborn took off from Sabishiro Beach, Japan, dropped their landing gear, and flew 4,860 mi to near Wenatchee, Wash., in 41 hr. 13 min. (Oct. 4–5).

1932 First woman's transatlantic solo. Amelia Earhart, flying a Pratt & Whitney Wasp-powered Lockheed Vega, flew alone from Harbor Grace, Newfoundland, to Ireland in approximately 15 hr. (May 20–21).

First westbound transatlantic solo. James A. Mollison, a British pilot, took a de Havilland Puss Moth from Portmarnock, Ireland, to Pennfield, New Brunswick (Aug. 18).

First woman airline pilot. Ruth Rowland Nichols, first woman to hold three international records at the same time—speed, distance, and altitude—was employed by N.Y.–New England Airways.

1933 First round-the-world solo. Wiley Post took a Lockheed Vega, *Winnie Mae,* 15,596 mi around the world in 7 days, 18 hr., 49½ min. (July 15–22).

1937 First successful helicopter flight. Hanna Reitsch, a German pilot, flew Dr. Heinrich Focke's FW-61 in free, fully controlled flight at Bremen

Amelia Earhart, 1897–1937.
Source: Library of Congress.

(July 4). Ms. Reitsch was also the first woman civil and military aviation test pilot.

First woman known to fly combat. Sabiha Gokcen, Turkish female army pilot, bombed and strafed Kurdish tribesmen during a rebellion.

1939 First turbojet flight. Just before their invasion of Poland, the Germans flew a Heinkel He-178 plane powered by a Heinkel S3B turbojet (Aug. 27).

1940 First wartime use of military gliders. German commandos made a successful glider assault on Belgium's Fort Eben-Emael during WWII (May 10).

1941–1945 Most combat missions flown by a pilot in any war. Captain Hans-Ulrich Rudel of Germany flew 2,530 combat missions during WWII while flying a JU-87 Stuka dive bomber. He survived the war.

1942–1945 Top-scoring fighter pilot of any war. German Luftwaffe ace Maj. Erich Hartmann scored 352 victories all while flying a Messerschmitt BF 109 during WWII. He was involved in 800 dogfights, and flew 1,425 missions. Maj. Hartmann survived the war.

1942 First enemy bombing of U.S. mainland. During WWII, a floatplane launched from a Japanese submarine off Cape Blanco, Ore., dropped incendiary bombs on the Oregon forest in two attempts to start forest fires and terrorize American civilians, but the bombs did little damage (Sept. 9 and 29).

First woman fighter pilot to shoot down an enemy aircraft. Soviet Lieutenant Lilya Litvyak, flying a Yak-1 fighter of the women's 586th Fighter Aviation Regiment, shot down two German planes over Stalingrad (Sept. 13).

First American jet plane flight. Robert Stanley, chief pilot for Bell Aircraft Corp., flew the Bell XP-59 *Airacomet* at Muroc Army Base, Calif. (Oct. 1).

1944 First production stage rocket-engine fighter plane. The German Messerschmitt Me 163B *Komet* (test flown 1941) became operational in June 1944. Some 350 of these delta-wing fighters were built before WWII in Europe ended.

1947 First piloted supersonic flight in an airplane. Capt. Charles E. Yeager, U.S. Air Force, flew the X-1 rocket-powered research plane built by Bell

Aircraft Corp., faster than the speed of sound at Muroc Air Force Base, Calif. (Oct. 14).

1949 **First round-the-world nonstop flight.** Capt. James Gallagher and USAF crew of 13 flew a Boeing B-50A Superfortress around the world nonstop from Ft. Worth, returning to same point: 23,452 mi in 94 hr., 1 min., with four aerial refuelings en route (Feb. 27–March 2).

1950 **First nonstop transatlantic jet flight.** Col. David C. Schilling (USAF) flew 3,300 mi from England to Limestone, Maine, in 10 hr., 1 min. (Sept. 22).

1951 **First solo across North Pole.** Charles F. Blair, Jr., flew a converted P-51 (May 29).

1952 **First jetliner service.** The De Havilland Comet flight was inaugurated by BOAC between London and Johannesburg, South Africa. Flight, including stops, took 23 hr., 38 min. (May 2).
First transatlantic helicopter flight. Capt. Vincent H. McGovern and 1st Lt. Harold W. Moore piloted two Sikorsky H-19s from Westover, Mass., to Prestwick, Scotland (3,410 mi). Trip was made in five stops, with a flying time of 42 hr., 25 min. (July 15–31).
First transatlantic round trip in same day. A British Canberra twin-jet bomber flew from Aldergrove, Northern Ireland, to Gander, Newfoundland, and back in 7 hr., 59 min. flying time (Aug. 26).

1955 **First transcontinental round trip in same day.** Lt. John M. Conroy piloted an F-86 Sabrejet across U.S. (Los Angeles–New York) and back—5,085 mi—in 11 hr., 33 min., 27 sec. (May 21).

1957 **First round-the-world nonstop jet plane flight.** Maj. Gen. Archie J. Old, Jr., USAF, led a flight of three Boeing B-52 bombers, powered with eight 10,000-pound-thrust Pratt & Whitney Aircraft J57 engines around the world in 45 hr., 19 min; distance 24,325 mi; average speed 525 mph (completed Jan. 18).

1958 **First transatlantic jet passenger service.** BOAC, New York to London (Oct. 4). Pan American started daily service, New York to Paris (Oct. 26).
First domestic jet passenger service. National Airlines inaugurated service between New York and Miami (Dec. 10).

1968 **Prototype of world's first supersonic airliner.** The Soviet-designed Tupolev Tu-144 made its first flight, Dec. 31. It first achieved supersonic speed on June 5, 1969.

1973 **First female pilot of a major U.S. scheduled airline.** Emily H. Warner became employed by Frontier Airlines on Jan. 29 as second officer on a Boeing 737.

1976 **First regularly scheduled commercial supersonic transport (SST) flights begin.** Air France and British Airways inaugurated service (Jan. 21). Air France flew the Paris–Rio de Janeiro route; B.A., the London–Bahrain. Both airlines began SST service to Washington, D.C. (May 24).

1977 **First successful human-powered aircraft.** Paul MacCready, an aeronautical engineer from Pasadena, Calif., was awarded the Kremer Prize for creating the world's first successful human-powered aircraft. The *Gossamer Condor* was flown by Bryan Allen over the required 3-mile course on Aug. 23.

1978 **First successful transatlantic balloon flight.** Three Albuquerque, N.M., men, Ben Abruzzo, Larry Newman, and Maxie Anderson, completed the crossing (Aug. 16.; landed, Aug. 17) in their helium-filled balloon, *Double Eagle II*.

1979 **First man-powered aircraft to fly across the English Channel.** The Kremer Prize for the Channel crossing was won by Bryan Allen, who flew the *Gossamer Albatross* from Folkestone, England, to Cap Gris-Nez, France, in 2 hr., 55 min. (June 12).

1980 **First successful balloon flight over the North Pole.** Sidney Conn and his wife, Eleanor, in hot-air balloon *Joy of Sound* (April 11).
First nonstop transcontinental balloon flight, and also record for longest overland voyage in a balloon. Maxie Anderson and his son, Kris, completed four-day flight from Fort Baker, Calif., to successful landing outside Matane, Quebec, in their helium-filled balloon, *Kitty Hawk* (May 12).
First long-distance solar-powered flight. Janice Brown, a 98-pound former teacher, flew a tiny experimental solar-powered aircraft, *Solar Challenger*, 6 mi in 22 min. near Marana, Ariz. (Dec. 3). The craft was powered by a 2.75-horsepower engine.

1981 **First solar-powered aircraft to fly across the English Channel.** Stephen R. Ptacek flew the 210-pound *Solar Challenger* at an average speed of 30 mph from Cormeilles-en-Vexin near Paris to the Royal Manston Air Force Base in southeast England in 5 hr., 30 min. (July 7).

1984 **First solo transatlantic balloon flight.** Joe W. Kittinger landed Sept. 18 near Savona, Italy, in his helium-filled balloon, *Rosie O'Grady's Balloon of Peace*, after a flight of 3,535 mi from Caribou, Maine.

1986 **First nonstop flight around the world without refueling.** From Edwards AFB, Calif., Dick Rutan and Jeana Yeager flew in *Voyager* around the world (24,986.727 mi), returning to Edwards in 216 hr., 3 min., 44 sec. (Dec. 14–23).

1987 **First transatlantic hot-air balloon flight.** Richard Branson and Per Lindstrand flew 2,789.6 mi from Sugarloaf Mt., Maine, to Ireland in the hot-air balloon *Virgin Atlantic Flyer* (July 2–4).

1991 **First transpacific hot-air balloon flight.** Richard Branson and Per Lindstrand flew about 6,700 mi from Miyakonyo, Japan, to 150 mi west of Yellowknife, Northwest Territories, Canada (Jan. 15–17).

1993 **First woman to copilot a commercial supersonic plane.** Barbara Harmer, British Airways, flew as first officer on the Concorde from London to New York City (March 25).

1995 **First solo transpacific balloon flight.** Steve Fossett made a flight of more than 5,430 mi from Seoul, South Korea, to Leader, Saskatchewan, Canada, in a helium-filled balloon. Also set record for distance (Feb. 18–21, 1995).

1999 **First nonstop round-the-world balloon flight.** Bertrand Piccard (Switzerland) and Brian Jones (UK) flew 28,431 mi (45,755 km) from Chateaux d'Oex, Switzerland, to Dakhla, Egypt, in 19 days, 21 hr., and 55 min. (March 1–21).

2001 **First solar-powered flight to shatter altitude records.** NASA's solar-powered propeller-driven plane *Helios* reached an altitude of 96,500 ft during a flight over Hawaii, breaking not only the 80,200-foot record for propeller-driven aircraft, but the 85,068-foot mark for all nonrocket aircraft as well (Aug. 13–14).

2002 **First solo nonstop round-the-world balloon flight.** Steve Fossett (U.S.) flew from Northam, West Australia, to Lake Yamma Yamma, Queensland, Australia, landing after 14 days, 19 hrs. He broke three balloon records along the way: fastest time around the world, measured by crossing 117° East longitude (13 days, 3 min.), longest distance flown solo (20,483.25 mi; 32,963.35 km), and longest time flown solo (355 hrs, 50 min.) (June 19–July 3).

2004 First non-stop 10,000-mile-plus passenger airline flight. Singapore Airlines launched a non-

stop 18 1/2 hour, 10,335-mile flight on the long-range Airbus 340-500 between Singapore to Newark, New Jersey (June 28–29).

2005 First nonstop solo flight around the world without refueling. From Salina, Kansas, Steve Fossett flew the Virgin Atlantic *Globalflyer* 22,878 mi around the world, arriving back in Kansas 67 hrs later (Feb. 28–March 3).

Absolute World Records

(maximum performance in any class)

Source: National Aeronautic Association

Speed Around the World, Nonstop, Nonrefueled

Speed (mph)	Date	Plane	Pilots	Place
115.65	Dec. 14–23, 1986	*Voyager*	Dick Rutan & Jeana Yeager (U.S.)	Edwards AFB, Calif.— Edwards AFB, Calif.

Distance, Great Circle Without Landing, also Distance, Closed Circuit Without Landing

Distance (mi)	Date	Plane	Pilots	Place
24,986.727	Dec. 14–23, 1986	*Voyager*	Dick Rutan & Jeana Yeager (U.S.)	Edwards AFB, Calif.— Edwards AFB, Calif.

Speed over a Straight Course

Speed (mph)	Date	Plane type	Pilot	Place
2,193.16	July 28, 1976	Lockheed SR-71A	Capt. Eldon W. Joersz (USAF)	Beale AFB, Calif.

Speed over a Closed Circuit

Speed (mph)	Date	Plane type	Pilot	Place
2,092.294	July 27, 1976	Lockheed SR-71A	Maj. Adolphus H. Bledsoe, Jr. (USAF)	Beale AFB, Calif.

Altitude

Height (ft)	Date	Plane type	Pilot	Place
123,523.58	Aug. 31, 1977	MIG-25, E-266M	Alexander Fedotov (USSR)	USSR

Altitude in Horizontal Flight

Height (ft)	Date		Pilot	Place
85,068.997	July 28, 1976		Capt. Robert C. Helt (USAF)	Beale AFB, Calif.

Altitude, Aircraft Launched from a Carrier Airplane

Height (ft)	Date	Plane type	Pilot	Place
314,750.00	July 17, 1962	N. American X-15-1	Maj. Robert White (USAF)	Edwards AFB, Calif.

World-Class Helicopter Records

Selected records. *Source:* National Aeronautic Association

Great Circle Distance Without Landing
International: 2,213.04 mi; 3,561.55 km.
Robert G. Ferry (U.S.) in Hughes YOH-6A helicopter powered by Allison T-63-A-5 engine; from Culver City, Calif., to Ormond Beach, Fla., April 6–7, 1966.

Distance, Closed Circuit Without Landing
International: 1,739.96 mi; 2,800.20 km.
Jack Schweibold (U.S.) in Hughes YOH-6A helicopter powered by Allison T-63-A-5 engine; Edwards Air Force Base, Calif., March 26, 1966.

Altitude without Payload
International: 40,820 ft; 12,442 m.
Jean Boulet (France) in Alouette SA 315-001 *Lama* powered by Artouste IIIB 735 KW engine; Istres, France, June 21, 1972.

Speed around the World, Eastbound
40.99 mph; 65.97 kph.
Joe Ronald Bower (U.S.) pilot, in Bell JetRanger III, powered by one Allison 250-C20J (317 shp), covered 23,800 mi in 24 days, 4 hr., 36 min. June 28–July 22, 1994.

Speed around the World, Westbound
57.01 mph; 91.75 kph.

Joe Ronald Bower (U.S.) pilot, John W. Williams (U.S.), co-pilot in Bell 430 powered by 2 Allison 250–C40, (811 shp), Aug. 17–Sept. 3, 1996.

Absolute World Records, Balloons

Selected records. *Source:* National Aeronautic Association
Altitude
113,739.9 ft; 34,668 m.
Cmdr. M.D. Ross (U.S.) and Lt. Cmdr. V.A. Prather, *Lee Lewis Memorial*, Gulf of Mexico, May 4, 1961.

Distance
25,360 mi; 40,814 km.
Bertrand Piccard (Switzerland) and Brian Jones (UK), *Cameron Balloons R-650*, Château d'Oex, Switzerland, to Dakhla, Egypt, March 1–21, 1999.

Duration
477 hr., 47 min.
Bertrand Piccard (Switzerland) and Brian Jones (UK), *Cameron Balloons R-650*, Château d'Oex, Switzerland, to Dakhla, Egypt, March 1–21, 1999.

Fastest time around the world
312 hr., 3 min.
Steve Fossett (U.S.), Spirit of Freedom, Northam, Western Australia to Lake Yamma Yamma, Queensland, Australia. Flight, June 19–July 3; record broken on July 2, 2002.

U.S. Postal Rates and Fees

Domestic Rates, last revised by the U.S. Postal Service on June 30, 2002

First-Class Mail

First-Class Mail includes all personal correspondence, all bills and statements of accounts, all matter sealed or otherwise closed against inspection, and matter wholly or partly in writing or typewriting. Any mailable items may be sent as First-Class Mail. Each piece must weigh 13 oz or less. Pieces over 13 oz can be sent as Priority Mail.

Single-Piece Letter/Flat Rates

1st oz	$0.37
Each additional oz	0.23

Weight not over (oz)	Rate	Weight not over (oz)	Rate
1*	$0.37	9	$2.21
2	0.60	10	2.44
3	0.83	11	2.67
4	1.06	12	2.90
5	1.29	13	3.13
6	1.52	Over 13 oz, see	
7	1.75	Priority Mail.	
8	1.98		

*Nonstandard surcharge may apply to pieces weighing 1 oz or less based on size.

Card Rates

Single postcard (commercial)	$0.23
Single postal card sold by United States Postal Service	0.25

Postcard Dimensions: Not larger than 4¼ by 6 in. by 0.016 in. thick. Not smaller than 3½ by 5 in. by 0.007 in. thick.

Express Mail

Express Mail is the fastest service, with next day delivery by 12 noon to most destinations. Express Mail is delivered 365 days a year—with no extra charge for Saturday, Sunday, or holiday delivery. Items must weigh 70 lbs or less and measure 108 in. or less in combined length and girth.

Customer Service—1-800-222-1811. Order Express Mail supplies and labels, arrange pickup service, obtain delivery information between ZIP Codes, and determine delivery status.

Post Office to Addressee Service

Up to 8 oz	$13.65
Up to 2 lbs	17.85
Up to 3 lbs	21.05
Up to 4 lbs	24.20
Up to 5 lbs	27.30
Up to 6 lbs	30.40
Up to 7 lbs	33.45
Over 7 lbs, see postmaster.	

Express Mail Flat-Rate Envelope

$13.65, regardless of weight or destination, for matter sent in a flat-rate envelope provided by the Postal Service.

Priority Mail

Priority Mail offers 2-day service to most domestic destinations. Items must weigh 70 lbs or less and measure 108 in. or less in combined length and girth. Items that weigh less than 15 lbs but measure more than 84 in. (combined length and girth) are charged the 15 lb rate ($11.05)*.

Single-Piece Rates*

Up to 1 lb	$3.85
Up to 2 lbs	3.95
Up to 3 lbs	4.75
Up to 4 lbs	5.30
Up to 5 lbs	5.85
Over 5 pounds, see postmaster.	

*Rates are given for zones local through 3.

Priority Mail Flat-Rate Envelope

$3.85, regardless of weight or destination, for matter sent in a flat-rate envelope provided by the Postal Service.

Media Mail (Book Rate)

Generally used for books (at least eight pages), film (16 mm or narrower), printed music, printed test materials, sound recordings, play scripts, printed educational charts, loose-leaf pages and binders consisting of medical information, and computer-readable media. Advertising restrictions apply. Packages must measure 108 in. or less in combined length and girth.

Weight not over (lbs)	Rate	Weight not over (lbs)	Rate
1	$1.42	9	$4.54
2	1.84	10	4.84
3	2.26	11	5.14
4	2.68	12	5.44
5	3.10	13	5.74
6	3.52	14	6.04
7	3.94	15	6.34
8	4.24	16	6.64

Special Services (Domestic Mail)

Certificate of Mailing

Provides evidence of mailing only. Certificate of mailing does not provide a record of delivery. Must be purchased at time of mailing. Available for First-Class Mail, Priority Mail, Parcel Post, Bound Printed Matter, and Media Mail.

Fee, in addition to postage—$0.90

Certified Mail

Provides the sender with a mailing receipt. A delivery record is maintained by the USPS. No insurance provided. Available with First-Class Mail and Priority Mail. For an additional fee, certified mail may be combined with restricted delivery or return receipt.

Fee, in addition to postage—$2.30

Insurance

Provides coverage against loss or damage. Coverage up to $5,000 for Parcel Post, Bound Printed Matter, and Media Mail matter as well as merchandise mailed at Priority Mail or First-Class Mail rates. Items must not be insured for more than their value. Insured mail must be presented to a retail employee at a post office or a rural carrier.

Liability	Fee, in addition to postage
$.01 to $50.00	$1.30
$50.01 to $100.00	2.20
$100.01 to $200.00	3.20
$200.01 to $300.00	4.20
$300.01 to $400.00	5.20
$400.01 to $500.00	6.20
$500.01 to $600.00	7.20
$600.01 to $5,000	*

*$7.00 plus $1.00 for each $100 or fraction over $600 in declared value.

Money Orders

Provides safe transmission of money. Available in amounts up to $1,000.
Fee up to $500, in addition to postage—$0.90
Fee up to $1,000, in addition to postage—$1.25

Registered Mail

Provides maximum protection and security for valuables. Provides sender with mailing receipt and a delivery record is maintained by the USPS. A record of mailing is maintained at the mailing post office. Available only for items paid at Priority Mail and First-Class Mail rates.

	Declared Value	Fee, in addition to postage
Without Insurance	$0.00	$ 7.50
With Insurance	$0.01 to $100	8.00
	$100.01 to $500.00	8.85
	$500.01 to $1,000.00	9.70
	$1,000.01 to $2,000.00	10.55

For higher values, consult your postmaster.

Restricted Delivery

Permits a mailer to direct delivery only to the addressee or addressee's authorized agent. The addressee must be an individual specified by name. Available for First-Class Mail, Priority Mail, Parcel Post, Bound Printed Matter, and Media Mail that is sent certified mail, COD, mail insured for more than $50, or registered mail.
Fee, in addition to postage—$3.50

Return Receipt

Available only for Express Mail, Certified Mail, COD, Insured Mail for more than $50.00, or Registered Mail.
Requested at time of mailing:
Showing to whom (signature), date, and addressee's address (in conjunction with another service) $1.75
Requested after mailing:
Showing to whom (signature) and date delivered $3.25

Special Handling

Provides preferential handling, but not preferential delivery, to extent practicable in dispatch and transportation. Available for First-Class Mail, Priority Mail, Parcel Post, Bound Printed Matter, and Media Mail.

Fee, in addition to postage:
Pieces weighing not more than 10 pounds—$5.95
Pieces weighing more than 10 pounds—$8.25

Collect on Delivery (COD)

Allows mailers to collect the price of goods and/or postage on merchandise ordered by addressee when it is delivered. Fees include insurance. Maximum amount $1,000; see postmaster for details.

Sizes for Domestic Mail

Mail must meet these standards:
• Thickness—No less than 0.007 in. thick. Pieces that are ¼ in. thick or less must be at least 3½ in. high, 5 in. long, and rectangular in shape.
• Combined length and girth—No more than 108 in.
• Weight—No more than 70 lbs.
Postcards must be:
• Minimum 3½ in. high, 5 in. long by .007 in. thick.
• Maximum 4¼ in. high, 6 in. long by .016 in. thick.

The Mail-Order Merchandise Rule

The mail-order rule adopted by the Federal Trade Commission in October 1975 provides that when you order by mail:
• You must receive the merchandise when the seller says you will.
• If you are not promised delivery within a certain time period, the seller must ship the merchandise to you no later than 30 days after your order comes in.
• If you don't receive it shortly after that 30-day period, you can cancel your order and get your money back.

ZIP Codes

The ZIP Code was instituted in 1963 and allows for electronic processing and delivery of mail. An envelope that does not include a ZIP Code in the delivery address must be manually sorted, which increases the cost of sorting the mail and causes mail to be delayed en route to the delivery address. ZIP Code directories are available for use or sale at your local post office, or you can look up ZIP Codes on-line: www.usps.gov/zip4/

In 1983, the Postal Service began to use an expanded ZIP Code called ZIP+4. It is composed of the original five-digit code plus a four-digit add-on. The four-digit add-on number identifies a geographic segment within the five-digit delivery area such as a city block, an office building, an individual high-volume receiver of mail, or any other unit that would aid efficient mail sorting and delivery.

Postal Information Websites

United States Postal Service: http://www.usps.gov/
ZIP Code Lookup: http://www.usps.gov/zip4/
U.S. Postal Service Rate Calculators:
   domestic: http://postcalc.usps.gov/
   international: http://ircalc.usps.gov/
   business: http://dbcalc.usps.gov/

International Postal Rates

Single Piece Letter-Post

Weight not over (oz)	Canada	Mexico	Western Europe and Israel	Australia, Japan, New Zealand	Other countries
1	$ 0.60	$ 0.60	$ 0.80	$ 0.80	$ 0.80
2	0.85	0.85	1.60	1.70	1.55
3	1.10	1.25	2.40	2.60	2.30
4	1.35	1.65	3.20	3.50	3.05
5	1.60	2.05	4.00	4.40	3.80
6	1.85	2.45	4.80	5.30	4.55
7	2.10	2.85	5.60	6.20	5.30
8	2.35	3.25	6.40	7.10	6.05
12	3.10	4.00	7.55	8.40	7.65
16	3.75	5.15	8.70	9.70	9.25
20	4.40	6.30	9.85	11.00	10.85
24	5.05	7.45	11.00	12.30	12.45
28	5.70	8.60	12.15	13.60	14.05
32	6.35	9.75	13.30	14.90	15.65
36	7.00	10.95	14.50	16.25	17.35
40	7.65	12.15	15.70	17.60	19.05
44	8.30	13.35	16.90	18.95	20.75
48	8.95	14.55	18.10	20.30	22.45
52	9.65	15.80	19.35	21.70	24.20
56	10.35	17.05	20.60	23.10	25.95
60	11.05	18.30	21.85	24.50	27.70
64	11.75	19.55	23.10	25.90	29.45

NOTE: Last revised by the U.S. Postal Service on June 30, 2002. Maximum weight: 64 oz. **Postcards and Postal Rates:** Canada and Mexico—$0.50; all others—$0.70.

U.S. Letter Rates Since the Civil War

The first U.S. postage stamps were issued on July 1, 1847. At that time, postal rates varied by distance traveled—under 300 miles, letters cost 5 cents per ½ oz; over 300 miles, letters cost 10 cents per ½ oz. (These rates fluctuated in the decade that followed.) Until prepayment became mandatory on April 1, 1855, Americans had the option to pay collect, which could entail higher rates. Since July 1, 1863, letters sent to all parts of the United States have been charged at the same rate.

July 1, 1863	3 cents per ½ oz.	Dec. 31, 1975	13 cents for 1st oz.
Oct. 1, 1883	2 cents per ½ oz.	May 29, 1978	15 cents for 1st oz.
July 1, 1885	2 cents per 1 oz.	March 22, 1981	18 cents for 1st oz.
Nov. 2, 1917	3 cents per 1 oz.	Nov. 1, 1981	20 cents for 1st oz.
July 1, 1919	2 cents per 1 oz.	Feb. 17, 1985	22 cents for 1st oz.
July 6, 1932	3 cents per 1 oz.	April 3, 1988	25 cents for 1st oz.
Aug. 1, 1958	4 cents per 1 oz.	Feb. 3, 1991	29 cents for 1st oz.
Jan. 7, 1963	5 cents per 1 oz.	Jan. 1, 1995	32 cents for 1st oz.
Jan. 7, 1968	6 cents per 1 oz.	Jan. 10, 1999	33 cents for 1st oz.
May 16, 1971	8 cents per 1 oz.	Jan. 7, 2001	34 cents for 1st oz.
March 2, 1974	10 cents per 1 oz.	June 30, 2002	37 cents for 1st oz.

State Abbreviations and State Postal Codes

State	Abbreviation	Postal code	State	Abbreviation	Postal code	State	Abbreviation	Postal code
Alabama	Ala.	AL	Kentucky	Ky.	KY	Ohio	Ohio	OH
Alaska	Alaska	AK	Louisiana	La.	LA	Oklahoma	Okla.	OK
Arizona	Ariz.	AZ	Maine	Maine	ME	Oregon	Ore.	OR
Arkansas	Ark.	AR	Maryland	Md.	MD	Pennsylvania	Pa.	PA
California	Calif.	CA	Massachusetts	Mass.	MA	Puerto Rico	P.R.	PR
Colorado	Colo.	CO	Michigan	Mich.	MI	Rhode Island	R.I.	RI
Connecticut	Conn.	CT	Minnesota	Minn.	MN	South Carolina	S.C.	SC
Delaware	Del.	DE	Mississippi	Miss.	MS	South Dakota	S.D.	SD
Dist. of Columbia	D.C.	DC	Missouri	Mo.	MO	Tennessee	Tenn.	TN
Florida	Fla.	FL	Montana	Mont.	MT	Texas	Tex.	TX
Georgia	Ga.	GA	Nebraska	Nebr.	NE	Utah	Utah	UT
Guam	Guam	GU	Nevada	Nev.	NV	Vermont	Vt.	VT
Hawaii	Hawaii	HI	New Hampshire	N.H.	NH	Virginia	Va.	VA
Idaho	Idaho	ID	New Jersey	N.J.	NJ	Virgin Islands	V.I.	VI
Illinois	Ill.	IL	New Mexico	N.M.	NM	Washington	Wash.	WA
Indiana	Ind.	IN	New York	N.Y.	NY	West Virginia	W.Va.	WV
Iowa	Iowa	IA	North Carolina	N.C.	NC	Wisconsin	Wis.	WI
Kansas	Kans.	KS	North Dakota	N.D.	ND	Wyoming	Wyo.	WY

Eastward, Ho! Skyscrapers Migrate to Asia

Fifteen years ago, the world's ten tallest buildings were all in North America; today all but two are in Asia

By RICHARD LACAYO TIME

On the morning of Sept. 11, 2001, Adrian D. Smith, a well-known architect in the Chicago office of Skidmore Owings & Merrill, was in a meeting with Donald Trump. The hyperbolic New York City developer was in Chicago to go over the design of a proposed Trump residential tower in that city that he had decided should be—what else?—the tallest building in the world, around 2,000 ft. In the midst of their meeting, the two men got word of the first plane that hit the World Trade Center. "When the second plane hit, we all rushed to the television to see what was happening," says Smith. "That was the end of the meeting." And also the end of the 2,000-ft tower. A few weeks later, Trump's people came back with a revised proposal—at 900 ft or so.

Born in the U.S.A.

The skyscraper was born in the U.S., and for most of the 20th century, it flourished here. Fifteen years ago, nine of the world's 10 tallest buildings were in the U.S. (The 10th was in Toronto.) Now just two are: the Sears Tower in Chicago and the Empire State Building in Manhattan. All the rest are in Asia. A combination of factors—a sluggish commercial real estate market, skepticism about the profitability of very tall buildings even in good times, the rise of urban thinking critical of skyscrapers, and the psychological fallout from 9/11—has discouraged today's American developers from going very, very high.

More subtly, for some time before 9/11, the tall building had been losing ground as a symbol of power, wealth, and importance, at least in Western countries, where museums, shops, and restaurants became more significant status indicators. But elsewhere in the world, extreme verticals are still entirely in fashion, especially for developing nations looking to announce themselves. Just last year there was a new claimant to the title of world's tallest building, the 1,670-ft Taipei 101—named for the number of its floors. After it was completed, Chinese authorities and the developer, who were determined not to let their least favorite neighbor get ahead in the vertical space race, not only greenlighted a much delayed project, the Shanghai World Financial Center, but insisted on additional stories so that the building will have more occupiable floors than the tower in Taiwan.

Asia Gains Ground . . . And Height

The Pacific Rim is not the only place where the new "supertalls" are going up. Coming soon is the Burj Dubai, in Dubai, one of the United Arab Emirates. It was designed by the same Adrian Smith who did Trump's tower. In 2008, when the Dubai building is complete, he says, it will rise to a height "of well over 2,000 ft." He won't say just how high. His clients don't want to tip their hand to other builders who have projects in the planning stages. If the others knew where the bar was set, they could easily pump their towers up a few feet higher—or more than a few feet. Architects and engineers agree that it's only a matter of time before a tower rises somewhere in Asia or the Middle East to 3,000 ft.—more than twice the height of either tower of the World Trade Center.

The right architectural language for those beanstalks is still up in the air. In many places Asia has become the last outpost of postmodernism, the ornamental style that American architects tried for a while in the 1980s, struggling to link the office tower to older traditions of Western building by tarting it up with Gothic spires and classical pediments. Postmodernism was an awkward undertaking, and it fell out of fashion when architects began finding more interesting ways beyond the stylistic endgame of modernism.

Not in Asia, however. Many Asian clients saw the plain glass-and-steel modernist box as a Western import, remote from their national traditions. They wanted silhouettes that would reflect local styles. So the Petronas Towers in Malaysia, until recently the tallest buildings in the world, evoke the minarets of a mosque expanded to sky-high proportions. The Jin Mao Tower in Shanghai, by Skidmore Owings & Merrill, is a highly elongated pagoda. So is Taipei 101, a giant knickknack of a building that pushes the postmodern idea to the edge of kitsch. Make that past the edge.

But more agreeable gestures are out there. Cesar Pelli, who designed the Petronas Towers, is also the architect behind Two International Finance Centre in Hong Kong, a 1,362-ft office tower executed in the art deco–flavored projectile form he has developed lately. And when it's completed, the Shanghai World Financial Center, by the American firm Kohn Pedersen Fox Associates, will be one of the most elegant buildings in the world, a chisel-shaped tower with a giant oculus cut into its tapering top. It could prove that architecture, not just construction, is headed to new heights. □

World's Tallest Buildings[1]

Rank	Building, city	Year	Stories	Height m	ft
1.	Taipei 101, Taipei, Taiwan	2004	101	509	1,670
2.	Petronas Tower 1, Kuala Lumpur, Malaysia	1998	88	452	1,483
3.	Petronas Tower 2, Kuala Lumpur, Malaysia	1998	88	452	1,483
4.	Sears Tower, Chicago	1974	110	442	1,450
5.	Jin Mao Building, Shanghai	1999	88	421	1,380
6.	Two International Finance Centre, Hong Kong	2003	88	415	1,362
7.	CITIC Plaza, Guangzhou, China	1996	80	391	1,283
8.	Shun Hing Square, Shenzhen, China	1996	69	384	1,260
9.	Empire State Building, New York	1931	102	381	1,250
10.	Central Plaza, Hong Kong	1992	78	374	1,227
11.	Bank of China, Hong Kong	1989	72	369	1,209
12.	Emirates Tower One, Dubai	1999	54	355	1,165
13.	Tuntex Sky Tower, Kaohsiung, Taiwan	1997	85	348	1,140
14.	Aon Centre, Chicago	1973	80	346	1,136
15.	The Center, Hong Kong	1998	73	346	1,135
16.	John Hancock Center, Chicago	1969	100	344	1,127
17.	Wuhan International Securities Building, Wuhan	UC05	68	331	1,087
18.	Shimao International Plaza, Shanghai	UC05	60	331	1,087
19.	Ryugyong Hotel, Pyongyang, N. Korea	1995	105	330	1,083
20.	Burj al Arab Hotel, Dubai	1999	60	321	1,053
21.	Chrysler Building, New York	1930	77	319	1,046
22.	Bank of America Plaza, Atlanta	1993	55	312	1,023
23.	U.S. Bank Tower, Los Angeles	1990	73	310	1,018
24.	Menara Telekom Headquarters, Kuala Lumpur	1999	55	310	1,017
25.	Emirates Tower Two, Dubai	2000	56	309	1,014
26.	AT&T Corporate Center, Chicago	1989	60	307	1,007
27.	JP Morgan Chase Tower, Houston	1982	75	305	1,002
28.	Baiyoke Tower II, Bangkok	1997	85	304	997
29.	Two Prudential Plaza, Chicago	1990	64	303	995
30.	Kingdom Centre, Riyadh	2002	41	302	992
31.	First Canadian Place, Toronto	1975	72	298	978
32.	Wells Fargo Plaza, Houston	1983	71	296	972
33.	Landmark Tower, Yokohama, Japan	1993	70	296	971
34.	311 South Wacker Drive, Chicago	1990	65	293	961
35.	SEG Plaza, Shenzhen	2000	71	292	957
36.	American International Building, New York	1932	67	290	952
37.	Key Tower, Cleveland	1991	57	289	947
38.	Plaza 66, Shanghai	2001	66	288	945
39.	One Liberty Place, Philadelphia	1987	61	288	945
40.	Sunjoy Tomorrow Square, Shanghai	2003	55	285	934
41.	Bank of America Center, Seattle	1984	76	284	933
42.	Cheung Kong Center, Hong Kong	1999	63	283	929
43.	Chongqing World Trade Center, Chongqing	UC05	60	283	929
44.	The Trump Building, New York	1930	71	283	927
45.	Bank of America Plaza, Dallas	1985	72	281	921
46.	United Overseas Bank Plaza, Singapore	1992	66	280	919
47.	Republic Plaza, Singapore	1995	66	280	919
48.	Overseas Union Bank Centre, Singapore	1986	63	280	919
49.	Citigroup Center, New York	1977	59	279	915
50.	Hong Kong New World Tower, Shanghai	2002	61	278	913
51.	Scotia Plaza, Toronto	1989	68	275	902
52.	Williams Tower, Houston	1983	64	275	901
53.	Wuhan World Trade Tower, Wuhan	1998	60	273	896
54.	Renaissance Tower, Dallas	1975	56	270	886
55.	Dapeng International Plaza, Guangzhou	2004	56	269	883
56.	21st Century Tower, Dubai	2003	55	269	883
57.	Al Faisaliah Center, Riyadh	2000	30	267	876
58.	900 North Michigan Ave., Chicago	1989	66	265	871
59.	Bank of America Corporate Center, Charlotte	1992	60	265	871
60.	SunTrust Plaza, Atlanta	1992	60	265	871
61.	Triumph Palace, Moscow	2004	61	264	866
62.	Shenzhen Special Zone Daily Tower, Shenzhen	1998	42	264	866
63.	Tower Palace Three, Tower G, Seoul	2004	73	264	865
64.	Trump World Tower, New York	2001	72	262	861
65.	Water Tower Place, Chicago	1976	74	262	859
66.	Aon Center, Los Angeles	1974	62	262	858
67.	BCE Place–Canada Trust Tower, Toronto	1990	53	261	856
68.	Post & Telecommunication Hub, Guangzhou	2002	66	260	853
69.	Transamerica Pyramid, San Francisco	1972	48	260	853
70.	G.E. Building, New York	1933	70	259	850
71.	Bank One Plaza, Chicago	1969	60	259	850
72.	Commerzbank Zentrale, Frankfurt	1997	56	259	850
73.	Two Liberty Place, Philadelphia	1990	58	258	848
74.	Philippine Bank of Communications, Makati	2000	55	258	848
75.	Park Tower, Chicago	2000	67	257	844
76.	Messeturm, Frankfurt	1990	64	257	843
77.	Sorrento 1, Hong Kong	2003	75	256	841
78.	U.S. Steel Tower, Pittsburgh	1970	64	256	841
79.	Mokdong Hyperion Tower A, Seoul	2003	69	256	840
80.	Rinku Gate Tower, Izumisano	1996	56	256	840
81.	The Harbourside, Hong Kong	2003	74	255	837
82.	Langham Place Office Tower, Hong Kong	2004	59	255	837
83.	Capital Tower, Singapore	2000	52	254	833
84.	Highcliff, Hong Kong	2003	73	253	831

Rank	Building, city	Year	Stories	Height m	ft
85.	Osaka World Trade Center, Osaka	1995	55	252	827
86.	Bank of Shanghai Headquarters, Shanghai	UC05	46	252	827
87.	Jiali Plaza, Wuhan	1997	61	251	824
88.	Rialto Tower, Melbourne	1985	63	251	823
89.	One Atlantic Center, Atlanta	1987	50	250	820
90.	Chelsea Tower, Dubai	2005	49	250	820
91.	Wisma 46, Jakarta	1995	46	250	820
92.	Korea Life Insurance Company, Seoul	1985	60	249	817
93.	CitySpire, New York	1989	75	248	814
94.	One Chase Manhattan Plaza, New York	1961	60	248	813
95.	State Tower, Bangkok	2001	68	247	811
96.	Bank One Tower, Indianapolis	1989	48	247	811
97.	Condé Nast Building, New York	1999	48	247	809
98.	MetLife, New York	1963	59	246	808
99.	Bloomberg Tower, New York	2004	55	246	806
100.	JR Central Towers, Nagoya	2000	51	245	804

NOTES: Height is measured from sidewalk level of main entrance to structural top of building. This includes spires, but does not include antennas or flag poles. UC = under construction, number indicates year of expected completion. 1. World Trade Center twin towers of New York City ranked fifth and sixth (at 1,368 ft and 1,362 ft) on this list until their destruction on Sept. 11, 2001. *Source:* Council on Tall Buildings and Urban Habitat, Lehigh University, 2005. Web: www.ctbuh.org.

World's Tallest Towers

Tower, city	Year	Height (m)	Height (ft)	Tower, city	Year	Height (m)	Height (ft)
Canadian National (CN) Tower, Toronto, Canada	1975	553	1,815	Central Radio & TV Tower, Beijing, China	1992	405	1,329
Ostankino Tower, Moscow, Russia	1967	537	1,762	Tianjin TV Tower, Tianjin, China	1991	415	1,362
Oriental Pearl Tower, Shanghai, China	1995	468	1,535	Kiev TV Tower, Kiev, Ukraine	1973	385	1,263
Milad Tower, Tehran, Iran	2005	435	1,427	Tashkent Tower, Tashkent, Uzbekistan	1985	375	1,230
Menara Kuala Lumpur, Kuala Lumpur, Malaysia	1996	421	1,403	Liberation Tower, Kuwait City, Kuwait	1996	372	1,221

NOTES: Height is from top to bottom, antennas included. A tower differs from a building in that the latter has floors, and is designed for residential, business, or manufacturing use. The structures listed here are principally telecommunications towers, and while they may have observation decks or restaurants, they do not have floors all the way up. Towers and buildings are freestanding structures; this list does not include masts supported by guy wires. The tallest mast currently standing is the KVLY-TV Mast in North Dakota, built in 1963; it is 629 m (2,063 ft) tall. The tallest mast of all time was the Warszawa Radio Mast near Konstantynów, Poland, built in 1974; it was 646 m (2,120 ft) tall before collapsing during renovation work in 1991. (Note that the name of a building or mast may include the word "tower," but that does not affect its status.) This list also does not include the Petronius Platform, built in 2000 in the Gulf of Mexico, which is 610 m (2,001 ft) tall without its spire, or 640 m (2,100 ft) with it. While it is the world's tallest freestanding structure, 535 m (1,754 ft) of it is underwater and it is partly supported by buoyancy. *Sources:* Structurae, Emporis, Wikipedia, and other sources.

Famous Structures

Ancient

The **Great Sphinx** of Egypt, one of the wonders of ancient Egyptian architecture, adjoins the pyramids of Giza and has a length of 240 ft. Built in the fourth dynasty, it is approximately 4,500 years old. A 10-year $2.5 million restoration project was completed in 1998. Other Egyptian buildings of note include the *Temples of Karnak, Edfu,* and *Abu Simbel* and the *Tombs at Beni Hassan.*

The **Parthenon*** of Greece, built on the Acropolis in Athens, was the chief temple to the goddess Athena. It was believed to have been completed by 438 B.C. The present temple remained intact until the 5th century A.D. Today, though the Parthenon is in ruins, its majestic proportions are still discernible.

Other great structures of the ancient Greek world were the *Temples* at Paestum (c. 540 and 420 B.C.); the famous *Erechtheum* (c. 421–405 B.C.), the *Temple of Athena Niké* (c. 426 B.C.), and the *Olympieum* (begun in the 6th century B.C.) in Athens; the *Athenian Treasury* at Delphi (c. 515 B.C.); and the *Theater* at Epidaurus (c. 325 B.C.).

The **Colosseum** (Flavian Amphitheater) of Rome, the largest and most famous of the Roman amphitheaters, was opened for use A.D. 80. Elliptical in shape, it consisted of three stories and an upper gallery, rebuilt in stone in its present form in the third century A.D. It was principally used for gladiatorial combat and could seat between 40,000 and 50,000 spectators.

The **Pantheon** at Rome, begun by Agrippa in 27 B.C. as a temple, was rebuilt in its present circular form by Hadrian (A.D. 118–128). Literally the Pantheon was intended as a temple of "all the gods." It is remarkable for its perfect preservation today, and has served continuously for 20 centuries as a place of worship.

Famous Roman triumphal arches, built to commemorate major military victories, include the **Arch of Titus** (c. A.D. 80) and the **Arch of Constantine** (c. A.D. 315).

Teotihuacán, located in central Mexico, was the largest city in the Americas at its height between A.D. 300 and 900. Built on a grid plan with a central avenue known as the Street of the Dead, it is the site of two enormous pyramid temples and the temple of the plumed serpent god Quetzalcoatl.

Later European

St. Mark's Cathedral in Venice (1063–1071), one of the great examples of Byzantine architecture, was begun in the 9th century. Partly destroyed by fire in 976, it was later rebuilt as a Byzantine edifice.

Other famous examples of Byzantine architecture are *St. Sophia* in Istanbul (532–537); *San Vitale* in Ravenna (542); and *Assumption Cathedral* in the Kremlin, Moscow (begun in 1475).

The cathedral group at Pisa (1067–1173), one of the most celebrated groups of structures built in Romanesque style, consists of the cathedral, the cathedral's baptistery, and the campanile (**Leaning Tower***). The campanile, a form of bell tower, is 180 ft high and now leans 13.5 ft out of the perpendicular.

Other examples of Romanesque architecture include the *Vézelay Abbey* in France (1130) and *Durham Cathedral* in England.

The **Alhambra** (1248–1354), located in Granada, Spain, is universally esteemed as one of the greatest masterpieces of Muslim architecture. Designed as a palace and fortress for the Moorish monarchs of Granada, it is surrounded by a heavily fortified wall more than a mile in perimeter.

The **Tower of London** is a group of buildings and towers covering 13 acres along the north bank of the Thames. The central *White Tower,* begun in 1078 during the reign of William the Conqueror, was originally a fortress and royal residence, but was later used as a prison. The *Bloody Tower* is associated with Anne Boleyn and other notables.

Westminster Abbey, in London, was begun in 1050 and completed in 1065. It was rebuilt and enlarged in several phases, beginning in 1245. With only two exceptions (Edward V and Edward VIII), every British monarch since William the Conqueror has been crowned in the abbey.

Notre-Dame de Paris (begun in 1163), one of the great examples of Gothic architecture, is a twin-towered church with a steeple over the crossing and immense flying buttresses supporting the masonry at the rear of the church.

Other famous Gothic structures are *Chartres Cathedral* (France; 12th century); *Sainte-Chapelle* (Paris, France; 1246–1248); *Reims Cathedral* (France; 13th–14th centuries; rebuilt after its almost complete destruction in World War I); *Rouen Cathedral* (France; 13th–16th centuries); *Salisbury Cathedral* (England; 1220–1260); *York Minster,* or the *Cathedral of St. Peter* (England; 1220–1472); *Milan Cathedral* (Italy; begun in 1386); and *Cologne Cathedral* (Germany; 13th–19th centuries; damaged in World War II but completely restored).

The **Duomo*** (cathedral) in Florence, with its pink, white, and green marble façade, has become a symbol of the city and the Renaissance. Construction began in 1296, and was completed nearly 200 years later, with the addition of Brunelleschi's massive dome. The adjacent baptistery is famous for its gilded bronze doors by Ghiberti.

The **Vatican** is a group of buildings in Rome comprising the official residence of the pope. The *Basilica of St. Peter,* the largest church in the Christian world, was begun in 1452, and it was rebuilt between 1506 and 1626. The *Sistine Chapel,* begun in 1473, is noted for frescoes by Michelangelo.

Other examples of Renaissance architecture are the *Palazzo Riccardi,* the *Palazzo Pitti,* and the *Palazzo Strozzi* in Florence; the *Palazzo Farnese* in Rome; the *Palazzo Grimani* (completed c. 1550) in Venice; the *Escorial* (1563–93) near Madrid; the *Town Hall* of Seville (1527–32); the *Louvre,* Paris; the *Château* at Blois, France; *St. Paul's Cathedral,* London (1675–1710; badly damaged in World War II); the *École Militaire,* Paris (1752); the *Pazzi Chapel,* Florence, designed by Brunelleschi (1429); and the *Palace of Fontainebleau* and the *Château de Chambord* in France.

The **Palace of Versailles** in France, containing the famous Hall of Mirrors, was built during the reign of Louis XIV in the 17th century and served as the royal palace until 1793. Built on the colossal scale typical of many works of baroque architecture, the palace is also noted for its gardens, which include some 1,400 fountains.

The **Eiffel Tower,** in Paris, was built for the Exposition of 1889 by Alexandre Gustave Eiffel. It is 984 ft high (1,056 ft including the television tower).

The **Guggenheim Bilbao Museum** (1993–97) in Bilbao, Spain, was designed by Frank Gehry. The undulating form of this riverfront building, clad in glass and gleaming sheets of titanium, has been compared to a fish, a boat, and water itself.

See also:
Architects
World's Tallest Buildings
Seven Wonders of the World

Asian, African, and American

The **Taj Mahal*** (1632–1650), at Agra, India, built by Shah Jahan as a tomb for his wife, is considered by some as the most perfect example of the Mogul style and by others as the most beautiful building in the world. Four slim white minarets flank the building, which is topped by a white dome; the entire structure is made of marble.

The **Dome of the Rock** (687–691) in Jerusalem is considered the first great work of Muslim architecture. It is noted for its beautiful mosaics of scrolling vines and flowers, and for its dome, which was originally covered in pure gold.

Another well-known Muslim edifice is the **Citadel,** located on an outcrop of limestone overlooking Cairo. Begun in 810, it was fortified (1176–1183) by Saladin during the Crusades.

Other famed Muslim edifices are the *Tombs of the Mamelukes* (15th century) in Cairo, the *Tomb of Humayun* in Delhi, the *Blue Mosque* (1468) at Tabriz, and the *Tamerlane Mausoleum* at Samarkand.

Angkor Wat, outside the city of Angkor Thom, Cambodia, is one of the most beautiful examples of Cambodian, or Khmer, architecture. The sanctuary was built during the 12th century.

The **Great Wall of China** (begun c. 214 B.C.), designed specifically as a defense against nomadic tribes, has large watch towers that could be called buildings. It was erected by Emperor Ch'in Shih Huang Ti and is 1,400 mi long. Built mainly of earth and stone, it varies in height between 18 and 30 ft.

The **Forbidden City** (1407–1420) in Beijing served as the seat of imperial power during the Ming and Qing dynasties (1368–1911). It is the world's largest palace complex, covering about 183 acres and including 9,999 buildings.

Typical of Chinese architecture are the pagodas, or temple towers. Among some of the better-known pagodas are the *Great Pagoda of the Wild Geese* at Sian (founded in 652) and *Nan t'a* (11th century) at Fang Shan.

The painted wooden **Torii,** or Gateway, at Miyajima Island, Japan, stands in the tidal flats opposite the historic Itsukushima Shrine. Built in the traditional Shinto style, with two columns supporting a concave crosspiece on top, the gate serves to welcome the spirits of the dead as they come from across the Inland Sea.

Other famous Japanese buildings include the Buddhist temples of **Horyuji** (7th century) and **Todaiji** (8th century) at Nara.

Machu Picchu is an ancient Inca fortress in the Andes Mountains of Peru. Thought to have been built and occupied from the mid-15th century, it is surrounded on three sides by stepped agricultural terraces, which are connected to the main plazas and buildings by thousands of stone steps.

United States

The **Chrysler Building** (1928–30) in New York City is one of the finest examples of art deco–style architecture. Built for automotive magnate Walter P. Chrysler, the building uses decorative elements borrowed from automobiles. At 1,046 ft it was briefly the world's tallest building.

The **Empire State Building** (1930–31) is one of the most popular tourist attractions in Manhattan. Features include a tiered structure that recalls ancient pyramids and a mast at the top for mooring dirigibles. Rising to 1,250 ft (not including the mast), it remained the tallest building in the world until the 1970s.

The elegant **Seagram Building** (1954–58), by Ludwig Mies van der Rohe, soars above an open plaza in Manhattan. Its slim steel frame is covered in amber-gray glass and costly bronze. It has been called the world's most imitated office building.

The **Cathedral of St. John the Divine,** in New York City, was begun in 1892 and is now two-thirds completed. When completed, it will be the largest cathedral in the world: 601 ft long, 146 ft wide at the nave, 320 ft wide at the transept. The east end is Romanesque-Byzantine style, and the nave and west end are Gothic.

The **Brooklyn Bridge** (1869–83) was the remarkable achievement of engineer John Roebling. The first steel-wire suspension bridge in the world, it has a main span of 1,596 ft.

The smooth, circular form of the **Guggenheim New York Museum** (1943–59), designed by Frank Lloyd Wright, is a Manhattan landmark. The main gallery space features a six-story concrete ramp that spirals up a glass-topped atrium.

The **Sears Tower** in Chicago is, at 1,450 ft, the tallest building in the United States. Constructed between 1974 and 1976 for Sears, Roebuck and Company, the structure is composed of 75-foot square tubes that rise to varying levels.

San Francisco's **Golden Gate Bridge,** completed in 1937, is one of the most recognizable structures in the United States. Designed by Joseph B. Strauss, this elegant suspension bridge has a main span of 4,200 ft.

The Seattle **Space Needle** was the futuristic centerpiece of the 1962 Seattle World's Fair. The 605-ft-tall Needle is topped by an observation deck and a revolving restaurant.

* Photos of these structures can be found in the Headline History section.

The Seven Wonders of the World

Since ancient times, people have put together many "seven wonders" lists. The content of these lists tends to vary, and none is definitive. The seven wonders that are most widely agreed upon as being in the original list are the **Seven Wonders of the Ancient World.** (* indicates photo can be found in the Headline History section.)

The **Pyramids of Egypt*** are three pyramids at Giza, outside modern Cairo. The largest pyramid, built by Khufu (Cheops), a king of the fourth dynasty, had an original estimated height of 482 ft (now approximately 450 ft). The base has sides 755 ft long. It contains 2,300,000 blocks; the average weight of each is 2.5 tons. Estimated date of completion is 2680 B.C. Of all the Ancient Wonders, the pyramids alone survive.

The **Hanging Gardens of Babylon** were supposedly built by Nebuchadnezzar around 600 B.C. to please his queen, Amuhia. They are also associated with the mythical Assyrian queen, Semiramis. Archeologists surmise that the gardens were laid out atop a vaulted building, with provisions for raising water. The terraces were said to rise from 75 to 300 ft.

The **Statue of Zeus (Jupiter) at Olympia** was made of gold and ivory by the Greek sculptor Phidias (5th century B.C.). Reputed to be 40 ft high, the statue has been lost without a trace, except for reproductions on coins.

The **Temple of Artemis (Diana) at Ephesus** was begun about 350 B.C., in honor of a non-Hellenic goddess who later became identified with the Greek goddess of the same name. The temple, with Ionic columns 60 ft high, was destroyed by invading Goths in A.D. 262.

The **Mausoleum at Halicarnassus** was erected by Queen Artemisia in memory of her husband, King Mausolus of Caria in Asia Minor, who died in 353 B.C. Some remains of the structure are in the British Museum. This shrine is the source of the modern word *mausoleum.*

The **Colossus at Rhodes** was a bronze statue of Helios (Apollo), about 105 ft high. The work of the sculptor Chares, who reputedly labored for 12 years before completing it in 280 B.C., it was destroyed during an earthquake in 224 B.C.

The **Pharos (Lighthouse) of Alexandria** was built by Sostratus of Cnidus during the 3rd century B.C. on the island of Pharos off the coast of Egypt. It was destroyed by an earthquake in the 13th century.

(Some lists include the Walls of Babylon in place of the second or seventh wonder.)

See also Greek and Roman Mythology, p. 468.

Notable Modern Bridges

Name	Location	Length of main span ft	Length of main span m	Year completed
Suspension	**United States**			
Verrazano-Narrows	Lower New York Bay	4,260	1,298	1964
Golden Gate	San Francisco Bay	4,200	1,280	1937
Mackinac	Mackinac Straits, Mich.	3,800	1,158	1957
George Washington	Hudson River at New York City	3,500	1,067	1931
Tacoma Narrows II	Puget Sound at Tacoma, Wash.	2,800	853	1950
San Francisco–Oakland Bay[1]	San Francisco Bay	2,310	704	1936
Bronx-Whitestone	East River, New York City	2,300	701	1939
Delaware Memorial[1]	Delaware River near Wilmington, Del.	2,150	655	1951, 1968
Seaway Skyway	St. Lawrence River at Ogdensburg, N.Y.	2,150	655	1960
Walt Whitman	Delaware River at Philadelphia	2,000	610	1957
Ambassador International	Detroit River at Detroit	1,850	564	1929
Throgs Neck	East River, New York City	1,800	549	1961
Benjamin Franklin	Delaware River at Philadelphia	1,750	533	1926
Bear Mountain	Hudson River at Peekskill, N.Y.	1,632	497	1924
William Preston Lane, Jr.[1]	Chesapeake Bay, Md.	1,600	488	1952, 1973
Williamsburg	East River, New York City	1,600	488	1903
Newport	Narragansett Bay at Newport, R.I.	1,600	488	1969
Brooklyn	East River, New York City	1,596	486	1883
Mid-Hudson	Poughkeepsie, N.Y.	1,495	457	1930
	International			
Akashi Kaikyo	Hyogo, Japan	6,529	1,990	1998
Izmit Bay	Marmara Sea, Turkey	5,472	1,668	UC
Storebælt	Denmark	5,328	1,624	1998
Humber	Humberside, England	4,626	1,410	1981
Jiangyin	Yangtze River, China	4,543	1,385	1999
Tsing Ma	Hong Kong	4,518	1,377	1997
Höga Kusten (High Coast)	Västernorrland, Sweden	3,969	1,210	1997
Minami Bisan-Seto	Japan	3,609	1,100	1988
Second Bosporus	Istanbul, Turkey	3,576	1,090	1988
First Bosporus	Istanbul, Turkey	3,524	1,074	1973
Third Kurushima	Japan	3,379	1,030	1999
Second Kurushima	Japan	3,346	1,020	1999
Ponte 25 de Abril	Tagus River at Lisbon, Portugal	3,323	1,013	1966
Forth Road	Queensferry, Scotland	3,300	1,006	1964
Kita Bisan-Seto	Japan	3,248	990	1988
Severn	Severn River at Beachley, England	3,240	988	1966
Yichang	Yangtze River, Hubei Province, China	3,150	960	2001
Shimotsui Straits	Japan	3,084	940	1988
Xiling Yangtze	Three Gorges Dam, China	2,952	900	1996
Cantilever	**United States**			
Commodore John Barry	Chester, Pa.	1,644	501	1974
Crescent City Connection[1]	Mississippi River, New Orleans, La.	1,576	480	1958, 1985
Transbay Bridge	San Francisco Bay	1,400	427	1936
Baton Rouge	Mississippi River, La.	1,235	376	1968
Tappan Zee	Hudson River at Tarrytown, N.Y.	1,212	369	1955
	International			
Quebec Railway	Quebec, Canada	1,800	549	1917
Forth Railway[1]	Queensferry, Scotland	1,710	521	1890
Minato Ohashi	Osaka, Japan	1,673	510	1974
Howrah	Hooghly River at Calcutta, India	1,500	457	1943
Steel Arch	**United States**			
New River Gorge	Fayetteville, W. Va.	1,700	518	1977
Bayonne	Kill Van Kull at Bayonne, N.J.	1,675	510	1931
Fremont	Portland, Ore.	1,255	383	1973
Roosevelt Lake	Roosevelt, Ariz.	1,080	329	1990
Glen Canyon	Page, Ariz.	1,028	313	1959
	International			
Lupu Bridge	Shanghai, China	1,800	550	2003
Sydney Harbor	Sydney, Australia	1,670	509	1932
Port Mann	Fraser River at Vancouver, British Columbia	1,200	366	1964
Yanjisha[2]	Guangzhou, China	1,181	360	2000
Thatcher Ferry	Panama Canal, Panama	1,128	344	1962

Name	Location	Length of main span ft	Length of main span m	Year completed
Cable-stayed	**United States**			
Clark	Alton, Ill.	1,360	415	1994
Dames Point	Jacksonville, Fla.	1,300	396	1988
Fred Hartman	Baytown, Tex.	1,250	381	1995
Sidney Lanier	Brunswick River, Ga.	1,250	381	2003
Hale Boggs Memorial	Luling, La.	1,222	373	1983
Sunshine Skyway	Tampa, Fla.	1,200	366	1987
	International			
Tatara	Honshu-Shikoku, Japan	2,920	890	1999
Pont de Normandie	Le Havre, France	2,808	856	1995
Second Nanjing	Yangtze River, Nanjing, China	2,060	628	2001
Wuhan Third Yangtze	Wuhan, Hubei Province, China	2,028	618	2000
Qingzhou Minjiang	Fuzhou, China	1,985	605	1996
Yang Pu	Shanghai, China	1,975	602	1993
Xupu	Shanghai, China	1,936	590	1997
Meiko Chuo	Aichi, Japan	1,936	590	1997
Rion-Antirion	Greece	1,837	560	2004
Skarnsundet	near Trondheim, Norway	1,739	530	1991
Queshi	Guangdong Province, China	1,700	518	1999
Tsurumi Tsubasa	Kanagawa, Japan	1,673	510	1995
Jingzhou	Yangtze River, Hubei Province, China	1,640	500	2002
Oresund	Denmark/Sweden	1,614	492	2000
Ikuchi	Honshu-Shikoku, Japan	1,608	490	1991
Higashi Kobe	Hyogo, Japan	1,591	485	1994
Zhanjiang Bay	Guangdong Province, China	1,575	480	1998
Ting Kau	Hong Kong	1,558	475	1997
Seohae Grand	South Korea	1,542	470	2000
Continuous Truss	**United States**			
Astoria	Columbia River, Ore.	1,232	376	1966
Croton Reservoir	Croton, N.Y.	1,052	321	1970
Ravenswood	Ohio River, Ravenswood, W. Va.	902	275	1981
Central	Ohio River, Newport, Ky.	850	259	1995
Braga Memorial	Taunton River at Somerset, Mass.	840	256	1965
Kingston-Rhinecliff	Kingston, N.Y.	800	244	1957
Mark Clark Expressway I-526	Cooper River at Charleston, S.C.	800	244	1992
	International			
Oshima	Oshima Island, Japan	1,066	325	1976
Tenmon	Kumamoto, Japan	984	300	1966
Kuronoseto	Nagashima-Kyushu, Japan	984	300	1974
Graf Spee	Germany	839	256	1936
Concrete Arch	**United States**			
Natchez Trace Pkwy.	Franklin, Tenn.	582	177	1994
Westinghouse	Pittsburgh, Pa.	460	140	1931
Jack's Run	Pittsburgh, Pa.	400	120	1930
Cappelen	Minneapolis, Minn.	400	120	1923
	International			
Wanxian	Wanxian, Sichuan Province, China	1,378	420	1997
Krk (I)	Krk, Croatia	1,280	390	1980
Jiangjiehe	Guizhou Province, China	1,083	330	1995
Gladesville	Parramatta River at Sydney, Australia	1,000	305	1964
Amizade	Paraná River at Foz do Iguassu, Brazil	951	290	1964
Bloukrans	Bloukrans River, South Africa	892	272	1983
Arrábida	Porto, Portugal	886	270	1963
Sandö	Angerman River at Kramfors, Sweden	866	264	1943
Confederation	Northumberland Strait, Canada	820	250	1997
Sibenik	Sibenik, Croatia	808	246	1966
Krk (II)	Krk, Croatia	800	244	1979
Fiumarella	Catanzaro, Italy	758	231	1961
Zaporozhe	Old Dnepr River, Ukraine	748	228	1952
Esla	Esla River at Zamora, Spain	645	197	1940
Segmental Construction	**United States**			
Jesse H. Jones Memorial	Houston Ship Channel, Tex.	750	228	1982

NOTES: UC = under construction in 2005. 1. Twin span. 2. Concrete-filled steel tubes. *Sources:* National Steel Bridge Alliance, Swedish Institute of Steel Construction, Structurae, Federal Highway Administration.

World's Highest Dams

Name	River, location	Structural height ft	Structural height m	Gross reservoir capacity Thousands of ac ft	Gross reservoir capacity Millions of cu m	Year completed
Rogun	Vakhsh, Tajikistan	1099	335	9,404	11,600	1985
Nurek	Vakhsh, Tajikistan	984	300	8,512	10,500	1980
Xiaowan	Lancang, China	958	292	12,161	15,000	UC
Grande Dixence	Dixence, Switzerland	935	285	324	400	1962
Inguri	Inguri, Georgia	892	272	801	1,100	1984
Vaiont	Vaiont, Italy	859	262	137	169	1961
Manuel M. Torres	Grijalva, Mexico	856	261	1,346	1,660	1981
Tehri	Bhagirathi, India	856	261	2,869	3,540	UC
Alvaro Obregon	Mextiquic, Mexico	853	260	n.a.	n.a.	1926
Mauvoisin	Drance de Bagnes, Switzerland	820	250	146	180	1957
Alberto Lleras	Orinoco, Colombia	797	243	811	1,000	1989
Mica	British Columbia, Canada	797	243	20,000	24,670	1972
Sayano-Shushenskaya	Yenisei, Russia	794	242	25,353	31,300	1980
Ertan	Yangtze/Yalong, China	787	240	4,702	5,800	1999
La Esmeralda	Batá, Colombia	778	237	661	815	1975
Kishau	Tons, India	774	236	1,946	2,400	1985
Oroville	Feather, Calif., U.S.	770	235	3,538	4,299	1968
El Cajón	Humuya, Honduras	768	234	4,580	5,650	1984
Chirkey	Sulak, Russia	764	233	2,252	2,780	1977
Shuibuya	Qingjiang, China	764	233	3,713	4,580	UC
Bhakra	Sutlej, India	741	226	8,002	9,870	1963
Luzzone	Brenno di Luzzone, Switzerland	738	225	71	87	1963
Hoover	Colorado, Ariz.-Nev.; U.S.	732	223	28,500	35,154	1936
Karun-4	Karun, Iran	728	222	1,880	2,320	UC
Contra	Verzasca, Switzerland	722	220	70	86	1965
Mratinje	Piva, Herzegovina	722	220	713	880	1973

NOTES: UC = under construction in 2005. n.a. = not available. *Sources:* International Commission on Large Dams, *World Register of Dams 2003*, and other sources.

World's Largest Dams

Dam	Location	Volume (thousands) cu m	Volume (thousands) cu yds	Year completed
Syncrude Tailings	Canada	540,000	706,320	UC
Chapetón	Argentina	296,200	387,410	UC
Pati	Argentina	238,180	274,026	UC
New Cornelia Tailings	United States	209,500	274,026	1973
Tarbela	Pakistan	121,720	159,210	1976
Kambaratinsk	Kyrgyzstan	112,200	146,758	UC
Fort Peck	Montana	96,049	125,628	1940
Lower Usuma	Nigeria	93,000	121,644	1990
Cipasang	Indonesia	90,000	117,720	UC
Atatürk	Turkey	84,500	110,522	1990
Yacyretá-Apipe	Paraguay/Argentina	81,000	105,944	1998
Guri (Raul Leoni)	Venezuela	78,000	102,014	1986
Rogun	Tajikistan	75,500	98,750	1985
Oahe	South Dakota	70,339	92,000	1963
Mangla	Pakistan	65,651	85,872	1967
Gardiner	Canada	65,440	85,592	1968
Afsluitdijk	Netherlands	63,400	82,927	1932
Oroville	California	59,639	78,008	1968
San Luis	California	59,405	77,700	1967
Nurek	Tajikistan	58,000	75,861	1980
Garrison	North Dakota	50,843	66,500	1956
Cochiti	New Mexico	48,052	62,850	1975
Tabka (Thawra)	Syria	46,000	60,168	1976
Bennett W.A.C.	Canada	43,733	57,201	1967
Tucuruí	Brazil	43,000	56,242	1984

NOTE: UC = under construction in 2005. China's Three Gorges dam on the Yangtze River, begun in 1993 and expected to be completed in 2009, will be the world's largest dam. *Source:* Department of the Interior, Bureau of Reclamation and *International Water Power and Dam Construction.*

Famous Ship Canals

Name	Location	Length (mi)[1]	Width (ft)	Depth (ft)	Locks	Year opened
Albert	Belgium	80.0	53.0	16.5	6	1939
Amsterdam-Rhine	Netherlands	45.0	164.0	41.0	3	1952
Beaumont–Port Arthur	United States	40.0	200.0	34.0	—	1916
Canal du Midi	France	149.0	n.a.	n.a.	100	1692
Chesapeake and Delaware	United States	14.0	450.0	35.0	—	1829
Erie Canal	United States	363.0	70.0	7.0	82	1825
Grand Canal	China	1,085.0	n.a.	n.a.	n.a.	7th cent.
Göta Canal	Sweden	240.0	n.a.	n.a.	58	1832
Houston	United States	50.0	(2)	40.0	—	1914
Kiel (Nord-Ostsee Kanal)	Germany	61.3	144.0	36.0	4	1895
Panama	Panama	50.7	110.0	41.0	12	1914
St. Lawrence Seaway	U.S. and Canada	2,400.0[3]	(4)	—	—	1959
Montreal to Prescott	U.S. and Canada	11.5	80.0	30.0	7	1959
Welland	Canada	27.5	80.0	27.0	8	1931
Sault Ste. Marie	Canada	1.2	60.0	16.8	1	1895
Sault Ste. Marie	United States	1.6	80.0	25.0	4	1915
Suez	Egypt	119.9[5]	1197.5	68.9	—	1869

1. Statute miles. 2. 300–400 ft. 3. From Montreal to Duluth. 4. 442–550 ft; there are 11.5 mi of locks, 80 ft wide and 30 ft deep. 5. From Port Said lighthouse to entrance channel in Suez roads. *Source:* American Society of Civil Engineers.

Notable Tunnels

Name	Location	Length mi	km	Year completed
Railroad, excluding subways				
Seikan	Tsugaru Strait, Japan	33.5	53.9	1988
Channel Tunnel[1]	English Channel, England-France	31.1	50.0	1994
Iwate Ichinohe	Tanigawa Mountains, Japan	16.0	25.8	2002
Daishimizu	Mikuni Mountain Range, Japan	13.8	22.2	1982
Simplon (I and II)	Alps, Switzerland-Italy	12.3	19.8	1906, 1922
Vereina	Klosters-Sagliains, Switzerland	11.8	19.1	1999
Shin Kanmon	Kanmon Strait, Japan	11.6	18.7	1975
Apennine	Bologna-Florence, Italy	11.5	18.5	1934
Qinling I-II	Qinling Mountains, China	11.5	18.5	2002
Rokkô	Rokkô Mountain, Japan	10.1	16.3	1972
Furka Base	Andermatt-Brig, Switzerland	9.6	15.4	1982
Haruna	Gunma Prefecture, Japan	9.5	15.4	1982
Severomuyskiy	Baikal-Amur, Russia	9.5	15.3	2001
Gorigamine	Takasaki-Nagano, Japan	9.4	15.2	1997
Monte Santomarco	Paola-Cosenza, Italy	9.3	15.0	1987
St. Gotthard	Swiss Alps	9.3	15.0	1882
Nakayama	Nakayama Pass, Hokkaido, Japan	9.2	14.9	1982
Lötschberg	Swiss Alps	9.1	14.6	1913
Mount MacDonald	Rogers Pass, Glacier Nat'l Park, Canada	9.1	14.6	1989
Romeriksporten	Oslo-Gardermoen airport, Norway	9.1	14.6	1999
Vehicular				
Laerdal	Laerdal–Aurland, Norway	15.2	24.5	2000
St. Gotthard	Alps, Switzerland	10.2	16.4	1980
Arlberg	Austrian Alps	8.7	14.0	1979
Fréjus	French Alps	8.0	12.9	1980
Mt. Blanc	Alps, France-Italy	7.0	11.3	1965
Gudvanga	Bergen-Oslo, Norway	7.1	11.4	1991
Folgefonn	Odda-Gjerde, Norway	6.9	11.2	2001
Kanetsu (southbound)	Tokyo-Niigata, Japan	6.9	11.0	1991
Kanetsu (northbound)	Tokyo-Niigata, Japan	6.8	10.9	1985
Gran Sasso d'Italia (E and W)	Abruzzo, Italy	6.3	10.2	1984, 1995
Aqualine Expressway	Tokyo Bay, Japan	5.9	9.5	1997
Mt. Ena	Japan Alps, Japan	5.3	8.5	1976[2]

1. Three-tunnel system including two rail tunnels (one carries passengers from England to France, the other from France to England) and a central service tunnel. 2. Parallel tunnel begun in 1976. *Sources:* American Society of Civil Engineers and International Bridge, Tunnel & Turnpike Association, and The World's Longest Tunnel Page, Web: home.no.net/lotsberg/.

See also World's Largest Subway Systems, p. 606.

Conversion Factors

To change	To	Multiply by	To change	To	Multiply by
acres	square feet	43,560	liters	quarts (liquid)	1.0567
acres	square miles	.001562	meters	feet	3.2808
atmospheres	cms. of mercury	76	meters	miles	.0006214
Btu	kilowatt-hour	.0002931	meters	yards	1.0936
Btu/hour	watts	.2931	metric tons	tons (long)	.9842
bushels	cubic inches	2150.4	metric tons	tons (short)	1.1023
centimeters	inches	.3937	miles	kilometers	1.6093
centimeters	feet	.03281	miles	feet	5280
cubic feet	cubic meters	.0283	miles (nautical)	miles (statute)	1.1516
cubic meters	cubic feet	35.3145	miles (statute)	miles (nautical)	.8684
cubic meters	cubic yards	1.3079	miles/hour	feet/minute	88
cubic yards	cubic meters	.7646	millimeters	inches	.0394
fathoms	feet	6.0	ounces (avdp)	grams	28.3495
feet	meters	.3048	ounces	pounds	.0625
feet	miles (nautical)	.0001645	ounces (troy)	ounces (avdp)	1.09714
feet	miles (statute)	.0001894	pecks	liters	8.8096
feet/second	miles/hour	.6818	pints (dry)	liters	.5506
furlongs	feet	660.0	pints (liquid)	liters	.4732
furlongs	miles	.125	pounds (ap or troy)	kilograms	.3732
gallons (U.S.)	liters	3.7853	pounds (avdp)	kilograms	.4536
grains	grams	.0648	pounds	ounces	16
grams	ounces (avdp)	.0353	quarts (dry)	liters	1.1012
grams	pounds	.002205	quarts (liquid)	liters	.9463
hectares	acres	2.4710	radians	degrees	57.30
hectoliters	bushels (U.S.)	2.8378	rods	meters	5.029
horsepower	watts	745.7	rods	feet	16.5
horsepower	Btu/hour	2,547	square feet	square meters	.0929
hours	days	.04167	square kilometers	square miles	.3861
inches	millimeters	25.4000	square meters	square feet	10.7639
inches	centimeters	2.5400	square miles	square kilometers	2.5900
kilograms	pounds (avdp or troy)	2.2046	square yards	square meters	.8361
kilometers	miles	.6214	tons (long)	metric tons	1.016
kilowatt-hour	Btu	3412	tons (short)	metric tons	.9072
knots	nautical miles/hour	1.0	tons (long)	pounds	2240
knots	statute miles/hour	1.151	tons (short)	pounds	2000
liters	gallons (U.S.)	.2642	watts	Btu/hour	3.4121
liters	pints (dry)	1.8162	watts	horsepower	.001341
liters	pints (liquid)	2.1134	yards	meters	.9144
liters	quarts (dry)	.9081	yards	miles	.0005682

NOTE: avdp = avoirdupois weight, ap = apothecaries' weight. *See also* p.539.

Fahrenheit and Celsius (Centigrade) Scales

°Celsius	°Fahrenheit	°Celsius	°Fahrenheit
−273.15	−459.67	30	86
−250	−418	35	95
−200	−328	40	104
−150	−238	45	113
−100	−148	50	122
−50	−58	55	131
−40	−40	60	140
−30	−22	65	149
−20	−4	70	158
−10	14	75	167
0	32	80	176
5	41	85	185
10	50	90	194
15	59	95	203
20	68	100	212
25	77		

Zero on the Fahrenheit scale represents the temperature produced by the mixing of equal weights of snow and common salt.

	°Fahrenheit	°Celsius
Boiling point of water	212°	100°
Freezing point of water	32°	0°
Absolute zero	−459.6°	−273.1°

Absolute zero is theoretically the lowest possible temperature, the point at which all molecular motion would cease.

To convert Fahrenheit to Celsius (Centigrade), subtract 32 and divide by 1.8.

To convert Celsius (Centigrade) to Fahrenheit, multiply by 1.8 and add 32.

Cardinal, Ordinal, and Nominal Numbers

Cardinal numbers, known as the "counting numbers," indicate quantity. **Ordinal numbers** indicate the order or rank of things in a set (e.g., sixth in line; fourth place). **Nominal numbers** name or identify something (e.g., a zip code or a player on a team.) They do not show quantity or rank.

Roman Numerals

Roman numerals are expressed by letters of the alphabet and are rarely used today except for formality or variety. There are four basic principles for reading Roman numerals:

1. A letter repeated once or twice repeats its value that many times (XXX = 30, CC = 200, etc.).
2. One or more letters placed after another letter of greater value increases the greater value by the amount of the smaller (VI = 6, LXX = 70, MCC = 1200, etc.).
3. A letter placed before another letter of greater value decreases the greater value by the amount

of the smaller (IV = 4, XC = 90, CM = 900, etc.). Several rules apply for subtraction: (a) only subtract powers of ten (I, X, or C, but not V or L); (b) only subtract one number from another; (c) do not subtract a number from one that is more than 10 times greater (that is, you can subtract 1 from 10 [IX] but not from 20—there is no such number as IXX).

4. A bar placed on top of a letter or string of letters increases the numeral's value by 1,000 times (XV = 15, $\overline{XV}$ = 15,000).

Letter	Value	Letter	Value	Letter	Value	Letter	Value	Letter	Value
I	1	VII	7	XL	40	C	100	$\overline{C}$	100,000
II	2	VIII	8	L	50	D	500	$\overline{D}$	500,000
III	3	IX	9	LX	60	M	1,000	$\overline{M}$	1,000,000
IV	4	X	10	LXX	70	V	5,000		
V	5	XX	20	LXXX	80	X	10,000		
VI	6	XXX	30	XC	90	L	50,000		

Mean and Median

The arithmetic mean, also called the average, of a series of quantities is obtained by finding the sum of the quantities and dividing it by the number of quantities. In the series 1, 3, 5, 18, 19, 20, 25, the mean or average is 13—in other words, 91 divided by 7.

The median of a series is that point which so divides it that half the quantities are on one side, half on the other. In the above series, the median is 18.

The median often better expresses the common-run, since it is not, as is the mean, affected by an excessively high or low figure. In the series 1, 3, 4, 7, 55, the median of 4 is a truer expression of the common-run than is the mean of 14.

Prime Numbers between 1 and 1,000

2	3	5	7	11	13	17	19	23
29	31	37	41	43	47	53	59	61	67
71	73	79	83	89	97	101	103	107	109
113	127	131	137	139	149	151	157	163	167
173	179	181	191	193	197	199	211	223	227
229	233	239	241	251	257	263	269	271	277
281	283	293	307	311	313	317	331	337	347
349	353	359	367	373	379	383	389	397	401
409	419	421	431	433	439	443	449	457	461
463	467	479	487	491	499	503	509	521	523
541	547	557	563	569	571	577	587	593	599
601	607	613	617	619	631	641	643	647	653
659	661	673	677	683	691	701	709	719	727
733	739	743	751	757	761	769	773	787	797
809	811	821	823	827	829	839	853	857	859
863	877	881	883	887	907	911	919	929	937
941	947	953	967	971	977	983	991	997	

World's Largest Known Prime Number

The largest currently known prime, $2^{25,964,951} - 1$, was found by Dr. Martin Nowak of Germany through the GIMPS project on Feb. 18, 2005. It has 7,816,230 digits. (You can actually buy a poster of the number!) The Electronic Frontier Foundation is offering a $100,000 award to whomever is the first to find a prime number with at least ten million digits; it seems likely that this will be claimed within the next few years.

Portraits and Designs of U.S. Paper Currency

Currency[1]	Portrait	Design on back	Currency[1]	Portrait	Design on back
$1	Washington	ONE between obverse and reverse of Great Seal of U.S.	$50[6]	Grant	U.S. Capitol
$2[2]	Jefferson	Monticello	$100[7]	Franklin	Independence Hall
$2[3]	Jefferson	"The Signing of the Declaration of Independence"	$500	McKinley	Ornate FIVE HUNDRED
			$1,000	Cleveland	Ornate ONE THOUSAND
$5[4]	Lincoln	Lincoln Memorial	$5,000	Madison	Ornate FIVE THOUSAND
$10[4]	Hamilton	U.S. Treasury Building	$10,000	Chase	Ornate TEN THOUSAND
$20[5]	Jackson	White House	$100,000[8]	Wilson	Ornate ONE HUNDRED THOUSAND

1. Denominations of $500 and higher were discontinued in 1969. 2. Discontinued in 1966. 3. New issue, April 1976. 4. New issue, May 2000. 5. New issue, fall 2003. 6. New issue, spring 2004. 7. New issue, March 1996. 8. For use only in transactions between Federal Reserve System and Treasury Department.

The 50 State Quarters Program Act

The 50 State Quarters Program Act began in 1999 and is expected to run until 2008, with five new quarters released every year over ten years. The quarters are being released in the order that the states joined the union. 700 million copies of each quarter will be produced. Each quarter will feature a different state design on the back.

State	Date of statehood	Issued	Design
Delaware	Dec. 7, 1787	1999	Caesar Rodney's horseback ride
Pennsylvania	Dec. 12, 1787	1999	Commonwealth statue, keystone, and outline of state
New Jersey	Dec. 18, 1787	1999	Washington crossing the Delaware River
Georgia	Jan. 2, 1788	1999	Peach, Live Oak, and outline of state
Connecticut	Jan. 9, 1788	1999	The Charter Oak
Massachusetts	Feb. 6, 1788	2000	Minuteman statue and outline of state
Maryland	April 28, 1788	2000	Maryland Statehouse and White Oak
South Carolina	May 23, 1788	2000	Palmetto tree, Carolina wren, and Yellow Jessamine
New Hampshire	June 21, 1788	2000	Old Man of the Mountain rock formation
Virginia	June 25, 1788	2000	First three ships to Jamestown
New York	July 26, 1788	2001	Statue of Liberty, state outline, the words "Gateway to Freedom," 11 stars
North Carolina	Nov. 21, 1789	2001	First flight at Kitty Hawk
Rhode Island	May 29, 1790	2001	A sailboat on the open sea, commemorating the "Ocean State"
Vermont	March 4, 1791	2001	Camel's Hump Mountain, maple trees with sap buckets
Kentucky	June 1, 1792	2001	Federal Hill, or "My Old Kentucky Home," race horse behind a fence
Tennessee	June 1, 1796	2002	Fiddle, trumpet, guitar, and musical score
Ohio	March 1, 1803	2002	Early airplane, astronaut, and state outline
Louisiana	April 30, 1812	2002	Pelican, horn with musical notes, and outline of Louisiana Purchase
Indiana	Dec. 11, 1816	2002	Race car and state outline
Mississippi	Dec. 10, 1817	2002	Blossoms and leaves of two magnolias
Illinois	Dec. 3, 1818	2003	Abraham Lincoln and state outline
Alabama	Dec. 14, 1819	2003	Helen Keller, with name in English and Braille
Maine	March 15, 1820	2003	The Pemaquid Point Light House and a schooner
Missouri	Aug. 10, 1821	2003	Lewis and Clark travelling down the Missouri River
Arkansas	June 15, 1836	2003	Rice stalks, a diamond, and a mallard, representing the "Natural State"
Michigan	Jan. 26, 1837	2004	Outline of state and Great Lakes
Florida	March 3, 1845	2004	Galleon, space shuttle, strip of land with palm trees, "Gateway to Discovery"
Texas	Dec. 29, 1845	2004	State outline and star encircled by lariat, representing the "Lone Star State"
Iowa	Dec. 28, 1846	2004	One-room schoolhouse, based on a Grant Wood painting
Wisconsin	May 29, 1848	2004	Cow's head, cheese, corn, and "Forward" motto
California	Sept. 9, 1850	2005	John Muir, Yosemite Valley, and California condor
Minnesota	May 11, 1858	2005	People fishing, a loon, and state outline with "Land of 10,000 Lakes"
Oregon	Feb. 14, 1859	2005	Crater Lake
Kansas	Jan. 29, 1861	2005	Buffalo and sunflowers
West Virginia	June 20, 1863	2005	New River Gorge, New River Gorge Bridge

Customary U.S. Weights and Measures

Linear Measure

12 inches (in.) = 1 foot (ft.)
3 feet = 1 yard (yd)
5½ yards = 1 rod (rd), pole, or perch (16½ ft.)
40 rods = 1 furlong (fur) = 220 yds = 660 ft.
8 furlongs = 1 statute mile (mi.) = 1,760 yds
  = 5,280 ft.
3 land miles = 1 league
5,280 feet = 1 statute or land mile
6,076.11549 feet = 1 international nautical mile

Area Measure

144 square inches = 1 sq ft.
9 square feet = 1 sq yd = 1,296 sq in.
30¼ square yards = 1 sq rd = 272¼ sq ft.
160 square rods = 1 acre = 4,840 sq yds
  = 43,560 sq ft.
640 acres = 1 sq mi.
1 mile square = 1 section (of land)
6 miles square = 1 township = 36 sections
  = 36 sq mi.

Cubic Measure

1,728 cubic inches = 1 cu ft.
27 cubic feet = 1 cu yd

Liquid Measure

When necessary to distinguish the liquid pint or quart from the dry pint or quart, the word "liquid" or the abbreviation "liq" should be used in combination with the name or abbreviation of the liquid unit.

4 gills (gi) = 1 pint (pt) (= 28.875 cu in.)
2 pints = 1 quart (qt) (= 57.75 cu in.)
4 quarts = 1 gallon (gal) (= 231 cu in.)
  = 8 pts = 32 gills

Apothecaries' Fluid Measure

60 minims (min.) = 1 fluid dram (fl dr) (= 0.2256 cu in.)
8 fluid drams = 1 fluid ounce (fl oz) (= 1.8047 cu in.)
16 fluid ounces = 1 pt (= 28.875 cu in.) = 128 fl drs
2 pints = 1 qt (= 57.75 cu in.) = 32 fl oz
  = 256 fl drs
4 quarts = 1 gal (= 231 cu in.) = 128 fl oz
  = 1,024 fl drs

Avoirdupois Weight

When necessary to distinguish the avoirdupois dram from the apothecaries' dram, or to distinguish the avoirdupois dram or ounce from the fluid dram or ounce, or to distinguish the avoirdupois ounce or pound from the troy or apothecaries' ounce or pound, the word "avoirdupois" or the abbreviation "avdp" should be used in combination with the name or abbreviation of the avoirdupois unit. (The "grain" is the same in avoirdupois, troy, and apothecaries' weights.)

$27^{11}/_{32}$ grains = 1 dram (dr)
16 drams = 1 oz = $437^{1}/_{2}$ grains
16 ounces = 1 lb = 256 drams = 7,000 grains
100 pounds = 1 hundredweight (cwt)[1]
20 hundredweights = 1 ton (tn) = 2,000 lbs[1]

In "gross" or "long" measure, the following values are recognized:

112 pounds = 1 gross or long cwt[1]
20 gross or long hundredweights = 1 gross or long ton
= 2,240 lbs[1]

1. When the terms "hundredweight" and "ton" are used unmodified, they are commonly understood to mean the 100-pound hundredweight and the 2,000-pound ton, respectively; these units may be designated "net" or "short" when necessary to distinguish them from the corresponding units in gross or long measure.

Dry Measure

When necessary to distinguish the dry pint or quart from the liquid pint or quart, the word "dry" should be used in combination with the name or abbreviation of the dry unit.

2 pints = 1 qt (= 67.2006 cu in.)
8 quarts = 1 peck (pk) (= 537.605 cu in.) = 16 pts
4 pecks = 1 bushel (bu) (= 2,150.42 cu in.) = 32 qts

Apothecaries' Weight

20 grains = 1 scruple (s ap)
3 scruples = 1 dram apothecaries' (dr ap)
= 60 grains
8 drams apothecaries' = 1 ounce apothecaries' (oz ap)
= 24 scruples = 480 grains
12 ounces apothecaries' = 1 pound apothecaries' (lb ap)
= 96 drams apothecaries'
= 288 scruples
= 5,760 grains

Units of Circular Measure

Second (″) = —
Minute (′) = 60 seconds
Degree (°) = 60 minutes
Right angle = 90 degrees
Straight angle = 180 degrees
Circle = 360 degrees

Troy Weight

24 grains = 1 pennyweight (dwt)
20 pennyweights = 1 ounce troy (oz t) = 480 grains
12 ounces troy = 1 pound troy (lb t)
= 240 pennyweights
= 5,760 grains

Gunter's or Surveyor's Chain Measure

7.92 inches = 1 link (li)
100 links = 1 chain (ch) = 4 rods = 66 ft.
80 chains = 1 statute mile = 320 rods = 5,280 ft.

The International System (Metric)

Source: Department of Commerce, National Bureau of Standards.

The International System of Units is a modernized version of the metric system, established by international agreement, that provides a logical and interconnected framework for all measurements in science, industry, and commerce. The system is built on a foundation of seven basic units, and all other units are derived from them. (Use of metric weights and measures was legalized in the United States in 1866, and our customary units of weights and measures are defined in terms of the meter and kilogram.)

Length. Meter. Up until 1983, the meter was defined as 1,650,763.73 wavelengths in a vacuum of the orange-red line of the spectrum of krypton-86. Since then, it is equal to the distance traveled by light in a vacuum in 1/299,792,45 of a second.

Time. Second. The second is defined as the duration of 9,192,631,770 cycles of the radiation associated with a specified transition of the cesium-133 atom.

Mass. Kilogram. The standard for the kilogram is a cylinder of platinum-iridium alloy kept by the International Bureau of Weights and Measures at Paris. A duplicate at the National Bureau of Standards serves as the mass standard for the United States. The kilogram is the only base unit still defined by a physical object.

Temperature. Kelvin. The kelvin is defined as the fraction 1/273.16 of the thermodynamic temperature of the triple point of water; that is, the point at which water forms an interface of solid, liquid, and vapor. This is defined as 0.01°C on the Centigrade or Celsius scale and 32.02°F on the Fahrenheit scale. The temperature 0 K is called "absolute zero."

Electric Current. Ampere. The ampere is defined as that current that, if maintained in each of two long parallel wires separated by one meter in free space, would produce a force between the two wires (due to their magnetic fields) of 2×10^{-7} newton for each meter of length. (A newton is the unit of force that when applied to one kilogram mass would experience an acceleration of one meter per second per second.)

Luminous Intensity. Candela. The candela is defined as the luminous intensity of 1/600,000 of a square meter of a cavity at the temperature of freezing platinum (2,042°K).

Amount of Substance. Mole. The mole is the amount of substance of a system that contains as many elementary entities as there are atoms in 0.012 kilogram of carbon-12.

Tables of Metric Weights and Measures

Linear Measure

10 millimeters (mm) = 1 centimeter (cm)	
10 centimeters = 1 decimeter (dm)	= 100 millimeters
10 decimeters = 1 meter (m)	= 1,000 millimeters
10 meters = 1 dekameter (dam)	
10 dekameters = 1 hectometer (hm)	= 100 meters
10 hectometers = 1 kilometer (km)	= 1,000 meters

Volume Measure

10 milliliters (ml) = 1 centiliter (cl)	
10 centiliters = 1 deciliter (dl)	= 100 milliliters
10 deciliters = 1 liter (l)	= 1,000 milliliters
10 liters = 1 dekaliter (dal)	
10 dekaliters = 1 hectoliter (hl)	= 100 liters
10 hectoliters = 1 kiloliter (kl)	= 1,000 liters

Area Measure

100 square millimeters (mm^2) = 1 sq centimeter (cm^2)
10,000 square centimeters = 1 sq meter (m^2)
= 1,000,000 sq millimeters
100 square meters = 1 are (a)
100 ares = 1 hectare (ha)
= 10,000 sq meters
100 hectares = 1 sq kilometer (km^2)
= 1,000,000 sq meters

Cubic Measure

1,000 cubic millimeters (mm^3) = 1 cu centimeter (cm^3)
1,000 cubic centimeters = 1 cu decimeter (dm^3)
= 1,000,000 cu millimeters
1,000 cubic decimeters = 1 cu meter (m^3)
= 1 stere
= 1,000,000 cu centimeters
= 1,000,000,000 cu millimeters

Weight

10 milligrams (mg) = 1 centigram (cg)	
10 centigrams = 1 decigram (dg)	= 100 milligrams
10 decigrams = 1 gram (g)	= 1,000 milligrams
10 grams = 1 dekagram (dag)	

10 dekagrams = 1 hectogram (hg)	= 100 grams
10 hectograms = 1 kilogram (kg)	= 1,000 grams
1,000 kilograms = 1 metric ton (t)	

Metric and U.S. Equivalents

1 angstrom[1] (light wave measurement)	0.1 nanometer 0.000 000 1 millimeter 0.000 000 004 inch
1 cable's length	120 fathoms 720 feet 219.456 meters
1 centimeter	0.3937 inch
1 decimeter	3.937 inches
1 dekameter	32.808 feet
1 fathom	6 feet 1.8288 meters
1 foot	0.3048 meter
1 furlong	10 chains (surveyor's) 660 feet 220 yards ⅛ statute mile 201.168 meters
1 inch	2.54 centimeters
1 kilometer	0.621 mile
1 league (land)	3 statute miles 4.828 kilometers

1 meter	39.37 inches 1.094 yards
1 micrometer	0.001 millimeter 0.000 039 37 inch
1 mil	0.001 inch 0.025 4 millimeter
1 mile (statute or land)	5,280 feet 1.609 kilometers
1 mile (nautical international)	1.852 kilometers 1.151 statute miles 0.999 U.S. nautical miles
1 millimeter	0.03937 inch
1 nanometer	0.001 micrometer or 0.000 000 039 37 inch
1 point (typography)	0.013 837 inch 1/72 inch (approximately) 0.351 millimeter
1 rod, pole, or perch	16½ feet 5.0292 meters
1 yard	0.9144 meter

Areas or Surfaces

1 acre	43,560 square feet 4,840 square yards 0.405 hectare
1 are	119.599 square yards 0.025 acre
1 hectare	2.471 acres
1 square centimeter	0.155 square inch
1 square decimeter	15.5 square inches
1 square foot	929.030 square centimeters
1 square inch	6.4516 square centimeters

1 square kilometer	0.386 square mile 247.105 acres
1 square meter	1.196 square yards 10.764 square feet
1 square mile	258.999 hectares
1 square millimeter	0.002 square inch
1 square rod, square pole or square perch	25.293 square meters
1 square yard	0.836 square meters

Capacities or Volumes

1 barrel, liquid	31 to 42 gallons[2]		1 quart, liquid (U.S.)	57.75 cubic inches 0.946 liter 0.833 British quart
1 bushel (U.S.) struck measure[3]	2,150.42 cubic inches 35.238 liters		1 quart (British)	69.354 cubic inches 1.032 U.S. dry quarts 1.201 U.S. liquid quarts
1 bushel, heaped (U.S.)	2,747.715 cubic inches 1.278 bushels, struck measure[4]		1 tablespoon, measuring	3 teaspoons 4 fluid drams ½ fluid ounce
1 cord (firewood)	128 cubic feet		1 teaspoon, measuring	⅓ tablespoon 1⅓ fluid drams
1 cubic centimeter	0.061 cubic inch		1 carat	200 milligrams 3.086 grains
1 cubic decimeter	61.024 cubic inches			
1 cubic foot	7.481 gallons 28.316 cubic decimeters		1 dram, apothecaries'	60 grains 3.888 grams
1 cubic inch	0.554 fluid ounce 4.433 fluid drams 16.387 cubic centimeters		1 dram, avoirdupois	27 1/32 (=27.344) grains 1.772 grams
1 cubic meter	1.308 cubic yards		1 grain	64.798 91 milligrams
1 cubic yard	0.765 cubic meter		1 gram	15.432 grains 0.035 avoirdupois ounce
1 cup, measuring	8 fluid ounces ½ liquid pint		1 kilogram	2.205 pounds
1 dram, fluid or liquid (U.S.)	⅛ fluid ounces 0.226 cubic inch 3.697 milliliters 1.041 British fluid drachms		1 microgram (μg—the Greek letter mu in combination with the letter g)	0.000 001 gram
1 dekaliter	2.642 gallons 1.135 pecks		1 milligram	0.015 grain
1 gallon (U.S.)	231 cubic inches 3.785 liters 0.833 British gallon 128 U.S. fluid ounces		1 ounce, avoirdupois	437.5 grains 0.911 troy or apothecaries' ounce 28.350 grams
1 gallon (British Imperial)	277.42 cubic inches 1.201 U.S. gallons 4.546 liters 160 British fluid ounces		1 ounce, troy or apothecaries'	480 grains 1.097 avoirdupois ounces 31.103 grams
1 hectoliter	26.418 gallons 2.838 bushels		1 pennyweight	1.555 grams
1 liter	1.057 liquid quarts 0.908 dry quart 61.024 cubic inches		1 point	0.01 carat 2 milligrams
1 milliliter	0.271 fluid dram 16.231 minims 0.061 cubic inch		1 pound, avoirdupois	7,000 grains 1.215 troy or apothecaries' pounds 453.592 37 grams
1 ounce, fluid or liquid (U.S.)	1.805 cubic inch 29.574 milliliters 1.041 British fluid ounces		1 pound, troy or apothecaries'	5,760 grains 0.823 avoirdupois pound 373.242 grams
1 peck	8.810 liters		1 ton, gross or long[5]	2,240 pounds 1.12 net tons 1.016 metric tons
1 pint, dry	33.600 cubic inches 0.551 liter		1 ton, metric	2,204.623 pounds 0.984 gross ton 1.102 net tons
1 pint, liquid	28.875 cubic inches 0.473 liter		1 ton, net or short	2,000 pounds 0.893 gross ton 0.907 metric ton
1 quart, dry (U.S.)	67.201 cubic inches 1.101 liters 0.969 British quart			

1. The angstrom is basically defined as 10^{-10} meter. 2. There is a variety of "barrels" established by law or usage. For example, federal taxes on fermented liquors are based on a barrel of 31 gallons; many state laws fix the "barrel for liquids" at 31½ gallons; one state fixes a 36-gallon barrel for cistern measurement; federal law recognizes a 40-gallon barrel for "proof spirits"; by custom, 42 gallons compose a barrel of crude oil or petroleum products for statistical purposes, and this equivalent is recognized "for liquids" by four states. 3. "Struck measure" refers to a struck, or level, bushel. It is the only official bushel measure in the UK. 4. Frequently recognized as 1¼ bushels, struck measure. 5. The gross or long ton is used commercially in the United States to only a limited extent, usually in restricted industrial fields. These units are the same as the British "ton."

Definitions of Gold Terminology

The term "fineness" defines a gold content in parts per thousand. For example, a gold nugget containing 885 parts of pure gold, 100 parts of silver, and 15 parts of copper would be considered 885-fine.

The word "karat" indicates the proportion of solid gold in an alloy based on a total of 24 parts. Thus, 14-karat (14K) gold indicates a composition of 14 parts of gold and 10 parts of other metals.

The term "gold-filled" is used to describe articles of jewelry made of base metal that are covered on one or more surfaces with a layer of gold alloy. No article having a gold alloy portion of less than one twentieth by weight may be marked "gold-filled." Articles may be marked "rolled gold plate" provided the proportional fraction and fineness designations are also shown.

Electroplated jewelry items carrying at least 7 millionths of an inch of gold on significant surfaces may be labeled "electroplate." Plate thicknesses less than this may be marked "gold-flashed" or "gold-washed."

Bolts and Screws: Conversion from Fractions of an Inch to Millimeters

Inch	mm	Inch	mm	Inch	mm	Inch	mm
1/64	0.40	17/64	6.75	33/64	13.10	49/64	19.45
1/32	0.79	9/32	7.14	17/32	13.50	25/32	19.84
3/64	1.19	19/64	7.54	35/64	13.90	51/64	20.24
1/16	1.59	5/16	7.94	9/16	14.29	13/16	20.64
5/64	1.98	21/64	8.33	37/64	14.69	53/64	21.03
3/32	2.38	11/32	8.73	19/32	15.08	27/32	21.43
7/64	2.78	23/64	9.13	39/64	15.48	55/64	21.83
1/8	3.18	3/8	9.53	5/8	15.88	7/8	22.23
9/64	3.57	25/64	9.92	41/64	16.27	57/64	22.62
5/32	3.97	13/32	10.32	21/32	16.67	29/32	23.02
11/64	4.37	27/64	10.72	43/64	17.06	59/64	23.42
3/16	4.76	7/16	11.11	11/16	17.46	15/16	23.81
13/64	5.16	29/64	11.51	45/64	17.86	61/64	24.21
7/32	5.56	15/32	11.91	23/32	18.26	31/32	24.61
15/64	5.95	31/64	12.30	47/64	18.65	63/64	25.00
1/4	6.35	1/2	12.70	3/4	19.05	1	25.40

Cooking Measurement Equivalents

1 tablespoon (tbsp) = 3 teaspoons (tsp)

1/16 cup = 1 tablespoon

1/8 cup = 2 tablespoons

1/6 cup = 2 tablespoons + 2 teaspoons

1/4 cup = 4 tablespoons

1/3 cup = 5 tablespoons + 1 teaspoon

3/8 cup = 6 tablespoons

1/2 cup = 8 tablespoons

2/3 cup = 10 tablespoons + 2 teaspoons

3/4 cup = 12 tablespoons

1 cup = 48 teaspoons

1 cup = 16 tablespoons

8 fluid ounces (fl oz) = 1 cup

1 pint (pt) = 2 cups

1 quart (qt) = 2 pints

4 cups = 1 quart

1 gallon (gal) = 4 quarts

16 ounces (oz) = 1 pound (lb)

1 milliliter (ml) = 1 cubic centimeter (cc)

1 inch (in) = 2.54 centimeters (cm)

Source: United States Dept. of Agriculture (USDA).

U.S.–Metric Cooking Conversions

U.S. to Metric

Capacity		Weight	
1/5 teaspoon	1 milliliter	1 oz	28 grams
1 teaspoon	5 ml	1 pound	454 grams
1 tablespoon	15 ml		
1 fluid oz	30 ml		
1/5 cup	47 ml		
1 cup	237 ml		
2 cups (1 pint)	473 ml		
4 cups (1 quart)	.95 liter		
4 quarts (1 gal.)	3.8 liters		

Metric to U.S.

Capacity		Weight	
1 milliliter	1/5 teaspoon	1 gram	.035 ounce
5 ml	1 teaspoon	100 grams	3.5 ounces
15 ml	1 tablespoon	500 grams	1.10 pounds
100 ml	3.4 fluid oz	1 kilogram	2.205 pounds
			= 35 ounces
240 ml	1 cup		
1 liter	34 fluid oz		
	= 4.2 cups		
	= 2.1 pints		
	= 1.06 quarts		
	= 0.26 gallon		

Prefixes and Multiples

Prefix	Symbol	Equivalent	Multiple/submultiple	Prefix	Symbol	Equivalent	Multiple/submultiple
yocto	y	septillionth part	10^{-24}	deka	da	tenfold	10
zepto	z	sextillionth part	10^{-21}	hecto	h	hundredfold	10^2
atto	a	quintillionth part	10^{-18}	kilo	k	thousandfold	10^3
femto	f	quadrillionth part	10^{-15}	mega	M	millionfold	10^6
pico	p	trillionth part	10^{-12}	giga	G	billionfold	10^9
nano	n	billionth part	10^{-9}	tera	T	trillionfold	10^{12}
micro	μ	millionth part	10^{-6}	peta	P	quadrillionfold	10^{15}
milli	m	thousandth part	10^{-3}	exa	E	quintillionfold	10^{18}
centi	c	hundredth part	10^{-2}	zetta	Z	sextillionfold	10^{21}
deci	d	tenth part	10^{-1}	yotta	Y	septillionfold	10^{24}

Common Formulas

CIRCUMFERENCE

Circle: $C = \pi d$, in which π is 3.1416 and d the diameter.

AREA

Triangle: $A = \dfrac{ab}{2}$, in which a is the base and b the height.

Square: $A = a^2$, in which a is one of the sides.

Rectangle: $A = ab$, in which a is the base and b the height.

Trapezoid: $A = \dfrac{h(a+b)}{2}$, in which h is the height, a the longer parallel side, and b the shorter.

Regular pentagon: $A = 1.720a^2$, in which a is one of the sides.

Regular hexagon: $A = 2.598a^2$, in which a is one of the sides.

Regular octagon: $A = 4.828a^2$, in which a is one of the sides.

Circle: $A = \pi r^2$, in which π is 3.1416 and r the radius.

VOLUME

Cube: $V = a^3$, in which a is one of the edges.

Rectangular prism: $V = abc$, in which a is the length, b the width, and c the depth.

Pyramid: $V = \dfrac{Ah}{3}$, in which A is the area of the base and h the height.

Cylinder: $V = \pi r^2 h$, in which π is 3.1416, r the radius of the base, and h the height.

Cone: $V = \dfrac{\pi r^2 h}{3}$, in which π is 3.1416, r the radius of the base, and h the height.

Sphere: $V = \dfrac{4 \pi r^3}{3}$, in which π is 3.1416 and r the radius.

TEMPERATURE SCALES

Degrees Fahrenheit to Degrees Celsius:
$$T_C = \frac{5}{9} (T_F - 32)$$

Degrees Celsius to Degrees Fahrenheit:
$$T_F = \frac{9}{5} T_C + 32$$

Degrees Celsius to Kelvins:
$$T_K = T_C + 273.15$$

MISCELLANEOUS

Distance in feet traveled by falling body:
$d = 16t^2$, in which t is the time in seconds.

Speed of sound in feet per second through any given temperature of air:
$V = \dfrac{1087 \sqrt{273 + t}}{16.52}$, in which t is the temperature Celsius.

Cost in cents of operation of electrical device:
$C = \dfrac{Wtc}{1000}$, in which W is the number of watts, t the time in hours, and c the cost in cents per kilowatt-hour.

Conversion of matter into energy (Einstein's Theorem): $E = mc^2$, in which E is the energy in ergs, m the mass of the matter in grams, and c the speed of light in centimeters per second:
$$(c^2 = 9 \times 10^{20})$$

Decimal Equivalents of Common Fractions

½	.5000	¹⁄₁₀	.1000	²⁄₇	.2857	³⁄₁₁	.2727	⁵⁄₉	.5556	⁷⁄₁₁	.6364
⅓	.3333	¹⁄₁₁	.0909	²⁄₉	.2222	⅘	.8000	⁵⁄₁₁	.4545	⁷⁄₁₂	.5833
¼	.2500	¹⁄₁₂	.0833	²⁄₁₁	.1818	⁴⁄₇	.5714	⁵⁄₁₂	.4167	⁸⁄₉	.8889
⅕	.2000	¹⁄₁₆	.0625	¾	.7500	⁴⁄₉	.4444	⁶⁄₇	.8571	⁸⁄₁₁	.7273
⅙	.1667	¹⁄₃₂	.0313	⅗	.6000	⁴⁄₁₁	.3636	⁶⁄₁₁	.5455	⁹⁄₁₀	.9000
¹⁄₇	.1429	¹⁄₆₄	.0156	³⁄₇	.4286	⅚	.8333	⅞	.8750	⁹⁄₁₁	.8182
⅛	.1250	⅔	.6667	⅜	.3750	⁵⁄₇	.7143	⁷⁄₉	.7778	¹⁰⁄₁₁	.9091
⅑	.1111	⅖	.4000	³⁄₁₀	.3000	⅝	.6250	⁷⁄₁₀	.7000	¹¹⁄₁₂	.9167

First Aid for Crossword Puzzlers

We cannot begin to list all the odd words you might encounter in your daily and Sunday crossword puzzles, for such words run into the thousands. But we have tried to include those that turn up most frequently, as well as many others that should be of help to you when you are unable to go any further.

We do not guarantee that the definitions in your puzzle will be exactly the same as ours, although we have checked every word with a standard dictionary and have followed its definition.

In nearly every case, we have used as the key word the principal noun of the definition, rather than any adjective, adjective phrase, or noun used as an adjective. And, to simplify your searching, we have grouped the words according to the number of spaces you have to fill.

Words of Two Letters

Ambary, DA
And (French, Latin), ET
Article (Arabic), AL
  (French), LA, LE, UN
  (Spanish), EL, LA, UN
At the (French), AU
  (Spanish), AL
Behold, LO
Bird: Hawaiian, OO
Birthplace: Abraham's, UR
Bone, OS
Buddha, FO
Butterfly: Peacock, IO
Champagne, AY
Chaos, NU
Chief: Burmese, BO
  Siamese, AT
Coin: Roman, AS
Concerning, RE
Dialect: Chinese, WU
Double (Egy. relig.), KA
Drama: Japanese, NO
Egg (comb. form), OO
Esker, OS

Eye (Scottish), EE
Factor: Amplification, MU
Fifty (Greek), NU
Fish: Carplike, ID
Force, OD
Forty (Greek), MU
From (French, Latin, Spanish), DE
  (Latin prefix), AB
From the (French), DU
God: Babylonian, EA, ZU
  Egyptian sun, RA
  Hindu unknown, KA
  Semitic, EL
Goddess: Babylonian, AI
  Greek Earth, GE
Gold (heraldry), OR
Gulf: Arctic, OB
Heart (Egy. relig.), AB
Indian: South American, GE
King: Of Bashan, OG
Language: Artificial, RO
  Assamese, AO
Lava: Hawaiian, AA

Letter: Greek, MU, NU, PI, XI
  Hebrew, HE, PE
Lily: Palm, TI
Measure: Chinese, HO, HU, KO, LI, MU, PU, TO, TU
  Japanese, GO, JO, MO, RI, SE, TO
  Netherlands, EL
  Portuguese, PE
  Siamese, WA
  Swedish, AM
  Type, EM, EN
  Vietnamese, LY
Monk: Buddhist, BO
Month: Jewish, AB
Mouth, OS
Mulberry: Indian, AL
Native: Burmese, WA
Note: Of scale, DO, FA, MI, LA, RE, TI
Of (French, Latin, Spanish), DE
Of the (French), DU

One (Scottish), AE
Pagoda: Chinese, TA
Plant: East Indian fiber, DA
Ridge: Sandy, AS, OS
River: Russian, OB
Sloth: Three-toed, AI
Soul (Egy. relig.), BA
Sound: Hindu mystic, OM
Suffix: Comparative, ER
To the: French, AU
  Spanish, AL
Tree: Buddhist sacred, BO
Tribe: Assamese, AO
Type: Jumbled, PI
Weight: Chinese, LI
  Danish, ES
  Japanese, MO
  Roman, AS
  Vietnamese, TA
Whirlwind: Faeroe Is., OE
Yes (German), JA
  (Italian, Spanish), SI
  (Russian), DA

Words of Three Letters

Adherent, IST
Again, BIS
Age, ERA
Antelope: African, GNU, KOB
Apricot: Japanese, UME
Article (German), DAS, DEM, DEN, DER, DES, DIE, EIN
  (French), LES, UNE
  (Spanish), LAS, LOS, UNA
Banana: Polynesian, FEI
Barge, HOY
Bass: African, IYO
Beak, NEB, NIB
Beard: Grain, AWN
Beetle: June, DOR
Being, ENS
Berry: Hawthorn, HAW
Beverage: Hawaiian, AVA
Bird: Australian, EMU
  Crowlike, JAY
  Extinct, MOA
  Fabulous, ROC
  Frigate, IWA
  Parson, POE, TUE, TUI
  Sea, AUK
Blackbird, ANI, ANO
Born, NEE
Bronze: Roman, AES
Bugle: Yellow, IVA
By way of, VIA
Canton: Swiss, URI
Cap: Turkish, FEZ
Catnip, NEP
Character: In "Faerie Queene," UNA
Coin (Money of account):
  Afghan, PUL
  Albanian, LEK
  Bulgarian, LEV, LEW

French, ECU, SOU
Guyanese, BIT
Indian, PIE
Japanese, SEN, YEN
Korean, WON
Lithuanian, LIT
Macao, Timor, AVO
Palestinian, MIL
Persian, PUL
Peruvian, SOL
Rumanian, BAN, LEU, LEY
Scandinavian, ORE
Siamese, ATT
Collection: Facts, ANA
Commune: Belgian, ANS, ATH
  Netherlands, EDE, EPE
Community: Russian, MIR
Constellation: Southern, ARA
Contraction: Poetic, EEN, EER, OER
Covering: Apex of roof, EPI
Crab: Fiddler, UCA
Crag: Rocky, TOR
Cry: Crow, rook, raven, CAW
Cup: Wine, AMA
Cymbal, Oriental, TAL, ZEL
Disease: Silkworm, UJI
Division: Danish territorial, AMT
  Geologic, EON
Doctrine, ISM
Dowry, DOT
Dry (French), SEC
Dynasty: Chinese, CHI, HAN, SUI, WEI, YIN
Eagle: Sea, ERN
Earth (comb. form), GEO
Egg: Louse, NIT
Eggs: Fish, ROE
Emmet, ANT

Enzyme, ASE
Equal (comb. form), ISO
Extension: building, ELL
Far (comb. form), TEL
Farewell, AVE
Fiber: Palm, TAL
Finial, EPI
Fish: Carplike, IDE
  Pikelike, GAR
Flatfish, DAB
Fleur-de-lis, LIS, LYS
Food: Hawaiian, POI
Formerly, NEE
Friend (French), AMI
Game: Card, LOO
Garment: Camel-hair, ABA
Gateway, DAR
Gazelle: Tibetan, GOA
Genus: Ducks, AIX
  Grasses, POA
  Grasses (maize), ZEA
  Herbs or shrubs, IVA
  Lizards, UTA
  Rodents (incl. house mice), MUS
  Ruminants (incl. cattle), BOS
  Swine, SUS
Gibbon: Malay, LAR
God: Assyrian, SIN
  Babylonian, ABU, ANU, BEL, HEA, SIN, UTU
  Irish sea, LER
  Phrygian, MEN
  Polynesian, ORO
Goddess: Babylonian, AYA
  Etruscan, UNI
  Hindu, SRI, UMA, VAC
  Teutonic, RAN

Governor: Algerian, DEY
  Turkish, BEY
Grampus, ORC
Grape, UVA
Grass: Meadow, POA
Gypsy, ROM
Hail, AVE
Hare: Female, DOE
Hawthorn, HAW
Hay: Spread for drying, TED
Herb: Japanese, UDO
  Perennial, PIA
  Used for blue dye, WAD
Herd: Whales, GAM, POD
Hero: Spanish, CID
High (music), ALT
Honey (pharm.), MEL
Humorist: American, ADE
I (Latin), EGO
I love (Latin), AMO
Indian: Algonquin, FOX, SAC, WEA
  Chimakuan, HOH
  Keresan, SIA
  Mayan, MAM
  Shoshonean, UTE
  Siouan, KAW, OTO
  South American, ITE, ONA, URO, URU, YAO
  Tierra del Fuego, ONA
  Wakashan, AHT
Ingot, PIG
Inlet: Narrow, RIA
Island: Cyclades, IOS
  Dodecanese, COS, KOS
  (French), ILE
  River, AIT
Jackdaw, DAW

John (Gaelic), IAN
Keelbill, ANI, ANO
Kiln, OST
King: British legendary, LUD
Kobold, NIS
Lace: To make, TAT
Lamprey, EEL
Language: Artificial, IDO
  Bantu, ILA
  Siamese, LAO, TAI
Leaf: Palm, OLA, OLE
Leaving, ORT
Left: Cause to turn, HAW
Letter: Greek, CHI, ETA, PHI,
  PSI, RHO, TAU
  Hebrew, MEM, NUN, SIN,
  TAV, VAU
Lettuce, COS
Life (comb. form), BIO
Lily: Palm, TOI
Lizard, EFT
Louse: Young, NIT
Love (Anglo-Irish), GRA
Lute: Oriental, TAR
Macaw: Brazilian, ARA
Marble, TAW
Match: Shooting (French), TIR
Meadow, LEA
Measure: Abyssinian, TAT
  Algerian, PIK
  Arabian, DEN, SAA
  Belgian, VAT
  Bulgarian, OKA, OKE
  Chinese, FEN, TOU, YIN
  Cloth, ELL
  Cyprus, OKA, OKE, PIK
  Czech, LAN, SAH
  Danish, FOD, MIL, POT
  Dominican Republic, ONA
  Dutch, old, AAM
  East Indian, KIT
  Egyptian, APT, HEN, PIK,
  ROB
  Electric, MHO, OHM
  Energy, ERG
  English, PIN
  Estonian, TUN
  French, POT
  German, AAM
  Greek, PIK
  Hebrew, CAB, HIN, KOR,
  LOG
  Hungarian, AKO
  Icelandic, FET
  Indian, GAZ, GUZ, JOW,
  KOS
  Japanese, BOO, CHO, KEN,
  RIN, SHO, SUN, TAN
  Malabar, ADY
  Metric (land), ARE
  Netherlands, KAN, KOP,
  MUD, VAT, ZAK
  Norwegian, FOT, POT
  Persian, GAZ, GUZ, MOU,
  ZAR, ZER
  Polish, CAL
  Rangoon, DHA, LAN
  Roman, PES, URN
  Russian, FUT, LOF
  Scottish, COP

Siamese, KEN, NIU, RAI,
  SAT, SEN, SOK, WAH, YOT
Somaliland, TOP
Spanish, PIE
Straits Settlements, PAU,
  TUN
Swedish, ALN, FOT, MIL,
  REF, TUM
Swiss, POT
Tunisian, SAA
Turkish, OKA, OKE, PIK
Vietnamese, GON, MAU,
  NGU, VUO, SAO, TAO, TAT
Wire, MIL
Württemberg, IMI
Yarn, LEA
Yugoslav, OKA, RIF
Milk, LAC
Milkfish, AWA
Moccasin, PAC
Money: Yap stone, FEI
Money of Account (also Coin):
  Anglo-Saxon, ORA, ORE
  French, SOU
  Indian, LAC
  Japanese, RIN
  Oman, GAJ
  Virgin Islands, BIT
Monkey: Capuchin, SAI
Morsel, ORT
Mother: Peer Gynt's, ASE
Mountain: Asia Minor, IDA
Mulberry: Indian, AAL, ACH,
  AWL
Muttonbird: New Zealand, OII
Nahoor, SNA
Native: Mindanao, ATA
Neckpiece, BOA
Newt, EFT
No (Scottish), NAE
Note: Guido's highest, ELA
  Of scale, SOL
Nursemaid: Oriental, AMA, IYA
Ocher: Yellow, SIL
One (Scottish), YIN
Ornament: Pagoda, TEE
Oven: Polynesian, UMU
Ox: Tibetan, YAK
Pagoda: Chinese, TAA
Parrot: Hawk, HIA
  New Zealand, KEA
Part: Footlike, PES
Particle: Electrified, ION
Pasha, DEY
Pass: Mountain, COL
Paste: Rice, AME
Pea: Indian split, DAL
Peasant: Philippine, TAO
Penpoint, NEB, NIB
Piece out, EKE
Pigeon, NUN
Pine: Textile screw, ARA
Pistol (slang), GAT
Pit: Baking, IMU
Plant: Pepper, AVA
Play: By Capek, RUR
Poem: Old French, DIT
Porgy: Japanese, TAI
Priest: Biblical high, ELI
Prince: Ethiopian, RAS

Pseudonym: Dickens', BOZ
Queen: Fairy, MAB
Quince: Bengal, BEL
Record: Ship's, LOG
Refuse: Flax (Scottish), PAB,
  POB
Resin, LAC
Resort, SPA
Revolver (slang), GAT
Right: Cause to turn, GEE
River: Scottish or English, DEE
  (Spanish), RIO
  Swiss, AAR
Room: Harem, ODA
Rootstock: Fern, ROI
Rose (Persian), GUL
Ruff: Female, REE
Rule: Indian, RAJ
Sailor, GOB, TAR
Saint: Female (abbr.), STE
  Islamic, PIR
Salt, SAL
Sash: Japanese, OBI
Scrap, ORT
Seed: Poppy, MAW
  Small, PIP
Self, EGO
Serpent: Vedic sky, AHI
Sesame, TIL
Sheep: Female, EWE
  Indian, SHA
  Male, RAM
Sheepfold (Scottish), REE
Shelter, LEE
Shield, ECU
Shooting match (French), TIR
Shrew: European, ERD
Shrub: Evergreen, YEW
Silkworm, ERI
Snake, ASP, BOA
Soak, RET
Son-in-law: Mohammed's, ALI
Sorrel: Wood, OCA
Spade: Long, narrow, LOY
Spirit: Malignant, KER
Spot: Playing-card, PIP
Spread for drying, TED
Spring: Mineral, SPA
Sprite: Water, NIX
Statesman: Japanese, ITO
Stern: Toward, AFT
Stomach: Bird's, MAW
Street (French), RUE
Summer (French), ETE
Sun, SOL
Swamp, BOG, FEN
Swan: Male, COB
Tea: Chinese, CHA
Temple: Shinto, SHA
Thing (law), RES
Title: Etruscan, LAR
  Monk's, FRA
  Portuguese, DOM
  Spanish, DON
  Turkish, AGA, BEY
Tool: Cutting, ADZ, AXE
  Mining, GAD
  Piercing, AWL
Tree: Candlenut, AMA
  Central American, EBO

East Indian, SAJ, SAL
Evergreen, YEW
Hawaiian, KOA, KOU
Indian, BEL, DAR
Linden, LIN
New Zealand, AKE
Philippine, DAO, TUA, TUI
Rubber, ULE
South American, APA
Tribe: New Zealand, ATI
Turmeric, REA
Twice, BIS
Twin: Siamese, ENG
Uncle (dialect), EAM, EME
Veil: Chalice, AER, AIR
Vessel: Wine, AMA
Vestment: Ecclesiastical, ALB
Vetch: Bitter, ERS
Victorfish, AKU
Vine: New Zealand, AKA
  Philippine, IYO
Wallaba, APA
Wapiti, ELK
Water (French), EAU
Waterfall, LIN
Watering place: Prussian, EMS
Weave: Designating plain,
  UNI
Weight: Bulgarian, OKA, OKE
  Burmese, MOO, VIS
  Chinese, FEN, HAO, KIN,
  SSU, TAN, YIN
  Cyprus, OKA, OKE
  Danish, LOD, ORT, VOG
  East Indian, TJI
  Egyptian, KAT, OKA, OKE
  English, for wool, TOD
  German, LOT
  Greek, MNA, OKA, OKE
  Indian, SER
  Japanese, FUN, KIN, RIN,
  SHI
  Korean, KON
  Malacca, KIP
  Mongolian, LAN
  Netherlands, ONS
  Norwegian, LOD
  Polish, LUT
  Rangoon, PAI
  Roman, BES
  Russian, LOT
  Siamese, BAT, HAP, PAI
  Swedish, ASS, ORT
  Turkish, OKA, OKE
  Vietnamese, CAN
  Yugoslav, OKA, OKE
Whales: Herd, GAM, POD
Wildebeest, GNU
Wing, ALA
Witticism, MOT
Wolframite, CAL
Worm: African, LOA
Wreath: Hawaiian, LEI
Yale, ELI
Yam: Hawaiian, HOI
Yes (French), OUI
Young: Bring forth, EAN
Z (letter), ZED

Words of Four Letters

Aborigine: Borneo, DYAK
Agave, ALOE
Animal: Footless, APOD
Ant: White, ANAI, ANAY
Antelope: African, ASSE, BISA, GUIB,
  KOBA, KUDU, ORYX, POKU, PUKU,
  TOPI, TORA
Apoplexy: Plant, ESCA
Apple, POME
Apricot, ANSU
Ardor, ELAN
Armadillo, APAR, PEBA, PEVA, TATU
Ascetic: Islamic, SUFI
Association: Chinese, TONG

Astronomer: Persian, OMAR
Avatar: Of Vishnu, RAMA
Axillary, ALAR
Band: Horizontal (heraldry), FESS
Barracuda, SPET
Bark: Mulberry, TAPA
Base: Column, DADO
Bearing (heraldry), ORLE
Beer: Russian, KVAS
Beige, ECRU
Being, ESSE
Beverage: Japanese rice, SAKE
Bird: Asian, MINA, MYNA
  Egyptian sacred, IBIS

Extinct, DODO, MAMO
Flightless, KIWI
Gull-like, TERN
Hawaiian, IIWI, MAMO
Parson, KOKO
Unfledged, EYAS
Birds: As class, AVES
Black, EBON
  (French), NOIR
Blackbird: European, MERL
Boat: Flat-bottomed, DORY
Bone: Forearm, ULNA
Bones, OSSA
Box, Japanese, INRO

Bravo (rare), EUGE
Buffalo: Indian wild, ARNA
Bull (Spanish), TORO
Burden, ONUS
Cabbage: Sliced, SLAW
Caliph: Islamic, OMAR
Canoe: Malay, PRAU, PROA
Cap: Military, KEPI
Cape, NESS
Capital: Ancient Irish, TARA
Case: Article, ETUI
Cat: Wild, BALU, EYRA
Chalcedony, SARD
Chamber: Indian ceremonial, KIVA
Channel: Brain, ITER
Cheese: Dutch, EDAM
Chest: Sepulchral stone, CIST
Chieftain: Arab, EMIR
Church: Part of, APSE, NAVE
 (Scottish), KIRK
Claim (law), LIEN
Cluster: Flower, CYME
Coin: Chinese, TAEL, YUAN
 German, MARK
 Indian, ANNA
 Iranian, RIAL
 Italian, LIRA
 Moroccan, OKIA
 Siamese, BAHT
 South American, PESO
 Spanish, DURO, PESO
 Turkish, PARA
Commune: Belgian, AATH
Composition: Musical, OPUS
Compound: Chemical, DIOL
Constellation: Southern, PAVO
Council: Russian, DUMA
Counsel, REDE
Covering: Seed, ARIL
Cross: Egyptian, ANKH
Cry: Bacchanalian, EVOE
Cup (Scottish), TASS
Cupbearer, SAKI
Dagger, DIRK
 Malay, KRIS
Dam: River, WEIR
Dash, ELAN
Date: Roman, IDES
Dawn: Pertaining to, EOAN
Dean: English, INGE
Decay: In fruit, BLET
Deer: Sambar, MAHA
Disease: Skin, ACNE
Disk: Solar, ATEN
Dog: Hunting, ALAN
Drink: Hindu intoxicating, SOMA
Duck, SMEE, SMEW, TEAL
Dynasty: Chinese, CHEN, CHIN, CHOU,
 CHOW, HSIA, MING, SUNG, TANG,
 TSIN
 Mongol, YUAN
Eagle: Biblical, GIER
 Sea, ERNE
Ear: Pertaining to, OTIC
Egyptian: Christian, COPT
Entrance: Mine, ADIT
Esau, EDOM
Escutcheon: Voided, ORLE
Eskers, OSAR
Evergreen: New Zealand, TAWA
Fairy: Persian, PERI
Family: Italian, ESTE
Far (comb. form), TELE
Farewell, VALE
Father (French), PERE
Fennel: Philippine, ANIS
Fever: Malarial, AGUE
Fiber: East Indian, JUTE
Firn, NEVE
Fish: Carplike, DACE
 Hawaiian, ULUA
 Herringlike, SHAD
 Mackerellike, CERO
 Marine, HAKE
 Sea, LING, MERO, OPAH
 Spiny-finned, GOBY

Food: Tropical, TARO
Foot: Metric, IAMB
Formerly, ERST
Founder: Of Carthage, DIDO
France: Southern, MIDI
Furze, ULEX
Gaelic, ERSE
Gaiter, SPAT
Game: Card, FARO, SKAT
Garlic: European wild, MOLY
Garment: Hindu, SARI
 Roman, TOGA
Gazelle, CORA
Gem, JADE, ONYX, OPAL, RUBY
Genus: Amphibians (incl. frogs), RANA
 Amphibians (incl. tree toads), HYLA
 Antelopes, ORYX
 Auks, ALCA, URIA
 Bees, APIS
 Birds (American ostriches), RHEA
 Birds (cranes), CRUS
 Birds (magpies), PICA
 Birds (peacocks), PAVO
 Cetaceans, INIA
 Ducks (incl. mallards), ANAS
 Fishes (burbots), LOTA
 Fishes (incl. bowfins), AMIA
 Geese (snow geese), CHEN
 Gulls, XEMA
 Herbs, ARUM, GEUM
 Insects (water scorpions), NEPA
 Lilies, ALOE
 Mammals (humans), HOMO
 Orchids, DISA
 Owls, ASIO, BUBO, OTUS
 Palms, NIPA
 Sea birds, SULA
 Sheep, OVIS
 Shrubs, Eurasian, ULEX
 Shrubs (hollies), ILEX
 Shrubs (incl. Virginia Willow), ITEA
 Shrubs, tropical, EVEA
 Snakes (sand snakes), ERYX
 Swans, OLOR
 Trees, chocolate, COLA
 Trees (ebony family), MABA
 Trees (incl. maples), ACER
 Trees (olives), OLEA
 Trees, tropical, EVEA
 Turtles, EMYS
Goat: Wild, IBEX, KRAS, TAHR, TAIR,
 THAR
God: Assyrian, ASUR
 Babylonian, ADAD, ADDU, ENKI,
 ENZU, IRRA, NABU, NEBO, UTUG
 Celtic, LLEU, LLEW
 Hindu, AGNI, CIVA, DEVA, DEWA,
 KAMA, RAMA, SIVA, VAYU
 Phrygian, ATYS
 Semitic, BAAL
 Teutonic, HLER
Goddess: Babylonian, ERUA, GULA
 Hawaiian, PELE
 Hindu, DEVI, KALI, SHRI, VACH
Gooseberry: Hawaiian, POHA
Gourd, PEPO
Grafted (heraldry), ENTE
Grandfather (obsolete), AIEL
Grandparents: Pertaining to, AVAL
Grass: Hawaiian, HILO
Gray (French), GRIS
Green (heraldry), VERT
Groom: Indian, SYCE
Half (prefix), DEMI, HEMI, SEMI
Hamlet, DORP
Hammerhead: Part of, PEEN
Handle, ANSA
Harp: Japanese, KOTO
Hartebeest, ASSE, TORA
Hautboy, OBOE
Hawk: Taken from nest (falconry), EYAS
Hearing (law), OYER
Heater: For liquids, ETNA
Herb: Aromatic, ANET, DILL
 Fabulous, MOLY
 Perennial, GEUM, SEGO

Pot, WORT
 Used for blue dye, WADE, WOAD
Hill: Flat-topped, MESA
 Sand, DENE, DUNE
Hoarfrost, RIME
Hog: Immature female, GILT
Holly, ILEX
House: Cow, BYRE
 (Spanish), CASA
Ice: Floating, FLOE
Image, ICON, IKON
Incarnation: Of Vishnu, RAMA
Indian: Algonquin, CREE, SAUK
 Central American, MAYA
 Iroquoian, ERIE
 Mexican, CORA
 Peruvian, CANA, INCA, MORO
 Shoshonean, HOPI
 Siouan, OTOE
 Southwestern, HOPI, PIMA, YUMA,
 ZUNI
Insect: Immature, PUPA
Instrument: Stringed, LUTE, LYRE
Ireland, EIRE, ERIN
Jacket: English, ETON
Jail (British), GAOL
Jar, OLLA
Judge: Islamic, CADI
Juniper: European, CADE
Kiln, OAST, OVEN
King: British legendary, LUDD, NUDD
Kiss, BUSS
Knife: Philippine, BOLO
Koran: Section of, SURA
Laborer: Spanish American, PEON
Lake: Mountain, TARN
 (Scottish), LOCH
Lamp: Miner's, DAVY
Landing place: Indian, GHAT
Language: Buddhist, PALI
 Japanese, AINU
Latvian, LETT
Layer: Of iris, UVEA
Leaf: Palm, OLAY, OLLA
Legislature: Ukrainian, RADA
Lemur, LORI
Leopard, PARD
Let it stand, STET
Letter: Greek, BETA, IOTA, ZETA
 Hebrew, AYIN, BETH, CAPH, KOPH,
 RESH, SHIN, TETH, YODH
 Papal, BULL
Lily, ALOE
Literature: Hindu sacred, VEDA
Lizard, GILA
 Monitor, URAN
Loquat, BIWA
Magistrate: Genoese or Venetian, DOGE
Man (Latin), HOMO
Mark: Omission, DELE
Marmoset: South American, MICO
Meadow: Fertile, VEGA
Measure: Electric, VOLT, WATT
 Force, DYNE
 Hebrew, OMER
 Printing, PICA
 Spanish or Portuguese, VARA
 Swiss land, IMMI
Medley, OLIO
Merganser, SMEW
Milk (French), LAIT
Molding, GULA
 Curved, OGEE
Mongoose: Crab-eating, URVA
Monk: Tibetan, LAMA
Monkey: African, MONA, WAAG
 Ceylonese, MAHA
 Cochin-China, DOUC
 South American, SAKI, TITI
Monkshood, ATIS
Month: Jewish, ADAR, ELUL, IYAR
Mother (French), MERE
Mountain: Thessaly, OSSA
Mouse: Meadow, VOLE
Mythology: Norse, EDDA
Nail (French), CLOU

Native: Philippine, MORO
Nest: Of pheasants, NIDE
Network, RETE
No (German), NEIN
Noble: Islamic, AMIR
Notice: Death, OBIT
Novel: By Zola, NANA
Nursemaid: Oriental AMAH, AYAH, EYAH
Nut: Philippine, PILI
Oak: Holm, ILEX
Oil (comb. form), OLEO
Ostrich: American, RHEA
Oven, KILN, OAST
Owl: Barn, LULU
Ox: Celebes wild, ANOE
  Extinct wild, URUS
Palm, ATAP, NIPA, SAGO
Parliament, DIET
Parrot: New Zealand, KAKA
Pass: Indian mountain, GHAT
Passage: Closing (music), CODA
Peach: Clingstone, PAVY
Peasant: Indian, RYOT
  Old English, CARL
Pepper: Australasian, KAVA
Perfume, ATAR
Persia, IRAN
Person: Extraordinary, ONER
Pickerel or pike, ESOX
Pitcher, EWER
Plant: Aromatic, NARD
  Century, ALOE
  Indigo, ANIL
  Pepper, KAVA
Platform: Raised, DAIS
Plum: Wild, SLOE
Pods: Vegetable, OKRA, OKRO
Poem: Epic, EPOS
Poet: Persian, OMAR
  Roman, OVID
Poison, BANE
  Arrow, INEE
Porkfish, SISI
Portico: Greek, STOA
Premium, AGIO
Priest: Islamic, IMAM
Prima donna, DIVA
Prong: Fork, TINE
Pseudonym: Lamb's, ELIA
Queen: Carthaginian, DIDO
  Hindu, RANI
Rabbit, CONY
Race: Of Japan, AINU
Rail: Ducklike, COOT
  North American, SORA
Redshank, CLEE
Refuse: After pressing, MARC
Regiment: Turkish, ALAI
Reliquary, ARCA
Resort: Italian, LIDO
Ridges: Sandy, ASAR, OSAR
River: German, ELBE, ODER
  Italian, ADDA
  Siberian, LENA
Road: Roman, ITER

Abode of dead: Babylonian, ARALU
Aborigine: Borneo, DAYAK
Aftersong, EPODE
Aloe, AGAVE
Animal: Footless, APODE
Ant, EMMET
Antelope: African, ADDAX, BEISA,
  CAAMA, ELAND, GUIBA, ORIBI,
  TIANG
  Goat, GORAL, SEROW
  Indian, SASIN
  Siberian, SAIGA
Arch: Pointed, OGIVE
Armadillo, APARA, POYOU, TATOU
Arrowroot, ARARU
Artery: Trunk, AORTA
Association: Russian, ARTEL
  Secret, CABAL
Author: English, READE

Rockfish: California, RENA
Rodent: Mouselike, VOLE
  South American, PACA
Rootstock, TARO
Salamander, NEWT
Salmon: Silver, COHO
  Young, PARR
Same (Greek), HOMO
  (Latin), IDEM
Sauce: Fish, ALEC
School: English, ETON
Seaweed, AGAR, ALGA, KELP
Secular, LAIC
Sediment, SILT
Seed: Dill, ANET
  Of vetch, TARE
Serf, ILOT
Sesame, TEEL
Settlement: Eskimo, ETAH
Shark: Atlantic, GATA
  European, TOPE
Sheep: Wild, UDAD
Sheltered, ALEE
Shield, EGIS
Ship: Jason's, ARGO
  Left side of, PORT
  Two-masted, BRIG
Shrine: Buddhist, TOPE
Shrub: New Zealand, TUTU
Sign: Magic, RUNE
Silkworm, ERIA
Skin: Beaver, PLEW
Skink: Egyptian, ADDA
Slave, ESNE
Sloth: Two-toed, UNAU
Smooth, LENE
Snow: Glacial, NEVE
Soapstone, TALC
Society: African secret, EGBO, PORO
Son: Of Seth, ENOS
Song (German), LIED
  Unaccompanied, GLEE
Sound: Lung, RALE
Sour, ACID
Sow: Young, GILT
Spike: Brad-shaped, BROB
Spirit: Buddhist evil, MARA
Stake: Poker, ANTE
Star: Temporary, NOVA
Starch: East Indian, SAGO
Stone: Precious, OPAL
Strap: Bridle, REIN
Strewn (heraldry), SEME
Sweetsop, ATES, ATTA
Sword: Fencing, EPEE, FOIL
Tambourine: African, TAAR
Tapir: Brazilian, ANTA
Tax, CESS
Tea: South American, MATE
Therefore (Latin), ERGO
Thing: Extraordinary, ONER
Three (dice, cards, etc.), TREY
Thrush: Hawaiian, OMAO
Tide, NEAP

Tipster: Racing, TOUT
Tissue, TELA
Title: Etruscan, LARS
  Hindu, BABU
  Indian, RAJA
  Islamic, EMIR, IMAM
  Persian, BABA
  Spanish, DONA
  Turkish, AGHA, BABA
Toad: Largest-known, AGUA
  Tree, HYLA
Tool: Cutting, ADZE
Track: Deer, SLOT
Tract: Sandy, DENE
Tree: Apple, SORB
  Central American, EBOE
  East Indian, TEAK
  Eucalyptus, YATE
  Guyanese and Trinidadian, MORA
  Javanese, UPAS
  Linden, LIME, LINN, TEIL, TILL
  Sandarac, ARAR
  Sassafras, AGUE
  Tamarisk salt, ATLE
Tribe: Moro, SULU
Trout, CHAR
Vessel: Arab, DHOW
Vestment: Ecclesiastical, COPE
Vetch, TARE
Vine: East Indian, SOMA
Violinist: Famous, AUER
Vortex, EDDY
Wampum, PEAG
Wapiti, STAG
Waste: Allowance for, TRET
Watchman: Indian, MINA
Water (Spanish), AGUA
Waterfall, LINN
Wavy (heraldry), ONDE, UNDE
Wax, CERE
  Chinese, PELA
Weed: Biblical, TARE
Weight: Ancient, MINA
  Danish (pl.), ESER
  East Asian, TAEL
  Greek, MINA
  Siamese, BAHT
Well done (rare), EUGE
Whale, CETE
  Killer, ORCA
  White, HUSE, HUSO
Whirlpool, EDDY
Wife: Of Geraint, ENID
Willow: Virginia, ITEA
Wine, PORT
Winged, ALAR
  (Heraldry), AILE
Wings, ALAE
Withered, SERE
Without (French), SANS
Wool: To comb, CARD
Work, OPUS
Wrong: Civil, TORT
Young: Bring forth, YEAN

Words of Five Letters

Automaton, GOLEM, ROBOT
Award: Motion-picture, OSCAR
Basket: Fishing, CREEL
Beer: Russian, KVASS
Bible: Islamic, KORAN, QUR'AN
Bird: Asian, MINAH, MYNAH
  Indian, SHAMA
  Larklike, PIPIT
  Loonlike, GREBE
  Oscine, VIREO
  South American, AGAMI
  Swimming, GREBE
Black: (French), NOIRE
  (Heraldry), SABLE
Blackbird: European, MERLE, OUSEL,
  OUZEL
Block: Glacial, SERAC
Blue (heraldry), AZURE
Boat: Eskimo, BIDAR, UMIAK

Bobwhite, COLIN, QUAIL
Bone (comb. form), OSTEO
  Leg, TIBIA
  Thigh, FEMUR
Broom: Twig, BESOM
Brother (French), FRERE
  Moses, AARON
Canoe: Eskimo, BIDAR, KAYAK
Cape: Papal, FANON, ORALE
Caravansary, SERAI
Card: Old playing, TAROT
Caterpillar: New Zealand, AWETO
Catkin, AMENT
Cavity: Stone, GEODE
Cephalopod, SQUID
Cetacean, WHALE
Chariot, ESSED
Cheek: Pertaining to, MALAR
Chieftain: Arab, EMEER

Child (Scottish), BAIRN
Cigar, CLARO
Coating: Seed, TESTA
Cockatoo: Palm, ARARA
Coin: Costa Rican, COLON
  Danish, KRONE
  Ecuadorian, SUCRE
  English, GROAT, PENCE
  French, FRANC
  German, KRONE, TALER
  Hungarian, PENGO
  Icelandic, KRONA
  Indian, RUPEE
  Iraqi, DINAR
  Norwegian, KRONE
  Polish, ZLOTY
  Russian, COPEC, KOPEK, RUBLE
  Swedish, KRONA
  Turkish, ASPER
  Yugoslav, DINAR
Collar: Papal, FANON, ORALE
  Roman, RABAT
Commune: Italian, TREIA
Composition: Choral, MOTET
Compound: Chemical, ESTER
Conceal (law), ELOIN
Council: Ecclesiastical, SYNOD
Court: Anglo-Saxon, GEMOT
  Inner, PATIO
Crest: Mountain, ARETE
Crown: Papal, TIARA
Cuttlefish, SEPIA
Date: Roman, NONES
Decree: Islamic, IRADE
  Russian, UKASE
Deposit: Loam, LOESS
Desert: Gobi, SHAMO
Devilfish, MANTA
Disease: Cereals, ERGOT
Disk, PATEN
Dog: Wild, DHOLE, DINGO
Dormouse, LEROT
Drum, TABOR
Duck: Sea, EIDER
Dynasty: Chinese, CHING, LIANG,
  SHANG
Earthquake, SEISM
Eel, ELVER, MORAY
Ermine: European, STOAT
Ether: Crystalline, APIOL
Fabric: Velvetlike, PANNE
Fabulist, AESOP
Family: Italian, CENCI
Fiber: West Indian, SISAL
Fig: Smyrna, ELEME, ELEMI
Figure: Of speech, TROPE
Finch: European, SERIN
Fish: American small, KILLY
Flower: Garden, ASTER
Friend (Spanish), AMIGO
Fruit: Tropical, MANGO
Fungus: Rye, ERGOT
Furze, GORSE
Gateway, TORAN, TORII
Gem, AGATE, BERYL, PEARL, TOPAZ
Genus: Barnacles, LEPAS
  Bears, URSUS
  Birds (loons), GAVIA
  Birds (nuthatches), SITTA
  Cats, FELIS
  Dogs, CANIS
  Fishes (chiros), ELOPS
  Fishes (perch), PERCA
  Geese, ANSER
  Grasses, STIPA
  Grasses (incl. oats), AVENA
  Gulls, LARUS
  Hares, rabbits, LEPUS
  Hawks, BUTEO
  Herbs, old world, INULA
  Herbs, trailing or climbing, APIOS
  Herbs, tropical, TACCA, URENA
  Horses, EQUUS
  Insects (olive flies), DACUS
  Lice, plant, APHIS
  Lichens, USNEA

Lizards, AGAMA
Moles, TALPA
Mollusks, OLIVA
Monkeys, CEBUS
Palms, ARECA·
Pigeons, GOURA
Plants (amaryllis family), AGAVE
Ruminants (goats), CAPRA
Shrubs, Asiatic, SABIA
Shrubs (heath), ERICA
Shrubs (incl. raspberry), RUBUS
Shrubs, tropical, IXORA, TREMA,
  URENA
Ticks, ARGAS
Trees (of elm family), TREMA, ULMUS
Trees, tropical, IXORA, TREMA
Goat: Bezoar, PASAN
God: Assyrian, ASHIR, ASHUR, ASSUR
  Babylonian, DAGAN, SIRIS
  Gaelic, DAGDA
  Hindu, BHAGA, INDRA, SHIVA
  Japanese, EBISU
  Philistine, DAGON
  Phrygian, ATTIS
  Teutonic, AEGIR, GYMIR
  Welsh, DYLAN
Goddess: Babylonian, ISTAR, NANAI
  Hindu, DURGA, GAURI, SHREE
Group: Of six, HEXAD
Grove: Sacred to Diana, NEMUS
Growing out, ENATE
Guitar: Hindu, SITAR
Gull: PEWEE, PEWIT
Hartebeest, CAAMA
Headdress: Jewish or Persian, TIARA
  Liturgical, MITER, MITRE
Heath, ERICA
Herb: Grasslike marsh, SEDGE
Heron, EGRET
Hog: Young, SHOAT, SHOTE
Image, EIKON
Indian: Cariban, ARARA
  Iroquoian, HURON
  Mexican, AZTEC, OPATA, OTOMI
  Muskhogean, CREEK
  Siouan, OSAGE, TETON
  Spanish American, ARARA, CARIB
Inflorescence: Racemose, AMENT
Insect: Immature, LARVA
Intrigue, CABAL
Iris: Yellow, SEDGE
Juniper, GORSE, RETEM
Kidneys: Pertaining to, RENAL
King: British legendary, LLUDD
Kite: European, GLEDE
Kobold, NISSE
Land: Cultivated, ARADA, ARADO
Landholder (Scottish), LAIRD, THANE
Language: Dravidian, TAMIL
Lariat, LASSO, REATA
Laughing, RIANT
Lawgiver: Athenian, DRACO, SOLON
Leaf: Calyx, SEPAL
  Fern, FROND
Lemur, LORIS
Letter: English, AITCH
  Greek, ALPHA, DELTA, GAMMA,
  KAPPA, OMEGA, SIGMA, THETA
  Hebrew, ALEPH, CHETH, GIMEL,
  SADHE, ZAYIN
Lichen, USNEA
Lighthouse, PHARE
Lizard: Old World, AGAMA
Loincloth, DHOTI
Louse: Plant, APHID
Macaw: Brazilian, ARARA
Mahogany: Philippine, ALMON
Mammal: Badgerlike, RATEL
  Civetlike, GENET
  Giraffelike, OKAPI
  Raccoonlike, COATI
Man (French), HOMME
Marble, AGATE
Mark: Insertion, CARET
Market place: Greek, AGORA
Marsupial: Australian, KOALA

Measure: Electric, FARAD, HENRY
  Energy, JOULE
  Metric, LITER, STERE
  Printing, AGATE
  Russian, VERST
Mixture: Smelting, MATTE
Mohicans: Last of, UNCAS
Molding: Convex, OVOLO, TORUS
Mole, TALPA
Monkey: African, PATAS
  Capuchin, SAJOU
  Howling, ARABA
Monkshood, ATEES
Month: Jewish, NISAN, SIVAN, TEBET
Museum (French), MUSEE
Musketeer, ATHOS
Native: Aleutian, ALEUT
  New Zealand, MAORI
Neckpiece: Ecclesiastical, AMICE
Nerve (comb. form), NEURO
·Nest: Eagle's or hawk's, AERIE
  Insect's, NIDUS
Net: Fishing, SEINE
Newsstand, KIOSK
Nitrogen, AZOTE
Noble: Islamic, AMEER
Nodule: Stone, GEODE
Nostrils, NARES
Notched irregularly, EROSE
Nymph: Islamic, HOURI
Official: Roman, EDILE
Oleoresin, ELEMI
Opening: Mouthlike, STOMA
Oration: Funeral, ELOGE
Ostiole, STOMA
Page: Left-hand, VERSO
  Right-hand, RECTO
Palm, ARECA, BETEL
Park: Colorado, ESTES
Perfume, ATTAR
Philosopher: Greek, PLATO
Pillar: Stone, STELA, STELE
Pinnacle: Glacial, SERAC
Plain, LLANO
Plant: Century, AGAVE
  Climbing, LIANA
  Dwarf, CUMIN
  East Asian perennial, RAMIE ·
  Medicinal, SENNA
  Mustard family, CRESS
Plate: Communion, PATEN
Poem: Lyric, EPODE
Point: Lowest, NADIR
Poplar, ABELE, ALAMO, ASPEN
Porridge: Spanish American, ATOLE
Post: Stair, NEWEL
Priest: Islamic, IMAUM
Protozoan, AMEBA
Queen: (French), REINE
  Hindu, RANEE
Rabbit, CONEY
Rail, CRAKE
Red (heraldry), GULES
Religion: Moslem, Muslim, ISLAM
Resin, ELEMI
Revoke (law), ADEEM
Rich man, MIDAS, NABOB
Ridge: Sandy, ESKAR, ESKER
River: French, LOIRE, SEINE
Rockfish: California, REINA
Rootstock: Fragrant, ORRIS
Ruff: Female, REEVE
Sack: Pack, KYACK
Salt: Ethereal, ESTER
Saltpeter, NITER, NITRE
Salutation: Eastern, SALAM
Sandpiper: Old World, TEREK
Scented, OLENT
School: Fish, SHOAL
  French public, LYCEE
Scriptures: Islamic, KORAN
Seaweeds, ALGAE
Seed: Aromatic, ANISE
Seraglio, HAREM, SERAI
Serf, HELOT
Sheep: Wild, AUDAD

Sheeplike, OVINE
Shield, AEGIS
Shoe: Wooden, SABOT
Shoots: Pickled bamboo, ACHAR
Shot: Billiard, CAROM, MASSE
Shrine: Buddhist, STUPA
Shrub: Burning bush, WAHOO
   Ornamental evergreen, TOYON
   Used in tanning, SUMAC
Silk: Watered, MOIRE
Sister (French), SOEUR
   (Latin), SOROR
Six: Group of, HEXAD
Skeleton: Marine, CORAL
Slave, HELOT
Snake, ABOMA, ADDER, COBRA,
   RACER
Soldier: French, POILU
   Indian, SEPOY
Sour, ACERB
Spirit: Air, ARIEL
Staff: Shepherd's, CROOK
Starwort, ASTER
Steel (German), STAHL
Stockade: Russian, ETAPE

Stop (nautical), AVAST
Storehouse, ETAPE
Subway: Parisian, METRO
Tapestry, ARRAS
Tea: Paraguayan, YERBA
Temple: Hawaiian, HEIAU
Terminal: Positive, ANODE
Theater: Greek, ODEON, ODEUM
Then (French), ALORS
Thread: Surgical, SETON
Thrush: Wilson's, VEERY
Title: Hindu, BABOO
   Indian, RAJAH, SAHEB, SAHIB
   Islamic, EMEER, IMAUM
Tree: Buddhist sacred, PIPAL
   East Indian cotton, SIMAL
   Hickory, PECAN
   Light-wooded, BALSA
   Malayan, TERAP
   Mediterranean, CAROB
   Mexican, ABETO
   Mexican pine, OCOTE
   New Zealand, MAIRE
   Philippine, ALMON
   Rain, SAMAN

South American, UMBRA
Tamarack, LARCH
Tamarisk salt, ATLEE
   West Indian, ACANA
Trout, CHARR
Troy, ILION, ILIUM
Twin: Siamese, CHANG
Vestment: Ecclesiastical, STOLE
Violin: Famous, AMATI, STRAD
Volcano: Mud, SALSE
Wampum, PEAGE
War cry: Greek, ALALA
Wavy (heraldry), UNDEE
Weight: Jewish, GERAH
Wen, TALPA
Wheat, SPELT
Wheel: Persian water, NORIA
Whitefish, CISCO
Willow, OSIER
Window: Bay, ORIEL
Wine, MEDOC, RHINE, TINTA, TOKAY
Winged, ALATE
Woman (French), FEMME
Year: Excess of solar over lunar, EPACT
Zoroastrian, PARSI

Words of Six or More Letters

Agave, MAGUEY
Alkaloid: Crystalline, ESERIN, ESERINE
Alligator, CAYMAN
Amphibole, EDENITE, URALITE
Ant: White, TERMITE
Antelope: African, DIKDIK, DUIKER,
   GEMSBOK, IMPALA, KOODOO
   European, CHAMOIS
   Indian, NILGAI, NILGAU, NILGHAI,
   NILGHAU
Ape: Asian or East Indian, GIBBON
Appendage: Leaf, STIPEL, STIPULE
Armadillo, PELUDO, TATOUAY
Arrowroot, ARARAO
Ascetic: Jewish, ESSENE
Ass: Asian wild, ONAGER
Avatar: Of Vishnu, KRISHNA
Babylonian, ELAMITE
Badge: Shoulder, EPAULET
Baldness, ALOPECIA
Barracuda, SENNET
Bark: Aromatic, SINTOC
Bearlike, URSINE
Beetle, ELATER
Bible: Zoroastrian, AVESTA
Bird: Sea, PETREL
   South American, SERIEMA
   Wading, AVOCET, AVOSET
Bone: Leg, FIBULA
Branched, RAMATE
Brother (Latin), FRATER
Bunting: European, ORTOLAN
Call: Trumpet, SENNET
Canoe: Eskimo, BAIDAR, OOMIAK
Caravansary, IMARET
Cat: Asian or African, CHEETAH
   Leopardlike, OCELOT
Cenobite: Jewish, ESSENE
Centerpiece: Table, EPERGNE
Cetacean, DOLPHIN, PORPOISE
Chariot, ESSEDA, ESSEDE
Chief: Seminole, OSCEOLA
Claim: Release as (law), REMISE
Clock: Water, CLEPSYDRA
Cloud, CUMULUS, NIMBUS
Coach: French hackney, FIACRE
Coin: Czech, KORUNA
   Dutch, GUILDER
   Ethiopian, TALARI
   Finnish, MARKKA
   German, THALER
   Greek, DRACHMA
   Haitian, GOURDE
   Honduran, LEMPIRA
   Hungarian, FORINT
   Indo-Chinese, PIASTER
   Panamanian, BALBOA
   Paraguayan, GUARANI
   Portuguese, ESCUDO

   Russian, COPECK, KOPECK,
   ROUBLE
   Spanish, PESETA
   Venezuelan, BOLIVAR
Communion: Last holy, VIATICUM
Conceal (law), ELOIGN
Confection, PRALINE
Construction: Sentence, SYNTAX
Convexity: Shaft of column, ENTASIS
Court: Anglo-Saxon, GEMOTE
Cow: Sea, DUGONG, MANATEE
Cylindrical, TERETE
Dagger, STILETTO
   Malay, CREESE, KREESE
Date: Roman, CALENDS, KALENDS
Deer, CARIBOU, WAPITI
Disease: Plant, ERINOSE
Doorkeeper, OSTIARY
Dragonflies: Order of, ODANATA
Drink: Of gods, NECTAR
Drum: TABOUR
   Moorish, ATABAL, ATTABAL
Duck: Fish-eating, MERGANSER
   Sea, SCOTER
Dynasty: Chinese, MANCHU
Eel, CONGER
Edit, REDACT
Envelope: Flower, PERIANTH
Eskimo, AMERIND
Ether: Crystalline, APIOLE
Excuse (law), ESSOIN
Eyespots, OCELLI
Fabric: ESTAMENE, ESTAMIN,
   ETAMINE
Falcon: European, KESTREL
Figure: Used as column, CARYATID,
   TELAMON
Fine: For punishment, AMERCE
Fish: Asian fresh-water, GOURAMI
   Pikelike, BARRACUDA
Five: Group of, PENTAD
Fly: African, TSETSE
Foot: Metric, ANAPEST, IAMBUS
Foxlike, VULPINE
Frying pan, SPIDER
Fur, KARAKUL
Galley: Greek or Roman, BIREME,
   TRIREME
Game: Card, ECARTE
Garment: Greek, CHLAMYS
Gateway, GOPURA, TORANA
Genus: Birds (ravens, crows), CORVUS
   Eels, CONGER
   Fishes, ANABAS
   Foxes, VULPES
   Herbs, ANEMONE
   Insects, CICADA
   Lemurs, GALAGO
   Mints (incl. catnip), NEPETA

   Mollusks, ANOMIA, ASTARTE,
   TEREDO
   Mollusks (incl. oysters), OSTREA
   Monkeys (spider monkeys), ATELES
   Thrushes (incl. robins), TURDUS
   Trees (of elm family), CELTIS
   Trees (inc. dogwood), CORNUS
   Trees, tropical American, SAPOTA
   Wrens, NANNUS
Gibbon, SIAMANG, WOUWOU
Gland: Salivary, RACEMOSE
Goat: Bezoar, PASANG
Goatlike, CAPRINE
God: Assyrian, ASHSHUR, ASSHUR
   Babylonian, BABBAR, MARDUK,
   MERODACH, NANNAR, NERGAL,
   SHAMASH
   Hindu, BRAHMA, KRISHNA, VISHNU
   Tahitian, TAAROA
Goddess: Babylonian, ISHTAR
   Hindu, CHANDI, HAIMAVATI,
   LAKSHMI, PARVATI, SARASVATI,
   SARASWATI
Government, POLITY
Governor: Persian, SATRAP
Grandson (Scottish), NEPOTE
Group: Of five, PENTAD
   Of nine, ENNEAD
   Of seven, HEPTAD
Hare: in first year, LEVERET
Harpsichord, SPINET
Herb: Alpine, EDELWEISS
   Chinese, GINSENG
   South African, FREESIA
Hermit, EREMITE
Hero: Legendary, PALADIN
Heron, BITTERN
Horselike, EQUINE
Hound: Short-legged, BEAGLE
House (French), MAISON
Idiot, CRETIN
Implement: Stone, NEOLITH
Incarnation: Hindu, AVATAR
Indian, APACHE, COMANCHE, PAIUTE,
   SENECA
Inn: Turkish, IMARET
Insects: Order of, DIPTERA
Instrument: Japanese banjolike,
   SAMISEN
   Musical, CLAVIER, SPINET
Interstice, AREOLA
Ironwood, COLIMA
Juniper: Old Testament, RAETAM
Kettledrum, ATABAL
King: Fairy, OBERON
Kneecap, PATELLA
Knife, MACHETE
Langur: Sumatran, SIMPAI
Legislature: Spanish, CORTES

Lemur: African, GALAGO
 Madagascar, AYEAYE
Letter: Greek, EPSILON, LAMBDA,
 OMICRON, UPSILON
 Hebrew, DALETH, LAMEDH, SAMEKH
Lighthouse, PHAROS
Lizard, IGUANA
Llama, ALPACA
Lockjaw, TETANUS
Locust, CICADA, CICALA
Macaw: Brazilian, MARACAN
Maid: Of Astolat, ELAINE
Mammal: Madagascar, TENDRAC,
 TENREC
Man (Spanish), HOMBRE
Marmoset: South American, TAMARIN
Marsupial, BANDICOOT, WOMBAT
Massacre, POGROM
Mayor: Spanish, ALCALDE
Measure: Electric, AMPERE, COULOMB,
 KILOWATT
Medicine: Quack, NOSTRUM
Member: Religious order, CENOBITE
Molasses, TREACLE
Monkey: African, GRIVET, NISNAS
 Asian, LANGUR
 Philippine, MACHIN
 South American, PINCHE, SAIMIRI,
 SAMIRI, SAPAJOU
Monster, CHIMERA, GORGON
 (Comb. form), TERATO
 Cretan, MINOTAUR
Month: Jewish, HESHVAN, KISLEV,
 SHEBAT, TAMMUZ, TISHRI, VEADAR
Mountain: Asia Minor, ARARAT
Mulct, AMERCE
Musketeer, ARAMIS, PORTHOS
Nearsighted, MYOPIC
Net, TRAMMEL
New York City, GOTHAM
Nine: Group of, ENNEAD
Nobleman: Spanish, GRANDEE
Official: Roman, AEDILE
Onyx: Mexican, TECALI
Order: Dragonflies, ODANATA
 Insects, DIPTERA
Organ: Plant, PISTIL

Ornament: Shoulder, EPAULET
Overcoat: Military, CAPOTE
Ox: Wild, BANTENG
Oxidation: Bronze or copper, PATINA
Paralysis: Incomplete, PARESIS
Pear: Alligator, AVOCADO
Persimmon: Mexican, CHAPOTE
Pipe: Peace, CALUMET
Plaid (Scottish), TARTAN
Plain, PAMPAS, STEPPE, TUNDRA
Plant: Buttercup family, ANEMONE
 Century, MAGUEY
 On rocks, LICHEN
Plowing: Fit for, ARABLE
Poem: Heroic, EPOPEE
 Six-lined, SESTET
Point: Highest, ZENITH
Potion: Love, PHILTER, PHILTRE
Protozoan, AMOEBA
Punish, AMERCE
Purple (heraldry), PURPURE
Queen: Fairy, TITANIA
Race: Skiing, SLALOM
Rat, BANDICOOT, LEMMING
Retort, RIPOST, RIPOSTE
Ring: Harness, TERRET
 Little, ANNULET
Rodent: Jumping, JERBOA
 Spanish American, AGOUTI, AGOUTY
Sailor: East Indian, LASCAR
Salmon: Young, GRILSE
Salutation: Eastern, SALAAM
Sandpiper, PLOVER
Sandy, ARENOSE
Sapodilla, SAPOTA, SAPOTE
Saw: Surgical, TREPAN
Seven: Group of, HEPTAD
Sexes: Common to both, EPICENE
Shawl: Mexican, SERAPE
Sheathing: Flower, SPATHE
Sheep: Wild, AOUDAD, ARGALI
Shipworm, TEREDO
Shoes: Mercury's winged, TALARIA
Shortening: Syllable, SYSTOLE
Shrub, SPIRAEA
Sickle-shaped, FALCATE

Silver (heraldry), ARGENT
Snake, ANACONDA
Speech: Loss of, APHASIA
Spiral, HELICAL
Staff: Bishop's, CROSIER, CROZIER
Stalk: Plant, PETIOLE
State: Swiss, CANTON
Studio, ATELIER
Swan: Young, CYGNET
Swimming, NATANT
Sword-shaped, ENSATE
Terminal: Negative, CATHODE
Third (music), TIERCE
Thrust: Fencing, RIPOST, RIPOSTE
Tile: Pertaining to, TEGULAR
Tomb: Empty, CENOTAPH
Tooth (comb. form), ODONTO
Tower: Islamic, MINARET
Tree: African timber, BAOBAB
 Black gum, TUPELO
 East Indian, MARGOSA
 Locust, ACACIA
 Malayan, SINTOC
 Marmalade, SAPOTE
Urn: Tea, SAMOVAR
Vehicle, LANDAU, TROIKA
Verbose, PROLIX
Viceroy: Egyptian, KHEDIVE
Vulture: American, CONDOR
Warehouse (French), ENTREPOT
Whale: White, BELUGA
Whirlpool, VORTEX
Will: Addition to, CODICIL
 Having left, TESTATE
Wind, CHINOOK, MONSOON, SIMOOM,
 SIMOON, SIROCCO
Window: In roof, DORMER
Wine, BARBERA, BURGUNDY,
 CABERNET, CHABLIS, CHIANTI,
 CLARET, MUSCATEL, RIESLING,
 SAUTERNE, SHERRY, ZINFANDEL
Wolfish, LUPINE
Woman: Boisterous, TERMAGANT
Woolly, LANATE
Workshop, ATELIER
Zoroastrian, PARSEE

Old Testament Names

We do not pretend that this list is all-inclusive. We list only those names that occur most often in crossword puzzles.

Aaron: First high priest of Jews; son of Amram; brother of Miriam and Moses; father of Abihu, Eleazar, Ithamar, and Nadab.
Abel: Son of Adam and Eve; slain by Cain.
Abigail: Wife of Nabal; later, wife of David.
Abihu: Son of Aaron.
Abimelech: King of Gerar.
Abner: Commander of army of Saul and Ishbosheth; slain by Joab.
Abraham (or Abram): Patriarch; forefather of the Jews; son of Terah; husband of Sarah; father of Isaac and Ishmael.
Absalom: Son of David and Maacah; revolted against David; slain by Joab.
Achish: King of Gath; gave refuge to David.
Achsa (or Achsah): Daughter of Caleb; wife of Othniel.
Adah: Wife of Lamech.
Adam: First man; husband of Eve; father of Cain, Abel, and Seth.
Adonijah: Son of David and Haggith.
Agag: King of Amalek; spared by Saul; slain by Samuel.
Ahasuerus: King of Persia; husband of Vashti and, later, Esther; sometimes identified with Xerxes the Great.
Ahijah: Prophet; foretold accession of Jeroboam.
Ahinoam: Wife of David.
Amasa: Commander of army of David; slain by Joab.
Amnon: Son of David and Ahinoam; raped Tamar; slain by Absalom.
Amram: Husband of Jochebed; father of Aaron, Miriam and Moses.
Asenath: Wife of Joseph.
Asher: Son of Jacob and Zilpah.

Balaam: Prophet; rebuked by his donkey for cursing God.
Barak: Jewish captain; associated with Deborah.
Baruch: Secretary to Jeremiah.
Bathsheba: Wife of Uriah; later, wife of David.
Belshazzar: Crown prince of Babylon.
Benaiah: Warrior of David; proclaimed Solomon King.
Ben-Hadad: Name of several kings of Damascus.
Benjamin: Son of Jacob and Rachel.
Bezaleel: Chief architect of Tabernacle.
Bilhah: Servant of Rachel; mistress of Jacob.
Bildad: Comforter of Job.
Boaz: Husband of Ruth; father of Obed.
Cain: Son of Adam and Eve; slayer of Abel; father of Enoch.
Cainan: Son of Enos.
Caleb: Spy sent out by Moses to visit Canaan; father of Achsa.
Canaan: Son of Ham.
Chilion: Son of Elimelech; husband of Orpah.
Cush: Son of Ham; father of Nimrod.
Dan: Son of Jacob and Bilhah.
Daniel: Prophet; saved from lions by God.
Deborah: Hebrew prophetess and judge; helped Israelites conquer Canaanites.
Delilah: Mistress and betrayer of Samson.
Elam: Son of Shem.
Eleazar: Son of Aaron; succeeded him as high priest.
Eli: High priest and judge; teacher of Samuel; father of Hophni and Phinehas.
Eliakim: Chief minister of Hezekiah.
Eliezer: Servant of Abraham.
Elihu: Comforter of Job.
Elijah (or Elias): Prophet; went to heaven in chariot of fire.

Elimelech: Husband of Naomi; father of Chilion and Mahlon.
Eliphaz: Comforter of Job.
Elisha (or Eliseus): Prophet; successor of Elijah.
Elkanah: Husband of Hannah; father of Samuel.
Enoch: Son of Cain.
Enoch: Father of Methuselah.
Enos: Son of Seth; father of Cainan.
Ephraim: Son of Joseph.
Esau: Son of Isaac and Rebecca; sold his birthright to his twin brother Jacob.
Esther: Jewish wife of Ahasuerus; saved Jews from Haman's plotting.
Eve: First woman; wife of Adam.
Ezra (or Esdras): Hebrew scribe and priest.
Gad: Son of Jacob and Zilpah.
Gehazi: Servant of Elisha.
Gideon: Israelite hero; defeated Midianites.
Goliath: Philistine giant; slain by David.
Hagar: Handmaid of Sarah; concubine of Abraham; mother of Ishmael.
Haggith: Mother of Adonijah.
Ham: Son of Noah; father of Cush, Mizraim, Phut, and Canaan.
Haman: Chief minister of Ahasuerus; hanged on gallows prepared for Mordecai.
Hannah: Wife of Elkanah; mother of Samuel.
Hanun: King of Ammonites.
Haran: Brother of Abraham; father of Lot.
Hazael: King of Damascus.
Hephzi-Bah: Wife of Hezekiah; mother of Mannaseh.
Hiram: King of Tyre.
Holofernes: General of Nebuchadnezzar; slain by Judith.
Hophni: Son of Eli.
Isaac: Hebrew patriarch; son of Abraham and Sarah; half brother of Ishmael; husband of Rebecca; father of Esau and Jacob.
Ishmael: Son of Abraham and Hagar; half brother of Isaac.
Issachar: Son of Jacob and Leah.
Ithamar: Son of Aaron.
Jabal: Son of Lamech and Adah.
Jabin: King of Hazor.
Jacob: Hebrew patriarch; founder of Israel; son of Isaac and Rebecca; husband of Leah and Rachel; father of sons Asher, Benjamin, Dan, Gad, Issachar, Joseph, Judah, Levi, Naphtali, Reuben, Simeon, and Zebulun, and daughter Dinah.
Jael: Slayer of Sisera.
Japheth: Son of Noah.
Jehoiada: High priest; husband of Jehoshabeath; revolted against Athaliah and made Joash King of Judah.
Jehoshabeath (or Jehosheba): Daughter of Jehoram of Judah; wife of Jehoiada.
Jephthah: Judge in Israel; sacrificed his only daughter because of vow.
Jesse: Son of Obed; father of David.
Jethro: Midianite priest; father of Zipporah.
Jezebel: Phoenician princess; wife of Ahab; mother of Ahaziah, Athaliah, and Jehoram.
Joab: Commander in chief under David; slayer of Abner, Absalom, and Amasa.
Job: Patriarch; underwent many afflictions; comforted by Bildad, Elihu, Eliphaz and Zophar.
Jochebed: Wife of Amram.
Jonah: Prophet; cast into sea and swallowed by great fish.
Jonathan: Son of Saul; friend of David.
Joseph: Son of Jacob and Rachel; sold into slavery by his brothers; husband of Asenath; father of Ephraim and Manassah.
Joshua: Successor of Moses; son of Nun.
Jubal: Son of Lamech and Adah.
Judah: Son of Jacob and Leah.
Judith: Slayer of Holofernes.
Kish: Father of Saul.

Laban: Father of Leah and Rachel.
Lamech: Son of Methuselah; father of Noah.
Lamech: Husband of Adah and Zillah; father of Jabal, Jubal, and Tubal-Cain.
Leah: Daughter of Laban; wife of Jacob; sister of Rachel.
Levi: Son of Jacob and Leah.
Lot: Son of Haran; escaped destruction of Sodom.
Maacah: Mother of Absalom and Tamar.
Mahlon: Son of Elimelech; first husband of Ruth.
Manasseh: Son of Joseph.
Melchizedek: King of Salem.
Methuselah: Patriarch; son of Enoch; father of Lamech.
Michal: Daughter of Saul; wife of David.
Miriam: Prophetess; daughter of Amram; sister of Aaron and Moses.
Mizraim: Son of Ham.
Mordecai: Uncle of Esther; with her aid, saved Jews from Haman's plotting.
Moses: Prophet and lawgiver; son of Amram; brother of Aaron and Miriam; husband of Zipporah.
Naaman: Syrian captain; cured of leprosy by Elisha.
Nabal: Husband of Abigail.
Naboth: Owner of vineyard; stoned to death because he would not sell it to Ahab.
Nadab: Son of Aaron.
Nahor: Father of Terah.
Naomi: Wife of Elimelech; mother-in-law of Ruth.
Naphtali: Son of Jacob and Bilhah.
Nathan: Prophet; reproved David for causing Uriah's death.
Nebuchadnezzar (or Nebuchadrezzar): King of Babylon; destroyer of Jerusalem.
Nehemiah: Jewish leader; empowered by Artaxerxes to rebuild Jerusalem.
Nimrod: Mighty hunter; son of Cush.
Noah: Patriarch; son of Lamech; escaped Deluge by building Ark; father of Ham, Japheth and Shem.
Nun (or Non): Father of Joshua.
Obed: Son of Boaz; father of Jesse.
Og: King of Bashan.
Orpah: Wife of Chilion.
Othniel: Kenezite; judge of Israel; husband of Achsa.
Phinehas: Son of Eleazer.
Phinehas: Son of Eli.
Phut (or Put): Son of Ham.
Potiphar: Egyptian official; bought Joseph.
Rachel: Wife of Jacob; mother of Joseph; sister of Leah.
Rebecca (or Rebekah): Wife of Isaac; mother of Esau and Jacob.
Reuben: Son of Jacob and Leah.
Ruth: Wife of Mahlon, later of Boaz; daughter-in-law of Naomi.
Samson: Judge of Israel; famed for strength; betrayed by Delilah.
Samuel: Hebrew judge and prophet; son of Elkanah.
Sarah (or Sara, Sarai): Wife of Abraham; mother of Isaac.
Sennacherib: King of Assyria.
Seth: Son of Adam; father of Enos.
Shem: Son of Noah; father of Elam.
Simeon: Son of Jacob and Leah.
Sisera: Canaanite captain; slain by Jael.
Tamar: Daughter of David and Maachah; raped by Amnon.
Terah: Son of Nahor; father of Abraham.
Tubal-Cain: Son of Lamech and Zillah.
Uriah: Husband of Bathsheba; sent to death in battle by David.
Vashti: Wife of Ahasuerus; set aside by him.
Zadok: High priest during David's reign.
Zebulun (or Zabulon): Son of Jacob and Leah.
Zillah: Wife of Lamech.
Zilpah: Servant of Leah; mistress of Jacob.
Zipporah: Daughter of Jethro; wife of Moses.
Zophar: Comforter of Job.

Kings of Judah and Israel

Kings Before Division of Kingdom

Saul: First King of Israel; son of Kish; father of Ish-Bosheth, Jonathan and Michal.
Ish-Bosheth (or Eshbaal): King of Israel; son of Saul.
David: King of Judah; later of Israel; son of Jesse; husband of Abigail, Ahinoam, Bathsheba, Michal, etc.; father of Absalom, Adonijah, Amnon, Solomon, Tamar, etc.
Solomon: King of Israel and Judah; son of David; father of Rehoboam.
Rehoboam: Son of Solomon; during his reign the kingdom was divided into Judah and Israel.

Kings of Judah (Southern Kingdom)

Rehoboam: First King.
Abijah (or Abijam or Abia): Son of Rehoboam.
Asa: Probably son of Abijah.
Jehoshaphat: Son of Asa.
Jehoram (or Joram): Son of Jehoshaphat; husband of Athaliah.
Ahaziah: Son of Jehoram and Athaliah.
Athaliah: Daughter of King Ahab of Israel and Jezebel; wife of Jehoram; only queen to occupy the throne of Judah.
Joash (or Jehoash): Son of Ahaziah.

Amaziah: Son of Joash.
Uzziah (or Azariah): Son of Amaziah.
Jotham: Regent, later King; son of Uzziah.
Ahaz: Son of Jotham.
Hezekiah: Son of Ahaz; husband of Hephzi-Bah.
Manasseh: Son of Hezekiah and Hephzi-Bah.
Amon: Son of Manasseh.
Josiah (or Josias): Son of Amon.
Jehoahaz (or Joahaz): Son of Josiah.
Jehoiakim: Son of Josiah.
Jehoiachin: Son of Jehoiakim.
Zedekiah: Son of Josiah; kingdom overthrown by Babylonians under Nebuchadnezzar.

Kings of Israel (Northern Kingdom)
Jeroboam I: Led secession of Israel.
Nadab: Son of Jeroboam I.
Baasha: Overthrew Nadab.
Elah: Son of Baasha.
Zimri: Overthrew Elah.
Omri: Overthrew Zimri.

Ahab: Son of Omri; husband of Jezebel.
Ahaziah: Son of Ahab.
Jehoram (or Joram): Son of Ahab.
Jehu: Overthrew Jehoram.
Jehoahaz (or Joahaz): Son of Jehu.
Jehoash (or Joash): Son of Jehoahaz.
Jeroboam II: Son of Jehoash.
Zechariah: Son of Jeroboam II.
Shallum: Overthrew Zechariah.
Menahem: Overthrew Shallum.
Pekahiah: Son of Menahem.
Pekah: Overthrew Pekahiah.
Hoshea: Overthrew Pekah; kingdom overthrown by Assyrians under Sargon II.

Prophets
Major. Isaiah, Jeremiah, Ezekiel, Daniel.
Minor. Hosea, Obadiah, Nahum, Haggai, Joel, Jonah, Habakkuk, Zechariah, Amos, Micah, Zephaniah, Malachi.

Greek and Roman Mythology

Most of the Greek deities were adopted by the Romans, although in many cases there was a change of name. In the list below, information is given under the Greek name; the name in parentheses is the Roman equivalent. However, all Latin names are listed with cross-references to the Greek ones. In addition, there are several deities that are exclusively Roman. **Bold** words within entries indicate cross references.

Achelous: River god; son of Oceanus and Tethys and said to be the father of the Sirens.
Acheron: One of several **Rivers of Underworld.**
Achilles: Greek warrior; slew Hector at Troy; slain by Paris, who wounded him in his vulnerable heel.
Actaeon: Hunter; surprised Artemis bathing; changed by her to stag; and killed by his dogs.
Admetus: King of Thessaly; his wife, Alcestis, offered to die in his place.
Adonis: Beautiful youth loved by Aphrodite.
Aeacus: One of three judges of dead in Hades; son of Zeus.
Aeëtes: King of Colchis; father of Medea; keeper of Golden Fleece.
Aegeus: Father of Theseus; believing Theseus killed in Crete, he drowned himself; Aegean Sea named for him.
Aegisthus: Son of Thyestes; slew Atreus; with Clytemnestra, his paramour, slew Agamemnon; slain by Orestes.
Aegyptus: Brother of Danaus; his sons, except Lynceus, slain by Danaides.
Aeneas: Trojan; son of Anchises and Aphrodite; after fall of Troy, led his followers eventually to Italy; loved and deserted Dido.
Aeolus: One of several **Winds.**
Aesculapius: See Asclepius.
Aeson: King of Ioclus; father of Jason; overthrown by his brother Pelias; restored to youth by Medea.
Aether: Personification of sky.
Aethra: Mother of Theseus.
Agamemnon: King of Mycenae; son of Atreus; brother of Menelaus; leader of Greeks against Troy; slain on his return home by Clytemnestra and Aegisthus.
Aglaia: One of several **Graces.**
Ajax: Greek warrior; killed himself at Troy because Achilles's armor was awarded to Odysseus.
Alcestis: Wife of Admetus; offered to die in his place but saved from death by Hercules.
Alcmene: Wife of Amphitryon; mother by Zeus of Hercules.
Alcyone: One of several **Pleiades.**
Alecto: One of several **Furies.**
Alectryon: Youth changed by Ares into cock.
Althaea: Wife of Oeneus; mother of Meleager.
Amazons: Female warriors in Asia Minor; supported Troy against Greeks.
Amor: See Eros.
Amphion: Musician; husband of Niobe; charmed stones to build fortifications for Thebes.
Amphitrite: Sea goddess; wife of Poseidon.
Amphitryon: Husband of Alcmene.
Anchises: Father of Aeneas.
Ancile: Sacred shield that fell from heavens; palladium of Rome.
Andraemon: Husband of Dryope.
Andromache: Wife of Hector.
Andromeda: Daughter of Cepheus; chained to cliff for monster to devour; rescued by Perseus.
Anteia: Wife of Proetus; tried to induce Bellerophon to elope with her.

Anteros: God who avenged unrequited love.
Antigone: Daughter of Oedipus; accompanied him to Colonus; performed burial rite for Polynices and hanged herself.
Antinoüs: Leader of suitors of Penelope; slain by Odysseus.
Aphrodite (Venus): Goddess of love and beauty; daughter of Zeus and Dione; mother of Eros.
Apollo: God of beauty, poetry, music; later identified with Helios as Phoebus Apollo; son of Zeus and Leto.
Aquilo: One of several **Winds.**
Arachne: Maiden who challenged Athena to weaving contest; changed to spider.
Ares (Mars): God of war; son of Zeus and Hera.
Argo: Ship in which Jason and followers sailed to Colchis for Golden Fleece.
Argus: Monster with hundred eyes; slain by Hermes; his eyes placed by Hera into peacock's tail.
Ariadne: Daughter of Minos; aided Theseus in slaying Minotaur; deserted by him on island of Naxos and married to Dionysus.
Arion: Musician; thrown overboard by pirates but saved by dolphin.
Artemis (Diana): Goddess of moon; huntress; twin sister of Apollo.
Asclepius (Aesculapius): Mortal son of Apollo; slain by Zeus for raising dead; later deified as god of medicine. Also known as Asklepios.
Astarte: Phoenician goddess of love; variously identified with Aphrodite, Selene, and Artemis.
Asterope: See Sterope.
Astraea: Goddess of Justice; daughter of Zeus and Themis.
Atalanta: Princess who challenged her suitors to a foot race; Hippomenes won race and married her.
Athena (Minerva): Goddess of wisdom; known poetically as Pallas Athene; sprang fully armed from head of Zeus.
Atlas: Titan; held world on his shoulders as punishment for warring against Zeus; son of Iapetus.
Atreus: King of Mycenae; father of Menelaus and Agamemnon; brother of Thyestes, three of whose sons he slew and served to him at banquet; slain by Aegisthus.
Atropos: One of several **Fates.**
Aurora: See Eos.
Auster: One of several **Winds.**
Avernus: Infernal regions; name derived from small vaporous lake near Vesuvius which was fabled to kill birds and vegetation.
Bacchus: See Dionysus.
Bellerophon: Corinthian hero; killed Chimera with aid of Pegasus; tried to reach Olympus on Pegasus and was thrown to his death.
Bellona: Roman goddess of war.
Boreas: One of several **Winds.**
Briareus: Monster of hundred hands; son of Uranus and Gaea.
Briseis: Captive maiden given to Achilles; taken by Agamemnon in exchange for loss of Chryseis, which caused Achilles to cease fighting, until death of Patroclus.
Cadmus: Brother of Europa; planter of dragon seeds from which first Thebans sprang.

Calliope: One of several **Muses.**

Calypso: Sea nymph; kept Odysseus on her island Ogygia for seven years.

Cassandra: Daughter of Priam; prophetess who was never believed; slain with Agamemnon.

Castor: One of **Dioscuri.**

Celaeno: One of several **Pleiades.**

Centaurs: Beings half man and half horse; lived in mountains of Thessaly.

Cephalus: Hunter; accidentally killed his wife Procris with his spear.

Cepheus: King of Ethiopia; father of Andromeda.

Cerberus: Three-headed dog guarding entrance to Hades.

Ceres: *See* Demeter.

Chaos: Formless void; personified as first of gods.

Charon: Boatman on Styx who carried souls of dead to Hades; son of Erebus.

Charybdis: Female monster; personification of whirlpool.

Chimera: Female monster with head of lion, body of goat, tail of serpent; killed by Bellerophon.

Chiron: Most famous of centaurs.

Chronos: Personification of time.

Chryseis: Captive maiden given to Agamemnon; his refusal to accept ransom from her father Chryses caused Apollo to send plague on Greeks besieging Troy.

Circe: Sorceress; daughter of Helios; changed Odysseus's men into swine.

Clio: One of several **Muses.**

Clotho: One of several **Fates.**

Clytemnestra: Wife of Agamemnon, whom she slew with aid of her paramour, Aegisthus; slain by her son Orestes.

Cocytus: One of several **Rivers of Underworld.**

Creon: Father of Jocasta; forbade burial of Polynices; ordered burial alive of Antigone.

Creüsa: Princess of Corinth, for whom Jason deserted Medea; slain by Medea, who sent her poisoned robe; also known as Glaüke.

Creusa: Wife of Aeneas; died fleeing Troy.

Cronus (Saturn): Titan; god of harvests; son of Uranus and Gaea; dethroned by his son Zeus.

Cupid: *See* Eros.

Cybele: Anatolian nature goddess; adopted by Greeks and identified with Rhea.

Cyclopes: Race of one-eyed giants (singular: Cyclops).

Daedalus: Athenian artificer; father of Icarus; builder of Labyrinth in Crete; devised wings attached with wax for him and Icarus to escape Crete.

Danae: Princess of Argos; mother of Perseus by Zeus, who appeared to her in form of golden shower.

Danaïdes: Daughters of Danaüs; at his command, all except Hypermnestra slew their husbands, the sons of Aegyptus.

Danaüs: Brother of Aegyptus; father of Danaïdes; slain by Lynceus.

Daphne: Nymph; pursued by Apollo; changed to laurel tree.

Decuma: One of several **Fates.**

Deino: One of several **Graeae.**

Demeter (Ceres): Goddess of agriculture; mother of Persephone.

Diana: *See* Artemis.

Dido: Founder and queen of Carthage; stabbed herself when deserted by Aeneas.

Diomedes: Greek hero; with Odysseus, entered Troy and carried off Palladium, sacred statue of Athena.

Diomedes: Owner of man-eating horses, which Hercules, as ninth labor, carried off.

Dione: Titan goddess; mother by Zeus of Aphrodite.

Dionysus (Bacchus): God of wine; son of Zeus and Semele.

Dioscuri: Twins Castor and Pollux; sons of Leda by Zeus.

Dis: *See* Pluto, Hades.

Dryads: Wood nymphs.

Dryope: Maiden changed to Hamadryad.

Echo: Nymph who fell hopelessly in love with Narcissus; faded away except for her voice.

Electra: Daughter of Agamemnon and Clytemnestra; sister of Orestes; urged Orestes to slay Clytemnestra and Aegisthus.

Electra: One of several **Pleiades.**

Elysium: Abode of blessed dead.

Endymion: Mortal loved by Selene.

Enyo: One of several **Graeae.**

Eos (Aurora): Goddess of dawn.

Epimetheus: Brother of Prometheus; husband of Pandora.

Erato: One of several **Muses.**

Erebus: Spirit of darkness; son of Chaos.

Erinyes: One of several **Furies.**

Eris: Goddess of discord.

Eros (Amor or Cupid): God of love; son of Aphrodite.

Eteocles: Son of Oedipus, whom he succeeded to rule alternately with Polynices; refused to give up throne at end of year; he and Polynices slew each other.

Eumenides: One of several **Furies.**

Euphrosyne: One of several **Graces.**

Europa: Mortal loved by Zeus, who, in form of white bull, carried her off to Crete.

Eurus: One of several **Winds.**

Euryale: One of several **Gorgons.**

Eurydice: Nymph; wife of Orpheus.

Eurystheus: King of Argos; imposed twelve labors on Hercules.

Euterpe: One of several **Muses.**

Fates: Goddesses of destiny; Clotho (Spinner of thread of life), Lachesis (Determiner of length), and Atropos (Cutter of thread); also called Moirae. Identified by Romans with their goddesses of fate; Nona, Decuma, and Morta; called Parcae.

Fauns: Roman deities of woods and groves.

Faunus: *See* Pan.

Favonius: One of several **Winds.**

Flora: Roman goddess of flowers.

Fortuna: Roman goddess of fortune.

Furies: Avenging spirits; Alecto, Megaera, and Tisiphone; known also as Erinyes or Eumenides.

Gaea: Goddess of earth; daughter of Chaos; mother of Titans; known also as Ge, Gea, Gaia, etc.

Galatea: Statue of maiden carved from ivory by Pygmalion; given life by Aphrodite.

Galatea: Sea nymph; loved by Polyphemus.

Ganymede: Beautiful boy; successor to Hebe as cupbearer of gods.

Glaucus: Mortal who became sea divinity by eating magic grass.

Golden Fleece: Fleece from ram that flew Phrixos to Colchis; Aeëtes placed it under guard of dragon; carried off by Jason.

Gorgons: Female monsters; Euryale, Medusa, and Stheno; had snakes for hair; their glances turned mortals to stone.

Graces: Beautiful goddesses: Aglaia (Brilliance), Euphrosyne (Joy), and Thalia (Bloom); daughters of Zeus.

Graeae: Sentinels for Gorgons.; Deino, Enyo, and Pephredo; had one eye among them, which passed from one to another.

Hades (Dis): Name sometimes given Pluto; also, abode of dead, ruled by Pluto.

Haemon: Son of Creon; promised husband of Antigone; killed himself in her tomb.

Hamadryads: Tree nymphs.

Harpies: Monsters with heads of women and bodies of birds.

Hebe (Juventas): Goddess of youth; cupbearer of gods before Ganymede; daughter of Zeus and Hera.

Hecate: Goddess of sorcery and witchcraft.

Hector: Son of Priam; slayer of Patroclus; slain by Achilles.

Hecuba: Wife of Priam.

Helen: Fairest woman in world; daughter of Zeus and Leda; wife of Menelaus; carried to Troy by Paris, causing Trojan War.

Heliades: Daughters of Helios; mourned for Phaëthon and were changed to poplar trees.

Helios (Sol): God of sun; later identified with Apollo.

Helle: Sister of Phrixos; fell from ram of Golden Fleece; water where she fell named Hellespont.

Hephaestus (Vulcan): God of fire; celestial blacksmith; son of Zeus and Hera; husband of Aphrodite.

Hera (Juno): Queen of heaven; wife of Zeus.

Hercules: Hero and strong man; son of Zeus and Alcmene; performed twelve labors or deeds to be free from bondage under Eurystheus; after death, his mortal share was destroyed, and he became immortal. Also known as Herakles or Heracles. Labors: (1) killing Nemean lion; (2) killing Lernaean Hydra; (3) capturing Erymanthian boar; (4) capturing Ceryneian hind; (5) killing man-eating Stymphalian birds; (6) procuring girdle of Hippolyte; (7) cleaning Augean stables; (8) capturing Cretan bull; (9) capturing man-eating horses of Diomedes; (10) capturing cattle of Geryon; (11) procuring golden apples of Hesperides; (12) bringing Cerberus up from Hades.

Hermes (Mercury): God of physicians and thieves; messenger of gods; son of Zeus and Maia.

Hero: Priestess of Aphrodite; Leander swam Hellespont nightly to see her; drowned herself at his death.

Hesperus: Evening star.

Hestia (Vesta): Goddess of hearth; sister of Zeus.

Hippolyte: Queen of Amazons; wife of Theseus.

Hippolytus: Son of Theseus and Hippolyte; falsely accused by Phaedra of trying to kidnap her; slain by Poseidon at request of Theseus.

Hippomenes: Husband of Atalanta, whom he beat in race by dropping golden apples, which she stopped to pick up.

Hyacinthus: Beautiful youth accidentally killed by Apollo, who caused flower to spring up from his blood.

Hydra: Nine-headed monster in marsh of Lerna; slain by Hercules.

Hygeia: Personification of health.

Hymen: God of marriage.

Hyperion: Titan; early sun god; father of Helios.

Hypermnestra: Daughter of Danaüs; refused to kill her husband Lynceus.

Hypnos (Somnus): God of sleep.

Iapetus: Titan; father of Atlas, Epimetheus, and Prometheus.

Icarus: Son of Daedalus; flew too near sun with wax-attached wings and fell into sea and was drowned.

Io: Mortal maiden loved by Zeus; changed by Hera into heifer.

Iobates: King of Lycia; sent Bellerophon to slay Chimera.

Iphigenia: Daughter of Agamemnon; offered as sacrifice to Artemis at Aulis; carried by Artemis to Tauris where she became priestess; escaped from there with Orestes.

Iris: Goddess of rainbow; messenger of Zeus and Hera.

Ismene: Daughter of Oedipus; sister of Antigone.

Iulus: Son of Aeneas.

Ixion: King of Lapithae; for making love to Hera he was bound to endlessly revolving wheel in Tartarus.

Janus: Roman god of gates and doors; represented with two opposite faces.

Jason: Son of Aeson; to gain throne of Ioclus from Pelias, went to Colchis and brought back Golden Fleece; married Medea; deserted her for Creüsa.

Jocasta: Wife of Laius; mother of Oedipus; unwittingly became wife of Oedipus; hanged herself when relationship was discovered.

Juno: See Hera.

Jupiter: See Zeus.

Juventas: See Hebe.

Lachesis: One of several **Fates.**

Laius: Father of Oedipus, by whom he was slain.

Laocoön: Priest of Apollo at Troy; warned against bringing wooden horse into Troy; destroyed with his two sons by serpents sent by Athena.

Lares: Roman ancestral spirits protecting descendants and homes.

Latona: See Leto.

Lavinia: Wife of Aeneas after defeat of Turnus.

Leander: Swam Hellespont nightly to see Hero; drowned in storm.

Leda: Mortal loved by Zeus in form of swan; mother of Helen, Clytemnestra, Dioscuri.

Lethe: One of several **Rivers of Underworld.**

Leto (Latona): Mother by Zeus of Artemis and Apollo.

Lucina: Roman goddess of childbirth; identified with Juno.

Lynceus: Son of Aegyptus; husband of Hypermnestra; slew Danaüs.

Maia: Daughter of Atlas; mother of Hermes.

Maia: One of several **Pleiades.**

Manes: Souls of dead Romans, particularly of ancestors.

Mars: See Ares.

Marsyas: Shepherd; challenged Apollo to music contest and lost; flayed alive by Apollo.

Medea: Sorceress; daughter of Aeëtes; helped Jason obtain Golden Fleece; when deserted by him for Creüsa, killed her children and Creüsa.

Medusa: One of several **Gorgons**, slain by Perseus, who cut off her head.

Megaera: One of several **Furies.**

Meleager: Son of Althaea; his life would last as long as brand burning at his birth; Althaea quenched and saved it but destroyed it when Meleager slew his uncles.

Melpomene: One of several **Muses.**

Memnon: Ethiopian king; made immortal by Zeus; son of Tithonus and Eos.

Menelaus: King of Sparta; son of Atreus; brother of Agamemnon; husband of Helen.

Mentor: Tutor of Telemachus and friend of Odysseus. In the *Odyssey*, on several occasions, Athena assumes form of Mentor to give advice to Telemachus or Odysseus

Mercury: See Hermes.

Merope: One of several **Pleiades.** Merope is said to have hidden in shame for loving a mortal.

Mezentius: Cruel Etruscan king; ally of Turnus against Aeneas; slain by Aeneas.

Midas: King of Phrygia; given gift of turning to gold all he touched.

Minerva: See Athena.

Minos: King of Crete; after death, one of three judges of dead in Hades; son of Zeus and Europa.

Minotaur: Monster, half man and half beast, kept in Labyrinth in Crete; slain by Theseus.

Mnemosyne: Goddess of memory; mother by Zeus of Muses.

Moirae: One of several **Fates.**

Momus: God of ridicule.

Morpheus: God of dreams.

Mors: See Thanatos.

Morta: One of several **Fates.**

Muses: Goddesses presiding over arts and sciences: Calliope (epic poetry), Clio (history), Erato (lyric and love poetry), Euterpe (music), Melpomene (tragedy), Polymnia or Polyhymnia (sacred poetry), Terpsichore (choral dance and song), Thalia (comedy and bucolic poetry), Urania (astronomy); daughters of Zeus and Mnemosyne.

Naiads: Nymphs of waters, streams, and fountains.

Napaeae: Wood nymphs.

Narcissus: Beautiful youth loved by Echo; in punishment for not returning her love, he was made to fall in love with his image reflected in pool; pined away and became flower.

Nemesis: Goddess of retribution.

Neoptolemus: Son of Achilles; slew Priam; also known as Pyrrhus.

Neptune: See Poseidon.

Nereids: Sea nymphs; attendants on Poseidon.

Nestor: King of Pylos; noted for wise counsel in expedition against Troy.

Nike: Goddess of victory.

Niobe: Daughter of Tantalus; wife of Amphion; her children slain by Apollo and Artemis; changed to stone but continued to weep her loss.

Nona: One of several **Fates.**

Notus: One of several **Winds.**

Nox: See Nyx.

Nymphs: Beautiful maidens; minor deities of nature.

Nyx (Nox): Goddess of night.

Oceanids: Ocean nymphs; daughters of Oceanus.

Oceanus: Eldest of Titans; god of waters.

Odysseus (Ulysses): King of Ithaca; husband of Penelope; wandered ten years after fall of Troy before arriving home.

Oedipus: King of Thebes; son of Laius and Jocasta; unwittingly murdered Laius and married Jocasta; tore his eyes out when relationship was discovered.

Oenone: Nymph of Mount Ida; wife of Paris, who abandoned her; refused to cure him when he was poisoned by arrow of Philoctetes at Troy.

Ops: See Rhea.

Oreads: Mountain nymphs.

Orestes: Son of Agamemnon and Clytemnestra; brother of Electra; slew Clytemnestra and Aegisthus; pursued by Furies until his purification by Apollo.

Orion: Hunter; slain by Artemis and made heavenly constellation.

Orpheus: Famed musician; son of Apollo and Muse Calliope; husband of Eurydice.

Pales: Roman goddess of shepherds and herdsmen.

Palinurus: Aeneas' pilot; fell overboard in his sleep and was drowned.

Pan (Faunus): God of woods and fields; part goat; son of Hermes.

Pandora: Opener of box containing human ills; mortal wife of Epimetheus.

Parcae: One of several **Fates.**

Paris: Son of Priam; gave apple of discord to Aphrodite, for which she enabled him to carry off Helen; slew Achilles at Troy; slain by Philoctetes.

Patroclus: Great friend of Achilles; wore Achilles' armor and was slain by Hector.

Pegasus: Winged horse that sprang from Medusa's body at her death; ridden by Bellerophon when he slew Chimera.

Pelias: King of Ioclus; seized throne from his brother Aeson; sent Jason for Golden Fleece; slain unwittingly by his daughters at instigation of Medea.

Pelops: Son of Tantalus; his father cooked and served him to gods; restored to life; Peloponnesus named for him.

Penates: Roman household gods.

Penelope: Wife of Odysseus; waited faithfully for him for many years while putting off numerous suitors.

Pephredo: One of several **Graeae.**

Periphetes: Giant; son of Hephaestus; slain by Theseus.

Persephone (Proserpine): Queen of infernal regions; daughter of Zeus and Demeter; wife of Pluto.

Perseus: Son of Zeus and Danaë; slew Medusa; rescued Andromeda from monster and married her.

Phaedra: Daughter of Minos; wife of Theseus; caused the death of her stepson, Hippolytus.

Phaethon: Son of Helios; drove his father's sun chariot and was struck down by Zeus before he set world on fire.

Philoctetes: Greek warrior who possessed Hercules' bow and arrows; slew Paris at Troy with poisoned arrow.

Phineus: Betrothed of Andromeda; tried to slay Perseus but turned to stone by Medusa's head.

Phlegethon: One of several **Rivers of Underworld.**

Phosphor: Morning star.

Phrixos: Brother of Helle; carried by ram of Golden Fleece to Colchis.

Pirithous: Son of Ixion; friend of Theseus; tried to carry off Persephone from Hades; bound to enchanted rock by Pluto.

Pleiades: Alcyone, Celaeno, Electra, Maia, Merope, Sterope or Asterope, Taygeta; seven daughters of Atlas; transformed into heavenly constellation, of which six stars are visible (Merope is said to have hidden in shame for loving a mortal).

Pluto (Dis): God of Hades; brother of Zeus.

Plutus: God of wealth.

Pollux: One of **Dioscuri.**

Polyhmnia: *See* Polymnia.

Polymnia (Polyhymnia): One of several **Muses.**

Polynices: Son of Oedipus; he and his brother Eteocles killed each other; burial rite, forbidden by Creon, performed by his sister Antigone.

Polyphemus: Cyclops; devoured six of Odysseus's men; blinded by Odysseus.

Polyxena: Daughter of Priam; betrothed to Achilles, whom Paris slew at their betrothal; sacrificed to shade of Achilles.

Pomona: Roman goddess of fruits.

Pontus: Sea god; son of Gaea.

Poseidon (Neptune): God of sea; brother of Zeus.

Priam: King of Troy; husband of Hecuba; ransomed Hector's body from Achilles; slain by Neoptolemus.

Priapus: God of regeneration.

Procris: Wife of Cephalus, who accidentally slew her.

Procrustes: Giant; stretched or cut off legs of victims to make them fit iron bed; slain by Theseus.

Proetus: Husband of Anteia; sent Bellerophon to Iobates to be put to death.

Prometheus: Titan; stole fire from heaven for man. Zeus punished him by chaining him to rock in Caucasus where vultures devoured his liver daily.

Proserpine: *See* Persephone.

Proteus: Sea god; assumed various shapes when called on to prophesy.

Psyche: Beloved of Eros; punished by jealous Aphrodite; made immortal and united with Eros.

Pygmalion: King of Cyprus; carved ivory statue of maiden which Aphrodite gave life as Galatea.

Pyramus: Babylonian youth; made love to Thisbe through hole in wall; thinking Thisbe slain by lion, killed himself.

Python: Serpent born from slime left by Deluge; slain by Apollo.

Quirinus: Roman war god.

Remus: Brother of Romulus; slain by him.

Rhadamanthus: One of three judges of dead in Hades; son of Zeus and Europa.

Rhea (Ops): Daughter of Uranus and Gaea; wife of Cronus; mother of Zeus; identified with Cybele.

Rivers of Underworld. Acheron (woe), Cocytus (wailing), Lethe (forgetfulness), Phlegethon (fire), Styx (across which souls of dead were ferried by Charon).

Romulus: Founder of Rome; he and Remus suckled in infancy by she-wolf; slew Remus; deified by Romans.

Sarpedon: King of Lycia; son of Zeus and Europa; slain by Patroclus at Troy.

Saturn: *See* Cronus.

Satyrs: Hoofed demigods of woods and fields; companions of Dionysus.

Sciron: Robber; forced strangers to wash his feet, then hurled them into sea where tortoise devoured them; slain by Theseus.

Scylla: Female monster inhabiting rock opposite Charybdis; menaced passing sailors.

Selene: Goddess of moon.

Semele: Daughter of Cadmus; mother by Zeus of Dionysus; demanded Zeus appear before her in all his splendor and was destroyed by his lightning bolts.

Sibyls: Various prophetesses; most famous, Cumaean sibyl, accompanied Aeneas into Hades.

Sileni: Minor woodland deities similar to satyrs (singular: silenus). Sometimes Silenus refers to eldest of satyrs, son of Hermes or Pan.

Silvanus: Roman god of woods and fields.

Sinis: Giant; bent pines, with which he hurled victims against side of mountain; slain by Theseus.

Sirens: Minor deities who lured sailors to destruction with their singing.

Sisyphus: King of Corinth; condemned in Tartarus to roll huge stone to top of hill; it always rolled back down again.

Sol: *See* Helios.

Somnus: *See* Hypnos.

Sphinx: Monster of Thebes; killed those who could not answer her riddle; slain by Oedipus. Name also refers to other monsters having body of lion, wings, and head and bust of woman.

Sterope (Asterope): One of several **Pleiades.**

Stheno: One of several **Gorgons.**

Styx: One of several **Rivers of Underworld.** The souls of the dead were ferried across the Styx by Charon.

Symplegades: Clashing rocks at entrance to Black Sea; Argo passed through, causing them to become forever fixed.

Syrinx: Nymph pursued by Pan; changed to reeds, from which he made his pipes.

Tantalus: Cruel king; father of Pelops and Niobe; condemned in Tartarus to stand chin-deep in lake surrounded by fruit branches; as he tried to eat or drink, water or fruit always receded.

Tartarus: Underworld below Hades; often refers to Hades.

Taygeta: One of several **Pleiades.**

Telemachus: Son of Odysseus; made unsuccessful journey to find his father.

Tellus: Roman goddess of earth.

Terminus: Roman god of boundaries and landmarks.

Terpsichore: One of several **Muses.**

Terra: Roman earth goddess.

Thalia: One of several **Graces.** Also one of several **Muses.**

Thanatos (Mors); God of death.

Themis: Titan goddess of laws of physical phenomena; daughter of Uranus; mother of Prometheus.

Theseus: Son of Aegeus; slew Minotaur; married and deserted Ariadne; later married Phaedra.

Thisbe: Beloved of Pyramus; killed herself at his death.

Thyestes: Brother of Atreus; Atreus killed three of his sons and served them to him at banquet.

Tiresias: Blind soothsayer of Thebes.

Tisiphone: One of several **Furies.**

Titans: Early gods from which Olympian gods were derived; children of Uranus and Gaea.

Tithonus: Mortal loved by Eos; changed into grasshopper.

Triton: Demigod of sea; son of Poseidon.

Turnus: King of Rutuli in Italy; betrothed to Lavinia; slain by Aeneas.

Ulysses: *See* Odysseus.

Urania: One of several **Muses.**

Uranus: Personification of Heaven; husband of Gaea; father of Titans; dethroned by his son Cronus.

Venus: *See* Aphrodite.

Vertumnus: Roman god of fruits and vegetables; husband of Pomona.

Vesta: *See* Hestia.

Vulcan: *See* Hephaestus.

Winds: Aeolus (keeper of winds), Boreas (Aquilo) (north wind), Eurus (east wind), Notus (Auster) (south wind), Zephyrus (Favonius) (west wind).

Zephyrus: One of several **Winds.**

Zeus (Jupiter): Chief of Olympian gods; son of Cronus and Rhea; husband of Hera.

Norse Mythology

Aesir: Chief gods of Asgard.

Andvari: Dwarf; robbed of gold and magic ring by Loki.

Angerbotha (Angrbotha): Giantess; mother by Loki of Fenrir, Hel, and Midgard serpent.

Asgard (Asgarth): Abode of gods.

Ask (Aske, Askr): First man; created by Odin, Hoenir, and Lothur.

Asynjur: Goddesses of Asgard.

Atli: Second husband of Gudrun; invited Gunnar and Hogni to his court, where they were slain; slain by Gudrun.

Audhumia (Audhumbla): Cow that nourished Ymir; created Buri by licking ice cliff.

Balder (Baldr, Baldur): God of light, spring, peace, joy; son of Odin; slain by Hoth at instigation of Loki.

Bifrost: Rainbow bridge connecting Midgard and Asgard.

Bragi (Brage): God of poetry; husband of Ithunn.

Branstock: Great oak in hall of Volsungs; into it, Odin thrust Gram, which only Sigmund could draw forth.

Brynhild: Valkyrie; wakened from magic sleep by Sigurd; married Gunnar, instigated death of Sigurd; killed herself and was burned on pyre beside Sigurd.

Bur (Bor): Son of Buri; father of Odin, Hoenir, and Lothur.

Buri (Bori): Progenitor of gods; father of Bur; created by Audhumla.

Embla: First woman; created by Odin, Hoenir, and Lothur.

Fafnir: Son of Rodmar, whom he slew for gold in Otter's skin; in form of dragon, guarded gold; slain by Sigurd.

Fenrir: Wolf; offspring of Loki; swallows Odin at Ragnarok and is slain by Vitharr.

Forseti: Son of Balder.

Frey (Freyr): God of fertility and crops; son of Njorth; originally one of **Vanir.**

Freya (Freyja): Goddess of love and beauty; sister of Frey; originally one of **Vanir.**

Frigg (Frigga): Goddess of sky; wife of Odin.

Garm: Watchdog of Hel; slays, and is slain by, Tyr at Ragnarok.

Gimle: Home of blessed after Ragnarok.

Giuki: King of Nibelungs; father of Gunnar, Hogni, Guttorm, and Gudrun.

Glathsehim (Gladsheim): Hall of gods in Asgard.

Gram (meaning "Angry"): Sigmund's sword; rewelded by Regin; used by Sigurd to slay Fafnir.

Greyfell: Sigmund's horse; descended from Sleipnir.

Grimhild: Mother of Gudrun; administered magic potion to Sigurd which made him forget Brynhild.

Gudrun: Daughter of Giuki; wife of Sigurd; later wife of Atli and Jonakr.

Gunnar: Son of Giuki, in his semblance Sigurd won Brynhild for him; slain at hall of Atli.

Guttorm: Son of Giuki; slew Sigurd at Brynhild's request.

Heimdall (Heimdallr): Guardian of Asgard.

Hel: Goddess of dead and queen of underworld; daughter of Loki.

Hiordis: Wife of Sigmund; mother of Sigurd.

Hoenir: One of creators of Ask and Embla; son of Bur.

Hogni: Son of Giuki; slain at hall of Atli.

Hoth (Hoder, Hodur): Blind god of night and darkness; slayer of Balder at instigation of Loki.

Ithunn (Ithun, Iduna): Keeper of golden apples of youth; wife of Bragi.

Jonakr: Third husband of Gudrun.

Jormunrek: Slayer of Swanhild; slain by sons of Gudrun.

Jotunnheim (Jotunheim): Abode of giants.

Lif and Lifthrasir: First man and woman after Ragnarok.

Loki: God of evil and mischief; instigator of Balder's death.

Lothur (Lodur): One of creators of Ask and Embla.

Midgard (Midgarth): Abode of mankind; the earth.

Midgard Serpent: Sea monster; offspring of Loki; slays, and is slain by, Thor at Ragnarok.

Mimir: Giant; guardian of well in Jotunnheim at root of Yggdrasill; knower of past and future.

Mjollnir: Magic hammer of Thor.

Nagifar: Ship to be used by giants in attacking Asgard at Ragnarok; built from nails of dead men.

Nanna: Wife of Balder.

Nibelungs: Dwellers in northern kingdom ruled by Giuki.

Niflheim (Nifelheim): Outer region of cold and darkness; abode of Hel.

Njorth: Father of Frey and Freya; originally one of **Vanir.**

Norns: Demigoddesses of fate: Urth (Urdur) (past), Verthandi (Verdandi) (present), Skuld (future).

Odin (Othin): Head of **Aesir;** creator of world with Vili and Ve; equivalent to Woden (Wodan, Wotan) in Teutonic mythology.

Otter: Son of Rodmar; slain by Loki; his skin filled with gold hoard of Andvari to appease Rodmar.

Ragnarok: Final destruction of present world in battle between gods and giants; some minor gods will survive, and Lif and Lifthrasir will repeople world.

Regin: Blacksmith; son of Rodmar, foster-father of Sigurd.

Rerir: King of Huns; son of Sigi.

Rodmar: Father of Regin, Otter, and Fafnir; demanded Otter's skin be filled with gold; slain by Fafnir, who stole gold.

Sif: Wife of Thor.

Siggeir: King of Goths; husband of Signy; he and his sons slew Volsung and his sons, except Sigmund; slain by Sigmund and Sinflotli.

Sigi: King of Huns; son of Odin.

Sigmund: Son of Volsung; brother of Signy, who bore him Sinflotli; husband of Hiordis, who bore him Sigurd.

Signy: Daughter of Volsung; sister of Sigmund; wife of Siggeir; mother by Sigmund of Sinflotli.

Sigurd: Son of Sigmund and Hiordis; wakened Brynhild from magic sleep; married Gudrun; slain by Guttorm at instigation of Brynhild.

Sigyn: Wife of Loki.

Sinflotli: Son of Sigmund and Signy.

Skuld: One of several **Norns.**

Sleipnir (Sleipner): Eight-legged horse of Odin.

Surt (Surtr): Fire demon; slays Frey at Ragnarok.

Svartalfaheim: Abode of dwarfs.

Swanhild: Daughter of Sigurd and Gudrun; slain by Jormunrek.

Thor: God of thunder; oldest son of Odin; equivalent to Germanic deity Donar.

Tyr: God of war; son of Odin; equivalent to Tiu in Teutonic mythology.

Ull (Ullr): Son of Sif; stepson of Thor.

Urth: One of several **Norns.**

Valhalla (Valhall): Great hall in Asgard where Odin received souls of heroes killed in battle.

Vali: Odin's son: Ragnarok survivor.

Valkyries: Virgins, messengers of Odin, who selected heroes to die in battle and took them to Valhalla; generally considered as nine in number.

Vanir: Early race of gods; three survivors, Njorth, Frey, and Freya, are associated with **Aesir.**

Ve: Brother of Odin; one of creators of world.

Verthandi: One of several **Norns.**

Vili: Brother of Odin; one of creators of world.

Vingolf: Abode of goddesses in Asgard.

Vitharr (Vithar): Son of Odin; survivor of Ragnarok.

Volsung: Descendant of Odin, and father of Signy, Sigmund; his descendants were called Volsungs.

Yggdrasill: Giant ash tree springing from body of Ymir and supporting universe; its roots extended to Asgard, Jotunnheim, and Niffleheim.

Ymir (Ymer): Primeval frost giant killed by Odin, Vili, and Ve; world created from his body; also, from his body sprang Yggdrasill.

Egyptian Mythology

Aaru: Abode of the blessed dead.

Amen (Amon, Ammdn): One of chief Theban deities; united with sun god under form of Amen-Ra; husband of Mut.

Amenti: Region of dead where souls were judged by Osiris.

Anubis: Guide of souls to Amenti; son of Osiris; jackal-headed.

Apis: Sacred bull, an embodiment of Ptah; identified with Osiris as Osiris-Apis or Serapis.

Geb (Keb, Seb): Earth god; father of Osiris; represented with goose on head.

Hathor (Athor): Goddess of love and mirth; cow-headed.

Horus: God of day; son of Osiris and Isis; hawk-headed.

Isis: Goddess of motherhood and fertility; sister and wife of Osiris.

Khepera: God of morning sun.

Khnemu (Khnum, Chnuphis, Chnemu, Chnum): Ram-headed god.

Khonsu (Khensu, Khuns): Son of Amen and Mut.

Mentu (Ment): Solar deity, sometimes considered god of war; falcon-headed.

Min (Khem, Chem): Principle of physical life.

Mut (Maut): Wife of Amen.

Nephthys: Goddess of the dead; sister and wife of Set.

Nu: Chaos from which world was created, personified as a god.

Nut: Goddess of heavens; consort of Geb.

Osiris: God of underworld and judge of dead; son of Geb and Nut; brother and husband of Isis.

Ptah (Phtha): Chief deity of Memphis.

Ra: God of the Sun, the supreme god; son of Nut; Pharaohs claimed descent from him; represented as lion, cat, or falcon.

Serapis: God uniting attributes of Osiris and Apis.

Set (Seth): God of darkness or evil; brother and enemy of Osiris; brother and husband of Nephthys.

Shu: Solar deity; son of Ra and Hathor.

Tem (Atmu, Atum, Tum): Solar deity.

Thoth (Dhouti): God of wisdom and magic; scribe of gods; ibis-headed.

A Concise Guide to Grammar and Style

This section discusses and illustrates the basic conventions of American capitalization, italicization, and punctuation.

Capitalization

Capitalize the following:

- **Proper nouns and adjectives derived from proper nouns:**

Marie Curie	China, Chinese
Smokey Robinson	Darwin, Darwinian

  But vocabulary words derived from proper nouns are generally lowercase:

china cups	plaster of paris
french fries	vienna sausage

- **The names of geographic divisions, regions, and localities and topographical features such as rivers, lakes, and mountains:**

North Pole	Gulf States
Middle East	Atlantic Ocean
Southern Hemisphere	Rocky Mountains
the North	Lake Tahoe
Lower East Side	Erie Canal

  Do not capitalize directions: She lives 10 miles north of Boston.

- **The names of nationalities, ethnic groups, tribes, and languages:**

Spanish	Bantu
Asian American	Creole

- **Titles when preceding a name:**

President Lincoln	Aunt Mary
Queen Victoria	Doctor Johnson
Senator Kennedy	Professor Davies

  Do not capitalize such terms elsewhere: a biography of the queen; the senator's speech; my aunt, Mary Wilson; the president's fundraising efforts; the residence of the vice president.

- **Epithets:** Ivan the Terrible; Lincoln is known as the Great Emancipator.

- **The names of political and judicial bodies, social organizations, councils, and departments:**

U.S. Senate	Rotary Club
Democratic Party	United Negro College Fund
State Department	U.S. Supreme Court

- **The names for periods, events, and documents of historical importance:**

Middle Ages	Constitution
Renaissance	Treaty of Versailles
Battle of Waterloo	Magna Carta

- **The names for streets, buildings, and monuments:**

Fifth Avenue	World Trade Center
Broadway	Statue of Liberty

- **The names for the supreme deity and sacred works:**

God, the Father Almighty	Bible
Yahweh	Talmud
Allah	Qu'ran

- **The names for religious denominations and their members:**

  Buddhism, Buddhists
  Catholicism, Catholics
  Judaism, Jews
  Methodist Church, Methodists
  Society of Friends, Quakers

- **The days of the week, months of the year, holidays, and holy days:**

Thursday	Labor Day
December	Passover

- **The pronoun I:**

  I told her I didn't want to go.

- **The first word in the salutation and complimentary close of a letter:**

  My dear Carol . . .
  Very truly yours . . .

- **The first word of a sentence:**

  Are you hungry? Lunch will be served soon.

- **The first word of a direct quotation, except when the quotation is split:**

  I asked, "Do you really like bats?"
  "Yes," said Holly, "they're so cute."

- **The first word and all the key words in the title of a literary or other artistic work:**

  The Bluest Eye (novel)
  A Streetcar Named Desire (play)
  "The Road Not Taken" (poem)
  Starry Night (painting)
  "Only the Lonely" (song)

- **The names of ships, aircraft, and space vehicles:**

  USS *Maine*
  The Spirit of St. Louis
  space shuttle *Challenger*

- **The names of constellations, planets, and stars:**

Milky Way	Saturn
the asteroid Juno	Little Dipper

- **The names of geologic eras, periods, epochs, and names of prehistoric divisions:**

Paleozoic Era	*Pleistocene*
Quaternary Period	*Stone Age*

- **The genus but not the species name in binomial nomenclature:**

  Canis familiaris (dog)
  Malus pumila (apple tree)

Italicization

Italicize the following (or underline if writing by hand or using a typewriter):

- **The titles of books, plays, book-length poems, magazines, and newspapers:**

  War and Peace   *TIME magazine*
  Twelfth Night   *National Geographic*
  Beowulf   *Miami Herald*

- **The titles of movies and radio and television programs:**

  Finding Nemo   *Law & Order*
  Car Talk   *Masterpiece Theater*

- **The titles of works of art, including paintings, sculptures, and major musical compositions:**

  Mona Lisa (painting)
  The Thinker (sculpture)
  Swan Lake (ballet)
  Porgy and Bess (opera)

  Do not italicize musical compositions named by number or key: Symphony No. 4; Quartet in E minor.

- **Words, letters, and numbers used as such:**

  How do you spell *ache*?
  Does your name end with a *c* or a *k*?
  The *6* looked like a *0*.

- **Foreign words and phrases that have not been assimilated into English:**

  Alex's *Weltanschauung* was gloomy.
  Ed made a *tarte au citron* for dessert.

- **Words and phrases that are being emphasized:**

  Paris was *the* place to be in the '20s.

- **The names of the plaintiff and defendant in legal citations:** *Johnson* v. *Smith.*

- **The names of ships, aircraft, and space vehicles:**

  USS *Maine*
  The Spirit of St. Louis
  space shuttle *Challenger*

- **The New Latin names of genera, species, subspecies, and varieties in botanical and zoological nomenclature:** *Quercus alba; Homo sapiens.*

Punctuation

End Marks

- **Use a period after a declarative or imperative statement:**

  I went to the library.
  Sign your name here.

- **Use a question mark after a direct question or to indicate uncertainty:**

  What is your name?
  Chaucer's dates are 1340?–1400.

  Do not use a question mark after an indirect question: I asked them what time they were leaving.

- **Use an exclamation point after an exclamatory or emphatic sentence or an interjection:**

  Give me a break!
  Hey! Ouch! Wow!

Comma

Use a comma:

- **To separate words in a list or series:**

  The baby likes grapes, bananas, and cantaloupe.

- **To separate two or more adjectives that come before a noun when *and* can be substituted without changing the meaning:**

  He had a kind, generous nature.
  The dog had thick, soft, shiny fur.

  Do not use the comma if the adjectives together express a single idea or the noun is a compound made up of an adjective and a noun:

  The kitchen had bright yellow curtains.
  A majestic bald eagle soared overhead.

- **To set off words or phrases in apposition to a noun:**

  George Eliot, the great 19th-century novelist, was born in 1819.

  Do not use commas when the appositive word or phrase is essential to the meaning of the sentence:

  The novelist George Eliot was born in 1819.

- **To set off nonessential phrases and clauses:**

  My French professor, who has an odd sense of humor, has been teaching for some 30 years.

  Do not use commas when the phrase or clause is essential to the meaning of the sentence:

  The professor who teaches my French class has an odd sense of humor.

- **To separate the independent clauses joined by a coordinating conjunction in a compound sentence:**

  He lives in New York, and she lives in London.
  Some people like golf, but others prefer tennis.

- **To set off interrupters such as *of course, however, I think,* and *by the way* from the rest of the sentence:**

  She knew, of course, that he was lying.
  By the way, I'll be away next week.

- **To set off an introductory word, phrase, or clause at the beginning of a sentence:**

  Yes, I'd like to go with you.
  After some years, we met again.
  Being tall, she often gets teased.

- **To set off a word in direct address:**

  Thanks, guys, for all your help.
  How was your trip, Kathy?

- **To set off a tag question:**

  You won't do that again, will you?

- **To introduce a short quotation:**

  The queen said, "Let them eat cake!"

- **To close the salutation in a personal letter and the complimentary close in a business or personal letter:**

  Dear Mary, . . . Sincerely, Fred

- **To set off titles and degrees:**

  Sarah Little, Ph.D.   Robert Johnson, Jr.

- **To separate sentence elements that might be read incorrectly without the comma:**

As they entered, in the shadows you could see a figure lurking.

- **To set off the month and day from the year in full dates:**

The conference will be held on August 6, 2001.

Do not use a comma when only the month and year appear:

The conference will be held in August 2001.

- **To set off the city and state in an address:**

Sam Green
10 Joy Street
Boston, MA 02116

If the address is inserted into text, add a second comma after the state:

Cincinnati, Ohio, is their home.

Colon

Use a colon:

- **To introduce a list, or words, phrases, and clauses that explain, enlarge upon, or summarize what has gone before:**

Please provide the following: your name, address, and phone number.

"No honest poet can ever feel quite sure of the permanent value of what he has written: He may have wasted his time and messed up his life for nothing."—T. S. Eliot

- **To introduce a long quotation:**

In 1780 John Adams wrote: "English is destined to be in the next and succeeding centuries more generally the language of the world than Latin was in the last or French is in the present age . . ."

- **To separate hour and minute(s) in standard time notation:**

The train arrives at 9:30.

- **To close the salutation in a business letter:**

Dear Sir or Madam:

Semicolon

Use a semicolon:

- **To separate the independent clauses in a compound sentence not joined by a conjunction:**

Only two seats were left; we needed three.

The situation is hopeful; the storm may lift soon.

- **To separate two independent clauses, the second of which begins with an adverb such as** *however, consequently, moreover,* **and** *therefore*:

We waited an hour; however, we couldn't hang around indefinitely.

- **To separate elements already punctuated with commas:**

Invitations were mailed to the various professors, associate professors, and assistant professors; the secretary of the department; and some of the grad students.

Dashes & Hyphens

- **Use a dash to indicate a sudden break in continuity or to set off an explanatory, a defining, or**

an emphatic phrase:

The sky grew dark—where were the kids?

Dairy foods—milk, cheese, yogurt—are a good source of calcium.

- **Use a hyphen to join the elements of a compound word or to join the elements of a compound modifier before a noun:**

well-wisher   ice-skating rink
fifty-three   college-age students

- **Use a hyphen to divide a word at the end of a line:**

Rasputin is one of history's most enigmatic and intriguing figures.

Brackets & Parentheses

- **Use brackets to set off words or letters in quoted matter that have been added by someone other than the author:**

"She [Willa Cather] is certainly one of the great American writers of the 20th century."

- **Use parentheses to set off nonessential information:**

We spent an hour (more or less) cleaning up.

Apostrophe

Use an apostrophe to indicate:

- **The possessive case of singular and plural nouns, indefinite pronouns, and proper nouns:**

my sister's son   somebody's lunch
my two sisters' sons   Charles's house
the children's toys   the Rosses' friends

- **The plural of letters, numbers, symbols, and words used as such:**

too many *thus*'s   ten *5*'s in a row
spelled with two *e*'s   delete some *&*'s

- **Missing letters in contractions and missing numbers in dates:**

I'm (I am)   class of '95
ma'am (madam)   winter of '97–'98

Quotation Marks

Use quotation marks:

- **To set off direct quotations:**

"Let's go to the beach," she suggested.

- **To set off titles of short stories, articles, chapters, essays, songs, poems, and individual radio and television programs:**

Chapter 9, "The New Englishes"
sang the "Star-Spangled Banner"
"The Apparent Trap" episode of *Frasier*

- **To set off words and phrases that are being used in an unusual or questionable way or might be preceded by** *so-called*:

Mari's "fine" was a day's volunteer work.

According to the article, bees appear to "remember" landmarks.

Commonly Mispronounced Words

aegis: *ee-jis*, not *ay-jis*
asterisk: *as-ter-isk*, not *as-ter-ik*
alumnae: *a-lum-nee*, not *a-lum-nay*
archipelago: *ar-ki-PEL-a-go*, not *arch-i-pel-a-go*
athlete: *ath-leet*, not *ath-a-leet*
candidate: *kan-di-dayt*, not *kan-i-dayt*
chimera: *kiy-MEER-a*, not *CHIM-er-a*
disastrous: *di-zas-tres*, not *di-zas-ter-es*
electoral: *e-LEK-tor-al*, not *e-lek-TOR-al*
etcetera: *et-set-er-a*, not *ek-set-er-a*
lambaste: *lam-bayst*, not *lam-bast*
larvae: *lar-vee*, not *lar-vay*
library: *li-brar-y*, not *li-bar-y*
mischievous: *MIS-che-vus*, not *mis-CHEE-vee-us*
mispronunciation: *mis-pro-nun-see-ay-shun*, not *mis-pro-nown-see-ay-shun*

nuclear: *noo-klee-ur*, not *noo-kyu-lur*
nuptial: *nup-shul*, not *nup-shoo-al*
primer: (schoolbook) *prim-mer*, not *pry-mer*
picture: *pik-cher*, not *pit-cher*
prescription: *prih-skrip-shun*, not *per-skrip-shun*
prerogative: *pre-rog-a-tive*, not *per-rog-a-tive*
peremptory: *per-emp-tuh-ree*, not *pre-emp-tuh-ree*
probably: *prob-a-blee*, not *pra-lee* or *prob-lee*
Realtor: *reel-ter*, not *ree-la-ter*
supposedly: *su-pos-ed-lee*, not *su-pos-ab-lee*
spurious: *spyoor-ee-us*, not *spur-ee-us*
ticklish: *tik-lish*, not *tik-i-lish*
triathlon: *try-ath-lon*, not *try-ath-a-lon*

National Spelling Bee

The National Spelling Bee was launched by the Louisville, Kentucky, *Courier-Journal* in 1925. With competitions, cash prizes, and a trip to the nation's capital, it was hoped the Bee would stimulate "general interest among pupils in a dull subject." The Scripps Howard News Service took over the Bee in 1941. Over the years the national finals have grown from a mere 9 contestants to about 270. In 2005, 13-year-old Poway, Calif., eighth-grader Anurag Kashyap took home more than $28,000 in cash and prizes for correctly spelling *appoggiatura*. Here are the winning words that made past spellers into national champions.

1925	gladiolus	1946	semaphore	1966	ratoon	1986	odontalgia
1926	abrogate	1947	chlorophyll	1967	chihuahua	1987	staphylococci
1927	luxuriance	1948	psychiatry	1968	abalone	1988	elegiacal
1928	albumen	1949	dulcimer	1969	interlocutory	1989	spoliator
1929	asceticism	1950	haruspex	1970	croissant	1990	fibranne
1930	fracas	1951	insouciant	1971	shalloon	1991	antipyretic
1931	foulard	1952	vignette	1972	macerate	1992	lyceum
1932	knack	1953	soubrette	1973	vouchsafe	1993	kamikaze
1933	propitiatory	1954	transept	1974	hydrophyte	1994	antediluvian
1934	deteriorating	1955	custaceology	1975	incisor	1995	xanthosis
1935	intelligible	1956	condominium	1976	narcolepsy	1996	vivisepulture
1936	interning	1957	schappe	1977	cambist	1997	euonym
1937	promiscuous	1958	syllepsis	1978	deification	1998	chiaroscurist
1938	sanitarium	1959	cacolet	1979	maculature	1999	logorrhea
1939	canonical	1960	troche	1980	elucubrate	2000	demarche
1940	therapy	1961	smaragdine	1981	sarcophagus	2001	succedaneum
1941	initials	1962	esquamulose	1982	psoriasis	2002	prospicience
1942	sacrilegious	1963	equipage	1983	Purim	2003	pococurante
1943	NO BEE	1964	sycophant	1984	luge	2004	autochthonous
1944	NO BEE	1965	eczema	1985	milieu	2005	appoggiatura
1945	NO BEE						

Most Widely Spoken Languages in the World

Language	Approx. number of speakers
1. Chinese (Mandarin)	1,075,000,000
2. English	514,000,000
3. Hindustani	496,000,000
4. Spanish	425,000,000
5. Russian	275,000,000
6. Arabic	256,000,000
7. Bengali	215,000,000
8. Portuguese	194,000,000
9. Malay-Indonesian	176,000,000
10. French	129,000,000

Source: Ethnologue, 13th Edition, and other sources.

Most Studied Foreign Languages in the U.S.[1]

Language	Fall 2002 enrollments	% change from 1998
1. Spanish	746,267	13.7 %
2. French	201,979	1.5
3. German	91,100	2.3
4. Italian	63,899	29.6
5. American Sign Language	60,781	432.2[2]
6. Japanese	52,238	21.1
7. Chinese	34,153	20.0
8. Latin	29,841	14.1
9. Russian	23,921	0.5
10. Ancient Greek[3]	20,376	24.2

1. By number of foreign language enrollments in U.S. institutions of higher education. 2. This is larger than the actual growth rate; it reflects past underreporting. 3. If combined, Biblical Hebrew and Modern Hebrew claim 10th place, with 22,802 enrolled and a 44% change. *Source:* Association of Departments of Foreign Languages at the Modern Language Association, *Foreign Language Enrollments in United States Institutions of Higher Education, Fall 2002.*

Easily Confused or Misused Words

affect / effect *Effect* is usually a noun that means a result or the power to produce a result: "The sound of the falling rain had a calming effect, nearly putting me to sleep." *Affect* is usually a verb that means to have an influence on: "His loud humming was affecting my ability to concentrate." Note that *effect* can also be a verb meaning to bring about or execute: "The speaker's somber tone effected a dampening in the general mood of the audience."

all right / alright Although *alright* is widely used, it is considered nonstandard English. As the *American Heritage Dictionary* notes, it's not "all right to use alright."

allusion / illusion *Allusion* is a noun that means an indirect reference: "The speech made allusions to the final report." *Illusion* is a noun that means a misconception: "The policy is designed to give an illusion of reform."

alternately / alternatively *Alternately* is an adverb that means in turn; one after the other: "We alternately spun the wheel in the game." *Alternatively* is an adverb that means on the other hand; one or the other: "You can choose a large bookcase or, alternatively, you can buy two small ones."

beside / besides *Beside* is a preposition that means next to: "Stand here beside me." *Besides* is an adverb that means also: "Besides, I need to tell you about the new products my company offers."

bimonthly / semimonthly *Bimonthly* is an adjective that means every two months: "I brought the cake for the bimonthly office party." *Bimonthly* is also a noun that means a publication issued every two months: "The company publishes several popular bimonthlies." *Semimonthly* is an adjective that means happening twice a month: "We have semimonthly meetings on the 1st and the 15th."

capital / capitol The city or town that is the seat of government is called the *capital*; the building in which the legislative assembly meets is the *capitol*. The term *capital* can also refer to an accumulation of wealth or to a capital letter.

cite / site *Cite* is a verb that means to quote as an authority or example: "I cited several eminent scholars in my study of water resources." It also means to recognize formally: "The public official was cited for service to the city." It can also mean to summon before a court of law: "Last year the company was cited for pollution violations." *Site* is a noun meaning location: "They chose a new site for the factory just outside town."

complement / compliment *Complement* is a noun or verb that means something that completes or makes up a whole: "The red sweater is a perfect complement to the outfit." *Compliment* is a noun or verb that means an expression of praise or admiration: "I received compliments about my new outfit."

comprise / compose According to the traditional rule, the whole comprises the parts, and the parts compose the whole. Thus, the board comprises five members, whereas five members compose (or make up) the board. It is also correct to say that the board is composed (not comprised) of five members.

connote / denote *Connote* is a verb that means to imply or suggest: "The word 'espionage' connotes mystery and intrigue." *Denote* is a verb that means

to indicate or refer to specifically: "The symbol for 'pi' denotes the number 3.14159."

discreet / discrete *Discreet* is an adjective that means prudent, circumspect, or modest: "Her discreet handling of the touchy situation put him at ease." *Discrete* is an adjective that means separate or individually distinct: "Each company in the conglomerate operates as a discrete entity."

disinterested / uninterested *Disinterested* is an adjective that means unbiased or impartial: "We appealed to the disinterested mediator to facilitate the negotiations." *Uninterested* is an adjective that means not interested or indifferent: "They seemed uninterested in our offer."

emigrant / immigrant *Emigrant* is a noun that means one who leaves one's native country to settle in another: "The emigrants spent four weeks aboard ship before landing in Los Angeles." *Immigrant* is a noun that means one who enters and settles in a new country: "Most of the immigrants easily found jobs." One emigrates *from* a place; one immigrates *to* another.

farther / further *Farther* is an adjective and adverb that means to or at a more distant point: "We drove 50 miles today; tomorrow, we will travel 100 miles farther." *Further* is an adjective and adverb that means to or at a greater extent or degree: "We won't be able to suggest a solution until we are further along in our evaluation of the problem." It can also mean in addition or moreover: "They stated further that they would not change the policy."

few / less *Few* is an adjective that means small in number. It is used with countable objects: "This department has few employees." *Less* is an adjective that means small in amount or degree. It is used with objects of indivisible mass: "Which jar holds less water?"

figuratively / literally *Figuratively* is an adverb that means metaphorically or symbolically: "Happening upon the shadowy figure, they figuratively jumped out of their shoes." *Literally* is an adverb that means actually: "I'm not exaggerating when I say I literally fell off my chair." It also means according to the exact meaning of the words: "I translated the Latin passage literally."

foreword / forward *Foreword* is a noun that means an introductory note or preface: "In my foreword I explained my reasons for writing the book." *Forward* is an adjective or adverb that means toward the front: "I sat in the forward section of the bus." "Please step forward when your name is called." *Forward* is also a verb that means to send on: "Forward the letter to the customer's new address."

founder / flounder In its primary sense *founder* means to sink below the surface of the water: "The ship foundered after colliding with an iceberg." By extension, *founder* means to fail utterly. *Flounder* means to move about clumsily, or to act with confusion. A good synonym for *flounder* is blunder: "After floundering through the first half of the course, Amy finally passed with the help of a tutor."

hanged / hung *Hanged* is the past tense and past participle of hang when the meaning is to execute by suspending by the neck: "They hanged the prisoner for treason." "The convicted killer was hanged at dawn." *Hung* is the past tense and participle of hang when the meaning is to suspend from above with no support from below: "I hung the painting on the wall." "The painting was hung at a crooked angle."

historic / historical In general usage, *historic* refers to what is important in history, while *historical* applies more broadly to whatever existed in the past whether it was important or not: "a historic summit meeting between the prime ministers;" "historical buildings torn down in the redevelopment."

i.e. / e.g. The abbreviation *e.g.* means for example (from Latin *exempli gratia*): "Her talents were legion and varied (e.g., deep sea diving, speed reading, bridge, and tango dancing)." The abbreviation *i.e.* means that is or in other words (from Latin *id est*): "The joy of my existence (i.e., my stamp collection) imbues my life with meaning."

it's / its *It's* is a contraction for it is, whereas *its* is the possessive form of it: "It's a shame that we cannot talk about its size."

laid / lain / lay *Laid* is the past tense and the past participle of the verb lay and not the past tense of lie. *Lay* is the past tense of the verb lie and *lain* is the past participle: "He laid his books down and lay down on the couch, where he has lain for an hour."

lend / loan Although some people feel *loan* should only be used as a noun, *lend* and *loan* are both acceptable as verbs in standard English: "Can you lend (loan) me a dollar?" However, only *lend* should be used in figurative senses: "Will you lend me a hand?"

nonplussed Meaning perplexed or bewildered, *nonplussed* is very often thought to mean just the opposite—calm, unruffled, cool-as-a-cucumber. A common mistake is to think the word means not "plussed," but no such word exists. *Nonplussed* originates from the Latin *non* (no) and *plus* (more, further), and means a state in which no more can be done—one is so perplexed that further action is impossible. "The lexicographer grew increasingly agitated and nonplussed by the frequency with which she noted the misuse of *nonplussed.*"

passed / past *Passed* is the past tense and past participle of *pass*. *Past* refers to time gone by; it is also a preposition meaning beyond. "In the past decade, I passed over countless opportunities; I was determined not to let them get past me again."

penultimate Meaning "next to last," *penultimate* is often mistakenly used to mean "the very last," or the ultimate: "The perfectionist was crestfallen when he was awarded the penultimate prize; the grand prize went to another."

principal / principle *Principal* is a noun that means a person who holds a high position or plays an important role: "The school principal has 20 years of teaching experience." *Principal* is also an adjective that means chief or leading: "The necessity of moving to another city was the principal reason I turned down the job offer." *Principle* is a noun that means a rule or standard: "They refused to compromise their principles."

stationary / stationery *Stationary* is an adjective that means fixed or unmoving: "They maneuvered around the stationary barrier in the road." *Stationery* is a noun that means writing materials: "We printed the letters on company stationery."

their / there / they're *Their* is the possessive form of they; *there* refers to place; and *they're* is the contraction of *they are*. "They're going there because their mother insisted they become proficient in Serbo-Croatian."

who's / whose *Who's* is the contraction of *who is*. *Whose* is the possessive form of *who*. "Who's going to figure out whose job it is to clean the stables?"

Some Basic Phrases in Other Languages

	The language itself	hello	good bye	please	thank you	English	yes	no	traditional toast
German	Deutsch	hallo	auf Wiedersehen	bitte	danke	Englisch	ja	nein	prosit
Dutch	Nederlands	hallo	tot ziens	alstublieft	dankjewel	engels	ja	nee	proost
Danish	dansk	hej	farvel	(1)	tak	engelsk	ja	nej	skål
Swedish	svenska	hej	hejdå	tack	tack	engelska	ja	nej	skål
French	français	bonjour	au revoir	s'il vous plaît	merci	anglais	oui	non	santé
Spanish	español	hola	adiós	por favor	gracias	inglés	sí	no	salud
Italian	italiano	ciao	arrivederci	per favore	grazie	inglese	si	no	salute
Hebrew	ivrit	shalom	lehitraot	bevakasha	toda	anglit	ken	lo	le-chaim
Irish	Gaeilge	fáilte	slán	le do thoil	go raibh maith agat	Béarla	sea[2]	ní ha[3]	slainte
Swahili	Kiswahili	(4)	kwa heri	tafadhali	asante	Kingereza	ndiyo	siyo	—
Japanese	nihongo	konnichiwa	sayonara	kudasai	arigatou	eigo	hai	iie	kanpai
Finnish	suomi	päivää	näkemiin	ole hyvä	kiitos	englanti	kyllä	ei	kippis
Indonesian	bahasa Indonesia	selamat pagi	selamat tinggal[5]	tolong	terima kasih	bahasa Inggris	ya	tidak	—

1. There is no single word or expression that directly corresponds to "please." Polite requests are made in different ways.
2. Literally, "it is." This can only be used in answering a question with the verb "to be." In Irish there is no word for "yes" or "no." Instead, the speaker repeats the verb from the question in the affirmative or the negative: Did you sleep well? I did. Are you coming? I am not. 3. Literally, "it is not." See above. 4. There is no single word for "hello." Which greeting is used will depend on the relative ages, number (singular or plural), and/or race of the speakers. For example, "hujambo," reply "sijambo," would be used by two people of similar age and race, whereas "jambo," reply "jambo," would be used by a white person and a black person. 5. Said by the person leaving; "selamat jalan" is said by the person staying.

Foreign Words and Phrases[1]

The English meanings given below are not necessarily literal translations.

ad absurdum (ad ab-sir'dum) [Lat.]: to the point of absurdity. "He tediously repeated his argument *ad absurdum.*"

ad infinitum (ad in-fun-eye'tum) [Lat.]: to infinity. "The lecture seemed to drone on *ad infinitum.*"

ad nauseam (ad noz'ee-um) [Lat.]: to a sickening degree. "The politician uttered one platitude after another *ad nauseam.*"

aficionado (uh-fish'ya-nah'doh) [Span.]: an ardent devotee. "I was surprised at what a baseball *aficionado* she had become."

angst (angkst) [Ger.]: dread and anxiety. "Sylvia's teenage *angst* was nothing compared to the parental *angst* experienced by the two individuals whose duty it was to raise her."

annus mirabilis (an'us muh-ra'buh-lis) [Lat.]: wonderful year. "Last year was the *annus mirabilis* for my company."

a priori (ah pree-or'ee) [Lat.]: based on theory rather than observation. "The fact that their house is in such disrepair suggests *a priori* that they are having financial difficulties."

au courant (oh' koo-rahn') [Fr.]: up-to-date. "The shoes, the hair, the clothes—every last detail of her dress, in fact—was utterly *au courant.*"

beau geste (boh zhest') [Fr.]: a fine or noble gesture, often futile. "My fellow writers supported me by writing letters of protest to the publisher, but their *beau geste* could not prevent the inevitable."

beau monde (boh' mond') [Fr.]: high society. "Such elegant decor would impress even the *beau monde.*"

bête noire (bet nwahr') [Fr.]: something or someone particularly disliked. "Talk of the good old college days way back when had become his *bête noire,* and he began to avoid his school friends."

bon mot (bon moe') [Fr.]: a witty remark or comment. "One *bon mot* after another flew out of his mouth, charming the audience."

bon vivant (bon vee-vahnt') [Fr.]: a person who lives luxuriously and enjoys good food and drink. "It's true he's quite the *bon vivant,* but when he gets down to business he conducts himself like a Spartan."

carpe diem (kar'pay dee'um) [Lat.]: seize the day. "So what if you have an 8:00 a.m. meeting tomorrow and various appointments? *Carpe diem!*"

carte blanche (kart blonsh') [Fr.]: unrestricted power to act on one's own. "I may have *carte blanche* around the office, but at home I'm a slave to my family's demands."

casus belli (kay'sus bel'eye) [Lat.]: an act justifying war. "The general felt that the banana republic's insolent remarks about our national honor were enough of a *casus belli* to launch an attack."

cause célèbre (koz suh-leb'ruh) [Fr.]: a widely known controversial case or issue. "The Sacco and Vanzetti trial became an international *cause célèbre* during the 1920s."

caveat emptor (kav'ee-ot emp'tor) [Lat.]: let the buyer beware. "Before you leap at that real estate deal, *caveat emptor!*"

comme ci comme ça (kom see' kom sah') [Fr.]: so-so. "The plans for the party strike me as *comme ci comme ça.*"

comme il faut (kom eel foe') [Fr.]: as it should be; fitting. "His end was truly *comme il faut.*"

coup de grâce (koo de grahss') [Fr.]: finishing blow. "After an already wildly successful day, the *coup de grâce* came when she won best all-around athlete."

cri de coeur (kree' de kur') [Fr.]: heartfelt appeal. "About to leave the podium, he made a final *cri de coeur* to his people to end the bloodshed."

de rigueur (duh ree-gur') [Fr.]: strictly required, as by etiquette, usage, or fashion. "Loudly proclaiming one's support for radical causes had become *de rigueur* among her crowd."

deus ex machina (day'us ex mahk'uh-nuh) [Lat.]: a contrived device to resolve a situation. "Stretching plausibility, the movie concluded with a *deus ex machina* ending in which everyone was rescued at the last minute."

dolce vita (dole'chay vee'tuh) [Ital.]: sweet life; the good life perceived as one of physical pleasure and self-indulgence. "My vacation this year is going to be two uninterrupted weeks of *dolce vita.*"

doppelgänger (dop'pul-gang-ur) [Ger.]: a ghostly double or counterpart of a living person. "I could not shake the sense that some shadowy *doppelgänger* echoed my every move."

enfant terrible (ahn-fahn' tay-reeb'luh) [Fr.]: an incorrigible child; an outrageously outspoken or bold person. "He played the role of *enfant terrible,* jolting us with his blunt assessment."

entre nous (ahn'truh noo') [Fr.]: between ourselves; confidentially. "*Entre nous,* their marriage is on the rocks."

ex cathedra (ex kuh-thee'druh) [Lat.]: with authority; used especially of those pronouncements of the pope that are considered infallible. "I resigned myself to obeying; my father's opinions were *ex cathedra* in our household."

ex post facto (ex' post fak'toh) [Lat.]: retroactively. "I certainly hope that the change in policy will be honored *ex post facto.*"

fait accompli (fate ah-kom-plee') [Fr.]: an accomplished fact, presumably irreversible. "There's no use protesting—it's a *fait accompli.*"

faux pas (foh pah') [Fr.]: a social blunder. "Suddenly, she realized she had unwittingly committed yet another *faux pas.*"

flagrante delicto (fla-grahn'tee di-lik'toh) [Lat.]: in the act. "The detective realized that without hard evidence he had no case; he would have to catch the culprit *flagrante delicto.*"

glasnost (glaz'nohst) [Rus.]: open and frank discussion; initiated by Mikhail Gorbachev in 1985 in the Soviet Union. "Once the old chairman retired, the spirit of *glasnost* pervaded the department."

hoi polloi (hoy' puh-loy') [Gk.]: the common people. "Marie Antoinette recommended cake to the *hoi polloi.*"

in loco parentis (in loh′koh pa-ren′tiss) [Lat.]: in the place of a parent. "The court appointed a guardian for the children, to serve *in loco parentis.*"

in medias res (in me′-dee-as rays) [Lat.]: in the middle of a sequence of occurences. "The film begin *in medias res,* with a panting, terrified man running through the night."

in situ (in sit′too) [Lat.]: situated in the original or natural position. "I prefer seeing statues *in situ* rather than in the confines of a museum."

in vino veritas (in vee′no vare′i-toss) [Lat.]: in wine there is truth. "By the end of the party, several of the guests had made a good deal of their private lives public, prompting the host to murmur to his wife, '*in vino veritas.*'"

ipso facto (ip′soh fak′toh) [Lat.]: by the fact itself. "An extremist, *ipso facto,* cannot become part of a coalition."

je ne sais quoi (zheh neh say kwah′) [Fr.]: I know not what; an elusive quality. "She couldn't explain it, but there was something *je ne sais quoi* about him that she found devastatingly attractive."

mano a mano (mah′no ah mah′no) [Span.]: directly or face-to-face in a confrontation or conflict. "'Stay out of it,' he admonished his friends, 'I want to handle this guy *mano a mano.*'"

mea culpa (may′uh kul′puh) [Lat.]: I am to blame. "His *mea culpa* was so offhand that I hardly think he meant it."

memento mori (muh-men′toh more′ee) [Lat.]: a reminder that you must die. "The skull rested on the mantlepiece as a *memento mori.*"

mise en scene (mee′ zahn sen) [Fr.]: the stage setting; surroundings. "The *mise en scene* for the sci-fi movie was molded, futuristic furniture and blinding klieg lights."

mot juste (moh zhoost′) [Fr.]: the exact, appropriate word. "'Rats!' screamed the defiant three-year-old, immensely proud of his *mot juste.*"

ne plus ultra (nee′ plus ul′truh) [Lat.]: the most intense degree of a quality or state. "Pulling it from the box, he realized he was face to face with the *ne plus ultra* of computers."

nom de plume (nom duh ploom′) [Fr.]: pen name. "Deciding it was time to sit down and begin a novel, the would-be writer spent the first several hours deciding upon a suitable *nom de plume.*"

persona non grata (per-soh′nuh non grah′tuh) [Lat.]: unacceptable or unwelcome person. "Once I was cut out of the will, I became *persona non grata* among my relatives."

prima facie (pry′ma fay′she) [Lat.]: at first sight, clear and evident. "Although her husband implored, 'I can explain!' the sight of another woman wrapped in his arms was *prima facie* evidence that he was a deceitful lout."

pro bono (pro boh′noh) [Lat.]: done or donated without charge; free. "The lawyer's *pro bono* work gave him a sense of value that his work on behalf of the corporation could not."

quid pro quo (kwid′ pro kwoh′) [Lat.]: something for something; an equal exchange. "She vowed that when she had the means, she would return his favors *quid pro quo.*"

sans souci (sahn soo-see′) [Fr.]: carefree. "After serveral glasses of champagne, their mood turned distinctly *sans souci.*"

savoir-faire (sav′wahr fair′) [Fr.]: the ability to say and do the correct thing. "She presided over the gathering with impressive *savoir-faire.*"

schadenfreude (shah den froy′deh) [Ger.]: pleasure at someone else's misfortunes. "*Schadenfreude* suffused the classroom after the insufferably supercilious class pet was caught cheating by the teacher."

sic transit gloria mundi (sick tran′sit glor′ee-uh mun′dee) [Lat.]: thus passes away the glory of the world. "Watching the aging former football quarterback lumber down the street, potbellied and dissipated, his friend shook his head in disbelief and muttered, '*sic transit gloria mundi.*'"

sine qua non (sin′ay kwah nohn′) [Lat.]: indispensable element or condition. "Lemon is the *sine qua non* of this recipe."

sotto voce (suh′tow voh′chee) [Ital.]: in a quiet voice, attempting not to be overheard. "While the others were distracted, he filled me in *sotto voce* on all the deliciously sordid details of the scandal."

sui generis (su′ee jen′e-ris) [Lat.]: unique. "Adjusting her pirate's hat and fringed hula skirt, Zelda sashayed into the party, knowing her fashion statement was *sui generis.*"

terra incognita (tare′uh in-kog-nee′tuh) [Lat.]: unknown territory. "When the conversation suddenly switched from contemporary fiction to medieval Albanian playwrights, he felt himself entering *terra incognita.*"

veni, vidi, vici (ven′ee vee′dee vee′chee) [Lat.]: I came, I saw, I conquered. "After the takeover the business mogul gloated, '*veni, vidi, vici.*'"

vox populi (voks pop′yoo-lie) [Lat.]: the voice of the people. "My sentiments echo those of the *vox populi.*"

Wanderjahr[2] (vahn′der-yahr) [Ger.]: a year or period of travel, especially following one's schooling. "The trio took off on their *Wanderjahr,* intent on visiting every museum between Edinburgh and Rome."

Weltanschauung[2] (velt′an-shou′ung) [Ger.]: a world view or philosophy of life. "His *Weltanschauung* gradually metamorphized from a grim and pessimistic one to a sunny, but no less complex, view."

Weltschmerz[2] (velt′shmerts) [Ger.]: sorrow over the evils of the world. "His poetry expressed a certain *Weltschmerz,* or world-weariness."

Zeitgeist[2] (zite′guyst) [Ger.]: the thought or sensibility characteristic of a particular period of time. "She blamed it on the *Zeitgeist,* which encouraged hedonistic excess."

---

1. Foreign words and phrases should be set in italics (or underlined if written in longhand) if their meanings are likely to be unknown to the reader. Whether the expression is familiar or unfamiliar, however, is a matter of judgment. In this list, all foreign words have been italicized for the sake of emphasis. 2. German nouns are capitalized. A familiar German expression that is not italicized, however, should be lowercased, following the English conventions of not capitalizing common nouns. "His proclivities leaned more to the occult than to the philosophical: a poltergeist he could understand; the *Zeitgeist* he could not."

Latin and Greek Word Elements

English is a living language, and it is growing all the time. One way that new words come into the language is when words are borrowed from other languages. New words are also created when words or word elements, such as roots, prefixes, and suffixes, are combined in new ways.

Many English words and word elements can be traced back to Latin and Greek. Often you can guess the meaning of an unfamiliar word if you know the meaning.

A **word root** is a part of a word. It contains the core meaning of the word, but it cannot stand alone. A **prefix** is also a word part that cannot stand alone. It is placed at the beginning of a word to change its meaning. A **suffix** is a word part that is placed at the end of a word to change its meaning. Often you can guess the meaning of an unfamiliar word if you know the meaning of its parts; that is, the root and any prefixes or suffixes that are attached to it.

Latin Roots, Prefixes, and Suffixes

Latin was the language spoken by the ancient Romans. As the Romans conquered most of Europe, the Latin language spread throughout the region. Over time, the Latin spoken in different areas developed into separate languages, including Italian, French, Spanish, and Portuguese. These languages are considered "sisters," as they all descended from Latin, their "mother" language.

In 1066 England was conquered by William, duke of Normandy, which is in northern France. For several hundred years after the Norman invasion, French was the language of court and polite society in England. It was during this period that many French words were borrowed into English. Linguists estimate that some 60% of our common everyday vocabulary today comes from French. Thus many Latin words came into English indirectly through French.

Many Latin words came into English directly, though, too. Monks from Rome brought religious vocabulary as well as Christianity to England beginning in the 6th century. From the Middle Ages onward many scientific, scholarly, and legal terms were borrowed from Latin.

During the 17th and 18th centuries, dictionary writers and grammarians generally felt that English was an imperfect language whereas Latin was perfect. In order to improve the language, they deliberately made up a lot of English words from Latin words. For example, fraternity, from Latin fraternitas, was thought to be better than the native English word brotherhood.

Many English words and word parts can be traced back to Latin and Greek. The following table lists some common Latin roots.

Latin root	Basic meaning	Example words
-dict-	to say	contradict, dictate, diction, edict, predict
-duc-	to lead, bring, take	deduce, produce, reduce
-gress-	to walk	digress, progress, transgress
-ject-	to throw	eject, inject, interject, project, reject, subject
-pel-	to drive	compel, dispel, impel, repel
-pend-	to hang	append, depend, impend, pendant, pendulum
-port-	to carry	comport, deport, export, import, report, support
-scrib-, -script-	to write	describe, description, prescribe, prescription, subscribe, subscription, transcribe, transcription
-tract-	to pull, drag, draw	attract, contract, detract, extract, protract, retract, traction
-vert-	to turn	convert, divert, invert, revert

From the example words in the above table, it is easy to see how roots combine with prefixes to form new words. For example, the root -tract-, meaning "to pull," can combine with a number of prefixes, including de- and re-. Detract means literally "to pull away" (de-, "away, off") and retract means literally "to pull back" (re-, "again, back"). The following table gives a list of Latin prefixes and their basic meanings.

Latin prefix	Basic meaning	Example words
co-	together	coauthor, coedit, coheir
de-	away, off; generally indicates reversal or removal in English	deactivate, debone, defrost, decompress, deplane
dis-	not, not any	disbelief, discomfort, discredit, disrepair, disrespect
inter-	between, among	international, interfaith, intertwine, intercellular, interject
non-	not	nonessential, nonmetallic, nonresident, nonviolence, nonskid, nonstop
post-	after	postdate, postwar, postnasal, postnatal
pre-	before	preconceive, preexist, premeditate, predispose, prepossess, prepay
re-	again; back, backward	rearrange, rebuild, recall, remake, rerun, rewrite
sub-	under	submarine, subsoil, subway, subhuman, substandard
trans-	across, beyond, through	transatlantic, transpolar

Words and word roots may also combine with suffixes. Here are examples of some important English suffixes that come from Latin:

Latin suffix	Basic meaning	Example words
-able, -ible	forms adjectives and means "capable or worthy of"	likable, flexible
-ation	forms nouns from verbs	creation, civilization, automation, speculation, information
-fy, -ify	forms verbs and means "to make or cause to become"	purify, acidify, humidify
-ment	forms nouns from verbs	entertainment, amazement, statement, banishment
-ty, -ity	forms nouns from adjectives	subtlety, certainty, cruelty, frailty, loyalty, royalty; eccentricity, electricity, peculiarity, similarity, technicality

Greek Roots, Prefixes, and Suffixes

The following table lists some common Greek roots.

Greek root	Basic meaning	Example words
-anthrop-	human	misanthrope, philanthropy, anthropomorphic
-chron-	time	anachronism, chronic, chronicle, synchronize, chronometer
-dem-	people	democracy, demography, demagogue, endemic, pandemic
-morph-	form	amorphous, metamorphic, morphology
-path-	feeling, suffering	empathy, sympathy, apathy, apathetic, psychopathic
-pedo-, -ped-	child, children	pediatrician, pedagogue
-philo-, -phil-	having a strong affinity or love for	philanthropy, philharmonic, philosophy
-phon-	sound	polyphonic, cacophony, phonetics

The following table gives a list of Greek prefixes and their basic meanings.

Greek prefix	Basic meaning	Example words
a-, an-	without	achromatic, amoral, atypical, anaerobic
anti-, ant-	opposite; opposing	anticrime, antipollution, antacid
auto-	self, same	autobiography, automatic, autopilot
bio-, bi-	life, living organism	biology, biophysics, biotechnology, biopsy
geo-	Earth; geography	geography, geomagnetism, geophysics, geopolitics
hyper-	excessive, excessively	hyperactive, hypercritical, hypersensitive
micro-	small	microcosm, micronucleus, microscope
mono-	one, single, alone	monochrome, monosyllable, monoxide
neo-	new, recent	neonatal, neophyte, neoconservatism, neofascism, neodymium
pan-	all	panorama, panchromatic, pandemic, pantheism
thermo-, therm-	heat	thermal, thermometer, thermostat

Words and word roots may also combine with suffixes. Here are examples of some important English suffixes that come from Greek:

Greek suffix	Basic meaning	Example words
-ism	forms nouns and means "the act, state, or theory of"	criticism, optimism, capitalism
-ist	forms agent nouns from verbs ending in -ize or nouns ending in -ism and is used like -er	conformist, copyist, cyclist
-ize	forms verbs from nouns and adjectives	formalize, jeopardize, legalize, modernize, emphasize, hospitalize, industrialize, computerize
-gram	something written or drawn, a record	cardiogram, telegram
-graph	something written or drawn; an instrument for writing, drawing, or recording	monograph, phonograph, seismograph
-logue, -log	speech, discourse; to speak	monologue, dialogue, travelogue
-logy	discourse, expression; science, theory, study	phraseology, biology, dermatology
-meter, -metry	measuring device; measure	spectrometer, geometry, kilometer, parameter, perimeter
-oid	forms adjectives and nouns and means "like, resembling" or "shape, form"	humanoid, spheroid, trapezoid
-phile	one that loves or has a strong affinity for; loving	audiophile, Francophile
-phobe, -phobia	one that fears a specified thing; an intense fear of a specified thing	agoraphobe, agoraphobia, xenophobe, xenophobia
-phone	sound; device that receives or emits sound; speaker of a language	homophone, geophone, telephone, Francophone

American Sign Language

Sign language for the deaf was first systematized in France during the 18th century by Abbot Charles-Michel l'Epée. French Sign Language (FSL) was brought to the United States in 1816 by Thomas Gallaudet, founder of the American School for the Deaf in Hartford, Conn. He developed American Sign Language (ASL), a language of gestures and hand symbols that express words and concepts.

In many respects, sign language is just like any spoken language, with a rich vocabulary and a highly organized, rule-governed grammar. But in sign language, information is processed through the eyes rather than the ears. Thus, facial expression and body movement play an important part in conveying information.

In spoken language, the relationship between most words and the objects and concepts they represent is arbitrary—there is nothing about the word "tree" that actually suggests a tree, either in the way it is spelled or pronounced. In the same way, in sign language most signs do not suggest, or imitate, the thing or idea they represent, and must be learned. Sign language may be acquired naturally as a child's first language, or it may be learned through study and practice.

"last year" or "one year ago"

Sign language shares other similarities with spoken languages. Like any living language, ASL grows and changes over time to accommodate native users' needs. ASL also has regional varieties, equivalent to spoken accents, with different signs being used in different parts of the country.

American Manual Alphabet

Along with sign language and lip reading, many deaf people also communicate with the manual alphabet, which uses finger positions that correspond to the letters of the alphabet to spell out words and names.

Braille Alphabet

Braille is a system of printing and writing for the blind created in 1824 by Louis Braille (1809–1852), a French inventor who went blind from an accident when he was three. Each character in Braille is made up of an arrangement of one-to-six raised points used in 63 possible combinations. Braille is read by passing the fingers over the raised characters. A universal Braille code for English-speaking countries was adopted in 1932.

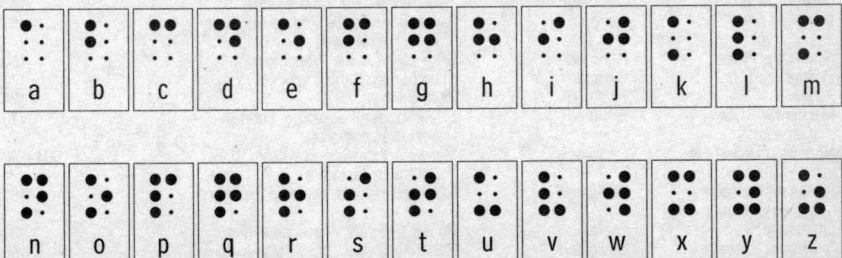

Explorations

Country or place	Event	Explorer	Date
AFRICA			
Sierra Leone	Explored	Hanno, Carthaginian seaman	c. 520 B.C.
Zaire River (Congo)	Mouth visited[1]	Diogo Cão, Portuguese explorer	c. 1484
Cape of Good Hope	Rounded	Bartolomeu Díaz, Portuguese explorer	1488
Gambia River	Explored	Mungo Park, Scottish explorer	1795
Sahara	Crossed	Dixon Denham and Hugh Clapperton, English explorers	1822–1823
Zambezi River	Explored[1]	David Livingstone, Scottish explorer	1851
Sudan	Explored	Heinrich Barth, German explorer	1852–1855
Victoria Falls	Explored[1]	David Livingstone, Scottish explorer	1855
Lake Tanganyika	Explored[1]	Richard Burton and John Speke, British explorers	1858
Lake Victoria, identified as the source of the Nile	Explored	John Speke, British explorer	1858
Zaire River (Congo)	Traced	Sir Henry M. Stanley, British explorer	1877
ASIA			
Punjab (India)	Invaded	Alexander the Great, king of Macedonia	327 B.C.
China	Explored	Marco Polo, Italian traveler	c. 1272
Tibet	Visited	Odoric of Pordenone, Italian monk	c. 1325
Southern China	Explored	Niccolò dei Conti, Venetian traveler	c. 1440
India	Explored (Cape route)	Vasco da Gama, Portuguese navigator	1498
Japan	Visited	St. Francis Xavier of Spain, missionary	1549
Arabia	Explored	Carsten Niebuhr, German explorer	1762
China	Explored	Ferdinand Richthofen, German scientist	1868
Mongolia	Explored	Nikolai M. Przhevalsky, Russian explorer	1870–1873
Central Asia	Explored	Sven Hedin, Swedish scientist	1890–1908
EUROPE			
Shetland Islands	Visited	Pytheas of Massilia (Marseille), Greek navigator and geographer	c. 325 B.C.
North Cape	Rounded	Ottar, Norwegian explorer	c. 870
Iceland	Colonized	Norwegian noblemen	c. 890–900
NORTH AMERICA			
Greenland	Colonized	Eric the Red, Norwegian	c. 985
Labrador, Newfoundland, Nova Scotia (?)	Explored[1]	Leif Eriksson, Norse explorer	1000
West Indies	Explored[1]	Christopher Columbus, Italian	1492
North America	Coast explored[1]	Giovanni Caboto (John Cabot), for British	1497
Pacific Ocean	Sighted[1]	Vasco Núñez de Balboa, Spanish explorer	1513
Florida	Explored	Ponce de León, Spanish explorer	1513
Mexico	Conquered	Hernando Cortés, Spanish adventurer	1519–1521
St. Lawrence River	Explored[1]	Jacques Cartier, French navigator	1534
Southwest United States	Explored	Francisco Coronado, Spanish explorer	1540–1542
Colorado River	Explored[1]	Hernando de Alarcón, Spanish explorer	1540
Mississippi River	Explored[1]	Hernando de Soto, Spanish explorer	1541
Frobisher Bay	Explored[1]	Martin Frobisher, English seaman	1576
Maine Coast	Explored	Samuel de Champlain, French explorer	1604
Jamestown, Va.	Settled	John Smith, English colonist	1607
Hudson River	Explored	Henry Hudson, English navigator	1609
Hudson Bay (Canada)	Explored[1]	Henry Hudson	1610
Baffin Bay	Explored[1]	William Baffin, English navigator	1616
Lake Michigan	Navigated	Jean Nicolet, French explorer	1634
Arkansas River	Explored[1]	Jacques Marquette and Louis Jolliet, French explorers	1673
Mississippi River	Explored	Sieur de La Salle, French explorer	1682
Bering Strait	Explored[1]	Vitus Bering, Danish explorer	1728
Alaska	Explored[1]	Vitus Bering	1741
Mackenzie River (Canada)	Explored[1]	Sir Alexander Mackenzie, Scottish-Canadian explorer	1789
Northwest United States	Explored	Meriwether Lewis and William Clark, American explorers	1804–1806
Northeast Passage (Arctic Ocean)	Navigated	Nils Nordenskjöld, Swedish explorer	1879
Greenland	Explored	Robert E. Peary, American explorer	1892
Northwest Passage	Navigated	Roald Amundsen, Norwegian explorer	1906

Country or place	Event	Explorer	Date
SOUTH AMERICA			
Continent	Explored	Christopher Columbus, Italian	1498
Brazil	Explored[1]	Pedro Alvarez Cabral, Portuguese	1500
Peru	Conquered	Francisco Pizarro, Spanish explorer	1532–1533
Amazon River	Explored	Francisco Orellana, Spanish explorer	1541
Cape Horn	Explored[1]	Willem C. Schouten, Dutch navigator	1615
OCEANIA			
Papua New Guinea	Explored	Jorge de Menezes, Portuguese explorer	1526
Australia	Explored	Abel Janszoon Tasman, Dutch navigator	1642
Tasmania	Explored[1]	Abel Janszoon Tasman	1642
Australia	Crossed	John McDouall Stuart, English explorer	1862
Australia	Explored	Robert Burke and William Wills, Australian explorers	1861
New Zealand	Sighted (and named)	Abel Janszoon Tasman, Dutch navigator	1642
New Zealand	Explored	James Cook, English navigator	1769
ARCTIC, ANTARCTIC, AND MISCELLANEOUS			
Africa, Middle East, Asia, and Europe	Explored	Ibn Batuta, greatest Arab traveler	1325–1349
Ocean exploration	Expedition	Ferdinand Magellan's ships circled globe for Spain	1519–1522
Galápagos Islands	Explored	Diego de Rivadeneira, Spanish captain	1535
Spitsbergen	Explored	Willem Barents, Dutch navigator	1596
Antarctic Circle	Crossed	James Cook, English navigator	1773
Antarctica	Explored[1]	Nathaniel Palmer, American whaler (archipelago), and Fabian Gottlieb von Bellingshausen, Russian admiral (mainland)	1820–1821
Antarctica	Explored	Charles Wilkes, American explorer	1840
North Pole	Reached[2]	Robert E. Peary, American explorer	1909
South Pole	Reached	Roald Amundsen, Norwegian explorer	1911

1. First European to reach the area. 2. Admiral Peary's claim to have reached the Pole has been disputed from the beginning—as was the claim made by his former colleague, Dr. Frederick Cook, who has been generally dismissed as a charlatan. The credit ultimately went to Peary, a claim officially backed by the U.S. Congress. But recent scholarship, including evidence culled from the journals and diaries of both Cook and Peary, has cast doubt on both explorers' veracity. If it is the case that neither reached the Pole, then the credit goes to Joseph Fletcher, who landed a U.S. Air Force C-47 plane there in 1952.

Geography Glossary

latitude lines Imaginary lines running horizontally around the globe. Also called parallels, latitude lines are equidistant from each other. Each degree of latitude is about 69 miles (110 km) apart. Zero degrees (0°) latitude is the equator, the widest circumference of the globe. Latitude is measured from 0° to 90° north and 0° to 90° south—90° north is the North Pole and 90° south is the South Pole.

longitude lines Imaginary lines, also called meridians, running vertically around the globe. Unlike latitude lines, longitude lines are not parallel. Meridians meet at the poles and are widest apart at the equator. Zero degrees longitude (0°) is called the prime meridian. The degrees of longitude run 180° east and 180° west from the prime meridian.

geographic coordinates Latitude and longitude lines form an imaginary grid over the Earth's surface. By combining longitude and latitude measurements, any location on earth can be determined. The units of measurement for geographic coordinates are degrees (°), minutes ('), and seconds ("). Like a circle, the Earth has 360 degrees. Each degree is divided into 60 minutes, which in turn is divided into 60 seconds. Latitude and longitude coordinates also include cardinal directions: north or south of the equator for latitude, and east or west of the prime meridian for longitude. The geographic coordinates of New York City, for example, are 40° N, 74° W, meaning that it is located 40 degrees north latitude and 74 degrees west longitude. Using min-

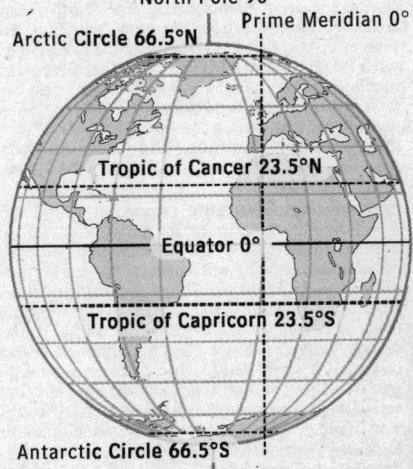

North Pole 90°
Prime Meridian 0°
Arctic Circle 66.5°N
Tropic of Cancer 23.5°N
Equator 0°
Tropic of Capricorn 23.5°S
Antarctic Circle 66.5°S
South Pole 90°

utes and seconds as well as degrees, the coordinates for New York would be 40°42′51″ N, 74°0′23″ W. (Latitude is always listed first.) A less common format for listing coordinates is in decimal degrees.

Mercator Projection | Robinson Projection

The Tropic of Cancer, for example, can be expressed in degrees and minutes (23°30′ N) or in decimal degrees (23.5° N).

hemisphere A hemisphere is half the Earth's surface. The four hemispheres are the Northern and Southern hemispheres, divided by the equator (0° latitude), and the Eastern and Western hemispheres, divided by the prime meridian (0° longitude) and the International Date Line (180°).

equator Zero degrees latitude. The Sun is directly overhead the equator at noon on the two equinoxes (March and Sept. 20 or 21). The equator divides the globe into the Northern and Southern hemispheres. The equator appears halfway between the North and South poles, at the widest circumference of the globe. It is 24,901.55 miles (40,075.16 km) long.

prime meridian Zero degrees longitude (0°). The prime meridian runs through the Royal Greenwich Observatory in Greenwich, England (the location was established in 1884 by international agreement). The prime meridian divides the globe into the Western and Eastern hemispheres. The Earth's time zones are measured from the prime meridian. The time at 0° is called Universal Time (UT) or Greenwich Mean Time (GMT). With the Greenwich meridian as the starting point, each 15° east and west marks a new time zone. The 24 time zones extend east and west around the globe for 180° to the International Date Line. When it is noon along the prime meridian, it is midnight along the International Date Line.

International Date Line Located at 180° longitude (180° E and 180° W are the same meridian). Regions to the east of the International Date Line are counted as being one calendar day earlier than the regions to the west. Although the International Date Line generally follows the 180° meridian (most of which lies in the Pacific Ocean), it does diverge in places. Since 180° runs through several countries, it would divide those countries not simply into two different time zones, but into two different calendar days. To avoid such unnecessary confusion, the date line dips and bends around countries to permit them to share the same time.

Tropic of Cancer A line of latitude located at 23°30' north of the equator. The Sun is directly overhead the Tropic of Cancer on the summer solstice in the Northern Hemisphere (June 20 or 21). It marks the northernmost point of the tropics, which falls between the Tropic of Cancer and the Tropic of Capricorn.

Tropic of Capricorn A line of latitude located at 23°30' south. The Sun is directly overhead the Tropic of Capricorn on the summer solstice in the Southern Hemisphere (Dec. 20 or 21). It marks the southernmost point of the tropics.

Arctic Circle A line of latitude located at 66°30' north, delineating the Northern Frigid Zone of the Earth.

Antarctic Circle A line of latitude located at 66°30' south, delineating the Southern Frigid Zone of the Earth.

globe The most accurate map of the Earth, duplicating its spherical shape and relative size.

map projections Two-dimensional representations of the three-dimensional Earth. Because projections attempt to present the spherical Earth on a flat plane, they inevitably produce distortions. Map projections are numerous and complex (e.g., there are a variety of cylindrical, conic, or azimuthal projections). Each projection has advantages and serves different purposes, and each produces different types of distortions in direction, distance, shape, and relative size of areas. One of the most famous projections is the Mercator, created by Geradus Mercator in 1569. It is a rectangular-shaped map in which all longitude and latitude lines are parallel and intersect at right angles (on a globe, meridians are not parallel, but grow narrower, eventually converging at the poles). Near the equator, the scale of the Mercator is accurate, but the farther one moves toward the poles, the greater the distortion—Antarctica in the far south and Greenland in the far north, for example, appear gigantic. The Mercator projection was used well into the 20th century, but has now been superseded by others, including the widely used Robinson projection. The Robinson projection is an elliptical-shaped map with a flat top and bottom. Developed in 1963 by Arthur H. Robinson, it is an orthophanic ("right appearing") projection, which attempts to reflect the spherical appearance of the Earth. The meridians, for example, are curved arcs, which gives the flat map a three-dimensional appearance. But to convey the likeness of a curved, three-dimensional globe, the Robinson projection must in fact distort shape, area, scale, and distance. The Albers, Lambert, Mollweide, and Winkel Tripel are some of the other commonly used map projections.

The Continents

A continent is defined as a large unbroken land mass completely surrounded by water, although in some cases continents are (or were in part) connected by land bridges. The seven continents are North America, South America, Europe, Asia, Africa, Australia, and Antarctica. The island groups in the Pacific are often called Oceania but this name does *not* imply that scientists consider them the remains of a continent.

Political considerations have often overridden geographical facts when it came to naming continents. Geographically, Europe, including the British Isles, is a large western peninsula of the continent of Asia; and many geographers, when referring to Europe and

Asia, speak of the Eurasian continent. But traditionally, Europe is counted as a separate continent, with the Ural and the Caucasus mountains forming the line of demarcation between Europe and Asia. To the south of Europe, Asia has an odd-shaped peninsula jutting westward, which has a large number of political subdivisions. The northern section is taken up by Turkey; to the south of Turkey there are Syria, Iraq, Israel, Jordan, Saudi Arabia, and a number of smaller Arab countries. All these are part of Asia. Traditionally, the island of Cyprus in the Mediterranean is also considered to be part of Asia. The Caribbean islands, Central America, and Greenland are considered part of North America.

Continental Drift and Plate-Tectonics Theory

Source: U.S. Dept. of the Interior, Geological Survey

According to the theory of continental drift, the world was made up of a single continent through most of geologic time. That continent eventually separated and drifted apart, forming into the seven continents we have today. The first comprehensive theory of continental drift was suggested by the German meteorologist Alfred Wegener in 1912. The hypothesis asserts that the continents consist of lighter rocks that rest on heavier crustal material—similar to the manner in which icebergs float on water. Wegener contended that the relative positions

of the continents are not rigidly fixed but are slowly moving—at a rate of about one yard per century.

According to the generally accepted plate-tectonics theory, scientists believe that Earth's surface is broken into a number of shifting slabs or plates, which average about 50 miles in thickness. These plates move relative to one another above a hotter, deeper, more mobile zone at average rates as great as a few inches per year. Most of the world's active volcanoes are located along or near the boundaries between shifting plates and are called plate-boundary volcanoes.

World Land Areas and Elevations

Area	Approximate land area sq. km	Approximate land area sq. mi.	Percentage of total land area	Elevation, feet and meters	
				Highest	Lowest
WORLD	148,647,000	57,393,000	100.0%	Mt. Everest, Tibet-Nepal, 29,035 ft. (8,850 m)[1]	Dead Sea, Israel-Jordan, 1,349 ft. below sea level (−411 m)
AFRICA	30,065,000	11,608,000	20.2	Mt. Kilimanjaro, Tanzania, 19,340 ft. (5,895 m)	Lake Assal, Djibouti, 512 ft. below sea level (−156 m)
ANTARCTICA	13,209,000	5,100,000	8.9	Vinson Massif, Ellsworth Mts., 16,066 ft. (4,897 m)	Lowest land point hidden within Bentley Subglacial Trench[2]
ASIA (includes the Middle East)	44,579,000	17,212,000	30.0	Mt. Everest, Tibet-Nepal, 29,035 ft. (8,850 m)	Dead Sea, Israel-Jordan, 1,349 ft. below sea level (−411 m)
AUSTRALIA (includes Oceania)	8,112,000	3,132,000	5.3	Mt. Kosciusko, Australia, 7,310 ft. (2,228 m)	Lake Eyre, Australia, 52 ft. below sea level (−12 m)
EUROPE (the Ural Mountains in Russia form the boundary between Europe and Asia)	9,938,000	3,837,000	6.7	Mt. Elbrus, Russia/Georgia, 18,510 ft. (5,642 m)	Caspian Sea, Russia/Kazakhstan 92 ft. below sea level (−28 m)
NORTH AMERICA (includes Central America and the Caribbean)	24,474,000	9,449,000	16.5	Mt. McKinley, Alaska, 20,320 ft. (6,194 m)	Death Valley, Calif., 282 ft. below sea level (−86 m)
SOUTH AMERICA	17,819,000	6,879,000	12.0	Mt. Aconcagua, Argentina, 22,834 ft. (6,960 m)	Valdes Peninsula, Argentina 131 ft. below sea level (−40 m)

1. The 1954 elevation of Everest, 29,028 ft. (8,848 m) was revised on Nov. 11, 1999, and now stands at 29,035 ft. (8,850 m).
2. Bentley Subglacial Trench itself (ice, not land) is −8,327 ft. below sea level (−2,538 m). *Source:* WorldAtlas.com.

Volcanoes of the World

Source: U.S. Dept. of the Interior, Geological Survey

About 550 volcanoes have erupted on Earth's surface since recorded history; about 60 are active each year. Far more have erupted unobserved on the ocean floor. Most volcanoes exist at the boundaries of Earth's crustal plates, such as the famous Ring of Fire that surrounds the Pacific Ocean plate. Fifty volcanoes have erupted in the United States since recorded history, and the United States ranks third, behind Indonesia and Japan, in the number of historically active volcanoes.

Volcanoes are built by the accumulation of their own eruptive products—lava, bombs (crusted over ash flows), and tephra (airborne ash and dust). A volcano is most commonly a conical hill or mountain built around a vent that connects with reservoirs of molten rock below the surface of Earth. The term *volcano* also refers to the opening or vent through which molten rock and gases are expelled.

Driven by buoyancy and gas pressure, the molten rock, which is lighter than the surrounding solid rock, forces its way upward and may ultimately break though zones of weaknesses in Earth's crust. If so, an eruption begins, and the molten rock may pour from the vent as nonexplosive lava flows, or it may shoot violently into the air as dense clouds of lava fragments. Larger fragments fall back around the vent, and accumulations of fall-back fragments may move downslope as ash flows under the force of gravity. Some of the finer ejected materials may be carried by the wind and fall to the ground many miles away. The finest ash particles may be injected miles into the atmosphere and carried many times around the world by stratospheric winds before settling out.

Molten rock below the surface of Earth that rises in volcanic vents is known as **magma,** but after it erupts from a volcano it is called lava. Originating many tens of miles beneath the ground, the ascending magma commonly contains some crystals, fragments of surrounding (unmelted) rocks, and dissolved gases, but it is primarily a liquid composed of oxygen, silicon, aluminum, iron, magnesium, calcium, sodium, potassium, titanium, and manganese. Upon cooling, the liquid magma solidifies to form an igneous or magmatic rock.

Lava is red-hot when it pours or blasts out of a vent but soon changes to dark red, gray, black, or some other color as it cools and solidifies. Very hot, gas-rich lava containing abundant iron and magnesium is fluid and flows like hot tar, whereas cooler, gas-poor lava high in silicon, sodium, and potassium flows sluggishly, like thick honey, or in other cases, like pasty, blocky masses.

All magmas contain dissolved gases, and as they rise to the surface to erupt, the confining pressures are reduced and the dissolved gases are liberated either quietly or explosively. If the lava is a thin fluid (not viscous), the gases may escape easily. But if the lava is thick and pasty (highly viscous), the gases will not move freely but will build up tremendous pressure and ultimately escape with explosive violence, throwing out great masses of solid rock as well as lava, dust, and ashes.

The violent separation of gas from lava may produce rock froth called **pumice.** Some of this froth is so light—because of the many gas bubbles—that it floats on water.   □

Recent Volcanic Activity

(**Bold** indicates activity in 2005)

Volcano	Year of last eruption or activity	Volcano	Year of last eruption or activity
Adatara, Honshu, Japan	1997	Egoni, Indonesia	2004
Akutan, Alaska	1996	Erta Ale, Ethiopia	2003
Ambrym Island, Vanuatu	2004	**Etna, Sicily, Italy**	**2005**
Amukta, Alaska	1996	Fernandina, Galápagos	1995
Anatahan, Mariana Islands	**2005**	Fogo, Cape Verde	1995
Arenal, Costa Rica	2003	**Fuego, Guatemala**	**2005**
Asama, Honshu, Japan	2003	**Fukutoku-Okanoba, Japan**	**2005**
Aso, Kyushu, Japan	2004	**Galeras, Colombia**	**2005**
Axial Seamount	1998	Gamalama, Indonesia	2003
Bandai, Honshu, Japan	2000	Grimsvotn, Iceland	1998
Bagana, Bougainville, Papua New Guinea	**2005**	Guagua Pichincha, Ecuador	2003
Barren Island, Indian Ocean	2003	Hachijo-Jima, Izu Islands, Japan	2002
Bezymianny, Kamchatka, Russia	**2005**	Hakkoda, Japan	1997
Bromo, Java, Indonesia	2000	Hekla, Iceland	2000
Mount Cameroon, Cameroon	2000	Mount Hili Aludo, Indonesia	1997
Canlaon, Philippines	2003	Hosho, Kyushu, Japan	1995
Cerro Azul, Galápagos Islands, Ecuador	1998	Ijen, Java, Indonesia	2001
Cerro Negro, Nicaragua	1999	Iwate-san, Honshu, Japan	1998
Chikurachki, Kuril Islands, Russia	2003	Jackson Segment, N. Gorda Ridge (nr. Oregon)	2001
Chiginagak, Alaska	1997		
Chuginadak, Alaska	**2005**	Kaba, Sumatra, Indonesia	2000
Mt. Cleveland, Chuginadak, Alaska	2001	**Mount Karangetang, Indonesia**	**2005**
Colima, Mexico	**2005**	**Karymsky, Kamchatka, Russia**	**ongoing**
Copahue, Argentina and Chile	2000	Kavachi Seamount, Solomon Islands	2004
Dukono, Indonesia	**2005**	Kelut, Java, Indonesia	2001
East Epi, Vanuatu	2004	Kick-'em-Jenny (nr. Grenada)	2003
Eastern Gemini Seamount, Vanuatu	1996	Kikai, Japan	2004

Volcano	Year of last eruption or activity	Volcano	Year of last eruption or activity
Kilauea, Hawaii	**ongoing**	Piton de la Fournaise, Réunion	2004
Kliuchevskoi, Kamchatka, Russia	**ongoing**	**Popocatepetl, Mexico**	**2005**
Komagatake, Hokkaido, Japan	2000	Rabaul, Papua New Guinea	2003
Korovin, Alaska	1998	**Reventador, Ecuador**	**2005**
Krakatau, Indonesia	2001	Rincon de la Vieja, Costa Rica	1998
Langila, New Britain	2004	Rotorua, New Zealand	2001
Lamongan, Indonesia	2003	Ruapehu, New Zealand	1999
Lascar, Chile	2003	Ruby Seamount, Mariana Islands	1995
Leroboleng, Indonesia	2003	**Mount St. Helens, Washington**	**2005**
Mount Lewotobi, Indonesia	2003	**Sakura-Jima, Japan**	**2005**
Llaima, Chile	2003	San Cristobal, Nicaragua	2001
Loihi Seamount, Hawaii	1996	**Santa Maria, Guatemala**	**2005**
Lokon, Sulawesi, Indonesia	2003	**Semeru, Java, Indonesia**	**2005**
Long Valley caldera, California	1996	**Sheveluch, Kamchatka, Russia**	**ongoing**
Lopevi, Central Islands, Vanuatu	2003	Shin-dake, Kuchinoerabujima Island, Japan	1999
La Madera, Nicaragua	1996	Shishaldin, Unimak Island, Alaska	2000
Manam, Papua New Guinea	**2005**	Soputan, Indonesia	2005
Maroa, New Zealand	2001	**Soufriere Hills, Montserrat, West Indies**	**2005**
Masaya, Nicaragua	2003	South Sister, Oregon	2001
Mauna Loa, Hawaii	2003	Stromboli, Italy	2002
Mayon, Philippines	2003	**Suwanose-Jima Ryukyu Islands, Japan**	**2005**
McDonald Island, Australia	1996	Tavurvur, Papua New Guinea	2000
Merapi, Indonesia	**2005**	Taal, Philippines	1999
Metis Shoal, Tonga	1995	**Talan, Indonesia**	**2005**
Momotombo, Nicaragua	1996	Telica, Nicaragua	1999
Monowai Seamount, Kermadec Islands	1997	Terceira, Azores	1999
		Tonga (unnamed volcano)	1999
Nyamuragira, Congo (Dem. Rep.)	**2005**	**Tungurahua, Ecuador**	**ongoing**
Nyiragongo, Congo (Dem. Rep.)	2003	**Ulawun, Papua New Guinea**	**2005**
Okmok, Alaska	1997	Usu, Japan	2000
Mount Oyama, Japan	2002	Veniaminof, Alaska	2004
Pacaya, Guatemala	**2005**	**Villarrica, Chile**	**2005**
Pago, Papua New Guinea	2004	White Island, New Zealand	2000
Papandayan, Java, Indonesia	2002	Yasur, Tanna Island, Vanuatu	2004
Pavlof, Alaska	1997	Yellowstone, Wyoming	1998
Peuet Sague, Indonesia	1998	Zacatecas, Mexico	1997
Piparo, Trinidad	1997		

As of Aug. 2005. *Source:* Volcano World. Web: volcano.und.edu/vw.html.

The Deadliest Volcanic Eruptions

Volcano	Year	Deaths	Major cause of deaths
Tambora, Indonesia	1815	92,000	Starvation
Krakatau, Indonesia	1883	36,417	Tsunami
Mount Pelee, Martinique	1902	29,025	Ash flows
Ruiz, Colombia	1985	25,000	Mudflows
Unzen, Japan	1792	14,300	Volcano collapse, tsunami
Laki, Iceland	1783	9,350	Starvation
Kelut, Indonesia	1919	5,110	Mudflows
Galunggung, Indonesia	1882	4,011	Mudflows
Vesuvius, Italy	1631	3,500	Mudflows, lava flows
Vesuvius, Italy	79	3,360	Ash flows, falls
Papandayan, Indonesia	1772	2,957	Ash flows
Lamington, Papua New Guinea	1951	2,942	Ash flows
El Chichon, Mexico	1982	2,000	Ash flows
Soufriere, St. Vincent	1902	1,680	Ash flows
Oshima, Japan	1741	1,475	Tsunami
Asama, Japan	1783	1,377	Ash flows, mudflows
Taal, Philippines	1911	1,335	Ash flows
Mayon, Philippines	1814	1,200	Mudflows
Agung, Indonesia	1963	1,184	Ash flows
Cotopaxi, Ecuador	1877	1,000	Mudflows
Pinatubo, Philippines	1991	800	Disease
Komagatake, Japan	1640	700	Tsunami
Ruiz, Colombia	1845	700	Mudflows
Hibok-Hibok, Philippines	1951	500	Ash flows

NOTE: All eruptions with more than 500 known human fatalities. Based on data in *Volcanic Hazards: A Sourcebook on the Effects of Eruptions* by Russell J. Blong (Academic Press, 1984). *Source:* Volcano World. Web: volcano.und.edu/vw.html.

Deadliest Earthquakes on Record

(50,000 deaths or more)

Date	Location	Deaths	Magnitude	Date	Location	Deaths	Magnitude
Jan. 23, 1556	Shansi, China	830,000	n.a.	Sept. 1290	Chihli, China	100,000	n.a.
Dec. 26, 2004	off west coast of northern Sumatra	283,106	9.0	Nov. 1667	Shemakha, Caucasia	80,000	n.a.
				Nov. 18, 1727	Tabriz, Iran	77,000	n.a.
July 27, 1976	Tangshan, China	255,000[1]	8.0	Nov. 1, 1755	Lisbon, Portugal	70,000	8.7
Aug. 9, 1138	Aleppo, Syria	230,000	n.a.	Dec. 25, 1932	Gansu, China	70,000	7.6
May 22, 1927	near Xining, China	200,000	8.3	May 31, 1970	Peru	66,000	7.8
Dec. 22, 856[2]	Damghan, Iran	200,000	n.a.	1268[4]	Silicia, Asia Minor	60,000	n.a.
Dec. 16, 1920	Gansu, China	200,000	8.6	Jan. 11, 1693	Sicily, Italy	60,000	n.a.
March 23, 893[2]	Ardabil, Iran	150,000	n.a.	May 30, 1935	Quetta, Pakistan	30,000– 60,000	7.5
Sept. 1, 1923	Kwanto, Japan	143,000	8.3				
Oct. 5, 1948	Ashgabat, Turkmenistan, USSR	110,000	7.3	Feb. 4, 1783	Calabria, Italy	50,000	n.a.
				June 20, 1990	Iran	50,000	7.7
Dec. 28, 1908	Messina, Italy	70,000– 100,000[3]	7.5				

1. Official. Estimated death toll as high as 655,000. 2. Note that these dates are prior to A.D. 1000. No digit is missing. 3. Estimated. 4. No date available. *Source:* National Earthquake Information Center, U.S. Geological Survey. Data compiled from several sources.

The Ten Largest[1] Earthquakes Since 1900

Location	Date	Magnitude[2]	Location	Date	Magnitude[2]
1. Chile	May 22, 1960	9.5	6. Off the coast of Ecuador	Jan. 31, 1906	8.8
2. Prince William Sound, Alaska	March 28, 1964[3]	9.2	7. Rat Islands, Aleutian Islands	Feb. 4, 1965	8.7
3. Andreanof Islands, Aleutian Islands	March 9, 1957	9.1	8. Northern Sumatra, Indonesia	March 28, 2005	8.7
4. Kamchatka	Nov. 4, 1952	9.0	9. India-China border	Aug. 15, 1950	8.6
5. Off western coast of Sumatra, Indonesia	Dec. 26, 2004	9.0	10. Kamchatka	Feb. 3, 1923	8.5

1. In terms of magnitude. 2. Moment magnitude. 3. March 28, 03:36:14 UT (March 27, 5:36 P.M. local time) *Source:* National Earthquake Information Center, U.S. Geological Survey.

The Severity of an Earthquake

Source: National Earthquake Information Center, U.S. Geological Survey

Earthquakes are the result of forces deep within Earth's interior that continuously affect its surface. The energy from these forces is stored in a variety of ways within the rocks. When this energy is released suddenly—by shearing movements along faults in the crust of Earth, for example—an earthquake results. The area of the fault where the sudden rupture takes place is called the focus or hypocenter of the earthquake. The point on Earth's surface directly above the focus is called the epicenter of the earthquake.

The severity of an earthquake can be expressed in terms of both intensity and magnitude. The two terms are quite different, however, and they are often confused. Intensity is based on the observed effects of ground shaking on people, buildings, and natural features. It varies from place to place within the disturbed region depending on the location of the observer with respect to the earthquake epicenter. Magnitude is related to the amount of seismic energy released at the hypocenter of the earthquake. It is based on the amplitude of the earthquake waves recorded on instruments, which have a common calibration. Magnitude is thus represented by a single, instrumentally determined value.

The Richter Magnitude Scale

Seismic waves are the vibrations from earthquakes that travel through Earth; they are recorded on instruments called seismographs. Seismographs record a zigzag trace that shows the varying amplitude of ground oscillations beneath the instrument. Sensitive seismographs, which greatly magnify these ground motions, can detect strong earthquakes from sources anywhere in the world. The time, location, and magnitude of an earthquake can be determined from the data recorded by seismograph stations.

The Richter magnitude scale was developed in 1935 by Charles F. Richter of the California Institute of Technology as a mathematical device to compare the size of earthquakes. The magnitude of an earthquake is determined from the logarithm of the amplitude of waves recorded by seismographs. Adjustments are included in the magnitude formula to compensate for the variation in the distance between the various seismographs and the epicenter of the earthquakes. On the Richter Scale, magnitude is expressed in whole numbers and decimal fractions. For example, a magnitude of 5.3 might be computed for a moderate earthquake, and a strong earthquake might be rated as magnitude 6.3.

Because of the logarithmic basis of the scale, each whole number increase in magnitude represents a tenfold increase in measured amplitude; as an estimate of energy, each whole number step in the magnitude scale corresponds to the release of about 31 times more energy than the amount associated with the preceding whole number value. Although the Richter Scale has no upper limit, the largest known shocks have had magnitudes in the 8.8 to 8.9 range.

Why Are There So Many Earthquake Magnitude Scales?

Earthquake size, as measured by the Richter Scale, is a well-known, but not well understood, concept. What is even less well understood is the proliferation of magnitude scales and their relation to Richter's original magnitude scale. Richter's magnitude scale was first created for measuring the size of earthquakes occurring in southern California, using relatively high-frequency data from nearby seismograph stations. This magnitude scale was referred to as ML, with the L standing for local.

As more seismograph stations were installed around the world, it became apparent that the method developed by Richter was strictly valid only for certain frequency and distance ranges. In order to take advantage of the growing number of globally distributed seismograph stations, new magnitude scales that are an extension of Richter's original idea were developed. These include body-wave magnitude, "mb," and surface-wave magnitude, "MS." Each is valid for a particular frequency range and type of seismic signal. In its range of validity each is equivalent to the Richter magnitude.

Because of the limitations of all three magnitude scales—ML, mb, and MS—a new, more uniformly

applicable extension of the magnitude scale, known as moment magnitude, or "MW," was developed. In particular, for very large earthquakes moment magnitude gives the most reliable estimate of earthquake size. New techniques that take advantage of modern telecommunications have recently been implemented, allowing reporting agencies to obtain rapid estimates of moment magnitude for significant earthquakes. So nowadays, when most seismologists announce a magnitude number, they are rarely referring to the Richter Scale.

The Modified Mercalli Intensity Scale

The effect of an earthquake on Earth's surface is called the intensity. The intensity scale consists of a series of certain key responses, such as people awakening, movement of furniture, damage to chimneys, and finally—total destruction. Although numerous intensity scales have been developed over the past several hundred years to evaluate the effects of earthquakes, the one currently used in the United States is the Modified Mercalli (MM) Intensity Scale. It was developed in 1931 by the American seismologists Harry Wood and Frank Neumann. This scale, composed of 12 increasing levels of intensity that range from imperceptible shaking to catastrophic destruction, is designated by Roman numerals. It does not have a mathematical basis; instead it is an arbitrary ranking based on observed effects. The Modified Mercalli Intensity value assigned to a specific site after an earthquake has a more meaningful measure of severity to the nonscientist than the magnitude because intensity refers to the effects actually experienced at that place.

See also Deadliest Tsunamis and Tsunami FAQ, p. 210.

Frequency of Earthquakes Worldwide

Descriptor	Magnitude	Annual average	Descriptor	Magnitude	Annual average
Great	8 or higher	1[1]	Light	4–4.9	c. 13,000
Major	7–7.9	17[2]	Minor	3–3.9	c. 130,000
Strong	6–6.9	134[2]	Very minor	2–2.9	c. 1,300,000
Moderate	5–5.9	1,319[2]			

1. Based on observations since 1900. 2. Based on observations since 1990. NOTE: The NEIC estimates that several million earthquakes occur in the world each year. Many go undetected because they hit remote areas or have very small magnitudes. *Source:* National Earthquake Information Center, U.S. Geological Survey.

Number of Earthquakes Worldwide, 2000–2005, and Mortality Figures

Magnitude	2000	2001	2002	2003	2004	2005
8.0–9.9	1	1	0	1	2	1
7.0–7.9	14	15	13	14	13	5
6.0–6.9	158	126	130	140	139	100
5.0–5.9	1,345	1,243	1,218	1,203	1,422	1,049
4.0–4.9	8,045	8,084	8,584	8,462	10,963	8,231
3.0–3.9	4,784	6,151	7,005	7,624	7,602	4,430
2.0–2.9	3,758	4,162	6,419	7,727	6,251	2,371
1.0–1.9	1,026	944	1,137	2,506	1,337	15
0.1–0.9	5	1	10	134	103	0
No magnitude	3,120	2,938	2,937	3,608	3,367	534
Total	22,256	23,534	27,454	31,419[1]	31,199[1]	17,159[1]
Estimated deaths	**231**	**21,357**	**1,685**	**33,819**	**284,012**	**1,952**

1. As of Aug. 4, 2005 *Source:* National Earthquake Information Center, U.S. Geological Survey. Web: neic.usgs.gov/neis/eqlists/eqstats.html

Major Earthquakes around the World, 2005

Date	Location	Magnitude[1]	Date	Location	Magnitude[1]
Feb. 5	Celebes Sea	7.1	June 13	Tarapaca, Chile	7.8
March 2	Banda Sea	7.1	June 15	Off coast of northern California	7.2
March 28	Northern Sumatra, Indonesia	8.7	July 24	Nicobar Islands, India	7.3

NOTE: A major earthquake is defined here as having a magnitude of 7.0 or more. 1. Unless otherwise indicated, magnitudes listed are moment magnitudes, the newest, most uniformly applicable magnitude scale. *Source:* National Earthquake Information Center, U.S. Geological Survey. Web: neic.usgs.gov/neis/bulletin/mag7.html

Estimated Deaths from Earthquakes, 2005[1]

Date	Region	Magnitude	Number killed	Date	Region	Magnitude	Number killed
Jan. 23	Sulawesi, Indonesia	6.2	1	May 3	Western Iran	4.9	4
Jan. 25	Turkey-Iraq Border Region	5.9	2	June 4	Eastern New Guinea region, Papua New Guinea	6.1	1
Feb. 2	Java, Indonesia	4.8	1				
Feb. 5	Celebes Sea	7.1	2	June 13	Tarapaca, Chile	.8	11
Feb. 22	Central Iran	6.4	612	July 5	South Africa	2.7	1
March 9	South Africa	5.0	2	July 25	Heilongjiang, China	5.0	1
March 20	Kyushu, Japan	6.6	1	**Total**			**1,952**
March 28	Northern Sumatra, Indonesia	8.7	1,313				

1. As of June 16, 2005. *Source:* National Earthquake Information Center, U.S. Geological Survey. Web: neic.usgs.gov/neis/bulletin/mag7.html

The World's 14 Highest Mountain Peaks (above 8,000 meters)

All 14 of the world's 8,000-meter peaks are located in the Himalaya or the Karakoram ranges in Asia. According to Everestnews.com, only 12 climbers have reached the summits of all 14: Reinhold Messner (Italy) was first, followed by Jerzy Kukuczka (Poland), Ehardt Loretan (Switzerland), Carlos Carsolio (Mexico), Krzysztof Wielicki (Poland), Juan Oiarzabal (Spain), Sergio Martini (Italy), Park Young Seok (Korea), Hang-Gil Um (Korea), Alberto Inurrategui (Spain), Han Wang Yong (Korea), and Ed Viesturs (U.S.).

Mountain	Location	Height Meters	Height Feet	First to summit (nationality)	Date
1. Everest[1]	Nepal/Tibet	8,850	29,035	Edmund Hillary (New Zealander, UK), Tenzing Norgay (Nepalese)	May 29, 1953
2. K2 (Godwin Austen)	Pakistan/China	8,611	28,250	A. Compagnoni, L. Lacedelli (Italian)	July 31, 1954
3. Kangchenjunga	Nepal/India	8,586	28,169	G. Band, J. Brown, N. Hardie, S. Streather (UK)	May 25, 1955
4. Lhotse	Nepal/Tibet	8,516	27,940	F. Luchsinger, E. Reiss (Swiss)	May 18, 1956
5. Makalu	Nepal/Tibet	8,463	27,766	J. Couzy, L. Terray, J. Franco, G. Magnone-Gialtsen, J. Bouier, S. Coupé, P. Leroux, A. Vialatte (French)	May 15, 1955
6. Cho Oyu	Nepal/Tibet	8,201	26,906	H. Tichy, S. Jöchler (Austrian), Pasang Dawa Lama (Nepalese)	Oct. 19, 1954
7. Dhaulagiri	Nepal	8,167	26,795	A. Schelbert, E. Forrer, K. Diemberger, P. Diener (Swiss), Nyima Dorji, Nawang Dorji (Nepalese)	May 13, 1960
8. Manaslu	Nepal	8,163	26,781	T. Imamishi, K. Kato, M. Higeta, (Japanese) G. Norbu (Nepalese)	May 9, 1956
9. Nanga Parbat	Pakistan	8,125	26,660	Hermann Buhl (Austrian)	July 3, 1953
10. Annapurna	Nepal	8,091	26,545	M. Herzog, L. Lachenal (French)	June 3, 1950
11. Gasherbrum I	Pakistan/China	8,068	26,470	P. K. Schoeing, A. J. Kauffman	July 4, 1958
12. Broad Peak	Pakistan/China	8,047	26,400	M. Schmuck, F. Wintersteller, K. Diemberger, H. Buhl (Austrian)	June 9, 1957
13. Gasherbrum II	Pakistan/China	8,035	26,360	F. Moravec, S. Larch, H. Willenpart (Austrian)	July 7, 1956
14. Shisha Pangma	Tibet	8,013	26,289	Hsu Ching and team of 9 (Chinese)	May 2, 1964

1. The 1955 elevation of Everest, 29,028 ft. (8,848 m), was revised on Nov. 11, 1999, and now stands at 29,035 ft. (8,850 m).

Highest Mountain Peaks of the World (continued from p. 492)

(*See* p. 502 for U.S. peaks.)

Mountain peak	Range	Location	ft.	m	Mountain peak	Range	Location	ft.	m
Annapurna II	Himalayas	Nepal	26,041	7,937	Gauri Sankar	Himalayas	Nepal/Tibet	23,440	7,145
Gyachung Kang	Himalayas	Nepal	25,910	7,897	Badrinath	Himalayas	India	23,420	7,138
Disteghil Sar	Karakoram	Pakistan	25,858	7,882	Nunkun	Himalayas	Kashmir	23,410	7,135
Himalchuli	Himalayas	Nepal	25,801	7,864	Lenin Peak	Pamirs	Tajikistan/Kyrgyzstan	23,405	7,134
Nuptse	Himalayas	Nepal	25,726	7,841	Pyramid	Himalayas	Nepal	23,400	7,132
Nanda Devi	Himalayas	India	25,663	7,824	Api	Himalayas	Nepal	23,399	7,132
Masherbrum	Karakoram	Kashmir[1]	25,660	7,821	Pauhunri	Himalayas	India/China	23,385	7,128
Rakaposhi	Karakoram	Pakistan	25,551	7,788	Trisul	Himalayas	India	23,360	7,120
Kanjut Sar	Karakoram	Pakistan	25,461	7,761	Korzhenevski Peak	Pamirs	Tajikistan	23,310	7,105
Kamet	Himalayas	India/Tibet	25,446	7,756	Kangto	Himalayas	Tibet	23,260	7,090
Namcha Barwa	Himalayas	Tibet	25,445	7,756	Nyainqen-tanglha	Nyainqen-tanglha Shan	China	23,255	7,088
Gurla Mandhata	Himalayas	Tibet	25,355	7,728	Trisuli	Himalayas	India	23,210	7,074
Ulugh Muz-tagh	Kunlun	Tibet	25,340	7,723	Dunagiri	Himalayas	India	23,184	7,066
Kungur	Muztagh Ata	China	25,325	7,719	Revolution Peak	Pamirs	Tajikistan	22,880	6,974
Tirich Mir	Hindu Kush	Pakistan	25,230	7,690	Aconcagua	Andes	Argentina	22,834	6,960
Saser Kangri	Karakoram	India	25,172	7,672	Ojos del Salado	Andes	Argentina/Chile	22,664	6,908
Makalu II	Himalayas	Nepal	25,120	7,657	Bonete	Andes	Argentina/Chile	22,546	6,872
Minya Konka (Gongga Shan)	Daxue Shan	China	24,900	7,590	Ama Dablam	Himalayas	Nepal	22,494	6,856
Kula Kangri	Himalayas	Bhutan	24,783	7,554	Tupungato	Andes	Argentina/Chile	22,310	6,800
Chang-tzu	Himalayas	Tibet	24,780	7,553	Moscow Peak	Pamirs	Tajikistan	22,260	6,785
Muztagh Ata	Muztagh Ata	China	24,757	7,546	Pissis	Andes	Argentina	22,241	6,779
Skyang Kangri	Himalayas	Kashmir	24,750	7,544	Mercedario	Andes	Argentina/Chile	22,211	6,770
Ismail Samani Peak (formerly Communism Peak)	Pamirs	Tajikistan	24,590	7,495	Huascarán	Andes	Peru	22,205	6,768
					Llullaillaco	Andes	Argentina/Chile	22,057	6,723
Jongsong Peak	Himalayas	Nepal	24,472	7,459	El Libertador	Andes	Argentina	22,047	6,720
Pobeda Peak	Tien Shan	Kyrgyzstan	24,406	7,439	Cachi	Andes	Argentina	22,047	6,720
Sia Kangri	Himalayas	Kashmir	24,350	7,422	Kailas	Himalayas	Tibet	22,027	6,714
Haramosh Peak	Karakoram	Pakistan	24,270	7,397	Incahuasi	Andes	Argentina/Chile	21,720	6,620
Istoro Nal	Hindu Kush	Pakistan	24,240	7,388	Yerupaja	Andes	Peru	21,709	6,617
Tent Peak	Himalayas	Nepal	24,165	7,365	Kurumda	Pamirs	Tajikistan	21,686	6,610
Chomo Lhari	Himalayas	Tibet/Bhutan	24,040	7,327	Galan	Andes	Argentina	21,654	6,600
Chamlang	Himalayas	Nepal	24,012	7,319	El Muerto	Andes	Argentina/Chile	21,463	6,542
Kabru	Himalayas	Nepal	24,002	7,316	Sajama	Andes	Bolivia	21,391	6,520
Alung Gangri	Himalayas	Tibet	24,000	7,315	Nacimiento	Andes	Argentina	21,302	6,493
Baltoro Kangri	Himalayas	Kashmir	23,990	7,312	Illampu	Andes	Bolivia	21,276	6,485
Muztagh Ata (K-5)	Kunlun	China	23,890	7,282	Illimani	Andes	Bolivia	21,201	6,462
Mana	Himalayas	India	23,860	7,273	Coropuna	Andes	Peru	21,083	6,426
Baruntse	Himalayas	Nepal	23,688	7,220	Laudo	Andes	Argentina	20,997	6,400
Nepal Peak	Himalayas	Nepal	23,500	7,163	Ancohuma	Andes	Bolivia	20,958	6,388
Amne Machin	Kunlun	China	23,490	7,160	Cuzco (Ausangate)	Andes	Peru	20,945	6,384

1. Kashmir is divided between India, Pakistan, and China, and the three countries dispute the boundaries. *Source:* National Geographic Society.

Climbing the Seven Summits

About 95 mountaineers have climbed all "Seven Summits"—the highest peak on each of the seven continents. The first was Dick Bass, an American businessman, on April 30, 1985. The seven summits are Mt. Everest (Asia) 29,035 ft., Mt. Aconcagua (South America) 22,834 ft., Mt. McKinley (North America) 20,320 ft., Mt. Kilimanjaro (Africa) 19,340 ft., Mt. Elbrus (Europe) 18,510 ft., Vinson Massif (Antarctica) 16,066 ft., and Kosciusko (Australia) 7,310 ft. Some climbers believe that the true Seven Summits should include Carstensz Pyramid (16,023 ft.) in Irian Jaya, Indonesia, rather than Australia's Kosciusko. Carstensz is the highest summit in Australia/Oceania, but strictly speaking, Oceania is not a continent.

Oceans and Seas

Name	Area sq. mi.	Area sq. km	Average depth ft.	Average depth m	Greatest known depth ft.	Greatest known depth m	Place of greatest known depth
Pacific Ocean	60,060,700	155,557,000	13,215	4,028	36,198	11,033	Mariana Trench
Atlantic Ocean	29,637,900	76,762,000	12,880	3,926	30,246	9,219	Puerto Rico Trench
Indian Ocean	26,469,500	68,556,000	13,002	3,963	24,460	7,455	Sunda Trench
Southern Ocean[1]	7,848,300	20,327,000	13,100–16,400	4,000–5,000	23,736	7,235	South Sandwich Trench
Arctic Ocean	5,427,000	14,056,000	3,953	1,205	18,456	5,625	77°45′N; 175°W
Mediterranean Sea[2]	1,144,800	2,965,800	4,688	1,429	15,197	4,632	Off Cape Matapan, Greece
Caribbean Sea	1,049,500	2,718,200	8,685	2,647	22,788	6,946	Off Cayman Islands
South China Sea	895,400	2,319,000	5,419	1,652	16,456	5,016	West of Luzon
Bering Sea	884,900	2,291,900	5,075	1,547	15,659	4,773	Off Buldir Island
Gulf of Mexico	615,000	1,592,800	4,874	1,486	12,425	3,787	Sigsbee Deep
Okhotsk Sea	613,800	1,589,700	2,749	838	12,001	3,658	146°10′E; 46°50′N
East China Sea	482,300	1,249,200	617	188	9,126	2,782	25°16′N; 125°E
Hudson Bay	475,800	1,232,300	420	128	600	183	Near entrance
Japan Sea	389,100	1,007,800	4,429	1,350	12,276	3,742	Central Basin
Andaman Sea	308,000	797,700	2,854	870	12,392	3,777	Off Car Nicobar Island
North Sea	222,100	575,200	308	94	2,165	660	Skagerrak
Red Sea	169,100	438,000	1,611	491	7,254	2,211	Off Port Sudan
Baltic Sea	163,000	422,200	180	55	1,380	421	Off Gotland

NOTE: For Caspian Sea, *see* Large Lakes of the World. 1. A decision by the International Hydrographic Organization in spring 2000 delimited a fifth world ocean. 2. Includes Black Sea and Sea of Azov.

Large Lakes of the World

Name and location	Area sq. mi.	Area km	Length mi.	Length km	Maximum depth ft.	Maximum depth m
Caspian Sea, Azerbaijan-Russia-Kazakhstan-Turkmenistan-Iran[1]	152,239	394,299	745	1,199	3,104	946
Superior, U.S.-Canada	31,820	82,414	383	616	1,333	406
Victoria, Tanzania-Uganda	26,828	69,485	200	322	270	82
Huron, U.S.-Canada	23,010	59,596	247	397	750	229
Michigan, U.S.	22,400	58,016	321	517	923	281
Aral, Kazakhstan-Uzbekistan	13,000	33,800	266	428	223	68
Tanganyika, Tanzania-Congo	12,700	32,893	420	676	4,708	1,435
Baikal, Russia	12,162	31,500	395	636	5,712	1,741
Great Bear, Canada	12,000	31,080	232	373	270	82
Nyasa, Malawi-Mozambique-Tanzania	11,600	30,044	360	579	2,316	706
Great Slave, Canada	11,170	28,930	298	480	2,015	614
Chad,[2] Chad-Niger-Nigeria	9,946	25,760	—	—	23	7
Erie, U.S.-Canada	9,930	25,719	241	388	210	64
Winnipeg, Canada	9,094	23,553	264	425	204	62
Ontario, U.S.-Canada	7,520	19,477	193	311	778	237
Balkhash, Kazakhstan	7,115	18,428	376	605	87	27
Ladoga, Russia	7,000	18,130	124	200	738	225
Onega, Russia	3,819	9,891	154	248	361	110
Titicaca, Bolivia-Peru	3,141	8,135	110	177	1,214	370
Nicaragua, Nicaragua	3,089	8,001	110	177	230	70
Athabaska, Canada	3,058	7,920	208	335	407	124
Rudolf, Kenya	2,473	6,405	154	248	—	—
Reindeer, Canada	2,444	6,330	152	245	—	—
Eyre, South Australia	2,400[3]	6,216	130	209	varies	varies
Issyk-Kul, Kyrgyzstan	2,394	6,200	113	182	2,297	700
Urmia,[2] Iran	2,317	6,001	81	130	49	15
Torrens, South Australia	2,200	5,698	130	209	—	—
Vänern, Sweden	2,141	5,545	87	140	322	98
Winnipegosis, Canada	2,086	5,403	152	245	59	18
Mobutu Sese Seko, Uganda	2,046	5,299	100	161	180	55
Nettilling, Baffin Island, Canada	1,950	5,051	70	113	—	—
Nipigon, Canada	1,870	4,843	72	116	—	—
Manitoba, Canada	1,817	4,706	140	225	22	7
Great Salt, U.S.	1,800	4,662	75	121	15–25	5–8
Kioga, Uganda	1,700	4,403	50	80	about 30	9

NOTE: Area more than 1,700 sq. mi. 1. The Caspian Sea is called "sea" because the Romans, finding it salty, named it *Mare Caspium*. Many geographers, however, consider it a lake because it is land-locked. 2. Figures represent high-water data. 3. Varies with the rainfall of the wet season. It has been reported to dry up almost completely on occasion.

Principal Rivers of the World

(See pp. 500–501 for other U.S. rivers.)

River	Source	Outflow	mi.	km
Nile	Tributaries of Lake Victoria, Africa	Mediterranean Sea	4,180	6,690
Amazon	Glacier-fed lakes, Peru	Atlantic Ocean	3,912	6,296
Mississippi-Missouri-Red Rock	Source of Red Rock, Montana	Gulf of Mexico	3,710	5,970
Chang Jiang (Yangtze)	Tibetan plateau, China	China Sea	3,602	5,797
Ob	Altai Mts., Russia	Gulf of Ob	3,459	5,567
Huang Ho (Yellow)	Eastern part of Kunlan Mts., West China	Gulf of Chihli	2,900	4,667
Yenisei	Tannu-Ola Mts., western Tuva, Russia	Arctic Ocean	2,800	4,506
Paraná	Confluence of Paranaiba and Grande rivers	Río de la Plata	2,795	4,498
Irtish	Altai Mts., Russia	Ob River	2,758	4,438
Zaire (Congo)	Confluence of Lualab and Luapula rivers, Congo	Atlantic Ocean	2,716	4,371
Heilong (Amur)	Confluence of Shilka (Russia) and Argun (Manchuria) rivers	Tatar Strait	2,704	4,352
Lena	Baikal Mts., Russia	Arctic Ocean	2,652	4,268
Mackenzie	Head of Finlay River, British Columbia, Canada	Beaufort Sea (Arctic Ocean)	2,635	4,241
Niger	Guinea	Gulf of Guinea	2,600	4,184
Mekong	Tibetan highlands	South China Sea	2,500	4,023
Mississippi	Lake Itasca, Minnesota	Gulf of Mexico	2,348	3,779
Missouri	Confluence of Jefferson, Gallatin, and Madison rivers, Montana	Mississippi River	2,315	3,726
Volga	Valdai plateau, Russia	Caspian Sea	2,291	3,687
Madeira	Confluence of Beni and Maumoré rivers, Bolivia–Brazil boundary	Amazon River	2,012	3,238
Purus	Peruvian Andes	Amazon River	1,993	3,207
São Francisco	Southwest Minas Gerais, Brazil	Atlantic Ocean	1,987	3,198
Yukon	Junction of Lewes and Pelly rivers, Yukon Territory, Canada	Bering Sea	1,979	3,185
St. Lawrence	Lake Ontario	Gulf of St. Lawrence	1,900	3,058
Rio Grande	San Juan Mts., Colorado	Gulf of Mexico	1,885	3,034
Brahmaputra	Himalayas	Ganges River	1,800	2,897
Indus	Himalayas	Arabian Sea	1,800	2,897
Danube	Black Forest, Germany	Black Sea	1,766	2,842
Euphrates	Confluence of Murat Nehri and Kara Su rivers, Turkey	Shatt-al-Arab	1,739	2,799
Darling	Central part of Eastern Highlands, Australia	Murray River	1,702	2,739
Zambezi	11°21′S, 24°22′E, Zambia	Mozambique Channel	1,700	2,736
Tocantins	Goiás, Brazil	Pará River	1,677	2,699
Murray	Australian Alps, New South Wales	Indian Ocean	1,609	2,589
Nelson	Head of Bow River, western Alberta, Canada	Hudson Bay	1,600	2,575
Paraguay	Mato Grosso, Brazil	Paraná River	1,584	2,549
Ural	Southern Ural Mts., Russia	Caspian Sea	1,574	2,533
Ganges	Himalayas	Bay of Bengal	1,557	2,506
Amu Darya (Oxus)	Nicholas Range, Pamir Mts., Turkmenistan	Aral Sea	1,500	2,414
Japurá	Andes, Colombia	Amazon River	1,500	2,414
Salween	Tibet, south of Kunlun Mts.	Gulf of Martaban	1,500	2,414
Arkansas	Central Colorado	Mississippi River	1,459	2,348
Colorado	Grand County, Colorado	Gulf of California	1,450	2,333
Dnieper	Valdai Hills, Russia	Black Sea	1,419	2,284
Ohio-Allegheny	Potter County, Pennsylvania	Mississippi River	1,306	2,102
Irrawaddy	Confluence of Nmai and Mali rivers, northeast Burma	Bay of Bengal	1,300	2,092
Orange	Lesotho	Atlantic Ocean	1,300	2,092
Orinoco	Serra Parima Mts., Venezuela	Atlantic Ocean	1,281	2,062
Pilcomayo	Andes Mts., Bolivia	Paraguay River	1,242	1,999
Xi Jiang (Si Kiang)	Eastern Yunnan Province, China	China Sea	1,236	1,989
Columbia	Columbia Lake, British Columbia, Canada	Pacific Ocean	1,232	1,983
Don	Tula, Russia	Sea of Azov	1,223	1,968
Sungari	China–North Korea boundary	Amur River	1,215	1,955
Saskatchewan	Canadian Rocky Mts.	Lake Winnipeg	1,205	1,939
Peace	Stikine Mts., British Columbia, Canada	Great Slave River	1,195	1,923
Tigris	Taurus Mts., Turkey	Shatt-al-Arab	1,180	1,899

Large Islands of the World

Island	Location and political affiliation	Area sq. mi.	Area sq. km
Greenland	North Atlantic (Danish)	839,999	2,175,597
New Guinea	Southwest Pacific (West Papua [Irian Jaya], Indonesia, western part; Papua New Guinea, eastern part)	309,000	800,311
Borneo	West mid-Pacific (Indonesian, south part; Brunei and Malaysian, north part)	287,300	744,108
Madagascar	Indian Ocean (Malagasy Republic)	227,000	587,931
Baffin	North Atlantic (Canadian)	195,926	507,451
Sumatra	Northeast Indian Ocean (Indonesian)	182,859	473,605
Honshu	Sea of Japan–Pacific (Japanese)	89,176	230,966
Great Britain	Off coast of NW Europe (England, Scotland, and Wales)	88,795	229,979
Victoria	Arctic Ocean (Canadian)	83,896	217,291
Ellesmere	Arctic Ocean (Canadian)	75,767	196,236
Sulawesi (Celebes)	West mid-Pacific (Indonesian)	73,057	189,218
South Island	South Pacific (New Zealand)	58,384	151,215
Java	Indian Ocean (Indonesian)	51,038	132,189
North Island	South Pacific (New Zealand)	44,702	115,778
Cuba	Caribbean Sea (republic)	42,803	110,860
Newfoundland	North Atlantic (Canadian)	42,031	108,860
Luzon	West mid-Pacific (Philippines)	40,420	104,688
Iceland	North Atlantic (republic)	39,800	103,082
Mindanao	West mid-Pacific (Philippines)	36,537	94,631
Ireland	West of Great Britain (republic, south part; United Kingdom, north part)	32,597	84,426
Hokkaido	Sea of Japan–Pacific (Japanese)	32,245	83,515
Sakhalin (Karafuto)	North of Japan (Russian)	29,500	76,405
Hispaniola	Caribbean Sea (Dominican Republic, east part; Haiti, west part)	29,300	75,887
Banks	Arctic Ocean (Canadian)	27,038	70,028
Tasmania	South of Australia (Australian)	26,200	67,858
Sri Lanka (Ceylon)	Indian Ocean (republic)	24,900	64,491
Devon	Arctic Ocean (Canadian)	21,331	55,247

NOTE: Australia is not included in this list because it is defined as a continent rather than an island.

Highest Waterfalls of the World

Name(s) (foreign)	Location	Height Feet	Height Meters
Angel (Salto Angel)	Canaima Nat'l Park, Venezuela	3,212	979
Tugela	Natal Nat'l Park, South Africa	2,800	850
Utigord (Utigordsfoss)	Norway	2,625	800
Monge (Mongefoss)	Marstein, Norway	2,540	774
Mutarazi (Mtarazi)	Nyanga Nat'l Park, Zimbabwe	2,499	762
Yosemite	Yosemite Nat'l Park, California, U.S.	2,425	739
Pieman	Alpine Nat'l Park, Victoria, Australia	2,346	715
Espelands (Espelandsfoss)	Hardanger Fjord, Norway	2,307	703[1]
Lower Mar Valley (Østra Mardolafoss)	Eikesdal, Norway	2,151	655[2]
Tyssestrengene	Odda, Norway	2,123	647[2]
Cuquenan (Salto Kukenan)	Kukenan Tepuy, Venezuela	2,000	610
Sentinel	Yosemite Nat'l Park, California, U.S.	2,000	610
Dudhsagar	Goa/Karnataka, India	1,969	600
Sutherland	Milford Sound, New Zealand	1,904	580
Kjell (Kjellfossen)	Gudvanger, Norway	1,841	561
Kahiwa	Molokai, Hawaii, U.S.	1,750	533
Takkakaw	Yoho Nat'l Park, B.C., Canada	1,650	503
Ribbon	Yosemite Nat'l Park, California, U.S.	1,612	491
King George VI	Guyana	1,600	488
Upper Mar Valley (Mardalsfossen)	nr. Eikesdal, Norway	1,536	468
Kaliuwaa (Sacred)	Pahu, Hawaii, U.S.	1,520	463
Della	Strathcona Provincial Park, B.C., Canada	1,444	440
Gavarnie	nr. Lourdes, France	1,384	422
Cachoeira da Fumaça (Glass or Smoke)	Chapada Diamantia Nat'l Park, Brazil	1,378	420
Giessbach	Bern, Switzerland	1,312	400
Krimmler	Hohe Tauern Nat'l Park, Austria	1,250	381
Vettis (Vettisfoss)	Jotunheimen, Norway	1,215	370
Papalaua	Molokai, Hawaii, U.S.	1,200	366
Tin Mine	Kosciusko Nat'l Park, Australia	1,182	360

1. Unofficial (estimated) height. Subject to revision. 2. Incorporated in hydroelectric scheme. Greatly diminished flow.
Sources: Merriam Webster's Geographical Dictionary, Third Edition (1997), www.britannica.com, www.waterfallsnorthwest.com, www.americanparknetwork.com, www.ga.gov.au/education/facts/landforms/waterfal.htm/, www.atlas.gc.ca/site/english/facts/waterfalls.html, The State of Hawaii Data Book 2001.

Polar Regions

Antarctica

The second smallest continent, mostly south of the Antarctic Circle.

Area: 14.2 million sq. km (5.5 million sq. mi.).

Geographic South Pole: Earth's southernmost point, at latitude 90°S, where all lines of longitude meet.

Magnetic South Pole: The magnetic South Pole shifts about 5 miles (km) a year and is now located at about 66°S and 139°E on the Adélie Coast of Antarctica.

Terrain: About 98% thick ice sheet and 2% barren rock; glaciers form ice shelves along about half of the coastline, and floating ice shelves constitute 11% of the area of the continent. **Ice sheet:** The continental ice sheet contains approximately 7 million cubic miles (30 million cu km) of ice, representing about 90% of the world's total. **Major ice shelves:** Amery, Filchner, Larsen, Ronne, Ross. Ice shelves make up about 10% of Antarctica's ice, and are floating sheets of ice attached to land that project out into coastal waters.

Climate: The coldest, windiest, driest continent.

Regions: East Antarctica (c. 3,000,000 sq. mi./ 7,770,000 sq. km), the largest portion of the continent, is a high, ice-covered plateau. West Antarctica (c. 2,500,000 sq. mi./6,475,000 sq. km), is an archipelago of mountainous islands connected by ice. A mountain range divides them.

Elevation extremes: *Lowest point:* Bentley Subglacial Trench –8,327 ft. below sea level (–2,538 m)—the lowest land elevation is hidden within the trench. *Highest point:* Vinson Massif 16,066 ft. (4,897 m), Ellsworth Mountains.

The Arctic

Region, primarily made up of the frozen Arctic Ocean, that surrounds the North Pole. Land masses include islands and the northern parts of the European, Asian, and North American continents.

Area: 14.056 million sq. km (5.4 million sq. mi.), largely frozen ocean.

Geographic North Pole: Northern end of Earth's axis, located at about latitude 90°N.

Magnetic North Pole: Continues to shift and is located at approximately 82°N and 114°W in the Queen Elizabeth Islands of northern Canada.

Terrain: Central surface covered by a perennial drifting polar icepack that averages about 3 meters in thickness; the icepack is surrounded by open seas during the summer, but more than doubles in size during the winter and extends to the encircling landmasses.

Climate: Polar climate characterized by persistent cold and relatively narrow annual temperature ranges; winters characterized by continuous darkness, cold and stable weather conditions, and clear skies; summers characterized by continuous daylight, damp and foggy weather, and weak cyclones with rain or snow.

Regions: The Arctic is divided by the summer isotherm, a climatic boundary between regions with summer temperatures averaging 50°F (or 10°C)—the subarctic—and colder regions (the true Arctic).

Elevation extremes: *Lowest point:* Fram Basin –4,665 m. *Highest point:* sea level 0 m.

Interesting Caves and Caverns of the World

Aggtelek. In village of same name, northern Hungary. Large stalactitic cavern about 5 mi. long.

Altamira Cave. Near Santander, Spain. Contains Stone Age animal paintings on roof and walls.

Antiparos. On island of same name in the Grecian Archipelago. Some stalactites are 20 ft. long. Brilliant colors and fantastic shapes.

Blue Grotto. On island of Capri, Italy. Sea cavern hollowed out in limestone by constant wave action. Now half filled with water because of sinking coast. Name derived from unusual blue light permeating the cave. Source of light is a submerged opening allowing light to pass through the water.

Carlsbad Caverns. Southeast New Mexico. Contains some of the largest and most impressive stalactites and stalagmites, particularly in the Lechuguilla Cave.

Fingal's Cave. On island of Staffa off coast of western Scotland. Penetrates about 200 ft. inland. Contains basaltic columns almost 40 ft. high.

Jenolan Caves. In Blue Mountain plateau, New South Wales, Australia. Beautiful stalactitic formations.

Kent's Cavern. Near Torquay, England. Source of much information on Paleolithic humans.

Lascaux Cave. Southwestern France. Features prehistoric cave paintings estimated to be tens of thousands of years old. Closed to the public.

Lubang Nasib Bagus. Sarawak, Malaysia. World's largest cave chamber: 2,300 ft. long, 1,480 ft. wide, and everywhere at least 230 ft. high.

Luray Caverns. Near Luray, Va. Has large stalactitic and stalagmitic columns of many colors.

Mogao Caves. Located along the old Silk Route in China, Mogao is composed of 492 cells and cave sanctuaries that are famous for their statues and wall paintings, spanning a thousand years of Buddhist art.

Mammoth Cave. This limestone cavern in central Kentucky is the longest cave system in the world. Cave area is about 10 mi. in diameter but has 345 mi. of irregular subterranean passageways at various levels, plus underground lakes and rivers.

Peak Cavern or Devil's Hole. Derbyshire, England. About 2,250 ft. into a mountain. Lowest part is about 600 ft. below the surface.

Postojna Grotto. Postojna, Slovenia. Largest cavern in Europe; numerous beautiful stalactites. Famous example of a karst cave—grooved and irregularly eroded limestone formations carved out by underground streams. Pivka River flows through part of it.

Singing Cave. Iceland. A lava cave; name derived from echoes of people singing in it.

Waitomo Cave. North Island, New Zealand. Glowworms on cave ceiling look like thousands of stars in the night sky.

Wind Cave. In Black Hills of South Dakota. Limestone caverns with stalactites and stalagmites almost entirely missing. Variety of crystal formations called "boxwork."

Wyandotte Cave. In Crawford County, southern Indiana. A limestone cavern with five levels of passages; one of the largest in North America. "Monumental Mountain," approximately 135 ft. high, is believed to be one of the world's largest underground "mountains."

Principal Deserts of the World

Deserts are arid regions, generally receiving less than ten inches of precipitation a year, or regions where the potential evaporation rate is twice as great as the precipitation.

The world's deserts are divided into four categories. **Subtropical deserts** are the hottest, with parched terrain and rapid evaporation. Although **cool coastal deserts** are located within the same latitudes as subtropical deserts, the average temperature is much cooler because of frigid offshore ocean currents. **Cold winter deserts** are marked by stark temperature differences from season to season, ranging from 100° F (38° C) in the summer to 10° F (−12° C) in the winter. **Polar regions** are also considered to be deserts because nearly all moisture in these areas is locked up in the form of ice.

Desert	Location	Size	Topography
SUBTROPICAL DESERTS			
Sahara	Morocco, Western Sahara, Algeria, Tunisia, Libya, Egypt, Mauritania, Mali, Niger, Chad, Ethiopia, Eritrea, Somalia	3.5 million sq. mi.	70% gravel plains, sand, and dunes. Contrary to popular belief, the desert is only 30% sand. The world's largest nonpolar desert gets its name from the Arabic word *Sahra'*, meaning desert
Arabian	Saudi Arabia, Kuwait, Qatar, United Arab Emirates, Oman, Yemen	1 million sq. mi.	Gravel plains, rocky highlands; one-fourth is the Rub al-Khali ("Empty Quarter"), the world's largest expanse of unbroken sand
Kalahari	Botswana, South Africa, Namibia	220,000 sq. mi.	Sand sheets, longitudinal dunes
Australian Desert			
Gibson	Australia (southern portion of the Western Desert)	120,000 sq. mi.	Sandhills, gravel, grass. These three regions of desert are collectively referred
Great Sandy	Australia (northern portion of the Western Desert)	150,000 sq. mi.	to as the Great Western Desert— otherwise known as "the Outback."
Great Victoria	Australia (southernmost portion of the Western Desert)	250,000 sq. mi.	Contains Ayers Rock, or Uluru, one of the world's largest monoliths
Simpson and Sturt Stony	Australia (eastern half of the continent)	56,000 sq. mi.	Simpson's straight, parallel sand dunes are the longest in the world—up to 125 mi. Encompasses the Stewart Stony Desert, named for the Australian explorer
Mojave	U.S.: Arizona, Colorado, Nevada, Utah, California	54,000 sq. mi.	Mountain chains, dry alkaline lake beds, calcium carbonate dunes
Sonoran	U.S.: Arizona, California; Mexico	120,000 sq. mi.	Basins and plains bordered by mountain ridges; home to the Saguaro cactus
Chihuahuan	Mexico; southwestern U.S.	175,000 sq. mi.	Shrub desert; largest in North America
Thar	India, Pakistan	175,000 sq. mi.	Rocky sand and sand dunes
COOL COASTAL DESERTS			
Namib	Angola, Namibia, South Africa	13,000 sq. mi.	Gravel plains
Atacama	Chile	54,000 sq. mi.	Salt basins, sand, lava; world's driest desert
COLD WINTER DESERTS			
Great Basin	U.S.: Nevada, Oregon, Utah	190,000 sq. mi.	Mountain ridges, valleys, 1% sand dunes
Colorado Plateau	U.S.: Arizona, Colorado, New Mexico, Utah, Wyoming	130,000 sq. mi.	Sedimentary rock, mesas, and plateaus— includes the Grand Canyon and is also called the "Painted Desert" because of the spectacular colors in its rocks and canyons
Patagonian	Argentina	260,000 sq. mi.	Gravel plains, plateaus, basalt sheets
Kara-Kum	Uzbekistan, Turkmenistan	135,000 sq. mi.	90% gray layered sand—name means "black sand"
Kyzyl-Kum	Uzbekistan, Turkmenistan, Kazakhstan	115,000 sq. mi.	Sands, rock—name means "red sand"
Iranian	Iran	100,000 sq. mi.	Salt, gravel, rock
Taklamakan	China	105,000 sq. mi.	Sand, dunes, gravel
Gobi	China, Mongolia	500,000 sq. mi.	Stony, sandy soil, steppes (dry grasslands)
POLAR			
Arctic	U.S., Canada, Greenland, Iceland, Norway, Sweden, Finland, Russia	5.4 million sq. mi.	Snow, glaciers, tundra
Antarctic	Antarctica	5.5 million sq. mi.	Ice, snow, bedrock

Latitude and Longitude of World Cities

(and time corresponding to 12:00 noon, Eastern Standard Time)

City	Latitude ° '	Longitude ° '	Time	City	Latitude ° '	Longitude ° '	Time
Aberdeen, Scotland	57 9 N	2 9 W	5:00 p.m.	La Paz, Bolivia	16 27 S	68 22 W	1:00 p.m.
Adelaide, Australia	34 55 S	138 36 E	2:30 a.m.[1]	Lima, Peru	12 0 S	77 2 W	12:00 noon
Algiers, Algeria	36 50 N	3 0 E	6:00 p.m.	Lisbon, Portugal	38 44 N	9 9 W	5:00 p.m.
Amsterdam, Netherlands	52 22 N	4 53 E	6:00 p.m.	Liverpool, England	53 25 N	3 0 W	5:00 p.m.
Ankara, Turkey	39 55 N	32 55 E	7:00 p.m.	London, England	51 32 N	0 5 W	5:00 p.m.
Asunción, Paraguay	25 15 S	57 40 W	1:00 p.m.	Madrid, Spain	40 26 N	3 42 W	6:00 p.m.
Athens, Greece	37 58 N	23 43 E	7:00 p.m.	Manchester, England	53 30 N	2 15 W	5:00 p.m.
Auckland, New Zealand	36 52 S	174 45 E	5:00 a.m.[1]	Manila, Philippines	14 35 N	120 57 E	1:00 a.m.[1]
Bangkok, Thailand	13 45 N	100 30 E	midnight	Marseilles, France	43 20 N	5 20 E	6:00 p.m.
Barcelona, Spain	41 23 N	2 9 E	6:00 p.m.	Mazatlán, Mexico	23 12 N	106 25 W	10:00 a.m.
Beijing, China	39 55 N	116 25 E	1:00 a.m.[1]	Mecca, Saudi Arabia	21 29 N	39 45 E	8:00 p.m.
Belém, Brazil	1 28 S	48 29 W	2:00 p.m.	Melbourne, Australia	37 47 S	144 58 E	3:00 a.m.[1]
Belfast, Northern Ireland	54 37 N	5 56 W	5:00 p.m.	Mexico City, Mexico	19 26 N	99 7 W	11:00 a.m.
Belgrade, Yugoslavia	44 52 N	20 32 E	6:00 p.m.	Milan, Italy	45 27 N	9 10 E	6:00 p.m.
Berlin, Germany	52 30 N	13 25 E	6:00 p.m.	Montevideo, Uruguay	34 53 S	56 10 W	2:00 p.m.
Birmingham, England	52 25 N	1 55 W	5:00 p.m.	Moscow, Russia	55 45 N	37 36 E	8:00 p.m.
Bogotá, Colombia	4 32 N	74 15 W	12:00 noon	Munich, Germany	48 8 N	11 35 E	6:00 p.m.
Bombay, India	19 0 N	72 48 E	10:30 p.m.	Nagasaki, Japan	32 48 N	129 57 E	2:00 a.m.[1]
Bordeaux, France	44 50 N	0 31 W	6:00 p.m.	Nagoya, Japan	35 7 N	136 56 E	2:00 a.m.[1]
Bremen, Germany	53 5 N	8 49 E	6:00 p.m.	Nairobi, Kenya	1 25 S	36 55 E	8:00 p.m.
Brisbane, Australia	27 29 S	153 8 E	3:00 a.m.[1]	Nanjing (Nanking), China	32 3 N	118 53 E	1:00 a.m.[1]
Brussels, Belgium	50 52 N	4 22 E	6:00 p.m.	Naples, Italy	40 50 N	14 15 E	6:00 p.m.
Bucharest, Romania	44 25 N	26 7 E	7:00 p.m.	New Delhi, India	28 35 N	77 12 E	10:30 p.m.
Budapest, Hungary	47 30 N	19 5 E	6:00 p.m.	Newcastle-on-Tyne, England	54 58 N	1 37 W	5:00 p.m.
Buenos Aires, Argentina	34 35 S	58 22 W	2:00 p.m.	Odessa, Ukraine	46 27 N	30 48 E	7:00 p.m.
Cairo, Egypt	30 2 N	31 21 E	7:00 p.m.	Osaka, Japan	34 32 N	135 30 E	2:00 a.m.[1]
Calcutta, India	22 34 N	88 24 E	10:30 p.m.	Oslo, Norway	59 57 N	10 42 E	6:00 p.m.
Canton, China	23 7 N	113 15 E	1:00 a.m.[1]	Panama City, Panama	8 58 N	79 32 W	12:00 noon
Cape Town, South Africa	33 55 S	18 22 E	7:00 p.m.	Paramaribo, Suriname	5 45 N	55 15 W	2:00 p.m.
Caracas, Venezuela	10 28 N	67 2 W	1:00 p.m.	Paris, France	48 48 N	2 20 E	6:00 p.m.
Cayenne, French Guiana	4 49 N	52 18 W	2:00 p.m.	Perth, Australia	31 57 S	115 52 E	1:00 a.m.[1]
Chihuahua, Mexico	28 37 N	106 5 W	10:00 a.m.	Plymouth, England	50 25 N	4 5 W	5:00 p.m.
Chongqing, China	29 46 N	106 34 E	1:00 a.m.[1]	Port Moresby, Papua New Guinea	9 25 S	147 8 E	3:00 a.m.[1]
Copenhagen, Denmark	55 40 N	12 34 E	6:00 p.m.	Prague, Czech Republic	50 5 N	14 26 E	6:00 p.m.
Córdoba, Argentina	31 28 S	64 10 W	2:00 p.m.	Rangoon, Myanmar	16 50 N	96 0 E	11:30 p.m.
Dakar, Senegal	14 40 N	17 28 W	5:00 p.m.	Reykjavík, Iceland	64 4 N	21 58 W	5:00 p.m.
Darwin, Australia	12 28 S	130 51 E	2:30 a.m.[1]	Rio de Janeiro, Brazil	22 57 S	43 12 W	2:00 p.m.
Djibouti, Djibouti	11 30 N	43 3 E	8:00 p.m.	Rome, Italy	41 54 N	12 27 E	6:00 p.m.
Dublin, Ireland	53 20 N	6 15 W	5:00 p.m.	Salvador, Brazil	12 56 S	38 27 W	2:00 p.m.
Durban, South Africa	29 53 S	30 53 E	7:00 p.m.	Santiago, Chile	33 28 S	70 45 W	1:00 p.m.
Edinburgh, Scotland	55 55 N	3 10 W	5:00 p.m.	St. Petersburg, Russia	59 56 N	30 18 E	8:00 p.m.
Frankfurt, Germany	50 7 N	8 41 E	6:00 p.m.	São Paulo, Brazil	23 31 S	46 31 W	2:00 p.m.
Georgetown, Guyana	6 45 N	58 15 W	1:00 p.m.	Shanghai, China	31 10 N	121 28 E	1:00 a.m.[1]
Glasgow, Scotland	55 50 N	4 15 W	5:00 p.m.	Singapore, Singapore	1 14 N	103 55 E	1:00 a.m.[1]
Guatemala City, Guatemala	14 37 N	90 31 W	11:00 a.m.	Sofia, Bulgaria	42 40 N	23 20 E	7:00 p.m.
Guayaquil, Ecuador	2 10 S	79 56 W	12:00 noon	Stockholm, Sweden	59 17 N	18 3 E	6:00 p.m.
Hamburg, Germany	53 33 N	10 2 E	6:00 p.m.	Sydney, Australia	34 0 S	151 0 E	3:00 a.m.[1]
Hammerfest, Norway	70 38 N	23 38 E	6:00 p.m.	Tananarive, Madagascar	18 50 S	47 33 E	8:00 p.m.
Havana, Cuba	23 8 N	82 23 W	12:00 noon	Teheran, Iran	35 45 N	51 45 E	8:30 p.m.
Helsinki, Finland	60 10 N	25 0 E	7:00 p.m.	Tokyo, Japan	35 40 N	139 45 E	2:00 a.m.[1]
Hobart, Tasmania	42 52 S	147 19 E	3:00 a.m.[1]	Tripoli, Libya	32 57 N	13 12 E	7:00 p.m.
Hong Kong, China	22 20 N	114 11 E	1:00 a.m.[1]	Venice, Italy	45 26 N	12 20 E	6:00 p.m.
Iquique, Chile	20 10 S	70 7 W	1:00 p.m.	Veracruz, Mexico	19 10 N	96 10 W	11:00 a.m.
Irkutsk, Russia	52 30 N	104 20 E	1:00 a.m.	Vienna, Austria	48 14 N	16 20 E	6:00 p.m.
Jakarta, Indonesia	6 16 S	106 48 E	midnight	Vladivostok, Russia	43 10 N	132 0 E	3:00 a.m.[1]
Johannesburg, South Africa	26 12 S	28 4 E	7:00 p.m.	Warsaw, Poland	52 14 N	21 0 E	6:00 p.m.
Kingston, Jamaica	17 59 N	76 49 W	12:00 noon	Wellington, New Zealand	41 17 S	174 47 E	5:00 a.m.[1]
Kinshasa, Congo	4 18 S	15 17 E	6:00 p.m.	Zürich, Switzerland	47 21 N	8 31 E	6:00 p.m.
Kuala Lumpur, Malaysia	3 8 N	101 42 E	1:00 a.m.[1]				

1. On the following day.

Miscellaneous Data for the United States

Highest point: Mount McKinley, Alaska   20,320 ft. (6,198 m)
Lowest point: Death Valley, Calif.   282 ft. (86 m) below sea level
Approximate mean elevation   2,500 ft. (763 m)
Points farthest apart (50 states): Log Point, Elliot Key, Fla.,
  and Kure Island, Hawaii   5,859 mi. (9,429 km)
Geographic center (50 states): in Butte County, S.D. (west of Castle Rock)   44°58'N lat.103°46'W long.
Geographic center (48 conterminous states): in Smith County, Kan. (near   39°50'N lat. 98°35'W long.
Lebanon)
Boundaries:
  Between Alaska and Canada   1,538 mi. (2,475 km)
  Between the 48 conterminous states and Canada (incl. the Great Lakes)   3,987 mi. (6,416 km)
  Between the United States and Mexico   1,933 mi. (3,111 km)

Source: U.S. Geological Survey.

Extreme Points of the United States (50 States)

Extreme point	Latitude	Longitude	Distance[1] mi.	km
Northernmost point: Point Barrow, Alaska	71°23' N	156°29' W	2,507	4,034
Easternmost point: West Quoddy Head, Maine	44°49' N	66°57' W	1,788	2,997
Southernmost point: Ka Lae (South Cape), Hawaii	18°55' N	155°41' W	3,463	5,573
Westernmost point: Cape Wrangell, Alaska (Attu Island)	52°55' N	172°27' E	3,625	5,833

1. From geographic center of United States (incl. Alaska and Hawaii), west of Castle Rock, S.D., 44°58' lat., 103°46' W long.
If measured from the prime meridian in Greenwich, England, Cape Wrangell, Attu Island, Alaska, would be the easternmost
point.

The Continental Divide

The Continental Divide is a ridge of high ground that runs irregularly north and south through the Rocky Mountains and separates eastward-flowing from westward-flowing streams. The waters that flow eastward empty into the Atlantic Ocean, chiefly by way of the Gulf of Mexico; those that flow westward empty into the Pacific. Every continent with the exception of Antarctica has a continental divide.

Rivers of the United States
(350 or more miles long)

Alabama-Coosa (600 mi.; 966 km): From junction of Oostanula and Etowah R. in Georgia to Mobile R.

Altamaha-Ocmulgee (392 mi.; 631 km): From junction of Yellow R. and South R., Newton Co. in Georgia to Atlantic Ocean.

Apalachicola-Chattahoochee (524 mi.; 843 km): From Towns Co. in Georgia to Gulf of Mexico in Florida.

Arkansas (1,459 mi.; 2,348 km): From Lake Co. in Colorado to Mississippi R. in Arkansas.

Brazos (923 mi.; 1,490 km): From junction of Salt Fork and Double Mountain Fork in Texas to Gulf of Mexico.

Canadian (906 mi.; 1,458 km): From Las Animas Co. in Colorado to Arkansas R. in Oklahoma.

Cimarron (600 mi.; 966 km): From Colfax Co. in New Mexico to Arkansas R. in Oklahoma.

Colorado (1,450 mi.; 2,333 km): From Rocky Mountain National Park in Colorado to Gulf of California in Mexico.

Colorado (862 mi.; 1,387 km): From Dawson Co. in Texas to Matagorda Bay.

Columbia (1,243 mi.; 2,000 km): From Columbia Lake in British Columbia to Pacific Ocean (entering between Oregon and Washington).

Colville (350 mi.; 563 km): From Brooks Range in Alaska to Beaufort Sea.

Connecticut (407 mi.; 655 km): From Third Connecticut Lake in New Hampshire to Long Island Sound in Connecticut.

Cumberland (720 mi.; 1,159 km): From junction of Poor and Clover Forks in Harlan Co. in Kentucky to Ohio R.

Delaware (390 mi.; 628 km): From Schoharie Co. in New York to Liston Point, Delaware Bay.

Gila (649 mi.; 1,044 km): From Catron Co. in New Mexico to Colorado R. in Arizona.

Green (360 mi.; 579 km): From Lincoln Co. in Kentucky to Ohio R. in Kentucky.

Green (730 mi.; 1,175 km): From Sublette Co. in Wyoming to Colorado R. in Utah.

Illinois (420 mi.; 676 km): From St. Joseph Co. in Indiana to Mississippi R. at Grafton in Illinois.

James (sometimes called *Dakota*) (710 mi.; 1,143 km): From Wells Co. in North Dakota to Missouri R. in South Dakota.

Kanawha-New (352 mi.; 566 km): From junction of North and South Forks of New R. in North Carolina, through Virginia and West Virginia (New R. becoming Kanawha R.), to Ohio R.

Kansas (743 mi.; 1,196 km): From source of Arikaree R. in Elbert Co., Colorado, to Missouri R. at Kansas City, Kansas.

Koyukuk (470 mi.; 756 km): From Brooks Range in Alaska to Yukon R.

Kuskokwim (724 mi.; 1,165 km): From Alaska Range in Alaska to Kuskokwim Bay.

Licking (350 mi.; 563 km): From Magoffin Co. in Kentucky to Ohio R. at Cincinnati in Ohio.

Little Missouri (560 mi.; 901 km): From Crook Co. in Wyoming to Missouri R. in North Dakota.

Milk (625 mi.; 1,006 km): From junction of forks in Alberta Province to Missouri R.

Mississippi (2,348 mi.; 3,779 km): From Lake Itasca in Minnesota to mouth of Southwest Pass in Louisiana.

Mississippi-Missouri-Red Rock (3,710 mi.; 5,970 km): From source of Red Rock R. in Montana to mouth of Southwest Pass in Louisiana.

Missouri (2,315 mi.; 3,726 km): From junction of Jefferson R., Gallatin R., and Madison R. in Montana to Mississippi R. near St. Louis.

Missouri-Red Rock (2,540 mi.; 4,090 km): From source of Red Rock R. in Montana to Mississippi R. near St. Louis.

Mobile-Alabama-Coosa (645 mi.; 1,040 km): From junction of Etowah R. and Oostanula R. in Georgia to Mobile Bay.

Neosho (460 mi.; 740 km): From Morris Co. in Kansas to Arkansas R. in Oklahoma.

Niobrara (431 mi.; 694 km): From Niobrara Co. in Wyoming to Missouri R. in Nebraska.

Noatak (350 mi.; 563 km): From Brooks Range in Alaska to Kotzebue Sound.

North Canadian (800 mi.; 1,290 km): From Union Co. in New Mexico to Canadian R. in Oklahoma.

North Platte (618 mi.; 995 km): From Jackson Co. in Colorado to junction with South Platte R. in Nebraska to form Platte R.

Ohio (981 mi.; 1,579 km): From junction of Allegheny R. and Monongahela R. at Pittsburgh to Mississippi R. between Illinois and Kentucky.

Ohio-Allegheny (1,306 mi.; 2,102 km): From Potter Co. in Pennsylvania to Mississippi R. at Cairo in Illinois.

Osage (500 mi.; 805 km): From east-central Kansas to Missouri R. near Jefferson City in Missouri.

Ouachita (605 mi.; 974 km): From Polk Co. in Arkansas to Red R. in Louisiana.

Pearl (411 mi.; 661 km): From Neshoba County in Mississippi to Gulf of Mexico (Mississippi-Louisiana).

Pecos (926 mi.; 1,490 km): From Mora Co. in New Mexico to Rio Grande in Texas.

Pee Dee-Yadkin (435 mi.; 700 km): From Watauga Co. in North Carolina to Winyah Bay in South Carolina.

Pend Oreille–Clark Fork (531 mi.; 855 km): Near Butte in Montana to Columbia R. on Washington-Canada border.

Platte (990 mi.; 1593 km): From source of Grizzly Creek in Jackson Co., Colorado, to Missouri R. south of Omaha, Nebraska.

Porcupine (569 mi.; 916 km): From Yukon Territory, Canada, to Yukon R. in Alaska.

Potomac (383 mi.; 616 km): From Garrett Co. in Maryland to Chesapeake Bay at Point Lookout in Maryland.

Powder (375 mi.; 603 km): From junction of forks in Johnson Co. in Wyoming to Yellowstone R. in Montana.

Red (1,290 mi.; 2,080 km): From source of Tierra Blanca Creek in Curry County, New Mexico, to Mississippi R. in Louisiana.

Red (also called *Red River of the North*) (545 mi.; 877 km): From junction of Otter Tail R. and Bois de Sioux R. in Minnesota to Lake Winnipeg in Manitoba, Canada.

Republican (445 mi.; 716 km): From junction of North Fork and Arikaree R. in Nebraska to junction with Smoky Hill R. in Kansas to form the Kansas R.

Rio Grande (1,900 mi.; 3,060 km): From San Juan Co. in Colorado to Gulf of Mexico.

Roanoke (380 mi.; 612 km): From junction of forks in Montgomery Co. in Virginia to Albemarle Sound in North Carolina.

Sabine (380 mi.; 612 km): From junction of forks in Hunt Co. in Texas to Sabine Lake between Texas and Louisiana.

Sacramento (377 mi.; 607 km): From Siskiyou Co. in California to Suisun Bay.

Saint Francis (425 mi.; 684 km): From Iron Co. in Missouri to Mississippi R. in Arkansas.

Salmon (420 mi.; 676 km): From Custer Co. in Idaho to Snake R.

San Joaquin (350 mi.; 563 km): From junction of forks in Madera Co. in California to Suisun Bay.

San Juan (360 mi.; 579 km): From Archuleta Co. in Colorado to Colorado R. in Utah.

Santee-Wateree-Catawba (538 mi.; 866 km): From McDowell Co. in North Carolina to Atlantic Ocean in South Carolina.

Smoky Hill (540 mi.; 869 km): From Cheyenne Co. in Colorado to junction with Republican R. in Kansas to form Kansas R.

Snake (1,038 mi.; 1,670 km): From Ocean Plateau in Wyoming to Columbia R. in Washington.

South Platte (424 mi.; 682 km): From Park Co. in Colorado to junction with North Platte R. in Nebraska to form Platte R.

Stikine (379 mi.; 610 km): From British Columbia in Canada to Stikine Strait near Wrangell, Alaska.

Susquehanna (444 mi.; 715 km): From Otsego Lake in New York to Chesapeake Bay in Maryland.

Tanana (659 mi.; 1,060 km): From Wrangell Mts. in Yukon Territory, Canada, to Yukon R. in Alaska.

Tennessee (652 mi.; 1,049 km): From junction of Holston R. and French Broad R. in Tennessee to Ohio R. in Kentucky.

Tennessee–French Broad (886 mi.; 1,417 km): From Transylvania Co. in North Carolina to Ohio R. at Paducah in Kentucky.

Tombigbee (525 mi.; 845 km): From junction of forks in Itawamba Co. in Mississippi to Mobile R. in Alabama.

Trinity (360 mi.; 579 km): From junction of forks in Dallas Co. in Texas to Galveston Bay.

Wabash (512 mi.; 824 km): From Darke Co. in Ohio to Ohio R. between Illinois and Indiana.

Washita (500 mi.; 805 km): From Hemphill Co. in Texas to Red R. in Oklahoma.

White (722 mi.; 1,160 km): From Madison Co. in Arkansas to Mississippi R.

Wisconsin (430 mi.; 692 km): From Vilas Co. in Wisconsin to Mississippi R.

Yellowstone (692 mi.; 1,110 km): From Park Co. in Wyoming to Missouri R. in North Dakota.

Yukon (1,979 mi.; 3,185 km): From source of McNeil R. in Yukon Territory, Canada, to Bering Sea in Alaska.

Coastline of the United States

State	Lengths, statute miles General coastline[1]	Lengths, statute miles Tidal shoreline[2]	State	Lengths, statute miles General coastline[1]	Lengths, statute miles Tidal shoreline[2]
Atlantic Coast:			**Gulf Coast:**		
Maine	228	3,478	Florida (Gulf)	770	5,095
New Hampshire	13	131	Alabama	53	607
Massachusetts	192	1,519	Mississippi	44	359
Rhode Island	40	384	Louisiana	397	7,721
Connecticut	—	618	Texas	367	3,359
New York	127	1,850	**Total Gulf Coast**	**1,631**	**17,141**
New Jersey	130	1,792	**Pacific Coast:**		
Pennsylvania	—	89	California	840	3,427
Delaware	28	381	Oregon	296	1,410
Maryland	31	3,190	Washington	157	3,026
Virginia	112	3,315	Hawaii	750	1,052
North Carolina	301	3,375	Alaska (Pacific)	5,580	31,383
South Carolina	187	2,876	**Total Pacific Coast**	**7,623**	**40,298**
Georgia	100	2,344	**Arctic Coast:**		
Florida (Atlantic)	580	3,331	Alaska (Arctic)	1,060	2,521
Total Atlantic Coast	**2,069**	**28,673**	**Total Arctic Coast**	**1,060**	**2,521**
			States Total	**12,383**	**88,633**

1. Figures are lengths of general outline of seacoast. Measurements are made with unit measure of 30 minutes of latitude on charts as near scale of 1:1,200,000 as possible. Coastline of bays and sounds is included to point where they narrow to width of unit measure, and distance across at such point is included. 2. Figures were obtained in 1939–1940 with recording instrument on the largest-scale maps and charts then available. Shoreline of outer coast, offshore islands, sounds, bays, rivers, and creeks is included to head of tidewater, or to point where tidal waters narrow to width of 100 feet. *Source:* Department of Commerce, National Oceanic and Atmospheric Administration, National Ocean Service.

Mountain Peaks in the United States Higher Than 14,000 Feet

Name	State	Height (ft.)	Name	State	Height (ft.)	Name	State	Height (ft.)
Mt. McKinley	Alaska	20,320	Castle Peak	Colo.	14,265	Windom Peak	Colo.	14,082
Mt. St. Elias	Alaska	18,008	Quandary Peak	Colo.	14,265	Mt. Columbia	Colo.	14,073
Mt. Foraker	Alaska	17,400	Mt. Evans	Colo.	14,264	Mt. Augusta	Alaska	14,070
Mt. Bona	Alaska	16,500	Longs Peak	Colo.	14,255	Missouri Mtn.	Colo.	14,067
Mt. Blackburn	Alaska	16,390	Mt. Wilson	Colo.	14,246	Humboldt Peak	Colo.	14,064
Mt. Sanford	Alaska	16,237	White Mtn.	Calif.	14,246	Mt. Bierstadt	Colo.	14,060
Mt. Vancouver	Alaska	15,979	North Palisade	Calif.	14,242	Sunlight Peak	Colo.	14,059
South Buttress	Alaska	15,885	Mt. Cameron	Colo.	14,238	Split Mtn.	Calif.	14,058
Mt. Churchill	Alaska	15,638	Mt. Shavano	Colo.	14,229	Handies Peak	Colo.	14,048
Mt. Fairweather	Alaska	15,300	Crestone Needle	Colo.	14,197	Culebra Peak	Colo.	14,047
Mt. Hubbard	Alaska	14,950	Mt. Belford	Colo.	14,197	Mt. Lindsey	Colo.	14,042
Mt. Bear	Alaska	14,831	Mt. Princeton	Colo.	14,197	Ellingwood Point	Colo.	14,042
East Buttress	Alaska	14,730	Mt. Yale	Colo.	14,196	Middle Palisade	Calif.	14,040
Mt. Hunter	Alaska	14,573	Mt. Bross	Colo.	14,172	Little Bear Peak	Colo.	14,037
Browne Tower	Alaska	14,530	Kit Carson Mtn.	Colo.	14,165	Mt. Sherman	Colo.	14,036
Mt. Alverstone	Alaska	14,500	Mt. Wrangell	Alaska	14,163	Redcloud Peak	Colo.	14,034
Mt. Whitney	Calif.	14,494[1]	Mt. Sill	Calif.	14,162	Mt. Langley	Calif.	14,027
University Peak	Alaska	14,470	Mt. Shasta	Calif.	14,162	Conundrum Peak	Colo.	14,022
Mt. Elbert	Colo.	14,433	El Diente Peak	Colo.	14,159	Mt. Tyndall	Calif.	14,019
Mt. Massive	Colo.	14,421	Point Success	Wash.	14,158	Pyramid Peak	Colo.	14,018
Mt. Harvard	Colo.	14,420	Maroon Peak	Colo.	14,156	Wilson Peak	Colo.	14,017
Mt. Rainier	Wash.	14,410	Tabeguache Mtn.	Colo.	14,155	Wetterhorn Peak	Colo.	14,015
Mt. Williamson	Calif.	14,370	Mt. Oxford	Colo.	14,153	North Maroon Peak	Colo.	14,014
La Plata Peak	Colo.	14,361	Mt. Sneffels	Colo.	14,150	San Luis Peak	Colo.	14,014
Blanca Peak	Colo.	14,345	Mt. Democrat	Colo.	14,148	Middle Palisade	Calif.	14,012
Uncompahgre Peak	Colo.	14,309	Capitol Peak	Colo.	14,130	Mt. Muir	Calif.	14,012
Crestone Peak	Colo.	14,294	Liberty Cap	Wash.	14,112	Mt. of the Holy Cross	Colo.	14,005
Mt. Lincoln	Colo.	14,286	Pikes Peak	Colo.	14,110	Huron Peak	Colo.	14,003
Grays Peak	Colo.	14,270	Snowmass Mtn.	Colo.	14,092	Thunderbolt Peak	Calif.	14,003
Mt. Antero	Colo.	14,269	Mt. Russell	Calif.	14,088	Sunshine Peak	Colo.	14,001
Torreys Peak	Colo.	14,267	Mt. Eolus	Colo.	14,083			

1. National Geodetic Survey. *Source:* U.S. Dept. of the Interior, Geological Survey.

Highest, Lowest, and Mean Elevations in the United States

State	Elevation (ft.)[1]	Highest point	Elevation (ft.)	Lowest point	Elevation (ft.)
Alabama	500	Cheaha Mountain	2,405	Gulf of Mexico	Sea level
Alaska	1,900	Mt. McKinley	20,320	Pacific Ocean	Sea level
Arizona	4,100	Humphreys Peak	12,633	Colorado River	70
Arkansas	650	Magazine Mountain	2,753	Ouachita River	55
California	2,900	Mt. Whitney	14,494	Death Valley	−282[2]
Colorado	6,800	Mt. Elbert	14,433	Arkansas River	3,350
Connecticut	500	Mt. Frissell, on south slope	2,380	Long Island Sound	Sea level
Delaware	60	Ebright Road, Del.–Pa. state line	448	Atlantic Ocean	Sea level
D.C.	150	Tenleytown, at Reno Reservoir	410	Potomac River	1
Florida	100	Sec. 30, T6N, R20W, Walton County	345	Atlantic Ocean	Sea level
Georgia	600	Brasstown Bald	4,784	Atlantic Ocean	Sea level
Hawaii	3,030	Puu Wekiu, Mauna Kea	13,796	Pacific Ocean	Sea level
Idaho	5,000	Borah Peak	12,662	Snake River	710
Illinois	600	Charles Mound	1,235	Mississippi River	279
Indiana	700	Franklin Township, Wayne County	1,257	Ohio River	320
Iowa	1,100	Sec. 29, T100N, R41W, Osceola County	1,670	Mississippi River	480
Kansas	2,000	Mt. Sunflower	4,039	Verdigris River	679
Kentucky	750	Black Mountain	4,139	Mississippi River	257
Louisiana	100	Driskill Mountain	535	New Orleans	−8[2]
Maine	600	Mt. Katahdin	5,267	Atlantic Ocean	Sea level
Maryland	350	Backbone Mountain	3,360	Atlantic Ocean	Sea level
Massachusetts	500	Mt. Greylock	3,487	Atlantic Ocean	Sea level
Michigan	900	Mt. Arvon	1,979	Lake Erie	572
Minnesota	1,200	Eagle Mountain	2,301	Lake Superior	600
Mississippi	300	Woodall Mountain	806	Gulf of Mexico	Sea level
Missouri	800	Taum Sauk Mountain	1,772	St. Francis River	230
Montana	3,400	Granite Peak	12,799	Kootenai River	1,800
Nebraska	2,600	Johnson Township, Kimball County	5,424	Missouri River	840
Nevada	5,500	Boundary Peak	13,140	Colorado River	479
New Hampshire	1,000	Mt. Washington	6,288	Atlantic Ocean	Sea level
New Jersey	250	High Point	1,803	Atlantic Ocean	Sea level
New Mexico	5,700	Wheeler Peak	13,161	Red Bluff Reservoir	2,842
New York	1,000	Mt. Marcy	5,344	Atlantic Ocean	Sea level
North Carolina	700	Mt. Mitchell	6,684	Atlantic Ocean	Sea level
North Dakota	1,900	White Butte	3,506	Red River	750
Ohio	850	Campbell Hill	1,549	Ohio River	455
Oklahoma	1,300	Black Mesa	4,973	Little River	289
Oregon	3,300	Mt. Hood	11,239	Pacific Ocean	Sea level
Pennsylvania	1,100	Mt. Davis	3,213	Delaware River	Sea level
Rhode Island	200	Jerimoth Hill	812	Atlantic Ocean	Sea level
South Carolina	350	Sassafras Mountain	3,560	Atlantic Ocean	Sea level
South Dakota	2,200	Harney Peak	7,242	Big Stone Lake	966
Tennessee	900	Clingmans Dome	6,643	Mississippi River	178
Texas	1,700	Guadalupe Peak	8,749	Gulf of Mexico	Sea level
Utah	6,100	Kings Peak	13,528	Beaverdam Wash	2,000
Vermont	1,000	Mt. Mansfield	4,393	Lake Champlain	95
Virginia	950	Mt. Rogers	5,729	Atlantic Ocean	Sea level
Washington	1,700	Mt. Rainier	14,410	Pacific Ocean	Sea level
West Virginia	1,500	Spruce Knob	4,861	Potomac River	240
Wisconsin	1,050	Timms Hill	1,951	Lake Michigan	579
Wyoming	6,700	Gannett Peak	13,804	Belle Fourche River	3,099
United States	**2,500**	**Mt. McKinley (Alaska)**	**20,320**	**Death Valley (California)**	**−282[2]**

1. Approximate mean elevation. 2. Below sea level. *Source:* U.S. Geological Survey.

Latitude and Longitude of U.S. and Canadian Cities
(and time corresponding to 12:00 noon, Eastern Standard Time)

City	Lat. °	Lat. ′	Long. °	Long. ′	Time	City	Lat. °	Lat. ′	Long. °	Long. ′	Time
Albany, N.Y.	42	40	73	45	12:00 noon	Memphis, Tenn.	35	9	90	3	11:00 a.m.
Albuquerque, N.M.	35	05	106	39	10:00 a.m.	Miami, Fla.	25	46	80	12	12:00 noon
Amarillo, Tex.	35	11	101	50	11:00 a.m.	Milwaukee, Wis.	43	2	87	55	11:00 a.m.
Anchorage, Alaska	61	13	149	54	8:00 a.m.	Minneapolis, Minn.	44	59	93	14	11:00 a.m.
Atlanta, Ga.	33	45	84	23	12:00 noon	Mobile, Ala.	30	42	88	3	11:00 a.m.
Austin, Tex.	30	16	97	44	11:00 a.m.	Montgomery, Ala.	32	21	86	18	11:00 a.m.
Baker, Ore.	44	47	117	50	9:00 a.m.	Montpelier, Vt.	44	15	72	32	12:00 noon
Baltimore, Md.	39	18	76	38	12:00 noon	Montreal, Que., Can.	45	30	73	35	12:00 noon
Bangor, Maine	44	48	68	47	12:00 noon	Moose Jaw, Sask.,	50	37	105	31	11:00 a.m.
Birmingham, Ala.	33	30	86	50	11:00 a.m.	Can.					
Bismarck, N.D.	46	48	100	47	11:00 a.m.	Nashville, Tenn.	36	10	86	47	11:00 a.m.
Boise, Idaho	43	36	116	13	10:00 a.m.	Nelson, B.C., Can.	49	30	117	17	9:00 a.m.
Boston, Mass.	42	21	71	5	12:00 noon	Newark, N.J.	40	44	74	10	12:00 noon
Buffalo, N.Y.	42	55	78	50	12:00 noon	New Haven, Conn.	41	19	72	55	12:00 noon
Calgary, Alba., Can.	51	1	114	1	10:00 a.m.	New Orleans, La.	29	57	90	4	11:00 a.m.
Carlsbad, N.M.	32	26	104	15	10:00 a.m.	New York, N.Y.	40	47	73	58	12:00 noon
Charleston, S.C.	32	47	79	56	12:00 noon	Nome, Alaska	64	25	165	30	8:00 a.m.
Charleston, W. Va.	38	21	81	38	12:00 noon	Oakland, Calif.	37	48	122	16	9:00 a.m.
Charlotte, N.C.	35	14	80	50	12:00 noon	Oklahoma City, Okla.	35	26	97	28	11:00 a.m.
Cheyenne, Wyo.	41	9	104	52	10:00 a.m.	Omaha, Neb.	41	15	95	56	11:00 a.m.
Chicago, Ill.	41	50	87	37	11:00 a.m.	Ottawa, Ont., Can.	45	24	75	43	12:00 noon
Cincinnati, Ohio	39	8	84	30	12:00 noon	Philadelphia, Pa.	39	57	75	10	12:00 noon
Cleveland, Ohio	41	28	81	37	12:00 noon	Phoenix, Ariz.	33	29	112	4	10:00 a.m.
Columbia, S.C.	34	0	81	2	12:00 noon	Pierre, S.D.	44	22	100	21	11:00 a.m.
Columbus, Ohio	40	0	83	1	12:00 noon	Pittsburgh, Pa.	40	27	79	57	12:00 noon
Dallas, Tex.	32	46	96	46	11:00 a.m.	Portland, Maine	43	40	70	15	12:00 noon
Denver, Colo.	39	45	105	0	10:00 a.m.	Portland, Ore.	45	31	122	41	9:00 a.m.
Des Moines, Iowa	41	35	93	37	11:00 a.m.	Providence, R.I.	41	50	71	24	12:00 noon
Detroit, Mich.	42	20	83	3	12:00 noon	Quebec, Que., Can.	46	49	71	11	12:00 noon
Dubuque, Iowa	42	31	90	40	11:00 a.m.	Raleigh, N.C.	35	46	78	39	12:00 noon
Duluth, Minn.	46	49	92	5	11:00 a.m.	Reno, Nev.	39	30	119	49	9:00 a.m.
Eastport, Maine	44	54	67	0	12:00 noon	Richfield, Utah	38	46	112	5	10:00 a.m.
Edmonton, Alb., Can.	53	34	113	28	10:00 a.m.	Richmond, Va.	37	33	77	29	12:00 noon
El Centro, Calif.	32	38	115	33	9:00 a.m.	Roanoke, Va.	37	17	79	57	12:00 noon
El Paso, Tex.	31	46	106	29	10:00 a.m.	Sacramento, Calif.	38	35	121	30	9:00 a.m.
Eugene, Ore.	44	3	123	5	9:00 a.m.	St. John, N.B., Can.	45	18	66	10	1:00 p.m.
Fargo, N.D.	46	52	96	48	11:00 a.m.	St. Louis, Mo.	38	35	90	12	11:00 a.m.
Flagstaff, Ariz.	35	13	111	41	10:00 a.m.	Salt Lake City, Utah	40	45	111	54	10:00 a.m.
Fort Worth, Tex.	32	43	97	19	11:00 a.m.	San Antonio, Tex.	29	23	98	33	11:00 a.m.
Fresno, Calif.	36	44	119	48	9:00 a.m.	San Diego, Calif.	32	42	117	10	9:00 a.m.
Grand Junction, Colo.	39	5	108	33	10:00 a.m.	San Francisco, Calif.	37	47	122	26	9:00 a.m.
Grand Rapids, Mich.	42	58	85	40	12:00 noon	San Jose, Calif.	37	20	121	53	9:00 a.m.
Havre, Mont.	48	33	109	43	10:00 a.m.	San Juan, P.R.	18	30	66	10	1:00 p.m.
Helena, Mont.	46	35	112	2	10:00 a.m.	Santa Fe, N.M.	35	41	105	57	10:00 a.m.
Honolulu, Hawaii	21	18	157	50	7:00 a.m.	Savannah, Ga.	32	5	81	5	12:00 noon
Hot Springs, Ark.	34	31	93	3	11:00 a.m.	Seattle, Wash.	47	37	122	20	9:00 a.m.
Houston, Tex.	29	45	95	21	11:00 a.m.	Shreveport, La.	32	28	93	42	11:00 a.m.
Idaho Falls, Idaho	43	30	112	1	10:00 a.m.	Sioux Falls, S.D.	43	33	96	44	11:00 a.m.
Indianapolis, Ind.	39	46	86	10	12:00 noon	Sitka, Alaska	57	10	135	15	8:00 a.m.
Jackson, Miss.	32	20	90	12	11:00 a.m.	Spokane, Wash.	47	40	117	26	9:00 a.m.
Jacksonville, Fla.	30	22	81	40	12:00 noon	Springfield, Ill.	39	48	89	38	11:00 a.m.
Juneau, Alaska	58	18	134	24	8:00 a.m.	Springfield, Mass.	42	6	72	34	12:00 noon
Kansas City, Mo.	39	6	94	35	11:00 a.m.	Springfield, Mo.	37	13	93	17	11:00 a.m.
Key West, Fla.	24	33	81	48	12:00 noon	Syracuse, N.Y.	43	2	76	8	12:00 noon
Kingston, Ont., Can.	44	15	76	30	12:00 noon	Tampa, Fla.	27	57	82	27	12:00 noon
Klamath Falls, Ore.	42	10	121	44	9:00 a.m.	Toledo, Ohio	41	39	83	33	12:00 noon
Knoxville, Tenn.	35	57	83	56	12:00 noon	Toronto, Ont., Can.	43	40	79	24	12:00 noon
Las Vegas, Nev.	36	10	115	12	9:00 a.m.	Tulsa, Okla.	36	09	95	59	11:00 a.m.
Lewiston, Idaho	46	24	117	2	9:00 a.m.	Vancouver, B.C., Can.	49	13	123	06	9:00 a.m.
Lincoln, Neb.	40	50	96	40	11:00 a.m.	Victoria, B.C., Can.	48	25	123	21	9:00 a.m.
London, Ont., Can.	43	2	81	34	12:00 noon	Virginia Beach, Va.	36	51	75	58	12:00 noon
Long Beach, Calif.	33	46	118	11	9:00 a.m.	Washington, D.C.	38	53	77	02	12:00 noon
Los Angeles, Calif.	34	3	118	15	9:00 a.m.	Wichita, Kan.	37	43	97	17	11:00 a.m.
Louisville, Ky.	38	15	85	46	12:00 noon	Wilmington, N.C.	34	14	77	57	12:00 noon
Manchester, N.H.	43	0	71	30	12:00 noon	Winnipeg, Man., Can.	49	54	97	7	11:00 a.m.

For more on U.S. geography, *see* National Parks, pp. 590–594.

2005 The year's theme music was a requiem, as headlines focused on the devastation wrought by Hurricane Katrina on the Gulf Coast, daily death counts from Iraq, and the passing of a beloved Pope

ALL PHOTOS: AP/WIDE WORLD PHOTOS

HURRICANE KATRINA: The category 4 hurricane slammed into the U.S. Gulf Coast on Aug. 29, devastating beachfront towns in Mississippi and Louisiana. When two levees in New Orleans were breached, 80% of the historic town was inundated, leaving as many as 125,000 survivors trapped in a city without food, power, or water. As looters ruled the streets, authorities were blamed for a tardy, poorly executed recovery effort.

NATION As George W. Bush's second term commenced, Americans focused on the twilight of a life and the dawn of a new Supreme Court

TAKE TWO: Republican George W. Bush earned a second term by defeating Democrat John Kerry, 51% to 48%. Above, the President leaves the White House on Jan. 20 for his second inauguration, with wife Laura and twin daughters Jenna (left) and Barbara.

ALBERTO GONZALES: The former White House counsel became the nation's first Hispanic Attorney General, although critics charged he had sanctioned U.S. torture.

CONDOLEEZZA RICE: President Bush named the National Security Adviser from his first term to replace retired general Colin Powell as Secretary of State.

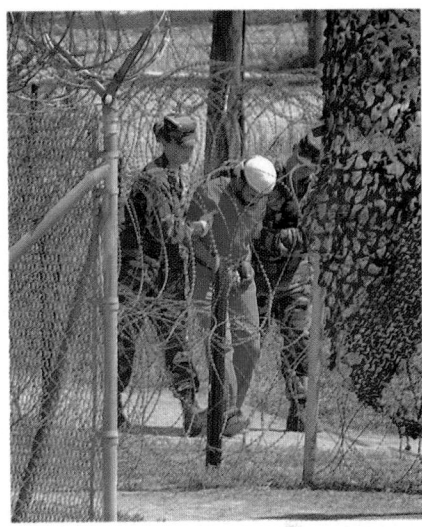

VACANCIES: After Chief Justice William Rehnquist died, President Bush nominated John Roberts to succeed him. Justice Sandra Day O'Connor resigned in July.

HORRORS? Bush Administration officials denied charges by Amnesty International that alleged terrorists held at Guantánamo Bay, Cuba, had been tortured and abused.

FLASHPOINT: Americans debated the fate of Terri Schiavo, 41, severely brain-damaged since 1990. Her ex-husband claimed she would have wanted her feeding tube removed; her parents disagreed. After the courts ruled for removal, Schiavo died on March 31.

WORLD Nations raced to aid suffering tsunami victims, while Britons, Iranians, Palestinians—and even Iraqis—went to the polls

BAD NEWS: On June 28 Iraq observed its first year of sovereignty following the 2003 U.S.-led invasion, but the nation remained deeply unstable. Insurgent attacks over the year brought more than 480 car bombings and 8,000 Iraqi casualties. With 140,000 U.S. troops still in the country, polls showed declining support for the war among Americans, while army enlistments lagged.

GOOD NEWS: Iraq held its first democratic national election since 1954 on Jan. 30. Eight million voters, 57% of those eligible, cast ballots, including many woman who voted for the first time, below. Minority Sunni Arabs boycotted the election, hampering efforts to unite the war-torn nation, which is sharply divided among squabbling Sunni and Shi'ite Arabs and Kurds.

MIDEAST MOVEMENT: Above, Mahmoud Abbas, a moderate, was elected president of the Palestinian Authority on Jan. 9. At left, Israelis living in the Gaza Strip protest Prime Minister Ariel Sharon's plan to withdraw from settlements in the region.

BATTLE IN BEIRUT: The Feb. 14 car-bomb murder of Lebanon's former prime minister Rafik Hariri, who opposed Syrian hegemony over his nation, triggered demonstrations by anti- and pro-Syrian factions. Syria withdrew all its 14,000 troops in Lebanon in April.

TIDE OF SUPPORT: The world mobilized to offer aid to survivors of the Dec. 26, 2004, tsunami that killed as many as 230,000 people across Southeast Asia. Above, children reach for food in Sri Lanka.

ODD COUPLE: Former presidents (and rivals) Bill Clinton, 58, and George H.W. Bush, 80, teamed up to lead the U.S. aid effort.

LONDON TERROR BOMBINGS: Four synchronized bomb blasts struck Britain's capital during the morning rush hour on July 7. The suicide attacks—three on underground commuter trains and one on a bus—killed more than 50 people and injured some 700.

THREE! Labour Party leader Tony Blair won a third term as Britain's prime minister in a June vote, but his majority in Parliament was sharply reduced.

NON! Residents of the Netherlands and France strongly rejected a proposed European Union constitution in May and June, raising questions about the Union's future.

NUCLEAR FEARS: South Koreans protest the policies of North Korea's Kim Jong Il, whose rogue nation, defying world opinion, continued to develop nuclear armaments.

RIGHT TURN: Mahmoud Ahmadinejad, an ultra-conservative Islamist and the mayor of Tehran, defeated moderate Hashemi Rafsanjani to become Iran's president.

SOCIETY A beloved pontiff died and a new pope was elected, while a royal wedding in Britain and a pop star's trial also made news

END OF AN ERA: An ailing Pope John Paul II, 84, meets with nuns in October 2004; he died six months later. Joseph Cardinal Ratzinger of Germany was elected pope and took the name Benedict XVI.

WHITE SMOKE: Members of the College of Cardinals walk through the Sistine Chapel as the electoral conclave begins on April 18. John Paul II had appointed 114 of the 117 electors, ensuring that his conservative views would affect the choice of his successor.

BEAT IT! In the year's most-watched celebrity trial, pop star Michael Jackson, 46, was found not guilty of charges of child molestation by a California jury.

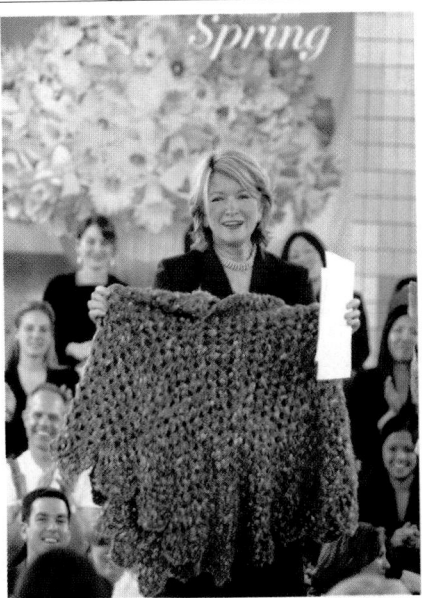

DUES PAID: Home maven Martha Stewart shows a poncho knit for her by a fellow prisoner as she returned from serving a five-month jail term in a securities case.

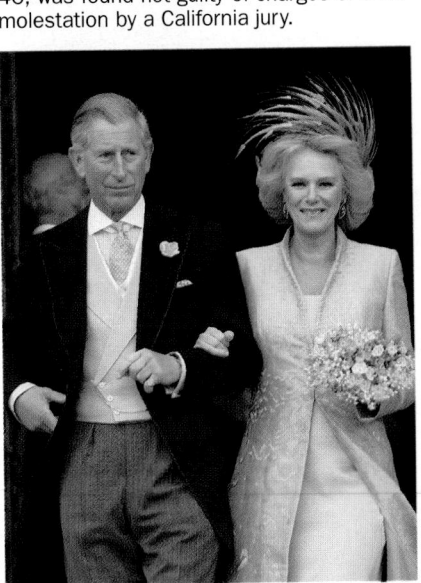

ROYAL WEDDING: Prince Charles, 56, the heir to the British throne, wed his longtime love interest, Camilla Parker Bowles, 57, in a civil ceremony on April 9.

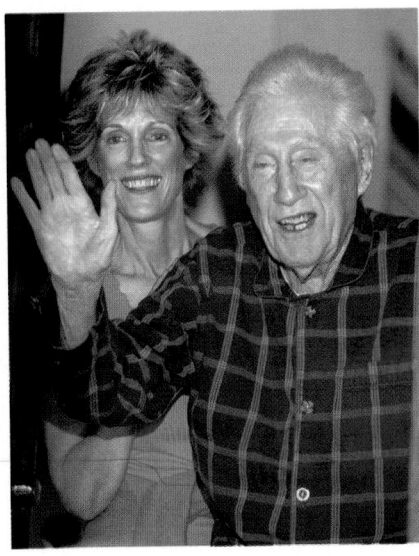

NAMED: Former FBI official Mark Felt, 91, revealed that he was "Deep Throat," the informer whose tips to reporters helped uncover crimes in the Nixon White House.

SCIENCE All eyes were trained on space, where a NASA probe explored a comet, while a U.S. shuttle crew weathered a rough flight

RETURN TO SPACE: The shuttle *Discovery* roared aloft on July 26 in NASA's first manned mission since the *Columbia* tragedy in 2003. But the flight was plagued by glitches: a large piece of insulating foam fell from the external fuel tank on launch, and materials protruding from the craft threatened re-entry and had to be removed in flight.

SMASHING SUCCESS: On July 4 an impactor probe launched from a NASA flyby spacecraft collided with Comet Tempel 1 on schedule in the Deep Impact mission, sending up a shower of ancient ice, dust, and gas to be studied by the flyby craft. Comets, flying time capsules, were formed early in the development of the solar system, some 4.5 billion years ago; studying their makeup helps scientists to understand conditions at that time.

SPORTS Football's New England Patriots and tennis's Venus Williams revisited old glories, while auto racing welcomed a fresh (female) face

BIG WHEEL: Although young (23) and tiny (100 lbs.), Danica Patrick revved up auto racing fans by finishing fourth at the Indianapolis 500, the best result yet for a woman.

REPATRIATED: Quarterback Tom Brady of the New England Patriots hoists the Super Bowl trophy, which the "Pats" won again, for the third time in four years.

COMEBACK: Venus Williams emerged from a slump, beating fellow American Lindsay Davenport in a classic match to win Britain's Wimbledon title for a third time.

ARTS Long-promised dreams took form as a 1975 Monty Python film came to Broadway and *Star Wars* fans saw the birth of Darth Vader

ORANGE CRUSH: Installation artists Christo and Jeanne-Claude erected 7,500 saffron "gates" for two weeks in New York City's Central Park, earning both cheers and jeers.

BRIT WITS: Monty Python ruled Broadway with *Spamalot*, a musical version of the comedy troupe's Holy Grail film romp.

YODA CODA: A statue of the Jedi master waits in line to see *Star Wars: Revenge of the Sith*, the last film in the popular series.

MILESTONES We bade farewell to timeless writers, a master of the modern, and the man who led us in late-night laughs for 29 years

PRINCE RAINIER: Monaco's ruler, shown with wife Grace Kelly in 1956, died at 81 after ruling for 55 years. He restored the vitality of his tiny nation on the Riviera.

JOHNNIE COCHRAN: The noted California attorney died at 67; he represented football star O.J. Simpson, found not guilty of murdering his wife Nicole in a 1995 trial.

SAUL BELLOW: The novelist, 89, who won the 1976 Nobel Prize for Literature, wed Chicago-style street smarts to a dazzling style in such works as *Humboldt's Gift*.

HUNTER S. THOMPSON: The reporter who invented "gonzo journalism" in such works as *Fear and Loathing in Las Vegas* took his life at 67 with a handgun on Feb. 20.

ARTHUR MILLER: In such works as *Death of a Salesman* (1949) and *The Crucible* (1953), the playwright, who died at 89, brought moral issues to life onstage.

PHILIP JOHNSON: The noted architect, 98, was an early advocate of stripped-down modern buildings but later helped pioneer postmodernism's flourishes.

JOHNNY CARSON: The genial Nebraskan, 79, earned a lasting place in American hearts by hosting NBC's *The Tonight Show* for 29 years until his retirement in 1992.

Afghanistan	Albania	Algeria	Andorra	Angola
Antigua & Barbuda	Argentina	Armenia	Australia	Austria
Azerbaijan	Bahamas	Bahrain	Bangladesh	Barbados
Belarus	Belgium	Belize	Benin	Bhutan
Bolivia	Bosnia-Herzegovina	Botswana	Brazil	Brunei
Bulgaria	Burkina Faso	Burundi	Cambodia	Cameroon
Canada	Cape Verde	Central African Republic	Chad	Chile
China	Colombia	Comoros	Congo, Dem. Republic of the	Congo, Rep. of
Costa Rica	Côte d'Ivoire	Croatia	Cuba	Cyprus
Czech Republic	Denmark	Djibouti	Dominica	Dominican Rep.

East Timor

Ecuador

Egypt

El Salvador

Equatorial Guinea

Eritrea

Estonia

Ethiopia

Fiji

Finland

France

Gabon

Gambia

Georgia

Germany

Ghana

Greece

Grenada

Guatemala

Guinea

Guinea-Bissau

Guyana

Haiti

Honduras

Hungary

Iceland

India

Indonesia

Iran

Iraq

Ireland

Israel

Italy

Jamaica

Japan

Jordan

Kazakhstan

Kenya

Kiribati

Korea, North

Korea, South

Kuwait

Kyrgyzstan

Laos

Latvia

Lebanon

Lesotho

Liberia

Libya

Liechtenstein

Lithuania

Luxembourg

Macedonia

Madagascar

Malawi

Malaysia

Maldives

Mali

Malta

Marshall Islands

Mauritania

Mauritius

Mexico

Micronesia

Moldova

Monaco

Mongolia

Morocco

Mozambique

Myanmar

Namibia

Nauru

Nepal

Netherlands

New Zealand

Nicaragua

Niger

Nigeria

Norway

Oman

Pakistan

Palau

Panama

Papua New
Guinea

Paraguay

Peru

Philippines

Poland

Portugal

Qatar

Romania

Russia

Rwanda

St. Kitts & Nevis

St. Lucia

St. Vincent &
The Grenadines

Samoa

San Marino

São Tomé &
Príncipe

Saudi Arabia

Senegal

Serbia &
Montenegro

Seychelles

Sierra Leone

Singapore

Slovakia

Slovenia

Solomon Islands

Somalia

South Africa

Spain

Sri Lanka

Sudan

Suriname

Swaziland

Sweden

Switzerland

Syria

Taiwan

Tajikistan

Tanzania

Thailand

Togo

Tonga

Trinidad &
Tobago

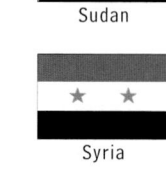

Tunisia

Turkey

Turkmenistan

Tuvalu

Uganda

Ukraine

United Arab
Emirates

United Kingdom

United States

Uruguay

Uzbekistan

Vanuatu

Vatican City

Venezuela

Vietnam

Yemen

Zambia

Zimbabwe

TIME ZONES
OF THE
WORLD

THE WORLD (Physical)

Robinson Projection
1:191,600,000

Elevation	
Meters	Feet
3,000	10,000
2,000	7,000
1,000	3,000
500	1,500
200	700
0	0

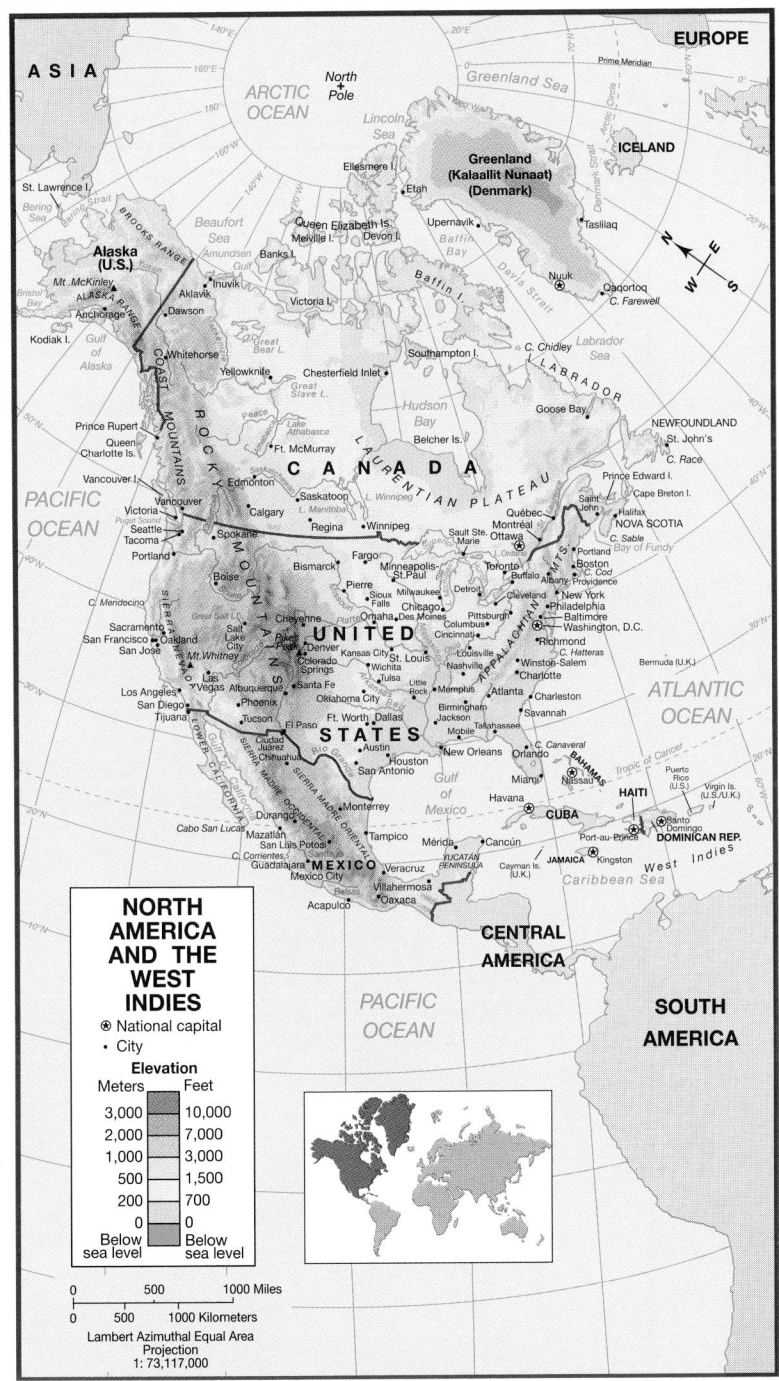

ARCTIC OCEAN

North Pole

ASIA

EUROPE

Greenland Sea

Lincoln Sea

Ellesmere I.

Greenland (Kalaallit Nunaat) (Denmark)

ICELAND

Etah

Upernavik

Tasiilaq

Alaska (U.S.)

Beaufort Sea

Queen Elizabeth Is.

Melville I.

Devon I.

Baffin Bay

St. Lawrence I.

Bering Sea

Mt. McKinley

ALASKA RANGE

Anchorage

Inuvik

Aklavik

Banks I.

Victoria I.

Nuuk

Qaqortoq

C. Farewell

Denmark Strait

Davis Strait

Kodiak I.

Gulf of Alaska

Dawson

Whitehorse

Yellowknife

Great Bear L.

Great Slave L.

Chesterfield Inlet

Southampton I.

C. Chidley

Labrador Sea

Prince Rupert

Queen Charlotte Is.

Peace R.

Lake Athabasca

Ft. McMurray

Hudson Bay

Belcher Is.

Goose Bay

NEWFOUNDLAND

St. John's

C. Race

Vancouver I.

Edmonton

C A N A D A

L. Winnipeg

LAURENTIAN PLATEAU

Prince Edward I.

Cape Breton I.

Victoria

Vancouver

Calgary

Saskatoon

L. Manitoba

Regina

Winnipeg

Québec

Saint John

NOVA SCOTIA

C. Sable

Seattle

Tacoma

Spokane

Sault Ste. Marie

Montréal

Ottawa

Portland

Boston

C. Cod

Bay of Fundy

Halifax

Portland

Boise

Fargo

Bismarck

Pierre

Minneapolis-St. Paul

Milwaukee

Detroit

Toronto

Buffalo

Albany

Providence

New York

Philadelphia

Baltimore

Washington, D.C.

C. Meridocino

Sacramento

San Francisco

Oakland

San Jose

Great Salt L.

Salt Lake City

Cheyenne

Denver

Omaha

Des Moines

Sioux Falls

Chicago

Cleveland

Pittsburgh

Columbus

Cincinnati

Richmond

C. Hatteras

Bermuda (U.K.)

ATLANTIC OCEAN

Mt. Whitney

Colorado Springs

Kansas City

St. Louis

Louisville

Nashville

Winston-Salem

Charlotte

PACIFIC OCEAN

Las Vegas

Los Angeles

San Diego

Tijuana

Phoenix

Tucson

Albuquerque

Santa Fe

Wichita

UNITED

Oklahoma City

Tulsa

Little Rock

Memphis

Atlanta

Charleston

Savannah

El Paso

Ciudad Juárez

Chihuahua

Rio Grande

Ft. Worth

Dallas

S T A T E S

Birmingham

Jackson

Mobile

Talahassee

Orlando

C. Canaveral

Austin

Houston

San Antonio

New Orleans

Gulf of Mexico

Miami

Nassau

BAHAMAS

Tropic of Cancer

Puerto Rico (U.S.)

Virgin Is. (U.S./U.K.)

Monterrey

Havana

CUBA

HAITI

Durango

Mazatlán

San Luis Potosí

Tampico

Mérida

Cancún

JAMAICA

Kingston

Port-au-Prince

Santo Domingo

DOMINICAN REP.

Cabo San Lucas

C. Corrientes

Guadalajara

MEXICO

Mexico City

Veracruz

YUCATÁN PENINSULA

Cayman Is. (U.K.)

West Indies

Caribbean Sea

Acapulco

Villahermosa

Oaxaca

Belize

CENTRAL AMERICA

PACIFIC OCEAN

SOUTH AMERICA

SIERRA MADRE OCCIDENTAL

SIERRA MADRE ORIENTAL

LOWER CALIFORNIA

Gulf of California

BROOKS RANGE

COAST MOUNTAINS

R O C K Y   M O U N T A I N S

SIERRA NEVADA

Columbia R.

Platte R.

Colorado R.

APPALACHIAN MTS.

LABRADOR

Amundsen Gulf

Bristol Bay

Puget Sound

NORTH AMERICA AND THE WEST INDIES

⊛ National capital

• City

Elevation

Meters	Feet
3,000	10,000
2,000	7,000
1,000	3,000
500	1,500
200	700
0	0
Below sea level	Below sea level

0   500   1000 Miles

0   500   1000 Kilometers

Lambert Azimuthal Equal Area Projection
1: 73,117,000

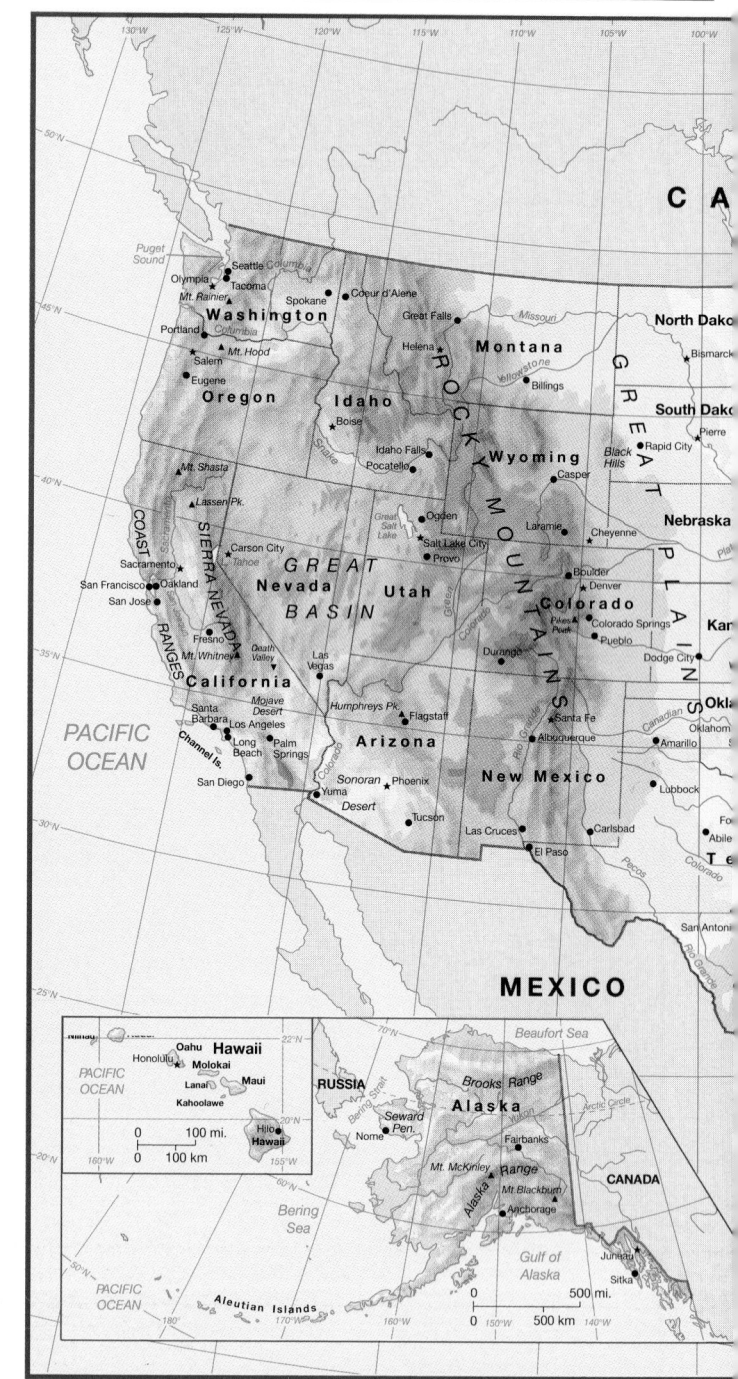

C A

Puget
Sound
Seattle   Columbia
Olympia   Tacoma
Mt. Rainier   Spokane   Coeur d'Alene
Washington   Great Falls
Portland   Columbia   Helena   **Montana**
Salem   Mt. Hood   Missouri   **North Dako**
Eugene   Bismarck
Oregon   **Idaho**   Billings
Boise   **South Dako**
Mt. Shasta   Idaho Falls   **Wyoming**   Black   Rapid City
Lassen Pk.   Pocatello   Hills   Pierre
                                    Casper
COAST   Carson City   Great   Ogden   Cheyenne   **Nebraska**
SIERRA NEVADA   Tahoe   Salt   Salt Lake City   Laramie   Platt
Sacramento   **GREAT**   Lake   Provo   Boulder
San Francisco   Oakland   **Nevada**   **BASIN**   **Utah**   Green   Denver   Kan
San Jose   **Colorado**   Colorado Springs
Fresno   Pikes Pk.   Pueblo
Mt. Whitney   Death   Las   Durango   Dodge City
RANGES   Valley   Vegas   Ar
California   Mojave   Okla
Santa   Desert   Humphreys Pk.   Flagstaff   Santa Fe   Oklahom
Barbara   Los Angeles   Albuquerque   Amarillo
Channel Is.   Long   Palm   **Arizona**   Rio Grande
PACIFIC   Beach   Springs   **New Mexico**   Lubbock
OCEAN   San Diego   Sonoran   Phoenix   Fo
Yuma   Desert   Las Cruces   Carlsbad   Abile
Tucson   Pecos   T e
El Paso   Colorado
San Antoni
MEXICO

G R E A T   P L A I N

R O C K Y   M O U N T A I N S

Hawaii inset:
Oahu   **Hawaii**
Honolulu   Molokai
PACIFIC   Lanai   Maui
OCEAN   Kahoolawe
Hilo
0   100 mi.   **Hawaii**
0   100 km

Beaufort Sea
RUSSIA   Bering Strait   Brooks Range   Arctic Circle
Seward   **Alaska**
Nome   Pen.
Fairbanks
Mt. McKinley   Range   **CANADA**
Alaska   Mt. Blackburn
Anchorage
Juneau
Gulf of   Sitka
Alaska
0   500 mi.
Bering   0   500 km
Sea
PACIFIC
OCEAN   Aleutian Islands

D A

90°W 85°W 80°W 75°W 70°W 65°W 60°W

Maine

Lake Superior

Duluth

Sault Ste. Marie

L. Champlain

Gulf of Maine

sota   Superior

Mt. Washington

Augusta

St. Paul

Green Bay

Montpelier

Portland

Eau Claire

Vt. N.H.

Portsmouth

Michigan

Concord

napolis

Wisconsin

Manchester

Rochester

Madison

Grand Rapids

Flint

Ontario

New York

Boston

Cape Cod

Albany

Rochester   Syracuse

Mass.

Worcester

Iowa

Cedar Rapids

Milwaukee Lansing

Kenosha

Chicago

Ann Arbor

Detroit

Buffalo

Hartford

Conn.

Providence

R.I.

New Haven

City

Rockford

Gary

Toledo

Erie

Pennsylvania

Newark

Long Island

New York

Des Moines

Rock Island

Fort Wayne

Akron

Reading

Trenton

New Jersey

ha

Illinois

Muncie

Springfield

Columbus

Harrisburg

Pittsburgh

Philadelphia

Atlantic City

Champaign

Indianapolis

Dayton

Wheeling

Baltimore

Dover

Delaware

Springfield

Indiana

Cincinnati

W.

Md.

Annapolis

Missouri

Louisville

Frankfort

Va.

Virginia

Washington, D.C.

Chesapeake Bay

Kansas City

St. Louis

Ohio

Lexington

Richmond

Williamsburg

Jefferson City

Kentucky

Winston-

Lynchburg

Norfolk

Virginia Beach

Missouri

Bowling Green

Salem

Durham

Cape Hatteras

Springfield

Knoxville

Nashville

Raleigh

North Carolina

Wilmington

Arkansas

Tennessee

Chattanooga

Charlotte

ATLANTIC OCEAN

Fort Smith

Memphis

Tennessee

Columbia

Little Rock

Athens

South Carolina

Birmingham

Atlanta

Augusta

Charleston

Georgia

Alabama

Macon

Savannah

Mississippi

Montgomery

Shreveport

Jackson

Albany

N

W   E

S

Louisiana

Mobile

Pensacola

Jacksonville

Tallahassee

St. Augustine

Baton Rouge

Daytona Beach

Port Arthur

New Orleans

Florida

Cape Canaveral

on

Orlando

Galveston

Tampa

L. Okeechobee

St. Petersburg

Gulf of Mexico

BAHAMAS

Fort Lauderdale

Miami

Florida Keys

Straits of Florida

UNITED STATES

⊕ National capital

★ State capital

● City

0   200   400 Miles

CUBA

Elevation

Meters		Feet
3,000		10,000
2,000		7,000
1,000		3,000
500		1,500
200		700
0		0

0   200   400 Kilometers

Albers Equal-Area Projection
1 : 26,044,000

CANADA
⊛ National capital
• Provincial capital
• City

Elevation
Meters / Feet
3,000 / 10,000
2,000 / 7,000
1,000 / 3,000
500 / 1,500
200 / 700
0 / 0

0   250   500 Miles
0   250   500 Kilometers

Lambert Conformal Conic
Projection
1:37,192,000

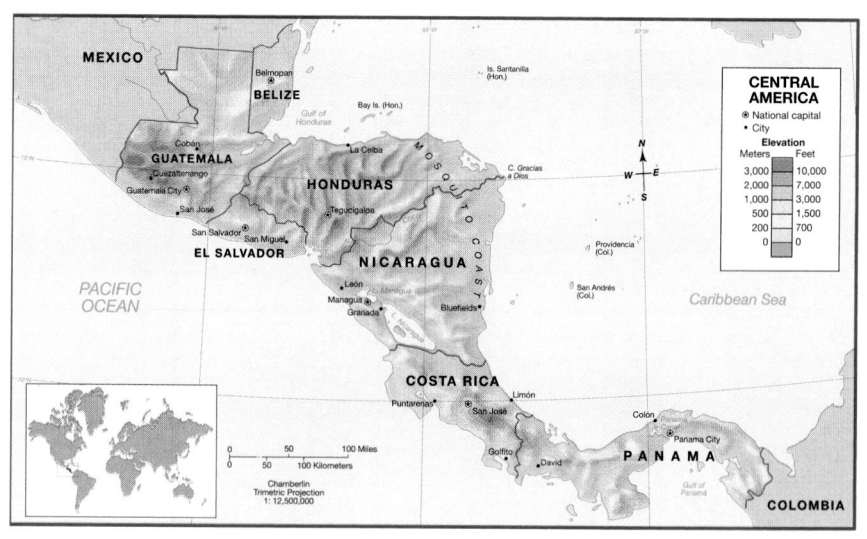

CENTRAL
AMERICA
⊛ National capital
• City

Elevation
Meters / Feet
3,000 / 10,000
2,000 / 7,000
1,000 / 3,000
500 / 1,500
200 / 700
0 / 0

0   50   100 Miles
0   50   100 Kilometers

Chamberlin
Trimetric Projection
1: 12,500,000

Galápagos Is. (Ecuador)
I. Marchena
I. San Salvador
I. Isabela
I. Santa Cruz
I. Fernandina
I. San Cristóbal
I. Sta. Maria
I. Española

WEST INDIES

Tropic of Cancer

Caribbean Sea
Neth. Antilles (Neth.)
Curaçao
I. de Margarita
Gulf of Venezuela
Gulf of Paria

CENTRAL AMERICA
Barranquilla
Cartagena
Maracaibo
Caracas
Morawhanna
Georgetown
New Amsterdam
Paramaribo
Devil's I.
Cayenne

ATLANTIC OCEAN

Gulf of Urabá
Monteria
Cúcuta
San Cristóbal
Ciudad Bolivar
GUYANA
SURINAME
French Guiana (Fr.)

VENEZUELA
Medellin
Manizales
Bucaramanga
Alto R.Tacuru
Bogotá
C. Corrientes
Mt.Tolima
Mt.Huila
Buenaventura
Cali

COLOMBIA
I. de Maracá
I. Caviana

I. Malpelo (Colombia)

Equator

ECUADOR
Quito
Mt. Cotopaxi
Mt. Chimborazo
Ambato
Cuenca
Guayaquil
Manaus
Belém
I. São Luis
Fortaleza
C. São Roque

Gulf of Guayaquil
Iquitos
PERU
Piura

BRAZIL
Recife

Trujillo
Mt. Huascarán

A N D E S

Callao
Lima
Cuzco
Salvador

El Misti
La Paz
Trinidad
BOLIVIA
Brasilia

PACIFIC OCEAN
Arequipa
Cochabamba
Santa Cruz

Potosi
Sucre
PARAGUAY
Belo Horizonte

Iquique
C. São Tomé
Rio de Janeiro

Antofagasta
San Miguel de Tucumán
Asunción
São Paulo
Santos

Tropic of Capricorn

San Felix (Chile)
San Ambrosio (Chile)
Mt. Ojos del Salado
Curitiba
I. de Santa Catarina
Pôrto Alegre

CHILE
Córdoba
Rivera

Viña del Mar
Valparaiso
Mt. Aconcagua
Mendoza
Salto
Paysandú
L. dos Patos
URUGUAY

Juan Fernández Is. (Chile)
I. Robinson Crusoe
Santiago
Rosario
Buenos Aires
Montevideo
L. Mirí

I. Alejandro Selkirk
Vol. Maipo
La Plata
Rio de la Plata
C. San Antonio

ANDES
Concepción
ARGENTINA
Mar del Plata

Negro
Bahia Blanca

SOUTH AMERICA

⊛ National capital
• City

Elevation

Meters	Feet
3,000	10,000
2,000	7,000
1,000	3,000
500	1,500
200	700
0	0

I. de Chiloé
Gulf of San Matías
Pen. Valdés
ATLANTIC OCEAN

Gulf of Corcovado
Archipiélago de los Chonos
Pen. Taitao
C. Tres Montes
Gulf of Penas
Gulf of San Jorge

Falkland Islands
(U.K.; claimed by Arg.)
Stanley

South Georgia (U.K.)

Strait of Magellan
Tierra del Fuego
I. de los Estados

I. Sta. Inés
Cape Horn

Antarctic Circle

0	300	600 Miles
0	300	600 Kilometers

Lambert Azimuthal
Equal-Area Projection
1: 43,697,000

ARCTIC OCEAN

Barents Sea

Denmark Strait

Jan Mayen (Norway)

North Cape

Hammerfest

Vardø

Iran

LAPLAND

Akureyri

ICELAND

Seydhisfjørdhur

Reykjavik

Norwegian Sea

Kiruna

Arctic Circle

Oulu

L. Oulu

Faroe Is. (Den.)

Trondheimsfjorden

Kristiansund

Trondheim

Ålesund

Sundsvall

Vaasa

Kuopio

FINLAND

Rockall (U.K.)

Tampere

Shetland Is. (U.K.)

Sognefjorden

Lillehammer

Bergen

Hardanger-fjorden

Oslo

Gävle

Turku

Helsinki

Espoo

Kotka

Ahvenanmaa (Finland)

G. of Finland

Stavanger

Arendal

Stockholm

Drammen

Vänern

Hebrides

C. Wrath

Orkney Is.

Moray Firth

Inverness

Kristiansand

Alborg

Visby

Gotland (Sw.)

UNITED KINGDOM

North Channel

SCOTLAND

Glasgow

Edinburgh

Göteborg

Öland

JUTLAND

Århus

DENMARK

Odense

Malmö

Baltic Sea

ATLANTIC OCEAN

Donegal

N. IRELAND

Belfast

Newcastle-upon-Tyne

North Sea

Galway

Irish Sea

Bradford

Copenhagen

Bornholm (Den.)

IRELAND

Limerick

Manchester

Leeds

Dublin

Liverpool

Sheffield

Cork

C.Clear

ENGLAND

Kiel

Lübeck

St. George's Channel

WALES

Birmingham

The Wash

Frisian Is.

Hamburg

Cardiff

NETHERLANDS

Bremen

Bristol

Amsterdam

London

The Hague

Utrecht

Hannover

Berlin

Southampton

Rotterdam

Essen

Dortmund

Magdeburg

Portsmouth

Antwerp

Düsseldorf

Leipzig

Dresden

Channel Is. (U.K.)

English Channel

Calais

Brussels

Liège

Cologne

Land's End

Lille

BELGIUM

Bonn

GERMANY

Brest

Cherbourg

Le Havre

LUX.

Frankfurt

EASTERN EUROPE

Rouen

Reims

Mannheim

Nantes

Versailles

Paris

Nuremberg

Orleans

Strasbourg

Stuttgart

FRANCE

Freiburg

Munich

Linz

Vienna

Basel

JURA MTS.

Salzburg

Bay of Biscay

Vichy

Bern

Zürich

Innsbruck

AUSTRIA

C. Ortegal

MASSIF CENTRAL

Lyon

Geneva

SWITZ.

Graz

CANTABRIAN MTS.

Bordeaux

Dordogne

Mt. Blanc

LIECHTENSTEIN

Bilbao

Grenoble

Turin

ALPS.

Venice

Trieste

Biarritz

Toulouse

Milan

PORTUGAL

PYRENEES

Nîmes

Marseille

Nice

MONACO

Genoa

Bologna

Ravenna

Porto

Braga

ANDORRA

G. of Lions

Pisa

Florence

SAN MARINO

Adriatic Sea

Coimbra

Salamanca

Saragossa

Corsica (Fr.)

ITALY

Siena

Perugia

APENNINES

Lisbon

SIERRA DE GUADARRAMA

Madrid

Barcelona

Ajaccio

VATICAN CITY

Rome

Sétubal

Toledo

Valencia

Majorca

Minorca

Sardinia (It.)

Mt. Vesuvius

Naples

Bari

Évora

SPAIN

Palma

Ibiza

Cagliari

Brindisi

SIERRA MORENA

Balearic Is.

Tyrrhenian Sea

C. St. Vincent

Córdoba

C. Nao

Seville

Granada

Reggio di Calabria

G. of Taranto

Cádiz

Málaga

Almería

Palermo

Messina

Mt. Etna

Ionian Sea

Gulf of Cádiz

Gibraltar (U.K.)

C. Palos

Catania

Sicily

Strait of Gibraltar

Cueta (Sp.)

C. Gata

C. Passero

Mediterranean Sea

Valletta

MALTA

AFRICA

WESTERN EUROPE

⊗ National capital

• City

Elevation

Meters		Feet
3,000		10,000
2,000		7,000
1,000		3,000
500		1,500
200		700
0		0

0   200   400 Miles

0   200   400 Kilometers

Azimuthal Equal-Area Projection
1: 31,019,000

Norwegian Sea
Barents Sea
Kolguyev I.
Cheshskaya Bay
C. Kanin
Murmansk
KOLA PENINSULA
Bay of Mezen
White Sea
Archangel
Arctic Circle
N. Dvina
Pechora
URAL MOUNTAINS
N
W E
S
Lake Onega
Kama Res.
Perm
Lake Ladoga
RUSSIA
Izhevsk
Ufa
Gulf of Finland
St. Petersburg
Tallinn
ESTONIA
Tartu
Lake Peipus
Novgorod
Lake Il'men
Rybinsk Res.
Yaroslavl
Tver
Volga
Nizhny Novgorod
Kazan
Kuybyshev Res.
Samara
Ural
Gulf of Riga
Riga
LATVIA
Liepaja
Moscow
Oka
Ryazan
Saratov
WESTERN EUROPE
Baltic Sea
LITHUANIA
Daugavpils
Kaunas
Smolensk
Volgograd Res.
Kaliningrad
RUSSIA
Vilnius
Vitsyebsk
Minsk
Mahilyow
Voronezh
Volgograd
Gdansk
Szczecin
Hrodna
Babruysk
BELARUS
Homyel
Belgorod
Tsimlyansk Res.
Astrakhan
POLAND
Poznan
Warsaw
Lodz
Kiev
Kharkiv
Luhansk
Don
Rostov-na-Donu
Caspian Sea
Wroclaw
Dnieper
Kremenchug Res.
CZECH
Prague
Pilzen
REP.
Olomouc
Ostrava
Cracow
Lviv
UKRAINE
Dnipropetrovsk
Donetsk
Brno
SLOVAKIA
Kosice
CARPATHIAN MTS.
Vinnytsya
Zaporizhzhya
Mariupol
Krasnodar
Grozny
Makhachkala
CAUCASUS MOUNTAINS
Bratislava
Miskolc
Debrecen
Balti
MOLDOVA
Kakhovka Res.
Gyor
Budapest
Cluj-Napoca
Iasi
Chisinau
Tighina
Tiraspol
Odesa
Sea of Azov
Sumgayit
SLOVENIA
Maribor
HUNGARY
Szeged
ROMANIA
CRIMEA
Sukhumi
GEORGIA
Tbilisi
Ljubljana
Pecs
Timisoara
Brasov
Kutaisi
Ganca
Baku
Rijeka
Zagreb
Novi Sad
TRANSYLVANIAN ALPS
Galati
Sevastopol
Simferopol
Batumi
ARMENIA
AZERBAIJAN
CROATIA
Banja Luka
Osijek
YUGOSLAVIA
Belgrade
Bucharest
Constanta
Black Sea
Gyumri
Yerevan
Split
BOSNIA & HERCEG.
Sarajevo
Nis
Danube
Ruse
Varna
AZER.
Mostar
Dubrovnik
Podgorica
Pristina
BALKAN MTS.
Sofia
BULGARIA
Burgas
Drava
L. Balaton
Adriatic Sea
Tirane
MACEDONIA
Skopje
Plovdiv
TURKEY
Istanbul
Bosporus
ALBANIA
Thessaloniki
Larissa
Mt. Olympus
Sea of Marmara
Dardanelles
ASIA
GREECE
Aegean Sea
Ionian Sea
Patras
Athens
Corinth
Piraeus
C. Akritas
C. Matapan
Sea of Crete
Rhodes (Gr.)
Heraklion
Crete (Gr.)
Mediterranean Sea
AFRICA

EASTERN EUROPE

⊛ National capital
• City

Elevation

Meters	Feet
3,000	10,000
2,000	7,000
1,000	3,000
500	1,500
200	700
0	0

0	200	400 Miles
0	200	400 Kilometers

Azimuthal Equal-Area Projection
1: 31,019,000

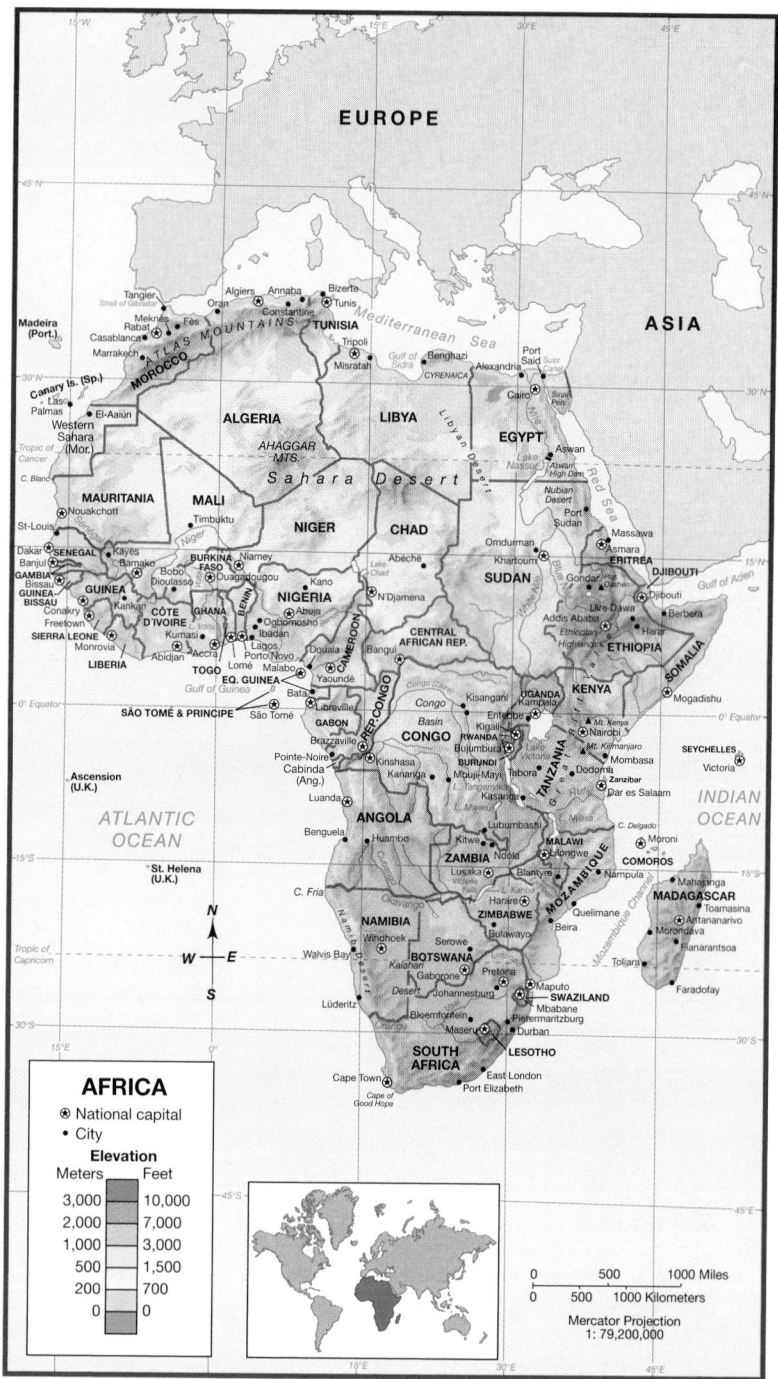

AFRICA

⊛ National capital
• City

Elevation

Meters	Feet
3,000	10,000
2,000	7,000
1,000	3,000
500	1,500
200	700
0	0

0   500   1000 Miles
0   500   1000 Kilometers

Mercator Projection
1: 79,200,000

NEAR AND MIDDLE EAST

⊛ National capital
• City

Elevation
Meters	Feet
4,000	13,000
3,000	10,000
2,000	7,000
1,000	3,000
500	1,500
200	700
0	0

0   250   500 Miles
0   250   500 Kilometers
Albers Equal-Area Projection
1:38,940,000

ASIA

EUROPE

AFRICA

Black Sea

Caspian Sea

Mediterranean Sea

Aegean Sea

Red Sea

Arabian Sea

Gulf of Oman

Gulf of Aden

Persian Gulf

UZBEKISTAN
TURKMENISTAN
TAJIKISTAN
AFGHANISTAN
PAKISTAN
IRAN
GEORGIA
ARMENIA
AZERBAIJAN
TURKEY
CYPRUS
SYRIA
LEBANON
ISRAEL
JORDAN
IRAQ
KUWAIT
SAUDI ARABIA
BAHRAIN
QATAR
UNITED ARAB EMIRATES
OMAN
YEMEN
EGYPT

HINDU KUSH
ELBURZ MTS.
ZAGROS MTS.
CAUCASUS MTS.
PONTIC MTS.
TAURUS MTS.
KURDISTAN
MESOPOTAMIA
TUWAYQ MTS.
ASIR
HEJAZ
Arabian Desert
Syrian Desert
Libyan Desert
Rub' al-Khali Desert
Garagum Desert
Qizilkum Desert

N
W ← → E
S

North Pole
ARCTIC OCE.
ATLANTIC OCEAN
Arctic Circle
Komsom
October Revolution I
Bolshevik
Chelyuski
Kara Sea
YAMAL PEN.
Gulf of Ob

E U R O P E

URAL MOUNTAINS
R U S S
Yekaterinburg
Chelyabinsk
Omsk
Krasnoyarsk
Novosibirsk
Oral
Aqtobe
Petropavl
URS-UST PLATEAU
Aral Sea
Aqmola
Temiratau
Qaraghandy Semey
Oskemen
SAY
KAZAKHSTAN

Mediterranean Sea
Black Sea
Izmir Bursa
Ankara
ASIA MINOR
TURKEY
Adana
CYPRUS
Nicosia
Gaziantep
LEBANON
Beirut
Aleppo
Tel Aviv
SYRIA
Damascus
Jerusalem
ISRAEL
Amman
Aqaba
JORDAN
Mt. Ararat
Tabriz
Al-Mosul
Baghdad
ZAGROS MTS.
Tehran
Mt. Damavand
IRAQ
UZBEKISTAN
Dashhowuz
Turkmenbashi
TURKMENISTAN
Ashgabat
Charjew
Mashhad
Syr Darya
Shymkent
Tashkent
Samarkand
Mary
Dushanbe
TAJIKISTAN
Bishkek
Almaty
Balkhash
Osh
TIAN SHAN
Kashgar
(Kashi)
KYRGYZSTAN
Ürümqi
U
He
Medina
KUWAIT
Kuwait
Abadan
Isfahan
IRAN
Herat
Kabul
AFGHANISTAN
Islamabad
Kandahar
Rawalpindi
KUNLUN MOUNTA
C
PLATEAU OF T
TIBET
SAUDI ARABIA
Riyadh
BAHRAIN
Manama
QATAR
Doha
Abu Dhabi
OMAN
UNITED ARAB EMIRATES
Muscat
Gulf of Oman
Shiraz
PAKISTAN
Faisalabad
Multan
Lahore
Delhi
New Delhi
Agra
Kanpur
NEPAL
Kathmandu
Mt. Everest
HIMALAYAS
BHUT
Brahmaputra
Jiddah
Mecca
ARABIAN DESERT
RUB AL-KHALI
Karachi
Hyderabad
THAR (GREAT INDIAN) DESERT
Ahmadabad
Ganges
Narmada
INDIA
Calcutta
BANGLADESH
Dhaka
Thin
Hodeida
San'a
YEMEN
OMAN
Aden
Gulf of Aden
Socotra
(Yemen)
Arabian Sea
Bombay
(Mumbai)
Nagpur
Godavari
DECCAN
Hyderabad
WESTERN GHATS
Krishna
PLATEAU
EASTERN GHATS
Bay of Bengal
AFRICA
Red Sea
Persian Gulf
Caspian Sea
Bangalore
Madras
(Chennai)
Minicoy
Gulf of Mannar
SRI LANKA
Colombo
Dondra Head
MALDIVES
Male
INDIAN OCEAN

50°E   60°E   70°E   80°E   90°E

ASIA

⊗ National capital
• City
⌇ Great Wall of China

Elevation

Meters	Feet
6,000	19,000
3,000	10,000
2,000	7,000
1,000	3,000
500	1,500
200	700
0	0

0   500   1000 Miles
0   500   1000 Kilometers
Lambert Azimuthal Equal-Area
Projection
1:61,016,000

OCEANIA

⊛ National capital
• City

Elevation

Meters	Feet
3,000	10,000
2,000	7,000
1,000	3,000
500	1,500
200	700
0	0

N
W — E
S

PACIFIC OCEAN

NORTH AMERICA

ASIA

Clipperton I. (Fr.)

Equator

Tropic of Capricorn

Easter I. (Chile)

Pitcairn I. (U.K.)

Marquesas Is.

P o l y n e s i a

Tuamotu Arch.

Society Is.   Tahiti
Papeete

Cook Is. (N.Z.)

Malden I. (Kiribati)

Jarvis I. (U.S.)

Kingman Reef (U.S.)

Kiritimati (Kiribati)

Starbuck I. (N.Z.)

Manihiki Atoll (N.Z.)

Palmyra I. (U.S.)

Hawaiian Islands

Oahu   Hawaii (U.S.)
Kauai   Hawaii

Midway Is. (U.S.)

International Date Line

Niue (N.Z.)

American Samoa (U.S.)
Pago Pago

WESTERN SAMOA
Apia

Tokelau Is. (N.Z.)

Wallis & Futuna (Fr.)

TONGA
Nuku'alofa

TUVALU
Funafuti

FIJI
Suva

K I R I B A T I

M i c r o n e s i a

Wake I. (U.S.)

Bonin Is. (Japan)

Volcano Is. (Japan)

Northern Mariana Islands (U.S.)

Guam (U.S.)

PALAU
Koror

FEDERATED STATES OF MICRONESIA
Palikir

MARSHALL ISLANDS
Majuro

Bikini Atoll

Tarawa I.
Bairiki

NAURU
Yaren

M e l a n e s i a

Admiralty Is.
Bismarck Arch.
New Ireland
New Britain

PAPUA NEW GUINEA
Port Moresby

Lae

Coral Sea Is. Terr. (Aust.)

SOLOMON ISLANDS
Honiara

VANUATU
Villa

New Caledonia (Fr.)
Noumea

Loyalty Is.

Coral Sea

Tropic of Cancer

NEW ZEALAND
Wellington

North Island

South Island

North Cape

East Cape

Auckland

Christchurch

Dunedin

Tasman Sea

AUSTRALIA

Darwin

Northern Territory

Western Australia

South Australia

Queensland

New South Wales

Victoria

Tasmania

Brisbane

Sydney   Canberra, A.C.T.

Melbourne

Adelaide

Perth

Cape Leeuwin

South East Cape

GREAT DIVIDING RANGE

GREAT SANDY DESERT

GIBSON DESERT

GREAT VICTORIA DESERT

Great Australian Bight

Timor Sea

Cape York Pen.

Gulf of Carpentaria

Townsville

Great Barrier Reef

INDIAN OCEAN

Tropic of Capricorn

Mercator Projection
1: 58,400,000

| 0 | 500 | 1,000 Miles |
| 0 | 500 | 1,000 Kilometers |

The New Science of Happiness

What makes the human heart sing? Researchers are taking a close look. What they've found may surprise you

By CLAUDIA WALLIS TIME

Sugary white sand gleams under the bright Yucatan sun, aquamarine water teems with tropical fish and lazy sea-turtles, cold Mexican beer beckons beneath the shady thatch of palapas—it's hard to imagine a sweeter spot than Akumal, Mexico, to contemplate the joys of being alive. And that was precisely the agenda when three leading psychologists gathered in this Mexican paradise in 1998 to plot a new direction for psychology.

For most of its history, psychology had concerned itself with all that ails the human mind: anxiety, depression, neurosis, obsessions, paranoia, delusions. The goal of practitioners was to bring patients from a negative, ailing state to a neutral normal, or, as University of Pennsylvania psychologist Martin Seligman puts it, "from a minus five to a zero." It was Seligman who had summoned the others to Akumal on Jan. 1, 1998—his first day as president of the American Psychological Association (APA)—to share a vision of a new goal for psychology. "I realized that my profession was half-baked. It wasn't enough for us to nullify disabling conditions and get to zero. We needed to ask, What are the enabling conditions that make human beings flourish? How do we get from zero to plus five?"

Every incoming APA president is asked to choose a theme for his or her yearlong term in office. Seligman was thinking big. He wanted to persuade substantial numbers in the profession to explore the region north of zero, to look at what actively made people feel fulfilled, engaged, and meaningfully happy. Mental health, he reasoned, should be more than the absence of mental illness. It should be something akin to a vibrant and muscular fitness of the human mind and spirit.

Over the decades, a few psychological researchers had ventured out of the dark realm of mental illness into the sunny land of the mentally hale and hearty. Some of Seligman's own research, for instance, had focused on optimism, a trait shown to be associated with good physical health, less depression and mental illness, longer life, and, yes, greater happiness. Perhaps the most eager explorer of this terrain was University of Illinois psychologist Edward Diener, a.k.a. Dr. Happiness. For more than two decades, basically ever since he got tenure and could risk entering an unfashionable field, Diener had been examining what does and does not make people feel satisfied with life. Seligman's goal was to shine a light on such work and encourage much, much more of it.

To help him realize his vision, Seligman invited Ray Fowler, then the long-reigning and influential CEO of the APA, to join him in Akumal. He also invited Hungarian-born psychologist Mihaly Csikszentmihalyi (pronounced "cheeks sent me high"), best known for exploring a happy state of mind

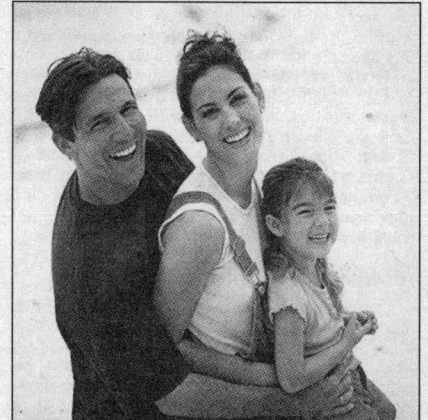
Stockbyte

called flow, the feeling of complete engagement in a creative or playful activity familiar to athletes, musicians, video-game enthusiasts—almost anyone who loses himself in a favorite pursuit. By the end of their week at the beach, the three had plans for the first-ever conference on positive psychology, to be held in Akumal a year later—it was to become an annual event—and a strategy for recruiting young talent to the nascent field. Within a few months, Seligman, who has a talent for popularizing and promoting his areas of interest, was approached by the Templeton Foundation in England, which proceeded to create lucrative awards for research in positive psych. The result: an explosion of research on happiness, optimism, positive emotions, and healthy character traits. Seldom has an academic field been brought so quickly and deliberately to life.

What Makes Us Happy

So, what has science learned about what makes the human heart sing? More than one might imagine—along with some surprising things about what doesn't ring our inner chimes. Take wealth, for instance, and all the delightful things that money can buy. Research by Diener, among others, has shown that once your basic needs are met, additional income does little to raise your sense of satisfaction with life. A good education? Sorry, Mom and Dad, neither education nor, for that matter, a high IQ paves the road to happiness. Youth? No, again. In fact, older people are more consistently satisfied with their lives than the young. And they're less prone to dark moods: a recent survey by the

Centers for Disease Control and Prevention found that people ages 20 to 24 are sad for an average of 3.4 days a month, as opposed to just 2.3 days for people ages 65 to 74. Marriage? A complicated picture: married people are generally happier than singles, but that may be because they were happier to begin with. Sunny days? Nope, although a 1998 study showed that Midwesterners think folks living in balmy California are happier and that Californians incorrectly believe this about themselves too.

On the positive side, religious faith seems to genuinely lift the spirit, though it's tough to tell whether it's the God part or the community aspect that does the heavy lifting. Friends? A giant yes. A 2002 study conducted at the University of Illinois by Diener and Seligman found that the most salient characteristics shared by the 10% of students with the highest levels of happiness and the fewest signs of depression were their strong ties to friends and family and commitment to spending time with them. "Word needs to be spread," concludes Diener. "It is important to work on social skills, close interpersonal ties, and social support in order to be happy."

Measuring Our Moods

Of course, happiness is not a static state. Even the happiest of people—the cheeriest 10%—feel blue at times. And even the bluest have their moments of joy. That has presented a challenge to social scientists trying to measure happiness. That, along with the simple fact that happiness is inherently subjective. To get around those challenges, researchers have devised several methods of assessment. Diener has created one of the most basic and widely used tools, the Satisfaction with Life Scale. Though some scholars have questioned the validity of this simple, five-question survey, Diener has found that it squares well with other measures of happiness, such as impressions from friends and family, expression of positive emotion, and low incidence of depression.

Researchers have devised other tools to look at more transient moods. Csikszentmihalyi pioneered a method of using beepers and, later, handheld computers to contact subjects at random intervals. A pop-up screen presents an array of questions: What are you doing? How much are you enjoying it? Are you alone or interacting with someone else? The method, called experience sampling, is costly, intrusive, and time consuming, but it provides an excellent picture of satisfaction and engagement at a specific time during a specific activity.

In December 2004, a team led by Nobel–prize-winning psychologist Daniel Kahneman of Princeton University unveiled a new tool for sizing up happiness: the day-reconstruction method. Participants fill out a long diary and questionnaire detailing everything they did on the previous day and whom they were with at the time and rating a range of feelings during each episode (happy, impatient, depressed, worried, tired, etc.) on a seven-point scale. The method was tested on a group of 900 women in Texas with some surprising results. It turned out that the five most positive activities for these women were (in descending order) sex, socializing, relaxing, praying or meditating, and eating. Exercising and watching TV were not far behind. But way down the list was "taking care of my children," which ranked below cooking and only slightly above housework.

Eight Steps Toward a More Satisfying Life

Want to lift your level of happiness? Here are some practical suggestions from University of California psychologist Sonja Lyubomirsky, based on research findings by her and others. Satisfaction (at least a temporary boost) guaranteed.

1. **Count your blessings.** One way to do this is with a "gratitude journal" in which you write down three to five things for which you are currently thankful—from the mundane (your peonies are in bloom) to the magnificent (a child's first steps). Do this once a week, say, on Sunday night. Keep it fresh by varying your entries as much as possible.

2. **Practice acts of kindness.** These should be both random (let that harried mom go ahead of you in the checkout line) and systematic (bring Sunday supper to an elderly neighbor). Being kind to others, whether friends or strangers, triggers a cascade of positive effects—it makes you feel generous and capable; gives you a greater sense of connection with others; and wins you smiles, approval, and reciprocated kindness—all happiness boosters.

3. **Savor life's joys.** Pay close attention to momentary pleasures and wonders. Focus on the sweetness of a ripe strawberry or the warmth of the sun when you step out from the shade. Some psychologists suggest taking "mental photographs" of pleasurable moments to review in less happy times.

4. **Thank a mentor.** If there's someone whom you owe a debt of gratitude for guiding you at one of life's crossroads, don't wait to express your appreciation—in detail and, if possible, in person.

5. **Learn to forgive.** Let go of anger and resentment by writing a letter of forgiveness to a person who has hurt or wronged you. Inability to forgive is associated with persistent rumination or dwelling on revenge, while forgiving allows you to move on.

6. **Invest time and energy in friends and family.** Where you live, how much money you make, your job title, and even your health have surprisingly small effects on your satisfaction with life. The biggest factor appears to be strong personal relationships.

7. **Take care of your body.** Getting plenty of sleep, exercising, stretching, smiling, and laughing can all enhance your mood in the short term. Practiced regularly, they can help make your daily life more satisfying.

8. **Develop strategies for coping with stress and hardships.** There is no avoiding hard times. Religious faith has been shown to help people cope, but so do the secular beliefs enshrined in axioms like "This too shall pass" and "That which doesn't kill me makes me stronger." The trick is that you have to believe them.

That may seem surprising, given that people frequently cite their children as their biggest source of delight—which was a finding of a TIME poll on happiness conducted late in 2004. When asked, "What one thing in life has brought you the greatest happiness?", 35% said it was their children or grandchildren or both. (Spouse was far behind at just 9%, and religion a runner-up at 17%.) The discrepancy with the study of Texas women points up one of the key debates in happiness research: Which kind of information is more meaningful—global reports of well-being ("My life is happy, and my children are my greatest joy") or more specific data on enjoyment of day-to-day experiences ("What a night! The kids were such a pain!")? The two are very different, and studies show they do not correlate well. Our overall happiness is not merely the sum of our happy moments minus the sum of our angry or sad ones.

This is true whether you are looking at how satisfied you are with your life in general or with something more specific, such as your kids, your car, your job, or your vacation. Kahneman likes to distinguish between the experiencing self and the remembering self. His studies show that what you remember of an experience is particularly influenced by the emotional high and low points and by how it ends. So, if you were to randomly beep someone on vacation in Italy, you might catch that person waiting furiously for a slow-moving waiter to take an order or grousing about the high cost of the pottery. But if you ask when it's over, "How was the vacation in Italy?", the average person remembers the peak moments and how he or she felt at the end of the trip.

The power of endings has been demonstrated in some remarkable experiments by Kahneman. One such study involved people undergoing a colonoscopy, an uncomfortable procedure in which a flexible scope is moved through the colon. While a control group had the standard procedure, half the subjects endured an extra 60 seconds during which the scope was held stationary; movement of the scope is typically the source of the discomfort. It turned out that members of the group that had the somewhat longer procedure with a benign ending found it less unpleasant than the control group, and they were more willing to have a repeat colonoscopy.

Asking people how happy they are, Kahneman contends, "is very much like asking them about the colonoscopy after it's over. There's a lot that escapes them." Kahneman therefore believes that social scientists studying happiness should pay careful attention to people's actual experiences rather than just survey their reflections. That, he feels, is especially relevant if research is to inform quality-of-life policies like how much money our society should devote to parks and recreation or how much should be invested in improving workers' commutes. "You cannot ignore how people spend their time," he says, "when thinking about well-being."

Seligman, in contrast, puts the emphasis on the remembering self. "I think we are our memories more than we are the sum total of our experiences," he says. For him, studying moment-to-moment experiences puts too much emphasis on transient pleasures and displeasures. Happiness goes deeper than that, he argues in his 2002 book *Authentic Happiness*. As a result of his research, he finds three components of happiness: pleasure ("the smiley-face piece"), engagement (the depth of involvement with one's family, work, romance, and hobbies), and meaning (using personal strengths to serve some larger end). Of those three roads to a happy, satisfied life, pleasure is the least consequential, he insists: "This is newsworthy because so many Americans build their lives around pursuing pleasure. It turns out that engagement and meaning are much more important."

Measure Your Happiness

How happy are you? Sure, you may think you know, but this little test will help you keep score. The Satisfaction with Life Scale was devised in 1980 by University of Illinois psychologist Edward Diener, a founding father of happiness research. Since then the scale has been used by researchers around the world.

Read the following five statements. Then use a 1-to-7 scale to rate your level of agreement.

1	2	3	4	5	6	7
Not at all true			Moderately true			Absolutely true

A. In most ways my life is close to my ideal. 1 2 3 4 5 6 7

B. The conditions of my life are excellent. 1 2 3 4 5 6 7

C. I am satisfied with my life. 1 2 3 4 5 6 7

D. So far I have gotten the important things I want in life. 1 2 3 4 5 6 7

E. If I could live my life over, I would change almost nothing. 1 2 3 4 5 6 7

TOTAL SCORE: _____

Scoring

31-35: extremely satisfied • **26-30:** very satisfied • **21-25:** slightly satisfied • **20:** neutral • **15-19:** slightly dissatisfied • **10-14:** dissatisfied • **5-9:** extremely dissatisfied

Can We Get Happier?

One of the biggest issues in happiness research is the question of how much our happiness is under our control. In 1996 University of Minnesota researcher David Lykken published a paper looking at the role of genes in determining one's sense of satisfaction in life. Lykken, now 76, gathered information on 4,000 sets of twins born in Minnesota from 1936 through 1955. After comparing happiness data on identical vs. fraternal twins, he came to the conclusion that about 50% of one's satisfaction with life comes from genetic programming. (Genes influence such traits as having a sunny, easygoing personality; dealing well with stress; and feeling low levels of anxiety and depression.) Lykken found that circumstantial factors like income, marital status, religion, and education contribute only about 8% to one's overall well-being. He attributes the remaining percentage to "life's slings and arrows."

Because of the large influence of our genes, Lykken proposed the idea that each of us has a happiness set point much like our set point for body weight. No matter what happens in our life—good, bad, spectacular, horrific—we tend to return in short order to our set range. A substantial body of research documents our tendency to return to the norm. A study of lottery winners done in 1978 found, for instance, that they did not wind up significantly happier than a control group. Even people who lose the use of their limbs to a devastating accident tend to bounce back, though perhaps not all the way to their base line.

In his extensive work on adaptation—the way we adjust to new circumstances—Edward Diener has found two life events that seem to knock people lastingly below their happiness set point: loss of a spouse and loss of a job. It takes five to eight years for a widow to regain her previous sense of well-being. Similarly, the effects of a job loss linger long after the individual has returned to the work force.

When he proposed his set-point theory eight years ago, Lykken came to a drastic conclusion. "It may be that trying to be happier is as futile as trying to be taller," he wrote. He has since come to regret that sentence. "I made a dumb statement in the original article," he tells TIME. "It's clear we can change our happiness levels widely—up or down."

Lykken's revisionist thinking coincides with the view of the positive-psychology movement, which has put a premium on research showing you can raise your level of happiness. For Seligman and like-minded researchers, that involves working on the three components of happiness—getting more pleasure out of life (which can be done by savoring sensory experiences, although, he warns, "you're never going to make a curmudgeon into a giggly person"), becoming more engaged in what you do, and finding ways of making your life feel more meaningful.

There are numerous ways to do that, they argue. At the University of California at Riverside, psychologist Sonja Lyubomirsky is using grant money from the National Institutes of Health to study different kinds of happiness boosters. One is the gratitude journal—a diary in which subjects write down things for which they are thankful. She has found that taking the time to conscientiously count their blessings once a week significantly increased subjects' overall satisfaction with life over a period of six weeks, whereas a control group that did not keep journals had no such gain.

Gratitude exercises can do more than lift one's mood. At the University of California at Davis, psychologist Robert Emmons found they improve physical health, raise energy levels, and, for patients

---

Feeling Good in the U.S.—Just How Happy Are We?

Based on their own assessment, Americans are overwhelmingly happy and optimistic people, regardless of income

Would you say you are happy...

	...most or all of the time	...some of the time	...not very often?
Under $35,000 a year	68%	24%	7%
$35,000 to $49,999	81%	14%	5%
$50,000 to $99,999	85%	13%	2%
Over $100,000 a year	88%	11%	1%
U.S. total	78%	16%	5%

Would you say that so far you have lived the best possible life that you could have, a very good life, a good life, a fair life, or a poor life?

Best possible	13%
Very good	37%
Good	33%
Fair	15%
Poor	2%

Do you consider yourself an optimist?

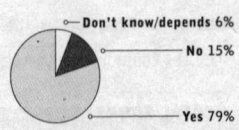

- Don't know/depends 6%
- No 15%
- Yes 79%

This TIME poll was conducted by telephone Dec. 13-14, 2004, among 1,009 adult Americans by SRBI Public Affairs. Margin of error is ±3 percentage points. "Not Sure" omitted for some questions.

with neuromuscular disease, relieve pain and fatigue. "The ones who benefited most tended to elaborate more and have a wider span of things they're grateful for," he notes.

Another happiness booster, say positive psychologists, is performing acts of altruism or kindness—visiting a nursing home, helping a friend's child with homework, mowing a neighbor's lawn, writing a letter to a grandparent. Doing five kind acts a week, especially all in a single day, gave a measurable boost to Lyubomirsky's subjects.

Seligman has tested similar interventions in controlled trials at Penn and in huge experiments conducted over the Internet. The single most effective way to turbocharge your joy, he says, is to make a "gratitude visit." That means writing a testimonial thanking a teacher, pastor, or grandparent—anyone to whom you owe a debt of gratitude—and then visiting that person to read him or her the letter of appreciation. "The remarkable thing," says Seligman, "is that people who do this just once are measurably happier and less depressed a month later. But it's gone by three months." Less powerful but more lasting, he says, is an exercise he calls three blessings—taking time each day to write down a trio of things that went well and why. "People are less depressed and happier three months later and six months later."

Seligman's biggest tip for lasting happiness is to figure out your strengths and find new ways to deploy them. Increasingly, his work, done in collaboration with Christopher Peterson at the University of Michigan, has focused on defining such human strengths and virtues as generosity, humor, gratitude, and zest. "As a professor, I don't like this," Seligman says, "but the cerebral virtues—curiosity, love of learning—are less strongly tied to happiness than interpersonal virtues like kindness, gratitude, and capacity for love."

Why do exercising gratitude, kindness, and other virtues provide a lift? "Giving makes you feel good about yourself," says Peterson. "When you're volunteering, you're distracting yourself from your own existence, and that's beneficial. More fuzzily, giving puts meaning into your life. You have a sense of purpose because you matter to someone else." Virtually all the happiness exercises being tested by positive psychologists, he says, make people feel more connected to others.

That seems to be the most fundamental finding from the science of happiness. "Almost every person feels happier when they're with other people," observes Mihaly Csikszentmihalyi. "It's paradoxical because many of us think we can hardly wait to get home and be alone with nothing to do, but that's a worst-case scenario. If you're alone with nothing to do, the quality of your experience really plummets."

But can a loner really become more gregarious through acts-of-kindness exercises? Can a dyed-in-the-wool pessimist learn to see the glass as half full?

Some psychologists simply doubt that personality is that flexible or that individuals can or should change their habitual coping styles. "If you're a pessimist who really thinks through in detail what might go wrong, that's a strategy that's likely to work very well for you," says Julie Norem, a psychology professor at Wellesley College and the author of *The Positive Power of Negative Thinking.* "In fact, you may be messed up if you try to substitute a positive attitude." She is worried that the messages of positive psychology reinforce "a lot of American biases" about how individual initiative and a positive attitude can solve complex problems.

Who's right? This is an experiment we can all do for ourselves. There's little risk in trying some extra gratitude and kindness, and the results—should they materialize—are their own reward. □

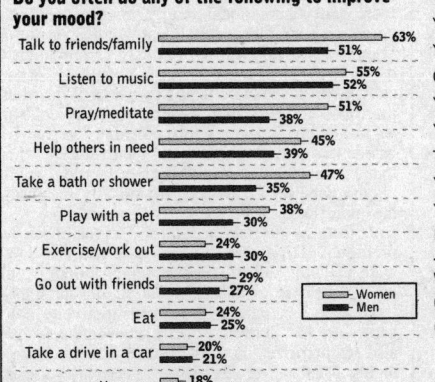

...And What Makes Us That Way?

Most people find happiness in family connections and friendships

Do you often do any of the following to improve your mood?

	Women	Men
Talk to friends/family	63%	51%
Listen to music	55%	52%
Pray/meditate	51%	38%
Help others in need	45%	39%
Take a bath or shower	47%	35%
Play with a pet	38%	30%
Exercise/work out	24%	30%
Go out with friends	29%	27%
Eat	24%	25%
Take a drive in a car	20%	21%
Have sex	18%	25%

What are your major sources of happiness?

Your relationship with your children	77%
Your friends and friendships	76%
Contributing to the lives of others	75%
Your relationships with spouse/partner or your love life	73%
Your degree of control over your life and destiny	66%
The things you do in your leisure time	64%
Your relationship with your parents	63%
Your religious or spiritual life and worship	62%
Holiday periods, such as Christmas and New Year's	50%

What one thing in your life has brought you the greatest happiness?

Top four answers

Children/grandchildren	35%
Family	17%
God/faith/religion	11%
Spouse	9%

This TIME poll was conducted by telephone Dec. 13-14, 2004, among 1,009 adult Americans by SRBI Public Affairs. Margin of error is ±3 percentage points. "Not Sure" omitted for some questions.

The Biology of Joy

Scientists know plenty about depression. Now they are starting to explore and understand the roots of positive emotion

By MICHAEL D. LEMONICK   TIME

Richard Davidson was in a lab observing a Buddhist Monk sink deep into serene meditation when he noticed something that sent his own pulse racing. Davidson, a professor of psychology and psychiatry at the University of Wisconsin, hurriedly double-checked the data streaming to his computer from electrodes attached to the monk's skull, but there was no mistake. Electrical activity in the left prefrontal lobe of the monk's brain was shooting up at a tremendous rate. "It was exciting," Davidson recalls. "We didn't expect to see anything quite that dramatic."

Davidson's excitement is all the more significant because he's known by colleagues as the king of happiness research. When he made the discovery five years ago, he had been studying the link between prefrontal-lobe activity and the sort of bliss deep meditators experience. But even for someone with his experience, watching the brain crackle with activity as a person entered a trancelike state was unprecedented. It made clear, says Davidson, who published the research study in the *Proceedings of the National Academy of Sciences* in 2004, that happiness isn't just a vague, ineffable feeling; it's a physical state of the brain—one that you can induce deliberately.

That's not all. As researchers have gained an understanding of the physical characteristics of a happy brain, they have come to see that those traits have a powerful influence on the rest of the body. People who rate in the upper reaches of happiness on psychological tests develop about 50% more antibodies than average in response to flu vaccines, and that, says Davidson, "is a very large difference." Others have discovered that happiness or related mental states like hopefulness, optimism, and contentment appear to reduce the risk or limit the severity of cardiovascular disease, pulmonary disease, diabetes, hypertension, colds, and upper-respiratory infections as well. According to a Dutch study of elderly patients published in November 2004, those upbeat mental states reduced an individual's risk of death 50% over the study's nine-year duration. Says Laura Kubzansky, a health psychologist at Harvard's School of Public Health, in a masterpiece of understatement: "There's clearly some kind of effect."

It makes sense that there should be. Doctors have known for years that clinical depression—the extreme opposite of happiness—can worsen heart disease, diabetes, and a host of other illnesses. But the neurochemistry of depression is much better known than that of happiness, mostly because the former has been studied more intensively and for much longer. Until about a decade ago, says Dacher Keltner, a psychologist at the University of California, Berkeley, "90% of emotion research focused on the negative, so there still are all of these interesting questions about the positive side."

A growing number of researchers exploring the physiology and neurology of happiness are starting

Royalty-Free Corbis

to answer those questions. Perhaps most fundamental of all is what happiness is, in a clinical sense. At this point, nobody can really say with precision. The word happiness, Davidson observes, "is kind of a placeholder for a constellation of positive emotional states. It's a state of well-being where individuals are typically not motivated to change their state. They're motivated to preserve it. It's associated with an active embracing of the world, but the precise characteristics and boundaries have really yet to be seriously characterized in scientific research."

Still, subjects can reliably tell researchers when they're feeling good, and two brain-imaging technologies—functional magnetic resonance imaging (MRI), which maps blood flow to active parts of the brain, and electroencephalograms, which sense the electrical activity of neuronal circuits—consistently point to the left prefrontal cortex as a prime locus of happiness.

That raises the chicken-and-egg question of whether the prefrontal cortex creates the sensation of happiness or whether it merely reflects one's more general emotional state. Davidson thinks the answer is both: "We're confident that this part of the brain is a proximal cause of at least certain kinds of happiness." That suggests some people are genetically predisposed to be happy by virtue of their busy prefrontal cortexes, and research in infants confirms it. Davidson measured left prefrontal activity in babies less than a year old and then subjected them to a test in which their mothers left the room briefly. "Some babies will just cry hysterically the instant the mom leaves," he says. "Others are more resilient." It turns out that the babies with the higher left prefrontal activity are the ones who don't cry. "We were actually able to predict which infants would cry in response to that brief but significant stress."

In short, as parents know instinctively, some babies are just born happy. But neuroscientists have also learned over the past decade that the brain is highly plastic. It rewires itself in response to experience, and that's especially true before the age of puberty. One might naively assume, therefore, that negative experiences might destroy a happy personality—and if they're extreme and frequent enough, that might be true. Davidson has learned, however, that mild to moderate doses of negative experience are beneficial. The reason, he believes, is that stressful events give us practice at bouncing back from unpleasant emotions. They're like an exercise to strengthen our happiness muscles or a vaccination against melancholy.

Exactly what is the physical difference, though, between a left prefrontal cortex that is predisposed to happiness and one that isn't? It almost certainly has in part to do with neurotransmitters, the chemicals that ferry signals from one neuron to the next. And while the prefrontal cortex is awash in many neurotransmitters, including dopamine, serotonin, glutamate, GABA, and more, Davidson believes dopamine may be especially important. People with a sensitive version of the receptor that accepts dopamine tend to have better moods, and researchers are actively studying the relationship of dopamine levels to feelings of euphoria and depression.

Dopamine pathways may be especially important in aspects of happiness associated with moving toward some sort of goal (monks achieving a meditative state as well as cigarette smokers allowed to light up after 24 hours of deprivation). But other neurochemicals may be more central to other kinds of happiness, including physical pleasure. "People have made progress differentiating the positive feeling you get when you approach a goal, which maps onto dopamine, and the sensory pleasure of enjoying something, which maps onto the opioid system," says Berkeley psychologist Keltner. "We're just beginning to apply a lens to all those parts of the nervous system in which the positive emotions are embodied. This is really neat territory."

Among those exploring that territory is Brian Knutson, an assistant professor of psychology and neuroscience at Stanford, who, like Davidson, uses MRI to monitor the brains of test subjects. The mental mode he studies is anticipation. "When people think of happiness," says Knutson, "they think of feeling good, but a big part of happiness is also looking forward to something." Knutson's research was inspired by the classic work of Ivan Pavlov, who trained dogs to salivate at the sound of a bell, which they associated with mealtime.

Instead of food, Knutson used money: a small cash payoff if subjects won a video game. "When we looked at their brains just before they got the reward," he says, "we saw this spark that clearly had to do with how positive the idea of making money was." The spark showed up not in the left prefrontal cortex but in what Knutson terms an old section, the nucleus accumbens, located in the subcortex, at the bottom of the brain. The bigger the prize, Knutson found, "the more activation." Knutson believes he is looking at the kind of happy feelings we experience as excitement. The primary focus of his work is to understand the neurophysiology of motivation and decision making—how emotion and reason work together as people make choices. But it could also be a key to mapping out the brain's broader happiness circuitry.

Understanding the neurophysiology of feeling good is one aspect of happiness research; another is understanding how positive emotion affects the rest of the body. As with the brain studies, the term happiness is too broad for a rigorous approach, so researchers tend to focus on specific aspects. Har-

vard psychologist Kubzansky has chosen to study optimism. In a large study she tracked 1,300 men for 10 years and found that heart-disease rates among men who called themselves optimistic were half the rates for men who didn't.

"It was a much bigger effect than we expected," she says—as big as the difference between smokers and nonsmokers. "We also looked at pulmonary function, since poor pulmonary function is predictive of a whole range of bad outcomes, including premature mortality, cardiovascular disease, and chronic obstructive pulmonary disease." Again, optimists did much better.

In a separate study, meanwhile, which has been accepted by the journal *Health Psychology*, Kubzansky, working with Duke psychologist and lead researcher Laura Richman, looked at hopefulness and curiosity—mental states that overlap with optimism in some ways. "We found them to be protective against hypertension, diabetes, and upper-respiratory infection," she says. Such protective effects may explain the longevity advantage found in that Dutch study of the elderly—an advantage for happy optimists that persisted even when researchers corrected for diet, education, and other factors.

Exactly how states of mind affect the body's biochemistry is still far from clear. One clue: in addition to reporting a positive mood when their left prefrontal cortexes are active, subjects in Davidson's experiments have lower levels of cortisol, a hormone produced by the adrenal gland in response to stress—and cortisol is known to depress immune function. Optimists may simply feel less stress than pessimists and thereby avoid the noxious biochemical cascades that stress is known to trigger. Another likely factor: optimistic, happy types seem to take better care of themselves than sad sacks do. Numerous studies—as well as common sense—suggest that to be the case.

In a series of studies begun in 1998, psychologist Robert Emmons of the University of California at Davis has found further evidence that happy people are better at health maintenance. Emmons randomly assigned 1,000 adults to one of three groups. The first group kept daily journals of their moods and rated them on a scale of 1 to 6. The second group did that and listed the things that annoyed or hassled them throughout their day. The third group kept a journal but added an activity that has repeatedly been shown to improve one's sense of satisfaction with life: they were asked to write down every day all the things for which they were grateful.

Despite being assigned randomly, the last group not only had the predicted jump in their overall feelings of happiness, says Emmons, but were also found to spend more time exercising, be more likely to have regular medical checkups, and routinely take preventive health actions like wearing sunscreen. Not surprisingly, the advantages were greatest when compared with the group that focused on life's hassles.

Such positive results gratify happiness researchers, who haven't been very successful in attracting federal dollars. Thanks to Keltner, Davidson, and others studying the biology of joy, the field has earned a degree of respectability that's long overdue—and that ultimately could make all of us a whole lot happier. □

How Full Is That Glass, Really?

Happiness—we seek it in wealth, status, pleasure, and entertainment. But it's all in the mind, right? Right

By ALICE PARK TIME

A positive outlook—a belief in your own future—is a trait associated with greater resilience. But who has got a firmer grip on reality: the glass-half-full optimist or the cold-eyed pessimist who focuses on obstacles ahead?

That's what psychologists Lauren Alloy and Lyn Abramson set out to find in the late 1970s when they began a seminal series of experiments exploring how mood affects the way people think. Back then most therapists took the Freudian view that depressed people—and by extension, pessimists—were out of touch with reality. It made sense, since depression was considered an aberrant mental state. Their work and subsequent research show that the relationship between cognition and mood is far more complex.

In carefully designed experiments, Alloy, then at Northwestern University, and Abramson, then at the State University of New York at Stony Brook, sat students in front of a panel featuring a green light and a button that they were told would activate the light when pressed. In fact, the amount of control students had over the light varied from 0% to 100%, with many points in between. When the students were asked how much control they thought they had over the light, the answers surprised the psychologists. Optimistic types (who scored low on tests for depressive symptoms) consistently overestimated their influence. By a lot. On average they believed they had 60% control even in sessions in which their button pressing had purely random effects. "The nondepressed had an illusion of control when in fact they had none," says Alloy. By contrast, more pessimistic students (those who had more depressive symptoms) judged their performance more accurately.

The finding that depressive types were "sadder but wiser," as the researchers put it, rocked conventional thinking in psychology. "Our demonstration was provocative because it was counter to theories of psychopathology," Abramson says. Clearly, nondepressed individuals were every bit as capable of distorting reality as the mentally ill were supposed to be.

In a second series of experiments with the light panel, the researchers tried to prove that mood really was the deciding factor in how students performed. To do so, they induced a depressed mood in nondepressed students by asking them to read a series of increasingly negative statements, beginning with a neutral idea such as "Today is neither better nor worse than any other day" and ending up with "I'd like to go to sleep and never wake up again." Similarly, they lifted the mood of depressed students by having them read positive statements. Sure enough, the students who were artificially "depressed" made more accurate judgments about their control over the light than students whose mood was happified.

Royalty-Free Corbis

"Basically, we could flip the entire phenomenon around," says Alloy.

Were happier folks deluded only about their power to control, or did they have similar illusions about other people? Alloy and Abramson tested that and found that happy people were much more accurate when observing others performing the light-panel task. The result was the opposite, however, with depressed people, who tended to overrate other people's performance. "That fits the theory that depressed people have a poor view of themselves but a better view of others," says Abramson.

In the years since Alloy and Abramson published their work, other researchers have built on their findings about how mood and outlook color all sorts of thinking tasks: making purchasing decisions, doing creative work, recognizing faces. In studies at the University of Utah, Lisa Aspinwall has found that when presented with an unsolvable problem, optimists spend less time on strategies that don't produce results. Pessimists, on the other hand, tend to ensnare themselves in one approach, sticking with it despite its futility. "Optimists didn't waste time and energy on something that couldn't be done, and these coping skills may be what helps them to handle stressful events in life situations as well," Aspinwall says.

That doesn't mean that pessimists are always at a disadvantage. Their negative filter can be advantageous in situations involving risk or critical judgment, such as buying a new home or filing taxes. So if you're picking an architect, it might be a good idea to go with an optimist, but you may want a pessimist for an accountant. □

Couch Potatoes, Arise!

It's not just a matter of looking svelte: exercise directly benefits your health. So what are you waiting for?

By JEFFREY KLUGER and CLAUDIA WALLIS TIME

There's nothing easier than falling out of shape, especially in the U.S. Americans may no longer lead the world in science, engineering, and productivity, but with TiVo on the flat-screen, Domino's at the door, and an arsenal of remotes within easy reach, we've got leisure time nailed.

Not only are a third of American adults obese, but a quarter of them—22% of men, 28% of women—admit that they spend virtually no leisure time getting exercise. The good news is that this is an improvement. In 1990, 31% admitted to being hopeless couch potatoes.

How many Americans get a moderate 30 minutes of exercise at least five times a week? In a TIME survey of more than 1,000 randomly selected American adults, 33% said they do. Federal surveys suggest that it's more like 26%, alhtough if you include data on activities such as gardening and cleaning, as opposed to just recreational exercise, the figure jumps to about 45%.

If you're one of the sedentary Americans who has wisely decided to get in shape, take heed: climbing off the couch and getting back into condition can be a dicey proposition. Trying to do it too fast can actually be dangerous. "Among those at greatest risk for heart-attack death is the habitually sedentary person who engages in unaccustomed physical activity," warns Barry Franklin, physiologist and chairman of the American Heart Association's Physical Activities Committee. Before starting even a minimal exercise program, therefore, you should call your doctor for a pre-workout O.K. or even a checkup.

Once you've been cleared for takeoff, the first step you take may be just that: a walking program that begins modestly and then builds up. Government guidelines recommend at least 30 minutes of moderate-intensity activities including walking most days of the week, but Franklin believes in starting even more slowly, if necessary. "I ask my patients if they could manage as little as eight to 10 minutes," he says. "Most of the time they say they can, and then come back having done 14 or 15."

Even that small start can yield big dividends. A good walking program may improve overall measures of physical health as much as 15% in just three months. Since the human body after age 25 experiences, on average, about a 1% falloff in fitness for every additional year of life, the numbers are easy to crunch. "That's a 15-year functional rejuvenation," Franklin says.

For folks aiming for more—weight loss, limberness, a competitive edge in sports—there are other avenues to becoming active again. Depending on how many years you've logged on the couch, high-impact activities such as jogging may not be for you—not if your creaky knees, ankles, and hips have anything to say about it. Best to get yourself

Royalty-Free Corbis

back in shape with a low-impact activity like swimming, cycling, or rowing.

Whatever you choose, begin with a shorter workout than you believe you can handle. "Consciously underdo," advises exercise physiologist Carl Foster of the University of Wisconsin-La Crosse. "We're all 19 behind our eyes, but if you jogged 10 miles a day when you were in college, that doesn't mean you can do it now." Besides, once you're comfortable with a more modest workout load, you can slowly increase it—about 10% a week, Foster recommends. Government guidelines suggest that if you're having trouble finding the time or energy for a full exercise session, you can still get significant health benefits from 30 to 60 minutes of exercise broken up into 10- or 15-minute segments throughout the day.

If you're interested in activities that require skill, be willing to bend the rules a little so you can keep up—allow the tennis ball to take an extra bounce, play half-speed hoops on just a portion of the court. Also, don't choose activities that are seasonal, expensive, or too solitary—each one a handy excuse for not sticking with your workout program. If you can afford it or if your gym or health club offers it, try to work with a personal trainer at least some of the time—someone who can rein you in when you're doing something wrong, applaud when you're doing something right, and, perhaps most important, make you feel guilty if you don't show up at all. Trainers are also good at knowing which muscle groups you need to strengthen for a sport you may be considering trying, and helping you exercise them into shape.

Finally, for all people new to workouts, it pays to continue to play it safe, even after your doctor has cleared you to exercise. Be alert for lightheadedness or pain or pressure in the chest. And if you can't speak reasonably comfortably while you're exercising, you're probably getting more winded than is good for you. "The risk from exercise is not too great, but it's there," says Foster. The benefits from doing it right, of course, are enormous. □

The Real Truth About Money

Why we remain keen for green even though it often gives us more social anxiety than satisfaction

By GREGG EASTERBROOK   TIME

Royalty-Free Corbis

If you made a graph of American life since the end of World War II, every line concerning money and the things that money can buy would soar upward, a statistical monument to materialism. Inflation-adjusted income per American has almost tripled. The size of the typical new house has more than doubled. A two-car garage was once a goal; now we're nearly a three-car nation. Designer everything, personal electronics, and other items that didn't even exist a half-century ago are now affordable. No matter how you chart the trends in earning and spending, everything is up, up, up. But if you made a chart of American happiness since the end of World War II, the lines would be as flat as a marble tabletop. In polls taken by the National Opinion Research Center in the 1950s, about one-third of Americans described themselves as "very happy." The center has conducted essentially the same poll periodically since then, and the percentage remains almost exactly the same today.

(In a December 2004 TIME poll on happiness that phrased the question differently, 17% of respondents said they were brimming with happiness "just about all the time," and about 60% said they were frequently happy.)

Yet if you charted the incidence of depression since 1950, the lines suggest a growing epidemic. Depending on what assumptions are used, clinical depression is 3 to 10 times as common today than two generations ago. A recent study by Ronald Kessler of Harvard Medical School estimated that each year, 1 in 15 Americans experience an episode of major depression—meaning not just a bad day but depression so debilitating that it's hard to get out of bed. Money jangles in our wallets and purses as never before, but we are basically no happier for it, and for many, more money leads to depression. How can that be?

Of course, our grandmothers, many of whom lived through the Depression and the war, told us that money can't buy happiness. We don't act as though we listened. Millions of us spend more time and energy pursuing the things money can buy than engaging in activities that create real fulfillment in life, like cultivating friendships, helping others, and developing a spiritual sense.

We say we know that money can't buy happiness. In the TIME poll, when people were asked about their major source of happiness, money ranked 14th. Still, we behave as though happiness is one wave of a credit card away. Too many Americans view expensive purchases as "shortcuts to well-being," says Martin Seligman, a psychologist at the University of Pennsylvania. But people are poor predictors of where those shortcuts will take them.

To be sure, there is ample evidence that being poor causes unhappiness. Studies by Ruut Veenhoven, a sociologist at Erasmus University in Rotterdam, show that the poor—those in Europe earning less than about $10,000 a year—are rendered unhappy by the relentless frustration and stress of poverty. But you knew that.

The surprise is that after a person's annual income exceeds $10,000 or so, Veenhoven found, money and happiness decouple and cease to have much to do with each other. The study, which has been replicated in the U.S., shows that Grandma had a point. Over the past two decades, in fact, an increasing body of social-science and psychological research has shown that there is no significant relationship between how much money a person earns and whether he or she feels good about life.

TIME's poll found that happiness tended to increase as income rose to $50,000 a year. (The median annual U.S. household income is around $43,000.) After that, more income did not have a dramatic effect. Edward Diener, a psychologist at the University of Illinois, interviewed members of the Forbes 400, the richest Americans. He found the Forbes 400 were only a tiny bit happier than the public as a whole. Because those with wealth often continue to feel jealousy about the possessions or prestige of other wealthy people, even large sums of money may fail to confer well-being.

That seems true because of a phenomenon that sociologists call reference anxiety—or, more popularly, keeping up with the Joneses. According to that thinking, most people judge their possessions in comparison with others'. People tend not to ask themselves, Does my house meet my needs? Instead they ask, Is my house nicer than my neighbor's? If you own a two-bedroom house and everyone around you owns a two-bedroom house, your reference anxiety will be low, and your two-bedroom house may seem fine. But if your two-bedroom house is surrounded by three- and four-bedroom houses, with someone around the corner doing a tear-down to build a McMansion, your reference anxiety may rise. Suddenly that two-bedroom house—one that your grandparents might have considered quite nice, even luxurious—doesn't seem enough. And so the money you spent on it stops providing you with a sense of well-being.

Our soaring reference anxiety is a product of the widening gap in income distribution. In other words, the rich are getting richer faster, and the rest of us are none too happy about it. During much of U.S. history, the majority lived in small towns or urban areas where conditions for most people were approximately the same—hence low reference anxiety. Also, most people knew relatively little about those who were living higher on the hog.

But in the past few decades, new economic forces have changed all that. Rapid growth in income for the top 5% of households has brought about a substantial cohort of people who live notably better than the middle class does, amplifying our reference anxiety. It all feeds middle-class anxiety, even when the middle is doing O.K. In nations with high levels

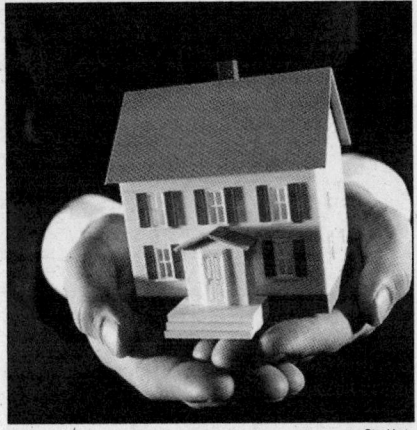

Stockbyte

of income equality like the Scandinavian countries, well-being tends to be higher than in nations with unequal wealth distribution such as the U.S. Meanwhile, television and the Web make it easier to know how the very well off live. (Never mind whether they're happy.) Want a peek inside Donald Trump's gold-plated world? Just click on the TV, and he'll show you. Wonder what Bill Gates's 66,000-sq ft megamansion is like? Just download the floor plan from the Internet!

Paradoxically, it is the very increase in money—which creates the wealth so visible in today's society—that triggers dissatisfaction. As material expectations keep rising, more money may engender only more desires. As men and women move up the economic ladder, most almost immediately stop feeling grateful for their elevated circumstances and focus on what they still don't have. Suppose you lived in a two-bedroom house for years and

dreamed of three bedrooms. You finally get that three-bedroom house. Will it bring you happiness? Not necessarily. Three bedrooms will become your new norm, and you'll begin to long for a four-bedroom abode.

That money never satisfies is suggested by this telling fact: polls show that Americans believe that, whatever their income level, they need more to live well. Even those making large sums said still larger sums were required. We seem conditioned to think we do not have enough, even if objectively our lives are comfortable.

Then again, if we think our lot is improving, happiness follows. Carol Graham, an economist at the Brookings Institution in Washington, found that people's expectations about the future may have more influence on their sense of well-being than their current state does. People living modestly but anticipating better days to come, Graham thinks, are likely to be happier than people living well but not looking forward to improvements in their living standards. Consider two people: one earns $50,000 a year and foresees a 10% raise, and the other makes $150,000 but does not expect any salary increase. The second person is much better off in financial terms, but the first is more likely to feel good about life.

And guess what? The U.S. hasn't had a decent raise in two decades. Income growth has almost come to a halt for the middle class. In real terms, although median household income is higher than ever, median household income has increased only around 15% since 1984. That means most people have never had it better but do not expect any improvement in the near future. People tend to focus on the negative part and ignore the positive.

Living standards, education levels, and other basic measures of U.S. social well-being have improved so much so quickly in the postwar era that another big leap seems improbable. If the typical new house is more than 2,300 sq ft, if more than half of high school graduates advance to college, if there are more cars and trucks in the U.S. than there are licensed drivers—all current statistics—then the country may need stability and equality more than it needs more money. But because we are all conditioned to think there's something wrong if we don't make more money each year, high standards of living in the U.S. may, paradoxically, have become an impediment to happiness. Fixated on always getting more, we fail to appreciate how much we have. Of course, in the grand scheme it's better that there are large numbers of Americans who are materially comfortable, if a bit whiny about it, than who are destitute. And never forget: 1 in 8 Americans are poor. Poverty remains a stark reality amid American affluence.

Psychology and sociology aside, there is a final reason money can't buy happiness: the things that really matter in life are not sold in stores. Love, friendship, family, respect, a place in the community, the belief that your life has purpose—those are the essentials of human fulfillment, and they cannot be purchased with cash. Everyone needs a certain amount of money, but chasing money rather than meaning is a formula for discontent. Too many Americans have made materialism and the cycle of work and spend their principal goals. Then they wonder why they don't feel happy. ☐

How to Live to Be 100—Happily

New research suggests that a long life is no accident. So what are the secrets of the world's centenarians?

By RICHARD CORLISS and
MICHAEL D. LEMONICK TIME

Margaret Dell is 96, but you'd need to check the birth date on her driver's license to believe it. Sporting a baseball cap with a Harley-Davidson logo on it, she is the designated driver for her seventysomething friends who no longer feel comfortable behind the wheel. Last winter a snowfall threatened to keep her from her appointed automotive rounds. She took a shovel and cleared a path to her car.

Driving keeps Dell young. That and knitting. She constantly knits. She makes baby booties and caps and blankets for friends and family whenever a baby arrives—the newborn getting an early blessing from the ageless. And every month, she donates several blankets to a charity for unwed mothers. Driving, knitting . . . and tennis. She plays two or three times a week. She has a much younger doubles partner who "covers the court. I'm a little afraid to run too much because of the circulation in my legs," she explains.

When she was in her 80s, she played in a doubles tournament that required that the ages of both partners add up to at least 100. Her partner was in his early 20s; they won the tournament.

A lifetime nonsmoker and nondrinker, Dell lives alone in a two-story house in Bethesda, Md., her bedroom on the second floor. "I could stay on the first floor, but I try to make myself walk up those stairs and keep going that way." She buys her own groceries. At home she likes a chicken or turkey sandwich for lunch. If she eats at the country club after tennis, she usually finishes only half and saves the rest for dinner. (The doggie bag is the senior citizen's medical-supply kit.)

Driving, tennis, knitting . . . and eating chocolates. She keeps them by her easy chair. "I am very bad about those Hershey Kisses," she confesses. "And I love those little Dove ice cream things. I take one before I go to bed." That's the only medication Dell will take without a fight. She's no fan of doctors. Some years back, she took a fall, and her doctor prescribed an MRI. "I just refused to go," she says. "They were having a party. It was my 90th birthday." And the party girl left his office. Fortunately, nothing was broken. But Dell knew that.

How does science explain someone like Margaret Dell? How can a woman closing in on the start of her second century be so robustly, almost defiantly, healthy, while men and women decades younger are languishing feebly in nursing homes, plagued with failing bodies and failing minds and wishing they hadn't been so unlucky as to live so long?

For most of human history, a long and healthy life has been shrugged off as a gift from the gods—or maybe the undeserved reward for a lifetime of plain cussedness. But to gerontologists, the vagaries of aging have become the focus of intense research.

Royalty-Free Corbis

Scientists are as obsessed with the question of why the superold survive and thrive as Ponce de León was with finding the Fountain of Youth. They want to understand why the Japanese islands of Okinawa are home to the world's largest population of centenarians, with almost 600 of its 1.3 million inhabitants living into their second century—many of them active and looking decades younger than their actual years. Like weekend visitors on the summer ferry to Martha's Vineyard, scientists and sociologists clog the boats to Sardinia and Nova Scotia, Canada, to see why those craggy locales harbor outsize clusters of the superold.

As well as studying these populations intensively to unlock their secrets, scientists have also taken a hard look at the very old in the U.S., most notably in the New England Centenarian Study, led by Dr. Thomas Perls, a geriatrician at Boston University, and in a major study under way at the National Institute on Aging. While the very old are happy to offer homespun explanations for their longevity—"I never took a drink"; "I drank a shot of whiskey every day"—experts are trying to unravel and understand the biological factors that allow some people to reach 100 while others drop off in their 70s or 80s.

Researchers are particularly interested in determining which factors allow up to 30% of those who reach 100 to do so in sufficient mental and physical health: a whopping 90% of centenarians, according to Perls, remain functionally independent up to age 92. "It's not 'the older you get, the sicker you get,' but 'the older you get, the healthier you've been,'" he says. "The advantage of living to 100 is not so much how you are at 100 but how you got there."

It's pretty obvious even to nonscientists that how you get there depends partly on the genes you are born with and partly on lifestyle—what and how much you eat, where you live, and what types of stress and trauma you experience. How much depends on each factor, though, was unknown until Swedish scientists tackled the problem in 1998. They did it by looking at the only set of people who share genes but not lifestyle: identical twins who were separated at birth and reared apart. If genes were most important, you would expect the twins to die at about the same age. In fact, they don't, and the average difference convinced the scientists that only about 20% to 30% of how long we live is genetically determined. The key factor is lifestyle.

"You could have Mercedes-Benz genes," says Dr. Bradley Willcox, of the Pacific Health Research Institute in Honolulu, "but if you never change the oil, you are not going to last as long as a Ford Escort that you take good care of. Those who have healthier genes and live healthier lives—those guys really survive for a long time."

Studies of Seventh-Day Adventists in Utah support this finding. Those unusually clean-living Americans are genetically diverse, but they avoid alcohol, caffeine, and tobacco—and they tend to live an average of eight years longer than their countrymen. "The lesson is pretty clear from my point of view in terms of what the average person should be doing," says Perls. "I strongly believe that with some changes in health-related behavior, each of us can earn the right to have at least 25 years beyond the age of 60—years of healthy life at good function. The disappointing news is that it requires work and willpower."

At least that's true for many Americans, whose fat- and calorie-packed diets and largely exercise-free lives are a prescription for heart disease and plenty of other ills. For Okinawans, by contrast, the traditional way of life seems tailor-made for living forever—one day at a time.

Each day, Seiryu Toguchi, 103, of Motobu, Okinawa, wakes at 6 a.m., in the house in which he was born, and opens the shutters. "It's a sign to my neighbors," he says, "that I am still alive." He does stretching exercises along with a radio broadcast, then eats breakfast: whole-grain rice and miso soup with vegetables. He puts in two hours of picking weeds in his 1,000-sq-ft field, whose crops are goya (a variety of bitter gourd), imo (a reddish-purple sweet potato), and okra. A fellow has to make a living, so Toguchi buys rice and meat with the profits from his produce.

Since his wife Kame's death seven years ago, at 93, he has done all the housework himself. He rejected his children's suggestion to come live with them because, he explains, "I enjoy my freedom." Although his doctors insist Toguchi is in excellent health, the farmer takes no chances. "If he feels that something is wrong," says his daughter Sumiko Sakihara, 74, "even in the middle of the night, he calls a taxi and goes to the hospital."

At 12:30 Toguchi eats lunch: goya stir-fry with egg and tofu. He naps for an hour or so, then spends two more hours in his field. After dinner he plays traditional songs—a favorite is "Spring When I Was 19"—on the three-stringed sanshin and makes an entry in his diary, as he has every night for the past decade. "This way," he says, "I won't forget my Chinese characters. It's fun. It keeps my mind sharp." For a nightcap he may have a sip of the wine he makes from aloe, garlic, and tumeric. And as he drifts off, he says, "my head is filled with all the things I want to do tomorrow."

Scientists working for the U.S. National Institutes of Health and Japan's Ministry of Health have been following oldsters like Toguchi since 1976 in the Okinawa Centenarian Study (OCS) and they've learned that he's typical. Elderly Okinawans tend to get plenty of physical and mental exercise. Their diets, moreover, are exemplary: low in fat and salt, and high in fruits and vegetables packed with fiber and antioxidant substances that protect against cancer, heart disease, and stroke. They consume more soy than any other population on earth: 60-120 g a day, compared to 30-50 g for the average Japanese, 10 for Chinese and virtually 0 g for the average American. Soy is rich in flavonoids—antioxidants strongly linked to low rates of cancer. This may be one of many reasons why the annual death rate from cancer in Okinawa is far below the U.S. rate.

But it's not just what Okinawans eat; it's how much. They practice a dietary philosophy known as *hara hachi bu*—literally, eight parts out of 10 full. Translation: they eat only to the point at which they are about 80% sated. That makes for a daily intake of no more than 1,800 calories, compared to the more than 2,500 that the average American man scarfs down. And as scientists have learned from lab

The Longevity Stakes: Where Do You Fit In?

RACE: On average, white U.S. males live to be 75 vs. 68 for blacks; for women, the racial gap is 80 vs. 75.

FAMILY: Married folk outlive singles (but men benefit more than women do); older siblings live longer than younger ones; mothers slightly outlive childless women.

ACHIEVEMENT: Americans with higher education live six years longer than high school dropouts;

Oscar winners outlive unsuccessful nominees by four years; CEOs outlive corporate VPs.

FAITH: The elderly who attend worship services weekly live longer than those who don't.

HEALTH: Smoking typically costs you 10 years; obesity costs an average of 7.1 years for females, 5.8 years for males; those who

sleep seven hours a night live longest; tall folk (6 ft to 6 ft 3 in. for men, 5 ft 7 in. to 5 ft 9 in. for women) average three more years than short people.

NATIONALITY: Japanese live longest: 81 years, Zambians shortest: 33 years; immigrants to the U.S. outlive natives by three years. ☐

animals, the simple act of calorie restriction can have significant effects on longevity.

Aging Okinawans also have a much lower incidence of dementia—Alzheimer's or other forms of senility—than their U.S. and European counterparts do. Part of that may also owe to diet; it's high in vitamin E, which seems to protect the brain. But perhaps just as important is a sense of belonging and purpose that provides a strong foundation for staying mentally alert well into old age. Okinawans maintain a sense of community, ensuring that every member, from youngest to oldest, is paid proper respect and feels equally valued. OCS data show that elderly Okinawans express a high level of satisfaction with life, something that is not as true in Western societies, where rates of suicide and depression are high among the elderly.

Need convincing evidence that our modern lifestyle can shorten lives? Look what happens when Okinawans move permanently off the island. They pick up the diet and cultural behaviors of their adopted country—and within a generation, their life-spans decrease and their rates of cancer and heart attack zoom. Even on the island, young males are following the seductive, virulent American style and renouncing imo for hamburgers. "Okinawan male life expectancy used to be No. 1 in Japan," says Dr. Makoto Suzuki, leader of the study of Okinawan elders. "It started to decline 10 years ago and hit 26th out of 47 prefectures in the 2000 census. I expect it to decline even further in the next census."

Oldsters in Sardinia, another wellspring of longevity, have many similarities to their Okinawan counterparts—except that the Sardinian ratio of centenarians is about equal for men and women (in most societies, 100-plus females outnumber males by 3 or 4 to 1). They maintain very active lives and powerful social networks; extended family and friends are available to share troubles and take some of the emotional burden out of life.

That makes perfect sense to Leonard Poon, director of the University of Georgia Gerontology Center. Since 1988 he has studied American centenarians—he calls them "expert survivors"—and compared them to people in their 80s ("master survivors") and to relative youngsters in their 60s. Poon found that out of 16 personality traits, the experts exhibited four coping mechanisms. First, he says, "centenarians are more dominant. They want to have their way," and they are not easily pushed around. Many are characterized by "suspiciousness. They do not take information on the superficial level" but will question an issue and think it through. They tend to be practical rather than idealistic. And in their approach to life, they are likely to be more relaxed. In other words, they are strong but not inflexible characters.

Poon also determined that people whose age reaches three figures tend to have a high level of cognition, demonstrating skill in everyday problem solving and learning. That's another reason exercise is important: to keep plenty of blood flowing to the brain as well as to stay in shape.

Like the Okinawans, Sardinians, and Nova Scotians, the U.S. centenarians enjoy a strong social-support system. Few Americans live in a village anymore, but having outlived family and friends of the same age, the superold find new helpers and confidants among people younger by a generation or more. Maintaining a connection with the world, with younger people, keeps their outlook youthful.

Even as medical science adds years to our collective lives, we chip away at them by doing things—stewing at our desk jobs, eating fatty processed foods, blowing a gasket in a freeway traffic jam, exercising no more than our fingers at the computer—that centenarians can't imagine. Most of them were born into an America as remote from today's metaphorically as the craggy villages of Sardinia, Okinawa, and Nova Scotia are geographically. In the early 1900s people walked miles to work not by choice but out of necessity; cars were still a luxury. People tilled the fields because their farmer parents needed cheap help. People ate what they grew because it was there. Most labor was manual then, and most nutrients were natural.

Any child of today who hopes to live into the 22nd century without the aid of medical miracles should look to the past, and consider the lessons today's centenarians took from the 19th century. There's a poetry of common sense in their scheme for immortality. Eat sensibly. Keep walking. Keep knitting. If you can't keep friends, make new ones. Plan so much invigorating work that there's just no time to die. And no regret when you do.   □

How Long Will You Live?

An average person living in an industrialized nation has the genetic makeup and environment to enable him or her to live to the age of 87.

INSTRUCTIONS: Start with 87 years. Depending on your answers to the questions below, add or subtract the appropriate number of years.

ATTITUDE: Are you optimistic? Do you generally approach life with good humor? Are you able to let go of things that are stressful?

If no, subtract 5 years.   _____

GENES: Do you have at least some family members who have lived into their 90s or later? Exceptional longevity runs strongly in families.

If yes, add 10 years.   _____

EXERCISE: Do you set aside at least 30 minutes a day, three days a week to exercise? Muscle-building exercises are particularly important.

If no, subtract 5 years.   _____

INTERESTS: Do you do things that are challenging to your brain regularly? It's important to take on activities that are novel and complex.

If yes, add 5 years.   _____

NUTRITION: do you have a diet that keeps you lean? carrying extra weight is not conducive to longevity.

If no, subtract 7 years.   _____

GET RID OF SMOKING: Do you smoke?

If yes, subtract 5 years.   _____

TOTAL   _____

Source: Adapted from: *Living to 100.*

Can Pets Make You Happy?

Of course they can—but better yet, they can also keep you healthy

By SORA SONG TIME

Royalty-Free Corbis

Like deities and tax law, your beloved pet works in mysterious ways. Science can't explain the power of the pooch or the karma of the kitty, but numerous studies have shown that furry companions—just by their presence—can help lower blood pressure and cholesterol levels, raise chances of survival after a heart attack, reduce loneliness and depression, and spread all-round good cheer.

Any owner will tell you how much joy a pet brings. For some, a critter provides more comfort than a spouse. A 2002 study by Karen Allen of the State University of New York at Buffalo measured stress

Most Popular Pet Names

Source: The American Society for the Prevention of Cruelty to Animals (ASPCA)

1. Max	4. Bear	7. Kitty	10. Brandy
2. Sam	5. Smokey	8. Molly	11. Ginger
3. Lady	6. Shadow	9. Buddy	12. Baby

levels and blood pressure in people—half of them pet owners—while they contended with performing 5 minutes of mental math or holding a hand in ice water. Subjects completed the tasks alone, with a spouse, a close friend, or with a pet. People with pets fared best. Those tested with their animal pals had smaller spikes in blood pressure and returned most quickly to baseline heart rates. With pets in the room, people also made fewer math errors than when figuring in front of spouses or friends

In another study, Allen put a group of hypertensive stockbrokers on blood-pressure-lowering drugs and told half of them to adopt a pet. Six months later, the new pet owners showed less than half the blood-pressure surge of their peers while performing stress-

ful tasks—and, again, made fewer math errors. It seems people feel less nervous around pets, says Allen, who thinks it may be because pets don't judge.

In part, it's that capacity for unconditional support that makes pets such good company. A study reported in the fall of 2004 suggests that having a pet dog not only buoys your spirits but may also help you trim your gut. Researchers at Northwestern Memorial Hospital spent a year studying 36 portly people and their equally pudgy dogs on joint diet-and-exercise programs; a separate control group of 56 people without pets was put on a solo program. On average, people lost about 11 lbs., or 5% of their body weight. Their canine sidekicks did even better, losing an average of 12 lbs., more than 15% of their body weight. Pup owners didn't lose any more weight than the pup-less but, say researchers, they got more exercise overall—mostly with their dogs— and found it rewarding instead of a chore.

No scientific study has deconstructed exactly why pets boost our well-being, but for most pet lovers that probably doesn't matter. It's enough to know that like many of the other basic joys in life, a pet's affection is simple, easy, and mercifully unconditional. □

Household Pet Ownership, 1990–2004

(as a percentage of total U.S. households)

	1990	1992	1994	1996	1998	2000	2002	2004
Dog	57.0%	58.0%	56.0%	59.0%	61.0%	62.0%	62.0%	63.0%
Cat	33.0	32.0	30.0	32.0	32.0	34.0	34.0	34.0
Freshwater fish	8.0	10.0	10.0	11.0	9.0	12.0	13.0	13.0
Bird	6.0	6.0	6.0	6.0	6.0	7.0	6.0	6.0
Small animal	4.0	5.0	5.0	5.0	4.0	5.0	5.0	5.0
Reptile	n.a.	n.a.	3.0	3.0	3.0	4.0	4.0	4.0
Equine	n.a.	n.a.	n.a.	n.a.	n.a.	n.a.	n.a.	4.0
Saltwater fish	.5	.7	.6	.6	.5	.7	.7	.7

n.a. = not available. *Source:* American Pet Products Manufacturers Association, *2005–2006 National Pet Owners Survey.*

Total Number of Pets Owned in the U.S., 2004

	Dog	Cat	Fish, freshwater	Fish, saltwater	Bird	Small animal	Reptile
Number of pet-owning households (in millions)	43.5	37.7	13.9	0.8	6.4	5.7	4.4
Average number of pets owned	1.7	2.4	10.0	12.0	2.6	3.2	2.5
Total number of pets (in millions)	73.9	90.5	139.0	9.6	16.6	18.2	11.0

Source: American Pet Products Manufacturers Association, *2005–2006 National Pet Owners Survey*

Thinking Outside the Pyramid

What's right—and wrong—with the new food trapezoid

By SANJAY GUPTA TIME

It's not really fair to blame the food pyramid that was retired in early 2005 for the millions of Americans who became obese since it was introduced in 1992. But the original pyramid—on which the federal school-meal program was based—certainly played a part. Not only was it confusing, measuring food in inscrutable serving sizes, but it also led millions of Americans down the doughnut path, recommending the intake of large quantities of carbohydrates without distinguishing between whole grains, which are good for you, and highly refined carbs that you might as well apply directly to the hips and gut.

So I was interested to see what the USDA would come up with after four years of deliberation and food-industry lobbying, not to mention $2.4 million taxpayer dollars. The result is not so much a pyramid as a trapezoid, with a cute little staircase running up the side to represent exercise and a vertical striped color scheme that's about as useful as an amber terror alert.

New Pyramid Gets Mixed Reviews

But once you get past the trapezoid, the so-called Food Guidance System is an improvement over the old pyramid. It replaces a one-size-fits-all meal plan with 12 different plans. To get to the information, however, it helps to have access to the Internet and to go to mypyramid.gov when it isn't overwhelmed by visitors. I gave it a try. I entered my age, sex, and exercise level and after about 10 minutes was rewarded with a recommended diet, measured helpfully in ounces and cups, that seemed tailor-made for me. I was less impressed after my CNN colleague Jack Cafferty pointed out that you can enter the data for two people with very different age and activity profiles and be given exactly the same diet.

The new scheme came under even harsher criticism from nutritionists, who complained that the government missed an opportunity to steer Americans away from the sugary, fatty, processed foods they consume in such quantities. "One of the biggest problems is it doesn't clearly say 'eat less,'" says Margo Wootan of the Center for Science in the Public Interest. It also says nothing about salt, saturated fat, or cholesterol. Nor does the USDA have a budget to promote its new pyramid. Instead, it is relying on word of mouth from doctors and nutritionists, and marketing campaigns paid for by the food industry. □

My Pyramid Plan

Age: 35, physical activity: 30 to 60 minutes per day

	Female	Male
Grains	6 ounces	9 ounces
Vegetables	2.5 cups	3.5 cups
Fruits	2 cups	2 cups
Milk	3 cups	3 cups
Meat and beans	5.5 ounces	6.5 ounces

NOTE: Results are based on a 2,000 calorie pattern for females, and a 2,600 calorie pattern for males.

2005 Food Pyramid

1992 Food Pyramid

Servings listed below are daily recommendations.

Measuring Body Mass

Body mass index (BMI) is a measure of body fat based on height and weight that applies to both adult men and adult women. To determine BMI, weight in kilograms is divided by height in meters, squared. To calculate your body mass index from the table below, locate your height in inches in the left-hand column, then follow it across until you locate your weight; the number at the very top is your body mass index. A BMI of less than 18.5 is considered underweight, 18.5 to 24.9 is considered normal weight, 25 to 29.9 is considered overweight, and one of 30 or above is considered obese.

Body Mass Index Chart

Height (inches)	19	20	21	22	23	24	25	26	27	28	29	30	31	32	33	34	35
									Body weight (pounds)								
58	91	96	100	105	110	115	119	124	129	134	138	143	148	153	158	162	167
59	94	99	104	109	114	119	124	128	133	138	143	148	153	158	163	168	173
60	97	102	107	112	118	123	128	133	138	143	148	153	158	163	168	174	179
61	100	106	111	116	122	127	132	137	143	148	153	158	164	169	174	180	185
62	104	109	115	120	126	131	136	142	147	153	158	164	169	175	180	186	191
63	107	113	118	124	130	135	141	146	152	158	163	169	175	180	186	191	197
64	110	116	122	128	134	140	145	151	157	163	169	174	180	186	192	197	204
65	114	120	126	132	138	144	150	156	162	168	174	180	186	192	198	204	210
66	118	124	130	136	142	148	155	161	167	173	179	186	192	198	204	210	216
67	121	127	134	140	146	153	159	166	172	178	185	191	198	204	211	217	223
68	125	131	138	144	151	158	164	171	177	184	190	197	203	210	216	223	230
69	128	135	142	149	155	162	169	176	182	189	196	203	209	216	223	230	236
70	132	139	146	153	160	167	174	181	188	195	202	209	216	222	229	236	243
71	136	143	150	157	165	172	179	186	193	200	208	215	222	229	236	243	250
72	140	147	154	162	169	177	184	191	199	206	213	221	228	235	242	250	258
73	144	151	159	166	174	182	189	197	204	212	219	227	235	242	250	257	265
74	148	155	163	171	179	186	194	202	210	218	225	233	241	249	256	264	272
75	152	160	168	176	184	192	200	208	216	224	232	240	248	256	264	272	279
76	156	164	172	180	189	197	205	213	221	230	238	246	254	263	271	279	287

Source: National Heart, Lung, and Blood Institute.

Age-Adjusted Percent Distributions of Body Mass Index (BMI) Among Persons 18 Years Old and Over, by Selected Characteristics, 2002

Selected characteristic	Under-weight	Healthy weight	Above healthy weight		
			Total	Over-weight	Obese
Total[1] (age-adjusted)	2.1%	39.6%	58.4%	35.0%	23.4%
Total[1] (unadjusted)	2.0	39.4	58.5	35.0	23.5
Age:[2]					
18 to 44 years	2.5	44.2	53.3	31.9	21.4
45 to 64 years	1.1	32.1	66.9	39.1	27.8
65 to 74 years	1.7	31.7	66.6	39.3	27.3
75 years and over	3.5	45.4	51.0	35.1	15.9
Sex:					
Male	1.1	32.0	66.9	43.1	23.8
Female	3.0	46.9	50.0	27.1	22.9
Race:					
White alone[4]	2.0	40.5	57.5	35.3	22.2
Black or African American alone[4]	1.7	29.4	68.9	34.1	34.8
American Indian or Alaska Native alone[4]	2.2[3]	36.1	61.7	30.4	31.3
Asian alone[4]	5.6	59.9	34.5	27.5	7.0
Native Hawaiian or other Pacific Islander alone[4]	—	33.2	66.8	36.4	30.4[3]
2 or more races[5]	2.6[3]	39.1	58.3	30.9	27.4
Hispanic or Latino origin status[6]:					
Hispanic or Latino	1.4	33.4	65.2	39.8	25.4
Not Hispanic or Latino	2.2	40.4	57.4	34.3	23.1
Education:[7]					
Less than a high school diploma	1.5	32.1	66.4	36.7	29.7
High school diploma or GED	2.0	34.6	63.4	35.9	27.5
Some college	1.7	36.1	62.2	36.4	25.8
Bachelors degree or higher	1.7	43.6	54.7	37.3	17.4

— Represents zero. 1. Total includes other races not shown separately and persons with unknown characteristics. 2. Estimates for age groups are not age adjusted. 3. Base figure too small to meet statistical standards for reliability of a derived figure. 4. Refers to persons who indicated only a single race group. 5. The "two or more races" refers to all persons who indicated more than one race group. 6. Persons of Hispanic or Latino origin may be of any race. 7. Education is shown only for persons 25 years old and over. Source: U.S. National Center for Health Statistics, Vital and Health Statistics, Series 10, Number 222, Summary Health Statistics for U.S. Adults: National Health Interview Survey, 2002. From Statistical Abstract of the United States: 2004–2005.

Percentage of U.S. Adults Engaging in Leisure Time, Transportation-Related, and Household-Related Physical Activity, 2003

Characteristic	Persons who meet recommended activity[1]	Persons not meeting recommended activity[2]	Persons who are physically inactive[3]
Total	46.0%	54.0%	24.3%
Male	48.2	51.8	22.0
Female	44.0	56.0	26.3
White, non-Hispanic	49.0	51.0	20.9
Black, non-Hispanic	36.3	63.7	32.7
Hispanic	37.5	62.5	36.0
Other	43.5	56.5	25.2
Males:			
18 to 29 years old	57.8	42.2	17.1
30 to 44 years old	48.7	51.3	20.7
45 to 64 years old	43.2	56.8	24.4
65 to 74 years old	45.7	54.3	24.9
75 years old and over	36.7	63.3	31.0
Females:			
18 to 29 years old	50.1	49.9	21.9
30 to 44 years old	47.7	52.3	23.4
45 to 64 years old	42.6	57.4	26.7
65 to 74 years old	37.1	62.9	31.2
75 years old and over	27.6	72.4	42.0
School years completed:			
Less than 12 years	33.8	66.2	45.7
12 years	43.1	56.9	30.5
Some college (13 to 15 years)	47.5	52.5	21.0
College (16 or more years)	51.9	48.1	13.1
Household income:			
Less than $10,000	34.7	65.3	42.2
$10,000 to $19,999	37.0	63.0	38.9
$20,000 to $34,999	43.6	56.4	29.4
$35,000 to $49,999	47.3	52.7	21.9
$50,000 and over	53.6	46.4	13.6

1. Recommended activity is physical activity at least 5 times/week x 30 minutes/time or vigorous physical activity for 20 minutes at a time at least 3 times/week. 2. Persons whose reported physical activity does not meet recommended level or report no leisure-time, transportation-related, or household-related physical activity. 3. Persons with no reported physical activity. *Source:* U.S. National Center for Chronic Disease Prevention and Health Promotion, "Nutrition and Physical Activity," and unpublished data. From *Statistical Abstract of the United States, 2004–2005.*

High School Students Engaged in Organized Physical Activity by Sex, Race, and Hispanic Origin, 2003

Characteristic	Enrolled in physical education class			Played on a sports team
	Total	Attended daily	Exercised 20 minutes or more per class[1]	
All students	**55.7%**	**28.4%**	**80.3%**	**57.6%**
Male	58.5	30.5	84.5	64.0
Female	52.8	26.4	75.3	51.0
White, non-Hispanic	53.7	24.9	81.5	60.8
Male	55.9	26.8	85.8	65.4
Female	51.5	23.1	76.6	55.9
Black, non-Hispanic	56.0	33.0	74.0	53.2
Male	63.1	37.1	80.0	67.5
Female	49.3	29.0	66.7	39.6
Hispanic	58.8	36.7	78.2	49.5
Male	61.4	39.5	82.5	56.2
Female	56.1	34.0	73.5	42.8

1. For students enrolled in physical education classes. *Source:* U.S. Centers for Disease Control and Prevention, Youth Risk Behavior Surveillance—United States, 2003, Morbidity and Mortality Weekly Report, Vol. 53, No. SS 02, May 21, 2004.

Recommended Daily Fat Intake

Total calories per day	Saturated fat in grams	Total fat in grams	Total calories per day	Saturated fat in grams	Total fat in grams
1,600	18 or less	53	2,500[1]	25 or less	80
2,000[1]	20 or less	65	2,800	31 or less	93
2,200	24 or less	73			

1. Percent daily values on nutrition facts labels are based on a 2,000 calorie diet. Values for 2,000 and 2,500 calories are rounded to the nearest 5 grams to be consistent with the nutrition facts label. *Source: Dietary Guidelines for Americans, 2005.* Web: www.health.gov.

Understanding AIDS

Acquired Immune Deficiency Syndrome, or AIDS, was first reported in mid-1981 in the United States; it is believed to have originated in Sub-Saharan Africa. The human immunodeficiency virus (HIV) that causes AIDS was identified in 1983, and by 1985 tests to detect the virus were available. The credit for discovering the AIDS virus is jointly shared by Dr. Robert Gallo, a researcher at the National Cancer Institute, and Luc Montagnier of the Pasteur Institute, France.

Destruction of Immune System

A fatal and incurable disease caused by HIV, AIDS attacks and destroys the immune system, gradually leaving the individual defenseless against illnesses that lead to death. These illnesses are referred to as "opportunistic" infections or diseases: in AIDS patients the most common are Pneumocystis carinii pneumonia (PCP), a parasitic infection of the lungs, and a type of cancer known as Kaposi's sarcoma (KS). Other opportunistic infections include unusually severe infections with yeast, cytomegalovirus, herpes virus, and parasites such as Toxoplasma or Cryptosporidia. Milder infections with these organisms do not suggest immune deficiencies. Symptoms of full-blown AIDS include a persistent cough, fever, and difficulty in breathing. Multiple purplish blotches and bumps on the skin may indicate Kaposi's sarcoma. The virus can also cause brain damage.

People infected with the virus can have a wide range of symptoms—from none to mild to severe. At least a fourth to a half of those infected with HIV will develop AIDS within four to ten years. Many experts think the percentage will grow much higher.

Transmission

Although the first reported cases involved homosexual men in Los Angeles who were infected through sexual contact, the principal mode of transmission throughout the world is through the exchange of bodily fluids during heterosexual intercourse. According to the World Health Organization, extensive spread of HIV appears to have begun in the late 1970s and early 1980s. It spread in men and women with multiple sexual partners in East and Central Africa and among homosexual and bisexual men in certain urban areas of the Americas, Australasia, and Western Europe.

In addition to sexual contact, AIDS has been spread by intravenous drug users sharing infected hypodermic needles. The virus can also be passed on through transfused blood or its components. It may also be transmitted from infected mother to infant before, during, or shortly after birth.

Two major types of HIV have been recognized, HIV-l and HIV-2. HIV-l is the dominant type worldwide. HIV-2 is found principally in West Africa but cases have been reported in East Africa, Europe, Asia, and Latin America. There are at least ten different genetic subtypes of HIV-l, but their biological and epidemiological significance is unclear at present. Both HIV-l and HIV-2 are transmitted in the same ways.

Pandemic

With no cure at present, prudence could save thousands of people who have yet to be exposed to the virus. Use of condoms lessens the possibility of transmission as does the elimination of sharing hypodermic needles. The fate of many will depend less on science than on the ability of large numbers of human beings to change their behavior in the face of growing danger.

The introduction of highly active antiretroviral therapy in 1996 was a turning point for those with access to sophisticated health-care systems. Although they can't cure HIV/AIDS, antiretrovirals (ARVs) and their use in combination, "cocktails," have dramatically reduced mortality and morbidity and prolonged and improved the lives of sufferers. However, 95% of people with HIV/AIDS live in developing countries, where access to these medicines remains unacceptably limited and the costs prohibitively expensive. Progress has recently been made in India, however, as Indian pharmaceutical companies are producing generic versions of ARVs and selling them for less than $1 a day. Officials estimate that about 12,000 Indians are currently taking such medications. Another obstacle is that not everyone can tolerate the potent medications and their side effects. Doctors are also reporting a significant increase of patients with drug-resistant HIV strains. Some 100 separate drugs are either in use or being tested for use against AIDS. Meanwhile, HIV has been spreading, with rising rates of infection in Eastern Europe, Russia, China, and Southeast Asia, prompting some scientists to grimly warn that the epidemic has only just begun.

On a global scale, men make up the majority of people living with HIV. However, in sub-Saharan Africa, women and girls account for about 57% of adults living with HIV. In the Caribbean, the figure hovers around 49%. The number of women living with HIV continues to increase in Eastern Europe, Asia, and Latin America.

Status of the World AIDS Epidemic, End of 2004

	Total	Adults	Children under 15 years
People newly infected with HIV in 2004	4.9 million	4.3 million	640,000
Number of people living with HIV/AIDS	39.4 million	37.2 million	2.2 million
AIDS deaths in 2004	3.1 million	2.6 million	510,000

Source: World Health Organization, UNAIDS. Web: www.unaids.org.

HIV/AIDS Statistics and Features by World Region, End 2002 and 2004

World region	Adults & children living with HIV	Adults & children newly infected with HIV	Adult prevalence rate	Adult & child deaths due to AIDS
Sub-Saharan Africa				
2004	23.4–28.4 million	2.7–3.8 million	6.9–8.3%	2.1–2.6 million
2002	22.5–27.3 million	2.6–3.6 million	7.0–8.4	1.9–2.3 million
North Africa & Middle East				
2004	230,000–1.5 million	34,000–350,000	0.1–0.7	12,000–72,000
2002	180,000–1.2 million	21,000–300,000	0.1–0.6	8,300–53,000
South & Southeast Asia				
2004	4.4–10.6 million	480,000–2.0 million	0.4–0.9	300,000–750,000
2002	3.9–9.7 million	430,000–2.0 million	0.4–0.9	260,000–650,000
East Asia				
2004	560,000–1.8 million	84,000–830,000	0.1–0.2	25,000–86,000
2002	380,000–1.2 million	36,000–360,000	0.1–0.2	18,000–63,000
Oceania				
2004	25,000–48,000	2,100–13,000	0.1–0.3	<1,700
2002	22,000–38,000	1,000–9,600	0.1–0.3	<1,000
Latin America				
2004	1.3–2.2 million	170,000–430,000	0.5–0.8	73,000–120,000
2002	1.1–2.0 million	140,000–320,000	0.4–0.7	58,000–96,000
Caribbean				
2004	270,000–780,000	27,000–140,000	1.5–4.1	24,000–61,000
2002	260,000–740,000	26,000–140,000	1.4–4.0	22,000–57,000
Eastern Europe & Central Asia				
2004	920,000–2.1 million	110,000–480,000	0.5–1.2	39,000–87,000
2002	670,000–1.5 million	94,000–440,000	0.4–0.8	27,000–58,000
Western & Central Europe				
2004	480,000–760,000	14,000–38,000	0.2–0.3	<8,500
2002	470,000–750,000	13,000–35,000	0.2–0.3	<8,000
North America				
2004	540,000–1.6 million	16,000–120,00	0.3–1.0	8,400–25,000
2002	500,000–1.6 million	16,000–120,000	0.3–1.0	8,400–25,000
Total				
2004	**35.9–44.3 million**	**4.3–6.4 million**	**1.0–1.3**	**2.8–3.5 million**
2002	**33.3–41.1 million**	**3.9–6.2 million**	**1.0–1.2**	**2.5–3.1 million**

Source: World Health Organization, UNAIDS. Web: www.unaids.org.

Reported Cases of Sexually Transmitted Disease in the U.S., 2003

More than 25 diseases are spread primarily through sexual activity. The latest estimates indicate that there are 15 million new sexually transmitted disease cases in the United States each year. Approximately one-fourth of these new infections are in teenagers. Nearly two-thirds of all STD cases occur in people younger than 25 years.

Disease	Total Male	Total Female	Total
Chlamydia	190,244	685,017	877,478
Gonorrhea	160,106	174,230	335,104
Primary syphilis	1,863	229	2,095
Secondary syphilis	4,093	988	5,082

Disease	Total Male	Total Female	Total
Early latent syphilis	5,664	2,691	8,361
Late and late latent syphilis	10,666	7,601	18,319
Neurosyphilis	420	121	541
Chancroid	25	29	54

Source: U.S. Centers for Disease Control and Prevention. Web: www.cdc.gov.

Leading Causes of Mortality Throughout the World, 2002

Rank	Cause	All countries Total deaths (in thousands)	All countries % of total
1.	Ischaemic heart disease	7,208	12.6%
2.	Cerebrovascular disease	5,509	9.7
3.	Lower respiratory infections	3,884	6.8
4.	HIV/AIDS	2,777	4.9
5.	Chronic obstructive pulmonary disease	2,748	4.8
6.	Diarrheal diseases	1,798	3.2

Rank	Cause	All countries Total deaths (in thousands)	All countries % of total
7.	Tuberculosis	1,566	2.7
8.	Malaria	1,272	2.2
9.	Cancer of trachea/bronchus/ lung	1,243	2.2
10.	Road traffic accidents	1,192	2.1%

Source: The World Health Report, 2003, The World Health Organization (WHO).

Estimated Persons Living in the U.S. with AIDS by Selected Characteristics: 1998 to 2002

Age and characteristic	1998	1999	2000	2001	2002
Total[1]	288,565	311,424	335,316	359,141	384,906
Age as of end of year					
Less than 13 years old	3,128	3,006	2,816	2,571	2,292
13 and 14 years old	372	438	513	642	732
15 to 24 years	4,657	4,675	4,951	5,204	5,653
35 to 44 years	130,403	141,434	151,476	158,962	165,348
45 to 54 years	66,105	77,334	89,716	102,991	116,927
55 to 64 years	16,033	19,330	23,030	27,462	33,201
65 years old and over	4,256	5,152	6,263	7,471	8,902
Race/ethnicity					
White, not Hispanic	113,267	120,094	126,851	133,461	140,835
Black, not Hispanic	115,644	126,499	138,129	149,808	162,412
Hispanic	55,980	60,767	65,823	70,865	76,052
Asian/Pacific Islander	2,314	2,578	2,858	3,189	3,574
American Indian/Alaska Native	989	1,074	1,198	1,316	1,450
Male adult/adolescent exposure category					
Males 13 years old and over, total	227,494	244,615	261,907	279,242	289,248
Male-to-male sexual contact	130,000	139,763	149,742	160,067	171,592
Injection drug use	55,735	59,199	62,743	65,729	68,636
Male-to-male sexual contact and injection drug use	20,256	21,212	21,931	22,679	23,495
Heterosexual contact	17,656	20,433	23,328	26,420	29,973
Other[2]	3,846	4,008	4,164	4,348	4,553
Female adult/adolescent exposure category					
Females 13 years old and over, total	57,338	63,023	39,579	79,035	82,764
Injection drug use	24,441	25,874	27,471	28,912	30,158
Heterosexual contact	31,175	35,295	40,072	44,895	50,174
Other[2]	1,722	1,854	2,036	2,227	2,432
Child (under 13 years old) total	3,731	3,784	3,827	3,864	3,893
Perinatal	3,577	3,635	3,680	3,716	3,748
Other[3]	154	149	147	147	145

1. Includes persons of unknown or multiple race and of unknown sex. 2. Includes hemophilia, blood transfusion, perinatal, and risk not reported or not identified. 3. Includes hemophilia, blood transfusion, and risk not reported or not identified. *Source:* U.S. Centers for Disease Control and Prevention, Atlanta, Ga., *HIV/AIDS Surveillance Report,* Volume 14. From: *Statistical Abstract of the United States: 2004–2005.*

Cancer: Estimated New Cases (2005) and Survival Rates in the U.S.

| | Estimated new cases, 2005 | | | Five-year relative survival rates[1] (percent) | | | | | |
| | | | | White | | Black | | All races | |
Site	Total	Male	Female	1983–1985	1992–1998	1983–1985	1992–1998	1983–1985	1992–1998
All sites[2]	1,372,910	710,040	662,870	54%	64%	40%	53%	52%	62%
Prostate	232,090	232,090	n.a.	76	98	64	93	75	97
Breast[3]	212,930	1,690	211,240	79	88	63	73	78	86
Lung	172,570	93,010	79,500	14	15	11	12	14	15
Colon	104,950	48,290	56,660	58	63	49	53	58	62
Bladder	63,210	47,010	16,200	78	82	60	65	78	82
Melanoma—skin	59,580	33,580	26,000	85	89	74	66	85	89
Non-Hodgkin lymphoma[4]	56,390	29,070	27,320	54	56	45	46	54	55
Uterine corpus	40,880	n.a.	40,880	85	86	54	61	83	84
Rectum	40,340	23,530	16,810	56	62	44	53	55	62
Kidney and renal pelvis	36,160	22,490	13,670	56	62	55	60	56	62
Leukemia[4]	34,810	19,640	15,170	42	47	34	38	41	46
Pancreas	32,180	16,100	16,080	3	4	5	4	3	4
Oral cavity and pharynx	29,370	19,100	10,270	55	59	35	35	53	56
Ovary	22,220	n.a.	22,220	40	53	42	53	41	53
Stomach	21,860	13,510	8,350	16	21	19	20	17	22
Uterine cervix	10,370	n.a.	10,370	71	72	60	60	69	71

NOTE: n.a. = not applicable. 1. The 5-year relative survival rate indicates that a person will not die from causes directly related to their cancer within 5 years. 2. Includes other sites not shown separately. 3. Survival rates for females only. 4. All types combined. *Sources:* American Cancer Society, U.S. National Institutes of Health, National Cancer Institute.

Americans Without Health Insurance[1] by Characteristic, 2003

Characteristic	Percent	Characteristic	Percent
Total	**15.6%**	$75,000 or more	8.2
Race and ethnicity		**Age**	
White	14.6	Under 18 years	11.4
Non-Hispanic	11.1	18 to 24 years	30.2
Black	19.6	25 to 34 years	26.4
Asian and Pacific Islander	18.8	35 to 44 years	18.1
Hispanic[2]	32.7	45 to 64 years	13.9
Household income		65 years and over	0.8
Less than $25,000	24.2	**Nativity**	
$25,000 to $49,999	19.9	Native	13.0
$50,000 to $74,999	12.5	Foreign born	34.5

1. For the entire year. 2. Hispanics may be of any race. *Source:* U.S. Census Bureau, *Current Population Reports, P60–223.* From: *Statistical Abstract of the United States: 2004–2005.*

Percent of Americans Without Health Insurance by State, 2002

State	Total	Percent children not covered	State	Total	Percent children not covered	State	Total	Percent children not covered
Alabama	12.7%	10.8%	Louisiana	18.4%	11.9%	Oklahoma	17.3%	11.6%
Alaska	18.7	13.3	Maine	11.3	7.9	Oregon	14.6	11.3
Arizona	16.8	14.7	Maryland	13.4	9.9	Pennsylvania	11.3	10.2
Arkansas	16.3	10.0	Massachusetts	9.9	5.9	Rhode Island	9.8	4.7
California	18.2	14.0	Michigan	11.7	6.9	South Carolina	12.5	6.9
Colorado	16.1	14.4	Minnesota	7.9	5.8	South Dakota	11.5	7.7
Connecticut	10.5	8.1	Mississippi	16.7	10.9	Tennessee	10.8	6.8
Delaware	9.9	9.8	Missouri	11.6	5.0	Texas	25.8	22.4
DC	13.0	8.6	Montana	15.3	15.0	Utah	13.4	9.3
Florida	17.3	14.5	Nebraska	10.2	5.6	Vermont	10.7	5.7
Georgia	16.1	12.3	Nevada	19.7	19.7	Virginia	13.5	12.3
Hawaii	10.0	7.4	New Hampshire	9.9	4.8	Washington	14.2	9.0
Idaho	17.9	13.6	New Jersey	13.9	9.7	West Virginia	14.6	10.3
Illinois	14.1	11.3	New Mexico	21.1	14.5	Wisconsin	9.8	4.6
Indiana	13.1	9.8	New York	15.8	9.9	Wyoming	17.7	14.2
Iowa	9.5	5.9	North Carolina	16.8	12.7			
Kansas	10.4	8.1	North Dakota	10.9	7.4	**Total U.S.**	**15.2**	**11.6**
Kentucky	13.6	12.6	Ohio	11.9	8.2			

NOTE: These estimates should not be used to rank the states. Results from different samplings could easily show different estimates and rankings because of small sampling sizes. *Source:* U.S. Census Bureau, *Current Population Survey, March 2003.*

Average Annual Expenditures Per Consumer for Health Care: 1990–2002

(in dollars, except percent)

Item	Health care, total					Percent distribution		
	Amount	Percent of total expenditures	Health insurance	Medical services	Drugs and medical supplies[1]	Health insurance	Medical services	Drugs and medical supplies[1]
1990	1,480	5.2%	581	562	337	39.3%	38.0%	22.8%
1995	1,732	5.4	860	512	360	49.7	29.6	20.8
1998	1,903	5.4	913	542	448	48.0	28.5	23.5
1999	1,959	5.3	923	558	479	47.1	28.5	24.5
2000	2,066	5.4	983	568	515	47.6	27.5	24.9
2001	2,182	5.5	1,061	573	549	48.6	26.3	25.2
2002	2,350	5.8	1,168	590	592	49.7	25.1	25.2
Age of reference person:								
Under 25 years old	640	2.6	285	196	160	44.5	30.6	25.0
25 to 34 years old	1,417	3.5	762	391	264	53.8	27.6	18.6
35 to 44 years old	1,980	4.1	1,023	556	402	51.7	28.1	20.3
45 to 54 years old	2,550	5.2	1,180	768	602	46.3	30.1	23.6
55 to 64 years old	3,007	6.8	1,356	863	788	45.1	28.7	26.2
65 to 74 years old	3,588	11.1	1,921	635	1,032	53.5	17.7	28.8
75 years old and over	3,584	15.1	1,849	527	1,207	51.6	14.7	33.7

1. Includes prescription and nonprescription drugs. 2. A complete reporter is a consumer unit providing values for at least one of the major sources of income. *Source:* U.S. Bureau of Labor Statistics, *Consumer Expenditure Survey,* annual. From: *Statistical Abstract of the United States: 2004—2005.*

U.S. Abortion Statistics, 1972–2001

	1972	1980	1985	1990	1995	1997	2000	2001
Reported no.								
legal abortions	586,760	1,297,606	1,328,570	1,429,247	1,210,883	1,186,039	857,475	853,485
Abortion ratio[1]	180	359	354	344	311	306	245	246
Abortion rate[2]	13	25	24	24	20	20	16	16
				Percentage distribution				
Age group (yrs)								
≤19	32.6%	29.2%	26.3%	22.4%	20.1%	20.1%	18.8%	18.1%
20–24	32.5	35.5	34.7	33.2	32.5	31.7	32.8	33.4
≥25	34.9	35.3	39.0	44.4	47.4	48.2	48.4	48.5
Marital status								
Married	29.7	23.1	19.3	21.7	19.7	19.0	18.7	18.4
Unmarried	70.3	76.9	80.7	78.3	80.3	81.0	81.3	81.6

NOTE: The number of areas reporting a given characteristic varied. 1. Number of legal induced abortions per 1,000 live births. 2. Number of legal induced abortions per 1,000 women aged 15–44 years. *Source:* U.S. Centers for Disease Control and Prevention. *Abortion Surveillance: Preliminary Analysis—United States, 2001.* Web: www.cdc.gov.

National Transplant Data

Registered U.S. Patients Waiting for Transplants

Total patients	88,176[1]	Lung	3,692	Pancreas	1,685
Kidney	61,623	Heart	3,187	Intestine	193
Liver	17,269	Kidney/Pancreas	2,462	Heart/Lung	164

NOTE: As of April 27, 2005. Patients can be listed with more than one transplant center, thus the number of registrations is greater than the actual number of patients. 1. Some patients are waiting for more than one organ; therefore the total number of patients is less than the sum of patients waiting for each organ. *Source:* United Network for Organ Sharing. Web: www.unos.org.

Number of U.S. Transplants Per Year, 1988–2004

	1988	1990	1995	2000	2004		1988	1990	1995	2000	2004
Heart	1,676	2,107	2,363	2,198	2,016	Liver	1,713	2,690	3,933	4,987	6,167
Heart/Lung	74	52	69	48	39	Lung	33	203	872	959	1,173
Intestine	—	5	46	81	152	Pancreas	79	69	109	472	603
Kidney	8,873	9,416	11,078	13,611	15,999	**Total:**					
Kidney/Pancreas	170	459	919	914	880	**All organs**	12,618	15,001	19,389	23,236	27,029

NOTE: Kidney-pancreas transplants are counted apart from kidney transplants and pancreas transplants and do not show up in the totals for the individual organs. Double kidney, double lung, and heart-lung transplants are each counted as one transplant. All other multi-organ transplants are included in the total for each individual organ. *Source:* National Organ Procurement and Transplantation Network.

Medical Practice Characteristics by Selected Specialty: 1990 to 2001

Specialty	1990	1995	1999	2001[2]	Specialty	1990	1995	1999	2001[2]
Mean patient visits per week					**Mean net income (in thousands)**				
All physicians[1]	120.9	107.6	106.7	107.2	All physicians[1]	$164.3	$195.5	n.a.	$205.7
General/family practice	146.0	133.7	122.9	126.6	General/family practice	102.7	131.2	n.a.	144.7
Internal medicine	112.0	99.7	103.0	102.7	Internal medicine	152.5	185.7	n.a.	196.1
Surgery	107.6	97.1	95.8	97.7	Surgery	236.4	269.4	n.a.	274.7
Pediatrics	134.0	125.9	120.5	111.0	Pediatrics	106.5	140.5	n.a.	137.8
Obstetrics/gynecology	120.0	94.0	101.8	101.2	Obstetrics/gynecology	207.3	244.3	n.a.	227.0
Mean hours in patient care per week					**Mean liability premium (in thousands)**				
All physicians[1]	53.3	51.3	51.6	52.8	All physicians[1]	$ 14.5	$ 15.0	n.a.	$ 18.4
General/family practice	55.0	52.9	50.6	50.7	General/family practice	7.8	9.0	n.a.	13.8
Internal medicine	55.7	53.9	54.2	56.2	Internal medicine	9.2	9.4	n.a.	13.7
Surgery	53.1	53.2	53.3	53.1	Surgery	22.8	23.3	n.a.	23.6
Pediatrics	52.4	50.4	49.5	49.4	Pediatrics	7.8	7.9	n.a.	11.6
Obstetrics/gynecology	60.4	54.6	59.0	59.3	Obstetrics/gynecology	34.3	38.6	n.a.	39.2

NOTE: n.a.= not available. 1. Includes other specialties not shown separately. 2. Mean net income and mean liability premium are 2000 data. *Source:* American Medical Association, Chicago Ill., *Physician Socioeconomic Statistics* (copyright). From: *Statistical Abstract of the United States: 2004–2005.*

Overview of Drug Use in the United States

Source: Substance Abuse and Mental Health Services Administration.

The *National Survey on Drug Use and Health,* an annual survey conducted by the Substance Abuse and Mental Health Services Administration (SAMHSA), estimates the prevalence of illicit drug use in the United States. Some of the more notable statistics from the 2003 study follow.

• An estimated 19.5 million Americans age 12 years or older were current users of illicit drugs in 2003, meaning they used an illicit drug at least once during the 30 days prior to being interviewed. This represents 8.2% of the population 12 years or older. There was no change in the overall rate of illicit drug use between 2002 and 2003.

• Marijuana is the most commonly used illicit drug, with 14.6 million users (a rate of 6.2%). An estimated 2.3 million persons (1.0%) were current cocaine users, 604,000 of whom used crack. Hallucinogens were used by 1.0 million persons, and there were an estimated 119,000 current heroin users. All of these 2003 estimates are similar to the estimates for 2002.

• The number of current users of Ecstasy (MDMA) decreased between 2002 and 2003, from 676,000 (0.3%) to 470,000 (0.2%). Although there were no significant changes in the past month use of other hallucinogens, there were significant declines in past year use of LSD (from 1 million to 558,000) and in past year overall hallucinogen use (from 4.7 million to 3.9 million) between 2002 and 2003, as well as in past year use of Ecstasy (from 3.2 million to 2.1 million).

• An estimated 6.3 million persons were current users of psychotherapeutic drugs taken nonmedically. This represents 2.7% of the population aged 12 or older. An estimated 4.7 million used pain relievers, 1.8 million used tranquilizers, 1.2 million used stimulants, and 0.3 million used sedatives. The 2003 estimates are all similar to the corresponding estimates for 2002.

• Rates of current illicit drug use varied significantly among the major racial/ethnic groups in 2003. Rates were highest among American Indians or Alaska Natives (12.1%), persons reporting two or more races (12.0%), and Native Hawaiians or Other Pacific Islanders (11.1%). Rates were 8.7% for blacks, 8.3% for whites, and 8.0% for Hispanics. Asians had the lowest rate at 3.8%.

• The rate of current illicit drug use among youths aged 12 to 17 did not change significantly between 2002 (11.6%) and 2003 (11.2%), and there were no changes for any specific illicit drug among this age group. However, there were decreases in the rates of past year use of LSD (1.3% to 0.6%), Ecstasy (2.2% to 1.3%), and methamphetamine (0.9% to 0.7%). In addition, there was a decline in past month marijuana use among youths aged 12 or 13, from 1.4% in 2002 to 1.0% in 2003.

• An estimated 18.2% of unemployed adults aged 18 or older were current illicit drug users in 2003 compared with 7.9% of those employed full time and 10.7% of those employed part time. However, most drug users were employed. Of the 16.7 million illicit drug users aged 18 or older in 2003, 12.4 million (74.3%) were employed either full or part time.

• An estimated 21.6 million Americans in 2003 were classified with substance dependence or abuse (9.1% of the total population aged 12 or older). Of these, 3.1 million were classified with dependence on or abuse of both alcohol and illicit drugs, 3.8 million were dependent on or abused illicit drugs but not alcohol, and 14.8 million were dependent on or abused alcohol but not illicit drugs.

• In 2003, an estimated 10.9 million persons reported driving under the influence of an illicit drug during the past year. This corresponds to 4.6% of the population aged 12 or older. The rates were 14.1% among young adults aged 18 to 25 and 3.1% among adults aged 26 or older. These rates were all similar to the 2002 rates.

Drug Use by Americans, 12 Years and Older

Type of drug	Ever used				Current user			
	1979	1990	2000	2003	1979	1990	2000	2003
Any illicit drug[1]	n.a.	n.a.	38.9%	46.4%	n.a.	n.a.	6.3 %	8.2%
Marijuana and hashish	27.9 %	30.5 %	34.2	40.6	13.2 %	5.4%	4.8	6.2
Cocaine	8.6	11.2	11.2	14.7	2.6	0.9	0.5	1.0
Crack	n.a.	n.a.	2.4	3.3	n.a.	n.a.	0.1	0.3
Hallucinogens	8.9	7.9	11.7	14.5	1.9	0.4	0.4	0.4
LSD	n.a.	n.a.	8.8	10.3	n.a.	n.a.	0.2	0.1
PCP	n.a.	n.a.	2.6	3.0	n.a.	n.a.	0.0	0.0
Ecstasy	n.a.	n.a.	2.9	4.6	n.a.	n.a.	n.a.	0.2
Heroin	1.3	0.8	1.2	1.6	0.1	n.a.	0.1	0.1
Stimulants[2]	n.a.	5.5	6.6	8.8	n.a.	0.6	0.4	0.5
Methamphetamine	n.a.	n.a.	4.0	5.2	n.a.	n.a.	0.2	0.3
Sedatives[2]	n.a.	2.8	3.2	4.0	n.a.	0.2	0.1	0.1
Tranquilizers[2]	n.a.	4.0	5.8	8.5	n.a.	0.6	0.4	0.8

NOTE: Current users are those who used drugs at least once within month prior to this study. n.a. = not available. 1. Any illicit drug indicates use at least once of marijuana/hashish, cocaine (including crack), heroin, hallucinogens (including LSD and PCP), inhalants, or any prescription-type psychotherapeutic used nonmedically. 2. Nonmedical use; does not include over-the-counter drugs. Source: U.S. Substance Abuse and Mental Health Services Administration (SAMHSA), Office of Applied Studies, *National Survey on Drug Use and Health, 2002 and 2003.* Web: www.oas.samhsa.gov.

A Snapshot of Annual High-Risk College Drinking Consequences

Source: National Institute on Alcohol Abuse and Alcoholism. Web: www.collegedrinkingprevention.gov/facts/snapshot.aspx.

The consequences of excessive and underage drinking affect virtually all college campuses, college communities, and college students, whether they choose to drink or not.

• **Death:** 1,400 college students between the ages of 18 and 24 die each year from alcohol-related unintentional injuries, including motor vehicle crashes (2002).

• **Injury:** 500,000 students between the ages of 18 and 24 are unintentionally injured under the influence of alcohol (2002).

• **Assault:** More than 600,000 students between the ages of 18 and 24 are assaulted by another student who has been drinking (2002).

• **Sexual abuse:** More than 70,000 students between the ages of 18 and 24 are victims of alcohol-related sexual assault or date rape (2002).

• **Unsafe sex:** 400,000 students between the ages of 18 and 24 had unprotected sex and more than 100,000 students between the ages of 18 and 24 report having been too intoxicated to know if they consented to having sex (2002).

• **Academic problems:** About 25% of college students report academic consequences of their drinking including missing class, falling behind, doing poorly on exams or papers, and receiving lower grades overall (1996, 2002).

• **Health problems/suicide attempts:** More than 150,000 students develop an alcohol-related health problem (2002) and between 1.2% and 1.5% of students indicate that they tried to commit suicide within the past year due to drinking or drug use (1998).

• **Drunk driving:** 2.1 million students between the ages of 18 and 24 drove under the influence of alcohol last year (2002).

• **Vandalism:** About 11% of college student drinkers report that they have damaged property while under the influence of alcohol (2002).

• **Property damage:** More than 25% of administrators from schools with relatively low drinking levels and over 50% from schools with high drinking levels say their campuses have a "moderate" or "major" problem with alcohol-related property damage (1995).

• **Police involvement:** About 5% of 4-year college students are involved with the police or campus security as a result of their drinking and an estimated 110,000 students between the ages of 18 and 24 are arrested for an alcohol-related violation such as public drunkenness or driving under the influence (2002).

• **Alcohol abuse and dependence:** 31% of college students met criteria for a diagnosis of alcohol abuse and 6% for a diagnosis of alcohol dependence in the past 12 months, according to questionnaire-based self-reports about their drinking (2002).

Alcohol Use in the Past Month, by Characteristics, 2003

	Type of alcohol use				Type of alcohol use		
Characteristic	Any alcohol use	Binge alcohol use	Heavy alcohol use	Characteristic	Any alcohol use	Binge alcohol use	Heavy alcohol use
Age				Black or African American	37.9%	19.0%	4.5%
12–17	17.7%	10.6%	2.6%	American Indian or Alaska Native	42.0	29.6	10.0
18–25	61.4	41.6	15.1	Native Hawaiian or other Pacific Islander	43.3	29.8	10.4
26 or older	52.5	21.0	5.9	Asian	39.8	11.0	2.3
Gender				Two or more races	44.4	21.8	6.1
Male	57.3	30.9	10.4	Hispanic or Latino	41.5	24.2	5.2
Female	43.2	14.8	3.4	**Total**	**50.1**	**22.6**	**6.8**
Hispanic origin and race							
Not Hispanic or Latino	51.3	22.4	7.0				
White	54.4	23.6	7.7				

Source: SAMHSA, Office of Applied Studies, *National Survey on Drug Use and Health, 2002 and 2003.* Web: www.oas.samhsa.gov.

Smoking Prevalence Among U.S. Adults, 1955–2002
(as a percent of population, 18 years of age and older)

Year	Overall population	Males	Females	Whites	Blacks
1955	—	56.9%	28.4%	—	—
1965	42.4%	51.9	33.9	42.1%	45.8%
1970	37.4	44.1	31.5	37.0	41.4
1980	33.2	37.6	29.3	32.9	36.9
1990	25.5	28.4	22.8	25.6	26.2
2000	23.3	25.7	21.0	24.1	23.2
2002	22.5	25.2	20.0	23.6	22.4

Source: U.S. Centers for Disease Control and Prevention. Web: www.cdc.gov.

Cigarette Use Among Americans by Characteristics, 2003

Characteristic	Lifetime	Past year	Past month	Characteristic	Lifetime	Past year	Past month
Age				African American	58.6%	28.8%	25.9%
12–17	31.0%	19.0%	12.2%	American Indian or Alaska Native	71.8	41.1	36.1
18–25	70.2	47.6	40.2	Native Hawaiian or Pacific Islander	55.0	38.6	33.1
26 or older	73.6	27.6	24.7	Asian	42.4	16.3	12.6
Gender				Two or more races	71.0	35.4	30.7
Male	73.2	32.4	28.1	Hispanic or Latino	56.8	26.5	21.4
Female	64.4	26.6	23.0	**Total**	**68.7**	**29.4**	**25.4**
Hispanic origin and race							
Not Hispanic	70.4	29.8	26.0				
White	74.0	30.6	26.6				

Source: SAMHSA, Office of Applied Studies, *National Survey on Drug Use and Health, 2002 and 2003.* Web: www.oas.samhsa.gov.

Blood Pressure Explained

Blood pressure is the force of blood against the walls of arteries. Blood pressure is recorded as two numbers—the systolic pressure (as the heart beats) over the diastolic pressure (as the heart relaxes between beats). The measurement is written one above or before the other, with the systolic number on top and the diastolic number on the bottom. For example, a blood pressure measurement of 120/80 mm Hg (millimeters of mercury) is expressed verbally as "120 over 80."

Normal blood pressure is less than 120 mm Hg systolic and less than 80 mm Hg diastolic.

When systolic and diastolic blood pressures fall into different categories, the higher category should be used to classify blood pressure level. For example, 160/80 mm Hg would be stage 2 hypertension (high blood pressure).

Category	Blood pressure level (mm Hg)	
	Systolic	Diastolic
Normal	< 120	< 80
Prehypertension	120–139	80–89
High blood pressure		
Stage 1 hypertension	140–159	90–99
Stage 2 hypertension	≥160	≥100

NOTE: < means less than; ≥ means greater than or equal to. *Source:* National Heart, Lung, and Blood Institute.

Blood Types

Human blood is grouped into four types: A, B, AB, and O. Each letter refers to a kind of antigen, or protein, on the surface of red blood cells. For example, the surface of red blood cells in Type A blood has antigens known as A-antigens.

Each blood type is also grouped by its Rhesus factor, or Rh factor. Blood is either Rh positive (Rh+) or Rh negative (Rh-). About 85% of Americans have Rh+ blood.

Rhesus refers to another type of antigen, or protein, on the surface of red blood cells. The name Rhesus comes from Rhesus monkeys, in which the protein was discovered.

Blood types become very important when a blood transfusion is necessary. In a blood transfusion, a patient must receive a blood type that is compatible with his or her own blood type—that is, the donated blood must be accepted by the patient's own blood.

If the blood types are not compatible, red blood cells will clump together, making clots that can block blood vessels and cause death.

Type O- blood is considered the "universal donor" because it can be donated to people of any blood type. Type AB+ blood is considered the "universal recipient" because people with this type can receive any blood type.

Blood type	Percent of Americans with this type	Who can receive this type
O+	37%	O+, A+, B+, AB+
O-	6	All blood types
A+	34	A+, AB+
A-	6	A+, A-, AB+, AB-
B+	10	B+, AB+
B-	2	B+, B-, AB+, AB-
AB+	4	AB+
AB-	1	AB+, AB-

America's Best Hospitals, 2005

The annual *U.S. News & World Report* list of the United States' best hospitals is prepared by the National Opinion Research Center at the University of Chicago. This year's list recognizes 16 hospitals, each of which excels in many specialties.

1. Johns Hopkins Hospital, Baltimore, Md.
2. Mayo Clinic, Rochester, Minn.
3. Massachusetts General Hospital, Boston, Mass.
4. Cleveland Clinic, Cleveland, Ohio
5. UCLA Medical Center, Los Angeles, Calif.
6. Barnes–Jewish Hospital, St. Louis, Mo.
7. New York Presbyterian Hospital, New York, N.Y.
8. Duke University Medical Center, Durham, N.C.
9. University of Washington Medical Center, Seattle, Wash.
10. University of California, San Francisco Medical Center, San Francisco, Calif.
11. University of Michigan Medical Center, Ann Arbor, Mich.
12. Brigham and Women's Hospital, Boston, Mass.
13. University of Pittsburgh Medical Center, Pittsburgh, Pa.
14. University of Chicago Hospitals, Chicago, Ill.
15. Hospital of the University of Pennsylvania, Philadelphia, Pa.
16. Stanford Hospital and Clinics, Stanford, Calif.

Who Is Playing Games—and Why

By **CHRIS TAYLOR** TIME

Imagine, if you will, the average games player. What do you see? A twitchy teenager mashing buttons on his controller, lost and alone in a violent on-screen world? Or a sad-sack Peter Pan type, the geek who never grew up? Sorry, you lose. The average American gamer is starting to look, well, pretty much like the average American. For the first time, according to a poll commissioned by AOL Games and obtained exclusively by TIME, roughly half of Americans ages 12 to 55 are tapping away at some kind of electronic game—whether on a console, a PC, a cell phone, or another handheld device—for an average of three hours every week.

The games you play say a lot about who you are. As you might expect, there are clear game-playing divisions along the fault lines of sex and age. Consoles like the Xbox and PlayStation 2 are predominantly the territory of twentysomething men, who prefer to picture themselves as sports stars (like Tiger Woods PGA Tour 2005) and racing drivers (Gran Turismo 4). Men 50 and older prefer martial games like Tom Clancy's Rainbow Six. Teenage girls are much more likely than boys to play games on their phone, while older women make up the majority of people playing card games such as Hearts online.

Women may favor more social games, but that doesn't make them any less ambitious. If you're playing the best-selling Sims games—and 60% of you are women—your goal is to have it all: great house, killer job, hypersmart, multigenerational family. Judge for yourself whether that's more constructive than having the most violent car crash.

Is it good for us, all this time spent in virtual worlds? Or is it as pernicious as television, sucking us ever further from reality? The AOL survey suggests we're in denial about the extent of our habit. One in 10 gamers claims to be addicted; 1 in 4 admits to losing a night of sleep to play games; and another quarter has been engrossed enough to skip meals. Club Pogo and Sims players average 18 and 20 hours a week on their games.

But don't think we're heading into a video-game version of The Matrix world with everyone plugged into his own pod. Quite the contrary: gamers appear to be more engaged with reality than other kinds of couch potatoes. According to a comprehensive survey by the Entertainment Software Association (ESA—whose members, of course, want you to think video games are wholesome), gamers spend an average of 23 hours a week volunteering and going to church, concerts, museums, and other cultural events. Hardcore gamers who play 11 hours a week or more spend even more time out in the cultural world (34 hours). "Anyone who still thinks gamers are single-minded loafers is living in a fantasy world," says Doug Lowenstein, president of the ESA. We're all Peter Pans now—and that's no bad thing. □

From Geek to Chic in 33 Years

Three decades after video games invaded our space, it's finally hip to be square

Top 10 Video Game Titles, 2004

Rank	Title	Plat-form	Publisher	Avg. retail price	Rank	Title	Plat-form	Publisher	Avg. retail price
1.	Grand Theft Auto: San Andreas	PS2	Take II Interactive	$49	6.	Pokemon Fire Red w/ Adapter	GBA	Nintendo of America	$32
2.	Halo 2*	XBX	Microsoft	52	7.	NBA Live 2005	PS2	Electronic Arts	33
3.	Madden NFL 2005*	PS2	Electronic Arts	49	8.	Spider-Man: The Movie 2	PS2	Activision	43
4.	ESPN NFL 2K5	PS2	Take II Interactive	19	9.	Halo	XBX	Microsoft	29
5.	Need for Speed: Underground 2	PS2	Electronic Arts	48	10.	ESPN NFL 2K5	XBX	Take II Interactive	19

*Includes Limited & Collector's Editions. *Source:* The NPD Group/NPD Funworld®/ Point-of-Sale.

Home Internet Connections by Technology, 2001 and 2003
(millions of households)

	2001	2003	Percent change		2001	2003	Percent change
Dial-up	44.2	38.6	−12.7%	Number of households with Internet	54.6	61.5	12.6%
DSL	3.3	9.3	181.8%				
Cable	6.6	12.6	90.9%	Total number of households	108.6	112.6	3.7%
Other*	0.5	0.9	80.0%				

*"Other" includes 0.4 million households with satellite and MMDS broadband in 2003. The 2003 individual home connection numbers do not add up to the category total due to rounding.

Internet Access and Usage in the U.S.

	Total adults	Any online/ Internet usage[1]	Have Internet access			Used the Internet in past 30 days		
			Home/ work/ other	Home	Work	Home/ work/ other	Home	Work
Total adults (thousands)	214,774	138,287	169,753	135,731	75,405	135,282	115,385	63,901
Percent	100.0%	100.0%	100.0%	100.0%	100.0%	100.0%	100.0%	100.0%
Men	48.1%	48.2%	48.4%	49.6%	50.8%	48.2%	49.0%	50.2%
Women	51.9	51.8	51.6	50.4	49.2	51.8	51.0	49.8
Education								
Graduated college plus	25.0	35.3	30.4	34.7	45.4	35.8	38.0	48.8
Attended college	27.2	33.6	30.9	31.8	32.0	33.8	33.5	31.6
Did not attend college	47.9	31.0	38.7	33.6	22.6	30.4	28.6	19.6
Age								
18–34	31.3	36.8	33.7	32.1	33.6	37.1	34.8	33.9
35–54	39.5	44.1	42.6	44.9	52.5	44.2	45.3	52.8
55+	29.2	19.1	23.7	23.0	13.9	18.7	20.0	13.3
Employment								
Full time	53.3	63.5	59.3	61.2	87.7	63.7	62.9	89.0
Part time	10.7	12.1	11.6	11.8	11.8	12.2	12.3	10.6
Occupation								
Professional	13.2	19.1	16.2	18.4	30.0	19.4	20.4	30.8
Mgmt./Bus./Finan. Ops.	9.3	13.1	11.4	12.9	20.7	13.3	13.8	22.8
Sales/Office	16.0	20.8	18.7	18.6	29.4	21.0	19.7	30.2
Nat. Res./Constr./Maint.	6.8	6.1	6.5	6.4	5.3	6.0	5.9	4.6
Other	18.8	16.5	18.1	16.8	14.0	16.3	15.5	11.3
Household income								
$150,000 or more	7.0	9.7	8.6	10.3	13.0	9.9	11.0	13.8
$75,000–149,999	24.6	33.2	29.6	34.2	40.8	33.5	35.5	42.9
$50,000–74,999	20.0	23.7	22.8	24.1	23.8	23.8	24.1	22.6
Less than $50,000	48.4	33.3	39.0	31.4	22.4	32.9	29.3	20.8

1. Any online/Internet usage is a net of those who looked at or used the Internet or any online service at home, work, or another place in the past 30 days. Source: MRI CyberStats, Spring 2005.

How Internet Access Has Changed

	2000	2002	2004		2000	2002	2004
Men	51%	60%	66%	**Household income**			
Women	46	56	61	< $30,000	31%	38%	44%
Race/Ethnicity[1]				$30,000–$50,000	52	65	69
White	50%	60%	67%	$50,000–$75,000	67	74	81
Black	34	45	43	$75,000+	78	86	89
Hispanic	43	54	59	**Education**			
Age				Did not graduate from high school	17%	23%	32%
				High school grad	34	45	52
18–29	69%	74%	78%	Some college	63	72	75
30–49	60	67	74	College plus	75	82	88
50–64	45	52	60	**Community type**			
65+	14	18	25	Rural	43%	49%	56%
				Suburban	54	63	68
				Urban	53	58	62

Margin of error is ±2.5% for 2000 and ±2% for 2002. *Source:* Pew Internet & American Life Project tracking survey, April 2000, March–May 2002, and May–June 2004. 1. The 2000 numbers for the race category are based on the March, April, and May–June 2000 data sets.

Growth of Daily Activities on the Internet in Recent Years

Activity	2000 (in millions)	2004 (in millions)	Activity	2000 (in millions)	2004 (in millions)
Go online	52	70	Do research for school or training	9	14
Use email	45	58			
Get news	19	35	Get travel information	6	10
Check the weather	14	25	Get health or medical information	6	7
Do research for a job	14	24			
Research a product before buying it	12	19	Look for religious and spiritual information	3	6
Look for political news or information	9	24	Buy a product	3	4
			Participate in online auction	3	4
Send instant message	10	15			

Source: Pew Internet & American Life Project.

Blog Readership

According to a 2004 survey by the Pew Internet & American Life Project, about 120 million U.S. adults use the Internet and about 32 million read blogs. However, only 38% of Internet users indicated they knew what the term *blog* means. A blog, a contraction of "web" and "log," is an online diary that people post for others to read. Blog readers make up 27% of all Internet users. Many blogs allow readers to post their own comments.

- 9% of Internet users said they read political blogs "frequently" or "sometimes" during the 2004 campaign.
- 7% of users say they have created a blog or web-based diary.
- 57% of bloggers are male.
- 48% are under age 30.
- Blog readership shot up 58% between February and November 2004.

Online Consumer Spending by Product, 2002–2004

Category	Online retail spending (billions of dollars)			Category	Online retail spending (billions of dollars)		
	2002	2003	2004		2002	2003	2004
Total	**$41.2**	**$52.6**	**$65.1**	Jewelry	$1.2	$1.4	$1.6
PCs	7.6	8.9	9.8	Grocery	1.1	1.7	2.4
Peripherals	2.3	2.6	2.7	Pets	0.2	0.4	0.5
Software	2.6	3.0	3.3	Toys	0.7	0.8	0.8
Consumer electronics	2.1	2.6	3.3	Sporting goods	0.9	1.3	1.6
Books	2.8	3.2	3.5	Flowers	0.8	1.0	1.2
Music	0.8	0.8	1.1	Specialty gifts	0.8	1.1	1.4
Videos	0.9	1.2	1.5	Furniture	0.3	0.5	0.6
Movie tickets	0.3	0.4	0.5	Large appliances	0.5	0.7	0.9
Event tickets	2.2	2.7	3.3	Housewares/small appliances	1.1	1.9	2.9
Over-the-counter drugs	0.1	0.2	0.3	Art and collectibles	0.5	0.6	0.8
Nutraceuticals	0.1	0.2	0.4	Home improvement	0.6	1.0	1.5
Medical supplies and contact lenses	0.2	0.3	0.4	Garden supplies	0.2	0.3	0.5
Personal care	0.2	0.4	0.8	Office products	1.2	1.8	2.6
Apparel	4.8	6.2	7.5	Auto parts	0.1	0.3	0.6
Footwear	0.8	1.0	1.3	Other	2.7	3.7	4.6

NOTE: (—) represents or rounds to zero. *Source:* Jupiter Media Metrix, Inc. From *Statistical Abstract of the United States: 2004.*

Top Domains/Websites

	Unique visitors[1] (thousands)		Unique visitors[1] (thousands)
Total Internet audience	**164,961**	13. Verizon Communications Corp.	27,827
1. Yahoo! sites	116,321	14. Lycos, Inc.	27,326
2. Time Warner Network	115,829	15 Intermix Media	26,672
3. MSN-Microsoft sites	111,519	16. The Weather Channel	25,233
4. Google sites	78,649	17. Vendare Media—New.net sites	24,180
5. eBay	63,825	18. AT&T Properties	23,158
6. Ask Jeeves	42,341	19. Expedia Travel	22,962
7. Amazon sites	39,066	20. Shopping.com sites	22,637
8. CNET Networks	33,494	21. Real.com Network	22,550
9. Viacom Online	32,077	22. Trip Network, Inc.	20,979
10. Monster Worldwide	29,918	23. Wal-Mart	19,736
11. New York Times Digital	29,762	24. Gorilla Nation Media	19,087
12. Walt Disney Internet Group (WDIG)	28,485	25. Weatherbug.com Property	18,807

NOTE: Audience: All persons at U.S. home/work/college/university locations. 1. Unique visitors over one-month period, April 2005. *Source:* comScore Media Metrix (comScore Media Metrix is a division of comScore Networks, Inc.).

Top General News Sites

	Unique visitors[1] (thousands)		Unique visitors[1] (thousands)
Total Internet audience	**164,961**	5. CNN	20,904
General News category	**94,375**	6. IBS Network	9,580
1. New York Times Digital	29,762	7. USATODAY sites	7,925
2. MSNBC	26,588	8. Knight Ridder Digital	7,619
3. Yahoo! News	25,093	9. Google News	7,050
4. AOL News	23,042	10. Tribune Newspapers	6,557

NOTE: Audience: All persons at U.S. home/work/college/university locations. 1. Unique visitors over one-month period, April 2005. *Source:* comScore Media Metrix (comScore Media Metrix is a division of comScore Networks, Inc.).

Top Travel Sites

	Unique visitors[1] (thousands)		Unique visitors[1] (thousands)
Total Internet audience	**164,961**	5. Hotels.com sites	9,430
Travel category	**72,983**	6. Priceline.com, Inc.	9,102
1. Expedia Travel	22,962	7. Yahoo! Travel	8,655
2. Trip Network, Inc.	20,979	8. Southwest.com	7,880
3. Orbitz.com	14,401	9. AOL Travel	7,693
4. Travelocity	12,940	10. TripAdvisor.com	5,921

NOTE: Audience: All persons at U.S. home/work/college/university locations. 1. Unique visitors over one-month period, April 2005. *Source:* comScore Media Metrix (comScore Media Metrix is a division of comScore Networks, Inc.).

Top Entertainment Sites

	Unique visitors[1] (thousands)		Unique visitors[1] (thousands)
Total Internet audience	**164,961**	5. Intermix Media	26,672
Entertainment category	**128,863**	6. Real.com Network	22,550
1. Viacom Online	32,077	7. MSN Entertainment	19,827
2. AOL Entertainment	31,389	8. Gorilla Nation Media	19,087
3. Yahoo! Music	29,903	9. Disney Online	17,502
4. WindowsMedia	27,693	10. Ticketmaster	13,832

NOTE: Audience: All persons at U.S. home/work/college/university locations. 1. Unique visitors over one-month period, April 2005. *Source:* comScore Media Metrix (comScore Media Metrix is a division of comScore Networks, Inc.).

Top Email Services (U.S.)

Brand or channel	Unique audience (thousands)	Brand or channel	Unique audience (thousands)
1. Yahoo! Mail	44,863	4. Google Gmail	4,326
2. AOL email	33,588	5. IncrediMail	2,677
3. MSN Hotmail	28,374	6. BellSouth Web Mail	1,962

Source: Nielsen//NetRatings, May 2005.

Top 10 U.S. Internet Advertisers, 2004

Advertisers	Impressions[1] (thousands)	Advertisers	Impressions[1] (thousands)
1. SBC Communications, Inc.	28,584,835	6. Apollo Group, Inc.	13,153,913
2. Netflix, Inc.	26,414,049	7. Ameritrade Holding Corp.	13,044,917
3. Dell Computer Corp.	22,276,192	8. United Online, Inc.	12,744,226
4. InterActiveCorp	20,736,020	9. Verizon Communications, Inc.	12,103,534
5. LowerMyBills.com, Inc.	18,981,676	10. Scottrade, Inc.	12,031,356

1. Impressions reported exclude house ads, which are ads that run on an advertiser's own Web property. *Source:* Nielsen//NetRatings AdRelevance, Dec. 2004.

Top Search Engines

	Searches (thousands)	Unique searchers[1] (thousands)		Searches (thousands)	Unique searchers[1] (thousands)
1. Google	1,986,795	71,928	4. AOL	194,558	19,866
2. Yahoo!	919,894	48,861	5. Ask Jeeves	87,282	11,727
3. MSN	515,926	40,560			

1. Unique visitors over one-month period, April 2005. *Source:* Nielsen//Net Ratings MegaView Search, April 2005.

Top 15 Countries in Internet Usage, 2004

	Internet users (thousands)	Share %		Internet users (thousands)	Share %
1. U.S.	185,550	19.86%	10. Brazil	22,320	2.39%
2. China	99,800	10.68	11. Russia	21,230	2.27
3. Japan	78,050	8.35	12. Canada	20,450	2.19
4. Germany	41,880	4.48	13. Mexico	13,880	1.49
5. India	36,970	3.96	14. Spain	13,440	1.44
6. UK	33,110	3.54	15. Australia	13,010	1.39
7. South Korea	31,670	3.39	**Top 15 Total**	**662,360**	**70.88**
8. Italy	25,530	2.73	**Worldwide Total**	**934,480**	**100.00**
9. France	25,470	2.73			

Source: Computer Industry Almanac, Inc. Web: www.c-i-a.com. Reprinted with permission.

Top 15 Countries in PCs-in-Use

Rank	Country	Year-end 2004 (millions)	2004 % share of total	Rank	Country	Year-end 2004 (millions)	2004 % share of total
1.	U.S.	223.81	27.22%	10.	Brazil	19.35	2.35%
2.	Japan	69.20	8.42	11.	Russia	19.01	2.31
3.	China	52.99	6.45	12.	Australia	13.72	1.67
4.	Germany	46.30	5.63	13.	India	13.03	1.58
5.	UK	35.89	4.37	14.	Mexico	11.21	1.36
6.	France	29.41	3.58	15.	Netherlands	11.11	1.35
7.	South Korea	26.20	3.19	**Total Top 15 Countries**		**616.27**	**74.96**
8.	Italy	22.65	2.75	**Total Worldwide**		**822.15**	**100.00**
9.	Canada	22.39	2.72				

Source: Computer Industry Almanac, Inc. Web: www.c-i-a.com. Reprinted with permission.

Computer Usage in the U.S.

(percent of U.S. adults in each group who use computers)

Men	73%	**Household income**	
Women	72	< $30,000	55%
Generation		$30,000–$49,999	82
Gen Y (ages 18–27)	85	$50,000–$74,999	92
Gen X (ages 28–39)	87	$75,000+	93
Trailing Boomers (ages 40–49)	84	**Community type**	
Leading Boomers (ages 50–58)	76	Urban	75
Matures (ages 59–68)	57	Suburban	76
After work (ages 69+)	24	Rural	61
Race and ethnicity		**Educational attainment**	
Whites	73	Less than high school	39
Blacks	62	High school graduate	67
Hispanics (English speaking)	75	Some college courses	84
		College graduate/graduate degree	91

Margin of error is ±2% *Source:* Pew Internet & American Life Project Tracking Survey, Feb. 3–March 1, 2004.

Households with Computers, 1998 and 2003

(percent of all households in specified group)

	1998	2003		1998	2003		1998	2003
U.S.	**42.1%**	**61.8%**	Ky.	35.9%	58.1%	Ohio	40.7%	58.8%
Ala.	34.3	53.9	La.	31.1	52.3	Okla.	37.8	55.4
Alaska	62.4	72.7	Maine	43.4	67.8	Ore.	51.3	67.0
Ariz.	44.3	64.3	Md.	46.3	66.0	Pa.	39.3	60.2
Ark.	29.8	50.0	Mass.	43.4	64.1	R.I.	41.0	62.3
Calif.	47.5	66.3	Mich.	44.0	59.9	S.C.	35.7	54.9
Colo.	55.3	70.0	Minn.	47.6	67.9	S.D.	41.6	62.1
Conn.	43.8	69.2	Miss.	25.7	48.3	Tenn.	37.5	56.7
Del.	40.5	59.5	Mo.	41.8	60.7	Tex.	40.9	59.0
DC	41.4	64.3	Mont.	40.9	59.5	Utah	60.1	74.1
Fla.	39.5	61.0	Neb.	42.9	66.1	Vt.	48.7	65.5
Ga.	35.8	60.6	Nev.	41.6	61.3	Va.	46.4	66.8
Hawaii	42.3	63.3	N.H.	54.2	71.5	Wash.	56.3	71.4
Idaho	50.0	69.2	N.J.	48.1	65.5	W.Va.	28.3	55.0
Ill.	42.7	60.0	N.M.	42.2	53.9	Wis.	43.0	63.8
Ind.	43.5	59.6	N.Y.	37.3	60.0	Wyo.	46.1	65.4
Iowa	41.4	64.7	N.C.	35.0	57.7			
Kans.	43.7	63.8	N.D.	40.2	61.2			

NOTE: As of October. *Source:* U.S. Department of Commerce, National Telecommunications and Information Administration, *Falling Through the Net: Defining the Digital Divide,* July 1999, and *A Nation Online,* 2004.

Top-Selling Software, 2004

Rank	Title	Unit volume share	Rank	Title	Unit volume share
	Total	100.0	5.	TurboTax 2003 Multi State 45	1.2
1.	TurboTax 2003 Deluxe	3.2	6.	Norton Antivirus 2005	1.1
2.	Norton Antivirus 2004	2.7	7.	Taxcut 2003 Deluxe	1.1
3.	Norton Internet Security 2004	1.3	8.	TurboTax 2003	1.0
4.	MS Office 2003 Student/Teacher Ed	1.2	9.	MS Windows XP Home Ed Upgr	0.9
			10.	The Sims 2	0.7

Source: NPD Group/NPDTechworld. Web: www.npd.com.

Top-Selling Education Software, 2004

Rank	Title	Unit volume share	Rank	Title	Unit volume share
	Total	100.0	7.	Jumpstart Advanced Kindergarten 2003	1.0
1.	Dora the Explorer Animal Adventures	2.3	8.	Mavis Beacon Teaches Typing 16.0	1.0
2.	Instant Immersion Spanish JC	1.9	9.	Jumpstart Advanced Third Grade 2003	1.0
3.	I Spy Fantasy	1.3	10.	Jumpstart Advanced Preschool 2003	1.0
4.	Strawberry Shortcake: Amazing Cookie Party	1.2			
5.	Snap! Typing JC	1.1			
6.	Instant Immersion Spanish	1.1			

Source: NPD Group/NPDTechworld. Web: www.npd.com.

Top 10 PC Game Titles, 2004

Rank	Title	Unit volume share	Rank	Title	Unit volume share
	Total	100.0	6.	The Sims 2 Special Edition	1.0
1.	The Sims 2	1.6	7.	Battlefield Vietnam	0.9
2.	Doom 3	1.3	8.	Call of Duty	0.9
3.	World of Warcraft	1.0	9.	Roller Coaster Tycoon 3	0.7
4.	Half-Life 2	1.0	10.	MS Zoo Tycoon: Complete Collection	0.7
5.	The Sims Deluxe	1.0			

Source: NPD Group/NPDTechworld. Web: www.npd.com.

The Revolution in Therapeutic Cloning

Looking for the frontier of biotechnology? South Korea leads the world in the creation of human embryonic stem cells

By **ALICE PARK**/SEOUL TIME

Seoul National University is the center of operations for Woo Suk Hwang, the South Korean scientist who made headlines in May 2005 when he announced that his team, using Dolly-the-sheep techniques, had created 11 human stem-cell lines perfectly matched to the DNA of human patients—a giant leap beyond anything any other lab has achieved. After hollowing out freshly harvested human eggs, researchers fused them with skin cells taken from nearly a dozen patients—ages 2 to 56, suffering from a variety of injuries and disorders—and grew them with unprecedented efficiency into early embryos lined with stem cells. The development, published online by the journal *Science*, takes doctors an important step closer to creating custom stem-cell treatments for everything from Alzheimer's disease to severed spinal cords.

A Controversial Breakthrough

Hwang's methods are controversial, however—particularly in the U.S.—and the White House immediately criticized the experiment. The process is called somatic cell nuclear transfer (SCNT), but most people know it colloquially as therapeutic cloning. "I am very concerned about cloning," President Bush said in response to the news. "I worry about a world in which cloning becomes accepted." Critics of embryonic cloning contend that because it involves the destruction of an embryo, it is tantamount to murder. As President Bush put it, he objects to "promot[ing] science which destroys life in order to save life."

Scientists, for their part, were singing a different tune. "It's a tremendous advance," says Paul Berg, a Nobel laureate from Stanford University and a major backer of California's independent stem-cell initiative. "The Koreans' work is incredibly impressive," says Stephen Minger, director of the stem-cell biology laboratory at King's College, London. "It is fantastic—a major, major breakthrough."

The crux of that breakthrough is this: each of the newly created stem-cell lines is genetically identical to one of Hwang's patients. That means any new tissue derived from that patient's cell line can be injected into that individual without triggering an immune reaction. If researchers can figure out how to fix the original defect, they may someday be able to generate replacement tissue that is custom designed to treat the patient's condition. Or at least that's the dream. No one knows yet whether those stem cells can be safely used in people.

Many scientists were astonished by how far the South Koreans had come. Only 15 months before this breakthrough, Hwang's group created a stir as the first—and so far the only—lab to generate human stem cells via SCNT. Back then it had to use 242 eggs before it was able to create a single, viable set of stem cells from a healthy woman. This time it was able to create 11 stem-cell lines using an average 17 eggs each. "The efficiency is exceptionally high—much higher than I would have thought possible," says Doug Melton, a stem-cell researcher at Harvard University and the Howard Hughes Medical Institute in Boston. "It's about what has been achieved in mouse cells after decades of work."

For Berg, Melton, and their American colleagues, there is a touch of envy blended with the praise. Stem-cell research in Asia—not just in South Korea but in China, Japan, and Singapore as well—is rapidly outdistancing the work being done in the U.S., reflecting, in large part, real differences in government policy. South Korea, for example, recently banned the use of cloning techniques for the creation of babies but fully supports Hwang's work—to the tune of $2 million a year. By contrast, researchers in the U.S. who want to study human embryonic stem cells are restricted to a handful of federally approved stem-cell lines—most of which, they say, are of such poor quality they cannot be used. Or scientists can forgo federal funding and look to state or private financing for their work. "In this country, we've been stumbling to create public policy," says Melton.

At the Cutting Edge

A veterinary scientist by training, Hwang says his pioneering work with human stem cells would not have been possible without an extensive animal-research program. Building on what he learned from his experiments on cows, pigs, and ducks, Hwang developed his own assembly line of nearly two dozen steps to improve the efficiency of human stem-cell production. "I wanted to develop a unique technique, not just mimic and modify what others had done," he says.

Hwang does not want his work in therapeutic cloning to be confused with reproductive cloning, which he deems "unsafe and unethical." He thinks cloning fully grown humans may be biologically impossible, given the many miscarriages and genetic anomalies that have bedeviled attempts to clone animals, and he doesn't like giving people the impression that therapies or treatment will be available anytime soon. Indeed, the most immediate benefit of Hwang's work will be to better understand how diseases develop. "Rather than having to study the patient or freshly dissected tissues from that patient, we can have a cell line of stem cells that can grow virtually forever," says Hans Keirstead, a neurobiologist at the University of California, Irvine. □

Roundup of Recent Science Discoveries, 2005

By Borgna Brunner

Omo Is Oldest

In 2003 the dating of an Ethiopian *Homo sapiens* fossil, "Herto Man," was hailed as a milestone in paleoanthropology. At 160,000 years old, Herto Man was a full 50,000 years older than any anatomically modern human ever discovered. But now, just two years later, Herto Man has already been replaced as humanity's forefather. And he was dethroned by a couple of skull fossils that have been kicking around, virtually ignored, for the last 40 years.

The skulls, called Omo I and Omo II, were discovered back in 1967 by paleontologist Richard Leakey, near the Omo River in southern Ethiopia. They were thought to be about 130,000 years old, but their dating was not considered definitive. Nor was their age a particularly burning issue at the time—when Leakey discovered the Omo skulls, he had been in hot pursuit of evidence of our earliest, prehuman ancestors, who preceded *Homo sapiens* by millions of years. As paleontologist John Fleagle of Stony Brook University put it, "The fact of the matter is, they wanted early hominids; modern humans were like chump change."

In the last several years, however, Fleagle and other researchers determined that the Omo skulls were worth another look. With the help of the latest dating technology, they announced in February that the skulls were an astonishing 195,000 years old, more than 65,000 years older than Herto. After four decades as a side show to Leakey's more spectacular discoveries, the Omo skulls have gone from "chump change" to our most revered elders. Omo is oldest, and Herto is history.

But does age really matter? In this case, it does in fact represent more than just paleontological one-upsmanship. The recalibration of the Omo fossils' ages was not simply undertaken because new technology made it possible, but because pinpointing the age of the earliest humans contributes important evidence to the "Out of Africa" theory—the debate over whether humanity originated in Africa and then migrated to other parts of the world, or whether, according to the subscribers of the multiregionalist theory, *Homo sapiens* developed independently in various parts of the world. The new dating of Omo, Fleagle contends, "places the first appearance of modern *Homo sapiens* in Africa many more thousands of years before our species appears on any other continent." The age of Herto strongly buttressed the "Out of Africa" case two years ago—that's why it was considered such a significant find. Given that the Omo skulls are 65,000 years older, they increase the gap between the emergence of humans in Africa and the much later *Homo sapiens* fossils found elsewhere in the world.

The Softer Side of *T. Rex*

In March paleontologists discovered the existence of soft tissue in a 68-million-year-old *Tyrannosaurus rex* fossil. An unprecedented find in a prehistoric creature—scientists had assumed no such tissue could survive more than 100,000 years—the soft tissue included cells and blood vessels.

The discovery was a serendipitous one. Because this *T. rex* fossil was located in a remote part of Montana (the Hell Creek formation, where about two dozen species of dinosaurs have been found) the fossil had to be removed by helicopter. According to paleontologist Jack Horner, who participated in the excavation, "we actually had to split the thighbone into two pieces to get it into the helicopter." When his colleague Mary Schweitzer later examined the hollow cavity of the broken bone in her North Carolina State University lab, she discovered the pliable tissue. Scientists predict the soft tissue will provide a gold mine of information about the physiology of dinosaurs.

Examination of the soft tissue has already yielded several exciting revelations. The tissue included medullary bone, a calcium-enriched substance temporarily present when birds are ready to produce eggshells and lay eggs. Not only does the presence of medullary bone reveal that this particular *T. rex* was female (paleontologists have never before determined the sex of a dinosaur), but the existence of medullary tissue also supports the widely held theory that modern birds descended from dinosaurs. According to Schweitzer, it "links the reproductive physiology of dinosaurs to birds very closely. It indicates that dinosaurs produced and shelled their eggs much more like modern birds than like modern crocodiles." Horner commented that "this is another piece to the puzzle and there are a lot of them. Anyone who would argue that birds and dinosaurs are not related—frankly, I'd put them in the Flat Earth Society group."

Mind over Matter

In 2001 Matt Nagle, a 25-year-old former football star from Weymouth, Mass., was stabbed in an unprovoked fight that severed his spinal cord. Paralyzed from the neck down, he lost even the ability to breathe on his own. But over the last year, this quadriplegic has performed a seemingly supernatural feat: he can control machines through his thoughts. Thanks to a chip implanted in his brain, Nagle has the ability to convey simple, motor-related thoughts to a computer, which then carries out his actions. He can now change channels on his TV, turn lights on and off, and play computer games simply by thinking about doing these things. In early 2005 he became the first human to reach and grasp objects using an artificial hand by thinking about moving his own paralyzed hand.

In June 2004 surgeons implanted a sensor called the Braingate Neural Interface System in the part of Nagle's brain that controls motor activity. Braingate channels the electrical signals from the brain that normally move through the spinal cord—which in Nagle's case is irreparably damaged—and sends them to wires attached to his skull. The wires convey the brain signals to a computer, which then interprets them and carries out the task.

Nagle is one of the pioneers in the exploding field of neuro-cybernetics, the science of using machines to carry out commands of the human brain. But he was not the first to turn his thoughts into action. Since 1996, a number of paralyzed patients have learned to move a computer cursor and even type messages—albeit laboriously—just by thinking about doing so. In the mid-1990s only a handful of labs were devoted to developing brain-machine interface (BMI) technology; today there are more then 60 labs throughout the world. Some are exploring systems that detect brain waves from outside the body; others, like Braingate, work with brain implants. Some of the most promising experiments have benefitted patients with "locked-in" syndrome—their brain functions normally but they've been robbed of all muscle control. BMI technology has allowed them to use their thoughts to regain rudimentary communication with the outside world.

The lead scientist on the Braingate experiment, John Donoghue of Brown University, believes that Nagle—and eventually other paralyzed people— will eventually regain some control over their environments through BMI technology. Ultimately, Donoghue hopes they'll regain control over their paralyzed limbs. "The technology required is very complex. There are still many issues to be resolved. But it's here. It's going to happen. Just look at Matt." This year four more volunteers will be added to the Braingate study, and researchers eventually hope to make the implant wireless. At the moment, Nagle can only use the BMI equipment a few times a week because it requires the help of technicians.

The researchers were fortunate to have selected the enormously resolute and optimistic Nagle as their first volunteer. Nagle had to spend months practicing intensively before the computers responded properly to his brain waves. And not only was there the real possibility that he might spend fruitless years involved in a failed experiment, but the brain implant also involved the risk of physical damage and psychiatric problems. "My mother was scared of what might happen, but what else can they do to me?" Nagle commented. "I was in a corner, and I had to come out fighting."

Earthlings Attack Comet

For the past 138 years, since its discovery in 1867, Comet Tempel 1 has had distant but harmonious relations with the inhabitants of planet Earth. But on July 4, somewhere between Mars and Jupiter, NASA's Deep Impact spacecraft blasted a gaping hole into the comet. The crash emitted the energy of 4.5 tons of TNT, releasing a tremendous plume of dust and gases. "There is a comet up in the sky wondering, what in the heck just happened," commented Charles Elachi, director of NASA's Jet Propulsion Laboratory. In an astonishingly tricky mission, Deep Impact traveled 268 million miles over six months to wreak havoc on the comet. According to NASA scientist Don Yeomans, "We hit it just exactly where we wanted to." More than 80 million people visited the NASA website in the 24 hours following the blast to witness the cosmic fireworks.

NASA assures us that there is, in fact, something scientifically redeemable about such violence. After our Sun and planets formed 4.6 billion years ago, comets were believed to have been formed out of the remaining dust and gases. By blasting a crater into the surface of Tempel 1 and uncovering its pristine interior, scientists hope to examine the primordial remnants of our solar system to gain insight into its formation. Some data is already available (for example, comets, once thought to resemble "dirty snowballs," are in fact more like "snowy dirtballs"), but it will take years until the more significant findings become available.

A Tenth Planet? Or Just Eight?

In recent years astronomers have discovered that our solar system is a great deal more crowded than we imagined. In 2004 alone, a dozen new moons circling Saturn were identified. Today's sophisticated telescopes have also uncovered a host of large objects inhabiting the frozen edges of our solar system—Varuna (2000), Ixion (2001), Quaoar (2002), and Sedna (2004) are among the most spectacular of what are called Kuiper Belt Objects (KBO), masses of rock and ice that appear beyond Neptune.

But just when we've grown accustomed, perhaps even a little jaded, by the steady parade of new moons and KBOs discovered each year, astronomers have succeeded in truly rattling our notion of the solar system: in July 2005 the California Institute of Technology and NASA announced the existence of a tenth planet. About 9 billion miles from the Sun resides 2003 UB313, estimated to be about one-and-a-half times the size of Pluto. "We are 100% confident that this is the first object bigger than Pluto ever found in the outer solar system," said Caltech astronomer Michael A. Brown, one of the three scientists responsible for the discovery.

The assertion of a tenth planet, however, is not without controversy, reviving the debate about what defines a planet and again calling into question whether the diminutive Pluto fits the bill. Some scientists consider the newly discovered object—along with Pluto—nothing more than a glorified Kuiper Belt Object. Alan Boss, a planet-formation theorist at the Carnegie Institution of Washington, contends that "to just call them planets does an injustice to the big guys in the solar system." But Brown maintains, "Pluto has been a planet for so long that the world is comfortable with that. It seems to me a logical extension that anything bigger than Pluto and farther out is a planet." When this long-standing controversy is finally resolved, it seems we will have either ten planets in our solar system, or just eight.

Given that 2003 UB313 is significantly larger than Pluto, why did it take so long to discover? According to Brown, its orbit lies 45 degrees from the plane on which the nine planets orbit the Sun, and until now "nobody look[ed] that high up in the sky." The object is so bright that even amateur astronomers can spot it fairly easily.

The object was first identified on Jan. 8, 2005, and Brown and his team had planned on announcing the discovery once they had accumulated more definitive data on the object's size, mass, and composition. But when someone hacked the team's website, threatening to preempt them, Brown and the others rushed to get the news out on July 29. Brown has already submitted a name for the planet to the International Astronomical Union, but he plans to keep it a secret until it is officially accepted. □

Major Discoveries About Human Ancestors

Living and extinct human beings and their near-human ancestors are called "hominids" and belong to the *Hominidae* family of primates. They should not be confused with "hominoids," which belong to the *Hominoidea* superfamily of primates and include apes and humans. Scientists theorize that the human and ape lines branched off from a common ancestor 8 million to 6 million years ago.

Years ago	Species	Discovered	Remarks
5.8–5.2 million	*Ardipithecus ramidus kadabba*	1997–1998 in Alayla, Ethiopia	May be oldest known human ancestor. About the size of modern chimpanzees, or 4 ft tall standing. May have walked upright
c. 4.4 million	*Ardipithecus ramidus ramidus*	1994 in Aramis, Ethiopia	Similar to *A. ramidus kadabba*
c. 4.2 million	*Australopithecus anamensis*	1995, two sites at Lake Turkana in Kenya: Kanapoi and Allia Bay	Possible ancestor of *A. afarensis* (Lucy). Walked upright
c. 3.2 million	*Australopithecus afarensis*	1974 at Hadar in the Afar triangle of eastern Ethiopia; Laetoli, Tanzania	Nicknamed "Lucy." Her skeleton was 3.5 ft (100 cm) tall. Had apelike skull. Walked fully upright. Lived in family groups throughout eastern Africa
c. 2.5 million	*Australopithecus africanus*	1924 at Taung, northern Cape Province, South Africa	Descendant of "Lucy." Lived in social groups
c. 2 million	*Australopithecus robustus*	1938 in Kromdraai, South Africa	Was related to *A. africanus*
c. 2 million	*Homo habilis* ("skillful" or "handy man")	1960 in Olduvai Gorge, Tanzania	First brain enlargement; is believed to have used stone tools
c. 1.8 million	*Homo erectus* ("upright man")	1891 at Trinil, Java, Indonesia	Brain size twice that of *australopithecine* species. "Java Man" may have been a direct ancestor of *Homo sapiens* or instead developed on a separate evolutionary track. He is the first hominid to use fire and the hand ax
c. 195,000	*Homo sapiens sapiens* ("knowing or wise man")	Discovered in 1964 (dated 2005) at Omo Kibish, Ethiopia	The Omo skull fossils are the oldest known anatomically modern humans

Scientific Classification

Classification, or taxonomy, is a system of categorizing living things. There are seven divisions in the system: (1) Kingdom; (2) Phylum or Division; (3) Class; (4) Order; (5) Family; (6) Genus; (7) Species.

Kingdom is the broadest division. While scientists currently disagree as to how many kingdoms there are, most support a five-kingdom (Animalia, Plantae, Protista, Monera, and Fungi) system. The lowest division is species, which consists of organisms that are capable of interbreeding to produce fertile offspring. Species are identified by two names (binomial nomenclature). The first name is the genus, the second is the species.

For example, a lion is *Panthera leo*, a tiger is *Panthera tigris*. The first word is always capitalized, the second is not, and both should be italicized. Humans, of course, are *Homo sapiens*. The full classification for a lion would be: Kingdom, Animalia (animals); Phylum, Chordata (vertebrate animals); Class, Mammalia (mammals); Order, Carnivora (meat eaters); Family, Felidae (all cats); Genus, Panthera (great cats); Species, leo (lions).

The Periodic Table

Although some elements, such as gold and iron, have been known to humans since prehistoric times, it wasn't until the 17th century that the first scientific discovery of an element (phosphorus) was made. Only 12 elements were known prior to 1700, but as more and more elements were discovered—by 1900 there were more than 80—scientists tried to find a way to organize them systematically, according to their physical and chemical properties.

Today, the periodic table (*see* next page) organizes the elements in horizontal rows, or periods, by order of increasing atomic number, which equals the number of protons in the atomic nucleus of each element. The elements are also organized in vertical columns, or groups, based on similar physical characteristics and chemical behavior. This arrangement developed side by side with atomic theory over about 200 years, and it continues to evolve as new elements are discovered.

Periodic Table of Elements

Notes: Elements 112, 113, 114, and 115 are under review. A temporary system of naming recommended by J. Chatt has been used above. 1. Mass number of the longest-lived isotope that is known. *Source:* International Union of Pure and Applied Chemistry (IUPAC). Web: http://www.chem.qmw.ac.uk/iupac/AtWt/.

The Elements

Elements are the building blocks of nature. Water, for example, is a compound consisting of the elements hydrogen and oxygen. Each element is a pure substance that cannot be split up into any simpler pure substance.

The smallest particle of an element that can exist is an atom. An atom consists of subatomic particles. The most important of these are protons, which have positive electrical charges; electrons, which have negative electrical charges; and neutrons, which are electrically neutral.

The atomic number of an element is the number of protons in one atom of the element. Each element

has a different atomic number. For example, the atomic numbers of hydrogen and oxygen are 1 and 8, respectively.

Elements with atomic numbers 1 (hydrogen) to 94 (plutonium) occur naturally on Earth. The remaining artificial elements have been created since 1940 by using nuclear reactors and particle accelerators. Element 100 is named fermium. Elements with atomic numbers 101 onward are known as the transfermium elements. They are also known as heavy elements because their atoms have very large masses compared with atoms of hydrogen, the lightest of all elements.

Chemical Elements

Element	Symbol	Atomic no.	Atomic wt.	Specific gravity	Melting point °C	Boiling point °C	No. of isotopes[1]	Discoverer	Year
Actinium	Ac	89	227[2]	10.07[3]	1051	3198	11	Debierne/Giesel	1899/1902
Aluminum	Al	13	26.981538	2.6989	660.32	2519	8	Wöhler	1827
Americium	Am	95	243[2]	13.67	1176	2011	13[4]	Seaborg et al.	1944
Antimony	Sb	51	121.76	6.61	630.63	1587	29	Early historic times	—
Argon	Ar	18	39.948	1.7837[5]	–189.35	–185.85	8	Rayleigh and Ramsay	1894
Arsenic (gray)	As	33	74.9216	5.73	817	603	14	Albertus Magnus	1250
Astatine	At	85	210[2]	—	302	—	21	Corson et al.	1940
Barium	Ba	56	137.327	3.5	727	1897	25	Davy	1808
Berkelium	Bk	97	247[2]	14.00[6]	1050 (α form)	—	8[4]	Seaborg et al.	1949
Beryllium	Be	4	9.012182	1.848	1287	2471	6	Vauquelin	1798
Bismuth	Bi	83	208.98038	9.747	271.40	1564	19	Geoffroy the Younger	1753
Bohrium	Bh	107	264[2]	—	—	—	—	Armbruster and Münzenberg	1981
Boron	B	5	10.811	2.37[7]	2075	4000	6	Gay-Lussac and Thénard; Davy	1808
Bromine	Br	35	79.904	3.12[5]	–7.2	58.8	19	Balard	1826
Cadmium	Cd	48	112.411	8.65	321.07	767	22	Stromeyer	1817
Calcium	Ca	20	40.078	1.55	842	1484	14	Davy	1808
Californium	Cf	98	251[2]	—	900	—	12[4]	Seaborg et al.	1950
Carbon	C	6	12.0107	1.8–3.5[8]	4492 (graphite)	3825	7	Prehistoric	—
Cerium	Ce	58	140.116	6.771	798	3443	19	Berzelius and Hisinger; Klaproth	1803
Cesium	Cs	55	132.90545	1.873	28.5	671	22	Bunsen and Kirchoff	1860
Chlorine	Cl	17	35.453	1.56[5]	–101.5	–34.04	11	Scheele	1774
Chromium	Cr	24	51.9961	7.18–7.20	1907	2671	9	Vauquelin	1797
Cobalt	Co	27	58.9332	8.9	1495	2927	14	Brandt	c.1735
Copper	Cu	29	63.546	8.96	1084.62	2562	11	Prehistoric	—
Curium	Cm	96	247[2]	13.51[3]	1345	3100	13[4]	Seaborg et al.	1944
Darmstadtium	Ds	110	281[2]	—	—	—	—	S. Hofmann et al.	1994
Dubnium	Db	105	262[2]	—	—	—	—	Ghiorso et al.	1970
Dysprosium	Dy	66	162.5	8.540	1412	2567	21	de Boisbaudran	1886
Einsteinium	Es	99	252[2]	—	860	—	12[4]	Ghiorso et al.	1952
Erbium	Er	68	167.259	9.045	1529	2868	16	Mosander	1843
Europium	Eu	63	151.964	5.283	822	1529	21	Demarcay	1901
Fermium	Fm	100	257[2]	—	1527	—	10[4]	Ghiorso et al.	1953
Fluorine	F	9	18.9984032	1.108[5]	–219.67	–188.12	6	Moissan	1886
Francium	Fr	87	223[2]	—	27	—	21	Perey	1939
Gadolinium	Gd	64	157.25	7.898	1313	3273	17	de Marignac	1880
Gallium	Ga	31	69.723	5.904	29.76	2204	14	de Boisbaudran	1875
Germanium	Ge	32	72.64	5.323	938.25	2833	17	Winkler	1886
Gold	Au	79	196.96655	19.32	1064.18	2856	21	Prehistoric	—
Hafnium	Hf	72	178.49	13.31	2233	4603	17	Coster and von Hevesy	1923
Hassium	Hs	108	277[2]	—	—	—	—	Armbruster and Münzenberg	1983
Helium	He	2	4.002602	0.1785[5]	–272.2	–268.934	5	Janssen	1868
Holmium	Ho	67	164.93032	8.781	1474	2700	29	Delafontäine and Soret	1878
Hydrogen	H	1	1.00794	0.070[5]	–259.34	–252.87	3	Cavendish	1766
Indium	In	49	114.818	7.31	156.60	2072	34	Reich and Richter	1863
Iodine	I	53	126.90447	4.93	113.7	184.4	24	Courtois	1811
Iridium	Ir	77	192.217	22.42	2446	4428	25	Tennant	1804
Iron	Fe	26	55.845	7.894	1538	2861	10	Prehistoric	—
Krypton	Kr	36	83.8	3.733[5]	–157.38	–153.22	23	Ramsay and Travers	1898
Lanthanum	La	57	138.9055	6.166	918	3464	19	Mosander	1839
Lawrencium	Lr	103	262[2]	—	1627	—	20[4]	Ghiorso et al.	1961
Lead	Pb	82	207.2	11.35	327.46	1749	29	Prehistoric	—

Element	Symbol	Atomic no.	Atomic wt.	Specific gravity	Melting point °C	Boiling point °C	No. of isotopes[1]	Discoverer	Year
Lithium	Li	3	6.941	0.534	180.50	1342	5	Arfvedson	1817
Lutetium	Lu	71	174.967	9.835	1663	3402	22	Urbain/ von Welsbach	1907
Magnesium	Mg	12	24.305	1.738	650	1090	8	Black	1755
Manganese	Mn	25	54.938049	7.21–7.44[9]	1246	2061	11	Gahn, Scheele, and Bergman	1774
Meitnerium	Mt	109	268[2]	—	—	—	—	GSI, Darmstadt, West Germany	1982
Mendelevium	Md	101	258[2]	—	827	—	3[4]	Ghiorso et al.	1955
Mercury	Hg	80	200.59	13.546	–38.83	356.73	26	Prehistoric	—
Molybdenum	Mo	42	95.94	10.22	2623	4639	20	Scheele	1778
Neodymium	Nd	60	144.24	6.80 & 7.004[10]	1021	3074	16	von Welsbach	1885
Neon	Ne	10	20.1797	0.89990 (g/10°C/1 atm)	–248.59	–246.08	8	Ramsay and Travers	1898
Neptunium	Np	93	237[2]	20.25	644		15[4]	McMillan and Abelson	1940
Nickel	Ni	28	58.6934	8.902	1455	2913	11	Cronstedt	1751
Niobium (Columbium)	Nb	41	92.90638	8.57	2477	4744	24	Hatchett	1801
Nitrogen	N	7	14.0067	0.808[5]	–210.00	–195.79	8	Rutherford	1772
Nobelium	No	102	259[2]	—	827	—	7[4]	Ghiorso et al.	1958
Osmium	Os	76	190.23	22.57	3033	5012	19	Tennant	1803
Oxygen	O	8	15.9994	1.14[5]	–218.79	–182.95	8	Priestley/Scheele	1774
Palladium	Pd	46	106.42	12.02	1554.9	2963	21	Wollaston	1803
Phosphorous (white)	P	15	30.973761	1.82	44.15	280.5	7	Brand	1669
Platinum	Pt	78	195.078	21.45	1768.4	3825	32	Ulloa/Wood	1735/1741
Plutonium	Pu	94	244[2]	19.84	640	3228	16[4]	Seaborg et al.	1940
Polonium	Po	84	209[2]	9.32	254	962	34	Curie	1898
Potassium	K	19	39.0983	0.862	63.5	759	10	Davy	1807
Praseodymium	Pr	59	140.90765	6.772	931	3520	15	von Welsbach	1885
Promethium	Pm	61	145[2]	—	1042	3000	14	Marinsky et al.	1945
Protactinium	Pa	91	231.03588	15.37[3]	1572	—	14	Hahn and Meitner	1917
Radium	Ra	88	226[2]	5.0?	700	—	15	Pierre and Marie Curie	1898
Radon	Rn	86	222[2]	4.4[5]	–71	–61.7	20	Dorn	1900
Rhenium	Re	75	186.207	21.02	3186	5596	21	Noddack, Berg, and Tacke	1925
Rhodium	Rh	45	102.9055	12.41	1964	3695	20	Wollaston	1803
Roentgenium[10]	Rg	111	272[2]	—	—	—	—	Hofmann et al.	1994
Rubidium	Rb	37	85.4678	1.532	39.30	688	20	Bunsen and Kirchoff	1861
Ruthenium	Ru	44	101.07	12.44	2334	4150	16	Klaus	1844
Rutherfordium	Rf	104	261[2]	—	—	—	—	Ghiorso et al.	1969
Samarium	Sm	62	150.36	7.536	1074	1794	17	Boisbaudran	1879
Scandium	Sc	21	44.95591	2.989	1541	2836	15	Nilson	1878
Seaborgium	Sg	106	266[2]	—	—	—	—	Ghiorso et al.	1974
Selenium (gray)	Se	34	78.96	4.79	220.5	685	20	Berzelius	1817
Silicon	Si	14	28.0855	2.33	1414	3265	8	Berzelius	1824
Silver	Ag	47	107.8682	10.5	961.78	2162	27	Prehistoric	—
Sodium	Na	11	22.98977	0.971	97.80	883	7	Davy	1807
Strontium	Sr	38	87.62	2.54	777	1382	18	Davy	1808
Sulfur	S	16	32.065	2.07[10]	95.3 (rhombic)	444.60	10	Prehistoric	—
Tantalum	Ta	73	180.9479	16.654	3017	5458	19	Ekeberg	1801
Technetium	Tc	43	98[2]	11.50[3]	2157	4265	23	Perrier and Segré	1937
Tellurium	Te	52	127.60	6.24	449.51	988	29	von Reichenstein	1782
Terbium	Tb	65	158.92534	8.234	1356	3230	24	Mosander	1843
Thallium	Tl	81	204.3833	11.85	304	1473	28	Crookes	1861
Thorium	Th	90	232.0381	11.72	1750	4788	12	Berzelius	1828
Thulium	Tm	69	168.93421	9.314	1545	1950	18	Cleve	1879
Tin (white)	Sn	50	118.71	7.31	231.93	2602	28	Prehistoric	—
Titanium	Ti	22	47.867	4.55	1668	3287	9	Gregor	1791
Tungsten	W	74	183.84	19.3	3422	5555	22	J. and F. d'Elhuyar	1783
Uranium	U	92	238.02891	19.05	1135	4131	15	Peligot	1841
Vanadium	V	23	50.9415	6.11	1910	3407	9	del Rio	1801
Xenon	Xe	54	131.293	3.52[5]	–111.79	–108.12	31	Ramsay and Travers	1898
Ytterbium	Yb	70	173.04	6.972	819	1196	16	Marignac	1878
Yttrium	Y	39	88.90585	4.457	1522	3345	21	Gadolin	1794
Zinc	Zn	30	65.39	7.133	419.5	907	15	Prehistoric	—
Zirconium	Zr	40	91.224	6.506[3]	1855	4409	20	Klaproth	1789

NOTES: Elements 112, 113, 114, 115, and 116 are under review and are thus not included. — means "approximately." < means "less than." 1. Isotopes are different forms of the same element having the same atomic number but different atomic weights. 2. Mass number of the longest-lived isotope that is known. 3. Calculated figure. 4. Artificially produced. 5. Liquid. 6. Estimated. 7. Amorphous. 8. Depending on whether amorphous, graphite, or diamond. 9. Depending on allotropic form. 10. In 2004, the International Union of Pure and Applied Chemistry named element 111 Roentgenium after the discoverer of x-rays, Wilhelm Roentgen.

Table of Geological Periods

It is generally assumed that planets are formed by the accretion of gas and dust in a cosmic cloud, but there is no way of estimating the length of this process. Our Earth acquired its present size, more or less, between 4 billion and 5 billion years ago. Life on Earth originated about 2 billion years ago, but there are no good fossil remains from periods earlier than the Cambrian, which began about 490 million years ago.

The known geological history of Earth since the Precambrian Time is subdivided into three eras, each of which includes a number of periods. They, in turn, are subdivided into epochs and stage ages.

In an epoch, a certain section may be especially well known because of rich fossil finds.

New Geological Period

In March 2004, geologists added a new time period to Earth's chronology—the Ediacaran Period. The Ediacaran Period lasted about 50 million years, from 600 million years ago to about 542 million years ago. It was the last period of the Precambrian's Neoproterozoic Era. Multicelled organisms first appeared during this time. This period is the first new one added in 120 years.

Precambrian Time

The Precambrian's lower limit is not defined, but ended about 542 million years ago. The Precambrian encompasses about 90% of the Earth's history.

Eonothem eon	Duration[1]	Eras	Events
Archaean (Greek *archaios* = ancient)	2,500?	Eoarchean (Greek *eos* = dawn + *archaios* = ancient) Paleoarchean (Greek *palaios* = old) Mesoarchean (Greek *mesos* = middle) Neoarchean (Greek *neo* = new)	Formation of oceans, atmosphere, and continents; bacteria
Proterozoic (Greek *proteros* = earlier + *zoön* = animal)	c. 2,000	Paleoproterozoic (Greek *palaios* = old) Mesoproterozoic (Greek *mesos* = middle) Neoproterozoic (Greek *neo* = new)	Oxygen build-up; multicelled organisms

1. In millions of years.

Paleozoic Era

This era began 542 million years ago and lasted about 291 million years. The name was compounded from Greek *palaios* (old) and *zoön* (animal).

Period	Duration[1]	Epochs	Events
Cambrian (*Cambria*, Latin name for Wales)	54	Lower Cambrian Middle Cambrian Upper Cambrian	Invertebrate sea life proliferating during this and the following period
Ordovician (Latin *Ordovices*, people of early Britain)	45	Lower Ordovician Upper Ordovician	Diverse marine life, including vertebrates; vascular plants
Silurian (Latin *Silures*, people of early Wales)	28	Lower Silurian Upper Silurian	Coral reefs; giant scorpions; first jawed fish
Devonian (Devonshire in England)	57	Lower Devonian Upper Devonian	Numerous fishes, other sea life; many plants, first trees; wingless insects
Carboniferous (Latin *carbo* = coal + *fero* = to bear)	60	Upper, Middle, and Lower Mississippian[2] Upper, Middle, and Lower Pennsylvanian[2]	Maximum coal formation in swampy forests; insects, amphibians, reptiles; fishes, clams, crustaceans
Permian (district of Perm in Russia)	48	Lower Permian Upper Permian	Large reptiles, amphibians; most species become extinct

1. In millions of years. 2. Mississippian and Pennsylvanian names are used only in the U.S.

Mesozoic Era

This era began 251 million years ago and lasted about 186 million years. The name was compounded from Greek *mesos* (middle) and *zoön* (animal). Popular name: Age of Reptiles.

Period	Duration[1]	Epochs	Events
Triassic (*trias* = triad)	51	Lower Triassic Middle Triassic Upper Triassic	Early dinosaurs, crocodiles, turtles; first mammals
Jurassic (Jura Mountains)	54	Lower Jurassic Middle Jurassic Upper Jurassic	Many seagoing reptiles; early large dinosaurs; later, flying reptiles (pterosaurs), earliest known birds
Cretaceous (Latin *creta* = chalk)	80	Lower Cretaceous Upper Cretaceous	Dinosaurs and other reptiles dominate; seed-bearing plants appear

1. In millions of years.

Cenozoic Era[1]

This era began 66 million years ago and includes the geological present. The name was compounded from Greek *kainos* (new) and *zoön* (animal). Popular name: Age of Mammals.

Period	Duration[2]	Epochs	Events
Paleogene (Greek *palaios* = old + *genes* = born)	42	Paleocene (Greek *palaios* = old + *kainos* = new). Eocene (Greek *eos* = dawn). Oligocene (Greek *oligos* = few).	Rich insect fauna, early bats, increasingly diverse varieties of mammals and birds
Neogene (Greek *neo* = new + *genes* = born)	23	Miocene (Greek *meios* = less + *kainos* = new). Pliocene (Greek *pleios* = more). Pleistocene (Greek *pleistos* = most) (popular name: Ice Age). Holocene (Greek *holos* = entire), the last 10,000 years to the present.	Further development of mammals and birds. Various forms of humans, including *Homo sapiens*

1. This table reflects the divisions used by the International Commission on Stratigraphy. The U.S. Geological Survey divides the Cenozoic Era into the Tertiary Period (with the Paleocene, Eocene, Oligocene, Miocene, and Pliocene Epochs) and the Quaternary Period (with the Pleistocene and Holocene Epochs). 2. In millions of years.

Branches of Science

Science describes an area of knowledge, typically about something in the physical world, that can be explained in terms of scientific observation or the scientific method. The scientific method is a discovery process that has evolved over several hundred years and can be summarized as follows:

- a phenomenon in the physical world is observed
- an explanation, or hypothesis, for the phenomenon is formed
- the hypothesis is tested by means of objective, reproducible experiments

If the results of the experiments support the hypothesis, it becomes accepted as scientific theory. Later, if new information is found to contradict the hypothesis, it may be revised or abandoned in favor of a new hypothesis, which is then subjected to additional experiments.

The sciences that describe the physical universe are categorized in different ways. The largest distinction in science is whether a science is pure, or theoretical, or whether it is applied, or practical. Pure science explains a phenomenon, while applied science determines how a particular phenomenon

may be put to use. In general, pure science is divided into the following categories:

- Physical sciences, which deal with matter and energy and allow us to describe the material universe in terms of weight, mass, volume, and other standard, objective measures.
- Earth sciences, which explain the phenomena of the Earth, its atmosphere, and the solar system to which it belongs.
- Life sciences, which describe living organisms, their internal processes, and their relationship to each other and the environment.

However, these three categories of pure science have areas of overlap, where one type of phenomenon may be associated with another. For example, light (studied in physics) is the energy source behind the (chemical) process of photosynthesis, or food production, in plants (studied in biology). For this reason, distinctions between pure sciences, and even between pure and applied sciences, can blur, and a new compound science can develop. An example of this is biochemistry, in which the chemical processes of living things (such as photosynthesis) are observed and explained.

Physical sciences	Life sciences	Earth sciences

Physics
  Kinetics
  Mechanics
  Electromagnetics
  Thermodynamics
	Biology
	  Botany
	  Zoology
		Geology
		Meteorology
		Astronomy

Chemistry
  Inorganic Chemistry
  Electrochemistry
  Analytical Chemistry		

Examples of Overlapping Sciences		

Physics + Chemistry =
  Physical Chemistry
	Biology + Chemistry =
	  Biochemistry
	  Organic Chemistry
		Geology + Chemistry =
		  Geochemistry

Astronomy + Physics =
  Astrophysics
	Biology + Geology =
	  Paleontology
		Geology + Astronomy =
		  Astrogeology

	Biology + Astronomy + Physics = Astronautics	

Inventions & Discoveries

See also Famous Firsts in Aviation, Nobel Prizes.

Adrenaline: (isolation of) John Jacob Abel, U.S., 1897.

Aerosol can: Erik Rotheim, Norway, 1926.

Air brake: George Westinghouse, U.S., 1868.

Air conditioning: Willis Carrier, U.S., 1911.

Airship: (non-rigid) Henri Giffard, France, 1852; (rigid) Ferdinand von Zeppelin, Germany, 1900.

Aluminum manufacture: (by electrolytic action) Charles M. Hall, U.S., 1866.

Anatomy, human: (*De fabrica corporis humani,* an illustrated systematic study of the human body) Andreas Vesalius, Belgium, 1543; (comparative: parts of an organism are correlated to the functioning whole) Georges Cuvier, France, 1799–1805.

Anesthetic: (first use of anesthetic—ether—on humans) Crawford W. Long, U.S., 1842.

Antibiotics: (first demonstration of antibiotic effect) Louis Pasteur, Jules-François Joubert, France, 1887; (discovery of penicillin, first modern antibiotic) Alexander Fleming, Scotland, 1928; (penicillin's infection-fighting properties) Howard Florey, Ernst Chain, England, 1940.

Antiseptic: (surgery) Joseph Lister, England, 1867.

Antitoxin, diphtheria: Emil von Behring, Germany, 1890.

Appliances, electric: (fan) Schuyler Wheeler, U.S., 1882; (flatiron) Henry W. Seely, U.S., 1882; (stove) Hadaway, U.S., 1896; (washing machine) Alva Fisher, U.S., 1906.

Aqualung: Jacques-Yves Cousteau, Emile Gagnan, France, 1943.

Aspirin: Dr. Felix Hoffman, Germany, 1899.

Astronomical calculator: The Antikythera device, Greece, first century B.C.. Found off island of Antikythera in 1900.

Atom: (nuclear model of) Ernest Rutherford, England, 1911.

Atomic structure: (formulated nuclear model of atom, Rutherford model) Ernest Rutherford, England, 1911; (proposed current concept of atomic structure, the Bohr model) Niels Bohr, Denmark, 1913.

Atomic theory: (ancient) Leucippus, Democritus, Greece, c. 500 B.C.; Lucretius, Rome c.100 B.C.; (modern) John Dalton, England, 1808.

Automobile: (first with internal combustion engine, 250 rpm) Karl Benz, Germany, 1885; (first with practical high-speed internal combustion engine, 900 rpm) Gottlieb Daimler, Germany, 1885; (first true automobile, not carriage with motor) René Panhard, Emile Lavassor, France, 1891; (carburetor, spray) Charles E. Duryea, U.S., 1892.

Autopilot: (for aircraft) Elmer A. Sperry, U.S., c.1910, first successful test, 1912, in a Curtiss flying boat.

Avogadro's law: (equal volumes of all gases at the same temperature and pressure contain equal number of molecules) Amedeo Avogadro, Italy, 1811.

Bacteria: Anton van Leeuwenhoek, The Netherlands, 1683.

Balloon, hot-air: Joseph and Jacques Montgolfier, France, 1783.

Barbed wire: (most popular) Joseph E. Glidden, U.S., 1873.

Bar codes (computer-scanned binary signal code): (retail trade use) Monarch Marking, U.S. 1970; (industrial use) Plessey Telecommunications, England, 1970.

Barometer: Evangelista Torricelli, Italy, 1643.

Bicycle: Karl D. von Sauerbronn, Germany, 1816; (first modern model) James Starley, England, 1884.

Big Bang theory: (the universe originated with a huge explosion) George LeMaitre, Belgium, 1927; (modified LeMaitre theory labeled "Big Bang") George A. Gamow,

---

Science Websites

National Science Foundation: www.nsf.gov
National Academy of Sciences: www.nas.edu
Science News Online: www.sciencenews.org
Popular Science: www.popsci.com
Periodic Table of Elements: www.infoplease.com/periodictable.php
Dinosauria Online: www.dinosauria.com
Discovery.com: www.discovery.com
Cosmology 101: http://map.gsfc.nasa.gov/m_uni.html
American Museum of Natural History: www.amnh.org
Newton (for K–12 teachers and students): www.newton.dep.anl.gov
Science Blog: www.scienceblog.com
The Smithsonian Web: www.si.edu
Scientific American: www.sciam.com

U.S., 1948; (cosmic microwave background radiation discovered, confirms theory) Arno A. Penzias and Robert W. Wilson, U.S., 1965.

Blood, circulation of: William Harvey, England, 1628.

Boyle's law: (relation between pressure and volume in gases) Robert Boyle, Ireland, 1662.

Braille: Louis Braille, France, 1829.

Bridges: (suspension, iron chains) James Finley, Pa., 1800; (wire suspension) Marc Seguin, Lyons, 1825; (truss) Ithiel Town, U.S., 1820.

Bullet: (conical) Claude Minié, France, 1849.

Calculating machine: (logarithms: made multiplying easier and thus calculators practical) John Napier, Scotland, 1614; (slide rule) William Oughtred, England, 1632; (digital calculator) Blaise Pascal, 1642; (multiplication machine) Gottfried Leibniz, Germany, 1671; (important 19th-century contributors to modern machine) Frank S. Baldwin, Jay R. Monroe, Dorr E. Felt, W. T. Ohdner, William Burroughs, all U.S.; ("analytical engine" design, included concepts of programming, taping) Charles Babbage, England, 1835.

Calculus: Isaac Newton, England, 1669; (differential calculus) Gottfried Leibniz, Germany, 1684.

Camera: (hand-held) George Eastman, U.S., 1888; (Polaroid Land) Edwin Land, U.S., 1948.

"Canals" of Mars: Giovanni Schiaparelli, Italy, 1877.

Carpet sweeper: Melville R. Bissell, U.S., 1876.

Car radio: William Lear, Elmer Wavering, U.S., 1929, manufactured by Galvin Manufacturing Co., "Motorola."

Cells: (word used to describe microscopic examination of cork) Robert Hooke, England, 1665; (theory: cells are common structural and functional unit of all living organisms) Theodor Schwann, Matthias Schleiden, 1838–1839.

Cement, Portland: Joseph Aspdin, England, 1824.

Chewing gum: (spruce-based) John Curtis, U.S., 1848; (chicle-based) Thomas Adams, U.S., 1870.

Cholera bacterium: Robert Koch, Germany, 1883.

Circuit, integrated: (theoretical) G.W.A. Dummer, England, 1952; (phase-shift oscillator) Jack S. Kilby, Texas Instruments, U.S., 1959.

Classification of plants: (first modern, based on comparative study of forms) Andrea Cesalpino, Italy, 1583; (classification of plants and animals by genera and species) Carolus Linnaeus, Sweden, 1737–1753.

Clock, pendulum: Christian Huygens, The Netherlands, 1656.

Coca-Cola: John Pemberton, U.S., 1886.

Combustion: (nature of) Antoine Lavoisier, France, 1777.

Compact disk: RCA, U.S., 1972.
Computers: (first design of analytical engine) Charles Babbage, 1830s; (ENIAC, Electronic Numerical Integrator and Calculator, first all-electronic, completed) John Presper Eckert, Jr., John Mauchly, U.S., 1945; (dedicated at University of Pennsylvania) 1946; (UNIVAC, Universal Automatic Computer, handled both numeric and alphabetic data) 1951; (personal computer) Steve Wozniak, U.S., 1976.
Concrete: (reinforced) Joseph Monier, France, 1877.
Condensed milk: Gail Borden, U.S., 1853.
Conditioned reflex: Ivan Pavlov, Russia, c.1910.
Conservation of electric charge: (the total electric charge of the universe or any closed system is constant) Benjamin Franklin, U.S., 1751–1754.
Contagion theory: (infectious diseases caused by living agent transmitted from person to person) Girolamo Fracastoro, Italy, 1546.
Continental drift theory: (geographer who pieced together continents into a single landmass on maps) Antonio Snider-Pellegrini, France, 1858; (first proposed in lecture) Frank Taylor, U.S. 1912; (first comprehensive detailed theory) Alfred Wegener, Germany, 1912.
Contraceptive, oral: Gregory Pincus, Min Chuch Chang, John Rock, Carl Djerassi, U.S., 1951.
Converter, Bessemer: William Kelly, U.S., 1851.
Cosmetics: Egypt, c. 4000 B.C.
Cosmic string theory: (first postulated) Thomas Kibble, UK, 1976.
Cotton gin: Eli Whitney, U.S., 1793.
Crossbow: China, c. 300 B.C.
Cyclotron: Ernest O. Lawrence, U.S., 1931.
Defibrillator: Dr. William Bennett Kouwenhoven, U.S., 1932; (implantable) M. Stephen Heilman, MD, Dr. Alois Langer, Morton Mower, MD, Michel Mirowski, MD, 1980.
Deuterium: (heavy hydrogen) Harold Urey, U.S., 1931.
Disease: (chemicals in treatment of) crusaded by Philippus Paracelsus, 1527–1541; (germ theory) Louis Pasteur, France, 1862–1877.
DNA: (deoxyribonucleic acid) Friedrich Meischer, Germany, 1869; (determination of double-helical structure) F. H. Crick, England and James D. Watson, U.S., 1953.
Dye: (aniline, start of synthetic dye industry) William H. Perkin, England, 1856.
Dynamite: Alfred Nobel, Sweden, 1867.
Electric cooking utensil: (first) patented by St. George Lane-Fox, England, 1874.
Electric generator (dynamo): (laboratory model) Michael Faraday, England, 1832; Joseph Henry, U.S., c.1832; (hand-driven model) Hippolyte Pixii, France, 1833; (alternating-current generator) Nikola Tesla, U.S., 1892.
Electric lamp: (arc lamp) Sir Humphrey Davy, England, 1801; (fluorescent lamp) A.E. Becquerel, France, 1867; (incandescent lamp) Sir Joseph Swann, England, Thomas A. Edison, U.S., contemporaneously, 1870s; (carbon arc street lamp) Charles F. Brush, U.S., 1879; (first widely marketed incandescent lamp) Thomas A. Edison, U.S., 1879; (mercury vapor lamp) Peter Cooper Hewitt, U.S., 1903; (neon lamp) Georges Claude, France, 1911; (tungsten filament) Irving Langmuir, U.S., 1915.
Electrocardiography: Demonstrated by Augustus Waller, Switzerland, 1887; (first practical device for recording activity of heart) Willem Einthoven, 1903, Netherlands.
Electromagnet: William Sturgeon, England, 1823.
Electron: Sir Joseph J. Thompson, England, 1897.
Electronic mail: Ray Tomlinson, U.S., 1972.
Elevator, passenger: (safety device permitting use by passengers) Elisha G. Otis, U.S., 1852; (elevator utilizing safety device) 1857.
E = mc²: (equivalence of mass and energy) Albert Einstein, Switzerland, 1907.

Thomas Alva Edison (1847–1931)
Library of Congress

Engine, internal combustion: No single inventor. Fundamental theory established by Sadi Carnot, France, 1824; (two-stroke) Etienne Lenoir, France, 1860; (ideal operating cycle for four-stroke) Alphonse Beau de Roche, France, 1862; (operating four-stroke) Nikolaus Otto, Germany, 1876; (diesel) Rudolf Diesel, Germany, 1892; (rotary) Felix Wankel, Germany, 1956.
Evolution: (organic) Jean-Baptiste Lamarck, France, 1809; (by natural selection) Charles Darwin, England, 1859.
Exclusion principle: (no two electrons in an atom can occupy the same energy level) Wolfgang Pauli, Germany, 1925.
Expanding universe theory: (first proposed) George LeMaitre, Belgium, 1927; (discovered first direct evidence that the universe is expanding) Edwin P. Hubble, U.S., 1929; (Hubble constant: a measure of the rate at which the universe is expanding) Edwin P. Hubble, U.S., 1929.
Falling bodies, law of: Galileo Galilei, Italy, 1590.
Fermentation: (microorganisms as cause of) Louis Pasteur, France, 1872.
Fiber optics: Narinder Kapany, England, 1955.
Fibers, man-made: (nitrocellulose fibers treated to change flammable nitrocellulose to harmless cellulose, precursor of rayon) Sir Joseph Swann, England, 1883; (rayon) Count Hilaire de Chardonnet, France, 1889; (Celanese) Henry and Camille Dreyfuss, U.S., England, 1921; (research on polyesters and polyamides, basis for modern man-made fibers) U.S., England, Germany, 1930s; (nylon) Wallace H. Carothers, U.S., 1935.
Frozen food: Clarence Birdseye, U.S., 1924.
Gene transfer: (recombinant DNA organism) Herbert Boyer, Stanley Cohen, U.S., 1973; (human) Steven Rosenberg, R. Michael Blaese, W. French Anderson, U.S., 1989.
Geometry, elements of: Euclid, Alexandria, Egypt, c. 300 B.C.; (analytic) René Descartes, France; and Pierre de Fermat, Switzerland, 1637.
Gravitation, law of: Sir Isaac Newton, England, c.1665 (published 1687).
Gunpowder: China, c.700.
Gyrocompass: Elmer A. Sperry, U.S., 1905.
Gyroscope: Jean Léon Foucault, France, 1852.
Halley's Comet: Edmund Halley, England, 1705.
Heart implanted in human, permanent artificial: Dr. Robert Jarvik, U.S., 1982.
Heart, temporary artificial: Willem Kolff, Netherlands, U.S., 1957.
Helicopter: (double rotor) Heinrich Focke, Germany, 1936; (single rotor) Igor Sikorsky, U.S., 1939.
Helium first observed on sun: Sir Joseph Lockyer, England, 1868.
Heredity, laws of: Gregor Mendel, Austria, 1865.
Holograph: Dennis Gabor, England, 1947.

Home videotape systems (VCR): (Betamax) Sony, Japan, 1975; (VHS) Matsushita, Japan, 1975.
Ice age theory: Louis Agassiz, Swiss-American, 1840.
Induction, electric: Joseph Henry, U.S., 1828.
Insulin: (first isolated) Sir Frederick G. Banting and Charles H. Best, Canada, 1921; (discovery first published) Banting and Best, 1922; (Nobel Prize awarded for purification for use in humans) John Macleod and Banting, 1923; (first synthesized), China, 1966.
Intelligence testing: Alfred Binet, Theodore Simon, France, 1905.
Interferon: Alick Isaacs, England, Jean Lindemann, Switzerland, 1957.
Isotopes: (concept of) Frederick Soddy, England, 1912; (stable isotopes) J. J. Thompson, England, 1913; (existence demonstrated by mass spectrography) Francis W. Aston, England, 1919.
Jet propulsion: (engine) Sir Frank Whittle, England, Hans von Ohain, Germany, 1936; (aircraft) *Heinkel He 178,* 1939.
Kinetic theory of gases: (molecules of a gas are in a state of rapid motion) Daniel Bernoulli, Switzerland, 1738.
Laser: (theoretical work on) Charles H. Townes, Arthur L. Schawlow, U.S., N. Basov, A. Prokhorov, U.S.S.R., 1958; (first working model) T. H. Maiman, U.S., 1960.
Lawn mower: Edwin Budding, John Ferrabee, England, 1830–1831.
LCD (liquid crystal display): Hoffmann-La Roche, Switzerland, 1970.
Lens, bifocal: Benjamin Franklin, U.S., c.1760.
Leyden jar: (prototype electrical condenser) Canon E. G. von Kleist of Kamin, Pomerania, 1745; independently evolved by Cunaeus and P. van Musschenbroek, University of Leyden, Holland, 1746, from where name originated.
Light, nature of: (wave theory) Christian Huygens, The Netherlands, 1678; (electromagnetic theory) James Clerk Maxwell, England, 1873.
Light, speed of: (theory that light has finite velocity) Olaus Roemer, Denmark, 1675.
Lightning rod: Benjamin Franklin, U.S., 1752.
Lock, cylinder: Linus Yale, U.S., 1851.
Locomotive:
(steam powered) Richard Trevithick, England, 1804; (first practical, due to multiple-fire-tube boiler) George Stephenson, England, 1829; (largest steam-powered) Union Pacific's "Big Boy," U.S., 1941.

Benjamin Franklin (1706–1790)

Loom: (horizontal, two-beamed) Egypt, c. 4400 B.C.; (Jacquard drawloom, pattern controlled by punch cards) Jacques de Vaucanson, France, 1745, Joseph-Marie Jacquard, 1801; (flying shuttle) John Kay, England, 1733; (power-driven loom) Edmund Cartwright, England, 1785.
Machine gun: (hand-cranked multibarrel) Richard J. Gatling, U.S., 1862; (practical single barrel, belt-fed) Hiram S. Maxim, Anglo-American, 1884.
Magnet, Earth is: William Gilbert, England, 1600.

Match: (phosphorus) François Derosne, France, 1816; (friction) Charles Sauria, France, 1831; (safety) J. E. Lundstrom, Sweden, 1855.
Measles vaccine: John F. Enders, Thomas Peebles, U.S., 1953.
Metric system: revolutionary government of France, 1790–1801.
Microphone: Charles Wheatstone, England, 1827.
Microscope: (compound) Zacharias Janssen, The Netherlands, 1590; (electron) Vladimir Zworykin et al., U.S., Canada, Germany, 1932–1939.
Microwave oven: Percy Spencer, U.S., 1947.
Motion, laws of: Isaac Newton, England, 1687.
Motion pictures: Thomas A. Edison, U.S., 1893.
Motion pictures, sound: Product of various inventions. First picture with synchronized musical score: *Don Juan,* 1926; with spoken dialogue: *The Jazz Singer,* 1927; both Warner Bros.
Motor, electric: Michael Faraday, England, 1822; (alternating-current) Nikola Tesla, U.S., 1892.
Motorcycle: (motor tricycle) Edward Butler, England, 1884; (gasoline-engine motorcycle) Gottlieb Daimler, Germany, 1885.
Moving assembly line: Henry Ford, U.S., 1913.
Neptune: (discovery of) Johann Galle, Germany, 1846.
Neptunium: (first transuranic element, synthesis of) Edward M. McMillan, Philip H. Abelson, U.S., 1940.
Neutron: James Chadwick, England, 1932.
Neutron-induced radiation: Enrico Fermi et al., Italy, 1934.
Nitroglycerin: Ascanio Sobrero, Italy, 1846.
Nuclear fission: Otto Hahn, Fritz Strassmann, Germany, 1938.
Nuclear reactor: Enrico Fermi, Italy, et al., 1942.
Ohm's law: (relationship between strength of electric current, electromotive force, and circuit resistance) Georg S. Ohm, Germany, 1827.
Oil well: Edwin L. Drake, U.S., 1859.
Oxygen: (isolation of) Joseph Priestley, England, 1774; Karl Scheele, Sweden, 1773.
Ozone: Christian Schönbein, Germany, 1839.
Pacemaker: (internal) Clarence W. Lillehie, Earl Bakk, U.S., 1957.
Paper: China, c.100 A.D.
Parachute: Louis S. Lenormand, France, 1783.
Pen: (fountain) Lewis E. Waterman, U.S., 1884; (ball-point, for marking on rough surfaces) John H. Loud, U.S., 1888; (ball-point, for handwriting) Lazlo Biro, Argentina, 1944.
Periodic law: (that properties of elements are functions of their atomic weights) Dmitri Mendeleev, Russia, 1869.
Periodic table: (arrangement of chemical elements based on periodic law) Dmitri Mendeleev, Russia, 1869.
Phonograph: Thomas A. Edison, U.S., 1877.
Photography: (first paper negative, first photograph, on metal) Joseph Nicéphore Niepce, France, 1816–1827; (discovery of fixative powers of hyposulfite of soda) Sir John Herschel, England, 1819; (first direct positive image on silver plate, the daguerreotype) Louis Daguerre, based on work with Niepce, France, 1839; (first paper negative from which a number of positive prints could be made) William Talbot, England, 1841. Work of these four men, taken together, forms basis for all modern photography. (First color images) Alexandre Becquerel, Claude Niepce de Saint-Victor, France, 1848–1860; (commercial color film with three emulsion layers, Kodachrome) U.S., 1935.
Photovoltaic effect: (light falling on certain materials can produce electricity) Edmund Becquerel, France, 1839.
Piano: (Hammerklavier) Bartolommeo Cristofori, Italy, 1709; (pianoforte with sustaining and damper pedals) John Broadwood, England, 1873.

Planetary motion, laws of: Johannes Kepler, Germany, 1609, 1619.

Plant respiration and photosynthesis: Jan Ingenhousz, Holland, 1779.

Plastics: (first material, nitrocellulose softened by vegetable oil, camphor, precursor to Celluloid) Alexander Parkes, England, 1855; (Celluloid, involving recognition of vital effect of camphor) John W. Hyatt, U.S., 1869; (Bakelite, first completely synthetic plastic) Leo H. Baekeland, U.S., 1910; (theoretical background of macromolecules and process of polymerization on which modern plastics industry rests) Hermann Staudinger, Germany, 1922; (polypropylene and low-pressure method for producing high-density polyethylene) Robert Banks, Paul Hogan, U.S., 1958.

Plate tectonics: Alfred Wegener, Germany, 1912–1915.

Plow, forked: Mesopotamia, before 3000 B.C.

Plutonium, synthesis of: Glenn T. Seaborg, Edwin M. McMillan, Arthur C. Wahl, Joseph W. Kennedy, U.S., 1941.

Polio, vaccine: (experimentally safe dead-virus vaccine) Jonas E. Salk, U.S., 1952; (effective large-scale field trials) 1954; (officially approved) 1955; (safe oral live-virus vaccine developed) Albert B. Sabin, U.S., 1954; (available in the U.S.) 1960.

Johann Gutenberg (c. 1400–1468)

Positron: Carl D. Anderson, U.S., 1932.

Pressure cooker: (early version) Denis Papin, France, 1679.

Printing: (block) Japan, c.700; (movable type) Korea, c.1400; Johann Gutenberg, Germany, c.1450; (lithography, offset) Aloys Senefelder, Germany, 1796; (rotary press) Richard Hoe, U.S., 1844; (linotype) Ottmar Mergenthaler, U.S., 1884.

Probability theory: René Descartes, France, and Pierre de Fermat, Switzerland, 1654.

Proton: Ernest Rutherford, England, 1919.

Prozac: (antidepressant fluoxetine) Bryan B. Malloy, Scotland, and Klaus K. Schmiegel, U.S., 1972; (released for use in U.S.) Eli Lilly & Company, 1987.

Psychoanalysis: Sigmund Freud, Austria, c.1904.

Pulsars: Antony Hewish and Jocelyn Bell Burnel, England, 1967.

Quantum theory: (general) Max Planck, Germany, 1900; (sub-atomic) Niels Bohr, Denmark, 1913; (quantum mechanics) Werner Heisenberg, Erwin Schrödinger, Germany, 1925.

Quarks: Jerome Friedman, Henry Kendall, Richard Taylor, U.S., 1967.

Quasars: Marten Schmidt, U.S., 1963.

Rabies immunization: Louis Pasteur, France, 1885.

Radar: (limited to one-mile range) Christian Hulsmeyer, Germany, 1904; (pulse modulation, used for measuring height of ionosphere) Gregory Breit, Merle Tuve, U.S., 1925; (first practical radar—radio detection and ranging) Sir Robert Watson-Watt, England, 1934–1935.

Radio: (electromagnetism, theory of) James Clerk Maxwell, England, 1873; (spark coil, generator of electromagnetic waves) Heinrich Hertz, Germany, 1886; (first practical system of wireless telegraphy) Guglielmo Marconi, Italy, 1895; (first long-distance telegraphic radio signal sent across the Atlantic) Marconi, 1901; (vacuum electron tube, basis for radio telephony) Sir John Fleming, England, 1904; (triode amplifying tube) Lee de Forest, U.S., 1906; (regenerative circuit, allowing long-distance sound reception) Edwin H. Armstrong, U.S., 1912; (frequency modulation—FM) Edwin H. Armstrong, U.S., 1933.

Radioactivity: (X-rays) Wilhelm K. Roentgen, Germany, 1895; (radioactivity of uranium) Henri Becquerel, France, 1896; (radioactive elements, radium and polonium in uranium ore) Marie Sklodowska-Curie, Pierre Curie, France, 1898; (classification of alpha and beta particle radiation) Pierre Curie, France, 1900; (gamma radiation) Paul-Ulrich Villard, France, 1900.

Radiocarbon dating, carbon-14 method: (discovered) Willard F. Libby, U.S., 1947; (first demonstrated) U.S., 1950.

Radio signals, extraterrestrial: first known radio noise signals were received by U.S. engineer, Karl Jansky, originating from the Galactic Center, 1931.

Radio waves: (cosmic sources, led to radio astronomy) Karl Jansky, U.S., 1932.

Razor: (safety, successfully marketed) King Gillette, U.S., 1901; (electric) Jacob Schick, U.S., 1928, 1931.

Reaper: Cyrus McCormick, U.S., 1834.

Refrigerator: Alexander Twining, U.S., James Harrison, Australia, 1850; (first with a compressor device) the Domelse, Chicago, U.S., 1913.

Refrigerator ship: (first) the *Frigorifique,* cooling unit designed by Charles Teller, France, 1877.

Relativity: (special and general theories of) Albert Einstein, Switzerland, Germany, U.S., 1905–1953.

Revolver: Samuel Colt, U.S., 1835.

Richter scale: Charles F. Richter, U.S., 1935.

Rifle: (muzzle-loaded) Italy, Germany, c.1475; (breech-loaded) England, France, Germany, U.S., c.1866; (bolt-action) Paul von Mauser, Germany, 1889; (automatic) John Browning, U.S., 1918.

Rocket: (liquid-fueled) Robert Goddard, U.S., 1926.

Roller bearing: (wooden for cartwheel) Germany or France, c.100 B.C.

Rotation of Earth: Jean Bernard Foucault, France, 1851.

Royal Observatory, Greenwich: established in 1675 by Charles II of England; John Flamsteed first Astronomer Royal.

Rubber: (vulcanization process) Charles Goodyear, U.S., 1839.

Saccharin: Constantine Fuhlberg, Ira Remsen, U.S., 1879.

Safety pin: Walter Hunt, U.S., 1849.

Saturn, ring around: Christian Huygens, The Netherlands, 1659.

"Scotch" tape: Richard Drew, U.S., 1929.

Screw propeller: Sir Francis P. Smith, England, 1836; John Ericsson, England, worked independently of and simultaneously with Smith, 1837.

Seat belt: (three point) Nils Bohlin, Sweden, 1962.

Seismograph: (first accurate) John Milne, England, 1880.

Sewing machine: Elias Howe, U.S., 1846; (continuous stitch) Isaac Singer, U.S., 1851.

Solar energy: First realistic application of solar energy using parabolic solar reflector to drive caloric engine on steam boiler, John Ericsson, U.S., 1860s.

Solar system, universe: (Sun-centered universe) Nicolaus Copernicus, Warsaw, 1543; (establishment of planetary orbits as elliptical) Johannes Kepler, Germany, 1609; (infinity of universe) Giordano Bruno, Italian monk, 1584.

Spectrum: (heterogeneity of light) Sir Isaac Newton, England, 1665–1666.

Spectrum analysis: Gustav Kirchhoff, Robert Bunsen, Germany, 1859.

Spermatozoa: Anton van Leeuwenhoek, The Netherlands, 1683.

Spinning: (spinning wheel) India, introduced to Europe in Middle Ages; (Saxony wheel, continuous spinning of wool or cotton yarn) England, c.1500–1600; (spinning jenny) James Hargreaves, England, 1764; (spinning frame) Sir Richard Arkwright, England, 1769; (spinning mule, completed mechanization of spinning, permitting production of yarn to keep up with demands of modern looms) Samuel Crompton, England, 1779.

Star catalog: (first modern) Tycho Brahe, Denmark, 1572.

Steam engine: (first commercial version based on principles of French physicist Denis Papin) Thomas Savery, England, 1639; (atmospheric steam engine) Thomas Newcomen, England, 1705; (steam engine for pumping water from collieries) Savery, Newcomen, 1725; (modern condensing, double acting) James Watt, England, 1782; (high-pressure) Oliver Evans, U.S., 1804.

Steamship: Claude de Jouffroy d'Abbans, France, 1783; James Rumsey, U.S., 1787; John Fitch, U.S., 1790; (high-pressure) Oliver Evans, U.S., 1804. All preceded Robert Fulton, U.S., 1807, credited with launching first commercially successful steamship.

Stethoscope: René Laënnec, France, 1819.

Sulfa drugs: (parent compound, para-aminobenzene-sulfanomide) Paul Gelmo, Austria, 1908; (antibacterial activity) Gerhard Domagk, Germany, 1935.

Superconductivity: (theory) John Bardeen, Leon Cooper, John Scheiffer, U.S., 1957.

Symbolic logic: George Boule, 1854; (modern) Bertrand Russell, Alfred North Whitehead, England, 1910–1913.

Samuel F. B. Morse (1791–1872)
Library of Congress

Tank, military: Sir Ernest Swinton, England, 1914.

Tape recorder: (magnetic steel tape) Valdemar Poulsen, Denmark, 1899.

Teflon: DuPont, U.S., 1943.

Telegraph: Samuel F. B. Morse, U.S., 1837.

Telephone: Alexander Graham Bell, U.S., 1876.

Telescope: Hans Lippershey, The Netherlands, 1608; (astronomical) Galileo Galilei, Italy, 1609; (reflecting) Isaac Newton, England, 1668.

Television: (Iconoscope–T.V. camera table) Vladimir Zworykin, U.S., 1923, and also kinescope (cathode ray tube) 1928; (mechanical disk-scanning method) successfully demonstrated by J.L. Baird, Scotland, C.F. Jenkins, U.S., 1926; (first all-electric television image) Philo T. Farnsworth, U.S., 1927; (color, mechanical disk) Baird, 1928; (color, compatible with black and white) George Valensi, France, 1938; (color, sequential rotating filter) Peter Goldmark, U.S., first introduced,

1951; (color, compatible with black and white) commercially introduced in U.S., National Television Systems Committee, 1953.

Thermodynamics: (first law: energy cannot be created or destroyed, only converted from one form to another) Julius von Mayer, Germany, 1842; James Joule, England, 1843; (second law: heat cannot of itself pass from a colder to a warmer body) Rudolph Clausius, Germany, 1850; (third law: the entropy of ordered solids reaches zero at the absolute zero of temperature) Walter Nernst, Germany, 1918.

Thermometer: (open-column) Galileo Galilei, c.1593; (clinical) Santorio Santorio, Padua, c.1615; (mercury, also Fahrenheit scale) Gabriel D. Fahrenheit, Germany, 1714; (centigrade scale) Anders Celsius, Sweden, 1742; (absolute-temperature, or Kelvin, scale) William Thompson, Lord Kelvin, England, 1848.

Tire, pneumatic: Robert W. Thompson, England, 1845; (bicycle tire) John B. Dunlop, Northern Ireland, 1888.

Toilet, flush: Product of Minoan civilization, Crete, c. 2000 B.C. Alleged invention by "Thomas Crapper" is untrue.

Tractor: Benjamin Holt, U.S., 1900.

Transformer, electric: William Stanley, U.S., 1885.

Transistor: John Bardeen, Walter H. Brattain, William B. Shockley, U.S., 1947.

Tuberculosis bacterium: Robert Koch, Germany, 1882.

Typewriter: Christopher Sholes, Carlos Glidden, U.S., 1867.

Uncertainty principle: (that position and velocity of an object cannot both be measured exactly, at the same time) Werner Heisenberg, Germany, 1927.

Uranus: (first planet discovered in recorded history) William Herschel, England, 1781.

Vaccination: Edward Jenner, England, 1796.

Vacuum cleaner: (manually operated) Ives W. McGaffey, U.S., 1869; (electric) Hubert C. Booth, England, 1901; (upright) J. Murray Spangler, U.S., 1907.

Van Allen (radiation) Belt: (around Earth) James Van Allen, U.S., 1958.

Video disk: Philips Co., The Netherlands, 1972.

Vitamins: (hypothesis of disease deficiency) Sir F. G. Hopkins, Casimir Funk, England, 1912; (vitamin A) Elmer V. McCollum, M. Davis, U.S., 1912–1914; (vitamin B) McCollum, U.S., 1915–1916; (thiamin, B_1) Casimir Funk, England, 1912; (riboflavin, B_2) D. T. Smith, E. G. Hendrick, U.S., 1926; (niacin) Conrad Elvehjem, U.S., 1937; (B_6) Paul Gyorgy, U.S., 1934; (vitamin C) C. A. Hoist, T. Froelich, Norway, 1912; (vitamin D) McCollum, U.S., 1922; (folic acid) Lucy Wills, England, 1933.

Voltaic pile: (forerunner of modern battery, first source of continuous electric current) Alessandro Volta, Italy, 1800.

Wallpaper: Europe, 16th and 17th century.

Wassermann test: (for syphilis) August von Wassermann, Germany, 1906.

Wheel: (cart, solid wood) Mesopotamia, c.3800–3600 B.C.

Windmill: Persia, c.600.

World Wide Web: (developed while working at CERN) Tim Berners-Lee, England, 1989; (development of Mosaic browser makes WWW available for general use) Marc Andreeson, U.S., 1993.

Xerography: Chester Carlson, U.S., 1938.

Yellow Fever: (transmission of) Walter Reed, U.S., 1900.

Zero: India, c. 600; (absolute zero temperature, cessation of all molecular energy) William Thompson, Lord Kelvin, England, 1848.

Zipper: W. L. Judson, U.S., 1891.

The National Inventors Hall of Fame

The National Inventors Hall of Fame, established in 1973 and located in Akron, Ohio, honors the women and men responsible for the great technological advances that make human, social, and economic progress possible. The Class of 2005 inductees have made accomplishments in medicine, engineering, computing, and more.

Matthias Baldwin, 1795–1866, *Steam Locomotive.* Baldwin was the first American to build steam locomotives of the same quality as were made in Europe. His "Old Ironsides" was the first locomotive to carry passengers. He later invented a series of improvements, including a powerful high-pressure steam engine.

C. Donald Bateman, 1932–, *Ground Proximity Warning System (GPWS).* In response to tragic airline crashes during the 1960s, Bateman invented a device that automatically warned pilots if their aircraft was approaching the ground or water.

Clarence Birdseye, 1886–1956, *Food Preservation.* During an expedition to Labrador, a young Birdseye observed native fishermen freezing their catch. He later observed that rapid freezing retained close to the original flavor and texture. Birdseye is credited with increasing the quality of the American diet by providing high quality foods for long-term preservation without drying, pickling, or canning.

Leopold Godowsky, Jr., 1900–1983, and **Leopold Mannes,** 1893–1964, *Color Film.* The duo affectionately known by colleagues and friends as "God and Man" were professional musicians who enjoyed photography as a hobby. In 1916 they started experimenting with color images by taking multiple black-and-white exposures through filters of various colors. They eventually invented a practical, high-quality color film released as Kodachrome film in 1936.

Robert Gundlach, 1926–, *Photocopying.* Gundlach devoted over three decades to transforming photocopiers into small, robust products that revolutionized xerography. As the field advanced, Gundlach invented ways to produce color copies and use digital technology. He has earned more than 150 patents; while most are related to xerography, they also include a snow-making machine, a comfortable backpack, and a water-based heat pump system.

Alec Jeffreys, 1950–, *Genetic Fingerprinting.* Jeffreys discovered a process that detects extremely variable DNA regions, enabling genetic fingerprinting. This made it possible to conclusively link suspects to the scene of a crime based on samples of blood, semen, skin, or hair. It also exonerated numerous people falsely convicted before genetic fingerprinting was invented.

Dean Kamen, 1951–, *Medication Infusion Pumps.* Kamen's first major innovation was the AutoSyringe, a wearable device that delivered precise doses of medication to diabetics and other patients with a variety of medical conditions. This gave patients greater freedom and control over their disease, dramatically improving their quality of life while reducing complications and painful daily injections. Among Kamen's other inventions are a portable peritoneal dialysis machine and the IBOT, a sophisticated wheelchair capable of climbing stairs.

Garrett Morgan, 1877–1963, *Safety Hood, Traffic Light.* Morgan's first well-known invention was the safety hood, a forerunner of the gas mask. When 32 workers in Cleveland, Ohio, were trapped during a tunnel collapse in 1916, Morgan and several volunteers using the masks were able to reach the trapped men and rescue several survivors. In 1923, Morgan patented his best-known invention, the three-way traffic signal, based on signs that signaled stop and go. He sold his patent rights to General Electric, which developed an electrical version.

Les Paul, 1915–, *Electric Guitar, Multi-Track Recording.* Paul's innovations led to his first solid-body electric guitar in 1946. He produced a series of extremely popular recordings—using advanced multi-track tape recorders he designed and built himself—that introduced the public to fast, multi-layered productions, in which he played as many as six musical parts simultaneously. Les Paul's work inspired a generation of musicians to embrace his guitar and recording techniques.

Jacob Rabinow, 1910–1999, *Optical Character Recognition (OCR).* Rabinow invented a process that allowed machine scanners to determine which letters or numbers were printed on a page. Over the years he crafted a series of improvements that made the process more reliable, eventually incorporating dictionaries into computer memories so the machines could determine the identity of a smudged or messy character.

Glenn T. Seaborg, 1912–1999, *Atomic Technology.* The nuclear chemist's best-known achievement was the synthesis and isolation of the radioactive element plutonium. He pioneered the creation of new exotic isotopes and elements by bombarding materials with atomic particles in particle accelerators, many of which his research team helped design. He was one of the most important participants in the Manhattan Project, which developed the atomic bomb during World War II.

Leo Sternbach, 1908–, *Benzodiazepines.* With the assistance of Lowell Randall and Earl Reeder, he discovered a new class of drugs, called benzodiazepines. Librium (1960) and Valium (1963), the first two drugs from this class, proved to be more effective at reducing stress and anxiety than previous tranquilizers, and had fewer side effects. Their success prompted further research, and several variants were developed, including Versed, Klonopin, Dalmane, Lexotan, Atavan, and Xanax.

Selman Waksman, 1888–1973, *Streptomycin.* A pioneer in microbiology, Waksman specialized in the study of microbes in soil. His most important find, streptomycin, provided the first effective treatment for tuberculosis, a disease that had ravaged mankind. Previously, tuberculosis victims were kept in sanitaria where their main treatment was fresh air and a healthy diet. Waksman's success inspired others to research antibiotics.

The 2005 Environmental Sustainability Index (ESI)

The ESI is a composite index tracking 21 indicators, including natural resources, pollution levels, and environmental management efforts, that characterize and influence environmental sustainability on a national scale. The United States ranks 45th. This high-middle ranking reflects high performance on issues such as water quality and environmental protection capacity and low performance on other issues, such as waste generation and greenhouse gas emissions.

ESI Rank	Country Name	ESI Rank	Country Name	ESI Rank	Country Name	ESI Rank	Country Name
1.	Finland	38.	Malaysia	75.	Indonesia	111.	Togo
2.	Norway	39.	Congo	76.	Spain	112.	Belgium
3.	Uruguay	40.	Netherlands	77.	Guinea-Bissau	113.	Dem. Rep. Congo
4.	Sweden	41.	Mali	78.	Kazakhstan	114.	Bangladesh
5.	Iceland	42.	Chile	79.	Sri Lanka	115.	Egypt
6.	Canada	43.	Bhutan	80.	Kyrgyzstan	116.	Guatemala
7.	Switzerland	44.	Armenia	81.	Guinea	117.	Syria
8.	Guyana	45.	United States	82.	Venezuela	118.	El Salvador
9.	Argentina	46.	Myanmar	83.	Oman	119.	Dominican Rep.
10.	Austria	47.	Belarus	84.	Jordan	120.	Sierra Leone
11.	Brazil	48.	Slovakia	85.	Nepal	121.	Liberia
12.	Gabon	49.	Ghana	86.	Benin	122.	South Korea
13.	Australia	50.	Cameroon	87.	Honduras	123.	Angola
14.	New Zealand	51.	Ecuador	88.	Côte d'Ivoire	124.	Mauritania
15.	Latvia	52.	Laos	89.	Serbia and Montenegro	125.	Philippines
16.	Peru	53.	Cuba			126.	Libya
17.	Paraguay	54.	Hungary	90.	Macedonia	127.	Vietnam
18.	Costa Rica	55.	Tunisia	91.	Turkey	128.	Zimbabwe
19.	Croatia	56.	Georgia	92.	Czech Republic	129.	Lebanon
20.	Bolivia	57.	Uganda	93.	South Africa	130.	Burundi
21.	Ireland	58.	Moldova	94.	Romania	131.	Pakistan
22.	Lithuania	59.	Senegal	95.	Mexico	132.	Iran
23.	Colombia	60.	Zambia	96.	Algeria	133.	China
24.	Albania	61.	Bosnia and Herzegovina	97.	Burkina Faso	134.	Tajikistan
25.	Central African Republic	62.	Israel	98.	Nigeria	135.	Ethiopia
				99.	Azerbaijan	136.	Saudi Arabia
26.	Denmark	63.	Tanzania	100.	Kenya	137.	Yemen
27.	Estonia	64.	Madagascar	101.	India	138.	Kuwait
28.	Panama	65.	United Kingdom	102.	Poland	139.	Trinidad and Tobago
29.	Slovenia	66.	Nicaragua	103.	Niger	140.	Sudan
30.	Japan	67.	Greece	104.	Chad	141.	Haiti
31.	Germany	68.	Cambodia	105.	Morocco	142.	Uzbekistan
32.	Namibia	69.	Italy	106.	Rwanda	143.	Iraq
33.	Russia	70.	Bulgaria	107.	Mozambique	144.	Turkmenistan
34.	Botswana	71.	Mongolia	108.	Ukraine	145.	Taiwan
35.	Papua New Guinea	72.	Gambia	109.	Jamaica	146.	North Korea
36.	France	73.	Thailand	110.	United Arab Emirates		
37.	Portugal	74.	Malawi				

Source: Esty, Daniel C., Marc Levy, Tanja Srebotnjak, and Alexander de Sherbinin (2005). *2005 Environmental Sustainability Index: Benchmarking National Environmental Stewardship.* New Haven: Yale Center for Environmental Law & Policy. www.yale.edu/esi.

World Energy Consumption and Carbon Dioxide Emissions, 1990–2025

Region	Energy consumption (quadrillion btu)				Carbon dioxide emissions (million metric tons)			
	1990	2001	2010	2025	1990	2001	2010	2025
Industrialized nations	182.8	211.5	236.3	281.4	10,462	11,634	12,938	15,643
Eastern Europe/Former Soviet Union	76.3	53.3	59.0	75.6	4,902	3,148	3,397	4,313
Developing nations								
Asia	52.5	85.0	110.6	173.4	3,994	6,012	7,647	11,801
Middle East	13.1	20.8	25.0	34.1	846	1,299	1,566	2,110
Africa	9.3	12.4	14.6	21.5	656	843	971	1,413
Central and South America	14.4	20.9	25.4	36.9	703	964	1,194	1,845
Total developing	89.3	139.2	175.5	265.9	6,200	9,118	11,379	17,168
Total world	348.4	403.9	470.8	622.9	21,563	23,899	27,715	37,124

Source: Energy Information Administration (EIA), 2003 and 2004. Web: www.eia.doe.gov/iea/.

Top World Oil Producers, Exporters, Consumers, and Importers, 2004

(millions of barrels per day)

Producers[1]	Total oil production	Exporters[2]	Net oil exports	Consumers[3]	Total oil consumption	Importers[4]	Net oil imports
1. *Saudi Arabia*	10.37	1. *Saudi Arabia*	8.73	1. United States	20.5	1. United States	11.8
2. Russia	9.27	2. Russia	6.67	2. China	6.5	2. Japan	5.3
3. United States	8.69	3. Norway	2.91	3. Japan	5.4	3. China	2.9
4. *Iran*	4.09	4. *Iran*	2.55	4. Germany	2.6	4. Germany	2.5
5. Mexico	3.83	5. *Venezuela*	2.36	5. Russia	2.6	5. South Korea	2.1
6. China	3.62	6. *United Arab*		6. India	2.3	6. France	2.0
7. Norway	3.18	*Emirates*	2.33	7. Canada	2.3	7. Italy	1.7
8. Canada	3.14	7. *Kuwait*	2.20	8. Brazil	2.2	8. Spain	1.6
9. *Venezuela*	2.86	8. *Nigeria*	2.19	9. South Korea	2.1	9. India	1.5
10. *United Arab*		9. Mexico	1.80	10. France	2.0	10. Taiwan	1.0
Emirates	2.76	10. *Algeria*	1.68	11. Mexico	2.0		
11. *Kuwait*	2.51	11. *Iraq*	1.48				
12. *Nigeria*	2.51	12. *Libya*	1.34				
13. United Kingdom	2.08	13. Kazakhstan	1.06				
14. *Iraq*	2.03	14. Qatar	1.02				

NOTE: OPEC members in italics. 1. Table includes all countries with total oil production exceeding 2 million barrels per day in 2004. Includes crude oil, natural gas liquids, condensate, refinery gain, and other liquids. 2. Includes all countries with net exports exceeding 1 million barrels per day in 2004. 3. Includes all countries that consumed more than 2 million barrels per day in 2004. 4. Includes all countries that imported more than 1 million barrels per day in 2004. *Source:* Energy Information Administration (EIA). www.eia.doe.gov/emeu/cabs/.

Greatest Oil Reserves by Country, 2005

Rank	Country	Proved reserves (billion barrels)	Rank	Country	Proved reserves (billion barrels)
1.	Saudi Arabia	261.9	6.	United Arab Emirates	97.8
2.	Canada	178.8[1]	7.	Venezuela	77.2
3.	Iran	125.8	8.	Russia	60.0
4.	Iraq	115.0	9.	Libya	39.0
5.	Kuwait	101.5	10.	Nigeria	35.3

NOTES: Proved reserves are estimated with reasonable certainty to be recoverable with present technology and prices. 1. Includes 174.5 billion barrels of oil sands reserves. *Source: Oil & Gas Journal,* Vol. 102, No. 47 (Dec. 10, 2004). From: U.S. Energy Information Administration. http://www.eia.doe.gov/emeu/international/petroleu.html.

Greatest Natural Gas Reserves by Country, 2005

Rank	Country	Proved reserves (trillion cu ft)	Rank	Country	Proved reserves (trillion cu ft)
1.	Russia	1,680.0	6.	United States	189.0
2.	Iran	940.0	7.	Nigeria	176.0
3.	Qatar	910.0	8.	Algeria	160.5
4.	Saudi Arabia	235.0	9.	Venezuela	151.0
5.	United Arab Emirates	212.1	10.	Iraq	110.0

NOTE: Proved reserves are estimated with reasonable certainty to be recoverable with present technology and prices. *Source: Oil & Gas Journal,* Vol. 102, No. 47 (Dec. 10, 2004). From: U.S. Energy Information Administration. http://www.eia.doe.gov/emeu/international/petroleu.html.

U.S. Emissions of Greenhouse Gases, 1990–2002

(million metric tons of gas for carbon dioxide and methane; thousand metric tons for nitrous oxide)

Gas	1990	1995	1996	1997	1998	1999	2000	2001	2002
Carbon dioxide	4,969.4	5,273.5	5,454.8	5,533.0	5,540.4	5,630.7	5,805.5	5,789.0	5,795.6
Methane	31.7	31.1	29.9	29.6	28.9	28.7	28.2	28.0	26.6
Nitrous oxide	1.2	1.3	1.2	1.2	1.2	1.2	1.2	1.2	1.1

Source: Compiled by the U.S. Energy Information Administration. Web: www.eia.doe.gov.

America's 25 Most Ozone-Polluted Metropolitan Areas, 2005

Ozone (see definition below) acts as a powerful respiratory irritant at the levels frequently found in most of the nation's urban areas during summer months. Symptoms include shortness of breath, chest pain when inhaling deeply, wheezing, and coughing. A study of a sample of longtime residents of Los Angeles, which has the highest and most frequent ozone problem in the nation, found that the group had a higher-than-expected loss of lung function over time.

Rank	Metropolitan area	Rank	Metropolitan area
1.	Los Angeles–Long Beach–Riverside, Calif.	13.	Hanford-Corcoran, Calif.
2.	Bakersfield, Calif.	13.	Cleveland-Akron-Elyria, Ohio
3.	Fresno-Madera, Calif.	15.	Knoxville-Sevierville–La Follette, Tenn.
4.	Visalia-Porterville, Calif.	15.	Modesto, Calif.
5.	Merced, Calif.	17.	Pittsburgh–New Castle, Pa.
6.	Houston-Baytown-Huntsville, Tex.	18.	Youngstown-Warren–East Liverpool, Ohio-Pa.
7.	Sacramento-Arden-Arcade-Truckee, Calif.-Nev.	19.	Columbus-Marion-Chillicothe, Ohio
8.	Dallas–Fort Worth, Tex.	20.	Detroit-Warren-Flint, Mich.
9.	New York–Newark-Bridgeport, N.Y.-N.J.-Conn.-Pa.	20.	Buffalo-Niagara-Cattaráugus, N.Y.
10.	Philadelphia-Camden-Vineland, Pa.-N.J.-Del.-Md.	22.	Sheboygan, Wis.
11.	Washington-Baltimore–Northern Va., DC-Md.-Va.-W. Va.	23.	Chicago-Naperville–Michigan City, Ill.-Ind.-Wis.
12.	Charlotte-Gastonia-Salisbury, N.C.-S.C.	24.	El Centro, Calif.
		25.	Lancaster, Pa.

Source: State of the Air: 2005, American Lung Association.

Major Air Pollutants

Pollutant	Sources	Effects
Ozone. A gas that can be found in two places. Near the ground (the troposphere), it is a major part of smog. The harmful ozone in the lower atmosphere should not be confused with the protective layer of ozone in the upper atmosphere (stratosphere), which screens out harmful ultraviolet rays.	Ozone is not created directly, but is formed when nitrogen oxides and volatile organic compounds mix in sunlight. That is why ozone is mostly found in the summer. Nitrogen oxides come from burning gasoline, coal, or other fossil fuels. There are many types of volatile organic compounds, and they come from sources ranging from factories to trees.	Ozone near the ground can cause a number of health problems. Ozone can lead to more frequent asthma attacks in people who have asthma and can cause sore throats, coughs, and breathing difficulty. It may even lead to premature death. Ozone can also hurt plants and crops.
Carbon monoxide. A gas that comes from the burning of fossil fuels, mostly in cars. It cannot be seen or smelled.	Carbon monoxide is released when engines burn fossil fuels. Emissions are higher when engines are not tuned properly, and when fuel is not completely burned. Cars emit a lot of the carbon monoxide found outdoors.	Carbon monoxide makes it hard for body parts to get the oxygen they need to run correctly. Exposure to carbon monoxide makes people feel dizzy and tired and gives them headaches.
Nitrogen dioxide. A reddish-brown gas that comes from the burning of fossil fuels. It has a strong smell at high levels.	Nitrogen dioxide mostly comes from power plants and cars. Nitrogen dioxide is formed in two ways—when nitrogen in the fuel is burned, or when nitrogen in the air reacts with oxygen at very high temperatures.	People who are exposed to nitrogen dioxide for a long time have a higher chance of getting respiratory infections. Nitrogen dioxide reacts in the atmosphere to form acid rain, which can harm plants and animals.
Particulate matter. Solid or liquid matter that is suspended in the air. To remain in the air, particles usually must be less than 0.1-mm wide and can be as small as 0.00005 mm.	Particulate matter can be divided into two types—coarse particles and fine particles. Coarse particles are formed from sources like road dust, sea spray, and construction. Fine particles are formed when fuel is burned in automobiles and power plants.	Particulate matter that is small enough can enter the lungs and cause health problems. Some of these problems include more frequent asthma attacks, respiratory problems, and premature death.
Sulfur dioxide. A corrosive gas that cannot be seen or smelled at low levels but can have a "rotten egg" smell at high levels.	Sulfur dioxide mostly comes from the burning of coal or oil in power plants. It also comes from factories that make chemicals, paper, or fuel. Like nitrogen dioxide, sulfur dioxide reacts in the atmosphere to form acid rain and particles.	Sulfur dioxide exposure can affect people who have asthma or emphysema by making it more difficult for them to breathe. It can also irritate people's eyes, noses, and throats. Sulfur dioxide can harm trees and crops, damage buildings, and make it harder for people to see long distances.

Pollutant	Sources	Effects
Lead. A blue-gray metal that is very toxic and is found in a number of forms and locations.	Outside, lead comes from cars in areas where unleaded gasoline is not used. Lead can also come from power plants and other industrial sources. Inside, lead paint is an important source of lead, especially in houses where paint is peeling.	High amounts of lead can be dangerous for small children and can lead to lower IQs and kidney problems. For adults, exposure to lead can increase the chance of having heart attacks or strokes.
Toxic air pollutants. A large number of chemicals that are known or suspected to cause cancer. Some important pollutants in this category include arsenic, asbestos, benzene, and dioxin.	Each toxic air pollutant comes from a slightly different source, but many are created in chemical plants or are emitted when fossil fuels are burned. Some toxic air pollutants, like asbestos and formaldehyde, can be found in building materials and can lead to indoor air problems. Many toxic air pollutants can also enter the food and water supplies.	Toxic air pollutants can cause cancer. Some toxic air pollutants can also cause birth defects. Other effects depend on the pollutant, but can include skin and eye irritation and breathing problems.
Stratospheric ozone depleters. Chemicals that can destroy the ozone in the stratosphere. These chemicals include chlorofluorocarbons (CFCs), halons, and other compounds that include chlorine or bromine.	CFCs are used in air conditioners and refrigerators, since they work well as coolants. They can also be found in aerosol cans and fire extinguishers. Other stratospheric ozone depleters are used as solvents in industry.	If the ozone in the stratosphere is destroyed, people are exposed to more radiation from the sun (ultraviolet radiation). This can lead to skin cancer and eye problems. Higher ultraviolet radiation can also harm plants and animals.
Greenhouse gases. Gases that stay in the air for a long time and warm up the planet by trapping sunlight. This is called the "greenhouse effect" because the gases act like the glass in a greenhouse. Some of the important greenhouse gases are carbon dioxide, methane, and nitrous oxide.	Carbon dioxide is the most important greenhouse gas. It comes from the burning of fossil fuels in cars, power plants, houses, and industry. Methane is released during the processing of fossil fuels, and also comes from natural sources like cows and rice paddies. Nitrous oxide comes from industrial sources and decaying plants.	The greenhouse effect can lead to changes in the climate of the planet. Some of these changes might include more temperature extremes, higher sea levels, changes in forest composition, and damage to land near the coast. Human health might be affected by diseases that are related to temperature or by damage to land and water.

Source: Jonathan Levy, Harvard School of Public Health. Based on information provided by the Environmental Protection Agency.

Top Ten Types of Debris Littering the Oceans

The 2003 International Coastal Cleanup enlisted more than 450,000 people in 91 countries in an effort that removed 7.5 million pounds of garbage from our oceans.

Rank	Debris items	Total number	Percent	Rank	Debris items	Total number	Percent
1.	Cigarettes/cigarette filters	1,922,830	29.5%	7.	Cups/plates/forks/ knives/spoons	317,447	4.9%
2.	Food wrappers/containers	632,161	9.7				
3.	Caps/lids	539,832	8.3	8.	Beverage cans	314,738	4.8
4.	Beverage bottles (plastic), 2 liters or less	438,763	6.7	9.	Straws/stirrers	273,105	4.2
				10.	Tobacco packaging/ wrappers	132,402	2.0
5.	Bags	354,294	5.4				
6.	Beverage bottles (glass)	328,239	5.0		**Totals**	**5,253,811**	**80.5**

Source: The Ocean Conservancy. Web: www.oceanconservancy.org.

America's Ten Most Endangered Rivers, 2005

Each year the organization American Rivers analyzes the condition of the nation's rivers to determine which are the most "endangered." Threats to these rivers include dams and channelizations that are harmful to fish or wildlife populations; depletion due to the rivers' use as a water supply for human populations; and coal mining operations that fill streams with coal and dirt. For more information, refer to the American Rivers website: www.amrivers.org.

Rank	River	State(s)	Rank	River	State(s)
1.	Susquehanna River	N.Y., Pa., Md.	6.	Santee River	S.C.
2.	McCrystal Creek	N.M.	7.	Little Miami River	Ohio
3.	Fraser River	Colo.	8.	Tuolumne River	Calif.
4.	Skykomish River	Wash.	9.	Price River	Utah
5.	Roan Creek	Tenn.	10.	Santa Clara River	Calif.

Animals and Nature

Animal Names: Male, Female, and Young

Animal	Male	Female	Young	Animal	Male	Female	Young	Animal	Male	Female	Young
Ass	Jack	Jenny	Foal	Duck	Drake	Duck	Duckling	Sheep	Ram	Ewe	Lamb
Bear	Boar	Sow	Cub	Elephant	Bull	Cow	Calf	Swan	Cob	Pen	Cygnet
Cat	Tom	Queen	Kitten	Fox	Dog	Vixen	Cub	Swine	Boar	Sow	Piglet
Cattle	Bull	Cow	Calf	Goose	Gander	Goose	Gosling	Tiger	Tiger	Tigress	Cub
Chicken	Rooster	Hen	Chick	Horse	Stallion	Mare	Foal	Whale	Bull	Cow	Calf
Deer	Buck	Doe	Fawn	Lion	Lion	Lioness	Cub	Wolf	Dog	Bitch	Pup
Dog	Dog	Bitch	Pup	Rabbit	Buck	Doe	Bunny				

Source: James G. Doherty, general curator, The Wildlife Conservation Society.

Gestation, Incubation, and Longevity of Selected Animals

Animal	Gestation or incubation, in days (average)	Longevity, in years (record exceptions)	Animal	Gestation or incubation, in days (average)	Longevity, in years (record exceptions)
Ass	365	18–20 (63)	Horse	329–345 (336)	20–25 (50+)
Bear	180–240[1]	15–30 (47)	Human	253–303	([2])
Cat	52–69 (63)	10–12 (26+)	Kangaroo	32–39[1]	4–6 (23)
Chicken	22	7–8 (14)	Lion	105–113 (108)	10 (29)
Cow	280	9–12 (39)	Monkey	139–270[1]	12–15[1] (29)
Deer	197–300[1]	10–15 (26)	Mouse	19–31[1]	1–3 (4)
Dog	53–71 (63)	10–12 (24)	Parakeet (Budgerigar)	17–20 (18)	8 (12+)
Duck	21–35[1] (28)	10 (15)	Pig	101–130 (115)	10 (22)
Elephant	510–730[1] (624)	30–40 (71)	Pigeon	11–19	10–12 (39)
Fox	51–63[1]	8–10 (14)	Rabbit	30–35 (31)	6–8 (15)
Goat	136–160 (151)	12 (17)	Rat	21	3 (5)
Groundhog	31–32	4–9	Sheep	144–152[1] (151)	12 (16)
Guinea pig	58–75 (68)	3 (6)	Squirrel	44	8–9 (15)
Hamster, golden	15–17	2 (8)	Whale	365–547[1]	n.a.
Hippopotamus	220–255 (240)	30 (49+)	Wolf	60–63	10–12 (16)

1. Depending on kind. 2. For human life expectancy charts, *see* Life Expectancy at Birth by Race and Sex, p. 192. *Source:* James G. Doherty, general curator, The Wildlife Conservation Society.

Speed of Animals

Most of the following measurements are for maximum speeds over approximate quarter-mile distances. Exceptions—which are included to give a wide range of animals—are the lion and elephant, whose speeds were clocked in the act of charging; the whippet, which was timed over a 200-yard course; the cheetah over a 100-yard distance; humans for a 15-yard segment of a 100-yard run; and the black mamba snake, six-lined race runner, spider, giant tortoise, three-toed sloth, and garden snail, which were measured over various small distances.

Animal	Speed (mph)	Animal	Speed (mph)	Animal	Speed (mph)
Peregrine falcon	200.00+	Zebra	40.00	White-tailed deer	30.00
Cheetah	70.00	Mongolian wild ass	40.00	Human	27.89
Pronghorn antelope	61.00	Greyhound	39.35	Elephant	25.00
Lion	50.00	Whippet	35.50	Black mamba snake	20.00
Thomson's gazelle	50.00	Jackal	35.00	Six-lined race runner	18.00
Wildebeest	50.00	Mule deer	35.00	Squirrel	12.00
Quarter horse	47.50	Rabbit (domestic)	35.00	Pig (domestic)	11.00
Cape hunting dog	45.00	Giraffe	32.00	Chicken	9.00
Elk	45.00	Reindeer	32.00	House mouse	8.00
Coyote	43.00	Cat (domestic)	30.00	Spider (*Tegenaria atrica*)	1.17
Gray fox	42.00	Kangaroo	30.00	Giant tortoise	0.17
Hyena	40.00	Grizzly bear	30.00	Three-toed sloth	0.15
Ostrich	40.00	Wart hog	30.00	Garden snail	0.03

Source: Natural History Magazine, March 1974, copyright 1974; The American Museum of Natural History; and James G. Doherty, general curator, The Wildlife Conservation Society.

Animal Group Terminology

Source: James G. Doherty, general curator, The Wildlife Conservation Society.

ants: colony
bears: sleuth, sloth
bees: grist, hive, swarm
birds: flight, volery
cats: clutter, clowder
cattle: drove
chicks: brood, clutch
clams: bed
cranes: sedge, seige
crows: murder
doves: dule
ducks: brace, team
elephants: herd
elks: gang
finches: charm

fish: school, shoal, draught
foxes: leash, skulk
geese: flock, gaggle, skein
gnats: cloud, horde
goats: trip
gorillas: band
hares: down, husk
hawks: cast
hens: brood
hogs: drift
horses: pair, team
hounds: cry, mute, pack
kangaroos: troop
kittens: kindle, litter
larks: exaltation

lions: pride
locusts: plague
magpies: tiding
mules: span
nightingales: watch
oxen: yoke
oysters: bed
parrots: company
partridges: covey
peacocks: muster, ostentation
pheasants: nest, bouquet
pigs: litter
ponies: string
quail: bevy, covey

rabbits: nest
seals: pod
sheep: drove, flock
sparrows: host
storks: mustering
swans: bevy, wedge
swine: sounder
toads: knot
turkeys: rafter
turtles: bale
vipers: nest
whales: gam, pod
wolves: pack, route
woodcocks: fall

Endangered and Threatened Species

Group	Endangered[1]		Threatened[2]		Total species	U.S. species with recovery plans
	U.S.	Foreign	U.S.	Foreign		
Mammals	68	251	10	20	349	54
Birds	77	175	13	6	271	76
Reptiles	14	64	22	16	116	33
Amphibians	11	8	10	1	30	15
Fishes	71	11	43	1	126	95
Clams	62	2	8	0	72	69
Snails	21	1	11	0	33	22
Insects	35	4	9	0	48	31
Arachnids	12	0	0	0	12	5
Crustaceans	18	0	3	0	21	13
Animal subtotal	**389**	**516**	**129**	**44**	**1,078**	**413**
Flowering plants	571	1	144	0	716	584
Conifers and cycads	2	0	1	2	5	3
Ferns and allies	24	0	2	0	26	26
Lichens	2	0	0	0	2	2
Plant subtotal	**599**	**1**	**147**	**2**	**749**	**615**
Total	**988**	**517**	**276**	**46**	**1,827**	**1,028**

NOTE: As of July 1, 2005. 1. *Endangered species* are those in danger of extinction. 2. *Threatened species* are those likely to become an endangered species within the foreseeable future. *Source:* U.S. Fish and Wildlife Service. Web: http://ecos.fws.gov/.

Water Supply of the World

The Antarctic Icecap is the largest supply of fresh water, representing nearly 2% of the world's total of fresh and salt water. As can be seen from the table below, the amount of water in our atmosphere is over 10 times as much as the water in all the rivers taken together. The fresh water actually available for human use in lakes and rivers and the accessible ground water amount to only about one-third of 1% of the world's total water supply.

	Surface area (sq mi)	Volume (cu mi)	Percentage of total[1]
Salt water			
The oceans	139,500,000	317,000,000	97.2%
Inland seas and saline lakes	270,000	25,000	0.008
Fresh water			
Freshwater lakes	330,000	30,000	0.009
All rivers (average level)	—	300	0.0001
Antarctic Icecap	6,000,000	6,300,000	1.9
Arctic Icecap and glaciers	900,000	680,000	0.21
Water in the atmosphere	197,000,000	3,100	0.001
Ground water within half a mile from surface	—	1,000,000	0.31
Deep-lying ground water	—	1,000,000	0.31
Total (rounded)	—	**326,000,000**	**100.00**

1. All figures are estimated. *Source:* Department of the Interior, Geological Survey.

The National Park System

Source: Department of the Interior, National Park Service.

The National Park System of the United States is administered by the National Park Service, a bureau of the Department of the Interior. Started with the establishment of Yellowstone National Park on March 1, 1872, the system includes not only the most extraordinary and spectacular scenic exhibits in the United States, but also a large number of sites distinguished for their historic or prehistoric importance, scientific interest, or superior recreational assets. The National Park System is made up of 388 areas covering more than 84 million acres in every state except Delaware. It also includes areas in the District of Columbia, American Samoa, Guam, Puerto Rico, and the Virgin Islands. A list of the areas follows, excluding those without "national" status. See also the excellent website of the Park Service: www.nps.gov.

NATIONAL PARKS

Name, location, and year authorized	Acreage	Outstanding characteristics
Acadia (Maine), 1919	47,548.94	Rugged seashore on Mt. Desert Island and adjacent mainland
Arches (Utah), 1971	76,518.98	Unusual stone arches, windows, pedestals caused by erosion
Badlands (S.D.), 1978	242,755.94	Arid land of fossils, prairie, bison, deer, bighorn sheep, antelope
Big Bend (Tex.), 1935	801,163.21	Mountains and desert bordering the Rio Grande
Biscayne (Fla.), 1980	172,924.07	Aquatic, coral reef park south of Miami
Black Canyon of the Gunnison (Colo.), 1999	30,243.53	Canyon with narrow opening, sheer walls, and startling depths
Bryce Canyon (Utah), 1924	35,835.08	Area of brilliantly colored, grotesque eroded rocks
Canyonlands (Utah), 1964	337,597.83	Colorful wilderness with impressive red-rock canyons, spires, arches
Capitol Reef (Utah), 1971	241,904.26	Highly colored sedimentary rock formations in high, narrow gorges
Carlsbad Caverns (N.M.), 1930	46,766.45	One of the world's largest known caves
Channel Islands (Calif.), 1980	249,561.00	Area is rich in marine mammals, sea birds, endangered species, and archeology
Congaree (S.C.), 2003	21,743.58	Contains the largest contiguous tract of old-growth bottomland hardwood forest remaining in the U.S.
Crater Lake (Ore.), 1902	183,224.05	Deep blue lake in heart of inactive volcano
Cuyahoga Valley (Ohio), 2000	32,860.73	Wilderness area offering recreational, historic, and cultural attractions, including scenic rail journeys
Death Valley (Calif.-Nev.), 1994	3,340,409.65	Largest desert, surrounded by high mountains, containing the lowest point in the Western Hemisphere
Denali (Alaska), 1917	4,740,911.72	Contains Mt. McKinley, N. America's highest mountain (20,320 ft)
Dry Tortugas (Fla.), 1992	64,701.22	Located 70 mi off Key West. Features an underwater nature trail
Everglades (Fla.), 1934	1,508,491.84	Subtropical area with abundant bird and animal life
Gates of the Arctic (Alaska), 1980	7,523,897.74	Diverse north central wilderness contains part of Brooks Range
Glacier (Mont.), 1910	1,013,572.41	Rocky Mountain scenery with many glaciers and lakes
Glacier Bay (Alaska), 1980	3,224,840.31	Popular for wildlife, whale-watching, glacier-calving, scenery
Grand Canyon (Ariz.), 1919	1,217,403.32	Mile-deep gorge, 4 to 18 mi wide, 217 mi long
Grand Teton (Wyo.), 1929	309,994.66	Picturesque range of high mountain peaks
Great Basin (Nev.), 1986	77,180.00	Exceptional scenic, biologic, geologic attractions
Great Smoky Mts. (N.C.-Tenn.), 1926	521,495.36	Highest mountain range east of Black Hills; luxuriant plant life
Guadalupe Mountains (Tex.), 1966	86,415.97	Contains highest point in Texas: Guadalupe Peak (8,751 ft)
Haleakala (Hawaii), 1916	29,830.15	World-famous 10,023-ft Haleakala volcano (dormant)
Hawaii Volcanoes (Hawaii), 1916	209,695.38	Spectacular volcanic area; luxuriant vegetation at lower levels
Hot Springs (Ark.), 1921	5,550.25	47 mineral hot springs said to have therapeutic value
Isle Royale (Mich.), 1931	571,790.11	Largest wilderness island in Lake Superior; moose, wolves, lakes
Joshua Tree (Calif.), 1994	784,162.05	Desert region featuring Joshua trees and a great variety of plants and animals
Katmai (Alaska), 1980	3,674,529.68	Expansion may ensure brown bear's preservation. Park is known for fishing, 1912 eruption of Novarupta, bears
Kenai Fjords (Alaska), 1980	669,982.99	Mountain goats, marine mammals, birdlife are features at this seacoast park near Seward
Kings Canyon (Calif.), 1890	461,901.20	Huge canyons; high mountains; giant sequoias
Kobuk Valley (Alaska), 1980	1,750,736.82	Native culture and anthropology center around the broad Kobuk River in northwest Alaska
Lake Clark (Alaska), 1980	2,619,733.21	Park provides scenic and wilderness recreation across Cook Inlet from Anchorage
Lassen Volcanic (Calif.), 1916	106,372.36	Exhibits of impressive volcanic phenomena
Mammoth Cave (Ky.), 1926	52,830.19	Vast limestone labyrinth with underground river

Name, location, and year authorized	Acreage	Outstanding characteristics
Mesa Verde (Colo.), 1906	52,121.93	Best-preserved prehistoric cliff dwellings in United States
Mount Rainier (Wash.), 1899	235,625.00	Single-peak glacial system; dense forests, flowered meadows
North Cascades (Wash.), 1968	504,780.94	Roadless Alpine landscape; jagged peaks; mountain lakes; glaciers
Olympic (Wash.), 1938	922,650.94	Finest Pacific Northwest rain forest; scenic mountain park
Petrified Forest (Ariz.), 1962	93,532.57	Extensive natural exhibit of petrified wood
Redwood (Calif.), 1968	112,512.97	Coastal redwood forests; contains world's tallest-known tree (369.2 ft)
Rocky Mountain (Colo.), 1915	265,765.03	Section of the Rocky Mountains; 107 named peaks over 10,000 ft
Saguaro (Ariz.), 1994	91,445.16	Giant saguaro cacti, unique to the Sonoran Desert, sometimes reach a height of 50 ft in this cactus forest
Sequoia (Calif.), 1890	404,051.17	Giant sequoias; magnificent High Sierra scenery, including Mt. Whitney
Shenandoah (Va.), 1926	199,038.07	Tree-covered mountains; scenic Skyline Drive
Theodore Roosevelt (N.D.), 1978	70,446.89	Scenic valley of Little Missouri River; T.R. Ranch; wildlife
Virgin Islands (U.S. V.I.), 1956	14,688.87	Beaches; lush hills; prehistoric Carib Indian relics
Voyageurs (Minn.), 1971	218,200.17	Wildlife, canoeing, fishing, hiking
Wind Cave (S.D.), 1903	28,295.03	Limestone caverns in Black Hills; bison herd
Wolf Trap Farm (Va.), 2003	130.28	The nation's first National Park for the Performing Arts
Wrangell–St. Elias (Alaska), 1980	8,323,147.59	Largest park system area has abundant wildlife, second highest peak in U.S. (Mt. St. Elias); adjoins Canadian park
Yellowstone (Wyo.-Mont.-Idaho), 1872	2,219,790.71	World's greatest geyser area; abundant falls, wildlife, canyons
Yosemite (Calif.), 1890	761,266.28	Mountains; inspiring gorges and waterfalls; giant sequoias
Zion (Utah), 1919	146,597.64	Multicolored gorge in heart of southern Utah desert

Name and location	Total acreage
National Historical Parks	
Adams (Mass.)	23.82
Appomattox Court House (Va.)	1,772.36
Boston (Mass.)	43.32
Cane River Creole (La.)	207.38
Cedar Creek and Belle Grove (Va.)	3,566.61
Chaco Culture (N.M.)	33,960,19
Chesapeake and Ohio Canal (Md.-W.Va.-DC)	19,575.25
Colonial (Va.)	9,452.41
Cumberland Gap (Ky.-Tenn.-Va.)	20,463.15
Dayton Aviation Heritage (Ohio)	86.46
George Rogers Clark (Ind.)	26.17
Harpers Ferry (W.Va.-Md.)	2,501.67
Hopewell Culture (Ohio)	1,169.96
Independence (Pa.)	44.80
Jean Lafitte (La.)	20,004.90
Kalaupapa (Hawaii)	10,778.88
Kaloko-Honokohau (Hawaii)	1,160.91
Keweenaw (Mich.)	1,869.40
Klondike Gold Rush (Alaska-Wash.)	13,191.35
Lowell (Mass.)	141.34
Lyndon B. Johnson (Tex.)	1,570.15
Marsh-Billings-Rockefeller (Vt.)	643.07
Minute Man (Mass.)	970.83
Morristown (N.J.)	1,711.36
Natchez (Miss.)	105.31
New Bedford Whaling (Mass.)	34.00
New Orleans Jazz (La.)	5.13
Nez Perce (Idaho)	2,494.59
Pecos (N.M.)	6,670.08
Pu'uhonua o Honaunau (Hawaii)	181.80
Rosie the Riveter/WWII Home Front (Calif.)	145.19
Salt River Bay (U.S. V.I.)	947.75
San Antonio Missions (Tex.)	825.92
San Francisco Maritime (Calif.)	49.86
San Juan Island (Wash.)	1,751.99
Saratoga (N.Y.)	3,392.42

Name and location	Total acreage
Sitka (Alaska)	113.17
Tumacácori (Ariz.)	46.28
Valley Forge (Pa.)	3,464.26
War in the Pacific (Guam)	2,036.98
Women's Rights (N.Y.)	7.44
National Monuments	
Agate Fossil Beds (Neb.)	3,055.22
Alibates Flint Quarries (Tex.)	1,370.97
Aniakchak (Alaska)	137,176.00
Aztec Ruins (N.M.)	317.80
Bandelier (N.M.)	33,676.67
Booker T. Washington (Va.)	223.92
Buck Island Reef (U.S. V.I.)	19,015.47
Cabrillo (Calif.)	159.94
Canyon de Chelly (Ariz.)	83,840.00
Cape Krusenstern (Alaska)	649,085.04
Capulin Volcano (N.M.)	792.84
Casa Grande Ruins (Ariz.)	472.50
Castillo de San Marcos (Fla.)	20.21
Castle Clinton (N.Y.)	1.00
Cedar Breaks (Utah)	6,154.60
Chiricahua (Ariz.)	11,984.73
Colorado (Colo.)	20,533.93
Craters of the Moon (Idaho)	304,727.05
Devils Postpile (Calif.)	798.46
Devils Tower (Wyo.)	1,346.91
Dinosaur (Utah-Colo.)	210,277.55
Effigy Mounds (Iowa)	2,526.39
Ellis Island (N.J.-N.Y.)	27.50
El Malpais (N.M.)	114,276.95
El Morro (N.M.)	1,278.72
Florissant Fossil Beds (Colo.)	5,998.09
Fort Frederica (Ga.)	241.42
Fort Matanzas (Fla.)	300.11
Fort McHenry (National Monument and Historic Shrine) (Md.)	43.26
Fort Pulaski (Ga.)	5,623.10
Fort Stanwix (N.Y.)	15.52

Name and location	Total acreage
Fort Sumter (S.C.)	199.57
Fort Union (N.M.)	720.60
Fossil Butte (Wyo.)	8,198.00
George Washington Birthplace (Va.)	550.23
George Washington Carver (Mo.)	210.00
Gila Cliff Dwellings (N.M.)	533.13
Governor's Island (N.Y.)	22.78
Grand Portage (Minn.)	709.97
Great Sand Dunes (Colo.)	42,272.18
Hagerman Fossil Beds (Idaho)	4,351.15
Hohokam Pima (Ariz.)	1,690.00
Homestead (Neb.)	195.11
Hovenweep (Utah-Colo.)	784.93
Jewel Cave (S.D.)	1,273.51
John Day Fossil Beds (Ore.)	14,056.73
Lava Beds (Calif.)	46,559.87
Little Bighorn Battlefield (Mont.)	765.34
Minidoka Internment (Idaho)	72.75
Montezuma Castle (Ariz.)	857.69
Muir Woods (Calif.)	553.55
Natural Bridges (Utah)	7,636.49
Navajo (Ariz.)	360.00
Ocmulgee (Ga.)	701.54
Oregon Caves (Ore.)	487.98
Organ Pipe Cactus (Ariz.)	330,688.86
Parashant (Ariz.)	n.a.
Petroglyph (N.M.)	7,231.63
Pinnacles (Calif.)	17,614.05
Pipe Spring (Ariz.)	40.00
Pipestone (Minn.)	281.78
Poverty Point (La.)	910.85
Rainbow Bridge (Utah)	160.00
Russell Cave (Ala.)	310.45
Salinas Pueblo Missions (N.M.)	1,071.42
Scotts Bluff (Neb.)	3,004.81
Statue of Liberty (N.Y.-N.J.)	58.38
Sunset Crater Volcano (Ariz.)	3,040.00
Timpanogos Cave (Utah)	250.00
Tonto (Ariz.)	1,120.00
Tuzigoot (Ariz.)	800.62
Virgin Islands Coral Reef (V.I.)	13,892.78
Walnut Canyon (Ariz.)	3,579.46
White Sands (N.M.)	143,732.92
Wupatki (Ariz.)	35,422.13
Yucca House (Colo.)	33.87

National Preserves

Aniakchak (Alaska)	465,603.00
Bering Land Bridge (Alaska)	2,697,393.11
Big Cypress (Fla.)	720,565.67
Big Thicket (Tex.)	97,168.03
Craters of the Moon (Idaho)	410,000.00
Denali (Alaska)	1,334,117.99
Gates of the Arctic (Alaska)	948,607.96
Glacier Bay (Alaska)	58,406.00
Great Sand Dunes (Colo.)	41,686.00
Jean Lafitte (La.)	20,004.90
Katmai (Alaska)	418,699.22
Lake Clark (Alaska)	1,410,291.99
Little River Canyon (Ala.)	13,632.96
Mojave (Calif.)	1,531,831.60
Noatak (Alaska)	6,569,904.43
Tallgrass Prairie (Kans.)	10,894.00
Wrangell-St. Elias (Alaska)	4,852,753.10
Yukon-Charley Rivers (Alaska)	2,526,512.31

Name and location	Total acreage

National Reserves

City of Rocks (Idaho)	14,107.19
Ebey's Landing (Nat'l Historical Reserve) (Wash.)	19,323.99
New Jersey Pinelands (N.J.)	1,100,000

National Military Parks

Chickamauga and Chattanooga (Ga.-Tenn.)	8,266.34
Fredericksburg and Spotsylvania (Va.)	8,361.92
Gettysburg (Pa.)	5,990.31
Guilford Courthouse (N.C.)	228.59
Horseshoe Bend (Ala.)	2,040.00
Kings Mountain (S.C.)	3,945.29
Pea Ridge (Ark.)	4,300.35
Shiloh (Tenn.)	4,024.88
Vicksburg (Miss.)	1,753.16

National Battlefields

Antietam (Md.)	3,244.37
Big Hole (Mont.)	1,010.61
Cowpens (S.C.)	841.56
Fort Donelson (Tenn.)	551.69
Fort Necessity (Pa.)	902.80
Monocacy (Md.)	1,647.01
Moores Creek (N.C.)	87.75
Petersburg (Va.)	2,659.19
Stones River (Tenn.)	709.36
Tupelo (Miss.)	1.00
Wilson's Creek (Mo.)	1,749.91

National Battlefield Parks

Kennesaw Mountain (Ga.)	2,884.14
Manassas (Va.)	5,067.92
Richmond (Va.)	2,151.94

National Battlefield Site

Brices Cross Roads (Miss.)	1.00

National Historic Sites

Abraham Lincoln Birthplace (Ky.)	344.50
Allegheny Portage Railroad (Pa.)	1,249.20
Andersonville (Ga.)	494.61
Andrew Johnson (Tenn.)	16.68
Bent's Old Fort (Colo.)	798.80
Boston African-American (Mass.)	0.59
Brown v. Board of Education (Kans.)	1.85
Carl Sandburg Home (N.C.)	263.65
Charles Pinckney (S.C.)	28.45
Chimney Rock (Nebr.)	83.36
Christiansted (U.S. V.I.)	27.15
Clara Barton (Md.)	8.59
Edgar Allan Poe (Pa.)	0.52
Edison (N.J.)	21.25
Eisenhower (Pa.)	690.46
Eleanor Roosevelt (N.Y.)	180.50
Eugene O'Neill (Calif.)	13.19
First Ladies (Ohio)	0.33
Ford's Theatre (Lincoln Museum) (DC)	0.29
Fort Bowie (Ariz.)	999.45
Fort Davis (Tex.)	473.87
Fort Laramie (Wyo.)	832.85
Fort Larned (Kan.)	718.39

Name and location	Total acreage
Fort Point (Calif.)	29.00
Fort Raleigh (N.C.)	512.93
Fort Scott (Kan.)	16.69
Fort Smith (Ark.-Okla.)	75.05
Fort Union Trading Post (N.D.-Mont.)	443.81
Fort Vancouver (Wash.)	208.89
Frederick Douglass (DC)	8.53
Frederick Law Olmsted (Mass.)	7.21
Friendship Hill (Pa.)	674.56
Gloria Dei Church (Pa.)	3.71
Golden Spike (Utah)	2,735.28
Grant-Kohrs Ranch (Mont.)	1,618.38
Hampton (Md.)	62.04
Harry S. Truman (Mo.)	6.67
Herbert Hoover (Iowa)	186.80
Home of F. D. Roosevelt (N.Y.)	799.98
Hopewell Furnace (Pa.)	848.06
Hubbell Trading Post (Ariz.)	160.09
James A. Garfield (Ohio)	7.82
Jamestown (Va.)	22.5
Jimmy Carter (Ga.)	70.86
John F. Kennedy (Mass.)	0.09
John Muir (Calif.)	344.73
Knife River Indian Villages (N.D.)	1,758.35
Lincoln Home (Ill.)	12.24
Little Rock Central High School (Ark.)	27.28
Longfellow (Mass.)	1.98
Lower East Side Tenement Museum (N.Y.)	n.a.
Maggie L. Walker (Va.)	1.29
Manzanar (Calif.)	813.81
Martin Luther King, Jr. (Ga.)	38.66
Martin Van Buren (N.Y.)	39.55
Mary McLeod Bethune Council House (DC)	0.07
Minuteman Missile (S.D.)	15.00
Nicodemus (Kans.)	161.35
Ninety Six (S.C.)	989.14
Palo Alto Battlefield (Tex.)	3,407.46
Pennsylvania Avenue (DC)	0.00
Puukohola Heiau (Hawaii)	86.24
Ronald Reagan Boyhood Home (Ill.)	1.01
Sagamore Hill (N.Y.)	83.02
Saint-Gaudens (N.H.)	148.15
Saint Paul's Church (N.Y.)	6.13
Salem Maritime (Mass.)	9.02
Sand Creek Massacre (Colo.)	12,583.34
San Juan (P.R.)	75.13
Saugus Iron Works (Mass.)	8.51
Sewall-Belmont House (DC)	0.35
Springfield Armory (Mass.)	54.93
Steamtown (Pa.)	62.48
Theodore Roosevelt Birthplace (N.Y.)	0.11
Theodore Roosevelt Inaugural (N.Y.)	1.03
Thomas Stone (Md.)	328.25
Touro Synagogue (R.I.)	0.23
Tuskegee Airmen (Ala.)	86.69
Tuskegee Institute (Ala.)	57.92
Ulysses S. Grant (Mo.)	9.60
Vanderbilt Mansion (N.Y.)	211.65
Washita Battlefield (Okla.)	315.20
Weir Farm (Conn.)	74.20
Whitman Mission (Wash.)	99.93
William Howard Taft (Ohio)	3.10

Name and location	Total acreage
National Memorials	
Arkansas Post (Ark.)	746.88
Arlington House, the Robert E. Lee Memorial (Va.)	27.91
Chamizal (Tex.)	54.90
Coronado (Ariz.)	4,750.22
David Berger (Ohio)	n.a.
De Soto (Fla.)	26.84
Father Marquette (Mich.)	52.00
Federal Hall (N.Y.)	0.45
Fort Caroline (Fla.)	138.39
Fort Clatsop (Ore.)	125.20
Franklin Delano Roosevelt (DC)	7.50
General Grant (N.Y.)	0.76
Hamilton Grange (N.Y.)	1.04
Jefferson National Expansion (Mo.)	192.83
John Ericsson (DC)	0.41
Johnstown Flood (Pa.)	164.12
Korean War Veterans (DC)	2.20
Lincoln Boyhood (Ind.)	199.65
Lincoln (DC)	107.43
Lyndon Baines Johnson Memorial Grove on the Potomac (DC)	17.00
Mount Rushmore (S.D.)	1,278.45
Oklahoma City (Okla.)	6.24
Perry's Victory and International Peace (Ohio)	25.39
Port Chicago Naval Magazine (Calif.)	n.a.
Roger Williams (R.I.)	4.56
Thaddeus Kosciuszko (Pa.)	0.02
Theodore Roosevelt Island (DC)	88.50
Thomas Jefferson (DC)	18.36
USS Arizona (Hawaii)	10.50
Vietnam Veterans (DC)	2.00
Washington Monument (DC)	106.01
World War II (DC)	7.20
Wright Brothers (N.C.)	428.44

National Seashores	
Assateague Island (Md.-Va.)	39,733.43
Canaveral (Fla.)	57,661.69
Cape Cod (Mass.)	43,604.94
Cape Hatteras (N.C.)	30,321.46
Cape Lookout (N.C.)	28,243.36
Cumberland Island (Ga.)	36,415.13
Fire Island (N.Y.)	19,579.47
Gulf Islands (Fla.-Miss.)	137,792.89
Padre Island (Tex.)	130,434.27
Point Reyes (Calif.)	71,067.66

National Lakeshores	
Apostle Islands (Wis.)	69,371.89
Indiana Dunes (Ind.)	15,044.47
Pictured Rocks (Mich.)	73,235.53
Sleeping Bear Dunes (Mich.)	71,194.71

National Park System Rivers	
Alagnak Wild River (Alaska)	30,665.45
Big South Fork National River (Ky.-Tenn.)	125,310.34
Bluestone National Scenic River (W.Va.)	4,309.51
Buffalo National River (Ark.)	94,293.31
Delaware National Scenic River (Pa.)	1,973.33
Great Egg Harbor Scenic and Recreational River (N.J.-Pa.)	43,311.42
Mississippi National River (Minn.)	53,775.00

Name and location	Total acreage
Missouri National Recreational River (Neb.)	45,350.00
New River Gorge National River (W.Va.)	70,465.89
Niobrara National Scenic River (Neb.)	5,992.96
Obed Wild and Scenic River (Tenn.)	5,173.69
Ozark National Scenic Riverways (Mo.)	80,785.04
Rio Grande Wild and Scenic River (Tex.)	9,600.00
St. Croix National Scenic Riverway (Minn.-Wis.)	67,460.31
Upper Delaware Scenic and Recreational River (Pa.)	74,999.56

National Historic Area

Aleutian WWII (Alaska)	81.00

National Heritage Areas

Cane River (La.)	116,000
Essex (Mass.)	352,000

National Recreation Areas

Amistad (Tex.)	58,500.00
Bighorn Canyon (Wyo.-Mont.)	120,296.22
Big South Fork (Ky.-Tenn.)	125,310.34
Boston Harbor Islands (Mass.)	1,482.25
Chattahoochee River (Ga.)	9,164.53
Chickasaw (Okla.)	9,888.83
Curecanti (Colo.)	41,972.42
Delaware Water Gap (Pa.-N.J.)	66,740.46
Gateway (N.Y.-N.J.)	26,606.63
Gauley River (W.Va.)	11,505.59
Glen Canyon (Ariz.-Utah)	1,254,306.19
Golden Gate (Calif.)	74,815.56
Lake Chelan (Wash.)	61,946.72
Lake Mead (Ariz.-Nev.)	1,495,664.00
Lake Meredith (Tex.)	44,977.63
Lake Roosevelt (Wash.)	100,390.31
Mississippi (Minn.)	53,775.00
Ross Lake (Wash.)	117,574.59
Santa Monica Mountains (Calif.)	153,672.77
Whiskeytown-Shasta-Trinity (Calif.)	42,503.46

National Heritage Corridors

Blackstone River Valley (Mass.-R.I.)	400,000
Delaware and Lehigh (Pa.)	n.a.
Erie Canalway (N.Y.)	3,087,360
Illinois and Michigan Canal (Ill.)	n.a.
Quinebaug and Shetucket Rivers Valley (Conn.)	694,000

Name and location	Total acreage

National Historic Trails[1]

Ala Kahakai	175
California	5,500
El Camino Real de Tierra Adentro	404
Juan Bautista de Anza	1,210
Lewis and Clark	3,700
Mormon Pioneer	1,300
Old Spanish	2,700
Oregon	2,170
Overmountain Victory	330
Pony Express	1,800
Santa Fe	900
Selma to Montgomery	54
Trail of Tears	2,200

1. Approx. length in miles, not area, is provided for trails. The actual length of publically accessible trails is often substantially less than that given.

National Scenic Trails[1]

Appalachian	2,174
Ice Age	1,000
Natchez Trace	444
North Country	4,000
Potomac Heritage	421.5

1. Approx. length in miles, not area, is provided for trails.

National Cemeteries[1]

Antietam (Md.)	11.36
Battleground (DC)	1.03
Chalmette Cemetery (La.)	17.5
Fort Donelson (Tenn.)	15.30
Fredericksburg (Va.)	12.00
Gettysburg (Pa.)	20.58
Poplar Grove (Va.)	8.72
Shiloh (Tenn.)	10.05
Stones River (Tenn.)	719.81
Vicksburg (Miss.)	116.28
Yorktown (Va.)	2.91

1. The National Cemeteries are not independent areas of the National Park System; each is part of a military park, battlefield, etc., except Battleground. Their acreage is kept separately. Arlington National Cemetery is under the Department of the Army.

Ten Most Visited National Parks, 2004

Rank	Name and location	Number of visitors	Rank	Name and location	Number of visitors
1.	Great Smoky Mountains National Park, Tenn.	9,167,046	6.	Yellowstone National Park, Wyo.-Mont.-Idaho	2,868,317
2.	Grand Canyon National Park, Ariz.	4,326,234	7.	Rocky Mountain National Park, Colo.	2,781,899
3.	Cuyahoga Valley National Park, Ohio	3,306,175	8.	Zion National Park, Utah	2,677,342
4.	Yosemite National Park, Calif.	3,280,911	9.	Grand Teton National Park, Wyo.	2,360,373
5.	Olympic National Park, Wash.	3,073,722	10.	Acadia National Park, Maine	2,207,847

Source: Based on data from the National Park Service. Web: www.nps.gov.

Hurricane Katrina

On August 29, 2005, the Category 4 Hurricane Katrina slammed into the U.S. Gulf Coast, breaching levees and inundating New Orleans while killing additional hundreds elsewhere in Louisiana and Mississippi. It was the third most intense hurricane to strike the U.S. mainland in recorded history. While the number of fatalities and amount of damage was unknown at press time, Katrina will certainly be recorded among the most devastating U.S. hurricanes. For updated information, see www.infoplease.com/spot/hurricanekatrina.html.

Atlantic Hurricane Names

Because hurricanes often occur at the same time, officials assign short, distinctive names to the storms to avoid confusion among weather stations, coastal bases, and ships at sea. Since 1953, Atlantic tropical storms have been named from lists created by the National Hurricane Center and now maintained and updated by the World Meteorological Organization. The lists featured only women's names until 1979, when men's and women's names were alternated. Six lists are used in rotation.

2005	2006	2007	2008	2009	2010
Arlene	Alberto	Andrea	Arthur	Ana	Alex
Bret	Beryl	Barry	Bertha	Bill	Bonnie
Cindy	Chris	Chantal	Cristobal	Claudette	Colin
Dennis	Debby	Dean	Dolly	Danny	Danielle
Emily	Ernesto	Erin	Edouard	Erika	Earl
Franklin	Florence	Felix	Fay	Fred	Fiona
Gert	Gordon	Gabrielle	Gustav	Grace	Gaston
Harvey	Helene	Humberto	Hanna	Henri	Hermine
Irene	Isaac	Ingrid	Ike	Ida	Igor
Jose	Joyce	Jerry	Josephine	Joaquin	Julia
Katrina	Kirk	Karen	Kyle	Kate	Karl
Lee	Leslie	Lorenzo	Laura	Larry	Lisa
Maria	Michael	Melissa	Marco	Mindy	Matthew
Nate	Nadine	Noel	Nana	Nicholas	Nicole
Ophelia	Oscar	Olga	Omar	Odette	Otto
Philippe	Patty	Pablo	Paloma	Peter	Paula
Rita	Rafael	Rebekah	Rene	Rose	Richard
Stan	Sandy	Sebastien	Sally	Sam	Shary
Tammy	Tony	Tanya	Teddy	Teresa	Tomas
Vince	Valerie	Van	Vicky	Victor	Virginie
Wilma	William	Wendy	Wilfred	Wanda	Walter

Source: National Hurricane Center, National Oceanic and Atmospheric Administration (NOAA).

Costliest Hurricanes in the United States (U.S. Mainland)[1]

Rank	Hurricane	Location	Year	Category[2]	Damage (in billions)	Rank	Hurricane	Location	Year	Category[2]	Damage (in billions)
1.	Andrew	Fla./La.	1992	5	$26.5	7.	Allison	Tex.	2001	TS[3]	$5.0
2.	Charley	Fla.	2004	4	15.0	8.	Floyd	Mid Atlantic/ NE U.S.	1999	2	4.5
3.	Ivan	Ala./Fla.	2004	3	14.2						
4.	Frances	Fla.	2004	2	8.9	9.	Isabel	Mid Atlantic	2003	2	3.4
5.	Hugo	S.C.	1989	4	7.0	10.	Fran	N.C.	1996	3	3.2
6.	Jeanne	Fla.	2004	3	6.9						

NOTE: Excludes 2005's Hurricane Katrina, which will likely top the list. Damages are listed in U.S. dollars and are not adjusted for inflation. 1. 1900–2004. 2. Saffir-Simpson Hurricane scale: Cat. 1 = weak; Cat. 5 = devastating. 3. Tropical storm intensity. *Source:* National Oceanic and Atmospheric Administration (NOAA).

Deadliest Hurricanes in the United States (U.S. Mainland)[1]

Rank	Hurricane	Year	Category[2]	Deaths	Rank	Hurricane	Year	Category[2]	Deaths
1.	Galveston, Tex.	1900	4	8,000[3]	6.	Audrey (SW La./N. Tex.)	1957	4	390
2.	Lake Okeechobee, Fla.	1928	4	1,836	7.	NE U.S.	1944	3	390[5]
3.	Florida Keys/S. Tex.	1919	4	600[4]	8.	Grand Isle, La.	1909	4	350
4.	New England	1938	3	600	9.	New Orleans, La.	1915	4	275
5.	Florida Keys	1935	5	408	10.	Galveston, Tex.	1915	4	275

NOTE: Excludes 2005's Hurricane Katrina, which will likely be ranked in the top 3. 1. 1900–2000. 2. Saffir-Simpson Hurricane scale: Cat. 1 = weak; Cat. 5 = devastating. 3. May actually have been as high as 10,000 to 12,000. 4. Over 500 of these lost on ships at sea; 600–900 estimated deaths. 5. Some 344 of these lost on ships at sea. *Source:* National Oceanic and Atmospheric Administration (NOAA).

Retired Hurricane Names

When hurricanes are particularly destructive, their names are retired from the list of usable names. Any country affected by a particularly terrible storm can request that the name be retired by petitioning the World Meteorological Organization. Below is a list of infamous hurricanes that have settled into retirement.

Name	Year	Location(s) affected	Name	Year	Location(s) affected
Agnes	1972	Florida, Northeast U.S.	Gilbert	1988	Lesser Antilles, Jamaica, Yucatan Peninsula, Mexico
Alicia	1983	North Texas			
Allen	1980	Antilles, Mexico, South Texas	Gloria	1985	North Carolina, Northeast U.S.
Allison[1]	2001	Texas	Hattie	1961	Belize, Guatemala
Andrew	1992	Bahamas, South Florida, and Louisiana	Hazel	1954	Antilles, North and South Carolina
Anita	1977	Mexico	Hilda	1964	Louisiana
Audrey	1957	Louisiana, North Texas	Hugo	1989	Antilles, South Carolina
Betsy	1965	Bahamas, Southeast Florida, Southeast Louisiana	Ione	1955	North Carolina
			Inez	1966	Lesser Antilles, Hispanola, Cuba, Florida Keys, Mexico
Beulah	1967	Antilles, Mexico, South Texas			
Bob	1991	North Carolina, Northeast U.S.	Iris	2001	Belize
Camille	1969	Louisiana, Mississippi, and Alabama	Isabel	2003	North Carolina, Northeast U.S.
Carla	1961	Texas	Isidore	2002	Western Cuba, Yucatan, Louisiana
Carmen	1974	Mexico	Ivan	2004	Windward Islands, Florida, Texas, Louisiana
Carol	1954	Northeast U.S.			
Celia	1970	South Texas	Janet	1955	Lesser Antilles, Belize, Mexico
Charley	2004	Florida, Cuba, Jamaica, South Carolina	Jeanne	2004	Caribbean, Bahamas, Florida
Cleo	1964	Lesser Antilles, Haiti, Cuba, Florida	Joan	1988	Curacao, Venezuela, Colombia, Nicaragua (crossed into Pacific and became Miriam)
Connie	1955	North Carolina			
David	1979	Lesser Antilles, Hispanola, Florida, and Eastern U.S.			
			Juan	2003	Nova Scotia
Diana	1990	Mexico	Keith	2000	Belize, Nicaragua, Mexico
Diane	1955	Mid-Atlantic U.S. and Northeast U.S.	Klaus	1990	Martinique
Donna	1960	Bahamas, Florida, and Eastern U.S.	Lenny	1999	Antilles
Dora	1964	Northeast Florida	Lili	2002	Lesser Antilles, Haiti, Jamaica, Cuba, Louisiana
Elena	1985	Mississippi, Alabama, Western Florida			
Ekiuse	1975	Antilles, Northwest Florida, Alabama	Luis	1995	Lesser Antilles
Fabian	2003	Bermuda	Marilyn	1995	Lesser Antilles, Puerto Rico
Flora	1963	Haiti, Cuba	Michelle	2001	Honduras, Nicaragua, Jamaica, Cayman Islands, Cuba
Floyd	1999	North Carolina, eastern seaboard			
Frances	2004	Caribbean, Florida, eastern United States	Mitch	1998	Central America, Nicaragua, Honduras
			Opal	1995	Central America, Mexico, Florida
Frederic	1979	Alabama and Mississippi	Roxanne	1995	Mexico

1. Tropical storm. *Source:* National Hurricane Center, National Oceanic and Atmospheric Administration (NOAA).

Most Intense[1] Hurricanes in the United States[2]
(U.S. Mainland)

Rank	Hurricane	Year	Category[3]	Rank	Hurricane	Year	Category[3]
1.	Florida Keys	1935	5	6.	Florida Keys/Tex.	1919	4
2.	Camille (Miss./La./Va.)	1969	5	7.	Lake Okeechobee, Fla.	1928	4
3.	Katrina (La./Miss.)[4]	2005	4	8.	Donna (Fla./Eastern U.S.)	1960	4
4.	Andrew (Fla./La.)	1992	5	9.	New Orleans, La.	1915	4
5.	Indianola, Tex.	1886	4	9.	Carla (Tex.)	1961	4

1. Intensity is for time of landfall. May have been stronger at other times. 2. 1851–2005. 3. Saffir-Simpson Hurricane scale: Cat. 1 = weak; Cat. 5 = devastating. 4. Preliminary data indicate that while Katrina's wind speed at landfall was slower than Andrew's (140 mph vs. 165), its barometric pressure was lower (27.11 inches vs. 27.23). The former is used to determine a hurricane's category; the latter, its intensity. *Sources:* NOAA and National Weather Service.

States with the Most Reported Deaths by Lightning, 1959–2004

Rank	State	Number of deaths		Rank	State	Number of deaths	
		1959–2004	1995–2004			1959–2004	1995–2004
1.	Florida	430	85	11.	Arkansas	118	8
2.	Texas	198	34	12.	Alabama	102	18
3.	North Carolina	182	17	13.	Georgia	100	19
4.	Ohio	137	22	13.	Michigan	100	11
5.	New York	135	7	15.	Mississippi	98	9
6.	Tennessee	134	10	15.	Oklahoma	98	10
7.	Louisiana	133	17	17.	Illinois	97	12
8.	Colorado	126	31	18.	South Carolina	91	14
9.	Maryland	123	7	19.	New Mexico	88	7
10.	Pennsylvania	121	12	20.	Kentucky	87	5

Source: National Severe Storms Laboratory, National Oceanic and Atmospheric Administration (NOAA).

The 15 Deadliest Tornadoes in the United States

Date	Location(s)	Deaths	Date	Location(s)	Deaths
1. March 18, 1925	Tri-State (Mo., Ill., Ind.)	689	9. June 8, 1953	Flint, Mich.	115
2. May 6, 1840	Natchez, Miss.	317	10. May 11, 1953	Waco, Tex.	114
3. May 27, 1896	St. Louis, Mo.	255	10. May 18, 1902	Goliad, Tex.	114
4. April 5, 1936	Tupelo, Miss.	216	12. March 23,	Omaha, Neb.	103
5. April 6, 1936	Gainesville, Ga.	203	1913		
6. April 9, 1947	Woodward, Okla.	181	13. May 26, 1917	Mattoon, Ill.	101
7. April 24, 1908	Amite La.; Purvis, Miss.	143	14. June 23, 1944	Shinnston, W. Va.	100
8. June 12, 1899	New Richmond, Wis.	117	15. April 18, 1880	Marshfield, Mo.	99

Source: Storm Prediction Center at the National Weather Service, National Oceanic and Atmospheric Administration (NOAA). Web: www.spc.noaa.gov/archive/tornadoes/t-deadly.html.

2004 Tornado Fatality Information

Tornado Fatalities by State

State	Deadly tornadoes	Fatalities
Illinois	2	9
Missouri	3	7
Florida	4	7
N. Carolina	1	3
Texas	2	2
Alabama	1	1
Georgia	1	1
Indiana	1	1
Louisiana	1	1
Mississippi	1	1
Nebraska	1	1
S. Carolina	1	1
Wisconsin	1	1
Total	**20**	**36**

By Intensity

Intensity	Deadly tornadoes	Fatalities
F0	1	1
F1	5	5
F2	4	8
F3	5	12
F4	2	4
F5	0	0
Unknown	3	6

Circumstances

Circumstance	Fatalities
Mobile home	11
Permanent home	21
Vehicle	2
Business	2

Source: Storm Prediction Center at the National Weather Service, National Oceanic and Atmospheric Administration (NOAA). Web: www.spc.noaa.gov/climo/torn/2004deadlytorn.html.

What Kind of Cloudy Is It?

Cloud	Descriptive Name	Height	Description
Cirrus	Mare's tails	4 miles +	thin, feathery
Cirrocumulus	Mackerel sky	4 miles +	small patches of white
Cirrostratus	Bedsheet clouds	4 miles +	thin, white sheets
Stratus*	High fogs	0-1 mile	low, gray blanket
Cumulus	Cauliflowers	¼-4 miles	flat-bottomed, white puffy
Cumulonimbus*	Thunderheads	¼-4 miles	mountains of heavy, dark clouds

*Indicates rain or snow clouds

Greatest Snowfalls in North America

	Place	Date	Inches	Centimeters
24 hours	Silver Lake, Colo.	April 14–15, 1921	76	195.6
1 month	Tamarack, Calif.	Jan. 1911	390	991
1 storm	Mt. Shasta Ski Bowl, Calif.	Feb. 13–19, 1959	189	480
1 season	Mount Baker, Wash.	1998–1999	1,140	2,895.6

Source: U.S. Army Corps of Engineers, Engineer Topographic Laboratories.

Recorded Weather Extremes, U.S. and Worldwide

Highest average annual mean temperature (world): Dallol, Ethiopia (Oct. 1960–Dec. 1966), 94° F (34.4° C). **(U.S.):** Key West, Fla. (30-year normal), 78.2° F (25.7° C).

Lowest average annual mean temperature (world): Plateau Station, Antarctica, –70° F (–56.7° C). **(U.S.):** Barrow, Alaska (30-year normal), 9.3° F (–12.6° C).

Greatest average yearly rainfall (world): Cherrapunji, India (74-year avg), 450 in. (1,143 cm). **(U.S.):** Mt. Waialeale, Kauai, Hawaii (32-year avg), 460 in. (1,168 cm).

Minimum average yearly rainfall (world): Arica, Chile (59-year avg), 0.03 in. (0.08 cm) (no rainfall for 14 consecutive years). **(U.S.):** Death Valley, Calif. (42-year avg), 1.63 in.

(4.14 cm). Bagdad, Calif., holds the U.S. record for the longest period with no measurable rain, 767 days, from Oct. 3, 1912 to Nov. 8, 1914.

Hottest summer average in Western Hemisphere (U.S.): Death Valley, Calif., 98° F (36.7° C).

Longest hot spell (world): Marble Bar, W. Australia, 100° F (37.8° C) (or above) for 162 consecutive days, Oct. 30, 1923 to Apr. 7, 1924.

Largest hailstone (U.S.): Aurora, Neb., 7 in. (17.8 cm) in diameter, 18.75 in. (47.6 cm) in circumference, June 22, 2003.

Costliest U.S. hailstorm: Denver, Colorado, July 11, 1990. Total damage was $625 million.

World and U.S. Extremes of Climate

Highest Recorded Temperatures

	Place	Date	Degrees Fahrenheit	Degrees Celsius
World (Africa)	El Azizia, Libya	Sept. 13, 1922	136	58
North America (U.S.)	Death Valley, Calif.	July 10, 1913	134	57
Asia	Tirat Tsvi, Israel	June 21, 1942	129	54
Australia	Cloncurry, Queensland	Jan. 16, 1889	128	53
Europe	Seville, Spain	Aug. 4, 1881	122	50
South America	Rivadavia, Argentina	Dec. 11, 1905	120	49
Canada	Midale and Yellow Grass, Saskatchewan, Canada	July 5, 1937	113	45
Oceania	Tuguegarao, Philippines	April 29, 1912	108	42
Persian Gulf (sea-surface)		Aug. 5, 1924	96	36
Antarctica	Vanda Station, Scott Coast	Jan. 5, 1974	59	15
South Pole		Dec. 27, 1978	7.5	−14

Lowest Recorded Temperatures

	Place	Date	Degrees Fahrenheit	Degrees Celsius
World (Antarctica)	Vostok	July 21, 1983	−129	−89
Asia	Oimekon, Russia	Feb. 6, 1933	−90	−68
	Verkhoyansk, Russia	Feb. 7, 1892	−90	−68
Greenland	Northice	Jan. 9, 1954	−87	−66
North America (excl. Greenland)	Snag, Yukon, Canada	Feb. 3, 1947	−81	−63
United States	Prospect Creek, Alaska	Jan. 23, 1971	−80	−62
U.S. (excl. Alaska)	Rogers Pass, Mont.	Jan. 20, 1954	−70	−56.5
Europe	Ust 'Shchugor, Russia	Jan.[1]	−67	−55
South America	Sarmiento, Argentina	June 1, 1907	−27	−33
Africa	Ifrane, Morocco	Feb. 11, 1935	−11	−24
Australia	Charlotte Pass, N.S.W.	June 29, 1994	−9	−22
Oceania	Mauna Kea, Hawaii	May 17, 1979	12	−11

1. Exact date unknown; lowest in 15-year period.

Greatest Rainfalls

	Place	Date	Inches	Centimeters
1 minute (World)	Unionville, Md.	July 4, 1956	1.23	3.1
20 minutes (World)	Curtea-de-Arges, Romania	July 7, 1889	8.1	20.5
42 minutes (World)	Holt, Mo.	June 22, 1947	12	30.5
12 hours (World)	Grand Ilet, La Réunion	Jan. 26, 1980	46	114
24 hours (World)	Foc-Foc, La Réunion	Jan. 7–8, 1966	72	182.5
24 hours (N. Hemisphere)	Paishih, Taiwan	Sept. 10–11, 1963	49	125
24 hours (Australia)	Bellenden Ker, Queensland	Jan. 4, 1979	44	114
24 hours (U.S.)	Alvin, Tex.	July 25–26, 1979	43	109
24 hours (Canada)	Ucluelet Brynnor Mines, British Columbia	Oct. 6, 1967	19	49
5 days (World)	Commerson, La Réunion	Jan. 23–28, 1980	156	395
1 month (World)	Cherrapunji, India	July 1861	366	930
12 months (World)	Cherrapunji, India	Aug. 1860–Aug. 1861	1,042	2,647
12 months (U.S.)	Kukui, Maui, Hawaii	Dec. 1981–Dec. 1982	739	1878

Lowest Average Annual Precipitation Extremes

Continent	Place	Lowest avg. (in.)	Elevation (ft)	Years of record
World (South America)	Arica, Chile	0.03	95	59
Africa	Wadi Halfa, Sudan	<0.10	410	39
Antarctica	Amundsen-Scott South Pole Station	0.80[1]	9,186	10
North America	Batagues, Mexico	1.20	16	14
Asia	Aden, Yemen	1.80	22	50
Australia	Mulka (Troudaninna), South Australia	4.05	160[2]	42
Europe	Astrakhan, Russia	6.40	45	25
Oceania	Puako, Hawaii, Hawaii	8.93	5	13

1. The value given is the average amount of solid snow accumulating in one year as indicated by snow markers. The liquid content of the snow is undetermined. 2. Approximate elevation. *Source:* U.S. Army Corps of Engineers, Engineer Topographic Laboratories.

Record Highest Temperatures by State

State	Temp. °F	Temp. °C	Date	Station	Elevation in feet
Alabama	112	44	Sept. 5, 1925	Centerville	345
Alaska	100	38	June 27, 1915	Fort Yukon	est. 420
Arizona	128	53	June 29, 1994	Lake Havasu City	505
Arkansas	120	49	Aug. 10, 1936	Ozark	396
California	134	57	July 10, 1913	Greenland Ranch	-178
Colorado	118	48	July 11, 1888	Bennett	5,484
Connecticut	106	41	July 15, 1995	Danbury	450
Delaware	110	43	July 21, 1930	Millsboro	20
D.C.	106	41	July 20, 1930	Washington	410
Florida	109	43	June 29, 1931	Monticello	207
Georgia	112	44	Aug. 20, 1983	Greenville	860
Hawaii	100	38	Apr. 27, 1931	Pahala	850
Idaho	118	48	July 28, 1934	Orofino	1,027
Illinois	117	47	July 14, 1954	E. St. Louis	410
Indiana	116	47	July 14, 1936	Collegeville	672
Iowa	118	48	July 20, 1934	Keokuk	614
Kansas	121	49	July 24, 1936[1]	Alton (near)	1,651
Kentucky	114	46	July 28, 1930	Greensburg	581
Louisiana	114	46	Aug. 10, 1936[1]	Plain Dealing	268
Maine	105	41	July 10, 1911[1]	North Bridgton	450
Maryland	109	43	July 10, 1936[1]	Cumberland & Frederick	623; 325
Massachusetts	107	42	Aug. 2, 1975	New Bedford & Chester	120; 640
Michigan	112	44	July 13, 1936	Mio	963
Minnesota	114	46	July 6, 1936[1]	Moorhead	904
Mississippi	115	46	July 29, 1930	Holly Springs	600
Missouri	118	48	July 14, 1954[1]	Warsaw & Union	705; 560
Montana	117	47	July 5, 1937	Medicine Lake	1,950
Nebraska	118	48	July 24, 1936[1]	Minden	2,169
Nevada	125	52	June 29, 1994	Laughlin	605
New Hampshire	106	41	July 4, 1911	Nashua	125
New Jersey	110	43	July 10, 1936	Runyon	18
New Mexico	122	50	June 27, 1994	Waste Isolat. Pilot Pit	3,418
New York	108	42	July 22, 1926	Troy	35
North Carolina	110	43	Aug. 21, 1983	Fayetteville	213
North Dakota	121	49	July 6, 1936	Steele	1,857
Ohio	113	45	July 21, 1934[1]	Gallipolis (near)	673
Oklahoma	120	49	June 27, 1994[1]	Tipton	1,350
Oregon	119	48	Aug. 10, 1898	Pendleton	1,074
Pennsylvania	111	44	July 10, 1936[1]	Phoenixville	100
Rhode Island	104	40	Aug. 2, 1975	Providence	51
South Carolina	111	44	June 28, 1954[1]	Camden	170
South Dakota	120	49	July 5, 1936	Gannvalley	1,750
Tennessee	113	45	Aug. 9, 1930[1]	Perryville	377
Texas	120	49	Aug. 12, 1936	Seymour	1,291
Utah	117	47	July 5, 1895	Saint George	2,880
Vermont	105	41	July 4, 1911	Vernon	310
Virginia	110	43	July 15, 1954	Balcony Falls	725
Washington	118	48	Aug. 5, 1961[1]	Ice Harbor Dam	475
West Virginia	112	44	July 10, 1936[1]	Martinsburg	435
Wisconsin	114	46	July 13, 1936	Wisconsin Dells	900
Wyoming	114	46	July 12, 1900	Basin	3,500

1. Also on earlier dates at the same or other places. *Source:* National Climatic Data Center, Asheville, N.C., and Storm Phillips, STORMFAX, INC.

Record Lowest Temperatures by State

State	Temp. °F	Temp. °C	Date	Station	Elevation in feet
Alabama	−27	−33	Jan. 30, 1966	New Market	760
Alaska	−80	−62	Jan. 23, 1971	Prospect Creek Camp	1,100
Arizona	−40	−40	Jan. 7, 1971	Hawley Lake	8,180
Arkansas	−29	−34	Feb. 13, 1905	Pond	1,250
California	−45	−43	Jan. 20, 1937	Boca	5,532
Colorado	−61	−52	Feb. 1, 1985	Maybell	5,920
Connecticut	−32	−36	Feb. 16, 1943	Falls Village	585
Delaware	−17	−27	Jan. 17, 1893	Millsboro	20
D.C.	−15	−26	Feb. 11, 1899	Washington	410
Florida	−2	−19	Feb. 13, 1899	Tallahassee	193
Georgia	−17	−27	Jan. 27, 1940	CCC Camp F-16	est. 1,000
Hawaii	12	−11	May 17, 1979	Mauna Kea	13,770
Idaho	−60	−51	Jan. 18, 1943	Island Park Dam	6,285
Illinois	−36	−38	Jan. 5, 1999	Congerville	635
Indiana	−36	−38	Jan. 19, 1994	New Whiteland	785
Iowa	−47	−44	Feb. 3, 1996	Elkader	770
Kansas	−40	−40	Feb. 13, 1905	Lebanon	1,812
Kentucky	−37	−38	Jan. 19, 1994	Shelbyville	730
Louisiana	−16	−27	Feb. 13, 1899	Minden	194
Maine	−48	−44	Jan. 19, 1925	Van Buren	510
Maryland	−40	−40	Jan. 13, 1912	Oakland	2,461
Massachusetts	−35	−37	Jan. 12, 1981	Chester	640
Michigan	−51	−46	Feb. 9, 1934	Vanderbilt	785
Minnesota	−60	−51	Feb. 2, 1996	Tower	1,460
Mississippi	−19	−28	Jan. 30, 1966	Corinth	420
Missouri	−40	−40	Feb. 13, 1905	Warsaw	700
Montana	−70	−57	Jan. 20, 1954	Rogers Pass	5,470
Nebraska	−47	−44	Feb. 12, 1899	Camp Clarke	3,700
Nevada	−50	−46	Jan. 8, 1937	San Jacinto	5,200
New Hampshire	−47	−44	Jan. 29, 1934	Mt. Washington	6,262
New Jersey	−34	−37	Jan. 5, 1904	River Vale	70
New Mexico	−50	−46	Feb. 1, 1951	Gavilan	7,350
New York	−52	−47	Feb. 18, 1979[1]	Old Forge	1,720
North Carolina	−34	−37	Jan. 21, 1985	Mt. Mitchell	6,525
North Dakota	−60	−51	Feb. 15, 1936	Parshall	1,929
Ohio	−39	−39	Feb. 10, 1899	Milligan	800
Oklahoma	−27	−33	Jan. 18, 1930	Watts	958
Oregon	−54	−48	Feb. 10, 1933[1]	Seneca	4,700
Pennsylvania	−42	−41	Jan. 5, 1904	Smethport	est. 1,500
Rhode Island	−23	−31	Jan. 11, 1942	Kingston	100
South Carolina	−19	−28	Jan. 21, 1985	Caesars Head	3,115
South Dakota	−58	−50	Feb. 17, 1936	McIntosh	2,277
Tennessee	−32	−36	Dec. 30, 1917	Mountain City	2,471
Texas	−23	−31	Feb. 8, 1933[1]	Seminole	3,275
Utah	−69	−56	Feb. 1, 1985	Peter's Sink	8,092
Vermont	−50	−46	Dec. 30, 1933	Bloomfield	915
Virginia	−30	−34	Jan. 22, 1985	Mountain Lake	3,870
Washington	−48	−44	Dec. 30, 1968	Mazama & Winthrop	2,120; 1,765
West Virginia	−37	−38	Dec. 30, 1917	Lewisburg	2,200
Wisconsin	−55	−48	Feb. 4, 1996	Couderay	1,300
Wyoming	−66	−54	Feb. 9, 1933	Riverside R.S.	6,500

1. Also on earlier dates at the same or other places. *Source:* National Climatic Data Center, Asheville, N.C., and Storm Phillips, STORMFAX, INC.

Climate of 100 Selected U.S. Cities

(For world cities, see p. 605)

| City | Average monthly temperature (°F)[1] | | | | Precipitation | | Snowfall[2] | |
| | Jan. | April | July | Oct. | Average annual | | Average annual | Number of years observed[4] |
					(in.)[1]	(days)[3]	(in.)[3]	
Albany, N.Y.	22.2	46.6	71.1	49.3	38.60	136	64.4	57
Albuquerque, N.M.	35.7	55.6	78.5	57.3	9.47	60	11.0	64
Anchorage, Alaska	15.8	36.3	58.4	34.1	16.08	115	70.8	39 / 60
Asheville, N.C.	35.8	54.1	73.0	55.2	47.07	126	15.3	39
Atlanta, Ga.	42.7	61.6	80.0	62.8	50.20	115	2.1	69 / 65
Atlantic City, N.J.	32.1	50.6	75.3	55.1	40.59	113	16.2	60 / 54
Austin, Texas	50.2	68.3	84.2	70.6	33.65	85	0.9	62 / 58
Baltimore, Md.	32.3	53.2	76.5	55.4	41.94	115	21.5	53
Baton Rouge, La.	50.1	66.6	81.7	68.1	63.08	110	0.2	52 / 46
Billings, Mont.	24.0	46.1	72.0	48.1	14.77	96	56.9	69
Birmingham, Ala.	42.6	61.3	80.2	62.9	53.99	117	1.5	60
Bismarck, N.D.	10.2	43.3	70.4	45.2	16.84	96	44.3	64
Boise, Idaho	30.2	50.6	74.7	52.8	12.19	89	20.6	64
Boston, Mass.	29.3	48.3	73.9	54.1	42.53	127	42.8	52 / 66
Bridgeport, Conn.	29.9	48.9	74.0	54.7	44.15	119	26.2	55 / 49
Buffalo, N.Y.	24.5	45.3	70.8	50.7	40.54	169	93.6	60
Burlington, Vt.	18.0	43.5	70.6	47.7	36.05	154	79.3	60
Caribou, Maine	9.5	38.1	65.6	42.8	37.44	161	112.1	64 / 63
Casper, Wyo.	22.3	42.7	70.0	45.7	13.03	94	77.8	53
Charleston, S.C.	47.9	64.2	81.7	66.2	51.53	114	0.7	61 / 57
Charleston, W.Va.	33.4	54.3	73.9	55.1	44.05	151	34.0	56 / 49
Charlotte, N.C.	41.7	60.9	80.3	61.7	43.51	112	5.6	64
Cheyenne, Wyo.	25.9	41.6	67.7	45.4	15.45	100	55.8	68
Chicago, Ill.	22.0	47.8	73.3	52.1	36.27	125	38.0	45 / 44
Cleveland, Ohio	25.7	47.6	71.9	52.2	38.71	155	57.6	62
Columbia, S.C.	44.6	63.2	82.0	63.7	48.27	109	1.9	56 / 55
Columbus, Ohio	28.3	52.0	75.1	54.7	38.52	137	28.2	64 / 56
Concord, N.H.	20.1	44.6	70.0	47.8	37.60	127	64.5	62
Dallas-Ft. Worth, Texas	44.1	65.0	85.0	67.2	34.73	79	2.6	50 / 45
Denver, Colo.	29.2	47.6	73.4	51.0	15.81	89	60.3	61
Des Moines, Iowa	20.4	50.6	76.1	52.8	34.72	108	33.3	64 / 60
Detroit, Mich.	24.5	48.1	73.5	51.9	32.89	135	41.3	45
Dodge City, Kan.	30.1	53.9	79.8	57.1	22.35	78	20.3	61
Duluth, Minn.	8.4	39.0	65.5	43.5	31.00	134	80.6	62 / 60
El Paso, Texas	45.1	64.6	83.3	64.9	9.43	49	5.3	64 / 57
Fairbanks, Alaska	-9.7	31.7	62.4	23.5	10.34	106	67.7	52
Fargo, N.D.	6.8	43.5	70.6	45.3	21.19	101	40.8	61
Grand Junction, Colo.	26.1	50.9	76.8	52.7	8.99	72	23.6	57
Grand Rapids, Mich.	22.4	46.3	71.4	49.9	37.13	144	73.3	40
Hartford, Conn.	25.7	48.9	73.7	51.9	46.16	128	49.6	49 / 46
Helena, Mont.	20.2	44.1	67.8	44.8	11.32	95	46.9	63 / 58
Honolulu, Hawaii	73.0	75.6	80.8	80.2	18.29	96	0.0	54 / 52
Houston, Texas	51.8	68.5	83.6	70.4	47.84	105	0.4	34 / 69
Indianapolis, Ind.	26.5	52.0	75.4	54.6	40.95	126	23.9	64 / 72
Jackson, Miss.	45.0	63.4	81.4	64.4	55.95	110	1.0	40 / 38
Jacksonville, Fla.	53.1	66.6	81.6	69.4	52.34	116	trace	62 / 60
Juneau, Alaska	25.7	40.8	56.8	42.3	58.33	223	97.0	59
Kansas City, Mo.	26.9	54.4	78.5	56.8	37.98	104	19.9	31 / 69
Knoxville, Tenn.	37.6	57.8	77.7	58.8	48.22	127	11.5	61 / 58
Las Vegas, Nev.	47.0	66.0	91.2	68.7	4.49	26	1.2	55 / 48
Lexington, Ky.	32.0	54.6	76.1	56.6	45.91	130	16.1	59 / 53
Little Rock, Ark.	40.1	61.4	82.4	63.3	50.93	104	5.2	61 / 56
Long Beach, Calif.	57.0	63.0	73.8	68.6	12.94	31	trace	59 / 52
Los Angeles, Calif.	57.1	60.8	69.3	66.9	13.15	35	trace	68 / 62
Louisville, Ky.	33.0	56.4	78.4	58.5	44.54	124	16.4	56
Madison, Wisc.	17.3	45.9	71.6	49.3	32.95	120	43.8	55
Memphis, Tenn.	39.9	62.1	82.5	63.8	54.65	107	5.1	53 / 49
Miami, Fla.	68.1	75.7	83.7	78.8	58.53	131	trace	61 / 59
Milwaukee, Wisc.	20.7	45.2	72.0	51.4	34.81	125	47.0	63
Minneapolis-St. Paul, Minn.	13.1	46.6	73.2	48.7	29.41	115	49.9	65 / 62
Mobile, Ala.	50.1	66.1	81.5	67.7	66.29	121	0.4	62 / 61
Montgomery, Ala.	46.6	64.3	81.8	65.4	54.77	108	0.4	59 / 52
Mt. Washington, N.H.	5.2	22.9	48.7	30.2	101.91	209	259.9	71
Nashville, Tenn.	36.8	58.5	79.1	59.9	48.11	119	10.1	62 / 58
Newark, N.J.	31.3	52.3	77.2	56.4	46.25	122	28.3	62
New Orleans, La.	52.6	68.2	82.7	70.0	64.16	114	0.2	55 / 51
New York, N.Y.	32.1	52.5	76.5	56.6	49.69	121	28.6	134 / 135
Norfolk, Va.	40.1	57.4	79.1	61.1	45.74	116	7.8	55 / 53

City	Average monthly temperature (°F)[1]				Precipitation		Snowfall[2]	Number of years observed[4]
					Average annual		Average annual (in.)[3]	
	Jan.	April	July	Oct.	(in.)[1]	(days)[3]		
Oklahoma City, Okla.	36.7	59.7	82.0	62.0	35.85	83	9.5	64
Olympia, Wash.	38.1	47.4	62.8	49.7	50.79	163	16.7	62 / 55
Omaha, Neb.	21.7	51.4	76.7	53.2	30.22	99	30.1	67 / 68
Philadelphia, Pa.	32.3	53.1	77.6	57.2	42.05	117	20.8	63 / 61
Phoenix, Ariz.	54.2	70.2	92.8	74.6	8.29	36	trace	64 / 62
Pittsburgh, Pa.	27.5	49.9	72.6	52.5	37.85	152	43.6	51
Portland, Maine	21.7	43.7	68.7	47.7	45.83	129	70.4	63
Portland, Ore.	39.9	51.2	68.1	54.3	37.07	153	6.5	63 / 55
Providence, R.I.	28.7	48.6	73.3	53.0	46.45	124	36.0	50
Raleigh, N.C.	39.7	59.1	78.8	60.0	43.05	113	7.5	59
Reno, Nev.	33.6	48.6	71.3	52.0	7.48	51	24.3	61 / 54
Richmond, Va.	36.4	57.1	77.9	58.3	43.91	114	13.8	66 / 64
Roswell, N.M.	40.0	60.5	80.8	61.4	13.34	54	11.7	31 / 51
Sacramento, Calif.	46.3	58.9	75.4	64.4	17.93	58	trace	64 / 50
Salt Lake City, Utah	29.2	50.0	77.0	52.5	16.50	91	58.7	75
San Antonio, Texas	50.3	68.6	84.3	70.7	32.92	82	0.7	61 / 58
San Diego, Calif.	57.8	62.6	70.9	67.6	10.77	41	trace	63 / 60
San Francisco, Calif.	49.4	56.2	62.8	61.0	20.11	63	trace	76 / 69
Savannah, Ga.	49.2	65.3	82.1	67.1	49.58	111	0.4	53 / 48
Seattle-Tacoma, Wash.	40.9	50.2	65.3	52.7	37.07	155	11.4	59 / 52
Sioux Falls, S.D.	14.0	45.7	73.0	48.0	24.69	98	41.2	58
Spokane, Wash.	27.3	46.5	68.6	47.2	16.67	112	48.6	56
Springfield, Ill.	25.1	52.8	76.3	55.5	35.56	113	23.2	56
St. Louis, Mo.	29.6	56.6	80.2	58.3	38.75	111	19.6	46 / 67
Tampa, Fla.	61.3	71.5	82.5	75.8	44.77	106	trace	57
Toledo, Ohio	23.9	48.3	73.0	51.8	33.21	134	37.1	48 / 43
Tucson, Ariz.	51.7	66.0	86.5	70.5	12.17	53	1.2	63
Tulsa, Okla.	36.4	60.8	83.5	62.6	42.42	91	10.2	64
Vero Beach, Fla.	63.0	71.5	81.7	76.4	51.93	126	trace	20 / 18
Washington, D.C.	34.9	56.1	79.2	58.8	39.35	113	17.1	62 / 60
Wichita, Kan.	30.2	55.3	81.0	58.6	30.38	85	15.9	50
Wilmington, Del.	31.5	52.4	76.6	55.8	42.81	117	21.1	56 / 53

1. Based on 30-year period 1971–2000. 2. Includes ice pellets and sleet; data since April 1988 also include hail. 3. Based on years observed, indicated in final column. 4. Through 2003. Where two figures are shown, the first figure is for precipitation data, the second for snowfall data. *Source:* National Oceanic and Atmospheric Administration (NOAA).

Revised Wind Chill Index

Source: The National Weather Service

The wind chill temperature index measures how cold people feel when outside. Wind chill is based on the rate of heat loss from exposed skin caused by wind and cold. As the wind increases, it draws heat from the body, driving down skin temperature and eventually the internal body temperature. The wind therefore makes it feel much colder. If the temperature is 0°F and the wind is blowing at 15 mph, the wind chill is −19°F. At this wind chill temperature, exposed skin can freeze in 30 minutes.

A revised wind chill table was introduced by the National Weather Service on Nov. 1, 2001. The new index was tested on human subjects and is based on heat loss from exposed skin. The old index, formulated in 1945 by Antarctic explorers, measured the cooling rate of water.

Wind speed (mph)	Temperature (°F)																	
	40	35	30	25	20	15	10	5	0	−5	−10	−15	−20	−25	−30	−35	−40	−45
5	36	31	25	19	13	7	1	−5	−11	−16	−22	−28	−34	−40	−46	−52	−57	−63
10	34	27	21	15	9	3	−4	−10	−16	−22	−28	−35	−41	−47	−53	−59	−66	−72
15	32	25	19	13	6	0	−7	−13	−19	−26	−32	−39	−45	−51	−58	−64	−71	−77
20	30	24	17	11	4	−2	−9	−15	−22	−29	−35	−42	−48	−55	−61	−68	−74	−81
25	29	23	16	9	3	−4	−11	−17	−24	−31	−37	−44	−51	−58	−64	−71	−78	−84
30	28	22	15	8	1	−5	−12	−19	−26	−33	−39	−46	−53	−60	−67	−73	−80	−87
35	28	21	14	7	0	−7	−14	−21	−27	−34	−41	−48	−55	−62	−69	−76	−82	−89
40	27	20	13	6	−1	−8	−15	−22	−29	−36	−43	−50	−57	−64	−71	−78	−84	−91
45	26	19	12	5	−2	−9	−16	−23	−30	−37	−44	−51	−58	−65	−72	−79	−86	−93
50	26	19	12	4	−3	−10	−17	−24	−31	−38	−45	−52	−60	−67	−74	−81	−88	−95
55	25	18	11	4	−3	−11	−18	−25	−32	−39	−46	−54	−61	−68	−75	−82	−89	−97
60	25	17	10	3	−4	−11	−19	−26	−33	−40	−48	−55	−62	−69	−76	−84	−91	−98

Frostbite Times: **Bold = 30 minutes**　*Italic = 10 Minutes*　***Bold italic = 5 minutes***

Formula: Wind Chill (°F) = $35.74 + 0.6215T − 35.75(V^{0.16}) + 0.4275T(V^{0.16})$
Where, T = Air Temperature (°F)　V = Wind Speed (mph)

See Weights and Measures, p. 452, for Fahrenheit and Celsius scales.

The World's Top Tourism Destinations

(international tourist arrivals)

2003 rank	Country	Arrivals (million)			2003 rank	Country	Arrivals (million)		
		2001	2002	2003			2001	2002	2003
1.	France	76.5	77.0	75.0	6.	United Kingdom	22.8	24.2	24.8
2.	Spain	49.5	52.3	52.5	7.	Austria	18.2	18.6	19.1
3.	United States	45.5	41.9	40.4	8.	Mexico	19.8	19.7	18.7
4.	Italy	39.1	39.8	39.6	9.	Germany	17.9	18.0	18.4
5.	China	33.2	36.8	33.0	10.	Canada	19.7	20.1	17.5

Source: World Tourism Organization (WTO). Web: www.world-tourism.org.

International Destinations of American Tourists, 2003

	All U.S. travelers	For leisure and visiting friends/ relatives	For business and conventions		All U.S. travelers	For leisure and visiting friends/ relatives	For business and conventions
Total number of travelers	24,452,000	19,782,000	7,018,000	**Leisure/recreational activities[1]**			
International destinations visited				Dining in restaurants	86%	86%	91%
Europe	42%	41%	50%	Shopping	75	79	67
Western Europe	40	39	47	Visit historical places	49	54	38
United Kingdom	13	12	20	Sightseeing in cities	41	46	30
France	8	8	8	Visit small towns/villages	41	46	26
Italy	7	7	5	Touring the countryside	34	39	21
Germany	6	6	9	Cultural sites	30	34	20
Spain	4	4	3	Art gallery, museum	27	30	20
Netherlands	3	4	4	Water sports/ sunbathing	25	30	12
Switzerland	3	2	3	Nightclub/dancing	24	26	17
Ireland	2	2	2	Guided tours	16	18	8
Austria	2	2	2	Concert, play, musical	13	15	10
Eastern Europe	4	4	4	Ethnic heritage sites	12	13	7
Caribbean	22	24	9	Amusement/ theme parks	10	11	6
Jamaica	6	7	3	Visit national parks	10	11	6
Bahamas	6	7	2	Casinos/gambling	9	10	4
Dominican Republic	4	4	1	Golf/tennis	7	7	7
South America	8	8	8	Environmental sites	6	7	4
Brazil	3	2	4	Camping/hiking	5	6	3
Central America	7	7	5	Cruises	5	5	2
Costa Rica	2	2	1	Sporting events	4	4	4
Africa	2	2	3	Hunting/fishing	3	4	2
Middle East	3	3	4	Ranch vacations	2	2	1
Asia	16	15	23				
Japan	4	4	7				
China	2	2	4				
South Korea	2	2	4				
Hong Kong	2	2	3				
Taiwan	2	2	4				
India	2	2	2				
Oceania	3	4	4				
Australia	2	2	3				

1. Multiple response. *Source:* U.S. Dept. of Commerce, ITA, Office of Travel & Tourism Industries.

Top States Visited by U.S. Tourists, 2003

1.	California	6.	North Carolina
2.	Florida	7.	Georgia
3.	Texas	8.	Virginia
4.	Pennsylvania	9.	Ohio
5.	New York	10.	Illinois

Source: Travel Industry Association of America; Travelscope®.

Season of U.S. Travel in 2003

(percent of trips)

Winter	20%
Spring	23%
Summer	33%
Fall	24%

Source: Travel Industry Association of America; Travelscope®.

Top U.S. States and Cities Visited by Overseas Travelers, 2003[1]

State/territory	Number of arrivals	U.S. city	Number of arrivals
1. New York	4.1 million	1. New York	4.0 million
2. Florida	4.1 million	2. Los Angeles	2.2 million
3. California	4.0 million	3. Miami	2.2 million
4. Hawaii	2.0 million	4. Orlando	1.8 million
5. Nevada	1.4 million	5. San Francisco	1.6 million
6. Guam	901,000	6. Oahu/Honolulu	1.6 million
7. Illinois	901,000	7. Las Vegas	1.3 million
8. Massachusetts	901,000	8. Metro DC area	901,000
9. Texas	901,000	9. Chicago	721,000
10. New Jersey	721,000	10. Boston	721,000
Top 10 state/territory total	**19.9 million**	**Top 10 city total**	**17.0 million**

NOTE: Includes travelers for business and pleasure, international travelers in transit through the United States, and students; excludes travel by international personnel and international businessmen employed in the United States. 1. Excludes visitors from Canada and Mexico. *Source:* U.S. Dept. of Commerce, Office of Travel and Tourism Industries/International Trade Administration.

America's Best Beaches, 2005

	Name	Location		Name	Location
1.	Fort DeSoto Park—North Beach	St. Petersburg, Fla.	6.	Coast Guard Beach	Cape Cod, Mass.
			7.	Coronado Beach	San Diego, Calif.
2.	Ocracoke Island	Outer Banks, N.C.	8.	Cape Florida State Park	Key Biscayne, Fla.
3.	Hanalei Bay	Kauai, Hawaii	9.	Main Beach	East Hampton, N.Y.
4.	Caladesi Island State Park	Clearwater, Fla.			
5.	Fleming Beach	Maui, Hawaii	10.	Hamoa Beach	Maui, Hawaii

NOTE: Released since 1991, 650 major public recreational beaches in the U.S. are rated according to 50 criteria. *Source:* Dr. Stephen P. Leatherman (a.k.a. Dr. Beach), author of *America's Best Beaches* and professor of environmental studies at Florida International University.

Top 25 Nationalities of Foreign Travelers to the U.S., 2004

Residence of travelers to the U.S.	Arrivals	Residence of travelers to the U.S.	Arrivals	Residence of travelers to the U.S.	Arrivals
1. Canada	13,849,000	10. Netherlands	424,872	19. Sweden	254,258
2. Mexico	11,906,000	11. Brazil	384,734	20. Switzerland	243,186
3. United Kingdom	4,302,737	12. Ireland	345,119	21. China	202,544
4. Japan	3,747,620	13. Spain	333,432	22. Belgium	175,997
5. Germany	1,319,904	14. Venezuela	330,285	23. Argentina	167,726
6. France	775,274	15. India	308,845	24. Hong Kong	123,335
7. South Korea	626,595	16. Taiwan	297,684	25. Austria	112,950
8. Australia	519,955	17. Colombia	295,371		
9. Italy	470,805	18. Israel	275,373		

Source: Office of Travel and Tourism Industries/International Trade Administration. Web: www.tia.org.

Current Travel Warnings for U.S. Citizens[1]

Travel warnings are issued when the State Department recommends that Americans avoid a certain country. The countries listed below are currently on that list. In addition to this list, the State Department issues Consular Information Sheets for every country of the world with information on such matters as the health conditions, crime, unusual currency or entry requirements, or any areas of instability.

Country	Most recent warning issued	Country	Most recent warning issued	Country	Most recent warning issued
Afghanistan	6/09/05	Iran	6/30/05	Pakistan	3/25/05
Algeria	7/21/05	Iraq	6/28/05	Philippines	3/23/05
Bosnia and Herzegovina	8/01/05	Israel, West Bank, and Gaza	6/20/05	Saudi Arabia	5/17/05
Burundi	12/07/04			Somalia	7/21/05
Central African Republic	4/19/05	Kenya	7/01/05	Sudan	8/05/05
Colombia	5/04/05	Kyrgyzstan	3/24/05	Uzbekistan	7/01/05
Côte d'Ivoire	2/08/05	Lebanon	4/21/05	Yemen	5/06/05
Dem. Rep. of the Congo	6/24/05	Liberia	3/03/05	Zimbabwe	3/16/05
Haiti	5/26/05	Nepal	6/24/05		
Indonesia	5/10/05	Nigeria	5/20/05		

NOTE: In the wake of the terrorist attacks on the World Trade Center and the Pentagon on Sept. 11, 2001, the State Department issued a worldwide caution for U.S. citizens traveling abroad. 1. As of August 2005. *Source:* U.S. Department of State. Web: http://travel.state.gov.

Average Number of Vacation Days Around the World Per Year

Italy	42 days	Brazil	34 days	Korea	25 days
France	37 days	United Kingdom	28 days	Japan	25 days
Germany	35 days	Canada	26 days	U.S.	13 days

Source: World Tourism Organization (WTO).

Average Daily Temperatures (°F) in Tourist Cities

(For U.S. cities, see Climate of Selected U.S. Cities, pp. 601–602)

Location	January High	January Low	April High	April Low	July High	July Low	October High	October Low
Acapulco (Mexico)	87	72	87	73	89	77	89	77
Amsterdam (Netherlands)	41	34	53	40	69	55	57	46
Athens (Greece)	54	42	67	52	90	72	74	60
Auckland (New Zealand)	73	60	67	56	56	46	63	52
Bangkok (Thailand)	89	69	94	78	91	77	89	76
Beijing (China)	35	15	68	44	87	71	67	44
Belgrade (Yugoslavia)	38	28	62	43	81	60	64	46
Berlin (Germany)	35	26	55	38	74	55	55	41
Bombay (India)	83	67	89	76	85	77	89	76
Cairo (Egypt)	65	47	83	57	96	70	86	65
Calcutta (India)	80	55	97	75	89	79	89	74
Cape Town (South Africa)	69	56	66	54	60	50	65	53
Caracas (Venezuela)	75	56	81	60	78	61	79	61
Copenhagen (Denmark)	36	29	50	37	72	55	53	42
Dublin (Ireland)	47	35	54	38	67	51	57	43
Glasgow (Scotland)	43	34	53	38	66	52	54	43
Hamilton (Bermuda)	68	58	71	59	85	73	79	69
Helsinki (Finland)	27	17	43	31	71	57	45	37
Hong Kong (China)	67	51	79	67	90	78	84	70
Istanbul (Turkey)	48	36	59	45	78	64	66	53
Jerusalem (Israel)	55	41	73	50	87	63	81	59
Kingston (Jamaica)	86	67	87	70	90	73	88	73
Lagos (Nigeria)	88	74	89	77	82	74	85	74
Lisbon (Portugal)	56	46	64	52	79	63	69	57
London (United Kingdom)	44	35	56	40	73	55	58	44
Madrid (Spain)	50	34	63	43	89	61	67	48
Mexico City (Mexico)	66	42	77	51	73	53	70	50
Montreal (Canada)	22	6	51	33	79	60	56	39
Moscow (Russia)	21	9	47	31	76	55	46	34
Nairobi (Kenya)	77	53	75	57	69	51	77	54
Nassau (Bahamas)	77	65	81	69	88	75	85	73
Oslo (Norway)	30	20	50	34	73	56	49	37
Paris (France)	42	32	60	41	76	55	59	44
Prague (Czech Republic)	34	25	55	40	74	58	54	44
Quebec (Canada)	19	3	45	30	77	58	51	37
Rio de Janeiro (Brazil)	84	73	80	69	75	63	77	66
Rome (Italy)	54	39	68	46	88	64	73	53
San José (Costa Rica)	75	58	79	62	77	62	77	60
San Juan (Puerto Rico)	81	70	83	72	86	76	86	75
Seoul (Korea)	33	17	62	42	84	70	67	47
Singapore	86	73	89	75	87	75	88	74
Stockholm (Sweden)	31	23	45	32	70	55	48	39
Sydney (Australia)	79	65	73	57	62	44	72	55
Taipei (Taiwan)	66	54	77	63	92	76	81	67
Tokyo (Japan)	48	31	64	48	84	71	70	56
Toronto (Canada)	30	17	51	35	79	60	57	42
Vancouver (Canada)	42	32	55	41	71	55	57	44
Vienna (Austria)	34	26	57	41	75	59	55	44
Zurich (Switzerland)	36	26	60	41	77	56	57	43

U.S. Passport Information

With a few exceptions, a passport is required for all U.S. citizens to depart and enter the United States and to enter most foreign countries.

Application for a passport may be made at a passport agency, many federal and state courts, probate courts, some county and municipal offices, and some post offices. The thirteen major cities with U.S. passport agencies are Boston, Chicago, Honolulu, Houston, Los Angeles, Miami, New Orleans, New York, Norwalk, Conn., Philadelphia, San Francisco, Seattle, and Washington, DC.

If you would like more information about obtaining or renewing a passport, visit the State Dept. website (http://travel.state.gov) or call the National Passport Information Center, 1-888-362-8668.

World's 25 Busiest Airports by Passengers and Cargo, 2004

Airport	Total passengers[1]	2003–2004 percent change	Airport	Total cargo[1]	2003–2004 percent change
1. Atlanta, Hartsfield (ATL)	83,578,906	5.7%	Memphis (MEM)	3,554,577	4.8%
2. Chicago, O'Hare (ORD)	75,373,888	7.1	Hong Kong (HKG)	3,132,449	15.7
3. London, Heathrow (LHR)	67,343,960	6.1	Tokyo, Narita (NRT)	2,373,133	10.1
4. Tokyo, Haneda (HND)	62,320,968	–0.9	Anchorage (ANC)	2,372,903	13.1
5. Los Angeles (LAX)	60,710,830	10.4	Seoul (ICN)	2,133,443	15.8
6. Dallas/Ft. Worth (DFW)	59,412,217	11.6	Los Angeles (LAX)	1,902,547	5.3
7. Frankfurt-Main (FRA)	51,098,271	5.7	Frankfurt-Main (FRA)	1,839,084	11.4
8. Paris, Charles de Gaulle (CDG)	50,860,561	5.5	Singapore (SIN)	1,795,646	10.0
9. Amsterdam, Schiphol (AMS)	42,541,180	6.5	Miami (MIA)	1,778,897	8.6
10. Denver (DEN)	42,393,693	13.0	Louisville (SDF)	1,739,029	7.5
11. Las Vegas (LAS)	41,436,571	14.3	Taipei (TPE)	1,701,020	13.4
12. Phoenix, Sky Harbor (PHX)	39,493,519	5.5	New York (JFK)	1,683,073	2.7
13. Madrid (MAD)	38,525,899	7.5	Chicago, O'Hare (ORD)	1,681,835	11.6
14. Bangkok (BKK)	37,960,169	25.8	Shanghai (PVG)	1,642,062	38.1
15. New York (JFK)	37,362,010	17.7	Paris, Charles de Gaulle (CDG)	1,637,610	9.4
16. Minneapolis/St. Paul (MSP)	36,748,577	10.7	Amsterdam, Schiphol (AMS)	1,467,205	8.4
17. Hong Kong (HKG)	36,713,000	36.1	London, Heathrow (LHR)	1,412,031	8.6
18. Houston (IAH)	36,490,828	6.8	Dubai (DXB)	1,169,256	22.2
19. Detroit (DTW)	35,199,307	7.8	Bangkok (BKK)	1,058,145	11.3
20. Beijing (PEK)	34,883,190	43.2	Indianapolis (IND)	1,000,262	9.3
21. San Francisco (SFO)	33,497,084	14.3	Newark (EWR)	920,104	5.0
22. Newark (EWR)	31,847,280	8.1	Osaka (KIX)	886,857	11.8
23. London, Gatwick (LGW)	31,461,523	4.8	Atlanta, Hartsfield (ATL)	864,650	7.9
24. Orlando (MCO)	31,110,852	13.9	Tokyo, Haneda (HND)	773,918	7.2
25. Tokyo, Narita (NRT)	31,106,264	17.2	Dallas/Ft. Worth (DFW)	754,764	12.2

NOTES: Total passengers enplaned and deplaned, passengers in transit counted once. Total cargo loaded and unloaded, freight and mail (in metric tons). 1. Results are preliminary. *Source:* Airports Council International World Headquarters, Geneva, Switzerland. Web: www.airports.org.

Getting to Work in the City

Commuting characteristics for the 15 largest U.S. cities by population, 2000

2000 rank	City of residence	Total workers 16 years and over	Means of transportation (%)					Worked at home	Average travel time to work (min.)
			Drove alone	Carpool	Public transit	Walked	Other means		
1.	New York, N.Y.	3,332,698	24.1%	6.4%	56.3%	9.3%	1.4%	2.5%	39.0
2.	Los Angeles, Calif.	1,592,463	67.1	14.9	9.5	2.9	1.6	4.0	28.1
3.	Chicago, Ill.	1,252,949	50.5	12.8	27.6	5.6	0.9	2.5	33.1
4.	Houston, Tex.	919,762	72.9	14.7	6.0	2.6	1.2	2.6	25.9
5.	Philadelphia, Pa.	587,156	47.6	10.4	28.0	10.4	1.7	1.9	29.2
6.	Phoenix, Ariz.	589,860	71.9	17.0	3.6	1.9	2.5	3.2	24.7
7.	San Diego, Calif.	579,615	78.5	10.4	4.6	2.3	1.2	2.9	22.6
8.	Dallas, Tex.	560,913	73.4	14.5	5.1	2.2	2.3	2.5	25.2
9.	San Antonio, Tex.	490,076	78.7	13.9	3.6	1.6	0.9	1.4	21.5
10.	Detroit, Mich.	317,179	76.4	12.8	6.2	2.3	1.2	1.0	24.2
11.	San Jose, Calif.	450,093	73.0	16.9	4.9	1.7	0.8	2.7	26.4
12.	Indianapolis, Ind.	407,377	81.9	10.2	2.2	2.5	1.5	1.7	21.6
13.	San Francisco, Calif.	419,601	41.1	9.3	32.1	8.8	3.9	4.8	29.6
14.	Jacksonville, Fla.	350,797	81.9	11.4	1.9	1.5	1.5	1.8	22.6
15.	Columbus, Ohio	353,192	82.5	9.3	3.0	2.0	0.7	2.5	20.7
	Total for U.S.	**127,448,586**	**76.3**	**11.2**	**5.2**	**2.7**	**1.4**	**3.2**	**24.3**

NOTES: Percentages may not add up to 100%, due to rounding. *Source:* U.S. Bureau of the Census. Web: www.census.gov/.

World's Largest Subway Systems

(by ridership)

City	Date system completed	Number of riders (year)	Length (km)	City	Date system completed	Number of riders (year)	Length (km)
Moscow	1935	3.2 bil (1997)	340	Paris	1900	1.2 bil (1998)	211
Tokyo	1927	2.6 bil (1997/98)	281+	Osaka	1933	957 mil (1997)	114
Seoul	1974	1.4 bil (1993)	278+	London	1863	866 mil (1999)	415
Mexico City	1969	1.4 bil (1996)	202	Hong Kong	1979	790 mil (1999)	82
New York City	1904	1.3 bil (2001)	371	St. Petersburg	1955	721 mil (1996)	110

Sources: Jane's Urban Transport Systems, 2002–2003 edition, and individual subway websites.

Major Causes of Traffic Congestion in the U.S.

Bottlenecks (traffic demand exceeds roadway capacity)	50% of total congestion	Work zones	15% of total congestion
		Bad weather	10% of total congestion
Traffic incidents	25% of total congestion	Poor signal timing	5% of total congestion

Source: American Highway Users Alliance, *Unclogging America's Arteries 1999-2004.* Web: www.highways.org.

America's 24 Worst Highway Bottlenecks

Rank	City	Freeway	Location	Vehicles per day	Annual hours of delay
1.	Los Angeles	US-101	US-101 (Ventura Fwy) at I-405 Interchange	318,000	27,144
2.	Houston	I-610	I-610 at I-10 Interchange (West)	295,000	25,181
3.	Chicago	I-90	I-90/94 at I-290 Interchange ("Circle Interchange")	293,671	25,068
4.	Phoenix	I-10	I-10 at SR-51/SR-202 Interchange ("Mini-Stack")	280,800	22,805
5.	Los Angeles	I-405	I-405 (San Diego Fwy) at I-10 Interchange	296,000	22,792
6.	Atlanta	I-75	I-75 at I-85 Interchange	259,128	21,045
7.	Washington (DC-Md.-Va.)	I-495	I-495 at I-270 Interchange	243,425	19,429
8.	Los Angeles	I-10	I-10 (Santa Monica Fwy) at I-5 Interchange	318,500	18,606
9.	Los Angeles	I-405	I-405 (San Diego Fwy) at I-605 Interchange	318,000	18,606
10.	Atlanta	I-285	I-285 at I-85 Interchange ("Spaghetti Junction")	266,000	17,072
11.	Chicago	I-94	I-94 (Dan Ryan Expwy) at I-90 Skyway Split (Southside)	260,403	16,713
12.	Phoenix	I-17	I-17 (Black Canyon Fwy) at I-10 Interchange (the "Stack") to Cactus Rd.	208,000	16,310
13.	Los Angeles	I-5	I-5 (Santa Ana Fwy) at SR-22/SR-57 Interchange ("Orange Crush")	308,000	16,304
14.	Providence	I-95	I-95 at I-195 Interchange	256,000	15,340
15.	Washington (DC-Md.-Va.)	I-495	I-495 at I-95 Interchange	185,125	15,035
16.	Tampa	I-275	I-275 at I-4 Interchange ("Malfunction Junction")	201,500	14,371
17.	Atlanta	I-285	I-285 at I-75 Interchange	239,193	14,333
18.	Seattle	I-5	I-5 at I-90 Interchange	301,112	14,306
19.	Chicago	I-290	I-290 (Eisenhower Expwy) Between Exits 17b and 23a	200,441	14,009
20.	Houston	I-45	I-45 (Gulf Freeway) at US-59 Interchange	250,299	13,944
21.	San Jose	US-101	US-101 at I-880 Interchange	244,000	12,249
22.	Las Vegas	US-95	US-95 at I-15 Interchange ("Spaghetti Bowl")	190,600	11,152
23.	San Diego	I-805	I-805 at I-15 Interchange	238,000	10,992
24.	Cincinnati	I-75	I-75, from Ohio River Bridge to I-71 Interchange	136,013	10,088

NOTE: In reviewing the list of bottleneck locations identified by this report, readers will note that none of the worst bottlenecks are in the New York City area. These are excluded because most of these bottlenecks are also the result of toll facilities, which are fundamentally different from other physical bottlenecks (such as freeway-to-freeway interchanges) that are prevalent around the country. Delay comparisons between toll facilities and other types of bottlenecks might not be consistent since different modeling techniques would be used. If objective field measurements of delay could be made at all locations around the country, several river crossings into Manhattan would no doubt be included in a list of the nation's worst bottlenecks. *Source:* American Highway Users Alliance, *Unclogging America's Arteries 1999-2004.* Web: www.highways.org.

U.S. Driving Fatalities, Total and Alcohol-Related

	Fatalities				Fatalities		
Year	Total	Alcohol-related	Percent	Year	Total	Alcohol-related	Percent
1982	43,945	26,173	60%	1993	40,150	17,908	45%
1983	42,589	24,635	58	1994	40,716	17,308	43
1984	44,257	24,762	56	1995	41,817	17,732	42
1985	43,825	23,167	53	1996	42,065	17,749	42
1986	46,087	25,017	54	1997	42,013	16,711	40
1987	46,390	24,094	52	1998	41,501	16,673	40
1988	47,087	23,833	51	1999	41,717	16,572	40
1989	45,582	22,424	49	2000	41,945	17,380	41
1990	44,599	22,587	51	2001	42,196	17,400	41
1991	41,508	20,159	49	2002	42,815	17,419	41
1992	39,250	18,290	47	2003	42,643	17,013	40

Source: National Highway Traffic Safety Administration.

Driving Laws, 2005

Currently all states plus DC have child safety seat laws and enforce a drinking age of 21. As of August 2005, all 50 states had blood alcohol concentration (bac) limits of 0.08, following concerted state and national efforts to lower the rate from 0.10. A national speed limit of 55 mph was imposed in 1974, and in 1987 it was modified to allow 65-mile-per-hour speeds on some rural freeways. The federal law was entirely repealed in 1995, giving states the right to set their own limits. As of April 2005, graduated licensing laws were in effect in 41 states plus DC, 38 of which prohibit young drivers from driving during high-risk nighttime and early morning hours.

State	Minimum age for driver's license[1]	Administrative license suspension[2]	Alcohol ignition interlock device[3]	Penalties include forfeiture[4]	Mandatory belt-use law seating positions	Motorcycle helmet law[5]	Maximum allowable speed limit 1995	Maximum allowable speed limit 2004
Alabama	17	90 days	no	no	front	yes	65	70
Alaska	16 + 6 mo.	90 days	yes	yes	all	18[6]	—	65
Arizona	16	90 days	yes	yes	front[7]	18	55	75
Arkansas	16	120 days	yes	yes	front	21	65	70
California	17	4 months	yes	yes	all	yes	55	70
Colorado	17	3 months	yes	no	front	no	65	75
Connecticut	16 + 10 mo.	90 days	no	no	front	18	55	65
Delaware	16 + 10 mo.	3 months	yes	no	all	19[8]	—	65
DC	18	2–90 days	no	no	all	yes	55	55
Florida	18	6 months	yes	yes	front[7]	21[9]	65	70
Georgia	18	1 year	yes	yes	front[7]	yes	55	70
Hawaii	16	3 months	yes	no	front[7]	18	—	60
Idaho	16	90 days	yes	no	all	18	65	75
Illinois	17	3 months	yes	yes	front[7]	no	65	65
Indiana	18	180 days	yes	no	front	18	65	65
Iowa	17	180 days	yes	no	front	no	55	65
Kansas	16	30 days	yes	no	front	18	65	70
Kentucky	16 + 6 mo.	—	yes	yes	all	21[9, 10]	65	65
Louisiana	17	90 days	yes	yes	front	yes	65	70
Maine	16 + 6 mo.	90 days	yes	yes	all	15[10]	65	65
Maryland	17 + 7 mo.	45 days	yes	no	front	yes	55	65
Massachusetts	18	90 days	no	no	all	yes	55	65
Michigan	17	—	yes	yes	front[7]	yes	55	70
Minnesota	16	90 days	yes	yes	front[7]	18[10]	65	70
Mississippi	16	90 days	yes	yes	front[7]	yes	65	70
Missouri	18	30 days	yes	yes	front[7]	yes	70	70
Montana	15	—	yes	yes	all	18	65	75
Nebraska	17	90 days	yes	no	front	yes	65	75
Nevada	16	90 days	yes	no	all	yes	55	75
New Hampshire	17 + 1 mo.	6 months	yes	no	—	no	65	65
New Jersey	18	—	yes	no	front[7]	yes	—	65
New Mexico	16 + 6 mo.	90 days	yes	no	all	18	65	75
New York	17	variable	yes	yes	all	yes	55	65
North Carolina	16 + 6 mo.	30 days	yes	yes	front	yes	55	70
North Dakota	16	91 days	yes	yes	front	18	65	75
Ohio	17	90 days	yes	yes	front	18[11]	65	65
Oklahoma	16	180 days	yes	yes	front	18	65	75
Oregon	17	90 days	yes	yes	all	yes	65	65
Pennsylvania	17	—	yes	yes	front[7]	21[11]	55	65
Rhode Island	17 + 6 mo.	—	yes	yes	all	21[6, 11]	55	65
South Carolina	16 + 6 mo.	—	yes	yes	all	21	65	70
South Dakota	16	—	no	no	front	18	65	75
Tennessee	17	—	yes	yes	front	yes	65	70
Texas	16 + 6 mo.	90 days	yes	yes	front[7]	21[9]	65	75
Utah	17	90 days	yes	no	all	18	55	75
Vermont	16 + 6 mo.	90 days	no	yes	all	yes	65	65
Virginia	18	7 days	yes	yes	front	yes	65	65
Washington	17	90 days	yes	yes	all	yes	55	70
West Virginia	17	6 months	yes	no	front[7]	yes	65	70
Wisconsin	16 + 9 mo.	6 months	yes	yes	front[7]	18[10]	65	65
Wyoming	16 + 6 mo.	90 days	no	no	all	19	65	75

1. Refers to minimum age for driver's license with no restrictions on unsupervised nighttime driving or carrying passengers. Driver education may be a prerequisite, and one may be limited to carrying only seat-belted passengers. 2. How long (or if) licenses can be suspended before conviction, if drivers fail or refuse to take a chemical test. 3. Legislation for instruments designed to prevent drivers from starting their cars when breath alcohol content is at or above a set point. 4. A multiple offender's vehicle may be seized and disposed. 5. Presence of law, or age below which riders are required to wear helmet. 6. All passengers required to wear helmet. 7. Required for certain ages at all seating positions. 8. Helmet must also be carried on the motorcycle, whether or not it is worn, for persons 19 and older. 9. Helmet optional for those over listed age if they have proper insurance. (In Texas, they may instead complete a training and safety course.) 10. Helmets must be worn by cyclists holding learners' permits. 11. First-year novices required to wear helmet. (In Penn., first two years, unless driver completes a safety course.) Source: Insurance Institute for Highway Safety. Web: www.hwysafety.org.

U.S. Seat Belt Use, 2004

State	Percent	State	Percent	State	Percent
Arizona	95.3%	Illinois	83.0%	Louisiana	75.0%
Hawaii	95.1	Connecticut	82.9	Ohio	74.1
Washington	94.2	Delaware	82.3	Idaho	74.0
Oregon	92.6	Minnesota	82.1	Wisconsin	72.4
Michigan	90.5	New Jersey	82.0	Maine	72.3
California	90.4	Pennsylvania	81.8	Tennessee	72.0
Puerto Rico	90.1	Montana	80.9	Wyoming	70.1
New Mexico	89.7	Oklahoma	80.3	South Dakota	69.4
Maryland	89.0	Alabama	80.0	Kansas	68.3
Dist. of Columbia	87.1	Vermont	79.9	North Dakota	67.4
Georgia	86.7	Virginia	79.9	Kentucky	66.0
Nevada	86.6	Colorado	79.3	South Carolina	65.7
Iowa	86.4	Nebraska	79.2	Arkansas	64.2
North Carolina	86.1	Alaska	76.7	Massachusetts	63.3
Utah	85.7	Florida	76.3	Mississippi	63.2
New York	85.0	Rhode Island	76.2	New Hampshire	n.a.
Indiana	83.4	Missouri	75.9	**Nationwide**	**80.0**
Texas	83.2	West Virginia	75.8		

NOTE: n.a. = not available. *Source:* National Highway Traffic Safety Administration, DOT HS 809 783, September 2004.

Most Popular Car Colors, 2003–2004
(Percentage of vehicles manufactured during 2003 and 2004 model years in North America)

Luxury	2004	2003	Sport/Compact	2004	2003
1. Silver and Gray	26%	41%	1. Silver	20%	20%
2. White Pearl	17	18	2. Red	17	16
3. White	12	13	3. Black	13	14
4. Black	12	11	4. Blue	13	14
5. Light Brown	11	<1	5. Lt. Brown	9	8
6. Red	9	4	6. White	9	9
7. Blue	9	4	7. Med./Dk. Gray	8	12
8. Yellow/Gold	4	4	8. Green	4	
9. Others	<1	4	9. Yellow	4	3
			10. Others	3	4

Full/Intermediate	2004	2003	SUV/Truck/Van	2004	2003
1. Silver	24%	25%	1. White/White Pearl	20%	22%
2. Lt. Brown	17	16	2. Silver	16	17
3. Red	12	9	3. Red	14	16
4. White	13	12	4. Black	12	12
5. Med./Dk. Gray	11	13	5. Blue	12	9
6. Black	9	9	6. Med./Dk. Gray	10	9
7. Blue	6	6	7. Lt. Brown	9	6
8. Green	5	5	8. Green	5	7
9. Yellow/Gold	1	2	9. Yellow/Gold	1	—
10. Others	2	3	10. Others	1	2

Source: DuPont Herberts Automotive Systems, Troy, Mich. 2004 DuPont Automotive Color Popularity Survey Results. Web: www.automotive.dupont.com.

Top-Selling Vehicles in the U.S., 2003

Rank	Vehicle	Number	Rank	Vehicle	Number
1.	Ford F-Series	821,865	6.	Ford Taurus	300,496
2.	Chevrolet Silverado	684,302	7.	Honda Civic	299,672
3.	Dodge Ram	449,371	8.	Ford Explorer	268,644
4.	Toyota Camry	413,296	9.	Chevrolet Impala	267,882
5.	Honda Accord	397,750	10.	Chevrolet Cavalier	256,550

Source: J. D. Power and Associates.

Most Stolen Cars, 2004

Rank	Year, make, model	Rank	Year, make, model	Rank	Year, make, model
1.	1999 Acura Integra	5.	2002 Audi S4	9.	1997 Acura Integra
2.	2002 BMW M Roadster	6.	1996 Acura Integra	10.	1992 Mercedes-Benz 600
3.	1998 Acura Integra	7.	1995 Acura Integra	11.	2001 Acura Integra
4.	1991 GMC V2500	8.	2004 Mercury Marauder	12.	1989 Chevrolet R25

NOTE: The most stolen vehicle report is based on total losses identified as stolen and not recovered. CCC does not include temporary auto-related thefts such as "joy-rides" or theft of car items such as stereos. *Source:* CCC Information Services, Inc.

Top AAA Cars, 2005

AAA evaluates more than 200 vehicles each year and selects the top-rated vehicle in each category, based on cost and type. Cars are rated according to value, fuel economy, braking, ride, handling, passenger environment, cargo space, and other criteria.

Category	Make/model	Category	Make/model
$50,000 or more	Jaguar XJ Long Wheelbase	Under $15,000	Mazda 3
$40,000–$50,000	Acura RL	SUV over $30,000	Volvo XC90
$35,000–$40,000	Lexus GS	SUV under $30,000	Ford Escape Hybrid
$30,000–$35,000	Volvo S80	Minivan	Honda Odyssey
$25,000–$30,000	Infiniti G35	Pickup Truck	Honda Ridgeline
$20,000–$25,000	Chrysler 300	Cool Car	Ford Mustang
$15,000–$20,000	Honda Accord		

Source: AAA. Web: www.aaa.com.

Most Expensive Cars, 2005

Rank	Make, model	Price	Rank	Make, model	Price
1.	Saleen S7	$562,700	6.	Maybach 57	$327,750
2.	Mercedes-Benz SLR McLaren	452,750	7.	Lamborghini Murciélago	281,000
3.	Porsche Carrera GT	443,000	8.	Aston Martin V12 Vanquish	256,350
4.	Maybach 62	377,750	9.	Ferrari 612 Scaglietti	254,150
5.	Rolls-Royce Phantom	320,000	10.	Ferrari 575M Maranello	225,090

NOTE: All base prices are for 2005 models. Includes only vehicles currently sold in the U.S. *Source:* Forbes.com.

Least and Most Polluting Cars, 2005

The *ACEEE's Green Book®*, a buyer's guide to environmentally friendly passenger vehicles, rates cars according to their emissions and fuel consumption, and publishes an annual list of the "greenest" and "meanest" (i.e., most polluting).

Greenest vehicles	MPG: city	MPG: hwy.	Green[1] score	Meanest vehicles	MPG: city	MPG: hwy.	Green[1] score
1. Honda Civic GX	30	34	57	1. Dodge Ram SRT10	9	12	11
2. Honda Insight	57	56	56	2. Ford Excursion	13	17	13
3. Toyota Prius	60	51	53	3. Hummer H2	13	17	13
4. Honda Civic Hybrid	47	48	51	4. Mercedes-Benz G55 AMG	12	14	13
5. Toyota Corolla	32	41	44	5. Lamborghini Murciélago	9	13	14
6. Toyota Echo	35	42	43	6. GMC Yukon XL K2500	13	17	14
7. Nissan Sentra	28	35	42	7. Chevrolet Suburban K2500	14	17	14
8. Honda Civic HX	36	44	42	8. Land Rover Range Rover	12	16	14
9. Pontiac Vibe/Toyota Matrix	30	36	41	9. Bentley Arnage	10	14	14
10. Mazda 3	28	35	41	10. Mercedes-Benz G500	13	14	15
11. Ford Escape Hybrid	36	31	40	11. Lamborghini Gallardo	9	15	15
12. Ford Focus/Focus Wagon	26	35	40	12. Dodge Ram 1500 Pickup	12	16	15

NOTE: MPG = miles per gallon. 1. The green score runs on a scale from 0 to 100. The top vehicle this year scored a 57, the average was 27, and the worst gas-guzzler scored 11. The score is based on automakers' test results for fuel economy and emissions as reported to the EPA, as well as an estimate of pollution from vehicle manufacturing, from the production and distribution of fuel, and from vehicle tailpipes. It also factors in air pollution. *Source:* American Council for an Energy-Efficient Economy (ACEEE). Web: www.greener.com.

Most and Least Knowledgeable U.S. Drivers

Based on the average scores on a 20-question driver's test commissioned by the GMAC Insurance Company, the most knowledgeable drivers in the U.S. are from Oregon and the least knowledgeable are from Rhode Island.

Rank	State	Rank	State	Rank	State	Rank	State	Rank	State
1.	Oregon	12.	North Dakota	21.	Colorado		New Mexico	41.	Florida
2.	Washington	13.	North Carolina	22.	Kansas	31.	Oklahoma	42.	Connecticut
3.	Iowa			23.	Michigan	32.	Texas	43.	California
4.	Idaho	14.	Indiana	24.	New Hampshire	33.	Utah	44.	Maryland
5.	Wyoming	15.	Alabama				Arizona	45.	District of Columbia
6.	Vermont		Nevada	25.	Tennessee	35.	Mississippi		New York
7.	Nebraska		Missouri	26.	Maine	36.	Delaware		
8.	Wisconsin	18.	Virginia	27.	Arkansas		Kentucky	47.	New Jersey
9.	Montana	19.	Ohio		South Carolina	38.	Pennsylvania	48.	Massachusetts
	West Virginia		South Dakota	29.	Georgia	39.	Louisiana	49.	Rhode Island
11.	Minnesota					40.	Illinois		

NOTE: Survey excludes Alaska and Hawaii. *Source:* General Motors Acceptance Corporation (GMAC) Insurance National Drivers Test administered to 5,000 licensed drivers nationwide.

Age and Gender Distribution of U.S. Licensed Drivers, 2003

	Male drivers		Female drivers		Total drivers	
Age	Number	Percent of total drivers	Number	Percent of total drivers	Number	Percent of total drivers
Under 16	19,027	0.0%	18,382	0.0%	37,409	0.0%
19 and under	4,746,340	4.8	4,516,877	4.6	9,263,217	4.7
20–24	8,493,837	8.6	8,242,994	8.4	16,736,831	8.5
25–29	8,669,799	8.8	8,394,229	8.6	17,064,028	8.7
30–34	9,622,899	9.8	9,302,556	9.5	18,925,455	9.6
35–39	9,960,238	10.1	9,724,146	9.9	19,684,384	10.0
40–44	10,653,505	10.8	10,606,207	10.8	21,259,712	10.8
45–49	10,135,650	10.3	10,206,178	10.4	20,341,828	10.4
50–54	8,916,619	9.1	9,001,861	9.2	17,918,480	9.1
55–59	7,482,632	7.6	7,502,345	7.7	14,984,977	7.6
60–64	5,680,012	5.8	5,702,436	5.8	11,382,448	5.8
65–69	4,370,011	4.4	4,407,404	4.5	8,777,415	4.5
70–74	3,613,116	3.7	3,749,487	3.8	7,362,603	3.8
75–79	2,894,252	2.9	3,173,326	3.2	6,067,578	3.1
80–84	1,856,730	1.9	2,103,187	2.1	3,959,917	2.0
85 and over	1,132,725	1.2	1,304,069	1.3	2,436,794	1.2
Total	**98,228,365**	**50.1**	**97,937,302**	**49.9**	**196,165,667**	**100.0**

Source: U.S. Department of Transportation, Federal Highway Administration, *Highway Statistics 2003.* Web: www.fhwa.dot.gov.

Licensed Drivers and Vehicle Registrations

Year	Resident population (millions)	Drivers (millions)	Motor vehicles (millions)	Year	Resident population (millions)	Drivers (millions)	Motor vehicles (millions)
1960	180	87	74	1982	232	150	160
1961	183	89	76	1983	234	154	164
1962	186	91	79	1984	236	155	166
1963	188	94	83	1985	239	157	172
1964	191	95	86	1986	241	159	176
1965	194	99	90	1987	243	161	179
1966	196	101	94	1988	246	163	184
1967	197	103	97	1989	248	166	187
1968	199	105	101	1990	248	167	189
1969	201	108	105	1991	252	169	188
1970	204	112	108	1992	255	173	190
1971	207	114	113	1993	258	173	194
1972	209	118	119	1994	260	175	198
1973	211	122	126	1995	263	177	202
1974	213	125	130	1996	265	180	206
1975	215	130	133	1997	268	183	208
1976	218	134	139	1998	270	185	208
1977	220	138	142	1999	273	187	216
1978	222	141	148	2000	281	191	218
1979	225	143	152	2001	281	191	226
1980	227	145	156	2002	288	195	230
1981	230	147	158	2003	291	196	231

Source: U.S. Department of Transportation, Federal Highway Administration, *Highway Statistics 2003.* Web: www.fhwa.dot.gov.

U.S. Railroad Ridership, 1988–2004

(millions)

	1988	1989	1990	1993	1995	1996	1997	1998	1999	2000	2001	2002	2003	2004
Amtrak system	21.5	21.4	22.2	22.1	20.7	19.7	20.2	21.1	21.5	22.5	23.5	23.4	24.0	25.0
Northeast Corridor	11.2	11.1	11.2	10.3	11.6	11.0	11.1	11.9	12.3	12.9	13.5	13.8	13.6	14.2
Intercity + West	10.3	10.3	11.0	11.8	9.1	8.7	9.1	9.2	9.2	9.6	10.0	9.6	10.4	10.8
Commuter trains[1]	15.4	17.4	18.0	32.9	42.2	45.9	48.5	54.0	58.3	61.6	n.a.	n.a.	n.a.	n.a.
Total	**36.9**	**38.8**	**40.2**	**55.0**	**62.9**	**65.6**	**68.7**	**75.1**	**79.8**	**84.1**	**n.a.**	**n.a.**	**n.a.**	**n.a.**

NOTE: n.a. = not available. 1. Includes only commuter trains run by Amtrak under contract. *Source:* National Assoc. of Railroad Passengers. Based on Amtrak annual reports. Web: www.narprail.org.

Road Mileages Between U.S. Cities

Cities[1]	Birmingham	Boston	Buffalo	Chicago	Cleveland	Dallas	Denver
Birmingham, Ala.	—	1,194	947	657	734	653	1,318
Boston, Mass.	1,194	—	457	983	639	1,815	1,991
Buffalo, N.Y.	947	457	—	536	192	1,387	1,561
Chicago, Ill.	657	983	536	—	344	931	1,050
Cleveland, Ohio	734	639	192	344	—	1,205	1,369
Dallas, Tex.	653	1,815	1,387	931	1,205	—	801
Denver, Colo.	1,318	1,991	1,561	1,050	1,369	801	—
Detroit, Mich.	754	702	252	279	175	1,167	1,301
El Paso, Tex.	1,278	2,358	1,928	1,439	1,746	625	652
Houston, Tex.	692	1,886	1,532	1,092	1,358	242	1,032
Indianapolis, Ind.	492	940	510	189	318	877	1,051
Kansas City, Mo.	703	1,427	997	503	815	508	616
Los Angeles, Calif.	2,078	3,036	2,606	2,112	2,424	1,425	1,174
Louisville, Ky.	378	996	571	305	379	865	1,135
Memphis, Tenn.	249	1,345	965	546	773	470	1,069
Miami, Fla.	777	1,539	1,445	1,390	1,325	1,332	2,094
Minneapolis, Minn.	1,067	1,402	955	411	763	969	867
New Orleans, La.	347	1,541	1,294	947	1,102	504	1,305
New York, N.Y.	983	213	436	840	514	1,604	1,780
Omaha, Nebr.	907	1,458	1,011	493	819	661	559
Philadelphia, Pa.	894	304	383	758	432	1,515	1,698
Phoenix, Ariz.	1,680	2,664	2,234	1,729	2,052	1,027	836
Pittsburgh, Pa.	792	597	219	457	131	1,237	1,411
St. Louis, Mo.	508	1,179	749	293	567	638	871
Salt Lake City, Utah	1,805	2,425	1,978	1,458	1,786	1,239	512
San Francisco, Calif.	2,385	3,179	2,732	2,212	2,540	1,765	1,266
Seattle, Wash.	2,612	3,043	2,596	2,052	2,404	2,122	1,373
Washington, D.C.	751	440	386	695	369	1,372	1,635

Cities[1]	Detroit	El Paso	Houston	Indianapolis	Kansas City	Los Angeles	Louisville
Birmingham, Ala.	754	1,278	692	492	703	2,078	378
Boston, Mass.	702	2,358	1,886	940	1,427	3,036	996
Buffalo, N.Y.	252	1,928	1,532	510	997	2,606	571
Chicago, Ill.	279	1,439	1,092	189	503	2,112	305
Cleveland, Ohio	175	1,746	1,358	318	815	2,424	379
Dallas, Tex.	1,167	625	242	*877	508	1,425	865
Denver, Colo.	1,310	652	1,032	1,051	616	1,174	1,135
Detroit, Mich.	—	1,696	1,312	290	760	2,369	378
El Paso, Tex.	1,696	—	756	1,418	936	800	1,443
Houston, Tex.	1,312	756	—	1,022	750	1,556	981
Indianapolis, Ind.	290	1,418	1,022	—	487	2,096	114
Kansas City, Mo.	760	936	750	487	—	1,609	519
Los Angeles, Calif.	2,369	800	1,556	2,096	1,609	—	2,128
Louisville, Ky.	378	1,443	981	114	519	2,128	—
Memphis, Tenn.	756	1,095	586	466	454	1,847	396
Miami, Fla.	1,409	1,957	1,237	1,225	1,479	2,757	1,111
Minneapolis, Minn.	698	1,353	1,211	600	466	2,041	716
New Orleans, La.	1,101	1,121	365	839	839	1,921	725
New York, N.Y.	671	2,147	1,675	729	1,216	2,825	785
Omaha, Nebr.	754	1,015	903	590	204	1,733	704
Philadelphia, Pa.	589	2,065	1,586	647	1,134	2,743	703
Phoenix, Ariz.	1,986	402	1,158	1,713	1,226	398	1,749
Pittsburgh, Pa.	288	1,778	1,395	360	847	2,456	416
St. Louis, Mo.	529	1,179	799	239	255	1,864	264
Salt Lake City, Utah	1,721	877	1,465	1,545	1,128	728	1,647
San Francisco, Calif.	2,475	1,202	1,958	2,299	1,882	403	2,401
Seattle, Wash.	2,339	1,760	2,348	2,241	1,909	1,150	2,355
Washington, D.C.	526	1,997	1,443	565	1,071	2,680	601

Cities[1]	Memphis	Miami	Minneapolis	New Orleans	New York	Omaha	Philadelphia
Birmingham, Ala.	249	777	1,067	347	983	907	894
Boston, Mass.	1,345	1,539	1,402	1,541	213	1,458	304
Buffalo, N.Y.	965	1,445	955	1,294	436	1,011	383
Chicago, Ill.	546	1,390	411	947	840	493	758
Cleveland, Ohio	773	1,325	763	1,102	514	819	432
Dallas, Tex.	470	1,332	969	504	1,604	661	1,515
Denver, Colo.	1,069	2,094	867	1,305	1,780	559	1,698
Detroit, Mich.	756	1,409	698	1,101	671	754	589
El Paso, Tex.	1,095	1,957	1,353	1,121	2,147	1,015	2,065
Houston, Tex.	586	1,237	1,211	365	1,675	903	1,586
Indianapolis, Ind.	466	1,225	600	839	729	590	647
Kansas City, Mo.	454	1,479	466	839	1,216	204	1,134
Los Angeles, Calif.	1,847	2,757	2,041	1,921	2,825	1,733	2,743
Louisville, Ky.	396	1,111	716	725	785	704	703
Memphis, Tenn.	—	1,025	854	401	1,134	658	1,045
Miami, Fla.	1,025	—	1,801	892	1,328	1,683	1,239
Minneapolis, Minn.	854	1,801	—	1,255	1,259	373	1,177
New Orleans, La.	401	892	1,255	—	1,330	1,043	1,241
New York, N.Y.	1,134	1,328	1,259	1,330	—	1,315	93
Omaha, Nebr.	658	1,683	373	1,043	1,315	—	1,233
Philadelphia, Pa.	1,045	1,239	1,177	1,241	93	1,233	—
Phoenix, Ariz.	1,464	2,359	1,644	1,523	2,442	1,305	2,360
Pittsburgh, Pa.	810	1,250	876	1,118	386	932	304
St. Louis, Mo.	295	1,241	559	696	968	459	886
Salt Lake City, Utah	1,556	2,571	1,243	1,743	2,282	967	2,200
San Francisco, Calif.	2,151	3,097	1,997	2,269	3,036	1,721	2,954
Seattle, Wash.	2,363	3,389	1,641	2,606	2,900	1,705	2,818
Washington, D.C.	902	1,101	1,114	1,098	229	1,170	140

Cities[1]	Phoenix	Pittsburgh	St. Louis	Salt Lake City	San Francisco	Seattle	Washington
Birmingham, Ala.	1,680	792	508	1,805	2,385	2,612	751
Boston, Mass.	2,664	597	1,179	2,425	3,179	3,043	440
Buffalo, N.Y.	2,234	219	749	1,978	2,732	2,596	386
Chicago, Ill.	1,729	457	293	1,458	2,212	2,052	695
Cleveland, Ohio	2,052	131	567	1,786	2,540	2,404	369
Dallas, Tex.	1,027	1,237	638	1,239	1,765	2,122	1,372
Denver, Colo.	836	1,411	871	512	1,266	1,373	1,635
Detroit, Mich.	1,986	288	529	1,721	2,475	2,339	526
El Paso, Tex.	402	1,778	1,179	877	1,202	1,760	1,997
Houston, Tex.	1,158	1,395	799	1,465	1,958	2,348	1,443
Indianapolis, Ind.	1,713	360	239	1,545	2,299	2,241	565
Kansas City, Mo.	1,226	847	255	1,128	1,882	1,909	1,071
Los Angeles, Calif.	398	2,456	1,864	728	403	1,150	2,680
Louisville, Ky.	1,749	416	264	1,647	2,401	2,355	601
Memphis, Tenn.	1,464	810	295	1,556	2,151	2,363	902
Miami, Fla.	2,359	1,250	1,241	2,571	3,097	3,389	1,101
Minneapolis, Minn.	1,644	876	559	1,243	1,997	1,641	1,114
New Orleans, La.	1,523	1,118	696	1,743	2,269	2,626	1,098
New York, N.Y.	2,442	386	968	2,282	3,036	2,900	229
Omaha, Nebr.	1,305	932	459	967	1,721	1,705	1,178
Philadelphia, Pa.	2,360	304	886	2,200	2,954	2,818	140
Phoenix, Ariz.	—	2,073	1,485	651	800	1,482	2,278
Pittsburgh, Pa.	2,073	—	599	1,899	2,653	2,517	241
St. Louis, Mo.	1,485	599	—	1,383	2,137	2,164	836
Salt Lake City, Utah	651	1,899	1,383	—	754	883	2,110
San Francisco, Calif.	800	2,653	2,137	754	—	817	2,864
Seattle, Wash.	1,482	2,517	2,164	883	817	—	2,755
Washington, D.C.	2,278	241	836	2,110	2,864	2,755	—

1. These figures represent estimates and are subject to change.

Air Distances Between U.S. Cities in Statute Miles

Cities	Birmingham	Boston	Buffalo	Chicago	Cleveland	Dallas	Denver
Birmingham, Ala.	—	1,052	776	578	618	581	1,095
Boston, Mass.	1,052	—	400	851	551	1,551	1,769
Buffalo, N.Y.	776	400	—	454	173	1,198	1,370
Chicago, Ill.	578	851	454	—	308	803	920
Cleveland, Ohio	618	551	173	308	—	1,025	1,227
Dallas, Tex.	581	1,551	1,198	803	1,025	—	663
Denver, Colo.	1,095	1,769	1,370	920	1,227	663	—
Detroit, Mich.	641	613	216	238	90	999	1,156
El Paso, Tex.	1,152	2,072	1,692	1,252	1,525	572	557
Houston, Tex.	567	1,605	1,286	940	1,114	225	879
Indianapolis, Ind.	433	807	435	165	263	763	1,000
Kansas City, Mo.	579	1,251	861	414	700	451	558
Los Angeles, Calif.	1,802	2,596	2,198	1,745	2,049	1,240	831
Louisville, Ky.	331	826	483	269	311	726	1,038
Memphis, Tenn.	217	1,137	803	482	630	420	879
Miami, Fla.	665	1,255	1,181	1,188	1,087	1,111	1,726
Minneapolis, Minn.	862	1,123	731	355	630	862	700
New Orleans, La.	312	1,359	1,086	833	924	443	1,082
New York, N.Y.	864	188	292	713	405	1,374	1,631
Omaha, Nebr.	732	1,282	883	432	739	586	488
Philadelphia, Pa.	783	271	279	666	360	1,299	1,579
Phoenix, Ariz.	1,456	2,300	1,906	1,453	1,749	887	586
Pittsburgh, Pa.	608	483	178	410	115	1,070	1,320
St. Louis, Mo.	400	1,038	662	262	492	547	796
Salt Lake City, Utah	1,466	2,099	1,699	1,260	1,568	999	371
San Francisco, Calif.	2,013	2,699	2,300	1,858	2,166	1,483	949
Seattle, Wash.	2,082	2,493	2,117	1,737	2,026	1,681	1,021
Washington, D.C.	661	393	292	597	306	1,185	1,494

Cities	Detroit	El Paso	Houston	Indianapolis	Kansas City	LosAngeles	Louisville
Birmingham, Ala.	641	1,152	567	433	579	1,802	331
Boston, Mass.	613	2,072	1,605	807	1,251	2,596	826
Buffalo, N.Y.	216	1,692	1,286	435	861	2,198	483
Chicago, Ill.	238	1,252	940	165	414	1,745	269
Cleveland, Ohio	90	1,525	1,114	263	700	2,049	311
Dallas, Tex.	999	572	225	763	451	1,240	726
Denver, Colo.	1,156	557	879	1,000	558	831	1,038
Detroit, Mich.	—	1,479	1,105	240	645	1,983	316
El Paso, Tex.	1,479	—	676	1,264	839	701	1,254
Houston, Tex.	1,105	676	—	865	644	1,374	803
Indianapolis, Ind.	240	1,264	865	—	453	1,809	107
Kansas City, Mo.	645	839	644	453	—	1,356	480
Los Angeles, Calif.	1,983	701	1,374	1,809	1,356	—	1,829
Louisville, Ky.	316	1,254	803	107	480	1,829	—
Memphis, Tenn.	623	976	484	384	369	1,603	320
Miami, Fla.	1,152	1,643	968	1,024	1,241	2,339	919
Minneapolis, Minn.	543	1,157	1,056	511	413	1,524	605
New Orleans, La.	939	983	318	712	680	1,673	623
New York, N.Y.	482	1,905	1,420	646	1,097	2,451	652
Omaha, Nebr.	669	878	794	525	166	1,315	580
Philadelphia, Pa.	443	1,836	1,341	585	1,038	2,394	582
Phoenix, Ariz.	1,690	346	1,017	1,499	1,049	357	1,508
Pittsburgh, Pa.	205	1,590	1,137	330	781	2,136	344
St. Louis, Mo.	455	1,034	679	231	238	1,589	242
Salt Lake City, Utah	1,492	689	1,200	1,356	925	579	1,402
San Francisco, Calif.	2,091	995	1,645	1,949	1,506	347	1,986
Seattle, Wash.	1,938	1,376	1,891	1,872	1,506	959	1,943
Washington, D.C.	396	1,728	1,220	494	945	2,300	476

Cities	Memphis	Miami	Minneapolis	New Orleans	New York	Omaha	Philadelphia
Birmingham, Ala.	217	665	862	312	864	732	783
Boston, Mass.	1,137	1,255	1,123	1,359	188	1,282	271
Buffalo, N.Y.	803	1,181	731	1,086	292	883	279
Chicago, Ill.	482	1,188	355	833	713	432	666
Cleveland, Ohio	630	1,087	630	924	405	739	360
Dallas, Tex.	420	1,111	862	443	1,374	586	1,299
Denver, Colo.	879	1,726	700	1,082	1,631	488	1,579
Detroit, Mich.	623	1,152	543	939	482	669	443
El Paso, Tex.	976	1,643	1,157	983	1,905	878	1,836
Houston, Tex.	484	968	1,056	318	1,420	794	1,341
Indianapolis, Ind.	384	1,024	511	712	646	525	585
Kansas City, Mo.	369	1,241	413	680	1,097	166	1,038
Los Angeles, Calif.	1,603	2,339	1,524	1,673	2,451	1,315	2,394
Louisville, Ky.	320	919	605	623	652	580	582
Memphis, Tenn.	—	872	699	358	957	529	881
Miami, Fla.	872	—	1,511	669	1,092	1,397	1,019
Minneapolis, Minn.	699	1,511	—	1,051	1,018	290	985
New Orleans, La.	358	669	1,051	—	1,171	847	1,089
New York, N.Y.	957	1,092	1,018	1,171	—	1,144	83
Omaha, Nebr.	529	1,397	290	847	1,144	—	1,094
Philadelphia, Pa.	881	1,019	985	1,089	83	1,094	—
Phoenix, Ariz.	1,263	1,982	1,280	1,316	2,145	1,036	2,083
Pittsburgh, Pa.	660	1,010	743	919	317	836	259
St. Louis, Mo.	240	1,061	466	598	875	354	811
Salt Lake City, Utah	1,250	2,089	987	1,434	1,972	833	1,925
San Francisco, Calif.	1,802	2,594	1,584	1,926	2,571	1,429	2,523
Seattle, Wash.	1,867	2,734	1,395	2,101	2,408	1,369	2,380
Washington, D.C.	765	923	934	966	205	1,014	123

Cities	Phoenix	Pittsburgh	St. Louis	Salt Lake City	San Francisco	Seattle	Washington
Birmingham, Ala.	1,456	608	400	1,466	2,013	2,082	661
Boston, Mass.	2,300	483	1,038	2,099	2,699	2,493	393
Buffalo, N.Y.	1,906	178	662	1,699	2,300	2,117	292
Chicago, Ill.	1,453	410	262	1,260	1,858	1,737	597
Cleveland, Ohio	1,749	115	492	1,568	2,166	2,026	306
Dallas, Tex.	887	1,070	547	999	1,483	1,681	1,185
Denver, Colo.	586	1,320	796	371	949	1,021	1,494
Detroit, Mich.	1,690	205	455	1,492	2,091	1,938	396
El Paso, Tex.	346	1,590	1,034	689	995	1,376	1,728
Houston, Tex.	1,017	1,137	679	1,200	1,645	1,891	1,220
Indianapolis, Ind.	1,499	330	231	1,356	1,949	1,872	494
Kansas City, Mo.	1,049	781	238	925	1,506	1,506	945
Los Angeles, Calif.	357	2,136	1,589	579	347	959	2,300
Louisville, Ky.	1,508	344	242	1,402	1,986	1,943	476
Memphis, Tenn.	1,263	660	240	1,250	1,802	1,867	765
Miami, Fla.	1,982	1,010	1,061	2,089	2,594	2,734	923
Minneapolis, Minn.	1,280	743	466	987	1,584	1,395	934
New Orleans, La.	1,316	919	598	1,434	1,926	2,101	966
New York, N.Y.	2,145	317	875	1,972	2,571	2,408	205
Omaha, Nebr.	1,036	836	354	833	1,429	1,369	1,014
Philadelphia, Pa.	2,083	259	811	1,925	2,523	2,380	123
Phoenix, Ariz.	—	1,828	1,272	504	653	1,114	1,983
Pittsburgh, Pa.	1,828	—	559	1,668	2,264	2,138	192
St. Louis, Mo.	1,272	559	—	1,162	1,744	1,724	712
Salt Lake City, Utah	504	1,668	1,162	—	600	701	1,848
San Francisco, Calif.	653	2,264	1,744	600	—	678	2,442
Seattle, Wash.	1,114	2,138	1,724	701	678	—	2,329
Washington, D.C.	1,983	192	712	1,848	2,442	2,329	—

Source: National Geodetic Survey.

Air Distances Between World Cities in Statute Miles

Cities	Berlin	Buenos Aires	Cairo	Calcutta	Cape Town	Caracas	Chicago
Berlin	—	7,402	1,795	4,368	5,981	5,247	4,405
Buenos Aires	7,402	—	7,345	10,265	4,269	3,168	5,598
Cairo	1,795	7,345	—	3,539	4,500	6,338	6,129
Calcutta	4,368	10,265	3,539	—	6,024	9,605	7,980
Cape Town	5,981	4,269	4,500	6,024	—	6,365	8,494
Caracas	5,247	3,168	6,338	9,605	6,365	—	2,501
Chicago	4,405	5,598	6,129	7,980	8,494	2,501	—
Hong Kong	5,440	11,472	5,061	1,648	7,375	10,167	7,793
Honolulu	7,309	7,561	8,838	7,047	11,534	6,013	4,250
Istanbul	1,078	7,611	768	3,638	5,154	6,048	5,477
Lisbon	1,436	5,956	2,363	5,638	5,325	4,041	3,990
London	579	6,916	2,181	4,947	6,012	4,660	3,950
Los Angeles	5,724	6,170	7,520	8,090	9,992	3,632	1,745
Manila	6,132	11,051	5,704	2,203	7,486	10,620	8,143
Mexico City	6,047	4,592	7,688	9,492	8,517	2,232	1,691
Montreal	3,729	5,615	5,414	7,607	7,931	2,449	744
Moscow	1,004	8,376	1,803	3,321	6,300	6,173	4,974
New York	3,965	5,297	5,602	7,918	7,764	2,132	713
Paris	545	6,870	1,995	4,883	5,807	4,736	4,134
Rio de Janeiro	6,220	1,200	6,146	9,377	3,773	2,810	5,296
Rome	734	6,929	1,320	4,482	5,249	5,196	4,808
San Francisco	5,661	6,467	7,364	7,814	10,247	3,904	1,858
Shanghai	5,218	12,201	5,183	2,117	8,061	9,501	7,061
Stockholm	504	7,808	2,111	4,195	6,444	5,420	4,278
Sydney	10,006	7,330	8,952	5,685	6,843	9,513	9,272
Tokyo	5,540	11,408	5,935	3,194	9,156	8,799	6,299
Warsaw	320	7,662	1,630	4,048	5,958	5,517	4,667
Washington, D.C.	4,169	5,218	5,800	8,084	7,901	2,059	597

Cities	Hong Kong	Honolulu	Istanbul	Lisbon	London	Los Angeles	Manila
Berlin	5,440	7,309	1,078	1,436	579	5,724	6,132
Buenos Aires	11,472	7,561	7,611	5,956	6,916	6,170	11,051
Cairo	5,061	8,838	768	2,363	2,181	7,520	5,704
Calcutta	1,648	7,047	3,638	5,638	4,947	8,090	2,203
Cape Town	7,375	11,534	5,154	5,325	6,012	9,992	7,486
Caracas	10,167	6,013	6,048	4,041	4,660	3,632	10,620
Chicago	7,793	4,250	5,477	3,990	3,950	1,745	8,143
Hong Kong	—	5,549	4,984	6,853	5,982	7,195	693
Honolulu	5,549	—	8,109	7,820	7,228	2,574	5,299
Istanbul	4,984	8,109	—	2,012	1,552	6,783	5,664
Lisbon	6,853	7,820	2,012	—	985	5,621	7,546
London	5,982	7,228	1,552	985	—	5,382	6,672
Los Angeles	7,195	2,574	6,783	5,621	5,382	—	7,261
Manila	693	5,299	5,664	7,546	6,672	7,261	—
Mexico City	8,782	3,779	7,110	5,390	5,550	1,589	8,835
Montreal	7,729	4,910	4,789	3,246	3,282	2,427	8,186
Moscow	4,439	7,037	1,091	2,427	1,555	6,003	5,131
New York	8,054	4,964	4,975	3,364	3,458	2,451	8,498
Paris	5,985	7,438	1,400	904	213	5,588	6,677
Rio de Janeiro	11,021	8,285	6,389	4,796	5,766	6,331	11,259
Rome	5,768	8,022	843	1,161	887	6,732	6,457
San Francisco	6,897	2,393	6,703	5,666	5,357	347	6,967
Shanghai	764	4,941	4,962	6,654	5,715	6,438	1,150
Stockholm	5,113	6,862	1,348	1,856	890	5,454	5,797
Sydney	4,584	4,943	9,294	11,302	10,564	7,530	3,944
Tokyo	1,794	3,853	5,560	6,915	5,940	5,433	1,866
Warsaw	5,144	7,355	863	1,715	899	5,922	5,837
Washington, D.C.	8,147	4,519	5,215	3,562	3,663	2,300	8,562

Cities	Mexico City	Montreal	Moscow	New York	Paris	Rio de Janeiro	Rome
Berlin	6,047	3,729	1,004	3,965	545	6,220	734
Buenos Aires	4,592	5,615	8,376	5,297	6,870	1,200	6,929
Cairo	7,688	5,414	1,803	5,602	1,995	6,146	1,320
Calcutta	9,492	7,607	3,321	7,918	4,883	9,377	4,482
Cape Town	8,517	7,931	6,300	7,764	5,807	3,773	5,249
Caracas	2,232	2,449	6,173	2,132	4,736	2,810	5,196
Chicago	1,691	744	4,974	713	4,134	5,296	4,808
Hong Kong	8,782	7,729	4,439	8,054	5,985	11,021	5,768
Honolulu	3,779	4,910	7,037	4,964	7,438	8,285	8,022
Istanbul	7,110	4,789	1,091	4,975	1,400	6,389	843
Lisbon	5,390	3,246	2,427	3,364	904	4,796	1,161
London	5,550	3,282	1,555	3,458	213	5,766	887
Los Angeles	1,589	2,427	6,003	2,451	5,588	6,331	6,732
Manila	8,835	8,186	5,131	8,498	6,677	11,259	6,457
Mexico City	—	2,318	6,663	2,094	5,716	4,771	6,366
Montreal	2,318	—	4,386	320	3,422	5,097	4,080
Moscow	6,663	4,386	—	4,665	1,544	7,175	1,474
New York	2,094	320	4,665	—	3,624	4,817	4,281
Paris	5,716	3,422	1,544	3,624	—	5,699	697
Rio de Janeiro	4,771	5,097	7,175	4,817	5,699	—	5,684
Rome	6,366	4,080	1,474	4,281	697	5,684	—
San Francisco	1,887	2,539	5,871	2,571	5,558	6,621	6,240
Shanghai	8,022	7,053	4,235	7,371	5,754	11,336	5,677
Stockholm	5,959	3,667	762	3,924	958	6,651	1,234
Sydney	8,052	9,954	9,012	9,933	10,544	8,306	10,136
Tokyo	7,021	6,383	4,647	6,740	6,034	11,533	6,135
Warsaw	6,365	4,009	715	4,344	849	6,467	817
Washington, D.C.	1,887	488	4,858	205	3,829	4,796	4,434

Cities	San Francisco	Shanghai	Stockholm	Sydney	Tokyo	Warsaw	Washington
Berlin	5,661	5,218	504	10,006	5,540	320	4,169
Buenos Aires	6,467	12,201	7,808	7,330	11,408	7,662	5,218
Cairo	7,364	5,183	2,111	8,952	5,935	1,630	5,800
Calcutta	7,814	2,117	4,195	5,685	3,194	4,048	8,084
Cape Town	10,247	8,061	6,444	6,843	9,156	5,958	7,901
Caracas	3,904	9,501	5,420	9,513	8,799	5,517	2,059
Chicago	1,858	7,061	4,278	9,272	6,299	4,667	597
Hong Kong	6,897	764	5,113	4,584	1,794	5,144	8,147
Honolulu	2,393	4,941	6,862	4,943	3,853	7,355	4,519
Istanbul	6,703	4,962	1,348	9,294	5,560	863	5,215
Lisbon	5,666	6,654	1,856	11,302	6,915	1,715	3,562
London	5,357	5,715	890	10,564	5,940	899	3,663
Los Angeles	347	6,438	5,454	7,530	5,433	5,922	2,300
Manila	6,967	1,150	5,797	3,944	1,866	5,837	8,562
Mexico City	1,887	8,022	5,959	8,052	7,021	6,365	1,887
Montreal	2,539	7,053	3,667	9,954	6,383	4,009	488
Moscow	5,871	4,235	762	9,012	4,647	715	4,858
New York	2,571	7,371	3,924	9,933	6,740	4,344	205
Paris	5,558	5,754	958	10,544	6,034	849	3,829
Rio de Janeiro	6,621	11,336	6,651	8,306	11,533	6,467	4,796
Rome	6,240	5,677	1,234	10,136	6,135	817	4,434
San Francisco	—	6,140	5,361	7,416	5,135	5,841	2,442
Shanghai	6,140	—	4,825	4,899	1,097	4,951	7,448
Stockholm	5,361	4,825	—	9,696	5,051	501	4,123
Sydney	7,416	4,899	9,696	—	4,866	9,696	9,758
Tokyo	5,135	1,097	5,051	4,866	—	5,249	6,772
Warsaw	5,841	4,951	501	9,696	5,249	—	4,457
Washington, D.C.	2,442	7,448	4,123	9,758	6,772	4,457	—

Source: Encyclopædia Britannica.

America's House Party

Record home prices are inflaming passions—and pocketbooks—as never before. Inside our raucous obsession with real estate

By JAMES PONIEWOZIK TIME

The stock market may be dragging, but home prices are soaring, fueling a national obsession with real estate. Your house is now your piggy bank, ATM, and 401(k). House gawking is a hobby, remodeling both entertainment and an investment. Folks brag about having bought their home in the '90s the way they used to brag about having bought Microsoft in the '80s. Even if you're not contemplating buying or selling anytime soon, the amazing lift in home values is changing the way we think about the roofs over our heads. Real estate isn't so much about nesting today as it is about nest feathering.

The house has always reflected its occupants' place in society. But now it also determines their place in society. The boom has divided haves from have-nots—owners from renters, hot markets from cold. The median U.S. home price jumped a stunning 15% between April 2004 and April 2005 and 55% over the past five years, according to the National Association of Realtors. The fact that houses are bought for pennies on the dollar magnifies the windfall. Say you put down 20% on a $150,000 house five years ago. At the average gain of 55%, that's an $82,500 gain on a $30,000 outlay, or a 275% return. In your face, S&P 500!

Average homeowners who bought in the '90s—not to mention those who have owned for decades—are now, like modern-day Clampetts, sitting atop newly discovered gushers of wealth. Many have borrowed against their fat cushions of equity. Some—like bettors taking chips off a blackjack table—have sold, trading down to smaller places or swapping a city apartment for a calmer, cheaper life in the country. Still others have stayed put and splurged.

House as Lifeboat

Past generations thought of their house as an investment, but a passive one. Burning the mortgage after 30 years promised a debt-free retirement and a little legacy for the next generation. But now people track their home values almost daily. And thanks to home-equity loans and refinancings, the home is an easily tapped source of cash. In 2004, U.S. homeowners took an estimated $139 billion out of the walls and floorboards through refinancings, compared with $26 billion in 2000, according to Freddie Mac. They put about 35% of that money into home improvements, spent 16% on consumer purchases, and used 26% to pay off debt (including credit cards for other consumer purchases), according to the Federal Reserve Board.

Of course, that's not free money. It's more debt, albeit at low interest. But you have to excuse homeowners for getting a little giddy. When they look at the rest of the economy, they see little else to be excited about. Employment has picked up, but wages haven't. Inflation has risen from the grave. The stock market is crawling to get back to where it was five years ago. Savings accounts throw off barely enough interest to feed a parking meter. Companies are cutting pensions, and politicians are making dire noises about Social Security. It's a scary message people are getting: We are heading toward a future in which we will need more money than ever to avert disaster, and there are fewer opportunities to get it. So people see their homes as their last, best hope for prosperity—as not just houses but also lifeboats.

Home Economics

Whether the market rises, plummets, or flattens, whether it happens over one year or five, it will not undo changes that the boom has wrought in the relationship between homeowner and home. The tech crash and the market slump didn't erase the culture of stocks.

Likewise, the deeper changes of the real estate boom are likely to stick, particularly the notion that the house is no longer just a home. By tapping their built-up home profits through refinancings and home-equity loans, owners have ensured that the home-as-piggy-bank will be with us for some time, and that may have wide implications for tomorrow's economy. □

Existing Home Sales, 2002–2004

Year	U.S.	Northeast	Midwest	South	West	Median sales price, U.S.
2002	5,631,000	950,000	1,346,000	2,065,000	1,269,000	$156,200
2003	6,183,000	1,022,000	1,468,000	2,282,000	1,404,000	$169,500
2004	6,784,000	1,114,000	1,549,000	2,542,000	1,577,000	$185,200

Source: National Association of REALTORS®.

2003 Median Value (Dollars) for All Owner-Occupied Housing Units

Rank		Estimate	Lower bound	Upper bound		Rank		Estimate	Lower bound	Upper bound
1.	California	$316,597	$313,883	$319,311		27.	Maine	$125,443	$122,021	$128,865
2.	Hawaii	302,315	250,250	354,380		28.	Ohio	116,375	112,437	120,313
3.	Massachusetts	300,767	296,228	305,306		29.	Idaho	114,580	111,548	117,612
4.	District of Columbia	246,310	239,308	253,312		30.	Montana	113,089	106,464	119,714
5.	New Jersey	240,145	237,389	242,901		31.	North Carolina	111,455	104,962	117,948
6.	Connecticut	215,496	211,728	219,264		32.	Wyoming	108,446	95,671	121,221
7.	Colorado	200,466	188,930	212,002		33.	Pennsylvania	106,966	105,449	108,483
8.	Rhode Island	199,745	196,347	203,143		34.	Missouri	106,763	103,041	110,485
9.	New Hampshire	198,288	194,811	201,765		35.	Tennessee	106,560	104,553	108,567
10.	New York	196,085	192,054	200,116		36.	New Mexico	105,911	98,327	113,495
11.	Washington	188,643	185,972	191,314		37.	South Carolina	105,667	100,224	111,110
12.	Maryland	180,942	176,552	185,332		38.	Indiana	104,833	99,300	110,366
13.	Oregon	166,847	163,930	169,764		39.	Kansas	98,893	94,583	103,203
14.	Alaska	165,363	161,072	169,654		40.	Nebraska	98,640	95,697	101,583
15.	Minnesota	165,294	161,342	169,246		41.	Texas	94,515	93,519	95,511
16.	Nevada	159,835	153,124	166,546		42.	South Dakota	92,791	87,459	98,123
17.	Illinois	157,564	155,280	159,848		43.	Kentucky	92,599	88,688	96,510
18.	Delaware	155,527	152,886	158,168		44.	Iowa	90,636	86,028	95,244
19.	Virginia	153,398	147,065	159,731		45.	Louisiana	90,168	87,469	92,867
20.	Utah	152,338	147,938	156,738		46.	Alabama	87,203	84,579	89,827
21.	Vermont	138,327	135,501	141,153		47.	Oklahoma	83,525	81,172	85,878
22.	Michigan	136,259	131,965	140,553		48.	Arkansas	79,902	76,531	83,273
23.	Arizona	134,699	132,130	137,268		49.	Mississippi	78,681	73,714	83,648
24.	Georgia	131,822	129,568	134,076		50.	North Dakota	78,577	75,867	81,287
25.	Wisconsin	129,575	123,631	135,519		51.	West Virginia	78,201	74,710	81,692
26.	Florida	129,344	125,166	133,522						

NOTE: Data based on 12 monthly samples during 2003. *Source:* U.S. Census Bureau, 2003 American Community Survey.

Economic Outlook Through 2012

Source: Bureau of Labor Statistics, *Monthly Labor Review,* Feb. 2004, www.bls.gov/opub/mlr/2001/11/art1abs.htm.

Every two years the Bureau of Labor Statistics (BLS) publishes its latest projections on the structure of the economy, labor force demographics, and future job growth. The following is a summary of the most recent BLS projections, which were released in Feb. 2004.

Recovery Predicted

After the boom of the 1990s, the U.S. economy suffered a number of serious setbacks, including the bursting of the technology bubble; the Sept. 11, 2001, terrorist attacks; significant losses of stock market wealth; a stagnant job market; corporate accounting scandals; and uncertainties related to the war in Iraq.

Although the economy has had difficulty shaking off a stubborn slowdown, recent statistical data suggest that we are now poised for a more sustained recovery. The BLS expects the gross domestic product (GDP) to reach $12.6 trillion in chained 1996 dollars by 2012, an increase of $3.2 trillion during the 2002–12 decade. This translates to an average annual rate of growth for real GDP of 3.0% over the period, 0.2% lower than the historical rate of 3.2% from 1992 to 2002.

A slower growth of civilian household employment, from 1.3% a year during the 1992–2002 period to 1.2% from 2002 to 2012, is expected to result in an increase of 17.3 million employees over the latter period, still greater than the increase of 15.8 million employees over the preceding 10-year period.

Consumer Spending to Grow

Personal consumption spending, which makes up two-thirds of economic activity, is expected to grow at an average annual rate of 2.8% from 2002 to 2012, sliding down from the historical high of 3.7% rate posted during the preceding 10-year period.

Consumer spending on durable goods, especially for cars and light trucks, was most notable during the past three years. Sales of autos roared to a peak of 17.2 million units in 2000, as the value of sales incentives reached a new high and buyers responded eagerly to the incentives.

Among consumer purchases of services, a major contributor to growth is health care expenditures. The growing number of elderly in the population, as well as advances in medical technology, has resulted in a greater demand for health services. Spending on medical services increased 2.5% per year during the 1992–2002 period. Over the coming 10 years, due to the importance of the demographic factors, spending on medical services is expected to continue to post solid gains at a growth rate of 3.0% annually.

Continued Trade Deficit

Globalization and international competition have played an important role in U.S. economic activity. With the world assumed to become more open to trade, the share of GDP accounted for by both exports and imports is expected to grow apace. A continued decline in the exchange rate will stimulate U.S. exports abroad and increase international competitiveness. Real exports are expected to grow at a 5.7% annual rate between 2002 and 2012. Both exports of goods and services also are expected to grow at the same rate of 5.7% annually per year during the projection period.

Imports are projected to grow at a rate of 5.2% annually over the 2002–12 period, much lower than the 8.7% annual rate of growth for imports over the 1992–2002 span. Imports of goods are expected to grow at 5.6% per year, and a 3.6% annual rate of growth is projected for imports of services during the 2002–12 period. As a result, net exports (exports minus imports) are expected to continue to make a negative contribution to the aggregate demand, reaching $734.6 billion in real terms by 2012. Although the bureau projects a continued increase in the trade surplus in services, the surplus in services still cannot offset the even larger deficit in goods.

Disposable Income on the Rise

On a per capita basis, nominal disposable income is expected to increase at an average annual rate of 4.3% from 2002 to 2012, reaching a level of $41,459 in the latter year—a gain of more than

$14,200 over the projection span. In real terms—that is, chained 1996 dollars—per capita income is projected to grow 1.7% per year from 2002 to 2012. Accordingly, real standard of living would rise over this period, at least measured on the basis of growth of disposable personal income.

Employment Outlook

Overall, civilian household employment is projected to increase by 1.2% per year from 2002 to 2012. The result is that about 17.3 million employed persons will be added to the economy over this 10-year period. Total employment measured on a nonfarm establishment basis is projected to grow at a rate of 1.6% between 2002 and 2012, from 130.4 million to 152.1 million, an increase of 21.7 million jobs.

Occupations with Highest Median Weekly Earnings Among Women, 2004

Rank	Occupation	Median weekly earnings	Rank	Occupation	Median weekly earnings
1.	Pharmacists	$1,432	6.	Computer programmers	$1,006
2.	Chief executives	1,310	7.	Physicians and surgeons	978
3.	Lawyers	1,255	8.	Human resource managers	958
4.	Computer and information systems managers	1,228	9.	Purchasing managers	946
5.	Computer software engineers	1,149	10.	Medical and health service managers	943

Source: U.S. Dept. of Labor, Women's Bureau. Web: www.dol.gov/wb.

10 Occupations with the Highest Median Earnings

Rank	Occupation
1.	Physicians and surgeons
2.	Dentists
3.	Chief executives
4.	Podiatrists
5.	Lawyers
6.	Engineering managers
7.	Optometrists
8.	Petroleum engineers
9.	Natural sciences managers
10.	Actuaries

Source: U.S. Census Bureau.

10 Occupations with the Lowest Median Earnings

Rank	Occupation
1.	Dishwashers
2.	Counter attendants, food concession
3.	Child-care workers
4.	Maids and housekeeping cleaners
5.	Dining room, cafeteria attendants, bartender helpers
6.	Food preparation workers
7.	Teacher assistants
8.	Restaurant hosts, hostesses
9.	Food prep and serving workers
10.	Waiters and waitresses

Source: U.S. Census Bureau.

Industries with the Fastest Wage and Salary Employment Growth, 2002–2012

Industry description	Thousands of jobs		Change, 2002–2012	Average annual rate of change, 2002–2012
	2002	2012		
Software publishers	256.0	429.7	173.7	5.3%
Management, scientific, and technical consulting services	731.8	1,137.4	405.6	4.5
Community care facilities for the elderly and residential care facilities	695.3	1,077.6	382.3	4.5
Computer systems design and related services	1,162.7	1,797.7	635.0	4.5
Employment services	3,248.8	5,012.3	1,763.5	4.4
Individual, family, community, and vocational rehabilitation services	1,269.3	1,866.6	597.3	3.9
Ambulatory health care services except offices of health practitioners	1,443.6	2,113.4	669.8	3.9
Water, sewage, and other systems	48.5	71.0	22.5	3.9
Internet services, data processing, and other information services	528.8	773.1	244.3	3.9
Child day-care services	734.2	1,050.3	316.1	3.6

Source: U.S. Department of Labor, Bureau of Labor Statistics.

Median Weekly Earnings of Selected Occupations, 2004

Occupation	Both sexes		Men		Women	
	Number of workers (in thousands)	Median weekly earnings	Number of workers (in thousands)	Median weekly earnings	Number of workers (in thousands)	Median weekly earnings
All occupations, 16 years and over	**101,224**	**$ 638**	**57,001**	**$ 713**	**44,223**	**$ 673**
Aircraft pilots and flight engineers	95	1,418	90	1,472	5	(¹)
Architects, except naval	142	1,141	105	1,242	38	(¹)
Biological scientists	109	929	60	946	49	(¹)
Brickmasons, blockmasons, and stonemasons	164	577	164	577	—	—
Bus drivers	366	500	215	588	152	440
Butchers and other meat, poultry, and fish processing workers	260	454	209	488	51	369
Carpenters	1,170	576	1,149	576	21	(¹)
Cashiers	1,355	322	339	380	1,016	313
Chemical engineers	65	1,221	55	1,242	10	(¹)
Chief executives	1,050	1,663	802	1,875	248	1,310
Child care workers	413	334	26	(¹)	387	334
Claims adjusters, appraisers, examiners, and investigators	257	762	85	052	171	677
Clergy	351	771	304	795	47	(¹)
Computer programmers	516	1,118	371	1,151	145	1,006
Computer scientists and systems analysts	604	1,027	418	1,092	186	902
Designers	480	714	250	818	230	646
Editors	110	856	56	946	54	759
Education administrators	651	1,019	246	1,172	405	905
Electricians	668	719	655	718	14	(¹)
Elementary and middle school teachers	2,206	806	435	917	1,772	776
Firefighters	263	933	250	942	13	(¹)
Hairdressers, hairstylists, and cosmetologists	291	398	24	(¹)	267	394
Hotel, motel, and resort desk clerks	67	349	27	(¹)	41	(¹)
Insurance underwriters	89	859	24	(¹)	65	772
Judges, magistrates, and other judicial workers	58	1,333	25	(¹)	33	(¹)
Lawyers	621	1,561	412	1,710	208	1,255
Machinists	408	670	392	679	16	(¹)
Marketing and sales managers	770	1,213	472	1,441	298	898
Medical scientists	83	1,025	38	(¹)	45	(¹)
Personal and home care aides	360	358	52	434	308	350
Personal financial advisers	229	1,062	167	1,170	61	773
Pharmacists	162	1,578	90	1,684	72	1,432
Physical therapists	121	925	50	955	70	900
Physician assistants	57	901	19	(¹)	38	(¹)
Physicians and surgeons	555	1,660	382	1,874	173	978
Police and sheriff's patrol officers	654	844	571	845	83	841
Postal service mail carriers	314	791	203	834	112	743
Preschool and kindergarten teachers	484	521	11	(¹)	473	515
Refuse and recyclable material collectors	67	508	62	512	5	(¹)
Registered nurses	1,800	904	148	1,031	1,651	895
Retail salespersons	1,865	496	1,100	597	766	386
Roofers	188	480	184	482	3	(¹)
Secondary school teachers	1,013	885	458	955	555	824
Security guards and gaming surveillance officers	641	457	502	471	138	418
Sewing machine operators	242	327	56	381	186	319
Social workers	620	698	148	720	472	689
Telemarketers	93	380	32	(¹)	61	355
Tellers	301	405	35	(¹)	265	401
Travel agents	69	576	10	(¹)	59	544
Writers and authors	86	760	42	(¹)	44	(¹)

NOTE: 1. Data not shown where base is less than 50,000. *Source:* U.S. Department of Labor, Bureau of Labor Statistics. Web: stats.bls.gov.

Farm and Nonfarm Labor Force, 1940–2004
(number in thousands)

	Civilian labor force employed				Civilian labor force employed		
Year	**Total**	**Agriculture**	**Nonagricultural industries**	**Year**	**Total**	**Agriculture**	**Nonagricultural industries**
1940[1]	47,520	9,540	37,980	1985	107,150	3,179	103,971
1945[1]	52,820	8,580	44,240	1990[2]	118,793	3,223	115,570
1950	58,918	7,160	51,758	1995	124,900	3,440	121,460
1955	62,170	6,450	55,722	2000[3]	136,891	2,464	134,427
1960[2]	65,778	5,458	60,318	2001	136,933	2,299	134,635
1965	71,088	4,361	66,726	2002	136,485	2,311	134,174
1970	78,678	3,463	75,215	2003	137,736	2,275	135,461
1975	85,846	3,408	82,438	2004	139,252	2,232	137,020
1980	99,302	3,364	95,938				

1. Data for persons age 14 and over. Beginning 1950, data relate to persons age 16 and over. 2. Not strictly comparable with data for prior years. 3. Beginning in Jan. 2000, data are not strictly comparable with data for 1999 and earlier years because of the revisions in the population controls used in the household survey. *Source:* U.S. Department of Labor, Bureau of Labor Statistics. Web: www.bls.gov/cps/cpsaat1.pdf.

Persons in the Labor Force, 1840–2004

	Labor force[1]			Labor force[1]	
Year	**Number (thousands)**	**Percent of working-age population**	**Year**	**Number (thousands)**	**Percent of working-age population**
1840	5,420	46.6%	1950	60,054	53.5%
1850	7,697	46.8	1960	69,877	55.3
1860	10,533	47.0	1970	82,049	58.2
1870	12,925	45.8	1980	106,085	62.0
1880	17,392	47.3	1990	125,182	65.3
1890	23,318	49.2	2000	140,863	67.2
1900	29,073	50.2	2001	141,815	66.9
1910	37,371	52.2	2002	144,863	66.6
1920	42,434	51.3	2003	146,510	66.2
1930	48,830	49.5	2004	147,401	66.0
1940	52,789	52.2			

1. For 1840 to 1930, the data relate to the population and gainful workers at age 10 and over; for 1940 to 1960, the data relate to the population and labor force at age 14 and over; for 1970 and 1980, the data relate to the population and labor force at age 16 and over. For 1940 to 1980, the data include the Armed Forces. *Source:* U.S. Department of Labor, Bureau of Labor Statistics. Web: data.bls.gov.

Employment Status by Race, 1975–2004

Year	Employment rate	Unemployment rate	Year	Employment rate	Unemployment rate
White			2000	60.8%	7.6%
1975	56.7%	7.8%	2001	59.7	8.7
1980	60.0	6.3	2002	58.1	10.3
1985	61.0	6.2	2003	57.4	10.8
1990	63.7	4.8	2004	57.2	10.4
1995	63.8	4.9			
2000	65.1	3.5	**Hispanic**[1]		
2001	64.4	4.2	1975	53.4	12.2
2002	63.4	5.1	1980	57.6	10.1
2003	63.0	5.2	1985	57.8	10.5
2004	63.1	4.8	1990	61.9	8.2
			1995	59.7	9.3
Black			2000	64.7	5.7
1975	50.1	14.8	2001	64.9	6.6
1980	52.3	14.3	2002	63.9	7.5
1985	53.4	15.1	2003	63.1	7.7
1990	56.7	11.4	2004	63.8	7.0
1995	57.1	10.4			

NOTE: Data apply to workers age 16 and older. 1. Hispanic persons may be of any race. *Source:* U.S. Department of Labor, Bureau of Labor Statistics. Web: data.bls.gov.

Employment Status by Sex, 1970–2004

| | | Civilian labor force | | | |
| | | Employed | | Unemployed | |
Year	Civilian noninstitutional population (in thousands)	Total (in thousands)	Percent of population	Total (in thousands)	Percent of labor force
Total both sexes					
1970	137,085	78,678	57.5%	4,093	4.9%
1975	153,153	85,846	56.1	7,929	8.5
1980	167,745	99,303	59.2	7,637	7.1
1985	178,206	107,150	60.1	8,312	7.2
1990	189,164	118,793	62.8	7,047	5.6
1995	198,584	124,900	62.9	7,404	5.6
2000	212,577	136,891	64.4	5,692	4.0
2002	217,570	136,485	62.7	8,378	5.8
2003	221,168	137,736	62.3	8,774	6.0
2004	223,357	139,252	62.3	8,149	5.5
Women					
1970	72,782	29,688	40.8	1,855	5.9
1975	80,860	33,989	42.0	3,486	9.3
1980	88,348	42,117	47.7	3,370	7.4
1985	93,736	47,259	50.4	3,791	7.4
1990	98,787	53,689	54.3	3,140	5.5
1995	103,406	57,523	55.6	3,421	5.6
2000	110,613	63,586	57.5	2,717	4.1
2002	112,985	63,582	56.3	3,781	5.6
2003	114,733	64,404	56.1	3,868	5.7
2004	115,647	64,728	56.0	3,694	5.4
Men					
1970	64,304	48,990	76.2	2,238	4.4
1975	72,291	51,857	71.7	4,442	7.9
1980	79,398	57,186	72.0	4,267	6.9
1985	84,469	59,891	70.9	4,521	7.0
1990	90,377	65,104	72.0	3,906	5.7
1995	95,178	67,377	70.8	3,983	5.6
2000	101,964	73,305	71.9	2,975	3.9
2002	104,585	72,903	69.7	4,597	5.9
2003	106,435	73,332	68.9	4,906	6.3
2004	107,710	74,524	69.2	4,456	5.6

Source: Current Population Survey, U.S. Department of Labor, Bureau of Labor Statistics. Web: www.bls.gov/cps/wlf-table1-2005.pdf.

Unemployment Rate by State, 2003 and 2004

	2003	2004		2003	2004		2003	2004
U.S.	**6.0%**	**5.5%**	Kansas	5.6%	5.5%	North Dakota	3.6%	3.4%
Alabama	5.8	5.6	Kentucky	6.2	5.3	Ohio	6.2	6.1
Alaska	7.7	7.5	Louisiana	6.3	5.7	Oklahoma	5.6	4.8
Arizona	5.7	5.0	Maine	5.0	4.6	Oregon	8.1	7.4
Arkansas	5.9	5.7	Maryland	4.5	4.2	Pennsylvania	5.7	5.5
California	6.8	6.2	Massachusetts	5.8	5.1	Puerto Rico	12.0	10.6
Colorado	6.2	5.5	Michigan	7.1	7.1	Rhode Island	5.4	5.2
Connecticut	5.5	4.9	Minnesota	4.9	4.7	South Carolina	6.7	6.8
Delaware	4.0	4.1	Mississippi	6.4	6.2	South Dakota	3.5	3.5
District of Columbia	7.2	8.2	Missouri	5.6	5.7	Tennessee	5.5	5.4
			Montana	4.4	4.4	Texas	6.7	6.1
Florida	5.3	4.8	Nebraska	4.0	3.8	Utah	5.7	5.2
Georgia	4.7	4.6	Nevada	5.1	4.3	Vermont	4.5	3.7
Hawaii	3.9	3.3	New Hampshire	4.5	3.8	Virginia	4.1	3.7
Idaho	5.3	4.7	New Jersey	5.9	4.8	Washington	7.4	6.2
Illinois	6.7	6.2	New Mexico	5.9	5.7	West Virginia	6.0	5.3
Indiana	5.3	5.2	New York	6.4	5.8	Wisconsin	5.6	4.9
Iowa	4.4	4.8	North Carolina	6.5	5.5	Wyoming	4.4	3.9

Source: U.S. Department of Labor, Bureau of Labor Statistics.

Overall Unemployment Rate in the Civilian Labor Force, 1920–2005

Year	Rate	Year	Rate	Year	Rate	Year	Rate	Year	Rate	Year	Rate
1920	5.2%	1946	3.9%	1966	3.8%	1986	7.0%	1996	5.4%	2005	
1928	4.2	1948	3.8	1968	3.6	1987	6.2	1997	4.9	Jan.	5.7%
1930	8.7	1950	5.3	1970	4.9	1988	5.5	1998	4.5	Feb.	5.8
1932	23.6	1952	3.0	1972	5.6	1989	5.3	1999	4.2	March	5.4
1934	21.7	1954	5.5	1974	5.6	1990	5.6	2000	4.0	April	4.9
1936	16.9	1956	4.1	1976	7.7	1991	6.8	2001	4.7	May	4.9
1938	19.0	1958	6.8	1978	6.1	1992	7.5	2002	5.8	June	5.0
1940	14.6	1960	5.5	1980	7.1	1993	6.9	2003	6.0	July	5.0
1942	4.7	1962	5.5	1982	9.7	1994	6.1	2004	5.5		
1944	1.2	1964	5.2	1984	7.5	1995	5.6				

NOTES: Estimates prior to 1940 are based on sources other than direct enumeration. Data prior to 1948 are for persons age 14 and over. Data beginning in 1948 are for persons age 16 and over. *Source:* U.S. Department of Labor, Bureau of Labor Statistics. Web: stats.bls.gov.

Mothers in the Labor Force, 1955–2004

	Percentage of mothers with children		
Year	Under 18 years	6 to 17 years	Under 6 years[1]
1955	27.0%	38.4%	18.2%
1965	35.0	45.7	25.3
1975	47.4	54.9	39.0
1980	56.6	64.3	46.8
1985	62.1	69.9	53.5
1990	66.7	74.7	58.2
1991	66.6	74.4	58.4
1992	67.2	75.9	58.0
1993	67.0	75.4	57.9
1994	68.4	76.0	60.3
1995	69.7	76.4	62.3
1996	70.2	77.2	62.3
1997	72.1	78.1	65.0
1998	72.3	78.4	65.2
1999	72.1	78.5	64.4
2000	72.9	79.0	65.3
2001	72.7	79.4	64.4
2002	72.2	78.6	64.1
2003	71.7	78.7	62.9
2004	70.7	77.5	62.2

1. May also have older children. NOTE: 1955 data are for April; 1965 and 1975–1994 data are for March. Data for 1994 and subsequent years are not directly comparable to previous years because of major revisions to the survey. *Source:* U.S. Department of Labor, Bureau of Labor Statistics. Web: data.bls.gov.

Women in the Labor Force, 1900–2004

Year	Number[1] (thousands)	% female population aged 16 and over[1]	% of labor force population aged 16 and over[1]
1900	5,319	18.8%	18.3%
1910	7,445	21.5	19.9
1920	8,637	21.4	20.4
1930	10,752	22.0	22.0
1940	12,845	25.4	24.3
1950	18,389	33.9	29.6
1960	23,240	37.7	33.4
1970	31,543	43.3	38.1
1980	45,487	51.5	42.5
1990[2]	56,829	57.5	45.2
1995[3]	60,944	58.9	46.1
2000	66,303	60.2	46.6
2001	66,848	60.1	46.5
2002	67,363	59.8	46.5
2003	68,272	59.5	47.0
2004	68,421	59.2	46.0

1. For 1900–1930, data relate to population and labor force age 10 and over; for 1940, to population and labor force age 14 and over; beginning 1950, to civilian population and labor force age 16 and over. 2. Data beginning in 1990 are not strictly comparable with data for prior years because population controls were adjusted. 3. Data beginning 1994 are not strictly comparable with data for prior years because of a major revision to survey methodology. *Source:* U.S. Department of Labor, Women's Bureau. Web: www.dol.gov.

Work Stoppages (Strikes) Involving 1,000 Workers or More

Year	Work stoppages	Workers involved (thousands)	Days idle (thousands)	Year	Work stoppages	Workers involved (thousands)	Days idle (thousands)
1950	424	1,698	30,390	1992	35	364	3,989
1960	222	896	13,260	1993	35	182	3,981
1970	381	2,468	52,761	1994	45	322	5,020
1975	235	965	17,563	1995	31	192	5,771
1980	187	795	20,844	1996	37	273	4,889
1984	62	376	8,499	1997	29	339	4,497
1985	54	324	7,079	1998	34	387	5,116
1986	69	533	11,861	1999	17	73	1,996
1987	46	174	4,481	2000	39	394	20,419
1988	40	118	4,381	2001	29	99	1,151
1989	51	452	16,996	2002	19	46	660
1990	44	185	5,926	2003	14	129	4,091
1991	40	392	4,584	2004	17	320	3,344

NOTE: Refers to stoppages that began in the year. Days idle is total for all stoppages in effect. Workers are counted more than once if they were involved in more than one stoppage during the year. *Source:* U.S. Department of Labor, Bureau of Labor Statistics. Web: data.bls.gov.

National Labor Organizations with Membership over 100,000

Members	Union[1]
2,679,396	National Education Association of the United States[2]
1,602,882	Service Employees International Union[3]
1,358,723	United Food and Commercial Workers International Union
1,350,000	American Federation of State, County, and Municipal Employees
1,328,000	International Brotherhood of Teamsters[3]
770,090	American Federation of Teachers
743,957	Laborers' International Union of North America
700,548	International Brotherhood of Electrical Workers
627,408	International Association of Machinists and Aerospace Workers
624,585	International Union, United Automobile, Aerospace, and Agricultural Implement Workers of America
557,136	Communications Workers of America
523,271	United Brotherhood of Carpenters and Joiners of America[2]
512,312	United Steelworkers of America
390,902	International Union of Operating Engineers
388,480	National Postal Mail Handlers Union
325,914	United Association of Journeymen and Apprentices of the Plumbing and Pipe-Fitting Industry of the U.S. and Canada
294,315	National Association of Letter Carriers
262,786	Paper, Allied-Industrial, and Chemical International Union
261,551	International Association of Fire Fighters
249,151	Hotel Employees and Restaurant Employees International Union

Members	Union[1]
239,147	American Postal Workers Union
209,876	Union of Needletrades, Industrial, and Textile Employees
204,282	American Federation of Government Employees
182,597	Amalgamated Transit Union
150,882	Office and Professional Employees International Union
149,808	American Nurses Association[2]
140,641	Sheet Metal Workers International Association
130,928	International Association of Bridge, Structural, Ornamental, and Reinforcing Iron Workers
115,511	International Brotherhood of Painters and Allied Trades
110,000	Transport Workers Union of America
109,917	Bakery, Confectionery, Tobacco Workers, and Grain Millers International Union
109,188	American Association of Classified School Employees[2]
108,205	International Union of Electronic, Electrical, Salaried, Machine, and Furniture Workers
104,102	International Alliance of Theatrical Stage Employees, Moving Picture Technicians, Artists, and Allied Crafts of the U.S. and Canada
101,810	The National Rural Letter Carriers' Association[2]
101,745	United Mine Workers of America
100,427	International Union of Bricklayers and Allied Craftworkers

1. Unless otherwise noted, unions are AFL-CIO affiliated. 2. Not AFL-CIO affiliated. 3. Severed ties with the AFL-CIO in July 2005. *Source:* U.S. Department of Labor.

Union Affiliation of Employed Wage and Salary Workers, 1983–2004

Year	Total employed (in thousands)	Percent of employed represented by unions	Year	Total employed (in thousands)	Percent of employed represented by unions
1983	88,290	23.3%	1995	110,038	16.7%
1985	94,521	20.5	2000	120,786	14.9
1990	104,876	18.2	2003	122,358	14.3
1993	106,101	17.6	2004	123,554	13.8

Source: U.S. Department of Labor, Bureau of Labor Statistics. Web: www.bls.gov.

Employed Wage and Salary Workers Represented by Unions, 2004

Occupation	Percent of workers	Industry	Percent of workers
Professional and related	20.9%	Public sector	40.7%
Natural resources, construction, and maintenance	19.4	Transportation and utilities	26.3
Production, transportation, and material moving	18.6	Manufacturing	13.9
		Information	15.4
Management, professional, and related	15.1	Education and health services	9.4
Service	12.3	Private sector	8.6
Sales and office	8.6		

Source: U.S. Bureau of Labor Statistics. Web: stats.bls.gov/cps/cpsaat42.pdf.

Union Membership Rates by State, 2004 Annual Averages
(U.S. Rate = 12.5%)

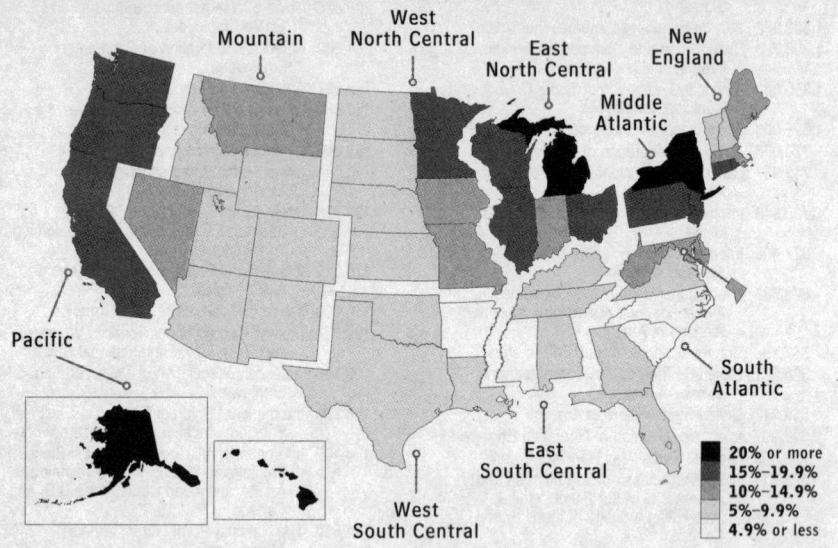

■	**20%** or more
■	**15%–19.9%**
■	**10%–14.9%**
■	**5%–9.9%**
□	**4.9%** or less

Source: Current Population Survey, Bureau of Labor Statistics. Web: www.bls.gov/news.release/pdf/union2.pdf

Per Capita Personal Income

Year	Amount	Year	Amount	Year	Amount	Year	Amount	Year	Amount	Year	Amount
1935	$ 474	1970	$ 3,893	1983	$12,352	1989	$18,176	1995	$23,562	2001	$30,575
1945	1,223	1975	5,851	1984	13,585	1990	19,188	1996	24,651	2002	30,804
1950	1,501	1979	8,638	1985	14,427	1991	19,652	1997	25,924	2003	31,472
1955	1,881	1980	9,910	1986	15,122	1992	20,576	1998	27,203	2004	32,937
1960	2,219	1981	10,949	1987	15,968	1993	21,231	1999	28,546		
1965	2,773	1982	11,731	1988	17,052	1994	22,086	2000	29,469		

Source: U.S. Department of Commerce, Bureau of Economic Analysis, *Survey of Current Business.* Web: www.bea.doc.gov/bea/regional/spi/.

Distribution of Household Income by Race

Income range	White			Black			Hispanic origin[1]		
	1972	1985	2003	1972	1985	2003	1972	1985	2003
Number of households (thousands)	60,618	76,576	91,962	6,809	9,797	13,629	2,655	5,213	11,693
Percent distribution									
Under $5,000	3.6%	2.9%	2.8%	8.3%	7.7%	6.9%	3.8%	4.9%	4.5%
$5,000 to $9,999	7.9	7.4	4.8	15.4	17.0	10.8	8.6	11.8	6.3
$10,000 to $14,999	7.5	7.3	6.6	13.0	11.2	9.7	12.1	11.4	8.1
$15,000 to $24,999	14.1	14.7	12.8	20.0	18.7	16.0	20.7	18.8	17.6
$25,000 to $34,999	15.0	13.8	11.8	15.6	13.4	13.3	20.5	15.4	15.8
$35,000 to $49,999	20.9	18.2	15.0	13.7	14.1	15.0	18.9	16.8	16.7
$50,000 to $74,999	19.7	19.2	18.5	10.9	11.4	14.6	11.4	13.1	15.9
$75,000 to $99,999	6.8	9.2	11.5	2.2	4.5	7.0	2.6	5.3	7.7
$100,000 and over	4.6	7.4	16.1	1.0	1.9	6.7	1.5	2.5	7.5
Median income	$36,510	$38,226	$45,631	$21,311	$22,742	$29,645	$27,552	$26,803	$32,997

1. Persons of Hispanic origin may be of any race. *Source:* U.S. Bureau of the Census: *Income, Poverty, and Health Insurance Coverage in the United States, 2003.*

Median Four-Person Family Income
(in current dollars)

Year	Income	Percent change	Year	Income	Percent change	Year	Income	Percent change
2003	$65,093	3.6%	1993	$45,161	2.1%	1983	$29,184	5.7%
2002	62,732	-0.9	1992	44,251	2.8	1982	27,619	5.1
2001	63,278	1.7	1991	43,056	4.6	1981	26,274	8.0
2000	62,228	3.7	1990	41,151	1.0	1980	24,332	8.6
1999	59,981	7.0	1989	40,763	4.4	1979	22,395	9.6
1998	56,061	5.1	1988	39,051	6.1	1978	20,428	9.1
1997	53,350	3.6	1987	36,812	6.0	1977	18,723	8.1
1996	51,518	3.7	1986	34,716	5.9	1976	17,315	9.3
1995	49,687	5.7	1985	32,777	5.4	1975	15,848	7.5
1994	47,012	4.1	1984	31,097	6.6			

Source: Income Statistics Branch/HHES Division, U.S. Bureau of the Census. Web: www.census.gov.

Federal Minimum Wage Rates, 1955–2005

Year	Value of the minimum wage Current dollars	Value of the minimum wage Constant (1996) dollars[1]	Year	Value of the minimum wage Current dollars	Value of the minimum wage Constant (1996) dollars[1]	Year	Value of the minimum wage Current dollars	Value of the minimum wage Constant (1996) dollars[1]	Year	Value of the minimum wage Current dollars	Value of the minimum wage Constant (1996) dollars[1]
1955	$0.75	$4.39	1968	$1.60	$7.21	1981	$3.35	$5.78	1994	$4.25	$4.50
1956	1.00	5.77	1969	1.60	6.84	1982	3.35	5.45	1995	4.25	4.38
1957	1.00	5.58	1970	1.60	6.47	1983	3.35	5.28	1996	4.75	4.75
1958	1.00	5.43	1971	1.60	6.20	1984	3.35	5.06	1997	5.15	5.03
1959	1.00	5.39	1972	1.60	6.01	1985	3.35	4.88	1998	5.15	4.96
1960	1.00	5.30	1973	1.60	5.65	1986	3.35	4.80	1999	5.15	4.85
1961	1.15	6.03	1974	2.00	6.37	1987	3.35	4.63	2000	5.15	4.69
1962	1.15	5.97	1975	2.10	6.12	1988	3.35	4.44	2001	5.15	4.56
1963	1.25	6.41	1976	2.30	6.34	1989	3.35	4.24	2002	5.15	4.49
1964	1.25	6.33	1977	2.30	5.95	1990	3.80	4.56	2003	5.15	4.39
1965	1.25	6.23	1978	2.65	6.38	1991	4.25	4.90	2004	5.15	4.28
1966	1.25	6.05	1979	2.90	6.27	1992	4.25	4.75	2005	5.15	4.15
1967	1.40	6.58	1980	3.10	5.90	1993	4.25	4.61			

1. Adjusted for inflation using the CPI-U (Consumer Price Index for All Urban Consumers). Source: U.S. Department of Labor. Web: http://www.dol.gov/esa/whd/flsa/.

State Minimum Wage Rates

State	Minimum wage	State	Minimum wage	State	Minimum wage
Federal minimum wage	**$5.15**	Kansas	$2.65	North Dakota	$5.15
Alabama	None	Kentucky	5.15	Ohio	4.25
Alaska	7.15	Louisiana	None	Oklahoma	5.15
Arizona	None	Maine	6.25	Oregon	7.05[1]
Arkansas	5.15	Maryland	5.15	Pennsylvania	5.15
California	6.75	Massachusetts	6.75	Rhode Island	6.75
Colorado	5.15	Michigan	5.15	South Carolina	None
Connecticut	7.10	Minnesota	5.15	South Dakota	5.15
Delaware	6.15	Mississippi	None	Tennessee	None
District of Columbia	6.15	Missouri	5.15	Texas	5.15
Florida	None	Montana	5.15	Utah	5.15
Georgia	5.15	Nebraska	5.15	Vermont	6.25
Hawaii	6.25	Nevada	5.15	Virginia	5.15
Idaho	5.15	New Hampshire	5.15	Washington	7.16[1]
Illinois	7.05[1]	New Jersey	5.15	West Virginia	5.15
Indiana	5.15	New Mexico	5.15	Wisconsin	5.15
Iowa	5.15	New York	5.15	Wyoming	5.15
		North Carolina	5.15		

NOTE: A state cannot reduce the requirements of the Fair Labor Standards Act (FLSA). Most states have adopted minimums, although many simply track the FLSA. Others are broader, for example, covering workers not covered under the FLSA or setting higher minimums than the federal rate. Some states set a state minimum lower than the federal rate. In that case, all workers in the state who are covered by the FLSA must receive the federal minimum. When state laws require a higher wage, employers must pay at least that higher rate to all workers covered by the state law, whether or not they also are covered by the federal law. Some minimum wage rates in this table apply only to large companies or employers with a certain dollar amount of receipts. Smaller companies may either have to pay a different minimum wage (which is not listed here) or there may be no minimum wage requirement at all. 1. Rate is indexed to inflation—adjusted every Jan. 1. Source: U.S. Department of Labor, Employment Standards Administration Wage and Hour Division and AFL-CIO.

Per Capita Personal Income by State

State	1980	1990	2000	2004	State	1980	1990	2000	2004
Alabama	$ 7,465	$14,899	$23,521	$27,795	Montana	$ 8,342	$14,743	$22,518	$26,857
Alaska	13,007	20,887	29,642	34,454	Nebraska	8,895	17,379	27,630	31,339
Arizona	8,854	16,262	24,988	28,442	Nevada	10,848	20,248	29,506	33,405
Arkansas	7,113	13,779	21,995	25,725	New Hampshire	9,150	20,231	33,169	37,040
California	11,021	20,656	32,149	35,019	New Jersey	10,966	24,182	37,118	41,332
Colorado	10,143	18,818	32,434	36,063	New Mexico	7,940	14,213	21,931	26,191
Connecticut	11,532	25,426	40,702	45,398	New York	10,179	22,322	34,689	38,228
Delaware	10,059	19,719	31,012	35,861	North Carolina	7,780	16,284	26,882	29,246
DC	12,251	24,643	38,838	51,803	North Dakota	8,642	15,320	24,708	31,398
Florida	9,246	18,785	27,764	31,455	Ohio	9,399	17,547	27,977	31,322
Georgia	8,021	17,121	27,794	30,051	Oklahoma	9,018	15,117	23,650	28,089
Hawaii	10,129	20,905	27,851	32,160	Oregon	9,309	17,201	27,660	29,971
Idaho	8,105	15,304	23,727	27,098	Pennsylvania	9,353	18,884	29,504	33,348
Illinois	10,454	20,159	31,856	34,351	Rhode Island	9,227	19,035	29,113	33,733
Indiana	8,914	16,815	26,933	30,094	South Carolina	7,392	15,101	24,000	27,172
Iowa	9,226	16,683	26,431	30,560	South Dakota	7,800	15,628	25,958	30,856
Kansas	9,880	17,639	27,374	30,811	Tennessee	7,711	15,903	25,946	30,005
Kentucky	7,679	14,751	24,085	27,709	Texas	9,439	16,747	27,752	30,222
Louisiana	8,412	14,279	23,090	27,581	Utah	7,671	14,063	23,436	26,606
Maine	7,760	17,041	25,380	30,566	Vermont	7,957	17,444	26,848	32,770
Maryland	10,394	22,088	33,482	39,247	Virginia	9,413	19,543	31,120	35,477
Massachusetts	10,103	22,248	37,704	41,801	Washington	10,256	19,268	31,230	35,299
Michigan	9,801	18,239	29,127	31,954	West Virginia	7,764	13,964	21,738	25,872
Minnesota	9,673	18,784	31,935	35,861	Wisconsin	9,364	17,399	28,100	32,157
Mississippi	6,573	12,578	20,900	24,650	Wyoming	11,018	16,905	27,372	34,306
Missouri	8,812	17,407	27,206	30,608	**United States**	**9,494**	**18,667**	**29,469**	**32,937**

NOTE: Per capita personal income was computed using midyear population estimates of the Bureau of the Census. *Source:* U.S. Department of Commerce, Bureau of Economic Analysis, *Survey of Current Business.* Web: www.bea.doc.gov/bea/regional/spi/.

Median Income of Households by Selected Characteristics, 2003

Characteristic	Number (thousands)	Median income	Characteristic	Number (thousands)	Median income
All households	**112,000**	**$43,318**	Black	13,969	$29,689
Type of household			Asian and Pacific Islander	4,235	55,262
Family households	76,217	53,991	Hispanic origin[1]	11,693	32,997
Married-couple families	57,719	62,405	**Age of householder**		
Female householder, no			15–24	6,610	27,053
husband present	13,781	29,307	25–34	19,159	44,779
Male householder, no			35–44	23,222	55,044
wife present	4,717	41,959	45–54	23,137	60,242
Nonfamily households	35,783	25,741	55–64	16,824	49,215
Female householder	19,647	21,313	65 and over	23,048	23,787
Male householder	16,136	31,928	**Earnings of full-time, year-round workers**		
Race and Hispanic origin of householder			Male	58,772	40,668
White	93,196	45,572	Female	41,908	30,724
Non-Hispanic	81,148	47,777			

1. Persons of Hispanic origin may be of any race. *Source:* U.S. Bureau of the Census, *Money Income in the United States: 2003.* Web: www.census.gov.

Consumer Credit Outstanding[1]
(in billions of dollars)

	Total	Commercial banks	Finance companies	Credit unions	Federal government and Sallie Mae	Savings institutions	Nonfinancial business	Pools of securitized assets[2]
1975	$ 168.7	$ 82.9	$ 32.7	$ 25.7	n.a	n.a.	n.a.	n.a.
1980	302.1	147.0	62.3	44.0	n.a	n.a.	n.a.	n.a.
1985	526.3	245.1	111.7	72.7	n.a.	n.a.	n.a.	n.a.
1990	751.9	347.1	133.3	93.1	n.a	n.a.	n.a.	n.a.
1995	1,122.8	502.0	152.1	131.9	n.a	$40.1	$85.1	$211.6
1999	1,426.2	499.8	181.6	167.9	n.a	61.5	80.3	435.1
2000	1,566.5	541.5	193.2	184.4	$104.0	64.6	82.7	500.1
2001	1,702.8	558.0	236.5	189.6	119.5	69.1	67.9	581.7
2002	1,762.3	587.4	232.3	195.7	129.6	68.6	56.9	621.4
2003	2,025.5	636.4	295.4	205.9	114.6	77.9	70.3	625.0
2004	2,140.4	697.4	365.6	215.4	98.4	91.3	65.9	606.6

1. Covers most short- and intermediate-term credit extended to individuals, excluding loans secured by real estate. 2. Outstanding balances of pools on which securities have been issued; these balances are no longer carried on the balance sheets of the loan originators. n.a. = not available. *Source:* Federal Reserve Board. Web http://www.federalreserve.gov/default.htm.

Poverty in the United States

Source: U.S. Bureau of the Census, Aug. 2004 supplement to the Current Population Survey (CPS). Web: www.census.gov.

The poverty rate in 2003 rose to 12.5%, up from 12.1% in 2002. About 35.9 million people were poor in 2003, 1.3 million more than in 2002. Both the number and rate have risen for three consecutive years, from 31.6 million and 11.3% in 2000, to 35.9 million and 12.5% in 2003.

For children under 18 years old, both the poverty rate and the number in poverty rose between 2002 and 2003, from 16.7% to 17.6%, and from 12.1 million to 12.9 million, respectively. The poverty rate of children under 18 remained higher than that of 18- to- 64-year-olds and that of seniors aged 65 and over (10.8% and 10.2%, respectively, both unchanged from 2002). In addition, children represented 35.9% of the people in poverty, compared with 25.4% of the total population.

The poverty rate for people reporting white as their only race was 10.5% in 2003, up from 10.2% in 2002. For blacks, neither the poverty rate nor the number in poverty changed significantly between 2002 and 2003. People who reported black as their only race, for example, had a poverty rate of 24.4% in 2003 and 24.1% in 2002. Among people who indicated Asian

as their only race, 11.8% were in poverty in 2003, higher than the 10.1% in 2002. The number in poverty also increased (from 1.2 million to 1.4 million).

The poverty rate and number of families in poverty increased to 10.0% and 7.6 million in 2003, up from 9.6% and 7.2 million in 2002. Married-couple families showed no change in either their poverty rate or their number in poverty (5.4% and 3.1 million in 2003). In contrast, the poverty rates and numbers in poverty increased for both female householders with no husband present (to 28.0% and 3.9 million in 2003, up from 26.5% and 3.6 million in 2002) and male householders with no wife present (to 13.5% and 640,000 in 2003, up from 12.1% and 560,000 in 2002).

In 2003, the poverty rates for the Northeast (11.3%), Midwest (10.7%), South (14.1%), and West (12.6%) all were unchanged from 2002, leaving the South with the highest rate. Two of the four regions showed increases in the number of people in poverty from 2002 to 2003: the number in the Midwest rose from 6.6 million to 6.9 million and the number in the South rose from 14.0 million to 14.5 million.

People and Families in Poverty by Selected Characteristics, 2002 and 2003

Characteristic	2003		2002	
	Number (thousands)	Percent[1]	Number (thousands)	Percent[1]
INDIVIDUALS				
Total	35,861	12.5%	34,570	12.1%
In families	25,684	10.8	24,534	10.4
Householder	7,607	10.0	7,229	9.6
Related children under 18	12,340	17.2	11,646	16.3
Related children under 6	4,654	19.8	4,296	18.5
In unrelated subfamilies	464	38.6	417	33.7
Reference person	191	37.6	167	31.7
Children under 18	271	41.7	241	35.4
Unrelated individual	9,713	20.4	9,618	20.4
Male	4,154	18.0	4,023	17.7
Female	5,559	22.6	5,595	22.9
Race[2] and Hispanic origin				
White	24,272	10.5	23,466	10.2
Non-Hispanic	15,902	8.2	15,567	8.0
Black	8,781	24.4	8,602	24.1
Asian	1,401	11.8	1,161	10.1
Hispanic[3]	9,051	22.5	8,555	21.8
Age				
Under 18	12,866	17.6	12,133	16.7
18–64	19,443	10.8	18,861	10.6
65 and over	3,552	10.2	3,576	10.4
Nativity				
Native	29,965	11.8	29,012	11.5
Foreign born	5,897	17.2	5,558	16.6
Naturalized citizen	1,309	10.0	1,285	10.0
Not a citizen	4,588	21.7	4,273	20.7
Region				
Northeast	6,052	11.3	5,871	10.9
Midwest	6,932	10.7	6,616	10.3
South	14,548	14.1	14,019	13.8
West	8,329	12.6	8,064	12.4
FAMILIES				
Total	7,607	10.0	7,229	9.6
Type of Family				
Married-couple	3,115	5.4	3,052	5.3
Female householder, no husband present	3,856	28.0	3,613	26.5
Male householder, no wife present	636	135	564	12.1

1. Percentage of total population. 2. Data for American Indians and Alaska Natives are not shown separately. 3. Hispanics may be of any race. *Source:* U.S. Census Bureau, *Current Population Survey,* 2003 and 2004 Annual Demographic Supplements.

Percent of People in Poverty by State, 2001–2003

State	3-year average 2001–2003	2-year average 2001–2002	2-year average 2002–2003	State	3-year average 2001–2003	2-year average 2001–2002	2-year average 2002–2003
United States	**12.1%**	**11.9%**	**12.3%**	Missouri	10.1	9.8%	10.3%
Alabama	15.1	15.2	14.7	Montana	14.0	13.4	14.3
Alaska	9.0	8.7	9.2	Nebraska	9.9	10.0	10.2
Arizona	13.9	14.1	13.5	Nevada	9.0	8.0	9.9
Arkansas	18.5	18.8	18.8	New Hampshire	6.0	6.1	5.8
California	12.9	12.8	13.1	New Jersey	8.2	8.0	8.3
Colorado	9.4	9.2	9.7	New Mexico	18.0	17.9	18.0
Connecticut	7.9	7.8	8.2	New York	14.2	14.1	14.2
Delaware	7.7	7.9	8.2	North Carolina	14.2	13.4	15.0
DC	17.3	17.6	16.9	North Dakota	11.7	12.7	10.6
Florida	12.7	12.6	12.6	Ohio	10.4	10.1	10.3
Georgia	12.0	12.1	11.5	Oklahoma	14.0	14.6	13.5
Hawaii	10.7	11.4	10.3	Oregon	11.7	11.3	11.7
Idaho	11.0	11.4	10.8	Pennsylvania	9.9	9.5	10.0
Illinois	11.8	11.5	12.7	Rhode Island	10.7	10.3	11.3
Indiana	9.2	8.8	9.5	South Carolina	14.0	14.7	13.5
Iowa	8.5	8.3	9.1	South Dakota	10.9	10.0	12.1
Kansas	10.3	10.1	10.4	Tennessee	14.3	14.5	14.4
Kentucky	13.7	13.4	14.3	Texas	15.8	15.3	16.3
Louisiana	16.9	16.9	17.2	Utah	9.8	10.2	9.5
Maine	11.8	11.9	12.5	Vermont	9.4	9.8	9.2
Maryland	7.7	7.3	8.0	Virginia	9.3	8.9	10.0
Massachusetts	9.7	9.5	10.1	Washington	11.4	10.8	11.8
Michigan	10.8	10.5	11.5	West Virginia	16.9	16.6	17.1
Minnesota	7.1	6.9	6.9	Wisconsin	8.8	8.2	9.2
Mississippi	17.9	18.9	17.2	Wyoming	9.1	8.8	9.4

Source: U.S. Census Bureau, Current Population Survey, 2002, 2003, and 2004 Annual Demographic Supplements. Web: www.census.gov.

Weighted Average Poverty Thresholds[1] for Families, 1960–2004

Calendar year	Individual[2]	Families of 2 persons or more					
		2 persons[2]	3 persons	4 persons	5 persons	6 persons	7 persons
1960	$1,490	$ 1,924	$ 2,359	$ 3,022	$ 3,560	$ 4,002	$ 4,921[3]
1965	1,582	2,048	2,514	3,223	3,797	4,264	5,248[3]
1970	1,954	2,525	3,099	3,968	4,680	5,260	6,468[3]
1975	2,724	3,506	4,293	5,500	6,499	7,316	9,022[3]
1980	4,190	5,363	6,565	8,414	9,966	11,269	12,761
1985	5,469	6,998	8,573	10,989	13,007	14,696	16,656
1990	6,652	8,509	10,419	13,359	15,792	17,839	20,241
1995	7,763	9,933	12,158	15,569	18,408	20,804	23,552
2000	8,959	11,531	13,470	17,761	21,419	24,636	28,347
2001	9,214	11,859	13,853	18,267	22,029	25,337	29,154
2002	9,359	12,047	14,480	18,244	21,469	24,038	26,924
2003	9,573	12,321	14,810	18,660	21,959	24,586	27,538
2004	9,827	12,649	14,776	19,484	23,497	27,025	31,096

1. Annual income. 2. Householder under 65 years. 3. For years before 1980, data are for families with seven persons or more. *Source:* U.S. Bureau of the Census. Web: www.census.gov.

Persons Below Poverty Level, 1975–2003

(in thousands)

Year	All persons	Percent	White	Percent	Black	Percent	Hispanic origin[1]	Percent	Asian and Pac. Isl.	Percent
1975	25,877	12.3%	17,770	9.7%	7,545	31.3%	2,991	26.9%	n.a.	n.a.
1980	29,272	13.0	19,699	10.2	8,579	32.5	3,491	25.7	n.a.	n.a.
1985	33,064	14.0	22,860	11.4	8,926	31.3	5,236	29.0	n.a.	n.a.
1990	33,585	13.5	22,326	10.7	9,837	31.9	6,006	28.1	858	12.2%
1995	36,425	13.8	24,423	11.2	9,872	29.3	8,574	30.3	1,411	14.6
2000	31,139	11.3	21,291	9.4	7,901	22.1	7,155	21.2	1,226	10.8
2001	32,907	11.7	22,739	9.9	8,136	22.7	7,997	21.4	1,275	10.2
2002	34,570	12.1	23,466	10.2	8,602	24.1	8,555	21.8	1,161[2]	10.1
2003	35,861	12.5	24,272	10.5	8,781	24.4	9,051	22.5	1,401	11.8

n.a. = not available. 1. Persons of Hispanic origin may be of any race. 2. For years 2002 and 2003, figures refer to people who reported Asian and did not report any other race category. *Source:* U.S. Bureau of the Census. Web: www.census.gov.

Food Insecurity and Hunger

(numbers in thousands)

| | | Food secure | | Food insecure | | | | | |
| | | | | Total | | Without hunger | | With hunger | |
Category	Total number[1]	Number	Percent	Number	Percent	Number	Percent	Number	Percent
Households:									
1998	103,309	91,121	88.2%	12,188	11.8%	8,353	8.1%	3,835	3.7%
1999	104,684	94,154	89.9	10,529	10.1	7,420	7.1	3,109	3.0
2000	106,043	94,942	89.5	11,101	10.5	7,786	7.3	3,315	3.1
2001	107,824	96,303	89.3	11,521	10.7	8,010	7.4	3,511	3.3
2002	108,601	96,543	88.9	12,058	11.1	8,259	7.6	3,799	3.5
2003	112,214	99,631	88.8	12,583	11.2	8,663	7.7	3,920	3.5
Households with children:									
1998	38,036	31,355	82.4	6,701	17.6	6,370	16.7	331	.9
1999	37,884	32,290	85.2	5,594	14.8	5,375	14.2	219	.6
2000	38,113	31,942	83.8	6,171	16.2	5,916	15.5	255	.7
2001	38,330	32,141	83.9	6,189	16.1	5,978	15.6	211	.6
2002	38,647	32,267	83.5	6,380	16.5	6,115	15.8	265	.7
2003	40,286	33,575	83.3	6,711	16.7	6,504	16.1	207	.5

1. Total households in each category exclude households whose food security status is unknown. In 2003, these represented 381,000 households. *Source:* Economic Research Service, U.S. Dept. of Agriculture, *Household Food Security in the United States, 2003.* Web: http://www.ers.usda.gov/publications/fanrr42/fanrr42b.pdf.

Food Stamp Households, 2002

| | Households | | | Participants | |
Household type	Number (in thousands)	Percent	Sex, race, and Hispanic origin	Number (in thousands)	Percent
Total	**8,201**	**100.0%**	**Total**	**19,041**	**100.0%**
With children	4,437	54.1	Male	7,769	40.8
Single-parent households	2,825	34.5	Female	11,269	59.2
Married-couple households	778	9.5	White, non-Hispanic	7,925	41.6
Other	834	18.8	Black, non-Hispanic	6,650	34.9
With elderly	1,537	18.7	Hispanic	3,467	18.2
Living alone	1,233	15.0	Asian	537	2.8
Not living alone	303	3.7	Native American	303	1.6
Disabled	2,213	27.0	Other	159	0.8
Living alone	1,300	15.8			
Not living alone	914	11.1			

Source: U.S. Dept. of Agriculture, Food and Nutrition Service, *Characteristics of Food Stamp Households: Fiscal Year 2002,* Dec. 2003. From *Statistical Abstract of the United States, 2004.*

Average Monthly Social Security Benefits, 1940–2003

| | Retired workers | | | Disabled workers | | | Non-disabled widow(er)s |
Year	Total	Men	Women	Total	Men	Women	
1940	$ 22.71	$ 23.26	$ 18.38	—	—	—	$ 20.36
1945	25.11	25.71	19.99	—	—	—	20.17
1950[1]	29.03	30.16	22.98	—	—	—	21.65
1955	69.74	75.86	56.05	—	—	—	49.68
1960	81.73	92.03	63.26	$ 91.16	$ 94.02	$ 78.91	62.12
1965[1]	82.69	90.89	68.78	93.26	97.89	80.27	73.81
1970	123.82	136.80	103.67	139.79	148.39	115.74	106.95
1975[2]	196.42	220.35	160.50	220.60	241.48	175.27	185.34
1980[2]	321.10	374.00	244.90	352.10	388.80	269.70	277.50
1985[3]	432.00	509.60	322.20	459.20	514.00	345.00	431.10
1990[3]	550.50	654.60	403.30	566.90	637.80	438.90	541.10
1995[3]	671.70	794.30	505.80	675.70	767.30	546.00	662.50
1999	757.71	904.62	697.50	754.12	846.48	629.63	776.07
2000	844.60	951.50	729.60	787.00	883.00	661.10	811.80
2001	874.50	984.90	755.90	814.90	913.80	688.70	840.80
2002	895.00	1,007.81	774.90	834.32	935.60	708.63	861.09
2003	922.10	1,038.90	797.50	861.70	965.90	734.40	888.30

1. Jan.–Aug. 2. Jan.–May. 3. Jan.–Nov. *Source:* Social Security Administration, *Social Security Bulletin: Annual Statistical Supplement, 2003.*

Social Security

Source: Social Security Administration, www.ssa.gov.

The original Social Security Act was passed in 1935 and is administered by the Social Security Administration and other agencies within the Department of Health and Human Services.

What Does Social Security Offer?

The Social Security contribution you pay gives you four different kinds of protection: (1) retirement benefits, (2) survivors' benefits, (3) disability benefits, and (4) Medicare hospital insurance benefits.

Retirement Benefits

If you were born earlier than 1938, you became eligible for the full amount of your retirement benefits at age 65. That age is gradually being increased: if you were born between 1943 and 1954, your full retirement age will be 66; it will be 67 if you were born 1960 onward. No matter when you were born, you will be able to retire at age 62 and get a smaller percentage of your full benefit.

The amount of the retirement benefit you are entitled to at your retirement age is the key to all other benefits under the program. The retirement benefit is based on covered earnings, which will be updated (indexed) to reflect the increases in average wages that have occurred since the earnings were paid. Your largest 35 years of adjusted earnings are averaged together and a formula is applied to the adjusted average to figure the benefit rate.

Survivor Benefits

This feature of the Social Security program gives your family valuable life-insurance protection. The amount of protection is again geared to what the worker would be entitled to if he had been at retirement age when he died. Your survivors could get:

1. A one-time cash payment of $255 for your spouse or minor children if you have enough work credits.
2. A benefit for each child until he or she reaches 18 (or 19, if the child is in full-time attendance at an elementary or secondary school), or at any age if disabled before 22.
3. A benefit for your widow(er), at any age, if she/he has your entitled children under 16 or disabled in care.
4. Your spouse or divorced spouse can get a widow's, widower's, or surviving divorced spouse's benefit starting at age 60. A widow or widower who first becomes entitled at retirement age or later will get 100% of his or her deceased spouse's basic amount (or the amount of the deceased spouse's reduced benefits).
5. Dependent parents can sometimes collect survivors' benefits. They are usually eligible if: (a) they were getting at least half their support from the deceased worker; (b) they have reached 62; (c) they are not eligible for a greater retirement benefit based on their own earnings; and (d) they have not married since the worker's death.

Disability Benefits

Disability benefits can be paid to several groups of people:

- Disabled workers under retirement age and their families.
- Persons disabled before age 22 who continue to be disabled. These benefits are payable as early as age 18 when a parent (or step-parent or grandparent under certain circumstances) receives Social Security retirement or disability benefits or when an insured parent dies.
- Disabled widows and widowers and (under certain conditions) disabled, surviving, and divorced spouses of workers who were insured at death. These benefits are payable as early as 50.

The SSA determines whether or not you qualify for disability benefits based on criteria including the severity of your condition and the earnings you continue to receive after you become disabled. To be considered for disability benefits, you should file a claim with a Social Security office as soon as you become disabled.

Medicare Program

Medicare is the nation's largest health insurance program. Generally, you are eligible for Medicare if you or your spouse worked for at least ten years in Medicare-covered employment and you are 65 years old and a citizen or permanent resident of the United States. You might also qualify for coverage if you are a younger person with a disability or with chronic kidney disease.

Medicare-covered services include:

- **Hospital insurance.** Financial assistance is available for necessary medical care and services furnished by Medicare-certified hospitals, skilled nursing facilities, home health agencies, and hospices.
- **Inpatient hospital care.** Medicare helps pay for up to 90 days of inpatient hospital care in each benefit period. Covered services include your semi-private room and meals, general nursing services, operating and recovery room costs, intensive care, drugs, laboratory tests, X rays, and all other necessary medical services and supplies.
- **Skilled nursing facility care.** If you meet certain conditions, Medicare will help pay for up to 100 days in a participating skilled nursing facility in each benefit period.
- **Home health care.** If you meet certain conditions, Medicare pays the full approved cost of covered home health care services. This includes part-time or intermittent skilled nursing services prescribed by a physician for treatment or rehabilitation of homebound patients.
- **Hospice care.** Medicare helps pay for hospice care for terminally ill beneficiaries who select the hospice care benefit.
- **Medical insurance (Part B).** Medicare Part B helps pay for doctor's services, outpatient hospital services (including emergency room visits), ambulance transportation, diagnostic tests, laboratory services, some preventive care such as mammography and Pap smear screening, outpatient therapy services, durable medical equipment and supplies, and a variety of other health services.

Gross Domestic Product or Expenditure, 1930–2004

(in billions of dollars)

Item	1930	1940	1950	1960	1970	1980	1990	2000	2004
Gross domestic product	$91.2	$101.4	$293.8	$526.4	$1,038.5	$2,789.5	$5,803.1	$9,817.0	$11,735.0
Personal consumption expenditures	70.1	71.3	192.2	331.7	648.5	1,757.1	3,839.9	6,739.4	8,229.9
Gross private domestic investment	10.8	13.6	54.1	78.9	152.4	479.3	861.0	1,735.5	1,927.3
Exports of goods and services	4.4	4.9	12.4	27.0	59.7	280.8	552.4	1,096.3	1,175.5
Imports of goods and services	4.1	3.4	11.6	22.8	55.8	293.8	630.3	1,475.8	1,781.6
Government[1]	10.0	15.0	46.8	111.6	233.8	566.2	1,180.2	1,721.6	2,183.9

1. Government consumption expenditures and gross investment. *Source:* U.S. Bureau of Economic Analysis, May 26, 2005. Web: www.bea.gov.

The Public Debt

Year	Gross debt amount	Year	Gross debt amount	Year	Gross debt amount	Year	Gross debt amount
1800	$82,976,294	1860	$ 64,842,288	1920	$ 25,952,456,406	1980	$ 930,210,000,000[1]
1805	82,312,151	1865	2,680,647,870	1925	20,516,193,888	1985	1,945,941,616,460
1810	53,173,218	1870	2,480,672,428	1930	16,185,309,831	1990	3,233,313,451,777
1815	99,833,660	1875	2,232,284,532	1935	28,700,892,625	1995	4,973,982,900,709
1820	91,015,566	1880	2,120,415,371	1940	42,967,531,038	2000	5,674,178,209,887
1825	83,788,433	1885	1,863,964,873	1945	258,682,187,410	2001	5,807,463,412,200
1830	48,565,407	1890	1,552,140,205	1950	257,357,352,351	2002	6,228,235,965,597
1835	33,733	1895	1,676,120,983	1955	280,768,553,189	2003	6,783,231,062,744
1840	3,573,344	1900	2,136,961,092	1960	290,216,815,242	2004	7,379,052,696,330
1845	15,925,303	1905	2,274,615,064	1965	320,904,110,042		
1850	63,452,774	1910	2,652,665,838	1970	389,158,403,690		
1855	35,586,957	1915	3,058,136,873	1975	576,649,000,000[1]		

NOTE: Figures as of Jan. 1 for years 1800–1840; as of July 1 for years 1845–1920; as of June 30 for years 1925–1950; as of Dec. 31 for years 1955–1985; as of Sept. 30 for years 1990–present. 1. Rounded to millions. *Source:* U.S. Department of the Treasury, The Public Debt Online. Web: www.publicdebt.treas.gov/opd/opdpdodt.htm.

Federal Outlays by Agency, 2003–2005

(in millions of dollars)

Department or agency	2003	2004	2005 (estimate)	Department or agency	2003	2004	2005 (estimate)
Legislative Branch	$ 3,427	$ 3,885	$ 4,083	National Aeronautics and Space Administration	$ 14,552	$ 15,189	$ 15,719
The Judiciary	5,123	5,392	5,741	National Science Foundation	4,736	5,118	5,641
Agriculture	72,374	71,769	94,912	Office of Personnel Management	54,135	56,535	60,964
Commerce	5,676	5,850	6,278	Small Business Administration	1,558	4,075	3,036
Defense—Military	388,870	437,116	444,068	Social Security Administration (On-budget)	46,333	49,005	55,750
Education	57,400	62,816	70,953	Social Security Administration (Off-budget)	461,401	481,200	503,298
Energy	19,385	19,972	22,178	Other Independent Agencies (On-budget)	14,450	10,034	20,681
Health and Human Services	505,345	543,389	585,772	Other Independent Agencies (Off-budget)	−5,245	−4,130	−1,010
Homeland Security	31,967	26,537	33,259	Allowances			34,899
Housing and Urban Development	37,474	45,019	42,614	Undistributed offsetting receipts	−210,450		
Interior	9,210	8,914	9,433	(On-budget)	(−117,303)		
Justice	21,539	28,954	21,171	(Off-budget)	(−93,147)	(−97,559)	(−102,906)
Labor	69,593	56,706	50,034	**Total outlays**	**$2,159,917**	**$2,292,215**	**$2,479,404**
State	9,261	10,934	11,934				
Transportation	50,807	54,547	58,215				
Treasury	366,987	374,817	402,972				
Veterans Affairs	56,891	59,554	68,046				
Corps of Engineers	4,751	4,838	4,891				
Other Defense—Civil Programs	39,883	41,730	43,460				
Environmental Protection Agency	8,061	8,334	7,862				
Executive Office of the President	387	3,308	5,765				
General Services Administration	573	−403	459				
International Assistance Programs	13,463	13,737	14,754				

Source: Budget of the United States Government, Fiscal Year 2006.

Receipts and Outlays of the Federal Government, 1789–2006
(in millions of dollars)

Year		Total			On-budget[1]	
	Receipts	Outlays	Surplus or deficit (−)	Receipts	Outlays	Surplus or deficit (−)
1789–1849	$ 1,160	$ 1,090	$ 70	$ 1,160	$ 1,090	$ 70
1850–1900	14,462	15,453	−991	14,462	15,453	−991
1905	544	567	−23	544	567	−23
1910	676	694	−18	676	694	−18
1915	683	746	−63	683	746	−63
1920	6,649	6,358	291	6,649	6,358	291
1925	3,641	2,924	717	3,641	2,924	717
1930	4,058	3,320	738	4,058	3,320	738
1935	3,609	6,412	−2,803	3,609	6,412	−2,803
1940	6,548	9,468	−2,920	5,998	9,482	−3,484
1945	45,159	92,712	−47,553	43,849	92,569	−48,720
1950	39,443	42,562	−3,119	37,336	42,038	−4,702
1955	65,451	68,444	−2,933	60,370	64,461	−4,091
1960	92,492	92,191	301	81,851	81,341	510
1965	116,817	118,228	−1,411	100,094	101,699	−1,605
1970	192,807	195,649	−2,842	159,348	168,042	−8,694
1975	279,090	332,332	−53,242	216,633	271,892	−55,260
1980	517,112	590,947	−73,835	403,903	476,618	−72,715
1985	734,088	946,423	−212,334	547,918	769,615	−221,698
1990	1,031,969	1,253,198	−221,229	750,314	1,028,133	−277,819
1995	1,351,830	1,515,837	−164,007	1,000,751	1,227,173	−226,422
2000	2,025,218	1,788,826	236,392	1,544,634	1,458,061	86,573
2002	1,853,173	2,010,975	−157,802	1,337,852	1,655,313	−317,461
2003	1,782,342	2,159,917	−377,575	1,258,500	1,796,908	−538,408
2004	1,880,071	2,292,215	−412,144	1,345,326	1,912,704	−567,378
2005[2]	2,052,845	2,479,404	−426,559	1,491,482	2,080,022	−588,540
2006[2]	2,177,550	2,567,617	−390,067	1,584,359	2,144,300	−559,941

NOTES: 1789–1842: federal fiscal year ended Dec. 31; 1844–1976: June 30; 1977–present: Sept. 30. 1. Excludes the Social Security surplus. For years prior to 1933, on-budget surplus was not calculated separately. 2. Estimated. *Source:* The Budget for Fiscal Year 2006.

The Federal Budget, 2003–2008
(in billions of dollars)

Description	Actual 2003	Actual 2004	Estimates			
			2005	2006	2007	2008
Receipts by source						
Individual income taxes	$ 793.7	$ 809.0	$ 893.7	$ 966.9	$1,071.1	$1,167.2
Corporate income taxes	131.8	189.4	226.5	220.3	229.8	243.4
Social insurance and retirement receipts	713.0	733.4	773.7	773.7	866.2	911.7
Excise taxes	67.5	69.9	74.0	75.6	77.2	79.0
Estate and gift taxes	22.0	24.8	23.8	26.1	23.5	24.3
Customs duties and fees	19.9	21.1	24.7	28.3	30.6	31.9
Miscellaneous receipts:						
Federal Reserve deposits	21.9	19.7	24.1	28.5	32.2	36.1
All other	12.7	12.9	12.3	13.1	13.4	13.4
Total receipts	**$1,782.3**	**$1,880.1**	**$2,052.8**	**$2,177.6**	**$2,344.2**	**$2,507.0**
Outlays by function						
National defense	404.9	455.9	465.9	447.4	448.9	466.1
International affairs	21.2	26.9	32.0	38,4	36.5	36.7
General science, space, and technology	20.9	23.1	24.0	24.0	24.8	25.2
Energy	−0.7	−0.2	1.4	2.1	1.4	1.3
Natural resources and environment	29.7	30.7	31.0	31.2	30.8	29.9
Agriculture	22.5	15.4	30.5	26.0	22.8	19.9
Commerce and housing credit	29.7	30.7	31.0	31.2	30.8	29.9
Transportation	67.1	64.6	68.5	70.7	71.2	72.5
Community and regional development	18.9	15.8	20.1	19.1	16.9	14.8
Education, training, employment, and social services	82.6	87.9	96.3	88.7	86.3	84.8
Health	219.6	240.1	257.5	268.4	282.7	301.9
Medicare	249.4	269.4	295.4	345.7	386.4	411.5
Income security	334.4	332.8	350.9	359.5	361.9	374.1
Social security	474.7	495.5	519.7	544.8	571.2	600.3
Veterans' benefits and services	57.0	59.8	68.2	68.4	67.6	72.5
Administration of justice	35.3	45.5	40.7	43.1	42.3	42.3
General government	23.1	21.8	18.9	17.8	19.1	17.9
Net interest	153.1	160.2	177.9	211.1	245.0	272.4
Allowances	—	—	34.9	24.2	17.7	2.5
Undistributed offsetting receipts	−54.4	−58.5	−65.0	−69.8	−77.6	−88.3
Total outlays	**$2,159.9**	**$2,292.2**	**$2,479.4**	**$2,567.6**	**$2,656.3**	**$2,757.8**

Source: Department of the Treasury and Office of Management and Budget.

Summary of Federal Government Expenditure, by State and Territory, Fiscal Year 2003

(in millions of dollars)

State and outlying area	Total	Retirement and disability	Other direct payments	Grants	Procurement	Salaries and wages
United States total	$2,061,486	$636,239	$446,119	$441,038	$327,413	$210,677
Alabama	36,871	12,232	7,698	6,649	7,067	3,224
Alaska	7,944	1,041	584	3,022	1,680	1,617
Arizona	37,801	12,022	6,653	7,235	8,557	3,335
Arkansas	18,340	7,038	4,558	4,541	864	1,339
California	219,706	61,236	49,480	51,329	37,050	20,611
Colorado	28,874	8,375	5,014	6,014	5,142	4,329
Connecticut	28,595	7,549	5,669	5,376	8,484	1,516
Delaware	5,061	1,945	1,201	1,181	245	489
District of Columbia	34,750	1,934	2,370	4,310	11,376	14,760
Florida	113,341	45,192	30,041	17,463	10,899	9,746
Georgia	51,910	16,666	11,426	10,561	5,243	8,015
Hawaii	11,269	3,014	1,502	1,911	1,978	2,864
Idaho	8,654	2,865	1,566	1,858	1,531	834
Illinois	73,020	24,786	20,232	15,720	5,729	6,553
Indiana	35,525	13,394	9,178	7,313	3,302	2,338
Iowa	17,550	6,780	4,654	3,877	1,109	1,129
Kansas	18,208	6,196	4,469	3,415	2,020	2,108
Kentucky	31,153	10,169	6,119	6,634	5,119	3,112
Louisiana	31,646	9,559	8,424	7,820	3,195	2,648
Maine	9,966	3,403	1,753	2,610	1,312	888
Maryland	57,646	13,306	9,161	8,632	16,216	10,331
Massachusetts	51,265	13,794	12,339	13,328	8,357	3,446
Michigan	57,870	22,042	15,556	12,970	3,884	3,418
Minnesota	27,580	9,627	6,514	6,914	2,406	2,120
Mississippi	21,741	6,923	4,904	5,318	2,626	1,970
Missouri	43,874	13,509	9,887	8,655	7,992	3,832
Montana	7,092	2,315	1,497	1,938	497	845
Nebraska	11,000	3,956	2,732	2,512	608	1,192
Nevada	11,637	4,708	2,280	1,955	1,472	1,222
New Hampshire	7,349	2,838	1,336	1,865	738	571
New Jersey	53,679	18,388	14,190	11,481	5,461	4,159
New Mexico	18,736	4,388	2,281	4,322	5,819	1,926
New York	137,898	40,506	33,524	47,575	7,758	8,535
North Carolina	51,766	18,806	11,012	11,613	3,794	6,541
North Dakota	5,726	1,447	1,627	1,537	398	717
Ohio	69,902	25,348	16,957	15,687	6,548	5,362
Oklahoma	25,254	8,772	5,505	5,136	2,488	3,353
Oregon	21,253	8,024	5,147	5,103	1,198	1,781
Pennsylvania	90,350	32,072	25,156	18,624	8,137	6,363
Rhode Island	8,036	2,535	1,791	2,234	659	817
South Carolina	28,038	10,106	5,486	5,969	3,614	2,863
South Dakota	6,202	1,809	1,641	1,698	381	673
Tennessee	42,602	13,744	8,922	9,057	7,522	3,357
Texas	140,451	39,149	29,117	28,423	29,823	13,939
Utah	13,500	3,892	2,051	2,845	2,665	2,047
Vermont	4,443	1,358	828	1,331	566	360
Virginia	82,454	19,553	9,420	7,886	30,839	14,756
Washington	43,368	13,587	8,513	8,881	6,629	5,758
West Virginia	14,226	5,663	3,048	3,562	665	1,289
Wisconsin	30,237	11,618	7,282	7,544	2,008	1,785
Wyoming	4,226	1,152	602	1,616	346	510
American Samoa	198	41	12	110	28	7
Micronesia	145	—	7	136	1	—
Guam	1,539	207	92	400	526	315
Marshall Islands	182	1	—	66	115	—
Northern Marianas	141	22	15	90	8	6
Palau	53	—	1	51	1	—
Puerto Rico	14,661	5,477	2,847	4,808	561	968
Virgin Islands	615	146	107	282	26	55
Undistributed	34,366	14	141	43	32,133	2,035

NOTE: Detail may not add to total due to rounding. *Source: U.S. Census Bureau, Consolidated Federal Funds Report for Fiscal Year 2003.* Web: www.census.gov.

U.S. Direct Investment in Other Countries, 2003
(in millions of dollars)

	All indus-tries	Mining	Util-ities	Manu-facturing	Whole-sale trade	Infor-mation	Banks	Finance, insur-ance	Services	Other indus-tries
All countries	$151,884	$9,816	$–213	$28,370	$12,802	$5,578	$693	$30,149	$4,497	$60,191
Canada	13,826	1,594	363	6,374	512	230	151	2,656	168	1,780
Europe	99,191	1,913	–1,506	16,237	10,162	5,064	1,011	17,185	1,591	47,534
Austria	316	(*)	0	423	–579	59	(D)	–10	25	(D)
Belgium	759	2	0	628	424	15	53	–292	–36	–36
Czech Republic	144	(*)	–15	154	25	(D)	(D)	44	–1	–2
Denmark	63	(D)	0	–102	(D)	(D)	0	(D)	(D)	(D)
Finland	329	0	0	–2	205	–10	0	(D)	43	(D)
France	1,504	8	(D)	–332	626	114	189	656	–74	(D)
Germany	8,676	43	13	285	2,038	207	504	276	154	5,157
Greece	63	–1	0	36	(D)	8	(D)	(D)	2	–58
Hungary	249	(*)	(D)	150	44	3	(D)	–2	3	(D)
Ireland	9,093	(D)	(*)	2,548	351	3,605	299	777	118	(D)
Italy	3,485	–31	–20	2,065	41	387	–109	177	151	823
Luxembourg	5,241	0	0	(D)	(D)	(D)	(D)	–572	(D)	6,033
Netherlands	14,968	228	(D)	2,093	2,169	320	7	2,602	–91	(D)
Norway	1,680	1,575	(*)	198	–148	–8	10	(D)	12	(D)
Poland	451	–2	5	495	–27	55	–177	27	14	61
Portugal	109	1	0	42	125	17	(*)	–13	–10	–52
Russia	237	75	0	55	8	(D)	13	3	–9	(D)
Spain	3,375	–49	2	1,173	(D)	188	53	–642	12	(D)
Sweden	3,000	0	0	(D)	227	–105	(D)	–166	24	(D)
Switzerland	14,444	3	0	5,087	2,081	–307	545	–290	34	7,291
Turkey	41	(*)	25	–105	56	–2	39	10	10	7
United Kingdom	30,455	139	743	2,115	981	499	–798	14,106	1,114	11,556
Other	508	–295	(D)	201	27	(D)	(D)	(D)	27	351
Latin America and Other Western Hemisphere	13,171	2,197	363	2,053	427	–630	–1	4,896	–100	3,967
South America	997	1,072	479	–660	112	–887	–98	–205	26	1,158
Argentina	207	–28	(D)	–421	(D)	–70	–182	185	–2	807
Brazil	–266	267	179	–742	–14	–518	67	–602	163	932
Chile	–246	156	(D)	85	37	–449	60	113	69	(D)
Colombia	195	1	1	69	27	(D)	(D)	47	–12	(D)
Ecuador	267	146	2	–31	(D)	(D)	(D)	(D)	(*)	12
Peru	463	421	(D)	10	24	(D)	(D)	6	–4	–10
Venezuela	440	175	117	321	70	(D)	(D)	69	–197	–126
Other	–63	–67	(D)	48	–6	18	–57	(D)	8	–10
Central America	6,545	174	128	1,888	–97	34	2,519	1,716	–16	199
Costa Rica	34	(*)	0	(D)	(D)	4	0	6	–1	15
Honduras	53	0	(*)	35	–8	(*)	(D)	1	0	(D)
Mexico	5,667	120	84	1,717	–88	8	2,327	1,640	–19	–122
Panama	686	55	(D)	(D)	61	(D)	(D)	71	3	296
Other	104	(*)	(D)	93	(D)	(D)	(D)	–3	1	(D)
Other Western Hemisphere	5,630	951	–244	825	412	222	–2,422	3,386	–110	2,610
Barbados	379	0	(D)	(D)	124	(D)	(D)	124	–7	82
Bermuda	1,832	30	17	(D)	547	68	0	2,242	(D)	–775
Dominican Republic	–56	0	(D)	–9	–7	(D)	(D)	–2	(*)	5
United Kingdom Islands, Caribbean	3,057	472	–264	442	–311	94	(D)	1,009	–59	(D)
Other	417	449	(D)	620	58	(D)	(D)	12	(D)	(D)
Africa	2,211	1,647	–5	–17	–96	60	–170	–29	34	787
Egypt	183	270	0	–106	–1	1	(D)	(D)	(*)	(D)
Nigeria	340	–145	0	16	–21	0	(D)	0	(D)	(D)
South Africa	89	–10	0	21	–79	124	(D)	–10	–20	(D)
Other	1,598	1,532	–5	52	5	–64	–61	(D)	(D)	(D)
Middle East	2,093	724	124	338	167	–188	60	189	70	609
Israel	517	(*)	(D)	205	115	(D)	(D)	(D)	106	(D)
Saudi Arabia	400	(D)	(D)	21	40	(D)	4	2	–12	(D)
United Arab Emirates	108	(D)	(D)	(D)	14	13	(D)	(D)	–2	(D)
Other	1,068	503	(D)	(D)	–2	1	(D)	(D)	–22	(D)

	All industries	Mining	Utilities	Manufacturing	Wholesale trade	Information	Banks	Finance, insurance	Services	Other industries
Asia and Pacific	$21,392	$1,742	$449	$3,385	$1,631	$1,043	$-359	$5,252	$2,733	$5,514
Australia	3,881	113	179	1,415	-16	-169	317	868	526	648
China	1,540	147	(D)	761	497	4	87	(D)	(D)	(D)
Hong Kong	1,725	0	(D)	477	298	51	-98	-485	163	(D)
India	243	11	54	53	128	-54	9	46	138	-143
Indonesia	72	970	141	-4	(D)	-64	-172	(D)	19	-800
Japan	5,800	(D)	0	-984	(*)	876	-430	3,820	(D)	(D)
Korea, Republic of	954	(*)	0	438	-17	37	-38	448	41	45
Malaysia	763	173	0	369	40	76	(D)	11	(D)	(D)
New Zealand	291	4	(*)	105	(D)	-30	(D)	82	31	(D)
Philippines	-325	-42	-1	-445	61	-24	(D)	36	15	(D)
Singapore	5,699	-25	2	804	(D)	307	-256	293	(D)	(D)
Taiwan	936	(*)	0	273	222	30	-13	331	-5	98
Thailand	-560	134	-32	86	(D)	3	11	(D)	(D)	(D)
Other	372	(D)	-22	35	(D)	(*)	-9	(D)	(*)	106

* Less than $500,000 (+/–). (D) Suppressed to avoid disclosure of data of individual companies. *Source:* U.S. Department of Commerce, Bureau of Economic Analysis. Web: http://www.bea.doc.gov/bea/di/di1usdbal.htm.

U.S. Contributions to International Organizations
(in millions of dollars)

Organization	2004	2005 (est.)	2006 (est.)
UN and affiliated agencies:			
Food and Agriculture Org.	$72	$83	$92
Int'l Atomic Energy Agency	68	70	84
Int'l Civil Aviation Org.	13	13	15
Int'l Labor Organization	60	65	63
Int'l Maritime Organization	1	1	1
Int'l Telecommunications Union	4	7	8
UN—Regular	317	362	439
UN—War Crimes Tribunals	17	31	37
Universal Postal Union	2	2	2
World Health Org.	94	96	96
World Intellectual Property Org.	1	1	1
World Meteorological Org.	11	10	11
UNESCO	56	72	72
UN—Capital Master Plan Loan Subsidy	—	6	—
UN—Capital Master Plan	—	—	10
Inter-American organizations:			
Inter-American Institute for Cooperation on Agriculture	17	17	17

Organization	2004	2005 (est.)	2006 (est.)
Organization of American States	$55	$56	$66
Pan American Health Org.	57	57	57
Regional organizations:			
Asia-Pacific Economic Cooperation	1	1	1
North Atlantic Assembly	1	1	1
North Atlantic Treaty Organization	28	45	63
Org. for Economic Cooperation and Development	77	67	92
South Pacific Commission	1	1	2
Other international organizations:			
Org. for the Prohibition of Chemical Weapons	18	25	30
World Trade Org./GATT	19	19	21
Other Int'l Organizations	10	9	11
Int'l Seabed Authority	—	—	1
Int'l Tribunal for the Law of the Sea	—	—	2
Int'l Coffee Org.	—	—	1

NOTE: All years are fiscal years. *Source:* Budget of the United States Government Fiscal Year 2006.

Producer Price Indexes by Major Commodity Groups

Commodity	2004	2003	2002	2000	1995	1990	1985	1980	1975	1970
All commodities	**146.7**	**138.1**	**131.1**	**132.7**	**124.7**	**116.3**	**103.2**	**89.8**	**58.4**	**38.1**
Farm products	123.3	111.5	99.0	99.5	107.4	112.2	95.1	102.9	77.0	45.8
Processed foods and feeds	151.2	143.4	136.2	133.1	127.0	121.9	103.5	95.9	72.6	44.6
Textile products and apparel	121.0	119.8	119.9	121.4	120.8	114.9	102.9	89.7	67.4	52.4
Hides, skins, and leather products	164.5	162.3	157.6	151.5	153.7	141.7	108.9	94.7	56.5	42.0
Fuels and related products and power	126.9	112.9	93.2	103.5	78.0	82.2	91.4	82.8	35.4	15.3
Chemicals and allied products	174.4	161.8	151.9	151.0	142.5	123.6	103.7	89.0	62.0	35.0
Rubber and plastic products	133.8	130.1	126.8	125.5	124.3	113.6	101.9	90.1	62.2	44.9
Lumber and wood products	195.6	177.4	173.3	178.2	178.1	129.7	106.6	101.5	62.1	39.9
Pulp, paper, and allied products	195.7	190.0	185.9	183.7	172.2	141.3	113.3	86.3	59.0	37.5
Metals and metal products	149.6	129.2	125.9	128.1	134.5	123.0	104.4	95.0	61.5	38.7
Machinery and equipment	122.1	121.9	122.9	124.0	126.6	120.7	107.2	86.0	57.9	40.0
Furniture and household durables	135.1	133.9	133.5	132.6	128.2	119.1	107.1	90.7	67:5	51.9
Nonmetallic mineral products	153.2	148.2	146.2	142.5	129.0	114.7	108.6	88.4	54.4	35.3
Transportation equipment	148.6	145.7	144.6	143.8	139.7	121.5	107.9	82.9	56.7	41.9

NOTES: 1982 = 100. *Source:* U.S. Department of Labor, Bureau of Labor Statistics, Division of Industrial Prices and Price Indexes. Web: data.bls.gov.

Consumer Price Index for All Urban Consumers

Group	2004	2003	2002	2001	2000	1995	1990	1985	1980	1975	1970	1965	1960	1950
All items	188.9	184.0	179.9	177.1	172.2	152.4	130.7	107.6	82.4	53.8	38.8	31.5	29.6	24.1
Food and beverages	186.6	180.5	176.8	173.6	168.4	148.9	132.1	105.6	86.7	60.2	40.1	n.a.	n.a.	n.a.
Housing	189.5	184.8	180.3	176.4	169.6	148.5	128.5	107.7	81.1	50.7	36.4	n.a.	n.a.	n.a.
Apparel	120.4	120.9	124.0	127.3	129.6	132.0	124.1	105.0	90.9	72.5	59.2	47.8	45.7	40.3
Transportation	163.1	157.6	152.9	154.3	153.3	139.1	120.5	106.4	83.1	50.1	37.5	31.9	29.8	22.7
Medical care	310.1	297.1	285.6	272.8	260.8	220.5	162.8	113.5	74.9	47.5	34.0	25.2	22.3	15.1

NOTES: 1982–1984 = 100. n.a. = not available. *Source:* U.S. Department of Labor, Bureau of Labor Statistics. Web: data.bls.gov.

Exports and Imports of Goods and Services, 1980–2010

Category	Billions of chained 1996 dollars				Average annual rate of change		
	1980	1990	2000	2010[1]	1980–1990	1990–2000	2000–2010[1]
Exports of goods and services	**$333.4**	**$575.7**	**$1,133.2**	**$2,393.7**	**5.6%**	**7.0%**	**7.8%**
Goods	238.9	393.2	836.1	1,821.2	5.1	7.8	8.1
Foods, feeds, and beverages	44.7	44.4	60.0	91.4	–0.1	3.1	4.3
Industrial supplies and materials	86.9	111.7	168.2	228.4	2.5	4.2	3.1
Capital goods, except autos	56.0	124.8	394.9	1,123.1	8.3	12.2	11.0
Computers	1.0	12.3	85.6	406.0	28.5	21.4	16.8
Civilian aircraft and parts	26.9	40.9	43.1	78.2	4.3	0.5	6.1
Other	48.5	79.1	271.5	740.4	5.0	13.1	10.6
Autos and parts	28.3	39.8	78.3	154.5	3.5	7.0	7.0
Consumer goods	25.1	48.1	89.8	182.7	6.7	6.4	7.4
Other merchandise exports	14.8	32.4	45.9	103.3	8.1	3.6	8.4
Services	89.0	183.4	299.3	591.7	7.5	5.0	7.1
Residual[2]	–31.8	–16.5	–8.6	–182.9	—	—	—
Imports of goods and services	**$326.3**	**$632.2**	**$1,532.3**	**$3,282.7**	**6.8%**	**9.3%**	**7.9%**
Goods	260.6	497.9	1,315.6	2,954.5	6.7	10.2	8.4
Foods, feeds, and beverages	20.9	30.4	49.4	61.9	3.8	5.0	2.3
Industrial supplies and materials	118.1	142.4	254.5	331.6	1.9	6.0	2.7
Petroleum and products	51.5	59.5	86.0	96.6	1.4	3.8	1.2
Other	55.0	83.6	167.9	234.8	4.3	7.2	3.4
Capital goods, except autos	18.5	88.8	451.7	1,428.6	17.0	17.7	12.2
Computers	0.2	11.6	152.6	670.2	50.1	29.4	15.9
Civilian aircraft and parts	6.0	13.5	23.9	36.7	8.5	5.8	4.4
Other	19.1	68.9	279.3	824.0	13.7	15.0	11.4
Autos and parts	52.5	101.6	192.5	322.8	6.8	6.6	5.3
Consumer goods	49.8	112.8	293.5	858.9	8.5	10.0	11.3
Other merchandise imports	12.4	35.2	80.9	148.0	11.0	8.7	6.2
Services	65.6	136.6	218.7	352.8	7.6	4.8	4.9
Residual[3]	–6.7	–21.5	–12.6	–323.9	—	—	—
Trade Deficit	**$ 7.1**	**$–56.5**	**$ –399.1**	**$ –889.1**	**—**	**21.6%**	**8.3%**

1. Projected. 2. The residual following the detailed categories for exports is the difference between the aggregate of "exports of goods and services" and the sum of the figures for those separate categories for exports of goods and services. 3. The residual following the detailed categories for imports is the difference between the aggregate of "imports of goods and services" and the sum of the figures for those separate categories for imports of goods and services. *Source:* Bureau of Labor Statistics, *Monthly Labor Review,* Nov. 2001.

The Shrinking Value of the Dollar

Year	Amount it took to equal $1 in 1913	Year	Amount it took to equal $1 in 1913	Year	Amount it took to equal $1 in 1913	Year	Amount it took to equal $1 in 1913
1913	$1.00	1945	$1.82	1975	$ 5.43	2001	$17.89
1920	2.02	1950	2.43	1980	8.32	2002	18.17
1925	1.77	1955	2.71	1985	10.87	2003	18.59
1930	1.69	1960	2.99	1990	13.20	2004	19.08
1935	1.38	1965	3.18	1995	15.39	2005	19.37
1940	1.41	1970	3.92	2000	17.39		

Source: Bureau of Labor Statistics. Web: http://stats.bls.gov/.

Imports and Exports of Leading Commodities
by Principal SITC Groupings (in millions of dollars)

Item	2004 Cumulative Exports	2004 Cumulative Imports	Item	2004 Cumulative Exports	2004 Cumulative Imports
Total balance of payment basis	$329,292	$570,728	Live animals	$ 113	$ 531
Net adjustments	–4,789	1,294	Meat and preparations	1,850	2,232
Selected commodities:			Metal manufactures, n.e.s.	5,062	8,432
ADP equipment; office machines	11,510	35,193	Metal ores; scrap	2,980	1,676
Airplane parts	6,054	1,986	Metalworking machinery	2,424	2,379
Airplanes	10,799	3,975	Mineral fuels, other	1,015	823
Alcoholic bev.,distilled	241	1,496	Natural gas	888	9,628
Aluminum	1,500	3,671	Nickel	185	782
Animal feeds	1,679	336	Oils/fats, vegetable	409	784
Basketware, etc.	2,159	3,585	Optical goods	1,047	1,436
Cereal flour	752	997	Paper and paperboard	4,400	6,420
Chemicals—medicinal	9,660	14,061	Petroleum preparations	3,580	14,015
Chemicals—organic	9,931	15,957	Photographic equipment	1,506	2,045
Chemicals—plastics	9,924	5,571	Platinum	217	1,584
Cigarettes	551	105	Pottery	45	634
Clothing	1,903	25,896	Power generating machinery	14,088	14,586
Coal	1,070	750	Printed materials	1,929	1,643
Coffee	3	774	Pulp and waste paper	1,865	1,162
Copper	853	1,775	Records/magnetic media	1,909	2,489
Cork, wood, lumber	1,651	3,774	Rice	597	112
Corn	2,711	104	Rubber tires and tubes	995	2,485
Cotton, raw and linters	2,492	8	Scientific instruments	13,579	11,206
Crude oil	77	48,920	Ships, boats	900	851
Electrical machinery	31,044	36,789	Silver and bullion	103	418
Fish and preparations	1,374	4,173	Soybeans	2,852	24
Footwear	191	6,619	Specialized ind. mach.	11,712	10,641
Furniture and bedding	1,664	11,411	Sugar	1	199
Gem diamonds	210	5,876	Television, VCR, etc.	7,984	32,062
General industrial machinery	14,073	18,631	Textile yarn, fabric	4,764	7,874
Glass	1,162	1,089	Tobacco, unmanufactured	488	253
Glassware	340	797	Toys/games/sporting goods	1,447	6,582
Gold, nonmonetary	1,688	1,574	Vegetables and fruits	3,524	5,856
Hides and skins	666	29	Vehicles	27,991	77,555
Iron and steel mill products	3,096	6,611	Watches/clocks/parts	113	1,300
Jewelry	968	3,156	Wheat	2,265	59
Lighting, plumbing	602	2,568	Wood manufactures	735	4,920
Liquefied propane/butane	169	1,125			

NOTES: SITC = Standard International Trade Classification. Details may not equal totals due to rounding. Data not seasonally adjusted. *Source:* U.S. Census Bureau, Foreign Trade Division. Web: http://www.census.gov/foreign-trade/PressRelease/current_press_release/exh15.txt.

Retail Prices of Selected Foods in U.S. Cities, 1890–1970

(in cents per unit indicated)

Year	Flour (5 lbs)	Bread (lb)	Round steak (lb)	Bacon (lb)	Butter (lb)	Eggs (doz.)	Milk (½ gal.)	Oranges (doz.)	Potatoes (10 lbs)	Coffee (lb)	Sugar (5 lbs)
1970	58.9¢	24.3¢	130.2¢	94.9¢	86.6¢	61.4¢	65.9¢	86.4¢	89.7¢	91.1¢	64.8¢
1965	58.1	20.9	108.4	81.3	75.4	52.7	52.6	77.8	93.7	83.3	59.0
1960	55.4	20.3	105.5	65.5	74.9	57.3	52.0	74.8	71.8	75.3	58.2
1955	53.8	17.7	90.3	65.9	70.9	60.6	46.2	52.8	56.4	93.0	52.1
1950	49.1	14.3	93.6	63.7	72.9	60.4	41.2	49.3	46.1	79.4	48.7
1945	32.1	8.8	40.6	41.1	50.7	58.1	31.2	48.5	49.3	30.5	33.4
1940	21.5	8.0	36.4	27.3	36.0	33.1	25.6	29.1	23.9	21.2	26.0
1935	25.3	8.3	36.0	41.3	36.0	37.6	23.4	22.0	19.1	25.7	28.2
1930	23.0	8.6	42.6	42.5	46.4	44.5	28.2	57.1	36.0	39.5	30.5
1925	30.5	9.3	36.2	47.1	55.2	55.4	27.8	57.1	36.0	50.4	35.0
1920	40.5	11.5	39.5	52.3	70.1	68.1	33.4	63.2	63.0	47.0	97.0
1915	21.0	7.0	23.0	26.9	35.8	34.1	17.6	n.a.	15.0	30.0	33.0
1910	18.0	n.a.	17.4	25.5	35.9	33.7	16.8	n.a.	17.0	n.a.	30.0
1905	16.0	n.a.	14.0	18.1	29.0	27.2	14.4	n.a.	17.0	n.a.	30.0
1900	12.5	n.a.	13.2	14.3	26.1	20.7	13.6	n.a.	14.0	n.a.	30.5
1895	12.0	n.a.	12.3	13.0	24.9	20.6	13.6	n.a.	14.0	n.a.	26.5
1890	14.5	n.a.	12.3	12.5	25.5	20.8	13.6	n.a.	16.0	n.a.	34.5

NOTE: n.a. = not available. *Source:* U.S. Bureau of the Census, *Historical Statistics of the United States, Colonial Times to 1970, Bicentennial Edition, Part 2.*

Per Capita Consumption of Principal Foods[1]

(in pounds unless otherwise noted)

Food	1990	1995	2000	2002	2003	Food	1990	1995	2000	2002	2003
Red meats[2,3,4]	112.3	115.1	113.5	114.0	111.9	Shortening	22.2	22.5	23.1	34.1	32.5
Beef	63.9	64.4	64.4	64.5	62.0	Lard and beef tallow	2.2	4.3	6.0	3.4	3.8
Veal	0.9	0.8	0.5	0.5	0.5	Salad and cooking					
Lamb & mutton	1.0	0.9	0.8	0.9	0.8	oils	25.3	26.9	35.2	37.7	37.3
Pork	46.4	49.0	47.7	48.2	48.5	Fruits and vegetables	656.0	694.3	707.7	683.6	691.5
Poultry[2,3,4]	56.3	62.9	66.5	70.7	71.2	Fruit	272.6	284.9	279.4	271.7	274.9
Chicken	42.4	48.8	52.9	56.8	57.5	Vegetables	383.5	409.4	428.3	412.0	416.6
Turkey	13.8	14.1	13.6	14.0	13.7	Peanuts (shelled)	6.0	5.7	5.8	5.8	6.3
Fish and shellfish	15.0	14.9	15.2	15.6	16.3	Tree nuts (shelled)	2.4	1.9	2.3	3.0	2.9
Eggs[4,5]	234.1	232.3	251.0	254.5	253.4	Flour and cereal					
Cheese	24.6	27.3	29.8	30.5	30.6	products[7]	181.0	192.8	199.9	191.3	194.0
Beverage milks	221.8	209.8	200.9	188.8	186.0	Wheat flour	136.0	141.8	146.3	136.7	125.5
Ice cream	15.8	15.7	16.5	16.7	16.7	Rice (milled basis)	15.8	18.9	19.7	19.2	20.1
All dairy products, milk equivalent,						Caloric sweeteners[8]	136.9	149.8	152.4	146.1	141.7
milkfat basis[6]	568.3	583.8	593.0	585.3	593.9	Coffee (green bean equiv.)	10.3	8.0	10.3	9.2	9.5
Fats and oils	63.0	66.3	74.5	90.1	87.9	Cocoa (chocolate					
Butter and margarine (product						liquor equiv.)	4.3	3.6	4.7	3.9	5.7
weight)	15.3	13.7	12.8	11.0	10.4						

1. In pounds, retail weight unless otherwise stated. Consumption normally represents total supply minus exports, nonfood use, and ending stocks. Calendar-year data, except fresh citrus fruits, peanuts, tree nuts, and rice, which are on crop-year basis. 2. Totals may not add up due to rounding. 3. Boneless, trimmed weight. Chicken series revised to exclude amount of ready-to-cook chicken going to pet food as well as some water leakage that occurs when chicken is cut up before packaging. 4. Excludes shipments to the U.S. territories. 5. Number per capita. 6. Includes condensed and evaporated milk and dry milk products. 7. Includes rye, corn, oats, and barley products. Excludes quantities used in alcoholic beverages, corn sweeteners, and fuel. 8. Dry weight equivalent. *Source:* U.S. Department of Agriculture, Economic Research Service. Web: www.usda.gov.

Credit Card Use, 1992–2001

General-purpose credit cards include Mastercard, Visa, Optima, and Discover. All dollar figures are given in constant 1998 dollars based on consumer price index data as published by the U.S. Bureau of Labor Statistics.

				Percent of cardholding families who:		
Age of family head and family income[1]	Percent having a general-purpose credit card	Percent having a balance after last month's bills	Median balance[2]	Almost always pay off the balance	Sometimes pay off the balance	Hardly ever pay off the balance
1992 total	62.4%	52.6%	$1,200	53.0%	19.6%	27.4%
1995 total	66.5	52.6	1,700	52.4	20.1	27.5
1998 total	67.5	54.7	2,000	53.8	19.3	26.9
2001 total	72.7	53.7	1,800	55.3	19.0	25.6
Under 35 years old	64.2	68.2	1,800	40.6	24.1	35.4
35–44 years old	76.9	62.9	2,000	47.0	22.8	30.2
45–54 years old	80.0	57.3	2,000	54.3	19.3	26.4
55–64 years old	76.0	48.2	2,000	59.8	17.8	22.3
65–74 years old	76.5	30.0	1,100	75.8	11.0	13.2
75 years old and over	59.7	24.2	700	81.2	9.3	9.4
Less than $10,000	28.5	67.4	1,000	45.3	23.0	31.7
$10,000–$24,999	56.1	57.0	1,000	49.5	19.9	30.6
$25,000–$49,999	76.1	61.3	1,700	46.7	19.7	33.6
$50,000–$99,999	87.9	53.9	2,000	55.2	20.8	24.0
$100,000 and more	95.8	36.1	3,000	75.2	13.9	10.9

1. Families include one-person units. 2. Among families having a balance. *Source:* Board of Governors of the Federal Reserve System, unpublished data. From *Statistical Abstract of the United States, 2003.*

Personal Consumption Expenditures

Category	Billions of chained 1996 dollars				Average annual rate of change (percent)		
	1980	1990	2000	2010 (projected)	1980–90	1990–2000	2000–2010 (projected)
Gross domestic product	$4,900.9	$6,707.9	$9,224.0	$12,835.6	3.2%	3.2%	3.4%
Personal consumption expenditures	3,193.0	4,474.5	6,257.8	8,786.5	3.4	3.4	3.5
Durable goods	279.8	487.1	895.5	1,455.4	5.7	6.3	5.0
New light vehicles	88.3	159.9	218.6	307.3	6.1	3.2	3.5
Other motor vehicles and parts	54.1	86.2	129.3	176.2	4.8	4.1	3.1
Personal computers	.0	1.6	108.8	802.4	(1)	52.1	22.1
Software	.0	.5	17.8	36.3	(1)	43.7	7.4
Furniture	95.5	160.4	294.6	483.2	5.3	6.3	5.1
Ophthalmic products	6.2	16.1	20.4	27.7	10.1	2.4	3.1
Other durable goods	53.5	80.8	152.9	256.1	4.2	6.6	5.3
Nondurable goods	1,065.8	1,369.6	1,849.9	2,635.5	2.5	3.1	3.6
Food and beverages	585.4	722.4	881.3	1,102.8	2.1	2.0	2.3
Clothing and shoes	124.0	197.2	335.3	511.0	4.7	5.5	4.3
Gasoline and motor oil	94.8	113.1	136.6	169.8	1.8	1.9	2.2
Fuel oil and coal	17.7	13.1	13.8	15.5	–3.0	.6	1.1
Tobacco products	65.6	52.0	42.8	46.5	–2.3	–1.9	.8
Drugs and medicines	54.5	80.3	139.9	316.6	4.0	5.7	8.5
Other nondurable goods	138.9	194.3	305.7	497.5	3.4	4.6	5.0
Services	1,858.4	2,616.2	3,527.7	4,784.5	3.5	3.0	3.1
Housing	541.5	696.2	850.1	1,070.2	2.5	2.0	2.3
Household operation	202.9	259.8	377.6	579.2	2.5	3.8	4.4
Electricity	66.7	83.2	103.9	137.7	2.2	2.2	2.9
Natural gas	31.1	29.5	32.8	30.8	–0.5	1.1	–0.6
Telephone	40.0	62.6	141.8	296.2	4.6	8.5	7.6
Other	66.2	85.9	100.8	142.5	2.6	1.6	3.5
Transportation services	124.7	173.4	251.3	318.5	3.4	3.8	2.4
Motor vehicle leases	—	5.5	37.6	49.1	(2)	21.2	2.7
Other	—	168.1	213.6	269.2	(2)	2.4	2.3
Medical services	487.6	710.9	903.9	1,174.9	3.8	2.4	2.7
Recreation services	79.7	145.0	227.0	408.1	6.2	4.6	6.0
Personal business services	242.8	363.2	554.8	759.0	4.1	4.3	3.2
Financial services	94.4	154.2	222.7	292.5	5.0	3.7	2.8
Other	147.4	209.0	332.4	467.4	3.6	4.7	3.5
Other services	170.8	267.0	362.3	488.3	4.6	3.1	3.0
Residual[3]	–35.6	–20.5	–68.7	–789.4			
Personal consumption expenditures + GDP	65.2	66.7	67.8	68.5			

NOTE: (—) Indicates data not available. 1. Undefined because of denominator with value zero. 2. Not applicable. 3. The residual is the difference between the first line and the sum of the most detailed lines. *Source:* Historical data, Bureau of Economic Analsysis; projected data, Bureau of Labor Statistics. *Monthly Labor Review,* Nov. 2002.

Average Prices of Selected Fuels and Electricity, 1980–2003

(In dollars per unit, except electricity, in cents per kWh. Represents price to end-users, except as noted.)

Type	1980	1990	1995	1996	1997	1998	1999	2000	2001	2002	2003
Crude oil, composite (bbl)[1]	28.07	22.22	17.23	20.71	19.04	12.52	17.51	28.26	22.95	24.1	28.5
Motor gasoline (gal.):[2]											
Unleaded regular	1.25	1.16	1.15	1.23	1.23	1.06	1.17	1.51	1.46	1.36	1.59
Unleaded premium	n.a.	1.35	1.34	1.41	1.42	1.25	1.36	1.69	1.66	1.56	1.78
No. 2 heating oil (gal.)	0.97	1.06	0.87	0.99	0.98	0.85	0.88	1.31	1.25	1.13	n.a.
No. 2 diesel fuel (gal.)	0.82	0.73	0.56	0.68	0.64	0.49	0.58	0.94	0.84	0.76	0.94
Residual fuel oil (gal.)	0.61	0.44	0.39	0.46	0.42	0.31	0.37	0.6	0.53	0.57	0.7
Natural gas, residential (1,000 cu/ft)	3.68	5.8	6.06	6.34	6.94	6.82	6.69	7.76	9.63	7.91	9.52
Electricity, residential (kWh)	5.36	7.83	8.4	8.36	8.43	8.26	8.16	8.24	8.62	8.46	8.74

NOTE: n.a. = not available. 1. Refiner acquisition cost. 2. Average, all service. *Source:* U.S. Energy Information Administration, *Monthly Energy Review.* From *Statistical Abstract of the United States, 2003.*

Farm Indexes

(1990–1992 = 100)

Year	Prices paid by farmers[1]	Prices rec'd by farmers[2]	Ratio[3]	Year	Prices paid by farmers[1]	Prices rec'd by farmers[2]	Ratio[3]
1975	47	73	155	1997	118	107	91
1980	75	98	131	1998	115	102	89
1985	86	91	106	1999	115	96	83
1990	99	104	105	2000	120	96	80
1991	100	100	99	2001	123	102	83
1992	101	98	97	2002	124	98	79
1993	103	101	98	2003	128	107	84
1994	106	100	94	2004	134	119	89
1995	109	102	93	2005	138	118	86
1996	115	112	98				

1. Commodities and services, interest, taxes, and wage rates. 2. All farm products. 3. Ratio of index of prices received by farmers to index of prices paid by farmers. May not compute directly due to rounding. *Source:* U.S. Department of Agriculture, National Agricultural Statistics Service. Web: www.usda.gov.

Number of Farms by State, 2001–2003

State	2001	2002	2003	State	2001	2002	2003
Alabama	46,000	45,000	45,000	Nebraska	50,000	49,400	48,500
Alaska	600	610	610	Nevada	3,050	3,000	3,000
Arizona	10,400	10,300	10,300	New Hampshire	3,300	3,400	3,400
Arkansas	48,000	47,500	47,500	New Jersey	9,800	9,900	9,900
California	81,000	79,700	78,500	New Mexico	17,800	17,700	17,500
Colorado	30,900	31,400	31,400	New York	37,500	37,000	37,000
Connecticut	4,200	4,200	4,200	North Carolina	55,000	54,200	53,500
Delaware	2,500	2,400	2,300	North Dakota	30,600	30,500	30,300
Florida	44,000	44,000	44,000	Ohio	78,000	77,800	77,600
Georgia	49,200	49,300	49,300	Oklahoma	84,000	83,500	83,500
Hawaii	5,500	5,500	5,500	Oregon	40,000	40,000	40,000
Idaho	24,500	25,000	25,000	Pennsylvania	58,500	58,200	58,200
Illinois	75,000	73,000	73,000	Rhode Island	830	850	850
Indiana	62,100	60,300	59,500	South Carolina	24,400	24,500	24,400
Iowa	92,000	90,600	90,000	South Dakota	32,000	31,800	31,600
Kansas	64,500	64,500	64,500	Tennessee	88,000	87,500	87,000
Kentucky	88,000	87,000	87,000	Texas	228,600	229,000	229,000
Louisiana	28,000	27,500	27,200	Utah	15,500	15,300	15,300
Maine	7,150	7,200	7,200	Vermont	6,600	6,600	6,500
Maryland	12,300	12,200	12,100	Virginia	47,900	47,600	47,500
Massachusetts	6,100	6,100	6,100	Washington	36,500	36,000	35,500
Michigan	53,000	53,300	53,300	West Virginia	20,800	20,800	20,800
Minnesota	81,000	80,900	80,000	Wisconsin	77,000	77,000	76,500
Mississippi	42,000	42,200	42,800	Wyoming	9,200	9,200	9,200
Missouri	108,000	107,000	106,000	**U.S. total**	**2,148,630**	**2,135,360**	**2,126,860**
Montana	27,800	27,900	28,000				

NOTE: A farm is any establishment from which $1,000 or more of agricultural products were sold or would normally be sold during the year. *Source:* U.S. Department of Agriculture. Web: www.usda.gov.

Number of Farms, Land in Farms, and Average-Size Farm: United States, 1990–2004

Year	Number of farms	Land in farms (1,000 acres)	Average farm size (acres)	Year	Number of farms	Land in farms (1,000 acres)	Average farm size (acres)
1990	2,145,820	986,850	460	1998	2,191,360	953,500	435
1991	2,116,760	981,736	464	1999	2,192,070	947,440	432
1992	2,107,840	978,503	464	2000	2,172,280	943,090	434
1993	2,201,590	968,845	440	2001	2,155,680	941,310	437
1994	2,197,690	965,935	440	2002	2,158,090	941,480	436
1995	2,196,400	962,515	438	2003	2,126,860	938,750	441
1996	2,190,500	958,675	438	2004	2,113,470	936,600	443
1997	2,190,510	956,010	436				

NOTE: A farm is any establishment from which $1,000 or more of agricultural products were sold or would normally be sold during the year. *Source:* U.S. Department of Agriculture. Web: www.usda.gov.

Largest Bankruptcies, 1980–Present

Company	Bankruptcy date	Total assets pre-bankruptcy (in millions)	Company	Bankruptcy date	Total assets pre-bankruptcy (in millions)
Worldcom, Inc.[1]	7/21/2002	$103,914	Kmart Corp.	1/22/2002	$14,600
Enron Corp.[2]	12/2/2001	63,392	FINOVA Group, Inc. (The)	3/7/2001	14,050
Conseco, Inc	12/18/2002	61,392	HomeFed Corp.	10/22/1992	13,885
Texaco, Inc.	4/12/1987	35,892	Southeast Banking Corp.	9/20/1991	13,390
Financial Corp. of America	9/9/1988	33,864	NTL, Inc.	5/8/2002	13,003
Global Crossing Ltd.	1/28/2002	30,185	Reliance Group Holdings, Inc.	6/12/2001	12,598
Pacific Gas and Electric Co.	4/6/2001	29,770			
UAL Corp.	12/9/2002	25,197	Imperial Corp. of America	2/28/1990	12,263
Adelphia Communications	6/25/2002	21,499	Federal-Mogul Corp.	10/1/2001	10,150
MCorp	3/31/1989	20,228	First City Bancorp. of Texas	10/31/1992	9,943
Mirant Corporation	7/14/2003	19,415	First Capital Holdings	5/30/1991	9,675
First Executive Corp.	5/13/1991	15,193	Baldwin-United	9/26/1983	9,383
Gibraltar Financial Corp.	2/8/1990	15,011			

1. Worldcom, Inc. assets taken from the audited annual report dated 12/31/2001. 2. The Enron assets were taken from the tax documents filed on 11/19/2001. The company has announced that the financials were under review at the time of filing for Chapter 11. *Source:* New Generation Research, Inc. Web: www.bankruptcydata.com.

Leading National Advertisers
(in millions; ranked by total U.S. advertising spending)

Rank	Advertiser	2004 ad dollars	Rank	Advertiser	2004 ad dollars
1.	General Motors Corp.	$3,997.4	14.	General Electric Co.	$1,819.0
2.	Procter & Gamble Co.	3,919.7	15.	Sony Corp.	1,665.3
3.	Time Warner	3,283.1	16.	Nissan Motor Co.	1,539.9
4.	Pfizer	2,957.3	17.	Altria Group	1,399.4
5.	SBC Communications	2,686.8	18.	McDonald's Corp.	1,388.9
6.	DaimlerChrysler	2,462.1	19.	L'Oreal	1,341.1
7.	Ford Motor Co.	2,458.0	20.	Unilever	1,319.1
8.	Walt Disney Co.	2,241.5	21.	Novartis	1,284.6
9.	Verizon Communications	2,197.3	22.	PepsiCo	1,262.2
10.	Johnson & Johnson	2,175.7	23.	Home Depot	1,255.9
11.	GlaxoSmithKline	1,828.3	24.	Merck & Co.	1,250.3
12.	Sears Holdings Corp.	1,823.0	25.	U.S. Government	1,228.5
13.	Toyota Motor Corp.	1,821.0			

Source: Advertising Age. Web: adage.com.

World Port Ranking, 2003

	Total cargo volume, metric tons (1,000s)				Container traffic (TEUs) (1,000s)[1]		
Rank	Port	Country	Tons	Rank	Port	Country	TEUs
1.	Singapore	Singapore	347,694	1.	Hong Kong	China	20,499
2.	Rotterdam	Netherlands	326,958	2.	Singapore	Singapore	18,411
3.	Shanghai	China	316,210	3.	Shanghai	China	11,280
4.	Hong Kong	China	207,612	4.	Shenzhen	China	10,615
5.	South Louisiana	United States	180,493	5.	Busan	South Korea	10,408
6.	Houston	United States	173,320	6.	Kaohsiung	Taiwan	8,843
7.	Chiba	Japan	169,000	7.	Los Angeles	United States	7,149
8.	Nagoya	Japan	168,378	8.	Rotterdam	Netherlands	7,107
9.	Guangzhou	China	167,720	9.	Hamburg	Germany	6,138
10.	Kwangyang	South Korea	165,089	10.	Antwerp	Belgium	5,445
11.	Busan	South Korea	162,460	11.	Dubai	United Arab Emirates	5,152
12.	Tianjin	China	161,820	12.	Port Kalang	Malaysia	4,840
13.	Ningbo	China	153,980	13.	Long Beach	United States	4,658
14.	Ulsan	South Korea	146,940	14.	Quingdao	China	4,239
15.	Antwerp	Belgium	142,875	15.	New York/New Jersey	United States	4,068
16.	Qingdao	China	140,900	16.	Tanjung Pelepas	Indonesia	3,487
17.	Kaohsiung	Taiwan	138,832	17.	Tokyo	Japan	3,314
18.	New York/New Jersey	United States	132,438	18.	Bremen/Bremerhafen	Germany	3,190
19.	Inchon	South Korea	131,018	19.	Laem Chabang	Thailand	3,181
20.	Dalian	China	126,020	20.	Gioia Tauro	Italy	3,149
21.	Yokohama	Japan	125,943	21.	Tianjin	China	3,015
22.	Qinhuangdao	China	125,620	22.	Ningbo	China	2,772
23.	Hamburg	Germany	106,536	23.	Guangzhou	China	2,762
24.	Marseilles	France	95,545	24.	Tanjung Priok	Indonesia	2,758
25.	Port Hedland	Australia	89,799	25.	Manila	Philippines	2,552

1. TEU denotes twenty-foot equivalent units. *Source:* American Association of Port Authorities. Web: www.aapa-ports.org.

United States' Largest Banks

(in millions of U.S. dollars)

Rank	Name (city, state)	Consolidated assets	Rank	Name (city, state)	Consolidated assets
1.	J. P. Morgan Chase & Company (New York, N.Y.)	$628,662	17.	ABN Amro North America Holding Company (Chicago, Ill.)	$61,259
2.	Bank of America Corp. (Charlotte, N.C.)	617,962	18.	Fifth Third Bancorp (Cincinnati, Ohio)	57,373
3.	Citigroup (New York, N.Y.)	582,123	19.	Citigroup (Sioux Falls, S.D.)	56,550
4.	Wachovia Corp. (Charlotte, N.C.)	353,541	20.	MBNA Corp. (Wilmington, Del.)	56,496
5.	Bank One Corp. (Chicago, Ill.)	256,787	21.	Comerica (Detroit, Mich.)	52,684
6.	Wells Fargo & Company (San Francisco, Calif.)	250,474	22.	Southtrust Corp. (Birmingham, Ala.)	51,885
7.	FleetBoston Financial Corp. (Providence, R.I.)	192,265	23.	M&T Bank Corp. (Buffalo, N.Y.)	49,202
8.	U.S. BC (Cincinnati, Ohio)	189,159	24.	Wells Fargo & Company (Minneapolis, Minn.)	48,802
9.	Suntrust Banks, Inc. (Atlanta, Ga.)	124,454	25.	National City Corp. (Cleveland, Ohio)	46,276
10.	HSBC North America Inc. (Buffalo, N.Y.)	92,958	26.	ABN Amro North America Holding Company (Troy, Mich.)	45,670
11.	Bank of New York Company, Inc. (New York, N.Y.)	89,258	27.	Amsouth Bancorporation (Birmingham, Ala.)	45,629
12.	State Street Corp. (Boston, Mass.)	80,435	28.	Regions Financial Corp. (Birmingham, Ala.)	45,248
13.	Keycorp (Cleveland, Ohio)	74,321	29.	Charter One Financial, Inc. (Cleveland, Ohio)	42,699
14.	BB&T Corp. (Winston-Salem, N.C.)	67,584	30.	National City Corp. (Indianapolis, Ind.)	42,549
15.	Bank One Corp. (Columbus, Ohio)	65,194			
16.	PNC Financial Services Group, Inc. (Pittsburgh, Pa.)	62,037			

NOTE: As of Dec. 31, 2004. *Source:* Federal Reserve System, National Information Center.

Largest U.S. Businesses

2004 rank	Company	Revenues ($ millions)	2004 rank	Company	Revenues ($ millions)
1.	Wal-Mart Stores	$288,189.0	26.	Procter & Gamble	$51,407.0
2.	Exxon Mobil	270,772.0	27.	Target	49,934.0
3.	General Motors	193,517.0	28.	Dell	49,205.0
4.	Ford Motor	172,233.0	29.	Costco Wholesale	48,107.0
5.	General Electric	152,363.0	30.	Johnson & Johnson	47,348.0
6.	ChevronTexaco	147,967.0	31.	Marathon Oil	45,444.0
7.	ConocoPhillips	121,663.0	32.	Time Warner	42,869.0
8.	Citigroup	108,276.0	33.	SBC Communications	41,098.0
9.	American Intl. Group	98,610.0	34.	Dow Chemical	40,161.0
10.	International Business Machines	96,293.0	35.	Albertson's	40,052.0
11.	Hewlett-Packard	79,905.0	36.	Morgan Stanley	39,549.0
12.	Berkshire Hathaway	74,382.0	37.	MetLife	39,535.0
13.	Home Depot	73,094.0	38.	Walgreen	37,508.2
14.	Verizon Communications	71,563.3	39.	United Technologies	37,445.0
15.	McKesson	69,506.1	40.	UnitedHealth Group	37,218.0
16.	Cardinal Health	65,130.6	41.	Microsoft	36,835.0
17.	Altria Group	64,440.0	42.	United Parcel Service	36,582.0
18.	Bank of America Corp.	63,324.0	43.	Lowe's	36,464.0
19.	State Farm Insurance	58,818.9	44.	Archer Daniels Midland	36,151.4
20.	J.P. Morgan Chase & Co.	56,931.0	45.	Sears Roebuck	36,099.0
21.	Kroger	56,434.4	46.	Safeway	35,822.9
22.	Valero Energy	53,918.6	47.	Lockheed Martin	35,526.0
23.	Amerisourcebergen	53,179.0	48.	Medco Health Solutions	35,351.9
24.	Pfizer	52,921.0	49.	Motorola	35,349.0
25.	Boeing	52,553.0	50.	Intel	34,209.0

Top NYSE Stocks by Dollar Value

2004 rank	Issue (symbol)	2004 dollar volume (in millions)	2004 rank	Issue (symbol)	2004 dollar volume (in millions)
1.	General Electric Company (GE)	$75,789.3	28.	Disney (Walt) Company (DIS)	$25,481.2
2.	Citigroup, Inc. (C)	63,386.1	29.	Verizon Communications (VZ)	25,039.0
3.	Pfizer, Inc (PFE)	61,151.9	30.	3M Company (MMM)	25,038.5
4.	Wal-Mart Stores (WMT)	57,866.4	31.	Time Warner, Inc. (TWX)	24,199.8
5.	Bank of America Corporation (BAC)	50,453.3	32.	Medtronic, Inc. (MDT)	23,841.0
6.	International Business Machines (IBM)	49,850.1	33.	PepsiCo, Inc. (PEP)	23,721.2
7.	Exxon Mobil Corporation (XOM)	48,748.4	34.	Schlumberger, Ltd. (SLB)	23,579.3
8.	Goldman Sachs Group (GS)	40,719.9	35.	SBC Communications (SBC)	23,554.5
9.	American Int'l Group, Inc. (AIG)	39,645.8	36.	General Motors Corporation (GM)	23,475.9
10.	J.P. Morgan Chase & Co. (JPM)	39,527.3	37.	United Technologies Corporation (UTX)	23,108.0
11.	Johnson & Johnson (JNJ)	38,395.3	38.	Guidant Corporation (GDT)	23,105.7
12.	Procter & Gamble Company (PG)	35,399.5	39.	Wyeth (WYE)	23,027.2
13.	Texas Instruments Inc. (TXN)	34,642.1	40.	American Express Company (AXP)	22,827.3
14.	Philip Morris Companies (MO)	34,564.2	41.	ONE (ONE)	22,740.8
15.	Merrill Lynch & Co. (MER)	30,610.6	42.	Tyco International (TYC)	22,611.6
16.	Merck & Co. (MRK)	30,103.6	43.	Newmont Mining Corporation (NEM)	22,585.1
17.	Morgan Stanley (MWD)	29,149.7	44.	AT&T Wireless Services, Inc. (AWE)	22,441.5
18.	Fannie Mae (FNM)	28,851.4	45.	Nokia Corporation (NOK)	22,181.2
19.	Home Depot, Inc. (HD)	27,514.9	46.	Lowes Companies, Inc. (LOW)	21,365.7
20.	ChevronTexaco Corporation (CVX)	27,263.0	47.	Boston Scientific Corporation (BSX)	21,270.7
21.	Coca-Cola Company (KO)	26,950.2	48.	Countrywide Financial Corporation (CFC)	20,940.8
22.	Genentech, Inc. (DNA)	26,649.2	49.	Lehman Brothers Holdings, Inc. (LEH)	20,880.0
23.	Motorola, Inc. (MOT)	26,567.4	50.	Caterpillar, Inc. (CAT)	20,706.4
24.	Viacom, Inc. (VIAB)	26,214.8			
25.	Hewlett-Packard Company (HPQ)	25,906.7			
26.	Wells Fargo & Company (WFC)	25,740.6			
27.	Eli Lilly and Company (LLY)	25,678.8			

Source: New York Stock Exchange.

Most Active Stocks on NYSE

2004 rank	Company name (symbol)	2004 share volume (in millions)	2004 rank	Company name (symbol)	2004 share volume (in millions)
1.	Lucent Technologies, Inc. (LU)	5,811.0	26.	Tyco International (TYC)	1,490.9
2.	Nortel Networks Corporation (NT)	4,808.5	27.	Viacom, Inc. (VIAB)	1,440.1
3.	Pfizer, Inc (PFE)	4,430.4	28.	Home Depot, Inc. (HD)	1,429.7
4.	General Electric Company (GE)	4,118.5	29.	Sprint FON Group (FON)	1,375.7
5.	Motorola, Inc. (MOT)	2,862.5	30.	Bank of America Corporation (BAC)	1,361.6
6.	Time Warner, Inc. (TWX)	2,712.8	31.	Johnson & Johnson (JNJ)	1,361.4
7.	Citigroup, Inc. (C)	2,649.8	32.	Taiwan Semiconductor (TSM)	1,345.9
8.	Texas Instruments, Inc. (TXN)	2,559.7	33.	Verizon Communications (VZ)	1,336.8
9.	EMC Corporation (EMC)	2,506.7	34.	American Int'l Group, Inc. (AIG)	1,329.7
10.	AT&T Wireless Services, Inc. (AWE)	2,350.0	35.	Philip Morris Companies (MO)	1,296.7
11.	Nokia Corporation (NOK)	2,325.5	36.	Coca-Cola Company (KO)	1,260.8
12.	Exxon Mobil Corporation (XOM)	2,278.5	37	Qwest Communications (Q)	1,231.3
13.	Hewlett-Packard Company (HPQ)	2,226.1	38.	National Semiconductor Corp. (NSM)	1,202.1
14.	Wal-Mart Stores (WMT)	2,037.8	39.	Bristol-Myers Squibb (BMY)	1,192.5
15.	J.P. Morgan Chase & Co. (JPM)	2,028.7	40.	Schering–Plough Corporation (SGP)	1,152.7
16.	Merck & Co. (MRK)	1,965.5	41.	AT&T Corporation (T)	1,124.4
17.	Agere Systems, Inc. (AGRA)	1,833.6	42.	Charles Schwab Corp. (SCH)	1,121.5
18.	Corning, Inc. (GLW)	1,740.8	43.	Boston Scientific Corp. (BSX)	1,080.7
19.	SBC Communications (SBC)	1,739.9	44.	Alcoa, Inc. (AA)	1,064.7
20.	Advanced Micro Devices, Inc. (AMD)	1,717.3	45.	Int'l Business Machines (IBM)	1,050.8
21.	Ford Motor Company (F)	1,707.4	46.	US Bancorp (USB)	1,046.5
22.	Liberty Media Corporation (L)	1,706.8	47.	Gap, Inc. (GPS)	1,043.9
23.	Micron Technology, Inc. (MU)	1,676.2	48.	Merrill Lynch & Co. (MER)	1,024.7
24.	Walt Disney Company (DIS)	1,645.5	49.	Morgan Stanley (MWD)	1,018.6
25.	Calpine Corporation (CPN)	1,520.5	50.	Wyeth (WYE)	989.0

Source: New York Stock Exchange.

Top NASDAQ Stocks by Market Value, 2004

Rank	Name	Symbol	Market value (in thousands)	Rank	Name	Symbol	Market value (in thousands)
1.	Microsoft Corporation	MSFT	$290,312,800	28.	Adobe Systems Incorporated	ADBE	$14,971,458
2.	Intel Corporation	INTC	147,894,970	29.	Apollo Group, Inc.	APOL	14,911,980
3.	Cisco Systems, Inc.	CSCO	127,217,157	30.	Juniper Networks, Inc.	JNPR	14,617,697
4.	Dell Inc.	DELL	104,688,571	31.	PACCAR Inc.	PCAR	13,981,227
5.	Amgen Inc.	AMGN	81,479,224	32.	Maxim Integrated Products, Inc.	MXIM	13,787,263
6.	eBay Inc.	EBAY	77,122,717	33.	Teva Pharmaceutical Industries Limited	TEVA	13,427,982
7.	Oracle Corporation	ORCL	70,362,554	34.	Genzyme Corporation	GENZ	13,325,265
8.	QUALCOMM Incorporated	QCOM	69,497,077	35.	Paychex, Inc.	PAYX	12,888,920
9.	Yahoo! Inc.	YHOO	51,803,180	36.	VERITAS Software Corporation	VRTS	12,051,812
10.	Comcast Corporation	CMCS	45,229,484	37.	Bed Bath & Beyond Inc.	BBBY	11,986,082
11.	Nextel Communications, Inc.	NXTL	32,459,626	38.	Network Appliance, Inc.	NTAP	11,918,771
12.	Applied Materials, Inc.	AMAT	29,039,784	39.	Linear Technology Corporation	LLTC	11,900,948
13.	Comcast Corporation	CMCS	27,959,582	40.	Google Inc.	GOOG	11,154,251
14.	Fifth Third Bancorp	FITB	26,549,159	41.	Biomet, Inc.	BMET	10,983,831
15.	Apple Computer, Inc.	AAPL	25,892,535	42.	Northern Trust Corporation	NTRS	10,649,173
16.	Starbucks Corporation	SBUX	24,782,238	43.	Xilinx, Inc.	XLNX	10,334,447
17.	Costco Wholesale Corporation	COST	22,707,776	44.	PeopleSoft, Inc.	PSFT	9,953,512
18.	Biogen Idec Inc.	BIIB	22,217,899	45.	Sirius Satellite Radio Inc.	SIRI	9,624,944
19.	Nasdaq-100 Trust, Series I	QQQQ	22,182,761	46.	Marvell Technology Group, Ltd.	MRVL	9,573,991
20.	Electronic Arts Inc.	ERTS	18,832,878	47.	KLA-Tencor Corporation	KLAC	9,104,154
21.	Sun Microsystems, Inc.	SUNW	18,126,974	48.	KMart Holding Corporation	KMRT	8,824,163
22.	Symantec Corporation	SYMC	18,119,842	49.	Autodesk, Inc.	ADSK	8,774,040
23.	Amazon.com, Inc.	AMZN	18,072,623	50.	Broadcom Corporation	BRCM	8,722,572
24.	IAC/InterActiveCorp	IACI	17,345,636				
25.	Staples, Inc.	SPLS	16,784,310				
26.	Research in Motion Limited	RIMM	15,469,987				
27.	Gilead Sciences, Inc.	GILD	15,147,731				

Source: The NASDAQ Stock Market, Inc.

Most Active NASDAQ Stocks, 2004

Rank	Name	Symbol	Total volume (in thousands)	Rank	Name	Symbol	Total volume (in thousands)
1.	Microsoft Corporation	MSFT	17,333,799	28.	Amgen Inc.	AMGN	2,138,481
2.	Sirius Satellite Radio Inc.	SIRI	17,020,339	29.	VERITAS Software Corporation	VRTS	2,110,613
3.	Intel Corporation	INTC	16,698,223	30.	Atmel Corporation	ATML	2,080,645
4.	Cisco Systems, Inc.	CSCO	13,951,370	31.	Comcast Corporation	CMCS	2,062,206
5.	Oracle Corporation	ORCL	11,479,446	32.	RF Micro Devices, Inc.	RFMD	2,046,572
6.	Sun Microsystems, Inc.	SUNW	10,367,515	33.	SanDisk Corporation	SNDK	2,026,718
7.	JDS Uniphase Corporation	JDSU	8,297,736	34.	Brocade Communications Systems, Inc.	BRCD	2,017,873
8.	Applied Materials, Inc.	AMAT	8,249,963	35.	Tellabs, Inc.	TLAB	1,872,902
9.	TASER International, Inc.	TASR	5,434,110	36.	Sanmina-SCI Corporation	SANM	1,824,221
10.	Yahoo! Inc.	YHOO	5,134,065	37.	Xilinx, Inc.	XLNX	1,818,146
11.	QUALCOMM Incorporated	QCOM	4,224,148	38.	Altera Corporation	ALTR	1,815,101
12.	Nasdaq-100 Trust, Series I	QQQQ	4,038,090	39.	PeopleSoft, Inc.	PSFT	1,807,957
13.	Dell Inc.	DELL	4,000,383	40.	Applied Micro Circuits Corporation	AMCC	1,797,555
14.	Ciena Corporation	CIEN	3,240,022	41.	KLA-Tencor Corporation	KLAC	1,778,156
15.	Nextel Communications, Inc.	NXTL	3,229,930	42.	Charter Communications, Inc.	CHTR	1,765,600
16.	Juniper Networks, Inc.	JNPR	3,121,345	43.	Vitesse Semiconductor Corporation	VTSS	1,731,019
17.	Conexant Systems, Inc.	CNXT	3,037,553	44.	Flextronics International Ltd.	FLEX	1,716,328
18.	Symantec Corporation	SYMC	2,750,416	45.	Novell, Inc.	NOVL	1,688,565
19.	Research in Motion Limited	RIMM	2,638,170	46.	Comcast Corporation	CMCS	1,645,749
20.	Broadcom Corporation	BRCM	2,571,582	47.	IAC/InterActiveCorp	IACI	1,622,758
21.	ADC Telecommunications, Inc.	ADCT	2,508,669	48.	PMC-Sierra, Inc.	PMCS	1,577,669
22.	eBay Inc.	EBAY	2,239,760	49.	Red Hat, Inc.	RHAT	1,561,654
23.	Apple Computer, Inc.	AAPL	2,194,588	50.	Maxim Integrated Products, Inc.	MXIM	1,502,289
24.	Siebel Systems, Inc.	SEBL	2,194,045				
25.	Amazon.com, Inc.	AMZN	2,173,082				
26.	Level 3 Communications, Inc.	LVLT	2,141,658				
27.	BEA Systems, Inc.	BEAS	2,140,614				

Source: The NASDAQ Stock Market, Inc.

Stolen Identity: A Consumer Nightmare

Source: Federal Trade Commission (FTC).

A new type of criminal has emerged—one who can wreak havoc with your finances and credit and destroy your good reputation. It's relatively easy for a determined thief to steal your name, your Social Security number, your credit card number, or some other bit of personal information without your knowledge and commit fraud in your name.

Unfortunately, you may not find out that your identity has been stolen until you receive bills for credit card accounts that you never opened, debts that you never incurred, or charges on your bills that you didn't sign for, authorize, or know anything about.

How Can This Happen?

When you make everyday transactions like writing a check at a store, charging purchases, renting a car, mailing your tax return, calling home on your cell phone, ordering new checks, or applying for a credit card, chances are that you don't give this a second thought. But crooks known as "identity thieves" may be paying attention. Each transaction requires you to share your personal information such as your bank and credit card account numbers, your Social Security number, name, address, and phone numbers. Despite your best efforts to control your personal information, skilled thieves can use a variety of methods, low- and high-tech, to gain access to your data.

How Your Identity Is Stolen

The Federal Trade Commission (FTC) has listed the following ways that imposters can get your personal information and take over your identity:

• They steal your wallet and purse containing your identification and credit and bank cards.
• They steal your mail, including your bank and credit card statements, pre-approved credit offers, telephone calling cards, and tax information.
• They complete a "change of address" form to divert your mail to another location.
• They rummage through your trash, or the trash of businesses, for personal data in a practice known as "dumpster diving."
• They fraudulently obtain your credit card report by posing as a landlord, employer, or someone else who may have a legitimate need for and a legal right to the information.
• They get your business or personnel records at work.
• They find personal information in your home.
• They use personal information you share on the Internet.
• They buy your personal information from "inside" sources. For example, an identity thief may pay a store employee for information about you that appears on an application for goods, services, or credit.

How Your Stolen Identity Is Used

The crooks call your credit card company and, pretending to be you, ask to change the mailing address on your credit card account. The imposter then runs up charges on your account. Because your bills are being sent to the new address, it may take some time before you realize that there is a problem.

Thieves can also open a new credit card account using your name, date of birth, and Social Security number. When they use the credit card and don't pay the bills, the delinquent account is reported on your credit report.

Other scenarios include establishing a phone or wireless service in your name, opening a bank account in your name and writing bad checks on it, and buying cars by taking out auto loans in your name.

Minimize Risk

Sign your credit cards upon receipt. Only carry cards that you need. Do not carry your Social Security card. Never write your PIN or Social Security number on anything you are going to throw away. Shred documents containing your Social Security number.

Do not release personal information such as your Social Security or bank account number over the phone unless you made the phone call and understand why the information is necessary.

Obtain an annual copy of your credit report from the three main credit bureaus and ensure the material is correct.

Be aware of credit card billing cycles. If you do not receive a bill on time, contact the company. A thief charging purchases to your account would likely change your billing address, so that it would take you longer to discover the fraud.

To thwart an identity thief who may pick through your trash or recycling bins to capture your personal information, tear or shred your charge receipts, copies of credit applications, insurance forms, physician statements, checks and bank statements, expired charge cards that you're discarding, and credit offers you get in the mail.

Try not to store financial information on your laptop unless absolutely necessary. If you do, use a strong password—a combination of letters (upper and lower case), numbers, and symbols. Don't use an automatic log-in feature that saves your user name and password so you don't have to enter them each time you log into or enter a site. And always log off when you're finished. That way, if your laptop gets stolen, it's harder for the thief to access your personal information.

Use a secure browser—software that encrypts or scrambles information you send over the

Internet—to guard the security of your online transactions. Be sure your browser has the most up-to-date encryption capabilities by using the latest version available from the manufacturer. You also can download some browsers for free over the Internet. When submitting information, look for the "lock" icon on the browser's status bar to be sure your information is secure during transmission.

Before you dispose of a computer, delete personal information. Deleting files using the keyboard or mouse commands may not be enough because the files may stay on the computer's hard drive, where they may be easily retrieved. Use a "wipe" utility program to overwrite the entire hard drive. It makes the files unrecoverable.

If You're a Victim

Do these three things immediately:

1) Contact the fraud departments of each of the three major credit bureaus and report that your identity has been stolen. Ask that a "fraud alert" be placed on your file and that no new credit be granted without your approval.

Main Credit Reporting Bureaus:

Equifax, P.O. Box 740241, Atlanta, GA 30374-0241, 888-766-0008
Experian, P.O. Box 9532, Allen, TX 75013, 888-397-3742

Trans Union, P.O. Box 6790, Fullerton, CA, 92834, 800-680-7289

2) For any accounts that have been fraudulently accessed or opened, contact the security departments of the appropriate creditors or financial institutions. Close these accounts. Put passwords (not your mother's maiden name) on any new accounts you open. If your checks have been stolen or misused, close the account and ask your bank to notify the appropriate check verification service. You can also contact these major check verification companies. Ask that retailers who use their databases not accept your checks.

Major Check Verification Companies:

TeleCheck, 800-710-9898
Certegy, Inc., 800-437-5120
International Check Services, 800-631-9656

3) File a report with your local police or the police where the identity theft took place. Get a copy of the report in case the bank, credit card company, or others need proof of the crime later on.

4) File a complaint with the FTC. To file a complaint, visit www.consumer.gov/idtheft, call the FTC's Identity Theft Hotline: toll-free 1-877-IDTHEFT (438-4338), or write: Identity Theft Clearinghouse, Federal Trade Commission, 600 Pennsylvania Avenue, NW, Washington, DC 20580.

How to Right a Wrong

Source: Federal Trade Commission (FTC).

Most companies want to make you happy so you'll come back and recommend them to your friends. But when you find a company that's not making the grade, how do you resolve the problem?

Mail and Telephone Order Sales

Shopping by phone or mail can be a convenient alternative to shopping at a store. But if your merchandise arrives late or not at all, you have some rights. By law, a company should ship your order within the time stated in its ads. If no time is promised, the company should ship your order within 30 days after receiving it. If the company is unable to ship within the promised time, they must give you an "option notice." This notice gives you the choice of agreeing to the delay or canceling your order and receiving a prompt refund. There is one exception to the 30-day rule. If a company doesn't promise a shipping time, and you're applying for credit to pay for your purchase, the company has 50 days to ship after receiving your order.

You're protected by the Fair Credit Billing Act (FCBA) when you use your credit card to pay for purchases.

Billing Errors

If you find an error on your credit or charge card statement, you can dispute the charge and withhold payment on the challenged amount while the charge

is in dispute. The error might be a charge for the wrong amount, for something you did not accept, or for an item that was not delivered as agreed. Of course, you still must pay any part of the bill that isn't in dispute, including the finance charges on the undisputed amount. If you decide to dispute a charge:

• Write to the creditor at the address indicated on the monthly statement for "billing inquiries." Include your name, address, credit card number, and a description of the billing error.

• Send your letter in a timely fashion. It must reach the creditor within 60 days after the first bill containing the error was mailed to you.

• The creditor must acknowledge your complaint in writing within 30 days after receiving it, unless the problem has been resolved. The creditor must resolve the dispute within two billing cycles (and not more than 90 days) after receiving the letter.

Unsatisfactory Goods or Services

You also may dispute charges for unsatisfactory goods or services. To take advantage of this protection, you must:

• have made the purchase in your home state or within 100 miles of your current billing address. The charge must be for more than $50.

• make a good-faith effort first to resolve the dispute with the seller. However, you are not required to use any special procedure to do so.

National Consumer Organizations

NOTE: For other organizations, *see* Societies & Associations, pp. 658–667.

AARP: Consumer Affairs Section, 601 E St. NW, Washington, DC 20049; 888-687-2277; Web: www.aarp.org.

Offers information on housing, insurance, funeral practices, eligibility for public benefits, financial security, transportation, and consumer protection issues on behalf of mid-life and older consumers.

Alliance Against Fraud in Telemarketing & Electronic Commerce (AAFTEC): c/o National Consumers League, 1701 K St. NW, Suite 1200, Washington, DC 20006; 202-835-3323; 202-835-0747 (fax); Web: www.fraud.org/aaft/aaftset.htm.

Combats telemarketing and Internet fraud through consumer education.

American Council on Consumer Interests (ACCI): 415 South Duff, Suite C., Ames, IA 50010-6600; 515-956-4666; 515-233-3101 (fax); Web: consumerinterests.org.

Provides research-based information on topics of consumer interest. Provides information about consumer publications, policies, and resources.

American Council on Science and Health (ACSH): 1995 Broadway, 2nd Fl., New York, NY 10023-5860; 212-362-7044; 212-362-4919 (fax); Web: www.acsh.org.

A consumer education consortium concerned with issues related to food, nutrition, chemicals, pharmaceuticals, lifestyle, the environment, and health.

American Savings Education Council (ASEC): 2121 K St. NW, Suite 600, Washington, DC 20037-1896; 202-659-0670; 202-775-6360 (fax); Web: www.asec.org.

Raises public awareness about what is needed to ensure long-term personal financial independence.

Better Business Bureau (BBB): 4200 Wilson Blvd., Suite 800, Arlington, VA 22203-1838; 703-276-0100; Web: www.bbb.org.

Offers a variety of consumer services including educational materials, information on charities and other organizations seeking public donations, and mediation and arbitration services.

Center for Auto Safety (CAS): 1825 Connecticut Ave. NW, Suite 330, Washington, DC 20009-5708; 202-328-7700; Web: www.autosafety.org.

Founded by Consumers Union and Ralph Nader in 1970 to advocate for auto safety and quality.

Center for Science in the Public Interest (CSPI): 1875 Connecticut Ave. NW, Suite 300, Washington, DC 20009; 202-332-9110; 202-265-4954 (fax); Web: www.cspinet.org.

Provides research, education, and advocacy on nutrition, health, food safety, and related issues.

Center for the Study of Services/Consumers' Checkbook: Consumers' Checkbook Headquarters, 733 15th St. NW, Suite 820, Washington, DC 20005; 800-213-7283; Web: www.checkbook.org.

Aids consumers in selecting doctors, hospitals, health plans, cars, and finding bargains.

Coalition Against Insurance Fraud: 1012 14th St. NW, Suite 200, Washington, DC 20005; 202-393-7330; 202-393-7329 (fax); Web: www.insurancefraud.org.

Organization of consumers, government agencies, and insurers dedicated to combating all forms of insurance fraud.

Congress Watch: 215 Pennsylvania Ave., SE, Washington, DC 20003; 202-546-4996; 202-547-7392 (fax); Web: www.citizen.org/congress.

An arm of Public Citizen, Congress Watch works for consumer-related legislation, regulation, and policies in such areas as campaign financing and health and safety.

Consumer Action (CA): 717 Market St., Suite 310, San Francisco, CA 94103-2109; 415-777-9635 (multilingual consumer complaint hotline); 415-777-9456 (voice/ttd); Web: www.consumer-action.org.

Advocates for credit, finance, HMO, and telecommunications issues.

Consumer Federation of America (CFA): 1424 16th St. NW, Suite 604, Washington, DC 20036; 202-387-6121; Web: www.consumerfed.org.

Composed of more than 260 organizations, CFA is a consumer advocacy and education organization. CFA focuses much of its advocacy in the areas of financial service, utilities, product safety, transportation, health care, and food safety.

Consumers Union of U.S., Inc. (CU): 101 Truman Ave., Yonkers, NY 10703-1057; 914-378-2000; Web: www.consumersunion.org.

Publisher of *Consumer Reports*. Researches and tests consumer goods and services.

Families USA Foundation: 1334 G St. NW, Washington, DC 20005; 202-628-3030; 202-347-2417 (fax); Web: www.familiesusa.org.

Advocates for high-quality, affordable healthcare.

Federal Communications Commission (FCC): 445 12th St. SW, Washington, DC 20554; 888-CALL-FCC or 888-225-5322; 866–418–0232 (fax); Web: www.fcc.gov.

Offers information to help consumers avoid unwanted telephone solicitations and to report other abusive techniques.

Federal Trade Commission (FTC): CRC-240, Washington, DC 20580; 1-877-FTC-HELP or 202-326-2222; Web: www.ftc.gov.

Enforces a variety of federal antitrust and consumer protection laws.

HALT: An Organization of Americans for Legal Reform: 1612 K St. NW, Suite 510, Washington, DC 20006; 202-887-8255, toll-free: 888-367-4258; 202-887-9699 (fax); Web: www.halt.org.

Helps consumers handle their legal affairs.

Housing and Urban Development (HUD): 451 7th St. SW, Washington, DC 20410; 202-708-1112; 800-347-3735 (fraud, waste, abuse complaints); Web: www.hud.gov/consumer/index.cfm.

Enforces federal laws and regulations that protect you from discrimination, fraud, and unscrupulous practices in buying and renting a home.

Internet Fraud Complaint Center (IFCC): Web: www.ifccfbi.gov.

Provides victims of Internet fraud a convenient, easy-to-use reporting mechanism that alerts authorities of a suspected criminal or civil violation. The IFCC is a partnership between the FBI and the National White Collar Crime Center.

Military Sentinel: Web: www.consumer.gov/military.

Allows members of the U.S. Armed Forces to enter consumer complaints directly into a database that is immediately accessible by over 500 law enforcement organizations throughout the United States, Canada, and Australia.

National Association of Consumer Agency Administrators (NACAA): Two Brentwood Commons, Suite 150, 750 Old Hickory Boulevard, Brentwood, Tennessee 37207; 1-866-SAY-NACAA or 615-371-6125; Web: www.nacaa.net.

A nonprofit association for administrators of government consumer-protection agencies. NACAA members work directly with consumers to solve problems, advance relevant legislation, and support consumer outreach and education.

National Community Reinvestment Coalition (NCRC): 733 15th St. NW, Suite 540, Washington, DC 20005; 202-628-8866; 202-628-9800 (fax); Web: www.ncrc.org.

Works toward ending discriminatory banking practices and increasing the flow of private capital and credit into underserved communities.

National Consumer Law Center (NCLC): 77 Summer St., 10th Fl., Boston, MA 02110-1006; 617-542-8010; 617-542-8028 (fax); Web: www.consumerlaw.org.

Focuses on the interests of low-income consumers in court, before administrative agencies, and before legislatures.

National Consumers League (NCL): 1701 K St. NW, Suite 1200, Washington, DC 20006; 202-835-3323; 202-835-0747 (fax); Web: nclnet.org.

Founded in 1899, NCL is America's pioneer consumer advocacy organization. It focuses on consumer health and safety protection as well as fairness in the marketplace and workplace.

National Council on Aging (NCOA): 300 D St. SW, Suite 801, Washington, DC 20024; 202-479-1200; 202-479-0735 (fax); Web: www.ncoa.org.

Advocates for public policies and provides programs and services that serve older persons.

National Foundation for Credit Counseling (NFCC): 801 Roeder Rd., Suite 900, Silver Spring, MD 20910; 301-589-5600; 301-495-5623 (fax); Web: www.nfcc.org.

Provides assistance with stressful financial situations.

National Fraud Information Center/Internet Fraud Watch (NFIC/IFW): c/o National Consumers League, 1701 K St. NW, Suite 1200, Washington, DC 20006; 800-876-7060; Web: www.fraud.org.

Helps to prevent telemarketing fraud and online and Internet fraud, and assists in filing complaints.

National Senior Citizens Law Center: 1101 14th St. NW, Suite 400, Washington, DC 20005; 202-289-6976; 202-289-7224 (fax); Web: www.nsclc.org.

Helps low-income and older Americans with legal services.

Public Citizen: 1600 20th St. NW, Washington, DC 20009; 202-588-1000; Web: www.citizen.org.

Represents consumer interests in Congress, the courts, government agencies, and the media. Its divisions include Auto Safety, Congress Watch, Critical Mass (Energy & Environment Program), Global Trade Watch, Health Research Group, and the Litigation Group.

U.S. Public Interest Research Group (U.S. PIRG): 218 D St. SE, Washington, DC 20003; 202-546-9707; 202-546-2461 (fax); Web: www.uspirg.org.

Advocates on issues such as the environment, product safety, financial privacy, and identity theft.

Women's Bureau, Dept. of Labor: 200 Constitution Ave. NW, Room S-3002, Washington, DC 20210; 800-827-5335, 202-693-6710; 202-693-6725 (fax); Web: www.dol.gov/wb.

Advocates for work issues such as sexual harassment, pregnancy discrimination, and child care.

Recalls

Several federal agencies enforce product-safety regulations and provide access to recall information. The central website providing access to recall information is www.recall.gov. Recalls are also posted regularly at www.pueblo.gsa.gov.

Appliances, children's products, clothing, electronics, furniture, household items, lighting, outdoor products, sports and exercise equipment: U.S. Consumer Product Safety Commission (CPSC); **Phone:** 800-638-2772; **Web:** www.cpsc.gov

Cars, child safety seats, motor vehicles and related equipment, tires: National Highway Traffic Safety Administration (NHTSA); **Phone:** 888-DASH-2-DOT; **Web:** www.nhtsa.dot.gov

Cosmetics, drugs, food, medical devices, pet and farm-animal feed, plasma and blood products, vaccines, veterinary products: Food and Drug Administration (FDA); **Phone:** 888-INFO-FDA; **Web:** www.fda.gov

Eggs, meat, poultry products: Food Safety and Inspection Service (FSIS); **Phone:** 888-674-6854; **Web:** www.fsis.usda.gov

Fungicides, pesticides, rodenticides, vehicle emissions: Environmental Protection Agency (EPA); **Phone:** 800-858-7378; **Web:** www.epa.gov

Recreational boats and boating equipment: U.S. Coast Guard (USCG); **Phone:** 800-368-5674; **Web:** www.uscgboating.org

Complaint Resources

Source: The Federal Citizen Information Center.

Here's a list of federal agencies where you can file a complaint against a company. The topic areas are arranged alphabetically.

Airline Baggage and Service: Aviation Consumer Protection Division, U.S. Department of Transportation, Room 4107, C-75, Washington, DC 20590; 202-366-2220; Email: airconsumer@ost.dot.gov.

Alcohol, Tobacco and Firearms: Bureau of Alcohol, Tobacco and Firearms, Office of Liaison and Public Information, 650 Massachusetts Ave. NW, Room 8290, Washington, DC 20226; Email: atfmail@atfhq.atf.treas.gov.

Auto Dealers: Federal Trade Commission, CRC-240, Washington, DC 20580; 877-FTC-HELP (382-4357).

Automobile—Vehicles and Equipment: U.S. Department of Transportation, National Highway Traffic Safety Administration, Office of Defects Investigation, NSA-10.01, 400 7th St. SW, Washington, DC 20590; 888-DASH-2-DOT (327-4236); 202-366-7882 (fax).

Banking—Federal Savings & Loan and Federal Savings Banks: Office of Thrift Supervision, 1700 G St. NW, Washington, DC 20552; 800-613-6743; 800-613-6743 (fax); Email: Customer.Assistance@occ.treas.gov.

Banking—Institutions with National or "NA" in the name: Customer Assistance Group, 1301 McKinney St., Suite 3710, Houston, TX 77010; 713-336-4301; 800-613-6743 (fax); Email: Customer.Assistance@occ.treas.gov.

Banking—State Chartered Banks: Federal Deposit Insurance Corporation, Compliance and Consumer Affairs, 550 17th St. NW, Washington, DC 20429; 800-934-3342.

Banking—All others in the Federal Reserve System: Alabama, Florida, Georgia, Louisiana, Mississippi, Tennessee: Consumer Complaints Supervision and Regulation Department, Federal Reserve Bank of Atlanta, 104 Marietta St. NW, Atlanta, GA 30303-2713; 404-589-7239. **Delaware, New Jersey, Pennsylvania:** Online complaint form: www.phil.frb.org/forms/consumercomplaint.htm. **All others:** Board of Governors of the Federal Reserve, Division of Consumer and Community Affairs, 20 & C Streets NW, Stop 801, Washington, DC 20551; 202-452-3693.

Cable Television Complaints: Federal Communications Commission, Cable Services Bureau, Consumer Protection and Competition Division, 445 12th St. SW, Washington, DC 20554; 888-CALL-FCC (225-5322).

Cell Phones, Pagers, Wireless: Federal Communications Commission, Wireless Telecommunications Bureau, Enforcement and Consumer Information Division, Informal Complaints and Public Inquiry Branch, 1270 Fairfield Rd., Gettysburg, PA 17325; 888-CALL-FCC or 888-TELL-FCC (TTY); 717-338-2694 (fax).

Consumer Products (except cars, food, drugs, cosmetics, and medicine): 800-638-2772.

Charities: Federal Trade Commission, CRC-240, Washington, DC 20580; 877-FTC-HELP (382-4357).

Cosmetics: Complaints Coordinator, Office of Cosmetics and Colors, 200 C St. SW (HFS-106), Washington, DC 20204; 800-270-8869 (automated phone system); 202-205-5098 (fax).

Companies (including finance, mortgage, credit card, and credit bureau): Federal Trade Commission, CRC-240, Washington, DC 20580; 877-FTC-HELP (382-4357).

Credit Unions: National Credit Union Administration, Office of Public & Congressional Affairs, 1775 Duke St., Alexandria, VA 22314-3428; 703-518-6330.

Food (except meat and poultry): Center for Food Safety and Applied Nutrition, Food and Drug Administration, 200 C St. SW, HFS-555, Washington, DC 20204; 301-443-1240 (emergency only).

Health Clubs and Exercise Equipment: Federal Trade Commission, CRC-240, Washington, DC 20580; 877-FTC-HELP (382-4357).

Home Improvement: Federal Trade Commission, CRC-240, Washington, DC 20580; 877-FTC-HELP (382-4357).

Investments: Securities and Exchange Commission, Office of Investor Education and Assistance, 450 5th St. NW, Washington, DC 20549-0213; 202-942-7040; 202-942-9634 (fax).

Meat and Poultry: Food Safety and Inspection Service, United States Department of Agriculture, Washington, DC 20250-3700; 800-535-4555 (voice), 202-720-3333 (Washington, DC area), 800-256-7072 (TDD/TTY).

Medicines, Drugs, Medical Devices, Medical Drugs, and Products Sold Online: MedWatch, The FDA Medical Products Reporting Program, Food and Drug Administration, 5600 Fishers La., Rockville, MD 20852-9787; 301-443-1240 (emergency only); 800-FDA-1088 (332-1088) to request a complaint form; 800-FDA-0178 (332-0178) to fax a complaint form.

Online Service, Auctions, Websites, E-commerce: Federal Trade Commission, CRC-240, Washington, DC 20580; 877-FTC-HELP (382-4357).

Retail Stores: Federal Trade Commission, CRC-240, Washington, DC 20580; 877-FTC-HELP (382-4357).

Spam or Junk Email: Federal Trade Commission, CRC-240, Washington, DC 20580; 877-FTC-HELP (382-4357); Forward spam or junk email: uce@ftc.gov.

Securities and Stocks: Securities and Exchange Commission, Office of Investor Education and Assistance, 450 5th St. NW, Washington, DC 20549-0213; 202-942-7040; 202-942-9634 (fax).

Telephone Service (Billing, Access, Service, Long Distance): Federal Communications Commission, Consumer Information Bureau, Consumer Complaints—Telephone, Washington, DC 20554; 888-CALL-FCC or 888-TELL-FCC (TTY).

Vaccines: 800-822-7967 or 301-217-9660.

Patents
Source: Department of Commerce, Patent and Trademark Office.

A patent, in the most general sense, is a document issued by a government, conferring some special right or privilege. The term is now restricted mainly to patents for inventions and, occasionally, land patents.

The grant of a patent for an invention gives the inventor the privilege, for a limited period of time, of excluding others from making, using, or selling a certain article.

In the United States, the law provides that a patent may be granted, for a term of 20 years from the date of application, to any person who has invented or discovered any new and useful art, machine, manufacture, or composition of matter, as well as any new and useful improvements thereof. A patent may also be granted to a person who has invented or discovered and asexually reproduced a new and distinct variety of plant (other than a tuber-propagated one) or has invented a new, original, and

ornamental design for an article of manufacture, for a term of 20 years and 14 years, respectively.

A patent is granted only upon receipt of a complete, regularly filed application and the appropriate fees, and upon determination that the invention is new, useful, and, in view of the prior art, unobvious to one skilled in the art. The disclosure must be of such nature as to enable others to reproduce the invention.

Patents are not granted for printed matter, for methods of doing business, or for devices for which claims contrary to natural laws are made. Applications for a perpetual-motion machine have been made from time to time, but until a working model is presented that actually fulfills the claim, no patent will be issued.

A complete application, which must be addressed to the Commissioner of Patents and Trademarks, Washington, DC 20231, consists of a specification with one or more claims; oath or declaration; drawing (whenever the nature of the case admits of it); and a basic filing fee of $380. The filing fee is not returned to the applicant if the patent is refused. If the patent is allowed, other fees are required. Phone 1-800-786-9199 for the latest fees.

Trademarks

Source: Department of Commerce, Patent and Trademark Office.

A trademark may be defined as a word, letter, device, or symbol, as well as any combination of these, that is used in connection with merchandise and that points distinctly to the origin of the goods.

Certificates of registration of trademarks are issued under the seal of the Patent and Trademark Office and may be registered by the owner if he or she is engaged in interstate or foreign commerce. Federal jurisdiction over trademarks arises under the commerce clause of the Constitution. Effective Nov. 16, 1989, applications to register may also be based on a "bona fide intention to use the mark in commerce." Trademarks may be registered by foreign owners who comply with U.S. law, as well as by citizens of foreign countries with which the United States has treaties relating to trademarks. U.S. citizens may register trademarks in foreign countries by complying with the laws of those countries. The right to registration and protection of trademarks in many foreign countries is guaranteed by treaties.

General jurisdiction in trademark cases involving federal registrations is given to federal courts. Adverse decisions of examiners on applications for registration are appealable to the Trademark Trial and Appeal Board, whose affirmances and decisions in *inter partes* proceedings are subject to court review. Before adopting a trademark, a person should make a search of prior marks to avoid unwittingly infringing upon them.

The duration of a trademark registration is ten years, but it may be renewed indefinitely for 10-year periods, provided the trademark is still in use at the time of expiration.

The application fee for registering is $325 per class.

Copyrights

Source: Excerpted from *Copyright Basics (Circular 1),* U.S. Copyright Office.

Copyright is a form of protection provided by the laws of the United States to the creators of "original works of authorship," including literary, dramatic, musical, artistic, and certain other intellectual works. This protection is available to both published and unpublished works. The 1976 Copyright Act generally gives the owner of a copyright the exclusive right to do and to authorize others to do the following:
• to reproduce the copyrighted work in copies or phonorecords;
• to prepare derivative works based upon the copyrighted work;
• to distribute copies or phonorecords of the copyrighted work to the public by sale or other transfer of ownership, or by rental, lease, or lending;
• to perform and/or display the copyrighted work publicly; and
• in the case of sound recordings, to perform the work publicly by means of a digital audio transmission.

It is illegal for anyone to violate these rights. However, these rights are not unlimited in scope. In some cases they are limited by the doctrine of "fair use," or by a "compulsory license" under which certain limited uses of copyrighted works are permitted in exchange for payment.

What Works Are Protected

Copyright protects "original works of authorship" that are fixed in a tangible form of expression. The fixation need not be directly perceptible so long as it may be communicated with the aid of a machine or device. Categories include:
• literary works;
• musical works, including any accompanying words;
• dramatic works, including any accompanying music;
• pantomimes and choreographic works;
• pictorial, graphic, and sculptural works;
• motion pictures and other audiovisual works;
• sound recordings; and
• architectural works.

These categories should be viewed quite broadly. For example, computer programs and most "compilations" are registrable as "literary works." Maps and architectural plans are registrable as "pictorial, graphic, and sculptural works."

What Is Not Protected

Several categories of material are generally not eligible for federal copyright protection. These include, among others:
• works that have not been fixed in a tangible form of expression—for example, choreographic works that have not been notated or recorded, or improvisational speeches or performances that have not been written or recorded;
• titles, names, short phrases, and slogans; familiar symbols or designs; mere variations of typographic ornamentation, lettering, or coloring; mere listings of ingredients or contents;
• ideas, procedures, methods, systems, processes, concepts, principles, discoveries, or devices, as distinguished from descriptions, explanations, or illustrations;
• works consisting entirely of information that is common property and containing no original authorship—for example, standard calendars, height and weight charts, tape measures and rulers, and lists or tables taken from public documents or other common sources.

U.S. Societies and Associations

Names are listed alphabetically according to key word in title; figure in parentheses is year of founding; other figure is membership.

The following is a partial list selected for general readership interest. For a more thorough list, *see* www.infoplease.com/ipa/A0004878. A comprehensive listing of approximately 23,000 national and international organizations can be found in the *Encyclopedia of Associations*, 41st ed., 2004, published by Gale Research Company, 835 Penobscot Building, 645 Griswold St., Detroit, Mich. 48226-4049, available in most public libraries.

AARP (American Association of Retired Persons) (1958): 601 E. St. N.W., Washington, D.C. 20049. 33,000,000. Phone: (888) 687-2277. www.aarp.org.

Abortion Federation, National (1977): 1755 Mass. Ave., Ste. 600, Washington, D.C. 20036. Phone: (202) 667-5881. www.prochoice.org.

Accountants, American Institute of Certified Public (1887): 1211 Avenue of the Americas, New York, N.Y. 10036-8775. 330,000. Phone: (212) 596-6200. www.aicpa.org.

ACSM: American Congress on Surveying and Mapping (1941): 6 Montgomery Village Ave., Ste. 403, Gaithersburg, Md. 20879. 8,000. Phone: (240) 632-9716. www.acsm.net.

Actors' Equity Association (1913): 165 W. 46th St., New York, N.Y. 10036. 40,000. Phone: (212) 869-8530. www.actorsequity.org.

Actuaries, Society of (1949): 475 N. Martingale, #600, Schaumburg, Ill. 60173-2226. 16,500. Phone: (847) 706-3500. www.soa.org.

Adirondack Mountain Club (1922): 814 Goggins Rd., Lake George, N.Y. 12845-4117. 22,000. Phone: (518) 668-4447. www.adk.org.

Aeronautic Association, National (1905): 1737 King Street, Ste. 220, Alexandria, Va. 22314. 300,000. Phone: (703) 527-0226. www.naa.aero.

Africa-American Institute, The (1953): 420 Lexington Ave., Ste. 1706, New York, N.Y. 10170-0002. Phone: (212) 949-5666. www.aaionline.org/

AFS Intercultural Programs—USA (American Field Service) (1947): 71 W. 23rd St., 17th Fl., New York, N.Y. 10010. 100,000. Phone: (212) 807-8686. www.afs.org.

Agricultural History Society (1919): University of Arkansas at Little Rock/Department of History, 2801 S. University Ave., Little Rock, Ark. 72204-1099. 1,400. Phone: (501) 569-8782. http://agriculturalhistory.ualr.edu/.

Agronomy, American Society of (1907): 677 S. Segoe Rd., Madison, Wis. 53711-1086. 11,400. Phone: (608) 273-8080; fax: (608) 273-2021. www.agronomy.org.

Air & Waste Management Association (1907): One Gateway Center, 3rd Flr., Pittsburgh, Pa. 15222. 14,000. Phone: (412) 232-3444. www.awma.org.

Aircraft Association, Experimental (1953): EAA Aviation Center, P.O. Box 3086, Oshkosh, Wis. 54903-3086. 170,000. Phone: (920) 426-4800. www.eaa.org.

Aircraft Owners and Pilots Association (1939): 421 Aviation Way, Frederick, Md. 21701-4798. 350,000. Phone: (301) 695-2000; fax: (301) 695-2375. www.aopa.org.

Air Force Association (1946): 1501 Lee Highway, Arlington, Va. 22209-1198. 150,000. Phone: (703) 247-5800. www.afa.org.

Air Line Pilots Association (1931): 1625 Massachusetts Ave. NW, Washington, DC 20036. 50,000. Phone: (703) 689-2270. www.alpa.org.

Al-Anon Family Group Headquarters, Inc. For families and friends of alcoholics. (1951): 1600 Corporate Landing Pkwy., Virginia Beach, Va. 23454-5617. 33,000 groups worldwide. Phone: (757) 563-1600. www.al-anon.org.

Alcoholics Anonymous (1935): A.A. World Services, Inc., P.O. Box 459, New York, N.Y. 10163. 2,160,013. Phone: (212) 870-3400. www.aa.org.

Alexander Graham Bell Association for the Deaf (1890): 3417 Volta Place N.W., Washington, D.C. 20007-2778. 6,200. Phone: (202) 337-5220 V, 337-5221 TTY; fax: (202) 337-8314. www.agbell.org.

Alzheimer's Association (1980): 225 N. Michigan Ave., Ste. 1700, Chicago, Ill. 60601-7633. 200 chapters. Phone: (312) 335-8700; (800) 272-3900. www.alz.org.

American Academy of Allergy, Asthma and Immunology (1943): 611 E. Wells St., Milwaukee, Wis. 53202. 5,000. Phone: (414) 272-6071. www.aaaai.org.

American Alliance for Health, Physical Education, Recreation and Dance (1885): 1900 Association Dr., Reston, Va. 20191. 26,000. Phone: (800) 213-7193. www.aahperd.org.

American Automobile Association (1902): 1000 AAA Dr., Heathrow, Fla. 32746-5063. Phone: (407) 444-7000. www.aaa.com.

American Civil Liberties Union (1920): 125 Broad St., 18th Flr., New York, N.Y. 10004-2400. 275,000. Phone: (212) 549-2500. www.aclu.org.

American Contract Bridge League (1927): 2990 Airways Blvd., Memphis, Tenn. 38116-3847. Phone: (901) 332-5586; fax: (901) 398-7754. www.acbl.org.

American Federation of Labor and Congress of Industrial Organizations (AFL-CIO) (1955): 815 16th St. N.W., Washington, D.C. 20006. 13,000,000. Phone: (202) 637-5000. www.aflcio.org.

American Federation of Musicians of the United States and Canada (1896): 1501 Broadway, Ste. 600, New York, N.Y. 10036. Phone: (212) 869-1330. www.afm.org.

American Forests (1875): P.O. Box 2000, Washington, D.C. 20013. 115,000. Phone: (202) 737-1944. www.americanforests.org.

American Foundry Society, Inc. (1896): 1695 North Penny Lane, Schaumburg, Ill. 60173-4555. 13,000. Phone: (800) 537-4237. www.afsinc.org.

American Friends Service Committee (1917): 1501 Cherry St., Philadelphia, Pa. 19102-1479. Phone: (215) 241-7000. www.afsc.org.

American Geographical Society, The (1851): 120 Wall St., Ste. 100, New York, N.Y. 10005-3904. 1,500. Phone: (212) 422-5456; fax: (212) 422-5480. email: amgeosoc@amergeog.org. www.amergeog.org.

American Geriatrics Society (1942): 350 Fifth Ave., Ste. 801, New York, N.Y. 10118. 6,000. Phone: (212) 308-1414; fax: (212) 832-8646. www.americangeriatrics.org.

American Heart Association (1924): 7272 Greenville Ave., Dallas, Tex. 75231-4596. 4,200,000 volunteers. Phone: (800) AHA-USA1. www.americanheart.org.

American Historical Association (1884): 400 A St. S.E., Washington, D.C. 20003-3889. 15,000. Phone: (202) 544-2422. www.historians.org.

American Indian Affairs, Association on (1923): 966 Hungerford Dr., Ste. 12-B, Rockville, Md. 20850. 40,000. Phone: (240) 314-7155. www.indian-affairs.org.

American Jewish Committee (1906): P.O. Box 705, New York, N.Y. 10105. 100,000. Phone: (212) 751-4000. www.ajc.org.

American Kennel Club (1884): 260 Madison Ave., New York, N.Y. 10016. 500+ member clubs. Phone: (212) 696-8200; (919) 233-9767 (customer service). www.akc.org.

American Legion, The (1919): 700 N. Pennsylvania St., Indianapolis, Ind. 46206. 3,000,000. Phone: (317) 630-1200. www.legion.org.

American Legion Auxiliary (1919): 777 N. Meridian St., 3rd Flr., Indianapolis, Ind. 46204. 1,000,000. Phone: (317) 955-3845. www.legion-aux.org.

American Mensa, Ltd. (1960): 1229 Corporate Drive West, Arlington, Tex. 76006–6103. 50,000. Phone: (817) 607-0060. www.us.mensa.org.

American Montessori Society (1960): 281 Park Avenue South, 6th Flr., New York, N.Y. 10010-6102. Phone: (212) 358-1250; fax: (212) 358-1256. www.amshq.org.

American Museum of Natural History (1869): Central Park West at 79th St., New York, N.Y. 10024-5192. 500,000. Phone: (212) 769-5606. www.amnh.org.

American Planning Association (1917) and American Institute of Certified Planners: Administrative Offices: 122 S. Michigan Ave., Chicago, Ill. 60603. 30,000. Phone: (312) 431-9100. www.planning.org.

Americans for Democratic Action, Inc. (1947): 1625 K St. N.W., Ste. 210, Washington, D.C. 20006. 70,000. Phone: (202) 785-5980. www.adaction.org.

American Society for Nutritional Sciences (1928): 9650 Rockville Pike, Ste. 4500, Bethesda, Md. 20814-3990. 3,600. Phone: (301) 530-7050. www.asns.org.

American Society for Public Administration (ASPA) (1939): 1120 G St. N.W., Ste. 700, Washington, D.C. 20005. 12,000. Phone: (202) 393-7878. www.aspanet.org.

American Universities, Association of (1900): 1200 New York Avenue NW, Ste. 550, Washington, D.C. 20005. Phone: (202) 408-7500. www.aau.edu.

American Water Resources Association (1964): 4 W. Federal St., P.O. Box 1626, Middleburg, Va. 20118-1626. Phone: (540) 687-8390. www.awra.org.

Amnesty International USA (1961): 5 Penn Plaza, New York, N.Y. 10001. 300,000. Phone: (212) 807-8400. www.amnestyusa.org.

AMVETS (American Veterans of World War II, Korea, and Vietnam) (1943): 4647 Forbes Blvd., Lanham, Md. 20706-4380. 250,000. Phone: (877) 7AMVETS. www.amvets.org.

Animals, The American Society for the Prevention of Cruelty to (ASPCA) (1866): 424 E. 92nd St., New York, N.Y. 10128-6804. 400,000+. Phone: (212) 876-7700. www.aspca.org.

Animals, The Fund For, Inc. (1967): 200 W. 57th St., New York, N.Y. 10019. 175,000. Phone: (212) 246-2096. www.fundforanimals.org.

Anthropological Association, American (1902): 2200 Wilson Blvd., Ste. 600, Arlington, Va. 22201. 11,500. Phone: (703) 528-1902. www.aaanet.org.

Anti-Defamation League (1913): 823 United Nations Plaza, New York, N.Y. 10017-3560. Phone: (212) 885-7700. www.adl.org.

Anti-Vivisection Society, The American (1883): 801 Old York Rd., #204, Jenkintown, Pa. 19046-1685. 15,000. Phone: (215) 887-0816; fax: (215) 887-2088. www.aavs.org.

Appraisers, American Society of (1936): 555 Herndon Parkway, Ste. 125, Herndon, Va. 20170. 6,500. Phone: (703) 478-2228. www.appraisers.org.

Arboriculture, International Society of (1924): P.O. Box 3129, Champaign, Ill. 61826-3129. 8,000.

Phone: (217) 355-9411; fax (217) 355-9516. email: isa@isa-arbor.com. www.isa-arbor.com/.

Archaeological Institute of America (1879): 656 Beacon St., Boston, Mass. 02215-2006. 11,000. Phone: (617) 353-9361. email: aia@aai.bu.edu. www.archaeological.org.

Architects, The American Institute of (1857): 1735 New York Ave. N.W., Washington, D.C. 20006-5292. 59,000. Phone: (202) 626-7300. www.aia.org.

Architectural Historians, Society of (1940): 1365 N. Astor St., Chicago, Ill. 60610-2144. 4,000. Phone: (312) 573-1365; fax: (312) 573-1141. www.sah.org.

Army, Association of the United States (1950): 2425 Wilson Blvd., Arlington, Va. 22201-3385. 100,000+. Phone: (800) 336-4570. www.ausa.org.

Arthritis Foundation (1948): P.O. Box 7669, Atlanta, Ga. 30357-0669. Over 150 local offices. Phone: (800) 283-7800. www.arthritis.org.

Arts, National Endowment for the (1965): 1100 Pennsylvania Ave. N.W., Washington, D.C. 20506. Phone: (202) 682-5400. arts.endow.gov.

ASM International ® (formerly the American Society for Metals) (1913): 9639 Kinsman Rd., Materials Park, Ohio 44073-0002. 44,000. Phone: (440) 338-5151; fax: (440) 338-4634. www.asm-intl.org.

Association for Investment Management and Research (1990): 560 Ray C. Hunt Dr., Charlottesville, Va. 22903-0668. 36,000. Phone: (800) 247-8132. www.aimr.com.

Astronomical Society, American (1899): 2000 Florida Ave., Ste. 400, Washington, D.C. 20009. 6,300. Phone: (202) 328-2010. www.aas.org.

Atheists, American (1963): P.O. Box 5733, Parsippany, N.J. 07054-6733. 40,000 families. Phone: (908) 276-7300. www.atheists.org.

Auctioneers Association, National (1949): 8880 Ballentine, Overland Park, Kan. 66214. 6,500. Phone: (913) 541-8084; fax: (913) 894-5281; email: publicrelations@auctioneers.org; www.auctioneers.org.

Audubon Society, National (1905): 700 Broadway, New York, N.Y. 10003-9562. 550,000. Phone: (212) 979-3000. www.audubon.org.

Authors League of America (1912): 330 W. 42nd St., 29th Flr., New York, N.Y. 10036-6902. 14,000. Phone: (212) 268-1208.

Autism Society of America (1965): 7910 Woodmont Ave., Ste. 300, Bethesda, Md. 20814-3067. 18,000+. Phone: (301) 657-0881; (800) 3AUTISM. www.autism-society.org.

Automobile Club, National (1924): 1151 East Hillsdale Blvd., Foster City, Calif. 94404. 200,000. Phone: (650) 294-7000. www.nationalautoclub.com.

Bar Association, American (1878): 321 North Clark Street, Chicago, Ill. 60610. 371,000. Phone: (312) 988-5000. www.abanet.org.

Barber Shop Quartet Singing in America, Society for the Preservation and Encouragement of (SPEBSQSA, Inc.) (1938): 7930 Sheridan Rd., Kenosha, Wis. 53143. 34,000. Phone: (800) 876-SING. www.spebsqsa.org.

Better Business Bureaus, Council of (1912): 4200 Wilson Blvd., Ste. 800, Arlington, Va. 22203-1838. Phone: (703) 276-0100; fax: (703) 525-8277. www.bbb.org.

Bible Society, American (1816): 1865 Broadway, New York, N.Y. 10023-7505. Phone: (800) 32-BIBLE; (212) 408-1200. www.americanbible.org.

Biblical Literature, Society of (1880): 825 Houston Mill Road, Ste. 350, Atlanta, Ga. 30329. 7,000 members, 1,200 subscribers. Phone: (404) 727-3100; fax: (404) 727-3101. www.sbl-site.org.

Big Brothers Big Sisters of America (1977): 230 N. 13th St., Philadelphia, Pa. 19107. Phone: (215) 567-7000. www.bbbsa.org.

Biochemistry and Molecular Biology, American Society for (1906): 9650 Rockville Pike, Bethesda, Md. 20814. 10,000. Phone: (301) 530-7145. www.asbmb.org.

Biological Sciences, American Institute of (1947): 1444 I St. N.W., Ste. 200, Washington, D.C. 20005. 6,000. Phone: (202) 628-1500. www.aibs.org.

Blind, American Council of the (1961): 1155 15th St. N.W., Ste. 1004, Washington, D.C. 20005. 40,000. Phone: (202) 467-5081. www.acb.org.

Blind, National Federation of the (1940): 1800 Johnson St., Baltimore, Md. 21230. 50,000. Phone: (410) 659-9314. www.nfb.org.

B'nai B'rith International (1843): 2020 K St. N.W., Washington, D.C. 20006. 500,000. Phone: (202) 857-6600. www.bnaibrith.org.

Booksellers Association, American (1900): 828 So. Broadway, Tarrytown, N.Y. 10591. 4,500. Phone: (914) 591-2665, (800) 637-0037. www.bookweb.org.

Boys & Girls Clubs of America (1906): 1230 West Peachtree St. N.W., Atlanta, Ga., 30309. 2,800,000 youth served. Phone: (404) 487-5700. www.bgca.org.

Boy Scouts of America (1910): 1325 W. Walnut Hill Lane, P.O. Box 152079, Irving, Tex. 75015-2079. 4.8 mil. www.scouting.org.

Brady Campaign, The (1974) (formerly Handgun Control, Inc.): 1225 Eye St. N.W., Ste. 1100, Washington, D.C. 20005. 380,000. Phone: (202) 898-0792. www.bradycampaign.org.

Broadcasters, National Association of (1922): 1771 N St. N.W., Washington, D.C. 20036-2891. Phone: (202) 429-5300. www.nab.org.

Brookings Institution, The (1916): 1775 Massachusetts Ave. N.W., Washington, D.C. 20036-2188. Phone: (202) 797-6000. www.brookings.org.

Business Education Association, National (1946): 1914 Association Dr., Reston, Va. 20191-1596. 16,000. Phone: (703) 860-8300; fax: (703) 620-4483. email: nbea@nbea.org; www.nbea.org.

Business Women's Association, American (1949): 9100 Ward Parkway, P.O. Box 8728, Kansas City, Mo. 64114-0728. 80,000. Phone: (800) 228-0007. fax: (816) 361-4991. email: abwa@abwahq.org. www.abwahq.org.

Camp Fire USA (1910): 4601 Madison Ave., Kansas City, Mo. 64112-1278. 629,000. Phone: (816) 756-1950. www.campfire.org.

Camping Association, The American (1910): 5000 State Rd. 67 N., Martinsville, Ind. 46151-7902. 5,500, 2,000+ camps. Phone: (765) 342-8456. www.acacamps.org.

Cancer Society, American (1913): 1599 Clifton Rd. N.E., Atlanta, Ga. 30329. Over 2 million volunteers. Phone: (800) ACS-2345 or check local listings. www.cancer.org.

CARE, Inc. (1945): 151 Ellis St. NE, Atlanta, Ga. 30303-2439. Programs in 62 developing countries. Phone: (404) 681-2552. www.care.org.

Carnegie Endowment for International Peace (1910): 1779 Massachusetts Ave., N.W., Washington, D.C. 20036–2103. Phone: (202) 483-7600; fax: (202) 483-1840. www.carnegieendowment.org.

Catholic Charities USA (1910): 1731 King St., Ste. 200, Alexandria, Va. 22314. 1,400 agencies and institutions. Phone: (703) 549-1390. www.catholiccharitiesusa.org.

Catholic Daughters of the Americas (1903): 10 W. 71st St., New York, N.Y. 10023. 115,000. Phone: (212) 877-3041. www.catholicdaughters.org

Catholic War Veterans of the U.S.A. Inc. (1935): 441 N. Lee St., Alexandria, Va. 22314. 35,000. Phone: (703) 549-3622. www.cwv.org.

Cerebral Palsy Associations, Inc., United (1949): 1660 L St. N.W., Ste. 700, Washington, D.C. 20036. 153 affiliates. Phone: (800) USA-5-UCP, (202) 776-0406, TTY (202) 973-7197. www.ucp.org.

Chamber of Commerce of the U.S. (1912): 1615 H St. N.W., Washington, D.C. 20062. 220,000. Phone: (202) 659-6000. www.uschamber.com.

Chemical Engineers, American Institute of (1908): 3 Park Ave., New York, N.Y. 10016-5991. 52,000. Phone: (212) 591-8100; (800) 242-4363. www.aiche.org.

Chemical Society, American (1876): 1155 16th St. N.W., Washington, D.C. 20036. 151,024. Phone: (800) 227-5558. www.chemistry.org.

Chess Federation, United States (1939): P.O. Box 3967, Crossville, Tenn. 38557. 50,000+. Phone: (931) 787-1234. www.uschess.org.

Child Labor Committee, National (1904): 1501 Broadway, Ste. 403, New York, N.Y. 10036. Phone: (212) 840-1801. www.kapow.org.

Children's Book Council (1945): 12 W. 37th St., 2nd Fl., New York, N.Y. 10018-7480. Phone: (212) 966-1990; fax: (212) 966-2073. email: staff@cbcbooks.org. www.cbcbooks.org.

Child Welfare League of America (1920): 440 First St. N.W., 3rd Fl., Washington, D.C. 20001-2085. 1,000 agencies. Phone: (202) 638-2952. www.cwla.org.

Chiropractic Association, American (1963): 1701 Clarendon Blvd., Arlington, Va. 22209. 22,000. Phone: (800) 986-4636; fax: (703) 243-2593. www.amerchiro.org.

Cities, National League of (1924): 1301 Pennsylvania Ave. N.W., Washington, D.C. 20004-1763. 18,000 cities and towns. Phone: (202) 626-3000. www.nlc.org.

Civil Air Patrol, National Headquarters (1941): 105 S. Hansell St., Bldg. 714, Maxwell AFB, Ala. 36112-6332. 53,000. Phone: (334) 953-4287. www.cap.gov.

Civil Engineers, American Society of (1852): 1801 Alexander Bell Dr., Reston, Va. 20191-4400. 123,000. Phone: (800) 548–ASCE (2723); (703) 295-6300. www.asce.org.

Clinical Pathologists, American Society of (1922): 2100 W. Harrison St., Chicago, Ill. 60612. 77,200. Phone: (312) 738-1336. www.ascp.org.

College Fund, United Negro (UNCF) (1944): 8260 Willow Oaks Corporate Dr., P.O. Box 10444, Fairfax, Va. 22031. 39 member institutions. Phone: (703) 205-3400, (800) 331-2244; fax: (703) 205-3576. www.uncf.org.

Colleges and Employers, National Association of (formerly College Placement Council) (1956): 62 Highland Ave., Bethlehem, Pa. 18017. 3,200. Phone: (800) 544-5272. www.naceweb.org.

Common Cause (1970): 1250 Connecticut Ave. N.W., Washington, D.C. 20036. 250,000. Phone: (202) 833-1200. www.commoncause.org.

Composers/USA, National Association of (1933): P.O. Box 49256, Barrington Station, Los Angeles, Calif. 90049. 600. Phone: (310) 541-8213. www.music-usa.org/nacusa/.

Congress of Racial Equality (CORE) (1942): 817 Broadway, 3rd Flr., New York, N.Y. 10003. Nationwide network of chapters. Phone: (212) 598-4000; fax: (212) 598-4141. www.core-online.org.

Conscientious Objectors, Central Committee for (1948): 1515 Cherry St., Philadelphia, Pa. 19102. Phone: (215) 563-8787.   405 14th St., #205, Oakland, Calif. 94612. Phone: (510) 465-1617. www.objector.org.

Conservation Engineers, Association of (1961): John Bruner, Box 21562, Cheyenne, Wyo. 82003. Phone: (307) 775-9269. www.conservation.state.mo.us/engineering/ace.

Consumer Federation of America (1968): 1424 16th St. N.W., Ste. 604, Washington, D.C. 20036. 260 member organizations. Phone: (202) 387-6121. www.consumerfed.org.

Consumers League, National (1899): 1701 K St. N.W., Ste. 1200, Washington, D.C. 20006. Phone: (202) 835-3323. www.natlconsumersleague.org.

Consumers Union (1936): 101 Truman Ave., Yonkers, N.Y. 10703-1057. 4.6 million subscribers to *Consumer Reports Magazine.* Phone: (914) 378-2000. www.consumersunion.org.

Country Music Association (1958): One Music Circle South, Nashville, Tenn. 37203. 6,000. Phone: (615) 244-2840. www.cmaworld.com.

Credit Management, National Association of (1896): 8840 Columbia 100 Parkway, Columbia, Md. 21045-2158. 30,000+ members. Phone: (410) 740-5560. www.nacm.org.

Credit Union National Association (1934): P.O. Box 431, Madison, Wis. 53701-0431. 51 state leagues representing 12,400 credit unions. Phone: (800) 356-9655. www.cuna.org.

Crime and Delinquency, National Council on (1907): 1970 Broadway, Ste. 500, Oakland, Calif. 94612. Phone: (510) 208-0500. www.nccd-crc.org.

CSA/USA, Celiac Sprue Association/United States of America, Inc., (1978): P.O. Box 31700, Omaha, Neb. 68131-0700. 6 regions in U.S., 74 chapters, 36 active resource units. Phone: (877) CSA-4CSA; fax: (402) 558-1347. www.csaceliacs.org.

Dairy Council, National (1915): 10255 W. Higgins Rd. Ste. 900, Rosemont, Ill. 60018. www.nationaldairycouncil.org.

Daughters of the American Revolution, National Society (1896): 1776 D St. N.W., Washington, D.C. 20006-5303. 172,000. Phone: (202) 628-1776. www.dar.org.

Deaf, National Association of the (1880): 814 Thayer Ave., Silver Spring, Md. 20910-4500. 51 state association affiliates. Phone: (301) 587-1788 V; (301) 587-1789 TTY. www.nad.org.

Defenders of Wildlife (1947): 1130 17th St. N.W., Washington, D.C. 20030. 200,000 members and supporters. Phone: (202) 682-9400. www.defenders.org.

Dental Association, American (1859): 211 E. Chicago Ave., Chicago, Ill. 60611. 141,000. Phone: (312) 440-2500. www.ada.org.

Diabetes Association, American (1940): 1701 N. Beauregard St., Alexandria, Va. 22311. Phone: (703) 549-1500; (800) 342-2383. www.diabetes.org/.

Dignity (1969): 1500 Massachusetts Ave. N.W., Ste. 8, Washington, D.C. 20005. 5,000. Phone: (202) 861-0017 and (800) 877-8797. www.dignityusa.org.

Disabled American Veterans (1920): 3725 Alexandria Pike, Cold Spring, Ky. 41076. 1,400,000. Phone: (859) 441-7300. www.dav.org.

Dowsers, Inc., The American Society of (1961): P.O. Box 24, Danville, Vt. 05828. 5,000. Phone: (800) 711-9530. email: ASD@dowsers.org. www.dowsers.org.

Ducks Unlimited, Inc. (1937): One Waterfowl Way, Memphis, Tenn. 38120. 600,000. Phone: (800) 45DUCKS. www.ducks.org.

Earthwatch (1971): 3 Clock Tower Place, Ste. 100, Box 75, Maynard, Mass. 01754. 75,000. Phone: (978) 461-0081. www.earthwatch.org.

Eastern Star, Order of, General Grand Chapter (1876): 1618 New Hampshire Ave. N.W., Washington, D.C. 20009-2549. 1,207,301. Phone: (202) 667-4737. www.easternstar.org.

Easter Seal Society, The National (1919): 230 W. Monroe, Ste. 1800, Chicago, Ill. 60606. 109 state and local affiliate societies operating 500 service sites. Phone: (312) 726-6200; (312) 726-4258 TTY. www.easter-seals.org.

Economic Association, American (1885): 2014 Broadway, Ste. 305, Nashville, Tenn. 37203. 22,000. 5,500 inst. subscribers. Phone: (615) 322-2595. www.vanderbilt.edu/AEA.

Edison Electric Institute (1933): 701 Pennsylvania Ave. N.W., Washington, D.C. 20004-2696. Phone: (202) 508-5000. www.eei.org.

Education, American Council on (ACE), (1918): One Dupont Circle N.W., Washington, D.C. 20036-1193.

1,600+ colleges and universities and 200+ higher education associations. Phone: (202) 939-9300. www.acenet.edu.

Educational Exchange, Council on International (1947): 7 Custom House St., 3rd Fl., Portland, Maine 04101. Phone: (800) 40-STUDY. www.ciee.org.

Educational Research Association, American (1916): 1230 17th St. N.W., Washington, D.C. 20036-3078. 22,000. Phone: (202) 223-9485. www.aera.net.

Education Association, National (1857): 1201 16th St. N.W., Washington, D.C. 20036-3290. 2.3 million. Phone: (202) 833-4000. www.nea.org.

Electrochemical Society, The (1902): 65 S. Main St., Pennington, N.J. 08534-2839. 7,000. Phone: (609) 737-1902; fax: (609) 737-2743. email: ecs@electrochem.org. www.electrochem.org.

Elks of the U.S.A., Benevolent and Protective Order of the (1868): 2750 N. Lakeview Ave., Chicago, Ill. 60614-1889. 1,300,000. Phone: (773) 755-4700. www.elks.org/default.cfm.

Energy Engineers, Association of (1977): 4025 Pleasantdale Rd., Ste. 420, Atlanta, Ga. 30340. 8,500. Phone: (770) 447-5083; fax: (770) 446-3969. email: info@aeecenter.org. www.aeecenter.org.

English-Speaking Union of the United States (1920): 144 E. 39th St., New York, N.Y. 10016. 18,000. Phone: (212) 817-1200. www.english-speakingunion.org.

Entomological Society of America (1889): 10001 Derekwood Lane, Ste. 100, Lanham, Md. 20706-4876. 7,400+. Phone: (301) 731-4535; fax: (301) 731-4538. email: esa@entsoc.org. www.entsoc.org.

Esperanto League for North America, The (1952): P.O. Box 1129, El Cerrito, Calif. 94530. Over 1,000. Phone: (800) 377-3726. www.esperanto-usa.org.

Equestrian Federation, United States (formerly American Horse Shows Association, Inc. and United States Equestrian Team) (1917): 4047 Iron Works Parkway, Lexington, Ky. 40511. 70,000+. Phone: (859) 258-2472. www.usef.org.

Exceptional Children, The Council for (1922): 1110 N. Glebe Rd., Ste. 300, Arlington, Va. 22201-5704. 54,000. Phone: (703) 620-3660 V; (703) 264-9446 TTY; fax: (703) 264-9494. email: cec@cec.sped.org. www.cec.sped.org.

Exploration Geophysicists, Society of (1930): 8801 South Yale, Tulsa, Okla. 74137-3575. 16,536. Phone: (918) 497-5500. www.seg.org.

Family and Consumer Sciences, American Association of (1909): 400 N. Columbus St., Ste. 202, Alexandria, Va. 22314. 14,500. Phone: (703) 706-4600. www.aafcs.org.

Family Campers & RVers (1949): 4804 Transit Rd., Bldg. 2, Depew, N.Y. 14043. Phone: (800) 245-9755. 42,000 families. www.fcrv.org.

Family, Career, and Community Leaders of America [evolved from Future Homemakers of America, Inc. (1945)]: 1910 Association Dr., Reston, Va. 20191-1584. 230,000. Phone: (703) 476-4900. www.fhahero.org.

Family Physicians, American Academy of (1947): 11400 Tomahawk Creek Pkwy., Leawood, Kans. 66211-2672. 88,000. Phone: (913) 906-6000. www.aafp.org.

Family Relations, National Council on (1938): 3989 Central Ave. N.E., #550, Minneapolis, Minn. 55421. 42,000 families. Phone: (888) 781-9331. www.ncfr.com.

Farm Bureau Federation, American (1919): 600 Maryland Ave., S.W., Ste. 800, Washington, D.C. 20024. 4.7 million member families. Phone: (202) 406-3600. www.fb.com.

Federal Bar Association (1920): 2215 M St. N.W., Washington, D.C. 20037. 15,000. Phone: (202) 785-1614; fax: (202) 785-1568. www.fedbar.org.

Federal Employees, National Federation of (1917): 1016 16th St. N.W., Washington, D.C. 20036. 150,000. Phone: (202) 862-4400. www.nffe.org.

Fellowship of Reconciliation (1915): 521 N. Broadway, Nyack, N.Y. 10960. 20,000. Phone: (845) 358-4601. www.forusa.org.

Female Executives, National Association for (1972): P.O. Box 3052, Langhorne, Pa. 19047. 150,000+. Phone: (800) 927-NAFE. www.nafe.com.

FFA Organization, National (1928): P.O. Box 68960, 6060 FFA Dr., Indianapolis, Ind. 46268. 457,278. Phone: (317) 802-6060. www.ffa.org.

Fire Protection Association, National (1896): One Batterymarch Park, Quincy, Mass. 02169-7471. 65,000+. Phone: (617) 770-3000. www.nfpa.org.

Flag Foundation, National (1968): Flag Plaza, 1275 Bedford Ave, Pittsburgh, Pa. 15219. 3,000+. Phone: (412) 261-1776. www.americanflags.org.

Fleet Reserve Association (1924): 125 N. West St., Alexandria, Va. 22314-2754. 162,000. Phone: (703) 683-1400. www.fra.org.

Foreign Policy Association (1918): 470 Park Ave. So., New York, N.Y. 10016-6819. Phone: (212) 481-8100. www.fpa.org.

Foreign Relations, Council on (1921): 58 E. 68th St., New York, N.Y. 10021. 3,400. Phone: (212) 434-9400. www.cfr.org.

Foreign Study, American Institute for (1964): River Plaza, 9 W. Broad St., Stamford, Conn. 06902-3788. Phone: (800) 727-2437. www.aifs.org.

Forensic Sciences, American Academy of (1948): 410 N. 21st St., Ste. 203., P.O. Box 669, Colorado Springs, Colo. 80901-0669. 4,315. Phone: (719) 636-1100; fax: (719) 636-1993. www.aafs.org.

Foresters, Society of American (1900): 5400 Grosvenor Lane, Bethesda, Md. 20814. 18,000. Phone: (301) 897-8720. www.safnet.org.

4-H Program (early 1900s): 1400 Independence Ave., S.W., Washington, D.C. 20250. 5.6 million. Phone: (202) 720-2908. www.4husa.org/.

Freedom of Information Center (1958): 133 Neff Annex, Univ. of Missouri, Columbia, Mo. 65211. Phone: (573) 882-4856. www.missouri.edu/~foiwww/

French Institute/Alliance Française (1898): 111 East 59th Street, New York, N.Y 10022. 9,000. Phone: (212) 355-6100. www.fiaf.org.

Friends of Animals Inc. (1957): 777 Post Rd., Darien, Conn. 06820. 120,000. Phone: (203) 656-1522. www.friendsofanimals.org/.

Friends of the Earth (1969): 1717 Massachusetts Avenue, N.W., Ste. 600, Washington, D.C. 20036-2002. 35,000. Phone: (877) 843-8687. www.foe.org.

Gamblers Anonymous: Box 17173, Los Angeles, Calif. 90017. Phone: (213) 386-8789. www.gamblersanonymous.org.

Gay and Lesbian Task Force, National (1973): 1325 Massachusetts Ave. N.W., Ste. 600, Washington, D.C. 20005. 35,000 members. Phone: (202) 393-5177. www.thetaskforce.org.

Genealogical Society, National (1903): 3108 Columbia Pike, Ste. 300, Arlington, Va. 22204-4304. 17,000+. Phone: (703) 525-0050; fax: (703) 525-0052. www.ngsgenealogy.org.

Geographers, Association of American (1904): 1710 16th St. N.W., Washington, D.C. 20009-3198. 7,000. Phone: (202) 234-1450; fax: (202) 234-2744. email: gaia@aag.org. www.aag.org.

Geographic Education, National Council for (1915): 206A Martin Hall, Jacksonville State University, Jacksonville, Ala. 36265-1602. 3,700. Phone: (256) 782-5293. www.ncge.org.

Geographic Society, National (1888): 1145 17th St. N.W., Washington, D.C. 20036-4688. 9,200,000. Phone: (800) 647-5463. www.nationalgeographic.com.

Geological Institute, American (1948): 4220 King St., Alexandria, Va. 22302-1502. 34 geoscience societies representing 100,000 geoscientists. Phone: (703) 379-2480. www.agiweb.org/.

Geological Society of America, Inc. (1888): P.O. Box 9140, Boulder, Colo. 80301-9140. 15,000. Phone: (303) 447-2020. www.geosociety.org.

German American National Congress, The (Deutsch-Amerikanischer National Kongress— D.A.N.K.) (1958): 4740 N. Western Ave., Chicago, Ill. 60625-2097. Phone: (773) 275-1100. www.dank.org.

Gideons International, The (1889): P.O. Box 140800, Nashville, Tenn. 37214-0800. 130,000. Phone: (615) 883-8533. www.gideons.org.

Gifted, The Association for the (1958): Oklahoma State Univ., 424 Willard Hall, Stillwater, Okla. 74078-3031. Phone: (405) 744-9441. www.cectag.org

Girl Scouts of the U.S.A. (1912): 420 Fifth Ave., New York, N.Y. 10018-2798. 2,500,000. Phone: (212) 852-8000. www.girlscouts.org.

Girls Incorporated (1945): 120 Wall St., 3rd. Flr., New York, N.Y. 10005. 350,000. Phone: (800) 374-4475. www.girlsinc.org.

Graphoanalysis Society, International (1929): 842 Fifth Ave., New Kensington, Pa. 15068. 10,000. Phone: (724) 472-9701. www.igas.com.

Gray Panthers (1970): 733 15th St. N.W., Ste. 437, Washington, D.C. 20005. Over 50 chapters (networks). Phone: (202) 737-1160. www.graypanthers.org.

Greenpeace (1971): 702 H St. N.W., Washington, D.C. 20001. 2.5 million. Phone: (800) 326-0959. www.greenpeaceusa.org.

Guide Dog Foundation for the Blind, Inc. (1946): 371 E. Jericho Turnpike, Smithtown, N.Y. 11787-2976. 100,000. Phone: (631) 265-2121; (800) 548-4337; fax: (631) 361-5192. www.guidedog.org.

Hadassah, The Women's Zionist Organization of America (1912): 50 West 58 St., New York, N.Y. 10019. 385,000. Phone: (800) 664-5646. www.hadassah.org.

Heating, Refrigerating and Air-Conditioning Engineers, Inc., American Society of (1959): 1791 Tullie Circle N.E., Atlanta, Ga. 30329. 50,000. Phone: (404) 636-8400. www.ashrae.org.

Helicopter Association International (1948): 1635 Prince St., Alexandria, Va. 22314. Phone: (703) 683-4646. www.rotor.com.

Historians, The Organization of American (1907): 112 N. Bryan St., Bloomington, Ind. 47408-4199. 12,000. Phone: (812) 855-7311. www.oah.org.

Historic Preservation, National Trust for (1949): 1785 Massachusetts Ave. N.W., Washington, D.C. 20036. 275,000. Phone: (202) 588-6000. www.nationaltrust.org.

Horse Council, Inc., American (1969): 1616 H St. N.W., 7th Fl., Washington, D.C. 20006. More than 190 organizations and 2,400 individuals. Phone: (202) 296-4031. www.horsecouncil.org.

Horticultural Association, National Junior (1935): 15 Railroad Ave., Homer City, Pa. 15748. Phone: (724) 479-3254. www.njha.org.

Horticultural Society, American (1922): 7931 East Boulevard Dr., Alexandria, Va. 22308. 22,000. Phone: (703) 768-5700 or (800) 777-7931; fax: (703) 768-8700. www.ahs.org.

Hostelling International—American Youth Hostels (1934): 8401 Colesville Rd., Ste. 600, Silver Spring, Md. 20910. 120,000. Phone: (301) 495-1240 for membership and reservations. www.hiayh.org.

Humane Association, American (1877): 63 Inverness Drive East, Englewood, Colo. 80112-5117. Phone: (303) 792-9900. www.americanhumane.org.

Humane Society of the United States (1954): 2100 L St. N.W., Washington, D.C. 20037. 5,000,000. Phone: (202) 452-1100. www.hsus.org.

Humanities, National Endowment for the (1965): 1100 Pennsylvania Ave. N.W., Washington, D.C. 20506. Phone: (202) 606-8400. www.neh.fed.us.

Hydrogen Energy, International Association for (1975): P.O. Box 248266, Coral Gables, Fla. 33124. 2,500. Phone: (305) 284-4666. www.iahe.org.

Industrial Engineers, Institute of (1948): 3577 Parkway Lane, Ste. 200, Norcross, Ga. 30092. 17,000+. Phone: (800) 494-0460. www.iienet.org.

Insurance and Financial Advisors, National Association of (1890): 2901 Telestar Court, Falls Church, Va. 22042–1205. 108,000. Phone: (877) TO-NAIFA. www.naifa.org..

Izaak Walton League of America (1922): 707 Conservation Lane, Gaithersburg, Md. 20878-2983. 50,000+. Phone: (800) 453-5463. www.iwla.org.

Jewish Community Centers Association (JCC) of North America (1917): 15 E. 26th St., New York, N.Y. 10010-1579. 275+ affiliated Jewish Community Centers, YM-YWHAs, and camps serving 1 million+ members. Phone: (212) 532-4949; fax: (212) 481-4174. email: info@jcca.org. www.jcca.org.

Jewish Congress, American (1918): Stephen Wise Congress House,15 East 84th St., New York, N.Y. 10028. 50,000. Phone: (212) 879-4500. www.ajcongress.org.

Jewish Historical Society, American (1892): 15 W. 16th St., New York, N.Y. 10011. 3,500. Phone: (212) 294-6160; fax: (212) 294-6161. email: ajhs@ajhs.org. www.ajhs.org.

Jewish War Veterans of the U.S.A. (1896): 1811 R St. N.W., Washington, D.C. 20009-1659. Phone: (202) 265-6280. www.jwv.org.

Jewish Women, National Council of (1893): 53 W. 23rd St., New York, N.Y. 10010. 90,000. Phone: (212) 645-4048. www.ncjw.org.

John Birch Society (1958): P.O. Box 8040, Appleton, Wis. 54912. Under 100,000. Phone: (920) 749-3780; fax: (920) 749-5062. www.jbs.org.

Journalists, Society of Professional (1909): 3909 N. Meridian St., Indianapolis, Ind. 46208. 13,500. Phone: (317) 927-8000. www.spj.org.

Judaism, American Council for (1943): P.O. Box 9009, Alexandria, Va. 22304. Phone: (703) 836-2546. www.acjna.org

Junior Achievement Inc. (1919): One Education Way, Colorado Springs, Colo. 80906. 5.2 million. Phone: (719) 540-8000; fax: (719) 540-6299. www.ja.org.

Junior Chamber of Commerce, The United States, Jaycees (1920): P.O. Box 7, Tulsa, Okla. 74102-0007. 113,000. Phone: (918) 584-2481; fax: (918) 584-4422. www.usjaycees.org.

Junior Leagues International, Inc., Association of (1921): 90 William Street, Ste. 200, New York, N.Y. 10038. 295 Leagues, 193,000+ members. Phone: (212) 951-8300. www.ajli.org.

Junior State of America (1934): 400 South El Camino Real, Ste. 300, San Mateo, Calif. 94402. 15,000. Phone: (650) 347-1600. www.jsa.org.

Kiwanis International (1915): 3636 Woodview Trace, Indianapolis, Ind. 46268. 316,000. Phone: (317) 875-8755. email: kiwanismail@kiwanis.org. www.kiwanis.org.

Knights of Columbus (1852): One Columbus Plaza, New Haven, Conn. 06510. 1,600,000. Phone: (203) 752-4000. www.kofc.org.

Knights Templar, Grand Encampment of (1816): 5097 N. Elston Ave., Ste. 101, Chicago, Ill. 60630-2460. 220,000. Phone: (773) 777-3300. www.knightstemplar.org.

La Leche League International (1956): 1400 N. Meacham Rd., Schaumburg, Ill. 60173-4808. 50,000. Phone: (847) 519-7730. www.lalecheleague.org.

Law, American Society of International (1906): 2223 Massachusetts Ave. N.W., Washington, D.C. 20008. 4,300. Phone: (202) 939-6000. www.asil.org.

League of Women Voters of the U.S. (1920): 1730 M St. N.W., Washington, D.C. 20036-4508. Phone: (202) 429-1965; fax: (202) 429-0854. www.lwv.org.

Legal Aid and Defender Association, National (1911): 1140 Connecticut Ave. N.W., Washington, D.C. 20036. 2,400. Phone: (202) 452-0620. www.nlada.org.

Legal Professionals, National Association of (1949): 314 East 3rd St., Ste. 210, Tulsa, Okla. 74120-2409. 6,000. Phone: (918) 582-5188. www.nals.org.

Leukemia & Lymphoma Society (1949): 1311 Mamaroneck Ave., White Plains, N.Y. 10605. Phone: (914) 949-5213. www.leukemia-lymphoma.org.

Library Association, American (1876): 50 E. Huron St., Chicago, Ill. 60611. 57,000. Phone: (800) 545-2433. www.ala.org.

Lions Clubs International (1917): 300 22nd St., Oak Brook, Ill. 60523-8842. 1,419,408. Phone: (630) 571-5466. www.lionsclubs.org.

Lung Association, American (1904): 61 Broadway, New York, N.Y. 10006. 99 constituent and affiliate associations. Phone: (212) 315-8700. www.lungusa.org.

Magazine Editors, American Society of (1963): 810 Seventh Ave., 24th Fl., New York, N.Y. 10019. 900. Phone: (212) 872-3737. www.magazine.org.

Management Accountants, Institute of (1919): 10 Paragon Dr., Montvale, N.J. 07645-1759. 80,000. Phone: (800) 638-4427. www.imanet.org.

Management Association, American (1923): 1601 Broadway, New York, N.Y. 10019. 700,000. Phone: (212) 586-8100. www.amanet.org.

Management Consultants, Institute of (1968): 2025 M St. N.W., Ste. 800, Washington, D.C. 20036–2557. 25 chapters. Phone: (202) 367-1134. www.imcusa.org

Manufacturers, National Association of (1895): 1331 Pennsylvania Ave. N.W., Washington, D.C. 20004-1790. Approx. 14,000. Phone: (202) 637-3000. www.nam.org.

Manufacturing Engineers, Society of: One SME Drive, Dearborn, Mich. 48121. Phone: (313) 271–1500 x 1078; fax: (313) 240–8251. www.sme.org.

March of Dimes Birth Defects Foundation (1938): 1275 Mamaroneck Ave., White Plains, N.Y. 10605. 104 chapters. Phone: (888) 663-4637. www.modimes.org.

Marine Corps Association (1913): 715 Broadway, Quantico, Va. 22134. 100,723. Phone: (703) 640-0136. www.mca-marines.org.

Marine Technology Society (1963): 5565 Sterrett Place, Ste. 108, Columbia, Md. 21044. 2,000+. Phone: (410) 884-5330; fax: (202) 429-9417. www.mtsociety.org.

Masons, Ancient and Accepted Scottish Rite, Northern Masonic Jurisdiction, Supreme Council 33 (1813): P.O. Box 519, Lexington, Mass. 02420-0519. 330,000. Phone: (781) 862-4410. www.supremecouncil.org/

Masons, Ancient and Accepted Scottish Rite, Southern Jurisdiction, Supreme Council (1801): 1733 16th St. N.W., Washington, D.C. 20009. 500,000. Phone: (202) 232-3579. www.srmason-sj.org/web

Mathematical Association of America (1915): P.O. Box 91112, Washington, D.C. 20090-1112. Phone: (800) 331-1622. www.maa.org.

Mathematical Society, American (1888): 201 Charles St., Providence, R.I. 02940-6248. Phone: (401) 455-4000. email: ams@ams.org. www.ams.org.

Mayflower Descendants, General Society of (1897): P.O. Box 3297, Plymouth, Mass. 02361. 24,500+. Phone: (508) 746-3188. www.mayflower.org.

Mechanical Engineers, American Society of (1880): 3 Park Ave., New York, N.Y. 10016-5990. 125,000. Phone: (800) 843-2763. www.asme.org.

Medical Association, American (1847): 515 N. State St., Chicago, Ill. 60610. 300,000 physicians. Phone: (312) 464-5000. www.ama-assn.org.

Mental Health Association, National (1909): 2001 N. Beauregard St., 12th Fl., Alexandria, Va., 22311. 340 affiliates. Phone: (703) 684-7722; (800) 969-NMHA; TTY (800) 433-5959; fax: (703) 684-5968. email: nmhainfo@aol.com. www.nmha.org

Meteorological Society, American (1919): 45 Beacon St., Boston, Mass. 02108-3693. 11,000+. Phone: (617) 227-2425. www.ametsoc.org.

Military Chaplains Association of the U.S.A. (1925): P.O. Box 7056, Arlington, Va. 22207-7056. 1,500. Phone: (703) 276-2189. www.mca-usa.org.

Mining, Metallurgical, and Petroleum Engineers, The American Institute of (1871): 8307 Shaffer Parkway, Littleton, Colo. 80127-4012. 4 Member Societies: Society for Mining, Metallurgy and Exploration; The Minerals, Metals & Materials Society; Iron & Steel Society; Society of Petroleum Engineers. Phone: (303) 948-4255; fax: (303) 948-4260. email: aime@aimehq.org. www.aimehq.org.

Model Aeronautics, Academy of (1936): 5161 East Memorial Dr., Muncie, Ind. 47302. 150,000. Phone: (765) 287-1256. www.modelaircraft.org/templates/ama/.

Modern Language Association of America (1883): 26 Broadway, 3rd Fl., New York, N.Y. 10004-1789. 30,000+. Phone: (646) 576-5000. www.mla.org.

Moose International, Inc. (1888): Rte. 31, Mooseheart, Ill. 60539. 1,600,000+. Phone: (630) 859-2000. www.mooseintl.org.

Mothers Against Drunk Driving (MADD) (1980): 511 E. John Carpenter Frwy., Ste. 700, Irving, Tex. 75062. 3 million members and supporters. Phone: (800) GET-MADD. www.madd.org.

Motion Picture Arts & Sciences, Academy of (1927): 8949 Wilshire Blvd., Beverly Hills, Calif. 90211-1972. Phone: (310) 247-3000. www.oscars.org.

Multiple Sclerosis Society, National (1946): 733 Third Ave., New York, N.Y. 10017. 350,000. Phone: (800) FIGHT-MS (344-4867). www.nationalmssociety.org.

Muscular Dystrophy Association (1950): 3300 East Sunrise Dr., Tucson, Ariz. 85718. 2,300,000 volunteers. Phone: (800) 572-1717. www.mdausa.org.

Museums, American Association of (1906): 1575 Eye St. N.W., Ste. 400, Washington, D.C. 20005. 16,000+. Phone: (202) 289-1818; fax: (202) 289-6578, TTY (202) 289-8439. www.aam-us.org.

Muzzle Loading Rifle Association, National (1933): P.O. Box 67, Friendship, Ind. 47021-0067. 25,000. Phone: (812) 667-5131. www.nmlra.org.

NAFSA: Association of International Educators (1948): 1307 New York Ave. N.W., 8th Flr., Washington, D.C. 20005-4701. 8,000+. Phone: (202) 737-3699. www.nafsa.org.

National Abortion and Reproductive Rights Action League (NARAL) (1969): 1156 15th St. N.W., Washington, D.C. 20005. 500,000. Phone: (202) 973-3000. www.naral.org.

National Association for the Advancement of Colored People (1909): 4805 Mt. Hope Dr., Baltimore, Md. 21215. 500,000+. Phone: (877) NAACP-98. www.naacp.org.

National Association of Insurance and Financial Advisors (1890): 2901 Telestar Court, Falls Church, Va. 22042-1205. 80,000. Phone: (703) 770-8100. www.naifa.org/index.html.

National Conference for Community and Justice, The (founded as The Natl. Conf. of Christians & Jews) (1927): 475 Park Avenue South, 19th Flr., New York, N.Y. 10016-6901. Phone: (212) 545-1300. www.nccj.org.

National Cooperative Business Association (formerly Cooperative League of the U.S.A.) (1916): 1401 New York Ave. N.W., Ste. 1100, Washington, D.C. 20005. Phone: (202) 638-6222. www.ncba.org.

National Council of La Raza (1968): 1111 16th St. N.W., Ste. 1126, Washington, D.C. 20036. 20,000+. Phone: (202) 785-1670. www.nclr.org.

National Council of the Churches of Christ in the USA (1950): 475 Riverside Drive, Rm. 850, New York, N.Y. 10115. 35 Protestant and Orthodox communions. Phone: (212) 870-2227. www.ncccusa.org.

National Grange of the Order of Patrons of Husbandry (1867): 1616 H St. N.W., Washington, D.C. 20006-4999. 300,000. Phone: (202) 628-3507; fax: (202) 347-1091. www.nationalgrange.org.

National Press Club (1908): National Press Bldg., 529 14th St. N.W., 13th Flr., Washington, D.C. 20045. 4,500+. Phone: (202) 662-7500. npc.press.org.

National PTA (National Congress of Parents and Teachers) (1897): 541 N. Fairbanks Ct., Ste. 1300, Chicago, Ill. 60611. 6.5 million. Phone: (800) 307-4782. email: info@pta.org. www.pta.org.

National Rifle Association of America (1871): 11250 Waples Mill Rd., Fairfax, Va. 22030. 3,300,000. Phone: (703) 267-1000. www.nra.org.

National Urban League, Inc. (1910): 120 Wall St., New York, N.Y. 10005. 115 affiliates in 34 states and D.C. Phone: (212) 558-5300. www.nul.org.

National Wildlife Federation (1936): 11100 Wildlife Center Dr., Reston, Va. 20190. 4,000,000+. Phone: (703) 438-6000. www.nwf.org.

Nature Conservancy, The (1951): 4245 N. Fairfax Dr., Ste. 100, Arlington, Va. 22203-1606. 900,000. Phone: (800) 628-6860. http://nature.org.

Naturopathic Physicians, American Association of (1986): 3201 New Mexico Ave. N.W., Ste. 350, Washington, D.C. 20016. 1,700. Phone: (866) 538-2267. www.naturopathic.org.

Naval Architects and Marine Engineers, The Society of (1893): 601 Pavonia Ave., Jersey City, N.J. 07306. 10,000+. Phone: (800) 798-2188; fax: (201) 798-4975. www.sname.org.

Naval Engineers, American Society of (1888): 1452 Duke St., Alexandria, Va. 22314. 6,800. Phone: (703) 836-6727; fax: (703) 836-7491. www.navalengineers.org.

Naval Institute, United States (1873): 291 Wood Rd., Annapolis, Md. 21402. 80,000+. Phone: (410) 268-6110. www.usni.org.

Navigation, The Institute of (1945): 3975 University Dr., Ste. 390, Fairfax, Va. 22030. 3,800. Phone: (703) 383-9688; fax: (703) 383-9689. email: membership@ion.org. www.ion.org.

Navy League of the United States (1902): 2300 Wilson Blvd., Arlington, Va. 22201-3308. 71,500. Phone: (703) 528-1775. www.navyleague.org.

NDIA (National Defense Industrial Association) (1997): 2111 Wilson Blvd., Ste. 400, Arlington, Va. 22201. 28,000 individual, 900 companies. Phone: (703) 522-1820. www.ndia.org.

Neurofibromatosis Foundation, Inc., The National (1978): 95 Pine St., 16th Flr., New York, N.Y. 10005. 38,000. Phone: (800) 323-7938; in N.Y. State (212) 344-NNFF; fax: (212) 747-0004. email: nnff@aol.com. www.nf.org.

Newspaper Association of America (1992): 1921 Gallows Rd., Ste. 600, Vienna, Va. 22182–3900. 70,000+ newspaper executives. Phone (703) 902-1600. www.naa.org.

Nondestructive Testing, Inc., The American Society for (1941): 1711 Arlingate Lane, P.O. Box 28518, Columbus, Ohio 43228-0518. 10,240. Phone: (800) 222-ASNT. www.asnt.org.

Nuclear Society, American (1954): 555 N. Kensington Ave., La Grange Park, Ill. 60526. 13,000. Phone: (708) 352-6611. www.ans.org.

Numismatic Association, American (1891): 818 N. Cascade Ave., Colorado Springs, Colo. 80903-3279. 28,000. Phone: (719) 632-2646. email: ana@money.org. www.money.org.

Nurses Association, American (1897): 8515 Georgia Ave., Ste. 400, Silver Spring, Md. 20910. 180,000. Phone: (800) 274-4ANA. www.ana.org.

Ocean Conservancy, The (formerly Center for Marine Conservation) (1972): 2029 K St. N.W., Washington, D.C. 20006. 120,000. Phone: (202) 429-5609. www.oceanconservancy.org/

Odd Fellows, Sovereign Grand Lodge, Independent Order of (1819): 422 Trade St., Winston-Salem, N.C. 27101. 460,000. Phone: (336) 725-5955. www.ioof.org.

Olympic Committee, United States (1921): One Olympic Plaza, Colorado Springs, Colo. 80909-5760. Phone: (719) 632-5551. www.olympic-usa.org.

Optimist International (1919): 4494 Lindell Blvd., St. Louis, Mo. 63108. 130,000+. Phone: (314) 371-6000. www.optimist.org.

Optometric Association, American (1898): 243 N. Lindbergh Blvd., St. Louis, Mo. 63141. 32,000. Phone: (314) 991-4100. www.aoanet.org.

Ornithologists' Union, American (1883): 1313 Dolley Madison Blvd., Ste. 402, McLean, Va. 22101. 4,000. Phone: (202) 357-2051. www.aou.org.

Overeaters Anonymous, Inc. (1960): World Service Office, P.O. Box 44020, Rio Rancho, N.M. 87174–4020. 150,000. Phone: (505) 891-2664. www.oa.org.

Parents, Families and Friends of Lesbians and Gays (1981): 1726 M St. N.W., Ste. 400, Washington, D.C. 20036. 77,000 households. Phone: (202) 467-8180. www.pflag.org.

Parents Without Partners (1957): 1650 South Dixie Hwy., Ste. 510, Boca Raton, Fla. 33432. 50,000+. Phone: (561) 391-8833. www.parentswithoutpartners.org.

Peace Action (a merger of SANE and the Nuclear Weapons Freeze Campaign) (1957): 1100 Wayne Ave., Ste. 1020, Silver Spring, Md. 20910. 55,000. Phone: (301) 565-4050. www.webcom.com/peaceact.

People For the American Way (1980): 2000 M St. N.W., Ste. 400, Washington, D.C. 20036. 300,000. Phone: (202) 467-4999. www.pfaw.org.

Petroleum Geologists, American Association of (1917): 1444 South Boulder Ave., Tulsa, Okla. 74119. 31,500. Phone: (918) 584-2555. www.aapg.org.

Pharmaceutical Association, American (1852): 2215 Constitution Ave. N.W., Washington, D.C. 20037-2985. 50,000+. Phone: (202) 628-4410. www.aphanet.org.

Philatelic Society, American (1886): 100 Match Factory Place, Bellefonte, Pa. 16823. 55,000+. Phone: (814) 933-3803. www.stamps.org.

Photogrammetry and Remote Sensing, American Society for (1934): 5410 Grosvenor Lane, Ste. 210, Bethesda, Md. 20814-2160. 7,000+. Phone: (301) 493-0290; fax: (301) 493-0208. email: asprs@asprs.org. www.asprs.org.

Photographic Society of America (1934): 3000 United Founders Blvd., Ste. 103, Oklahoma City, Okla. 73112-3940. Phone: (405) 843-1437. www.psa-photo.org.

Physical Society, The American (1899): One Physics Ellipse, College Park, Md. 20740-3844. 41,000. Phone: (301) 209-3200. www.aps.org.

Physical Therapy Association, American (APTA) (1921): 1111 N. Fairfax St., Alexandria, Va. 22314-1488. 66,000+. Phone: (703) 684-2782. www.apta.org.

Physics, American Institute of (1931): One Physics Ellipse, College Park, Md. 20740-3843. 125,000. Phone: (301) 209-3100. www.aip.org.

Pilot International (1921): Pilot International Headquarters, 244 College St., P.O. Box 4844, Macon, Ga. 31208-4844. 25,000. Phone: (478) 743-7403. www.pilotinternational.org.

Planetary Society, The (1980): 65 N. Catalina Ave., Pasadena, Calif. 91106-2301. 100,000. Phone: (626) 793-5100. www.planetary.org.

Planned Parenthood® Federation of America, Inc., (1916): 434 West 33rd St. New York, N.Y. 10001. 150 affiliates. Phone: (212) 541-7800; fax: (212) 245-1845. www.plannedparenthood.org.

Plastics Engineers, Society of (1942): P.O. Box 403, 14 Fairfield Dr., Brookfield, Conn. 06804-0403. 32,000+. Phone: (203) 775-0471. www.4spe.org.

Police and Concerned Citizens, American Federation of (1966): American Police Hall of Fame, 6350 Horizon Dr., Titusville, Fla. 32780. 100,000. Phone: (321) 264-0911. www.aphf.org/p14_afop.html.

Police, International Association of Chiefs of (1893): 515 N. Washington St., Alexandria, Va. 22314-2357. 19,000+. Phone: (703) 836-6767. www.theiacp.org.

Political and Social Science, American Academy of (1889): 3814 Walnut St., Philadelphia, Pa. 19104-6197. Phone: (215) 746-6500. www.aapss.org/.

Political Science, Academy of (1880): 475 Riverside Dr., Ste. 1274, New York, N.Y. 10115-1274. 8,500. Phone: (212) 870-2500. www.psqonline.org.

Population Connection (formerly Zero Population Growth) (1968): 1400 Sixteenth St. N.W., Ste. 320, Washington, D.C. 20036. 55,000. Phone: (202) 332-2200. http://www.populationconnection.org/.

Prevent Blindness America (1908): 211 West Wacker Dr., Ste. 1700, Chicago, Ill. 60606. 21 affiliates and divisions. Phone: (800) 331-2020. www.preventblindness.org.

Professional Engineers, National Society of (1934): 1420 King St., Alexandria, Va. 22314-2794. 60,000. Phone: (703) 684-2800; fax: (703) 836-4875. www.nspe.org.

Professional Photographers of America, Inc. (1880): 229 Peachtree St. N.W., #2200, Atlanta, Ga. 30303-2206. 14,000. Phone: (404) 522-8600. www.ppa.com.

Psychiatric Association, American (1844): 1000 Wilson Blvd., Ste. 1825, Arlington, Va. 22209-3901. 40,537. Phone: (703) 907-7300. www.psych.org.

Psychoanalytic Association, The American (1911): 309 E. 49th St., New York, N.Y. 10017. 3,000+ psychoanalysts. Phone: (212) 752-0450; fax: (212) 593-0571. www.apsa.org.

Psychological Association, American (1892): 750 First St. N.E., Washington, D.C. 20002–4242. 159,000. Phone: (202) 336 5500; (202) 336-6123 TTY. www.apa.org.

Public Health Association, American (1872): 800 I St. N.W., Washington, D.C. 20001-3710. 50,000+. Phone: (202) 777-2742. www.apha.org.

Puppeteers of America (1937): P.O. Box 330, West Liberty, Iowa 52776. Phone: (888) 568-6235. www.puppeteers.org

Quality, The American Society for (1946): 600 N. Plankinton Ave., Milwaukee, Wis. 53203. 135,000+. Phone: (414) 272-8575. www.asq.org.

Railroads, Association of American (1934): 50 F St. N.W., Washington, D.C. 20001-1564. Phone: (202) 639-2100. www.aar.org.

Recording Arts & Sciences, Inc., National Academy of (1957): 3402 Pico Blvd., Santa Monica, Calif. 90405. 13,000. Phone: (310) 392-3777. www.grammy.com.

Red Cross, American (1881): 2025 E Street N.W., Washington, D.C. 20006. Approx. 1,650 chapters. Phone: (202) 303-4498. www.redcross.org.

Rehabilitation Association, National (1925): 633 S. Washington St., Alexandria, Va. 22314. 12,000. Phone: (703) 836-0850; TDD: (703) 836-0849. www.nationalrehab.org.

Reserve Officers Association of the United States (1922): 1 Constitution Ave. N.E., Washington, D.C. 20002-5655. 93,000. Phone: (800) 809-9448. www.roa.org.

Retired Federal Employees, National Association (1921): 606 N. Washington St., Alexandria, Va. 22314. 400,000+. Phone: (703) 838-7760. www.narfe.org.

Reye's Syndrome Foundation, National (1974): P.O. Box 829, Bryan, Ohio 43506-0829. Phone: (800) 233-7393; fax: (419) 636-9897. email: nsrf@reyessyndrome.org. www.reyessyndrome.org.

RID-USA (Remove Intoxicated Drivers) (1978): Box 520, Schenectady, N.Y. 12301. Phone: (518) 372-0034/(518) 393-HELP; fax: (518) 370-4917. www.crisny.org/not-for-profit/ridusa/.

Right to Life, Committee, Inc., National (1973): 512 10th St. N.W., Washington, D.C. 20004. Phone: (202) 626-8800. www.nrlc.org

Rotary International (1905): One Rotary Center, 1560 Sherman Ave., Evanston, Ill. 60201. 1.2 million in 161 countries and 35 geographical regions. Phone: (847) 866-3000. www.rotary.org.

SAE (Society of Automotive Engineers) (1905): 400 Commonwealth Dr., Warrendale, Pa. 15096-0001. 80,000. Phone: (724) 776-4841. www.sae.org.

Safety Council, National (1913): 1121 Spring Lake Dr., Itasca, Ill. 60143-3201. Phone: (630) 285-1121. www.nsc.org.

Salvation Army, The (1865): National Headquarters, 615 Slaters Lane, P.O. Box 269, Alexandria, Va. 22313. 453,150. Phone: (703) 684-5500. www.salvationarmyusa.org.

Save-the-Redwoods League (1918): 114 Sansome St., Rm 1200, San Francisco, Calif. 94104-3823. 45,000. Phone: (415) 362-2352. www.savetheredwoods.org.

Science, American Association for the Advancement of (1848): 1200 New York Ave. N.W., Washington, D.C. 20005. 143,000. Phone: (202) 326-6400. www.aaas.org.

Science and Health, American Council on (1978): 1995 Broadway, 2nd Flr., New York, N.Y. 10023-5860. Phone: (212) 362-7044; fax: (212) 362-4919. email: acsh@acsh.org. www.acsh.org.

Science Fiction Society, World (1939): P.O. Box 426159, Kendall Square Station, Cambridge, Mass. 02142. email: mpc@wsfs.org www.wsfs.org.

Scientists, Federation of American (FAS) (1945): 1717 K St. N.W., Ste. 209, Washington, D.C. 20036. 4,000. Phone: (202) 546-3300. www.fas.org.

SCRABBLE® Association, National (1978): P.O. Box 700, 403 Front Street Garden, Greenport, N.Y. 11944. 10,000. Phone: (631) 477-0033. www.scrabble-assoc.com

Screen Actors Guild (1933): 5757 Wilshire Blvd., Los Angeles, Calif. 90036-3600. 96,000. Phone: (323) 954-1600. www.sag.com.

Sculpture Society, National (1893): 237 Park Ave., New York, N.Y. 10017. 4,000. Phone: (212) 764-5645. www.nationalsculpture.org

Seeing Eye Inc., The (1929): P.O. Box 375, Morristown, N.J. 07963-0375. Phone: (973) 539-4425. www.seeingeye.org

Senior Citizens, National Alliance of (1974): 2525 Wilson Blvd., Arlington, Va. 22201. 117,000. Fax: (703) 528-4380.

Shrine of North America and Shriners Hospitals for Children, The (1872 and 1922): 2900 Rocky Point Drive, Tampa, Fla. 33607-1460. 525,000. Phone: (813) 281-0300. www.shrinershq.org.

Sierra Club (1892): 85 2nd Street, San Francisco, Calif. 94105-3441. 700,000+. Phone: (415) 977-5500. www.sierraclub.org.

SIETAR INTERNATIONAL (The International Society for Intercultural Education, Training and Research) (1974): 8835 S.W. Canyon Lane, Ste. 238, Portland, Ore. 97225. 12,500. Phone: (503) 297-4622. www.sietarinternational.org.

Simon Wiesenthal Center (1977): 1399 South Roxbury, Los Angeles, Calif. 90035. 400,000 member families. Phone: (800) 900-9036. www.wiesenthal.org.

Small Business Association, National (1937): 1156 15th St. N.W., Washington, D.C. 20005. 65,000+. Phone: (202) 293-8830; fax: (202) 872-8543. www.nsba.biz.

Social Work Education, Council on (1952): 1725 Duke St., Ste. 500, Alexandria, Va. 22314. Phone: (703) 683-8080; fax: (703) 683-8099. www.cswe.org.

Social Workers, National Association of (1955): 750 First St. N.E., Ste. 700, Washington, D.C. 20002-4241. Phone: (202) 408-8600. www.naswdc.org.

Society for Integrative and Comparative Biology (formerly the American Society of Zoologists) (1890): 1313 Dolley Madison Blvd. #402, McLean, Va. 22101. 2,100. Phone: (703) 790-1745; (800) 955-1236. email: SICB@BurkInc.com www.sicb.org.

Soil and Water Conservation Society (1945): 945 S.W. Ankeny Rd., Ankeny, Iowa 50021. 10,000. Phone: (515) 289-2331; fax: (515) 289-1227. www.swcs.org.

Songwriters Guild of America, The (1931): 1500 Harbor Blvd., Weehawken, N.J. 07087-6732. Phone: (201) 867-7603. www.songwritersguild.com

Sons of Italy in America, Order (1905): 219 E St. N.E., Washington, D.C. 20002. 500,000. Phone: (202) 547-2900. www.osia.org.

Sons of the American Revolution, National Society of the (1889): 1000 S. 4th St., Louisville, Ky. 40203. 26,000. Phone: (502) 589-1776. www.sar.org.

Soroptimist International of the Americas (1921): 1709 Spruce St., Philadelphia, Pa. 19103-6103. 100,000. Phone: (215) 893-9000. www.soroptimist.org/

Southern Early Childhood Association (formerly SACUS) (1948): P.O. Box 55930, Little Rock, Ark. 72215-5930. 21,000. Phone: (800) 305-7322; fax: (501) 227-5297. email: seca@aristotle.net. www.southernearlychildhood.org.

Space Society, National (1974): 1620 I (Eye) St. N.W., Ste. 615, Washington, D.C. 20006. Phone: (202) 429-1600; fax: (202) 463-8497. www.nss.org/.

Special Olympics International, Inc. (1968): 1133 19th St. N.W., Washington, D.C., 20036. 1,000,000. Phone: (202) 628-3630. www.specialolympics.org.

Speech-Language-Hearing Association, American (1925): 10801 Rockville Pike, Rockville, Md. 20852. 99,000+. Phone & TTY: (800) 638-8255. www.asha.org.

Sports Car Club of America Inc. (1944): P.O. Box 19400, Topeka, Kans. 66619-0400. 55,000. Phone: (800) 770-2055. www.scca.org.

Statistical Association, American (1839): 1429 Duke St., Alexandria, Va. 22314-3415. 19,000. Phone: (888) 231-3473. www.amstat.org.

Student Association, United States (1947): 1413 K Street N.W., 9th Flr., Washington, D.C. 20005. 350 schools (3.5 million students). Phone: (202) 347-8772. www.usstudents.org.

Surgeons, American College of (1913): 633 North Saint Clair, Chicago, Ill. 60611-3211. 56,000+. Phone: (312) 202-5000. www.facs.org.

Symphony Orchestra League, American (1942): 33 W. 60th St., 5th Fl., New York, N.Y. 10023-7905. 5,500. Phone: (212) 262-5161. www.symphony.org.

TASH: The Association for Persons with Severe Handicaps (1974): 29 W. Susquehanna Ave., Ste. 210, Baltimore, Md. 21204. 8,500. Phone: (410) 828-8274. www.tash.org.

Tax Foundation (1937): 1900 M St. N.W., Ste. 550, Washington, D.C. 20036. Phone: (202) 464-6200; fax: (202) 464-6201. email: taxfnd@intr.net. www.taxfoundation.org

Teachers, American Federation of (1916): 555 New Jersey Ave. N.W., Washington, D.C., 20001. 900,000+. Phone: (202) 879-4400. www.aft.org.

Testing & Materials, American Society for (1898): 100 Barr Harbor Dr., W. Conshohocken, Pa. 19428-2959. 35,000. Phone: (610) 832-9585. www.astm.org.

The Arc (1950): 1010 Wayne Ave., Ste. 650, Silver Spring, Md. 20910. A national organization on mental retardation. 140,000 members, 1,200 state and local chapters. Phone: (301) 565-3842. www.thearc.org.

Theosophical Society in America, The (1875): P.O. Box 270, Wheaton, Ill. 60189-0270. 4,400. Phone: (630) 668-1571. www.theosophical.org.

Tin Can Sailors, Inc. (1976): P.O. Box 100, Somerset, Mass. 02726. 20,900. Phone: (800) 223-5535. www.destroyers.org.

Toastmasters International (1924): P.O. Box 9052, Mission Viejo, Calif. 92690-7052. 170,000. Phone: (949) 858-8255; fax: (949) 858-1207. www.toastmasters.org.

TOUGHLOVE America (1979): 127 Manhattan Ave., Hermosa Beach, Calif. 90254. 500 registered groups. www.toughlove.com.

TransAfrica Forum (1981): 1426 21st St. N.W., Washington, D.C. 20036. Phone: (202) 223-1960; fax: (202) 223-1966. www.transafricaforum.org.

Travel Agents, American Society of (ASTA) (1931): 1101 King St., Alexandria, Va. 22314. 26,000. Phone: (703) 739-2782. www.astanet.com.

Travelers Aid International (1851): 1612 K St. N.W., Ste. 506, Washington, D.C. 20006. 45 agencies, 500+ corporate representatives. Phone: (202) 546-1127; fax: (202) 546-9112. www.travelersaid.org.

Tuberous Sclerosis Association, Inc., National (1974): 801 Roeder Rd., Ste. 750, Silver Spring, Md. 20910. 5,000. Phone: (800) 225-6872; fax: (301) 562-9870. www.tsalliance.org.

UFOs, National Investigations Committee on (1967): 21601 Devonshire St. #217, Chatsworth, Calif. 91311-8415. Phone: (818) 882-0052. www.nicufo.org.

UNICEF, U.S. Committee for (1947): 333 E. 38th St., New York, N.Y. 10016. 20,000 volunteers. Phone: (800) 4UNICEF. www.unicefusa.org.

Union of Concerned Scientists (1969): 2 Brattle Square, Cambridge, Mass. 02238. 70,000. Phone: (617) 547-5552. www.ucsusa.org.

United Daughters of the Confederacy® (1894): 328 N. Boulevard, Richmond, Va. 23220-4057. 24,000. Phone: (804) 355-1636. www.hqudc.org.

United Jewish Communities (formerly United Jewish Appeal) (1939): P.O. Box 30, Old Chelsea Station, New York, N.Y. 10113. Phone: (212) 284-6500. www.ujc.org.

United Way of America (1918): 701 N. Fairfax St., Alexandria, Va. 22314-2045. 1,400 local United Ways. Phone: (703) 836-7112. http://national.unitedway.org.

University Women, American Association of (1881): 1111 16th St. N.W., Washington, D.C. 20036. 150,000. Phone: (800) 326-AAUW (2289); TDD: (202) 785-7777. www.aauw.org.

USO (United Service Organizations) (1941): World Headquarters, 2111 Wilson Boulevard, Ste. 1200, Arlington, Va. 22201. 121 centers worldwide. Phone: (703) 908-6400. www.uso.org.

Veterans Committee, American (AVC) (1944): 554 Madison Ave., New York, N.Y. 10022-3201. 15,000. www.usmm.net/avc-mast45.html

Veterans of Foreign Wars of the U.S. (1899): 406 W. 34th St., Kansas City, Mo. 64111. VFW and Auxiliary, 2.1 million. Phone: (816) 756-3390. www.vfw.org.

Veterinary Medical Association, American (1863): 1931 N. Meacham Rd., Ste. 100, Schaumburg, Ill. 60173. 62,000. Phone: (847) 925-8070. www.avma.org.

Volunteers of America (1896): 1660 Duke St., Alexandria, Va. 22314-3421. 40,000+ volunteers. Phone: (703) 341-5000; (800) 899-0089. www.voa.org.

War Resisters League (1923): 339 Lafayette St., New York, N.Y. 10012. 12,000. Phone: (212) 228-0450; fax: (212) 228-6193. www.warresisters.org.

Washington Legal Foundation (1977): 2009 Massachusetts Ave. N.W., Washington, D.C. 20036. 100,000. Phone: (202) 588-0302. www.wlf.org.

Water Quality Association (1974): 4151 Naperville Rd., Lisle, Ill. 60532. 2,200. Phone: (630) 505-0160. www.wqa.org.

Welding Society, American (1919): 550 N.W. LeJeune Rd., Miami, Fla. 33126. 50,000. Phone: (305) 443-9353; (800) 443-9353. www.aws.org.

Wildlife Fund (U.S.), World (1961): 1250 24th St. N.W., Washington, D.C. 20037. 1.2 million. Phone: (202) 293-4800. www.wwf.org.

Woman's Christian Temperance Union, National (1874): 1730 Chicago Ave., Evanston, Ill. 60201-4585. Under 20,000. Phone: (847) 864-1397. www.wctu.org.

Women, National Organization for (NOW) (1966): 1100 H St. N.W., 2nd fl., Washington, D.C. 20005. 500,000. Phone: (202) 628-8669. www.now.org.

Women Police, The International Association of (1915): P.O. Box 2710 Phoenix, Ariz. 85002. 3,000. Phone: (602) 382-8751. www.iawp.org.

Women's American ORT (1927): 250 Park Ave. South, New York, N.Y. 10003. Chapters throughout the U.S. Phone: (800) 51–WAORT. www.waort.org.

Women's Educational and Industrial Union (1877): One Washington Mall, Boston, Mass. 02108. 1,500. Phone: (617) 536-5651; fax: (617) 247-8826. www.weiu.org.

Women's International League for Peace and Freedom (1915): 1213 Race St., Philadelphia, Pa. 19107–1691. 10,000. Phone: (215) 563-7110. www.wilpf.org.

World Future Society (1966): 7910 Woodmont Ave., Ste. 450, Bethesda, Md. 20814. 30,000. Phone: (301) 656-8274; fax: (301) 951-0394. www.wfs.org.

World Health, American Association for (1953): 1825 K St. N.W., Washington, D.C. 20006. Phone: (202) 466-5883; fax: (202) 466-5896. email: AAWHstaff@aol.com. www.thebody.com/aawh/aawhpage.html.

World Peace, International Association of Educators for (1967): P.O. Box 3282, Mastin Lake Station, Huntsville, Ala. 35810-0282. 102 countries. Phone: (256) 534-5501. www.iaewp.org.

World Peace Foundation (1910): 79 John F. Kennedy St., Cambridge, Mass. 02138. Phone: (617) 496-9812; fax: (617) 491-8588. www.worldpeacefoundation.org

Worldwatch Institute (1974): 1776 Massachusetts Ave. N.W., Washington, D.C. 20036-1904. Global environmental research organization. Phone: (202) 452-1999; fax: (202) 296-7365. email: worldwatch@worldwatch.org. www.worldwatch.org.

Writers Union, National (1981): 113 University Place, 6th Flr., New York, N.Y. 10003. 6,500. Phone: (212) 254-0279. www.nwu.org.

YMCA of the USA (1844): 101 N. Wacker Dr., Chicago, Ill. 60606. 16.9 million. Phone: (312) 977-0031. www.ymca.net.

Young Women's Christian Association of the U.S.A. (1858 in U.S.A., 1855 in England): 1015 18th St., N.W., Ste. 1110, Washington, D.C 20036. 2,000,000. Phone: (202) 467 0801. www.ywca.org.

Zionist Organization of America (1897): 4 E. 34th St., New York, N.Y. 10016. 50,000. Phone: (212) 481-1500; fax: (212) 481-1515. www.zoa.org.

I n any broad overview of history, arbitrary compartmentalization of facts is self-defeating (and makes locating interrelated people, places, and things that much harder). Therefore, Headline History is designed as a "timeline"—a chronology that highlights both the march of time and interesting, sometimes surprising, juxtapositions.

See also related sections of the almanac, particularly Inventions and Discoveries, U.S. Government and History, and Countries of the World.

B.C.

Before Christ (B.C.) or Before the Common Era (B.C.E.)

4.5 billion B.C. Planet Earth formed.

3 billion B.C. First signs of primeval life (bacteria and blue-green algae) appear in oceans.

600 million B.C. Earliest date to which fossils can be traced.

4.4 million B.C. Earliest known hominid fossils (*Ardipithecus ramidus*) found in Aramis, Ethiopia, 1994.

4.2 million B.C. *Australopithecus anamensis* found in Lake Turkana, Kenya, 1995.

3.2 million B.C. *Australopithecus afarensis* (nicknamed "Lucy") found in Ethiopia, 1974.

2.5 million B.C. *Homo habilis* ("Skillful Man"). First brain expansion; is believed to have used stone tools.

1.8 million B.C. *Homo erectus* ("Upright Man"). Brain size twice that of *Australopithecine* species.

1.7 million B.C. *Homo erectus* leaves Africa.

100,000 B.C. First modern *Homo sapiens* in South Africa.

70,000 B.C. Neanderthal man (use of fire and advanced tools).

35,000 B.C. Neanderthal man replaced by later groups of *Homo sapiens* (i.e., Cro-Magnon man, etc.).

18,000 B.C. Cro-Magnons replaced by later cultures.

15,000 B.C. Migrations across Bering Straits into the Americas.

10,000 B.C. Semi-permanent agricultural settlements in Old World.

10,000–4,000 B.C. Development of settlements into cities and development of skills such as the wheel, pottery, and improved methods of cultivation in Mesopotamia and elsewhere.

5500–3000 B.C. Predynastic Egyptian cultures develop (5500–3100 B.C.); begin using agriculture (c. 5000 B.C.). Earliest known civilization arises in Sumer (4500–4000 B.C.). Earliest recorded date in Egyptian calendar (4241 B.C.). First year of Jewish calendar (3760 B.C.). First phonetic writing appears (c. 3500 B.C.). Sumerians develop a city-state civilization (c. 3000 B.C.). Copper used by Egyptians and Sumerians. Western Europe is neolithic, without metals or written records.

3000–2000 B.C. Pharaonic rule begins in Egypt. King Khufu (Cheops), 4th dynasty (2700–2675 B.C.), completes construction of the Great Pyramid at Giza (c. 2680 B.C.). The Great Sphinx of Giza (c. 2540 B.C.) is built by King Khafre. Earliest Egyptian mummies. Papyrus. Phoenician settlements on coast of what is now Syria and Lebanon. Semitic tribes settle in Assyria. Sargon, first Akkadian king, builds Mesopotamian empire. The Gilgamesh epic (c. 3000 B.C.). Abraham leaves Ur (c. 2000 B.C.). Systematic astronomy in Egypt, Babylon, India, China.

3000–1500 B.C. The most ancient civilization on the Indian subcontinent, the sophisticated and extensive Indus Valley civilization, flourishes in what is today Pakistan. In Britain, Stonehenge erected according to some unknown astronomical rationale. Its three main phases of construction are thought to span c. 3000–1500 B.C.

2000–1500 B.C. Hyksos invaders drive Egyptians from Lower Egypt (17th century B.C.). Amosis I frees Egypt from Hyksos (c. 1600 B.C.). Assyrians rise to power—cities of Ashur and Nineveh. Twenty-four-character alphabet in Egypt. Israelites enslaved in Egypt. Cuneiform inscriptions used by Hittites. Peak of Minoan culture on Isle of Crete—earliest form of written Greek. Hammurabi, king of Babylon, develops oldest existing code of laws (18th century B.C.).

Ra, Egyptian Sun God
(3000–2000 B.C.)

The Great Pyramid at Giza
(c. 2680 B.C.)

Stonehenge
(c. 3000–1500 B.C.)

**Pythagoras
(582?–507? B.C.)**

**Buddha
(563?–483? B.C.)**

1500–1000 B.C. Ikhnaton develops monotheistic religion in Egypt (c. 1375 B.C.). His successor, Tutankhamen, returns to earlier gods. Moses leads Israelites out of Egypt into Canaan—Ten Commandments. Greeks destroy Troy (c. 1193 B.C.). End of Greek civilization in Mycenae with invasion of Dorians. Chinese civilization develops under Shang Dynasty. Olmec civilization in Mexico—stone monuments; picture writing.

1000–900 B.C. Solomon succeeds King David, builds Jerusalem temple. After Solomon's death, kingdom divided into Israel and Judah. Hebrew elders begin to write Old Testament books of Bible. Phoenicians colonize Spain with settlement at Cadiz.

900–800 B.C. Phoenicians establish Carthage (c. 810 B.C.). The *Iliad* and the *Odyssey*, perhaps composed by Greek poet Homer.

800–700 B.C. Prophets Amos, Hosea, Isaiah. First recorded Olympic games (776 B.C.). Legendary founding of Rome by Romulus (753 B.C.). Assyrian king Sargon II conquers Hittites, Chaldeans, Samaria (end of Kingdom of Israel). Earliest written music. Chariots introduced into Italy by Etruscans.

700–600 B.C. End of Assyrian Empire (616 B.C.)—Nineveh destroyed by Chaldeans (Neo-Babylonians) and Medes (612 B.C.). Founding of Byzantium by Greeks (c. 660 B.C.). Building of the Acropolis in Athens. Solon, Greek lawgiver (640–560 B.C.). Sappho of Lesbos, Greek poet (fl. c. 610–580 B.C.). Lao-tse, Chinese philosopher and founder of Taoism (born c. 604 B.C.).

600–500 B.C. Babylonian King Nebuchadnezzar builds empire, destroys Jerusalem (586 B.C.). Babylonian Captivity of the Jews (starting 587 B.C.). Hanging Gardens of Babylon. Cyrus the Great of Persia creates great empire, conquers Babylon (539 B.C.), frees the Jews. Athenian democracy develops. Aeschylus, Greek dramatist (525–465 B.C.). Pythagoras, Greek philosopher and mathematician (582?–507? B.C.). Confucius (551–479 B.C.) develops ethical and social philosophy in China. The *Analects* or Lun-yü ("collected sayings") are compiled by the second generation of Confucian disciples. Buddha (563?–483? B.C.) founds Buddhism in India.

SOME ANCIENT CIVILIZATIONS

Name	Approximate dates	Location	Major cities
Akkadian	2350–2230 B.C.	Mesopotamia, parts of Syria, Asia Minor, Iran	Akkad, Ur, Erich
Assyrian	1800–889 B.C.	Mesopotamia, Syria	Assur, Nineveh, Calah
Babylonian	1728–1686 B.C. (old) 625–539 B.C. (new)	Mesopotamia, Syria, Palestine	Babylon
Cimmerian	750–500 B.C.	Caucasus, northern Asia Minor	—
Egyptian	2850–715 B.C.	Nile valley	Thebes, Memphis, Tanis
Etruscan	900–396 B.C.	Northern Italy	—
Greek	900–200 B.C.	Greece	Athens, Sparta, Thebes, Mycenae, Corinth
Hittite	1640–1200 B.C.	Asia Minor, Syria	Hattusas, Nesa
Indus Valley	3000–1500 B.C.	Pakistan, Northwestern India	—
Lydian	700–547 B.C.	Western Asia Minor	Sardis, Miletus
Mede	835–550 B.C.	Iran	Media
Minoan	3000–1100 B.C.	Crete	Knossos
Persian	559–330 B.C.	Iran, Asia Minor, Syria	Persepolis, Pasargadae
Phoenician	1100–332 B.C.	Palestine (colonies: Gibraltar, Carthage, Sardinia)	Tyre, Sidon, Byblos
Phrygian	1000–547 B.C.	Central Asia Minor	Gordion
Roman	500 B.C.–A.D. 300	Italy, Mediterranean region, Asia Minor, western Europe	Rome, Byzantium
Scythian	800–300 B.C.	Caucasus	—
Sumerian	3200–2360 B.C.	Mesopotamia	Ur, Nippur

500–400 B.C. Greeks defeat Persians: battles of Marathon (490 B.C.), Thermopylae (480 B.C.), Salamis (480 B.C.). Peloponnesian Wars between Athens and Sparta (431–404 B.C.)—Sparta victorious. Pericles comes to power in Athens (462 B.C.). Flowering of Greek culture during the Age of Pericles (450–400 B.C.). The Parthenon is built in Athens as a temple of the goddess Athena (447–432 B.C.). Ictinus and Callicrates are the architects and Phidias is responsible for the sculpture. Sophocles, Greek dramatist (496?–406 B.C.). Hippocrates, Greek "Father of Medicine" (born 460 B.C.). Xerxes I, king of Persia (rules 485–465 B.C.).

400–300 B.C. Pentateuch—first five books of the Old Testament evolve in final form. Philip of Macedon, who believed himself to be a descendant of the Greek people, assassinated (336 B.C.) after subduing the Greek city-states; succeeded by son, Alexander the Great (356–323 B.C.), who destroys Thebes (335 B.C.), conquers Tyre and Jerusalem (332 B.C.), occupies Babylon (330 B.C.), invades India, and dies in Babylon. His empire is divided among his generals; one of them, Seleucis I, establishes Middle East empire with capitals at Antioch (Syria) and Seleucia (in Iraq). Trial and execution of Greek philosopher Socrates (399 B.C.). Dialogues recorded by his student, Plato (c. 427–348 or 347 B.C.). Euclid's work on geometry (323 B.C.). Aristotle, Greek philosopher (384–322 B.C.). Demosthenes, Greek orator (384–322 B.C.). Praxiteles, Greek sculptor (400–330 B.C.).

300–251 B.C. First Punic War (264–241 B.C.): Rome defeats the Carthaginians and begins its domination of the Mediterranean. Temple of the Sun at Teotihuacán, Mexico (c. 300 B.C.). Invention of Mayan calendar in Yucatán—more exact than older calendars. First Roman gladiatorial games (264 B.C.). Archimedes, Greek mathematician (287–212 B.C.).

250–201 B.C. Second Punic War (219–201 B.C.): Hannibal, Carthaginian general (246–142 B.C.), crosses the Alps (218 B.C.), reaches gates of Rome (211 B.C.), retreats, and is defeated by Scipio Africanus at Zama (202 B.C.). Great Wall of China built (c. 215 B.C.).

200–151 B.C. Romans defeat Seleucid King Antiochus III at Thermopylae (191 B.C.)—beginning of Roman world domination. Maccabean revolt against Seleucids (167 B.C.).

150–101 B.C. Third Punic War (149–146 B.C.): Rome destroys Carthage, killing 450,000 and enslaving the remaining 50,000 inhabitants. Roman armies conquer Macedonia, Greece, Anatolia, Balearic Islands, and southern France. Venus de Milo (c. 140 B.C.). Cicero, Roman orator (106–43 B.C.).

100–51 B.C. Julius Caesar (100–44 B.C.) invades Britain (55 B.C.) and conquers Gaul (France) (c. 50 B.C.). Spartacus leads slave revolt against Rome (71 B.C.). Romans conquer Seleucid empire. Roman general Pompey conquers Jerusalem (63 B.C.). Cleopatra on Egyptian throne (51–31 B.C.). Chinese develop use of paper (c. 100 B.C.). Virgil, Roman poet (70–19 B.C.). Horace, Roman poet (65–8 B.C.).

50–1 B.C. Caesar crosses Rubicon to fight Pompey (50 B.C.). Herod made Roman governor of Judea (37 B.C.). Caesar murdered (44 B.C.). Caesar's nephew, Octavian, defeats Mark Antony and Cleopatra at Battle of Actium (31 B.C.), and establishes Roman empire as Emperor Augustus; rules 27 B.C.–A.D. 14. Pantheon built for the first time under Agrippa, 27 B.C. Ovid, Roman poet (43 B.C.–A.D. 18).

A.D.
Christian Era (A.D.) or the Common Era (C.E.)

1–49 Birth of Jesus Christ (variously given from 4 B.C. to A.D. 7). After Augustus, Tiberius becomes emperor (dies, A.D. 37), succeeded by Caligula (assassinated, A.D. 41), who is followed by Claudius. Crucifixion of Jesus (probably A.D. 30). Han dynasty in China founded by Emperor Kuang Wu Ti. Buddhism introduced to China.

50–99 Claudius poisoned (A.D. 54), succeeded by Nero (commits suicide, A.D. 68). Missionary journeys of Paul the Apostle (A.D. 34–60). Jews revolt against Rome; Jerusalem destroyed (A.D. 70). Roman persecutions of Christians begin (A.D. 64). Colosseum built in Rome (A.D. 71–80). Trajan (rules A.D. 98–116); Roman empire extends to Mesopotamia, Arabia, Balkans. First Gospels of St. Mark, St. John, St. Matthew.

Confucius
(551–479 B.C.)

Parthenon
(447–432 B.C.)

Plato
(427?–348 or 347 B.C.)

Augustus Caesar
(63 B.C.–A.D. 14)

Roman Aqueduct
Montpellier, France

Mayan Pyramid at Chichén Itzá

Celtic Cross

Japanese Pagoda

Viking Ship (c. 900)

100–149 Hadrian rules Rome (A.D. 117–138); codifies Roman law, rebuilds Pantheon, establishes postal system, builds wall between England and Scotland. Jews revolt under Bar Kokhba (A.D. 122–135); final Diaspora (dispersion) of Jews begins.

150–199 Marcus Aurelius rules Rome (A.D. 161–180). Oldest Mayan temples in Central America (c. A.D. 200).

200–249 Goths invade Asia Minor (c. A.D. 220). Roman persecutions of Christians increase. Persian (Sassanid) empire re-established. End of Chinese Han dynasty.

250–299 Increasing invasions of the Roman empire by Franks and Goths. Buddhism spreads in China. Classic period of Mayan civilization (A.D. 250–900); develop hieroglyphic writing, advances in art, architecture, science.

300–349 Constantine the Great (rules A.D. 312–337) reunites eastern and western Roman empires, with new capital (Constantinople) on site of Byzantium (A.D. 330); issues Edict of Milan legalizing Christianity (A.D. 313); becomes a Christian on his deathbed (A.D. 337). Council of Nicaea (A.D. 325) defines orthodox Christian doctrine. First Gupta dynasty in India (c. A.D. 320).

350–399 Huns (Mongols) invade Europe (c. A.D. 360). Theodosius the Great (rules A.D. 392–395)—last emperor of a united Roman empire. Roman empire permanently divided in A.D. 395: western empire ruled from Rome; eastern empire ruled from Constantinople.

400–449 Western Roman empire disintegrates under weak emperors. Alaric, king of the Visigoths, sacks Rome (A.D. 410). Attila, Hun chieftain, attacks Roman provinces (A.D. 433). St. Patrick returns to Ireland (A.D. 432) and brings Christianity to the island. St. Augustine's *City of God* (A.D. 411).

450–499 Vandals destroy Rome (A.D. 455). Western Roman empire ends as Odoacer, German chieftain, overthrows last Roman emperor, Romulus Augustulus, and becomes king of Italy (A.D. 476). Ostrogothic kingdom of Italy established by Theodoric the Great (A.D. 493). Clovis, ruler of the Franks, is converted to Christianity (A.D. 496). First schism between western and eastern churches (A.D. 484).

500–549 Eastern and western churches reconciled (519). Justinian I, the Great (483–565), becomes Byzantine emperor (527), issues his first code of civil laws (529), conquers North Africa, Italy, and part of Spain. Plague spreads through Europe (542 *et seq.*). Arthur, semi-legendary king of the Britons (killed, c. 537). Boëthius, Roman scholar (executed, 524).

550–599 Beginnings of European silk industry after Justinian's missionaries smuggle silkworms out of China (553). Mohammed, founder of Islam (570–632). Buddhism in Japan (c. 560). St. Augustine of Canterbury brings Christianity to Britain (597). After killing about half the population, plague in Europe subsides (594).

600–649 Mohammed flees from Mecca to Medina (the *Hegira*); first year of the Muslim calendar (622). Muslim empire grows (634). Arabs conquer Jerusalem (637), conquer Persians (641).

650–699 Arabs attack North Africa (670), destroy Carthage (697). Venerable Bede, English monk (672–735).

700–749 Arab empire extends from Lisbon to China (by 716). Charles Martel, Frankish leader, defeats Arabs at Tours/Poitiers, halting Arab advance in Europe (732). Charlemagne (742–814). Introduction of pagodas in Japan from China.

750–799 Charlemagne becomes king of the Franks (771). Caliph Harun al-Rashid rules Arab empire (786–809): the "golden age" of Arab culture. Vikings begin attacks on Britain (790), land in Ireland (795). City of Machu Picchu flourishes in Peru.

800–849 Charlemagne crowned first Holy Roman Emperor in Rome (800). Charlemagne dies (814), succeeded by his son, Louis the Pious, who divides France among his sons (817). Arabs conquer Crete, Sicily, and Sardinia (826–827).

850–899 Norsemen attack as far south as the Mediterranean but are thwarted (859), discover Iceland (861). Alfred the Great becomes king of Britain (871), defeats Danish invaders (878). Russian nation founded by Vikings under Prince Rurik, establishing capital at Novgorod (855–879).

900–949 Beginning of Mayan Post-Classical period (900–1519). Vikings discover Greenland (c. 900). Arab Spain under Abd ar-Rahman III becomes center of learning (912–961). Otto I becomes King of Germany (936).

950–999 Mieczyslaw I becomes first ruler of Poland (960). Eric the Red establishes first Viking colony in Greenland (982). Hugh Capet elected King of France in 987; Capetian dynasty to rule until 1328. Musical notation systematized (c.

990). Vikings and Danes attack Britain (988–999). Otto I crowned Holy Roman Emperor by Pope John XII (962).

1000–1099 (A.D.)

c. 1000–1300 Classic Pueblo period of Anasazi culture; cliff dwellings.

c. 1000 Hungary and Scandinavia converted to Christianity. Viking raider Leif Eriksson discovers North America, calls it Vinland. *Beowulf,* Old English epic.

c. 1008 Murasaki Shikibu finishes *The Tale of Genji,* the world's first novel.

1009 Muslims destroy Holy Sepulchre in Jerusalem.

1013 Danes control England. Canute takes throne (1016), conquers Norway (1028), dies (1035); kingdom divided among his sons: Harold Harefoot (England), Sweyn (Norway), Hardecanute (Denmark).

1040 Macbeth murders Duncan, king of Scotland.

1053 Robert Guiscard, Norman invader, establishes kingdom in Italy, conquers Sicily (1072).

1054 Final separation between Eastern (Orthodox) and Western (Roman) churches.

1055 Seljuk Turks, Asian nomads, move west, capture Baghdad, Armenia (1064), Syria, and Palestine (1075).

1066 William of Normandy invades England, defeats last Saxon king, Harold II, at Battle of Hastings, crowned William I of England ("the Conqueror").

1068 Construction on the cathedral in Pisa, Italy, begins.

1073 Emergence of strong papacy when Gregory VII is elected. Conflict with English and French kings and German emperors will continue throughout medieval period.

1095 At Council of Clermont, Pope Urban II calls for a holy war to wrest control of Jerusalem from Muslims, which launches the First Crusade (1096), one of at least 8 European military campaigns between 1095 and 1291 to regain the Holy Land.

1100–1199 (A.D.)

1100–1300 Construction of Cathedral at Chartres, France.

1144 Second Crusade begins.

c. 1150 Angkor Wat is completed.

1150–1167 Universities of Paris and Oxford founded in France and England.

1162 Thomas á Becket named Archbishop of Canterbury, murdered by Henry II's men (1170). Troubadours (wandering minstrels) glorify romantic concepts of feudalism.

1169 Ibn-Rushd begins translating Aristotle's works.

1189 Richard I ("the Lionhearted") succeeds Henry II in England, killed in France (1199), succeeded by King John. Third Crusade.

1200–1299 (A.D.)

1200–1204 Fourth Crusade.

1211 Genghis Khan invades China, captures Peking (1214), conquers Persia (1218), invades Russia (1223), dies (1227).

1212 Children's Crusade.

1215 King John forced by barons to sign Magna Carta at Runneymede, limiting royal power.

1217 Fifth Crusade.

1228 Sixth Crusade.

Mesa Verde Cliff Dwellings (c. 1000–1300)

Cathedral and Tower at Pisa

Chartres Cathedral

King John (1167–1216)

THE CRUSADES (1096–1291)

In 1095 at Council of Clermont, Pope Urban II calls for war to rescue Holy Land from Muslim infidels. The *First Crusade* (1096) is assembled in response to Emperor Alexius I. The Christians capture Antioch (1098) and Jerusalem (1099). They establish the Crusader States, ruled by Europeans. It is the only successful crusade. The *Second Crusade* begins after the Seljuk Turks recapture Edessa, one of the Crusader States, in 1144. It is led by King Louis VIII of France and Holy Roman Emperor Conrad III. Crusaders perish in Asia Minor (1147).

Saladin controls Egypt (1171), unites Islam in holy war *(jihad)* against Christians, recaptures Jerusalem (1187). *Third Crusade* (1189) under kings of France, England, and Germany fails to reduce Saladin's power. *Fourth Crusade* (1200–1204)—French knights sack Greek Christian Constantinople, establish Latin empire in Byzantium. Greeks reestablish Orthodox faith (1262).

Children's Crusade (1212)—only one of 30,000 French children and about 200 of 20,000 German children survive to return home. Other Crusades—*Fifth,* against Egypt (1217), *Sixth* (1228), *Seventh* (1248), *Eighth* (1270). Mamelukes conquer Acre; end of the Crusades (1291).

**Thomas Aquinas
(1225–1274)**

**The Duomo in
Florence**

**Joan of Arc
(1412–1431)**

**Michelangelo's David
(1504)**

**Balboa
(1475–1517)**

1231 The Inquisition begins as Pope Gregory IX assigns Dominicans responsibility for combating heresy. Torture used (1252). Ferdinand and Isabella establish Spanish Inquisition (1478). Tourquemada, Grand Inquisitor, forces conversion or expulsion of Spanish Jews (1492). Forced conversion of Moors (1499). Inquisition in Portugal (1531). First Protestants burned at the stake in Spain (1543). Spanish Inquisition abolished (1834).

1241 Mongols defeat Germans in Silesia, invade Poland and Hungary, withdraw from Europe after Ughetai, Mongol leader, dies.

1248 Seventh Crusade.

1251 Kublai Khan governs China, becomes ruler of Mongols (1259), establishes Yuan dynasty in China (1280), invades Burma (1287), dies (1294).

1260 Chartres cathedral consecrated.

1270 Eighth Crusade.

1271 Marco Polo of Venice travels to China, in court of Kublai Khan (1275–1292), returns to Genoa (1295) and writes *Travels.*

1273 Thomas Aquinas stops work on *Summa Theologica,* the basis of all Catholic theological teaching; never completes it.

1295 English King Edward I summons the Model Parliament.

1300–1399 (A.D.)

1312–1337 Mali Empire reaches its height in Africa under King Mansa Musa.

c. 1325 The beginning of the Renaissance in Italy: writers Dante, Petrarch, Boccaccio; painter Giotto. Development of *Noh* drama in Japan. Aztecs establish Tenochtitlán on site of modern Mexico City. Peak of Muslim culture in Spain. Small cannon in use.

1337–1453 Hundred Years' War—English and French kings fight for control of France.

1347–1351 At least 25 million people die in Europe's "Black Death" (bubonic plague).

1368 Ming Dynasty begins in China.

1376–1382 John Wycliffe, pre-Reformation religious reformer, and followers translate Latin Bible into English.

1378 The Great Schism (to 1417)—rival popes in Rome and Avignon, France, fight for control of Roman Catholic Church.

c. 1387 Chaucer's *Canterbury Tales.*

1398 Tamerlane, the Mongol conqueror, begins last great conquest—Delhi.

1400–1499 (A.D.)

1407 Casa di San Giorgio, one of the first public banks, founded in Genoa.

1415 Henry V defeats French at Agincourt. Jan Hus, Bohemian preacher and follower of Wycliffe, burned at stake in Constance as heretic.

1418–1460 Portugal's Prince Henry the Navigator sponsors exploration of Africa's coast.

1420 Brunelleschi begins work on the Duomo in Florence.

1428 Joan of Arc leads French against English, captured by Burgundians (1430) and turned over to the English, burned at the stake as a witch after ecclesiastical trial (1431).

1438 Incas rule in Peru.

1450 Florence becomes center of Renaissance arts and learning under the Medicis.

1453 Turks conquer Constantinople, end of the Byzantine empire, beginning of the Ottoman empire.

1455 The Wars of the Roses, civil wars between rival noble factions, begin in England (to 1485). Having invented printing with movable type at Mainz, Germany, Johann Gutenberg completes first Bible.

1462 Ivan the Great rules Russia until 1505 as first czar; ends payment of tribute to Mongols.

1492 Moors conquered in Spain by troops of Ferdinand and Isabella. Columbus becomes first European to encounter Caribbean islands, returns to Spain (1493). Second voyage to Dominica, Jamaica, Puerto Rico (1493–1496). Third voyage to Orinoco (1498). Fourth voyage to Honduras and Panama (1502–1504).

1497 Vasco da Gama sails around Africa and discovers sea route to India (1498). Establishes Portuguese colony in India (1502). John Cabot, employed by England, reaches and explores Canadian coast. Michelangelo's *Bacchus* sculpture.

1500–1599 (A.D.)

1501 First black slaves in America brought to Spanish colony of Santo Domingo.

c. 1503 Leonardo da Vinci paints the *Mona Lisa.* Michelangelo sculpts the *David* (1504).

1506 St. Peter's Church started in Rome; designed and decorated by such artists and architects as Bramante, Michelangelo, da Vinci, Raphael, and Bernini before its completion in 1626.

1509 Henry VIII ascends English throne. Michelangelo paints the ceiling of the Sistine Chapel.

1513 Balboa becomes the first European to encounter the Pacific Ocean. Machiavelli writes *The Prince*.

1517 Turks conquer Egypt, control Arabia. Martin Luther posts his 95 theses denouncing church abuses on church door in Wittenberg—start of the Reformation in Germany.

1519 Ulrich Zwingli begins Reformation in Switzerland. Hernando Cortes conquers Mexico for Spain. Charles I of Spain is chosen Holy Roman Emperor Charles V. Portuguese explorer Ferdinand Magellan sets out to circumnavigate the globe.

**Martin Luther
(1483–1546)**

1520 Luther excommunicated by Pope Leo X. Suleiman I ("the Magnificent") becomes Sultan of Turkey, invades Hungary (1521), Rhodes (1522), attacks Austria (1529), annexes Hungary (1541), Tripoli (1551), makes peace with Persia (1553), destroys Spanish fleet (1560), dies (1566). Magellan reaches the Pacific, is killed by Philippine natives (1521). One of his ships under Juan Sebastián del Cano continues around the world, reaches Spain (1522).

1524 Verrazano, sailing under the French flag, explores the New England coast and New York Bay.

1527 Troops of the Holy Roman Empire attack Rome, imprison Pope Clement VII—the end of the Italian Renaissance. Castiglione writes *The Courtier*. The Medici family expelled from Florence.

**Henry VIII
(1491–1547)**

1532 Pizarro marches from Panama to Peru, kills the Inca chieftain, Atahualpa, of Peru (1533). Machiavelli's *The Prince* published posthumously.

1535 Reformation begins as Henry VIII makes himself head of English Church after being excommunicated by Pope. Sir Thomas More executed as traitor for refusal to acknowledge king's religious authority. Jacques Cartier sails up the St. Lawrence River, basis of French claims to Canada.

1536 Henry VIII executes second wife, Anne Boleyn. John Calvin establishes Reformed and Presbyterian form of Protestantism in Switzerland, writes *Institutes of the Christian Religion*. Danish and Norwegian Reformations. Michelangelo's *Last Judgment*.

1541 John Knox leads Reformation in Scotland, establishes Presbyterian church there (1560).

**Queen Elizabeth I
(1533–1603)**

1543 Publication of *On the Revolution of Heavenly Bodies* by Polish scholar Nicolaus Copernicus—giving his theory that the earth revolves around the sun.

1545 Council of Trent to meet intermittently until 1563 to define Catholic dogma and doctrine, reiterate papal authority.

1547 Ivan IV ("the Terrible") crowned as czar of Russia, begins conquest of Astrakhan and Kazan (1552), battles nobles (boyars) for power (1564), kills his son (1580), dies, and is succeeded by his weak and feeble-minded son, Fyodor I.

1553 Roman Catholicism restored in England by Queen Mary I.

1556 Akbar the Great becomes Mogul emperor of India, conquers Afghanistan (1581), continues wars of conquest (until 1605).

**William Shakespeare
(1564–1616)**

1558 Queen Elizabeth I ascends the throne (rules to 1603). Restores Protestantism, establishes state Church of England (Anglicanism). Renaissance will reach height in England—Shakespeare, Marlowe, Spenser.

1561 Persecution of Huguenots in France stopped by Edict of Orleans. French religious wars begin again with massacre of Huguenots at Vassy. St. Bartholomew's Day Massacre—thousands of Huguenots murdered (1572). Amnesty granted (1573). Persecution continues periodically until Edict of Nantes (1598) gives Huguenots religious freedom (until 1685).

1568 Protestant Netherlands revolts against Catholic Spain; independence will be acknowledged by Spain in 1648.

1570 Japan permits visits of foreign ships. Queen Elizabeth I excommunicated by Pope. Turks attack Cyprus and war on Venice. Turkish fleet defeated at Battle of Lepanto by Spanish and Italian fleets (1571). Peace of Constantinople (1572) ends Turkish attacks on Europe.

**Rembrandt van Rijn
(1606–1669)**

1580 Francis Drake returns to England after circumnavigating the globe; knighted by Queen Elizabeth I (1581). Montaigne's *Essays* published.

1582 Pope Gregory XIII implements the Gregorian calendar.

Catherine de Medici
(1519–1589)

1583 William of Orange rules the Netherlands; assassinated on orders of Philip II of Spain (1584).

1587 Mary, Queen of Scots, executed for treason by order of Queen Elizabeth I. Monteverdi's *First Book of Madrigals.*

1588 Defeat of the Spanish Armada by English. Henry, King of Navarre and Protestant leader, recognized as Henry IV, first Bourbon king of France. Converts to Roman Catholicism in 1593 in attempt to end religious wars.

1590 Henry IV enters Paris, wars on Spain (1595), marries Marie de Medici (1600), assassinated (1610). Spenser's *The Faerie Queen.* El Greco's *St. Jerome.* Galileo's experiments with falling objects.

1598 Boris Godunov becomes Russian czar. Tycho Brahe describes his astronomical experiments.

1600–1699 (A.D.)

1600 Giordano Bruno burned as a heretic. English East India Company established.

1603 Ieyasu rules Japan, moves capital to Edo (Tokyo). Shakespeare's *Hamlet.*

1605 Cervantes's *Don Quixote de la Mancha,* the first modern novel.

1607 Jamestown, Virginia, established—first permanent English colony on American mainland. Pocahontas, daughter of Chief Powhatan, saves life of John Smith.

1609 Samuel de Champlain establishes French colony of Quebec. The *Relation,* the first newspaper, debuts in Germany.

1610 Galileo sees the moons of Jupiter through his telescope.

1611 Gustavus Adolphus elected King of Sweden. King James Version of the Bible published in England. Rubens paints his *Descent from the Cross.*

1614 John Napier discovers logarithms.

1618 Start of the Thirty Years' War—Protestants revolt against Catholic oppression; Denmark, Sweden, and France will invade Germany in later phases of war. Kepler proposes last of three laws of planetary motion.

1619 A Dutch ship brings the first African slaves to British North America.

1620 Pilgrims, after three-month voyage in *Mayflower,* land at Plymouth Rock. Francis Bacon's *Novum Organum.*

1623 New Netherland founded by Dutch West India Company.

1630 Massachusetts Bay Colony.

1632 Maryland founded by Lord Baltimore.

1633 Inquisition forces Galileo (astronomer) to recant his belief in Copernican theory.

1642 English Civil War. Cavaliers, supporters of Charles I, against Roundheads, parliamentary forces. Oliver Cromwell defeats Royalists (1646). Parliament demands reforms. Charles I offers concessions, brought to trial (1648), beheaded (1649). Cromwell becomes Lord Protector (1653). Rembrandt paints his *Night Watch.*

1643 Taj Mahal completed.

1644 End of Ming Dynasty in China—Manchus come to power. Descartes's *Principles of Philosophy.*

1648 End of the Thirty Years' War. German population about half of what it was in 1618 because of war and pestilence.

1658 Cromwell dies; son Richard resigns and Puritan government collapses.

1660 English Parliament calls for the restoration of the monarchy; invites Charles II to return from France.

1661 Charles II is crowned King of England. Louis XIV begins personal rule as absolute monarch; starts to build Versailles.

1664 British take New Amsterdam from the Dutch. English limit "Nonconformity" with reestablished Anglican Church. Isaac Newton's experiments with gravity.

1665 Great Plague in London kills 75,000.

1666 Great Fire of London. Molière's *Misanthrope.*

1667 Milton's *Paradise Lost,* widely considered the greatest epic poem in English.

1682 Pennsylvania founded by William Penn.

1683 War of European powers against the Turks (to 1699). Vienna withstands three-month Turkish siege; high point of Turkish advance in Europe.

1684 Gottfried Wilhelm Leibniz's calculus published.

1685 James II succeeds Charles II in England, calls for freedom of conscience (1687). Protestants fear restoration of Catholicism and demand "Glorious Revolution." William of Orange invited to England and James II escapes

Galileo
(1564–1642)

Pocahontas
(c. 1595–1617)

Taj Mahal

John Milton
(1608–1674)

to France (1688). William III and his wife, Mary, crowned. In France, Edict of Nantes of 1598, granting freedom of worship to Huguenots, is revoked by Louis XIV; thousands of Protestants flee.

1689 Peter the Great becomes Czar of Russia—attempts to westernize nation and build Russia as a military power. Defeats Charles XII of Sweden at Poltava (1709). Beginning of the French and Indian Wars (to 1763), campaigns in America linked to a series of wars between France and England for domination of Europe.

1690 William III of England defeats former king James II and Irish rebels at Battle of the Boyne in Ireland. John Locke's *Human Understanding*.

Sir Isaac Newton
(1642–1727)

1700–1799 (A.D.)

1701 War of the Spanish Succession begins—the last of Louis XIV's wars for domination of the continent. The Peace of Utrecht (1714) will end the conflict and mark the rise of the British Empire. Called Queen Anne's War in America, it ends with the British taking New Foundland, Acadia, and Hudson's Bay Territory from France, and Gibraltar and Minorca from Spain.

1704 Deerfield (Mass.) Massacre of English colonists by French and Indians. Bach's first cantata. Jonathan Swift's *Tale of a Tub*. *Boston News Letter*—first newspaper in America.

1707 United Kingdom of Great Britain formed—England, Wales, and Scotland joined by parliamentary Act of Union.

1729 Bach's *St. Matthew Passion*. Isaac Newton's *Principia* translated from Latin into English.

1732 Benjamin Franklin begins publishing *Poor Richard's Almanack*. James Oglethorpe and others found Georgia.

Frederick the Great
(1712–1786)

1735 John Peter Zenger, New York editor, acquitted of libel in New York, establishing press freedom.

1740 Capt. Vitus Bering, Dane employed by Russia, discovers Alaska. Frederick II "the Great" crowned king of Prussia.

1746 British defeat Scots under Stuart Pretender Prince Charles at Culloden Moor. Last battle fought on British soil.

1751 Publication of the *Encyclopédie* begins in France, the "bible" of the Enlightenment.

1755 Samuel Johnson's *Dictionary* first published. Great earthquake in Lisbon, Portugal—over 60,000 die. U.S. postal service established.

1756 Seven Years' War (French and Indian Wars in America) (to 1763), in which Britain and Prussia defeat France, Spain, Austria, and Russia. France loses North American colonies; Spain cedes Florida to Britain in exchange for Cuba. In India, over 100 British prisoners die in "Black Hole of Calcutta."

Samuel Johnson
(1709–1784)

1757 Beginning of British Empire in India as Robert Clive, British commander, defeats Nawab of Bengal at Plassey.

1759 British capture Quebec from French. Voltaire's *Candide*. Haydn's *Symphony No. 1*.

THE REVOLUTIONARY WAR

Conflicts increase between colonists and Britain on western frontier because of royal edict limiting western expansion (1763) and regulation of colonial trade and increased taxation of colonies (Writs of Assistance allow search for illegal shipments, 1761; Sugar Act, 1764; Currency Act, 1764; Stamp Act, 1765; Quartering Act, 1765; Duty Act, 1767). Boston Massacre (1770). Lord North attempts conciliation (1770). Boston Tea Party (1773), followed by punitive measures passed by Parliament—the "Intolerable Acts."

First Continental Congress (1774) sends "Declaration of Rights and Grievances" to King George III, urges colonies to form Continental Association. Paul Revere's ride and Lexington and Concord battle between Massachusetts Minutemen and British (1775).

Second Continental Congress (1775), while sending "olive branch" to the king, begins to raise army, appoints Washington commander-in-chief, and seeks alliance with France. Some colonial legislatures urge their delegates to vote for independence. Declaration of Independence **(July 4, 1776)**.

Major Battles of the Revolutionary War: *Long Island:* Howe defeats Putnam's division of Washington's Army in Brooklyn Heights, but Americans escape across East River (1776). *Trenton and Princeton:* Washington defeats Hessians at Trenton, British at Princeton. Howe winters in Philadelphia; Washington at Valley Forge (1777–1778). Burgoyne surrenders British army to General Gates at *Saratoga* (1777).

France recognizes American independence (1778). The War moves south: Savannah captured by British (1778); Charleston occupied (1780); Americans fight successful guerrilla actions under Marion, Pickens, and Sumter. In the West, George Rogers Clark attacks Forts Kaskaskia and Vincennes (1778–1779), defeating British in the region. Cornwallis surrenders at *Yorktown*, Virginia **(Oct. 19, 1781)**. By 1782, Britain is eager for peace because of conflicts with European nations. *Peace of Paris* (1783): Britain recognizes American independence.

Benjamin Franklin
(1706–1790)

George Washington
(1732–1799)

Alexander Hamilton
(1755–1804)

Ludwig van Beethoven
(1770–1827)

1762 Catherine II ("the Great") becomes czarina of Russia. Jean Jacques Rousseau's *Social Contract.* Mozart tours Europe as six-year-old prodigy.

1765 James Watt invents the steam engine. Britain imposes the Stamp Act on the American colonists.

1769 Sir William Arkwright patents a spinning machine—an early step in the Industrial Revolution.

1770 The Boston Massacre.

1772 Joseph Priestley and Daniel Rutherford independently discover nitrogen. Partition of Poland—in 1772, 1793, and 1795, Austria, Prussia, and Russia divide land and people of Poland, end its independence.

1773 The Boston Tea Party.

1774 First Continental Congress drafts "Declaration of Rights and Grievances."

1775 The American Revolution begins with battle of Lexington and Concord. Second Continental Congress. Priestley discovers hydrochloric and sulfuric acids.

1776 Declaration of Independence. Gen. George Washington crosses the Delaware Christmas night. Adam Smith's *Wealth of Nations.* Edward Gibbon's *Decline and Fall of the Roman Empire.* Thomas Paine's *Common Sense.* Fragonard's *Washerwoman.* Mozart's *Haffner Serenade.*

1778 Capt. James Cook discovers Hawaii. Franz Mesmer uses hypnotism.

1781 Immanuel Kant's *Critique of Pure Reason.* Herschel discovers Uranus.

1783 Revolutionary War ends with Treaty of Paris. William Blake's poems. Beethoven's first printed works.

1784 Crimea annexed by Russia. John Wesley's *Deed of Declaration,* the basic work of Methodism.

1785 Russians settle Aleutian Islands.

1787 The Constitution of the United States signed. Lavoisier's work on chemical nomenclature. Mozart's *Don Giovanni.*

1788 French *Parlement* presents grievances to Louis XVI who agrees to convening of Estates-General in 1789—not called since 1613. Goethe's *Egmont.* Laplace's *Laws of the Planetary System.*

1789 French Revolution begins with the storming of the Bastille. In U.S., Washington elected president with all 69 votes of the Electoral College, takes oath of office in New York City. Vice President: John Adams. Secretary of State: Thomas Jefferson. Secretary of Treasury: Alexander Hamilton.

1790 H.M.S. *Bounty* mutineers settle on Pitcairn Island. Aloisio Galvani experiments on electrical stimulation of the muscles. Philadelphia temporary capital of U.S. as Congress votes to establish new capital on Potomac. U.S. population about 3,929,000, including 698,000 slaves. Lavoisier formulates *Table of 31 chemical elements.*

1791 U.S. Bill of Rights ratified. Boswell's *Life of Johnson.*

1792 Mary Wollstonecraft's *Vindication of the Rights of Woman.*

1793 Louis XVI and Marie Antoinette executed. Reign of Terror begins in France. Eli Whitney invents the cotton gin, spurring the growth of the cotton industry and helping to institutionalize slavery in the U.S. South.

1794 Kosciusko's uprising in Poland quelled by the Russians. In U.S., Whiskey Rebellion in Pennsylvania as farmers object to liquor taxes. Reign of Terror ends with execution of Robespierre.

1796 Napoléon Bonaparte, French general, defeats Austrians. In the U.S., Washington's Farewell Address **(Sept. 17);** John Adams elected president; Thomas Jefferson, vice president. Edward Jenner introduces smallpox vaccination.

1798 Napoleon extends French conquests to Rome and Egypt. U.S. Navy Department established.

FRENCH REVOLUTION (1789–1799)

Revolution begins when Third Estate (Commons) delegates swear not to disband until France has a constitution. Paris mob storms Bastille, symbol of royal power **(July 14, 1789).** National Assembly votes for Constitution, Declaration of the Rights of Man, a limited monarchy, and other reforms (1789–1790). Legislative Assembly elected, Revolutionary Commune formed, and French Republic proclaimed (1792). War of the First Coalition—Austria, Prussia, Britain, Netherlands, and Spain fight to restore French nobility (1792–1797).

Start of series of wars between France and European powers that will last, almost without interruption, for 23 years. Louis XVI and Marie Antoinette executed. Committee of Public Safety begins Reign of Terror as political control measure. Interfactional rivalry leads to mass killings. Danton and Robespierre executed. Third French Constitution sets up Directory government (1795). Napoleon abolishes the Directory, establishes the Consulate, becomes the First Consul of France (1799).

1799 Rosetta Stone discovered in Egypt. Napoleon leads coup that overthrows Directory, establishes the Consulate, becomes First Consul—one of three who rule France together.

1800–1899 (A.D.)

1800 Napoleon conquers Italy, firmly establishes himself as First Consul in France. In the U.S., federal government moves to Washington, D.C. Robert Owen's social reforms in England. William Herschel discovers infrared rays. Alessandro Volta produces electricity.

1801 Austria makes temporary peace with France. United Kingdom of Great Britain and Ireland established with one monarch and one parliament; Catholics excluded from voting.

Napoléon Bonaparte (1769–1821)

1803 U.S. negotiates Louisiana Purchase from France: for $15 million, U.S. doubles its domain, increasing its territory by 827,000 sq mi (2,144,500 sq km), from Mississippi River to Rockies and from Gulf of Mexico to British North America.

1804 Haiti declares independence from France; first black nation to gain freedom from European colonial rule. Napoleon transforms the Consulate of France into an empire, proclaims himself emperor of France, systematizes French law under *Code Napoleon*. In the U.S., Alexander Hamilton is mortally wounded in duel with Aaron Burr. Lewis and Clark expedition begins exploration of what is now northwest U.S.

1805 Lord Nelson defeats the French-Spanish fleets in the Battle of Trafalgar. Napoleon victorious over Austrian and Russian forces at the Battle of Austerlitz.

Edgar Allan Poe (1809–1849)

1807 Robert Fulton makes first successful steamboat trip on *Clermont* between New York City and Albany.

1808 French armies occupy Rome and Spain, extending Napoleon's empire. Britain begins aiding Spanish guerrillas against Napoleon in Peninsular War. In the U.S., Congress bars importation of slaves. Beethoven's *Fifth* and *Sixth Symphonies* performed.

1812 Napoleon's Grand Army invades Russia in June. Forced to retreat in winter, most of Napoleon's 600,000 men are lost. In the U.S., war with Britain declared over freedom of the seas for U.S. vessels (War of 1812). USS *Constitution* sinks British frigate.

Richard Wagner (1813–1883)

1814 French defeated by allies (Britain, Austria, Russia, Prussia, Sweden, and Portugal) in War of Liberation. Napoleon exiled to Elba, off Italian coast. Bourbon king Louis XVIII takes French throne. George Stephenson builds first practical steam locomotive.

1815 Napoleon returns: "Hundred Days" begin. Napoleon defeated by Wellington at Waterloo, banished again to St. Helena in South Atlantic. Congress of Vienna: victorious allies change the map of Europe. War of 1812 ends with Treaty of Ghent.

1819 Simón Bolívar liberates New Granada (now Colombia, Venezuela, and Ecuador) as Spain loses hold on South American countries; named president of Colombia.

1820 Missouri Compromise—Missouri admitted as slave state but slavery barred in rest of Louisiana Purchase north of 36°30′ N.

Harriet Beecher Stowe (1811–1896)

1821 Guatemala, Panama, and Santo Domingo proclaim independence from Spain.

1822 Greeks proclaim a republic and independence from Turkey. Turks invade Greece. Russia declares war on Turkey (1828). Greece also aided by France and Britain. War ends and Turks recognize Greek independence (1829). Brazil becomes independent of Portugal. Schubert's *Eighth Symphony* ("The Unfinished").

1823 U.S. Monroe Doctrine warns European nations not to interfere in Western Hemisphere.

1824 Mexico becomes a republic, three years after declaring independence from Spain. Bolívar liberates Peru, becomes its president. Beethoven's *Ninth Symphony*.

1825 First passenger-carrying railroad in England.

1826 Joseph-Nicéphore Niepce takes the world's first photograph.

Walt Whitman (1819–1892)

WAR OF 1812

British interference with American trade, impressment of American seamen, and "War Hawks" drive for western expansion lead to war. American attacks on Canada foiled; U.S. Commodore Perry wins battle of Lake Erie (1813). British capture and burn Washington (1814) but fail to take Fort McHenry at Baltimore. Andrew Jackson repulses assault on New Orleans after Treaty of Ghent ends war (1815). War settles little but strengthens U.S. as independent nation.

**Dred Scott
(1795?–1858)**

**Charles Darwin
(1809–1882)**

**Frederick Douglass
(1817–1895)**

**Harriet Tubman
(c. 1820–1913)**

**Samuel Clemens
(Mark Twain)
(1835–1910)**

1830 French invade Algeria. Louis Philippe becomes "Citizen King" as revolution forces Charles X to abdicate. Church of Jesus Christ of Latter-day Saints formed in U.S. by Joseph Smith.

1831 Polish revolt against Russia fails. Belgium separates from the Netherlands. In U.S., Nat Turner leads unsuccessful slave rebellion.

1833 Slavery abolished in British Empire.

1834 Charles Babbage invents "analytical engine," precursor of computer. McCormick patents reaper.

1836 Boer farmers start "Great Trek"—Natal, Transvaal, and Orange Free State founded in South Africa. Mexican army besieges Texans in Alamo. Entire garrison, including Davy Crockett and Jim Bowie, wiped out. Texans gain independence from Mexico after winning Battle of San Jacinto. Dickens's *Pickwick Papers.*

1837 Victoria becomes queen of Great Britain. Mob kills Elijah P. Lovejoy, Illinois abolitionist publisher.

1839 First Opium War (to 1842) between Britain and China, over importation of drug into China.

1840 Lower and Upper Canada united.

1841 U.S. President Harrison dies (**April 4**) one month after inauguration; John Tyler becomes first vice president to succeed to presidency.

1842 Crawford Long uses first anesthetic (ether).

1843 Wagner's opera *The Flying Dutchman.*

1844 Democratic convention calls for annexation of Texas and acquisition of Oregon ("Fifty-four-forty-or-fight"). Five Chinese ports opened to U.S. ships. Samuel F. B. Morse patents telegraph.

1845 Congress adopts joint resolution for annexation of Texas. Edgar Allan Poe publishes *The Raven and Other Poems.*

1846 U.S. declares war on Mexico. California and New Mexico annexed by U.S. Brigham Young leads Mormons to Great Salt Lake. W. T. Morton uses ether as anesthetic. Sewing machine patented by Elias Howe. Frederick Douglass launches abolitionist newspaper *The North Star.* Failure of potato crop causes famine in Ireland.

1848 Revolt in Paris: Louis Philippe abdicates; Louis Napoleon elected president of French Republic. Revolutions in Vienna, Venice, Berlin, Milan, Rome, and Warsaw. Put down by royal troops in 1848–1849. U.S.-Mexico War ends; Mexico cedes claims to Texas, California, Arizona, New Mexico, Utah, Nevada. U.S. treaty with Britain sets Oregon Territory boundary at 49th parallel. Karl Marx and Friedrich Engels's *Communist Manifesto.* Harriet Tubman escapes from slavery and joins the Underground Railroad. Women's Rights Convention in Seneca Falls, N.Y.

1849 California gold rush begins.

1850 Henry Clay opens great debate on slavery, warns South against secession.

1851 Herman Melville's *Moby-Dick.*

1852 South African Republic established. Louis Napoleon proclaims himself Napoleon III ("Second Empire"). Harriet Beecher Stowe's *Uncle Tom's Cabin.*

1853 Crimean War begins as Turkey declares war on Russia. Commodore Perry reaches Tokyo.

1854 Britain and France join Turkey in war on Russia. In U.S., Kansas-Nebraska Act permits local option on slavery; rioting and bloodshed. Japanese allow American trade. Antislavery men in Michigan form Republican Party. Tennyson's *Charge of the Light Brigade.* Thoreau's *Walden.*

1855 Armed clashes in Kansas between pro- and anti-slavery forces. Florence Nightingale nurses wounded in Crimea. Walt Whitman's *Leaves of Grass.*

1856 Flaubert's *Madame Bovary.*

1857 Supreme Court, in Dred Scott decision, rules that a slave is not a citizen. Financial crisis in Europe and U.S. Great Mutiny (Sepoy Rebellion) begins in India. India placed under crown rule as a result.

1858 Pro-slavery constitution rejected in Kansas. Abraham Lincoln makes strong antislavery speech in Springfield, Ill.: "This Government cannot endure permanently half slave and half free." Lincoln-Douglas debates. First trans-Atlantic telegraph cable completed by Cyrus W. Field.

1859 John Brown raids Harpers Ferry; is captured and hanged. Work begins on Suez Canal. Unification of Italy starts under leadership of Count Cavour, Sardinian premier. Joined by France in war against Austria. Jean-Joseph-Étienne Lenoir builds first practical internal-combustion engine. Edward Fitzgerald's translation of *The Rubaiyat of Omar Khayyam.* Charles Darwin's *Origin of Species.* J. S. Mill's *On Liberty.*

1860 South Carolina secedes from the Union.

1861 U.S. Civil War begins as attempts at compromise fail. Mississippi, Florida, Alabama, Georgia, Louisiana, and Texas secede; with South Carolina, they form the Confederate States of America, with Jefferson Davis as president. Virginia, Arkansas, Tennessee, North Carolina secede and join Confederacy. First Battle of Bull Run (Manassas). Congress creates Colorado, Dakota, and Nevada territories; adopts income tax; Lincoln inaugurated. Serfs emancipated in Russia. Pasteur's theory of germs. Independent Kingdom of Italy proclaimed under Sardinian king Victor Emmanuel II.

1862 Several major Civil War battles: Battle of Shiloh, Second Battle of Bull Run (Manassas), Battle of Antietam. Salon des Refusés introduces impressionism.

1863 French capture Mexico City; proclaim Archduke Maximilian of Austria emperor. Battle of Gettysburg.

1864 Gen. Sherman's Atlanta campaign and "march to the sea."

1865 Gen. Lee surrenders to Grant at Appomattox; the Civil War is over. Lincoln fatally shot at Ford's Theater by John Wilkes Booth. Vice President Johnson sworn as successor. Booth caught and dies of gunshot wounds; four conspirators are hanged. Joseph Lister begins antiseptic surgery. Gregor Mendel's *Law of Heredity*. Lewis Carroll's *Alice's Adventures in Wonderland*.

1866 Alfred Nobel invents dynamite (patented in Britain, 1867). Seven Weeks' War: Austria defeated by Prussia and Italy.

1867 Austria-Hungary Dual Monarchy established. French leave Mexico; Maximilian executed. Dominion of Canada established. U.S. buys Alaska from Russia for $7,200,000. South African diamond field discovered. Japan ends 675–year shogun rule. Volume I of Marx's *Das Kapital*. Strauss's *Blue Danube*.

1868 Revolution in Spain; Queen Isabella deposed, flees to France. In U.S., Fourteenth Amendment giving civil rights to blacks is ratified. Georgia under military government after legislature expels blacks.

1869 First U.S. transcontinental rail route completed. James Fisk and Jay Gould's attempt to control gold market causes Black Friday panic. Suez Canal opens. Mendeleev's periodic table of elements.

1870 Franco-Prussian War (to 1871): Napoleon III capitulates at Sedan. Revolt in Paris; Third Republic proclaimed.

1871 France surrenders Alsace-Lorraine to Germany; war ends. German Empire proclaimed with Prussian King as Kaiser Wilhelm I. Fighting with Apaches begins in American West. Boss Tweed corruption exposed in New York. The Chicago Fire, with 250 deaths and $196-million damage. Stanley meets Livingstone in Africa.

1872 Congress gives amnesty to most Confederates. Jules Verne's *Around the World in 80 Days*.

**Abraham Lincoln
(1809–1865)**

**Robert E. Lee
(1807–1870)**

**William Tecumseh
Sherman
(1820–1891)**

THE CIVIL WAR

Apart from the matter of slavery, the Civil War arose out of both the economic and political rivalry between an agrarian South and an industrial North and the issue of the right of states to secede from the Union.

1861 After South Carolina secedes **(Dec. 20, 1860),** Mississippi, Florida, Alabama, Georgia, Louisiana, and Texas follow, forming the Confederate States of America, with Jefferson Davis as president **(Jan.–March).** War begins as Confederates fire on Fort Sumter **(April 12).** Lincoln calls for 75,000 volunteers. Southern ports blockaded by superior Union naval forces. Virginia, Arkansas, Tennessee, and North Carolina secede to complete 11-state Confederacy. Union army advancing on Richmond repulsed at first Battle of Bull Run (Manassas) **(July).**

1862 Edwin M. Stanton named secretary of war **(Jan.).** Grant wins first important Union victory in West, at Fort Donelson; Nashville falls **(Feb.).** Ironclads, Union's *Monitor* and Confederate's *Virginia (Merrimac)* duel at Hampton Roads **(March).** New Orleans falls to Union fleet under Farragut; city occupied **(April).** Grant's army escapes defeat at Shiloh. Memphis falls as Union gunboats control upper Mississippi **(June).** Confederate general Robert E. Lee victorious at second Battle of Bull Run (Manassas) **(Aug.).** Union army under McClellan halts Lee's attack on Washington in the Battle of Antietam **(Sept.).** Lincoln removes

McClellan for lack of aggressiveness. Burnside's drive on Richmond fails at Fredericksburg **(Dec.).** Union forces under Rosecrans chase Bragg through Tennessee; battle of Murfreesboro **(Oct.–Jan. 1863).**

1863 Lee defeats Hooker at Chancellorsville; "Stonewall" Jackson, Confederate general, dies **(May).** Confederate invasion of Pennsylvania stopped at Gettysburg by George Meade—Lee loses 20,000 men—the greatest battle of the war **(July).** That and the Union victory at Vicksburg mark the war's turning point. Union general George H. Thomas, the "Rock of Chickamauga," holds Bragg's forces on Georgia-Tennessee border **(Sept.).** Sherman, Hooker, and Thomas drive Bragg back to Georgia. Tennessee restored to the Union **(Nov.).**

1864 Ulysses S. Grant named commander-in-chief of Union forces **(March).** In the Wilderness campaign, Grant forces Lee's Army of Northern Virginia back toward Richmond **(May–June).** Sherman's Atlanta campaign and "march to the sea" **(May–Sept.).** Farragut's victory at Mobile Bay **(Aug.).** Hood's Confederate army defeated at Nashville. Sherman takes Savannah **(Dec.).**

1865 Sheridan defeats Confederates at Five Forks; Confederates evacuate Richmond **(April).** On April 9, Lee surrenders to Grant at Appomattox.

Johannes Brahms
(1833–1897)

Chief Joseph
(c. 1840–1904)

Statue of Liberty

Marie Curie
(1867–1934)

1873   Economic crisis in Europe. U.S. establishes gold standard.

1875   First Kentucky Derby.

1876   Sioux kill Gen. George A. Custer and 264 troopers at Little Big Horn River. Alexander Graham Bell patents the telephone.

1877   After presidential election of 1876, electoral commission gives disputed electoral college votes to Rutherford B. Hayes despite Tilden's popular majority. Russo-Turkish war (ends in 1878 with power of Turkey in Europe broken). Reconstruction ends in the American South. Thomas Edison patents phonograph. The Nez Perce leader Chief Joseph is forced to surrender. Tchaikovsky's *Swan Lake.*

1878   Congress of Berlin revises Treaty of San Stefano, ending Russo-Turkish War; makes extensive redivision of southeast Europe. First commercial telephone exchange opened in New Haven, Conn.

1879   Thomas A. Edison invents electric light.

1880   U.S.-China treaty allows U.S. to restrict immigration of Chinese labor.

1881   President Garfield fatally shot by assassin; Vice President Arthur succeeds him. Charles J. Guiteau convicted and executed (1882).

1882   Terrorism in Ireland after land evictions. Britain invades and conquers Egypt. Germany, Austria, and Italy form Triple Alliance. In U.S., Congress adopts Chinese Exclusion Act. Rockefeller's Standard Oil Trust is first industrial monopoly. In Berlin, Robert Koch announces discovery of tuberculosis germ.

1883   Congress creates Civil Service Commission. Brooklyn Bridge and Metropolitan Opera House completed.

1884   Berlin West Africa Conference held in Berlin (lasting until **Feb. 1885**), at which the major European nations discuss expansion in Africa.

1885   British general Charles G. "Chinese" Gordon killed at Khartoum in Egyptian Sudan. World's first skyscraper built in Chicago.

1886   Bombing at Haymarket Square, Chicago, kills seven policemen and injures many others. Eight alleged anarchists accused—three imprisoned, one commits suicide, four hanged. (In 1893, Illinois governor Altgeld, critical of trial, pardons three survivors.) Statue of Liberty dedicated. Geronimo, Apache Indian chief, surrenders.

1887   Queen Victoria's Golden Jubilee. Sir Arthur Conan Doyle's first Sherlock Holmes story, *A Study in Scarlet.*

1888   Historic March blizzard in northeast U.S.—many perish, property damage exceeds $25 million. George Eastman's box camera (the Kodak). J. B. Dunlop invents pneumatic tire. Jack the Ripper murders in London.

1889   Second (Socialist) International founded in Paris. Indian Territory in Oklahoma opened to settlement. Thousands die in Johnstown, Pa. flood. Eiffel Tower built for the Paris exposition. Mark Twain's *A Connecticut Yankee in King Arthur's Court.*

1890   Congress votes to pass Sherman Antitrust Act. Sioux chief Sitting Bull arrested and killed by police on Pine Ridge reservation; two weeks later, U.S. troops kill over 200 Sioux at Battle of Wounded Knee.

1892   Battle between steel strikers and Pinkerton guards at Homestead, Pa.; union defeated after militia intervenes. Silver mine strikers in Idaho fight non-union workers; U.S. troops dispatched. Diesel engine patented.

1893   New Zealand becomes first country in the world to grant women the vote.

1894   Sino-Japanese War begins (ends in 1895 with China's defeat). In France, Capt. Alfred Dreyfus convicted on false treason charge (pardoned in 1906). In U.S., Jacob S. Coxey of Ohio leads "Coxey's Army" of unemployed on Washington. Eugene V. Debs calls general strike of rail workers to support Pullman Company strikers; strike broken, Debs jailed for six months. Edison's kinetoscope given first public showing in New York City.

1895   X-rays discovered by German physicist Wilhelm Roentgen. Auguste and Louis Lumière premiere motion pictures at a café in Paris.

SPANISH-AMERICAN WAR (1898–1899)

War fires stoked by "jingo journalism" as American people support Cuban rebels against Spain. American business sees economic gain in Cuban trade and resources and American power zones in Latin America. Outstanding events: Submarine mine sinks U.S. battleship *Maine* in Havana Harbor **(Feb. 15)**; 260 killed; responsibility never fixed. Congress declares independence of Cuba **(April 19)**. Spain declares war on U.S. **(April 24)**; Congress **(April 25)** formally declares nation has been at war with Spain since **April 21**. Commodore George Dewey wins seven-hour battle of Manila Bay **(May 1)**. Spanish fleet destroyed off Santiago, Cuba **(July 3)**; city surrenders **(July 17)**. Treaty of Paris (ratified by Senate 1899) ends war. U.S. given Guam and Puerto Rico and agrees to pay Spain $20 million for Philippines. Cuba independent of Spain; under U.S. military control for three years until **May 20, 1902**. Yellow fever is eradicated and political reforms achieved.

1896 Supreme Court's *Plessy* v. *Ferguson* decision—"separate but equal" doctrine. Alfred Nobel's will establishes prizes for peace, science, and literature. Marconi receives first wireless patent in Britain. William Jennings Bryan delivers "Cross of Gold" speech at Democratic Convention in Chicago. First modern Olympic games held in Athens, Greece.

1897 Theodor Herzl launches Zionist movement.

1898 Chinese "Boxers," anti-foreign organization, established. They stage uprisings against Europeans in 1900; U.S. and other Western troops relieve Peking legations. U.S. Battleship *Maine* is sunk in Havana Harbor. Spanish-American War begins. U.S. destroys Spanish fleet near Santiago, Cuba. Pierre and Marie Curie discover radium and polonium.

Sigmund Freud
(1856–1939)

1899 Boer War (or South African War): conflict between British and Boers (descendants of Dutch settlers of South Africa). Causes rooted in longstanding territorial disputes and in friction over political rights for English and other "uitlanders" following 1886 discovery of vast gold deposits in Transvaal. (British victorious as war ends in 1902.) Casualties: 5,774 British dead, about 4,000 Boers. Union of South Africa established in 1908 as confederation of colonies; becomes British dominion in 1910.

1900 Hurricane ravages Galveston, Tex.; 6,000–8,000 dead. Fauvist movement in painting begins, led by Henri Matisse. Sigmund Freud's *The Interpretation of Dreams*. Carrie Chapman Catt succeeds Susan B. Anthony as president of National Woman Suffrage Association.

Carrie Chapman Catt
(1859–1947)

1901 Queen Victoria dies, and is succeeded by her son, Edward VII. As President McKinley begins second term, he is shot fatally by anarchist Leon Czolgosz. Theodore Roosevelt sworn in as successor.

1902 Enrico Caruso's first gramophone recording. Aswan Dam completed.

1903 Wright brothers, Orville and Wilbur, fly first powered, controlled, heavier-than-air plane at Kitty Hawk, N.C. Henry Ford organizes Ford Motor Company. The Boston Red Sox win the first World Series against the Pittsburgh Pirates. W.E.B. Du Bois publishes *The Souls of Black Folk*.

1904 Russo-Japanese War begins—competition for Korea and Manchuria. *Entente Cordiale:* Britain and France settle their international differences. General theory of radioactivity by Rutherford and Soddy. New York City subway opens.

Albert Einstein
(1879–1955)

1905 In Russo-Japanese War, Port Arthur surrenders to Japanese; Russia suffers other defeats. President Roosevelt mediates Treaty of Portsmouth, N.H., which recognizes Japan's control of Korea and restores southern Manchuria to China. The Russian Revolution of 1905 begins on "Bloody Sunday" when troops fire onto a defenseless group of demonstrators in St. Petersburg. Strikes and riots follow. Sailors on battleship *Potemkin* mutiny; reforms, including first Duma (parliament), established by Czar Nicholas II's "October Manifesto." Albert Einstein's special theory of relativity and other key theories in physics. Franz Lehar's *Merry Widow*.

1906 San Francisco earthquake and three-day fire; more than 500 dead. Roald Amundsen, Norwegian explorer, fixes magnetic North Pole.

1907 Second Hague Peace Conference, of 46 nations, adopts 10 conventions on rules of war. Financial panic of 1907 in U.S. Mahler begins work on "Song of the Earth." Oklahoma becomes 46th state. Picasso's *Les Demoiselles d'Avignon* introduces cubism.

Vladimir Lenin
(1870–1924)

1908 Earthquake kills 150,000 in southern Italy and Sicily. U.S. Supreme Court, in Danbury Hatters' case, outlaws secondary union boycotts. Model T produced by Ford Motor Company.

1909 North Pole reportedly reached by American explorers Robert E. Peary and Matthew Henson. The National Association for the Advancement of Colored People is founded in New York by prominent black and white intellectuals and led by W.E.B. Du Bois.

1910 Boy Scouts of America incorporated. Angel Island, in San Francisco Bay, becomes immigration center for Asians entering U.S.

1911 First use of aircraft as offensive weapon in Turkish-Italian War. Italy defeats Turks and annexes Tripoli and Libya. Chinese Republic proclaimed after revolution overthrows Manchu dynasty. Sun Yat-sen named president. Mexican Revolution: Porfirio Diaz, president since 1877, replaced by Francisco Madero. Triangle Shirtwaist Company fire in New York; 146 killed. Amundsen reaches South Pole. Ernest Rutherford discovers the structure of the atom. Richard Strauss's *Der Rosenkavalier.* Irving Berlin's *Alexander's Ragtime Band.*

Robert Peary
(1856–1920)

W.E.B. Du Bois
(1868–1963)

Woodrow Wilson
(1856–1924)

Bessie Smith
(1894–1937)

1912   Balkan Wars (1912–1913) resulting from territorial disputes: Turkey defeated by alliance of Bulgaria, Serbia, Greece, and Montenegro; London peace treaty (1913) partitions most of European Turkey among the victors. In second war (1913), Bulgaria attacks Serbia and Greece and is defeated after Romania intervenes and Turks recapture Adrianople. *Titanic* sinks on maiden voyage; over 1,500 drown. New Mexico and Arizona admitted as states.

1913   Suffragists demonstrate in London. Garment workers strike in New York and Boston; win pay raise and shorter hours. Henry Ford develops first moving assembly line. 16th Amendment (income tax) and 17th (popular election of U.S. senators) adopted. Bill creating U.S. Federal Reserve System becomes law. Stravinsky's *The Rite of Spring*. Woodrow Wilson becomes 28th U.S. president. Armory Show introduces modern art to U.S.; Duchamp's *Nude Descending a Staircase* shocks public.

1914   World War I begins: Austrian Archduke Francis Ferdinand and wife Sophie are assassinated; Austria declares war on Serbia, Germany on Russia and France, Britain on Germany. Panama Canal officially opened. Congress sets up Federal Trade Commission, passes Clayton Antitrust Act. U.S. Marines occupy Veracruz, Mexico, intervening in civil war to protect American interests.

1915   *Lusitania* sunk by German submarine. Second Battle of Ypres. U.S. banks lend $500 million to France and Britain. Genocide of estimated 600,000 to 1 million Armenians by Turkish soldiers. D. W. Griffith's film *Birth of a Nation*. Albert Einstein's *General Theory of Relativity.*

1916   Congress expands armed forces. Battle of Verdun. Battle of the Somme. Tom Mooney arrested for San Francisco bombing (pardoned in 1939). Pershing fails in raid into Mexico in quest of rebel Pancho Villa. U.S. buys Virgin Islands from Denmark for $25 million. President Wilson re-elected with "he kept us out of war" slogan. "Black Tom" explosion at munitions dock in Jersey City, N.J., $40,000,000 damages; traced to German saboteurs. Margaret Sanger opens first birth control clinic. Easter Rebellion in Ireland put down by British troops. Jeannette Rankin becomes first woman elected to Congress.

1917   First U.S. combat troops in France as U.S. declares war on Germany **(April 6).** Third Battle of Ypres. Russian Revolution of 1917—climax of long unrest under czars. February Revolution—Nicholas II forced to abdicate, liberal government created. Kerensky becomes prime minister and forms provisional government **(July).** In October Revolution, Bolsheviks seize power in armed coup d'état led by Lenin and Trotsky. Kerensky flees. Balfour Declaration promises Jewish homeland in Palestine. U.S. declares war on Austria-Hungary **(Dec. 7).** Armistice between

---

WORLD WAR I (1914–1918)

Imperial, territorial, and economic rivalries led to the "Great War" between the Central Powers (Austria-Hungary, Germany, Bulgaria, and Turkey) and the Allies (U.S., Britain, France, Russia, Belgium, Serbia, Greece, Romania, Montenegro, Portugal, Italy, and Japan). About 10 million combatants killed, 20 million wounded.

1914 Austrian Archduke Francis Ferdinand and wife assassinated in Sarajevo by Serbian nationalist, Gavrilo Princip **(June 28).** Austria declares war on Serbia **(July 28).** Germany declares war on Russia **(Aug. 1),** on France **(Aug. 3),** invades Belgium **(Aug. 4).** Britain declares war on Germany **(Aug. 4).** Germans defeat Russians in Battle of Tannenberg on Eastern Front **(Aug.).** First Battle of the Marne **(Sept.).** German drive stopped 25 miles from Paris. By end of year, war on the Western Front is "positional" in the trenches.

1915 German submarine blockade of Great Britain begins **(Feb.).** Dardanelles Campaign—British land in Turkey **(April),** withdraw from Gallipoli **(Dec.–Jan. 1916).** Germans use gas at second Battle of Ypres **(April–May).** *Lusitania* sunk by German submarine—1,198 lost, including 128 Americans **(May 7).** On Eastern Front, German and Austrian "great offensive" conquers all of Poland and Lithuania; Russians lose 1 million men (by Oct. 1). "Great Fall Offensive" by Allies results in little change from 1914 **(Sept.–Oct.).** Britain and France declare war on Bulgaria **(Oct. 14).**

1916 Battle of Verdun—Germans and French each lose about 350,000 men **(Feb.).** Extended submarine

warfare begins **(March).** British-German sea battle of Jutland **(May);** British lose more ships, but German fleet never ventures forth again. On Eastern Front, the Brusilov offensive demoralizes Russians, costs them 1 million men **(June–Sept.).** Battle of the Somme—British lose over 400,000; French, 200,000; Germans, about 450,000; all with no strategic results **(July–Nov.).** Romania declares war on Austria-Hungary **(Aug. 27).** Bucharest captured **(Dec.).**

1917 U.S. declares war on Germany **(April 6).** Submarine warfare at peak **(April).** On Italian Front, Battle of Caporetto—Italians retreat, losing 600,000 prisoners and deserters **(Oct.–Dec.).** On Western Front, Battles of Arras, Champagne, Ypres (third battle), etc. First large British tank attack **(Nov.).** U.S. declares war on Austria-Hungary **(Dec. 7).** Armistice between new Russian Bolshevik government and Germans **(Dec. 15).**

1918 Great offensive by Germans **(March–June).** Americans' first important battle role at Château-Thierry—as they and French stop German advance **(June).** Second Battle of the Marne **(July–Aug.)**—start of Allied offensive at Amiens, St. Mihiel, etc. Battles of the Argonne and Ypres panic German leadership **(Sept.–Oct.).** British offensive in Palestine **(Sept.).** Germans ask for armistice **(Oct. 4).** British armistice with Turkey **(Oct.).** German Kaiser abdicates **(Nov.).** Hostilities cease on Western Front **(Nov. 11).**

new Russian Bolshevik government and Germans **(Dec. 15).** Sigmund Freud's *Introduction to Psychoanalysis*.

1918 Russian revolutionaries execute the former czar and his family. Russian Civil War between Reds (Bolsheviks) and Whites (anti-Bolsheviks); Reds win in 1920. Allied troops (U.S., British, French) intervene **(March);** leave in 1919. Second Battle of the Marne **(July–Aug.)** German Kaiser abdicates **(Nov.);** hostilities cease on the Western Front. Japanese hold Vladivostok until 1922. Worldwide influenza epidemic strikes; by 1920, nearly 20 million are dead. In U.S. alone, 500,000 perish.

1919 Third International (Comintern) establishes Soviet control over international Communist movements. Paris peace conference. Versailles Treaty, incorporating Woodrow Wilson's draft Covenant of League of Nations, signed by Allies and Germany; rejected by U.S. Senate. Congress formally ends war in 1921. 18th (Prohibition) Amendment adopted. Alcock and Brown make first trans-Atlantic nonstop flight. Mahatma Gandhi initiates satyagraha ("truth force") campaigns, beginning his nonviolent resistance movement against British rule in India.

Mahatma Gandhi
(1869–1948)

1920 League of Nations holds first meeting at Geneva, Switzerland. U.S. Dept. of Justice "red hunt" nets thousands of radicals; aliens deported. Women's suffrage (19th) amendment ratified. Treaty of Sèvres dissolves Ottoman Empire. First Agatha Christie mystery. Sinclair Lewis's *Main Street*.

1921 Reparations Commission fixes German liability at 132 billion gold marks. German inflation begins. Major treaties signed at Washington Disarmament Conference limit naval tonnage and pledge to respect territorial integrity of China. In U.S., Nicola Sacco and Bartolomeo Vanzetti, Italian-born anarchists, convicted of armed robbery murder; case stirs worldwide protests; they are executed in 1927.

William Butler Yeats
(1865–1939)

1922 Mussolini marches on Rome; forms Fascist government. Irish Free State, a self-governing dominion of British Empire, officially proclaimed. Kemal Atatürk, founder of modern Turkey, overthrows last sultan. James Joyce's *Ulysses*.

1923 Adolf Hitler's "Beer Hall Putsch" in Munich fails; in 1924 he is sentenced to five years in prison where he writes *Mein Kampf;* released after eight months. Occupation of Ruhr by French and Belgian troops to enforce reparations payments. Widespread Ku Klux Klan violence in U.S. Earthquake destroys third of Tokyo. George Gershwin's *Rhapsody in Blue*. Bessie Smith, known as "the Empress of the Blues," makes her first record. Irish poet William Butler Yeats wins Nobel Prize in Literature.

Robert Frost
(1874–1963)

1924 Death of Lenin; Stalin wins power struggle, rules as Soviet dictator until death in 1953. Italian Fascists murder Socialist leader Giacomo Matteotti. Interior Secretary Albert B. Fall and oilmen Harry Sinclair and Edward L. Doheny are charged with conspiracy and bribery in the Teapot Dome scandal, involving fraudulent leases of naval oil reserves. In 1931, Fall is sentenced to year in prison; Doheny and Sinclair acquitted of bribery. Nathan Leopold and Richard Loeb convicted in "thrill killing" of Bobby Franks in Chicago; defended by Clarence Darrow; sentenced to life imprisonment. (Loeb killed by fellow convict in 1936; Leopold paroled in 1958, dies in 1971.) Robert Frost wins first of four Pulitzers.

1925 Nellie Tayloe Ross elected governor of Wyoming; first woman governor elected in U.S. Locarno conferences seek to secure European peace by mutual guarantees. John T. Scopes convicted and fined for teaching evolution in a public school in Tennessee "Monkey Trial"; sentence set aside. John Logie Baird, Scottish inventor, transmits human features by television. Hitler publishes Volume I of *Mein Kampf*.

Pablo Picasso
(1881–1973)

1926 General strike in Britain brings nation's activities to standstill. U.S. marines dispatched to Nicaragua during revolt; they remain until 1933. Gertrude Ederle of U.S. is first woman to swim English Channel. Ernest Hemingway's *The Sun Also Rises*.

1927 German economy collapses. Socialists riot in Vienna; general strike follows acquittal of Nazis for political murder. Trotsky expelled from Russian Communist Party. Charles A. Lindbergh flies first successful solo nonstop flight from New York to Paris. Ruth Snyder and Judd Gray convicted of murder of Albert Snyder; they are executed at Sing Sing prison in 1928. Philo T. Farnsworth demonstrates working television model. Georges Lemaître proposes Big Bang Theory. Babe Ruth hits 60 home runs in the season; record stands for next 34 years. *The Jazz Singer,* with Al Jolson, first part-talking motion picture.

Babe Ruth
(George Herman Ruth)
(1895–1948)

Benito Mussolini
(1883–1945)

Joseph Stalin
(1879–1953)

Adolf Hitler
(1889–1945)

1928 Kellogg-Briand Pact, outlawing war, signed in Paris by 65 nations. Alexander Fleming discovers penicillin. Richard E. Byrd starts expedition to Antarctic; returns in 1930. Anthropologist Margaret Mead publishes *Coming of Age in Samoa. Oxford English Dictionary* published after 44 years of research.

1929 Trotsky expelled from USSR Lateran Treaty establishes independent Vatican City. In U.S., stock market prices collapse, with U.S. securities losing $26 billion—first phase of Depression and world economic crisis. St. Valentine's Day gangland massacre in Chicago. Edwin Powell Hubble proposes theory of expanding universe.

1930 Britain, U.S., Japan, France, and Italy sign naval disarmament treaty. Nazis gain in German elections. Cyclotron developed by Ernest O. Lawrence, U.S. physicist. Pluto discovered by astronomers.

1931 Spain becomes a republic with overthrow of King Alfonso XIII. German industrialists finance 800,000-strong Nazi party. British parliament enacts statute of Westminster, legalizing dominion equality with Britain. Mukden Incident begins Japanese occupation of Manchuria. In U.S., Hoover proposes one-year moratorium of war debts. Harold C. Urey discovers heavy hydrogen. Gangster Al Capone sentenced to 11 years in prison for tax evasion (freed in 1939; dies in 1947). Notorious Scottsboro trial begins, exposing depth of Southern racism. "The Star Spangled Banner" officially becomes national anthem.

1932 Nazis lead in German elections with 230 Reichstag seats. Famine in USSR. In U.S., Congress sets up Reconstruction Finance Corporation to stimulate economy. Veterans march on Washington—most leave after Senate rejects payment of cash bonuses; others removed by troops under Douglas MacArthur. U.S. protests Japanese aggression in Manchuria. Amelia Earhart is first woman to fly Atlantic solo. Charles A. Lindbergh's baby son kidnapped, killed. (Bruno Richard Hauptmann arrested in 1934, convicted in 1935, executed in 1936.)

1933 Hitler appointed German chancellor, gets dictatorial powers. Reichstag fire in Berlin; Nazi terror begins. Germany and Japan withdraw from League of Nations. Giuseppe Zangara executed for attempted assassination of president-elect Roosevelt in which Chicago mayor Cermak is fatally shot. Roosevelt inaugurated ("the only thing we have to fear is fear itself"); launches New Deal. Prohibition repealed. USSR recognized by U.S.

1934 Chancellor Dollfuss of Austria assassinated by Nazis. Hitler becomes führer. USSR admitted to League of Nations. Dionne sisters, first quintuplets to survive beyond infancy, born in Canada. Mao Zedong begins the Long March north with 100,000 soldiers.

1935 Saar incorporated into Germany after plebiscite. Nazis repudiate Versailles Treaty, introduce compulsory military service. Mussolini invades Ethiopia; League of Nations invokes sanctions. Roosevelt opens second phase of

---

THE HOLOCAUST (1933–1945)

"Holocaust" is the term describing the Nazi annihilation of about 6 million Jews (two thirds of the pre-World War II European Jewish population), including 4,500,000 from Russia, Poland, and the Baltic; 750,000 from Hungary and Romania; 290,000 from Germany and Austria; 105,000 from The Netherlands; 90,000 from France; 54,000 from Greece.

The Holocaust was unique in its being *genocide*—the systematic destruction of a people solely because of religion, race, ethnicity, nationality, or sexual preference—on an unmatched scale. Along with the Jews, another 9 to 10 million people—Gypsies, Slavs (Poles, Ukrainians, and Belarussians), homosexuals, and the disabled—were exterminated.

1933 Hitler named German Chancellor **(Jan.)**. Dachau, first concentration camp, established **(March)**. Boycotts against Jews begin **(April)**.

1935 Anti-Semitic Nuremberg Laws passed by Reichstag; Jews lose citizenship and civil rights **(Sept.)**.

1937 Buchenwald concentration camp opens **(July)**.

1938 Extension of anti-Semitic laws to Austria after annexation **(March)**. *Kristallnacht* (Night of Broken Glass)—anti-Semitic riots and destruction of Jewish institutions in Germany and Austria **(Nov. 9)**. 26,000 Jews sent to concentration camps; Jewish children expelled from schools **(Nov. 9–10)**. Expropriation of Jewish property and businesses **(Dec.)**.

1940 As war continues, Einsatzgruppen (mobile killing squads) follow German army into conquered lands, rounding up and massacring Jews and other "undesirables."

1941 Goering instructs Heydrich to carry out the "final solution to the Jewish question" **(July 31)**. Deportation of German Jews begins; massacres of Jews in Odessa and Kiev **(Nov.)**; and in Riga and Vilna **(Dec.)**.

1942 Mass killings using Zyklon-B begin at Auschwitz-Birkenau **(Jan.)**. Nazi leaders attend Wannsee Conference to coordinate the "final solution" **(Jan. 20)**. 100,000 Jews from Warsaw Ghetto deported to Treblinka death camp **(July)**.

1943 Warsaw Ghetto uprisings **(Jan. and April)**; Ghetto exterminated **(May)**.

1944 476,000 Hungarian Jews sent to Auschwitz **(May–June)**. D-day **(June 6)**. Soviet Army liberates Maidanek death camp **(July)**. Nazis try to hide evidence of death camps **(Nov.)**.

1945 As Allies advance, Nazis force concentration camp inmates on death marches. Americans liberate Buchenwald and British liberate Bergen-Belsen camps **(April)**. Nuremberg War Crimes Trial **(Nov. 1945–Oct. 1946)**.

New Deal in U.S., calling for social security, better housing, equitable taxation, and farm assistance. Huey Long assassinated in Louisiana.

1936 Germans occupy Rhineland. Italy annexes Ethiopia. Rome-Berlin Axis proclaimed (Japan to join in 1940). Trotsky exiled to Mexico. King George V dies; succeeded by son, Edward VIII, who soon abdicates to marry an American-born divorcée, and is succeeded by brother, George VI. Spanish civil war begins. Hundreds of Americans join the "Lincoln Brigades." (Franco's fascist forces defeat Loyalist forces by 1939, when Madrid falls.) War between China and Japan begins, to continue through World War II. Japan and Germany sign anti-Comintern pact; joined by Italy in 1937.

1937 Hitler repudiates war guilt clause of Versailles Treaty; continues to build German power. Italy withdraws from League of Nations. U.S. gunboat *Panay* sunk by Japanese in Yangtze River. Japan invades China, conquers most of coastal area. Amelia Earhart lost somewhere in Pacific on round-the-world flight. Picasso's *Guernica* mural.

1938 Hitler marches into Austria; political and geographical union of Germany and Austria proclaimed. Munich Pact—Britain, France, and Italy agree to let Germany partition Czechoslovakia. Douglas "Wrong-Way" Corrigan flies from New York to Dublin. Fair Labor Standards Act establishes minimum wage. Orson Welles's radio broadcast *War of the Worlds*.

1939 Germany invades Poland; occupies Bohemia and Moravia; renounces pact with England and concludes 10-year non-aggression pact with USSR. Russo-Finnish War begins; Finns to lose one-tenth of territory in 1940 peace treaty. World War II begins. In U.S., Roosevelt submits $1,319-million defense budget, proclaims U.S. neutrality, and declares limited emergency. Einstein writes FDR about feasibility of atomic bomb. New York World's Fair opens. DAR refuses to allow Marian Anderson to perform. *Gone with the Wind* premieres.

Dorothea Lange's photo "Migrant Mother" (1936) documented the Great Depression (1929–1940)

Amelia Earhart (1897–1937)

WORLD WAR II (1939-1945)

Axis powers (Germany, Italy, Japan, Hungary, Romania, Bulgaria) *versus* Allies (U.S., Britain, France, USSR, Australia, Belgium, Brazil, Canada, China, Denmark, Greece, Netherlands, New Zealand, Norway, Poland, South Africa, Yugoslavia).

1939 Germany invades Poland and annexes Danzig; Britain and France give Hitler ultimatum **(Sept. 1)**, declare war **(Sept. 3)**. Disabled German pocket battleship *Admiral Graf Spee* blown up off Montevideo, Uruguay, on Hitler's orders **(Dec. 17)**. Limited activity ("Sitzkrieg") on Western Front.

1940 Nazis invade Netherlands, Belgium, and Luxembourg **(May 10)**. Chamberlain resigns as Britain's prime minister; Churchill takes over **(May 10)**. Germans cross French frontier **(May 12)** using air/tank/ infantry "Blitzkrieg" tactics. Dunkerque evacuation— about 335,000 out of 400,000 Allied soldiers rescued from Belgium by British civilian and naval craft **(May 26–June 3)**. Italy declares war on France and Britain; invades France **(June 10)**. Germans enter Paris; city undefended **(June 14)**. France and Germany sign armistice at Compiègne **(June 22)**. Nazis bomb Coventry, England **(Nov. 14)**.

1941 Germans launch attacks in Balkans. Yugoslavia surrenders—General Mihajlovic continues guerrilla warfare; Tito leads left-wing guerrillas **(April 17)**. Nazi tanks enter Athens; remnants of British Army quit Greece **(April 27)**. Hitler attacks Russia **(June 22)**. Atlantic Charter—FDR and Churchill agree on war aims **(Aug. 14)**. Japanese attacks on Pearl Harbor, Philippines, Guam force U.S. into war; U.S. Pacific fleet crippled **(Dec. 7)**. U.S. and Britain declare war on Japan. Germany and Italy declare war on U.S.; Congress declares war on those countries **(Dec. 11)**.

1942 British surrender Singapore to Japanese **(Feb. 15)**. Roosevelt orders Japanese and Japanese Americans in western U.S. to be exiled to "relocation centers," many for the remainder of the war **(Feb. 19)**. U.S. forces on Bataan peninsula in Philippines surrender **(April 9)**. U.S. and Filipino troops on Corregidor island in Manila Bay surrender to Japanese **(May 6)**. Village of Lidice in Czechoslovakia razed by Nazis

(June 10). U.S. and Britain land in French North Africa **(Nov. 8)**.

1943 Casablanca Conference—Churchill and FDR agree on unconditional surrender goal **(Jan. 14–24)**. German 6th Army surrenders at Stalingrad—turning point of war in Russia **(Feb. 1–2)**. Remnants of Nazis trapped on Cape Bon, ending war in Africa **(May 12)**. Mussolini deposed; Badoglio named premier **(July 25)**. Allied troops land on Italian mainland after conquest of Sicily **(Sept. 3)**. Italy surrenders **(Sept. 8)**. Nazis seize Rome **(Sept. 10)**. Cairo Conference: FDR, Churchill, Chiang Kai-shek pledge defeat of Japan, free Korea **(Nov. 22–26)**. Teheran Conference: FDR, Churchill, Stalin agree on invasion plans **(Nov. 28–Dec. 1)**.

1944 U.S. and British troops land at Anzio on west Italian coast and hold beachhead **(Jan. 22)**. U.S. and British troops enter Rome **(June 4)**. D-Day—Allies launch Normandy invasion **(June 6)**. Hitler wounded in bomb plot **(July 20)**. Paris liberated **(Aug. 25)**. Athens freed by Allies **(Oct. 13)**. Americans invade Philippines **(Oct. 20)**. Germans launch counteroffensive in Belgium—Battle of the Bulge **(Dec. 16)**.

1945 Yalta Agreement signed by FDR, Churchill, Stalin—establishes basis for occupation of Germany, returns to Soviet Union lands taken by Germany and Japan; USSR agrees to friendship pact with China **(Feb. 11)**. Mussolini killed at Lake Como **(April 28)**. Admiral Doenitz takes command in Germany; suicide of Hitler announced **(May 1)**. Berlin falls **(May 2)**. Germany signs unconditional surrender terms at Rheims **(May 7)**. Allies declare V-E Day **(May 8)**. Potsdam Conference—Truman, Churchill, Atlee (after **July 28**), Stalin establish council of foreign ministers to prepare peace treaties; plan German postwar government and reparations **(July 17–Aug. 2)**. A-bomb dropped on Hiroshima by U.S. **(Aug. 6)**. USSR declares war on Japan **(Aug. 8)**. Nagasaki hit by A-bomb **(Aug. 9)**. Japan agrees to surrender **(Aug. 14)**. V-J Day— Japanese sign surrender terms aboard battleship *Missouri* **(Sept. 2)**.

**Franklin Delano
Roosevelt
(1882–1945)**

**Winston Churchill
(1874–1965)**

**Harry S. Truman
(1884–1972)**

Atomic Bomb

**Anne Frank
(1929–1945)**

1940 Hitler invades Norway, Denmark (**April 9**), the Netherlands, Belgium, Luxembourg (**May 10**), and France (**May 12**). Churchill becomes Britain's prime minister. Trotsky assassinated in Mexico (**Aug. 20**). Estonia, Latvia, and Lithuania annexed by USSR. U.S. trades 50 destroyers for leases on British bases in Western Hemisphere. Selective Service Act signed. The first official network television broadcast is put out by NBC.

1941 Germany attacks the Balkans and Russia. Japanese surprise attack on U.S. fleet at Pearl Harbor brings U.S. into World War II; U.S. and Britain declare war on Japan. Manhattan Project (atomic bomb research) begins. Roosevelt enunciates "four freedoms," signs Lend-Lease Act, declares national emergency, promises aid to USSR. Orson Welles's *Citizen Kane.*

1942 Declaration of United Nations signed in Washington (**Jan. 1**). Nazi leaders attend Wannsee Conference to coordinate the "final solution to the Jewish question," the systematic genocide of Jews known as the Holocaust. Women's military services established. Enrico Fermi achieves nuclear chain reaction. More than 120,000 Japanese and persons of Japanese ancestry living in western U.S. moved to "relocation centers," some for the duration of the war (Executive Order 9066). Coconut Grove nightclub fire in Boston kills 492 (**Nov. 28**).

1943 Churchill and Roosevelt hold Casablanca Conference (**Jan. 14–23**). Mussolini deposed. President freezes prices, salaries, and wages to prevent inflation. Income tax withholding introduced.

1944 Allies invade Normandy on D-Day (**June 6**). G.I. Bill of Rights enacted. Bretton Woods Conference creates International Monetary Fund and World Bank (**July 1–22**). Dumbarton Oaks Conference—U.S., British Commonwealth, and USSR propose establishment of United Nations (**Aug. 21–Oct. 7**). Battle of the Bulge (**Dec. 16**). Gunnar Myrdal's *An American Dilemma.*

1945 Yalta Conference (Roosevelt, Churchill, Stalin) plans final defeat of Germany (**Feb. 4–11**). FDR dies (**April 12**). Hitler commits suicide (**April 30**); Germany surrenders (**May 7**); **May 8** is declared V-E Day. Potsdam Conference (Truman, Churchill, Stalin) establishes basis of German reconstruction (**July–Aug.**). U.S. drops atomic bombs on Japanese cities of Hiroshima (**Aug. 6**) and Nagasaki (**Aug. 9**). Japan signs official surrender on V-J Day (**Sept. 2**). United Nations established (**Oct. 24**). First electronic computer, ENIAC, built.

1946 First meeting of UN General Assembly opens in London (**Jan. 10**). Winston Churchill's "Iron Curtain" speech warns of Soviet expansion (**March 5**). League of Nations dissolved (**April**). Italy abolishes monarchy (**June**). Verdict in Nuremberg war trial: 12 Nazi leaders (including 1 tried in absentia) sentenced to hang; 7 imprisoned; 3 acquitted (**Oct. 1**). Goering commits suicide a few hours before 10 other Nazis are executed (**Oct. 15**). Juan Perón becomes president of Argentina. Benjamin Spock's childcare classic published.

1947 Britain nationalizes coal mines (**Jan. 1**). Peace treaties for Italy, Romania, Bulgaria, Hungary, Finland signed in Paris (**Feb. 10**). Soviet Union rejects U.S. plan for UN atomic-energy control (**March 4**). Truman proposes Truman Doctrine, which was to aid Greece and Turkey in resisting communist expansion (**March 12**). Marshall Plan for European recovery proposed—a coordinated program to help European nations recover from ravages of war (**June**). (By the time it ended in 1951, this "European Recovery Program" had cost $13 billion.) India and Pakistan gain independence from Britain (**Aug. 15**). U.S. Air Force pilot Chuck Yeager becomes first person to break the sound barrier (**Oct. 14**). Jackie Robinson joins the Brooklyn Dodgers. Anne Frank's *The Diary of a Young Girl* published.

1948 Gandhi assassinated in New Delhi by Hindu fanatic (**Jan. 30**). Burma (**Jan. 4**) and Ceylon (**Feb. 4**) granted independence by Britain. Communists seize power in Czechoslovakia (**Feb. 23–25**). Organization of American States (OAS) Charter signed at Bogotá, Colombia (**April 30**). Nation of Israel proclaimed; British end mandate at midnight; Arab armies attack (**May 14**). Berlin blockade begins (**June 24**), prompting Allied airlift (**June 26**). (Blockade ends **May 12, 1949**; airlift continues until **Sept. 30, 1949**.) Stalin and Tito break (**June 28**). Independent Republic of Korea is proclaimed, following election supervised by UN (**Aug. 15**). Verdict in Japanese war trial: 18 imprisoned (**Nov. 12**); Tojo and six others hanged (**Dec. 23**). United States of Indonesia established as Dutch and Indonesians settle conflict (**Dec. 27**). Alger Hiss, former

U.S. State Department official, indicted on perjury charges after denying passing secret documents to communist spy ring; convicted in second trial (1950) and sentenced to five-year prison term. Truman ends racial segregation in military. Alfred Kinsey publishes *Sexual Behavior in the American Male.* Tennessee Williams's *A Streetcar Named Desire* wins Pulitzer.

1949 Cease-fire in Palestine (**Jan. 7**). Truman proposes Point Four Program to help world's less developed areas (**Jan. 20**). Israel signs armistice with Egypt (**Feb. 24**). Start of North Atlantic Treaty Organization (NATO)—treaty signed by 12 nations (**April 4**). Federal Republic of Germany (West Germany) established (**May 23**). First successful Soviet atomic test (**July 14**). Communist People's Republic of China formally proclaimed by Chairman Mao Zedong (**Oct. 1**). German Democratic Republic (East Germany) established under Soviet rule (**Oct. 7**). South Africa institutionalizes apartheid.

Tennessee Williams
(1911–1983)

1950 Brink's robbery in Boston; almost $3 million stolen (**Jan. 17**). Truman orders development of hydrogen bomb (**Jan. 31**). Robert Schuman proposes Schuman Plan to pool European coal and steel (**May 9**). Korean War begins when North Korean Communist forces invade South Korea (**June 25**). Assassination attempt on President Truman by Puerto Rican nationalists (**Nov. 1**). McCarthyism begins.

1951 Julius and Ethel Rosenberg sentenced to death for passing atomic secrets to Russians (**March**). Spurred by Schuman Plan, six nations form European Coal and Steel Community (**April**); effective 1952. Japanese peace treaty signed in San Francisco by 49 nations (**Sept. 8**). Color television introduced in U.S. Libya gains independence (**Dec. 24**).

Woody Guthrie
(1912–1967)

1952 George VI dies; his daughter becomes Elizabeth II (**Feb. 6**). AEC announces "satisfactory" experiments in hydrogen-weapons research; eyewitnesses tell of blasts near Enewetak (**Nov.**). Ralph Ellison's *The Invisible Man.*

1953 Gen. Dwight D. Eisenhower inaugurated president of United States (**Jan. 20**). Stalin dies (**March 5**). Malenkov becomes Soviet premier; Beria, minister of interior; Molotov, foreign minister (**March 6**). Dag Hammarskjöld begins term as UN secretary-general (**April 10**). James Watson and Francis Crick publish their discovery of the molecular model of DNA (**April–May**). Edmund Hillary of New Zealand and Tenzing Norgay of Nepal reach top of Mt. Everest (**May 29**). East Berliners rise against Communist rule; quelled by tanks (**June 17**). Egypt becomes republic ruled by military junta (**June 18**). Julius and Ethel Rosenberg executed in Sing Sing prison (**June 19**). Korean armistice signed (**July 27**). Moscow announces explosion of hydrogen bomb (**Aug. 20**). Tito becomes president of Yugoslavia. James Watson, Francis Crick, and Rosalind Franklin discover structure of DNA. Ernest Hemingway wins Pulitzer for *The Old Man and the Sea.*

Dwight D. Eisenhower
(1890–1969)

1954 First atomic submarine *Nautilus* launched (**Jan. 21**). Five U.S. congressmen shot on floor of House as Puerto Rican nationalists fire from spectators' gallery; all five recover (**March 1**). Soviet Union grants sovereignty to East Germany (**March 23**). *Army* v. *McCarthy* inquiry—Senate subcommittee report blames both sides (**April 22–June 17**). Dien Bien Phu, French military outpost in Vietnam, falls to Vietminh army (**May 7**). U.S. Supreme Court (in *Brown* v. *Board of Education of Topeka*) unanimously bans racial segregation in public schools (**May 17**). Eisenhower launches world atomic pool without Soviet Union (**Sept. 6**). Eight-nation Southeast Asia defense treaty (SEATO) signed at Manila (**Sept. 8**). Dr. Jonas Salk starts inoculating children against polio. Algerian War of Independence against France begins (**Nov.**); France struggles to maintain colonial rule until 1962 when it agrees to Algeria's independence. William Faulkner's *A Fable* wins Pulitzer.

Dag Hammarskjöld
(1905–1961)

KOREAN WAR (1950–1953)

1950 North Korean Communist forces invade South Korea (**June 25**). UN calls for cease-fire and asks UN members to assist South Korea (**June 27**). Truman orders U.S. forces into Korea (**June 27**). North Koreans capture Seoul (**June 28**). Gen. Douglas MacArthur designated commander of unified UN forces (**July 8**). Pusan Beachhead—UN forces counterattack and capture Seoul (**Aug.–Sept.**), capture Pyongyang, North Korean capital (**Oct.**). Chinese Communists enter war (**Oct. 26**), force UN retreat toward 38th parallel (**Dec.**).

1951 Gen. Matthew B. Ridgway replaces MacArthur after he threatens Chinese with massive retaliation (**April 11**). Armistice negotiations (**July**) continue with interruptions until **June 1953**.

1953 Armistice signed (**July 27**). Chinese troops withdraw from North Korea (**Oct. 26, 1958**), but over 200 violations of armistice noted to **1959**.

**Fidel Castro
(1926–)**

**John H. Glenn, Jr.
(1921–)**

**Martin Luther King, Jr.
(1929–1968)**

**John F. Kennedy
(1917–1963)**

1955 Nikolai A. Bulganin becomes Soviet premier, replacing Malenkov (**Feb. 8**). Churchill resigns; Anthony Eden succeeds him (**April 6**). West Germany becomes a sovereign state (**May 5**). Western European Union (WEU) comes into being (**May 6**). Warsaw Pact, east European mutual defense agreement, signed (**May 14**). Argentina ousts Perón (**Sept. 19**). President Eisenhower suffers coronary thrombosis in Denver (**Sept. 24**). Rosa Parks refuses to sit at the back of the bus. Martin Luther King, Jr., leads black boycott of Montgomery, Ala., bus system (**Dec. 1**); desegregated service begins **Dec. 21, 1956**. AFL and CIO become one organization—AFL-CIO (**Dec. 5**). Tennessee Williams's *Cat on a Hot Tin Roof* wins Pulitzer.

1956 Nikita Khrushchev, First Secretary of USSR Communist Party, denounces Stalin's excesses (**Feb. 24**). First aerial H-bomb tested over Namu islet, Bikini Atoll—10 million tons TNT equivalent (**May 21**). Workers' uprising against Communist rule in Poznan, Poland, is crushed (**June 28–30**); rebellion inspires Hungarian students to stage a protest against Communism in Budapest (**Oct. 23**). Egypt takes control of Suez Canal (**July 26**). Hungarian rebellion forces Soviet troops to withdraw from Budapest (**Oct.**). Israel launches attack on Egypt's Sinai peninsula and drives toward Suez Canal (**Oct. 29**). Imre Nagy announces Hungary's withdrawal from Warsaw Pact (**Nov. 1**); Soviet troops enter and reclaim Budapest (**Nov. 4**). British and French invade Port Said on the Suez Canal (**Nov. 5**). Cease-fire forced by U.S. pressure stops British, French, and Israeli advance (**Nov. 6**). Morocco gains independence. Ingmar Bergman's *The Seventh Seal*. Woody Guthrie composes "This Land is Your Land." Allen Ginsberg's *Howl*.

1957 Eisenhower Doctrine calls for aid to Mideast countries which resist armed aggression from Communist-controlled nations (**Jan. 5**). The "Little Rock Nine" integrate Arkansas high school. Eisenhower sends troops to quell mob and protect school integration (**Sept. 24**). Russians launch *Sputnik I*, first Earth-orbiting satellite—the Space Age begins (**Oct. 4**).

1958 European Economic Community (Common Market) becomes effective (**Jan. 1**). Army's Jupiter-C rocket fires first U.S. Earth satellite, *Explorer I*, into orbit (**Jan. 31**). Egypt and Syria merge into United Arab Republic (**Feb. 1**). Khrushchev becomes premier of Soviet Union as Bulganin resigns (**Mar. 27**). Gen. Charles de Gaulle becomes French premier (**June 1**), remaining in power until 1969. Eisenhower orders U.S. Marines into Lebanon at request of President Chamoun, who fears overthrow (**July 15**). New French constitution adopted (**Sept. 28**), de Gaulle elected president of 5th Republic (**Dec. 21**).

1959 Cuban President Batista resigns and flees—Castro takes over (**Jan. 1**). Tibet's Dalai Lama escapes to India (**Mar. 31**). St. Lawrence Seaway opens, allowing ocean ships to reach Midwest (**April 25**). Alaska and Hawaii become states. Leakeys discover hominid fossils.

1960 American U-2 spy plane, piloted by Francis Gary Powers, shot down over Russia (**May 1**). Khrushchev kills Paris summit conference because of U-2 (**May 16**). Top Nazi murderer of Jews, Adolf Eichmann, captured by Israelis in Argentina (**May 23**)—executed in Israel in 1962. Powers sentenced to prison for 10 years (**Aug. 19**)—freed in **February 1962** in exchange for Soviet spy. Communist China and Soviet Union split in conflict over Communist ideology. Senegal, Ghana, Nigeria, Madagascar, and Zaire (Belgian Congo) gain independence. Cuba begins confiscation of $770 million of U.S. property (**Aug. 7**). There are 900 U.S. military advisers in South Vietnam.

1961 U.S. breaks diplomatic relations with Cuba (**Jan. 3**). Robert Frost recites "The Gift Outright" at John F. Kennedy's inauguration as president of U.S. (**Jan. 20**). Moscow announces putting first man in orbit around Earth, Maj. Yuri A. Gagarin (**April 12**). Cuba invaded at Bay of Pigs by an estimated 1,200 anti-Castro exiles aided by U.S.; invasion crushed (**April 17**). First U.S. spaceman, Navy Cmdr. Alan B. Shepard, Jr., rockets 116.5 miles up in 302-mile trip (**May 5**). Virgil Grissom becomes second American astronaut, making 118-mile-high, 303-mile-long rocket flight over Atlantic (**July 21**). Gherman Stepanovich Titov is launched in Soviet spaceship *Vostok II:* makes 17½ orbits in 25 hours, covering 434,960 miles before landing safely (**Aug. 6**). East Germans erect Berlin Wall between East and West Berlin to halt flood of refugees (**Aug. 13**). USSR fires 50-megaton hydrogen bomb, biggest explosion in history (**Oct. 29**). There are 2,000 U.S. military advisers in South Vietnam.

1962 Lt. Col. John H. Glenn, Jr., is first American to orbit Earth—three times in 4 hr 55 min **(Feb. 20)**. France transfers sovereignty to new republic of Algeria **(July 3)**. Cuban missile crisis—USSR to build missile bases in Cuba; Kennedy orders Cuban blockade, lifts blockade after Russians back down **(Aug.–Nov.)**. James H. Meredith, escorted by federal marshals, registers at University of Mississippi **(Oct. 1)**. Pope John XXIII opens Second Vatican Council **(Oct. 11)**—Council holds four sessions, finally closing **Dec. 8, 1965**. Cuba releases 1,113 prisoners of 1961 invasion attempt **(Dec. 24)**. Burundi, Jamaica, Western Samoa, Uganda, and Trinidad and Tobago become independent. William Faulkner wins Pulitzer for *The Reivers*. Rachel Carson's *Silent Spring*.

James H. Meredith (1933–)

1963 France and West Germany sign treaty of cooperation ending four centuries of conflict **(Jan. 22)**. Michael E. De Bakey implants artificial heart in human for first time at Houston hospital; plastic device functions and patient lives for four days **(April 21)**. Pope John XXIII dies **(June 3)**—succeeded **June 21** by Cardinal Montini, who becomes Paul VI. U.S. Supreme Court rules no locality may require recitation of Lord's Prayer or Bible verses in public schools **(June 17)**. U.K.'s Profumo scandal **(June)**. Civil rights rally held by 200,000 blacks and whites in Washington, D.C.; Martin Luther King delivers "I have a dream" speech **(Aug. 28)**. Washington-to-Moscow "hot line" communications link opens, designed to reduce risk of accidental war **(Aug. 30)**. President Kennedy shot and killed by sniper in Dallas, Tex. Lyndon B. Johnson becomes president same day **(Nov. 22)**. Lee Harvey Oswald, accused assassin of President Kennedy, is shot and killed by Jack Ruby, Dallas nightclub owner **(Nov. 24)**. Kenya achieves independence. Betty Friedan publishes *The Feminine Mystique*. There are 15,000 U.S. military advisers in South Vietnam.

Betty Friedan (1921–)

VIETNAM WAR

U.S., South Vietnam, and Allies versus North Vietnam and National Liberation Front (Viet Cong).

1950 President Truman sends 35-man military advisory group to aid French fighting to maintain colonial power in Vietnam.

1954 After defeat of French at Dien Bien Phu, Geneva Agreements **(July)** provide for withdrawal of French and Vietminh to either side of demarcation zone (DMZ) pending reunification elections, which are never held. Presidents Eisenhower and Kennedy (from 1954 onward) send civilian advisers and, later, military personnel to train South Vietnamese.

1960 Communists form National Liberation Front in South.

1960–1963 U.S. military advisers in South Vietnam rise from 900 to 15,000.

1963 Ngo Dinh Diem, South Vietnam's premier, slain in coup **(Nov. 1)**.

1964 North Vietnamese torpedo boats reportedly attack U.S. destroyers in Gulf of Tonkin **(Aug. 2)**. President Johnson orders retaliatory air strikes. Congress approves Gulf of Tonkin resolution **(Aug. 7)** authorizing president to take "all necessary measures" to win in Vietnam, allowing for the war's expansion.

1965 U.S. planes begin combat missions over South Vietnam. In **June,** 23,000 American advisers committed to combat. By end of year over 184,000 U.S. troops in area.

1966 B-52s bomb DMZ, reportedly used by North Vietnam for entry into South **(July 31)**.

1967 South Vietnam National Assembly approves election of Nguyen Van Thieu as president **(Oct. 21)**.

1968 U.S. has almost 525,000 men in Vietnam. In Tet offensive **(Jan.–Feb.),** Viet Cong guerrillas attack Saigon, Hue, and some provincial capitals. In My Lai massacre, American soldiers kill 300 Vietnamese villagers **(March 16)**. President Johnson orders halt to U.S. bombardment of North Vietnam **(Oct. 31)**. Saigon and N.L.F. join U.S. and North Vietnam in Paris peace talks.

1969 President Nixon announces Vietnam peace offer **(May 14)**—begins troop withdrawals **(June)**. Viet Cong forms Provisional Revolutionary Government. U.S. Senate calls for curb on commitments **(June 25)**. Ho Chi Minh, 79, North Vietnam president, dies **(Sept. 3)**; collective leadership chosen. Some 6,000 U.S. troops pulled back from Thailand and 1,000 marines from Vietnam (announced **Sept. 30**). Massive demonstrations in U.S. protest or support war policies **(Oct. 15)**.

1970 U.S. troops invade Cambodia in order to destroy North Vietnamese sanctuaries **(May 1)**.

1971 Congress bars use of combat troops, but not air power, in Laos and Cambodia **(Jan. 1)**. South Vietnamese troops, with U.S. air cover, fail in Laos thrust. Many American ground forces withdrawn from Vietnam combat. *New York Times* publishes Pentagon papers, classified material on expansion of war **(June)**.

1972 Nixon responds to North Vietnamese drive across DMZ by ordering mining of North Vietnam ports and heavy bombing of Hanoi-Haiphong area **(April 1)**. Nixon orders "Christmas bombing" of North to get North Vietnamese back to conference table **(Dec.)**.

1973 President orders halt to offensive operations in North Vietnam **(Jan. 15)**. Representatives of North and South Vietnam, U.S., and N.L.F. sign peace pacts in Paris, ending longest war in U.S. history **(Jan. 27)**. Last American troops departed in their entirety **(March 29)**.

1974 Both sides accuse each other of frequent violations of cease-fire agreement.

1975 Full-scale warfare resumes. South Vietnam premier Nguyen Van Thieu resigns **(April 21)**. South Vietnamese government surrenders to North Vietnam; U.S. Marine embassy guards and U.S. civilians and dependents evacuated **(April 30)**. More than 140,000 Vietnamese refugees leave by air and sea, many to settle in U.S. Provisional Revolutionary Government takes control **(June 6)**.

1976 Election of National Assembly paves way for reunification of North and South.

The Beatles

Malcolm X
(1925–1965)

Thurgood Marshall
(1908–1993)

Lyndon B. Johnson
(1908–1973)

Richard Nixon
(1913–1994)

1964 U.S. Supreme Court rules that congressional districts should be roughly equal in population (**Feb. 17**). Jack Ruby convicted of murder in slaying of Lee Harvey Oswald; sentenced to death by Dallas jury (**March 14**)—conviction reversed **Oct. 5, 1966**; Ruby dies **Jan. 3, 1967**, before second trial can be held. Three civil rights workers—Schwerner, Goodman, and Cheney—murdered in Mississippi (**June**). Twenty-one arrests result in trial and conviction of seven by federal jury. Nelson Mandela sentenced to life imprisonment (**June 11**). Congress approves Gulf of Tonkin resolution (**Aug. 7**). President's Commission on the Assassination of President Kennedy issues Warren Report concluding that Lee Harvey Oswald acted alone. The Beatles appear on *The Ed Sullivan Show.*

1965 Rev. Dr. Martin Luther King, Jr., and more than 2,600 other blacks arrested in Selma, Ala., during three-day demonstrations against voter-registration rules (**Feb. 1**). Malcolm X, black-nationalist leader, shot to death at Harlem rally in New York City (**Feb. 21**). U.S. Marines land in Dominican Republic as fighting persists between rebels and Dominican army (**April 28**). Medicare, senior citizens' government medical assistance program, begins (**July 1**). Blacks riot for six days in Watts section of Los Angeles: 34 dead, over 1,000 injured, nearly 4,000 arrested, fire damage put at $175 million (**Aug. 11–16**). Power failure in Ontario plant blacks out parts of eight states of northeast U.S. and two provinces of southeast Canada (**Nov. 9**). Ralph Nader's *Unsafe at Any Speed.*

1966 Black teenagers riot in Watts, Los Angeles; two men killed and at least 25 injured (**March 15**). Supreme Court decides *Miranda* v. *Arizona.*

1967 Three Apollo astronauts—Col. Virgil I. Grissom, Col. Edward White II, and Lt. Cmdr. Roger B. Chaffee—killed in spacecraft fire during simulated launch (**Jan. 27**). Biafra secedes from Nigeria (**May 30**). Israeli and Arab forces battle; six-day war ends with Israel occupying Sinai Peninsula, Golan Heights, Gaza Strip, and east bank of Suez Canal (**June 5**). Red China announces explosion of its first hydrogen bomb (**June 17**). Racial violence in Detroit; 7,000 National Guardsmen aid police after night of rioting. Similar outbreaks occur in New York City's Spanish Harlem, Rochester, N.Y., Birmingham, Ala., and New Britain, Conn. (**July 23**). Thurgood Marshall sworn in as first black U.S. Supreme Court justice (**Oct. 2**). Dr. Christiaan N. Barnard and team of South African surgeons perform world's first successful human heart transplant (**Dec. 3**)—patient dies 18 days later.

1968 North Korea seizes U.S. Navy ship *Pueblo;* holds 83 on board as spies (**Jan. 23**). Tet offensive, turning point in Vietnam war (**Jan.–Feb.**). My Lai massacre (**March 16**). President Johnson announces he will not seek or accept presidential renomination (**March 31**). Martin Luther King, Jr., civil rights leader, is slain in Memphis (**April 4**)—James Earl Ray, indicted in murder, captured in London on **June 8.** In 1969 Ray pleads guilty and is sentenced to 99 years. Sen. Robert F. Kennedy is shot and critically wounded in Los Angeles hotel after winning California primary (**June 5**)—dies **June 6.** Sirhan B. Sirhan convicted 1969. Czechoslovakia is invaded by Russians and Warsaw Pact forces to crush liberal regime (**Aug. 20**).

1969 Richard M. Nixon is inaugurated 37th president of the U.S. (**Jan. 20**). Stonewall riot in New York City marks beginning of gay rights movement (**June 28**). *Apollo 11* astronauts—Neil A. Armstrong, Edwin E. Aldrin, Jr., and Michael Collins—take man's first walk on moon (**July 20**). Sen. Edward M. Kennedy pleads guilty to leaving scene of fatal accident at Chappaquiddick, Mass. (**July 18**), in which Mary Jo Kopechne was drowned—gets two-month suspended sentence (**July 25**). Woodstock Festival (**Aug. 15–17**). *Sesame Street* debuts. Internet (ARPA) goes online.

1970 Biafra surrenders after 32-month fight for independence from Nigeria (**Jan. 15**). Rhodesia severs last tie with British crown and declares itself a racially segregated republic (**March 1**). U.S. troops invade Cambodia (**May 1**). Four students at Kent State University in Ohio slain by National Guardsmen at demonstration protesting incursion into Cambodia (**May 4**). Senate repeals Gulf of Tonkin resolution (**June 24**).

1971 Supreme Court rules unanimously that busing of students may be ordered to achieve racial desegregation (**April 20**). Anti-war militants attempt to disrupt government business in Washington (**May 3**)—police and military units arrest as many as 12,000; most are later released. *Pentagon Papers* published (**June**). Twenty-sixth Amendment to U.S. Constitution lowers voting age to 18. UN seats Communist China and expels Nationalist China (**Oct. 25**).

1972 President Nixon makes unprecedented eight-day visit to Communist China and meets with Mao Zedong (**Feb. 21–27**). Britain takes over direct rule of Northern Ireland in bid for peace (**March 24**). Gov. George C. Wallace of Alabama is shot by Arthur H. Bremer at Laurel, Md., political rally (**May 15**). Five men are apprehended by police in attempt to bug Democratic National Committee headquarters in Washington, D.C.'s Watergate complex—start of the Watergate scandal (**June 17**). Supreme Court rules that death penalty is unconstitutional (**June 29**). Eleven Israeli athletes at Olympic Games in Munich are killed after eight members of an Arab terrorist group invade Olympic Village; five guerrillas and one policeman are also killed (**Sept. 5**). "Christmas bombing" of North Vietnam (**Dec. 25**).

1973 Great Britain, Ireland, and Denmark enter European Economic Community (**Jan. 1**). Supreme Court rules on *Roe* v. *Wade* (**Jan. 22**). Vietnam War ends with signing of peace pacts (**Jan. 27**). Nixon, on national TV, accepts responsibility, but not blame, for Watergate; accepts resignations of advisers H. R. Haldeman and John D. Ehrlichman, fires John W. Dean III as counsel (**April 30**). Greek military junta abolishes monarchy and proclaims republic (**June 1**). U.S. bombing of Cambodia ends, marking official halt to 12 years of combat activity in Southeast Asia (**Aug. 15**). Chile's Marxist president, Salvadore Allende, is overthrown (**Sept. 11**). Fourth and biggest Arab-Israeli conflict begins as Egyptian and Syrian forces attack Israel as Jews mark Yom Kippur, holiest day in their calendar (**Oct. 6**). Spiro T. Agnew resigns as vice president and then, in federal court in Baltimore, pleads no contest to charges of evasion of income taxes on $29,500 he received in 1967, while governor of Maryland. He is fined $10,000 and put on three years' probation (**Oct. 10**). In the "Saturday Night Massacre," Nixon fires special Watergate prosecutor Archibald Cox and Deputy Attorney General William D. Ruckelshaus; Attorney General Elliot L. Richardson resigns (**Oct. 20**). Egypt and Israel sign U.S.-sponsored cease-fire accord (**Nov. 11**). Duke Ellington's autobiography, *Music Is My Mistress,* is published.

1974 Patricia Hearst, 19-year-old daughter of publisher Randolph Hearst, kidnapped by Symbionese Liberation Army (**Feb. 5**). House Judiciary Committee adopts three articles of impeachment charging President Nixon with obstruction of justice, failure to uphold laws, and refusal to produce material subpoenaed by the committee (**July 30**). Richard M. Nixon announces he will resign the next day, the first president to do so (**Aug. 8**). Vice President Gerald R. Ford of Michigan is sworn in as 38th president of the U.S. (**Aug. 9**). Ford grants "full, free, and absolute pardon" to ex-president Nixon (**Sept. 8**).

1975 John N. Mitchell, H. R. Haldeman, John D. Ehrlichman found guilty of Watergate cover-up (**Jan. 1**); sentenced to 30 months to 8 years in jail (**Feb. 21**). Pol Pot and Khmer Rouge take over Cambodia (**April**). American merchant ship *Mayaguez,* seized by Cambodian forces, is rescued in operation by U.S. Navy and Marines, 38 of whom are killed (**May 15**). *Apollo* and *Soyuz* spacecraft take off for U.S.-Soviet link-up in space (**July 15**). President Ford escapes assassination attempt in Sacramento, Calif. (**Sept. 5**). President Ford escapes second assassination attempt in 17 days (**Sept. 22**).

1976 Supreme Court rules that blacks and other minorities are entitled to retroactive job seniority (**March 24**). Ford signs Federal Election Campaign Act (**May 11**). Supreme Court rules that death penalty is not inherently cruel or unusual and is a constitutionally acceptable form of punishment (**July 3**). Nation celebrates bicentennial (**July 4**). Israeli airborne commandos attack Uganda's Entebbe Airport and free 103 hostages held by pro-Palestinian hijackers of Air France plane; one Israeli and several Ugandan soldiers killed in raid (**July 4**). Mysterious disease that eventually claims 29 lives strikes American Legion convention in Philadelphia (**Aug. 4**). Jimmy Carter elected U.S. president (**Nov. 2**).

1977 First woman Episcopal priest ordained (**Jan. 1**). Scientists identify previously unknown bacterium as cause of mysterious "legionnaire's disease" (**Jan. 18**). Carter pardons Vietnam draft evaders (**Jan. 21**). Scientists report using bacteria in lab to make insulin (**May 23**). Supreme Court rules that states are not required to spend Medicaid funds on elective abortions (**June 20**). Deng Xiaoping, purged Chinese leader, restored to power as "Gang of Four" is expelled from Communist Party (**July 22**). South African activist Stephen Biko dies in police custody

Mao Zedong
(1893–1976)

Duke Ellington
(1899–1974)

Gerald R. Ford
(1913–)

Jimmy Carter
(1924–)

**Pope John Paul II
(1920–2005)**

**Anwar Sadat
(1918–1981)**

**Ayatollah Ruhollah
Khomeini
(1900–1989)**

**Ronald Reagan
(1911–2004)**

**Sandra Day O'Connor
(1930–)**

(**Sept. 12**). Nuclear-proliferation pact, curbing spread of nuclear weapons, signed by 15 countries, including U.S. and USSR (**Sept. 21**).

1978 President chooses Federal Appeals Court Judge William H. Webster as F.B.I. Director (**Jan. 19**). Rhodesia's prime minister Ian D. Smith and three black leaders agree on transfer to black majority rule (**Feb. 15**). U.S. Senate approves Panama Canal neutrality treaty (**March 16**); votes treaty to turn canal over to Panama by year 2000 (**April 18**). Former Italian premier Aldo Moro kidnapped by left wing terrorists, who kill five bodyguards (**March 16**); he is found slain (**May 9**). Californians in referendum approve Proposition 13 for nearly 60% slash in property tax revenues (**June 6**). Supreme Court, in Bakke case, bars quota systems in college admissions but affirms constitutionality of programs giving advantage to minorities (**June 28**). Pope Paul VI, dead at 80, mourned (**Aug. 6**); new Pope, John Paul I, 65, dies unexpectedly after 34 days in office (**Sept. 28**); succeeded by Karol Cardinal Wojtyla of Poland as John Paul II (**Oct. 16**). "Framework for Peace" in Middle East signed by Egypt's president Anwar Sadat and Israeli premier Menachem Begin after 13-day conference at Camp David led by President Carter (**Sept. 17**). Jim Jones's followers commit mass suicide in Jonestown, Guyana (**Nov. 18**).

1979 Oil spills pollute ocean waters in Atlantic and Gulf of Mexico (**Jan. 1, June 8, July 21**). Ohio agrees to pay $675,000 to families of dead and injured in Kent State University shootings (**Jan. 4**). Vietnam and Vietnam-backed Cambodian insurgents announce fall of Phnom Penh, Cambodian capital, and collapse of Pol Pot regime (**Jan. 7**). Shah leaves Iran after year of turmoil (**Jan. 16**); revolutionary forces under Muslim leader, Ayatollah Ruhollah Khomeini, take over (**Feb. 1** *et seq.*). Nuclear power plant accident at Three Mile Island, Pa., releases radiation (**March 28**). Conservatives win British election; Margaret Thatcher new prime minister (**May 3**). Carter and Brezhnev sign SALT II agreement (**June 14**). Nicaraguan president Gen. Anastasio Somoza Debayle resigns and flees to Miami (**July 17**); Sandinistas form government (**July 19**). Earl Mountbatten of Burma, 79, British World War II hero, and three others killed by blast on fishing boat off Irish coast (**Aug. 27**); two I.R.A. members accused (**Aug. 30**). Iranian militants seize U.S. embassy in Teheran and hold hostages (**Nov. 4**). Soviet invasion of Afghanistan stirs world protests (**Dec. 27**).

1980 Six U.S. embassy aides escape from Iran with Canadian help (**Jan. 29**). F.B.I.'s undercover operation "Abscam" (for Arab scam) implicates public officials (**Feb. 2**). U.S. breaks diplomatic ties with Iran (**April 7**). Eight U.S. servicemen are killed and five are injured as helicopter and cargo plane collide in abortive desert raid to rescue American hostages in Teheran (**April 25**). Supreme Court upholds limits on federal aid for abortions (**June 30**). Shah of Iran dies at 60 (**July 27**). Anastasio Somoza Debayle, ousted Nicaragua ruler, and two aides assassinated in Asunción, Paraguay capital (**Sept. 17**). Iraq troops hold 90 square miles of Iran after invasion; 8-year Iran-Iraq war begins (**Sept. 19**). Ronald Reagan elected president in Republican sweep (**Nov. 4**). Three U.S. nuns and lay worker found shot in El Salvador (**Dec. 4**). John Lennon of the Beatles shot dead in New York City (**Dec. 8**). Smallpox eradicated.

1981 Ronald Reagan takes oath as 40th president (**Jan. 20**). U.S.-Iran agreement frees 52 hostages held in Teheran since 1979 (**Jan. 20**); hostages welcomed back in U.S. (**Jan. 25**). President Reagan wounded by gunman, with press secretary and two law-enforcement officers (**March 30**). Pope John Paul II wounded by gunman (**May 14**). Reagan nominates Judge Sandra Day O'Connor, 51, of Arizona, as first woman on Supreme Court (**July 7**). More than 110 die in collapse of aerial walkways in lobby of Hyatt Regency Hotel in Kansas City; 188 injured (**July 18**). Air controllers strike, disrupting flights (**Aug. 3**); government dismisses strikers (**Aug. 11**). AIDS is first identified.

1982 British overcome Argentina in Falklands war (**April 2–June 15**). Israel invades Lebanon in attack on P.L.O. (**June 4**). John W. Hinckley, Jr., found not guilty because of insanity in shooting of President Reagan (**June 21**). Alexander M. Haig, Jr., resigns as secretary of state (**June 25**). Equal Rights Amendment fails ratification (**June 30**). Princess

Grace, 52, dies of injuries when car plunges off mountain road; daughter Stephanie, 17, suffers serious injuries (**Sept. 14**). Lebanese Christian Phalangists kill hundreds of people in two Palestinian refugee camps in West Beirut (**Sept. 15**). Leonid Brezhnev, Soviet leader, dies at 75 (**Nov. 10**). Yuri V. Andropov, 68, chosen as successor (**Nov. 15**). Permanent artificial heart implanted in human for first time in Dr. Barney B. Clark, 61, at University of Utah Medical Center in Salt Lake City (**Dec. 2**).

1983 Pope John Paul II signs new Roman Catholic code incorporating changes brought about by Second Vatican Council (**Jan. 25**). Second space shuttle, *Challenger,* makes successful maiden voyage, which includes the first U.S. space walk in nine years (**April 4**). U.S. Supreme Court declares many local abortion restrictions unconstitutional (**June 15**). Sally K. Ride, 32, first U.S. woman astronaut in space as a crew member aboard space shuttle *Challenger* (**June 18**). U.S. admits shielding former Nazi Gestapo chief Klaus Barbie, 69, the "butcher of Lyon," wanted in France for war crimes (**Aug. 15**). Benigno S. Aquino, Jr., 50, political rival of Philippines president Marcos, slain in Manila (**Aug. 21**). South Korean Boeing 747 jetliner bound for Seoul apparently strays into Soviet airspace and is shot down by a Soviet SU-15 fighter after it had tracked the airliner for two hours; all 269 aboard are killed, including 61 Americans (**Aug. 30**). Terrorist explosion kills 237 U.S. Marines in Beirut (**Oct. 23**). U.S. and Caribbean allies invade Grenada (**Oct. 25**).

1984 Bell System broken up (**Jan. 1**). France gets first deliveries of Soviet natural gas (**Jan. 1**). Syria frees captured U.S. Navy pilot, Lieut. Robert C. Goodman, Jr. (**Jan. 3**). U.S. and Vatican exchange diplomats after 116-year hiatus (**Jan. 10**). Reagan orders U.S. Marines withdrawn from Beirut international peacekeeping force (**Feb. 7**). Yuri V. Andropov dies at 69; Konstantin U. Chernenko, 72, named Soviet Union leader (**Feb. 9**). Italy and Vatican agree to end Roman Catholicism as state religion (**Feb. 18**). Reagan ends U.S. role in Beirut by relieving Sixth Fleet from peacekeeping force (**March 30**). Congress rebukes President Reagan on use of federal funds for mining Nicaraguan harbors (**April 10**). Soviet Union withdraws from summer Olympic games in U.S., and other bloc nations follow (**May 7** *et seq.*). José Napoleón Duarte, moderate, elected president of El Salvador (**May 11**). Three hundred slain as Indian Army occupies Sikh Golden Temple in Amritsar (**June 6**). Thirty-ninth Democratic National Convention, in San Francisco, nominates Walter F. Mondale and Geraldine A. Ferraro (**July 16–19**). Thirty-third Republican National Convention, at Dallas, renominates President Reagan and Vice President Bush (**Aug. 20–25**). Brian Mulroney and Conservative party win Canadian election in landslide (**Sept. 4**). Indian prime minister Indira Gandhi assassinated by two Sikh bodyguards; 1,000 killed in anti-Sikh riots; son Rajiv succeeds her (**Oct. 31**). President Reagan re-elected in landslide with 59% of vote (**Nov. 6**). Toxic gas leaks from Union Carbide plant in Bhopal, India, killing 2,000 and injuring 150,000 (**Dec. 3**).

1985 Ronald Reagan, 73, takes oath for second term as 40th president (**Jan. 20**). General Westmoreland settles libel action against CBS (**Feb. 18**). Prime Minister Margaret Thatcher addresses Congress, endorsing Reagan's policies (**Feb. 20**). USSR leader Chernenko dies at 73 and is replaced by Mikhail Gorbachev, 54 (**March 11**). Two Shi'ite Muslim gunmen capture TWA airliner with 133 aboard, 104 of them Americans (**June 14**); 39 remaining hostages freed in Beirut (**June 30**). Supreme Court, 5–4, bars public school teachers from parochial schools (**July 1**). Arthur James Walker, 50, retired naval officer, convicted by federal judge of participating in Soviet spy ring operated by his brother, John Walker (**Aug. 9**). P.L.O. terrorists hijack *Achille Lauro,* Italian cruise ship, with 80 passengers, plus crew (**Oct. 7**); American, Leon Klinghoffer, killed (**Oct. 8**); Italian government toppled by political crisis over hijacking (**Oct. 16**). John A. Walker and son, Michael I. Walker, 22, sentenced in Navy espionage case (**Oct. 28**). Reagan and Gorbachev meet at summit (**Nov. 19**); agree to step up arms control talks and renew cultural contacts (**Nov. 21**). Terrorists seize Egyptian Boeing 737 airliner after takeoff from Athens (**Nov. 23**); 59 dead as Egyptian forces storm plane on Malta (**Nov. 24**). U.S. budget-balancing bill enacted (**Dec. 12**).

1986 Spain and Portugal join European Economic Community (**Jan. 1**). President freezes Libyan assets in U.S. (**Jan. 8**). Supreme Court bars racial bias in trial jury selection (**Jan. 14**). *Voyager 2* spacecraft reports secrets of Uranus (**Jan. 26**). Space shuttle *Challenger* explodes after launch at Cape Canaveral, Fla., killing all seven aboard (**Jan. 28**). Haiti president

Indira Gandhi
(1917–1984)

Corazon Aquino
(1933–)

Mikhail S. Gorbachev
(1931–)

Margaret Thatcher
(1925–)

Sally K. Ride
(1951–)

**William Rehnquist
(1924–2005)**

**George Bush
(1924–)**

**Benazir Bhutto
(1953–)**

**Yoweri Museveni
(1944–)**

Jean-Claude Duvalier flees to France **(Feb. 7).** President Marcos flees Philippines after ruling 20 years, as newly elected Corazon Aquino succeeds him **(Feb. 26).** Prime Minister Olof Palme of Sweden shot dead **(Feb. 28).** Austrian president Kurt Waldheim's service as Nazi army officer revealed **(March 3).** Union Carbide agrees to settlement with victims of Bhopal gas leak in India **(March 22).** Halley's comet yields information on return visit **(April 10).** U.S. planes attack Libyan "terrorist centers" **(April 14).** Desmond Tutu elected archbishop in South Africa **(April 14).** Major nuclear accident at Soviet Union's Chernobyl power station alarms world **(April 26** *et seq.***).** Ex-Navy analyst, Jonathan Jay Pollard, 31, guilty as spy for Israel **(June 4).** Supreme Court reaffirms abortion rights **(June 11).** World Court rules U.S. broke international law in mining Nicaraguan waters **(June 27).** Supreme Court voids automatic provisions of budget-balancing law **(July 7).** Jerry A. Whitworth, ex-Navy radioman, convicted as spy **(July 24);** he is also part of Walker family spy ring. Muslim captors release Rev. Lawrence Martin Jenco **(July 26).** Senate Judiciary Committee approves William H. Rehnquist as chief justice of U.S. **(Aug. 14).** House votes arms appropriations bill rejecting administration's "Star Wars" policy **(Aug. 15).** Three Lutheran church groups in U.S. set to merge **(Aug. 29).** Congress overrides Reagan veto of stiff sanctions against South Africa **(Sept. 29** and **Oct. 2).** Congress approves immigration bill barring hiring of illegal aliens, with amnesty provision **(Oct. 17).** Reagan signs $11.7-billion budget reduction measure **(Oct. 21).** He approves sweeping revision of U.S. tax code **(Oct. 22).** Democrats triumph in elections, gaining eight seats to win Senate majority **(Nov. 4).** Secret initiative to send arms to Iran revealed **(Nov. 6** *et seq.***);** Reagan denies exchanging arms for hostages and halts arms sales **(Nov. 19);** diversion of funds from arms sales to Nicaraguan Contras revealed **(Nov. 25).**

1987 William Buckley, U.S. hostage in Lebanon, reported slain **(Jan. 20).** Supreme Court rules Rotary Clubs must admit women **(May 4).** Iraqi missiles kill 37 in attack on U.S. frigate *Stark* in Persian Gulf **(May 17);** Iraqi president apologizes **(May 18).** Prime Minister Thatcher wins rare third term in Britain **(June 11).** Supreme Court justice Lewis F. Powell, Jr., retires **(June 26).** Klaus Barbie, 73, Gestapo wartime chief in Lyon, sentenced to life by French court for war crimes **(July 4).** Oliver North, Jr., tells congressional inquiry higher officials approved his secret Iran-Contra operations **(July 7–10).** Admiral John M. Poindexter, former National Security Adviser, testifies he authorized use of Iran arms sale profits to aid Contras **(July 15–22).** Secretary of State George P. Shultz testifies he was deceived repeatedly on Iran-Contra affair **(July 23–24).** Defense Secretary Caspar W. Weinberger tells inquiry of official deception and intrigue **(July 31, Aug. 3).** Reagan says Iran arms-Contra policy went astray and accepts responsibility **(Aug. 12).** Severe earthquake strikes Los Angeles, leaving 100 injured and six dead **(Oct. 1).** Senate, 58–42, rejects Robert H. Bork as Supreme Court justice **(Oct. 23).**

1988 U.S. and Canada reach free trade agreement **(Jan. 2).** Robert C. McFarlane, former National Security Adviser, pleads guilty in Iran-Contra case **(March 11).** U.S. Navy ship shoots down Iranian airliner in Persian Gulf, mistaking it for jet fighter; 290 killed **(July 3).** Terrorists kill nine tourists on Aegean cruise **(July 11).** Democratic convention nominates Gov. Michael Dukakis of Massachusetts for president and Texas senator Lloyd Bentsen for vice president **(July 17** *et seq.***).** Republicans nominate George Bush for president and Indiana senator Dan Quayle for vice president **(Aug. 15** *et seq.***).** Plane blast kills Pakistani president Mohammad Zia ul-Haq **(Aug. 17).** Republicans sweep 40 states in election. Bush beats Dukakis **(Nov. 8).** Benazir Bhutto, first Islamic woman prime minister, chosen to lead Pakistan **(Dec. 1).** Pan-Am 747 explodes from terrorist bomb and crashes in Lockerbie, Scotland, killing all 259 aboard and 11 on ground **(Dec. 21).**

1989 U.S. planes shoot down two Libyan fighters over international waters in Mediterranean **(Jan. 4).** Emperor Hirohito of Japan dead at 87 **(Jan. 7).** George Herbert Walker Bush inaugurated as 41st U.S. president **(Jan. 20).** Iran's Ayatollah Khomeini declares author Salman Rushdie's book *The Satanic Verses* offensive and sentences him to death **(Feb. 14).** Ruptured tanker *Exxon Valdez* sends 11 million gallons of crude oil into Alaska's Prince William Sound **(March 24).** Tens of thousands of Chinese students take over Beijing's Tiananmen Square in rally for democracy **(April 19** *et seq.***).** U.S. jury convicts Oliver North in Iran-Contra affair (**May 4**). More than one million in Beijing demonstrate for democracy; chaos spreads across nation (**mid-May** *et seq.*). Mikhail S. Gorbachev named Soviet president (**May 25**). Thousands killed in Tiananmen Square as Chinese leaders take hard line toward demonstrators (**June 4** *et seq.*). Army general Colin R. Powell is first black chairman of Joint Chiefs of Staff (**Aug. 9**). P. W. Botha quits as South Africa's president (**Aug. 14**). *Voyager 2* spacecraft speeds by Neptune after making startling discoveries about the planet and its moons (**Aug. 29**). Deng Xiaoping resigns from China's leadership (**Nov. 9**). After 28 years, Berlin Wall is open to West (**Nov. 11**). Czech Parliament ends Communists' dominant role (**Nov. 30**). Romanian uprising overthrows Communist government (**Dec. 15** *et seq.*); President Ceausescu and wife executed (**Dec. 25**). U.S. troops invade Panama, seeking capture of Gen. Manuel Noriega (**Dec. 20**); resistance to U.S. collapses (**Dec. 24**). Dalai Lama wins Nobel Peace Prize.

François Mitterrand
(1916–1996)

1990   World Wide Web debuts, popularizes Internet. Gen. Manuel Noriega surrenders in Panama (**Jan. 3**). Yugoslav Communists end 45-year monopoly of power (**Jan. 22**). Soviet Communists relinquish sole power (**Feb. 7**). South Africa frees Nelson Mandela, imprisoned 27½ years (**Feb. 11**). Violeta Barrios de Chamorro inaugurated as Nicaraguan president. Hubble Space Telescope launched (**April 25**). U.S.-Soviet summit reaches accord on armaments (**June 1**). Western Alliance ends cold war and proposes joint action with Soviet Union and Eastern Europe (**July 6**). U.S. Appeals Court overturns Oliver North's Iran-Contra conviction (**July 20**). Iraqi troops invade Kuwait and seize petroleum reserves, setting off Persian Gulf War (**Aug. 2** *et seq.*). East and West Germany reunited (**Oct. 3**). Republicans set back in midterm elections (**Nov. 8**). Gorbachev assumes emergency powers (**Nov. 17**). Leaders of 34 nations in Europe and North America proclaim a united Europe (**Nov. 21**). Margaret Thatcher resigns as British prime minister (**Nov. 22**); John Major succeeds her (**Nov. 28**). Lech Walesa wins Poland's runoff presidential election (**Dec. 9**). Haiti elects leftist priest as president in first democratic election (**Dec. 17**).

General Colin Powell
(1937–)

1991   U.S. and Allies at war with Iraq (**Jan. 15**). Warsaw Pact dissolves military alliance (**Feb. 25**). Cease-fire ends Persian Gulf War; UN forces are victorious (**April 3**). Europeans end sanctions on South Africa (**April 15**). Supreme Court limits death row appeals (**April 16**). Winnie Mandela sentenced in kidnapping (**May 13**). William H. Webster retires as director of CIA; Robert H. Gates succeeds him (**May 14**). France agrees to sign 1968 treaty banning spread of atomic weapons (**June 3**). Communist government of Albania resigns (**June 4**). Jiang Qing, widow of Mao, commits suicide (**June 4**). South African Parliament repeals apartheid laws (**June 5**). Warsaw Pact dissolved (**July 1**). Boris N. Yeltsin inaugurated as first freely elected president of Russian Republic (**July 10**). Bush-Gorbachev summit negotiates strategic arms reduction treaty (**July 31**). China accepts nuclear nonproliferation treaty (**Aug. 10**). Lithuania, Estonia, and Latvia win independence (**Aug. 25**); Bush recognizes them (**Sept. 2**). Haitian

---

THE PERSIAN GULF WAR (JAN. 16, 1991–APRIL 6, 1991)

1990 Iraq invades its tiny neighbor, Kuwait, after talks break down over oil production and debt repayment. Iraqi president Saddam Hussein later annexes Kuwait and declares it a 19th province of Iraq (**Aug. 2**). President Bush believes that Iraq intends to invade Saudi Arabia and take control of the region's oil supplies. He begins organizing a multinational coalition to seek Kuwait's freedom and restoration of its legitimate government. The UN Security Council authorizes economic sanctions against Iraq. Bush orders U.S. troops to protect Saudi Arabia at the Saudis' request and "Operation Desert Shield" begins (**Aug. 6**). 230,000 American troops arrive in Saudi Arabia to take defensive action, but when Iraq continues a huge military buildup in Kuwait, the President orders an additional 200,000 troops deployed to prepare for a possible offensive action by the U.S.-led coalition forces. He subsequently obtains a UN Security Council resolution setting a **Jan. 15, 1991** deadline for Iraq to withdraw unconditionally from Kuwait (**Nov. 8**).

1991 Bush wins congressional approval for his position with the most devastating air assault in history

against military targets in Iraq and Kuwait (**Jan. 16**). He rejects a Soviet-Iraq peace plan for a gradual withdrawal that does not comply with all the UN resolutions and gives Iraq an ultimatum to withdraw from Kuwait by noon **Feb. 23** (**Feb. 22**). The president orders the ground war to begin (**Feb. 24**). In a brilliant and lightning-fast campaign, U.S. and coalition forces smash through Iraq's defenses and defeat Saddam Hussein's troops in only four days of combat. Allies enter Kuwait City (**Feb. 26**). Iraqi army sets fire to over 500 of Kuwait's oil wells as final act of destruction to Kuwait's infrastructure. Bush orders a unilateral cease-fire 100 hours after the ground offensive started (**Feb. 27**). Allied and Iraqi military leaders meet on battlefield to discuss terms for a formal cease-fire to end the Gulf War. Iraq agrees to abide by all of the UN resolutions (**Mar. 3**). The first Allied prisoners of war are released (**Mar. 4**). Official cease-fire accepted and signed (**April 6**). 532,000 U.S. forces served in Operation Desert Storm. There were a total of 147 U.S. battle deaths during the Gulf War, 145 nonbattle deaths, and 467 wounded in action.

Hubble Space Telescope

Lech Walesa
(1943–)

Toni Morrison
(1931–)

Ruth Bader Ginsburg
(1933–)

Boris Yeltsin
(1931–)

troops seize president in uprising **(Sept. 30)**. U.S. suspends assistance to Haiti **(Oct. 1)**. Professor Anita Hill accuses Judge Clarence Thomas of sexual harassment **(Oct. 6)**; Senate, 52–48, confirms Thomas for Supreme Court after stormy hearings **(Oct. 15)**. Israel and Soviet Union resume relations after 24 years **(Oct. 18)**. U.S. indicts two Libyans in 1988 bombing of Pan Am Flight 103 over Lockerbie, Scotland **(Nov. 15)**. Anglican envoy Terry Waite and U.S. Prof. Thomas M. Sutherland freed by Lebanese **(Nov. 18)**. Last three U.S. hostages freed in Lebanon **(Dec. 2–4)**. Soviet Union breaks up after President Gorbachev's resignation; constituent republics form Commonwealth of Independent States **(Dec. 25)**.

1992 Yugoslav Federation broken up **(Jan. 15)**. Bush and Yeltsin proclaim formal end to cold war **(Feb. 1)**. U.S. lifts trade sanctions against China **(Feb. 21)**. U.S. recognizes three former Yugoslav republics **(April 7)**. Gen. Noriega, former Panama leader, convicted in U.S. court **(April 9)**. Four police officers acquitted in Los Angeles beating of Rodney King; rioting erupts in South-Central Los Angeles **(April 29 et seq.)**. Caspar W. Weinberger indicted in Iran-Contra affair **(June 16)**. Last Western hostages freed in Lebanon **(June 17)**. Supreme Court reaffirms right to abortion **(June 29)**. Democrats nominate Bill Clinton and Al Gore **(July 1)**. Gen. Noriega sentenced to 40 years on drug charges **(July 10)**. Court clears *Exxon Valdez* skipper **(July 10)**. Israeli Parliament approves Yitzhak Rabin's coalition government, dominated by Labor Party **(July 13)**. Police officers acquitted in April on criminal charges in Rodney King beating are indicted on federal civil rights charges **(Aug. 5)**. North American trade compact announced **(Aug. 12)**. Republicans renominate Bush and Quayle **(Aug. 20)**. UN expels Serbian-dominated Yugoslavia **(Sept. 22)**. Senate ratifies second Strategic Arms Limitation Treaty **(Oct. 1)**. Top Japanese leader, Shin Kanemaru, resigns in scandal **(Oct. 14)**. Bill Clinton elected president, Al Gore vice president; Democrats keep control of Congress **(Nov. 3)**. Russian Parliament approves START treaty **(Nov. 4)**. U.S. forces leave Philippines, ending nearly a century of American military presence **(Nov. 24)**. Czechoslovak Parliament approves separation into two nations **(Nov. 25)**. UN approves U.S.-led force to guard food for Somalia **(Dec. 3)**. Prince and Princess of Wales agree to separate **(Dec. 9)**. Bush pardons former Reagan administration officials involved in Iran-Contra affair **(Dec. 24)**.

1993 Vaclav Havel elected as Czech president **(Jan. 26)**. Clinton agrees to compromise on military's ban on homosexuals **(Jan. 29)**. U.S. begins airlift of supplies to besieged Bosnia towns **(Feb. 28)**. Federal agents besiege Texas Branch Davidian religious cult after six are killed in raid **(March 1 et seq.)**. Five arrested, sixth sought in bombing of World Trade Center in New York **(March 29)**. Two police officers convicted on federal civil rights charges in Rodney King beating **(April 17)**; sentenced **(Aug. 4)**. Fire kills 72 as cult standoff in Texas ends with federal assault **(April 19)**. President of Sri Lanka assassinated **(May 1)**. British Commons approves European unity pact **(May 20)**. Twenty-two UN troops killed in Somalia **(June 5)**. Ruth Bader Ginsburg appointed to Supreme Court **(June 14)**. Iraq accepts UN weapons monitoring **(July 19)**. Vincent W. Foster, Jr., senior White House lawyer, commits suicide **(July 22)**. Midwest flood damage expected to exceed $10 billion **(July 24)**. Israeli-Palestinian accord reached **(Aug. 28)**. U.S. agents blamed in Waco, Tex., siege **(Oct. 1)**. Yeltsin's forces crush revolt in Russian Parliament **(Oct. 4 et seq.)**. China breaks nuclear test moratorium **(Oct. 5)**. Canada's opposition Liberal Party regains power in landslide **(Oct. 25)**. Europe's Maastricht Treaty takes effect, creating European Union **(Nov. 1)**. Jean Chretien sworn in as Canada's 20th prime minister **(Nov. 4)**. House of Representatives approves North American Free Trade Agreement **(Nov. 17)**; Senate follows **(Nov. 21)**. South Africa adopts majority rule constitution **(Nov. 18)**. Clinton signs Brady bill regulating firearms purchases **(Nov. 30)**. Toni Morrison wins Nobel prize for literature.

1994 Serbs' heavy weapons pound Sarajevo **(Jan. 5–6)**. Olympic figure skater Nancy Kerrigan attacked **(Jan. 6)**; three arrested in attack **(Jan. 13)**. Major earthquake jolts Los Angeles; 51 dead **(Jan. 17 et seq.)**. Clinton ends trade embargo on Vietnam **(Feb. 9)**. Aldrich Ames, high C.I.A. official, charged with spying for Soviets **(Feb. 22)**. Four convicted in World Trade Center bombing **(March 4)**. Mexican presidential candidate assassinated **(March 23)**. Rwandan genocide of Tutsis by Hutus begins; estimated 800,000 slaughtered in c. 100 days **(April 6)**. South Africa holds first interracial national election **(April 29)**;

Nelson Mandela elected president. Israel and Palestinians sign accord **(May 4).** Clinton accused of sexual harassment while governor of Arkansas **(May 6).** Congress votes protection for women's health clinics **(May 12).** O. J. Simpson arrested in killings of wife, Nicole Brown Simpson, and friend, Ronald Goldman **(June 18).** Supreme Court approves limit on abortion protests **(June 30).** Senate confirms Stephen G. Breyer for Supreme Court **(July 29).** Women's health clinic doctor shot dead outside Florida clinic **(July 29).** Major league baseball players strike **(Aug. 13).** "Carlos the Jackal," international terrorist, captured **(Aug. 15).** IRA declares cease-fire in Northern Ireland **(Aug. 31).** Small plane crashes into White House **(Sept. 12).** Baseball owners end season and cancel World Series **(Sept. 14).** Powerful earthquake strikes Japan **(Oct. 4).** Aristide returns to joyous Haiti **(Oct. 4).** U.S. sends forces to Persian Gulf **(Oct. 7).** Ulster Protestants declare cease-fire **(Oct. 13).** Israel and Jordan sign peace treaty **(Oct. 17).** Reagan, 83, reveals he has Alzheimer's disease **(Nov. 6).** G.O.P. wins control of House and Senate **(Nov. 8).** Aristide forms Haitian government with prime minister and full cabinet **(Nov. 9).** Clinton orders Bosnian arms embargo ended **(Nov. 10).** Newt Gingrich named House Speaker **(Dec. 5).** Bentsen resigns as Treasury Secretary **(Dec. 6).** Russians attack secessionist Republic of Chechnya **(Dec. 11** *et seq.***).** John Salvi kills two at Massachusetts Planned Parenthood clinic **(Dec. 30).**

Nelson Mandela
(1918–)

1995 Republicans take control of Congress **(Jan. 4).** More than 5,000 dead in Japanese earthquake **(Jan. 17** *et seq.***).** Criminal trial of O. J. Simpson opens in California **(Jan. 24).** U.S. rescues Mexico's economy with $20-billion aid program **(Feb. 21).** Senate rejects balanced-budget amendment **(March 2).** Nerve gas attack in Tokyo subway kills eight and injures thousands. The Aum Shinrikyo ("Supreme Truth") cult is to blame **(March 20).** Major League Baseball strike ends **(April 2).** Appeals court upholds woman's plea to enter Citadel military academy **(April 13).** UN Council votes easier sanctions for Iraq **(April 14).** Scores killed as terrorist's car bomb blows up block-long Oklahoma City federal building **(April 19);** Timothy McVeigh, 27, Army veteran, arrested as suspect **(April 21);** authorities seek second suspect, link right-wing paramilitary groups to bombing **(April 22).** Death toll 2,000 in Rwanda massacre **(April 22).** Fighting escalates in Bosnia and Croatia **(May 1).** U.S. shuttle docks with Russian space station **(June 27).** F.B.I. suspends four in Idaho siege inquiry **(Aug. 11).** France explodes nuclear device in Pacific; wide protests ensue **(Sept. 5).** Senator Bob Packwood of Oregon resigns under pressure for sexual and official misconduct **(Sept. 6).** Israelis and Palestinians agree on transferring West Bank to Arabs **(Sept. 24).** Los Angeles jury finds O. J. Simpson not guilty of murder charges **(Oct. 3).** Pope John Paul II visits U.S. on whirlwind tour **(Oct. 4–8).** Warring parties agree on cease-fire in Bosnia **(Oct. 5).** Million Man March draws hundreds of thousands of black men to capital **(Oct. 16).** Quebec narrowly rejects independence from Canada **(Oct. 30).** Israeli prime minister Yitzhak Rabin slain by Jewish extremist at peace rally **(Nov. 4).** U.S. servicemen admit rape of Japanese schoolgirl in Okinawa **(Nov. 7).** Nigeria hangs writer Ken Saro-Wiwa and eight other minority rights advocates **(Nov. 10).** Irish voters approve end to constitutional ban on divorce **(Nov. 24).** Combatants sign Bosnia peace treaty **(Dec. 14).** House move stalls Congress–White House negotiations to avert government shutdown **(Dec. 20).** Seamus Heaney wins Nobel prize for literature.

Jean-Bertrand Aristide
(1953–)

Dalai Lama
(1935–)

Yitzhak Rabin
(1922–1995)

1996 U.S. budget crisis in fourth month **(Jan 3).** Clinton approves resumption of many government operations **(Jan. 6).** Senate ratifies major arms reduction treaty **(Jan. 26).** France announces end to nuclear tests **(Jan. 29).** At least 73 dead in Sri Lankan suicide bombing **(Feb. 1).** Suicide bombers kill 59 in Israel **(March 4).** Bob Dole sweeps Republican primaries **(March 5).** Britain alarmed by deadly cow disease **(March 20** *et seq.***).** UN tribunal charges war crimes by Bosnian Muslims and Croats **(March 22).** Commerce Secretary Ronald H. Brown killed in plane crash **(April 3).** FBI arrests suspected Unabomber **(April 3).** Clinton signs line-item veto bill **(April 9).** President blocks ban on late-term abortions **(April 10).** ValuJet crashes in Everglades; all 110 aboard killed **(May 11).** Chechnya peace treaty signed **(May 27).** Israel elects Benjamin Netanyahu as prime minister **(May 31).** China agrees to world ban

Seamus Heaney
(1939–)

Ella Fitzgerald
(1918–1996)

Madeleine Albright
(1937–)

Kofi Annan
(1938–)

Hale-Bopp Comet

Princess Diana
(1961–1997)

on atomic testing (**June 6**). Leaders in Balkans sign accord on arms limits (**June 14**). Jazz great Ella Fitzgerald dies (**June 15**). Truck bomb kills 19 at U.S. base in Saudi Arabia (**June 25**). Boris Yeltsin is reelected in Russian election (**July 3**). Prince Charles and Princess Diana agree on divorce (**July 12**). 747 airliner crashes in Atlantic off Long Island; all 230 aboard perish (**July 17**). Bomb mars Summer Olympic games in Atlanta (**July 25**). Clinton signs bill to raise minimum wage (**Aug. 2**). Congress passes welfare reform bill (**Aug. 2**); approved by Clinton (**Aug. 22**). Republican convention opens in San Diego (**Aug. 12**); Bob Dole and Jack Kemp nominated (**Aug. 14**). Democrats convene in Chicago (**Aug. 26**). Iraqis strike at Kurdish enclave (**Aug. 31**); after warning, U.S. attacks Iraq's southern air defenses (**Sept. 2–3**); Iraq halts attacks on U.S. planes enforcing flight exclusion zones in north and south (**Sept. 13**). Violence flares in Jerusalem over Israel opening tourist tunnel (**Sept. 24**). Taliban Muslim fundamentalists capture Afghan capital (**Sept. 27**). Ethnic violence breaks out in Zairian refugee camps (**Oct. 13**); thousands of refugees from Rwanda and Burundi abandon camps (**Oct. 21**). Clinton-Gore ticket wins national election; Republicans retain control of Congress (**Nov. 5**). Mid-air collision in India kills 342 (**Nov. 12**). Texaco settles racial bias suit (**Nov. 15**). Hundreds of thousands of Hutu refugees return to Rwanda (**Nov. 15–18**). Clinton appoints Madeleine Albright as first female U.S. secretary of state (**Dec. 5**). Kofi Annan named UN secretary-general (**Dec. 13**). FBI agent charged with spying for Moscow (**Dec. 18**). Thousands march in Belgrade in continuing protest against president's annulment of election results (**Dec. 26**).

1997 Two Hutu sentenced to death in Rwandan genocide (**Jan. 3**). Floods cause wide damage in U.S. West (**Jan. 5**). Newt Gingrich reelected as House Speaker (**Jan. 7**). Hebron agreement signed; Israel gives up large part of West Bank city of Hebron (**Jan. 16**). U.S. shuttle joins Russian space station (**Jan. 17**). Gingrich found guilty of ethics violations (**Jan. 17**). President Clinton starts second term (**Jan. 20**). U.S., U.K., and France agree to freeze Nazis' gold loot (**Feb. 3**). O. J. Simpson found liable in civil suit (**Feb. 5**). Deng Xiaoping, Chinese leader, dead at 92 (**Feb. 19**). Israeli government approves establishment of Jewish settlement in East Jerusalem, a setback in Middle East peace process (**Feb. 26**). Tornadoes wreak havoc in Arkansas, Ohio, and Kentucky (**March 3**). State of anarchy in Albania when third of population loses savings because of pyramid schemes (**March 13**). Hale-Bopp comet is the closest it will be to Earth until 4397 (**March 22**). Heaven's Gate cult members commit mass suicide in California (**March 27**). U.S. Appeals Court upholds California ban on affirmative action (**April 8**). U.S. judge upholds California marijuana law (**April 11**). Tiger Woods breaks multiple records in Masters golf tournament (**April 13**). Fire kills 300 pilgrims outside Mecca (**April 15**). Senate, 74–26, approves chemical-weapons treaty (**April 24**). Thousands flee North Dakota flood (**April 27**). Sergeant Major of the Army, Gene C. McKinney, charged in sex cases (**May 7**). Russian president Yeltsin signs Chechnya peace treaty (**May 12**). U.S.-Russian spaceship linkup in orbit ends (**May 21**). U.S. jobless rate for May reported 4.8%, lowest since 1973 (**June 6**). European Union bolsters currency merger (**June 16**). Congress votes major tax cuts (**June 26**). Hong Kong returns to Chinese rule (**June 30**). U.S. spacecraft begins exploration of Mars (**July 4**). Andrew Cunanan murders fashion designer Gianni Versace (**July 15**). Khmer Rouge hold trial of longtime leader Pol Pot (**July 25**). White House and GOP agree on measure to balance budget (**July 28**). U.S. spacecraft transmits thousands of pictures from Mars (**Aug. 8**). Clinton exercises new line-item veto (**Aug. 11**). Timothy J. McVeigh sentenced to death for Oklahoma City bombing (**Aug. 14**). Princess Diana, 36, killed with two others in Paris car crash (**Aug. 31**). Three Islamic suicide bombers kill four persons in Jerusalem (**Sept. 4**). Mother Teresa dead at 87 (**Sept. 5**). Swiss plan first payment to Holocaust victims (**Sept. 17**). Militant Taliban leaders seize Kabul (**Sept. 27**). Iraq expels all U.S. members of UN arms-inspection team (**Oct. 29**). GOP victorious in off-year elections (**Nov. 4**). Pakistani convicted in 1993 CIA killings (**Nov. 10**). Two convicted in New York World Trade Center bombing (**Nov. 12**). Egyptian Islamic militants kill 62 at Luxor tourist site (**Nov. 17**). FBI ends 16-month investigation of crash of Flight 800 off Long Island; denies sabotage (**Nov. 18**). European Union plans to admit six nations (**Dec. 13**). U.S. company launches first commercial spy satellite (**Dec. 24**). Paris court convicts "Carlos the Jackal" of murder (**Dec. 24**).

1998 Ramzi Ahmed Yousef sentenced to life for 1993 World Trade Center bombing **(Jan. 9)**. Pope John Paul II visits Cuba **(Jan. 21–25)**. President accused in White House sex scandal; denies allegations of affair with White House intern, Monica Lewinsky **(Jan. 21 et seq.)**. President outlines first balanced budget in 30 years **(Feb. 3)**. U.S. plane cuts ski cable in Italy and sends car plunging; 20 killed **(Feb. 3)**. Thousands dead in Afghanistan quake **(Feb. 4 et seq.)**. U.S. court rules line-item veto unconstitutional **(Feb. 12)**. Serbs battle ethnic Albanians in Kosovo **(March 5 et seq.)**. U.S. drops condemnation of China's human rights record **(March 13)**. Hindu nationalist Vajpayee becomes India's prime minister **(March 19)**. FDA approves Viagra, male impotence drug **(March 27)**. Federal judge in Arkansas throws out Paula Jones case **(April 1)**. Landmark peace settlement, the Good Friday Accord, reached in Northern Ireland **(April 10)**. U.S. trade deficit biggest in decade **(April 17)**. Europeans agree on single currency, the euro **(May 3)**. Unabomber, Theodore Kaczynski, sentenced to four life terms **(May 4)**. India conducts three atomic tests despite worldwide disapproval **(May 11, 13)**. Indonesian dictator Suharto steps down after 32 years in power **(May 21)**. Pakistan stages five nuclear tests in response to India's **(May 29, 30)**. Serbs renew attack on Kosovo rebels **(June 1)**. Life sentence meted out to Terry Nichols, convicted in Oklahoma City bombing fatal to 168 **(June 4)**. Nigerian dictator Sani Abacha dies **(June 8)**. Congress votes to overhaul IRS **(July 9)**. Iraq ends cooperation with UN arms inspectors **(Aug. 5)**. U.S. embassies in Kenya and Tanzania bombed **(Aug. 7)**. Clinton admits to affair with White House intern in televised address to nation **(Aug. 17)**. Russia fights to avert financial collapse **(Aug. 17)**. U.S. cruise missiles hit suspected terrorist bases in Sudan and Afghanistan **(Aug. 20)**. North Korea fires missile across Japan **(Aug. 31)**. Swissair jet crashes; kills 229 **(Sept. 2)**. Starr Report by independent counsel outlines case for impeachment proceedings against president **(Sept. 11)**. Senate sustains veto of bill to outlaw late-term abortions **(Sept. 18)**. Iran lifts death threat against Salman Rushdie **(Sept. 24)**. German chancellor Helmut Kohl defeated by Gerhard Schröder **(Sept. 27)**. U.S. budget surplus largest in three decades **(Oct. 5)**. Matthew Shepard, gay Wyoming student, fatally beaten in hate crime **(Oct. 6)**. NATO, on verge of air strikes, reaches settlement with Milosevic on Kosovo **(Oct. 12)**. Former Chilean dictator Pinochet arrested in London **(Oct. 16)**. Wye Mills Agreement between Netanyahu and Arafat moves Middle East peace talks forward **(Oct. 23)**. More than 10,000 die in Central American hurricane, Mitch **(Nov. 1)**. Democrats unexpectedly gain five House seats in national election; Republicans keep control of House and Senate **(Nov. 3)**. House Speaker Gingrich to step down **(Nov. 9)**. House panel drafts impeachment charges; votes along party lines to approve four articles **(Dec. 11–12)**. Clinton orders air strikes on Iraq **(Dec. 16–19)**. House impeaches President Clinton along party lines on two charges, perjury and obstruction of justice **(Dec. 19)**.

1999 U.S. agrees to ease restrictions on Cuba **(Jan. 4)**. Dennis Hastert elected to replace Newt Gingrich as Speaker of the House **(Jan. 6)**. NBA ends 191-day labor dispute **(Jan. 6)**. International Olympic Committee expels six members as bribery scandal widens **(Jan. 24)**. King Hussein of Jordan dies **(Feb. 7)**. Senate acquits President Clinton of impeachment charges **(Feb. 12)**. Gen. Olusegun Obasanjo elected president of Nigeria **(Feb. 28)**. First nonstop balloon flight around world completed in 20 days by Bertrand Piccard (Switzerland) and Brian Jones (UK) **(March 1–20)**. Marine pilot acquitted in killing of 20 in 1998 Italian ski gondola accident; Italians outraged **(March 4)**. U.S. accuses China of stealing nuclear secrets **(March 5)**. Joe DiMaggio dies at age 84 **(March 8)**. Czech Republic, Poland, and Hungary join NATO **(March 12)**. NATO launches air strikes on Serbia to end attacks against ethnic Albanians in Kosovo **(March 24)**. Dr. Jack Kevorkian convicted of second-degree murder in assisted-suicide case **(March 26)**. "Melissa" computer virus spreads through the Internet **(March 27)**. Libya hands over two suspects in 1988 Pan Am jet bombing **(April 5)**. Two Colo. students go on shooting spree in Columbine High School, killing 15, including themselves **(April 20)**. NATO bombs mistakenly hit Chinese embassy in Belgrade **(May 7)**. Citadel graduates its first woman **(May 8)**. Crime rate in U.S. falls for seventh consecutive year **(May 16)**. Ehud Barak defeats Benjamin Netanyahu in Israeli prime minister election **(May 17)**. U.S. inspects suspected nuclear weapons site in North Korea, finds nothing **(May 20–24)**. Serbs

Mother Teresa
(1910–1997)

100

Euro 100

Mars Sojourner Rover

William J. Clinton
(1946–)

Gerhard Schröder
(1944–)

**Thabo Mbeki
(1942–)**

**Eileen Collins
(1956–)**

**Hillary Clinton
(1947–)**

**Vladimir Putin
(1952–)**

sign agreement to pull troops out of Kosovo after 11 weeks of NATO air attacks (**June 9**). Nelson Mandela retires as president of South Africa; succeeded by Thabo Mbeki (**June 16**). Britain's Prince Edward marries Sophie Rhys-Jones (**June 19**). Kurd leader Abdullah Ocalan sentenced to death for treason in Turkey (**June 29**). White supremacist goes on shooting spree in Midwest, killing three including self and wounding eight (**July 2–5**). U.S. soccer team tops China for women's World Cup (**July 10**). Taiwanese leader Lee Teng-hui challenges "One China" policy (**July 11**). Serial killer Rafael Reséndez-Ramirez surrenders himself to U.S. authorities (**July 13**). John F. Kennedy, Jr., wife Carolyn Bessette Kennedy, and sister-in-law Lauren Bessette killed in plane crash off coast of Martha's Vineyard (**July 16**). Col. Eileen Collins becomes first female to head a space shuttle mission (**July 16**). Falun Gong meditation sect banned by Chinese government (**July 22**). Day-trader kills 9 and wounds 13 in two Atlanta brokerage offices before committing suicide (**July 29**). Yeltsin replaces Prime Minister Stepashin with Vladimir Putin in fourth government shakeup in 17 months (**Aug. 9**). Islamic militants declare independence for Dagestan and announce holy war against Russia (**Aug. 10**). White supremacist opens fire at Jewish community center in LA, wounding five and killing one as he flees (**Aug. 10**). More than 17,000 people die in 7.4 earthquake in Turkey (**Aug. 17**). Attorney General Janet Reno reopens investigation of 1993 Waco, Tex., stand-off (**Aug. 25**). People of East Timor vote for independence from Indonesia (**Aug. 31**). Israeli prime minister Ehud Barak and PLO leader Yasir Arafat announce peace accord (**Sept. 4**). Larry Gene Ashbrook goes on rampage in Tex. church, killing seven and himself (**Sept. 15**). NASA accidentally loses $125 million spacecraft as it orbits Mars (**Sept. 23**). Dozens of people exposed to radiation in Japan's worst nuclear accident (**Sept. 30**). Russia sends ground troops to Chechnya as conflict with Islamic militants intensifies (**Oct. 1**). World population reaches six billion milestone (**Oct. 11**). Military coup led by Gen. Pervez Musharraf overthrows Pakistani government (**Oct. 12**). Tobacco companies admit to harm caused by cigarette smoking (**Oct. 13**). Senate rejects 1996 nuclear test-ban treaty; international leaders upset by U.S. stand (**Oct. 13**). Indonesia elects Muslim leader Abdurrahman Wahid president (**Oct. 20**). Pro golfer Payne Stewart and five others killed in plane crash (**Oct. 25**). EgyptAir flight crashes over Atlantic, killing all 217 on board (**Oct. 31**). Judge finds Microsoft to be a monopoly (**Nov. 5**). U.S. and China reach landmark trade agreement (**Nov. 15**). China launches first spacecraft (**Nov. 21**). Five-year-old Cuban refugee Elián González gets caught in politically charged custody battle (**Nov. 25**). World Trade Organization conference disrupted by violent protests in Seattle (**Nov. 29** *et seq.*). New Northern Ireland government begins self-rule for first time in 25 years (**Dec. 2**). Muslim terrorists hijack Indian Airlines jet with 189 on board (**Dec. 24**).

2000 Socialist president, Ricardo Lagos, elected in Chile (**Jan. 16**). George W. Bush and Al Gore take Iowa caucuses in U.S. presidential race (**Jan. 22**). Austria at center of European dispute after conservative People's Party forms coalition with the far-right Freedom Party, headed by xenophobe Jörg Haider (**Feb. 3**). First Lady Hillary Clinton officially enters N.Y. Senate race (**Feb. 6**). Hijackers seize Afghan plane; release hostages in Stansted, England (**Feb. 6–12**). Britain ends self-rule in Northern Ireland after Irish Republican Army misses disarmament deadline (**Feb. 11**). NEAR spacecraft becomes first to orbit an asteroid (**Feb. 14**). Wary investors cause stock plunge; beginning of the end of the Internet stock boom (**Feb. 25**). Reformists win control of Iranian parliament for first time since 1979 Islamic revolution (**Feb. 26**). Gun maker Smith & Wesson limits the manufacture and distribution of handguns in light of lawsuits (**March 17**). Mass murder or suicide of hundreds in Ugandan doomsday cult (**March 18**). Acting Russian president Vladimir V. Putin formally chosen for post (**March 25**). Microsoft loses antitrust suit; appeal expected (**April 3**). Controversial Osprey plane crash kills 19 marines (**April 8**). Cuban boy Elián González reunited with father after federal raid of Miami relatives' home (**April 22**). Vermont approves same-sex unions (**April 25**). "I love you" virus disrupts computers worldwide (**May 4**). South Carolina removes Confederate battle flag from capitol dome (**May 18**). Chile ends Augusto Pinochet's immunity, clearing way for trial on murder and torture charges during years as dictator (**May 24**). Israeli troops withdraw from Lebanese security zone after 22 years of occupation (**May 24**). Former Indonesian president Suharto under house arrest, charged with corruption and abuse of power (**May 29**). Britain restores parliamentary powers to Northern Ireland after Sinn Fein agrees to disarm (**June 4**). Presidents of North and South Korea sign peace accord, ending half-century of antagonism (**June 15**). British find 58 bodies of illegal Asian immigrants suffocated in Dutch truck that transported them (**June 20**). Elián González returns to Cuba with father (**June 23**). U.S. navy resumes shelling exercises of Puerto Rico's Vieques Island, used as a training site (**June 25**). Human genome deciphered; expected to revolutionize the practice of medicine (**June 26**). Iraq believed to resume missile program (**June 30**). Vicente Fox Quesada elected president of Mexico (**July 2**). Bashar al-Assad succeeds late father, Hafez al-Assad, as Syrian president (**July 10**). Concorde crash kills 113 near Paris (**July 25**). Republican convention picks Texas governor George W. Bush as presidential candidate; Dick Cheney for vice presidential spot (**Aug. 2**). Democratic convention selects Vice President Al Gore and Sen. Joseph I. Lieberman to head ticket (**Aug. 14**). Los Alamos scientist Wen Ho Lee, accused of stealing sensitive nuclear weapons data, freed after serving nine months in prison (**Sept. 13**). Olympic Games open in Australia (**Sept. 15**). Six-year Whitewater investigation of the Clintons ends without indictments (**Sept. 20**). Yugoslav opposition claims victory; incumbent Slobodan Milosevic denies results (**Sept. 25**). Danish voters reject euro (**Sept. 26**). Abortion pill, RU-486, wins U.S. approval (**Sept. 28**). Palestinians and Israelis clash, spurred by visit of right-wing Israeli leader Ariel Sharon to a joint Jewish/Muslim holy site; "Al Aksa intifada" continues unabated (**Sept. 30** *et seq.*). Nationwide uprising overthrows Yugoslavian president Milosevic (**Oct. 5**). Vojislav Kostunica sworn in as Yugoslav president (**Oct. 7**). 17 U.S. sailors on navy destroyer *Cole* die in Yemen terrorist explosion (**Oct. 12**). U.S. presidential election closest in decades; Bush's slim lead in Florida leads to automatic recount in that state (**Nov. 7–8**). Republicans file federal suit to block manual recount of Florida presidential election ballots sought by Democrats (**Nov. 11**). Philippine president Joseph Estrada impeached after receiving gambling payoffs (**Nov. 13**). Florida Supreme Court rules hand count of presidential ballots may continue (**Nov. 21**). Global warming talks collapse at Hague conference (**Nov. 25**). Florida Secretary of State Katherine Harris certifies Bush as winner by 537 votes (**Nov. 26**). Mad Cow disease alarms Europe (**Nov. 30** *et seq.*). Israeli prime minister Ehud Barak resigns (**Dec. 9**). U.S. Supreme Court orders halt to manual recount of presidential votes in Florida (**Dec. 9**). Supreme Court seals Bush victory by 5–4; rules there can be no further recounting (**Dec. 12**).

2001 Congo president Laurent Kabila assassinated by bodyguard (**Jan. 16**). In final days of presidency, Bill Clinton issues controversial pardons, including one for Marc Rich, billionaire fugitive financier (**Jan. 20**). George W. Bush is sworn in as 43rd president (**Jan. 20**). Earthquake kills thousands in India (**Jan. 26** *et seq.*). Libyan convicted in Flight 103 bombing over Lockerbie, Scotland (**Jan. 31**). Right-winger Ariel Sharon wins election in Israel (**Feb. 6**). U.S. submarine *Greeneville* sinks Japanese fishing boat, killing 9 (**Feb. 9**). FBI agent Robert Hanssen is charged with spying for Russia for 15 years (**Feb. 20**). The long-simmering resentment of Macedonia's ethnic Albanians erupts into violence (**March 15** *et seq.*). British livestock epidemic, foot-and-mouth disease, reaches crisis levels (**March 23**). Bush abandons global-warming treaty (Kyoto Protocol), angering European leaders (**March 30**). U.S. spy plane and Chinese jet collide. The 24 crew members of the U.S. plane are detained for 11 days; U.S. issues a formal statement of regret (**April 2** *et seq.*). Race riots in Cincinnati continue for several days following a shooting of an unarmed black man by a white police officer (**April 7** *et seq.*). U.S. millionaire Dennis Tito becomes first space tourist, visiting the International Space Station aboard a Russian booster (**April 28**). Former Klansman Thomas E. Blanton convicted of 1963 murder of four black girls in Birmingham, Ala. (**May 1**). After a Palestinian suicide bomber kills 5 and wounds more than 100 in a Netanya shopping mall, Israeli warplanes retaliate by bombing West Bank and Gaza strip (**May 18**). Four are declared guilty in 1998 terrorist bombings of U.S. embassies in Kenya and Tanzania (**May 29**). Balance of the Senate shifts after Jim Jeffords of Vermont changes his party affiliation from Republican to Independent. The move strips Republicans of control of the Senate and gives Democrats the narrowest of majorities (50–49–1) (**June 5**). Bush signs new tax-cut law, cutting taxes by $1.35 trillion over

Vicente Fox Quesada
(1942–)

Vojislav Kostunica
(1944–)

Yasir Arafat
(1929–2004)

Ariel Sharon
(1928–)

**Mohammad Khatami
(1943–)**

World Trade Center

**Hamid Karzai
(1957–)**

**Jacques Chirac
(1932–)**

11 years, the largest tax cut in 2 decades (**June 7**). Mohammad Khatami, Iran's moderate president, is reelected in a landslide (**June 9**). Oklahoma City bomber Timothy McVeigh executed (**June 11**). Syrian forces evacuate Beirut area after decades of occupation (**June 19**). Former Yugoslav president Slobodan Milosevic is delivered to UN tribunal in The Hague to await war-crimes trial (**June 29**). Without U.S., 178 nations reach agreement on climate accord, which rescues, though dilutes, 1997 Kyoto Protocol (**July 23**). Bush allows stem cell research, approving federal funds for studies using existing strains of stem cells (**Aug. 9**). After six months of fighting, a peace agreement is signed between rebels and the Macedonian government (**Aug. 13**). Budget surplus dwindles; some blame the slowing economy and the Bush tax cut (**Aug. 22**). Terrorists attack United States. Hijackers ram jetliners into twin towers of New York City's World Trade Center and the Pentagon. A fourth hijacked plane crashes 80 mi outside of Pittsburgh. Toll of dead is more than 3,000. Within days, Islamic militant Osama bin Laden and the al-Qaeda terrorist network are identified as the parties behind the attacks (**Sept. 11**). Anthrax scare rivets nation, as anthrax-laced letters are sent to various media and government officials. Several die after handling the letters (**October 5** *et seq.*). In response to Sept. 11 terrorist attacks, U.S. and British forces launch bombing campaign against Taliban government and al-Qaeda terrorist camps in Afghanistan. Bombings continue on a daily basis (**Oct. 7** *et seq.*). Irish Republican Army announces that it has begun to dismantle its weapons arsenal, marking a dramatic leap forward in Northern Ireland peace process (**Oct. 23**). Plane crash kills 260 in Queens, N.Y. (**Nov. 12**). Afghani factions create a post-Taliban government (**Nov. 27**). Enron Corp., one of world's largest energy companies, files for bankruptcy (**Dec. 2**). Israel condemns the Palestinian Authority as a "terror-supporting entity" and severs ties with leader Yasir Arafat following mounting violence against Israelis. The Israeli Army begins bombing Palestinian areas (**Dec. 4** *et seq.*). Taliban regime in Afghanistan collapses after two months of bombing by American warplanes and fighting by Northern Alliance ground troops (**Dec. 9**). Hamid Karzai, new interim Afghan leader, is sworn in (**Dec. 22**).

2002 The euro currency debuts in 12 European countries (**Jan. 2**). U.S. takes Taliban and al-Qaeda prisoners to Guantanamo Bay (**Jan. 10**). Defrocked priest John Geoghan convicted of child molestation; church's role in cover-up sparks national outrage (**Jan. 18**). U.S. reporter Daniel Pearl kidnapped in Pakistan (**Jan. 23**). Kenneth L. Lay, chairman of bankrupt energy trader Enron, resigns; company under federal investigation for hiding debt and misrepresenting earnings (**Jan. 24**). President Bush's first State of Union address labels Iran, Iraq, and North Korea "an axis of evil" (**Jan. 29**). Queen Elizabeth II of England marks 50 years as monarch (**Feb 6**). The trial of Slobodan Milosevic on charges of crimes against humanity opens at The Hague (**Feb. 12**). American Taliban soldier John Walker Lindh charged with supporting terrorism (**Feb. 13**). Reporter Pearl confirmed dead in Pakistan (**Feb. 21**). Angolan UNITA rebel leader Jonas Savimbi killed in battle (**Feb. 22**). Tamil Tigers and Sri Lankan government sign a cease-fire agreement (**Feb. 22**). Hundreds in India die in Hindu-Muslim clashes (**March 2**). U.S. and Afghan troops launch Operation Anaconda against remaining al-Qaeda and Taliban fighters in Afghanistan (**March 2**). Saudi peace proposal—offering Israel normal relations with all Arab nations in return for withdrawal from occupied territories—approved at Arab League summit (**March 28**). Israeli tanks and warplanes attack West Bank towns of Nablus, Jenin, Bethlehem, and others in response to string of Palestinian suicide attacks. In the first three months of 2002, 14 suicide bombers killed dozens of Israeli civilians and wounded hundreds (**March 29–April 21**). Israeli prime minister Sharon calls for exile of Palestinian leader Yasir Arafat (**April 2**). UNITA Rebels and Angolan government sign a cease-fire ending 30 years of civil war (**April 4**). International Criminal Court wins UN ratification, but U.S. refuses to ratify (**April 11**). Venezuelan president Hugo Chavez ousted in coup, then reinstated (**April 12, 14**). U.S. and Russia reach landmark arms agreement to cut both countries' nuclear arsenals by up to two-thirds over the next ten years (**May 13**). East Timor becomes a new nation (**May 20**). In letter to Director, FBI lawyer Coleen Rowley criticizes FBI for thwarting terrorist efforts (**May 21**). Dirty bomb plot foiled with arrest of Jose Padilla (**June 10**). U.S. abandons 31-year-old Antiballistic Missile treaty (**June

13). At national conference, U.S. bishops recommend zero tolerance policy for priests who abuse children **(June 14).** Arthur Andersen firm convicted of destroying documents relating to former client Enron Corp. **(June 15).** Bush announces U.S. will not recognize an independent Palestinian state until Yasir Arafat is replaced **(June 24).** WorldCom, after admitting to misstating profits, files for bankruptcy—largest claim in U.S. history **(July 21).** Pennsylvania miners rescued after spending 77 hours in a dark, flooded mine shaft **(July 28).** Bush signs corporate reform bill in response to spate of corporate scandals **(July 30).** Bush addresses United Nations, calls for a "regime change" in Iraq **(Sept. 12).** Tyco executives L. Dennis Kozlowski and Mark Swartz indicted in stock-fraud scheme **(Sept. 12).** Terrorist bomb in Bali kills hundreds **(Oct. 12).** Government suspended in Northern Ireland in protest of suspected IRA spy ring **(Oct. 14).** Former ImClone Executive Sam Waksal pleads guilty to charges including fraud and perjury **(Oct. 15).** North Korea admits to developing nuclear arms in defiance of treaty **(Oct. 16).** Vatican calls for softening of U.S. bishops' abuse policy **(Oct. 18).** Chechen rebels take 763 hostages in Moscow theater; Russian authorities release a gas into theater, killing 116 hostages and freeing remaining survivors **(Oct. 23–26).** Snipers prey upon DC suburbs, killing ten and wounding others **(Oct. 2–24).** Police arrest two sniper suspects, John Allen Muhammad and John Lee Malvo **(Oct. 24).** CIA kills six al-Qaeda members in Yemen **(Nov. 4).** Republicans retake the Senate in midterm elections; gain additional House seats **(Nov. 5).** UN Security Council passes unanimous resolution calling on Iraq to disarm or else face "serious consequences" **(Nov. 8).** China's Jiang Zemin officially retires as general secretary; Hu Jintao named as his successor **(Nov. 14).** UN arms inspectors return to Iraq **(Nov. 18).** EPA relaxes Clean Air Act **(Nov. 22).** Bush signs legislation creating cabinet-level Department of Homeland Security **(Nov. 25).** Boston archbishop Cardinal Bernard Law resigns over growing child sexual abuse scandal in the Catholic Church **(Dec. 13).** Trent Lott steps down as Republican leader after furor over pro-segregationist remark **(Dec. 20).** Sen. Bill Frist unanimously elected Republican leader of the Senate **(Dec. 23).**

Tony Blair
(1953–)

2003 North Korea withdraws from treaty on the nonproliferation of nuclear weapons **(Jan. 10).** Illinois governor George Ryan commutes 167 death row sentences, calling capital punishment flawed **(Jan. 11).** White House announces huge deficits expected to top $200 billion in 2003 **(Jan. 15).** The UN's report on Iraqi weapons inspections is highly critical, but not damning **(Jan. 27).** In State of the Union address, Bush announces that he is ready to attack Iraq even without a UN mandate **(Jan. 28).** Ariel Sharon elected Israeli prime minister **(Jan. 29).** Space shuttle *Columbia* explodes, killing all seven astronauts **(Feb. 1).** Nine-week general strike in Venezuela calling for President Chavez's resignation ends in defeat **(Feb. 2).** U.S. Secretary of State Powell presents Iraq war rationale to UN, citing Iraqi weapons as imminent threat to world security **(Feb. 5).** Massive peace demonstrations take place around the world, protesting potential invasion of Iraq **(Feb. 15).** UN Security Council members France, Germany, and Russia insist that "the military option should only be a last resort" concerning Iraq **(Feb. 24).** Serbian prime minister Zoran Djindjic assassinated **(March 12).** Hu Jintao succeeds Chinese president Jiang Zemin **(March 15).** The United States and Britain launch war against Iraq **(March 19).** Baghdad falls to U.S. troops **(April 9).** European Union expands by ten nations **(April 16).** First Palestinian prime minister, Mahmoud Abbas, sworn in **(April 29).** U.S.-backed "road map" for peace proposed for Middle East **(April 30).** The United States declares official end to combat operations in Iraq **(May 1).** U.S. diplomat Paul Bremer becomes civil administrator of occupied Iraq **(May 12).** Terrorists strike in Saudi Arabia, killing 34 at Western compound; al-Qaeda suspected **(May 12).** Bush signs ten-year, $350-billion tax-cut package, the third-largest tax cut in U.S. history **(May 28).** Burmese opposition leader Aung San Suu Kyi again placed under house arrest by military regime **(May 30).** Eric Rudolph, Olympic bombing suspect, arrested **(May 31).** International Atomic Energy Agency (IAEA) discovers Iran's concealed nuclear activities and calls for intensified inspections **(June 18).** In one of the most important rulings on the issue of affirmative action in 25 years, the U.S. Supreme Court decisively upholds the use of affirmative action in higher education **(June 23).** Palestinian militant groups announce cease-fire toward Israel **(June 29).**

Hugo Chavez
(1954–)

Hu Jintao
(1942–)

Luiz Ignácio Lula
da Silva
(1945–)

George W. Bush
(1946–)

Saddam Hussein
(1937–)

Donald H. Rumsfeld
(1932–)

Paul Martin
(1938–)

Secretary of Defense Donald Rumsfeld announces price of Iraq war is about $3.9 billion a month, nearly double the April estimate (**July 9**). Iraq's interim governing council is inaugurated (**July 13**). Saddam Hussein's sons killed in firefight (**July 22**). Mutinous troops attempt unsuccessful coup in Philippines (**July 27**). Terrorist bombing at Indonesian hotel kills ten (**Aug. 6**). Liberia's autocratic president Charles Taylor forced to leave civil war–ravaged country (**Aug. 11**). NATO assumes control of peacekeeping force in Afghanistan (**Aug. 11**). Libya accepts blame for 1988 bombing of flight over Lockerbie, Scotland; agrees to pay $2.7 billion to the families of the 270 victims (**Aug. 15**). Suicide bombing destroys UN headquarters in Baghdad, killing 24, including top envoy Sergio Vieira de Mello (**Aug. 19**). Palestinian suicide bombing in Jerusalem kills 20 Israelis, including 6 children (**Aug. 19**). Venezuelan opposition files petition for referendum to recall President Hugo Chavez (**Aug. 20**). After Israel retaliates for suicide bombing by killing top member of Hamas, militant Palestinian groups formally withdraw from cease-fire in effect since June 29 (**Aug. 24**). Investigation into the loss of space shuttle *Columbia* cites egregious organizational problems at NASA (**Aug. 25**). Congressional Budget Office predicts federal deficit of $480 billion in 2004 and $5.8 trillion by 2013 (**Aug. 26**). Palestinian prime minister Mahmoud Abbas resigns; "road map" to peace effectively collapses (**Sept. 6**). California governor Gray Davis ousted in recall vote; actor Arnold Schwarzenegger elected in his place (**Oct. 7**). UN votes in favor of a resolution ordering Israel to end construction of security barrier dividing Israeli and Palestinian areas (**Oct. 24**). Bush signs bill banning so-called partial-birth abortion procedure (**Nov. 5**). President Bush signs $87.5 billion emergency package for post-war Iraq reconstruction; this supplements $79 billion approved in April (**Nov. 5**). New Palestinian prime minister Ahmed Qurei takes office (**Nov. 12**). Alabama chief justice Roy S. Moore forced from office after his refusal to remove monument of the Ten Commandments (**Nov. 13**). The Bush administration reverses policy, agrees to transfer power to an interim Iraqi government sooner than originally planned (**Nov. 14**). Suicide bombers attack two synagogues in Istanbul, Turkey, killing 25 (**Nov. 15**). Massachusetts Supreme Court rules in favor of gay marriage (**Nov. 18**). Another terrorist attack in Istanbul kills 26; al-Qaeda suspected in both (**Nov. 20**). Georgian president Eduard Shevardnadze resigns after weeks of protests (**Nov. 23**). John A. Muhammad, convicted in the 2002 Washington, DC, area shootings, receives death sentence (**Nov. 24**). President Bush eliminates steel tariffs after WTO says U.S. violated trade laws (**Dec. 4**). Paul Martin succeeds Jean Chretien as Canadian prime minister (**Dec. 12**). Saddam Hussein is captured by American troops (**Dec. 13**). Libyan leader Muammar Qaddafi announces he will give up weapons program (**Dec. 19**).

2004 Former Enron CFO Andrew Fastow pleads guilty to defrauding Enron (**Jan. 13**). Bush proposes ambitious space program that includes flights to the Moon, Mars, and beyond (**Jan. 14**). Iraq weapons investigator David Kay resigns, says there's no evidence of weapons of mass destruction, one of the Bush administration's chief reasons for launching war in Iraq (**Jan. 23**). About one third of Iran's Parliament steps down to protest hard-line Guardian Council's banning of more than 2,000 reformists from running in parliamentary elections (**Feb. 1**). A. Q. Khan, founder of Pakistan's nuclear program, admits he sold nuclear-weapons designs to other countries, including North Korea, Iran, and Libya (**Feb. 4**). Armed rebels in Haiti force President Aristide to resign and flee the country (**Feb. 29**). John Kerry secures Democratic nomination after winning nine out of ten primaries and caucuses (**March 2**). Spain is rocked by terrorist attacks, killing more than 200. Al Qaeda takes responsibility (**March 11**). Spain's governing Popular Party loses election to opposition Socialists. Outcome seen as a reaction to terrorist attacks days before and Popular Party's support of the U.S.-led war in Iraq (**March 14**). North Atlantic Treaty Organization formally admits seven new countries: Bulgaria, Estonia, Latvia, Lithuania, Romania, Slovakia, and Slovenia (**March 29**). U.S. troops launch offensive in Falluja in response to killing and mutilation on March 31 of four U.S. civilian contractors. (**April 5–May 1**). Israeli prime minister Sharon announces plan to unilaterally withdraw from Gaza Strip (**April 12**). Greek Cypriots reject UN reunification plan with Turkish Cypriots (**April 24**). U.S. media release graphic photos of American soldiers abusing and sexually humiliating

Iraqi prisoners at Abu Ghraib prison. Images spark outrage around the world (**April 30**). Gay marriages begin in Massachusetts, the first state in the country to legalize such unions (**May 17**). Sudan rebels (SPLA) and government reach accord to end 21-year civil war. However, separate war in western Darfur region between Arab militias and black Africans continues unabated (**May 26**). U.S. hands over power to Iraqi interim government; Iyad Allawi becomes prime minister (**June 28**). In *Rasul* v. *Bush*, Supreme Court rules that "enemy combatants" held at Guantánamo Bay, Cuba, are legally entitled to file petitions for writs of habeas corpus; and in *Hamdi* v. *Rumsfeld*, court rules that the detention of a U.S. citizen held as an enemy combatant is invalid, rejecting government's claim that the executive branch has unreviewable authority in time of war (**June 28**). Israeli Supreme Court orders removal of part of security barrier dividing Israeli and Palestinian lands (**June 30**). Senate Intelligence Committee reports that intelligence on Iraq's weapons programs was "overstated" and flawed (**July 5**). Sept. 11 commission harshly criticizes government's handling of terrorist attacks (**July 22**). Democratic National Convention in Boston nominates John Kerry for president (**July 26–29**). Security Council demands Sudanese government disarm militias in Darfur that are massacring civilians (**July 30**). Florida hit by hurricanes Bonnie (**Aug. 12**) and Charley (**Aug. 13**). Summer Olympics take place in Athens, Greece (**Aug. 13–29**). Venezuelan president Hugo Chavez survives recall referendum (**Aug. 16**). Pentagon-sponsored Schlesinger report rejects idea that Abu Ghraib prison abuse was work of a few aberrant soldiers, and asserts there were "fundamental failures throughout all levels of command" (**Aug. 24**). Republican Convention in New York renominates President Bush (**Aug. 30–Sept. 2**). Chechen terrorists take about 1,200 schoolchildren and others hostage in Beslan, Russia; 340 people die when militants detonate explosives (**Sept. 1–3**). Hurricane Ivan ravages U.S. south (**Sept. 15**). U.S.'s final report on Iraq's weapons finds no WMDs (**Sept. 16**). UN Atomic Energy Agency tells Iran to stop enriching uranium; a nascent nuclear weapons program suspected (**Sept. 18**). Bush eases trade restrictions on Libya (**Sept. 20**). Congress extends tax cuts due to expire at the end of 2005 (**Sept. 23**). Hurricane Jeanne hits Florida (**Sept. 26**). 380 tons of explosives reported missing in Iraq (**Oct. 25**). Bush reelected president (**Nov. 2**). U.S. troops launch attack on Falluja, stronghold of the Iraqi insurgency (**Nov. 8**). Yasir Arafat dies in Paris (**Nov. 11**). Ukraine presidential election declared fraudulent (**Nov. 21**). Red Cross alleges abuse at U.S.-run Guantánamo prison (**Nov. 30**). Hamid Karzai inaugurated as Afghanistan's first popularly elected president (**Dec. 7**). Missile test fails; setback for Bush administration's missile defense system (**Dec. 15**). Massive protests by supporters of opposition candidate Viktor Yushchenko's lead to a new Ukrainian election; Yushchenko eventually declared prime minister (**Dec. 26**). Enormous tsunami devastates Asia; at least 225,000 killed (**Dec. 26**).

Viktor Yushchenko
(1954–)

For 2005 chronology, *see* Current Events pp. 35–44.

A Profile of the World

Source: The World Factbook, 2005

Geography

Age: 4.55 billion years old.

Total area: 510.072 million sq km (196.940 million sq mi). **Land area:** 148.94 million sq km (57.506 million sq mi). **Water area:** 361.132 million sq km (139.434 million sq mi). **Coastline:** 356,000 km (221,208 mi). **Note:** 70.8% of the world is water, 29.2% is land.

Terrain: Highest elevation is Mt. Everest at 8,850 m (29,035 ft) and lowest land depression is the Dead Sea at –411 m (–1,349 ft) below sea level. The greatest ocean depth is the Mariana Trench at –10,924 m (–35,840 ft) in the Pacific Ocean.

Land use: *Arable land:* 10.73%. *Permanent crops:* 1%. *Other:* 88.27% (2001 est.). *Irrigated land:* 2,714,320 sq km (1,048,005 sq mi).

People

Population: 6,458,141,043 (Aug. 3, 2005 est.).

Growth rate: 1.14% (2005 est.).

Birth rate: 20.15 births/1,000 population (2005 est.).

Death rate: 8.78 deaths/1,000 population (2005 est.).

Sex ratio (at birth): 1.06 males/female (2005 est.).

Infant mortality rate: 50.11 deaths/1,000 live births (2004 est.).

Life expectancy at birth: *Total population:* 64.33 years. *Male:* 62.73 years. *Female:* 66.04 years (2005 est.).

Total fertility rate: 2.6 children born per woman (2005 est.).

Literacy: Age 15 and over who can read and write (1995 est.). *Total population:* 77%. *Male:* 83%. *Female:* 71%.

Government and Economy

Political divisions: 193 sovereign nations, 61 dependent areas, and 6 disputed territories.

Economy: Global output (GWP) rose by 4.9% in 2004, led by China (9.1%), Russia (6.7%), and India (6.2%). Growth results posted by the major industrial countries varied from a small gain in Italy (1.3%) to a strong gain by the United States (4.4%). The developing nations also varied in their growth results, with many countries facing population increases that erode gains in output. The addition of 75 million people each year to an already overcrowded globe is exacerbating the problems of pollution, desertification, underemployment, epidemics, and famine. Because of their own internal problems and priorities, the industrialized countries devote insufficient resources to deal effectively with the poorer areas of the world, which, at least from an economic point of view, are becoming further marginalized.

GWP/PPP: $55.5 trillion (2004 est.).

GWP—real growth rate: 4.9% (2004 est.).

GWP/PPP—per capita: $8,800 (2004 est.).

GWP composition: agriculture 4%, industry 32%, services 64% (2004 est.).

Inflation rate (consumer price index): developed countries 1% to 4% typically; developing countries 5% to 60% typically (2004 est.).

Unemployment rate: 30% combined unemployment and underemployment in many nonindustrialized countries; developed countries typically 4%–12% unemployment.

Exports: $8.819 trillion (f.o.b., 2003 est.).

Imports: $8.754 trillion (f.o.b., 2003 est.).

External debt: $12.7 trillion (2004 est.)

Military expenditures: roughly 2% of GWP (1999 est.).

Territories, Colonies, and Dependencies

Source: The World Factbook, 2005

The following is a list of dependencies—territories under the jurisdiction of another country.

Under Australian Jurisdiction (6)
Ashmore and Cartier Islands
Christmas Island
Cocos (Keeling) Islands
Coral Sea Islands
Heard Island and McDonald Islands
Norfolk Island

Under Danish Jurisdiction (2)
Faeroe Islands
Greenland

Under Dutch Jurisdiction (2)
Aruba
Netherlands Antilles

Under French Jurisdiction (16)
Bassas da India
Clipperton Island
Europa Island
French Guiana
French Polynesia
French Southern and Antarctic Lands
Glorioso Islands
Guadeloupe
Juan de Nova Island
Martinique
Mayotte
New Caledonia
Réunion
Saint Pierre and Miquelon
Tromelin Island
Wallis and Futuna

Under New Zealand Jurisdiction (3)
Cook Islands
Niue
Tokelau

Under Norwegian Jurisdiction (3)
Bouvet Island
Jan Mayen
Svalbard

Under UK Jurisdiction (15)
Anguilla
Bermuda
British Indian Ocean Territory
British Virgin Islands
Cayman Islands
Falkland Islands
Gibraltar
Guernsey
Jersey
Isle of Man
Montserrat
Pitcairn Islands
Saint Helena
South Georgia and the South Sandwich Islands
Turks and Caicos Islands

Under U.S. Jurisdiction (14)
American Samoa
Baker Island
Guam
Howland Island
Jarvis Island
Johnston Atoll
Kingman Reef
Midway Islands
Navassa Island
Northern Mariana Islands
Palmyra Atoll
Puerto Rico
Virgin Islands
Wake Island

Disputed Territories (6): Antarctica, Gaza Strip, Paracel Islands, Spratly Islands, West Bank, Western Sahara

Country Statistics at a Glance

Country rankings of the type presented below cannot pretend to be definitive; instead they aspire only to provide the reader with an approximation of the high and low ends on a particular scale. Country data vary enormously depending on the sources, and the absence of reliable data on some countries requires their omission, which further skews the results.

LARGEST COUNTRIES[1] (in sq mi):* 2004

1.	Russia	6,592,735
2.	Canada	3,855,081
3.	United States	3,717,792
4.	China	3,705,386
5.	Brazil	3,286,470
6.	Australia	2,967,893
7.	India	1,269,338
8.	Argentina	1,068,296
9.	Kazakhstan	1,049,150
10.	Sudan	967,493

SMALLEST COUNTRIES[1] (in sq mi):* 2004

1.	Vatican City	0.17
2.	Monaco	0.75
3.	Nauru	8.11
4.	Tuvalu	10.0
5.	San Marino	23.6
6.	Liechtenstein	62.0
7.	Marshall Islands	70.0
8.	Saint Kitts and Nevis	101.0
9.	Maldives	116.0
10.	Malta	122.0

HIGHEST POPULATION DENSITY[2] (per sq mi): 2005

1.	Monaco	43,046
2.	Singapore	16,548
3.	Malta	3,266
4.	Maldives	3,014
5.	Bahrain	2,681
6.	Bangladesh	2,596
7.	Barbados	1,678
8.	Taiwan	1,648
9.	Nauru	1,609
10.	Mauritius	1,562

LOWEST POPULATION DENSITY[2] (per sq mi): 2005

1.	Western Sahara	2.7
2.	Mongolia	4.6
3.	Namibia	6.4
4.	Australia	6.8
5.	Suriname	7.0
6.	Botswana	7.1
7.	Iceland	7.5
8.	Mauritania	7.8
9.	Libya	8.5
	Canada	8.5

HIGHEST GDP PER CAPITA[3] (PPP in U.S. dollars): 2004

1.	Luxembourg	$58,900
2.	United States	40,100
3.	Norway	40,000
4.	San Marino	34,600
5.	Switzerland	33,800
6.	Denmark	32,200
7.	Iceland	31,900
	Ireland	31,900
9.	Canada	31,500
10.	Austria	31,300

LOWEST GDP PER CAPITA[3] (PPP in U.S. dollars): 2004

1.	East Timor	$400
2.	Burundi	600
	Malawi	600
	Sierra Leone	600
	Somalia	600
6.	Comoros	700
	Congo, Dem. Rep. of	700
	Guinea-Bissau	700
	Tanzania	700
10.	Afghanistan	800

HIGHEST INFLATION:[3] 2004

1.	Zimbabwe	133.0%
2.	Dominican Republic	55.0
3.	Angola	43.8
4.	Iraq	25.4
5.	Suriname	23.0
6.	Venezuela	22.4
7.	Haiti	22.0
8.	Zambia	18.3
9.	Guinea	18.0
10.	Belarus	17.4

LOWEST INFLATION:[3] 2004

1.	Nauru	−3.6%
2.	Barbados	−0.5
3.	St. Vincent and the Grenadines	−0.4
4.	Japan	−0.1
5.	Israel	0.0
6.	Oman	0.2
7.	Brunei	0.3
8.	Antigua and Barbuda	0.4
	Macedonia	0.4
10.	Finland	0.7
	Sweden	0.7

HIGHEST INFANT MORTALITY RATE[2] (deaths per 1,000 births): 2005

1.	Western Sahara	191.2
2.	Angola	163.1
3.	Afghanistan	143.6
4.	Sierra Leone	130.8
5.	Mozambique	128.9
6.	Liberia	121.7
7.	Niger	116.8
8.	Mali	116.7
9.	Somalia	110.8
10.	Tajikistan	107.2

LOWEST INFANT MORTALITY RATE[2] (deaths per 1,000 births): 2005

1.	Singapore	2.3
2.	Sweden	2.8
3.	Iceland	3.3
	Japan	3.3
5.	Finland	3.6
6.	Norway	3.7
7.	Czech Republic	3.9
	Malta	3.9
9.	Andorra	4.0
10.	Germany	4.2

HIGHEST LIFE EXPECTANCY[2] (in years): 2005

1.	Andorra	83.5
2.	San Marino	81.6
	Singapore	81.6
4.	Japan	81.2
5.	Australia	80.4
	Sweden	80.4
	Switzerland	80.4
8.	Iceland	80.2
9.	Canada	80.1
10.	Italy	79.7

LOWEST LIFE EXPECTANCY[2] (in years): 2005

1.	Botswana	33.9
2.	Swaziland	35.6
3.	Angola	36.6
4.	Lesotho	36.7
5.	Zimbabwe	36.7
6.	Malawi	37.0
7.	Zambia	39.7
8.	Mozambique	40.3
9.	Central African Rep.	41.0
10.	Niger	42.1

NOTE: Only countries for which statistics were available in sources 1, 2, or 3 figure in these lists. *Size refers to the total area of a country, which includes the land area plus bodies of water. *Sources:* 1. Information Please Database. 2. U.S. Census Bureau, International Database. 3. *The World Factbook, 2005.*

World Population Growth, Year 1 to 2050

Year	Population	Year	Population	Year	Population	Year	Population	Year	Population
1	200 million	1900	1.6 billion	1970	3.7 billion	1995	5.7 billion	2030	8.1 billion
1000	275 million	1950	2.55 billion	1975	4 billion	2000	6.1 billion	2040	8.6 billion
1500	450 million	1955	2.8 billion	1980	4.5 billion	2005	6.45 billion	2050	9 billion
1750	700 million	1960	3 billion	1985	4.85 billion	2010	6.8 billion		
1850	1.2 billion	1965	3.3 billion	1990	5.3 billion	2020	7.5 billion		

Source: Matt Rosenberg, Geography Editor, About.com. Web: http://geography.about.com.

World's 50 Most Populous Countries: 2005

Rank	Country	Population	Rank	Country	Population	Rank	Country	Population
1.	China	1,306,313,812	19.	Thailand	65,444,371	35.	Canada	32,805,041
2.	India	1,080,264,388	20.	France	60,656,178	36.	Morocco	32,725,847
3.	United States	295,734,134	21.	United Kingdom	60,441,457	37.	Algeria	32,531,853
4.	Indonesia	241,973,879	22.	Congo, Dem.		38.	Afghanistan	29,928,987
5.	Brazil	186,112,794		Rep. of	60,085,004	39.	Peru	27,925,628
6.	Pakistan	162,419,946	23.	Italy	58,103,033	40.	Nepal	27,676,547
7.	Bangladesh	144,319,628	24.	Korea, South	48,422,644	41.	Uganda	27,269,482
8.	Russia	143,420,309	25.	Ukraine	47,425,336	42.	Uzbekistan	26,851,195
9.	Nigeria	128,771,988	26.	South Africa	44,344,136	43.	Saudi Arabia	26,417,599
10.	Japan	127,417,244	27.	Colombia	42,954,279	44.	Iraq	26,074,906
11.	Mexico	106,202,903	28.	Myanmar		45.	Venezuela	25,375,281
12.	Philippines	87,857,473		(Burma)	42,909,464	46.	Malaysia	23,953,136
13.	Vietnam	83,535,576	29.	Spain	40,341,462	47.	Korea, North	22,912,177
14.	Germany	82,431,390	30.	Sudan	40,187,486	48.	Taiwan	22,894,384
15.	Egypt	77,505,756	31.	Argentina	39,537,943	49.	Romania	22,329,977
16.	Ethiopia	73,053,286	32.	Poland	38,635,144	50.	Ghana	21,029,853
17.	Turkey	69,660,559	33.	Tanzania	36,766,356			
18.	Iran	68,017,860	34.	Kenya	33,829,590			

Source: U.S. Census Bureau, International Database.

Most Populous Cities of the World

Rank	City[1]	Population	Year	Rank	City[1]	Population	Year
1.	Mumbai (Bombay), India	11,914,398	2001c	11.	Jakarta, Indonesia	8,389,443	2000c
2.	Shanghai, China	10,996,500	2003e	12.	Tokyo, Japan	8,340,000	2003e
3.	São Paulo, Brazil	10,677,019	2003e	13.	New York City, U.S.	8,085,742	2003e
4.	Seoul, South Korea	10,207,296	2002e	14.	Teheran, Iran	7,796,257	2004e
5.	Moscow, Russia	10,101,500	2001c	15.	Cairo, Egypt	7,629,866	2004e
6.	Delhi, India	9,817,439	2001c	16.	London, U.K.	7,172,036	2001c
7.	Karachi, Pakistan	9,339,023	1998c	17.	Lima, Peru	7,029,928	2004e
8.	Istanbul, Turkey	8,831,805	2000c	18.	Bogotá, Colombia	6,712,247	2001e
9.	Beijing, China	8,689,000	2001e	19.	Bangkok, Thailand	6,320,174	2000c
10.	Mexico City, Mexico	8,591,309	2000c	20.	Rio de Janeiro, Brazil	5,974,081	2003e

NOTES: "c" = census figure; "e" = estimated. 1. Refers to the city proper, as opposed to an urban agglomeration, which would also count the surrounding urban areas in the total. *Source:* GeoHive. Web: http://www.geohive.com/charts/city_notagg.php.

World's Most Populous Urban Agglomerations:[1] 2005

Rank	Name	Est. population	Rank	Name	Est. population
1.	Tokyo, Japan	35,327,000	11.	Dhaka, Bangladesh	12,560,000
2.	Mexico City, Mexico	19,013,000	12.	Los Angeles–Long	
3.	New York–Newark, U.S.	18,498,000		Beach–Santa Ana, U.S.	12,146,000
4.	Mumbai (Bombay), India	18,336,000	13.	Karachi, Pakistan	11,819,000
5.	São Paulo, Brazil	18,333,000	14.	Rio de Janeiro, Brazil	11,469,000
6.	Delhi, India	15,334,000	15.	Osaka–Kobe, Japan	11,286,000
7.	Calcutta, India	14,299,000	16.	Cairo, Egypt	11,146,000
8.	Buenos Aires, Argentina	13,349,000	17.	Lagos, Nigeria	11,135,000
9.	Jakarta, Indonesia	13,194,000	18.	Beijing, China	10,849,000
10.	Shanghai, China	12,665,000	19.	Metro Manila, Philippines	10,677,000
			20.	Moscow, Russia	10,672,000

NOTES: The definitions of agglomerations vary significantly from city to city, hence the difficulty of compiling an accurate, comparative list of the world's most populous urban areas. 1. Includes metropolitan areas and surrounding urban agglomerations. Agglomerations include a central city and bordering urban areas. Some agglomerations have more than one central city (e.g., Tokyo includes Yokohama and Kawasaki). *Source:* Population Division of the Department of Economic and Social Affairs of the United Nations Secretariat (2004). *World Urbanization Prospects: The 2003 Revision.* Web: http://www.unpopulation.org.

Area and Population of Countries

(mid-2005 estimates)

Country	Area (in sq km)	Population	Country	Area (in sq km)	Population
Afghanistan	647,500	29,928,987	Grenada	344	89,502
Albania	28,748	3,563,112	Guatemala	108,890	14,655,189
Algeria	2,381,740	32,531,853	Guinea	245,857	9,467,866
Andorra	468	70,549	Guinea-Bissau	36,120	1,416,027
Angola	1,246,700	11,190,786	Guyana	214,970	765,283
Antigua and Barbuda	443	68,722	Haiti	27,750	8,121,622
Argentina	2,766,890	39,537,943	Honduras	112,090	6,975,204
Armenia	29,800	2,982,904	Hungary	93,030	10,006,835
Australia	7,686,850	20,090,437	Iceland	103,000	296,737
Austria	83,858	8,184,691	India	3,287,590	1,080,264,388
Azerbaijan	86,600	7,911,974	Indonesia	1,919,440	241,973,879
Bahamas, The	13,940	301,790	Iran	1,648,000	68,017,860
Bahrain	665	688,345	Iraq	437,072	26,074,906
Bangladesh	144,000	144,319,628	Ireland	70,280	4,015,676
Barbados	431	279,254	Israel	20,770	6,276,883
Belarus	207,600	10,300,483	Italy	301,230	58,103,033
Belgium	30,510	10,364,388	Jamaica	10,991	2,731,832
Belize	22,966	279,457	Japan	377,835	127,417,244
Benin	112,620	7,460,025	Jordan	92,300	5,759,732
Bhutan	47,000	2,232,291	Kazakhstan	2,717,300	15,185,844
Bolivia	1,098,580	8,857,870	Kenya	582,650	33,829,590
Bosnia and Herzegovina	51,129	4,025,476	Kiribati	811	103,092
Botswana	600,370	1,640,115	Korea, North	120,540	22,912,177
Brazil	8,511,965	186,112,794	Korea, South	98,480	48,422,644
Brunei	5,770	372,361	Kuwait	17,820	2,335,648
Bulgaria	110,910	7,450,349	Kyrgyzstan	198,500	5,146,281
Burkina Faso	274,200	13,925,313	Laos	236,800	6,217,141
Burundi	27,830	6,370,609	Latvia	64,589	2,290,237
Cambodia	181,040	13,607,069	Lebanon	10,400	3,826,018
Cameroon	475,440	16,380,005	Lesotho	30,355	1,867,035
Canada	9,984,670	32,805,041	Liberia	111,370	3,482,211
Cape Verde	4,033	418,224	Libya	1,759,540	5,765,563
Central African Republic	622,984	3,799,897	Liechtenstein	160	33,717
Chad	1,284,000	9,826,419	Lithuania	65,200	3,596,617
Chile	756,950	15,980,912	Luxembourg	2,586	468,571
China	9,596,960	1,306,313,812	Macedonia	25,333	2,045,262
Colombia	1,138,910	42,954,279	Madagascar	587,040	18,040,341
Comoros	2,170	671,247	Malawi	118,480	12,158,924
Congo, Republic of the	342,000	3,039,126	Malaysia	329,750	23,953,136
Congo, Democratic			Maldives	300	349,106
Republic of the	2,345,410	60,085,004	Mali	1,240,000	12,291,529
Costa Rica	51,100	4,016,173	Malta	316	398,534
Côte d'Ivoire	322,460	17,298,040	Marshall Islands	181.3	59,071
Croatia	56,542	4,495,904	Mauritania	1,030,700	3,086,859
Cuba	110,860	11,346,670	Mauritius	2,040	1,230,602
Cyprus	9,250	780,133	Mexico	1,972,550	106,202,903
Czech Republic	78,866	10,241,138	Micronesia,		
Denmark	43,094	5,432,335	Federated States of	702	108,105
Djibouti	23,000	476,703	Moldova	33,843	4,455,421
Dominica	754	69,029	Monaco	1.95	32,409
Dominican Republic	48,730	8,950,034	Mongolia	1,565,000	2,791,272
East Timor	15,007	1,040,880	Morocco	446,550	32,725,847
Ecuador	283,560	13,363,593	Mozambique	801,590	19,406,703
Egypt	1,001,450	77,505,756	Myanmar (Burma)	678,500	42,909,464
El Salvador	21,040	6,704,932	Namibia	825,418	2,030,692
Equatorial Guinea	28,051	535,881	Nauru	21	13,048
Eritrea	121,320	4,561,599	Nepal	140,800	27,676,547
Estonia	45,226	1,332,893	Netherlands	41,526	16,407,491
Ethiopia	1,127,127	73,053,286	New Zealand	268,680	4,035,461
Fiji	18,270	893,354	Nicaragua	129,494	5,465,100
Finland	337,030	5,223,442	Niger	1,267,000	11,665,937
France	547,030	60,656,178	Nigeria	923,768	128,771,988
Gabon	267,667	1,389,201	Norway	324,220	4,593,041
Gambia, The	11,300	1,593,256	Oman	212,460	3,001,583
Georgia	69,700	4,677,401	Pakistan	803,940	162,419,946
Germany	357,021	82,431,390	Palau	458	20,303
Ghana	239,460	21,029,853	Panama	78,200	3,039,150
Greece	131,940	10,668,354	Papua New Guinea	462,840	5,545,268

Country	Area (in sq km)	Population	Country	Area (in sq km)	Population
Paraguay	406,750	6,347,884	Swaziland	17,363	1,173,900
Peru	1,285,220	27,925,628	Sweden	449,964	9,001,774
Philippines	300,000	87,857,473	Switzerland	41,290	7,489,370
Poland	312,685	38,635,144	Syria	185,180	18,448,752
Portugal	92,391	10,566,212	Taiwan	35,980	22,894,384
Qatar	11,437	863,051	Tajikistan	143,100	7,163,506
Romania	237,500	22,329,977	Tanzania	945,087	36,766,356
Russia	17,075,200	143,420,309	Thailand	514,000	65,444,371
Rwanda	26,338	8,440,820	Togo	56,785	5,681,519
St. Kitts and Nevis	261	38,958	Tonga	748	112,422
St. Lucia	616	166,312	Trinidad and Tobago	5,128	1,088,644
St. Vincent and the Grenadines	389	117,534	Tunisia	163,610	10,074,951
Samoa	2,944	177,287	Turkey	780,580	69,660,559
San Marino	61.2	28,880	Turkmenistan	488,100	4,952,081
São Tomé and Príncipe	1,001	187,410	Tuvalu	26	11,636
Saudi Arabia	1,960,582	26,417,599	Uganda	236,040	27,269,482
Senegal	196,190	11,126,832	Ukraine	603,700	47,425,336
Serbia and Montenegro	102,350	10,829,175	United Arab Emirates	82,880	2,563,212
Seychelles	455	81,188	United Kingdom	244,820	60,441,457
Sierra Leone	71,740	6,017,643	United States	9,629,091	295,734,134
Singapore	692.7	4,425,720	Uruguay	176,220	3,415,920
Slovakia	48,845	5,431,363	Uzbekistan	447,400	26,851,195
Slovenia	20,273	2,011,070	Vanuatu	12,200	205,754
Solomon Islands	28,450	538,032	Vatican City	0.44	921
Somalia	637,657	8,591,629	Venezuela	912,050	25,375,281
South Africa	1,219,912	44,344,136	Vietnam	329,560	83,535,576
Spain	504,782	40,341,462	Western Sahara	266,000	273,000
Sri Lanka	65,610	20,064,776	Yemen	527,970	20,727,063
Sudan	2,505,810	40,187,486	Zambia	752,614	11,261,795
Suriname	163,270	438,144	Zimbabwe	390,580	12,746,990

Source: U.S. Census Bureau, International Database, and The World Factbook, 2005.

The Death Penalty Worldwide

According to Amnesty International, during 2004 more than 3,797 people were executed in 25 countries, and more than 7,395 people were sentenced to death in 64 countries. For U.S. figures, see p. 386.

Death Penalty Outlawed (year)[1]
Andorra (1990)
Angola (1992)
Armenia (2003)
Australia (1984)
Austria (1950)
Azerbaijan (1998)
Belgium (1996)
Bermuda (1999)
Bhutan (2004)
Bosnia-Herzegovina (1997)
Bulgaria (1998)
Cambodia (1989)
Canada (1976)
Cape Verde (1981)
Colombia (1910)
Costa Rica (1877)
Côte d'Ivoire (2000)
Croatia (1990)
Cyprus (1983)
Czech Republic (1990)
Denmark (1933)
Djibouti (1995)
Dominican Republic (1966)
East Timor (1999)
Ecuador (1906)
Estonia (1998)
Finland (1949)
France (1981)
Georgia (1997)
Germany (1987)

Greece (1993)
Guinea-Bissau (1993)
Haiti (1987)
Honduras (1956)
Hungary (1990)
Iceland (1928)
Ireland (1990)
Italy (1947)
Kiribati (1979)
Liechtenstein (1987)
Lithuania (1998)
Luxembourg (1979)
Macedonia (1991)
Malta (1971)
Marshall Islands (1986)
Mauritius (1995)
Mexico (2005)
Micronesia (1986)
Moldova (1995)
Monaco (1962)
Mozambique (1990)
Namibia (1990)
Nepal (1990)
Netherlands (1870)
New Zealand (1961)
Nicaragua (1979)
Niue (n.a.)
Norway (1905)
Palau (n.a.)
Panama (1903)
Paraguay (1992)
Poland (1997)
Portugal (1867)

Romania (1989)
Samoa (2004)
San Marino (1848)
São Tomé and Príncipe (1990)
Senegal (2004)
Serbia and Montenegro (2002)
Seychelles (1993)
Slovak Republic (1990)
Slovenia (1989)
Solomon Islands (1966)
South Africa (1995)
Spain (1978)
Sweden (1921)
Switzerland (1942)
Turkey (2002)
Turkmenistan (1999)
Tuvalu (1978)
Ukraine (1999)
United Kingdom (1973)
Uruguay (1907)
Vanuatu (1980)
Vatican City (1969)
Venezuela (1863)

Death Penalty Outlawed for Ordinary Crimes[2] (year)
Albania (2000)
Argentina (1984)

Bolivia (1997)
Brazil (1979)
Chile (2001)
Cook Islands (n.a.)
El Salvador (1983)
Fiji (1979)
Israel (1954)
Latvia (1999)
Peru (1979)

De Facto Ban on Death Penalty[3] (year)[4]
Algeria (1993)
Benin (1987)
Brunei Darussalam (1957)
Burkina Faso (1988)
Central African Republic (1981)
Congo (Republic) (1982)
Gambia (1981)
Grenada (1978)
Kenya (n.a.)
Madagascar (1958)
Maldives (1952)
Mali (1980)
Mauritania (1987)
Morocco (1993)
Myanmar (1993)
Nauru (1968)
Niger (1976)
Papua New Guinea (1950)
Russia (1999)

Sri Lanka (1976)
Suriname (1982)
Togo (n.a.)
Tonga (1982)
Tunisia (1990)

Death Penalty Permitted
Afghanistan
Antigua and Barbuda
Bahamas
Bahrain
Bangladesh
Barbados
Belarus
Belize
Botswana
Burundi
Cameroon
Chad
China (People's Republic)
Comoros
Congo (Democratic Republic)
Cuba
Dominica
Egypt
Equatorial Guinea
Eritrea
Ethiopia
Gabon
Ghana
Guatemala
Guinea

Guyana	Kuwait	Oman	Singapore	Uganda
India	Kyrgyzstan	Pakistan	Somalia	United Arab
Indonesia	Laos	Palestinian Authority	Sudan	Emirates
Iran	Lebanon	Philippines	Swaziland	United States
Iraq	Lesotho	Qatar	Syria	Uzbekistan
Jamaica	Liberia	Rwanda	Taiwan	Vietnam
Japan	Libya	St. Kitts and Nevis	Tajikistan	Yemen
Jordan	Malawi	St. Lucia	Tanzania	
Kazakhstan	Malaysia	St. Vincent and the	Thailand	Zambia
Korea, North	Mongolia	Grenadines	Trinidad and Tobago	Zimbabwe
Korea, South	Nigeria	Saudi Arabia		
		Sierra Leone		

NOTE: n.a. = date not available. 1. If death penalty was outlawed for ordinary crimes before it was outlawed in all cases, the earlier date is given. 2. Death penalty is permitted only for exceptional crimes, such as crimes committed under military law or in wartime. 3. Death penalty is sanctioned by law but has not been the practice for ten or more years. 4. Year of last execution. *Source:* Amnesty International.

Infant Mortality and Life Expectancy for Selected Countries, 2005

Country	Infant mortality[1]	Life expectancy[2]	Country	Infant mortality[1]	Life expectancy[2]	Country	Infant mortality[1]	Life expectancy[2]
Albania	21.5	77.2	Germany	4.2	78.7	Pakistan	72.4	63.0
Angola	191.2	36.6	Greece	5.5	79.1	Panama	20.5	71.9
Australia	4.7	80.4	Guatemala	35.9	65.1	Peru	31.9	69.5
Austria	4.7	78.9	Hungary	8.6	72.4	Poland	8.5	74.4
Bangladesh	62.6	62.1	India	56.3	64.3	Portugal	5.0	77.5
Brazil	29.6	71.7	Iran	41.6	70.0	Russia	15.4	67.1
Canada	4.8	80.1	Ireland	5.4	77.6	Slovakia	7.4	74.5
Chile	8.8	76.6	Israel	7.0	79.3	South Africa	61.8	43.3
China	24.2	72.3	Italy	5.9	79.7	Spain	4.4	79.5
Costa Rica	9.9	76.8	Japan	3.3	81.2	Sri Lanka	14.3	73.2
Cyprus	7.2	77.7	Kenya	61.5	48.0	Sweden	2.8	80.4
Czech Republic	3.9	76.0	Korea, South	7.0	75.8	Switzerland	4.4	80.4
Denmark	4.6	77.6	Mexico	20.9	75.2	Syria	29.5	70.0
Ecuador	23.7	76.2	Mozambique	130.8	40.3	United Kingdom	5.2	78.4
Egypt	32.6	71.0	New Zealand	5.8	78.7	United States	6.5	77.7
Finland	3.6	78.3	Nigeria	98.8	46.7	Venezuela	22.2	74.3
France	4.3	79.6	Norway	3.7	79.4	Zimbabwe	67.7	36.7

1. Infant deaths per 1,000 live births. 2. Life expectancy at birth, in years, both sexes. *Source:* U.S. Census Bureau, International Database.

Crude Birth and Death Rates for Selected Countries
(per 1,000 population)

	Birth rate							Death rate						
Country	2005	2004	2003	1990	1985	1980	1975	2005	2004	2003	1990	1985	1980	1975
Australia	12.3	12.4	12.6	15.4	15.7	15.3	16.9	7.4	7.4	7.3	7.0	7.5	7.4	7.9
Austria	8.8	8.9	9.4	11.6	11.6	12.0	12.5	9.7	9.6	9.7	10.6	11.9	12.2	12.8
Belgium	10.5	10.6	10.4	12.6	11.5	12.7	12.2	10.2	10.2	10.1	10.6	11.2	11.6	12.2
Czech Republic[1]	9.1	9.1	9.0	13.4	14.5	16.4	19.6	10.5	10.5	10.7	11.7	11.8	12.1	11.5
France	12.2	12.3	12.5	13.5	13.9	14.8	14.1	9.1	9.1	9.1	9.3	10.1	10.2	10.6
Germany[2]	8.3	8.4	8.6	11.4	9.6	10.0	9.7	10.6	10.4	10.3	11.2	11.5	11.6	12.1
Greece	9.7	9.7	9.8	10.2	11.7	15.4	15.7	10.2	10.1	9.9	9.3	9.4	9.1	8.9
Ireland	14.5	14.5	14.6	15.1	17.6	21.9	21.5	7.8	7.9	7.9	9.1	9.4	9.7	10.6
Israel	18.2	18.4	18.7	22.2	23.5	24.1	28.2	6.2	6.2	6.2	6.2	6.6	6.7	7.1
Italy	8.9	9.1	9.2	9.8	10.1	11.2	14.8	10.3	10.2	10.1	9.4	9.5	9.7	9.9
Japan	9.5	9.6	9.6	9.9	11.9	13.7	17.2	8.9	8.8	8.6	6.7	6.2	6.2	6.4
Mauritius	15.6	15.8	16.1	21.0	18.8	27.0	25.1	6.8	6.8	6.8	6.5	6.8	7.2	8.1
Netherlands	11.1	11.4	11.3	13.3	12.3	12.8	13.0	8.7	8.7	8.7	8.6	8.5	8.1	8.3
New Zealand	13.9	14.0	14.1	18.0	15.6	—	18.4	7.5	7.5	7.5	7.9	8.4	—	8.1
Norway	11.7	11.9	12.2	14.3	12.3	12.5	14.1	9.4	9.5	9.7	10.7	10.7	10.1	9.9
Panama	22.0	20.4	20.8	23.9	26.6	26.8	32.3	5.3	6.4	6.2	—	—	—	—
Poland	9.7	10.6	10.5	14.3	18.2	19.5	18.9	9.8	10.0	10.0	10.2	10.3	9.8	8.7
Portugal	10.8	10.9	11.4	11.8	12.8	16.4	19.1	10.4	10.4	10.2	10.4	9.6	9.9	10.4
Romania	10.7	10.7	10.8	13.6	15.8	—	—	11.7	11.7	12.2	10.6	10.9	—	—
Switzerland	9.8	9.8	9.6	12.5	11.6	11.3	12.3	8.5	8.4	8.8	9.5	9.2	9.2	8.7
Tunisia	15.5	15.7	16.5	25.8	31.3	35.2	36.6	5.1	5.0	5.0	—	—	—	—
United Kingdom	10.8	10.9	11.0	13.9	13.3	13.5	12.5	10.2	10.2	10.2	11.2	11.8	11.8	11.9
United States	14.1	14.1	14.1	16.7	15.7	16.2	14.0	8.2	8.3	8.4	8.6	8.7	8.9	8.9

1. Data prior to 1994 pertain to the former Czechoslovakia. 2. All data pertaining to Germany prior to 1990 are for West Germany. NOTE: (—) = not available. *Source:* United Nations, *Monthly Bulletin of Statistics, June 1997.* Data for 2003, 2004, and 2005 from the U.S. Census Bureau, International Database.

Freedom in the World, 2005

Since 1978, Freedom House has published Freedom in the World, an annual comparative assessment of the state of political rights and civil liberties around the world. Widely used by policy makers, journalists, and scholars, the 600-page survey is considered the definitive report on freedom around the globe. The 2005 ratings reflect global events from Dec. 1, 2003, through Nov. 30, 2004.

According to the survey, 89 countries are free. Their 2.8 billion inhabitants (44% of the world's population) enjoy a broad range of rights. Fifty-four countries representing 1.2 billion people (19%) are considered partly free. Political rights and civil liberties are more limited in these countries, in which corruption, dominant ruling parties, or, in some cases, ethnic or religious strife is often the norm. The survey finds that 49 countries are not free. The 2.4 billion inhabitants (37%) of these countries, nearly three-fifths of whom live in China, are denied most basic political rights and civil liberties. In 2004, Russia was the only country to register a negative category change, moving from partly free to not free.

FREE[1]
Ranking: 1
Andorra
Australia
Austria
Bahamas
Barbados
Belgium
Canada
Cape Verde
Chile
Costa Rica
Cyprus
Czech Republic
Denmark
Dominica
Estonia
Finland
France
Germany
Hungary
Iceland
Ireland
Italy
Kiribati
Liechtenstein
Luxembourg
Malta
Marshall Islands
Mauritius
Micronesia
Nauru
Netherlands
New Zealand
Norway
Palau
Poland
Portugal
San Marino
Slovakia
Slovenia
Spain
Sweden
Switzerland

Tuvalu
United Kingdom
United States
Uruguay

Ranking: 1.5
Belize
Bulgaria
Greece
Grenada
Japan
Latvia
Monaco
Panama
St. Kitts and Nevis
St. Lucia
St. Vincent and the
   Grenadines
South Africa
South Korea
Suriname
Taiwan

Ranking: 2
Antigua and
   Barbuda
Argentina
Benin
Botswana
Croatia
Dominican Republic
Ghana
Guyana
Israel
Lithuania
Mali
Mexico
Mongolia
Samoa
São Tomé and
   Príncipe
Vanuatu

Ranking: 2.5
Brazil
El Salvador

India
Jamaica
Lesotho
Namibia
Peru
Philippines
Romania
Senegal
Serbia and
   Montenegro
Thailand

PARTLY FREE[1]
Ranking: 3
Albania
Bolivia
East Timor
Ecuador
Honduras
Kenya
Macedonia
Madagascar
Nicaragua
Niger
Papua New Guinea
Paraguay
Seychelles
Solomon Islands
Sri Lanka
Trinidad and Tobago
Turkey

Ranking: 3.5
Bosnia and
   Herzegovina
Fiji
Georgia
Indonesia
Moldova
Mozambique
Sierra Leone
Tanzania
Ukraine
Venezuela

Ranking: 4
Bangladesh
Colombia
Comoros
The Gambia
Guatemala
Guinea-Bissau
Malawi
Malaysia
Nigeria
Tonga
Zambia

Ranking: 4.5
Armenia
Burkina Faso
Congo, Rep. of
Gabon
Jordan
Kuwait
Liberia
Morocco
Singapore
Uganda

Ranking: 5
Bahrain
Burundi
Djibouti
Ethiopia
Nepal
Yemen

NOT FREE[1]
Ranking: 5.5
Afghanistan
Algeria
Angola
Azerbaijan
Bhutan
Brunei
Cambodia
Central African
   Republic
Chad
Egypt

Guinea
Kazakhstan
Kyrgyzstan
Lebanon
Maldives
Mauritania
Oman
Pakistan
Qatar
Russia
Rwanda
Tajikistan
Togo
Tunisia

Ranking: 6
Cameroon
Congo, Dem. Rep. of
Côte d'Ivoire
Iran
Iraq
Swaziland
United Arab
   Emirates

Ranking: 6.5
Belarus
China
Equatorial Guinea
Eritrea
Haiti
Laos
Somalia
Uzbekistan
Vietnam
Zimbabwe

Ranking: 7
Cuba
Libya
Myanmar (Burma)
North Korea
Saudi Arabia
Sudan
Syria
Turkmenistan

1. Countries are ranked according to political rights and civil liberties on a scale from 1 (most free) to 7 (least free). Source: *Freedom in the World, 2005*, published by Freedom House. www.freedomhouse.org/research/survey2005.htm.

Global Trends in Freedom

Year under review	Free countries	Partly free countries	Not free countries	Year under review	Free countries	Partly free countries	Not free countries
1974	41 (27%)	48 (32%)	63 (41%)	1994	76 (40%)	61 (32%)	54 (28%)
1984	53 (32%)	59 (35%)	55 (33%)	2004	89 (46%)	54 (28%)	49 (26%)

Source: *Freedom in the World*, an annual comparative assessment of the state of political rights and civil liberties around the world, published by Freedom House. www.freedomhouse.org/research/survey2005.htm.

The 2004 Transparency International Corruption Perceptions Index

According to the annual survey by the Berlin-based organization Transparency International, the world's least corrupt country is seen as being Finland and the countries perceived as most corrupt are Bangladesh and Haiti. The index defines corruption as the abuse of public office for private gain, and measures the degree to which corruption is perceived to exist among a country's public officials and politicians. It is a composite index, drawing on 18 surveys from 12 independent institutions, which gathered the opinions of businesspeople and country analysts. Because of the absence of reliable data, only 146 of the world's countries are included in the survey. The scores range from 10 (squeaky clean) to zero (highly corrupt). A score of 5.0 is the number Transparency International considers the borderline figure distinguishing countries that do and do not have a serious corruption problem. Countries that have improved their rating since the 2003 index were Austria, Botswana, Czech Republic, El Salvador, France, the Gambia, Germany, Jordan, Switzerland, Tanzania, Thailand, Uganda, United Arab Emirates, and Uruguay. Countries that have a worse rating since 2003 include Bahrain, Belize, Cyprus, Dominican Republic, Jamaica, Kuwait, Luxembourg, Mauritius, Oman, Poland, Saudi Arabia, Senegal, and Trinidad and Tobago.

Country rank	Country	2004 CPI Score	Country rank	Country	2004 CPI Score	Country rank	Country	2004 CPI Score
1.	Finland	9.7		El Salvador	4.2		Serbia and Montenegro	2.7
2.	New Zealand	9.6		Trinidad and Tobago	4.2	102.	Eritrea	2.6
3.	Denmark	9.5	54.	Bulgaria	4.1		Papua New Guinea	2.6
	Iceland	9.5		Mauritius	4.1		Philippines	2.6
5.	Singapore	9.3		Namibia	4.1		Uganda	2.6
6.	Sweden	9.2	57.	Latvia	4.0		Vietnam	2.6
7.	Switzerland	9.1		Slovakia	4.0		Zambia	2.6
8.	Norway	8.9	59.	Brazil	3.9	108.	Albania	2.5
9.	Australia	8.8	60.	Belize	3.8		Argentina	2.5
10.	Netherlands	8.7		Colombia	3.8		Libya	2.5
11.	United Kingdom	8.6	62.	Cuba	3.7		Palestinian Authority	2.5
12.	Canada	8.5		Panama	3.7	112.	Ecuador	2.4
13.	Austria	8.4	64.	Ghana	3.6		Yemen	2.4
	Luxembourg	8.4		Mexico	3.6	114.	Congo, Rep. of	2.3
15.	Germany	8.2		Thailand	3.6		Ethiopia	2.3
16.	Hong Kong	8.0	67.	Croatia	3.5		Honduras	2.3
17.	Belgium	7.5		Peru	3.5		Moldova	2.3
	Ireland	7.5		Poland	3.5		Sierra Leone	2.3
	United States	7.5		Sri Lanka	3.5		Uzbekistan	2.3
20.	Chile	7.4	71.	China	3.4		Venezuela	2.3
21.	Barbados	7.3		Saudi Arabia	3.4		Zimbabwe	2.3
22.	France	7.1		Syria	3.4	122.	Bolivia	2.2
	Spain	7.1	74.	Belarus	3.3		Guatemala	2.2
24.	Japan	6.9		Gabon	3.3		Kazakhstan	2.2
25.	Malta	6.8		Jamaica	3.3		Kyrgyzstan	2.2
26.	Israel	6.4	77.	Benin	3.2		Niger	2.2
27.	Portugal	6.3		Egypt	3.2		Sudan	2.2
28.	Uruguay	6.2		Mali	3.2		Ukraine	2.2
29.	Oman	6.1		Morocco	3.2	129.	Cameroon	2.1
	United Arab Emirates	6.1		Turkey	3.2		Iraq	2.1
31.	Botswana	6.0	82.	Armenia	3.1		Kenya	2.1
	Estonia	6.0		Bosnia and Herzegovina	3.1		Pakistan	2.1
	Slovenia	6.0		Madagascar	3.1	133.	Angola	2.0
34.	Bahrain	5.8	85.	Mongolia	3.0		Congo, Dem. Rep. of	2.0
35.	Taiwan	5.6		Senegal	3.0		Côte d'Ivoire	2.0
36.	Cyprus	5.4	87.	Dominican Republic	2.9		Georgia	2.0
37.	Jordan	5.3		Iran	2.9		Indonesia	2.0
38.	Qatar	5.2		Romania	2.9		Tajikistan	2.0
39.	Malaysia	5.0	90.	The Gambia	2.8		Turkmenistan	2.0
	Tunisia	5.0		India	2.8	140.	Azerbaijan	1.9
41.	Costa Rica	4.9		Malawi	2.8		Paraguay	1.9
42.	Hungary	4.8		Mozambique	2.8	142.	Chad	1.7
	Italy	4.8		Nepal	2.8		Myanmar (Burma)	1.7
44.	Kuwait	4.6		Russia	2.8	144.	Nigeria	1.6
	Lithuania	4.6		Tanzania	2.8	145.	Bangladesh	1.5
	South Africa	4.6	97.	Algeria	2.7		Haiti	1.5
47.	South Korea	4.5		Lebanon	2.7			
48.	Seychelles	4.4		Macedonia	2.7			
49.	Greece	4.3		Nicaragua	2.7			
	Suriname	4.3						
51.	Czech Republic	4.2						

Source: Transparency International, 2004. Web: www.transparency.org.

World's Ten Most Corrupt Leaders[1]

Name	Position	Funds embezzled[2]
1. Mohamed Suharto	President of Indonesia (1967–1998)	$15–35 billion
2. Ferdinand Marcos	President of the Philippines (1972–1986)	5–10 billion
3. Mobutu Sese Seko	President of Zaire (1965–1997)	5 billion
4. Sani Abacha	President of Nigeria (1993–1998)	2–5 billion
5. Slobodan Milosevic	President of Serbia/Yugoslavia (1989–2000)	1 billion
6. Jean-Claude Duvalier	President of Haiti (1971–1986)	300–800 million
7. Alberto Fujimori	President of Peru (1990–2000)	600 million
8. Pavlo Lazarenko	Prime Minister of Ukraine (1996–1997)	114–200 million
9. Arnoldo Alemán	President of Nicaragua (1997–2002)	100 million
10. Joseph Estrada	President of the Philippines (1998–2001)	78–80 million

1. Defined as former political leaders who have been accused of embezzling the most funds from their countries over the past two decades. 2. All sums are estimates of alleged embezzlement and appear in U.S. dollars. *Source:* Transparency International Global Corruption Report 2004.

The Bribe Payers' Index

The Bribe Payers' Index ranks the 21 leading exporting countries according to the degree to which their companies are perceived to be paying bribes abroad to senior public officials. According to the latest survey, published by Transparency International in 2002, the countries most likely to offer bribes are Russia, China, Taiwan, and South Korea. All of these countries have laws criminalizing corrupt payments to foreign officials.

Most and Least Livable Countries: UN Human Development Index, 2004

The Human Development Index (HDI), published annually by the UN, ranks nations according to their citizens' quality of life rather than strictly by a nation's traditional economic figures. The criteria for calculating rankings include life expectancy, educational attainment, and adjusted real income.

"Most Livable" Countries, 2004		"Least Livable" Countries, 2004	
1. Norway	11. Switzerland	1. Sierra Leone	11. Chad
2. Sweden	12. United Kingdom	2. Niger	12. Angola
3. Australia	13. Finland	3. Burkina Faso	13. Malawi
4. Canada	14. Austria	4. Mali	14. Zambia
5. Netherlands	15. Luxembourg	5. Burundi	15. Côte d'Ivoire
6. Belgium	16. France	6. Guinea-Bissau	16. Tanzania
7. Iceland	17. Denmark	7. Mozambique	17. Benin
8. United States	18. New Zealand	8. Ethiopia	18. Guinea
9. Japan	19. Germany	9. Central African Republic	19. Rwanda
10. Ireland	20. Spain	10. Congo, Dem. Rep. of the	20. East Timor

Source: Human Development Report, 2004, United Nations. Web: hdr.undp.org.

Kingdoms and Monarchs of the World

Country	Monarch	Type of monarchy	Country	Monarch	Type of monarchy
Bahrain	King Hamad bin Isa al-Khalifa	Constitutional	Monaco	Prince Albert II	Constitutional
			Morocco	King Muhammad VI	Constitutional
Belgium	King Albert II	Constitutional	Nepal	King Gyandendra	Absolute[2]
Bhutan	King Jigme Singye Wangchuck	Transitional[1]	Netherlands	Queen Beatrix	Constitutional
			Norway	King Harald V	Constitutional
Brunei	Sultan Haji Hassanal Bolkiah	Constitutional	Oman	Sultan Qabus ibn Sa'id	Absolute
			Qatar	Emir Sheik Hamad ibn Khalifa al-Thani	Constitutional
Cambodia	King Norodom Sihamoni	Constitutional			
Denmark	Queen Margrethe II	Constitutional	Samoa	Malietoa Tanumafili II	Constitutional
Japan	Emperor Akihito	Constitutional	Saudi Arabia	King Abdullah	Absolute
Jordan	King Abdullah II	Constitutional	Spain	King Juan Carlos I	Parliamentary
Kuwait	Sheik Jaber al-Ahmad al-Sabah	Constitutional	Swaziland	King Mswati III	Absolute
			Sweden	King Carl XVI Gustaf	Constitutional
Lesotho	King Letsie III	Constitutional	Thailand	King Bhumibol Adulyadej	Constitutional
Liechtenstein	Prince Hans Adam II	Constitutional	Tonga	King Taufa'ahau Tupou IV	Constitutional
Luxembourg	Grand Duke Henri	Constitutional	United Kingdom	Queen Elizabeth II[3]	Constitutional[4]
Malaysia	King Syed Sirajuddin	Constitutional			

1. Bhutan is in the process of becoming a constitutional monarchy. 2. Constitutional monarchy suspended in 2002, when King Gyanendra assumed power. 3. Queen Elizabeth II is also the Sovereign of 15 countries in the Commonwealth of Nations: Antigua and Barbuda, Australia, the Bahamas, Barbados, Belize, Canada, Grenada, Jamaica, New Zealand, Papua New Guinea, St. Kitts and Nevis, St. Lucia, St. Vincent and the Grenadines, the Solomon Islands, and Tuvalu. 4. Also parliamentary democracy.

World's 50 Poorest Countries, 2004
UN list of least developed countries[1]

Afghanistan, Angola, Bangladesh, Benin, Bhutan, Burkina Faso, Burundi, Cambodia, Cape Verde, Central African Republic, Chad, Comoros, Democratic Republic of Congo, Djibouti, Equatorial Guinea, Eritrea, Ethiopia, Gambia, Guinea, Guinea-Bissau, Haiti, Kiribati, Laos, Lesotho, Liberia, Madagascar, Malawi, Maldives, Mali, Mauritania, Mozambique, Myanmar, Nepal, Niger, Rwanda, Samoa, São Tomé and Príncipe, Senegal, Sierra Leone, Solomon Islands, Somalia, Sudan, East Timor, Togo, Tuvalu, Uganda, Tanzania, Vanuatu, Yemen, Zambia.

1. The UN classifies countries as "least developed" based on three criteria: (1) annual gross domestic product (GDP) below $900 per capita; (2) quality of life, based on life expectancy at birth, per capita calorie intake, primary and secondary school enrollment rates, and adult literacy; and (3) economic vulnerability, based on instability of agricultural productions and exports, inadequate diversification, and economic smallness. Half or more of the population in the 50 least developed countries listed above are estimated to live at or below the absolute poverty line of U.S. $1 dollar per day.

Gap Between Rich and Poor: World Income Inequality
Percentage share of income (poorest and richest 20% of population)

To understand how many inhabitants of a country are poor, it is not enough to know a country's per capita income. The number of poor people in a country and the average quality of life depend on how equally or unequally income is distributed across the population. In Brazil and Hungary, for example, per capita income levels are quite comparable, but the incidence of poverty in Brazil is much higher. In Hungary the richest 20% of the population receives about four times more income than the poorest 20%, whereas in Brazil the richest 20% receives 30 times more than the poorest 20%.

	Countries with greatest inequality	Gini index	Lowest 20%	Highest 20%		Countries with greatest equality	Gini Index	Lowest 20%	Highest 20%
1.	Sierra Leone	62.9	1.1%	63.4%	1.	Slovak Republic	19.5	11.9%	31.4%
2.	Central African Republic	61.3	2.0	65.0	2.	Belarus	21.7	11.4	33.3
3.	Swaziland	60.9	2.7	64.4	3.	Hungary	24.4	10.0	34.4
4.	Brazil	60.7	2.2	64.1	4.	Denmark	24.7	9.6	34.5
5.	Nicaragua	60.3	2.3	63.6	5.	Japan	24.9	10.6	35.7
6.	South Africa	59.3	2.9	64.8	6.	Sweden	25.0	9.6	34.5
7.	Paraguay	57.7	1.9	60.7	7.	Czech Republic	25.4	10.3	35.9
8.	Colombia	57.1	3.0	60.9	8.	Finland	25.6	10.0	35.8
9.	Chile	56.7	3.3	61.0	9.	Norway	25.8	9.7	35.8
10.	Honduras	56.3	2.2	59.4	10.	Bulgaria	26.4	10.1	36.8
11.	Guinea-Bissau	56.2	2.1	58.9	11.	Luxembourg	26.9	9.4	36.5
12.	Lesotho	56.0	2.8	60.1	12.	Italy	27.3	8.7	36.3
13.	Guatemala	55.8	3.8	60.6	13.	Slovenia	28.4	9.1	37.7
14.	Burkina Faso	55.1	4.6	60.4	14.	Belgium	28.7	8.3	37.3
15.	Mexico	53.1	3.5	57.4	15.	Egypt	28.9	9.8	39.0
16.	Zambia	52.6	3.3	56.6	15.	Rwanda	28.9	9.7	39.1
17.	Hong Kong, China	52.2	4.4	57.1	17.	Croatia	29.0	8.8	38.0
17.	El Salvador	52.2	3.3	56.4	17.	Ukraine	29.0	8.8	37.8
19.	Papua New Guinea	50.9	4.5	56.5	19.	Germany	30.0	8.2	38.5
20.	Nigeria	50.6	4.4	55.7	20.	Austria	31.0	6.9	38.0
21.	Mali	50.5	4.6	56.2	21.	Romania	31.1	8.0	39.5
21.	Niger	50.5	2.6	53.3	22.	Pakistan	31.2	9.5	41.1
23.	Gambia, The	50.2	4.0	55.3	23.	Canada	31.5	7.5	39.3
24.	Zimbabwe	50.1	4.7	55.7	24.	Korea, South	31.6	7.5	39.3
25.	Venezuela	49.5	3.0	53.2	25.	Poland	31.6	7.8	39.7

NOTE: Countries are ranked according to the Gini index (or coefficient), a measure of income inequality within a country. A country's Gini rating is between 0 and 100, with 0 indicating perfect equality and 100 indicating absolute inequality. (The U.S. rates 40.8 on the Gini index—the poorest 20% of its population receives 5.2% of income; the richest 20% receives 46.4%.)
Source: World Development Index 2002, The World Bank.

Per Capita Foreign Aid Assistance by World's Wealthiest Countries, 2002

Country	Per capita government aid	Per capita private giving	Country	Per capita government aid	Per capita private giving
Australia	14¢	3¢	Japan	20¢	0.4¢
Austria	18	2	Netherlands	57	4
Belgium	28	2	New Zealand	8	1
Canada	17	2	Norway	1.02	24
Denmark	64	1	Portugal	9	0.1
Finland	24	1	Spain	11	1
France	25	1	Sweden	61	1
Greece	7	0.1	Switzerland	35	7
Germany	18	3	United Kingdom	23	2
Ireland	28	6	United States	13	5
Italy	11	0.2			

Source: © Center for Global Development and Carnegie Endowment for International Peace. From "Ranking the Rich," *Foreign Policy,* May/June 2004. Reprinted with permission.

Income Tax by Country, 2003

Country	Single person without children	One-earner family with two children	Country	Single person without children	One-earner family with two children
Australia	24.0%	15.6%	South Korea	6.8%	6.2%
Austria	28.9	8.9	Luxembourg	22.5	−2.6
Belgium	40.6	20.3	Mexico	4.4	4.4
Canada	24.6	14.5	Netherlands	34.0	23.3
Czech Republic	24.1	6.3	New Zealand	20.6	20.4
Denmark	42.4	29.7	Norway	28.8	18.3
Finland	31.2	22.8	Poland	31.2	29.2
France	26.8	15.1	Portugal	16.6	5.6
Germany	41.9	19.5	Slovak Republic	19.1	6.6
Greece	15.9	15.9	Spain	18.5	9.7
Hungary	25.5	4.8	Sweden	30.8	21.6
Iceland	25.3	3.6	Switzerland	21.2	8.5
Ireland	16.4	−2.6	Turkey	29.9	29.9
Italy	27.2	14.2	United Kingdom	24.3	10.3
Japan	17.4	13.2	United States	24.1	9.1

Source: Organization for Economic Cooperation and Development, Paris, France, *Taxing Wages, 2001–2002* (copyright). From *Statistical Abstract of the United States: 2004–2005*.

Economic Statistics by Country, 2004

Country	GDP/PPP	GDP/PPP per capita	Real growth rate (%)	Inflation (%)
Afghanistan	$21.5 billion[1]	$ 800[1]	7.5%	10.3[1]%
Albania	17.46 billion	4,900	5.6	3.2
Algeria	212.3 billion	6,600	6.1	3.1
Andorra	1.9 billion[1]	26,800[1]	2.0[1]	4.3[2]
Angola	23.17 billion	2,100	11.7	43.8
Antigua and Barbuda	750 million[3]	11,000[3]	3.0[3]	0.4[2]
Argentina	483.5 billion	12,400	8.3	6.1
Armenia	13.65 billion	4,600	9.0	3.5
Australia	611.7 billion	30,700	3.5	2.3
Austria	255.9 billion	31,300	1.9	1.8
Azerbaijan	30.01 billion	3,800	9.8	4.6
Bahamas, The	5.295 billion	17,700	3.0	1.2
Bahrain	13.01 billion	19,200	5.6	2.1
Bangladesh	275.7 billion	2,000	4.9	6.0
Barbados	4.569 billion	16,400	2.3	−0.5[1]
Belarus	70.5 billion	6,800	6.4	17.4
Belgium	316.2 billion	30,600	2.6	1.9
Belize	1.778 billion	6,500	3.5	2.9
Benin	8.338 billion	1,200	5.0	2.8
Bhutan	2.9 billion[1]	1,400[1]	5.3[1]	3.0[3]
Bolivia	22.33 billion	2,600	3.7	4.9
Bosnia and Herzegovina	26.21 billion	6,500	5.0	1.1
Botswana	15.05 billion	9,200	3.5	7.0
Brazil	1.492 trillion	8,100	5.1	7.6
Brunei	6.842 billion[1]	23,600[1]	3.2[1]	0.3[1]
Bulgaria	61.63 billion	8,200	5.3	6.1
Burkina Faso	15.74 billion	1,200	4.8	2.4
Burundi	4.001 billion	600	3.0	8.5
Cambodia	26.99 billion	2,000	5.4	3.1
Cameroon	30.17 billion	1,900	4.9	1.0
Canada	1.023 trillion	31,500	2.4	1.9
Cape Verde	600 million[3]	1,400[3]	5.0	1.5
Central African Republic	4.248 billion	1,100	0.5	3.6[4]
Chad	15.66 billion	1,600	38.0	8.0
Chile	169.1 billion	10,700	5.8	2.4
China	7.262 trillion	5,600	9.1	4.1
Colombia	281.1 billion	6,600	3.6	5.9
Comoros	441 million[3]	700[3]	2.0[3]	3.5[4]
Congo, Dem. Rep. of	42.74 billion	700	7.5	14.0[1]
Congo, Rep. of	2.324 billion	800	3.7	1.8
Costa Rica	$37.97 billion	$ 9,600	3.9%	11.5%
Côte d'Ivoire	24.78 billion	1,500	−1.0	1.4
Croatia	50.33 billion	11,200	3.7	2.5
Cuba	33.92 billion	3,000	3.0	3.1
Cyprus*	15.71 billion	20,300	3.2	2.4[1]
	4.54 billion	7,135	2.6	12.6[1]
Czech Republic	172.2 billion	16,800	3.7	3.2
Denmark	174.4 billion	32,200	2.1	1.4
Djibouti	619 million[3]	1,300[3]	3.5[3]	2.0[3]
Dominica	384 million[1]	5,500[1]	−1.0[1]	1.0[4]
Dominican Republic	55.68 billion	6,300	1.7	55.0
East Timor	370 million	400	1.0	4.0[1]
Ecuador	49.51 billion	3,700	5.8	2.0
Egypt	316.3 billion	4,200	4.5	9.5
El Salvador	32.35 billion	4,900	1.8	5.4
Equatorial Guinea	1.27 billion[3]	2,700[3]	20.0[3]	8.5
Eritrea	4.154 billion	900	2.5	10.0
Estonia	19.23 billion	14,300	6.0	3.0
Ethiopia	54.89 billion	800	11.6	2.4
Fiji	5.173 billion	5,900	3.6	1.6[3]
Finland	151.2 billion	29,000	3.0	0.7
France	1.737 trillion	28,700	2.1	2.3
Gabon	7.966 billion	5,900	1.9	1.5
Gambia, The	2.799 billion	1,800	6.0	7.0
Georgia	14.45 billion	3,100	9.5	5.5
Germany	2.362 trillion	28,700	1.7	1.6
Ghana	48.27 billion	2,300	5.4	13.0
Greece	226.4 billion	21,300	3.7	2.9
Grenada	440 million[3]	5,000[3]	2.5[3]	2.8[4]
Guatemala	59.47 billion	4,200	2.6	7.2
Guinea	19.5 billion	2,100	1.0	18.0
Guinea-Bissau	1.008 billion	700	2.6	4.0[3]
Guyana	2.899 billion	3,800	1.9	4.5
Haiti	12.05 billion	1,500	−3.5	22.0
Honduras	18.79 billion	2,800	4.2	7.0
Hungary	149.3 billion	14,900	3.9	7.0
Iceland	9.373 billion	31,900	1.8	4.0
India	3.319 trillion	3,100	6.2	4.2
Indonesia	827.4 billion	3,500	4.9	6.1
Iran	516.7 billion	7,700	6.3	15.5
Iraq	89.8 billion	3,500	52.3	25.4

Country	GDP/PPP	GDP/PPP per capita	Real growth rate (%)	Inflation (%)
Ireland	$126.4 billion	$31,900	5.1 %	2.2 %
Israel	129 billion	20,800	3.9	0.0
Italy	1.609 trillion	27,700	1.3	2.3
Jamaica	11.13 billion	4,100	1.9	12.4
Japan	3.745 trillion	29,400	2.9	-0.1
Jordan	25.5 billion	4,500	5.1	3.2
Kazakhstan	118.4 billion	7,800	9.1	6.9
Kenya	34.68 billion	1,100	2.2	9.0
Kiribati	79 million[4]	800[4]	1.5[4]	2.5[4]
Korea, North	30 billion	1,400	1.0	n.a.[1]
Korea, South	925.1 billion	19,200	4.6	3.6
Kuwait	48 billion	21,300	6.8	2.3
Kyrgyzstan	8.495 billion	1,700	6.0	3.2
Laos	11.28 billion	1,900	6.0	12.3
Latvia	26.53 billion	11,500	7.6	6.0
Lebanon	18.83 billion	5,000	4.0	2.0
Lesotho	5.892 billion	3,200	3.3	5.3
Liberia	2.903 billion	900	21.8	15.0[1]
Libya	37.48 billion	6,700	4.9	2.9
Liechtenstein	825 million[5]	25,000[5]	11.0[5]	1.0[4]
Lithuania	45.23 billion	12,500	6.6	1.1
Luxembourg	27.27 billion	58,900	2.3	2.4
Macedonia	14.4 billion	7,100	1.3	0.4
Madagascar	14.56 billion	800	5.5	7.5
Malawi	7.41 billion	600	4.0	12.0
Malaysia	229.3 billion	9,700	7.1	1.3
Maldives	1.25 billion[3]	3,900[3]	2.3[3]	1.0[3]
Mali	11 billion	900	4.0	4.5[3]
Malta	7.223 billion	18,200	1.0	2.9
Marshall Islands	115 million[4]	1,600[4]	1.0[4]	2.0[4]
Mauritania	5.534 billion	1,800	3.0	7.0[1]
Mauritius	15.68 billion	12,800	4.7	4.5
Mexico	1.006 trillion	9,600	4.1	5.4
Micronesia, Federated States of	277 million[3]	2,000[3]	1.0[3]	1.0[3]
Moldova	8.581 billion	1,900	6.8	11.5
Monaco	870 million[2]	27,000[2]	0.9[2]	1.9[2]
Mongolia	5.332 billion	1,900	10.6	11.0
Morocco	134.6 billion	4,200	4.4	2.1
Mozambique	23.38 billion	1,200	8.2	12.8
Myanmar (Burma)	74.3 billion	1,700	-1.3	17.2
Namibia	14.76 billion	7,300	4.8	4.2
Nauru	60 million[4]	5,000[4]	n.a.	-3.6[6]
Nepal	39.53 billion	1,500	3.0	2.9[3]
Netherlands	481.1 billion	29,500	1.2	1.4
New Zealand	92.51 billion	23,200	4.8	2.4
Nicaragua	12.34 billion	2,300	4.0	9.3
Niger	9.716 billion	900	3.5	3.0[3]
Nigeria	125.7 billion	1,000	6.2	16.5
Norway	183 billion	40,000	3.3	1.0
Oman	38.09 billion	13,100	1.2	0.2
Pakistan	347.3 billion	2,200	6.1	4.8
Palau	174 million[4]	9,000[4]	1.0[4]	3.4[2]
Panama	20.57 billion	6,900	6.0	2.0
Papua New Guinea	11.99 billion	2,200	0.9	4.2
Paraguay	29.93 billion	4,800	2.8	5.1
Peru	155.3 billion	5,600	4.5	3.8
Philippines	430.6 billion	5,000	5.9	5.5
Poland	$463 billion	$12,000	5.6%	3.4 %
Portugal	188.7 billion	17,900	1.1	2.1
Qatar	19.49 billion	23,200	8.7	3.0
Romania	171.5 billion	7,700	8.1	9.6
Russia	1.408 trillion	9,800	6.7	11.5
Rwanda	10.43 billion	1,300	0.9	7.0
St. Kitts and Nevis	339 million[3]	8,800[3]	-1.9[3]	1.7[4]
St. Lucia	866 million[3]	5,400[3]	3.3[3]	3.0[4]
St. Vincent and the Grenadines	342 million[3]	2,900[3]	0.7[3]	-0.4[4]
Samoa	1 billion[3]	5,600[3]	5.0[3]	4.0[4]
San Marino	940 million[4]	34,600[4]	7.5[4]	3.3[4]
São Tomé and Príncipe	214 million[1]	1,200[1]	6.0	14.0
Saudi Arabia	310.2 billion	12,000	5.0	0.8
Senegal	18.36 billion	1,700	3.2	0.8
Serbia and Montenegro	26.27 billion	2,400	6.5	8.8
Seychelles	626 million[3]	7,800[3]	1.5	5.0
Sierra Leone	3.335 billion	600	6.0	1.0[3]
Singapore	120.9 billion	27,800	8.1	1.7
Slovakia	78.89 billion	14,500	5.3	7.5
Slovenia	39.41 billion	19,600	3.9	3.3
Solomon Islands	800 million[3]	1,700[3]	5.8[1]	10.0[1]
Somalia	4.597 billion	600	2.8	n.a.
South Africa	491.4 billion	11,100	3.5	4.5
Spain	937.6 billion	23,300	2.6	3.2
Sri Lanka	80.58 billion	4,000	5.2	5.8
Sudan	76.19 billion	1,900	6.4	9.0
Suriname	1.885 billion	4,300	4.2	23.0[1]
Swaziland	6.018 billion	5,100	2.5	5.4
Sweden	255.4 billion	28,400	3.6	0.7
Switzerland	251.9 billion	33,800	1.8	0.9
Syria	60.44 billion	3,400	2.3	2.1
Taiwan	576.2 billion	25,300	6.0	1.7
Tajikistan	7.95 billion	1,100	10.5	8.0
Tanzania	23.71 billion	700	5.8	5.4
Thailand	524.8 billion	8,100	6.1	2.8
Togo	8.684 billion	1,600	3.0	1.0
Tonga	244 million[3]	2,300[3]	1.5[3]	10.3[3]
Trinidad and Tobago	11.48 billion	10,500	5.7	3.3
Tunisia	70.88 billion	7,100	5.1	4.1
Turkey	508.7 billion	7,400	8.2	9.3
Turkmenistan	27.6 billion	5,700	7.5	9.0
Tuvalu	12.2 million[2]	1,100[2]	3.0[2]	5.0[2]
Uganda	39.39 billion	1,500	5.0	3.5
Ukraine	299.1 billion	6,300	12.0	12.0
UAE	63.67 billion	25,200	5.7	3.2
UK	1.782 trillion	29,600	3.2	1.4
U.S.	11.75 trillion	40,100	4.4	2.5
Uruguay	49.27 billion	14,500	10.2	7.6
Uzbekistan	47.59 billion	1,800	4.4	3.0
Vanuatu	580 million[1]	2,900[1]	1.1[1]	3.1[1]
Venezuela	145.2 billion	5,800	16.8	22.4
Vietnam	227.2 billion	2,700	7.7	9.5
Yemen	16.25 billion	800	1.9	12.2
Zambia	9.409 billion	900	4.6	18.3
Zimbabwe	24.37 billion	1,900	-8.2	133.0

NOTES: Definitions: Gross domestic product (GDP): The value of all goods and services produced domestically. Purchasing power parity (PPP): The PPP method involves the use of standardized international dollar price weights, which are applied to the GDP produced in a given economy. The data derived from the 1998 method provide a better comparison of economic well-being between countries than conversions at official currency exchange rates. n.a. = not available. *First line of figures for Greek Cyprus, second for Turkish Cyprus. 1. 2003 est. 2. 2000 est. 3. 2002 est. 4. 2001 est. 5. 1999 est. 6. 1993 est. Source: The World Factbook, 2005.

Largest Military Expenditures, 2004

(Military expenditure: in MER[1] dollar terms)

Rank	Country	Spending level[2] ($ billions)	Per capita ($)	World share (%)	Rank	Country	Spending level[2] ($ billions)	Per capita ($)	World share (%)
1.	United States	$455.3	$1,533	47%	10.	South Korea	$ 15.5	$ 323	2%
2.	United Kingdom	47.4	798	5	11.	India	15.1	14	2
3.	France	46.2	764	5	12.	Israel	10.7	1,627	1
4.	Japan	42.4	332	4	13.	Canada	10.6	336	1
5.	China[3]	35.4	27	4	14.	Turkey	10.1	140	1
6.	Germany	33.9	411	3	15.	Australia	10.1	507	1
7.	Italy	27.8	484	3		Subtotal,			
8.	Russia[3]	19.4	136	2		top 15	$799.2		82%
9.	Saudi Arabia	19.3	775	2		World	$975.0	153	100%

1. MER = market exchange rate. 2. Spending figures are in U.S. dollars, at constant (2003) prices and exchange rates. 3. Estimated figure. *Source: SIPRI Yearbook 2005,* Stockholm International Peace Research Institute.

Significant Ongoing Armed Conflicts, 2005

Main warring parties	Year began[1]	Main warring parties	Year began[1]
Middle East		**Africa**	
U.S. and UK vs. Iraq	2003	Algeria vs. Armed Islamic Group (GIA)	1991
Israel vs. Palestinian Authority/Hamas/Hezbollah/ Palestinian separatists	1948	Côte d'Ivoire vs. rebels	2002
Asia		Democratic Republic of Congo and allies vs. Rwanda, Uganda, and indigenous rebels	1997
Afghanistan: U.S., UK, and Coalition Forces vs. al-Qaeda and Taliban	2001	Somalia vs. rival clans	1991
		Sudan vs. Darfur rebel groups	2003
India vs. Kashmiri separatist groups/Pakistan	1948	Uganda vs. Lord's Resistance Army (LRA)	1986
India vs. Assam insurgents (various)	1979	**Europe**	
Indonesia vs. Christians and Muslims in Molucca Islands	1977	Russia vs. Chechen separatists	1994
		Latin America	
Indonesia vs. Papua (Irian Jaya) separatists	1969	Colombia vs. National Liberation Army (ELN)	1978
Nepal vs. Maoist rebels	1995	Colombia vs. Revolutionary Armed Forces of Colombia (FARC)	1978
Philippines vs. Mindanaoan separatists (MILF/ASG)	1971	Colombia vs. Autodefensas Unidas de Colombia (AUC)	1990

NOTE: As of Aug. 2004. 1. Where multiple parties and long-standing but sporadic conflict are concerned, date of first combat deaths is given. *Sources:* Project Ploughshares, www.ploughshares.ca, and news sources.

Recently Suspended Armed Conflicts

Main warring parties	Years of conflict	Main warring parties	Years of conflict
Indonesia vs. Aceh separatists	1976–2005	Chad vs. Muslim separatists (MDJT)	1998–2002
Sudan vs. Sudanese People's Liberation Army[1]	1983–2004	Burundi: Tuti vs. Hutu[1]	1988–2001
		Taliban vs. Northern Alliance	1995–2001
Solomon Islands vs. Malaitan Eagle Force and Isatabu Freedom Movement	1998–2003	Indonesia vs. East Timor	1975–2000
Liberia vs. LURD rebels	2000–2003	Tajikistan vs. United Tajik Opposition (UTO)	1992–2000
Angola vs. UNITA	1975–2002	Ethiopia vs. Eritrea	1998–2000
Sri Lanka vs. Tamil Eelan[1]	1978–2002	Fiji vs. insurgents	2000
Sierra Leone vs. RUF	1991–2002		

1. Cease-fire remains tenuous. *Sources:* Project Ploughshares, www.ploughshares.ca, and news sources.

Countries with Nuclear Weapons Capability

Acknowledged: Britain, China, France, India, Pakistan, Russia, United States

Unacknowledged: Israel

Seeking: North Korea,[1] Iran[2]

Abandoned: South Africa—Constructed but then voluntarily dismantled six uranium bombs. Belarus, Kazakhstan, Ukraine—When Soviet Union broke up, these former states possessed nuclear warheads that they have since given up.

1. In Dec. 2002, North Korea revealed that it had violated its 1994 agreement to freeze its nuclear weapons program and has been developing a nuclear bomb. On April 24, 2003, North Korea announced it possessed a nuclear bomb but this claim has not been verified. 2. In Aug. 2005, U.S. intelligence estimated that Iran would possess nuclear weapons in the next decade. *Source:* U.S. State Department and *TIME* magazine.

See also UN peacekeeping missions, p. 908

Principal Sources of Refugees, 2004

These countries have generated the greatest number of refugees and asylum seekers. It does not include persons granted permanent status in other countries.

Country	Number	Country	Number	Country	Number
Former Palestine	2,985,500	Somalia	324,900	Nepal	101,400
Afghanistan	2,088,200	Vietnam	310,300	Sri Lanka	88,200
Sudan	703,500	Colombia	263,600	Croatia	70,400
Myanmar	691,800	Angola	223,300	Philippines	66,200
Burundi	482,200	Eritrea	204,200	Rwanda	59,300
Congo (Dem. Rep. of)	469,100	China	158,100	Tajikistan	56,200
Iraq	366,100	Bhutan	120,500	Chad	54,200
Liberia	328,300	North Korea	101,900	Ethiopia	52,100

Source: World Refugee Survey, 2005, U.S. Committee on Refugees.

Internally Displaced Persons, 2004

Table includes countries in which persecution, armed conflict, or widespread violence has internally displaced the largest numbers of civilians. Although internally displaced persons share many characteristics with refugees, they are not protected by international refugee law because they remain inside their own countries.

Country	Number	Country	Number	Country	Number
Sudan	5,300,000–6,700,000	Indonesia	500,000	Lebanon	300,000
Colombia	2,900,000	Liberia	464,000	Georgia	260,000
Congo (Dem. Rep. of)	2,330,000	Algeria	400,000–600,000	Serbia and Montenegro	225,000–251,000
Uganda	1,330,000	Somalia	400,000	Central African Republic	200,000
Iraq	1,000,000	Kenya	360,000		
Myanmar	550,000–800,000	Sri Lanka	353,000	Nigeria	200,000–250,000
Azerbaijan	528,000	Turkey	350,000–1,000,000	Jordan	168,000
Côte d'Ivoire	500,000–800,000	Russia	339,000		
India	500,000	Bosnia and Herzegovina	309,200		

Source: World Refugee Survey, 2005, U.S. Committee on Refugees.

The Failed States Index

FOREIGN POLICY and the Fund for Peace have ranked 60 troubled countries that are in danger of collapse. The countries are ranked according to twelve social, economic, political, and military indicators, including economic decline and inequality, demographic pressures, war, and corruption. Below are the top 20 most vulnerable countries.

1. Côte D'Ivoire
2. Dem. Rep. of the Congo
3. Sudan
4. Iraq
5. Somalia
6. Sierra Leone
7. Chad
8. Yemen
9. Liberia
10. Haiti
11. Afghanistan
12. Rwanda
13. North Korea
14. Colombia
15. Zimbabwe
16. Guinea
17. Bangladesh
18. Burundi
19. Dominican Rep.
20. Central African Rep.

Source: FOREIGN POLICY www.foreignpolicy.com, 2005.

U.S.-Designated Foreign Terrorist Organizations[1]

Name and base of operations	Goals and targets	Est. strength	Year founded	Activities
Abu Nidal Organization (ANO) a.k.a. Fatah; Iraq	Targets U.S., UK, France, Israel, moderate Palestinians, the PLO, Arab countries	A few hundred	1974	Attacks in 20 countries, killing or injuring 900. Leader Abu Nidal died in 2002
Abu Sayyaf Group; Philippines, Malaysia	Aims to create Islamic state in Philippines; profit-driven terror	200–500	1991	Kidnappings, bombings, assassinations, and extortion
Al-Aqsa Martyrs Brigade; West Bank, Gaza Strip, Israel	Aims to drive out Israelis and to establish a Palestinian state	Unknown	2000	Shootings, suicide operations (first Palestinian female suicide bombing)
Ansar al-Islam (AI); Iraqi Kurds and Arabs	Aims to create an Islamic state in Iraq; allied with al-Qaeda	500–1,000	2001	Ambushes and attacks
Armed Islamic Group (GIA); Algeria	Aims to replace Algerian regime with an Islamic state	Less than 100	1992	Massacred thousands of civilians, targeted foreigners
Asbat al-Ansar; Lebanon	Aims to create Islamic state, opposes peace with Israel	300	1990s	Assassinations, bombings of Western targets, failed coup

Name and base of operations	Goals and targets	Est. strength	Year founded	Activities
Aum Shinrikyo (Aum); Japan, Russia	Claims U.S. will start WWIII with Japan, beginning Armageddon	1,950	1987	Chemical attacks on Tokyo subways, no recent activity
Basque Fatherland and Liberty (ETA); Spain, France	Targets Spanish and French government interests, tourists	Unknown	1959	Since 1960, more than 850 killed, hundreds injured
Communist Party of the Philippines/New People's Army (CPP/NPA); Philippines	Targets Philippine security forces, politicians, judges, government informers, NPA rebels	Less than 9,000	1969	Assassinations, murders, attacks on U.S. personnel and interests
Continuity Irish Republican Army (CIRA); Northern Ireland, Irish Republic	Targets British military, Northern Ireland security forces, Loyalist paramilitary groups	Less than 50	1990s	Bombings, assassinations, kidnappings, hijackings, extortion, robberies
Gama'a al-Islamiyya (Islamic Group); Egypt	Aims to replace Egypt's government with an Islamic state	Unknown	1973	1993 World Trade Center bombings, attacks on tourists
HAMAS (Islamic Resistance Movement); West Bank, Gaza Strip, Israel	Aims to replace Israel with Palestinian Islamic state using political and violent means	Unknown	1987	Large-scale suicide bombings and attacks against Israelis and Palestinian collaborators
Harakat ul-Mujahidin (HUM); Pakistan	Targets Indian troops, Kashmiri civilians, and Western interests	Several hundred	1985	Linked to al-Qaeda, hijacked Indian airliner in 1999
Hezbollah (Party of God); Lebanon, worldwide cells	Dedicated to eliminating Israel, is anti-U.S. and anti-Israel	A few hundred	1982	Suicide bombings, hijacked 1985 TWA Flight 847
Islamic Movement of Uzbekistan (IMU); South Asia, Tajikistan, Iran	Aims to remove Karimov, establish an Islamic state, and fight anti-Islamic opponents	Less than 500	1991	Car bombs, taking foreign hostages, most active in Kyrgyzstan and Tajikistan
Jaish-e-Mohammed (JEM) (Army of Mohammed); Pakistan	Aims to unite Kashmir with Pakistan, targets Indian government and political leaders	Several hundred	2000	Murder of U.S. journalist, Indian Parliament bombing, anti-Christian attacks
Jemaah Islamiya organization (JI); cells span Southeast Asia	Plotted against tourist spots, U.S., Israeli, British, and Australian diplomatic buildings	Unknown	1990s	Bombings in Indonesia and Philippines
Al-Jihad (AJ); Cairo, Egypt, Yemen, Afghanistan, Pakistan, Lebanon, UK	Aims to replace the Egyptian government with Islamic state, attack U.S., Israeli interests	Several hundred	1970s	Attacks on Egyptian government personnel, assassinated Anwar Sadat
Kahane Chai (Kach); Israel, West Bank	Organizes protests against the Israeli government	Unknown	1994	Threats made to Arabs, Palestinians, and Israeli officials
Kongra-Gel (KGK), a.k.a. Kurdistan Workers' Party (PKK) and KADEK; Turkey, Europe, Middle East	Targets Turkish security forces, officials, and villagers who oppose organization	4,000–5,000	1974	Attacked diplomatic and commercial facilities, bombed tourist sites
Lashkar-e- Tayyiba (LT) (Army of the Righteous); Pakistan	Targets Indian troops and civilians in Kashmir	Several thousand	1989	Attacks on border security forces and Indian Parliament
Lashkar i Jhangvi (LJ); Pakistan, Afghanistan	Anti-Shi'ite group aims to create a Muslim state in Pakistan	Less than 100	1996	Armed attacks, bombings, attempted assassinations
Liberation Tigers of Tamil Eelam (LTTE); Sri Lanka	Targets key personnel, senior political and military leaders	8,000–10,000	1976	Assassinations, suicide bombers: "The Black Tigers"
Libyan Islamic Fighting Group (LIFG); Libya, United Kingdom, other countries	Pledged to overthrow un-Islamic government of Libyan president Muammar al-Qaddafi	Several hundred	1990s	Suicide bombings, assassination attempt against Qaddafi, clashes with Libyan security forces
Mujahedin-e Khalq Organization (MEK); Iraq	Largest armed Iranian opposition to the present government, advocates a secular Iranian regime	Over 3,000	1960s	Assassinations, terrorist bombings, foreign military-aided assaults, large-scale overseas attacks
National Liberation Army (ELN); Colombia, Venezuela	Targets foreign employees from large corporations	3,000	1965	Kidnapping, hijacking, bombing, and extortion
Palestine Islamic Jihad (PIJ); Israel, West Bank, Gaza Strip	Targets Israeli military and civilians, opposes secularism	Unknown	1970s	Suicide bombings, attacks on Israeli interests
Palestine Liberation Front (PLF); Iraq	Known for aerial attacks against Israel	Unknown	1970s	Attacked Italian ship *Achille Lauro*, murdered a U.S. citizen

Name and base of operations	Goals and targets	Est. strength	Year founded	Activities
Popular Front for the Liberation of Palestine (PFLP); Syria, Lebanon, Israel, West Bank, Gaza Strip	Targets Israel's "illegal occupation" of Palestine and opposes negotiations with Israel	Unknown	1967	International terrorist acts in the 1970s, attacks against Israel and moderate Arab targets since 1978
Popular Front for the Liberation of Palestine–General Command (PFLP-GC); Syria	Attacks in Europe and the Middle East. Targets Israel, West Bank, and Gaza Strip	Several hundred	1968	Unusual attacks: hot air balloons, hang gliders, Lebanese guerrilla operations
Al-Qaeda; Afghanistan until 2001, Southeast Asia, Middle East, worldwide cells	Targets "non-Islamic" regimes and U.S. citizens	Several thousand	1980s	Bombings of embassies and USS Cole; September 11, 2001, U.S. attacks
Real IRA; Northern Ireland, UK, Irish Republic	Targets civilians, military, police, and Protestant communities	Less than 100	1998	Bombings, assassinations, robberies
Revolutionary Armed Forces of Colombia (FARC); Colombia	Targets Colombian political, military, and economic interests, also foreign citizens	9,000–12,000	1964	Bombings, mortar attacks, kidnappings, extortion, guerrilla warfare, and drug trafficking
Revolutionary Nuclei (formerly ELA); Athens, Greece	Targets U.S. and European interests and government buildings in Greece	Believed small	1995	Arson attacks, low-level bombings, usually striking in early-morning hours
Revolutionary Organization 17 November; Athens, Greece	Seeks removal of U.S. bases, Turkish military, and the severing of NATO and EU ties	Believed small	1975	Assassinations, bombings, improvised rocket attacks, supported by bank robberies
Revolutionary People's Liberation Army/Front (DHKP-C); Turkey	Anti-U.S., anti-NATO, and anti-Turkish establishment group	Unknown	1978	Attacks on U.S. interests, suicide bombings
Salafist Group for Call and Combat (GSPC); Algeria	Military and government targets, pledges to avoid civilians	Several hundred	1992	Attacks military, police, and government convoys
Shining Path (Sendero Luminoso, SL); Peru	Aims to build communist regime, targets political enemies	300	1960s	30,000 dead, assassinations, bombings, village raids
Tanzim Qa'idat al-Jihad fi Bilad al-Rafidayn (QJBR) a.k.a. Al-Zarqawi Network and Al-Qaeda in Iraq; Iraq	Aims to expel Coalition forces and establish Islamic state in Iraq, then move to Syria, Lebanon, Israel, and Jordan	Unknown	2003	Many bombings, killing hundreds; assassination of key Iraqi political figures; beheadings of Americans
United Self-Defense Forces of Colombia (AUC); Colombia	Targets "insurgents" from FARC and ELN	8,000–11,000	1997	Assassinations, guerrilla warfare, and drug trafficking

1. As of April 2005, the U.S. State Department has designated these groups as Foreign Terrorist Organizations (FTOs). *Source:* U.S. Department of State, Office of Counterterrorism, Center for Defense Information, Terrorism Project.

Telephones and Computers by Country, 2002
(rates per 100 persons)

Country	Telephone main lines	Cellular phone subscribers	Personal computers[1]	Country	Telephone main lines	Cellular phone subscribers	Personal computers[1]
Australia	53.86	63.98	56.51	Italy	48.07	93.87	23.07
Austria	48.88	78.62	36.93	Japan	55.83	63.65	38.22
Belgium	49.44	78.56	24.14	Korea, South	48.86	67.95	55.58
Brazil	22.32	20.06	7.48	Mexico	14.67	25.45	8.20
Canada	63.55	37.72	48.70	Netherlands	61.77	74.47	46.66
China	16.69	16.09	2.76	Norway	73.44	84.36	52.83
Colombia	17.94	10.62	4.93	Pakistan	2.50	0.85	n.a.
Czech Republic	36.23	84.88	17.74	Poland	n.a.	36.26	10.56
Ecuador	11.02	12.06	3.11	Russia	24.22	12.01	8.87
Egypt	11.49	6.68	1.66	Saudi Arabia	15.11	22.80	13.67
Finland	52.35	86.74	44.17	Singapore	46.29	79.56	62.20
France	56.89	64.70	34.71	South Africa	10.66	30.39	7.26
Germany	65.09	72.75	43.13	Spain	50.62	82.42	19.60
Guatemala	7.05	13.15	1.44	Switzerland	74.42	78.93	70.87
Hungary	36.12	67.60	10.84	Taiwan	58.17	106.15	39.46
India	3.98	1.22	0.72	Thailand	10.50	26.04	3.98
Indonesia	3.65	5.52	1.19	United			
Iraq	2.78	0.08	0.83	Kingdom	59.06	84.07	40.57
Israel	45.30	95.45	24.26	United States	64.58	48.81	65.89

— Represents or rounds to zero. n.a. = Not available. 1. In many countries mainframe computers are used extensively, and thousands of users can be connected to a single mainframe computer; thus the number of PCs understates the total use of computers. *Source:* International Telecommunications Union, Geneva, Switzerland, *World Telecommunication Indicators,* (copyright). From *Statistical Abstract of the United States: 2004–2005.*

Major sources: The World Factbook 2005; Center for International Research, U.S. Bureau of the Census; *The Columbia Encyclopedia; The World Book Encyclopedia; Encyclopædia Britannica;* U.S. State Dept.; and various newspapers
(Information as of Aug.–Sept. 2005; for updated country information, see www.infoplease.com/countries.html.)

Definitions: Gross domestic product (GDP): the value of all goods and services produced domestically; purchasing power parity (PPP): the PPP method involves the use of standardized international dollar price weights, which are applied to the GDP produced in a given economy. The data derived from the PPP method provide a better comparison of economic well-being between countries than conversions at official currency exchange rates. Literacy rates and population figures are supplied by the U.S. Census Bureau.

Afghanistan

ISLAMIC REPUBLIC OF AFGHANISTAN

National name: Jomhuri-ye Eslami-ye Afghanestan
President: Hamid Karzai (2002)
Area: 250,000 sq mi (647,500 sq km)
Population (2005 est.): 29,928,987 (growth rate: 4.8%); birth rate: 47.0/1000; infant mortality rate: 163.1/1000; life expectancy: 42.9; density per sq mi: 120
Capital and largest city (2003 est.): Kabul, 2,206,300. **Other large cities:** Kandahar, 349,300; Mazar-i-Sharif, 246,900; Charikar, 202,600; Herat, 171,500. **Monetary unit:** Afghani. **Languages:** Pashtu, Dari Persian, other Turkic and minor languages. **Ethnicity/race:** Pashtun 42%, Tajik 27%, Hazara 9%, Uzbek 9%, minor ethnic groups (Chahar Aimaks, Turkmen, Baloch, and others). **Religion:** Islam (Sunni 80%, Shiite 19%), other 1%. **Literacy rate:** 36% (1999 est.)
Economic summary: GDP/PPP (2003 est.): $21.5 billion; per capita $800. **Real growth rate:** 7.5%. **Inflation:** 10.3%. **Unemployment:** n.a. **Arable land:** 12%. **Agriculture:** opium, wheat, fruits, nuts, wool, mutton, sheepskins, lambskins. **Labor force** (2001 est): 11.8 million; agriculture 80%, industry 10%, services 10%. **Natural resources:** natural gas, petroleum, coal, copper, chromite, talc, barites, sulfur, lead, zinc, iron ore, salt, precious and semiprecious stones. **Industries:** small-scale production of textiles, soap, furniture, shoes, fertilizer, cement; handwoven carpets; natural gas, coal, copper. **Exports:** $446 million (FY03–04): opium, fruits and nuts, handwoven carpets, wool, cotton, hides and pelts, precious and semiprecious gems. **Imports:** $3.759 billion (FY03–04): capital goods, food, textiles, petroleum products. **Major trading partners:** U.S., France, India, Pakistan, South Korea, Japan, Germany, Turkmenistan, Kenya (2003).

Geography Afghanistan, approximately the size of Texas, is bordered on the north by Turkmenistan, Uzbekistan, and Tajikistan, on the extreme northeast by China, on the east and south by Pakistan, and by Iran on the west. The country is split east to west by the Hindu Kush mountain range, rising in the east to heights of 24,000 ft (7,315 m). With the exception of the southwest, most of the country is covered by high snow-capped mountains and is traversed by deep valleys.

Government In June 2002 a multiparty republic replaced an interim government that had been established in Dec. 2001, following the fall of the Islamic Taliban government.

History Darius I and Alexander the Great were the first to use Afghanistan as the gateway to India. Islamic conquerors arrived in the 7th century, and Genghis Khan and Tamerlane followed in the 13th and 14th centuries.

In the 19th century, Afghanistan became a battleground in the rivalry between imperial Britain and czarist Russia for control of Central Asia. Three Anglo-Afghan wars (1839–1842, 1878–1880, and 1919) ended inconclusively. In 1893 Britain established an unofficial border, the Durand Line, separating Afghanistan from British India, and London granted full independence in 1919. Emir Amanullah founded an Afghan monarchy in 1926.

During the cold war, King Mohammed Zahir Shah developed close ties with the Soviet Union, accepting extensive economic assistance from Moscow. He was deposed in 1973 by his cousin Mohammed Daoud, who proclaimed a republic. Daoud was killed in a 1978 coup, and Noor Taraki took power, setting up a Marxist regime. He, in turn, was executed in Sept. 1979, and Hafizullah Amin became president. Amin was killed in Dec. 1979, as the Soviets launched a full-scale invasion of Afghanistan and installed Babrak Karmal as president.

The Soviets, and the Soviet-backed Afghan government, were met with fierce popular resistance. Guerrilla forces, calling themselves *mujahideen,* pledged a jihad, or holy war, to expel the invaders. Initially armed with outdated weapons, the mujahideen became a focus of U.S. cold war strategy against the Soviet Union, and with Pakistan's help, Washington began funneling sophisticated arms to the resistance. Moscow's troops were soon bogged down in a no-win conflict with determined Afghan fighters. In 1986 Karmal resigned, and was replaced by Mohammad Najibullah. In April 1988 the USSR, U.S., Afghanistan, and Pakistan signed accords calling for an end to outside aid to the warring factions. In return, a Soviet withdrawal took place in Feb. 1989, but the pro-Soviet government of President Najibullah was left in the capital, Kabul.

By mid-April 1992 Najibullah was ousted as Islamic rebels advanced on the capital. Almost immediately, the various rebel groups began fighting one another for control. Amid the chaos of competing factions, a group calling itself the Taliban—consisting of Islamic students—seized control of Kabul in Sept. 1996. It imposed harsh fundamentalist laws, including stoning for adultery and severing hands for theft. Women were prohibited from work and school, and they were required to cover themselves from head to foot in public. By fall 1998 the Taliban controlled about 90% of the country and, with its scorched-earth tactics and human rights abuses, had turned itself into an international pariah. Only three countries—Pakistan, Saudi Arabia, and the UAR—recognized the Taliban as Afghanistan's legitimate government.

On Aug. 20, 1998, U.S. cruise missiles struck a terrorist training complex in Afghanistan believed to have been financed by Osama bin Laden, a wealthy Islamic radical sheltered by the Taliban. The U.S. asked for the deportation of Bin Laden, whom it believed was involved in the bombing of the U.S. embassies in

Kenya and Tanzania on Aug. 7, 1998. The UN also demanded the Taliban hand over Bin Laden for trial.

In Sept. 2001, legendary guerrilla leader Ahmed Shah Masoud was killed by suicide bombers, a seeming death knell for the anti-Taliban forces, a loosely connected group referred to as the Northern Alliance. Days later, terrorists attacked New York's World Trade Center towers and the Pentagon, and Bin Laden emerged as the primary suspect in the tragedy.

On Oct. 7, after the Taliban repeatedly and defiantly refused to turn over Bin Laden, the U.S. and its allies began daily air strikes against Afghan military installations and terrorist training camps. Five weeks later, with the help of U.S. air support, the Northern Alliance managed with breathtaking speed to take the key cities of Mazar-i-Sharif and Kabul, the capital. On Dec. 7, the Taliban regime collapsed entirely when its troops fled their last stronghold, Kandahar. However, al-Qaeda members and other mujahideen from various parts of the Islamic world who had earlier fought alongside the Taliban persisted in pockets of fierce resistance, forcing U.S. and allied troops to maintain a presence in Afghanistan. Osama bin Laden and Taliban leader Mullah Muhammad Omar remained at large.

In Dec. 2001, Hamid Karzai, a Pashtun (the dominant ethnic group in the country) and the leader of the powerful 500,000-strong Populzai clan, was named head of Afghanistan's interim government; in June 2002, he formally became president. The U.S. maintained about 12,000 troops to combat the remnants of the Taliban and al-Qaeda, and about 31 nations have also contributed NATO-led peacekeeping forces. But attacks on American-led forces have intensified since the war, and warlords continue to maintain tight regional control. In a highly aggressive and uncharacteristic move, Karzai attempted to rein in one of the most powerful warlords, Ismail Khan, by removing him from the governorship of Herat, a western province, in Sept. 2004. Violent protests followed Khan's ouster.

Afghanistan's *loya jirga,* or grand assembly, ratified a new constitution on Jan. 4, 2004. Low voter registration and the ongoing threat posed by insurgents prompted President Karzai to postpone elections scheduled for June 2004.

Sixteen candidates, including Karzai, were on the ballot in the Oct. 9, 2004, presidential election. Voter turnout was high, and violence was minimal. Karzai was declared the winner in November, taking 55.4% of the vote. He was inaugurated in December.

In May 2005, 17 people were killed during anti-American protests prompted by a report in *Newsweek* that American guards at the prison at Guantánamo Bay, Cuba, had desecrated the Koran. Although *Newsweek,* under intense pressure from the White House, retracted the story, FBI documents from 2002 and 2003, released in late May 2005, revealed that detainees at Guantánamo Bay complained that interrogators had abused the Koran. One complaint said guards flushed a Koran down a toilet.

The Taliban continued to attack U.S. troops throughout 2005, making it the deadliest year for U.S. troops since the war ended in 2001. The insurgents intensified their attacks over the summer—an attempt to disrupt September's parliamentary elections. In June, insurgents shot down a Chinook helicopter, killing eight Navy Seals and eight other Special Operations troops who were on a mission to rescue four Navy Seals.

U.S. and Afghan troops fought back, however, killing about 100 Taliban fighters and capturing dozens in July and August.

Albania

REPUBLIC OF ALBANIA

National name: Republika e Shqiperise
President: Alfred Moisiu (2002)
Prime Minister: Sali Berisha (2005)
Area: 11,100 sq mi (28,748 sq km)
Population (2005 est.): 3,563,112 (growth rate: 0.5%); birth rate: 15.1/1000; infant mortality rate: 21.5/1000; life expectancy: 77.2; density per sq mi: 321
Capital and largest city (2003 est.): Tirana, 353,400. **Other large cities:** Durres, 113,900; Elbasan, 97,000. **Monetary unit:** Lek. **Languages:** Albanian (Tosk is the official dialect), Greek. **Ethnicity/race:** Albanian 95%, Greeks 3%, other 2%: Vlachs, Gypsies, Serbs, and Bulgarians (1989 est.). **Religions:** Islam 70%, Albanian Orthodox 20%, Roman Catholic 10% (est.). **Literacy rate:** 87% (2003 est.)
Economic summary: GDP/PPP (2004 est.): $17.46 billion; per capita $4,900. **Real growth rate:** 5.6%. **Inflation:** 3.2%. **Unemployment:** 14.8% officially; may be as high as 30% (2001 est.). **Arable land:** 21%. **Agriculture:** wheat, corn, potatoes, vegetables, fruits, sugar beets, grapes; meat, dairy products. **Labor force:** 1.09 million (not including 352,000 emigrant workers); agriculture 57%, nonagricultural private sector 20%, public sector 23%. **Industries:** food processing, textiles and clothing; lumber, oil, cement, chemicals, mining, basic metals, hydropower. **Natural resources:** petroleum, natural gas, coal, chromium, copper, timber, nickel, hydropower. **Exports:** $552.4 million (f.o.b., 2004 est.): textiles and footwear; asphalt, metals and metallic ores, crude oil; vegetables, fruits, tobacco. **Imports:** $2.076 billion (f.o.b., 2004 est.): machinery and equipment, foodstuffs, textiles, chemicals. **Major trading partners:** Italy, Greece, Germany, Turkey (2003).

Geography Albania is situated on the eastern shore of the Adriatic Sea, with Montenegro and Serbia to the north, Macedonia to the east, and Greece to the south. Slightly larger than Maryland, Albania is composed of two major regions: a mountainous highland region (north, east, and south) constituting 70% of the land area, and a western coastal lowland region that contains nearly all of the country's agricultural land and is the most densely populated part of Albania.

Government Emerging democracy.

History A part of Illyria in ancient times and later of the Roman Empire, Albania was ruled by the Byzantine Empire from 535 to 1204. An alliance (1444–1466) of Albanian chiefs failed to halt the advance of the Ottoman Turks, and the country remained under at least nominal Turkish rule for more than four centuries, until it proclaimed its independence on Nov. 28, 1912.

Largely agricultural, Albania is one of the poorest countries in Europe. A battlefield in World War I, after the war it became a republic in which a conservative Muslim landlord, Ahmed Zogu, proclaimed himself president in 1925 and king (Zog I) in 1928. He ruled until Italy annexed Albania in 1939. Communist guerrillas under Enver Hoxha seized power in 1944, near the end of World War II. Hoxha was a devotee of Stalin, emulating the Soviet leader's repressive tactics, imprisoning or executing landowners and others who did not conform to the socialist ideal. Hoxha eventually broke with Soviet communism in 1961 because of differences with Khrushchev and then aligned himself with Chinese communism, which he also abandoned in 1978 after the death of Mao. From then on Albania went its own way to forge its individual version of the socialist state and became one of the most isolated—and economically underdeveloped—countries in the world. Hoxha was succeeded by Ramiz Alia in 1982.

Elections in March 1991 gave the Communists a decisive majority. But a general strike and street demonstrations soon forced the all-Communist cabinet to resign. In June 1991 the Communist Party of Labor renamed itself the Socialist Party and renounced its past ideology. The opposition Democratic Party won a landslide victory in the 1992 elections, and Sali Berisha, a former cardiologist, became Albania's first elected president. The following year, ex-Communists, including Ramiz Alia and former prime minister Fatos Nano, were imprisoned on corruption charges.

But Albania's experiment with democratic reform and a free-market economy went disastrously awry in March 1997, when large numbers of its citizens invested in shady get-rich-quick pyramid schemes. When five of these schemes collapsed in the beginning of the year, robbing Albanians of an estimated $1.2 billion in savings, Albanians' rage turned against the government, which appeared to have sanctioned the nationwide swindle. Rioting broke out, the country's fragile infrastructure collapsed, and gangsters and rebels overran the country, plunging it into virtual anarchy. A multinational protection force eventually restored order and set up the elections that formally ousted President Sali Berisha.

In spring 1999, Albania was heavily involved in the affairs of its fellow ethnic Albanians to the north, in Kosovo. Albania served as an outpost for NATO troops and took in approximately 440,000 Kosovar refugees, about half the total number of ethnic Albanians who were driven from their homes in Kosovo.

Ilir Meta, elected prime minister in 1999, rapidly moved forward in his first years to modernize the economy, privatize business, fight crime, and reform the judiciary and tax systems. He resigned in Jan. 2002, frustrated by political infighting. In June 2002, former general Alfred Moisiu was elected president, endorsed by both the Socialists (headed by Fatos Nano) and the Democrats (led by Sali Berisha) in an effort to end the unproductive political fractiousness that has stalemated the government. The political duel between Nano and Berisha continued on, however, and little improvement was evident in the standard of living for Albanians. In 2005 elections, Berisha replaced Nano as prime minister.

Algeria

PEOPLE'S DEMOCRATIC REPUBLIC OF ALGERIA

National name: Al Jumhuriyah al Jaza'iriyah ad Dimuqratiyah ash Sha'biyah
President: Abdel-Aziz Bouteflika (1999)
Prime Minister: Ahmed Ouyahia (2003)
Area: 919,590 sq mi (2,381,740 sq km)
Population (2005 est.): 32,531,853 (growth rate: 1.2%); birth rate: 17.1/1000; infant mortality rate: 31.0/1000; life expectancy: 73.0; density per sq mi: 35
Capital and largest city (2003 est.): Algiers, 3,917,000 (metro. area), 1,742,800 (city proper). **Other large cities:** Oran, 752,200; Constantine, 530,100; Batna, 278,100; Annaba, 246,700. **Monetary unit:** Dinar.
Languages: Arabic (official), French, Berber dialects.
Ethnicity/race: Arab-Berber 99%, European less than 1%. **Religion:** Islam (Sunni) 99% (state religion), Christian and Jewish 1%.
Economic summary: GDP/PPP (2004 est.): $212.3 billion; per capita $6,600. **Real growth rate:** 6.1%. **Inflation:** 3.1%. **Unemployment:** 25.4%. **Arable land:** 3%. **Agriculture:** wheat, barley, oats, grapes, olives, citrus, fruits; sheep, cattle. **Labor force:** 9.91 million;

agriculture 14%, industry 13.4%, construction and public works 10%, trade 14.6%, government 32%, other 16% (2003 est.). **Industries:** petroleum, natural gas, light industries, mining, electrical, petrochemical, food processing. **Natural resources:** petroleum, natural gas, iron ore, phosphates, uranium, lead, zinc. **Exports:** $32.16 billion (f.o.b., 2004 est.): petroleum, natural gas, and petroleum products 97%. **Imports:** $15.25 billion (f.o.b., 2004 est): capital goods, foodstuffs, consumer goods. **Major trading partners:** Italy, U.S., France, Spain, Canada, Belgium, Brazil, Germany, China, Turkey (2003).

Geography Nearly four times the size of Texas, Algeria is bordered on the west by Morocco and Western Sahara and on the east by Tunisia and Libya. The Mediterranean Sea is to the north, and to the south are Mauritania, Mali, and Niger. The Saharan region, which is 85% of the country, is almost completely uninhabited. The highest point is Mount Tahat in the Sahara, which rises 9,850 ft (3,000 m).

Government Parliamentary republic.

History Excavations in Algeria have indicated that *Homo erectus* resided there between 500,000 and 700,000 years ago. Phoenician traders settled on the Mediterranean coast in the 1st millennium B.C. As ancient Numidia, Algeria became a Roman colony, part of what was called Mauretania Caesariensis, at the close of the Punic Wars (145 B.C.). Conquered by the Vandals about A.D. 440, it fell from a high state of civilization to virtual barbarism, from which it partly recovered after an invasion by Arabs about 650. Christian during its Roman period, the indigenous Berbers were then converted to Islam. Falling under the control of the Ottoman Empire by 1536, Algiers served for three centuries as the headquarters of the Barbary pirates. Ostensibly to rid the region of the pirates, the French occupied Algeria in 1830 and made it a part of France in 1848.

Algerian independence movements led to the uprisings of 1954–1955, which developed into full-scale war. In 1962, French president Charles de Gaulle began the peace negotiations, and on July 5, 1962, Algeria was proclaimed independent. In Oct. 1963, Ahmed Ben Bella was elected president, and the country became Socialist. He began to nationalize foreign holdings and aroused opposition. He was overthrown in a military coup on June 19, 1965, by Col. Houari Boumédienne, who suspended the constitution and sought to restore economic stability. After his death, Boumédienne was succeeded by Col. Chadli Bendjedid in 1978. Berbers rioted in 1980 when Arabic was made the country's only official language. Algeria entered a major recession after world oil prices plummeted in the 1980s.

The fundamentalist Islamic Salvation Front (Front Islamique du Salut; FIS) won the largest number of votes in the country's first-ever parliamentary elections in Dec. 1991. To thwart the electoral results, the army canceled the general election, which plunged the country into a bloody civil war. An estimated 100,000 people have been massacred by Islamic terrorists since war began in Jan. 1992. The undeclared civil war escalated in its brutality and senselessness in 1997–1998. Islamic extremists, who had originally focused their attacks on government officials and then shifted to intellectuals and journalists, abandoned political motivations entirely and targeted defenseless villagers. The mass slaughters were as savage as they were random, and the government was markedly ineffectual in stemming the violence.

Abdel-Aziz Bouteflika's ascension to the presidency in April 1999 was initially expected to bring peace and some economic improvement to this desperate war-torn country. Bouteflika, however, remains locked in power struggles with the military, whose support is crucial. Despite the appearance of democracy, Algeria remains in essence a military dictatorship. In 2001 violence by Islamic militants was again on the rise, and the long-disaffected Berber minority engaged in several large-scale protests.

Algeria's most destructive earthquake in two decades struck near the capital on May 21, 2003, killing over 2,000 people and injuring many more thousands.

In April 2004 presidential elections, praised by international monitors for their fairness, incumbent Bouteflika won 85% of the vote. Bouteflika stated that his second term would be devoted to solving the three-year-old crisis in the Berber region of Kabylia, freeing women from restrictive family codes, and bringing about "true national reconciliation" caused by the civil war. The country's dire economic situation has improved slightly, but Algeria still faces a high unemployment rate.

Andorra

PRINCIPALITY OF ANDORRA

National name: Principat d'Andorra
Head of Government: Albert Pintat Santolària (2005)
Chiefs of State (Coprinces): Frederic de Saint-Sernin for France and Nemesi Marques Oste for Spain
Area: 181 sq mi (468 sq km)
Population (2005 est.): 70,549 (growth rate: 1.0%); birth rate: 9.0/1000; infant mortality rate: 4.0/1000; life expectancy: 83.5; density per sq mi: 390
Capital and largest city (2003 est.): Andorra la Vella, 23,000. **Monetary units:** Euro. **Languages:** Catalán (official), French, Castilian, Portuguese. **Ethnicity/race:** Spanish 43%, Andorran 33%, Portuguese 11%, French 7%, other 6% (1998). **Religion:** Roman Catholic (predominant). **Literacy rate:** 100%
Economic summary: GDP/PPP (2003 est.): $1.9 billion; per capita $26,800. **Real growth rate:** 2%. **Inflation:** 4.3% (2000). **Unemployment:** 0% (1996 est.). **Arable land:** 2%. **Agriculture:** small quantities of rye, wheat, barley, oats, vegetables; sheep. **Labor force:** 33,000 (2001 est.); agriculture 1%, industry 21%, services 78% (2000 est.). **Industries:** tourism (particularly skiing), cattle raising, timber, banking. **Natural resources:** hydropower, mineral water, timber, iron ore, lead. **Exports:** $58 million (f.o.b., 1998): tobacco products, furniture. **Imports:** $1.077 billion (1998): consumer goods, food, electricity. **Major trading partners:** Spain, France, U.S. (2000).

Geography Andorra is nestled high in the Pyrénées Mountains on the French-Spanish border.

Government A parliamentary coprincipality composed of the bishop of Urgel (Spain) and the president of France. Their representatives are listed above. The principality was internationally recognized as a sovereign state in 1993.

History An autonomous and semi-independent coprincipality, Andorra has been under the joint suzerainty of the French state and the Spanish bishops of Urgel since 1278. It maintains closer ties to Spain, however, and Catalán is its official language. In the late 20th century, Andorra became a popular tourist and winter sports destination and a wealthy international commercial center because of its banking facilities, low taxes, and lack of customs duties. In 1990 Andorra approved a customs union treaty with the EU permitting free movement of industrial goods between

the two, but with Andorra applying the EU's external tariffs to third countries. Andorra became a member of the UN in 1993 and a member of the Council of Europe in 1994.

Angola

REPUBLIC OF ANGOLA

National name: Republica de Angola
President: José Eduardo dos Santos (1979)
Prime Minister: Fernando da Piedade Dias dos Santos (2003)
Area: 481,351 sq mi (1,246,700 sq km)
Population (2005 est.): 11,190,786 (growth rate: 1.9%); birth rate: 44.6/1000; infant mortality rate: 191.2/1000; life expectancy: 36.6; density per sq mi: 23
Capital and largest city (2003 est.): Luanda, 2,297,200. **Other large cities:** Huambo, 171,000; Lubango, 136,000. **Monetary unit:** New Kwanza. **Languages:** Portuguese (official), Bantu and other African languages. **Ethnicity/race:** Ovimbundu 37%, Kimbundu 25%, Bakongo 13%, mestico (mixed European and Native African) 2%, European 1%, other 22%. **Religions:** Indigenous 47%, Roman Catholic 38%, Protestant 15% (1998 est.). **Literacy rate:** 42% (1998 est.)
Economic summary: GDP/PPP (2004 est.): $23.17 billion; per capita $2,100. **Real growth rate:** 11.7%. **Inflation:** 43.8%. **Unemployment:** extensive unemployment and underemployment affecting more than half the population (2001 est.). **Arable land:** 2%. **Agriculture:** bananas, sugarcane, coffee, sisal, corn, cotton, manioc (tapioca), tobacco, vegetables, plantains; livestock; forest products; fish. **Labor force:** 5.41 million; agriculture 85%, industry and services 15% (2003 est.). **Industries:** petroleum; diamonds, iron ore, phosphates, feldspar, bauxite, uranium, and gold; cement; basic metal products; fish processing; food processing; brewing; tobacco products; sugar; textiles, ship repair. **Natural resources:** petroleum, diamonds, iron ore, phosphates, copper, feldspar, gold, bauxite, uranium. **Exports:** $12.76 billion (f.o.b., 2004 est.): crude oil, diamonds, refined petroleum products, gas, coffee, sisal, fish and fish products, timber, cotton. **Imports:** $4.896 billion (f.o.b., 2004 est.): machinery and electrical equipment, vehicles and spare parts; medicines, food, textiles, military goods. **Major trading partners:** U.S., China, Taiwan, France, Portugal, South Africa, Netherlands, Brazil, UK (2003).

Geography Angola, more than three times the size of California, extends for more than 1,000 mi (1,609 km) along the South Atlantic in southwest Africa. The Democratic Republic of the Congo and the Republic of Congo are to the north and east, Zambia is to the east, and Namibia is to the south. A plateau averaging 6,000 ft (1,829 m) above sea level rises abruptly from the coastal lowlands. Nearly all the land is desert or savanna, with hardwood forests in the northeast.

Government Angola underwent a transition from a one-party socialist state to a nominally multiparty democracy in 1992.

History The original inhabitants of Angola are thought to have been Khoisan speakers. After 1000, large numbers of Bantu speakers migrated to the region and became the dominant group. Angola derives its name from the Bantu kingdom of Ndongo, whose name for its king is *ngola*.

Explored by the Portuguese navigator Diego Cão in 1482, Angola became a link in trade with India and Southeast Asia. Later it was a major source of slaves for Portugal's New World colony of Brazil. Development of the interior began after the Berlin Conference in 1885 fixed the colony's borders, and British and Portuguese investment fostered mining, railways, and agriculture.

Following World War II, independence movements began but were sternly suppressed by Portuguese military forces. The major nationalist organizations were the Popular Movement for the Liberation of Angola (MPLA), a Marxist party; National Front for the Liberation of Angola (FNLA); and the National Union for the Total Independence of Angola (UNITA). After 14 years of war, Portugal finally granted independence to Angola in 1975. The MPLA, which had led the independence movement, has controlled the government ever since. But no period of peace followed Angola's long war for independence. UNITA disputed the MPLA's ascendancy, and civil war broke out almost immediately. With the Soviet Union and Cuba supporting the Marxist MPLA, and the United States and South Africa supporting the anti-Communist UNITA, the country became a cold war battleground.

With the waning of the cold war and the withdrawal of Cuban troops in 1989, the MPLA began to make the transition to a multiparty democracy. Despite shifting ideologies, the civil war continued, with UNITA's charismatic rebel leader, Jonas Savimbi, armed and sustained by his control of approximately 80% of the country's diamond trade. Free elections took place in 1992, with incumbent president José Eduardo dos Santos and the MPLA winning the UN-certified election over Savimbi and UNITA. Savimbi then withdrew, charging election fraud, and the civil war resumed.

Four years of relative peace took place between 1994 and 1998, when the UN, at a cost of $1.6 billion, oversaw the 1994 Lusaka peace accord. In 1997 it was agreed that a coalition government with UNITA would be implemented. But Savimbi violated the accord repeatedly by refusing to give up his strongholds, failing to demobilize his army, and retaking territory. As a result, the government suspended coalition rule in Sept. 1998, and the country again plunged into civil war. Angola's citizens continued to suffer. The hostilities affected an estimated 4 million people, about a third of the total population, and there were almost 2 million refugees.

On Feb. 22, 2002, government troops killed Jonas Savimbi, and his exhausted troops were ready to lay down their arms. Six weeks later, on April 4, rebel leaders signed a cease-fire deal with the government, signaling the end of 30 years of civil war. Within another five weeks, 80% of the rebels had been disarmed. While peace finally seemed secure, more than a half-million Angolans were faced with starvation. Thousands of Angolan refugees returned to their country in 2003, where their prospects are bleak.

Angola is the second-largest oil producer in sub-Saharan Africa, yet its people are among the continent's poorest. The corruption of the dos Santos government bears much of the blame. According to the International Monetary Fund, more than $4 billion in oil receipts have disappeared from Angola's treasury in the last six years.

Antigua and Barbuda

Sovereign: Queen Elizabeth II (1952)
Governor-General: James Beethoven Carlisle (1993)
Prime Minister: Baldwin Spencer (2004)
Land area: 171 sq mi (443 sq km)
Population (2005 est.): 68,722 (growth rate: 0.6%); birth rate: 17.3/1000; infant mortality rate: 19.5/1000; life expectancy: 71.9; density per sq mi: 402
Capital and largest city (2003 est.): St. John's, 23,500.
Other large cities: English Harbour, 2,900; Codrington (capital of Barbuda), est. pop. 870.

Monetary unit: East Caribbean dollar. **Languages:** English (official), local dialects. **Ethnicity/race:** black, British, Portuguese, Lebanese, Syrian. **Religions:** Christian (predominantly Anglican and other Protestant; some Roman Catholic). **Literacy rate:** 89% (1960 est.)
Economic summary: GDP/PPP (2002 est.): $750 million; per capita $11,000. **Real growth rate:** 3%. **Inflation:** 0.4% (2000 est.). **Unemployment:** 11% (2001 est.). **Arable land:** 18%. **Agriculture:** cotton, fruits, vegetables, bananas, coconuts, cucumbers, mangoes, sugarcane; livestock. **Labor force:** 30,000; commerce and services 82%, industry 11%, agriculture 7% (1983). **Industries:** tourism, construction, light manufacturing (clothing, alcohol, household appliances). **Natural resources:** negl.; pleasant climate fosters tourism. **Exports:** $689 million (2002): petroleum products 48%, manufactures 23%, machinery and transport equipment 17%, food and live animals 4%, other 8%. **Imports:** $692 million (2002 est.): food and live animals, machinery and transport equipment, manufactures, chemicals, oil. **Major trading partners:** Germany, UK, U.S., Singapore, Poland, UK, Trinidad and Tobago (2003). **Member of Commonwealth of Nations**

Geography Antigua, the larger of the two main islands, is 108 sq mi (280 sq km). The island dependencies of Redonda (an uninhabited rocky islet) and Barbuda (a coral island formerly known as Dulcina) are 0.5 sq mi (1.30 sq km) and 62 sq mi (161 sq km), respectively.

Government Constitutional monarchy.

History Antigua was explored by Christopher Columbus in 1493 and named for the Church of Santa Maria de la Antigua in Seville. Antigua was colonized by Britain in 1632; Barbuda was first colonized in 1678. The country joined the West Indies Federation in 1958. With the breakup of the federation, it became one of the West Indies Associated States in 1967, self-governing its internal affairs. Full independence was granted Nov. 1, 1981.

The Bird family has controlled the islands since Vere C. Bird founded the Antigua Labor Party in the mid-1940s. While tourism and financial services have turned the country into one of the more prosperous in the Caribbean, law enforcement officials have charged that Antigua and Barbuda is a major center of money laundering, drug trafficking, and arms smuggling. Several scandals tainted the Bird family, especially the 1995 conviction of Prime Minister Lester Bird's brother, Ivor, for cocaine smuggling. In 2000, Antigua and 35 other offshore banking centers agreed to reforms meant to prevent money laundering.

In March 2004, the Bird political dynasty came to an end when labor activist Baldwin Spencer defeated Lester Bird, who had been prime minister since 1994. In 2005, income tax, which had been eliminated in 1975, was reintroduced to help alleviate Antigua's deficit.

Argentina
ARGENTINE REPUBLIC

National name: República Argentina
President: Néstor Kirchner (2003)
Area: 1,068,296 sq mi (2,766,890 sq km)
Population (2005 est.): 39,537,943 (growth rate: 1.0%); birth rate: 16.9/1000; infant mortality rate: 15.2/1000; life expectancy: 75.9; density per sq mi: 37
Capital and largest city (2003 est.): Buenos Aires, 13,076,300 (metro. area), 12,116,400 (city proper).
Other large cities: Córdoba, 1,486,200; Rosario, 1,276,900; Mendoza, 988,600; Mar del Plata, 683,700.

Monetary unit: Peso. **Languages:** Spanish (official), English, Italian, German, French. **Ethnicity/race:** white (mostly Spanish and Italian) 97%; mestizo, Amerindian, other 3%. **Religions:** Roman Catholic 92%, Protestant 2%, Jewish 2%, other 4%. **Literacy rate:** 96.2% (1995 est.)
Economic summary: GDP/PPP (2004 est.): $483.5 billion; per capita $12,400. **Real growth rate:** 8.3%. **Inflation:** 6.1%. **Unemployment:** 14.8%. **Arable land:** 12%. **Agriculture:** sunflower seeds, lemons, soybeans, grapes, corn, tobacco, peanuts, tea, wheat; livestock. **Labor force:** 15.04 million; agriculture n.a., industry n.a., services n.a. **Industries:** food processing, motor vehicles, consumer durables, textiles, chemicals and petrochemicals, printing, metallurgy, steel. **Natural resources:** fertile plains of the pampas, lead, zinc, tin, copper, iron ore, manganese, petroleum, uranium. **Exports:** $33.78 billion (f.o.b., 2004 est.): edible oils, fuels and energy, cereals, feed, motor vehicles. **Imports:** $22.06 billion (f.o.b., 2004 est.): machinery and equipment, motor vehicles, chemicals, metal manufactures, plastics. **Major trading partners:** Brazil, Chile, U.S., China, Spain, Germany (2003).

Geography Second in South America only to Brazil in size and population, Argentina is a plain, rising from the Atlantic to the Chilean border and the towering Andes peaks. Aconcagua (22,834 ft, 6,960 m) is the highest peak in the world outside Asia. Argentina is also bordered by Bolivia and Paraguay on the north, and by Uruguay and Brazil on the east.

Government Republic.

History First explored in 1516 by Juan Díaz de Solis, Argentina developed slowly under Spanish colonial rule. Buenos Aires was settled in 1580; the cattle industry was thriving as early as 1600. Invading British forces were expelled in 1806–1807, and after Napoléon conquered Spain (1808), the Argentinians set up their own government in 1810. On July 9, 1816, independence was formally declared.

As it had in World War I, Argentina proclaimed neutrality at the outbreak of World War II, but in the closing phase declared war on the Axis powers on March 27, 1945. Juan D. Perón, an army colonel, emerged as the strongman of the postwar era, winning the presidential elections of 1946 and 1951. Perón's political strength was reinforced by his second wife—Eva Duarte de Perón (Evita)—and her popularity with the working classes. Although she never held a government post, Evita acted as de facto minister of health and labor, establishing a national charitable organization, and awarding generous wage increases to the unions, who responded with political support for Perón. Opposition to Perón's increasing authoritarianism led to a coup by the armed forces, which sent Perón into exile in 1955, three years after Evita's death. Argentina entered a long period of military dictatorships with brief intervals of constitutional government.

The former dictator returned to power in 1973 and his third wife, Isabel Martínez de Perón, was elected vice president. After Perón's death in 1974, she became the hemisphere's first woman chief of state, assuming control of a nation teetering on economic and political collapse. In 1975, terrorist acts by left- and right-wing groups killed some 700 people. The cost of living rose 355%, while strikes and demonstrations were constant. On March 24, 1976, a military junta led by army commander Lt. Gen. Jorge Rafael Videla seized power and imposed martial law.

The military began the "dirty war" to restore order and eradicate its opponents. The Argentine Commission for Human Rights, in Geneva, has charged the junta with 2,300 political murders, over 10,000 political arrests, and the disappearance of 20,000 to 30,000 people. While violence declined, the economy remained in chaos. In March 1981 Videla was deposed by Field Marshal Roberto Viola, who in turn was succeeded by Lt. Gen. Leopoldo Galtieri.

On April 2, 1982, Galtieri invaded the British-held Falkland Islands, known as Las Islas Malvinas (Malvinas Islands) in Spanish, in what was seen as an attempt to increase his popularity. Great Britain, however, won a decisive victory, and Galtieri resigned in disgrace three days after Argentina's surrender. Maj. Gen. Reynaldo Bignone took over June 14, amid increasing prodemocratic public sentiment. As the 1983 elections approached, inflation hit 900% and Argentina's crippling foreign debt reached unprecedented levels.

In the presidential election of Oct. 1983, Raúl Alfonsín, leader of the Radical Civic Union, handed the Peronist Party its first defeat since its founding. Growing unemployment and quadruple-digit inflation, however, led to a Peronist victory in the elections of May 1989. Alfonsín resigned a month later in the wake of riots over high food prices, in favor of the new Peronist president, Carlos Menem. In 1991, Menem promoted economic austerity measures that deregulated businesses and privatized state-owned industries. But beginning in Sept. 1998, eight years into Menem's two-term presidency, Argentina entered its worst recession in a decade. Menem's economic policies, tolerance of corruption, and pardoning of military leaders involved in the dirty war eventually lost him the support of the poor and the working class who had elected him.

In Dec. 1999 Fernando de la Rua became president. Despite the introduction of several tough economic austerity plans, by 2001 the recession slid into its third year. The IMF gave Argentina $13.7 billion in emergency aid in Jan. 2001 and $8 billion in Aug. 2001. The international help was not enough, however, and by the end of 2001, Argentina verged on economic collapse. Rioters protesting government austerity measures forced de la Rua to resign in Dec. 2001. Argentina then defaulted on its $155 billion foreign debt payments, the largest such default in history.

After more instability, Congress named Eduardo Duhalde president on Jan. 1, 2002. Duhalde soon announced an economic plan devaluing the Argentine peso, which had been pegged to the dollar for a decade. The devaluation plunged the banking industry into crisis and wiped out much of the savings of the middle class, plunging millions of Argentinians into poverty.

In July 2002, former junta leader Galtieri and 42 other military officers were arrested and charged with the torture and execution of 22 leftist guerrillas during Argentina's 7-year military dictatorship. In recent years, judges have found legal loopholes allowing them to circumvent the blanket amnesty laws passed in 1986 and 1987, which have allowed many accused of atrocities during the dirty war to walk free. In June 2005, the Supreme Court ruled that these amnesty laws were unconstitutional.

Peronist Néstor Kirchner, the former governor of Santa Cruz, became Argentina's president in May 2003, after former president Carlos Menem abandoned the race. Kirchner has vowed to aggressively reform the courts, police, and armed services and to prosecute perpetrators of the dirty war. Argentina's economy has been rebounding since its near collapse in 2001, with an impressive growth rate of about 8% since President Kirchner took office. In March 2005, Kirchner announced that the country's debt had been successfully restructured.

Armenia

REPUBLIC OF ARMENIA

National Name: Hayastani Hanrapetut'yun
President: Robert Kocharian (1998)
Prime Minister: Andranik Markarian (2000)
Area: 11,506 sq mi (29,800 sq km)
Population (2005 est.): 2,982,904 (growth rate: –0.3%); (Armenian, 93%; others, Kurds, Ukrainians, and Russians); birth rate: 11.8/1000; infant mortality rate: 23.3/1000; life expectancy: 71.5; density per sq mi: 259
Capital and largest city (2003 est.): Yerevan, 1,462,700 (metro. area), 1,267,600 (city proper). **Other large cities:** Vanadzor, 147,400; Gyumri (Leninakan), 125,300; Abovian, 59,300. **Monetary unit:** Dram. **Languages:** Armenian 96%, Russian 2%, other 2%. **Ethnicity/race:** Armenian 93%, Russian 2%, Azeri 1%, other (mostly Yezidi Kurds) 4% (2002). Note: as of the end of 1993, virtually all Azeris had emigrated from Armenia. **Religion:** Armenian Apostolic 94%, other Christian 4%, Yezidi 2%. **Literacy rate:** 99% (1989 est.)
Economic summary: GDP/PPP (2004 est.): $13.65 billion; per capita $4,600. **Real growth rate:** 9%. **Inflation:** 3.5%. **Unemployment:** 30%. Note: official rate is 10.9% for 2000. **Arable land:** 18%. **Agriculture:** fruit (especially grapes), vegetables; livestock. **Labor force:** 1.4 million (2001); agriculture 45%, industry 25%, services 30% (2002 est.). **Industries:** diamond-processing, metal-cutting machine tools, forging-pressing machines, electric motors, tires, knitted wear, hosiery, shoes, silk fabric, chemicals, trucks, instruments, microelectronics, jewelry manufacturing, software development, food processing, brandy. **Natural resources:** small deposits of gold, copper, molybdenum, zinc, alumina. **Exports:** $850 million (f.o.b., 2004 est.): diamonds, mineral products, foodstuffs, energy. **Imports:** $1.3 billion (f.o.b., 2004 est.): natural gas, petroleum, tobacco products, foodstuffs, diamonds. **Major trading partners:** Belgium, UK, Israel, Russia, Iran, U.S., Germany, UAE, Italy, Ukraine (2003).

Geography Armenia is located in the southern Caucasus and is the smallest of the former Soviet republics. It is bounded by Georgia on the north, Azerbaijan on the east, Iran on the south, and Turkey on the west. Contemporary Armenia is a fraction of the size of ancient Armenia. A land of rugged mountains and extinct volcanoes, its highest point is Mount Aragats, 13,435 ft (4,095 m).

Government Republic.

History One of the world's oldest civilizations, Armenia once included Mount Ararat, which biblical tradition identifies as the mountain that Noah's ark rested on after the flood. It was the first country in the world to officially embrace Christianity as its religion (c. A.D. 300).

In the 6th century B.C., Armenians settled in the kingdom of Urartu (the Assyrian name for Ararat), which was in decline. Under Tigrane the Great (fl. 95–55 B.C.) the Armenian empire reached its height and became one of the most powerful in Asia, stretching from the Caspian to the Mediterranean Seas. Throughout most of its long history, however, Armenia has been invaded by a succession of empires. Under constant threat of domination by foreign forces, Armenians became both cosmopolitan as well as fierce protectors of their culture and tradition.

Over the centuries Armenia was conquered by Greeks, Romans, Persians, Byzantines, Mongols, Arabs, Ottoman Turks, and Russians. From the 16th century through World War I major portions of Armenia were controlled by their most brutal invader, the Ottoman Turks, under whom the Armenians experienced discrimination, religious persecution, heavy taxation, and armed attacks. In response to Armenian nationalist stirrings, the Turks massacred thousands of Armenians in 1894 and 1896. The most horrific massacre took place in April 1915 during World War I, when the Turks ordered the deportation of the Armenian population to the deserts of Syria and Mesopotamia. According to the majority of historians, between 600,000 and 1.5 million Armenians were murdered or died of starvation. The Armenian massacre is considered the first genocide in the 20th century. Turkey denies that a genocide took place and claims that a much smaller number died in a civil war.

After the Turkish defeat in World War I, the independent Republic of Armenia was established on May 28, 1918, but survived only until Nov. 29, 1920, when it was annexed by the Soviet Army. On March 12, 1922, the Soviets joined Georgia, Armenia, and Azerbaijan to form the Transcaucasian Soviet Socialist Republic, which became part of the USSR. In 1936, after a reorganization, Armenia became a separate constituent republic of the USSR. Armenia declared its independence from the collapsing Soviet Union on Sept. 23, 1991.

In 1988, Armenia became involved in a territorial dispute with Azerbaijan over the enclave of Nagorno-Karabakh, to which both laid claim. The majority of the enclave were Armenian Christians who wanted to secede from Azerbaijan and either become part of Armenia or gain full independence. War broke out between Armenia and Azerbaijan over the region from 1992–1994, resulting in 30,000 casualties. Armenia effectively controls the region today, although no formal resolution exists.

An Armenian diaspora has existed throughout the nation's history, and Armenian emigration has been particularly heavy since independence from the Soviet Union. An estimated 60% of the total 8 million Armenians worldwide live outside the country, with 1 million each in the U.S. and Russia. Other significant Armenian communities are located in Georgia, France, Iran, Lebanon, Syria, Argentina, and Canada.

Australia

COMMONWEALTH OF AUSTRALIA

Sovereign: Queen Elizabeth II (1952)
Governor-General: Michael Jeffery (2003)
Prime Minister: John Howard (1996)
Area: 2,967,893 sq mi (7,686,850 sq km)
Population (2005 est.): 20,090,437 (growth rate: 0.9%); birth rate: 12.3/1000; infant mortality rate: 4.7/1000; life expectancy: 80.4; density per sq mi: 7
Capital (2003 est.): Canberra, 327,700. **Largest cities:** Sydney, 4,250,100; Melbourne, 3,610,800; Brisbane, 1,545,700; Perth, 1,375,200; Adelaide, 1,087,600. **Monetary unit:** Australian dollar. **Languages:** English, native languages. **Ethnicity/race:** Caucasian 92%, Asian 7%, aboriginal (353,000) and other 1%. **Religions:** Anglican 26.1%, Roman Catholic 26%, other Christian 24.3%. **Literacy rate:** 100% (1980 est.)
Economic summary: GDP/PPP (2004 est.): $611.7 billion; per capita $30,700. **Real growth rate:** 3.5%. **Inflation:** 2.3%. **Unemployment:** 5.1% (Dec. 2004 est.). **Arable land:** 7%. **Agriculture:** wheat, barley, sugarcane, fruits; cattle, sheep, poultry. **Labor force:** 10.35 million; agriculture 3.6%, industry 26.4%, services 70%. **Industries:** mining, industrial and transportation equipment, food processing, chemicals, steel. **Natural resources:** bauxite, coal, iron ore, copper, tin, silver, uranium, nickel, tungsten, mineral sands, lead, zinc, diamonds, natural gas, petroleum. **Exports:** $86.89

billion (2004 est.): coal, gold, meat, wool, alumina, iron ore, wheat, machinery and transport equipment. **Imports:** $98.1 billion (2004 est.): machinery and transport equipment, computers and office machines, telecommunication equipment and parts; crude oil and petroleum products. **Major trading partners:** Japan, U.S., China, South Korea, New Zealand, UK, Germany (2003). **Member of Commonwealth of Nations**

Geography The continent of Australia, with the island state of Tasmania, is approximately equal in area to the United States (excluding Alaska and Hawaii). Mountain ranges run from north to south along the east coast, reaching their highest point in Mount Kosciusko (7,308 ft; 2,228 m). The western half of the continent is occupied by a desert plateau that rises into barren, rolling hills near the west coast. The Great Barrier Reef, extending about 1,245 mi (2,000 km), lies along the northeast coast. The island of Tasmania (26,178 sq mi; 67,800 sq km) is off the southeast coast.

Government Democracy. Symbolic executive power is vested in the British monarch, who is represented throughout Australia by the governor-general.

History The first inhabitants of Australia were the Aborigines, who migrated there at least 40,000 years ago from Southeast Asia. There may have been between a half million to a full million Aborigines at the time of European settlement; today there are about 350,000.

Dutch, Portuguese, and Spanish ships sighted Australia in the 17th century; the Dutch landed at the Gulf of Carpentaria in 1606. In 1616 the territory became known as New Holland. The British arrived in 1688, but it was not until Captain James Cook's voyage in 1770 that Great Britain claimed possession of the vast island, calling it New South Wales. A British penal colony was set up at Port Jackson (what is now Sydney) in 1788, and about 161,000 transported English convicts were settled there until the system was suspended in 1839.

Free settlers and former prisoners established six colonies: New South Wales (1786), Tasmania (then Van Diemen's Land) (1825), Western Australia (1829), South Australia (1834), Victoria (1851), and Queensland (1859). Various gold rushes attracted settlers, as did the mining of other minerals. Sheep farming and grain soon became important economic enterprises. The six colonies became states and in 1901 federated into the Commonwealth of Australia with a constitution that incorporated British parliamentary and U.S. federal traditions. Australia became known for its liberal legislation: free compulsory education, protected trade unionism with industrial conciliation and arbitration, the secret ballot, women's suffrage, maternity allowances, and sickness and old-age pensions.

Australia fought alongside Britain in World War I, notably with the Australia and New Zealand Army Corps (ANZAC) in the Dardanelles campaign (1915). Participation in World War II brought Australia closer to the United States. Parliamentary power in the second half of the 20th century shifted between three political parties: the Australian Labour Party, the Liberal Party, and the National Party. Australia relaxed its discriminatory immigration laws in the 1960s and 1970s, which favored Northern Europeans. Thereafter, about 40% of its immigrants came from Asia, diversifying a population that was predominantly of English and Irish heritage. An Aboriginal movement grew in the 1960s that gained full citizenship and improved education for the country's poorest socioeconomic group.

In March 1996 the opposition Liberal Party–National Party coalition easily won the national elections, removing the Labour Party after 13 years in power. Pressure from the new, conservative One Nation Party threatened to reduce the gains made by Aborigines and to limit immigration.

In Sept. 1999, Australia led the international peacekeeping force sent to restore order in East Timor after pro-Indonesian militias began massacring civilians to thwart East Timor's referendum on independence. Australia's relations with East Timor have soured since then over a dispute over oil reserves claimed by both countries.

In Nov. 1999, Australia's 11.6 million voters rejected a referendum that would have ended Australia's formal allegiance to the British Crown. The referendum would have replaced the British governor-general with an Australian president chosen by Parliament. Although the vast majority of Australians do not consider themselves monarchists, they rejected the referendum because it did not provide for direct, popular elections but instead gave Parliament the power to select the president.

In 2000, Prime Minister Howard instituted a new tax system, lowering income and corporate taxes, and adding sales taxes on goods and services.

John Howard won a third term in Nov. 2001, primarily as the result of his tough policy against illegal immigration. It has also brought him considerable criticism: refugees attempting to enter Australia—most of them from Afghanistan, Iran, and Iraq and numbering about 5,000 annually—have been imprisoned in bleak detention camps and subjected to a lengthy immigration process. Asylum-seekers have staged riots and hunger strikes. Howard has also dealt with refugees with the "Pacific solution," which reroutes boat people from Australian shores to camps in Papua New Guinea and Nauru. In 2004, however, the government began easing its policies on immigration.

Prime Minister Howard sent 2,000 Australian troops to fight alongside American and British troops in the 2003 Iraq war, despite strong opposition among Australians. There were no Australian casualties. Australia released the Flood report in 2004, an assessment of prewar intelligence on Iraq, which described the evidence supporting Iraq's possession of weapons of mass destruction as "thin, ambiguous, and incomplete." But like similar U.S. and UK intelligence reports, it cleared the government of manipulating the intelligence.

In July 2003, Australia successfully restored order to the Solomon Islands, which had descended into lawlessness during a brutal civil war.

Australia has been the victim of two significant terrorist attacks in recent years: the 2002 Bali, Indonesia, bombings by a group with ties to al-Qaeda in which 202 died, many of whom were Australians, and the 2004 attack on the Australian embassy in Indonesia, which killed ten.

In Oct. 2004, Howard won a fourth term as prime minister.

Australian External Territories

Norfolk Island (13.36 sq mi; 34.6 sq km) was placed under Australian administration in 1914. Population 1,828 (July 2005 est.). Formerly a notorious penal colony, Norfolk Island became home to the entire population of Pitcairn Island in 1856. The 194 residents of tiny Pitcairn—all of whom were the descendants of the mutineers from the HMS *Bounty* and their Tahitian wives—embarked on the 3,700-mile journey to Norfolk because of overpopulation. Many Norfolk residents can trace their genealogy directly to the adventurers from *Bounty*.

Ashmore and Cartier Islands (1.93 sq mi), situated in the Indian Ocean off the northwest coast of Australia, came under Australian administration in 1934.

Heard Island and the McDonald Islands (159 sq mi; 412 sq km), lying in the sub-Antarctic, were placed under Australian administration in 1947. The islands are uninhabited.

Christmas Island (52 sq mi; 135 sq km) is situated in the Indian Ocean. It came under Australian administration in 1958. Most of the island is now a national park. The population is 361 (2005 est.).

Coral Sea Islands (400,000 sq mi; 1,036,000 sq km, but only a few sq mi of land) became a territory of Australia in 1969. There is no permanent population on the islands.

Cocos (Keeling) Islands are made up of a group of 27 small coral islands in two separate atolls in the Indian Ocean, 1,721 mi (2,768 km) northwest of Perth. West Island is the largest, about 6.2 mi (10 km) long. The islands became an Australian territory in 1955. In April 1984 the residents voted to merge with Australia. The population of the Cocos is 628 (July 2005 est.).

Austria

REPUBLIC OF AUSTRIA

National name: Republik Österreich
President: Heinz Fischer (2004)
Chancellor: Wolfgang Schüssel (2000)
Area: 32,378 sq mi (83,858 sq km)
Population (2005 est.): 8,184,691 (growth rate: 0.1%); birth rate 8.8/1000; infant mortality rate: 4.7/1000; life expectancy: 78.9; density per sq mi: 253
Capital and largest city (2003 est.): Vienna, 2,041,300 (metro area), 1,523,600 (city proper). **Other large cities:** Graz, 219,500; Linz, 185,300; Salzburg, 145,500; Innsbruck, 115,600. **Monetary units:** Euro (formerly schilling). **Languages:** German 98% (official nationwide); Slovene, Croatian, Hungarian (each official in one region). **Ethnicity/race:** German 88.5%, recent immigrant groups 10% (includes Turks, Bosnians, Serbians, Croatians), indigenous minorities 1.5% (includes Croatians, Slovenes, Hungarians, Czechs, Slovaks, Roma) (2001). **Religions:** Roman Catholic 74%, Protestant 5%, Islam 4%, other 17%. **Literacy rate:** 98%
Economic summary: GDP/PPP (2004 est.): $255.9 billion; per capita $31,300. **Real growth rate:** 1.9%. **Inflation:** 1.8%. **Unemployment:** 4.4%. **Arable land:** 17%. **Agriculture:** grains, potatoes, sugar beets, wine, fruit; dairy products, cattle, pigs, poultry; lumber. **Labor force:** 3.45 million; services 67%, industry and crafts 29%, agriculture and forestry 4%. **Industries:** construction, machinery, vehicles and parts, food, metals, chemicals, lumber and wood processing, paper and paperboard, communications equipment, tourism. **Natural resources:** oil, coal, lignite, timber, iron ore, copper, zinc, antimony, magnesite, tungsten, graphite, salt, hydropower. **Exports:** $102.7 billion (f.o.b., 2004): machinery and equipment, motor vehicles and parts, paper and paperboard, metal goods, chemicals, iron and steel; textiles, foodstuffs. **Imports:** $101.2 billion (f.o.b., 2004 est.): machinery and equipment, motor vehicles, chemicals, metal goods, oil and oil products; foodstuffs. **Major trading partners:** Germany, Italy, Switzerland, U.S., UK, France, Hungary, Netherlands (2003).

Geography Slightly smaller than Maine, Austria includes much of the mountainous territory of the eastern Alps (about 75% of the area). The country contains many snowfields, glaciers, and snowcapped peaks, the highest being the Grossglockner (12,530 ft;

3,819 m). The Danube is the principal river. Forests and woodlands cover about 40% of the land.

Government Federal republic.

History Settled in prehistoric times, the central European land that is now Austria was overrun in pre-Roman times by various tribes, including the Celts. After the fall of the Roman Empire, of which Austria was part, the area was invaded by Bavarians and Slavic Avars. Charlemagne conquered the area in 788 and encouraged colonization and Christianity. In 1252, Ottokar, king of Bohemia, gained possession, only to lose the territories to Rudolf of Hapsburg in 1278. Thereafter, until World War I, Austria's history was largely that of its ruling house, the Hapsburgs. Austria emerged from the Congress of Vienna in 1815 as the continent's dominant power. The *Ausgleich* of 1867 provided for a dual sovereignty, the empire of Austria and the kingdom of Hungary, under Franz Joseph I, who ruled until his death on Nov. 21, 1916. The Austrian-Hungarian minority rule of this immensely diverse empire, which included German, Czech, Romanian, Serbian, and many other lands, became increasingly difficult in an age of emerging nationalist movements. When Archduke Francis Ferdinand was assassinated by a Serbian nationalist in Sarajevo in 1914, World War I, as well as the destruction of the Austro-Hungarian Empire, began.

During World War I, Austria-Hungary was one of the Central powers with Germany, Bulgaria, and Turkey, and the conflict left the country in political chaos and economic ruin. Austria, shorn of Hungary, was proclaimed a republic in 1918, and the monarchy was dissolved in 1919. A parliamentary democracy was set up by the constitution of Nov. 10, 1920. To check the power of Nazis advocating union with Germany, Chancellor Engelbert Dolfuss in 1933 established a dictatorship, but he was assassinated by the Nazis on July 25, 1934. Kurt von Schuschnigg, his successor, struggled to keep Austria independent, but on March 12, 1938, German troops occupied the country, and Hitler proclaimed its *Anschluss* (union) with Germany, annexing it to the Third Reich.

After World War II, the U.S. and Britain declared the Austrians a "liberated" people, but the Russians prolonged the occupation. Finally Austria concluded a state treaty with the USSR and the other occupying powers and regained its independence on May 15, 1955. The second Austrian republic, established Dec. 19, 1945, on the basis of the 1920 constitution (amended in 1929), was declared by the federal Parliament to be permanently neutral.

On June 8, 1986, former UN secretary-general Kurt Waldheim was elected to the ceremonial office of president in a campaign marked by controversy over his alleged links to Nazi war crimes in Yugoslavia. Austria became a member of the European Union in 1995, but it retained its strict constitutional neutrality and forbade the stationing of foreign troops on its soil.

In Feb. 2000 the conservative People's Party formed a coalition with the far-right Freedom Party, headed by Jörg Haider. A nationalist against immigration, Haider had made several controversial remarks praising some Nazi policies, which he has since recanted. His gradual rise to power was credited to voters weary of decades of stasis under the rule of the Social Democrats. The European Union condemned Austria's new coalition, froze diplomatic contacts, and imposed sanctions, accusing Haider of being a racist, xenophobe, and Nazi-sympathizer. Given the controversy, Haider chose not to join the government, but he continued to wield influence from the sidelines.

In Sept. 2002, the coalition between the People's Party and the Freedom Party dissolved after a shake-up in the Freedom Party, instigated by Haider. In Nov. 2002, the People's Party made large gains in general elections. After failed coalition talks with other parties, the People's Party again formed a government with the Freedom Party in Feb. 2003. A government plan to overhaul the country's pension program led to widespread strikes in May and June 2003—the first national strikes in decades.

In 2004, Heinz Fischer, known as the "left conscience" of the Social Democrat Party, was elected to the largely ceremonial role of president.

Azerbaijan

REPUBLIC OF AZERBAIJAN

National Name: Azarbaycan Respublikasi
President: Ilham Aliyev (2003)
Prime Minister: Artur Rasizade (2003)
Area: 33,436 sq mi (86,600 sq km)
Population (2005 est.): 7,911,974 (growth rate: 0.6%); birth rate: 20.4/1000; infant mortality rate: 81.7/1000; life expectancy: 63.4; density per sq mi: 237
Capital and largest city (2003 est.): Baku, 2,118,600 (metro area), 1,235,400 (city proper), a port on the Caspian Sea. **Other large cities (2004 est.):** Ganja, 303,000; Sumgait, 280,500. **Monetary unit:** Manat. **Languages:** Azerbaijani Turkic 89%, Russian 3%, Armenian 2%, other 6% (1995 est.). **Ethnicity/race:** Azeri 90%, Dagestani 3.2%, Russian 2.5%, Armenian 2%, other 2.3% (1998 est.). Note: almost all Armenians live in the separatist Nagorno-Karabakh region. **Religions:** Islam 93.4%, Russian Orthodox 2.5%, Armenian Orthodox 2.3%, other 1.8% (1995 est.). **Literacy rate:** 97% (1989 est.)
Economic summary: GDP/PPP (2004 est.): $30.01 billion; per capita $3,800. **Real growth rate:** 9.8%. **Inflation:** 4.6%. **Unemployment:** 1.2% (official rate). **Arable land:** 19%. **Agriculture:** cotton, grain, rice, grapes, fruit, vegetables, tea, tobacco; cattle, pigs, sheep, goats. **Labor force:** 5.09 million; agriculture and forestry 32%, industry and construction 15%, services 53% (1997). **Industries:** petroleum and natural gas, petroleum products, oilfield equipment; steel, iron ore, cement; chemicals and petrochemicals; textiles. **Natural resources:** petroleum, natural gas, iron ore, nonferrous metals, alumina. **Exports:** $3.168 billion (f.o.b., 2004 est.): oil and gas 90%, machinery, cotton, foodstuffs. **Imports:** $3.622 billion (f.o.b., 2004 est.): machinery and equipment, oil products, foodstuffs, metals, chemicals. **Major trading partners:** Italy, Czech Republic, Germany, France, Turkey, Georgia, Russia, UK, U.S., Kazakhstan (2003).

Geography Azerbaijan is located on the western shore of the Caspian Sea at the southeast extremity of the Caucasus. The region is a mountainous country, and only about 7% of it is arable land. The Kura River Valley is the area's major agricultural zone.

Government Constitutional republic.

History Northern Azerbaijan was known as Caucasian Albania in ancient times. The area was the site of many conflicts involving Arabs, Kazars, and Turks. After the 11th century, the territory became dominated by Turks and eventually was a stronghold of the Shiite Muslim religion and Islamic culture. The territory of Soviet Azerbaijan was acquired by Russia from Persia through the Treaty of Gulistan in 1813 and the Treaty of Turkamanchai in 1828.

After the Bolshevik Revolution, Azerbaijan declared its independence from Russia in May 1918. The republic was reconquered by the Red Army in 1920, and was annexed into the Transcaucasian Soviet Socialist Republic in 1922. It was later reestablished as a separate Soviet Republic on Dec. 5, 1936. Azerbaijan declared independence from the collapsing Soviet Union on Aug. 30, 1991.

Since 1988, Azerbaijan and Armenia have been feuding over the enclave of Nagorno-Karabakh. The majority of the enclave's inhabitants are Armenian Christians agitating to secede from the predominantly Muslim Azerbaijan and join with Armenia. War broke out in 1988 when Nagorno-Karabakh tried to break away and annex itself to Armenia, and 30,000 died before a cease-fire agreement was reached in 1994, with Armenia regaining its hold over the disputed enclave. Final plans on the status of Nagorno-Karabakh have yet to be determined.

The country's economic troubles are expected to be transformed through Western investment in Azerbaijan's oil resources, an untapped reserve whose estimated worth is trillions of dollars. Since 1994, the Azerbaijan state oil company (SOCAR) has signed several billion-dollar agreements with international oil companies. Azerbaijan's pro-Western stance and its careful economic management have made it the most attractive of the oil-rich Caspian countries for foreign investment. In the years since its independence, the country has undergone rapid privatization, and the IMF gave it high marks as one of the most successful economic overhauls ever. In Sept. 2002, construction of the 1,100-mile Baku-Tblisi-Ceyhan pipeline (a route through Georgia and Turkey) began. Major investors are Britain's BP (33%), Azerbaijan's SOCAR (25%), the U.S.'s Unocal (8.9%), and Norway's Statoil (8.7%). In May 2005, the first section of the pipeline opened.

In 2003, President Heydar Aliyev, who was seriously ill, chose his son as the new prime minister, paving the way for his eventual succession. The opposition protested strenuously. In October elections, the president's son, Ilham Aliyev, was elected president. Heydar Aliyev died in December.

Bahamas

COMMONWEALTH OF THE BAHAMAS

Sovereign: Queen Elizabeth II (1952)
Governor-General: Ivy Dumont (2001)
Prime Minister: Perry Christie (2002)
Area: 5,382 sq mi (13,940 sq km)
Population (2005 est.): 301,790 (growth rate: 0.7%); birth rate: 17.9/1000; infant mortality rate: 25.2/1000; life expectancy: 65.5; density per sq mi: 56
Capital and largest city (2003 est.): Nassau, 222,200. **Monetary unit:** Bahamian dollar. **Languages:** English (official), Creole (among Haitian immigrants). **Ethnicity/race:** black 85%, white 12%, Asian and Hispanic 3%. **Religions:** Baptist 32%, Anglican 20%, Roman Catholic 19%, Methodist 6%, Church of God 6%, other Protestant 12%. **Literacy rate:** 98.2% (1995 est.)
Economic summary: GDP/PPP (2004 est.): $5.295 billion; per capita $17,700. **Real growth rate:** 3%. **Inflation:** 1.2%. **Unemployment:** 10.2%. **Arable land:** 1%. **Agriculture:** citrus, vegetables; poultry. **Labor force:** 156,000 (1999); tourism 40%, other services 50%, industry 5%, agriculture 5% (1995 est.). **Industries:** tourism, banking, cement, oil transshipment, salt, rum, aragonite, pharmaceuticals, spiral-welded steel pipe. **Natural resources:** salt, aragonite, timber, arable land. **Exports:** $636 million (2003 est.): mineral products and salt, animal products, rum, chemicals; fruit and vegetables. **Imports:** $1.63 billion (2003): machinery and transport

equipment, manufactures, chemicals, mineral fuels; food and live animals. **Major trading partners:** U.S., Spain, Germany, France, Poland, Switzerland, Peru, Paraguay, South Korea, Italy, Brazil, Japan, Venezuela (2003). **Member of Commonwealth of Nations**

Geography The Bahamas are an archipelago of about 700 islands and 2,400 uninhabited islets and cays lying 50 mi off the east coast of Florida. They extend for about 760 mi (1,223 km). Only about 30 of the islands are inhabited; the most important is New Providence (80 sq mi; 207 sq km), on which the capital, Nassau, is situated. Other islands include Grand Bahama, Abaco, Eleuthera, Andros, Cat Island, and San Salvador (or Watling's Island).

Government Parliamentary democracy.

History The Arawak Indians were the first inhabitants of the Bahamas. Columbus's first encounter with the New World was on Oct. 12, 1492, when he landed on the Bahamian island of San Salvador. The British first built settlements on the islands in the 17th century. In the early 18th century, the Bahamas were a favorite pirate haunt.

The Bahamas were a Crown colony from 1717 until they were granted internal self-government in 1964. The islands moved toward greater autonomy in 1968 after the overwhelming victory in general elections of the Progressive Liberal Party, led by Prime Minister Lynden O. Pindling, over the predominantly white United Bahamians Party. With its new mandate from the black population (85% of Bahamians), Pindling's government negotiated a new constitution with Britain under which the colony became the Commonwealth of the Bahama Islands in 1969. On July 10, 1973, the Bahamas became an independent nation.

Once heavily reliant on agriculture and fishing, the Bahamas has diversified its economy into tourism, financial services, and international shipping. While it enjoys a per capita income that is among the top 30 in the world, there is a big gap between the urban middle class and poor farmers. In addition, the nation is vulnerable to hurricanes, which regularly inflict serious damage.

Bahrain

KINGDOM OF BAHRAIN

National Name: Mamlakat al Bahrayn
King: Hamad ibn Isa al-Khalifah (1999)
Prime Minister: Khalifah ibn Sulman al-Khalifah (1970)
Area: 257 sq mi (665 sq km)
Population (2005 est.): 688,345 (growth rate: 1.5%); birth rate: 18.1/1000; infant mortality rate: 17.3/1000; life expectancy: 74.2; density per sq mi: 2,681
Capital and largest city (2003 est.): Al-Manámah, 527,000 (metro area), 149,900 (city proper). **Monetary unit:** Bahrain dinar. **Languages:** Arabic, English, Farsi, Urdu. **Ethnicity/race:** Bahraini 63%, Asian 19%, other Arab 10%, Iranian 8%. **Religion:** Islam (Shiite 70%, Sunni 30%). **Literacy rate:** 89% (2003 est.)
Economic summary: GDP/PPP (2004 est): $13.01 billion; per capita $19,200. **Real growth rate:** 5.6%. **Inflation:** 2.1%. **Unemployment:** 15% (1998 est.). **Arable land:** 3%. **Agriculture:** fruit, vegetables; poultry, dairy products; shrimp, fish. **Labor force:** 370,000; note: 44% of the population in the 15–64 age group is non-national; industry, commerce, and service 79%, government 20%, agriculture 1% (1997 est.).
Industries: petroleum processing and refining, aluminum smelting, iron pelletization, fertilizers, offshore banking, ship repairing; tourism. **Natural resources:** oil, associated and nonassociated natural gas, fish, pearls.
Exports: $8.205 billion (2004 est.): petroleum and petroleum products, aluminum, textiles. **Imports:** $5.87 billion (2004 est.): crude oil, machinery, chemicals. **Major trading partners:** U.S., South Korea, Saudi Arabia, Japan, UK, Germany (2003).

Geography Bahrain, which means "two seas," is an archipelago in the Persian Gulf off the coast of Saudi Arabia. The islands for the most part are level expanses of sand and rock. A causeway connects Bahrain to Saudi Arabia.

Government Constitutional monarchy.

History Known in ancient times as Dilmun, Bahrain was an important center of trade by the 3rd millennium B.C. The islands were ruled by the Persians in the 4th century A.D., and then by Arabs until 1541, when the Portuguese invaded them. Persia again claimed Bahrain in 1602. In 1783 Ahmad ibn al-Khalifah took over, and the al-Khalifahs remain the ruling family today. Bahrain became a British protectorate in 1820. It did not gain full independence until Aug. 14, 1971.

Although oil was discovered in Bahrain in the 1930s, it was relatively little compared to other Gulf states, and the wells are expected to be the first in the region to dry up. Sheik Isa ibn Sulman al-Khalifah, who became emir in 1961, was determined to diversify his country's economy, and he set about establishing Bahrain as a major financial center. The country provides its people with free medical care, education, and old-age pensions.

Conflicts between the Shiites and Sunnis are a continuing problem in Bahrain. The Sunni minority, to which the ruling al-Khalifah family belongs, controls nearly all the power and wealth in the country. Shiite Muslims have continued to agitate for more representation in government, and minor violent clashes have led to about two dozen deaths since 1994.

Bahrain has been an important Western ally, serving as a Western air base during the Persian Gulf War in 1991 and the Iraq war in 2003. It continues to serve as the base of the United States' Fifth Fleet, which patrols the Gulf.

The emir, Sheik Isa ibn Sulman al-Khalifah, died in 1999 after four decades of rule. He was succeeded by his son, Sheik Hamad ibn Isa al-Khalifah, who gave himself the title of king but also began a sweeping democratization of the country: censorship has been relaxed and draconian laws repealed, exiles have been repatriated, and the stateless Bidoons have been granted citizenship. In a Feb. 2001 referendum, which permitted women to vote for the first time, Bahrainis overwhelmingly supported the transformation of the traditional monarchy into a constitutional one. In Oct. 2002, Bahrain had its first parliamentary election since 1973.

Bangladesh

PEOPLE'S REPUBLIC OF BANGLADESH

President: Iajuddin Ahmed (2002)
Prime Minister: Khaleda Zia (2001)
Area: 55,598 sq mi (144,000 sq km)
Population (2005 est.): 144,319,628 (growth rate: 2.1%); birth rate: 30.0/1000; infant mortality rate: 62.6/1000; life expectancy: 62.1; density per sq mi: 2,596
Capital and largest city (2003 est.): Dhaka, 10,356,500 (metro.area), 8,942,300 (city proper). **Other large cities:** Chittagong, 2,592,400; Khulna, 1,211,500. **Monetary unit:** Taka. **Principal languages:** Bangla (official), English. **Ethnicity/race:** Bengali 98%, tribal groups, non-Bengali Muslims (1998). **Religions:** Islam 83%, Hindu 16%, other 1%. **Literacy rate:** 43% (2003 est.)

Economic summary: GDP/PPP (2004 est.): $275.7 billion; per capita $2,000. **Real growth rate:** 4.9%. **Inflation:** 6%. **Unemployment:** 40% (includes underemployment). **Arable land:** 62%. **Agriculture:** rice, jute, tea, wheat, sugarcane, potatoes, tobacco, pulses, oilseeds, spices, fruit; beef, milk, poultry. **Labor force:** 65.49 million; note: extensive export of labor to Saudi Arabia, Kuwait, UAE, Oman, Qatar, and Malaysia; agriculture 63%, services 26%, industry 11% (FY95/96). **Industries:** cotton textiles, jute, garments, tea processing, paper newsprint, cement, chemical fertilizer, light engineering, sugar. **Natural resources:** natural gas, arable land, timber, coal. **Exports:** $7.478 billion (2004 est.): garments, jute and jute goods, leather, frozen fish and seafood (2001). **Imports:** $10.03 billion (2004 est.): machinery and equipment, chemicals, iron and steel, textiles, foodstuffs, petroleum products, cement (2000). **Major trading partners:** U.S., Germany, UK, France, India, China, Singapore, Japan, Hong Kong (2003). **Member of Commonwealth of Nations**

Geography Bangladesh, on the northern coast of the Bay of Bengal, is surrounded by India, with a small common border with Myanmar in the southeast. The country is low-lying riverine land traversed by the many branches and tributaries of the Ganges and Brahmaputra Rivers. Tropical monsoons and frequent floods and cyclones inflict heavy damage in the delta region.

Government Parliamentary democracy.

History What is now called Bangladesh is part of the historic region of Bengal, the northeast portion of the Indian subcontinent. Bangladesh consists primarily of East Bengal (West Bengal is part of India and its people are primarily Hindu) plus the Sylhet district of the Indian state of Assam.

The earliest reference to the region was to a kingdom called Vanga, or Banga (c. 1000 B.C.). Buddhists ruled for centuries, but by the 10th century Bengal was primarily Hindu. In 1576, Bengal became part of the Mogul Empire, and the majority of East Bengalis converted to Islam. Bengal was ruled by British India from 1757 until Britain withdrew in 1947, and Pakistan was founded out of the two predominantly Muslim regions of the Indian subcontinent. For almost 25 years after independence from Britain, its history was part of Pakistan's (*see* Pakistan).

West Pakistan and East Pakistan were united by religion (Islam), but their peoples were separated by culture, physical features, and 1,000 miles of Indian territory.

Tension between East and West Pakistan developed from the outset because of their vast geographic, economic, and cultural differences. East Pakistan's Awami League, a political party founded by the Bengali nationalist Sheik Mujibur Rahman in 1949, sought independence from West Pakistan. Although 56% of the population resided in East Pakistan, the West held the lion's share of political and economic power. In 1970 East Pakistanis secured a majority of the seats in the National Assembly. President Yahya Khan postponed the opening of the National Assembly in an attempt to circumvent East Pakistan's demand for greater autonomy. As a consequence East Pakistan seceded, and the independent state of Bangladesh, or Bengali nation, was proclaimed on March 26, 1971. Civil war broke out, and with the help of Indian troops in the last few weeks of the war, East Pakistan defeated West Pakistan on Dec. 16, 1971. An estimated 1 million Bengalis were killed in the fighting or later slaughtered. Ten million more took refuge in India. In Feb.

1974, Pakistan agreed to recognize the independent state of Bangladesh.

Founding president Sheikh Mujibur was assassinated in 1975, as was the next president, Zia ur-Rahman. On March 24, 1982, Gen. Hossain Mohammad Ershad, army chief of staff, took control in a bloodless coup but was forced to resign on Dec. 6, 1990, amid violent protests and numerous allegations of corruption. A succession of prime ministers governed in the 1990s, including Khaleda Zia, wife of the assassinated president Zia ur-Rahman, and Sheikh Hasina Wazed, the daughter of Sheik Mujibur.

Prime Minister Sheikh Hasina completed her five-year term as prime minister in July 2000—the first leader to do so since the country gained independence from Pakistan in 1974. In Oct. 2001 elections, Khaleda Zia again won the prime ministership.

A grenade attack in the northeast killed Awami League leader and finance minister Shah AMS Kibria and four other party officials in Jan. 2005. In response, the opposition organized a three-day general strike. Two people died and dozens were wounded when about 400 small bombs exploded simultaneously across the country on Aug. 17, 2005. An outlawed Islamic group, Jamatul Myjahideen Bangladesh, claimed responsibility.

Barbados

Sovereign: Queen Elizabeth II (1952)
Governor-General: Sir Clifford Husbands (1996)
Prime Minister: Owen Arthur (1994)
Area: 166 sq mi (431 sq km)
Population (2005 est.): 279,254 (growth rate: 0.3%); birth rate: 12.8/1000; infant mortality rate: 12.5/1000; life expectancy: 71.4; density per sq mi: 1,678
Capital and largest city (2003 est.): Bridgetown, 98,900. **Monetary unit:** Barbados dollar. **Language:** English. **Ethnicity/race:** black 90%, white 4%, Asian and mixed 6%. **Religions:** Protestant 67% (Anglican 40%, Pentecostal 8%, Methodist 7%, other 12%), Roman Catholic 4%, none 17%, other 12%. **Literacy rate:** 97% (1995 est.)
Economic summary: GDP/PPP (2004 est.): $4.569 billion; per capita: $16,400. **Real growth rate:** 2.3%. **Inflation:** –0.5%. **Unemployment:** 10.7% (2003 est.). **Arable land:** 37%. **Agriculture:** sugarcane, vegetables, cotton. **Labor force:** 128,500 (2001 est.); services 75%, industry 15%, agriculture 10% (1996 est.). **Industries:** tourism, sugar, light manufacturing, component assembly for export. **Natural resources:** petroleum, fish, natural gas. **Exports:** $206 million (2002): sugar and molasses, rum, other foods and beverages, chemicals, electrical components. **Imports:** $1.039 billion (2002): consumer goods, machinery, foodstuffs, construction materials, chemicals, fuel, electrical components. **Major trading partners:** U.S., Trinidad and Tobago, UK, Jamaica, St. Lucia, St. Vincent and the Grenadines, Japan (2003). **Member of Commonwealth of Nations**

Geography An island in the Atlantic about 300 mi (483 km) north of Venezuela, Barbados is only 21 mi long (34 km) and 14 mi across (23 km) at its widest point. It is circled by fine beaches and narrow coastal plains. The highest point is Mount Hillaby (1,105 ft; 337 m) in the north-central area.

Government Parliamentary democracy.

History Barbados is thought to have been originally inhabited by Arawak Indians. By the time Europeans explored the island, however, it was uninhabited. The Portuguese were the first Europeans to set foot on the island, but it was the British who first established a colony there in 1627. Colonists first cultivated tobacco and cotton, but by the 1640s they had switched to sugar, which was enormously profitable. Slaves were brought in from Africa to work sugar plantations, and eventually the population was about 90% black. A slave revolt took place in 1816; slavery was abolished in the British Empire in 1834.

Barbados was the administrative headquarters of the Windward Islands until it became a separate colony in 1885. Barbados was a member of the Federation of the West Indies from 1958 to 1962. Britain granted the colony independence on Nov. 30, 1966, and it became a parliamentary democracy within the Commonwealth.

Since independence, Barbados has been politically stable. However, local anger over rulings by the final appeals court, appointed by Queen Elizabeth, led to the creation in 1997 of a constitutional commission to consider abandoning all ties to Great Britain. In May 2003, Prime Minister Arthur won a third term.

Belarus

REPUBLIC OF BELARUS

National Name: Respublika Byelarus'
President: Alyaksandr Lukashenka (1994)
Prime Minister: Syarhey Sidorski (2003)
Area: 80,154 sq mi (207,600 sq km)
Population (2005 est.): 10,300,483 (growth rate: –0.1%); birth rate: 10.8/1000; infant mortality rate: 13.4/1000; life expectancy: 68.7; density per sq mi: 129
Capital and largest city (2003 est.): Mensk (Minsk), 1,769,500. **Other large cities:** Gomel, 502,200; Mogilyov, 374,000; Vitebsk, 355,800; Grodno, 314,100; Brest, 306,300; Bobruysk, 228,100. **Monetary unit:** Belorussian ruble. **Languages:** Belorussian (White Russian), Russian, other. **Ethnicity/race:** Belorussian 81.2%, Russian 11.4%, Polish, Ukrainian, and other 7.4%. **Religion:** Eastern Orthodox 80%, other (including Roman Catholic, Protestant, Jewish, and Muslim) 20% (1997 est.). **Literacy rate:** 100% (2003 est.)
Economic summary: GDP/PPP (2004 est.): $70.5 billion; per capita $6,800. **Real growth rate:** 6.4%. **Inflation:** 17.4%. **Unemployment:** 2% officially registered unemployed (2004); large number of underemployed workers. **Arable land:** 30%. **Agriculture:** grain, potatoes, vegetables, sugar beets, flax; beef, milk. **Labor force:** 4.305 million (Dec. 31, 2003); agriculture 14%, industry 34.7%, services 51.3% (2003 est.). **Industries:** metal-cutting machine tools, tractors, trucks, earthmovers, motorcycles, televisions, chemical fibers, fertilizer, textiles, radios, refrigerators. **Natural resources:** forests, peat deposits, small quantities of oil and natural gas, granite, dolomitic limestone, marl, chalk, sand, gravel, clay. **Exports:** $11.47 billion (f.o.b., 2004 est.): machinery and equipment, mineral products, chemicals, metals; textiles, foodstuffs. **Imports:** $13.57 billion (f.o.b., 2004 est.): mineral products, machinery and equipment, chemicals, foodstuffs, metals. **Major trading partners:** Russia, UK, Poland, Germany, Netherlands, Ukraine (2003).

Geography Much of Belarus (formerly the Belorussian Soviet Socialist Republic of the USSR, and then Byelorussia) is a hilly lowland with forests, swamps, and numerous rivers and lakes. There are wide rivers emptying into the Baltic and Black Seas. Its forests cover over one-third of the land and its peat marshes are a valuable natural resource. The largest lake is Narach, 31 sq mi (79.6 sq km).

Government Republic.

History In the 5th century A.D., Belarus (also known as White Russia) was colonized by east Slavic tribes. Kiev dominated it from the 9th to 12th centuries. After the destruction of Kiev by the Mongols in the 13th century, the territory was conquered by the dukes of Lithuania, although it retained a degree of autonomy. Belarus became part of the Grand Duchy of Lithuania, which merged with Poland in 1569. Following the partitions of Poland in 1772, 1793, and 1795, in which Poland was divided among Russia, Prussia, and Austria, Belarus became part of the Russian empire.

Following World War I, Belarus proclaimed itself a republic, only to find itself occupied by the Red Army soon after its March 1918 announcement. The Polish-Soviet War of 1918–1921 was fought to decide the fate of Belarus. West Belarus was ceded to Poland; the larger eastern part formed the Belorussian SSR, and was then joined to the USSR in 1922. In 1939, the Soviet Union took back West Belarus from Poland under the secret protocol of the Nazi-Soviet Nonaggression Pact and incorporated it into the Belorussian Soviet Socialist Republic. Occupied by the Nazis in World War II, Belarus was one of the war's most devastated battlefields.

When the Chernobyl nuclear power plant in Ukraine exploded in 1986, 70% of its radioactivity fell on the Belorussian SSR. Cancer and other illnesses have multiplied as a result.

Belarus declared its sovereignty in July 1990 and its independence in Aug. 1991. It became a cofounder of the Commonwealth of Independent States (CIS) in Dec. 1991. In Jan. 1994, the country's Parliament ousted its reform-minded leader, Stanislav Shushkevich, in protest against his support for market economics. He was replaced by Alyaksandr Lukashenka, who over the next two years greatly expanded the powers of the presidency. Lukashenka sought to renew ties with Russia, and, with much fanfare, Belarus and Russia signed a treaty in April 1997 aimed at significantly increasing cooperation between the two states, stopping just short of union. The Russian financial crisis that began in fall 1998 severely affected Belarus's Soviet-style planned economy.

The EU and the U.S. have denounced the increasingly oppressive political atmosphere and human rights violations in Belarus under the Soviet-style authoritarianism of President Lukashenka. In 1999, the year Lukashenka was to step down, he rigged a national referendum allowing him to cancel the elections and remain president. Lukashenka's government has been accused of running a death squad that has killed dozens, including opposition party members and underworld figures. After harassing the opposition and curtailing their campaign activities, Lukashenka won reelection in the Sept. 9, 2001, presidential race. In 2004, the Council of Europe strongly criticized the Belarus government for blocking investigation into the disappearance of four dissidents in 1999 and 2000.

Belgium

KINGDOM OF BELGIUM

National name: Royaume de Belgique—Koninkrijk België
Sovereign: King Albert II (1993)
Prime Minister: Guy Verhofstadt (1999)
Area: 11,780 sq mi (30,510 sq km)
Population (2005 est.): 10,364,388 (growth rate: 0.2%); birth rate: 10.5/1000; infant mortality rate: 4.7/1000; life expectancy: 78.6; density per sq mi: 880
Capital and largest city (2003 est.): Brussels, 1,750,600 (metro area), 981,200 (city proper). **Other large cities:** Antwerp, 952,600 (metro area), 450,000

(city proper); Ghent, 226,900; Charleroi, 201,200; Liège, 185,700; Bruges, 117,200. **Monetary units:** Euro (formerly Belgian franc). **Languages:** Dutch (Flemish) 60%, French 40%, German less than 1% (all official). **Ethnicity/race:** Fleming, Walloon, mixed, or other . **Religion:** Roman Catholic 75%, Protestant or other 25%. **Literacy rate:** 98% (2003 est.)

Economic summary: GDP/PPP (2004 est.): $316.2 billion; per capita $30,600. **Real growth rate:** 2.6%. **Inflation:** 1.9%. **Unemployment:** 12% (first half, 2004 est.). **Arable land:** 23%. **Agriculture:** sugar beets, fresh vegetables, fruits, grain, tobacco; beef, veal, pork, milk. **Labor force:** 4.75 million; agriculture 1.3%, industry 24.5%, services 74.2% (2003 est.). **Industries:** engineering and metal products, motor vehicle assembly, transportation equipment, scientific instruments, processed food and beverages, chemicals, basic metals, textiles, glass, petroleum. **Natural resources:** coal, natural gas, construction materials, silica sand, carbonates. **Exports:** $255.7 billion (f.o.b., 2003 est.): machinery and equipment, chemicals, diamonds, metals and metal products, foodstuffs. **Imports:** $235 billion (f.o.b., 2003 est.): machinery and equipment, chemicals, diamonds, pharmaceuticals, foodstuffs, transportation equipment, oil products. **Major trading partners:** Germany, France, Netherlands, UK, U.S., Italy, Ireland (2003).

Geography Located in western Europe, Belgium has about 40 mi of seacoast on the North Sea, at the Strait of Dover, and is approximately the size of Maryland. The Meuse and the Schelde, Belgium's principal rivers, are important commercial arteries.

Government Parliamentary democracy under a constitutional monarch. Under the 1994 constitution, autonomy was granted to the Walloon region (Wallonia), the Flemish region (Flanders), and the bilingual Brussels-Capital region; autonomy was also guaranteed for the Flemish-, French-, and German-speaking "communities." The central government retains responsibility for foreign policy, defense, taxation, and social security.

History Belgium occupies part of the Roman province of Belgica, named after the Belgae, a people of ancient Gaul. The area was conquered by Julius Caesar in 57–50 B.C., then was overrun by the Franks in the 5th century A.D. It was part of Charlemagne's empire in the 8th century, then in the next century was absorbed into Lotharingia and later into the duchy of Lower Lorraine. In the 12th century it was partitioned into the duchies of Brabant and Luxembourg, the bishopric of Liège, and the domain of the count of Hainaut, which included Flanders. In the 15th century, most of the low countries (currently the Netherlands, Belgium and Luxembourg) passed to the duchy of Burgundy and were subsequently inherited by Emperor Charles V. When the latter abdicated in 1555, they went to his son Philippe II, King of Spain. While the northern part, now the Netherlands, gained its independence in the following decades, the southern part remained under Spanish control until 1713, when it was transferred to Austria. During the wars that followed the French Revolution, Belgium was occupied and later annexed to France. But with the downfall of Napoléon, the Congress of Vienna in 1815 reunited the Low Countries under the rule of the King of Holland.

Germany's invasion of Belgium in 1914 set off World War I. The Treaty of Versailles (1919) gave the areas of Eupen, Malmédy, and Moresnet to Belgium. Leopold III succeeded Albert, king during World War I, in 1934. In World War II, Belgium was overwhelmed by Nazi Germany, and Leopold III was held prisoner.

When he returned at the government's invitation after a narrowly favorable referendum, riots broke out in several cities. He abdicated on July 16, 1951, and his son, Baudouin, became king. Because of growing opposition to Belgian rule in its African colonies, Belgium granted independence to the Congo (now Democratic Republic of the Congo) in 1960 and to Ruanda-Urundi (now the nations of Rwanda and Burundi) in 1962.

Since 1958, when the European Economic Community was born, Brussels, the country's capital, has gradually established itself as the de facto capital of what has now become the European Union (EU), a role that became official in Dec. 2000 when the European Council of heads of government decided to hold all its regular meetings in Brussels. As a result, the city has become home not only to nearly 20,000 European civil servants, but to an even more numerous community of lobbyists, lawyers, and other professionals drawn to the EU's main decision center.

Growing divisions between Flemings and Walloons, and devolution along linguistic lines, culminated in the revised constitution of 1994, which turned Belgium into a federal state with significant autonomy for its three regions and its three language "communities."

In the 1990s Belgium's public life was shaken by a number of serious scandals. In 1991, a former deputy prime minister and socialist leader was murdered in a contract killing that took several years to be elucidated. In 1998, along with two other major Belgian politicians, former NATO secretary-general Willy Claes was convicted of bribery. The Dutroux child sex-and-murder affair in 1996 led to national outrage, compounded by the realization that less official negligence and inefficiency could have saved the lives of several children. It fueled pressure for reform of the political, judicial, and police systems. In 1999, a public health scandal involving Dioxin, a cancer-causing chemical, resulted in the unexpected electoral defeat of Christian-Democratic prime minister Jean-Luc Dehaene.

In June 1999, the new prime minister, Guy Verhofstadt of the Liberal Party, cobbled together a coalition of liberals, socialists and greens, which was continued, without the green parties, after the May 2003 election. His government passed extremely liberal social policies, including the legalization of gay marriage and euthanasia, and the partial decriminalization of marijuana. Against the wishes of the Prime Minister's Party, a parliamentary majority also extended voting rights at local elections to all foreign residents.

In Nov. 2004, a Belgian court ruled that the far-right party Vlaams Blok, a nationalist and anti-immigration party that accounts for over 20% of the vote in Flanders, was guilty of violating antiracism laws, and thus ineligible for funding or television access. The party has since changed its name to Vlaam Belang ("Flemish interest") and attempted to cleanse its party program.

Belize

Sovereign: Queen Elizabeth II (1952)
Governor-General: Sir Colville Young (1993)
Prime Minister: Said Musa (1998)
Area: 8,867 sq mi (22,966 sq km)
Population (2005 est.): 279,457 (growth rate: 2.3%); birth rate: 29.3/1000; infant mortality rate: 25.7/1000; life expectancy: 67.5; density per sq mi: 32
Capital (2003 est.): Belmopan, 8,700. **Largest city:** Belize City, 52,600. **Monetary unit:** Belize dollar.
Languages: English (official), Spanish, Mayan, Garifuna (Carib), Creole. **Ethnicity/race:** mestizo 48.7%, Creole 24.9%, Maya 10.6%, Garifuna 6.1%, other 9.7%.

Religions: Roman Catholic 49.6%, Protestant 27% (Anglican 5.3%, Methodist 3.5%, Mennonite 4.1%, Seventh-Day Adventist 5.2%, Pentecostal 7.4%, Jehovah's Witnesses 1.5%), none 9.4%, other 14%. **Literacy rate:** 94% (2003 est.)

Economic summary: GDP/PPP (2004 est.): $1.778 billion; per capita $6,500. **Real growth rate:** 3.5%. **Inflation:** 2.9%. **Unemployment:** 12.9% (2003). **Arable land:** 3%. **Agriculture:** bananas, coca, citrus, sugar; fish, cultured shrimp; lumber; garments. **Labor force:** 90,000; note: shortage of skilled labor and all types of technical personnel; agriculture 27%, industry 18%, services 55% (2001 est.). **Industries:** garment production, food processing, tourism, construction. **Natural resources:** arable land potential, timber, fish, hydropower. **Exports:** $401.4 million (f.o.b., 2004 est.): sugar, bananas, citrus, clothing, fish products, molasses, wood. **Imports:** $579.9 million (f.o.b., 2004 est.): machinery and transport equipment, manufactured goods; fuels, chemicals, pharmaceuticals; food, beverages, tobacco. **Major trading partners:** U.S., UK, France, Mexico, Cuba (2003). **Member of Commonwealth of Nations**

Geography Belize is situated on the Caribbean Sea, south of Mexico and east and north of Guatemala in Central America. In area, it is about the size of New Hampshire. Most of the country is heavily forested with various hardwoods. Mangrove swamps and cays along the coast give way to hills and mountains in the interior. The highest point is Victoria Peak, 3,681 ft (1,122 m).

Government Parliamentary democracy within the British Commonwealth.

History The Mayan civilization spread into the area of Belize between 1500 B.C. and A.D. 300 and flourished until about 1200. Several major archeological sites—notably Caracol, Lamanai, Lubaantun, Altun Ha, and Xunantunich—reflect the advanced civilization and much denser population of that period. European contact began in 1502 when Columbus sailed along the coast. The first recorded European settlement was begun by shipwrecked English seamen in 1638. Over the next 150 years, more English settlements were established. This period was also marked by piracy, indiscriminate logging, and sporadic attacks by Indians and neighboring Spanish settlements. Both Spain and Britain lay claim to the land until Britain defeated the Spanish in the battle of St. George's Cay (1798). It became a colony of Great Britain in 1840, known as British Honduras, and a Crown colony in 1862. Full internal self-government was granted in Jan. 1964. In 1973, the country changed its name to Belize.

Belize became independent on Sept. 21, 1981. But Guatemala, which had made claims on the territory since the 1800s, refused to recognize it. British troops remained in the country to defend it. Although the dispute between Guatemala and Great Britain remained unresolved, Guatemala recognized Belize's sovereignty in Sept. 1991. Guatemala, however, still claims more than half of Belize's territory.

Prime Minister Said Musa was reelected to a second term in 2003.

Benin

REPUBLIC OF BENIN

National name: Republique du Benin
President: Mathieu Kérékou (1996)
Area: 43,483 sq mi (112,620 sq km)
Population (2005 est.): 7,460,025 (growth rate: 2.8%); birth rate: 42.0/1000; infant mortality rate: 85.0/1000; life expectancy: 50.5; density per sq mi: 172

Capital (2003 est.): Porto-Novo (official), 231,600. **Largest cities:** Cotonou (de facto capital) 734,600; Parakou 205,300; Djougou, 184,200. **Monetary unit:** CFA Franc. **Languages:** French (official), Fon, Yoruba, tribal languages. **Ethnicity/race:** African 99% (42 ethnic groups, most important being Fon, Adja, Yoruba, Bariba), Europeans 5,500. **Religions:** indigenous 50%, Christian 30%, Islam 20%. **Literacy rate:** 41% (2000)

Economic summary: GDP/PPP (2004 est.): $8.338 billion; per capita $1,200. **Real growth rate:** 5%. **Inflation:** 2.8%. **Unemployment:** n.a. **Arable land:** 18%. **Agriculture:** cotton, corn, cassava (tapioca), yams, beans, palm oil, peanuts, livestock (2001). **Labor force:** n.a. **Industries:** textiles, food processing, chemical production, construction materials (2001). **Natural resources:** small offshore oil deposits, limestone, marble, timber. **Exports:** $720.9 million (f.o.b., 2004 est.): cotton, crude oil, palm products, cocoa. **Imports:** $934.5 million (f.o.b., 2004 est.): foodstuffs, capital goods, petroleum products. **Major trading partners:** China, India, Thailand, Ghana, Niger, Indonesia, Nigeria, Italy, France, UK, Côte d'Ivoire, Thailand (2003).

Geography This West African nation on the Gulf of Guinea, between Togo on the west and Nigeria on the east, is about the size of Tennessee. It is bounded also by Burkina Faso and Niger on the north. The land consists of a narrow coastal strip that rises to a swampy, forested plateau and then to highlands in the north. A hot and humid climate blankets the entire country.

Government Republic under a multiparty democratic rule.

History The Abomey kingdom of the Dahomey, or Fon, peoples was established in 1625. A rich cultural life flourished, and Dahomey's wooden masks, bronze statues, tapestries, and pottery are world renowned. One of the smallest and most densely populated regions in Africa, Dahomey was annexed by the French in 1893 and incorporated into French West Africa in 1904. It became an autonomous republic within the French Community in 1958, and on Aug. 1, 1960, Dahomey was granted its independence within the Community.

Gen. Christophe Soglo deposed the first president, Hubert Maga, in an army coup in 1963. He dismissed the civilian government in 1965, proclaiming himself chief of state. A group of young army officers seized power in Dec. 1967, deposing Soglo. In Dec. 1969, Benin had its fifth coup of the decade, with the army again taking power. In May 1970, a three-man presidential commission with a six-year term was created to take over the government. In May 1972, yet another army coup ousted the triumvirate and installed Lt. Col. Mathieu Kérékou as president. Between 1974 and 1989 Dahomey embraced socialism, and changed its name to the People's Republic of Benin. The name *Benin* commemorates an African kingdom that flourished from the 15th to the 17th century in what is now southwest Nigeria. In 1990, Benin abandoned Marxist ideology, began moving toward multiparty democracy, and changed its name again, to the Republic of Benin.

By the end of the 1980s, Benin's economy was near collapse. As its oil boom ended, Nigeria expelled 100,000 Beninese migrant workers and closed the border with Benin. Kérékou's socialist collectivization of Benin's agriculture and the ballooning bureaucracy further damaged the economy. By 1988, international financial institutions feared Benin would default on its loans and pressured Kérékou to make financial reforms.

Kérékou subsequently embarked on a major privatization campaign, cut the government payroll, and reduced social services, prompting student and labor union unrest. Fearing a revolution, Kérékou agreed to a new constitution and free elections. In 1991, Nicéphore Soglo, an economist and former director of the International Bank for Reconstruction and Development, was elected president. Although he enjoyed widespread support at first, Soglo gradually became unpopular as austerity measures reduced living standards and a 50% currency devaluation in 1994 caused inflation. Kérékou defeated Soglo in the 1996 elections and was easily reelected in March 2001.

Bhutan

KINGDOM OF BHUTAN

Ruler: King Jigme Singye Wangchuck (1972)
Prime Minister: Lyonpo Yeshey Zimba (2004)
Area: 18,147 sq mi (47,000 sq km)
Population (2005 est.): 2,232,291 (growth rate: 2.1%); birth rate: 34.0/1000; infant mortality rate: 100.4/1000; life expectancy: 54.4; density per sq mi: 123
Capital and largest city (2003 est.): Thimphu (official), 60,200. **Monetary unit:** Ngultrum. **Languages:** Dzongkha (official), Tibetan dialects (among Bhotes), Nepalese dialects (among Nepalese). **Ethnicity/race:** Bhote 50%, ethnic Nepalese 35%, indigenous or migrant tribes 15%. **Religions:** Lamaistic Buddhist 75%, Indian- and Nepalese-influenced Hinduism 25%. **Literacy rate:** 42% (1995 est.)
Economic summary: GDP/PPP (2003 est.): $2.9 billion; per capita $1,400. **Real growth rate:** 5.3%. **Inflation:** 3% (2002 est.). **Unemployment:** n.a. **Arable land:** 3%. **Agriculture:** rice, corn, root crops, citrus, grains; dairy products, eggs. **Labor force:** n.a.; note: massive lack of skilled labor (1997 est.); agriculture 93%, services 5%, industry and commerce 2%. **Industries:** cement, wood products, processed fruits, alcoholic beverages, calcium carbide. **Natural resources:** timber, hydropower, gypsum, calcium carbide.
Exports: $154 million (f.o.b., 2000 est.): electricity (to India), cardamom, gypsum, timber, handicrafts, cement, fruit, precious stones, spices. **Imports:** $196 million (c.i.f., 2000 est.): fuel and lubricants, grain, machinery and parts, vehicles, fabrics, rice. **Major trading partners:** India, Bangladesh, Philippines, Japan, Austria (2003).

Geography Mountainous Bhutan, half the size of Indiana, is situated on the southeast slope of the Himalayas, bordered on the north and east by Tibet and on the south and west and east by India. The landscape consists of a succession of lofty and rugged mountains and deep valleys. In the north, towering peaks reach a height of 24,000 ft (7,315 m).

Government Monarchy.

History Although archeological exploration of Bhutan has been limited, evidence of civilization in the region dates back to at least 2000 B.C. Aboriginal Bhutanese, known as Monpa, are believed to have migrated from Tibet. The traditional name of the country since the 17th century has been Drukyul, Land of the Drokpa (Dragon People), a reference to the dominant branch of Tibetan Buddhism that is still practiced in the Himalayan kingdom.

British troops invaded the region in 1865 and negotiated an agreement under which Britain agreed to pay an annual allowance to the Bhutanese monarchy on condition of good behavior. A treaty between India and the seat of government, Thimphu, in 1949 increased this subsidy and placed Bhutan's foreign affairs under Indian control. Until the 1960s Bhutan was largely isolated from the rest of the world, and its people carried on a tranquil, traditional way of life, farming and trading, which had

remained intact for centuries. After China invaded Tibet, however, Bhutan strengthened its ties and contact with India in an effort to avoid Tibet's fate. New roads and other connections to India began to end its isolation. In the 1960s Bhutan also undertook social modernization, abolishing slavery and the caste system, emancipating women, and enacting land reform. In 1985, Bhutan made its first diplomatic links with non-Asian countries.

A pro-democracy campaign emerged in 1991, which the government claimed was composed largely of Nepali immigrants. As a result, some 100,000 Nepali civil servants were either evicted or encouraged to emigrate. Most of them crossed the border back into Nepal, where they were housed in UN-administered refugee camps. Several rounds of talks aimed at deciding which country should claim the refugees have yielded few results, and the refugees have continued to languish in the camps for more than a decade.

In 1998, King Jigme Singye Wangchuck voluntarily curtailed his powerful monarchy by yielding to the formerly rubber-stamp legislature, giving it the right to remove him from leadership and appoint his cabinet. King Wangchuck moved closer to diluting the absolute monarchy in March 2005, with the release of a draft constitution, which outlined plans for the country to shift to a two-party democracy. The proposed constitution will be put to a referendum before it is adopted.

In Dec. 2004, Bhutan became the first nation in the world to ban the sale of tobacco and smoking in public.

Bolivia

REPUBLIC OF BOLIVIA

National name: República de Bolivia
President: Eduardo Rodriguez (interim) (2005)
Area: 424,162 sq mi (1,098,580 sq km)
Population (2005 est.): 8,857,870 (growth rate: 1.5%); birth rate: 23.8/1000; infant mortality rate: 53.1/1000; life expectancy: 65.5; density per sq mi: 21
Historic and judicial capital (2003 est.): Sucre, 204,200; **Administrative capital:** La Paz, 1,576,100 (metro. area), 830,500 (city proper). **Other large cities:** Santa Cruz, 1,168,700; Cochabamba, 815,800; El Alto, 728,500; Oruro, 211,700. **Monetary unit:** Boliviano. **Languages:** Spanish, Quechua, Aymara (all official). **Ethnicity/race:** Quechua 30%, mestizo 30%, Aymara 25%, white 15%. **Religion:** Roman Catholic 95%, Protestant (Evangelical Methodist) 5%. **Literacy rate:** 87% (2003 est.)
Economic summary: GDP/PPP (2004 est.): $22.33 billion; per capita $2,600. **Real growth rate:** 3.7%. **Inflation:** 4.9%. **Unemployment:** 9.2% in urban areas with widespread underemployment (2003 est.). **Arable land:** 3%. **Agriculture:** soybeans, coffee, coca, cotton, corn, sugarcane, rice, potatoes; timber. **Labor force:** 3.8 million; agriculture n.a., industry n.a., services n.a. **Industries:** mining, smelting, petroleum, food and beverages, tobacco, handicrafts, clothing. **Natural resources:** tin, natural gas, petroleum, zinc, tungsten, antimony, silver, iron, lead, gold, timber, hydropower. **Exports:** $1.986 billion (f.o.b., 2004 est.): natural gas, soybeans and soy products, crude petroleum, zinc ore, tin. **Imports:** $1.595 billion (f.o.b., 2004 est.): petroleum products, plastics, paper, aircraft and aircraft parts, prepared foods, automobiles, insecticides, soybeans. **Major trading partners:** Brazil, Venezuela, Colombia, U.S., Peru, Argentina, Chile (2003).

Geography Landlocked Bolivia is equal in size to California and Texas combined. Brazil forms its eastern border; its other neighbors are Peru and Chile on the west and Argentina and Paraguay on the south.

The western part, enclosed by two chains of the Andes, is a great plateau—the Altiplano, with an average altitude of 12,000 ft (3,658 m). Almost half the population lives on the plateau, which contains Oruro, Potosí, and La Paz. At an altitude of 11,910 ft (3,630 m), La Paz is the highest administrative capital city in the world. The Oriente, a lowland region ranging from rain forests to grasslands, comprises the northern and eastern two-thirds of the country. Lake Titicaca, at an altitude of 12,507 ft (3,812 m), is the highest commercially navigable body of water in the world.

Government Republic.

History Famous since Spanish colonial days for its mineral wealth, modern Bolivia was once a part of the ancient Incan empire. After the Spaniards defeated the Incas in the 16th century, Bolivia's predominantly Indian population was reduced to slavery. The remoteness of the Andes helped protect the Bolivian Indians from the European diseases that decimated other South American Indians. But the existence of a large indigenous group forced to live under the thumb of their colonizers created a stratified society of haves and have-nots that continues to this day. Income inequality between the largely impoverished Indians who make up two-thirds of the country and the light-skinned, European elite remains vast.

By the end of the 17th century the mineral wealth had begun to dry up. The country won its independence in 1825 and was named after Simón Bolívar, the famous liberator. Hampered by internal strife, Bolivia lost great slices of territory to three neighboring nations. Several thousand square miles and its outlet to the Pacific were taken by Chile after the War of the Pacific (1879–1884). In 1903, a piece of Bolivia's Acre Province, rich in rubber, was ceded to Brazil. And in 1938, after losing the Chaco War of 1932–1935 to Paraguay, Bolivia gave up its claim to nearly 100,000 sq mi of the Gran Chaco. Political instability ensued.

In 1965, a guerrilla movement mounted from Cuba and headed by Maj. Ernesto (Ché) Guevara began a revolutionary war. With the aid of U.S. military advisers, the Bolivian army smashed the guerrilla movement, capturing and killing Guevara on Oct. 8, 1967. A string of military coups followed before the military returned the government to civilian rule in 1982, when Hernán Siles Zuazo became president. At that point, Bolivia was regularly shut down by work stoppages and had the lowest per capita income in South America.

In June 1993, free-market advocate Gonzalo Sánchez de Lozada was elected president. He was succeeded by former general Hugo Bánzer, an ex-dictator turned democrat who became president for the second time in Aug. 1997. Bánzer made significant progress in wiping out illicit coca production and drug trafficking, which pleased the United States. However, the eradication of coca, a major crop in Bolivia since Incan times, plunged many Bolivian farmers into abject poverty. Although Bolivia sits on South America's second-largest natural gas reserves as well as considerable oil, the country has remained one of the poorest on the continent.

In Aug. 2002, Gonzalo Sánchez de Lozada again became president, pledging to continue economic reforms and to create jobs. In Feb. 2003, rioting took place in protest against a proposed income tax, which the government then withdrew. In October Sánchez resigned after two months of rioting and strikes over a gas-exporting project that protesters believed would benefit foreign companies more than Bolivians. His

vice president, Carlos Mesa, best known as a journalist and historian with little experience in government, replaced him.

Despite continued unrest, Mesa remained popular during his first two years as president. In a July 2004 referendum on the future of the country's significant natural gas reserves—the second largest in South America—Bolivians overwhelmingly supported Mesa's plan to exert more control over foreign gas companies. The referendum skirted the issue of nationalizing gas companies and ridding the country of foreign oil investment, which is what many leftist groups have called for. Mesa thereby managed to satisfy the strong antiprivatization sentiment among Bolivians without shutting the door on some limited form of privatization in the future.

But rising fuel prices in Jan. 2005 led to massive protests by tens of thousands of impoverished farmers and miners, and by March Mesa offered to resign, saying his ability to govern was paralyzed by the unrest. The two common demands of the various protest groups were the nationalization of the oil and gas industries and the formation of a constituent assembly to replace the National Congress that will redraft the constitution. His resignation was rejected, but after months of continuing protests, he resigned on June 6. Supreme Court justice Eduardo Rodriguez took over as interim president.

Bosnia and Herzegovina

National Name: Bosna i Hercegovina
Presidency, Chairman of the (rotating): Borislav Paravac (2004)
Prime Minister: Adnan Terzic (2002)
Area: 19,741 sq mi (51,129 sq km)
Population (2005 est.): 4,025,476 (all data dealing with population are subject to considerable error because of the dislocations caused by military action and ethnic cleansing) (growth rate: 0.4%); birth rate: 12.5/1000; infant mortality rate: 21.1/1000; life expectancy: 72.8; density per sq mi: 204
Capital and largest city (2003 est.): Sarajevo, 581,500 (unofficial). **Other large cities:** Banja Luka, 189,700; Tuzla 119,200; Mostar, 90,800. **Monetary unit:** Marka.
Languages: Bosnian, Croatian, Serbian (all official).
Ethnicity/race: Bosniak 48%, Serb 37.1%, Croat 14.3%, other 0.6% (2000) . **Religions:** Muslim 40%, Orthodox 31%, Roman Catholic 15%, other 14%.
Literacy rate: n.a.
Economic summary: GDP/PPP (2004 est.): $26.21 billion; per capita $6,500. **Real growth rate:** 5%.
Inflation: 1.1%. **Unemployment:** 44% officially; however, gray economy may reduce actual unemployment to near 20%. **Arable land:** 14%.
Agriculture: wheat, corn, fruits, vegetables; livestock.
Labor force: 1.026 million (2001); agriculture n.a., industry n.a., services n.a. **Industries:** steel, coal, iron ore, lead, zinc, manganese, bauxite, vehicle assembly, textiles, tobacco products, wooden furniture, tank and aircraft assembly, domestic appliances, oil refining (2001). **Natural resources:** coal, iron ore, bauxite, copper, lead, zinc, chromite, cobalt, manganese, nickel, clay, gypsum, salt, sand, forests, hydropower. **Exports:** $1.7 billion (f.o.b., 2004 est.): metals, clothing, wood products. **Imports:** $5.2 billion (f.o.b., 2004 est.): machinery and equipment, chemicals, fuels, foodstuffs.
Major trading partners: Italy, Croatia, Germany, Slovenia, Hungary, Austria (2003).

Geography Bosnia and Herzegovina make up a triangular-shaped republic, about half the size of Kentucky, on the Balkan peninsula. The Bosnian region in the north is mountainous and covered with thick forests. The Herzegovina region in the south is largely rugged, flat farmland. It has a narrow coastline without natural harbors stretching 13 mi (20 km) along the Adriatic Sea.

Government Emerging democracy, with a rotating, tripartite presidency divided between predominantly Serb, Croatian, and Bosnian political parties.

History Since the time of the Roman Empire, the Balkans has been a crossroads of religions and civilizations. The ethnic groups now known as Bosnians, Croats, and Serbs are largely the result of different religious and cultural identities created by contact with neighboring empires that expanded and contracted in the Balkans over centuries. With minor differences, these groups speak the same language, called Serbo-Croatian or sometimes Bosnian.

Called Illyricum in ancient times, the area now called Bosnia and Herzegovina was conquered by the Romans in the 2nd and 1st centuries B.C. and folded into the Roman province of Dalmatia. In the 4th and 5th centuries A.D. Goths overran that portion of the declining Roman Empire and occupied the area until the 6th century, when the Byzantine Empire claimed it. Slavs began settling the region during the 7th century. Around 1200, Bosnia won independence from Hungary and endured as an independent Christian state for some 260 years.

The expansion of the Ottoman Empire into the Balkans introduced another cultural, political, and religious framework. The Turks defeated the Serbs at the famous battle of Kosovo in 1389. They conquered Bosnia in 1463. During the roughly 450 years Bosnia and Herzegovina were under Ottoman rule, many Christian Slavs became Muslim. A Bosnian Islamic elite gradually developed and ruled the country on behalf of the Turkish overlords. As the borders of the Ottoman Empire began to shrink in the 19th century, Muslims from elsewhere in the Balkans migrated to Bosnia. Bosnia also developed a sizable Jewish population, with many Jews settling in Sarajevo after their expulsion from Spain in 1492. However, through the 19th century the term *Bosnian* commonly included residents of all faiths. A relatively secular society, intermarriage among religious groups was not unknown.

Neighboring Serbia and Montenegro fought against the Ottoman Empire in 1876 and were aided by the Russians, their fellow Slavs. At the Congress of Berlin in 1878, following the end of the Russo-Turkish War (1877–1878), Austria-Hungary was given a mandate to occupy and govern Bosnia and Herzegovina, in an effort by Europe to ensure that Russia did not dominate the Balkans. Although the provinces were still officially part of the Ottoman Empire, they were annexed by the Austro-Hungarian Empire on Oct. 7, 1908. As a result, relations with Serbia, which had claims on Bosnia and Herzegovina, became embittered. The hostility between the two countries climaxed in the assassination of Austrian archduke Franz Ferdinand in Sarajevo on June 28, 1914, by a Serbian nationalist. This event precipitated the start of World War I (1914–1918). Bosnia and Herzegovina were annexed to Serbia as part of the newly formed Kingdom of Serbs, Croats, and Slovenes on Oct. 26, 1918. The name was later changed to Yugoslavia in 1929.

When Germany invaded Yugoslavia in 1941, Bosnia and Herzegovina were made part of Nazi-controlled Croatia. During the German and Italian occupation, Bosnian and Herzegovinian resistance fighters fought a fierce guerrilla war against the Ustachi, the Croatian Fascist troops. At the end of World War II, Bosnia and Herzegovina were reunited into a single state as one of the six republics of the newly reestablished Communist Yugoslavia under Marshall Tito. His authoritarian control kept the ethnic enmities of his patchwork nation in check. Tito died in 1980, and with growing economic dissatisfaction and the fall of the iron curtain over the next decade, Yugoslavia began to splinter.

In Dec. 1991, Bosnia and Herzegovina declared independence from Yugoslavia and asked for recognition by the European Union (EU). In a March 1992 referendum, Bosnian voters chose independence, and President Izetbegovic declared the nation an independent state. Unlike the other former Yugoslav states, which were generally composed of a dominant ethnic group, Bosnia was an ethnic tangle of Muslims (44%), Serbs (31%), and Croats (17%), and this mix contributed to the duration and savagery of its fight for independence.

Both the Croatian and Serbian presidents had planned to partition Bosnia between themselves. Attempting to carve out their own enclaves, the Serbian minority, with the help of the Serbian Yugoslav army, took the offensive and laid siege, particularly on Sarajevo, and began its ruthless campaigns of ethnic cleansing, which involved the expulsion or massacre of Muslims. Croats also began carving out their own communities. By the end of Aug. 1992, rebel Bosnian Serbs had conquered over 60% of Bosnia. The war did not begin to wane until NATO stepped in, bombing Serb positions in Bosnia in Aug. and Sept. 1995. Serbs entered the UN safe havens of Tuzla, Zepa, and Srebrenica, where they murdered thousands. About 250,000 died in the war between 1992 and 1995.

U.S.-sponsored peace talks in Dayton, Ohio, led to an agreement in 1995 that called for a Muslim-Croat federation and a Serb entity within the larger federation of Bosnia. Sixty thousand NATO troops were to supervise its implementation. Fighting abated and orderly elections were held in Sept. 1996. President Alija Izetbegovic, a Bosnian Muslim, or Bosniak, won the majority of votes to become the leader of the three-member presidency, each representing one of the three ethnic groups.

But this alliance of unreconstructed enemies had little success in creating a working government or keeping violent clashes in check. The terms of the Dec. 1995 Dayton Peace Accord were largely ignored by Bosnian Serbs, with its former president, archnationalist Radovan Karadzic, still in de facto control of the Serbian enclave. Many indicted war criminals, including Karadzic, remain at large. NATO proved to be a largely ineffective peacekeeping force.

The crucial priorities facing postwar Bosnian leaders were rebuilding the economy, resettling the estimated 1 million refugees still displaced, and establishing a working government. Progress on these goals has been minimal, and a massive corruption scandal uncovered in 1999 severely tested the goodwill of the international community.

In 1994, the UN's International Criminal Tribunal for the former Yugoslavia opened in The Hague, Netherlands. In Aug. 2001, Radislav Drstic, a Bosnian Serb general, was found guilty of genocide in the killing of up to 8,000 Bosnian Muslims in Srebrenica in 1995. It was the first genocide conviction in Europe since the UN genocide treaty was drawn up in 1951. In 2001, the trial of former Serbian president Slobodan Milosevic began (and continues today). He was charged with crimes against humanity.

Under pressure from Paddy Ashdown, the international administrator of Bosnia authorized under the Dayton Accord, Bosnian Serb leaders finally admitted in June 2004 that Serbian troops were responsible for the massacre of up to 8,000 Bosnian Muslims in Srebrenica in 1995. Until then, Serb leaders had refused to acknowledge guilt in the worst civilian massacre since World War II. Thus far, only 13 individuals have been indicted by the UN International Criminal Tribunal for their role in the killings, and Bosnian Serb Army commander Ratko Mladic, who orchestrated the massacre, remains at large. In August, a small, largely symbolic step was taken toward unifying the country when a world-famous 14th-century Ottoman bridge in Mostar was rebuilt. Destroyed during the war, the bridge now once again spans the Croatian and Bosnian sections of the city.

In Dec. 2004, the European Union officially took over NATO's peacekeeping mission in Bosnia. It is the largest peacekeeping operation the EU has undertaken. In March 2005, Ashdown, the international administrator, sacked Dragan Covic, the Croat member of the presidency, charging him with corruption and abuse of office. Covic became the third member of the Bosnian presidency forced to resign since the tripartite presidency was established.

Botswana

REPUBLIC OF BOTSWANA

President: Festus Mogae (1998)
Area: 231,803 sq mi (600,370 sq km)
Population (2005 est.): 1,640,115 (growth rate: 0.0%); birth rate: 23.3/1000; infant mortality rate: 54.6/1000; life expectancy: 33.9; density per sq mi: 7
Capital and largest city (2003 est.): Gaborone, 195,000. **Monetary unit:** Pula. **Languages:** English (official), Setswana. **Ethnicity/race:** Tswana (or Setswana) 79%, Kalanga 11%, Basarwa 3%, other (including Kgalagadi and white) 7%. **Religions:** indigenous beliefs 85%, Christian 15%. **Literacy rate:** 80% (2003 est.)
Economic summary: GDP/PPP (2004 est.): $15.05 billion; per capita $9,200. **Real growth rate:** 3.5%. **Inflation:** 7%. **Unemployment:** 23.8%. **Arable land:** 1%. **Agriculture:** livestock, sorghum, maize, millet, beans, sunflowers, groundnuts. **Labor force:** 264,000 formal sector employees (2000). **Industries:** diamonds, copper, nickel, salt, soda ash, potash; livestock processing; textiles. **Natural resources:** diamonds, copper, nickel, salt, soda ash, potash, coal, iron ore, silver. **Exports:** $2.94 billion (f.o.b., 2004 est.): diamonds, copper, nickel, soda ash, meat, textiles. **Imports:** $2.255 billion (f.o.b., 2004 est.): foodstuffs, machinery, electrical goods, transport equipment, textiles, fuel and petroleum products, wood and paper products, metal and metal products. **Major trading partners:** European Free Trade Association (EFTA), Southern African Customs Union (SACU), Zimbabwe (2000). **Member of Commonwealth of Nations**

Geography Twice the size of Arizona, Botswana is in south-central Africa, bounded by Namibia, Zambia, Zimbabwe, and South Africa. Most of the country is near-desert, with the Kalahari occupying the western part of the country. The eastern part is hilly, with salt lakes in the north.

Government Parliamentary republic.

History The earliest inhabitants of the region were the San, who were followed by the Tswana. About half the country today is ethnic Tswana. The term for the country's people, *Batswana,* refers to national rather than ethnic origin.

Encroachment by the Zulu in the 1820s and by Boers from Transvaal in the 1870s and 1880s threatened the peace of the region. In 1885, Britain established the area as a protectorate, then known as Bechuanaland. In 1961, Britain granted a constitution to the country. Self-government began in 1965, and on Sept. 30, 1966, the country became independent. Botswana is Africa's oldest democracy.

The new country maintained good relations with its white-ruled neighbors but gradually changed its policies, harboring rebel groups from South Rhodesia as well as some from South Africa.

Although Botswana is rich in diamonds, it has high unemployment and stratified socioeconomic classes. In 1999 it suffered its first budget deficit in 16 years because of a slump in the international diamond market. Yet it remains one of the wealthiest as well as most stable countries on the continent.

After 17 years in power, President Ketumile Masire retired in 1997, and Festus Mogae, an Oxford-educated economist, became the new president. Mogae has won high marks from the international financial community for continuing to privatize Botswana's mining and industrial operations.

Although Botswana's economic outlook remains strong, the devastation that AIDS has caused threatens to destroy the country's future. In 2001, Botswana had the highest rate of HIV infection in the world: 350,000 of its 1.6 million people were infected, and half of the population between 25 and 29 was dying of the disease. In 2002, however, Botswana, with the help of international donors, launched an ambitious national campaign that provided free antiviral drugs to anyone who needed them. By March 2004, Botswana no longer had the world's highest HIV infection rate. But with 37.5% of the population infected, the country remains on the brink of catastrophe.

President Mogae won a second and final four-year term in Oct. 2004.

Brazil

FEDERATIVE REPUBLIC OF BRAZIL

National name: República Federativa do Brasil
President: Luiz Inácio Lula da Silva (2003)
Area: 3,286,470 sq mi (8,511,965 sq km)
Population (2005 est.): 186,112,794 (growth rate: 1.1%); birth rate: 16.8/1000; infant mortality rate: 29.6/1000; life expectancy: 71.7; density per sq mi: 57
Capital (2003 est.): Brasília, 2,160,100. **Largest cities:** São Paulo, 18,847,400 (metro. area), 10,195,000 (city proper); Rio de Janeiro, 11,437,100 (metro. area), 6,119,800 (city proper); Salvador, 2,590,400; Belo Horizonte, 2,347,500; Recife, 1,485,500; Porto Alegre, 1,372,700. **Monetary unit:** Real. **Languages:** Portuguese (official), Spanish, English, French. **Ethnicity/race:** white (includes Portuguese, German, Italian, Spanish, Polish) 55%, mixed white and black 38%, black 6%, other (includes Japanese, Arab, Amerindian) 1%. **Religion:** Roman Catholic 80%. **Literacy rate:** 80% (2003 est.)
Economic summary: GDP/PPP (2004 est.): $1.492 trillion; per capita $8,100. **Real growth rate:** 5.1%. **Inflation:** 7.6%. **Unemployment:** 11.5%. **Arable land:** 7%. **Agriculture:** coffee, soybeans, wheat, rice, corn, sugarcane, cocoa, citrus; beef. **Labor force:** 89 million; agriculture 20%, industry 14%, services 66% (2003 est.). **Industries:** textiles, shoes, chemicals, cement, lumber, iron ore, tin, steel, aircraft, motor vehicles and parts, other machinery and equipment. **Natural resources:** bauxite, gold, iron ore, manganese, nickel, phosphates, platinum, tin, uranium, petroleum, hydropower, timber. **Exports:** $95 billion (f.o.b., 2004 est.): transport equipment, iron ore, soybeans, footwear, coffee, autos. **Imports:** $61 billion

(f.o.b., 2004 est.): machinery, electrical and transport equipment, chemical products, oil. **Major trading partners:** U.S., Argentina, China, Netherlands, Germany, Japan (2003).

Geography Brazil covers nearly half of South America and is the continent's largest nation. It extends 2,965 mi (4,772 km) north-south, 2,691 mi (4,331 km) east-west, and borders every nation on the continent except Chile and Ecuador. Brazil may be divided into the Brazilian Highlands, or plateau, in the south and the Amazon River Basin in the north. Over a third of Brazil is drained by the Amazon and its more than 200 tributaries. The Amazon is navigable for ocean steamers to Iquitos, Peru, 2,300 mi (3,700 km) upstream. Southern Brazil is drained by the Plata system—the Paraguay, Uruguay, and Paraná Rivers.

Government Federal republic.

History Brazil is the only Latin American nation that derives its language and culture from Portugal. The native inhabitants mostly consisted of the nomadic Tupí-Guaraní Indians. Adm. Pedro Alvares Cabral claimed the territory for Portugal in 1500. The early explorers brought back a wood that produced a red dye, *pau-brasil,* from which the land received its name. Portugal began colonization in 1532 and made the area a royal colony in 1549.

During the Napoleonic Wars, King João VI, fearing the advancing French armies, fled Portugal in 1808 and set up his court in Rio de Janeiro. João was drawn home in 1820 by a revolution, leaving his son as regent. When Portugal tried to reimpose colonial rule, the prince declared Brazil's independence on Sept. 7, 1822, becoming Pedro I, emperor of Brazil. Harassed by his Parliament, Pedro I abdicated in 1831 in favor of his five-year-old son, who became emperor in 1840 (Pedro II). The son was a popular monarch, but discontent built up, and in 1889, following a military revolt, he abdicated. Although a republic was proclaimed, Brazil was ruled by military dictatorships until a revolt permitted a gradual return to stability under civilian presidents.

President Wenceslau Braz cooperated with the Allies and declared war on Germany during World War I. In World War II, Brazil again cooperated with the Allies, welcoming Allied air bases, patrolling the South Atlantic, and joining the invasion of Italy after declaring war on the Axis powers.

After a military coup in 1964, Brazil had a series of military governments. Gen. João Baptista de Oliveira Figueiredo became president in 1979 and pledged a return to democracy in 1985. The election of Tancredo Neves on Jan. 15, 1985, the first civilian president since 1964, brought a nationwide wave of optimism, but when Neves died several months later, Vice President José Sarney became president. Collor de Mello won the election of late 1989, pledging to lower hyperinflation with free-market economics. When Collor faced impeachment by Congress because of a corruption scandal in Dec. 1992 and resigned, Vice President Itamar Franco assumed the presidency.

A former finance minister, Fernando Cardoso, won the presidency in the Oct. 1994 election with 54% of the vote. Cardoso sold off inefficient government-owned monopolies in the telecommunications, electrical power, port, mining, railway, and banking industries.

In Jan. 1999, the Asian economic crisis spread to Brazil. Rather than prop up the currency through financial markets, Brazil opted to let the currency float, which sent the real plummeting—at one time as much as 40%. Cardoso was highly praised by the international community for quickly turning around his country's economic crisis. Despite his efforts, however, the economy continued to slow throughout 2001, and the country also faced an energy crisis. The IMF offered Brazil an additional aid package in Aug. 2001. And in Aug. 2002, to ensure that Brazil would not be dragged down by neighboring Argentina's catastrophic economic problems, the IMF agreed to lend Brazil a phenomenal $30 billion over fifteen months.

In Jan. 2003, Luiz Inácio Lula da Silva, a former trade union leader and factory worker widely known by the name Lula, became Brazil's first working-class president. As leader of Brazil's only Socialist party, the Workers' Party, Lula pledged to increase social services and improve the lot of the poor. But he also recognized that a distinctly non-socialist program of fiscal austerity was needed to rescue the economy. The president's first major legislative success was a plan to reform the country's debt-ridden pension system, which operated under an annual $20 billion deficit. Civil servants staged massive strikes opposing this and other reforms. Although public debt and inflation remained a problem in 2004, Brazil's economy showed signs of growth and unemployment was down. Polls in Aug. 2004 demonstrated that the majority of Brazilians supported Lula's tough economic reform efforts.

In 2005, an unfolding bribery scandal weakened Lula's administration and led to the resignation of several high government officials. Lula issued a televised apology in August, and promised "drastic measures" to reform the political system.

Brunei

BRUNEI DARUSSALAM

National Name: Negara Brunei Darussalam
Sultan: Haji Hassanal Bolkiah (1967)
Area: 2,228 sq mi (5,770 sq km)
Population (2005 est.): 372,361 (growth rate: 1.9%); birth rate: 19.0/1000; infant mortality rate: 12.6/1000; life expectancy: 74.8; density per sq mi: 167
Capital and largest city (2003 est.): Bandar Seri Begawan, 78,000. **Other large cities:** Kuala Belait 27,800, Seria 23,400. **Monetary unit:** Brunei dollar. **Languages:** Malay (official), English, Chinese. **Ethnicity/race:** Malay 67%, Chinese 15%, indigenous 6%, other 12%. **Religions:** Islam (official religion) 67%, Buddhist 13%, Christian 10%, indigenous beliefs and other 10%. **Literacy rate:** 92% (2003 est.)
Economic summary: GDP/PPP (2003 est.): $6.842 billion; per capita $23,600. **Real growth rate:** 3.2%. **Inflation:** 0.3%. **Unemployment:** 3.2% (2002 est.). **Arable land:** 1%. **Agriculture:** rice, vegetables, fruits, chickens, water buffalo. **Labor force:** 158,000; note: includes foreign workers and military personnel; temporary residents make up 40% of labor force (2002 est.); government 48%, production of oil, natural gas, services, and construction 42%, agriculture, forestry, and fishing 10% (1999 est.). **Industries:** petroleum, petroleum refining, liquefied natural gas, construction. **Natural resources:** petroleum, natural gas, timber. **Exports:** $7.7 billion (f.o.b., 2003 est.): crude oil, natural gas, refined products. **Imports:** $5.2 billion (c.i.f., 2003): machinery and transport equipment, manufactured goods, food, chemicals. **Major trading partners:** Japan, South Korea, Thailand, Australia, U.S., China, Singapore, Malaysia, Hong Kong, Australia.

Geography About the size of Delaware, Brunei is an independent sultanate on the northwest coast of the island of Borneo in the South China Sea, wedged between the Malaysian states of Sabah and Sarawak.

Government Constitutional sultanate.

History Brunei was trading with China during the 6th century, and, through allegiance to the Javanese Majapahit kingdom (13th. to 15th century), it came under Hindu influence. In the early 15th century, with the decline of the Majapahit kingdom and widespread conversion to Islam, Brunei became an independent sultanate. It was a powerful state from the 16th to the 19th century, ruling over the northern part of Borneo and adjacent island chains. But it fell into decay and lost Sarawak in 1841, becoming a British protectorate in 1888 and a British dependency in 1905. Japan occupied Brunei during World War II; it was liberated by Australia in 1945.

The sultan regained control over internal affairs in 1959, but Britain retained responsibility for the state's defense and foreign affairs until 1984, when the sultanate became fully independent. Sultan Bolkiah was crowned in 1967 at the age of 22, succeeding his father, Sir Omar Ali Saifuddin, who had abdicated. During his reign, exploitation of the rich Seria oilfield had made the sultanate wealthy. Brunei has one of the highest per capita incomes in Asia, and the sultan is believed to be one of the richest men in the world. In Aug. 1998, Oxford-educated Prince Al-Muhtadee Billah was inaugurated as heir to the 500-year-old monarchy.

Sultan Bolkiah began taking cautious steps toward democratic reform in Sept. 2004, when he reinstated parliament for the first time since Brunei gained independence in 1984. He was widely praised in May 2005 when he fired four members of his cabinet, including the education minister, whose plan to expand religious education angered many parents.

Bulgaria

REPUBLIC OF BULGARIA

President: Georgi Purvanov (2002)
Prime Minister: Sergei Stanishev (2005)
Area: 42,822 sq mi (110,910 sq km)˙
Population (2005 est.): 7,450,349 (growth rate: –0.9%); birth rate: 9.7/1000; infant mortality rate: 20.6/1000; life expectancy: 72.0; density per sq mi: 174
Capital and largest city (2003 est.): Sofia, 1,088,700.
Other large cities: Plovdiv, 338,200; Varna, 312,300; Burgas, 192,000; Ruse, 161,000. **Monetary unit:** Lev.
Languages: Bulgarian; secondary languages strongly correspond to ethnic breakdown. **Ethnicity/race:** Bulgarian 83.9%, Turk 9.4%, Roma 4.7%, other (including Macedonian, Armenian, Tatar, Circassian) 2%. **Religions:** Bulgarian Orthodox 82.6%, Islam 12.2%, Roman Catholic 1.7%, Jewish 0.1%, Protestant, Gregorian-Armenian, and other 3.4% (1998). **Literacy rate:** 99% (2003 est.)
Economic summary: GDP/PPP (2004 est.): $61.63 billion; per capita $8,200. **Real growth rate:** 5.3%. **Inflation:** 6.1%. **Unemployment:** 12.7%. **Arable land:** 40%. **Agriculture:** vegetables, fruits, tobacco, livestock, wine, wheat, barley, sunflowers, sugar beets. **Labor force:** 3.398 million; agriculture 11%, industry 32.7%, services 56.3% (3rd quarter 2004 est.). **Industries:** electricity, gas and water; food, beverages and tobacco; machinery and equipment, base metals, chemical products, coke, refined petroleum, nuclear fuel. **Natural resources:** bauxite, copper, lead, zinc, coal, timber, arable land. **Exports:** $9.134 billion (f.o.b., 2004 est.): clothing, footwear, iron and steel, machinery and equipment, fuels. **Imports:** $12.23 billion (f.o.b., 2004 est.): machinery and equipment; metals and ores; chemicals and plastics; fuels, minerals, and raw materials. **Major trading partners:** Italy, Germany, . Greece, Turkey, France, U.S., Russia (2003).

Geography Bulgaria shares borders with Serbia, Macedonia, Romania, Greece, and Turkey. Two moun-

tain ranges and two great valleys mark the topography of Bulgaria, a country the size of Tennessee and situated on the Black Sea. The Maritsa is Bulgaria's principal river, and the Danube also flows through the country.

Government Parliamentary democracy.

History The Thracians lived in what is now known as Bulgaria from about 3500 B.C. They were incorporated into the Roman Empire by the first century A.D. At the decline of the empire, the Goths, Huns, Bulgars, and Avars invaded. The Bulgars, who crossed the Danube from the north in 679, took control of the region. Although the country bears the name of the Bulgars, the Bulgar language and culture died out, replaced by a Slavic language, writing, and religion. In 865, Boris I adopted Orthodox Christianity. The Bulgars twice conquered most of the Balkan peninsula between 893 and 1280. But in 1396 they were invaded by the Ottoman Empire, which made Bulgaria a Turkish province until 1878. Ottoman rule was harsh and inescapable, given Bulgaria's proximity to its oppressor. In 1878, Russia forced Turkey to give Bulgaria its independence after the Russo-Turkish War (1877–1878). But the European powers, fearing Russia's and Bulgaria's dominance in the Balkans, intervened at the Congress of Berlin (1878), limiting Bulgaria's territory and fashioning it into a small principality ruled by Alexander of Battenburg, the nephew of the Russian czar.

Alexander was succeeded in 1887 by Prince Ferdinand of Saxe-Coburg-Gotha, who declared a kingdom independent of the Ottoman Empire on Oct. 5, 1908. In the First Balkan War (1912–1913), Bulgaria and the other members of the Balkan League fought against Turkey to regain Balkan territory. Angered by the small portion of Macedonia it received after the battle—it considered Macedonia an integral part of Bulgaria—the country instigated the Second Balkan War (June–Aug. 1913) against Turkey as well as its former allies. Bulgaria lost the war and all the territory it had gained in the First Balkan War. Bulgaria joined Germany in World War I in the hope of again gaining Macedonia. After this second failure, Ferdinand abdicated in favor of his son in 1918. Boris III squandered Bulgaria's resources and assumed dictatorial powers in 1934–1935. Bulgaria fought on the side of the Nazis in World War II, but after Russia declared war on Bulgaria on Sept. 5, 1944, Bulgaria switched sides. Three days later, on Sept. 9, 1944, a Communist coalition took control of the country and set up a government under Kimon Georgiev.

A Soviet-style People's Republic was established in 1947 and Bulgaria acquired the reputation of being the most slavishly loyal to Moscow of all the East European Communist countries. The general secretary of the Bulgarian Communist Party, Todor Zhikov, resigned in 1989 after 35 years in power. His successor, Peter Mladenov, purged the Politburo, ended the Communist monopoly on power, and held free elections in May 1990 that led to a surprising victory for the Communist Party, renamed the Bulgarian Socialist Party (BSP). Mladenov was forced to resign in July 1990.

In Oct. 1991, the Union of Democratic Forces won, forming Bulgaria's first non-Communist government since 1946. Power shifted back and forth between the pro-Western Union of Democratic Forces (UDF) and the BSP during the 1990s. The economy continued to deteriorate amid growing concern over the spread of organized crime. A new UDF government, led by Prime Minister Ivan Kostov, was elected in 1997 to overhaul the economic system and institute reforms aimed at stemming corruption. Progress on both fronts remained slow. As a result, the UDF lost the July 2001 election to the former king of Bulgaria, leader of the Simeon II National Movement (SNM). The new prime minister, Simeon Saxe-Coburg-Gotha (Simeon II), had been dethroned 55 years earlier (at age nine) during the Communist takeover of the country. Bulgaria became a member of NATO in 2004. In 2005, the EU approved its membership for 2007, subject to the implementation of reforms, especially the cleaning up of corruption and organized crime.

In June 2005 general elections, no party received a clear majority, and a coalition government was formed with Socialist Party leader Sergei Stanishev as the new prime minister.

Burkina Faso

President: Blaise Compaoré (1987)
Prime Minister: Paramanga Ernest Yonli (2000)
Area: 105,869 sq mi (274,200 sq km)
Population (2005 est.): 13,925,313 (growth rate: 2.5%); birth rate: 44.2/1000; infant mortality rate: 97.6/1000; life expectancy: 43.9; density per sq mi: 132
Capital and largest city (2003 est.): Ouagadougou, 962,100. **Monetary unit:** CFA Franc. **Languages:** French (official); native African (Sudanic) languages 90%. **Ethnicity/race:** Mossi (over 40%), Gurunsi, Senufo, Lobi, Bobo, Mande, Fulani. **Religions:** Islam 50%, indigenous beliefs 40%, Christian (mainly Roman Catholic) 10%. **Literacy rate:** 27% (2003 est.)
Economic summary: GDP/PPP (2004 est.): $15.74 billion; per capita $1,200. **Real growth rate:** 4.8%. **Inflation:** 2.4%. **Unemployment:** n.a. **Arable land:** 14%. **Agriculture:** cotton, peanuts, shea nuts, sesame, sorghum, millet, corn, rice; livestock. **Labor force:** 5 million; note: a large part of the male labor force migrates annually to neighboring countries for seasonal employment (2003). **Industries:** cotton lint, beverages, agricultural processing, soap, cigarettes, textiles, gold. **Natural resources:** manganese, limestone, marble; small deposits of gold, phosphates, pumice, salt. **Exports:** $418.6 million (f.o.b., 2004 est.): cotton, livestock, gold. **Imports:** $866.3 million (f.o.b., 2004 est.): capital goods, food products, petroleum. **Major trading partners:** Singapore, China, Thailand, Italy, Ghana, Colombia, France, Côte d'Ivoire, Togo, Belgium (2003).

Geography Slightly larger than Colorado, Burkina Faso, formerly known as Upper Volta, is a landlocked country in West Africa. Its neighbors are Côte d'Ivoire, Mali, Niger, Benin, Togo, and Ghana. The country consists of extensive plains, low hills, high savannas, and a desert area in the north.

Government Parliamentary.

History Burkina Faso was originally inhabited by the Bobo, Lobi, and Gurunsi peoples, with the Mossi and Gurma peoples immigrating to the region in the 14th century. The lands of the Mossi empire became a French protectorate in 1897, and by 1903 France had subjugated the other ethnic groups. Called Upper Volta by the French, it became a separate colony in 1919, was partitioned among Niger, the Sudan, and Côte d'Ivoire in 1932, and was reconstituted in 1947. An autonomous republic within the French Community, Upper Volta became independent on Aug. 5, 1960.

President Maurice Yameogo was deposed on Jan. 3, 1966, by a military coup led by Col. Sangoulé Lamizana, who dissolved the National Assembly and suspended the constitution. Constitutional rule returned in 1978 with the election of an Assembly and a presidential vote in June in which Gen. Lamizana won by a narrow margin over three other candidates.

On Nov. 25, 1980, Col. Sayé Zerbo led a bloodless coup that toppled Lamizana. In turn, Maj. Jean-Baptist Ouedraogo ousted Zerbo on Nov. 7, 1982. But the real revolutionary change occurred the following year when a 33-year-old flight commander, Thomas Sankara, took control. A Marxist-Leninist, he challenged the traditional Mossi chiefs, advocated women's liberation, and allied the country with North Korea, Libya, and Cuba. To sever ties to the colonial past, Sankara changed the name of the country in 1984 to Burkina Faso, which combines two of the nation's languages and means "the land of upright men."

While Sankara's investments in schools, food production, and clinics brought some improvement in living standards, foreign investment declined, many businesses left the country, and unhappy labor unions began strikes. On Oct. 15, 1987, formerly loyal soldiers assassinated Sankara. His best friend and ally Blaise Compaoré became president. Compaoré immediately set about "rectifying" Sankara's revolution. In 1991 he agreed to economic reforms proposed by the World Bank. A new constitution paved the way for elections in 1991, which Compaoré won easily, although opposition parties boycotted. In 1998, he was reelected by a landslide. A coup against the president was foiled in 2003.

Burma (Myanmar)

SEE MYANMAR.

Burundi

REPUBLIC OF BURUNDI

National name: Republika y'u Burundi
President: Pierre Nkurunziza (2005)
Area: 10,745 sq mi (27,830 sq km)
Population (2005 est.): 6,370,609 (growth rate: 2.2%); birth rate: 39.7/1000; infant mortality rate 69.3/1000; life expectancy: 43.5; density per sq mi: 593
Capital and largest city (2003 est.): Bujumbura, 331,700. **Other large city:** Gitega, 45,700. **Monetary unit:** Burundi franc. **Languages:** Kirundi and French (official), Swahili. **Ethnicity/race:** Hutu (Bantu) 85%, Tutsi (Hamitic) 14%, Twa (Pygmy) 1%. **Religions:** Roman Catholic 62%, indigenous 23%, Islam 10%, Protestant 5%. **Literacy rate:** 52% (2003 est.)
Economic summary: GDP/PPP (2004 est.): $4.001 billion; per capita $600. **Real growth rate:** 3%. **Inflation:** 8.5%. **Unemployment:** n.a. **Arable land:** 35%. **Agriculture:** coffee, cotton, tea, corn, sorghum, sweet potatoes, bananas, manioc (tapioca); beef, milk, hides. **Labor force:** 2.99 million (2002); agriculture 93.6%, industry 2.3%, services 4.1% (2002 est.). **Industries:** light consumer goods such as blankets, shoes, soap; assembly of imported components; public works construction; food processing. **Natural resources:** nickel, uranium, rare earth oxides, peat, cobalt, copper, platinum (not yet exploited), vanadium, arable land, hydropower, niobium, tantalum, gold, tin, tungsten, kaolin, limestone. **Exports:** $31.84 million (f.o.b., 2004 est.): coffee, tea, sugar, cotton, hides. **Imports:** $138.2 million (f.o.b., 2004 est.): capital goods, petroleum products, foodstuffs. **Major trading partners:** Switzerland, UK, Rwanda, Netherlands, Kenya, Tanzania, Uganda, Zambia, France, India, Japan, China (2003).

Geography Wedged between Tanzania, the Democratic Republic of the Congo, and Rwanda in east-central Africa, Burundi occupies a high plateau divided by several deep valleys. It is equal in size to Maryland.

Government Republic.

History The original inhabitants of Burundi were the Twa, a Pygmy people who now make up only 1% of the population. Today the population is divided between the Hutu (approximately 85%) and the Tutsi, approximately 14%. While the Hutu and Tutsi are considered to be two separate ethnic groups, scholars point out that they speak the same language, have a history of intermarriage, and share many cultural characteristics. Traditionally, the differences between the two groups were occupational rather than ethnic. Agricultural people were considered Hutu, while the cattle-owning elite were identified as Tutsi. Supposedly Tutsi were tall and thin, while Hutu were short and square, but in fact it is often impossible to tell one from the other. The 1933 requirement by the Belgians that everyone carry an identity card indicating tribal ethnicity as Tutsi or Hutu increased the distinction. Since independence, the landowning Tutsi aristocracy has dominated Burundi.

Burundi was once part of German East Africa. Belgium won a League of Nations mandate in 1923, and subsequently Burundi, with Rwanda, was transferred to the status of a United Nations trust territory. In 1962, Burundi gained independence and became a kingdom under Mwami Mwambutsa IV, a Tutsi. A Hutu rebellion took place in 1965, leading to brutal Tutsi retaliations. Mwambutsa was deposed by his son, Ntaré V, in 1966. Ntaré in turn was overthrown the same year in a military coup by Premier Michel Micombero, also a Tutsi. In 1970–1971, a civil war erupted, leaving more than 100,000 Hutu dead.

On Nov. 1, 1976, Lt. Col. Jean-Baptiste Bagaza led a coup and assumed the presidency. He suspended the constitution and announced that a 30-member Supreme Revolutionary Council would be the governing body. In Sept. 1987 Bagaza was overthrown by Maj. Pierre Buyoya, who became president. Ethnic hatred again flared in Aug. 1988, and about 20,000 Hutu were slaughtered. Buyoya, however, began reforms to heal the country's ethnic rift. The Burundi Democracy Front's candidate, Melchior Ndadaye, won the country's first democratic presidential elections, held on June 2, 1993. Ndadaye, the first Hutu to assume power in Burundi, was killed within months during a coup. The second Hutu president, Cyprien Ntaryamira, was killed on April 6, 1994, when a plane carrying him and the Rwandan president was shot down. As a result, Hutu youth gangs began massacring Tutsi; the Tutsi-controlled army retaliated by killing Hutus.

The frequency of ethnic clashes increased, developing into a low-intensity civil war. A six-nation regional proposal to send troops into Burundi to maintain peace and order was devised in July 1996. Distrustful of the scheme, the Tutsi-dominated army led a coup deposing the Hutu president and installed Maj. Pierre Buyoya that month. More than 300,000 people were killed in the civil war since 1993, with the Tutsi-dominated army and the Hutu rebel forces responsible for the slaughter. After several aborted cease-fires, a 2001 peace plan included a power-sharing agreement that has been relatively successful: Buyoya, a Tutsi, governed the new transitional government for the first 18 months; then, in April 2003, a Hutu president, Domitien Ndayizeye, assumed power. In Aug. 2005, former Hutu rebel leader Pierre Nkurunziza was elected president by Parliament. The peaceful transfer of power to a democratically elected leader seemed to indicate that Burundi's 12-year civil war may truly be at an end.

Cambodia
KINGDOM OF CAMBODIA

National Name: Preahreacheanacha Kampuchea
King: Norodom Sihamoni (2004)
Prime Minister: Hun Sen (1998)
Area: 69,900 sq mi (181,040 sq km)
Population (2005 est.): 13,607,069 (growth rate: 1.8%); birth rate: 27.1/1000; infant mortality rate: 71.5/1000; life expectancy: 58.9; density per sq mi: 195
Capital and largest city (2003 est.): Phnom Penh, 1,169,800. **Monetary unit:** Riel. **Languages:** Khmer (official), French, English. **Ethnicity/race:** Khmer 90%, Vietnamese %, Chinese 1%, other 4%. **Religions:** Theravada Buddhist 95%, others 5%. **Literacy rate:** 70% (2003 est.)
Economic summary: GDP/PPP (2004 est.): $26.99 billion; per capita $2,000. **Real growth rate:** 5.4%. **Inflation:** 3.1%. **Unemployment:** 2.5% (2000 est.). **Arable land:** 21%. **Agriculture:** rice, rubber, corn, vegetables, cashews, tapioca. **Labor force:** 7 million; agriculture 75% (2004 est.). **Industries:** tourism, garments, rice milling, fishing, wood and wood products, rubber, cement, gem mining, textiles. **Natural resources:** oil and gas, timber, gemstones, some iron ore, manganese, phosphates, hydropower potential. **Exports:** $2.311 billion (f.o.b., 2004 est.): clothing, timber, rubber, rice, fish, tobacco, footwear. **Imports:** $3.129 billion (f.o.b., 2004 est.): petroleum products, cigarettes, gold, construction materials, machinery, motor vehicles, pharmaceutical products. **Major trading partners:** U.S., Germany, UK, Thailand, Hong Kong, Singapore, China, Vietnam, Taiwan, South Korea (2003).

Geography Situated on the Indochinese peninsula, Cambodia is bordered by Thailand and Laos on the north and Vietnam on the east and south. The Gulf of Thailand is off the western coast. The size of Missouri, the country consists chiefly of a large alluvial plain ringed by mountains and on the east is the Mekong River. The plain is centered around Lake Tonle Sap, which is a natural storage basin of the Mekong.

Government Multiparty liberal democracy under a constitutional monarchy.

History The area that is present-day Cambodia came under Khmer rule about 600, when the region was at the center of a vast empire that stretched over most of Southeast Asia. Under the Khmers, who were Hindus, a magnificent temple complex was constructed at Angkor. Buddhism was introduced in the 12th century during the rule of Jayavaram VII. However, the kingdom, then known as Kambuja, fell into decline after Jayavaram's reign and was nearly annihilated by Thai and Vietnamese invaders. Its power steadily diminished until 1863, when France colonized the region, joining Cambodia, Laos, and Vietnam into a single protectorate known as French Indochina.

The French quickly usurped all but ceremonial powers from the monarch, Norodom. When he died in 1904, the French passed over his sons and handed the throne to his brother, Sisowath. Sisowath and his son ruled until 1941, when Norodom Sihanouk was elevated to power. Sihanouk's coronation, along with the Japanese occupation during the war, worked to reinforce a sentiment among Cambodians that the region should be free from outside control. After World War II, Cambodians sought independence, but France was reluctant to part with its colony. Cambodia was granted independence within the French Union in 1949. But the French-Indochinese War provided an opportunity for Sihanouk to gain full military control of the country. He abdicated in 1955 in favor of his parents, remaining head of the government, and when his father died in 1960, Sihanouk became chief of state without returning to the throne. In 1963, he sought a guarantee of Cambodia's neutrality from all parties in the Vietnam War.

However, North Vietnamese and Vietcong troops had begun using eastern Cambodia as a safe haven from which to launch attacks into South Vietnam, making it increasingly difficult to stay out of the war. An indigenous Communist guerrilla movement known as the Khmer Rouge also began to put pressure on the government in Phnom Penh. On March 18, 1970, while Sihanouk was abroad, anti-Vietnamese riots broke out and Sihanouk was overthrown by Gen. Lon Nol. The Vietnam peace agreement of 1973 stipulated withdrawal of foreign forces from Cambodia, but fighting continued between Hanoi-backed insurgents and U.S.-supplied government troops.

Combat climaxed in April 1975 when the Lon Nol regime was overthrown by Pol Pot, leader of the Khmer Rouge forces. The four years of nightmarish Khmer Rouge rule led to the state-sponsored extermination of citizens by its own government. Between 1 million and 2 million people were massacred on the "killing fields" of Cambodia or worked to death through forced labor. Pol Pot's radical vision of transforming the country into a Marxist agrarian society led to the virtual extermination of the country's professional and technical classes.

Pol Pot was ousted by Vietnamese forces on Jan. 8, 1979, and a new pro-Hanoi government led by Heng Samrin was installed. Pol Pot and 35,000 Khmer Rouge fighters fled into the hills of western Cambodia, where they were joined by forces loyal to the ousted Sihanouk in a guerrilla movement aimed at overthrowing the Heng Samrin government. The Vietnamese plan originally called for a withdrawal by early 1990 and a negotiated political settlement. The talks became protracted, however, and a UN agreement was not signed until 1992, when Sihanouk was appointed leader of an interim Supreme National Council convened to run the country until elections could be held in 1993.

Free elections in May 1993 saw the defeat of Heng Samrin's successor, Hun Sen, who refused to accept the outcome of the vote and insisted instead on a power-sharing agreement. Under the arrangement, Hun Sen and Sihanouk's son, Prince Norodom Ranariddh, would act as co–prime ministers. The Khmer Rouge stronghold in the western jungles splintered in 1997, with factions either battling each other or defecting. Ranariddh and Hun Sen both courted Khmer Rouge factions in an effort to shore up their power. In early July, Hun Sen took advantage of the charged political atmosphere to depose Ranariddh, the country's only popularly elected leader. Hun Sen later launched a brutal purge, executing more than 40 political opponents. Shortly after the July coup, the Khmer Rouge organized a show trial of their notorious leader, Pol Pot, who had not been seen by the West in more than two decades. He was sentenced to house arrest for his crimes against humanity. He died on April 15, 1998. In the July 1998 election, Hun Sen defeated opposition leaders Sam Rainsy and Prince Ranariddh, but the opposition parties accused him of voter fraud. Cambodia was able to regain its UN seat, lost nearly a year earlier as a result of Hun Sen's coup.

Elections in July 2003 resulted in a stalemate—none of the parties won the two-thirds majority required to govern alone. Ranariddh refused to form a coalition with Hun Sen, calling him an autocrat and accusing him of corruption. After months of negotiations, Rana-

riddh and Hun Sen agreed in June 2004 to form a coalition, with Hun Sen remaining prime minister. In August, Cambodia's parliament ratified the country's entry into the World Trade Organization.

In March 2003 the UN and Cambodia announced that after five years they had finally agreed on a system to try senior Khmer Rouge officials on charges of genocide. Cambodia's lower house of parliament ratified the agreement in October 2004. UN members pledged about $38 million in April 2005 to fund the tribunal. Among those expected to stand trial are Ta Mok, alias The Butcher, and Kang Kech Iev, alias Duch, who ran the notorious Tuol Sleng prison.

King Norodom Sihanouk announced in Oct. 2004 that he had abdicated. Days later, the government formed the Throne Council, a nine-member panel responsible for naming a new king. The king indicated that he selected his son Prince Norodom Sihamoni to be his successor. Prince Sihamoni, a ballet dancer and choreographer, lives in France and has kept a distance from Cambodian politics.

In February 2005, opposition leader Sam Rainsy and two other members of parliament faced charges of defamation when parliament voted to strip them of their immunity. Sam Rainsy had accused the government of planning to kill political opponents.

Cameroon
REPUBLIC OF CAMEROON

National name: République du Cameroun
President: Paul Biya (1982)
Prime Minister: Ephraïm Inoni (2004)
Area: 183,567 sq mi (475,440 sq km)
Population (2005 est.): 16,380,005 (growth rate: 1.9%); birth rate: 34.7/1000; infant mortality rate: 68.3/1000; life expectancy: 47.8; density per sq mi: 89
Capital: Yaoundé, 1,395,200 (metro. area), 1,154,400 (city proper). **Largest city:** Douala, 1,490,500 (metro. area), 1,274.300 (city proper). **Monetary unit:** CFA Franc. **Languages:** French, English (both official); 24 major African language groups. **Ethnicity/race:** Cameroon Highlanders 31%, Equatorial Bantu 19%, Kirdi 11%, Fulani 10%, Northwest Bantu 8%, Eastern Nigritic 7%, other African 13%, non-African less than 1%. **Religions:** indigenous beliefs 40%, Christian 40%, Islam 20%. **Literacy rate:** 79% (2003 est.)
Economic summary: GDP/PPP (2004 est.): $30.17 billion; per capita $1,900. **Real growth rate:** 4.9%. **Inflation:** 1%. **Unemployment:** 30% (2001 est.). **Arable land:** 13%. **Agriculture:** coffee, cocoa, cotton, rubber, bananas, oilseed, grains, root starches; livestock; timber. **Labor force:** 6.68 million; agriculture 70%, industry and commerce 13%, other 17%. **Industries:** petroleum production and refining, aluminum production, food processing, light consumer goods, textiles, lumber, ship repair. **Natural resources:** petroleum, bauxite, iron ore, timber, hydropower. **Exports:** $2.445 billion (f.o.b., 2004 est.): crude oil and petroleum products, lumber, cocoa beans, aluminum, coffee, cotton. **Imports:** $1.979 billion (f.o.b., 2004 est.): machinery, electrical equipment, transport equipment, fuel, food. **Major trading partners:** Spain, Italy, France, Netherlands, U.S., Nigeria, Japan, China, Germany (2003).

Geography Cameroon is a Central African nation on the Gulf of Guinea, bordered by Nigeria, Chad, the Central African Republic, the Republic of Congo, Equatorial Guinea, and Gabon. It is nearly twice the size of Oregon. Mount Cameroon (13,350 ft; 4,069 m), near the coast, is the highest elevation in the country. The main rivers are the Benue, Nyong, and Sanaga.

Government After a 1972 plebiscite, a unitary republic was formed out of East and West Cameroon to replace the former federal republic.

History Bantu speakers were among the first groups to settle Cameroon, followed by the Muslim Fulani in the 18th and 19th centuries. The land escaped colonial rule until 1884, when treaties with tribal chiefs brought the area under German domination. After World War I, the League of Nations gave the French a mandate over 80% of the area, and the British 20% adjacent to Nigeria. After World War II, when the country came under a UN trusteeship in 1946, self-government was granted, and the Cameroon People's Union emerged as the dominant party by campaigning for reunification of French and British Cameroon and for independence. Accused of being under Communist control, the party waged a campaign of revolutionary terror from 1955 to 1958, when it was crushed. In British Cameroon, unification was also promoted by the leading party, the Kamerun National Democratic Party, led by John Foncha.

France set up Cameroon as an autonomous state in 1957, and the next year its legislative assembly voted for independence by 1960. In 1959 a fully autonomous government of Cameroon was formed under Ahmadou Ahidjo. Cameroon became an independent republic on Jan. 1, 1960. In 1961 the southern part of the British territory joined the new Federal Republic of Cameroon and the northern section voted for unification with Nigeria. The president of Cameroon since independence, Ahmadou Ahidjo was replaced in 1982 by the prime minister, Paul Biya. Both administrations have been authoritarian.

With the expansion of oil, timber, and coffee exports, the economy has continued to improve, although corruption is prevalent, and environmental degradation remains a concern. In June 2000 the World Bank agreed to provide more than $200 million to build a $3.7 billion pipeline connecting the oil fields in neighboring Chad with the Cameroon coast.

Canada

Sovereign: Queen Elizabeth II (1952)
Governor-General: Adrienne Clarkson (1999)
Prime Minister: Paul Martin (2003)
Area: 3,855,081 sq mi (9,984,670 sq km)
Population (2005 est.): 32,805,041 (growth rate: 0.9%); birth rate: 10.8/1000; infant mortality rate: 4.8/1000; life expectancy: 80.1; density per sq mi: 9
Capital (2003 est.): Ottawa, Ontario, 1,089,100 (metro. area), 852,100 (city proper). **Largest cities (metropolitan areas):** Toronto, 5,508,000, 4,494,200 (city proper); Montreal, 3,248,000; Vancouver, 1,865,300; Calgary, 1,089,100; Edmonton, 966,200; Quebec, 689,400; Winnipeg, 675,800; Hamilton, 636,900; London, 439,400; Kitchener, 426,200.
Monetary unit: Canadian dollar. **Languages:** English 59.3%, French 23.2% (both official); other 17.5%.
Ethnicity/race: British Isles origin 28%, French origin 23%, other European 15%, indigenous Indian and Inuit 2%, other, mostly Asian, African, Arab 6%, mixed background 26%. **Religions:** Roman Catholic 46%, Protestant 36%, other 18% (based on 1991 census). **Literacy rate:** 97% (1986 est.)
Economic summary: GDP/PPP (2004 est.): $1.023 trillion; per capita $31,500. **Real growth rate:** 2.4%. **Inflation:** 1.9%. **Unemployment:** 7%. **Arable land:** 5%. **Agriculture:** wheat, barley, oilseed, tobacco, fruits, vegetables; dairy products; forest products; fish. **Labor force:** 17.37 million (2004); services 74%, manufacturing 15%, construction 5%, agriculture 3%, other 3% (2000). **Industries:** transportation

equipment, chemicals, processed and unprocessed minerals, food products; wood and paper products; fish products, petroleum and natural gas. **Natural resources:** iron ore, nickel, zinc, copper, gold, lead, molybdenum, potash, diamonds, silver, fish, timber, wildlife, coal, petroleum, natural gas, hydropower. **Exports:** $315.6 billion (f.o.b., 2004 est.): motor vehicles and parts, industrial machinery, aircraft, telecommunications equipment; chemicals, plastics, fertilizers; wood pulp, timber, crude petroleum, natural gas, electricity, aluminum. **Imports:** $256.1 billion (f.o.b., 2004 est.): machinery and equipment, motor vehicles and parts, crude oil, chemicals, electricity, durable consumer goods. **Major trading partners:** U.S., Japan, UK, China (2003).

Geography Covering most of the northern part of the North American continent and with an area larger than that of the United States, Canada has an extremely varied topography. In the east the mountainous maritime provinces have an irregular coastline on the Gulf of St. Lawrence and the Atlantic. The St. Lawrence plain, covering most of southern Quebec and Ontario, and the interior continental plain, covering southern Manitoba and Saskatchewan and most of Alberta, are the principal cultivable areas. They are separated by a forested plateau rising from Lakes Superior and Huron.

Westward toward the Pacific, most of British Columbia, the Yukon, and part of western Alberta are covered by parallel mountain ranges, including the Rockies. The Pacific border of the coast range is ragged with fjords and channels. The highest point in Canada is Mount Logan (19,850 ft; 6,050 m), which is in the Yukon. The two principal river systems are the Mackenzie and the St. Lawrence. The St. Lawrence, with its tributaries, is navigable for over 1,900 mi (3,058 km).

Government Canada is a federation of ten provinces (Alberta, British Columbia, Manitoba, New Brunswick, Newfoundland and Labrador, Nova Scotia, Ontario, Prince Edward Island, Quebec, and Saskatchewan) and three territories (Northwest Territories, Yukon, and as of April 1, 1999, Nunavut). Formally considered a constitutional monarchy, Canada is governed by its own House of Commons. While the governor-general is officially the representative of Queen Elizabeth II, in reality the governor-general acts only on the advice of the Canadian prime minister.

History The first inhabitants of Canada were native Indian peoples, primarily the Inuit (Eskimo). The Norse explorer Leif Eriksson probably reached the shores of Canada (Labrador or Nova Scotia) in 1000, but the history of the white man in the country actually began in 1497, when John Cabot, an Italian in the service of Henry VII of England, reached Newfoundland or Nova Scotia. Canada was taken for France in 1534 by Jacques Cartier. The actual settlement of New France, as it was then called, began in 1604 at Port Royal in what is now Nova Scotia; in 1608, Quebec was founded. France's colonization efforts were not very successful, but French explorers by the end of the 17th century had penetrated beyond the Great Lakes to the western prairies and south along the Mississippi to the Gulf of Mexico. Meanwhile, the English Hudson's Bay Company had been established in 1670. Because of the valuable fisheries and fur trade, a conflict developed between the French and English; in 1713, Newfoundland, Hudson Bay, and Nova Scotia (Acadia) were lost to England. During the Seven Years' War (1756–1763), England extended its conquest, and the British general James Wolfe won his famous victory

Canadian Prime Ministers Since 1867

Term	Prime Minister	Party	Term	Prime Minister	Party
1867–1873	Sir John A. Macdonald	Conservative	1930–1935	Richard B. Bennett	Conservative
1873–1878	Alexander Mackenzie	Liberal	1935–1948	W. L. Mackenzie King	Liberal
1878–1891	Sir John A. Macdonald	Conservative	1948–1957	Louis S. St. Laurent	Liberal
1891–1892	Sir John J. C. Abbott	Conservative	1957–1963	John G. Diefenbaker	Conservative
1892–1894	Sir John S. D. Thompson	Conservative	1963–1968	Lester B. Pearson	Liberal
1894–1896	Sir Mackenzie Bowell	Conservative	1968–1979	Pierre Elliott Trudeau	Liberal
1896	Sir Charles Tupper	Conservative	1979–1980	Charles Joseph Clark	Conservative
1896–1911	Sir Wilfrid Laurier	Liberal	1980–1984	Pierre Elliott Trudeau	Liberal
1911–1917	Sir Robert L. Borden	Conservative	1984	John Turner	Liberal
1917–1920	Sir Robert L. Borden	Unionist	1984–1993	Brian Mulroney	Conservative
1920–1921	Arthur Meighen	Unionist	1993	Kim Campbell	Conservative
1921–1926	W. L. Mackenzie King	Liberal	1993–2003	Jean Chrétien	Liberal
1926	Arthur Meighen	Conservative	2003–	Paul Martin	Liberal
1926–1930	W. L. Mackenzie King	Liberal			

over Gen. Louis Montcalm outside Quebec on Sept. 13, 1759. The Treaty of Paris in 1763 gave England control.

At that time the population of Canada was almost entirely French, but in the next few decades, thousands of British colonists emigrated to Canada from the British Isles and from the American colonies. In 1849, the right of Canada to self-government was recognized. By the British North America Act of 1867, the dominion of Canada was created through the confederation of Upper and Lower Canada, Nova Scotia, and New Brunswick. In 1869, Canada purchased from the Hudson's Bay Company the vast middle west (Rupert's Land) from which the provinces of Manitoba (1870), Alberta (1905), and Saskatchewan (1905) were later formed. In 1871, British Columbia joined the dominion, and in 1873, Prince Edward Island followed. The country was linked from coast to coast in 1885 by the Canadian Pacific Railway.

During the formative years between 1866 and 1896, the Conservative Party, led by Sir John A. Macdonald, governed the country, except during the years 1873–1878. In 1896 the Liberal Party took over and, under Sir Wilfrid Laurier, an eminent French Canadian, ruled until 1911. By the Statute of Westminster in 1931 the British dominions, including Canada, were formally declared to be partner nations with Britain, "equal in status, in no way subordinate to each other," and bound together only by allegiance to a common Crown.

Newfoundland became Canada's tenth province on March 31, 1949, following a plebiscite. Canada also includes three territories—the Yukon Territory, the Northwest Territories, and the newest territory, Nunavut. This new territory includes all of the Arctic north of the mainland, Norway having recognized Canadian sovereignty over the Sverdrup Islands in the Arctic in 1931.

The Liberal Party, led by William Lyon Mackenzie King, dominated Canadian politics from 1921 until 1957, when it was succeeded by the Progressive Conservatives. The Liberals, under the leadership of Lester B. Pearson, returned to power in 1963. Pearson remained prime minister until 1968, when he retired and was replaced by a former law professor, Pierre Elliott Trudeau. Trudeau maintained Canada's defensive alliance with the United States but began moving toward a more independent policy in world affairs.

Faced with an increasingly violent separatist movement in the predominantly French province of Quebec, Trudeau introduced the Official Languages Bill, which encouraged bilingualism in the federal government; he also gave an economic portfolio to a French-speaking minister, Jean Chrétien. Both measures increased the power of French-speaking politicians in the federal government.

In 1976, the Parti Québécois (PQ) won the provincial Quebec elections, and René Lévesque became premier. The Quebec government passed Bill 101 in 1977, which established numerous rules promoting the French-speaking culture; for example, only French was to be used for commercial signs and for most public school instruction. Many of Bill 101's provisions have since been amended, striking more of a compromise; commercial signs, for example, may now be in French and English, provided that the French lettering is twice the size of the English. Quebec held a referendum in May 1980 on whether it should seek independence from Canada; it was defeated by 60% of the voters.

Resolving a dispute that had occupied Trudeau since the beginning of his tenure, Queen Elizabeth II signed the Constitution Act (also called the Canada Act) in Ottawa on April 17, 1982, thereby cutting the last legal tie between Canada and Britain. The constitution retains Queen Elizabeth as queen of Canada and keeps Canada's membership in the Commonwealth. This constitution was accepted by every province except Quebec.

In the national election on Sept. 4, 1984, the Progressive Conservative Party scored an overwhelming victory, fundamentally changing the country's political landscape. The Conservatives, led by Brian Mulroney, won the highest political majority in Canadian history.

Population by Provinces and Territories

Province	2005	2004
	(in thousands)	
Alberta	3,236.9	3,190.4
British Columbia	4,232.5	4,182.9
Manitoba	1,176.1	1,167.5
New Brunswick	751.2	751.2
Newfoundland and Labrador	515.9	517.9
Nova Scotia	936.9	936.9
Ontario	12,483.0	12,347.4
Prince Edward Island	137.8	137.9
Quebec	7,577.1	7,527.4
Saskatchewan	995.1	994.9
Northwest Territories	43.0	43.0
Yukon Territory	31.3	31.0
Nunavut	29.7	29.3

NOTE: As of April 1, 2005. *Source: Statistics Canada.*

The dominant foreign issue was a free-trade pact with the U.S., a treaty bitterly opposed by the Liberal and New Democratic Parties. The conflict led to elections in Nov. 1988 that solidly reelected Mulroney and gave him a mandate to proceed with the agreement.

The issue of separatist sentiments in French-speaking Quebec flared up again in 1990 with the failure of the Meech Lake Accord. The accord was designed to bring Quebec into the constitution while easing its residents' fear of losing their identity within the English-speaking majority by giving it status as a "distinct society."

The economy continued to be mired in a long recession that many blamed on the free-trade agreement. Brian Mulroney's popularity continued to decline, causing him to resign before the next election. In June 1993 the governing Progressive Conservative Party chose Defense Minister Kim Campbell as its leader, making her the first female prime minister in Canadian history. The national election in Oct. 1993 resulted in the reemergence of the Liberal Party and the installation of Jean Chrétien as prime minister.

The Quebec referendum on secession in Oct. 1995 yielded a narrow rejection of the proposal, and separatists vowed to try again. Since then, however, the Quebec Liberal Party has replaced the Bloc Québecois as the ruling party.

On April 1, 1999, the Northwest Territories were officially divided to create a new territory in the east that would be governed by Canada's Inuits, who make up 85% of the area's population.

In July 2000, Stockwell Day of the new right-wing Canadian Alliance Party unexpectedly emerged as the leader of Canada's opposition. In Nov. 2000 elections, however, Prime Minister Jean Chrétien of the Liberal Party won a landslide victory for a third five-year term. After the election, the conservatives rapidly lost steam.

In recent years, Canada has introduced some of the world's most liberal social policies. Medical marijuana for the terminally or chronically ill was legalized in 2001; the country began legally dispensing marijuana by prescription in July 2003. In 2003, Ontario and British Columbia legalized same-sex marriage; and more provinces and territories followed in 2004. In July 2005, Canada legalized gay marriage throughout the country, becoming one of four nations (along with Belgium, the Netherlands, and Spain) to do so.

Canada-U.S. relations were strained in 2003 when Canada refused to join Washington's coalition supporting the war in Iraq. In December, Canada was incensed when the U.S. included it on a list of countries banned from bidding on future reconstruction contracts in Iraq. Despite Canada's opposition to the war in Iraq, it had contributed $240 million to reconstruction efforts in Iraq and sent 2,000 soldiers to Afghanistan. Relations with the United States improved in Jan. 2004 after President Bush reversed the policy.

In Dec. 2003, Chrétien stepped down and handed the prime ministership to the new leader of Canada's Liberal Party, former finance minister Paul Martin. Chrétien had announced in 2002 that he would not seek a fourth term—conflict between Chrétien and Martin had divided and weakened the Liberal Party in recent years. A financial scandal uncovered in Feb. 2004 under Chrétien's rule further diminished the party's standing. In June 2004, Martin was reelected prime minister, but the Liberal Party lost its majority in Parliament, which it had dominated for 11 years. In 2005, a scandal involving the misappropriation of government funds by the Liberal Party threatened the stability of Martin's government. Martin himself was not implicated in the scandal.

Cape Verde

REPUBLIC OF CAPE VERDE

National name: República de Cabo Verde
President: Pedro Pires (2001)
Prime Minister: José Maria Neves (2001)
Area: 1,557 sq mi (4,033 sq km)
Population (2005 est.): 418,224 (growth rate: 0.7%); birth rate: 25.3/1000; infant mortality rate: 47.8/1000; life expectancy: 70.5; density per sq mi: 269
Capital and largest city (2003 est.): Praia, 99,400.
Other large city: Mindelo, 66,100. **Monetary unit:** Cape Verdean escudo. **Languages:** Portuguese, Criuolo. **Ethnicity/race:** Creole (mulatto) 71%, African 28%, European 1%. **Religion:** Roman Catholic (infused with indigenous beliefs), Protestant (mostly Church of the Nazarene). **Literacy rate:** 77% (2003 est.)
Economic summary: GDP/PPP (2002 est.): $600 million; per capita $1,400. **Real growth rate:** 5%. **Inflation:** 1.5%. **Unemployment:** 21% (2000 est.). **Arable land:** 10%. **Agriculture:** bananas, corn, beans, sweet potatoes, sugarcane, coffee, peanuts; fish. **Labor force:** n.a. **Industries:** food and beverages, fish processing, shoes and garments, salt mining, ship repair. **Natural resources:** salt, basalt rock, limestone, kaolin, fish, clay, gypsum. **Exports:** $61.11 million (f.o.b., 2004 est.): fuel, shoes, garments, fish, hides. **Imports:** $387.3 million (f.o.b., 2004 est.): foodstuffs, industrial products, transport equipment, fuels. **Major trading partners:** Portugal, France, U.S., UK, Netherlands (2003).

Geography Cape Verde, only slightly larger than Rhode Island, is an archipelago in the Atlantic 385 mi (500 km) west of Senegal.

The islands are divided into two groups: Barlavento in the north, composed of Santo Antão (291 sq mi; 754 sq km), Boa Vista (240 sq mi; 622 sq km), São Nicolau (132 sq mi; 342 sq km), São Vicente (88 sq mi; 246 sq km), Sal (83 sq mi; 298 sq km), and Santa Luzia (13 sq mi; 34 sq km); and Sotavento in the south, consisting of São Tiago (383 sq mi; 992 sq km), Fogo (184 sq mi; 477 sq km), Maio (103 sq mi; 267 sq km), and Brava (25 sq mi; 65 sq km). The islands are mostly mountainous, with the land deeply scarred by erosion. There is an active volcano on Fogo.

Government Republic.

History Uninhabited on their discovery in 1456, the Cape Verde islands became part of the Portuguese empire in 1495. A majority of today's inhabitants are of mixed Portuguese and African ancestry.

Positioned on the great trade routes between Africa, Europe, and the New World, the islands became a prosperous center for the slave trade but suffered economic decline after the slave trade was abolished in 1876. In the 20th century, Cape Verde served as a shipping port.

In 1951, Cape Verde's status changed from a Portuguese colony to an overseas province, and in 1961 the inhabitants became full Portuguese citizens. An independence movement led by the African Party for the Independence of Guinea-Bissau (another former Portuguese colony) and Cape Verde (PAIGC) was founded in 1956. Following the 1974 coup in Portugal, after which Portugal began abandoning its colonial empire, the islands became independent (July 5, 1975).

On Jan. 13, 1991, the first multiparty elections since independence resulted in the ruling African Party for the Independence of Cape Verde (PAICV) losing its majority to the Movement for Democracy Party (MPD). The MPD candidate, Antonio Monteiro, won the subsequent presidential election, and was easily reelected in 1996. In 2001, Pedro Pires became president.

In an effort to take advantage of its proximity to cross-Atlantic sea and air lanes, the government has embarked on a major expansion of its port and airport capacities. It is also modernizing its fish processing industry. These projects are being partly paid for by the EU and the World Bank, making Cape Verde one of the largest per-capita aid recipients in the world. Disenchantment with the government's privatization program, continued high unemployment, and widespread poverty helped defeat the MPD in elections held in Jan. 2001. The PAICV swept back into power and José Maria Neves became prime minister.

Central African Republic

National name: République Centrafricaine
President: Gen. François Bozizé (2003)
Prime Minister: Elie Doté (2005)
Area: 240,534 sq mi (622,984 sq km)
Population (2005 est.): 3,799,897 (growth rate: 1.5%); birth rate: 35.2/1000; infant mortality rate: 91.0/1000; life expectancy: 41.0; density per sq mi: 16
Capital and largest city (2003 est.): Bangui, 810,000 (metro. area), 669,800 (city proper). **Monetary unit:** CFA Franc. **Languages:** French (official), Sangho (lingua franca, national), tribal languages. **Ethnicity/ race:** Baya 33%, Banda 27%, Mandjia 13%, Sara 10%, Mboum 7%, M'Baka 4%, Yakoma 4%, other 2%. **Religions:** indigenous beliefs 35%, Protestant and Roman Catholic (both with animist influence) 25% each, Islam 15%. **Literacy rate:** 51% (2003 est.)
Economic summary: GDP/PPP (2004 est.): $4.248 billion; per capita $1,100. **Real growth rate:** 0.5%. **Inflation:** 3.6% (2001 est.). **Unemployment:** 8% (23% for Bangui) (2001 est.). **Arable land:** 3%. **Agriculture:** cotton, coffee, tobacco, manioc (tapioca), yams, millet, corn, bananas; timber. **Labor force:** n.a. **Industries:** diamond mining, logging, brewing, textiles, footwear, assembly of bicycles and motorcycles. **Natural resources:** diamonds, uranium, timber, gold, oil, hydropower. **Exports:** $172 million (f.o.b., 2002 est.): diamonds, timber, cotton, coffee, tobacco. **Imports:** $136 million (f.o.b., 2002 est.): food, textiles, petroleum products, machinery, electrical equipment, motor vehicles, chemicals, pharmaceuticals. **Major trading partners:** Belgium, Italy, Spain, France, Indonesia, Cameroon, U.S. (2003).

Geography Situated about 500 mi (805 km) north of the equator, the Central African Republic is a landlocked nation bordered by Cameroon, Chad, the Sudan, the Democratic Republic of the Congo, and the Republic of Congo. The Ubangi and the Shari are the largest of many rivers.

Government Multiparty republic since 1991.

History From the 16th to 19th century, the people of this region were ravaged by slave traders. The Banda, Baya, Ngbandi, and Azande make up the largest ethnic groups.

The French occupied the region in 1894. As the colony of Ubangi-Shari, what is now the Central African Republic was united with Chad in 1905. In 1910 it was joined with Gabon and the Middle Congo to become French Equatorial Africa. After World War II a rebellion in 1946 forced the French to grant self-government. In 1958 the territory voted to become an autonomous republic within the French Community, and on Aug. 13, 1960, President David Dacko proclaimed the republic's independence from France. Dacko moved the country politically into Beijing's orbit, but he was overthrown in a coup on Dec. 31, 1965, by Col. Jean-Bédel Bokassa, army chief of staff.

On Dec. 4, 1976, the Central African Republic became the Central African Empire. Marshal Jean-Bédel Bokassa, who had ruled the republic since he took power in 1965, was declared Emperor Bokassa I. Brutality and excess characterized his regime. He was overthrown in a coup on Sept. 20, 1979. Former president David Dacko returned to power and changed the country's name back to the Central African Republic. An army coup on Sept. 1, 1981, deposed President Dacko again.

In 1991, President André Kolingba, under pressure, announced a move toward parliamentary democracy. In elections held in Aug. 1993, Prime Minister Ange-Félix Patassé defeated Kolingba. Part of Patassé's popularity rested on his pledge to pay the back salaries of the military and civil servants.

A 1994 economic upturn was too small to effectively improve the catastrophic financial condition of the nation. Patassé was unable to pay the salaries due to government workers, and the military revolted in 1996. At Patassé's request, French troops suppressed the uprising. In 1998 the United Nations sent an all-African peacekeeping force to the country. In elections held in Sept. 1999, amid widespread charges of massive fraud, Patassé easily defeated Kolingba. Patassé survived a coup attempt in May 2001, but two years later, in March 2003, he was overthrown by Gen. François Bozizé. After two years of military rule, presidential elections were held, and Bozizé won in what international monitors called a free and fair election.

Chad

REPUBLIC OF CHAD

National name: République du Tchad
President: Idriss Déby (1990)
Prime Minister: Pascal Yoadimnadji (2005)
Area: 495,752 sq mi (1,284,000 sq km)
Population (2005 est.): 9,826,419 (growth rate: 3.0%); birth rate: 46.0/1000; infant mortality rate: 93.8/1000; life expectancy: 47.9; density per sq mi: 20
Capital and largest city (2003 est.): N'Djamena, 609,600. **Monetary unit:** CFA Franc. **Languages:** French, Arabic (both official); Sara; more than 120 languages and dialects. **Ethnicity/race:** 200 distinct groups. North and center, mostly Muslim: Arabs, Gorane (Toubou, Daza, Kreda), Zaghawa, Kanembou, Ouaddai, Baguirmi, Hadjerai, Fulbe, Kotoko, Hausa, Boulala, and Maba. South, mostly Christian or animist: Sara (Ngambaye, Mbaye, Goulaye), Moundang, Moussei, Massa. **Religions:** Islam 51%, Christian 35%, animist 7%, other 7%. **Literacy rate:** 48% (2003 est.)
Economic summary: GDP/PPP (2004 est.): $15.66 billion; per capita $1,600. **Real growth rate:** 38%. **Inflation:** 8%. **Unemployment:** n.a. **Arable land:** 3%. **Agriculture:** cotton, sorghum, millet, peanuts, rice, potatoes, manioc (tapioca); cattle, sheep, goats, camels. **Labor force:** n.a.; agriculture more than 85% (subsistence farming, herding, and fishing). **Industries:** oil, cotton textiles, meatpacking, beer brewing, natron (sodium carbonate), soap, cigarettes, construction materials. **Natural resources:** petroleum (unexploited but exploration under way), uranium, natron, kaolin, fish (Lake Chad), gold, limestone, sand and gravel, salt. **Exports:** $365 million (f.o.b., 2003 est.): cotton, cattle, gum arabic. **Imports:** $500.7 million (f.o.b., 2004 est.): machinery and transportation equipment, industrial goods, petroleum products, foodstuffs, textiles. **Major trading partners:** U.S., Germany, Portugal, France, Morocco, Cameroon, Netherlands (2003).

Geography A landlocked country in north-central Africa, Chad is about 85% the size of Alaska. Its neighbors are Niger, Libya, the Sudan, the Central African Republic, Cameroon, and Nigeria. Lake Chad, from which the country gets its name, lies on the western border with Niger and Nigeria. In the north is a desert that runs into the Sahara.

Government Republic.

History The area around Lake Chad has been inhabited since at least 500 B.C. In the 8th century A.D. Berbers began migrating to the area. Islam arrived in 1085, and by the 16th century a trio of rival kingdoms flourished: the Kanem-Bornu, Baguirmi, and Ouaddaï. In 1883–1893, all three kingdoms came under the rule of the Sudanese conqueror Rabih al-Zubayr. In 1900, Rabih was overthrown by the French, who absorbed these kingdoms into the colony of French Equatorial Africa, as part of Ubangi-Shari (now the Central African Republic), in 1913. In 1946, the territory, now known as Chad, became an autonomous republic within the French Community. An independence movement led by the first premier and president, François (later Ngarta) Tombalbaye, achieved complete independence on Aug. 11, 1960. Tombalbaye was killed in the 1975 coup and succeeded by Gen. Félix Malloum, who faced a Libyan-financed civil war throughout his tenure in office. In 1977, Libya seized a strip of Chadian land and launched an invasion two years later.

Nine rival groups meeting in Lagos, Nigeria, in March 1979 agreed to form a provisional government headed by Goukouni Oueddei, a former rebel leader. Fighting broke out again in Chad in March 1980, when Defense Minister Hissen Habré challenged Goukouni and seized the capital. Libyan president Muammar al-Qaddafi, in Jan. 1981, proposed a merger of Chad with Libya. The Libyan proposal was rejected and Libyan troops withdrew from Chad that year, but in 1983 they poured back into the northern part of the country in support of Goukouni. France, in turn, sent troops into southern Chad in support of Habré. Government troops then launched an offensive in early 1987 that drove the Libyans out of most of the country.

In 1990, Idriss Déby, a former defense minister and head of the Patriotic Salvation Movement, overthrew Habré, suspended the constitution, and dissolved the legislature. In 1994 a new constitution was drafted and an amnesty for political prisoners was declared. Déby won multiparty elections in 1996 and was reelected in 2001. His rule has been marked by repression and corruption. Déby has faced about a half-dozen insurgencies since taking office.

In June 2000 the World Bank agreed to provide more than $200 million to build a $3.7-billion pipeline connecting the oil fields in Chad to those in Cameroon. Oil revenues are estimated to earn $2.5 billion over the next 30 years. Human rights groups are concerned they will only benefit the oil companies and the political elite in Cameroon and Chad. The World Bank, however, has forced Chad to agree to spend 80% of the resulting oil revenues on education, health, infrastructure, and other social welfare projects desperately needed by this impoverished country. In Nov. 2004, Chad received its first oil check. In the next 25 years Chad is expected to make $80 million per year, increasing the government treasury by 50%.

In 2004, hundreds of thousands of refugees fled to Chad to escape the fighting in Sudan's Darfur region, where they face hunger and disease in desperately undersupplied refugee camps.

In 2005, more than 77% of voters approved a referendum that would allow President Déby to run for a third term.

Chile

REPUBLIC OF CHILE

National name: República de Chile
President: Ricardo Lagos (2000)
Area: 292,258 sq mi (756,950 sq km)
Population (2005 est.): 15,980,912 (growth rate: 1.0%); birth rate: 15.4/1000; infant mortality rate: 8.8/1000; life expectancy: 76.6; density per sq mi: 55
Capital and largest city (2003 est.): Santiago, 5,333,100 (metro. area), 4,372,800 (city proper). **Other large cities:** Viña del Mar, 303,100; Valparaíso, 274,100; Talcahuano, 252,800; Temuco, 247,200; Concepción, 217,600. **Monetary unit:** Chilean Peso.
Language: Spanish. **Ethnicity/race:** white and white-Amerindian 95%, Amerindian 3%, other 2%. **Religions:** Roman Catholic 89%, Protestant 11%, small Jewish and Muslim populations. **Literacy rate:** 96% (2003 est.)
Economic summary: GDP/PPP (2004 est.): $169.1 billion; per capita $10,700. **Real growth rate:** 5.8%. **Inflation:** 2.4%. **Unemployment:** 8.5%. **Arable land:** 3%. **Agriculture:** grapes, apples, pears, onions, wheat, corn, oats, peaches, garlic, asparagus, beans, beef, poultry, wool; fish; timber. **Labor force:** 6.2 million; agriculture 13.6%, industry 23.4%, services 63% (2003). **Industries:** copper, other minerals, foodstuffs, fish processing, iron and steel, wood and wood products, transport equipment, cement, textiles. **Natural resources:** copper, timber, iron ore, nitrates, precious metals, molybdenum, hydropower. **Exports:** $29.2 billion (f.o.b., 2004 est.): copper, fruit, fish products, paper and pulp, chemicals, wine. **Imports:** $22.53 billion (f.o.b., 2004 est.): petroleum and petroleum products, chemicals, electrical and telecommunications equipment, industrial machinery, vehicles, natural gas. **Major trading partners:** U.S., Japan, China, South Korea, Mexico, Italy, Argentina, Brazil (2003).

Geography Situated south of Peru and west of Bolivia and Argentina, Chile fills a narrow 1,800-mile (2,897 km) strip between the Andes and the Pacific. One-third of Chile is covered by the towering ranges of the Andes. In the north is the driest place on Earth, the Atacama Desert, and in the center is a 700-mile-long (1,127 km) thickly populated valley with most of Chile's arable land. At the southern tip of Chile's mainland is Punta Arenas, the southernmost city in the world, and beyond that lies the Strait of Magellan and Tierra del Fuego, an island divided between Chile and Argentina. The southernmost point of South America is Cape Horn, a 1,390-foot (424 m) rock on Horn Island in the Wollaston group, which belongs to Chile. Chile also claims sovereignty over 482,628 sq mi (1,250,000 sq km) of Antarctic territory; the Juan Fernández Islands, about 400 mi (644 km) west of the mainland; and Easter Island, about 2,000 mi (3,219 km) west.

Government Republic.

History Chile was originally under the control of the Incas in the north and the nomadic Araucanos in the south. In 1541, a Spaniard, Pedro de Valdivia, founded Santiago. Chile won its independence from Spain in 1818 under Bernardo O'Higgins and an Argentinian, José de San Martin. O'Higgins, dictator until 1823, laid the foundations of the modern state with a two-party system and a centralized government.

The dictator from 1830 to 1837, Diego Portales, fought a war with Peru in 1836–1839 that expanded Chilean territory. Chile fought the War of the Pacific with Peru and Bolivia from 1879 to 1883, winning Antofagasta, Bolivia's only outlet to the sea, and extensive areas from Peru. Pedro Montt led a revolt that overthrew José Balmaceda in 1891 and established a parliamentary dictatorship lasting until a new constitution was adopted in 1925. Industrialization began before World War I and led to the formation of Marxist groups. Juan Antonio Ríos, president during World War II, was originally pro-Nazi but in 1944 led his country into the war on the side of the Allies.

In 1970, Salvador Allende became the first president in a non-Communist country freely elected on a Marxist program. Allende quickly established relations with Cuba and the People's Republic of China, introduced Marxist economic and social reforms, and nationalized many private companies, including U.S.-owned ones. In Sept. 1973, Allende was overthrown and killed in a military coup covertly sponsored by the CIA, ending a 46-year era of constitutional government in Chile.

The coup was led by a four-man junta headed by Army Chief of Staff Augusto Pinochet, who eventually assumed the office of president. Committed to "exterminat[ing] Marxism," the junta suspended Parliament, banned political activity, and severely curbed civil liberties. Pinochet's brutal dictatorship led to the imprisonment, torture, execution, and expulsion of thousands of Chileans. The economy, in tatters under Allende's socialist revolution, gradually improved after Chile's return to privatization under Pinochet. In 1989, Pinochet lost a plebiscite on whether he should remain in power. He stepped down in Jan. 1990 in favor of Patricio Aylwin, who was elected in Dec. 1989 as the head of a 17-party coalition. In Dec. 1993, Eduardo Frei Ruiz-Tagle, the candidate of a center-left coalition and son of a previous president, was elected president.

Pinochet, who had retained his post as army commander in chief after the 1989 plebiscite, retired in March 1998. In Oct. 1998, he was arrested and detained in England on an extradition request issued by a Spanish judge who sought Pinochet in connection with the disappearance of Spanish citizens during his rule. British courts ultimately denied his extradition, and Pinochet returned to Chile in March 2000, where the courts eventually ruled that he was mentally unfit to stand trial. In 2004, however, Chile's Supreme Court stripped him of immunity, and he is expected to face trial for at least some of the abuses that occurred during his 17-year rule.

Ricardo Lagos became president in March 2000, the first Socialist to run the country since Allende. Chile's economic growth slowed to 3% for 2001, partly the result of a drop in international copper prices and the economic turmoil in neighboring Argentina. In 2003 there were several minor financial scandals involving insider information and bribery. In response, Lagos introduced new reforms promising greater transparency. In 2004, Chile passed a law permitting divorce for the first time.

China

PEOPLE'S REPUBLIC OF CHINA

National name: Zhonghua Renmin Gongheguo
President: Hu Jintao (2003)
Prime Minister: Wen Jiabao (2003)
Area: 3,705,386 sq mi (9,596,960 sq km)[1]
Population (2005 est.): 1,306,313,812 (growth rate: 0.6%); birth rate: 13.1/1000; infant mortality rate: 24.2/1000; life expectancy: 72.3; density per sq mi: 353
Capital (2003 est.): Beijing, 9,376,200 (metro. area), 6,619,000 (city proper). **Largest cities:** Shanghai, 12,039,900 (metro. area), 9,005,600 (city proper); Tianjin (Tientsin), 4,333,900; Wuhan, 3,959,700; Shenyang (Mukden), 3,574,100; Guangzhou,

3,473,800; Haerbin, 2,904,900; Xian, 2,642,100; Chungking (Chongquing), 2,370,100; Chengdu, 2,011,000; Hong Kong (Xianggang), 1,361,200.
Monetary unit: Yuan/Renminbi. **Languages:** Standard Chinese (Mandarin/Putonghua), Yue (Cantonese), Wu (Shanghaiese), Minbei (Fuzhou), Minnan (Hokkien-Taiwanese), Xiang, Gan, Hakka dialects, minority languages. **Ethnicity/race:** Han Chinese 91.9%, Zhuang, Uygur, Hui, Yi, Tibetan, Miao, Manchu, Mongol, Buyi, Korean, and other nationalities 8.1%.. **Religions:** Officially atheist; Christian 3%–4%; Daoist (Taoist), Buddhist, Muslim 1%–2%. (2002 est.). Literacy rate: 86% (2003 est.)
Economic summary: GDP/PPP (2004 est.): $7.262 trillion; per capita $5,600. **Real growth rate:** 9.1% (official data). **Inflation:** 4.1%. **Unemployment:** urban unemployment roughly 9.8%; substantial unemployment and underemployment in rural areas. **Arable land:** 15%. **Agriculture:** rice, wheat, potatoes, corn, peanuts, tea, millet, barley, apples, cotton, oilseed, pork, fish. **Labor force:** 760.8 million (2003); agriculture 49%, industry 22%, services 29% (2003 est.). **Industries:** mining and ore processing, iron, steel, aluminum, and other metals; coal; machine building; armaments; textiles and apparel; petroleum; cement; chemicals; fertilizers; consumer products, including footwear, toys, and electronics; food processing; transportation equipment, including automobiles, rail cars and locomotives, ships, and aircraft; telecommunications equipment, commercial space launch vehicles and satellites. **Natural resources:** coal, iron ore, petroleum, natural gas, mercury, tin, tungsten, antimony, manganese, molybdenum, vanadium, magnetite, aluminum, lead, zinc, uranium, hydropower potential (world's largest). **Exports:** $583.1 billion (f.o.b., 2004 est.): machinery and equipment, plastics, optical and medical equipment, iron and steel. **Imports:** $552.4 billion (f.o.b., 2004 est.): machinery and equipment, oil and mineral fuels, plastics, optical and medical equipment, organic chemicals, iron and steel. **Major trading partners:** U.S., Hong Kong, Japan, South Korea, Germany, Taiwan (2003).

1. Including Manchuria and Tibet.

Geography The greater part of the country is mountainous. Its principal ranges are the Tien Shan, the Kunlun chain, and the Trans-Himalaya. In the southwest is Tibet, which China annexed in 1950. The Gobi Desert lies to the north. China proper consists of three great river systems: the Yellow River (Huang He), 2,109 mi (5,464 km) long; the Yangtze River (Chang Jiang), the third-longest river in the world at 2,432 mi (6,300 km); and the Pearl River (Zhu Jiang), 848 mi (2,197 km) long.

Government Communist state.

History The earliest recorded human settlements in what is today called China were discovered in the Huang He basin and date from about 5000 B.C. During the Shang dynasty (1500–1000 B.C.), the precursor of modern China's ideographic writing system developed, allowing the emerging feudal states of the era to achieve an advanced stage of civilization, rivaling in sophistication any society found at the time in Europe, the Middle East, or the Americas. It was following this initial flourishing of civilization, in a period known as the Chou dynasty (1122–249 B.C.), that Lao-tse, Confucius, Mo Ti, and Mencius laid the foundation of Chinese philosophical thought.

The feudal states, often at war with one another, were first united under Emperor Ch'in Shih Huang Ti, during whose reign (246–210 B.C.) work was begun on the Great Wall of China, a monumental bulwark against invasion from the West. Although the Great Wall symbolized China's desire to protect itself from the outside world, under the Han dynasty (206 B.C.–A.D. 220), the civilization conducted extensive commercial trading with the West.

In the T'ang dynasty (618–907)—often called the golden age of Chinese history—painting, sculpture, and poetry flourished, and woodblock printing, which enabled the mass production of books, made its earliest known appearance. The Mings, last of the native rulers (1368–1644), overthrew the Mongol, or Yuan, dynasty (1271–1368) established by Kublai Khan. The Mings in turn were overthrown in 1644 by invaders from the north, the Manchus.

China remained largely isolated from the rest of the world's civilizations, closely restricting foreign activities. By the end of the 18th century only Canton (location of modern-day Hong Kong) and the Portuguese port of Macao were open to European merchants. But with the first Anglo-Chinese War in 1839–1842, a long period of instability and concessions to Western colonial powers began. Following the war, several ports were opened up for trading, and Hong Kong was ceded to Britain. Treaties signed after further hostilities (1856–1860) weakened Chinese sovereignty and gave foreigners immunity from Chinese jurisdiction. European powers took advantage of the disastrous Sino-Japanese War of 1894–1895 to gain further trading concessions from China. Peking's response, the Boxer Rebellion (1900), was suppressed by an international force.

The death of Empress Dowager Tzu Hsi in 1908 and the accession of the infant emperor Hsüan T'ung (Pu-Yi) were followed by a nationwide rebellion led by Dr. Sun Yat-sen, who overthrew the Manchus and became the first president of the Provisional Chinese Republic in 1911. Dr. Sun resigned in favor of Yuan Shih-k'ai, who suppressed the Republicans in a bid to consolidate his power. Yuan's death in June 1916 was followed by years of civil war between rival militarists and Dr. Sun's Republicans. Nationalist forces, led by General Chiang Kai-shek and with the advice of Communist experts, soon occupied most of China, setting up the Kuomintang regime in 1928. Internal strife continued, however, and Chiang eventually broke with the Communists.

On Sept. 18, 1931, Japan launched an invasion of Manchuria, capturing the province. Tokyo set up a puppet state dubbed Manchukuo and installed the last Manchu emperor, Henry Pu-Yi (Hsüan T'ung), as its nominal leader. Japanese troops moved to seize China's northern provinces in July 1937 but were resisted by Chiang, who had been able to use the Japanese invasion to unite most of China behind him. Within two years, however, Japan had seized most of the nation's eastern ports and railways. The Kuomintang government retreated first to Hankow and then to Chungking, while the Japanese set up a puppet government at Nanking, headed by Wang Jingwei.

Japan's surrender to the Western Allies in 1945 touched off civil war between the Kuomintang forces under Chiang and Communists led by Mao Zedong, who had been battling since the 1930s for control of China. Despite U.S. aid, the Kuomintang were overcome by the Soviet-supported Communists, and Chiang and his followers were forced to flee the mainland, establishing a government-in-exile on the island of Formosa (Taiwan). The Mao regime proclaimed the People's Republic of China on Oct. 1, 1949, with Beijing as the new capital and Zhou Enlai as premier.

After the Korean War began in June 1950, China led the Communist bloc in supporting North Korea, and on Nov. 26, 1950, the Mao regime sent troops to assist the North in its efforts to capture the South.

In an attempt to restructure China's primarily agrarian economy, Mao undertook the "Great Leap Forward" campaign in 1958, a disastrous program that aimed to combine the establishment of rural communes with a crash program of village industrialization. The Great Leap forced the abandonment of farming activities, leading to widespread famine in which more than 20 million people died of malnutrition.

In 1959, a failed uprising against China's invasion and occupation of Tibet forced Tibetan Buddhism's spiritual leader, the Dalai Lama, and 100,000 of his followers to flee to India. The invasion of Tibet and a perceived rivalry for the leadership of the world Communist movement caused a serious souring of relations between China and the USSR, former allies. In 1965 Tibet was formally made an autonomous region of China. China's harsh religious and cultural persecution of Tibetans, which continues to this day, has spawned growing international protest.

The failure of the Great Leap Forward touched off a power struggle within the Chinese Communist Party between Mao and his supporters and a reformist faction including future premier Deng Xiaoping. Mao moved to Shanghai, and from that base he and his supporters waged what they called the Cultural Revolution. Beginning in the spring of 1966, Mao ordered the closing of schools and the formation of ideologically pure Red Guard units, dominated by youths and students. The Red Guards campaigned against "old ideas, old culture, old habits, and old customs." Millions died as a series of violent purges were carried out. By early 1967, the Cultural Revolution had succeeded in bolstering Mao's position as China's paramount leader.

Anxious to exploit the Sino-Soviet rift, the Nixon administration made a dramatic announcement in July 1971 that National Security Adviser Henry Kissinger had secretly visited Beijing and reached an agreement whereby Nixon would visit China. The movement toward reconciliation, which signaled the end of the U.S. containment policy toward China, provided momentum for China's admission to the UN. Despite U.S. opposition to expelling Taiwan (Nationalist China), the world body overwhelmingly voted to oust Taiwan in favor of Beijing's Communist government.

President Nixon went to Beijing for a week early in 1972, meeting Mao as well as Zhou. The summit ended with a historic communiqué on Feb. 28, in which both nations promised to work toward improved relations. Full diplomatic relations were barred by China as long as the U.S. continued to recognize the legitimacy of Nationalist China.

Following Zhou's death on Jan. 8, 1976, his successor, Vice Premier Deng Xiaoping, was supplanted within a month by Hua Guofeng, former minister of public security. Hua became permanent premier in April. In Oct. he was named successor to Mao as chairman of the Communist Party. But Mao's death on Sept. 10 unleashed the bitter intraparty rivalries that had been suppressed since the Cultural Revolution. Old opponents of Mao launched a campaign against his widow, Jiang Qing, and three of her "radical" colleagues. The so-called Gang of Four was denounced for having undermined the party, the government, and the economy. They were tried and convicted in 1981. Meanwhile, in 1977, Deng Xiaoping was reinstated as deputy premier, chief of staff of the army, and member of the Central Committee of the Politburo.

Beijing and Washington announced full diplomatic relations on Jan. 1, 1979, and the Carter administration abrogated the Taiwan defense treaty. Deputy Premier Deng sealed the agreement with a visit to the U.S. that coincided with the opening of embassies in both capitals on March 1. On Deng's return from the U.S., Chinese troops invaded and briefly occupied an area along Vietnam's northern border. The action was seen as a response to Vietnam's invasion of Cambodia and ouster of the Khmer Rouge government, which China had supported.

In 1981, Deng protégé Hu Yaobang replaced Hua Guofeng as party chairman. Deng became chairman of the Central Committee's military commission, giving him control over the army. The body's 215 members concluded the session with a statement holding Mao Zedong responsible for the "grave blunder" of the Cultural Revolution.

Under Deng Xiaoping's leadership, meanwhile, China's Communist ideology went through a massive reinterpretation, and sweeping economic changes were set in motion in the early 1980s. The Chinese scrapped the personality cult that idolized Mao Zedong, muted Mao's old call for class struggle and exportation of the Communist revolution, and imported Western technology and management techniques to replace the Marxist tenets that had slowed modernization. Deng concluded an agreement for the return of Hong Kong following the expiration of Britain's 99-year lease on the territory on July 1, 1997.

The removal of Hu Yaobang as party chairman in Jan. 1987 signaled a hard-line resurgence within the party. Hu—who had become a hero to many reform-minded Chinese—was replaced by former premier Zhao Ziyang. With the death of Hu in April 1989, the ideological struggle spilled into the streets of the capital, as student demonstrators occupied Beijing's Tiananmen Square in May, calling for democratic reforms. Less than a month later, the demonstrations were crushed in a bloody crackdown as troops and tanks moved into the square and fired on protesters, killing several hundred.

In annual sessions of the rubber-stamp National People's Congress in 1992 and 1993, the government called for accelerating the drive for economic reform, but the sessions were widely seen as an effort to maintain China's moves toward a market economy while retaining political authoritarianism. At the session in 1993, Communist Party leader Jiang Zemin was elected president, while hard-liner Li Peng was reelected to another five-year term as prime minister. Since 1993, the Chinese economy has continued to grow rapidly.

Deng Xiaoping's death in Feb. 1997 left a younger generation in charge of managing the enormous country. In 1998, Prime Minister Zhu Rongji introduced a sweeping program to privatize state-run businesses and further liberalize the nation's economy, a move lauded by Western economists.

On July 1, 1997, when Britain's lease on the New Territories expired, Hong Kong returned to Chinese sovereignty, and in 1999, the Portuguese colony of Macao also was returned to Chinese rule.

In Aug. 1999, China rounded up thousands of members of the Falun Gong sect, a highly popular religious movement that combines elements of Buddhism, Taoism, and martial arts. China, which has now outlawed the sect, was thought to consider the apolitical spiritual group threatening because its numbers exceeded the membership of the Chinese Communist Party.

China was admitted to the World Trade Organization in Nov. 2001. Its entry ended a 15-year debate over whether China is entitled to the full trading rights of capitalist countries.

In Nov. 2002, Vice President Hu Jintao became general secretary of the Communist Party at the 16th Party Congress, succeeding President Jiang. But Jiang retained various positions of power, including head of the Central Military Commission, and filled the Politburo Standing Committee with his protégés. Jiang thus positioned himself to rule as éminence grise for the next several years. Hu Jintao assumed the presidency in March 2003.

On Sept. 24, 2004, former president Jiang Zemin stepped down as China's military chief, thus completing the transfer of power to President Hu that had begun nearly two years earlier.

Tension between China and Taiwan intensified in March 2005, when China passed an antisecession law that said the country could use force if Taiwan moved toward achieving independence. Taiwan president Chen Shui-bian called the bill a "law of aggression."

Lien Chan, who heads Taiwan's opposition Nationalist Party, traveled to China in April and met with President Hu. It was the first meeting between Nationalist and Communist Party leaders since 1949, when the defeated Nationalists retreated to Taiwan. Lien called the visit a "journey of peace." In May, Hu met with another Taiwanese opposition leader, James Soong, chairman of the People First Party. In a joint communiqué intended to restart negotiations between Taiwan and China, they agreed to a principle of "two sides of the strait, one China."

Relations between China and Japan reached new lows in April, when the Chinese government condoned a series of anti-Japanese protests, sparked by the release of new Japanese textbooks that whitewashed the atrocities committed by Japan during World War II. After three weeks of demonstrations, the Chinese government ordered an end to the protests. Japanese prime minister Junichiro Koizumi apologized for Japan's abuses, saying, "Japan, through its colonial rule and aggression, caused tremendous damage and suffering to the people of many countries."

Relations further deteriorated in May, when Wu Yi, China's vice-premier, shunned Japanese prime minister Junichiro Koizumi during a brief visit to Japan that was intended to mend relations. Chinese officials said she canceled their planned meeting to protest laudatory comments about the Yasukuni shrine made by Japanese officials. The shrine, which honors some of Japan's most notorious war criminals, has been a constant source of animosity between the countries.

In June 2005, the China National Oil Corporation (Cnoc) bid $18.5 billion to take over the U.S. oil company Unocal. The Chinese firm withdrew the bid in August amid strong resistance from U.S. officials.

After months of pressure from the Bush administration, China announced in July that it will no longer peg the yuan to the dollar. Instead, it is linked to a fluctuating group of foreign currencies.

In July, China hosted a fourth round of six-nation talks about dismantling North Korea's nuclear weapons program. The talks ended in deadlock.

Hong Kong

Status: Special Administrative Region of China
Chief Executive: Donald Tsang (2005)
Area: 422 sq mi (1,092 sq km)
Population (2005 est.): 6,898,686 (growth rate: 0.6%); birth rate: 7.3/1000; infant mortality rate: 3.0/1000; life expectancy: 81.5; density per sq mi: 16,362

Hong Kong consists of the island of Hong Kong (32 sq mi; 83 sq km), Stonecutters' Island, Kowloon Peninsula, and the New Territories on the adjoining mainland. The island of Hong Kong was ceded to Britain in 1841. Stonecutters' Island and Kowloon were annexed in 1860, and the New Territories, which are mainly agricultural lands, were leased from China in 1898 for 99 years. On July 1, 1997, Hong Kong was returned to China. The vibrant capitalist enclave retains its status as a free port, with its laws to remain unchanged for 50 years. Chief Executive Tung Chee-hwa formulated a policy agenda based on the concept of "one country, two systems," thus preserving Hong Kong's economic independence.

In a series of massive demonstrations in July 2003, more than 500,000 people took to the streets of Hong Kong to protest proposed anti-subversion laws that curtailed civil rights. Surprisingly, Tung Chee-hwa scrapped the law in September. After pro-democracy parties handed pro-China parties a stunning defeat in November elections, China quickly moved to stifle the democracy movement. In April 2004, Beijing officials banned popular elections for Hong Kong's chief executive, scheduled for 2007, and also postponed indefinitely the expansion of the number of popularly elected legislators. Hundreds of thousands of protesters took to the streets again in July, this time boldly calling for democracy and criticizing the Chinese government. Pro-democracy candidates took about 60% of the popular vote in Sept. 2004 elections, but Beijing's legislative system granted them only 40% of the seats in the legislature.

Tung Chee-hwa stepped down in March 2005, citing health reasons. Many observers speculated that he was forced to resign. His deputy, Donald Tsang, became acting chief executive. Days after his resignation, Tung was named vice-chairman of the Chinese People's Political Consultative Conference, a group that advises Parliament.

Macao

Status: Special Administrative Region of China
Chief Executive: Edmund Ho (1999)
Area: 10 sq mi (25.4 sq km)
Population (2005 est.): 449,198 (growth rate: 0.9%); birth rate: 8.5/1000; infant mortality rate: 4.4/1000; life expectancy: 82.1; density per sq mi: 45,804

Colonized by the Portuguese in 1557, Macao was the oldest European outpost in China. In 1987, Portugal and China reached an agreement to return Macao to Chinese rule on Dec. 20, 1999. They agreed on provisions to ensure the autonomy of Macao, including its right to elect local leaders, the right of its residents to travel freely, and the right to maintain its way of life for 50 years after the start of Chinese rule.

Colombia

REPUBLIC OF COLOMBIA

National name: República de Colombia
President: Alvaro Uribe (2002)
Area: 439,733 sq mi (1,138,910 sq km)
Population (2005 est.): 42,954,279 (growth rate: 1.5%); birth rate: 20.8/1000; infant mortality rate: 21.0/1000; life expectancy: 71.7; density per sq mi: 98
Capital and largest city (2003 est.): Santafé de Bogotá, 6,837,800. **Other large cities:** Cali, 2,283,200; Medellín, 1,957,800; Barranquilla, 1,330,400; Cartagena, 901,500. **Monetary unit:** Colombian Peso. **Language:** Spanish. **Ethnicity/race:** mestizo 58%, white 20%, mulatto 14%, black 4%, mixed black-Amerindian 3%, Amerindian 1%.

Religion: Roman Catholic 90%. **Literacy rate:** 93% (2003 est.)
Economic summary: GDP/PPP (2004 est.): $281.1 billion; per capita $6,600. **Real growth rate:** 3.6%. **Inflation:** 5.9%. **Unemployment:** 13.6%. **Arable land:** 2%. **Agriculture:** coffee, cut flowers, bananas, rice, tobacco, corn, sugarcane, cocoa beans, oilseed, vegetables; forest products; shrimp. **Labor force:** 20.7 million; services 46%, agriculture 30%, industry 24% (1990). **Industries:** textiles, food processing, oil, clothing and footwear, beverages, chemicals, cement; gold, coal, emeralds. **Natural resources:** petroleum, natural gas, coal, iron ore, nickel, gold, copper, emeralds, hydropower. **Exports:** $15.5 billion (f.o.b., 2004 est.): petroleum, coffee, coal, apparel, bananas, cut flowers. **Imports:** $15.34 billion (f.o.b., 2004 est.): iindustrial equipment, transportation equipment, consumer goods, chemicals, paper products, fuels, electricity. **Major trading partners:** U.S., Ecuador, Venezuela, Brazil, Mexico, China, Japan, Germany (2003).

Geography Colombia is bordered on the northwest by Panama, on the east by Venezuela and Brazil, and on the southwest by Peru and Ecuador. Through the western half of the country, three Andean ranges run north and south. The eastern half is a low, jungle-covered plain, drained by spurs of the Amazon and Orinoco Rivers, inhabited mostly by isolated tropical-forest Indian tribes. The fertile plateau and valley of the eastern range are the most densely populated parts of the country.

Government Republic.

History Little is known about the various Indian tribes who inhabited Colombia before the Spanish arrived. In 1510 Spaniards founded Darien, the first permanent European settlement on the American mainland. In 1538 they established the colony of New Granada, the area's name until 1861.

After a 14-year struggle, during which time Simón Bolívar's Venezuelan troops won the battle of Boyacá in Colombia on Aug. 7, 1819, independence was attained in 1824. Bolívar united Colombia, Venezuela, Panama, and Ecuador in the Republic of Greater Colombia (1819–1830), but he lost Venezuela and Ecuador to separatists. Two political parties dominated the region: the Conservatives believed in a strong central government and a powerful church; the Liberals believed in a decentralized government, strong regional power, and a less influential role for the church. Bolívar was himself a Conservative, while his vice president, Francisco de Paula Santander, was the founder of the Liberal Party.

Santander served as president between 1832 and 1836, a period of relative stability, but by 1840 civil war erupted. Other periods of Liberal dominance (1849–1857 and 1861–1880), which sought to disestablish the Roman Catholic Church, were marked by insurrection. Nine different governments followed, each rewriting the constitution. In 1861 the country was called the United States of New Granada; in 1863 it became the United States of Colombia; and in 1885, it was named the Republic of Colombia.

In 1899 a brutal civil war broke out, the War of a Thousand Days, that lasted until 1902. The following year, Colombia lost its claims to Panama because it refused to ratify the lease to the U.S. of the Canal Zone. Panama declared its independence in 1903.

The Conservatives held power until 1930, when revolutionary pressure put the Liberals back in power. The Liberal administrations of Enrique Olaya Herrera and Alfonso López (1930–1938) were marked by social reforms that failed to solve the country's problems, and in 1946, a period of insurrection and banditry broke out, referred to as La Violencia, which claimed hundreds of thousands of lives by 1958. Laureano Gómez (1950–1953); the army chief of staff, Gen. Gustavo Rojas Pinilla (1953–1956); and a military junta (1956–1957) sought to curb disorder by repression.

Marxist guerrilla groups organized in the 1960s and 1970s, most notably the May 19th Movement (M-19), the National Liberation Army (ELN), and the Revolutionary Armed Forces of Colombia (FARC), plunging the country into violence and instability. In the 1970s and 1980s, Colombia became one of the international centers for illegal drug production and trafficking, and at times the drug cartels (the Medillin and Cali cartels were the most notorious) virtually controlled the country. Colombia provides 75% of the world's illegal cocaine. In the 1990s, numerous right-wing paramilitary groups also formed, made up of drug traffickers and landowners. The umbrella group for these paramilitaries is the United Self-Defense Forces of Colombia (AUC).

Belisario Betancur Cuartas, a Conservative who assumed the presidency in 1982, unsuccessfully attempted to stem the guerrilla violence. In an official war against drug trafficking, Colombia became a public battleground with bombs, killings, and kidnappings. By 1989, homicide had become the leading cause of death in the nation. Elected president in 1990, César Gaviria Trujillo proposed lenient punishment in exchange for surrender by the leading drug dealers. Ernesto Samper of the Liberal Party became president in 1994. In 1996 he was accused of accepting campaign contributions from drug traffickers, but the House of Representatives absolved him of the charges.

Andrés Pastrana Arango was elected president in 1998, pledging to clean up corruption. In Dec. 1999 the Colombian military reported that 2,787 people were kidnapped that year—the largest number in the world—and blamed rebels. The murder rate soared in 1999, with some 23,000 people reported killed by leftist guerrillas, right-wing paramilitaries, drug traffickers, and common criminals. The violence has created more than 100,000 refugees, while 2 million Colombians have fled the country in recent years.

In Aug. 2000, the U.S. government approved "Plan Colombia," pledging $1.3 billion to fight drug trafficking. Pastrana used the plan to undercut drug production and prevent guerrilla groups from benefiting from drug sales. In Aug. 2001, Pastrana signed "war legislation," which expanded the rights of the military in dealing with rebels.

Alvaro Uribe of the Liberal Party easily won the presidential election in May 2002. He took office in August, pledging to get tough on the rebels and drug traffickers by increasing military spending and seeking U.S. military cooperation. An upsurge in violence accompanied his inauguration, and Uribe declared a state of emergency within a week. In his first year, Uribe beefed up Colombia's security forces with the help of U.S. special forces, launched an aggressive campaign against the drug trade, and passed several economic reform bills.

In May 2004, the UN announced that Colombia's 39-year-long drug war had created the worst humanitarian crisis in the Western Hemisphere. More than 2 million people have been forced to leave their homes and several Indian tribes are close to extinction. Colombia now has the third-largest displaced population in the world, with only Sudan and the Congo having more. Uribe has produced some impressive results in fixing his country's ills, however. According to his defense minister, during 2003 more than 16,000 suspected leftist guerrillas and right-wing paramilitary

vigilantes either surrendered, were apprehended, or were killed. Since 2003, the right-wing paramilitary group AUC has been involved in peace talks with the government, but despite demobilizing 4,000 troops, the vigilante group seemed as vigorous as ever in 2005. Although the two other major armed groups, left-wing FARC and ELN, continue to finance themselves through kidnapping and drug trafficking, governmental efforts have been successful in significantly reducing the kidnapping rate.

By 2005, the United States had invested $3 billion into Plan Colombia, the joint U.S.-Colombia coca antinarcotics plan begun in 2000. While officials say the program has eradicated more than a million acres of coca plants, Colombian drug traffickers are still managing to supply 90% of the cocaine used in the U.S. and 50% of the heroin—the same percentages supplied five years ago, when the program began.

Comoros

UNION OF THE COMOROS

National Name: Union des Comores
President: Azali Assoumani (2002)
Area: 838 sq mi (2,170 sq km)
Population (2005 est.): 671,247 (growth rate: 2.9%); birth rate: 37.5/1000; infant mortality rate: 74.9/1000; life expectancy: 62.0; density per sq mi: 801
Capital and largest city (2003 est.): Moroni (on Grande Comoro), 60,200. **Monetary unit:** Franc. **Languages:** Arabic and French (both official), Shikomoro (Swahili/Arabic blend). **Ethnicity/race:** Antalote, Cafre, Makoa, Oimatsaha, Sakalava. **Religions:** Sunni Muslim 98%, Roman Catholic 2%. **Literacy rate:** 57% (2003 est.)
Economic summary: GDP/PPP: (2002 est.) $441 million; per capita $700. **Real growth rate:** 2% (2001 est.). **Unemployment:** 20% (1996 est.). **Arable land:** 36%. **Agriculture:** vanilla, cloves, perfume essences, copra, coconuts, bananas, cassava (tapioca). **Labor force:** 144,500 (1996 est.): agriculture 80%. **Industries:** tourism, perfume distillation. **Natural resources:** negl. **Exports:** $28 million (f.o.b., 2002 est.): vanilla, ylang-ylang, cloves, perfume oil, copra. **Imports:** $88 million (f.o.b., 2002 est.): rice and other foodstuffs, consumer goods; petroleum products, cement, transport equipment. **Major trading partners:** France, Germany, U.S., Singapore, Japan, South Africa, UAE, Kenya, Mauritius (2003).

Geography The Comoros Islands—Grande Comoro (Ngazidja), Anjouan, Mohéli, and Mayotte (which is not part of the country and retains ties to France)—constitute an archipelago of volcanic origin in the Indian Ocean, 190 mi off the coast of Mozambique.

Government Emerging republic.

History Comoros was frequented by travelers from Africa, Madagascar, Indonesia, and Arabia before the first Europeans encountered the islands. Arabic influence has been the strongest.

France colonized Mayotte in 1843 and by 1904 had annexed the remainder of the archipelago. In a 1974 referendum, 95% of the population voted for independence. The exception was Mayotte, which, with its Christian majority, voted against joining the other mainly Islamic islands in independence. Today it remains a French overseas territory.

The remaining Comoros islands declared themselves independent on July 6, 1975, with Ahmed Abdallah as president. A month after independence, he was overthrown by Justice Minister Ali Soilih. This was only the beginning of Comoros's chronic instability: the country has gone through more than 20 coups since independence and has experienced several attempts at secession. Orchestrating at least four of these coups was a group of white mercenaries known as Les Affreux (The Terrible Ones), and their notorious leader, Frenchman "Colonel" Bob Denard. Denard fled Comoros in 1989, when 3,000 French soldiers were sent after him.

The island of Anjouan declared independence on Aug. 3, 1997, after months of protests and clashes with security forces. The secessionists wanted a return to French rule, contending that independence from France has brought economic disaster and political chaos. Mohéli, the smallest island, also seceded. But France refused to support the secession of either island. In Sept. 1997, President Mohamed Taki's forces attempted to retake Anjouan but failed.

In 1999, Col. Azali Assoumani led a coup, overthrowing interim president Tadjidine. He promised interim military rule would end in a year, a pledge the Organization of African Unity would continue to remind him of. After years of aborted peace talks, a new constitution was approved in March 2002, and the three islands were reunited. Each island elected its own president, and in May a federal president was elected from Grande Comoro, former military coup leader Azali. In Feb. 2003, a coup against Azali was thwarted.

A power-sharing agreement signed in Dec. 2003 gave the individual islands semi-autonomous status and led to elections in March and April 2004. A National Assembly was sworn in July 2004.

Congo, Democratic Republic of the

National Name: Republique Democratique du Congo
President: Joseph Kabila (2001)
Area: 905,563 sq mi (2,345,410 sq km)
Population (2005 est.): 60,085,004 (growth rate: 3.0%); birth rate: 44.4/1000; infant mortality rate: 92.9/1000; life expectancy: 49.4; density per sq mi: 66
Capital and largest city (2003 est.): Kinshasa, 6,541,300. **Other large cities:** Lubumbashi, 1,105,900; Mbuji-Mayi, 938,000; Kolwezi, 832,400; Kisangani, 523,000. **Monetary unit:** Congolese franc. **Languages:** French (official), Lingala, Kingwana, Kikongo, Tshiluba. **Ethnicity/race:** over 200 African ethnic groups, the majority are Bantu; the four largest tribes—Mongo, Luba, Kongo (all Bantu), and the Mangbetu-Azande (Hamitic)—make up about 45% of the population. **Religions:** Roman Catholic 50%, Protestant 20%, Kimbanguist 10%, Islam 10%; other syncretic and indigenous 10%. **Literacy rate:** 66% (2003 est.)
Economic summary: GDP/PPP (2004 est.): $42.74 billion; per capita $700. **Real growth rate:** 7.5%. **Inflation:** 14% (2003 est.). **Unemployment:** n.a. **Arable land:** 3%. **Agriculture:** coffee, sugar, palm oil, rubber, tea, quinine, cassava (tapioca), palm oil, bananas, root crops, corn, fruits; wood products. **Labor force:** 14.51 million (1993 est.). **Industries:** mining (diamonds, copper, zinc), mineral processing, consumer products (including textiles, footwear, cigarettes, processed foods and beverages), cement, commercial ship repair. **Natural resources:** cobalt, copper, cadmium, petroleum, industrial and gem diamonds, gold, silver, zinc, manganese, tin, germanium, uranium, radium, bauxite, iron ore, coal, hydropower, timber. **Exports:** $1.417 billion (f.o.b., 2002 est.): diamonds, copper, crude oil, coffee, cobalt. **Imports:** $933 million (f.o.b., 2002 est.): foodstuffs, mining and other machinery, transport equipment, fuels. **Major trading partners:** Belgium, U.S., Zimbabwe, Finland, South Africa, France, Germany, Kenya, Netherlands (2003).

Geography The Congo, in west-central Africa, is bordered by the Republic of Congo, the Central African Republic, the Sudan, Uganda, Rwanda, Burundi, Tanzania, Zambia, Angola, and the Atlantic Ocean. It is one-quarter the size of the U.S. The principal rivers are the Ubangi and Bomu in the north and the Congo in the west, which flows into the Atlantic. The entire length of Lake Tanganyika lies along the eastern border with Tanzania and Burundi.

Government Dictatorship.

History Formerly the Belgian Congo, this territory was inhabited by ancient Negrito peoples (Pygmies), who were pushed into the mountains by Bantu and Nilotic invaders. The American correspondent Henry M. Stanley navigated the Congo River in 1877 and opened the interior to exploration. Commissioned by King Leopold II of the Belgians, Stanley made treaties with native chiefs that enabled the king to obtain personal title to the territory at the Berlin Conference of 1885.

Leopold accumulated a vast personal fortune from ivory and rubber through Congolese slave labor; 10 million people are estimated to have died from forced labor, starvation, and outright extermination during Leopold's colonial rule. His brutal exploitation of the Congo eventually became an international cause célèbre, prompting Belgium to take over administration of the Congo, which remained a colony until agitation for independence forced Brussels to grant freedom on June 30, 1960. In elections that month, two prominent nationalists won: Patrice Lumumba of the leftist Mouvement National Congolais became prime minister and Joseph Kasavubu of the ABAKO Party became head of state. But within weeks of independence, the Katanga Province, led by Moise Tshombe, seceded from the new republic, and another mining province, South Kasai, followed. Belgium sent paratroopers to quell the civil war, and with Kasavubu and Lumumba of the national government in conflict, the United Nations flew in a peacekeeping force.

Kasavubu staged an army coup in 1960 and handed Lumumba over to the Katangan forces. A UN investigating commission found that Lumumba had been killed by a Belgian mercenary in the presence of Tshombe, who was then the president of Katanga. U.S. and Belgian involvement in the assassination have been alleged. In a possibly related development, Dag Hammarskjold, UN secretary-general, died in a plane crash en route to a peace conference with Tshombe on Sept. 17, 1961.

Tshombe rejected a national reconciliation plan submitted by the UN in 1962. Tshombe's troops fired on the UN force in December, and in the ensuing conflict Tshombe capitulated on Jan. 14, 1963. The peacekeeping force withdrew, and, in a complete about-face, Kasavubu named Tshombe premier in order to fight a spreading rebellion. Tshombe used foreign mercenaries, and with the help of Belgian paratroops airlifted by U.S. planes, defeated the most serious opposition, a Communist-backed regime in the northeast.

Kasavubu abruptly dismissed Tshombe in 1965 but was then himself ousted by Gen. Joseph-Desiré Mobutu, army chief of staff. The new president nationalized the Union Minière, the Belgian copper mining enterprise that had been a dominant force in the Congo since colonial days. Mobutu eliminated opposition to win the election in 1970. In 1975, he nationalized much of the economy, barred religious instruction in schools, and decreed the adoption of African names. He changed the country's name to Zaire and his own to Mobuto Sese Seko, which means "the all-powerful warrior who, because of his endurance and inflexible will to win, will go from conquest to conquest leaving fire in his wake." In 1977, invaders from Angola calling themselves the Congolese National Liberation Front pushed into Shaba and threatened the important mining center of Kolwezi. France and Belgium provided military aid to defeat the rebels.

Laurent Kabila and his long-standing but little-known guerrilla movement launched a seven-month campaign that ousted Mobutu in May 1997, ending one of the world's most corrupt and megalomaniacal regimes. The last of the CIA-nurtured cold war despots, Mobutu deftly courted France and the U.S., which used Zaire as a launching pad for covert operations against bordering countries, particularly Marxist Angola. Mobutu's disastrous policies drove his country into economic collapse while he siphoned off millions of dollars for himself.

The country was renamed the Democratic Republic of the Congo in 1997, which had been its name before Mobutu changed it to Zaire in 1971. But elation over Mobutu's downfall faded as Kabila's own autocratic style emerged, and he seemed devoid of a clear plan for reconstructing the country. He stymied UN human rights investigations and continued to depend on foreign troops for border skirmishes rather than establish a strong national army. Many Congolese dismissed him as a puppet ruler who allowed his country to be overrun by outsiders, particularly the Rwandans. At the same time, he alienated many of his former supporters who helped him to power, including Rwanda and Uganda.

In Aug. 1998, Congolese rebel forces, backed by Kabila's former allies, Rwanda and Uganda, gained control of a large portion of the country until Angolan, Namibian, and Zimbabwean troops came to Kabila's aid. In 1999, the Lusaka Accord was signed by all six of the countries involved, as well as by most, but not all, of the various rebel groups.

In Jan. 2001, Kabila was assassinated, allegedly by one of his bodyguards. His young and inexperienced son Joseph became the new president. He demonstrated a willingness to engage in talks to end the civil war. In April 2002, the government agreed to a power-sharing arrangement with Ugandan-supported rebels, and in July, the presidents of the Congo and Rwanda signed an accord: Rwanda promised to withdraw its 35,000 troops from the eastern Congolese border; the Congo would in turn disarm the thousands of Hutu militiamen in its territory, who threatened Rwandan security. In Sept. 2002, Uganda also signed a peace agreement with the nation. But the warring parties were slow to depart; most had been looting the Congo of its natural resources and had little incentive to end the war. More than 2.5 million people are estimated to have died in the Congo's complex four-year civil war, which involved seven foreign armies and numerous rebel groups that often fought among themselves.

Despite the peace agreement and power-sharing plan signed between the main parties in the Congolese war, the fighting and killing continued. In April 2003, hundreds of civilians were massacred in the eastern province of Ituri in an ethnic conflict. In June a French force with a UN mandate was deployed to defend the population from further tribal fighting. Joseph Kabila signed a new constitution in April, and on July 17, 2003, Congo's new power-sharing government was inaugurated. The government includes 4 vice presidents and 36 ministers, 16 of which are former rebels. But in 2004, peace was dangerously insecure. In May, an insurgency in Bukavu erupted, other areas of Congo grew restive, and Rwanda continued to support various rebel groups fighting the government. By the end of 2004, the death toll from the conflict had reached 3.8 million.

Despite instability, political progress continued. In May 2005, a new constitution was adopted by the National Assembly. Voter registration followed, and the next step will be a referendum to ratify the constitution.

Congo, Republic of

National name: République du Congo
President: Denis Sassou-Nguesso (1997)
Area: 132,046 sq mi (342,000 sq km)
Population (2005 est.): 3,039,126 (growth rate: 1.3%); birth rate: 27.9/1000; infant mortality rate: 92.4/1000; life expectancy: 49.0; density per sq mi: 23
Capital and largest city (2003 est.): Brazzaville, 1,169,900. **Other large city:** Pointe-Noire, 544,200.
Monetary unit: CFA Franc. **Languages:** French (official), Lingala, Monokutuba, Kikongo, many local languages and dialects. **Ethnicity/race:** Kongo 48%, Sangha 20%, M'Bochi 12%, Teke 17%, Europeans (mostly French) and other 3%. **Religions:** Christian 50%, animist 48%, Islam 2%. **Literacy rate:** 84% (2003 est.)
Economic summary: GDP/PPP (2004 est.): $2.324 billion; per capita $800. **Real growth rate:** 3.7%. **Inflation:** 1.8%. **Unemployment:** n.a. **Arable land:** 1%. **Agriculture:** cassava (tapioca), sugar, rice, corn, peanuts, vegetables, coffee, cocoa; forest products. **Labor force:** n.a. **Industries:** petroleum extraction, cement, lumber, brewing, sugar, palm oil, soap, flour, cigarettes. **Natural resources:** petroleum, timber, potash, lead, zinc, uranium, copper, phosphates, natural gas, hydropower. **Exports:** $2.224 billion (f.o.b., 2004): petroleum, lumber, plywood, sugar, cocoa, coffee, diamonds. **Imports:** $749.3 million (f.o.b., 2004 est.): capital equipment, construction materials, foodstuffs. **Major trading partners:** China, Taiwan, U.S., South Korea, Trinidad and Tobago, France, Italy, India, Belgium (2003).

Geography The Congo is situated in west-central Africa astride the equator. It borders Gabon, Cameroon, the Central African Republic, the Democratic Republic of the Congo, and the Angola exclave of Cabinda, with a short stretch of coast on the South Atlantic. Its area is nearly three times that of Pennsylvania. Most of the inland is tropical rain forest, drained by tributaries of the Congo River.

Government Dictatorship.

History In precolonial times, the region now called the Republic of Congo was dominated by three kingdoms: Kongo (originating about 1000), the Loango (flourishing in the 17th century), and Tio. After the Portuguese located the Congo River in 1482, commerce was carried on with the tribes, especially the slave trade.

The Frenchman Pierre Savorgnan de Brazza signed a treaty with Makoko, ruler of the Bateke people, in 1880, thus establishing French control. It was first called French Congo, and after 1905 Middle Congo. With Gabon and Ubangi-Shari, it became the colony of French Equatorial Africa in 1910. Abuse of laborers led to public outcry against the French colonialists as well as rebellions among the Congolese, but the exploitation of the native workers continued until 1930. During World War II the colony joined Chad in supporting the Free French cause against the Vichy government. The Congo proclaimed its independence without leaving the French Community in 1960, calling itself the Republic of Congo.

Congo's second president, Alphonse Massemba-Débat, instituted a Marxist-Leninist government. In 1968, Maj. Marien Ngouabi overthrew him but kept Congo on a Socialist course. He was sworn in for a second five-year term in 1975. A four-man commando squad assassinated Ngouabi on March 18, 1977. Col. Joachim Yhombi-Opango, army chief of staff, assumed the presidency on April 4. Yhombi-Opango resigned on Feb. 4, 1979, and was replaced by Col. Denis Sassou-Nguesso.

In July 1990 the leaders of the ruling party voted to end the one-party system. A national political conference, hailed as a model for sub-Saharan Africa, renounced Marxism in 1991 and scheduled the country's first free elections for 1992. Pascal Lissouba became the country's first democratically elected president.

Political and ethnic tensions intensified in 1993 after legislative elections, when the opposition's rejection of the results developed into violence. A peace agreement was signed between the government and the opposition in Aug. 1994. A four-month civil war (June 5–Oct. 15, 1997) devastated Brazzaville, the capital. Buttressed by military aid from Angola, former Marxist dictator Denis Sassou-Nguesso overthrew President Lissouba. In late 1999 a peace agreement was signed between Sassou-Nguesso, who comes from the north, and the rebels representing the populous south. The postwar period has been traumatic for the desperately poor country.

In March 2002, President Sassou-Nguesso was reelected with 89.4% of the vote. His opponents were either barred from the country or withdrew from the election.

The so-called Ninja rebels continued to battle government forces, each attempting to gain or maintain control of the country's rich oil reserves and each seemingly unconcerned about the toll this new outbreak of violence took on civilians. In May 2003, the government and Ninja rebels signed an agreement to end hostilities.

Costa Rica

REPUBLIC OF COSTA RICA

National name: República de Costa Rica
President: Abel Pacheco (2002)
Area: 19,730 sq mi (51,100 sq km)
Population (2005 est.): 4,016,173 (growth rate: 1.5%); birth rate: 18.6/1000; infant mortality rate: 9.9/1000; life expectancy: 76.8; density per sq mi: 204
Capital and largest city (2003 est.): San José, 1,527,300 (metro. area), 337,200 (city proper). **Monetary unit:** Colón. **Languages:** Spanish (official), English. **Ethnicity/race:** white (including mestizo) 94%, black 3%, Amerindian 1%, Chinese 1%, other 1%. **Religion:** Roman Catholic 76.3%, Evangelical 13.7%, Jehovah's Witnesses 1.3%, other Protestant 0.7%, other 4.8%, none 3.2%. **Literacy rate:** 96% (2003 est.)
Economic summary: GDP/PPP (2004 est.): $37.97 billion; per capita $9,600. **Real growth rate:** 3.9%. **Inflation:** 11.5%. **Unemployment:** 6.6%. **Arable land:** 4%. **Agriculture:** coffee, pineapples, bananas, sugar, corn, rice, beans, potatoes; beef; timber. **Labor force:** 1.81 million; agriculture 20%, industry 22%, services 58% (1999 est.). **Industries:** microprocessors, food processing, textiles and clothing, construction materials, fertilizer, plastic products. **Natural resource:** hydropower. **Exports:** $6.184 billion (2004 est.): coffee, bananas, sugar; pineapples; textiles, electronic components, medical equipment. **Imports:** $7.842 billion (2004 est.): raw materials, consumer goods, capital equipment, petroleum. **Major trading partners:** U.S., Guatemala, Nicaragua, Mexico, Venezuela (2003).

Geography This Central American country lies between Nicaragua to the north and Panama to the south. Its area slightly exceeds that of Vermont and New Hampshire combined. It has a narrow Pacific coastal region. Cocos Island (10 sq mi; 26 sq km), about 300 mi (483 km) off the Pacific Coast, is under Costa Rican sovereignty.

Government Democratic republic.

History Costa Rica was inhabited by an estimated 25,000 Indians when Columbus explored it in 1502. Few of the Indians survived the Spanish conquest, which began in 1563. The region grew slowly and was administered as a Spanish province. Costa Rica achieved independence in 1821 but was absorbed for two years by Agustín de Iturbide in his Mexican empire. It became a republic in 1848. Except for the military dictatorship of Tomás Guardia from 1870 to 1882, Costa Rica has enjoyed one of the most democratic governments in Latin America.

In the 1970s, rising oil prices, falling international commodity prices, and inflation hurt the economy. Efforts have since been made to reduce reliance on coffee, banana, and beef exports. Tourism is now a major business. Oscar Arias Sanchez, who became president in 1986, was awarded the Nobel Peace Prize in 1987 for his role in negotiating settlements to both the Nicaraguan and the Salvadoran civil wars.

José Maria Figueres Olsen of the National Liberation Party became president in 1994. He opposed economic suggestions made by the International Monetary Fund, instead favoring greater government intervention in the economy. The World Bank subsequently withheld $100 million of financing. In 1998, Miguel Angel Rodríguez of the Social Christian Unity Party became president, pledging economic reforms, such as privatization. In 2000, Costa Rica and Nicaragua resolved a long-standing dispute over navigation of the San Juan River, which forms their border. A psychiatrist, Abel Pacheco, also of the Social Christian Unity Party, won the presidency in elections held in April 2002. In May 2003, several national strikes took place, by energy and telecommunications workers over privatization, and by teachers over their salaries.

Costa Rica has a reputation as one of the most stable, prosperous, and least corrupt Latin American countries. But in fall 2004, three former Costa Rican presidents (Jose Maria Figueres Olsen, Miguel Angel Rodríguez, and Rafael Angel Calderon) were investigated on corruption charges.

Côte d'Ivoire

REPUBLIC OF CÔTE D'IVOIRE

National name: République de Côte d'Ivoire
President: Laurent Gbagbo (2000)
Prime Minister: Seydou Diarra (2003)
Area: 124,502 sq mi (322,460 sq km)
Population (2005 est.): 17,298,040 (growth rate: 2.1%); birth rate: 35.5/1000; infant mortality rate: 90.8/1000; life expectancy: 48.6; density per sq mi: 139
Capital (2003 est.): Yamoussoukro (official), 185,600. **Largest city:** Abidjan (administrative capital), 4,113,600 (metro. area), 3,427,500 (city proper). **Monetary unit:** CFA Franc. **Languages:** French (official) and African languages (Diaula esp.). **Ethnicity/race:** Akan 42.1%, Voltaiques (Gur) 17.6%, Northern Mandes 16.5%, Krous 11%, Southern Mandes 10%, other 2.8% (includes 130,000 Lebanese and 14,000 French) (1998). **Religions:** indigenous 25%–40%, Islam 35%–40%, Christian 20%–30% (2001). **Literacy rate:** 51% (2003 est.)
Economic summary: GDP/PPP (2004 est.): $24.78 billion; per capita $1,500. **Real growth rate:** –1%. **Inflation:** 1.4%. **Unemployment:** 13% in urban areas (1998). **Arable land:** 10%. **Agriculture:** coffee, cocoa beans, bananas, palm kernels, corn, rice, manioc

(tapioca), sweet potatoes, sugar, cotton, rubber; timber. **Labor force:** 6.7 million; 68% agricultural. **Industries:** foodstuffs, beverages; wood products, oil refining, truck and bus assembly, textiles, fertilizer, building materials, electricity, ship construction and repair. **Natural resources:** petroleum, natural gas, diamonds, manganese, iron ore, cobalt, bauxite, copper, hydropower. **Exports:** $5.124 billion (f.o.b., 2004 est.): cocoa, coffee, timber, petroleum, cotton, bananas, pineapples, palm oil, fish. **Imports:** $3.36 billion (f.o.b., 2004 est.): fuel, capital equipment, foodstuffs. **Major trading partners:** France, Netherlands, U.S., Spain, Nigeria, UK (2003).

Geography Côte d'Ivoire (also known as the Ivory Coast), in western Africa on the Gulf of Guinea, is a little larger than New Mexico. Its neighbors are Liberia, Guinea, Mali, Burkina Faso, and Ghana. The country consists of a coastal strip in the south, dense forests in the interior, and savannas in the north.

Government Presidential/parliamentary democracy until Dec. 1999, when a coup installed a military dictatorship.

History Côte d'Ivoire was originally made up of numerous isolated settlements; today it represents more than sixty distinct tribes, including the Baoule, Bete, Senoufou, Agni, Malinke, Dan, and Lobi. Côte d'Ivoire attracted both French and Portuguese merchants in the 15th century who were in search of ivory and slaves. French traders set up establishments early in the 19th century, and in 1842, the French obtained territorial concessions from local tribes, gradually extending their influence along the coast and inland. The area was organized as a territory in 1893, became an autonomous republic in the French Union after World War II, and achieved independence on Aug. 7, 1960. Côte d'Ivoire formed a customs union in 1959 with Dahomey (Benin), Niger, and Burkina Faso. The nation's economy is one of the most developed in sub-Saharan Africa. It is the world's largest exporter of cocoa and one of the largest exporters of coffee.

From independence until his death in 1993, Felix Houphouët-Boigny served as president. Massive protests by students, farmers, and professionals forced the president to legalize opposition parties and hold the first contested presidential election in Oct. 1990, which Houphouët-Boigny won with 81% of the vote.

Beginning in Sept. 1998, thousands of demonstrators protested a constitutional revision that granted President Henri Konan Bédié greatly enhanced powers. Bédié also promoted the concept of *ivoirité,* which, roughly translated, means "pure Ivoirian pride." Although its defenders describe *ivoirité* as a term of positive national pride, it has led to a dangerous xenophobia, with numerous ethnic Malians and Burkinans being driven out of the country in 1999.

President Bédié was overthrown in the country's first military coup in Dec. 1999, and Gen. Robert Guei assumed control of the country. As a result, the majority of foreign aid to the country ceased.

In what were seen as the first steps toward reasserting democracy, voters overwhelmingly approved a draft constitution in July 2000. However, the document permitted only those of "pure Ivoirian" stock to run for president, thereby excluding nearly 40% of the population. Guei, who had promised to stay in power only to "sweep the house clean," instead decided to run for president in Oct. 2000 elections. Gen. Guei ran against a civilian opposition candidate, Laurent Gbagbo. Each declared victory in an election most believe to have been rife with fraud. Popular outcry against Guei soon turned violent, forcing him to leave the country, and

Gbagbo assumed the presidency. Many observers questioned his mandate, however, since the popular opposition leader Alassane Ouattara had been excluded from the election on the specious grounds that he was not a pure-blooded Ivoirian. It was not until June 2002 that Ouattara was finally granted full Ivoirian citizenship, allowing him to run for president. Hundreds have died in violence sparked by the dispute.

Mutineering soldiers attempted a coup on Sept. 19, 2002. Guei and Interior Minister Doudou were killed in fighting between government soldiers and the rebels. President Gbagbo accused Guei of staging the coup. Fighting continued, even after a French-brokered peace accord was signed on Jan. 25, 2003, calling for the government to share power with the rebels. President Gbagbo's supporters found such a plan unacceptable, and there was rioting in the capital. The war was finally declared officially over in July. The peace, supported by 4,000 UN-sponsored French peacekeeping troops, was fragile, however. Pro-government and rebel militias remained armed, and in 2004, Northern and Muslim rebels still controlled half the country.

In Nov. 2004, the civil war again erupted; in May 2005, another peace deal was signed.

Croatia

REPUBLIC OF CROATIA

National Name: Republika Hrvatska
President: Stipe Mesic (2000)
Prime Minister: Ivo Sanader (2003)
Area: 21,831 sq mi (56,542 sq km)
Population (2005 est.): 4,495,904 (growth rate: 0.0%); birth rate: 9.6/1000; infant mortality rate: 6.8/1000; life expectancy: 74.5; density per sq mi: 206
Capital and largest city (2003 est.): Zagreb, 685,500.
Other large cities: Split, 173,600; Rijeka, 142,500; Osijek, 89,600. **Monetary unit:** Kuna. **Languages:** Croatian 96% (official), other 4% (including Italian, Hungarian, Czech, Slovak, German). **Ethnicity/race:** Croat 89.6%, Serb 4.5%, Bosniak 0.5%, Hungarian 0.4%, Slovene 0.3%, Czech 0.2%, Roma 0.2%, Albanian 0.1%, Montenegrin 0.1%, others 4.1% (2001). **Religions:** Roman Catholic 87.8%, Orthodox 4.4%, Muslim 1.3%, Protestant 0.3%, others and unknown 6.2% (2001) . **Literacy rate:** 99% (2003 est.)
Economic summary: GDP/PPP (2004 est.): $50.33 billion; per capita $11,200. **Real growth rate:** 3.7%. **Inflation:** 2.5%. **Unemployment:** 13.8%. **Arable land:** 26%. **Agriculture:** wheat, corn, sugar beets, sunflower seed, barley, alfalfa, clover, olives, citrus, grapes, soybeans, potatoes; livestock, dairy products. **Labor force:** 1.71 million; agriculture 2.7%, industry 32.8%, services 64.5% (2004). **Industries:** chemicals and plastics, machine tools, fabricated metal, electronics, pig iron and rolled steel products, aluminum, paper, wood products, construction materials, textiles, shipbuilding, petroleum and petroleum refining, food and beverages; tourism. **Natural resources:** oil, some coal, bauxite, low-grade iron ore, calcium, natural asphalt, silica, mica, clays, salt, hydropower. **Exports:** $7.845 billion (f.o.b., 2004 est.): transport equipment, textiles, chemicals, foodstuffs, fuels. **Imports:** $16.7 billion (f.o.b., 2004 est.): machinery, transport and electrical equipment, chemicals, fuels and lubricants, foodstuffs. **Major trading partners:** Italy, Bosnia and Herzegovina, Germany, Slovenia, Austria, France, Russia (2003).

Geography Croatia is a former Yugoslav republic on the Adriatic Sea. It is about the size of West Virginia. Part of Croatia is a barren, rocky region lying in the Dinaric Alps. The Zagorje region north of the capital, Zagreb, is a land of rolling hills, and the fertile agricultural region of the Pannonian Plain is bordered by the Drava, Danube, and Sava Rivers in the east. Over one-third of Croatia is forested.

Government Presidential/parliamentary democracy.

History Croatia, at one time the Roman province of Pannonia, was settled in the 7th century by the Croats. They converted to Christianity between the 7th and 9th centuries and adopted the Roman alphabet under the suzerainty of Charlemagne. In 925, the Croats defeated Byzantine and Frankish invaders and established their own independent kingdom, which reached its peak during the 11th century. A civil war ensued in 1089, which later led to the country being conquered by the Hungarians in 1091. The signing of the *Pacta Conventa* by Croatian tribal chiefs and the Hungarian king in 1102 united the two nations politically under the Hungarian monarch, but Croatia retained its autonomy.

Following the defeat of the Hungarians by the Turks at the battle of Mohács in 1526, Croatia (along with Hungary) elected Austrian archduke Ferdinand of Hapsburg as their king. After the establishment of the Austro-Hungarian kingdom in 1867, Croatia became part of Hungary until the collapse of Austria-Hungary in 1918 following its defeat in World War I. On Oct. 29, 1918, Croatia proclaimed its independence and joined in union with Montenegro, Serbia, and Slovenia to form the Kingdom of Serbs, Croats, and Slovenes. The name was changed to Yugoslavia in 1929.

When Germany invaded Yugoslavia in 1941, Croatia became a Nazi puppet state. Croatian Fascists, the Ustachi, slaughtered countless Serbs and Jews during the war. After Germany was defeated in 1945, Croatia was made into a republic of the newly reconstituted Communist nation of Yugoslavia; however, Croatian nationalism persisted. After Yugoslavian leader Tito's death in 1980, Croatia's demands for independence began multiplying.

In 1990, free elections were held, and the Communists were defeated by a nationalist party led by Franjo Tudjman. In June 1991, the Croatian Parliament passed a declaration of independence from Yugoslavia. Six months of intensive fighting with the Serbian-dominated Yugoslavian army followed, claiming thousands of lives and wreaking mass destruction.

A UN cease-fire was arranged on Jan. 2, 1992. The UN Security Council in February approved sending a 14,000-member peacekeeping force to monitor the agreement and protect the minority Serbs in Croatia. In a 1993 referendum the Serb-occupied portion of Croatia (Krajina) resoundingly voted for integration with Serbs in Bosnia and Serbia proper. Although the Zagreb government and representatives of Krajina signed a cease-fire in March 1994, further negotiations broke down. In a lightning-quick operation, the Croatian army retook western Slavonia in May 1995. Similarly, in August, the central Croatian region of Krajina, held by Serbs, was returned to Zagreb's control.

Announcing on television in 1999 that "national issues are more important than democracy," President Tudjman continued to alienate Croatians with his authoritarian rule, out-of-touch nationalism, and disastrous handling of the war-shattered economy. In Dec. 1999, Tudjman died. Less than a month later, his Croatian Democratic Union (HDZ) Party was defeated by a reformist center-left coalition headed by Ivica Racan. But in Nov. 2003 elections, a right-wing coalition led by the nationalist HDZ once again assumed power. The new prime minister, Ivo Sanader, claims that his party is now far less nationalist and far more moderate than its earlier incarnation under Tudjman. In 2003, Croatia formally submitted its application to join the EU. President Mesic was reelected in Jan. 2005.

Cuba

REPUBLIC OF CUBA

National name: República de Cuba
President: Fidel Castro (1976)
Area: 42,803 sq mi (110,860 sq km)
Population (2005 est.): 11,346,670 (growth rate: 0.3%); birth rate: 12.0/1000; infant mortality rate: 6.3/1000; life expectancy: 77.2; density per sq mi: 265
Capital and largest city (2003 est.): Havana, 2,686,000 (metro. area), 2,343,700 (city proper). **Other large cities:** Santiago de Cuba, 554,400; Camagüey, 354,400; Holguin, 319,300; Guantánamo, 274,300; Santa Clara, 251,800. **Monetary unit:** Cuban Peso. **Language:** Spanish. **Ethnicity/race:** mulatto 51%, white 37%, black 11%, Chinese 1%. **Religion:** nominally 85% Roman Catholic before Castro assumed power. **Literacy rate:** 97% (2003 est.)
Economic summary: GDP/PPP (2004 est.): $33.92 billion; per capita $3,000. **Real growth rate:** 3%. **Inflation:** 3.1%. **Unemployment:** 2.5%. **Arable land:** 33%. **Agriculture:** sugar, tobacco, citrus, coffee, rice, potatoes, beans; livestock. **Labor force:** 4.55 million; agriculture 24%, industry 25%, services 51% (1999). **Industries:** sugar, petroleum, tobacco, construction, nickel, steel, cement, agricultural machinery, pharmaceuticals. **Natural resources:** cobalt, nickel, iron ore, copper, manganese, salt, timber, silica, petroleum, arable land. **Exports:** $2.104 billion (f.o.b., 2004 est.): sugar, nickel, tobacco, fish, medical products, citrus, coffee. **Imports:** $5.296 billion (f.o.b., 2004 est.): petroleum, food, machinery and equipment, chemicals. **Major trading partners:** Netherlands, Canada, Russia, Spain, China, Venezuela, Italy, U.S., Mexico, France (2003).

Geography The largest island of the West Indies group (equal in area to Pennsylvania), Cuba is also the westernmost—just west of Hispaniola (Haiti and the Dominican Republic), and 90 mi (145 km) south of Key West, Fla., at the entrance to the Gulf of Mexico. The island is mountainous in the southeast and south-central area (Sierra Maestra). It is flat or rolling elsewhere. Cuba also includes numerous smaller islands, islets, and cays.

Government Communist state.

History Arawak (or Taino) Indians inhabiting Cuba when Columbus landed on the island in 1492 died from diseases brought by sailors and settlers. By 1511, Spaniards under Diego Velásquez had established settlements. Havana's superb harbor made it a common transit point to and from Spain.

In the early 1800s, Cuba's sugarcane industry boomed, requiring massive numbers of black slaves. A simmering independence movement turned into open warfare from 1867 to 1878. Slavery was abolished in 1886. In 1895, the poet José Marti led the struggle that finally ended Spanish rule, thanks largely to U.S. intervention in 1898 after the sinking of the battleship *Maine* in Havana harbor.

An 1899 treaty made Cuba an independent republic under U.S. protection. The U.S. occupation, which ended in 1902, suppressed yellow fever and brought large American investments. The 1901 Platt Amendment allowed the U.S. to intervene in Cuba's affairs, which it did four times from 1906 to 1920. Cuba terminated the amendment in 1934.

In 1933 a group of army officers, including army sergeant Fulgencio Batista, overthrew President Gerardo Machado. Batista became president in 1940, running a corrupt police state.

In 1956, Fidel Castro Ruz launched a revolution from his camp in the Sierra Maestra mountains. Castro's brother Raul and Ernesto (Ché) Guevara, an Argentine physician, were his top lieutenants. Many anti-Batista landowners supported the rebels. The U.S. ended military aid to Cuba in 1958, and on New Year's Day 1959, Batista fled into exile and Castro took over the government.

The U.S. initially welcomed what looked like a democratic Cuba, but a rude awakening came within a few months when Castro established military tribunals for political opponents and jailed hundreds. Castro disavowed Cuba's 1952 military pact with the U.S., confiscated U.S. assets, and established Soviet-style collective farms. The U.S. broke relations with Cuba on Jan. 3, 1961, and Castro formalized his alliance with the Soviet Union. Thousands of Cubans fled the country.

In 1961 a U.S.-backed group of Cuban exiles invaded Cuba. Planned during the Eisenhower administration, the invasion was given the go-ahead by President John Kennedy, although he refused to give U.S. air support. The landing at the Bay of Pigs on April 17, 1961, was a fiasco. The invaders did not receive popular Cuban support and were easily repulsed by the Cuban military.

A Soviet attempt to install medium-range missiles in Cuba—capable of striking targets in the United States with nuclear warheads—provoked a crisis in 1962. Denouncing the Soviets for "deliberate deception," on Oct. 22 Kennedy said that the U.S. would blockade Cuba so the missiles could not be delivered. Six days later Soviet premier Nikita Khrushchev ordered the missile sites dismantled and returned to the USSR, in return for a U.S. pledge not to attack Cuba.

The U.S. established limited diplomatic ties with Cuba on Sept. 1, 1977, making it easier for Cuban Americans to visit the island. Contact with the more affluent Cuban Americans prompted a wave of discontent in Cuba, producing a flood of asylum seekers. In response, Castro opened the port of Mariel to a "freedom flotilla" of boats from the U.S., allowing 125,000 to flee to Miami. After the refugees arrived, it was discovered their ranks were swelled with prisoners, mental patients, homosexuals, and others unwanted by the Cuban government.

Cuba fomented Communist revolutions around the world, especially in Angola, where thousands of Cuban troops were sent in the 1980s.

Russian aid, which had long supported Cuba's failing economy, ended when Communism collapsed in eastern Europe in 1990. Cuba's foreign trade also plummeted, producing a severe economic crisis. In 1993, Castro permitted limited private enterprise, allowed Cubans to possess convertible currencies, and encouraged foreign investment in its tourist industry. In March 1996, the U.S. tightened its embargo with the Helms-Burton Act.

Christmas became an official holiday in 1997 for the first time since the revolution, in response to Pope John Paul II's 1998 visit to Cuba, which raised hopes for greater religious freedom.

In June 2000, Castro won a publicity bonanza when the Clinton administration sent Elian Gonzalez, a young Cuban boy found clinging to an inner tube near Miami, back to Cuba. The U.S. Cuban community had demanded that the boy remain in Miami rather than be returned to his father in Cuba. By many accounts, the influential Cuban Americans lost public sympathy by pitting political ideology against familial bonds.

In March and April 2003, Castro sent nearly 80 dissidents to prison with long sentences, prompting an international condemnation of Cuba's harsh crackdown on human rights.

The Bush administration tightened its embargo in June 2004, allowing Cuban Americans to return to the island only once every three years (instead of every year) and restricting the amount of U.S. cash that can be spent there to $50 per day. In response, Cuba banned the use of dollars, which had been legal currency in the country for more than a decade.

Cyprus

REPUBLIC OF CYPRUS

National name: Kypriaki Dimokratia—Kibris Cumhuriyeti
President: Tassos Papadopoulos (2003)
Area: 3,571 sq mi (9,250 sq km)
Population (2005 est.): 780,133 (growth rate: 0.5%); birth rate: 12.6/1000; infant mortality rate: 7.2/1000; life expectancy: 77.7; density per sq mi: 218
Capital and largest city (2003 est.): Lefkosia (Nicosia) (in government-controlled area), 197,600. **Monetary unit:** Cyprus pound. **Languages:** Greek, Turkish (both official); English. **Ethnicity/race:** Current: Greek 77%, Turkish 18% (each concentrated almost exclusively in separate areas); other 5% (2001). **Religions:** Greek Orthodox 78%, Islam 18%, Maronite, Armenian Apostolic, and other 4%. **Literacy rate:** 98% (2003 est.)
Economic summary: GDP/PPP: Greek Cypriot area (2004 est.): $15.71 billion; $20,300 per capita; Turkish Cypriot area (2004 est.): $4.54 billion; $7,135 per capita. **Real growth rate:** Greek Cypriot area: 3.2%; Turkish Cypriot area: 2.6%. **Inflation:** Greek Cypriot area: 2.4%; Turkish Cypriot area: 12.6% (2003 est.). **Unemployment:** Greek Cypriot area: 3.2%; Turkish Cypriot area: 5.6%. **Arable land:** 8%. **Agriculture:** citrus, vegetables, barley, grapes, olives, vegetables, poultry, pork, lamb, kids, dairy, cheese. **Labor force:** Greek Cypriot area: 330,000; Turkish Cypriot area: 95,025; Greek Cypriot area: agriculture 4.9%, industry 19.4%, services 75.6%; Turkish Cypriot area: agriculture 15.1%, industry 27%, services 57.9% (2003 est.). **Industries:** tourism, food and beverage processing; cement and gypsum production; ship repair and refurbishment; textiles; light chemicals; metal products; wood, paper, stone, and clay products. **Natural resources:** copper, pyrites, asbestos, gypsum, timber, salt, marble, clay earth pigment. **Exports:** Greek Cypriot area: $1.094 billion (f.o.b., 2004 est.): citrus, potatoes, pharmaceuticals, cement, clothing, and cigarettes; Turkish Cypriot area: $49.3 million (f.o.b., 2004 est.): citrus, potatoes, textiles. **Imports:** Greek Cypriot area: $5.258 billion (f.o.b., 2004 est.): consumer goods, petroleum and lubricants, intermediate goods, machinery, transport equipment; Turkish Cypriot area: $415.2 million (f.o.b., 2004 est.): vehicles, fuel, cigarettes, food, minerals, chemicals, machinery. **Major trading partners:** UK, Greece, Lebanon, Italy, Germany, Japan, France, China, U.S. (2003). **Member of Commonwealth of Nations**

Geography The third-largest island in the Mediterranean (one and one-half times the size of Delaware), Cyprus lies off the southern coast of Turkey and the western shore of Syria. The highest peak is Mount Olympus at 6,406 ft (1,953 m).

Government Republic. Mediation efforts by the UN seek to reunify the Greek and Turkish areas of the island under one federated system of government.

History Cyprus was the site of early Phoenician and Greek colonies. For centuries its rule passed through many hands. It fell to the Turks in 1571, and a large Turkish colony settled on the island.

In World War I, at the outbreak of hostilities with Turkey, Britain annexed the island. It was declared a Crown colony in 1925. The Greek population, which regarded Greece as its mother country, sought self-determination and union *(enosis)* with Greece. In 1955, a guerrilla war against British rule was launched by the National Organization of Cypriot Combatants (EOKA). In 1958, Greek Cypriot nationalist leader Archbishop Markarios began calling for Cypriot independence rather than union with Greece. During this period, Turkish Cypriots began demanding that the island be partitioned between the Greek and Turkish populations.

Cyprus became an independent nation on Aug. 16, 1960, after Greek and Turkish Cypriots agreed on a constitution, which excluded both the possibility of partition as well as of union with Greece. Markarios became the country's first president.

Fighting between Greek and Turkish Cypriots flared up in the early 1960s, and a UN peacekeeping force was sent to the island in 1965. On July 15, 1974, Archbishop Markios was overthrown in a military coup led by the Cypriot National Guard. On July 20, Turkey invaded Cyprus, asserting its right to protect the Turkish Cypriot minority. Turkey gained control of 30% of northern Cyprus, and displaced some 180,000 Greek Cypriots. A UN-sponsored cease-fire was established on July 22, and Turkish troops were permitted to remain in the north. In Dec. 1974, Makarios again assumed the presidency. The following year, the island was partitioned into Greek and Turkish territories separated by a UN-occupied buffer zone.

Turkish Cypriots proclaimed a separate state under Rauf Denktash in the northern part of the island on Nov. 15, 1983, naming it the "Turkish Republic of Northern Cyprus." The UN Security Council, in its Resolution 541 of Nov. 18, 1983, declared this action illegal and called for withdrawal. No country except Turkey has recognized this entity.

In 1988, George Vassiliou, a conservative and critic of UN proposals to reunify Cyprus, became president. The purchase of missiles capable of reaching the Turkish coast evoked threats of retaliation from Turkey in 1997, and Cyprus's plans to deploy more missiles in Aug. 1999 again raised Turkey's ire.

The continued strife between Greek Cypriots and Turkish Cypriots threatened Cyprus's potential EU membership—it had met all the economic standards—and provided a great incentive to both sides to resolve their differences. UN-sponsored talks between the Greek and Turkish leaders, Kleridas and Denktash, continued intensively in 2002, but without resolution. In Dec. 2002, the EU invited Cyprus to join in 2004, provided the UN plan was accepted by February 2003. Without reunification, only Greek Cyprus was to be welcomed into the EU. But just weeks before the UN deadline, President Kleridas was defeated by right-wing candidate Tassos Papadopoulos, a hard-liner on reunification. The UN deadline passed, and the UN declared that the talks had failed. In April 2004, dual referendums were held, with the Greek side overwhelmingly rejecting the most recent UN reunification plan, and the Turkish side voting in favor. In May, Greek Cyprus alone became a part of the EU.

In April 2005, Turkish Cyprus elected Mehmet Ali Talat as their president, ousting longtime leader Rauf Denktash, who staunchly opposed reunification. Talat supports reunification, but Greek Cyprus's president, Papadopoulos, remains set against it.

Czech Republic

National name: Ceska Republika
President: Vaclav Klaus (2003)
Prime Minister: Jiri Paroubek (2005)
Area: 30,450 sq mi (78,866 sq km)
Population (2005 est.): 10,241,138 (growth rate: –0.1%); birth rate: 9.1/1000; infant mortality rate: 3.9/1000; life expectancy: 76.0; density per sq mi: 336

Capital and largest city (2003 est.): Prague, 1,378,700 (metro. area), 1,169,800 (city proper). **Other large cities:** Brno, 376,400; Ostrava, 317,700; Plzen, 164,900; Olomouc, 102,900. **Monetary unit:** Koruna. **Language:** Czech. **Ethnicity/race:** Czech 81.2%, Moravian 13.2%, Slovak 3.1%, Polish 0.6%, German 0.5%, Silesian 0.4%, Roma (Gypsy) 0.3%, Hungarian 0.2%, other 0.5% (1991). **Religions:** atheist 39.8%, Roman Catholic 39.2%, Protestant 4.6%, Orthodox 3%, other 13.4%. **Literacy rate:** 100% (1999 est.)
Economic summary: GDP/PPP (2004 est.): $172.2 billion; per capita $16,800. **Real growth rate:** 3.7%. **Inflation:** 3.2%. **Unemployment:** 10.6%. **Arable land:** 40%. **Agriculture:** wheat, potatoes, sugar beets, hops, fruit; pigs, poultry. **Labor force:** 5.25 million; agriculture 4%, industry 38%, services 58% (2002 est.) **Industries:** metallurgy, machinery and equipment, motor vehicles, glass, armaments. **Natural resources:** hard coal, soft coal, kaolin, clay, graphite, timber. **Exports:** $66.51 billion (f.o.b., 2004 est.): machinery and transport equipment 52%, chemicals 5%, raw materials and fuel 9% (2003). **Imports:** $68.19 billion (f.o.b., 2004 est.): machinery and transport equipment 46%, raw materials and fuels 15%, chemicals 10% (2003). **Major trading partners:** Germany, Slovakia, Austria, UK, Poland, France, Italy, Netherlands, China, Russia (2003).

Geography The Czech Republic's central European landscape is dominated by the Bohemian Massif, which rises to heights of 3,000 ft (900 m) above sea level. This ring of mountains encircles a large elevated basin, the Bohemian Plateau. The principal rivers are the Elbe and the Vltava.

Government Parliamentary democracy.

History Probably about the 5th century A.D., Slavic tribes from the Vistula basin settled in the region of Bohemia, Moravia, and Silesia. The Czechs founded the kingdom of Bohemia and the Premyslide dynasty, which ruled Bohemia and Moravia from the 10th to the 16th century. One of the Bohemian kings, Charles IV, Holy Roman Emperor, made Prague an imperial capital and a center of Latin scholarship. The Hussite movement founded by Jan Hus (1369?–1415) linked the Slavs to the Reformation and revived Czech nationalism, previously under German domination. A Hapsburg, Ferdinand I, ascended the throne in 1526. The Czechs rebelled in 1618, precipitating the Thirty Years' War (1618–1648). Defeated in 1620, they were ruled for the next 300 years as part of the Austrian empire. Full independence from the Hapsburgs was not achieved until the end of World War I, following the collapse of the Austrian-Hungarian Empire.

A union of the Czech lands and Slovakia was proclaimed in Prague on Nov. 14, 1918, and the Czech nation became one of the two component parts of the newly formed Czechoslovakian state. In March 1939, German troops occupied Czechoslovakia, and Czech Bohemia and Moravia became German protectorates for the duration of World War II. The former government returned in April 1945 when the war ended and the country's pre-1938 boundaries were restored. When elections were held in 1946, Communists became the dominant political party and gained control of the Czechoslovakian government in 1948. Thereafter, the former democracy was turned into a Soviet-style state.

Nearly 42 years of Communist rule ended with the nearly bloodless "velvet revolution" in 1989. Václav Havel, a leading playwright and dissident, was elected president of Czechoslovakia in 1989. Havel, imprisoned twice by the Communist regime and his plays banned, became an international symbol for human rights, democracy, and peaceful dissent. The return of democratic political reform saw a strong Slovak nationalist movement emerge by the end of 1991, which sought independence for Slovakia. When the general elections of June 1992 failed to resolve the continuing coexistence of the two republics within the federation, Czech and Slovak political leaders agreed to separate their states into two fully independent nations. On Jan. 1, 1993, the Czechoslovakian federation was dissolved and two separate independent countries were established—the Czech Republic and Slovakia. The Czech Republic joined NATO in March 1999.

In Aug. 2002, severe flooding caused 70,000 people in Prague and 200,000 nationwide to be evacuated.

President Václav Havel left office in Feb. 2003, after 13 years as president. Over the years, Havel lost some of his immense popularity with the Czechs, who became disenchanted with his failings as a political leader. But internationally Havel has remained a towering figure of moral authority and courage. In March, Vaclav Klaus became the Czech Republic's second president. A conservative economist, he and Havel often clashed. In May 2004, the Czech Republic joined the EU. In April 2005, Jiri Paroubek became the third prime minister appointed in nine months.

Denmark

KINGDOM OF DENMARK

National name: Kongeriget Danmark
Sovereign: Queen Margrethe II (1972)
Prime Minister: Anders Fogh Rasmussen (2001)
Area: 16,639 sq mi (43,094 sq km)[1]
Population (2005 est.): 5,432,335 (growth rate: 0.3%); birth rate: 11.4/1000; infant mortality rate: 4.6/1000; life expectancy: 77.6; density per sq mi: 326
Capital and largest city (2003 est.): Copenhagen, 1,094,400. **Other large cities:** Århus, 220,700; Odense, 144,600; Ålborg, 120,600. **Monetary unit:** Krone. **Languages:** Danish, Faroese, Greenlandic (Inuit dialect), German; English is the predominant second language. **Ethnicity/race:** Scandinavian, Inuit, Faroese, German, Turkish, Iranian, Somali. **Religions:** Evangelical Lutheran 95%, other Protestant and Roman Catholic 3%, Muslim 2%. **Literacy rate:** 100%
Economic summary: GDP/PPP (2004 est.): $174.4 billion; per capita $32,200. **Real growth rate:** 2.1%. **Inflation:** 1.4%. **Unemployment:** 6.2%. **Arable land:** 54%. **Agriculture:** barley, wheat, potatoes, sugar beets; pork, dairy products; fish. **Labor force:** 2.87 million; services 79%, industry 17%, agriculture 4% (2002 est.). **Industries:** iron, steel, nonferrous metals, chemicals, food processing, machinery and transportation equipment, textiles and clothing, electronics, construction, furniture and other wood products, shipbuilding and refurbishment, windmills. **Natural resources:** petroleum, natural gas, fish, salt, limestone, stone, gravel and sand. **Exports:** $73.06 billion (f.o.b., 2004 est.): machinery and instruments, meat and meat products, dairy products, fish, chemicals, furniture, ships, windmills. **Imports:** $63.45 billion (f.o.b., 2004 est.): machinery and equipment, raw materials and semimanufactures for industry, chemicals, grain and foodstuffs, consumer goods. **Major trading partners:** Germany, Sweden, UK, U.S., Norway, France, Netherlands, Italy (2003).

1. Excluding Faroe Islands and Greenland.

Geography Smallest of the Scandinavian countries (half the size of Maine), Denmark occupies the Jutland peninsula, a lowland area. The country also consists of several islands in the Baltic Sea; the two largest are Sjælland, the site of Copenhagen, and Fyn.

Government Constitutional monarchy.

History From 10,000 to 1500 B.C., the population of present-day Denmark evolved from a society of hunters and fishers into one of farmers. Called Jutland by the end of the 8th century, its mariners were among the Vikings, or Norsemen, who raided western Europe and the British Isles from the 9th to 11th century.

The country was Christianized by Saint Ansgar and Harald Blaatand (Bluetooth)—the first Christian king—in the 10th century. Harald's son, Sweyn, conquered England in 1013. Sweyn's son, Canute the Great, who reigned from 1014 to 1035, united Denmark, England, and Norway under his rule; the southern tip of Sweden was part of Denmark until the 17th century. On Canute's death, civil war tore apart the country until Waldemar I (1157–1182) reestablished Danish hegemony over the north.

In 1282, the nobles won the Great Charter, and Eric V was forced to share power with Parliament and a Council of Nobles. Waldemar IV (1340–1375) restored Danish power, checked only by the Hanseatic League of north German cities allied with ports from Holland to Poland. Denmark, Norway, and Sweden united under the rule of his daughter Margrethe in 1397. But Sweden later achieved autonomy and in 1523, under Gustavus I, independence.

Denmark supported Napoléon, for which it was punished at the Congress of Vienna in 1815 by the loss of Norway to Sweden. In 1864, the Prussians under Bismarck and the Austrians made war on Denmark as an initial step in the unification of Germany. Denmark was neutral in World War I.

In 1940, Denmark was invaded by the Nazis. King Christian X reluctantly cautioned his fellow Danes to accept the occupation, but there was widespread resistance against the Nazis. Denmark was the only occupied country in World War II to save all its Jews from extermination, by smuggling them out of the country.

Beginning in 1944, Denmark's relationship with its territories changed substantially. In that year, Iceland declared its independence from Denmark, ending a union that had existed since 1380. In 1948, the Faroe Islands, which had also belonged to Denmark since 1380, were granted home rule, and in 1953, Greenland officially became a territory of Denmark.

In 2001, the dominant Social-Democrat Party lost to Anders Fogh Rasmussen of the center-right Liberal Party, which formed a coalition with the Conservative Party. Prime Minister Fogh Rasmussen, author of *From Socialist to Minimalist State*, is a strong proponent of privatization, deregulation, and limited government. Immigration to Denmark fell dramatically in 2002, after Fogh Rasmussen instituted Europe's most restrictive laws for asylum seekers. Because of Denmark's social welfare benefits, the country had become a much-sought-after haven for refugees.

Denmark was a strong ally to the U.S. during the Iraq war, one of five countries to contribute combat troops (the others were the U.S., UK, Australia, and Poland).

In Feb. 2005, Fogh Rasmussen won a second term as prime minister.

Outlying Territories of Denmark

Faroe Islands
Status: Autonomous part of Denmark
Chief of State: Queen Margrethe II (1972)
High Commissioner: Birgit Kleis (2001)
Prime Minister: Jóannes Eidesgaard (2004)
Area: 540 sq mi (1,399 sq km)
Population (2005 est.): 46,962 (growth rate: 0.6%); birth rate: 14.0/1000; infant mortality rate: 6.2/1000; life expectancy: 79.2; density per sq mi: 87

Capital and largest city (2003 est.): Tórshavn, 17,300.
  Monetary unit: Faroese krone. **Languages:** Faroese,
  Danish (both official). **Ethnicity/race:** Scandinavian.
  Religion: Evangelical Lutheran. **Literacy rate:** n.a.

This group of 18 islands, of which 17 are inhabited,
is located in the North Atlantic about 200 mi (322 km)
northwest of the Shetland Islands. They were settled by
the Vikings, the ancestors of the modern-day Faroese,
in the 8th century. The Faroese language is derived
from Old Norse. The islands joined Denmark in 1386
and have been part of the Danish kingdom ever since.
The Faroes have had home rule, under Danish authority, since 1948.

Greenland

Status: Autonomous part of Denmark
Chief of State: Queen Margrethe II (1972)
High Commissioner: Gunnar Martens (1995)
Premier: Jonathan Motzfeldt (1997)
Area: 836,326 sq mi (incl. 677,851 sq mi covered by
  icecap) (2,166,086 sq km)
Population (2005 est.): 56,375 (growth rate: 0%); birth
  rate: 15.9/1000; infant mortality rate: 15.8/1000; life
  expectancy: 69.7; density per sq mi: 0.07
Capital and largest city (2003 est.): Godthaab, 14,100.
  Monetary unit: Krone. **Languages:** Greenlandic (East
  Inuit), Danish, English. **Ethnicity/race:** Greenlander
  88% (Eskimos and Greenland-born whites), Danish
  and other 12% (2000). **Religion:** Evangelical
  Lutheran. **Literacy rate:** n.a.

The Inuit are believed to have crossed from North
America to northwest Greenland, the world's largest
island, between 4000 B.C. and A.D. 1000. Greenland was
colonized in 985–986 by Eric the Red. The Norse
settlements declined in the 14th century, however,
mainly as a result of a cooling in Greenland's climate,
and in the 15th century they became extinct. In 1721,
Greenland was recolonized by the Royal Greenland
Trading Company of Denmark.

Greenland was under U.S. protection during World
War II, but it maintained Danish sovereignty. A definitive agreement for the joint defense of Greenland
within the framework of NATO was signed in 1951. A
large U.S. air base at Thule in the far north was completed in 1953. Under 1953 amendments to the Danish
constitution, Greenland became part of Denmark, with
two representatives in the Danish Folketing. On May 1,
1979, Greenland gained home rule, with its own local
Parliament (Landsting).

Djibouti

REPUBLIC OF DJIBOUTI

National name: Jumhouriyya Djibouti
President: Ismail Omar Guelleh (1999)
Prime Minister: Dileita Mohamed Dileita (2001)
Area: 8,880 sq mi (23,000 sq km)
Population (2005 est.): 476,703 (growth rate: 2.1%);
  birth rate: 40.0/1000; infant mortality rate: 104.1/1000;
  life expectancy: 43.1; density per sq mi: 54
Capital (1995 est.): Djibouti, 383,000. **Monetary unit:**
  Djibouti franc. **Languages:** French and Arabic (both
  official), Somali, Afar. **Ethnicity/race:** Somali 60%,
  Afar 35%, French, Arab, Ethiopian, and Italian 5%.
  Religions: Islam 94%, Christian 6%. **Literacy rate:**
  68% (2003 est.)
Economic summary: GDP/PPP (2002 est.): $619
  million; per capita $1,300. **Real growth rate:** 3.5%.
  Inflation: 2%. **Unemployment:** 50% (2004 est.).
  Arable land: 0.04%. **Agriculture:** fruits, vegetables;
  goats, sheep, camels, animal hides. **Labor:** 282,000
  (2000). **Industries:** construction, agricultural
  processing, salt. **Natural resources:** geothermal
  areas, gold, clay, granite, limestone, marble, salt,

diatomite, gypsum, pumice, petroleum. **Exports:** $155
million (f.o.b., 2002 est.): reexports, hides and skins,
coffee (in transit). **Imports:** $665 million (f.o.b., 2002
est.): foods, beverages, transport equipment,
chemicals, petroleum products. **Major trading
partners:** Somalia, Yemen, Ethiopia, Saudi Arabia,
China, India, France, UK, U.S. (2003).

Geography Djibouti lies in northeast Africa on the
Gulf of Aden at the southern entrance to the Red Sea.
It borders on Ethiopia, Eritrea, and Somalia. The
country, the size of Massachusetts, is mainly a stony
desert, with scattered plateaus and highlands.

Government Republic with a unicameral legislature.

History Ablé immigrants from Arabia migrated to
what is now Djibouti in about the 3rd century B.C. Their
descendants are the Afars, one of the two main ethnic
groups that make up Djibouti today. Somali Issas
arrived thereafter. Islam came to the region in 825.

Djibouti was acquired by France between 1843 and
1886 through treaties with the Somali sultans. Small,
arid, and sparsely populated, it is important chiefly
because of the capital city's port, the terminal of the
Djibouti–Addis Ababa railway that carries 60% of
Ethiopia's foreign trade. Originally known as French
Somaliland, the colony voted in 1958 and 1967 to
remain under French rule. It was renamed the Territory
of the Afars and Issas in 1967 and took the name of its
capital city on June 27, 1977, when France transferred
sovereignty to the new independent nation of Djibouti.
On Sept. 4, 1992, voters approved in referendum a new
multiparty constitution. In 1991, conflict between the
Afars and the Issa-dominated government erupted and
the continued warfare has ravaged the country.

The dictatorial president, Hassan Gouled Aptidon,
who had run the country since its independence, finally
stepped aside in 1999, and Ismail Omar Guelleh was
elected president. In March 2000, the main Afars rebel
group signed a peace accord with the government. The
fighting, severe drought, and presence of tens of thousands of refugees from its war-torn neighbors, Ethiopia
and Somalia, have severely strained Djibouti's agricultural capacity.

In April 2000 experts estimated some 150,000
people, or more than one-quarter of the population,
needed food aid. The United Nations agreed to spend
$2.7 million to increase the city of Djibouti's port
facilities since it is a crucial regional grain terminus. In
2002, Djibouti became a key U.S. military base used to
combat terrorism. In 2005, President Guelleh, the only
candidate, was reelected.

Dominica

COMMONWEALTH OF DOMINICA

President: Nicholas Liverpool (2003)
Prime Minister: Roosevelt Skerrit (2004)
Area: 291 sq mi (754 sq km)
Population (2005 est.): 69,029 (growth rate: -0.3%);
  birth rate: 15.7/1000; infant mortality rate: 14.2/1000;
  life expectancy: 74.7; density per sq mi: 237
Capital and largest city (2003 est.): Roseau, 20,000.
  Monetary unit: East Caribbean dollar. **Languages:**
  English (official) and French patois. **Ethnicity/race:**
  black, mixed black and European, European, Syrian,
  Carib Amerindian. **Religions:** Roman Catholic 77%,
  Protestant 15% (Methodist 5%, Pentecostal 3%,
  Seventh-Day Adventist 3%, Baptist 2%, other 2%),
  none 2%, other 6%. **Literacy rate:** 94% (2003 est.)
Economic summary: GDP/PPP (2003 est.): $384
  million; per capita $5,500. **Real growth rate:** -1%.
  Inflation: 1% (2001 est.). **Unemployment:** 23% (2000

est.). **Arable land:** 7%. **Labor force:** 25,000 (1999 est); agriculture 40%, industry and commerce 32%, services 28%. **Agriculture:** bananas, citrus, mangoes, root crops, coconuts, cocoa; forest and fishery potential not exploited. **Industries:** soap, coconut oil, tourism, copra, furniture, cement blocks, shoes. **Natural resources:** timber, hydropower, arable land. **Exports:** $39 million (f.o.b., 2003 est.): bananas, soap, bay oil, vegetables, grapefruit, oranges. **Imports:** $98.2 million (f.o.b., 2003 est.): manufactured goods, machinery and equipment, food, chemicals. **Major trading partners:** UK, Jamaica, U.S., Antigua and Barbuda, Guyana, Japan, Trinidad and Tobago, China, South Korea (2003). **Member of Commonwealth of Nations**

Geography Dominica (pronounced Dom-in-EEK-a) is a mountainous island of volcanic origin of the Lesser Antilles in the Caribbean, south of Guadeloupe and north of Martinique.

Government Parliamentary democracy.

History Explored by Columbus in 1493, Dominica was claimed by Britain and France until 1763, when it was formally ceded to Britain. Along with other Windward Isles, it became a self-governing member of the West Indies Associated States in free association with Britain in 1967.

Dissatisfaction over the slow pace of reconstruction after Hurricane David devastated the island in Sept. 1979 brought a landslide victory to Mary Eugenia Charles of the Freedom Party in July 1980. The Freedom Party won again in 1985 and 1990. The opposition United Workers' Party won in June 1995. In 1997 Dominica became the first Caribbean country to participate in the work of Green Globe, aiming to make Dominica a model ecotourism destination. Although the island is poorer than some of its Caribbean neighbors, Dominica has a relatively low crime rate and does not have the extremes of wealth and poverty evident on other islands. Economic austerity measures, including higher taxes, were introduced in 2002. Massive protests followed.

In parliamentary elections in 2005, Prime Minister Roosevelt Skerrit's Dominica Labour Party won 12 of 21 seats.

Dominican Republic

National name: República Dominicana
President: Leonel Fernández (2004)
Area: 18,815 sq mi (48,730 sq km)
Population (2005 est.): 8,950,034 (growth rate: 1.3%); birth rate: 23.3/1000; infant mortality rate: 32.4/1000; life expectancy: 67.3; density per sq mi: 476
Capital and largest city (2003 est.): Santo Domingo, 2,851,300 (metro. area), 2,252,400 (city proper).
Other large city: Santiago de los Caballeros, 501,900. **Monetary unit:** Dominican Peso. **Language:** Spanish. **Ethnicity/race:** white 16%, black 11%, mixed 73%. **Religion:** Roman Catholic 95%. **Literacy rate:** 85% (2003 est.)
Economic summary: GDP/PPP (2004 est.): $55.68 billion; per capita $6,300. **Real growth rate:** 1.7%. **Inflation:** 55%. **Unemployment:** 17%. **Arable land:** 23%. **Agriculture:** sugarcane, coffee, cotton, cocoa, tobacco, rice, beans, potatoes, corn, bananas; cattle, pigs, dairy products, beef, eggs. **Labor force:** 2.3 million to 2.6 million (2000 est); services and government 58.7%, industry 24.3%, agriculture 17% (1998 est.). **Industries:** tourism, sugar processing, ferronickel and gold mining, textiles, cement, tobacco. **Natural resources:** nickel, bauxite, gold, silver. **Exports:** $5.446 billion (f.o.b., 2004 est.): ferronickel, sugar, gold, silver, coffee, cocoa, tobacco, meats,

consumer goods. **Imports:** $8.093 billion (f.o.b., 2004 est.): foodstuffs, petroleum, cotton and fabrics, chemicals and pharmaceuticals. **Major trading partners:** U.S., Canada, Haiti, Venezuela, Mexico, Colombia (2003).

Geography The Dominican Republic in the West Indies occupies the eastern two-thirds of the island of Hispaniola, which it shares with Haiti. Its area equals that of Vermont and New Hampshire combined. Duarte Peak, at 10,417 ft (3,175 m), is the highest point in the West Indies.

Government Representative democracy.

History The Dominican Republic was explored by Columbus on his first voyage in 1492. He named it La Española, and his son, Diego, was its first viceroy. The capital, Santo Domingo, founded in 1496, is the oldest European settlement in the Western Hemisphere.

Spain ceded the colony to France in 1795, and Haitian blacks under Toussaint L'Ouverture conquered it in 1801. In 1808 the people revolted and captured Santo Domingo the next year, setting up the first republic. Spain regained title to the colony in 1814. In 1821 Spanish rule was overthrown, but in 1822 the colony was reconquered by the Haitians. In 1844 the Haitians were thrown out, and the Dominican Republic was established, headed by Pedro Santana. Uprisings and Haitian attacks led Santana to make the country a province of Spain from 1861 to 1865.

President Buenaventura Báez, faced with an economy in shambles, attempted to have the country annexed to the U.S. in 1870, but the U.S. Senate refused to ratify a treaty of annexation. Disorder continued until the dictatorship of Ulíses Heureaux; in 1916, when chaos broke out again, the U.S. sent in a contingent of marines, who remained until 1934.

A sergeant in the Dominican army trained by the marines, Rafaél Leonides Trujillo Molina, overthrew Horacio Vásquez in 1930 and established a dictatorship that lasted until his assassination in 1961, 31 years later. In 1962, Juan Bosch of the leftist Dominican Revolutionary Party, became the first democratically elected president in four decades.

In 1963, a military coup ousted Bosch and installed a civilian triumvirate. Leftists rebelled against the new regime in April 1965, and U.S. president Lyndon Johnson sent in marines and troops. After a cease-fire in May, a compromise installed Hector Garcia-Godoy as provisional president. In 1966, right-wing candidate Joaquin Balaguer won in free elections against Bosch, and U.S. and other foreign troops withdrew.

In 1978 the army suspended the counting of ballots when Balaguer trailed in a fourth-term bid. After a warning from President Jimmy Carter, however, Balaguer accepted the victory of Antonio Guzmán of the Dominican Revolutionary Party. In 1982 elections, Salvador Jorge Blanco of the Dominican Revolutionary Party defeated Balaguer and Bosch. Balaguer was again elected president in May 1986 and remained in office for the next ten years.

In 1996, U.S.-raised Leonel Fernández secured more than 51% of the vote through an alliance with Balaguer. The first item on the president's agenda was the partial sale of some state-owned enterprises. Fernández was praised for ending decades of isolationism and improving ties with other Caribbean countries, but he was criticized for not fighting corruption or alleviating the poverty that affects 60% of the population.

In Aug. 2000 the center-left Hipólito Mejía was elected president amid popular discontent over power outages in the recently privatized electric industry. In 2001 the army was deployed in major cities to fight rising crime. In May 2004 presidential elections, the previous president, Leonel Fernández (1996–2000), won 57% of the vote, defeating incumbent Mejía. He vowed to institute austerity measures to rescue the country from its current economic crisis.

East Timor

DEMOCRATIC REPUBLIC OF TIMOR-LESTE

National name: Republika Demokratika Timor Lorosa'e/ Republica Democratica de Timor-Leste
President: José Alexandre (Xanana) Gusmão (2002)
Prime Minister: Mari Alkatiri (2002)
Area: 5,794 sq mi (15,007 sq km)
Population (2005 est.): 1,040,880 (growth rate: 2.1%); birth rate: 27.2/1000; infant mortality rate: 47.4/1000; life expectancy: 65.9; density per sq mi: 180
Capital and largest city (2003 est.): Dili, 50,800.
Monetary unit: U.S. dollar. **Languages:** Tetum, Portuguese (official); Bahasa Indonesia, English; other indigenous languages, including Tetum, Galole, Mambae, and Kemak. **Ethnicity/race:** Austronesian (Malayo-Polynesian), Papuan, small Chinese minority.
Religions: Roman Catholic 90%, Islam 4%, Protestant 3%, Hindu 0.5%, Buddhist, animist (1992 est.).
Literacy rate: 48% (2001)
Economic summary: GDP/PPP (2004 est.): $370 million; per capita $400. **Real growth rate:** 1%. **Inflation:** 4% (2003 est.). **Unemployment:** 50% (including underemployment) (1992 est.). **Arable land:** 5%. **Agriculture:** coffee, rice, maize, cassava, sweet potatoes, soybeans, cabbage, mangoes, bananas, vanilla. **Labor force:** n.a. **Industries:** printing, soap manufacturing, handicrafts, woven cloth. **Natural resources:** gold, petroleum, natural gas, manganese, marble. **Exports:** $8 million (2004 est.): coffee, sandalwood, marble; note—the potential for oil and vanilla exports. **Imports:** $167 million (2004 est.): food, gasoline, kerosene, machinery. **Major trading partners:** Portugal, Taiwan, Germany, U.S., Indonesia, Australia, Singapore, Vietnam, Portugal, Malaysia, China.

Geography East Timor is located in the eastern part of Timor, an island in the Indonesian archipelago that lies between the South China Sea and the Indian Ocean. East Timor includes the enclave of Oecussi, which is located within West Timor (Indonesia). After Indonesia, East Timor's closest neighbor is Australia, 400 mi to the south. It is semiarid and mountainous.

Government Republic.

History Timor was first colonized by the Portuguese in 1520. The Dutch, who claimed many of the surrounding islands, took control of the western portion of the island in 1613. Portugal and the Netherlands fought over the island until an 1860 treaty divided Timor, granting Portugal the eastern half of the island as well as the western enclave of Oecussi (the first Portuguese settlement on the island). Australia and Japan fought each other on the island during World War II; nearly 50,000 East Timorese died during the subsequent Japanese occupation.

In 1949, the Netherlands gave up its colonies in the Dutch West Indies, including West Timor, and the nation of Indonesia was born. East Timor remained under Portuguese control until 1975, when the Portuguese abruptly pulled out after 455 years of colonization. The sudden Portuguese withdrawal left the island vulnerable. On July 16, 1976, 9 days after the Democratic Republic of East Timor was declared an independent nation, Indonesia invaded and annexed it. Although no country except Australia officially recognized the annexation, Indonesia's invasion was sanc-

tioned by the United States and other western countries, who had cultivated Indonesia as a trading partner and cold-war ally (Fretilin, the East Timorese political party spearheading independence, was Marxist at the time).

Indonesia's invasion and its brutal occupation of East Timor—small, remote, and desperately poor—largely escaped international attention. East Timor's resistance movement was violently suppressed by Indonesian military forces, and more than 200,000 Timorese were reported to have died from famine, disease, and fighting since the annexation. Indonesia's human rights abuses finally began receiving international notice in the 1990s, and in 1996 two East Timorese activists, Bishop Carlos Filipe Ximenes Belo and José Ramos-Horta, received the Nobel Peace Prize for their efforts to gain freedom peacefully.

After Indonesia's hard-line president Suharto left office in 1998, his successor, B. J. Habibie, unexpectedly announced his willingness to hold a referendum on East Timorese independence, reversing 25 years of Indonesian intransigence. As the referendum on self-rule drew closer, fighting between separatist guerrillas and pro-Indonesian paramilitary forces in East Timor intensified. The UN-sponsored referendum had to be rescheduled twice because of violence. On Aug. 30, 1999, 78.5% of the population voted to secede from Indonesia. But in the days following the referendum, pro-Indonesian militias and Indonesian soldiers retaliated by razing towns, slaughtering civilians, and forcing a third of the population out of the province. After enormous international pressure, Indonesia finally agreed to allow UN forces into East Timor on Sept. 12. Led by Australia, an international peacekeeping force began restoring order to the ravaged region.

The UN Transitional Authority in East Timor (UNTAET) then governed the territory for nearly three years. On May 20, 2002, nationhood was declared. Charismatic rebel leader José Alexandre Gusmão, who was imprisoned by Indonesia from 1992 to 1999, was overwhelmingly elected the nation's first president on April 14, 2002. The president has a largely symbolic role; real power rests with the Parliament and Prime Minister Mari Alkatiri, also a former guerrilla leader.

The first new country of the millennium, East Timor is also one of the world's poorest. Its meager infrastructure was destroyed by the Indonesian militias in 1999 and the economy, primarily made up of subsistence farming and fishing, is in shambles. East Timor's offshore gas and oil reserves promised the only real hope for lifting it out of poverty, but a dispute with Australia over the rights to the oil reserves in the East Timor Sea thwarted those efforts. The oil and gas fields lie much closer to East Timor than to Australia, but a 1989 deal between Indonesia and Australia set the maritime boundary along Australia's continental shelf, which gives it control of 85% of the sea and most of the oil. Under these terms, Australia was to receive 82% of the oil revenues and East Timor just 18%. Finally, after years of wrangling, the two countries agreed in May 2005 to defer the redrawing of the border for 50 years and to split the oil and gas revenues down the middle.

Relations between East Timor and Indonesia thawed slightly in April 2005, when Indonesian President Susilo Bambang Yudhoyono made his first visit to East Timor. After five years of talks, the two countries agreed on a border between East Timor and Indonesian-controlled West Timor.

Ecuador

REPUBLIC OF ECUADOR

National name: República del Ecuador
President: Alfredo Palacio (2005)
Area: 109,483 sq mi (283,560 sq km)
Population (2005 est.): 13,363,593 (growth rate: 1.2%);
  birth rate: 22.7/1000; infant mortality rate: 23.7/1000;
  life expectancy: 76.2; density per sq mi: 122
Capital (2003 est.): Quito 1,780,700 (metro. area),
  1,443,900 (city proper). **Largest cities:** Guayaquil,
  2,597,600 (metro. area), 2,013,500 (city proper);
  Cuenca, 285,700. **Monetary unit:** U.S. dollar.
Languages: Spanish (official), Quechua, other
  Amerindian languages. **Ethnicity/race:** mestizo (mixed
  Amerindian and white) 65%, Amerindian 25%, Spanish
  7%, black 3%. **Religion:** Roman Catholic 95%.
Literacy rate: 93% (2003 est.)
Economic summary: GDP/PPP (2004 est.): $49.51
  billion; per capita $3,700. **Real growth rate:** 5.8%.
  Inflation: 2%. **Unemployment:** 11.1%,
  underemployment 47%. **Arable land:** 6%.
  Agriculture: bananas, coffee, cocoa, rice, potatoes,
  manioc (tapioca), plantains, sugarcane; cattle, sheep,
  pigs, beef, pork, dairy products; balsa wood; fish,
  shrimp . **Labor force:** 4.53 million (urban); agriculture
  8%, industry 24%, services 68% (2001). **Industries:**
  petroleum, food processing, textiles, wood products,
  chemicals. **Natural resources:** petroleum, fish, timber,
  hydropower. **Exports:** $7.56 billion (2004 est.):
  petroleum, bananas, cut flowers, shrimp. **Imports:**
  $7.65 billion (2004 est.): vehicles, medicinal products,
  telecommunications equipment, electricity. **Major
  trading partners:** U.S., Colombia, Germany,
  Venezuela, Brazil, Chile, Japan (2003).

Geography Ecuador, about equal in area to Nevada,
is in the northwest part of South America fronting on
the Pacific. To the north is Colombia and to the east
and south is Peru. Two high and parallel ranges of the
Andes, traversing the country from north to south, are
topped by tall volcanic peaks. The highest is Chimborazo at 20,577 ft (6,272 m). The Galápagos Islands (or
Colón Archipelago: 3,029 sq mi; 7,845 sq km), in the
Pacific Ocean about 600 mi (966 km) west of the
South American mainland, became part of Ecuador in
1832.

Government Republic.

History The tribes in the northern highlands of Ecuador formed the Kingdom of Quito around 1000. It was
absorbed, by conquest and marriage, into the Inca
Empire. Spanish conquistador Francisco Pizarro conquered the land in 1532, and through the 17th century
a Spanish colony thrived by exploitation of the Indians. The first revolt against Spain occurred in 1809. In
1819, Ecuador joined Venezuela, Colombia, and
Panama in a confederacy known as Greater Colombia.

When Greater Colombia collapsed in 1830, Ecuador
became independent. Revolts and dictatorships followed; it had 48 presidents during the first 131 years of
the republic. Conservatives ruled until the revolution of
1895 ushered in nearly a half century of Radical Liberal rule, during which the church was disestablished
and freedom of worship, speech, and press was introduced. Although it was under military rule in the
1970s, the country did not experience the violence and
repression characteristic of other Latin American military regimes. Its last 30 years of democracy, however,
have been largely ineffectual because of a weak executive branch and a strong, fractious Congress.

Peru invaded Ecuador in 1941 and seized a large
tract of Ecuadorian territory in the disputed Amazon
region. In 1981 and 1995 war broke out again. In May
1999, Ecuador and Peru signed a treaty ending the
nearly 60-year border dispute.

In 1998, Ecuador experienced one of its worst economic crises. El Niño caused $3 billion in damage; the
price of its principal export, oil, plunged; and its inflation rate, 43%, was the highest in Latin America. In
1999, the government was near bankruptcy, the currency lost 40% of its value against the dollar, and the
poverty rate soared to 70%, doubling in five years. The
president's economic austerity plan was protested with
massive strikes in March 1999.

President Jamil Mahuad was overthrown in Jan.
2000, in the first military coup in Latin America in a
decade. The junta gave power to the vice president,
Gustavo Noboa. Faced with the worst economic crisis
in Ecuador's history, Noboa restructured Ecuador's foreign debt, adopted the U.S. dollar as the national currency, and continued privatization of state-owned
industries, generating enormous opposition. In Feb.
2001, the government cut fuel prices after violent protests by Indians, who are among Ecuador's most disad-
vantaged people.

Within two years, Ecuador's economy had
rebounded from the brink of collapse. The economy
grew by 5.4% for 2001, the highest rate in Latin
America. Inflation was 22%, down from 91% in 2000,
and the budget was balanced. But chronic corruption
among senior government officials, as well as among
the courts and the judiciary, has continued.

Lucio Gutiérrez, a leftist colonel best known for
orchestrating the 2000 coup against President Jamil
Mahuad, was elected to the presidency in 2003 on an
anticorruption platform. He became Ecuador's sixth
president in seven years. His attempts to introduce aus-
tere fiscal reforms, however, quickly alienated his
political base, and numerous national strikes took place
over 2003. But some economic improvements were
seen in 2003: the GDP grew by an estimated 2.7%, and
inflation dropped to a remarkable 6%.

In November, President Gutiérrez narrowly escaped
impeachment for the alleged misuse of government
funds. In December he removed 27 of the 31 justices
of the Supreme Court, claiming the judges had supported the impeachment attempt and were sympathetic
to the opposition parties. He replaced them with judges
who supported the government. In April, the new
Supreme Court overturned corruption charges against
an exiled former president, Abdala Bucaram, who was
an ally of Gutiérrez. Outraged by what was seen as
Gutiérrez's attempts to control the judiciary branch,
tens of thousands of Ecuadorians took to the street and
protested. The protesters accused Gutiérrez of corruption, mismanagement, and an authoritarian style of
governing, and polls indicated that just 5% of the
people still supported him. On April 20, Gutiérrez was
ousted by the Ecuadorian Congress, and his estranged
deputy, Alfredo Palacio, took over as president. He
became the country's seventh president in eight years.

Egypt

ARAB REPUBLIC OF EGYPT

National name: Jumhuriyat Misr al-Arabiyah
President: Hosni Mubarak (1981)
Prime Minister: Ahmed Nazif (2004)
Area: 386,660 sq mi (1,001,450 sq km)
Population (2005 est.): 77,505,756 (growth rate: 1.8%);
  birth rate: 23.3/1000; infant mortality rate: 32.6/1000;
  life expectancy: 71.0; density per sq mi: 200
Capital and largest city (2003 est.): Cairo, 15,892,400
  (metro. area), 7,937,700 (city proper). **Other large
  cities:** Alexandria, 3,891,000; Giza, 2,597,600 (part of
  Cairo metro. area); Shubra el Khema, 1,018,000 (part

of Cairo metro. area); El Mahalla el Kubra, 462,300.
Monetary unit: Egyptian pound. **Languages:** Arabic (official), English and French widely understood by educated classes. **Ethnicity/race:** Eastern Hamitic stock (Egyptians, Bedouins, and Berbers) 99%, Greek, Nubian, Armenian, other European (primarily Italian and French) 1%. **Religions:** Islam (mostly Sunni) 94%, Coptic Christian and other 6%. **Literacy rate:** 58% (2003 est.)

Economic summary: GDP/PPP (2004 est.): $316.3 billion; per capita $4,200. **Real growth rate:** 4.5%. **Inflation:** 9.5%. **Unemployment:** 10.9% **Arable land:** 3%. **Agriculture:** cotton, rice, corn, wheat, beans, fruits, vegetables; cattle, water buffalo, sheep, goats. **Labor force:** 20.71 million; agriculture 32%, industry 17%, services 51% (2001 est.). **Industries:** textiles, food processing, tourism, chemicals, hydrocarbons, construction, cement, metals. **Natural resources:** petroleum, natural gas, iron ore, phosphates, manganese, limestone, gypsum, talc, asbestos, lead, zinc. **Exports:** $11 billion (f.o.b., 2004 est.): crude oil and petroleum products, cotton, textiles, metal products, chemicals. **Imports:** $19.21 billion (f.o.b., 2004 est.): machinery and equipment, foodstuffs, chemicals, wood products, fuels. **Major trading partners:** U.S., Italy, UK, Germany, France, China, Saudi Arabia (2003).

Geography

Egypt, at the northeast corner of Africa on the Mediterranean Sea, is bordered on the west by Libya, on the south by the Sudan, and on the east by the Red Sea and Israel. It is nearly one and one-half times the size of Texas. Egypt is divided into two unequal, extremely arid regions by the landscape's dominant feature, the northward-flowing Nile River. The Nile starts 100 mi (161 km) south of the Mediterranean and fans out to a sea front of 155 mi between the cities of Alexandria and Port Said.

Government

Republic.

History

Egyptian history dates back to about 4000 B.C., when the kingdoms of upper and lower Egypt, already highly sophisticated, were united. Egypt's golden age coincided with the 18th and 19th dynasties (16th to 13th century B.C.), during which the empire was established. Persia conquered Egypt in 525 B.C., Alexander the Great subdued it in 332 B.C., and then the dynasty of the Ptolemies ruled the land until 30 B.C., when Cleopatra, last of the line, committed suicide and Egypt became a Roman, then Byzantine, province. Arab caliphs ruled Egypt from 641 until 1517, when the Turks took it for their Ottoman Empire.

Napoléon's armies occupied the country from 1798 to 1801. In 1805, Mohammed Ali, leader of a band of Albanian soldiers, became pasha of Egypt. After completion of the Suez Canal in 1869, the French and British took increasing interest in Egypt. British troops occupied Egypt in 1882, and British resident agents became its actual administrators, though it remained under nominal Turkish sovereignty. In 1914, this fiction was ended, and Egypt became a protectorate of Britain.

Egyptian nationalism, led by Zaghlul Pasha and the Wafd party, forced Britain to relinquish its claims on the country. Egypt became an independent sovereign state on Feb. 28, 1922, with Fu'ad I as its king. In 1936, by an Anglo-Egyptian treaty of alliance, all British troops and officials were to be withdrawn, except from the Suez Canal Zone. When World War II started, Egypt remained neutral.

When Israel declared independence in 1948, Egypt and other Arab countries attacked; by 1949, however, Israel had rebuffed them.

Tensions grew between the Wafd party and the monarchy following independence, and in 1952, the army,

led by Gen. Mohammed Naguib, seized power. Three days later, King Farouk abdicated in favor of his infant son. The monarchy was abolished and a republic proclaimed on June 18, 1953, with Naguib becoming president and prime minister. He relinquished the prime ministership in 1954 to Gamal Abdel Nasser, leader of the ruling military junta. Nasser also assumed the presidency in 1956.

Nasser's policies embroiled his country in continual conflict. In 1956, the U.S. and Britain withdrew their pledges of financial aid for the building of the Aswan High Dam. In response, Nasser nationalized the Suez Canal and expelled British oil and embassy officials. The Soviet Union then agreed to finance the dam, and would come to exert increasing influence over Egypt in the coming decade. Israel, barred from the canal and exasperated by terrorist raids, invaded the Gaza Strip and the Sinai Peninsula. Britain and France, after demanding Egyptian evacuation of the canal zone, attacked Egypt on Oct. 31, 1956. Worldwide pressure forced Britain, France, and Israel to halt the hostilities. A UN emergency force occupied the canal zone, and all troops were evacuated in the spring of 1957.

From 1956 to 1961, Egypt and Syria united to form a single country called the United Arab Republic (UAR). Syria ended this relationship in 1961 after a military coup, but Egypt continued to call itself the UAR until 1971.

In 1967, border tensions between Egypt and Israel led to the Six-Day War. On June 5, Israel launched an air assault, and within days had annexed the Sinai Peninsula, the East Bank of the Jordan River, and the Golan Heights. A UN cease-fire on June 10 saved the Arabs from complete rout. Nasser declared the 1967 cease-fire void along the canal in April 1969 and began a war of attrition. On Sept. 28, 1970, Nasser died of a heart attack. Anwar el-Sadat, an associate of Nasser and a former newspaper editor, became the next president.

In July 1972, Sadat ordered the expulsion of Soviet "advisers and experts" from Egypt because the Russians had not provided the sophisticated weapons he felt were needed to retake territory lost to Israel in 1967.

The fourth Arab-Israeli War broke out on Oct. 6, 1973, during the Jewish holiday of Yom Kippur. Egypt swept deep into the Sinai, while Syria strove to throw Israel off the Golan Heights. A UN-sponsored truce was accepted on Oct. 22. In Jan. 1974, both sides agreed to a settlement negotiated by the U.S. that gave Egypt a narrow strip along the entire Sinai bank of the Suez Canal. In June, President Nixon made the first visit by a U.S. president to Egypt and full diplomatic relations were established. The Suez Canal was reopened on June 5, 1975.

In the most audacious act of his career, Sadat flew to Jerusalem at the invitation of Prime Minister Menachem Begin on Nov. 20, 1977, to discuss a permanent peace settlement. The Arab world reacted with fury. Egypt and Israel signed a formal peace treaty on March 26, 1979. The pact ended 30 years of war and established diplomatic and commercial relations.

By mid-1980, two-thirds of the Sinai had been transferred back to Egypt, but Sadat halted further talks with Israel in Aug. 1980 because of continued Israeli settlement of the West Bank. On Oct. 6, 1981, Sadat was assassinated by extremist Muslim soldiers at a parade in Cairo. Vice-President Hosni Mubarak, a former air force chief of staff, succeeded him. Israel completed the return of the Sinai to Egyptian control on April 25, 1982. Israel's invasion of Lebanon in June brought a marked cooling in Egyptian-Israeli relations, but not a disavowal of the peace treaty.

The government has concentrated much of its time and attention in recent years on combating Islamic extremists, who have in particular targeted Copts (Egyptian Christians). In 1997, a terrorist attack on foreign tourists killed 70. During the 1990s, about 26,000 Islamic militants were imprisoned and dozens were executed.

At least 90 people died in a series of car bomb explosions at popular Red Sea resort Sharm el Sheik in July 2005. Two militant groups claimed responsibility.

In July 2005, President Mubarak announced he would seek a fifth six-year term. Earlier in the year Mubarak had amended the constitution to allow for multiparty elections, the first in Egyptian history. Few believe that any of Egypt's 21 fledgling opposition parties have any chance of defeating Mubarak, who has ruled Egypt since 1981.

El Salvador

REPUBLIC OF EL SALVADOR

National name: República de El Salvador
President: Antonio Saca (2004)
Area: 8,124 sq mi (21,040 sq km)
Population (2005 est.): 6,704,932 (growth rate: 1.8%); birth rate: 27.0/1000; infant mortality rate: 25.1/1000; life expectancy: 71.2; density per sq mi: 825
Capital and largest city (2003 est.): San Salvador, 1,791,700 (metro. area), 504,700 (city proper). **Other large cities:** Santa Ana, 167,200; San Miguel, 145,100; Zacatecoluca, 36,700. **Monetary units:** Colón; U.S. dollar. **Languages:** Spanish, Nahua (among some Amerindians). **Ethnicity/race:** mestizo 90%, white 9%, Amerindian 1%. **Religions:** Catholics 83%; growing population of evangelical Protestants (1992). **Literacy rate:** 80% (2003 est.)
Economic summary: GDP/PPP (2004 est.): $32.35 billion; per capita $4,900. **Real growth rate:** 1.8%. **Inflation:** 5.4%. **Unemployment:** 6.3%—but the economy has much underemployment. **Arable land:** 32%. **Agriculture:** coffee, sugar, corn, rice, beans, oilseed, cotton, sorghum; shrimp; beef, dairy products. **Labor force:** 2.75 million; agriculture 17.1%, industry 17.1%, services 65.8% (2003 est.). **Industries:** food processing, beverages, petroleum, chemicals, fertilizer, textiles, furniture, light metals. **Natural resources:** hydropower, geothermal power, petroleum, arable land. **Exports:** $3.249 billion (2004 est.): offshore assembly exports, coffee, sugar, shrimp, textiles, chemicals, electricity. **Imports:** $5.968 billion (2004 est.): raw materials, consumer goods, capital goods, fuels, foodstuffs, petroleum, electricity. **Major trading partners:** U.S., Guatemala, Honduras, Mexico (2003).

Geography Situated on the Pacific coast of Central America, El Salvador has Guatemala to the west and Honduras to the north and east. It is the smallest of the Central American countries, with an area equal to that of Massachusetts, and it is the only one without an Atlantic coastline. Most of the country is on a fertile volcanic plateau about 2,000 ft (607 m) high.

Government Republic.

History The Pipil Indians, descendants of the Aztecs, likely migrated to the region in the 11th century. In 1525, Pedro de Alvarado, a lieutenant of Cortés, conquered El Salvador.

El Salvador, with the other countries of Central America, declared its independence from Spain on Sept. 15, 1821, and was part of a federation of Central American states until that union dissolved in 1838. For decades after its independence, El Salvador experienced numerous revolutions and wars against other Central American republics. From 1931 to 1979 El Salvador was ruled by a series of military dictatorships.

In 1969, El Salvador invaded Honduras after Honduran landowners deported several thousand Salvadorans. The four-day war became known as the "football war" because it broke out during a soccer game between the two countries.

In the 1970s discontent with societal inequalities, a poor economy, and the repressive measures of dictatorship led to civil war between the government, ruled since 1961 by the right-wing National Conciliation Party (PCN), and leftist antigovernment guerrilla units, whose leading group was the Farabundo Martí National Liberation Front (FMLN). The U.S. intervened on the side of the military dictatorship, despite its scores of human rights violations. Between 1979 and 1981, about 30,000 people were killed by rightwing death squads backed by the military. José Napoleón Duarte—a moderate civilian who was president from 1984 to 1989—offered an alternative to the political extremes of right and left, but Duarte was unable to end the war. In 1989, Alfredo Cristiani of the right-wing Nationalist Republican Alliance (ARENA) was elected. On Jan. 16, 1992, the government signed a peace treaty with the guerrilla forces, formally ending the 12-year civil war that had killed 75,000.

In 1998, Hurricane Mitch devastated the country, leaving 200 dead and over 30,000 homeless. In Jan. and Feb. 2001, major earthquakes struck El Salvador, damaging about 20% of the nation's housing. An even worse disaster beset the country in the summer when a severe drought destroyed 80% of the country's crops, causing famine in the countryside.

In 2004, Antonio Saca of ARENA was elected president. The nation ratified a free-trade agreement (CAFTA) with the U.S. in 2005.

Equatorial Guinea

REPUBLIC OF EQUATORIAL GUINEA

National name: Républica de Guinea Ecuatorial
President: Col. Teodoro Obiang Nguema Mbasogo (1979)
Prime Minister: Miguel Abia Biteo Borico (2004)
Area: 10,830 sq mi (28,051 sq km)
Population (2005 est.): 535,881 (growth rate: 2.4%); birth rate: 36.2/1000; infant mortality rate: 85.1/1000; life expectancy: 55.6; density per sq mi: 49
Capital and largest city (2003 est.): Malabo, 92,900.
Monetary unit: CFA Franc. **Languages:** Spanish, French (both official); pidgin English, Fang, Bubi, Ibo. **Ethnicity/race:** Bioko (primarily Bubi, some Fernandinos), Río Muni (primarily Fang), Europeans less than 1,000, mostly Spanish. **Religions:** nominally Christian and predominantly Roman Catholic, pagan practices. **Literacy rate:** 86% (2003 est.)
Economic summary: GDP/PPP (2002 est.): $1.27 billion; per capita $2,700. **Real growth rate:** 20%. **Inflation:** 8.5% (2004 est.). **Unemployment:** 30% (1998 est.). **Arable land:** 5%. **Agriculture:** coffee, cocoa, rice, yams, cassava (tapioca), bananas, palm oil nuts; livestock; timber. **Labor force:** n.a. **Industries:** petroleum, fishing, sawmilling, natural gas. **Natural resources:** petroleum, natural gas, timber, gold, bauxite, diamonds, tantalum, sand and gravel, clay. **Exports:** $2.77 billion (f.o.b., 2004 est.): petroleum, methanol, timber, cocoa. **Imports:** $1.167 billion (f.o.b., 2004 est.): petroleum sector equipment, other equipment. **Major trading partners:** U.S., Spain, China, Canada, Italy, UK, France, Côte d'Ivoire, Spain, Norway (2003).

Geography Equatorial Guinea, formerly Spanish Guinea, consists of Río Muni (10,045 sq mi; 26,117 sq km), on the western coast of Africa, and several islands in the Gulf of Guinea, the largest of which is Bioko (formerly Fernando Po) (785 sq mi; 2,033 sq km). The other islands are Annobón, Corisco, Elobey Grande, and Elobey Chico. The total area is twice that of Connecticut.

Government Dictatorship.

History The mainland was originally inhabited by Pygmies. The Fang and Bubi migrated there in the 17th century and to the main island of Fernando Po (now called Bioko) in the 19th century. In the 18th century, the Portuguese ceded land to the Spanish that included Equatorial Guinea. From 1827 to 1844, Britain administered Fernando Po, but it was then reclaimed by Spain. Río Muni, the mainland, was not occupied by the Spanish until 1926. Spanish Guinea, as it was then called, gained independence from Spain on Oct. 12, 1968. It is Africa's only Spanish-speaking country.

From the outset, President Francisco Macías Nguema, considered the father of independence, began a brutal reign, destroying the economy of the fledgling country and abusing human rights. Calling himself the "Unique Miracle," Nguema is considered one of the worst despots in African history. In 1971, the U.S. State Department reported that his regime was "characterized by abandonment of all government functions except internal security, which was accomplished by terror; this led to the death or exile of up to one-third of the population." In 1979, Nguema was overthrown and executed by his nephew, Lieut. Col. Teodoro Obiang Nguema Mbasogo. Obiang has been gradually modernizing the country but has retained many of his uncle's dictatorial practices, including the amassing of personal wealth by siphoning it from the public coffers. In 2003, state radio compared him to God.

A recent offshore oil boom resulted in the economy's growth by 71.2% in 1997, the first year of the petroleum bonanza, and it has sustained this phenomenal rate of growth. It is unlikely, however, that the country's new wealth will benefit the average citizen—the president's family and cronies control the industry.

In 2004, a plot by about 60 foreign white mercenaries to overthrow the government was thwarted when their plane made a stop in Zimbabwe.

Eritrea

STATE OF ERITREA

National name: Hagere Ertra
President: Isaias Afwerki (1993)
Area: 46,842 sq mi (121,320 sq km)
Population (2005 est.): 4,561,599 (growth rate: 2.5%); birth rate: 38.6/1000; infant mortality rate: 74.9/1000; life expectancy: 52.2; density per sq mi: 97
Capital and largest city (2003 est.): Asmara, 899,000 (metro. area), 400,000 (city proper). **Other large cities:** the ports of Massawa, 30,700; and Assab, 56,300. **Monetary unit:** Nakfa. **Languages:** Afar, Arabic, Tigre and Kunama, Tigrinya, other Cushitic languages. **Ethnicity/race:** ethnic Tigrinya 50%, Tigre and Kunama 40%, Afar 4%, Saho (Red Sea coast dwellers) 3%. **Religions:** Islam, Eritrean Orthodox Christianity, Roman Catholic, Protestant. **Literacy rate:** 59% (2003 est.)
Economic summary: GDP/PPP (2004 est.): $4.154 billion; per capita $900. **Real growth rate:** 2.5%. **Inflation:** 10%. **Unemployment:** n.a. (2003 est.). **Arable land:** 5%. **Agriculture:** sorghum, lentils, vegetables, corn, cotton, tobacco, coffee, sisal; livestock, goats; fish. **Labor force:** n.a.: agriculture 80%, industry and services 20%. **Industries:** food processing, beverages, clothing and textiles, salt, cement, commercial ship repair. **Natural resources:** gold, potash, zinc, copper, salt, possibly oil and natural gas, fish. **Exports:** $64.44 million (f.o.b., 2004 est.):

livestock, sorghum, textiles, food, small manufactures (2000). **Imports:** $622 million (f.o.b., 2004 est.): machinery, petroleum products, food, manufactured goods (2000). **Major trading partners:** Malaysia, Italy, France, U.S., Turkey, UK, Russia (2003).

Geography Eritrea was formerly the northernmost province of Ethiopia and is about the size of Indiana. Much of the country is mountainous. Its narrow Red Sea coastal plain is one of the hottest and driest places in Africa. The cooler central highlands have fertile valleys that support agriculture. Eritrea is bordered by the Sudan on the north and west, the Red Sea on the north and east, and Ethiopia and Djibouti on the south.

Government A transitional government committed to a democratic system.

History Eritrea was part of the first Ethiopian kingdom of Aksum until its decline in the 8th century. It came under the control of the Ottoman Empire in the 16th century, and later of the Egyptians. The Italians captured the coastal areas in 1885, and the Treaty of Uccialli (May 2, 1889) gave Italy sovereignty over part of Eritrea. The Italians named their colony after the Roman name for the Red Sea, *Mare Erythraeum,* and ruled it up until World War II. The British captured Eritrea in 1941 and later administered it as a UN Trust Territory until it became federated with Ethiopia on Sept. 15, 1952. It was made an Ethiopian province on Nov. 14, 1962. A civil war broke out against the Ethiopian government, led by rebel groups who opposed the union and wanted independence for Eritrea. Fighting continued over the next 32 years.

In 1991, the Ethiopian People's Revolutionary Democratic Front deposed the country's hard-line Communist dictator Mengistu. Without Mengistu's troops to battle, the Eritrean People's Liberation Front was able to gain control of Asmara, the Eritrean capital, and form a provisional government. In 1993, a referendum on Eritrean independence was held, supported by the UN and the new Ethiopian government. Eritrean voters almost unanimously opted for an independent republic. Ethiopia recognized Eritrea's sovereignty on May 3, 1993, and sought a new era of cooperation between the two countries.

The cooperation did not last long. Following Eritrea's independence, Eritrea and Ethiopia disagreed about the exact demarcation of their borders, and in May 1998 border clashes broke out. After an eight-month lull that both sides used to reinforce their 600-mile common border, war broke out in earnest. Both impoverished countries spent millions of dollars on warplanes and weapons, about 80,000 people were killed, and refugees were legion. The war essentially ended in a stalemate, and a formal peace agreement was signed in Dec. 2000. The United Nations has supplied more than 4,000 troops to continue patrolling the buffer zone between the two nations. An international boundary commission ruled on the disputed border between the two countries on April 13, 2002. Ethiopia disputed the new border, escalating tensions once again. In 2003, resolution of the border question was postponed indefinitely.

Estonia

REPUBLIC OF ESTONIA

National name: Eesti Vabariik
President: Arnold Rüütel (2001)
Prime Minister: Andrus Ansip (2005)
Area: 17,462 sq mi (45,226 sq km)
Population (2005 est.): 1,332,893 (growth rate: –0.7%);

birth rate: 9.9/1000; infant mortality rate: 7.9/1000; life expectancy: 71.8; density per sq mi: 76
Capital and largest city (2003 est.): Tallinn, 379,000. **Other large city:** Tartu, 100,100. **Monetary unit:** Kroon. **Languages:** Estonian (official), Russian, Ukrainian, Finnish, other. **Ethnicity/race:** Estonian 65.3%, Russian 28.1%, Ukrainian 2.5%, Belorussian 1.5%, Finn 1%, other 1.6% (1998). **Religions:** Evangelical Lutheran, Russian Orthodox, Estonian Orthodox, Baptist, Methodist, Seventh-Day Adventist, Roman Catholic, Pentecostal, Word of Life, Jewish. **Literacy:** 100% (2003 est.)
Economic summary: GDP/PPP (2004 est.): $19.23 billion; per capita $14,300. **Real growth rate:** 6%. **Inflation:** 3%. **Unemployment:** 9.6%. **Arable land:** 16%. **Agriculture:** potatoes, vegetables; livestock and dairy products; fish. **Labor force:** 660,000; industry 20%, agriculture 11%, services 69% (1999 est.). **Industries:** engineering, electronics, wood and wood products, textile; information technology, telecommunications. **Natural resources:** oil shale, peat, phosphorite, clay, limestone, sand, dolomite, arable land, sea mud. **Exports:** $5.701 billion (f.o.b., 2004 est.): machinery and equipment 33%, wood and paper 15%, textiles 14%, food products 8%, furniture 7%, metals, chemical products (2001). **Imports:** $7.318 billion (f.o.b., 2004 est.): machinery and equipment 33.5%, chemical products 11.6%, textiles 10.3%, foodstuffs 9.4%, transportation equipment 8.9% (2001). **Major trading partners:** Finland, Sweden, Russia, Germany, Latvia, Lithuania, Ukraine, China, Japan (2003).

Geography Estonia is mainly a lowland country that is bordered by the Baltic Sea, Latvia, and Russia. It has numerous lakes and forests and many rivers, most draining northward into the Gulf of Finland or eastward into Lake Peipus, its largest lake.

Government Parliamentary democracy.

History Estonians resisted the assaults of Vikings, Danes, Swedes, and Russians before the 13th century. In 1346, the Danes, who possessed northern Estonia, sold the land to the Teutonic Knights of Germany, who already possessed Livonia (southern Estonia and Latvia). The Teutonic Knights reduced the Estonians to serfdom. In 1526, the Swedes took over, and the power of the German (Balt) landowning class was reduced. But after 1721, when Russia succeeded Sweden as the ruling power under the Peace of Nystad, the Estonians were subject to a double bondage—the Balts and the czarist officials. The oppression lasted until the closing months of World War I, when Estonia finally achieved independence after a victorious war (1918–1920). But shortly after the start of World War II, the nation was occupied by Russian troops and incorporated as the 16th republic of the USSR in 1940. Germany occupied the nation from 1941 to 1944, when it was retaken by the Soviets.

Estonia declared independence from the Soviet Union in March 1990. Soviet resistance ensued, but after recognition by European and other countries, the Soviet Union acknowledged Estonian nationhood on Sept. 6, 1991. UN membership followed on Sept. 17, 1991. The newly independent nation embraced free-market reforms. Fueled by foreign investments, economic advances continued. At the end of 1998, Estonia relaxed the strict citizenship requirements that kept the country's Russian speakers—about one-third of the population—from gaining citizenship. This reform eased the way for Estonia's entry into the European Union, which took place in 2004, the year it also joined NATO.

Ethiopia

FEDERAL DEMOCRATIC REPUBLIC OF ETHIOPIA

National name: Ityop'iya Federalawi Demokrasiyawi Ripeblik
President: Girma Woldegiorgis (2001)
Prime Minister: Meles Zenawi (1995)
Area: 435,184 sq mi (1,127,127 sq km)
Population (2005 est.): 73,053,286 (growth rate: 2.4%); birth rate: 38.6/1000; infant mortality rate: 95.3/1000; life expectancy: 48.8; density per sq mi: 168
Capital and largest city (2003 est.): Addis Ababa, 2,716,200. **Monetary unit:** Birr. **Languages:** Amharic (official), Tigrigna, Orominga, Guaragigna, Somali, Arabic, English, over 70 others. **Ethnicity/race:** Oromo 40%, Amhara and Tigrean 32%, Sidamo 9%, Shankella 6%, Somali 6%, Afar 4%, Gurage 2%, other 1%. **Religions:** Islam 45%–50%, Ethiopian Orthodox 35%–40%, animist 12%, other 3%–8%. **Literacy rate:** 43% (2003 est.)
Economic summary: GDP/PPP (2004 est.): $54.89 billion; per capita $800. **Real growth rate:** 11.6%. **Inflation:** 2.4%. **Unemployment:** n.a. **Arable land:** 11%. **Agriculture:** cereals, pulses, coffee, oilseed, sugarcane, potatoes, qat; hides, cattle, sheep, goats. **Labor force:** n.a.; agriculture and animal husbandry 80%, government and services 12%, industry and construction 8% (1985). **Industries:** food processing, beverages, textiles, chemicals, metals processing, cement. **Natural resources:** small reserves of gold, platinum, copper, potash, natural gas, hydropower. **Exports:** $562.8 million (f.o.b., 2004 est.): coffee, qat, gold, leather products, live animals, oilseeds. **Imports:** $2.104 billion (f.o.b., 2004 est.): food and live animals, petroleum and petroleum products, chemicals, machinery, motor vehicles, cereals, textiles. **Major trading partners:** Djibouti, Germany, Saudi Arabia, Japan, Italy, U.S., China (2003).

Geography Ethiopia is in east-central Africa, bordered on the west by the Sudan, the east by Somalia and Djibouti, the south by Kenya, and the northeast by Eritrea. It has several high mountains, the highest of which is Ras Dashan at 15,158 ft (4,620 m). The Blue Nile, or Abbai, rises in the northwest and flows in a great semicircle before entering the Sudan. Its chief reservoir, Lake Tana, lies in the northwest.

Government Federal republic.

History Archeologists have found the oldest known human ancestors in Ethiopia, including *Ardipithecus ramidus kadabba* (c. 5.8–5.2 million years old) and *Australopithecus anamensis* (c. 4.2 million years old). Originally called Abyssinia, Ethiopia is sub-Saharan Africa's oldest state, and its Solomonic dynasty claims descent from King Menelik I, traditionally believed to have been the son of the queen of Sheba and King Solomon. The current nation is a consolidation of smaller kingdoms that owed feudal allegiance to the Ethiopian emperor.

Hamitic peoples migrated to Ethiopia from Asia Minor in prehistoric times. Semitic traders from Arabia penetrated the region in the 7th century B.C. Its Red Sea ports were important to the Roman and Byzantine Empires. Coptic Christianity was brought to the region in A.D. 341, and a variant of it became Ethiopia's state religion. Ancient Ethiopia reached its peak in the 5th century, then was isolated by the rise of Islam and weakened by feudal wars.

Modern Ethiopia emerged under Emperor Menelik II, who established its independence by routing an Italian invasion in 1896. He expanded Ethiopia by conquest. Disorders that followed Menelik's death brought his daughter to the throne in 1917, with his cousin, Tafari Makonnen, as regent and heir apparent. When the empress died in 1930, Tafari was crowned Emperor Haile Selassie I.

Haile Selassie, called the "Lion of Judah," outlawed slavery and tried to centralize his scattered realm, in which 70 languages were spoken. In 1931, he created a constitution, revised in 1955, that called for a Parliament with an appointed senate, an elected chamber of deputies, and a system of courts. But basic power remained with the emperor.

Fascist Italy invaded Ethiopia on Oct. 3, 1935, forcing Haile Selassie into exile in May 1936. Ethiopia was annexed to Eritrea, then an Italian colony, and to Italian Somaliland, forming Italian East Africa. In 1941, British troops routed the Italians, and Haile Selassie returned to Addis Ababa. In 1952, Eritrea was incorporated into Ethiopia.

On Sept. 12, 1974, Haile Selassie was deposed, the constitution suspended, and Ethiopia proclaimed a Socialist state under a collective military dictatorship called the Provisional Military Administrative Council (PMAC), also known as the Derg. U.S. aid stopped, and Cuban and Soviet aid began. Lt. Col. Mengistu Hailè Mariam became head of state in 1977. During this period Ethiopia fought against Eritrean secessionists as well as Somali rebels, and the government fought against its own people in a campaign called the "red terror." Thousands of political opponents were killed. Mengistu remained leader until 1991, when his greatest supporter, the Soviet Union, dismantled itself.

A group called the Ethiopian People's Revolutionary Democratic Front seized the capital in 1991, and in May a separatist guerrilla organization, the Eritrean People's Liberation Front, took control of the province of Eritrea. The two groups agreed that Eritrea would have an internationally supervised referendum on independence. This election took place in April 1993 with almost unanimous support for Eritrean independence. Ethiopia accepted and recognized Eritrea as an independent state within a few days. Sixty-eight leaders of the former military government were put on trial in April 1996 on charges that included genocide and crimes against humanity.

Since Eritrea's independence, Eritrea and Ethiopia had disagreed about the exact demarcation of their borders, and in May 1998 Eritrea initiated border clashes that developed into a full-scale war that left more than 80,000 dead and further destroyed both countries' ailing economies. After a costly and bloody two-year war, a permanent cease-fire was reached in June 2000—Ethiopia had the upper hand when the fighting ceased—and a formal peace agreement was signed in Dec. 2000. The United Nations has provided more than 4,000 peacekeeping forces to patrol the buffer zone between the two nations. An international commission defined a new border between the two countries in April 2002. Ethiopia disputed the new border, escalating tensions between the two countries once again. In 2003, the border question was put on hold indefinitely.

In 2003, in an effort to solve its chronic shortage of food and to lessen its dependence on international aid, Ethiopia began relocating 2 million farmers from their parched highland homes to areas with more fertile soil in the western part of the country. The largest relocation program in African history, however, has turned into a disaster. The majority of those resettled are still unable to support themselves, and, most alarmingly, much of the fertile regions where the farmers have been resettled are rife with malaria.

Fiji

REPUBLIC OF THE FIJI ISLANDS

President: Ratu Josefa Iloilo (2000)
Prime Minister: Laisenia Qarase (2001)
Area: 7,054 sq mi (18,270 sq km)
Population (2005 est.): 893,354 (growth rate: 1.4%); birth rate: 22.7/1000; infant mortality rate: 12.6/1000; life expectancy: 69.5; density per sq mi: 127
Capital and largest city (2003 est.): Suva (on Viti Levu), 177,300. **Monetary unit:** Fiji dollar.
Languages: English (official), Fijian, Hindustani.
Ethnicity/race: Fijian 51%, Indian 44%, European, other Pacific Islanders, overseas Chinese, and other 5% (1998). **Religions:** Christian 52% (Methodist 37%, Roman Catholic 9%), Hindu 38%, Islam 8%, other 2%. **Literacy rate:** 94% (2003 est.).
Economic summary: GDP/PPP (2004 est.): $5.173 billion; per capita $5,900. **Real growth rate:** 3.6%. **Inflation:** 1.6% (2002 est.). **Unemployment:** 7.6% (1999). **Arable land:** 11%. **Agriculture:** sugarcane, coconuts, cassava (tapioca), rice, sweet potatoes, bananas; cattle, pigs, horses, goats; fish. **Labor force:** 137,000 (1999); agriculture, including subsistence agriculture 70% (2001 est.). **Industries:** tourism, sugar, clothing, copra, gold, silver, lumber, small cottage industries. **Natural resources:** timber, fish, gold, copper, offshore oil potential, hydropower. **Exports:** $609 million (f.o.b., 2002): sugar, garments, gold, timber, fish, molasses, coconut oil. **Imports:** $835 million (c.i.f., 2002): manufactured goods, machinery and transport equipment, petroleum products, food, chemicals. **Major trading partners:** U.S., Australia, UK, Samoa, Japan, Singapore, New Zealand (2003).

Geography Fiji consists of 332 islands in the southwest Pacific Ocean about 1,960 mi (3,152 km) from Sydney, Australia. About 110 of these islands are inhabited. The two largest are Viti Levu (4,109 sq mi; 10,642 sq km) and Vanua Levu (2,242 sq mi; 5,807 sq km).

Government Republic.

History Fiji, which had been inhabited since the second millennium B.C., was explored by the Dutch and the British in the 17th and 18th centuries. In 1874, an offer of cession by the Fijian chiefs was accepted, and Fiji was proclaimed a possession and dependency of the British Crown. In the 1880s large-scale cultivation of sugarcane began. Over the next 40 years, more than 60,000 indentured laborers from India were brought to the island to work the plantations. By 1920, all indentured servitude had ended. Racial conflict between Indians and the indigenous Fijians has been central to the small island's history.

Fiji became independent on Oct. 10, 1970. In Oct. 1987, Brig. Gen. Sitiveni Rabuka staged a coup to prevent an Indian-dominated coalition party from taking power. The military coup caused an exodus of thousands of Fijians of Indian origin who suffered ethnic discrimination at the hands of the government.

A new constitution, which took effect in July 1998, provided for a multiracial cabinet and raised the prospect of a coalition government. The previous constitution had guaranteed dominance to ethnic Fijians. In 1999, Fiji's first ethnic Indian prime minister, Mahendra Chaudhry, took office.

Continuing ethnic tensions, partly fueled by economic problems, plunged Fiji into a national nightmare in 2000. On May 19, a group of armed soldiers entered the Parliament and took three dozen people hostage, including President Chaudhry. George Speight, a part-Fijian businessman, led the insurrection, and he demanded that the 1998 constitution be rewritten to allow dominance of ethnic Fijians. The standoff lasted two months. In July 2000, Speight and other coup leaders were taken into custody and charged with treason. In Feb. 2002, Speight was sentenced to death, but his sentence was commuted.

Although the coup was eventually foiled, deposed prime minister Chaudhry and his democratically elected government were not restored to power. Instead, the military and the Great Council of Chiefs, a group of 50 traditional Fijian leaders, appointed an interim government dominated by ethnic Fijians. Elections were held in 2001, but no party achieved a majority. Interim prime minister Laisenia Qarase's Fijian United Party won 31 of 71 seats, and Qarase was sworn in as prime minister in September. His cabinet consisted entirely of ethnic Fijians, but a court ruled in 2002 that ethnic Indians must be included. In July 2003, Fiji's Supreme Court unanimously upheld that decision, declaring Qarase's government unconstitutional. In 2004, political infighting stalled the implementation of a new multiethnic cabinet.

Much to Prime Minister Qarase's displeasure, Vice President Ratu Jope Seniloli and four other prominent figures were convicted for their part in the 2000 coup and imprisoned in Aug. 2004. In 2005, Qarase backed a highly controversial bill that included an amnesty clause for the 2000 coup leaders. The bill was supported by the Great Council of Chiefs and the ethnic Fijian establishment but vehemently rejected by the opposition (led by former prime minister Chaudhry, who was deposed in the coup) as well as the military. In July 2005 the country's military commander warned that if the bill was passed, the army might remove the government.

Finland

REPUBLIC OF FINLAND

National name: Suomen Tasavalta—Republiken Finland
President: Tarja Halonen (2000)
Prime Minister: Matti Vanhanen (2003)
Area: 130,127 sq mi (337,030 sq km)
Population (2005 est.): 5,223,442 (growth rate: 0.2%); birth rate: 10.5/1000; infant mortality rate: 3.6/1000; life expectancy: 78.3; density per sq mi: 40
Capital and largest city (2003 est.): Helsinki, 1,162,900 (metro. area), 582,600 (city proper). **Other large cities:** Espoo, 229,500; Tampere, 201,200; Vantaa, 189,200; Turku, 178,100. **Monetary unit:** Euro (formerly markka). **Languages:** Finnish 93.4%, Swedish 5.9% (both official); small Sami- (Lapp) and Russian-speaking minorities. **Ethnicity/race:** Finn 93%, Swede 6%, Sami (Lapp) 0.11%, Romany (Gypsy) 0.12%, Tatar 0.02%. **Religions:** Evangelical Lutheran 89%, Greek Orthodox 1%, none 9%, other 1%. **Literacy rate:** 100% (1980 est.)
Economic summary: GDP/PPP (2004 est.): $151.2 billion; per capita $29,000. **Real growth rate:** 3%. **Inflation:** 0.7%. **Unemployment:** 8.9%. **Arable land:** 7%. **Agriculture:** barley, wheat, sugar beets, potatoes; dairy cattle; fish. **Labor force:** 2.66 million; public services 32%, industry 22%, commerce 14%, finance, insurance, and business services 10%, agriculture and forestry 8%, transport and communications 8%, construction 6%. **Industries:** metals and metal products, electronics, machinery and scientific instruments, shipbuilding, pulp and paper, foodstuffs, chemicals, textiles, clothing. **Natural resources:** timber, iron ore, copper, lead, zinc, chromite, nickel, gold, silver, limestone. **Exports:** $61.04 billion (f.o.b., 2004 est.): machinery and equipment, chemicals, metals; timber, paper, pulp (1999). **Imports:** $45.17 billion (f.o.b., 2004 est.): foodstuffs, petroleum and petroleum products, chemicals, transport equipment, iron and steel, machinery, textile yarn and fabrics, grains (1999). **Major trading partners:** Germany, Sweden, U.S., UK, Russia, Netherlands, Denmark, France (2003).

Geography Finland is three times the size of Ohio. It is heavily forested and contains thousands of lakes, numerous rivers, and extensive areas of marshland. Except for a small highland region in the extreme northwest, the country is a lowland less than 600 ft (180 m) above sea level. Off the southwest coast are the Swedish-populated Åland Islands (581 sq mi; 1,505 sq km), which have had an autonomous status since 1921.

Government Republic.

History The first inhabitants of Finland were the Sami (Lapp) people. When Finnish speakers migrated to Finland in the first millennium B.C., the Sami were forced to move northward to the arctic regions, with which they are traditionally associated. The Finns' repeated raids on the Scandinavian coast impelled Eric IX, the Swedish king, to conquer the country in 1157. It was made a part of the Swedish kingdom and converted to Christianity.

By 1809 the whole of Finland was conquered by Alexander I of Russia, who set up Finland as a grand duchy. The period of Russification (1809–1914) sapped Finnish political power and made Russian the country's official language. When Russia became engulfed by the March Revolution of 1917, Finland seized the opportunity to declare independence on Dec. 6, 1917.

The USSR attacked Finland on Nov. 30, 1939, after Finland refused to give into Soviet territorial demands. The Finns staged a strong defense for three months before being forced to cede the Soviets 16,000 sq mi (41,440 sq km). Under German pressure, the Finns joined the Nazis against Russia in 1941, but they were defeated again and forced to cede the Petsamo area to the USSR. In 1948, a treaty of friendship and mutual assistance was signed by the two nations. Finland continued to pursue a foreign policy of nonalignment throughout the cold war era.

Running on a platform to revitalize the economy, Ahtisaari, a Social Democrat, won the country's first direct presidential election in a runoff in Feb. 1994. Previously, presidents had been chosen by electors. Finland became a member of the European Union in Jan. 1995. On Jan. 1, 1999, Finland, along with ten other European countries, adopted the euro as its currency. In 2000, Tarja Halonen, who had been Finland's foreign minister, became its first woman president.

Since 1998, Finland has been judged to be the world's least corrupt country, according to the annual corruption survey by the Berlin-based organization Transparency International. In April 2003, Finland appointed its first female prime minister, making it the only country in Europe with both a female president and prime minister. But Prime Minister Jaatteenmaki resigned after only two months in office when it was revealed that she had used leaked classified information against her rival in the election (she was acquitted of the charges the following year). In June, Defense Minister Matti Vanhanen was selected by Parliament to replace her.

France

FRENCH REPUBLIC

National name: République Française
President: Jacques Chirac (1995)
Prime Minister: Dominique de Villepin (2005)
Area: 211,208 sq mi (547,030 sq km)
Population (2005 est.): 60,656,178 (growth rate: 0.4%);

birth rate: 12.2/1000; infant mortality rate: 4.3/1000; life expectancy: 79.6; density per sq mi: 287
Capital and largest city (2003 est.): Paris, 11,330,700 (metro. area), 2,110,400 (city proper). **Other large cities:** Marseille, 820,700; Lyon, 443,900; Toulouse, 411,800; Nice, 332,000; Nantes, 282,300; Strasbourg, 272,600; Bordeaux, 217,000. **Monetary unit:** Euro (formerly French franc). **Languages:** French 100%, rapidly declining regional dialects (Provençal, Breton, Alsatian, Corsican, Catalan, Basque, Flemish). **Ethnicity/race:** Celtic and Latin with Teutonic, Slavic, North African, Southeast Asian, and Basque minorities. **Religions:** Roman Catholic 83%–88%, Protestant 2%, Islam 5%–10%, Jewish 1%. **Literacy rate:** 99% (1980 est.)
Economic summary: GDP/PPP (2004 est.): $1.737 trillion; per capita $28,700. **Real growth rate:** 2.1%. **Inflation:** 2.3%. **Unemployment:** 10.1%. **Arable land:** 34%. **Agriculture:** wheat, cereals, sugar beets, potatoes, wine grapes; beef, dairy products; fish. **Labor force:** 27.7 million; services 71.5%, industry 24.4%, agriculture 4.1% (1999). **Industries:** machinery, chemicals, automobiles, metallurgy, aircraft, electronics; textiles, food processing; tourism. **Natural resources:** coal, iron ore, bauxite, zinc, uranium, antimony, arsenic, potash, feldspar, fluorospar, gypsum, timber, fish. **Exports:** $419 billion (f.o.b., 2004 est.): machinery and transportation equipment, aircraft, plastics, chemicals, pharmaceutical products, iron and steel, beverages. **Imports:** $419.7 billion (f.o.b., 2004 est.): machinery and equipment, vehicles, crude oil, aircraft, plastics, chemicals. **Major trading partners:** Germany, Spain, UK, Italy, Belgium, Netherlands, U.S. (2003).

Geography France is about 80% the size of Texas. In the Alps near the Italian and Swiss borders is western Europe's highest point—Mont Blanc (15,781 ft; 4,810 m). The forest-covered Vosges Mountains are in the northeast, and the Pyrénées are along the Spanish border. Except for extreme northern France, the country may be described as four river basins and a plateau. Three of the streams flow west—the Seine into the English Channel, the Loire into the Atlantic, and the Garonne into the Bay of Biscay. The Rhône flows south into the Mediterranean. For about 100 mi (161 km), the Rhine is France's eastern border. In the Mediterranean, about 115 mi (185 km) east-southeast of Nice, is the island of Corsica (3,367 sq mi; 8,721 sq km).

Government Fifth republic.

History Archeological excavations indicate that France has been continuously settled since Paleolithic times. The Celts, who were later called *Gauls* by the Romans, migrated from the Rhine valley into what is now France. In about 600 B.C. Greeks and Phoenicians established settlements along the Mediterranean, most notably at Marseille. Julius Caesar conquered part of Gaul in 57–52 B.C., and it remained Roman until Franks invaded in the 5th century A.D.

The Treaty of Verdun (843) divided the territories corresponding roughly to France, Germany, and Italy among the three grandsons of Charlemagne. Charles the Bald inherited *Francia Occidentalis,* which became an increasingly feudalized kingdom. By 987, the crown passed to Hugh Capet, a princeling who controlled only the Ile-de-France, the region surrounding Paris. For 350 years, an unbroken Capetian line added to its domain and consolidated royal authority until the accession in 1328 of Philip VI, first of the Valois line. France was then the most powerful nation in Europe, with a population of 15 million.

The missing pieces in Philip Valois's domain were the French provinces still held by the Plantagenet kings

of England, who also claimed the French crown. Beginning in 1338, the Hundred Years' War eventually settled the contest. After France's victory in the final battle, Castillon (1453), the Valois were the ruling family, and the English had no French possessions left except Calais. Once Burgundy and Brittany were added, the Valois dynasty's holdings resembled modern France. Protestantism spread throughout France in the 16th century and led to civil wars. Henry IV, of the Bourbon dynasty, issued the Edict of Nantes (1598), granting religious tolerance to the Huguenots (French Protestants). Absolute monarchy reached its apogee in the reign of Louis XIV (1643–1715), the Sun King, whose brilliant court was the center of the Western world.

After a series of costly foreign wars that weakened the government, the French Revolution plunged France into a bloodbath beginning in 1789 with the establishment of the First Republic and ending with a new authoritarianism under Napoléon Bonaparte, who had successfully defended the infant republic from foreign attack and then made himself first consul in 1799 and emperor in 1804. The Congress of Vienna (1815) sought to restore the pre-Napoléonic order in the person of Louis XVIII, but industrialization and the middle class, both fostered under Napoléon, built pressure for change, and a revolution in 1848 drove Louis Philippe, last of the Bourbons, into exile. Prince Louis Napoléon, a nephew of Napoléon I, declared the Second Empire in 1852 and took the throne as Napoléon III. His opposition to the rising power of Prussia ignited the Franco-Prussian War (1870–1871), which ended in his defeat, his abdication, and the creation of the Third Republic.

A new France emerged from World War I as the continent's dominant power. But four years of hostile occupation had reduced northeast France to ruins. Beginning in 1919, French foreign policy aimed at keeping Germany weak through a system of alliances, but it failed to halt the rise of Adolf Hitler and the Nazi war machine. On May 10, 1940, Nazi troops attacked, and, as they approached Paris, Italy joined with Germany. The Germans marched into an undefended Paris and Marshal Henri Philippe Pétain signed an armistice on June 22. France was split into an occupied north and an unoccupied south, Vichy France, which became a totalitarian German puppet state with Pétain as its chief. Allied armies liberated France in Aug. 1944, and a provisional government in Paris headed by Gen. Charles de Gaulle was established. The Fourth Republic was born on Dec. 24, 1946. The empire became the French Union; the National Assembly was strengthened and the presidency weakened; and France joined NATO. A war against Communist insurgents in French Indochina, now Vietnam, was abandoned after the defeat of French forces at Dien Bien Phu in 1954. A new rebellion in Algeria threatened a military coup, and on June 1, 1958, the Assembly invited de Gaulle to return as premier with extraordinary powers. He drafted a new constitution for a Fifth Republic, adopted on September 28, which strengthened the presidency and reduced legislative power. He was elected president on Dec. 21, 1958.

France next turned its attention to decolonization in Africa; the French protectorates of Morocco and Tunisia had received independence in 1956. French West Africa was partitioned and the new nations were granted independence in 1960. Algeria, after a long civil war, finally became independent in 1962. Relations with most of the former colonies remained amicable. De Gaulle took France out of the NATO military command in 1967 and expelled all foreign-controlled troops from the country. De Gaulle's government was weakened by massive protests in May 1968 when student rallies became violent and millions of factory workers engaged in wildcat strikes across France. After normalcy was reestablished in 1969, de Gaulle's successor, Georges Pompidou, modified Gaullist policies to include a classical laissez-faire attitude toward domestic economic affairs. The conservative, pro-business climate contributed to the election of Valéry Giscard d'Estaing as president in 1974.

Socialist François Mitterrand attained a stunning victory in the May 10, 1981, presidential election.

Rulers of France

Name	Born	Ruled[1]	Name	Born	Ruled[1]
Carolingian Dynasty			Louis XV the Well-Beloved	1710	1715–1774
Pepin the Short	c. 714	751–768	Louis XVI	1754	1774–1792[13]
Charlemagne[2]	742	768–814	Louis XVII (Louis Charles de	1785	1793–1795
Louis I the Pious[3]	778	814–840	France)[14]		
Charles I the Bald[4]	823	840–877	**First Republic**		
Louis II the Stammerer	846	877–879	National Convention	—	1792–1795
Louis III[5]	c. 863	879–882	Directory (Directoire)	—	1795–1799
Carloman[5]	?	879–884	**Consulate**		
Charles II the Fat[6]	839	884–887[7]	Napoléon Bonaparte[15]	1769	1799–1804
Eudes (Odo), count of Paris	?	888–898	**First Empire**		
Charles III the Simple[8]	879	893–923[9]	Napoléon I	1769	1804–1815[16]
Robert I[10]	c. 865	922–923	**Restoration of House of Bourbon**		
Rudolf (Raoul), duke of Burgundy	?	923–936	Louis XVIII le Désiré	1755	1814–1824
Louis IV d'Outremer	c. 921	936–954	Charles X	1757	1824–1830[17]
Lothair	941	954–986	**Bourbon-Orleans Line**		
Louis V the Sluggard	c. 967	986–987	Louis Philippe ("Citizen King")	1773	1830–1848[18]
Capetian Dynasty			**Second Republic**		
Hugh Capet	c. 940	987–996	Louis Napoléon[19]	1808	1848–1852
Robert II the Pious[11]	c. 970	996–1031	**Second Empire**		
Henry I	1008	1031–1060	Napoléon III (Louis Napoléon)	1808	1852–1870[20]
Philip I	1052	1060–1108	**Third Republic (Presidents)**		
Louis VI the Fat	1081	1108–1137	Louis Adolphe Thiers	1797	1871–1873
Louis VII the Young	c.1121	1137–1180	Marie E. P. M. de MacMahon	1808	1873–1879
Philip II (Philip Augustus)	1165	1180–1223	François P. J. Grévy	1807	1879–1887
Louis VIII the Lion	1187	1223–1226	Sadi Carnot	1837	1887–1894
Louis IX (St. Louis)	1214	1226–1270	Jean Casimir-Périer	1847	1894–1895
Philip III the Bold	1245	1270–1285	François Félix Faure	1841	1895–1899
Philip IV the Fair	1268	1285–1314	Émile Loubet	1838	1899–1906
Louis X the Quarreler	1289	1314–1316	Clement Armand Fallières	1841	1906–1913
John I[12]	1316	1316	Raymond Poincaré	1860	1913–1920
Philip V the Tall	1294	1316–1322	Paul E. L. Deschanel	1856	1920–1920
Charles IV the Fair	1294	1322–1328	Alexandre Millerand	1859	1920–1924
House of Valois			Gaston Doumergue	1863	1924–1931
Philip VI	1293	1328–1350	Paul Doumer	1857	1931–1932
John II the Good	1319	1350–1364	Albert Lebrun	1871	1932–1940
Charles V the Wise	1337	1364–1380	**Vichy Government (Chief of State)**		
Charles VI the Well-Beloved	1368	1380–1422	Henri Philippe Pétain	1856	1940–1944
Charles VII	1403	1422–1461	**Provisional Government (Presidents)**		
Louis XI	1423	1461–1483	Charles de Gaulle	1890	1944–1946
Charles VIII	1470	1483–1498	Félix Gouin	1884	1946–1946
Louis XII the Father of the People	1462	1498–1515	Georges Bidault	1899	1946–1947
Francis I	1494	1515–1547	**Fourth Republic (Presidents)**		
Henry II	1519	1547–1559	Vincent Auriol	1884	1947–1954
Francis II	1544	1559–1560	René Coty	1882	1954–1959
Charles IX	1550	1560–1574	**Fifth Republic (Presidents)**		
Henry III	1551	1574–1589	Charles de Gaulle	1890	1959–1969
House of Bourbon			Georges Pompidou	1911	1969–1974
Henry IV of Navarre	1553	1589–1610	Valéry Giscard d'Estaing	1926	1974–1981
Louis XIII	1601	1610–1643	François Mitterrand	1916	1981–1995
Louis XIV the Great	1638	1643–1715	Jacques Chirac	1932	1995–

1. For kings and emperors through the Second Empire, year of end of rule is also that of death, unless otherwise indicated. 2. Crowned Emperor of the West in 800. His brother, Carloman, ruled as king of the Eastern Franks from 768 until his death in 771. 3. Holy Roman Emperor, 814–840. 4. Holy Roman Emperor, 875–877 as Charles II. 5. Ruled jointly, 879–882. 6. Holy Roman Emperor, 881–887, as Charles III. 7. Died 888. 8. King, 893–898, in opposition to Eudes. 9. Died 929. 10. Not counted in regular line of kings of France by some authorities. Elected by nobles but killed in Battle of Soissons. 11. Sometimes called Robert I. 12. Posthumous son of Louis X; lived for only five days. 13. Executed 1793. 14. Titular king only. He died in prison according to official reports, but many pretenders appeared during the Bourbon restoration. 15. As first consul, Napoléon held the power of government. In 1804, he became emperor. 16. Abdicated first time, June 1814. Reentered Paris, March 1815, after escape from Elba; Louis XVIII fled to Ghent. Abdicated second time, June 1815. He named as his successor his son, Napoléon II, who was not acceptable to the Allies. He died 1821. 17. Died 1836. 18. Died 1850. 19. President; became emperor in 1852. 20. Died 1873.

The victors immediately moved to carry out campaign pledges to nationalize major industries, halt nuclear testing, suspend nuclear power plant construction, and impose new taxes on the rich. The Socialists' policies during Mitterrand's first two years created a 12% inflation rate, a huge trade deficit, and devaluations of the franc. In March 1986, a center-right coalition led by Jacques Chirac won a slim majority in legislative elections. Chirac became prime minister, initiating a period of "cohabitation" between him and the Socialist president, Mitterrand. Mitterrand's decisive reelection in 1988 led to Chirac being replaced as prime minister by Michel Rocard, a Socialist. Relations, however, cooled with Rocard, and in May 1991 Edith Cresson—also a Socialist—became France's first female prime minister. But Cresson's unpopularity forced Mitterrand to replace Cresson with a more well-liked Socialist, Pierre Bérégovoy, who eventually was embroiled in a scandal and committed suicide. Mitterrand did succeed in helping to draft the Maastricht Treaty and, after winning a slim victory in a referendum, confirming close economic and security ties between France and the European Union (EU).

On his third try Chirac won the presidency in May 1995, campaigning vigorously on a platform to reduce unemployment. Elections for the National Assembly in 1997 gave the Socialist coalition a majority. Shortly after becoming president, Chirac resumed France's nuclear testing in the South Pacific, despite widespread international protests as well as rioting in the countries affected by it. Socialist leader Lionel Jospin became prime minister in 1997. In the spring of 1999, the country took part in the NATO air strikes in Kosovo, despite some internal opposition.

Jean-Marie Le Pen, leader of the right-wing anti-immigrant National Front Party, shocked France in April 2002 with his second-place finish in the first round of France's presidential election. He took 17% of the vote, eliminating Lionel Jospin, the Socialist prime minister, who tallied 16%. Jospin, stunned by the result, announced that he was retiring from politics and threw his support behind incumbent president Jacques Chirac, who won with an overwhelming 82.2% of the vote in the runoff election. Chirac's center-right coalition won an absolute majority in Parliament. In July 2002, Chirac survived an assassination attempt by a right-wing extremist.

During the fall 2002 and winter 2003 diplomatic wrangling at the United Nations over Iraq, France repeatedly defied the U.S. and Britain by calling for more weapons inspections and diplomacy before resorting to war. Relations between the U.S. and France have remained severely strained over Iraq.

France sent peacekeeping forces to assist two African countries in 2002 and 2003, Côte d'Ivoire and the Democratic Republic of the Congo.

Prime Minister Raffarin's plan to overhaul the national pension system sparked numerous strikes across France in May and June 2003, involving tens of thousands of sanitation workers, teachers, transportation workers, and air traffic controllers. In August, a deadly heat wave killed an estimated 10,000 people, mostly elderly. The catastrophe occurred during two weeks of 104°F (40°C) temperatures.

In 2004, the French government passed a law banning the wearing of Muslim headscarves and other religious symbols in schools. The government maintained that the wearing of conspicuous religious symbols threatened the country's secular identity; others contended it curtailed religious freedom.

In March 2004 regional elections, the Socialist Party made enormous gains over Chirac's Union for a Popular Movement (UMP) Party. Unpopular economic reforms are credited for the UMP's defeat.

On May 29, 2005, French voters rejected the European Union constitution by a 55%–45% margin. Reasons given for rejecting the constitution included concerns about forfeiting too much French sovereignty to a centralized European government and alarm at the EU's rapid addition of 10 new members in 2004, most from eastern Europe. In response, President Chirac, who strongly supported the constitution, replaced Prime Minister Jean-Pierre Raffarin with Dominique de Villepin, a former foreign minister.

Overseas Departments

Overseas Departments elect representatives to the National Assembly, and the same administrative organization as that of continental France applies to them.

French Guiana (including Inini)
Status: Overseas Department
Prefect: Henri Masse (1999)
Area: 35,135 sq mi (91,000 sq km)
Population (2006 est.): 195,506 (growth rate: 2.1%); birth rate 20.7/1000; infant mortality rate 12.1/1000; life expectancy: 77.1; density per sq mi: 6
Capital and largest city (2003 est.): Cayenne, 60,500.
Monetary unit: Franc. **Language:** French. **Ethnicity/race:** black or mulatto 66%, white 12%, East Indian, Chinese, Amerindian 12%, other 10%. **Religion:** Roman Catholic. **Literacy rate:** 83% (1982 est.)
Economic summary: GDP/PPP (2003 est.): $1.551 billion; per capita $8,300. **Real growth rate:** n.a. **Inflation:** 1.5% (2002 est.). **Unemployment:** 22% (2001). **Arable land:** 0.14%. **Agriculture:** corn, rice, manioc (tapioca), sugar, cocoa, vegetables, bananas; cattle, pigs, poultry. **Labor force:** 58,800 (1997); services, government, and commerce 60.6%, industry 21.2%, agriculture 18.2% (1980). **Industries:** construction, shrimp processing, forestry products, rum, gold mining. **Natural resources:** bauxite, timber, gold (widely scattered), cinnabar, kaolin, fish. **Exports:** $155 million (f.o.b., 2002 est.): shrimp, timber, gold, rum, rosewood essence, clothing. **Imports:** $625 million (c.i.f., 2002 est.): food (grains, processed meat), machinery and transport equipment, fuels and chemicals. **Major trading partners:** France, Switzerland, U.S., Trinidad and Tobago, Italy (2002 est.)

French Guiana, lying north of Brazil and east of Suriname on the northeast coast of South America, was variously settled by the Spanish, Dutch, and French. The Treaty of Breda awarded France the territory in 1667. The French used it as a penal colony between 1852 and 1939, which included the infamous Devil's Island. In 1947 it became an overseas department of France. Since then, many indigenous French Guianians have called for increased autonomy, although only around 5% favor independence from France, partly due to the vast subsidies from the French government. The European Space Center at Kourou has brought a corner of French Guiana into the modern world and attracted a sizable expatriate workforce.

Guadeloupe
Status: Overseas Department
Prefect: Paul Girot de Langlade (2004)
Area: 687 sq mi (1,780 sq km)
Population (2005 est.): 448,713 (growth rate: 0.9%); birth rate: 15.4/1000; infant mortality rate: 8.6/1000; life expectancy: 77.9; density per sq mi: 653

Capital (2003 est.): Basse-Terre, 12,900. **Largest city:** Abymes, 65,700. **Monetary unit:** Franc. **Languages:** French 99% (official), Creole patois. **Ethnicity/race:** black or mulatto 90%, white 5%, East Indian, Lebanese, Chinese less than 5%. **Religions:** Roman Catholic 95%, Hindu and pagan African 4%, Protestant 1%. **Literacy rate:** 98% (1977 est.)
Economic summary: GDP/PPP (2003 est.): $3.513 billion; per capita $7,900. **Real growth rate:** n.a. **Inflation:** n.a. **Unemployment:** 27.8% (1998). **Arable land:** 11%. **Agriculture:** bananas, sugarcane, tropical fruits and vegetables; cattle, pigs, goats. **Labor force:** 125,900 (1997). **Industries:** construction, cement, rum, sugar, tourism. **Natural resources:** cultivable land, beaches and climate that foster tourism. **Exports:** $140 million (f.o.b., 1997): bananas, sugar, rum. **Imports:** $1.7 billion (c.i.f., 1997): foodstuffs, fuels, vehicles, clothing and other consumer goods, construction materials. **Major trading partners:** France, Martinique, U.S., Germany, Japan, Netherlands Antilles (1999).

Guadeloupe, in the West Indies about 300 mi (483 km) southeast of Puerto Rico, was explored by Columbus in 1493. It consists of the twin islands of Basse-Terre and Grande-Terre and five dependencies—Marie-Galante, Les Saintes, La Désirade, St. Barthélemy, and the northern three-fifths of St. Martin. The volcano Soufrière (4,813 ft; 1,467 m), also called La Grande Soufrière, is the highest point on Guadeloupe.

French colonization began in 1635, and in 1674 Guadeloupe became part of the domain of France. In 1946, it became an overseas department of France.

Martinique

Status: Overseas Department
Prefect: Michel Cadot (2000)
Area: 425 sq mi (1,100 sq km)
Population (2005 est.): 432,900 (growth rate: 0.8%); birth rate: 14.1/1000; infant mortality rate: 7.1/1000; life expectancy: 79.0; density per sq mi: 1,019
Capital and largest city (2003 est.): Fort-de-France, 170,300 (metro. area), 96,400 (city proper). **Other large cities:** Le Lamentin, 36,400; Schoelcher, 21,400; Sainte-Marie, 20,600. **Monetary unit:** Franc. **Languages:** French, Creole patois. **Ethnicity/race:** African and African-white-Indian mixture 90%, white 5%, East Indian, Lebanese, Chinese less than 5%. **Religions:** Roman Catholic 85%, Protestant 10.5%, Muslim 0.5%, Hindu 0.5%, other 3.5% (1997). **Literacy rate:** 97.7% (2003 est.)
Economic summary: GDP/PPP (2003 est.): $6.117 billion; per capita $14,400. **Real growth rate:** n.a. **Inflation:** 3.9% (1990). **Unemployment:** 27.2% (1998). **Arable land:** 10%. **Agriculture:** pineapples, avocados, bananas, flowers, vegetables, sugarcane. **Labor force:** 165,900 (1998); agriculture 10%, industry 17%, services 73% (1997). **Industries:** construction, rum, cement, oil refining, sugar, tourism. **Natural resources:** coastal scenery and beaches, cultivable land. **Exports:** $250 million (f.o.b., 1997): refined petroleum products, bananas, rum, pineapples (2001 est.). **Imports:** $2 billion (c.i.f., 1997): petroleum products, crude oil, foodstuffs, construction materials, vehicles, clothing and other consumer goods. **Major trading partners:** France, Guadeloupe, Venezuela, Germany, Italy, U.S. (2000).

Martinique, a mountainous island lying in the Lesser Antilles about 300 mi (483 km) northeast of Venezuela, was probably explored by Columbus in 1502 and was taken for France in 1635. Martinique became a domain of the French crown in 1674. It became an overseas department of France in 1946.

Réunion

Status: Overseas Department
Prefect: Laurent Cayrel (2005)
Area: 972 sq mi (2,517 sq km)
Population (2005 est.): 776,948 (growth rate: 1.4%); birth rate: 19.3/1000; infant mortality rate: 7.8/1000; life expectancy: 74.0; density per sq mi: 799
Capital and largest city (2003 est.): Saint-Denis, 142,600. **Other large cities:** Saint-Paul, 95,100; Saint-Pierre, 74,700; Le Tampon, 65,400. **Monetary unit:** Franc. **Languages:** French (official), Creole. **Ethnicity/race:** French, African, Malagasy, Chinese, Pakistani, Indian. **Religions:** Roman Catholic 86%, Hindu, Muslim, Buddhist (1995). **Literacy rate:** 89% (2003 est.)
Economic summary: GDP/PPP (2004 est.): $4.57 billion; per capita $6,000. **Real growth rate:** 2.5%. **Inflation:** n.a. **Unemployment:** 36% (1999 est.). **Arable land:** 14%. **Agriculture:** sugarcane, vanilla, tobacco, tropical fruits, vegetables, corn. **Labor force:** 309,900 (2000); agriculture 13%, industry 12%, services 75% (2000). **Industries:** sugar, rum, cigarettes, handicraft items, flower oil extraction. **Natural resources:** fish, arable land, hydropower. **Exports:** $214 million (f.o.b., 1997): sugar 63%, rum and molasses 4%, perfume essences 2%, lobster 3%, (1993). **Imports:** $2.5 billion (c.i.f., 1997): manufactured goods, food, beverages, tobacco, machinery and transportation equipment, raw materials, and petroleum products. **Major trading partners:** France, Japan, Comoros, Bahrain, Germany, Italy (2000).

Of volcanic origin, Réunion consists mostly of rugged mountains and short torrential rivers. It is located about 450 mi (724 km) east of Madagascar, in the Indian Ocean. First explored by Portuguese navigators in the 16th century, the island of Réunion, then uninhabited, was taken as a French possession in 1642. African slaves were imported first to work coffee and then sugar plantations; with the abolition of slavery in 1848, indentured laborers from Indochina, India, and East Africa were brought in. In 1947, Réunion became an overseas department of France.

Overseas Territories and Countries

Overseas Territories are comparable to Departments except that their administrative organization includes a locally elected government.

French Polynesia

Status: Overseas Country
High Commissioner: Jean Aribaud (1999)
President: Oscar Temaru (2004)
Area: 1,609 sq mi (4,167 sq km)
Population (2005 est.): 270,485 (growth rate: 1.5%); birth rate: 16.9/1000; infant mortality rate: 8.4/1000; life expectancy: 75.9 density per sq mi: 168
Capital (2003 est.): Papeete (on Tahiti), 111,400 (metro. area), 30,200 (city proper). **Monetary unit:** Pacific financial community franc. **Languages:** French, Tahitian (both official). **Ethnicity/race:** Polynesian 78%, Chinese 12%, local French 6%, metropolitan French 4%. **Religions:** Protestant 54%, Roman Catholic 30%, other 10%, no religion 6%. **Literacy rate:** 98% (1977)
Economic summary: GDP/PPP (2003 est.): $4.58 billion; per capita $17,500 . **Real growth rate:** n.a. **Inflation:** 1.5% (2002 est.). **Unemployment:** 11.8% (1994). **Arable land:** 1%. **Agriculture:** coconuts, vanilla, vegetables, fruits; poultry, beef, dairy products, coffee. **Labor force:** 70,000 (1996); agriculture 13%, industry 19%, services 68% (2002). **Industries:** tourism, pearls, agricultural processing, handicrafts, phosphates. **Natural**

resources: timber, fish, cobalt, hydropower. **Exports:** $244 million (f.o.b., 2002): cultured pearls, coconut products, mother-of-pearl, vanilla, shark meat (1997). **Imports:** $1.341 billion (f.o.b., 2002): fuels, foodstuffs, machinery and equipment. **Major trading partners:** France, Japan, U.S., Australia, New Zealand (2003).

The term *French Polynesia* is applied to the scattered French possessions in the South Pacific—Mangareva (Gambier), Makatea, the Marquesas Islands, Rapa, Rurutu, Rimatara, the Society Islands, the Tuamotu Archipelago, Tubuai, Raivavae, and the island of Clipperton—which were organized into a single colony in 1903. There are 120 islands, of which 25 are uninhabited. The principal and most populous island—Tahiti, in the Society group—was claimed by the French in 1768. The indigenous people are mostly Maoris.

The Pacific Nuclear Test Center on the atoll of Mururoa, 744 mi (1,200 km) from Tahiti, was completed in 1966. In 1975 worldwide opposition forced the French to move the testing underground on Fangataufa. To compensate the residents for the nuclear weapons tests from 1995 to 1996, France offered a 10-year $194-million annual compensation package. An independence movement continues to flourish in French Polynesia. In 2004, France changed its status from a French Overseas Territory to an Overseas Country, which gave French Polynesia more autonomy over local affairs.

New Caledonia and Dependencies

Status: Overseas Territory
President: Marie-Noëlle Thémereau (2004)
High Commissioner: Thierry Lataste (1998)
Area: 7,359 sq mi (19,060 sq km)
Population (2005 est.): 216,494 (growth rate: 1.3%); birth rate: 18.5/1000; infant mortality rate: 7.7/1000; life expectancy: 74.0; density per sq mi: 29
Capital (2003 est.): Nouméa, 134,500 (metro. area), 86,400 (city proper). **Monetary unit:** Pacific financial community franc. **Languages:** French (official), 33 Melanesian and Polynesian dialects. **Ethnicity/race:** Kanak (Melanesian) 42.5%, European 37.1%, Wallisian 8.4%, Polynesian 3.8%, Indonesian 3.6%, Vietnamese 1.6%, other 3%. **Religions:** Roman Catholic 60%, Protestant 30%. **Literacy rate:** 91% (1976 est.)
Economic summary: GDP/PPP (2003 est.): $3.158 billion; per capita $15,000 (2002 est.). **Real growth rate:** n.a. **Inflation:** –0.6% (2000 est.). **Unemployment:** 19% (1996). **Arable land:** 0.4%. **Agriculture:** vegetables; beef, deer, other livestock products. **Labor force:** 79,395 (including 15,018 unemployed, 1996); agriculture 7%, industry 23%, services 70% (1999 est.). **Industries:** nickel mining and smelting. **Natural resources:** nickel, chrome, iron, cobalt, manganese, silver, gold, lead, copper. **Exports:** $448 million (f.o.b., 2002): ferronickels, nickel ore, fish. **Imports:** $1.007 billion (f.o.b., 2002): chemicals, machinery and equipment, fuels, chemicals, foodstuffs. **Major trading partners:** Japan, France, Taiwan, Spain, South Korea, Australia, Italy, Singapore, New Zealand (2003).

New Caledonia (6,466 sq mi; 16,747 sq km), about 1,070 mi (1,722 km) northeast of Sydney, Australia, was explored by Capt. James Cook in 1774 and annexed by France in 1853. The government also administers the Isle of Pines, the Loyalty Islands (Uvéa, Lifu, and Maré), the Belep Islands, the Huon Island group, and Chesterfield Islands. The native people are Melanesians called the Kanak. In 1984, the French National Assembly passed a law that granted internal autonomy to New Caledonia. In 1998 the

Nouméa Accords postponed discussions about independence for the territory until at least 2013.

Southern and Antarctic Lands

Status: Overseas Territory
Administrator: Michel Champon (2005)
Area: 3,023 sq mi (7,829 sq km, excluding Adélie Land)
Capital: Port-au-Français

This territory is uninhabited except for the personnel of scientific bases. It consists of Adélie Land (166,752 sq mi; 431,888 sq km) on the Antarctic mainland (which the U.S. does not recognize) and the following islands in the southern Indian Ocean: the Kerguelen and Crozet archipelagos and the islands of Saint-Paul and New Amsterdam.

Wallis and Futuna Islands

Status: Overseas Territory
Administrator: Xavier de Furst (2005)
Area: 106 sq mi (274 sq km)
Population (2005 est.): 16,025 (growth rate: n.a.); birth rate: n.a.; infant mortality rate: n.a.; life expectancy: n.a.; density per sq mi: 151
Capital (2003 est.): Mata-Utu, 1,300. **Languages:** French, Wallisian. **Ethnicity/race:** Polynesian. **Religion:** Roman Catholic. **Literacy rate:** 50% (1969 est.)
Economic summary: GDP/PPP (2004 est.): $60 million; per capita $3,800. **Real growth rate:** n.a. **Inflation:** n.a. **Unemployment:** n.a. **Arable land:** 5%. **Agriculture:** breadfruit, yams, taro, bananas; pigs, goats. **Labor force:** n.a.; agriculture, livestock, and fishing 80%, government 4% (2001 est.). **Industries:** copra, handicrafts, fishing, lumber. **Natural resources:** negl. **Exports:** $250,000 (f.o.b., 1999): copra, chemicals, construction materials. **Imports:** $300,000 (f.o.b., 1999): chemicals, machinery, passenger ships, consumer goods. **Major trading partners:** Italy, Croatia, U.S., Denmark France, Australia, New Zealand.

The two island groups in the South Pacific between Fiji and Samoa were settled by French missionaries at the beginning of the 19th century. A protectorate was established in the 1880s. There is a French-appointed high administrator, a 20-member Territorial Assembly, and a deputy and a senator to the French national Parliament. The three traditional Polynesian kings also help decide internal policy matters. Following a referendum by the Polynesian inhabitants, the status was changed to that of an Overseas Territory in 1961.

Territorial Collectivities

The Territorial Collectivity status was created in 1976 for Mayotte; it was conceived as being midway between an Overseas Territory and an Overseas Department.

Saint Pierre and Miquelon

Status: Territorial Collectivity
Prefect: Albert Dupuy (2005)
Area: 93 sq mi (242 sq km)
Population (2005 est.): 7,012; density per sq mi: 75
Capital (2003 est.): Saint Pierre, 5,900. **Language:** French (official). **Ethnicity/race:** Basques and Bretons (French fishermen). **Religion:** Roman Catholic 99%. **Literacy rate:** 99% (1982 est.)
Economic summary: GDP/PPP (2003 est.): $48.3 million, supplemented by annual payments from France of about $60 million; per capita $7,000 (2001 est.). **Real growth rate:** n.a. **Inflation:** 2.1% (1991–1996 average). **Unemployment:** 9.8% (1997). **Arable land:** 13%. **Agriculture:** vegetables; poultry, cattle,

sheep, pigs; fish. **Labor force:** 3,261 (1999); fishing 18%, industry (mainly fish processing) 41%, services 41% (1996 est.). **Industries:** fish processing and supply base for fishing fleets; tourism. **Natural resources:** fish, deepwater ports. **Exports:** $10 million (f.o.b., 2002): fish and fish products, soybeans, animal feed, mollusks and crustaceans, fox and mink pelts. **Imports:** $106 million (f.o.b., 2002): meat, clothing, fuel, electrical equipment, machinery, building materials. **Major trading partners:** U.S., Ecuador, France, Canada, Belgium, Italy (2003).

The sole remnant of the French colonial empire in North America, these islands were first occupied by the French in 1604. Their importance arises from their proximity to the Grand Banks, located 10 mi south of Newfoundland, making them the center of the French Atlantic cod fisheries.

Mayotte

Status: Territorial Collectivity
Prefect: Jean-Paul Kihl (2004)
Area: 144 sq mi (374 sq km)
Population (2005 est.): 193,633 (growth rate: 3.9%); birth rate: 41.6/1000; infant mortality rate: 62.4/1000; life expectancy: 61.4; density per sq mi: 1,341
Capital (2003 est.): Dzaoudzi 15,100. **Largest city:** Mamoudzou, 45,700. **Languages:** Mahorian (a Swahili dialect), French (official language) spoken by 35% of the population. **Religions:** Islam 97%, Christian (mostly Roman Catholic)
Economic summary: GDP/PPP (2003 est.): $466.8 million; per capita $2,600. **Real growth rate:** n.a. **Inflation:** n.a. **Unemployment:** 38% (1999). **Arable land:** n.a. **Agriculture:** vanilla, ylang-ylang (perfume essence), coffee, copra. **Labor force:** 48,800 (2000). **Industries:** newly created lobster and shrimp industry, construction. **Natural resources:** negl. **Exports:** $3.44 million (f.o.b., 1997): ylang-ylang (perfume essence), vanilla, copra, coconuts, coffee, cinnamon. **Imports:** $141.3 million (f.o.b., 1997): food, machinery and equipment, transportation equipment, metals, chemicals. **Major trading partners:** France, Comoros, Réunion, Africa, Southeast Asia (2000 est.).

France gained colonial control over Mayotte in 1843. It is the most populous of the four Comoros Islands in the Indian Ocean off Mozambique in Africa. Mayotte chose to remain a French dependency rather than join the other Comoran islands in declaring independence in 1975. Comoros laid claim to Mayotte shortly after independence and continues to do so. In July 2000, 70% of voters opted to accept greater autonomy but remain a part of France.

French Possessions

Bassas da India (0.1 sq mi, 0.2 sq km), a French possession since 1897, is an uninhabited volcanic atoll off the southeastern coast of Africa in the Mozambique channel.

Clipperton Island (2 sq mi, 6 sq km) is an uninhabited atoll named for a pirate who used it as a hideout in the 18th century. Located in the Pacific Ocean southwest of Mexico, it was claimed by France in 1855, seized by Mexico in 1897, and ultimately awarded to France in 1935.

Europa Island (11 sq mi, 28 sq km), a French possession since 1897, is located off the southeastern coast of Africa in the southern Mozambique channel. A small French military garrison resides there.

Glorioso Islands (2 sq mi, 5 sq km), a French possession since 1892, is composed of two coral islands (Ile Glorieuse and Ile du Lys) and three rock islets. Uninhabited except for a military garrison on Ile Glo-

rieuse, the islands are located off Southern Africa, northwest of Madagascar.

Juan de Nova Island (1.7 sq mi, 4.4 sq km) is named after a famous 15th century Spanish explorer and has been a French possession since 1897. Located off southern Africa in the Mozambique Channel, the island is inhabited by a small French garrison.

Tromelin Island (0.4 sq mi, 1 sq km), a possession of France since 1814, is located in the Indian Ocean, east of Madagascar. It currently serves as a sea turtle sanctuary and a meteorological station.

Gabon

GABONESE REPUBLIC

National name: République Gabonaise
President: El Hadj Omar Bongo Ondimba (1967)
Premier: Jean-François Ntoutoume-Emane (1999)
Area: 103,346 sq mi (267,667 sq km)
Population (2005 est.): 1,389,201 (growth rate: 2.5%); birth rate: 36.2/1000; infant mortality rate: 53.6/1000; life expectancy: 55.8; density per sq mi: 13
Capital and largest city (2003 est.): Libreville, 661,600. **Other large cities:** Port-Gentil, 116,200; Franceville, 41,300. **Monetary unit:** CFA Franc. **Languages:** French (official), Fang, Myene, Bateke, Bapounou/ Eschira, Bandjabi. **Ethnicity/race:** Bantu tribes, including four major tribal groupings: Fang, Punu, Nzeiby, Mbede (Obamba/Bateke); other Africans and Europeans 11.3%, including 0.8% French and 0.8% persons of dual nationality. **Religions:** Christian 55%–75%, animist, Islam less than 1%. **Literacy rate:** 63% (1995 est.)
Economic summary: GDP/PPP (2004 est.): $7.966 billion; per capita $5,900. **Real growth rate:** 1.9%. **Inflation:** 1.5%. **Unemployment:** 21% (1997 est.). **Arable land:** 1%. **Agriculture:** cocoa, coffee, sugar, palm oil, rubber; cattle; okoume (a tropical softwood); fish. **Labor force:** 650,000; agriculture 60%, services 25%, industry 15%. **Industries:** petroleum extraction and refining; manganese, and gold mining; chemicals; ship repair; food and beverage; textile; lumbering and plywood; cement. **Natural resources:** petroleum, natural gas, diamond, niobium, manganese, uranium, gold, timber, iron ore, hydropower. **Exports:** $3.71 billion (f.o.b., 2004 est.): crude oil 77%, timber, manganese, uranium (2001). **Imports:** $1.225 billion (f.o.b., 2004 est.): machinery and equipment, foodstuffs, chemicals, construction materials. **Major trading partners:** U.S., France, China, UK (2003). **Member of French Community**

Geography This West African country with the Atlantic as its western border is also bounded by Equatorial Guinea, Cameroon, and the Congo. Its area is slightly less than Colorado's. Most of the country is covered by a dense tropical forest.

Government Republic.

History The earliest humans in Gabon were believed to be the Babinga, or Pygmies, dating back to 7000 B.C., who were later followed by Bantu groups from southern and eastern Africa. Now there are many tribal groups in the country, the largest being the Fang peoples, who constitute 25% of the population.

Gabon was first explored by the Portuguese navigator Diego Cam in the 15th century. In 1472, the Portuguese explorers encountered the mouth of the Como River and named it "Rio de Gabao," river of Gabon, which later became the name of the country. The Dutch began arriving in 1593, and the French in 1630. In 1839, the French founded their first settlement on the left bank of the Gabon estuary and gradually occupied the hinterland during the second half of the 19th century. The land became a French territory in 1888, an autonomous republic within the French Union after World War II, and an independent republic on Aug. 17, 1960.

Albert-Bernard Bongo became Gabon's second president in 1967. He changed his name to Omar in 1973, upon converting to Islam. Strikes and riots led to a transitional constitution in May 1990 legalizing political parties and calling for free elections. In its first multiparty election in Dec. 1993, Bongo received just over 51% of the vote, while the opposition candidate alleged fraud and tried to establish a rival government.

In Dec. 1998, President Bongo, who had ruled the country for 31 years, was elected for an additional 7. Gabon lacks roads, schools, and adequate health care, yet the oil-rich country has lined the pockets of its ruler, who, according to the French weekly *L'Autre Afrique*, is said to own more real estate in Paris than any other foreign leader. Despite his reputation for corruption and authoritarianism, Bongo has a strong national following. In July 2003, the country's constitution was changed, allowing Bongo to be reelected indefinitely; that year, he changed his name again, to El Hadj Omar Bongo Ondimba.

Gambia, The

REPUBLIC OF THE GAMBIA

President: Yahya Jammeh (1994)
Area: 4,363 sq mi (11,300 sq km)
Population (2005 est.): 1,593,256 (growth rate: 2.9%); birth rate: 39.9/1000; infant mortality rate: 72.0/1000; life expectancy: 55.2; density per sq mi: 365
Capital (2003 est.): Banjul, 46,700. **Largest city:** Serekunda, 344,100. **Monetary unit:** Dalasi.
Languages: English (official), Mandinka, Wolof, Fula, other indigenous. **Ethnicity/race:** African 99% (Mandinka 42%, Fula 18%, Wolof 16%, Jola 10%, Serahuli 9%, other 4%), non-African 1%. **Religions:** Islam 90%, Christian 9%, indigenous 1%. **Literacy rate:** 40% (2003 est.)
Economic summary: GDP/PPP (2004 est.): $2.799 billion; per capita $1,800. **Real growth rate:** 6%. **Inflation:** 7%. **Unemployment:** n.a. (2002 est.). **Arable land:** 25%. **Agriculture:** rice, millet, sorghum, peanuts, corn, sesame, cassava (tapioca), palm kernels; cattle, sheep, goats. **Labor force:** 400,000 (1996); agriculture 75%, industry, commerce, and services 19%, government 6%. **Industries:** processing peanuts, fish, and hides; tourism; beverages; agricultural machinery assembly, woodworking, metalworking; clothing. **Natural resources:** fish, titanium (rutile and ilmenite), tin, zircon, silica sand, clay, petroleum. **Exports:** $114.4 million (f.o.b., 2004 est.): peanut products, fish, cotton lint, palm kernels, reexports. **Imports:** $180.9 million (f.o.b., 2004 est.): foodstuffs, manufactures, fuel, machinery and transport equipment. **Major trading partners:** UK, India, China, Germany, Belgium, Malaysia, Italy, Senegal, Brazil, U.S., Netherlands (2003). **Member of Commonwealth of Nations**

Geography Situated on the Atlantic coast in westernmost Africa and surrounded on three sides by Senegal, Gambia is twice the size of Delaware. The Gambia River flows for 200 mi (322 km) through Gambia on its way to the Atlantic. The country, the smallest on the continent, averages only 20 mi (32 km) in width.

Government Republic.

History Since the 13th century, the Wolof, Malinke, and Fulani peoples settled in what is now the Gambia. The Portuguese were the first European explorers, encountering the Gambia River in 1455, and in 1681 the French founded an enclave at Albredabut. During the 17th century, Gambia was settled by various com-

panies of English merchants. Slavery was the chief source of revenue before it was abolished in 1807. Gambia became a British Crown colony in 1843 and an independent nation within the Commonwealth of Nations on Feb. 18, 1965. Full independence was approved in a 1970 referendum, and on April 24 of that year Gambia proclaimed itself a republic.

Dauda Kairaba Jawara served as Gambia's president from 1970 to 1994. A military coup led by Capt. Yahya Jammeh deposed the president in July 1994, suspended the constitution, and banned existing political parties. Jammeh promised new elections, which were held in Sept. 1996, and he won 55% of the vote against his nearest rival, Ousseynou Darboe. In April 1997, he completed the promised return to civilian rule. Censorship of the press and other repressive measures continue to mar the country's transition to democracy.

Unrest plagued Gambia throughout much of 2000. In January Jammeh crushed a coup attempt staged by some of his own bodyguards, and in April violent student protests rocked the country. The peanut export system collapsed in the same year from mismanagement, leaving farmers unpaid and unable to sell a bumper crop of the country's main commodity. In 2001, Jammeh lifted the ban against various opposition parties he had outlawed after his 1994 coup. He was reelected in Oct. 2001 with 53% of the vote. In Dec. 2004, Gambia passed a media law that allows the state to jail journalists found guilty of libel and sedition.

Georgia

GEORGIA

National name: Sak'art'velo
President: Mikhail Saakashvili (2004)
Prime Minister: Zurab Nogaideli (2005)
Minister of State: Avtandil Jorbenadze (2001)
Area: 26,911 sq mi (69,700 sq km)
Population (2005 est.): 4,677,401 (growth rate: –0.4%); birth rate: 10.2/1000; infant mortality rate: 18.6/1000; life expectancy: 75.9; density per sq mi: 174
Capital and largest city (2003 est.): Tbilisi, 1,440,000 (metro. area), 1,240,200 (city proper). **Other large cities:** Kutaisi, 268,800; Batoumi, 145,400; and Sokhumi, 110,300. **Monetary unit:** Lari. **Languages:** Georgian 71% (official), Russian 9%, Armenian 7%, Azerbaijani 6%, other 7% (Abkhaz is the official language in Abkhazia). **Ethnicity/race:** Georgian 70.1%, Armenian 8.1%, Russian 6.3%, Azeri 5.7%, Ossetian 3%, Abkhaz 1.8%, other 5%. **Religions:** Georgian Orthodox 65%, Islam 11%, Russian Orthodox 10%, Armenian Orthodox 8%, unknown 6%. **Literacy rate:** 99% (1999 est.)
Economic summary: GDP/PPP (2004 est.): $14.45 billion; per capita $3,100. **Real growth rate:** 9.5%. **Inflation:** 5.5%. **Unemployment:** 17% (2001 est.). **Arable land:** 11%. **Agriculture:** citrus, grapes, tea, hazelnuts, vegetables; livestock. **Labor force:** 2.1 million (2001 est.); industry 20%, agriculture 40%, services 40% (1999 est.). **Industries:** steel, aircraft, machine tools, electrical appliances, mining (manganese and copper), chemicals, wood products, wine. **Natural resources:** forests, hydropower, manganese deposits, iron ore, copper, minor coal and oil deposits; coastal climate and soils allow for important tea and citrus growth. **Exports:** $909.4 million (2004 est.): scrap metal, machinery, chemicals; fuel reexports; citrus fruits, tea, wine. **Imports:** $1.806 billion (2004 est.): fuels, machinery and parts, transport equipment, grain and other foods, pharmaceuticals. **Major trading partners:** Russia, Turkey, Turkmenistan, Armenia, Switzerland, Ukraine, UK, Azerbaijan, U.S., Germany, France (2003).

Geography Georgia is bordered by the Black Sea in the west, by Turkey and Armenia in the south, by Azerbaijan in the east, and Russia in the north. The republic also includes the Abkhazia and Ajara autonomous republics and South Ossetia.

Government Republic.

History Georgia became a kingdom about 4 B.C. and Christianity was introduced in A.D. 337. During the reign of Queen Tamara (1184–1213), its territory included the whole of Transcaucasia. During the 13th century, Tamerlane and the Mongols decimated its population. From the 16th century on, the country was the scene of a struggle between Persia and Turkey. In the 18th century it became a vassal to Russia in exchange for protection from the Turks and Persians.

Georgia joined Azerbaijan and Armenia in 1917 to establish the anti-Bolshevik Transcaucasian Federation and on its dissolution in 1918 proclaimed its independence. In 1922, Georgia, Armenia, and Azerbaijan were annexed by the USSR and formed the Transcaucasian Soviet Socialist Republic. In 1936, Georgia became a separate Soviet republic. Under Soviet rule it was transformed from an agrarian country to a largely industrial urban society.

Georgia proclaimed its independence from the USSR on April 6, 1991. In Jan. 1992, its leader, Zviad Gamsakhurdia, was sacked and later accused of dictatorial policies, the jailing of opposition leaders, human rights abuses, and clamping down on the media. A ruling military council was established by the opposition until a civilian authority could be restored. In 1992, Eduard Shevardnadze, the Soviet Union's foreign minister under Gorbachev, became president.

In 1992–1993, the government engaged in armed conflict with separatists in the breakaway province of Abkhazia. In 1994, Russia and Georgia signed a cooperation treaty that authorized Russia to keep three military bases in Georgia and allowed Russians to train and equip the Georgian army. In 1996, Georgia and its breakaway region of South Ossetia agreed to a cessation of hostilities in their six-year conflict. With little progress in resolving the Abkhazia situation, however, Parliament in April 1997 voted overwhelmingly to threaten Russia with loss of its military bases should it fail to extend Russian military control over the separatist region. In 1998, the U.S. and Britain began an operation to remove nuclear material from Georgia, dangerous remains from its Soviet years. A darling of the West since his days as the Soviet Union's foreign minister, Shevardnadze was viewed far less favorably by his own people, who were frustrated by unemployment, poverty, cronyism, and rampant corruption. In the 2000 presidential elections, Shevardnadze was reelected with 80% of the vote, though international observers determined the election was marred by irregularities.

In 2002, U.S. troops trained Georgia's military in antiterrorism measures in the hopes that Georgian troops would subdue Muslim rebels fighting in the country. Tensions between Georgia and Russia were strained over the Pankisi Gorge, a lawless region of Georgia that Russia said had become a haven for Islamic militants and Chechen rebels.

In May 2003, work began on the Georgian section of the enormously ambitious Baku-Tbilisi-Ceyhan oil pipeline, which runs from Azerbaijan through Georgia to Turkey.

Massive demonstrations began after the preliminary results of the Nov. 2, 2003, parliamentary elections. The opposition party (and international monitors) claimed that the elections were rigged in favor of Shevardnadze and the political parties who supported him. After more than three weeks of massive protests, She-

vardnadze resigned on Nov. 30. Georgians compared the turn of events to Czechoslovakia's velvet revolution. In Jan. 2004 presidential elections, Mikhail Saakashvili, the key opposition leader, won in a landslide. The 36-year-old lawyer built his reputation as a reformer committed to ending corruption.

Saakashvili's first major challenge was asserting control over the breakaway region of Ajaria. Its leader, Aslan Abashidze, refused to recognize the new Georgian president, but after several months of confrontations, was forced to resign and leave the country in May 2004. Efforts to reintegrate the two other breakaway regions he inherited, South Ossetia and Abkhazia, have proven more difficult. Saakashvili had offered South Ossetia autonomy and financial aid but not independence, an offer the region's leaders have rejected.

Germany

FEDERAL REPUBLIC OF GERMANY

National name: Bundesrepublik Deutschland
President: Horst Köhler (2004)
Chancellor: Gerhard Schröder (1998)
Area: 137,846 sq mi (357,021 sq km)
Population (2005 est.): 82,431,390 (growth rate: 0%); birth rate: 8.3/1000; infant mortality rate: 4.2/1000; life expectancy: 78.7; density per sq mi: 598
Capital and largest city (2003 est.): Berlin (capital since Oct. 3, 1990), 3,933,300 (metro. area), 3,274,500 (city proper). **Other large cities:** Hamburg, 1,686,100; Munich, 1,185,400; Cologne, 965,300; Frankfurt, 648,000; Essen, 588,800; Dortmund, 587,600; Stuttgart, 581,100; Düsseldorf, 568,900; Bremen, 527,900; Hanover, 516,300; Duisburg, 513,400. **Monetary unit:** Euro (formerly Deutsche mark). **Language:** German. **Ethnicity/race:** German 91.5%, Turkish 2.4%, Italian 0.7%, Greek 0.4%, Polish 0.4%, other 4.6%. **Religions:** Protestant 34%, Roman Catholic 34%, Islam 3.7%, Unaffiliated or other 28.3%. **Literacy rate:** 99% (1977 est.)
Economic summary GDP/PPP (2004 est.): $2.362 trillion; per capita $28,700. **Real growth rate:** 1.7%. **Inflation:** 1.6%. **Unemployment:** 10.6%. **Arable land:** 34%. **Agriculture:** potatoes, wheat, barley, sugar beets, fruit, cabbages; cattle, pigs, poultry. **Labor force:** 42.63 million; industry 33.4%, agriculture 2.8%, services 63.8% (1999). **Industries:** among the world's largest and most technologically advanced producers of iron, steel, coal, cement, chemicals, machinery, vehicles, machine tools, electronics, food and beverages; shipbuilding; textiles. **Natural resources:** iron ore, coal, potash, timber, lignite, uranium, copper, natural gas, salt, nickel, arable land. **Exports:** $893.3 billion (f.o.b., 2004 est.): machinery, vehicles, chemicals, metals and manufactures, foodstuffs, textiles. **Imports:** $716.7 billion (f.o.b., 2004 est.): machinery, vehicles, chemicals, foodstuffs, textiles, metals. **Major trading partners:** France, U.S., UK, Italy, Netherlands, Austria, Belgium, Spain, China (2003).

Geography Located in central Europe, Germany is made up of the North German Plain, the Central German Uplands (Mittelgebirge), and the Southern German Highlands. The Bavarian plateau in the southwest averages 1,600 ft (488 m) above sea level, but it reaches 9,721 ft (2,962 m) in the Zugspitze Mountains, the highest point in the country. Germany's major rivers are the Danube, the Elbe, the Oder, the Weser, and the Rhine. Germany is about the size of Montana.

Government Federal republic.

History The Celts are believed to have been the first inhabitants of Germany. They were followed by German tribes at the end of the 2nd century B.C. German invasions destroyed the declining Roman Empire in the 4th and 5th centuries A.D. One of the tribes, the Franks, attained supremacy in western Europe under Charlemagne, who was crowned Holy Roman Emperor in 800. By the Treaty of Verdun (843), Charlemagne's lands east of the Rhine were ceded to the German Prince Louis. Additional territory acquired by the Treaty of Mersen (870) gave Germany approximately the area it maintained throughout the Middle Ages. For several centuries after Otto the Great was crowned king in 936, German rulers were also usually heads of the Holy Roman Empire.

By the 14th century, the Holy Roman Empire was little more than a loose federation of the German princes who elected the Holy Roman Emperor. In 1438, Albert of Hapsburg became emperor, and for the next several centuries the Hapsburg line ruled the Holy Roman Empire until its decline in 1806. Relations between state and church were changed by the Reformation, which began with Martin Luther's 95 theses, and came to a head in 1547, when Charles V scattered the forces of the Protestant League at Mühlberg. The Counter-Reformation followed. A dispute over the succession to the Bohemian throne brought on the Thirty Years' War (1618–1648), which devastated Germany and left the empire divided into hundreds of small principalities virtually independent of the emperor.

Meanwhile, Prussia was developing into a state of considerable strength. Frederick the Great (1740–1786) reorganized the Prussian army and defeated Maria Theresa of Austria in a struggle over Silesia. After the defeat of Napoléon at Waterloo (1815), the struggle between Austria and Prussia for supremacy in Germany continued, reaching its climax in the defeat of Austria in the Seven Weeks' War (1866) and the formation of the Prussian-dominated North German Confederation (1867). The architect of this new German unity was Otto von Bismarck, a conservative, monarchist, and militaristic Prussian prime minister. He unified all of Germany in a series of three wars against Denmark (1864), Austria (1866), and France (1870–1871). On Jan. 18, 1871, King Wilhelm I of Prussia was proclaimed German emperor in the Hall of Mirrors at Versailles. The North German Confederation, created in 1867, was abolished, and the Second German Reich, consisting of the North and South German states, was born. With a powerful army, an efficient bureaucracy, and a loyal bourgeoisie, Chancellor Bismarck consolidated a powerful centralized state.

Wilhelm II dismissed Bismarck in 1890 and embarked upon a "New Course," stressing an intensified colonialism and a powerful navy. His chaotic foreign policy culminated in the diplomatic isolation of Germany and the disastrous defeat in World War I (1914–1918). The Second German Empire collapsed following the defeat of the German armies in 1918, the naval mutiny at Kiel, and the flight of the kaiser to the Netherlands. The Social Democrats, led by Friedrich Ebert and Philipp Scheidemann, crushed the Communists and established a moderate state, known as the Weimar Republic, with Ebert as president. President Ebert died on Feb. 28, 1925, and on April 26, Field Marshal Paul von Hindenburg was elected president. The mass of Germans regarded the Weimar Republic as a child of defeat, imposed on a Germany whose legitimate aspirations to world leadership had been thwarted by a world conspiracy. Added to this were a crippling currency debacle, a tremendous burden of reparations, and acute economic distress.

Adolf Hitler, an Austrian war veteran and a fanatical nationalist, fanned discontent by promising a Greater Germany, abrogation of the Treaty of Ver-

sailles, restoration of Germany's lost colonies, and the destruction of the Jews, whom he scapegoated as the reason for Germany's downfall and depressed economy. When the Social Democrats and the Communists refused to combine against the Nazi threat, President von Hindenburg made Hitler the chancellor on Jan. 30, 1933. With the death of von Hindenburg on Aug. 2, 1934, Hitler repudiated the Treaty of Versailles and began full-scale rearmament. In 1935, he withdrew Germany from the League of Nations, and the next year he reoccupied the Rhineland and signed the Anti-Comintern pact with Japan, at the same time strengthening relations with Italy. Austria was annexed in March 1938. By the Munich agreement in Sept. 1938, he gained the Czech Sudetenland, and in violation of this agreement he completed the dismemberment of Czechoslovakia in March 1939. His invasion of Poland on Sept. 1, 1939, precipitated World War II.

Hitler established death camps to carry out "the final solution to the Jewish question." By the end of the war, Hitler's Holocaust had killed 6 million Jews, as well as Gypsies, homosexuals, Communists, the handicapped, and others not fitting the Aryan ideal. After some dazzling initial successes in 1939–1942, Germany surrendered unconditionally to Allied and Soviet military commanders on May 8, 1945. On June 5 the four-nation Allied Control Council became the de facto government of Germany.

(For details of World War II and of the Holocaust, see Headline History, World War II.)

At the Berlin (or Potsdam) Conference (July 17–Aug. 2, 1945) President Truman, Premier Stalin, and Prime Minister Clement Attlee of Britain set forth the guiding principles of the Allied Control Council: Germany's complete disarmament and demilitarization, destruction of its war potential, rigid control of industry, and decentralization of the political and economic structure. Pending final determination of territorial questions at a peace conference, the three victors agreed to the ultimate transfer of the city of Königsberg (now Kaliningrad) and its adjacent area to the USSR and to the administration by Poland of former German territories lying generally east of the Oder-Neisse Line. For purposes of control, Germany was divided into four national occupation zones.

The Western powers were unable to agree with the USSR on any fundamental issues. Work of the Allied Control Council was hamstrung by repeated Soviet vetoes; and finally, on March 20, 1948, Russia walked out of the Council. Meanwhile, the U.S. and Britain had taken steps to merge their zones economically (Bizone); on May 31, 1948, the U.S., Britain, France, and the Benelux countries agreed to set up a German state comprising the three Western zones. The USSR reacted by clamping a blockade on all ground communications between the Western zones and West Berlin, an enclave in the Soviet zone. The Western Allies countered by organizing a gigantic airlift to fly supplies into the beleaguered city. The USSR was finally forced to lift the blockade on May 12, 1949.

The Federal Republic of Germany was proclaimed on May 23, 1949, with its capital at Bonn. In free elections, West German voters gave a majority in the Constituent Assembly to the Christian Democrats, with the Social Democrats largely making up the opposition. Konrad Adenauer became chancellor, and Theodor Heuss of the Free Democrats was elected the first president.

The East German states adopted a more centralized constitution for the Democratic Republic of Germany, put into effect on Oct. 7, 1949. The USSR thereupon dissolved its occupation zone but Soviet troops remained. The Western Allies declared that the East

German Republic was a Soviet creation undertaken without self-determination and refused to recognize it. Soviet forces created a state controlled by the secret police with a single party, the Socialist Unity (Communist) Party.

Agreements in Paris in 1954 giving the Federal Republic full independence and complete sovereignty came into force on May 5, 1955. Under the agreement, West Germany and Italy became members of the Brussels treaty organization created in 1948 and renamed the Western European Union. West Germany also became a member of NATO. In 1955, the USSR recognized the Federal Republic. The Saar territory, under an agreement between France and West Germany, held a plebiscite and despite economic links to France, elected to rejoin West Germany on Jan. 1, 1957.

The division between West Germany and East Germany was intensified when the Communists erected the Berlin Wall in 1961. In 1968, the East German Communist leader, Walter Ulbricht, imposed restrictions on West German movements into West Berlin. The Soviet-bloc invasion of Czechoslovakia in Aug. 1968 added to the tension. West Germany signed a treaty with Poland in 1970, renouncing force and setting Poland's western border at the Oder-Neisse Line. It subsequently resumed formal relations with Czechoslovakia in a pact that "voided" the Munich treaty that gave Nazi Germany the Sudetenland. By 1973, normal relations were established between East and West Germany and the two states entered the United Nations.

West German chancellor Willy Brandt, winner of a Nobel Peace Prize for his foreign policies, was forced to resign in 1974 when an East German spy was discovered to be one of his top staff members. Succeeding him was a moderate Social Democrat, Helmut Schmidt. Schmidt staunchly backed U.S. military strategy in Europe, staking his political fate on placing U.S. nuclear missiles in Germany unless the Soviet Union reduced its arsenal of intermediate missiles. He also strongly opposed nuclear freeze proposals.

Helmut Kohl of the Christian Democrat Party became chancellor in 1982. An economic upswing in 1986 led to Kohl's reelection. The fall of the Communist government in East Germany left only Soviet objections to German reunification to be dealt with. On the night of Nov. 9, 1989, the Berlin Wall was dismantled, making reunification all but inevitable. In July 1990, Kohl asked Soviet leader Gorbachev to drop his objections in exchange for financial aid from (West) Germany. Gorbachev agreed, and on Oct. 3, 1990, the German Democratic Republic acceded to the Federal Republic and Germany became a united and sovereign state for the first time since 1945.

A reunited Berlin serves as the official capital of unified Germany, although the government would continue to have administrative functions in Bonn during the 12-year transition period. The issues of the cost of reunification and the modernization of the former East Germany were serious considerations facing the reunified nation.

In its most important election in decades, on Sept. 27, 1998, Germans chose Social Democrat Gerhard Schröder as chancellor over Christian Democrat incumbent Helmut Kohl, ending a 16-year-long rule that oversaw the reunification of Germany and symbolized the end of the cold war in Europe. A centrist, Schröder campaigned for "the new middle" and promised to rectify Germany's high unemployment rate of 10.6%.

Tension between the old-style left-wing and the more pro-business pragmatists within Schröder's government came to a head with the abrupt resignation of Finance Minister Oskar Lafontaine in March 1999, who was also chairman of the ruling Social Democratic Party. Lafontaine's plans to raise taxes on industry and raise German wages—already nearly the highest in the world—went against the more centrist policies of Schröder. Hans Eichel was chosen to become the next finance minister.

Germany joined the other NATO allies in the military conflict in Kosovo in 1999. Before the Kosovo crisis, Germans had not participated in an armed conflict since World War II. Germany agreed to take 40,000 Kosovar refugees, the most of any NATO country.

In Dec. 1999, former chancellor Helmut Kohl and other high officials in the Christian Democrat Party (CDU) admitted accepting tens of millions of dollars in illegal donations during the 1980s and 1990s. The enormity of the scandal led to the virtual dismemberment of the CDU in early 2000, a party that had long been a stable conservative force in German politics.

In July 2000, Schröder managed to pass significant tax reforms that would lower the top income-tax rate from 51% to 42% by 2005. He also eliminated the capital gains tax on companies selling shares in other companies, a measure that was expected to spur mergers. In May 2001, the German Parliament authorized the payment of $4.4 billion in compensation to 1.2 million surviving Nazi-era slave laborers.

Schröder was narrowly reelected in Sept. 2002, defeating conservative businessman Edmund Stoiber. Schröder's Social Democrats and coalition partner, the Greens, won a razor-thin majority in Parliament. Schröder's deft handling of Germany's catastrophic floods in August and his tough stance against U.S. plans for a preemptive attack on Iraq buoyed him in the weeks leading up to the election. Germany's continued reluctance to support the U.S. call for military action against Iraq severely strained its relations with Washington.

Germany's recession continued in 2003: for the previous three years Europe's biggest economy had the lowest growth rate among EU countries. In Aug. 2003, Schröder unfurled an ambitious fiscal reform package and called his proposal "the most significant set of structural reforms in the social history of Germany." The reforms reduced some of the benefits of Germany's generous social welfare system, including national health insurance and unemployment compensation.

Gerhard Schröder's Social Democratic Party (SPD) suffered a devastating defeat in local elections in May 2005, ending the party's 39-year reign in Germany's most populous state, North Rhine–Westphalia. The election was seen as a referendum on Schröder's economic reform programs, which have done little to rejuvenate the economy and have angered many Germans accustomed to their country's generous social welfare programs. The reforms have reduced such programs as unemployment benefits at a time when unemployment has reached an alarming 12%. Schröder engineered early elections, for Sept. 2005 instead of Sept. 2006, and seemed to be taking a gamble that when given the bald choice between the SPD and the conservative CDU and its leader, Angela Merkel, the electorate would continue to support him.

Ghana

REPUBLIC OF GHANA

President: John Agyekum Kufuor (2001)
Area: 92,456 sq mi (239,460 sq km)
Population (2005 est.): 21,029,853 (growth rate: 1.3%); birth rate: 24.0/1000; infant mortality rate: 51.4/1000; life expectancy: 56.0; density per sq mi: 227
Capital and largest city (2003 est.): Accra, 2,825,800 (metro. area), 1,661,400 (city proper). **Other large**

cities: Kumasi, 645,100; Tamale, 279,600. **Monetary unit:** Cedi. **Languages:** English (official), African languages (including Akan, Moshi-Dagomba, Ewe, and Ga). **Ethnicity/race:** black African 98.5% (major tribes: Akan 44%, Moshi-Dagomba 16%, Ewe 13%, Ga 8%, Gurma 3%, Yoruba 1%), European and other 1.5% (1998). **Religions:** Christian 63%, indigenous beliefs 21%, Islam 16%. **Literacy rate:** 75% (2003 est.)
Economic summary: GDP/PPP (2004 est.): $48.27 billion; per capita $2,300. **Real growth rate:** 5.4%. **Inflation:** 13%. **Unemployment:** 20% (1997 est.). **Arable land:** 16%. **Agriculture:** cocoa, rice, coffee, cassava (tapioca), peanuts, corn, shea nuts, bananas; timber. **Labor force:** 10.24 million; agriculture 60%, industry 15%, services 25% (1999 est.). **Industries:** mining, lumbering, light manufacturing, aluminum smelting, food processing, cement, small commercial shipbuilding. **Natural resources:** gold, timber, industrial diamonds, bauxite, manganese, fish, rubber, hydropower, petroleum, silver, salt, limestone. **Exports:** $3.01 billion (f.o.b., 2004 est.): gold, cocoa, timber, tuna, bauxite, aluminum, manganese ore, diamonds. **Imports:** $3.699 billion (f.o.b., 2004 est.): capital equipment, petroleum, foodstuffs. **Major trading partners:** Netherlands, UK, France, Germany, Japan, Italy, Turkey, U.S., Nigeria, China, India (2003). **Member of Commonwealth of Nations**

Geography A West African country bordering on the Gulf of Guinea, Ghana is bounded by Côte d'Ivoire to the west, Burkina Faso to the north, Togo to the east, and the Atlantic Ocean to the south. It compares in size to Oregon, and its largest river is the Volta.

Government Constitutional democracy.

History Several major civilizations flourished in the general region of what is now Ghana. The ancient empire of Ghana (located 500 mi northwest of the contemporary state) reigned until the 13th century. The Akan peoples established the next major civilization, beginning in the 13th century, and then the Ashanti Empire flourished in the 18th and 19th centuries.

Called the Gold Coast, the area was first seen by Portuguese traders in 1470. They were followed by the English (1553), the Dutch (1595), and the Swedes (1640). British rule over the Gold Coast began in 1820, but it was not until after quelling the severe resistance of the Ashanti in 1901 that it was firmly established. British Togoland, formerly a colony of Germany, was incorporated into Ghana by referendum in 1956. Created as an independent country on March 6, 1957, Ghana, as the result of a plebiscite, became a republic on July 1, 1960.

Premier Kwame Nkrumah attempted to take leadership of the Pan-African Movement, holding the All-African People's Congress in his capital, Accra, in 1958 and organizing the Union of African States with Guinea and Mali in 1961. But he oriented his country toward the Soviet Union and China and built an autocratic rule over all aspects of Ghanaian life. In Feb. 1966, while Nkrumah was visiting Beijing and Hanoi, he was deposed by a military coup led by Gen. Emmanuel K. Kotoka.

A series of military coups followed and on June 4, 1979, Flight Lt. Jerry Rawlings overthrew Lt. Gen. Frederick Akuffo's military rule. Rawlings permitted the election of a civilian president to go ahead as scheduled the following month, and Hilla Limann, candidate of the People's National Party, took office. Rawlings's three-month rule was one of Ghana's bloodiest periods, with executions of numerous government officials and business leaders. Two years later Rawlings staged another coup, charging the civilian government with corruption. As chairman of the Provisional National Defense Council, Rawlings scrapped the constitution, instituted an austerity program, and reduced budget deficits over the next decade. He then returned the country to civilian rule and won the presidency in multiparty elections in 1992 and again in 1996. Since then, Ghana has been widely viewed as one of Africa's most stable democracies.

A major cocoa producer, Ghana has been hurt by slumps in cocoa prices. In July 2000, Ghana and neighboring countries began destroying massive amounts of cocoa to drive up the price. Together they produce 70% of the world's cocoa. Since gold is Ghana's largest source of foreign exchange, fluctuating prices have hammered the economy, and mining companies cut 10,000 jobs in 1999. Saudi Arabian investors rescued Ashanti Goldfields, the largest company in sub-Saharan Africa, from near collapse in Feb. 2000.

In Jan. 2001, John Agyekum Kufuor was elected president. In 2002, he set up a National Reconciliation Commission to review human rights abuses during the country's period of military rule. He was reelected in Dec. 2004.

Greece

HELLENIC REPUBLIC

National name: Elliniki Dimokratia
President: Karolos Papoulias (2005)
Prime Minister: Kostas Karamanlis (2004)
Area: 50,942 sq mi (131,940 sq km)
Population (2005 est.): 10,668,354 (growth rate: 0.2%); birth rate: 9.7/1000; infant mortality rate: 5.5/1000; life expectancy: 79.1; density per sq mi: 209
Capital (2003 est.): Athens, 3,247,000 (metro. area), 747,300 (city proper). **Other large cities:** Thessaloníki, 361,200; Piraeus, 179,300; Patras, 167,000. **Monetary unit:** Euro (formerly drachma). **Languages:** Greek 99% (official), English, French. **Ethnicity/race:** Greek 98%, other 2%; note: the Greek government states there are no ethnic divisions in Greece. **Religions:** Greek Orthodox 98%, Islam 1.3%, other 0.7%. **Literacy rate:** 98% (2003 est.)
Economic summary: GDP/PPP (2004 est.): $226.4 billion; per capita $21,300. **Real growth rate:** 3.7%. **Inflation:** 2.9%. **Unemployment:** 10%. **Arable land:** 21%. **Agriculture:** wheat, corn, barley, sugar beets, olives, tomatoes, wine, tobacco, potatoes; beef, dairy products. **Labor force:** 4.4 million; agriculture 12%, industry 20%, services 68% (2004 est.). **Industries:** tourism; food and tobacco processing, textiles; chemicals, metal products; mining, petroleum. **Natural resources:** lignite, petroleum, iron ore, bauxite, lead, zinc, nickel, magnesite, marble, salt, hydropower potential. **Exports:** $15.5 billion (f.o.b., 2004 est.): food and beverages, manufactured goods, petroleum products, chemicals, textiles. **Imports:** $54.28 billion (f.o.b., 2004 est.): machinery, transport equipment, fuels, chemicals. **Major trading partners:** Germany, Italy, UK, U.S., Bulgaria, Cyprus, France, Russia, South Korea, Netherlands, Japan (2003).

Geography Located in southern Europe, Greece forms an irregular-shaped peninsula in the Mediterranean with two additional large peninsulas projecting from it: the Chalcidice and the Peloponnese. The Greek Islands are generally subdivided into two groups, according to location: the Ionian Islands (including Corfu, Cephalonia, and Leucas) west of the mainland and the Aegean Islands (including Euboea, Samos, Chios, Lesbos, and Crete) to the east and south. North-central Greece, Epirus, and western Macedonia are all mountainous. The main chain of the Pindus Mountains extends from northwest Greece to the Peloponnese. Mount Olympus, rising to 9,570 ft (2,909 m), is the highest point in the country.

Government Parliamentary republic.

History Indo-European peoples, including the Mycenaeans, began entering Greece about 2000 B.C. and set up sophisticated civilizations. About 1200 B.C., the Dorians, another Indo-European people, invaded Greece, and a dark age followed, known mostly through the Homeric epics. At the end of this time, classical Greece began to emerge (c. 750 B.C.) as a loose composite of city-states with a heavy involvement in maritime trade and a devotion to art, literature, politics, and philosophy. Greece reached the peak of its glory in the 5th century B.C., but the Peloponnesian War (431–404 B.C.) weakened the nation, and it was conquered by Philip II and his son Alexander the Great of Macedonia, who considered themselves Greek. By the middle of the 2nd century B.C., Greece had declined to the status of a Roman province. It remained within the eastern Roman Empire until Constantinople fell to the Crusaders in 1204. In 1453, the Turks took Constantinople and by 1460, Greece was a province in the Ottoman Empire. The Greek war of independence (immortalized by the poet Byron) began in 1821, and by 1827 Greece won independence with sovereignty guaranteed by Britain, France, and Russia.

The protecting powers chose Prince Otto of Bavaria as the first king of modern Greece in 1832 to reign over an area only slightly larger than the Peloponnese peninsula. Chiefly under the next king, George I, chosen by the protecting powers in 1863, Greece acquired much of its present territory. During his 57-year reign, a period in which he encouraged parliamentary democracy, Thessaly, Epirus, Macedonia, Crete, and most of the Aegean islands were added from the disintegrating Turkish empire. Unfavorable economic conditions forced about one-sixth of the entire Greek population to emigrate (mostly to the U.S.) in the late 19th and early 20th centuries. An unsuccessful war against Turkey after World War I brought down the monarchy, which was replaced by a republic in 1923.

Two military dictatorships and a financial crisis brought back the exiled king, George II, but only until 1941, when Italian and German invaders overcame tough Greek resistance. After British and Greek troops liberated the country in Oct. 1944, Communist guerrillas staged a long military campaign against the government; the Greek civil war, infamous for its brutality, began in Dec. 1944 and continued until Oct. 16, 1949, when the Communist guerrillas conceded defeat. The Greek government received U.S. aid under the Truman Doctrine, the predecessor of the Marshall Plan, to fight against the Communists.

Greece was a charter member of the UN and became a member of the North Atlantic Treaty Organization (NATO) in 1951. A military junta seized power in April 1967, sending young King Constantine II into exile. Col. George Papadopoulos, a leader of the junta, gradually attempted to modify his hard-line right-wing image. A coup ousted Papadopoulos in Nov. 1973.

A referendum in Dec. 1974, five months after the demise of the military dictatorship, ended the Greek monarchy and established a republic. Former premier Karamanlis returned from exile to become premier of Greece's first civilian government since 1967. Greece has continued to be ruled by freely elected civilian governments ever since. On Jan. 1, 1981, Greece became the 10th member of the European Union. Andreas Papandreou, son of former premier George Papandreou, founded the Panhellenic Socialist Movement (PASOK) and became Greece's first Socialist premier (1981–1989).

Greece continued to experience tensions with Turkey over a disputed, unpopulated 10-acre island and over Cyprus, which is divided into Greek and Turkish sectors.

The pro-Western Socialist prime minister Kostas Simitis (1996–2004) was credited with reviving the Greek economy. Still, *The Economist* magazine estimated in 2001 that it would be at least another 15 years before the per capita GDP in Greece comes close to the current EU average.

In the summer of 2002, the government was finally able to crack down on the 17 November (17N) terrorist organization, which had eluded the Greek authorities for the previous 27 years. The radical leftist group was responsible for more than 20 assassinations of American, British, and Greek diplomats, military personnel, and businessmen. Greece was criticized for decades by the international community for being soft on terrorism, and confidence in its ability to provide adequate security during the 2004 Olympics was weak. In parliamentary elections in March 2004, the conservative New Democracy Party swept to power, defeating Pasok, the ruling Socialist Party. The new prime minister, Kostas Karamanlis, vowed to deliver a safe and successful Olympics, and in spite of last-minute construction, the Athens Olympics was widely hailed as a triumph. It cost Greece $10 billion to hold the games.

Grenada

Sovereign: Queen Elizabeth II (1952)
Governor-General: Sir Daniel Williams (1996)
Prime Minister: Keith C. Mitchell (1995)
Area: 133 sq mi (344 sq km)
Population (2005 est.): 89,502 (growth rate 0.2%); birth rate: 22.3/1000; infant mortality rate: 14.6/1000; life expectancy: 64.5; density per sq mi: 674
Capital and largest city (2003 est.): St. George's, 4,300. **Monetary unit:** East Caribbean dollar.
Languages: English (official), French patois.
Ethnicity/race: black 82%, mixed black and European 13%, European and East Indian 5%, and trace of Arawak/Carib Amerindian. **Religions:** Roman Catholic 53%, Anglican 13.8%, other Protestant 33.2%.
Literacy rate: 90% (1970 est.)
Economic summary: GDP/PPP (2002 est.): $440 million; per capita $5,000. **Real growth rate:** 2.5%. **Inflation:** 2.8% (2001 est.). **Unemployment:** 12.5% (2000). **Arable land:** 6%. **Agriculture:** bananas, cocoa, nutmeg, mace, citrus, avocados, root crops, sugarcane, corn, vegetables. **Labor force:** 42,300 (1996); services 62%, agriculture 24%, industry 14% (1999 est.). **Industries:** food and beverages, textiles, light assembly operations, tourism, construction. **Natural resources:** timber, tropical fruit, deepwater harbors. **Exports:** $46 million (2002 est.): bananas, cocoa, nutmeg, fruit and vegetables, clothing, mace. **Imports:** $208 million (2002 est.): food, manufactured goods, machinery, chemicals, fuel. **Major trading partners:** U.S., Germany, Netherlands, St. Lucia, Antigua and Barbuda, UK, Dominica, Trinidad and Tobago, Japan (2003). **Member of Commonwealth of Nations**

Geography Grenada (the first "a" is a long vowel) is the most southerly of the Windward Islands, about 100 mi (161 km) from the Venezuelan coast. It is a volcanic island traversed by a mountain range, the highest peak of which is Mount St. Catherine (2,756 ft; 840 m).

Government Constitutional monarchy. A governor-general represents the sovereign, Elizabeth II.

History The Arawak Indians were the first to inhabit Grenada, but they were all eventually massacred by the Carib Indians. When Columbus arrived in 1498 he encountered the Caribs, who continued to rule over the island for another 150 years. The French gained control of the island in 1672 and held on to it until 1762, when the British invaded. Black slaves were granted freedom in 1833. After more than 200 years of British rule, most recently as part of the West Indies Associated States, Grenada became independent on Feb. 7, 1974, with Eric M. Gairy as prime minister.

In 1979, the Marxist New Jewel Movement staged a coup, and its leader, Maurice Bishop, became prime minister. Bishop, a protégé of Cuba's President Castro, was killed in a military coup on Oct. 19, 1983.

In an effort to establish order on the island and eliminate the Cuban military presence, U.S. president Ronald Reagan ordered an invasion of Grenada on Oct. 25, 1983, involving over 1,900 U.S. troops and a small military force from Barbados, Dominica, Jamaica, St. Lucia, and St. Vincent. The troops met strong resistance from Cuban military personnel on the island but soon occupied it. After a gradual withdrawal of peacekeeping forces, a centrist coalition led by Herbert A. Blaize won a parliamentary majority in 1984. The New National Party (NNP), led by Keith C. Mitchell, won a majority in the 1995 parliamentary elections. He won reelection again in 1999 and 2003.

In Sept. 2004, Grenada suffered the most damage of any country from Hurricane Ivan, which killed 39 and left thousands homeless. In July 2005, Hurricane Emily wreaked further destruction.

Guatemala

REPUBLIC OF GUATEMALA

National name: República de Guatemala
President: Oscar Berger (2004)
Area: 42,042 sq mi (108,890 sq km)
Population (2005 est.): 14,655,189 (growth rate: 2.6%); birth rate: 34.1/1000; infant mortality rate: 35.9/1000; life expectancy: 65.1; density per sq mi: 349
Capital and largest city (2003 est.): Guatemala City, 2,655,900 (metro. area), 1,128,800 (city proper). **Other large cities:** Mixco, 287,600; Villa Nueva, 138,900. **Monetary unit:** Quetzal. **Languages:** Spanish 60%, Amerindian languages 40% (23 officially recognized Amerindian languages, including Quiche, Cakchiquel, Kekchi, Mam, Garifuna, and Xinca). **Ethnicity/race:** Mestizo (Ladino)—mixed Amerindian-Spanish ancestry—55%, Amerindian (Mayan) or predominantly Amerindian 43%, whites and others 2%. **Religions:** Roman Catholic, Protestant, indigenous Mayan beliefs. **Literacy rate:** 71% (2003 est.)
Economic summary: GDP/PPP (2004 est.): $59.47 billion; per capita $4,200. **Real growth rate:** 2.6%. **Inflation:** 7.2%. **Unemployment:** 7.5% (2003 est.). **Arable land:** 13%. **Agriculture:** sugarcane, corn, bananas, coffee, beans, cardamom; cattle, sheep, pigs, chickens. **Labor force:** 3.68 million; agriculture 50%, industry 15%, services 35% (1999 est.). **Industries:** sugar, textiles and clothing, furniture, chemicals, petroleum, metals, rubber, tourism. **Natural resources:** petroleum, nickel, rare woods, fish, chicle, hydropower. **Exports:** $2.911 billion (f.o.b., 2004 est.): coffee, sugar, petroleum, apparel, bananas, fruits and vegetables, cardamom. **Imports:** $7.77 billion (f.o.b., 2004 est.): fuels, machinery and transport equipment, construction materials, grain, fertilizers, electricity. **Major trading partners:** U.S., El Salvador, Mexico, South Korea, China (2003).

Geography The northernmost of the Central American nations, Guatemala is the size of Tennessee. Its neighbors are Mexico on the north and west, and Belize, Honduras, and El Salvador on the east. The country consists of three main regions—the cool highlands with the heaviest population, the tropical area along the Pacific and Caribbean coasts, and the tropical jungle in the northern lowlands (known as the Petén).

Government Constitutional democratic republic.

History Once the site of the impressive ancient Mayan civilization, Guatemala was conquered by Spanish conquistador Pedro de Alvarado in 1524 and became a republic in 1839 after the United Provinces of Central America collapsed. From 1898 to 1920, dictator Manuel Estrada Cabrera ran the country, and from 1931 to 1944, Gen. Jorge Ubico Castaneda served as strongman.

After Ubico's overthrow in 1944 by the "October Revolutionaries," a group of left-leaning students and professionals, liberal-democratic coalitions led by Juan José Arévalo (1945–1951) and Jacobo Arbenz Guzmán (1951–1954) instituted social and political reforms that strengthened the peasantry and urban workers at the expense of the military and big landowners, like the U.S.-owned United Fruit Company. With covert U.S. backing, Col. Carlos Castillo Armas led a coup in 1954, and Arbenz took refuge in Mexico. A series of repressive regimes followed, and by 1960 the country was plunged into a civil war between military governments, right-wing vigilante groups, and leftist rebels that would last 36 years, the longest civil war in Latin American history. Death squads murdered an estimated 50,000 leftists and political opponents during the 1970s. In 1977, the U.S. cut off military aid to the country because of its egregious human rights abuses. The indigenous Mayan Indians were singled out for special brutality by the right-wing death squads. By the end of the war, 200,000 citizens were dead.

A succession of military juntas dominated during the civil war, until a new constitution was passed and civilian Marco Vinicio Cerezo Arévalo was elected and took office in 1986. He was followed by Jorge Serrano Elías in 1991. In 1993, Serrano moved to dissolve Congress and the Supreme Court and suspend constitutional rights, but the military deposed Serrano and allowed the inauguration of Ramiro de Leon Carpio, the former attorney general for human rights. A peace agreement was finally signed in Dec. 1996 by President Álvaro Arzú Irigoyen.

In 1999, a Guatemalan truth commission blamed the army for 93% of the atrocities and the rebels (the Guatemalan National Revolutionary Unit) for 3%. The former guerrillas apologized for their crimes, and President Clinton apologized for U.S. support of the right-wing military governments. The army has not acknowledged its guilt. Alfonso Portillo Cabrera, closely associated with the former dictatorship of Efrain Rios Montt (1982–1983), became president in Jan. 2000. In Aug. 2000, Portillo apologized for the former government's human rights abuses and pledged to prosecute those responsible and compensate victims.

In July 2003, the country's highest court ruled that former coup leader and military dictator Rios Montt, responsible for the massacre of tens of thousands of civilians during the civil war, was eligible to run for president in November. The ruling conflicted with the constitution, which bans anyone who seized power in a coup from running for the presidency. But in November, Rios Montt was soundly defeated by two candidates, conservative Oscar Berger and center-leftist Alvaro Colom. In the runoff election in December, Berger was elected president.

In 2004, Guatemala experienced an alarmingly violent crime wave. More than 2,000 murders took place, which were blamed on crime gangs and bands of teenagers.

In 2005, the government ratified a free-trade agreement (CAFTA) with the U.S.

Guinea

REPUBLIC OF GUINEA

National name: République de Guinée
President: Lansana Conté (1984)
Prime Minister: Cellou Dalein Diallo (2004)
Area: 94,925 sq mi (245,857 sq km)
Population (2005 est.): 9,467,866 (growth rate: 2.4%); birth rate: 42.0/1000; infant mortality rate: 90.4/1000; life expectancy: 49.9; density per sq mi: 100
Capital and largest city (2003 est.): Conakry, 1,767,200. **Monetary unit:** Guinean franc.
Languages: French (official), native tongues (Malinké, Susu, Fulani). **Ethnicity/race:** Peuhl 40%, Malinke 30%, Susu 20%, smaller tribes 10%. **Religions:** Islam 85%, Christian 8%, indigenous 7%. **Literacy rate:** 36% (1995 est.)
Economic summary: GDP/PPP (2004 est.): $19.5 billion; per capita $2,100. **Real growth rate:** 1%. **Inflation:** 18%. **Unemployment:** n.a. (2002 est.). **Arable land:** 4%. **Agriculture:** rice, coffee, pineapples, palm kernels, cassava (tapioca), bananas, sweet potatoes; cattle, sheep, goats; timber. **Labor force:** 3 million (1999); agriculture 80%, industry and services 20% (2000 est.). **Industries:** bauxite, gold, diamonds; alumina refining; light manufacturing and agricultural processing industries. **Natural resources:** bauxite, iron ore, diamonds, gold, uranium, hydropower, fish. **Exports:** $709.2 million (f.o.b., 2004 est.): bauxite, alumina, gold, diamonds, coffee, fish, agricultural products. **Imports:** $641.5 million (f.o.b., 2004 est.): petroleum products, metals, machinery, transport equipment, textiles, grain and other foodstuffs. **Major trading partners:** South Korea, Spain, U.S., Russia, France, Ireland, Belgium, Germany, Ukraine, China, Italy, Netherlands, UK, Côte d'Ivoire, India (2003).

Geography Guinea, in West Africa on the Atlantic, is also bordered by Guinea-Bissau, Senegal, Mali, Côte d'Ivoire, Liberia, and Sierra Leone. Slightly smaller than Oregon, the country consists of a coastal plain, a mountainous region, a savanna interior, and a forest area in the Guinea Highlands. The highest peak is Mount Nimba at 5,748 ft (1,752 m).

Government Republic.

History Beginning in 900, the Susu migrated from the north and began settling in the area that is now Guinea. The Susu civilization reached its height in the 13th century. Today the Susu make up about 20% of Guinea's population. From the 16th to the 19th century, the Fulani Empire dominated the region. In 1849, the French claimed it as a protectorate. First called Rivières du Sud, the protectorate was rechristened French Guinea, and finally, in 1895, it became part of French West Africa.

Guinea achieved independence on Oct. 2, 1958, and became an independent state with Sékou Touré as president. Under Touré, the country was the first avowedly Marxist state in Africa. Diplomatic relations with France were suspended in 1965, with the Soviet Union replacing France as the country's chief source of economic and technical assistance.

Prosperity came in 1960 after the start of exploitation of bauxite deposits. Touré was reelected to a seven-year term in 1974 and again in 1981. He died after 26 years as president in March 1984. A week later, a military regime headed by Col. Lansana Conté took power.

In 1989, President Conté announced that Guinea would move to a multiparty democracy, and in 1991, voters approved a new constitution. In Dec. 1993 elections, the president's Unity and Progress Party took almost 51% of the vote. In 2001, a government referendum was passed that eliminated presidential term limits, thus allowing Conté to run for a third term in 2003. Despite the trappings of multiparty rule, Conté has ruled the country with an iron fist.

Guinea has had ongoing difficulties with its neighbor Liberia, which was embroiled in a long civil war during the 1990s and again in 2000–2003. Guinea had taken sides against rebel leader Charles Taylor in Liberia's civil war and was part of the Nigerian-led ECOMOG forces that intervened in the crisis. As a consequence, President Conté's relations with Taylor remained sour after Taylor became Liberia's president in 1997. The fighting in Liberia spilled over the border into Guinea on several occasions. Sierra Leone's recent civil war also caused problems for neighboring Guinea. Already burdened by an inadequate infrastructure and a weak economy, an influx of nearly 300,000 refugees from Sierra Leone has overwhelmed the country.

In Dec. 2003 President Conté was reelected to a third term. In April 2004, after two months on the job, Prime Minister Lonseny Fall resigned and went into exile, claiming that the president would not allow him to govern effectively. President Conté is in poor health, and many fear a power struggle should he die or be deposed.

Guinea-Bissau

REPUBLIC OF GUINEA-BISSAU

National name: República da Guiné-Bissau
President: João Bernardo Vieira (2005)
Prime Minister: Carlos Gomes Júnior (2004)
Area: 13,946 sq mi (36,120 sq km)
Population (2005 est.): 1,416,027 (growth rate: 2.0%); birth rate: 37.6/1000; infant mortality rate: 107.2/1000; life expectancy: 47.0; density per sq mi: 102
Capital and largest city (2003 est.): Bissau, 296,900.
Monetary unit: CFA Franc. **Languages:** Portuguese (official), Criolo, African languages. **Ethnicity/race:** African 99% (Balanta 30%, Fula 20%, Manjaca 14%, Mandinga 13%, Papel 7%), European and mulatto less than 1%. **Religions:** indigenous beliefs 50%, Islam 45%, Christian 5%. **Literacy rate:** 42% (2002 est.)
Economic summary: GDP/PPP (2004 est.): $1.008 billion; per capita $700. **Real growth rate:** 2.6%. **Inflation:** 4% (2002 est.). **Unemployment:** n.a. (1998). **Arable land:** 11%. **Agriculture:** rice, corn, beans, cassava (tapioca), cashew nuts, peanuts, palm kernels, cotton; timber; fish. **Labor force:** 480,000 (1999); agriculture 82% (2000 est.). **Industries:** agricultural products processing, beer, soft drinks. **Natural resources:** fish, timber, phosphates, bauxite, clay, granite, limestone, unexploited deposits of petroleum. **Exports:** $54 million (f.o.b., 2002 est.): cashew nuts, shrimp, peanuts, palm kernels, sawn lumber. **Imports:** $104 million (f.o.b., 2002 est.): foodstuffs, machinery and transport equipment, petroleum products. **Major trading partners:** India, Nigeria, Italy, Senegal, Portugal, China, Spain (2003).

Geography A neighbor of Senegal and Guinea in West Africa, on the Atlantic coast, Guinea-Bissau is about half the size of South Carolina. The country is a low-lying coastal region of swamps, rain forests, and mangrove-covered wetlands, with about 25 islands off the coast.

Government Republic.

History The land now known as Guinea-Bissau was once the kingdom of Gabú, which was part of the larger Mali Empire. After 1546 Gabú became more autonomous, and at least portions of the kingdom existed until 1867. The first European to encounter Guinea-Bissau was the Portuguese explorer Nuño Tristão in 1446; colonists in the Cape Verde Islands obtained trading rights in the territory, and it became a center of the Portuguese slave trade. In 1879, the connection with the islands was broken.

The African Party for the Independence of Guinea-Bissau and Cape Verde (another Portuguese colony) was founded in 1956, and guerrilla warfare by nationalists grew increasingly effective. By 1974 the rebels controlled most of the countryside, where they formed a government that was soon recognized by scores of countries. The military coup in Portugal in April 1974 brightened the prospects for freedom, and in August the Lisbon government signed an agreement granting independence to the province. The new republic took the name Guinea-Bissau.

In Nov. 1980, João Bernardo Vieira headed a military coup that deposed Luis Cabral, president since 1974. In his 19 years of rule, Vieira was criticized for crony capitalism and corruption and for failing to alleviate the poverty of Guinea-Bissau, one of the world's poorest countries. Vieira also brought in troops from Senegal and the Republic of Guinea to help fight against an insurgency movement, a highly unpopular act. In May 1999 rebels deposed Vieira.

Following a period of military rule, Kumba Yalá, a former teacher and popular leader of Guinea-Bissau's independence movement, was elected president in 2000. In Sept. 2003 he was deposed in a military coup. Yalá's increasingly repressive measures and refusal to hold elections were cited as causes. In 2005, former president Vieira returned from six years of exile in Portugal and won the presidency in the July 2005 elections.

Guyana

COOPERATIVE REPUBLIC OF GUYANA

President: Bharrat Jagdeo (1999)
Prime Minister: Samuel Hinds (1999)
Area: 83,000 sq mi (214,970 sq km)
Population (2005 est.): 765,283 (growth rate: 0.3%); birth rate: 18.4/1000; infant mortality rate: 33.3/1000; life expectancy: 65.5; density per sq mi: 9
Capital and largest city (2003 est.): Georgetown, 227,700. **Monetary unit:** Guyanese dollar.
Languages: English (official), Amerindian dialects, Creole, Hindi, Urdu. **Ethnicity/race:** East Indian 50%; black 36%; Amerindian 7%; white, Chinese, and mixed 7%. **Religions:** Christian 50%, Hindu 35%, Islam 10%, other 5%. **Literacy rate:** 99% (2003 est.)
Economic summary: GDP/PPP (2004 est.): $2.899 billion; per capita $3,800. **Real growth rate:** 1.9%. **Inflation:** 4.5%. **Unemployment:** 9.1% (2000) (understated). **Arable land:** 2%. **Labor force:** 418,000 (2001 est.); agriculture n.a., industry n.a., services n.a. **Agriculture:** sugar, rice, wheat, vegetable oils; beef, pork, poultry, dairy products; fish, shrimp. **Industries:** bauxite, sugar, rice milling, timber, textiles, gold mining. **Natural resources:** bauxite, gold, diamonds, hardwood timber, shrimp, fish. **Exports:** $570.2 million (f.o.b., 2004 est.): sugar, gold, bauxite/alumina, rice, shrimp, molasses, rum, timber. **Imports:** $650.1 million (f.o.b., 2004 est.): manufactures, machinery, petroleum, food. **Major trading partners:** Canada, U.S., UK, Portugal, Belgium, Jamaica, Trinidad and Tobago, Italy, Cuba (2003). **Member of Commonwealth of Nations**

Geography Guyana is the size of Idaho and is situated on the northern coast of South America east of Venezuela, west of Suriname, and north of Brazil. A tropical forest covers more than 80% of the country.

Government Republic.

History The Warrou people were the indigenous inhabitants of Guyana. The Dutch, English, and French established colonies in what is now known as Guyana, but by the early 17th century the majority of the settlements were Dutch. During the Napoleonic wars Britain took over the Dutch colonies of Berbice, Demerara, and Essequibo, which became British Guiana in 1831.

Slavery was outlawed in 1834, and the great need for plantation workers led to a large wave of immigration, primarily of East Indians. Today, about half of the population is of East Indian descent and about 36% are of African descent.

In 1889, Venezuela voiced its claim to a large swath of Guyanese territory, but ten years later an international tribunal ruled the land belonged to British Guiana.

British Guiana became a Crown colony in 1928, and in 1953 it was granted home rule. In 1950, Cheddi Jagan, who was Indian-Guyanese, and Forbes Burnham, who was Afro-Guyanese, created the colony's first political party, the Progressive People's Party (PPP), which was dedicated to gaining the colony's independence. In the 1953 elections, Cheddi Jagan was elected chief minister. The British, however, alarmed by Jagan's Marxist views, suspended the constitution and government within months and installed an interim government. In 1955, the PPP split, with Burnham breaking off to create the People's National Congress (PNC). The leftist Jagan of the PPP and the more moderate Burnham of the PNC were to dominate Guyanan politics for decades to come. In 1961, Britain granted the colony autonomy, and Jagan became prime minister (1961–1964). Strikes and rioting weakened Jagan's rule, much of it believed to be the result of covert CIA operations. In 1964, Burnham succeeded Jagan as prime minister, a position he retained after the country gained full independence on May 26, 1966. With independence, the country returned to its traditional name, Guyana.

In 1978, the country gained worldwide attention when American religious cult leader Jim Jones and 900 of his followers committed mass suicide in Jonestown, Guyana.

Burnham ruled Guyana until his death in 1985 (from 1980 to 1985, after a change in the constitution, he served as president). Guyana's first independent decades were marked by continued racial unrest between Indian-Guyanese and Afro-Guyanese as well as economic malaise.

Desmond Hoyte of the PNC became president in 1985, but in 1992 the PPP reemerged, winning a majority in the general election. Jagan became president, and the former Marxist succeeded in reviving the economy. After his death in 1997, his wife, Janet Jagan, was elected president. Former finance minister Bharrat Jagdeo assumed the presidency in 1999.

Guyana's potential economic development was hurt in 2000 as border disputes with both Venezuela to the west and Suriname to the east heated up. Suriname and Guyana have been unable to resolve the border dispute in an oil-rich coastal area. Venezuela's president Hugo Chavez has revived the 19th-century claim to more than half of Guyana's territory.

In March 2001, Bharrat Jagdeo won a second term in elections that underscored Guyana's bitter racial tensions. The reelection of Jagdeo, an ethnic East Indian, caused rioting among Afro-Guyanese, who claimed widespread election fraud.

In Jan.–Feb. 2005, the country experienced its worst natural disaster. More than a third of the country's population was affected by devastating flooding.

Haiti

REPUBLIC OF HAITI

National name: République d'Haïti
President: Boniface Alexandre (interim) (2004)
Prime Minister: Gérard Latortue (interim) (2004)
Area: 10,714 sq mi (27,750 sq km)
Population (2005 est.): 8,121,622 (growth rate: 2.3%); birth rate: 36.6/1000; infant mortality rate: 73.5/1000; life expectancy: 52.9; density per sq mi: 758
Capital and largest city (2003 est.): Port-au-Prince, 1,764,000 (metro. area), 1,119,000 (city proper). **Monetary unit:** Gourde. **Languages:** Creole and French (both official). **Ethnicity/race:** black 95%, mulatto and white 5%. **Religions:** Roman Catholic 80%, Protestant 16% (Baptist 10%, Pentecostal 4%, Adventist 1%, other 1%), other 3%, none 1%. Note: roughly half the population practices Vaudou. **Literacy rate:** 53% (2003 est.)
Economic summary: GDP/PPP (2004 est.): $12.05 billion; per capita $1,500. **Real growth rate:** −3.5%. **Inflation:** 22%. **Unemployment:** widespread unemployment and underemployment; more than two-thirds of the labor force do not have formal jobs (2002 est.). **Arable land:** 28%. **Agriculture:** coffee, mangoes, sugarcane, rice, corn, sorghum, wood. **Labor force:** 3.6 million; note: shortage of skilled labor, unskilled labor abundant (1995); agriculture 66%, services 25%, industry 9%. **Industries:** sugar refining, flour milling, textiles, cement, light assembly industries based on imported parts. **Natural resources:** bauxite, copper, calcium carbonate, gold, marble, hydropower. **Exports:** $338.1 million (f.o.b., 2004 est.): manufactures, coffee, oils, cocoa, mangoes. **Imports:** $1.085 billion (f.o.b., 2004 est.): food, manufactured goods, machinery and transport equipment, fuels, raw materials. **Major trading partners:** U.S., Dominican Republic, Canada, Colombia (2003).

Geography Haiti, in the West Indies, occupies the western third of the island of Hispaniola, which it shares with the Dominican Republic. About the size of Maryland, Haiti is two-thirds mountainous, with the rest of the country marked by great valleys, extensive plateaus, and small plains.

Government Republic with an elected government.

History Explored by Columbus on Dec. 6, 1492, Haiti's native Arawaks fell victim to Spanish rule. In 1697, Haiti became the French colony of Saint-Dominique, which became a leading sugarcane producer dependent on slaves. In 1791, an insurrection erupted among the slave population of 480,000, resulting in a declaration of independence by Pierre-Dominique Toussaint l'Ouverture in 1801. Napoléon Bonaparte suppressed the independence movement, but it eventually triumphed in 1804 under Jean-Jacques Dessalines, who gave the new nation the Arawak name *Haiti*. It was the world's first independent black republic.

The revolution wrecked Haiti's economy. Years of strife between the light-skinned mulattos who dominated the economy and the majority black population, plus disputes with neighboring Santo Domingo, continued to hurt the nation's development. After a succession of dictatorships a bankrupt Haiti accepted a U.S. customs receivership from 1905 to 1941. Occupation by U.S. Marines from 1915 to 1934 brought stability. Haiti's high population growth made it the most densely populated nation in the hemisphere.

In 1949, after four years of democratic rule by President Dumarsais Estimé, dictatorship returned under Gen. Paul Magloire, who was succeeded by François Duvalier, nicknamed "Papa Doc," in 1957. Duvalier's secret police, the "Tontons Macoutes," ensured political stability with brutal efficiency. Upon Duvalier's death in 1971, his son, Jean-Claude, or "Baby Doc," succeeded as ruler of the poorest nation in the Western Hemisphere. In the early 1980s, Haiti became one of the first countries to face an AIDS epidemic. Fear of the disease caused tourists to stay away, and the tourist industry collapsed, causing rising unemployment. Unrest generated by the economic crisis forced Baby Doc to flee the country in 1986.

Throughout the 1990s the international community tried to establish democracy in Haiti. The country's first elected chief executive, Jean-Bertrand Aristide, a leftist Roman Catholic priest who seemed to promise a new era in Haiti, took office in Feb. 1991. The military, however, took control in a coup nine months later. A UN peacekeeping force, led by the U.S.—Operation Uphold Democracy—arrived in 1994. Aristide was restored to office and René Preval became his successor in 1996 elections. U.S. soldiers and UN peacekeepers left in 2000. Haiti's government, however, remained ineffectual and its economy was in ruins. Haiti has the highest rates of AIDS, malnutrition, and infant mortality in the region.

In 2000, former president Aristide was reelected president in elections boycotted by the opposition and questioned by many foreign observers. The U.S. and other countries threatened Haiti with sanctions unless democratic procedures were strengthened. Aristide, once a charismatic champion of democracy, grew more authoritarian and seemed incapable of improving the lot of his people. Violent protests rocked the country in Jan. 2004, the month of Haiti's bicentennial, with protesters demanding that Aristide resign. By February, a full-blown armed revolt was under way, and Aristide's hold on power continued to slip. The protests, groups of armed rebels, and French and American pressure led to the ousting of Aristide on Feb. 29. Thereafter a U.S.-led international force of 2,300 entered the chaos-engulfed country to attempt to restore order, and an interim government took over. In September, Hurricane Jeanne ravaged Haiti, killing more than 2,400 people. Lawlessness and gang violence were widespread, and the interim government had no control over parts of the country, which were run by armed former soldiers.

Honduras

REPUBLIC OF HONDURAS

National name: República de Honduras
President: Ricardo Maduro (2002)
Area: 43,278 sq mi (112,090 sq km)
Population (2005 est.): 6,975,204 (growth rate: 2.2%); birth rate: 30.4/1000; infant mortality rate: 29.3/1000; life expectancy: 65.6; density per sq mi: 161
Capital and largest city (2003 est.): Tegucigalpa, 1,436,000 (metro. area), 1,248,300 (city proper). **Monetary unit:** Lempira. **Languages:** Spanish (official), Amerindian dialects; English widely spoken in business. **Ethnicity/race:** mestizo 90%, Amerindian 7%, black 2%, white 1%. **Religions:** Roman Catholic 97%, growing population of evangelical Protestants. **Literacy rate:** 76% (2003 est.)
Economic summary: GDP/PPP (2004 est.): $18.79 billion; per capita $2,800. **Real growth rate:** 4.2%. **Inflation:** 7%. **Unemployment:** 28.5%. **Arable land:** 10%. **Agriculture:** bananas, coffee, citrus; beef; timber; shrimp. **Labor force:** 2.47 million; agriculture 34%, industry 21%, services 45% (2001 est.).

Industries: sugar, coffee, textiles, clothing, wood products. **Natural resources:** timber, gold, silver, copper, lead, zinc, iron ore, antimony, coal, fish, hydropower. **Exports:** $1.457 billion (f.o.b., 2004 est.): coffee, shrimp, bananas, gold, palm oil, fruit, lobster, lumber. **Imports:** $3.332 billion (f.o.b., 2004 est.): machinery and transport equipment, industrial raw materials, chemical products, fuels, foodstuffs (2000). **Major trading partners:** U.S., El Salvador, Guatemala, Mexico (2003).

Geography Honduras, in the north-central part of Central America, has a Caribbean as well as a Pacific coastline. Guatemala is to the west, El Salvador to the south, and Nicaragua to the east. The second-largest country in Central America, Honduras is slightly larger than Tennessee. Generally mountainous, the country is marked by fertile plateaus, river valleys, and narrow coastal plains.

Government Democratic constitutional republic.

History During the first millennium, Honduras was inhabited by the Maya. Columbus explored the country in 1502. Honduras, with four other Central American nations, declared its independence from Spain in 1821 to form a federation of Central American states. In 1838, Honduras left the federation and became independent. Political unrest rocked Honduras in the early 1900s, resulting in an occupation by U.S. Marines. Dictator Gen. Tiburcio Carias Andino established a strong government in 1932.

In 1969, El Salvador invaded Honduras after Honduran landowners deported several thousand Salvadorans. Five thousand people ultimately died in what is called "the football war" because it broke out during a soccer game between the two countries. By threatening economic sanctions and military intervention, the Organization of American States (OAS) induced El Salvador to withdraw. After a decade of military rule, parliamentary democracy returned with the election of Roberto Suazo Córdova as president in 1982. However, Honduras faced severe economic problems and tensions along its border with Nicaragua. "Contra" rebels, waging a guerrilla war against the Sandinista regime in Nicaragua, used Honduras as a training and staging area. The U.S. also used Honduras for military exercises and built bases to train Honduran and Salvadoran troops.

In 1997, Carlos Flores Facussé of the Liberal Party was elected president. He began to reform the economy and modernize the government. In recent years, Honduras has faced high unemployment, inflation, and economic over-dependence on coffee and bananas. In Oct. 1998, Hurricane Mitch killed some 13,000 Hondurans, left 2 million homeless, and caused more than $5 billion in damage.

In 2002, Ricardo Maduro became president, promising to lessen crime and corruption, but his hard-line efforts, growing increasingly more repressive, have not improved these problems.

In March 2005, the nation's Congress ratified a free-trade agreement (CAFTA) with the U.S.

Hungary

REPUBLIC OF HUNGARY

National name: Magyar Köztársaság
President: László Sólyom (2005)
Prime Minister: Ferenc Gyurcsány (2004)
Area: 35,919 sq mi (93,030 sq km)
Population (2005 est.): 10,006,835 (growth rate: –0.3%); birth rate: 9.8/1000; infant mortality rate: 8.6/1000; life expectancy: 72.4; density per sq mi: 279

Capital and largest city (2003 est.): Budapest, 2,597,000 (metro. area), 1,769,500 (city proper). **Other large cities:** Debrecen, 210,500; Miskolc, 182,600; Szeged, 173,200; Pécs, 163,900. **Monetary unit:** Forint. **Languages:** Magyar (Hungarian) 98.2%, other 1.8%. **Ethnicity/race:** Hungarian 89.9%, Roma 4%, German 2.6%, Serb 2%, Slovak 0.8%, Romanian 0.7%. **Religions:** Roman Catholic 67.5%, Calvinist 20%, Lutheran 5%, atheist and others 7.5%. **Literacy rate:** 99% (2003 est.)

Economic summary: GDP/PPP (2004 est.): $149.3 billion; per capita $14,900. **Real growth rate:** 3.9%. **Inflation:** 7%. **Unemployment:** 5.9%. **Arable land:** 50%. **Agriculture:** wheat, corn, sunflower seed, potatoes, sugar beets; pigs, cattle, poultry, dairy products. **Labor force:** 4.17 million; agriculture 6.2%, industry 27.1%, services 66.7% (2002). **Industries:** mining, metallurgy, construction materials, processed foods, textiles, chemicals (especially pharmaceuticals), motor vehicles. **Natural resources:** bauxite, coal, natural gas, fertile soils, arable land. **Exports:** $54.62 billion (f.o.b., 2004 est.): machinery and equipment 61.1%, other manufactures 28.7%, food products 6.5%, raw materials 2%, fuels and electricity 1.6% (2003). **Imports:** $58.68 billion (f.o.b., 2004 est.): machinery and equipment 51.6%, other manufactures 35.7%, fuels and electricity 7.7%, food products 3.1%, raw materials 2.0% (2003). **Major trading partners:** Germany, Austria, Italy, France, UK, Netherlands, China, Russia, Japan (2003).

Geography This central European country is the size of Indiana. Most of Hungary is a fertile, rolling plain lying east of the Danube River and drained by the Danube and Tisza rivers. In the extreme northwest is the Little Hungarian Plain. South of that area is Lake Balaton (250 sq mi; 648 sq km).

Government Parliamentary democracy.

History By 14 B.C., western Hungary was part of the Roman Empire's provinces of Pannonia and Dacia. The area east of the Danube was never part of the Roman Empire and was largely occupied by various Germanic and Asiatic peoples. In 896 all of Hungary was invaded by the Magyars, who founded a kingdom. Christianity was accepted during the reign of Stephen I (St. Stephen), 977–1038. A devastating invasion by the Mongols killed half of Hungary's population in 1241. The peak of Hungary's great period of medieval power came during the reign of Louis I the Great (1342–1382), whose dominions touched the Baltic, Black, and Mediterranean seas. War with the Turks broke out in 1389, and for more than 100 years the Turks advanced through the Balkans. When the Turks smashed a Hungarian army in 1526, western and northern Hungary accepted Hapsburg rule to escape Turkish occupation. Transylvania became independent under Hungarian princes. Intermittent war with the Turks was waged until a peace treaty was signed in 1699.

After the suppression of the 1848 revolt, led by Louis Kossuth, against Hapsburg rule, the dual monarchy of Austria-Hungary was set up in 1867. The dual monarchy was defeated with the other Central Powers in World War I. After a short-lived republic in 1918, the chaotic Communist rule of 1919 under Béla Kun ended with the Romanians occupying Budapest on Aug. 4, 1919. When the Romanians left, Adm. Nicholas Horthy entered the capital with a national army. The Treaty of Trianon of June 4, 1920, by which the Allies parceled out Hungarian territories, cost Hungary 68% of its land and 58% of its population.

In World War II, Hungary allied with Germany, which aided the country in recovering lost territories. Following the German invasion of Russia on June 22,

1941, Hungary joined the attack against the Soviet Union, but withdrew in defeat from the eastern front by May 1943. Germany occupied the country for the remainder of the war and set up a puppet government. Hungarian Jews and Gypsies were sent to death camps. The German regime was driven out by the Soviets in 1944–1945.

By the Treaty of Paris (1947), Hungary had to give up all territory it had acquired since 1937 and to pay $300 million in reparations to the USSR, Czechoslovakia, and Yugoslavia. In 1948, the Communist Party, with the support of Soviet troops, seized control. Hungary was proclaimed a People's Republic and one-party state in 1949. Industry was nationalized, the land collectivized into state farms, and the opposition terrorized by the secret police. The terror, modeled after that of the USSR, reached its height with the trial and life imprisonment of József Cardinal Mindszenty, the leader of Hungary's Roman Catholics, in 1948. On Oct. 23, 1956, an anti-Communist revolution broke out in Budapest. To cope with it, the Communists set up a coalition government and called former prime minister Imre Nagy back to head the government. But he and most of his ministers sympathized with the anti-Communist opposition, and he declared Hungary a neutral power, withdrawing from the Warsaw Treaty and appealing to the United Nations for help. One of his ministers, János Kádár, established a counterregime and asked the USSR to send in military power. Soviet troops and tanks suppressed the revolution in bloody fighting after 190,000 people had fled the country. Under Kádár (1956–1988), Communist Hungary maintained more liberal policies in the economic and cultural spheres, and Hungary became the most liberal of the Soviet-bloc nations of eastern Europe. Continuing his program of national reconciliation, Kádár emptied prisons, reformed the secret police, and eased travel restrictions.

In 1989, Hungary's Communists abandoned their monopoly on power voluntarily, and the constitution was amended in Oct. 1989 to allow for a multiparty state. The last Soviet troops left Hungary in June 1991, thereby ending almost 47 years of military presence. The transition to a market economy proved difficult. In April 1999, Hungary became part of NATO, and in May 2004, it joined the EU. In 2005, László Sólyom was selected president in 2005, a largely ceremonial post.

Iceland

REPUBLIC OF ICELAND

National name: Lydveldid Island
President: Ólafur Ragnar Grímsson (2004)
Prime Minister: Halldór Ásgrímsson (2004)
Area: 39,768 sq mi (103,000 sq km)[1]
Population (2005 est.): 296,737 (growth rate: 0.9%); birth rate: 13.7/1000; infant mortality rate: 3.3/1000; life expectancy: 80.2; density per sq mi: 7
Capital and largest city (2003 est.): Reykjavik, 184,200 (metro. area), 114,800 (city proper). **Monetary unit:** Icelandic króna. **Languages:** Icelandic, English, Nordic languages, German widely spoken. **Ethnicity/race:** homogeneous mixture of Norse/Celtic descendants 94%, population of foreign origin 6%. **Religions:** Church of Iceland (Evangelical Lutheran) 87.1%, other Protestant 4.1%, Roman Catholic 1.7%, other 7.1% (2002). **Literacy rate:** 100% (1997 est.)
Economic summary: GDP/PPP (2004 est.): $9.373 billion; per capita $31,900. **Real growth rate:** 1.8%. **Inflation:** 4%. **Unemployment:** 3.1%. **Arable land:** 0.07%. **Agriculture:** potatoes, green vegetables, mutton, dairy products, fish. **Labor force:** 158,100; agriculture, fishing and fish processing 10.3%, industry

18.3%, services 71.4% (2003). **Industries:** fish processing; aluminum smelting, ferrosilicon production, geothermal power; tourism. **Natural resources:** fish, hydropower, geothermal power, diatomite. **Exports:** $2.902 billion (f.o.b., 2004 est.): fish and fish products 70%, aluminum, animal products, ferrosilicon, diatomite. **Imports:** $3.307 billion (2004 est.): machinery and equipment, petroleum products; foodstuffs, textiles. **Major trading partners:** UK, Germany, Netherlands, U.S., Spain, Denmark, Norway, France, Sweden, Italy (2003).

1. Including some offshore islands.

Geography Iceland, an island about the size of Kentucky, lies in the north Atlantic Ocean east of Greenland and just touches the Arctic Circle. It is one of the most volcanic regions in the world. More than 13% is covered by snowfields and glaciers, and most of the people live in the 7% of the island that is made up of fertile coastland. The Gulf Stream keeps Iceland's climate milder than one would expect from an island near the Arctic Circle.

Government Constitutional republic.

History The earliest inhabitants of Iceland were Irish hermits, who left the island upon the arrival of the pagan Norse people in the late 9th century. A constitution drawn up c. 930 created a form of democracy and provided for an *Althing*, the world's oldest practicing legislative assembly. The island's early history was preserved in the Icelandic sagas of the 13th century.

In 1262–1264, Iceland came under Norwegian rule and passed to ultimate Danish control through the unification of the kingdoms of Norway, Sweden, and Denmark (the Kalmar Union) in 1397.

In 1874, Icelanders obtained their own constitution, and in 1918, Denmark recognized Iceland, via the Act of Union, as a separate state with unlimited sovereignty. It remained, however, nominally under the Danish monarchy.

During the German occupation of Denmark in World War II, British, then American, troops occupied Iceland and used it for a strategic air base. While officially neutral, Iceland cooperated with the Allies throughout the conflict. On June 17, 1944, after a popular referendum, the Althing proclaimed Iceland an independent republic.

The country joined the North Atlantic Treaty Organization in 1949 and subsequently received an American air force base in 1951. In 1970, it was admitted to the European Free Trade Association. Iceland unilaterally extended its territorial fishing limit from 3 to 200 nautical miles in 1972, precipitating a dispute with the UK known as the "cod wars," which ended in 1976 when the UK recognized the new limits. In 1980, the Icelanders elected a woman to the office of the presidency, the first elected female chief of state (i.e., president as distinct from prime minister) in the world. After the recession of the early 1990s, Iceland's economy rebounded.

At the International Whaling Commission meeting in July 2001, Iceland refused to agree to the continuation of the moratorium on commercial whaling that had been in effect since 1986. In 2003, after a 14-year lull, the country began hunting whales for scientific research.

In May 2003, David Oddsson was reelected, making him the longest-serving prime minister in Europe. In 2004, in a prearranged agreement made between the two parties of the coalition government, Oddsson and Foreign Minister Halldór Ásgrímsson switched positions.

India

REPUBLIC OF INDIA

National name: Bharat
President: A.P.J. Abdul Kalam (2002)
Prime Minister: Manmohan Singh (2004)
Area: 1,269,338 sq mi (3,287,590 sq km)
Population (2005 est.): 1,080,264,388 (growth rate:
1.4%); birth rate: 22.3/1000; infant mortality rate:
56.3/1000; life expectancy: 64.3; density per sq mi: 851
Capital (2003 est.): New Delhi, 17,037,900 (metro.
  area), 10,203,700 (city proper). **Largest cities:**
Bombay (Mumbai), 17,012,100 (metro. area),
12,383,100 (city proper); Calcutta (Kolkata), 14,090,200
(metro. area), 4,760,800 (city proper); Bangalore,
4,461,100; Madras (Chennai), 4,382,100; Ahmedabad,
3,653,700; Hyderabad, 3,585,600; Kanpur, 2,631,800.
Monetary unit: Rupee. **Principal languages:** Hindi
(official), English (official), Bengali, Gujarati, Kashmiri,
Malayalam, Marathi, Oriya, Punjabi, Tamil, Telugu,
Urdu, Kannada, Assamese, Sanskrit, Sindhi (all
recognized by the constitution). Dialects, 1,600+.
Ethnicity/race: Indo-Aryan 72%, Dravidian 25%,
Mongoloid and other 3% (2000). **Religions:** Hindu
81.3%, Islam 12%, Christian 2.3%, Sikh 1.9%, other
(including Buddhists, Jains, and Parsis) 2.5%. **Literacy
rate:** 60% (2003 est.)
Economic summary: GDP/PPP (2004 est.): $3.319
trillion; per capita $3,100. **Real growth rate:** 6.2%.
Inflation: 4.2%. **Unemployment:** 9.2%. **Arable land:**
54%. **Agriculture:** rice, wheat, oilseed, cotton, jute,
tea, sugarcane, potatoes; cattle, water buffalo, sheep,
goats, poultry; fish. **Labor force:** 482.2 million;
agriculture 60%, services 23%, industry 17% (1999).
Industries: textiles, chemicals, food processing, steel,
transportation equipment, cement, mining, petroleum,
machinery, software. **Natural resources:** coal
(fourth-largest reserves in the world), iron ore,
manganese, mica, bauxite, titanium ore, chromite,
natural gas, diamonds, petroleum, limestone, arable
land. **Exports:** $69.18 billion (f.o.b., 2004 est.): textile
goods, gems and jewelry, engineering goods,
chemicals, leather manufactures. **Imports:** $89.33
billion (f.o.b., 2004 est.): crude oil, machinery, gems,
fertilizer, chemicals. **Major trading partners:** U.S.,
UAE, Hong Kong, UK, China, Germany, Belgium
(2003). **Member of Commonwealth of Nations**

Geography One-third the area of the United States,
the Republic of India occupies most of the subcontinent of India in southern Asia. It borders on China in
the northeast. Other neighbors are Pakistan on the
west, Nepal and Bhutan on the north, and Burma and
Bangladesh on the east.
The country can be divided into three distinct geographic regions: the Himalayan region in the north,
which contains some of the highest mountains in the
world, the Gangetic Plain, and the plateau region in the
south and central part. Its three great river systems
have extensive deltas and all rise in the Himalayas: the
Ganges, the Indus, and the Brahmaputra.

Government Federal republic.

History One of the earliest civilizations, the Indus
Valley civilization flourished on the Indian subcontinent from c. 2600 B.C. to c. 2000 B.C. It is generally
accepted that the Aryans entered India c. 1500 B.C.
from the northwest, finding a land that was already
home to an advanced civilization. They introduced
Sanskrit and the Vedic religion, a forerunner of Hinduism. Buddhism was founded in the 6th century B.C.
and was spread throughout northern India, most notably by one of the great ancient kings of the Mauryan

dynasty, Asoka (c. 269–232 B.C.), who also unified
most of the Indian subcontinent for the first time.
In 1526, Muslim invaders founded the great Mogul
Empire, centered on Delhi, which lasted, at least in
name, until 1857. Akbar the Great (1542–1605)
strengthened and consolidated this empire. The long
reign of his great-grandson, Aurangzeb (1618–1707),
represents both the greatest extent of the Mogul
Empire and the beginning of its decay.
Vasco da Gama, the Portuguese explorer, landed in
India in 1498, and for the next 100 years the Portuguese had a virtual monopoly on trade with the subcontinent. Meanwhile, the English founded the East India
Company, which set up its first factory at Surat in 1612
and began expanding its influence, fighting the Indian
rulers and the French, Dutch, and Portuguese traders
simultaneously.
Bombay, taken from the Portuguese, became the seat
of English rule in 1687. The defeat of French and
Mogul armies by Lord Clive in 1757 laid the foundation
of the British Empire in India. The East India Company
continued to suppress native uprisings and extend British rule until 1858, when the administration of India
was formally transferred to the British Crown following
the Sepoy Mutiny of native troops in 1857–1858.
After World War I, in which the Indian states sent
more than 6 million troops to fight beside the Allies,
Indian nationalist unrest rose to new heights under the
leadership of a Hindu lawyer, Mohandas K. Gandhi,
called Mahatma Gandhi. His philosophy of civil disobedience called for nonviolent noncooperation against
British authority. He soon became the leading spirit of
the Indian National Congress Party, which was the
spearhead of revolt. In 1919, the British gave added
responsibility to Indian officials, and in 1935, India was
given a federal form of government and a measure of
self-rule.
In 1942, with the Japanese pressing hard on the eastern borders of India, the British War Cabinet tried and
failed to reach a political settlement with nationalist
leaders. The Congress Party took the position that the
British must quit India. Fearing mass civil disobedience, the government of India carried out widespread
arrests of Congress leaders, including Gandhi.
Gandhi was released in 1944 and negotiations for a
settlement were resumed. Finally, in Aug. 1947, India
gained full independence. The victory was soured,
however, by the partitioning of the predominantly
Muslim regions of the north into the separate nation
of Pakistan. The Muslim League, led by Mohammed
Ali Jinnah, demanded a separate nation for the Muslim minority to prevent Hindu political and social
domination. Indian Hindus, however, had hoped for a
unified rather than balkanized Indian subcontinent.
Lord Mountbatten as viceroy partitioned India along
religious lines and split the provinces of Bengal and
the Punjab, which both nations claimed. The partition
of Pakistan and India led to the largest migration in
human history, with 17 million people fleeing across
the borders in both directions to escape the bloody
riots occurring among sectarian groups. Armed conflict also broke out over rival claims to the princely
states of Jammu and Kashmir.
Jawaharlal Nehru, nationalist leader and head of the
Congress Party, was made prime minister. In 1949, a
constitution was approved, making India a sovereign
republic. Under a federal structure the states were organized on linguistic lines. The dominance of the Congress Party contributed to stability. In 1956, the republic absorbed former French settlements. Five years
later, the republic forcibly annexed the Portuguese
enclaves of Goa, Damao, and Diu.

Nehru died in 1964. His successor, Lal Bahadur Shastri, died on Jan. 10, 1966. Nehru's daughter, Indira Gandhi, became prime minister, and she continued his policy of nonalignment.

In 1971, the Pakistani army moved in to quash the independence movement in East Pakistan that was supported by India, and some 10 million Bengali refugees poured across the border into India, creating social, economic, and health problems. After numerous border incidents, India invaded East Pakistan and in two weeks forced the surrender of the Pakistani army. East Pakistan was established as an independent state and renamed Bangladesh.

In May 1975, the 300-year-old kingdom of Sikkim became a full-fledged Indian state. Situated in the Himalayas, Sikkim was a virtual dependency of Tibet until the early 19th century. Under an 1890 treaty between China and Great Britain, it became a British protectorate and was made an Indian protectorate after Britain quit the subcontinent.

In the summer of 1975, the world's largest democracy veered suddenly toward authoritarianism when a judge in Allahabad, Indira Gandhi's home constituency, found Gandhi's landslide victory in the 1971 elections invalid because civil servants had illegally aided her campaign. Amid demands for her resignation, Gandhi decreed a state of emergency on June 26 and ordered mass arrests of her critics, including all opposition party leaders except the Communists.

Despite strong opposition to her repressive measures, particularly resentment against compulsory birth control programs, in 1977 Gandhi announced parliamentary elections for March. At the same time, she freed most political prisoners. The landslide victory of Morarji R. Desai unseated Gandhi, but she staged a spectacular comeback in the elections of Jan. 1980.

In 1984, Gandhi ordered the Indian army to root out a band of Sikh holy men and gunmen who were using the most sacred shrine of the Sikh religion, the Golden Temple in Amritsar, as a base for terrorist raids in a violent campaign for greater political autonomy in the strategic Punjab border state. The perceived sacrilege to the Golden Temple kindled outrage among many of India's 14 million Sikhs and brought a spasm of mutinies and desertions by Sikh officers and soldiers in the army.

On Oct. 31, 1984, Indira Gandhi was assassinated by two men identified by police as Sikh members of her bodyguard. The ruling Congress Party chose her older son, Rajiv Gandhi, to succeed her as prime minister for four years. While running for reelection, Rajiv Gandhi was assassinated on May 22, 1991, by Tamil militants who objected to India's mediation of the civil war in Sri Lanka.

The ruling Congress Party lost the parliamentary elections of May 1996, and its waning resulted in a period of political instability. The Hindu nationalist Bharatiya Janata Party (BJP) then became the dominant force in politics, with Atal Bihari Vajpayee as prime minister.

In May 1998, India set off five nuclear tests, surprising the international community, which widely condemned India's pronuclear stance. Despite international urging for restraint, Pakistan responded by conducting several nuclear tests of its own two weeks later. India has resisted signing the Comprehensive Test Ban Treaty for nuclear weapons and has been slapped with sanctions by the U.S. and other countries. Less than a year later, in April 1999, both India and Pakistan tested nuclear-capable ballistic missiles.

India and Pakistan have held various talks about the disputed territory of Kashmir, which is the issue at the base of their chronic antagonism and their displays of nuclear strength. India controls two-thirds of this Himalayan region, which is the only Indian state that is predominantly Muslim.

The Indian Air Force launched air strikes on May 26, 1999, and later sent in ground troops against Islamic guerrilla forces in Kashmir. India blamed Pakistan for orchestrating violence in Kashmir by sending soldiers and mercenaries across the so-called Line of Control that divides Kashmir between India and Pakistan. Pakistan countered that the guerrillas were independent Kashmiri freedom fighters struggling for India's ouster from the region. Most international sources agreed with India's assumption that Pakistan was arming the soldiers. In Aug. 1999, Pakistan was forced to withdraw, but fighting continued sporadically during the coming year.

In Oct. 2001, violence again broke out in the region when a suicide bombing by a Pakistan-based militant organization killed 38 in India-controlled Kashmir. India retaliated with heavy shelling across the Line of Control. India, angered by Washington's sudden coziness to Pakistan following the Sept. 11 attacks, took the opportunity to point out that while Pakistan might be helping the U.S. fight terrorism on the Afghan front, it was simultaneously supporting terrorism on its own borders with India. On Dec. 13, 2001, suicide bombers attacked the Indian Parliament, killing 14 people. Indian officials blamed the deadly attack on Islamic militants supported by Pakistan.

Hope for a peaceful solution to the conflict in Kashmir was raised Nov. 2002, when a newly elected coalition government in India-controlled Jammu and Kashmir vowed to reach out to separatists and to improve conditions in the state. But hopes were dashed in March 2003, following the slaughter of 24 Hindus in Indian-controlled Kashmir. Officials blamed the massacre on Islamic militants. Days after the violence, both India and Pakistan test-fired short-range missiles capable of carrying nuclear warheads. Two bombs exploded in Bombay in August, killing more than 50 people and injuring about 150. Indian officials blamed Lashkar-e-Taiba, a Pakistan-based militant Islamic group. But in Nov. 2003, India and Pakistan declared their first formal cease-fire in 14 years. The cease-fire applied to the entire Line of Control dividing Kashmir. Relations have continued to thaw between the two countries. Three rounds of bilateral talks took place in 2004. While no real progress on the stalemate was made, both governments have agreed to implement confidence-building measures. In addition, the two sides agreed to open a bus service in April 2005 between the two capitals of Kashmir—Srinagar on the Indian side and Pakistan's Muzaffarabad. Despite an attempt by armed militants to foil the opening by setting fire to the Tourism Reception Center, a building that held the first passengers, families that have been separated by the Line of Control since 1947 were reunited when buses successfully crossed the Peace Bridge.

In one of the most dramatic political upsets in modern Indian history, the Indian National Congress Party, led by Sonia Gandhi, prevailed in parliamentary elections in May 2004, prompting Prime Minister Atal Bihari Vajpayee to resign. Although the country prospered economically under Vajpayee's rule, a substantial number of India's poor felt they had not benefitted from India's economic growth. Sonia Gandhi, the Italian-born widow of former prime minister Rajiv Gandhi, dealt a further shock to the country when she refused to become prime minister. The BJP had vociferously protested Gandhi's expected elevation to prime minister because of her foreign birth. The Congress Party instead chose former finance minister Manmohan Singh, who became India's first Sikh prime minister.

On Dec. 26, 2004, a tremendously powerful tsunami ravaged 12 Asian countries. Nearly 11,000 people perished in India.

President Bush announced in March 2005 that he would allow American companies to provide India with several types of modern combat weapons, including F-16 and F-18 fighter jets. The announcement was seen as an attempt to balance Bush's offer to sell Pakistan about two dozen F-16s.

President Bush and Manmohan Singh reached an agreement in July 2005 that would allow India to seek outside help in developing its civilian nuclear power program while maintaining its nuclear weapons. In addition, India would submit the civilian program, but not its weapons program, to inspections. The accord departs from an "atoms for peace" program that dates to the Eisenhower, administration, which bans countries with nuclear weapons from buying nuclear fuel and equipment from foreign countries.

Monsoon rains in late July and early August 2005 caused devastating landslides and floods that killed about 900 people in and around Bombay.

Indonesia

REPUBLIC OF INDONESIA

National name: Republik Indonesia
President: Susilo Bambang Yudhoyono (2004)
Area: 741,096 sq mi (1,919,440 sq km)
Population (2005 est.): 241,973,879 (growth rate: 1.5%); birth rate: 20.7/1000; infant mortality rate; 35.6/1000; life expectancy: 69.6; density per sq mi: 327
Capital and largest city (2003 est.): Jakarta, 17,891,000 (metro. area), 8,827,900 (city proper).
Other large cities: Surabaya, 3,038,800; Bandung, 2,733,500; Medan, 2,204,300; Semarang, 1,267,100.
Monetary unit: Rupiah. **Languages:** Bahasa Indonesia (official), English, Dutch, Javanese, and more than 580 other languages and dialects.
Ethnicity/race: Javanese 45%, Sundanese 14%, Madurese 7.5%, coastal Malays 7.5%, other 26%.
Religions: Islam 88%, Protestant 5%, Roman Catholic 3%, Hindu 2%, Buddhist 1%, other 1%. **Literacy rate:** 89% (2003 est.)
Economic summary: GDP/PPP (2004 est.): $827.4 billion; per capita $3,500. **Real growth rate:** 4.9%. **Inflation:** 6.1%. **Unemployment:** 9.2%. **Arable land:** 11%. **Agriculture:** rice, cassava (tapioca), peanuts, rubber, cocoa, coffee, palm oil, copra, poultry, beef, pork, eggs. **Labor force:** 111.5 million; agriculture 45%, industry 16%, services 39% (1999 est.)
Industries: petroleum and natural gas, textiles, apparel, footwear, mining, cement, chemical fertilizers, plywood, rubber, food, tourism. **Natural resources:** petroleum, tin, natural gas, nickel, timber, bauxite, copper, fertile soils, coal, gold, silver. **Exports:** $69.86 billion (f.o.b., 2004 est.): oil and gas, electrical appliances, plywood, textiles, rubber. **Imports:** $45.07 billion (f.o.b., 2004 est.): machinery and equipment; chemicals, fuels, foodstuffs. **Major trading partners:** Japan, U.S., Singapore, South Korea, China, Thailand, Australia, Saudi Arabia (2003).

Geography Indonesia is an archipelago in Southeast Asia consisting of 17,000 islands (6,000 inhabited) and straddling the equator. The largest islands are Sumatra, Java (the most populous), Bali, Kalimantan (Indonesia's part of Borneo), Sulawesi (Celebes), the Nusa Tenggara islands, the Moluccas Islands, and Irian Jaya (also called West Papua), the western part of New Guinea. Its neighbor to the north is Malaysia and to the east is Papua New Guinea.

Indonesia, part of the "ring of fire," has the largest number of active volcanoes in the world. Earthquakes are frequent. Wallace's line, a zoological demarcation between Asian and Australian flora and fauna, divides Indonesia.

Government Republic.

History The 17,000 islands that make up Indonesia were home to a diversity of cultures and indigenous beliefs when the islands came under the influence of Hindu priests and traders in the first and second centuries A.D. Muslim invasions began in the 13th century, and most of the archipelago had converted to Islam by the 15th century. Portuguese traders arrived early in the next century but were ousted by the Dutch around 1595. The Dutch United East India Company established posts on the island of Java, in an effort to control the spice trade.

After Napoléon subjugated the Netherlands in 1811, the British seized the islands but returned them to the Dutch in 1816. In 1922, Indonesia was made an integral part of the Dutch kingdom. During World War II, Japan seized the islands. Tokyo was primarily interested in Indonesia's oil, which was vital to the war effort, and tolerated fledgling nationalists such as Sukarno and Mohammed Hatta. After Japan's surrender, Sukarno and Hatta proclaimed Indonesian independence on Aug. 17, 1945. Allied troops, mostly British Indian forces, fought nationalist militias to reassert the prewar status quo until the arrival of Dutch troops.

In Nov. 1946, a draft agreement on forming a Netherlands-Indonesian Union was reached, but differences in interpretation resulted in more fighting between Dutch and nationalist forces. Following a bitter war for independence, leaders on both sides agreed to terms of a union on Nov. 2, 1949. The transfer of sovereignty took place in Amsterdam on Dec. 27, 1949. In Feb. 1956, Indonesia abrogated the union and began seizing Dutch property in the islands.

In 1963, Netherlands New Guinea (the Dutch portion of the island of New Guinea) was transferred to Indonesia and renamed West Irian, which became Irian Jaya in 1973 and West Papua in 2000. Hatta and Sukarno, the cofathers of Indonesian independence, split over Sukarno's concept of "guided democracy," and under Sukarno's rule the Indonesian Communist Party (PKI) steadily increased its influence.

Sukarno was named president for life in 1966. Sukarno enjoyed mass support for his policies, but a growing power struggle between the military and the PKI loomed over his government. After an attempted military coup was put down by army chief of staff General Suharto and officers loyal to him, Suharto's forces killed hundreds of thousands of suspected Communists in a massive purge aimed at undermining Sukarno's rule.

Suharto took over the reins of government and gradually eased Sukarno out of office, completing his consolidation of power in 1967. Under Suharto the military assumed an overarching role in national affairs, and relations with the West were enhanced. Indonesia's economy improved dramatically and national elections were permitted, although the opposition was so tightly controlled as to virtually choke off dissent.

In 1975, Indonesia invaded the former Portuguese half of the island of Timor; it seized the territory in 1976. A separatist movement developed at once. Unlike the rest of Indonesia, which had been a Dutch colony, East Timor was governed by the Portuguese for 400 years, and while 90% of Indonesians are Muslim, the East Timorese are primarily Catholic. More than 200,000 Timorese are reported to have died from famine, disease, and fighting since the annexation. In 1996, two East Timorese resistance activists, Bishop Carlos Filipe Ximenes Belo and José Ramos-Horta, received the Nobel Peace Prize.

In the summer of 1997, Indonesia suffered a major economic setback, along with most other Asian economies. Banks failed and the value of Indonesia's currency, the rupiah, plummeted. Antigovernment demonstrations and riots broke out, directed mainly at the country's prosperous ethnic Chinese. As the economic crisis deepened, student demonstrators occupied the national Parliament, demanding Suharto's ouster. On May 21, 1998, Suharto stepped down, ending 32 years of rule, and handed over power to Vice President B. J. Habibie.

June 7, 1999, marked Indonesia's first free parliamentary election since 1955. The ruling Golkar Party took a backseat to the Indonesian Democratic Party-Struggle (PDI-P), led by Megawati Sukarnoputri, the daughter of Sukarno, Indonesia's first president.

The ethnic, religious, and political tensions kept in check during Suharto's 32 years of authoritarian rule erupted in the months following his downfall. Rioting and violence shook the provinces of Aceh, Ambon (in the Moluccas), Borneo, and Irian Jaya. But nowhere was the violence more brutal and unjust than in East Timor. Habibie unexpectedly ended 25 years of Indonesian intransigence by announcing in Feb. 1999 that he was willing to hold a referendum on East Timorese independence. Twice rescheduled because of violence, a UN-organized referendum took place on Aug. 30, 1999, with 78.5% of the population voting to secede from Indonesia. In the days following the election, pro-Indonesian militias and Indonesian soldiers massacred civilians and forced a third of the population out of the region. After enormous international pressure, the government, which was either unwilling or unable to stop the violent rampage, finally agreed to allow UN forces into East Timor on Sept. 12, 1999. East Timor achieved independence on May 20, 2002.

On Oct. 20, 1999, in a surprising upset, the Indonesian Parliament elected Abdurrahman Wahid as the new president of Indonesia, defeating Megawati Sukarnoputri, the popular leader of the Indonesian Democratic Party-Struggle. Wahid was a Sufi cleric as well as an adept politician with a reputation for honesty and moderation.

In the fall of 2000 and winter of 2001, President Wahid came under increasing criticism for corruption and incompetence. He was blamed for not stopping ethnic clashes and killings in Aceh, Irian Jaya, the Moluccas Islands, and especially in Borneo, where the Dayak people turned against Madurese immigrants, slaughtering hundreds. Wahid was forced from power in July 2001, and Vice President Megawati Sukarnoputri assumed the helm.

A terrorist bombing on Oct. 12, 2002, at a nightclub in Bali killed more than 200 people, mostly tourists. In 2003, Amrozi bin Nurhasyim and Imam Samudra, members of Jemaah Islamiyah, an Islamic terrorist group linked with al-Qaeda, were sentenced to death for their roles in the bombing. But the radical Muslim cleric Abu Bakar Bashir, believed to be the head of Jemaah Islamiyah, was only given a light three-year sentence on lesser charges, causing parts of the international community to question Indonesia's commitment to fighting terrorism. Authorities arrested Bashir in April 2004—on the same day he was set to be released from prison—claiming they had new evidence that proved he is in fact the leader of Jemaah Islamiyah

and that he approved the Bali bombing. In March 2005, he was found not guilty of terrorism charges in the bombings of Jakarta's Marriott Hotel in 2003 and the Bali nightclub. He was, however, convicted of a lesser charge.

In May 2003, President Megawati declared military rule in Aceh and launched an offensive intended to destroy the Free Aceh Movement. The invasion marked the end of a cease-fire that was signed in Dec. 2002 between the Indonesian government and Aceh separatists. The government and the separatists signed a peace treaty in Aug. 2005, ending the 30-year war that had claimed 15,000 people. As part of the accord, the rebels will surrender their arms and the government will gradually withdraw its troops. In addition, the Acehnese agreed to give up their demand for independence in exchange for the right to establish political parties.

Megawati's PDI-P Party fared poorly in April 2004 elections, placing second behind the Golkar Party of former president Suharto. In July, retired general Susilo Bambang Yudhoyono placed first in the country's first direct presidential elections, but he did not garner enough votes to win outright. However, he soundly defeated Megawati in the September runoff.

On Dec. 26, 2004, a magnitude 9.0 earthquake, whose epicenter was off the west coast of the Indonesian island of Sumatra, caused a tremendously powerful tsunami in the Indian Ocean that devastated 12 Asian countries. At least 225,000 people died in the disaster, and millions were left homeless. Indonesia was the heaviest hit, with more than 150,000 casualties. Many of the deaths occurred in the war-torn province of Aceh.

Iran

ISLAMIC REPUBLIC OF IRAN

National name: Jomhuri-ye Eslami-ye Iran
Chief of State: Ayatollah Ali Khamenei (1989)
President: Mahmoud Ahmadinejad (2005)
Area: 636,293 sq mi (1,648,000 sq km)
Population (2005 est.): 68,017,860 (growth rate: 0.9%); birth rate: 16.8/1000; infant mortality rate: 41.6/1000; life expectancy: 70.0; density per sq mi: 107
Capital and largest city (2003 est.): Teheran, 11,224,800 (metro. area), 7,893,700 (city proper). **Other large cities:** Mashad, 2,061,100; Isfahan, 1,378,600; Tabriz, 1,213,400. **Monetary unit:** Rial.
Languages: Persian and Persian dialects 58%, Turkic and Turkic dialects 26%, Kurdish 9%, Luri 2%, Balochi 1%, Arabic 1%, Turkish 1%, other 2%. **Ethnicity/race:** Persian 51%, Azerbaijani 24%, Gilaki and Mazandarani 8%, Kurd 7%, Arab 3%, Lur 2%, Baloch 2%, Turkmen 2%, other 1%. **Religions:** Islam 98% (Shi'a 89%, Sunni 9%); Zoroastrian, Jewish, Christian, and Baha'i 2%.
Literacy rate: 79% (2003 est.)
Economic summary: GDP/PPP (2004 est.): $516.7 billion; per capita $7,700. **Real growth rate:** 6.3%. **Inflation:** 15.5%. **Unemployment:** 11.2%. **Arable land:** 9%. **Agriculture:** wheat, rice, other grains, sugar beets, fruits, nuts, cotton; dairy products, wool; caviar. **Labor force:** 23 million; note: shortage of skilled labor; agriculture 30%, industry 25%, services 45% (2001 est.). **Industries:** petroleum, petrochemicals, textiles, cement and other construction materials, food processing (particularly sugar refining and vegetable oil production), metal fabrication, armaments. **Natural resources:** petroleum, natural gas, coal, chromium, copper, iron ore, lead, manganese, zinc, sulfur. **Exports:** $38.79 billion (f.o.b., 2004 est.): petroleum 80%, chemical and petrochemical products, fruits and nuts, carpets. **Imports:** $31.3 billion (f.o.b., 2004 est.):

industrial raw materials and intermediate goods, capital goods, foodstuffs and other consumer goods, technical services, military supplies. **Major trading partners:** Japan, China, Italy, Taiwan, Turkey, South Korea, Germany, France, UAE, Russia (2003).

Geography Iran, a Middle Eastern country south of the Caspian Sea and north of the Persian Gulf, is three times the size of Arizona. It shares borders with Iraq, Turkey, Azerbaijan, Turkmenistan, Armenia, Afghanistan, and Pakistan.

The Elburz Mountains in the north rise to 18,603 ft (5,670 m) at Mount Damavend. From northwest to southeast, the country is crossed by a desert 800 mi (1,287 km) long.

Government Iran has been an Islamic theocracy since the Pahlavi monarchy regime was overthrown on Feb. 11, 1979.

History The region now called Iran was occupied by the Medes and the Persians in the 1500s B.C., until the Persian king Cyrus the Great overthrew the Medes and became ruler of the Achaemenid (Persian) Empire, which reached from the Indus to the Nile at its zenith in 525 B.C. Persia fell to Alexander in 331–330 B.C. and a succession of other rulers: the Seleucids (312–302 B.C.), the Greek-speaking Parthians (247 B.C.–A.D. 226), the Sasanians (224–c. 640), and the Arab Muslims (in 641). By the mid-800s Persia had become an international scientific and cultural center. In the 12th century it was invaded by the Mongols. The Safavid dynasty (1501–1722), under whom the dominant religion became Shiite Islam, followed, and was then replaced by the Qajar dynasty (1794–1925).

During the Qajar dynasty, the Russians and the British fought for economic control of the area, and during World War I, Iran's neutrality did not stop it from becoming a battlefield for Russian and British troops. A coup in 1921 brought Reza Kahn to power. In 1925, he became shah and changed his name to Reza Shah Pahlavi. He subsequently did much to modernize the country and abolished all foreign extraterritorial rights.

The country's pro-Axis allegiance in World War II led to Anglo-Russian occupation of Iran in 1941 and deposition of the shah in favor of his son, Mohammed Reza Pahlavi. Pahlavi's Westernization programs alienated the clergy, and his authoritarian rule led to massive demonstrations during the 1970s, to which the shah responded with the imposition of martial law in Sept. 1978. The shah and his family fled Iran on Jan. 16, 1979; and the exiled cleric Ayatollah Ruhollah Khomeini returned to establish an Islamic theocracy. Khomeini proceeded with his plans for revitalizing Islamic traditions. He urged women to return to the veil; banned alcohol, Western music, and mixed bathing; shut down the media; closed universities; and eliminated political parties.

Revolutionary militants invaded the U.S. embassy in Teheran on Nov. 4, 1979, seized staff members as hostages, and precipitated an international crisis. Khomeini refused all appeals, even a unanimous vote by the UN Security Council demanding immediate release of the hostages. Iranian hostility toward Washington was reinforced by the Carter administration's economic boycott and deportation order against Iranian students in the U.S., the break in diplomatic relations, and ultimately an aborted U.S. raid in April 1980 aimed at rescuing the hostages.

As the first anniversary of the embassy seizure neared, Khomeini and his followers insisted on their original conditions: guarantee by the U.S. not to interfere in Iran's affairs, cancellation of U.S. damage claims against Iran, release of $8 billion in frozen Iranian assets, an apology, and the return of the assets held by the former imperial family. These conditions were largely met and the 52 American hostages were released on Jan. 20, 1981, ending 444 days in captivity.

The sporadic war with Iraq regained momentum in 1982, as Iran launched an offensive in March and regained much of the border area occupied by Iraq in late 1980. The stalemated war dragged on well into 1988. Although Iraq expressed its willingness to stop fighting, Iran stated that it would not end the war until Iraq agreed to pay for war damages and to punish the Iraqi government leaders involved in the conflict. On July 20, 1988, Khomeini, after a series of Iranian military reverses, agreed to cease-fire negotiations with Iraq. A cease-fire went into effect on Aug. 20, 1988. Khomeini died in June 1989 and Ayatollah Ali Khamenei succeeded him as the supreme leader.

By early 1991 the Islamic revolution appeared to have lost much of its militancy. Attempting to revive a stagnant economy, President Rafsanjani took measures to decentralize the command system and introduce free-market mechanisms.

Mohammed Khatami, a little-known moderate cleric, former newspaperman, and national librarian, won the presidential election with 70% of the vote on May 23, 1997, a stunning victory over the conservative ruling elite. Khatami supported greater social and political freedoms, but his steps toward liberalizing the strict clerical rule governing the country put him at odds with the supreme leader, Ayatollah Khamenei.

Signaling a seismic change in Iran's political environment, reform candidates won the overwhelming majority of seats in Feb. 2000 parliamentary elections, thereby wresting control from hard-liners, who had dominated the Parliament since the 1979 Islamic revolution. The Parliament's reformist transformation greatly buttressed the efforts of Khatami in constructing a nation of "lasting pluralism and Islamic democracy." Khatami has walked a jittery tightrope between student groups and other liberals pressuring him to introduce bolder freedoms, and Iran's military and conservative clerical elite (including Khamenei), who have expressed growing impatience with the president's liberalizing measures.

In June 2001 presidential elections, Khatami won reelection with a stunning 77% of the vote. Khatami's new cabinet, composed of 20 moderates, disappointed liberals who had hoped he would step up the pace of reform. Friction between Iran's reformers and conservatives increased in 2002.

Iran cooperated in the fight against global terrorism after the Sept. 11 bombings, assisting its war-torn neighbor Afghanistan in restoring peace. But U.S. president Bush announced in Jan. 2002 that Iran was part of an "axis of evil," calling it one of the most active state sponsors of international terrorism.

By 2003, Iran was fanning much of the world's suspicions that it had illegal nuclear ambitions. In June 2003, the International Atomic Energy Agency (IAEA) criticized Iran's concealment of much of its nuclear facilities and called on the country to permit more rigorous inspections of its nuclear sites. In Aug. 2003, the IAEA found traces of highly enriched uranium in a nuclear facility; in the face of this evidence and intense international pressure, Iran reluctantly agreed in December to suspend its uranium enrichment program and allow for thorough IAEA inspections.

On Dec. 26, the most destructive earthquake of 2003 devastated the historic city of Bam, killing an estimated 28,000 to 30,000 of its 80,000 residents.

On Feb. 20, conservatives won a landslide victory in parliamentary elections, a devastating setback for Iran's reformist movement. The hard-line Guardian Council had disqualified more than 2,500 reformist candidates, including more than 80 who were already members of the 290-seat Parliament.

The IAEA again censured the country in June 2004 for failing to fully cooperate with nuclear inspections. Neither U.S. threats nor Europe's coaxing managed to halt Iran's alarming defiance.

In June 2005, former Teheran mayor Mahmoud Ahmadinejad, a hard-line conservative, won the presidential election with 62% of the vote. It was a surprising defeat for Akbar Hashemi Rafsanjani, a former president (1989–1997), who had been expected to win. Ahmadinejad was highly popular among Iran's rural poor, who responded to his pledge to fight corruption among the country's elite. Under Ahmadinejad, most international observers expected Iran to take a sharply conservative turn. Unlike his successor, Mohammed Khatami, who frequently clashed with the country's supreme leader, Ahmadinejad is a devout follower of Ayatollah Ali Khamenei. In Aug. 2005, he rejected an EU disarmament plan that was backed by the U.S. and had been under negotiation for two years.

Iraq

REPUBLIC OF IRAQ

National name: Al Jumhuriyah al Iraqiyah
President: Jalal Talabani (2005)
Prime Minister: Ibrahim al-Jaafari (2005)
Area: 168,753 sq mi (437,072 sq km)
Population (2005 est.): 26,074,906 (growth rate: 2.7%); birth rate: 32.5/1000; infant mortality rate: 50.2/1000; life expectancy: 68.7; density per sq mi: 155
Capital and largest city (2003 est.): Baghdad, 6,777,300 (metro. area), 5,772,000 (city proper).
  Largest cities: Mosul, 1,791,600; Basra, 1,377,000; Irbil, 864,900; Kirkuk, 755,700. **Monetary unit:** U.S. dollar. **Languages:** Arabic (official), Kurdish (official in Kurdish regions), Assyrian, Armenian. **Ethnicity/race:** Arab 75%–80%, Kurdish 15%–20%, Turkoman, Assyrian, or other 5%. **Religions:** Islam 97% (Shiite 60%–65%, Sunni 32%–37%), Christian or other 3%. **Literacy rate:** 40% (2003 est.)
Economic summary: GDP/PPP (2004 est.): $89.8 billion; per capita $3,500. **Real growth rate:** 52.3%. **Inflation:** 25.4%. **Unemployment:** 25%–30%. **Arable land:** 13%. **Agriculture:** wheat, barley, rice, vegetables, dates, cotton; cattle, sheep, poultry. **Labor force:** 6.7 million; agriculture n.a.; industry n.a.; services n.a. **Industries:** petroleum, chemicals, textiles, construction materials, food processing, fertilizer, metal fabrication/processing. **Natural resources:** petroleum, natural gas, phosphates, sulfur. **Exports:** $10.1 billion (f.o.b., 2004 est.): crude oil (83.9%), crude materials excluding fuels (8.0%), food and live animals (5.0%). **Imports:** $9.9 billion (f.o.b., 2004 est.): food, medicine, manufactures. **Major trading partners:** U.S., Canada, Italy, Taiwan, Jordan, Turkey, Vietnam, Germany, UK (2003).

Geography Iraq, a triangle of mountains, desert, and fertile river valley, is bounded on the east by Iran, on the north by Turkey, on the west by Syria and Jordan, and on the south by Saudi Arabia and Kuwait. It is twice the size of Idaho. The country has arid desert land west of the Euphrates, a broad central valley between the Euphrates and the Tigris, and mountains in the northeast.

Government The dictatorship of Saddam Hussein collapsed on April 9, 2003, after U.S. and British forces invaded the country. Sovereignty was returned to Iraq on June 28, 2004.

History From earliest times Iraq was known as Mesopotamia—the land between the rivers—for it embraces a large part of the alluvial plains of the Tigris and Euphrates rivers.

An advanced civilization existed by 4000 B.C. Sometime after 2000 B.C. the land became the center of the ancient Babylonian and Assyrian empires. Mesopotamia was conquered by Cyrus the Great of Persia in 538 B.C., and by Alexander in 331 B.C. After an Arab conquest in 637–640, Baghdad became the capital of the ruling caliphate. The country was cruelly pillaged by the Mongols in 1258, and during the 16th, 17th, and 18th centuries was the object of repeated Turkish-Persian competition.

Nominal Turkish suzerainty imposed in 1638 was replaced by direct Turkish rule in 1831. In World War I, Britain occupied most of Mesopotamia and was given a mandate over the area in 1920. The British renamed the area Iraq and recognized it as a kingdom in 1922. In 1932, the monarchy achieved full independence. Britain again occupied Iraq during World War II because of its pro-Axis stance in the initial years of the war.

Iraq became a charter member of the Arab League in 1945, and Iraqi troops took part in the Arab invasion of Palestine in 1948.

At age 3, King Faisal II succeeded his father, Ghazi I, who was killed in an automobile accident in 1939. Faisal and his uncle, Crown Prince Abdul-Illah, were assassinated in July 1958 in a swift revolutionary coup that ended the monarchy and brought to power a military junta headed by Abdul Karem Kassim. Kassim reversed the monarchy's pro-Western policies, attempted to rectify the economic disparities between rich and poor, and began to form alliances with Communist countries.

Kassim was overthrown and killed in a coup staged on March 8, 1963, by the military and the Baath Socialist Party. The Baath Party advocated secularism, pan-Arabism, and socialism. The following year, the new leader, Abdel Salam Arif, consolidated his power by driving out the Baath Party. He adopted a new constitution in 1964. In 1966, he died in a helicopter crash. His brother, Gen. Abdel Rahman Arif, assumed the presidency, crushed the opposition, and won an indefinite extension of his term in 1967.

Arif's regime was ousted in July 1968 by a junta led by Maj. Gen. Ahmed Hassan al-Bakr of the Baath Party. Bakr and his second-in-command, Saddam Hussein, imposed authoritarian rule in an effort to end the decades of political instability that followed World War II. One of the world's leading producers of oil, Iraq used its oil revenues to develop one of the strongest military forces in the region.

On July 16, 1979, President Bakr was succeeded by Saddam Hussein, whose regime steadily developed an international reputation for repression, human rights abuses, and terrorism.

A long-standing territorial dispute over control of the Shatt-al-Arab waterway between Iraq and Iran broke into full-scale war on Sept. 20, 1980, when Iraq invaded western Iran. The eight-year war cost the lives of an estimated 1.5 million people and finally ended in a UN-brokered cease-fire in 1988. Poison gas was used by both Iran and Iraq.

In July 1990, President Hussein asserted spurious territorial claims on Kuwaiti land. A mediation attempt by Arab leaders failed, and on Aug. 2, 1990, Iraqi troops invaded Kuwait and set up a puppet government. The UN unsuccessfully imposed trade sanctions against Iraq to pressure it to withdraw. On Jan. 18, 1991, UN forces, under the leadership of U.S. general Norman Schwarzkopf, launched the Gulf War (Operation Desert Storm), liberating Kuwait in less than a week.

The war did little to dwarf Iraq's resilient dictator. Rebellions by both Shiites and Kurds, encouraged by the U.S., were brutally crushed. In 1991, the UN set up a northern no-fly zone to protect Iraq's Kurdish population; in 1992 a southern no-fly zone was established as a buffer between Iraq and Kuwait and to protect Shiites.

The UN Security Council imposed sanctions beginning in 1990 that barred Iraq from selling oil except in exchange for food and medicine. The sanctions against Iraq failed to crush its leader but caused catastrophic suffering among its people—the country's infrastructure was in ruins, and disease, malnutrition, and the infant mortality rate skyrocketed.

The UN weapons inspections team mandated to ascertain that Iraq had destroyed all its nuclear, chemical, biological, and ballistic arms after the war was continually thwarted by Saddam Hussein. In Nov. 1997, he expelled the American members of the UN inspections team, a standoff that stretched on until Feb. 1998. But in Aug. 1998, Hussein again put a halt to the inspections. On Dec. 16, the United States and Britain began Operation Desert Fox, four days of intensive air strikes. From then on, the U.S. and Britain conducted hundreds of air strikes on Iraqi targets within the no-fly zones. The sustained low-level warfare continued unabated into 2003.

After the Sept. 11, 2001, terrorist attacks, President Bush began calling for a "regime change" in Iraq, describing the nation as part of an "axis of evil." The alleged existence of weapons of mass destruction, the thwarting of UN weapons inspections, Iraq's alleged links to terrorism, and Saddam Hussein's despotism and human rights abuses were the major reasons cited for necessitating a preemptive strike against the country. The Arab world and much of Europe condemned the hawkish and unilateral U.S. stance. The UK, however, declared its intention to support the U.S. in military action. On Sept. 12, 2002, Bush addressed the UN, challenging the organization to swiftly enforce its own resolutions against Iraq, or else the U.S. would act on its own. On Nov. 8, the UN Security Council unanimously approved a resolution imposing tough new arms inspections on Iraq. On Nov. 26, new inspections of Iraq's military holdings began.

The UN's formal report at the end of Jan. 2003 was not promising, with chief weapons inspector Hans Blix lamenting that "Iraq appears not to have come to a genuine acceptance, not even today, of the disarmament that was demanded of it." While the Bush administration felt the report cemented its claim that a military solution was imperative, several permanent members of the UN Security Council—France, Russia, and China—urged that the UN inspectors be given more time to complete their task. Bush and Blair continued to call for war, insisting that they would go ahead with a "coalition of the willing" if not with UN support. All diplomatic efforts ceased by March 17, when President Bush delivered an ultimatum to Saddam Hussein to leave the country within 48 hours or face war.

On March 20, the war against Iraq began at 5:30 A.M. Baghdad time (9:30 P.M. EST, March 19) with the launch of Operation Iraqi Freedom. By April 9, U.S. forces took control of the capital, signaling the collapse of Saddam Hussein's regime. Although the war had been officially declared over on May 1, 2003, Iraq remained enveloped in violence and chaos. Iraqis began protesting almost immediately against the delay in self-rule and the absence of a timetable to end the U.S. occupation. In July, the U.S. administrator for Iraq, Paul Bremer, appointed an Iraqi governing council.

Months of searching for Iraq's weapons of mass destruction yielded no hard evidence, and both administrations and their intelligence agencies came under fire. There were also mounting allegations that the existence of these weapons was exaggerated or distorted as a pretext to justify the war. In fall 2003, President Bush recast the rationale for war, no longer citing the danger of weapons of mass destruction, but instead describing Iraq as "the central front" in the war against terrorism. A free and democratic Iraq, he contended, would serve as a model for the rest of the Middle East.

Continued instability in 2003 kept 140,000 American troops (at a cost of $4 billion a month), as well as 11,000 British and 10,000 coalition troops in Iraq. The U.S. launched several tough military campaigns to subdue Iraqi resistance, which also had the effect of further alienating the populace. The rising violence prompted the Bush administration to reverse its Iraq policy in Nov. 2003: the transfer of power to an interim government would take place in July 2004, much earlier than originally planned.

After eight months of searching, the U.S. military captured Saddam Hussein on Dec. 13. The deposed leader was found hiding in a hole near his hometown of Tikrit and surrendered without a fight.

In Jan. 2004, the CIA's chief weapons inspector, David Kay, stated that U.S. intelligence about Iraq's weapons of mass destruction "was almost all wrong." When the final report on the existence of weapons of mass destruction in Iraq was issued in Oct. 2004, Kay's successor, Charles Duelfer, confirmed that there was no evidence of an Iraqi weapons production program.

The turmoil and violence in Iraq increased throughout 2004. Suicide bombings, kidnappings, and beheadings targeted civilians, Iraqi security forces, foreign workers, and coalition soldiers. By April, a number of separate uprisings had spread throughout the Sunni triangle and in the Shiite-dominated south. In September alone there were 2,300 attacks by insurgents. In October, U.S. officials estimated there were between 8,000 and 12,000 hard-core insurgents and a total of more than 20,000 "active sympathizers." Loosely divided into Baathists, nationalists, and Islamists, all but about 1,000 were thought to be indigenous fighters.

Reconstruction efforts, hampered by bureaucracy and security concerns, had also fallen woefully short of U.S. expectations: by September, just 6% ($1 billion) of the reconstruction money approved by the U.S. Congress in 2003 had in fact been used. Electricity and clean water were still below prewar levels, and half of Iraq's employable population was still without work. With few palpable signs of reconstruction to generate goodwill toward the U.S., American troops often faced a hostile populace. In April, the U.S. reversed its policy of banning Baath Party officials from positions of responsibility—the U.S. had fired all high-ranking members and disbanded the Iraqi army, affecting about 400,000 positions, depleting Iraq of its skilled workforce, and further embittering the Sunni population.

In late April, the appalling physical and sexual abuse and humiliation of Iraqi prisoners at Abu Ghraib prison near Baghdad came to light when photographs were released by the U.S. media. The images sparked outrage around the world. In August, the Schlesinger report's investigation into Abu Ghraib (the furthest reaching of many Pentagon-sponsored reports on the subject) called the prisoner abuse acts of "brutality and purposeless sadism," rejected the idea that the abuse was simply the work of a few aberrant soldiers, and asserted that there were "fundamental failures throughout all levels of command, from the soldiers on the ground to Central Command and to the Pentagon."

On June 28, 2004, sovereignty was officially returned to Iraq. Former exile and Iraqi Government Council member Iyad Allawi became prime minister of the Iraqi interim government, and Ghazi al-Yawar, a Sunni Muslim, was chosen president.

On July 9, the Senate Intelligence Committee released a unanimous bipartisan "Report on Pre-War Intelligence on Iraq," concluding that "most of the major key judgments" on Iraq's weapons of mass destruction were "either overstated, or were not supported by, the underlying intelligence report." The report also stated that there was no "established formal relationship" between al-Qaeda and Saddam Hussein. The following week, Britain's Butler report on pre-Iraq intelligence echoed the American findings.

On Oct. 25, 380 tons of powerful explosives were reported missing from a military installation called Al Qaqaa sometime after the U.S.-led war began in March 2003. Before the U.S. invasion, the enormous cache of missing explosives had been monitored and safeguarded by the International Atomic Energy Agency.

Iraq's Jan. 30, 2005, elections to select a 275-seat National Assembly went ahead as scheduled, and a total of 8.5 million people voted, representing about 58% of those Iraqis eligible to vote. A coalition of Shiites, the United Iraq Alliance, received 48% of the vote, the Kurdish parties received 26% of the vote, and the Sunnis just 2%—most Sunni leaders had called for a boycott. In April, Jalal Talabani, a Kurd, became president, and Ibrahim al-Jaafari, a relgious Shiite, became prime minister.

The elections did not stem the insurgency, which continued to rage in 2005. The violence grew increasingly sectarian, with Sunni insurgents targeting Shiite and Kurdish civilians in suicide bombings. According to a British-based antiwar group, the death rate for Iraqi civilians reached almost 25,000 in the two years since the war began (no official U.S. or Iraqi tally of civilian casualties exists). By mid-August 2005, 1,860 U.S. soldiers had died and more than 14,000 had been wounded.

The U.S. and Iraqi governments agreed that no firm timetable for the withdrawal of U.S. troops should be set. Withdrawal would take place as Iraqi police and security forces grew strong enough to assume responsibility for the country's stability. But the training of Iraqi security forces had been far below what had been expected. A July 2005 Pentagon report stated that only "a small number" of Iraqi security forces are capable of fighting the insurgency without American help. These security forces are also a favorite target of the insurgents.

In Aug. 2005, after three months of fractious negotiations, Iraqi lawmakers completed a draft constitution that will be voted on in a national referendum on Oct. 15. Shiites and Kurds supported a decentralized government with autonomous regions in the Kurdish north and the Shiite south; the minority Sunnis wanted strong centralization, fearing that they will otherwise be deprived of the oil wealth of the north and south. That issue, as well as the role of Islam in government and women's rights, remained unresolved in the final draft. In the end, the minority Sunnis denounced the document and vowed to defeat it at the referendum stage. Given that the insurgency is largely fueled by Sunnis,

their disaffection from the political process is likely to bring more divisiveness and violence.

For an updated profile of Iraq, *see* www.infoplease.com/iraqprofile.

Ireland

National name: Éire
President: Mary McAleese (1997)
Taoiseach (Prime Minister): Bertie Ahern (1997)
Area: 27,135 sq mi (70,280 sq km)
Population (2005 est.): 4,015,676 (growth rate: 1.2%); birth rate: 14.5/1000; infant mortality rate: 5.4/1000; life expectancy: 77.6; density per sq mi: 148
Capital (2003 est.): Dublin, 1,018,500. **Other large cities:** Cork, 193,400; Limerick, 84,900; Galway, 67,200. **Monetary units:** Euro (formerly Irish pound [punt]). **Languages:** English, Irish (Gaelic). **Ethnicity/race:** Celtic, English. **Religions:** Roman Catholic 91.6%, Anglican 2.5%, other 5.9%. **Literacy rate:** 98% (1981 est.)
Economic summary: GDP/PPP (2004 est.): $126.4 billion; per capita $31,900. **Real growth rate:** 5.1%. **Inflation:** 2.2%. **Unemployment:** 4.3%. **Arable land:** 15%. **Agriculture:** turnips, barley, potatoes, sugar beets, wheat; beef, dairy products. **Labor force:** 1.92 million; agriculture 8%, industry 29%, services 64% (2002 est.). **Industries:** steel, lead, zinc, silver, aluminum, barite, and gypsum mining processing; food products, brewing, textiles, clothing; chemicals, pharmaceuticals; machinery, rail transportation equipment, passenger and commercial vehicles, ship construction and refurbishment; glass and crystal; software, tourism. **Natural resources:** zinc, lead, natural gas, barite, copper, gypsum, limestone, dolomite, peat, silver. **Exports:** $103.8 billion (f.o.b., 2004 est.): machinery and equipment, computers, chemicals, pharmaceuticals; live animals, animal products. **Imports:** $60.65 billion (f.o.b., 2004 est.): data processing equipment, other machinery and equipment, chemicals, petroleum and petroleum products, textiles, clothing. **Major trading partners:** U.S., UK, Belgium, Germany, France, Netherlands, Italy (2003)

Geography Ireland is situated in the Atlantic Ocean and separated from Great Britain by the Irish Sea. Half the size of Arkansas, it occupies the entire island except for the six counties that make up Northern Ireland. Ireland resembles a basin—a central plain rimmed with mountains, except in the Dublin region. The mountains are low, with the highest peak, Carrantuohill in County Kerry, rising to 3,415 ft (1,041 m). The principal river is the Shannon, which begins in the north-central area, flows south and southwest for about 240 mi (386 km), and empties into the Atlantic.

Government Republic.

History In the Stone and Bronze Ages, Ireland was inhabited by Picts in the north and a people called the Erainn in the south, the same stock, apparently, as in all the isles before the Anglo-Saxon invasion of Britain. About the 4th century B.C., tall, red-haired Celts arrived from Gaul or Galicia. They subdued and assimilated the inhabitants and established a Gaelic civilization. By the beginning of the Christian Era, Ireland was divided into five kingdoms—Ulster, Connacht, Leinster, Meath, and Munster. Saint Patrick introduced Christianity in 432, and the country developed into a center of Gaelic and Latin learning. Irish monasteries, the equivalent of universities, attracted intellectuals as well as the pious and sent out missionaries to many parts of Europe and, some believe, to North America.

Norse depredations along the coasts, starting in 795, ended in 1014 with Norse defeat at the Battle of Clontarf by forces under Brian Boru. In the 12th century, the pope gave all of Ireland to the English Crown as a papal fief. In 1171, Henry II of England was acknowledged "Lord of Ireland," but local sectional rule continued for centuries, and English control over the whole island was not reasonably absolute until the 17th century. In the Battle of the Boyne (1690), the Catholic King James II and his French supporters were defeated by the Protestant King William III (of Orange). An era of Protestant political and economic supremacy began.

By the Act of Union (1801), Great Britain and Ireland became the "United Kingdom of Great Britain and Ireland." A steady decline in the Irish economy followed in the next decades. The population had reached 8.25 million when the great potato famine of 1846–1848 took many lives and drove more than 2 million people to immigrate to North America.

In the meantime, anti-British agitation continued along with demands for Irish home rule. The advent of World War I delayed the institution of home rule and resulted in the Easter Rebellion in Dublin (April 24–29, 1916), in which Irish nationalists unsuccessfully attempted to throw off British rule. Guerrilla warfare against British forces followed proclamation of a republic by the rebels in 1919. The Irish Free State was established as a dominion on Dec. 6, 1922, with six northern counties remaining as part of the United Kingdom. A civil war ensued between those supporting the Anglo-Irish Treaty that established the Irish Free State and those repudiating it because it led to the partitioning of the island. The Irish Republican Army (IRA), led by Eamon de Valera, fought against the partition but lost. De Valera joined the government in 1927 and became prime minister in 1932. In 1937 a new constitution changed the nation's name to Éire. Ireland remained neutral in World War II.

In 1948, De Valera was defeated by John A. Costello, who demanded final independence from Britain. The Republic of Ireland was proclaimed on April 18, 1949, and withdrew from the Commonwealth. From the 1960s onwards two antagonistic currents dominated Irish politics. One sought to bind the wounds of the rebellion and civil war. The other was the effort of the outlawed Irish Republican Army and more moderate groups to bring Northern Ireland into the republic. The "troubles"—the violence and terrorist acts between Republicans and Unionists in both the Republic of Ireland and Northern Ireland—would plague the island for the remainder of the century and beyond.

Under the First Programme for Economic Expansion (1958–1963), economic protection was dismantled and foreign investment encouraged. This prosperity brought profound social and cultural changes to what had been one of the poorest and least technologically advanced countries in Europe. Ireland joined the European Economic Community (now the EU) in 1973. In the 1990 presidential election, Mary Robinson was elected the republic's first woman president. The election of a candidate with socialist and feminist sympathies was regarded as a watershed in Irish political life, reflecting the changes taking place in Irish society. Irish voters approved the Maastricht Treaty, which paved the way for the establishment of the EU, by a large majority in a referendum held in 1992. In 1993, the Irish and British governments signed a joint peace initiative (the Downing Street Declaration), in which they pledged to seek mutually agreeable political structures in Northern Ireland and between the two islands.

A referendum on allowing divorce under certain conditions—hitherto constitutionally forbidden—was narrowly passed in Nov. 1995.

In 1998 hope for a solution to the troubles in Northern Ireland seemed palpable. A landmark settlement, the Good Friday Agreement of April 10, 1998, called for Protestants to share political power with the minority Catholics and gave the Republic of Ireland a voice in Northern Irish affairs. The resounding commitment to the settlement was demonstrated in a dual referendum on May 22: the North approved the accord by a vote of 71% to 29%, and in the Irish Republic 94% favored it. After numerous stops and starts, the new government in Northern Ireland was formed on Dec. 2, 2000, but it has been suspended four times since then (and has remained suspended since Oct. 2002) primarily because of Sinn Fein's reluctance to disarm its military wing, the IRA. In 2005, however, the IRA renounced armed struggle, and peace again seemed possible.

Despite a number of recent corruption and bribery scandals, most of which involved the centrist Fianna Fáil Party of Prime Minister Bertie Ahern, the party won 81 of 166 seats in May 2002. Ahern became the first Irish prime minister in 33 years to be elected to a second successive term.

Once a country plagued with high unemployment, high inflation, slow growth, and a large public debt, Ireland has undergone an extraordinary economic transformation in the last 15 years. Formerly an agriculture-based economy, the "Celtic Tiger" has become a leader in high-tech industries and in some years its economy has grown as much as 10%.

See also Northern Ireland, under United Kingdom.

Israel

STATE OF ISRAEL

National name: Medinat Yisra'el
President: Moshe Katsav (2000)
Prime Minister: Ariel Sharon (2001)
Area: 8,019 sq mi (20,770 sq km)
Population (2005 est.): 6,276,883 (growth rate: 1.2%); birth rate: 18.2/1000; infant mortality rate: 7.0/1000; life expectancy: 79.3; density per sq mi: 783
Capital and largest city (2003 est.): Jerusalem,[1] 695,500. **Other large cities:** Tel Aviv, 365,300; Haifa, 280,200. **Monetary unit:** Shekel. **Languages:** Hebrew (official), Arabic, English. **Ethnicity/race:** Jewish 80.1% (Europe/Americas/Oceania-born 32.1%, Israel-born 20.8%, Africa-born 14.6%, Asia-born 12.6%), non-Jewish 19.9% (mostly Arab) (1996 est.). **Religions:** Judaism 80.1%, Islam 14.6% (mostly Sunni), Christian 2.1%, others 3.2% (1996 est.). **Literacy rate:** 95% (2003 est.)
Economic summary: GDP/PPP (2004 est.): $129 billion; per capita $20,800. **Real growth rate:** 3.9%. **Inflation:** 0%. **Unemployment:** 10.7%. **Arable land:** 16%. **Agriculture:** citrus, vegetables, cotton; beef, poultry, dairy products. **Labor force:** 2.68 million; public services 31.2%, manufacturing 20.2%, finance and business 13.1%, commerce 12.8%, construction 7.5%, personal and other services 6.4%, transport, storage, and communications 6.2%, agriculture, forestry, and fishing 2.6% (1996). **Industries:** high-technology projects (including aviation, communications, computer-aided design and manufactures, medical electronics, fiber optics), wood and paper products, potash and phosphates, food, beverages, and tobacco, caustic soda, cement, construction, metals products, chemical products, plastics, diamond cutting, textiles and footwear. **Natural resources:** timber, potash, copper ore, natural gas, phosphate rock, magnesium bromide,

clays, sand. **Exports:** 34.41 billion (f.o.b., 2004 est.): machinery and equipment, software, cut diamonds, agricultural products, chemicals, textiles and apparel. **Imports:** $36.84 billion (f.o.b., 2004 est.): raw materials, military equipment, investment goods, rough diamonds, fuels, grain, consumer goods. **Major trading partners:** U.S., Belgium, Hong Kong, Germany, UK, Switzerland, Italy (2003).

1. Israel proclaimed Jerusalem as its capital in 1950, but the U.S., like nearly all other countries, maintains its embassy in Tel Aviv.

Geography Israel, slightly larger than Massachusetts, lies at the eastern end of the Mediterranean Sea. It is bordered by Egypt on the west, Syria and Jordan on the east, and Lebanon on the north. Its maritime plain is extremely fertile. The southern Negev region, which comprises almost half the total area, is largely a desert. The Jordan, the only important river, flows from the north through Lake Hule (Waters of Merom) and Lake Kinneret (Sea of Galilee or Sea of Tiberias), finally entering the Dead Sea, 1,349 ft (411 m) below sea level—the world's lowest land elevation.

Government Parliamentary democracy.

History Palestine, considered a holy land by Jews, Muslims, and Christians, and homeland of the modern state of Israel, was known as Canaan to the ancient Hebrews. Palestine's name derives from the Philistines, a people who occupied the southern coastal part of the country in the 12th century B.C.

A Hebrew kingdom established in 1000 B.C. was later split into the kingdoms of Judah and Israel; they were subsequently invaded by Assyrians, Babylonians, Egyptians, Persians, Romans, and Alexander the Great of Macedonia. By A.D. 135, few Jews were left in Palestine; most lived in the scattered and tenacious communities of the Diaspora. Palestine became a center of Christian pilgrimage after the emperor Constantine converted to that faith. The Arabs took Palestine from the Byzantine empire in 634–640. Interrupted only by Christian Crusaders, Muslims ruled Palestine until the 20th century. During World War I, British forces defeated the Turks in Palestine and governed the area under a League of Nations mandate from 1923.

As part of the 19th-century Zionist movement, Jews had begun settling in Palestine as early as 1820. This effort to establish a Jewish homeland received British approval in the Balfour Declaration of 1917. During the 1930s, Jews persecuted by the Hitler regime poured into Palestine. The postwar acknowledgment of the Holocaust—Hitler's genocide of 6 million Jews—increased international interest in and sympathy for the cause of Zionism. However, Arabs in Palestine and surrounding countries bitterly opposed prewar and postwar proposals to partition Palestine into Arab and Jewish sectors. The British mandate to govern Palestine ended after the war, and, in 1947, the UN voted to partition Palestine. When the British officially withdrew on May 14, 1948, the Jewish National Council proclaimed the State of Israel.

U.S. recognition came within hours. The next day, Arab forces from Egypt, Jordan, Syria, Lebanon, and Iraq invaded the new nation. By the cease-fire on Jan. 7, 1949, Israel had increased its original territory by 50%, taking western Galilee, a broad corridor through central Palestine to Jerusalem, and part of modern Jerusalem. Chaim Weizmann and David Ben-Gurion became Israel's first president and prime minister. The new government was admitted to the UN on May 11, 1949.

The next clash with Arab neighbors came when Egypt nationalized the Suez Canal in 1956 and barred Israeli shipping. Coordinating with an Anglo-French force, Israeli troops seized the Gaza Strip and drove through the Sinai to the east bank of the Suez Canal, but withdrew under U.S. and UN pressure. In the Six-Day War of 1967, Israel made simultaneous air attacks against Syrian, Jordanian, and Egyptian air bases, totally defeating the Arabs. Expanding its territory by 200%, Israel at the cease-fire held the Golan Heights, the West Bank of the Jordan River, Jerusalem's Old City, and all of the Sinai and the east bank of the Suez Canal.

In the face of Israeli reluctance even to discuss the return of occupied territories, the fourth Arab-Israeli War erupted on Oct. 6, 1973, with a surprise Egyptian and Syrian assault on the Jewish high holy day of Yom Kippur. Initial Arab gains were reversed when a cease-fire took effect two weeks later, but Israel suffered heavy losses.

A dramatic breakthrough in the tortuous history of Mideast peace efforts occurred on Nov. 9, 1977, when Egypt's president Anwar Sadat declared his willingness to talk peace. Prime Minister Menachem Begin, on Nov. 15, extended an invitation to the Egyptian leader to address the Knesset in Jerusalem. Sadat's arrival in Israel four days later raised worldwide hopes, but a peace agreement between Egypt and Israel was long in coming. On March 14, 1979, the Knesset approved a final peace treaty, and 12 days later, Begin and Sadat signed the document, together with President Jimmy Carter, in a White House ceremony. Israel began its withdrawal from the Sinai, which it had annexed from Egypt, on May 25.

Although Israel withdrew its last settlers from the Sinai in April 1982, the fragile Mideast peace was shattered on June 9, 1982, by a massive Israeli assault on southern Lebanon, where the Palestinian Liberation Organization was entrenched. The PLO had long plagued Israelis with terrorist actions. Israel destroyed PLO strongholds in Tyre and Sidon and reached the suburbs of Beirut on June 10. A U.S.-mediated accord between Lebanon and Israel, signed on May 17, 1983, provided for Israeli withdrawal from Lebanon. Israel eventually withdrew its troops from the Beirut area but kept them in southern Lebanon, where occasional skirmishes would continue. Lebanon, under pressure from Syria, canceled the accord in March 1984.

A continual source of tension has been the relationship between the Jews and the Palestinians living within Israeli territories. Most Arabs fled the region when the state of Israel was declared, but those who remain now make up almost one-fifth of the population of Israel. They are about two-thirds Muslim, as well as Christian and Druze. Palestinians living on the West Bank and the Gaza Strip fomented the riots begun in 1987, known as the *intifada*. Violence heightened as Israeli police cracked down and Palestinians retaliated. Continuing Jewish settlement of lands designated for Palestinians has added to the unrest.

In 1988, the leader of the PLO, Yasir Arafat, reversed decades of PLO polemic by acknowledging Israel's right to exist. He stated his willingness to enter negotiations to create a Palestinian political entity that would coexist with the Israeli state.

In 1991, Israel was struck by Iraqi missiles during the Persian Gulf War. The Israelis did not retaliate in order to preserve the international coalition against Iraq. In 1992, Yitzhak Rabin became prime minister. He halted the disputed Israeli settlement of the occupied territories.

Highly secretive talks in Norway resulted in the landmark Oslo Accord between the PLO and the Israeli government in 1993. The accord stipulated a five-year plan in which Palestinians of the West Bank and the Gaza Strip would gradually become self-governing. Arafat became president of the new Palestinian Authority. In 1994, Israel signed a peace treaty with Jordan; Israel still has no formal peace agreement with Syria or Lebanon.

On Nov. 4, 1995, Prime Minister Rabin was slain by a Jewish extremist, jeopardizing the tenuous progress toward peace. Shimon Peres succeeded him until May 1996 elections for the Knesset gave Israel a new hardline prime minister, Benjamin Netanyahu, by a razorthin margin. Netanyahu reversed or stymied much of the Oslo Agreement, contending that it offered too many concessions too fast and jeopardized Israelis' safety.

Israeli-Palestinian peace negotiations in 1997 were repeatedly undermined by both sides. Although the Hebron Accord was signed in January, calling for the withdrawal of Israeli troops from the city, the construction of new Jewish settlements on the West Bank in March profoundly upset progress toward peace.

Terrorism erupted again in 1997 when radical Hamas suicide bombers claimed the lives of more than 20 Israeli civilians. Netanyahu, accusing Palestinian Authority president Arafat of lax security, retaliated with draconian sanctions against Palestinians working in Israel, including the withholding of millions of dollars in tax revenue, a blatant violation of the Oslo Agreement. Netanyahu also persisted in authorizing right-wing Israelis to build new settlements in mostly Arab East Jerusalem. Arafat, meanwhile, seemed unwilling or unable to curb the violence of extremist Arabs.

An Oct. 1998 summit at Wye Mills, Md., generated the first real progress in the stymied Middle East peace talks in 19 months, with Netanyahu and Arafat settling several important interim issues called for by the 1993 Oslo Peace Agreement. The peace accord, however, began unraveling almost immediately. By the end of April 1999, Israel had made 41 air raids on Hezbollah guerrillas in Lebanon. The guerrillas were fighting against Israeli troops and their allies, the South Lebanon Army militia, who occupied a security zone set up in 1985 to guard Israel's borders. Public pressure in Israel to withdraw the troops grew.

Labor Party leader Ehud Barak won the 1999 election and announced that he planned not only to pursue peace with the Palestinians, but to establish relations with Syria and end the low-grade war in southern Lebanon with the Iranian-armed Hezbollah guerrillas. In Dec. 1999, Israeli-Syrian talks resumed after a nearly four-year hiatus. By Jan. 2000, however, talks had broken down when Syria demanded a detailed discussion of the return of all of the Golan Heights. In Feb., new Hezbollah attacks on Israeli troops in southern Lebanon led to Israel's retaliatory bombing as well as Barak's decision to pull out of Lebanon. Israeli troops pulled out of Lebanon on May 24, 2000, after 18 consecutive years of occupation.

Peace talks in July 2000 at Camp David between Barak and Arafat ended unsuccessfully, despite President Clinton's strongest efforts—the status of Jerusalem was the primary sticking point. In September, Likud Party leader Ariel Sharon visited the compound called Temple Mount by Jews and Haram al-Sharif by Muslims, a fiercely contested site that is sacred to both Jews and Muslims. The visit set off the worst violence in years, killing around 400 people, mostly Palestinians. The violence (dubbed the Al-Aksa intifada) and the stalled peace process fueled growing concerns about Israeli security, paving the way for hard-liner Sharon's stunning landslide victory over Barak in Feb. 2001. Violence on both sides continued at an alarming rate. Palestinians carried out some of the most horrific

suicide bombings and terrorist attacks in years (Hamas and the Al-Aksa Martyr Brigade claimed responsibility for the majority of them), killing Israeli civilians at cafés, bus stops, and supermarkets. In retaliation, Israel unleashed bombing raids on Palestinian territory and sent troops and tanks to occupy West Bank and Gaza cities.

In 2003, in an attempt to restart the stalled Israeli-Palestinian peace process, Israel and the United States resolved to circumvent Arafat, whom Sharon called "irrelevant" and an obstacle. Under U.S. pressure, Arafat reluctantly appointed a prime minister in April, who was to replace him in negotiating the peace process, Mahmoud Abbas, formerly Arafat's second-in-command. On May 1, the "Quartet" (the U.S., UN, EU, and Russia) unfurled the "road map" for peace, which envisioned the creation of a Palestinian state by 2005. Although Sharon publicly acknowledged the need for a Palestinian state and Abbas committed himself to ending Palestinian violence, the road map quickly led nowhere, with neither side honoring their obligations. Sharon also persisted in building the highly controversial security barrier dividing Israeli and Palestinian areas (in October, a UN resolution condemning the barrier passed 144–4, with only the U.S., Israel, Micronesia, and the Marshall Islands supporting it). Hopes for the road map were shattered in the fall of 2003 as Palestinian attacks on Israeli civilians continued, and Israel stepped up its "targeted killings" of Palestinian militants.

In Dec. 2003, Sharon announced a startling plan—the unilateral withdrawal from the Gaza Strip. In turn, Israel was to hold on to large blocks of land in the West Bank and reject the "right of return" for Palestinian refugees. Some speculated that by giving up Gaza, Sharon was tightening Israel's hold on the West Bank—he continued to approve construction of new houses in West Bank settlements, a clear violation of the "road map." Sharon's Likud Party, however, furiously rejected his Gaza plan—that Sharon, the architect of the Jewish settlements in Gaza and the West Bank, would be the very man calling for their abandonment was viewed as an enormous betrayal. Undaunted, Sharon continued to shore up political support for the plan—while bridling against its unilateral nature, many Labor Party members supported the withdrawal—and on Oct. 26, he succeeded in winning the endorsement of the Knesset.

In May 2004, the UN Security Council condemned Israel's attack on the Rafah refugee camp in the Gaza Strip, the largest Israeli military operation in Gaza in decades. About 40 Palestinians, half of whom were civilians, were killed while participating in a protest march, and more than 1,000 Palestinians were left homeless after bulldozers razed their homes. The Israeli military claimed the razing was necessary to secure the border between Egypt and the Gaza Strip.

In July, in response to a ruling by Israel's Supreme Court about the construction of the West Bank barrier, Israel revised the route so that it did not cut into Palestinian land—the UN estimated that the original route would have taken almost 15% of West Bank territory for Israel.

Yasir Arafat's death in Nov. 2004 significantly altered the political landscape. Mahmoud Abbas was easily elected the Palestinian president in Jan. 2005, and at a summit in February, Abbas and Sharon agreed to an unequivocal cease-fire. A continued danger to this cease-fire were Palestinian militant groups, over whom Abbas has had little control.

On Aug. 15, the withdrawal of some 8,000 Israeli settlers began. The evacuation involved 21 Gaza settlements as well as four of the more isolated of the West

Bank's 120 settlements. Tens of thousands of Israelis protested the withdrawal, but the majority of Israelis supported the pullout, many viewing it as Israel's just and humane response toward the Palestinians and a significant step toward real security and peace for Israelis.

Italy

ITALIAN REPUBLIC

National name: Repubblica Italiana
President: Carlo Azeglio Ciampi (1999)
Prime Minister: Silvio Berlusconi (2001)
Area: 116,305 sq mi (301,230 sq km)
Population (2005 est.): 58,103,033 (growth rate: 0.1%); birth rate: 8.9/1000; infant mortality rate: 5.9/1000; life expectancy: 79.7; density per sq mi: 500
Capital and largest city (2003 est.): Rome, 3,550,900 (metro. area), 2,455,600 (city proper). **Other large cities:** Milan, 1,180,700; Naples, 991,700; Turin, 856,000; Palermo, 651,500; Genoa, 602,500; Bologna, 369,300; Florence, 351,600; Bari, 311,900; Catania, 305,900; Venice, 265,700. **Monetary unit:** Euro (formerly lira). **Languages:** Italian (official); German-, French-, and Slovene-speaking minorities. **Ethnicity/ race:** Italian (includes small clusters of German-, French-, and Slovene-Italians in the north and Albanian- and Greek-Italians in the south). **Religions:** Roman Catholic (predominant), Protestant, Jewish, Islamic. **Literacy rate:** 99% (2003 est.)
Economic summary: GDP/PPP (2004 est.): $1.609 trillion; per capita $27,700. **Real growth rate:** 1.3%. **Inflation:** 2.3%. **Unemployment:** 8.6%. **Arable land:** 28%. **Agriculture:** fruits, vegetables, grapes, potatoes, sugar beets, soybeans, grain, olives; beef, dairy products; fish. **Labor force:** 24.27 million; services 63%, industry 32%, agriculture 5% (2001). **Industries:** tourism, machinery, iron and steel, chemicals, food processing, textiles, motor vehicles, clothing, footwear, ceramics. **Natural resources:** mercury, potash, marble, sulfur, natural gas and crude oil reserves, fish, coal, arable land. **Exports:** $336.4 billion (f.o.b., 2004 est.): engineering products, textiles and clothing, production machinery, motor vehicles, transport equipment, chemicals; food, beverages and tobacco; minerals and nonferrous metals. **Imports:** $329.3 billion (f.o.b., 2004 est.): engineering products, chemicals, transport equipment, energy products, minerals and nonferrous metals, textiles and clothing; food, beverages and tobacco. **Major trading partners:** Germany, France, U.S., Spain, UK, Netherlands, Belgium (2003).

Geography Italy, slightly larger than Arizona, is a long peninsula shaped like a boot, surrounded on the west by the Tyrrhenian Sea and on the east by the Adriatic. It is bounded by France, Switzerland, Austria, and Slovenia to the north. The Apennine Mountains form the peninsula's backbone; the Alps form its northern boundary. The largest of its many northern lakes is Garda (143 sq mi; 370 sq km); the Po, its principal river, flows from the Alps on Italy's western border and crosses the Lombard plain to the Adriatic Sea. Several islands form part of Italy; the largest are Sicily (9,926 sq mi; 25,708 sq km) and Sardinia (9,301 sq mi; 24,090 sq km).

Government Republic.

History The migrations of Indo-European peoples into Italy probably began about 2000 B.C. and continued down to 1000 B.C. From about the 9th century B.C. until it was overthrown by the Romans in the 3rd century B.C., the Etruscan civilization dominated the area. By 264 B.C. all Italy south of Cisalpine Gaul was under

the leadership of Rome. For the next seven centuries, until the barbarian invasions destroyed the western Roman Empire in the 4th and 5th centuries A.D., the history of Italy is largely the history of Rome. From 800 on, the Holy Roman Emperors, Roman Catholic popes, Normans, and Saracens all vied for control over various segments of the Italian peninsula. Numerous city-states, such as Venice and Genoa, whose political and commercial rivalries were intense, and many small principalities flourished in the late Middle Ages. Although Italy remained politically fragmented for centuries, it became the cultural center of the Western world from the 13th to the 16th century.

In 1713, after the War of the Spanish Succession, Milan, Naples, and Sardinia were handed over to the Hapsburgs of Austria, which lost some of its Italian territories in 1735. After 1800, Italy was unified by Napoléon, who crowned himself king of Italy in 1805; but with the Congress of Vienna in 1815, Austria once again became the dominant power in a disunited Italy. Austrian armies crushed Italian uprisings in 1820–1821 and 1831. In the 1830s, Giuseppe Mazzini, a brilliant liberal nationalist, organized the Risorgimento (Resurrection), which laid the foundation for Italian unity. Disappointed Italian patriots looked to the House of Savoy for leadership. Count Camille di Cavour (1810–1861), prime minister of Sardinia in 1852 and the architect of a united Italy, joined England and France in the Crimean War (1853–1856), and in 1859 helped France in a war against Austria, thereby obtaining Lombardy. By plebiscite in 1860, Modena, Parma, Tuscany, and the Romagna voted to join Sardinia. In 1860, Giuseppe Garibaldi conquered Sicily and Naples and turned them over to Sardinia. Victor Emmanuel II, king of Sardinia, was proclaimed king of Italy in 1861. The annexation of Venetia in 1866 and of papal Rome in 1870 marked the complete unification of peninsular Italy into one nation under a constitutional monarchy.

Italy declared its neutrality upon the outbreak of World War I on the ground that Germany had embarked upon an offensive war. In 1915, Italy entered the war on the side of the Allies but obtained less territory than it expected in the postwar settlement. Benito ("Il Duce") Mussolini, a former Socialist, organized discontented Italians in 1919 into the Fascist Party to "rescue Italy from Bolshevism." He led his Black Shirts in a march on Rome and, on Oct. 28, 1922, became prime minister. He transformed Italy into a dictatorship, embarking on an expansionist foreign policy with the invasion and annexation of Ethiopia in 1935 and allying himself with Adolf Hitler in the Rome-Berlin Axis in 1936. When the Allies invaded Italy in 1943, Mussolini's dictatorship collapsed; he was executed by Partisans on April 28, 1945, at Dongo on Lake Como. Following the armistice with the Allies (Sept. 3, 1943), Italy joined the war against Germany as a cobelligerent. A June 1946 plebiscite rejected monarchy and a republic was proclaimed. The peace treaty of Sept. 15, 1947, required Italian renunciation of all claims in Ethiopia and Greece and the cession of the Dodecanese islands to Greece and of five small Alpine areas to France. The Trieste area west of the new Yugoslav territory was made a free territory (until 1954, when the city and a 90-square-mile zone were transferred to Italy and the rest to Yugoslavia).

Italy became an integral member of NATO and the European Economic Community (later the EU) as it successfully rebuilt its postwar economy. A prolonged outbreak of terrorist activities by the left-wing Red Brigades threatened domestic stability in the 1970s, but by the early 1980s the terrorist groups had been suppressed. "Revolving door" governments, political instability, scandal, and corruption characterized Italian politics in the 1980s and 1990s.

Italy adopted the euro as its currency in Jan. 1999. Treasury Secretary Carlo Ciampi, who is credited with the economic reforms that permitted Italy to enter the European Monetary Union, was elected president in May 1999. Italy joined its NATO partners in the Kosovo crisis. Aviano Air Base in northern Italy was a crucial base for launching air strikes into Kosovo and Yugoslavia.

In June 2001, Silvio Berlusconi, a conservative billionaire, was sworn in as prime minister. He pledged to reduce unemployment, cut taxes, revamp the educational system, and reform the bureaucracy. His critics were alarmed by the apparent massive conflict of interest of a prime minister who also owned 90% of Italy's media. He was accused of Mafia connections and was under indictment for tax fraud and bribery. Found guilty in three out of four of his trials, he was acquitted in all of them on appeal. Several other cases are pending.

In Nov. 2002, Giulio Andreotti, who served as Italy's prime minister numerous times between 1972 and 1992, was sentenced to 24 years for ordering the Mafia to murder a journalist in 1979. At 84, however, he was deemed too old for prison.

In 2003, Parliament passed an immunity law for top government officials that meant the latest corruption trial involving Berlusconi—he is accused of bribing judges in 1985—would be suspended while he remained in office.

At the end of 2003, Italian food giant Parmalat was accused of a massive accounting fraud scheme—$5 billion the company claimed was in fact nonexistent.

In March, U.S. troops in Iraq shot an Italian intelligence officer, who had just rescued an Italian hostage from militants. Italy sharply disputed the U.S. military's explanation, which fully exonerated the soldiers involved, contending in its own report that the American soldiers' "inexperience and stress" led to the erroneous killing. With polls already indicating that more than 70% of Italians were opposed to Italian troops in Iraq, Berlusconi announced that he was likely to withdraw all 3,000 Italian troops in the fall.

In April 2005, regional elections had disastrous results for Berlusconi's center-right coalition—it lost in 12 out of 14 regional votes. The dismal state of the economy was blamed for the poor showing. Berlusconi's coalition collapsed and he resigned on April 20. He formed a new government days later.

Jamaica

Sovereign: Queen Elizabeth II (1952)
Governor-General: Sir Howard Cooke (1991)
Prime Minister: Percival J. Patterson (1992)
Area: 4,244 sq mi (10,991 sq km)
Population (2005 est.): 2,731,832 (growth rate: 0.7%); birth rate: 16.6/1000; infant mortality rate: 12.4/1000; life expectancy: 76.3; density per sq mi: 644
Capital and largest city (2003 est.): Kingston, 937,700 (metro. area), 590,500 (city proper). **Monetary unit:** Jamaican dollar. **Languages:** English, Jamaican Creole. **Ethnicity/race:** black 90.9%, East Indian 1.3%, white 0.2%, Chinese 0.2%, mixed 7.3%, other 0.1%. **Religions:** Protestant 61.3% (Church of God 21.2%, Baptist 8.8%, Anglican 5.5%, Seventh-Day Adventist 9%, Pentecostal 7.6%, Methodist 2.7%, United Church 2.7%, Brethren 1.1%, Jehovah's Witness 1.6%, Moravian 1.1%), Roman Catholic 4%, other including some spiritual cults 34.7%. **Literacy rate:** 88% (2003 est.)

Economic summary: GDP/PPP (2004 est.): $11.13 billion; per capita $4,100. **Real growth rate:** 1.9%. **Inflation:** 12.4%. **Unemployment:** 15%. **Arable land:** 16%. **Agriculture:** sugarcane, bananas, coffee, citrus, yams, vegetables, poultry, goats, milk, crustaceans, and mollusks. **Labor force:** 1.14 million; agriculture 20.1%, industry 16.6%, services 63.4% (2003). **Industries:** tourism, bauxite/alumina, textiles, agro processing, wearing apparel, light manufactures, rum, cement, metal, paper, chemical products, telecommunications. **Natural resources:** bauxite, gypsum, limestone. **Exports:** $1.679 billion (f.o.b., 2004 est.): alumina, bauxite, sugar, bananas, rum, coffee, yams, beverages, chemicals, wearing apparel, mineral fuels. **Imports:** $3.624 billion (f.o.b., 2004 est.): food and other consumer goods, industrial supplies, fuel, parts and accessories of capital goods, machinery and transport equipment, construction materials. **Major trading partners:** U.S., Canada, UK, France, Norway, Germany, China, Netherlands, Trinidad and Tobago, Venezuela, Japan (2003).
Member of Commonwealth of Nations

Geography Jamaica is an island in the West Indies, 90 mi (145 km) south of Cuba and 100 mi (161 km) west of Haiti. It is a little smaller than Connecticut. The island is made up of coastal lowlands, a limestone plateau, and the Blue Mountains, a group of volcanic hills, in the east.

Government Constitutional parliamentary democracy.

History Jamaica was inhabited by Arawak Indians when Columbus explored it in 1494 and named it St. Iago. It remained under Spanish rule until 1655, when it became a British possession. Buccaneers operated from Port Royal, also the capital, until it fell into the sea in an earthquake in 1692. Disease decimated the Arawaks, so black slaves were imported to work on the sugar plantations. During the 17th and 18th centuries the British were consistently harassed by the Maroons, armed bands of freed slaves roaming the countryside. Abolition of the slave trade (1807), emancipation of the slaves (1833), and a drop in sugar prices eventually led to a depression that resulted in an uprising in 1865. The following year Jamaica became a Crown colony, and conditions improved considerably. Introduction of bananas reduced dependence on sugar.

On May 5, 1953, Jamaica gained internal autonomy, and, in 1958, it led in organizing the West Indies Federation. A nationalist labor leader, Sir Alexander Bustamente, later campaigned to withdraw from the federation. After a referendum, Jamaica became independent on Aug. 6, 1962. Michael Manley, of the socialist People's National Party, became prime minister in 1972.

The Labour Party defeated Manley in 1980 and its capitalist-oriented leader, Edward P. G. Seaga, became prime minister. He encouraged private investment and began an austerity program. Like other Caribbean countries, Jamaica was hard-hit by the 1981–1982 recession. Devaluation of the Jamaican dollar made Jamaican products more competitive on the world market and the country achieved record growth in tourism and agriculture. While manufacturing also grew, food prices rose as much as 75% and thousands of Jamaicans fell deeper into poverty.

In 1989, Manley was reelected, but he resigned in 1992 and was replaced by P. J. Patterson. In May 1997, the government signed a "Ship-Rider Agreement," allowing U.S. authorities to enter Jamaican waters and search vessels with the Jamaican government's permission in order to fight drug trafficking. In 2001, violence between politically connected gangs escalated in Kingston, promoting fears that the tourist industry could suffer. In Oct. 2002, Patterson won his third term in office.

In Sept. 2004, Hurricane Ivan, the worst storm to hit the island in decades, destroyed thousands of homes.

Japan

National name: Nippon
Emperor: Akihito (1989)
Prime Minister: Junichiro Koizumi (2001)
Area: 145,882 sq mi (377,835 sq km)
Population (2005 est.): 127,417,244 (growth rate: 0.1%); birth rate: 9.5/1000; infant mortality rate: 3.3/1000; life expectancy: 81.2; density per sq mi: 873
Capital and largest city (2003 est.): Tokyo, 31,139,900 (metro. area), 8,240,100 (city proper). **Other large cities:** Yokohama, 3,494,900 (part of Tokyo metro. area); Osaka, 2,597,000; Nagoya, 2,189,700; Sapporo, 1,848,000; Kobe, 1,529,900 (part of Osaka metro. area); Kyoto, 1,470,600 (part of Osaka metro. area); Fukuoka, 1,368,900; Kawasaki, 1,276,200 (part of Tokyo metro. area); Hiroshima, 1,132,700. **Monetary unit:** Yen.
Language: Japanese. **Ethnicity/race:** Japanese 99%, other 1% (mostly Korean). **Religions:** Shintoist and Buddhist 84%, other 16% (including Christian 0.7%).
Literacy rate: 99% (1995 est.)
Economic summary: GDP/PPP (2004 est.): $3.745 trillion; per capita $29,400. **Real growth rate:** 2.9%. **Inflation:** –0.1%. **Unemployment:** 4.7%. **Arable land:** 12%. **Agriculture:** rice, sugar beets, vegetables, fruit, pork, poultry, dairy products, eggs, fish. **Labor force:** 66.97 million; services 70%, industry 25%, agriculture 5% (2002 est.). **Industries:** among world's largest and technologically advanced producers of motor vehicles, electronic equipment, machine tools, steel and nonferrous metals, ships, chemicals, textiles, processed foods. **Natural resources:** negligible mineral resources, fish. **Exports:** $538.8 billion (f.o.b., 2004 est.): transport equipment, motor vehicles, semiconductors, electrical machinery, chemicals. **Imports:** $401.8 billion (f.o.b., 2004 est.): machinery and equipment, fuels, foodstuffs, chemicals, textiles, raw materials (2001). **Major trading partners:** U.S., China, South Korea, Taiwan, Hong Kong, Indonesia (2003).

Geography An archipelago in the Pacific, Japan is separated from the east coast of Asia by the Sea of Japan. It is approximately the size of Montana. Japan's four main islands are Honshu, Hokkaido, Kyushu, and Shikoku. The Ryukyu chain to the southwest was U.S.-occupied from 1945 to 1972, when it reverted to Japanese control, and the Kurils to the northeast are Russian-occupied.

Government Constitutional monarchy with a parliamentary government.

History Legend attributes the creation of Japan to the sun goddess, from whom the emperors were descended. The first of them was Jimmu, supposed to have ascended the throne in 660 B.C., a tradition that constituted official doctrine until 1945.

Recorded Japanese history begins in approximately A.D. 400, when the Yamato clan, eventually based in Kyoto, managed to gain control of other family groups in central and western Japan. Contact with Korea introduced Buddhism to Japan at about this time. Through the 700s Japan was much influenced by China, and the Yamato clan set up an imperial court similar to that of China. In the ensuing centuries, the authority of the imperial court was undermined as powerful gentry families vied for control.

At the same time, warrior clans were rising to prominence as a distinct class known as samurai. In 1192, the Minamoto clan set up a military government under their leader, Yoritomo. He was designated shogun (military dictator). For the following 700 years, shoguns from a succession of clans ruled in Japan, while the imperial court existed in relative obscurity.

First contact with the West came in about 1542, when a Portuguese ship off course arrived in Japanese waters. Portuguese traders, Jesuit missionaries, and Spanish, Dutch, and English traders followed. Suspicious of Christianity and of Portuguese support of a local Japanese revolt, the shoguns of the Tokugawa period (1603–1867) prohibited all trade with foreign countries; only a Dutch trading post at Nagasaki was permitted. Western attempts to renew trading relations failed until 1853, when Commodore Matthew Perry sailed an American fleet into Tokyo Bay. Trade with the West was forced upon Japan under terms less than favorable to the Japanese. Strife caused by these actions brought down the feudal world of the shoguns. In 1868, the emperor Meiji came to the throne, and the shogun system was abolished.

Japan quickly made the transition from a medieval to a modern power. An imperial army was established with conscription, and parliamentary government was formed in 1889. The Japanese began to take steps to extend their empire. After a brief war with China in 1894–1895, Japan acquired Formosa (Taiwan), the Pescadores Islands, and part of southern Manchuria. China also recognized the independence of Korea (Chosen), which Japan later annexed (1910).

In 1904–1905, Japan defeated Russia in the Russo-Japanese War, gaining the territory of southern Sakhalin (Karafuto) and Russia's port and rail rights in Manchuria. In World War I, Japan seized Germany's Pacific islands and leased areas in China. The Treaty of Versailles then awarded Japan a mandate over the islands.

At the Washington Conference of 1921–1922, Japan agreed to respect Chinese national integrity, but, in 1931, it invaded Manchuria. The following year, Japan set up this area as a puppet state, "Manchukuo," under Emperor Henry Pu-Yi, the last of China's Manchu dynasty. On Nov. 25, 1936, Japan joined the Axis. The invasion of China came the next year, followed by the Pearl Harbor attack on the U.S. on Dec. 7, 1941. Japan won its first military engagements during the war, extending its power over a vast area of the Pacific. Yet, after 1942, the Japanese were forced to retreat, island by island, to their own country. The dropping of atomic bombs on the cities of Hiroshima and Nagasaki in 1945 by the United States finally brought the government to admit defeat. Japan surrendered formally on Sept. 2, 1945, aboard the battleship *Missouri* in Tokyo Bay. Southern Sakhalin and the Kuril Islands reverted to the USSR, and Formosa (Taiwan) and Manchuria to China. The Pacific islands remained under U.S. occupation.

Gen. Douglas MacArthur was appointed supreme commander of the U.S. occupation of postwar Japan (1945–1952). In 1947, a new constitution took effect. The emperor became largely a symbolic head of state. The U.S. and Japan signed a security treaty in 1951, allowing for U.S. troops to be stationed in Japan. In 1952, Japan regained full sovereignty, and, in 1972, the U.S. returned to Japan the Ryuku Islands, including Okinawa.

Japan's postwar economic recovery was nothing short of remarkable. New technologies and manufacturing were undertaken with great success. A shrewd trade policy gave Japan larger shares in many Western markets, an imbalance that caused some tensions with the U.S. The close involvement of Japanese government in the country's banking and industry produced accusations of protectionism. Yet economic growth continued through the 1970s and 1980s, eventually making Japan the world's second-largest economy (after the U.S.).

During the 1990s, Japan suffered an economic downturn prompted by scandals involving government officials, bankers, and leaders of industry. Japan succumbed to the Asian economic crisis in 1998, experiencing its worst recession since World War II. These setbacks led to the resignation of Prime Minister Ryutaro Hashimoto in July 1998. He was replaced by Keizo Obuchi. In 1999, Japan seemed to make slight progress in an economic recovery. Prime Minister Obuchi died of a stroke in May 2000 and was succeeded by Yoshiro Mori, whose administration was dogged by scandal and blunders from the outset.

Despite attempts to revive the economy, fears that Japan would slide back into recession increased in early 2001. The embattled Mori resigned in April 2001 and was replaced by Liberal Democrat Junichiro Koizumi—the country's 11th prime minister in 13 years. Koizumi enjoyed fleeting popularity; after two years in office the economy remained in a slump and his attempts at reform were thwarted.

At an unprecedented summit meeting in North Korea in Sept. 2002, President Kim Jong Il apologized to Koizumi for North Korea's kidnapping of Japanese citizens during the 1970s and 1980s, and Koizumi pledged a generous aid package—both significant steps toward normalizing relations.

Koizumi was overwhelmingly reelected in Sept. 2003 and promised to push ahead with tough economic reforms.

Relations between Japan and China reached new lows in April 2005, when thousands of Chinese, with tacit government approval, took to the streets to protest the publication of Japanese textbooks that whitewashed the atrocities committed by Japan during World War II. After three weeks of demonstrations, the Chinese government ordered an end to the protests and Japanese prime minister Koizumi apologized for Japan's abuses. "Japan, through its colonial rule and aggression, caused tremendous damage and suffering."

Relations further deteriorated in May, when Wu Yi, China's vice-premier, shunned Koizumi during a brief visit to Japan that was intended to mend relations. Chinese officials said she canceled their planned meeting to protest laudatory comments about the Yasukuni shrine made by Japanese officials. The shrine, which honors some of Japan's most notorious war criminals, has been a constant source of animosity between the countries.

In August, Koizumi called for early elections, when the upper house of Parliament rejected his proposal to privatize the postal service—a reform he has long advocated. In addition to delivering mail, Japan's postal service also functions as a savings bank and has about $3 trillion in assets. Koizumi won a landslide victory in September, with his Liberal Democrat party securing its biggest majority since 1986.

Jordan

THE HASHEMITE KINGDOM OF JORDAN

National name: Al-Mamlaka al-Urduniya al-Hashimiyah
Ruler: King Abdullah II (1999)
Prime Minister: Adnan Badran (2004)
Area: 35,637 sq mi (92,300 sq km) excludes West Bank
Population (2005 est.): 5,759,732 (growth rate: 2.6%); birth rate: 21.8/1000; infant mortality rate: 17.4/1000; life expectancy: 78.2; density per sq mi: 162
Capital and largest city (2003 est.): Amman, 2,677,500 (metro. area), 1,293,200. **Other large cities:** Zarka, 512,200; Irbid, 267,200; As-Salt, 200,400. **Monetary unit:** Jordanian dinar. **Languages:** Arabic (official),

English. **Ethnicity/race:** Arab 98%, Circassian 1%, Armenian 1%. **Religions:** Islam (Sunni) 92%, Christian 6% (mostly Greek Orthodox), other 2%. **Literacy rate:** 91% (2003 est.)
Economic summary: GDP/PPP (2004 est.): $25.5 billion; per capita $4,500. **Real growth rate:** 5.1%. **Inflation:** 3.2%. **Unemployment:** 15% official rate; actual rate is approximately 30%. **Arable land:** 3%. **Agriculture:** wheat, barley, citrus, tomatoes, melons, olives; sheep, goats, poultry. **Labor force:** 1.41 million; services 82.5%, industry 12.5%, agriculture 5% (2001 est.). **Industries:** phosphate mining, pharmaceuticals, petroleum refining, cement, potash, inorganic chemicals, light manufacturing, tourism. **Natural resources:** phosphates, potash, shale oil. **Exports:** $3.2 billion (f.o.b., 2004 est.): clothing, phosphates, fertilizers, potash, vegetables, manufactures, pharmaceuticals. **Imports:** $7.6 billion (f.o.b., 2004 est.): crude oil, machinery, transport equipment, food, live animals, manufactured goods. **Major trading partners:** U.S., Iraq, Switzerland, India, Saudi Arabia, China, Germany (2003).

Geography The Middle East kingdom of Jordan is bordered on the west by Israel and the Dead Sea, on the north by Syria, on the east by Iraq, and on the south by Saudi Arabia. It is comparable in size to Indiana. Arid hills and mountains make up most of the country. The southern section of the Jordan River flows through the country.

Government Constitutional hereditary monarchy.

History In biblical times, the country that is now Jordan contained the lands of Edom, Moab, Ammon, and Bashan. Together with other Middle Eastern territories, Jordan passed in turn to the Assyrians, the Babylonians, the Persians, and, about 330 B.C., the Seleucids. Conflict between the Seleucids and the Ptolemies enabled the Arabic-speaking Nabataeans to create a kingdom in southeast Jordan. In A.D. 106 it became part of the Roman province of Arabia and in 633–636 was conquered by the Arabs. In the 16th century, Jordan submitted to Ottoman Turkish rule and was administered from Damascus. Taken from the Turks by the British in World War I, Jordan (formerly known as Transjordan) was separated from the Palestine mandate in 1920, and in 1921, placed under the rule of Abdullah ibn Hussein.

In 1923, Britain recognized Jordan's independence, subject to the mandate. In 1946, grateful for Jordan's loyalty in World War II, Britain abolished the mandate. That part of Palestine occupied by Jordanian troops was formally incorporated by action of the Jordanian Parliament in 1950. King Abdullah was assassinated in 1951. His son Talal, who was mentally ill, was deposed the next year. Talal's son Hussein, born on Nov. 14, 1935, succeeded him.

From the beginning of his reign, Hussein had to steer a careful course between his powerful neighbor to the west, Israel, and rising Arab nationalism, frequently a direct threat to his throne. Riots erupted when he joined the Central Treaty Organization (the Baghdad Pact) in 1955, and he incurred further unpopularity when Britain, France, and Israel attacked the Suez Canal in 1956, forcing him to place his army under nominal command of the United Arab Republic of Egypt and Syria. The 1961 breakup of the UAR eased Arab national pressure on Hussein, who was the first to recognize Syria after it reclaimed its independence. Jordan was swept into the 1967 Arab-Israeli War, however, and lost the old city of Jerusalem and all of its territory west of the Jordan River, the West Bank. Embittered Palestinian guerrilla forces virtually took over sections of Jordan in the aftermath of defeat, and open warfare broke out between the Palestinians and government forces in 1970.

Despite intervention of Syrian tanks, Hussein's Bedouin army defeated the Palestinians. The Jordanians drove out the Syrians and 12,000 Iraqi troops who had been in the country since the 1967 war. Ignoring protests from other Arab states, Hussein, by mid-1971, crushed Palestinian strength in Jordan and shifted the problem to Lebanon, where many of the guerrillas had fled. As Egypt and Israel neared final agreement on a peace treaty early in 1979, Hussein met with Yasir Arafat, the PLO leader, on March 17, and issued a joint statement of opposition. Although the U.S. pressed Jordan to break Arab ranks on the issue, Hussein elected to side with the great majority, cutting ties with Cairo and joining the boycott against Egypt.

Jordan's stance during the Persian Gulf War strained relations with the U.S. and led to the termination of U.S. aid. The signing of a national charter by King Hussein and leaders of the main political groups in June 1991 meant political parties were permitted in exchange for acceptance of the constitution and the monarchy. King Hussein's decision to join the Middle East peace talks in mid-1991 helped restore his country's relations with the U.S.

In July 1994, King Hussein and the Israeli prime minister Yitzhak Rabin signed a declaration ending the state of belligerency between the two countries. A peace agreement between the two countries was signed on Oct. 26, 1994, although a clause in it calling the king the "custodian" of Islamic holy shrines in Jerusalem angered the PLO. In the wake of the agreement, Jordan's relations with the U.S. and with the moderate Arab states, including Saudi Arabia, warmed. In 1997, Jordan, determined to attract foreign investment, began negotiating with the United States about membership in the World Trade Organization. In Jan. 1999, King Hussein unexpectedly deposed his brother, Prince Hassan, who had been heir apparent for 34 years, and named his eldest son as the new crown prince. A month later, King Hussein died of cancer, and Abdullah, 37, a popular military leader with little political experience, became king.

The first parliamentary elections under King Abdullah took place in June 2003 and resulted in a two-thirds majority for the king's supporters. In 2005, the king, unhappy with the slow progress on reforms, replaced his cabinet.

Kazakhstan

REPUBLIC OF KAZAKHSTAN

National name: Qazaqstan Respublikasy
President: Nursultan A. Nazarbayev (1990)
Prime Minister: Daniyal Akhmetov (2003)
Area: 1,049,150 sq mi (2,717,300 sq km)
Population (2005 est.): 15,185,844 (growth rate: 0.3%); birth rate: 15.8/1000; infant mortality rate: 29.2/1000; life expectancy: 66.5; density per sq mi: 14
Capital (2003 est.): Astana, 288,200 (formerly Aqmola; capital since 1997). **Largest cities:** Almaty (former capital), 1,045,900; Karaganda, 404,600; Shymkent, 333,500; Taraz, 305,700; Pavlodar, 299,500; Ust-Kamenogorsk, 288,000; Aqtöbe, 234,400.
Monetary unit: Tenge. **Languages:** Kazak (Qazaq, state language) 64.4%; Russian (official, used in everyday business) 95% (2001 est.). **Ethnicity/race:** Kazak (Qazaq) 53.4%, Russian 30%, Ukrainian 3.7%, Uzbek 2.5%, German 2.4%, Tatar 1.4%, other 6.6% (1999). **Religions:** Islam 47%, Russian Orthodox 44%, Protestant 2%, other 7%. **Literacy rate:** 98% (1999 est.)

Economic summary: GDP/PPP (2004 est.): $118.4 billion; per capita $7,800. **Real growth rate:** 9.1%. **Inflation:** 6.9%. **Unemployment:** 8%. **Arable land:** 8%. **Agriculture:** grain (mostly spring wheat), cotton; livestock. **Labor force:** 7.95 million; industry 30%, agriculture 20%, services 50% (2002 est.). **Industries:** oil, coal, iron ore, manganese, chromite, lead, zinc, copper, titanium, bauxite, gold, silver, phosphates, sulfur, iron and steel; tractors and other agricultural machinery, electric motors, construction materials. **Natural resources:** major deposits of petroleum, natural gas, coal, iron ore, manganese, chrome ore, nickel, cobalt, copper, molybdenum, lead, zinc, bauxite, gold, uranium. **Exports:** $18.47 billion (f.o.b., 2004 est.): oil and oil products 58%, ferrous metals 24%, chemicals 5%, machinery 3%, grain, wool, meat, coal (2001). **Imports:** $13.07 billion (f.o.b., 2004 est.): machinery and equipment 41%, metal products 28%, foodstuffs 8% (2001). **Major trading partners:** Bermuda, Russia, Switzerland, China, Italy, Germany, U.S. (2003).

Geography Kazakhstan lies in the north of the central Asian republics and is bounded by Russia in the north, China in the east, Kyrgyzstan and Uzbekistan in the south, and the Caspian Sea and part of Turkmenistan in the west. It has almost 1,177 mi (1,894 km) of coastline on the Caspian Sea. Kazakhstan is slightly more than twice the size of Texas. The territory is mostly steppe land with hilly plains and plateaus.

Government Republic.

History The indigenous Kazakhs were a nomadic Turkic people who belonged to several divisions of Kazakh hordes. They grouped together in settlements and lived in dome-shaped tents made of felt called *yurts*. Their tribes migrated seasonally to find pastures for their herds of sheep, horses, and goats. Although they had chiefs, the Kazakhs were rarely united as a single nation under one great leader. Their tribes fell under Mongol rule in the 13th century and they were dominated by Tartar khanates until the area was conquered by Russia in the 18th century.

The area became part of the Kirgiz Autonomous Republic formed by the Soviet authorities in 1920, and in 1925 this entity's name was changed to the Kazakh Autonomous Soviet Socialist Republic (Kazakh ASSR). After 1927, the Soviet government began forcing the nomadic Kazakhs to settle on collective and state farms, and the Soviets continued the czarist policy of encouraging large numbers of Russians and other Slavs to settle in the region.

Owing to the region's intensive agricultural development and its use as a testing ground for nuclear weapons by the Soviet government, serious environmental problems developed by the late 20th century. Along with the other central Asian republics, Kazakhstan obtained its independence from the collapsing Soviet Union in 1991. Kazakhstan proclaimed its membership in the Commonwealth of Independent States on Dec. 21, 1991, along with ten other former Soviet republics. In 1993, the country overwhelmingly approved the Nuclear Non-Proliferation Treaty. President Nursultan Nazarbayev restructured and consolidated many operations of the government in 1997, eliminating a third of the government ministries and agencies. In 1997, the national capital was changed from Almaty, the largest city, to Astana (formerly Aqmola).

In Jan. 1999, Nazarbayev was sworn into office for another seven years, although the election was widely criticized when an opposition leader was disqualified on a technicality. Despite his authoritarianism, Nazarbayev, who has ruled Kazakhstan since 1989 (when it was still part of the Soviet Union), is a widely popular leader. Kazakhstan has the potential for becoming one of central Asia's richest countries because of its huge mineral and oil resources and its liberalized economy, which encourages Western investment. In 2000, oil was discovered in Kazakhstan's portion of the Caspian Sea. It is believed to be the largest oil find in 30 years. In March 2001, a pipeline opened to transport oil from the Tengiz fields to the Russian Black Sea port of Novorossiysk. In 2004, Kazakhstan signed a deal allowing China to build an oil pipeline to the Chinese border.

But as its economic outlook blossoms, Kazakhstan's scarce democratic principles continue to wither. In the past several years, the president has harassed the independent media, arrested opposition leaders, and passed a law making it virtually impossible for new political parties to form.

Kenya

REPUBLIC OF KENYA

National name: Jamhuri ya Kenya
President: Mwai Kibaki (2002)
Area: 224,961 sq mi (582,650 sq km)
Population (2005 est.): 33,829,590 (growth rate: 2.6%); birth rate: 40.1/1000; infant mortality rate: 61.5/1000; life expectancy: 48.0; density per sq mi: 150
Capital and largest city (2003 est.): Nairobi, 3,064,800 (metro. area), 2,411,900 (city proper). **Other large city:** Mombasa, 712,600. **Monetary unit:** Kenya shilling.
Languages: English (official), Swahili (national), and several other languages spoken by 25 ethnic groups.
Ethnicity/race: Kikuyu 22%; Luhya 14%; Luo 13%; Kalenjin 12%; Kamba 11%; Kisii 6%; Meru 6%; other African 15%; Asian, European, and Arab 1%. **Religions:** Protestant 45%, Roman Catholic 33%, indigenous beliefs 10%, Islam 10%, others 2% (note: estimates vary widely). **Literacy rate:** 85% (2003 est.)
Economic summary: GDP/PPP (2004 est.): $34.68 billion; per capita $1,100. **Real growth rate:** 2.2%. **Inflation:** 9%. **Unemployment:** 40% (2001 est.). **Arable land:** 8%. **Agriculture:** tea, coffee, corn, wheat, sugarcane, fruit, vegetables; dairy products, beef, pork, poultry, eggs. **Labor force:** 11.4 million; agriculture 75% (2003 est.). **Industries:** small-scale consumer goods (plastic, furniture, batteries, textiles, soap, cigarettes, flour), agricultural products; oil refining, aluminum, steel, lead, cement; commercial ship repair, tourism. **Natural resources:** limestone, soda ash, salt, gemstones, fluorspar, zinc, diatomite, gypsum, wildlife, hydropower. **Exports:** $2.589 billion (f.o.b., 2004 est.): tea, horticultural products, coffee, petroleum products, fish, cement. **Imports:** $4.19 billion (f.o.b., 2004 est.): machinery and transportation equipment, petroleum products, motor vehicles, iron and steel, resins and plastics. **Major trading partners:** Uganda, UK, U.S., Netherlands, Pakistan, Egypt, Tanzania, UAE, Saudi Arabia, South Africa, China, India, Japan, Germany (2003). **Member of Commonwealth of Nations**

Geography Kenya lies across the equator in east-central Africa, on the coast of the Indian Ocean. It is twice the size of Nevada. Kenya borders Somalia to the east, Ethiopia to the north, Tanzania to the south, Uganda to the west, and Sudan to the northwest. In the north, the land is arid; the southwest corner is in the fertile Lake Victoria Basin; and a length of the eastern depression of the Great Rift Valley separates western highlands from those that rise from the lowland coastal strip.

Government Republic.

History Paleontologists believe people may first have inhabited Kenya about 2 million years ago. In the 700s, Arab seafarers established settlements along the coast, and the Portuguese took control of the area in the early 1500s. More than 40 ethnic groups reside in Kenya. Its largest group, the Kikuyu, migrated to the region at the beginning of the 18th century.

The land became a British protectorate in 1890 and a Crown colony in 1920, when it went by the name British East Africa. Nationalist stirrings began in the 1940s, and in 1952 the Mau Mau movement, made up of Kikuyu militants, rebelled against the government. The fighting lasted until 1956.

On Dec. 12, 1963, Kenya became fully independent. Jomo Kenyatta, a nationalist leader during the independence struggle who had been jailed by the British, became its first president.

From 1964 to 1992, the country was ruled as a one-party state by the Kenya African National Union (KANU), first under Kenyatta and then under Daniel arap Moi. Demonstrations and riots pressured Moi to allow for multiparty elections in 1992.

The economy did not flourish under Moi's rule. In the 1990s, Kenya's infrastructure began disintegrating and official graft was rampant, contributing to the withdrawal of much foreign aid. In early 1995, President Moi moved against the opposition and ordered the arrest of anyone who insulted him.

A series of disasters plagued Kenya in 1997 and 1998: severe flooding destroyed roads, bridges, and crops; epidemics of malaria and cholera overwhelmed the ineffectual health care system; and ethnic clashes erupted between the Kikuyu and Kalenjin ethnic groups in the Rift Valley.

On Aug. 7, 1998, the U.S. embassy in Nairobi was bombed by terrorists, killing 243 and injuring more than 1,000. The embassy in neighboring Tanzania was bombed the same day, killing 10.

In a successful effort to win back IMF and World Bank funding, which had been suspended because of Kenya's corruption and poor economic practices, President Moi appointed his high-profile critic and political opponent, Richard Leakey, as head of the civil service in 1999. A third-generation white Kenyan, son of paleontologists Louis and Mary Leakey, he had been a highly effective reformer as head of the Kenya Wildlife Service. But after 20 months during which he made a promising start at cleaning up Kenya's corrupt bureaucracy, Leakey was sacked by Moi. Kenya is regularly ranked among the ten most corrupt countries in the world, according to the watchdog group Transparency International.

An anticorruption law, sponsored by the ruling party, failed to pass in Parliament in Aug. 2001 and imperiled Kenya's chances for international aid. Opposition leaders called the law a cynical ploy meant to give the appearance of reform; the proposed law, they contended, was in fact too weak and full of loopholes to make a dent in corruption.

Opposition leader Mwai Kibaki won the Dec. 2002 presidential election, defeating Moi's protégé, Uhuru Kenyatta (term limits prevented Moi, in power for 24 years, from running again). Kibaki promised to put an end to the country's rampant corruption. In his first few months, Kibaki did initiate a number of reforms—ordering a crackdown on corrupt judges and police and instituting free primary school education—and international donors opened their coffers again.

But by 2004, disappointment in Kibaki set in when little further progress was evident, and a long-awaited new constitution, meant to limit the president's power, still had not been delivered. Kibaki made no real progress on his mandate to stem corruption, which became glaringly evident when his anticorruption minister, John Githongo, resigned in Feb. 2005, frustrated that he was prevented from investigating a number of scandals. In July 2005, Parliament finally approved a draft of a constitution, but many criticized it for not curbing the president's powers to a greater degree.

Kiribati

REPUBLIC OF KIRIBATI

President: Anote Tong (2003)
Area: 313 sq mi (811 sq km)
Population (2005 est.): 103,092 (growth rate: 2.3%); birth rate: 30.9/1000; infant mortality rate: 48.5/1000; life expectancy: 61.7; density per sq mi: 329
Capital and largest city (2003 est.): Tarawa, 26,600. **Monetary unit:** Australian dollar. **Languages:** English (official), I-Kiribati (Gilbertese). **Ethnicity/race:** predominantly Micronesian, some Polynesian. **Religions:** Roman Catholic 52%, Protestant (Congregational) 40%, some Seventh-Day Adventist, Muslim, Baha'i, Latter-day Saints, and Church of God (1999). **Literacy rate:** n.a.
Economic summary: GDP/PPP (2001 est.): $79 million, supplemented by a nearly equal amount from external sources; per capita $800. **Real growth rate:** 1.5%. **Inflation:** 2.5%. **Unemployment:** 2%; underemployment 70% (1992 est.). **Arable land:** 3%. **Agriculture:** copra, taro, breadfruit, sweet potatoes, vegetables; fish. **Labor force:** 7,870 economically active, not including subsistence farmers (2001 est.). **Industries:** fishing, handicrafts. **Natural resources:** phosphate (production discontinued in 1979). **Exports:** $35 million (f.o.b. 2002): copra 62%, coconuts, seaweed, fish. **Imports:** $83 million (c.i.f., 2002): foodstuffs, machinery and equipment, miscellaneous manufactured goods, fuel. **Major trading partners:** Japan, Australia, U.S., Thailand, Fiji, New Zealand (2003). **Member of Commonwealth of Nations**

Geography Kiribati, formerly the Gilbert Islands, consists of three widely separated main groups of southwest Pacific islands: the Gilberts on the equator, the Phoenix Islands to the east, and the Line Islands farther east. Ocean Island, producer of phosphates until it was mined out in 1981, is also included in the 2 million square miles of ocean. Most of the islands of Kiribati are low-lying coral atolls built on a submerged volcanic chain and encircled by reefs.

Government Republic.

History Kiribati was first settled by early Austronesian-speaking peoples long before the 1st century A.D. Fijians and Tongans arrived about the 14th century and subsequently merged with the older groups to form the traditional I-Kiribati Micronesian society and culture. The islands were first sighted by British and American ships in the late 18th and early 19th centuries, and the first British settlers arrived in 1837. A British protectorate since 1892, the Gilbert and Ellice Islands became a Crown colony in 1915–1916. Kiritimati (Christmas) Atoll became a part of the colony in 1919; the Phoenix Islands were added in 1937.

Tarawa and others of the Gilbert group were occupied by Japan during World War II. Tarawa was the site of one of the bloodiest battles in U.S. Marine Corps history when Marines landed in Nov. 1943 to dislodge the Japanese defenders. The Gilbert Islands and Ellice Islands (now Tuvalu) were separated in 1975 and granted internal self-government by Britain. Kiribati became independent on July 12, 1979.

Kiribati's 1995 act of moving the international date line far to the east, so that it encompassed Kiribati's

Line Islands group, courted controversy. The move, which fulfilled one of President Tito's campaign promises, was intended to enable Kiribati to become the first country to see the dawn on Jan. 1, 2000, and welcome the new millennium—an event of significance for tourism. In 1999, Kiribati gained UN membership.

In 2002, Kiribati passed a controversial law enabling it to shut down newspapers. The legislation followed the launching of Kiribati's first successful nongovernment-run newspaper. Anote Tong of the opposition party, Boutokaan Te Koaua, was elected president in 2003.

Korea, North

DEMOCRATIC PEOPLE'S REPUBLIC OF KOREA

National name: Choson Minjujuui Inmin Konghwaguk
Head of State: Kim Jong Il (1994)
Prime Minister: Hong Song Nam (1997)
Area: 46,540 sq mi (120,540 sq km)
Population (2005 est.): 22,912,177 (growth rate: 0.9%); birth rate: 16.1/1000; infant mortality rate: 24.0/1000; life expectancy: 71.4; density per sq mi: 492
Capital and largest city (2003): Pyongyang, 3,222,000 (metro. area), 2,767,900. **Monetary unit:** Won. **Language:** Korean. **Ethnicity/race:** racially homogeneous; small Chinese community, a few ethnic Japanese. **Religions:** Buddhism and Confucianism; religious activities almost nonexistent. **Literacy rate:** 99% (1990 est.)
Economic summary: GDP/PPP (2004 est.): $30.88 billion; per capita $1,400. **Real growth rate:** 1%. **Inflation:** n.a. (2003 est.). **Unemployment:** n.a. (2003). **Arable land:** 21%. **Agriculture:** rice, corn, potatoes, soybeans, pulses; cattle, pigs, pork, eggs. **Labor force:** 9.6 million; agricultural 36%, nonagricultural 64%. **Industries:** military products; machine building, electric power, chemicals; mining (coal, iron ore, magnesite, graphite, copper, zinc, lead, and precious metals), metallurgy; textiles, food processing; tourism. **Natural resources:** coal, lead, tungsten, zinc, graphite, magnesite, iron ore, copper, gold, pyrites, salt, fluorspar, hydropower. **Exports:** $1.2 million (f.o.b., 2003 est.): minerals, metallurgical products, manufactures (including armaments); textiles and fishery products. **Imports:** $2.1 billion (c.i.f., 2003): petroleum, coking coal, machinery and equipment; textiles, grain. **Major trading partners:** China, South Korea, Japan, Thailand (2003).

Geography Korea is a 600-mile (966 km) peninsula jutting out from Manchuria and China (and a small portion of the USSR). North Korea occupies an area slightly smaller than Pennsylvania north of the 38th parallel.

The country is almost completely covered by a series of north-south mountain ranges separated by narrow valleys. The Yalu River forms part of the northern border with Manchuria.

Government Authoritarian socialist; one-man dictatorship.

History The ancient history of the Korean peninsula can be traced to the Neolithic Age, when Turkic-Manchurian-Mongol peoples migrated into the region from China. The first agriculturally based settlements appeared around 6000 B.C. Some of the larger communities of this era were established along the Han-gang River near modern-day Seoul, others near Pyongyang and Pusan. According to ancient lore, Korea's earliest civilization, known as Choson, was founded in 2333 B.C. by Tan-gun.

In the 17th century, Korea became a vassal state of China and was cut off from outside contact until the Sino-Japanese War of 1894–1895. Following Japan's victory, Korea was granted independence. By 1910, Korea had been annexed by Japan, which developed the country but never won over the Korean nationalists, who continued to agitate for independence.

After Japan's surrender at the conclusion of World War II, the Korean peninsula was partitioned into two occupation zones, divided at the 38th parallel. The USSR controlled the north, with the U.S. taking charge of the south. In 1948, the division was made permanent with the establishment of the separate regimes of North and South Korea. The Democratic People's Republic of Korea (North Korea) was established on May 1, 1948, with Kim Il Sung as president.

Hoping to unify the Koreas under a single Communist government, the North launched a surprise invasion of South Korea on June 25, 1950. In the following days, the UN Security Council condemned the attack and demanded an immediate withdrawal.

President Harry S. Truman ordered U.S. air and naval units into action to enforce the UN order. The British government followed suit, and soon a UN multinational command was set up to aid the South Koreans.

The North Korean invaders swiftly seized Seoul and surrounded the allied forces in the peninsula's southeast corner near Pusan. In a desperate bid to reverse the military situation, UN Commander Gen. Douglas MacArthur ordered an amphibious landing at Inchon on Sept. 15 and routed the North Korean army. MacArthur's forces pushed north across the 38th parallel, approaching the Yalu River.

Prompted by this successful counteroffensive, Communist China entered the war, forcing the UN troops into a headlong retreat. Seoul was lost again, then regained. Ultimately, the war stabilized near the 38th parallel but dragged on for two years while negotiations took place. An armistice was agreed to on July 27, 1953.

Kim Il Sung's death on July 8, 1994, introduced a period of uncertainty, as his son, Kim Jong Il, assumed the leadership mantle. Negotiations over the country's suspected possession of atomic weapons dragged on, but an agreement was reached in June 1995 that included a provision for providing the North with a South Korean nuclear reactor.

The nuclear standoffs that characterized the mid-1990s were overshadowed when famine struck the nation's 24 million inhabitants in 1998 and 1999. Two years of floods had been followed by severe droughts in 1997 and 1998, causing devastating crop failures. Because of a lack of fuel and machinery parts, and weather conditions that encouraged parasites, only 10% of North Korea's rice fields could be worked. The staggering food crisis necessitated foreign aid. In the fall of 1999, the severe famine, which claimed an estimated 2 million to 3 million lives, had begun to wane.

In Sept. 1998, North Korea launched a test missile over Japan, claiming it was simply a scientific satellite. This launch alarmed Japan—and much of the rest of the world—about North Korea's intentions regarding reentry into the nuclear arms race. In 1999, North Korea agreed to allow the United States to conduct ongoing inspections of a suspected nuclear development site, Kumchangri, which North Korea admitted had been devised for "a sensitive military purpose." In exchange, the U.S. would increase food aid and initiate a program for bringing potato production to the country.

Antagonism between North and South Korea erupted into open aggression twice within six months in late 1998 and 1999, with South Korea hitting one North

Korean vessel and sinking two others that were discovered trespassing in South Korean waters. Tension with South Korea eased dramatically in June 2000, when South Korea's president, Kim Dae Jung, met with North Korea's President Kim Jong Il in Pyongyang. The summit marked the first-ever meeting of the two countries' leaders. But efforts toward reconciliation fizzled thereafter, and various minor military skirmishes followed.

In Jan. 2002, President Bush described North Korea as part of an "axis of evil." Such open hostility marked a dramatic shift in U.S. policy toward North Korea from the Clinton administration's policy of engagement.

North Korea stunned the world in late 2002 with two admissions. In September, the government acknowledged that it had kidnapped about a dozen Japanese in the 1970s and 1980s for the purposes of training North Korean spies. In October, confronted with U.S. intelligence, North Korea admitted that it had violated a 1994 agreement freezing its nuclear-weapons program and had in fact been developing nuclear bombs. Since 2002, North Korea has vacillated between affirming and denying that it already has nuclear weapons.

In late December 2002, North Korea expelled UN weapons inspectors from the country and announced it could no longer agree to the terms of the nuclear Non-Proliferation Treaty (NPT), officially withdrawing from it in January 2003. During talks with China and the U.S. in April, North Korea announced that it had already produced nuclear weapons and threatened to test or export them. In July, North Korean officials reported that the country had reprocessed enough plutonium to build six nuclear bombs. Kim has regularly used threats and hostile acts to try to wring aid from the international community, but it was difficult to decipher how he expected to accomplish his aims—economic aid and a safeguard against U.S. attack—through such brinkmanship. Refusing to bow to North Korea's demands, the United States informed the nation's diplomats that it would not begin to negotiate until North Korea first dismantled its nuclear program. China took on the role of mediator between North Korea and the U.S., urging less inflexibility on both sides. A modest breakthrough occurred when officials from the U.S., North Korea, China, Russia, South Korea, and Japan met in Aug. 2003 in Beijing, although nothing substantive resulted. Six-nation negotiations in Feb. and June 2004 were also inconclusive, and a fourth round of talks in Aug. 2005 were deadlocked as well.

Korea, South

REPUBLIC OF KOREA

National name: Taehan Min'guk
President: Roh Moo Hyun (2003)
Prime Minister: Lee Hae-chan (2004)
Area: 38,023 sq mi (98,480 sq km)
Population (2005 est.): 48,422,644 (growth rate: 0.4%); birth rate: 10.1/1000; infant mortality rate: 7.0/1000; life expectancy: 75.8; density per sq mi: 1,274
Capital and largest city (2003 est.): Seoul, 19,969,100 (metro. area), 9,630,600 (city proper). **Other large cities:** Pusan, 3,504,900; Inchon, 2,479,600 (part of Seoul metro. area); Taegu, 2,369,800. **Monetary unit:** Won. **Languages:** Korean, English widely taught.
Ethnicity/race: homogeneous (except for about 20,000 Chinese). **Religions:** no affiliation 46%, Christian 26%, Buddhist 26%, Confucianist 1%, other 1%. **Literacy rate:** 98% (2003 est.)
Economic summary: GDP/PPP (2004 est.): $925.1 billion; per capita $19,200. **Real growth rate:** 4.6%. **Inflation:** 3.6%. **Unemployment:** 3.6%. **Arable land:**

17%. **Agriculture:** rice, root crops, barley, vegetables, fruit; cattle, pigs, chickens, milk, eggs; fish. **Labor force:** 22.9 million; agriculture 8%, industry 19%, services 73% (2004 est.). **Industries:** electronics, telecommunications, automobile production, chemicals, shipbuilding, steel. **Natural resources:** coal, tungsten, graphite, molybdenum, lead, hydropower potential. **Exports:** $250.6 billion (f.o.b., 2004 est.): semiconductors, wireless telecommunications equipment, motor vehicles, computers, steel, ships, petrochemicals. **Imports:** $214.2 billion (f.o.b., 2004 est.): machinery, electronics and electronic equipment, oil, steel, transport equipment, organic chemicals, plastics. **Major trading partners:** China, U.S., Japan, Hong Kong, Saudi Arabia (2003).

Geography Slightly larger than Indiana, South Korea lies below the 38th parallel on the Korean peninsula. It is mountainous in the east; in the west and south are many harbors on the mainland and offshore islands.

Government Republic.

History South Korea came into being after World War II, the result of a 1945 agreement reached by the Allies at the Potsdam Conference, making the 38th parallel the boundary between a northern zone of the Korean peninsula to be occupied by the USSR and southern zone to be controlled by U.S. forces. (For details, *see* Korea, North.)

Elections were held in the U.S. zone in 1948 for a National Assembly, which adopted a republican constitution and elected Syngman Rhee as the nation's president. The new republic was proclaimed on Aug. 15 and was recognized as the legal government of Korea by the UN on Dec. 12, 1948.

On June 25, 1950, North Korean Communist forces launched a massive surprise attack on South Korea, quickly overrunning the capital, Seoul. U.S. armed intervention was ordered on June 27 by President Harry S. Truman, and on the same day the UN invoked military sanctions against North Korea. Gen. Douglas MacArthur was named commander of the UN forces. U.S. and South Korean troops fought a heroic holding action, but by the first week of August they were forced back to a 4,000-square-mile beachhead in southeast Korea. There they stood off superior North Korean forces until Sept. 15, when a major UN amphibious assault was launched deep behind Communist lines at Inchon, the port of Seoul.

By Sept. 30, UN forces were in complete control of South Korea. They then crossed the 38th parallel and pursued retreating Communist forces into North Korea. In late October, UN forces neared the Sino-Korean border, several hundred thousand Chinese Communist troops entered the conflict, pushing MacArthur's forces back to the border between North and South Korea. By the time truce talks began on July 10, 1951, UN forces had crossed over the parallel again and were driving back into North Korea. Cease-fire negotiations dragged on for two years before an armistice was finally signed at Panmunjom on July 27, 1953, leaving a devastated Korea in need of large-scale rehabilitation. No official peace treaty has ever been signed between the former combatants.

President Syngman Rhee, after 12 years in office, was forced to resign in 1960 amid rising discontent with his autocratic leadership. Po Sun Yun was elected to succeed him, but political instability continued. In 1961, Gen. Park Chung Hee seized power and subsequently began a program of economic reforms designed to stimulate the nation's economy. The U.S. stepped up military aid, strengthening South Korea's armed forces to 600,000 men. Park's assassination on Oct. 26, 1979, by Kim Jae Kyu, head of the Korean Central Intelligence Agency, brought a liberalizing trend as new president Choi Kyu Hah freed imprisoned dissidents.

The release of opposition leader Kim Dae Jung in Feb. 1980 sparked antigovernment demonstrations that turned into riots, which were brutally suppressed by authorities. Kim, the most visible leader of the opposition, was imprisoned again. Choi resigned on Aug. 16. Chun Doo Hwan, head of a military Special Committee for National Security Measures, was the sole candidate when the electoral college confirmed him as president on Aug. 27. In 1986–1987, South Korea's opposition demanded that the president be selected by direct popular vote. After weeks of protest and rioting, Chun agreed to the demand. A split in the opposition led to Roh Tae Woo's election on Dec. 16, 1987.

In Aug. 1996 Roh was convicted on bribery charges, and Chun was convicted for bribery as well as his role in the 1979 coup and the 1980 crackdown on rioters. In 1997, an accumulation of corrupt business practices and bad loans led to a series of bankruptcies and a massive devaluation of South Korea's currency. The political instability that followed helped former dissident Kim Dae Jung become the first South Korean president ever to be elected from the political opposition.

In 1998 the Asian economic crisis bottomed out in South Korea. The nation began rebounding in 1999, the only sizable Asian economy to do so.

Antagonism between North and South Korea erupted into open aggression in 1998 and 1999. Tensions eased dramatically in June 2000, when President Kim Dae Jung met with the North's president, Kim Jong Il, in Pyongyang. The summit marked the first-ever meeting of the countries' leaders. President Kim Dae Jung won the Nobel Peace Prize in Oct. 2000 for his Sunshine Policy, which included initiating peace and reconciliation with North Korea.

Roh Moo Hyun of the ruling Millennium Democratic Party became president in February 2003 and promptly faced daunting problems. His vow to pursue his predecessor's Sunshine Policy toward North Korea was put to the test as the North continued to taunt the world with boasts about its nuclear capabilities. In addition, many South Koreans had begun to resent U.S. influence over their country. In March 2004, the conservative National Assembly voted overwhelmingly to impeach Roh, claiming he had violated election laws. More than 70% of the public, however, condemned the move, and thousands of his supporters took to the streets to protest. South Koreans showed their disapproval of Roh's impeachment at the polls in April, when they gave the liberal pro-Roh Uri Party a majority in the National Assembly. The Constitutional Court dismissed the impeachment in May, and Roh was reinstated as president.

In September 2004, officials told the International Atomic Energy Agency that in 2000, a group of rogue scientists had produced a small amount of weapons-grade uranium, a violation of several treaties.

Researchers stunned the world in May 2005, when they announced they had devised a new procedure to produce human stem-cell lines from a cloned human embryo.

After four days of inter-Korean talks in May, officials from South Korea agreed to send North Korea 200,000 tons of fertilizer, and the two sides agreed they would "cooperate for the peace on the Korean Peninsula." In July, China hosted a fourth round of disarmament talks with the U.S., South Korea, China, Japan, and Russia. The talks ended in a deadlock.

Kuwait

STATE OF KUWAIT

National name: Dawlat al-Kuwayt
Emir: Sheik Jaber al-Ahmad al-Sabah (1977)
Prime Minister: Sheik Sabah al-Ahmad al-Sabah (2003)
Area: 6,880 sq mi (17,820 sq km)
Population (2005 est.): 2,335,648 (growth rate: 3.4%);
birth rate: 21.9/1000; infant mortality rate: 9.9/1000; life
expectancy: 77.0; density per sq mi: 339
Capital (2003 est.): Kuwait, 1,709,800 (metro. area),
32,600 (city proper). **Largest city:** as-Salimiyah,
146,900. **Monetary unit:** Kuwaiti dinar. **Languages:**
Arabic (official), English. **Ethnicity/race:** Kuwaiti 45%,
other Arab 35%, South Asian 9%, Iranian 4%, other
7%. **Religions:** Islam 85% (Sunni 70%, Shiite 30%);
Christian, Hindu, Parsi, and other 15%. **Literacy rate:**
84% (2003 est.)
Economic summary: GDP/PPP (2004 est.): $48 billion;
per capita $21,300. **Real growth rate:** 6.8%.
Inflation: 2.3%. **Unemployment:** 2.2%. **Arable land:**
1%. **Agriculture:** practically no crops; fish. **Labor
force:** 1.42 million; note: non-Kuwaitis represent about
80% of the labor force; agriculture n.a., industry n.a.,
services n.a. **Industries:** petroleum, petrochemicals,
cement, shipbuilding and repair, desalination, food
processing, construction materials. **Natural
resources:** petroleum, fish, shrimp, natural gas.
Exports: $27.42 billion (f.o.b., 2004 est.): oil and
refined products, fertilizers. **Imports:** $11.12 billion
(f.o.b., 2004 est.): food, construction materials,
vehicles and parts, clothing. **Major trading partners:**
Japan, South Korea, U.S., Singapore, Taiwan,
Pakistan, Germany, China, UK, Saudi Arabia, Italy,
France (2003).

Geography   Kuwait is situated northeast of Saudi
Arabia at the northern end of the Persian Gulf, south
of Iraq. It is slightly larger than Hawaii. The low-lying
desert land is mainly sandy and barren.

Government   Kuwait is a constitutional monarchy,
governed by the al-Sabah family.

History   Kuwait is believed to have been part of an
early civilization in the 3rd millennium B.C. and to
have traded with Mesopotamian cities. Archeological
and historical traces disappeared around the first millennium B.C. At the beginning of the 18th century A.D.,
the 'Anizah tribe of central Arabia founded Kuwait
City, which became an autonomous sheikdom by
1756. 'Abd Rahim of the al-Sabah became the first
sheik, and his descendants continue to rule Kuwait
today. In the late 18th and early 19th centuries, the
sheikdom belonged to the fringes of the Ottoman
Empire. Kuwait obtained British protection in 1897
when the sheik feared that the Turks would expand
their hold over the area. In 1961, Britain ended the
protectorate, giving Kuwait independence, but agreed
to give military aid on request. Iraq immediately
threatened to occupy the area, and the British sent
troops to defend Kuwait. Soon afterward the Arab
League sent in troops, replacing the British. Iraq's
claim was dropped when the Arab League recognized
Kuwait's independence on July 20, 1961. Kuwait typically followed a neutral and mediatory policy among
Arab states.

Oil was discovered there in the 1930s, and Kuwait
proved to have 20% of the world's known oil
resources. Since 1946 it has been the world's second-
largest oil exporter. The sheik, who receives half of the
profits, devotes most of them to the education, welfare,
and modernization of his kingdom. In 1966, Sheik
Sabah designated a relative, Jaber al-Ahmad al-Sabah,
as his successor. By 1968, the sheikdom had established a model welfare state, and it sought to establish
dominance among the sheikdoms and emirates of the
Persian Gulf.

In July 1990, Iraqi president Saddam Hussein
blamed Kuwait for falling oil prices. After a failed
Arab mediation attempt to solve the dispute peacefully,
Iraq invaded Kuwait on Aug. 2, 1990, set up a pro-
Iraqi provisional government, and drained Kuwait of
its economic resources. A coalition of Arab and Western military forces drove Iraqi troops from Kuwait in a
mere four days, from Feb. 23–27, 1991, ending the
Persian Gulf War. The emir returned to his country
from Saudi Arabia in mid-March. Martial law, in effect
since the end of the Gulf War, ended in late June. The
U.S. sent 2,400 troops to the country in Aug. 1992,
ostensibly as part of a training exercise, though it was
widely interpreted as a show of strength to Saddam
Hussein. Iraqi "training" maneuvers near the Kuwaiti
border in Oct. 1994 renewed fears of aggression in the
country. A Kuwaiti appeal brought the quick deployment of U.S. and British troops and equipment.

In 1999, the emir gave women the right to vote and
run for Parliament, but later that year Parliament
defeated the ruler's decree. Kuwaiti society has grown
increasingly conservative under the influence of
Islamic fundamentalists. In 2003, traditionalists won a
sweeping victory in parliamentary elections. The emir
and crown prince (who served as prime minister) are
elderly and ailing; in July 2003, the country's de facto
leader, foreign minister Sabah al-Ahmad al-Sabah,
replaced the crown prince as prime minister.

In May 2005, Kuwait abandoned its 1999 ban on
women's suffrage, and in June a woman was appointed
to the cabinet. Saudi Arabia is now the only country
with suffrage that does not allow its women to vote.

Kyrgyzstan

THE KYRGYZ REPUBLIC

National name: Kyrgyz Respublikasy
President: Kurmanbek Bakiev (2005)
Prime Minister: Felix Kulov (2005)
Area: 76,641 sq mi (198,500 sq km)
Population (2005 est.): 5,146,281; (Kyrgyz, 52.4%;
Russian, 18%; Uzbek, 12.9%; Ukrainian, 2.5%;
German, 2.4%; other, 11.8%) (growth rate: 1.3%); birth
rate: 22.5/1000; infant mortality rate: 35.6/1000; life
expectancy: 68.2; density per sq mi: 67
Capital and largest city (2003 est.): Bishkek (formerly
Frunze), 824,900. **Other large city:** Osh 225,600.
Monetary unit: Som. **Languages:** Kyrgyz, Russian
(both official). **Ethnicity/race:** Kyrgyz 64.9%, Uzbek
13.8%, Russian 12.5%, Dungan 1.1%, Ukrainian 1%,
Uygur 1%, other 5.7% (1999). **Religions:** Islam, 75%;
Russian Orthodox, 20%; other, 5%. **Literacy rate:**
97% (1989 est.)
Economic summary: GDP/PPP (2004 est.): $8.495
billion; per capita $1,700. **Real growth rate:** 6%.
Inflation: 3.2%. **Unemployment:** 18%. **Arable land:**
7%. **Agriculture:** tobacco, cotton, potatoes,
vegetables, grapes, fruits and berries; sheep, goats,
cattle, wool. **Labor force:** 2.7 million (2000);
agriculture 55%, industry 15%, services 30% (2000
est.). **Industries:** small machinery, textiles, food
processing, cement, shoes, sawn logs, refrigerators,
furniture, electric motors, gold, rare earth metals.
Natural resources: abundant hydropower; significant
deposits of gold and rare earth metals; locally
exploitable coal, oil, and natural gas; other deposits of
nepheline, mercury, bismuth, lead, and zinc. **Exports:**
$646.7 million (f.o.b., 2004 est.): cotton, wool, meat,
tobacco; gold, mercury, uranium, natural gas,
hydropower; machinery; shoes. **Imports:** $775.1

million (f.o.b., 2004 est.): oil and gas, machinery and equipment, chemicals, foodstuffs. **Major trading partners:** UAE, Switzerland, Russia, Kazakhstan, Canada, China, U.S., Uzbekistan, Germany (2003).

Geography Kyrgyzstan (formerly Kirghizia) is a rugged country with the Tien Shan mountain range covering approximately 95% of the whole territory. The mountaintops are perennially covered with snow and glaciers. Kyrgyzstan borders Kazakhstan on the north and northwest, Uzbekistan in the southwest, Tajikistan in the south, and China in the southeast. The republic is the same size in area as the state of Nebraska.

Government Constitutional republic.

History The native Kyrgyz are a Turkic people who in ancient times first settled in the Tien Shan mountains. They were traditionally pastoral nomads. There was extensive Russian colonization in the 1900s and Russian settlers were given much of the best agricultural land. This led to an unsuccessful and disastrous revolt by the Kyrgyz people in 1916. Kyrgyzstan became part of the Soviet Federated Socialist Republic in 1924, and was made an autonomous republic in 1926. It became a constituent republic of the USSR in 1936. The Soviets forced the Kyrgyz to abandon their nomadic culture and brought modern farming and industrial production techniques into their society.

Kyrgyzstan proclaimed its independence from the Soviet Union on Aug. 31, 1991. On Dec. 21, 1991, Kyrgyzstan joined the Commonwealth of Independent States. The country joined the UN and the IMF in 1992 and adopted a shock-therapy economic program. Voters endorsed market reforms in a referendum held in Jan. 1994, and in 1996, referendum voters overwhelmingly endorsed proposed constitutional changes that enhanced the power of the president.

There is an ethnic and economic divide between the more developed north with its Kyrgyz population and the impoverished south, which is made up of Uzbeks and a diverse group of other ethnicities. About 50% of the entire population lived below the poverty line in 2003.

Since 1999, several groups of radical Islamic gunmen, believed to be from Uzbekistan or Tajikistan, have led raids and kidnappings from camps in Kyrgyzstan's mountains.

In elections held on Oct. 30, 2000, President Askar Akayev easily won reelection with nearly 75% of the vote. The election, however, was marred by allegations of fraud, diminishing Kyrgyzstan's claim to be the centerpiece of central Asian democracy. Once a popular leader, Akayev's standing has diminished as a result of accusations of nepotism and corruption.

In 2001, Kyrgyzstan permitted troops from the U.S. and seven other nations to be stationed in the country in support of efforts to fight against the Taliban and al-Qaeda in neighboring Afghanistan. In 2002, construction of a large U.S. airbase began outside of Bishkek. In Feb. 2003, a controversial referendum expanded Akayev's powers, and in June Parliament granted him lifelong immunity from prosecution.

February and March 2005 parliamentary elections were judged by international observers and opposition leaders to be flawed, and they set off violent protests in the country. On March 24, as the protests spread to the capital, President Akayev fled the country, and he announced his resignation on April 4. Opposition leader Kurmanbek Bakiev served as interim president and prime minister until the July 10 election, in which he won the presidency with 88.7% of the vote. Felix Kulov became the prime minister. An opposition leader, he had been imprisoned by former president Akayev until the March 24 coup.

Laos

LAO PEOPLE'S DEMOCRATIC REPUBLIC

National name: Sathalanalat Paxathipatai Paxaxon Lao
President: Khamtai Siphandon (2001)
Prime Minister: Boungnang Vorachith (2001)
Area: 91,428 sq mi (236,800 sq km)
Population (2005 est.): 6,217,141 (growth rate: 2.4%); birth rate: 36.0/1000; infant mortality rate: 85.2/1000; life expectancy: 55.1; density per sq mi: 68
Capital and largest city (2003 est.): Vientiane, 194,200. **Monetary unit:** New Kip. **Languages:** Lao (official), French, English, various ethnic languages. **Ethnicity/race:** Lao Loum (lowland) 68%, Lao Theung (upland) 22%, Lao Soung (highland) including the Hmong ("Meo") and the Yao (Mien) 9%, ethnic Vietnamese/Chinese 1%. **Religions:** Buddhist 60%, animist and other 40% (including Christian 1.5%). **Literacy rate:** 53% (2003 est.)
Economic summary: GDP/PPP (2004 est.): $11.28 billion; per capita $1,900. **Real growth rate:** 6%. **Inflation:** 12.3%. **Unemployment:** 5.7% (1997 est.). **Arable land:** 4%. **Agriculture:** sweet potatoes, vegetables, corn, coffee, sugarcane, tobacco, cotton, tea, peanuts, rice, water buffalo, pigs, cattle, poultry. **Labor force:** 2.6 million (2001 est.); agriculture 80% (1997 est.). **Industries:** tin and gypsum mining, timber, electric power, agricultural processing, construction, garments, tourism. **Natural resources:** timber, hydropower, gypsum, tin, gold, gemstones. **Exports:** $365.5 million (2004 est.): garments, wood products, coffee, electricity, tin. **Imports:** $579.5 million (f.o.b., 2004 est.): machinery and equipment, vehicles, fuel, consumer goods. **Major trading partners:** Thailand, Vietnam, France, Germany, China (2003).

Geography A landlocked nation in Southeast Asia occupying the northwest portion of the Indochinese peninsula, Laos is surrounded by China, Vietnam, Cambodia, Thailand, and Burma. It is twice the size of Pennsylvania. Laos is a mountainous country, especially in the north, where peaks rise above 9,000 ft (2,800 m). Dense forests cover the northern and eastern areas. The Mekong River, which forms the boundary with Burma and Thailand, flows through the country for 932 mi (1,500 km) of its course.

Government Communist state.

History The Lao people migrated into Laos from southern China from the 8th century onward. In the 14th century, the first Laotian state was founded, the Lan Xang kingdom, which ruled Laos until it split into three separate kingdoms in 1713. During the 18th century the three kingdoms came under Siamese (Thai) rule, and, in 1893, became a French protectorate. Its territory was incorporated into the union of Indochina. A strong nationalist movement developed during World War II, but France reestablished control in 1946 and made the king of Luang Prabang constitutional monarch of all Laos. France granted semiautonomy in 1949 and then, spurred by the Viet Minh rebellion in Vietnam, full independence within the French Union in 1950.

In 1951, Prince Souphanouvong organized the Pathet Lao, a Communist independence movement, in North Vietnam. Viet Minh and Pathet Lao forces invaded central Laos, and civil war resulted. By the Geneva agreements of 1954 and an armistice of 1955, two northern provinces were given to the Pathet Lao; the rest went to the royal regime. Full sovereignty was given to the kingdom by the Paris agreements of Dec. 29, 1954. In 1957, Prince Souvanna Phouma, the royal prime minister, and Pathet Lao leader Prince Souphanouvong, the prime minister's half-brother, agreed to reestablishment of a unified government, with Pathet Lao participation and integration of Pathet Lao forces into the royal army. The agreement broke down in 1959, and armed conflict began anew.

In 1960, the struggle became three-way as Gen. Phoumi Nosavan, controlling the bulk of the royal army, set up in the south a pro-Western revolutionary government headed by Prince Boun Oum. General Phoumi took Vientiane in December, driving Souvanna Phouma into exile in Cambodia. The Soviet bloc supported Souvanna Phouma. In 1961, a ceasefire was arranged and the three princes agreed to a coalition government headed by Souvanna Phouma.

But North Vietnam, the U.S. (in the form of CIA personnel), and China remained active in Laos after the settlement. North Vietnam used a supply line (Ho Chi Minh Trail) running down the mountain valleys of eastern Laos into Cambodia and South Vietnam, particularly after the U.S.–South Vietnamese incursion into Cambodia in 1970 stopped supplies via Cambodian seaports.

An agreement reached in 1973 revived the coalition government. The Communist Pathet Lao seized complete power in 1975, installing Souphanouvong as president and Kaysone Phomvihane as prime minister. Since then other parties and political groups have been moribund and most of their leaders have fled the country. The monarchy was abolished on Dec. 2, 1975, when the Pathet Lao ousted a coalition government and King Sisavang Vatthana abdicated.

The Supreme People's Assembly in Aug. 1991 adopted a new constitution that dropped all references to socialism but retained the one-party state. In addition to implementing market-oriented policies, the country has passed laws governing property, inheritance, and contracts.

During the 1990s, the country began making more diplomatic overtures toward its neighbors. In 1995, the U.S. announced a lifting of its ban on aid to the nation. By most international estimates, Laos is one of the 10 poorest countries in the world. The subsistence farmers who make up more than 80% of the population have been plagued with bad agricultural conditions—alternately floods and drought—since 1993.

Since March 2000, Vientiane has been rocked by a series of unexplained blasts. The activity has been widely attributed to a group of Hmong tribesmen based in the north. The anti-Communist rebel group has been protesting the government's reluctance to embrace democratic reforms. Others attribute the bombs to rival factions in the government or military.

In Feb. 2002 parliamentary elections, 165 out of 166 candidates were members of the governing Lao People's Revolutionary Party.

A group of international banks agreed in May 2005 to fund a $1.6 billion hydroelectric dam on the Nam Theun River. Officials estimate exports of electricity will bring Laos $2 billion in revenue each year.

Latvia

THE REPUBLIC OF LATVIA

National name: Latvijas Republika
President: Vaira Vike-Freiberga (1999)
Prime Minister: Aigars Kalvitis (2004)
Area: 24,938 sq mi (64,589 sq km)
Population (2005 est.): 2,290,237 (growth rate: –0.7%); birth rate: 9.0/1000; infant mortality rate: 9.6/1000; life expectancy: 71.0; density per sq mi: 92
Capital and largest city (2003 est.): Riga, 867,700 (metro. area), 706,200 (city proper). **Other large cities:** Daugavpils, 111,700; Liepaja, 82,300.
Monetary unit: Lats. **Languages:** Latvian (official), Lithuanian, Russian, other. **Ethnicity/race:** Latvian 57.7%, Russian 29.6%, Belorussian 4.1%, Ukrainian 2.7%, Polish 2.5%, Lithuanian 1.4%, other 2% (2002). **Religions:** Lutheran, Roman Catholic, Russian Orthodox. **Literacy:** 100% (2003 est.)
Economic summary: GDP/PPP (2004 est.): $26.53 billion; per capita $11,500. **Real growth rate:** 7.6%. **Inflation:** 6%. **Unemployment:** 8.8%. **Arable land:** 30%. **Agriculture:** grain, sugar beets, potatoes, vegetables; beef, pork, milk, eggs; fish. **Labor force:** 1.17 million; agriculture 15%, industry 25%, services 60% (2000 est.). **Industries:** buses, vans, street and railroad cars, synthetic fibers, agricultural machinery, fertilizers, washing machines, radios, electronics, pharmaceuticals, processed foods, textiles; note: dependent on imports for energy and raw materials. **Natural resources:** peat, limestone, dolomite, amber, hydropower, wood, arable land. **Exports:** $3.569 billion (f.o.b., 2004 est.): wood and wood products, machinery and equipment, metals, textiles, foodstuffs. **Imports:** $5.97 billion (f.o.b., 2004 est.): machinery and equipment, chemicals, fuels, vehicles. **Major trading partners:** UK, Germany, Sweden, Lithuania, Estonia, Denmark, Russia, Finland, Poland, Italy (2003).

Geography   Latvia borders Estonia on the north, Lithuania in the south, the Baltic Sea with the Gulf of Riga in the west, Russia in the east, and Belarus in the southeast. Latvia is largely a fertile lowland with numerous lakes and hills to the east.

Government   Parliamentary democracy.

History   Baltic tribespeople settled along the Baltic Sea and, lacking a centralized government, fell prey to more powerful peoples. In the 13th century they were overcome by the Livonian Brothers of the Sword, a German order of knights whose mission was to conquer and Christianize the Baltic region. The land became part of the state of Livonia until 1561. Germans made up the ruling class of Livonia and Baltic tribes made up the peasantry. German became the official language of the region.

Poland conquered the territory in 1562 and occupied it until Sweden took over the land in 1629, ruling over it until 1721. Then the land passed to Russia. From 1721 until 1918, the Latvians remained Russian subjects, although they preserved their language, customs, and folklore.

The Russian Revolution of 1917 gave them their opportunity for freedom, and the Latvian republic was proclaimed on Nov. 18, 1918. The republic lasted little more than 20 years. Plagued by political instability, Latvia essentially became a dictatorship under President Karlis Ulmanis. It was occupied by Russian troops in 1939 and incorporated into the Soviet Union in 1940. German armies occupied the nation from 1941 to 1944. Of the 70,000 Jews living in Latvia during World War II, 95% were massacred. In 1944, Russia again took control of Latvia.

Latvia was one of the most economically well-off and industrialized parts of the Soviet Union. When a coup against Soviet president Mikhail Gorbachev failed in 1991, the Baltic nations saw an opportunity to free themselves from Soviet domination and, following the actions of Lithuania and Estonia, Latvia declared its independence on Aug. 21, 1991. European and most other nations quickly recognized their independence, and on Sept. 2, 1991, President Bush announced full diplomatic recognition for Latvia, Estonia, and Lithuania. The Soviet Union recognized Latvia's independence on Sept. 6, and UN membership followed on Sept. 17, 1991.

Because Latvians' ethnic identity had been quashed throughout its history by foreign rulers, the new Latvian republic set up strict citizenship laws, limiting citizenship to ethnic Latvians and to those who had lived in the region before Soviet rule in 1940. This denied about 452,000 of the country's 740,000 ethnic Russians of citizenship.

Latvia's bid to join the European Union required that it speed up naturalization of minorities, in particular its large number of Russians. In 1998, a referendum passed easing the citizenship rules, although it was still necessary to be competent in the Latvian language, which many believe is unreasonable to expect of older or poorly educated ethnic Russians. To aid in admission to NATO, Parliament in 2002 passed a law no longer requiring parliamentary candidates to speak Latvian. In June 2003, President Vike-Freiberga easily won reelection. In Dec. 2004, Aigars Kalvitis became prime minister, forming the twelfth government since Latvia's independence from Russia. The nation became a member of both the EU and NATO in 2004.

Lebanon

REPUBLIC OF LEBANON

National name: Al-Joumhouriya al-Lubnaniya
President: Emile Lahoud (1998)
Prime Minister: Fouad Siniora (2005)
Area: 4,015 sq mi (10,400 sq km)
Population (2005 est.): 3,826,018 (growth rate: 1.3%); birth rate: 18.9/1000; infant mortality rate: 24.5/1000; life expectancy: 72.6; density per sq mi: 953
Capital and largest city (2003 est.): Beirut, 1,916,100 (metro. area), 1,171,000 (city proper). **Other large cities:** Tripoli, 212,900; Sidon, 149,000. **Monetary unit:** Lebanese pound. **Languages:** Arabic (official), French, English, Armenian. **Ethnicity/race:** Arab 95%, Armenian 4%, other 1%. **Religions:** Islam 70% (including Shi'a, Sunni, Druze, Isma'ilite, Alawite, Nusayri), Christian 30% (including Orthodox Christian, Catholic, Protestant), Jewish negl. **Literacy rate:** 87% (2003 est.)
Economic summary: GDP/PPP (2004 est.): $18.83 billion; per capita $5,000. **Real growth rate:** 4%. **Inflation:** 2%. **Unemployment:** 18% (1997 est.). **Arable land:** 17%. **Agriculture:** citrus, grapes, tomatoes, apples, vegetables, potatoes, olives, tobacco; sheep, goats. **Labor force:** 2.6 million; note: in addition, there are as many as 1 million foreign workers (2001 est.); services n.a.; industry n.a.; agriculture n.a. **Industries:** banking, food processing, jewelry, cement, textiles, mineral and chemical products, wood and furniture products, oil refining, metal fabricating. **Natural resources:** limestone, iron ore, salt, water-surplus state in a water-deficit region, arable land. **Exports:** $1.783 billion (f.o.b., 2004 est.): authentic jewelry, inorganic chemicals, miscellaneous consumer goods, fruit, tobacco, construction minerals, electric power machinery and switchgear, textile fibers, paper. **Imports:** $8.162 billion (f.o.b., 2004 est.): petroleum products, cars, medicinal products, clothing, meat and live animals, consumer goods, paper, textile fabrics, tobacco. **Major trading partners:** Switzerland, UAE, Saudi Arabia, U.S., Turkey, France, Germany, Italy, Syria, China, UK (2003).

Geography Lebanon lies at the eastern end of the Mediterranean Sea north of Israel and west of Syria. It is four-fifths the size of Connecticut. The Lebanon Mountains, which parallel the coast on the west, cover most of the country, while on the eastern border is the Anti-Lebanon range. Between the two lies the Bekaa Valley, the principal agricultural area.

Government Republic.

History After World War I, France was given a League of Nations mandate over Lebanon and its neighbor Syria, which together had previously been a single political unit in the Ottoman Empire. France divided them in 1920 into separate colonial administrations, drawing a border that separated predominantly Muslim Syria from the kaleidoscope of religious communities in Lebanon, where Maronite Christians were then dominant. After 20 years of the French mandate regime, Lebanon's independence was proclaimed on Nov. 26, 1941, but full independence came in stages. Under an agreement between representatives of Lebanon and the French National Committee of Liberation, most of the powers exercised by France were transferred to the Lebanese government on Jan. 1, 1944. The evacuation of French troops was completed in 1946.

According to the National Pact, different religious communities are represented in the government by having a Maronite Christian president, a Sunni Muslim prime minister, and a Shiite National Assembly speaker. The arrangement worked for two decades.

Civil war broke out in 1958, with Muslim factions led by Kamal Jumblat and Saeb Salam rising in insurrection against the Lebanese government headed by President Camille Chamoun, a Maronite Christian favoring close ties to the West. At Chamoun's request, President Eisenhower, on July 15, sent U.S. troops to reestablish the government's authority.

Clan warfare between various religious factions in Lebanon goes back centuries. The hodgepodge includes Maronite Christians, who, since independence, have dominated the government; Sunni Muslims, who have prospered in business and shared political power; the Druze, who hold a faith incorporating aspects of Islam and Gnosticism; and Shiite Muslims.

A new—and bloodier—Lebanese civil war that broke out in 1975 resulted in the addition of still another ingredient in the brew—the Syrians. In the fighting between Lebanese factions, 40,000 Lebanese were estimated to have been killed and 100,000 wounded between March 1975 and Nov. 1976. At that point, Syrian troops intervened at the request of the Lebanese and brought large-scale fighting to a halt. In 1977 the civil war again flared up and continued until 1990, decimating the country.

Palestinian guerrillas staging raids on Israel from Lebanese territory drew punitive Israeli raids on Lebanon and two large-scale Israeli invasions, in 1978 and again in 1982. In the first invasion, the Israelis entered the country in March 1978 and withdrew that June, after the UN Security Council created a 6,000-man peacekeeping force for the area called UNIFIL. As the UN departed, the Israelis turned their strongholds over to a Christian militia that they had organized, instead of to the UN force.

The second Israeli invasion came on June 6, 1982, after an assassination attempt by Palestinian terrorists on the Israeli ambassador in London. As a base of the PLO, Lebanon became the Israelis' target. Nearly 7,000 Palestinians were dispersed to other Arab nations. The violence seemed to have come to an end when, on Sept. 14, Bashir Gemayel, the 34-year-old president-elect, was killed by a bomb that destroyed the headquarters of his Christian Phalangist Party. Following his assassination, Christian militiamen massacred about 1,000 Palestinians in the Israeli-controlled Sabra and Shatila refugee camps, but Israel denied responsibility.

The massacre in the refugee camps prompted the return of a multinational peacekeeping force. Its mandate was to support the central Lebanese government, but it soon found itself drawn into the struggle for power between different Lebanese factions. The country was engulfed in chaos and instability. During their stay in Lebanon, 241 U.S. Marines and about 60 French soldiers were killed, most of them in suicide bombings of the Marine and French army compounds on Oct. 23, 1983. The multinational force withdrew in the spring of 1984. In 1985, the majority of Israeli troops withdrew from the country, but Israel left some troops along a buffer zone on the southern Lebanese border, where they engaged in ongoing skirmishes with Palestinian groups. The Palestinian terrorist group Hezbollah, or "Party of God," was formed in the 1980s during Israel's second invasion of Lebanon. With financial backing from Iran, it has launched attacks against Israel for more than 20 years.

In July 1986, Syrian observers took up a position in Beirut to monitor a peacekeeping agreement. The agreement broke down and fighting between Shiite and Druze militia in West Beirut became so intense that Syrian troops mobilized in Feb. 1987, suppressing militia resistance. In 1991 a treaty of friendship was signed with Syria, which in effect gave Syria control over Lebanon's foreign relations. In early 1991, the Lebanese government, backed by Syria, regained control over the south and disbanded various militias, thereby ending the 16-year civil war, which had destroyed much of the infrastructure and industry of Lebanon.

In June 1999, just before Israeli prime minister Benjamin Netanyahu left office, Israel bombed southern Lebanon, its most severe attack on the country since 1996. In May 2000, Israel's new prime minister, Ehud Barak, withdrew Israeli troops after 18 consecutive years of occupation.

In the summer of 2001, Syria withdrew nearly all of its 25,000 troops from Beirut and surrounding areas. About 14,000 troops, however, remained in the countryside. With the continuation of Israeli-Palestinian violence in 2002, Hezbollah again began building up forces along the Lebanese-Israeli border.

In Aug. 2004, in a stark reminder of Syria's continuing iron grip on Lebanon, Syria insisted that Lebanon's pro-Syrian president, Émile Lahoud, remain in office beyond the constitutional limit of one six-year term. Despite outrage in the country, the Lebanese Parliament did Syria's bidding, permitting Lahoud to serve for three more years.

A UN Security Council resolution in Sept. 2004 demanded that Syria remove the troops it had stationed in Lebanon for the past 28 years. Syria responded by moving about 3,000 troops from the vicinity of Beirut to eastern Lebanon, a gesture that was viewed by many as merely cosmetic. As a result of the crisis, Prime Minister Rafik Hariri (1992–1998, 2000–2004), largely responsible for Lebanon's economic rebirth in the past decade, resigned. On Feb. 14, 2005, he was killed by a car bomb. Many suspected Syria of involvement and large protests ensued, calling for Syria's withdrawal from the country. After two weeks of protests by Sunni Muslim, Christian, and Druze parties, pro-Syrian prime minister Omar Karami resigned on Feb. 28. Several days later, Syria made a vague pledge to withdraw its troops but failed to announce a timetable. On March 8, the militant group Hezbollah sponsored a massive pro-Syrian rally, primarily made up of Shiites, that greatly outnumbered previous anti-Syrian protests. Hundreds of thousands gathered to thank Syria for its involvement in Lebanon. The pro-Syrian demonstrations led to President Lahoud's reappointment of Karami as prime minister on March 9. But thereafter an anti-Syrian protest—twice the size of the Hezbollah protest—

followed. In mid-March, Syria withdrew 4,000 troops and redeployed the remaining 10,000 to Lebanon's Bekaa Valley, which borders Syria. In April, Omar Karami resigned a second time after failing to form a government. Lebanon's new prime minister, Najib Mikati—a compromise candidate between the pro-Syrian and anti-Syrian groups—announced that new elections would be held in May. On April 26, after 29 years of occupation, Syria withdrew all of its troops.

In May and June 2005, Syria held four rounds of parliamentary elections. An anti-Syrian alliance led by Saad al-Hariri, the 35-year-old son of assassinated former prime minister leader Rafik Hariri, won 72 out of 128 seats. Former finance minister Fouad Siniora, who was closely associated with Hariri, became prime minister.

Lesotho

KINGDOM OF LESOTHO

Sovereign: King Letsie III (1996)
Prime Minister: Pakalitha Mosisili (1998)
Area: 11,720 sq mi (30,355 sq km)
Population (2005 est.): 1,867,035 (growth rate: 0.1%); birth rate: 26.5/1000; infant mortality rate: 84.2/1000; life expectancy: 36.7; density per sq mi: 159
Capital and largest city (2003 est.): Maseru 173,700. **Monetary unit:** Maluti. **Languages:** English, Sesotho (both official); Zulu, Xhosa. **Ethnicity/race:** Sotho 99.7%, Europeans, Asians, and other 0.3%. **Religions:** Christian 80%, indigenous beliefs 20%. **Literacy rate:** 85% (2003 est.)
Economic summary: GDP/PPP (2004 est.): $5.892 billion; per capita $3,200. **Real growth rate:** 3.3%. **Inflation:** 5.3%. **Unemployment:** 45% (2002). **Arable land:** 11%. **Agriculture:** corn, wheat, pulses, sorghum, barley; livestock. **Labor force:** 838,000 (2000); 86% of resident population engaged in subsistence agriculture; roughly 35% of the active male wage earners work in South Africa. **Industries:** food, beverages, textiles, apparel assembly, handicrafts; construction; tourism. **Natural resources:** water, agricultural and grazing land, diamonds, sand, clay, building stone. **Exports:** $484.5 million (f.o.b., 2004 est.): manufactures 75% (clothing, footwear, road vehicles), wool and mohair, food and live animals (2000). **Imports:** $730.9 million (f.o.b., 2004 est.): food; building materials, vehicles, machinery, medicines, petroleum products (2000). **Major trading partners:** U.S., Canada, Belgium/Luxembourg, Hong Kong, Taiwan, China, Germany (2003). **Member of Commonwealth of Nations**

Geography Mountainous Lesotho, the size of Maryland, is surrounded by the Republic of South Africa.

Government Parliamentary constitutional monarchy.

History Lesotho (formerly Basutoland) was constituted a native state under British protection by a treaty signed with the native chief Moshoeshoe in 1843. It was annexed to Cape Colony in 1871, but in 1884 it was restored to direct control by the Crown. The colony of Basutoland became the independent nation of Lesotho on Oct. 4, 1966, with King Moshoeshoe II as sovereign.

In the 1970 elections, Ntsu Mokhehle, head of the Basutoland Congress Party, claimed a victory, but Prime Minister Leabua Jonathan declared a state of emergency, suspended the constitution, and arrested Mokhehle. King Moshoeshoe II was briefly exiled, but returned after a compromise with Jonathan: the new constitution would name him head of state but forbid his participation in politics.

After the king refused to approve the replacement in Feb. 1990 of individuals dismissed by Justin Metsino Lekhanya, the chairman of the Military Council, the latter stripped the king of his executive power. Then in early March, Lekhanya sent the king into exile. In November, the king was dethroned, and his son was sworn in as King Letsie III.

Lekhanya was himself forced to resign in April 1991, and Col. Ramaema became the new chairman in May. In Jan. 1995, the crown reverted to the father of Letsie III, Moshoeshoe II. Letsie again became crown prince. In 1996, however, King Moshoeshoe died in an automobile accident, and Letsie again assumed the throne.

In fall 1998, hundreds of demonstrators protested for weeks in front of the king's palace, claiming voting fraud in the May elections that put Prime Minister Pakalitha Mosisili in power. They demanded that the government step down and hold new elections. Troops from South Africa and Botswana entered the country to stop the riots and put down an army mutiny.

Lesotho faces one of the highest rates of HIV infection in the world, leading some demographers to predict that the country's population will begin declining in several years if current trends continue.

Liberia

REPUBLIC OF LIBERIA

President: Gyude Bryant (2003)
Area: 43,000 sq mi (111,370 sq km)
Population (2005 est.): 3,482,211 (growth rate: 2.6%); birth rate: 44.2/1000; infant mortality rate: 128.9/1000; life expectancy: 47.7; density per sq mi: 81
Capital and largest city (2003 est.): Monrovia, 1,348,900 (metro. area), 550,200 (city proper).
Monetary unit: Liberian dollar. **Languages:** English 20% (official), some 20 ethnic-group languages.
Ethnicity/race: indigenous African tribes 95% (including Kpelle, Bassa, Gio, Kru, Grebo, Mano, Krahn, Gola, Gbandi, Loma, Kissi, Vai, Bella, Mandingo, and Mende), Americo-Liberians 2.5% (descendants of former U.S. slaves), Congo People 2.5% (descendants of former Caribbean slaves).
Religions: traditional 40%, Christian 40%, Islam 20%. **Literacy rate:** 58% (2003 est.)
Economic summary: GDP/PPP (2004 est.): $2.903 billion; per capita $900. **Real growth rate:** 21.8%. **Inflation:** 15% (2003 est.). **Unemployment:** 85% (2003 est.). **Arable land:** 4%. **Agriculture:** rubber, coffee, cocoa, rice, cassava (tapioca), palm oil, sugarcane, bananas; sheep, goats; timber. **Labor force:** agriculture 70%, industry 8%, services 22% (2000 est.). **Industries:** rubber processing, palm oil processing, timber, diamonds. **Natural resources:** iron ore, timber, diamonds, gold, hydropower. **Exports:** $1.079 billion (f.o.b., 2002 est.): rubber, timber, iron, diamonds, cocoa, coffee. **Imports:** $5.051 billion (f.o.b., 2002 est.): fuels, chemicals, machinery, transportation equipment, manufactured goods; foodstuffs. **Major trading partners:** Germany, Poland, Greece, U.S., France, Thailand, China, South Korea, Japan, Singapore, Spain (2003).

Geography Lying on the Atlantic in the southern part of West Africa, Liberia is bordered by Sierra Leone, Guinea, and Côte d'Ivoire. It is comparable in size to Tennessee. Most of the country is a plateau covered by dense tropical forests, which thrive under an annual rainfall of about 160 in. a year.

Government Republic.

History Africa's first republic, Liberia was founded in 1822 as a result of the efforts of the American Colonization Society to settle freed American slaves in West Africa. The society contended that the immigration of blacks to Africa was an answer to the problem of slavery as well as to what it felt was the incompatibility of the races. Over the course of forty years, about 12,000 slaves were voluntarily relocated. Originally called Monrovia, the colony became the Free and Independent Republic of Liberia in 1847.

The English-speaking Americo-Liberians, descendants of former American slaves, make up only 5% of the population, but have historically dominated the intellectual and ruling class. Liberia's indigenous population is composed of 16 different ethnic groups.

The government of Africa's first republic was modeled after that of the United States, and Joseph Jenkins Roberts of Virginia was elected the first president. Ironically, Liberia's constitution denied indigenous Liberians equal rights with the lighter-skinned American emigrants and their descendants.

After 1920, considerable progress was made toward opening up the interior, a process that was speeded in 1951 by the establishment of a 43-mile (69-km) railroad to the Bomi Hills from Monrovia. In July 1971, while serving his sixth term as president, William V. S. Tubman died following surgery and was succeeded by his longtime associate, Vice President William R. Tolbert, Jr.

Tolbert was ousted in a military coup on April 12, 1980, by Master Sgt. Samuel K. Doe, backed by the U.S. government. Doe's rule was characterized by corruption and brutality. A rebellion led by Charles Taylor, a former Doe aide, and the National Patriotic Front of Liberia (NPFL), started in Dec. 1989; the following year, Doe was assassinated. The Economic Community of West African States (ECOWAS) negotiated with the government and the rebel factions and attempted to restore order, but the civil war raged on. By April 1996, factional fighting by the country's warlords had destroyed any last vestige of normalcy and civil society. The civil war finally ended in 1997.

In what was considered by international observers to be a free election, Charles Taylor won 75% of the presidential vote in July 1997. The country had next to no health care system, and the capital was without electricity and running water. Taylor supported Sierra Leone's brutal Revolutionary United Front (RUF) in the hopes of toppling his neighbor's government, and in exchange for diamonds, which enriched his personal coffers. As a consequence, the UN issued sanctions.

In 2002, rebels—Liberians United for Reconciliation and Democracy (LURD)—intensified their attacks on Taylor's government. By June 2003, LURD and other rebel groups controlled two-thirds of the country. Finally, on Aug. 11, Taylor stepped down and went into exile in Nigeria. Gyude Bryant, a businessman seen as a coalition builder, was selected by the various factions as the new president. By the time he was exiled, Taylor had bankrupted his own country, siphoning off $100 million. According to the *New York Times*, Taylor left Liberia the world's poorest nation. In 2004, international donors promised more than $500 million in aid.

On the second anniversary of Taylor's ouster, he was still a free man living in Nigeria, where he had been offered sanctuary.

Libya

GREAT SOCIALIST PEOPLE'S LIBYAN ARAB JAMAHIRIYA

National name: Al Jumahiriyah al Arabiyah al Libiyah ash Shabiyah al Ishtirakiyah al Uzma
Chief of State: Col. Muammar al-Qaddafi (1969)
Prime Minister: Mubarak Abdallah al-Shamikh (2000)
Area: 679,358 sq mi (1,759,540 sq km)

Population (2005 est.): 5,765,563 (growth rate: 2.3%);
　birth rate: 26.8/1000; infant mortality rate: 24.6/1000;
　life expectancy: 76.5; density per sq mi: 8
Capital and largest city (2003 est.): Tripoli, 2,357,800
　(metro. area), 1,269,700 (city proper). **Other large
　city:** Benghazi, 734,900. **Monetary unit:** Libyan dinar.
　Languages: Arabic, Italian, and English widely
　understood in major cities. **Ethnicity/race:** Berber and
　Arab 97%, Greeks, Maltese, Italians, Egyptians,
　Pakistanis, Turks, Indians, Tunisians. **Religion:** Islam
　(Sunni) 97%. **Literacy rate:** 83% (2003 est.)
Economic summary: GDP/PPP (2004 est.): $37.48
　billion; per capita $6,700. **Real growth rate:** 4.9%.
　Inflation: 2.9%. **Unemployment:** 30%. **Arable land:**
　1%. **Agriculture:** wheat, barley, olives, dates, citrus,
　vegetables, peanuts, soybeans; cattle. **Labor force:**
　1.59 million; services and government 54%, industry
　29%, agriculture 17% (1997 est.). **Industries:**
　petroleum, iron and steel, food processing, textiles,
　handicrafts, cement. **Natural resources:** petroleum,
　natural gas, gypsum. **Exports:** $18.65 billion (f.o.b.,
　2004 est.): crude oil, refined petroleum products,
　natural gas. **Imports:** $7.224 billion (f.o.b., 2004 est.):
　machinery, transport equipment, semifinished goods,
　food, consumer products (1999). **Major trading
　partners:** Italy, Spain, Germany, Turkey, France, UK,
　Tunisia (2003).

Geography　Libya stretches along the northeast coast
of Africa between Tunisia and Algeria on the west and
Egypt on the east; to the south are the Sudan, Chad,
and Niger. It is one-sixth larger than Alaska. A greater
part of the country lies within the Sahara. Along the
Mediterranean coast and farther inland is arable plateau land.

Government　Military dictatorship.

History　The first inhabitants of Libya were Berber
tribes. In the 7th century B.C., Phoenicians colonized
the eastern section of Libya, called Cyrenaica, and
Greeks colonized the western portion, called Tripolitania. Tripolitania was for a time under Carthaginian
control. It became part of the Roman Empire from 46
B.C. to A.D. 436, after which it was sacked by the Vandals. Cyrenaica belonged to the Roman Empire from
the 1st century B.C. until its decline, after which it was
invaded by Arab forces in 642. Beginning in the 16th
century, both Tripolitania and Cyrenaica nominally
became part of the Ottoman Empire.

Tripolitania was one of the outposts for the Barbary
pirates who raided Mediterranean merchant ships or
required them to pay tribute. In 1801, the pasha of Tripoli raised the price of tribute, which led to the Tripoli-
tan war with the United States. When the peace treaty
was signed on June 4, 1805, U.S. ships no longer had
to pay tribute to Tripoli.

Following the outbreak of hostilities between Italy
and Turkey in 1911, Italian troops occupied Tripoli.
Italian sovereignty was recognized in 1912. Libyans
continued to fight the Italians until 1914, by which
time Italy controlled most of the land. Italy formally
united Tripolitania and Cyrenaica in 1934 as the colony
of Libya.

Libya was the scene of much desert fighting during
World War II. After the fall of Tripoli on Jan. 23,
1943, it came under Allied administration. In 1949,
the UN voted that Libya should become independent,
and in 1951 it became the United Kingdom of Libya.
Oil was discovered in the impoverished country in
1958 and eventually transformed its economy.

On Sept. 1, 1969, 27-year-old Col. Muammar
al-Qaddafi deposed the king and revolutionized the
country, making it a pro-Arabic, anti-Western, Islamic
republic with socialist leanings. It was also rabidly
anti-Israeli. A notorious firebrand, Qaddafi aligned
himself with dictators, such as Uganda's Idi Amin,
and fostered anti-Western terrorism.

On Aug. 19, 1981, two U.S. Navy F-14s shot down
two Soviet-made SU-22s of the Libyan air force that
had attacked them in air space above the Gulf of Sidra.
On March 24, 1986, U.S. and Libyan forces skir-
mished in the Gulf of Sidra, and two Libyan patrol
boats were sunk. Qaddafi's troops also supported
rebels in Chad but suffered major military reverses in
1987. A two-year-old U.S. covert policy to destabilize
the Libyan government ended in failure in Dec. 1990.

On Dec. 21, 1988, a Boeing 747 exploded in flight
over Lockerbie, Scotland, the result of a terrorist bomb,
killing all 259 people aboard and 11 on the ground.
This and other acts of terrorism, including the bombing
of a Berlin discotheque in 1986 and the downing of a
French UTA airliner in 1989 that killed 170, turned
Libya into a pariah in the eyes of the west. Two Libyan
intelligence agents were indicted in the Lockerbie
bombing, but Qaddafi refused to hand them over, leading to UN-approved trade and air traffic embargoes in
1992. In 1999, Libya finally surrendered the two men,
who were tried in the Netherlands in 2000–2001. One
was found guilty of mass murder; the other defendant
was found innocent. Libya had hoped its fainthearted
cooperation would lead to suspended sanctions, which
had severely affected the Libyan economy. The UN did
suspend its sanctions, but they were not formally
removed for another four years, until Sept. 2003, when
Libya finally admitted its guilt in the Lockerbie bombing and agreed to pay $2.7 billion to the families. In
2004, Libya also agreed to compensate the families of
the victims of the UTA airliner bombing ($170 million)
and the Berlin disco bombing ($35 million).

After months of secret talks with the U.S. and Britain, Qaddafi surprised the world in Dec. 2003 by
announcing he would give up the pursuit of weapons of
mass destruction and submit to full UN weapons
inspections. After inspections at four secret sites, the
International Atomic Energy Agency concluded that
Libya's progress on a nuclear bomb had been in the
very nascent stages. In June 2004, the U.S. and Libya
restored diplomatic relations after a 24-year hiatus.

Liechtenstein

PRINCIPALITY OF LIECHTENSTEIN

National name: Fuerstentum Liechtenstein
Ruler: Prince Hans Adam II (1989)
Head of Government: Otmar Hasler (2001)
Area: 62 sq mi (160 sq km)
Population (2005 est.): 33,717 (growth rate: 0.8%); birth
　rate: 10.4/1000; infant mortality rate: 4.7/1000; life
　expectancy: 79.5; density per sq mi: 546
Capital and largest city (2003 est.): Vaduz, 5,300.
　Monetary unit: Swiss franc. **Languages:** German
　(official), Alemannic dialect. **Ethnicity/race:** Alemannic
　86%; Italian, Turkish, and other 14%. **Religions:**
　Roman Catholic, 76.2%, Protestant, 7%; unknown,
　10.6%; other, 6.2% (2002). **Literacy rate:** 100% (1981
　est.)
Economic summary: GDP/PPP (1999 est.): $825 million;
　per capita $25,000. **Real growth rate:** 11%. **Inflation:**
　1% (2001). **Unemployment:** 1.3% (Sept. 2002). **Arable
　land:** 25%. **Agriculture:** wheat, barley, corn, potatoes;
　livestock, dairy products. **Labor force:** 29,000 of whom
　19,000 are foreigners; 13,000 commute from Austria,
　Switzerland, and Germany to work each day (Dec.
　2001); industry 47.4%, services 51.3%, agriculture 1.3%.
　Industries: electronics, metal manufacturing, dental
　products, ceramics, pharmaceuticals, food products,
　precision instruments, tourism, optical instruments.

Natural resources: hydroelectric potential, arable land.
Exports: $2.47 billion (1996): small specialty machinery, connectors for audio and video, parts for motor vehicles, dental products, hardware, prepared foodstuffs, electronic equipment, optical products. **Imports:** $917.3 million (1996): agricultural products, raw materials, machinery, metal goods, textiles, foodstuffs, motor vehicles. **Major trading partners:** EU (Germany, Austria, France, Italy, UK), U.S., Switzerland.

Geography Tiny Liechtenstein, not quite as large as Washington, DC, lies on the east bank of the Rhine River south of Lake Constance between Austria and Switzerland. It consists of low valley land and Alpine peaks. Falknis (8,401 ft; 2,561 m) and Naafkopf (8,432 ft; 2,570 m) are the tallest.

Government Hereditary constitutional monarchy.

History The Liechtensteiners are descended from the Alemanni tribe that came into the region after A.D. 500. Founded in 1719, Liechtenstein was a member of the German Confederation from 1815 to 1866, when it became an independent principality. It abolished its army in 1868 and has managed to stay neutral and undamaged in all European wars since then. Liechtenstein still claims 1,600 sq km of Czech territory (the royal family's ancestral home) confiscated in 1918; the Czech Republic insists that restitution does not go back before Feb. 1948, when the Communists seized power. In a referendum on July 1, 1984, male voters granted women the right to vote in national (but not local) elections.

Blacklisted in 2000 as a center for money laundering, Liechtenstein toughened its laws and made major efforts to clean up its financial practices. In 2002, the country was removed from the OECD's (Organization of Economic Cooperation and Development) blacklist.

In March 2003, Liechtenstein's people overwhelmingly voted to give its prince more powers, including the right to dismiss governments and approve judicial nominees. Prince Hans Adam II had threatened to leave the country if his demands for more authority were not met. Before the vote, he had already possessed more power than any other European monarch.

In Aug. 2003 he announced that he would give up the day-to-day ruling of the country in one year's time. In Aug. 2004, his son, Prince Alois, 36, became regent of Liechtenstein, while Hans Adam II remained the official head of state.

Lithuania

REPUBLIC OF LITHUANIA

National name: Lietuvos Respublika
President: Valdas Adamkus (2004)
Prime Minister: Algirdas Brazauskas (2001)
Area: 25,174 sq mi (65,200 sq km)
Population (2005 est.): 3,596,617 (growth rate: –0.3%); birth rate: 8.6/1000; infant mortality rate: 6.9/1000; life expectancy: 74.0; density per sq mi: 143
Capital and largest city (2003 est.): Vilnius, 543,500.
Other large cities: Kaunas, 379,800; Klaipéda, 193,400. **Monetary unit:** Litas. **Languages:** Lithuanian (official), Polish, Russian. **Ethnicity/race:** Lithuanian 80.6%, Russian 8.7%, Polish 7%, Belorussian 1.6%, other 2.1%. **Religions:** Roman Catholic (primarily); others include Lutheran, Russian Orthodox, Protestant, evangelical Christian Baptist, Islam, Judaism. **Literacy:** 100% (2003 est.)
Economic summary: GDP/PPP (2004 est.): $45.23 billion; per capita $12,500. **Real growth rate:** 6.6%. **Inflation:** 1.1%. **Unemployment:** 8%. **Arable land:** 45%. **Agriculture:** grain, potatoes, sugar beets, flax, vegetables; beef, milk, eggs; fish. **Labor force:** 1.63

million; industry 30%, agriculture 20%, services 50% (1997 est.). **Industries:** metal-cutting machine tools, electric motors, television sets, refrigerators and freezers, petroleum refining, shipbuilding (small ships), furniture making, textiles, food processing, fertilizers, agricultural machinery, optical equipment, electronic components, computers, amber. **Natural resources:** peat, arable land. **Exports:** $8.88 billion (f.o.b., 2004 est.): mineral products 23%, textiles and clothing 16%, machinery and equipment 11%, chemicals 6%, wood and wood products 5%, foodstuffs 5% (2001). **Imports:** $11.02 billion (f.o.b., 2004 est.): mineral products 21%, machinery and equipment 17%, transport equipment 11%, chemicals 9%, textiles and clothing 9%, metals 5% (2001). **Major trading partners:** Switzerland, Russia, Germany, Latvia, UK, France, Denmark, Estonia, Sweden, Poland, Italy (2003).

Geography Lithuania is situated on the eastern shore of the Baltic Sea and borders Latvia on the north, Belarus on the east and south, and Poland and the Kaliningrad region of Russia on the southwest. It is a country of gently rolling hills, many forests, rivers and streams, and lakes. Its principal natural resource is agricultural land.

Government Parliamentary democracy.

History The Liths, or Lithuanians, united in the 12th century under the rule of Mindaugas, who became king in 1251. Through marriage, one of the later Lithuanian rulers became the king of Poland (Ladislaus II) in 1386, uniting the countries. In 1410, the Poles and Lithuanians defeated the powerful Teutonic Knights at Tannenberg. From the 14th to the 16th century, Poland and Lithuania made up one of medieval Europe's largest empires, stretching from the Black Sea almost to Moscow. The two countries formed a confederation for almost 200 years, and in 1569 they formally united. Russia, Prussia, and Austria partitioned Poland in 1772, 1792, and 1795. As a consequence, Lithuania came under Russian rule after the last partition. Russia attempted to immerse Lithuania in Russian culture and language, but anti-Russian sentiment continued to grow. Following World War I and the collapse of Russia, Lithuania declared independence (1918), under German protection.

The republic was then annexed by the Soviet Union in 1940. From June 1941 to 1944, it was occupied by German troops, with whom Lithuania served in World War II. Some 240,000 Jews were massacred in Lithuania during the Nazi years. In 1944, the Soviets again annexed Lithuania.

The Lithuanian independence movement reemerged in 1988. In 1990, Vytautas Landsbergis, the non-Communist head of the largest Lithuanian popular movement (Sajudis), was elected president. On the same day, the Supreme Council rejected Soviet rule and declared the restoration of Lithuania's independence, the first Baltic republic to take this action. Confrontation with the Soviet Union ensued along with economic sanctions, but they were lifted after both sides agreed to a face-saving compromise.

Lithuania's independence was quickly recognized by major European and other nations, including the United States. The Soviet Union finally recognized the independence of the Baltic states on Sept. 6, 1991. UN admittance followed on Sept. 17, 1991. Successful implementation of structural and legislative reforms in Lithuania attracted greater direct foreign investments by the mid-1990s.

In late 2002, Lithuania was accepted for membership in the EU and NATO, and it joined both in 2004. In Jan. 2003 Rolandas Paksas defeated the incumbent,

Valdas Adamkus, in the presidential election. It was a surprising upset, given that Adamkus had helped bring about his country's entry into NATO and the European Union. In April 2004, President Paksas was removed from office after his conviction for dealings with Russian mobsters. It was Lithuania's worst political crisis since independence from the Soviet Union. In July 2004, Valdas Adamkus was again elected president.

Luxembourg

GRAND DUCHY OF LUXEMBOURG

National name: Grand-Duché de Luxembourg
Ruler: Grand Duke Henri (2000)
Prime Minister: Jean-Claude Juncker (1995)
Area: 998 sq mi (2,586 sq km)
Population (2005 est.): 468,571 (growth rate: 1.3%); birth rate: 12.1/1000; infant mortality rate: 4.8/1000; life expectancy: 78.7; density per sq mi: 469
Capital and largest city (2003 est.): Luxembourg, 78,800. **Monetary unit:** Euro (formerly Luxembourg franc). **Languages:** Luxermbourgish (national) French, German (both administrative). **Ethnicity/race:** Celtic base (with French and German blend), Portuguese, Italian, Slavs (from Montenegro, Albania, and Kosovo), and European (guest and worker residents). **Religions:** Roman Catholic 87%; Protestant, Jewish, Islamic 13% (2000). **Literacy rate:** 100% (2003 est.)
Economic summary: GDP/PPP (2004 est.): $27.27 billion; per capita $58,900. **Real growth rate:** 2.3%. **Inflation:** 2.4%. **Unemployment:** 4.5% (Dec., 2004 est.). **Arable land:** 23%. **Agriculture:** barley, oats, potatoes, wheat, fruits, wine grapes; livestock products. **Labor force:** 293,700 (of whom 105,000 are foreign cross-border workers primarily from France, Belgium, and Germany); agriculture 1%, industry 13%, services 86% (2004 est.). **Industries:** banking, iron and steel, food processing, chemicals, metal products, engineering, tires, glass, aluminum, information technology, tourism and banking. **Natural resources:** iron ore (no longer exploited), arable land. **Exports:** $13.4 billion (f.o.b., 2003): machinery and equipment, steel products, chemicals, rubber products, glass. **Imports:** $16.3 billion (c.i.f., 2003): minerals, metals, foodstuffs, quality consumer goods. **Major trading partners:** Germany, France, Belgium, UK, Italy, Spain, Netherlands, China (2003).

Geography Luxembourg is about half the size of Delaware. The Ardennes Mountains extend from Belgium into the northern section of Luxembourg. The rolling plateau of the fertile Bon Pays is in the south.

Government Constitutional monarchy.

History Luxembourg, once part of Charlemagne's empire, became an independent state in 963, when Siegfried, count of Ardennes, became sovereign of Lucilinburhuc ("Little Fortress"). In 1060, Conrad, a descendant of Siegfried, took the title count of Luxembourg. From the 15th to the 18th century, Spain, France, and Austria held the duchy in turn. The Congress of Vienna in 1815 made it a Grand Duchy and gave it to William I, king of the Netherlands. In 1839, the Treaty of London ceded the western part of Luxembourg to Belgium. The eastern part, continuing in personal union with the Netherlands and a member of the German Confederation, became autonomous in 1848 and a neutral territory by decision of the London Conference of 1867, governed by its grand duke. Germany occupied the duchy in World Wars I and II. Allied troops liberated the enclave in 1944.

Luxembourg joined NATO in 1949, the Benelux Economic Union (with Belgium and the Netherlands) in 1948, and the European Economic Community (later the EU) in 1957. In 1961, Prince Jean, son and heir of Grand Duchess Charlotte, was made head of state, acting for his mother. She abdicated in 1964, and Prince Jean became grand duke. Grand Duchess Charlotte died in 1985. Luxembourg's Parliament approved the Maastricht Accord, paving the way for the economic unity of the EU in July 1992. Crown Prince Henri was sworn in as grand duke in Oct. 2000, replacing his father, Jean, who had been head of state for 26 years. In 2002, the euro became the country's new currency. In 2005, the nation voted to approve the EU constitution, despite the constitution's recent defeats in France and the Netherlands.

Macedonia

REPUBLIC OF MACEDONIA[1]

National Name: Republika Makedonija
President: Branko Crvenkovski (2004)
Prime Minister: Vlado Buckovski (2004)
Area: 9,928 sq mi (25,713 sq km)
Population (2005 est.): 2,045,262 (growth rate: 0.3%); birth rate: 12.0/1000; infant mortality rate: 10.1/1000; life expectancy: 73.7; density per sq mi: 209
Capital and largest city (2003 est.): Skopje, 587,300 (metro. area), 452,500 (city proper). **Other large cities:** Bitola, 84,400; Kumanovo, 78,900; Prilep, 56,900. **Monetary unit:** Denar. **Languages:** Macedonian 68%, Albanian 25% (both official); Turkish 3%, Serbo-Croatian 2%, other 2%. **Ethnicity/race:** Macedonian 64.2%, Albanian 25.2%, Turkish 3.8%, Roma (Gypsy) 2.7%, Serb 1.8%, other 2.3% (2002). **Religions:** Macedonian Orthodox 70%, Islam 29%, other 1% (1994)
Economic summary: GDP/PPP (2004 est.): $14.4 billion; per capita $7,100. **Real growth rate:** 1.3%. **Inflation:** 0.4%. **Unemployment:** 37.7% (3rd qtr., 2004 est.). **Arable land:** 22%. **Agriculture:** wheat, grapes, rice, tobacco, corn, millet, cotton, sesame, mulberry leaves, citrus, vegetables; beef, pork, poultry, mutton. **Labor force:** 855,000; agriculture n.a., industry n.a., services n.a. **Industries:** coal, metallic chromium, lead, zinc, ferronickel, textiles, wood products, tobacco, food processing, buses, steel. **Natural resources:** low-grade iron ore, copper, lead, zinc, chromite, manganese, nickel, tungsten, gold, silver, asbestos, gypsum, timber, arable land. **Exports:** $1.629 billion (f.o.b., 2004 est.): food, beverages, tobacco; miscellaneous manufactures, iron and steel. **Imports:** $2.677 billion (f.o.b., 2004 est.): machinery and equipment, chemicals, fuels; food products, automobiles. **Major trading partners:** Serbia and Montenegro, Germany, Greece, Croatia, U.S., Slovenia, Bulgaria, Turkey (2003).

1. The UN recognized the Republic of Macedonia on April 8, 1993, under the temporary name the Former Yugoslav Republic of Macedonia. The U.S. recognized Macedonia as a state in Feb. 1994.

Geography Macedonia is a landlocked state in the heart of the Balkans and is slightly smaller than the state of Vermont. It is a mountainous country with small basins of agricultural land. The Vardar is the largest and most important river.

Government Parliamentary democracy.

History The Republic of Macedonia occupies the western half of the ancient Kingdom of Macedonia. Historic Macedonia was defeated by Rome and became a Roman province in 148 B.C. After the Roman Empire was divided in A.D. 395, Macedonia was intermittently ruled by the Byzantine Empire until Turkey took possession of the land in 1371. The Ottoman Turks dominated Macedonia for the next five centuries, until 1913. During the 19th and 20th centuries, there was a constant struggle by the Balkan powers to possess Macedonia for its economic wealth and its strategic military corridors. The Treaty of San Stefano in 1878, ending the Russo-Turkish War, gave the largest part of Macedonia to Bulgaria. Bulgaria lost much of its Macedonian territory when it was defeated by the Greeks and Serbs in the Second Balkan War of 1913. Most of Macedonia went to Serbia and the remainder was divided among Greece and Bulgaria.

In 1918, Serbia, which included much of Macedonia, joined in union with Croatia, Slovenia, and Montenegro to form the Kingdom of Serbs, Croats, and Slovenes, which was renamed Yugoslavia in 1929. Bulgaria joined the Axis powers in World War II and occupied parts of Yugoslavia, including Macedonia, in 1941. During the occupation of their country, Macedonian resistance fighters fought a guerrilla war against the invading troops. The Yugoslavian federation was reestablished after the defeat of Germany in 1945, and in 1946, the government removed the Vardar territory of Macedonia from Serbian control and made it an autonomous Yugoslavian republic. Later, when President Tito recognized the Macedonian people as a separate nation, Macedonia's distinct culture and language were able to flourish, no longer suppressed by outside rule.

On Sept. 8, 1991, Macedonia declared its independence from Yugoslavia and asked for recognition from the European Union nations. It became a member of the UN in 1993 under the provisional name of the Former Yugoslav Republic of Macedonia (FYROM) because Greece vociferously protested Macedonia's right to the name, which is also the name of a large northern province of Greece. To Greece, the use of the name implies Macedonia's interest in territorial expansion into the Greek province. Greece has imposed two trade embargoes against the country as a result.

Tensions between ethnic Albanians and Macedonians continued to rise during the Kosovo crisis, during which more than 140,000 refugees streamed into the country from neighboring Kosovo. Most of the refugees returned to Kosovo in 2000.

The long-simmering resentment of Macedonia's ethnic Albanians erupted into violence in March 2001, prompting the government to send troops into the heavily Albanian western section of the country. The rebels sought greater autonomy within Macedonia. In Aug. 2001, after six months of fighting, the rebels and the Macedonian government signed a peace agreement that allowed a British-led NATO force to enter the country and disarm the guerrillas. In Nov. 2001, Macedonia's Parliament agreed to constitutional amendments giving broader rights to its Albanian minority. Albanian became one of the country's two official languages.

In Sept. 2002 elections, a center-left coalition ousted the governing coalition, which had been embroiled in previous years' guerrilla insurgency. Branko Crvenkovski of the Together for Macedonia coalition became the new prime minister. In Feb. 2004, President Boris Trajkovski was killed in a plane crash. Prime Minister Crvenkovski was then elected president, and former interior minister Hari Kostov became prime minister. In August, Parliament approved legislation redrawing internal borders and giving ethnic Albanians more local autonomy in regions where Albanians predominate. After just five months on the job, Prime Minister Kostov resigned, frustrated over disputes with his coalition. Defense Minister Vlado Buckovski assumed the post in December.

Madagascar

REPUBLIC OF MADAGASCAR

National name: Repoblikan'i Madagasikara
President: Marc Ravalomanana (2002)
Prime Minister: Jacques Sylla (2002)
Area: 226,656 sq mi (587,040 sq km)
Population (2005 est.): 18,040,341 (growth rate: 3.0%); birth rate: 41.7/1000; infant mortality rate: 76.8/1000; life expectancy: 57.0; density per sq mi: 80
Capital and largest city (2003 est.): Antananarivo, 1,390,800. **Monetary unit:** Malagasy franc.
Languages: Malagasy and French (both official).
Ethnicity/race: Malayo-Indonesian (Merina and related Betsileo), Côtiers (mixed African, Malayo-Indonesian, and Arab ancestry—Betsimisaraka, Tsimihety, Antaisaka, Sakalava), French, Indian, Creole, Comoran. **Religions:** indigenous beliefs 52%, Christian 41%, Islam 7%.
Literacy rate: 69% (2003 est.)
Economic summary: GDP/PPP (2004 est.): $14.56 billion; per capita $800. **Real growth rate:** 5.5%. **Inflation:** 7.5%. **Unemployment:** 5.9% (1998). **Arable land:** 5%. **Agriculture:** coffee, vanilla, sugarcane, cloves, cocoa, rice, cassava (tapioca), beans, bananas, peanuts; livestock products. **Labor force:** 7.3 million (2000). **Industries:** meat processing, soap, breweries, tanneries, sugar, textiles, glassware, cement, automobile assembly plant, paper, petroleum, tourism. **Natural resources:** graphite, chromite, coal, bauxite, salt, quartz, tar sands, semiprecious stones, mica, fish, hydropower. **Exports:** $868.2 million (f.o.b., 2004 est.): coffee, vanilla, shellfish, sugar; cotton cloth, chromite, petroleum products. **Imports:** $1.147 billion (f.o.b., 2004 est.): capital goods, petroleum, consumer goods, food. **Major trading partners:** France, U.S., Germany, Mauritius, China, South Africa, Iran, India (2003).

Geography Madagascar lies in the Indian Ocean off the southeast coast of Africa opposite Mozambique. The world's fourth-largest island, it is twice the size of Arizona. The country's low-lying coastal area gives way to a central plateau. The once densely wooded interior has largely been cut down.

Government Multiparty republic.

History The Malagasy are of mixed Malayo-Indonesian and African-Arab ancestry. Indonesians are believed to have migrated to the island about 700. King Andrianampoinimerina (1787–1810) ruled the major kingdom on the island, and his son, Radama I (1810–1828), unified much of the island. The French made the island a protectorate in 1885, and then, in 1894–1895, ended the monarchy, exiling Queen Rànavàlona III to Algiers. A colonial administration was set up, to which the Comoro Islands were attached in 1908, and other territories later. In World War II, the British occupied Madagascar, which retained ties to Vichy France.

An autonomous republic within the French Community since 1958, Madagascar became an independent member of the community in 1960. In May 1973, an army coup led by Maj. Gen. Gabriel Ramanantsoa ousted Philibert Tsiranana, president since 1959. Comdr. Didier Ratsiraka, named president on June 15, 1975, announced that he would follow a socialist course and, after nationalizing banks and insurance companies, declared all mineral resources nationalized. Repression and censorship characterized his regime. Ratsiraka was reelected in 1989 in a suspicious election that led to riots as well as the formation of a multiparty system in 1990. In 1991, Ratsiraka agreed to share power with the democratically minded opposition leader, Albert Zafy, who then overwhelmingly won the presidential elections in Feb. 1993. But Zafy was impeached by Parliament for abusing his constitutional powers during an economic crisis and lost the 1996 presidential election to Ratsiraka, who became president in Feb. 1997.

The Dec. 2001 presidential election between incumbent president Didier Ratsiraka and Marc Ravalomanana, the mayor of Antananarivo, proved inconclusive and a runoff vote was scheduled. But Ravalomanana claimed the election was rigged, and in Feb. 2002 he declared himself president. In response, Ratsiraka proclaimed martial law and set up a rival capital in Toamasina. Madagascar in effect found itself with two presidents and two capitals. After a recount in April, the High Constitutional Court declared Ravalomanana was the winner with 51.5% of the vote. Ratsiraka, after first refusing to accept the outcome, fled to France in July, and Madagascar's six-month civil war ended.

In Oct. 2004, the World Bank and the International Monetary Fund agreed to write off half of Madagascar's debt.

Malawi

REPUBLIC OF MALAWI

President: Bingu wa Mutharika (2004)
Area: 45,745 sq mi (118,480 sq km)
Population (2005 est.): 12,158,924 (growth rate: 2.1%); birth rate: 44.0/1000; infant mortality rate: 103.3/1000; life expectancy: 37.0; density per sq mi: 266
Capital (2003 est.): Lilongwe, 499,200. **Largest city:** Blantyre, 547,500. **Monetary unit:** Kwacha.
Languages: English and Chichewa (both official), others important regionally. **Ethnicity/race:** Chewa, Nyanja, Tumbuko, Yao, Lomwe, Sena, Tonga, Ngoni, Ngonde, Asian, European. **Religions:** Protestant 55%, Roman Catholic 20%, Islam 20%, indigenous beliefs 3%, other 2%. **Literacy rate:** 63% (2003 est.)
Economic summary: GDP/PPP (2004 est.): $7.41 billion; per capita $600. **Real growth rate:** 4%. **Inflation:** 12%. **Unemployment:** n.a. (2003 est.). **Arable land:** 23%. **Agriculture:** tobacco, sugarcane, cotton, tea, corn, potatoes, cassava (tapioca), sorghum, pulses; groundnuts, Macadamia nuts; cattle, goats. **Labor force:** 4.5 million (2001 est.); agriculture 90% (2003 est.). **Industries:** tobacco, tea, sugar, sawmill products, cement, consumer goods. **Natural resources:** limestone, arable land, hydropower, unexploited deposits of uranium, coal, and bauxite. **Exports:** $503.4 million (f.o.b., 2004 est.): tobacco 60%, tea, sugar, cotton, coffee, peanuts, wood products, apparel. **Imports:** $521.1 million (f.o.b., 2004 est.): food, petroleum products, semimanufactures, consumer goods, transportation equipment. **Major trading partners:** South Africa, U.S., Germany, Egypt, Portugal, Japan, Netherlands, South Africa, India, Tanzania (2003). **Member of Commonwealth of Nations**

Geography Malawi is a landlocked country about the size of Pennsylvania. Located in southeast Africa, it is surrounded by Mozambique, Zambia, and Tanzania. Lake Malawi, formerly Lake Nyasa, occupies most of the country's eastern border. The north-south Rift Valley is flanked by mountain ranges and high plateau areas.

Government Multiparty democracy.

History Early human inhabitants of what is now Malawi date to 8000–2000 B.C. Bantu-speaking peoples migrated there between the 1st and 4th centuries A.D. A large slave trade took place in the 18th and 19th centuries and brought Islam to the region. At the

same time, missionaries introduced Christianity. Several major kingdoms were established in the precolonial period: the Maravi in 1480, the Ngonde in 1600, and the Chikulamayembe in the 18th century.

The first European to make extensive explorations in the area was David Livingstone in the 1850s and 1860s. In 1884, Cecil Rhodes's British South African Company received a charter to develop the country. The company came into conflict with the Arab slavers in 1887–1889. Britain annexed what was then called the Nyasaland territory in 1891 and made it a protectorate in 1892. Sir Harry Johnstone, the first high commissioner, used Royal Navy gunboats to wipe out the slavers.

Between 1951 and 1953, Britain combined Nyasaland with the colonies of Northern and Southern Rhodesia to form a federation, a move protested by black Africans who were wary of alignment with the ultra conservative white-minority rule in South Rhodesia.

On July 6, 1964, Nyasaland became the independent nation of Malawi. Two years later, it became a republic within the Commonwealth of Nations. Dr. Hastings K. Banda became Malawi's first prime minister (a title later changed to president). In his first month as ruler, he declared, "one party, one leader, one government, and no nonsense about it." In 1971, he became president for life, further consolidating his authoritarian rule. In addition to allowing former colonialists to retain considerable power in the country, he maintained warm relations with the white-minority government of South Africa. These policies drew heavy criticism from citizens of Malawi and other African nations. In 1992, Banda faced violent protests.

Bakili Muluzi of the United Democratic Front (UDF) won the country's first free election in May 1994, ending Banda's 30-year rule. In 1999, Muluzi was reelected. While Malawi was no longer the repressive society it was under Banda, Muluzi's government was tainted by corruption scandals. Senior officials are believed to have sold off 160,000 tons of reserve maize in 2000, despite the signs of a coming famine. In 2002 and 2003, the country faced severe food shortages, with more than 3 million people suffering.

In May 2004, Bingu wa Mutharika, an economist and crony of Muluzi, was elected president in elections that were widely considered irregular.

In 2005, Malawi faced its worst food shortage in over a decade, with more than 4 million people, 34% of the population, without adequate food supplies.

Malaysia

Head of State: King Syed Sirajuddin Syed Putra Jamalullail (2001)
Prime Minister: Abdullah Badawi (2003)
Area: 127,316 sq mi (329,750 sq km)
Population (2005 est.): 23,953,136 (growth rate: 1.8%); birth rate: 23.1/1000; infant mortality rate: 17.7/1000; life expectancy: 72.2; density per sq mi: 188
Capital and largest city (2003 est.): Kuala Lumpur, 3,688,200 (metro. area), 1,403,400. **Other large cities:** Kelang, 683,200; Johor Bharu, 682,100. **Monetary unit:** Ringgit. **Languages:** Bahasa Melayu (Malay, official), English, Chinese dialects (Cantonese, Mandarin, Hokkien, Hakka, Hainan, Foochow), Tamil, Telugu, Malayalam, Panjabi, Thai; several indigenous languages (including Iban, Kadazan) in East Malaysia. **Ethnicity/race:** Malay and other indigenous 58%, Chinese 24%, Indian 8%, others 10% (2000). **Religions:** Muslim, Buddhist, Daoist, Hindu, Christian, Sikh; Shamanism (East Malaysia). **Literacy rate:** 89% (2003 est.)
Economic summary: GDP/PPP (2004 est.): $229.3 billion; per capita $9,700. **Real growth rate:** 7.1%. **Inflation:** 1.3%. **Unemployment:** 3%. **Arable land:** 5%. **Agriculture:** Peninsular Malaysia—rubber, palm oil,

cocoa, rice; Sabah—subsistence crops, rubber, timber, coconuts, rice; Sarawak—rubber, pepper; timber. **Labor force:** 10.49 million; agriculture 14.5%, industry 36%, services 49.5% (2000 est.). **Industries:** Peninsular Malaysia—rubber and oil palm processing and manufacturing, light manufacturing industry, electronics, tin mining and smelting, logging and processing timber; Sabah—logging, petroleum production; Sarawak—agriculture processing, petroleum production and refining, logging. **Natural resources:** tin, petroleum, timber, copper, iron ore, natural gas, bauxite. **Exports:** $123.5 billion (f.o.b., 2004 est.): electronic equipment, petroleum and liquefied natural gas, wood and wood products, palm oil, rubber, textiles, chemicals. **Imports:** $99.3 billion (f.o.b., 2004 est.): electronics, machinery, petroleum products, plastics, vehicles, iron and steel products, chemicals. **Major trading partners:** U.S., Singapore, Japan, China, Hong Kong, Thailand, South Korea, Germany (2003). **Member of Commonwealth of Nations**

Geography Malaysia is on the Malay Peninsula in southeast Asia. The nation also includes Sabah and Sarawak on the island of Borneo to the east. Its area slightly exceeds that of New Mexico.

Most of Malaysia is covered by forest, with a mountain range running the length of the peninsula. Extensive forests provide ebony, sandalwood, teak, and other woods.

Government Constitutional monarchy.

History The ancestors of the people that now inhabit the Malaysian peninsula first migrated to the area between 2500 and 1500 B.C. Those living in the coastal regions had early contact with Chinese and Indians; seafaring traders from India brought with them Hinduism, which was blended with the local animist beliefs. As Muslims conquered India, they spread the religion of Islam to Malaysia. In the 15th century A.D., Islam acquired a firm hold on the region when the Hindu ruler of the powerful city-state of Malacca, Parameswara Dewa Shah, converted to Islam.

British and Dutch interest in the region grew in the 1800s, with the British East India Company establishment of a trading settlement on the island of Singapore. Trade soared, with Singapore's population growing from only 5,000 in 1820 to nearly 100,000 in just 50 years. In the 1880s, Britain formally established protectorates in Malaysia. At about the same time, rubber trees were introduced from Brazil. With the mass production of automobiles, rubber became a valuable export, and laborers were brought in from India to work the rubber plantations.

Following the Japanese occupation of Malaysia during World War II, a growing nationalist movement prompted the British to establish the semiautonomous Federation of Malaya in 1948. But Communist guerrillas took to the jungles to begin a war of national liberation against the British, who declared a state of emergency to quell the insurgency, which lasted until 1960.

The independent state of Malaysia came into existence on Sept. 16, 1963, as a federation of Malaya, Singapore, Sabah (North Borneo), and Sarawak. In 1965, Singapore withdrew from the federation to become a separate nation. Since 1966, the 11 states of former Malaya have been known as West Malaysia, and Sabah and Sarawak have been known as East Malaysia.

By the late 1960s Malaysia was torn by communal rioting directed against Chinese and Indians, who controlled a disproportionate share of the country's wealth. Beginning in 1968, the government moved to achieve greater economic balance through a national economic policy.

In the 1980s, Dr. Mohamad Mahathir succeeded Datuk Hussein as prime minister. Mahathir instituted economic reforms that would transform Malaysia into one of the so-called Asian Tigers. Throughout the 1990s, Mahathir embarked on a massive project to build a new capital from scratch in an attempt to bypass congested Kuala Lumpur.

Beginning in 1997 and continuing through the next year, Malaysia suffered from the Asian currency crisis. Instead of following the economic prescriptions of the International Monetary Fund and World Bank, the prime minister opted for fixed exchange rates and capital controls. In late 1999, Malaysia was on the road to economic recovery, and it appeared Mahathir's measures were working.

Mahathir sacked his heir apparent, Anwar Ibrahim, from his posts as deputy prime minister and finance minister in Sept. 1998, after a disagreement over how to deal with the country's economic problems. In defiance, Anwar launched a reform movement attacking the government. The prime minister then jailed Anwar, who was beaten and convicted on trumped-up charges of corruption and sodomy.

In Oct. 2003, Mahathir retired after 22 years in office. His rule led to his country's enormous economic growth but was also characterized by repression and human rights abuses. Malaysia's new prime minister, Abdullah Badawi, has a more statesmanlike reputation, and in his first year in office he made headway on reducing corruption and instituting reforms. In March 2004, the ruling National Front coalition won an astonishing 90% of parliamentary seats, and Abdullah was reelected on his own merits.

Malaysia's high court overturned Anwar's sodomy conviction in Sept. 2004, and the former deputy prime minister was released after serving six years in prison. The international community praised Abdullah for not interfering with the court's ruling.

Maldives

REPUBLIC OF MALDIVES

National name: Dhivehi Raajjeyge Jumhooriyyaa
President: Maumoon Abdul Gayoom (1978)
Area: 116 sq mi (300 sq km)
Population (2005 est.): 349,106 (growth rate: 2.8%); birth rate: 35.4/1000; infant mortality rate: 56.5/1000; life expectancy: 64.1; density per sq mi: 3,014
Capital and largest city (2003 est.): Malé, 81,600.
  Monetary unit: Rufiya. **Languages:** Maldivian Dhivehi (official); English spoken by most government officials.
  Ethnicity/race: South Indians, Sinhalese, Arabs.
  Religion: Islam (Sunni). **Literacy rate:** 97% (2003 est.)
Economic summary: GDP/PPP (2002 est.): $1.25 billion; per capita $3,900. **Real growth rate:** 2.3%. **Inflation:** 1%. **Unemployment:** negl. (2003 est.). **Arable land:** 13%. **Agriculture:** coconuts, corn, sweet potatoes; fish. **Labor force:** 88,000 (2000); agriculture 22%, industry 18%, services 60% (1995). **Industries:** fish processing, tourism, shipping, boat-building, coconut processing, garments, woven mats, rope, handicrafts, coral and sand mining. **Natural resources:** fish. **Exports:** $90 million (f.o.b., 2002 est.): fish, clothing. **Imports:** $392 million (f.o.b., 2002 est.): petroleum products, ships, foodstuffs, textiles, clothing, intermediate and capital goods. **Major trading partners:** U.S., Thailand, Sri Lanka, Japan, UK, Indonesia, Singapore, India, Malaysia, UAE (2003).

Geography The Republic of Maldives is a group of atolls in the Indian Ocean about 417 mi (671 km) southwest of Sri Lanka. Its 1,190 coral islets stretch over an area of 35,200 square mi (90,000 sq km). With concerns over global warming and the shrinking of the polar ice caps, Maldives is directly threatened, as none of its islands rises more than six feet above sea level.

Government Republic.

History The Maldives (formerly called the Maldive Islands) were first settled in the 5th century B.C. by Buddhist seafarers from India and Sri Lanka. According to tradition, Islam was adopted in A.D. 1153. Originally the islands were under the suzerainty of Ceylon (now Sri Lanka). They came under British protection in 1887 and were a dependency of the then-colony of Ceylon until 1948. An independence agreement with Britain was signed July 26, 1965. For centuries a sultanate, the islands adopted a republican form of government in 1952, but the sultanate was restored in 1954. In 1968, however, as the result of a referendum, a republic was again established in the recently independent country. Ibrahim Nasir, the authoritarian president since 1968, was removed from office and replaced by the more progressive Maumoon Abdul Gayoom in 1978. Gayoom was elected to a sixth five-year term in 2003.

On Dec. 26, 2004, a tremendously powerful tsunami in the Indian Ocean devastated 12 Asian countries. The Maldives reported 82 deaths and suffered enormous damage: 14 of the archipelago's islands became uninhabitable, requiring its inhabitants to be permanently evacuated, and another 79 islands were left without safe drinking water.

Parliament voted in June 2005 to shift to a multiparty democracy. President Gayoom indicated that he supported the move.

Mali

REPUBLIC OF MALI

National name: République de Mali
President: Amadou Toumani Touré (2002)
Prime Minister: Ousmane Issoufi Maïga (2004)
Area: 478,764 sq mi (1,240,000 sq km)
Population (2005 est.): 12,291,529 (growth rate: 2.7%); birth rate: 46.8/1000; infant mortality rate: 116.8/1000; life expectancy: 45.1; density per sq mi: 26
Capital and largest city (2003 est.): Bamako, 1,323,200 (metro. area), 935,400. **Monetary unit:** CFA Franc. **Languages:** French (official), Bambara 80%, numerous African languages. **Ethnicity/race:** Mande 50% (Bambara, Malinke, Sarakole), Peul 17%, Voltaic 12%, Tuareg and Moor 10%, Songhai 6%, other 5%. **Religions:** Islam 90%, indigenous beliefs 9%, Christian 1%. **Literacy rate:** 46% (2003 est.)
Economic summary: GDP/PPP (2004 est.): $11 billion; per capita $900. **Real growth rate:** 4%. **Inflation:** 4.5% (2002 est.). **Unemployment:** 14.6% urban areas; 5.3% rural areas (2001 est.). **Arable land:** 4%. **Agriculture:** cotton, millet, rice, corn, vegetables, peanuts; cattle, sheep, goats. **Labor force:** 3.93 million (2001 est.); agriculture and fishing 80% (2001 est.). **Industries:** food processing; construction; phosphate and gold mining. **Natural resources:** gold, phosphates, kaolin, salt, limestone, uranium, hydropower note: bauxite, iron ore, manganese, tin, and copper deposits are known but not exploited. **Exports:** $915 million (f.o.b., 2002 est.): cotton, gold, livestock. **Imports:** $927 million (f.o.b., 2002 est.): petroleum, machinery and equipment, construction materials, foodstuffs, textiles. **Major trading partners:** Thailand, China, India, Italy, Bangladesh, UK, Taiwan, France, Senegal, Côte d'Ivoire (2003).

Geography Most of Mali, in West Africa, lies in the Sahara. A landlocked country four-fifths the size of Alaska, it is bordered by Guinea, Senegal, Mauritania, Algeria, Niger, Burkina Faso, and the Côte d'Ivoire. The only fertile area is in the south, where the Niger and Senegal rivers provide irrigation.

Government Republic.

History Caravan routes have passed through Mali since A.D. 300. The Malinke Empire ruled regions of Mali from the 12th to the 16th century, and the Songhai Empire reigned over the Timbuktu-Gao region in the 15th century. Morocco conquered Timbuktu in 1591, and ruled over it for two centuries. Subjugated by France by the end of the 19th century, the land became a colony in 1904 (named French Sudan in 1920) and in 1946 became part of the French Union. On June 20, 1960, it became independent and, under the name of Sudanese Republic, was joined with the Republic of Senegal in the Mali federation. However, Senegal seceded from the federation on Aug. 20, 1960, and the Sudanese Republic then changed its name to the Republic of Mali on Sept. 22.

In the 1960s, Mali concentrated on economic development, continuing to accept aid from both Soviet bloc and Western nations, as well as international agencies. In the late 1960s, it began retreating from close ties with China. But a purge of conservative opponents brought greater power to President Modibo Keita, and in 1968, the influence of the Chinese and their Malian sympathizers increased. The army overthrew the government on Nov. 19, 1968, and brought Mali under military rule for the next 20 years. Mali and Burkina Faso fought a brief border war from Dec. 25 to 29, 1985. In 1991, dictator Moussa Traoré was overthrown, and Mali made a peaceful transition to democracy. In 1992, Alpha Konaré became Mali's first democratically elected president.

Mali's second multiparty national elections took place in May 1997, with President Konaré winning reelection.

Konaré won international praise for his efforts to revive Mali's faltering economy. His adherence to International Monetary Fund guidelines increased foreign investment and helped make Mali the second-largest cotton producer in Africa. Konaré was also the chairman of the 15-nation ECOWAS (the Economic Community of West African States), which in recent years has concentrated on brokering peace in Sierra Leone, Liberia, and Guinea. Konaré retired after serving the two five-year terms permitted by the constitution.

In June 2002, Amadou Toumani Touré was elected president. A highly popular and respected public figure, he engineered the 1991 coup that freed the country from military rule. In 2004, he appointed Ousmane Issoufi Maïga as the new prime minister.

In 2005 a severe locust infestation and drought threatened about 10% of the population with starvation.

Malta

MALTA

National name: Repubblika ta' Malta
President: Eddie Fenech Adami (2004)
Prime Minister: Lawrence Gonzi (2004)
Area: 122 sq mi (316 sq km)
Population (2005 est.): 398,534 (growth rate: 0.4%); birth rate: 10.2/1000; infant mortality rate: 3.9/1000; life expectancy: 78.9; density per sq mi: 3,266
Capital (2003 est.): Valletta, 194,200 (metro. area) 6,900 (city proper). **Largest city:** Birkirkara, 21,600. **Monetary unit:** Maltese lira. **Languages:** Maltese and English (both official). **Ethnicity/race:** Maltese (descendants of ancient Carthaginians and Phoenicians, with strong elements of Italian and other Mediterranean stock). **Religion:** Roman Catholic 98%. **Literacy rate:** 93% (2003 census)
Economic summary: GDP/PPP (2004 est.): $7.223 billion; per capita $18,200. **Real growth rate:** 1%. **Inflation:** 2.9%. **Unemployment:** 7% (2003 est.).

Arable land: 28%. **Agriculture:** potatoes, cauliflower, grapes, wheat, barley, tomatoes, citrus, cut flowers, green peppers; pork, milk, poultry, eggs. **Labor force:** 160,000 (2002 est); industry 24%, services 71%, agriculture 5% (1999 est.). **Industries:** tourism; electronics, shipbuilding and repair, construction; food and beverages, textiles, footwear, clothing, tobacco. **Natural resources:** limestone, salt, arable land. **Exports:** $2.625 billion (f.o.b., 2004 est.): machinery and transport equipment, manufactures. **Imports:** $3.407 billion (f.o.b., 2004 est.): machinery and transport equipment, manufactured and semimanufactured goods; food, drink, and tobacco. **Major trading partners:** Singapore, U.S., UK, Germany, France, China, Italy, Japan, South Korea (2003). **Member of Commonwealth of Nations**

Geography The five Maltese islands—Malta, Gozo, Comino, Comminotto, and Filflawith—have a combined land area smaller than Philadelphia. Malta is located in the Mediterranean Sea, about 60 mi (97 km) south of the southeast tip of Sicily.

Government Republic.

History The strategic importance of Malta was recognized by the Phoenicians, who occupied it, as did, in turn, the Greeks, Carthaginians, and Romans. The apostle Paul was shipwrecked there in A.D. 60. With the division of the Roman Empire in A.D. 395, Malta was assigned to the eastern portion dominated by Constantinople. Between 870 and 1090, it came under Arab rule. In 1091, the Norman noble Roger I, then ruler of Sicily, came to Malta with a small retinue and defeated the Arabs. The Knights of St. John (Malta), who obtained the three habitable Maltese islands of Malta, Gozo, and Comino from Charles V in 1530, reached their highest fame when they withstood an attack by superior Turkish forces in 1565. Napoléon seized Malta in 1798, but the French forces were ousted by British troops the next year, and British rule was confirmed by the Treaty of Paris in 1814.

Malta was heavily attacked by German and Italian aircraft during World War II but was never invaded by the Axis powers. It became an independent nation on Sept. 21, 1964, and a republic on Dec. 13, 1974, but it remained in the British Commonwealth. In 1979, when its alliance with Great Britain ended, Malta sought to guarantee its neutrality through agreements with other countries. Although Malta applied for membership in the European Union, when the Labour Party won the election in Oct. 1996, it froze Malta's EU application and withdrew from the NATO Partnership for Peace program in an effort to maintain its neutrality. When the Nationalist Party won the Sept. 1998 elections, however, it revived the EU accession bid, and in May 2004 Malta joined the EU. In July 2005, it ratified the proposed EU constitution.

Marshall Islands

REPUBLIC OF THE MARSHALL ISLANDS

President: Kessai H. Note (2000)
Total land area: 70 sq mi (181.3 sq km), includes the atolls of Bikini, Eniwetok, and Kwajalein
Population (2005 est.): 59,071 (growth rate: 2.3%); birth rate: 33.5/1000; infant mortality rate: 29.4/1000; life expectancy: 70.0; density per sq mi: 844
Capital and largest city (2003 est.): Majuro, 20,500.
Languages: Marshallese (two major dialects from the Malayo-Polynesian family), English (both official); Japanese. **Ethnicity/race:** Micronesian. **Religion:** Christian (mostly Protestant). **Literacy rate:** 94% (1999)
Economic summary: GDP/PPP (2001 est.): $115 million; per capita $1,600. **Real growth rate:** 1%. **Inflation:** 2%.

Unemployment: 30.9% (1999 est.). **Arable land:** 17%. **Agriculture:** coconuts, tomatoes, melons, taro, breadfruit, fruits; pigs, chickens. **Labor force:** 28,700 (1996 est) agriculture 21.4%, industry 20.9%, services 57.7%. **Industries:** copra, tuna processing, tourism, craft items from shell, wood, and pearls. **Natural resources:** coconut products, marine products, deep seabed minerals. **Exports:** $9 million (f.o.b., 2000): copra cake, coconut oil, handicrafts, fish. **Imports:** $54 million (f.o.b., 2000): foodstuffs, machinery and equipment, fuels, beverages and tobacco. **Major trading partners:** U.S., Japan, Australia, China, NZ, Singapore, Fiji, Philippines (2000).

Geography The Marshall Islands, east of the Carolines, are divided into two chains: the western, or Ralik, group, including the atolls Jaluit, Kwajalein, Wotho, Bikini, and Eniwetok; and the eastern, or Ratak, group, including the atolls Mili, Majuro, Maloelap, Wotje, and Likiep. The islands are of the coralreef type and rise only a few feet above sea level. The Marshall Islands comprise an area slightly larger than Washington, DC.

Government Constitutional government in free association with the U.S.

History Micronesian peoples were the first inhabitants of the archipelago. The islands were explored by the Spanish in the 16th century and were named for a British captain in 1788. Germany unsuccessfully attempted to colonize the islands in 1885. Japan claimed them in 1914, but after several battles during World War II, the U.S. seized them from the Japanese. In 1947, the UN made the island group, along with the Mariana and Caroline archipelagos, a U.S. trust territory.

U.S. nuclear testing took place between 1946 and 1958 on the islands of Bikini and Eniwetok. The people of Bikini were removed to another island, and a total of 23 U.S. atomic and hydrogen bomb tests were conducted. Despite clean-up attempts, the islands remain uninhabited today because of nuclear contamination. The U.S. paid the islands $183.7 million in damages in 1983, and in 1999, the U.S. approved a one-time $3.8-million payment to the relocated people of Bikini atoll.

The United States and the Marshall Islands signed a Compact of Free Association in 1986, which meant the islands became self-governing but would receive U.S. military and economic aid, roughly $65 million a year. The Marshall Islands were admitted to the UN on Sept. 17, 1991.

Kwajalein atoll is the site of an American military base and has been used for missile defense testing since the 1960s.

In 2000, Kessai Note became the first commoner to become president—his predecessors had been island chiefs. He ran on an anticorruption ticket and is attempting to make his small nation more self-sufficient. In 2003, the U.S. and the Marshall Islands agreed on a new Compact of Free Association, an extension of the lease to use the Kwajalein military base in exchange for economic aid. In Jan. 2004, Parliament reelected President Note.

Mauritania

ISLAMIC REPUBLIC OF MAURITANIA

National name: Al Jumhuriyah al Islamiyah al Muritaniyah
President: Col. Ely Ould Mohamed Vall (2005)
Prime Minister: Sidi Mohamed Ould Boubacar (2005)
Area: 397,953 sq mi (1,030,700 sq km)
Population (2005 est.): 3,086,859 (growth rate: 2.9%); birth rate: 41.4/1000; infant mortality rate: 70.9/1000;

life expectancy: 52.7; density per sq mi: 8
Capital and largest city (2003 est.): Nouakchott, 661,400. **Monetary unit:** Ouguiya. **Languages:** Hassaniya Arabic, Wolof (both official); Pulaar, Soninke, French. **Ethnicity/race:** mixed Maur/black 40%, Maur 30%, black 30%. **Religion:** Islam 100%. **Literacy rate:** 42% (2003 est.)
Economic summary: GDP/PPP (2004 est.): $5.534 billion; per capita $1,800. **Real growth rate:** 3%. **Inflation:** 7% (2003 est.). **Unemployment:** 20%. **Arable land:** 0.5%. **Agriculture:** dates, millet, sorghum, rice, corn; cattle, sheep. **Labor force:** 786,000 (2001); agriculture 50%, services 40%, industry 10% (2001 est.). **Industries:** fish processing, mining of iron ore and gypsum. **Natural resources:** iron ore, gypsum, copper, phosphate, diamonds, gold, oil, fish. **Exports:** $541 million (f.o.b., 2002): iron ore, fish and fish products, gold. **Imports:** $860 million (f.o.b., 2002): machinery and equipment, petroleum products, capital goods, foodstuffs, consumer goods. **Major trading partners:** France, Japan, Spain, Italy, Belgium, Germany, Russia, Côte d'Ivoire, China, UK, Netherlands (2003).

Geography Mauritania, three times the size of Arizona, is situated in northwest Africa with about 350 mi (592 km) of coastline on the Atlantic Ocean. It is bordered by Morocco on the north, Algeria and Mali on the east, and Senegal on the south. The country is mostly desert, with the exception of the fertile Senegal River valley in the south and grazing land in the north.

Government Military rule. The legal system is based on Islam.

History Mauritania was first inhabited by blacks and Berbers, and it was a center for the Berber Almoravid movement in the 11th century, which sought to spread Islam through western Africa. It was first explored by the Portuguese in the 15th century, but by the 19th century the French gained control. They organized the area into a territory in 1904, and in 1920 it became one of the colonies that constituted French West Africa. In 1946, it became a French Overseas territory.

Mauritania became an independent nation on Nov. 28, 1960, and was admitted to the United Nations in 1961 over the strenuous opposition of Morocco, which claimed the territory. In the late 1960s, the government sought to make Arab culture dominant. Racial and ethnic tensions between Moors, Arabs, Berbers, and blacks were frequent.

Mauritania and Morocco divided the territory of Spanish Sahara (later called Western Sahara) between them after the Spanish departed in 1975, with Mauritania controlling the southern third. The Polisario Front, indigenous Saharawi rebels, fought for the territory against both Mauritania and Morocco. Increased military spending and rising casualties in the region helped bring down the civilian government of Ould Daddah in 1978. A succession of military rulers followed. In 1979, Mauritania withdrew from Western Sahara.

In 1984, Col. Maaouye Ould Sidi Ahmed Taya took control of the government. He relaxed Islamic law, fought corruption, instituted economic reforms urged by the International Monetary Fund, and held the country's first multiparty parliamentary elections in 1986. Although the 1991 constitution set up a multiparty democracy, politics remains based on ethnic and racial lines. The primary conflict is between blacks, who dominate southern regions, and the Moorish-Arabic north, which runs the country. Racial tensions reached a peak in 1989 when Mauritania went to war with Senegal in a dispute over the border. As each country

repatriated citizens of the other, critics accused Mauritania of taking the opportunity to expel thousands of blacks.

Although Mauritania officially abolished slavery in 1980, the nation continues to tolerate the enslavement of blacks by North African Arabs. In 1993, the U.S. State Department estimated that there were more than 90,000 chattel slaves in the country.

In 1992, Taya won the nation's first multiparty presidential election, which opponents charged was rigged. Taya's attempts to restructure the economy provoked periodic protests, the most serious of which were the bread riots in Nouakchott in 1995.

In 2002, the government banned a political party, Action for Change (AC), which has campaigned for greater rights for blacks, calling it racist and violent. Two other opposition parties have been banned in the past few years. The IMF granted Mauritania debt relief in June 2002, wiping out $1.1 billion, half of Mauritania's overall debt.

Coup attempts in June 2003 and Aug. 2004 were thwarted. Taya's crackdown on Islamists and his support for Israel and the U.S. were believed to have sparked the attempts to overthrow him. In Aug. 2005, however, President Taya was deposed by military officers while out of the country.

Mauritius

REPUBLIC OF MAURITIUS

President: Anerood Jugnauth (2003)
Prime Minister: Navin Ramgoolam (2005)
Area: 788 sq mi (2,040 sq km)
Population (2005 est.): 1,230,602 (growth rate: 0.8%); birth rate: 15.6/1000; infant mortality rate: 15.0/1000; life expectancy: 72.4; density per sq mi: 1,562
Capital and largest city (2003 est.): Port Louis, 577,200 (metro. area), 143,800 (city proper).
Monetary unit: Mauritian rupee. **Languages:** English, French (both official); Creole, Hindi, Urdu, Hakka, Bojpoori. **Ethnicity/race:** Indo-Mauritian 68%, Creole 27%, Sino-Mauritian 3%, Franco-Mauritian 2%. **Religions:** Hindu 52%, Christian 28.3% (Roman Catholic 26%, Protestant 2.3%), Islam 16.6%, other 3.1%. **Literacy rate:** 86% (2003 est.)
Economic summary: GDP/PPP (2004 est.): $15.68 billion; per capita $12,800. **Real growth rate:** 4.7%. **Inflation:** 4.5%. **Unemployment:** 10.8%. **Arable land:** 49%. **Agriculture:** sugarcane, tea, corn, potatoes, bananas, pulses; cattle, goats; fish. **Labor force:** 560,000; construction and industry 36%, services 24%, agriculture and fishing 14%, trade, restaurants, hotels 16%, transportation and communication 7%, finance 3% (1995). **Industries:** food processing (largely sugar milling), textiles, clothing; chemicals, metal products, transport equipment, nonelectrical machinery; tourism. **Natural resources:** arable land, fish. **Exports:** $2.012 billion (f.o.b., 2004 est.): clothing and textiles, sugar, cut flowers, molasses. **Imports:** $2.245 billion (f.o.b., 2004 est.): manufactured goods, capital equipment, foodstuffs, petroleum products, chemicals. **Major trading partners:** UK, France, U.S., Madagascar, South Africa, China, India (2003).
Member of Commonwealth of Nations

Geography Mauritius is a mountainous island in the Indian Ocean east of Madagascar.

Government Parliamentary democracy within the British Commonwealth.

History After a brief Dutch settlement, French immigrants who came in 1715 named the island Île de France and established the first road and harbor infrastructure, as well as the sugar industry, under the leadership of Gov. Mahe de Labourdonnais. Blacks from

Africa and Madagascar came as slaves to work in the sugarcane fields. In 1810, the British captured the island and in 1814, by the Treaty of Paris, it was ceded to Great Britain along with its dependencies.

Indian immigration, which followed the abolition of slavery in 1835, rapidly changed the fabric of Mauritian society, and the country flourished with the increased cultivation of sugarcane. The opening of the Suez Canal in 1869 heralded the decline of Mauritius as a port of call for ships rounding the southern tip of Africa, bound for South and East Asia. The economic instability of the price of sugar, the main crop, in the first half of the 20th century brought civil unrest, then economic, administrative, and political reforms. Mauritius became independent on March 12, 1968.

The effects of Cyclone Claudette in 1979 and of falling world sugar prices in the early 1980s led the government to initiate a vigorous program of agricultural diversification and to develop the processing of imported goods for the export market. The country formally broke ties with the British Crown in March 1992, becoming a republic within the Commonwealth.

In addition to sugarcane, textile production and tourism are the leading industries. Primary education is free, and Mauritius boasts one of the highest literacy rates in sub-Saharan Africa.

With a complicated ethnic mix—about 30% of the population is of African descent and the remainder is mostly of Indian descent, both Hindu and Muslim—political allegiances are organized according to class and ethnicity.

In Feb. 2002, Mauritius went through four presidents in succession. Two resigned within days of each other, each after refusing to sign a controversial anti-terrorism law that severely curtails the rights of suspects. The law, supported by the prime minister, was ultimately signed by a third, interim president. At the end of February, a fourth president, Karl Offman, was elected by Parliament.

In Oct. 2003, Paul Berenger, a white Mauritian of French ancestry, became the first non-Hindu prime minister in the history of Mauritius. Berenger and the previous prime minister, Aneerood Jugnauth, formed a coalition during Sept. 2000 elections. Under their agreement, Jugnauth served as prime minister for three years and Berenger assumed the prime ministership for the remaining two years of the term. Jugnauth then became president in 2003, and in July 2005, Navin Ramgoolam, prime minister from 1995 to 2000, again assumed that office.

Mexico

UNITED MEXICAN STATES

Official name: Estados Unidos Mexicanos
President: Vicente Fox Quesada (2000)
Area: 761,602 sq mi (1,972,550 sq km)
Population (2005 est.): 106,202,903 (growth rate: 1.2%); birth rate: 21.0/1000; infant mortality rate: 20.9/1000; life expectancy: 75.2; density per sq mi: 139
Capital and largest city (2003 est.): Mexico City, 21,233,900 (metro. area), 8,681,400 (city proper).
Other large cities: Ecatepec, 1,731,900 (part of Mexico City metro. area); Guadalajara, 1,665,800; Puebla, 1,345,500; Nezahualcóyotl, 1,250,700 (part of Mexico City metro. area); Monterrey, 1,135,000.
Monetary unit: Mexican peso. **Languages:** Spanish, various Mayan, Nahuatl, and other regional indigenous languages. **Ethnicity/race:** mestizo (Amerindian-Spanish) 60%, Amerindian or predominantly Amerindian 30%, white 9%, other 1%.
Religions: nominally Roman Catholic 89%, Protestant 6%, other 5%. **Literacy rate:** 92% (2003 est.)

Economic summary: GDP/PPP (2004 est.): $1.006 trillion; per capita $9,600. **Real growth rate:** 4.1%. **Inflation:** 5.4%. **Unemployment:** 3.2% plus underemployment of perhaps 25%. **Arable land:** 13%. **Agriculture:** corn, wheat, soybeans, rice, beans, cotton, coffee, fruit, tomatoes; beef, poultry, dairy products; wood products. **Labor force:** 34.73 million; agriculture 18%, industry 24%, services 58% (2003). **Industries:** food and beverages, tobacco, chemicals, iron and steel, petroleum, mining, textiles, clothing, motor vehicles, consumer durables, tourism. **Natural resources:** petroleum, silver, copper, gold, lead, zinc, natural gas, timber. **Exports:** $182.4 billion (f.o.b., 2004 est.): manufactured goods, oil and oil products, silver, fruits, vegetables, coffee, cotton. **Imports:** $190.8 billion (f.o.b., 2004 est.): metalworking machines, steel mill products, agricultural machinery, electrical equipment, car parts for assembly, repair parts for motor vehicles, aircraft, and aircraft parts. **Major trading partners:** U.S., Canada, Germany, China, Japan (2003).

Geography Mexico is bordered by the United States to the north and Belize and Guatemala to the southeast. Mexico is about one-fifth the size of the United States. Baja California in the west is an 800-mile (1,287-km) peninsula and forms the Gulf of California. In the east are the Gulf of Mexico and the Bay of Campeche, which is formed by Mexico's other peninsula, the Yucatán. The center of Mexico is a great, high plateau, open to the north, with mountain chains on the east and west and with ocean-front lowlands lying outside them.

Government Federal republic.

History At least three great civilizations—the Mayas, the Olmecs, and later the Toltecs—preceded the wealthy Aztec Empire, conquered in 1519–1521 by the Spanish under Hernando Cortés. Spain ruled Mexico as part of the viceroyalty of New Spain for the next 300 years until Sept. 16, 1810, when the Mexicans first revolted. They won independence in 1821.

From 1821 to 1877, there were two emperors, several dictators, and enough presidents and provisional executives to make a new government on the average of every nine months. Mexico lost Texas (1836), and after defeat in the war with the U.S. (1846–1848), it lost the area that is now California, Nevada, and Utah, most of Arizona and New Mexico, and parts of Wyoming and Colorado under the Treaty of Guadalupe Hidalgo. In 1855, the Indian patriot Benito Juárez began a series of reforms, including the disestablishment of the Catholic Church, which owned vast property. The subsequent civil war was interrupted by the French invasion of Mexico (1861) and the crowning of Maximilian of Austria as emperor (1864). He was overthrown and executed by forces under Juárez, who again became president in 1867.

The years after the fall of the dictator Porfirio Diaz (1877–1880 and 1884–1911) were marked by bloody political-military strife and trouble with the U.S., culminating in the punitive U.S. expedition into northern Mexico (1916–1917) in unsuccessful pursuit of the revolutionary Pancho Villa. Since a brief civil war in 1920, Mexico has enjoyed a period of gradual agricultural, political, and social reforms. The Partido Nacional Revolucionario (PNR; National Revolutionary Party), dominated by revolutionary and reformist politicians from northern Mexico, was established in 1929; it continued to control Mexico throughout the 20th century and was renamed the Partido Revolucionario Institucional (PRI; Institutional Revolutionary Party) in 1946. Relations with the U.S. were disturbed in 1938 when all foreign oil wells were expropriated, but a compensation agreement was reached in 1941.

Following World War II, the government emphasized economic growth. During the mid-1970s, under the leadership of President José López Portillo, Mexico became a major petroleum producer. By the end of Portillo's term, however, Mexico had accumulated a huge external debt because of the government's unrestrained borrowing on the strength of its petroleum revenues. The collapse of oil prices in 1986 cut Mexico's export earnings. In Jan. 1994, Mexico joined Canada and the United States in the North American Free Trade Agreement (NAFTA), which will phase out all tariffs over a 15-year period, and in Jan. 1996, it became a founding member of the World Trade Organization (WTO).

In 1995, the U.S. agreed to prevent the collapse of Mexico's private banks. In return, the U.S. won virtual veto power over much of Mexico's economic policy. In 1997, in what observers called the freest elections in Mexico's history, the PRI lost control of the lower legislative house and the mayoralty of Mexico City in a stunning upset. To increase democracy, President Ernesto Zedillo said in 1999 that he would break precedent and not personally choose the next PRI presidential nominee. Several months later, Mexico held its first presidential primary, which was won by former interior secretary Francisco Labastida, Zedillo's closest ally among the candidates.

In elections held on July 2, 2000, the PRI lost the presidency, ending 71 years of one-party rule. Vicente Fox Quesada, of the conservative National Action Party (PAN), took 43% of the vote to Labastida's 36%. Fox vowed tax reform, an overhaul of the legal system, and a reduction in power of the central government. By 2002, however, Fox had made little headway on his ambitious reform agenda. Disfavor with Fox was evident in 2003 parliamentary elections, when the PRI rebounded, winning 224 of the 500 seats in the lower house. After the elections, Fox admitted publicly that many Mexicans were disappointed with his government thus far.

In 2004, a two-year investigation into the "dirty war," which Mexico's authoritarian government waged against its opponents in the 1960s and 1970s, led to an indictment—later dropped—against former president Luis Echeverria for ordering the 1971 shooting of student protesters.

An attempt to bring criminal charges against Andrés Manuel López Obrador, the enormously popular leftist mayor of Mexico City, were dropped in May 2005 after a huge public rally in favor of the mayor took place. López Obrador was accused of a technical offense, breaching a court order involving the construction of an access road in the city, which could have blocked his intended run for the presidency in 2006. Many believe that the charges were politically motivated, so that López Obrador could not run against the deeply unpopular incumbent, Vicente Fox.

Micronesia

FEDERATED STATES OF MICRONESIA

President: Joseph J. Urusemal (2003)
Total area: 271 sq mi (702 sq km). Land area, same (includes islands of Pohnpei, Yap, Chuuk, and Kosrae)
Population (2005 est.): 108,105 (growth rate: –0.1); birth rate: 25.1/1000; infant mortality rate: 30.2/1000; life expectancy: 69.8; density per sq mi: 399
Capital (2003 est.): Palikir 11,600. **Languages:** English (official, common), Chukese, Pohnpeian, Yapase, Kosrean, Ulithian, Woleaian, Nukuoro, Kapingamarangi. **Ethnicity/race:** nine ethnic Micronesian and Polynesian groups. **Religions:**

Roman Catholic 50%, Protestant 47%. **Literacy rate:** 89% (1980 est.)
Economic summary: GDP/PPP (2002 est.): $277 million; note: GDP is supplemented by grant aid, averaging perhaps $100 million annually; per capita $2,000. **Real growth rate:** 1%. **Inflation:** 1%. **Unemployment:** 16% (1999 est.). **Arable land:** 6%. **Agriculture:** black pepper, tropical fruits and vegetables, coconuts, cassava (tapioca), betel nuts, sweet potatoes; pigs, chickens. **Labor force:** n.a.; two-thirds are government employees. **Industries:** tourism, construction, fish processing, specialized aquaculture, craft items from shell, wood, and pearls. **Natural resources:** forests, marine products, deep-seabed minerals. **Exports:** $22 million (f.o.b., FY99/00 est.): fish, garments, bananas, black pepper. **Imports:** $149 million (f.o.b., FY99/00 est.): food, manufactured goods, machinery and equipment, beverages. **Major trading partners:** Japan, U.S., Guam, Australia (2000).

Geography The Federated States of Micronesia is composed of the island states of Yap, Chuuk (Truk), Pohnpei (Ponape), and Kosrae, all in the Caroline Islands. The islands vary geologically from high mountainous islands to low coral atolls, with volcanic outcroppings on Pohnpei, Kosrae, and Chuuk. They are located 3,200 mi (5,150 km) west-southwest of Hawaii, in the north Pacific Ocean.

Government Constitutional government in free association with the United States since Nov. 1986.

History The islands, inhabited by Micronesian and Polynesian peoples, were colonized by Spain in the 17th century. Germany purchased them from Spain in 1898. They were occupied by the Japanese in 1914, but American forces seized them from the Japanese during World War II. On April 2, 1947, the United Nations Security Council created the Trust Territory of the Pacific Islands. The trust placed the Northern Mariana, Caroline, and Marshall Islands under the administration of the United States.

The Micronesian Federation (FMA) became self-governing in 1979. In 1983, the FMA voted to accept a Compact of Free Association with the U.S., and in Nov. 1986, the U.S. government declared the Trust Territory agreements no longer in effect—thereby granting the Federated States of Micronesia full independence. In Nov. 2002 the compact was renewed for another 20 years.

The FMA was admitted to the United Nations on Sept. 17, 1991. In July 1993, the country became a member of the International Monetary Fund. Micronesia, as well as many other South Pacific countries, is alarmed by the effect continued global warming will have on its islands—the consequent rise in the level of the oceans threatens low-lying islands with flooding and, eventually, with submergence.

In 2004, Yap was ravaged by Typhoon Sudel, and much of its infrastructure was destroyed.

Moldova

REPUBLIC OF MOLDOVA

National name: Republica Moldova
President: Vladimir Voronin (2001)
Prime Minister: Vasile Tarlev (2001)
Area: 13,067 sq mi (33,843 sq km)
Population (2005 est.): 4,455,421 (growth rate: 0.2%); birth rate: 15.3/1000; infant mortality rate: 40.4/1000; life expectancy: 65.2; density per sq mi: 341
Capital and largest city (2003 est.): Chisinau, 772,500 (metro. area), 709,900 (city proper). **Other large cities:** Tiraspol, 209,800; Beltsy, 175,400; Bendery

(Tighina), 144,900. **Monetary unit:** Leu. **Languages:** Moldovan (official; virtually the same as Romanian), Russian, Gagauz (a Turkish dialect). **Ethnicity/race:** Moldavian/Romanian 64.5%, Ukrainian 13.8%, Russian 13%, Gagauz 3.5%, Jewish 1.5%, Bulgarian 2%, other 1.7% (1989 est.). **Religions:** Eastern Orthodox 98%, Jewish 1.5%, Baptist and other 0.5% (2000). **Literacy rate:** 99% (2003 est.)

Economic summary: GDP/PPP (2004 est.): $8.581 billion; per capita $1,900. **Real growth rate:** 6.8%. **Inflation:** 11.5%. **Unemployment:** 8% (roughly 25% of working age Moldovans are employed abroad) (2002 est.). **Arable land:** 55%. **Agriculture:** vegetables, fruits, wine, grain, sugar beets, sunflower seed, tobacco; beef, milk. **Labor force:** 1.36 million; agriculture 40%, industry 14%, services 46% (1998). **Industries:** food processing, agricultural machinery, foundry equipment, refrigerators and freezers, washing machines, hosiery, sugar, vegetable oil, shoes, textiles. **Natural resources:** lignite, phosphorites, gypsum, arable land, limestone. **Exports:** $1.03 billion (f.o.b., 2004 est.): foodstuffs, textiles, machinery. **Imports:** $1.83 billion (f.o.b., 2004 est.): mineral products and fuel 32%, machinery and equipment, chemicals, textiles (2000). **Major trading partners:** Russia, Romania, Italy, Germany, Ukraine, Belarus, U.S. (2003).

Geography Moldova (formerly Moldavia) is a landlocked republic of hilly plains lying east of the Carpathian Mountains between the Prut and Dniester (Dnestr) rivers. The country is sandwiched between Romania and Ukraine. The area is a very fertile region with rich black soil (chernozem) covering three-quarters of the territory.

Government Democratic republic.

History Most of what is now Moldova was the independent principality of Moldavia in the 14th century. In the 16th century it came under Ottoman Turkish rule. Russia acquired Moldavian territory in 1791, and more in 1812 (the Treaty of Bucharest) when Turkey gave up the province of Bessarabia[1] to Russia. Turkey held the rest of Moldavia but it was passed to Romania in 1918. Russia did not recognize the cession of this territory.

In 1924, the USSR established Moldavia as an Autonomous Soviet Socialist Republic. As a result of the Nazi-Soviet Nonaggression Pact of 1939, Romania was forced to cede all of Bessarabia to the Soviet Union in 1940. The Soviets merged the Moldavia ASSR with the Romanian-speaking districts of Bessarabia to form the Moldavian Soviet Socialist Republic. During World War II, Romania joined Germany in the attack on the Soviet Union and reconquered Bessarabia. But Soviet troops retook the territory in 1944 and reestablished the Moldavian SSR.

For many years, Romania and the USSR disputed each other's territorial claims over Bessarabia. Following the aborted coup against Soviet president Mikhail Gorbachev, Moldavia proclaimed its independence in Sept. 1991 and changed its name to the Romanian spelling, Moldova.

Conflict between ethnic Romanians and the Russian-Ukrainian majority in Trans-Dniester erupted upon independence. Trans-Dniester separatists (primarily ethnic Russians and Ukrainians) fought for independence from Moldova in 1992; about 1,500 died in the conflict. Unrest continues in Trans-Dniester. In the south, Gagauz, which is composed mostly of Turkic Christians, has also attempted secession.

The Russian financial crisis in fall 1998 severely affected Moldova, which relied on Russia for 60% of its foreign trade. Economic disaster caused an exodus

of an estimated 600,000 Moldovans. Moldova is considered the poorest country in Europe. In Feb. 2001, the Communist Party won an overwhelming victory in parliamentary elections, and its leader, Vladimir Voronin, became prime minister. Voronin has attempted to forge closer relations with Moscow, thus sparking protests among those who advocate for closer cultural and ethnic ties to Romania.

In parliamentary elections in March 2005, the Communist Party—formerly aligned with Russia but recently becoming more pro-Western—won 46% of the vote. In April, President Voronin was reelected president, and he in turn reappointed Prime Minister Vasile Tarlev.

In June 2005, Ukraine proposed a peace plan for the Trans-Dniester that would involve free elections and autonomy for the region as well as the withdrawal of Russian troops. Moldova's Parliament has approved the plan.

1. The area between the Prut and Dniester rivers.

Monaco

PRINCIPALITY OF MONACO

National name: Principauté de Monaco
Ruler: Prince Albert II (2005)
Minister of State: Patrick Leclercq (2000)
Area: 0.75 sq mi (465 acres) (1.95 sq km)
Population (2005 est.): 32,409 (growth rate: 0.4%); birth rate: 9.3/1000; infant mortality rate: 5.4/1000; life expectancy: 79.6; density per sq mi: 43,046
Capital (2003 est.): Monaco, 1,400. **Largest city:** Monte Carlo, 15,400. **Monetary unit:** Euro. **Languages:** French (official), English, Italian, Monégasque. **Ethnicity/race:** French 47%, Monegasque 16%, Italian 16%, other 21%. **Religion:** Roman Catholic 90%. **Literacy rate:** 99% (2003 est.)
Economic summary: GDP/PPP (2000 est.): $870 million; $27,000 per capita. **Real growth rate:** 0.9%. **Inflation:** 1.9%. **Unemployment:** 22% (1999). **Arable land:** 0%. **Agriculture:** none. **Labor force:** 30,540 (Jan. 1994). **Natural resources:** none. **Industries:** tourism, construction, small-scale industrial and consumer products. **Exports:** n.a. **Imports:** n.a. Full customs integration with France, which collects and rebates Monegasque trade duties; also participates in EU.

Geography Monaco is a tiny, hilly wedge driven into the French Mediterranean coast; it is 9 mi east of Nice, France.

Government Constitutional monarchy.

History The Phoenicians, and after them the Greeks, had a temple on the Monacan headland honoring Hercules. The principality took its name from *Monoikos,* the Greek surname for this mythological strong man. After being independent for 800 years, Monaco was annexed to France in 1793 and was placed under Sardinia's protection in 1815. By the Franco-Monegasque treaty of 1861, Monaco went under French guardianship but continued to be independent. A treaty made with France in 1918 contained a clause providing that, in the event that the male Grimaldi dynasty should die out, Monaco would become an autonomous state under French protection.

Monaco has a tourist business that attracts as many as 1.5 million visitors a year and is famous for its beaches and casinos, especially world-famous Monte Carlo. It had gaming tables as early as 1856.

Prince Rainier III, born on May 31, 1923, succeeded his grandfather, Louis II, on the latter's death, on May 9, 1949. Rainier was married, in 1956, to American actress Grace Kelly and they subsequently had three children. Their son, Prince Albert Louis Pierre (b. 1958) is heir to the throne. Immensely popular, Princess Grace died on Sept. 14, 1982, of injuries received in a car accident near Monte Carlo. She was 52.

Monaco's practice of providing a tax shelter for French businessmen resulted in a 1962 dispute between the countries. A compromise was reached by which French citizens with less than five years' residence in Monaco were taxed at French rates, and taxes were imposed on Monegasque companies doing more than 25% of their business outside the principality. The country was admitted to the UN in May 1993, making it the smallest country represented there. It celebrated the 700th anniversary of the Grimaldi reign in 1997. In 2002, the constitution was revised to ensure that the Grimaldis retain the throne even if Crown Prince Albert has no heir. On April 6, 2005, Prince Rainier, Europe's longest-reigning monarch, died, and Prince Albert II succeeded him.

Mongolia

National name: Mongol Uls
President: Nambariin Enkhbayar (2005)
Prime Minister: Tsakhiagiyn Elbegdorj (2004)
Area: 604,247 sq mi (1,565,000 sq km)
Population (2005 est.): 2,791,272 (growth rate: 1.5%); birth rate: 21.5/1000; infant mortality rate: 53.8/1000; life expectancy: 64.5; density per sq mi: 5
Capital and largest city (2003 est.): Ulaan Baatar, 804,200. **Monetary unit:** Tugrik. **Languages:** Mongolian, 90%; also Turkic and Russian (1999). **Ethnicity/race:** Mongol (predominantly Khalkha) 85%, Turkic (of which Kazak is the largest group) 7%, Tungusic 4.6%, other (including Chinese and Russian) 3.4% (1998). **Religions:** Tibetan Buddhist Lamaism 96%, Islam (primarily in the southwest), Shamanism, and Christian 4% (1998). **Literacy rate:** 99% (2003 est.)
Economic summary: GDP/PPP (2004 est.): $5.332 billion; per capita $1,900. **Real growth rate:** 10.6%. **Inflation:** 11%. **Unemployment:** 6.7% (2003). **Arable land:** 1%. **Agriculture:** wheat, barley, vegetables, forage crops, sheep, goats, cattle, camels, horses. **Labor force:** 1.488 million (2003); primarily herding/agricultural. **Industries:** construction and construction materials; mining (coal, copper, molybdenum, fluorspar, and gold); oil; food and beverages; processing of animal products, cashmere and natural fiber manufacturing. **Natural resources:** oil, coal, copper, molybdenum, tungsten, phosphates, tin, nickel, zinc, wolfram, fluorspar, gold, silver, iron, phosphate. **Exports:** $853 million (f.o.b., 2004 est.): copper, apparel, livestock, animal products, cashmere, wool, hides, fluorspar, other nonferrous metals. **Imports:** $1 billion (c.i.f., 2004 est.): machinery and equipment, fuel, cars, food products, industrial consumer goods, chemicals, building materials, sugar, tea. **Major trading partners:** China, U.S., Russia, Singapore, Australia, UK, South Korea, Japan, Germany (2003).

Geography Mongolia lies in central Asia between Siberia on the north and China on the south. It is slightly larger than Alaska.

The productive regions of Mongolia—a tableland ranging from 3,000 to 5,000 ft (914 to 1,524 m) in elevation—are in the north, which is well drained by numerous rivers, including the Hovd, Onon, Selenga, and Tula. Much of the Gobi Desert falls within Mongolia.

Government Parliamentary republic now in transition from Communism.

History Nomadic tribes that periodically plundered agriculturally based China from the west are recorded in Chinese history dating back more than 2,000 years.

It was to protect China from these marauding peoples that the Great Wall was constructed around 200 B.C. The name *Mongol* comes from a small tribe whose leader, Ghengis Khan, began a conquest that would eventually encompass an enormous empire stretching from Asia to Europe, as far west as the Black Sea and as far south as India and the Himalayas. But by the 14th century, the kingdom was in serious decline, with invasions from a resurgent China and internecine warfare.

The State of Mongolia was formerly known as Outer Mongolia. It contains the original homeland of the historic Mongols, whose power reached its zenith during the 13th century under Kublai Khan. The area accepted Manchu rule in 1689, but after the Chinese Revolution of 1911 and the fall of the Manchus in 1912, the northern Mongol princes expelled the Chinese officials and declared independence under the Khutukhtu, or "Living Buddha."

In 1921, Soviet troops entered the country and facilitated the establishment of a republic by Mongolian revolutionaries in 1924. China also made a claim to the region but was too weak to assert it. Under the 1945 Chinese-Russian Treaty, China agreed to give up Outer Mongolia, which, after a plebiscite, became a nominally independent country.

Allied with the USSR in its dispute with China, Mongolia began mobilizing troops along its borders in 1968 when the two powers became involved in border clashes on the Kazakh-Sinkiang frontier to the west and at the Amur and Ussuri rivers. A 20-year treaty of friendship and cooperation, signed in 1966, entitled Mongolia to call on the USSR for military aid in the event of invasion.

In 1989, the Mongolian democratic revolution began, led by Sanjaasurengiyn Zorig. Free elections held in Aug. 1990 produced a multiparty government, though it was still largely Communist. As a result, Mongolia has moved only gradually toward a market economy. With the collapse of the USSR, however, Mongolia was deprived of Soviet aid. Primarily in reaction to the economic turmoil, the Communist Mongolian People's Revolutionary Party (MPRP) won a significant majority in parliamentary elections in 1992. In 1996, however, the Democratic Alliance, an electoral coalition, defeated the MPRP, breaking with Communist rule for the first time since 1921. But in 1997, a former Communist and chairman of the People's Revolutionary Party, Natsagiyn Bagabandi, was elected president, further strengthening the hand of the anti-reformers.

Disagreement within Mongolia's ruling coalition over the pace and direction of market reforms in April 1998 caused a shake-up that thrust Tsakhiagiyn Elbegdorj, a pro-reform politician, into the prime minister's position. But parliamentary cross-purposes led to his resignation, and a succession of prime ministers followed.

Bagabandi was reelected president in 2001. In the 2004 elections, however, the MPRP was dealt a stunning blow, reducing its number of seats in Parliament from 72 to 36. The opposition Motherland Democratic Coalition took 34 seats, and in August, its leader, Tsakhiagiyn Elbegdorj, was appointed prime minister to lead a coalition government.

MPRP candidate Nambariin Enkhbayar was elected president in May 2005. He won 53.4% of the vote, thereby avoiding a runoff election. His closest rival, Mendsaikhan Enkhsaikhan of the Democratic Party, took 20%. Enkhbayar was Mongolia's prime minister from 1990 to 1994.

Morocco

KINGDOM OF MOROCCO

National name: al-Mamlaka al-Maghrebia
Ruler: King Muhammed VI (1999)
Prime Minister: Driss Jettou (2002)
Area: 172,413 sq mi (446,550 sq km)
Population (2005 est.): 32,725,847 (growth rate: 1.6%);
birth rate: 22.3/1000; infant mortality rate: 41.6/1000;
life expectancy: 70.7; density per sq mi: 190
Capital (2003 est.): Rabat, 1,636,600. **Largest cities:**
Casablanca, 3,397,000; Fez, 941,800; Marrakech,
755,200. **Monetary unit:** Dirham. **Languages:** Arabic
(official), Berber dialects, French often used for
business, government, and diplomacy. **Ethnicity/race:**
Arab-Berber 99.1%, Jewish 0.2%, other 0.7%.
Religions: Islam 98.7%, Christian 1.1%, Jewish 0.2%.
Literacy rate: 52% (2003 est.)
Economic summary: GDP/PPP (2004 est.): $134.6
billion; per capita $4,200. **Real growth rate:** 4.4%.
Inflation: 2.1%. **Unemployment:** 12.1%. **Arable land:**
20%. **Agriculture:** barley, wheat, citrus, wine,
vegetables, olives; livestock. **Labor force:** 11.02
million; agriculture 40%, services 45%, industry 15%
(2003 est.). **Industries:** phosphate rock mining and
processing, food processing, leather goods, textiles,
construction, tourism. **Natural resources:** phosphates,
iron ore, manganese, lead, zinc, fish, salt. **Exports:**
$9.754 billion (f.o.b., 2004 est.): clothing, fish,
inorganic chemicals, transistors, crude minerals,
fertilizers (including phosphates), petroleum products,
fruits, vegetables. **Imports:** $15.63 billion (f.o.b. 2004
est.): crude petroleum, textile fabric,
telecommunications equipment, wheat, gas and
electricity, transistors, plastics. **Major trading
partners:** France, Spain, UK, Germany, Italy, U.S.,
Saudi Arabia, Russia (2003).

Geography Morocco, about one-tenth larger than
California, lies across the Strait of Gibraltar on the
Mediterranean and looks out on the Atlantic from the
northwest shoulder of Africa. Algeria is to the east and
Mauritania to the south. On the Atlantic coast there is
a fertile plain. The Mediterranean coast is mountainous. The Atlas Mountains, running northeastward from
the south to the Algerian frontier, average 11,000 ft
(3,353 m) in elevation.

Government Constitutional monarchy.

History Morocco has been the home of the Berbers
since the second millennium B.C. In A.D. 46, Morocco
was annexed by Rome as part of the province of Mauritania until the Vandals overran this portion of the
declining empire in the 5th century. The Arabs
invaded circa 685, bringing Islam. The Berbers joined
them in invading Spain in 711, but then they revolted
against the Arabs, resenting their secondary status. In
1086, Berbers took control of large areas of Moorish
Spain until they were expelled in the 13th century.

The land was rarely unified and was usually ruled by
small tribal states. Conflicts between Berbers and Arabs
were chronic. Portugal and Spain began invading
Morocco, which helped to unify the land in defense. In
1660, Morocco came under the control of the Alawite
dynasty. It is a sherif dynasty—descended from the
prophet Muhammed—and rules Morocco to this day.

During the 17th and 18th centuries Morocco was one
of the Barbary states, the headquarters of pirates who
pillaged Mediterranean traders. European powers
showed interest in colonizing the country beginning in
1840, and there were frequent clashes with the French
and Spanish. Finally, in 1904, France and Spain concluded a secret agreement that divided Morocco into
zones of French and Spanish influence, with France
controlling almost all of Morocco and Spain controlling
the small southwest portion, which became known as
Spanish Sahara. Morocco grew into an even greater
object of European rivalry by the turn of the century,
almost leading to a European war in 1905 when Germany attempted to gain a foothold in the mineral-rich
country. By the terms of the Algeciras Conference
(1906), the sultan of Morocco maintained control of his
lands and France's privileges were curtailed. The conference was an indication of what was to come in World
War I, with Germany and Austria-Hungary lining up on
one side of the territorial dispute, and France, Britain,
and the United States on the other.

In 1912, the sultan of Morocco, Moulay Abd
al-Hafid, permitted the French protectorate status.
Nationalism expanded during World War II. Sultan
Muhammed V was deposed by the French in 1953 and
replaced by his uncle, but nationalist agitation forced
his return in 1955. In 1956, France and Spain recognized the independence and sovereignty of Morocco.
At his death on Feb. 26, 1961, Muhammed V's son
succeeded him as King Hassan II. In the 1990s, King
Hassan promulgated "Hassanian democracy," which
allowed for significant political freedom while at the
same time retaining ultimate power for the monarch. In
Aug. 1999, King Hassan II died after 38 years on the
throne and his son, Prince Sidi Muhammed, was
crowned King Muhammed VI. Since then Muhammed
VI has pledged to make the political system more
open, allow freedom of expression, and support economic reform. He has also advocated giving more
rights to women, a position opposed by Islamic fundamentalists. The entrenched political elite and the military have also been leery of some reform proposals.
With about 20% of the population living in dire poverty, economic expansion is a prime goal.

Morocco's occupation of Western Sahara (formerly
Spanish Sahara) has been repeatedly criticized by the
international community. In the 1970s, tens of thousands of Moroccans crossed the border into Spanish
Sahara to back their government's contention that the
northern part of the territory was historically part of
Morocco. Spain, which had controlled the territory
since 1912, withdrew in 1976, creating a power
vacuum that was filled by Morocco in the north and
Mauritania in the south. When Mauritania withdrew in
Aug. 1979, Morocco overran the remainder of the territory. A rebel group, the Polisario Front, has fought
against Morocco since 1976 for the independence of
Western Sahara on behalf of the indigenous Saharawis.
The Polisario and Morocco agreed in Sept. 1991 to a
UN-negotiated cease-fire, which was contingent on a
referendum regarding independence. For the past
decade, however, Morocco has opposed the referendum. In 2002, King Muhammed VI reasserted that he
"will not renounce an inch of" Western Sahara.

On May 16, 2003, terrorists believed to be associated with al-Qaeda killed 33 people in several simultaneous attacks. Four bombs targeted Jewish, Spanish,
and Belgian buildings in Casablanca. In the 2004 terrorist bombings in Madrid, Spain, numerous Moroccans were implicated.

Mozambique

REPUBLIC OF MOZAMBIQUE

National name: República de Moçambique
President: Armando Guebuza (2005)
Prime Minister: Luisa Diogo (2004)
Area: 309,494 sq mi (801,590 sq km)
Population (2005 est.): 19,406,703 (growth rate: 1.5%);
birth rate: 35.8/1000; infant mortality rate: 130.8/1000;
life expectancy: 40.3; density per sq mi: 63

Capital and largest city (2003 est.): Maputo, 1,691,000 (metro. area), 1,114,000 (city proper). **Monetary unit:** Metical. **Languages:** Portuguese (official), Bantu languages. **Ethnicity/race:** indigenous tribal groups 99.66% (Shangaan, Chokwe, Manyika, Sena, Makua, and others), Europeans 0.06%, Euro-Africans 0.2%, Indians 0.08%. **Religions:** indigenous beliefs 50%, Christian 30%, Islam 20%. **Literacy rate:** 48% (2003 est.)

Economic summary: GDP/PPP (2004 est.): $23.38 billion; per capita $1,200. **Real growth rate:** 8.2%. **Inflation:** 12.8%. **Unemployment:** 21% (1997 est.). **Arable land:** 5%. **Agriculture:** cotton, cashew nuts, sugarcane, tea, cassava (tapioca), corn, coconuts, sisal, citrus and tropical fruits, potatoes, sunflowers; beef, poultry. **Labor force:** 9.2 million (2000 est.); agriculture 81%, industry 6%, services 13% (1997 est.). **Industries:** food, beverages, chemicals (fertilizer, soap, paints), aluminum, petroleum products, textiles, cement, glass, asbestos, tobacco. **Natural resources:** coal, titanium, natural gas, hydropower, tantalum, graphite. **Exports:** $689.4 million (f.o.b., 2004 est.): aluminum, prawns, cashews, cotton, sugar, citrus, timber; bulk electricity. **Imports:** $972.9 million (f.o.b., 2004 est.): machinery and equipment, vehicles, fuel, chemicals, metal products, foodstuffs, textiles. **Major trading partners:** Belgium, South Africa, Italy, Spain, Germany, Zimbabwe, Australia, U.S. (2003).

Geography Mozambique stretches for 1,535 mi (2,470 km) along Africa's southeast coast. It is nearly twice the size of California. Tanzania is to the north; Malawi, Zambia, and Zimbabwe to the west; and South Africa and Swaziland to the south. The country is generally a low-lying plateau broken up by 25 sizable rivers that flow into the Indian Ocean. The largest is the Zambezi, which provides access to central Africa.

Government Multiparty republic.

History Bantu speakers migrated to Mozambique in the first millennium, and Arab and Swahili traders settled the region thereafter. It was explored by Vasco da Gama in 1498 and first colonized by Portugal in 1505. By 1510, the Portuguese had control of all of the former Arab sultanates on the east African coast. Portuguese colonial rule was repressive.

Guerrilla activity began in 1963 and became so effective by 1973 that Portugal was forced to dispatch 40,000 troops to fight the rebels. A cease-fire was signed in Sept. 1974, and after having been under Portuguese colonial rule for 470 years, Mozambique became independent on June 25, 1975. The first president, Samora Moises Machel, had been the head of the National Front for the Liberation of Mozambique (FRELIMO) in its ten-year guerrilla war for independence. He died in a plane crash in 1986 and was succeeded by his foreign minister, Joaquim Chissanó.

On Jan. 25, 1985, after a decade of independence, the government was locked in a paralyzing war with antigovernment guerrillas, the Mozambique National Resistance (MNR, or Renamo), who were backed by the white minority government in South Africa. The guerrilla movement weakened President Chissanó's attempts to institute socialism, which he then decided to abandon in 1989. A new constitution was drafted calling for three branches of government and granting civil liberties. A cease-fire agreement signed in Oct. 1992 between the government and the MNR ended 16 years of civil war.

In multiparty elections in 1994, President Chissanó won. In Nov. 1995 the country was the first nonformer British colony to become a member of the British Commonwealth. The president's disciplined economic plan was highly successful, winning the country foreign confidence and aid. While Mozambique posted some of the world's largest economic growth rates in the late 1990s, it has suffered enormous setbacks because of natural disaster, such as the enormous damage caused by severe flooding in the winters of 2000 and 2001. Hundreds died and thousands were displaced.

In 2002 Chissanó announced he would not seek a third term. FRELIMO's candidate, independence hero Armando Guebuza, was elected president and sworn in on Feb. 2, 2005.

Myanmar

UNION OF MYANMAR

National name: Pyidaungsu Myanmar Naingngandau
Head of State: Senior Gen. Than Shwe (1992)
Prime Minister: Lt. Gen. Soe Win (2004)
Area: 261,969 sq mi (678,500 sq km)
Population (2005 est.): 42,909,464 (growth rate: 0.4%); birth rate: 18.1/1000; infant mortality rate: 67.2/1000; life expectancy: 56.2; density per sq mi: 164
Capital and largest city (2003 est.): Rangoon (Yangon), 4,344,100. **Other large city:** Mandalay, 1,147,400. **Monetary unit:** Kyat. **Languages:** Burmese, minority languages. **Ethnicity/race:** Burman 68%, Shan 9%, Karen 7%, Rakhine 4%, Chinese 3%, Mon 2%, Indian 2%, other 5%. **Religions:** Buddhist 89%, Christian 4% (Baptist 3%, Roman Catholic 1%), Islam 4%, Animist 1%, other 2%. **Literacy rate:** 83% (1995 est.)
Economic summary: GDP/PPP (2004 est.): $74.3 billion; per capita $1,700. **Real growth rate:** –1.3%. **Inflation:** 17.2%. **Unemployment:** 5.2%. **Arable land:** 15%. **Agriculture:** rice, pulses, beans, sesame, groundnuts, sugarcane; hardwood; fish and fish products. **Labor force:** 27.01 million; agriculture 70%, industry 7%, services 23% (2001 est.). **Industries:** agricultural processing; knit and woven apparel; wood and wood products; copper, tin, tungsten, iron; construction materials; pharmaceuticals; fertilizer; cement. **Natural resources:** petroleum, timber, tin, antimony, zinc, copper, tungsten, lead, coal, some marble, limestone, precious stones, natural gas, hydropower. **Exports:** $2.137 billion (f.o.b., 2004 est.): clothing, gas, wood products, pulses, beans, fish, rice. **Imports:** $1.754 billion (f.o.b., 2004 est.): fabric, petroleum products, plastics, machinery, transport equipment, construction materials, crude oil; food products. **Major trading partners:** Thailand, India, U.S., China, Japan, Singapore, South Korea, Malaysia (2003).

Geography Slightly smaller than Texas, Myanmar occupies the Thailand/Cambodia portion of the Indochinese peninsula. India lies to the northwest and China to the northeast. Bangladesh, Laos, and Thailand are also neighbors. The Bay of Bengal touches the southwest coast. The fertile delta of the Irrawaddy River in the south contains a network of intercommunicating canals and nine principal river mouths.

Government Military regime.

History The ethnic origins of modern Myanmar (known historically as Burma) are a mixture of Indo-Aryans, who began pushing into the area around 700 B.C., and the Mongolian invaders under Kublai Khan who penetrated the region in the 13th century. Anawrahta (1044–1077) was the first great unifier of Myanmar.

In 1612, the British East India Company sent agents to Burma, but the Burmese doggedly resisted efforts of British, Dutch, and Portuguese traders to establish posts along the Bay of Bengal. Through the Anglo-Burmese War in 1824–1826 and two subsequent wars, the British East India Company expanded to the whole of Burma. By 1886, Myanmar was annexed to India, then became a separate colony in 1937.

During World War II, Burma was a key battleground; the 800-mile Burma Road was the Allies' vital supply line to China. The Japanese invaded the country in Dec. 1941, and by May 1942 had occupied most of it, cutting off the Burma Road. After one of the most difficult campaigns of the war, Allied forces liberated most of Burma prior to the Japanese surrender in Aug. 1945.

Burma became independent on Jan. 4, 1948. In 1962, left-wing general Ne Win staged a coup, banned political opposition, suspended the constitution, and introduced the "Burmese way of socialism." After 25 years of economic hardship and repression, the Burmese people held massive demonstrations in 1987 and 1988. These were brutally quashed by the State Law and Order Council (SLORC). In 1989, the military government officially changed the name of the country to Myanmar. (The U.S. State Department does not recognize the name Myanmar or the military regime that represents it.)

In May 1990 elections, the opposition National League for Democracy (NLD) won in a landslide. But the military, or SLORC, refused to recognize the election results. The leader of the opposition, Aung San Suu Kyi, was awarded the Nobel Peace Prize in 1991, which focused world attention on SLORC's repressive policies. Daughter of the assassinated general Aung San, who was revered as the father of Burmese independence, Suu Kyi remained under house arrest from 1989 until 1995. A new constitution was drafted in 1994 that called for an elected executive branch but appeared designed specifically to forbid Suu Kyi from becoming president. Suu Kyi continued to protest against the government, but almost every move she made was answered with a counterblow from SLORC.

Although the ruling junta has maintained a tight grip on Myanmar since 1988, it has not been able to subdue an insurgency in the country's south that has gone on for decades. The ethnic Karen movement has sought an independent homeland along Myanmar's southern border with Thailand. In Jan. 2004, the military government and the insurgents from the Karen National Union agreed to end the fighting, but they stopped short of signing a cease-fire.

From 2000 to 2002, Suu Kyi was again placed under house arrest. In spring 2003, the government cracked down once again on the democracy movement, detaining Suu Kyi and shuttering NLD headquarters. The regime opened a constitutional convention in May 2004, but many observers doubted its legitimacy.

In October 2004, the government arrested Prime Minister Gen. Khin Nyunt and charged him with corruption. He had angered the leadership of the junta with his recent experiments with reform, first by freeing Suu Kyi from house arrest and later for proposing a seven-step "road map to democracy."

A series of coordinated bomb attacks in May 2005 killed about a dozen people and wounded more than 100 in Rangoon. The military junta blamed the Karen National Union and the Shan State Army. The ethnic rebel groups, however, denied any involvement.

Namibia

REPUBLIC OF NAMIBIA

President: Hifikepunye Pohamba (2005)
Prime Minister: Nahas Angula (2005)
Area: 318,694 sq mi (825,418 sq km)
Population (2005 est.): 2,030,692 (growth rate: 0.7%); birth rate: 25.2/1000; infant mortality rate: 49.0/1000; life expectancy: 43.9; density per sq mi: 6
Capital and largest city (2003 est.): Windhoek, 221,000. **Summer capital:** Swakopmund, 26,200.
Monetary unit: Namibian dollar. **Languages:** English 7% (official), Afrikaans common language of most of the population and about 60% of the white population, German 32%, indigenous languages: Oshivambo, Herero, Nama. **Ethnicity/race:** black 87.5%, white 6%, mixed 6.5%. Note: about 50% of the population belong to the Ovambo tribe and 9% to the Kavangos tribe; other ethnic groups are: Herero 7%, Damara 7%, Nama 5%, Caprivian 4%, Bushmen 3%, Baster 2%, Tswana 0.5%. **Religions:** Christian 80%–90% (Lutheran at least 50%), indigenous beliefs 10%–20%. **Literacy rate:** 84% (2003 est.)
Economic summary: GDP/PPP (2004 est.): $14.76 billion; per capita $7,300. **Real growth rate:** 4.8%. **Inflation:** 4.2%. **Unemployment:** 35% (1998). **Arable land:** 1%. **Agriculture:** millet, sorghum, peanuts; livestock; fish. **Labor force:** 840,000; agriculture 47%, industry 25%, services, 28% (1999 est.). **Industries:** meatpacking, fish processing, dairy products; mining (diamond, lead, zinc, tin, silver, tungsten, uranium, copper). **Natural resources:** diamonds, copper, uranium, gold, lead, tin, lithium, cadmium, zinc, salt, vanadium, natural gas, hydropower, fish; note: suspected deposits of oil, coal, and iron ore. **Exports:** $1.356 billion (f.o.b., 2004 est.): diamonds, copper, gold, zinc, lead, uranium; cattle, processed fish, karakul skins. **Imports:** $1.473 billion (f.o.b., 2004 est.): foodstuffs; petroleum products and fuel, machinery and equipment, chemicals. **Major trading partners:** EU, U.S. (2001).

Geography Namibia is bounded on the north by Angola and Zambia, on the east by Botswana, and on the east and south by South Africa. It is for the most part a portion of the high plateau of southern Africa, with a general elevation of from 3,000 to 4,000 ft.

Government Republic.

History The San peoples may have inhabited what is now Namibia more than 2,000 years ago. The Bantu-speaking Herero migrated there in the 1600s. The Ovambo, the largest ethnic group today, migrated in the 1800s.

In the late 15th century, the Portuguese explorer Bartolomeu Dias became the first European to visit Namibia. Formerly called South-West Africa, the territory became a German colony in 1884. Between 1904 and 1908, German troops massacred tens of thousands of Herero, who had revolted against colonial domination. In 1915, during World War I, Namibian territory was taken over by South African forces. In 1921, it became a mandated territory of the League of Nations, under the administration of South Africa.

Upon the dissolution of the League of Nations in 1946, South Africa refused to accept United Nations authority and replace its mandate with a UN trusteeship. A black Marxist separatist group, the South West African People's Organization (SWAPO), formed in 1960 and began small-scale guerrilla attacks aimed at achieving independence. In 1966, the UN called for South Africa's withdrawal from the territory, and officially renamed it Namibia in 1968. South Africa refused to obey. Under a 1974 Security Council resolution, South Africa was required to begin the transfer of power or face UN action. Prime Minister Balthazar J. Vorster rejected UN supervision, claiming that his government was prepared to negotiate Namibian independence, but not with SWAPO, which the UN had recognized as the "sole legitimate representative" of the Namibian people.

South Africa handed over limited powers to a new, multiracial administration in 1985 (the previous government had enforced South Africa's apartheid laws).

Installation of the new government ended South Africa's direct rule, but South Africa retained an effective veto over the new government's decisions. Finally, in 1988 South Africa agreed to a plan for independence. SWAPO leader Sam Nujoma was elected president, and on March 21, 1990, Namibia achieved independence.

Nujoma was reelected in 1994 and again in 1999, after the constitution was amended to allow him to seek a third term. Nujoma announced in Nov. 2001 that he would not seek reelection when his term expired in 2004. In Nov. 2004, Hifikepunye Pohamba of SWAPO was elected president with 76% of the vote. He took office on March 21, 2005.

In 2004, Germany issued a formal apology for the massacre of Herero by German colonial troops between 1904 and 1908.

Nauru

REPUBLIC OF NAURU

President: Ludwig Scotty (2004)
Area: 8.11 sq mi (21 sq km)
Population (2005 est.): 13,048 (growth rate: 1.8%); birth rate: 25.1/1000; infant mortality rate: 9.9/1000; life expectancy: 62.7; density per sq mi: 1,609
Capital and largest city (2003 est.): Yaren, 4,900.
Monetary unit: Australian dollar. **Languages:** Nauruan (official), English. **Ethnicity/race:** Nauruan 58%, other Pacific Islander 26%, Chinese 8%, European 8%. **Religions:** Christian (two-thirds Protestant, one-third Roman Catholic). **Literacy rate:** n.a
Economic summary: GDP/PPP (2001 est.): $60 million; per capita $5,000. **Real growth rate:** n.a. **Inflation:** −3.6% (1993). **Unemployment:** 90%. **Arable land:** 0%. **Agriculture:** coconuts. **Labor force:** employed in mining phosphates, public administration, education, and transportation. **Industries:** phosphate mining, offshore banking, coconut products. **Natural resources:** phosphates, fish. **Exports:** $640,000 (f.o.b., 2004): phosphates. **Imports:** $19.8 million (c.i.f., 2004 est.): food, fuel, manufactures, building materials, machinery. **Major trading partners:** Japan, India, South Korea, Australia, Indonesia, U.S. (2003). **Special relationship within the Commonwealth of Nations**

Geography Nauru (pronounced NAH-oo-roo) is an island in the Pacific just south of the equator, about 2,500 mi (4,023 km) southwest of Honolulu. Phosphate mining has virtually destroyed the tiny nation's ecology, turning its tropical vegetation into a barren, rocky wasteland.

Government Republic.

History In 1798, a British navigator became the first European to visit the island. Germany annexed it in 1888, and by the turn of the century, phosphate, a lucrative fertilizer, began to be mined. The island was placed under joint Australian, New Zealand, and British mandate after World War I. The Japanese occupied the island during World War II and forced 1,200 Nauruans—roughly two-thirds of the population—to relocate. In 1947, it became a UN trusteeship administered by Australia. By 1967, the phosphate mining industry finally was under the control of the islanders, and on Jan. 31, 1968, Nauru became one of the world's smallest independent republics. For a period of time, Nauru's phosphate made the tiny country's per capita income the highest in the world, after Saudi Arabia.

As its phosphate stores began to run out (by 2006, its reserves will be exhausted), the island was reduced to an environmental wasteland. Nauru appealed to the International Court of Justice to compensate for the damage from almost a century of phosphate strip-mining by foreign companies. In 1993, Australia offered Nauru an out-of-court settlement of $2.5 million Australian dollars annually for 20 years. New Zealand and the UK additionally agreed to pay a one-time settlement of $12 million each. Declining phosphate prices, the high cost of maintaining an international airline, and the government's financial mismanagement combined to make the economy collapse in the late 1990s. By the millennium Nauru was virtually bankrupt.

In 2000, the G7 nations put pressure on the country to review its banking system, which is used by Russian criminals for money laundering.

Since Sept. 2001, Nauru has accepted three boatloads of Asian refugees destined for Australia. Australia compensated the island with $20 million and other financial incentives for taking this refugee problem off its hands. The detention camps, which held more than 400 asylum seekers in 2003, are said to be extremely bleak and lack medical care.

Bernard Dowiyogo, elected in 2003 as president for the seventh time (nonsequentially), died in March 2003 following emergency heart surgery. Ludwig Scotty, a senior cabinet minister, was elected in May 2003 elections. In August of that year, Scotty was sacked in a no-confidence vote, and René Harris, who has twice served as president, was elected to the post. But, given Nauru's tumultuous politics, by June 2004 Scotty had again regained the presidency.

Nepal

KINGDOM OF NEPAL

Ruler: King Gyanendra Bir Bikram Shah Deva (2001)
Prime Minister: vacant
Area: 54,363 sq mi (140,800 sq km)
Population (2005 est.): 27,676,547 (growth rate: 2.2%); birth rate: 31.4/1000; infant mortality rate: 67.0/1000; life expectancy: 59.8; density per sq mi: 509
Capital and largest city (2003 est.): Kathmandu, 1,203,100 (metro. area), 729,000 (city proper). **Other large cities:** Biratnagar, 174,600; Lalitpur, 169,100.
Monetary unit: Nepalese rupee. **Languages:** Nepali 90% (official), over 40 other languages and major dialects, English (1995). **Ethnicity/race:** Brahmin, Chetri, Newar, Gurung, Magar, Tamang, Rai, Limbu, Sherpa, Tharu, and others (1995). **Religions:** Hindu 86.2%, Buddhist 7.8%, Islam 3.8%, other 2.2% (1995). **Literacy rate:** 45% (2003 est.)
Economic summary: GDP/PPP (2004 est.): $39.53 billion; per capita $1,500. **Real growth rate:** 3%. **Inflation:** 2.9% (2002 est.). **Unemployment:** 47% (2001 est.). **Arable land:** 22%. **Agriculture:** rice, corn, wheat, sugarcane, root crops; milk, water buffalo meat. **Labor force:** 10 million (1996 est.); note: severe lack of skilled labor; agriculture 81%, services 16%, industry 3%. **Industries:** tourism, carpet, textile; small rice, jute, sugar, and oilseed mills; cigarette; cement and brick production. **Natural resources:** quartz, water, timber, hydropower, scenic beauty, small deposits of lignite, copper, cobalt, iron ore. **Exports:** $568 million (f.o.b., 2002 est.), but does not include unrecorded border trade with India: carpets, clothing, leather goods, jute goods, grain. **Imports:** $1.419 billion (f.o.b., 2002 est.): gold, machinery and equipment, petroleum products, fertilizer. **Major trading partners:** India, U.S., Germany, China, UAE, Singapore (2003).

Geography A landlocked country the size of Arkansas, lying between India and the Tibetan Autonomous Region of China, Nepal contains Mount Everest (29,035 ft; 8,850 m), the tallest mountain in the world. Along its southern border, Nepal has a strip of level land that is partly forested, partly cultivated. North of that is the slope of the main section of the Himalayan range, including Everest and many other peaks higher than 8,000 m.

Government In Nov. 1990, King Birendra promulgated a new constitution and introduced a multiparty parliamentary democracy in Nepal. King Gyanendra dissolved the government in 2002 and has since ruled as an absolute monarch.

History The first civilizations in Nepal, which flourished around the 6th century B.C., were confined to the fertile Kathmandu Valley where the present-day capital of the same name is located. It was in this region that Prince Siddhartha Gautama was born c. 563 B.C. Gautama achieved enlightenment as Buddha and spawned Buddhist belief.

Nepali rulers' early patronage of Buddhism largely gave way to Hinduism, reflecting the increased influence of India, around the 12th century. Though the successive dynasties of the Gopalas, the Kiratis, and the Licchavis expanded their rule, it was not until the reign of the Malla kings from 1200–1769 that Nepal assumed the approximate dimensions of the modern state.

The kingdom of Nepal was unified in 1768 by King Prithvi Narayan Shah, who had fled India following the Moghul conquests of the subcontinent. Under Shah and his successors Nepal's borders expanded as far west as Kashmir and as far east as Sikkim (now part of India). A commercial treaty was signed with Britain in 1792 and again in 1816 after more than a year of hostilities with the British East India Company.

In 1923, Britain recognized the absolute independence of Nepal. Between 1846 and 1951, the country was ruled by the Rana family, which always held the office of prime minister. In 1951, however, the king took over all power and proclaimed a constitutional monarchy. Mahendra Bir Bikram Shah became king in 1955. After Mahendra died of a heart attack in 1972, Prince Birendra, at 26, succeeded to the throne.

In 1990, a prodemocracy movement forced King Birendra to lift the ban on political parties. The first free election in three decades provided a victory for the liberal Nepali Congress Party in 1991, although the Communists made a strong showing. A small but growing Maoist guerrilla movement, seeking to overthrow the constitutional monarchy and install a Communist government, began operating in the countryside in 1996.

On June 1, 2001, King Birendra was shot and killed by his son, Crown Prince Dipendra. Angered by his family's disapproval of his choice of a bride, he also killed his mother and several other members of the royal family before shooting himself. Prince Gyanendra, the younger brother of King Birendra, was then crowned king.

King Gyanendra dismissed the government in October 2002, calling it corrupt and ineffective. He declared a state of emergency in November and ordered the army to crack down on the Maoist guerrillas. The rebels intensified their campaign, and the government responded with equal intensity, killing hundreds of Maoists, the largest toll since the insurgency began in 1996. In Aug. 2003, the Maoist rebels withdrew from peace talks with the government and ended a cease-fire that had been signed in Jan. 2003. The following August, the rebels blockaded Kathmandu for a week, cutting off shipments of food and fuel to the capital.

King Gyanendra fired the entire government in Feb. 2005 and declared a state of emergency. Many of the country's politicians were placed under house arrest, phone and Internet lines were cut, and the airports were closed. International organizations condemned the act and called for democracy to be reestablished. King Gyanendra said the government was making no progress toward elections and had not pursued a peace process with Maoist rebels. The day after the shake-up, he appointed a new 10-member cabinet. King Gyanendra lifted the state of emergency in late April, but many of the restrictions on civil liberties have continued.

The Netherlands

KINGDOM OF THE NETHERLANDS

National name: Koninkrijk der Nederlanden
Sovereign: Queen Beatrix (1980)
Prime Minister: Jan Peter Balkenende (2002)
Area: 16,033 sq mi (41,526 sq km)
Population (2005 est.): 16,407,491 (growth rate: 0.5%); birth rate: 11.1/1000; infant mortality rate: 5.0/1000; life expectancy: 78.8; density per sq mi: 1,023
Capital and largest city (2003 est.): Amsterdam (official), 737,900; The Hague (administrative capital), 465,900. **Other large cities:** Rotterdam, 600,700; Utrecht, 263,900; Eindhoven, 206,900. **Monetary units:** Euro (formerly guilder). **Languages:** Dutch, Frisian (both official). **Ethnicity/race:** Dutch 83%, other 17% (9% of non-Western origin, mainly Turks, Moroccans, Antilleans, Surinamese, and Indonesians) (1999 est.). **Religions:** Roman Catholic 31%, Protestant 21%, Islam 4.4%, other 3.6%, unaffiliated 40% (1998). **Literacy rate:** 99% (2000 est.)
Economic summary: GDP/PPP (2004 est.): $481.1 billion; per capita $29,500. **Real growth rate:** 1.2%. **Inflation:** 1.4%. **Unemployment:** 6%. **Arable land:** 27%. **Agriculture:** grains, potatoes, sugar beets, fruits, vegetables; livestock. **Labor force:** 7.53 million; services 73%, industry 23%, agriculture 4% (1998 est.). **Industries:** agroindustries, metal and engineering products, electrical machinery and equipment, chemicals, petroleum, construction, microelectronics, fishing. **Natural resources:** natural gas, petroleum, arable land. **Exports:** $293.1 billion (f.o.b, 2004 est.): machinery and equipment, chemicals, fuels; foodstuffs. **Imports:** $252.7 billion (f.o.b, 2004 est.): machinery and transport equipment, chemicals, fuels; foodstuffs, clothing. **Major trading partners:** Germany, Belgium, France, UK, Italy, U.S., UK, China (2003).

Geography The Netherlands, on the coast of the North Sea, is twice the size of New Jersey. Part of the great plain of north and west Europe, the Netherlands has maximum dimensions of 190 by 160 mi (360 by 257 km) and is low and flat except in Limburg in the southeast, where some hills rise up to 322 m (1056 ft). About half the country's area is below sea level, making the famous Dutch dikes a requisite for the use of much of the land. Reclamation of land from the sea through dikes has continued through recent times. All drainage reaches the North Sea, and the principal rivers—Rhine, Maas (Meuse), and Schelde—have their sources outside the country.

Government Constitutional monarchy.

History Julius Caesar found the low-lying Netherlands inhabited by Germanic tribes—the Nervii, Frisii, and Batavi. The Batavi on the Roman frontier did not submit to Rome's rule until 13 B.C., and then only as allies.

The Franks controlled the region from the 4th to the 8th century, and it became part of Charlemagne's empire in the 8th and 9th centuries. The area later passed into the hands of Burgundy and the Austrian Hapsburgs and finally in the 16th century came under Spanish rule.

When Philip II of Spain suppressed political liberties and the growing Protestant movement in the Netherlands, a revolt led by William of Orange broke out in 1568. Under the Union of Utrecht (1579), the seven northern provinces became the United Provinces of the Netherlands. War between the United Provinces and Spain continued into the 17th century, but in 1648 Spain finally recognized Dutch independence.

The Dutch East India Company was established in 1602, and by the end of the 17th century Holland was one of the great sea and colonial powers of Europe.

The nation's independence was not completely established until after the Thirty Years' War (1618–1648), when the country's rise as a commercial and maritime power began. In 1688, the English Parliament invited William of Orange, stadtholder, and his wife, Mary Stuart, to rule England as William III and Mary II. William then used the combined resources of England and the Netherlands to wage war on Louis XIV's France. In 1814, all the provinces of Holland and Belgium were merged into one kingdom, but in 1830 the southern provinces broke away to form the kingdom of Belgium. A liberal constitution was adopted by the Netherlands in 1848. The country remained neutral during World War I.

In spite of its neutrality in World War II, the Netherlands was invaded by the Nazis in May 1940, and the Dutch East Indies were later taken by the Japanese. The nation was liberated in May 1945. In 1948, after a reign of 50 years, Queen Wilhelmina abdicated and was succeeded by her daughter Juliana.

In 1949, after a four-year war, the Netherlands granted independence to the Dutch East Indies, which became the Republic of Indonesia. The Netherlands also joined NATO that year. The Netherlands joined the European Economic Community (later, the EU) in 1958. In 1999, it adopted the single European currency, the euro.

In 1963, it turned over the western half of New Guinea to Indonesia, ending 300 years of Dutch presence in Asia. Attainment of independence by Suriname on Nov. 25, 1975, left the Netherlands Antilles and Aruba as the country's only overseas territories.

The Netherlands has extremely liberal social policies: prostitution is legal, and it became the first nation in the world to legalize same-sex marriage (2000) and euthanasia (2002).

Wim Kok's government resigned in April 2002 after a report concluded that Dutch UN troops failed to prevent a massacre of Bosnian Muslims by Bosnian Serbs in a UN safe haven near Srebrenica in 1995. Explaining his action, the popular prime minister said, "The international community is big and anonymous. We are taking the consequences of the international community's failure in Srebrenica."

The country's normally bland political scene was further rocked with the May 2002 assassination of Pim Fortuyn, a right-wing anti-immigrant politician. Days later, his party, Lijst Pim Fortuyn, placed second in national elections, behind Jan Peter Balkenende's Christian Democrats. Leading the country into a marked shift to the right, Balkenende formed a three-way center-right coalition government with his Christian Democrats, Lijst Pim Fortuyn, and the People's Party for Freedom and Democracy. Balkenende became prime minister in July 2002.

In 2005, just days after French voters rejected the EU constitution in a referendum, the Netherlands followed suit.

Netherlands Autonomous Countries

Netherlands Antilles

Status: Part of the Kingdom of the Netherlands
Governor: Frits Goedgedrag (2002)
Prime Minister: Etienne Ys (2004)
Area: 371 sq mi (960 sq km)
Population (2005 est.): 219,958 (growth rate: 0.8%); birth rate: 15.0/1000; infant mortality rate: 10.0/1000; life expectancy: 75.8; density per sq mi: 593
Capital and largest city (2003 est.): Willemstad, 60,100. **Monetary unit:** Netherlands Antillean guilder. **Languages:** Dutch (official), Papiamento predominates, English widely spoken, Spanish. **Ethnicity/race:** mixed black 85%, Carib Amerindian, white, East Asian. **Religions:** Roman Catholic, Protestant, Jewish, Seventh-Day Adventist. **Literacy rate:** 97% (2003 est.)
Economic summary: GDP/PPP (2003 est.): $2.45 billion; per capita $11,400. **Real growth rate:** 0.5%. **Inflation:** 2.1%. **Unemployment:** 15.6% (2002 est.). **Arable land:** 10%. **Agriculture:** aloes, sorghum, peanuts, vegetables, tropical fruit. **Labor force:** 89,000 (2000); agriculture 1%, industry 13%, services 86% (2000 est.). **Industries:** tourism (Curaçao, Sint Maarten, and Bonaire), petroleum refining (Curaçao), petroleum transshipment facilities (Curaçao and Bonaire), light manufacturing (Curaçao). **Natural resources:** phosphates (Curaçao only), salt (Bonaire only). **Exports:** $1.579 billion (f.o.b., 2002): petroleum products. **Imports:** $2.233 billion (f.o.b., 2002): crude petroleum, food, manufactures. **Major trading partners:** U.S., Venezuela, The Bahamas, Singapore, Honduras, Guatemala, Netherlands (2003).

The Netherlands Antilles are composed of two groups of Caribbean islands 500 mi (805 km) apart: the first group, composed of Curaçao (173 sq mi; 448 sq km) and Bonaire (95 sq mi; 246 sq km), is located about 40 mi (64 km) off the Venezuelan coast. Originally inhabited by Arawak Indians, these two islands as well as Aruba were claimed by Spain in 1527 and then by the Dutch in 1643. The Dutch Lesser Antilles to the north—Saint Eustatius, the southern part of St. Martin (Dutch: Sint Maarten), and Saba—make up the remainder of the island federation. First inhabited by the Carib Indians, St. Martin was explored by Columbus in 1493. In 1845, the six islands (then including Aruba) officially formed the Netherlands Antilles. In 1994, the islands voted to preserve their federation with the Netherlands.

Aruba

Status: Part of the Kingdom of the Netherlands
Governor: Fredis Refunjol (2004)
Prime Minister: Nelson O. Oduber (2001)
Area: 75 sq mi (193 sq km)
Population (2005 est.): 71,566 (growth rate: 0.5%); birth rate: 11.3/1000; infant mortality rate: 5.9/1000; life expectancy: 79.1; density per sq mi: 960
Capital and largest city (2003 est.): Oranjestad, 20,700. **Monetary unit:** Aruban guilder/florin. **Languages:** Dutch (official), Papiamento, English, Spanish. **Ethnicity/race:** mixed European/Caribbean Indian 80%. **Religions:** Roman Catholic 82%, Protestant 8%, Hindu, Muslim, Confucian, Jewish. **Literacy rate:** 97% (2003 est.)
Economic summary: GDP/PPP (2002 est.): $1.94 billion; per capita $28,000. **Real growth rate:** –1.5%. **Inflation:** 3.2%. **Unemployment:** 0.6% (2003 est.). **Arable land:** 11% aloe plantations included (0.01%). **Agriculture:** aloes; livestock; fish. **Labor force:** 41,500 (1997 est.); most employment is in wholesale and retail trade and repair, followed by hotels and

restaurants; oil refining. **Industries:** tourism, transshipment facilities, oil refining. **Natural resources:** negl.; white sandy beaches. **Exports:** $128 million (including oil reexports) (f.o.b., 2002): live animals and animal products, art and collectibles, machinery and electrical equipment, transport equipment. **Imports:** $841 million (f.o.b., 2002 est.): machinery and electrical equipment, crude oil for refining and reexport, chemicals; foodstuffs. **Major trading partners:** Netherlands, Panama, Colombia, Netherlands Antilles, Venezuela, U.S. (2003).

Aruba, an island slightly larger than Washington, DC, lies 18 mi (28.9 km) off the coast of Venezuela in the southern Caribbean.

The Arawak Indians were the first inhabitants of Aruba. Spain explored the island in 1499, and more than a century later the Netherlands (1636) claimed the island. After a brief rule by the British, the Dutch again took control of the island in 1816, and it officially became part of the Netherlands Antilles in 1845.

On Jan. 1, 1986, Aruba seceded from the federation, but it decided in 1994 to indefinitely postpone the transition to full independence. The Netherlands controls Aruba's defense and foreign affairs, but all internal affairs are handled by an island government directing its own civil service, judiciary, revenue, and currency.

New Zealand

Sovereign: Queen Elizabeth II (1952)
Governor-General: Dame Silvia Cartwright (2001)
Prime Minister: Helen Clark (1999)
Area: 103,737 sq mi (268,680 sq km) (excluding dependencies)
Population (2005 est.): 4,035,461 (growth rate: 1.0%); birth rate: 13.9/1000; infant mortality rate: 5.8/1000; life expectancy: 78.7; density per sq mi: 39
Capital (2003 est.): Wellington, 342,500 (metro. area), 165,100 (city proper). **Largest cities:** Auckland, 369,300 (metro. area), 359,500 (city proper); Christchurch, 334,100. **Monetary unit:** New Zealand dollar. **Languages:** English, Maori (both official) . **Ethnicity/race:** New Zealand European 74.5%, Maori 9.7%, other European 4.6%, Pacific Islander 3.8%, Asian and others 7.4%. **Religions:** Anglican 24%, Presbyterian 18%, Roman Catholic 15%, Methodist 5%, Baptist 2%, other Protestant 3%, unspecified or none 33% (1986). **Literacy rate:** 99% (1980 est.)
Economic summary: GDP/PPP (2004 est.): $92.51 billion; per capita $23,200. **Real growth rate:** 4.8%. **Inflation:** 2.4%. **Unemployment:** 4.2%. **Arable land:** 6%. **Agriculture:** wheat, barley, potatoes, pulses, fruits, vegetables; wool, beef, lamb and mutton, dairy products; fish. **Labor force:** 2.05 million: services 65%, industry 25%, agriculture 10% (1995). **Industries:** food processing, wood and paper products, textiles, machinery, transportation equipment, banking and insurance, tourism, mining. **Natural resources:** natural gas, iron ore, sand, coal, timber, hydropower, gold, limestone. **Exports:** $19.85 billion (2004 est.): dairy products, meat, wood and wood products, fish, machinery. **Imports:** $19.77 billion (2004 est.): machinery and equipment, vehicles and aircraft, petroleum, electronics, textiles, plastics. **Major trading partners:** Australia, U.S., Japan, China, UK, Germany (2003). **Member of Commonwealth of Nations**

Geography New Zealand, about 1,250 mi (2,012 km) southeast of Australia, consists of two main islands and a number of smaller outlying islands so scattered that they range from the tropical to the antarctic. The country is the size of Colorado. New Zealand's two main components are the North Island and the South Island, separated by Cook Strait. The North Island (44,281 sq mi; 115,777 sq km) is 515 mi (829 km) long and volcanic in its south-central part. This area contains many hot springs and beautiful geysers. South Island (58,093 sq mi; 151,215 sq km) has the Southern Alps along its west coast, with Mount Cook (12,316 ft; 3754 m) the highest point. Other inhabited islands include Stewart Island, the Chatham Islands, and Great Barrier Island.

Government Parliamentary democracy.

History Maoris were the first inhabitants of New Zealand, arriving on the islands in about 1000. Maori oral history maintains that the Maoris came to the island in seven canoes from other parts of Polynesia. In 1642, New Zealand was explored by Abel Tasman, a Dutch navigator. British captain James Cook made three voyages to the islands, beginning in 1769. Britain formally annexed the islands in 1840.

The Treaty of Waitangi (Feb. 6, 1840) between the British and several Maori tribes promised to protect Maori land if the Maoris recognized British rule. Encroachment on the land by British settlers was relentless, however, and skirmishes between the two groups intensified.

From the outset, the country has been in the forefront in instituting social welfare legislation. New Zealand was the world's first country to give women the right to vote (1893). It adopted old-age pensions (1898); a national child welfare program (1907); social security for the elderly, widows, and orphans, along with family benefit payments; minimum wages; a 40-hour workweek and unemployment and health insurance (1938); and socialized medicine (1941).

New Zealand fought with the Allies in both world wars as well as in Korea. In 1999, it became part of the UN peacekeeping force sent to East Timor.

In recent years, New Zealand has introduced extremely liberal social policies. In June 2003, Parliament legalized prostitution 60–59, and in Dec. 2004, same-sex unions were recognized and given the same rights as married couples.

Cook Islands and Overseas Territories

The Cook Islands (93 sq mi; 241 sq km) were placed under New Zealand administration in 1901. They achieved self-governing status in association with New Zealand in 1965. **Population (July 2005 est.):** 21,388.

Niue (100 sq mi; 259 sq km) was formerly administered as part of the Cook Islands. It was placed under separate New Zealand administration in 1901 and achieved self-governing status in association with New Zealand in 1974. The capital is Alofi. **Population (2005 est.):** 2,166.

Tokelau (3.86 sq mi; 10 sq km) was formerly administered as part of the Gilbert and Ellice Islands colony. It was placed under New Zealand administration in 1925. **Population (2005 est.):** 1,405.

Nicaragua

REPUBLIC OF NICARAGUA

National name: República de Nicaragua
President: Enrique Bolaños (2002)
Area: 49,998 sq mi (129,494 sq km)
Population (2005 est.): 5,465,100 (growth rate: 1.9%); birth rate: 24.9/1000; infant mortality rate: 29.1/1000; life expectancy: 70.3; density per sq mi: 109
Capital and largest city (2003 est.): Managua, 1,390,500 (metro. area), 1,146,000 (city proper). **Monetary unit:** Gold cordoba. **Languages:** Spanish (official); English and indigenous languages on Atlantic

coast. **Ethnicity/race:** mestizo 69%, white 17%, black 9%, Amerindian 5%. **Religions:** Roman Catholic 85%, Protestant. **Literacy rate:** 68% (2003 est.).
Economic summary: GDP/PPP (2004 est.): $12.34 billion; per capita $2,300. **Real growth rate:** 4%. **Inflation:** 9.3%. **Unemployment:** 7.8% plus considerable underemployment of 46.5% (2003 est.). **Arable land:** 16%. **Agriculture:** coffee, bananas, sugarcane, cotton, rice, corn, tobacco, sesame, soya, beans; beef, veal, pork, poultry, dairy products. **Labor force:** 1.93 million; agriculture 30.5%, industry 17.3%, services 52.2% (2003 est.). **Industries:** food processing, chemicals, machinery and metal products, textiles, clothing, petroleum refining and distribution, beverages, footwear, wood. **Natural resources:** gold, silver, copper, tungsten, lead, zinc, timber, fish. **Exports:** $750 million (f.o.b., 2004 est.): coffee, beef, shrimp and lobster, tobacco, sugar, gold, peanuts. **Imports:** $2.02 billion (f.o.b., 2004 est.): consumer goods, machinery and equipment, raw materials, petroleum products. **Major trading partners:** U.S., El Salvador, Costa Rica, Honduras, Mexico, Guatemala, Venezuela, Japan (2003).

Geography Largest but most sparsely populated of the Central American nations, Nicaragua borders on Honduras to the north and Costa Rica to the south. It is slightly larger than New York State. Nicaragua is mountainous in the west, with fertile valleys. Two big lakes, Nicaragua and Managua, are connected by the Tipitapa River. The Pacific coast is volcanic and very fertile. The swampy Caribbean coast is aptly called the "Mosquito Coast."

Government Republic.

History Nicaragua, which derives its name from the chief of the area's leading Indian tribe at the time of the Spanish Conquest, was first settled by the Spanish in 1522. The country won independence in 1838. For the next century, Nicaragua's politics were dominated by the competition for power between the Liberals, who were centered in the city of León, and the Conservatives, centered in Granada.

To back up its support of the new Conservative government in 1909, the U.S. sent a small detachment of Marines to Nicaragua from 1912 to 1925. The Bryan-Chamorro Treaty of 1916 (terminated in 1970) gave the U.S. an option on a canal route through Nicaragua and naval bases. U.S. Marines were sent again to quell disorder after the 1924 elections. A guerrilla leader, Gen. César Augusto Sandino, fought the U.S. troops from 1927 until their withdrawal in 1933.

After ordering Sandino's assassination, Gen. Anastasio Somoza García was dictator from 1936 until his own assassination in 1956. He was succeeded by his son Luis, who alternated with trusted family friends in the presidency until his death in 1967. He was succeeded by his brother, Maj. Gen. Anastasio Somoza Debayle. The Somozas ruled Nicaragua with an iron fist, reducing its dependence on banana exports, exiling political foes, and amassing a family fortune.

Sandinista guerrillas, leftists who took their name from Sandino, launched an offensive in 1979. After seven weeks of fighting, Somoza fled the country on July 17, 1979. The Sandinistas assumed power two days later. On Jan. 23, 1981, the Reagan administration suspended U.S. aid, charging that Nicaragua, with the aid of Cuba and the Soviet Union, was supplying arms to rebels in El Salvador. The Sandinistas denied the charges. Later that year, Nicaraguan guerrillas known as "Contras" began a war to overthrow the Sandinistas. Elections were finally held on Nov. 4, 1984, with Daniel Ortega, the Sandinista junta coordinator, winning the presidency. The war intensified in 1986–1987.

Negotiations sponsored by the Contadora (neutral Latin American) nations foundered, but Costa Rican president Oscar Arias promoted a treaty signed by Central American leaders in Aug. 1987.

Violetta Barrios de Chamorro, owner of the opposition paper *La Prensa*, led a broad anti-Sandinista coalition to victory in the 1990 elections, ending 11 years of Sandinista rule. Enthusiasm for Chamorro gradually faded. Business groups were dissatisfied with the pace of reforms; Sandinistas, upset with what they regarded as the dismantling of their earlier achievements, threatened to take up arms again; and many people were disillusioned over governmental corruption.

Former Managua mayor and Conservative candidate Arnoldo Alemán won the 1996 election. Former Sandinista leader Daniel Ortega was his closest rival.

In 1998, Hurricane Mitch killed more than 9,000 people, left 2 million people homeless, and caused $10 billion in damages. Many people fled to the U.S., which offered Nicaraguans an immigration amnesty program until July 1999. Nicaragua remains one of the poorest countries in the Western Hemisphere.

In the Nov. 2001 presidential elections, Enrique Bolaños, the ruling Liberal Party leader, defeated Ortega, who was attempting a comeback.

In Aug. 2002, former president Arnoldo Alemán was charged with fraud and embezzlement, and in 2003 he was sent to prison for 20 years. Current president Bolaños triumphantly called it the "frying of the Big Fish." The anticorruption watchdog, Transparency International, ranks Alemán among the most corrupt leaders of the past two decades.

The country received an enormous show of support from the international community in 2004 when the IMF and World Bank forgave $4.5 billion of Nicaragua's debt.

Niger

REPUBLIC OF NIGER

National name: République du Niger
President: Tandja Mamadou (1999)
Prime Minister: Hama Amadou (1999)
Area: 489,189 sq mi (1,267,000 sq km)
Population (2005 est.): 11,665,937 (growth rate: 2.6%); birth rate: 48.3/1000; infant mortality rate: 121.7/1000; life expectancy: 42.1; density per sq mi: 24
Capital and largest city (2003 est.): Niamey, 748,600.
Other large cities: Zinder, 202,300; Maradi, 189,000.
Monetary unit: CFA Franc. **Languages:** French (official), Hausa, Djerma. **Ethnicity/race:** Hausa 56%, Djerma 22%, Fula 8.5%, Tuareg 8%, Beri Beri (Kanouri) 4.3%, Arab, Toubou, and Gourmantche 1.2%, about 1,200 French expatriates. **Religions:** Islam 80%, indigenous beliefs and Christian 20%.
Literacy rate: 18% (2003 est.)
Economic summary: GDP/PPP (2004 est.): $9.716 billion; per capita $900. **Real growth rate:** 3.5%. **Inflation:** 3% (2002 est.). **Unemployment:** n.a. (2002 est.). **Arable land:** 4%. **Agriculture:** cowpeas, cotton, peanuts, millet, sorghum, cassava (tapioca), rice; cattle, sheep, goats, camels, donkeys, horses, poultry. **Labor force:** 70,000 receive regular wages or salaries (2002 est); agriculture 90%, industry and commerce 6%, government 4%. **Industries:** uranium mining, cement, brick, soap, textiles, food processing, chemicals, slaughterhouses. **Natural resources:** uranium, coal, iron ore, tin, phosphates, gold, petroleum. **Exports:** $280 million (f.o.b., 2002 est.): uranium ore, livestock, cowpeas, onions. **Imports:** $400 million (f.o.b., 2002 est.): foodstuffs, machinery, vehicles and parts, petroleum, cereals. **Major trading partners:** France, Nigeria, Japan, Spain, Côte d'Ivoire, China, U.S. (2003).

Geography Niger, in West Africa's Sahara region, is four-fifths the size of Alaska. It is surrounded by Mali, Algeria, Libya, Chad, Nigeria, Benin, and Burkina Faso. The Niger River in the southwest flows through the country's only fertile area. Elsewhere the land is semiarid.

Government Republic, emerging from military rule.

History The nomadic Tuaregs were the first inhabitants in the Sahara region. The Hausa (14th century), the Zerma (17th century), the Gobir (18th century), and Fulani (19th century) also established themselves in the region now called Niger.

Niger was incorporated into French West Africa in 1896. There were frequent rebellions, but when order was restored in 1922, the French made the area a colony. In 1958, the voters approved the French constitution and voted to make the territory an autonomous republic within the French Community. The republic adopted a constitution in 1959 but the next year withdrew from the Community, proclaiming its independence.

During the 1970s, the country's economy flourished from uranium production, but when uranium prices fell in the 1980s, its brief period of prosperity ended. The drought of 1968–1975 devastated the country. An estimated 2 million people were starving in Niger, but 200,000 tons of imported food, half U.S.-supplied, substantially ended famine conditions.

The 1974 army coup ousted President Hamani Diori, who had held office since 1960. The new president, Lt. Col. Seyni Kountché, chief of staff of the army, installed a 12-man military government. A predominantly civilian government was formed by Kountché in 1976.

In 1993, the country's first multiparty election resulted in the presidency of Ousmane Mahamane, who was then deposed in a Jan. 1996 coup. In July, the military leader of the coup, Ibrahim Baré Maïnassara, was declared president in a rigged election. Considered a corrupt and ineffectual president, Maïnassara was assassinated in April 1999 by his own guards. The National Reconciliation Council, responsible for the coup, kept its promise and held democratic elections; in Nov. 1999, Tandja Mamadou was elected president. As a result, foreign aid, primarily from France, was restored.

The nomadic Tuaregs, of Berber and Arab descent, have a fiercely insular culture and share little affinity with the black African majority of Niger. Conflict between the Tuaregs and the other tribes of Niger first surfaced in the early 20th century. Cease-fires between the government and various Tuareg rebel groups went into effect in 1995 and 1997. The impoverished Tuaregs have received little of the economic aid they were promised, which is not surprising given Niger's political instability and desperate poverty.

Niger found itself a pawn in the war against Iraq when both the U.S. and Britain claimed that Iraq sought to buy uranium from Niger, citing this as evidence that Saddam Hussein was reconstituting his country's nuclear weapons program. While the U.S. evidence for the Iraq-Niger uranium connection was exposed as a forgery, Britain's Butler report, released in July 2004, concluded the claim was "credible," based on separate evidence. But the final report of the Iraqi Survey Group in Sept. 2004—the U.S. report assessing evidence of Iraq's weapons of mass destruction—concluded that the "ISG has not found evidence to show that Iraq sought uranium from abroad after 1991."

Under pressure, Niger criminalized slavery in 2003, but about 43,000 people are still thought to be held as slaves. In March 2005, a public ceremony freeing 7,000 slaves was planned, but at the last minute the government reversed itself, denying that slavery existed in the country.

In 2005, Niger faced its worst locust infestation in 15 years as well as a severe drought. The UN reported that 3.6 million citizens were suffering from malnutrition. President Tandja, however, claimed the food crisis was propaganda invented by the country's political opposition.

Nigeria

FEDERAL REPUBLIC OF NIGERIA

President: Olusegun Obasanjo (1999)
Area: 356,667 sq mi (923,768 sq km)
Population (2005 est.): 128,771,988 (growth rate: 2.4%); birth rate: 40.6/1000; infant mortality rate: 98.8/1000; life expectancy: 46.7; density per sq mi: 361
Capital (2003 est.): Abuja, 590,400 (metro. area), 165,700 (city proper). **Largest cities:** Lagos (2003 est.), 9,529,700 (metro. area), 8,349,700 (city proper); Kano, 3,329,900; Ibadan, 3,139,500; Kaduna, 1,510,300. **Monetary unit:** Naira. **Languages:** English (official), Hausa, Yoruba, Ibo, Fulani, and more than 200 others. **Ethnicity/race:** More than 250 ethnic groups, including Hausa and Fulani 29%, Yoruba 21%, Ibo 18%, Ijaw 10%, Kanuri 4%, Ibibio 3.5%, Tiv 2.5%. **Religions:** Islam 50%, Christian 40%, indigenous beliefs 10%. **Literacy rate:** 68% (2003 est.)
Economic summary: GDP/PPP (2004 est.): $125.7 billion; per capita $1,000. **Real growth rate:** 6.2%. **Inflation:** 16.5%. **Unemployment:** n.a. **Arable land:** 31%. **Agriculture:** cocoa, peanuts, palm oil, corn, rice, sorghum, millet, cassava (tapioca), yams, rubber; cattle, sheep, goats, pigs; timber; fish. **Labor force:** 55.67 million; agriculture 70%, industry 10%, services 20% (1999 est.). **Industries:** crude oil, coal, tin, columbite, palm oil, peanuts, cotton, rubber, wood, hides and skins, textiles, cement and other construction materials, food products, footwear, chemicals, fertilizer, printing, ceramics, steel, small commercial ship construction and repair. **Natural resources:** natural gas, petroleum, tin, columbite, iron ore, coal, limestone, lead, zinc, arable land. **Exports:** $33.99 billion (f.o.b., 2004 est.): petroleum and petroleum products 95%, cocoa, rubber. **Imports:** $17.14 billion (f.o.b., 2004 est.): machinery, chemicals, transport equipment, manufactured goods, food and live animals. **Major trading partners:** U.S., India, Brazil, Spain, France, Japan, UK, Germany, China (2003). **Member of Commonwealth of Nations**

Geography Nigeria, one-third larger than Texas and the most populous country in Africa, is situated on the Gulf of Guinea in West Africa. Its neighbors are Benin, Niger, Cameroon, and Chad. The lower course of the Niger River flows south through the western part of the country into the Gulf of Guinea. Swamps and mangrove forests border the southern coast; inland are hardwood forests.

Government Multiparty government transitioning from military to civilian rule.

History The first inhabitants of what is now Nigeria were thought to have been the Nok people (500 B.C.–c. A.D. 200). The Kanuri, Hausa, and Fulani peoples subsequently migrated there. Islam was introduced in the 13th century, and the empire of Kanem controlled the area from the end of the 11th century to the 14th.

The Fulani Empire ruled the region from the beginning of the 19th century until the British annexed Lagos in 1851 and seized control of the rest of the region by 1886. It formally became the Colony and Protectorate of Nigeria in 1914. During World War I, native troops of the West African frontier force joined with French forces to defeat the German garrison in the Cameroons.

On Oct. 1, 1960, Nigeria gained independence, becoming a member of the Commonwealth of Nations and joining the United Nations. Organized as a loose federation of self-governing states, the independent nation faced the overwhelming task of unifying a country with 250 ethnic and linguistic groups.

Rioting broke out in 1966, and military leaders, primarily of Ibo ethnicity, seized control. In July, a second military coup put Col. Yakubu Gowon in power, a choice unacceptable to the Ibos. Also in that year, the Muslim Hausas in the north massacred the predominantly Christian Ibos in the east, many of whom had been driven from the north. Thousands of Ibos took refuge in the eastern region, which declared its independence as the Republic of Biafra on May 30, 1967. Civil war broke out. In Jan. 1970, after 31 months of civil war, Biafra surrendered to the federal government.

Gowon's nine-year rule was ended in 1975 by a bloodless coup that made Army Brig. Muritala Rufai Mohammed the new chief of state. The return of civilian leadership was established with the election of Alhaji Shehu Shagari as president in 1979. An oil boom in the 1970s buoyed the economy and by the 1980s Nigeria was considered an exemplar of African democracy and economic well-being.

The military again seized power in 1984, only to be followed by another military coup the following year. Maj. Gen. Ibrahim Babangida announced that the country would be returned to civilian rule, but after the presidential election of June 12, 1993, he voided the results. Nevertheless, Babangida resigned as president in August. In November the military, headed by defense minister Sani Abacha, seized power again.

Corruption and notorious governmental inefficiency as well as a harshly repressive military regime characterized Abacha's reign over this oil-rich country, turning it into an international pariah. A UN fact-finding mission in 1996 reported that Nigeria's "problems of human rights are terrible and the political problems are terrifying." During the 1970s, Nigeria had the 33rd highest per-capita income in the world, but by 1997 it had dropped to the 13th poorest. The hanging of writer Ken Saro-Wiwa in 1995 because he protested against the government was condemned around the world.

As leader of the multination peacekeeping force ECOMOG, Nigeria has established itself as West Africa's superpower, intervening militarily in the civil wars of Liberia and Sierra Leone. But Nigeria's costly war efforts have been unpopular with its own people, who feel Nigeria's limited economic resources are being unnecessarily drained.

Abacha died of a heart attack in 1998 and was succeeded by another military ruler, Gen. Abdulsalam Abubakar, who pledged to step aside for an elected leader by May 1999. The suspicious death of opposition leader Mashood Abiola, who had been imprisoned by the military ever since he legally won the 1993 presidential election, was a crushing blow to democratic proponents. In Feb. 1999, free presidential elections led to an overwhelming victory for Gen. Olusegun Obasanjo, a former member of the military elite who was imprisoned for three years for criticizing the military rule. Obasanjo's commitment to democracy, his anticorruption drives, and his desire to recover billions allegedly stolen by the family and cronies of Abacha initially gained him high praise from the populace as well as the international community. But within two years, the hope of reform seemed doomed as economic mismanagement and rampant corruption persisted. Obasanjo's priorities in 2001 were symbolized by his plans to build a $330 million national soccer stadium, an extravagance that exceeded the combined budget for both health and education. In April 2003, he was reelected.

Nigeria's stability has been repeatedly threatened by fighting between fundamentalist Muslims and Christians over the spread of Islamic law (sharia) across the heavily Muslim north. One-third of Nigeria's 36 states is ruled by sharia law. More than 10,000 people have died in religious clashes since military rule ended in 1999.

In 2003, after religious and political leaders in the Kano region banned polio immunization—contending that it sterilized girls and spread HIV—an outbreak of polio spread through Nigeria, entering neighboring countries the following year. The Kano region lifted its ten-month ban against vaccination in July 2004. On Aug. 24, there were 602 polio cases worldwide, 79% of which were in Nigeria.

In Sept. 2004, violence broke out in the Niger Delta, Nigeria's oil-producing region. A rebel group, the Niger Delta People's Volunteer Force, threatened to shut down oil production unless the desperately impoverished local residents, the Ijaw people, begin to see some benefit from Nigeria's oil riches. The conflict caused world oil prices to soar.

Norway

KINGDOM OF NORWAY

National name: Kongeriket Norge
Sovereign: King Harald V (1991)
Prime Minister: Kjell Magne Bondevik (2001)
Area: 125,181 sq mi (324,220 sq km)
Population (2005 est.): 4,593,041 (growth rate: 0.4%); birth rate: 11.7/1000; infant mortality rate: 3.7/1000; life expectancy: 79.4; density per sq mi: 37
Capital and largest city (2003 est.): Oslo, 791,500. **Other large cities:** Bergen, 211,200; Stavanger, 168,600; Trondheim, 144,000. **Monetary unit:** Norwegian krone. **Languages:** Bokmål Norwegian, Nynorsk Norwegian (both official); small Sami- and Finnish-speaking minorities. **Ethnicity/race:** Norwegian, Sami 20,000. **Religions:** Evangelical Lutheran 86% (state church), other Protestant and Roman Catholic 3%, other 1%, none and unknown 10%. **Literacy rate:** 100% (2003 est.)
Economic summary: GDP/PPP (2004 est.): $183 billion; per capita $40,000. **Real growth rate:** 3.3%. **Inflation:** 1%. **Unemployment:** 4.3%. **Arable land:** 3%. **Agriculture:** barley, wheat, potatoes; pork, beef, veal, milk; fish. **Labor force:** 2.38 million; services 74%, industry 22%, agriculture, forestry, and fishing 4% (1995). **Industries:** petroleum and gas, food processing, shipbuilding, pulp and paper products, metals, chemicals, timber, mining, textiles, fishing. **Natural resources:** petroleum, copper, natural gas, pyrites, nickel, iron ore, zinc, lead, fish, timber, hydropower. **Exports:** $76.64 billion (f.o.b., 2004 est.): petroleum and petroleum products, machinery and equipment, metals, chemicals, ships, fish. **Imports:** $45.96 billion (f.o.b., 2004 est.): machinery and equipment, chemicals, metals, foodstuffs. **Major trading partners:** UK, Germany, Netherlands, U.S., France, Sweden, Denmark, China (2003).

Geography Norway is situated in the western part of the Scandinavian peninsula. It extends about 1,100 mi (1,770 km) from the North Sea along the Norwegian Sea to more than 300 mi (483 km) above the Arctic Circle, the farthest north of any European country. It is slightly larger than New Mexico. Nearly 70% of Norway is uninhabitable and covered by mountains, glaciers, moors, and rivers. The hundreds of deep fjords that cut into the coastline give Norway an over-all oceanfront of more than 12,000 mi (19,312 km). Galdhø Peak, at 8,100 ft (2,469 m), is Norway's high-est point and the Glåma (Glomma) is the principal river, at 372 mi (598 km) long.

Government Constitutional monarchy.

History Norwegians, like the Danes and Swedes, are of Teutonic origin. The Norsemen, also known as Vikings, ravaged the coasts of northwest Europe from the 8th to the 11th century and were ruled by local chieftains. Olaf II Haraldsson became the first effec-tive king of all Norway in 1015 and began converting the Norwegians to Christianity. After 1442, Norway was ruled by Danish kings until 1814, when it was united with Sweden—although retaining a degree of independence and receiving a new constitution—in an uneasy partnership. In 1905, the Norwegian Parlia-ment arranged a peaceful separation and invited a Danish prince to the Norwegian throne—King Haakon VII. A treaty with Sweden provided that all disputes be settled by arbitration and that no fortifications be erected on the common frontier.

When World War I broke out, Norway joined with Sweden and Denmark in a decision to remain neutral and to cooperate in the joint interest of the three coun-tries. In World War II, Norway was invaded by the Germans on April 9, 1940. It resisted for two months before the Nazis took complete control. King Haakon and his government fled to London, where they estab-lished a government-in-exile. Maj. Vidkun Quisling, who served as Norway's prime minister during the war, was the most notorious of the Nazi collaborators. The word for traitor, *quisling*, bears his name. He was executed by the Norwegians on Oct. 24, 1945. Despite severe losses in the war, Norway recovered quickly as its economy expanded. It joined NATO in 1949.

In the late 20th century, the Labor Party and the Conservative Party seesawed for control, each some-times having to lead minority governments. An impor-tant debate was over Norway's membership in the European Union. In an advisory referendum held in Nov. 1994, voters rejected seeking membership for their nation in the EU. The country became the second-largest net oil exporter after Saudi Arabia in 1995. Nor-way continued to experience rapid economic growth into the new millennium.

In March 2000, Prime Minister Kjell Magne Bond-evik resigned after Parliament voted to build the coun-try's first gas-fired power stations. Bondevik had objected to the project, asserting that the plants would emit too much carbon dioxide. Labor Party leader Jens Stoltenberg succeeded Bondevik. Stoltenberg and the Labor Party were defeated in Sept. 2001 elections, and no party emerged with a clear majority. After a month of talks, the Conservatives, the Christian People's Party, and the Liberals formed a coalition with Bonde-vik as prime minister. The governing coalition was backed by the far-right Progress Party.

For several years running, the UN's Human Devel-opment Index has rated Norway the world's "most liv-able" country. The index ranks nations according to their citizens' quality of life.

Dependencies of Norway

Svalbard (23,957 sq mi; 62,049 sq km), in the Arc-tic Ocean about 360 mi north of Norway, consists of the Spitsbergen group and several smaller islands, including Bear Island, Hope Island, King Charles Land, and White Island (or Gillis Land). The capital is Longyear-byen. It came under Norwegian administration in 1925. **Population:** 2,701 (2005 est.). 62% of the population is Russian and Ukrainian; 38% is Norwegian. Coal mining is the major economic activity.

Bouvet Island (23 sq mi; 58.5 sq km), an island nature reserve in the South Atlantic about 1,600 mi south-southwest of the Cape of Good Hope, came under Norwegian administration in 1928. It is uninhab-ited.

Jan Mayen Island (144 sq mi; 373 sq km), in the Arctic Ocean between Norway and Greenland, came under Norwegian administration in 1929. There are no permanent inhabitants, just workers at the navigation base and weather/radio station.

Oman

SULTANATE OF OMAN

National name: Saltanat Uman
Sultan: Qabus ibn Sa'id (1970)
Area: 82,031 sq mi (212,460 sq km)[1]
Population (2005 est.): 3,001,583 (growth rate: 3.3%); birth rate: 36.7/1000; infant mortality rate: 19.5/1000; life expectancy: 73.1; density per sq mi: 37
Capital (2003 est.): Muscat, 797,000 (metro.area), 54,800 (city proper). **Monetary unit:** Omani rial.
Languages: Arabic (official), English, Baluchi, Urdu, Indian dialects. **Ethnicity/race:** Arab, Baluchi, South Asian (Indian, Pakistani, Sri Lankan, Bangladeshi), African. **Religions:** Islam: Ibadhi 75%, Sunni, Shi'a; Hindu. **Literacy rate:** 76% (2003 est.)
Economic summary: GDP/PPP (2004 est.): $38.09 billion; per capita $13,100. **Real growth rate:** 1.2%. **Inflation:** 0.2%. **Unemployment:** 15%. **Arable land:** 0.12%. **Agriculture:** dates, limes, bananas, alfalfa, vegetables; camels, cattle; fish. **Labor force:** 920,000 (2002 est.); agriculture n.a., industry n.a., services n.a. **Industries:** crude oil production and refining, natural and liquefied natural gas (LNG) production, construction, cement, copper, steel, chemicals, optic fiber. **Natural resources:** petroleum, copper, asbestos, some marble, limestone, chromium, gypsum, natural gas. **Exports:** $13.14 billion (f.o.b., 2004 est.): petroleum, reexports, fish, metals, textiles. **Imports:** $6.373 billion (f.o.b., 2004 est.): machinery and transport equipment, manufactured goods, food, livestock, lubricants. **Major trading partners:** South Korea, China, Japan, Thailand, UAE, Iran, U.S., UK, Germany, India (2003).

1. Excluding the Kuria Muria Islands.

Geography Oman is a 1,000-mile-long (1,700-km) coastal plain at the southeast tip of the Arabian penin-sula lying on the Arabian Sea and the Gulf of Oman. It is bordered by the United Arab Emirates, Saudi Ara-bia, and Yemen. The country is the size of Kansas.

Government Absolute monarchy.

History Arabs migrated to Oman from the 9th cen-tury B.C. onward, and conversion to Islam occurred in the 7th century A.D. Muscat, the capital of the geo-graphical area known as Oman, was occupied by the Portuguese from 1508 to 1648. Then it fell to Ottoman Turks, but in 1741 Ahmad ibn Sa'id forced them out. The descendants of Sultan Ahmad rule Oman today.

Ahmad expanded his empire to East Africa, and for a time the Omani capital was in Zanzibar. After 1861, however, Zanzibar fell from Omani control.

The sultans and imams of Oman clashed continu-ously throughout the 20th century until 1959, when the last Ibadi imam was evicted from the country. In a pal-ace coup on July 23, 1970, the sultan, Sa'id bin Taimur, who had ruled since 1932, was overthrown by his son, Qabus ibn Sa'id, who promised to establish a modern government and use newfound oil wealth to aid the people of this very isolated state. Oman joined the Arab League and the United Nations in 1971.

A long border dispute with Yemen was resolved in Oct. 1992; in 1997, the countries agreed to new maps defining the border.

In 1997, Sultan Qabus granted women the right to be elected to the country's consultative body, the Shura Council (Majlis al-Shura). In 2003, the sultan extended voting rights to everyone over 21; previously, voters were selected from among the elite, and only about a quarter of the population was allowed to vote.

Pakistan

ISLAMIC REPUBLIC OF PAKISTAN

President: Gen. Pervez Musharraf (2001)
Prime minister (caretaker): Shaukat Aziz (2004)
Area: 310,401 sq mi (803,940 sq km)[1]
Population (2005 est.): 162,419,946 (growth rate: 2.0%); birth rate: 30.4/1000; infant mortality rate: 72.4/1000; life expectancy: 63.0; density per sq mi: 523
Capital (2003 est.): Islamabad, 601,600. **Largest cities:** Karachi, 10,573,200; Lahore, 5,756,100; Faisalabad (Lyallpur), 2,247,700; Rawalpindi, 1,598,600; Gujranwala, 1,384,100. **Monetary unit:** Pakistan rupee. **Principal languages:** Punjabi 48%, Sindhi 12%, Siraiki (a Punjabi variant) 10%, Pashtu 8%, Urdu (official) 8%, Balochi 3%, Hindko 2%, Brahui 1%, English, Burushaski, and others 8%. **Ethnicity/race:** Punjabi, Sindhi, Pashtun (Pathan), Baloch, Muhajir (immigrants from India and their descendants). **Religions:** Islam 97% (Sunni 77%, Shiite 20%); Christian, Hindu, and other 3%. **Literacy rate:** 46% (2003 est.)
Economic summary GDP/PPP (2004 est.): $347.3 billion; per capita $2,200. **Real growth rate:** 6.1%. **Inflation:** 4.8% (FY03/04 est.). **Unemployment:** 8.3% plus substantial underemployment. **Arable land:** 28%. **Agriculture:** cotton, wheat, rice, sugarcane, fruits, vegetables; milk, beef, mutton, eggs. **Labor force:** 45.43 million; note: extensive export of labor, mostly to the Middle East, and use of child labor; agriculture 42%, industry 20%, services 38% (2004 est.). **Industries:** textiles and apparel, food processing, pharmaceuticals, construction materials, paper products, fertilizer, shrimp. **Natural resources:** land, extensive natural gas reserves, limited petroleum, poor quality coal, iron ore, copper, salt, limestone. **Exports:** $15.07 billion (f.o.b., 2004 est.): textiles (garments, bed linen, cotton cloth, and yarn), rice, leather goods, sports goods, chemicals, manufactures, carpets and rugs. **Imports:** $14.01 billion (f.o.b., 2004 est.): petroleum, petroleum products, machinery, plastics, transportation equipment, edible oils, paper and paperboard, iron and steel, tea. **Major trading partners:** U.S., UAE, UK, Germany, Hong Kong, Saudi Arabia, China, Japan, Kuwait, U.S., Malaysia, Singapore (2003).

1. Excluding Kashmir and Jammu.

Geography Pakistan is situated in the western part of the Indian subcontinent, with Afghanistan and Iran on the west, India on the east, and the Arabian Sea on the south. The name *Pakistan* is derived from the Urdu words *Pak* (meaning pure) and *stan* (meaning country). It is nearly twice the size of California.

The northern and western highlands of Pakistan contain the towering Karakoram and Pamir mountain ranges, which include some of the world's highest peaks: K2 (28,250 ft; 8,611 m) and Nanga Parbat (26,660 ft; 8,126 m). The Baluchistan Plateau lies to the west, and the Thar Desert and an expanse of alluvial plains, the Punjab and Sind, lie to the east. The 1,000-mile-long (1,609 km) Indus River and its tribu-

taries flow through the country from the Kashmir region to the Arabian Sea.

Government Military rule was instituted in Oct. 1999; a nominal democracy was declared in June 2001 by the ruling military leader, Pervez Musharraf.

History Pakistan was one of the two original successor states to British India, which was partitioned along religious lines in 1947. For almost 25 years following independence, it consisted of two separate regions, East and West Pakistan, but now it is made up only of the western sector. Both India and Pakistan have laid claim to the Kashmir region; this territorial dispute led to war in 1949, 1965, 1971, and 1999, and remains unresolved today.

What is now Pakistan was in prehistoric times the Indus Valley civilization (c. 2500–1700 B.C.). A series of invaders—Aryans, Persians, Greeks, Arabs, Turks, and others—controlled the region for the next several thousand years. Islam, the principal religion, was introduced in 711. In 1526, the land became part of the Mogul Empire, which ruled most of the Indian subcontinent from the 16th to the mid-18th century. By 1857, the British became the dominant power in the region. With Hindus holding most of the economic, social, and political advantages, the Muslim minority's dissatisfaction grew, leading to the formation of the nationalist Muslim League in 1906 by Mohammed Ali Jinnah (1876–1949). The league supported Britain in the Second World War while the Hindu nationalist leaders, Nehru and Gandhi, refused. In return for the league's support of Britain, Jinnah expected British backing for Muslim autonomy. Britain agreed to the formation of Pakistan as a separate dominion within the Commonwealth in Aug. 1947, a bitter disappointment to India's dream of a unified subcontinent. Jinnah became governor-general. The partition of Pakistan and India along religious lines resulted in the largest migration in human history, with 17 million people fleeing across the borders in both directions to escape the sectarian violence accompanying the partition.

Pakistan became a republic on March 23, 1956, with Maj. Gen. Iskander Mirza as the first president. Military rule prevailed for the next two decades. Tensions between East and West Pakistan existed from the outset. Separated by more than a thousand miles, the two regions shared few cultural and social traditions other than religion. To the growing resentment of East Pakistan, the West monopolized the country's political and economic power. In 1970, East Pakistan's Awami League, led by the Bengali leader Sheik Mujibur Rahman, secured a majority of the seats in the National Assembly. President Yahya Khan postponed the opening of the National Assembly to skirt East Pakistan's demand for greater autonomy, provoking civil war. The independent state of Bangladesh, or Bengali nation, was proclaimed on March 26, 1971. Indian troops entered the war in its last weeks fighting on the side of the new state. Pakistan was defeated on Dec. 16, 1971, and President Yahya Khan stepped down. Zulfikar Ali Bhutto took over Pakistan and accepted Bangladesh as an independent entity. In 1976, formal relations between India and Pakistan resumed.

Pakistan's first elections under civilian rule took place in March 1977, and the overwhelming victory of Bhutto's Pakistan People's Party (PPP) was denounced as fraudulent. A rising tide of violent protest and political deadlock led to a military takeover on July 5 by Gen. Mohammed Zia ul-Haq. Bhutto was tried and convicted for the 1974 murder of a political opponent, and despite worldwide protests he was executed on April 4, 1979, touching off riots by his supporters. Zia declared himself president on Sept. 16, 1978, and ruled by martial law until Dec. 30, 1985, when a measure of representative government was restored. On Aug. 19, 1988, Zia was killed in a midair explosion of a Pakistani Air Force plane. Elections at the end of 1988 brought longtime Zia opponent Benazir Bhutto, daughter of Zulfikar Bhutto, into office as prime minister.

In the 1990s, Pakistan saw a shaky succession of governments—Benazir Bhutto was prime minister twice and Nawaz Sharif three times, until he was deposed in a coup on Oct. 12, 1999, by Gen. Pervez Musharraf. The Pakistani public, familiar with military rule for 25 of the nation's 52-year history, generally viewed the coup as a positive step and hoped it would bring a badly needed economic upswing.

To the surprise of much of the world, two new nuclear powers emerged in May 1998 when India, followed by Pakistan just weeks later, conducted nuclear tests. Fighting with India again broke out in the disputed territory of Kashmir in May 1999.

Close ties with Afghanistan's Taliban government thrust Pakistan into a difficult position following the Sept. 11 terrorist attacks on the U.S. Under U.S. pressure, Pakistan broke with its neighbor to become the United States' chief ally in the region. In return, President Bush ended sanctions (instituted after Pakistan's testing of nuclear weapons in 1998), rescheduled its debt, and helped to bolster the legitimacy of the rule of Pervez Musharraf, who appointed himself president in 2001.

On Dec. 13, 2001, suicide bombers attacked the Indian Parliament, killing 14 people, including 5 assailants. Indian officials blamed the attack on Islamic militants supported by Pakistan. Both sides assembled hundreds of thousands of troops along their common border, bringing the two nuclear powers to the brink of war.

In April 2002, voters overwhelmingly approved a referendum to extend Musharraf's presidency for another five years. The vote, however, outraged opposing political parties and human rights groups that said the process was rigged. In August, he unveiled 29 constitutional amendments that strengthened his grip on the country.

Pakistani officials dealt a heavy blow to al-Qaeda in March 2003, arresting Khalid Shaikh Mohammed, the top aide to Osama bin Laden, who organized the 2001 terrorist attacks against the U.S. The search for bin Laden intensified in northern Pakistan following Mohammed's arrest.

In Nov. 2003, Pakistan and India declared the first formal cease-fire in Kashmir in 14 years. In April 2005, a bus service began between the two capitals of Kashmir—Srinagar on the Indian side and Pakistan's Muzaffarabad—uniting families that had been separated by the Line of Control since 1947.

Abdul Qadeer Khan, the father of Pakistan's nuclear bomb, was exposed in Feb. 2004 for having sold nuclear secrets to North Korea, Iran, and Libya. Musharraf had him apologize publicly, and then pardoned him. While much of the world reviled him for this unconscionable act of nuclear proliferation, the scientist remains a national hero in Pakistan. Khan claimed that he alone and not Pakistan's military or government was involved in the selling of these ultraclassified secrets; few in the international community have accepted this explanation.

President Musharraf declared in December 2004 that he would retain his post as head of the army, a reversal of an earlier promise.

President Bush said in March 2005 that the U.S. would sell Pakistan F-16 fighter jets. Pakistan had been trying to buy the planes since 1990 but had been repeatedly denied because of its nuclear-weapons programs. In what was considered an attempt to balance the offer to Pakistan, Bush also would allow American companies to provide India with several types of modern combat weapons, including F-16s and F-18s.

Pakistani officials announced that three of the four suicide bombers who attacked London's transit system in July 2005 had visited Pakistan in 2004. Days later, about 200 suspected Islamic militants were detained after a series of raids on mosques and madrassas. Despite the move, many have questioned President Musharraf's sincerity in rooting out militants and remnants of the Taliban. Indeed, during the summer of 2005, violence intensified in the mountainous North and South Waziristan regions, which border Afghanistan, suggesting that the insurgents are regrouping.

Palau

REPUBLIC OF PALAU

National name: Beluu er a Belau
President: Tommy Remengesau (2001)
Total area: 177 sq mi (458 sq km)
Population (2005 est.): 20,303 (growth rate: 1.4%); birth rate: 18.4/1000; infant mortality rate: 14.8/1000; life expectancy: 70.1; density per sq mi: 115
Capital and largest city (2003 est.): Koror, 11,100.
Monetary unit: U.S. dollar used. **Languages:** Palauan, English, Sonsoralese, Tobi, Angaur (all official), Filipino, Chinese, Carolinian, Japanese, and other Asian languages.. **Ethnicity/race:** Palauan (Micronesian with Malayan and Melanesian admixtures) 70%, Asian (mainly Filipinos, followed by Chinese, Taiwanese, and Vietnamese) 28%, white 2% (2000 est.). **Religions:** Christian (Roman Catholics 49%, Seventh-Day Adventists, Jehovah's Witnesses, the Assembly of God, the Liebenzell Mission, and Latter-Day Saints), Modekngei (one-third observes this indigenous religion). **Literacy rate:** 92% (1980 est.)
Economic summary: GDP/PPP (2001 est.): $174 million; note: GDP numbers reflect U.S. spending; per capita $9,000. **Real growth rate:** 1%. **Inflation:** 3.4% (2000 est.). **Unemployment:** 2.3% (2000 est.). **Arable land:** 9%. **Agriculture:** coconuts, copra, cassava (tapioca), sweet potatoes. **Labor force:** 9,845 (2000); agriculture 20%, industry n.a., services n.a. (1990). **Industries:** tourism, craft items (from shell, wood, pearls), construction, garment making. **Natural resources:** forests, minerals (especially gold), marine products, deep-seabed minerals. **Exports:** $18 million (f.o.b., 2001 est.): shellfish, tuna, copra, garments. **Imports:** $99 million (f.o.b., 2001 est.): machinery and equipment, fuels, metals; foodstuffs. **Major trading partners:** U.S., Japan, Singapore, Guam, South Korea (2000).

Geography The Palau island chain consists of about 200 islands located in the western Pacific Ocean, 528 mi (650 km) southeast of the Philippines. Only eight of the islands are permanently inhabited.

Government Constitutional republic.

History The original settlers of Palau are believed to have arrived from Indonesia as early as 2500 B.C. The Palau islands' position on the western threshold of Oceania and their proximity to Southeast Asia have led to the population being a mixture of Malay, Melanesian, Filipino, and Polynesian ancestry.

Explored by the Spanish navigator Ruy López de Villalobos in 1543, the islands remained under nominal Spanish ownership for more than 300 years before Spain sold them to Germany in 1899. Japan occupied Palau during World War I and received a mandate over them from the League of Nations in 1920. They remained in Japanese control and served as an important naval base until the U.S. seized them during World War II. After the war they became a UN trusteeship (1947), administered by the U.S. Palau signed a Compact of Free Association with the U.S. in 1992, requiring the United States to provide economic aid in exchange for the right to build and maintain U.S. military facilities in Palau. Palau became a sovereign state in 1994. In 2000, former vice president Tommy Remengesau won the presidential election.

Palestinian State (proposed)

WEST BANK AND GAZA STRIP

President: Mahmoud Abbas (2005)
Prime Minister: Ahmed Qurei (2003)
Area: West Bank: 2,263 sq mi (5,860 sq km); Gaza Strip: 139 sq mi (360 sq km)
Population (2005 est.): West Bank: 2,385,615, Gaza Strip: 1,376,289 (growth rate: West Bank: 3.1%, Gaza Strip: 3.8%); birth rate: West Bank: 32.4/1000, Gaza Strip: 40.0/1000; infant mortality rate: West Bank: 19.6/1,000, Gaza Strip: 22.9/1000; life expectancy: West Bank: 73.1, Gaza Strip: 71.8; density per sq mi: West Bank: 1,054, Gaza Strip: 9,902. NOTE: figures above include approximately 8,000 Israeli settlers who evacuated the Gaza Strip in Aug. 2005.
Capital: Undetermined. **Large cities (2003 est.):** Gaza, 1,331,600 (metro. area), 407,600 (city proper); Hebron, 137,000; Nablus, 115,400. **Monetary units:** New Israeli shekels, Jordanian dinars, U.S. dollars.
Languages: Arabic, Hebrew, English. **Ethnicity/race:** West Bank: Palestinian Arab and other 83%, Jewish 17%; Gaza Strip: Palestinian Arab and other.
Religions: West Bank: Islam 75% (predominantly Sunni), Jewish 17%, Christian and other 8%; Gaza Strip: Islam 98.7% (predominantly Sunni), Christian 0.7%.
Economic summary: Gaza Strip: GDP/PPP (2003 est.): $768 million; $600 per capita. **Real growth rate:** 4.5%. **Inflation:** 2.2% (2001 est., includes West Bank). **Unemployment:** 50% (includes West Bank). **Arable land:** 29%. **Agriculture:** olives, citrus, vegetables; beef, dairy products. **Labor force:** 725,000 (2004); agriculture 14%, industry 19%, services 66% (2004). **Industries:** generally small family businesses that produce textiles, soap, olive-wood carvings, and mother-of-pearl souvenirs; the Israelis have established some small-scale modern industries in an industrial center. **Natural resources:** arable land, natural gas. **Exports:** $205 million (f.o.b., 2002, includes West Bank): citrus, flowers (Gaza Strip); olives, fruit, vegetables, limestone (West Bank). **Imports:** $1.9 billion (c.i.f., 2002, includes West Bank): food, consumer goods, construction materials. **Major trading partners:** Israel, Egypt, West Bank. **West Bank: GDP/PPP** (2003 est.): $1.7 billion; $800 per capita. **Real growth rate:** 6%. **Arable land:** 16.9%. **Agriculture:** olives, citrus, vegetables; beef, dairy products. **Labor force:** 364,000 (2004); agriculture 15%, industry 25%, services 60% (2004 est.). **Natural resource:** arable land. **Major trading partners:** Israel, Jordan, Gaza Strip (2000).

Geography The West Bank is located to the east of Israel and the west of Jordan. The Gaza Strip is located between Israel and Egypt on the Mediterranean coast.

Government The Palestinian Authority (PA), with Arafat its elected leader, took control of the newly non-Israeli-occupied areas, assuming governmental duties in 1994.

History The history of the proposed modern Palestinian state, which is expected to be formed from the territories of the West Bank and Gaza Strip, began with the British Mandate of Palestine. From Sept. 29, 1923, until May 14, 1948, Britain controlled the region, but by 1947, Britain had appealed to the UN to solve the complex problem of competing Palestinian and Jewish claims to the land. In Aug. 1947, the UN proposed dividing Palestine into a Jewish state, an Arab state, and a small international zone. Arabs rejected the idea. As soon as Britain pulled out of Palestine in 1948, neighboring Arab nations invaded, intent on crushing the newly declared State of Israel. Israel emerged victorious, affirming its sovereignty. The remaining areas of Palestine were divided between Transjordan (now Jordan), which annexed the West Bank, and Egypt, which gained control of the Gaza Strip.

Through a series of political and social policies, Jordan sought to consolidate its control over the political future of Palestinians and to become their speaker. Jordan even extended citizenship to Palestinians in 1949; Palestinians constituted about two-thirds of the country's population. In the Gaza Strip, administered by Egypt from 1948–1967, poverty and unemployment were high, and most of the Palestinians lived in refugee camps.

In the Arab-Israeli war of 1967, Israel, over a period of six days, defeated the military forces of Egypt, Syria, and Jordan and annexed the territories of East Jerusalem, the Golan Heights, the West Bank, the Gaza Strip, and all of the Sinai peninsula. The Palestinian Liberation Organization (PLO), formed in 1964, was a terrorist organization bent on Israel's annihilation. Palestinian rioting, demonstrations, and terrorist acts against Israelis became chronic. In 1974, PLO leader Yasir Arafat addressed the UN General Assembly, the first stateless government to do so. Violence again escalated in 1987 during the *intifada* ("shaking off"), a new era in Palestinian mass mobilization. In 1988, Yasir Arafat publicly eschewed terrorism and officially recognized the state of Israel.

In 1993, highly secretive talks in Norway between the PLO and the Israeli government resulted in the Oslo Agreement. The accord stipulated a five-year plan in which Palestinians of the West Bank and the Gaza Strip would gradually become self-governing. On Sept. 13, 1993, Arafat and Israeli prime minister Yitzak Rabin signed the historic "Declaration of Principles." As part of the agreement, Israel pulled out of the Gaza Strip and Jericho in the West Bank in 1994. The Palestinian Authority (PA), with Arafat as its elected leader, took control of the newly non-Israeli-occupied areas, assuming all governmental duties.

Intensive negotiations between Barak and Arafat in 2000 remained deadlocked over Israeli-occupied East Jerusalem, which Arafat insisted must be the capital of the future Palestinian state. At the end of September, however, the stalemate disintegrated into the worst violence between Israelis and Palestinians in years, provoked by Likud hard-liner Ariel Sharon's visit to the compound called Temple Mount by Jews and Haram al-Sharif by Muslims, a fiercely contested site that is sacred to both faiths. The intensified violence, which included an unprecedented number of Palestinian suicide attacks against Israeli civilians and the inevitable Israeli military reprisals, was dubbed the al-Aksa intifada. In four years (2000–2004), the intifada had led to the deaths of almost 4,000, including nearly 3,000 Palestinians.

For five months in 2002, Israeli troops surrounded Yasir Arafat at the Palestinian Authority headquarters in Ramallah. Prime Minister Sharon, blaming Arafat directly for inciting terror, called for his expulsion from the territories. Washington echoed Israel's view that Arafat had become "irrelevant" and announced that the U.S. would not recognize an independent Palestinian state until Arafat was replaced. Throughout the summer, Palestinian suicide bombings (Hamas and the Al-Aksa Martyr Brigade claimed responsibility for the majority of them) and Israeli reprisals continued.

In March 2003, Arafat agreed to political reforms— his government, to the disillusionment of many Palestinians, was rife with corruption. He also agreed to share power with a prime minister. Mahmoud Abbas, second-in-command of the PLO, assumed the post on April 30. Unlike Arafat, Abbas emphatically rejected the Palestinian intifada, but he had no influence or control over Palestinian militant groups the way Arafat did. On May 1, the Quartet (the U.S., UN, EU, and Russia) unfurled its "road map" for peace, which called on both sides to make concessions and end the wave of deadly violence. But the road map quickly led nowhere: Abbas, with little real political power, could not disable terrorist organizations, and Israel did not dismantle settlements, much less prevent new ones from cropping up. Sharon also continued to build the controversial security barrier that divides Israeli and Palestinian areas. Abbas resigned in September, and Arafat appointed a new prime minister, Ahmed Qurei.

In Dec. 2003, Sharon announced a startling plan— the unilateral withdrawal from the Gaza Strip. In turn, Israel was to hold on to large blocks of land in the West Bank and reject the "right of return" for Palestinian refugees. Some speculated that by giving up Gaza, Sharon was tightening Israel's hold on the West Bank; he continued to approve construction of new houses in West Bank settlements, a clear violation of the "road map."

On March 22, 2004, Israel assassinated Sheik Ahmed Yassin, the founder and spiritual leader of Hamas. Outrage and protest throughout the Arab world followed. Since September 2003, Israel has killed more than 20 Hamas officials and has vowed to destroy the entire leadership. Within months, Israel had assassinated Yassin's successor as well.

In July 2004, Israel revised the route of its security barrier so that it no longer cut into Palestinian land. The UN estimated that the original route would have taken almost 15% of West Bank territory for Israel. The new route will attempt to ensure that Palestinians aren't subject to undue hardships, such as separating villagers from their farmland.

On November 10, Yasir Arafat died, marking the end of an era in Palestinian affairs. He was buried in his West Bank compound in Ramallah. On Jan. 9, former prime minister Mahmoud Abbas (also known as Abu Mazen) was easily elected president with 62% of the vote. His ascension significantly altered the political landscape. At a summit on Feb. 8, 2005, Abbas and Israeli prime minister Sharon made the most promising move toward peace in the four years since the intifada began. Both sides agreed to an unequivocal cease-fire, pledging to "end all acts of violence against all Israelis and Palestinians everywhere." The most immediate danger to this cease-fire were Palestinian militant groups, over whom Abbas has next to no control.

On Aug. 15, the withdrawal of some 8,000 Israeli settlers from Gaza began. The evacuation involved 21 Gaza settlements as well as four of the more isolated of the West Bank's 120 settlements. About 25% of Gaza's land had been occupied by the 8,000 settlers. Gaza, which has the world's highest population density, will replace the settlers' one-family houses with apartment buildings. A group of American philanthropists purchased 800 acres of greenhouses from the departing settlers and donated them to the Palestinians, providing employment and revenue.

Panama

REPUBLIC OF PANAMA

National name: República de Panamá
President: Martín Torrijos (2004)
Area: 30,193 sq mi (78,200 sq km)
Population (2005 est.): 3,039,150 (growth rate: 1.3%); birth rate: 20.0/1000; infant mortality rate: 20.5/1000; life expectancy: 71.9; density per sq mi: 101
Capital and largest city (2003 est.): Panama City, 1,053,500 (metro. area), 437,200 (city proper). **Other large cities:** San Miguelito, 309,500; Colón, 44,400. **Monetary units:** balboa; U.S. dollar. **Languages:** Spanish (official), English 14%, many bilingual. **Ethnicity/race:** mestizo 70%, Amerindian and mixed (West Indian) 14%, white 10%, Indian 6%. **Religions:** Roman Catholic 85%, Protestant 15%. **Literacy rate:** 93% (2003 est.)
Economic summary: GDP/PPP (2004 est.): $20.57 billion; per capita $6,900. **Real growth rate:** 6%. **Inflation:** 2%. **Unemployment:** 12.6%. **Arable land:** 7%. **Agriculture:** bananas, rice, corn, coffee, sugarcane, vegetables; livestock; shrimp. **Labor force:** 1.32 million; note: shortage of skilled labor, but an oversupply of unskilled labor; agriculture 20.8%, industry 18%, services 61.2% (1995 est.). **Industries:** construction, brewing, cement and other construction materials, sugar milling. **Natural resources:** copper, mahogany forests, shrimp, hydropower. **Exports:** $5.699 billion (f.o.b., 2004 est.): bananas, shrimp, sugar, coffee, clothing (1999). **Imports:** $7.164 billion (f.o.b., 2004 est.): capital goods, foodstuffs, consumer goods, chemicals. **Major trading partners:** U.S., Nigeria, Germany, South Korea, El Salvador, Peru, Costa Rica, Belgium, Japan, China, Singapore (2003).

Geography The southernmost of the Central American nations, Panama is south of Costa Rica and north of Colombia. The Panama Canal bisects the isthmus at its narrowest and lowest point, allowing passage from the Caribbean Sea to the Pacific Ocean. Panama is slightly smaller than South Carolina. It is marked by a chain of mountains in the west, moderate hills in the interior, and a low range on the east coast. There are extensive forests in the fertile Caribbean area.

Government Constitutional democracy.

History Explored by Columbus in 1502 and by Balboa in 1513, Panama was the principal shipping point to and from South and Central America in colonial days. In 1821, when Central America revolted against Spain, Panama joined Colombia, which had already declared its independence. For the next 82 years, Panama attempted unsuccessfully to break away from Colombia. Between 1850 and 1900 Panama had 40 administrations, 50 riots, 5 attempted secessions, and 13 U.S. interventions. After a U.S. proposal for canal rights over the narrow isthmus was rejected by Colombia, Panama proclaimed its independence with U.S. backing in 1903.

For canal rights in perpetuity, the U.S. paid Panama $10 million and agreed to pay $250,000 each year, which was increased to $430,000 in 1933 and to $1,930,000 in 1955. In exchange, the U.S. got the Canal Zone—a 10-mile-wide strip across the isthmus—and considerable influence in Panama's affairs. On Sept. 7, 1977, Gen. Omar Torrijos Herrera and President Jimmy Carter signed treaties giving

Panama gradual control of the canal, phasing out U.S. military bases, and guaranteeing the canal's neutrality.

Nicolas Ardito Barletta, Panama's first directly elected president in 16 years, was inaugurated on Oct. 11, 1984, for a five-year term. He was a puppet of strongman Gen. Manuel Noriega, a former CIA operative and head of the secret police. Noriega replaced Barletta with vice president Eric Arturo Delvalle a year later. In 1988, Noriega was indicted in the U.S. for drug trafficking, but when Delvalle attempted to fire him, Noriega forced the National Assembly to replace Delvalle with Manuel Solis Palma. In Dec. 1989, the assembly named Noriega "maximum leader" and declared the U.S. and Panama to be in a state of war. In Dec. 1989, 24,000 U.S. troops seized control of Panama City in an attempt to capture Noriega after a U.S. soldier was killed in Panama. On Jan. 3, 1990, Noriega surrendered himself to U.S. custody and was transported to Miami, where he was later convicted of drug trafficking. Guillermo Endara, who probably would have won an election suppressed earlier by Noriega, was installed as president.

On Dec. 31, 1999, the U.S. formally handed over control of the Panama Canal to Panama. Meanwhile, Colombian rebels and paramilitary forces have made periodic incursions into Panamanian territory, raising security concerns. Panama has also faced increased drug and arms smuggling.

In May 2004 presidential elections, Martín Torrijos Herrara, the son of former dictator Omar Torrijos, won 47.5% of the vote. He took office in September.

Panama Canal. In 1524, King Charles V of Spain ordered a survey of a waterway across the isthmus in consideration of building a canal. In 1878, the Colombian government gave a construction concession to the French Canal Company. The effort ended in bankruptcy nine years later, and the U.S. ultimately paid the French $40 million for their rights and assets. The U.S. project, built on territory controlled by the United States, began in 1904 and was completed in 1914.

Papua New Guinea

INDEPENDENT STATE OF PAPUA NEW GUINEA

Sovereign: Queen Elizabeth II (1952)
Governor-General: Paulias Matane (2004)
Prime Minister: Sir Michael Somare (2002)
Area: 178,703 sq mi (462,840 sq km)
Population (2005 est.): 5,545,268 (growth rate: 2.3%); birth rate: 29.9/1000; infant mortality rate: 51.5/1000; life expectancy: 64.9; density per sq mi: 31
Capital and largest city (2003 est.): Port Moresby, 324,900. **Monetary unit:** Kina. **Languages:** Tok Pisin (Melanesian Pidgin, the lingua franca), Hiri Motu (in Papua region), English 1–2%; 715 indigenous languages. **Ethnicity/race:** Melanesian, Papuan, Negrito, Micronesian, Polynesian. **Religions:** Roman Catholic 22%, Lutheran 16%, Presbyterian/Methodist/ London Missionary Society 8%, Anglican 5%, Evangelical Alliance 4%, Seventh-Day Adventist 1%, other Protestant 10%, indigenous beliefs 34%.
Literacy rate: 66% (2003 est.)
Economic summary: GDP/PPP (2004 est.): $11.99 billion; per capita $2,200. **Real growth rate:** 0.9%. **Inflation:** 4.2%. **Unemployment:** n.a. **Arable land:** 0.5%. **Agriculture:** coffee, cocoa, coconuts, palm kernels, tea, rubber, sweet potatoes, fruit, vegetables, poultry, pork. **Labor force:** 3.32 million; agriculture 85%, industry n.a., services n.a. **Industries:** copra crushing, palm oil processing, plywood production, wood chip production; mining of gold, silver, and copper; crude oil production; construction, tourism. **Natural resources:** gold, copper, silver, natural gas, timber, oil, fisheries. **Exports:** $2.437 billion (f.o.b., 2004 est.): oil, gold, copper ore, logs, palm oil, coffee, cocoa, crayfish, prawns. **Imports:** $1.353 billion (f.o.b., 2004 est.): machinery and transport equipment, manufactured goods, food, fuels, chemicals. **Major trading partners:** Australia, Japan, China, Singapore, New Zealand (2003). **Member of Commonwealth of Nations**

Geography Papua New Guinea occupies the eastern half of the island of New Guinea, just north of Australia, and many outlying islands. The Indonesian province of West Papua (Irian Jaya) is to the west. To the north and east are the islands of Manus, New Britain, New Ireland, and Bougainville, all part of Papua New Guinea. About one-tenth larger than California, its mountainous interior has only recently been explored. Two major rivers, the Sepik and the Fly, are navigable for shallow-draft vessels.

Government Constitutional monarchy with parliamentary democracy.

History The first inhabitants of the island New Guinea were Papuan, Melanesian, and Negrito tribes, who altogether spoke more than 700 distinct languages. The eastern half of New Guinea was first explored by Spanish and Portuguese explorers in the 16th century. In 1828, the Dutch formally took possession of the western half of the island (now the province of West Papua [Irian Jaya], Indonesia). In 1885, Germany formally annexed the northern coast and Britain took similar action in the south. In 1906, Britain transferred its rights to British New Guinea to a newly independent Australia, and the name of the territory was changed to the Territory of Papua. Australian troops invaded German New Guinea (called Kaiser-Wilhelmsland) in World War I and gained control of the territory under a League of Nations mandate. New Guinea and some of Papua were invaded by Japanese forces in 1942. After being liberated by the Australians in 1945, it became a United Nations trusteeship, administered by Australia. The territories were combined and called the Territory of Papua and New Guinea.

Australia granted limited home rule in 1951. Autonomy in internal affairs came nine years later, and in Sept. 1975, Papua New Guinea achieved complete independence from Britain.

A violent nine-year secessionist movement took place on the island of Bougainville. In 1989, guerrillas of the Bougainville Revolutionary Army (BRA) shut down the island's Australian-owned copper mine, a major source of revenue for the country. The rebels believed that Bougainville deserved a greater share of the earnings for its copper. In 1990, the BRA declared Bougainville's independence, whereupon the government blockaded the island until Jan. 1991, when a peace treaty was signed. In 1997, Papua New Guinea's government hired South African mercenary soldiers to fight on Bougainville in order to end the long-running crisis, but this action led to massive demonstrations and the mercenary contract was rescinded. In April 1998, a cease-fire was declared.

On July 17, 1998, an earthquake-triggered tsunami off the northern coast of Papua New Guinea killed at least 1,500 people and left thousands more injured and homeless.

In Aug. 2004, Australia sent several hundred policemen to train the country's police force to fight the soaring crime rate. But in May 2005, the Australians withdrew after Papua New Guinea's Supreme Court ruled their presence unconstitutional.

Paraguay

REPUBLIC OF PARAGUAY

National name: República del Paraguay
President: Nicanor Duarte Frutos (2003)
Area: 157,046 sq mi (406,750 sq km)
Population (2005 est.): 6,347,884 (growth rate: 2.5%);
birth rate: 29.4/1000; infant mortality rate: 25.6/1000;
life expectancy: 74.9; density per sq mi: 40
Capital and largest city (2003 est.): Asunción,
1,482,200 (metro. area), 525,100. **Other large cities:**
Ciudad del Este, 239,500; San Lorenzo, 210,000.
Monetary unit: Guaraní. **Languages:** Spanish,
Guaraní (both official). **Ethnicity/race:** mestizo 95%.
Religions: Roman Catholic 90%, Mennonite, other
Protestant. **Literacy rate:** 94% (2003 est.)
Economic summary: GDP/PPP (2004 est.): $29.93
billion; per capita $4,800. **Real growth rate:** 2.8%.
Inflation: 5.1%. **Unemployment:** 15.1%. **Arable land:**
8%. **Agriculture:** cotton, sugarcane, soybeans, corn,
wheat, tobacco, cassava (tapioca), fruits, vegetables;
beef, pork, eggs, milk; timber. **Labor force:** 2.66
million; agriculture 45%. **Industries:** sugar, cement,
textiles, beverages, wood products, steel, metallurgy,
electric power. **Natural resources:** hydropower,
timber, iron ore, manganese, limestone. **Exports:**
$2.936 billion (f.o.b., 2004 est.): soybeans, feed,
cotton, meat, edible oils, electricity, wood, leather.
Imports: $3.33 billion (f.o.b., 2004 est.): road vehicles,
consumer goods, tobacco, petroleum products,
electrical machinery. **Major trading partners:** Brazil,
Uruguay, Switzerland, Argentina, China (2003).
International conflicts: unruly region at convergence
of Argentina-Brazil-Paraguay borders is locus of
money laundering, smuggling, arms and drug
trafficking, and harbors Islamist militants.

Geography California-size Paraguay is surrounded
by Brazil, Bolivia, and Argentina in south-central
South America. Eastern Paraguay, between the Paraná
and Paraguay rivers, is upland country with the thick-
est population settled on the grassy slope that inclines
toward the Paraguay River. The greater part of the
Chaco region to the west is covered with marshes,
lagoons, dense forests, and jungles.

Government Constitutional republic.

History Indians speaking Guaraní—the most common language in Paraguay today, after Spanish—were
the country's first inhabitants. In 1526 and again in
1529, Sebastian Cabot explored Paraguay when he
sailed up the Paraná and Paraguay rivers. From 1608
until their expulsion from the Spanish dominions in
1767, the Jesuits maintained an extensive establishment in the south and east of Paraguay. In 1811, Paraguay revolted against Spanish rule and became a
nominal republic under two consuls.

Paraguay was governed by three dictators during the
first 60 years of independence. The third, Francisco
López, waged war against Uruguay, Brazil, and Argentina in 1865–1870, a conflict in which half the male
population was killed. A new constitution in 1870,
designed to prevent dictatorships and internal strife,
failed to do so, and not until 1912 did a period of comparative economic and political stability begin. The
Chaco War (1932–1935) with Bolivia won Paraguay
more western territory.

After World War II, politics became particularly
unstable. Alfredo Stroessner was dictator from 1954
until 1989, during which he was accused of the torture
and murder of thousands of political opponents.
Despite Paraguay's human rights record, the U.S. continuously supported Stroessner.

Stroessner was overthrown by army leader Gen.
Andres Rodriguez in 1989. Rodriguez went on to win
Paraguay's first multicandidate election in decades.
Paraguay's new constitution went into effect in 1992.
In 1993, Juan Carlos Wasmosy, a wealthy business-
man and the candidate of the governing Colorado
Party, won a five-year term in free elections.

Raúl Cubas Grau was elected president in May
1998. In 1999, Cubas was forced from office for his
alleged involvement in the assassination of Vice President Luis María Argaña. The vice president had criticized Cubas for refusing to jail his mentor, Gen. Lino
Oviedo, who had been convicted of leading a failed
1996 coup against Wasmosy.

Luis Ángel González Macchi, who was appointed
caretaker president after Cubas stepped down, undertook a governmental overhaul, and for the first time
since Stroessner was overthrown, political and economic power was no longer entirely within the hands
of the corrupt and military-backed Colorado Party. The
U.S. has accused the Colorado Party of smuggling,
money laundering, trafficking Bolivian cocaine, and
supporting international terrorist organizations.

In Aug. 2000, the opposition Liberal Party won its
first major victory in more than 50 years with the election of Julio Cesar Franco as vice president. He narrowly defeated the son of the previous vice president,
Argaña. Paraguay's government sought to clean up the
political system by bringing to trial political and military figures suspected of human rights violations, corruption, or other crimes.

In 2002, antigovernment rioters demanded that
President González Macchi resign, blaming him for
Paraguay's protracted recession since the late 1990s. In
Dec. 2002, González Macchi was accused of mishan-
dling $16 million in state funds. He was acquitted in an
impeachment trial in Feb. 2003. Former journalist
Nicanor Duarte Frutos became president on August 15,
2003. He has pledged to clean up the pervasive corruption in his nearly bankrupt country.

Peru

REPUBLIC OF PERU

National name: República del Perú
President: Alejandro Toledo (2001)
Prime Minister: Pedro Pablo Kuczynski (2005)
Area: 496,223 sq mi (1,285,220 sq km)
Population (2005 est.): 27,925,628 (growth rate: 1.4%);
birth rate: 20.9/1000; infant mortality rate: 31.9/1000;
life expectancy: 69.5; density per sq mi: 56
Capital and largest city (2003 est.): Lima, 8,113,000
(metro. area). **Other large cities:** Arequipa, 837,300;
Trujillo, 725,200; Chiclayo, 598,400. **Monetary unit:**
Nuevo sol (1991). **Languages:** Spanish, Quéchua
(both official); Aymara; many minor Amazonian
languages. **Ethnicity/race:** Amerindian 45%, mestizo
37%, white 15%, black, Japanese, Chinese, and other
3%. **Religion:** Roman Catholic 90%. **Literacy rate:**
91% (2003 est.)
Economic summary: GDP/PPP (2004 est.): $155.3
billion; per capita $5,600. **Real growth rate:** 4.5%.
Inflation: 3.8%. **Unemployment:** 9.6% in metropolitan
Lima; widespread underemployment. **Arable land:** 3%.
Agriculture: coffee, cotton, sugarcane, rice, potatoes,
corn, plantains, grapes, oranges, coca; poultry, beef,
dairy products; fish. **Labor force:** 11 million; agriculture
9%, industry 18%, services 73% (2001). **Industries:**
mining and refining of minerals and metals, petroleum
extraction and refining, natural gas, fishing and fish
processing, textiles, clothing, food processing, steel,
metal fabrication. **Natural resources:** copper, silver,
gold, petroleum, timber, fish, iron ore, coal, phosphate,

potash, hydropower, natural gas. **Exports:** $12.3 billion (f.o.b., 2004 est.): copper, gold, zinc, crude petroleum and petroleum products, coffee. **Imports:** 9.6 billion (f.o.b., 2004 est.): petroleum and petroleum products, plastics, machinery, vehicles, iron and steel, wheat, paper. **Major trading partners:** U.S., UK, China, Switzerland, Chile, Spain, Brazil, Colombia (2003).

Geography Peru, in western South America, extends for nearly 1,500 mi (2,414 km) along the Pacific Ocean. Colombia and Ecuador are to the north, Brazil and Bolivia to the east, and Chile to the south. Five-sixths the size of Alaska, Peru is divided by the Andes Mountains into three sharply differentiated zones. To the west is the coastline, much of it arid, extending 50 to 100 mi (80 to 160 km) inland. The mountain area, with peaks over 20,000 ft (6,096 m), lofty plateaus, and deep valleys, lies centrally. Beyond the mountains to the east is the heavily forested slope leading to the Amazonian plains.

Government Constitutional republic.

History Peru was once part of the great Incan Empire and later the major vice-royalty of Spanish South America. It was conquered in 1531–1533 by Francisco Pizarro. On July 28, 1821, Peru proclaimed its independence, but the Spanish were not finally defeated until 1824. For a hundred years thereafter, revolutions were frequent; a new war was fought with Spain in 1864–1866, and an unsuccessful war was fought with Chile from 1879 to 1883 (the War of the Pacific).

Peru emerged from 20 years of dictatorship in 1945 with the inauguration of President José Luis Bustamente y Rivero after the first free election in many decades. But he served for only three years and was succeeded in turn by Gen. Manuel A. Odria, Manuel Prado y Ugarteche, and Fernando Belaúnde Terry. On Oct. 3, 1968, Belaúnde was overthrown by Gen. Juan Velasco Alvarado. In 1975, Velasco was replaced in a bloodless coup by his prime minister, Gen. Francisco Morales Bermudez, who promised to restore civilian government. In elections held on May 18, 1980, Belaúnde Terry, the last civilian president, was elected president again. The Maoist guerrilla group Shining Path, or Sendero Luminoso, began their brutal campaign to overthrow the government. The military's subsequent crackdown led to further civilian human rights abuses and disappearances. A smaller rebel group, Tupac Amaru, also fought against the government.

Peru's fragile democracy survived. In 1985, Belaúnde Terry was the first elected president to turn over power to a constitutionally elected successor since 1945. Alberto Fujimori won the 1990 elections. Citing continuing terrorism, drug trafficking, and corruption, Fujimori dissolved Congress, suspended the constitution, and imposed censorship in April 1992. By September, most of Shining Path had been vanquished. A new constitution was approved in 1993.

Fujimori was reelected in 1995, and again in May 2000 to a third five-year term, after his opponent, Alejandro Toledo, withdrew from the contest, charging fraud. In Sept. 2000, Fujimori's intelligence chief, Vladimiro Montesinos, was videotaped bribing a congressman. Fujimori announced he would dismantle the powerful National Intelligence Service, which has been accused of human rights violations. Two months later, he stunned his nation by resigning during a trip to Japan. Revelations that Fujimori secretly held Japanese citizenship—and could not be extradited to face corruption charges—enraged the populace.

In 2001, the centrist Alejandro Toledo was elected president with 53% of the vote, narrowly defeating former president Alan García. His rags-to-riches story

and mixed Indian and Latino heritage made him popular among the poor. Inheriting a country wracked by economic troubles and corruption, Toledo did little, however, to restore confidence in the government. Early in his presidency, he gave himself a significant pay raise while at the same time calling for economic austerity. In June 2002, a popular revolt took place in the cities of Arequipa and Tacna and in other areas of southern Peru after the sale of two state-run electricity firms to a Belgian company, Tractebel. Toledo had specifically promised during his campaign not to sell these firms. Opinion polls have revealed that more than 60% of Peruvians are adamantly opposed to privatization and foreign investment, which in the past has led to price increases, mass layoffs, corruption, and few discernible benefits for the populace. To quell the rioting, Toledo suspended the decision to privatize, apologized publicly, and reshuffled his government.

In Aug. 2003, a truth commission report revealed that 69,000 people were killed during the 1980–2000 wars between rebel groups and the government, about twice the original estimate. The deaths were carried out by the rebels (54%) as well as the military (30%); other militias were responsible for the remainder.

Since Toledo took office in 2001, the economy has grown annually by about 4%, but this growth, centered on mining and the gas industry, has not yet created new jobs. A series of scandals and political missteps have made Toledo Latin America's least popular leader. According to a variety of polls taken between 2003 and 2005, his approval rating has ranged from 8%–14%.

The Philippines

REPUBLIC OF THE PHILIPPINES

National name: Republika ng Pilipinas
President: Gloria Macapagal Arroyo (2001)
Area: 115,830 sq mi (300,000 sq km)
Population (2005 est.): 87,857,473 (growth rate: 1.8%); birth rate: 25.3/1000; infant mortality rate: 23.5/1000; life expectancy: 69.9; density per sq mi: 759
Capital and largest city (2003 est.): Manila, 13,790,900 (metro. area), 10,232,900 (city proper). **Other large cities:** Quezon City (2000 est.), 1,669,776 (part of Manila metro. area); Cebu (2003 est.), 761,900.
Monetary unit: Peso. **Languages:** Filipino (based on Tagalog), English (both official); eight major dialects: Tagalog, Cebuano, Ilocano, Hiligaynon or Ilonggo, Bicol, Waray, Pampango, and Pangasinense.
Ethnicity/race: Christian Malay 91.5%, Muslim Malay 4%, Chinese 1.5%, other 3%. **Religions:** Roman Catholic 83%, Protestant 9%, Islam 5%, Buddhist and other 3%. **Literacy rate:** 96% (2003 est.)
Economic summary: GDP/PPP (2004 est.): $430.6 billion; per capita $5,000. **Real growth rate:** 5.9%. **Inflation:** 5.5%. **Unemployment:** 11.7%. **Arable land:** 19%. **Agriculture:** sugarcane, coconuts, rice, corn, bananas, cassavas, pineapples, fish, mangoes, pork, eggs, beef. **Labor force:** 35.86 million; agriculture 36%, industry 16%, services 48% (2004 est.). **Industries:** electronics assembly, garments, footwear, pharmaceuticals, chemicals, wood products, food processing, petroleum refining, fishing. **Natural resources:** timber, petroleum, nickel, cobalt, silver, gold, salt, copper. **Exports:** $38.63 billion (f.o.b., 2004 est.): electronic equipment, machinery and transport equipment, garments, optical instruments, coconut products, fruits and nuts, copper products, chemicals. **Imports:** 37.5 billion (f.o.b., 2004 est.): raw materials, machinery and equipment, fuels, vehicles and vehicle parts, plastic, chemicals, grains. **Major trading partners:** U.S., Japan, Hong Kong, Netherlands, Taiwan, Malaysia, Singapore, China, South Korea (2003).

Geography The Philippine Islands are an archipelago of over 7,000 islands lying about 500 mi (805 km) off the southeast coast of Asia. The overall land area is comparable to that of Arizona. Only about 7% of the islands are larger than one square mile, and only one-third have names. The largest are Luzon in the north (40,420 sq mi; 104,687 sq km), Mindanao in the south (36,537 sq mi; 94,631 sq km), and Samar (5,124 sq mi; 13,271 sq km). The islands are of volcanic origin, with the larger ones crossed by mountain ranges. The highest peak is Mount Apo (9,690 ft; 2,954 m) on Mindanao.

Government Republic.

History Ferdinand Magellan, the Portuguese navigator in the service of Spain, explored the Philippines in 1521. Twenty-one years later, a Spanish exploration party named the group of islands in honor of Prince Philip, who was later to become Philip II of Spain. Spain retained possession of the islands for the next 350 years.

The Philippines were ceded to the U.S. in 1899 by the Treaty of Paris after the Spanish-American War. Meanwhile, the Filipinos, led by Emilio Aguinaldo, had declared their independence. They initiated guerrilla warfare against U.S. troops that persisted until the capture of Aguinaldo in 1901. By 1902, peace was established except among the Islamic Moros on the southern island of Mindanao.

The first U.S. civilian governor-general was William Howard Taft (1901–1904). The Jones Law (1916) provided for the establishment of a Philippine legislature composed of an elective Senate and House of Representatives. The Tydings-McDuffie Act (1934) provided for a transitional period until 1946, at which time the Philippines would become completely independent. Under a constitution approved by the people of the Philippines in 1935, the Commonwealth of the Philippines came into being with Manuel Quezon y Molina as president.

On Dec. 8, 1941, the islands were invaded by Japanese troops. Following the fall of Gen. Douglas MacArthur's forces at Bataan and Corregidor, Quezon established a government-in-exile that he headed until his death in 1944. He was succeeded by Vice President Sergio Osmeña. U.S. forces under MacArthur reinvaded the Philippines in Oct. 1944 and, after the liberation of Manila in Feb. 1945, Osmeña reestablished the government.

The Philippines achieved full independence on July 4, 1946. Manuel A. Roxas y Acuña was elected its first president, succeeded by Elpidio Quirino (1948–1953), Ramón Magsaysay (1953–1957), Carlos P. García (1957–1961), Diosdado Macapagal (1961–1965), and Ferdinand E. Marcos (1965–1986).

Under Marcos, civil unrest broke out in opposition to the leader's despotic rule. Martial law was declared on Sept. 21, 1972, and Marcos proclaimed a new constitution that ensconced himself as president. Martial law was officially lifted on Jan. 17, 1981, but Marcos and his wife, Imelda, retained broad powers.

In an attempt to rescure American support, Marcos set presidential elections for Feb. 7, 1986. With the support of the Catholic Church, Corazon Aquino declared her candidacy. Marcos was declared the official winner, but independent observers reported widespread election fraud and vote rigging. Anti-Marcos protests exploded in Manila, Defense Minister Juan Enrile and Lt. Gen. Fidel Ramos defected to the opposition, and Marcos lost virtually all support; he was forced to flee into exile and entered the U.S. on Feb. 25, 1986.

The Aquino government survived coup attempts by Marcos supporters and other right-wing elements, including one in November by Enrile. Legislative elections on May 11, 1987, gave pro-Aquino candidates a large majority. Negotiations on renewal of leases for U.S. military bases threatened to sour relations between the two countries. Volcanic eruptions from Mount Pinatubo, however, severely damaged Clark Air Base, and in July 1991, the U.S. decided simply to abandon it.

In elections in May 1992, Gen. Fidel Ramos, who had the support of the outgoing Aquino, won the presidency in a seven-way race. In Sept. 1992, the U.S. Navy turned over the Subic Bay naval base to the Philippines, ending its long-standing U.S. military presence.

Meanwhile, the separatist Moro National Liberation Front was fighting a protracted war for an Islamic homeland on Mindanao, the southernmost of the two main islands. The Philippine army also battled another rebel group, the Moro Islamic Liberation Front. In Aug. 2001, both rebel groups signed unity agreements with the Philippine government. Frequent and violent clashes with these and other terrorist groups have continued, however. Abu Sayyaf, a small group of guerrillas that has been fighting since the 1970s for an independent Islamic state and reportedly has links to Osama bin Laden, gained international notoriety throughout 2000 and 2001 with its spree of kidnappings and murders. The Philippine military has also battled the New People's Army, a group of Communist guerrillas that have targeted Philippine security forces since 1969. International officials reported in June 2003 that Jemaah Islamiyah, an affiliate of al-Qaeda, was training recruits in Mindanao, in the southern Philippines. About 120,000 people have died in the conflicts with rebel groups, and more than 3 million have been displaced.

In May 1998, 61-year-old former action film star Joseph Estrada was elected president of the Philippines. Within two years, however, the Philippine Senate began to impeach Estrada on corruption charges. Massive street demonstrations and the loss of political support eventually forced Estrada from office. Vice President Gloria Macapagal Arroyo, daughter of former president Diosdado Macapagal, became president in Jan. 2001.

In July 2003, dozens of mutinous soldiers took over a Manila shopping complex, protesting low pay and demanding the resignation of President Arroyo and the defense secretary. The demonstration ended peacefully.

In May 2004 elections, President Arroyo narrowly defeated film star Fernando Poe. Poe alleged voter fraud and warned of a revolt by his supporters.

Police killed three top members of Abu Sayyaf while quelling a March 2005 prison uprising in Manila. In all, 22 people, including 20 prisoners and two guards, died in the violence.

President Gloria Macapagal Arroyo faced a political crisis in the summer of 2005, after admitting to calling an election official during 2004's presidential race. A taped phone conversation between Arroyo and the official seemed to suggest that she had tried to use her power to influence the outcome. Several members of her cabinet quit and joined the opposition and tens of thousands of protesters in calling for her resignation. In a televised address, Arroyo apologized for the "lapse of judgement" and said, "my intent was not to influence the outcome of the election and it did not." The opposition filed an impeachment motion in July. In addition, Arroyo's husband, who had been accused of taking bribes from a gambling syndicate, said in July that he was moving abroad indefinitely.

In her state of the nation address in July, Arroyo proposed replacing the country's presidential system of government with a parliamentary one.

Poland

REPUBLIC OF POLAND

National name: Rzeczpospolita Polska
President: Aleksander Kwasniewski (1995)
Prime Minister: Marek Belka (2004)
Area: 120,728 sq mi (312,685 sq km)
Population (2005 est.): 38,635,144 (growth rate: 0%); birth rate: 10.8/1000; infant mortality rate: 8.5/1000; life expectancy: 74.4; density per sq mi: 320
Capital and largest city (2003 est.): Warsaw, 2,201,900 (metro. area), 1,607,600 (city proper). **Other large cities:** Lodz, 778,200; Krakow, 733,100; Wroclaw, 632,200; Poznan, 581,200; Gdansk, 456,700; Szczecin, 415,700. **Monetary unit:** Zloty. **Language:** Polish. **Ethnicity/race:** Polish 96.7%, German 0.4%, Belorussian 0.1% Ukrainian 0.1%, other 2.7% (2002). **Religions:** Roman Catholic 95% (about 75% practicing), Eastern Orthodox, Protestant, and other 5%. **Literacy rate:** 100% (2003 est.)
Economic summary: GDP/PPP (2004 est.): $463 billion; per capita $12,000. **Real growth rate:** 5.6%. **Inflation:** 3.4%. **Unemployment:** 19.5%. **Arable land:** 46%. **Agriculture:** potatoes, fruits, vegetables, wheat; poultry, eggs, pork. **Labor force:** 17.02 million; agriculture 16.1%, industry 29%, services 54.9% (2002). **Industries:** machine building, iron and steel, coal mining, chemicals, shipbuilding, food processing, glass, beverages, textiles. **Natural resources:** coal, sulfur, copper, natural gas, silver, lead, salt, amber, arable land. **Exports:** $75.98 billion (f.o.b., 2004 est.): machinery and transport equipment 37.8%, intermediate manufactured goods 23.7%, miscellaneous manufactured goods 17.1%, food and live animals 7.6% (2003). **Imports:** $81.61 billion (f.o.b., 2004 est.): machinery and transport equipment 38%, intermediate manufactured goods 21%, chemicals 14.8%, minerals, fuels, lubricants, and related materials 9.1% (2003). **Major trading partners:** Germany, France, Italy, UK, Netherlands, Czech Republic, Russia, China (2003).

Geography Poland, a country the size of New Mexico, is in north-central Europe. Most of the country is a plain with no natural boundaries except the Carpathian Mountains in the south and the Oder and Neisse rivers in the west. Other major rivers, which are important to commerce, are the Vistula, Warta, and Bug.

Government Democratic republic.

History Great (north) Poland was founded in 966 by Mieszko I, who belonged to the Piast dynasty. The tribes of southern Poland then formed Little Poland. In 1047, both Great Poland and Little Poland united under the rule of Casimir I the Restorer. Poland merged with Lithuania by royal marriage in 1386. The Polish-Lithuanian state reached the peak of its power between the 14th and 16th century, scoring military successes against the (Germanic) Knights of the Teutonic Order, the Russians, and the Ottoman Turks.

Lack of a strong monarchy enabled Russia, Prussia, and Austria to carry out a first partition of the country in 1772, a second in 1792, and a third in 1795. For more than a century thereafter, there was no Polish state, just Austrian, Prussian, and Russian sectors, but the Poles never ceased their efforts to regain their inde-

pendence. The Polish people revolted against foreign dominance throughout the 19th century. Poland was formally reconstituted in Nov. 1918, with Marshal Josef Pilsudski as chief of state. In 1919, Ignace Paderewski, the famous pianist and patriot, became the first prime minister. In 1926, Pilsudski seized complete power in a coup and ruled dictatorially until his death on May 12, 1935.

Despite a ten-year nonaggression pact signed in 1934, Hitler attacked Poland on Sept. 1, 1939. Soviet troops invaded from the east on Sept. 17, and on Sept. 28, a German-Soviet agreement divided Poland between the USSR and Germany. Wladyslaw Raczkiewicz formed a government-in-exile in France, which moved to London after France's defeat in 1940. All of Poland was occupied by Germany after the Nazi attack on the USSR in June 1941. Nazi Germany's occupation policy in Poland was designed to eradicate Polish culture through mass executions and to exterminate the country's large Jewish minority.

The Polish government-in-exile was replaced with the Communist-dominated Polish Committee of National Liberation by the Soviet Union in 1944. Moving to Lublin after that city's liberation, it proclaimed itself the Provisional Government of Poland. Some former members of the Polish government in London joined with the Lublin government to form the Polish Government of National Unity, which Britain and the U.S. recognized. On Aug. 2, 1945, in Berlin, President Harry S. Truman, Joseph Stalin, and Prime Minister Clement Attlee of Britain established a new de facto western frontier for Poland along the Oder and Neisse rivers. (The border was finally agreed to by West Germany in a nonaggression pact signed on Dec. 7, 1970.) On Aug. 16, 1945, the USSR and Poland signed a treaty delimiting the Soviet-Polish frontier. Under these agreements, Poland was shifted westward. In the east, it lost 69,860 sq mi (180,934 sq km); in the west, it gained (subject to final peace-conference approval) 38,986 sq mi (100,973 sq km).

A new constitution in 1952 made Poland a "people's democracy" of the Soviet type. In 1955, Poland became a member of the Warsaw Treaty Organization, and its foreign policy became identical to that of the USSR. The government undertook persecution of the Roman Catholic Church as a remaining source of opposition. Wladyslaw Gomulka was elected leader of the United Workers (Communist) Party in 1956. He denounced the Stalinist terror, ousted many Stalinists, and improved relations with the church. Most collective farms were dissolved, and the press became freer. A strike that began in shipyards and spread to other industries in Aug. 1980 produced a stunning victory for workers when the economically hard-pressed government accepted for the first time in a Marxist state the right of workers to organize in independent unions.

Led by Solidarity, an independent union founded by an electrician, Lech Walesa, workers launched a drive for liberty and improved conditions. A national strike for a five-day workweek in Jan. 1981 led to the dismissal of Prime Minister Pinkowski and the naming of the fourth prime minister in less than a year, Gen. Wojciech Jaruzelski. Martial law was declared on Dec. 13, when Walesa and other Solidarity leaders were arrested. It formally ended in 1984 but the government retained emergency powers. Increasing opposition to the government because of the failing economy led to a new wave of strikes in 1988. Unable to quell the dissent entirely, the government relegalized Solidarity and allowed it to compete in elections.

Solidarity members won a stunning victory in 1989, taking almost all the seats in the Senate and all of the 169 seats they were allowed to contest in the Sejm. This gave them substantial influence in the new government. Tadeusz Mazowiecki was appointed prime minister. Lech Walesa won the presidential election of 1990 with 74% of the vote. In 1991, the first fully free parliamentary election since World War II resulted in representation for 29 political parties. Efforts to turn Poland into a market economy, however, led to economic difficulties and widespread discontent. In the second democratic parliamentary election of Sept. 1993, voters returned power to ex-Communists and their allies. Solidarity's popularity and influence continued to wane. In 1995, Aleksander Kwasniewski, leader of the successor to the Communist Party, the Democratic Left, won the presidency over Walesa in a landslide.

In 1999, Poland became part of NATO, along with the Czech Republic and Hungary.

In Sept. 2001 parliamentary elections, former Communists, reconstituted as the center-left Democratic Left Alliance, won 41% of the vote. The election seemed to mark the demise of Solidarity, which did not win a single seat.

Poland was a staunch supporter of the United States and Britain during the Iraq war and sent 200 troops to Iraq (60 were combat soldiers). In Sept. 2003, Poland became the leader of a 9,000-strong multinational stabilizing force in Iraq. It contributed 2,000 of its own soldiers. In April 2005, Poland announced it would withdraw all troops from Iraq at the end of the year.

On May 1, 2004, Poland joined the EU. Prime Minister Leszek Miller resigned on May 2, 2004. His popularity had plummeted to 10% because of the country's continued economic troubles and a number of corruption scandals. Former finance minister Marek Belka succeeded him.

Portugal

PORTUGUESE REPUBLIC

National name: República Portuguesa
President: Jorge Sampaio (1996)
Prime Minister: José Sócrates (2005)
Area: 35,672 sq mi (92,391 sq km)
Population (2005 est.): 10,566,212 (growth rate: 0.4%); birth rate: 10.8/1000; infant mortality rate: 5.0/1000; life expectancy: 77.5; density per sq mi: 296
Capital and largest city (2003 est.): Lisbon, 2,618,100 (metro. area), 559,400. **Other large city:** Oporto, 264,200. **Monetary unit:** Euro (formerly escudo). **Languages:** Portuguese (official), Mirandese (official, but locally used). **Ethnicity/race:** homogeneous Mediterranean stock; less than 100,000 citizens of black African descent who immigrated to mainland during decolonization; East Europeans have entered since 1990. **Religions:** Roman Catholic 94%, Protestant 6%. **Literacy rate:** 93% (2003 est.).
Economic summary: GDP/PPP (2004 est.): $188.7 billion; per capita $17,900. **Real growth rate:** 1.1%. **Inflation:** 2.1%. **Unemployment:** 6.5%. **Arable land:** 22%. **Agriculture:** grain, potatoes, olives, grapes; sheep, cattle, goats, poultry, beef, dairy products. **Labor force:** 5.48 million; services 60%, industry 30%, agriculture 10% (1999 est.). **Industries:** textiles and footwear; wood pulp, paper, and cork; metals and metalworking; oil refining; chemicals; fish canning; rubber and plastic products; ceramics; electronics and communications equipment; rail transportation equipment; aerospace equipment; ship construction and refurbishment; wine; tourism. **Natural resources:** fish, forests (cork), tungsten, iron ore, uranium ore,

marble, arable land, hydropower. **Exports:** $37.68 billion (f.o.b., 2004 est.): clothing and footwear, machinery, chemicals, cork and paper products, hides. **Imports:** $52.1 billion (f.o.b., 2004 est.): machinery and transport equipment, chemicals, petroleum, textiles, agricultural products. **Major trading partners:** Spain, Germany, France, UK, U.S., Italy, Belgium, Netherlands (2003). **International disputes:** Portugal has periodically reasserted claims to territories around the town of Olivenza, Spain.

Geography Portugal occupies the western part of the Iberian Peninsula and is slightly smaller than Indiana. The country is crossed by three large rivers that rise in Spain, flow into the Atlantic and divide the country into three geographic areas. The Minho River, part of the northern boundary, cuts through a mountainous area that extends south to the vicinity of the Douro River. South of the Douro, the mountains slope to the plains around the Tejo River. The remaining division is the southern one of Alentejo. The Azores stretch over 340 mi (547 km) in the Atlantic and consist of nine islands with a total area of 902 square mi (2,335 sq km). Madeira, consisting of two inhabited islands, Madeira and Porto Santo, and two groups of uninhabited islands, lie in the Atlantic about 535 mi (861 km) southwest of Lisbon.

Government Parliamentary democracy.

History An early Celtic tribe, the Lusitanians, are believed to have been the first inhabitants of Portugal. The Roman Empire conquered the region in about 140 B.C. Toward the end of the Roman Empire, the Visigoths had invaded the entire Iberian Peninsula.

Portugal won its independence from Moorish Spain in 1143. King John I (1385–1433) unified his country at the expense of the Castilians and the Moors of Morocco. The expansion of Portugal was brilliantly coordinated by John's son, Prince Henry the Navigator. In 1488, Bartolomeu Dias reached the Cape of Good Hope, proving that Asia was accessible by sea. In 1498, Vasco da Gama reached the west coast of India. By the middle of the 16th century, the Portuguese Empire extended to West and East Africa, Brazil, Persia, Indochina, and the Malayan peninsula.

In 1581, Philip II of Spain invaded Portugal and held it for 60 years, precipitating a catastrophic decline in Portuguese commerce. Courageous and shrewd explorers, the Portuguese proved to be inefficient and corrupt colonizers. By the time the Portuguese monarchy was restored in 1640, Dutch, English, and French competitors had begun to seize the lion's share of the world's colonies and commerce. Portugal retained Angola and Mozambique in Africa, and Brazil (until 1822).

The corrupt King Carlos, who ascended the throne in 1889, made João Franco the prime minister with dictatorial power in 1906. In 1908, Carlos and his heir were shot dead on the streets of Lisbon. The new king, Manoel II, was driven from the throne in the revolution of 1910, and Portugal became a French-style republic. Traditionally friendly to Britain, Portugal fought in World War I on the Allied side in Africa as well as on the Western Front. Weak postwar governments and a revolution in 1926 brought Antonio de Oliveira Salazar to power. As minister of finance (1928–1940) and prime minister (1932–1968), Salazar ruled Portugal as a virtual dictator. He kept Portugal neutral in World War II but gave the Allies naval and air bases after 1943. Portugal joined NATO as a founding member in 1949 but did not gain admission to the United Nations until 1955.

Portugal's foreign and colonial policies met with increasing difficulty both at home and abroad beginning in the 1950s. In fact, the bloodiest and most protracted wars against colonialism in Africa were fought against the Portuguese. Portugal lost the tiny remnants of its Indian empire—Goa, Daman, and Diu—to Indian military occupation in 1961, the year an insurrection broke out in Angola. For the next 13 years, Salazar, who died in 1970, and his successor, Marcello Caetano, fought independence movements amid growing world criticism. Leftists in the armed forces, weary of a losing battle, launched a successful revolution on April 25, 1974. After the 1974 revolution, the new military junta gave up its territories, beginning with Portuguese Guinea in Sept. 1974, which became the Republic of Guinea-Bissau. The decolonization of the Cape Verde Islands and Mozambique was effected in July 1975. Angola achieved independence later that same year, thus ending a colonial involvement in that continent that had begun in 1415. Full-scale international civil war, however, followed Portugal's departure from Angola, and Indonesia forcibly annexed independent East Timor. Also in 1975, the government nationalized banking, transportation, heavy industries, and the media. Portugal continued to experience social, economic, and political upheavals for the next decade.

Portugal was admitted to the European Economic Community (now European Union) on Jan. 1, 1986, and on Feb. 16, Mario Soares became the country's first civilian president in 60 years. Aníbal Cavaço Silva, an advocate of free-market economics and the Social Democratic candidate, had been elected as prime minister in 1985, signaling a more politically stable era. General elections in Oct. 1995 went to the Socialist Party, which fell just short of an absolute majority in the assembly. Lisbon mayor Jorge Sampaio, a Socialist, won the race for president in Jan. 1996. Portugal's Socialist government continued to take advantage of rosy economic conditions in 1997, and in 1999, Portugal became a founding member of the European Economic and Monetary Union (EMU).

Portugal gave up its last colony, Macao, on Dec. 20, 1999, turning the small Asian seaport over to China.

In 2002, center-right Social Democrat leader José Manuel Durão Barroso became prime minister, after the Socialist Party suffered defeats. In the summer of 2003, more than a thousand people died during an unprecedented heat wave that caused fires to ravage Portugal's forests. Prime Minister Barroso resigned in July 2004 to become president of the European Commission. Pedro Santana Lopes, the new leader of the Social Democrats, succeeded him as prime minister. In Feb. 2005 elections, the Socialist Party won 45% of the vote, and José Sócrates became prime minister.

Qatar

STATE OF QATAR

National name: Dawlat Qatar
Emir: Sheik Hamad bin Khalifa al-Thani (1995)
Prime Minister: Abdullah bin Khalifa al-Thani (1996)
Area: 4,416 sq mi (11,437 sq km)
Population (2005 est.): 863,051 (growth rate: 2.6%);
  birth rate: 15.5/1000; infant mortality rate: 18.6/1000;
  life expectancy: 73.7; density per sq mi: 195
Capital (2003 est.): Doha, 550,700 (metro. area),
  318,500 (city proper). **Monetary unit:** Qatari riyal.
Languages: Arabic (official); English a common
  second language. **Ethnicity/race:** Arab 40%, Pakistani
  18%, Indian 18%, Iranian 10%, other 14%. **Religion:**
  Islam 95%. **Literacy rate:** 83% (2003 est.)
Economic summary: GDP/PPP (2004 est.): $19.49

billion; per capita $23,200. **Real growth rate:** 8.7%.
Inflation: 3%. **Unemployment:** 2.7% (2001). **Arable
land:** 2%. **Agriculture:** fruits, vegetables; poultry, dairy
products, beef; fish. **Labor force:** 140,000. **Industries:**
crude oil production and refining, ammonia, fertilizers,
petrochemicals, steel reinforcing bars, cement,
commercial ship repair. **Natural resources:** petroleum,
natural gas, fish. **Exports:** $15 billion (f.o.b., 2004 est.):
liquefied natural gas (LNG), petroleum products,
fertilizers, steel. **Imports:** $6.15 billion (f.o.b., 2004
est.): machinery and transport equipment, food,
chemicals. **Major trading partners:** Japan, South
Korea, Singapore, U.S., Germany, UK, Italy, UAE,
Saudi Arabia (2003).

Geography Qatar (pronounced KAH-ter) occupies a small peninsula that extends into the Persian Gulf from the east side of the Arabian Peninsula. Saudi Arabia is to the west and the United Arab Emirates to the south. The country is mainly barren.

Government Constitutional monarchy.

History Qatar was once controlled by the sheikhs of Bahrain, but in 1867, war broke out between the people and their absentee rulers. To keep the peace in the Gulf, the British installed Muhammad ibn Thani al-Thani, head of a leading Qatari family, as the region's ruler. In 1893, the Ottoman Turks made incursions into Qatar, but the emir successfully deflected them. In 1916, the emir agreed to allow Qatar to become a British protectorate.

Oil was discovered in the 1940s, bringing wealth to the country in the 1950s and 1960s. About 85% of Qatar's income from exports comes from oil. Its people have one of the highest per capita incomes in the world. In 1971, Qatar was to join the other emirates of the Trucial Coast to become part of the United Arab Emirates. But both Qatar and Bahrain decided against the merger and instead formed independent nations.

Qatar permitted the international forces to use Qatar as a base during the 1991 Persian Gulf War. A border dispute erupted with Saudi Arabia that was settled in Dec. 1992. A territorial dispute with Bahrain over the Hawar Islands remains unresolved, however. In 1994, Qatar signed a defense pact with the U.S., becoming the third Gulf state to do so.

In June 1995, Crown Prince Hamad bin Khalifa al-Thani deposed his father, primarily because the king was out of step with the country's economic reforms. The emir was not stripped of his title, and much of the power was already in his son's hands. The new emir lifted press censorship and instituted other liberal reforms, including democratic elections and women's suffrage (1999). In 2003 Crown Prince Jassim, who declared he had never wanted to be king, abdicated in favor of his younger brother, Prince Tamim.

Qatar is the home of Al Jazeera, the immensely popular and controversial Arabic satellite television network.

Qatar introduced its first constitution on June 9, 2005. It guarantees freedom of expression, assembly, and religion, and calls for a 45-seat Parliament. Thirty of the seats will be filled in democratic elections; the emir will appoint the remaining seats.

Romania

President: Traian Basescu (2004)
Prime Minister: Calin Popescu-Tariceanu (2004)
Area: 91,699 sq mi (237,500 sq km)
Population (2005 est.): 22,329,977 (growth rate: –0.1%);
  birth rate: 10.7/1000; infant mortality rate: 26.4/1000;
  life expectancy: 71.3; density per sq mi: 244
Capital and largest city (2003 est.): Bucharest,

2,210,800 (metro. area), 1,906,800 (city proper).
Other large cities: Iasi, 320,000; Cluj-Napoca, 316,400; Timisoara, 316,100; Constanta, 309,000; Craiova, 301,100, Galati, 297,100; Brasov, 282,500.
Monetary unit: Leu. **Languages:** Romanian (official), Hungarian, German. **Ethnicity/race:** Romanian 89.5%, Hungarian 6.6%, Roma (Gyspy) 2.5%, Ukrainian 0.3%, German 0.3%, Russian 0.2%, Turkish 0.2%, other 0.4% (2002). **Religions:** Romanian Orthodox 87%, Protestant 6.8%, Roman Catholic 5.6%, other (mostly Islam) 0.4%, unaffiliated 0.2% (2002). **Literacy rate:** 98% (2003 est.)
Economic summary: GDP/PPP (2004 est.): $171.5 billion; per capita $7,700. **Real growth rate:** 8.1%. **Inflation:** 9.6%. **Unemployment:** 6.3%. **Arable land:** 41%. **Agriculture:** wheat, corn, barley, sugar beets, sunflower seed, potatoes, grapes; eggs, sheep. **Labor force:** 9.66 million; agriculture 31.6%, industry 30.7%, services 37.7% (2004). **Industries:** textiles and footwear, light machinery and auto assembly, mining, timber, construction materials, metallurgy, chemicals, food processing, petroleum refining. **Natural resources:** petroleum (reserves declining), timber, natural gas, coal, iron ore, salt, arable land, hydropower. **Exports:** $23.54 billion (f.o.b., 2004 est.): textiles and footwear, metals and metal products, machinery and equipment, minerals and fuels, chemicals, agricultural products. **Imports:** $28.43 billion (f.o.b., 2004 est.): machinery and equipment, fuels and minerals, chemicals, textile and products, basic metals, agricultural products. **Major trading partners:** Italy, Germany, France, UK, Turkey, Russia (2003).

Geography Romania is in southeast Europe and is slightly smaller than Oregon. The Carpathian Mountains divide Romania's upper half from north to south and connect near the center of the country with the Transylvanian Alps, running east and west. North and west of these ranges lies the Transylvanian plateau, and to the south and east are the plains of Moldavia and Walachia. In its last 190 mi (306 km), the Danube River flows through Romania only. It enters the Black Sea in northern Dobruja, just south of the border with Ukraine.

Government Republic.

History Most of Romania was the Roman province of Dacia from about A.D. 100 to 271. From the 3rd to the 12th century, wave after wave of barbarian conquerors overran the native Daco-Roman population. Subjection to the first Bulgarian empire (8th–10th century) brought Eastern Orthodox Christianity to the Romanians. In the 11th century, Transylvania was absorbed into the Hungarian Empire. By the 16th century, the main Romanian principalities of Moldavia and Walachia had become satellites within the Ottoman Empire, although they retained much independence. After the Russo-Turkish War of 1828–1829, they became Russian protectorates. The nation became a kingdom in 1881 after the Congress of Berlin.

At the start of World War I, Romania proclaimed its neutrality, but it later joined the Allied side and in 1916 declared war on the Central Powers. The armistice of Nov. 11, 1918, gave Romania vast territories from Russia and the Austro-Hungarian Empire, doubling its size. The areas acquired included Bessarabia, Transylvania, and Bukovina. The Banat, a Hungarian area, was divided with Yugoslavia. King Carol II was crowned in 1930 and transformed the throne into a royal dictatorship. In 1938, he abolished the democratic constitution of 1923. In 1940, the country was reorganized along Fascist lines, and the Fascist Iron Guard became the

nucleus of the new totalitarian party. On June 27, the Soviet Union occupied Bessarabia and northern Bukovina. King Carol II dissolved Parliament, granted the new prime minister, Ion Antonescu, full power, abdicated his throne, and went into exile.

Romania subsequently signed the Axis Pact on Nov. 23, 1940, and the following June joined in Germany's attack on the Soviet Union, reoccupying Bessarabia. About 270,000 Jews were massacred in Fascist Romania. Following the invasion of Romania by the Red Army in Aug. 1944, King Michael led a coup that ousted the Antonescu government. An armistice with the Soviet Union was signed in Moscow on Sept. 12, 1944. A Communist-dominated government bloc won elections in 1946, Michael abdicated on Dec. 30, 1947, and in 1955 Romania joined the Warsaw Treaty Organization and the United Nations.

Running a neo-Stalinist police state from 1967–1989, Nicolae Ceausescu wound the iron curtain tightly around Romania, turning a moderately prosperous country into one at the brink of starvation. To repay his $10 billion foreign debt in 1982, he ransacked the Romanian economy of everything that could be exported, leaving the country with desperate shortages of food, fuel, and other essentials. An army-assisted rebellion in Dec. 1989 led to Ceausescu's overthrow, trial, and execution.

An ex-Communist, Ion Iliescu of the National Salvation Front, served as president from 1990–1995. Emil Constantinescu of the Democratic Convention Party served as president from 1996–2000. The post-Communist governments' conflicted and halfhearted attempts to change to a free-market economy have been largely unrealized. In 2000 former president Iliescu returned to power with a landslide victory, easily defeating a xenophobic nationalist opponent. Discrimination against the Magyars (ethnic Hungarians) and the Roma (Gypsies) continues, fueled by several ultranationalist political parties.

The country applied for membership in the EU in June 1995. Economic reform has proceeded at a glacial pace, and growing dissatisfaction with the government's inefficiencies and economic policies led to a wave of protests by workers, students, and others that peaked in 1997, and again in 1999, when coal miners striked.

Romania joined NATO in 2004, and in 2005 the EU approved the entry of Romania in 2007. Final acceptance into the EU will require a number of reforms, including increased law enforcement and environmental measures, and the protection of the rights of the Roma (Gypsy) minority.

Russia

RUSSIAN FEDERATION

National name: Rossiyskaya Federatsiya
President: Vladimir Putin (2000)
Prime Minister: Mikhail Fradkov (2004)
Area: 6,592,735 sq mi (17,075,200 sq km)
Population (2005 est.): 143,420,309 (growth rate: –0.4%); birth rate: 9.8/1000; infant mortality rate: 15.4/1000; life expectancy: 67.1; density per sq mi: 22
Capital and largest city (2003 est.): Moscow, 11,970,500 (metro. area), 8,368,200 (city proper).
Other large cities: St. Petersburg, 4,582,300; Novosibirsk, 1,395,500; Nizhny Novgorod, 1,340,900; Yekaterinburg, 1,256,600; Samara, 1,146,800; Kazan, 1,113,600; Ufa, 1,096,600; Chelyabinsk, 1,080,000; Perm, 998,800; Volgograd, 984,200. **Monetary unit:** Ruble. **Languages:** Russian, others. **Ethnicity/race:** Russian 81.5%, Tatar 3.8%, Ukrainian 3%, Chuvash 1.2%, Bashkir 0.9%, Byelorussian 0.8%, Moldavian

0.7%, other 8.1% (1989). **Religions:** Russian Orthodox, Islam, others. **Literacy rate:** 100% (2003 est.)

Economic summary: GDP/PPP (2004 est.): $1.408 trillion; per capita $9,800. **Real growth rate:** 6.7%. **Inflation:** 11.5%. **Unemployment:** 8.3%, plus considerable underemployment. **Arable land:** 7%. **Agriculture:** grain, sugar beets, sunflower seed, vegetables, fruits; beef, milk. **Labor force:** 71.83 million; agriculture 12.3%, industry 22.7%, services 65% (2002 est.). **Industries:** complete range of mining and extractive industries producing coal, oil, gas, chemicals, and metals; all forms of machine building from rolling mills to high-performance aircraft and space vehicles; defense industries including radar, missile production, and advanced electronic components, shipbuilding; road and rail transportation equipment; communications equipment; agricultural machinery, tractors, and construction equipment; electric power generating and transmitting equipment; medical and scientific instruments; consumer durables, textiles, foodstuffs, handicrafts. **Natural resources:** wide natural resource base including major deposits of oil, natural gas, coal, and many strategic minerals, timber; note: formidable obstacles of climate, terrain, and distance hinder exploitation of natural resources. **Exports:** $162.5 billion (2004 est.): petroleum and petroleum products, natural gas, wood and wood products, metals, chemicals, and a wide variety of civilian and military manufactures. **Imports:** $92.91 billion (2004 est.): machinery and equipment, consumer goods, medicines, meat, sugar, semifinished metal products. **Major trading partners:** Germany, Netherlands, Italy, China, Belarus, Ukraine, U.S., Switzerland, Kazakhstan, France (2003).

Geography The Russian Federation is the largest of the 21 republics that made up the Commonwealth of Independent States. It occupies most of eastern Europe and north Asia, stretching from the Baltic Sea in the west to the Pacific Ocean in the east, and from the Arctic Ocean in the north to the Black Sea and the Caucasus in the south. It is bordered by Norway and Finland in the northwest; Estonia, Latvia, Belarus, Ukraine, Poland, and Lithuania in the west; Georgia and Azerbaijan in the southwest; and Kazakhstan, Mongolia, China, and North Korea along the southern border.

Government Constitutional federation.

History Tradition says the Viking Rurik came to Russia in 862 and founded the first Russian dynasty in Novgorod. The various tribes were united by the spread of Christianity in the 10th and 11th centuries; Vladimir "the Saint" was converted in 988. During the 11th century, the grand dukes of Kiev held such centralizing power as existed. In 1240, Kiev was destroyed by the Mongols, and the Russian territory was split into numerous smaller dukedoms. Early dukes of Moscow extended their dominion over other Russian cities through their office of tribute collector for the Mongols and because of Moscow's role as an administrative and trade center.

In the late 15th century, Duke Ivan III acquired Novgorod and Tver and threw off the Mongol yoke. Ivan IV—the Terrible (1533–1584), first Muscovite czar—is considered to have founded the Russian state. He crushed the power of rival princes and boyars (great landowners), but Russia remained largely medieval until the reign of Peter the Great (1689–1725), grandson of the first Romanov czar, Michael (1613–1645). Peter made extensive reforms aimed at westernization and, through his defeat of Charles XII of Sweden at the Battle of Poltava in 1709, he extended Russia's boundaries to the west. Catherine the Great (1762–1796) con-

tinued Peter's westernization program and also expanded Russian territory, acquiring the Crimea, Ukraine, and part of Poland. During the reign of Alexander I (1801–1825), Napoléon's attempt to subdue Russia was defeated (1812–1813), and new territory was gained, including Finland (1809) and Bessarabia (1812). Alexander originated the Holy Alliance, which for a time crushed Europe's rising liberal movement.

Alexander II (1855–1881) pushed Russia's borders to the Pacific and into central Asia. Serfdom was abolished in 1861, but heavy restrictions were imposed on the emancipated class. Revolutionary strikes, following Russia's defeat in the war with Japan, forced Nicholas II (1894–1917) to grant a representative national body (Duma), elected by narrowly limited suffrage. It met for the first time in 1906 but had little influence on Nicholas.

World War I demonstrated czarist corruption and inefficiency, and only patriotism held the poorly equipped army together for a time. Disorders broke out in Petrograd (renamed Leningrad and now St. Petersburg) in March 1917, and defection of the Petrograd garrison launched the revolution. Nicholas II was forced to abdicate on March 15, 1917, and he and his family were killed by revolutionists on July 16, 1918. A provisional government under the successive prime ministerships of Prince Lvov and a moderate, Alexander Kerensky, lost ground to the radical, or Bolshevik, wing of the Socialist Democratic Labor Party. On Nov. 7, 1917, the Bolshevik Revolution, engineered by Vladimir Lenin and Leon Trotsky, overthrew the Kerensky government, and authority was vested in a Council of People's Commissars, with Lenin as prime minister.

The humiliating Treaty of Brest-Litovsk (March 3, 1918) concluded the war with Germany, but civil war and foreign intervention delayed Communist control of all Russia until 1920. A brief war with Poland in 1920 resulted in Russian defeat.

Emergence of the USSR The Union of Soviet Socialist Republics was established as a federation on Dec. 30, 1922. The death of Lenin on Jan. 21, 1924, precipitated an intraparty struggle between Joseph Stalin, general secretary of the party, and Trotsky, who favored swifter socialization at home and fomentation of revolution abroad. Trotsky was dismissed as commissar of war in 1925 and banished from the Soviet Union in 1929. He was murdered in Mexico City on Aug. 21, 1940, by a political agent. Stalin further consolidated his power by a series of purges in the late 1930s, liquidating prominent party leaders and military officers. Stalin assumed the prime ministership on May 6, 1941.

The term *Stalinism* has become the definition of an inhumane, draconian socialism. Stalin sent millions of Soviets who did not conform to the Stalinist ideal to forced-labor camps, and he persecuted his country's vast number of ethnic groups—reserving particular vitriol for Jews and Ukrainians. Soviet historian Roy Medvedev estimated that about 20 million died from starvation, executions, forced collectivization, and life in the labor camps under Stalin's rule.

Soviet foreign policy, at first friendly toward Germany and antagonistic toward Britain and France and then, after Hitler's rise to power in 1933, becoming anti-Fascist and pro–League of Nations, took an abrupt turn on Aug. 24, 1939, with the signing of a nonaggression pact with Nazi Germany. The next month, Moscow joined in the German attack on Poland, seizing territory later incorporated into the Ukrainian and Belorussian SSRs. The Russo-Finnish War (1939–1940) added territory to the Karelian SSR set up on

Rulers of Russia Since 1533

Name	Ruled[1]	Name	Ruled[1]	Name	Ruled[1]
Ivan IV the Terrible	1533–1584	Ivan VI	1740–1741[6]	**POLITICAL LEADERS OF USSR**	
Theodore I	1584–1598	Elizabeth	1741–1762	Vladimir Ilyich Lenin	1917–1924
Boris Godunov	1598–1605	Peter III	1762–1762	Aleksei Rykov	1924–1930
Theodore II	1605–1605	Catherine II the Great	1762–1796	Vyacheslav Molotov	1930–1941
Demetrius I[2]	1605–1606	Paul I	1796–1801	Joseph Stalin[8]	1941–1953
Basil IV Shuiski	1606–1610[3]	Alexander I	1801–1825	Georgi M. Malenkov	1953–1955
"Time of Troubles"	1610–1613	Nicholas I	1825–1855	Nikolai A. Bulganin	1955–1958
Michael Romanov	1613–1645	Alexander II	1855–1881	Nikita S. Khrushchev	1958–1964
Alexis I	1645–1676	Alexander III	1881–1894	Leonid I. Brezhnev	1964–1982
Theodore III	1676–1682	Nicholas II	1894–1917[7]	Yuri V. Andropov	1982–1984
Ivan V[4]	1682–1689[5]	**PROVISIONAL GOVERNMENT**		Konstantin U.	1984–1985
Peter I the Great[4]	1682–1725	**(PREMIERS)**		Chernenko	
Catherine I	1725–1727	Prince Georgi Lvov	1917–1917	Mikhail S. Gorbachev	1985–1991
Peter II	1727–1730	Alexander Kerensky	1917–1917	**PRESIDENTS OF RUSSIA**	
Anna	1730–1740			Boris Yeltsin	1991–1999
				Vladimir Putin	2000–

1. For czars through Nicholas II, year of end of rule is also that of death, unless otherwise indicated. 2. Also known as Pseudo-Demetrius. 3. Died 1612. 4. Ivan V and Peter I the Great ruled jointly until 1689, when Ivan was deposed. 5. Died 1696. 6. Died 1764. 7. Killed 1918. 8. General secretary of Communist Party, 1924–1953.

March 31, 1940; the annexation of Bessarabia and Bukovina from Romania became part of the new Moldavian SSR on Aug. 2, 1940; and the annexation of the Baltic republics of Estonia, Latvia, and Lithuania in June 1940 created the 14th, 15th, and 16th Soviet republics. The Soviet-German collaboration ended abruptly with a lightning attack by Hitler on June 22, 1941, which seized 500,000 sq mi of Russian territory before Soviet defenses, aided by U.S. and British arms, could halt it. The Soviet resurgence at Stalingrad from Nov. 1942 to Feb. 1943 marked the turning point in a long battle, ending in the final offensive of Jan. 1945. Then, after denouncing a 1941 nonaggression pact with Japan in April 1945, when Allied forces were nearing victory in the Pacific, the Soviet Union declared war on Japan on Aug. 8, 1945, and quickly occupied Manchuria, Karafuto, and the Kuril Islands.

After the war, the Soviet Union, United States, Great Britain, and France divided Berlin and Germany into four zones of occupation, which led to immediate antagonism between the Soviet and Western powers, culminating in the Berlin blockade in 1948. The USSR's tightening control over a cordon of Communist states, running from Poland in the north to Albania in the south, was dubbed the "iron curtain" by Churchill and would later lead to the Warsaw Pact. It marked the beginning of the cold war, the simmering hostility that pitted the world's two superpowers, the U.S. and the USSR—and their competing political ideologies—against each other for the next 45 years. Stalin died on March 6, 1953.

The new power emerging in the Kremlin was Nikita S. Khrushchev (1958–1964), first secretary of the party. Khrushchev formalized the eastern European system into a Council for Mutual Economic Assistance (Comecon) and a Warsaw Pact Treaty Organization as a counterweight to NATO. The Soviet Union exploded a hydrogen bomb in 1953, developed an intercontinental ballistic missile by 1957, sent the first satellite into space (Sputnik I) in 1957, and put Yuri Gagarin in the first orbital flight around Earth in 1961. Khrushchev's downfall stemmed from his decision to place Soviet nuclear missiles in Cuba and then, when challenged by the U.S., backing down and removing the weapons. He was also blamed for the ideological break with China after 1963. Khrushchev was forced into retirement on Oct. 15, 1964, and was replaced by Leonid I. Brezhnev as first secretary of the party and Aleksei N. Kosygin as premier.

U.S. president Jimmy Carter and Brezhnev signed the SALT II treaty in Vienna on June 18, 1979, setting ceilings on each nation's arsenal of intercontinental ballistic missiles. The U.S. Senate refused to ratify the treaty because of the invasion of Afghanistan by Soviet troops on Dec. 27, 1979. On Nov. 10, 1982, Leonid Brezhnev died. Yuri V. Andropov, who had formerly headed the KGB, became his successor but died less than two years later, in Feb. 1984. Konstantin U. Chernenko, a 72-year-old party stalwart who had been close to Brezhnev, succeeded him. After 13 months in office, Chernenko died on March 10, 1985. Chosen to succeed him as Soviet leader was Mikhail S. Gorbachev, who led the Soviet Union in its long-awaited shift to a new generation of leadership. Unlike his immediate predecessors, Gorbachev did not also assume the title of president but wielded power from the post of party general secretary.

Gorbachev introduced sweeping political and economic reforms, bringing *glasnost* and *perestroika*, "openness" and "restructuring," to the Soviet system. He established much warmer relations with the West, ended the Soviet occupation of Afghanistan, and announced that the Warsaw Pact countries were free to pursue their own political agendas. Gorbachev's revolutionary steps ushered in the end of the cold war, and in 1990 he was awarded the Nobel Peace Prize for his contributions to ending the 45-year conflict between East and West.

The Soviet Union took much criticism in early 1986 over the April 24 meltdown at the Chernobyl nuclear plant and its reluctance to give out any information on the accident.

Dissolution of the USSR Gorbachev's promised reforms began to falter, and he soon had a formidable political opponent agitating for even more radical restructuring. Boris Yeltsin, president of the Russian SSR, began challenging the authority of the federal government and resigned from the Communist Party along with other dissenters in 1990. On Aug. 29, 1991, an attempted coup d'état against Gorbachev was orchestrated by a group of hardliners. Yeltsin's defiant actions during the coup—he barricaded himself in the Russian Parliament and called for national strikes—resulted in Gorbachev's reinstatement. But from then on, power had effectively shifted from Gorbachev to Yeltsin and away from centralized power to greater power for the individual Soviet republics. In his last months as the head of the Soviet Union, Gorbachev dissolved the Communist Party and proposed the formation of the Commonwealth of Independent States (CIS), which, when implemented, gave most of the Soviet Socialist Republics their independence, binding them together in a loose, primarily economic federation. Russia and ten other former Soviet republics joined the CIS on Dec. 21, 1991. Gorbachev resigned on Dec. 25, and Yeltsin, who had been the driving force behind the Soviet dissolution, became president of the newly established Russian Republic.

At the start of 1992, Russia embarked on a series of dramatic economic reforms, including the freeing of prices on most goods, which led to an immediate downturn. A national referendum on confidence in Yeltsin and his economic program took place in April 1993. To the surprise of many, the president and his shock-therapy program won by a resounding margin. In September, Yeltsin dissolved the legislative bodies left over from the Soviet era.

The president of the southern republic of Chechnya accelerated his region's drive for independence in 1994. In December, Russian troops closed the borders and sought to squelch the independence drive. The Russian military forces met firm and costly resistance. In May 1997, the two-year war formally ended with the signing of a peace treaty that adroitly avoided the issue of Chechen independence.

In March 1998 Yeltsin dismissed his entire government and replaced Prime Minister Viktor Chernomyrdin with fuel and energy minister Sergei Kiriyenko. On Aug. 28, 1998, amid the Russian stock market's free fall, the Russian government halted trading of the ruble on international currency markets. This financial crisis led to a long-term economic downturn and to political upheaval. Yeltsin then sacked Kiriyenko and reappointed Chernomyrdin. The Duma rejected Chernomyrdin and on Sept. 11 elected foreign minister Yevgeny Primakov as prime minister. The repercussions of Russia's financial emergency were felt throughout the Commonwealth of Independent States.

Impatient with Yeltsin's increasingly erratic behavior, the Duma attempted to impeach him in May 1999. But the impeachment motion was quickly quashed and soon Yeltsin was on the ascendancy again. In keeping with his capricious style, Yeltsin dismissed Primakov and substituted Interior Minister Sergei Stepashin. Just three months later, however, Yeltsin ousted Stepashin and replaced him with Vladimir Putin on Aug. 9, 1999, announcing that in addition to serving as prime minister, the former KGB agent was his choice as a successor in the 2000 presidential election.

In 1999, the former Russian satellites of Poland, Hungary, and the Czech Republic joined NATO, raising Russia's hackles. The desire of Lithuania, Latvia, and Estonia, all of which were once part of the Soviet Union, to join the organization in the future further antagonized Russia.

Just three years after the bloody 1994–1996 Chechen-Russian war ended in devastation and stalemate, the fighting started again in 1999, with Russia launching air strikes and following up with ground troops. By the end of November, Russian troops had surrounded Chechnya's capital, Grozny, and about 215,000 Chechen refugees had fled to neighboring Ingushetia. Russia maintained that a political solution was impossible until Islamic militants in Chechnya had been vanquished.

In a decision that took Russia and the world by surprise, Boris Yeltsin resigned on Dec. 31, 1999, and Vladimir Putin became the acting president.

In Feb. 2000, after almost five months of fighting, Russian troops captured Grozny. The control of Grozny was a political as well as a military victory for Putin, whose hard-line stance against Chechnya greatly contributed to his political popularity.

On March 26, 2000, Putin won the presidential election with about 53% of the vote. Putin moved to centralize power in Moscow and attempted to limit the power and influence of both the regional governors and wealthy business leaders. Although Russia remained economically stagnant, Putin brought his nation a measure of political stability it never had under the mercurial and erratic Yeltsin.

In Aug. 2000 the Russian government was severely criticized for its handling of the *Kursk* disaster, a nuclear submarine accident that left 118 sailors dead.

Russia was initially alarmed in 2001 when the U.S. announced its rejection of the Anti-Ballistic Missile Treaty of 1972, which for 30 years had been viewed as a crucial force in keeping the nuclear arms race under control. But Putin was eventually placated by Bush's reassurances, and in May 2002, the U.S. and Russian leaders announced a landmark pact to cut both countries' nuclear arsenals by up to two-thirds over the next ten years.

On Oct. 23, 2002, Chechen rebels seized a crowded Moscow theater and detained 763 people, including 3 Americans. Armed and wired with explosives, the rebels demanded that the Russian government end the war in Chechnya. Government forces stormed the theater the next day, after releasing a gas into the theater that killed not only all the rebels but more than 100 hostages.

In March 2003, Chechens voted in a referendum that approved a new regional constitution making Chechnya a separatist republic within Russia. Agreeing to the constitution meant abandoning claims for complete independence, and the new powers accorded the republic were little more than cosmetic. During 2003, there were 11 bomb attacks against Russia that were believed to have been orchestrated by Chechen rebels.

In April 2003 reformist politician Sergei Yushenkov became the third outspoken critic of the Kremlin to be assassinated in five years. Just hours before he was gunned down, Yushenkov had officially registered his new political party, Liberal Russia. In Nov. 2003, billionaire Mikhail Khodorkovsky, president of the Yukos oil company, was arrested on charges of fraud and tax evasion. Khodorkovsky supported liberal opposition parties, which led many to suspect that President Putin may have engineered his arrest. On May 31, 2005, Khodorkovsky was sentenced to nine years in prison.

Putin was reelected president in March 2004, with 70% of the vote. International election observers considered the process less than democratic.

On May 9, Chechnya's Moscow-backed leader, Akhmad Kadyrov, was killed in a bombing. The assassination undermined Russian claims that Chechnya had been growing more secure. At the end of August, another Russian-supported leader, Alu Alkhanov, was elected president of Chechnya with 73.5% of the vote. Chechen terrorist attacks occurred before and after the elections. On Sept. 1–3, dozens of heavily armed guerrillas seized a school in Beslan, near Chechnya, and held about 1,100 young schoolchildren, teachers, and parents hostage. Hundreds of hostages were killed, including about 156 children. Chechen warlord Shamil Basayev claimed responsibility. In the aftermath of the horrific attack, Putin announced that he would radically restructure the government to fight terrorism more effectively. The world community expressed deep concern that Putin's plans would consolidate his power and roll back democracy in Russia.

In Sept. 2004, Russia endorsed the Kyoto Protocol on climate change. It was the final endorsement needed to put the protocol into effect worldwide.

Former Chechen president and rebel leader Aslan Maskhadov was killed by Russian special forces on March 8, 2005. Putin hailed it as a victory in his fight against terrorism.

Rwanda

REPUBLIC OF RWANDA

National name: Republika y'u Rwanda
President: Paul Kagame (2000)
Prime Minister: Bernard Makuza (2000)
Area: 10,169 sq mi (26,338 sq km)
Population (2005 est.): 8,440,820 (growth rate: 2.4%); birth rate: 40.6/1000; infant mortality rate: 91.2/1000; life expectancy: 47.0; density per sq mi: 830
Capital and largest city (2003 est.): Kigali, 298,100.
Monetary unit: Rwanda franc. **Languages:** Kinyarwanda, French, and English (all official); Kiswahili in commercial centers. **Ethnicity/race:** Hutu 84%, Tutsi 15%, Twa (Pygmoid) 1%. **Religions:** Roman Catholic 56.5%, Protestant 26%, Adventist 11.1%, Islam 4.6%, indigenous beliefs 0.1%, none 1.7% (2001). **Literacy rate:** 70% (2003 est.).
Economic summary: GDP/PPP (2004 est.): $10.43 billion; per capita $1,300. **Real growth rate:** 0.9%. **Inflation:** 7%. **Unemployment:** n.a. **Arable land:** 41%. **Agriculture:** coffee, tea, pyrethrum (insecticide made from chrysanthemums), bananas, beans, sorghum, potatoes; livestock. **Labor force:** 4.6 million (2000); agriculture 90%. **Industries:** cement, agricultural products, small-scale beverages, soap, furniture, shoes, plastic goods, textiles, cigarettes. **Natural resources:** gold, cassiterite (tin ore), wolframite (tungsten ore), methane, hydropower, arable land. **Exports:** $69.78 million (f.o.b., 2004 est.): coffee, tea, hides, tin ore. **Imports:** $260 million (f.o.b., 2004 est.): foodstuffs, machinery and equipment, steel, petroleum products, cement and construction material. **Major trading partners:** Indonesia, Germany, China, Kenya, Belgium, Uganda, France (2003).

Geography Rwanda, in east-central Africa, is surrounded by the Democratic Republic of the Congo, Uganda, Tanzania, and Burundi. It is slightly smaller than Maryland. Steep mountains and deep valleys cover most of the country. Lake Kivu in the northwest, at an altitude of 4,829 ft (1,472 m), is the highest lake in Africa. Extending north of it are the Virunga Mountains, which include the volcano Karisimbi (14,187 ft; 4,324 m), Rwanda's highest point.

Government Republic.

History The original inhabitants of Rwanda were the Twa, a Pygmy people who now make up only 1% of the population. While the Hutu and Tutsi are often considered to be two separate ethnic groups, scholars point out that they speak the same language, have a history of intermarriage, and share many cultural characteristics. Traditionally, the differences between the two groups were occupational rather than ethnic. Agricultural people were considered Hutu, while the cattle-owning elite were identified as Tutsi. Supposedly Tutsi were tall and thin, while Hutu were short and square, but is often impossible to tell one from the other. The 1933 requirement by the Belgians that everyone carry an identity card indicating tribal ethnicity as Tutsi or Hutu enhanced the distinction. Since independence, repeated violence in both Rwanda and Burundi has increased ethnic differentiation between the groups.

Rwanda, which became a part of German East Africa in 1890, was first visited by European explorers in 1854. During World War I, it was occupied in 1916 by Belgian troops. After the war, it became a Belgian League of Nations mandate, along with Burundi, under the name of Ruanda-Urundi. The mandate was made a UN trust territory in 1946. Until the Belgian Congo achieved independence in 1960, Ruanda-Urundi was administered as part of that colony. Belgium at first maintained Tutsi dominance but eventually encouraged power sharing between Hutu and Tutsi. Ethnic tensions led to civil war, forcing many Tutsi into exile. When Ruanda became the independent nation of Rwanda on July 1, 1962, it was under Hutu rule.

In Oct. 1990, the Rwandan Patriotic Front (RPF), Tutsi rebels in exile in Uganda, invaded in an attempt to overthrow the Hutu-led Rwandan government. Peace accords were signed in Aug. 1993, calling for a coalition government. But after the downing of a plane in April 1994 that killed the presidents of both Rwanda and Burundi, deep-seated ethnic violence erupted. (Who is responsible for shooting down the plane is unclear. One theory suggests it was Hutu extremists who rejected the Hutu-Tutsi power-sharing plan proposed by President Juvénal Habyarimana, a Hutu moderate. In 2004, a French judge asserted that it was the current Tutsi president, Paul Kagame, who has vehemently denied the charge.)

The presidential guard began murdering Tutsi opposition leaders, and soon policemen and soldiers began attempting to murder the entire Tutsi population. In 100 days, beginning in April 1994, Hutu rampaged through the country and slaughtered an estimated 800,000 Tutsi and their moderate Hutu sympathizers. A 30,000-member militia group, the Interahamwe, led much of the murderous spree, but, goaded by radio propaganda, ordinary Hutu joined in massacring their Tutsi neighbors. Although the genocidal slaughter seemed a spontaneous eruption of hatred, it has in fact been shown to have been carefully orchestrated by the Hutu government.

In response, the Tutsi rebel force, the Rwandan Patriotic Front, swept across the country in a 14-week civil war, routing the largely Hutu government. Despite horrific reports of genocide, no country came to the Tutsi's assistance. The UN, already stationed in Rwanda at the time of the killing, withdrew entirely after ten of its soldiers were killed.

In the aftermath of the genocide, an estimated 1.7 million Hutu fled across the border into neighboring Zaire (now the Democratic Republic of the Congo). Although Tutsi rebels took control of the government, they permitted a Hutu, Pasteur Bizimungu, to serve as president, attempting to deflect accusations of a resurgence in Tutsi elitism and to foster national unity. Paul Kagame, the Tutsi rebel leader, became vice president and éminence grise.

Amid the legitimate refugees from the genocide were Hutu militiamen, who began waging guerrilla warfare from refugee camps in Zaire. The Hutu guerrillas in Zaire, as well as Zaire's threat to exile their own ethnic Tutsi, led to Rwanda's support of rebel forces, headed by Laurent Kabila, bent on overthrowing Zaire's Mobutu Sese Seko. But Rwanda soon grew disenchanted with Kabila's new regime. The Kabila government was not able to prevent the raids from Hutu guerrillas that continued to traumatize the country and destabilize the region. In Aug. 1998, a little more than a year after Kabila took over, a rebellion began against his reign, instigated by Rwanda and Uganda.

Refugee problems, continued massacres, and the horrific legacy of genocide continued to haunt the national psyche. In Sept. 1998, a UN tribunal sentenced Jean Kambanda, a former prime minister of

Rwanda, to life in prison for his part in the 1994 genocide. He became the first person in history to be convicted for the crime of genocide, first defined in the 1948 Genocide Convention after World War II. By 2001, eight others had also been convicted of the same charge. The UN tribunal, however, was criticized for its inefficiency and slow pace. In Dec. 1999, an independent report, commissioned by the UN, took Kofi Annan and other UN officials to task for not intervening effectively in the genocide.

In April 2000, President Bizimungu resigned and Vice President Paul Kagame became the first Tutsi president of the nation. It was Kagame's rebel force that seized Rwanda's capital and put an end to the genocide in 1994.

Rwanda continued fighting against the Democratic Republic of the Congo throughout its four-year civil war. Finally, in July 2002, the two countries signed a peace accord: Rwanda promised to withdraw its 35,000 troops from the Congolese border; Congo in turn agreed to disarm the thousands of Hutu militiamen in its territory, who threatened Rwandan security.

In May 2003, 93% of Rwandans voted to approve a new constitution that instituted a balance of political power between Hutu and Tutsi. No party, for example, can hold more than half the seats in Parliament. It also outlawed the incitement of ethnic hatred. In Aug. 26 presidential elections, the first since the Rwandan genocide, Paul Kagame, who had served as president since 2000, won a landslide victory. In June 2004, Pasteur Bizimungu, the Hutu who had served as president between 1994 and 2000 (then–vice president Kagame held the real power), was sentenced to 15 years in prison on charges of inciting ethnic hatred. Many considered the trial politically motivated.

St. Kitts and Nevis

FEDERATION OF ST. KITTS AND NEVIS

Sovereign: Queen Elizabeth II (1952)
Governor-General: Sir Cuthbert Sebastian (1996)
Prime Minister: Denzil Douglas (1995)
Area: St. Kitts, 65 sq mi (168 sq km); Nevis, 36 sq mi (93 sq km)
Population (2005 est.): 38,958 (growth rate: 0.4%); birth rate: 18.1/1000; infant mortality rate: 14.5/1000; life expectancy: 72.2; density per sq mi: 387
Capital (2003 est.): Basseterre (on St. Kitts), 11,500. **Largest town on Nevis:** Charlestown, 1,300. **Monetary unit:** East Caribbean dollar. **Language:** English. **Ethnicity/race:** predominantly black; some British, Portuguese, and Lebanese. **Religions:** Anglican, other Protestant, Roman Catholic. **Literacy rate:** 97% (1980 est.)
Economic summary: GDP/PPP (2002 est.): $339 million; per capita $8,800. **Real growth rate:** –1.9%. **Inflation:** 1.7% (2001 est.). **Unemployment:** 4.5% (1997). **Arable land:** 19%. **Agriculture:** sugarcane, rice, yams, vegetables, bananas; fish. **Labor force:** 18,170 (June 1995). **Industries:** sugar processing, tourism, cotton, salt, copra, clothing, footwear, beverages. **Natural resources:** arable land. **Exports:** $70 million (2002 est.): machinery, food, electronics, beverages, tobacco. **Imports:** $195 million (2002 est.): machinery, manufactures, food, fuels. **Major trading partners:** U.S., UK, Canada, Germany, Italy, Trinidad and Tobago, Denmark (2003).

Geography St. Kitts, the larger of the two islands, is roughly oval in shape except for a long, narrow peninsula to the southeast. Its highest point is Mount Liamuiga (3,792 ft [1,156 m]). The Narrows, a 2-mile- (3-km-) wide channel, separates the two islands. The circularly shaped Nevis is surrounded by coral reefs and the island is almost entirely a single mountain, Nevis Peak (3,232 ft [985 m]). A volcanic mountain chain dominates the center of both islands.

Government Constitutional monarchy.

History When Christopher Columbus explored the islands in 1493, they were inhabited by the Carib people. Today, most of the inhabitants are the descendants of African slaves. The British settled on St. Kitts—formerly St. Christopher—in 1623, and on Nevis in 1628. The French settled on St. Kitts in 1627, and an Anglo-French rivalry lasted for more than 100 years. After a decisive British victory over the French at Brimstone Hill in 1782, the islands came under permanent British control. The islands, along with nearby Anguilla, were united in 1882. They joined the West Indies federation in 1958 and remained in that association until its dissolution in 1962. St. Kitts–Nevis–Anguilla became an associated state of the United Kingdom in 1967. Anguilla seceded in 1980, and St. Kitts and Nevis gained independence on Sept. 19, 1983.

A drop in world sugar prices hurt the nation's economy through the mid-1980s, and the government sought to reduce the islands' dependence on sugar production and to diversify the economy, promoting tourism and financial services. In 1990, the prime minister of Nevis announced that he intended to seek an end to the federation with St. Kitts by 1992, but a local election in June 1992 postponed the idea. In Aug. 1998, 62% of the population voted for Nevis to secede, but the vote fell short of the two-thirds majority required.

The country had been blacklisted by various international financial agencies for improprieties in its offshore financial services industry, but by 2002 it had been removed from all such lists.

St. Lucia

Sovereign: Queen Elizabeth II (1952)
Governor-General: Dame Pearlette Louisy (1997)
Prime Minister: Kenny D. Anthony (1997)
Area: 238 sq mi (616 sq km)
Population (2005 est.): 166,312 (growth rate: 1.3%); birth rate: 20.1/1000; infant mortality rate: 13.5/1000; life expectancy: 73.6; density per sq mi: 699
Capital and largest city (2003 est.): Castries, 60,300. **Monetary unit:** East Caribbean dollar. **Languages:** English (official), French patois. **Ethnicity/race:** black 90%, mixed 6%, East Indian 3%, white 1%. **Religions:** Roman Catholic 90%, Anglican 3%, other Protestant 7%. **Literacy rate:** 67% (1980 est.)
Economic summary: GDP/PPP (2002 est.): $866 million; per capita $5,400. **Real growth rate:** 3.3%. **Inflation:** 3% (2001 est.). **Unemployment:** 20% (2003 est.). **Arable land:** 7%. **Agriculture:** bananas, coconuts, vegetables, citrus, root crops, cocoa. **Labor force:** 43,800 (2001 est); agriculture 21.7%, services 53.6%, industry, commerce, and manufacturing 24.7%. **Industries:** clothing, assembly of electronic components, beverages, corrugated cardboard boxes, tourism, lime processing, coconut processing. **Natural resources:** forests, sandy beaches, minerals (pumice), mineral springs, geothermal potential. **Exports:** $66 million (2002 est.): bananas 41%, clothing, cocoa, vegetables, fruits, coconut oil. **Imports:** $267 million (2002 est.): food 23%, manufactured goods 21%, machinery and transportation equipment 19%, chemicals, fuels. **Major trading partners:** UK, U.S., Antigua and Barbuda, Dominica, Trinidad and Tobago, Venezuela (2003). **Member of Commonwealth of Nations**

Geography One of the Windward Islands of the eastern Caribbean, St. Lucia lies just south of Martinique. It is of volcanic origin. A chain of wooded mountains runs from north to south and from them flow many streams into fertile valleys.

Government Parliamentary democracy. A governor-general represents the sovereign, Queen Elizabeth II.

History The first inhabitants of St. Lucia were the Arawak Indians, who were forced off the island by the Caribs. Explored by Spain and then France, St. Lucia became a British territory in 1814 and one of the Windward Islands in 1871. With other Windward Islands, St. Lucia was granted home rule in 1967 as one of the West Indies Associated States. On Feb. 22, 1979, St. Lucia achieved full independence in ceremonies boycotted by the opposition St. Lucia Labour Party, which had advocated a referendum before cutting ties with Britain. The United Workers Party (UWP), then in power, called for new elections and was defeated by the St. Lucia Labour Party (SLP). The UWP was returned to power in the elections of 1982, 1987, and 1992.

Kenny Anthony became prime minister in 1997, when his St. Lucia Labour Party won 16 of the 17 parliamentary seats.

The 1999 European Union decision to end its preferential treatment of bananas imported from former colonies has led St. Lucia to try to diversify its agricultural crops. In 2002, tropical storm Lili devastated the banana crop.

St. Vincent and the Grenadines

Sovereign: Queen Elizabeth II (1952)
Governor-General: Frederick Ballantyne (2002)
Prime Minister: Ralph Gonsalves (2001)
Area: 150 sq mi (389 sq km)
Population (2005 est.): 117,534 (growth rate: 0.3%); birth rate: 16.3/1000; infant mortality rate: 14.8/1000; life expectancy: 73.6; density per sq mi: 783
Capital and largest city (2003 est.): Kingstown, 17,600.
Monetary unit: East Caribbean dollar. **Languages:** English, French patois. **Ethnicity/race:** black 66%, mixed 19%, East Indian 6%, Carib Amerindian 2%, other 7%. **Religions:** Anglican 47%, Methodist 28%, Roman Catholic 13%, Hindu, Seventh-Day Adventist, other Protestant. **Literacy rate:** 96% (1970 est.)
Economic summary: GDP/PPP (2002 est.): $342 million; per capita $2,900. **Real growth rate:** 0.7%. **Inflation:** –0.4% (2001 est.). **Unemployment:** 15% (2001 est.). **Arable land:** 18%. **Agriculture:** bananas, coconuts, sweet potatoes, spices, small numbers of cattle, sheep, pigs, goats, fish. **Labor force:** 67,000 (1984 est.); agriculture 26%, industry 17%, services 57% (1980 est.). **Industries:** food processing, cement, furniture, clothing, starch. **Natural resources:** hydropower, cropland. **Exports:** $38 million (2002 est.): bananas 39%, eddoes and dasheen (taro), arrowroot starch, tennis racquets. **Imports:** $174 million (2002 est.): foodstuffs, machinery and equipment, chemicals and fertilizers, minerals and fuels. **Major trading partners:** UK, U.S., Barbados, Trinidad and Tobago, Saint Lucia, Antigua and Barbuda (2003). **Member of Commonwealth of Nations**

Geography St. Vincent, chief island of the chain, is 18 mi (29 km) long and 11 mi (18 km) wide and is located 100 mi (161 km) west of Barbados. The island is mountainous and well forested. St. Vincent is dominated by the volcano Mount Soufrière, which rises to 4,048 ft (1,234 m). The Grenadines, a chain of nearly 600 islets with a total area of only 17 sq mi (27 sq km), extend for 60 mi (96 km) between St. Vincent and Grenada. The main islands in the Grenadines are Bequia, Balliceau, Canouan, Mayreau, Mustique, Isle D'Quatre, Petit Saint Vincent, and Union Island.

Government Parliamentary democracy.

History The Carib Indians inhabited St. Vincent before the Europeans arrived, and the island still sports a sizable number of Carib artifacts. Explored by Columbus in 1498, and alternately claimed by Britain and France, St. Vincent became a British colony by the Treaty of Paris in 1763. In 1773, the island was divided between the Caribs and the British, but conflicts between the groups persisted. In 1776, the Caribs revolted and were subdued. Thereafter the British deported most of them to islands in the Gulf of Honduras. Sugarcane cultivation brought thousands of African slaves and, later, Portuguese and East Indian laborers.

The islands belonged to the West Indies Federation from 1958 until its dissolution in 1962, won home rule in 1969 as part of the West Indies Associated States, and achieved full independence Oct. 26, 1979. Prime Minister Milton Cato's government quelled a brief rebellion on Dec. 8, 1979, attributed to economic problems following the eruption of Mount Soufrière in April 1979 (which had caused the evacuation of the northern two-thirds of the island). The eruption, followed by Hurricane Allen in 1980, seriously damaged the nation's economy, particularly the important banana crop, in the 1980s. But by the 1990s the economy had begun to rebound. With the 1999 decision by the European Union to end its preferential treatment of bananas imported from former colonies, St. Vincent sought to diversify its economy, primarily through expanding tourism.

In 2001 elections, the Unity Labour Party (ULP) won a landslide upset, and Ralph Gonsalves, a lawyer, became the new prime minister.

Samoa

INDEPENDENT STATE OF SAMOA

Head of State: Malietoa Tanumafili II (1963)
Prime Minister: Tuilaepa Sailele Malielegaoi (1998)
Area: 1,137 sq mi (2,944 sq km)
Population (2005 est.): 177,287 (growth rate: –0.2%); birth rate: 15.9/1000; infant mortality rate: 27.7/1000; life expectancy: 70.7; density per sq mi: 156
Capital and largest city (2003 est.): Apia, 35,900.
Monetary unit: Tala. **Languages:** Samoan, English. **Ethnicity/race:** Samoan 92.6%, Euronesians 7% (persons of European and Polynesian blood), Europeans 0.4%. **Religion:** Christian 99.7% (about half associated with the London Missionary Society; includes Congregational, Roman Catholic, Methodist, Latter-Day Saints, Seventh-Day Adventist). **Literacy rate:** 100% (2003 est.)
Economic summary: GDP/PPP (2002 est.): $1 billion; per capita $5,600. **Real growth rate:** 5%. **Inflation:** 4% (2001 est.). **Unemployment:** n.a.; note: substantial underemployment. **Arable land:** 21%. **Agriculture:** coconuts, bananas, taro, yams, coffee, cocoa. **Labor force:** 90,000 (2000 est.). **Industries:** food processing, building materials, auto parts. **Natural resources:** hardwood forests, fish, hydropower. **Exports:** $14 million (f.o.b. 2002): fish, coconut oil and cream, copra, taro, automotive parts, garments, beer. **Imports:** $113 million (f.o.b. 2002): machinery and equipment, industrial supplies, foodstuffs. **Major trading partners:** Australia, Indonesia, U.S., New Zealand, Fiji, Japan, Taiwan, Singapore (2003).

Geography Samoa, formerly Western Samoa, is in the South Pacific Ocean about 2,200 mi (3,540 km) south of Hawaii. The larger islands in the Samoan chain, Upolu and Savai'i, are mountainous and of volcanic origin. There is little level land except in the coastal areas, where most cultivation takes place.

Government Constitutional monarchy under a native chief.

History Polynesians, possibly from Tonga, first settled in the Samoan islands about 1000 B.C. Samoa was explored by Dutch and French traders in the 18th century. Toward the end of the 19th century, conflicting interests of the U.S., Britain, and Germany resulted in an 1899 treaty that recognized the paramount interests of the U.S. in those islands west of 171°W (American Samoa) and Germany's interests in the other islands (Western Samoa).

New Zealand seized Western Samoa from Germany in 1914, and in 1946 it became a UN trust territory administered by New Zealand. A resistance movement to both German and New Zealand rule, known as the *Mau* ("strongly held view") movement, helped to edge the islands toward independence on Jan. 1, 1962. A constitutional monarchy, Samoa has a legislative assembly whose members are from the *matai*, or titled class.

Barraged regularly by cyclones that have wreaked havoc on the country's primarily agrarian economy, Samoa has begun stepping up its tourism industry—not such a difficult undertaking in this archetypal South Pacific paradise.

A referendum in 1990 gave most women the right to vote for the first time. In 1997, a new constitutional amendment changed the country's name to Samoa. In 2002, the prime minister of New Zealand apologized to Samoa for the injustices that occurred under New Zealand rule. In 2004, Australia announced it would give Samoa $7 million to train its security forces.

San Marino

REPUBLIC OF SAN MARINO

National name: Repubblica di San Marino
Captains Regent: Fausta Simona Morganti and Cesare Antonio Gasperoni (2005)
Area: 24 sq mi (61.2 sq km)
Population (2005 est.): 28,880 (growth rate: 1.3%); birth rate: 10.2/1000; infant mortality rate: 5.7/1000; life expectancy: 81.6; density per sq mi: 1,222
Capital (2003 est.): San Marino, 4,300. **Largest city:** Serravalle, 8,700. **Monetary unit:** Euro. **Language:** Italian. **Ethnicity/race:** Sammarinese, Italian. **Religion:** Roman Catholic. **Literacy rate:** 96% (1976 est.)
Economic summary: GDP/PPP (2001 est.): $940 million; per capita $34,600. **Real growth rate:** 7.5%. **Inflation:** 3.3%. **Unemployment:** 2.6%. **Arable land:** 17%. **Agriculture:** wheat, grapes, corn, olives; cattle, pigs, horses, beef, cheese, hides. **Labor force:** 18,500 (1999); services 57%, industry 42%, agriculture 1% (2000 est.). **Industries:** tourism, banking, textiles, electronics, ceramics, cement, wine. **Natural resource:** building stone. **Exports:** trade data are included with the statistics for Italy: building stone, lime, wood, chestnuts, wheat, wine, baked goods, hides, ceramics. **Imports:** trade data are included with the statistics for Italy: wide variety of consumer manufactures, food.

Geography One-tenth the size of New York City, San Marino is surrounded by Italy. It is situated in the Apennines, a little inland from the Adriatic Sea near Rimini.

Government Republic.

History According to tradition, San Marino was founded about A.D. 350 and had the good luck for centuries to stay out of the many wars and feuds on the Italian peninsula. It is the oldest republic in the world. San Marino has survived, completely intact, attacks by other self-governing Italian city-states, the Napoleonic Wars, the unification of Italy, and two world wars. Those born in San Marino remain citizens and can vote no matter where they live. It joined the United Nations in 1992.

São Tomé and Príncipe

DEMOCRATIC REPUBLIC OF SÃO TOMÉ AND PRÍNCIPE

National name: República Democrática de São Tomé e Príncipe
President: Fradique de Menezes (2003)
Prime Minister: Maria do Carmo Silveira (2005)
Area: 386 sq mi (1,001 sq km)
Population (2005 est.): 187,410 (growth rate: 3.2%); birth rate: 40.8/1000; infant mortality rate: 43.1/1000; life expectancy: 67.0; density per sq mi: 485
Capital and largest city (2003 est.): São Tomé, 53,300. **Monetary unit:** Dobra. **Language:** Portuguese (official). **Ethnicity/race:** mestico (mixed European and native African), angolares (descendants of Angolan slaves), forros (descendants of freed slaves), servicais (contract laborers from Angola, Mozambique, and Cape Verde), tongas (children of servicais born on the islands), Europeans (primarily Portuguese). **Religions:** Christian 80% (Roman Catholic, Evangelical Protestant, Seventh-Day Adventist). **Literacy rate:** 79% (1991 est.)
Economic summary: GDP/PPP (2003 est.): $214 million; per capita $1,200. **Real growth rate:** 6%. **Inflation:** 14% (2004 est.). **Unemployment:** n.a. **Arable land:** 6%. **Agriculture:** cocoa, coconuts, palm kernels, copra, cinnamon, pepper, coffee, bananas, papayas, beans; poultry; fish. **Labor force:** n.a.; population mainly subsistence agriculture and fishing; note: shortages of skilled workers. **Industries:** light construction, textiles, soap, beer; fish processing; timber. **Natural resources:** fish, hydropower. **Exports:** $6.7 million (f.o.b., 2004 est.): cocoa 80%, copra, coffee, palm oil. **Imports:** $41 million (f.o.b., 2004 est.): machinery and electrical equipment, food products, petroleum products. **Major trading partners:** Netherlands, Canada, Germany, Philippines, Belgium, France, UK, Portugal, Italy (2003).

Geography The tiny volcanic islands of São Tomé and Príncipe lie in the Gulf of Guinea about 150 mi (240 km) off West Africa. São Tomé (about 330 sq mi; 859 sq km) is covered by a dense mountainous jungle, out of which have been carved large plantations. Príncipe (about 40 sq mi; 142 sq km) consists of jagged mountains. Other islands in the republic are Pedras Tinhosas and Rolas. About 95% of the population lives on São Tomé.

Government Republic.

History São Tomé and Príncipe, believed to have been originally uninhabited, were explored by Portuguese navigators in 1471 and settled by the end of the century. Intensive cultivation by slave labor made the islands a major producer of sugar during the 17th century, but output declined until the introduction of coffee and cocoa in the 19th century brought new prosperity. The island of São Tomé was the world's largest producer of cocoa in 1908, and the crop is still its most important. Working conditions for laborers, however, were horrendous, and in 1909 British and German chocolate manufacturers boycotted São Tomé cocoa in protest. An exile liberation movement was formed in 1953 after Portuguese landowners quelled labor riots by killing several hundred African workers.

The Portuguese revolution of 1974 brought the end of the overseas empire, and on July 12, 1975, Lisbon granted São Tomé independence. Manuel Pinto da Costa, leader of the only legal political party (Movement for the Liberation of São Tomé and Príncipe [MLSTP]), became president and Miguel Trovoada served as prime minister. After a 1978 coup attempt failed, Trovoada was accused of participating in the conspiracy and exiled. In 1990 a new constitution instituted multiparty rule. Trovoada returned and in March 1991 was voted president in the country's first free elections. Príncipe became autonomous in 1995.

Protests and unrest erupted throughout the 1990s over unemployment and soaring inflation. One of Africa's poorest countries, São Tomé has what is believed to be enormous untapped off-shore oil reserves—an estimated 6 billion barrels that are expected to begin flowing by 2007 or 2008. Businessman Fradique de Menezes won the presidential election in 2001. In July 2003, a military coup deposed Menezes while he was out of the country. International pressure resulted in Menezes's restoration to the presidency a week later.

Saudi Arabia

KINGDOM OF SAUDI ARABIA

National name: Al-Mamlaka al-'Arabiya as-Sa'udiya
Sovereign: King Abdullah (2005)
Area: 756,981 sq mi (1,960,582 sq km)
Population (2005 est.): 26,417,599 (growth rate: 2.3%); birth rate: 29.6/1000; infant mortality rate: 13.2/1000; life expectancy: 75.5; density per sq mi: 35
Capital and largest city (2003 est.): Riyadh, 3,724,100. **Other large cities:** Jeddah, 2,745,000; Makkah (Mecca), 1,614,800. **Monetary unit:** Riyal. **Language:** Arabic. **Ethnicity/race:** Arab 90%, Afro-Asian 10%. **Religion:** Islam 100%. **Literacy rate:** 79% (2003 est.)
Economic summary: GDP/PPP (2004 est.): $310.2 billion; per capita $12,000. **Real growth rate:** 5%. **Inflation:** 0.8%. **Unemployment:** 25% (unofficial estimate). **Arable land:** 2%. **Agriculture:** wheat, barley, tomatoes, melons, dates, citrus; mutton, chickens, eggs, milk. **Labor force:** 6.62 million; note: 35% of the population in the 15–64 age group is nonnational; agriculture 12%, industry 25%, services 63% (1999 est.). **Industries:** crude oil production, petroleum refining, basic petrochemicals, ammonia, industrial gases, sodium hydroxide (caustic soda), cement, construction, fertilizer, plastics, commercial ship repair, commercial aircraft repair. **Natural resources:** petroleum, natural gas, iron ore, gold, copper. **Exports:** $113 billion (f.o.b., 2004 est.): petroleum and petroleum products 90%. **Imports:** $36.21 billion (f.o.b., 2004 est.): machinery and equipment, foodstuffs, chemicals, motor vehicles, textiles. **Major trading partners:** U.S., Japan, South Korea, China, Taiwan, Singapore, Germany, UK, France (2003).

Geography Saudi Arabia occupies most of the Arabian Peninsula, with the Red Sea and the Gulf of Aqaba to the west and the Persian Gulf to the east. Neighboring countries are Jordan, Iraq, Kuwait, Qatar, the United Arab Emirates, the Sultanate of Oman, Yemen, and Bahrain, connected to the Saudi mainland by a causeway. Saudi Arabia contains the world's largest continuous sand desert, the Rub Al-Khali, or Empty Quarter. Its oil region lies primarily in the eastern province along the Persian Gulf.

Government Saudi Arabia was an absolute monarchy until 1992, at which time the Saud royal family introduced the country's first constitution. The legal system is based on the sharia (Islamic law).

History Saudi Arabia is not only the homeland of the Arab peoples—it is thought that the first Arabs originated on the Arabian Peninsula—but also the homeland of Islam, the world's second-largest religion. Muhammad founded Islam there, and it is the location of the two holy pilgrimage cities of Mecca and Medina. The Islamic calendar begins in 622, the year of the hegira, or Muhammad's flight from Mecca. A succession of invaders attempted to control the peninsula, but by 1517 the Ottoman Empire dominated, and in the middle of the 18th century, it was divided into separate principalities. In 1745 Muhammad ibn 'Abd al-Wahhab began calling for the purification and reform of Islam, and the Wahhabi movement swept across Arabia. By 1811, Wahhabi leaders had waged a jihad—a holy war—against other forms of Islam on the peninsula and succeeded in uniting much of it. By 1818, however, the Wahhabis had been driven out of power again by the Ottomans and their Egyptian allies.

The kingdom of Saudi Arabia is almost entirely the creation of King Ibn Saud (1882–1953). A descendant of Wahhabi leaders, he seized Riyadh in 1901 and set himself up as leader of the Arab nationalist movement. By 1906 he had established Wahhabi dominance in Nejd and conquered Hejaz in 1924–1925. The Hejaz and Nejd regions were merged to form the kingdom of Saudi Arabia in 1932, which was an absolute monarchy ruled by sharia. A year later the region of Asir was incorporated into the kingdom.

Oil was discovered in 1936, and commercial production began during World War II. This oil-derived wealth allowed the country to provide free health care and education while not collecting any taxes from its people. Saudi Arabia was neutral until nearly the end of the war, but it was permitted to be a charter member of the United Nations. The country joined the Arab League in 1945 and took part in the 1948–1949 war against Israel. Saudi Arabia still does not recognize the state of Israel. On Ibn Saud's death in 1953, his eldest son, Saud, began an 11-year reign marked by an increasing hostility toward the radical Arabism of Egypt's Gamal Abdel Nasser. In 1964, the ailing Saud was deposed and replaced by the prime minister, Crown Prince Faisal, who gave vocal support but no military help to Egypt in the 1967 Arab-Israeli War.

Faisal's assassination by a deranged kinsman in 1975 shook the Middle East, but it failed to alter his kingdom's course. His successor was his brother, Prince Khalid. Khalid gave influential support to Egypt during negotiations on Israeli withdrawal from the Sinai Desert. King Khalid died of a heart attack in 1982, and he was succeeded by his half-brother, Prince Fahd bin 'Abdulaziz, who had exercised the real power throughout Khalid's reign. King Fahd chose his half-brother Abdullah as crown prince.

Saudi Arabia and the smaller oil-rich Arab states on the Persian Gulf, fearful that they might become Ayatollah Ruhollah Khomeini's next targets if Iran conquered Iraq, made large financial contributions to the Iraqi war effort during the 1980s. At the same time, cheating by other members of the Organization of Petroleum Exporting Countries (OPEC), competition from nonmember oil producers, and conservation efforts by consuming nations combined to drive down the world price of oil. At the time Saudi Arabia had one-third of all known oil reserves, but falling demand and rising production outside OPEC combined to reduce its oil revenues from $120 billion in 1980 to less than $25 billion in 1985, threatening the country with domestic unrest and undermining its influence in the Gulf area.

At the start of 1996, King Fahd passed authority to Crown Prince Abdullah, after suffering an incapacitating stroke. In 1998 the country's oil income fell by 40% because of a worldwide decline in prices, and it entered its first recession in six years.

In 2000, Saudi Arabia, along with other OPEC nations experiencing a recession, decided to reduce production to raise oil prices. In 2001, OPEC cut oil production three additional times.

Saudi Arabia's relations with the U.S. were strained after the Sept. 11, 2001, terrorist attacks—15 of the 19 suicide bombers involved were Saudis. Despite the monarchy's close ties to the West, much of the extremely influential religious establishment has supported anti-Americanism and Islamic militancy. In Aug. 2003, following the U.S.-led war on Iraq in March and April 2003, the United States withdrew its troops stationed in Saudi Arabia. The U.S. had maintained troops in the country for the past decade, a source of great controversy in the strongly conservative Islamic country. One of the major reasons given for the Sept. 11 attacks by Saudi terrorist Osama bin Laden was the presence of U.S. troops in the home of Islam's holiest sites, Medina and Mecca. On May 12, 2003, suicide bombers killed 34, including eight Americans, at housing compounds for Westerners in Riyadh. Al-Qaeda was suspected. Saudi Arabia's commitment to antiterrorist measures was again called into question by the U.S. and other countries. In July, the U.S. Congress bitterly criticized Saudi Arabia's alleged financing of terrorist organizations. While the Saudi government arrested a sizable number of suspected terrorists, little was done to quell Islamic militancy in the kingdom. Several attacks against Westerners took place in 2003 and 2004.

In Feb. 2005, Saudi Arabia held its first elections ever: municipal council elections to choose half of the new council members in Riyadh. The other half continued to be appointed, in keeping with the previous Saudi system. Women were not eligible to vote, and less than a third of eligible voters registered.

In Aug. 2005, King Fahd bin 'Abdulaziz died. His half-brother Abdullah, who had been the de facto ruler of the country for the past decade, assumed the throne.

Senegal

REPUBLIC OF SENEGAL

National name: République du Sénégal
President: Abdoulaye Wade (2000)
Prime Minister: Macky Sall (2004)
Area: 75,749 sq mi (196,190 sq km)
Population (2005 est.): 11,126,832 (growth rate: 2.5%); birth rate: 35.2/1000; infant mortality rate: 55.5/1000; life expectancy: 56.8; density per sq mi: 147
Capital and largest city (2003 est.): Dakar, 2,476,400.
Monetary unit: CFA Franc. **Languages:** French (official); Wolof, Pulaar, Jola, Mandinka. **Ethnicity/race:** Wolof 43.3%, Fulani 23.8%, Serer 14.7%, Diola 3.7%, Mandingo 3%, Soninke 1.1%, European and Lebanese 1%, other 9.4%. **Religions:** Islam 94%, Christian 5% (mostly Roman Catholic), indigenous 1%.
Literacy rate: 40% (2003 est.)
Economic summary: GDP/PPP (2004 est.): $18.36 billion; per capita $1,700. **Real growth rate:** 3.2%. **Inflation:** 0.8%. **Unemployment:** 48% (urban youth 40%) (2001 est.). **Arable land:** 13%. **Agriculture:**

peanuts, millet, corn, sorghum, rice, cotton, tomatoes, green vegetables; cattle, poultry, pigs; fish. **Labor force:** 4.65 million; agriculture 70%. **Industries:** agricultural and fish processing, phosphate mining, fertilizer production, petroleum refining, construction materials, ship construction and repair. **Natural resources:** fish, phosphates, iron ore. **Exports:** $1.374 billion (f.o.b., 2004 est.): fish, groundnuts (peanuts), petroleum products, phosphates, cotton. **Imports:** $2.128 billion (f.o.b., 2004 est.): foods and beverages, capital goods, fuels. **Major trading partners:** India, France, Mali, Italy, Côte d'Ivoire, Spain, Nigeria, Thailand (2003).

Geography   The capital of Senegal, Dakar, is the westernmost point in Africa. The country, slightly smaller than South Dakota, surrounds Gambia on three sides and is bordered on the north by Mauritania, on the east by Mali, and on the south by Guinea and Guinea-Bissau.

Senegal is mainly a low-lying country, with a semi-desert area in the north and northeast and forests in the southwest. The largest rivers include the Senegal in the north and the Casamance in the southern tropical climate region.

Government   Multiparty democractic republic.

History   The Toucouleur people, among the early inhabitants of Senegal, converted to Islam in the 11th century, although their religious beliefs retained strong elements of animism. The Portuguese had some stations on the banks of the Senegal River in the 15th century, and the first French settlement was made at St.-Louis in 1659. Gorée Island became a major center for the Atlantic slave trade through the 1700s, and millions of Africans were shipped from there to the New World. The British took parts of Senegal at various times, but the French gained possession in 1840 and made it part of French West Africa in 1895. In 1946, together with other parts of French West Africa, Senegal became an overseas territory of France. On June 20, 1960, it formed an independent republic federated with Mali, but the federation collapsed within four months.

Although Senegal is neither a large nor a strategically located country, it has nonetheless played a prominent role in African politics since its independence. As a black nation that is more than 90% Muslim, Senegal has been a diplomatic and cultural bridge between the Islamic and black African worlds. Senegal has also maintained closer economic, political, and cultural ties to France than probably any other former French African colony.

Senegal's first president, Léopold Sédar Senghor, towered over the country's political life until his voluntary retirement in 1981. He replaced multiparty democracy with an authoritarian regime. An acclaimed poet, Senghor sought to become a "black-skinned Frenchman," a quest he ultimately discovered to be impossible. An advocate of "African socialism," Senghor increased government involvement in the economy through a series of four-year plans.

In 1973 Senegal and six other nations created the West African Economic Community. When rising oil prices and fluctuations in the price of peanuts, a major export crop, ruined the economy in the 1970s, Senghor reversed course. He emphasized new industries such as tourism and fishing. Politically, the so-called passive revolution allowed limited opposition.

When the economy continued to stagnate, and with it Senghor's popularity, he resigned after 20 years at the helm in favor of his protégé, Abdou Diouf. Diouf, who led the country for the next 20 years, initiated further economic and political liberalization, including the sale of government companies and permitting the existence of political parties. In March 2000, opposition party challenger Abdoulaye Wade won 60% of the vote in multiparty elections. Diouf stepped aside in what was hailed as a rare smooth transition of power in Africa. In Jan. 2001, the Senegalese voted in a new constitution that legalized opposition parties and granted women equal property rights with men.

In Sept. 2002, 1,863 passengers were killed when the state-owned *Joola* ferry sank. The government accepted responsibility for the disaster.

The president removed Prime Minister Idrissa Seck in April 2004. Seck was considered Wade's rival.

Serbia and Montenegro

National name: Srbija i Crna Gora
Federal President: Svetozar Marovic (2003)
Presidents: Boris Tadic, Serbia (2004); Filip Vujanovic, Montenegro (2003)
Prime Ministers: Vojislav Kostunica, Serbia (2004); Milo Djukanovic, Montenegro (2002)
Area: 39,517 sq mi (102,350 sq km)
Population (2005 est.): 10,829,175 (growth rate: 0.0%); birth rate: 12.1/1000; infant mortality rate: 12.9/1000; life expectancy: 74.7; density per sq mi: 274
Capital and largest city (2003 est.): Belgrade, 1,717,800 (metro. area), 1,285,200 (city proper).
Other large cities: Pristina, 204,500; Novi Sad, 191,300; Nis, 174,000. **Monetary unit:** Yugoslav new dinar. **Languages:** Serbian (official) 95%, Albanian 5%. **Ethnicity/race:** Serbs 62.6%, Albanians 16.5%, Montenegrins 5%, Hungarians 3.3%, other 12.6% (1991). **Religions:** Orthodox 65%, Islam 19%, Roman Catholic 4%, Protestant 1%, other 11%. **Literacy rate:** 93% (1991)
Economic summary: GDP/PPP (2004 est.): $26.27 billion; per capita $2,400. **Real growth rate:** 6.5%. **Inflation:** 8.8%. **Unemployment:** 30%; unemployment is approximately 50% in Kosovo. **Arable land:** 33%. **Agriculture:** cereals, fruits, vegetables, tobacco, olives; cattle, sheep, goats. **Labor force:** 3.2 million; agriculture n.a., industry n.a., services n.a. **Industries:** machine building (aircraft, trucks, and automobiles; tanks and weapons; electrical equipment; agricultural machinery); metallurgy (steel, aluminum, copper, lead, zinc, chromium, antimony, bismuth, cadmium); mining (coal, bauxite, nonferrous ore, iron ore, limestone); consumer goods (textiles, footwear, foodstuffs, appliances); electronics, petroleum products, chemicals, and pharmaceuticals. **Natural resources:** oil, gas, coal, antimony, copper, lead, zinc, nickel, gold, pyrite, chrome, hydropower, arable land. **Exports:** $3.245 billion (f.o.b., 2004 est.): manufactured goods, food and live animals, raw materials. **Imports:** $9.538 billion (f.o.b., 2004 est.): machinery and transport equipment, fuels and lubricants, manufactured goods, chemicals, food and live animals, raw materials. **Major trading partners:** Italy, Germany, Austria, France, Greece, Slovenia, Hungary, Bulgaria (2003).

Geography Serbia and Montenegro together are about the size of the state of Kentucky. They are largely mountainous. The northeast section of Serbia is part of the rich, fertile Danubian Plain drained by the Danube, Tisa, Sava, and Morava river systems. Montenegro is a jumbled mass of mountains, containing also some grassy slopes and fertile river valleys.

Government In Feb. 2003, the Federal Republic of Yugoslavia was renamed Serbia and Montenegro. The former Yugoslavia, once an often volatile union of six republics, splintered in the 1990s from a brutal ten-year civil war. The renaming reflects the two remain-

ing republics, Serbia and Montenegro. The new government is a loose union, linked only by a small joint administration in charge of defense and foreign affairs.

History Renamed Serbia and Montenegro in 2003, the former Yugoslavia was formed on Dec. 4, 1918, from the patchwork of Balkan states and territories. World War I began there with the assassination of Archduke Franz Ferdinand of Austria at Sarajevo on June 28, 1914. The new kingdom of Serbs, Croats, and Slovenes included the former kingdoms of Serbia and Montenegro; Bosnia-Herzegovina, previously administered jointly by Austria and Hungary; Croatia-Slavonia, a semiautonomous region of Hungary; and Dalmatia, formerly administered by Austria. King Peter I of Serbia became the first monarch; his son, Alexander I, succeeded him on Aug. 16, 1921. Croatian demands for a federal state forced Alexander to assume dictatorial powers in 1929 and to change the country's name to Yugoslavia. Serbian dominance continued despite his efforts, amid the resentment of other regions. A Macedonian associated with Croatian dissidents assassinated Alexander in Marseilles, France, on Oct. 9, 1934, and his cousin, Prince Paul, became regent for the king's son, Prince Peter.

Paul's pro-Axis policy brought Yugoslavia to sign the Axis Pact on March 25, 1941, and opponents overthrew the government two days later. On April 6 the Nazis occupied the country, and the young king and his government fled. Two guerrilla armies—the Chetniks under Draza Mihajlovic supporting the monarchy and the Partisans under Tito (Josip Broz) leaning toward the USSR—fought the Nazis for the duration of the war. In 1943, Tito established an Executive National Committee of Liberation to function as a provisional government. Tito won the election held in the fall of 1945 while monarchists boycotted the vote. A new Assembly abolished the monarchy and proclaimed the Federal People's Republic of Yugoslavia, with Tito as prime minister. Tito ruthlessly eliminated the opposition and broke with the Soviet bloc in 1948. Yugoslavia followed a middle road, combining orthodox Communist control of politics and general overall economic policy with a varying degree of freedom in the arts, travel, and individual enterprise. Tito became president in 1953 and president-for-life under a revised constitution adopted in 1963.

After Tito's death on May 4, 1980, a rotating presidency designed to avoid internal dissension was put into effect immediately, and the feared clash of Yugoslavia's multiple nationalities and regions appeared to have been averted. In May 1991 Croatian voters supported a referendum calling for their republic to become an independent nation. A similar referendum passed in December in Slovenia. In June the respective Parliaments in both republics passed declarations of independence. Ethnic violence flared up almost immediately. The largely Serbian-led Yugoslav military pounded breakaway Bosnia and Herzegovina, leading the UN Security Council in May 1992 to impose economic sanctions on the Belgrade government.

Despite rampant inflation reaching approximately 3,000% per month in Dec. 1993, the Serbian government of Slobodan Milosevic maintained its effective control over the remainder of Yugoslavia. Trade sanctions were lifted in Dec. 1995 following the signing of the Dayton Accords. In June 1996, the UN Security Council lifted its heavy weapons embargo. Large groups of demonstrators in 1996–1997 engaged in several months of daily protests after Milosevic refused to recognize opposition victories in local elections and in elections in Montenegro. Constitutionally barred from another term as president of Serbia,

Milosevic became president of the Federal Republic of Yugoslavia (Serbia and Montenegro) in July 1997.

In Feb. 1998 the Yugoslav army and Serbian police began fighting against the separatist Kosovo Liberation Army, but their scorched-earth tactics were concentrated on ethnic Albanian civilians—Muslims who make up 90% of Kosovo's population. More than 900 Kosovars were killed in the fighting, and the hundreds of thousands forced to flee their homes were without adequate food and shelter. Although Serbs make up only 10% of Kosovo's population, the region figures strongly in Serbian nationalist mythology.

NATO was reluctant to intervene because Kosovo—unlike Bosnia in 1992—was legally a province of Yugoslavia. The proof of civilian massacres finally gave NATO the impetus to intervene for the first time ever in the dealings of a sovereign nation with its own people. After months of negotiations led nowhere, on March 24, 1999, NATO began launching air strikes. Weeks of daily bombings destroyed significant Serbian military targets, yet Milosevic showed no signs of relenting. In fact, Serbian militia stepped up civilian massacres and deportations in Kosovo, and by the end of the conflict, the UN high commissioner for refugees estimated that at least 850,000 people had fled Kosovo. The refugee crisis put a heavy burden on neighboring countries such as Albania and Macedonia. As effective as NATO airpower might have been against Serbian targets, it was utterly helpless in preventing Serb soldiers and paramilitaries from wreaking havoc on Kosovo's civilians. The initial reason NATO gave for involvement in Kosovo was to avoid a wider Balkan war, but once Serbia began accelerating its campaign of ethnic cleansing in Kosovo, NATO's reason for fighting changed to preventing a human rights calamity. Yet without a concomitant change in military strategy—sending in ground troops—many wondered whether there would be any Kosovars left to save. NATO's hesitation in committing to a land battle—and therefore putting its troops at greater risk—ultimately paid off. Serbia finally agreed to sign a UN-approved peace agreement with NATO on June 3, ending the 11-week war.

In the Sept. 2000 federal elections, Vojislav Kostunica, a law professor and political outsider, won the presidency in spite of widespread reports of fraud and voter intimidation. His election formally ended the autocratic rule of Milosevic, who had entangled his country in almost continuous war, first with the breakaway republics of Croatia and Bosnia (1991–1995) and then in the Serbian province of Kosovo in 1998. He had dragged Yugoslavia into economic collapse and relegated it to pariah status throughout much of the world. When Milosevic refused to honor the election results and demanded a runoff election, the country erupted in massive public demonstrations, ultimately forcing Milosevic to step down on Oct. 5. But Kostunica was quick to assert himself as a true-believing Serb nationalist with no plans for becoming the darling of the West.

In 2001, Milosevic was turned over to the United Nations International Criminal Tribunal for the former Yugoslavia in The Hague, charged with genocide and crimes against humanity. His lengthy trial continued through 2005.

In March 2002, the nation agreed to form a new state, replacing Yugoslavia with a loose federation called Serbia and Montenegro, which went into effect in Feb. 2003. The new arrangement was made to placate Montenegro's restive stirrings for independence and allowed Montenegro to hold a referendum on independence after three years. In May 2003, Filip Vujanovic, a strong advocate of Montenegran independence, was elected Montenegro's president.

The prime minister of the Serbian state, Zoran Djindjic, a reformer who helped bring about the fall of Milosevic, was assassinated in March 2003. Extreme nationalists, organized crime, and Serbia's own police and security services were implicated.

On March 17, 2004, Mitrovica, in Kosovo, experienced the worst ethnic violence in the region since the 1999 war. At least 19 people were killed, another 500 were injured, and about 4,000 Serbs lost their homes. NATO sent in an extra 1,000 troops to restore order.

In June 2004, Democratic Party leader Boris Tadic was elected Serbian president, defeating a nationalist candidate. Tadic plans to work toward gaining EU membership for Serbia.

Seychelles

REPUBLIC OF SEYCHELLES

President: James Michel (2004)
Area: 176 sq mi (455 sq km)
Population (2005 est.): 81,188 (growth rate: 0.4%); birth rate: 16.2/1000; infant mortality rate: 15.5/1000; life expectancy: 71.8; density per sq mi: 462
Capital and largest city (2003 est.): Victoria, 23,000.
Monetary unit: Seychelles rupee. **Languages:** Seselwa Creole, English, French (all official). **Ethnicity/race:** mixed French, African, Indian, Chinese, and Arab. **Religions:** Roman Catholic 86.6%, Anglican 6.8%, other Christian 2.5%, other 4.1%. **Literacy rate:** 58% (1971 est.)
Economic summary: GDP/PPP (2002 est.): $626 million; per capita $7,800. **Real growth rate:** 1.5% (2004 est.). **Inflation:** 5% (2004 est.). **Unemployment:** n.a. **Arable land:** 2%. **Agriculture:** coconuts, cinnamon, vanilla, sweet potatoes, cassava (tapioca), bananas; broiler chickens; tuna fish. **Labor force:** 30,900 (1996); industry 19%, services 71%, agriculture 10% (1989). **Industries:** fishing; tourism; processing of coconuts and vanilla, coir (coconut fiber) rope, boat building, printing, furniture; beverages. **Natural resources:** fish, copra, cinnamon trees. **Exports:** $256.2 million (f.o.b., 2004 est.): canned tuna, frozen fish, cinnamon bark, copra, petroleum products (reexports). **Imports:** $393.4 million (f.o.b., 2004 est.): machinery and equipment, foodstuffs, petroleum products, chemicals. **Major trading partners:** UK, France, Italy, Germany, Saudi Arabia, South Africa, Spain, Singapore (2003). **Member of Commonwealth of Nations**

Geography The Seychelles consist of an archipelago of about 100 islands in the Indian Ocean northeast of Madagascar. The principal islands are Mahé (55 sq mi; 142 sq km), Praslin (15 sq mi; 38 sq km), and La Digue (4 sq mi; 10 sq km). The Aldabra, Farquhar, and Desroches groups are included in the territory of the republic.

Government Socialist multiparty republic.

History The Seychelles were uninhabited when the British East India Company were the first visitors to the archipelago in 1609. Thereafter, they became a favorite pirate haven. The French claimed the islands in 1756 and administered them as part of the colony of Mauritius. The British gained control of the islands through the Treaty of Paris (1814) and changed the islands' name from the French Séchelles to the Anglicized Seychelles.

The islands became self-governing in 1975 and independent on June 29, 1976. They have remained a member of the Commonwealth of Nations. Their first president, James Mancham, was overthrown in 1977 by the prime minister, France-Albert René. At first René created a Socialist state with a one-party system, but later he reintroduced a multiparty system as well as various reforms.

To increase revenue, in 1996 the government quietly initiated an Economic Citizenship Program that provides foreigners with the opportunity to obtain a Seychelles passport upon payment of $25,000. A new law in late 1995 had granted immunity from criminal prosecution to anyone investing $10 million in the country.

In elections held in March 1998, President France-Albert René was reelected with 66.6% of the vote.

In Sept. 2001, President René was reelected for another five years, defeating Wavel Ramkalawan, an Anglican priest. In April 2004, he stepped down after 27 years in power. His vice president, James Michel, who had also served in the government for 27 years, assumed the presidency.

Sierra Leone

REPUBLIC OF SIERRA LEONE

President: Ahmad Tejan Kabbah (1998)
Area: 27,699 sq mi (71,740 sq km)
Population (2005 est.): 6,017,643 (growth rate: 2.2%); birth rate: 42.8/1000; infant mortality rate: 143.6/1000; life expectancy: 42.5; density per sq mi: 217
Capital and largest city (2003 est.): Freetown, 1,051,000. **Monetary unit:** Leone. **Languages:** English (official), Mende (southern vernacular), Temne (northern vernacular), Krio (lingua franca). **Ethnicity/ race:** 20 native African tribes 90% (Temne 30%, Mende 30%, other 30%); Creole (Krio) 10%; refugees from Liberia's recent civil war, small numbers of Europeans, Lebanese, Pakistanis, and Indians. **Religions:** Islam 60%, indigenous 30%, Christian 10%. **Literacy rate:** 31% (1995 est.)
Economic summary: GDP/PPP (2004 est.): $3.335 billion; per capita $600. **Real growth rate:** 6%. **Inflation:** 1% (2002 est.). **Unemployment:** n.a. **Arable land:** 7%. **Agriculture:** rice, coffee, cocoa, palm kernels, palm oil, peanuts; poultry, cattle, sheep, pigs; fish. **Labor force:** 1.369 million (1981 est.). **Industries:** diamond mining; small-scale manufacturing (beverages, textiles, cigarettes, footwear); petroleum refining, small commercial ship repair. **Natural resources:** diamonds, titanium ore, bauxite, iron ore, gold, chromite. **Exports:** $49 million (f.o.b., 2002 est.): diamonds, rutile, cocoa, coffee, fish (1999). **Imports:** $264 million (f.o.b., 2002 est.): foodstuffs, machinery and equipment, fuels and lubricants, chemicals (1995). **Major trading partners:** Belgium, Germany, UK, U.S., Côte d'Ivoire, France, Netherlands, Ukraine (2003). **Member of Commonwealth of Nations**

Geography Sierra Leone, on the Atlantic Ocean in West Africa, is half the size of Illinois. Guinea, in the north and east, and Liberia, in the south, are its neighbors. Mangrove swamps lie along the coast, with wooded hills and a plateau in the interior. The eastern region is mountainous.

Government Constitutional democracy.

History The Bulom people were thought to have been the earliest inhabitants of Sierra Leone, followed by the Mende and Temne peoples in the 15th century and thereafter the Fulani. The Portuguese were the first Europeans to explore the land and gave Sierra Leone its name, which means "lion mountains." Freetown, on the coast, was ceded to English settlers in 1787 as a home for blacks discharged from the British armed forces and also for runaway slaves who had found asylum in London. In 1808 the coastal area became a British colony, and in 1896 a British protectorate was proclaimed over the hinterland.

Sierra Leone became an independent nation on April 27, 1961. A military coup overthrew the civilian government in 1967, which was in turn replaced by civilian rule a year later. The country declared itself a republic on April 19, 1971.

A coup attempt early in 1971 led to then prime minister Siaka Stevens calling in troops from neighboring Guinea's army, which remained for two years. Stevens turned the government into a one-party state under the aegis of the All People's Congress Party in April 1978. In 1992 rebel soldiers overthrew Stevens's successor, Joseph Momoh, calling for a return to a multiparty system. In 1996, another military coup ousted the country's military leader and president. Nevertheless, a multiparty presidential election proceeded in 1996, and People's Party candidate Ahmad Tejan Kabbah won with 59.4% of the vote, becoming Sierra Leone's first democratically elected president.

But a violent military coup ousted President Kabbah's civilian government in May 1997. The leader of the coup, Lieut. Col. Johnny Paul Koroma, assumed the title Head of the Armed Forces Revolutionary Council (AFRC). Koroma began a reign of terror, destroying the economy and murdering enemies. The Commonwealth of Nations demanded the reinstatement of Kabbah, and ECOMOG, the Nigerian-led peacekeeping force, intervened. On March 10, 1998, after ten months in exile, Kabbah resumed his rule over Sierra Leone. The ousted junta and other rebel forces continued to wage attacks, many of which included the torture, rape, and brutal maimings of thousands of civilians, including countless children; amputation by machete was the horrific signature of the rebels. In addition to political power, the rebels were after control of Sierra Leone's rich diamond fields.

In Jan. 1999, rebels and Liberian mercenaries stormed the capital, demanding the release of the imprisoned Revolutionary United Front (RUF) leader, Foday Sankoh. ECOMOG regained control of Freetown, but President Kabbah later released Sankoh so he could participate in peace negotiations. Pressured by Nigeria and the U.S., among other countries, Kabbah agreed to an untenable power-sharing agreement in July 1999, which made Sankoh vice president of the country—and in charge of the diamond mines. The accord dissolved in May 2000 after the RUF abducted about 500 UN peacekeepers and attacked Freetown. Sankoh was captured and died in government custody in 2003, while awaiting trial for war crimes.

The conflict was officially declared over in Jan. 2002. An estimated 50,000 people were killed in the decadelong civil war. The UN installed its largest peacekeeping force in the country (17,000 troops). President Kabbah was reelected with 70% of the vote in May 2002. In 2004, the disarmament of 70,000 soldiers was completed, and a UN-sponsored war crimes tribunal opened. For the past several years, the UN has listed Sierra Leone as the world's "least livable" country, based on its poverty and the poor quality of life endured by its citizens.

Singapore

REPUBLIC OF SINGAPORE

President: S. R. Nathan (1999)
Prime Minister: Lee Hsien Loong (2004)
Area: 267 sq mi (692.7 sq km)
Population (2005 est.): 4,425,720 (growth rate: 1.6%); birth rate: 9.5/1000; infant mortality rate: 2.3/1000; life expectancy: 81.6; density per sq mi: 16,548
Capital and largest city (2003 est.): Singapore, 3,438,600. **Monetary unit:** Singapore dollar. **Languages:** Malay (national), Mandarin Chinese, Tamil, English (all official). **Ethnicity/race:** Chinese 76.7%, Malay 14%, Indian 7.9%, other 1.4%. **Religions:** Buddhist (Chinese), Islam (Malays),

Christian, Hindu, Sikh, Taoist, Confucianist. **Literacy rate:** 93% (2003 est.)
Economic summary: GDP/PPP (2004 est.): $120.9 billion; per capita $27,800. **Real growth rate:** 8.1%. **Inflation:** 1.7%. **Unemployment:** 3.4%. **Arable land:** 2%. **Agriculture:** rubber, copra, fruit, orchids, vegetables, poultry, eggs, fish, ornamental fish. **Labor force:** 2.18 million; manufacturing 18%, construction 6%, transportation and communication 11%, financial, business, and other services 49%, other 16% (2003). **Industries:** electronics, chemicals, financial services, oil drilling equipment, petroleum refining, rubber processing and rubber products, processed food and beverages, ship repair, offshore platform construction, life sciences, entrepôt trade. **Natural resources:** fish, deepwater ports. **Exports:** $174 billion (f.o.b., 2004 est.): machinery and equipment (including electronics), consumer goods, chemicals, mineral fuels. **Imports:** $155.2 billion (2004 est.): machinery and equipment, mineral fuels, chemicals, foodstuffs. **Major trading partners:** Malaysia, U.S., Hong Kong, China, Japan, Taiwan, Thailand, South Korea (2003). **Member of Commonwealth of Nations**

Geography The Republic of Singapore consists of the main island of Singapore, off the southern tip of the Malay Peninsula between the South China Sea and the Indian Ocean, and 58 nearby islands.

Government Parliamentary republic.

History Inhabitants of the Malaysian peninsula and the island of Singapore first migrated to the area between 2500 and 1500 B.C. (*see* Malaysia). British and Dutch interest in the region grew with the spice trade, and the trading post of Singapore was founded in 1819 by Sir Stamford Raffles. It was made a separate Crown colony of Britain in 1946, when the former colony of the Straits Settlements was dissolved. The other two settlements on the peninsula—Penang and Malacca—became part of the Union of Malaya, and the small island of Labuan was transferred to North Borneo. The Cocos (or Keeling) Islands and Christmas Island were transferred to Australia in 1955 and in 1958, respectively.

Singapore attained full internal self-government in 1959, and Lee Kwan Yew, an economic visionary with an authoritarian streak, took the helm as prime minister. On Sept. 16, 1963, Singapore joined Malaya, Sabah (North Borneo), and Sarawak in the Federation of Malaysia. It withdrew from the federation on Aug. 9, 1965, and a month later proclaimed itself a republic.

Under Lee, Singapore developed into one of the cleanest, safest, and most economically prosperous cities in Asia. However, Singapore's strict rules of civil obedience also drew criticism from those who said the nation's prosperity was achieved at the expense of individual freedoms.

S. R. Nathan was declared president without an election when he was certified as the only candidate eligible to run in 1999 elections. In Aug. 2004, Lee Hsien Loong became the country's third prime minister since Singapore gained independence from Britain in 1965.

Slovakia

SLOVAK REPUBLIC

National name: Slovenska Republika
President: Ivan Gasparovic (2004)
Prime Minister: Mikulás Dzurinda (1998)
Area: 18,859 sq mi (48,845 sq km)
Population (2005 est.): 5,431,363 (growth rate: 0.2%); birth rate: 10.6/1000; infant mortality rate: 7.4/1000; life expectancy: 74.5; density per sq mi: 288
Capital and largest city (2003 est.): Bratislava,

428,800. **Other large city:** Kosice, 233,600. **Monetary unit:** Koruna. **Languages:** Slovak (official), Hungarian. **Ethnicity/race:** Slovak 85.7%, Hungarian 10.6%, Roma 1.6%, Czech, Moravian, Silesian 1%, Ruthenian and Ukrainian 0.6%, German 0.1%, Polish 0.1%, other 0.2% (1996). **Religions:** Roman Catholic 60.3%, atheist 9.7%, Protestant 8.4%, Orthodox 4.1%, other 17.5%. **Literacy rate:** n.a
Economic summary: GDP/PPP (2004 est.): $78.89 billion; per capita $14,500. **Real growth rate:** 5.3%. **Inflation:** 7.5%. **Unemployment:** 13.1%. **Arable land:** 30%. **Agriculture:** grains, potatoes, sugar beets, hops, fruit; pigs, cattle, poultry; forest products. **Labor force:** 2.2 million (3rd qtr., 2004 est.); agriculture 5.8%, industry 29.3%, construction 9%, services 55.9% (2003). **Industries:** metal and metal products; food and beverages; electricity, gas, coke, oil, nuclear fuel; chemicals and manmade fibers; machinery; paper and printing; earthenware and ceramics; transport vehicles; textiles; electrical and optical apparatus; rubber products. **Natural resources:** brown coal and lignite; small amounts of iron ore, copper and manganese ore; salt; arable land. **Exports:** $29.25 billion (f.o.b., 2004 est.): vehicles 25.9%, machinery and electrical equipment 21.3%, base metals 14.6%, chemicals and minerals 10.1%, plastics 5.4%. **Imports:** $29.67 billion (f.o.b., 2004 est.): machinery and transport equipment 41.1%, intermediate manufactured goods 19.3%, fuels 12.3%, chemicals 9.8%, miscellaneous manufactured goods 10.2% (2003). **Major trading partners:** Germany, Czech Republic, Austria, Italy, Poland, U.S., Hungary, Russia (2003).

Geography Slovakia is located in central Europe. The land has rugged mountains, rich in mineral resources, with vast forests and pastures. The Carpathian Mountains dominate the topography of Slovakia, with lowland areas in the southern region. Slovakia is about twice the size of the state of Maryland.

Government Parliamentary democracy.

History Present-day Slovakia was settled by Slavic Slovaks about the 6th century. They were politically united in the Moravian Empire in the 9th century. In 907, the Germans and the Magyars conquered the Moravian state, and the Slovaks fell under Hungarian control from the 10th century up until 1918. When the Hapsburg-ruled empire collapsed in 1918 following World War I, the Slovaks joined the Czech lands of Bohemia, Moravia, and part of Silesia to form the new joint state of Czechoslovakia. In March 1939, Germany occupied Czechoslovakia, established a German "protectorate," and created a puppet state out of Slovakia with Monsignor Josef Tiso as prime minister. The country was liberated from the Germans by the Soviet army in the spring of 1945, and Slovakia was restored to its prewar status and rejoined to a new Czechoslovakian state.

After the Communist Party took power in Feb. 1948, Slovakia was again subjected to a centralized Czech-dominated government, and antagonism between the two republics developed. In Jan. 1969, the nation became the Slovak Socialist Republic of Czechoslovakia.

Nearly 42 years of Communist rule for Slovakia ended when Vaclav Havel became president of Czechoslovakia in 1989 and democratic political reform began. However, with the demise of Communist power, a strong Slovak nationalist movement resurfaced, and the rival relationship between the two states increased. By the end of 1991, discussions between Slovak and Czech political leaders turned to whether the Czech and Slovak republics should continue to coexist within the federal structure or be divided into two independent states.

After the general election in June 1992, it was decided that two fully independent republics would be created. The Republic of Slovakia came into existence on Jan. 1, 1993. The Parliament in February elected Michal Kovac as president.

Populist Vladimir Meciar, who served three times as Slovakia's prime minister, exhibited increasingly authoritarian behavior and was cited as the reason Slovakia was for a time eliminated from consideration for both the EU and NATO. Slovakia's very low influx of foreign capital during Meciar's tenure was the result of his government's lack of transparency. Meciar was unseated in 1998 elections by the reformist government of Mikulás Dzurinda. In April 2000 Meciar was arrested and charged with paying illegal bonuses to his cabinet ministers while in office. A three-week standoff with police preceded the arrest, ending only when police commandos blew open the door on Meciar's house and seized him. He was also questioned about his alleged involvement in the 1995 kidnapping of the son of Slovakia's former president, Michal Kovac.

Dzurinda has improved Slovakia's reputation in the West, but his tough economic measures have made him unpopular within the country. Former prime minister Meciar has proven oddly resilient. In Sept. 2002 elections, the ruling coalition held onto power, despite Meciar coming out ahead in the vote. In April 2004, Meciar ran for the presidency against his former right-hand man, Ivan Gasparovic. Gasparovic, however, won the largely ceremonial post by a wide majority. In 2004, Slovakia joined the EU and NATO. In May 2005, it ratified the EU constitution.

Slovenia

REPUBLIC OF SLOVENIA

National name: Republika Slovenija
President: Janez Drnovsek (2002)
Prime Minister: Janez Jansa (2004)
Area: 7,827 sq mi (20,273 sq km)
Population (2005 est.): 2,011,070 (growth rate: 0.0%); birth rate: 8.9/1000; infant mortality rate: 4.5/1000; life expectancy: 76.1; density per sq mi: 257
Capital and largest city (2003 est.): Ljubljana, 258,000. **Other large city:** Maribor, 92,400. **Monetary unit:** Slovenian tolar. **Languages:** Slovenian 92%, Serbo-Croatian 6.2%, other 1.8%. **Ethnicity/race:** Slovene 92%, Croat 1%, Serb 0.5%, Hungarian 0.4%, Bosniak 0.3%, other 5.8% (1991). **Religions:** Roman Catholic 70.8% (including 2% Uniate), Lutheran 1%, Islam 1%, atheist 4.3%, other 22.9%. **Literacy rate:** 100% (2003 est.)
Economic summary: GDP/PPP (2004 est.): $39.41 billion; per capita $19,600. **Real growth rate:** 3.9%. **Inflation:** 3.3%. **Unemployment:** 6.4%. **Arable land:** 9%. **Agriculture:** potatoes, hops, wheat, sugar beets, corn, grapes; cattle, sheep, poultry. **Labor force:** 870,000; agriculture 6%, industry 40%, services 55% (2002). **Industries:** ferrous metallurgy and aluminum products, lead and zinc smelting, electronics (including military electronics), trucks, electric power equipment, wood products, textiles, chemicals, machine tools. **Natural resources:** lignite coal, lead, zinc, mercury, uranium, silver, hydropower, forests. **Exports:** $14.97 billion (f.o.b., 2004 est.): manufactured goods, machinery and transport equipment, chemicals, food. **Imports:** $16.07 billion (f.o.b., 2004 est.): machinery and transport equipment, manufactured goods, chemicals, fuels and lubricants, food. **Major trading partners:** Germany, Italy, Croatia, Austria, France, Bosnia and Herzegovina (2003).

Geography Slovenia occupies an area about the size of the state of Massachusetts. It is largely a mountainous republic and almost half of the land is forested, with hilly plains spread across the central and eastern regions. Mount Triglav, the highest peak, rises to 9,393 ft (2,864 m).

Government Parliamentary democractic republic.

History Slovenia was originally settled by Illyrian and Celtic peoples. It became part of the Roman Empire in the first century B.C.

The Slovenes were a south Slavic group that settled in the region in the 6th century A.D. During the 7th century, the Slavs established the Slavic state of Samu, which owed its allegiance to the Avars, who dominated the Hungarian plain until Charlemagne defeated them in the late 8th century.

When the Hungarians were defeated by the Turks in 1526, Hungary accepted Austrian Hapsburg rule in order to escape Turkish domination; the Hapsburg monarchy was the first to include all of the Slovene regions. Thus, Slovenia and Croatia became part of the Austro-Hungarian kingdom when the dual monarchy was established in 1867. Like Croatia and unlike the other Balkan states, it is primarily Roman Catholic.

Following the defeat and collapse of Austria-Hungary in World War I, Slovenia declared its independence. It formally joined with Montenegro, Serbia, and Croatia on Dec. 4, 1918, to form the new nation called the Kingdom of the Serbs, Croats, and Slovenes. The name was later changed to Yugoslavia in 1929.

During World War II, Germany occupied Yugoslavia, and Slovenia was divided among Germany, Italy, and Hungary. For the duration of the war many Slovenes fought a guerrilla war against the Nazis under the leadership of the Croatian-born Communist resistance leader, Marshal Tito. After the final defeat of the Axis powers in 1945, Slovenia was again made into a republic of the newly established Communist nation of Yugoslavia.

In the 1980s, Slovenia agitated for greater autonomy and occasionally threatened to secede. It introduced a multiparty system and in 1990 elected a non-Communist government. Slovenia declared its independence from Yugoslavia on June 25, 1991. The Serbian-dominated Yugoslavian army tried to keep Slovenia in line and some brief fighting took place, but the army then withdrew its forces. Unlike Croatia and Bosnia, Slovenia was able to sever itself from Yugoslavia with relatively little violence. With recognition of its independence granted by the European Community in 1992, the country began realigning its economy and society toward western Europe. Slovenia joined the EU and NATO in 2004.

In a surprise upset, the center-right Slovenian Democrats (SDS) leader Janez Jansa won in Oct. 2004 elections. Prime Minister Anton Rop, of the Liberal Democratic Party (LDS), conceded defeat. LDS had been in power for most of the previous 12 years.

Solomon Islands

Sovereign: Queen Elizabeth II (1952)
Governor-General: Nathaniel Waena (2004)
Prime Minister: Sir Allan Kemakeza (2001)
Area: 10,985 sq mi (28,450 sq km)
Population (2005 est.): 538,032 (growth rate: 2.7%); birth rate: 30.7/1000; infant mortality rate: 21.3/1000; life expectancy: 72.7; density per sq mi: 49
Capital and largest city (2003 est.): Honiara (on Guadalcanal), 54,600. **Monetary unit:** Solomon Islands dollar. **Languages:** English 1%–2% (official),

Melanesian pidgin (lingua franca), 120 indigenous languages. **Ethnicity/race:** Melanesian 93%, Polynesian 4%, Micronesian 1.5%, European 0.8%, Chinese 0.3%, other 0.4%. **Religions:** Anglican 45%, Roman Catholic 18%, United (Methodist/Presbyterian) 12%, Baptist 9%, Seventh-Day Adventist 7%, other Protestant 5%, indigenous beliefs 4%. **Literacy rate:** n.a
Economic summary: GDP/PPP (2002 est.): $800 million; per capita $1,700. **Real growth rate:** 5.8% (2003 est.). **Inflation:** 10% (2003 est.). **Unemployment:** n.a. **Arable land:** 0.6%. **Agriculture:** cocoa beans, coconuts, palm kernels, rice, potatoes, vegetables, fruit; cattle, pigs; timber; fish. **Labor force:** 26,840 (1999); agriculture 75%, industry 5%, services 20% (2000 est.). **Industries:** fish (tuna), mining, timber. **Natural resources:** fish, forests, gold, bauxite, phosphates, lead, zinc, nickel. **Exports:** $74 million (f.o.b., 2003 est.): timber, fish, copra, palm oil, cocoa. **Imports:** $67 million (f.o.b., 2003): food, equipment, manufactured goods, fuels, chemicals. **Major trading partners:** China, South Korea, Japan, Philippines, Thailand, Singapore, Australia, India, New Zealand, Fiji, Papua New Guinea (2003). **Member of British Commonwealth**

Geography   A scattered archipelago of about 1,000 mountainous islands and low-lying coral atolls, the Solomon Islands lie east of Papua New Guinea and northeast of Australia in the south Pacific. The islands include Guadalcanal, Malaita, Santa Isabel, San Cristóbal, Choiseul, New Georgia, and the Santa Cruz group.

Government   Parliamentary democracy.

History   It is thought that people have lived in the Solomon Islands since at least 2000 b.c. Explored in 1568 by Alvaro de Mendana of Spain, the Solomons were not visited again for about 200 years. In 1886, Great Britain and Germany divided the islands between them, but later Britain was given control of the entire territory. The Japanese invaded the islands in World War II, and they were the scene of some of the bloodiest battles in the Pacific theater, most famously the battle of Guadalcanal. The British gained control of the island again in 1945. In 1976 the islands became self-governing and gained independence in 1978.

Since early 1999, the Isatabu Freedom Movement, a militia group made up of indigenous Isatabus from Guadalcanal, have expelled more than 20,000 Malaitans from the island. The Malaitans had migrated from nearby Malaita, and many secured jobs in the capital, Honiara, stirring resentment among Isatabus that has grown steadily since independence. In response to the ethnic violence and expulsions, a rival Malaitan militia group was founded, the Malaita Eagle Force. In June 2000, the Malaita Eagle Force stole police weapons, forced Prime Minister Bartholomew Ulufa'alu to resign, and seized control of Honiara. The rival groups agreed to a cease-fire in June 2000, barely averting a civil war. Although a peace agreement has been signed and elections have taken place, the country continues to suffer from lawlessness. In July 2003, at the request of the prime minister, a 2,250-strong international peacekeeping force led by Australia arrived on the island to restore order, disarm the militias, and expel the "thieves, drunkards, and extortionists" from the notoriously corrupt police force. Australia's intervention was highly successful, and two years after troops arrived, the country remained relatively stable.

Somalia

National name: Soomaaliya
President: Abdullahi Yusuf Ahmed (2004)
Prime Minister: Ali Muhammad Ghedi (2004)
Area: 246,199 sq mi (637,657 sq km)
Population (2005 est.): 8,591,629 (growth rate: 3.4%); birth rate: 45.6/1000; infant mortality rate: 116.7/1000; life expectancy: 48.1; density per sq mi: 35
Capital and largest city (2003 est.): Mogadishu, 1,208,800. **Monetary unit:** Somali shilling.
Languages: Somali (official), Arabic, English, Italian.
Ethnicity/race: Somali 85%, Bantu and others 15% (including Arabs 30,000). **Religion:** Islam (Sunni).
Literacy rate: 38% (2001 est.)
Economic summary: GDP/PPP (2004 est.): $4.597 billion; per capita $600. **Real growth rate:** 2.8%. **Inflation:** n.a. (businesses print their own money). **Unemployment:** n.a. **Arable land:** 2%. **Agriculture:** cattle, sheep, goats; bananas, sorghum, corn, coconuts, rice, sugarcane, mangoes, sesame seeds, beans; fish. **Labor force:** 3.7 million (very few are skilled laborers); agriculture (mostly pastoral nomadism) 71%, industry and services 29%. **Industries:** a few light industries, including sugar refining, textiles, wireless communication. **Natural resources:** uranium and largely unexploited reserves of iron ore, tin, gypsum, bauxite, copper, salt, natural gas, likely oil reserves. **Exports:** $79 million (f.o.b., 2002 est.): livestock, bananas, hides, fish, charcoal, scrap metal. **Imports:** $344 million (f.o.b., 2002 est.): manufactures, petroleum products, foodstuffs, construction materials, qat. **Major trading partners:** UAE, Yemen, India, Oman, China, Nigeria, Djibouti, Kenya, Brazil (2003).

Geography   Somalia, situated in the Horn of Africa, lies along the Gulf of Aden and the Indian Ocean. It is bounded by Djibouti in the northwest, Ethiopia in the west, and Kenya in the southwest. In area it is slightly smaller than Texas. Generally arid and barren, Somalia has two chief rivers, the Shebelle and the Juba.

Government   Between Jan. 1991 and Aug. 2000, Somalia had no working government. A fragile parliamentary government was formed in 2000, but it expired in 2003 without establishing control of the country. In 2004, a new transitional Parliament was instituted and elected a president.

History   From the 7th to the 10th century, Arab and Persian trading posts were established along the coast of present-day Somalia. Nomadic tribes occupied the interior, occasionally pushing into Ethiopian territory. In the 16th century, Turkish rule extended to the northern coast, and the Sultans of Zanzibar gained control in the south.

After British occupation of Aden in 1839, the Somali coast became its source of food. The French established a coal-mining station in 1862 at the site of Djibouti, and the Italians planted a settlement in Eritrea. Egypt, which for a time claimed Turkish rights in the area, was succeeded by Britain. By 1920, a British and an Italian protectorate occupied what is now Somalia. The British ruled the entire area after 1941, with Italy returning in 1950 to serve as United Nations trustee for its former territory.

By 1960, Britain and Italy granted independence to their respective sectors, enabling the two to join as the Republic of Somalia on July 1, 1960. Somalia broke diplomatic relations with Britain in 1963 when the British granted the Somali-populated Northern Frontier District of Kenya to the Republic of Kenya.

On Oct. 15, 1969, President Abdi Rashid Ali Shermarke was assassinated and the army seized power. Maj. Gen. Mohamed Siad Barre, as president of a renamed Somali Democratic Republic, leaned heavily toward the USSR. In 1977, Somalia openly backed rebels in the easternmost area of Ethiopia, the Ogaden Desert, which had been seized by Ethiopia at the turn of the century. Somalia acknowledged defeat in an eight-month war against the Ethiopians that year, having lost much of its 32,000-man army and most of its tanks and planes. President Siad Barre fled the country in late Jan. 1991. His departure left Somalia in the hands of a number of clan-based guerrilla groups, none of which trusted each other.

Africa's worst drought of the century occurred in 1992, and, coupled with the devastation of civil war, Somalia was plunged into a severe famine that killed 300,000. U.S. troops were sent in to protect the delivery of food in Dec. 1992, and in May 1993 the UN took control of the relief efforts from the U.S. The warlord Mohamed Farah Aidid ambushed UN troops and dragged American bodies through the streets, causing an about-face in U.S. willingness to involve itself in the fate of this lawless country. The last of the U.S. troops departed in late March, leaving 19,000 UN troops behind.

Since 1991 Somalia has been engulfed in anarchy. Years of peace negotiations between the various factions were fruitless, and warlords and militias ruled over individual swaths of land. In 1991, a breakaway nation, the Somaliland Republic, proclaimed its independence. Since then several warlords have set up their own ministates in Puntland and Jubaland. Although internationally unrecognized, these states have been peaceful and stable.

In Aug. 2000, a Parliament convened in nearby Djibouti and elected Somalia's first government in nearly a decade. After its first year in office, the government still controlled only 10% of the country, and in Aug. 2003, its mandate expired. In Oct. 2002, new talks to establish a government began; in Aug. 2004 a 275-member transitional Parliament was inaugurated for a five-year term. Parliament selected a national president in September, Abdullahi Yusuf Ahmed, the president of the breakaway region of Puntland. The new government, however, spent its first year operating out of Kenya—Somalia remained too violent and unstable, and lawmakers were unable to agree on what city should serve as the seat of government.

South Africa

REPUBLIC OF SOUTH AFRICA

President: Thabo Mbeki (1999)

Area: 471,008 sq mi (1,219,912 sq km)

Population (2005 est.): 44,344,136 (growth rate: –0.3%); birth rate: 18.5/1000; infant mortality rate: 61.8/1000; life expectancy: 43.3; density per sq mi: 94

Administrative capital (2003 est.): Pretoria, 1,541,300 (metro. area), 1,249,700 (city proper); **Legislative capital and largest city:** Cape Town, 3,140,600 (metro. area), 2,733,000 (city proper); **Judicial capital:** Bloemfontein, 378,000. No decision has been made to relocate the seat of government. South Africa is demarcated into nine provinces, consisting of the Gauteng, Northern Province, Mpumalanga, North West, KwaZulu/Natal, Eastern Cape, Western Cape, Northern Cape, and Free State. Each province has its own capital. **Other large cities:** Durban/Pinetown, 2,396,100; Johannesburg, 1,675,200; East Rand, 1,378,792 (part of Johannesburg metro. area, 2000 est.). **Monetary unit:** Rand. **Languages:** Afrikaans,

English, Ndebele, Pedi, Sotho, Swazi, Tsonga, Tswana, Venda, Xhosa, Zulu (all 11 official). **Ethnicity/race:** black 75.2%, white 13.6%, Colored 8.6%, Indian 2.6%. **Religions:** Christian 68% (includes most whites and Coloreds, about 60% of blacks, and about 40% of Indians), indigenous beliefs and animist 28.5%, Islam 2%, Hindu 1.5% (60% of Indians). **Literacy rate:** 86% (2003 est.)

Economic summary: GDP/PPP (2004 est.): $491.4 billion; per capita $11,100. **Real growth rate:** 3.5%. **Inflation:** 4.5%. **Unemployment:** 26.2% (includes workers no longer looking for employment). **Arable land:** 12%. **Agriculture:** corn, wheat, sugarcane, fruits, vegetables; beef, poultry, mutton, wool, dairy products. **Labor force:** 16.63 million economically active; agriculture 30%, industry 25%, services 45% (1999 est.). **Industries:** mining (world's largest producer of platinum, gold, chromium); automobile assembly, metalworking, machinery, textile, iron and steel, chemicals, fertilizer, foodstuffs, commercial ship repair. **Natural resources:** gold, chromium, antimony, coal, iron ore, manganese, nickel, phosphates, tin, uranium, gem diamonds, platinum, copper, vanadium, salt, natural gas. **Exports:** $41.97 billion (f.o.b., 2004 est.): gold, diamonds, platinum, other metals and minerals, machinery and equipment (1998 est.). **Imports:** $39.42 billion (f.o.b., 2004 est.): machinery and equipment, chemicals, petroleum products, scientific instruments, foodstuffs (2000 est.). **Major trading partners:** UK, U.S., Japan, Germany, China, Italy, India, Saudi Arabia, France (2003).

Geography South Africa, on the continent's southern tip, is bordered by the Atlantic Ocean on the west and by the Indian Ocean on the south and east. Its neighbors are Namibia in the northwest, Zimbabwe and Botswana in the north, and Mozambique and Swaziland in the northeast. The kingdom of Lesotho forms an enclave within the southeast part of South Africa, which occupies an area nearly three times that of California.

The southernmost point of Africa is Cape Agulhas, located in the Western Cape Province about 100 mi (161 km) southeast of the Cape of Good Hope.

Government Republic.

History The San people were the first settlers; the Khoikhoi and Bantu-speaking tribes followed. The Dutch East India Company landed the first European settlers on the Cape of Good Hope in 1652, launching a colony that by the end of the 18th century numbered only about 15,000. Known as Boers or Afrikaners, and speaking a Dutch dialect known as Afrikaans, the settlers as early as 1795 tried to establish an independent republic.

After occupying the Cape Colony in that year, Britain took permanent possession in 1815 at the end of the Napoleonic Wars, bringing in 5,000 settlers. Anglicization of government and the freeing of slaves in 1833 drove about 12,000 Afrikaners to make the "great trek" north and east into African tribal territory, where they established the republics of the Transvaal and the Orange Free State.

The discovery of diamonds in 1867 and gold nine years later brought an influx of "outlanders" into the republics and spurred Cape Colony prime minister Cecil Rhodes to plot annexation. Rhodes's scheme of sparking an "outlander" rebellion, to which an armed party under Leander Starr Jameson would ride to the rescue, misfired in 1895, forcing Rhodes to resign. What British expansionists called the "inevitable" war with the Boers broke out on Oct. 11, 1899. The defeat of the Boers in 1902 led in 1910 to the Union of South Africa, composed of four provinces, the two former republics, and the old Cape and Natal colonies. Louis Botha, a Boer, became the first prime minister. Organized political activity among Africans started with the establishment of the African National Congress in 1912.

Jan Christiaan Smuts brought the nation into World War II on the Allied side against Nationalist opposition, and South Africa became a charter member of the United Nations in 1945, but he refused to sign the Universal Declaration of Human Rights. Apartheid—racial separation—dominated domestic politics as the Nationalists gained power and imposed greater restrictions on Bantus (black Africans), Asians, and Coloreds (in South Africa the term meant any nonwhite person). Black voters were removed from the voter rolls in 1936. Over the next half-century, the nonwhite population of South Africa was forced out of designated white areas. The Group Areas Acts of 1950 and 1986 forced about 1.5 million Africans to move from cities to rural townships, where they lived in abject poverty under repressive laws.

South Africa declared itself a republic in 1961 and severed its ties with the Commonwealth, which strongly objected to the country's racist policies. The white supremacist National Party, which had first come to power in 1948, would continue its rule for the next three decades.

In 1960, 70 black protesters were killed during a peaceful demonstration in Sharpesville. The African National Congress (ANC), the principal antiapartheid organization, was banned that year, and in 1964 its leader, Nelson Mandela, was sentenced to life imprisonment. Black protests against apartheid grew stronger and more violent. In 1976, an uprising in the black township of Soweto spread to other black townships and left 600 dead. Beginning in the 1960s, international opposition to apartheid intensified. The UN imposed sanctions, and many countries divested their South African holdings.

Apartheid's grip on South Africa began to give way when F. W. de Klerk replaced P. W. Botha as president in 1989. De Klerk removed the ban on the ANC and released its leader, Nelson Mandela, after 27 years of imprisonment. The Inkatha Freedom Party, a black opposition group led by Mangosuthu Buthelezi, which was seen as collaborating with the apartheid system, frequently clashed with the ANC during this period.

In 1991, a multiracial forum led by de Klerk and Mandela, the Convention for a Democratic South Africa (CODESA), began working on a new constitution. In 1993, an interim constitution was passed, which dismantled apartheid and provided for a multiracial democracy with majority rule. The peaceful transition of South Africa from one of the world's most repressive societies into a democracy is one of the 20th century's most remarkable success stories. Mandela and de Klerk were jointly awarded the Nobel Peace Prize in 1993.

The 1994 election, the country's first multiracial one, resulted in a massive victory for Mandela and his ANC. The new government included six ministers from the National Party and three from the Inkatha Freedom Party. A new national constitution was approved and adopted in May 1996.

In 1997 the Truth and Reconciliation Commission, chaired by Desmond Tutu, began hearings regarding human rights violations between 1960 and 1993. The commission promised amnesty to those who confessed their crimes under the apartheid system. In 1998, F. W. de Klerk, P. W. Botha, and leaders of the ANC appeared before the commission, and the nation contin-

ued to grapple with its enlightened but often painful and divisive process of national recovery.

Nelson Mandela, whose term as president cemented his reputation as one of the world's most farsighted and magnanimous statesmen, retired in 1999. On June 2, 1999, Thabo Mbeki, the pragmatic deputy president and leader of the ANC, was elected president in a landslide, having already assumed many of Mandela's governing responsibilities.

In his first term, Mbeki wrestled with a slumping economy and a skyrocketing crime rate. South Africa, the country with the highest number of HIV-positive people in the world (6.5 million in 2005), has been hampered in fighting the epidemic by its president's highly controversial views. Mbeki has denied the link between HIV and AIDS and claimed that the West has exaggerated the epidemic to boost drug profits. The international community as well as most South African leaders, including Nelson Mandela and Desmond Tutu, have condemned Mbeki's stance. In Aug. 2003, after years of delay, Mbeki reversed his hands-off AIDS policy, but the government's deep ambivalence toward combating the epidemic persists.

As expected, on April 15, 2004, the African National Congress won South Africa's general election in a landslide, taking about 70% of the vote, and Thabo Mbeki was sworn in for a second term.

Spain

KINGDOM OF SPAIN

National name: Reino de España
Ruler: King Juan Carlos I (1975)
Prime Minister: José Luis Rodríguez Zapatero (2004)
Area: 194,896 sq mi (504,782 sq km)[1]
Population (2005 est.): 40,341,462 (growth rate: 0.2%); birth rate: 10.1/1000; infant mortality rate: 4.4/1000; life expectancy: 79.5; density per sq mi: 207
Capital and largest city (2003 est.): Madrid, 5,130,000 (metro. area), 3,169,400 (city proper). **Other large cities:** Barcelona, 1,528,800; Valencia, 741,100; Seville, 679,100. **Monetary units:** Euro (formerly peseta). **Languages:** Castilian Spanish 74% (official nationwide); Catalan 17%, Galician 7%, Basque 2% (each official regionally). **Ethnicity/race:** composite of Mediterranean and Nordic types. **Religions:** Roman Catholic 94%, other 6%. **Literacy rate:** 98% (2003 est.)
Economic summary: GDP/PPP (2004 est.): $937.6 billion; per capita $23,300. **Real growth rate:** 2.6%. **Inflation:** 3.2%. **Unemployment:** 10.4%. **Arable land:** 26%. **Agriculture:** grain, vegetables, olives, wine grapes, sugar beets, citrus; beef, pork, poultry, dairy products; fish. **Labor force:** 19.33 million; agriculture 5.3%, manufacturing, mining, and construction 30.1%, services 64.6% (2004 est.). **Industries:** textiles and apparel (including footwear), food and beverages, metals and metal manufactures, chemicals, shipbuilding, automobiles, machine tools, tourism, clay and refractory products, footwear, pharmaceuticals, medical equipment. **Natural resources:** coal, lignite, iron ore, uranium, mercury, pyrites, fluorspar, gypsum, zinc, lead, tungsten, copper, kaolin, potash, hydropower, arable land. **Exports:** $172.5 billion (f.o.b., 2004 est.): machinery, motor vehicles; foodstuffs, pharmaceuticals, medicines, other consumer goods. **Imports:** $222 billion (f.o.b., 2004 est.): machinery and equipment, fuels, chemicals, semifinished goods; foodstuffs, consumer goods; measuring and medical control instruments. **Major trading partners:** France, Germany, Italy, Portugal, UK, U.S., Netherlands (2003).

1. Including the Balearic and Canary Islands.

Geography Spain occupies 85% of the Iberian Peninsula, which it shares with Portugal, in southwest Europe. Africa is less than 10 mi (16 km) south at the Strait of Gibraltar. A broad central plateau slopes to the south and east, crossed by a series of mountain ranges and river valleys. Principal rivers are the Ebro in the northeast, the Tajo in the central region, and the Guadalquivir in the south. Off Spain's east coast in the Mediterranean are the Balearic Islands (1,936 sq mi; 5,014 sq km), the largest of which is Majorca. Sixty mi (97 km) west of Africa are the Canary Islands (2,808 sq mi; 7,273 sq km).

Government Parliamentary monarchy.

History Spain, originally inhabited by Celts, Iberians, and Basques, became a part of the Roman Empire in 206 B.C., when it was conquered by Scipio Africanus. In A.D. 412, the barbarian Visigothic leader Ataulf crossed the Pyrenees and ruled Spain, first in the name of the Roman emperor and then independently. In 711, the Muslims under Tariq entered Spain from Africa and within a few years completed the subjugation of the country. In 732, the Franks, led by Charles Martel, defeated the Muslims near Poitiers, thus preventing the further expansion of Islam in southern Europe. Internal dissension of Spanish Islam invited a steady Christian conquest from the north.

Aragon and Castile were the most important Spanish states from the 12th to the 15th century, consolidated by the marriage of Ferdinand II.and Isabella I in 1469. The last Muslim stronghold, Granada, was captured in 1492. Roman Catholicism was established as the official state religion and most Jews (1492) and Muslims (1502) were expelled. In the era of exploration, discovery, and colonization, Spain amassed tremendous wealth and a vast colonial empire through the conquest of Mexico by Cortés (1519–1521) and Peru by Pizarro (1532–1533). The Spanish Hapsburg monarchy became for a time the most powerful in the world. In 1588, Philip II sent his invincible Armada to invade England, but its destruction cost Spain its supremacy on the seas and paved the way for England's colonization of America. Spain then sank rapidly to the status of a second-rate power under the rule of weak Hapsburg kings, and it never again played a major role in European politics. The War of the Spanish Succession (1701–1714) resulted in Spain's loss of Belgium, Luxembourg, Milan, Sardinia, and Naples. Its colonial empire in the Americas and the Philippines vanished in wars and revolutions during the 18th and 19th centuries.

In World War I, Spain maintained a position of neutrality. In 1923, Gen. Miguel Primo de Rivera became dictator. In 1930, King Alfonso XIII revoked the dictatorship, but a strong antimonarchist and republican movement led to his leaving Spain in 1931. The new constitution declared Spain a workers' republic, broke up the large estates, separated church and state, and secularized the schools. The elections held in 1936 returned a strong Popular Front majority, with Manuel Azaña as president.

On July 18, 1936, a conservative army officer in Morocco, Francisco Franco Bahamonde, led a mutiny against the government. The civil war that followed lasted three years and cost the lives of nearly a million people. Franco was aided by Fascist Italy and Nazi Germany, while Soviet Russia helped the Loyalist side. Several hundred leftist Americans served in the Abraham Lincoln Brigade on the side of the republic. The war ended when Franco took Madrid on March 28, 1939. Franco became head of the state, national chief of the Falange Party (the governing party), and prime minister and caudillo (leader). In a referendum in 1947, the Spanish people approved a Franco-drafted succession law declaring Spain a monarchy again. Franco, however, continued as chief of state.

In 1969, Franco and the *Cortes* ("states") designated Prince Juan Carlos Alfonso Victor María de Borbón (who married Princess Sophia of Greece on May 14, 1962) to become king of Spain when the provisional government headed by Franco came to an end. Franco died of a heart attack on Nov. 20, 1975, after more than a year of ill health, and Juan Carlos was proclaimed king on Nov. 22.

Under pressure from Catalonian and Basque nationalists, Prime Minister Adolfo Suárez granted home rule to these regions in 1979. Basque separatists committed hundreds of terrorist bombings and kidnappings that continue to the present. With the overwhelming election of Prime Minister Felipe González Márquez and his Spanish Socialist Workers Party in the Oct. 20, 1982, parliamentary elections, the Franco past was finally buried.

Spain entered NATO in 1982. A treaty admitting Spain, along with Portugal, to the European Economic Community, now the European Union, took effect on Jan. 1, 1986. General elections in March 1996 produced a victory for the conservative Popular Party, and its leader, José María Aznar, became prime minister. He and his party easily won reelection in 2000.

In Aug. 2002, Batasuna, the political wing of the Basque terrorist organization ETA, was banned. The wisdom of driving the party underground instead of permitting it a legitimate political outlet has been questioned.

Aznar's backing of the U.S. war in Iraq was highly unpopular—90% of Spaniards opposed the war. (Spain sent no troops to Iraq during the war but contributed 1,300 peacekeeping forces during the reconstruction period.) Yet Aznar's Popular Party did extremely well in municipal elections in May 2003. The country's relative prosperity and the prime minister's tough stance against the ETA were thought to be responsible for the strong showing.

On March 11, 2004, Spain suffered its most horrific terrorist attack: 202 people were killed and 1,400 were injured in bombings at Madrid's railway station. The government at first blamed ETA, but soon evidence emerged that al-Qaeda was responsible. When record numbers of voters went to the polls days later, Aznar's Popular Party experienced a stinging defeat, and José Luis Rodríguez Zapatero of the Socialist Party became the new prime minister. Many Spaniards blamed Aznar's staunch support of the U.S. and the war in Iraq for making Spain an al-Qaeda target. Others were angered by what they saw as the government's politically motivated position that ETA was to blame for the attacks at the same time that links to al-Qaeda were emerging. By April, a dozen suspects, most of them Moroccan, were arrested for the bombings. On April 4, several suspects blew themselves up during a police raid to avoid capture. In May, the new prime minister made good on his campaign promise, recalling Spain's 1,300 soldiers from Iraq, much to the displeasure of the United States, which said Spain was appeasing terrorists.

In June 2005, despite strong opposition from the Catholic Church, Spain legalized gay marriage. (Three other countries permit same-sex marriage: Belgium, the Netherlands, and Canada.)

Sri Lanka

DEMOCRATIC SOCIALIST REPUBLIC OF SRI LANKA

President: Chandrika B. Kumaratunga (1994)
Prime Minister: Mahinda Rajapakse (2004)
Area: 25,332 sq mi (65,610 sq km)
Population (2005 est.): 20,064,776 (growth rate: 0.8%); birth rate: 15.6/1000; infant mortality rate: 14.3/1000; life expectancy: 73.2; density per sq mi: 792
Capital and largest city (2003 est.): Colombo, 2,436,000 (metro. area), 656,100 (city proper); **Legislative and judicial capital:** Sri Jayawardenepura Kotte, 118,300. **Other large cities:** Dehiwala-Mount Lavinia 214,300; Moratuwa, 181,000; Kandy, 112,400. **Monetary unit:** Sri Lanka rupee. **Languages:** Sinhala 74% (official and national), Tamil 18% (national), other 8%; English is commonly used in government and spoken competently by about 10%. **Ethnicity/race:** Sinhalese 74%, Tamil 18%, Moor 7%, Burgher, Malay, and Vedda 1%. **Religions:** Buddhist 70%, Hindu 15%, Christian 8%, Islam 7% (1999). **Literacy rate:** 92% (2003 est.)
Economic summary: GDP/PPP (2004 est.): $80.58 billion; per capita $4,000. **Real growth rate:** 5.2%. **Inflation:** 5.8%. **Unemployment:** 7.8%. **Arable land:** 14%. **Agriculture:** rice, sugarcane, grains, pulses, oilseed, spices, tea, rubber, coconuts; milk, eggs, hides, beef. **Labor force:** 7.26 million; services 45%, agriculture 38%, industry 17% (1998 est.). **Industries:** rubber processing, tea, coconuts, and other agricultural commodities; telecommunications, insurance, and banking; clothing, cement, petroleum refining, textiles, tobacco. **Natural resources:** limestone, graphite, mineral sands, gems, phosphates, clay, hydropower. **Exports:** $5.306 billion (f.o.b., 2004 est.): textiles and apparel; tea and spices; diamonds, emeralds, rubies; coconut products; rubber manufactures, fish. **Imports:** $7.265 billion (f.o.b., 2004 est.): textile fabrics, mineral products, petroleum, foodstuffs, machinery and transportation equipment. **Major trading partners:** U.S., UK, India, Germany, Hong Kong, Singapore, Japan, China, South Korea, Taiwan, Malaysia (2003). **Member of Commonwealth of Nations**

Geography An island in the Indian Ocean off the southeast tip of India, Sri Lanka is about half the size of Alabama. Most of the land is flat and rolling; mountains in the south-central region rise to over 8,000 ft (2,438 m).

Government Republic.

History Indo-Aryan emigration from India in the 5th century B.C. came to form the largest ethnic group on Sri Lanka today, the Sinhalese. Tamils, the second-largest ethnic group on the island, were originally from the Tamil region of India and emigrated between the 3rd century B.C. and A.D. 1200. Until colonial powers controlled Ceylon (the country's name until 1972), Sinhalese and Tamil rulers fought for dominance over the island. The Tamils, primarily Hindus, claimed the northern section of the island and the Sinhalese, who are predominantly Buddhist, controlled the south. In 1505 the Portuguese took possession of Ceylon until the Dutch India Company usurped control (1658–1796). The British took over in 1796, and Ceylon became an English Crown colony in 1802. The British developed coffee, tea, and rubber plantations. On Feb. 4, 1948, after pressure from Ceylonese nationalist leaders (which briefly unified the Tamil and Sinhalese), Ceylon became a self-governing dominion of the Commonwealth of Nations.

S.W.R.D. Bandaranaike became prime minister in 1956 and championed Sinhalese nationalism, making Sinhala the country's only official language and including state support of Buddhism, further marginalizing the Tamil minority. He was assassinated in 1959 by a Buddhist monk. His widow, Sirimavo Bandaranaike, became the world's first female prime minister in 1960. The name *Ceylon* was changed to *Sri Lanka* ("resplendent island") on May 22, 1972.

The Tamil minority's mounting resentment toward the Sinhalese majority's monopoly on political and economic power, exacerbated by cultural and religious differences, erupted in bloody violence in 1983. Tamil rebel groups, the strongest of which were the Liberation Tigers of Tamil Eelam, or Tamil Tigers, began fighting for a separate nation.

President Ranasinghe Premadasa was assassinated at a May Day political rally in 1993, when a Tamil rebel detonated explosives strapped to himself. Tamil extremists have frequently resorted to terrorist attacks against civilians. The next president, Chandrika Kumaratunga, vowed to restore peace to the country. In Dec. 1999, she was herself wounded in a terrorist attack. By early 2000, 18 years of war had claimed the lives of more than 64,000, mostly civilians.

After Dec. 2001 elections, Ranil Wickremesinghe, a longtime bitter rival of President Kumaratunga, was sworn in as prime minister. Wickremesinghe's victory precipitated a formal cease-fire with the Tamil rebels, signed in Feb. 2002. In September talks, the government lifted its ban on the group, and the Tigers dropped their demand for an independent Tamil state. Another significant breakthrough came in December when the Tigers and the government struck a power-sharing deal that would give the rebels regional autonomy. But negotiations in 2003 achieved little.

Intense political rivalry threatened the peace process. In Nov. 2003, President Kumaratunga, convinced that Prime Minister Wickremesinghe was too soft in his negotiations with the Tigers, wrested away some of his powers. In Feb. 2004, the president dissolved Parliament and called for elections in the hope of further eroding the power of the prime minister. The gamble paid off for Kumaratunga—her United People's Freedom Alliance won April's parliamentary elections; and Wickremesinghe was replaced by a new prime minister, Mahinda Rajapakse, a high-ranking member of Kumaratunga's party.

On Dec. 26, 2004, a tremendously powerful tsunami ravaged 12 Asian countries. About 38,000 people were reported killed in Sri Lanka. President Kumaratunga and the Tamil Tigers reached a deal in June 2005 to share about $4.5 billion in international aid to rebuild the country after the devastating tsunami. But intensifying violence in the eastern part of the country threatened the cease-fire and jeopardized the aid package.

Sri Lanka seemed on the brink of returning to war in Aug. 2005, when Foreign Minister Lakshman Kadirgamar was assassinated and the government declared a state of emergency. The government accused the Tamil Tigers of the killing.

Sudan

REPUBLIC OF THE SUDAN

National name: Jamhuryat as-Sudan
President: Lt. Gen. Omar Hassan Ahmad al-Bashir (1989)
Area: 967,493 sq mi (2,505,810 sq km)
Population (2005 est.): 40,187,486 (growth rate: 2.6%); birth rate: 35.2/1000; infant mortality rate: 62.5/1000; life expectancy: 58.5; density per sq mi: 42
Capital (2003 est.): Khartoum, 5,717,300 (metro. area), 1,397,900 (city proper). **Largest cities:** Omdurman, 2,103,900; Port Sudan, 450,400. **Monetary unit:** Dinar. **Languages:** Arabic (official), Nubian, Ta Bedawie, diverse dialects of Nilotic, Nilo-Hamitic,

Sudanic languages, English. **Ethnicity/race:** black 52%, Arab 39%, Beja 6%, foreigners 2%, other 1%. **Religions:** Islam (Sunni) 70% (in north), indigenous 25%, Christian 5% (mostly in south and Khartoum). **Literacy rate:** 61% (2003 est.)

Economic summary: GDP/PPP (2004 est.): $76.19 billion; per capita $1,900. **Real growth rate:** 6.4%. **Inflation:** 9%. **Unemployment:** 18.7% (2002 est.). **Arable land:** 7%. **Agriculture:** cotton, groundnuts (peanuts), sorghum, millet, wheat, gum arabic, sugarcane, cassava (tapioca), mangos, papaya, bananas, sweet potatoes, sesame; sheep, livestock. **Labor force:** 11 million (1996 est.); agriculture 80%, industry and commerce 7%, government 13% (1998 est.). **Industries:** oil, cotton ginning, textiles, cement, edible oils, sugar, soap distilling, shoes, petroleum refining, pharmaceuticals, armaments, automobile/light truck assembly. **Natural resources:** petroleum; small reserves of iron ore, copper, chromium ore, zinc, tungsten, mica, silver, gold, hydropower. **Exports:** $3.395 billion (f.o.b., 2004 est.): oil and petroleum products; cotton, sesame, livestock, groundnuts, gum arabic, sugar. **Imports:** $3.496 billion (f.o.b., 2004 est.): foodstuffs, manufactured goods, refinery and transport equipment, medicines and chemicals, textiles, wheat. **Major trading partners:** China, Saudi Arabia, UAE, UK, Germany, India, France (2003).

Geography Sudan, in northeast Africa, is the largest country on the continent, measuring about one-fourth the size of the United States. Its neighbors are Chad and the Central African Republic on the west, Egypt and Libya on the north, Ethiopia and Eritrea on the east, and Kenya, Uganda, and Democratic Republic of the Congo on the south. The Red Sea washes about 500 mi of the eastern coast. It is traversed from north to south by the Nile.

Government Military government.

History What is now northern Sudan was in ancient times the kingdom of Nubia, which came under Egyptian rule after 2600 B.C. An Egyptian and Nubian civilization called Kush flourished until A.D. 350. Missionaries converted the region to Christianity in the 6th century, but an influx of Muslim Arabs, who had already conquered Egypt, eventually controlled the area and replaced Christianity with Islam. During the 1500s a people called the Funj conquered much of Sudan, and several other black African groups settled in the south, including the Dinka, Shilluk, Nuer, and Azande. Egyptians again conquered Sudan in 1874, and after Britain occupied Egypt in 1882, it took over Sudan in 1898, ruling the country in conjunction with Egypt. It was known as the Anglo-Egyptian Sudan between 1898 and 1955.

The 20th century saw the growth of Sudanese nationalism, and in 1953 Egypt and Britain granted Sudan self-government. Independence was proclaimed on Jan. 1, 1956. Since independence, Sudan has been ruled by a series of unstable parliamentary governments and military regimes. Under Maj. Gen. Gaafar Mohamed Nimeiri, Sudan instituted fundamentalist Islamic law in 1983. This exacerbated the rift between the Arab North, the seat of the government, and the black African animists and Christians in the South. Differences in language, religion, ethnicity, and political power erupted in an unending civil war between government forces, strongly influenced by the National Islamic Front (NIF) and the southern rebels, whose most influential faction is the Sudan People's Liberation Army (SPLA). Human rights violations, religious persecution, and allegations that Sudan had been a safe haven for terrorists isolated the country from most of the international community. In 1995, the UN imposed sanctions against it.

On Aug. 20, 1998, the United States launched cruise missiles that destroyed a pharmaceutical manufacturing facility in Khartoum which allegedly manufactured chemical weapons. The U.S. contended that the Sudanese factory was financed by Islamic militant Osama bin Laden.

Since 1999 international attention has been focused on evidence that slavery is widespread throughout Sudan. Arab raiders from the north of the country have enslaved thousands of southerners, who are black. The Dinka people have been the hardest-hit. Some sources point out that the raids intensified in the 1980s along with the civil war between North and South.

Ever since Lt. Gen. Omar Bashir's military coup in 1989, the de facto ruler of Sudan had been Hassan el-Turabi, a cleric and political leader who is a major figure in the pan-Arabic Islamic fundamentalist resurgence. In 1999, however, Bashir ousted Turabi and placed him under house arrest. (He was freed in Oct. 2003.) Since then Bashir has made overtures to the West, and in Sept. 2001, the UN lifted its six-year-old sanctions. The U.S., however, still officially considers Sudan a terrorist state.

A cease-fire was declared between the Sudanese government and the Sudan People's Liberation Army (SPLA) in July 2002. During peace talks, which continued through 2003, the government agreed to a power-sharing government for six years, to be followed by a referendum on self-determination for the South. Fighting on both sides continued throughout the peace negotiations. In May 2004, a deal between the government and the SPLA was signed, ending 20 years of brutal civil war that resulted in the deaths of 2 million people.

Just as Sudan's civil war seemed to be coming to an end, another war intensified in the northwestern Darfur region. After the government quelled a rebellion in Darfur in Jan. 2004, it allowed pro-government militias called the Janjaweed to carry out massacres against black villagers and rebel groups in the region. These Arab militias, believed to have been armed by the government, have killed more than 30,000 and displaced more than 1 million. While the war in the South was fought against black Christians and animists, the Darfur conflict is being fought against black Muslims. Although the international community has reacted with alarm to the humanitarian disaster—unmistakably the world's worst—it has been ineffective in persuading the Sudanese government to rein in the Janjaweed. Despite the EU and the U.S. describing the killing as genocide, and despite a UN Security Council resolution demanding that Sudan stop the Arab militias, the killing has continued throughout 2005.

On Jan. 9, 2005, after three years of negotiations, the peace deal between the Southern rebels, led by John Garang of the SPLA, and the Khartoum government to end the two-decades-long civil war was signed, giving roughly half of Sudan's oil wealth to the South, as well as nearly complete autonomy and the right to secede after six years. But just two weeks after Garang was sworn in as first vice president as part of the power-sharing agreement, he was killed in a helicopter crash during bad weather. Rioting erupted in Khartoum, killing nearly 100. Garang's deputy, Salva Kiir, was quickly sworn in as the new vice president, and both North and South vowed that the peace agreement would hold.

Suriname

REPUBLIC OF SURINAME

National name: Republiek Suriname
President: Ronald Venetiaan (2000)
Prime Minister: Jules Ajodhia (2000)
Area: 63,039 sq mi (163,270 sq km)
Population (2005 est.): 438,144 (growth rate: 0.2%);
birth rate: 18.4/1000; infant mortality rate: 23.6/1000;
life expectancy: 69.0; density per sq mi: 7
Capital and largest city (2003 est.): Paramaribo,
217,300. **Monetary unit:** Surinamese dollar.
Languages: Dutch (official), Surinamese (lingua franca),
English widely spoken, Hindustani, Javanese. **Ethnicity/
race:** East Indians (also known locally as Hindustanis)
37%, Creole (mixed white and black) 31%, Javanese
15%, "Bush Negroes" (also known as Maroons) 10%,
Amerindian 2%, Chinese 2%, Europeans 1%, other 2%.
Religions: Hindu 27.4%, Protestant 25.2%
(predominantly Moravian), Roman Catholic 22.8%, Islam
19.6%, indigenous 5%. **Literacy rate:** 93% (1995 est.)
Economic summary: GDP/PPP (2004 est.): $1.885
billion; per capita $4,300. **Real growth rate:** 4.2%.
Inflation: 23% (2003 est.). **Unemployment:** 17%
(2000). **Arable land:** 0.4%. **Agriculture:** paddy rice,
bananas, palm kernels, coconuts, plantains, peanuts;
beef, chickens; forest products; shrimp. **Labor force:**
104,000 (2003); agriculture n.a., industry n.a., services
n.a. **Industries:** bauxite and gold mining, alumina
production, oil, lumbering, food processing, fishing.
Natural resources: timber, hydropower, fish, kaolin,
shrimp, bauxite, gold, and small amounts of nickel,
copper, platinum, iron ore. **Exports:** $495 million (f.o.b.,
2002): alumina, crude oil, lumber, shrimp and fish, rice,
bananas. **Imports:** $604 million (f.o.b., 2002): capital
equipment, petroleum, foodstuffs, cotton, consumer
goods. **Major trading partners:** U.S., Norway, Belgium,
France, Iceland, Italy, Netherlands, Trinidad and Tobago,
China, Japan (2003).

Geography Suriname lies on the northeast coast of
South America, with Guyana to the west, French Guiana to the east, and Brazil to the south. It is about
one-tenth larger than Michigan. The principal rivers
are the Corantijn on the Guyana border, the Marowijne
in the east, and the Suriname, on which the capital city
of Paramaribo is situated.

Government Constitutional democracy.

History Suriname's earliest inhabitants were the
Surinen Indians, after whom the country is named. By
the 16th century they had been supplanted by other
South American Indians. Spain explored Suriname in
1593, but by 1602 the Dutch began to settle the land,
followed by the English. The English transferred sovereignty to the Dutch in 1667 (the Treaty of Breda) in
exchange for New Amsterdam (New York). Colonization was confined to a narrow coastal strip, and until
the abolition of slavery in 1863, African slaves furnished the labor for the coffee and sugarcane plantations. Escaped African slaves fled into the interior,
reconstituted their western African culture, and came
to be called "Bush Negroes" by the Dutch. After 1870,
East Indian laborers were imported from British India
and Javanese from the Dutch East Indies.

Known as Dutch Guiana, the colony was integrated
into the kingdom of the Netherlands in 1948. Two years
later Dutch Guiana was granted home rule, except for
foreign affairs and defense. After race rioting over
unemployment and inflation, the Netherlands granted
Suriname complete independence on Nov. 25, 1975. A
coup d'état in 1980 brought military rule. During much
of the 1980s Suriname was under the repressive control
of Lieut. Col. Dési Bouterse. The Netherlands stopped
all aid in 1982 when Suriname soldiers killed 15 journalists, politicians, lawyers, and union officials. Defense
spending increased significantly, and the economy suffered. A guerrilla insurgency by the Jungle Commando
(a Bush Negro guerrilla group) threatened to destabilize
the country and was harshly suppressed by Bouterse.
Free elections were held on May 25, 1991, depriving
the military of much of its political power. In 1992 a
peace treaty was signed between the government and
several guerrilla groups. In March 1997, the president
announced new economic measures, including eliminating import tariffs on most basic goods, coupled with
strict price controls. Later that year, the Netherlands
said it would prosecute Bouterse for cocaine trafficking.

Public discontent over the 70% inflation rate
prompted President Jules Wijdenbosch to hold elections in May 2000, one year ahead of schedule. The
New Front for Democracy and Development, a coalition led by former president Ronald Venetiaan, won the
election. Suriname has earned a reputation as a center
for drug trafficking; in 1998, former dictator Bouterse
was sentenced in absentia in the Netherlands for transporting cocaine.

In Aug. 2005, after two rounds of national elections
ended in deadlock, Venetiaan was reelected to another
term in a special election of lawmakers.

Swaziland

KINGDOM OF SWAZILAND

Ruler: King Mswati III (1986)
Prime Minister: Barnabas Sibusiso Dlamini (1996)
Area: 6,704 sq mi (17,363 sq km)
Population (2005 est.): 1,173,900 (growth rate: 0.3%);
birth rate: 27.7/1000; infant mortality rate: 69.3/1000;
life expectancy: 35.6; density per sq mi: 175
Capital (2003 est.): Mbabane 69,000. **Largest city:**
Manzini, 75,000. **Monetary unit:** Lilangeni.
Languages: English, siSwati (both official). **Ethnicity/
race:** African 97%, European 3%. **Religions:** Zionist
(a blend of Christianity and indigenous ancestral
worship) 40%; Roman Catholic 20%; Muslim 10%;
Anglican, Bahai, Methodist, Mormon, Jewish, and
other 30%. **Literacy rate:** 82% (2003 est.)
Economic summary: GDP/PPP (2004 est.): $6.018
billion; per capita $5,100. **Real growth rate:** 2.5%.
Inflation: 5.4%. **Unemployment:** 34% (2000 est.).
Arable land: 10%. **Agriculture:** sugarcane, cotton,
corn, tobacco, rice, citrus, pineapples, sorghum,
peanuts; cattle, goats, sheep. **Labor force:** 383,200
(2000). **Industries:** mining (coal, raw asbestos), wood
pulp, sugar, soft drink concentrates, textile and
apparel. **Natural resources:** asbestos, coal, clay,
cassiterite, hydropower, forests, small gold and
diamond deposits, quarry stone, talc. **Exports:** $900.1
million (f.o.b., 2004 est.): soft drink concentrates,
sugar, wood pulp, cotton yarn, refrigerators, citrus and
canned fruit. **Imports:** $1.14 million (f.o.b., 2004 est.):
motor vehicles, machinery, transport equipment,
foodstuffs, petroleum products, chemicals. **Major
trading partners:** South Africa, EU, U.S.,
Mozambique, Japan, Singapore (2004). **Member of
Commonwealth of Nations**

Geography Swaziland, which is about 85% the size
of New Jersey, is surrounded by South Africa and
Mozambique. The country is largely mountainous.

Government Absolute monarchy.

History Bantu peoples migrated southwest to the area
of Mozambique in the 16th century. A number of clans
broke away from the main body in the 18th century and
settled in Swaziland. In the 19th century these clans
organized as a tribe, partly because they were in constant conflict with the Zulu. Their ruler, Mswazi,

appealed to the British in the 1840s for help against the Zulu. The British and the Transvaal governments guaranteed the independence of Swaziland in 1881.

South Africa held Swaziland as a protectorate from 1894 to 1899, but after the Boer War, in 1902, Swaziland was transferred to British administration. The paramount chief was recognized as the native authority in 1941. In 1963, the territory was constituted a protectorate, and on Sept. 6, 1968, it became the independent nation of Swaziland.

Since 1986, King Mswati III has ruled as sub-Saharan Africa's last absolute monarch. Political parties are banned and the king appoints 10 of the 65 members of Parliament as well as the prime minister. King Mswati can veto any law passed by the legislature and frequently rules by decree.

In 2002, hundreds of thousands of Swazis faced starvation. Two years of drought as well as bad planning and poor agricultural practices were blamed for the crisis. The government came under criticism for buying the king a $50 million luxury jet—a quarter of the national budget—while famine loomed. In 2002, the country's judges resigned en masse in protest of the government's refusal to comply with court decisions. In April 2003, the government information minister announced that the media were banned from making negative remarks about the government—criticism of the king's new luxury jet in particular would not be tolerated. In 2004, a third year of drought befell the country. International donor agencies and human rights groups condemned the king's plans to build new multimillion-dollar palaces for each of his 11 wives (12 by 2005) while his people faced starvation and the country's AIDS epidemic spiraled out of control. About 30% of the population is infected.

Although the king signed the country's first constitution in Aug. 2005, the document essentially maintains the status quo: opposition parties remain banned and the king retains ultimate power.

Sweden

KINGDOM OF SWEDEN

National name: Konungariket Sverige
Sovereign: King Carl XVI Gustaf (1973)
Prime Minister: Göran Persson (1996)
Area: 173,731 sq mi (449,964 sq km)
Population (2005 est.): 9,001,774 (growth rate: 0.2%); birth rate: 10.4/1000; infant mortality rate: 2.8/1000; life expectancy: 80.4; density per sq mi: 52
Capital and largest city (2003 est.): Stockholm, 1,622,300 (metro. area), 1,251,900 (city proper).
Other large cities: Göteborg, 506,600; Malmö, 245,300; Uppsala, 127,300. **Monetary unit:** Krona.
Language: Swedish, small Sami- and Finnish-speaking minorities. **Ethnicity/race:** indigenous population: Swedes and Finnish and Sami minorities; foreign-born or first-generation immigrants: Finns, Yugoslavs, Danes, Norwegians, Greeks, Turks. **Religions:** Lutheran 87%, Roman Catholic, Orthodox, Baptist, Muslim, Jewish, Buddhist. **Literacy rate:** 99% (1979 est.)
Economic summary: GDP/PPP (2004 est.): $255.4 billion; per capita $28,400. **Real growth rate:** 3.6%. **Inflation:** 0.7%. **Unemployment:** 5.6%. **Arable land:** 7%. **Agriculture:** barley, wheat, sugar beets; meat, milk. **Labor force:** 4.46 million; agriculture 2%, industry 24%, services 74% (2000 est.). **Industries:** iron and steel, precision equipment (bearings, radio and telephone parts, armaments), wood pulp and paper products, processed foods, motor vehicles. **Natural resources:** zinc, iron ore, lead, copper, silver, timber, uranium, hydropower. **Exports:** $121.7 billion

(f.o.b., 2004 est.): machinery 35%, motor vehicles, paper products, pulp and wood, iron and steel products, chemicals. **Imports:** $97.97 billion (f.o.b., 2004 est.): machinery, petroleum and petroleum products, chemicals, motor vehicles, iron and steel; foodstuffs, clothing. **Major trading partners:** U.S., Germany, Norway, UK, Denmark, Finland, Netherlands, France, Belgium (2003).

Geography Sweden, which occupies the eastern part of the Scandinavian Peninsula, is the fourth-largest country in Europe and is one-tenth larger than California. The country slopes eastward and southward from the Kjölen Mountains along the Norwegian border, where the peak elevation is Kebnekaise at 6,965 ft (2,123 m) in Lapland. In the north are mountains and many lakes. To the south and east are central lowlands and south of them are fertile areas of forest, valley, and plain. Along Sweden's rocky coast, chopped up by bays and inlets, are many islands, the largest of which are Gotland and Öland.

Government Constitutional monarchy.

History The earliest historical mention of Sweden is found in Tacitus's *Germania*, where reference is made to the powerful king and strong fleet of the Sviones. In the 11th century, Olaf Sköttkonung became the first Swedish king to be baptized as a Christian. Around 1400, an attempt was made to unite Sweden, Norway, and Denmark into one kingdom, but this led to bitter strife between the Danes and the Swedes. In 1520, the Danish king Christian II conquered Sweden and in the "Stockholm Bloodbath" put leading Swedish personages to death. Gustavus Vasa (1523–1560) broke away from Denmark and fashioned the modern Swedish state. He also confiscated property from the Roman Catholic Church in Sweden to pay Sweden's war debts. The king justified his actions on the basis of Martin Luther's doctrines, which were being accepted nationwide with royal encouragement. The Lutheran Swedish church was eventually adopted as the state church.

Sweden played a leading role in the second phase (1630–1635) of the Thirty Years' War (1618–1648). By the Treaty of Westphalia (1648), Sweden obtained western Pomerania and some neighboring territory on the Baltic. In 1700, a coalition of Russia, Poland, and Denmark united against Sweden and by the Peace of Nystad (1721) forced it to relinquish Livonia, Ingria, Estonia, and parts of Finland. Sweden emerged from the Napoleonic Wars with the acquisition of Norway from Denmark and with a new royal dynasty stemming from Marshal Jean Bernadotte of France, who became King Charles XIV (1818–1844). The artificial union between Sweden and Norway led to an uneasy relationship, and the union was finally dissolved in 1905. Sweden maintained a position of neutrality in both world wars.

An elaborate structure of welfare legislation, imitated by many larger nations, began with the establishment of old-age pensions in 1911. Economic prosperity based on its neutralist policy enabled Sweden, together with Norway, to pioneer in public health, housing, and job security programs. Forty-four years of Socialist government ended in 1976 with the election of a Conservative coalition headed by Thorbjörn Fälldin. The Socialists were returned to power in the election of 1982, but Prime Minister Olof Palme, a Socialist, was assassinated by a gunman on Feb. 28, 1986, leaving Sweden stunned. Palme's Socialist domestic policies were carried out by his successor, Ingvar Carlsson. Elections in Sept. 1991 ousted the Social Democrats (Socialists) from power. The new coalition of four conservative parties pledged to reduce taxes and the welfare state but not alter Sweden's traditional neutrality. In Sept. 1994 the Social Democrats emerged again after three years as the opposition party.

In a 1994 referendum voters approved joining the European Union. Although supportive of a European monetary union, Sweden decided not to adopt the euro when it debuted in 1999 and rejected it again overwhelmingly in a referendum in Sept. 2003.

The Social Democrat Party, and its leader, Prime Minister Göran Persson, easily won reelection in Sept. 2002. The center-left Social Democrats have run the government for six out of the last seven decades.

Switzerland

SWISS CONFEDERATION

National name: Schweiz/Suisse/Svizzera/Svizra
President: Samuel Schmid (2004)
Area: 15,942 sq mi (41,290 sq km)
Population (2005 est.): 7,489,370 (growth rate: 0.5%); birth rate: 9.8/1000; infant mortality rate: 4.4/1000; life expectancy: 80.4; density per sq mi: 470
Capital (2003 est.): Bern, 122,700. **Largest cities:** Zurich, 971,800 (metro. area), 348,100 (city proper); Geneva, 178,900; Basel, 162,800; Lausanne, 117,400.
Monetary unit: Swiss franc. **Languages:** German 63.7%, French 12.9%, Italian 7.6%, Romansch 0.6% (all official); other 8.9%. **Ethnicity/race:** German 65%, French 18%, Italian 10%, Romansch 1%, other 6%. **Religions:** Roman Catholic 46.1%, Protestant 40%, other 5%, no religion 8.9% (1990). **Literacy rate:** 99% (1980 est.)
Economic summary: GDP/PPP (2004 est.): $251.9 billion; per capita $33,800. **Real growth rate:** 1.8%. **Inflation:** 0.9%. **Unemployment:** 3.4%. **Arable land:** 10%. **Agriculture:** grains, fruits, vegetables; meat, eggs. **Labor force:** 3.77 million; services 69%, industry 26%, agriculture 5% (1998). **Industries:** machinery, chemicals, watches, textiles, precision instruments. **Natural resources:** hydropower potential, timber, salt. **Exports:** $130.7 billion (f.o.b., 2004 est.): machinery, chemicals, metals, watches, agricultural products. **Imports:** $121.1 billion (f.o.b., 2004 est.): machinery, chemicals, vehicles, metals; agricultural products, textiles. **Major trading partners:** Germany, U.S., France, Italy, UK, Netherlands, Austria (2003).

Geography Switzerland, in central Europe, is the land of the Alps. Its tallest peak is the Dufourspitze at 15,203 ft (4,634 m) on the Swiss side of the Italian border, one of 10 summits of the Monte Rosa massif. The tallest peak in all of the Alps, Mont Blanc (15,771 ft; 4,807 m), is actually in France. Most of Switzerland is composed of a mountainous plateau bordered by the great bulk of the Alps on the south and by the Jura Mountains on the northwest. The country's largest lakes—Geneva, Constance (Bodensee), and Maggiore—straddle the French, German-Austrian, and Italian borders, respectively. The Rhine, navigable from Basel to the North Sea, is the principal inland waterway.

Government Federal republic.

History Called Helvetia in ancient times, Switzerland in 1291 was a league of cantons in the Holy Roman Empire. Fashioned around the nucleus of three German forest districts of Schwyz, Uri, and Unterwalden, the Swiss Confederation slowly added new cantons. In 1648 the Treaty of Westphalia gave Switzerland its independence from the Holy Roman Empire.

French revolutionary troops occupied the country in 1798 and named it the Helvetic Republic, but Napoléon in 1803 restored its federal government. By 1815, the French- and Italian-speaking peoples of Switzerland had been granted political equality.

In 1815, the Congress of Vienna guaranteed the neutrality and recognized the independence of Switzerland. In the revolutionary period of 1847, the Catholic cantons seceded and organized a separate union called the *Sonderbund*, but they were defeated and rejoined the federation.

In 1848, the new Swiss constitution established a union modeled on that of the U.S. The federal constitution of 1874 established a strong central government while giving large powers of control to each canton. National unity and political conservatism grew as the country prospered from its neutrality. Its banking system became the world's leading repository for international accounts.

Strict neutrality was its policy in both world wars. Geneva was the seat of the League of Nations (later the European headquarters of the United Nations) and of a number of international organizations.

Allegations in the 1990s concerning secret assets of Jewish Holocaust victims deposited in Swiss banks led to international criticism and the establishment of a fund to reimburse the victims and their families.

Surprisingly, women were not given the right to vote or to hold office until 1971. Switzerland's first woman president—as well as the first Jew to assume the position—was Ruth Dreifuss in 1999.

In Sept. 2000, the Swiss voted against a plan to cut the number of foreigners in the country to 18% of the population (in 2000 foreigners made up 19.3%). Since 1970, four similar anti-immigration plans have failed.

On Sept 10, 2002, the Swiss abandoned their longheld neutrality to become the 190th member of the UN.

In Oct. 2003, Switzerland took a turn to the right when the far-right Swiss People's Party (SVP) had the strongest showing in parliamentary elections, garnering 28% of the vote. Its virulently anti-immigration, anti-EU leader, Christopher Blocher, was given a cabinet position.

In a 2005 referendum, Switzerland supported future EU membership.

Syria

SYRIAN ARAB REPUBLIC

National name: Al-Jumhuriyah al-'Arabiyah as-Suriyah
President: Bashar al-Assad (2000)
Prime Minister: Muhammad Naji al-Otari (2003)
Area: 71,498 sq mi (185,180 sq km)
Population (2005 est.): 18,448,752 (growth rate: 2.3%); birth rate: 28.3/1000; infant mortality rate: 29.5/1000; life expectancy: 70.0; density per sq mi: 258
Capital (2003 est.): Damascus, 2,381,800 (metro. area), 1,861,900. **Largest cities:** Aleppo, 2,492,100 (metro. area), 1,933,700 (city proper); Homs, 751,500; Latakia, 417,100; Hama, 380,200. **Monetary unit:** Syrian pound. **Languages:** Arabic (official); Kurdish, Armenian, Aramaic, Circassian widely understood; French, English somewhat understood. **Ethnicity/race:** Arab 90.3%, Kurds, Armenians, and other 9.7%. **Religions:** Islam (Sunni) 74%, Alawite, Druze, and other Islamic sects 16%; Christian (various sects) 10%; Jewish (tiny communities in Damascus, Al Qamishli, and Aleppo). **Literacy rate:** 77% (2003 est.)
Economic summary: GDP/PPP (2004 est.): $60.44 billion; per capita $3,400. **Real growth rate:** 2.3%. **Inflation:** 2.1%. **Unemployment:** 20% (2002 est.). **Arable land:** 25%. **Agriculture:** wheat, barley, cotton, lentils, chickpeas, olives, sugar beets; beef, mutton,

eggs, poultry, milk. **Labor force:** 5.12 million; agriculture 30%, industry 27%, services 43% (2002 est.). **Industries:** petroleum, textiles, food processing, beverages, tobacco, phosphate rock mining. **Natural resources:** petroleum, phosphates, chrome and manganese ores, asphalt, iron ore, rock salt, marble, gypsum, hydropower. **Exports:** $6.086 billion (f.o.b., 2004 est.): crude oil, petroleum products, fruits and vegetables, cotton fiber, clothing, meat and live animals, wheat. **Imports:** $5.042 billion (f.o.b., 2004 est.): machinery and transport equipment, electric power machinery, food and livestock, metal and metal products, chemicals and chemical products, plastics, yarn, paper. **Major trading partners:** Germany, Italy, UAE, Lebanon, France, Croatia, U.S., China, Turkey (2003).

Geography Slightly larger than North Dakota, Syria lies at the eastern end of the Mediterranean Sea. It is bordered by Lebanon and Israel on the west, Turkey on the north, Iraq on the east, and Jordan on the south. Coastal Syria is a narrow plain, in back of which is a range of coastal mountains, and still farther inland a steppe area. In the east is the Syrian Desert and in the south is the Jebel Druze Range. The highest point in Syria is Mount Hermon (9,232 ft; 2,814 m) on the Lebanese border.

Government Republic under a military regime since March 1963.

History Ancient Syria was conquered by Egypt about 1500 B.C., and after that by Hebrews, Assyrians, Chaldeans, Persians, and Alexander the Great of Macedonia. From 64 B.C. until the Arab conquest in A.D. 636, it was part of the Roman Empire except during brief periods. The Arabs made it a trade center for their extensive empire, but it suffered severely from the Mongol invasion in 1260 and fell to the Ottoman Turks in 1516. Syria remained a Turkish province until World War I.

A secret Anglo-French pact of 1916 put Syria in the French zone of influence. The League of Nations gave France a mandate over Syria after World War I, but the French were forced to put down several nationalist uprisings. In 1930, France recognized Syria as an independent republic but still subject to the mandate. After nationalist demonstrations in 1939, the French high commissioner suspended the Syrian constitution. In 1941, British and Free French forces invaded Syria to eliminate Vichy control. During the rest of World War II, Syria was an Allied base. Again in 1945, nationalist demonstrations broke into actual fighting, and British troops had to restore order. Syrian forces met a series of reverses while participating in the Arab invasion of Palestine in 1948. In 1958, Egypt and Syria formed the United Arab Republic, with Gamal Abdel Nasser of Egypt as president. However, Syria became independent again on Sept. 29, 1961, following a revolution.

In the Arab-Israeli War of 1967, Israel quickly vanquished the Syrian army. Before acceding to the UN cease-fire, the Israeli forces took control of the fortified Golan Heights. Syria joined Egypt in attacking Israel in Oct. 1973 in the fourth Arab-Israeli War, but was pushed back from initial successes on the Golan Heights and ended up losing more land. However, in the settlement worked out by U.S. secretary of state Henry A. Kissinger in 1974, the Syrians recovered all the territory lost in 1973.

In the mid-1970s Syria sent some 20,000 troops to support Muslim Lebanese in their armed conflict with Christian militants supported by Israel during the civil war in Lebanon. Syrian troops frequently clashed with Israeli troops during Israel's 1982 invasion of Lebanon and remained thereafter as occupiers of large portions of Lebanon.

In 1990, President Assad ruled out any possibility of legalizing opposition political parties. In Dec. 1991 voters approved a fourth term for Assad, giving him 99.98% of the vote.

In the 1990s, the slowdown in the Israeli-Palestinian peace process was echoed in the lack of progress in Israeli-Syrian relations. Confronted with a steadily strengthening strategic partnership between Israel and Turkey, Syria took steps to construct a countervailing alliance by improving relations with Iraq, strengthening ties with Iran, and collaborating more closely with Saudi Arabia. In Dec. 1999, Israeli-Syrian talks resumed after a nearly four-year hiatus, but they soon broke down over discussions about the Golan Heights.

On June 10, 2000, President Hafez al-Assad died. He had ruled with an iron fist since taking power in a military coup in 1970. His son, Bashar al-Assad, an ophthalmologist by training, succeeded him. He has emulated his father's autocratic rule.

In the summer of 2001, Syria withdrew nearly all of its 25,000 troops from Beirut. Syrian soldiers, however, remained in the Lebanese countryside.

In April 2003, shortly after the Iraq war seemed to be winding down, the Bush administration turned its ire on Syria, calling the country a rogue nation that harbored members of Saddam Hussein's regime and possessed chemical weapons.

In March 2004, Syrian Kurds rioted and clashed with police for several days after a brawl at a soccer game. It was Syria's worst unrest in decades.

The U.S. imposed economic sanctions on the country in May, accusing it of continuing to support terrorism.

In Sept. 2004, a UN Security Council resolution asked Syria to withdraw its 15,000 remaining troops from Lebanon. Syria responded by moving about 3,000 troops from the vicinity of Beirut to eastern Lebanon, a gesture viewed by many as merely cosmetic.

On Feb. 14, 2004, Lebanon's former prime minister Rafiq Hariri was assassinated. Many implicated Syria in the death of the popular and independent leader, who staunchly opposed Syrian involvement in Lebanon. Huge Lebanese protests called for Syria's withdrawal from the country, a demand backed by the U.S., EU, and UN. In addition to the anti-Syrian demonstrations, however, there were a number of massive pro-Syrian rallies in Lebanon sponsored by the Shiite militant group Hezbollah. By the end of April, Syria had withdrawn all its troops, ending a 29-year occupation.

Taiwan

REPUBLIC OF CHINA

National name: Zhonghua Minguo
President: Chen Shui-bian (2000)
Prime Minister: Frank Hsieh (2005)
Area: 13,892 sq mi (35,980 sq km)
Population (2005 est.): 22,894,384 (growth rate: 0.6%); birth rate: 12.6/1000; infant mortality rate: 6.4/1000; life expectancy: 77.3; density per sq mi: 1,648
Capital and largest city (2003 est.): Taipei, 7,871,900 (metro. area), 2,722,600 (city proper). **Other large cities:** Kaohsiung, 1,514,900; Tai Chung, 1,069,900; Tainan, 755,800; Keelung, 410,500. **Monetary unit:** Taiwan dollar. **Languages:** Chinese (Mandarin, official), Taiwanese (Min), Hakka dialects. **Ethnicity/race:** Taiwanese (including Hakka) 84%, mainland Chinese 14%, aborigine 2%. **Religions:** mixture of Buddhist, Confucian, and Taoist 93%, Christian 4.5%,

other 2.5%. **Literacy rate:** 86% (1980)
Economic summary: GDP/PPP (2004 est.): $576.2
billion; per capita $25,300. **Real growth rate:** 6%.
Inflation: 1.7%. **Unemployment:** 4.5%. **Arable land:**
24%. **Agriculture:** rice, corn, vegetables, fruit, tea;
pigs, poultry, beef, milk; fish. **Labor force:** 10.22
million; agriculture 8%, industry 35%, services 57%
(2001 est.). **Industries:** electronics, petroleum refining,
armaments, chemicals, textiles, iron and steel,
machinery, cement, food processing, vehicles,
consumer products, pharmaceuticals. **Natural
resources:** small deposits of coal, natural gas,
limestone, marble, asbestos. **Exports:** $170.5 billion
(f.o.b., 2004 est.): computer products and electrical
equipment, metals, textiles, plastics and rubber
products, chemicals (2002). **Imports:** $165.4 billion
(f.o.b., 2003 est.): machinery and electrical equipment
44.5%, minerals, precision instruments (2002). **Major
trading partners:** China, including Hong Kong, U.S.,
Japan, South Korea (2004).

Geography The Republic of China today consists
of the island of Taiwan, an island 100 mi (161 km)
off the Asian mainland in the Pacific; two off-shore
islands, Kinmen (Quemoy) and Matsu; and the
nearby islets of the Pescadores chain. It is slightly
larger than the combined areas of Massachusetts
and Connecticut.

Government Multiparty democracy.

History Taiwan was inhabited by aborigines of
Malayan descent when Chinese from the areas now designated as Fukien and Kwangtung began settling it in
the 7th century, becoming the majority. The Portuguese
explored the area in 1590, naming it "the Beautiful"
(Formosa). In 1624 the Dutch set up forts in the south,
the Spanish in the north. The Dutch forced out the
Spanish in 1641 and controlled the island until 1661,
when Chinese general Koxinga took it over and established an independent kingdom. The Manchus seized
the island in 1683 and held it until 1895, when it passed
to Japan after the first Sino-Japanese War. Japan developed and exploited Formosa. It was the target of heavy
American bombing during World War II, and at the
close of the war the island was restored to China.

After the defeat of its armies on the mainland, the
Nationalist government of Generalissimo Chiang Kai-
shek retreated to Taiwan in Dec. 1949. Chiang dominated the island, even though only 15% of the population consisted of the 1949 immigrants, the
Kuomintang. He maintained a 600,000-man army in
the hope of eventually recovering the mainland.
Beijing viewed the Taiwanese government with suspicion and anger, referring to Taiwan as a breakaway
province of China.

The UN seat representing all of China was held by
the Nationalists for over two decades before being lost
in Oct. 1971, when the People's Republic of China was
admitted and Taiwan was forced to abdicate its seat to
Beijing.

Chiang died at 87 of a heart attack on April 5, 1975.
His son, Chiang Ching-kuo, continued as prime minister and was a dominant figure in the Taipei regime. In
April 1991, President Lee Teng-hui formally declared
an end to emergency rule, which had existed since
Chiang's forces originally occupied the island. In the
first full election in many decades, the governing Kuomintang in Dec. 1991 won 71% of the vote, affirming
the island's opposition to reunification with China. In
Feb. 1993 the president, himself a native Taiwanese,
nominated Lien Chan, another native, to be prime minister, marking a further generational shift away from
the mainland exiles.

In the island's first free presidential election, voters
defied mainland intimidation and gave 54% of the vote
to incumbent president Lee Teng-hui.

President Lee Teng-hui rankled mainland China by
announcing in July 1999 that he was abandoning the
longstanding "One China" policy that had kept the
peace between the small island and its powerful neighbor and that he would from then on deal with China on
a "state-to-state basis." China, which had vowed to
someday unite Taiwan with the mainland, retaliated by
conducting submarine warfare exercises and missile
tests near the island in an effort to intimidate its tiny
brazen neighbor, as it had once before in 1996.

In the March 2000 presidential race, voters elected
pro-independence candidate Chen Shui-bian of the
Democratic Progressive Party, ending more than 50
years of Nationalist rule.

The day before the March 20, 2004, elections, President Chen Shui-bian and Vice President Annette Lu
survived an assassination attempt. Chen won the election over Lien Chan by just 30,000 votes out of 13
million cast. The country's first-ever referendum failed
because less than 50% of eligible voters weighed in on
its questions. The referendum asked if Taiwan should
arm itself with additional defensive weapons if China
does not withdraw its missiles and if Taiwan should
continue to negotiate with China.

Tension between China and Taiwan intensified in
March 2005, when China passed an antisecession law
that said the country could use force if Taiwan moved
toward achieving independence. "The state shall
employ non-peaceful means and other necessary measures to protect China's sovereignty and territorial
integrity," the legislation stated. Taiwan president Chen
Shui-bian called the bill a "law of aggression." Hundreds of thousands of Taiwanese took to the streets to
protest the bill.

In 2005, China met with several Taiwanese opposition leaders in an effort to undermine Taiwan's defiant
president. Lien Chan, who heads the opposition
Nationalist Party, traveled to China in April and met
with President Hu Jintao. It was the first meeting
between Nationalist and Communist Party leaders
since 1949, when the defeated Nationalists retreated to
Taiwan. Lien called the visit a "journey of peace." In
May, Hu met with another opposition leader, James
Soong, chairman of the People First Party. In a joint
communiqué intended to restart negotiations between
Taiwan and China, they agreed to a principle of "two
sides of the strait, one China."

Tajikistan

REPUBLIC OF TAJIKISTAN

National name: Jumhurii Tojikiston
President: Imomali Rakhmonov (1992)
Prime Minister: Akil Akilov (1999)
Area: 55,251 sq mi (143,100 sq km)
Population (2005 est.): 7,163,506 (growth rate: 2.2%);
birth rate: 32.6/1000; infant mortality rate: 110.8/1000;
life expectancy: 64.6; density per sq mi: 130
Capital and largest city (2003 est.): Dushanbe, 817,100
(metro. area), 590,300 (city proper). **Other large city:**
Khodzhent (Leninabad), 156,500. **Monetary unit:**
somoni. **Languages:** Tajik (official), Russian widely used
in government and business. **Ethnicity/race:** Tajik
64.9%, Uzbek 25%, Russian 3.5% (declining because of
emigration); other 6.6%. **Religions:** Islam: Sunni 85%,
Shiite 5%; other 10% (2003 est.). **Literacy rate:** 99%
(2003 est.)
Economic summary: GDP/PPP (2004 est.): $7.95 billion;
per capita $1,100. **Real growth rate:** 10.5%. **Inflation:**
8%. **Unemployment:** 40% (2002 est.). **Arable land:**

7%. **Agriculture:** cotton, grain, fruits, grapes, vegetables; cattle, sheep, goats. **Labor force:** 3.187 million (2000); agriculture 67%, industry 8%, services 25% (2000 est.). **Industries:** aluminum, zinc, lead, chemicals and fertilizers, cement, vegetable oil, metal-cutting machine tools, refrigerators and freezers. **Natural resources:** hydropower, some petroleum, uranium, mercury, brown coal, lead, zinc, antimony, tungsten, silver, gold. **Exports:** $1.13 billion (f.o.b., 2004 est.): aluminum, electricity, cotton, fruits, vegetable oil, textiles. **Imports:** $1.3 billion (f.o.b., 2004 est.): electricity, petroleum products, aluminum oxide, machinery and equipment, foodstuffs. **Major trading partners:** Netherlands, Turkey, Latvia, Switzerland, Uzbekistan, Russia, Iran, Kazakhstan, Ukraine, Azerbaijan, Romania (2003).

Geography Ninety-three percent of Tajikistan's territory is mountainous, and the mountain glaciers are the source of its rivers. Tajikistan is an earthquake-prone area. The republic is bounded by China in the east, Afghanistan to the south, and Uzbekistan and Kyrgyzstan to the west and north. The central Asian republic also includes the Gorno-Badakh Shan Autonomous region. Tajikistan is slightly larger than the state of Illinois.

Government Republic.

History The Tajiks, whose language is nearly identical with Persian, were part of the ancient Persian Empire that was ruled by Darius I and later conquered by Alexander the Great (333 B.C.). In the 7th and 8th centuries, Arabs conquered the region and brought Islam. The Tajiks were successively ruled by Uzbeks and then Afghans until claimed by Russia in the 1860s. In 1924, Tajikistan was consolidated into a newly formed Tajik Autonomous Soviet Socialist Republic, which was administratively part of the Uzbek SSR until the Tajik ASSR gained full-fledged republic status in 1929.

Tajikistan declared its sovereignty in Aug. 1990. In 1991, the republic's Communist leadership supported the attempted coup against Soviet president Mikhail Gorbachev. Tajikistan joined with ten other former Soviet republics in the Commonwealth of Independent States on Dec. 21, 1991. A parliamentary republic was proclaimed and presidential rule abolished in Nov. 1992. After independence, Tajikistan experienced sporadic conflict as the Communist-dominated government struggled to combat an insurgency by Islamic and democratic opposition forces. Despite continued international efforts to end the civil war, periodic fighting continued. About 60,000 people lost their lives in Tajikistan's civil war. The conflict ended officially on June 27, 1997, with the signing in Moscow of peace accords between the government of President Imomali Rakhmonov and the United Tajik Opposition (UTO), a coalition of largely Islamic groups. Since then, however, peace has been tenuous, marred regularly by killing sprees by various opposition groups.

A referendum in June 2003 extended the president's term in office for an additional 14 years. Opposition parties cried foul. In 2005 parliamentary elections, the president's governing party received 80% of the votes; international monitors pronounced them irregular.

Tanzania

UNITED REPUBLIC OF TANZANIA
President: Benjamin William Mkapa (1995)
Prime Minister: Frederick Tluway Sumaye (1995)
Area: 364,898 sq mi (945,087 sq km)[1]
Population (2005 est.): 36,766,356 (growth rate: 1.8%);

birth rate: 38.2/1000; infant mortality rate: 98.5/1000; life expectancy: 45.2; density per sq mi: 101
Administrative capital and largest city (2003 est.): Dar es Salaam, 2,489,800; **Official capital:** Dodoma, 164,500. **Monetary unit:** Tanzanian shilling. **Languages:** Swahili, English (both official); Arabic; many local languages. **Ethnicity/race:** native African 99% (includes 95% Bantu, consisting of well over 100 tribes), Asian, European, and Arab 1%. **Religions:** mainland: Christian 30%, Islam 35%, indigenous 35%; Zanzibar: more than 99% Islam. **Literacy rate:** 78% (2003 est.)
Economic summary: GDP/PPP (2004 est.): $23.71 billion; per capita $700. **Real growth rate:** 5.8%. **Inflation:** 5.4%. **Unemployment:** n.a. **Arable land:** 5%. **Agriculture:** coffee, sisal, tea, cotton, pyrethrum (insecticide made from chrysanthemums), cashew nuts, tobacco, cloves, corn, wheat, cassava (tapioca), bananas, fruits, vegetables; cattle, sheep, goats. **Labor force:** 19 million; agriculture 80%, industry and services 20% (2002 est.). **Industries:** agricultural processing (sugar, beer, cigarettes, sisal twine), diamond, gold and iron mining, soda ash, oil refining, shoes, cement, apparel, wood products, fertilizer, salt. **Natural resources:** hydropower, tin, phosphates, iron ore, coal, diamonds, gemstones, gold, natural gas, nickel. **Exports:** $1.248 billion (f.o.b., 2004 est.): gold, coffee, cashew nuts, manufactures, cotton. **Imports:** $1.972 billion (f.o.b., 2004 est.): consumer goods, machinery and transportation equipment, industrial raw materials, crude oil. **Major trading partners:** India, Japan, Netherlands, UK, Germany, South Africa, China, Zambia, UAE, Kenya (2003). **Member of Commonwealth of Nations**

1. Including Zanzibar.

Geography Tanzania is in East Africa on the Indian Ocean. To the north are Uganda and Kenya; to the west, Burundi, Rwanda, and Congo; and to the south, Mozambique, Zambia, and Malawi. Its area is three times that of New Mexico. Tanzania contains three of Africa's best-known lakes—Victoria in the north, Tanganyika in the west, and Nyasa in the south. Mount Kilimanjaro in the north, 19,340 ft (5,895 m), is the highest point on the continent. The island of Zanzibar is separated from the mainland by a 22-mile channel.

Government Republic.

History Arab traders first began to colonize the area in 700. Portuguese explorers reached the coastal regions in 1500 and held some control until the 17th century, when the sultan of Oman took power. With what are now Burundi and Rwanda, Tanganyika became the colony of German East Africa in 1885. After World War I, it was administered by Britain under a League of Nations mandate and later as a UN trust territory.

Although not mentioned in old histories until the 12th century, Zanzibar was always believed to have had connections with southern Arabia. The Portuguese made it one of their tributaries in 1503 and later established a trading post, but they were driven from Oman by Arabs in 1698. Zanzibar was declared independent of Oman in 1861 and, in 1890, it became a British protectorate.

Tanganyika became independent on Dec. 9, 1961; Zanzibar on Dec. 10, 1963. On April 26, 1964, the two nations merged into the United Republic of Tanganyika and Zanzibar. The name was changed to Tanzania six months later.

An invasion by Ugandan troops in Nov. 1978 was followed by a counterattack in Jan. 1979, in which 5,000 Tanzanian troops were joined by 3,000 Ugandan exiles opposed to President Idi Amin. Within a month, full-scale war developed. Tanzanian president Julius Nyerere kept troops in Uganda in open support of former Ugandan president Milton Obote, despite protests from opposition groups, until the national elections in Dec. 1980.

In Nov. 1985, Nyerere stepped down as president. Ali Hassan Mwinyi, his vice president, succeeded him. Running unopposed, Mwinyi was elected president in October. Shortly thereafter plans were announced to study the benefits of instituting a multiparty democracy, and in Oct. 1995 the country's first multiparty elections since independence took place.

On Aug. 7, 1998, the U.S. embassy in Dar es Salaam was bombed by terrorists, killing ten. The same day an even more devastating explosion destroyed the U.S. embassy in neighboring Kenya.

Since taking office in 1995 President Benjamin William Mkapa has sought to increase economic productivity while dealing with serious pollution problems and deforestation. With more than one million people infected with HIV, AIDS care and prevention have been major public health issues. On foreign policy, Tanzania has taken a leading diplomatic role in East Africa, hosting peace talks for the factions fighting in neighboring Burundi. The UN International Criminal Tribunal for Rwanda (ICTR) is located in the town of Arusha. In Oct. 2000, Mkapa was easily reelected. In 2002, opposition leaders and foreign donors criticized the president's costly new $21 million personal jet.

Thailand

KINGDOM OF THAILAND

Ruler: King Bhumibol Adulyadej (1946)
Prime Minister: Thaksin Shinawatra (2001)
Area: 198,455 sq mi (514,000 sq km)
Population (2005 est.): 65,444,371 (growth rate: 0.9%); birth rate: 15.7/1000; infant mortality rate: 20.5/1000; life expectancy: 71.6; density per sq mi: 330
Capital and largest city (2003 est.): Bangkok, 8,838,500 (metro. area), 6,610,800 (city proper). **Other large cities:** Nonthaburi, 304,700; Chiang Mai, 175,500. **Monetary unit:** baht. **Languages:** Thai (Siamese), English (secondary language of the elite), ethnic and regional dialects. **Ethnicity/race:** Thai 75%, Chinese 14%, other 11%. **Religions:** Buddhist 95%, Islam 3.8%, Christian 0.5%, Hindu 0.1%, other 0.6% (1991). **Literacy rate:** 96% (2003 est.)
Economic summary: GDP/PPP (2004 est.): $524.8 billion; per capita $8,100. **Real growth rate:** 6.1%. **Inflation:** 2.8%. **Unemployment:** 1.5% (Nov. 2004 est.). **Arable land:** 29%. **Agriculture:** rice, cassava (tapioca), rubber, corn, sugarcane, coconuts, soybeans. **Labor force:** 36.43 million (Nov. 2004 est.); agriculture 49%, industry 14%, services 37% (2000 est.). **Industries:** tourism, textiles and garments, agricultural processing, beverages, tobacco, cement, light manufacturing such as jewelry, electric appliances and components, computers and parts, integrated circuits, furniture, plastics, world's second-largest tungsten producer, and third-largest tin producer. **Natural resources:** tin, rubber, natural gas, tungsten, tantalum, timber, lead, fish, gypsum, lignite, fluorite, arable land. **Exports:** $87.91 billion (f.o.b., 2004 est.): textiles and footwear, fishery products, rice, rubber, jewelry, automobiles, computers and electrical appliances. **Imports:** $80.84 billion (f.o.b., 2004 est.): capital goods, intermediate goods and raw materials, consumer goods, fuels. **Major trading partners:** U.S., Japan, Singapore, China, Hong Kong, Malaysia, Taiwan (2003).

Geography Thailand occupies the western half of the Indochinese peninsula and the northern two-thirds of the Malay Peninsula in southeast Asia. Its neighbors are Burma (Myanmar) on the north and west, Laos on the north and northeast, Cambodia on the east, and Malaysia on the south. Thailand is about the size of France.

Government Constitutional monarchy.

History The Thais first began settling their present homeland in the 6th century, and by the end of the 13th century ruled most of the western portion. During the next 400 years, they fought sporadically with the Cambodians to the east and the Burmese to the west. Formerly called Siam, Thailand has never experienced foreign colonization. The British gained a colonial foothold in the region in 1824, but by 1896 an Anglo-French accord guaranteed the independence of Thailand. A coup in 1932 demoted the monarchy to titular status and established representative government with universal suffrage.

At the outbreak of World War II, Japanese forces attacked Thailand. After five hours of token resistance Thailand yielded to Japan on Dec. 8, 1941, subsequently becoming a staging area for the Japanese campaign against Malaya. Following the demise of a pro-Japanese puppet government in July 1944, Thailand repudiated the declaration of war it had been forced to make in 1942 against Britain and the U.S.

By the late 1960s the nation's problems largely stemmed from conflicts brewing in neighboring Cambodia and Vietnam. Although Thailand had received $2 billion in U.S. economic and military aid since 1950 and had sent troops (paid by the U.S.) to Vietnam while permitting U.S. bomber bases on its territory, the collapse of South Vietnam and Cambodia in spring 1975 brought rapid changes in the country's diplomatic posture. At the Thai government's insistence, the U.S. agreed to withdraw all 23,000 U.S. military personnel remaining in Thailand by March 1976.

Three years of civilian government ended with a military coup on Oct. 6, 1976. Political parties, banned after the coup, gained limited freedom in 1980. In the same year, the National Assembly elected Gen. Prem Tinsulanonda as prime minister. Prem continued as prime minister following the 1983 and 1986 elections.

Fleeing from Laos, Vietnam, and the murderous regime of Cambodia's Pol Pot, refugees flooded into Thailand in 1978 and 1979. Despite efforts by the United States and other Western countries to resettle them, a total of 130,000 Laotians and Vietnamese were living in camps along the Cambodian border in mid-1980.

On April 3, 1981, a military coup against the Prem government failed. Another coup attempt on Sept. 9, 1985, was crushed by loyal troops after ten hours of fighting in Bangkok. In Feb. 1991, yet another coup yielded another junta, which declared a state of emergency and abolished the constitution. A scandal over a land-reform program caused the fall of the government in May 1995. A succession of governments followed.

Following several years of unprecedented economic growth, Thailand's economy, once one of the strongest in the region, collapsed under the weight of foreign debt in 1997. The Thai economy's downfall set off a chain reaction in the region, sparking the Asian currency crisis. The Thai government quickly accepted restructuring guidelines as a condition of the International Monetary Fund's $17 billion bailout. Thailand's economy, while far from completely recovered, continued to improve over the next several years.

Thaksin Shinawatra, head of the Thai Rak Thai Party, became prime minister in Jan. 2001. The hugely popular Thaksin, a billionaire telecommunications mogul, was indicted in Dec. 2000 on corruption charges but acquitted in August 2001.

Violence has plagued Thailand's Muslim-dominated southern provinces since the beginning of 2004, with armed insurgents attacking police stations, security stations, and military depots. Nearly 800 people have been killed in the attacks, which officials attribute to Islamic militants. The violence intensified in July 2005, prompting Thaksin to declare a state of emergency in the south.

On Dec. 26, 2004, a tremendously powerful tsunami ravaged 12 Asian countries. Thailand reported about 5,300 casualties.

Thaksin made history in the Feb. 2005 elections, becoming the first prime minister to serve two consecutive terms. His Thai Rak Thai Party won in a landslide. He was criticized during his first term for alleged corruption, for failing to control the insurgency in the south, and for an ineffective response to Thailand's avian flu outbreak, but his deft handling of the tsunami crisis increased his popularity in the days leading up to the election.

Togo

TOGOLESE REPUBLIC

National name: République Togolaise
President: Faure Gnassingbe (2005)
Prime Minister: Edem Kodjo (2005)
Area: 21,925 sq mi (56,785 sq km)
Population (2005 est.): 5,681,519 (growth rate: 2.2%); birth rate: 33.5/1000; infant mortality rate: 66.6/1000; life expectancy: 52.6; density per sq mi: 259
Capital and largest city (2003 est.): Lomé, 749,700 (metro. area), 676,400 (city proper). **Monetary unit:** CFA Franc. **Languages:** French (official, commerce); Ewé, Mina (south); Kabyé, Cotocoli (north); and many dialects. **Ethnicity/race:** native African (37 tribes; largest and most important are Ewe, Mina, and Kabre) 99%, European and Syrian-Lebanese less than 1%. **Religions:** Indigenous beliefs 51%, Christian 29%, Islam 20%. **Literacy rate:** 61% (2003 est.)
Economic summary: GDP/PPP (2004 est.): $$8.684 billion; per capita $1,600. **Real growth rate:** 3%. **Inflation:** 1%. **Unemployment:** n.a. (2003 est.). **Arable land:** 46%. **Agriculture:** coffee, cocoa, cotton, yams, cassava (tapioca), corn, beans, rice, millet, sorghum; livestock; fish. **Labor force:** 1.74 million (1996); agriculture 65%, industry 5%, services 30% (1998 est.). **Industries:** phosphate mining, agricultural processing, cement; handicrafts, textiles, beverages. **Natural resources:** phosphates, limestone, marble, arable land. **Exports:** $663.1 million (f.o.b., 2004 est.): reexports, cotton, phosphates, coffee, cocoa. **Imports:** $824.9 million (f.o.b., 2004 est.): machinery and equipment, foodstuffs, petroleum products. **Major trading partners:** Burkina Faso, Ghana, Netherlands, Benin, Mali, Taiwan, France, Côte d'Ivoire, Germany, Italy, South Africa, China (2003).

Geography Togo, twice the size of Maryland, is on the south coast of West Africa bordering on Ghana to the west, Burkina Faso to the north, and Benin to the east. The Gulf of Guinea coastline, only 32 mi long (51 km), is low and sandy. The only port is at Lomé. The Togo hills traverse the central section.

Government Republic transitioning to multiparty democratic rule.

History The Voltaic peoples and the Kwa were the earliest known inhabitants. The Ewe followed in the 14th century and the Ane in the 18th century. The Danish claimed the land in the 18th century, but by 1884 it was established as a German colony (Togo-

land). The area was split between the British and the French under League of Nations mandates after World War I and subsequently administered as UN trusteeships. The British portion voted for incorporation with Ghana. The French portion became Togo, which declared its independence on April 27, 1960.

Togo's first democratically elected president, Sylvano Olympius, was overthrown in 1963. He was shot and killed by Sgt. Etienne Eyadema while he attempted to scale the walls of the American Embassy to seek asylum. The government of Nicolas Grunitzky was overthrown in a bloodless coup on Jan. 13, 1967, led by Lt. Col. Etienne Eyadema (now called Gen. Gnassingbé Eyadema). A National Reconciliation Committee was set up to rule the country, but in April, Eyadema dissolved the committee and took over as president. He suspended the constitution, banned political parties, and created a cult of personality around his presidency—his official biography describes him as a "force of nature." Under pressure from the West, Eyadema legalized opposition parties in 1993, but the first multiparty presidential election in Aug. 1993 (which gave Eyadema more than 96% of the vote) was considered fraudulent, as was his 1998 reelection. In Feb. 2005, Eyadema died—he had been Africa's longest-serving ruler (38 years). A day after his death, the military installed his son, Faure Gnassingbe, to serve out his term. Gnassingbe took office on Feb. 7 amid strong international condemnation. Under internal and external pressure, Gnassingbe stepped down later that month and agreed to elections on April 24. Violent protests surrounded the elections, and these protests grew when the results were announced: Gnassingbe won 60% of the vote while main opposition candidate Bob Akitani received 38%. On May 4, Gnassingbe was sworn into office.

Tonga

KINGDOM OF TONGA

Sovereign: King Taufa'ahau Tupou IV (1965)
Prime Minister: Prince Lavaka Ata Ulukalala (2000)
Area: 289 sq mi (748 sq km)
Population (2005 est.): 112,422 (growth rate: 2.0%); birth rate: 25.2/1000; infant mortality rate: 12.6/1000; life expectancy: 69.5; density per sq mi: 389
Capital and largest city (2003 est.): Nuku'alofa, 24,500. **Monetary unit:** Pa'anga. **Languages:** Tongan (an Austronesian language), English. **Ethnicity/race:** Polynesian, European (about 300). **Religion:** Christian (Free Wesleyan Church claims over 30,000 adherents). **Literacy rate:** 99% (1996 est.)
Economic summary: GDP/PPP (2002 est.): $244 million; per capita $2,300. **Real growth rate:** 1.5%. **Inflation:** 10.3%. **Unemployment:** 13.3% (1996 est.). **Arable land:** 24%. **Agriculture:** squash, coconuts, copra, bananas, vanilla beans, cocoa, coffee, ginger, black pepper; fish. **Labor force:** 33,910 (1996); agriculture 65% (1997 est.). **Industries:** tourism, fishing. **Natural resources:** fish, fertile soil. **Exports:** $27 million (f.o.b., 2002 est.): squash, fish, vanilla beans, root crops. **Imports:** $86 million (f.o.b., 2002 est.): foodstuffs, machinery and transport equipment, fuels, chemicals. **Major trading partners:** U.S., Japan, New Zealand, Fiji, Australia (2003). **Member of Commonwealth of Nations**

Geography Situated east of the Fiji Islands in the South Pacific, Tonga (also called the Friendly Islands) consists of some 150 islands, of which 36 are inhabited. Most of the islands contain active volcanic craters; others are coral atolls.

Government Hereditary constitutional monarchy.

History Polynesians have lived on Tonga for at least 3,000 years. The Dutch were the first to explore the islands, landing on Tafahi in 1616. British explorer James Cook landed on islands in 1773 and 1777 and dubbed them the Friendly Islands. The current royal dynasty of Tonga was founded in 1831 by Taufa'ahau Tupou, who took the name George I. He consolidated the kingdom by conquest and in 1875 granted a constitution. In 1900, his great-grandson, George II, signed a treaty of friendship with Britain, and the country became a British protected state. The treaty was revised in 1959. Tonga became independent on June 4, 1970.

The government is largely controlled by the king, his nominees, and a small group of hereditary nobles. In the 1990s a movement began aimed at curtailing the powers of the monarchy, and the Tongan Pro-Democracy Movement (TPDM) has continued to gain in popular support. In 1999, Tonga gained UN membership.

The king's official court jester, American Jesse Bogdonoff, a former salesman of magnets to relieve back pain, was sued by the government in 2002 for squandering $26 million of Tonga's money (40% of its annual revenue) in unsound investment schemes. In 2004, he agreed to pay a $1 million settlement.

The king, who celebrated his 85th birthday in 2003, has grown increasingly authoritarian and has curtailed press freedom. In July and August 2005, 3,000 civil servants went on strike, demanding better pay. Throughout 2005, discontent with economic and social inequities intensified throughout the kingdom.

Trinidad and Tobago

REPUBLIC OF TRINIDAD AND TOBAGO

President: Maxwell Richards (2003)
Prime Minister: Patrick Manning (2001)
Area: 1,980 sq mi (5,128 sq km)
Population (2005 est.): 1,088,644 (growth rate: –0.7%); birth rate: 12.8/1000; infant mortality rate: 24.3/1000; life expectancy: 68.9; density per sq mi: 550
Capital and largest city (2003 est.): Port-of-Spain, 263,800 (metro. area), 45,300 (city proper). **Monetary unit:** Trinidad and Tobago dollar. **Languages:** English (official), Hindi, French, Spanish, Chinese. **Ethnicity/ race:** East Indian (a local term—primarily immigrants from northern India) 40.3%, black 39.5%, mixed 18.4%, white 0.6%, Chinese and other 1.2%. **Religions:** Roman Catholic 29.4%, Hindu 23.8%, Anglican 10.9%, Islam 5.8%, Presbyterian 3.4%, other 26.7%. **Literacy rate:** 99% (2003 est.).
Economic summary: GDP/PPP (2004 est.): $11.48 billion; per capita $10,500. **Real growth rate:** 5.7%. **Inflation:** 3.3%. **Unemployment:** 10.4%. **Arable land:** 15%. **Agriculture:** cocoa, sugarcane, rice, citrus, coffee, vegetables; poultry. **Labor force:** 590,000; construction and utilities 12.4%, manufacturing, mining, and quarrying 14%, agriculture 9.5%, services 64.1% (1997 est.). **Industries:** petroleum, chemicals, tourism, food processing, cement, beverage, cotton textiles. **Natural resources:** petroleum, natural gas, asphalt. **Exports:** $6.671 billion (f.o.b., 2004 est.): petroleum and petroleum products, chemicals, steel products, fertilizer, sugar, cocoa, coffee, citrus, flowers. **Imports:** $4.65 billion (f.o.b., 2004 est.): machinery, transportation equipment, manufactured goods, food, live animals. **Major trading partners:** U.S., Jamaica, France, Venezuela, Brazil, Germany, UK, Republic of the Congo, Japan (2003). **Member of Commonwealth of Nations**

Geography Trinidad and Tobago lie in the Caribbean Sea off the northeast coast of Venezuela. Trinidad, the larger at 1,864 sq mi (4,828 sq km), is mainly flat and rolling, with mountains in the north that reach a height of 3,085 ft (940 m) at Mount Aripo. Tobago, at just 116 sq mi (300 sq km), is heavily forested with hardwood trees.

Government Parliamentary democracy.

History When Trinidad was explored by Columbus in 1498, it was inhabited by the Arawaks; Carib Indians inhabited Tobago. Trinidad remained in Spanish possession, despite raids by other European nations, until it was ceded to Britain in 1802. Tobago passed between Britain and France several times, but it was ultimately given to Britain in 1814. Slavery was abolished in 1834. Between 1845 and 1917, thousands of indentured workers were brought from India to work on sugarcane plantations. In 1889 Trinidad and Tobago were made a single colony.

Partial self-government was instituted in 1925, and from 1958 to 1962 the nation was part of the West Indies Federation. On Aug. 31, 1962, it became independent and on Aug. 1, 1976, Trinidad and Tobago became a republic, remaining within the Commonwealth. While the country is a stable democracy and enjoys the highest living standards in the Caribbean thanks to oil revenue, tension between East Indians and blacks has underlined much of political life. In 1970 rioting and an army mutiny against the East Indian population prompted a state of emergency, which lasted for two years.

Eric Williams, "Father of the Nation" and leader of the People's National Movement (PNM), which is largely supported by blacks, governed from 1956 until his death in 1981. In Dec. 1986 the multiracial National Alliance for Reconstruction (NAR), based in Tobago, won a parliamentary majority, promising to sell most state-owned companies, reorganize the civil service, and reduce dependence on oil.

In 1990, to protest the NAR government, some 100 radical black Muslims blew up the police station in an attempted coup, in which the prime minister and other officials were held hostage for six days. The NAR was defeated in 1991, and the PNM returned to power. In 1995, the East Indian–based party, the United National Congress (UNC), led by Basdeo Panday, formed a coalition government with the NAR. In 2000, Panday narrowly won another term.

In Dec. 2001 elections, the governing UNC Party and the PNM Party gained 18 seats each. The two parties agreed to allow President Robinson to select the prime minister to end the impasse. But when Robinson selected Patrick Manning of the PNM because of his "moral and spiritual values," the opposition angrily called for new elections. In the Oct. 2002 elections, Manning's party declared victory. Maxwell Richards, a university dean, was selected president by Parliament in 2003.

Tunisia

TUNISIAN REPUBLIC

National name: Al-Jumhuriyah at-Tunisiyah
President: Zine al-Abidine Ben Ali (1987)
Prime Minister: Mohamed Ghannouchi (1999)
Area: 63,170 sq mi (163,610 sq km)
Population (2005 est.): 10,074,951 (growth rate: 1.0%); birth rate: 15.5/1000; infant mortality rate: 24.8/1000; life expectancy: 74.9; density per sq mi: 159
Capital and largest city (2003 est.): Tunis, 1,660,300

(metro. area), 699,700 (city proper). **Monetary unit:** Tunisian dinar. **Languages:** Arabic (official, commerce), French (commerce). **Ethnicity/race:** Arab-Berber 98%, European 1%, Jewish and other 1%. **Religions:** Islam (Sunni) 98%, Christian 1%, Jewish and other 1%. **Literacy rate:** 74% (2003 est.) **Economic summary: GDP/PPP** (2004 est.): $70.88 billion; per capita $7,100. **Real growth rate:** 5.1%. **Inflation:** 4.1%. **Unemployment:** 13.8%. **Arable land:** 18%. **Agriculture:** olives, olive oil, grain, dairy products, tomatoes, citrus fruit, beef, sugar beets, dates, almonds. **Labor force:** 3.55 million; note: shortage of skilled labor; services 55%, industry 23%, agriculture 22% (1995 est.). **Industries:** petroleum, mining (particularly phosphate and iron ore), tourism, textiles, footwear, agribusiness, beverages. **Natural resources:** petroleum, phosphates, iron ore, lead, zinc, salt. **Exports:** $9.926 billion (f.o.b., 2004 est.): textiles, mechanical goods, phosphates and chemicals, agricultural products, hydrocarbons. **Imports:** $11.52 billion (f.o.b., 2004 est.): textiles, machinery and equipment, hydrocarbons, chemicals, food. **Major trading partners:** France, Italy, Germany, Spain, Libya (2003).

Geography Tunisia, at the northernmost bulge of Africa, thrusts out toward Sicily to mark the division between the eastern and western Mediterranean Sea. Twice the size of South Carolina, it is bordered on the west by Algeria and by Libya on the south. Coastal plains on the east rise to a north-south escarpment that slopes gently to the west. The Sahara Desert lies in the southernmost part. Tunisia is more mountainous in the north, where the Atlas range continues from Algeria.

Government Republic.

History Tunisia was settled by the Phoenicians in the 12th century B.C. By the sixth and fifth centuries B.C., the great city-state of Carthage (derived from the Phoenician name for "new city") dominated much of the western Mediterranean. The three Punic Wars between Rome and Carthage (the second was the most famous, pitting the Roman general Scipio Africanus against Carthage's Hannibal) led to the complete destruction of Carthage by 146 B.C.

Except for an interval of Vandal conquest in A.D. 439–533, Carthage was part of the Roman Empire until the Arab conquest of 648–669. It was then ruled by various Arab and Berber dynasties, followed by the Turks, who took it in 1570–1574 and made it part of the Ottoman Empire until the 19th century. In the late 16th century, it was a stronghold for the Barbary pirates. French troops occupied the country in 1881, and the bey, the local Tunisian ruler, signed a treaty acknowledging it as a French protectorate.

Nationalist agitation forced France to recognize Tunisian independence and sovereignty in 1956. The Constituent Assembly deposed the bey on July 25, 1957, declared Tunisia a republic, and elected Habib Bourguiba as president. Bourguiba maintained a pro-Western foreign policy that earned him enemies. Tunisia refused to break relations with the U.S. during the Arab-Israeli War in June 1967. Concerned with Islamic fundamentalist plots against the state, the government stepped up efforts to eradicate the movement, including censorship and frequent detention of suspects.

In 1987, the aged Bourguiba was declared mentally unfit to continue as president and was removed from office in a bloodless coup. He was succeeded by Gen. Zine al-Abidine Ben Ali, whose tenure has been marked by repression, a poor human rights record, the rise in Islamic fundamentalism, and growing anti-Western sentiments among the populace. Ben Ali was reelected in Oct. 1999 with 99% of the vote in an election criticized by many human rights observers. In May 2000 Ben Ali's Constitutional Democratic Assembly Party swept local elections with 92% of the vote, in a contest many opposition leaders boycotted. However, Tunisia's economy continued to improve in the late 1990s, making the country one of the most attractive in Africa for foreign investors. In May 2002, a referendum passed that ended the three-term limit for the presidency. It permitted Ben Ali, who has served as president for more than 15 years, to run for two more terms. Opposition parties protested. In Oct. 2004, the president was reelected with 94% of the vote.

Turkey

REPUBLIC OF TURKEY

National name: Türkiye Cumhuriyeti
President: Ahmet Necdet Sezer (2000)
Prime Minister: Recep Tayyip Erdogan (2003)
Area: 301,382 sq mi (incl. 9,121 in Europe) (780,580 sq km)
Population (2005 est.): 69,660,559 (growth rate: 1.1%); birth rate: 16.8/1000; infant mortality rate: 41.0/1000; life expectancy: 72.4; density per sq mi: 231
Capital (2003 est.): Ankara, 3,582,000 (metro. area), 3,456,100 (city proper). **Largest cities:** Istanbul, 10,048,900 (metro. area), 9,419,000 (city proper); Izmir, 2,398,200; Bursa, 1,288,900; Adana, 1,219,900; Gaziantep, 979,500. **Monetary unit:** Turkish lira (YTL). **Languages:** Turkish (official), Kurdish, Arabic, Armenian, Greek. **Ethnicity/race:** Turkish 80%, Kurdish 20% (estimated). **Religions:** Islam (mostly Sunni) 99.8%, other 0.2% (mostly Christians and Jews). **Literacy rate:** 87% (2003 est.)
Economic summary: GDP/PPP (2004 est.): $508.7 billion; per capita $7,400. **Real growth rate:** 8.2%. **Inflation:** 9.3%. **Unemployment:** 9.3% (plus underemployment of 4.0%). **Arable land:** 31%. **Agriculture:** tobacco, cotton, grain, olives, sugar beets, pulse, citrus; livestock. **Labor force:** 25.3 million; note: about 1.2 million Turks work abroad; agriculture 35.9%, industry 22.8%, services 41.2% (3rd quarter, 2004). **Industries:** textiles, food processing, autos, mining (coal, chromite, copper, boron), steel, petroleum, construction, lumber, paper. **Natural resources:** antimony, coal, chromium, mercury, copper, borate, sulfur, iron ore, arable land, hydropower. **Exports:** $69.46 billion (f.o.b., 2004 est.): apparel, foodstuffs, textiles, metal manufactures, transport equipment. **Imports:** $94.5 billion (f.o.b., 2004 est.): machinery, chemicals, semifinished goods, fuels, transport equipment. **Major trading partners:** Germany, U.S., UK, Italy, France, Russia, Switzerland (2003).

Geography Turkey is at the northeast end of the Mediterranean Sea in southeast Europe and southwest Asia. To the north is the Black Sea and to the west is the Aegean Sea. Its neighbors are Greece and Bulgaria to the west, Russia and Ukraine to the north (through the Black Sea), Georgia, Armenia, Azerbaijan, and Iran to the east, and Syria and Iraq to the south. The Dardanelles, the Sea of Marmara, and the Bosporus divide the country. Turkey in Europe comprises an area about equal to the state of Massachusetts. Turkey in Asia is about the size of Texas. Its center is a treeless plateau rimmed by mountains.

Government Republican parliamentary democracy.

History Anatolia (Turkey in Asia) was occupied in about 1900 B.C. by the Indo-European Hittites and, after the Hittite Empire's collapse in 1200 B.C., by Phrygians and Lydians. The Persian Empire occupied the area in the 6th century B.C., giving way to the Roman Empire, then later the Byzantine Empire. The Ottoman Turks first appeared in the early 13th century, subjugating Turkish and Mongol bands pressing against the eastern borders of Byzantium and making the Christian Balkan states their vassals. They gradually spread through the Near East and Balkans, capturing Constantinople in 1453 and storming the gates of Vienna two centuries later. At its height, the Ottoman Empire stretched from the Persian Gulf to western Algeria. Lasting for 600 years, the Ottoman Empire was not only one of the most powerful empires in the history of the Mediterranean region, but it generated a great cultural outpouring of Islamic art, architecture, and literature.

After the reign of Sultan Süleyman I the Magnificent (1494–1566), the Ottoman Empire began to decline politically, administratively, and economically. By the 18th century, Russia was seeking to establish itself as the protector of Christians in Turkey's Balkan territories. Russian ambitions were checked by Britain and France in the Crimean War (1854–1856), but the Russo-Turkish War (1877–1878) gave Bulgaria virtual independence and Romania and Serbia liberation from their nominal allegiance to the sultan. Turkish weakness stimulated a revolt of young liberals known as the Young Turks in 1909. They forced Sultan Abdul Hamid to grant a constitution and install a liberal government. However, reforms were no barrier to further defeats in a war with Italy (1911–1912) and the Balkan Wars (1912–1913). Turkey sided with Germany in World War I, and, as a result, lost territory at the conclusion of the war.

Turkey's current boundaries were drawn in 1923 at the Conference of Lausanne, and Turkey became a republic with Kemal Atatürk as the first president. The Ottoman sultanate and caliphate were abolished, and modernization, reform, and industrialization began under Atatürk's direction. He secularized Turkish society, reducing Islam's dominant role and replacing Arabic with the Latin alphabet for writing the Turkish language. After Atatürk's death in 1938, parliamentary government and a multiparty system gradually took root in Turkey, despite periods of instability and brief intervals of military rule. Neutral during most of World War II, Turkey, on Feb. 23, 1945, declared war on Germany and Japan, but it took no active part in the conflict. Turkey became a full member of NATO in 1952, was a signatory in the Balkan Entente (1953), joined the Baghdad Pact (1955; later CENTO), joined the Organization for European Economic Cooperation (OEEC) and the Council of Europe, and became an associate member of the European Common Market in 1963.

Turkey invaded Cyprus by sea and air on July 20, 1974, following the failure of diplomatic efforts to resolve conflicts between Turkish and Greek Cypriots. Turkey unilaterally announced a cease-fire on Aug. 16, after having gained control of 40% of the island. Turkish Cypriots established their own state in the north on Feb. 13, 1975. In July 1975, after a 30-day warning, Turkey took control of all the U.S. installations except the joint defense base at Incirlik, which it reserved for "NATO tasks alone."

The establishment of military government in Sept. 1980 stopped the slide toward anarchy and brought some improvement in the economy. A Constituent Assembly, consisting of the six-member National Security Council and members appointed by them, drafted a new constitution that was approved by an overwhelming (91.5%) majority of the voters in a Nov. 6, 1982, referendum. Martial law was gradually lifted. The military, however, effectively continues to control the country.

About 12 million Kurds, roughly 20% of Turkey's population, live in the southeast region of Turkey. Turkey, however, does not officially recognize Kurds as a minority group and is therefore exempted from protecting their rights. Oppression of Kurds and Kurdish culture led to the emergence in 1984 of the Kurdistan Workers' Party (PKK), a militant Kurdish terrorist campaign under the leadership of Abdullah Ocalan. Although the guerrilla movement sought independence at first, by the late 1980s the rebel Kurds were willing to accept an autonomous state or a federation with Turkey. About 35,000 have died in clashes between the military and the PKK during the 1980s and 1990s. On Feb. 16, 1999, Ocalan was captured. He was tried and convicted of treason and separatism on June 2, 1999, and sentenced to death.

On Aug. 17, 1999, western Turkey was devastated by an earthquake (magnitude 7.4) that left more than 17,000 dead and 200,000 homeless. Another huge earthquake struck in November.

Construction on a $3 billion 1,000-mile oil pipeline running from Baku, Azerbaijan, to the Mediterranean port city of Ceyhan began in Sept. 2002. The pipeline is expected to bolster the economy.

In Nov. 2002 elections, the recently formed Justice and Development Party (AK) won. Its leader, Recep Tayyip Erdogan, was barred from becoming prime minister, however, because of a conviction for "inciting religious hatred" by reciting an Islamic poem at a rally in 1998. Another popular AK leader, Abdullah Gul, served as prime minister until Turkish law was amended to permit Erdogan to run for a seat in Parliament again, which he easily won. Gul resigned as prime minister, making way for Erdogan.

In March 2003, U.S.-Turkish relations were severely strained when Turkey's parliament narrowly failed to pass a resolution permitting the U.S. to use Turkish bases as a launching pad for the pending war against Iraq. Turkish opinion polls reported that an overwhelming 90% of Turks were against war in Iraq, but the U.S. had promised the country much-needed economic aid.

In Nov. 2003, two terrorist attacks rocked Istanbul. On Nov. 17, truck bombs exploded near two synagogues; on Nov. 22, the British Consulate and a British bank were targeted. More than 50 were killed and hundreds were wounded in the attacks; al-Qaeda is believed to be responsible.

In an effort to make itself more attractive to potential EU membership, Turkey has begun revamping some of its repressive laws and policies. In 2003, its Parliament passed a law reducing the military's role in political life, and offered partial amnesty to PKK members, many of whom have sought refuge in northern Iraq. In 2004, Turkish state television broadcast the first Kurdish language program and the government freed four Kurdish activists from prison. Turkey also abolished the death penalty in all but exceptional cases.

Turkmenistan

President-for-Life: Saparmurad A. Niyazov (1990)
Area: 188,455 sq mi (488,100 sq km)
Population (2005 est.): 4,952,081 (growth rate: 1.8%); birth rate: 27.7/1000; infant mortality rate: 73.1/1000; life expectancy: 61.4; density per sq mi: 26
Capital and largest city (2003 est.): Ashgabat, 727,700. **Other large cities:** Chardzhou, 213,500; Tashauz, 160,400. **Monetary unit:** Manat.
Languages: Turkmen 72%; Russian 12%; Uzbek 9%; other 7%. **Ethnicity/race:** Turkmen 85%, Uzbek 5%,

Russian 4%, other 6% (2003). **Religions:** Islam 89%, Eastern Orthodox 9%, unknown 2%. **Literacy rate:** 98% (1989 est.)
Economic summary: GDP/PPP (2004 est.): $27.6 billion; per capita $5,700. **Real growth rate:** 7.5% (IMF est.). **Inflation:** 9%. **Unemployment:** 60%. **Arable land:** 4%. **Agriculture:** cotton, grain; livestock. **Labor force:** 2.32 million (2003 est.); agriculture 48.2%, industry 13.8%, services 37% (2003 est.). **Industries:** natural gas, oil, petroleum products, textiles, food processing. **Natural resources:** petroleum, natural gas, coal, sulfur, salt. **Exports:** $4 billion (f.o.b., 2004 est.): gas, crude oil, petrochemicals, cotton fiber, textiles. **Imports:** $2.85 billion (f.o.b., 2004 est.): machinery and equipment, chemicals, foodstuffs. **Major trading partners:** Ukraine, Italy, Iran, Turkey, Russia, UAE, Germany, China (2003).

Geography Turkmenistan (formerly Turkmenia) is bounded by the Caspian Sea in the west, Kazakhstan in the north, Uzbekistan in the east, and Iran and Afghanistan in the south. About nine-tenths of Turkmenistan is desert, chiefly the Kara-Kum. One of the world's largest sand deserts, it is approximately 138,966 sq mi (360,000 sq km).

Government One-party republic.

History Turkmenistan was once part of the ancient Persian Empire. The Turkmen people were originally pastoral nomads and some of them continued this way of life up into the 20th century, living in transportable dome-shaped felt tents. The territory was ruled by the Seljuk Turks in the 11th century. The Mongols of Ghenghis Khan conquered the land in the 13th century and dominated the area for the next two centuries until they were deposed in the late 15th century by invading Uzbeks. Prior to the 19th century, Turkmenia was divided into two lands, one belonging to the khanate of Khiva and the other belonging to the khanate of Bukhara. In 1868, the khanate of Khiva was made part of the Russian Empire and Turkmenia became known as the Transcaspia Region of Russian Turkistan. Turkmenistan was later formed out of the Turkistan Autonomous Soviet Socialist Republic, founded in 1922, and was made an independent Soviet Socialist Republic on May 13, 1925. It was the poorest of the Soviet republics.

Turkmenistan declared its sovereignty in Aug. 1990 and became a member of the Commonwealth of Independent States on Dec. 21, 1991, together with ten other former Soviet republics. It established a government more authoritarian than those functioning in the other newly independent central Asian republics. President Saparmurad A. Niyazov, also called the Turkmenbashi (Leader of All Turkmens), has attempted to create a cult of personality through extravagant self-promotion. Cities, aftershave, and a meteor now bear his name. In 2002, he renamed all the months of the calendar—April is now named after his mother. Niyazov was voted president-for-life by his rubber-stamp Parliament in 1999.

In the 1990s, Turkmenistan exported gas through a Russian pipeline, bringing in about $1 billion per year. But in 1993, Russia closed down Turkmenistan's only pipeline because it competed with Russia's own gas exportation. Turkmenistan was limited to exporting gas to its impoverished central Asian neighbors, who were unable to pay their bills. The nation then opened a pipeline route to Iran, generally agreed to be the most economical route for exporting Caspian oil, and thus ruffled the feathers of Iran's enemy, the U.S. So far, the new plan has not brought in money, and the country is living off loans from Western countries, such as Germany, who hope to partner with the oil-rich, money-poor country. In 2003, Russia agreed to buy 60 billion cubic meters of gas from Turkmenistan annually. At the time of the deal, Turkmenistan began to restrict the rights of its ethnic Russian citizens, infuriating Russia.

An alleged assassination attempt against Niyazov in Nov. 2002 (thought by outsiders to have been staged) resulted in the conviction of 46 opposition leaders and critics of the government.

In recent years, the country's educational system has degenerated significantly—the number of years of school required has been reduced, the curriculum has grown increasingly vocational, and substantial classroom time is devoted to political propaganda, including the president's own book, *Rukhnama* (Book of the Soul).

Tuvalu

Sovereign: Queen Elizabeth II (1952)
Governor-General: Filoimea Telito (2005)
Prime Minister: Maatia Toafa (2004)
Area: 10 sq mi (26 sq km)
Population (2005 est.): 11,636 (growth rate: 1.5%); birth rate: 21.9/1000; infant mortality rate: 20.0/1000; life expectancy: 68.0; density per sq mi: 1,159
Capital and largest city (2003 est.): Funafuti, 5,300.
Monetary unit: Australian dollar. **Languages:** Tuvaluan, English, Samoan, Kiribati (on the island of Nui). **Ethnicity/race:** Polynesian 96%, Micronesian 4%. **Religions:** Church of Tuvalu (Congregationalist) 97%, Seventh-Day Adventist 1.4%, Baha'i 1%, other 0.6%. **Literacy rate:** n.a
Economic summary: GDP/PPP (2000 est.): $12.2 million; per capita $1,100. **Real growth rate:** 3%. **Inflation:** 5%. **Unemployment:** n.a. **Arable land:** 0%. **Agriculture:** coconuts; fish. **Labor force:** 7,000 (2001 est.); people make a living mainly through exploitation of the sea, reefs, and atolls and from wages sent home by those working abroad (mostly workers in the phosphate industry and sailors). **Industries:** fishing, tourism, copra. **Natural resource:** fish. **Exports:** $1 million (f.o.b., 2002): copra, fish. **Imports:** $79 million (c.i.f., 2002): food, animals, mineral fuels, machinery, manufactured goods. **Major trading partners:** UK, Poland, Australia, Philippines, Fiji, Germany, Japan, New Zealand (2003). **Member of Commonwealth of Nations**

Geography Tuvalu consists of nine small islands scattered over 500,000 sq mi of the western Pacific, just south of the equator. The islands include Niulakita, Nukulaelae, Funafuti, Nukufetau, Vaitupu, Nui, Niutao, Nanumaga (Nanumanga), and Nanumea.

Government Constitutional monarchy with a parliamentary democracy.

History Formerly the Ellice Islands, Tuvalu's first Polynesian settlers were probably Samoans or Tongans. The Ellice Islands became a British protectorate in 1892 and were annexed by Britain in 1915–1916 as part of the Gilbert and Ellice Islands Colony. The Ellice Islands were separated from the Gilberts in 1975, given home rule, and renamed Tuvalu. Full independence was granted on Sept. 30, 1978, but Tuvalu remained part of the Commonwealth. In 1979, the U.S. gave Tuvalu four islands that had been U.S. territory.

In 1997, the government adopted a strong stance on the need to control emissions of greenhouse gases in order to ensure the survival of low-lying island nations, which are threatened by rising sea levels—Tuvalu's highest point is just 16 ft above sea level. In 2000, Tuvalu became a member of the United Nations. Tuvalu reportedly makes millions of dollars each year by leasing its highly marketable .tv Internet domain.

Uganda

REPUBLIC OF UGANDA

President: Yoweri Museveni (1986)
Prime Minister: Apolo Nsibambi (1999)
Area: 91,135 sq mi (236,040 sq km)
Population (2005 est.): 27,269,482 (growth rate: 3.3%); birth rate: 47.4/1000; infant mortality rate: 67.8/1000; life expectancy: 51.6; density per sq mi: 299
Capital and largest city (2003 est.): Kampala, 1,461,600 (metro. area), 1,244,000 (city proper).
Monetary unit: Ugandan new shilling. **Languages:** English (official), Ganda or Luganda, other Niger-Congo languages, Nilo-Saharan languages, Swahili, Arabic. **Ethnicity/race:** Baganda 17%, Ankole 8%, Basoga 8%, Iteso 8%, Bakiga 7%, Langi 6%, Rwanda 6%, Bagisu 5%, Acholi 4%, Lugbara 4%, Batoro 3%, Bunyoro 3%, Alur 2%, Bagwere 2%, Bakonjo 2%, Jopodhola 2%, Karamojong 2%, Rundi 2%, non-African (European, Asian, Arab) 1%, other 8%. **Religions:** Roman Catholic 33%, Protestant 33%, Islam 16%, indigenous beliefs 18%. **Literacy rate:** 70% (2003 est.)
Economic summary: GDP/PPP (2004 est.): $39.39 billion; per capita $1,500. **Real growth rate:** 5%. **Inflation:** 3.5%. **Unemployment:** n.a. **Arable land:** 26%. **Agriculture:** coffee, tea, cotton, tobacco, cassava (tapioca), potatoes, corn, millet, pulses; beef, goat meat, milk, poultry, cut flowers. **Labor force:** 12.41 million; agriculture 82%, industry 5%, services 13% (1999 est.). **Industries:** sugar, brewing, tobacco, cotton textiles, cement, steel production. **Natural resources:** copper, cobalt, hydropower, limestone, salt, arable land. **Exports:** $621.7 million (f.o.b., 2004 est.): coffee, fish and fish products, tea; gold, cotton, flowers, horticultural products. **Imports:** $1.306 billion (f.o.b., 2004 est.): capital equipment, vehicles, petroleum, medical supplies; cereals. **Major trading partners:** Kenya, Switzerland, Netherlands, UK, South Africa, India, Japan, UAE, U.S., China (2003).
Member of the Commonwealth of Nations

Geography Uganda, twice the size of Pennsylvania, is in East Africa. It is bordered on the west by Congo, on the north by the Sudan, on the east by Kenya, and on the south by Tanzania and Rwanda. The country, which lies across the equator, is divided into three main areas—swampy lowlands, a fertile plateau with wooded hills, and a desert region. Lake Victoria forms part of the southern border.

Government Multiparty democractic republic.

History About 500 B.C. Bantu-speaking peoples migrated to the area now called Uganda. By the 14th century, three kingdoms dominated, Buganda (meaning "state of the Gandas"), Bunyoro, and Ankole. Uganda was first explored by Europeans as well as Arab traders in 1844. An Anglo-German agreement of 1890 declared it to be in the British sphere of influence in Africa, and the Imperial British East Africa Company was chartered to develop the area. The company did not prosper financially, and in 1894 a British protectorate was proclaimed. Few Europeans permanently settled in Uganda, but it attracted many Indians, who became important players in Ugandan commerce. Uganda became independent on Oct. 9, 1962. Sir Edward Mutesa, the king of Buganda (Mutesa II), was elected the first president, and Milton Obote the first

prime minister, of the newly independent country. With the help of a young army officer, Col. Idi Amin, Prime Minister Obote seized control of the government from President Mutesa four years later.

On Jan. 25, 1971, Colonel Amin deposed President Obote. Obote went into exile in Tanzania. Amin expelled Asian residents and launched a reign of terror against Ugandan opponents, torturing and killing tens of thousands. In 1976, he had himself proclaimed "President for Life." In 1977, Amnesty International estimated that 300,000 may have died under his rule, including church leaders and recalcitrant cabinet ministers.

After Amin held military exercises on the Tanzanian border in 1978, angering Tanzania's president, Julius Nyerere, a combined force of Tanzanian troops and Ugandan exiles loyal to former president Obote invaded Uganda and chased Amin into exile in Saudi Arabia in 1979. After a series of interim administrations, President Obote led his People's Congress Party to victory in 1980 elections that opponents charged were rigged. On July 27, 1985, army troops staged a coup and took over the government. Obote fled into exile. The military regime installed Gen. Tito Okello as chief of state.

The National Resistance Army (NRA), an anti-Obote group led by Yoweri Museveni, kept fighting after it had been excluded from the new regime. It seized Kampala on Jan. 29, 1986, and Museveni was declared president. Museveni has transformed the ruins of Idi Amin and Milton Obote's Uganda into an economic miracle, preaching a philosophy of self-sufficiency and anticorruption. Western countries have flocked to assist him in the country's transformation. Nevertheless, it remains one of Africa's poorest countries. A ban on political parties was lifted in 1996, and the incumbent Museveni won 72% of the vote, reflecting his popularity due to the country's economic recovery.

Uganda has waged an enormously successful campaign against AIDS, dramatically reducing the rate of new infections through an intensive public health and education campaign. Museveni won reelection in March 2001 with 70% of the vote, following a nasty and spirited campaign.

Close ties with Rwanda (many Rwandan Tutsi exiles helped Museveni come to power) led to the cooperation of Uganda and Rwanda in the ousting of Zaire's Mobutu Sese Seko in 1997, and a year later, in efforts to unseat his successor, Laurent Kabila, whom both countries originally supported but from whom they grew estranged. But in 1999, Uganda and Rwanda quarreled over strategy in the Democratic Republic of the Congo, and began fighting each other. The two countries mended their differences in 2002. Uganda also signed a peace accord with the Congo in Sept. 2002 and finally withdrew its remaining troops from the country in May 2003.

In 2004, Uganda continued its 17-year battle against the Lord's Resistance Army (LRA), an extremist rebel group based in Sudan. Between 8,000 and 10,000 children have been abducted by the LRA and form the army of "prophet" Joseph Kony, whose aim is to take over Uganda and run it according to his vision of Christianity. Up to 1.5 million people in northern Uganda have been displaced because of the fighting and the fear that their children will be abducted.

In July 2005, Parliament amended the constitution to eliminate term limits, thus allowing President Museveni another term in office. In August, a multiparty political system was reinstituted after a 19-year absence.

Ukraine

National name: Ukrayina
President: Viktor Yushchenko (2005)
Prime Minister: Yuri Yekhanurov (acting)(2005)
Area: 233,089 sq mi (603,700 sq km)
Population (2005 est.): 47,425,336 (growth rate: –0.6%);
birth rate: 10.5/1000; infant mortality rate: 20.3/1000;
life expectancy: 66.8; density per sq mi: 203
Capital (2003 est.): Kyiv (Kiev), 3,296,100 (metro. area),
2,588,400 (city proper). **Other large cities:** Kharkiv,
1,435,200; Odessa, 1,022,300; Donetske, 984,900;
Lvov, 700,100. **Monetary unit:** Hryvna. **Language:**
Ukrainian, Russian, Romanian, Polish, Hungarian.
Ethnicity/race: Ukrainian 77.8%, Russian 17.3%,
Belorussian 0.6%, Moldovan 0.5%, Crimean Tatar
0.5%, Bulgarian 0.4%, Hungarian 0.3%, Romanian
0.3%, Polish 0.3%, Jewish 0.2%, other 1.8% (2001).
Religions: Ukrainian Orthodox (Moscow Patriarchate,
Kiev Patriarchate), Ukrainian Autocephalous Orthodox,
Ukrainian Catholic (Uniate), Protestant, Jewish.
Literacy rate: 100% (2003 est.)
Economic summary: GDP/PPP (2004 est.): $299.1
billion; per capita $6,300. **Real growth rate:** 12%.
Inflation: 12%. **Unemployment:** 3.5% officially
registered; large number of unregistered or
underemployed workers. **Arable land:** 56%.
Agriculture: grain, sugar beets, sunflower seeds,
vegetables; beef, milk. **Labor force:** 21.11 million;
industry 32%, agriculture 24%, services 44% (1996).
Industries: coal, electric power, ferrous and
nonferrous metals, machinery and transport
equipment, chemicals, food processing (especially
sugar). **Natural resources:** iron ore, coal,
manganese, natural gas, oil, salt, sulfur, graphite,
titanium, magnesium, kaolin, nickel, mercury, timber,
arable land. **Exports:** $32.91 billion (2004 est.):
ferrous and nonferrous metals, fuel and petroleum
products, chemicals, machinery and transport
equipment, food products. **Imports:** $31.45 billion
(2004 est.): energy, machinery and equipment,
chemicals. **Major trading partners:** Russia, Germany,
Italy, China, Turkmenistan (2003).

Geography Located in southeast Europe, the country consists largely of fertile black soil steppes. Mountainous areas include the Carpathians in the southwest and the Crimean chain in the south. Ukraine is bordered by Belarus on the north, by Russia on the north and east, by the Black Sea on the south, by Moldova and Romania on the southwest, and by Hungary, Slovakia, and Poland on the west.

Government Constitutional republic.

History Ukraine was known as "Kievan Rus" (from which *Russia* is a derivative) up until the 16th century. In the 9th century, Kiev was the major political and cultural center in eastern Europe. Kievan Rus reached the height of its power in the 10th century and adopted Byzantine Christianity. The Mongol conquest in 1240 ended Kievan power. From the 13th to the 16th century, Kiev was under the influence of Poland and western Europe. The negotiation of the Union of Brest-Litovsk in 1596 divided the Ukrainians into Orthodox and Ukrainian Catholic faithful. In 1654, Ukraine asked the czar of Moscovy for protection against Poland, and the Treaty of Pereyasav signed that year recognized the suzerainty of Moscow. The agreement was interpreted by Moscow as an invitation to take over Kiev, and the Ukrainian state was eventually absorbed into the Russian Empire.

After the Russian Revolution, Ukraine declared its independence from Russia on Jan. 28, 1918, and several years of warfare ensued with several groups. The Red Army finally was victorious over Kiev, and in 1920 Ukraine became a Soviet republic. In 1922, Ukraine became one of the founders of the Union of Soviet Socialist Republics. In the 1930s, the Soviet government's enforcement of collectivization met with peasant resistance, which in turn prompted the confiscation of grain from Ukrainian farmers by Soviet authorities; the resulting famine took an estimated 5 million lives. Ukraine was one of the most devastated Soviet republics after World War II. (For details on World War II, *see* Headline History, World War II.) On April 26, 1986, the nation's nuclear power plant at Chernobyl was the site of the world's worst nuclear accident. On Oct. 29, 1991, the Ukrainian Parliament voted to shut down the reactor within two years' time and asked for international assistance in dismantling it.

When President Leonid Kravchuk was elected by the Ukrainian Parliament in 1990, he vowed to seek Ukrainian sovereignty. Ukraine declared its independence on Aug. 24, 1991. In Dec. 1991, Ukrainian, Russian, and Belorussian leaders cofounded a new Commonwealth of Independent States with the capital to be situated in Minsk, Belarus. The new country's government was slow to reform the Soviet-era state-run economy, which was plagued by declining production, rising inflation, and widespread unemployment in the years following independence. The U.S. announced in Jan. 1994 that an agreement had been reached with Russia and Ukraine for the destruction of Ukraine's entire nuclear arsenal. In Oct. 1994, Ukraine began a program of economic liberalization and moved to reestablish central authority over Crimea. In 1995, Crimea's separatist leader was removed and the Crimean constitution revoked.

In June 1996, the last strategic nuclear warhead was removed to Russia. Also that month Parliament approved a new constitution that allowed for private ownership of land. An agreement was signed in May 1997 on the future of the Black Sea fleet, by which Ukrainian and Russian ships will share the port of Sevastopol for 20 years.

The Russian financial crisis in fall 1998 led to severe problems for the Ukrainian economy, which is dependent on Russia for 40% of its foreign trade. Ukraine remains saddled with its Soviet-era economy, and most of its major industries are still under state control. Corruption is rampant, and as a result, Western investors have shown only minimal interest. The election of the reform-minded Viktor Yushchenko as prime minister in Dec. 1999, however, was greeted with optimism by the West. He was also highly popular among Ukrainians. But in April 2001, he was dismissed in a no-confidence vote engineered by Communist hard-liners and Ukrainian big business.

In the winter of 2001 violent demonstrations rocked Ukraine, with protesters demanding the resignation and impeachment of authoritarian president Leonid Kuchma. Critics accused Kuchma of involvement in the murder of a journalist critical of government corruption. Kuchma was recorded on tape urging that the journalist be disposed of.

In 2004, Kuchma announced he would be retiring. A presidential election pitted Viktor Yushchenko, the former reformist prime minister, against Viktor Yanukovich, the current prime minister and Kuchma's chosen successor. The campaign was an especially dirty one. Yushchenko was nearly fatally poisoned with dioxin and had to be hospitalized for several weeks shortly before the election. His doctors predict that the poisoning will affect his health for years to come. In the Nov. 21 runoff election, Prime Minister Yanukovich received 49.5% of the vote and Yushchenko 46.5%. International monitors declared the elections massively fraudulent.

Hundreds of thousands of Yushchenko's supporters took to the streets of the capital and other cities in protest, and what became known as the Orange Revolution (after Yushchenko's signature campaign color) continued full strength over the next two weeks. On Dec. 3, the Supreme Court invalidated the election results. On Dec. 8, Parliament voted in favor of an overhaul of Ukraine's political system, amending the constitution to reform election laws and transferring some presidential powers to the Parliament. In the final presidential runoff on Dec. 26, Yushchenko won 52% of the vote to Yanukovich's 44.2%. On Jan. 23, 2005, Viktor Yushchenko was sworn in. Fellow reformist Yulia Timoshenko became the prime minister. But within the year Yushchenko's reformist reputation was tarnished by his administration's infighting and allegations of corruption. He fired Prime Minster Timoshenko and her entire cabinet in Aug. 2005. The crisis has naturally shaken the public's belief in the Orange Revolution.

United Arab Emirates

National name: Al-Imarat al-'Arabiyah al-Muttahidah
President: Sheikh Khalifa bin Zayed Al Nahyan (2004)
Prime Minister: Sheikh Maktoum bin Rashid al-Maktoum (1990)
Area: 32,000 sq mi (82,880 sq km)
Population (2005 est.): 2,563,212 (growth rate: 1.5%); birth rate: 18.8/1000; infant mortality rate: 14.5/1000; life expectancy: 75.2; density per sq mi: 80
Capital (2003 est.): Abu Dhabi, 539,800. **Largest city:** Dubai, 1,511,700 (metro. area), 906,100 (city proper). **Monetary unit:** U.A.E. dirham. **Languages:** Arabic (official), Persian, English, Hindi, Urdu. **Ethnicity/race:** Emiri 19%, other Arab and Iranian 23%, South Asian 50%, other expatriates (includes Westerners and East Asians) 8% (1982). **Religions:** Islam 96% (Sunni 80%, Shiite 16%), Christian, Hindu, and other 4%. **Literacy rate:** 78% (2003 est.)
Economic summary: GDP/PPP (2004 est.): $63.67 billion; per capita $25,200. **Real growth rate:** 5.7%. **Inflation:** 3.2%. **Unemployment:** 2.4% (2001). **Arable land:** 0.6%. **Agriculture:** dates, vegetables, watermelons; poultry, eggs, dairy products; fish. **Labor force:** 2.36 million; note: 73.9% of the population in the 15–64 age group is nonnational; services 78%, industry 15%, agriculture 7% (2000 est.). **Industries:** petroleum, fishing, aluminum, cement, fertilizers, commercial ship repair, petrochemicals, construction materials, some boatbuilding, handicrafts, textiles. **Natural resources:** petroleum, natural gas. **Exports:** $69.48 billion (f.o.b., 2004 est.): crude oil 45%, natural gas, reexports, dried fish, dates. **Imports:** $45.66 billion (f.o.b., 2004 est.): machinery and transport equipment, chemicals, food. **Major trading partners:** Japan, South Korea, Iran, China, India, Germany, U.S., France, UK (2003).

Geography The United Arab Emirates, in the eastern part of the Arabian Peninsula, extends along part of the Gulf of Oman and the southern coast of the Persian Gulf. The nation is the size of Maine. Its neighbors are Saudi Arabia to the west and south, Qatar to the north, and Oman to the east. Most of the land is barren and sandy.

Government Federation formed in 1971 by seven emirates known as the Trucial States—Abu Dhabi (the largest), Dubai, Sharjah, Ajman, Fujairah, Ras al-Khaimah, and Umm al-Qaiwain.

History Originally the area was inhabited by a seafaring people who were converted to Islam in the 7th century. Later, a dissident sect, the Carmathians, established a powerful sheikdom, and its army conquered Mecca. After the sheikdom disintegrated, its people became pirates. Threatening the Sultanate of Muscat and Oman early in the 19th century, the pirates provoked the intervention of the British, who in 1820 enforced a partial truce and in 1853 a permanent truce. Thus what had been called the Pirate Coast was renamed the Trucial Coast. The British provided the nine Trucial states with protection but did not formally administer them as a colony.

The British withdrew from the Persian Gulf in 1971, and the Trucial states became a federation called the United Arab Emirates (UAE). Two of the Trucial states, Bahrain and Oman, chose not to join the federation, reducing the number of states to seven.

The country signed a military defense agreement with the U.S. in 1994 and one with France in 1995.

After the Sept. 11 terrorist attacks on the U.S., the UAE was identified as a major financial center used by al-Qaeda in transferring money to the hijackers. The nation immediately cooperated with the U.S., freezing accounts tied to suspected terrorists and strongly clamping down on money laundering. The U.S. stationed troops in the UAE during the 2003 Iraq war.

Sheikh Zayed bin Sultan Al Nahyan, the founder of the UAE and ruler of the federation since 1971, died in November 2004. His son succeeded him.

United Kingdom

UNITED KINGDOM OF GREAT BRITAIN AND NORTHERN IRELAND

Sovereign: Queen Elizabeth II (1952)
Prime Minister: Tony Blair (1997)
Area: 94,525 sq mi (244,820 sq km)
Population (2005 est.): 60,441,457 (growth rate: 0.3%); birth rate: 10.8/1000; infant mortality rate: 5.2/1000; life expectancy: 78.4; density per sq mi: 639
Capital and largest city (2003 est.): London, 11,219,000 (metro. area), 7,417,700 (city proper). **Other large cities:** Glasgow, 1,099,400; Birmingham, 971,800; Liverpool, 461,900; Edinburgh, 460,000; Leeds, 417,000; Bristol, 406,500; Manchester, 390,700; Bradford, 288,400. **Monetary unit:** Pound sterling (£). **Languages:** English, Welsh, Scots Gaelic. **Ethnicity/race:** English 81.5%; Scottish 9.6%; Irish 2.4%; Welsh 1.9%; Ulster 1.8%; West Indian, Indian, Pakistani, and other 2.8%. **Religions:** Anglican and Roman Catholic 40 million, Muslim 1.5 million, Presbyterian 800,000, Methodist 760,000, Sikh 500,000, Hindu 500,000, Jewish 350,000. **Literacy rate:** 99% (2000 est.)
Economic summary: GDP/PPP (2004 est.): $1.782 trillion; per capita $29,600. **Real growth rate:** 3.2%. **Inflation:** 1.4%. **Unemployment:** 4.8%. **Arable land:** 23%. **Agriculture:** cereals, oilseed, potatoes, vegetables; cattle, sheep, poultry; fish. **Labor force:** 29.78 million; agriculture 1.5%, industry 19.1%, services 79.5% (2004). **Industries:** machine tools, electric power equipment, automation equipment, railroad equipment, shipbuilding, aircraft, motor vehicles and parts, electronics and communications equipment, metals, chemicals, coal, petroleum, paper and paper products, food processing, textiles, clothing, and other consumer goods. **Natural resources:** coal, petroleum, natural gas, tin, limestone, iron ore, salt, clay, chalk, gypsum, lead, silica, arable land. **Exports:** $347.2 billion (f.o.b., 2004 est.): manufactured goods, fuels, chemicals; food, beverages, tobacco. **Imports:** $439.4 billion (f.o.b., 2004 est.): manufactured goods, machinery, fuels; foodstuffs. **Major trading partners:** U.S., Germany, France, Netherlands, Ireland, Belgium, Spain, Italy (2003).

Geography The United Kingdom, consisting of Great Britain (England, Wales, and Scotland) and Northern Ireland, is twice the size of New York State. England, in the southeast part of the British Isles, is separated from Scotland on the north by the granite Cheviot Hills; from them the Pennine chain of uplands extends south through the center of England, reaching its highest point in the Lake District in the northwest. To the west along the border of Wales—a land of steep hills and valleys—are the Cambrian Mountains, while the Cotswolds, a range of hills in Gloucestershire, extend into the surrounding shires.

Important rivers flowing into the North Sea are the Thames, Humber, Tees, and Tyne. In the west are the Severn and Wye, which empty into the Bristol Channel and are navigable, as are the Mersey and Ribble.

Government The United Kingdom is a constitutional monarchy and parliamentary democracy, with a queen and a Parliament that has two houses: the House of Lords, with 574 life peers, 92 hereditary peers, and 26 bishops; and the House of Commons, which has 651 popularly elected members. Supreme legislative power is vested in Parliament, which sits for five years unless dissolved sooner. The House of Lords was stripped of most of its power in 1911, and now its main function is to revise legislation. In Nov. 1999 hundreds of hereditary peers were expelled in an effort to make the body more democratic. The executive power of the Crown is exercised by the cabinet, headed by the prime minister.

Ruler Queen Elizabeth II, born April 21, 1926, elder daughter of King George VI and Queen Elizabeth, succeeded to the throne upon the death of her father on Feb. 6, 1952. On Nov. 20, 1947, she married Prince Philip, duke of Edinburgh, born June 10, 1921. Their children are Prince Charles (heir apparent), born Nov. 14, 1948; Princess Anne, born Aug. 15, 1950; Prince Andrew, born Feb. 19, 1960; and Prince Edward, born March 10, 1964. Prince William Arthur Philip Louis, son of Prince Charles and the late Princess of Wales and second in line to the throne, was born June 21, 1982. A second son, Prince Henry Charles Albert David, was born Sept. 15, 1984, and is third in line.

History Stonehenge and other examples of prehistoric culture are all that remain of the earliest inhabitants of Britain. Celtic peoples followed. Roman invasions of the 1st century B.C. brought Britain into contact with continental Europe. When the Roman legions withdrew in the 5th century A.D., Britain fell easy prey to the invading hordes of Angles, Saxons, and Jutes from Scandinavia and the Low Countries. The invasions had little effect on the Celtic peoples of Wales and Scotland. Seven large Anglo-Saxon kingdoms were established, and the original Britons were forced into Wales and Scotland. It was not until the 10th century that the country finally became united under the kings of Wessex. Following the death of Edward the Confessor (1066), a dispute about the succession arose, and William, Duke of Normandy, invaded England, defeating the Saxon king, Harold II, at the Battle of Hastings (1066). The Norman conquest introduced Norman French law and feudalism.

The reign of Henry II (1154–1189), first of the Plantagenets, saw an increasing centralization of royal power at the expense of the nobles, but in 1215 King John (1199–1216) was forced to sign the Magna Carta, which awarded the people, especially the nobles, certain basic rights. Edward I (1272–1307) continued the conquest of Ireland, reduced Wales to subjection, and made some gains in Scotland. In 1314, however, English forces led by Edward II were ousted from Scotland after the Battle of Bannockburn. The late 13th and early 14th centuries saw the development of a separate House of Commons with tax-raising powers. Edward III's claim to the throne of France led to the Hundred Years' War (1338–1453) and the loss of almost all the large English territory in France. In England, the great poverty and discontent caused by the war were intensified by the Black Death, a plague that reduced the population by about one-third. The Wars of the Roses (1455–1485), a struggle for the throne between the House of York and the House of Lancaster, ended in the victory of Henry Tudor (Henry VII) at Bosworth Field (1485).

During the reign of Henry VIII (1509–1547), the church in England asserted its independence from the Roman Catholic Church. Under Edward VI and Mary, the two extremes of religious fanaticism were reached, and it remained for Henry's daughter, Elizabeth I (1558–1603), to set up the Church of England on a moderate basis. In 1588, the Spanish Armada, a fleet sent out by Catholic King Philip II of Spain, was defeated by the English and destroyed during a storm. During Elizabeth's reign, England became a world power. Elizabeth's heir was a Stuart—James VI of Scotland—who joined the two crowns as James I (1603–1625). The Stuart kings incurred large debts and were forced either to depend on Parliament for taxes or to raise money by illegal means. In 1642, war broke out between Charles I and a large segment of the Parliament; Charles was defeated and executed in 1649, and the monarchy was then abolished. After the death in 1658 of Oliver Cromwell, the lord protector, the Puritan Commonwealth fell to pieces and Charles II was placed on the throne in 1660. The struggle between the king and Parliament continued, but Charles II knew when to compromise. His brother, James II (1685–1688), possessed none of Charles II's ability and was ousted by the Revolution of 1688, which confirmed the primacy of Parliament. James's daughter, Mary, and her husband, William of Orange, then became the rulers.

Queen Anne's reign (1702–1714) was marked by the Duke of Marlborough's victories over France at Blenheim, Oudenarde, and Malplaquet in the War of the Spanish Succession. England and Scotland meanwhile were joined by the Act of Union (1707). Upon the death of Anne, the distant claims of the elector of Hanover were recognized, and he became king of Great Britain and Ireland as George I. The unwillingness of the Hanoverian kings to rule resulted in the formation by the royal ministers of a cabinet, headed by a prime minister, which directed all public business. Abroad, the constant wars with France expanded the British Empire all over the globe, particularly in North America and India. This imperial growth was checked by the revolt of the American colonies (1775–1781). Struggles with France broke out again in 1793 and during the Napoleonic Wars, which ended at Waterloo in 1815.

The Victorian era, named after Queen Victoria (1837–1901), saw the growth of a democratic system of government that had begun with the Reform Bill of 1832. The two important wars in Victoria's reign were the Crimean War against Russia (1853–1856) and the Boer War (1899–1902), the latter enormously extending Britain's influence in Africa. Increasing uneasiness at home and abroad marked the reign of Edward VII (1901–1910). Within four years after the accession of George V in 1910, Britain entered World War I when Germany invaded Belgium. The nation was led by coalition cabinets, headed first by Herbert Asquith and then, starting in 1916, by the

Rulers of England and Great Britain

Name	Born	Ruled[1]	Name	Born	Ruled[1]
SAXONS[2]			Henry VI	1421	1422–1461[5]
Egbert[3]	c. 775	802–839	**HOUSE OF YORK**		
Ethelwulf	?	839–858	Edward IV	1442	1461–1483[5]
Ethelbald	?	858–860	Edward V	1470	1483–1483
Ethelbert	?	860–865	Richard III	1452	1483–1485
Ethelred I	?	865–871	**HOUSE OF TUDOR**		
Alfred the Great	849	871–899	Henry VII	1457	1485–1509
Edward the Elder	c. 870	899–924	Henry VIII	1491	1509–1547
Athelstan	895	924–939	Edward VI	1537	1547–1553
Edmund I the Deed-doer	921	939–946	Jane (Lady Jane Grey)[6]	1537	1553–1553
Edred	c. 925	946–955	Mary I ("Bloody Mary")	1516	1553–1558
Edwy the Fair	c. 943	955–959	Elizabeth I	1533	1558–1603
Edgar the Peaceful	c. 943	959–975	**HOUSE OF STUART**		
Edward the Martyr	c. 962	975–978	James I[7]	1566	1603–1625
Ethelred II the Unready	968	978–1016	Charles I	1600	1625–1649
Edmund II Ironside	c. 993	1016	**COMMONWEALTH**		
DANES			Council of State	—	1649–1653
Canute	995	1016–1035	Oliver Cromwell[8]	1599	1653–1658
Harold I Harefoot	c.1016	1035–1040	Richard Cromwell[8]	1626	1658–1659[9]
Hardecanute	c.1018	1040–1042	**RESTORATION OF HOUSE OF STUART**		
SAXONS			Charles II	1630	1660–1685
Edward the Confessor	c.1004	1042–1066	James II	1633	1685–
Harold II	c.1020	1066			1688[10]
HOUSE OF NORMANDY			William III[11]	1650	1689–1702
William I the Conqueror	1027	1066–1087	Mary II[11]	1662	1689–1694
William II Rufus	c.1056	1087–1100	Anne	1665	1702–1714
Henry I Beauclerc	1068	1100–1135	**HOUSE OF HANOVER**		
Stephen of Boulogne	c.1100	1135–1154	George I	1660	1714–1727
HOUSE OF PLANTAGENET			George II	1683	1727–1760
Henry II	1133	1154–1189	George III	1738	1760–1820
Richard I Coeur de Lion	1157	1189–1199	George IV	1762	1820–1830
John Lackland	1167	1199–1216	William IV	1765	1830–1837
Henry III	1207	1216–1272	Victoria	1819	1837–1901
Edward I Longshanks	1239	1272–1307	**HOUSE OF SAXE-COBURG[12]**		
Edward II	1284	1307–1327	Edward VII	1841	1901–1910
Edward III	1312	1327–1377	**HOUSE OF WINDSOR[12]**		
Richard II	1367	1377–1399[4]	George V	1865	1910–1936
HOUSE OF LANCASTER			Edward VIII	1894	1936[13]
Henry IV Bolingbroke	1367	1399–1413	George VI	1895	1936–1952
Henry V	1387	1413–1422	Elizabeth II	1926	1952–

1. Year of end of rule is also that of death, unless otherwise indicated. 2. Dates for Saxon kings are still controversial. 3. Became king of West Saxons in 802; considered (from 828) first king of all England. 4. Died 1400. 5. Henry VI reigned again briefly 1470–1471. 6. Nominal queen for 9 days; not counted as queen by some authorities. She was beheaded in 1554. 7. Ruled in Scotland as James VI (1567–1625). 8. Lord Protector. 9. Died 1712. 10. Died 1701. 11. Joint rulers (1689–1694). 12. Name changed from Saxe-Coburg to Windsor in 1917. 13. Was known after his abdication as the Duke of Windsor; died 1972.

Welsh statesman David Lloyd George. Postwar labor unrest culminated in the general strike of 1926.

King Edward VIII succeeded to the throne on Jan. 20, 1936, at his father's death, but he abdicated on Dec. 11, 1936 (in order to marry an American divorcée, Wallis Warfield Simpson), in favor of his brother, who became George VI.

The efforts of Prime Minister Neville Chamberlain to stem the rising threat of Nazism in Germany failed with the German invasion of Poland on Sept. 1, 1939, which was followed by Britain's entry into World War II on Sept. 3. Allied reverses in the spring of 1940 led to Chamberlain's resignation and the formation of another coalition war cabinet by the Conservative leader, Winston Churchill, who led Britain through most of World War II. Churchill resigned shortly after V-E Day, May 8, 1945, but then formed a "caretaker" government that remained in office until after the parliamentary elections in July, which the Labour Party won overwhelmingly. The new government, formed by Clement R. Attlee, began a moderate socialist program.

In 1951, Churchill again became prime minister at the head of a Conservative government. George VI died on Feb. 6, 1952, and was succeeded by his daughter, Elizabeth II. Churchill stepped down in 1955 in favor of Sir Anthony Eden, who resigned on grounds of ill health in 1957 and was succeeded by Harold Macmillan and Sir Alec Douglas-Home. In 1964, Harold Wilson led the Labour Party to victory. A lagging economy brought the Conservatives back to power in 1970. Prime Minister Edward Heath won Britain's admission to the European Community. Margaret Thatcher became Britain's first woman prime minister as the Conservatives won 339 seats on May 3, 1979.

An Argentine invasion of the Falkland Islands on April 2, 1982, involved Britain in a war 8,000 mi from the home islands. Argentina had long claimed the Falklands, known as the *Malvinas* in Spanish, which had been occupied by the British since 1832. Britain won a decisive victory within six weeks when more than 11,000 Argentine troops on the Falklands surrendered on June 14, 1982.

British Prime Ministers Since 1770

Name	Term	Name	Term
Lord North (Tory)	1770–1782	William E. Gladstone (Liberal)	1886–1886
Marquis of Rockingham (Whig)	1782–1782	Marquis of Salisbury (Conservative)	1886–1892
Earl of Shelburne (Whig)	1782–1783	William E. Gladstone (Liberal)	1892–1894
Duke of Portland (Coalition)	1783–1783	Earl of Rosebery (Liberal)	1894–1895
William Pitt, the Younger (Tory)	1783–1801	Marquis of Salisbury (Conservative)	1895–1902
Henry Addington (Tory)	1801–1804	Arthur James Balfour (Conservative)	1902–1905
William Pitt, the Younger (Tory)	1804–1806	Sir H. Campbell-Bannerman (Liberal)	1905–1908
Baron Grenville (Whig)	1806–1807	Herbert H. Asquith (Liberal)	1908–1915
Duke of Portland (Tory)	1807–1809	Herbert H. Asquith (Coalition)	1915–1916
Spencer Perceval (Tory)	1809–1812	David Lloyd George (Coalition)	1916–1922
Earl of Liverpool (Tory)	1812–1827	Andrew Bonar Law (Conservative)	1922–1923
George Canning (Tory)	1827–1827	Stanley Baldwin (Conservative)	1923–1924
Viscount Goderich (Tory)	1827–1828	James Ramsay MacDonald (Labour)	1924–1924
Duke of Wellington (Tory)	1828–1830	Stanley Baldwin (Conservative)	1924–1929
Earl Grey (Whig)	1830–1834	James Ramsay MacDonald (Labour)	1929–1931
Viscount Melbourne (Whig)	1834–1834	James Ramsay MacDonald (Coalition)	1931–1935
Sir Robert Peel (Tory)	1834–1835	Stanley Baldwin (Coalition)	1935–1937
Viscount Melbourne (Whig)	1835–1841	Neville Chamberlain (Coalition)	1937–1940
Sir Robert Peel (Tory)	1841–1846	Winston Churchill (Coalition)	1940–1945
Earl Russell (Whig)	1846–1852	Clement R. Attlee (Labour)	1945–1951
Earl of Derby (Tory)	1852–1852	Sir Winston Churchill (Conservative)	1951–1955
Earl of Aberdeen (Coalition)	1852–1855	Sir Anthony Eden (Conservative)	1955–1957
Viscount Palmerston (Liberal)	1855–1858	Harold Macmillan (Conservative)	1957–1963
Earl of Derby (Conservative)	1858–1859	Sir Alec Frederick Douglas-Home	1963–1964
Viscount Palmerston (Liberal)	1859–1865	(Conservative)	
Earl Russell (Liberal)	1865–1866	Harold Wilson (Labour)	1964–1970
Earl of Derby (Conservative)	1866–1868	Edward Heath (Conservative)	1970–1974
Benjamin Disraeli (Conservative)	1868–1868	Harold Wilson (Labour)	1974–1976
William E. Gladstone (Liberal)	1868–1874	James Callaghan (Labour)	1976–1979
Benjamin Disraeli (Conservative)	1874–1880	Margaret Thatcher (Conservative)	1979–1990
William E. Gladstone (Liberal)	1880–1885	John Major (Conservative)	1990–1997
Marquis of Salisbury (Conservative)	1885–1886	Tony Blair (Labour)	1997–

Although there were continuing economic problems and foreign policy disputes, an upswing in the economy in 1986–1987 led Thatcher to call elections in June, and she won a near-unprecedented third consecutive term. The unpopularity of Thatcher's poll tax together with an uncompromising position toward further European integration eroded support within her own party. When John Major won the Conservative Party leadership in November, Thatcher resigned, paving the way for Major to form a government.

Eighteen years of Conservative rule ended in May 1997 when Tony Blair and the Labour Party triumphed in the British elections. Blair has been compared to former U.S. president Bill Clinton for his youthful, telegenic personality and centrist views. He produced constitutional reform that partially decentralized the UK, leading to the formation of separate Parliaments in Wales and Scotland by 1999. Britain turned over its colony Hong Kong to China in July 1997.

Blair's controversial meeting in Oct. 1997 with Sinn Fein's president, Gerry Adams, was the first meeting in 76 years between a British prime minister and a Sinn Fein leader. It infuriated numerous factions but was a symbolic gesture in support of the nascent peace talks in Northern Ireland. In 1998 the Good Friday Agreement, strongly supported by Tony Blair, led to the first promise of peace between Catholics and Protestants since the beginning of the so-called Troubles.

Along with the U.S., Britain launched air strikes against Iraq in Dec. 1998 after Saddam Hussein expelled UN arms inspectors. In the spring of 1999, Britain spearheaded the NATO operation in Kosovo, which resulted in Yugoslavian president Slobodan Milosevic's withdrawal from the territory.

In Feb. 2001, foot-and-mouth disease broke out among British livestock, prompting other nations to ban British meat imports and forcing the slaughter of thousands of cattle, pigs, and sheep in an effort to stem the highly contagious disease. The episode cost farmers and the tourist industry billions of dollars.

In June 2001, Blair won a second landslide victory, with the Labour Party capturing 413 seats in Parliament.

Britain became the staunchest ally of the U.S. after the Sept. 11 attacks. British troops joined the U.S. in the bombing campaign against Afghanistan in Oct. 2001, after the Taliban-led government refused to turn over the prime suspect in the terrorist attacks, Osama bin Laden.

Blair again proved himself to be the strongest international supporter of the U.S. in Sept. 2002, when he became President Bush's major ally in calling for a war against Iraq. Blair maintained that military action was justified because Iraq was developing weapons of mass destruction that were a direct threat to its enemies. He continued to support the Bush administration's hawkish policies despite significant opposition in his own party and the British public. In March 2003, a London *Times* newspaper poll indicated that only 19% of respondents approved of military action without a UN mandate. As the inevitability of the U.S. strike on Iraq grew nearer, Blair announced that he would join the U.S. in fighting Iraq with or without a second UN resolution. Three of his ministers resigned as a result. Britain entered the war on March 20, supplying 45,000 troops.

In the aftermath of the war, Blair came under fire from government officials for allegedly exaggerating

Iraq's possession of weapons of mass destruction. In July 2003 Blair announced that "history would forgive" the UK and U.S. "if we are wrong" and that the end to the "inhuman carnage and suffering" caused by Saddam Hussein was justification enough for the war. The arguments about the war grew so vociferous between the Blair government and the BBC that a prominent weapons scientist, David Kelly, who was caught in the middle, committed suicide. In Jan. 2004, the Hutton Report exonerated the Blair administration of any misconduct concerning the weapons inspections and concluded that it had not "sexed-up" the intelligence dossier, an accusation put forth by BBC reporter Andrew Gilligan. The report strongly criticized the BBC for its "defective" editorial policies, and as a consequence, the BBC's top management resigned.

In July 2004, the Butler Report on pre–Iraq war British intelligence was released. It echoed the findings of the U.S. Senate Intelligence Committee of the week before that the intelligence had vastly exaggerated Saddam Hussein's threat. The famous claim that Iraq's chemical and biological weapons "are deployable within 45 minutes of an order to use them" was especially singled out as highly misleading. But like the U.S. report, it cleared the government of any role in manipulating the intelligence.

On May 5, 2005, Blair won a historic third term as the country's prime minister. Despite this victory, Blair's party was severely hurt in the elections. The Labour Party won just 36% of the national vote, the lowest percentage by a ruling party in British history. The Conservative Party won 33%, and the Liberal Democrats 22%. Blair acknowledged that the reason for the poor showing was Britain's involvement in the war in Iraq, which was widely unpopular. A number of political analysts believe Blair will not serve out his new five-year term. Many expect him to resign in the next several years and turn over the reins of the Labour Party to Gordon Brown, the chancellor of the exchequer, whose policies many credit in creating Britain's strong and stable economy.

On July 7, 2005, London suffered a terrorist bombing, Britain's worst attack since World War II. Four bombs exploded in three subway stations and on one double-decker bus during the morning rush hour, killing 52 and wounding more than 700. Four Muslim men, three of them British-born, were identified as the suicide bombers. On July 21, terrorists attempted another attack on the transit system, but the bombs failed to explode. A leaked document by a top British government official warned Prime Minister Blair more than a year before the bombings that Britain's engagement in Iraq was fueling Islamic extremism, but Blair has repeatedly denied such a link, contending that the bombings were the result of an "evil ideology" that had taken root before the Iraq war. Blair has proposed legislation that would toughen the country's antiterrorism measures.

Northern Ireland

Status: Part of United Kingdom
First Minister: (suspended Oct. 14, 2002)
Area: 5,452 sq mi (14,121 sq km)
Population (1998 est.): 1,688,600
Capital and largest city (2003 est.): Belfast, 484,800 (metro. area), 246,200 (city proper). **Monetary unit:** British pound sterling (£). **Language:** English. **Religions:** Presbyterian, Church of Ireland, Roman Catholic, Methodist.

Geography Northern Ireland is composed of 26 districts, derived from the boroughs of Belfast and Londonderry and the counties of Antrim, Armagh, Down, Fermanagh, Londonderry, and Tyrone. Together they are commonly called Ulster, though the territory does not include the entire ancient province of Ulster. It is slightly larger than Connecticut.

Government Northern Ireland is an integral part of the United Kingdom (it has 12 representatives in the British House of Commons), but under the terms of the Government of Ireland Act in 1920, it had a semiautonomous government. In 1972, however, after three years of sectarian violence between Protestants and Catholics that resulted in more than 400 dead and thousands injured, Britain suspended the Ulster Parliament. The Ulster counties were governed directly from London after an attempt to return certain powers to an elected assembly in Belfast.

As a result of the Good Friday Agreement of 1998, a new coalition government was formed on Dec. 2, 1999, with the British government formally transferring governing power to the Northern Irish Parliament. David Trimble, Protestant leader of the Ulster Unionist Party (UUP) and winner of the 1998 Nobel Peace Prize, became first minister. The government has been suspended four times since then; it has remained suspended since Oct. 14, 2002.

History Ulster was part of Catholic Ireland until the reign of Elizabeth I (1558–1603) when, after suppressing three Irish rebellions, the Crown confiscated lands in Ireland and settled the Scots Presbyterians in Ulster. Another rebellion in 1641–1651, brutally crushed by Oliver Cromwell, resulted in the settlement of Anglican Englishmen in Ulster. Subsequent political policy favoring Protestants and disadvantaging Catholics encouraged further Protestant settlement in Northern Ireland.

Northern Ireland did not separate from the South until William Gladstone presented, in 1886, his proposal for home rule in Ireland. The Protestants in the North feared domination by the Catholic majority. Industry, moreover, was concentrated in the North and dependent on the British market. When World War I began, civil war threatened between the regions. Northern Ireland, however, did not become a political entity until the six counties accepted the Home Rule Bill of 1920. This set up a semiautonomous Parliament in Belfast and a Crown-appointed governor advised by a cabinet of the prime minister and 8 ministers, as well as a 12-member representation in the House of Commons in London.

When the Republic of Ireland gained sovereignty in 1922, relations improved between North and South, although the Irish Republican Army (IRA), outlawed in recent years, continued the struggle to end the partition of Ireland. In 1966–1969, rioting and street fighting between Protestants and Catholics occurred in Londonderry, fomented by extremist nationalist Protestants, who feared the Catholics might attain a local majority, and by Catholics demonstrating for civil rights. These confrontations became known as "the Troubles."

The religious communities, Catholic and Protestant, became hostile armed camps. British troops were brought in to separate them but themselves became a target of Catholics, particularly by the IRA, which by this time had turned into a full-fledged terrorist movement. The goal of the IRA was to eject the British and unify Northern Ireland with the Irish Republic to the south. The Protestants remained tenaciously loyal to the United Kingdom, and various Protestant terrorist organizations pursued the Unionist cause through violence. Various attempts at representational government and power-sharing foundered during the 1970s, and both sides were further polarized. Direct rule from London and the presence of British troops failed to stop the violence.

In Oct. 1977, the 1976 Nobel Peace Prize was awarded to Mairead Corrigan and Betty Williams, founders of the Community of Peace People, a nonsectarian organization dedicated to creating peace in Northern Ireland. Intermittent violence continued, however, and on Aug. 27, 1979, an IRA bomb killed Lord Mountbatten as he was sailing off southern Ireland. This incident heightened tensions. Catholic protests over the death of IRA hunger striker Bobby Sands in 1981 fueled more violence. Riots, sniper fire, and terrorist attacks killed more than 3,200 people between 1969 and 1998. Among the attempts at reconciliation undertaken during the 1980s was the Anglo-Irish Agreement (1985), which, to the dismay of Unionists, marked the first time the Republic of Ireland had been given an official consultative role in the affairs of the province.

In 1997, Northern Ireland made a significant step in the direction of stemming sectarian strife. The first formal peace talks began on Oct. 6 with representatives of eight major Northern Irish political parties participating, a feat that in itself required three years of negotiations. Two smaller Protestant parties, including extremist Ian Paisley's Democratic Unionists, boycotted the talks. For the first time, Sinn Fein, the political wing of the IRA, won two seats in the British Parliament, which went to Sinn Fein president Gerry Adams and his second-in-command, Martin McGuinness. Although the election strengthened the IRA's political legitimacy, it was the IRA's resumption of the 17-month cease-fire, which had collapsed in Feb. 1996, that gained them a place at the negotiating table.

A landmark settlement, the Good Friday Agreement of April 10, 1998, came after 19 months of intensive negotiations. The accord called for Protestants to share political power with the minority Catholics, and it gave the Republic of Ireland a voice in Northern Irish affairs. In turn, Catholics were to suspend the goal of a united Ireland—a territorial claim that was the raison d'être of the IRA and was written into the Irish Republic's constitution—unless the largely Protestant North voted in favor of such an arrangement, an unlikely occurrence.

The resounding commitment to the settlement was demonstrated in a dual referendum on May 22, 1998: the North approved the accord by a vote of 71% to 29%, and in the Irish Republic 94% favored it. In October, the Nobel Peace Prize was awarded to John Hume and David Trimble, leaders of the largest Catholic and Protestant political parties, an incentive for all sides to ensure that this time the peace would last.

In Dec. 1998 the rival Northern Ireland politicians agreed on the organization and contents of the new coalition government, but in June 1999 the peace process again hit an impasse when the IRA refused to disarm prior to the Assembly of Northern Ireland's new provincial cabinet. Sinn Fein insisted that the IRA would only begin giving up its illegal weapons after the formation of the new government; Unionists demanded disarmament first. As a result, the Ulster Unionists boycotted the Assembly session that would have nominated the cabinet to run the new coalition government. The nascent Northern Irish government was stillborn in July 1999.

Subsequent talks on the agreement, which would have ended three decades of direct rule from London, seemed to go nowhere. Finally, at the end of November, David Trimble, leader of the Ulster Unionists, abandoned the seemingly sacrosanct "no guns, no government" position and took a difficult leap of faith in agreeing to form a government prior to Sinn Fein's disarmament. If the IRA did not begin the destruction of

their weapons by Jan. 31, 2000, however, the Ulster Unionists threatened they would withdraw from the Northern Irish Parliament, shutting down the new government. With this compromise in place, this government was quickly formed, and on Dec. 2, 1999, the British government formally transferred governing power to the Northern Irish Parliament. David Trimble became first minister. Two leaders of Sinn Fein, Gerry Adams and Martin McGuinness, received seats in the 4-party 12-member Parliament. But by the deadline, Sinn Fein had made little progress toward disarmament and claimed it had not made any such commitment. As a result, the British government suspended Parliament on Feb. 12, 2000, and once again imposed direct rule. In July 2001, after issuing one last ultimatum to the IRA to begin destroying its weapons stores, Ulster Unionist leader Trimble resigned his post as first minister.

Following Trimble's departure, the IRA offered another vague and open-ended disarmament plan, only to withdraw it. But on Oct. 23, days before Britain was to suspend the Assembly, Sinn Fein leader Gerry Adams dramatically announced that the IRA had indeed begun disarming. As a result, Trimble was reelected as first minister.

On April 8, 2002, international weapons inspectors announced that the IRA had put more stockpiled munitions "beyond use," the euphemistic phrase applied to disarmament in the negotiations. British and Irish leaders hoped that Protestant paramilitary groups would also begin to surrender their weapons. The Council on Foreign Relations has estimated that Protestant paramilitary groups have been responsible for 30% of the civilian deaths in the Northern Irish conflict. The two main Protestant vigilante groups are the Ulster Volunteer Force (UVF) and the Ulster Defence Association (UDA). Strongest during the 1970s, their ranks have since diminished. While Protestant paramilitaries have observed a cease-fire since the IRA declared one, none of these groups have made any moves toward surrendering their weapons as stipulated by the Good Friday Accord.

On Oct. 14, the British government again assumed direct rule of Northern Ireland, after the Unionists threatened to quit the Assembly in protest of suspected spying activity by the IRA. In March and April 2003, negotiations were again under way to reinstate the Northern Ireland Assembly. But Sinn Fein's vague language, weakly pledging that its "strategies and disciplines will not be inconsistent with the Good Friday Agreement," caused Tony Blair to challenge Sinn Fein once and for all to make a clear, unambiguous pledge to renounce using the paramilitary for political means. According to the *New York Times* (April 24, 2003), "virtually every newspaper in Britain and Ireland has editorialized in favor of full disarmament, and the Irish government, traditionally sympathetic to Sinn Fein, is almost as adamant about the matter as London is."

In Nov. 2003 legislative elections, the Ulster Unionists and other moderates lost out to Northern Ireland's extremist parties: Ian Paisley's Democratic Unionists and Sinn Fein. Power sharing between these antithetical parties was out of the question.

A $50 million bank robbery in Dec. 2004 was linked to the IRA, and Sinn Fein's legitimacy as a political organization suffered a severe setback. The brutal murder in Jan. 2005 of Belfast Catholic Robert McCartney by the IRA, and the campaign by his five sisters to hold the IRA accountable, further tarnished the IRA's standing, even in Catholic communities that had once been IRA strongholds. The IRA's subsequent offer to kill the men responsible for McCartney's murder only generated more outrage.

On July 28, 2005, the IRA announced that it was entering a new era in which it would unequivocally relinquish violence. The statement said that IRA members have been "instructed to assist the development of purely political and democratic programs through exclusively political means" and that "all IRA units have been ordered to dump arms" and "to complete the process to verifiably put its arms beyond use."

Scotland

Status: Part of United Kingdom
First Minister: Jack McConnell (2001)
Area: 30,414 sq mi (78,772 sq km)
Population (1996 est.): 5,128,000; density per sq mi: 168.6
Capital (2003 est.): Edinburgh, 663,700 (metro. area), 460,000 (city proper). **Largest city:** Glasgow, 1,361,000 (metro. area), 1,099,400 (city proper). **Monetary unit:** British pound sterling (£). **Languages:** English, Scots Gaelic. **Religions:** Church of Scotland (established church—Presbyterian), Roman Catholic, Scottish Episcopal Church, Baptist, Methodist

Geography Scotland occupies the northern third of the island of Great Britain. It is bounded by England in the south and on the other three sides by water: by the Atlantic Ocean on the west and north and by the North Sea on the east. Scotland is divided into three physical regions—the Highlands; the Central Lowlands, containing two-thirds of the population; and the Southern Uplands. The western Highland coast is intersected throughout by long, narrow sea lochs, or fjords. Scotland also includes the Outer and Inner Hebrides and other islands off the west coast and the Orkney and Shetland Islands off the north coast.

Government England and Scotland have shared a monarch since 1603 and a Parliament since 1707, but in May 1999, Scotland elected its own Parliament for the first time in three centuries. The new Scottish legislature was in part the result of British prime minister Tony Blair's campaign promise to permit devolution, the transfer of local powers from London to Edinburgh. In a Sept. 1997 referendum, 74% of Scotland voted in favor of their own Parliament, which controls most domestic affairs, including health, education, and transportation, and has powers to legislate and raise taxes. Queen Elizabeth opened the new Parliament on July 2, 1999.

History The first inhabitants of Scotland were the Picts, a Celtic tribe. Between A.D. 82 and A.D. 208, the Romans invaded Scotland, naming it Caledonia. Roman influence over the land, however, was minimal.

The Scots, a Celtic tribe from Ireland, migrated to the west coast of Scotland in about 500. Kenneth McAlpin, king of the Scots, ascended the throne of the Pictish kingdom in about 843, thereby uniting the various Scots and Pictish tribes under one kingdom called Dal Riada. By the 11th century, the monarchy had extended its borders to include much of what is Scotland today.

English influence in the region expanded when Malcolm III, king of Scotland from 1057–1093, married an English princess. England's appetite for Scottish land began to grow over the 12th and 13th centuries, and in 1296 King Edward I of England successfully invaded Scotland. The following year Robert the Bruce led a revolt for independence, was crowned king of Scotland (Robert I) in 1306, and after years of war defeated the English in 1314 at the Battle of Bannockburn. In 1328 the English finally recognized Scottish independence.

In the 16th century John Knox introduced the Scottish reformation, and the Presbyterian Church replaced Catholicism as the official religion. In 1567, Mary, queen of Scots, a Catholic, was forced to abdicate the Scottish throne and was later executed by Elizabeth I of England. Mary's son, James VI, was raised as a Protestant, and in 1603 he succeeded Elizabeth on the English throne as King James I of England. James thus became ruler of both Scotland and England, though the countries remained separate. In 1707, after a century of turmoil, Scotland and England passed the Act of Union, which united Scotland, England, and Wales under one rule as the Kingdom of Great Britain. The House of Hanover replaced the Stuart lineage on the throne in 1714, which caused a rebellion among Scots who still supported the Stuarts. The Jacobites, as the rebels were called, led two uprisings, in 1715 and again in 1745.

With the advent of the Industrial Revolution, Scotland, whose chief product had been textiles, began developing the industries of shipbuilding, coal mining, iron, and steel. In the late 20th century Scotland concentrated on electronics and high-tech industries. The North Sea has also become an important source of oil and gas.

In May 1999, Scotland elected its first separate Parliament in three centuries. Labour won the largest number of seats, defeating the Scottish National Party (SNP), which supports Scotland's independence from Britain.

Wales

Status: Part of United Kingdom
First Secretary: Rhodri Morgan (2000)
Area: 8,019 sq mi (20,768 sq km)
Population (1993 est.): 2,906,500
Capital and largest city (2003 est.): Cardiff, 676,400 (metro. area), 280,800 (city proper). **Monetary unit:** British pound sterling (£). **Languages:** English, Welsh. **Religions:** Calvinistic Methodist, Church of Wales (disestablished—Anglican), Roman Catholic

Geography Wales lies west of England and is separated from England by the Cambrian Mountains. It is bordered on the northwest, west, and south by the Irish Sea and on the northeast and east by England. Wales is generally hilly; the Snowdon range in the northern part culminates in Mount Snowdon (3,560 ft, 1,085 m), Wales's highest peak.

Government Until 1999, Wales was ruled solely by the UK government and a secretary of state. In the referendum of Sept. 18, 1997, Welsh citizens voted to establish a National Assembly. Wales will remain part of the UK, and the secretary of state for Wales and members of Parliament from Welsh constituencies will continue to have seats in Parliament. Unlike Scotland, which in 1999 voted to have its own Parliament, the National Assembly will not be able to legislate and raise taxes. Wales will, however, control most of its local affairs. The Welsh National Assembly officially opened on July 1, 1999.

History The prehistoric peoples of Wales left behind megaliths and other impressive monuments. They were followed by settlements of Celts in the region. The Romans occupied the region from the 1st to the 5th century A.D. Thereafter Angles, Saxons, and Jutes invaded the British island, but they left Wales virtually untouched. Beginning in the 8th century, the various Welsh tribes fought with their Anglo-Saxon neighbors to the east, but the Welsh were able to thwart attempted invasions. After William the Conqueror subdued England in 1066, however, his Norman armies marched into Wales in 1093 and occupied portions of it. By 1282, the English conquest of Wales was complete, and in 1284, the Statute of Rhuddlan formalized

England's sovereignty over Wales. In 1301, King Edward I gave his son, who later became Edward II, the title Prince of Wales, a gesture meant to indicate the unity and relationship between the two lands. With the exception of Edward II, all subsequent British monarchs have given this title to their eldest son.

In 1400, the Welsh prince Owen Glendower led a revolt against the English, expelling them from much of Wales in just four years. By 1410, however, his rebellion was crushed. In 1485, Henry VII became king of England. A Welshman and the first in the Tudor line, Henry's reign, and those of subsequent Tudors, made English rule more palatable to the Welsh. His son, King Henry VIII, joined England and Wales under the Act of Union in 1536.

The Industrial Revolution transformed Wales and threatened the traditional livelihood of farmers and shepherds. In the 20th century, the economy of Wales was based primarily on coal production. After World War I, coal prices dropped; this, coupled with the Great Depression, fueled high unemployment rates and economic uncertainty.

In recent years, a resurgence of the Welsh language and culture has demonstrated a stronger national identity among the Welsh, and politically the country moved toward greater self-government (devolution). In 1999, with the strong support of Britain's prime minister, Tony Blair, Wales opened the Welsh National Assembly, the first real self-government Wales has had in more than 600 years.

Overseas Territories and Crown Dependencies of the United Kingdom

Anguilla
Status: Overseas territory
Governor: Alan Huckle (2004)
Chief Minister: Osbourne Fleming (2000)
Area: 39.38 sq mi (102 sq km)
Population (2005 est.): 13,254 (growth rate: 1.8%); birth rate: 14.3/1000; infant mortality rate: 21.0/1000; life expectancy: 77.1; density per sq mi: 337
Capital (2003 est.): The Valley, 830. **Monetary unit:** East Caribbean dollar. **Ethnicity/race:** black African. **Literacy:** 95% (1984 est.)
Economic summary: GDP/PPP (2002 est.): $112 million; per capita $7,500. **Real growth rate:** 2.8%. **Inflation:** 2.3%. **Unemployment:** 8% (2002). **Arable land:** 0%. **Agriculture:** small quantities of tobacco, vegetables; cattle raising. **Labor force:** 6,049 (2001); commerce 36%, services 29%, construction 18%, transportation and utilities 10%, manufacturing 3%, agriculture/fishing/forestry/mining 4% (2000 est.). **Industries:** tourism, boatbuilding, offshore financial services. **Natural resources:** salt, fish, lobster. **Exports:** $2.6 million (1999): lobster, fish, livestock, salt, concrete blocks, rum. **Imports:** $80.9 million (1999); fuels, foodstuffs, manufactures, chemicals, trucks, textiles. **Major trading partners:** UK, U.S., Puerto Rico, St.-Martin (2000).

Anguilla was first colonized in 1650 by English settlers from St. Christopher (St. Kitts) and has since remained a British territory. It was originally part of the West Indies Associated States as a component of the St. Kitts–Nevis–Anguilla Federation. In 1967, Anguilla declared its independence from the federation but Britain did not recognize this action. In Feb. 1969, Anguilla voted to cut all ties with Britain and become an independent republic. In March, Britain landed troops on the island and, on March 30, a truce was signed. In July 1971, Anguilla became a dependency of Britain and two months later Britain ordered the withdrawal of all its troops. A new constitution for Anguilla, effective in Feb. 1976, provided for separate administration and a government of elected representatives. The Associated State of St. Kitts–Nevis-Anguilla ended in 1980, and in 1982 a new Anguillan constitution took effect.

Bermuda
Status: Overseas territory
Governor: Sir John Vereker (2002)
Prime Minister: Alex Scott (2003)
Area: 21 sq mi (53.3 sq km)
Population (2005 est.): 65,365 (growth rate: 0.6%); birth rate: 11.6/1000; infant mortality rate: 8.5/1000; life expectancy: 77.8; density per sq mi: 3,176
Capital (2003 est.): Hamilton, 970. **Monetary unit:** Bermuda dollar. **Ethnicity/race:** black African 58%, white and other 42%. **Literacy rate:** 98% (1970 est.)
Economic summary: GDP/PPP (2003 est.): $2.33 billion; per capita $36,000. **Real growth rate:** 2%. **Inflation:** 3.3% (mid-2003 est.). **Unemployment:** 5% (2002 est.). **Arable land:** 20%. **Agriculture:** bananas, vegetables, citrus, flowers; dairy products. **Labor force:** 37,472 (2000); clerical 22%, services 20%, laborers 17%, professional and technical 17%, administrative and managerial 13%, sales 8%, agriculture and fishing 3%. **Industries:** tourism, international business, light manufacturing. **Natural resources:** limestone, pleasant climate fostering tourism. **Exports:** $879 million (2002): reexports of pharmaceuticals. **Imports:** $5.523 billion (2002): machinery and transport equipment, construction materials, chemicals, food and live animals. **Major trading partners:** France, Norway, UK, Kazakhstan, U.S. (2003).

Bermuda is an archipelago of about 360 small islands, 580 mi (934 km) east of North Carolina. The largest is (Great) Bermuda, or Main Island. Explored by Juan de Bermúdez, a Spaniard, the islands were settled in 1612 by an offshoot of the Virginia Company. Bermuda became a Crown colony in 1684.

In 1968, Bermuda was granted a new constitution, its first prime minister, and autonomy, except for foreign relations, defense, and internal security. The predominantly white United Bermuda Party has retained power in four elections against the opposition—the black-led Progressive Labour Party—although Bermuda's population is 58% black. U.S. air and navy bases, which had been leased in 1941 for 99-year terms, closed in 1995, along with Canadian, British army, and Royal Navy bases. In a referendum held in Aug. 1995, nearly three-fourths of those voting opposed independence.

British Indian Ocean Territory
Status: Overseas territory
Commissioner: John White (1998)
Administrative headquarters: Victoria, Seychelles
Area: 85 sq mi (220 sq km)

This territory, consisting of the Chagos Archipelago and other small island groups, was formed in 1965 by agreement with Mauritius and the Seychelles. One of its islands, Diego Garcia (17 sq mi), is a joint U.S.-UK refueling and support station that was used during the Persian Gulf War (1991), the war against Afghanistan (1991), and the second Iraq war (2003). The island's small native population, known as the Ilois, were forced to relocate (1967–1973) to Mauritius and the Seychelles, where the majority of these former agricultural workers live in poverty in urban slums. In 2000, a British court ruled that the immigration order was invalid but upheld the island's military status. The Ilois sued the British government for compensation and the right to repatriation, but in Oct. 2003 a British judge ruled that although the Ilois had been treated "shamefully" by the government, their claims were unfounded. In 2004 the British government issued an "Order of Council" prohibiting islanders from ever returning to Diego Garcia.

British Virgin Islands
VIRGIN ISLANDS
Status: Overseas territory
Governor: Tom Macan (2002)
Chief Minister: Orlando Smith (2003)
Area: 59 sq mi (153 sq km)
Population (2005 est.): 22,643 (growth rate: 2.0%); birth rate: 14.9/1000; infant mortality rate: 17.3/1000; life expectancy: 76.5; density per sq mi: 383
Capital (2003 est.): Road Town (on Tortola): 9,100.
Monetary unit: U.S. dollar. **Literacy rate:** 97.8% (1991 est.)
Economic summary: GDP/PPP (2004 est.): $2.498 billion; per capita $38,500. **Real growth rate:** 1%. **Inflation:** 2.5% (2003). **Unemployment:** 3% (1995). **Arable land:** 20%. **Agriculture:** fruits, vegetables; livestock, poultry; fish. **Labor force:** 12,770. **Industries:** tourism, light industry, construction, rum, concrete block, offshore financial center. **Natural resources:** negl. **Exports:** $25.3 million (2002): rum, fresh fish, fruits, animals; gravel, sand. **Imports:** $187 million (2002 est.): building materials, automobiles, foodstuffs, machinery. **Major trading partners:** Virgin Islands (U.S.), Puerto Rico, U.S.

Some 36 islands (more than 20 are uninhabited) in the Caribbean Sea northeast of Puerto Rico and west of the Leeward Islands, the British Virgin Islands are economically interdependent with the U.S. Virgin Islands to the south. The principal islands are Tortola, Virgin Gorda, Anegada, and Jost Van Dyke. When Christopher Columbus explored the islands in 1493, he found the Carib people living there. By 1596 most of the Caribs had fled or been killed.

The British Virgin Islands were annexed in 1672. The English planters' slave-based sugar plantations declined after slavery was abolished in the first half of the 19th century. The islands received a separate administration in 1956 as a Crown colony. Tourism is the islands' mainstay.

Cayman Islands
Status: Overseas territory
Governor: Stuart Jack (2005)
Area: 101 sq mi (262 sq km)
Population (2005 est.): 44,270 (growth rate: 2.6%); birth rate: 12.9/1000; infant mortality rate: 8.2/1000; life expectancy: 80.0; density per sq mi: 438
Capital (2003 est.): George Town (on Grand Cayman), 29,400. **Monetary unit:** Cayman Islands dollar. **Literacy rate:** 98% (1970 est.)
Economic summary: GDP/PPP (2004 est.): $1.391 billion; per capita $32,300. **Real growth rate:** 1.7% (2002 est.). **Inflation:** 2.8% (2002). **Unemployment:** 4.1% (1997). **Arable land:** 4%. **Agriculture:** vegetables, fruit; livestock, turtle farming. **Labor force:** 19,820 (1995); agriculture 1.4%, industry 12.6%, services 86% (1995). **Industries:** tourism, banking, insurance and finance, construction, construction materials, furniture. **Natural resources:** fish, climate and beaches that foster tourism. **Exports:** $1.2 million (1999): turtle products, manufactured consumer goods. **Imports:** $457.4 million (1999): foodstuffs, manufactured goods. **Major trading partners:** U.S., Trinidad and Tobago, UK, Netherlands Antilles, Japan.

The Caymans consist of three islands—Grand Cayman (76 sq mi; 197 sq km), Cayman Brac (22 sq mi; 57 sq km), and Little Cayman (20 sq mi; 52 sq km)—situated about 180 mi (290 km) northwest of Jamaica. They were dependencies of Jamaica until 1959, when they became a unit territory within the Federation of the West Indies. In 1962, upon the dissolution of the federation, the Cayman Islands became a British dependency, and a new constitution approved in 1972 provided for a greater degree of autonomy. Tourism and finance are the Cayman Islands' major industries. For a time, the Cayman Islands were blacklisted by the Paris-based Financial Action Task Force (FATF) for its allegedly loose policy concerning money laundering. It was removed from the list in 2001.

Channel Islands: Jersey and Guernsey
Status: Crown dependencies
Lieutenant Governor of Jersey: Sir Michael Wilkes (1995)
Lieutenant Governor of Guernsey: Vice Adm. Sir John Coward (1994)
Area: 45 sq mi (116 sq km) (Jersey), 30 sq mi (78 sq km) (Guernsey)
Populations (2005 est.): Jersey, 90,812; Guernsey, 65,228
Capital of Jersey (2003 est.): St. Helier, 28,600
Capital of Guernsey (2003 est.): St. Peter Port, 16,600.
Monetary units: Guernsey pound; Jersey pound

This group of islands, lying in the English Channel off the northwest coast of France, belonged to the Duchy of Normandy until it passed to the English Crown with the Norman conquest of 1066. It was the only British possession occupied by Germany during World War II. English and French are commonly spoken (though use of the latter is declining), and a Norman-French patois survives.

For administrative purposes, the islands are divided into the Bailiwick of Jersey (45 sq mi; 116 sq km), including the Ecrehous rocks and Les Minquiers, and the Bailiwick of Guernsey (30 sq mi; 78 sq km), including Alderney (3 sq mi; 7.8 sq km), Sark (2 sq mi; 5.2 sq km), Herm, Jethou, Brechou, and other smaller islands. The Channel Islands enjoy tax sovereignty, and their exports are protected by British tariff barriers. Financial services, tourism, market gardening, and dairy farming are important industries.

Falkland Islands
Status: Overseas territory
Governor: Howard Pearce (2002)
Chief Executive: A. M. Gurr
Area: 4,700 sq mi (12,173 sq km)
Population (July 2003 est.): 2,967
Capital (2003 est.): Stanley (on East Falkland), 2,100.
Monetary unit: Falkland Island pound
Economic summary: GDP/PPP (2002 est.): $75 million; per capita $25,000. **Real growth rate:** n.a. **Inflation:** 3.6% (1998). **Unemployment:** full employment; labor shortage (2001). **Arable land:** 0%. **Agriculture:** fodder and vegetable crops; sheep, dairy products. **Labor force:** 1,100 (est.); agriculture 95% (mostly sheepherding and fishing). **Industries:** fish and wool processing; tourism. **Natural resources:** fish, squid, wildlife, calcified seaweed, sphagnum moss. **Exports:** $82 million (2002): wool, hides, meat. **Imports:** $53 million (2002): fuel, food and drink, building materials, clothing. **Major trading partners:** Spain, UK, U.S., Italy (2003).

This sparsely inhabited dependency consists of a group of islands in the South Atlantic, about 250 mi (402 km) east of the South American mainland. The largest islands are East Falkland and West Falkland. The English captain John Strong made the first recorded landing in the Falklands in 1690. The islands passed among the French, Spanish, and British until 1820, when the Argentine government proclaimed its sovereignty. In 1833 a British force expelled the few remaining Argentine officials from the island without firing a shot, and in 1841 a British civilian lieutenant-governor was appointed for the Falklands. Colonial status was granted to the Falklands in 1892. Argentina, calling the islands *Las Islas Malvinas*, regularly protested Britain's occupation of the islands. On April 2, 1982, Argentina's military government invaded the Falklands. The Falkland Islands war ended ten weeks later with the surrender of the Argentine forces at Stanley to British troops, who had forcibly reoccupied the islands. Argentina still claims the islands. But an agreement between Argentina and the United Kingdom in 1995 sought to defuse licensing and sovereignty conflicts that would dampen foreign interest in exploiting the Falkland Islands' potential oil reserves.

Gibraltar

Status: Overseas territory
Governor: Francis Richards (2003)
Chief Minister: Peter Caruana (1996)
Area: 2.51 sq mi (6.5 sq km)
Population (2005 est.): 27,884 (growth rate: 0.2%); birth rate: 10.9/1000; infant mortality rate: 5.1/1000; life expectancy: 79.7; density per sq mi: 11,111. **Monetary unit:** Gibraltar pound. **Literacy rate:** above 80% (2003 est.)
Economic summary: GDP/PPP (2000 est.): $769 million; per capita $27,900. **Real growth rate:** n.a. **Inflation:** 1.5% (1998). **Unemployment:** 2% (2001 est.). **Arable land:** 0%. **Agriculture:** none. **Labor force:** 14,800 (including non-Gibraltar laborers); services 60%, industry 40%, agriculture negl. **Industries:** tourism, banking and finance, ship repairing, tobacco. **Natural resources:** negl. **Exports:** $136 million (2002): (principally reexports) petroleum 51%, manufactured goods 41%, other 8%. **Imports:** $1.743 billion (c.i.f., 2002): fuels, manufactured goods, and foodstuffs. **Major trading partners:** Germany, France, UK, Turkmenistan, Switzerland, Spain, Russia, Italy, Netherlands, Romania (2003).

Gibraltar, at the south end of the Iberian Peninsula, is a rocky promontory commanding the western entrance to the Mediterranean. Aside from its strategic importance, it is also a free port, naval base, and coaling station. It was captured by the Moorish leader Tarik, crossing from Africa into Spain in 711, and its name is derived from the Arabic, *Jabal-al-Tarik* (Mount of Tarik). In the 15th century, it passed to the Moorish ruler of Granada and later became Spanish. It was captured by an Anglo-Dutch force in 1704 during the War of the Spanish Succession and passed to Great Britain by the Treaty of Utrecht in 1713. Since then Spain has continually laid claim to it. Most of the inhabitants of Gibraltar are of Spanish, Italian, and Maltese descent, and in 1981 Gibraltarians were granted full British citizenship. Spanish efforts to recover Gibraltar culminated in a referendum in 1967, in which the residents voted overwhelmingly to retain their link with Britain. In response, Spain sealed Gibraltar's land border between 1969 and 1985. In 2002, Britain and Spain discussed sharing the sovereignty of Gibraltar. In reaction, the government of Gibraltar held a referendum in Nov. 2002 in which the population voted almost unanimously against shared sovereignty.

Isle of Man

Status: Crown dependency
Lieutenant Governor: Ian David Macfadyen (2000)
Chief Minister: Donald James Gelling (1996)
Area: 221 sq mi (572 sq km)
Population (2005 est.): 75,049 (growth rate: 0.5%); birth rate: 11.2/1000; infant mortality rate: 5.9/1000; life expectancy: 78.3; density per sq mi: 340
Capital (2003 est.): Douglas, 25,400. **Monetary unit:** Isle of Man pound

The Isle of Man is situated in the Irish Sea, equidistant from Scotland, Ireland, and England. Among its earliest inhabitants were Celts, and their language, Manx, which is closely related to Irish and Scottish Gaelic, remained the everyday speech of the people until the first half of the 19th century. Manx now has no native speakers. Norse (Viking) invasions began about 800, and the island was a dependency of Norway until 1266. During this period the Isle of Man came under a Scandinavian system of government that has remained practically unchanged ever since. The island entered the control of England in 1341. After allowing a succession of feudal lords to rule the island, the British Parliament purchased sovereignty over the island in 1765. The Isle of Man continues to be administered according to its own laws by a government composed of the lieutenant governor, a legislative council, and a House of Keys, one of the most ancient legislative assemblies in the world.

Montserrat

Status: Overseas territory
Governor: Deborah Barnes Jones (2004)
Chief Minister: John Osborne (2001)
Area: 39 sq mi (102 sq km)
Population (2005 est.): 9,341 (growth rate: 1.0%); birth rate: 17.6/1000; infant mortality rate: 7.3/1000; life expectancy: 78.7; density per sq mi: 237
Capital (2003 est.): Plymouth. The city was abandoned in 1997 due to volcanic activity. Interim government buildings have been built at Brades Estate, in the Carr's Bay/Little Bay vicinity at the northwest end of Montserrat. **Monetary unit:** East Caribbean dollar
Economic summary: GDP/PPP (2002 est.): $29 million; per capita $3,400. **Real growth rate:** –1%. **Inflation:** 2.6% (2002 est.). **Unemployment:** 6% (1998 est.). **Arable land:** 20%. **Agriculture:** cabbages, carrots, cucumbers, tomatoes, onions, peppers; livestock products. **Labor force:** 4,521; note: recently lowered by flight of people from volcanic activity (2000 est); agriculture n.a., industry n.a., services n.a. **Industries:** tourism, rum, textiles, electronic appliances. **Natural resources:** negl. **Exports:** $700,000 (2001): electronic components, plastic bags, apparel, hot peppers, live plants, cattle. **Imports:** $17 million (2001): machinery and transportation equipment, foodstuffs, manufactured goods, fuels, lubricants, and related materials. **Major trading partners:** U.S., Antigua and Barbuda, UK, Trinidad and Tobago, Japan, Canada.

The island of Montserrat is in the Lesser Antilles of the West Indies. Until 1956, it was a division of the Leeward Islands. In 1958 Montserrat joined the Federation of the West Indies, remaining a member until that organization's dissolution in 1962. Unlike most other British West Indies possessions, Montserrat, with its weak economy, has not vigorously sought independence. The Soufrière Hills volcano began erupting in 1995, and the situation continued to worsen through 1998, with the capital, Plymouth, destroyed and the southern and central parts of the British colony having been evacuated. Thousands had moved to nearby Antigua, Britain, or other parts of the Caribbean. In 2004, the U.S. Dept. of Homeland Security announced that it was revoking the "temporary protected status" of its

292 Montserrat refugees, a number of whom have lived in the U.S. for years and rebuilt their lives there. A *Washington Post* editorial called the decision "absurd and cruel."

Pitcairn Island

Status: Overseas territory
Governor: Richard Fell (nonresident) (2001)
Island Mayor: Jay Warren (2004)
Area: 18.15 sq mi (47 sq km)
Population (2004): 47; density per sq mi: 3
Capital: Adamstown

Pitcairn Island, in the South Pacific about midway between Australia and South America, consists of the island of Pitcairn and the three uninhabited islands of Henderson, Duicie, and Oeno. Pitcairn was settled in 1790 by British mutineers from the ship *Bounty*, commanded by Capt. William Bligh. One of the most remote islands in the world, it was annexed as a British colony in 1838. Overpopulation forced removal of the settlement to Norfolk Island in 1856, but about 40 persons soon returned.

The descendants of First Mate Fletcher Christian, the eight other mutineers, and the dozen or so Tahitians who accompanied them still inhabit the island. In addition to English, the residents of Pitcairn speak a dialect that is a mixture of Tahitian and 18th-century English.

In 2004, a sex-abuse scandal brought the obscure island worldwide media attention. Four men were convicted of multiple sex offenses against women and young girls and received jail sentences ranging from two to six years; two others were sentenced to community service. Jay Warren, the island's magistrate, was found innocent.

St. Helena

Status: Overseas territory
Governor: David Hollamby (1999)
Area: 158 sq mi (410 sq km)
Population (2005 est.): 7,460 (growth rate: 0.6%); birth rate: 12.3/1000; infant mortality rate: 19.0/1000; life expectancy: 77.8; density per sq mi: 47
Capital (2003 est.): Jamestown, 1,500. **Monetary unit:** Pound sterling. **Literacy rate:** 97% (1987 est.)

St. Helena is a remote volcanic island in the South Atlantic about 1,100 mi (1,770 km) from the west coast of Africa. It is famous as Napoléon's place of exile (1815–1821). The island was discovered in 1502 by João da Nova, a Spanish navigator in the service of Portugal. It was taken for England in 1659 by the East India Company and was brought under the direct government of the Crown in 1834. After the opening of the Suez Canal in 1870, St. Helena's importance as a port of call diminished. About two-thirds of the colony's budget is provided by the United Kingdom in the form of a subsidy.

St. Helena has two dependencies: Ascension (34 sq mi; 88 sq km), an island about 700 mi (1,127 km) northwest of St. Helena; and Tristan da Cunha (40 sq mi; 104 sq km), a group of six islands about 1,500 mi (2,414 km) south-southwest of St. Helena.

South Georgia and the South Sandwich Islands

Status: Overseas territory
Commissioner: Donald A. Lamont (1999)
Area: 1,506 sq mi (3,903 sq km)
Population: no indigenous inhabitants

The islands are located in the South Atlantic Ocean, east of the tip of South America, approximately 1,000 km east of the Falkland Islands, from which they are administered. In addition to South Georgia Island and the nine South Sandwich Islands, the island group includes Shag Rocks, Black Rock, Clerke Rocks, and Bird Island. A small military garrison on South Georgia withdrew in March 2001 and was replaced by a permanent group of scientists from the British Antarctic Survey.

Turks and Caicos Islands

Status: Overseas territory
Governor: Richard Tauwhare (2005)
Chief Minister: Michael Misick (2003)
Area: 166 sq mi (430 sq km)
Population (2005 est.): 20,556 (growth rate: 2.9%); birth rate: 22.2/1000; infant mortality rate: 15.7/1000; life expectancy: 74.5; density per sq mi: 124
Capital (2003 est.): Cockburn Town, 5,000. **Monetary unit:** U.S. dollar. **Literacy rate:** 98% (1970 est.)
Economic summary: GDP/PPP (2002 est.): $216 million; per capita $11,500. **Real growth rate:** 4.9% (2000 est.). **Inflation:** 4% (1995). **Unemployment:** 10% (1997 est.). **Arable land:** 2%. **Agriculture:** corn, beans, cassava (tapioca), citrus fruits; fish. **Labor force:** 4,848 (1990 est.); about 33% in government and 20% in agriculture and fishing; significant numbers in tourism, financial, and other services (1997 est.). **Industries:** tourism, offshore financial services. **Natural resources:** spiny lobster, conch. **Exports:** $169.2 million (2000): lobster, dried and fresh conch, conch shells. **Imports:** $175.6 million (2000): food and beverages, tobacco, clothing, manufactures, construction materials. **Major trading partners:** U.S., UK.

These two groups of islands are near the Bahamas in the Caribbean. The principal islands in the Turks group are Grand Turk and Salt Cay; the principal islands in the Caicos group are South Caicos, East Caicos, Middle (or Grand) Caicos, North Caicos, Providenciales, and West Caicos. The islands were not settled by Europeans until 1678, when British colonists from Bermuda established a salt-panning industry. The islands were at first placed under the Bahamian government, but in 1874 they became dependencies of the colony of Jamaica. Following Jamaica's independence, they became a British Crown colony. The salt production industry, the islands' economic mainstay, ceased in 1964 and gave way to tourism, offshore financial services, and fishing.

United States

THE UNITED STATES OF AMERICA

President: George W. Bush (2001)
Vice President: Richard B. Cheney (2001)
Area (2003): 3,717,792 sq mi (9,629,091 sq km)
Population (2005 est.): 295,734,134
Population (2000 census): 280,562,489 (change 1990–2000: 13.2%) (growth rate: 0.9%); birth rate: 14.1/1000; infant mortality rate: 6.5/1000; life expectancy: 77.7; density per sq mi: 80
Capital (2003 est.): Washington, DC, 570,898. **Largest cities (2003 est.):** New York, 8,085,742 (city proper); Los Angeles, 3,819,951; Chicago, 2,869,121; Houston, 2,009,960; Philadelphia, 1,479,339; Phoenix, 1,388,416; San Diego, 1,266,753; San Antonio, 1,214,725; Dallas, 1,208,318; Detroit, 911,402.
Monetary unit: dollar. **Languages:** English, sizable Spanish-speaking minority. **Ethnicity/race:** White: 211,460,626 (75.1%); Black: 34,658,190 (12.3%); Asian: 10,242,998 (3.6%); American Indian and Alaska Native: 2,475,956 (0.9%); Native Hawaiian and other Pacific Islander: 398,835 (0.1%); other race: 15,359,073 (5.5%); Hispanic origin:[1] 35,305,818 (12.5%). **Religions:** Protestant 56%; Roman Catholic

28%; Jewish 2%; other 4%; none 10% (1989).
Literacy rate: 97% (1979 est.)
Economic summary: GDP/PPP (2004 est.): $11.75 trillion; per capita $40,100. **Real growth rate:** 4.4%. **Inflation:** 2.5%. **Unemployment:** 5.5%. **Arable land:** 19%. **Agriculture:** wheat, corn, other grains, fruits, vegetables, cotton; beef, pork, poultry, dairy products; forest products; fish. **Labor force:** 147.4 million (includes unemployed): farming, forestry, and fishing 0.7%, manufacturing, extraction, transportation, and crafts 22.7%, managerial, professional, and technical 34.9%, sales and office 25.5%, other services 16.3%; note: figures exclude the unemployed (2004). **Industries:** leading industrial power in the world, highly diversified and technologically advanced; petroleum, steel, motor vehicles, aerospace, telecommunications, chemicals, electronics, food processing, consumer goods, lumber, mining. **Natural resources:** coal, copper, lead, molybdenum, phosphates, uranium, bauxite, gold, iron, mercury, nickel, potash, silver, tungsten, zinc, petroleum, natural gas, timber. **Exports:** $795 billion (f.o.b., 2004 est.): agricultural products 9.2% (soybeans, fruit, corn), industrial supplies 26.8% (organic chemicals); capital goods 49.0% (transistors, aircraft, motor vehicle parts, computers, telecommunications equipment), consumer goods 15.0% (automobiles, medicines) (2003). **Imports:** $1.476 trillion (f.o.b., 2004 est.): agricultural products 4.9%, industrial supplies 32.9% (crude oil 8.2%), capital goods 30.4% (computers, telecommunications equipment, motor vehicle parts, office machines, electric power machinery), consumer goods 31.8% (automobiles, clothing, medicines, furniture, toys) (2003). **Major trading partners:** Canada, Mexico, Japan, UK, China, Germany (2003).

1. Persons of Hispanic origin can be of any race.

Government Federal republic.

The president is elected for a four-year term and may be reelected only once. The bicameral Congress consists of the 100-member Senate, elected to a six-year term with one-third of the seats becoming vacant every two years, and the 435-member House of Representatives, elected every two years. The minimum voting age is 18. (*See also* Profile of the United States, U.S. States, U.S. Cities, U.S. Statistics, and U.S. Government and History.)

U.S. Territories and Outlying Areas

Puerto Rico

COMMONWEALTH OF PUERTO RICO
Status: Commonwealth
Governor: Aníbal Acevedo Vilá (2005)
Capital and largest city (2002 est.): San Juan, 433,412. **Other large cities:** Bayamón, 224,670; Ponce, 186,112; Carolina, 187,468
Land area: 3,515 sq mi (9,104 sq km)
Population (2005 est.): 3,916,632 (growth rate: 0.5%); birth rate: 13.9/1000; infant mortality rate: 8.2/1000; life expectancy: 77.6; density per sq mi: 1,114. **Monetary unit:** U.S. dollar. **Languages:** Spanish and English (both official). **Ethnicity/race:** Almost entirely Hispanic. **Religions:** Roman Catholic 85%, Protestant denominations and other 15%. **Literacy rate:** 94% (2001)
Economic summary: GDP/PPP (2004 est.): $68.95 billion; per capita $17,700. **Real growth rate:** 2.7%. **Inflation:** 6.5% (2003 est.). **Unemployment:** 12% (2002). **Arable land:** 4%. **Agriculture:** sugarcane, coffee, pineapples, plantains, bananas, livestock products, chickens. **Labor force:** 1.3 million (2000); agriculture 3%, industry 20%, services 77% (2000 est.). **Industries:** pharmaceuticals,

electronics, apparel, food products, tourism. **Natural resources:** some copper and nickel; potential for onshore and offshore oil. **Exports:** $46.9 billion (f.o.b., 2001): chemicals, electronics, apparel, canned tuna, rum, beverage concentrates, medical equipment. **Imports:** $29.1 billion (c.i.f., 2001): chemicals, machinery and equipment, clothing, food, fish, petroleum products. **Major trading partners:** U.S., UK, Netherlands, Dominican Republic, Ireland, Japan (2002 est.).

The Commonwealth of Puerto Rico is located in the Caribbean Sea, about 1,000 mi east-southeast of Miami, Fla. A possession of the United States, it consists of the island of Puerto Rico plus the adjacent islets of Vieques, Culebra, and Mona. Puerto Rico has a mountainous, tropical ecosystem with very little flat land and few mineral resources.

Puerto Rico's governor is elected directly for a four-year term. A bicameral legislature consists of a 27-member Senate and a 51-member House of Representatives, all elected for four-year terms. From 1940 to 1968, Puerto Rican politics was dominated by a party advocating voluntary association with the U.S. Since then, the New Progressive Party, a party favoring U.S. statehood, has won five of the last eight gubernatorial elections. Puerto Ricans have twice voted to determine their political status. In 1967, the outcome was Commonwealth 60%; statehood 39%; independence 1%. In 1993, Commonwealth dropped to 48.6%; statehood rose to 46.3%; independence polled 4.4%; and 0.6% of the ballots were blank or spoiled.

Under the Commonwealth formula, residents of Puerto Rico lack voting representation in Congress and do not participate in presidential elections. As U.S. citizens, Puerto Ricans are subject to military service and most federal laws. Residents of the Commonwealth pay no federal income tax on locally generated earnings, but Puerto Rico government income-tax rates are set at a level that closely parallels federal-plus-state levies on the mainland.

When Christopher Columbus arrived there in 1493, the island was inhabited by the peaceful Arawak Indians, who were being challenged by the warlike Carib Indians. Puerto Rico remained economically undeveloped until 1830, when sugarcane, coffee, and tobacco plantations were gradually developed. After Puerto Ricans began to press for independence, Spain granted the island broad powers of self-government in 1897. But during the Spanish-American War of 1898 American troops invaded the island and Spain ceded it to the U.S. Since then, Puerto Rico has remained an unincorporated U.S. territory. Its people were granted American citizenship under the Jones Act in 1917; were permitted to elect their own governor, beginning in 1948; and now fully administer their internal affairs under a constitution approved by the U.S. Congress in 1952. In spite of broad popular support for the autonomy of the Commonwealth government and a rapidly modernizing industrial society, there were expressions of dissatisfaction. Puerto Rican extremists dramatized their desire for independence with an attempt to assassinate President Truman on Nov. 1, 1950, and on March 1, 1954, they wounded five congressmen in an attack on the U.S. Capitol.

A self-help program of economic development and social welfare (called "Operation Bootstrap") was forged in the 1940s by four-time governor Luis Muñoz Marín. In a little more than four decades, much of the island's crushing poverty was eliminated. This was done partly through the development of manufacturing and service industries, the latter related to an enormous growth in tourism. Also, many Puerto Ricans migrated to large cities on the mainland U.S.

Puerto Rico is a major hub of Caribbean commerce, finance, tourism, and communications. San Juan is one of the world's busiest cruise-ship ports, and Puerto Rico's standard of living continues to be among the highest in the Western hemisphere. Its future political status, however, remains unclear. On March 4, 1998, the U.S. House of Representatives passed a bill that called for binding elections in Puerto Rico to decide the island's permanent political status.

Since the 1940s, the U.S. Navy has used Vieques island as a bombing range. Protests against the exercises grew in recent years, and in a July 2001 referendum, residents of the island voted overwhelmingly to close the base. The navy withdrew from Vieques in May 2003.

The Nov. 2, 2004, gubernatorial elections led to a two-month recount and a court challenge. On Jan. 2, 2005, Aníbal Acevedo Vilá of the Popular Democratic Party was declared governor. He received 48.4% of the vote, and his main challenger, Pedro Rossello of the New Progressive Party, 48.2%. Acevedo supports the existing U.S. territorial status of the island; Rossello supports statehood for Puerto Rico.

Guam
TERRITORY OF GUAM
Status: Territory
Governor: Felix Camacho (2003)
Capital (2000 est.): Agaña, 1,100
Land area: 212 sq mi (549 sq km)
Population (2005 est.): 168,564 (growth rate: 1.5%); birth rate: 19.0/1000; infant mortality rate: 6.9/1000; life expectancy: 78.4; density per sq mi: 795. **1996 est. net migration:** 3 migrants per 1,000 population. **Languages:** English and Chamorro; note: most residents are bilingual; Japanese also widely spoken. **Ethnicity/race:** Chamorro 37%, Filipino 26%, Caucasian 10%, Chinese, Japanese, Korean, and other, 27%. **Religions:** Roman Catholic 85%, other 15% (1999 est.). **Literacy rate:** 99% (1990 est.). **Monetary unit:** U.S. dollar
Economic summary: GDP/PPP (2000 est.): $3.2 billion; per capita $21,000. **Real growth rate:** n.a. **Inflation:** 0% (1999 est.). **Unemployment:** 15% (2000 est.). **Arable land:** 9%. **Agriculture:** fruits, copra, vegetables; eggs, pork, poultry, beef. **Labor force:** 60,000 (2000 est.); federal and territorial government 26%, private 74% (trade 24%, other services 40%, industry 10%) (2000 est.). **Industries:** U.S. military, tourism, construction, transshipment services, concrete products, printing and publishing, food processing, textiles. **Natural resources:** fishing (largely undeveloped), tourism (especially from Japan). **Exports:** $38 million (f.o.b., 2002 est.): mostly transshipments of refined petroleum products; construction materials, fish, food and beverage products. **Imports:** $462 million (f.o.b., 2002 est.): petroleum and petroleum products, food, manufactured goods. **Major trading partners:** Japan, South Korea, Singapore, Hong Kong (2003).

Guam is the largest and southernmost island in the Marianas Archipelago. The island is divided into a northern coralline limestone plateau and a southern chain of volcanic hills. Today Guam is an unincorporated, organized territory of the United States. The people of Guam have been U.S. citizens since 1950. They have been represented in the U.S. Congress since 1973 by a nonvoting delegate, but they do not participate in presidential elections. The executive branch includes a popularly elected governor, who serves a four-year term. The legislative branch is a 21-member unicameral legislature whose members are elected every two years.

Guam was probably explored by the Portuguese navigator Ferdinand Magellan (sailing for Spain) in 1521. The island was formally claimed by Spain in 1565, and its people were forced into submission and conversion to Roman Catholicism beginning in 1668. After the Spanish-American War of 1898, Spain ceded Guam to the United States. From 1899 to 1949, the U.S. Navy administered Guam, except during the Japanese occupation from 1941–1944. Guam was liberated by American military forces in the summer of 1944. Guam's economy is based on tourism and U.S. military spending (U.S. naval and air force bases occupy one-third of the land on Guam).

U.S. Virgin Islands
UNITED STATES VIRGIN ISLANDS
Status: Territory
Governor: Charles Turnbull (1999)
Capital (2000 est.): Charlotte Amalie (on St. Thomas), 11,004
Land area: 136 sq mi (352 sq km)
Population (2005 est.): 108,708 (growth rate: −0.1%); birth rate: 14.2/1000; infant mortality rate: 8.0/1000; life expectancy: 78.9; density per sq mi: 800. **Languages:** English (official), but Spanish and French are also spoken. **Ethnicity/race:** West Indian 74% (45% born in the Virgin Islands and 29% born elsewhere in the West Indies), U.S. mainland 13%, Puerto Rican 5%, other 8%, black 80%, white 15%, other 5%, 14% of Hispanic origin. **Religions:** Baptist 42%, Roman Catholic 34%, Episcopalian 17%, other 7%. **Literacy rate:** n.a. **Monetary unit:** U.S. dollar
Economic summary: GDP/PPP (2002 est.): $2.5 billion; per capita $17,200. **Real growth rate:** 2%. **Inflation:** 2.2% (2003). **Unemployment:** 9.3% (2003 est.). **Arable land:** 12%. **Agriculture:** fruit, vegetables, sorghum; Senepol cattle. **Labor force:** 48,900 (2003 est.); agriculture 1%, industry 19%, services 80% (2003 est.). **Industries:** tourism, petroleum refining, watch assembly, rum distilling, construction, pharmaceuticals, textiles, electronics. **Natural resources:** sun, sand, sea, surf. **Exports:** $n.a.: refined petroleum products. **Imports:** $n.a.: crude oil, foodstuffs, consumer goods, building materials. **Major trading partners:** U.S., Puerto Rico.

The Virgin Islands, consisting of nine main islands and some 75 islets, were explored by Columbus in 1493. They were originally inhabited by the Carib Indians. Since 1666, England has held six of the main islands; the remaining three (St. Croix, St. Thomas, and St. John), as well as about 50 of the islets, were eventually acquired by Denmark, which named them the Danish West Indies. In 1917, these islands were purchased by the U.S. from Denmark for $25 million.

Congress granted U.S. citizenship to Virgin Islanders in 1927. Universal suffrage was given in 1936 to all persons who could read and write English. The governor was elected by popular vote for the first time in 1970; previously he had been appointed by the U.S. president. A unicameral 15-person legislature serves the Virgin Islands, and congressional legislation gave the islands a nonvoting representative in Congress. Residents of the islands substantially enjoy the same rights as those enjoyed by mainlanders, but they may not vote in presidential elections.

Tourism is the primary economic activity, accounting for most of the GDP and 70% of employment. All goods made in the Virgin Islands qualify for duty-free entry into the United States.

American Samoa

TERRITORY OF AMERICAN SAMOA

Status: Territory
Governor: Togiola Tulafono (2003)
Capital (2003 est.): Pago Pago, 4,100
Land area: 77 sq mi (199 sq km)
Population (2005 est.): 57,881 (growth rate: –0.1%); birth rate: 23.1/1000; infant mortality rate: 9.3/1000; life expectancy: 75.8; density per sq mi: 753. **Languages:** Samoan (closely related to Hawaiian and other Polynesian languages) and English; most people are bilingual. **Ethnicity/race:** Samoan (Polynesian) 89%, Tongan 4%, Caucasian 2%, other 5%. **Religions:** Christian Congregationalist 50%, Roman Catholic 20%, Protestant denominations and other 30%. **Literacy rate:** 97% (1980 est.). **Monetary unit:** U.S. dollar
Economic summary: GDP/PPP (2000 est.): $500 million; per capita $8,000. **Real growth rate:** n.a. **Inflation:** n.a. **Unemployment:** 6% (2000). **Arable land:** 10%. **Agriculture:** bananas, coconuts, vegetables, taro, breadfruit, yams, copra, pineapples, papayas; dairy products, livestock. **Labor force:** 14,000 (1996); government 33%, tuna canneries 34%, other 33% (1990). **Industries:** tuna canneries (largely supplied by foreign fishing vessels), handicrafts. **Natural resources:** pumice, pumicite. **Exports:** $30 million (2002): canned tuna 93%. **Imports:** $123 million (2002): materials for canneries 56%, food 8%, petroleum products 7%, machinery and parts 6%. **Major trading partners:** Samoa, Japan, Canada, Australia, New Zealand, UK, South Korea (2003).

American Samoa, a group of five volcanic islands and two coral atolls located some 2,600 mi south of Hawaii in the South Pacific, is an unincorporated, unorganized territory of the U.S. It includes the eastern Samoan islands of Tutuila, Aunu'u, and Rose; three islands (Ta'u, Olosega, and Ofu) of the Manu'a group; and Swains Island. Around 1000 B.C. Proto-polynesians established themselves in the islands, and their descendants are one of the few remaining Polynesian societies. The Dutch navigator Jacob Roggeveen sighted the Manu'a Islands in 1722. American Samoa has been a territory of the United States since April 17, 1900, when the High Chiefs of Tutuila signed the first of two Deeds of Cession for the islands to the U.S. (Congress ratified the Deeds in 1929.) Swains Island, which is privately owned, came under U.S. administration in 1925.

Until World War II the United States operated a coaling station and naval base in Pago Pago. During the war, the islands were an important U.S. Marines staging area. In 1960 American Samoa ratified its territorial constitution and has since developed a modern, self-governing political system. American Samoans elect a governor, lieutenant governor, and legislature. The legislature (Fono) consists of two houses: the Senate, selected by village chiefs (matai) for four-year terms, and the House of Representatives, elected by the general population for two-year terms. The people of American Samoa are U.S. nationals, not U.S. citizens, but many have become naturalized American citizens. American Samoa does 80%–90% of its foreign trade with the U.S. Canned tuna is the primary export, earning $300 million annually. Transfers from the U.S. government add substantially to American Samoa's economic well-being.

Northern Mariana Islands

COMMONWEALTH OF THE NORTHERN MARIANA ISLANDS

Status: Commonwealth
Governor: Juan N. Babautu (2002)
Capital: Chalan Kanoa (on Saipan)
Total area: 184 sq mi (477 sq km)
Population (2005 est.): 80,362 (growth rate: 2.6%); birth rate: 19.5/1000; infant mortality: 7.1/1000; life expectancy: 75.9; density per sq mi: 436. **Languages:** English (official), Chamorro, Carolinian. **Ethnicity/race:** Chamorro, Carolinian, other Micronesian, Caucasian, Japanese, Chinese, Korean. **Religion:** Primarily Roman Catholic. **Literacy rate:** 97% (1980 est.). **Monetary unit:** U.S. dollar
Economic summary: GDP/PPP (2000 est.): $900 million; note: GDP numbers reflect U.S. spending; per capita $12,500. **Real growth rate:** n.a. **Inflation:** 1.2% (1997 est.). **Unemployment:** n.a. **Arable land:** 13%. **Agriculture:** coconuts, fruits, vegetables; cattle. **Labor force:** 6,006 total indigenous labor force; 2,699 unemployed; 28,717 foreign workers (June 1995). **Industries:** tourism, construction, garments, handicrafts. **Natural resources:** arable land, fish. **Exports:** $ n.a.: garments. **Imports:** $ n.a.: food, construction equipment and materials, petroleum products. **Major trading partners:** U.S., Japan (2000).

The Northern Mariana Islands, east of the Philippines and south of Japan, include the islands of Rota, Saipan, Tinian, Pagan, Guguan, Agrihan, and Aguijan. Although sighted by Ferdinand Magellan in 1521 as he sailed for Spain, the islands were not settled by Europeans until 1668, when missionaries converted the indigenous Chamorro people to Catholicism. They were ruled successively by Spain, Germany, and Japan before they became a UN Trusteeship (administered by the U.S.) after World War II. The Commonwealth of the Northern Mariana Islands (CNMI) became part of the United States in Nov. 1986. Spanish cultural traditions remain strong.

In recent years, Saipan's garment industry has been accused of exploiting thousands of Asian immigrants. Saipan's territorial status enables its employers to claim their clothing is "Made in the USA," while paying workers low wages and sidestepping import duties and tariffs.

Midway Islands

Status: Territory
Total area: 2 sq mi (5 sq km)
Population (July 2003 est.): no indigenous inhabitants; approx. 40 U.S. Fish and Wildlife Service staff.

The Midway Islands consist of a circular atoll, 6 mi in diameter, that encloses two islands. Lying about 1,150 mi west-northwest of Hawaii, the islands were first explored by Captain N. C. Brooks on July 5, 1859, in the name of the U.S. The atoll was declared a U.S. possession in 1867, and in 1903 Theodore Roosevelt made it a naval reservation. The island was renamed "Midway" by the U.S. Navy in recognition of its geographic location on the route between California and Japan. Air traffic across the Pacific increased the island's importance in the mid-1930s; the San Francisco–Manila mail route included a regular stop on Midway. Its military importance was soon recognized, and the navy began building an air and submarine base there in 1940. The Battle of Midway, which took place from June 3–6, 1942, was considered a turning point in World War II. After the war, the strategic importance of the island declined; the Midway stop for commercial air traffic was eliminated in 1950, and the air base closed in 1992.

Wake Island

Status: Territory
Total area: 2.51 sq mi (6.5 sq km)
Comparative size: about 11 times the size of the Mall in Washington, DC
Population (July 2003 est.): no indigenous inhabitants; 200 civilian contractors.
Economy: The economic activity is limited to providing services to U.S. military personnel and contractors on the island. All food and manufactured goods must be imported.

Wake Island, about halfway between Midway and Guam, is an atoll consisting of the three islets of Wilkes, Peale, and Wake. The islets were discovered by the British in 1796 and annexed by the U.S. in 1899. In 1938, Pan American Airways established a seaplane base, and Wake Island was used as a commercial base for several years. On Dec. 8, 1941, it was attacked by the Japanese, who took possession on Dec. 23. It was surrendered by the Japanese on Sept. 4, 1945.

Johnston Atoll

Status: Territory
Land area: 1.08 sq mi (2.8 sq km); density per sq mi: 1,111
Population (Jan. 2004 est.): no indigenous inhabitants; 396 U.S. military and civilian personnel

Johnston is a coral atoll about 700 mi southwest of Hawaii. It consists of four small islands—Johnston Island, Sand Island, Hikina Island, and Akau Island—which lie on a 9-mile-long reef. The atoll was discovered by Capt. Charles James Johnston of HMS *Cornwallis* in 1807. In 1858 it was claimed by Hawaii, and it later became a U.S. possession. Johnston Atoll was used by the U.S. Air Force to conduct test launchings of nuclear missiles and contains a landfill of plutonium-contaminated waste. More than four million pounds of chemical weapons have been destroyed on Johnston since 1990, and the U.S. military has been fined several times since then for improperly handing VX and sarin gas and releasing the deadly substances on the atoll. The military is gradually departing and the atoll will be turned into a wildlife refuge. However, the U.S. Fish and Wildlife Service, the atoll's inheritor, is concerned about the possibility of eventual radioactive leakage.

Baker, Howland, and Jarvis Islands

Status: Territory
These Pacific islands were claimed by the United States under the Guano Act of 1856 on May 13, 1936. Guano, composed of phosphates, was used as fertilizer in the 19th century, and its collection was highly lucrative. Through the Guano Act the U.S. gained 79 tiny territories around the world; it still controls eight of them. Baker Island is an atoll with an area of approximately one square mile about 1,650 mi from Hawaii. Howland Island, 36 mi to the northwest, is 1 mile long and half a mile wide. On their round-the-world flight in 1937, Amelia Earhart and Fred J. Noonan were headed for Howland when they disappeared. Jarvis Island is several hundred miles to the east.

Kingman Reef

Status: Territory
Kingman Reef, located about 1,000 mi south of Hawaii, was discovered by Capt. E. Fanning in 1798 but named for Capt. W. E. Kingman, who rediscovered

it in 1853. Triangular in shape, it is about 9.5 mi long. A U.S. possession since 1922, Kingman Reef is a Naval Defensive Sea Area and Airspace Reservation and is closed to the public.

Navassa Island

Status: Territory
Navassa Island is located in the Caribbean Sea, 99.4 mi (160 km) south of the U.S. naval base at Guantánamo, Cuba, between Cuba, Haiti, and Jamaica. The island has a total area of 2.01 sq mi (5.2 sq km). It was claimed for the U.S. in 1857 under the Guano Act. The Navassa Phosphate Company mined the island until 1900, enlisting hundreds of freed American slaves to dig out several tons of guano. Working conditions were so brutal that the laborers revolted in 1889, killing their supervisors. The island is also claimed by Haiti.

Palmyra Atoll

Status: Territory
Palmyra Atoll is an incorporated territory of the U.S. and privately owned. The atoll has a total area of 4.6 sq mi (11.9 sq km) and is located in the North Pacific Ocean, 994 mi (1,600 km) southwest of Honolulu. It was a U.S. military base during World War II but was not attacked.

Uruguay

ORIENTAL REPUBLIC OF URUGUAY

National name: República Oriental del Uruguay
President: Tabaré Vázquez (2005)
Area: 68,039 sq mi (176,220 sq km)
Population (2005 est.): 3,415,920 (growth rate: 0.5%); birth rate: 14.1/1000; infant mortality rate: 11.9/1000; life expectancy: 76.1; density per sq mi: 50
Capital and largest city (2003 est.): Montevideo, 1,745,100 (metro. area), 1,347,600 (city proper).
Monetary unit: Uruguay peso. **Languages:** Spanish, Portunol, or Brazilero. **Ethnicity/race:** white 88%, mestizo 8%, black 4%. **Religions:** Roman Catholic 66%, Protestant 2%, Jewish 1%, nonprofessing or other 31%. **Literacy rate:** 98% (2003 est.)
Economic summary: GDP/PPP (2004 est.): $49.27 billion; per capita $14,500. **Real growth rate:** 10.2%. **Inflation:** 7.6%. **Unemployment:** 13%. **Arable land:** 7%. **Agriculture:** rice, wheat, corn, barley; livestock; fish. **Labor force:** 1.56 million; agriculture 14%, industry 16%, services 70%. **Industries:** food processing, electrical machinery, transportation equipment, petroleum products, textiles, chemicals, beverages. **Natural resources:** arable land, hydropower, minor minerals, fisheries. **Exports:** $2.2 billion (f.o.b., 2003 est.): meat, rice, leather products, wool, fish, dairy products. **Imports:** $2.071 billion (f.o.b., 2003): machinery, chemicals, road vehicles, crude petroleum. **Major trading partners:** Brazil, U.S., Argentina, Germany, China, Mexico, Italy, Russia (2003).

Geography Uruguay, on the east coast of South America south of Brazil and east of Argentina, is comparable in size to Oklahoma. The country consists of a low, rolling plain in the south and a low plateau in the north. It has a 120-mile (193 km) Atlantic shoreline, a 235-mile (378 km) frontage on the Rio de la Plata, and 270 mi (435 km) on the Uruguay River, its western boundary.

Government Constitutional republic.

History Prior to European settlement, Uruguay was inhabited by indigenous people, the Charrúas. Juan Díaz de Solis, a Spaniard, visited Uruguay in 1516, but the Portuguese were first to settle it when they founded the town of Colonia del Sacramento in 1680. After a long struggle, Spain wrested the country from Portugal in 1778, by which time almost all of the indigenous people had been exterminated. Uruguay revolted against Spain in 1811, only to be conquered in 1817 by the Portuguese from Brazil. Independence was reasserted with Argentine help in 1825, and the republic was set up in 1828.

A revolt in 1836 touched off nearly 50 years of factional strife, including an inconclusive civil war (1839–1851) and a war with Paraguay (1865–1870), accompanied by occasional armed intervention by Argentina and Brazil. Uruguay, made prosperous by meat and wool exports, founded a welfare state early in the 20th century under President José Batlle y Ordóñez, who ruled from 1903 to 1929. A decline began in the 1950s as successive governments struggled to maintain a large bureaucracy and costly social benefits. Economic stagnation and left-wing terrorist activity followed.

A military coup ousted the civilian government in 1973. The military dictatorship that followed used fear and terror to demoralize the population, taking thousands of political prisoners. After ruling for 12 years, the brutal military regime permitted election of a civilian government in Nov. 1984 and relinquished rule in March 1985; full political and civil rights were then restored.

Subsequent leaders contended with high inflation and a mammoth national debt. Presidential and legislative elections in Nov. 1994 resulted in a narrow victory for the center-right Colorado Party and its presidential candidate, Julio Sanguinetti Cairolo, who had been president in 1985–1990. He pushed for constitutional and economic reforms aimed at reducing inflation and the size of the public sector, including tax increases and privatization. In Nov. 1999 Jorge Batlle, of the Colorado Party, won the presidency.

In 2002, Uruguay entered its fourth year of recession. Economic troubles in neighboring Argentina caused a staggering 90% drop in tourism. Batlle also faced a sizable budget deficit, a growing public debt, and a weakening of the peso on international markets. The country's economic outlook began improving in 2003. In a Dec. 2003 referendum, 60% of the electorate voted against opening up the state oil monopoly to foreign investment. In Oct. 2004, Tabaré Vázquez of the socialist Broad Front won 50.7% of the vote; he took office in March 2005. It was the left's first national victory in Uruguay.

Uzbekistan

REPUBLIC OF UZBEKISTAN

National name: Ozbekiston Respublikasi
President: Islam A. Karimov (1990)
Prime Minister: Shavkat Mirziyayev (2003)
Area: 172,741 sq mi (447,400 sq km)
Population (2005 est.): 26,851,195 (growth rate: 1.7%); birth rate: 26.2/1000; infant mortality rate: 71.1/1000; life expectancy: 64.2; density per sq mi: 155
Capital and largest city (2003 est.): Tashkent, 3,457,500 (metro. area), 2,155,400 (city proper).
Other large cities: Samarkand, 374,900; Andijon, 354,500. **Monetary unit:** Uzbekistani sum.
Languages: Uzbek 74.3%, Russian 14.2%, Tajik 4.4%, other 7.1%. **Ethnicity/race:** Uzbek 80%, Russian 5.5%, Tajik 5%, Kazak 3%, Karakalpak 2.5%, Tatar 1.5%, other 2.5% (1996 est.). **Religions:** Islam (mostly Sunnis) 88%, Eastern Orthodox 9%, other 3%. Literacy rate: 99% (2003 est.)
Economic summary: GDP/PPP (2004 est.): $47.59 billion; per capita $1,800. **Real growth rate:** 4.4%.

Inflation: 3%. **Unemployment:** 0.6% officially, plus another 20% underemployed. **Arable land:** 11%.
Agriculture: cotton, vegetables, fruits, grain; livestock.
Labor force: 14.64 million; agriculture 44%, industry 20%, services 36% (1995). **Industries:** textiles, food processing, machine building, metallurgy, gold petroleum, natural gas, chemicals. **Natural resources:** natural gas, petroleum, coal, gold, uranium, silver, copper, lead and zinc, tungsten, molybdenum.
Exports: $3.7 billion (f.o.b., 2004 est.): cotton 41.5%, gold 9.6%, energy products 9.6%, mineral fertilizers, ferrous metals, textiles, food products, automobiles (1998 est.). **Imports:** $2.82 billion (f.o.b., 2004 est.): machinery and equipment 49.8%, foodstuffs 16.4%, chemicals, metals (1998 est.). **Major trading partners:** Russia, China, Ukraine, Tajikistan, Bangladesh, Turkey, Japan, Kazakhstan, U.S., South Korea, Germany (2003).

Geography Uzbekistan is situated in central Asia between the Amu Darya and Syr Darya Rivers, the Aral Sea, and the slopes of the Tien Shan Mountains. It is bounded by Kazakhstan in the north and northwest, Kyrgyzstan and Tajikistan in the east and southeast, Turkmenistan in the southwest, and Afghanistan in the south. The republic also includes the Karakalpakstan Autonomous Republic, with its capital, Nukus (1992 est. pop., 182,000). The country is about one-tenth larger in area than the state of California.

Government Republic; authoritarian presidential rule.

History The Uzbekistan land was once part of the ancient Persian Empire and was later conquered by Alexander the Great in the 4th century B.C. During the 8th century, the nomadic Turkic tribes living there were converted to Islam by invading Arab forces who dominated the area. The Mongols under Ghengis Khan took over the region from the Seljuk Turks in the 13th century, and it later became part of Tamerlane the Great's empire and that of his successors until the 16th century. The Uzbeks invaded the territory in the early 16th century and merged with the other inhabitants in the area. Their empire broke up into separate Uzbek principalities, the khanates of Khiva, Bukhara, and Kokand. These city-states resisted Russian expansion into the area but were conquered by the Russian forces in the mid-19th century.

The territory was made into the Uzbek Republic in 1924 and became the independent Uzbekistan Soviet Socialist Republic in 1925. Under Soviet rule, Uzbekistan concentrated on growing cotton with the help of irrigation, mechanization, and chemical fertilizers and pesticides, causing serious environmental damage.

In June 1990, Uzbekistan was the first central Asian republic to declare that its own laws had sovereignty over those of the central Soviet government. Uzbekistan became fully independent and joined with ten other former Soviet republics on Dec. 21, 1991, in the Commonwealth of Independent States.

Vozrozhdeniye, an island in the Aral Sea, was a secret test site for biological weapons during the Soviet era. In 1988, the Soviets attempted to bury the evidence on the island, a frightening legacy that Uzbekistan inherited upon independence. U.S. scientists have confirmed that the island contains live anthrax and other deadly poisons.

President Karimov, a former Communist Party boss, is an autocrat who has brutally suppressed political parties and religious freedom and maintained rule with an iron fist. In 1999, after a bus hijacking, he declared, "I am prepared to rip off the heads of 200 people, to sacrifice their lives, in order to save peace and calm in the republic." The country's thousands of political and religious prisoners are subject to appalling conditions and horrific torture, including being boiled alive.

In 1999, the country battled against militant Islamic groups bent on the overthrow of the secular government. Fighting against the Islamic Movement of Uzbekistan (IMU) continued for the next several years.

In 2001, Uzbekistan provided the U.S. and UK with a base to fight against Taliban and al-Qaeda forces in neighboring Afghanistan and became the United States' main regional partner in the war on terror. Karimov linked his own battle against the Islamic opposition to the global fight on terrorism. He also exploited the real threat of Islamicism by labeling all of his opponents as Islamic extremists. As a strategic partner, the U.S. has been reluctant to take a firm stand regarding Uzbekistan's dismal human rights record. According to a report in the *New York Times* in May 2005, the U.S. has sent clandestine planeloads of accused terrorists to Uzbekistan as part of its controversial "rendition" program, the delivery of prisoners to countries with abusive interrogation tactics that are prohibited in the United States.

On May 13, 2005, unarmed antigovernment demonstrators in the city of Andijan were killed in a military crackdown; the number of casualties is still disputed, but it may be as many as 1,000. Earlier, a number of protesters had stormed a prison and released about 2,000 prisoners to protest what they saw as the rigged trial of 23 businessmen. The government claimed the men were Islamic terrorists; the protesters insisted the 23 were antigovernment civic leaders whom the government saw as a threat to its authority. After the U.S. called for an inquiry into the massacre and supported the airlift of Uzbek refugees escaping the violence, President Karimov ordered the U.S. air base in Uzbekistan shut down.

Vanuatu

REPUBLIC OF VANUATU

President: Kalkot Mataskelekele (2004)
Prime Minister: Ham Lini (2004)
Area: 4,710 sq mi (12,200 sq km)
Population (2005 est.): 205,754 (growth rate: 1.5%); birth rate: 23.1/1000; infant mortality rate: 55.2/1000; life expectancy: 62.5; density per sq mi: 44
Capital and largest city (2003 est.): Port Vila, 35,300.
Monetary unit: Vatu. **Languages:** Bislama (a Melanesian pidgin English), English, French (all 3 official); more than 100 local languages. **Ethnicity/race:** indigenous Melanesian 98%, French, Vietnamese, Chinese, other Pacific Islanders.
Religions: Presbyterian 36.7%, Anglican 15%, Roman Catholic 15%, indigenous beliefs 7.6%, Seventh-Day Adventist 6.2%, Church of Christ 3.8%, other 15.7% (including Jon Frum Cargo cult). **Literacy rate:** 53% (1979 est.)
Economic summary: GDP/PPP (2003 est.): $580 million; per capita $2,900. **Real growth rate:** 1.1%. **Inflation:** 3.1%. **Unemployment:** n.a. **Arable land:** 2%. **Agriculture:** copra, coconuts, cocoa, coffee, taro, yams, coconuts, fruits, vegetables; fish, beef. **Labor force:** n.a.; agriculture 65%, services 30%, industry 5% (2000 est.). **Industries:** food and fish freezing, wood processing, meat canning. **Natural resources:** manganese, hardwood forests, fish. **Exports:** $26.6 million (f.o.b., 2003): copra, beef, cocoa, timber, kava, coffee. **Imports:** $138 million (c.i.f., 2002): machinery and equipment, foodstuffs, fuels. **Major trading partners:** Thailand, Indonesia, Japan, Australia, Poland, Singapore, New Zealand, Fiji (2003).

Geography Vanuatu is an archipelago of 83 islands lying between New Caledonia and Fiji in the South Pacific. Largest of the islands is Espiritu Santo (875 sq mi; 2,266 sq km); others are Efate, Malekula, Malo, Pentecost, and Tanna.

Government Republic.

History The first settlers are believed to have arrived approximately 3,500 years ago from New Guinea and the Solomon Islands by canoe. The islands were sighted by Pedro Fernandes de Queiros of Portugal in 1606 and were charted by the British navigator James Cook in 1774, who named the archipelago New Hebrides, after the northern Scottish islands. Competing British and French claims to the islands led to the formation of a condominium government, allowing for joint British-French rule in 1906. The islands' plantation economy, based on imported Vietnamese labor, was prosperous until the 1920s, when markets for its products declined. Diseases brought by missionaries, sandalwood traders, and others helped reduce the population from approximately 1 million in 1800 to 45,000 in 1935. The islands served as a major Allied base in World War II. After the war, the indigenous Melanesians began lobbying for independence, which in 1980 the country achieved. It was then renamed Vanuatu.

A brief rebellion by French settlers and plantation workers on Espiritu Santo took place in May 1980. Britain, France, and Papua New Guinea sent soldiers, who quelled the revolt, which the new government said was financed by the Phoenix Foundation, a right-wing U.S. group.

In July 2002, former prime minister Barak Sope was convicted of forgery. Alfred Maseng was elected president in April 2004, but he was forced to step down when his criminal record was revealed. In Aug. 2004, Kalkot Mataskelekele was selected from 16 candidates as the new president. He is the country's first president to hold a university degree.

Vatican City (Holy See)

National name: Stato della Città del Vaticano (Santa Sede)
Ruler: Benedict XVI (2005)
Area: 0.17 sq mi (0.44 sq km)
Population (July 2003 est.): 911; density per sq mi: 5,362. **Monetary unit:** Euro. **Languages:** Italian, Latin, French, various other languages. **Ethnicity/race:** Italian, Swiss, other. **Religion:** Roman Catholic.
Labor force: dignitaries, priests, nuns, guards, and 3,000 lay workers who live outside the Vatican.
Budget (2001): Revenues: $173.5 million; expenditures: $176.6 million, including capital expenditures.

Geography The Vatican City State is situated on the Vatican hill, on the right bank of the Tiber River, within the city of Rome.

Government The pope has full legal, executive, and judicial powers. Executive power over the area is in the hands of a commission of cardinals appointed by the pope. The College of Cardinals is the pope's chief advisory body, and upon his death the cardinals elect his successor for life.

History The Vatican City State, sovereign and independent, is the survivor of the papal states that in 1859 comprised an area of some 17,000 sq mi (44,030 sq km). During the struggle for Italian unification, from 1860 to 1870, most of this area became part of Italy. By an Italian law of May 13, 1871, the temporal power of the pope was abrogated, and the territory of the papacy was confined to the Vatican and Lateran palaces and the villa of Castel Gandolfo. The popes consistently refused to recognize this arrangement. The Lateran Treaty of Feb. 11, 1929, between the Vatican and the kingdom of Italy, established the autonomy of the Holy See.

The first session of Ecumenical Council Vatican II was opened by John XXIII on Oct. 11, 1962, to plan and set policies for the modernization of the Roman Catholic Church. Pope Paul VI continued the council, presiding over the last three sessions. Vatican II, as it is called, revolutionized some of the church's practices. Power was decentralized, giving bishops a larger role, the liturgy was vernacularized, and laymen were given a larger part in church affairs.

On Aug. 26, 1978, Cardinal Albino Luciani was chosen by the College of Cardinals to succeed Paul VI, who had died of a heart attack on Aug. 6. The new pope took the name John Paul I. Only 34 days after his election, John Paul I died of a heart attack, ending the shortest reign in 373 years. On Oct. 16, Cardinal Karol Wojtyla, 58, was chosen pope and took the name John Paul II. Pope John Paul II became the first Polish pope and the first non-Italian pope since the 16th century.

On May 13, 1981, a Turkish terrorist shot the pope in St. Peter's Square, the first assassination attempt against the pontiff in modern times. The pope later met and forgave him. On June 3, 1985, the Vatican and Italy ratified a new church-state treaty, known as a concordat, replacing the Lateran Treaty of 1929. The new accord affirmed the independence of Vatican City but ended a number of privileges that the Catholic Church had in Italy, including its status as the state religion.

On April 2, 2005, John Paul died. He was the third-longest reigning pope (26 years). A champion of the poor, he is credited by many with hastening the fall of communism in Poland and other eastern bloc countries. His vitality and charisma energized the world's one billion Catholics. His rule was characterized by conservatism regarding church doctrine, particularly on issues such as birth control, women's roles in the church, and homosexuality. The pope also remained circumspect about the U.S. church's sexual abuse scandals in 2002. He was the Vatican's greatest ambassador, traveling to 129 countries. John Paul canonized 482 saints and beatified 1,338 people, which was believed to be more than all his predecessors combined.

On April 19, German cardinal Joseph Ratzinger was named the new pope. Pope Benedict XVI is known as an accomplished scholar of theology and is considered an archconservative in his religious views. He served as Pope John Paul II's closest associate and is expected to continue the policy of a "strong Rome." The church's power will not become more decentralized but remain firmly in the hands of Rome.

For a list of all the popes, see pp. 367–369.

Venezuela

BOLIVARIAN REPUBLIC OF VENEZUELA

National name: República Bolivariana de Venezuela
President: Hugo Chavez (1999)
Area: 352,143 sq mi (912,050 sq km)
Population (2005 est.): 25,375,281 (growth rate: 1.4%); birth rate: 18.9/1000; infant mortality rate: 22.2/1000; life expectancy: 74.3; density per sq mile: 72
Capital (2003 est.): Caracas, 3,517,300 (metro. area), 1,741,400 (city proper). **Largest cities:** Maracaibo, 1,889,000 (metro. area), 1,854,300 (city proper);

Valencia, 1,515,400; Barquisimeto, 948,900. **Monetary unit:** Bolivar. **Languages:** Spanish (official), numerous indigenous dialects. **Ethnicity/race:** Spanish, Italian, Portuguese, Arab, German, African, indigenous people. **Religions:** Roman Catholic 96%, Protestant 2%, other 2%. **Literacy rate:** 93% (2003 est.)
Economic summary: GDP/PPP (2004 est.): $145.2 billion; per capita $5,800. **Real growth rate:** 16.8%. **Inflation:** 22.4%. **Unemployment:** 17.1%. **Arable land:** 3%. **Agriculture:** corn, sorghum, sugarcane, rice, bananas, vegetables, coffee; beef, pork, milk, eggs; fish. **Labor force:** 12.25 million; services 64%, industry 23%, agriculture 13% (1997 est.). **Industries:** petroleum, iron ore mining, construction materials, food processing, textiles, steel, aluminum, motor vehicle assembly. **Natural resources:** petroleum, natural gas, iron ore, gold, bauxite, other minerals, hydropower, diamonds. **Exports:** $35.84 billion (f.o.b., 2004 est.): petroleum, bauxite and aluminum, steel, chemicals, agricultural products, basic manufactures. **Imports:** $14.98 billion (f.o.b., 2004 est.): raw materials, machinery and equipment, transport equipment, construction materials. **Major trading partners:** U.S., Netherlands Antilles, Dominican Republic, Colombia, Brazil, Mexico (2003).

Geography Venezuela, a third larger than Texas, occupies most of the northern coast of South America on the Caribbean Sea. It is bordered by Colombia to the west, Guyana to the east, and Brazil to the south. Mountain systems break Venezuela into four distinct areas: (1) the Maracaibo lowlands; (2) the mountainous region in the north and northwest; (3) the Orinoco basin, with the llanos (vast grass-covered plains) on its northern border and great forest areas in the south and southeast; and (4) the Guiana Highlands, south of the Orinoco, accounting for nearly half the national territory.

Government Federal republic.

History When Columbus explored Venezuela on his third voyage in 1498, the area was inhabited by Arawak, Carib, and Chibcha Indians. A subsequent Spanish explorer gave the country its name, meaning "Little Venice." Caracas was founded in 1567. Simón Bolívar, who led the liberation from Spain of much of the continent, was born in Caracas in 1783. With Bolívar taking part, Venezuela was one of the first South American colonies to revolt in 1810, winning independence in 1821. Federated at first with Colombia and Ecuador as the Republic of Greater Colombia, Venezuela became a republic in 1830. A period of unstable dictatorships followed. Antonio Guzman Blanco governed from 1870 to 1888, developing an infrastructure, expanding agriculture, and welcoming foreign investment.

Gen. Juan Vicente Gómez was dictator from 1908 to 1935, when Venezuela became a major oil exporter. A military junta ruled after his death. Leftist Dr. Rómulo Betancourt and the Democratic Action Party won a majority of seats in a Constituent Assembly to draft a new constitution in 1946. A well-known writer, Rómulo Gallegos, candidate of Betancourt's party, became Venezuela's first democratically elected president in 1947. Within eight months, Gallegos was overthrown by a military-backed coup led by Marcos Peréz Jiménez, who was ousted himself in 1958. Since 1959, Venezuela has been one of the most stable democracies in Latin America. Betancourt served from 1959–1964, while Rafael Caldera Rodríguez, president from 1969 to 1974, legalized the Communist Party and established diplomatic relations with Moscow.

Venezuela benefited from the oil boom of the early 1970s. In 1974, President Carlos Andrés Pérez took office, and in 1976 Venezuela nationalized foreign-owned oil and steel companies, offering compensation. Luis Herrera Campíns took office in 1978. Declining world oil prices sent Venezuela's economy into a tailspin, increasing the country's foreign debt. Pérez was reelected to a nonconsecutive term in 1988 and launched an unpopular austerity program. Military officers staged two unsuccessful coup attempts in 1992, while the following year Congress impeached Pérez on corruption charges. President Rafael Caldera Rodríguez was elected in Dec. 1993 to face the 1994 collapse of half of the country's banking sector, falling oil prices, foreign debt repayment, and inflation. In 1997, the government announced an expansion of gold and diamond mining to reduce reliance on oil.

Leftist president Hugo Chavez took office in 1999, pledging political and economic reforms to give the poor a greater share of the country's oil wealth. A constituent Assembly was formed to rewrite the constitution in July 1999, followed by the creation of a constitutional Assembly made up of Chavez's allies that replaced the democratically elected Congress. Chavez's assumption of greater power prompted charges that he is establishing a left-wing dictatorship.

Chavez was reelected to a six-year term in July 2000. Troops were called in to quell serious protests over the election in several cities. In 2000 Chavez visited other OPEC countries, becoming the first foreign head of state to visit Iraq since the 1991 Gulf War. He is close to President Fidel Castro of Cuba, which receives Venezuelan oil at reduced prices.

In Dec. 2001, business and labor organizations held a work stoppage to protest Chavez's increasingly authoritarian government. In April 2002, tensions reached a boiling point as workers reduced oil production to protest Chavez policies. Following a massive anti-Chavez demonstration during which 12 people were killed, a coalition of business and military leaders forced Chavez from power. But international criticism of the coup, especially in Latin America, and an outpouring of support from the president's followers returned Chavez to power just two days later. After the coup, Chavez remained highly popular among the poor, despite the desperate state of the economy. Venezuelan labor unions, business organizations, the media, and a good part of the military remained substantially less enchanted.

Beginning in early Dec. 2002, a general strike was called by business and labor leaders. By Jan. 2003 it had virtually brought the economy, including the oil industry, to a halt. Strike leaders pledged to continue until Chavez resigned or agreed to early elections. But in Feb. 2003, after nine weeks, the strikers conceded defeat. In Aug. 2003, a petition with 3.2 million signatures was delivered to the country's election commission, demanding a recall referendum on Chavez. The Chavez government challenged the referendum process rigorously, and petitions submitted in Sept. 2003 and Feb. 2004 were rejected as invalid. The electoral board finally accepted a petition in June 2004 and scheduled the referendum for August 15. Chavez, who had been shoring up his standing with the Venezuelan poor during the delays, won the referendum with an overwhelming 58% of the vote. The opposition alleged fraud, but international observers confirmed that there had been no irregularities. Chavez's hand was clearly strengthened, and by the spring of 2005, his popularity rating reached 70%, due in large part to his social spending programs.

Vietnam
SOCIALIST REPUBLIC OF VIETNAM

National name: Công Hòa Xa Hôi Chú Nghia Viêt Nam
President: Tran Duc Luong (1997)
Prime Minister: Phan Van Khai (1997)
Area: 127,243 sq mi (329,560 sq km)
Population (2005 est.): 83,535,576 (growth rate: 1.0%); birth rate: 17.1/1000; infant mortality rate: 25.9/1000; life expectancy: 70.6; density per sq mi: 657
Capital (2003 est.): Hanoi, 2,543,700 (metro. area), 1,396,500 (city proper). **Largest cities:** Ho Chi Minh City (Saigon), 5,894,100 (metro. area), 3,415,300 (city proper); Haiphong, 581,600; Da Nang, 452,700; Hué 271,900; Nha Trang, 270,100; Qui Nho'n, 199,700.
Monetary unit: Dong. **Languages:** Vietnamese (official); English (increasingly favored as a second language); some French, Chinese, Khmer; mountain area languages (Mon-Khmer and Malayo-Polynesian).
Ethnicity/race: Vietnamese 85%–90%, Chinese, Hmong, Thai, Khmer, Cham, mountain groups.
Religions: Buddhist, Hoa Hao, Cao Dai, Christian (predominantly Roman Catholic, some Protestant), indigenous beliefs, Muslim. **Literacy rate:** 94% (2003 est.)
Economic summary: GDP/PPP (2004 est.): $227.2 billion; per capita $2,700. **Real growth rate:** 7.7%. **Inflation:** 9.5%. **Unemployment:** 1.9%. **Arable land:** 20%. **Agriculture:** paddy rice, coffee, fish and seafood, rubber, cotton, tea, pepper, soybeans, cashews, sugar cane, peanuts, bananas, poultry. **Labor force:** 42.98 million; agriculture 63%, industry and services 37% (2000 est.). **Industries:** food processing, garments, shoes, machine building, mining, cement, chemical fertilizer, glass, tires, oil, coal, steel, paper. **Natural resources:** phosphates, coal, manganese, bauxite, chromate, offshore oil and gas deposits, forests, hydropower. **Exports:** $23.72 billion (f.o.b., 2004 est.): crude oil, marine products, rice, coffee, rubber, tea, garments, shoes. **Imports:** $26.31 billion (f.o.b., 2004 est.): machinery and equipment, petroleum products, fertilizer, steel products, raw cotton, grain, cement, motorcycles. **Major trading partners:** U.S., Japan, Australia, China, Germany, Singapore, UK, Taiwan, South Korea, Thailand, Hong Kong (2003).

Geography Vietnam occupies the eastern and southern part of the Indochinese peninsula in Southeast Asia, with the South China Sea along its entire coast. China is to the north and Laos and Cambodia are to the west. Long and narrow on a north-south axis, Vietnam is about twice the size of Arizona. The Mekong River delta lies in the south.

Government Communist state.

History The Vietnamese are descendants of nomadic Mongols from China and migrants from Indonesia. According to mythology, the first ruler of Vietnam was Hung Vuong, who founded the nation in 2879 B.C. China ruled the nation then known as Nam Viet as a vassal state from 111 B.C. until the 15th century, an era of nationalistic expansion, when Cambodians were pushed out of the southern area of what is now Vietnam.

A century later, the Portuguese were the first Europeans to enter the area. France established its influence early in the 19th century, and within 80 years it conquered the three regions into which the country was then divided—Cochin-China in the south, Annam in the central region, and Tonkin in the north.

France first unified Vietnam in 1887, when a single governor-generalship was created, followed by the first physical links between north and south—a rail and road system. Even at the beginning of World War II, however, there were internal differences among the three regions. Japan took over military bases in Vietnam in 1940, and a pro-Vichy French administration remained until 1945. Veteran Communist leader Ho Chi Minh organized an independence movement known as the Vietminh to exploit the confusion surrounding France's weakened influence in the region. At the end of the war, Ho's followers seized Hanoi and declared a short-lived republic, which ended with the arrival of French forces in 1946.

Paris proposed a unified government within the French Union under the former Annamite emperor, Bao Dai. Cochin-China and Annam accepted the proposal, and Bao Dai was proclaimed emperor of all Vietnam in 1949. Ho and the Vietminh withheld support, and the revolution in China gave them the outside help needed for a war of resistance against French and Vietnamese troops armed largely by a United States worried about cold war Communist expansion.

A bitter defeat at Dien Bien Phu in northwest Vietnam on May 5, 1954, broke the French military campaign and resulted in the division of Vietnam. In the new South, Ngo Dinh Diem, prime minister under Bao Dai, deposed the monarch in 1955 and made himself president. Diem used strong U.S. backing to create an authoritarian regime that suppressed all opposition but could not eradicate the Northern-supplied Communist Viet Cong.

Skirmishing grew into a full-scale war, with escalating U.S. involvement. A military coup, U.S.-inspired in the view of many, ousted Diem on Nov. 1, 1963, and a kaleidoscope of military governments followed. The most savage fighting of the war occurred in early 1968 during the Vietnamese New Year, known as Tet. Although the so-called Tet Offensive ended in a military defeat for the North, its psychological impact changed the course of the war.

U.S. bombing and an invasion of Cambodia in the summer of 1970—an effort to destroy Viet Cong bases in the neighboring state—marked the end of major U.S. participation in the fighting. Most American ground troops were withdrawn from combat by mid-1971 when the U.S. conducted heavy bombing raids on the Ho Chi Minh Trail—a crucial North Vietnamese supply line. In 1972, secret peace negotiations led by Secretary of State Henry A. Kissinger took place, and a peace settlement was signed in Paris on Jan. 27, 1973.

By April 9, 1975, Hanoi's troops marched within 40 miles of Saigon, the South's capital. South Vietnam's president Thieu resigned on April 21 and fled. Gen. Duong Van Minh, the new president, surrendered Saigon on April 30, ending a war that claimed the lives of 1.3 million Vietnamese and 58,000 Americans.

In 1977, border clashes between Vietnam and Cambodia intensified, as well as accusations by its former ally Beijing that Chinese residents of Vietnam were being subjected to persecution. Beijing cut off all aid and withdrew 800 technicians.

Hanoi was also preoccupied with a continuing war in Cambodia, where 60,000 Vietnamese troops had invaded and overthrown the country's Communist leader Pol Pot and his pro-Chinese regime. In early 1979, Vietnam was conducting a two-front war: defending its northern border against a Chinese invasion and supporting its army in Cambodia, which was still fighting Pol Pot's Khmer Rouge guerrillas. Hanoi's Marxist policies combined with the destruction of the country's infrastructure during the decades of fighting devastated Vietnam's economy. However, it started to pick up in 1986 under *Doi Moi* (economic renovation), an effort at limited privatization. Vietnamese troops began limited withdrawals from Laos and

Cambodia in 1988, and Vietnam supported the Cambodian peace agreement signed in Oct. 1991.

The U.S. lifted a Vietnamese trade embargo in Feb. 1994 that had been in place since U.S. involvement in the war. Full diplomatic relations were announced between the two countries in July 1995. In April 1997, a pact was signed with the U.S. concerning repayment of the $146 million wartime debt incurred by the South Vietnamese government, and the following year the nation began a drive to eliminate inefficient bureaucrats and streamline the approval process for direct foreign investment. Efforts of reform-minded officials toward political and economic change have been thwarted by Vietnam's ruling Communist Party. In April 2001, however, the progressive Nong Duc Manh was appointed general secretary of the ruling Communist Party, succeeding Le Kha Phieu. Even with a reformer at the helm of the party, change has been slow and cautious.

In Nov. 2001, Vietnam's National Assembly approved a trade agreement that opened U.S. markets to Vietnam's goods and services. Tariffs on Vietnam's products dropped to about 4% from rates as high as 40%. Vietnam in return opened its state markets to foreign competition.

The government highlighted its efforts to crack down on corruption and crime with the June 2003 conviction of notorious criminal syndicate boss Truong Van Cam, known as Nam Cam. He was sentenced to death, along with 155 other defendants, and executed in June 2004.

Prime Minister Phan Van Khai visited the United States in June 2005, becoming the first Vietnamese leader to do so since the Vietnam War ended. He met with President Bush and several business leaders, including Microsoft chairman Bill Gates. The U.S. is Vietnam's largest trading partner, buying about $7 billion in Vietnamese goods each year.

(For a Vietnam War chronology, *see* Headline History, p. 685.)

Western Sahara (proposed state)

WESTERN SAHARA

Area: 102,703 sq mi (266,000 sq km)
Population (2005 est.): 273,008 (growth rate: n.a.); birth rate: n.a.; infant mortality rate: n.a.; life expectancy: n.a.; density per sq mi: n.a.
Largest city (2003 est.): El Aaiun 198,200. **Monetary unit:** Tala. **Languages:** Hassaniya Arabic, Moroccan Arabic. **Ethnicity/race:** Saharawi, Arab, Berber. **Religion:** Islam
Economic summary: GDP/PPP: n.a. **Arable land:** 0.02%. **Agriculture:** fruits and vegetables (grown in the few oases); camels, sheep, goats (kept by nomads). **Labor force:** 12,000; animal husbandry and subsistence farming 50%. **Industries:** phosphate mining, handicrafts. **Natural resources:** phosphates, iron ore. **Exports:** n.a.: phosphates 62%. **Imports:** n.a.: fuel for fishing fleet, foodstuffs. **Major trading partners:** Morocco claims and administers Western Sahara, so trade partners are included in overall Moroccan accounts.

Geography Located in northern Africa on the Atlantic Ocean, Western Sahara is surrounded by Algeria to the east, Morocco to the north, and Mauritania to the south. About the size of Colorado, it is mostly low, flat desert with some small mountains in the south and northeast.

Government Legal status of the territory is disputed and sovereignty unresolved; a UN referendum on the issue is planned. The territory is contested by Morocco and the Polisario Front, which in Feb. 1976, formally proclaimed a government-in-exile of the Saharawi Arab Democratic Republic, now officially recognized by about 55 countries.

History Little is known about Western Sahara before the 4th century B.C., when trade with Europe began. During the Middle Ages it was occupied first by Berbers and then by the Arabic-speaking Muslim Bedouins. In the 19th century the Spanish laid claim to the southern coastal region, called Rio de Oro, and later occupied the northern interior region, Saguia el Hamra, in 1934. The Spanish formally united the two regions, and it became known as Spanish Sahara in 1958. Both Morocco and Mauritania sought to control the territory, and when the Spanish departed in 1976 they divided the territory between them. In the meantime, the indigenous Saharawis began fighting for independence. In 1976, the insurgents, called the Polisario Front, declared a government-in-exile (the Saharawi Arab Democratic Republic) from their base in Algeria. Mauritania reached a peace agreement with the Polisario in 1979, but Morocco then seized the land given up by Mauritania and now exerts administrative control over the entire region. The Polisario Front fought Morocco to a stalemate and agreed in Sept. 1991 to a cease-fire, which was contingent on a referendum regarding independence. For more than a decade, however, the UN has failed to hold the referendum; disputes over voter eligibility have been the major stumbling block, as well as Morocco's opposition to the referendum. In Aug. 2001, former secretary of state James A. Baker, special UN envoy to the Western Sahara, proposed that instead of a referendum on independence, Western Sahara consider becoming an autonomous region of Morocco. The Polisario rejected the new proposal, which it saw as a reversal of the UN's decadelong promise to hold a referendum on self-determination. In 2002, King Mohammed VI of Morocco reasserted that he will not "renounce an inch of" the Western Sahara.

In August 2003, a UN Security Council resolution adopted a new peace plan that would turn Western Sahara into a semiautonomous region of Morocco for five years, after which a referendum would be held to determine independence, autonomy, or integration into Morocco. The Polisario agreed to the plan; Morocco refused to consider it. In June 2004, a frustrated James Baker resigned after seven years as UN envoy. His successor has vowed to achieve a resolution. The UN has spent more than $600 million on peacekeeping efforts in Western Sahara over the last 13 years.

In Aug. 2005, the Polisario freed the last Moroccan prisoners it had been holding. The 404 men had been imprisoned for almost 20 years and were the world's longest-held prisoners of war.

Yemen

REPUBLIC OF YEMEN

National name: Al-Jumhuriyah al-Yamaniyah
President: Ali Abdullah Saleh (1990)
Prime Minister: Abdul Qader Bajamal (2001)
Area: 203,849 sq mi (527,970 sq km)
Population (2005 est.): 20,727,063 (growth rate: 3.5%); birth rate: 43.1/1000; infant mortality rate: 61.5/1000; life expectancy: 61.8; density per sq mi: 102
Capital and largest city (2003 est.): Sanaá, 1,778,900. **Other large cities:** Aden, 568,700; Hodiedah, 426,100; Tiaz, 317,600. **Monetary unit:** Rial.
Language: Arabic. **Ethnicity/race:** predominantly Arab; but also Afro-Arab, South Asians, Europeans.
Religions: Islam (including Sunni and Shiite), small numbers of Jewish, Christian, and Hindu. **Literacy rate:** 50% (2003 est.)
Economic summary: GDP/PPP (2004 est.): $16.25 billion; per capita $800. **Real growth rate:** 1.9%. **Inflation:** 12.2%. **Unemployment:** 35% (2003 est.). **Arable land:** 3%. **Agriculture:** grain, fruits, vegetables, pulses, qat (mildly narcotic shrub), coffee, cotton; dairy products, livestock (sheep, goats, cattle, camels), poultry; fish. **Labor force:** 5.98 million. **Industries:** crude oil production and petroleum refining; small-scale production of cotton textiles and leather goods; food processing; handicrafts; small aluminum products factory; cement; commercial ship repair. **Natural resources:** petroleum, fish, rock salt, marble, small deposits of coal, gold, lead, nickel, copper, fertile soil in west. **Exports:** $4.468 billion (f.o.b., 2004 est.): crude oil, coffee, dried and salted fish. **Imports:** $3.734 billion (f.o.b., 2004 est.): food and live animals, machinery and equipment, chemicals. **Major trading partners:** China, Thailand, South Korea, Malaysia, Singapore, UAE, Saudi Arabia, India, U.S., Kuwait, France (2003).

Geography Formerly divided into two nations, the People's Democratic Republic of Yemen and the Yemen Arab Republic, the Republic of Yemen occupies the southwest tip of the Arabian Peninsula on the Red Sea opposite Ethiopia and extends along the southern part of the Arabian Peninsula on the Gulf of Aden and the Indian Ocean. Saudi Arabia is to the north and Oman is to the east. The country is about the size of France. A 700-mile (1,130-km) narrow coastal plain in the south gives way to a mountainous region and then a plateau area.

Government Parliamentary republic.

History The history of Yemen dates back to the Minaean (1200–650 B.C.) and Sabaean (750–115 B.C.) kingdoms. Ancient Yemen (centered around the port of Aden) engaged in the lucrative myrrh and frankincense trade. It was invaded by the Romans (1st century A.D.) as well as the Ethiopians and Persians (6th century A.D.). In A.D. 628 it converted to Islam and in the 10th century came under the control of the Rassite dynasty of the Zaidi sect, which remained involved in North Yemeni politics until 1962. The Ottoman Turks nominally occupied the area from 1538 to the decline of their empire in 1918.

The northern portion of Yemen was ruled by imams until a pro-Egyptian military coup took place in 1962. The junta proclaimed the Yemen Arab Republic, and after a civil war in which Egypt's Nasser and the USSR supported the revolutionaries and King Saud of Saudi Arabia and King Hussein of Jordan supported the royalists, the royalists were finally defeated in mid-1969.

The southern port of Aden, strategically located at the opening of the Red Sea, was colonized by Britain in 1839, and by 1937, with an expansion of its territory, it was known as the Aden Protectorate. In the 1960s the Nationalist Liberation Front (NLF) fought against British rule, which led to the establishment of the People's Republic of Southern Yemen on Nov. 30, 1967. In 1979, under strong Soviet influence, the country became the only Marxist state in the Arab world.

The Republic of Yemen was established on May 22, 1990, when pro-Western Yemen and the Marxist Yemen Arab Republic merged after 300 years of separation to form the new nation. The poverty and decline in Soviet economic support in the south was an important incentive for the merger. The new president, Ali Abdullah Saleh, was elected by the Parliaments of both countries.

Differences over power sharing and the pace of integration between the north and the south came to a head in 1994, resulting in a civil war. The north's superior forces quickly overwhelmed the south in May and early June despite the south's brief declaration of succession. The victorious north presented a reconciliation plan providing for a general amnesty and pledges to protect political democracy.

The president's party, the General People's Congress, won an enormous victory in the April 1997 parliamentary elections, the first since the civil war. In 1998–1999, a militant Islamic group, the Aden-Abyan Islamic Army, kidnapped several groups of Western tourists, which led to the deaths of several during a poorly orchestrated rescue attempt. The group's leader, Zein al-Abidine al-Mihdar, threatened to continue attacks on tourists and government officials. The goal of the militants is to overthrow the government and turn Yemen into an Islamic state.

On Oct. 12, 2000, 17 Americans died and 37 were wounded when suicide bombers attacked the U.S. Navy destroyer *Cole*, which was refueling in Aden, Yemen. The U.S. has had numerous clashes with Yemeni authorities during the investigation of the terrorist act. After the Sept. 11 terrorist attacks on the U.S., however, Yemen increased its cooperation with the U.S. and assisted in antiterrorism measures. In Oct. 2002, a French tanker, the *Limburg*, was also the victim of a terrorist attack off the coast of Yemen. Ten suspects of the *Cole* bombing escaped from prison in April 2003; seven, including the two suspected masterminds of the attack, were recaptured in 2004. Fifteen militants were convicted in Aug. 2004 on a variety of charges, including the attack on the *Limburg*. In September, two key al-Qaeda operatives involved in the *Cole* bombing were sentenced to death, and Yemeni troops killed dissident Shiite cleric Hussein al-Houthi. In spring 2005 several hundred of al-Houthi's followers were killed in clashes with the government.

Yugoslavia

SEE SERBIA AND MONTENEGRO.

Zaire

SEE CONGO, DEMOCRATIC REPUBLIC OF.

Zambia

REPUBLIC OF ZAMBIA

President: Levy Mwanawasa (2002)
Area: 290,584 sq mi (752,614 sq km)
Population (2005 est.): 11,261,795 (growth rate: 2.1%); birth rate: 41.4/1000; infant mortality rate: 88.3/1000; life expectancy: 39.7; density per sq mi: 39
Capital and largest city (2003 est.): Lusaka, 1,773,300 (metro. area), 1,265,000 (city proper). **Other large cities:** Ndola, 349,300; Kitwe, 306,200; Kabwe, 219,600, Chingola, 151,100. **Monetary unit:** Kwacha.
Languages: English (official); major vernaculars: Bemba, Kaonda, Lozi, Lunda, Luvale, Nyanja, Tonga; about 70 other indigenous languages. **Ethnicity/race:** African 98.7%, European 1.1%, other 0.2%.
Religions: Christian 50%–75%, Islam and Hindu 24%–49%, indigenous beliefs 1%. **Literacy rate:** 81% (2003 est.)
Economic summary: GDP/PPP (2004 est.): $9.409 billion; per capita $900. **Real growth rate:** 4.6%. **Inflation:** 18.3%. **Unemployment:** 50% (2000 est.). **Arable land:** 7%. **Agriculture:** corn, sorghum, rice, peanuts, sunflower seed, vegetables, flowers, tobacco, cotton, sugarcane, cassava (tapioca); cattle, goats, pigs, poultry, milk, eggs, hides; coffee. **Labor force:** 4.63 million; agriculture 85%, industry 6%, services 9%. **Industries:** copper mining and processing, construction, foodstuffs, beverages, chemicals, textiles, fertilizer, horticulture. **Natural resources:** copper, cobalt, zinc, lead, coal, emeralds, gold, silver, uranium, hydropower. **Exports:** $1.548 billion (f.o.b., 2004 est.): copper/cobalt 64%, cobalt, electricity, tobacco, flowers, cotton. **Imports:** $1.519 billion (f.o.b., 2004 est.): machinery, transportation equipment, petroleum products, electricity, fertilizer; foodstuffs, clothing. **Major trading partners:** UK, South Africa, Tanzania, Switzerland, Zimbabwe, UAE (2003). **International conflicts:** dormant dispute remains where Botswana, Namibia, Zambia, and Zimbabwe boundaries converge.

Geography Zambia, a landlocked country in south-central Africa, is about one-tenth larger than Texas. It is surrounded by Angola, Zaire, Tanzania, Malawi, Mozambique, Zimbabwe, Botswana, and Namibia. The country is mostly a plateau that rises to 8,000 ft (2,434 m) in the east.

Government Republic.

History Early humans inhabited present-day Zambia between one and two million years ago. Today the country is made up almost entirely of Bantu-speaking peoples. Empire builder Cecil Rhodes obtained mining concessions in 1889 from King Lewanika of the Barotse and sent settlers to the area soon thereafter. The region was ruled by the British South Africa Company, which Rhodes established, until 1924, when the British government took over the administration.

From 1953 to 1964, Northern Rhodesia was federated with Southern Rhodesia (now Zimbabwe) and Nyasaland (now Malawi) in the Federation of Rhodesia and Nyasaland. On Oct. 24, 1964, Northern Rhodesia became the independent nation of Zambia.

Kenneth Kaunda, the first president, kept Zambia within the Commonwealth of Nations. The country's economy, dependent on copper exports, was threatened when Rhodesia declared its independence from British rule in 1965 and defied UN sanctions, which Zambia supported, an action that deprived Zambia of its trade route through Rhodesia. The U.S., Britain, and Canada organized an airlift in 1966 to ship gasoline into Zambia.

In 1972 Kaunda outlawed all opposition political parties. The world copper market collapsed in 1975. The Zambian economy was devastated—it had been the third-largest miner of copper in the world after the United States and Soviet Union. With a soaring debt and inflation rate in 1991, riots took place in Lusaka, resulting in a number of killings. Mounting domestic pressure forced Kaunda to move Zambia toward multiparty democracy. National elections on Oct. 31, 1991, brought a stunning defeat to Kaunda. The new president, Frederick Chiluba, called for sweeping economic reforms, including privatization and the establishment of a stock market. He was reelected in Nov. 1996. Chiluba declared martial law in 1997 and arrested Kaunda following a failed coup attempt. The 1999 slump in world copper prices again depressed the economy because copper provides 80% of Zambia's export earnings.

In 2001 Chiluba contemplated changing the constitution to allow him to run for another presidential term. After protests he relented and selected Levy Mwanawasa, a former vice president with whom he had fallen out, as his successor. Mwanawasa became president in Jan. 2002; opposition parties protested over alleged fraud. In June 2002, Mwanawasa, once seen as a pawn of Chiluba, accused the former president of stealing millions from the government while in office. Chiluba was arrested and charged in Feb. 2003.

Although the country faced the threat of famine in 2002, the president refused to accept any international donations of food that had been genetically modified, which Mwanawasa considered "poison." In Aug. 2003, impeachment proceedings against the president for corruption were rejected by Parliament. In April 2005, the World Bank approved a $3.8 billion debt relief package for the country.

Zimbabwe

REPUBLIC OF ZIMBABWE

President: Robert Mugabe (1980)
Area: 150,803 sq mi (390,580 sq km)
Population (2005 est.): 12,746,990 (growth rate: 0.5%); birth rate: 29.7/1000; infant mortality rate: 67.7/1000; life expectancy: 36.7; density per sq mi: 85
Capital and largest city (2003 est.): Harare, 2,331,400 (metro. area), 1,919,700 (city proper). **Other large cities:** Bulawayo, 965,000; Chitungwiza, 411,700.
Monetary unit: Zimbabwean dollar. **Languages:** English (official), Shona, Ndebele (Sindebele), numerous minor tribal dialects. **Ethnicity/race:** African 98% (Shona 82%, Ndebele 14%, other 2%), mixed and Asian 1%, white less than 1%. **Religions:** syncretic (part Christian, part indigenous beliefs) 50%, Christian 25%, indigenous beliefs 24%, Muslim and other 1%. **Literacy rate:** 91% (2003 est.).
Economic summary: GDP/PPP (2004 est.): $24.37 billion; per capita $1,900. **Real growth rate:** –8.2%. **Inflation:** 133%. **Unemployment:** 70% (2002 est.). **Arable land:** 8%. **Agriculture:** corn, cotton, tobacco, wheat, coffee, sugarcane, peanuts; sheep, goats, pigs. **Labor force:** 4.23 million; agriculture 66%, services 24%, industry 10% (1996). **Industries:** mining (coal, gold, platinum, copper, nickel, tin, clay, numerous metallic and nonmetallic ores), steel, wood products, cement, chemicals, fertilizer, clothing and footwear, foodstuffs, beverages. **Natural resources:** coal, chromium ore, asbestos, gold, nickel, copper, iron ore, vanadium, lithium, tin, platinum group metals. **Exports:** $1.409 billion (f.o.b., 2004 est.): cotton, tobacco, gold, ferroalloys, textiles/clothing. **Imports:** $1.599 billion (f.o.b., 2004 est.): machinery and transport equipment, other manufactures, chemicals, fuels. **Major trading partners:** Zambia, South Africa, China, Germany, Japan, Democratic Republic of the Congo (2003). **International disputes:** dormant dispute remains where Botswana, Namibia, Zambia, and Zimbabwe boundaries converge.

Geography Zimbabwe, a landlocked country in south-central Africa, is slightly smaller than California. It is bordered by Botswana on the west, Zambia on the north, Mozambique on the east, and South Africa on the south.

Government Parliamentary democracy.

History The remains of early humans, dating back 500,000 years, have been discovered in present-day Zimbabwe. The land's earliest settlers, the Khoisan, date back to 200 B.C. After a period of Bantu domination, the Shona people ruled, followed by the Nguni and Zulu peoples. By the mid-19th century the descendants of the Nguni and Zulu, the Ndebele, had established a powerful warrior kingdom.

The first British explorers, colonists, and missionaries arrived in the 1850s, and the massive influx of foreigners led to the establishment of the territory Rhodesia, named after Cecil Rhodes of the British South Africa Company. In 1923, European settlers voted to become the self-governing British colony of Southern Rhodesia. After a brief federation with Northern Rhodesia (now Zambia) and Nyasaland (now Malawi) in the post–World War II period, Southern Rhodesia (also known as Rhodesia) chose to remain a colony when its two partners voted for independence in 1963.

On Nov. 11, 1965, the conservative white-minority government of Rhodesia declared its independence from Britain. The country resisted the demands of black Africans, and Prime Minister Ian Smith withstood British pressure, economic sanctions, and guerrilla attacks in his effort to uphold white supremacy. On March 1, 1970, Rhodesia formally proclaimed itself a republic. Heightened guerrilla war and a withdrawal of South African military aid in 1976 marked the beginning of the collapse of Smith's 11 years of resistance.

Black nationalist movements were led by Bishop Abel Muzorewa of the African National Congress and Ndabaningi Sithole, who were moderates, and guerrilla leaders Robert Mugabe of the Zimbabwe African National Union (ZANU) and Joshua Nkomo of the Zimbabwe African People's Union (ZAPU), who advocated revolution.

On March 3, 1978, Smith, Muzorewa, Sithole, and Chief Jeremiah Chirau signed an agreement to transfer power to the black majority by Dec. 31, 1978. They formed an Executive Council, with chairmanship rotating but with Smith retaining the title of prime minister. Blacks were named to each cabinet ministry, serving as coministers with the whites already holding these posts. African nations and rebel leaders immediately denounced the action, but Western governments were more reserved, although none granted recognition to the new regime.

The white minority finally consented to hold multiracial elections in 1980, and Robert Mugabe won a landslide victory. The country achieved independence on April 17, 1980, under the name Zimbabwe. Mugabe eventually established a one-party socialist state, but by 1990 he had instituted multiparty elections and in 1991 deleted all references to Marxism-Leninism and scientific socialism from the constitution. Parliamentary elections in April 1995 gave Mugabe's party a stunning victory with 63 of the 65 contested seats, and in 1996 Mugabe won another six-year term as president.

In 2000, veterans of Zimbabwe's war for independence in the 1970s began squatting on land owned by white farmers in an effort to reclaim land taken under British colonization—one-third of Zimbabwe's arable land was owned by 4,000 whites. In Aug. 2002, Mugabe ordered all white commercial farmers to leave their land without compensation. Mugabe's support for the squatters and his repressive rule has led to foreign sanctions against Zimbabwe. Once heralded as a champion of the anticolonial movement, Mugabe is now viewed by much of the international community as an authoritarian ruler responsible for egregious human rights abuses and for running the economy of his country into the ground.

In March 2002, Zimbabwe was suspended from the Commonwealth of Nations. That month Mugabe was reelected president for another six years in a blatantly rigged election whose results were enforced by the president's militia. In 2003, inflation hit 300%, the country faced severe food shortages, and the farming system had been destroyed. In 2004, the IMF estimated that the country had grown one-third poorer in the last five years.

Parliamentary elections in March 2005 were judged by international monitors to be egregiously flawed. In April, Zimbabwe was reelected to the UN Commission on Human Rights, outraging numerous countries and human rights groups. In mid-2005, Zimbabwe demolished its urban slums and shantytowns, leaving 700,000 people homeless.

United Nations

Preamble of the United Nations Charter

The Charter of the United Nations was adopted at the San Francisco Conference of 1945. The complete text is available on the UN website, www.un.org/aboutun/charter.

We the peoples of the United Nations determined to save succeeding generations from the scourge of war, which twice in our lifetime has brought untold sorrow to mankind, and

To reaffirm faith in fundamental human rights, in the dignity and worth of the human person, in the equal rights of men and women and of nations large and small, and

To establish conditions under which justice and respect for the obligations arising from treaties and other sources of international law can be maintained, and

To promote social progress and better standards of life in larger freedom, and for these ends

To practice tolerance and live together in peace with one another as good neighbors, and

To unite our strength to maintain international peace and security, and

To insure, by the acceptance of principles and the institution of methods, that armed force shall not be used, save in the common interest, and

To employ international machinery for the promotion of the economic and social advancement of all peoples, have resolved to combine our efforts to accomplish these aims.

Accordingly, our respective Governments, through representatives assembled in the city of San Francisco, who have exhibited their full powers found to be in good and due form, have agreed to the present Charter of the United Nations and do hereby establish an international organization to be known as the United Nations.

Principal Organs of the United Nations

Secretariat

This is the directorate on UN operations, apart from political decisions. The staff works under the secretary-general, whom it assists and advises.

Secretaries-General
Kofi Annan, Ghana, Jan. 1, 1997
Boutros Boutros-Ghali, Egypt, 1992–1996
Javier Pérez de Cuéllar, Peru, 1982–1991
Kurt Waldheim, Austria, 1972–1981
U Thant, Burma (Myanmar), 1961–1971
Dag Hammarskjöld, Sweden, 1953–1961
Trygve Lie, Norway, 1946–1953

General Assembly

The General Assembly is the world's forum for discussing matters affecting world peace and security, and for making recommendations concerning them. It has no power to enforce decisions. It is composed of the 51 original member nations and those admitted since, totaling 191. On important questions, including international peace and security, a two-thirds majority of those present and voting is required. Decisions on other questions are made by a simple majority. Emphasis is given to questions relating to international peace and security brought before it by members, the Security Council, or nonmembers. It also maintains a broad program of international cooperation in economic, social, cultural, educational, and health fields, and for assisting in human rights and freedoms.

International Court of Justice

The International Court of Justice is the UN's principal judicial organ. Based in The Hague, Netherlands, the Court pursues two primary objectives:

(1) settling legal disputes submitted by states in accordance with international law, and (2) advising on legal questions brought by authorized international organs and agencies. The Court consists of 15 judges elected to 9-year terms by the United Nations General Assembly and the Security Council during independent sittings.

Security Council

The Security Council is the primary instrument for establishing and maintaining international peace. Its main purpose is to prevent war by settling disputes between nations. Under the charter, the council is permitted to dispatch a UN force to stop aggression. All member nations undertake to make available armed forces, assistance, and facilities to maintain international peace and security (*see* p. 908 for list of UN Peacekeeping Operations).

The Security Council has 15 members. There are five permanent members: the United States, the Russian Federation, Britain, France, and China; and ten temporary members elected by the General Assembly for two-year terms, from five different regions of the world. Voting on procedural matters requires a nine-vote majority to carry. However, on questions of substance, the vote of each of the five permanent members is required. As of Jan. 2005, the ten elected nonpermanent members were Algeria, Argentina, Benin, Brazil, Denmark, Greece, Japan, the Philippines, Romania, and Tanzania. In Jan. 2006 the terms of Algeria, Benin, Brazil, the Philippines, and Romania will expire.

Economic and Social Council

This council is composed of 54 members elected by the General Assembly to three-year terms. It works under the authority of the General Assembly and seeks to promote progress in terms of higher standards of living, full employment, and economic and social viability; it also seeks solutions to international socioeconomic, health, and other problems through international and cultural cooperation. Finally, it advocates for the universal respect for and observance of human rights and fundamental freedoms for all.

Trusteeship Council

The UN charter originally established the Trusteeship Council as a main organ of the UN and entrusted it with the administration of territories placed under the trusteeship system.

The Trusteeship Council suspended operations on Nov. 1, 1994, after the October independence of Palau, the last UN territory.

UN Peacekeeping Missions

Since 1948 there have been 60 UN peacekeeping operations, of which 47 have been created by the United Nations Security Council since 1988. Close to 130 nations have contributed personnel at various times, and 105 are currently providing peacekeepers. As of May 31, 2005, there were 16 peacekeeping operations underway with a total of 66,058 personnel, and the top contributors of military and civilian personnel to current missions were Pakistan (9,880), Bangladesh (7,932), India (6,001), and Nepal (3,562).

Current UN Peacekeeping Operations

Region/Country	Began	Region/Country	Began
AFRICA		**ASIA**	
Western Sahara	April 1991	India/Pakistan	Jan. 1949
Sierra Leone	Oct. 1999	**EUROPE**	
Democratic Republic	Nov. 1999	Cyprus	March 1964
of the Congo		Georgia	Aug. 1993
Ethiopia and Eritrea	July 2000	Kosovo	June 1999
Côte d'Ivoire	May 2003	**MIDDLE EAST**	
Liberia	Oct. 2003	Middle East	May 1948
Burundi	May 2004	Golan Heights	June 1974
Sudan	March 2005	Lebanon	March 1978
AMERICA			
Haiti	April 2004		

Completed UN Peacekeeping Operations

Region/Country	Duration	Region/Country	Duration
AFRICA		**AMERICAS**	
Congo	July 1960–June 1964	Dominican Republic	May 1965–Oct. 1966
Angola	Dec. 1988–May 1991	Central America	Nov. 1989–Jan. 1992
Namibia	April 1989–March 1990	Observer Group	
Angola	May 1991–Feb. 1995	El Salvador	July 1991–April 1995
Somalia	April 1992–March 1993	Haiti	Sept. 1993–June 1996
Mozambique	Dec. 1992–Dec. 1994	Haiti	July 1996–July 1997
Somalia	March 1993–March 1995	Guatemala	Jan.–May 1997
Rwanda/Uganda	June 1993–Sept. 1994	Haiti	Aug.–Nov. 1997
Liberia	Sept. 1993–Sept. 1997	Haiti	Dec. 1997–March 2000
Rwanda	Oct. 1993–March 1996	**ASIA**	
Chad/Libya	May–June 1994	West New Guinea	Oct. 1962–April 1963
Angola	Feb. 1995–June 1997	India/Pakistan	Sept. 1965–March 1966
Angola	June 1997–Feb. 1999	Afghanistan/Pakistan	May 1988–March 1990
Sierra Leone	July 1998–Oct. 1999	Cambodia	Oct. 1991–March 1992
Central African Republic	April 1998–Feb. 2000	Cambodia	March 1992–Sept. 1993
MIDEAST		Tajikistan	Dec. 1994–May 2000
Middle East—1st UN	Nov. 1956–June 1967	East Timor	Oct. 1999–May 2002
Emergency Force		East Timor	May 2002–May 2005
Lebanon	June–Dec. 1958	**EUROPE**	
Yemen	July 1963–Sept. 1964	Former Yugoslavia	Feb. 1992–March 1995
Middle East—2nd UN	Oct. 1973–July 1979	Croatia	March 1995–Jan. 1996
Emergency Force		Former Yugoslavia	March 1995–Feb. 1999
Iran/Iraq	Aug. 1988–Feb. 1991	Rep. of Macedonia	
Iraq/Kuwait	April 1991–Oct. 2003	Bosnia & Herzegovina	Dec. 1995–Dec. 2002
		Croatia	Jan. 1996–Jan. 1998
		Prevlaka Peninsula	Feb. 1996–Dec. 2002
		Croatia	Jan. 1998–Oct. 1998

Source: United Nations Dept. of Public Information.

Members of the United Nations (191 nations)

Country	Joined UN[1]	Country	Joined UN[1]	Country	Joined UN[1]
Afghanistan	1946	Georgia	1992	Norway	1945
Albania	1955	Germany	1973	Oman	1971
Algeria	1962	Ghana	1957	Pakistan	1947
Andorra	1993	Greece	1945	Palau	1994
Angola	1976	Grenada	1974	Panama	1945
Antigua and Barbuda	1981	Guatemala	1945	Papua New Guinea	1975
Argentina	1945	Guinea	1958	Paraguay	1945
Armenia	1992	Guinea-Bissau	1974	Peru	1945
Australia	1945	Guyana	1966	Philippines	1945
Austria	1955	Haiti	1945	Poland	1945
Azerbaijan	1992	Honduras	1945	Portugal	1955
Bahamas	1973	Hungary	1955	Qatar	1971
Bahrain	1971	Iceland	1946	Romania	1955
Bangladesh	1974	India	1945	Russian Federation	1945
Barbados	1966	Indonesia	1950	Rwanda	1962
Belarus	1945	Iran	1945	St. Kitts and Nevis	1983
Belgium	1945	Iraq	1945	St. Lucia	1979
Belize	1981	Ireland	1955	St. Vincent and the	
Benin	1960	Israel	1949	Grenadines	1980
Bhutan	1971	Italy	1955	Samoa, Western	1976
Bolivia	1945	Jamaica	1962	San Marino	1992
Bosnia and Herzegovina	1992	Japan	1956	São Tomé and Príncipe	1975
Botswana	1966	Jordan	1955	Saudi Arabia	1945
Brazil	1945	Kazakhstan	1992	Senegal	1960
Brunei Darussalam	1984	Kenya	1963	Serbia and Montenegro[6]	2000
Bulgaria	1955	Kiribati	1999	Seychelles	1976
Burkina Faso	1960	North Korea	1991	Sierra Leone	1961
Burma (Myanmar)	1948	South Korea	1991	Singapore	1965
Burundi	1962	Kuwait	1963	Slovakia[3]	1993
Cambodia	1955	Kyrgyzstan	1992	Slovenia	1992
Cameroon	1960	Laos	1955	Solomon Islands	1978
Canada	1945	Latvia	1991	Somalia	1960
Cape Verde	1975	Lebanon	1945	South Africa	1945
Central African Republic	1960	Lesotho	1966	Spain	1955
Chad	1960	Liberia	1945	Sri Lanka	1955
Chile	1945	Libya	1955	Sudan	1956
China[2]	1945	Liechtenstein	1990	Suriname	1975
Colombia	1945	Lithuania	1991	Swaziland	1968
Comoros	1975	Luxembourg	1945	Sweden	1946
Congo	1960	Macedonia[5]	1993	Switzerland[4]	2002
Congo, Dem. Rep.	1960	Madagascar	1960	Syria	1945
Costa Rica	1945	Malawi	1964	Tajikistan	1992
Côte d'Ivoire	1960	Malaysia	1957	Tanzania	1961
Croatia	1992	Maldives	1965	Thailand	1946
Cuba	1945	Mali	1960	Togo	1960
Cyprus	1960	Malta	1964	Tonga	1999
Czech Republic[3]	1993	Marshall Islands	1991	Trinidad and Tobago	1962
Denmark	1945	Mauritania	1961	Tunisia	1956
Djibouti	1977	Mauritius	1968	Turkey	1945
Dominica	1978	Mexico	1945	Turkmenistan	1992
Dominican Republic	1945	Micronesia	1991	Tuvalu	2000
East Timor[4]	2002	Moldova	1992	Uganda	1962
Ecuador	1945	Monaco	1993	Ukraine	1945
Egypt	1945	Mongolia	1961	United Arab Emirates	1971
El Salvador	1945	Morocco	1956	United Kingdom	1945
Equatorial Guinea	1968	Mozambique	1975	United States	1945
Eritrea	1993	Namibia	1990	Uruguay	1945
Estonia	1991	Nauru	1999	Uzbekistan	1992
Ethiopia	1945	Nepal	1955	Vanuatu	1981
Fiji	1970	Netherlands	1945	Venezuela	1945
Finland	1955	New Zealand	1945	Vietnam	1977
France	1945	Nicaragua	1945	Yemen, Republic of	1947
Gabon	1960	Niger	1960	Zambia	1964
Gambia	1965	Nigeria	1960	Zimbabwe	1980

1. The UN officially came into existence on Oct. 24, 1945. 2. On Oct. 25, 1971, the UN voted membership to the People's Republic of China, which replaced the Republic of China (Taiwan) in the world body. 3. Czechoslovakia was an original member of the United Nations from Oct. 24, 1945. As of Dec. 31, 1992, it ceased to exist and the Czech Republic and Slovakia as successor states were admitted Jan. 19, 1993. 4. Newest members. 5. The General Assembly on April 8, 1993, decided to admit the state provisionally being referred to as "The Former Yugoslav Republic of Macedonia" pending settlement of the difference that has arisen over its name. 6. The Socialist Federal Republic of Yugoslavia was a charter member; after its dissolution, the Federal Republic of Yugoslavia was admitted Nov. 1, 2000. On Feb. 4, 2003, the name of the Federal Republic of Yugoslavia was changed to Serbia and Montenegro.

U.S. Representatives to the United Nations

Year	Ambassador	Year	Ambassador
1946	Edward R. Stettinius, Jr.	1977–1979	Andrew Young
1946–1947	Herschel V. Johnson (acting)	1979–1981	Donald McHenry
1947–1953	Warren R. Austin	1981–1985	Jeane J. Kirkpatrick
1953–1960	Henry Cabot Lodge, Jr.	1985–1989	Vernon A. Walters
1960–1961	James J. Wadsworth	1989–1992	Thomas J. Pickering
1961–1965	Adlai E. Stevenson	1992–1993	Edward J. Perkins
1965–1968	Arthur J. Goldberg	1993–1996	Madeleine K. Albright
1968	George W. Ball	1997–1998	Bill Richardson
1968–1969	James Russell Wiggins	1998–1999	A. Peter Burleigh (acting)
1969–1971	Charles W. Yost	1999–2001	Richard Holbrooke
1971–1973	George H. W. Bush	2001	James B. Cunningham (acting)
1973–1975	John A. Scali	2001–2004	John D. Negroponte
1975–1976	Daniel P. Moynihan	2004–2005	John Danforth
1976–1977	William W. Scranton	2005–	John Bolton

Selected International Organizations

Arab League (AL)
Members: (21 plus the Palestine Liberation Organization) Algeria, Bahrain, Comoros, Djibouti, Egypt, Iraq, Jordan, Kuwait, Lebanon, Libya, Mauritania, Morocco, Oman, Qatar, Saudi Arabia, Somalia, Sudan, Syria, Tunisia, UAE, Yemen, Palestine Liberation Organization

Association of Southeast Asian Nations (ASEAN)
Members: (10) Brunei, Cambodia, Indonesia, Laos, Malaysia, Myanmar (Burma), Philippines, Singapore, Thailand, Vietnam
Associate Member: (1) Papua New Guinea

Group of 8 (G-8)
Members: (9) Canada, EU (as one member), France, Germany, Italy, Japan, Russia, UK, U.S.

Commonwealth of Nations
Members: (54) Antigua and Barbuda, Australia, the Bahamas, Bangladesh, Barbados, Belize, Botswana, Brunei, Cameroon, Canada, Cyprus, Dominica, Fiji, the Gambia, Ghana, Grenada, Guyana, India, Jamaica, Kenya, Kiribati, Lesotho, Malawi, Malaysia, Maldives, Malta, Mauritius, Mozambique, Namibia, Nauru, New Zealand, Nigeria, Pakistan, Papua New Guinea, Saint Kitts and Nevis, Saint Lucia, Saint Vincent and the Grenadines, Samoa, Seychelles, Sierra Leone, Singapore, Solomon Islands, South Africa, Sri Lanka, Swaziland, Tanzania, Tonga, Trinidad and Tobago, Tuvalu, Uganda, UK, Vanuatu, Zambia, Zimbabwe (suspended)

Commonwealth of Independent States (CIS)
Members: (12) Armenia, Azerbaijan, Belarus, Georgia, Kazakhstan, Kyrgyzstan, Moldova, Russia, Tajikistan, Turkmenistan, Ukraine, Uzbekistan

European Union (EU)
Members: (25) Austria, Belgium, Denmark, Finland, France, Germany, Greece, Ireland, Italy, Luxembourg, Netherlands, Portugal, Spain, Sweden, UK. **New Members in 2004:** Cyprus, Czech Republic, Estonia, Hungary, Latvia, Lithuania, Malta, Poland, Slovakia, Slovenia

North Atlantic Treaty Organization (NATO)
Members: (26) Belgium, Canada, Czech Republic, Denmark, France, Germany, Greece, Hungary, Iceland, Italy, Luxembourg, Netherlands, Norway, Poland, Portugal, Spain, Turkey, UK, U.S. **New members in 2004:** Bulgaria, Estonia, Latvia, Lithuania, Romania, Slovakia, Slovenia

African Union (AU)[1]
Members: (53) Algeria, Angola, Benin, Botswana, Burkina Faso, Burundi, Cameroon, Cape Verde, Central African Republic, Chad, Comoros, Congo, Côte d'Ivoire, Democratic Republic of the Congo, Djibouti, Egypt, Equatorial Guinea, Eritrea, Ethiopia, Gabon, The Gambia, Ghana, Guinea, Guinea-Bissau, Kenya, Lesotho, Liberia, Libya, Madagascar, Malawi, Mali, Mauritania, Mauritius, Mozambique, Namibia, Niger, Nigeria, Rwanda, São Tomé and Principe, Senegal, Seychelles, Sierra Leone, Somalia, South Africa, Sudan, Swaziland, Tanzania, Togo, Tunisia, Uganda, Western Sahara, Zambia, Zimbabwe

Organization of Petroleum Exporting Countries (OPEC)
Members: (11) Algeria, Indonesia, Iran, Iraq, Kuwait, Libya, Nigeria, Qatar, Saudi Arabia, UAE, Venezuela

1. The Organization of African Unity (OAU), the African Union's predecessor, was formally disbanded on July 8, 2002. The AU was inaugurated July 9, 2002. The 53 member nations remain the same.

Foreign Embassies in the United States

Source: U.S. Department of State.

Embassy of Afghanistan, 2341 Wyoming Ave., N.W.,Washington, D.C. 20008. Phone: 202-483-6410.

Embassy of the Republic of Albania, 2100 S St., N.W., Washington, D.C. 20008. Phone: 202-223-4942.

Embassy of the Democratic & Popular Republic of Algeria, 2118 Kalorama Rd., N.W., Washington, D.C. 20008. Phone: 202-265-2800.

Embassy of Andorra/Permanent Mission to the UN, 2 United Nations Plaza, 25th flr., New York, N.Y. 10017. Phone: 212-750-8064.

Embassy of the Republic of Angola, 2100–2108 16th St., N.W., Washington, D.C. 20009. Phone: 202-785-1156.

Embassy of Antigua & Barbuda, 3216 New Mexico Ave., N.W., Washington, D.C. 20016. Phone: 202-362-5122.

Embassy of the Argentine Republic, 1600 New Hampshire Ave., N.W., Washington, D.C. 20009. Phone: 202-238-6401.

Embassy of the Republic of Armenia, 2225 R Street, N.W., Washington, D.C. 20008. Phone: 202-319-1976.

Embassy of Australia, 1601 Massachusetts Ave., N.W., Washington, D.C. 20036. Phone: 202-797-3000.

Embassy of Austria, 3524 International Court, N.W., Washington, D.C. 20008-3027. Phone: 202-895-6700.

Embassy of the Republic of Azerbaijan, 2741 34th St., N.W., Washington, D.C. 20008. Phone: 202-337-3500.

Embassy of the Commonwealth of the Bahamas, 2220 Massachusetts Ave., N.W., Washington, D.C. 20008. Phone: 202-319-2660.

Embassy of the Kingdom of Bahrain, 3502 International Dr., N.W., Washington, D.C. 20008. Phone: 202-342-1111.

Embassy of the People's Republic of Bangladesh, 3510 International Drive, N.W., Washington, D.C. 20008. Phone: 202-244-0183.

Embassy of Barbados, 2144 Wyoming Ave., N.W., Washington, D.C. 20008. Phone: 202-939-9200.

Embassy of the Republic of Belarus, 1619 New Hampshire Ave., N.W., Washington, D.C. 20009. Phone: 202-986-1604.

Embassy of Belgium, 3330 Garfield St., N.W., Washington, D.C. 20008. Phone: 202-333-6900.

Embassy of Belize, 2535 Massachusetts Ave., N.W., Washington, D.C. 20008. Phone: 202-332-9636.

Embassy of the Republic of Benin, 2124 Kalorama Road, N.W., Washington, D.C. 20008. Phone: 202-232-6656.

Bhutan Permanent Mission to the UN, 2 UN Plaza, 27th Floor, New York NY 10017. Phone: 212-826-1919.

Embassy of Bolivia, 3014 Massachusetts Ave., N.W., Washington, D.C. 20008. Phone: 202-483-4410.

Embassy of Bosnia and Herzegovina, 2109 E St. N.W., Washington, D.C. 20037. Phone: 202-337-1500.

Embassy of Botswana, 1531-1533 New Hampshire Ave., N.W., Washington, D.C. 20036. Phone: 202-244-4990.

Brazilian Embassy, 3006 Massachusetts Ave., N.W., Washington, D.C. 20008. Phone: 202-238-2700.

Embassy of Brunei Darussalam, 3520 International Court, N.W., Washington, D.C. 20008. Phone: 202-237-1838.

Embassy of the Republic of Bulgaria, 1621 22nd St., N.W., Washington, D.C. 20008. Phone: 202-387-0174.

Embassy of Burkina Faso, 2340 Massachusetts Ave., N.W., Washington, D.C. 20008. Phone: 202-332-5577.

Embassy of the Republic of Burundi, 2233 Wisconsin Ave., N.W., Suite 212, Washington, D.C. 20007. Phone: 202-342-2574.

Embassy of the Kingdom of Cambodia, 4530 16th St., N.W., Washington, D.C. 20011. Phone: 202-726-7742.

Embassy of the Republic of Cameroon, 2349 Massachusetts Ave., N.W., Washington, D.C. 20008. Phone: 202-265-8790.

Embassy of Canada, 501 Pennsylvania Ave., N.W., Washington, D.C. 20001. Phone: 202-682-1740.

Embassy of the Republic of Cape Verde, 3415 Massachusetts Ave., N.W., Washington, D.C. 20007. Phone: 202-965-6820.

Embassy of Central African Republic, 1618 22nd St. N.W., Washington, D.C. 20008. Phone: 202-483-7800.

Embassy of the Republic of Chad, 2002 R St., N.W., Washington, D.C. 20009. Phone: 202-462-4009.

Embassy of Chile, 1732 Massachusetts Ave., N.W., Washington, D.C. 20036. Phone: 202-785-1746.

Embassy of the People's Republic of China, 2300 Connecticut Ave., N.W., Washington, D.C. 20008. Phone: 202-328-2500.

Embassy of Colombia, 2118 Leroy Pl., N.W., Washington, D.C. 20008. Phone: 202-387-8338.

Embassy of the Federal and Islamic Republic of Comoros, c/o Permanent Mission of the Federal and Islamic Republic of Comoros to the United Nations, 420 E. 50th St., New York, N.Y. 10022. Phone: 212-972-8010.

Embassy of the Democratic Republic of Congo, 1800 New Hampshire Ave., N.W., Washington, D.C. 20009. Phone: 202-234-7690.

Embassy of the Republic of Congo, 4891 Colorado Ave., N.W., Washington, D.C. 20011. Phone: 202-726-5500.

Embassy of Costa Rica, 2114 S St., N.W., Washington, D.C. 20008. Phone: 202-234-2945.

Embassy of the Republic of Côte d'Ivoire, 2424 Massachusetts Ave., N.W., Washington, D.C. 20007. Phone: 202-797-0300.

Embassy of the Republic of Croatia, 2343 Massachusetts Ave., N.W., Washington, D.C. 20008-2853. Phone: 202-588-5899.

Cuban Interests Section, 2630 16th St., N.W., Washington, D.C. 20009. Phone: 202-797-8518.

Embassy of the Republic of Cyprus, 2211 R St. N.W., Washington, D.C. 20008. Phone: 202-462-5772.

Embassy of the Czech Republic, 3900 Spring of Freedom St., N.W., Washington, D.C. 20008. Phone: 202-274-9100.

Royal Danish Embassy, 3200 Whitehaven St., N.W., Washington, D.C. 20008. Phone: 202-234-4300.

Embassy of the Republic of Djibouti, 1156 15th St., N.W., Suite 515, Washington, D.C. 20005. Phone: 202-331-0270.

Embassy of the Commonwealth of Dominica, 3216 New Mexico Ave., N.W., Washington, D.C. 20016. Phone: 202-364-6781.

Embassy of the Dominican Republic, 1715 22nd St., N.W., Washington, D.C. 20008. Phone: 202-332-6280.

Embassy of Ecuador, 2535 15th St., N.W., Washington, D.C. 20009. Phone: 202-234-7200.

Embassy of the Arab Republic of Egypt, 3521 International Court, N.W., Washington, D.C. 20008. Phone: 202-895-5463.

Embassy of El Salvador, 2308 California St., N.W., Washington, D.C. 20008. Phone: 202-265-9671.

Embassy of Equatorial Guinea, 2020 16th Street, N.W., Washington, D.C. 20009. Phone: 202-518-5700.

Embassy of the State of Eritrea, 1708 New Hampshire Ave., N.W., Washington, D.C., 20009. Phone: 202-319-1991.

Embassy of Estonia, 2131 Massachusetts Ave., N.W., Washington, D.C. 20008. Phone: 202-588-0101.

Embassy of Ethiopia, 3506 International Dr., N.W., Washington, D.C. 20008. Phone: 202-364-1200.

European Union Delegation, 2300 M St., N.W., Washington, D.C. 20037. Phone: 202-862-9500.

Embassy of Fiji, 2233 Wisconsin Ave., N.W., Suite 240, Washington, D.C. 20007. Phone: 202-337-8320.

Embassy of Finland, 3301 Massachusetts Ave., N.W., Washington, D.C. 20008. Phone: 202-298-5800.

Embassy of France, 4101 Reservoir Rd., N.W., Washington, D.C. 20007. Phone: 202-944-6000.

Embassy of the Gabonese Republic, 2034 20th St., N.W., Suite 200, Washington, D.C. 20009. Phone: 202-797-1000.

Embassy of the Republic of the Gambia, 1156 15th St., N.W., Suite 905, Washington, D.C. 20005. Phone: 202-785-1399.

Embassy of the Republic of Georgia, 1101 15th St., N.W., Suite 602, Washington, D.C. 20005. Phone: 202-387-2390.

Embassy of Germany, 4645 Reservoir Rd., N.W., Washington, D.C. 20007-1998. Phone: 202-298-4000.

Embassy of Ghana, 3512 International Dr., N.W., Washington, D.C. 20008. Phone: 202-686-4520.

Embassy of Greece, 2211 Massachusetts Ave., N.W., Washington, D.C. 20008. Phone: 202-939-1306.

Embassy of Grenada, 1701 New Hampshire Ave., N.W., Washington, D.C. 20009. Phone: 202-265-2561.

Embassy of Guatemala, 2220 R St., N.W., Washington, D.C. 20008. Phone: 202-745-4952.

Embassy of the Republic of Guinea, 2112 Leroy Pl., N.W., Washington, D.C. 20008. Phone: 202-986-4300.

Embassy of the Republic of Guinea-Bissau, 15929 Yukon Lane, Rockville, MD 20855. Phone: 301-947-3958.

Embassy of Guyana, 2490 Tracy Pl., N.W., Washington, D.C. 20008. Phone: 202-265-6900.

Embassy of the Republic of Haiti, 2311 Massachusetts Ave., N.W., Washington, D.C. 20008. Phone: 202-332-4090.

Apostolic Nunciature of the Holy See, 3339 Massachusetts Ave., N.W., Washington, D.C. 20008. Phone: 202-333-7121.

Embassy of Honduras, 3007 Tilden St., N.W., Suite 4M, Washington, D.C. 20008. Phone: 202-966-7702.

Embassy of the Republic of Hungary, 3910 Shoemaker St., N.W., Washington, D.C. 20008. Phone: 202-362-6730.

Embassy of Iceland, 1156 15th St., N.W., Suite 1200, Washington, D.C. 20005-1704. Phone: 202-265-6653.

Embassy of India, 2107 Massachusetts Ave., N.W., Washington, D.C. 20008. Phone: 202-939-7000.

Embassy of the Republic of Indonesia, 2020 Massachusetts Ave., N.W., Washington, D.C. 20036. Phone: 202-775-5200.

Iranian Interests Section, 2209 Wisconsin Ave., N.W., Washington, D.C. 20007. Phone: 202-965-4990.

Embassy of the Republic of Iraq, 1801 P St., N.W., Washington, D.C. 20036. Phone: 202-483-7500.

Embassy of Ireland, 2234 Massachusetts Ave., N.W., Washington, D.C. 20008. Phone: 202-462-3939.

Embassy of Israel, 3514 International Dr., N.W., Washington, D.C. 20008. Phone: 202-364-5500.

Embassy of Italy, 3000 Whitehaven St., N.W., Washington, D.C. 20008. Phone: 202-612-4400.

Embassy of Jamaica, 1520 New Hampshire Ave., N.W., Washington, D.C. 20036. Phone: 202-452-0660.

Embassy of Japan, 2520 Massachusetts Ave., N.W., Washington, D.C. 20008. Phone: 202-238-6700.

Embassy of the Hashemite Kingdom of Jordan, 3504 International Dr., N.W., Washington, D.C. 20008. Phone: 202-966-2664.

Embassy of the Republic of Kazakhstan, 1401 16th St., N.W., Washington, D.C. 20036. Phone: 202-232-5488.

Embassy of the Republic of Kenya, 2249 R St., N.W., Washington, D.C. 20008. Phone: 202-387-6101.

Embassy of the Republic of Korea, 2450 Massachusetts Ave., N.W., Washington, D.C. 20008. Phone: 202-939-5600.

Kuwait Information Office, 2600 Virginia Ave., N.W., Suite 404, Washington, D.C. 20037. Phone: 202-338-0211.

Embassy of the Kyrgyz Republic, 1732 Wisconsin Ave., Washington, D.C. 20007. Phone: 202-338-5141.

Embassy of the Lao People's Democratic Republic, 2222 S St., N.W., Washington, D.C. 20008. Phone: 202-332-6416.

Embassy of Latvia, 4325 17th St., N.W., Washington, D.C. 20011. Phone: 202-726-8213.

Embassy of Lebanon, 2560 28th St., N.W., Washington, D.C. 20008. Phone: 202-939-6300.

Embassy of the Kingdom of Lesotho, 2511 Massachusetts Ave., N.W., Washington, D.C. 20008. Phone: 202-797-5533.

Embassy of the Republic of Liberia, 5201 16th St., N.W., Washington, D.C. 20011. Phone: 202-723-0437.

Embassy of the Republic of Lithuania, 2622 16th St., N.W., Washington, D.C. 20009. Phone: 202-234-5860.

Embassy of the Grand Duchy of Luxembourg, 2200 Massachusetts Ave., N.W., Washington, D.C. 20008. Phone: 202-265-4171.

Embassy of the Republic of Macedonia, 1101 30th St., N.W., Suite 302, Washington, D.C. 20007. Phone: 202-337-3063.

Embassy of the Republic of Madagascar, 2374 Massachusetts Ave., N.W., Washington, D.C. 20008. Phone: 202-265-5525.

Embassy of Malawi, 1156 15th St., N.W., Suite 320, Washington, D.C. 20005. Phone: 202-721-0270.

Embassy of Malaysia, 3516 International Ct., N.W., Washington, D.C. 20008. Phone: 202-572-9700.

Embassy of the Republic of Mali, 2130 R St., N.W., Washington, D.C. 20008. Phone: 202-332-2249.

Embassy of Malta, 2017 Connecticut Ave., N.W., Washington, D.C. 20008. Phone: 202-462-3611.

Embassy of the Republic of the Marshall Islands, 2433 Massachusetts Ave., N.W., Washington, D.C. 20008. Phone: 202-234-5414.

Embassy of the Islamic Republic of Mauritania, 2129 Leroy Pl., N.W., Washington, D.C. 20008. Phone: 202-232-5700.

Embassy of the Republic of Mauritius, 4301 Connecticut Ave., N.W., Suite 441, Washington, D.C. 20008. Phone: 202-244-1491.

Embassy of Mexico, 1911 Pennsylvania Ave., N.W., Washington, D.C. 20006. Phone: 202-728-1600.

Embassy of the Federated States of Micronesia, 1725 N St., N.W., Washington, D.C. 20036. Phone: 202-223-4383.

Embassy of the Republic of Moldova, 2101 S St., N.W., Washington, D.C. 20008. Phone: 202-667-1130

Embassy of Mongolia, 2833 M St., N.W., Washington, D.C. 20007. Phone: 202-333-7117.

Embassy of the Kingdom of Morocco, 1601 21st St., N.W., Washington, D.C. 20009. Phone: 202-462-7979.

Embassy of the Republic of Mozambique, 1990 M St., N.W., Suite 570, Washington, D.C. 20036. Phone: 202-293-7146.

Embassy of the Union of Myanmar (Burma), 2300 S St., N.W., Washington, D.C. 20008. Phone: 202-332-4350.

Embassy of the Republic of Namibia, 1605 New Hampshire Ave., N.W., Washington, D.C. 20009. Phone: 202-986-0540.

Embassy of Nepal, 2131 Leroy Pl., N.W., Washington, D.C. 20008. Phone: 202-667-4550.

Embassy of the Netherlands, 4200 Linnean Ave., N.W., Washington, D.C. 20008. Phone: 202-244-5300.

Embassy of New Zealand, 37 Observatory Circle, N.W., Washington, D.C. 20008. Phone: 202-328-4800.

Embassy of Nicaragua, 1627 New Hampshire Ave., N.W., Washington, D.C. 20009. Phone: 202-939-6570.

Embassy of the Republic of Niger, 2204 R St., N.W., Washington, D.C. 20008. Phone: 202-483-4224.

Embassy of the Federal Republic of Nigeria, 3519 International Ct., N.W., Washington, D.C. 20008. Phone: 202-986-8400.

Royal Embassy of Norway, 2720 34th St., N.W., Washington, D.C. 20008. Phone: 202-333-6000.

Embassy of the Sultanate of Oman, 2535 Belmont Rd., N.W., Washington, D.C. 20008. Phone: 202-387-1980.

Embassy of the Islamic Republic of Pakistan, 3517 International Ct., N.W., Washington, D.C. 20008. Phone: 202-243-6500.

Embassy of the Republic of Palau, 1700 Pennsylvania Ave., N.W., Suite 400, Washington, D.C. 20006. Phone: 202-452-6814.

Embassy of the Republic of Panama, 2862 McGill Terrace, N.W., Washington, D.C. 20008. Phone: 202-483-1407.

Embassy of Papua New Guinea, 1779 Massachusetts Ave., N.W., Suite 805, Washington, D.C. 20036. Phone: 202-745-3680.

Embassy of Paraguay, 2400 Massachusetts Ave., N.W., Washington, D.C. 20008. Phone: 202-483-6960.

Embassy of Peru, 1700 Massachusetts Ave., N.W., Washington, D.C. 20036. Phone: 202-833-9860.

Embassy of the Philippines, 1600 Massachusetts Ave., N.W., Washington, D.C. 20036. Phone: 202-467-9300.

Embassy of the Republic of Poland, 2640 16th St., N.W., Washington, D.C. 20009. Phone: 202-234-3800.

Embassy of Portugal, 2125 Kalorama Rd., N.W., Washington, D.C. 20008. Phone: 202-328-8610.

Embassy of the State of Qatar, 2555 M St., N.W., Washington, D.C. 20037. Phone: 202-274-1603.

Embassy of Romania, 1607 23rd St., N.W., Washington, D.C. 20008. Phone: 202-332-2879.

Embassy of the Russian Federation, 2650 Wisconsin Ave., N.W., Washington, D.C. 20007. Phone: 202-298-5700.

Embassy of the Republic of Rwanda, 1714 New Hampshire Ave., N.W., Washington, D.C. 20009. Phone: 202-232-2882.

Embassy of Saint Kitts and Nevis, 3216 New Mexico Ave., N.W., Washington, D.C. 20016. Phone: 202-686-2636.

Embassy of Saint Lucia, 3216 New Mexico Ave., N.W., Washington, D.C. 20016. Phone: 202-364-6792.

Embassy of Saint Vincent and the Grenadines, 3216 New Mexico Ave., N.W., Washington, D.C. 20016. Phone: 202-364-6730.

Royal Embassy of Saudi Arabia, 601 New Hampshire Ave., N.W., Washington, D.C. 20037. Phone: 202-337-4076.

Embassy of the Republic of Senegal, 2112 Wyoming Ave., N.W., Washington, D.C. 20008. Phone: 202-234-0540.

Embassy of Serbia and Montenegro, 2134 Kalorama Rd., N.W., Washington, D.C. 20008. Phone: 202-332-0333.

Permanent Mission of Seychelles to the United Nations, 800 Second Ave., Suite 400C, New York, N.Y. 10017. Phone: 212-972-1785.

Embassy of Sierra Leone, 1701 19th St., N.W., Washington, D.C. 20009. Phone: 202-939-9261.

Embassy of the Republic of Singapore, 3501 International Pl., N.W., Washington, D.C. 20008. Phone: 202-537-3100.

Embassy of the Slovak Republic, 3523 International Ct., N.W., Washington, D.C. 20008. Phone: 202-237-1054.

Embassy of the Republic of Slovenia, 1525 New Hampshire Ave., N.W., Washington, D.C. 20036. Phone: 202-667-5363.

Embassy of the Republic of South Africa, 3051 Massachusetts Ave., N.W., Washington, D.C. 20008.

Phone: 202-232-4400.

Embassy of Spain, 2375 Pennsylvania Ave., N.W., Washington, D.C. 20037. Phone: 202-728-2330.

Embassy of Sri Lanka, 2148 Wyoming Ave., N.W., Washington, D.C. 20008. Phone: 202-483-4025.

Embassy of the Republic of the Sudan, 2210 Massachusetts Ave., N.W., Washington, D.C. 20008. Phone: 202-338-8565.

Embassy of the Republic of Suriname, 4301 Connecticut Ave., N.W., Suite 460, Washington, D.C. 20008. Phone: 202-244-7488.

Embassy of the Kingdom of Swaziland, 1712 New Hampshire Ave., N.W., Washington, D.C. 20009. Phone: 202-234-5002.

Embassy of Sweden, 1501 M St., N.W., Suite 900, Washington, D.C. 20005. Phone: 202-467-2600.

Embassy of Switzerland, 2900 Cathedral Ave., N.W., Washington, D.C. 20008. Phone: 202-745-7900.

Embassy of the Syrian Arab Republic, 2215 Wyoming Ave., N.W., Washington, D.C. 20008. Phone: 202-232-6313.

Taipei Economic and Cultural Representation Office (Taiwan), 4201 Wisconsin Ave., N.W., Washington, D.C. 20016. Phone: 202-895-1800.

Embassy of the United Republic of Tanzania, 2139 R St., N.W., Washington, D.C. 20008. Phone: 202-939-6123.

Royal Thai Embassy, 1024 Wisconsin Ave., N.W., Washington, D.C. 20007. Phone: 202-944-3600.

Embassy of the Republic of Togo, 2208 Massachusetts Ave., N.W., Washington, D.C. 20008. Phone: 202-234-4212.

Embassy of the Republic of Trinidad and Tobago, 1708 Massachusetts Ave., N.W., Washington, D.C. 20036. Phone: 202-467-6490.

Embassy of Tunisia, 1515 Massachusetts Ave., N.W., Washington, D.C. 20005. Phone: 202-862-1850.

Embassy of the Republic of Turkey, 2525 Massachusetts Ave., N.W., Washington, D.C. 20008. Phone: 202-612-6700.

Embassy of Turkmenistan, 2207 Massachusetts Ave., N.W., Washington, D.C. 20008. Phone: 202-588-1500.

Embassy of the Republic of Uganda, 5911 16th St., N.W., Washington, D.C. 20011. Phone: 202-726-7100.

Embassy of Ukraine, 3350 M St., N.W., Washington, D.C. 20007. Phone: 202-349-3398.

Embassy of the United Arab Emirates, 3522 International Ct., N.W., Washington, D.C. 20008. Phone: 202-243-2400.

United Kingdom of Great Britain & Northern Ireland— British Embassy, 3100 Massachusetts Ave., N.W., Washington, D.C. 20008. Phone: 202-588-7800.

Embassy of Uruguay, 1913 I St., N.W., Washington, D.C. 20006. Phone: 202-331-1313.

Embassy of the Republic of Uzbekistan, 1746 Massachusetts Ave., N.W., Washington, D.C. 20036. Phone: 202-887-5300.

Embassy of the Republic of Venezuela, 1099 30th St., N.W., Washington D.C. 20007. Phone: 202-342-2214.

Embassy of the Socialist Republic of Vietnam, 1233 20th St., N.W., Suite 400, Washington, D.C. 20036. Phone: 202-861-0737.

Embassy of the Republic of Yemen, 2319 Wyoming Ave., N.W., Washington, D.C. 20008. Phone: 202-965-4760.

Embassy of the Republic of Zambia, 2419 Massachusetts Ave., N.W., Washington, D.C. 20008. Phone: 202-265-9717.

Embassy of the Republic of Zimbabwe, 1608 New Hampshire Ave., N.W., Washington, D.C. 20009. Phone: 202-332-7100.

Diplomatic Personnel to and from the U.S.

Country	U.S. Representative to[1]	Rank	Representative from[1]	Rank
Afghanistan	Ronald Neumann	Amb.	Seyyed Tayeb Jawad	Amb.
Albania	Marcie Berman Ries	Amb.	Fatos Tarifa	Amb.
Algeria	Richard W. Erdman	Amb.	Amine Kherbi	Amb.
Andorra	George Argyros	Amb.	Jelena V. Pia Comella	Cd'A
Angola	Cynthia G. Efird	Amb.	Josefina Pitra Diakité	Amb.
Antigua and Barbuda	Mary E. Kramer[2]	Amb.	Deborah Mae Lovell	Amb.
Argentina	Lino Gutierrez	Amb.	Jose Octavio Bordon	Amb.
Armenia	John Marshall Evans	Amb.	Tatoul Markarian	Amb.
Australia	John Thomas Schieffer	Amb.	Peter Baxter	Cd'A
Austria	Lyons Brown, Jr.	Amb.	Eva Nowotny	Amb.
Azerbaijan	Reno L. Harnish	Amb.	Hafiz Pashayev	Amb.
Bahamas	John D. Rood	Cd'A.	Joshua Sears	Amb.
Bahrain	William T. Monroe	Amb.	Yasser G. Shaheen	Cd'A
Bangladesh	Harry K. Thomas, Jr.	Amb.	Shamsher M. Chowdhury	Amb.
Barbados	Mary E. Kramer[2]	Amb.	Michael Ian King	Amb.
Belarus	George A. Krol	Amb.	Mikhail Khvostov	Amb.
Belgium	Tom C. Korologos	Cd'A	Frans van Daele	Amb.
Belize	Russell F. Freeman	Amb.	Lisa M. Shoman	Amb.
Benin	Wayne Neill	Amb.	Segbe Cyrille Oguin	Amb.
Bermuda	Antoinette R. Becker	ACG	—	—
Bolivia	David N. Greenlee	Amb.	Jaime Aparicio Otero	Amb.
Bosnia-Herzegovina	Douglas L. McElhaney	Amb.	Igor Davidovic	Amb.
Botswana	Joseph Huggins	Amb.	Lapologang Caesar Lekoa	Amb.
Brazil	John J. Danilovich	Amb.	Roberto Abdenur	Amb.
Brunei	Gene B. Christy	Amb.	Pengiran Indera Negara P. A. Puteh	Amb.
Bulgaria	James W. Pardew	Amb.	Elena Poptodorova	Amb.
Burkina Faso	Anthony J. Holmes	Amb.	Tertius Zongo	Amb.
Burundi	James Howard Yellin	Amb.	Antoine Ntamobwa	Amb.
Cambodia	Charles Aaron Ray	Amb.	Sereywath Ek	Amb.
Cameroon	R. Niels Marquardt	Amb.	Jerome Mendouga	Amb.
Canada	Paul Cellucci	Amb.	Frank McKenna	Amb.
Cape Verde	Donald C. Johnson	Amb.	Jose Brito	Amb.
Central African Republic	—	—	Emmanuel Touaboy	Amb.
Chad	Marc Wall	Amb.	Mahamoud Adam Bechir	Amb.
Chile	Craig A. Kelly	Amb.	Andrés Bianchi	Amb.
China	Clark J. Randt, Jr.	Amb.	Zhou Wenzhong	Amb.
Colombia	William B. Wood	Amb.	Luis Alberto Moreno	Amb.
Comoros	John Price[4]	Amb.	Mahmoud M. Aboud	Amb.
Congo, Dem. Rep. of	Aubrey Hooks	Amb.	Faida Mitifu	Amb.
Congo, Rep. of	Robin R. Sanders	Amb.	Serge Mombouli	Amb.
Costa Rica	Douglas M. Barnes	Cd'A	Tomás Dueñas	Amb.
Côte d'Ivoire	Aubrey Hooks	Amb.	Daouda Diabate	Amb.
Croatia	Ralph Frank	Amb.	Neven Jurica	Amb.
Cuba	James C. Cason	P.O.	Dagoberto Rodriguez Barrera	P.O.
Cyprus	Michael Klosson	Amb.	Euripides L. Evriviades	Amb.
Czech Republic	William J. Cabaniss, Jr.	Amb.	Martin Palous	Amb.
Denmark	Sally M. Light	Cd'A	Ulrik Andreas Federspiel	Amb.
Djibouti	Marguerita D. Ragsdale	Amb.	Roble Olhaye	Amb.
Dominica	Mary E. Kramer[2]	Amb.	Swinburne Lestrade	Amb.
Dominican Republic	Hans H. Hertell	Amb.	Flavio Dario Espinal	Amb.
East Timor	Grover Joseph Rees III	Amb.	Jose Luis Guterrés	Amb.
Ecuador	Kristie Anne Kenney	Amb.	Andres Horacio Teran Parral	Cd'A
Egypt	C. David Welch	Amb.	M. Nabil Fahmy	Amb.
El Salvador	H. Douglas Barclay	Amb.	Rene A. León Rodríguez	Amb.
Equatorial Guinea	George M. Staples	Amb.	Teodoro Biyoga Nsuea	Amb.
Eritrea	Scott DeLisi	Amb.	Girma Asmerom	Amb.
Estonia	Aldona Zofia Wos	Amb.	Juri Luik	Amb.
Ethiopia	Aurelia A. Brazeal	Amb.	Kassahun Ayele	Amb.
EU Delegation	Rockwell Schnabel	Amb.	John Bruton	Amb.
Fiji	David L. Lyon[3]	Amb.	Paula Bolaqace Navunisaravj	S.S.
Finland	Earle I. Mack	Amb.	Jukka Valtasaari	Amb.
France	Alejandro Wolff	Cd'A	Jean-David Levitte	Amb.
Gabon	R. Barrie Walkley	Amb.	Jules Marius Ogouebandja	Amb.
Gambia, The	Joseph D. Stafford III	Amb.	Dodou Bammy Jagne	Amb.
Georgia	Richard M. Miles	Amb.	Levan Mikeladze	Amb.
Germany	Daniel R. Coats	Amb.	Wolfgang Friedrich Ischinger	Amb.

Country	U.S. Representative to[1]	Rank	Representative from[1]	Rank
Ghana	Mary Carlin Yates	Amb.	Fritz Kwabena Poku	Amb.
Greece	Charles P. Ries	Amb.	Georges Savvaides	Amb.
Grenada	Mary E. Kramer[2]	Amb.	Denis G. Antoine	Amb.
Guatemala	John Randle Hamilton	Amb.	Jose Guillermo Castillo	Amb.
Guinea	Jackson McDonald	Amb.	Alpha Oumar Raflou Barry	Amb.
Guinea-Bissau	Richard Roth	Amb.	Henrique Adriano Da Silva	Cd'A.
Guyana	Roland W. Bullen	Amb.	Bayney Karran	Amb.
Haiti	James B. Foley	Amb.	Raymond Joseph	Cd'A
Holy See	Brent Hardt	Cd'A	Gabriel Montalvo	Pap. Nun.
Honduras	Larry Leon Palmer	Amb.	Mario Miguel Canahuati	Amb.
Hong Kong	James Keith	C.G.	—	—
Hungary	George Herbert Walker III	Amb.	András Simonyi	Amb.
Iceland	James I. Gadsden	Amb.	Helgi Ágústsson	Amb.
India	David C. Mulford	Amb.	Ronen Sen	Amb.
Indonesia	B. Lynn Pascoe	Amb.	Soemadi D. M. Brotodiningrat	Amb.
Iran	—	—	—	—
Iraq	Zalmay Khalilzad	Amb.	Aid Ahmad	Cd'A
Ireland	James C. Kenny	Amb.	Noel Fahey	Amb.
Israel	Daniel C. Kurtzer	Amb.	Daniel Ayalon	Amb.
Italy	Melvin F. Sembler	Amb.	Sergio Vento	Amb.
Jamaica	Sue McCourt Cobb	Amb.	Gordon Shirley	Amb.
Japan	J. Thomas Schieffer	Amb.	Ryozo Kato	Amb.
Jordan	Edward William Gnehm, Jr.	Amb.	Karim Tawiq Kawar	Amb.
Kazakhstan	John M. Ordway	Amb.	Kanat B. Saudabayev	Amb.
Kenya	William M. Bellamy	Amb.	Leonard Njogu Ngaithe	Amb.
Kiribati, Republic of	David L. Lyon[3]	Amb.	—	—
Korea, South	Mark Minton	Cd'A	Seok-Hyun Hong	Amb.
Kuwait	Richard LeBaron	Amb.	Salem Abdullah Al-Jaber Al-Sabah	Amb.
Kyrgyz Republic	Stephen M. Young	Amb.	Zamira Sydykova	Amb.
Laos	Patricia M. Haslach	Amb.	Phanthong Phommahaxay	Amb.
Latvia	Catherine Todd Bailey	Amb.	Maris Riekstins	Amb.
Lebanon	Vincent Martin Battle	Amb.	Farid Abboud	Amb.
Lesotho	Robert G. Loftis	Amb.	Molelekeng E. Rapolaki	Amb.
Liberia	John William Blaney III	Amb.	Charles A. Minor	Amb.
Liechtenstein	Pamela Willeford[5]	Amb.	Claudia Fritsche	Amb.
Lithuania	Stephen D. Mull	Amb.	Vygaudas Usackas	Amb.
Luxembourg	Peter Terpeluk, Jr.	Amb.	Arlette Conzemius-Paccourd	Amb.
Macedonia	Lawrence Edward Butler	Amb.	Nikola Dimitrov	Amb.
Madagascar	James D. McGee	Amb.	Narisoa Rajaonarivony	Amb.
Malawi	Stephen Browning	Amb.	Bernardo Sande	Amb.
Malaysia	Christopher J. LaFleur	Amb.	Ghazzali bin Sheikh Abdul Khalid	Amb.
Maldives	Jeffrey J. Lunstead[6]	Amb.	Mohamed Latheef	Amb.
Mali	Vicki Huddlestone	Amb.	Abdoulaye Diop	Amb.
Malta	William Grant	Cd'A	John Lowell	Amb.
Marshall Islands	Michael J. Senko	Amb.	Banny de Brum	Amb.
Mauritania	Joseph E. LeBaron	Amb.	Tijani Ould M. E. Kerim	Amb.
Mauritius	John Price[4]	Amb.	Usha Jeetah	Amb.
Mexico	Antonio O. Garza, Jr.	Amb.	Carlos Alberto de Icaza Gonzalez	Amb.
Micronesia	Suzanne K. Hale	Amb.	Jesse B. Marehalau	Amb.
Moldova	Heather M. Hodges	Amb.	Mihai Manoli	Amb.
Mongolia	Pamela J. Slutz	Amb.	Ravdan Bold	Amb.
Morocco	Thomas T. Riley	Amb.	Aziz Mekouar	Amb.
Mozambique	Helen La Lime	Amb.	Armando A. Panguene	Amb.
Myanmar (Burma)	Carmen M. Martinez	Cd'A	Daw Yin Yin Myint	Cd'A
Namibia	Joyce A. Barr	Amb.	Hopelong Uushona Ipinge	Amb.
Nauru	David L. Lyon[3]	Amb.	Vinci Niel Clodumar	Amb.
Nepal	James F. Moriarty	Amb.	Kedar Bhakta Shrestha	Amb.
Netherlands	Clifford M. Sobel	Amb.	Boudewijn Johannes Van Eenen-naam	Amb.
Netherlands Antilles	Deborah A. Bolton	C.G.	—	—
New Zealand	Charles S. Swindells	Amb.	John Wood	Amb.
Nicaragua	Barbara Calandra Moore	Amb.	Salvador Stadthagen	Amb.
Niger	Dennise Mathieu	Amb.	Fatima Djibo Sidikou	Cd'A
Nigeria	John Campbell	Amb.	George Achulike Obiozor	Amb.
Norway	John Doyle Ong	Amb.	Knut Vollebaek	Amb.
Oman	Richard Lewis Baltimore III	Amb.	Mohamed Ali Al-Khusaiby	Amb.
Pakistan	Ryan C. Crocker	Amb.	Jehangir Karamat	Amb.

Country	U.S. Representative to[1]	Rank	Representative from[1]	Rank
Palau	Francis J. Ricciardone, Jr.	Amb.	Hersey Kyota	Amb.
Panama	Linda Ellen Watt	Amb.	Federico A. Humbert Arias	Amb.
Papua New Guinea	Robert W. Fitts	Amb.	Evan Jeremy Paki	Amb.
Paraguay	John F. Keane	Amb.	James Spalding Hellmers	Amb.
Peru	J. Curtis Struble	Amb.	Eduardo Ferrero Costa	Amb.
Philippines	Francis J. Ricciardone, Jr.	Amb.	Albert del Rosario	Amb.
Poland	Victor Ashe	Amb.	Boguslaw Wind	Cd'A
Portugal	John N. Palmer	Amb.	Pedro M. Dos Reis Alves Catarino	Amb.
Qatar	Chase Untermeyer	Amb.	Bader Omar Al-Dafa	Amb.
Romania	Thomas L. Delare	Amb.	Sorin Dumitru Ducaru	Amb.
Russia	William Burns	Amb.	Yuriy Viktorovich Ushakov	Amb.
Rwanda	Margaret K. McMillion	Amb.	Zac Nsenga	Amb.
Saint Kitts and Nevis	Mary E. Kramer[2]	Amb.	Izben Cordinal Williams	Amb.
Saint Lucia	Mary E. Kramer[2]	Amb.	Sonia Merlyn Johnny	Amb.
Saint Vincent and the Grenadines	Mary E. Kramer[2]	Amb.	Ellsworth I. A. John	Amb.
Samoa, Western	Charles J. Swindells	Amb.	Aliioaiga Feturi Elisaia	Amb.
São Tomé and Príncipe, Dem. Rep. of	R. Barrie Walkley	Amb.	Domingos Augusto Ferreira	UN PM
Saudi Arabia	James Curtis Oberwetter	Amb.	Bandar bin Sultan	Amb.
Senegal	Richard Roth	Amb.	Amadou Lamine Ba	Amb.
Serbia and Montenegro	Michael C. Polt	Amb.	Ivan Vujacic	Amb.
Seychelles	John Price	Amb.	Emile Patrick Jeremie Bonnelame	Amb.
Sierra Leone	Thomas N. Hull	Amb.	Ibrahim M. Kamara	Amb.
Singapore	Franklin L. Lavin	Amb.	Heng Chee Chan	Amb.
Slovakia	Scott N. Thayer	Cd'A	Rastislav Kacer	Amb.
Slovenia	Thomas B. Robertson	Amb.	Samuel Zbogar	Amb.
Solomon Islands	Robert W. Fitts	Amb.	Colin David Beck	Amb.
South Africa	Jendayi Frazer	Amb.	Barbara Joyce Mosima Masekela	Amb.
Spain	George L. Argyros	Amb.	Carlos Westendorp	Amb.
Sri Lanka	Jeffrey J. Lunstead[6]	Amb.	Bernard Goonetilleke	Amb.
Sudan	Gerard M. Gallucci	Cd'A	Khidr Haroun Ahmed	Amb.
Suriname	Marsha E. Barnes	Amb.	Henry Lothar Illes	Amb.
Swaziland	Lewis W. Lucke	Amb.	Mary Madzandza Kanya	Amb.
Sweden	M. Teel Bivins	Amb.	Jan Eliasson	Amb.
Switzerland	Pamela Willeford[5]	Amb.	Christian Blickenstorfer	Amb.
Syria	Margaret Scobey	Amb.	Imad Mustafa	Amb.
Tajikistan	Richard E. Hoagland	Amb.	Khamrokhon Zaripov	Amb.
Tanzania	Robert V. Royall	Amb.	Andrew Mhando Daraja	Amb.
Thailand	Ralph L. "Skip" Boyce	Amb.	Kasit Piromya	Amb.
Togo	Gregory Engle	Amb.	Akoussoulelou Bodjona	Amb.
Tonga	David L. Lyon[3]	Amb.	Fekitamoeloa Utoikamanu	Amb.
Trinidad and Tobago	Roy L. Austin	Amb.	Marina Annette Valere	Amb.
Tunisia	William J. Hudson	Amb.	Mohamed Nejib Hachana	Amb.
Turkey	Eric S. Edelman	Amb.	Osman Faruk Logoglu	Amb.
Turkmenistan	Tracey A. Jacobson	Amb.	Meret Bairamovich Orazov	Amb.
Tuvalu	David L. Lyon[3]	Amb.	—	—
Uganda	Jimmy Kolker	Amb.	Edith Grace Ssempala	Amb.
Ukraine	John E. Herbst	Amb.	Mykhailo B. Reznik	Amb.
United Arab Emirates	Michele J. Sison	Amb.	Al Asri Saeed Ahmed Al Dhahri	Amb.
United Kingdom	William S. Farish	Amb.	David G. Manning	Amb.
Uruguay	Martin J. Silverstein	Amb.	Carlos Gianelli Derois	Amb.
Uzbekistan	Jon Purnell	Amb.	Abdulaziz Kamilov	Amb.
Vanuatu	Robert W. Fitts	Amb.	—	—
Venezuela	William R. Brownfield	Amb.	Bernardo Alvarez Herrera	Amb.
Vietnam	Michael W. Marine	Amb.	Nguyen Tam Chien	Amb.
Yemen	Thomas C. Krajeski	Amb.	Abdulwahab A. Al-Hajjri	Amb.
Zambia	Martin George Brennan	Amb.	Inonge Mbikusita-Lewanika	Amb.
Zimbabwe	Chistopher William Dell	Amb.	Simbi Veke Mubako	Amb.

NOTE: ACG=Acting Consul General; Amb.=Ambassador; Cd'A=Charge d'Affaires; C.G.=Consul General; Pap. Nun.=Papal Nuncio; P.O.=Principal Officer; UN PM=head of Permanent Mission to U.N.; S.S.=Second Secretary 1. As of June 2005. 2. The U.S. embassy in Barbados currently serves seven independent nations of the Eastern Caribbean (Barbados, Antigua and Barbuda, Dominica, Grenada, St. Kitts and Nevis, St. Lucia, and St. Vincent and the Grenadines) and provides consular services to American citizens in the nearby European dependent territories. 3. Ambassador to Fiji, Republic of Kiribati, Nauru, Tonga, and Tuvalu. 4. Ambassador to Comoros and Mauritius. 5. Ambassador to Liechtenstein and Switzerland. 6. Ambassador to the Maldives and Sri Lanka. *Sources:* U.S. Department of State, CIA World Factbook.

The Olympic Games

1896 Athens, Greece	1948 London, Great Britain (S)	1984 Sarajevo, Yugoslavia (W)
1900 Paris, France	1952 Oslo, Norway (W)	1984 Los Angeles, United States (S)
1904 St. Louis, United States	1952 Helsinki, Finland (S)	1988 Calgary, Canada (W)
1906 Athens, Greece	1956 Cortina d'Ampezzo, Italy (W)	1988 Seoul, South Korea (S)
1908 London, Great Britain	1956 Melbourne, Australia (S)	1992 Albertville, France (W)
1912 Stockholm, Sweden	1960 Squaw Valley, United States (W)	1992 Barcelona, Spain (S)
1920 Antwerp, Belgium	1960 Rome, Italy (S)	1994 Lillehammer, Norway (W)
1924 Chamonix, France (W)	1964 Innsbruck, Austria (W)	1996 Atlanta, United States (S)
1924 Paris, France (S)	1964 Tokyo, Japan (S)	1998 Nagano, Japan (W)
1928 St. Moritz, Switzerland (W)	1968 Grenoble, France (W)	2000 Sydney, Australia (S)
1928 Amsterdam, Netherlands (S)	1968 Mexico City, Mexico (S)	2002 Salt Lake City, United States (W)
1932 Lake Placid, United States (W)	1972 Sapporo, Japan (W)	2004 Athens, Greece (S)
1932 Los Angeles, United States (S)	1972 Munich, Germany (S)	2006 Turin, Italy (W)
1936 Garmisch-Partenkirchen, Germany (W)	1976 Innsbruck, Austria (W)	2008 Beijing, China (S)
	1976 Montreal, Canada (S)	2010 Vancouver, Canada (W)
1936 Berlin, Germany (S)	1980 Lake Placid, United States (W)	2012 London, Great Britain (S)
1948 St. Moritz, Switzerland (W)	1980 Moscow, USSR (S)	

(W)—Site of Winter Games. (S)—Site of Summer Games.

The first Olympic Games of which there is record were held in 776 B.C., and consisted of one event, a great foot race of about 200 yards held on a plain by the River Alpheus (now the Ruphia) just outside the little town of Olympia in Greece. It was from that date the Greeks began to keep their calendar by "Olympiads," the four-year spans between the celebrations of the famous games.

The modern Olympic Games, which started in Athens in 1896, are the result of the devotion of a French educator, Baron Pierre de Coubertin, to the idea that, since young people and athletics have gone together through the ages, education and athletics might go hand-in-hand toward a better international understanding.

The principal organization responsible for the staging of the Games is the International Olympic Committee (IOC). Other important roles are played by the National Olympic Committees in each participating country, international sports federations, and the organizing committee of the host city.

The Olympic motto is "Citius, Altius, Fortius"—"Faster, Higher, Stronger." The Olympic symbol is five interlocking circles colored blue, yellow, black, green, and red, on a white background, representing the five continents. At least one of those colors appears in the national flag of every country.

Beginning in 1994, the IOC decided to change the format of having both the Summer and Winter Games in the same year. Summer and Winter Olympics now alternate every two years.

In Feb. 1998 the IOC announced that new sports added to the games must include women's events.

At the 2005 Singapore meeting the IOC decided to eliminate baseball and softball from the 2012 Olympics, the first sports to be dropped since polo in 1936.

Summer Games: Gold Medals

TRACK AND FIELD–MEN

100-Meter Dash

1896	Thomas Burke, United States	12.00
1900	Francis W. Jarvis, United States	10.80
1904	Archie Hahn, United States	11.00
1906	Archie Hahn, United States	11.20
1908	Reginald Walker, South Africa	10.80
1912	Ralph Craig, United States	10.80
1920	Charles Paddock, United States	10.80
1924	Harold Abrahams, Great Britain	10.60
1928	Percy Williams, Canada	10.80
1932	Eddie Tolan, United States	10.30
1936	Jesse Owens, United States	10.30[1]
1948	Harrison Dillard, United States	10.30
1952	Lindy Remigino, United States	10.40
1956	Bobby Morrow, United States	10.50
1960	Armin Hary, Germany	10.20
1964	Robert Hayes, United States	10.00
1968	James Hines, United States	09.90
1972	Valery Borzow, USSR	10.14
1976	Hasely Crawford, Trinidad and Tobago	10.06
1980	Allan Wells, Britain	10.25
1984	Carl Lewis, United States	09.99
1988	Carl Lewis, United States	09.92[2]
1992	Linford Christie, Great Britain	09.96
1996	Donovan Bailey, Canada	09.84[3]
2000	Maurice Greene, United States	09.87
2004	Justin Gatlin, United States	09.85

1. Wind assisted. 2. Lewis was awarded the gold medal when Ben Johnson of Canada, the original winner in 09.79s, was stripped of the medal after testing positive for steroid use. 3. World record.

200-Meter Dash

1900	John Tewksbury, United States	22.20
1904	Archie Hahn, United States	21.60
1908	Robert Kerr, Canada	22.60
1912	Ralph Craig, United States	21.70
1920	Allan Woodring, United States	22.00
1924	Jackson Scholz, United States	21.60
1928	Percy Williams, Canada	21.80
1932	Eddie Tolan, United States	21.20
1936	Jesse Owens, United States	20.70
1948	Melvin E. Patton, United States	21.10
1952	Andrew Stanfield, United States	20.70
1956	Bobby Morrow, United States	20.60

1960	Livio Berruti, Italy	20.50
1964	Henry Carr, United States	20.30
1968	Tommie Smith, United States	19.80
1972	Vallery Borzov, USSR	20.00
1976	Don Quarrie, Jamaica	20.23
1980	Pietro Mennea, Italy	20.19
1984	Carl Lewis, United States	19.80
1988	Joe DeLoach, United States	19.75
1992	Mike Marsh, United States	20.01
1996	Michael Johnson, United States	19.32[1]
2000	Konstantinos Kenteris, Greece	20.09
2004	Shawn Crawford, United States	19.79

1. World record.

400-Meter Dash

1896	Thomas Burke, United States	54.20
1900	Maxwell Long, United States	49.40
1904	Harry Hillman, United States	49.20
1906	Paul Pilgrim, United States	53.20
1908	Wyndham Halswelle, Great Britain (walkover)	50.00
1912	Charles Reidpath, United States	48.20
1920	Bevil Rudd, South Africa	49.60
1924	Eric Liddell, Great Britain	47.60
1928	Ray Barbuti, United States	47.80
1932	William Carr, United States	46.20
1936	Archie Williams, United States	46.50
1948	Arthur Wint, Jamaica, B.W.I.	46.20
1952	George Rhoden, Jamaica, B.W.I.	45.90
1956	Charles Jenkins, United States	46.70
1960	Otis Davis, United States	44.90
1964	Mike Larrabee, United States	45.10
1968	Lee Evans, United States	43.80
1972	Vincent Matthews, United States	44.66
1976	Alberto Juantorena, Cuba	44.26
1980	Viktor Markin, USSR	44.60
1984	Alonzo Babers, United States	44.27
1988	Steve Lewis, United States	43.87
1992	Quincy Watts, United States	43.50
1996	Michael Johnson, United States	43.49
2000	Michael Johnson, United States	43.84
2004	Jeremy Wariner, United States	44.00

800-Meter Run

1896	Edwin Flack, Australia	2:11.00
1900	Alfred Tysoe, Great Britain	2:01.40
1904	James Lightbody, United States	1:56.00
1906	Paul Pilgrim, United States	2:01.20
1908	Mel Sheppard, United states	1:52.80
1912	Ted Meredith, United States	1:51.90
1920	Albert Hill, Great Britain	1:53.40
1924	Douglas Lowe, Great Britain	1:52.40
1928	Douglas Lowe, Great Britain	1:51.80
1932	Thomas Hampson, Great Britain	1:49.80
1936	John Woodruff, United States	1:52.90
1948	Malvin Whitfield, United States	1:49.20
1952	Malvin Whitfield, United States	1:49.20
1956	Tom Courtney, United States	1:47.70
1960	Peter Snell, New Zealand	1:46.30
1964	Peter Snell, New Zealand	1:45.10
1968	Ralph Doubell, Australia	1:44.30
1972	David Wottle, United States	1:45.90
1976	Alberto Juantorena, Cuba	1:43.50
1980	Steve Ovett, Britain	1:45.40
1984	Joaquin Cruz, Brazil	1:43.00
1988	Paul Ereng, Kenya	1:43.45
1992	William Tanui, Kenya	1:43.66
1996	Vebjoern Rodal, Norway	1:42.58
2000	Nils Schumann, Germany	1:45.08
2004	Yuriy Borzakovskiy, Russia	1:44.45

1,500-Meter Run

1896	Edwin Flack, Australia	4:33.20
1900	Charles Bennett, Great Britain	4:06.00
1904	James Lightbody, United States	4:05.40
1906	James Lightbody, United States	4:12.00
1908	Mel Sheppard, United States	4:03.40

1912	Arnold Jackson, Great Britain	3:56.80
1920	Albert Hill, Great Britain	4:01.80
1924	Paavo Nurmi, Finland	3:53.60
1928	Harry Larva, Finland	3:53.20
1932	Luigi Becali, Italy	3:51.20
1936	Jack Lovelock, New Zealand	3:47.80
1948	Henri Eriksson, Sweden	3:49.80
1952	Joseph Barthel, Luxembourg	3:45.20
1956	Ron Delany, Ireland	3:41.20
1960	Herb Elliott, Australia	3:35.60
1964	Peter Snell, New Zealand	3:38.10
1968	Kipchoge Keino, Kenya	3:34.90
1972	Pekka Vasala, Finland	3:36.30
1976	John Walker, New Zealand	3:39.17
1980	Sebastian Coe, Britain	3:38.40
1984	Sebastian Coe, Britain	3:32.53
1988	Peter Rono, Kenya	3:35.96
1992	Fermin Cacho Ruiz, Spain	3:40.12
1996	Noureddine Morceli, Algeria	3:35.78
2000	Noah Ngeny, Kenya	3:32.07
2004	Hicham El Guerrouj, Morocco	3:34.18

5,000-Meter Run

1912	Hannes Kolehmainen, Finland	14:36.60
1920	Joseph Guillemot, France	14:55.60
1024	Paavo Nurmi, Finland	14:31.20
1928	Willie Ritola, Finland	14:38.00
1932	Lauri Lehtinen, Finland	14:30.00
1936	Gunnar Hockert, Finland	14:22.20
1948	Gaston Reiff, Belgium	14:17.60
1952	Emil Zatopek, Czechoslovakia	14:06.60
1956	Vladimir Kuts, USSR	13:39.60
1960	Murray Halberg, New Zealand	13:43.40
1964	Bob Schul, United States	13:48.80
1968	Mohamed Gammoudi, Tunisia	14:05.00
1972	Lasse Viren, Finland	13:26.40
1976	Lasse Viren, Finland	13:24.76
1980	Miruts Yifter, Ethiopia	13:21.00
1984	Saud Aouita, Morocco	13:05.59
1988	John Ngugi, Kenya	13:11.70
1992	Dieter Baumann, Germany	13:12.52
1996	Venuste Niyongabo, Burundi	13:07.96
2000	Millon Wolde, Ethiopia	13:35.49
2004	Hicham El Guerrouj, Morocco	13:14.39

10,000-Meter Run

1912	Hannes Kolehmainen, Finland	31:20.80
1920	Paavo Nurmi, Finland	31:45.80
1924	Willie Ritola, Finland	30:23.20
1928	Paavo Nurmi, Finland	30:18.80
1932	Janusz Kusocinski, Poland	30:11.40
1936	Ilmari Salminen, Finland	30:15.40
1948	Emil Zatopek, Czechoslovakia	29:59.60
1952	Emil Zatopek, Czechoslovakia	29:17.00
1956	Vladimir Kuts, USSR	28:45.60
1960	Peter Bolotnikov, USSR	28:32.20
1964	Billy Mills, United States	28:24.40
1968	Nartali Temu, Kenya	29:27.40
1972	Lasse Viren, Finland	27:38.40
1976	Lasse Viren, Finland	27:40.38
1980	Miruts Yifter, Ethiopia	27:42.70
1984	Alberto Cova, Italy	27:47.50
1988	Mly Brahim Boutaib, Morocco	27:21.46
1992	Khalid Skah, Morocco	27:47.70
1996	Haile Gebrselassie, Ethiopia	27:07.34
2000	Haile Gebrselassie, Ethiopia	27:18.20
2004	Kenenisa Bekele, Ethiopia	27:05.10

Marathon

1896	Spiridon Loues, Greece	2:58:50.00
1900	Michel Teato, France	2:59:45.00
1904	Thomas Hicks, United States	3:28:53.00
1906	William J. Sherring, Canada	2:51:23.65
1908	John J. Hayes, United States	2:55:18.40
1912	Kenneth McArthur, South Africa	2:36:54.80
1920	Hannes Kolehmainen, Finland	2:32:35.80

1924	Albin Stenroos, Finland	2:41:22.60
1928	A. B. El Quafi, France	2:32:57.00
1932	Juan Zabala, Argentina	2:31:36.00
1936	Kitei Son, Japan	2:29:19.20
1948	Delfo Cabrera, Argentina	2:34:51.60
1952	Emil Zatopek, Czechoslovakia	2:23:30.20
1956	Alain Mimoun, France	2:25:00.00
1960	Abebe Bikila, Ethiopia	2:15:16.20
1964	Abebe Bikila, Ethiopia	2:12:11.20
1968	Mamo Wold, Ethiopia	2:20:26.40
1972	Frank Shorter, United States	2:12:19.80
1976	Walter Cierpinski, East Germany	2:09:55.00
1980	Walter Cierpinski, East Germany	2:11:30.00
1984	Carlos Lopes, Portugal	2:09:21.00
1988	Gelindo Bordin, Italy	2:10:47.00
1992	Hwang Young-Cho, South Korea	2:13:23.00
1996	Josia Thugwane, South Africa	2:12:36.00
2000	Gezahgne Abera, Ethiopia	2:10:11.00
2004	Stefano Baldini, Italy	2:10:55.00

110-Meter Hurdles

1896	Thomas Curtis, United States	17.60
1900	Alvin Kraenzlein, United States	15.40
1904	Frederick Schule, United States	16.00
1906	R.G. Leavitt, United States	16.20
1908	Forrest Smithson, United States	15.00
1912	Frederick Kelly, United States	15.10
1920	Earl Thomson, Canada	14.80
1924	Daniel Kinsey, United States	15.00
1928	Sydney Atkinson, South Africa	14.80
1932	George Saling, United States	14.60
1936	Forrest Towns, United States	14.20
1948	William Porter, United States	13.90
1952	Harrison Dillard, United States	13.70
1956	Lee Calhoun, United States	13.50
1960	Lee Calhoun, United States	13.80
1964	Hayes Jones, United States	13.60
1968	Willie Davenport, United States	13.30
1972	Rodney Milburn, United States	13.24
1976	Guy Drut, France	13.30
1980	Thomas Munkelt, East Germany	13.20
1984	Roger Kingdom, United States	13.20
1988	Roger Kingdom, United States	12.98
1992	Mark McCoy, Canada	13.12
1996	Allen Johnson, United States	12.95
2000	Anier Garcia, Cuba	13.00
2004	Xiang Liu, China	12.91

200-Meter Hurdles

1900	Alvin Kraenzlein, United States	25.40
1904	Harry Hillman, United States	24.60

400-Meter Hurdles

1900	John Tewksbury, United States	57.60
1904	Harry Hillman, United States	53.00
1908	Charles Bacon, United States	55.00
1920	Frank Loomis, United States	54.00
1924	F. Morgan Taylor, United States	52.60
1928	Lord David Burghley, Great Britain	53.40
1932	Robert Tisdall, Ireland	51.80[1]
1936	Glenn Hardin, United States	52.40
1948	Roy Cochran, United States	51.10
1952	Charles Moore, United States	50.80
1956	Glenn Davis, United States	50.10
1960	Glenn Davis, United States	49.30
1964	Rex Cawley, United States	49.60
1968	David Hemery, Great Britain	48.10
1972	John Akii-Bua, Uganda	47.80
1976	Edwin Moses, United States	47.64
1980	Volker Beck, East Germany	48.70
1984	Edwin Moses, United States	47.75
1988	Andre Phillips, United States	47.19
1992	Kevin Young, United States	46.78
1996	Derrick Adkins, United States	47.54
2000	Angelo Taylor, United States	47.50
2004	Felix Sanchez, Dominican Republic	47.63

1. Record not allowed.

2,500-Meter Steeplechase

1900	George Orton, United States	7:34.00
1904	James Lightbody, United States	7:39.60

3,000-Meter Steeplechase

1920	Percy Hodge, Great Britain	10:00.40
1924	Willie Ritola, Finland	09:33.60
1928	Toivo Loukola, Finland	09:21.80
1932	Volmari Iso-Hollo, Finland	10:33.40[1]
1936	Volmari Iso-Hollo, Finland	09:03.80
1948	Thure Sjoestrand, Sweden	09:04.60
1952	Horace Ashenfelter, United States	08:45.40
1956	Chris Brasher, Great Britain	08:41.20
1960	Zdzislaw Krzyskowiak, Poland	08:34.20
1964	Gaston Roelants, Belgium	08:30.80
1968	Amos Biwott, Kenya	08:51.00
1972	Kipchoge Keino, Kenya	08:23.60
1976	Anders Gardervd, Sweden	08:08.02
1980	Bronislaw Malinowski, Poland	08:09.70
1984	Julius Korir, Kenya	08:11.80
1988	Julius Karluki, Kenya	08:05.51
1992	Matthew Birir, Kenya	08:08.84
1996	Joseph Keter, Kenya	08:07.12
2000	Reuben Kosgei, Kenya	08:21.43
2004	Ezekiel Kemboi, Kenya	08:05.81

1. About 3,450 meters-extra lap by error.

10,000-Meter Walk

1912	George Goulding, Canada	46:28.40
1920	Ugo Frigerio, Italy	48:06.20
1924	Ugo Frigerio, Italy	47:49.00
1948	John Mikaelsson, Sweden	45:13.20
1952	John Mikaelsson, Sweden	45:02.80

20,000-Meter Walk

1956	Leonid Spirin, USSR	1:31:27.40
1960	Vladimir Golubnichy, USSR	1:34:07.20
1964	Ken Mathews, Great Britain	1:29:34.00
1968	Vladimir Golubnichy, USSR	1:33:58.40
1972	Peter Frenkel, East Germany	1:26:42.40
1976	Daniel Bautista, Mexico	1:24:40.60
1980	Maurizio Damiliano, Italy	1:23:35.50
1984	Ernesto Conto, Mexico	1:23.13.00
1988	Jozef Pribilinec, Czechoslovakia	1:19:57.00
1992	Daniel Plaza, Spain	1:21:45.00
1996	Jefferson Perez, Ecuador	1:20:07.00
2000	Robert Korzeniowski, Poland	1:18:59.00
2004	Ivano Brugnetti, Italy	1:19:40.00

50,000-Meter Walk

1932	Thomas W. Green, Great Britain	4:50:10.00
1936	Harold Whitlock, Great Britain	4:30:41.10
1948	John Ljunggren, Sweden	4:41:52.00
1952	Giuseppe Dordoni, Italy	4:28:07.80
1956	Norman Read, New Zealand	4:30:42.80
1960	Donald Thompson, Great Britain	4:25:30.00
1964	Abdon Pamich, Italy	4:11:12.40
1968	Christoph Hohne, East Germany	4:20:13.60
1972	Bern Kannernberg, West Germany	3:56:11.60
1980	Hartwig Guader, East Germany	3:49:24.00
1984	Raul Gonzalez, Mexico	3:37:26.00
1988	Viacheslau Ivanenko, USSR	3:48:29.00
1992	Andrei Perlov, Unified Team[1]	3:50:13.00
1996	Robert Korzeniowski, Poland	3:43:30.00
2000	Robert Korzeniowski, Poland	3:42:22.00
2004	Robert Korzeniowski, Poland	3:38:46.00

1. Former Soviet Union team.

400-Meter Relay (4x100)

1912	Great Britain	42.40
1920	United States	42.20
1924	United States	41.00
1928	United States	41.00
1932	United States	40.00
1936	United States	39.80
1948	United States	40.60
1952	United States	40.10
1956	United States	39.50

1960	Germany	39.50
1964	United States	39.00
1968	United States	38.20
1972	United States	38.19
1976	United States	38.33
1980	USSR	38.26
1984	United States	37.83
1988	USSR	38.19
1992	United States	37.40[1]
1996	Canada	37.69
2000	United States	37.61
2004	Great Britain	38.07

1. World record.

1,600-Meter Relay (4x400)

1912	United States	3:16.60
1920	Great Britain	3:22.20
1924	United States	3:16.00
1928	United States	3:14.20
1932	United States	3:08.20
1936	Great Britain	3:09.00
1948	United States	3:10.40
1952	Jamaica, B.W.I.	3:03.90
1956	United States	3:04.80
1960	United States	3:02.20
1964	United States	3:00.70
1968	United States	2:56.10
1972	Kenya	2:59.80
1976	United States	2:58.65
1980	USSR	3:01.10
1984	United States	2:57.91
1988	United States	2:56.16
1992	United States	2:55.74[1]
1996	United States	2:55.99
2000	United States	2:56.35
2004	United States	2:55.91

1. World record.

Team Race

		Pts
1900	Great Britain (5,000 meters)	26
1904	United States (4 miles)	27
1908	Great Britain (3 miles)	6
1912	United States (3,000 meters)	9
1920	United States (3,000 meters)	10
1924	Finland (3,000 meters)	9

Standing High Jump

1900	Ray Ewry, United States	5 ft 5 in
1904	Ray Ewry, United States	4 ft 11 in
1906	Ray Ewry, United States	5 ft 1.625 in
1908	Ray Ewry, United States	5 ft 2 in
1912	Platt Adams, United States	5 ft 4.125 in

Running High Jump

1896	Ellery Clark, United States	5 ft 11.25 in
1900	Irving Baxter, United States	6 ft 2.75 in
1904	Samuel Jones, United States	5 ft 11 in
1906	Con Leahy, Ireland	5 ft 9.875 in
1908	Harry Porter, United States	6 ft 3 in
1912	Alma Richards, United States	6 ft 4 in
1920	Richmond Landon, United States	6 ft 4.25 in
1924	Harold Osborn, United States	6 ft 5.9375 in
1928	Robert W. King, United States	6 ft 4.375 in
1932	Duncan McNaughton, Canada	6 ft 5.625 in
1936	Cornelius Johnson, United States	6 ft 7.9375 in
1948	John Winter, Australia	6 ft 6 in
1952	Walter David, United States	6 ft 8.9375 in
1956	Charles Damas, United States	6 ft 11.25 in
1960	Robert Shavlakadze, USSR	7 ft 1 in
1964	Valeri Brumel, USSR	7 ft 1.75 in
1968	Dick Fosbury, United States	7 ft 4.25 in
1972	Yuri Tarmak, USSR	7 ft 3.75 in
1976	Jacek Wszola, Poland	7 ft 4.5 in
1980	Gerd Wessig, East Germany	7 ft 8.75 in
1984	Dietmar Mogenburg, West Germany	7 ft 8.5 in
1988	Guennadi Avdeenko, USSR	7 ft 0.5 in
1992	Javier Sotomayor, Cuba	7 ft 8.5 in

1996	Charles Austin, United States	7 ft 10 in
2000	Sergey Kliugin, Russia	7 ft 8.5 in
2004	Stefan Holm, Sweden	7 ft 8.91 in

Long Jump

1896	Ellery Clark, United States	20 ft 9.75 in
1900	Alvin Kraenzlein, United States	23 ft 6.875 in
1904	Myer Prinstein, United States	24 ft 1 in
1906	Myer Prinstein, United States	23 ft 7.5 in
1908	Frank Irons, United States	24 ft 6.5in
1912	Albert Gutterson, United States	24 ft 11.25 in
1920	William Petterssen, Sweden	23 ft 5.5 in
1924	DeHart Hubbard, United States	24 ft 5.125 in
1928	Edward B. Hamm, United States	25 ft 4.75 in
1932	Edward Gordon, United States	25 ft 0.75 in
1936	Jesse Owens, United States	26 ft 5.3125 in
1948	Willie Steele, United States	25 ft 8 in
1952	Jerome Biffle, United States	24 ft 10 in
1956	Gregory Bell, United States	25 ft 8.25 in
1960	Ralph Boston, United States	26 ft 7.75 in
1964	Lynn Davies, Great Britain	26 ft 5.75 in
1968	Bob Beamon, United States	29 ft 2.5 in
1972	Randy Williams, United States	27 ft 0.5 in
1976	Arnie Robinson, United States	24 ft 7.75 in
1980	Lutz Dombrowski, E. Germany	28 ft 0.25 in
1984	Carl Lewis, United States	28 ft 0.25 in
1988	Carl Lewis, United States	28 ft 7.25 in
1992	Carl Lewis, United States	28 ft 5.5 in
1996	Carl Lewis, United States	27 ft 10.75 in
2000	Ivan Pedroso, Cuba	28 ft 0.75 in
2004	Dwight Phillips, United States	28 ft 2.19 in

Triple Jump

1896	James B. Connolly, United States	45 ft
1900	Myer Prinstein, United States	47 ft 4.25 in
1904	Myer Prinstein, United States	47 ft
1906	P.G. O'Connor, Ireland	46 ft 2 in
1908	Timothy Ahearne, Great Britain	48 ft 1.25 in
1912	Gustaf Lindblom, Sweden	48 ft 5.125 in
1920	Vilho Tuulos, Finland	47 ft 6.875 in
1924	Archie Winter, Australia	50 ft 11.125 in
1928	Mikio Oda, Japan	49 ft 10.8125 in
1932	Chuhei Nambu, Japan	51 ft 7 in
1936	Naoto Tajima, Japan	52 ft 5.875 in
1948	Arne Ahman, Sweden	50 ft 6.25 in
1952	Adhemar da Silva, Brazil	53 ft 2.5 in
1956	Adhemar da Silva, Brazil	53 ft 7.5 in
1960	Jozef Schmidt, Poland	55 ft 1.75 in
1964	Jozef Schmidt, Poland	55 ft 3.25 in
1968	Viktor Saneyev, USSR	57 ft 0.75 in
1972	Viktor Saneyev, USSR	56 ft 11 in
1976	Viktor Saneyev, USSR	56 ft 8.75 in
1980	Jaak Uudmae, USSR	56 ft 11.125 in
1984	Al Joyner, United States	56 ft 7.5 in
1988	Hristo Markov, Bulgaria	57 ft 9.25 in
1992	Mike Conley, United States	59 ft 7.5 in
1996	Kenny Harrison, United States	59 ft 4.25 in
2000	Jonathan Edwards, Great Britain	58 ft 1.25 in
2004	Christian Olsson, Sweden	58 ft 4.39 in

Pole Vault

1896	William Hoyt, United States	10 ft 9.75 in
1900	Irving Baxter, United States	10 ft 9.875 in
1904	Charles Dvorak, United States	11 ft 6 in
1906	Fernand Gouder, France	11 ft 6 in
1908	Alfred Gilbert, United States, and Edward Cook, United States (tie)	12 ft 2 in
1912	Harry Babcock, United States	12 ft 11.5 in
1920	Frank Foss, United States	13 ft 5.5625 in
1924	Lee Barnes, United States	12 ft 11.5 in
1928	Sabin W. Carr, United States	13 ft 9.375 in
1932	William Miller, United States	14 ft 1.875 in
1936	Earle Meadows, United States	14 ft 3.25 in
1948	Guinn Smith, United States	14 ft 0.25 in
1952	Robert Richards, United States	14 ft 11.125 in
1956	Robert Richards, United States	14 ft 11.5 in

1960	Don Bragg, United States	15 ft 5.125 in
1964	Fred Hansen, United States	16 ft 8.75 in
1968	Bob Seagren, United States	17 ft 8.5 in
1972	Wolfgang Nordwig, East Germany	18 ft 0.5 in
1976	Tadeusz Slusarski, Poland	18 ft 0.5 in
1980	Wladyslaw Kozakiewics, Poland	18 ft 11.5 in
1984	Pierre Quinon, France	18 ft 10.25 in
1988	Sergei Bubka, USSR	19 ft 4.25 in
1992	Maxim Tarassov, Unified Team[1]	19 ft 0.25 in
1996	Jean Galfione, France	19 ft 5.25 in
2000	Nick Hysong, United States	19 ft 4.25 in
2004	Tim Mack, United States	19 ft 6.25 in

1. Former Soviet Union team.

16-lb Shot-Put

1896	Robert Garrett, United States	36 ft 9.75 in
1900	Richard Sheldon, United States	46 ft 3.125 in
1904	Ralph Rose, United States	48 ft 7 in
1906	Martin Sheridan, United States	40 ft 4.8 in
1908	Ralph Rose, United States	46 ft 7.5 in
1912	Pat McDonald, United States	50 ft 4 in
1920	Ville Porhola, Finland	48 ft 7.125 in
1924	Clarence Houser, United States	49 ft 2.5 in
1928	John Kuck, United States	52 ft 11.6875 in
1932	Leo Sexton, United States	52 ft 6.1875 in
1936	Hans Woellke, Germany	53 ft 1.75 in
1948	Wilbur Thompson, United States	56 ft 2 in
1952	Parry O'Brien, United States	57 ft 1.5 in
1956	Parry O'Brien, United States	60 ft 11 in
1960	Bill Nieder, United States	64 ft 6.75 in
1964	Dallas Long, United States	66 ft 8.25 in
1968	Randy Matson, United States	67 ft 4.75 in
1972	Wladyslaw Komar, Poland	69 ft 6 in
1976	Udo Beyer, East Germany	69 ft 0.75 in
1980	Vladmir Klselyov, USSR	70 ft 0.5 in
1984	Alessandro Andrei, Italy	69 ft 9 in
1988	Uhf Timmerman, East Germany	73 ft 8.75 in
1992	Michael Stulze, United States	71 ft 2.5 in
1996	Randy Barnes, United States	70 ft 11.25 in
2000	Arsi Harju, Finland	69 ft 10.25 in
2004	Yuriy Bilonog, Ukraine	69 ft 5.07 in

Discus Throw

1896	Robert Garrett, United States	95 ft 7.5 in
1900	Rudolf Bauer, Hungary	118 ft 2.875 in
1904	Martin Sheridan, United States	128 ft 10.5 in
1906	Martin Sheridan, United States	136 ft 0.3 in
1908	Martin Sheridan, United States	134 ft 2 in
1912	Armas e, Finland	145 ft 0.5625 in
1920	Elmer Niklander, Finland	146 ft 7 in
1924	Clarence Houser, United States	151 ft 5.25 in
1928	Clarence Houser, United States	155 ft 2.8 in
1932	John Anderson, United States	162 ft 4.875 in
1936	Ken Carpenter, United States	165 ft 7.375 in
1948	Adolfo Consolini, Italy	173 ft 2 in
1952	Simeon Iness, United States	180 ft 6.5 in
1956	Al Oerter, United States	184 ft 10.5 in
1960	Al Oerter, United States	194 ft 2 in
1964	Al Oerter, United States	200 ft 1.5 in
1968	Al Oerter, United States	212 ft 6 in
1972	Ludvik Danek, Czechoslovakia	211 ft 3 in
1976	Mac Wilkins, United States	221 ft 5 in
1980	Viktor Rashchupkin, USSR	218 ft 8 in
1984	Rolf Dannenberg, West Germany	218 ft 6 in
1988	Jurgen Schult, East Germany	225 ft 9.25 in
1992	Romas Ubartas, Lithuania	213 ft 7.75 in
1996	Lars Riedel, Germany	227 ft 8 in
2000	Virgilijus Alekna, Lithuania	227 ft 4 in
2004	Virgilijus Alekna, Lithuania	229 ft 3.57 in

Javelin Throw

1906	Eric Lemming, Sweden	175 ft 6 in
1908	Eric Lemming, Sweden	179 ft 10.5 in
1912	Eric Lemming, Sweden	198 ft 11.25 in
1920	Jonni Myyra, Finland	215 ft 9.75 in
1924	Jonni Myyra, Finland	206 ft 6.75 in

1928	Eric Lundquist, Sweden	218 ft 6.125 in
1932	Matti Jarvinen, Finland	238 ft 7 in
1936	Gerhard Stoeck, Germany	235 ft 8.3125 in
1948	Kaj Rautavaara, Finland	228 ft 10.5 in
1952	Cy Young, United States	242 ft 0.75 in
1956	Egil Danielsen, Norway	281 ft 2.25 in
1960	Viktor Tsibuelnko, USSR	277 ft 8.375 in
1964	Pauli Nevala, Finland	271 ft 2.25 in
1968	Janis Lusis, USSR	295 ft 7 in
1972	Klaus Wolfermann, West Germany	296 ft 10 in
1976	Miklos Nemeth, Hungary	310 ft 4 in
1980	Dainis Kula, USSR	299 ft 2.375 in
1984	Arto Haerkoenen, Finland	284 ft 8 in
1988	Tapio Korjus, Finland	276 ft 6 in
1992	Jan Zelezny, Czechoslovakia	294 ft 2 in
1996	Jan Zelezny, Czech Republic	289 ft 3 in
2000	Jan Zelezny, Czech Republic	295 ft 9.5 in
2004	Andreas Thorkildsen, Norway	283 ft 9.51 in

16-lb Hammer Throw

1900	John Flanagan, United States	167 ft 4 in
1904	John Flanagan, United States	168 ft 1 in
1908	John Flanagan, United States	170 ft 4.25 in
1912	Matt McGrath, United States	179 ft 7.125 in
1920	Pat Ryan, United States	173 ft 5.625 in
1924	Fred Tootell, United States	174 ft 10.25 in
1928	Patrick O'Callaghan, Ireland	168 ft 7.5 in
1932	Patrick O'Callaghan, Ireland	176 ft 11.125 in
1936	Karl Hein, Germany	185 ft 4 in
1948	Imre Nemeth, Hungary	183 ft 11.5 in
1952	Jozsef Csermak, Hungary	197 ft 11.5625 in
1956	Harold Connolly, United States	207 ft 2.75 in
1960	Vasily Rudenkov, USSR	220 ft 1.625 in
1964	Romuald Klim, USSR	228 ft 9.5 in
1968	Gyula Zsivotzky, Hungary	240 ft 8 in
1972	Anatoly Bondarchuk, USSR	247 ft 8.5 in
1976	Yuri Sedykh, USSR	254 ft 4 in
1980	Yuri Sedykh, USSR	(81.80m) 268 ft 4.5 in
1984	Juha Tiainen, Finland	256 ft 2 in
1988	Sergei Litvinov, USSR	278 ft 2.5 in
1992	Andrey Abduvaliyev, Unified Team[1]	270 ft 9.5 in
1996	Balazs Kiss, Hungary	266 ft 6 in
2000	Szymon Ziolkowski, Poland	262 ft 6 in
2004	Koji Murofushi, Japan	272 ft 0.17 in

1. Former Soviet Union team.

Decathlon

1912	Jim Thorpe, United States	—
	Hugo Wieslander, Sweden	—
1920	Helge Lovland, Norway	6,804.35 pts.
1924	Harold Osborn, United States	7,710.775 pts.
1928	Paavo Yrjola, Finland	8,053.29 pts.
1932	James Bausch, United States	8,462.23 pts.
1936	Glenn Morris, United States	7,900 pts.[1]
1948	Robert B. Mathias, United States	7,139 pts.
1952	Robert B. Mathias, United States	7,887 pts.
1956	Milton Campbell, United States	7,937 pts.
1960	Rafer Johnson, United States	8,392 pts.
1964	Willi Holdorf, Germany	7,887 pts.[1]
1968	Bill Toomey, United States	8,193 pts.
1972	Nikolai Avilov, USSR	8,454 pts.
1976	Bruce Jenner, United States	8,618 pts.
1980	Daley Thompson, Great Britain	8,495 pts.
1984	Daley Thompson, Great Britain	8,797 pts.
1988	Christian Schenk, East Germany	8,488 pts.
1992	Robert Zmelik, Czechoslovakia	8,611 pts.
1996	Dan O'Brien, United States	8,824 pts.
2000	Erki Nool, Estonia	8,641 pts.
2004	Roman Sebrle, Czech Republic	8,893 pts.

1. Point system revised.

TRACK AND FIELD–WOMEN

100-Meter Dash
1928	Elizabeth Robinson, United States	12.20
1932	Stella Walsh, Poland	11.90
1936	Helen Stephens, United States	11.50
1948	Fanny Blankers-Koen, Netherlands	11.90
1952	Marjorie Jackson, Australia	11.50
1956	Betty Cuthbert, Australia	11.50
1960	Wilma Rudolph, United States	11.00
1964	Wyomia Tyus, United States	11.40
1968	Wyomia Tyus, United States	11.00
1972	Renate Stecher, East Germany	11.07
1976	Annegret Richter, West Germany	11.08
1980	Lyudmila Kondratyeva, USSR	11.06
1984	Evelyn Ashford, United States	10.97
1988	Florence Griffith-Joyner, United States	10.54
1992	Gail Devers, United States	10.82
1996	Gail Devers, United States	10.94
2000	Marion Jones, United States	10.75
2004	Yuliya Nesterenko, Belarus	10.93

200-Meter Dash
1948	Fanny Blankers-Koen, Netherlands	24.40
1952	Marjorie Jackson, Australia	23.70
1956	Betty Cuthbert, Australia	23.40
1960	Wilma Rudolph, United States	24.00
1964	Edith McGuire, United States	23.00
1968	Irena Szewinska, Poland	22.50
1972	Renate Stecher, East Germany	22.40
1976	Baerbel Eckert, East Germany	22.37
1980	Barbara Wockel, East Germany	22.03
1984	Valerie Brisco-Hooks, United States	21.81
1988	Florence Griffith-Joyner, United States	21.34
1992	Gwen Torrence, United States	21.81
1996	Marie-Jose Perec, France	22.12
2000	Marion Jones, United States	21.84
2004	Veronica Campbell, Jamaica	22.05

400-Meter Dash
1964	Betty Cuthbert, Australia	52.00
1968	Colette Besson, France	52.00
1972	Monika Zehrt, East Germany	51.08
1976	Irena Szewinska, Poland	49.29
1980	Marita Koch, East Germany	48.88
1984	Valerie Brisco-Hooks, United States	48.83
1988	Olga Bryzguina, USSR	48.65
1992	Marie Jose-Perec, France	48.83
1996	Marie Jose-Perec, France	48.25
2000	Cathy Freeman, Australia	49.11
2004	Tonique Williams-Darling, Bahamas	49.41

800-Meter Run
1928	Lina Radke, Germany	2:16.80
1960	Ljudmila Shevcova, USSR	2:04.30
1964	Ann Packer, Great Britain	2:01.10
1968	Madeline Manning, United States	2:00.90
1972	Hildegard Falck, West Germany	1:58.60
1976	Tatiana Kazankina, USSR	1:54.94
1980	Nadezhda Olizarenko, USSR	1:53.50
1984	Doina Melinte, Romania	1:57.60
1988	Sigrun Wodars, East Germany	1:56.10
1992	Ellen Van Langen, Netherlands	1:55.54
1996	Svetlana Masterkova, Russia	1:57.73
2000	Maria Mutola, Mozambique	1:56.15
2004	Kelly Holmes, Great Britain	1:56.38

1,500-Meter Run
1972	Ludmila Bragina, USSR	4:01.40
1976	Tatiana Kazankina, USSR	4:05.48
1980	Tatiana Kazankina, USSR	3:56.60
1984	Gabriella Dorio, Italy	4:03.25
1988	Paula Ivan, Romania	3:53.96
1992	Hassiba Boulmerka, Algeria	3:55.30
1996	Svetlana Masterkova, Russia	4:00.83
2000	Nouria Merah-Benida, Algeria	4:05.10
2004	Kelly Holmes, Great Britain	3:57.90

5,000-Meter Run
1996	Wang, Jun-Xia, China	14:59.88
2000	Gabriela Szabo, Romania	14:40.79
2004	Meseret Defar, Ethiopia	14:45.65

10,000-Meter Run
1992	Derartu Tulu, Ethiopia	31:60.02
1996	Fernanda Ribeiro, Portugal	31:01.63
2000	Derartu Tulu, Ethiopia	30:17.49
2004	Huina Xing, China	30:24.36

Marathon
1984	Joan Benoit, United States	2:24:52
1988	Rose Mota, Portugal	2:25.40
1992	Valentina Yegorova, Unified Team	2:32.41
1996	Fatuma Roba, Ethiopia	2:26.05
2000	Naoko Takahashi, Japan	2:23.14
2004	Mizuki Noguchi, Japan	2:26.20

80-Meter Hurdles
1932	Mildred Didrikson, United States	11.70
1936	Trebisonda Valla, Italy	11.70
1948	Fanny Blankers-Koen, Netherlands	11.20
1952	Shirley S. de la Hunty, Australia	10.90
1956	Shirley S. de la Hunty, Australia	10.70
1960	Irina Press, USSR	10.80
1964	Karin Balzer, Germany	10.50[1]
1968	Maureen Caird, Australia	10.30

1. Wind assisted.

100-Meter Hurdles
1972	Annelie Ehrhardt, East Germany	12.59
1976	Johanna Schaller, East Germany	12.77
1980	Vera Komisova, USSR	12.56
1984	Benita Fitzgerald-Brown, United States	12.84
1988	Jordanka Donkova, Bulgaria	12.38
1992	Paraskevi Patoulidou, Greece	12.64
1996	Ludmila Engquist, Sweden	12.58
2000	Olga Shishigina, Kazakhstan	12.65
2004	Joanna Hayes, United States	12.37

400-Meter Hurdles
1984	Nawai El Moutawakel, Morocco	54.61
1988	Debra Flintoff-King, Australia	53.17
1992	Sally Gunnell, Great Britain	53.23
1996	Deon Hemmings, Jamaica	52.82
2000	Irina Privalova, Russia	53.02
2004	Fani Halkia, Greece	52.82

400-Meter Relay (4 × 100)
1928	Canada	48.40
1932	United States	47.00
1936	United States	46.90
1948	Netherlands	47.50
1952	United States	45.90
1956	Australia	44.50
1960	United States	44.50
1964	Poland	43.60
1968	United States	42.80
1972	West Germany	42.81
1976	East Germany	42.50
1980	East Germany	41.60
1984	United States	41.65
1988	United States	41.98
1992	United States	42.11
1996	United States	41.95
2000	Bahamas	41.95
2004	Jamaica	41.73

1,600-Meter Relay (4 × 400)
1972	East Germany	3:23.00
1976	East Germany	3:19.23
1980	USSR	3:20.20
1984	United States	3:18.29
1988	USSR	3:15.18
1992	Unified Team[1]	3:20.20
1996	United States	3:20.91
2000	United States	3:22.62
2004	United States	3:19.01

1. Former Soviet Union team.

10,000-Meter Walk
1992	ChenYue-Ling, China	44:32
1996	Yelena Nikolayeva, Russia	41:49

20,000-Meter Walk
2000	Liping Wang, China	1:29:05
2004	Athanasia Tsoumeleka, Greece	1:29:12

Running High Jump
1928	Ethel Catherwood, Canada	5 ft 3 in
1932	Jean Shiley, United States	5 ft 5.25 in
1936	Ibolya Csak, Hungary	5 ft 3 in
1948	Alice Coachman, United States	5 ft 6.125 in
1952	Ester Brand, South Africa	5 ft 5.75 in
1956	Mildred McDaniel, United States	5 ft 9.25 in
1960	Iolanda Balas, Romania	6 ft 0.75 in
1964	Iolanda Balas, Romania	6 ft 2.75 in
1968	Miloslava Rezkova, Czechoslovakia	5 ft 11.75 in
1972	Ulrike Meyfarth, West Germany	6 ft 3.625 in
1976	Rosemarie Ackerman, E. Germany	6 ft 4 in
1980	Sara Simeoni, Italy	6 ft 5.5 in
1984	Ulrike Meyfarth, West Germany	6 ft 7.5 in
1988	Louise Ritter, United States	6 ft 8 in
1992	Heike Henkel, Germany	6 ft 7.5 in
1996	Stefka Kostadinova, Bulgaria	6 ft 8.75 in
2000	Yelena Yelesina, Russia	6 ft 7 in
2004	Yelena Slesarenko, Russia	6 ft 9.1 in

Long Jump
1948	Olga Gyarmati, Hungary	18 ft 8.25 in
1952	Yvette Williams, New Zealand	20 ft 5.75 in
1956	Elzbieta Krzesinska, Poland	20 ft 9.75 in
1960	Vera Krepkina, USSR	20 ft 10.75 in
1964	Mary Rand, Great Britain	22 ft 2 in
1968	Viorica Ciscopoleanu, Romania	22 ft 4.5 in
1972	Heidemarie Rosendahl, West Germany	22 ft 3 in
1976	Angela Voigt, East Germany	22 ft 0.5 in
1980	Tatiana Kolpakova, USSR	23 ft 2 in
1984	Anisoara Stanciu, Romania	22 ft 10 in
1988	Jackie Joyner-Kersee, United States	24 ft 3.5 in
1992	Heike Drechsler, Germany	23 ft 5.25 in
1996	Chioma Ajunwa, Nigeria	23 ft 4.5 in
2000	Heike Drechsler, Germany	22 ft 11.25 in
2004	Tatyana Lebedeva, Russia	23 ft 2.35 in

Triple Jump
1996	Inessa Kravets, Ukraine	50 ft 1.5 in
2000	Tereza Marinova, Bulgaria	49 ft 10.5 in
2004	Francoise Mbango Etone, Cameroon	50 ft 2.36 in

Shot-Put
1948	Micheline Ostermeyer, France	45 ft 1.5 in
1952	Galina Zybina, USSR	50 ft 1.5 in
1956	Tamara Tishkyevich, USSR	54 ft 5 in
1960	Tamara Press, USSR	56 ft 9.875 in
1964	Tamara Press, USSR	59 ft 6 in
1968	Margitta Gummel, East Germany	64 ft 4 in
1972	Nadezhda Chizhova, USSR	69 ft
1976	Ivanka Christova, Bulgaria	69 ft 5 in
1980	Ilona Sluplanek, East Germany	73 ft 6 in
1984	Claudia Losch, West Germany	67 ft 2.25 in
1988	Natalya Lisovskaya, USSR	72 ft 11.5 in
1992	Svetlana Kriveleva, Unified Team[1]	69 ft 1.25 in
1996	Astrid Kumbernuss, Germany	67 ft 5.5 in
2000	Yanina Korolchik, Belarus	67 ft 5.5 in
2004	Yumileidi Cumba, Cuba	64 ft 3.26 in

1. Former Soviet Union team.

Discus Throw
1928	Helena Konopacka, Poland	129 ft 11.875 in
1932	Lillian Copeland, United States	133 ft 2 in
1936	Gisela Mauermayer, Germany	156 ft 3.175 in
1948	Micheline Ostermeyer, France	137 ft 6.5 in
1956	Olga Fikotova, Czechoslovakia	176 ft 1.5 in
1960	Nina Ponomareva, USSR	180 ft 8.25 in
1964	Tamara Press, USSR	187 ft 10.75 in
1968	Lia Manoliu, Romania	191 ft 2.5 in
1972	Faina Melnik, USSR	218 ft 7 in

1976	Evelin Schlaak, East Germany	226 ft 4 in
1980	Evelin Jahl, East Germany	229 ft 6.5 in
1984	Ria Stalman, Netherlands	214 ft 5 in
1988	Martina Hellmann, East Germany	237 ft 2.25 in
1992	Maritza Marten, Cuba	229 ft 10.25 in
1996	Ilke Wyludda, Germany	228 ft 6.5 in
2000	Ellina Zvereva, Belarus	224 ft 5 in
2004	Natalya Sadova, Russia	219 ft 10.58 in

Javelin Throw
1932	Mildred Didrikson, United States	143 ft 4 in
1936	Tilly Fleischer, Germany	148 ft 2.75 in
1948	Herma Bauma, Austria	149 ft 6 in
1952	Dana Zatopek, Czechoslovakia	165 ft 7 in
1956	Inessa Janzeme, USSR	176 ft 8 in
1960	Elvira Ozolina, USSR	183 ft 8 in
1964	Mihaela Penes, Romania	198 ft 7.5 in
1968	Angela Nemeth, Hungary	198 ft
1972	Ruth Fuchs, East Germany	209 ft 7 in
1976	Ruth Fuchs, East Germany	216 ft 4 in
1980	Maria Colon, Cuba	224 ft 5 in
1984	Tessa Sanderson, Britain	228 ft 2 in
1988	Petra Felke, East Germany	245 ft
1992	Silke Renke, Germany	224 ft 2.5 in
1996	Heli Rantanen, Finland	222 ft 11 in
2000	Trine Hattestad, Norway	226 ft 1 in
2004	Osleidys Menendez, Cuba	234 ft 8.14 in

Hammer Throw
2000	Kamila Skolimowska, Poland	233 ft 5.75 in
2004	Olga Kuzenkova, Russia	246 ft 1.54 in

Pole Vault
2000	Stacy Dragila, United States	15 ft 1 in
2004	Yelena Isinbayeva, Russia	16 ft 1.31 in[1]

1. World record.

Pentathlon
1964	Irina Press, USSR	5,246 pts.
1968	Ingrid Becker, West Germany	5,098 pts.
1972	Mary Peters, Britain	4,801 pts.
1976	Siegrun Siegl, East Germany	4,745 pts.
1980	Nadyeszhda Tkachenko, USSR	5,083 pts.
1984	Daniele Masala, Italy	5,469 pts.
1988	Jackie Joyner-Kersee, United States	7,291 pts.

Heptathlon
1992	Jackie Joyner-Kersee, United States	7,044 pts.
1996	Ghada Shouaa, Syria	6,780 pts.
2000	Denise Lewis, Great Britain	6,584 pts.
2004	Carolina Kluft, Sweden	6,952 pts.

SWIMMING–MEN

50-Meter Freestyle
1988	Matt Biondi, United States	22.14
1992	Alexander Popov, Unified Team[1]	21.91
1996	Alexander Popov, Russia	22.13
2000	Anthony Ervin and Gary Hall, Jr., United States	21.98
2004	Gary Hall, Jr., United States	21.93

1. Former Soviet Union team.

100-Meter Freestyle
1896	Alfred Hajos, Hungary	1:22.20
1904	Zoltan de Halmay, Hungary	1:02.80[1]
1906	Charles Daniels, United States	1:13.00
1908	Charles Daniels, United States	1:05.60
1912	Duke P. Kahanamoku, United States	1:03.40
1920	Duke P. Kahanamoku, United States	1:01.40
1924	John Weissmuller, United States	0:59.00
1928	John Weissmuller, United States	0:58.60
1932	Yasuji Miyazaki, Japan	0:58.20
1936	Ferenc Csik, Hungary	0:57.60
1948	Walter Ris, United States	0:57.30
1952	Clarke Scholes, United States	0:57.40
1956	Jon Henricks, Australia	0:55.40
1960	John Devitt, Australia	0:55.20
1964	Don Schollander, United States	0:53.40

1968	Michael Wenden, Australia	0:52.20
1972	Mark Spitz, United States	0:51.22
1976	Jim Montgomery, United States	0:49.99
1980	Jorg Woithe, East Germany	0:50.40
1984	Rowdy Gaines, United States	0:49.80
1988	Matt Biondi, United States	0:48.63
1992	Alexander Popov, Unified Team[2]	0:49.02
1996	Alexander Popov, Russia	0:48.74
2000	Pieter van den Hoogenband, Netherlands	0:48.30
2004	Pieter van den Hoogenband, Netherlands	0:48.17

1. 100 yards. 2. Former Soviet Union team.

200-Meter Freestyle

1900	Frederick Lane, Australia	2:25.20
1904	Charles Daniels, United States	2:44.20[1]
1968	Michael Wenden, Australia	1:55.20
1972	Mark Spitz, United States	1:52.78
1976	Bruce Furniss, United States	1:50.29
1980	Sergei Kopliakov, USSR	4:49.81
1984	Michael Gross, West Germany	1:47.44
1988	Duncan Armstrong, Australia	1:47.25
1992	Evgueni Sadovyi, Unified Team[2]	1:46.70
1996	Danyon Loader, New Zealand	1:47.63
2000	Pieter van den Hoogenband, Netherlands	1:45.35[3]
2004	Ian Thorpe, Australia	1:44.71

1. 220 yards 2. Former Soviet Union team. 3. World record.

400-Meter Freestyle

1896	Paul Neumann, Austria	8:12.60[1]
1904	Charles Daniels, United States	6:16.20[2]
1906	Otto Sheff, Austria	6:23.80
1908	Henry Taylor, Great Britain	5:36.80
1912	George Hodgson, Canada	5:24.40
1920	Norman Ross, United States	5:26.80
1926	John Weissmuller, United States	5:04.20
1928	Albert Zorilla, Argentina	5:01.60
1932	Clarence Crabbe, United States	4:48.40
1936	Jack Medica, United States	4:44.50
1948	William Smith, United States	4:41.00
1952	Jean Boiteux, France	4:30.70
1956	Murray Rose, Australia	4:27.30
1960	Murray Rose, Australia	4:18.30
1964	Don Schollander, United States	4:12.20
1968	Mike Burton, United States	4:09.00
1972	Bradford Cooper, Australia	4:00.27[3]
1976	Brian Goodell, United States	3:51.93
1980	Vladimir Salnikov, USSR	3:51.31
1984	George DiCarlo, United States	3:51.23
1988	Uwe Dassier, East Germany	3:46.95
1992	Evgueni Sadovyi, Unified Team	3:45.00[4]
1996	Danyon Loader, New Zealand	3:47.97
2000	Ian Thorpe, Australia	3:40.59[4]
2004	Ian Thorpe, Australia	3:43.10

1. 500 meters. 2. 440 yards. 3. Rich DeMont, United States, won but was disqualified following day for medical reasons. 4. World record.

1,500-Meter Freestyle

1904	Emil Rausch, Germany	27:18.20[1]
1906	Henry Taylor, Great Britain	28:28.00[2]
1908	Henry Taylor, Great Britain	22:48.40
1912	George Hodgson, Canada	22:00.00
1920	Norman Ross, United States	22:23.20
1924	Andrew Charlton, Australia	20:06.60
1928	Arne Borg, Sweden	19:51.80
1932	Kusuo Kitamura, Japan	19:12.40
1936	Noboru Terada, Japan	19:13.70
1948	James McLane, United States	19:18.50
1952	Ford Konno, United States	18:30.00
1956	Murray Rose, Australia	17:58.90
1960	Jon Konrads, Australia	17:19.60
1964	Robert Windle, Australia	17:01.70
1968	Michael Burton, United States	16:38.90
1972	Michael Burton, United States	15:52.58
1976	Brian Goodell, United States	15:02.40
1980	Vladimir Salnikov, USSR	14:58.27
1984	Michael O'Brien, United States	15:05.20
1988	Vladimir Salnikov, USSR	15:00.40
1992	Kieren Perkins, Australia	14:43.48
1996	Kieren Perkins, Australia	14:56.40
2000	Grant Hackett, Australia	14:48.33
2004	Grant Hackett, Australia	14:43.40

1. One mile. 2. 1,600 meters

100-Meter Backstroke

1904	Walter Brack, Germany	1:16.80[1]
1908	Arno Bieberstein, Germany	1:24.60
1912	Harry Hebner, United States	1:21.20
1920	Warren Kealoha, United States	1:15.20
1924	Warren Kealoha, United States	1:13.20
1928	George Kojac, United States	1:08.20
1932	Masaji Kiyokawa, Japan	1:08.60
1936	Adolph Kiefer, United States	1:05.90
1948	Allen Stack, United States	1:06.40
1952	Yoshinobu Oyakawa, United States	1:05.40
1956	David Thiele, Australia	1:02.20
1960	David Thiele, Australia	1:01.90
1968	Roland Matthes, East Germany	0:58.70
1972	Roland Matthes, East Germany	0:56.58
1976	John Naber, United States	0:55.49
1980	Bengt Baron, Sweden	0:56.53
1984	Rick Carey, United States	0:55.79
1988	Daichi Suzuki, Japan	0:55.05
1992	Mark Tewksbury, Canada	0:53.98
1996	Jeff Rouse, United States	0:54.10
2000	Lenny Krayzelburg, United States	0:53.72
2004	Aaron Peirsol, United States	0:54.06

1. 100 yards

200-Meter Backstroke

1900	Ernst Hoppenberg, Germany	2:47.00
1964	Jed Graef, United States	2:10.30
1968	Roland Matthes, East Germany	2:09.60
1972	Roland Matthes, East Germany	2:02.82
1976	John Naber, United States	1:59.19
1980	Sandor Wladar, Hungary	2:01.93
1984	Rick Carey, United States	2:00.23
1988	Igor Polianski, USSR	1:59.37
1992	Martin Lopez Zubero, Spain	1:58.47
1996	Brad Bridgewater, United States	1:58.54
2000	Lenny Krayzelburg, United States	1:56.76
2004	Aaron Peirsol, United States	1:54.95

100-Meter Breaststroke

1968	Donald McKenzie, United States	1:07.70
1972	Nobutaka Taguchi, Japan	1:04.94
1976	John Hencken, United States	1:03.11
1980	Duncan Goodhew, Britain	1:03.34
1984	Steve Lindquist, United States	1:01.65
1988	Adrian Moorhouse, Great Britain	1:02.04
1992	Nelson Diebel, United States	1:01.50
1996	Fred Deburghgraeve, Belgium	1:00.60[1]
2000	Domenico Fioravanti, Italy	1:00.46
2004	Kosuke Kitajima, Japan	1:00.08

1. World record.

200-Meter Breaststroke

1908	Frederick Holman, Great Britain	3:09.20
1912	Walter Bathe, Germany	3:01.80
1920	Haken Malmroth, Sweden	3:04.40
1924	Robert Skelton, United States	2:56.60
1928	Yoshiyuki Tsuruta, Japan	2:48.80
1932	Yoshiyuki Tsuruta, Japan	2:45.40
1936	Tetsuo Hamuro, Japan	2:41.50
1948	Joseph Verdeur, United States	2:39.30
1952	John Davies, Australia	2:34.40
1956	Masaura Furukawa, Japan	2:34.70
1960	Bill Muliken, United States	2:37.40
1964	Ian O'Brien, Australia	2:07.80
1968	Felipe Munoz, Mexico	2:28.70
1972	John Hencken, United States	2:21.55
1976	David Willkie, Britain	2:15.11
1980	Robertas Zulpa, USSR	2:15.85

1984	Victor Davis, Canada	2:13.34
1988	Jozef Szabo, Hungary	2:13.52
1992	Mike Barrowman, United States	2:10.16
1996	Norbert Rozsa, Hungary	2:12.57
2000	Domenico Fioravanti, Italy	2:10.87
2004	Kosuke Kitajima, Japan	2:09.44

100-Meter Butterfly

1968	Douglas Russell, United States	55.90
1972	Mark Spitz, United States	54.27
1976	Matt Vogel, United States	54.35
1980	Par Arvidsson, Sweden	54.92
1984	Michael Gross, West Germany	53.08
1988	Anthony Nesty, Surinam	53.00
1992	Pablo Morales, United States	53.32
1996	Denis Pankratov, Russia	52.27[1]
2000	Lars Froelander, Sweden	52.00
2004	Michael Phelps, United States	51.25
1. World record.		

200-Meter Butterfly

1956	Bill Yorzyk, United States	2:19.30
1960	Mike Troy, United States	2:12.80
1964	Kevin Berry, Australia	2:06.60
1968	Carl Robie, United States	2:08.70
1972	Mark Spitz, United States	2:00.70
1976	Mike Bruner, United States	1:59.23
1980	Sergei Fesenko, USSR	1:59.76
1984	Jon Sieben, Australia	1:57.00
1988	Michael Gross, East Germany	1:56.94
1992	Mel Stewart, United States	1:56.26
1996	Denis Pankratov, Russia	1:56.51
2000	Tom Malchow, United States	1:55.35
2004	Michael Phelps, United States	1:54.04

200-Meter Individual Medley

1968	Charles Hickcox, United States	2:12.00
1972	Gunnar Larsson, Sweden	2:07.17
1988	Tamas Darnyi, Hungary	2:00.17
1992	Tamas Darnyi, Hungary	2:00.76
1996	Attila Czene, Hungary	1:59.91
2000	Massimiliano Rosolino, Italy	1:58.98
2004	Michael Phelps, United States	1:57.14

400-Meter Individual Medley

1964	Dick Roth, United States	4:45.40
1968	Charles Hickcox, United States	4:48.40
1972	Gunnar Larsson, Sweden	4:31.98
1976	Rod Strachan, United States	4:23.68
1980	Aleksandr Sidorenko, USSR	4:22.80
1984	Alex Baumann, Canada	4:17.41
1988	Tamas Darnyi, Hungary	4:14.75
1992	Tamas Darnyi, Hungary	4:14.23
1996	Tom Dolan, United States	4:14.90
2000	Tom Dolan, United States	4:11.76
2004	Michael Phelps, United States	4:08.26[1]
1. World record.		

400-Meter Freestyle Relay (4 × 100)

1964	United States	3:32.20
1968	United States	3:31.70
1972	United States	3:26.42
1988	United States	3:16.52
1992	United States	3:16.74
1996	United States	3:15.41
2000	Australia	3:13.67
2004	South Africa	3:13.17[1]
1. World record.		

800-Meter Freestyle Relay (4 × 200)

1908	Great Britain	10:55.60
1912	Australia	10:11.20
1920	United States	10:04.40
1924	United States	09:53.40
1928	United States	09:36.20
1932	Japan	08:58.40
1936	Japan	08:51.50
1948	United States	08:46.10
1952	United States	08:31.10

1956	Australia	08:23.60
1960	United States	08:10.20
1964	United States	07:52.10
1968	United States	07:52.30
1972	United States	07:35.78
1976	United States	07:23.22
1980	USSR	07:23.50
1984	United States	07:16.59
1988	United States	07:12.51
1992	Unified Team[1]	07:11.95
1996	United States	07:14.84
2000	Australia	07:07.05[2]
2004	United States	07:07.33
1. Former Soviet Union team. 2. World record.		

400-Meter Medley Relay (4 × 100)

1960	United States	4:05.40
1964	United States	3:58.40
1968	United States	3:54.90
1972	United States	3:48.16
1976	United States	3:42.22
1980	Australia	3:45.70
1984	United States	3:39.30
1988	United States	3:36.93
1992	United States	3:36.93
1996	United States	3:34.84
2000	United States	3:33.73
2004	United States	3:30.68[1]
1. World record.		

Springboard Dive		**Points**
1908	Albert Zuerner, Germany	85.50
1912	Paul Guenther, Germany	79.23
1920	Louis Kuehn, United States	675.00
1924	Albert White, United States	696.40
1928	Pete Desjardins, United States	185.04
1932	Michael Galitzen, United States	161.38
1936	Richard Degener, United States	163.57
1948	Bruce Harlan, United States	163.64
1952	David Browning, United States	205.59
1956	Robert Clotworthy, United States	159.56
1960	Gary Tobian, United States	170.00
1964	Ken Sitzberger, United States	159.90
1968	Bernard Wrightson, United States	170.15
1972	Vladimir Vasin, USSR	594.09
1976	Phil Boggs, United States	619.05
1980	Alexsandr Portnov, USSR	905.02
1984	Greg Louganis, United States	754.41
1988	Greg Louganis, United States	730.80
1992	Mark Lenzi, United States	676.53
1996	Xiong Ni, China	701.46
2000	Xiong Ni, China	708.72
2004	Bo Peng, China	787.38

Platform Dive		**Points**
1904	G.E. Sheldon, United States	12.75
1906	Gottlob Walz, Germany	156.00
1908	Hialmar Johansson, Sweden	83.75
1912	Erik Adlerz, Sweden	73.94
1920	Clarence Pinkston, United States	100.67
1924	Albert White, United States	487.30
1928	Pete Desjardins, United States	98.74
1932	Harold Smith, United States	124.80
1936	Marshall Wayne, United States	113.58
1948	Samuel Lee, United States	130.05
1952	Samuel Lee, United States	156.28
1956	Joaquin Capilla, Mexico	152.44
1960	Bob Webster, United States	165.56
1964	Bob Webster, United States	148.58
1968	Klaus Dibiasi, Italy	164.18
1972	Klaus Dibiasi, Italy	504.12
1976	Klaus Dibiasi, Italy	600.51
1980	Falk Hoffman, East Germany	835.65
1984	Greg Louganis, United States	710.91
1988	Greg Louganis, United States	638.61
1992	Sun, Shu-Wei, China	677.31

1996	Dmitri Saoutine, Russia	692.34
2000	Tian Liang, China	724.53
2004	Jia Hu, China	748.08

Synchronized 3m Springboard Dive   **Points**

2000	Xiao Hailiang and Xiong Ni, China	365.58
2004	Nikolaos Siranidis and Thomas Bimis, Greece	353.34

Synchronized 10m Platform Dive   **Points**

2000	Igor Loukachine and Dmitri Saoutine, Russia	365.04
2004	Liang Tian and Jinghui Yang, China	383.88

SWIMMING–WOMEN

50-Meter Freestyle

1988	Kristin Otto, East Germany	25.49
1992	Yang, Wen-Yi, China	24.79
1996	Amy Van Dyken, United States	24.87
2000	Inge de Bruijn, Netherlands	24.32
2004	Inge de Bruijn, Netherlands	24.58

100-Meter Freestyle

1912	Fanny Durack, Australia	1:22.20
1920	Ethelda Bleibtrey, United States	1:13.60
1924	Ethel Lackie, United States	1:12.40
1928	Albina Osipowich, United States	1:11.00
1932	Helene Madison, United States	1:06.80
1936	Hendrika Mastenbroek, Netherlands	1:05.90
1948	Greta Andersen, Denmark	1:06.30
1952	Katalin Szoke, Hungary	1:06.80
1956	Dawn Fraser, Australia	1:02.00
1960	Dawn Fraser, Australia	1:01.20
1964	Dawn Fraser, Australia	0:59.50
1968	Marge Jan Henne, United States	1:00.00
1972	Sandra Neilson, United States	0:58.59
1976	Kornelia Ender, East Germany	0:55.65
1980	Barbara Krause, East Germany	0:54.79
1984	Carrie Steinseifer, United States	0:55.92
1988	Kristin Otto, East Germany	0:54.93
1992	Zhuang Yong, China	0:54.64
1996	Le Jingyi, China	0:54.50
2000	Inge de Bruijn, Netherlands	0:58.83
2004	Jodie Henry, Australia	0:53.84

200-Meter Freestyle

1968	Debbie Meyer, United States	2:10.50
1972	Shane Gould, Australia	2:03.56
1976	Kornelia Ender, East Germany	1:59.26
1980	Barbara Krause, East Germany	1:58.33
1984	Mary Wayle, United States	1:59.23
1988	Heike Friedrich, East Germany	1:57.65
1992	Nicole Haislett, United States	1:57.90
1996	Claudia Poll, Costa Rica	1:58.16
2000	Susie O'Neill, Australia	1:58.24
2004	Camelia Potec, Romania	1:58.03

400-Meter Freestyle

1920	Ethelda Bleibtrey, United States	4:34.00[1]
1924	Martha Norelius, United States	6:02.20
1928	Martha Norelius, United States	5:42.80
1932	Helene Madison, United States	5:28.50
1936	Hendrika Mastenbroek, Netherlands	5:26.40
1948	Ann Curtis, United States	5:17.80
1952	Valerie Gyenge, Hungary	5:12.10
1956	Lorraine Crapp, Australia	4:54.60
1960	Chris von Saltza, United States	4:50.60
1964	Ginny Duenkel, United States	4:43.30
1968	Debbie Meyer, United States	4:31.80
1972	Shane Gould, Australia	4:19.04
1976	Petra Thumer, East Germany	4:09.89
1980	Ines Diers, East Germany	4:08.76
1984	Tiffany Cohen, United States	4:07.10
1988	Janet Evans, United States	4:03.85
1992	Dagmar Hase, Germany	4:07.18
1996	Michelle Smith, Ireland	4:07.25
2000	Brooke Bennett, United States	4:05.80

2004	Laure Manaudou, France	4:05.34

1. 300 meters.

800-Meter Freestyle

1968	Debbie Meyer, United States	9:24.00
1972	Keena Rothhammer, United States	8:53.68
1976	Petra Thumer, East Germany	8:37.14
1980	Michelle Ford, Australia	8:28.90
1984	Tiffany Cohen, United States	8:24.95
1988	Janet Evans, United States	8:20.20
1992	Janet Evans, Unites States	8:25.52
1996	Brooke Bennett, Unites States	8:27.89
2000	Brooke Bennett, United States	8:19.67
2004	Ai Shibata, Japan	8:24.54

100-Meter Backstroke

1924	Sybil Bauer, United States	1:23.20
1928	Marie Braun, Netherlands	1:22.00
1932	Eleanor Holm, United States	1:19.40
1936	Dina Senff, Netherlands	1:18.90
1948	Karen Harup, Denmark	1:14.40
1952	Joan Harrison, South Africa	1:14.30
1956	Judy Grinham, Great Britain	1:12.90
1960	Lynn Burke, United States	1:09.30
1964	Cathy Ferguson, United States	1:07.70
1968	Kaye Hall, United States	1:06.20
1972	Melissa Belote, United States	1:05.78
1976	Ulrike Richter, East Germany	1:01.83
1980	Rica Reinisch, East Germany	1:00.86
1984	Theresa Andrews, United States	1:02.55
1988	Kristin Otto, East Germany	1:00.89
1992	Krisztina Egerszegi, Hungary	1:00.68
1996	Beth Botsford, United States	1:01.19
2000	Diana Mocanu, Romania	1:00.21
2004	Natalie Coughlin, United States	1:00.37

200-Meter Backstroke

1968	Pokey Watson, United States	2:24.80
1972	Melissa Belote, United States	2:19.19
1976	Ulrike Richter, East Germany	2:13.43
1980	Rica Reinisch, East Germany	2:11.77
1984	Jolanda DeRover, Netherlands	2:12.38
1988	Krisztina Egerszegi, Hungary	2:09.29
1992	Krisztina Egerszegi, Hungary	2:07.06
1996	Krisztina Egerszegi, Hungary	2:07.83
2000	Diana Mocanu, Romania	2:08.16
2004	Kirsty Coventry, Zimbabwe	2:09.19

100-Meter Breaststroke

1968	Djurdjica Bjedov, Yugoslavia	1:15.80
1972	Catherine Carr, United States	1:13.58
1976	Hannelore Anke, East Germany	1:11.16
1980	Ute Geweniger, East Germany	1:10.22
1984	Petra Van Staveren, Netherlands	1:09.88
1988	Tainia Dangalakova, Bulgaria	1:07.95
1992	Elena Roudkovskaia, Unified Team	1:08.00
1996	Penny Heyns, South Africa	1:07.73
2000	Megan Quann, United States	1:07.05
2004	Xuejuan Luo, China	1:06.64

200-Meter Breaststroke

1924	Lucy Morton, Great Britain	3:33.20
1928	Hilde Schrader, Germany	3:12.60
1932	Clare Dennis, Australia	3:06.30
1936	Hideko Maehata, Japan	3:03.60
1948	Nel van Vliet, Netherlands	2:57.20
1952	Eva Szekely, Hungary	2:51.70
1956	Ursula Happe, Germany	2:53.10
1960	Anita Lonsbrough, Great Britain	2:49.50
1964	Galina Prozumenschikova, USSR	2:46.40
1968	Sharon Wichman, United States	2:44.40
1972	Beverly Whitfield, Australia	2:41.71
1976	Marina Koshevaia, USSR	2:33.35
1980	Lina Kachushite, USSR	2:29.54
1984	Anne Ottenbrite, Canada	2:30.38
1988	Silke Hoerner, East Germany	2:26.71
1992	Kyoko Iwasaki, Japan	2:26.65
1996	Penny Heyns, South Africa	2:25.41

2000	Agnes Kovacs, Hungary	2:24.35
2004	Amanda Beard, United States	2:23.37

100-Meter Butterfly

1956	Shelley Mann, United States	1:11.00
1960	Carolyn Schuler, United States	1:09.50
1964	Sharon Stouder, United States	1:04.70
1968	Lynn McClements, Australia	1:05.50
1972	Mayumi Aoki, Japan	1:03.34
1976	Kornelia Ender, East Germany	1:00.13
1980	Caren Metschuck, East Germany	1:00.42
1984	Mary Meagher, United States	0:59.26
1988	Kristin Otto, East Germany	0:59.00
1992	Qian Hong, China	0:58.62
1996	Amy Van Dyken, United States	0:59.13
2000	Inge de Bruijn, Netherlands	0:56.61[1]
2004	Petria Thomas, Australia	0:57.72

1. World record.

200-Meter Butterfly

1968	Ada Kok, Netherlands	2:24.70
1972	Karen Moe, United States	2:15.57
1976	Andrea Pollack, East Germany	2:11.41
1980	Ines Geissler, East Germany	2:10.44
1984	Mary Meagher, United States	2:06.90
1988	Kathleen Nord, East Germany	2:09.51
1992	Summer Sanders, United States	2:06.67
1996	Susan O'Neill, Australia	2:07.76
2000	Misty Hyman, United States	2:05.88
2004	Otylia Jedrzejczak, Poland	2:06.05

200-Meter Individual Medley

1968	Claudia Kolb, United States	2:24.70
1972	Shane Gould, Australia	2:23.07
1984	Tracy Caulkins, United States	2:12.64
1988	Daniela Hunger, East Germany	2:12.59
1992	Lin Lee, China	2:11.55[1]
1996	Michelle Smith, Ireland	2:13.93
2000	Yana Klochkova, Ukraine	2:10.68
2004	Yana Klochkova, Ukraine	2:11.14

1. World record.

400-Meter Individual Medley

1964	Donna de Varona, United States	5:18.70
1968	Claudia Kolk, United States	5:08.50
1972	Gail Neall, Australia	5:02.97
1976	Ulrike Tauber, East Germany	4:42.77
1980	Petra Schneider, East Germany	4:36.29
1984	Tracy Caulkins, United States	4:39.21
1988	Janet Evans, United States	4:37.76
1992	Krisztina Egerszegi, Hungary	4:36.54
1996	Michelle Smith, Ireland	4:39.18
2000	Yana Klochkova, Ukraine	4:33.59[1]
2004	Yana Klochkova, Ukraine	4:34.83

1. World record.

400-Meter Freestyle Relay (4 × 100)

1912	Great Britain	5:52.80
1920	United States	5:11.60
1924	United States	4:58.80
1928	United States	4:47.60
1932	United States	4:38.00
1936	Netherlands	4:36.00
1948	United States	4:29.20
1952	Hungary	4:24.40
1956	Australia	4:17.10
1960	United States	4:08.90
1964	United States	4:03.80
1968	United States	4:02.50
1972	United States	3:55.19
1976	United States	3:44.82
1980	East Germany	3:42.71
1984	United States	3:44.43
1988	East Germany	3:40.63
1992	United States	3:39.46
1996	United States	3:39.29
2000	United States	3:36.61
2004	Australia	3:35.94[1]

1. World record.

800-Meter Freestyle Relay (4 × 200)

1996	United States	7:59.87
2000	United States	7:57.80
2004	United States	7:53.42[1]

1. World record.

400-Meter Medley Relay (4 × 100)

1960	United States	4:41.10
1964	United States	4:33.90
1968	United States	4:28.30
1972	United States	4:20.75
1976	East Germany	4:07.95
1980	East Germany	4:06.67
1984	United States	4:08.34
1988	East Germany	4:03.74
1992	United States	4:02.54
1996	United States	4:02.88
2000	United States	3:58.30
2004	Australia	3:57.32[1]

1. World record.

Springboard Dive	**Points**
1920 Aileen Riggin, United States	539.90
1924 Elizabeth Becker, United States	474.50
1928 Helen Meany, United States	78.62
1932 Georgia Coleman, United States	87.52
1936 Marjorie Gestring, United States	89.27
1948 Victoria M. Draves, United States	108.74
1952 Patricia McCormick, United States	147.30
1956 Patricia McCormick, United States	142.36
1960 Ingrid Kramer, Germany	155.81
1964 Ingrid Kramer Engel, Germany	145.00
1968 Sue Gossick, United States	150.77
1972 Micki King, United States	450.03
1976 Jennifer Chandler, United States	506.19
1980 Irina Kalinina, USSR	725.91
1984 Sylvie Bernier, Canada	530.70
1988 Gao Min, China	580.23
1992 Gao Min, China	572.40
1996 Fu Ming-Xia, China	547.68
2000 Fu Ming-Xia, China	609.42
2004 Jingjing Guo, China	633.15

Platform Dive	**Points**
1912 Greta Johansson, Sweden	39.90
1920 Stefani Fryland, Denmark	34.60
1924 Caroline Smith, United States	166.00
1928 Elizabeth B. Pinkston, United States	31.60
1932 Dorothy Poynton, United States	40.26
1936 Dorothy Poynton Hill, United States	33.92
1948 Victoria M. Draves, United States	68.87
1952 Patricia McCormick, United States	79.37
1956 Patricia McCormick, United States	84.85
1960 Ingrid Kramer, Germany	91.28
1964 Lesley Bush, United States	99.80
1968 Milena Duchkova, Czechoslovakia	109.59
1972 Ulrika Knape, Sweden	390.00
1976 Elena Vaytsekhovskaia, USSR	406.59
1980 Martina Jaschke, East Germany	596.25
1984 Zhou Ji-Hong, China	435.51
1988 Xu Yan-Mei, China	445.20
1992 Fu Ming-Xia, China	461.43
1996 Fu Ming-Xia, China	521.58
2000 Laura Wilkinson, United States	543.75
2004 Chantelle Newbery, Australia	590.31

Synchronized 3m Springboard Dive	**Points**
2000 Vera Ilina and Ioulia Pakhalina, Russia	332.64
2004 Minxia Wu and Jingjing Guo, China	336.90

Synchronized 10m Platform Dive	**Points**
2000 Li Na and Sang Xue, China	345.12
2004 Lishi Lao and Ting Li, China	352.14

DISTRIBUTION OF MEDALS—2004 SUMMER GAMES

(Athens, Greece)

Country	Gold	Silver	Bronze	Total	Country	Gold	Silver	Bronze	Total
United States	35	39	29	103	Jamaica	2	1	2	5
Russia	27	27	38	92	Uzbekistan	2	1	2	5
China	32	17	14	63	Croatia	1	2	2	5
Australia	17	16	16	49	Egypt	1	1	3	5
Germany	14	16	18	48	Switzerland	1	1	3	5
Japan	16	9	12	37	Azerbaijan	1	0	4	5
France	11	9	13	33	North Korea	0	4	1	5
Italy	10	11	11	32	Georgia	2	2	0	4
South Korea	9	12	9	30	Indonesia	1	1	2	4
Great Britain	9	9	12	30	Latvia	0	4	0	4
Cuba	9	7	11	27	Mexico	0	3	1	4
Ukraine	9	5	9	23	Slovenia	0	1	3	4
Netherlands	4	9	9	22	Morocco	2	1	0	3
Romania	8	5	6	19	Chile	2	0	1	3
Spain	3	11	5	19	Lithuania	1	2	0	3
Hungary	8	6	3	17	Zimbabwe	1	1	1	3
Greece	6	6	4	16	Belgium	1	0	2	3
Belarus	2	6	7	15	Portugal	0	2	1	3
Canada	3	6	3	12	Estonia	0	1	2	3
Bulgaria	2	1	9	12	Bahamas	1	0	1	2
Brazil	4	3	3	10	Israel	1	0	1	2
Turkey	3	3	4	10	Finland	0	2	0	2
Poland	3	2	5	10	Serbia/Montenegro	0	2	0	2
Thailand	3	1	4	8	Nigeria	0	0	2	2
Denmark	2	0	6	8	Venezuela	0	0	2	2
Kazakhstan	1	4	3	8	Cameroon	1	0	0	1
Czech Republic	1	3	4	8	Dominican Rep.	1	0	0	1
Sweden	4	1	2	7	Ireland	1	0	0	1
Austria	2	4	1	7	United Arab Emirates	1	0	0	1
Ethiopia	2	3	2	7					
Kenya	1	4	2	7	Hong Kong	0	1	0	1
Norway	5	0	1	6	India	0	1	0	1
Iran	2	2	2	6	Paraguay	0	1	0	1
Slovakia	2	2	2	6	Colombia	0	0	1	1
Argentina	2	0	4	6	Eritrea	0	0	1	1
South Africa	1	3	2	6	Mongolia	0	0	1	1
New Zealand	3	2	0	5	Syria	0	0	1	1
Taiwan	2	2	1	5	Trinidad/Tobago	0	0	1	1

BOXING

(U.S. winners only)

NOTE: U.S. boycotted Olympics in 1980.

Flyweight-112 pounds (51 kg)

1904	George Finnegan	1952	Nate Brooks
1920	Frank De Genaro	1976	Leo Randolph
1924	Fidel La Barba	1984	Steve McCrory

Bantamweight-119 (54 kg)

| 1904 | O. L. Kirk | 1988 | Kennedy McKinney |

Featherweight-126 pounds (57 kg)

| 1904 | O. L. Kirk | 1984 | Meldrick Taylor |
| 1924 | Jackie Fields | | |

Lightweight-132 pounds (60 kg)

1904	H. J. Spanger	1976	Howard Davis
1920	Samuel Mosberg	1984	Pernell Whitaker
1968	Ronnie Harris	1992	Oscar De La Hoya

Light Welterweight-140 pounds (63.5 kg)

| 1952 | Charles Adkins | 1976 | Ray Leonard |
| 1972 | Ray Seales | 1984 | Jerry Page |

Welterweight-148 pounds (67 kg)

| 1904 | Al Young | 1984 | Mark Breland |
| 1932 | Edward Flynn | | |

Light Middleweight-157 pounds (71 kg)

| 1960 | Wilbert McClure | 1996 | David Reid |
| 1984 | Frank Tate | | |

Middleweight-165 pounds (75 kg)

1904	Charles Mayer	1960	Eddie Cook
1932	Carmen Barth	1976	Michael Spinks
1952	Floyd Patterson		

Light Heavyweight-179 pounds (81 kg)

1920	Edward Eagan	1976	Leon Spinks
1952	Norvel Lee	1988	Andrew Maynard
1956	James Boyd	2004	Andre Ward
1960	Cassius Clay		

Heavyweight-201 pounds (91 kg)

1904	Sam Berger	1968	George Foreman
1952	Edward Sanders	1984	Henry Tilman
1956	Pete Rademacher	1988	Ray Mercer
1964	Joe Frazier		

Super Heavyweight (unlimited)

| 1984 | Tyrell Biggs |

BASKETBALL–MEN

1904	United States
1936	United States
1948	United States
1952	United States
1956	United States
1960	United States
1964	United States
1968	United States
1972	USSR

1976	United States
1980	Yugoslavia
1984	United States
1988	USSR
1992	United States
1996	United States
2000	United States
2004	Argentina

BASKETBALL–WOMEN

1976	USSR
1980	USSR
1984	United States
1988	United States

1992	Unified Team[1]
1996	United States
2000	United States
2004	United States

1. Former Soviet Union team.

Other 2004 Summer Olympic Games Champions

Archery
Men's individual—Marco Galiazzo, Italy
Men's team—South Korea
Women's individual—Sung Hyun Park, South Korea
Women's team—South Korea

Badminton
Men's singles—Taufik Hidayat, Indonesia
Men's doubles—South Korea (Dong Moon Kim, Tae Kwon Ha)
Women's singles—Ning Zhang, China
Women's doubles—China (Jiewen Zhang, Wei Yang)
Mixed doubles—China (Jun Zhang, Ling Gao)

Baseball
Men—Cuba

Beach Volleyball
Women—United States (Kerri Walsh, Misti May)
Men—Brazil (Ricardo Santos, Emanuel Rega)

Boxing
Light flyweight—Yan Bhartelemy Varela, Cuba
Flyweight—Yuriorkis Gamboa Toledano, Cuba
Bantamweight—Guillermo Rigondeaux Ortiz, Cuba
Featherweight—Alexei Tichtchenko, Russia
Lightweight—Mario Cesar Kindelan Mesa, Cuba
Light welterweight—Manus Boonjumnong, Thailand
Welterweight—Bakhtiyar Artayev, Kazakhstan
Middleweight—Gaydarbek Gaydarbekov, Russia
Light heavyweight—Andre Ward, United States
Heavyweight—Odlanier Solis Fonte, Cuba
Super heavyweight—Alexander Povetkin, Russia

Cycling—Men
Individual sprint (track)—Ryan Bayley, Australia
Individual pursuit (track)—Bradley Wiggins, Great Britain
Team pursuit (track)—Australia
Team sprint (track)—Germany
1 km time trial (track)—Chris Hoy, Great Britain
Individual points race (track)—Mikhail Ignatyev, Russia

Keirin (track)—Ryan Bayley, Australia
Madison (track)—Australia
Individual time trial (road)—Tyler Hamilton, United States
Road race—Paolo Bettini, Italy
Mountain bike—Julien Absalon, France

Cycling—Women
Sprint (track)—Lori-Ann Muenzer, Canada
Individual pursuit (track)—Sarah Ulmer, New Zealand
500m time trial (track)—Anna Meares, Australia
Points race (track)—Olga Slyusareva, Russia
Individual time trial (road)—Leontien Zijlaard-Van Moorsel, Netherlands
Road race—Sara Carrigan, Australia
Mountain bike—Gunn-Rita Dahle, Norway

Equestrian
Individual three-day—Leslie Law, Great Britain
Three-day team event—France
Individual dressage—Anky van Grunsven, Netherlands
Team dressage—Germany
Individual jumping—Cian O'Connor, Ireland
Team jumping—Germany

Fencing—Men
Individual epee—Marcel Fischer, Switzerland
Individual foil—Brice Guyart, France
Individual sabre—Aldo Montano, Italy
Team epee—France
Team foil—Italy
Team sabre—France

Fencing—Women
Individual epee—Timea Nagy, Hungary
Individual foil—Valentina Vezzali, Italy
Individual sabre—Mariel Zagunis, United States
Team epee—Russia

Field Hockey
Men—Australia
Women—Germany

Gymnastics (Artistic)—Men
All-around—Paul Hamm, United States
Floor exercise—Kyle Shewfelt, Canada
Pommel horse—Haibin Teng, China
Rings—Dimosthenis Tampakos, Greece
Horizontal bar—Igor Cassina, Italy
Parallel bars—Valeri Goncharov, Ukraine
Vault—Gervasio Deferr, Spain
Team—Japan

Gymnastics (Artistic)—Women
All-around—Carly Patterson, United States
Uneven bars—Emilie Lepennec, France
Balance beam—Catalina Ponor, Romania
Floor exercise—Catalina Ponor, Romania
Vault—Monica Rosu, Romania
Team—Romania

Gymnastics (Rhythmic)
Individual—Alina Kabaeva, Russia
Team—Russia

Judo—Men
Extra-lightweight (60kg)—Tadahiro Nomura, Japan
Half-lightweight (66kg)—Masato Uchishiba, Japan
Lightweight (73kg)—Won Hee Lee, South Korea
Half-middleweight (81kg)—Ilias Iliadis, Greece
Middleweight (90kg)—Zurab Zviadauri, Georgia
Half-heavyweight (100kg)—Ihar Makarau, Belarus
Heavyweight (100kg+)—Keiji Suzuki, Japan

Judo—Women
Extra-lightweight (48kg)—Ryoko Tani, Japan
Half-lightweight (52kg)—Dongmei Xian, China
Lightweight (57kg)—Yvonne Boenisch, Germany
Half-middleweight (63kg)—Ayumi Tanimoto, Japan
Middleweight (70kg)—Masae Ueno, Japan
Half-heavyweight (78kg)—Noriko Anno, Japan
Heavyweight (78kg+)—Maki Tsukada, Japan

Kayak-Canoe—Men
Kayak pairs 500m—Germany
Canoe singles 500m—Andreas Dittmer, Germany
Canoe pairs 500m—China
Kayak singles 500m—Adam Van Koeverden, Canada
Kayak singles 1,000m—Eirik Veraas Larsen, Norway
Kayak fours 1,000m—Hungary
Canoe singles 1,000m—David Cal, Spain
Canoe pairs 1,000m—Germany
Canoe slalom pairs—Slovakia

Kayak slalom singles—Benoit Peschier, France
Canoe slalom singles—Tony Estanguet, France

Kayak—Women
Pairs 500m—Hungary
Singles 500m—Natasa Janics, Hungary
Fours 500m—Germany
Slalom singles—Elena Kaliska, Slovakia

Modern Pentathlon
Men—Andrey Moiseev, Russia
Women—Zsuzsanna Voros, Hungary

Rowing—Men
Single sculls—Olaf Tufte, Norway
Lightweight double sculls—Poland
Heavyweight double sculls—France
Quadruple sculls—Russia
Coxless pair—Australia
Lightweight coxless four—Denmark
Heavyweight coxless four—Great Britain
Eight—United States

Rowing—Women
Single sculls—Katrin Rutschow-Stomporowski, Germany
Lightweight double sculls—Romania
Heavyweight double sculls—New Zealand
Quadruple sculls—Germany
Coxless pair—Romania
Eight—Romania

Sailing
Open Tornado—Austria
Open 49er—Spain
Open Laser—Brazil
Men's Star—Brazil
Men's Mistral—Israel
Men's Finn—Great Britain
Men's 470—United States
Women's Mistral—France
Women's Europe—Norway
Women's Yngling—Great Britain
Women's 470—Greece

Shooting—Men
Skeet—Andrea Benelli, Italy
Rifle 3-position—Zhanbo Jia, China
Rapid fire pistol—Ralf Schumann, Germany
Rifle prone—Matt Emmons, United States
Running target—Manfred Kurzer, Germany (World record)

Double trap—Ahmed Almaktoum, United Arab Emirates
50m pistol—Mikhail Nestruev, Russia
Air rifle—Qinan Zhu, China
Trap—Alexei Alipov, Russia
Air pistol—Yifu Wang, China

Shooting—Women
Rifle 3-position—Lioubov Galkina, Russia
Skeet—Diana Igaly, Hungary
25m Pistol—Mariya Grozdeva, Bulgaria
Double trap—Kim Rhode, United States
Trap—Suzanne Balogh, Australia
Air pistol—Olena Kostevych, Ukraine
Air rifle—Li Du, China

Soccer
Men—Argentina
Women—United States

Softball
United States

Synchronized Swimming
Duet—Russia
Team—Russia

Table Tennis
Men's singles—Seung Min Ryu, South Korea
Men's doubles—China
Women's singles—Zhang Yining, China
Women's doubles—China

Taekwondo
Men 58kg—Mu Yen Chu, Taiwan
Men 68kg—Hadi Saei Bonehkohal, Iran
Men 80kg—Steven Lopez, United States
Men 80kg+—Dae Sung Moon, South Korea
Women 49kg—Shih Hsin Chen, Taiwan
Women 57kg—Ji Won Jang, South Korea
Women 67kg—Wei Luo, China
Women 67kg+—Zhong Chen, China

Team Handball
Men—Croatia
Women—Denmark

Tennis
Men's singles—Nicolas Massu, Chile
Men's doubles—Chile
Women's singles—Justine Henin-Hardenne, Belgium
Women's doubles—China

Trampoline
Men—Yuri Nikitin, Russia
Women—Anna Dogonadze, Germany

Triathlon
Men—Hamish Carter, New Zealand
Women—Kate Allen, Austria

Volleyball
Men—Brazil
Women—China

Water Polo
Men—Hungary
Women—Italy

Weightlifting—Men
56kg—Halil Mutlu, Turkey
62kg—Zhiyong Shi, China
69kg—Guozheng Zhang, China
77kg—Taner Sagir, Turkey
85kg—George Asanidze, Georgia
94kg—Milen Dobrev, Bulgaria
105kg—Dmitry Berestov, Russia
105kg+—Hossein Reza Zadeh, Iran

Weightlifting—Women
48kg—Taylan Nurcan, Turkey
53kg—Udomporn Polsak, Thailand
58kg—Yanqing Chen, China
63kg—Natalia Skakun, Ukraine
69kg—Chunhong Liu, China
75kg—Pawina Thongsuk, Thailand
75kg+—Gonghong Tang, China

Wrestling—Men's Freestyle
55kg—Mavlet Batirov, Russia
60kg—Yandro Miguel Quintana, Cuba
66kg—Elbrus Tedeyev, Ukraine
74kg—Buvaysa Saytiev, Russia
84kg—Cael Sanderson, United States
96kg—Khadjimourat Gatsalov, Russia
120kg—Artur Taymazov, Uzbekistan

Wrestling—Women's Freestyle
48kg—Irini Merleni, Ukraine
55kg—Saeori Yoshida, Japan
63kg—Kaori Icho, Japan
72kg—Xu Wang, China

Wrestling—Men's Greco-Roman
55kg—Istvan Majoros, Hungary
60kg—Ji Hyun Jung, South Korea
66kg—Farid Mansurov, Azerbaijan
74kg—Alexandr Dokturishivili, Uzbekistan
84kg—Alexei Michine, Russia
96kg—Karam Ibrahim, Egypt
120kg—Khasan Baroev, Russia

Winter Games: Gold Medals

FIGURE SKATING—MEN

1908 Ulrich Salchow, Sweden
1920 Gillis Grafström, Sweden
1924 Gillis Grafström, Sweden
1928 Gillis Grafström, Sweden
1932 Karl Schäfer, Austria
1936 Karl Schäfer, Austria
1948 Dick Button, United States
1952 Dick Button, United States
1956 Hayes Alan Jenkins, United States
1960 David Jenkins, United States
1964 Manfred Schnelldorfer, Germany

1968 Wolfgang Schwarz, Austria
1972 Ondrej Nepela, Czechoslovakia
1976 John Curry, Great Britain
1980 Robin Cousins, Great Britain
1984 Scott Hamilton, United States
1988 Brian Boitano, United States
1992 Viktor Petrenko, Unified Team*
1994 Alexei Urmanov, Russia
1998 Ilia Kulik, Russia
2002 Alexei Yagudin, Russia

*Former Soviet Union team.

FIGURE SKATING–WOMEN

1908	Madge Syers, Britain	
1920	Magda Julin-Mauroy, Sweden	
1924	Herma Planck-Szabò, Austria	
1928	Sonja Henie, Norway	
1932	Sonja Henie, Norway	
1936	Sonja Henie, Norway	
1948	Barbara Ann Scott, Canada	
1952	Jeanette Altwegg, Great Britain	
1956	Tenley Albright, United States	
1960	Carol Heiss, United States	
1964	Sjoukje Dijkstra, Netherlands	
1968	Peggy Fleming, United States	
1972	Beatrix Schuba, Austria	
1976	Dorothy Hamill, United States	
1980	Anett Pötzsch, East Germany	
1984	Katarina Witt, East Germany	
1988	Katarina Witt, East Germany	
1992	Kristi Yamaguchi, United States	
1994	Oksana Baiul, Ukraine	
1998	Tara Lipinski, United States	
2002	Sarah Hughes, United States	

SPEED SKATING–MEN

(U.S. winners only)

500 Meters

1924	Charles Jewtraw	44.00
1932	Jack Shea	43.40
1952	Ken Henry	43.20
1964	Terry McDermott	40.10
1980	Eric Heiden	38.03
2002	Casey FitzRandolph	69.23[1]

1,000 Meters

1976	Peter Mueller	1:19.32
1980	Eric Heiden	1:15.18
1994	Dan Jansen	1:12.43[2]

1,500 Meters

1932	Jack Shea	2:57.50
1980	Eric Heiden	1:55.44
2002	Derek Parra	1:43.95[2]

5,000 Meters

1932	Irving Jaffee	9:40.80
1980	Eric Heiden	7:02.29

10,000 Meters

1932	Irving Jaffee	19:13.60
1980	Eric Heiden	14:28.13

1. Combined time of two races. 2. World record.

SPEED SKATING–WOMEN

(U.S. winners only)

500 Meters

1972	Anne Henning	43.33
1976	Sheila Young	42.76
1988	Bonnie Blair	39.10
1992	Bonnie Blair	40.33
1994	Bonnie Blair	39.25

1,000 Meters

1992	Bonnie Blair	1:21.90
1994	Bonnie Blair	1:18.74
2002	Chris Witty	1:13.83[1]

1,500 Meters

1972	Dianne Holum	2:20.85

1. World record.

SKIING, ALPINE–MEN

Downhill

1948	Henri Oreiller, France	2:55.00
1952	Zeno Colò, Italy	2:30.80
1956	Toni Sailer, Austria	2:52.20
1960	Jean Vuarnet, France	2:06.00
1964	Egon Zimmermann, Austria	2:18.16
1968	Jean-Claude Killy, France	1:59.85
1972	Bernhard Russi, Switzerland	1:51.43
1976	Franz Klammer, Austria	1:45.73
1980	Leonhard Stock, Austria	1:45.50
1984	Bill Johnson, United States	1:45.59
1988	Pirmin Zurbriggen, Switzerland	1:59.63
1992	Patrick Ortlieb, Austria	1:50.37
1994	Tommy Moe, United States	1:45.75
1998	Jean-Luc Cretier, France	1:50.11
2002	Fritz Strobl, Austria	1:39.13

Slalom

1948	Edi Reinalter, Switzerland	2:10.30
1952	Othmar Schneider, Austria	2:00.00
1956	Toni Sailer, Austria	3:14.70
1960	Ernst Hinterseer, Austria	2:08.90
1964	Pepi Stiegler, Austria	2:11.13
1968	Jean-Claude Killy, France	1:39.73
1972	Francisco Ochoa, Spain	1:49.27
1976	Piero Gros, Italy	2:03.29
1980	Ingemar Stenmark, Sweden	1:44.26
1984	Phil Mahre, United States	1:39.41
1988	Alberto Tomba, Italy	1:39.47
1992	Finn Christian Jagge, Norway	1:44.39
1994	Thomas Stangassinger, Austria	2:02.02
1998	Hans-Petter Buraas, Norway	1:49.31
2002	Jean-Pierre Vidal, France	1:41.06

Giant Slalom

1952	Stein Eriksen, Norway	2:25.00
1956	Toni Sailer, Austria	3:00.10
1960	Roger Staub, Switzerland	1:48.30
1964	François Bonlieu, France	1:46.71
1968	Jean-Claude Killy, France	3:29.28
1972	Gustav Thöni, Italy	3:09.62
1976	Heini Hemmi, Switzerland	3:26.97
1980	Ingemar Stenmark, Sweden	2:40.74
1984	Max Julen, Switzerland	2:41.18
1988	Alberto Tomba, Italy	2:06.37
1992	Alberto Tomba, Italy	2:06.98
1994	Markus Wasmeier, Germany	2:52.46
1998	Hermann Maier, Austria	2:38.51
2002	Stephan Eberharter, Austria	2:23.28

Super Giant Slalom

1988	Frank Piccard, France	1:39.66
1992	Kjetil Andre Aamdt, Norway	1:13.04
1994	Markus Wasmeier, Germany	1:32.53
1998	Hermann Maier, Austria	1:34.84
2002	Kjetil Andre Aamodt, Norway	1:21.58

Men's Combined (Downhill and Slalom)

		Points
1936	Franz Pfnür, Germany	99.25
1948	Henri Oreiller, France	3.27
1952–1984	Not held	
1988	Hubert Strolz, Austria	36.55
1992	Josef Polig, Italy	14.58
		Time
1994	Lasse Kjus, Norway	3:17.53
1998	Mario Reiter, Austria	3:08.06
2002	Kjetil Andre Aamodt, Norway	3:17.56

SKIING, ALPINE–WOMEN

Downhill

1948	Hedy Schlunegger, Switzerland	2:28.30
1952	Trude Jochum-Beiser, Austria	1:47.10
1956	Madeleine Berthod, Switzerland	1:40.70
1960	Heidi Biebl, Germany	1:37.60
1964	Christl Haas, Austria	1:55.39
1968	Olga Pall, Austria	1:40.87
1972	Marie-Theres Nadig, Switzerland	1:36.68
1976	Rosi Mittermaier, West Germany	1:46.16
1980	Annemarie Moser-Pröll, Austria	1:37.52
1984	Michela Figini, Switzerland	1:13.36
1988	Marina Kiehl, West Germany	1:25.86
1992	Kerrin Lee-Gartner, Canada	1:52.55

1994	Katja Seizinger, Germany	1:35.93
1998	Katja Seizinger, Germany	1:28.89
2002	Carole Montillet, France	1:39.56

Slalom

1948	Gretchen Fraser, United States	1:57.20
1952	Andrea Mead Lawrence, United States	2:10.60
1956	Renée Colliard, Switzerland	1:52.30
1960	Anne Heggtveit, Canada	1:49.60
1964	Christine Goitschel, France	1:29.86
1968	Marielle Goitschel, France	1:25.86
1972	Barbara Cochran, United States	1:31.24
1976	Rosi Mittermaier, West Germany	1:30.54
1980	Hanni Wenzel, Liechtenstein	1:25.09
1984	Paoletta Magoni, Italy	1:36.47
1988	Vreni Schneider, Switzerland	1:36.69
1992	Petra Kronberger, Austria	1:32.68
1994	Vreni Schneider, Switzerland	1:56.01
1998	Hilde Gerg, Germany	1:32.40
2002	Janica Kostelic, Croatia	1:46.10

Giant Slalom

1952	Andrea Mead Lawrence, United States	2:06.80
1956	Ossi Reichert, Germany	1:56.50
1960	Yvonne Rügg, Switzerland	1:39.90
1964	Marielle Goitschel, France	1:52.24
1968	Nancy Greene, Canada	1:51.97
1972	Marie-Theres Nadig, Switzerland	1:29.90
1976	Kathy Kreiner, Canada	1:29.13
1980	Hanni Wenzel, Liechtenstein	2:41.66
1984	Debbie Armstrong, United States	2:20.98
1988	Vreni Schneider, Switzerland	2:06.49
1992	Pernilla Wiberg, Sweden	2:12.74
1994	Deborah Compagnoni, Italy	2:30.97
1998	Deborah Compagnoni, Italy	2:50.59
2002	Janica Kostelic, Croatia	2:30.01

Super Giant Slalom

1988	Sigrid Wolf, Austria	1:19.03
1992	Deborah Compagnoni, Italy	1:21.22
1994	Diann Roffe-Steinrotter, United States	1:22.15
1998	Picabo Street, United States	1:18.02
2002	Daniela Ceccarelli, Italy	1:13.59

Combined (Downhill and Slalom)   **Points**

1936	Christl Cranz, Germany	97.06
1948	Trude Beiser, Austria	6.58
1952–1984 Not held		
1988	Anita Wachter, Austria	29.25
1992	Petra Kronberger, Austria	2.55

                                Time

1994	Pernilla Wiberg, Sweden	3:05.16
1998	Katja Seizinger, Germany	2:40.74
2002	Janica Kostelic, Croatia	2:43.28

ICE HOCKEY

MEN

1920	Canada	1976	USSR
1924	Canada	1980	United States
1928	Canada	1984	USSR
1932	Canada	1988	USSR
1936	Great Britain	1992	Unified Team*
1948	Canada	1994	Sweden
1952	Canada	1998	Czech Republic
1956	USSR	2002	Canada
1960	United States		
1964	USSR	**WOMEN**	
1968	USSR	1998	United States
1972	USSR	2002	Canada
		*Former Soviet Union	
		team.	

2002 Men's Championship
Canada 5, United States 2
2002 Women's Championship
Canada 3, United States 2

FREESTYLE SKIING—MEN

Moguls

1992	Edgar Grospiron, France
1994	Jean-Luc Brassard, Canada
1998	Jonny Moseley, United States
2002	Janne Lahtela, Finland

Aerials

1994	Andreas Schoenbaechler, Switzerland
1998	Eric Bergoust, United States
2002	Ales Valenta, Czech Republic

FREESTYLE SKIING—WOMEN

Moguls

1992	Donna Weinbrecht, United States
1994	Stine Lise Hattestad, Norway
1998	Tae Satoya, Japan
2002	Kari Traa, Norway

Aerials

1994	Lina Cherjazova, Uzbekistan
1998	Nikki Stone, United States
2002	Alisa Camplin, Australia

DISTRIBUTION OF MEDALS
2002 WINTER OLYMPIC GAMES

(Salt Lake City, Utah)

Country	Gold	Silver	Bronze	Total
Germany	12	16	7	35
United States	10	13	11	34
Norway	11	7	6	24
Canada	6	3	8	17
Austria	2	4	10	16
Russia	6	6	4	16
Italy	4	4	4	12
France	4	5	2	11
Switzerland	3	2	6	11
China	2	2	4	8
Netherlands	3	5	0	8
Finland	4	2	1	7
Sweden	0	2	4	6
Croatia	3	1	0	4
Korea	2	2	0	4
Bulgaria	0	1	2	3
Estonia	1	1	1	3
Great Britain	1	0	2	3
Australia	2	0	0	2
Czech Republic	1	0	1	2
Japan	0	1	1	2
Poland	0	1	1	2
Spain	0	0	1	1
Belarus	0	0	1	1
Slovenia	0	0	1	1

2002 UNITED STATES MEDALISTS

Alpine Skiing
Men's Combined—SILVER—Bode Miller
Men's Giant Slalom—SILVER—Bode Miller

Bobsleigh
Four-Man—SILVER—Todd Hayes, Bill Schuffenhauer,
   Garrett Hines, Randy Jones
Four-Man—BRONZE—Mike Kohn, Doug Sharp, Brian
   Shimer, Dan Steele
Women—GOLD—Jill Bakken, Vonetta Flowers

Figure Skating
Women—GOLD—Sarah Hughes
Women—BRONZE—Michelle Kwan
Men—BRONZE—Timothy Goebel

Freestyle Skiing
Men's Aerials—SILVER—Joe Pack
Men's Moguls—SILVER—Travis Mayer
Women's Moguls—SILVER—Shannon Bahrke

Hockey
Men—SILVER—Tom Barrasso, Brian Rolston, Mike York, Tony Amonte, Chris Chelios, Chris Drury, Mike Dunham, Bill Guerin, Brett Hull, John LeClair, Brian Leetch, Mike Modano, Brian Rafalski, Jeremy Roenick, Gary Suter, Keith Tkachuk, Doug Weight, Scott Young, Tom Poti, Mike Richter, Phil Housley, Adam Deadmarsh, Aaron Miller
Women—Silver—Chris Bailey, Laurie Baker, Karyn Bye, Julie Chu, Natalie Darwitz, Sara DeCosta, Tricia Dunn, Cammi Granato, Courtney Kennedy, Andrea Kilbourne, Katie King, Shelley Looney, Sue Merz, Allison Mleczko, Tara Mounsey, Jenny Potter, Angela Ruggiero, Sara Tueting, Lyndsay Wall, Krissy Wendell

Luge
Men's Doubles—SILVER—Brian Martin, Mark Grimmette
Men's Doubles—BRONZE—Clay Ives, Chris Thorpe

Short Track Speed Skating
Men's 1,000 m—SILVER—Apolo Anton Ohno
Men's 1,500 m—GOLD—Apolo Anton Ohno
Men's 500 m—BRONZE—Rusty Smith

Skeleton
Men—GOLD—Jim Shea
Women—GOLD—Tristan Gale
Women—SILVER—Lea Ann Parsley

Snowboarding
Men's Halfpipe—GOLD—Ross Powers
Men's Halfpipe—SILVER—Danny Kass
Men's Halfpipe—BRONZE—Jarret Thomas
Men's Parallel Giant Slalom—BRONZE—Chris Klug
Women's Halfpipe—GOLD—Kelly Clark

Speed Skating
Women's 1,000 m—GOLD—Chris Witty
Women's 1,000 m—BRONZE—Jennifer Rodriguez
Women's 1,500 m—BRONZE—Jennifer Rodriguez
Men's 1,000 m—BRONZE—Joey Cheek
Men's 1,500 m—GOLD—Derek Parra
Men's 500 m—GOLD—Casey FitzRandolph
Men's 500 m—BRONZE—Kip Carpenter
Men's 5,000 m—SILVER—Derek Parra

Other 2002 Winter Olympic Games Champions

Biathlon
Men's 10 km Sprint—Ole Einar Bjoerndalen, Norway
Men's 12.5 km Pursuit—Ole Einar Bjoerndalen, Norway
Men's 20 km Individual—Ole Einar Bjoerndalen, Norway
Men's 4 × 7.5 km Relay—Norway
Women's 10 km Pursuit—Olga Pyleva, Russia
Women's 15 km Individual—Andrea Henkel, Germany
Women's 4 × 7.5 km Relay—Germany
Women's 7.5 km Sprint—Kati Wilhelm, Germany

Bobsledding
2-man—Germany
4-man—Germany
Women—United States

Cross-Country Skiing
Men's 10 km Free Pursuit—Johann Muehlegg, Spain
Men's 15 km Classical—Andrus Veerpalu, Estonia
Men's 30 km Free Mass Start—Johann Muehlegg, Spain
Men's 4 × 10 km Relay—Norway
Men's 50 km Classical—Mikhail Ivanov, Russia
Men's Sprint—Tor Arne Hetland, Norway
Women's 10 km Classical—Bente Skari, Norway
Women's 15 km Free Mass Start—Stefania Belmondo, Italy
Women's 30 km Classical—Gabriella Paruzzi, Italy
Women's 4 × 5 km Relay—Germany
Women's 5 km Free Pursuit—Olga Danilova, Russia
Women's Sprint—Julija Tchepalova, Russia

Curling
Men—Norway
Women—Germany

Figure Skating
Pairs—David Pelletier and Jamie Sale, Canada; Elena Berezhnaya and Anton Sikharulidze, Russia
Ice dancing—Marina Anissina and Gwendal Peizerat, France

Skeleton
Men—Jim Shea, United States
Women—Tristan Gale, United States

Luge
Men's Doubles—Germany
Men's Singles—Armin Zoeggeler, Italy
Women's Singles—Sylke Otto, Germany

Nordic Combined
Individual 15 km—Samppa Lajunen, Finland
Sprint 7.5 km—Samppa Lajunen, Finland
Team 4 × 5 km Relay—Finland

Short Track Speed Skating
Women's 1,000 km—Yang Yang (A), China
Women's 1,500 km—Gi-Hyun Ko, Korea
Women's 3,000 km Relay—Korea
Women's 500 m—Yang Yang (A), China
Men's 1,000 m—Steven Bradbury, Australia
Men'1 1,500 m—Apolo Anton Ohno, United States
Men's 500 m—Marc Gagnon, Canada
Men's 5,000 m Relay—Canada

Ski Jumping
Individual K120—Simon Ammann, Switzerland
Individual K90—Simon Ammann, Switzerland
Team K120-Germany

Snowboarding
Men's Halfpipe—Ross Powers, United States
Men' Parallel Giant Slalom—Philipp Schoch, Switzerland
Women's Halfpipe—Kelly Clark, United States
Women's Parallel Giant Slalom—Isabelle Blanc, France

Speed Skating
Women's 1,500 m—Anni Friesinger, Germany
Women's 3,000 m—Claudia Pechstein, Germany
Women's 500 m—Catriona LeMay Doan, Canada
Women's 5,000 m—Claudia Pechstein, Germany
Men's 1,000 m—Gerard van Velde, Netherlands
Men's 10,000 m—Jochem Uytdehaage, Netherlands
Men's 5,000 m—Jochem Uytdehaage, Netherlands

Football

The pastime of kicking around a ball goes back beyond the limits of recorded history. Ancient savage tribes played football of a primitive kind. There was a ball-kicking game played by Athenians, Spartans, and Corinthians 2,500 years ago, which the Greeks called *Episkuros*. The Romans had a somewhat similar game called *Harpastum* and are supposed to have carried the game with them when they invaded the British Isles in the first century B.C.

Undoubtedly the game known in the United States as football traces directly to the English game of rugby, though the modifications have been many. Informal football was played on college lawns well over a century ago, and an annual freshman-sophomore series of "scrimmages" began at Yale in 1840. The first formal intercollegiate football game was the Princeton-Rutgers contest at New Brunswick, N.J., on Nov. 6, 1869, with Rutgers winning by 6 goals to 4.

In those days, games were played with 25, 20, 15, or 11 men on a side. In 1880, there was a convention at which Walter Camp of Yale persuaded the delegates to agree to 11 players on a side.

The first professional game was played in 1895 at Latrobe, Pa. The National Football League was founded in 1920, as the American Professional Football Association (the name changed to NFL in 1922). The All-American Conference went into action in 1946. At the end of the 1949 season the two circuits merged, retaining the name of the older league. In 1960, the American Football League began operations. In 1970, the leagues merged. The United States Football League played its first season in 1983, from March to July. It suspended spring operations after the 1985 season, and planned a 1986 move to fall, but suspended operations again.

In March 1991, another effort at spring football was launched. This time the ten-team World League of American Football had the backing of the National Football League. After two seasons it was suspended. The league returned in 1995, with six teams in Europe. In 1998, it was renamed the NFL Europe League.

In 2002 the NFL divisions were realigned. National and American Conferences were split into four divisions with four teams per division. Scheduling has also been changed and every team will meet every other team at least once every four years.

College Football

NATIONAL COLLEGE FOOTBALL CHAMPIONS

Prior to 1998, the National Collegiate Athletic Association recognized as unofficial champion the team selected each year by press association polls of writers and coaches. After 1998, the Bowl Championship Series (BCS) was implemented to determine the NCAA champs, using polls, computer rankings, schedule, record, and quality win factors. Changes made in the 2004 season narrowed down the process, with the system employing the AP media poll, the USA Today/ESPN coaches poll, and a computer average. The championship game rotates among the major bowl games. The 2004 title game took place at the FedEx Orange Bowl, where Southern California defeated Oklahoma, 55–19; in 2005, the Rose Bowl hosts the title game.

1936 Minnesota	1952 Mich. State	1965 Alabama and	1977 Notre Dame	1991 Miami (Fla.) and
1937 Pittsburgh	1953 Maryland	Mich. State	1978 Alabama and	Washington
1938 Texas Christian	1954 Ohio State and	1966 Notre Dame	So. Calif.	1992 Alabama
1939 Texas A & M	UCLA	1967 So. Calif.	1979 Alabama	1993 Florida State
1940 Minnesota	1955 Oklahoma	1968 Ohio State	1980 Georgia	1994 Nebraska
1941 Minnesota	1956 Oklahoma	1969 Texas	1981 Clemson	1995 Nebraska
1942 Ohio State	1957 Auburn and	1970 Texas and	1982 Penn State	1996 Univ. of Florida
1943 Notre Dame	Ohio State	Nebraska	1983 Miami (Fla.)	1997 Michigan and
1944 Army	1958 Louisiana State	1971 Nebraska	1984 Brigham Young	Nebraska
1945 Army	1959 Syracuse	1972 So. Calif.	1985 Oklahoma	1998 Tennessee
1946 Notre Dame	1960 Minnesota	1973 Notre Dame	1986 Penn State	1999 Florida State
1947 Notre Dame	1961 Alabama	and U. of Ala.	1987 Miami (Fla.)	2000 Oklahoma
1948 Michigan	1962 So. Calif.	1974 Oklahoma and	1988 Notre Dame	2001 Miami (Fla.)
1949 Notre Dame	1963 Texas	So. Calif.	1989 Miami (Fla.)	2002 Ohio State
1950 Oklahoma	1964 Alabama	1975 Oklahoma	1990 Colorado and	2003 Louisiana State
1951 Tennessee		1976 Pittsburgh	Georgia Tech	and So. Calif.[1]
				2004 So. Calif.

1. USC was ranked number 1 in the polls and number-2-ranked Louisiana State won the Sugar Bowl. Had LSU and USC met in the Sugar Bowl, there would have been only one champion.

RECORD OF ANNUAL MAJOR COLLEGE FOOTBALL BOWL GAMES

Rose Bowl (at Pasadena, Calif.)

1902 Michigan 49, Stanford 0	1920 Harvard 7, Oregon 6	1928 Stanford 7, Pittsburgh 6
1916 Washington State 14, Brown 0	1921 California 28, Ohio State 0	1929 Georgia Tech 8, California 7
1917 Oregon 14, Pennsylvania 0	1922 Washington and Jefferson 0,	1930 So. Calif. 47, Pittsburgh 14
1918 Mare Island Marines 19, Camp	California 0	1931 Alabama 24, Wash. State 0
Lewis 7	1923 So. Calif. 14, Penn State 3	1932 So. Calif. 21, Tulane 12
1919 Great Lakes 17, Mare Island	1924 Navy 14, Washington 14	1933 So. Calif. 35, Pittsburgh 0
Marines 0	1925 Notre Dame 27, Stanford 10	1934 Columbia 7, Stanford 0
	1926 Alabama 20, Washington 19	1935 Alabama 29, Stanford 13
	1927 Alabama 7, Stanford 7	1936 Stanford 7, So. Methodist 0

1937 Pittsburgh 21, Washington 0
1938 California 13, Alabama 0
1939 So. Calif. 7, Duke 3
1940 So. Calif. 14, Tennessee 0
1941 Stanford 21, Nebraska 13
1942 Oregon State 20, Duke 16[1]
1943 Georgia 9, UCLA 0
1944 So. Calif. 29, Washington 0
1945 So. Calif. 25, Tennessee 0
1946 Alabama 34, So. Calif. 14
1947 Illinois 45, UCLA 14
1948 Michigan 49, So. Calif. 0
1949 Northwestern 20, California 14
1950 Ohio State 17, California 14
1951 Michigan 14, California 6
1952 Illinois 40, Stanford 7
1953 So. Calif. 7, Wisconsin 0
1954 Michigan State 28, UCLA 20
1955 Ohio State 20, So. Calif. 7
1956 Michigan State 17, UCLA 14
1957 Iowa 35, Oregon State 19
1958 Ohio State 10, Oregon 7
1959 Iowa 38, California 12
1960 Washington 44, Wisconsin 8
1961 Washington 17, Minnesota 7
1962 Minnesota 21, UCLA 3
1963 So. Calif. 42, Wisconsin 37
1964 Illinois 17, Washington 7
1965 Michigan 34, Oregon State 7
1966 UCLA 14, Michigan State 12
1967 Purdue 14, So. Calif. 13
1968 So. Calif. 14, Indiana 3
1969 Ohio State 27, So. Calif. 16
1970 So. Calif. 10, Michigan 3
1971 Stanford 27, Ohio State 17
1972 Stanford 13, Michigan 12
1973 So. Calif. 42, Ohio State 17
1974 Ohio State 42, So. Calif. 21
1975 So. Calif. 18, Ohio State 17
1976 UCLA 23, Ohio State 10
1977 So. Calif. 14, Michigan 6
1978 Washington 27, Michigan 20
1979 So. Calif. 17, Michigan 10
1980 So. Calif. 17, Ohio State 16
1981 Michigan 23, Washington 6
1982 Washington 28, Iowa 0
1983 UCLA 24, Michigan 14
1984 UCLA 45, Illinois 9
1985 So. Calif. 20, Ohio St. 17
1986 UCLA 45, Iowa 28
1987 Arizona State 22, Michigan 15
1988 Michigan State 20, So. Calif. 17
1989 Michigan 22, So. Calif. 14
1990 So. Calif. 17, Michigan 10
1991 Washington 46, Iowa 34
1992 Washington 34, Michigan 14
1993 Michigan 38, Washington 31
1994 Wisconsin 21, UCLA 16
1995 Penn State 38, Oregon 20
1996 So. Calif. 41,
        Northwestern 32
1997 Ohio State 20, Arizona State 17
1998 Michigan 21, Washington
        State 16
1999 Wisconsin 38, UCLA 31
2000 Wisconsin 17, Stanford 9
2001 Washington 34, Purdue 24
2002 Miami 37, Nebraska 14
2003 Oklahoma 34, Washington
        State 14

2004 So. Calif. 28, Michigan 14
2005 Michigan 37, Texas 38
1. Played at Durham, N.C.

Orange Bowl (at Miami)

1933 Miami (Fla.) 7, Manhattan 0
1934 Duquesne 33, Miami (Fla.) 7
1935 Bucknell 26, Miami (Fla.) 0
1936 Catholic 20, Mississippi 19
1937 Duquesne 13, Mississippi
        State 12
1938 Auburn 6, Michigan State 0
1939 Tennessee 17, Oklahoma 0
1940 Georgia Tech 21, Missouri 7
1941 Mississippi State 14, George-
        town 7
1942 Georgia 40, Texas Christian 26
1943 Alabama 37, Boston College 21
1944 Louisiana State 19, Texas
        A & M 14
1945 Tulsa 26, Georgia Tech 12
1946 Miami (Fla.) 13, Holy Cross 6
1947 Rice 8, Tennessee 0
1948 Georgia Tech 20, Kansas 14
1949 Texas 41, Georgia 28
1950 Santa Clara 21, Kentucky 13
1951 Clemson 15, Miami (Fla.) 14
1952 Georgia Tech 17, Baylor 14
1953 Alabama 61, Syracuse 6
1954 Oklahoma 7, Maryland 0
1955 Duke 34, Nebraska 7
1956 Oklahoma 20, Maryland 6
1957 Colorado 27, Clemson 21
1958 Oklahoma 48, Duke 21
1959 Oklahoma 21, Syracuse 6
1960 Georgia 14, Missouri 0
1961 Missouri 21, Navy 14
1962 Louisiana State 25, Colorado 7
1963 Alabama 17, Oklahoma 0
1964 Nebraska 13, Auburn 7
1965 Texas 21, Alabama 17
1966 Alabama 39, Nebraska 28
1967 Florida 27, Georgia Tech 12
1968 Oklahoma 26, Tennessee 24
1969 Penn State 15, Kansas 14
1970 Penn State 10, Missouri 3
1971 Nebraska 17, Louisiana
        State 12
1972 Nebraska 38, Alabama 6
1973 Nebraska 40, Notre Dame 6
1974 Penn State 16, Louisiana
        State 9
1975 Notre Dame 13, Alabama 11
1976 Oklahoma 14, Michigan 6
1977 Ohio State 27, Colorado 10
1978 Arkansas 31, Oklahoma 6
1979 Oklahoma 31, Nebraska 24
1980 Oklahoma 24, Florida State 7
1981 Oklahoma 18, Florida State 17
1982 Clemson 22, Nebraska 15
1983 Nebraska 21, Louisiana
        State 20
1984 Miami (Fla.) 31, Nebraska 30
1985 Washington 28, Oklahoma 17
1986 Oklahoma 25, Penn State 10
1987 Oklahoma 42, Arkansas 8
1988 Miami (Fla.) 20, Oklahoma 14
1989 Miami (Fla.) 23, Nebraska 3
1990 Notre Dame 21, Colorado 6
1991 Colorado 10, Notre Dame 9
1992 Miami (Fla.) 22, Nebraska 0
1993 Florida State 27, Nebraska 14
1994 Florida State 18, Nebraska 16
1995 Nebraska 24, Miami (Fla.) 17

1996 Florida State 31, Notre
        Dame 26
1997 Nebraska 41, Virginia Tech 21
1998 Nebraska 42, Tennessee 17
1999 Florida 31, Syracuse 10
2000 Michigan 35, Alabama 34
2001 Oklahoma 13, Florida State 2
2002 Florida 56, Maryland 23
2003 So. Calif. 38, Iowa 17
2004 Miami 16, Florida State 14
2005 So. Calif. 55, Oklahoma 19

Sugar Bowl (at New Orleans)

1935 Tulane 20, Temple 14
1936 Texas Christian 3, Louisiana
        State 2
1937 Santa Clara 21, Louisiana
        State 14
1938 Santa Clara 6, Louisiana
        State 0
1939 Texas Christian 15, Carnegie
        Tech 7
1940 Texas A & M 14, Tulane 13
1941 Boston College 19,
        Tennessee 13
1942 Fordham 2, Missouri 0
1943 Tennessee 14, Tulsa 7
1944 Georgia Tech 20, Tulsa 18
1945 Duke 29, Alabama 26
1946 Oklahoma A & M 33, St. Mary's
        (Calif.) 13
1947 Georgia 20, North Carolina 10
1948 Texas 27, Alabama 7
1949 Oklahoma 14, North Carolina 6
1950 Oklahoma 35, Louisiana State 0
1951 Kentucky 13, Oklahoma 7
1952 Maryland 28, Tennessee 13
1953 Georgia Tech 24, Mississippi 7
1954 Georgia Tech 42, West
        Virginia 19
1955 Navy 21, Mississippi 0
1956 Georgia Tech 7, Pittsburgh 0
1957 Baylor 13, Tennessee 7
1958 Mississippi 39, Texas 7
1959 Louisiana State 7, Clemson 0
1960 Mississippi 21, Louisiana
        State 0
1961 Mississippi 14, Rice 6
1962 Alabama 10, Arkansas 3
1963 Mississippi 17, Arkansas 13
1964 Alabama 12, Mississippi 7
1965 Louisiana State 13,
        Syracuse 10
1966 Missouri 20, Florida 18
1967 Alabama 34, Nebraska 7
1968 Louisiana State 20,
        Wyoming 13
1969 Arkansas 16, Georgia 2
1970 Mississippi 27, Arkansas 22
1971 Tennessee 34, Air Force
        Academy 13
1972 Oklahoma 40, Auburn 22
1973 Oklahoma 14, Penn State 0
1974 Notre Dame 24, Alabama 23
1975 Nebraska 13, Florida 10
1976 Alabama 13, Penn State 6
1977 Pittsburgh 27, Georgia 3
1978 Alabama 35, Ohio State 6
1979 Alabama 14, Penn State 7
1980 Alabama 24, Arkansas 9
1981 Georgia 17, Notre Dame 10
1982 Pittsburgh 24, Georgia 20
1983 Penn State 27, Georgia 23
1984 Auburn 9, Michigan 7

1985	Nebraska 28, Louisiana State 10
1986	Tennessee 35, Miami (Fla.) 7
1987	Nebraska 30, Louisiana State 15
1988	Syracuse 16, Auburn 16 (tie)
1989	Florida State 13, Auburn 7
1990	Miami (Fla.) 33, Alabama 25
1991	Tennessee 23, Virginia 22
1992	Notre Dame 39, Florida 28
1993	Alabama 34, Miami (Fla.) 13
1994	Florida 41, West Virginia 7
1995	Florida State 23, Florida 17
1996	Virginia Tech 28, Texas 10
1997	Florida 52, Florida State 20
1998	Florida State 31, Ohio State 14
1999	Ohio State 24, Texas A & M 14
2000	Florida State 46, Virginia Tech 29
2001	Miami (Fla.) 37, Florida 20
2002	Louisiana State 47, Illinois 34
2003	Georgia 26, Florida State 13
2004	Louisiana State 21, Oklahoma 14
2005	Auburn 16, Virginia Tech 13

Cotton Bowl (at Dallas)

1937	Texas Christian 16, Marquette 6
1938	Rice 28, Colorado 14
1939	St. Mary's (Calif.) 20, Texas Tech. 13
1940	Clemson 6, Boston College 3
1941	Texas A & M 13, Fordham 12
1942	Alabama 29, Texas A & M 21
1943	Texas 14, Georgia Tech 7
1944	Randolph Field 7, Texas 7
1945	Oklahoma A & M 34, Texas Christian 0
1946	Texas 40, Missouri 27
1947	Louisiana State 0, Arkansas 0
1948	So. Methodist 13, Penn State 13
1949	So. Methodist 21, Oregon 13
1950	Rice 27, North Carolina 13
1951	Tennessee 20, Texas 14
1952	Kentucky 20, Texas Christian 7
1953	Texas 16, Tennessee 0
1954	Rice 28, Alabama 6
1955	Georgia Tech 14, Arkansas 6
1956	Mississippi 14, Texas Christian 13
1957	Texas Christian 28, Syracuse 27
1958	Navy 20, Rice 7
1959	Air Force 0, Texas Christian 0
1960	Syracuse 23, Texas 14
1961	Duke 7, Arkansas 6
1962	Texas 12, Mississippi 7
1963	Louisiana State 13, Texas 0

1964	Texas 28, Navy 6
1965	Arkansas 10, Nebraska 7
1966	Louisiana State 14, Arkansas 7
1967	Georgia 24, So. Methodist 9
1968	Texas A & M 20, Alabama 16
1969	Texas 36, Tennessee 13
1970	Texas 21, Notre Dame 17
1971	Notre Dame 24, Texas 11
1972	Penn State 30, Texas 6
1973	Texas 17, Alabama 13
1974	Nebraska 19, Texas 3
1975	Penn State 41, Baylor 20
1976	Arkansas 31, Georgia 10
1977	Houston 30, Maryland 21
1978	Notre Dame 38, Texas 10
1979	Notre Dame 35, Houston 34
1980	Houston 17, Nebraska 14
1981	Alabama 30, Baylor 2
1982	Texas 14, Alabama 12
1983	So. Meth. 7, Pittsburgh 3
1984	Georgia 10, Texas 9
1985	Boston College 45, Houston 28
1986	Texas A & M 36, Auburn 16
1987	Ohio State 28, Texas A & M 12
1988	Texas A & M 35, Notre Dame 10
1989	UCLA 17, Arkansas 3
1990	Tennessee 31, Arkansas 27
1991	Miami (Fla.) 46, Texas 3
1992	Florida State 10, Texas A & M 2
1993	Notre Dame 28, Texas A & M 3
1994	Notre Dame 24, Texas A & M 21
1995	So. Calif. 55, Texas Tech 14
1996	Colorado 38, Oregon 6
1997	Brigham Young 19, Kansas State 15
1998	UCLA 29, Texas A & M 23
1999	Texas 38, Mississippi State 11
2000	Arkansas 27, Texas 6
2001	Kansas State 35, Tennessee 21
2002	Oklahoma 10, Arkansas 3
2003	Texas 35, Louisiana State 20
2004	Mississippi 31, Oklahoma State 28
2005	Tennessee 38, Texas A & M 7

Gator Bowl (at Jacksonville, Fla.)

1953	Florida 14, Tulsa 13
1954	Texas Tech 35, Auburn 13
1955	Auburn 33, Baylor 13
1956	Vanderbilt 25, Auburn 13
1957	Georgia Tech 21, Pittsburgh 14
1958	Tennessee 3, Texas A & M 0
1959	Mississippi 7, Florida 3
1960	Arkansas 14, Georgia Tech 7
1961	Florida 13, Baylor 12

1962	Penn State 30, Georgia Tech 15
1963	Florida 17, Penn State 7
1964	No. Carolina 35, Air Force 0
1965	Florida State 36, Oklahoma 19
1966	Georgia Tech 31, Texas Tech 21
1967	Tennessee 18, Syracuse 12
1968	Penn State 17, Florida State 17 (tie)
1969	Missouri 35, Alabama 10
1970	Florida 14, Tennessee 13
1971	Auburn 35, Mississippi 28
1972	Georgia 7, North Carolina 3
1973	Auburn 24, Colorado 3
1974	Texas Tech 28, Tennessee 19
1975	Auburn 27, Texas 3
1976	Maryland 13, Florida 0
1977	Notre Dame 20, Penn State 9
1978	Pittsburgh 34, Clemson 3
1979	Clemson 17, Ohio State 15
1980	North Carolina 17, Michigan 15
1981	Pittsburgh 37, South Carolina 9
1982	North Carolina 31, Arkansas 27
1983	Florida State 31, West Virginia 12
1984	Florida 14, Iowa 6
1985	Oklahoma State 21, South Carolina 14
1986	Florida State 34, Oklahoma State 23
1987	Clemson 27, Stanford 21
1988	Louisiana State 30, South Carolina 13
1989	Georgia 34, Mich. State 27
1990	Clemson 27, West Virginia 7
1991	Michigan 35, Mississippi 3
1992	Oklahoma 38, Virginia 14
1993	Florida 27, No. Carolina St. 10
1994	Alabama 24, No. Carolina 10
1995	Tennessee 45, Virginia Tech 23
1996	Syracuse 41, Clemson 0
1997	North Carolina 20, West Virginia 13
1998	North Carolina 42, Virginia Tech 3
1999	Georgia Tech 35, Notre Dame 28
2000	Miami (Fla.) 28, Georgia Tech 13
2001	Virginia Tech 41, Clemson 20
2002	Florida State 30, Virginia Tech 17
2003	North Carolina State 28, Notre Dame 6
2004	Maryland 41, West Virginia 7
2005	Florida State 30, West Virginia 18

RESULTS OF OTHER 2004–2005 BOWL GAMES

Fiesta Bowl—Utah 35, Pittsburgh 7
Outback Bowl—Georgia 24, Wisconsin 21
Capital One Bowl—Iowa 30, Louisiana State 25
New Orleans Bowl—Southern Mississippi 31, North Texas 10
Champs Sports Bowl—Georgia Tech 51, Syracuse 14
GMAC Bowl—Bowling Green 52, Memphis 35
Fort Worth Bowl—Cincinnati 32, Marshall 14
Las Vegas Bowl—Wyoming 24, UCLA 21
Hawaii Bowl—Hawaii 59, Alabama-Birmingham 40
MPC Computers Bowl—Fresno State 37, Virginia 34
Motor City Bowl—Connecticut 39, Toledo 10
Independence Bowl—Iowa State 17, Miami (Ohio) 13

Insight Bowl—Oregon State 38, Notre Dame 21
Alamo Bowl—Ohio State 33, Oklahoma State 7
Houston Bowl—Colorado 33, Texas-El Paso 28
Holiday Bowl—Texas Tech 45, California 31
Continental Tire Bowl—Boston College 37, North Carolina 24
Emerald Bowl—Navy 34, New Mexico 19
Silicon Valley Classic—Northern Illinois 34, Troy 21
Liberty Bowl—Louisville 44, Boise State 40
Peach Bowl—Miami 27, Florida 10
Sun Bowl—Arizona State 27, Purdue 23
Music City Bowl—Minnesota 20, Alabama 16

HEISMAN MEMORIAL TROPHY WINNERS

The Heisman Memorial Trophy is presented annually by the Downtown Athletic Club of New York City to the nation's outstanding college football player, as determined by a poll of sportswriters and sportscasters.

1935 Jay Berwanger, Chicago	1959 Billy Cannon, Louisiana State	1984 Doug Flutie, Boston College
1936 Larry Kelley, Yale	1960 Joe Bellino, Navy	1985 Bo Jackson, Auburn
1937 Clinton Frank, Yale	1961 Ernie Davis, Syracuse	1986 Vinny Testaverde, Miami
1938 Davey O'Brien, Texas Christian	1962 Terry Baker, Oregon State	1987 Tim Brown, Notre Dame
1939 Nile Kinnick, Iowa	1963 Roger Staubach, Navy	1988 Barry Sanders, Oklahoma State
1940 Tom Harmon, Michigan	1964 John Huarte, Notre Dame	1989 Andre Ware, Houston
1941 Bruce Smith, Minnesota	1965 Mike Garrett, So. Calif.	1990 Ty Detmer, Brigham Young
1942 Frank Sinkwich, Georgia	1966 Steve Spurrier, Florida	1991 Desmond Howard, Michigan
1943 Angelo Bertelli, Notre Dame	1967 Gary Beban, UCLA	1992 Gino Torretta, Miami
1944 Leslie Horvath, Ohio State	1968 O. J. Simpson, So. Calif.	1993 Charlie Ward, Florida State
1945 Felix Blanchard, Army	1969 Steve Owens, Oklahoma	1994 Rashaan Salaam, Colorado
1946 Glenn Davis, Army	1970 Jim Plunkett, Stanford	1995 Eddie George, Ohio State
1947 Johnny Lujack, Notre Dame	1971 Pat Sullivan, Auburn	1996 Danny Wuerffel, Florida
1948 Doak Walker, So. Methodist	1972 Johnny Rodgers, Nebraska	1997 Charles Woodson, Michigan
1949 Leon Hart, Notre Dame	1973 John Cappelletti, Penn State	1998 Ricky Williams, Texas
1950 Vic Janowicz, Ohio State	1974-75 Archie Griffin, Ohio State	1999 Ron Dayne, Wisconsin
1951 Dick Kazmaier, Princeton	1976 Tony Dorsett, Pittsburgh	2000 Chris Weinke, Florida State
1952 Billy Vessels, Oklahoma	1977 Earl Campbell, Texas	2001 Eric Crouch, University of
1953 Johnny Lattner, Notre Dame	1978 Billy Sims, Oklahoma	Nebraska
1954 Alan Ameche, Wisconsin	1979 Charles White, So. Calif.	2002 Carson Palmer, So. Calif.
1955 Howard Cassady, Ohio State	1980 George Rogers, South Carolina	2003 Jason White, Oklahoma
1956 Paul Hornung, Notre Dame	1981 Marcus Allen, So. Calif.	2004 Matt Leinart, So. Calif.
1957 John Crow, Texas A & M	1982 Herschel Walker, Georgia	
1958 Pete Dawkins, Army	1983 Mike Rozier, Nebraska	

2004 NCAA CHAMPIONSHIP PLAYOFFS

DIVISION I-AA
Quarterfinals
(Dec. 4, 2004)
Sam Houston State 35, Eastern
  Washington 34
Montana 47, New Hampshire 17
William & Mary 44, Delaware 38 (2
  OT)
James Madison 14, Furman 13

Semifinals
(Dec. 10–11, 2004)
Montana 34, Sam Houston State 13
James Madison 48, William & Mary 34

Championship
(Dec. 17, 2004)
James Madison 31, Montana 21

DIVISION II
Quarterfinals
(Nov. 27, 2004)
North Dakota 19, Grand Valley State
  15
Pittsburg State 50, Northwest Missouri
  State 36
West Chester 48, East Stroudsburg 38
Valdosta State 38, Albany State (Ga.)
  24

Semifinals
(Dec. 4, 2004)
Pittsburg State 31, North Dakota 19
Valdosta State 45, West Chester 21

Championship
(Dec. 11, 2004)
Valdosta State 36, Pittsburg State 31

DIVISION III
Quarterfinals
(Dec. 4, 2004)
Linfield 56, Occidental 27
Rowan 56, Delaware Valley 7
Mary Hardin-Baylor 52, Washington &
  Jefferson 16
Mount Union 38, Carthage 20

Semifinals
(Dec. 11, 2004)
Linfield 52, Rowan 0
Mary Hardin-Baylor 38, Mount Union
  35

Championship
(Dec. 18, 2004)
Linfield 28, Mary Hardin-Baylor 21

2004 NATIONAL ASSOCIATION OF INTERCOLLEGIATE ATHLETICS CHAMPIONSHIPS

Quarterfinals
(Nov. 27, 2004)
St. Francis (Ind.) 48, Hastings (Nebr.) 17
Georgetown (Ky.) 46, MidAmerica Nazarene (Kans.) 27
Carroll (Mont.) 56, Dickinson State (N.D.) 17
Azusa Pacific (Calif.) 24, Sioux Falls (S.D.) 3

Semifinals
(Dec. 4, 2004)
St. Francis 12, Georgetown 7
Carroll 14, Azusa Pacific 10
Championship
(Dec. 18, 2004)
Carroll 15, St. Francis 13

COLLEGE FOOTBALL HALL OF FAME

(South Bend, Indiana)
NOTE: Date given is player's last year of competition

Players

Abell, Earl—Colgate, 1915
Agase, Alex—Purdue/Illinois, 1946
Agganis, Harry—Boston Univ., 1952
Albert, Frank—Stanford, 1941
Aldrich, Chas. (Ki)—Texas Christian,
  1938
Aldrich, Malcolm—Yale, 1921
Alexander, Joseph—Syracuse, 1920
Allen, Marcus—So. Calif., 1981
Alworth, Lance—Arkansas, 1961
Ameche, Alan (Horse)—Wisconsin, 1954

Amling, Warren—Ohio State, 1946
Anderson, Bob P.—Army, 1959
Anderson, Dick—Colorado, 1967
Anderson, Donny—Texas Tech, 1965
Anderson, H. (Hunk)—Notre Dame, 1921
Arnett, Jon—So. Calif., 1956
Atkins, Doug—Tennessee, 1952
Babich, Bob—Miami-Ohio, 1968
Bacon, C. Everett—Wesleyan, 1912
Bagnell, Francis (Reds)—Pennsylvania,
  1950

Bailey, Johnny—Texas A&M, 1989
Baker, Hobart (Hobey)—Princeton, 1913
Baker, John—So. Calif., 1931
Baker, Terry—Oregon State, 1962
Ballin, Harold—Princeton, 1914
Banker, Bill—Tulane, 1929
Banonis, Vince—Detroit, 1941
Barber, Mike—Marshall (W. Va.), 1988
Barnes, Stanley—So. Calif., 1921
Barrett, Charles—Cornell, 1915
Baston, Bert—Minnesota, 1916

Battles, Cliff—W. Va. Wesleyan, 1931
Baugh, Sammy—Texas Christian, 1936
Baughan, Maxie—Georgia Tech, 1959
Baumgartner, Kirk—Wisconsin-Stevens Point, 1989
Bausch, James—Kansas, 1930
Beagle, Ron—Navy, 1955
Beasley, Terry—Auburn, 1971
Beban, Gary—UCLA, 1967
Bechtol, Hub—Texas Tech, 1946
Beck, Ray—Georgia Tech, 1951
Beckett, John—Oregon, 1913
Bednarik, Chuck—Pennsylvania 1948
Behm, Forrest—Nebraska,.1940
Bell, Bobby—Minnesota, 1962
Bell, Ricky—Southern California, 1976
Bellino, Joe—Navy, 1960
Below, Marty—Wisconsin, 1923
Benbrook, A.—Michigan, 1911
Bennett, Cornelius—Alabama, 1986
Bentrim, Jeff—North Dakota State, 1986
Bertelli, A.—Notre Dame, 1943
Berry, Charlie—Lafayette, 1924
Berwanger, John (Jay)—Chicago, 1935
Bettencourt, Larry—St. Mary's, 1927
Biletnikoff, Fred—Florida State, 1964
Blanchard, Felix (Doc)—Army, 1946
Blazine, Tony—Ill. Wesleyan, 1934
Bock, Ed—Iowa State, 1938
Bomar, Lynn—Vanderbilt, 1924
Bomeisler, Doug (Bo)—Yale, 1913
Booth, Albie—Yale, 1931
Bork, George—Northern Illinois, 1963
Borries, Fred—Navy, 1934
Bosely, Bruce—West Virginia, 1955
Bosseler, Don—Miami (Fla.), 1956
Bottari, Vic—California, 1939
Bowden, Murry—Dartmouth, 1970
Boynton, Ben—Williams, 1920
Bozis, Al—Georgetown, 1941
Bradshaw, Terry—Louisiana Tech, 1969
Brewer, Charles—Harvard, 1895
Bright, John—Drake, 1951
Brodie, John—Stanford, 1956
Brooke, George—Pennsylvania, 1895
Brosky, Al—Illinois, 1952
Brown, Bob—Nebraska, 1963
Brown, George—Navy/San Diego State, 1947
Brown, Gordon—Yale, 1900
Brown, Jim—Syracuse, 1956
Brown, John, Jr.—Navy, 1913
Brown, Johnny Mack—Alabama, 1925
Brown, Raymond (Tay)—So. Calif., 1932
Brown, Tom—Minnesota, 1960
Browner, Ross—Notre Dame, 1977
Bruner, Teel—Centre College (Ky.), 1985
Buchanan, Buck—Grambling State, 1962
Budde, Brad—So. Calif., 1979
Bunker, Paul—Army, 1902
Burford, Chris—Stanford, 1959
Burris, Kurt—Oklahoma, 1954
Burton, Ron—Northwestern, 1956
Butkus, Dick—Illinois, 1964
Butler, Kevin—Georgia, 1984
Butler, Robert—Wisconsin, 1912
Cafego, George—Tennessee, 1939
Cagle, Chris—SW La./Army, 1929
Cain, John—Alabama, 1932
Calip, Brad—East Central (Okla.), 1984
Cameron, Eddie—Wash. & Lee, 1924
Campbell, David C.—Harvard, 1901
Campbell, Earl—Texas, 1977
Cannon, Billy—Louisiana State, 1959
Cannon, Jack—Notre Dame, 1929
Cappelletti, John—Penn State, 1973
Carideo, Frank—Notre Dame, 1930
Caroline, J.C.—Illinois, 1954
Carney, Charles—Illinois, 1921
Carpenter, Bill—Army, 1959
Carpenter, C. Hunter—VPI, 1905
Carroll, Charles—Washington, 1928

Carson, Harry—So. Carolina State, 1975
Carter, Anthony—Michigan, 1982
Casanova, Tommy—Louisiana State, 1971
Casey, Edward L.—Harvard, 1919
Cason, Rod—Angelo State, 1971
Cassady, Howard—Ohio State, 1955
Casillas, Tony—Oklahoma, 1985
Chamberlain, Guy—Nebraska, 1915
Chapman, Sam—Cal.-Berkeley, 1938
Chappuis, Bob—Michigan, 1947
Christman, Paul—Missouri, 1940
Cichy, Joe—North Dakota State, 1970
Clark, Earl (Dutch)—Colo. College, 1929
Cleary, Paul—So. Calif., 1947
Clevenger, Zora—Indiana, 1903
Cloud, Jack—William & Mary, 1948
Cochran, Gary—Princeton, 1895
Cody, Josh—Vanderbilt, 1920
Coleman, Don—Mich. State, 1951
Conerly, Chuck—Mississippi, 1947
Connor, George—Notre Dame, 1947
Cooper, Bill—Muskingum (Ohio), 1960
Corbin, W.—Yale, 1888
Corbus, William—Stanford, 1933
Cowan, Hector—Princeton, 1889
Covert, Jimbo—Pittsburgh, 1983
Coy, Edward H. (Tad)—Yale, 1909
Crawford, Brad—Franklin (Ind.), 1977
Crawford, Fred—Duke, 1933
Crow, John D.—Texas A & M, 1957
Crowley, James—Notre Dame, 1924
Csonka, Larry—Syracuse, 1967
Curtis, Tom—Michigan, 1969
Cutter, Slade—Navy, 1934
Czarobski, Ziggie—Notre Dame, 1947
Dale, Carroll—Virginia Tech, 1959
Dalrymple, Gerald—Tulane, 1931
Dalton, John—Navy, 1912
Daly, Charles—Harvard/Army, 1902
Daniell, Averell—Pittsburgh, 1936
Daniell, James—Ohio State, 1941
Davies, Tom—Pittsburgh, 1921
Davis, Anthony—So. Calif., 1974
Davis, Ernest—Syracuse, 1961
Davis, Glenn—Army, 1946
Davis, Harold—Westminster (Pa.), 1956
Davis, Robert T.—Georgia Tech, 1947
Dawkins, Pete—Army, 1958
Delaney, Joe—Northwestern State, 1980
Deery, Tom—Widener, 1981
DeLong, Steve—Tennessee, 1964
Dement, Kenneth—SE Missouri, 1954
Den Herder, Vern—Central (Iowa), 1970
De Rogatis, Al—Duke, 1940
DesJardien, Paul—Chicago 1914
Devino, Aubrey—Iowa, 1921
DeWitt, John—Princeton, 1903
Dial, Buddy—Rice, 1958
Dicus, Chuck—Arkansas, 1970
Dierdorf, Dan—Michigan, 1970
Ditka, Mike—Pittsburgh, 1960
Dobbs, Glenn—Tulsa, 1942
Dodd, Bobby—Tennessee, 1930
Donan, Holland—Princeton, 1950
Donchess, Joseph—Pittsburgh, 1929
Dorney, Keith—Penn State, 1978
Dorsett, Tony—Pittsburgh, 1976
Dougherty, Nathan—Tennessee, 1909
Dove, Bob—Notre Dame, 1942
Drahos, Nick—Cornell, 1940
Driscoll, Paddy—Northwestern, 1917
Drury, Morley—So. Calif., 1927
Dryer, Fred—San Diego State, 1968
Dudek, Joe—Plymouth State, 1985
Duden, Dick—Navy, 1945
Dudley, William (Bill)—Virginia, 1941
Duncan, Randy—Iowa, 1958
Easley, Ken—UCLA, 1980
Eckersall, Walter—Chicago, 1906
Edwards, Turk—Washington State, 1931
Edwards, William—Princeton, 1900
Eichenlaub, R.—Notre Dame, 1913

Eisenhauer, Steve—Navy, 1953
Elking, Larry—Baylor, 1964
Elliott, Chalmers—Purdue, 1944 & Mich., 1947
Elliott, Pete—Michigan, 1948
Elmendorf, Dave—Texas A & M, 1970
Elway, John—Stanford, 1982
Emanuel, Frank—Tennessee, 1965
Evans, Ray—Kansas, 1947
Exendine, Albert—Carlisle, 1908
Falaschi, Nello—Santa Clara, 1937
Fears, Tom—Santa Clara/UCLA, 1947
Feathers, Beattie—Tennessee, 1933
Fenimore, Robert—Oklahoma State, 1947
Fenton, G.E. (Doc)—Louisiana State, 1910
Ferguson, Bob—Ohio State, 1961
Ferraro, John—So. Calif., 1944
Fesler, Wesley—Ohio State, 1930
Fincher, Bill—Georgia Tech, 1920
Fischer, Bill—Notre Dame, 1948
Fish, Hamilton—Harvard, 1909
Fisher, Robert—Harvard, 1911
Flowers, Abe—Georgia Tech, 1920
Flowers, Charlie—Mississippi, 1959
Floyd, George—Eastern Kentucky, 1981
Fortmann, Daniel—Colgate, 1935
Fralic, Bill—Pittsburgh, 1984
Francis, Sam—Nebraska, 1936
Franck, George (Sonny)—Minnesota, 1940
Franco, Edmund (Ed)—Fordham, 1937
Frank, Clint—Yale, 1937
Franz, Rodney—California, 1949
Frederickson, Tucker—Auburn, 1964
Friedman, Benny—Michigan, 1926
Gabriel, Roman—North Carolina St., 1961
Gain, Bob—Kentucky, 1950
Galiffa, Arnold—Army, 1949
Galimore, Willie—Florida A & M, 1956
Gallarneau, Hugh—Stanford, 1941
Gamble, Kenny—Colgate, 1987
Garbisch, Edgar—Army, 1924
Garrett, Mike—So. Calif., 1965
Gelbert, Charles—Pennsylvania, 1896
Geyer, Forest—Oklahoma, 1915
Gibbs, Jake—Mississippi, 1960
Giel, Paul—Minnesota, 1953
Gifford, Frank—So. Calif., 1951
Gilbert, Chris—Texas, 1968
Gilbert, Walter—Auburn, 1936
Gilmer, Harry—Alabama, 1947
Gipp, George—Notre Dame, 1920
Gladchuk, Chet—Boston College, 1940
Glass, Bill—Baylor, 1956
Glover, Rich—Nebraska, 1972
Goldberg, Marshall—Pittsburgh, 1938
Goodreault, Gene—Boston College, 1940
Gordon, Walter—California, 1918
Governale, Paul—Columbia, 1942
Grabowski, Jim—Illinois, 1965
Graham, Otto—Northwestern, 1943
Gradishar, Randy—Ohio State, 1973
Grange, Harold (Red)—Illinois, 1925
Grayson, Roberty—Stanford, 1935
Green, Charles—Wittenberg, 1964
Green, Darrell—Texas A&I, 1982
Green, Hugh—Pittsburgh, 1980
Green, Joe—North Texas State, 1968
Green, Tim—Syracuse, 1985
Griese, Bob—Purdue, 1966
Griffin, Archie—Ohio State, 1975
Grinnell, William—Tufts, 1934
Groom, Jerry—Notre Dame, 1950
Guglielmi, Ralph—Notre Dame, 1954
Gulick, Merel—Hobart, 1929
Guy, Ray—So. Mississippi, 1972
Guyon, Joe—Georgia Tech, 1919
Hadl, John—Kansas, 1961
Hale, Edwin—Mississippi Col., 1921

Hall, Parker—Mississippi, 1938
Ham, Jack—Penn State, 1970
Hamilton, Robert (Bones)—Stanford, 1935
Hamilton, Tom—Navy, 1925
Hannah, John—Alabama, 1972
Hanson, Vic—Syracuse, 1926
Harder, Pat—Wisconsin, 1942
Hardwick, H. (Tack)—Harvard, 1914
Hare, T. Truxton—Pennsylvania, 1900
Harley, Chick—Ohio State, 1919
Harmon, Tom—Michigan, 1940
Harpster, Howard—Carnegie Tech, 1928
Harris, Wayne—Arkansas, 1960
Hart, Edward J. Princeton, 1911
Hart, Leon—Notre Dame, 1949
Hartman, Bill—Georgia, 1937
Haslett, Jim—Indiana (Pa.), 1978
Hawkins, Frank—Nevada, 1980
Haynes, Michael—Arizona State, 1975
Hazel, Homer—Rutgers, 1924
Healey, Ed—Dartmouth, 1916
Heffelfiner, W. (Pudge)—Yale, 1891
Hein, Mel—Washington State, 1930
Heinrich, Don—Washington, 1952
Hendricks, Ted—Miami, 1968
Henley, Garney—Huron, 1959
Henry, Wilbur—Wash. & Jefferson, 1919
Herschberger, Clarence—Chicago, 1899
Herwig, Robert—California, 1937
Heston, Willie—Michigan, 1904
Hickman, Herman—Tennessee, 1931
Hickok, William—Yale, 1895
Hicks, John—Ohio State, 1973
Hill, Dan—Duke, 1938
Hillebrand, A.R. (Doc)—Princeton, 1900
Hinkey, Frank—Yale, 1894
Hinkle, Carl—Vanderbilt, 1937
Hinkle, Clark—Bucknell, 1932
Hirsch, Elroy—Wisconsin/Michigan, 1943
Hitchcock, James—Auburn, 1932
Hoage, Terry—Georgia, 1983
Hoffman, Frank—Notre Dame, 1931
Hogan, James J.—Yale, 1904
Holland, Jerome (Brud)—Cornell, 1938
Holleder, Don—Army, 1955
Hollenbeck, William—Pennsylvania, 1908
Holovak, Michael—Boston College, 1942
Holt, Pierce—Angelo State, 1980
Holub, E.J.—Texas Tech, 1960
Hornung, Paul—Notre Dame, 1956
Horrell, Edwin—California, 1924
Horvath, Les—Ohio State, 1944
Houston, Jim—Ohio State, 1959
Howe Arthur—Yale, 1911
Howell, Millard (Dixie)—Alabama, 1934
Huarte, John—Notre Dame, 1964
Hubbard, Cal—Centenary, 1926
Hubbard, John—Amherst, 1906
Hubert, Allison—Alabama, 1925
Huff, Robert Lee (Sam)—W. Va., 1955
Humble, Weldon G.—Rice, 1946
Hunley, Ricky—Arizona, 1983
Hunt, Jackie—Marshall, 1941
Hunt, Joel—Texas A & M, 1927
Huntington, Ellery—Colgate, 1914
Hutson, Don—Alabama, 1934
Ingram, James—Navy, 1906
Iacavazzi, Cosmo—Princeton, 1964
Isbell, Cecil—Purdue, 1937
Jablonsky, Harvey—Wash. U./Army, 1933
Jackson, Bo—Auburn, 1985
Jackson, Keith—Oklahoma, 1987
Janowicz, Vic—Ohio State, 1951
Jefferson, John—Arizona State, 1977
Jenkins, Darold—Missouri, 1941
Jensen, Jack—Cal.-Berkeley, 1948
Joesting, Herbert—Minnesota, 1927
Johnson, Billy—Widener, 1973
Johnson, Gary—Grambling State, 1974

Johnson, James—Carlisle, 1903
Johnson, Robert—Tennessee, 1967
Johnson, Ron—Michigan, 1968
Jones, Brent—Santa Clara, 1985
Jones, Calvin—Iowa, 1955
Jones, Gormer—Ohio State, 1935
Jones, Stan—Maryland, 1953
Jordan, Lee Roy—Alabama, 1962
Juhan, Frank—Univ. of South, 1910
Justice, Charlie—North Carolina, 1949
Kaer, Mort—So. Calif., 1926
Kapp, Joe—California, 1958
Karras, Alex—Iowa, 1957
Kavanaugh, Kenneth—Louisiana State, 1939
Kaw, Edgar—Cornell, 1922
Kazmaier, Richard—Princeton, 1951
Keck, James—Princeton, 1921
Kelley, Larry—Yale, 1936
Kelly, William—Montana, 1926
Kenna, Ed—Syracuse, 1966
Kern, George—Boston College, 1941
Ketcham, Henry—Yale, 1913
Keyes, Leroy—Purdue, 1968
Killinger, William—Penn State, 1922
Kilmer, Billy—UCLA, 1960
Kimbrough, John—Texas A & M, 1940
Kinard, Frank—Mississippi, 1937
Kinard, Terry—Clemson, 1982
Kiner, Steve—Tennessee, 1969
King, Philip—Princeton, 1893
Kinnick, Nile—Iowa, 1939
Kipke, Harry—Michigan, 1923
Kirkpatrick, John Reed—Yale, 1910
Kitzmiller, John—Oregon, 1929
Koch, Barton—Baylor, 1931
Kitner, Malcolm—Texas, 1942
Kramer, Ron—Michigan, 1956
Kroll, Alex—Rutgers, 1961
Krueger, Charlie—Texas A & M, 1957
Kwalick, Ted—Penn State, 1968
Lach, Steve—Duke, 1941
Lane, Myles—Dartmouth, 1927
Lanier, Sr., Willie—Morgan State, 1966
Lattner, Joseph J.—Notre Dame, 1953
Lauricella, Hank—Tennessee, 1952
Lautenschlaeger—Tulane, 1925
Layden, Elmer—Notre Dame, 1924
Layne, Bobby—Texas, 1947
Lea, Langdon—Princeton, 1895
Leaks, Roosevelt—Texas, 1974
LeBaron, Eddie—Univ. of Pacific, 1949
LeClair, Jim—North Dakota, 1971
Leech, James—Va. Mil. Inst., 1920
Lester, Darrell—Texas Christian, 1935
Levias, Jerry—Southern Methodist, 1968
Lewis, D. D.—Mississippi State, 1968
Lewis, Leo—Lincoln (Mo.), 1954
Lilly, Bob—Texas Christian, 1960
Little, Floyd—Syracuse, 1966
Lio, Augie—Georgetown, 1940
Lockbaum, Gordie—Holy Cross, 1987
Locke, Gordon—Iowa, 1922
Lomax, Neil—Portland (Ore.) State, 1980
Long, Chuck—Iowa, 1985
Long, Mel—Toledo, 1971
Loria, Frank—Virginia Tech, 1967
Lott, Ronnie—So. Calif., 1980
Lourie, Don—Princeton, 1921
Lucas, Richard—Penn State, 1959
Luckman, Sid—Columbia, 1938
Lujack, John—Notre Dame, 1947
Lund, J. L. (Pug)—Minnesota, 1934
Lynch, Jim—Notre Dame, 1966
MacAfee, Ken—Notre Dame, 1977
Macomber, Bart—Illinois, 1915
MacLeod, Robert—Dartmouth, 1938
Maegle, Dick—Rice, 1954
Mahan, Edward W.—Harvard, 1915
Majors, John—Tennessee, 1956
Mallory, William—Yale, 1893
Mancha, Vaughn—Alabama, 1947

Mandich, James—Michigan, 1969
Mann, Gerald—So. Methodist, 1927
Manning, Archie—Mississippi, 1970
Manske, Edgar—Northwestern, 1933
Marinaro, Ed—Cornell, 1971
Marino, Dan—Pittsburgh, 1982
Markov, Vic—Washington, 1937
Marshall, Robert—Minnesota, 1907
Martin, Jim—Notre Dame, 1949
Matson, Ollie—San Fran. U., 1952
Matthews, Ray—Texas Christian, 1928
Maulbetsch, John—Michigan, 1914
Mauthe, J. L. (Pete)—Penn State, 1912
Maxwell, Robert—Chicago/Swarthmore, 1906
May, Mark—Pittsburgh, 1980
McAfee, George—Duke, 1939
McCallum, Napoleon—Navy, 1985
McCauley, Don—North Carolina, 1970
McClung, Thomas L.—Yale, 1891
McColl, William F.—Stanford, 1951
McCormick, James B.—Princeton, 1907
McDonald, Tom—Oklahoma, 1956
McDowall, Jack—No. Carolina State, 1927
McElhenny, Hugh—Washington, 1951
McEver, Gene—Tennessee, 1931
McEwan, John—Minn./Army, 1916
McFadden, J. B.—Clemson, 1939
McFadin, Bud—Texas, 1950
McGee, Mike—Duke, 1959
McGinley, Edward—Pennsylvania, 1924
McGovern, J.—Minnesota, 1910
McGraw, Thurman—Colorado State, 1949
McGriff, Tyrone—Florida A & M, 1979
McKeever, Mike—So. Calif., 1960
McKenzie, Reggie—Michigan, 1971
McLaren, George—Pittsburgh, 1918
McMahon, Jim—Brigham Young, 1981
McMillan, Dan—So. Calif./California, 1922
McMillin, A. N. (Bo)—Centre, 1921
McWhorter, Robert—Georgia, 1913
Mercer, Leroy—Pennsylvania, 1912
Meredith, Don—So. Methodist, 1959
Merritt, Frank—Army, 1943
Metzger, Bert—Notre Dame, 1930
Meyland, Wayne—Nebraska, 1967
Michaels, Lou—Kentucky, 1957
Michels, John—Tennessee, 1952
Mickal, Abe—Louisiana State, 1935
Miller, Creighton—Notre Dame, 1943
Miller, Don—Notre Dame, 1925
Miller, Edgar (Rip)—Notre Dame, 1924
Miller, Eugene—Penn State, 1913
Miller, Fred—Notre Dame, 1928
Millner, Wayne—Notre Dame, 1935
Milstead, Century—Wabash/Yale, 1923
Minds, John—Pennsylvania, 1897
Minisi, Anthony—Navy/Pennsylvania, 1947
Mitchell, Lydell—Penn State, 1971
Modzelewski, Dick—Maryland, 1952
Moffatt, Alex—Princeton, 1884
Molinski, Ed—Tennessee, 1940
Montgomery, Cliff—Columbia, 1933
Montgomery, Wilbert—Abilene Christian, 1976
Moomaw, Donn—UCLA, 1952
Morley, William—Columbia, 1903
Morris, George—Georgia Tech, 1952
Morris, Larry—Georgia Tech, 1954
Morton, Craig—California, 1964
Morton, William—Dartmouth, 1931
Moscrip, Monk—Stanford, 1935
Muller, Harold (Brick)—Calif., 1922
Musso, Johnny—Alabama, 1971
Nagurski, Bronko—Minnesota, 1929
Neighbors, Billy—Alabama, 1961
Nevers, Ernie—Stanford, 1925
Newell, Marshall—Harvard, 1893
Newman, Harry—Michigan, 1932

Newsome, Ozzie—Alabama, 1977
Nielsen, Gifford—Brigham Young, 1976
Nix, Dwayne, Texas A&M-Kingsville, 1968
Nobis, Tommy—Texas, 1965
Nomellini, Leo—Minnesota, 1949
Oberland, Andrew—Dartmouth, 1925
O'Brien, Davey—Texas Christian, 1938
O'Brien, Ken—Cal.-Davis, 1982
O'Dea, Pat—Wisconsin, 1899
Odell, Robert—Pennsylvania, 1943
O'Hearn, J.—Cornell, 1915
Olds, Robin—Army, 1942
Oliphant, Elmer—Purdue/Army, 1917
Olsen, Merlin—Utah State, 1961
Onkotz, Dennis—Penn State, 1969
Oosterbaan, Ben—Michigan, 1927
O'Rourke, Charles—Boston College, 1940
Orsi, John—Colgate, 1931
Osgood, W. D.—Cornell/Pennsylvania, 1895
Osmanski, William—Holy Cross, 1938
Outland, John—Kansas/Pennsylvania, 1899
Owen, George—Harvard, 1922
Owens, Jim—Oklahoma, 1949
Owens, Steve—Oklahoma, 1969
Page, Alan—Notre Dame, 1966
Palumbo, Joe—U. of Virginia, 1951
Pardee, Jack—Texas A & M, 1956
Parilli, Vito (Babe)—Kentucky, 1951
Parker, Clarence (Ace)—Duke, 1936
Parker, Jackie—Miss. State, 1953
Parker, James—Ohio State, 1956
Payton, Walter—Jackson State, 1974
Pazzetti, V. J.—Wesleyan/Lehigh, 1912
Peabody, Endicott—Harvard, 1941
Peck, Robert—Pittsburgh, 1916
Pellegrini, Bob—Maryland, 1955
Pennock, Stanley B.—Harvard, 1914
Pfann, George—Cornell, 1923
Phillips, H. D.—Univ. of South, 1904
Phillips, Loyd—Arkansas, 1966
Pingel, John—Michigan State, 1938
Pihos, Pete—Indiana, 1945
Pinckert, Ernie—So. Calif., 1931
Plunkett, Jim—Stanford, 1970
Poe, Arthur—Princeton, 1899
Pollard, Fritz—Brown, 1916
Poole, Barney—Miss./Army, 1947
Powell, Marvin—So. Calif., 1976
Pregulman, Merv—Michigan, 1943
Price, Eddie—Tulane, 1949
Pritchard, Ron—Arizona State, 1968
Pruitt, Greg—Oklahoma, 1972
Pugh, Larry—Westminster, Pa., 1964
Pund, Henry—Georgia Tech, 1928
Ramsey, Gerrard—Wm. & Mary, 1942
Rauch, John—Georgia, 1948
Reasons, Gary—Northwestern State (La.), 1983
Redell, Bill—Occidental, 1963
Redman, Rick—Washington, 1964
Reeds, Claude—Oklahoma, 1913
Reid, Mike—Penn State, 1970
Reid, Steve—Northwestern, 1936
Reid, William—Harvard, 1900
Reifsnyder, Bob—Navy, 1958
Renfro, Mel—Oregon, 1963
Rentner, Ernest—Northwestern, 1932
Reppert, Scott—Lawrence (Wis.), 1982
Ressler, Glenn—Penn State, 1964
Reynolds, Robert—Nebraska, 1952
Reynolds, Robert—Stanford, 1935
Rhino, Randy—Georgia Tech, 1974
Rhome, Jerry—Tulsa, 1964
Richardson, Willie—Jackson State (Miss.), 1962
Richter, Les—California, 1951
Richter, Pat—Wisconsin, 1962
Riley, John—Northwestern, 1931
Rimington, Dave—Nebraska, 1982

Rinehart, Charles—Lafayette, 1897
Ritchie, Richard—Texas A & M, 1977
Ritcher, Jim—No. Carolina St., 1979
Roberts, Calvin—Gustavus Adolphus (Minn.), 1952
Roberts, J. D.—Oklahoma, 1953
Robeson, Paul—Rutgers, 1918
Robinson, Dave—Penn State, 1962
Robinson, Jerry—UCLA, 1978
Rocker, Tracy—Auburn, 1988
Rodgers, Ira—West Virginia, 1919
Rodgers, Johnny—Nebraska, 1972
Rogers, Edward L.—Minnesota, 1903
Rogers, George—South Carolina, 1980
Roland, Johnny—Missouri, 1965
Romig, Joe—Colorado, 1961
Rosenberg, Aaron—So. Calif., 1934
Ross, Dan—Northeastern, 1978
Rote, Kyle—So. Methodist, 1950
Routt, Joe—Texas A & M, 1937
Salmon, Louis—Notre Dame, 1904
Sanders, Barry—Oklahoma State, 1988
Sarkisian, Alex—Northwestern, 1948
Sauer, George—Nebraska, 1933
Savitsky, George—Pennsylvania, 1947
Saxon, Jimmy—Texas, 1961
Sayers Gale—Kansas, 1964
Scarbath, Jack—Maryland, 1952
Scarlett, Hunter—Pennsylvania, 1909
Schloredt, Bob—Washington, 1960
Schmidt, Joe—Pittsburgh, 1952
Schoonover, Wear—Arkansas, 1929
Schreiner, Dave—Wisconsin, 1942
Schultz, Adolf (Germany)—Mich., 1908
Schwab, Frank—Lafayette, 1922
Schwartz, Marchmont—Notre Dame, 1931
Schwegler, Paul—Washington, 1931
Scott, Clyde—Arkansas, 1949
Scott, Freddie—Amherst, 1973
Scott, Richard—Navy, 1947
Scott, Tom—Virginia, 1953
Seibels, Henry—Sewanee, 1899
Sellers, Ron—Florida State, 1968
Selmon, Lee Roy—Oklahoma, 1975
Sewell, Harley—Texas, 1952
Shakespeare, Bill—Notre Dame, 1935
Shell, Donnie—So. Carolina St., 1973
Shelton, Murray—Cornell, 1915
Shevlin, Tom—Yale, 1905
Shively, Bernie—Illinois, 1926
Simons, Claude—Tulane, 1934
Sims, Billy—Oklahoma, 1979
Simpson, O. J.—So. Calif., 1968
Singletary, Mike—Baylor, 1980
Sington, Fred—Alabama, 1930
Sinkwich, Frank—Georgia, 1942
Sisemore, Jerry—Texas, 1972
Sitko, Emil—Notre Dame, 1949
Skladany, Joe—Pittsburgh, 1933
Slater, F.F. (Duke)—Iowa, 1921
Smith, Billy Ray—Arkansas, 1982
Smith, Bruce—Minnesota, 1941
Smith, Bubba—Michigan State, 1966
Smith, Ernie—So. Calif., 1932
Smith, Harry—So. Calif., 1939
Smith, Jim Ray—Baylor, 1954
Smith, John (Clipper)—Notre Dame, 1927
Smith, Riley—Alabama, 1935
Smith, Vernon—Georgia, 1931
Snow, Neil—Michigan, 1901
Spani, Gary—Kansas State, 1977
Sparlis, Al—UCLA, 1945
Spears, Clarence W.—Dartmouth, 1915
Spears, W.D.—Vanderbilt, 1927
Sprackling, William—Brown, 1911
Sprague, M. (Bud)—Texas/Army, 1928
Spurrier, Steve—Florida, 1966
Stafford, Harrison—Texas, 1932
Stagg, Amos Alonzo—Yale, 1889
Stanfill, Bill—Georgia, 1968
Starcevich, Max—Washington, 1936

Staubach, Roger—Navy, 1963
Steffen, Walter—Chicago, 1908
Steffy, Joe—Army, 1947
Stein, Herbert—Pittsburgh, 1921
Steuber, Robert—Missouri, 1943
Stevens, Mal—Yale, 1923
Stevenson, Ben—Tuskegee (Ala.), 1930
Stevenson, Vincent—Pennsylvania, 1905
Stillwagon, Jim—Ohio State, 1970
Stinchcomb, Gaylord—Ohio State, 1920
Strom, Brock—Air Force, 1959
Stromberg, William—Johns Hopkins, 1981
Strong, Ken—New York Univ., 1928
Strupper, George—Georgia Tech, 1917
Stuhldreher, Harry—Notre Dame, 1924
Stydahar, Joe—West Virginia, 1935
Suffridge, Robert—Tennessee, 1940
Suhey, Steve—Penn State, 1947
Sullivan, Pat—Auburn, 1971
Sundstrom, Frank—Cornell, 1923
Swann, Lynn—So. Calif., 1973
Swanson, Clarence—Nebraska, 1921
Swiacki, Bill—Holy Cross/Colombia, 1947
Swink, Jim—Texas Christian, 1956
Talboom, Eddie—Wyoming, 1950
Taliafarro, George—Indiana, 1948
Tarkenton, Fran—Georgia, 1960
Tatum, Jack—Ohio State, 1970
Tavener, John—Indiana, 1944
Taylor, Bruce—Boston Univ., 1969
Taylor, Charles—Stanford, 1942
Theismann, Joe—Notre Dame, 1970
Thomas, Aurelius—Ohio State, 1957
Thompson, Joe—Pittsburgh, 1907
Thomsen, Lynn—Austana, 1986
Thorne, Samuel B.—Yale, 1906
Thorpe, Jim—Carlisle, 1912
Ticknor, Ben—Harvard, 1930
Tigert, John—Vanderbilt, 1904
Tinsley, Gaynell—Louisiana State, 1936
Tipton, Eric—Duke, 1938
Tonnemaker, Clayton—Minnesota, 1949
Torrey, Robert—Pennsylvania, 1906
Totten, Willie—Miss. Valley State, 1985
Trautman, Randy—Boise State, 1981
Travis, Ed Tarkio—Missouri, 1920
Trippi, Charles—Georgia, 1946
Tryon, J. Edward—Colgate, 1925
Tubbs, Jerry—Oklahoma, 1956
Utay, Joe—Texas A & M, 1907
Van Brocklin, Norm—Oregon, 1948
Van Pelt, Brad—Michigan State, 1972
Van Sickel, Dale—Florida, 1929
Van Surdam, Henderson—Wesleyan, 1905
Very, Dexter—Penn State, 1912
Vessels, Billy—Oklahoma, 1952
Vick, Ernie—Michigan, 1921
Wagner, Huber—Pittsburgh, 1913
Walker, Doak—So. Methodist, 1949
Walker, Herschel—Georgia, 1982
Wallace, Bill—Rice, 1935
Walsh, Adam—Notre Dame, 1924
Warburton, I. (Cotton)—So. Calif., 1934
Ward, Robert (Bob)—Maryland, 1951
Ware, Andre—Houston, 1989
Warner, William—Cornell, 1903
Washington, Joe—Oklahoma, 1975
Washington, Ken—UCLA, 1939
Weatherall, Jim—Oklahoma, 1951
Webster, George—Mich. State, 1966
Wedemeyer, Herman J.—St. Mary's, 1947
Weekes, Harold—Columbia, 1902
Wehrli, Roger—Missouri, 1968
Weiner, Art—North Carolina, 1949
Weir, Ed—Nebraska, 1925
Welch, Gus—Carlisle, 1914
Weller, John—Princeton, 1935
Wendell, Percy—Harvard, 1913
West, D. Belford—Colgate, 1919

Westfall, Bob—Michigan, 1941
Weyand, Alex—Army, 1915
Wharton, Charles—Pennsylvania, 1896
Wheeler, Arthur—Princeton, 1894
White, Byron (Whizzer)—Colorado, 1937
White, Charles—So. Calif., 1979
White, Danny—Arizona State, 1973
White, Ed—California-Berkeley, 1968
White, Randy—Maryland, 1974
White, Reggie—Tennessee, 1983
Whitmire, Don—Alabama/Navy, 1944
Wickhorst, Frank—Navy, 1926
Widseth, Ed—Minnesota, 1936
Wiggin, Paul—Stanford, 1956
Wildung, Richard—Minnesota, 1942

Williams, Bob—Notre Dame, 1950
Williams, David—Illinois, 1985
Williams, Doug—Grambling, 1977
Williams, James—Rice, 1949
Willis, William—Ohio State, 1945
Wilson, George—Washington, 1925
Wilson, George—Lafayette, 1928
Wilson, Harry—Penn State/Army, 1923
Wilson, Marc—Brigham Young, 1979
Winslow, Kellen—Missouri, 1978
Wistert, Albert A.—Michigan, 1942
Wistert, Al—Michigan, 1942
Wistert, Frank (Whitey)—Michigan, 1933
Wood, Barry—Harvard, 1931
Wojciechowicz, Alex—Fordham, 1936

Wyant, Andrew—Bucknell/Chicago, 1894
Wyatt, Bowden—Tennessee, 1938
Wyckoff, Clint—Cornell, 1896
Yarr, Tom—Notre Dame, 1931
Yary, Ron—So. Calif., 1968
Yoder, Lloyd—Carnegie Tech, 1926
Young, Charles—So. Calif., 1972
Young, Claude (Buddy)—Illinois, 1946
Young, Harry—Wash. & Lee, 1916
Young, Steve—Brigham Young, 1983
Young, Walter—Oklahoma, 1938
Youngblood, Jack—Florida, 1970
Youngblood, Jim—Tennessee, 1972
Zarnas, Gus—Ohio State, 1937

Coaches

Bill Alexander
Dr. Ed Anderson
Ike Armstrong
Chris Ault
Earl Banks
Harry Baujan
Thomas Beck
Matty Bell
Hugo Bezdek
Dana X. Bible
Bernie Bierman
Bob Blackman
Earl (Red) Blaik
Frank Broyles
Earle Bruce
Paul "Bear" Bryant
Harold Burry
Jim Butterfield
James "Wally" Butts
Charles W. Caldwell
Walter Camp
Len Casanova
Marino Casem
Frank Cavanaugh
Jerry Claiborne
Richard Colman
Don Coryell
Carmen Cozza
Fritz Crisler
Duffy Daugherty
Bob Devaney
Dan Devine
Doug Dickey
Gil Dobie

Bobby Dodd
Terry Donahue
Michael Donohue
Vince Dooley
Gus Dorais
Pat Dye
Bill Edwards
LaVell Edwards
Charles (Rip) Engle
Forest Evashevski
Don Faurot
Hayden Fry
Joseph Fusco
Jake Gaither
Sid Gillman
Ernest Godfrey
Ray Graves
Andy Gustafson
Jack Harding
Edward K. Hall
Richard Harlow
Jesse Harper
Roger Harring
Percy Haughton
Woody Hayes
John W. Heisman
R.A. (Bob) Higgins
Paul Hoernemann
Orin E. Hollingberry
Frank Howard
Marcelino (Chelo) Huerta
William Ingram
Don James

Morley Jennings
Howard Jones
L. (Biff) Jones
Thomas (Tad) Jones
Ralph (Shug) Jordan
Bob Keade
Andy Kerr
Roy Kidd
Chuck Klausing
Frank Kush
Frank Leahy
George E. Little
Lou Little
El (Slip) Madigan
Fred Martinelli
Dave Maurer
Charley McClendon
Herbert McCracken
Daniel McGugin
John McKay
Allyn McKeen
DeOrmond (Tuss)
  McLaughry
John Merritt
L.R. (Dutch) Meyer
Bernie Moore
Scrappy Moore
Jack Mollenkopf
Ray Morrison
Darrell Mudra
Arnett "Ace" Mumford
George A. Munger
Clarence Munn
Frank Murray

William Murray
Ed (Hooks) Mylin
Earle (Greasy) Neale
Jess Neely
Don Nehlen
David Nelson
Robert Neyland
Billy Nicks
Homer Norton
Frank (Buck) O'Neill
Tom Osborne
Bennie Owen
Ara Parseghian
Doyt Perry
James Phalea
Tommy Prothro
John Ralston
Harold "Tubby" Ray-
  mond
Charlie Richard
E.N. Robinson
Knute Rockne
E. L. (Dick) Romney
William W. Roper
Darrell Royal
Ad Rutschman
Henry (Red) Sanders
George F. Sanford
Bo Schembechler
Ron Schipper
Francis A. Schmidt
Floyd (Ben)
  Schwartzwalder
Clark Shaughnessy

Buck Shaw
Edgar Sherman
Andrew L. Smith
Carl Snavely
Jim Sochor
Amos A. Stagg
Gilbert Steinke
Dick Strahm
Jock Sutherland
Barry Switzer
James Tatum
Grant Teaff
Frank W. Thomas
Lee Tressell
Thad Vann
John H. Vaught
Wallace Wade
Lynn Waldorf
Glenn (Pop) Warner
Frank Waters
George Welsh
Frosty Westering
E.E. (Tad) Wieman
John W. Wilce
Bud Wilkinson
Henry L. Williams
George W. Woodruff
Warren Woodson
Bowden Wyatt
Bill Yeoman
Fielding H. Yost
Jim Young
Robert Zuppke

Professional Football
SUPER BOWLS I–XXXIX

Game	Date	Winner	Loser	Site	Attendance
XXXIX	Feb. 6, 2005	New England (AFC) 24	Philadelphia (NFC) 21	Alltel Stadium, Jacksonville, Fla.	78,125
XXXVIII	Feb. 1, 2004	New England (AFC) 32	Carolina (NFC) 29	Reliant Stadium, Houston, Tex.	71,525
XXXVII	Jan. 26, 2003	Tampa Bay (NFC) 48	Oakland Raiders (AFC) 21	Qualcomm Stadium, San Diego, Calif.	67,603
XXXVI	Feb. 3, 2002	New England (AFC) 20	St. Louis (NFC) 17	Superdome, New Orleans	72,922
XXXV	Jan. 28, 2001	Baltimore (AFC) 34	New York Giants (NFC) 7	Raymond James Stadium, Tampa, Fla.	71,921
XXXIV	Jan. 30, 2000	St. Louis (NFC) 23	Tennessee (AFC) 16	Georgia Dome, Atlanta, Ga.	72,625
XXXIII	Jan. 31, 1999	Denver (AFC) 34	Atlanta (NFC) 19	Pro Player Stadium, Miami, Fla.	74,803
XXXII	Jan. 25, 1998	Denver (AFC) 31	Green Bay (NFC) 24	Qualcomm Stadium, San Diego, Calif.	68,912
XXXI	Jan. 26, 1997	Green Bay (NFC) 35	New England (AFC) 21	Superdome, New Orleans, La.	72,301
XXX	Jan. 28, 1996	Dallas (NFC) 27	Pittsburgh (AFC) 17	Sun Devil Stadium, Tempe, Ariz.	76,347
XXIX	Jan. 29, 1995	San Francisco (NFC) 49	San Diego (AFC) 26	Joe Robbie Stadium, Miami, Fla.	74,107
XXVIII	Jan. 30, 1994	Dallas (NFC) 30	Buffalo (AFC) 13	Georgia Dome, Atlanta, Ga.	72,817
XXVII	Jan. 31, 1993	Dallas (NFC) 52	Buffalo (AFC) 17	Rose Bowl, Pasadena, Calif.	98,374
XXVI	Jan. 26, 1992	Washington (NFC) 37	Buffalo (AFC) 24	Metrodome, Minneapolis, Minn.	63,130
XXV	Jan. 27, 1991	Giants (NFC) 20	Buffalo (AFC) 19	Tampa Stadium, Tampa, Fla.	73,813
XXIV	Jan. 28, 1990	San Francisco (NFC) 55	Denver (AFC) 10	Superdome, New Orleans	72,919
XXIII	Jan. 22, 1989	San Francisco (NFC) 20	Cincinnati (AFC) 16	Joe Robbie Stadium, Miami, Fla.	75,179
XXII	Jan. 31, 1988	Washington (NFC) 42	Denver (AFC) 10	Jack Murphy Stadium, San Diego, Calif.	73,302
XXI	Jan. 25, 1987	Giants (NFC) 39	Denver (AFC) 20	Rose Bowl, Pasadena, Calif.	101,063
XX	Jan. 26, 1986	Chicago (NFC) 46	New England (AFC) 10	Superdome, New Orleans	73,818
XIX	Jan. 20, 1985	San Francisco (NFC) 38	Miami (AFC) 16	Stanford Stadium, Palo Alto, Calif.	84,059
XVIII	Jan. 22, 1984	Los Angeles Raiders (AFC) 38	Washington (NFC) 9	Tampa Stadium, Tampa, Fla	72,920

Game	Date	Winner	Loser	Site	Attendance
XVII	Jan. 30, 1983	Washington (NFC) 27	Miami (AFC) 17	Rose Bowl, Pasadena, Calif.	103,667
XVI	Jan. 24, 1982	San Francisco (NFC) 26	Cincinnati (AFC) 21	Silverdome, Pontiac, Mich.	81,270
XV	Jan. 25, 1981	Oakland (AFC) 27	Philadelphia (NFC) 10	Superdome, New Orleans	75,500
XIV	Jan. 20, 1980	Pittsburgh (AFC) 31	Los Angeles (NFC) 19	Rose Bowl, Pasadena	103,985
XIII	Jan. 21, 1979	Pittsburgh (AFC) 35	Dallas (NFC) 31	Orange Bowl, Miami	79,484
XII	Jan. 15, 1978	Dallas (NFC) 27	Denver (AFC) 10	Superdome, New Orleans	75,583
XI	Jan. 9, 1977	Oakland (AFC) 32	Minnesota (NFC) 14	Rose Bowl, Pasadena	103,424
X	Jan. 18, 1976	Pittsburgh (AFC) 21	Dallas (NFC) 17	Orange Bowl, Miami	80,187
IX	Jan. 12, 1975	Pittsburgh (AFC) 16	Minnesota (NFC) 6	Tulane Stadium, New Orleans	80,997
VIII	Jan. 13, 1974	Miami (AFC) 24	Minnesota (NFC) 7	Rice Stadium, Houston	71,882
VII	Jan. 14, 1973	Miami (AFC) 14	Washington (NFC) 7	Memorial Coliseum, Los Angeles	90,182
VI	Jan. 16, 1972	Dallas (NFC) 24	Miami (AFC) 3	Tulane Stadium, New Orleans	81,591
V	Jan. 17, 1971	Baltimore (AFC) 16	Dallas (NFC) 13	Orange Bowl, Miami	79,204
IV	Jan. 11, 1970	Kansas City (AFL) 23	Minnesota (NFL) 7	Tulane Stadium, New Orleans	80,562
III	Jan. 12, 1969	New York (AFL) 16	Baltimore (NFL) 7	Orange Bowl, Miami	75,389
II	Jan. 14, 1968	Green Bay (NFL) 33	Oakland (AFL) 14	Orange Bowl, Miami	75,546
I	Jan. 15, 1967	Green Bay (NFL) 35	Kansas City (AFL) 10	Memorial Coliseum, Los Angeles	61,946

NOTE: Super Bowls I to IV were played before the American Football League and National Football League merged into the NFL, which was divided into two conferences, the NFC and AFC.

NATIONAL FOOTBALL LEAGUE FINAL STANDINGS 2004

AMERICAN FOOTBALL CONFERENCE

	W	L	T	Pct	PF	PA
East						
New England Patriots[1]	14	2	0	.875	437	260
New York Jets[2]	10	6	0	.625	333	261
Buffalo Bills	9	7	0	.562	395	284
Miami Dolphins	4	12	0	.250	275	354
North						
Pittsburgh Steelers[1]	15	1	0	.938	372	251
Baltimore Ravens	9	7	0	.562	317	268
Cincinnati Bengals	8	8	0	.500	374	372
Cleveland Browns	4	12	0	.250	276	390
South						
Indianapolis Colts[1]	12	4	0	.750	522	351
Jacksonville Jaguars	9	7	0	.562	261	280
Houston Texans	7	9	0	.438	309	339
Tennessee Titans	5	11	0	.312	344	439
West						
San Diego Chargers[1]	12	4	0	.750	446	313
Denver Broncos[2]	10	6	0	.625	381	304
Kansas City Chiefs	7	9	0	.438	483	435
Oakland Raiders	5	11	0	.312	320	442

1. Division champion. 2. Wild card qualifier. **Wild card:** Jan. 8, 2005: New York 20, San Diego 17; Jan. 9: Indianapolis 49, Denver 24. **Division:** Jan. 15, 2005: Pittsburgh 20, New York 17; Jan. 16: New England 20, Indianapolis 3. **Conference:** Jan. 23: New England 41, Pittsburgh 27.

NATIONAL FOOTBALL CONFERENCE

	W	L	T	Pct	PF	PA
East						
Philadelphia Eagles[1]	13	3	0	.812	386	260
New York Giants	6	10	0	.375	303	347
Dallas Cowboys	6	10	0	.375	293	405
Washington Redskins	6	10	0	.375	240	265
North						
Green Bay Packers[1]	10	6	0	.625	424	380
Minnesota Vikings[2]	8	8	0	.500	405	395
Detroit Lions	6	10	0	.375	296	350
Chicago Bears	5	11	0	.312	231	331
South						
Atlanta Falcons[1]	11	5	0	.688	340	337
New Orleans Saints	8	8	0	.500	348	405
Carolina Panthers	7	9	0	.438	355	339
Tampa Bay Buccaneers	5	11	0	.312	301	304
West						
Seattle Seahawks[1]	9	7	0	.562	371	373
St. Louis Rams[2]	8	8	0	.500	319	392
Arizona Cardinals	6	10	0	.375	284	322
San Francisco 49ers	2	14	0	.125	259	452

1. Division champion. 2. Wild card qualifier. **Wild card:** Jan. 8, 2005: St. Louis 26, Seattle 20; Jan. 9: Minnesota 31, Green Bay 17. **Division:** Jan. 15, 2005: Atlanta 47, St. Louis 17; Jan. 16: Philadelphia 27, Minnesota 14. **Conference:** Jan. 23: Philadelphia 27, Atlanta 10.

LEAGUE CHAMPIONSHIP—SUPER BOWL XXXIX

(Feb. 6, 2005, Alltel Stadium, Jacksonville, Fla. Attendance: 78,125. Time: 3:38)

Scoring

	1st Q	2nd Q	3rd Q	4th Q	Final
New England	0	7	7	10	24
Philadelphia	0	7	7	7	21

2nd: PHI—TD: 6-yd pass from McNabb to Smith (Akers kick), 9:55. NE—TD: 4-yd pass from Brady to Givens (Vinatieri kick), 1:10.

3rd: NE—TD: 2-yd pass from Brady to Vrabel (Vinatieri kick), 11:04. PHI—TD: 10-yd pass from McNabb to Westbrook (Akers kick), 3:35.

4th: NE—TD: 2-yd run by Dillon (Vinatieri kick), 13:44. NE—FG: 22-yd by Vinatieri, 8:40. PHI—TD: 30-yd pass from McNabb to Lewis (Akers kick), 1:48.

MVP: Deion Branch, New England wide receiver.

Individual Statistics

Passing: NE—Brady 23–33 for 236 yds. PHI: McNabb 30–51 for 357 yds.

Rushing: NE—Dillon 18 for 75 yds, Faulk 8 for 38 yds, Pass 1 for 0, Brady, 1 for −1 yds. PHI—Westbrook 15 for 44 yds, Levens 1 for 1 yd, McNabb 1 for 0 yd.

Receiving: NE—Branch 11 for 133 yds, Dillon 3 for 31 yds, Givens 3 for 19 yds, Faulk 2 for 27 yds, Brown 2 for 17 yds, Vrabel 1 for 2 yds, Graham 1 for 7 yds. PHI—Owens 9 for 122 yds, Westbrook 7 for 60 yds, Pinkston 4 for 82 yds, Lewis 4 for 53 yds, Smith 4 for 27 yds, Mitchell 1 for 11 yds, Parry 1 for 2 yds.

Field goals: NE—Vinatieri 1–1.

Punting: NE—Miller 7. PHI—Johnson 5.

Kickoff Returns: NE—Johnson 2, Pass 1, Fauria 1. PHI—Reed 4, Hood 1.

Punt Returns: NE—Johnson 1, Brown 3. PHI—Westbrook 3, downed 1, out of bounds 1.

Statistics of the Game

	Patriots	Eagles		Patriots	Eagles
First downs	21	24	Completions–attempts	23–33	30–51
3rd down efficiency	4–12–33	9–16–56	Yards per pass	6.3	5.9
Total offense (net yards)	331	369	Had intercepted	0	3
Plays	63	72	Punts–number and average	7–45.1	5–42.8
Average gain	5.3	5.1	Return–yardage	31	19
Rushing yards (net)	112	45	Penalties–number and yards	7–47	3–35
Rushes	28	17	Fumbles–number and lost	1–1	2–1
Average per rush	4.0	2.6	Time of possession	31:37	28:23
Passing yards (net)	219	324			

NATIONAL LEAGUE CHAMPIONS

Year	Champion	(W-L-T)	Year	Champion	(W-L-T)	Year	Champion	(W-L-T)
1920	Akron Pros	(6–0–3)	1925	Chicago Cardinals	(11-2-1)	1928	Providence Steam Roller	(8-1-2)
1921	Chicago Staleys	(10-1-1)	1926	Frankford Yellow Jackets	(14-1-1)	1929	Green Bay Packers	(12-0-1)
1922	Canton Bulldogs	(10-0-2)	1927	New York Giants	(11-1-1)	1930	Green Bay Packers	(10-3-1)
1923	Canton Bulldogs	(11-0-1)				1931	Green Bay Packers	(12-2-0)
1924	Cleveland Bulldogs	(7-1-1)				1932	Chicago Bears	(7-1-6)

Year	Eastern Conference winners (W-L-T)	Western Conference winners (W-L-T)	League champion playoff results
1933	New York Giants (11-3-0)	Chicago Bears (10-2-1)	Chicago Bears 23, New York 21
1934	New York Giants (8-5-0)	Chicago Bears (13-0-0)	New York 30, Chicago Bears 13
1935	New York Giants (9-3-0)	Detroit Lions (7-3-2)	Detroit 26, New York 7
1936	Boston Redskins (7-5-0)	Green Bay Packers (10-1-1)	Green Bay 21, Boston 6
1937	Washington Redskins (8-3-0)	Chicago Bears (9-1-1)	Washington 28, Chicago Bears 21
1938	New York Giants (8-2-1)	Green Bay Packers (8-3-0)	New York 23, Green Bay 17
1939	New York Giants (9-1-1)	Green Bay Packers (9-2-0)	Green Bay 27, New York 0
1940	Washington Redskins (9-2-0)	Chicago Bears (8-3-0)	Chicago Bears 73, Washington 0
1941	New York Giants (8-3-0)	Chicago Bears (10-1-1)[1]	Chicago Bears 37, New York 9
1942	Washington Redskins (10-1-1)	Chicago Bears (11-0-0)	Washington 14, Chicago Bears 6
1943	Washington Redskins (6-3-1)[1]	Chicago Bears (8-1-1)	Chicago Bears 41, Washington 21
1944	New York Giants (8-1-1)	Green Bay Packers (8-2-0)	Green Bay 14, New York 7
1945	Washington Redskins (8-2-0)	Cleveland Rams (9-1-0)	Cleveland 15, Washington 14
1946	New York Giants (7-3-1)	Chicago Bears (8-2-1)	Chicago Bears 24, New York 14
1947	Philadelphia Eagles (8-4-0)[1]	Chicago Cardinals (9-3-0)	Chicago Cardinals 28, Philadelphia 21
1948	Philadelphia Eagles (9-2-1)	Chicago Cardinals (11-1-0)	Philadelphia 7, Chicago Cardinals 0
1949	Philadelphia Eagles (11-1-0)	Los Angeles Rams (8-2-2)	Philadelphia 14, Los Angeles 0
1950[2]	Cleveland Browns (10-2-0)[1, 3]	Los Angeles Rams (9-3-0)[1]	Cleveland 30, Los Angeles 28
1951[2]	Cleveland Browns (11-1-0)	Los Angeles Rams (8-4-0)	Los Angeles 24, Cleveland 17
1952[2]	Cleveland Browns (8-4-0)	Detroit Lions (9-3-0)[1]	Detroit 17, Cleveland 7
1953	Cleveland Browns (11-1-0)	Detroit Lions (10-2-0)	Detroit 17, Cleveland 16
1954	Cleveland Browns (9-3-0)	Detroit Lions (9-2-1)	Cleveland 56, Detroit 10
1955	Cleveland Browns (9-2-1)	Los Angeles Rams (8-3-1)	Cleveland 38, Los Angeles 14
1956	New York Giants (8-3-1)	Chicago Bears (9-2-1)	New York 47, Chicago Bears 7
1957	Cleveland Browns (9-2-1)	Detroit Lions (8-4-0)[1]	Detroit 59, Cleveland 14
1958	New York Giants (9-3-0)[1]	Baltimore Colts (9-3-0)	Baltimore 23, New York 17[4]
1959	New York Giants (10-2-0)	Baltimore Colts (9-3-0)	Baltimore 31, New York 16
1960	Philadelphia Eagles (10-2-0)	Green Bay Packers (8-4-0)	Philadelphia 17, Green Bay 13
1961	New York Giants (10-3-1)	Green Bay Packers (11-3-0)	Green Bay 37, New York 0
1962	New York Giants (12-2-0)	Green Bay Packers (13-1-0)	Green Bay 16, New York 7
1963	New York Giants (11-3-0)	Chicago Bears (11-1-2)	Chicago 14, New York 10
1964	Cleveland Browns (10-3-1)	Baltimore Colts (12-2-0)	Cleveland 27, Baltimore 0
1965	Cleveland Browns (11-3-0)	Green Bay Packers (11-3-1)[1]	Green Bay 23, Cleveland 12
1966	Dallas Cowboys (10-3-1)	Green Bay Packers (12-2-0)	Green Bay 34, Dallas 27
1967	Dallas Cowboys (9-5-0)[1]	Green Bay Packers (9-4-1)[1]	Green Bay 21, Dallas 17
1968	Cleveland Browns (10-4-0)[1]	Baltimore Colts (13-1-0)[1]	Baltimore 34, Cleveland 0
1969	Cleveland Browns (10-3-1)[1]	Minnesota Vikings (12-2-0)[1]	Minnesota 27, Cleveland 7

1. Won divisional playoff. 2. League was divided into American and National Conferences, 1950–1952 and again in 1970, when leagues merged. 3. Cleveland Browns and San Francisco 49ers joined league after All-America Football Conference (1946–1949) folded. 4. Won at 8:15 of sudden death overtime period.

NATIONAL CONFERENCE CHAMPIONS

Year	Eastern Division	Central Division	Western Division	Champion
1970	Dallas Cowboys (10-4-0)	Minnesota Vikings (12-2-0)	San Francisco 49ers (10-3-1)	Dallas
1971	Dallas Cowboys (11-3-0)	Minnesota Vikings (11-3-0)	San Francisco 49ers (9-5-0)	Dallas
1972	Washington Redskins (11-3-0)	Green Bay Packers (10-4-0)	San Francisco 49ers (8-5-1)	Washington
1973	Dallas Cowboys (10-4-0)	Minnesota Vikings (12-2-0)	Los Angeles Rams (12-2-0)	Minnesota
1974	St. Louis Cardinals (10-4-0)	Minnesota Vikings (10-4-0)	Los Angeles Rams (10-4-0)	Minnesota
1975	St. Louis Cardinals (11-3-0)	Minnesota Vikings (12-2-0)	Los Angeles Rams (12-2-0)	Dallas[1]
1976	Dallas Cowboys (11-3-0)	Minnesota Vikings (11-2-1)	Los Angeles Rams (10-3-1)	Minnesota
1977	Dallas Cowboys (12-2-0)	Minnesota Vikings (9-5-0)	Los Angeles Rams (10-4-0)	Dallas

Year	Eastern Division	Central Division	Western Division	Champion
1978	Dallas Cowboys (12-4-0)	Minnesota Vikings (8-7-1)	Los Angeles Rams (12-4-0)	Dallas
1979	Dallas Cowboys (11-5-0)	Tampa Bay Buccaneers (10-6-0)	Los Angeles Rams (9-7-0)	Los Angeles
1980	Philadelphia Eagles (12-4-0)	Minnesota Vikings (9-7-0)	Atlanta Falcons (12-4-0)	Philadelphia
1981	Dallas Cowboys (12-4-0)	Tampa Bay Buccaneers (9-7-0)	San Francisco 49ers (13-3-0)	San Francisco
1982[2]				Washington
1983	Washington Redskins (14-2-0)	Detroit Lions (8-8-0)	San Francisco 49ers (10-6-0)	Washington
1984	Washington Redskins (11-5-0)	Chicago Bears (10-6-0)	San Francisco 49ers (15-1-0)	San Francisco
1985	Dallas Cowboys (10-6-0)	Chicago Bears (15-1-0)	Los Angeles Rams (11-5-0)	Chicago
1986	New York Giants (14-2-0)	Chicago Bears (14-2-0)	San Francisco 49ers (10-5-1)	New York
1987	Washington Redskins (11-4-0)	Chicago Bears (11-4-0)	San Francisco 49ers (13-2-0)	Washington
1988	Philadelphia Eagles (10-6-0)	Chicago Bears (12-4-0)	San Francisco 49ers (10-6-0)	San Francisco
1989	New York Giants (12-4-0)	Minnesota Vikings (10-6-0)	San Francisco 49ers (14-2-0)	San Francisco
1990	New York Giants (13-3-0)	Chicago Bears (11-5-0)	San Francisco 49ers (14-2-0)	New York
1991	Washington (14-2-0)	Detroit Lions (12-4-0)	New Orleans Saints (11-5-0)	Washington
1992	Dallas Cowboys (13-3-0)	Minnesota Vikings (11-5-0)	San Francisco 49ers (14-2-0)	Dallas
1993	Dallas Cowboys (12-4-0)	Detroit Lions (10-6-0)	San Francisco 49ers (10-6-0)	Dallas
1994	Dallas Cowboys (12-4-0)	Minnesota Vikings (10-6-0)	San Francisco 49ers (13-3-0)	San Francisco
1995	Dallas Cowboys (12-4-0)	Green Bay Packers (11-5-0)	San Francisco 49ers (11-5-0)	Dallas
1996	Dallas Cowboys (10-6-0)	Green Bay Packers (13-3-0)	Carolina Panthers (12-4-0)	Green Bay
1997	New York Giants (10-5-1)	Green Bay Packers (13-3-0)	San Francisco 49ers (13-3-0)	Green Bay
1998	Dallas Cowboys (10-6-0)	Minnesota Vikings (15-1-0)	Atlanta Falcons (14-2-0)	Atlanta
1999	Washington Redskins (10-6-0)	Tampa Bay Buccaneers (11-5-0)	St. Louis Rams (13-3-0)	St. Louis
2000	New York Giants (12-4-0)	Minnesota Vikings (11-5-0)	New Orleans Saints (10-6-0)	New York
2001	Philadelphia Eagles (11-5-0)	Chicago Bears (13-3-0)	St. Louis Rams (14-2-0)	St. Louis

Year	East	North	South	West	Champion
2002	Philadelphia (12-4-0)	Green Bay (12-4-0)	Tampa Bay (12-4-0)	San Francisco (10-6-0)	Tampa Bay
2003	Philadelphia (12-4-0)	Green Bay (10-6-0)	Carolina (11-5-0)	St. Louis (12-4-0)	Carolina
2004	Philadelphia (13-3-0)	Green Bay (10-6-0)	Atlanta (11-5-0)	Seattle (9-7-0)	Philadelphia

1. Wild card. 2. Schedule reduced to 9 games from usual 16, with no standings kept in Eastern, Central, and Western Divisions because of 57-day player strike. Washington Redskins won conference title and also had best regular-season record (8-1-0).

AMERICAN LEAGUE CHAMPIONS

Year	Eastern Division (W-L-T)	Western Division (W-L-T)	League champion, playoff results
1960	Houston Oilers (10-4-0)	Los Angeles Chargers (10-4-0)	Houston 24, Los Angeles 16
1961	Houston Oilers (10-3-1)	San Diego Chargers (12-2-0)	Houston 10, San Diego 3
1962	Houston Oilers (11-3-0)	Dallas Texans (11-3-0)	Dallas 20, Houston 17[1]
1963	Boston Patriots (8-6-1)[2]	San Diego Chargers (11-3-0)	San Diego 51, Boston 10
1964	Buffalo Bills (12-2-0)	San Diego Chargers (8-5-1)	Buffalo 20, San Diego 7
1965	Buffalo Bills (10-3-1)	San Diego Chargers (9-2-3)	Buffalo 23, San Diego 0
1966	Buffalo Bills (9-4-1)	Kansas City Chiefs (11-2-1)	Kansas City 31, Buffalo 7
1967	Houston Oilers (9-4-1)	Oakland Raiders (13-1-0)	Oakland 40, Houston 7
1968	New York Jets (11-3-0)	Oakland Raiders (12-2-0)[2]	New York 27, Oakland 23
1969	New York Jets (10-4-0)	Oakland Raiders (12-1-1)	Kansas City 17, Oakland 7[3]

1. Won at 2:45 of second sudden death overtime period. 2. Won divisional playoff. 3. Kansas City defeated New York, 13-6, and Oakland defeated Houston, 56-7, in interdivisional playoffs.

AMERICAN CONFERENCE CHAMPIONS

Year	Eastern Division	Central Division	Western Division	Champion
1970	Baltimore Colts (11-2-1)	Cincinnati Bengals (8-6-0)	Oakland Raiders (8-4-2)	Baltimore
1971	Miami Dolphins (10-3-1)	Cleveland Browns (9-5-0)	Kansas City Chiefs (10-3-1)	Miami
1972	Miami Dolphins (14-0-0)	Pittsburgh Steelers (11-3-0)	Oakland Raiders (10-3-1)	Miami
1973	Miami Dolphins (12-2-0)	Cincinnati Bengals (10-4-0)	Oakland Raiders (9-4-1)	Miami
1974	Miami Dolphins (11-3-0)	Pittsburgh Steelers (10-3-1)	Oakland Raiders (12-2-0)	Pittsburgh
1975	Baltimore Colts (10-4-0)	Pittsburgh Steelers (12-2-0)	Oakland Raiders (12-2-0)	Pittsburgh
1976	Baltimore Colts (11-3-0)	Pittsburgh Steelers (10-4-0)	Oakland Raiders (13-1-0)	Oakland
1977	Baltimore Colts (10-4-0)	Pittsburgh Steelers (9-5-0)	Denver Broncos (12-2-0)	Denver
1978	New England Patriots (11-5-0)	Pittsburgh Steelers (14-2-0)	Denver Broncos (10-6-0)	Pittsburgh
1979	Miami Dolphins (10-6-0)	Pittsburgh Steelers (12-4-0)	San Diego Chargers (12-4-0)	Pittsburgh
1980	Buffalo Bills (11-5-0)	Cleveland Browns (11-5-0)	San Diego Chargers (11-5-0)	Oakland[1]
1981	Miami Dolphins (11-4-1)	Cincinnati Bengals (12-4-0)	San Diego Chargers (10-6-0)	Cincinnati
1982[2]				Miami
1983	Miami Dolphins (12-4-0)	Pittsburgh Steelers (10-6-0)	Los Angeles Raiders (12-4-0)	Los Angeles
1984	Miami Dolphins (14-2-0)	Pittsburgh Steelers (9-7-0)	Denver Broncos (13-3-0)	Miami
1985	Miami Dolphins (12-4-0)*	Cleveland Browns (8-8)	Los Angeles Raiders (12-4-0)	New England[1]
1986	New England Patriots (11-5-0)	Cleveland Browns (12-4-0)	Denver Broncos (11-5-0)	Denver
1987	Indianapolis Colts (9-6-0)	Cleveland Browns (10-5-0)	Denver Broncos (10-4-1)	Denver
1988	Buffalo Bills (12-4-0)	Cincinnati Bengals (12-4-0)	Seattle Seahawks (9-7-0)	Cincinnati
1989	Buffalo Bills (9-7-0)	Cleveland Browns (9-6-1)	Denver Broncos (11-5-0)	Denver
1990	Buffalo Bills (13-3-0)	Cincinnati Bengals (9-7-0)	Los Angeles Raiders (12-4-0)	Buffalo
1991	Buffalo Bills (13-3-0)	Houston Oilers (11-5-0)	Denver Broncos (12-4-0)	Buffalo
1992	Miami Dolphins (11-5-0)	Pittsburgh Steelers (11-5-0)	San Diego Chargers (11-5-0)	Buffalo[1]

Year	Eastern Division	Central Division	Western Division	Champion
1993	Buffalo Bills (12-4-0)	Houston Oilers (12-4-0)	Kansas City Chiefs (11-5-0)	Buffalo
1994	Miami Dolphins (10-6-0)	Pittsburgh Steelers (12-4-0)	San Diego Chargers (11-5-0)	San Diego
1995	Buffalo Bills (10-6-0)	Pittsburgh Steelers (11-5-0)	Kansas City Chiefs (13-3-0)	Pittsburgh
1996	New England Patriots (11-5-0)	Pittsburgh Steelers (10-6-0)	Denver Broncos (13-3-0)	New England
1997	New England Patriots (10-6-0)	Pittsburgh Steelers (11-5-0)	Kansas City Chiefs (13-3-0)	Denver[1]
1998	New York Jets (12-4-0)	Jacksonville Jaguars (11-5-0)	Denver Broncos (14-2-0)	Denver
1999	Indianapolis Colts (13-3-0)	Jacksonville Jaguars (14-2-0)	Seattle Seahawks (9-7-0)	Tennessee[1]
2000	Miami Dolphins (11-5-0)	Tennessee Titans (13-3-0)	Oakland Raiders (12-4-0)	Baltimore[1]
2001	New England Patriots (11-5-0)	Pittsburgh Steelers (13-3-0)	Oakland Raiders (10-6-0)	New England

Year	East	North	South	West	Champion
2002	N.Y. Jets (9-7-0)	Pittsburgh (10-5-1)	Tennessee (11-5-0)	Oakland (11-5-0)	Oakland
2003	New England (14-2-0)	Baltimore (10-6-0)	Indianapolis (12-4-0)	Kansas City (13-3-0)	New England
2004	New England (14-2-0)	Pittsburgh (15-1-0)	Indianapolis (12-4-0)	San Diego (10-6-0)	New England

1. Wild card. 2. Schedule reduced to 9 games from usual 16, with no standings kept in Eastern, Central, and Western Divisions, because of 57-day player strike. Miami Dolphins won the conference title, but the Los Angeles Raiders had best regular-season record (8-1-0).

NFL INDIVIDUAL LIFETIME, SEASON, AND GAME RECORDS

(American Football League records were incorporated into NFL records after merger of the leagues.)

Players listed in boldface were active during the 2004 season. The NFL does not recognize records from the All-American Football Conference (AAFC), which existed from 1946 to 1949. The 49ers, Browns, and Colts merged with the NFL in 1949.

All-Time Scoring Leaders
(Through 2004)

Rank	Player	Touch-downs	Player	Points
1.	**Jerry Rice**	207	**Gary Anderson**	2,448
2.	**Emmitt Smith**	175	**Morten Andersen**	2,358
3.	Marcus Allen	144	George Blanda	2,002
4.	**Marshall Faulk**	135	Norm Johnson	1,736
5.	Cris Carter	130	Nick Lowery	1,711
6.	Jim Brown	126	Jan Stenerud	1,699
7.	Walter Payton	125	Eddie Murray	1,594
8.	John Riggins	116	Al Del Greco	1,584
9.	Lenny Moore	111	**John Carney**	1,537
10.	Barry Sanders	109	**Matt Stover**	1,481

All-Time Leading Receivers
(Through 2004)

Rank	Player	Number of receptions	Player	Yards
1.	**Jerry Rice**	1,549	**Jerry Rice**	22,895
2.	Cris Carter	1,101	**Tim Brown**	14,934
3.	**Tim Brown**	1,094	James Lofton	14,004
4.	Andre Reed	951	Cris Carter	13,899
5.	Art Monk	940	Henry Ellard	13,777
6.	Irving Fryar	851	Andre Reed	13,198
7.	**Marvin Harrison**	845	Steve Largent	13,089
8.	Larry Centers	827	Irving Fryar	12,785
9.	Steve Largent	819	Art Monk	12,721
10.	Shannon Sharpe	815	Charlie Joiner	12,146

All-Time Leading Passers (Through 2004)

Rank	Player	Yards	Player	Number completed	Player	Number of touchdowns
1.	Dan Marino	61,361	Dan Marino	4,967	Dan Marino	420
2.	John Elway	51,475	**Brett Favre**	4,306	**Brett Favre**	376
3.	**Brett Favre**	49,734	John Elway	4,123	Fran Tarkenton	342
4.	Warren Moon	49,325	Warren Moon	3,988	John Elway	300
5.	Fran Tarkenton	47,003	Fran Tarkenton	3,686	Warren Moon	291
6.	**Vinny Testaverde**	44,475	**Vinny Testaverde**	3,631	Johnny Unitas	290
7.	Dan Fouts	43,040	**Drew Bledsoe**	3,449	Joe Montana	273
8.	Joe Montana	40,551	Joe Montana	3,409	**Vinny Testaverde**	268
9.	Johnny Unitas	40,239	Dan Fouts	3,297	Dave Krieg	261
10.	**Drew Bledsoe**	39,808	Dave Krieg	3,105	Sonny Jurgensen	255

All-Time Interception Leaders
(Through 2004)

		Amount
1.	Paul Krause	81
2.	Emlen Tunnell	79
3.	Rod Woodson	71
4.	Dick Lane	68
5.	Ken Riley	65
6.	Ronnie Lott	63
7.	Dave Brown	62
	Dick LeBeau	62
9.	Emmitt Thomas	58
10.	Mel Blount	57
	Bobby Boyd	57
	Johnny Robinson	57
	Everson Walls	57
	Eugene Robinson	57

All-Time Sack Leaders
(Through 2004)

		Amount
1.	Bruce Smith	200
2.	Reggie White	198
3.	Kevin Greene	160
4.	Chris Doleman	150
5.	John Randle	137
	Richard Dent	137
7.	Lawrence Taylor	132
	Leslie O'Neal	132
9.	Rickey Jackson	128
10.	Derrick Thomas	126

All-Time Leading Rushers
(Through 2004)

		Yards
1.	**Emmitt Smith**	18,355
2.	Walter Payton	16,726
3.	Barry Sanders	15,269
4.	**Curtis Martin**	13,366
5.	**Jerome Bettis**	13,294
6.	Eric Dickerson	13,259
7.	Tony Dorsett	12,739
8.	Jim Brown	12,312
9.	Marcus Allen	12,243
10.	Franco Harris	12,120

Scoring

Most points scored, lifetime—2,448, Gary Anderson, Pittsburgh, 1982–94; Philadelphia, 1995–96; San Francisco, 1997; Minnesota, 1998–2002; Tennessee, 2003.

Most points, season—176, Paul Hornung, Green Bay, 1960 (15 td, 41 pat, 15 fg).

Most points, game—40, Ernie Nevers, Chicago Cardinals, 1929 (6 td, 4 pat).

Most touchdowns, lifetime—207, Jerry Rice, San Francisco, 1985–2000; Oakland 2001–2003; Seattle 2004.

Most points after touchdown, lifetime—943, George Blanda, Chicago Bears, 1949–58; Baltimore, 1950; Houston, 1960–66; Oakland, 1967–75.

Most field goals, lifetime—538, Gary Anderson, Pittsburgh, 1982–94; Philadelphia, 1995–96; San Francisco, 1997; Minnesota, 1998–2002; Tennessee, 2003–04.

Most field goals, season—39, Olindo Mare, Miami, 1999; Jeff Wilkins, St. Louis, 2003.

Most field goals, game—7, Jim Bakken, St. Louis, 1967; Rich Karlis, Minnesota, 1989; and Chris Boniol, Dallas, 1996.

Longest field goal—63 yards, Tom Dempsey, New Orleans, 1970; Jason Elam, Denver, 1998.

Rushing

Most yards gained, lifetime—18,355, Emmitt Smith, Dallas Cowboys, 1990–2002; Arizona, 2003–04.

Most yards gained, season—2,105, Eric Dickerson, Los Angeles, 1984.

Most yards gained, game—278, Corey Dillon, Cincinnati, 2000.

Most touchdowns, lifetime—164, Emmitt Smith, Dallas, 1990–2002; Arizona, 2003–04.

Most touchdowns, season—25, Emmitt Smith, Dallas, 1995.

Most touchdowns, game—6, Ernie Nevers, Chicago Cardinals, 1929.

Longest run from scrimmage—99 yards, Tony Dorsett, Dallas, 1983.

Receiving

Most pass receptions, lifetime—1,549, Jerry Rice, San Francisco, 1985–2000; Oakland 2001–2003; Seattle 2004.

Most pass receptions, season—123, Herman Moore, Detroit, 1995.

Most pass receptions, game—20, Terrell Owens, San Francisco, 2000.

Most yards gained, pass receptions, lifetime—22,895, Jerry Rice, San Francisco, 1985–2000; Oakland 2001–2003; Seattle 2004.

Most yards gained, receptions, season—1,848, Jerry Rice, San Francisco, 1995.

Most yards gained, receptions, game—336, Flipper Anderson, Los Angeles Rams, 1989.

Most touchdown receptions, lifetime—197, Jerry Rice, San Francisco, 1985–2000; Oakland 2001–2003; Seattle 2004.

Most touchdown pass receptions, season—22, Jerry Rice, San Francisco, 1987.

Most touchdown pass receptions, game—5, Bob Shaw, Chicago Cards, 1950; Kellen Winslow, San Diego, 1981; Jerry Rice, San Francisco, 1990.

Interceptions

Most pass interceptions, lifetime—81, Paul Krause, Washington, 1964-67; Minnesota, 1968–79.

Most pass interceptions, season—14, Richard (Night Train) Lane, Detroit, 1952.

Most pass interceptions, game—4, by 18 players.

Longest pass interception return—104 yards, James Willis, Philadelphia, 1996.

Kicking

Highest average punting, lifetime—45.1 yards, Sammy Baugh, Washington, 1937–52.

Longest punt return—103 yards, Robert Bailey, L.A. Rams, 1994.

Longest kick-off return—106 yards, Roy Green, St. Louis, 1979; Al Carmichael, Green Bay, 1956; Noland Smith, Kansas City, 1967.

Passing

Most touchdown passes, lifetime—420, Dan Marino, Miami, 1983–99.

Most touchdown passes, season—49, Peyton Manning, Indianapolis, 2004.

Most touchdown passes, game—7, Sid Luckman, Chicago Bears, 1943; Adrian Burk, Philadelphia, 1954; George Blanda, Houston, 1961; Y. A. Tittle, N.Y. Giants, 1962; Joe Kapp, Minnesota, 1969.

Longest pass completion—99 yards, Frank Filchock (to Andy Farkas), Washington, 1939; George Izo (to Bob Mitchell), Washington, 1963; Karl Sweetan (to Pat Studstill), Detroit, 1966; Sonny Jurgensen (to Gerry Allen), Washington, 1968; Jim Plunkett (to Cliff Branch) L.A. Raiders, 1983; Ron Jaworski (to Mike Quick), Philadelphia, 1985; Stan Humphries (to Tony Martin), San Diego, 1994; Brett Favre (to Robert Brooks), Green Bay, 1995; Trent Green (to Marc Boerigter) Kansas City, 2002; Jeff Garcia (to Andre Davis) Cleveland, 2004.

Most passes completed, lifetime—4,967, Dan Marino, Miami, 1983–99.

Most passes completed, season—404, Warren Moon, 1991.

Most passes completed, game—45, Drew Bledsoe, New England, 1994.

Most yards gained, lifetime—61,361, Dan Marino, Miami, 1983–99.

Most yards gained, season—5,084, Dan Marino, Miami, 1984.

Most yards gained, game—554, Norm Van Brocklin, Los Angeles, 1951.

PRO FOOTBALL HALL OF FAME

(National Football Museum, Canton, Ohio)

Teams named are those with which player is best identified; figures in parentheses indicate number of playing seasons.

Adderley, Herb, defensive back, Packers, Cowboys (12)	1961–72
Allen, George, coach, Rams, Redskins (12)	1966–77
Allen, Marcus, running back, Raiders, Chiefs (16)	1982–97
Alworth, Lance, wide receiver, Chargers, Cowboys (12)	1961–72
Atkins, Doug, defensive end, Browns, Bears, Saints (17)	1953–69
Badgro, Morris, end, N.Y. Yankees, Giants, Brooklyn Dodgers (8)	1927, 1930–36
Barney, Lem, defensive back, Lions (11)	1967–78
Battles, Cliff, back, Redskins (6)	1932–37
Baugh, Sammy, quarterback, Redskins (16)	1936–52
Bednarik, Chuck, center-lineback, Eagles (14)	1949–62
Bell, Bert, NFL founder, Eagles and Steelers, NFL Commissioner	1946–59
Bell, Bobby, linebacker, Chiefs (12)	1963–74
Berry, Raymond, end, Colts (13)	1955–67
Bethea, Elvin, defensive end, Oilers (16)	1968–83
Bidwell, Charles W., owner, Chicago Cardinals	1933–47
Biletnikoff, Fred, wide receiver, Raiders (14)	1965–78

Blanda, George, quarterback-kicker, Bears,
  Oilers, Raiders (27)   1949–75
Blount, Mel, cornerback, Pittsburgh Steelers (14)   1970–83
Bradshaw, Terry, quarterback, Pittsburgh Steelers (14)   1970–83
Brown, Bob, tackle, Eagles, Rams, Raiders (10)   1964–73
Brown, Jim, fullback, Browns (9)   1957–65
Brown, Paul E., coach, Browns (1946–62),
  Bengals (1968–75)   1946–75
Brown, Roosevelt, tackle, Giants (13)   1953–65
Brown, Willie, cornerback, Broncos, Raiders (16)   1963–78
Buchanan, Buck, tackle, Chiefs (11)   1963–73
Buoniconti, Nick, linebacker, Patriots, Dolphins (14)   1962–74, 1976
Butkus, Dick, linebacker, Bears (9)   1965–73
Campbell, Earl, running back, Oilers, Saints (8)   1978–85
Canadeo, Tony, back, Packers (11)   1941–52
Carr, Joe, NFL president (18)   1921–39
Casper, Dave, tight end, Raiders, Oilers, Vikings (11)   1974–84
Chamberlin, Guy, end, 4 teams (9)   1919–27
Christiansen, Jack, defensive back, Lions (8)   1951–58
Clark, Earl (Dutch), quarterback, Spartans, Lions (7)   1931–38
Connor, George, tackle, linebacker, Bears (8)   1948–55
Conzelman, Jimmy, quarterback, 5 teams (10), owner, Detroit
  Panthers   1921–48
Creekmur, Lou, offensive tackle/guard, Lions (10)   1950–59
Csonka, Larry, back, Dolphins, Giants (11)   1968–79
Davis, Al, owner, Raiders, coach, general manager   1963–
Davis, Willie, defensive end, Packers (10)   1960–69
Dawson, Len, quarterback, Steelers, Browns,
  Texans, Chiefs (19)   1957–75
DeLamielleure, guard, Bills, Browns (13)   1973–84
Dickerson, Eric, running back, Rams, Colts, Raiders,
  Falcons (11)   1983–93
Dierdorf, Dan, tackle/center, Cardinals (13)   1971–83
Ditka, Mike, tight end, Bears, Eagles, Cowboys (12)   1961–72
Donovan, Art, defensive tackle, Colts (12)   1950–61
Dorsett, Tony, running back, Cowboys, Broncos (12)   1977–88
Driscoll, John (Paddy), quarterback, Cards, Bears (11)   1919–29
Dudley, Bill, back, Steelers, Lions, Redskins (9)   1942–53
Edwards, Albert Glen (Turk), tackle, Redskins (9)   1932–40
Eller, Carl, defensive end, Vikings, Seahwaks (16)   1964–79
Elway, John, quarterback, Broncos (16)   1983–98
Ewbank, Weeb, coach, Colts, Jets (20)   1954–73
Fears, Tom, end, Rams (9); coach, Saints   1948–56
Finks, Jim, administrator/general manager,
  Vikings, Bears, Saints   1964–93
Flaherty, Ray, end, Yankees, Giants (9); coach,
  Redskins, Yankees (14)   1928–49
Ford, Len, end, defensive end, Browns, Packers (11)   1948–58
Fouts, Dan, quarterback, Chargers (15)   1973–87
Fortmann, Daniel J., guard, Bears (8)   1936–43
Friedman, Benny, quarterback, Bulldogs, Wolverines,
  Giants, Dodgers (13)   1927–34
Gatski, Frank, offensive lineman, Browns (12)   1946–57
George, Bill, linebacker, Bears, Rams (15)   1952–66
Gibbs, Joe, coach, Redskins (11)   1981–92
Gifford, Frank, back, Giants (12)   1952–64
Gillman, Sid, coach, Rams, Chargers, Oilers (18)   1955–70, 1973–74
Graham, Otto, quarterback, Browns (10)   1946–55
Grange, Harold (Red), back, Bears, Yankees (9)   1925–34
Grant, Bud, coach, Vikings (18)   1967–85
Greene, Joe, defensive tackle, Steelers (13)   1968–81
Gregg, Forrest, tackle, Packers (15)   1956–71
Griese, Bob, quarterback, Dolphins (14)   1967–80
Groza, Lou, place-kicker, tackle, Browns (21)   1946–67
Guyon, Joe, back, 6 teams (8)   1919–27
Halas, George, NFL founder, owner and coach, Staleys
  and Bears, end (11)   1919–27
Ham, Jack, linebacker, Steelers (13)   1970–82
Hampton, Dan, defensive end, defensive tackle, Bears (12)   1979–90
Hannah, John, guard, Patriots (13)   1973–85
Harris, Franco, running back, Steelers, Seahawks (13)   1972–84
Haynes, Mike, defensive back, Patriots, Raiders (10)   1976–85
Healey, Ed, tackle, Bears (8)   1920–27
Hein, Mel, center, Giants (15)   1931–45
Hendricks, Ted, linebacker, Colts, Packers, Raiders (15)   1969–83
Henry, Wilbur (Pete), tackle, Bulldogs, Giants (8)   1920–28
Herber, Arnie, quarterback, Packers, Giants (13)   1930–45
Hewitt, Bill, end, Bears, Eagles (9)   1932–43
Hinkle, Clarke, fullback, Packers (10)   1932–41

Hirsch, Elroy (Crazy Legs), back, end, Rams (12)   1946–57
Hornung, Paul, running back, Packers (9)   1957–62, 1964–66
Houston, Ken, defensive back, Oilers, Redskins (14)   1967–80
Hubbard, R. (Cal), tackle, Giants, Packers (9)   1927–36
Huff, Sam, linebacker, Giants, Redskins (13)   1956–67, 1969
Hunt, Lamar, founder A.F.L., owner Texans, Chiefs   1959–
Hutson, Don, end, Packers (11)   1935–45
Johnson, John Henry, back, 49ers, Lions,
  Steelers, Oilers (13)   1954–66
Johnson, Jimmy, cornerback, 49ers (16)   1961–76
Joiner, Charlie, receiver, Oilers, Bengals, Chargers (18)   1969–86
Jones, David (Deacon), defensive end, Rams,
  Chargers, Redskins (14)   1961–74
Jones, Stan, defensive tackle, Bears, Redskins (13)   1954–66
Jordan, Henry, defensive tackle, Browns, Packers (13)   1957–69
Jurgensen, Sonny, quarterback, Eagles, Redskins (18)   1957–74
Kelly, Jim, quarterback, Bills (11)   1986–96
Kelly, Leroy, running back, Browns (10)   1964–73
Kiesling, Walt, guard, 6 teams (13)   1926–38
Kinard, Frank (Bruiser), tackle, Dodgers (9)   1938–47
Krause, Paul, safety, Redskins, Vikings (16)   1964–79
Lambeau, Earl (Curly), NFL founder, coach,
  end, back, Packers (11)   1919–53
Lambert, Jack, linebacker, Steelers (11)   1974–84
Landry, Tom, coach, Cowboys (29)   1960–88
Lane, Richard (Night Train), defensive back,
  Rams, Cardinals, Lions (14)   1952–65
Langer, Jim, center, Dolphins, Vikings (12)   1970–81
Lanier, Willie, linebacker, Chiefs (11)   1967–77
Largent, Steve, receiver, Seahawks (14)   1976–89
Lary, Yale, defensive back, punter, Lions (11)   1952–64
Laveill, Dante, end, Browns (11)   1946–56
Layne, Bobby, quarterback, Bears, Lions, Steelers (15)   1948–62
Leemans, Alphonse (Tuffy), back, Giants (8)   1936–43
Levy, Marv, coach, Chiefs, Bills (17)   1978–97
Lilly, Bob, defensive tackle, Cowboys (14)   1961–74
Little, Larry, guard, Dolphins, Chargers (14)   1967–80
Lofton, James, wide receiver, Packers, Raiders, Bills,
  Rams, Eagles (16)   1978–93
Lombardi, Vince, coach, Packers, Redskins (11)   1959–70
Long, Howie, defensive end, Raiders (13)   1981–93
Lott, Ronnie, cornerback, safety, 49ers, Raiders, Jets (14)   1981–94
Luckman, Sid, quarterback, Bears (12)   1939–50
Lyman, Roy (Link), tackle, Bulldogs, Bears (11)   1922–34
Mack, Tom, guard, Rams (13)   1966–78
Mackey, John, tight end, Colts, Chargers (10)   1963–72
Mara, Tim, NFL founder, owner, Giants   1925–59
Mara, Wellington, NFL executive, owner, Giants   1937–
Marchetti, Gino, defensive end, Colts (14)   1952–66
Marino, Dan, quarterback, Dolphins (17)   1983–99
Marshall, George P., NFL founder, owner, Redskins   1932–65
Matson, Ollie, back, Cardinals, Rams, Lions, Eagles (14)   1952–66
Maynard, Don, receiver, Giants, Jets, Cardinals (15)   1958–73
McAfee, George, back, Bears (8)   1940–50
McCormack, Mike, tackle, N.Y. Yanks,
  Cleveland Browns (10)   1951–62
McDonald, Tommy, wide receiver, Eagles, Cowboys,
  Rams, Falcons, Browns (12)   1957–68
McElhenny, Hugh, back, 49ers, Vikings, Giants (13)   1952–64
McNally, John (Blood), back, 7 teams (15)   1925–39
Michalske, August, guard, Yankees, Packers (11)   1926–37
Millner, Wayne, end, Redskins (7)   1936–45
Mitchell, Bobby, wide receiver, Browns, Redskins (11)   1958–68
Mix, Ron, tackle, Chargers (11)   1960–71
Montana, Joe, quarterback, 49ers, Chiefs (15)   1979–94
Moore, Lenny, back, Colts (12)   1956–67
Motley, Marion, fullback, Browns, Steelers (9)   1946–55
Munchak, Mike, guard, Oilers (12)   1982–93
Munoz, Anthony, tackle, Bengals (13)   1980–92
Musso, George, guard-tackle, Bears (12)   1933–44
Nagurski, Bronko, fullback, Bears (9)   1930–43
Namath, Joe, quarterback, Jets, Rams (13)   1965–77
Neale, Earle (Greasy), coach, Eagles   1941–50
Nevers, Ernie, fullback, Chicago Cardinals (5)   1926–31
Newsome, Ozzie, tight end, Browns (13)   1978–90
Nitschke, Ray, linebacker, Packers (15)   1958–72
Noll, Chuck, coach, Steelers (23)   1969–81
Nomellini, Leo, defensive tackle, 49ers (14)   1950–63
Olsen, Merlin, defensive tackle, Rams (15)   1962–76

Otto, Jim, center, Raiders (15)	1960–74
Owen, Steve, tackle, Giants (9), coach, Giants (13)	1924–53
Page, Alan, defensive tackle, Vikings, Bears (15)	1967–81
Parker, Clarence (Ace), quarterback, Dodgers (7)	1937–46
Parker, Jim, guard, tackle, Colts (11)	1957–67
Payton, Walter, running back, Bears (13)	1977–89
Perry, Joe, fullback, 49ers, Colts (16)	1948–63
Pihos, Pete, end, Eagles (9)	1947–55
Pollard, Fritz, halfback, coach, Akron Pros-Indians, Milwaukee Badgers, Hammond Pros, Gilberton Cadamounts, Providence Steam Roller (8)	1919–25
Ray, Hugh (Shorty), NFL advisor	1938–52
Reeves, Dan, owner, Rams	1941–71
Renfro, Mel, cornerback, safety, Cowboys (14)	1964–77
Riggins, John, running back, Jets, Redskins (14)	1971–84
Ringo, Jim, center, Packers (15)	1953–67
Robustelli, Andy, defensive end, Rams, Giants (14)	1951–64
Rooney, Art, NFL founder, owner, Steelers	1933–88
Rooney, Dan, contributor, Steelers	1955–
Rozelle, Pete, commissioner, NFL	1960–89
St. Claire, Bob, tackle, 49ers (11)	1953–63
Sanders, Barry, running back, Lions (10)	1989–98
Sayers, Gale, back, Bears (7)	1965–71
Schmidt, Joe, linebacker, Lions (13)	1953–65
Schramm, Tex, administrator, Rams, Cowboys (42)	1947–89
Selmon, Lee Roy, defensive end, Buccaneers (13)	1976–84
Shaw, Billy, guard, Bills (9)	1961–69
Shell, Art, tackle, Raiders (15)	1968–82
Shula, Don, coach, Colts, Dolphins (33)	1963–95
Simpson, O.J., back, Bills, 49ers (11)	1969–79
Singletary, Mike, linebacker, Bears (12)	1981–92
Slater, Jackie, tackle, Rams (20)	1976–95
Smith, Jackie, tight end, Cardinals, Cowboys (16)	1963–78
Stallworth, John, wide receiver, Steelers (14)	1974–87
Starr, Bart, quarterback, coach, Packers (16)	1956–71
Staubach, Roger, quarterback, Cowboys (11)	1969–79
Stautner, Ernie, defensive tackle, Steelers (14)	1950–63
Stenerud, Jan, placekicker, Chiefs, Packers, Vikings (19)	1967–85

Stephenson, Dwight, center, Dolphins (8)	1980–87
Stram, Hank, coach, Texans/Chiefs, Saints (17)	1960–74, 1976–77
Strong, Ken, back, Giants, Yankees (14)	1929–47
Stydahar, Joe, tackle, Bears (9); coach, Rams, Cardinals (5)	1936–54
Swann, Lynn, wide receiver, Steelers (9)	1974–82
Tarkenton, Fran, quarterback, Vikings, Giants (18)	1961–78
Taylor, Charlie, wide receiver, Redskins (14)	1964–77
Taylor, Jim, fullback, Packers, Saints (10)	1958–67
Taylor, Lawrence, linebacker, Giants (13)	1981–93
Thorpe, Jim, back, 7 teams (12)	1915–28
Tittle, Y.A., quarterback, Colts, 49ers, Giants (17)	1948–64
Trafton, George, center, Bears (13)	1920–32
Trippi, Charley, back, Chicago Cardinals (9)	1947–55
Tunnell, Emlen, defensive back, Giants, Packers (14)	1948–61
Turner, Clyde (Bulldog), center, Bears (13)	1940–52
Unitas, John, quarterback, Colts (18)	1956–73
Upshaw, Gene, guard, Raiders (15)	1967–81
Van Brocklin, Norm, quarterback, Rams, Eagles (12)	1949–60
Van Buren, Steve, back, Eagles (8)	1944–51
Walker, Doak, running back, def. back, kicker, Lions (6)	1950–55
Walsh, Bill, coach, 49ers (10)	1979–88
Warfield, Paul, wide receiver, Browns, Dolphins (13)	1964–74, 1976–77
Waterfield, Bob, quarterback, Rams (8)	1945–52
Webster, Mike, center, Steelers, Chiefs (17)	1974–90
Weinmeister, Arnie, tackle, N.Y. Yankees, Giants (6)	1948–53
White, Randy, defensive tackle, Cowboys (14)	1975–88
Wilcox, Dave, linebacker, 49ers (11)	1964–74
Willis, Bill, guard, Browns (8)	1946–53
Wilson, Larry, defensive back, Cardinals (13)	1960–72
Winslow, Kellen, tight end, Chargers (9)	1979–87
Wood, Willie, safety, Packers (12)	1960–71
Wojciechowicz, Alex, center, Lions, Eagles (13)	1938–50
Yary, Ron, tackle, Vikings, Rams (15)	1968–82
Young, Steve, quarterback, Buccaneers, 49ers (15)	1985–99
Youngblood, Jack, defensive end, Rams (14)	1971–84

Basketball

Basketball is one of the few sports whose exact origin is definitely known. In the winter of 1891–1892, Dr. James Naismith, an instructor in the YMCA Training College (now Springfield College) at Springfield, Mass., deliberately invented the game of basketball in order to provide indoor exercise and competition for the students between the closing of the football season and the opening of the baseball season. He affixed peach baskets overhead on the walls at opposite ends of the gymnasium and organized teams to play his new game in which the purpose was to toss an association (soccer) ball into one basket and prevent the opponents from tossing the ball into the other basket. Because Dr. Naismith had eighteen available players when he invented the game, the first rule was: "There shall be nine players on each side." Later the number of players became optional, depending upon the size of the available court, but the five-player standard was adopted when the game spread over the country. U.S. soldiers brought basketball to Europe in World War I, and it soon became a worldwide sport.

College Basketball

NCAA CHAMPIONS

1939 Oregon	1951 Kentucky	1964 UCLA	1983 North Carolina State	1996 Kentucky
1940 Indiana	1952 Kansas	1965 UCLA		1997 Arizona
1941 Wisconsin	1953 Indiana	1966 Texas Western	1984 Georgetown	1998 Kentucky
1942 Stanford	1954 La Salle	1967–73 UCLA	1985 Villanova	1999 Connecticut
1943 Wyoming	1955 San Francisco	1974 North Carolina State	1986 Louisville	2000 Michigan State
1944 Utah	1956 San Francisco		1987 Indiana	2001 Duke
1945 Oklahoma A & M	1957 North Carolina	1975 UCLA	1988 Kansas	2002 Maryland
	1958 Kentucky	1976 Indiana	1989 Michigan	2003 Syracuse
1946 Oklahoma A & M	1959 California	1977 Marquette	1990 UNLV	2004 Connecticut
	1960 Ohio State	1978 Kentucky	1991 Duke	2005 North Carolina
1947 Holy Cross	1961 Cincinnati	1979 Michigan State	1992 Duke	
1948 Kentucky	1962 Cincinnati	1980 Louisville	1993 North Carolina	
1949 Kentucky	1963 Loyola (Chicago)	1981 Indiana	1994 Arkansas	
1950 C.C.N.Y.		1982 North Carolina	1995 UCLA	

NATIONAL INVITATION TOURNAMENT (NIT) CHAMPIONS

1938 Temple	1953 Seton Hall	1965 St. John's	1978 Texas	1992 Virginia
1939 Long Island U.	1954 Holy Cross	(N.Y.C.)	1979 Indiana	1993 Minnesota
1940 Colorado	1955 Duquesne	1966 Brigham Young	1980 Virginia	1994 Villanova
1941 Long Island U.	1956 Louisville	1967 So. Illinois	1981 Tulsa	1995 Virginia Tech
1942 West Virginia	1957 Bradley	1968 Dayton	1982 Bradley	1996 Nebraska
1943–44 St. John's	1958 Xavier (Cincin-	1969 Temple	1983 Fresno State	1997 Michigan
(N.Y.C.)	nati)	1970 Marquette	1984 Michigan	1998 Minnesota
1945 DePaul	1959 St. John's	1971 North Carolina	1985 UCLA	1999 California
1946 Kentucky	(N.Y.C.)	1972 Maryland	1986 Ohio State	2000 Wake Forest
1947 Utah	1960 Bradley	1973 Virginia Tech	1987 So. Mississippi	2001 Tulsa
1948 St. Louis	1961 Providence	1974 Purdue	1988 Connecticut	2002 Memphis
1949 San Francisco	1962 Dayton	1975 Princeton	1989 St. John's	2003 St. John's
1950 C.C.N.Y.	1963 Providence	1976 Kentucky	(N.Y.C.)	(N.Y.C.)
1951 Brigham Young	1964 Bradley	1977 St. Bonaven-	1990 Vanderbilt	2004 Michigan
1952 La Salle		ture	1991 Stanford	2005 South Carolina

MEN'S NCAA BASKETBALL CHAMPIONSHIPS, 2005

Division I

First Round—Austin
Eastern Kentucky 64, Kentucky 72
Iowa 64, Cincinnati 76
Niagara 67, Oklahoma 84
Texas-El Paso 54, Utah 60
Vermont 60, Syracuse 57
Delaware State 46, Duke 57
Old Dominion 81, Michigan State 89
Mississippi State 93, Stanford 70

First Round—Albuquerque
Pittsburgh 71, Pacific 79
Montana 77, Washington 88
Chattanooga 54, Wake Forest 70
Winthrop 64, Gonzaga 74
Creighton 61, West Virginia 63
UCLA 66, Texas Tech 78
George Washington 68, Georgia Tech 80
Louisiana-Lafayette 62, Louisville 68

First Round—Chicago
Pennsylvania 65, Boston College 85
Nevada 61, Texas 57
Utah State 53, Arizona 66
Fairleigh Dickinson 55, Illinois 67
Univ. of Ala.-Birmingham 82, Louisiana State 68
Wisconsin-Milwaukee 83, Alabama 73
St. Mary's 56, Southern Illinois 65
Southeastern Louisiana 50, Oklahoma State 63

First Round—Syracuse
North Carolina State 75, Charlotte 63
Iowa State 64, Minnesota 53
Central Florida 71, Connecticut 77
Northern Iowa 52, Wisconsin 57
Bucknell 64, Kansas 63
Ohio 62, Florida 67
New Mexico 47, Villanova 55
Oakland 68, North Carolina 96

Second Round—Austin
Oklahoma 58, Utah 67
Cincinnati 60, Kentucky 69
Vermont 61, Michigan State 72
Mississippi State 55, Duke 63

Second Round—Albuquerque
Gonzaga 69, Texas Tech 71
West Virginia 111, Wake Forest 105
Washington 97, Pacific 79
Georgia Tech 54, Louisville 76

Second Round—Chicago
Illinois 71, Nevada 59
Boston College 75, Wisconsin-Milwaukee 83
Arizona 85, Univ. of Ala.-Birmingham 63
Southern Illinois 77, Oklahoma State 85

Second Round—Syracuse
North Carolina State 65, Connecticut 62
Bucknell 62, Wisconsin 71
Villanova 76, Florida 65
Iowa State 65, North Carolina 92

Third Round—Austin
Michigan State 78, Duke 68
Utah 52, Kentucky 62

Third Round—Albuquerque
Louisville 93, Washington 79
West Virginia 65, Texas Tech 60

Third Round—Chicago
Wisconsin-Milwaukee 63, Illinois 77
Arizona 79, Oklahoma State 78

Third Round—Syracuse
North Carolina State 56, Wisconsin 65
Villanova 66, North Carolina 67

Regional Finals
Austin—Michigan State 94, Kentucky 88
Albuquerque—West Virginia 85, Louisville 93
Chicago—Arizona 89, Illinois 90
Syracuse—Wisconsin 82, North Carolina 88

Final Four
(April 2, 2005, St. Louis, Mo.)
Louisville 57, Illinois 72
Michigan State 71, North Carolina 87

National Final
(April 4, 2005, St. Louis, Mo.)
North Carolina 75, Illinois 70

Division II
Championship
Virginia Union 63, Bryant 58

Division III
Championship
Wisconsin-Stevens Point 73, Rochester 49

LEADING NCAA DIVISION I MEN, 2004–2005

POINTS PER GAME

	FGM	3FG	FT	PTS	PPG
Keydren Clark, St. Peter's	230	109	152	721	25.8
Taylor Coppenrath, Vermont	271	9	226	777	25.1
Juan Mendez, Niagara	221	39	224	705	23.5
Rob Monroe, Quinnipiac	173	72	171	589	22.7
Bo McCalebb, New Orleans	261	25	132	679	22.6

FIELD-GOAL PERCENTAGE

	G	FGM	FGA	FG%
Bruce Brown, Hampton	30	178	269	66.2
Nate Harris, Utah State	32	172	264	65.2
Eric Williams, Wake Forest	33	201	319	63.0
Chad McKnight, Morehead State	27	155	246	63.0
Aaron Andrews, Morgan State	28	140	224	62.5

REBOUNDING

	G	REB	RPG
Paul Millsap, Louisiana Tech	29	360	12.4
Andrew Bogut, Utah	35	427	12.2
Lance Allred, Weber State	29	348	12.0
Michael Harris, Rice	31	363	11.7
Dwayne Jones, St. Joseph's	36	418	11.6

ASSISTS

	G	AST	APG
Damitrius Coleman, Mercer	28	224	8.0
Will Funn, Portland State	28	224	8.0
Marcus Williams, Connecticut	31	243	7.8
Walker Russell, Jacksonville State	29	211	7.3
Jose Juan Barea, Northeastern	30	218	7.3

FREE-THROW PERCENTAGE

	G	FT	FTA	FT%
Blake Ahearn, SW Missouri State	32	90	95	94.7
J. J. Redick, Duke	33	196	209	93.8
Vince Greene, Illinois State	30	81	88	92.0
Salim Stoudamire, Arizona	36	122	134	91.0
Jamaal Hilliard, Lafayette	28	91	100	91.0

THREE-PT FIELD-GOAL PERCENTAGE

	G	3FG	3FGA	3FG%
Salim Stoudamire, Arizona	36	120	238	50.4
Will Whittington, Marist	28	97	197	49.2
Dennis Trammell, Ball State	23	59	122	48.4
Chris Lofton, Tennessee	31	93	200	46.5
Drake Diener, DePaul	31	85	184	46.2

NCAA DIVISION I SINGLE-GAME SCORING MARKS[1]

	Year	Pts		Year	Pts
Kevin Bradshaw, US Int'l vs. Loyola-CA	1991	72	Anthony Roberts, Oral Rbts. vs. Oregon	1977	65
Pete Maravich, LSU vs. Alabama	1970	69	Scott Haffner, Evansville vs. Dayton	1989	65
Calvin Murphy, Niagara vs. Syracuse	1969	68	Pete Maravich, LSU vs. Kentucky	1970	64
Jay Handlan, Wash. & Lee vs. Furman	1951	66	Johnny Neumann, Ole Miss vs. LSU	1971	63
Pete Maravich, LSU vs. Tulane	1969	66	Hersey Hawkins, Bradley vs. Detroit	1988	63
Anthony Roberts, Oral Rbts. vs. N.C. A.&T.	1977	66			

1. Scored against a Division I opponent.

NCAA DIVISION I INDIVIDUAL CAREER RECORDS

SCORING—TOTAL POINTS

	Yrs	Last	Gm	Pts
Pete Maravich, LSU	3	1970	83	3,667
Freeman Williams, Port. St.	4	1978	106	3,249
Lionel Simmons, La Salle	4	1990	131	3,217
Alphonso Ford, Miss. Val. St.	4	1993	109	3,165
Harry Kelly, Texas Southern	4	1983	110	3,066
Hersey Hawkins, Bradley	4	1988	125	3,008
Oscar Robertson, Cincinnati	3	1960	88	2,973
Danny Manning, Kansas	4	1988	147	2,951
Alfredrick Hughes, Loyola-Ill.	4	1985	120	2,914
Elvin Hayes, Houston	3	1968	93	2,884

SCORING—AVERAGE POINTS

	Yrs	Last	Pts	Avg
Pete Maravich, LSU	3	1970	3,667	44.2
Austin Carr, Notre Dame	3	1971	2,560	34.6
Oscar Robertson, Cinn.	3	1960	2,973	33.8
Calvin Murphy, Niagara	3	1970	2,548	33.1
Dwight Lamar, SW La.	2	1973	1,862	32.7
Frank Selvy, Furman	3	1954	2,538	32.5
Rick Mount, Purdue	3	1970	2,323	32.3
Darrell Floyd, Furman	3	1956	2,281	32.1
Nick Werkman, Seton Hall	3	1964	2,273	32.0
Willie Humes, Idaho St.	2	1971	1,510	31.5

BLOCKED SHOTS—AVERAGE

	Yrs	Last	No	Avg
Keith Closs, Cen. Conn. St.	2	1996	317	5.87
Adonal Foyle, Colgate	3	1997	492	5.66
David Robinson, Navy	2	1987	351	5.24
Wojciech Mydra, La.-Monroe	4	2002	535	4.65
Shaquille O'Neal, LSU	3	1992	412	4.58

Note: minimum 225 blocked shots.

ASSISTS—TOTAL

	Yrs	Last	Gm	No
Bobby Hurley, Duke	4	1993	140	1,076
Chris Corchiani, N.C. State	4	1991	124	1,038
Ed Cota, N. Carolina	4	2000	138	1,030
Keith Jennings, E. Tenn. St.	4	1991	127	983
Steve Blake, Maryland	4	2003	138	972
Sherman Douglas, Syracuse	4	1989	138	960
Tony Miller, Marquette	4	1995	123	956
Greg Anthony, Portland/UNLV	4	1991	138	950
Doug Gottlieb, ND/Okla St.	4	2000	124	947
Gary Payton, Oregon St.	4	1990	120	939

STEALS—AVERAGE

	Yrs	Last	No	Avg
Desmond Cambridge, Alabama A&M	3	2002	330	3.93
Mookie Blaylock, Oklahoma	2	1989	281	3.80
Ronn McMahon, Eastern Wash.	3	1990	225	3.52
Eric Murdock, Providence	4	1991	376	3.21
Van Usher, Tennessee Tech	3	1992	270	3.18

Note: minimum 225 steals.

REBOUNDS—TOTAL, SINCE 1973

	Yrs	Last	Gm	No
Tim Duncan, Wake Forest	4	1997	128	1,570
Derrick Coleman, Syracuse	4	1990	143	1,537
Malik Rose, Drexel	4	1996	120	1,514
Ralph Sampson, Virginia	4	1983	132	1,511
Pete Padgett, Nevada-Reno	4	1976	104	1,464
Lionel Simmons, La Salle	4	1990	131	1,429
Anthony Bonner, St. Louis	4	1990	133	1,424
Tyrone Hill, Xavier-Ohio	4	1990	126	1,380
Popeye Jones, Murray St.	4	1992	123	1,374
Michael Brooks, La Salle	4	1980	114	1,372

WOMEN'S NCAA CHAMPIONSHIPS, 2005

Division I

First Round—Chattanooga
Louisiana State 70, Stetson 36
Arizona 72, Oklahoma 69
DePaul 79, Virginia Tech 78
Liberty 78, Penn State 70
Georgia 75, Rice 49
Texas 64, Oral Roberts 47
Boston College 65, Houston 43
Duke 80, Canisius 48

First Round—Tempe
North Carolina 97, Coppin State 62
George Washington 60, Mississippi 57
Arizona State 87, Eastern Kentucky 65
Notre Dame 61, UC-Santa Barbara 51
Virginia 79, Old Dominion 57
Minnesota 64, St. Francis (Pa.) 33
Oregon 58, Texas Christian Univ. 55
Baylor 91, Illinois State 70

First Round—Philadelphia
Tennessee 94, Western Carolina 43
Purdue 68, New Mexico 56
Middle Tennessee 60, North Carolina State 58
Texas Tech 69, Texas-Arlington 49
Temple 66, Louisiana Tech 61
Rutgers 62, Hartford 37
Maryland 65, Wisconsin-Green Bay 55
Ohio State 86, Holy Cross 45

First Round—Kansas City
Michigan State 73, Alcorn State 41
Southern California 65, Louisville 49
Vanderbilt 67, Montana 44
Kansas State 70, Bowling Green 60
Florida State 87, Richmond 54
Connecticut 95, Dartmouth 47
Utah 73, Iowa State 61
Stanford 94, Santa Clara 57

Second Round—Chattanooga
Louisiana State 76, Arizona 43
Liberty 88, DePaul 79
Georgia 70, Texas 68
Duke 70, Boston College 65

Second Round—Tempe
North Carolina 71, George Washington 47
Arizona State 70, Notre Dame 61
Minnesota 73, Virginia 58
Baylor 69, Oregon 46

Second Round—Philadelphia
Tennessee 75, Purdue 54
Texas Tech 80, Middle Tennessee 69
Rutgers 61, Temple 54
Ohio State 75, Maryland 65

Second Round—Kansas City
Michigan State 61, Southern California 59
Vanderbilt 63, Kansas State 60
Connecticut 70, Florida State 52
Stanford 88, Utah 62

Third Round—Chattanooga
Louisiana State 90, Liberty 48
Duke 63, Georgia 57
Third Round—Tempe
North Carolina 79, Arizona State 72
Baylor 64, Minnesota 57
Third Round—Philadelphia
Tennessee 75, Texas Tech 59
Rutgers 64, Ohio State 58
Third Round—Kansas City
Michigan State 76, Vanderbilt 64
Stanford 76, Connecticut 59
Regional Finals
Chattanooga—Louisiana State 59, Duke 49
Tempe—Baylor 72, North Carolina 63
Philadelphia—Tennessee 59, Rutgers 49
Kansas City—Michigan State 76, Stanford 69
Final Four
(April 3, 2005, Indianapolis, Ind.)
Michigan State 68, Tennessee 64
Baylor 68, Louisiana State 57
National Championship
(April 5, 2005, Indianapolis, Ind.)
Baylor 84, Michigan State 62

Division II
Championship
Washburn 70, Seattle Pacific 53

Division III
Championship
Millikin 70, Randolph-Macon 50

LEADING NCAA DIVISION I WOMEN, 2004–2005

POINTS PER GAME

	FGM	3FG	FT	PTS	PPG
Tan White, Mississippi State	241	61	138	681	23.5
Emily Faurholt, Idaho	241	46	169	697	23.2
Tori Talbert, Texas State	208	0	144	560	22.4
Tamara James, Miami (Fla.)	242	39	124	647	22.3
Beth Swink, St. Francis (Pa.)	255	1	177	688	22.2

FIELD-GOAL PERCENTAGE

	G	FGM	FGA	FG%
Katie Feenstra, Liberty	32	230	343	67.1
Amber Jackson, San Jose State	30	205	311	65.9
Ashley Earley, Vanderbilt	32	240	375	64.0
LaToya Davis, Texas Tech	31	157	256	61.3
Becky O'Neil, Weber State	29	145	237	61.2

THREE-POINT FIELD-GOAL PERCENTAGE

	G	3FG	3FGA	3FG%
K. C. Cowgill, SW Missouri State	33	74	139	53.2
Ashley Cazee, Eastern Ky.	28	56	113	49.6
Matea Pender, Univ. of Md. Baltimore County	28	62	127	48.8
Jill Marano, La Salle	28	57	123	46.3
Kate Endress, Ball State	29	70	152	46.1

FREE-THROW PERCENTAGE

	G	FT	FTA	FT%
Kristin Iwanaga, California	29	85	91	93.4
Nefertiti Walker, Stetson	31	80	87	92.0
Melissa Yeagley, Iona	26	83	92	90.2
Megan Duffy, Notre Dame	33	137	153	89.5
Tynisha Alexander, Tennessee Tech	29	109	122	89.3

REBOUNDS PER GAME

	G	REB	RPG
Sancho Lyttle, Houston	30	362	12.1
Sandora Irvin, Texas Christian	33	390	11.8
Nakeya Downing, Southeastern La.	27	318	11.8
Khara Smith, DePaul	31	364	11.7
Sugiery Monsac, Robert Morris	30	348	11.6

ASSISTS PER GAME

	G	AST	APG
Yolanda Paige, West Virginia	34	297	8.7
Temeka Johnson, Louisiana State	36	278	7.7
Erin Grant, Texas Tech	31	218	7.0
Corrie Mizusawa, Oregon	30	209	7.0
Anesia Smith, Maryland	32	214	6.7

OTHER TOURNAMENTS, 2004–2005

MEN
NIT—South Carolina 60, St. Joseph's 57
NAIA Div. I—John Brown (Ark.) 65, Azusa Pacific (Calif.) 55
NAIA Div. II—Walsh (Ohio) 81, Concordia (Nebr.) 70

WOMEN
NIT—Southwest Missouri State 78, West Virginia 70
NAIA Div. I—Union (Tenn.) 67, Oklahoma City 63
NAIA Div. II—Morningside 75, Cedarville 65

Professional Basketball

The NBA divisions were realigned beginning in the 2004–2005 season. The Eastern Conference now has three divisions: the Atlantic (Boston, New Jersey, New York, Philadelphia, Toronto), the Central (Chicago, Cleveland, Detroit, Indiana, Milwaukee), and the Southeast (Atlanta, Charlotte, Miami, Orlando, Washington). The Western Conference divisions are: the Southwest (Dallas, Houston, Memphis, New Orleans, San Antonio), the Northwest (Denver, Minnesota, Portland, Seattle, Utah), and the Pacific (Golden State, Los Angeles Clippers, Los Angeles Lakers, Phoenix, Sacramento).

NATIONAL BASKETBALL ASSOCIATION CHAMPIONS

The National Basketball Association was originally the Basketball Association of America. It took its current name in 1949 when it merged with the National Basketball League.

Year	Eastern Conference	Western Conference	Winner (Series)
1947	Philadelphia Warriors	Chicago Stags	Philadelphia Warriors (4–1)
1948	Philadelphia Warriors	Baltimore Bullets	Baltimore Bullets (4–2)
1949	Washington Capitols	Minneapolis Lakers	Minneapolis Lakers (4–2)
1950	Syracuse Nationals	Minneapolis Lakers	Minneapolis Lakers (4–2)
1951	New York Knickerbockers	Rochester Royals	Rochester Royals (4–3)
1952	New York Knickerbockers	Minneapolis Lakers	Minneapolis Lakers (4–3)
1953	New York Knickerbockers	Minneapolis Lakers	Minneapolis Lakers (4–1)
1954	Syracuse Nationals	Minneapolis Lakers	Minneapolis Lakers (4–3)
1955	Syracuse Nationals	Ft. Wayne Pistons	Syracuse Nationals (4–3)
1956	Philadelphia Warriors	Ft. Wayne Pistons	Philadelphia Warriors (4–1)
1957	Boston Celtics	St. Louis Hawks	Boston Celtics (4–3)
1958	Boston Celtics	St. Louis Hawks	St. Louis Hawks (4–2)
1959	Boston Celtics	Minneapolis Lakers	Boston Celtics (4–0)
1960	Boston Celtics	St. Louis Hawks	Boston Celtics (4–3)
1961	Boston Celtics	St. Louis Hawks	Boston Celtics (4–1)
1962	Boston Celtics	Los Angeles Lakers	Boston Celtics (4–3)
1963	Boston Celtics	Los Angeles Lakers	Boston Celtics (4–2)
1964	Boston Celtics	San Francisco Warriors	Boston Celtics (4–1)
1965	Boston Celtics	Los Angeles Lakers	Boston Celtics (4–1)
1966	Boston Celtics	Los Angeles Lakers	Boston Celtics (4–3)
1967	Philadelphia 76ers	San Francisco Warriors	Philadelphia 76ers (4–2)
1968	Boston Celtics	Los Angeles Lakers	Boston Celtics (4–2)
1969	Boston Celtics	Los Angeles Lakers	Boston Celtics (4–3)
1970	New York Knickerbockers	Los Angeles Lakers	New York Knickerbockers (4–3)
1971	Baltimore Bullets	Milwaukee Bucks	Milwaukee Bucks (4–0)
1972	New York Knickerbockers	Los Angeles Lakers	Los Angeles Lakers (4–1)
1973	New York Knickerbockers	Los Angeles Lakers	New York Knickerbockers (4–1)
1974	Boston Celtics	Milwaukee Bucks	Boston Celtics (4–3)
1975	Washington Bullets	Golden State Warriors	Golden State Warriors (4–0)
1976	Boston Celtics	Phoenix Suns	Boston Celtics (4–2)
1977	Philadelphia 76ers	Portland Trail Blazers	Portland Trail Blazers (4–2)
1978	Washington Bullets	Seattle SuperSonics	Washington Bullets (4–3)
1979	Washington Bullets	Seattle SuperSonics	Seattle SuperSonics (4–1)
1980	Philadelphia 76ers	Los Angeles Lakers	Los Angeles Lakers (4–2)
1981	Boston Celtics	Houston Rockets	Boston Celtics (4–2)
1982	Philadelphia 76ers	Los Angeles Lakers	Los Angeles Lakers (4–2)
1983	Philadelphia 76ers	Los Angeles Lakers	Philadelphia 76ers (4–0)
1984	Boston Celtics	Los Angeles Lakers	Boston Celtics (4–3)
1985	Boston Celtics	Los Angeles Lakers	Los Angeles Lakers (4–2)
1986	Boston Celtics	Houston Rockets	Boston Celtics (4–2)
1987	Boston Celtics	Los Angeles Lakers	Los Angeles Lakers (4–2)
1988	Detroit Pistons	Los Angeles Lakers	Los Angeles Lakers (4–3)
1989	Detroit Pistons	Los Angeles Lakers	Detroit Pistons (4–0)
1990	Detroit Pistons	Portland Trail Blazers	Detroit Pistons (4–1)
1991	Chicago Bulls	Los Angeles Lakers	Chicago Bulls (4–1)
1992	Chicago Bulls	Portland Trail Blazers	Chicago Bulls (4–2)
1993	Chicago Bulls	Phoenix Suns	Chicago Bulls (4–2)
1994	New York Knickerbockers	Houston Rockets	Houston Rockets (4–3)
1995	Orlando Magic	Houston Rockets	Houston Rockets (4–0)
1996	Chicago Bulls	Seattle SuperSonics	Chicago Bulls (4–2)
1997	Chicago Bulls	Utah Jazz	Chicago Bulls (4–2)

Year	Eastern Conference	Western Conference	Winner (Series)
1998	Chicago Bulls	Utah Jazz	Chicago Bulls (4–2)
1999	New York Knickerbockers	San Antonio Spurs	San Antonio Spurs (4–1)
2000	Indiana Pacers	Los Angeles Lakers	Los Angeles Lakers (4–2)
2001	Philadelphia 76ers	Los Angeles Lakers	Los Angeles Lakers (4–1)
2002	New Jersey Nets	Los Angeles Lakers	Los Angeles Lakers (4–0)
2003	New Jersey Nets	San Antonio Spurs	San Antonio Spurs (4–2)
2004	Detroit Pistons	Los Angeles Lakers	Detroit Pistons (4–1)
2005	Detroit Pistons	San Antonio Spurs	San Antonio Spurs (4–3)

INDIVIDUAL NBA SCORING CHAMPIONS

Season	Player, Team	G	FG	3FG[1]	FT	Pts	Avg
1953–54	Neil Johnston, Philadelphia Warriors	72	591	—	577	1,759	24.4
1954–55	Neil Johnston, Philadelphia Warriors	72	521	—	589	1,631	22.7
1955–56	Bob Pettit, St. Louis Hawks	72	646	—	557	1,849	25.7
1956–57	Paul Arizin, Philadelphia Warriors	71	613	—	591	1,817	25.6
1957–58	George Yardley, Detroit Pistons	72	673	—	655	2,001	27.8
1958–59	Bob Pettit, St. Louis Hawks	72	719	—	667	2,105	29.2
1959–60	Wilt Chamberlain, Philadelphia Warriors	72	1,065	—	577	2,707	37.6
1960–61	Wilt Chamberlain, Philadelphia Warriors	79	1,251	—	531	3,033	38.4
1961–62	Wilt Chamberlain, Philadelphia Warriors	80	1,597	—	835	4,029	50.4
1962–63	Wilt Chamberlain, San Francisco Warriors	80	1,463	—	660	3,586	44.8
1963–64	Wilt Chamberlain, San Francisco Warriors	80	1,204	—	540	2,948	36.9
1964–65	Wilt Chamberlain, San Francisco Warriors/Phila. 76ers	73	1,063	—	408	2,534	34.7
1965–66	Wilt Chamberlain, Philadelphia 76ers	79	1,074	—	501	2,649	33.5
1966–67	Rick Barry, San Francisco Warriors	78	1,011	—	753	2,775	35.6
1967–68	Dave Bing, Detroit Pistons	79	835	—	472	2,142	27.1
1968–69	Elvin Hayes, San Diego Rockets	82	930	—	467	2,327	28.4
1969–70	Jerry West, Los Angeles Lakers	74	831	—	647	2,309	31.2
1970–71	Lew Alcindor,[2] Milwaukee Bucks	82	1,063	—	470	2,596	31.7
1971–72	Kareem Abdul-Jabbar, Milwaukee Bucks	81	1,159	—	504	2,822	34.8
1972–73	Nate Archibald, Kansas City/Omaha Kings	80	1,028	—	663	2,719	34.0
1973–74	Bob McAdoo, Buffalo Braves	74	901	—	459	2,261	30.8
1974–75	Bob McAdoo, Buffalo Braves	82	1,095	—	641	2,831	34.5
1975–76	Bob McAdoo, Buffalo Braves	78	934	—	559	2,427	31.1
1976–77	Pete Maravich, New Orleans Jazz	73	886	—	501	2,273	31.1
1977–78	George Gervin, San Antonio Spurs	82	864	—	504	2,232	27.2
1978–79	George Gervin, San Antonio Spurs	80	947	—	471	2,365	29.6
1979–80	George Gervin, San Antonio Spurs	78	1,024	32	505	2,585	33.1
1980–81	Adrian Dantley, Utah Jazz	80	909	2	632	2,452	30.7
1981–82	George Gervin, San Antonio Spurs	79	993	10	555	2,551	32.3
1982–83	Alex English, Denver Nuggets	82	959	2	406	2,326	28.4
1983–84	Adrian Dantley, Utah Jazz	79	802	1	813	2,418	30.6
1984–85	Bernard King, New York Knicks	55	691	1	426	1,809	32.9
1985–86	Dominique Wilkins, Atlanta Hawks	78	888	13	527	2,366	30.3
1986–87	Michael Jordan, Chicago Bulls	82	1,098	12	833	3,041	37.1
1987–88	Michael Jordan, Chicago Bulls	82	1,069	7	723	2,868	35.0
1988–89	Michael Jordan, Chicago Bulls	81	966	27	674	2,633	32.5
1989–90	Michael Jordan, Chicago Bulls	82	1,034	92	593	2,753	33.6
1990–91	Michael Jordan, Chicago Bulls	82	990	29	571	2,580	31.5
1991–92	Michael Jordan, Chicago Bulls	80	943	27	491	2,404	30.1
1992–93	Michael Jordan, Chicago Bulls	78	992	81	476	2,541	32.6
1993–94	David Robinson, San Antonio Spurs	80	840	10	693	2,383	29.8
1994–95	Shaquille O'Neal, Orlando Magic	79	930	0	455	2,315	29.3
1995–96	Michael Jordan, Chicago Bulls	82	916	111	548	2,491	30.4
1996–97	Michael Jordan, Chicago Bulls	82	920	111	480	2,431	29.6
1997–98	Michael Jordan, Chicago Bulls	82	881	30	565	2,357	28.7
1998–99	Allen Iverson, Philadelphia 76ers	48	435	58	356	1,284	26.8
1999–2000	Shaquille O'Neal, L.A. Lakers	79	956	0	432	2,344	29.7
2000–01	Allen Iverson, Philadelphia 76ers	71	762	98	585	2,207	31.1
2001–02	Allen Iverson, Philadelphia 76ers	60	665	78	475	1,883	31.4
2002–03	Tracy McGrady, Orlando Magic	75	829	173	576	2,407	32.1
2003–04	Tracy McGrady, Orlando Magic	67	653	174	398	1,878	28.0
2004–05	Allen Iverson, Philadelphia 76ers	75	771	104	656	2,302	30.7

NOTE: Decided by total points through 1968–69, and per-game average since. 1. 3-point field goals were not used before the 1979–80 season. 2. (Kareem Abdul-Jabbar).

NBA INDIVIDUAL RECORDS, GAME

(Through 2004–2005 season)

Most points, game—100, Wilt Chamberlain, Philadelphia vs. New York, 1962

Most free throws, game—28, Wilt Chamberlain, Philadelphia vs. New York, 1962; 28, Adrian Dantley, Utah vs. Houston, 1984

Most field goals, game—36, Wilt Chamberlain, Philadelphia vs. New York, 1962

Most assists, game—30, Scott Skiles, Orlando vs. Denver, 1990

Most rebounds, game—55, Wilt Chamberlain, Philadelphia vs. Boston, 1960

Most 3-pt. field goals, game—11, Dennis Scott, Orlando vs. Atlanta, 1996

Most blocked shots, game—17, Elmore Smith, Los Angeles vs. Portland, 1973

Most steals, game—11, Larry Kenon, San Antonio vs. Kansas City, 1976; 11, Kendall Gill, New Jersey vs. Miami, 1999

NBA MOST VALUABLE PLAYERS

1956 Bob Pettit, St. Louis
1957 Bob Cousy, Boston
1958 Bill Russell, Boston
1959 Bob Pettit, St. Louis
1960 Wilt Chamberlain, Philadelphia
1961–63 Bill Russell, Boston
1964 Oscar Robertson, Cincinnati
1965 Bill Russell, Boston
1966–68 Wilt Chamberlain, Philadelphia
1969 Wes Unseld, Baltimore
1970 Willis Reed, New York
1971–72 Lew Alcindor
(Kareem Abdul-Jabbar), Milwaukee
1973 Dave Cowens, Boston
1974 Kareem Abdul-Jabbar, Milwaukee
1975 Bob McAdoo, Buffalo

1976–77 Kareem Abdul-Jabbar, L.A. Lakers
1978 Bill Walton, Portland
1979 Moses Malone, Houston
1980 Kareem Abdul-Jabbar, L.A. Lakers
1981 Julius Erving, Philadelphia
1982 Moses Malone, Houston
1983 Moses Malone, Philadelphia
1984 Larry Bird, Boston
1985 Larry Bird, Boston
1986 Larry Bird, Boston
1987 Magic Johnson, L.A. Lakers
1988 Michael Jordan, Chicago
1989 Magic Johnson, L.A. Lakers
1990 Magic Johnson, L.A. Lakers
1991 Michael Jordan, Chicago

1992 Michael Jordan, Chicago
1993 Charles Barkley, Phoenix
1994 Hakeem Olajuwon, Houston
1995 David Robinson, San Antonio
1996 Michael Jordan, Chicago
1997 Karl Malone, Utah
1998 Michael Jordan, Chicago
1999 Karl Malone, Utah
2000 Shaquille O'Neal, L.A. Lakers
2001 Allen Iverson, Philadelphia
2002 Tim Duncan, San Antonio
2003 Tim Duncan, San Antonio
2004 Kevin Garnett, Minnesota
2005 Steve Nash, Phoenix

NBA LIFETIME LEADERS

(through 2005 season)
Players in bold face active in 2004–2005 season

POINTS	Yrs	Gm	Pts	Avg
Kareem Abdul-Jabbar	20	1,560	38,387	24.6
Karl Malone	19	1,476	36,928	25.0
Michael Jordan	15	1,072	32,292	30.1
Wilt Chamberlain	14	1,045	31,419	30.1
Moses Malone	19	1,329	27,409	20.6
Elvin Hayes	16	1,303	27,313	21.0
Hakeem Olajuwon	18	1,238	26,946	21.8
Oscar Robertson	14	1,040	26,710	25.7
Dominique Wilkins	15	1,074	26,668	24.8
John Havlicek	16	1,270	26,395	20.8

SCORING AVERAGE
Minimum of 400 games or 10,000 points

	Yrs	Gm	Pts	Avg
Michael Jordan	15	1,072	32,292	30.1
Wilt Chamberlain	14	1,045	31,419	30.1
Allen Iverson	9	610	16,738	27.4
Elgin Baylor	14	846	23,149	27.4
Jerry West	14	932	25,192	27.0
Shaquille O'Neal	13	882	23,583	26.7
Bob Pettit	11	792	20,880	26.4
George Gervin	10	791	20,708	26.2
Oscar Robertson	14	1,040	26,710	25.7
Karl Malone	19	1,476	36,928	25.0

FIELD GOALS MADE

	Yrs	FG	Att	Pct
Kareem Abdul-Jabbar	20	15,837	28,307	.559
Karl Malone	19	13,528	26,210	.516
Wilt Chamberlain	14	12,681	23,497	.540
Michael Jordan	15	12,192	24,537	.497
Elvin Hayes	16	10,976	24,272	.452
Hakeem Olajuwon	18	10,749	20,991	.512
Alex English	15	10,659	21,036	.507
John Havlicek	16	10,513	23,930	.439
Dominique Wilkins	15	9,963	21,589	.461
Patrick Ewing	15	9,702	19,241	.504

FREE THROWS

	Yrs	FT	Att	Pct
Karl Malone	19	9,787	13,188	.742
Moses Malone	19	8,531	11,090	.769
Oscar Robertson	14	7,694	9,185	.838
Michael Jordan	15	7,327	8,772	.835
Jerry West	14	7,160	8,801	.814
Dolph Schayes	16	6,979	8,274	.843
Adrian Dantley	15	6,832	8,351	.818
Kareem Abdul-Jabbar	20	6,712	9,304	.721
Charles Barkley	16	6,349	8,643	.735
Reggie Miller	18	6,237	7,026	.888

3–PT FIELD GOALS MADE

Reggie Miller	2,560
Dale Ellis	1,719
Glen Rice	1,559
Tim Hardaway	1,542
Ray Allen	1,486

TOTAL MINUTES PLAYED

Kareem Abdul-Jabbar	57,446
Karl Malone	54,852
Elvin Hayes	50,000
Wilt Chamberlain	47,859
John Stockton	47,764

REBOUNDS

Wilt Chamberlain	23,924	Karl Malone	14,968
Bill Russell	21,620	Robert Parish	14,715
Kareem Abdul-Jabbar	17,440	Nate Thurmond	14,464
Elvin Hayes	16,279	Walt Bellamy	14,241
Moses Malone	16,212	Wes Unseld	13,769

BLOCKED SHOTS

Hakeem Olajuwon	3,830
Kareem Abdul-Jabbar	3,189
Dikembe Mutombo	3,097
Mark Eaton	3,064
David Robinson	2,954

STEALS

John Stockton	3,265
Michael Jordan	2,514
Gary Payton	2,331
Maurice Cheeks	2,310
Scottie Pippen	2,307

ASSISTS

John Stockton	15,806	**Gary Payton**	8,508
Mark Jackson	10,334	**Rod Strickland**	7,987
Magic Johnson	10,141	Maurice Cheeks	7,392
Oscar Robertson	9,887	**Jason Kidd**	7,283
Isiah Thomas	9,061	Lenny Wilkens	7,211

NATIONAL BASKETBALL ASSOCIATION FINAL STANDINGS, 2004–2005

EASTERN CONFERENCE

Atlantic Division	W	L	Pct	GB
Boston Celtics[1]	45	37	.549	—
Philadelphia 76ers[2]	43	39	.524	2
New Jersey Nets[2]	42	40	.512	3
Toronto Raptors	33	49	.402	12
New York Knicks	33	49	.402	12

Central Division	W	L	Pct	GB
Detroit Pistons[1]	54	28	.659	—
Chicago Bulls[2]	47	35	.573	7
Indiana Pacers[2]	44	38	.537	10
Cleveland Cavaliers	42	40	.512	12
Milwaukee Bucks	30	52	.366	24

Southeast Division	W	L	Pct	GB
Miami Heat[1]	59	23	.720	—
Washington Wizards[2]	45	37	.549	14
Orlando Magic	36	46	.439	23
Charlotte Bobcats	18	64	.220	41
Atlanta Hawks	13	69	.159	46

WESTERN CONFERENCE

Northwest Division	W	L	Pct	GB
Seattle SuperSonics[1]	52	30	.634	—
Denver Nuggets[2]	49	33	.598	3
Minnesota Timberwolves	44	38	.537	8
Portland Trail Blazers	27	55	.329	25
Utah Jazz	26	56	.317	26

Pacific Division	W	L	Pct	GB
Phoenix Suns[1]	62	20	.756	—
Sacramento Kings[2]	50	32	.610	12
L.A. Clippers	37	45	.451	25
L.A. Lakers	34	48	.415	28
Golden State Warriors	34	48	.415	28

Southwest Division	W	L	Pct	GB
San Antonio Spurs[1]	59	23	.720	—
Dallas Mavericks[2]	58	24	.707	1
Houston Rockets[2]	51	31	.622	8
Memphis Grizzlies[2]	45	37	.549	14
New Orleans Hornets	18	64	.220	41

1. Division champion. 2. Playoff qualifier.

NBA PLAYOFFS, 2005

EASTERN CONFERENCE

First Round
(Best of 7)
Miami Heat defeated New Jersey Nets, 4 games to 0
Detroit Pistons defeated Philadelphia 76ers, 4 games to 1
Indiana Pacers defeated Boston Celtics, 4 games to 3
Washington Wizards defeated Chicago Bulls, 4 games to 2

Conference Semifinals
(Best of 7)
Miami Heat defeated Washington Wizards, 4 games to 0
Detroit Pistons defeated Indiana Pacers, 4 games to 2

Conference Finals
(Best of 7)
Detroit Pistons defeated Miami Heat, 4 games to 3

WESTERN CONFERENCE

First Round
(Best of 7)
Phoenix Suns defeated Memphis Grizzlies, 4 games to 0
San Antonio Spurs defeated Denver Nuggets, 4 games to 1
Seattle SuperSonics defeated Sacramento Kings, 4 games to 1
Dallas Mavericks defeated Houston Rockets, 4 games to 3

Conference Semifinals
(Best of 7)
Phoenix Suns defeated Dallas Mavericks, 4 games to 2
San Antonio Spurs defeated Seattle SuperSonics, 4 games to 2

Conference Finals
(Best of 7)
San Antonio Spurs defeated Phoenix Suns, 4 games to 1

NBA CHAMPIONSHIPS

San Antonio Spurs defeated Detroit Pistons, 4 games to 3
Tim Duncan, San Antonio, named Finals MVP

June 9—San Antonio 84, Detroit 69
June 12—San Antonio 97, Detroit 76
June 14—Detroit 96, San Antonio 79
June 16—Detroit 102, San Antonio 71

June 19—San Antonio 96, Detroit 95
June 21—Detroit 95, San Antonio 86
June 23—San Antonio 81, Detroit 74

NBA INDIVIDUAL LEADERS, 2004–2005 SEASON

POINTS PER GAME
Minimum of 49 games played

	Gm	Pts	PPG
Allen Iverson, Philadelphia	75	2,302	30.7
Kobe Bryant, L.A. Lakers	66	1,819	27.6
LeBron James, Cleveland	80	2,175	27.2
Dirk Norwitzki, Dallas	78	2,032	26.1
Amare Stoudemire, Phoenix	80	2,080	26.0
Tracy McGrady, Houston	78	2,003	25.7
Gilbert Arenas, Washington	80	2,038	25.5
Vince Carter, New Jersey	77	1,886	24.5
Dwyane Wade, Miami	77	1,854	24.1
Ray Allen, Seattle	78	1,867	23.9

ASSISTS PER GAME
Minimum of 49 games played

	Gm	Ast	APG
Steve Nash, Phoenix	75	861	11.5
Brevin Knight, Charlotte	66	591	9.0
Jason Kidd, New Jersey	66	545	8.3
Stephen Marbury, New York	82	668	8.1
Allen Iverson, Philadelphia	75	596	7.9
LeBron James, Cleveland	80	577	7.2
Steve Francis, Orlando	78	547	7.0
Andre Miller, Denver	82	569	6.9
Mike Bibby, Sacramento	80	541	6.8
Dwyane Wade, Miami	77	520	6.8

REBOUNDS PER GAME
Minimum of 49 games played

	Gm	Reb	RPG
Kevin Garnett, Minnesota	82	1,108	13.5
Ben Wallace, Detroit	74	902	12.2
Shawn Marion, Phoenix	81	915	11.3
Emeka Okafor, Charlotte	73	795	10.9
Troy Murphy, Golden State	70	756	10.8
Shaquille O'Neal, Miami	73	760	10.4
Kurt Thomas, New York	80	831	10.4
Dwight Howard, Orlando	82	823	10.0
Dirk Nowitzki, Dallas	78	757	9.7
Tyson Chandler, Chicago	80	775	9.7

FIELD GOAL PERCENTAGE
Minimum of 288 field goals made

	FGM	FGA	Pct
Shaquille O'Neal, Miami	658	1,095	.601
Amare Stoudemire, Phoenix	747	1,336	.559
Yao Ming, Houston	538	975	.552
Udonis Haslem, Miami	346	641	.540
Eddy Curry, Chicago	393	730	.538
Ruben Patterson, Portland	319	601	.531
Mark Blount, Boston	327	618	.529
Brad Miller, Sacramento	319	609	.524
Carlos Boozer, Utah	361	693	.521
Dwight Howard, Orlando	352	677	.520

FREE-THROW PERCENTAGE
Minimum of 120 free throws made

	FTM	FTA	Pct
Reggie Miller, Indiana	250	268	.933
Earl Boykins, Denver	279	303	.921
Peja Stojakovic, Sacramento	253	275	.920
Damon Stoudamire, Portland	182	199	.915
Chauncey Billups, Detroit	343	382	.898
Steve Nash, Phoenix	211	238	.887
Like Ridnour, Seattle	159	180	.883
Ray Allen, Seattle	378	428	.883
Austin Croshere, Indiana	226	256	.883
Danny Fortson, Seattle	227	258	.880

3-POINT FIELD GOAL PERCENTAGE
Minimum of 55 3-point field goals made

	3FGM	3FGA	Pct
Fred Holberg, Minnesota	70	145	.483
Joe Johnson, Phoenix	177	370	.478
Cuttino Mobley, Sacramento	150	342	.439
Mike Miller, Memphis	140	323	.433
Damon Jones, Miami	225	521	.432
Steve Nash, Phoenix	94	218	.431
Jon Barry, Houston	71	165	.430
Chauncey Billups, Detroit	165	387	.426
Eric Piatkowski, Chicago	57	134	.425
Jason Terry, Dallas	103	245	.420

BLOCKED SHOTS PER GAME
Minimum of 49 games played or 96 blocked shots

	Gm	Blk	BPG
Andrei Kirilenko, Utah	41	136	3.32
Marcus Camby, Denver	66	199	3.02
Tim Duncan, San Antonio	66	174	2.64
Theo Ratliff, Portland	63	158	2.51
Ben Wallace, Detroit	74	176	2.38
Shaquille O'Neal, Miami	73	171	2.34
Joel Przybilla, Portland	76	163	2.14
Zydrunas Ilgauskas, Cleveland	78	165	2.12
Elton Brand, L.A. Clippers	81	169	2.09
Adonal Foyle, Golden State	78	159	2.04

STEALS PER GAME
Minimum of 49 games played or 120 steals

	Gm	Stl	SPG
Larry Hughes, Washington	61	176	2.89
Allen Iverson, Philadelphia	75	180	2.40
LeBron James, Cleveland	80	177	2.21
Shawn Marion, Phoenix	81	163	2.01
Brevin Knight, Charlotte	66	131	1.98
Gilbert Arenas, Washington	80	139	1.74
Tracy McGrady, Houston	78	135	1.73
Andre Iguodala, Philadelphia	82	138	1.68
Gerald Wallace, Charlotte	70	117	1.67
Paul Pierce, Boston	82	133	1.62

Women's Professional Basketball

WOMEN'S NATIONAL BASKETBALL ASSOCIATION, 2005 SEASON

Eastern Conference

	W	L	Pct	GB	Home	Road
Connecticut Sun	26	8	.765	—	14–3	12–5
Indiana Fever	21	13	.618	5	14–3	7–10
New York Liberty	18	16	.529	8	10–7	8–9
Detroit Shock	16	18	.471	10	12–5	4–13
Washington Mystics	16	18	.471	10	10–7	6–11
Charlotte Sting	6	28	.176	20	5–12	1–16

NOTE: GB refers to Games Behind leader.

Western Conference

	W	L	Pct	GB	Home	Road
Sacramento Monarchs	25	9	.735	—	15–2	10–7
Seattle Storm	20	14	.588	5	14–3	6–11
Houston Comets	19	15	.559	6	11–6	8–9
Los Angeles Sparks	17	17	.500	8	11–6	6–11
Phoenix Mercury	16	18	.471	9	11–6	5–12
Minnesota Lynx	14	20	.412	11	11–6	3–14
San Antonio Silver Stars	7	27	.206	18	5–12	2–15

2005 WNBA LEAGUE LEADERS

POINTS PER GAME

	Gm	Pts	PPG
Sheryl Swoopes, Houston	33	614	18.6
Lauren Jackson, Seattle	34	597	17.6
Chamique Holdsclaw, Los Angeles	33	561	17.0
Diana Taurasi, Phoenix	33	527	16.0
Deanna Nolan, Detroit	33	524	15.9

REBOUNDS PER GAME

	Gm	Reb	RPG
Cheryl Ford, Detroit	33	322	9.8
Lauren Jackson, Seattle	34	313	9.2
Tamika Catchings, Indiana	34	264	7.8
Lisa Leslie, Los Angeles	34	248	7.3
Taj McWilliams-Franklin, Connecticut	34	248	7.3

ASSISTS PER GAME

	Gm	Ast	APG
Sue Bird, Seattle	30	176	5.9
Temeka Johnson, Washington	34	177	5.2
Lindsay Whalen, Connecticut	34	172	5.1
Shannon Johnson, San Antonio	34	158	4.6
Diana Taurasi, Phoenix	33	150	4.5

BLOCKS PER GAME

	Gm	Blk	BPG
Margo Dydek, Connecticut	31	71	2.29
Vanessa Hayden, Minnesota	31	68	2.19
Lisa Leslie, Los Angeles	34	71	2.09
Lauren Jackson, Seattle	34	67	1.97
Ruth Riley, Detroit	33	46	1.39
Cheryl Ford, Detroit	33	46	1.39
Elena Baranova, New York	33	46	1.39

STEALS PER GAME

	Gm	Stl	SPG
Tamika Catchings, Indiana	34	90	2.65
Sheryl Swoopes, Houston	33	66	2.00
Lisa Leslie, Los Angeles	34	67	1.97
Tully Bevilaqua, Indiana	31	60	1.94
Nykesha Sales, Connecticut	34	61	1.79

FIELD GOAL PERCENTAGE

	FGM	FGA	FG%
Michelle Snow, Houston	152	276	.551
Ann Wauters, New York	151	279	.541
DeMya Walker, Sacramento	125	234	.534
Janell Burse, Seattle	127	243	.523
Wendy Palmer-Daniel, San Antonio	125	242	.517

3-POINT FIELD GOAL PERCENTAGE

	3FGM	3FGA	3FG%
Laurie Koehn, Washington	35	75	.467
Doneeka Hodges, Los Angeles	31	69	.449
Kara Lawson, Sacramento	36	81	.444
Sue Bird, Seattle	45	103	.437
Allison Feaster, Charlotte	37	86	.430

FREE THROW PERCENTAGE

	FTM	FTA	FT%
Becky Hammon, New York	118	131	.901
Janet Arcain, Houston	83	94	.883
Betty Lennox, Seattle	76	87	.874
Tamika Whitmore, Los Angeles	92	106	.868
Penny Taylor, Phoenix	102	118	.864

Sports Personalities

A name in parentheses is the original name or form of name. Localities are places of birth. Dates of birth appear as month/day/year. **Boldface** years in parentheses are dates of (**birth–death**).

Information has been gathered from many sources, including the individuals themselves. However, the almanac cannot guarantee the accuracy of every individual item.

Aaron, Hank (Henry) (baseball); Mobile, Ala., 2/5/34
Abdul-Jabbar, Kareem (Lewis Ferdinand Alcindor, Jr.) (basketball); New York City, 4/16/47
Adu, Freddy (soccer); Tema, Ghana, 6/2/89
Affleck, Francis (auto racing) (**1951–1985**)
Agassi, Andre (tennis); Las Vegas, Nev., 4/29/70
Aikman, Troy (football); West Covina, Calif., 11/21/66
Ali, Muhammad (Cassius Clay) (boxing); Louisville, Ky., 1/18/42
Allen, Dick (Richard Anthony) (baseball); Wampum, Pa., 3/8/42
Allen, George (football) (**1918–1990**)
Allison, Bobby (Robert Arthur) (auto racing); Miami, Fla., 12/3/37
Allison, Davey (auto racing); Hueytown, Ala. (**1961–1993**)
Alston, Walter (baseball); Venice, Ohio (**1911–1984**)
Alworth, Lance (football); Houston, 8/3/40
Ameche, Alan (football); Houston (**1933–1988**)
Anderson, Sparky (George) (baseball); Bridgewater, S.D., 2/22/34
Andretti, Mario (auto racing); Montona, Trieste, Italy, 2/28/40
Anthony, Earl (bowling); Kent, Wash. (**1939–2001**)
Appling, Luke (baseball); High Point, N.C. (**1907–1990**)
Arcaro, Eddie (George Edward) (jockey); Cincinnati (**1916–1997**)
Armstrong, Lance (bicycling); Plano, Tex., Sept. 18, 1971
Ashe, Arthur (tennis); Richmond, Va. (**1943–1993**)
Ashford, Evelyn (track & field); Shreveport, La., 4/15/57
Austin, Tracy (tennis); Palos Verdes, Calif., 12/12/62
Averill, Earl (baseball); Everett, Wash. (**1915–1983**)
Babashoff, Shirley (swimming); Whittier, Calif., 1/31/57
Baer, Max (boxing); Omaha, Neb. (**1909–1959**)
Bailey, Donovan (track); Canada, 12/16/67
Banks, Ernie (baseball); Dallas, 1/31/31
Bannister, Roger (runner); Harrow, England, 3/24/29
Barkley, Charles (basketball); Leeds, Ala., 2/20/63
Barry, Rick (Richard) (basketball); Elizabeth, N.J., 3/28/44
Bauer, Hank (Henry) (baseball); East St. Louis, Ill., 7/31/22
Baugh, Sammy (football); Temple, Tex., 3/17/14
Baylor, Elgin (basketball); Washington, D.C., 9/16/34
Beamon, Bob (long jumper); New York City, 8/29/46
Becker, Boris (tennis); Leiman, W. Germany, 11/22/67

Beckham, David (soccer); Leytonstone, England, 5/2/75
Bee, Clair (basketball); Cleveland, Ohio (**1896–1983**)
Beliveau, Jean (hockey); Three Rivers, Quebec, Canada, 8/31/31
Belle, Albert (baseball); Shreveport, La., 8/25/66
Beman, Deane (golf); Washington, D.C., 4/22/38
Bench, Johnny (Johnny Lee) (baseball); Oklahoma City, 12/7/47
Berg, Patty (Patricia Jane) (golf); Minneapolis, 2/13/18
Berra, Yogi (Lawrence) (baseball); St. Louis, 5/12/25
Biletnikoff, Frederick (football); Erie, Pa., 2/23/43
Bing, Dave (basketball); Washington, D.C., 11/24/43
Bird, Larry (basketball); French Lick, Ind., 12/7/56
Blaik, Earl H. (football); Detroit (**1897–1989**)
Blanda, George Frederick (football); Youngwood, Pa., 9/17/27
Bledsoe, Drew (football); Walla Walla, Wash., 2/14/72
Blue, Vida (baseball); Mansfield, La., 7/28/49
Bodine, Brett (auto racing); Chemung, N.Y., 1/11/59
Bodine, Geoff (auto racing); Chemung, N.Y., 4/18/49
Boggs, Wade (baseball); Omaha, Neb., 6/15/58
Bonds, Barry (baseball); Riverside, Calif., 7/24/64
Borg, Björn (tennis); Stockholm, Sweden, 6/6/56
Boros, Julius (golf); Fairfield, Conn. (**1920–1994**)
Bossy, Mike (hockey); Montreal, 1/22/57
Boston, Ralph (long jumper); Laurel, Miss., 5/9/39
Bourque, Ray (hockey); Montreal, Que., 12/28/60
Bradley, Bill (William Warren) (basketball); Crystal City, Mo., 7/28/43
Bradley, Pat (golf); Westford, Mass., 3/24/51
Bradshaw, Terry (football); Shreveport, La., 9/2/48
Breedlove, Craig (Norman) (speed driving); Los Angeles, 3/23/38
Brett, George (baseball); Glendale, W. Va., 5/15/53
Brock, Louis Clark (baseball); El Dorado, Ark., 6/18/39
Brown, Jim (football); St. Simon Island, Ga., 2/17/36
Brumel, Valeri (high jumper); Tolbuzino, Siberia (**1942–2003**)
Bryant, Paul "Bear" (football); Morro Bottom, Ark. (**1913–1983**)
Bryant, Rosalyn Evette (track); Chicago, 1/7/56
Burton, Michael (swimming); Des Moines, Iowa, 7/3/47
Butkus, Dick (Richard Marvin) (football); Chicago, 12/9/42
Calipari, John (basketball); Moon, Pa., 2/10/59

Campanella, Roy (baseball); Homestead, Pa. **(1921–1993)**
Campbell, Earl (football); Tyler, Tex., 3/29/55
Canseco, Jose (baseball); Havana, Cuba, 7/2/64
Caponi, Donna Maria (golf); Detroit, 1/29/45
Cappelletti, Gino (football); Keewatin, Minn., 3/26/34
Capriati, Jennifer (tennis); New York City, 3/29/76
Carew, Rod (Rodney Cline) (baseball); Gatun, Panama, 10/1/45
Carlos, John (sprinter); New York City, 6/5/45
Carlton, Steven Norman (baseball); Miami, Fla., 12/22/44
Carner, Joanne Gunderson, Mrs. Don (golf); Kirkland, Wash., 3/4/39
Casals, Rosemary (tennis); San Francisco, 9/16/48
Casper, Billy (golf); San Diego, Calif., 6/24/31
Caulkins, Tracy (swimming); Winona, Minn., 1/11/63
Cauthen, Steve (jockey); Covington, Ky., 5/1/60
Chamberlain, Wilt (Wilton) (basketball); Philadelphia **(1936–1999)**
Chandler, A. B. (Happy) (baseball); Louisville, Ky. **(1898–1991)**
Chandler, Spud (baseball); Commerce, Ga. **(1907–1990)**
Chang, Michael (tennis); Hoboken, N.J., 2/22/72
Chapot, Frank (equestrian); Camden, N.J., 2/24/34
Chastain, Brandi (soccer); San Jose, Calif., 7/21/68
Chinaglia, Giorgio (soccer); Carrara, Italy, 1/24/47
Clarke, Bobby (Robert Earle) (hockey); Flin Flon, Manitoba, Canada, 8/13/49
Clemens, Roger (baseball); Dayton, Ohio, 8/4/62
Clemente, Roberto Walker (baseball); Carolina, Puerto Rico **(1934–1972)**
Cobb, Ty (Tyrus Raymond) (baseball); Narrows, Ga. **(1886–1961)**
Cochran, Barbara Ann (skiing); Claremont, N.H., 1/14/51
Cochran, Marilyn (skiing); Burlington, Vt., 2/7/50
Cochran, Robert (skiing); Claremont, N.H., 12/11/51
Coe, Sebastian Newbold (track); London, England, 9/29/56
Coffey, Paul (hockey); Weston, Ont., 6/1/61
Colavito, Rocky (Rocco Domenico) (baseball); New York City, 8/10/33
Coleman, Derrick (basketball); Mobile, Ala., 6/21/67
Comaneci, Nadia (gymnast); Onesti, Romania, 11/12/61
Conigliaro, Tony (baseball); Revere, Mass. **(1945–1990)**
Connors, Jimmy (James Scott) (tennis); East St. Louis, Ill., 9/2/52
Cooper, Cynthia (basketball); Chicago, 4/14/63
Cordero, Angel (jockey); Santurce, Puerto Rico, 5/8/42
Cosell, Howard (broadcaster); Winston-Salem, N.C. **(1918–1995)**
Courier, Jim (tennis); Sanford, Fla., 8/17/70
Cournoyer, Yvan Serge (hockey); Drummondville, Quebec, Canada, 11/22/43
Court, Margaret Smith (tennis); Albury, New South Wales, Australia, 7/16/42
Cousy, Bob (basketball); New York City, 8/9/28
Crabbe, Buster (swimming); Scottsdale, Ariz. **(1908–1983)**
Crenshaw, Ben (golf); Austin, Tex., 1/11/52
Cronin, Joe (baseball executive); San Francisco **(1906–1984)**
Cruyff, Johan (soccer); Amsterdam, Netherlands, 4/25/47
Csonka, Larry (Lawrence Richard) (football); Stow, Ohio, 12/25/46
Dancer, Stanley (harness racing); New Egypt, N.J., 7/25/27
Dark, Alvin (baseball); Comanche, Okla., 1/7/22
Davenport, Willie (track); Troy, Ala. **(1943–2002)**
Dawson, Andre (baseball); Miami, Fla., 7/10/54
Dawson, Leonard Ray (football); Alliance, Ohio, 6/20/35
Dean, Dizzy (Jay Hanna) (baseball); Lucas, Ark. **(1911–1974)**
DeBusschere, Dave (basketball); Detroit **(1940–2003)**
De La Hoya, Oscar (boxing); East Los Angeles, Calif., 2/4/73
Delvecchio, Alex Peter (hockey); Fort William, Ontario, Canada, 12/4/31
Demaret, Jim (golf); Houston **(1910–1983)**
Dempsey, Jack (William H.) (boxing); Manassa, Colo. **(1895–1983)**
De Stéfano, Alfredo (soccer); Buenos Aires, 7/4/26
DeVicenzo, Roberto (golf); Buenos Aires, 4/14/23
Dibbs, Edward George (tennis); Brooklyn, New York, 2/23/51
Dietz, James W. (rowing); New York, N.Y., 1/12/49
DiMaggio, Joe (baseball); Martinez, Calif. **(1914–1999)**
Dionne, Marcel (hockey); Drummondville, Quebec, Canada, 8/3/51
Dorsett, Tony (football); Rochester, Pa., 4/7/54
Dryden, Kenneth (hockey); Hamilton, Ontario, Canada, 8/4/47
Drysdale, Don (baseball); Van Nuys, Calif. **(1936–1993)**
Duran, Roberto (boxing); Panama City, 6/16/51
Durocher, Leo (baseball); West Springfield, Mass. **(1906–1991)**
Durr, Francois (tennis); Algiers, Algeria, 12/25/42
Earnhardt, Dale (auto racing); Concord, N.C. **(1951–2001)**
Earnhardt, Dale, Jr. (auto racing); Concord, N.C., 10/10/74
Eckersley, Dennis (baseball); Oakland, Calif., 10/3/54
Elder, Lee (golf); Dallas, 7/14/34
Elliott, Bill (auto racing); Dawsonville, Ga., 10/8/55
Elway, John (football); Port Angeles, Wash., 6/28/60
Emerson, Roy (tennis); Kingsway, Australia, 11/3/36
Ender, Kornelia (swimming); Plauen, East Germany, 10/25/58
Erving, Julius ("Dr. J") (basketball); Roosevelt, N.Y., 2/22/50
Esposito, Phil (Philip Anthony) (hockey); Sault Ste. Marie, Ontario, Canada, 2/20/42
Evans, Lee (runner); Mandena, Calif., 2/25/47

Evert, Chris (Christine Marie) (tennis); Fort Lauderdale, Fla., 12/21/54
Ewbank, Weeb (football); Richmond, Ind. **(1907–1998)**
Ewing, Patrick (basketball); Kingston, Jamaica, 8/5/62
Favre, Brett (football); Gulfport, Miss., 10/10/69
Feller, Robert (Bob) (baseball); Van Meter, Iowa, 11/3/18
Feuerbach, Allan Dean (track); Preston, Iowa, 1/12/48
Finley, Charles O. (sportsman); Ensley, Ala. **(1918–1996)**
Fischer, Bobby (chess); Chicago, 3/9/43
Fitzsimmons, Bob (Robert Prometheus) (boxing); Cornwall, England **(1862–1917)**
Fleming, Peggy Gale (ice skating); San Jose, Calif., 7/27/48
Ford, Whitey (Edward) (baseball); New York City, 10/21/28
Foreman, George (boxing); Marshall, Tex., 1/10/49
Fosbury, Richard (high jumper); Portland, Ore., 3/6/47
Fox, Nellie (Jacob Nelson) (baseball); St. Thomas, Pa. **(1927–1975)**
Foxx, James Emory (baseball); Sudlersville, Md. **(1907–1967)**
Foyt, A. J. (auto racing); Houston, 1/16/35
Frazier, Joe (boxing); Beaufort, S.C., 1/12/44
Frazier, Walt (basketball); Atlanta, 3/29/45
Freeman, Cathy (track & field); Mackay, Queensland, Australia, 2/16/73
Frick, Ford C. (baseball); Wawaka, Ind. **(1894–1978)**
Furniss, Bruce (swimming); Fresno, Calif., 5/27/57
Gable, Dan (wrestling); Waterloo, Iowa, 10/25/45
Gabriel, Roman (football); Wilmington, N.C., 8/5/40
Gallagher, Michael Donald (skiing); Yonkers, N.Y., 10/3/41
Garvey, Steve (baseball); Tampa, Fla., 12/22/48
Gehrig, Lou (Henry Louis) (baseball); New York City **(1903–1941)**
Gehringer, Charlie (baseball); Fowlerville, Mich. **(1903–1993)**
Geoffrion, "Boom Boom" (Bernie) (hockey); Montreal, Quebec, Canada, 2/14/31
Gerulaitis, Vitas (tennis); Brooklyn, N.Y. **(1954–1994)**
Gervin, George (basketball); Long Beach, Calif., 4/27/52
Giacomin, Ed (hockey); Sudbury, Ontario, Canada, 6/6/39
Giamatti, A. Bartlett (baseball); South Hadley, Mass. **(1938–1989)**
Gibson, Bob (baseball); Omaha, Neb., 11/9/35
Gifford, Frank (football); Santa Monica, Calif., 8/16/30
Gilbert, Rod (Rodrique) (hockey); Montreal, 7/1/41
Gilmore, Artis (basketball); Chipley, Fla., 9/21/49
Glance, Harvey (track); Phenix City, Ala., 3/28/57
Gonzalez, Pancho (tennis); Los Angeles **(1928–1995)**
Goodell, Brian Stuart (swimming); Stockton, Calif., 4/2/59
Gooden, Dwight (baseball); Tampa, Fla., 11/16/64
Goodrich, Gail (basketball); Los Angeles, 4/23/43
Goolagong, Cawley, Evonne (tennis); Griffith, Australia, 7/31/51
Gordon, Jeff (auto racing); Vallejo, Calif., 8/4/71
Gossage, "Goose" (Rich) (baseball); Colorado Springs, Colo., 4/5/51
Graf, Steffi (tennis); Mannheim, W. Germany, 6/14/69
Graham, David (golf); Windson, Australia, 5/23/46
Graham, Otto Everett (football); Waukegan, Ill. **(1921–2003)**
Grange, Red (Harold) (football); Forksville, Pa. **(1904–1991)**
Green, Hubert (golf); Birmingham, Ala., 12/28/46
Greene, Charles E. (sprinter); Pine Bluff, Ark., 3/21/45
Greene, "Mean" (Joe) (football); Temple, Tex., 9/24/46
Gretzky, Wayne (hockey); Brantford, Ont., 1/26/61
Griese, Bob (Robert Allen) (football); Evansville, Ind., 2/3/45
Griffey, Ken, Jr. (baseball); Donora, Pa., 11/21/69
Grove, Lefty (Robert Moses) (baseball); Lonaconing, Md. **(1900–1975)**
Groza, Lou (football); Martins Ferry Ohio **(1924–2000)**
Guidry, Ronald Ames (baseball); Lafayette, La., 8/28/50
Gwynn, Tony (baseball); Los Angeles, Calif., 5/9/60
Halas, George (football); Chicago **(1895–1983)**
Hall, Gary (swimming); Fayetteville, N.C., 8/7/51
Hall, Gary, Jr. (swimming); Cincinnati, Ohio, 9/26/74
Hamill, Dorothy (figure skating); Chicago, 7/26/56
Hamilton, Scott (figure skating); Bowling Green, Ohio, 8/28/58
Hamm, Mia (soccer); Selma, Ala., 3/17/72
Hammond, Kathy (runner); Sacramento, Calif., 11/2/51
Hardaway, Anfernee (basketball); Memphis, Tenn., 7/18/72
Harding, Tonya (figure skating); Portland, Ore., 11/12/70
Harris, Franco (football); Ft. Dix, N.J., 3/7/50
Hartack, William, Jr. (jockey); Colver, Pa., 12/9/32
Hasek, Dominik (hockey); Pardubice, Czechoslavakia, 1/29/65
Haughton, William (harness racing); Gloversville, N.Y. **(1923–1986)**
Havlicek, John (basketball); Martins Ferry, Ohio, 4/8/40
Hayes, Elvin (basketball); Rayville, La., 11/17/45
Hayes, Woody (football); Upper Arlington, Ohio **(1913–1987)**
Heiden, Eric (speed skating); Madison, Wis., 6/14/58
Hencken, John (swimming); Culver City, Calif., 5/29/54
Henderson, Rickey (baseball); Chicago, 12/25/58
Henie, Sonja (ice skater); Oslo **(1912–1969)**
Herman, Floyd Caves (Babe) (baseball); Buffalo, N.Y. **(1903–1987)**
Hernandez, Keith (baseball); San Francisco, 10/20/53
Hershiser, Orel (baseball); Buffalo, N.Y., 9/16/58
Hickcox, Charles (swimming); Phoenix, Ariz., 2/6/47
Hines, James (sprinter); Dumas, Ark., 9/10/46
Hingis, Martina (tennis); Kosice, Slovakia, 9/30/80
Hodges, Gil (baseball); Princeton, Ind. **(1924–1972)**

Hogan, Ben (golf); Dublin, Tex. (1912–1997)
Holmes, Larry (boxing); Cuthert, Ga., 11/3/49
Holyfield, Evander (boxing); Atlanta, Ga., 10/19/62
Hornsby, Rogers (baseball); Winters, Tex. (1896–1963)
Hornung, Paul (football); Louisville, Ky., 12/23/35
Houk, Ralph (baseball); Lawrence, Kans., 8/9/19
Howard, Elston (baseball); St. Louis (1929–1980)
Howe, Gordon (hockey); Floral, Sask., Canada, 3/31/28
Howell, Jim Lee (football); Lonoke, Ark. (1914–1995)
Howser, Dick (baseball); Miami, Fla. (1937–1987)
Hubbell, Carl (baseball); Carthage, Mo. (1903–1988)
Huff, Sam (Robert Lee) (football); Morgantown, W. Va., 10/4/34
Hull, Bobby (hockey); Point Anne, Ontario, Canada, 1/3/39
Hunter, "Catfish" (Jim) (baseball); Hertford, N.C. (1946–1999)
Hutson, Donald (football); Pine Bluff, Ark. (1913–1997)
Irwin, Hale (golf); Joplin, Mo., 6/3/45
Jacobs, Helen Hull (tennis); Globe, Ariz. (1908–1997)
Jackson, Phil (basketball coach); Deer Lodge, Mont., 9/17/45
Jackson, Reggie (baseball); Wyncote, Pa., 5/18/46
Jagr, Jaromir (hockey); Kladno, Czechoslovakia, 2/15/72
James, LeBron (basketball); Akron, Ohio, 12/30/1984
Jeffries, James J. (boxing); Carroll, Ohio (1875–1953)
Jenkins, Ferguson Arthur (baseball); Chatham, Ontario, Canada,
12/13/43
Jenner, (W.) Bruce (track); Mt. Kisco, N.Y., 10/28/49
Jezek, Linda (swimming); Palo Alto, Calif., 3/10/60
Johnson, Anthony (rowing); Washington, D.C., 11/16/40
Johnson, Jack (John Arthur) (boxing); Galveston, Tex. (1876–1946)
Johnson, Jimmy (football); Port Arthur, Tex., 8/14/43
Johnson, "Magic" (Earvin) (basketball); E. Lansing, Mich., 8/14/59
Johnson, Michael (track); Dallas, 8/13/67
Johnson, Rafer (decathlon); Hillsboro, Tex., 8/18/35
Johnson, Randy (baseball); Walnut Creek, Calif., 9/10/63
Johnson, Wilham Julius (Judy) (baseball); Wilmington, Del. (1899–1989)
Jones, Cobi (soccer); Detroit, 6/16/70
Jones, Deacon (David) (football); Eatonville, Fla., 12/9/38
Jones, Marion (track & field); Los Angeles, 10/12/75
Jordan, Michael (basketball); Brooklyn, N.Y., 2/17/63
Joyner, Florence Griffith (sprinter); Mojave Desert, Calif. (1959–1998)
Joyner-Kersee, Jackie (track); East St. Louis, Ill., 3/3/62
Juantorena, Alberto (track); Santiago, Cuba, 12/3/50
Jurgensen, Sonny (football); Wilmington, N.C., 8/23/34
Justice, Dave (baseball); Cincinnati, Ohio, 4/14/66
Kaat, Jim (baseball); Zeeland, Mich., 11/7/38
Kaline, Al (Albert) (baseball); Baltimore, 12/19/34
Keino, Kipchoge (runner); Kapchemoiymo, Kenya, 1/17/40
Kelly, Leroy (football); Philadelphia, 5/20/42
Kelly, Red (Leonard Patrick) (hockey); Simcoe, Ontario, Canada, 7/9/27
Kerrigan, Nancy (figure skating); Woburn, Mass., 10/13/69
Killebrew, Harmon (baseball); Payette, Idaho, 6/29/36
Killy, Jean-Claude (skiing); Saint-Cloud, France, 8/30/43
Kilmer, Bill (William Orland) (football); Topeka, Kans., 9/5/39
King, Billie Jean (Bille Jean Moffitt) (tennis); Long Beach, Calif.,
11/22/43
Kinsella, John (swimming); Oak Park, Ill., 8/26/52
Kluszewski, Ted (baseball); Argo, Ill. (1924–1988)
Kodes, Jan (tennis); Prague, Czechoslovakia, 3/1/46
Kolb, Claudia (swimming); Hayward, Calif., 12/19/49
Korbut, Olga (gymnast); Grodno, Byelorussia, USSR, 5/16/55
Koufax, Sandy (Sanford) (baseball); Brooklyn, N.Y., 12/30/35
Kramer, Jack (tennis); Las Vegas, Nev., 8/1/21
Kramer, Jerry (football); Jordan, Mont., 1/23/36
Krayzelburg, Lenny (swimming); Odessa, Ukraine, 9/28/75
Kuenn, Harvey (baseball); West Allis, Wis. (1930–1988)
Kuhn, Bowie Kent (baseball); Takoma Park, Md., 10/28/26
Kwan, Michelle (figure skating); Torrance, Calif., 7/7/80
Lafleur, Guy Damien (hockey); Thurso, Quebec, Canada, 9/20/51
Laird, Ronald (walker); Louisville, Ky., 5/31/35
Lalas, Alexi (soccer); Birmingham, Mich., 6/1/70
Lamonica, Daryle (football); Fresno, Calif., 7/17/41
Landis, Kenesaw Mountain (1st baseball commissioner); Millville, Ohio
(1866–1944)
Landry, Tom (football); Mission, Tex. (1924–2000)
Landy, John (runner, governor of Victoria); Australia, 4/12/30
Larrieu, Francie (track); Palo Alto, Calif., 11/28/52
La Russa, Tony (baseball); Tampa, Fla., 10/4/44
Lasorda, Tom (baseball); Norristown, Pa., 9/22/27
Laver, Rod (tennis); Rockhampton, Australia, 8/9/38
Layne, Bobby (football); Lubbock, Texas (1926–1986)
Leetch, Brian (hockey); Corpus Christi, Tex., 3/3/68
Lemieux, Mario (hockey); Montreal, Quebec, Canada, 10/5/65
Lendl, Ivan (tennis); Prague, 3/7/60
Leonard, Benny (Benjamin Leiner) (boxing); New York City (1896–1947)
Leonard, Sugar Ray (boxing); Wilmington, N.C., 5/17/56
Lewis, Carl (track); Willingboro, N.J., 7/1/61
Lindros, Eric (hockey); London, Ont., 2/28/73
Lipinski, Tara (figure skating); Philadelphia, 6/10/82

Liquori, Marty (runner); Montclair, N.J., 9/11/49
Little, Lou (football); Leominster, Mass. (1893–1979)
Littler, Gene (golf); La Jolla, Calif., 7/21/30
Lobo, Rebecca (basketball); Southwick, Mass., 10/6/73
Lombardi, Vince (football); Brooklyn, N.Y. (1913–1970)
Longden, Johnny (horse racing); Wakefield, England (1907–2003)
Lopat, Eddie (baseball); New York City (1918–1992)
Lopez, Al (baseball); Tampa, Fla., 8/20/08
Lopez, Nancy (golf); Torrance, Calif., 1/6/57
Louis, Joe (Joe Louis Barrow) (boxing); Lafayette, Ala. (1914–1981)
Lukas, D. Wayne (horse racing); Antigo, Wis., 9/2/35
Lynn, Frederic Michael (baseball); Chicago , 2/3/52
Lynn, Janet (figure skating); Rockford, Ill., 4/6/53
Mack, Connie (Cornelius Alexander McGillicuddy) (baseball executive);
East Brookfield, Mass. (1862–1956)
Mackey, John (football); New York City, 9/24/41
Maddux, Greg (baseball); San Angelo, Texas, 4/14/66
Mahovlich, Frank (Francis William) (hockey); Timmins, Ontario,
Canada, 1/10/38
Mahre, Phil (skiing); White Pass, Wash., 5/10/57
Malone, Karl (basketball); Summerfield, La., 7/24/63
Malone, Moses (basketball); Petersburg, Va., 3/23/55
Mandlikova, Hana (tennis); Prague, Czechoslovakia, 2/62
Mann, Carol (golf); Buffalo, N.Y., 2/3/41
Manning, Madeline (runner); Cleveland, 1/11/48
Mantle, Mickey Charles (baseball); Spavinaw, Okla. (1931–1995)
Maradona, Diego (soccer); Villa Fiorito, Argentina, 10/30/60
Maravich, "Pistol Pete" (Peter) Aliquippa, Pa. (1948–1988)
Marble, Alice (tennis); Palm Springs, Calif. (1913–1990)
Marciano, Rocky (boxing); Brockton, Mass. (1923–1969)
Marichal, Juan (baseball); Laguna Verde, Montecristi, Dominican
Republic, 10/20/37
Marino, Dan (football); Pittsburgh, Pa., 9/15/61
Maris, Roger (baseball); Hibbing, Minn. (1934–1985)
Martin, Billy (Alfred Manuel) (baseball); Berkeley, Calif. (1928–1989)
Martin, Christy (boxing); Mullers, W.Va., 6/12/68
Martin, Rick (Richard Lionel) (hockey); Verdun, Quebec, Canada,
7/26/51
Martinez, Pedro (baseball); Manoguayabo, Dominican Republic,
10/25/71
Mathews, Ed (Edwin) (baseball); Texarkana, Tex. (1931–2001)
Mattingly, Don (baseball); Evansville, Ind., 4/20/61
Matson, Randy (shot putter); Kilgore, Tex., 3/5/45
Mays, Willie (baseball); Westfield, Ala., 5/6/31
McAdoo, Bob (basketball); Greensboro, N.C., 9/25/51
McCarthy, Joe (Joseph Vincent) (baseball); Philadelphia (1887–1978)
McCovey, Willie Lee (baseball); Mobile, Ala., 1/10/38
McDonald, Lanny (hockey); Hanna, Alberta, Canada, 2/16/53
McDowell, Jack (baseball); Van Nuys, Calif., 1/16/66
McEnroe, John Patrick, Jr. (tennis); Wiesbaden, Germany, 2/16/59
McGraw, John Joseph (baseball); Truxton, N.Y. (1873–1934)
McGwire, Mark (baseball); Pomona, Calif., 10/1/63
McLain, Dennis (baseball); Chicago, 3/24/44
McMillan, Kathy Laverne (track); Raeford, N.C., 11/7/57
Merrill, Janice (track); New London, Conn., 6/18/62
Messier, Mark (hockey); Edmonton, Alberta, Canada, 1/18/61
Meyer, Deborah (swimming); Haddonfield, N.J., 8/14/52
Meyers, Ann (basketball); San Diego, Calif., 3/26/55
Middlecoff, Cary (golf); Halls, Tenn. (1921–1998)
Mikita, Stan (hockey); Sokolce, Czechoslovakia, 5/20/40
Milburn, Rodney, Jr. (hurdler); Opelousas, La. (1950–1997)
Miller, Cheryl (basketball); Riverside, Calif., 1/3/64
Miller, Johnny (golf); San Francisco, 4/29/47
Miller, Reggie (basketball); Riverside, Calif., 8/24/65
Montana, Joe (football); New Eagle, Pa., 6/11/56
Montgomery, Jim (swimming); Madison, Wis., 1/24/55
Montgomery, Tim (track); Gaffney, S.C., 1/25/75
Moody, Helen Wills (tennis); Centerville, Calif. (1906–1998)
Moore, Archie (boxing); Benoit, Miss. (1913–1998)
Morgan, Joe Leonard (baseball); Bonham, Tex., 9/19/43
Morrall, Earl (football); Muskegon, Mich., 5/17/34
Morton, Craig L. (football); Flint, Mich., 2/5/43
Mosconi, Willie (pocket billiards); Philadelphia (1913–1993)
Moses, Edwin Corley (track); Dayton, Ohio, 8/31/55
Mungo, Van Lingo (baseball); Pageland, S.C. (1911–1985)
Munson, Thurman (baseball); Akron, Ohio (1947–1979)
Murphy, Calvin (basketball); Norwalk, Conn., 5/9/48
Murray, Eddie (baseball); Los Angeles, 2/24/56
Musial, Stan (baseball); Donora, Pa., 11/21/20
Myers, Linda (archery); York, Pa., 6/19/47
Naber, John (swimming); Evanston, Ill., 1/20/56
Namath, Joe (Joseph William) (football); Beaver Falls, Pa., 5/31/43
Nastase, Ilie (tennis); Bucharest, 7/19/46
Navratilova, Martina (tennis); Prague, 10/18/56
Nehemiah, Renaldo (track); Newark, N.J., 3/24/59
Nelson, Cindy (skiing); Lutsen, Minn., 8/19/55
Newcombe, John (tennis); Sydney, Australia, 5/23/44

Niekro, Phil (baseball); Lansing, Ohio, 4/1/39
Nicklaus, Jack (golf); Columbus, Ohio, 1/21/40
Norman, Gregory (golf); Mount Isa, Australia, 2/10/55
Oerter, Al (discus thrower); New York City, 9/19/36
Olajuwon, Hakeem (basketball); Lagos, Nigeria, 1/21/63
Oldfield, Barney (racing driver); Fulton County, Ohio **(1878–1946)**
Oliva, Tony (Pedro) (baseball); Pinar Del Rio, Cuba, 7/20/40
Olsen, Merlin Jay (football); Logan, Utah, 9/15/40
O'Malley, Walter (baseball executive); New York City **(1903–1979)**
O'Neal, Shaquille (basketball); Newark, N.J., 3/6/72
Orantes, Manuel (tennis); Granada, Spain, 2/6/49
Orr, Bobby (hockey); Parry Sound, Ontario, Canada, 3/20/48
Ovett, Steve (track); Brighton, England, 10/9/55
Owens, Jesse (track); Decatur, Ala. **(1913–1980)**
Paige, Satchel (Leroy) (baseball); Mobile, Ala. **(1906–1982)**
Palmer, Arnold (golf); Latrobe, Pa., 9/10/29
Palmer, James Alvin (baseball); New York City, 10/15/45
Parcells, Bill (football coach); Englewood, N.J., 8/22/41
Parent, Bernard Marcel (hockey); Montreal, Quebec, Canada, 4/3/45
Park, Brad (Douglas Bradford) (hockey); Toronto, Ontario, Canada, 7/6/48
Parseghian, Ara (football); Akron, Ohio, 5/21/23
Pasarell, Charles (tennis); San Juan, Puerto Rico, 2/12/44
Patterson, Floyd (boxing); Waco, N.C., 1/4/35
Peete, Calvin (golf); Detroit, Mich., 7/18/43
Pelé (Edson Arantes do Nascimento) (soccer); Tres Coracoes, Brazil, 10/23/40
Perry, Gaylord (baseball); Williamston, N.C., 9/15/38
Perry, Jim (baseball); Williamston, N.C., 10/30/36
Pettit, Bob (basketball); Baton Rouge, La., 12/12/32
Petty, Richard Lee (auto racing); Randleman, N.C., 7/2/37
Pincay, Laffit, Jr. (jockey); Panama City, Panama, 12/29/46
Pippen, Scottie (basketball); Trenton, N.J., 9/25/65
Plager, Barclay (ice hockey); Kirkland Lake, Ontario, Canada **(1941–1988)**
Plante, Jacques (hockey); Sahwinigan Falls, Quebec, Canada **(1929–1986)**
Player, Gary (golf); Johannesburg, South Africa, 11/1/35
Plunkett, Jim (football); San Jose, Calif., 12/5/47
Potvin, Denis Charles (hockey); Hull, Quebec, Canada, 10/29/53
Powell, Asafa (track); Linstead, Jamaica, 11/11/82
Powell, Boog (John) (baseball); Lakeland, Fla., 8/17/41
Powell, Mike (track); Philadelphia, 11/10/63
Prefontaine, Steve Roland (runner); Coos Bay, Ore. **(1951–1975)**
Prince, Bob (baseball announcer); Pittsburgh **(1917–1985)**
Proell, Annemarie Moser (Alpine skier); Kleinarl, Austria, 3/27/53
Rafter, Patrick (tennis); Brisbane, Australia, 12/28/72
Ralston, Dennis (tennis); Bakersfield, Calif., 7/27/42
Rankin, Judy Torluemke (golf); St. Louis, Mo., 2/18/45
Raschi, Vic (baseball); West Springfield, Mass. **(1919–1988)**
Ratelle, Jean (Joseph Gilbert Yvon Jean) (hockey); St. Jean, Quebec, Canada, 10/29/53
Rawls, Betsy (Elizabeth Earle) (golf); Spartanburg, S.C., 5/4/28
Reed, Willis (basketball); Hico, La., 6/25/42
Reese, Pee Wee (Harold) (baseball); Ekron, Ky. **(1919–1999)**
Resch, Glenn "Chico" (hockey); Moose Jaw, Saskatchewan, Canada, 7/10/48
Rice, Jerry (football); Crawford, Miss., 10/13/62
Richard, Maurice (hockey); Montreal **(1921–2000)**
Riessen, Martin (tennis); Hinsdale, Ill., 12/4/41
Rigney, William (baseball); Alameda, Calif. **(1918–2001)**
Rios, Marcelo (tennis); Santiago, Chile, 12/26/75
Ripken, Cal, Jr. (baseball); Havre de Grace, Md., 8/24/60
Rizzuto, Phil (baseball); New York City, 9/25/18
Robertson, Oscar (basketball); Charlotte, Tenn., 11/24/38
Robinson, Arnie (track); San Diego, 4/7/48
Robinson, Brooks (baseball); Little Rock, Ark., 5/18/37
Robinson, David (basketball); Key West, Fla., 8/6/65
Robinson, Frank (baseball); Beaumont, Tex., 8/31/35
Robinson, Jackie (baseball); Cairo, Ga. **(1919–1972)**
Robinson, Larry Clark (hockey); Marvelville, Ontario, Canada, 6/2/51
Robinson, "Sugar" Ray (boxing); Detroit **(1921–1989)**
Rockne, Knute Kenneth (football); Voss, Norway **(1888–1931)**
Rockwell, Martha (skiing); Providence, R.I., 4/26/44
Rodman, Dennis (basketball); Trenton, N.J., 5/13/61
Ronaldo (soccer); Bento Ribeiro, Brazil, 9/22/76
Rono, Henry (track); Kiptaragon, Kenya, 2/12/52
Rooney, Art (football); Pittsburgh, Pa. **(1901–1988)**
Rose, Pete (Peter Edward) (baseball); Cincinnati, 4/14/41
Rosenbloom, Maxie (boxing); New York City **(1904–1976)**
Rosewall, Ken (tennis); Sydney, Australia, 11/2/34
Rote, Kyle (football); San Antonio **(1928–2002)**
Roush, Edd (baseball); Oakland City, Ind. **(1893–1988)**
Rozelle, Pete (Alvin Ray) (commissioner of National Football League); South Gate, Calif. **(1926–1996)**
Rudolph, Wilma Glodean (sprinter); St. Bethlehem, Tenn. **(1940–1994)**
Russell, Bill (basketball); Monroe, La., 2/12/34

Ruth, Babe (George Herman Ruth) (baseball); Baltimore **(1895–1948)**
Rutherford, Johnny (auto racing); Fort Worth, 3/12/38
Ryan, Nolan (Lynn Nolan, Jr.) (baseball); Refugio, Tex., 1/31/47
Ryon, Luann (archery); Long Beach, Calif., 1/13/53
Ryun, Jim (runner); Wichita, Kan., 4/29/47
Salazar, Alberto (track); Havana, 8/7/58
Sampras, Pete (tennis); Washington, D.C., 8/12/71
Samuels, Howard (horse racing soccer); New York City **(1920–1984)**
Sanders, Barry (football); Wichita, Kan., 7/16/68
Sanders, Deion (baseball/football); Ft. Myers, Fla., 8/9/67
Santana, Manuel (Manuel Santana Martinez) (tennis); Chamartin, Spain, 5/10/38
Sayers, Gale (football); Wichita, Kan., 5/30/43
Schmidt, Mike (baseball); Dayton, Ohio, 9/27/49
Schoendienst, Red (Albert) (baseball); Germantown, Ill., 2/2/23
Schollander, Donald (swimming); Charlotte, N.C., 4/30/46
Scurry, Briana (soccer); Minneapolis, Minn., 9/7/71
Seagren, Bob (Robert Lloyd) (pole vaulter); Pomona, Calif., 10/17/46
Seau, Junior (football); Oceanside, Calif., 1/19/69
Seaver, Tom (baseball); Fresno, Calif., 11/17/44
Seidler, Maren (track); Brooklyn, N.Y., 6/11/51
Seles, Monica (tennis); Novi Sad, Yugoslavia, 12/2/73
Selke, Frank (ice hockey); Canada **(1893–1985)**
Sewell, Joe (baseball); Titus, Ala. **(1898–1990)**
Shepherd, Lee (auto racing) **(1945–1985)**
Shero, Fred (hockey); Camden, N.J. **(1925–1990)**
Shoemaker, Willie (jockey); Fabens, Tex. **(1931–2003)**
Shore, Eddie (ice hockey); Saskatchewan, Canada **(1902–1985)**
Shorter, Frank (runner); Munich, Germany, 10/31/47
Shriver, Pam (tennis); Baltimore, 7/4/62
Shula, Don (Donald Francis) (football); Grand River, Ohio, 1/4/30
Silvester, Jay (discus thrower); Tremonton, Utah, 2/27/37
Simpson, O.J. (Orenthal James) (football); San Francisco, 7/9/47
Sims, Billy (football); St. Louis, 9/18/55
Smith, Bubba (Charles Aaron) (football); Orange, Tex., 2/28/45
Smith, Emmitt (football); Pensacola, Fla., 5/15/69
Smith, Ozzie (baseball); Mobile, Ala., 12/26/54
Smith, Ronnie Ray (sprinter); Los Angeles, 3/28/49
Smith, Stanley Roger (tennis); Pasadena, Calif., 12/14/46
Smith, Tommie (sprinter); Clarksville, Tex., 6/5/44
Smoke, Marcia Jones (canoeing); Oklahoma City, 7/18/41
Snead, Sam (golf); Hot Springs, Va. **(1912–2002)**
Sneva, Tom (auto racing); Spokane, Wash., 6/1/48
Snider, Duke (Edwin) (baseball); Los Angeles, 9/19/26
Solomon, Harold (tennis); Washington, D.C., 9/17/52
Sorenstam, Annika (golf); Stockholm, Sweden, 10/9/70
Sosa, Sammy (Samuel) (baseball); San Pedro de Macoris, Dominican Republic, 11/12/68
Spahn, Warren (baseball); Buffalo, N.Y. **(1921–2003)**
Speaker, Tristram (baseball); Hubbard City, Tex. **(1888–1958)**
Spencer, Brian (ice hockey); Fort St. James, British Columbia **(1949–1988)**
Spinks, Leon (boxing); St. Louis, 7/11/53
Spitz, Mark (swimming); Modesto, Calif., 2/10/50
Stabler, Kenneth (football); Foley, Ala., 12/25/45
Stagg, Amos Alonzo (football); West Orange, N.J. **(1862–1965)**
Stargell, Willie (Wilver Dornell) (baseball); Earlsboro, Okla. **(1941–2001)**
Starr, Bart (football); Montgomery, Ala., 1/9/34
Staub, "Rusty" (Daniel) (baseball); New Orleans, 4/4/44
Staubach, Roger (football); Cincinnati, 2/5/42
Steinkraus, William C. (equestrian); Cleveland, 10/12/25
Stenerud, Jan (football); Fetsund, Norway, 11/26/42
Stengel, Casey (Charles Dillon) (baseball); Kansas City, Mo. **(1891–1975)**
Stenmark, Ingemar (Alpine skier); Tarnaby, Sweden, 3/18/56
Stevens, Scott (hockey); Completon, New Brunswick, 5/4/66
Stockton, Richard LaClede (tennis); New York City, 2/18/51
Stones, Dwight Edwin (track); Los Angeles, 12/6/53
Strawberry, Darryl (baseball); Los Angeles, 3/12/62
Street, Picabo (skiing); Triumph, Idaho, 4/3/71
Sullivan, John Lawrence (boxing); Boston **(1858–1918)**
Summitt, Pat (basketball); Henrietta, Tenn., 6/14/52
Sutton, Don (Donald Howard) (baseball); Clio, Ala., 4/2/45
Swann, Lynn (football); Alcoa, Tenn., 3/7/52
Swoopes, Sheryl (basketball); Brownfield, Tex., 3/25/71
Tanner, Leonard Roscoe III (tennis); Chattanooga, Tenn., 10/15/51
Tarkenton, Fran (francis) (football); Richmond, Va., 2/3/40
Tebbetts, Birdie (George R.) (baseball); Nashua, N.H. **(1914–1999)**
Theismann, Joe (football); New Brunswick, N.J., 9/9/46
Thomas, Frank (baseball); Columbus, Ga., 5/27/68
Thomas, Isiah (basketball); Chicago, Ill., 4/30/61
Thomas, Thurman (football); Houston, 5/16/66
Thompson, David (basketball); Shelby, N.C., 7/13/54
Thorpe, Ian (swimming); Sydney, New South Wales, Australia, 10/13/82
Thorpe, Jim (James Francis) (all-around athlete); nr. Prague, Okla. **(1888–1953)**
Tilden, William Tatem II (tennis); Philadelphia **(1893–1953)**

Tittle, Y. A. (Yelberton Abraham) (football); Marshall, Tex., 10/24/26
Toomey, William (decathlon); Philadelphia, 1/10/39
Trevino, Lee (golf); Dallas, 12/1/39
Trottier, Bryan (hockey); Val Marie, Sask., Canada, 7/17/56
Tunney, Gene (James J.) (boxing); New York City **(1898–1978)**
Tyson, Mike (boxing); Brooklyn, N.Y., 6/30/66
Tyus, Wyomia (runner); Griffin, Ga., 8/29/45
Ueberroth, Peter (baseball); Evanston, Ill., 9/2/37
Unitas, John (football); Pittsburgh **(1933–2002)**
Unser, Al (auto racing); Albuquerque, N.M., 5/29/39
Unser, Bobby (auto racing); Albuquerque, N.M., 2/20/34
Valenzuela, Fernando (baseball); Sonora, Mexico, 11/1/60
Valvano, Jim (basketball); New York City **(1946–1993)**
Van Brocklin, Norm (football); Eagle Butte, S.D. **(1926–1983)**
Vaughn, Mo (baseball); Norwalk, Conn., 12/15/67
Vilas, Guillermo (tennis); Mar del Plata, Argentina, 8/17/52
Viola, Frank (baseball); Hempstead, N.Y., 4/19/60
Viren, Lasse (track); Myrskyla, Finland, 7/22/49
Vitale, Dick (basketball); E. Rutherford, N.J., 6/9/39
Wade, Virginia (tennis); Bournemouth, England, 7/10/45
Wagner, Honus (John Peter Honus) (baseball); Carnegie, Pa. **(1867–1955)**
Waitz, Grete (Andersen) (running); Oslo, Norway, 10/1/53
Walcott, Jersey Joe (Arnold Cream) (boxing); Merchantville, N.J. **(1914–1994)**
Wallace, Rusty (auto racing); St. Louis, Mo., 8/14/56
Walsh, Adam (football); Churchville, Iowa **(1901–1985)**
Walton, Bill (basketball); La Mesa, Calif., 11/5/52
Waltrip, Darrell (auto racing); Owensboro, Ky., 2/5/47
Waterfield, Bob (football); Burbank, Calif **(1921–1983)**
Watson, Martha Rae (track); Long Beach, Calif., 8/19/46
Watson, Tom (golf); Kansas City, Mo., 9/4/49

Weaver, Earl (baseball); St. Louis, 8/14/30
Weiskopf, Tom (golf); Massillon, Ohio, 11/9/42
Weiss, George (baseball executive); New Haven, Conn. **(1895–1972)**
Weissmuller, Johnny (swimmer and actor); Freidorf, Romania **(1904–1984)**
West, Jerry (basketball); Cheylan, W. Va., 5/28/38
White, Reggie (football); Chattanooga, Tenn. **(1961–2004)**
White, Willye B. (long jumper); Money, Miss., 1/1/36
Whitworth, Kathy (golf); Monahans, Tex., 9/27/39
Wie, Michelle (golf); Honolulu, Hawaii, 10/11/89
Wilkens, Mac Maurice (track); Eugene, Ore., 11/15/50
Wilkins, Lennie (basketball) 11/25/37
Wilkinson, Bud (football); Minneapolis **(1916–1994)**
Williams, Dick (baseball); St. Louis, 5/7/29
Williams, Serena (tennis); Saginaw, Mich., 9/26/81
Williams, Ted (baseball); San Diego **(1918–2002)**
Williams, Venus (tennis); Lynnwood, Calif., 6/17/80
Wills, Maury (baseball); Washington, D.C., 10/2/32
Winfield, Dave (baseball); St. Paul, Minn., 10/3/51
Wohlhuter, Richard C. (runner); Geneva, Ill., 12/23/45
Wood, "Smokey Joe" (Joseph) (baseball); Kansas City, Mo. **(1890–1985)**
Woods, Tiger (Eldrick) (golf); Long Beach, Calif., 12/30/75
Wottle, David James (runner); Canton, Ohio, 8/7/50
Wright, Mickey (Mary Kathryn) (golf); San Diego, 2/14/35
Yarborough, Cale (William Caleb) (auto racing); Timmonsville, S.C., 3/27/39
Yastrzemski, Carl (baseball); Southampton, N.Y., 8/22/39
Young, Cy (Denton True) (baseball); Gilmore, Ohio **(1867–1955)**
Young, Sheila (speed skater, bicycle racer); Detroit, 10/14/50
Young, Steve (football); Salt Lake City, Utah, 10/11/61
Zaharias, Babe Didrikson (golf); Port Arthur, Tex. **(1913–1956)**

Sullivan Awards

JAMES E. SULLIVAN MEMORIAL AWARD WINNERS
(Amateur Athlete of the Year Chosen in Amateur Athletic Union Poll)

Year	Winner	Sport	Year	Winner	Sport
1930	Robert Tyre Jones, Jr.	Golf	1968	Debbie Meyer	Swimming
1931	Bernard E. Berlinger	Track and field	1969	Bill Toomey	Decathlon
1932	James A. Bausch	Track and field	1970	John Kinsella	Swimming
1933	Glenn Cunningham	Track and field	1971	Mark Spitz	Swimming
1934	William R. Bonthron	Track and field	1972	Frank Shorter	Marathon
1935	W. Lawson Little, Jr.	Golf	1973	Bill Walton	Basketball
1936	Glenn Morris	Track and field	1974	Rick Wohlhuter	Track and field
1937	J. Donald Budge	Tennis	1975	Tim Shaw	Swimming
1938	Donald R. Lash	Track and field	1976	Bruce Jenner	Track and field
1939	Joseph W. Burk	Rowing	1977	John Naber	Swimming
1940	J. Gregory Rice	Track and field	1978	Tracy Caulkins	Swimming
1941	Leslie MacMitchell	Track and field	1979	Kurt Thomas	Gymnastics
1942	Cornelius Warmerdam	Track and field	1980	Eric Heiden	Speed skating
1943	Gilbert L. Dodds	Track and field	1981	Carl Lewis	Track and field
1944	Ann Curtis	Swimming	1982	Mary Decker Tabb	Track and field
1945	Felix (Doc) Blanchard	Football	1983	Edwin Moses	Track and field
1946	Y. Arnold Tucker	Football	1984	Greg Louganis	Diving
1947	John B. Kelly, Jr.	Rowing	1985	Joan Benoit-Samuelson	Marathon
1948	Robert B. Mathias	Track and field	1986	Jackie Joyner-Kersee	Heptathlon
1949	Richard T. Button	Figure skating	1987	Jim Abbott	Baseball
1950	Fred Wilt	Track and field	1988	Florence Griffith-Joyner	Track and field
1951	Robert E. Richards	Track and field	1989	Janet Evans	Swimming
1952	Horace Ashenfelter	Track and field	1990	John Smith	Wrestling
1953	Sammy Lee	Diving	1991	Mike Powell	Track and field
1954	Malvin Whitfield	Track and field	1992	Bonnie Blair	Speed skating
1955	Harrison Dillard	Track and field	1993	Charles Ward	Football/Basketball
1956	Patricia McCormick	Diving	1994	Dan Jansen	Speed skating
1957	Bobby Jo Morrow	Track and field	1995	Bruce Baumgartner	Wrestling
1958	Glenn Davis	Track and field	1996	Michael Johnson	Track and field
1959	Parry O'Brien	Track and field	1997	Peyton Manning	Football
1960	Rafer Johnson	Track and field	1998	Chamique Holdsclaw	Basketball
1961	Wilma Rudolph Ward	Track and field	1999	Kelly and Coco Miller	Basketball
1962	Jim Beatty	Track and field	2000	Rulon Gardner	Wrestling
1963	John Pennel	Track and field	2001	Michelle Kwan	Figure skating
1964	Don Schollander	Swimming	2002	Sarah Hughes	Figure skating
1965	Bill Bradley	Basketball	2003	Michael Phelps	Swimming
1966	Jim Ryun	Track and field	2004	Paul Hamm	Gymnastics
1967	Randy Matson	Track and field			

Hockey

Ice hockey, by birth and upbringing a Canadian game, is an offshoot of field hockey. Some historians say that the first ice hockey game was played in Montreal in Dec. 1879 between two teams composed almost exclusively of McGill University students, but others assert that earlier hockey games took place in Kingston, Ontario, or Halifax, Nova Scotia. In the Montreal game of 1879, there were fifteen players on a side, who used an assortment of crude sticks to keep the puck in motion. Early rules allowed nine men on a side, but the number was reduced to seven in 1886 and later to six.

The first governing body of the sport was the Amateur Hockey Association of Canada, organized in 1887. In the winter of 1894–1895, a group of college students from the United States visited Canada and saw hockey played. They became enthusiastic about the game and introduced it as a winter sport when they returned home. The first professional league was the International Hockey League, which operated in northern Michigan in 1904–1906.

Until 1910, professionals and amateurs were allowed to play together on "mixed teams," but this arrangement ended with the formation of the first "big league," the National Hockey Association, in eastern Canada in 1910. The Pacific Coast League was organized in 1911 for western Canadian hockey. The league included Seattle and later other American cities. The National Hockey League replaced the National Hockey Association in 1917. Boston, in 1924, was the first American city to join that circuit. The league expanded to include western cities in 1967. The Stanley Cup was competed for by "mixed teams" from 1894 to 1910, thereafter by professionals. It was awarded to the winner of the NHL playoffs from 1926–1967 and now to the league champion. The World Hockey Association was organized in Oct. 1972 and was dissolved after the 1978–1979 season when the NHL absorbed four of the teams.

Hockey, once considered a cold-weather sport, has increased its fan base to the southern and western part of the United States. In 1996, Florida and Colorado battled in the Stanley Cup Finals, the San Jose Sharks sold out all 41 of their home games, and the second team in two years (Winnipeg) migrated from Canada to the Southwest region of the U.S. (Phoenix).

The Nashville Predators joined the league in the 1998–1999 season. The 1999–2000 season introduced the Atlanta Thrashers and the 2000–2001 season saw the new Columbus Blue Jackets and the Minnesota Wild.

The collective agreement between the NHL and the NHL Players Association (NHLPA) expired on Sept. 15, 2004, and a lockout began. A major sticking point was the salary cap the league wanted and the NHLPA was adamantly against. After many bargaining sessions, the 2004–2005 season was finally canceled on Feb. 16, 2005. The NHL and NHLPA finally came to terms on July 22, 2005. Among the points agreed on was a 24% salary rollback on player contracts, renegotiating six-year contracts after the fourth year, upper and lower salary caps, and NHL participation in the Olympics. In an attempt to revitalize the game, new rule changes were also adopted, chief among them the adoption of the shootout, making tied games a thing of the past.

STANLEY CUP WINNERS
Emblematic of World Professional Championship; NHL Championship after 1967

1893 Montreal A.A.A.	1925 Victoria Cougars	1962–64 Toronto Maple Leafs
1894 Montreal A.A.A.	1926 Montreal Maroons	1965–66 Montreal Canadiens
1895 Montreal Victorias	1927 Ottawa Senators	1967 Toronto Maple Leafs
1896 (Feb.) Winnipeg Victorias	1928 N.Y. Rangers	1968–69 Montreal Canadiens
1896 (Dec.) Montreal Victorias	1929 Boston Bruins	1970 Boston Bruins
1897–99 Montreal Victorias	1930–31 Montreal Canadiens	1971 Montreal Canadiens
1899–1900 Montreal Shamrocks	1932 Toronto Maple Leafs	1972 Boston Bruins
1901 Winnipeg Victorias	1933 N.Y. Rangers	1973 Montreal Canadiens
1902 Montreal A.A.A.	1934 Chicago Blackhawks	1974–75 Philadelphia Flyers
1903–05 Ottawa Silver Seven	1935 Montreal Maroons	1976–79 Montreal Canadiens
1906 Montreal Wanderers	1936–37 Detroit Red Wings	1980–83 N.Y. Islanders
1907 (Jan.) Kenora Thistles	1938 Chicago Blackhawks	1984–85 Edmonton Oilers
1907 (March) Montreal Wanderers	1939 Boston Bruins	1986 Montreal Canadiens
1908 Montreal Wanderers	1940 N.Y. Rangers	1987–88 Edmonton Oilers
1909 Ottawa Senators	1941 Boston Bruins	1989 Calgary Flames
1910 Montreal Wanderers	1942 Toronto Maple Leafs	1990 Edmonton Oilers
1911 Ottawa Senators	1943 Detroit Red Wings	1991–92 Pittsburgh Penguins
1912–13 Quebec Bulldogs	1944 Montreal Canadiens	1993 Montreal Canadiens
1914 Toronto Blueshirts	1945 Toronto Maple Leafs	1994 N.Y. Rangers
1915 Vancouver Millionaires	1946 Montreal Canadiens	1995 N.J. Devils
1916 Montreal Canadiens	1947–49 Toronto Maple Leafs	1996 Colorado Avalanche
1917 Seattle Metropolitans	1950 Detroit Red Wings	1997–98 Detroit Red Wings
1918 Toronto Arenas	1951 Toronto Maple Leafs	1999 Dallas Stars
1919 No champion	1952 Detroit Red Wings	2000 N.J. Devils
1920–21 Ottawa Senators	1953 Montreal Canadiens	2001 Colorado Avalanche
1922 Toronto St. Patricks	1954–55 Detroit Red Wings	2002 Detroit Red Wings
1923 Ottawa Senators	1956–60 Montreal Canadiens	2003 N.J. Devils
1924 Montreal Canadiens	1961 Chicago Blackhawks	2004 Tampa Bay Lightning

NHL CHAMPIONS

Wales Trophy

1939–41 Boston	1963 Toronto	1974 Boston	1987 Philadelphia	1998 Washington
1942 New York	1964 Montreal	**Eastern Conference[1]**	1988 Boston	1999 Buffalo
1943 Detroit	1965 Detroit	1975 Buffalo	1989 Montreal	2000–01 New
1944–47 Montreal	1966 Montreal	1976–79 Montreal	1990 Boston	Jersey
1948 Toronto	1967 Chicago	1980 Buffalo	1991–92 Pittsburgh	2002 Carolina
1948–55 Detroit	**Eastern Division**	1981 Montreal	1993 Montreal	2003 New Jersey
1956 Montreal	1968–69 Montreal	1982–84 N.Y.	1994 N.Y. Rangers	2004 Tampa Bay
1957 Detroit	1970 Chicago	Islanders	1995 New Jersey	
1958–62 Montreal	1971–72 Boston	1985 Philadelphia	1996 Florida	
	1973 Montreal	1986 Montreal	1997 Philadelphia	

1. Prior to 1994 was the Wales Conference.

CAMPBELL BOWL

Western Division

1968–70 St. Louis	1980 Philadelphia	1991 Minnesota	1999–2000 Dallas
1971–73 Chicago	1981 N.Y. Islanders	1992 Chicago	2001 Colorado
1974 Philadelphia	1982–85 Edmonton	1993 Los Angeles	2002 Detroit
Western Conference[2]	1986 Calgary	1994 Vancouver	2003 Anaheim
1975–77 Philadelphia	1987–88 Edmonton	1995 Detroit	2004 Calgary
1978–79 N.Y. Islanders	1989 Calgary	1996 Colorado	
	1990 Edmonton	1997–98 Detroit	

2. Prior to 1994 was the Campbell Conference.

NATIONAL HOCKEY LEAGUE YEARLY TROPHY WINNERS

The Hart Trophy—Most Valuable Player

1924 Frank Nighbor, Ottawa
1925 Billy Burch, Hamilton
1926 Nels Stewart, Montreal Maroons
1927 Herb Gardiner, Montreal Canadiens
1928 Howie Morenz, Montreal Canadiens
1929 Roy Worters, N.Y. Americans
1930 Nels Stewart, Montreal Maroons
1931–32 Howie Morenz, Montreal Canadiens
1933 Eddie Shore, Boston
1934 Aurel Joliat, Montreal Canadiens
1935–36 Eddie Shore, Boston
1937 Babe Siebert, Montreal Canadiens
1938 Eddie Shore, Boston
1939 Toe Blake, Montreal Canadiens
1940 Ebbie Goodfellow, Detroit
1941 Bill Cowley, Boston
1942 Tommy Anderson, N.Y. Americans
1943 Bill Cowley, Boston
1944 Babe Pratt, Toronto
1945 Elmer Lach, Montreal Canadiens
1946 Max Bentley, Chicago
1947 Maurice Richard, Montreal Canadiens
1948 Buddy O'Connor, N.Y. Rangers
1949 Sid Abel, Detroit
1950 Chuck Rayner, N.Y. Rangers
1951 Milt Schmidt, Boston
1952–53 Gordie Howe, Detroit
1954 Al Rollins, Chicago
1955 Ted Kennedy, Toronto
1956 Jean Belveau, Montreal Canadiens
1957–58 Gordie Howe, Detroit
1959 Andy Bathgate, N.Y. Rangers
1960 Gordie Howe, Detroit

1961 Bernie Geoffrion, Montreal Canadiens
1962 Jacques Plante, Montreal Canadiens
1963 Gordon Howe, Detroit
1964 Jean Beliveau, Montreal Canadiens
1965–66 Bobby Hull, Chicago
1967–68 Stan Mikita, Chicago
1969 Phil Esposito, Boston
1970–72 Bobby Orr, Boston
1973 Bobby Clarke, Philadelphia
1974 Phil Esposito, Boston
1975–76 Bobby Clarke, Philadelphia
1977–78 Guy Lafleur, Montreal
1979 Bryan Trottier, N.Y. Islanders
1980–87 Wayne Gretzky, Edmonton
1988 Mario Lemieux, Pittsburgh
1989 Wayne Gretzky, Los Angeles
1990 Mark Messier, Edmonton
1991 Brett Hull, St. Louis
1992 Mark Messier, N.Y. Rangers
1993 Mario Lemieux, Pittsburgh
1994 Sergei Fedorov, Detroit
1995 Eric Lindros, Philadelphia
1996 Mario Lemieux, Pittsburgh
1997–98 Dominik Hasek, Buffalo
1999 Jaromir Jagr, Pittsburgh
2000 Chris Pronger, St. Louis
2001 Joe Sakic, Colorado
2002 Jose Theodore, Montreal
2003 Peter Forsberg, Colorado
2004 Martin St. Louis, Tampa Bay

Vezina Trophy—Leading Goalkeeper

1956–60 Jacques Plante, Montreal
1961 Johnny Bower, Toronto
1962 Jacques Plante, Montreal
1963 Glenn Hall, Chicago
1964 Charlie Hodge, Montreal
1965 Terry Sawchuk—Johnny Bower, Toronto

1966 Gump Worsley—Charlie Hodge, Montreal
1967 Glen Hall—Denis Dejordy, Chicago
1968 Gump Worsley—Rogie Vachon, Montreal
1969 Glenn Hall—Jacques Plante, St. Louis
1970 Tony Esposito, Chicago
1971 Ed Giacomin—Gilles Villemure, N.Y. Rangers
1972 Tony Esposito—Gary Smith, Chicago
1973 Ken Dryden, Montreal
1974 Bernie Parent, Philadelphia and Tony Esposito, Chicago
1975 Bernie Parent, Philadelphia
1976 Ken Dryden, Montreal
1977–79 Ken Dryden—Bunny Larocque, Montreal
1980 Bob Sauve—Don Edwards, Buffalo
1981 Richard Sevigny—Denis Herron—Bunny Larocque, Montreal
1982 Billy Smith, N.Y. Islanders
1983 Pete Peeters, Boston
1984 Tom Barrasso, Buffalo
1985 Pelle Lindbergh, Philadelphia
1986 John Vanbiesbrouck, N.Y. Rangers
1987 Ron Hextall, Philadelphia
1988 Grant Fuhr, Edmonton
1989–90 Patrick Roy, Montreal
1991 Ed Belfour, Chicago
1992 Patrick Roy, Montreal
1993 Ed Belfour, Chicago
1994–95 Dominik Hasek, Buffalo
1996 Jim Carey, Washington
1997–99 Dominik Hasek, Buffalo
2000 Olaf Kolzig, Washington
2001 Dominik Hasek, Buffalo
2002 Jose Theodore, Montreal
2003–04 Martin Brodeur, New Jersey

James Norris Trophy—Defenseman

1954   Red Kelly, Detroit
1955–58 Doug Harvey, Montreal
1959   Tom Johnson, Montreal
1960–62 Doug Harvey, Montreal, N.Y. Rangers (62)
1963–65 Pierre Pilote, Chicago
1966   Jacques Laperriere, Montreal
1967   Harry Howell, N.Y. Rangers
1968–75 Bobby Orr, Boston
1976   Denis Potvin, N.Y. Islanders
1977   Larry Robinson, Montreal
1978–79 Denis Potvin, N.Y. Islanders
1980   Larry Robinson, Montreal
1981   Randy Carlyle, Pittsburgh
1982   Doug Wilson, Chicago
1983–84 Rod Langway, Washington
1985–86 Paul Coffey, Edmonton
1987–88 Ray Bourque, Boston
1989   Chris Chelios, Montreal
1990–91 Ray Bourque, Boston
1992   Brian Leetch, N.Y. Rangers
1993   Chris Chelios, Chicago
1994   Ray Bourque, Boston
1995   Paul Coffey, Detroit
1996   Chris Chelios, Chicago
1997   Brian Leetch, N.Y. Rangers
1998   Rob Blake, Los Angeles
1999   Al MacInnis, St. Louis
2000   Chris Pronger, St. Louis
2001–2003 Nicklas Lidstrom, Detroit
2004   Scott Niedermayer, New Jersey

Lady Byng Trophy—Sportsmanship

1960   Don McKenney, Boston
1961   Red Kelly, Toronto
1962–63 Dave Keon, Toronto
1964   Ken Wharram, Chicago
1965   Bobby Hull, Chicago
1966   Alex Delvecchio, Detroit
1967–68 Stan Mikita, Chicago
1969   Alex Delvecchio, Detroit
1970   Phil Goyette, St. Louis
1971   Johnny Bucyk, Boston
1972   Jean Ratelle, N.Y. Rangers
1973   Gilbert Perreault, Buffalo
1974   Johnny Bucyk, Boston
1975   Marcel Dionne, Detroit
1976   Jean Ratelle, N.Y. Rangers, Boston

1977   Marcel Dionne, Los Angeles
1978   Butch Goring, Los Angeles
1979   Bob MacMillan, Atlanta
1980   Wayne Gretzky, Edmonton
1981   Rick Kehoe, Pittsburgh
1982   Rick Middleton, Boston
1983–84 Mike Bossy, N.Y. Islanders
1985   Jari Kurri, Edmonton
1986   Mike Bossy, N.Y. Islanders
1987   Joey Mullen, Calgary
1988   Mats Naslund, Montreal
1989   Joey Mullen, Calgary
1990   Brett Hull, St. Louis
1991–92 Wayne Gretzky, Los Angeles
1993   Pierre Turgeon, N.Y. Islanders
1994   Wayne Gretzky, Los Angeles
1995   Ron Francis, Pittsburgh
1996–97 Paul Kariya, Anaheim
1998   Ron Francis, Pittsburgh
1999   Wayne Gretzky, N.Y. Rangers
2000   Pavol Demitra, St. Louis
2001   Joe Sakic, Colorado
2002   Ron Francis, Carolina
2003   Alexander Mogilny, Toronto
2004   Brad Richards, Tampa Bay

Calder Trophy—Rookie

1962   Bobby Rousseau, Montreal
1963   Kent Douglas, Toronto
1964   Jacques Laperriere, Montreal
1965   Roger Crozier, Detroit
1966   Brit Selby, Toronto
1967   Bobby Orr, Boston
1968   Derek Sanderson, Boston
1969   Danny Grant, Minnesota
1970   Tony Esposito, Chicago
1971   Gilbert Perreault, Buffalo
1972   Ken Dryden, Montreal
1973   Steve Vickers, N.Y. Rangers
1974   Denis Potvin, N.Y. Islanders
1975   Eric Vail, Atlanta
1976   Bryan Trottier, N.Y. Islanders
1977   Willi Plett, Atlanta
1978   Mike Bossy, N.Y. Islanders
1979   Bobby Smith, Minnesota
1980   Ray Bourque, Boston
1981   Peter Stastny, Quebec
1982   Dale Hawerchuk, Winnipeg
1983   Steve Larmer, Chicago
1984   Tom Barrasso, Buffalo
1985   Mario Lemieux, Pittsburgh
1986   Gary Suter, Calgary

1987   Luc Robitaille, Los Angeles
1988   Joe Nieuwendyk, Calgary
1989   Brian Leetch, N.Y. Rangers
1990   Sergei Makarov, Calgary
1991   Ed Belfour, Chicago
1992   Pavel Bure, Vancouver
1993   Teemu Selanne, Winnipeg
1994   Martin Brodeur, N.J. Devils
1995   Peter Forsberg, Quebec
1996   Daniel Alfredsson, Ottawa
1997   Bryan Berard, N.Y. Islanders
1998   Sergei Samsonov, Boston
1999   Chris Drury, Colorado
2000   Scott Gomez, New Jersey
2001   Evgeni Nabokov, San Jose
2002   Dany Heatley, Atlanta
2003   Barret Jackman, St. Louis
2004   Andrew Raycroft, Boston

Art Ross Trophy—Leading Scorer

1955   Bernie Geoffrion, Montreal
1956   Jean Beliveau, Montreal
1957   Gordie Howe, Detroit
1958–59 Dickie Moore, Montreal
1960   Bobby Hull, Chicago
1961   Bernie Geoffrion, Montreal
1962   Bobby Hull, Chicago
1963   Gordie Howe, Detroit
1964–65 Stan Mikita, Chicago
1966   Bobby Hull, Chicago
1967–68 Stan Mikita, Chicago
1969   Phil Esposito, Boston
1970   Bobby Orr, Boston
1971–74 Phil Esposito, Boston
1975   Bobby Orr, Boston
1976–78 Guy Lafleur, Montreal
1979   Bryan Trottier, N.Y. Islanders
1980   Marcel Dionne, Los Angeles
1981–87 Wayne Gretzky, Edmonton
1988–89 Mario Lemieux, Pittsburgh
1990–91 Wayne Gretzky, Los Angeles
1992–93 Mario Lemieux, Pittsburgh
1994   Wayne Gretzky, Los Angeles
1995   Jaromir Jagr, Pittsburgh
1996–97 Mario Lemieux, Pittsburgh
1998–2001 Jaromir Jagr, Pittsburgh
2002   Jarome Iginla, Calgary
2003   Peter Forsberg, Colorado
2004   Martin St. Louis, Tampa Bay

OTHER NHL AWARDS—2004

Frank Selke Trophy (Top defensive forward)—Kris Draper, Detroit

King Clancy Trophy (Humanitarian community involvement)—Jarome Iginla, Calgary

Jack Adams Award (Coach of the Year)—John Tortorella, Tampa Bay

Bill Masterson Trophy (Perseverance, sportsmanship, and dedication to hockey)—Bryan Berard, Chicago

Maurice Richard Trophy (Goal-scoring leader)—Rick Nash, Columbus; Ilya Kovalchuk, Atlanta; and Jarome Iginla, Calgary

2004 STANLEY CUP CHAMPIONSHIP FINALS

Tampa Bay Lightning defeated Calgary Flames, 4 games to 3.

May 25—Calgary 4, TAMPA BAY 1
May 27—TAMPA BAY 4, Calgary 1
May 29—CALGARY 3, Tampa Bay 0
May 31—Tampa Bay 1, CALGARY 0

June 3—Calgary 3, TAMPA BAY 2 (OT)
June 5—Tampa Bay 3, CALGARY 2 (OT)
June 7—TAMPA BAY 2, Calgary 1

Conn Smythe Trophy for most valuable player in the playoffs: Brad Richards, Tampa Bay

NATIONAL HOCKEY LEAGUE FINAL STANDINGS OF THE CLUBS: 2003–2004

EASTERN CONFERENCE

Atlantic Division

	W	L	T	Pts	GF	GA
Philadelphia Flyers[1]	40	21	15	101	229	186
New Jersey Devils[2]	43	25	12	100	213	164
N.Y. Islanders[2]	38	29	11	91	237	210
N.Y. Rangers	27	40	7	69	206	250
Pittsburgh Penguins	23	47	8	58	190	303

Northeast Division

	W	L	T	Pts	GF	GA
Boston Bruins[1]	41	19	15	104	209	188
Toronto Maple Leafs[2]	45	24	10	103	242	204
Ottawa Senators[2]	43	23	10	102	262	189
Montreal Canadiens[2]	41	30	7	93	208	192
Buffalo Sabres	37	34	7	85	220	221

Southeast Division

	W	L	T	Pts	GF	GA
Tampa Bay Lightning[1]	46	22	8	106	245	192
Atlanta Thrashers	33	37	8	78	214	243
Carolina Hurricanes	28	34	14	76	172	209
Florida Panthers	28	35	15	75	188	221
Washington Capitals	23	46	10	59	186	253

WESTERN CONFERENCE

Central Division

	W	L	T	Pts	GF	GA
Detroit Red Wings[1]	48	21	11	109	255	189
St. Louis Blues[2]	39	30	11	91	191	198
Nashville Predators[2]	38	29	11	91	216	217
Columbus Blue Jackets	25	45	8	62	177	238
Chicago Blackhawks	20	43	11	59	188	259

Northwest Division

	W	L	T	Pts	GF	GA
Vancouver Canucks[1]	43	24	10	101	235	194
Colorado Avalanche[1]	40	22	13	100	236	198
Calgary Flames[1]	42	30	7	94	200	176
Edmonton Oilers	36	29	12	89	221	208
Minnesota Wild	30	29	20	83	188	183

Pacific Division

	W	L	T	Pts	GF	GA
San Jose Sharks[1]	43	21	12	104	219	183
Dallas Stars[2]	41	26	13	97	194	175
Los Angeles Kings	28	29	16	81	205	217
Anaheim Mighty Ducks	29	35	10	76	184	213
Phoenix Coyotes	22	36	18	68	188	245

1. Clinched division. 2. Playoff qualifier.

NHL LEADING SCORERS: 2003–2004

	Gm	G	A	Pts
Martin St. Louis, Tampa Bay	82	38	56	94
Ilya Kovalchuk, Atlanta	81	41	46	87
Joe Sakic, Colorado	81	33	54	87
Markus Naslund, Vancouver	78	35	49	84
Marian Hossa, Ottawa	81	36	46	82

NHL LEADING GOALTENDERS: 2003–2004

(Minimum 26 games played)

	Gm	GAA	W	L	T
Miikka Kiprusoff, Calgary	38	1.69	24	10	4
Dwayne Roloson, Minnesota	48	1.88	19	18	11
Marty Turco, Dallas	73	1.98	37	21	13
Martin Brodeur, New Jersey	75	2.03	38	26	11
Robert Esche, Philadelphia	40	2.04	21	11	7

NHL CAREER SCORING LEADERS

(Through 2003–2004 season)

		Yrs	Gm	G	A	Pts
1.	Wayne Gretzky	20	1,487	894	1,963	2,857
2.	**Mark Messier**	25	1,756	694	1,193	1,887
3.	Gordie Howe	26	1,767	801	1,049	1,850
4.	**Ron Francis**	24	1,731	549	1,249	1,798
5.	Marcel Dionne	18	1,348	731	1,040	1,771
6.	**Steve Yzerman**	21	1,453	678	1,043	1,721
7.	**Mario Lemieux**	16	889	683	1,018	1,701
8.	Phil Esposito	18	1,282	717	873	1,590
9.	Ray Bourque	22	1,612	410	1,169	1,579
10.	Paul Coffey	21	1,409	396	1,135	1,531

Players active during 2003–2004 season in **bold** type.

NHL CAREER GOALTENDING WINS LEADERS

(Through 2003–2004 season)

		Yrs	Gm	W	L	T
1.	Patrick Roy	20	1,029	551	315	131
2.	Terry Sawchuk	21	971	447	330	172
3.	Jacques Plante	18	837	435	247	146
4.	**Ed Belfour**	16	856	435	281	111
5.	Tony Esposito	16	886	423	306	152
6.	Glenn Hall	18	906	407	326	163
7.	Grant Fuhr	19	868	403	295	114
8.	**Martin Brodeur**	12	740	403	217	105
9.	**Curtis Joseph**	15	798	396	289	90
10.	Mike Vernon	19	781	385	273	92

Players active during 2003–2004 season in **bold** type.

College Hockey

2005 FROZEN FOUR—MEN

First Round

Boston College 5, Mercyhurst 4
North Dakota 4, Boston University 0
Cornell 3, Ohio State 2
Minnesota 1, Maine 0 (OT)
Colorado College 6, Colgate 5
Michigan 4, Wisconsin 1
New Hampshire 3, Harvard 2 (OT)
Denver 4, Bemidji State 3 (OT)

Second Round

North Dakota 6, Boston College 3
Minnesota 2, Cornell 1
Colorado College 4, Michigan 3
Denver 4, New Hampshire 2

Semifinals

North Dakota 4, Minnesota 2
Denver 6, Colorado College 2

Final

Denver 4, North Dakota 1

2005 FROZEN FOUR—WOMEN

Regionals
Minnesota 6, Providence 1
Dartmouth 4, Wisconsin 3
Harvard 5, Mercyhurst 4 (3 OT)
St. Lawrence 3, Minnesota–Duluth 2 (OT)

Semifinals
Minnesota 7, Dartmouth 2
Harvard 4, St. Lawrence 1

Final
Minnesota 4, Harvard 3

Bowling

The game of bowling in the United States is an indoor development of the more ancient outdoor game that survives as lawn bowling. The outdoor game is prehistoric in origin and probably goes back to primitive man and round stones that were rolled at some target. It is believed that a game something like nine-pins was popular among the Dutch, Swiss, and Germans as long ago as A.D. 1200. The game was played outdoors with an alley consisting of a single plank 12 to 18 inches wide, along which a ball was rolled toward three rows of three pins each placed at the far end of the alley.

It is supposed that the Dutch settlers of New Amsterdam (New York City), brought their bowling games with them. About a century ago the game of nine-pins was flourishing in the United States but was so corrupted by gambling on matches that it was barred by law in New York and Connecticut. Since the law barred "nine-pins," a tenth pin was added, thus legally making it a new game.

Various organizations were formed to make rules for bowling and supervise competition in the United States, but none was successful until the American Bowling Congress (ABC), organized Sept. 9, 1895, became the ruling body. On Jan. 1, 2005, the ABC joined the Women's International Bowling Congress, Young American Bowling Alliance, and USA Bowling to become the United States Bowling Congress (USBC). In 2000, three former Microsoft executives bought the ailing Professional Bowlers Association for $5 million.

AMERICAN BOWLING CONGRESS CHAMPIONS

Year	Singles	All events	Year	Singles	All events
1959	Ed Lubanski	Ed Lubanski	1984	Bob Antczak and Neal Young	
1960	Paul Kulbaga	Vince Lucci		(tie)	Bob Goike
1961	Lyle Spooner	Luke Karen	1985	Glen Harbison	Barry Asher
1962	Andy Renaldo	Billy Young	1986	Jess Mackey	Ed Marazka
1963	Fred Delello	Bus Owalt	1987	Terry Taylor	Ryan Schafer
1964	Jim Stefanich	Les Zikes, Jr.	1988	Steve Hutkowski	Rick Steelsmith
1965	Ken Roeth	Tom Hathaway	1989	Paul Tetreault	George Hall
1966	Don Chapman	John Wilcox	1990	Bob Hochrein	Mike Neumann
1967	Frank Perry	Gary Lewis	1991	Ed Deines	Tom Howery
1968	Wayne Kowalski	Vince Mazzanti	1992	Bob Youker and Gary	
1969	Greg Campbell	Eddie Jackson		Blatchford (tie)	Mike Tucker
1970	Jake Yoder	Mike Berlin	1993	Dan Bock	Jeff Nimke
1971	Al Cohn	Al Cohn	1994	John Weltzien	Thomas Holt
1972	Bill Pointer	Mac Lowry	1995	Matt Surina	Jeff Kwiatkowski
1973	Ed Thompson	Ron Woolet	1996	Donald Scudder, Jr.	Scott Kurtz
1974	Gene Krause	Bob Hart	1997	John Socha	Jeff Richgels
1975	Jim Setser	Bobby Meadows	1998	John Gaines	Chris Barnes
1976	Mike Putzer	Jim Lindquist	1999	Dan Winter	Thomas A. Jones
1977	Frank Gadaleto	Bud Debenham	2000	Garran Hein	Roy Daniels
1978	Rich Mersek	Chris Cobus	2001	Nicholas Hoagland	D. J. Archer
1979	Rick Peters	Bob Basacchi	2002	Mark Millsap	Stephen A. Hardy
1980	Mike Eaton	Steve Fehr	2003	Ron R. Bahr	Steve P. Kloempken
1981	Rob Vital	Rod Toft	2004	John Janawicz	John Janawicz
1982	Bruce Bohm	Rich Wonders	2005	David Adam	Scott Craddock
1983	Rick Kendrick	Tony Cariello			

PROFESSIONAL BOWLERS ASSOCIATION

PBA World Championship[1]

1960	Don Carter	1972	Johnny Guenther	1987	Randy Pedersen	1998	Pete Weber
1961	Dave Soutar	1973–75	Earl Anthony	1988	Brian Voss	1999	Tim Criss
1962	Carmen Salvino	1976	Paul Colwell	1989	Pete Weber	2000	Norm Duke
1963	Billy Hardwick	1977	Tommy Hudson	1990	Jim Pencak	2001	Walter Ray
1964	Bob Strampe	1978	Warren Nelson	1991	Mike Miller		Williams, Jr.
1965	Dave Davis	1979	Mike Aulby	1992	Eric Forkel	2002	Doug Kent
1966	Wayne Zahn	1980	Johnny Petraglia	1993	Ron Palombi	2003	Walter Ray
1967	Dave Davis	1981–83	Earl Anthony	1994	David Traber		Williams, Jr.
1968	Wayne Zahn	1984	Bob Chamberlain	1995	Scott Alexander	2004	Tom Baker
1969–70	Mike McGrath	1985	Mike Aulby	1996	Butch Soper	2005	Patrick Allen
1971	Mike Lemongello	1986	Tom Crites	1997	Rich Steelsmith		

1. Formerly National Championship Tournament.

BOWLING PROPRIETORS' ASSOCIATION OF AMERICA—MEN

United States Open[1]

1971 Mike Lemongello	1980 Steve Martin	1989 Mike Aulby	1998 Walter Ray
1972 Don Johnson	1981 Marshall Holman	1990 Ron Palumbi, Jr.	Williams, Jr.
1973 Mike McGrath	1982 Dave Husted	1991 Pete Weber	1999 Bob Learn, Jr.
1974 Larry Laub	1983 Gary Dickinson	1992 Robert Lawrence	2000 Robert Smith
1975 Steve Neff	1984 Mark Roth	1993 Del Ballard, Jr.	2001 Mika Koivuniemi
1976 Paul Moser	1985 Marshall Holman	1994 Justin Hromek	2002– Walter Ray
1977 Johnny Petraglia	1986 Steve Cook	1995 Dave Husted	2003[2] Williams, Jr.
1978 Nelson Burton, Jr.	1987 Del Ballard	1996 Dave Husted	2004 Pete Weber
1979 Joe Berardi	1988 Pete Weber	1997 Not held	2005 Chris Barnes

1. Replaced All-Star tournament and is rolled as part of PBA tour. 2. 2002 and 2003 tournaments combined.

WOMEN'S INTERNATIONAL BOWLING CONGRESS CHAMPIONS

Year	Singles	All events	Year	Singles	All events
1959	Mae Bolt	Pat McBride	1985	Polly Schwarzel	Aleta Sill
1960	Marge McDaniels	Judy Roberts	1986	Dana Stewart	Robin Romeo and Maria
1961	Elaine Newton	Evelyn Teal			Lewis (tie)
1962	Martha Hoffman	Flossie Argent	1987	Regi Junak	Leanne Barrette
1963	Dot Wilkinson	Helen Shablis	1988	Michelle Meyer-Welty	Lisa Wagner
1964	Jean Havlish	Jean Havlish	1989	Lorraine Anderson	Nancy Fehn
1965	Doris Rudell	Donna Zimmerman	1990	Dana Miller-Mackie and	Carol Norman
1966	Gloria Bouvia	Kate Helbig		Paula Carter (tie)	
1967	Gloria Paeth	Carol Miller	1991	Debbie Kuhn	Debbie Kuhn
1968	Norma Parks	Susie Reichley	1992	Patty Ann	Mitsuko Tokimoto
1969	Joan Bender	Helen Duval	1993	Karen Collurs and Kari	Bertha Blackshur and
1970	Dorothy Fothergill	Dorothy Fothergill		Murph (tie)	Sharon Davis (tie)
1971	Mary Scruggs	Lorrie Nichols	1994	Vicki Fifield	Wendy Macpherson-
1972	D. D. Jacobson	Mildred Martorella			Papanos
1973	Bobby Buffaloe	Toni Calvery	1995	Beth Owen	Beth Owen
1974	Shirley Garms	Judy C. Soutar	1996	Cindy Berlanga	Lorrie Nichols
1975	Barbara Leicht	Virginia Norton	1997	Jean Schmidt	Kendra Cameron
1976	Bev Shonk	Betty Morris	1998	Nellie Glandon	Liz Johnson
1977	Akiko Yamaga	Akiko Yamaga	1999	Maggie Matheson	Marlene Walls
1978	Mae Bolt	Annese Kelly	2000	Cathy Krasner	Carolyn Dorin-Ballard
1979	Betty Morris	Betty Morris	2001	Lisa Wagner	Jonquay Armon
1980	Betty Morris	Cheryl Robinson	2002	Theresa Smith	Cara Honeychurch
1981	Virginia Norton	Virginia Norton	2003	Michelle Feldman	Michelle Feldman
1982	Gracie Freeman	Aleta Rzepecki	2004	Sharon Smith	Kim Adler
1983	Aleta Rzepecki	Virginia Norton	2005	Leanne Barrette	Leanne Barrette
1984	Freida Gates	Shinobu Saitoh			

WIBC QUEENS TOURNAMENT CHAMPIONS

1961 Janet Harman	1973 Dorothy Fothergill	1985 Aleta Sill	1997 Sandra-Jo Shiery-
1962 Dorothy Wilkinson	1974 Judy Soutar	1986 Cora Fiebig	Odom
1963 Irene Monterosso	1975 Cindy Powell	1987 Cathy Almeida	1998 Lynda Norry
1964 D.D. Jacobson	1976 Pamela Buckner	1988 Wendy Macpherson	1999 Leanne Barrette
1965 Betty Kuczynski	1977 Dana Stewart	1989 Carol Gianotti	2000 Wendy Macpherson
1966 Judy Lee	1978 Loa Boxberger	1990 Patty Ann	2001 Carolyn Dorin-Ballard
1967 Mildred Martorella	1979 Donna Adamek	1991 Dede Davidson	2002 Kim Terrell
1968 Phyllis Massey	1980 Donna Adamek	1992 Cindy Coburn-Carroll	2003 Wendy Macpherson
1969 Ann Feigel	1981 Katsuko Sugimoto	1993 Jan Schmidt	2004 Marianne DiRupo
1970 Mildred Martorella	1982 Katsuko Sugimoto	1994 Anne Marie Duggan	2005 Tennelle Milligan
1971 Mildred Martorella	1983 Aleta Rzepecki	1995 Sandy Postma	
1972 Dorothy Fothergill	1984 Kazue Inahashi	1996 Lisa Wagner	

OTHER PBA TOURNAMENTS, 2005

Geico Open—Mika Koivuniemi 200, Parker Bohn III 196
El Paso Classic—Parker Bohn III 288, Robert Smith 235
Dallas Open—Patrick Allen 267, Brad Angelo 183
Birmingham Open—Patrick Allen 218, Mike DeVaney 216
Atlanta Classic—Norm Duke 246, Ryan Shafer 226
Jackson Hewitt Tax Service Open—Amleto Monacelli 215, David Traber 195

Cambridge Credit Classic—Tommy Jones 266, Tony Reyes 217
Baby Ruth Real Deal Classic—Mika Koivuniemi 267, Jim Pratt 226
Banquet Open—Tommy Jones 219, Liz Johnson 192
Dexter Tournament of Champions—Steve Jaros 248, Norm Duke 242

OTHER USBC CHAMPIONS, 2005

Collegiate Singles—Men: P. J. Haggerty, Fresno State; Women: Kelly Zapf, Kansas

Intercollegiate Bowling Championships—Men: Lindenwood; Women: Wichita State

Storm National Mixed Team Challenge—Two Balls and Three Bags, Oswego, Ill.

ABC/WIBC Senior Championships:

Division A (70 yrs +)—Men: Bob Webb, Burnsville, N.C.; Women: Frances Johnson, Waterford, Mich.

Division B (ages 65–69)—Men: Dick Taylor, Downey, Calif; Women: Shirley Jones, Greeley, Colo.

Division C (ages 60–64)—Men: Harry Velez, Athol, Idaho; Women: Rozina Smith, Winnipeg, Manitoba

Division D (ages 55–59)—Men: Rye Young, Lakewood, Colo.; Women: Libby Hall, Joliet, Ill.

Pepsi Youth Championship, Div. I—Boys: Ryan Appel, Saskatoon, Saskatchewan; Girls: Tammy Vaneski, McDonald, Pa.

Junior Gold Bowling National Championships—Men: Chris Bolosan, Newport News, Va.; Women: Stefanie Nation, Miami, Fla.

WIBC Senior Queens—Shirley Levens, Titusville, Fla.

ABC Senior Masters—Vince Mazzanti, Jr., Levittown, Pa.

Skiing

HISTORY OF SKIING IN THE UNITED STATES

The Norwegians, Swedes, Lapps, and other inhabitants of northern lands used skis for many centuries before skiing became a sport. Emigrants from these countries brought skis to the United States with them. The first skier of record in the United States was a mailman by the name of "Snowshoe" Thompson, born and raised in Telemarken, Norway, who came to the United States and, beginning in 1850, used skis through 20 successive winters in carrying mail from northern California to Carson Valley, Idaho.

Ski clubs sprang up over 100 years ago where there were Norwegian and Swedish settlers in Wisconsin and Minnesota, and ski contests were held in that territory in 1886. On Feb. 21, 1904, at Ishpenning, Mich., a small group of skiers organized the National Ski Association. In 1961 it was renamed the United States Ski Association. In the 1990s it became the United States Ski and Snowboard Association and included freestyle and disabled skiing.

ALPINE SKIING

2005 Orowheat U.S. Alpine Championships
(April 1–April 5, 2005, Mammoth Mountain, Calif.)

Men

Downhill—1. Steve Nyman, Orem, Utah; 2. J. J. Johnson, Park City, Utah; 3. John Kucera, Canada

Super G—1. Daron Rahlves, Sugar Bowl, Calif.; 2. John Kucera, Canada; 3. Bode Miller, Franconia, N.H.

Slalom—1. Ted Ligety, Park City, Utah; 2. Jimmy Cochran, Keene, N.H.; 3. Brad Spence, Canada

Giant Slalom—1. Erik Schlopy, Park City, Utah; 2. Dane Spencer, Boise, Idaho; 3. Evan Weiss, Seattle, Wash.

Combined—1. Ted Ligety, Park City, Utah; 2. Steve Nyman, Orem, Utah; 3. Jimmy Cochran, Keene, N.H.

Women

Downhill—1. Jonna Mendes, Heavenly, Calif.; 2. (tie) Caroline Lalive, Steamboat Springs, Colo., and Julia Mancuso, Olympic Valley, Calif.

Super G—1. Bryna McCarty, Concord, Vt.; 2. Julia Mancuso, Olympic Valley, Calif.; 3. Allison Forsyth, Canada

Slalom—1. Sarah Schleper, Vail, Colo.; 2. Kristina Koznick, Eagan, Minn.; 3. Julia Mancuso, Olympic Valley, Calif.

Giant Slalom—1. Julia Mancuso, Olympic Valley, Calif.; 2. Allison Forsyth, Canada; 3. Kristina Koznick, Eagan, Minn.

Combined —1. Julia Mancuso, Olympic Valley, Calif.; 2. Chelsea Marshall, Pittsfield, Vt.; 3. Courtney Hammond, Mercer Island, Wash.

2005 Alpine World Cup Champions

Men	Pts	Women	Pts
Overall—Bode Miller, United States	1,648	Overall—Anja Paerson, Sweden	1,359
Downhill—Michael Walchhofer, Austria	681	Downhill—Renate Goetschl, Austria	567
Slalom—Benjamin Raich, Austria	552	Slalom—Tanja Poutiainen, Finland	570
Giant Slalom—Benjamin Raich, Austria	423	Giant Slalom—Tanja Poutiainen, Finland	461
Super G—Bode Miller, United States	470	Super G—Michaela Dorfmeister, Austria	493
Combined—Benjamin Raich, Austria	100	Combined—Janica Kostelic, Croatia	100

2005 The Hartford U.S. Disabled Alpine Championships
(March 24–27, 2005, Vail, Colo.)

Skiers are placed in categories appropriate to their disability. There are 3 blind classes, 11 standing classes, and 5 sitting classes. When several classes combine in competition, a factor system is used to calculate results.

Men

Downhill—**Blind:** Andy Parr. **Sitting:** Christopher Devlin-Young. **Standing:** James Lagerstrom.

Super G—**Blind:** Andy Parr. **Sitting:** Christopher Devlin-Young. **Standing:** Clay Timothy Fox.

Giant Slalom—**Blind:** Andy Parr. **Sitting:** Tyler Walker. **Standing:** Clay Timothy Fox.

Slalom—**Sitting:** Christopher Devlin-Young. **Standing:** Monte Meier.

Women

Downhill— **Sitting:** Laurie Stephens. **Standing:** Allison Jones.

Super G—**Sitting:** Laurie Stephens. **Standing:** Reinhild Möller.

Giant Slalom—**Sitting:** Laurie Stephens. **Standing:** Reinhild Möller.

Slalom—**Sitting:** Stephani Victor. **Standing:** Reinhild Möller.

FREESTYLE SKIING

2005 Freestyle Skiing World Cup Champions
Men
Aerials—Jeret Peterson, United States
Moguls—Jeremy Bloom, United States
Ski-Cross—Tomas Kraus, Czech Republic
Overall—Jeremy Bloom, United States
Women
Aerials—Nina Li, China
Moguls—Jennifer Heil, Canada
Ski-Cross—Ophelie David, France
Overall—Nina Li, China

2005 Sprint U.S. Freestyle Championships
(March 24–26, 2005, Park City, Utah)
Men
Moguls—Nate Roberts, Park City, Utah
Aerials—Ryan St. Onge, Steamboat Springs, Colo.
Dual Moguls—Nate Roberts, Park City, Utah
Women
Moguls—Jillian Vogtli, Ellicotville, N.Y.
Aerials—Lacy Schnoor, Draper, Utah
Dual Moguls—Shelly Robertson, Reno, Nev.

SNOWBOARDING
2005 World Cup Snowboard Champions

Men
Parallel Slalom—Philipp Schoch, Switzerland
Snowboard Cross—Xavier Delerue, France
Halfpipe—Mathieu Crepel, France
Big Air—Jukka Eratuli, Finland

Women
Parallel Slalom—Daniela Meuli, Switzerland
Snowboard Cross—Doresia Krings, Austria
Halfpipe—Mero Narita, Japan

2005 Burton U.S. Snowboard Open
(March 15–20, 2005, Stratton, Vt.)

Men
Slopestyle—Risto Mattila
Halfpipe—Danny Kass
Rail Jam—Eddie Wall

Women
Slopestyle—Janna Meyen
Halfpipe—Gretchen Bleiler
Rail Jam—Leanne Pelosi

NORDIC SKIING/SKI JUMPING/CROSS COUNTRY
2005 U.S. Ski Jumping/Nordic Combined Championships
(March 25–27, 2005, Steamboat Springs, Colo.)

Men
Normal Hill (K90m)—1. Todd Lodwick, Steamboat Springs, Colo.; 2. Clint Jones, Steamboat Springs, Colo.; 3. Tommy Schwall, Steamboat Springs, Colo.
Large Hill (K114m)—1. Todd Lodwick, Steamboat Springs, Colo.; 2. Clint Jones, Steamboat Springs, Colo.; 3. Tommy Schwall, Steamboat Springs, Colo.
Nordic Combined (K114m jumping–7.5k race)—1. Todd Lodwick, Steamboat Springs, Colo.; 2. Jed Hinkley, Andover, N.H.; 3. Bill Demong, Vermontville, N.Y.

Women
Normal Hill (K90m)—1. Jessica Jerome, Park City, Utah; 2. Lindsey Van, Park City, Utah; 3. Alissa Johnson, Park City, Utah
Large Hill (K114m)—1. Lindsey Van, Park City, Utah; 2. Jessica Jerome, Park City, Utah; 3. Alissa Johnson, Park City, Utah

2005 Chevrolet U.S. Cross Country Championships
(Jan. 3–10, 2005, Soldier Hollow, Utah)

Men
30km Freestyle—Andrew Johnson, Greensboro, Vt.
10km Classic—Justin Freeman, Andover, N.H.
10km Freestyle—James Southam, Anchorage, Alaska
Classic Sprints—Torin Koos, Leavenworth, Wash.
Pursuit—Andrew Johnson, Greensboro, Vt.

Women
15km Freestyle—Rebecca Dussault, Gunnison, Colo.
5km Classic—Wendy Wagner, Park City, Utah
5km Freestyle—Rebecca Dussault, Gunnison, Colo.
Classic Sprints—Lindsay Williams, St. Paul, Minn.
Pursuit—Rebecca Dussault, Gunnison, Colo.

Speed Skating

WORLD SPEED SKATING RECORDS (LONG TRACK)

(As of Aug. 16, 2005)

Distance	Time	Skater	Place	Date
Men				
500 m	34.32	Hiroyasu Shimizu, Japan	Salt Lake City	March 10, 2001
1,000 m	1:07.18	Gerard van Velde, Netherlands	Salt Lake City	Feb. 16, 2002
1,500 m	1:43.33	Shani Davis, United States	Salt Lake City	Jan. 9, 2005
3,000 m	3:39.02	Chad Hendrick, United States	Calgary, Canada	March 10, 2005
5,000 m	6:14.66	Jochem Uytdehaage, Netherlands	Salt Lake City	Feb. 9, 2002
10,000 m	12:58.92	Jochem Uytdehaage, Netherlands	Salt Lake City	Feb. 22, 2002
Women				
500 m	37.22	Catriona LeMay Doan, Canada	Calgary, Canada	Dec. 9, 2001
1,000 m	1:13.83	Chris Witty, United States	Salt Lake City	Feb. 17, 2002
1,500 m	1:53.87	Cindy Klassen, Canada	Salt Lake City	Jan. 9, 2005
3,000 m	3:57.70	Claudia Pechstein, Germany	Salt Lake City	Feb. 10, 2002
5,000 m	6:46.91	Claudia Pechstein, Germany	Salt Lake City	Feb. 23, 2002

WORLD SPEED SKATING RECORDS (SHORT TRACK)

(As of April 20, 2005)

Distance	Time	Skater	Place	Date
Men				
500 m	41.184	Jean-Francois Monette, Canada	Calgary, Canada	Oct. 18, 2003
1,000 m	1:24.674	Jiajun Li, China	Bormio, Italy	Feb. 14, 2004
1,500 m	2:10.639	Hyun-Soo Ahn, South Korea	Marquette, Mich.	Oct. 24, 2003
3,000 m	4:32.646	Hyun-Soo Ahn, South Korea	Beijing, China	Dec. 7, 2003
5,000 m relay	6:39.990[1]	Canada	Beijing, China	March 13, 2005
Women				
500 m	43.671	Evgenia Radanova, Bulgaria	Calgary, Canada	Oct. 19, 2001
1,000 m	1:30.483	Chun-Sa Byun, South Korea	Budapest, Hungary	Jan. 12, 2003
1,500 m	2:18.861	Eun-Ju Jung, South Korea	Beijing, China	Jan. 11, 2004
3,000 m	5:02.180	Lee-Kyung Chun, South Korea	Gjövik, Norway	March 19, 1995
3,000 m relay	4:11.742	Republic of Korea	Calgary, Canada	Oct. 19, 2003

1. Awaiting International Skating Union ratification.

WORLD SINGLE DISTANCE SPEED SKATING CHAMPIONSHIPS, 2005

(March 3–6, 2005, Inzell, Germany)

Men	Time	Women	Time
500 m—Joji Kato, Japan	35.45	500 m—Manli Wang, China	38.29
1,000 m—Even Wetten, Norway	1:10.10	1,000 m—Barbara de Loor, Netherlands	1:18.24
1,500 m—Rune Stordal, Norway	1:50.69	1,500 m—Cindy Klassen, Canada	1:58.49
5,000 m—Chad Hedrick, United States	6:25.61	3,000 m—Cindy Klassen, Canada	4:10.37
10,000 m—Bob de Jong, Netherlands	13:25.64	5,000 m—Anni Friesinger, Germany	7:18.32
Team pursuit—Netherlands	3:53.83	Team pursuit—Germany	3:05.81

WORLD SHORT TRACK CHAMPIONSHIPS, 2005

(March 11–13, 2005, Beijing, China)

Men	Time	Women	Time
500 m—Francois-Louis Tremblay, Canada	42.106	500 m—Yang Yang (A), China	45.038
1,000 m—Apolo Anton Ohno, United States	1:30.066	1,000 m—Choi Eun-Kyung, South Korea	1:31.085
1,500 m—Ahn Hyun-Soo, South Korea	2:14.396	1,500 m—Jin Sun-Yu, South Korea	2:20.461
3,000 m—Apolo Anton Ohno, United States	5:13.719	3,000 m—Kang Yun-Mi, South Korea	5:21.039
5,000 m relay—Canada	6:39.990	3,000 m Relay—Canada	4:20.767
Overall—Ahn Hyun-Soo, South Korea	89 pts.	Overall—Jin Sun-Yu, South Korea	76 pts

Figure Skating

WORLD CHAMPIONS

Men

1960	Alain Giletti, France
1961	No competition
1962	Donald Jackson, Canada
1963	Don McPherson, Canada
1964	Manfred Schnelldorfer, West Germany
1965	Alain Calmat, France
1966–68	Emmerich Danzer, Austria
1969–70	Tim Wood, United States
1971–73	Ondrej Nepela, Czechoslovakia
1974	Jan Hoffman, East Germany
1975	Sergei Yolkov, USSR
1976	John Curry, Britain
1977	Vladimir Kovalev, USSR
1978	Charles Tickner, United States
1979	Vladimir Kovalev, USSR
1980	Jan Hoffman, East Germany
1981–84	Scott Hamilton, United States
1985	Alexandr Fadeev, USSR
1986	Brian Boitano, United States
1987	Brian Orser, Canada
1988	Brian Boitano, United States
1989–91	Kurt Browning, Canada
1992	Viktor Petrenko, Unified Team
1993	Kurt Browning, Canada
1994–95	Elvis Stojko, Canada
1996	Todd Eldredge, United States
1997	Elvis Stojko, Canada
1998–2000	Alexei Yagudin, Russia
2001	Evgeni Plushenko, Russia
2002	Alexei Yagudin, Russia
2003–04	Evgeni Plushenko, Russia
2005	Stephane Lambiel, Switzerland

Women

1956–60	Carol Heiss, United States
1961	No competition
1962–64	Sjoukje Dijkstra, Netherlands
1965	Petra Burka, Canada
1966–68	Peggy Fleming, United States
1969–70	Gabriele Seyfert, East Germany
1971–72	Beatrix Schuba, Austria
1973	Karen Magnusson, Canada
1974	Christine Errath, East Germany
1975	Dianne de Leeuw, Netherlands
1976	Dorothy Hamill, United States
1977	Linda Fratianne, United States
1978	Anett Poetzsch, East Germany
1979	Linda Fratianne, United States
1980	Anett Poetzsch, East Germany
1981	Denise Beillmann, Switzerland
1982	Elaine Zayak, United States
1983	Rosalynn Sumners, United States
1984–85	Katarina Witt, East Germany
1986	Debi Thomas, United States

1987–88	Katarina Witt, East Germany	1995	Chen Lu, China	2000–01	Michelle Kwan, United States
1989	Midori Ito, Japan	1996	Michelle Kwan, United States	2002	Irina Slutskaya, Russia
1990	Jill Trenary, United States	1997	Tara Lipinski, United States	2003	Michelle Kwan, United States
1991–92	Kristi Yamaguchi, United States	1998	Michelle Kwan, United States	2004	Shizuka Arakawa, Japan
1993	Oksana Baiul, Ukraine	1999	Maria Butyrskaya, Russia	2005	Irina Slutskaya, Russia
1994	Yuka Sato, Japan				

U.S. CHAMPIONS

Men

1946–52	Richard Button
1953–56	Hayes Jenkins
1957–60	David Jenkins
1961	Bradley Lord
1962	Monty Hoyt
1963	Tommy Liz
1964	Scott Allen
1965	Gary Visconti
1966	Scott Allen
1967	Gary Visconti
1968–70	Tim Wood
1971	John M. Petkevich
1972	Ken Shelley
1973–75	Gordon McKellen
1976	Terry Kubicka
1977–80	Charles Tickner
1981–84	Scott Hamilton
1985–88	Brian Boitano
1989	Christopher Bowman
1990–91	Todd Eldredge
1992	Christopher Bowman
1993–94	Scott Davis
1995	Todd Eldredge
1996	Rudy Galindo
1997–98	Todd Eldredge
1999–2000	Michael Weiss
2001	Timothy Goebel
2002	Todd Eldredge
2003	Michael Weiss
2004–2005	Johnny Weir

Women

1943–48	Gretchen Merrill
1949–50	Yvonne Sherman
1951	Sonya Klopfer
1952–56	Tenley Albright
1957–60	Carol Heiss
1961	Laurence Owen
1962	Barbara Roles Pursley
1963	Lorraine Hanlon
1964–68	Peggy Fleming
1969–73	Janet Lynn
1974–76	Dorothy Hamill
1977–80	Linda Fratianne
1981	Elaine Zayak
1982–84	Rosalynn Sumners
1985	Tiffany Chin
1986	Debi Thomas
1987	Jill Trenary
1988	Debi Thomas
1989–90	Jill Trenary
1991	Tonya Harding
1992	Kristi Yamaguchi
1993	Nancy Kerrigan
1994	Tonya Harding
1995	Nicole Bobek
1996	Michelle Kwan
1997	Tara Lipinski
1998–2005	Michelle Kwan

2005 STATE FARM U.S. CHAMPIONSHIPS
(Jan. 9–16, 2005, Portland, Ore.)

Men's singles
1. Johnny Weir, SC of New York
2. Timothy Goebel, Winterhurst FSC
3. Evan Lysacek, DuPage FSC

Pairs
1. Kathryn Orscher, SC of Hartford and Garrett Lucash, Charter Oak FSC
2. Rena Inoue and John Baldwin, both All Year FSC
3. Marcy Hinzmann, Winterhurst FSC and Aaron Parchem, Detroit SC

Women's singles
1. Michelle Kwan, Los Angeles FSC
2. Sasha Cohen, Orange County FSC
2. Kimberly Meissner, Univ. of Delaware FSC

Dance
1. Tanith Belbin and Benjamin Agosto, both Arctic FSC
2. Melissa Gregory, SC of New York and Denis Petukhov, Skokie Valley SC
3. Lydia Manon, Arctic FSC and Ryan O'Meara, Coyotes SC of Arizona

2005 WORLD CHAMPIONSHIPS
(March 14–20, 2005, Moscow, Russia)

Men's singles
1. Stephane Lambiel, Switzerland
2. Jeffrey Buttle, Canada
3. Evan Lysacek, United States

Women's singles
1. Irina Slutskaya, Russia
2. Sasha Cohen, United States
3. Carolina Kostner, Italy

Pairs
1. Tatiana Totmianina and Maxim Marinin, Russia
2. Maria Petrova and Alexei Tikhonov, Russia
3. Dan Zhang and Hao Zhang, China

Dance
1. Tatiana Navka and Roman Kostomarov, Russia
2. Tanith Belbin and Benjamin Agosto, United States
3. Elena Grushina and Ruslan Goncharov, Ukraine

Swimming

WORLD LONG COURSE RECORDS—MEN

(Through Aug. 8, 2005)

Distance	Record	Holder	Country	Date
Freestyle				
50 m	0:21.64	Alexander Popov	Russia	June 16, 2000
100 m	0:47.84	Pieter van den Hoogenband	Netherlands	Sept. 19, 2000
200 m	1:44.06	Ian Thorpe	Australia	July 25, 2001
400 m	3:40.08	Ian Thorpe	Australia	July 30, 2002
800 m	7:38.65	Grant Hackett	Australia	July 27, 2005
1,500 m	14:34.56	Grant Hackett	Australia	July 29, 2001

Distance	Record	Holder	Country	Date
Backstroke				
50 m	0:24.80	Thomas Rupprath	Germany	July 27, 2003
100 m	0:53.17	Aaron Peirsol	United States	April 2, 2004
200 m	1:54.66	Aaron Peirsol	United States	July 29, 2005
Breaststroke				
50 m	0:27.18	Oleg Lisogor	Ukraine	Aug. 2, 2002
100 m	0:59.30	Brendan Hansen	United States	July 8, 2004
200 m	2:09.04	Brendan Hansen	United States	July 11, 2004
Butterfly				
50 m	0:22.96	Roland Schoeman	South Africa	July 25, 2005
100 m	0:50.40	Ian Crocker	United States	July 30, 2005
200 m	1:53.93	Michael Phelps	United States	July 22, 2003
Individual medley				
200 m	1:55.94	Michael Phelps	United States	Aug. 9, 2003
400 m	4:08.26	Michael Phelps	United States	Aug. 14, 2004
Medley relay				
400 m	3:30.68	Olympic Team	United States	Aug. 21, 2004
Freestyle relay				
400 m	3:13.17	Olympic Team	South Africa	Aug. 15, 2004
800 m	7:04.66	National Team	Australia	July 27, 2001

NOTE: International Swimming Federation (FINA) discontinued acceptance of records in yards in 1968. *Source:* FINA.

WORLD LONG COURSE RECORDS—WOMEN
(Through Aug. 8, 2005)

Distance	Record	Holder	Country	Date
Freestyle				
50 m	0:24.13	Inge de Bruijn	Netherlands	Sept. 22, 2000
100 m	0:53.52	Jodie Henry	Australia	Aug. 18, 2004
200 m	1:56.64	Franziska van Almsick	Germany	Aug. 3, 2002
400 m	4:03.85	Janet Evans	United States	Sept. 22, 1988
800 m	8:16.22	Janet Evans	United States	Aug. 20, 1989
1,500 m	15:52.10	Janet Evans	United States	March 26, 1988
Backstroke				
50 m	0:28.25	Sandra Voelker	Germany	June 17, 2000
100 m	0:59.58	Natalie Coughlin	United States	Aug. 13, 2002
200 m	2:06.62	Kristina Egerszegi	Hungary	Aug. 25, 1991
Breaststroke				
50 m	0:30.45	Jade Edmiston	Australia	July 31, 2005
100 m	1:06.20	Jessica Hardy	United States	July 25, 2005
200 m	2:21.72	Leisel Jones	Australia	July 29, 2005
Butterfly				
50 m	0:25.57	Anna-Karin Kammerling	Sweden	July 30, 2000
100 m	0:56.61	Inge de Bruijn	Netherlands	Sept. 17, 2000
200 m	2:05.61	Otylia Jedrzejczak	Poland	July 28, 2005
Individual medley				
200 m	2:09.72	Yanyan Wu	China	Oct. 17, 1997
400 m	4:33.59	Yana Klochkova	Ukraine	Sept. 16, 2000
Medley relay				
400 m	3:57.32	Olympic Team	Australia	Aug. 21, 2004
Freestyle relay				
400 m	3:35.94	Olympic Team	Australia	Aug. 14, 2004
800 m	7:53.42	Olympic Team	United States	Aug. 18, 2004

NOTE: International Swimming Federation (FINA) discontinued acceptance of records in yards in 1968. *Source:* FINA.

AMERICAN LONG COURSE SWIMMING RECORDS
(Through Aug. 8, 2005)

MEN

Distance	Record	Holder	Date
Freestyle			
50 m	0:21.76	Gary Hall, Jr.	Aug. 15, 2000
100 m	0:48.17	Jason Lezak	July 10, 2004
200 m	1:45.32	Michael Phelps	Aug. 16, 2004
400 m	3:44.11	Klete Keller	Aug. 14, 2004
800 m	7:48.09	Larsen Jensen	July 25, 2003
1,500 m	14:45.29	Larsen Jensen	Aug. 21, 2004
Backstroke			
50 m	0:24.99	Lenny Krayzelburg	Aug. 28, 1999
100 m	0:53.17	Aaron Peirsol	April 2, 2005
200 m	1:54.66	Aaron Peirsol	July 29, 2005

MEN

Distance	Record	Holder	Date
Breaststroke			
50 m	0:27.39	Ed Moses	March 31, 2001
100 m	0:59.30	Brendan Hansen	July 8, 2004
200 m	2:09.04	Brendan Hansen	July 11, 2004
Butterfly			
50 m	0:23.47	Ian Crocker	July 20, 2003
100 m	0:50.40	Ian Crocker	July 30, 2005
200 m	1:53.93	Michael Phelps	July 22, 2003
Individual medley			
200 m	1:55.94	Michael Phelps	Aug. 9, 2003

MEN

Distance	Record	Holder	Date
400 m	4:08.26	Michael Phelps	Aug. 14, 2004

Medley relay

Distance	Record	Holder	Date
400 m	3:30.68	U.S. Olympic Team	Aug. 21, 2004

Freestyle relay

Distance	Record	Holder	Date
400 m	3:13.86	U.S. Olympic Team	Sept. 16, 2000
800 m	7:07.33	U.S. Olympic Team	Aug. 17, 2004

WOMEN

Distance	Record	Holder	Date
Freestyle			
50 m	0:24.63	Dara Torres	Sept. 23, 2000
100 m	0:53.99	Natalie Coughlin	Aug. 29, 2002
200 m	1:57.41	Lindsay Benko	July 24, 2003
400 m	4:03.85	Janet Evans	Sept. 22, 1988
800 m	8:16.22	Janet Evans	Aug. 20, 1989
1,500 m	15:52.10	Janet Evans	March 26, 1988
Backstroke			
50 m	0:28.49	Natalie Coughlin	July 23, 2001
100 m	0:59.58	Natalie Coughlin	Aug. 13, 2002

Source: United States Swim Team, FINA.

WOMEN

Distance	Record	Holder	Date
200 m	2:08.53	Natalie Coughlin	Aug. 16, 2002
Breaststroke			
50 m	0:31.34	Megan Quann	Aug. 11, 2000
100 m	1:06.20	Jessica Hardy	July 25, 2005
200 m	2:22.44	Amanda Beard	July 12, 2004
Butterfly			
50 m	0:26.00	Jenny Thompson	July 26, 2003
100 m	0:57.58	Dara Torres	Aug. 9, 2000
200 m	2:05.88	Misty Hyman	Sept. 20, 2000
Individual medley			
200 m	2:11.24	Katie Hoff	April 1, 2005
400 m	4:34.95	Kaitlin Sandeno	Aug. 14, 2004
Medley relay			
400 m	3:58.30	U.S. Olympic Team	Sept. 23, 2000
Freestyle relay			
400 m	3:36.39	U.S. Olympic Team	Aug. 14, 2004
800 m	7:53.42	U.S. Olympic Team	Aug. 18, 2004

UNITED STATES SUMMER NATIONAL CHAMPIONSHIPS, 2005
(Irvine, Calif., Aug. 3–7, 2005)

Men	Time
50 m freestyle—Ben Wildman-Tobriner	0:22.13
100 m freestyle—Roland Schoeman	0:48.38
200 m freestyle—Michael Phelps	1:46.40
400 m freestyle—Klete Keller	3:46.20
800 m freestyle—Klete Keller	7:56.66
1,500 m freestyle—Charles Peterson	15:19.03
100 m backstroke—Randall Bal	0:54.09
200 m backstroke—Christian DeJong	1:58.25
100 m breaststroke—Matthew Lowe	1:01.64
200 m breaststroke—Matthew Lowe	2:14.40
100 m butterfly—Roland Schoeman	0:53.08
200 m butterfly—Michael Phelps	1:55.26
200 m individual medley—Timothy Liebhold	2:01.75
400 m individual medley—Robert Margalis	4:18.66
400 m medley relay—Tucson Ford Dealers	3:42.23
400 m freestyle relay—Club Wolverine	3:19.38
800 m freestyle relay—Club Wolverine	7:12.35

Women	Time
50 m freestyle—Amanda Weir	0:25.45
100 m freestyle—Amanda Weir	0:54.47
200 m freestyle—Britta Reimer	1:59.73
400 m freestyle—Britta Reimer	4:10.13
800 m freestyle—Kate Ziegler	8:31.11
1,500 m freestyle—Kate Ziegler	16:14.52
100 m backstroke—Helen Silver	1:02.64
100 m breaststroke—Jessica Hardy	1:07.45
200 m breaststroke—Rebecca Soni	2:26.27
100 m butterfly—Elaine Breeden	59.20
200 m butterfly—Elaine Breeden	2:09.85
200 m individual medley—Ariana Kukors	2:14.57
400 m individual medley—Ariana Kukors	4:43.32
400 m medley relay—Palo Alto Stanford	4:10.00
400 m freestyle relay—California Aquatic	3:44.99
800 m freestyle relay—California Aquatic	8:13.29

FINA WORLD CHAMPIONSHIPS, 2005
(Montreal, Canada, July 17–31, 2005)

Men	Time
50 m freestyle—Roland Schoeman, South Africa	0:21.69
100 m freestyle—Filippo Magnini, Italy	0:48.12
200 m freestyle—Michael Phelps, United States	1:45.20
400 m freestyle—Grant Hackett, Australia	3:42.91
800 m freestyle—Grant Hackett, Australia	7:38.65
1,500 m freestyle—Grant Hackett, Australia	14:42.58
50 m backstroke—Aristeidis Grigoriadis, Greece	0:24.95
100 m backstroke—Aaron Peirsol, United States	0:53.62
200 m backstroke—Aaron Peirsol, United States	1:54.66
50 m breaststroke—Mark Warnecke, Germany	0:27.63
100 m breaststroke—Brendan Hansen, United States	0:59.37

Men	Time
200 m breaststroke—Brendan Hansen, United States	2:09.85
50 m butterfly—Roland Schoeman, South Africa	0:22.96
100 m butterfly—Ian Crocker, United States	0:50:40
200 m butterfly—Pawel Korzeniowski, Poland	1:55.02
200 m individual medley—Michael Phelps, United States	1:56.68
400 m individual medley—Laszlo Cseh, Hungary	4:09.63
4×100 m medley relay—United States	3:31.85
4×100 m freestyle relay—United States	3:13.77
4×200 m freestyle relay—United States	7:06.58

Women	Time
50 m freestyle—Lisbeth Lenton, Australia	0:24.59
100 m freestyle—Jodie Henry, Australia	0:54.18
200 m freestyle—Solenne Figues, France	1:58.60
400 m freestyle—Laure Manaudou, France	4:06.44
800 m freestyle—Kate Ziegler, United States	8:25.31
1,500 m freestyle—Kate Ziegler, United States	16:00.41
50 m backstroke—Giaan Rooney, Australia	0:28.63
100 m backstroke—Kirsty Coventry, Zimbabwe	1:00.24
200 m backstroke—Kirsty Coventry, Zimbabwe	2:08.52
50 m breaststroke—Jade Edmistone, Australia	0:30.45
100 m breaststroke—Leisel Jones, Australia	1:06.25
200 m breaststroke—Leisel Jones, Australia	2:21.72
50 m butterfly—Danni Miatke, Australia	0:26.11

Women	Time
100 m butterfly—Jessicah Schipper, Australia	0:57.23
200 m butterfly—Otylia Jedrzejczak, Poland	2:05.61
200 m individual medley—Katie Hoff, United States	2:10.41
400 m individual medley—Katie Hoff, United States	4:36.07
4×100 m medley relay—Australia	3:57.47
4×100 m freestyle relay—Australia	3:37.32
4×200 m freestyle relay—United States	7:53.70

Boxing

Whether it be called pugilism, prize fighting, or boxing, there is no tracing "the Sweet Science" to any definite source. Tales of rivals exchanging blows for fun, fame, or money go back to earliest recorded history and classical legend. There was a mixture of boxing and wrestling called the "pancratium" in the ancient Olympic Games; in such contests rivals belabored one another with hands fortified by heavy leather wrappings that were sometimes studded with metal. More than one Olympic competitor lost his life in this brutal exercise.

There was little law or order in pugilism until Jack Broughton, one of the early champions of England, drew up a set of rules for the game in 1743. Broughton, called "the father of English boxing," also is credited with having invented boxing

gloves. However, these gloves—or "mufflers" as they were called—were used only in teaching "the manly art of self-defense" or in training bouts. All professional championship fights were contested with bare knuckles until 1892, when John L. Sullivan lost the heavyweight championship of the world to James J. Corbett in New Orleans in a bout in which both contestants wore regulation gloves.

The Broughton Rules were superseded by the London Prize Ring Rules of 1838. In 1884 the eighth marquis of Queensberry, with the help of John G. Chambers, put forward the Queensberry Rules, a code that called for gloved contests. Amateurs took to the Queensberry Rules more quickly than the professionals did.

HISTORY OF WORLD HEAVYWEIGHT CHAMPIONSHIP FIGHTS (WBC, WBA, IBF)
(Bouts in which a new champion was crowned)

Date	Where held	Winner, weight (age)	Loser, weight (age)	Rounds
Sept. 7, 1892	New Orleans, La.	James J. Corbett, 178 (26)	John L. Sullivan, 212 (33)	21
March 17, 1897	Carson City, Nev.	Bob Fitzsimmons, 167 (34)	James J. Corbett, 183 (30)	KO 14
June 9, 1899	Coney Island, N.Y.	James J. Jeffries, 206 (24)[1]	Bob Fitzsimmons, 167 (37)	KO 11
July 3, 1905	Reno, Nev.	Marvin Hart 190 (28)	Jack Root 171 (29)	TKO 12
Feb. 23, 1906	Los Angeles	Tommy Burns, 180 (24)[2]	Marvin Hart, 188 (29)	20
Dec. 26, 1908	Sydney, Australia	Jack Johnson, 196 (30)	Tommy Burns, 176 (27)	KO 14
April 5, 1915	Havana, Cuba	Jess Willard, 230 (33)	Jack Johnson, 205½ (37)	KO 26
July 4, 1919	Toledo, Ohio	Jack Dempsey, 187 (24)	Jess Willard, 245 (37)	KO 3
Sept. 23, 1926	Philadelphia	Gene Tunney, 189 (28)[3]	Jack Dempsey, 190 (31)	10
June 12, 1930	New York	Max Schmeling, 188 (24)	Jack Sharkey, 197 (27)	WF 4
June 21, 1932	Long Island City	Jack Sharkey, 205 (29)	Max Schmeling, 188 (26)	15
June 29, 1933	Long Island City	Primo Carnera, 260½ (26)	Jack Sharkey, 201 (30)	KO 6
June 14, 1934	Long Island City	Max Baer, 209½ (25)	Primo Carnera, 263¼ (27)	KO 11
June 13, 1935	Long Island City	Jim Braddock, 193¾ (29)	Max Baer, 209½ (26)	15
June 22, 1937	Chicago	Joe Louis, 197¼ (23)	Jim Braddock, 197 (31)	KO 8
June 22, 1949	Chicago	Ezzard Charles, 181¾ (27)[4]	Joe Walcott, 195½ (35)	15
Sept. 27, 1950	New York	Ezzard Charles, 184½ (29)[5]	Joe Louis, 218 (36)	15
July 18, 1951	Pittsburgh	Joe Walcott, 194 (37)	Ezzard Charles, 182 (30)	KO 7
Sept. 23, 1952	Philadelphia	Rocky Marciano, 184 (29)[6]	Joe Walcott, 196 (38)	KO13
Nov. 30, 1956	Chicago	Floyd Patterson, 182¼ (21)	Archie Moore, 187¾ (42)	KO 5
June 26, 1959	New York	Ingemar Johansson, 196 (26)	Floyd Patterson, 182 (24)	KO 3
June 20, 1960	New York	Floyd Patterson, 190 (25)	Ingemar Johansson, 194¾ (27)	KO 5
Sept. 25, 1962	Chicago	Sonny Liston, 214 (28)	Floyd Patterson, 189 (27)	KO 1
Feb. 25, 1964	Miami Beach, Fla.	Cassius Clay (Muhammad Ali), 210 (22)[7]	Sonny Liston, 218 (30)	KO 7
March 4, 1968	New York	Joe Frazier, 204½ (24)[8]	Buster Mathis, 243½ (23)	KO 11
April 27, 1968	Oakland, Calif.	Jimmy Ellis, 197 (28)[9]	Jerry Quarry, 195 (22)	15
Feb. 16, 1970	New York	Joe Frazier, 205 (26)[10]	Jimmy Ellis, 201 (29)	KO 5
Jan. 22, 1973	Kingston, Jamaica	George Foreman, 217½ (24)	Joe Frazier, 214 (29)	KO 2
Oct. 30, 1974	Kinshasa, Zaire	Muhammad Ali, 216½ (32)	George Foreman, 220 (26)	KO 8
Feb. 15, 1978	Las Vegas, Nev.	Leon Spinks, 197 (25)	Muhammad Ali, 224½ (36)	15
June 9, 1978	Las Vegas, Nev.	Larry Holmes, 212 (28)[11]	Ken Norton, 220 (32)	15
Sept. 15, 1978	New Orleans	Muhammad Ali, 221 (36)[12]	Leon Spinks, 201 (25)	15
Oct. 20, 1979	Pretoria, S. Africa	John Tate, 240 (24)[13]	Gerrie Coetzee, 222 (24)	15
March 31, 1980	Knoxville, Tenn.	Mike Weaver, 207½ (27)	John Tate, 232 (25)	KO 15

Date	Where held	Winner, weight (age)	Loser, weight (age)	Rounds
Dec. 10, 1982	Las Vegas, Nev.	Michael Dokes, 216 (24)	Mike Weaver, 209½ (30)	KO 1
Sept. 23, 1983	Richfield, Ohio	Gerrie Coetzee, 215 (28)	Michael Dokes, 217 (25)	KO 10
March 9, 1984	Las Vegas, Nev.	Tim Witherspoon, 220½ (26)[14]	Greg Page, 239½ (25)	12
Aug. 31, 1984	Las Vegas, Nev.	Pinklon Thomas, 216 (26)	Tim Witherspoon, 217 (26)	12
Nov. 9, 1984	Las Vegas, Nev.	Larry Holmes, 221½ (35)[15]	James Smith, 227 (31)	KO 12
Dec. 1, 1984	Sun City, S. Africa	Greg Page, 236 (25)[16]	Gerry Coetzee, 217 (29)	KO 8
April 29, 1985	Buffalo, N.Y.	Tony Tubbs, 229 (26)[16]	Greg Page, 239½ (26)	15
Sept. 21,1985	Las Vegas, Nev.	Michael Spinks, 200 (29)	Larry Holmes, 221 (35)	15
Jan. 17, 1986	Atlanta, Ga.	Tim Witherspoon, 227 (28)	Tony Tubbs, 229 (27)	15
Nov. 23, 1986	Las Vegas, Nev.	Mike Tyson, 217 (20)[17]	Trevor Berbick, 220 (29)	KO 2
Dec. 12, 1986	New York	James Smith, 230 (33)[16]	Tim Witherspoon, 218 (29)	KO 1
March 7, 1987	Las Vegas, Nev.	Mike Tyson, 217 (20)[16]	James Smith, 230 (33)	12
Feb. 10, 1990	Tokyo	James "Buster" Douglas, 231½ (29)[18]	Mike Tyson, 220 (23)	KO 10
Oct. 25, 1990	Las Vegas, Nev.	Evander Holyfield, 208 (28)	James "Buster" Douglas, 246 (30)	KO 3
Nov. 13, 1992	Las Vegas, Nev.	Riddick Bowe, 235 (25)[19]	Evander Holyfield, 205 (30)	12
Nov. 6, 1993	Las Vegas, Nev.	Evander Holyfield, 217 (30)	Riddick Bowe, 246 (26)	12
April 22, 1994	Las Vegas, Nev.	Michael Moorer, 214 (26)	Evander Holyfield, 214 (31)[20]	12
Sept 24, 1994	London	Oliver McCall, 228 (29)[21]	Lennox Lewis, 238 (28)	2
Nov. 5, 1994	Las Vegas, Nev.	George Foreman, 250 (45)[22]	Michael Moorer, 222 (26)	10
April 8, 1995	Las Vegas, Nev.	Bruce Seldon, 232 (28)[23]	Tony Tucker, 238 (36)	7
Dec.9, 1995	Stuttgart, Ger.	Frans Botha, 227 (28)[24]	Axel Schulz, 222 (27)	12
March 16, 1996	Las Vegas, Nev.	Mike Tyson, 220 (29)[25]	Frank Bruno, 247 (34)	3
June 22, 1996	Dortmund, Ger.	Michael Moorer, 222 (28)	Axel Schulz, 222 (27)	12
Sept. 7, 1996	Las Vegas, Nev.	Mike Tyson, 219 (30)	Bruce Seldon, 229 (29)	1
Nov. 9, 1996	Las Vegas, Nev.	Evander Holyfield, 215 (34)[23]	Mike Tyson, 222 (30)	11
Feb. 7, 1997	Las Vegas, Nev.	Lennox Lewis, 251 (31)[25]	Oliver McCall, 237 (30)	5
Nov. 8, 1997	Las Vegas, Nev.	Evander Holyfield, 214 (35)[26]	Michael Moorer, 223 (30)	8
Nov. 13, 1999	Las Vegas, Nev.	Lennox Lewis, 240 (33)[23, 27]	Evander Holyfield, 217 (36)	12
Aug. 12, 2000	Las Vegas, Nev.	Evander Holyfield, 221 (37)[23]	John Ruiz, 224 (24)	12
March 3, 2001	Las Vegas, Nev.	John Ruiz, 227 (27)[23]	Evander Holyfield, 217 (38)	12
Apr. 21, 2001	South Africa	Hasim Rahman, 237 (28)[25, 26]	Lennox Lewis, 253 (35)	KO 5
Nov. 17, 2001	Las Vegas, Nev.	Lennox Lewis, 246 (36)[25, 26, 28]	Hasim Rahman, 236 (29)	KO 4
Dec. 14, 2002	Atlantic City, N.J.	Chris Byrd, 214 (32)[26]	Evander Holyfield, 220 (40)	12
March 1, 2003	Las Vegas, Nev.	Roy Jones, Jr., 193 (34)[23]	John Ruiz, 226 (31)	12
April 17, 2004	New York	John Ruiz, 240 (32)[23]	Fres Oquendo, 222 (31)	11
April 24, 2004	Los Angeles, Calif.	Vitali Klitschko, 245 (33)[25]	Corrie Sanders, 235 (32)	8
April 30, 2005	New York	James Toney, 233 (37)[29]	John Ruiz, 241 (33)	12

1. Jeffries retired as champion in March 1905. He named Marvin Hart and Jack Root as leading contenders and agreed to referee their fight in Reno, Nev., on July 3, 1905, with the stipulation that he would term the winner the champion. Hart, 190 (28), knocked out Root, 171 (29), in the 12th round. 2. Burns claimed the title after defeating Hart. 3. Tunney retired as champion after defeating Tom Heeney on July 26, 1928. 4. After Louis announced his retirement as champion on March 1, 1949, Charles won recognition from the National Boxing Association as champion by defeating Walcott. 5. Charles gained undisputed recognition as champion by defeating Louis, who came out of retirement. 6. Retired as champion April 27, 1956. 7. The World Boxing Association (WBA) later withdrew its recognition of Clay as champion and declared the winner of a bout between Ernie Terrell and Eddie Machen would gain its version of the title. Terrell, 199 (25), won a 15-round decision from Machen, 192 (32), in Chicago on March 5, 1965. Clay, 212¼ (25) and Terrell, 212½ (27), met in Houston on Feb. 6, 1967, Clay winning a 15-round decision. 8. Winner recognized by N.Y., Mass., Maine, Ill., Tex. and Pa. to fill vacated title when Clay was stripped of championship for failing to accept U.S. induction. 9. Bout was final of eight-man tournament to fill Clay's place and is recognized by World Boxing Association. 10. Bout settled controversy over title. 11. Holmes won World Boxing Council title after WBC had withdrawn recognition of Spinks, March 18, 1978, and awarded its title to Norton. WBC said Spinks had reneged on agreement to fight Norton. 12. Ali regained World Boxing Association championship. 13. Tate won WBA title after Ali retired and left it vacant. 14. Tim Witherspoon and Greg Page fought for the WBC heavyweight title vacated by Larry Holmes, who could not come to agreement on a deal to fight Page, the No. 1 contender. Holmes declared he would fight under the banner of the International Boxing Federation (IBF). Several dates were set and postponed for fights between Holmes and Gerry Coetzee, the WBA champ, the latest being Nov. 16, 1984. 15. First fight under banner of International Boxing Federation. 16. New WBA champion. 17. New WBC champion. 18. New undisputed champion. 19. The WBC stripped Bowe of its version of the title in December 1992 and named Lennox Lewis champion. 20. After the loss, Holyfield retired. 21. New WBC champion. Lennox Lewis had been named champion in 1992 and had won three title defenses before losing to McCall. 22. For combined WBA/IBF titles. Later WBA stripped Foreman of the title for failing to fight no. 1 contender Tony Tucker. IBF also stripped Foreman on June 29, 1995. 23. New WBA champion. 24. IBF title later tested positive for steroids and was stripped of the title. 25. New WBC champion. 26. New IBF champion. 27. Surrendered WBA title to fight Michael Grant in unsanctioned bout. 28. Lewis surrendered his IBF title in 2002. 29. Originally a unanimous decision in Toney's favor, the bout was changed to "no contest" after Toney tested positive for a banned substance. Ruiz retained the title.

OTHER WORLD BOXING TITLEHOLDERS

Light Heavyweight

(Through Aug. 23, 2005)

1903	Jack Root, George Gardner	1939	Melio Bettina
1903–05	Bob Fitzsimmons	1939–41	Billy Conn[2]
1905–12	Philadelphia Jack O'Brien[1]	1941	Anton Christoforidis (NBA)
1912–16	Jack Dillon	1941–48	Gus Lesnevich
1916–20	Battling Levinsky	1948–50	Freddie Mills
1920–22	Georges Carpentier	1950–52	Joey Maxim
1923	Battling Siki	1952–61	Archie Moore[3]
1923–25	Mike McTigue	1961–63	Harold Johnson
1925–26	Paul Berlenbach	1963–65	Willie Pastrano
1926–27	Jack Delaney[2]	1965–66	José Torres
1927	Mike McTigue	1966–67	Dick Tiger
1927–29	Tommy Loughran	1968	Dick Tiger, Bob Foster
1930	Jimmy Slattery	1969–70	Bob Foster
1930–34	Maxie Rosenbloom	1971	Vicente Rondon (WBA), Bob Foster (WBC)
1934–35	Bob Olin	1972–73	Bob Foster (WBA, WBC)
1935–39	John Henry Lewis		

1974	John Conteh (WBA), Bob Foster (WBC)[1, 4]
1975–76	Victor Galindez (WBA), John Conteh (WBC)
1977	Victor Galindez (WBA), John Conteh (WBC),[4] Miguel Cuello (WBC)
1978	Victor Galindez (WBA), Mike Rossman (WBA), Miguel Cuello (WBC), Mate Parlov (WBC), Marvin Johnson (WBC)
1979	Mike Rossman (WBA), Victor Galindez (WBA), Marvin Johnson (WBA), Matthew (Franklin) Saad Muhammad (WBC)

1980	Matthew Saad Muhammad (WBC), Marvin Johnson (WBA), Eddie (Gregory) Mustafa Muhammad (WBA)
1981	Matthew Saad Muhammad (WBC), Eddie Mustafa Muhammad (WBA), Michael Spinks (WBA), Dwight Braxton (WBC)
1982	Dwight Braxton (WBC), Michael Spinks (WBA)
1983	Michael Spinks (undisputed)
1984	Michael Spinks (undisputed)
1985	Michael Spinks (undisputed)[5]
1986	Marvin Johnson (WBA), Dennis Andries (WBC)
1987	Thomas Hearns (WBC), Virgil Hill (WBA), Bobby Czyz (IBF)
1988	Charles Williams (IBF), Virgil Hill (WBA), Donny LaLonde (WBC), Sugar Ray Leonard (WBC)
1989	Dennis Andries (WBC), Virgil Hill (WBA), Charles Williams (IBF), Jeff Harding (WBC)
1990	Virgil Hill (WBA), Charles Williams (IBF), Jeff Harding (WBC), Dennis Andries (WBC)
1991	Virgil Hill (WBA), Thomas Hearns (WBA), Dennis Andries (WBC), Charles Williams (IBF)
1992	Charles Williams (IBF), James Waring (IBF), Jeff Harding (WBC)
1993	Virgil Hill (WBA), Jeff Harding (WBC), Henry Maske (IBF)
1994	Virgil Hill (WBA), Mike McCallum (WBC), Henry Maske (IBF)
1995	Virgil Hill (WBA), Fabio Tiozzo (WBC), Henry Maske (IBF)
1996–97	Virgil Hill (WBA), Fabio Tiozzo (WBC), Henry Maske (IBF)
1998	Roy Jones (WBA, WBC), Reggie Johnson (IBF)
1999–2001	Roy Jones (WBA, WBC, IBF)
2002	Bruno Girard (WBA), Roy Jones (WBC, IBF)
2003	Vacant (WBA), Antonio Tarver (WBC, IBF)
2004	Antonio Tarver (WBC), Fabrice Tiozzo (WBA), Glen Johnson (IBF)
2005	Tomasz Adamek (WBC), Fabrice Tiozzo (WBA), Clinton Woods (IBF)

1. Retired. 2. Abandoned title. 3. NBA withdrew recognition in 1961, New York Commission in 1962; recognized thereafter only by California and Europe. 4. WBC withdrew recognition. 5. Spinks relinquished title in 1985 to fight for heavyweight title.

Middleweight

1867–72	Tom Chandler
1872–81	George Rooke
1881–82	Mike Donovan[1]
1884–91	Jack (Nonpareil) Dempsey

1891–97	Bob Fitzsimmons[2]
1908	Stanley Ketchel, Billy Papke
1908–10	Stanley Ketchel[3]
1913	Frank Klaus
1913–14	George Chip
1914–17	Al McCoy
1917–20	Mike O'Dowd
1920–23	Johnny Wilson
1923–26	Harry Greb
1926	Tiger Flowers
1926–31	Mickey Walker[2]
1931–41	Gorilla Jones, Ben Jeby, Marcel Thil, Lou Brouillard, Vince Dundee, Teddy Yarosz, Babe Risko, Freddy Steele, Al Hostak, Solly Kreiger, Fred Apostoli, Cerferino Garcia, Ken Overlin, Billy Soose, Tony Zale[4]
1941–47	Tony Zale
1947–48	Rocky Graziano
1948	Tony Zale
1948–49	Marcel Cerdan
1949–51	Jake LaMotta
1951–52	Ray Robinson[1]
1952	Ray Robinson, Randy Turpin
1953–55	Carl Olson
1955–57	Ray Robinson[5]
1957	Gene Fullmer, Ray Robinson
1957–58	Carmen Basilio
1958–60	Ray Robinson[6]
1959–62	Gene Fullmer (NBA)
1960–61	Paul Pender[7]
1961–62	Terry Downes[1]
1962	Paul Pender[1]
1962–63	Dick Tiger
1963–65	Joey Giardello
1965–66	Dick Tiger
1966	Emile Griffith
1967	Nino Benvenuti, Emile Griffith
1968	Emile Griffith, Nino Benvenuti
1969	Nino Benvenuti
1970	Nino Benvenuti, Carlos Monzon
1971–73	Carlos Monzon
1974–75	Carlos Monzon (WBA), Rodrigo Valdez (WBC)
1976	Carlos Monzon (WBA, WBC), Rodrigo Valdez (WBC)
1977	Carlos Monzon (WBA, WBC),[1] Rodrigo Valdez (WBA, WBC)
1978	Rodrigo Valdez, Hugo Corro
1979	Hugo Corro, Vito Antuofermo
1980	Vito Antuofermo, Alan Minter, Marvin Hagler
1981	Marvin Hagler
1982–86	Marvin Hagler (undisputed)
1987	Marvin Hagler (undisputed), Sugar Ray Leonard (undisputed)
1988	Sumbu Kalambay (WBA), Thomas Hearns (WBC), Iran Barkley (WBC), Frank Tate (IBF), Michael Nunn (IBF), James Kinchen (NABF)

1989	Michael Nunn (IBF), Mike McCallum (WBA), Iran Barkley (WBC), Roberto Duran (WBC)
1990	Michael McCallum (WBA), Michael Nunn (IBF), Iran Barkley (WBC)
1991	Michael Nunn (IBF), James Toney (IBF), Michael McCallum (WBA)
1992	James Toney (IBF), Julian Jackson (WBC), Reggie Johnson (WBA)
1993	Reggie Johnson (WBA), Gerald McClellan (WBC), Roy Jones (IBF)
1994	Julian Jackson (WBA), Gerald McClellan (WBC), Roy Jones (IBF)
1995	Jorge Castro (WBA), Julian Jackson (WBC), Bernard Hopkins (IBF)
1996	William Joppy (WBA), Keith Holmes (WBC), Bernard Hopkins (IBF)
1997	Shinji Takehara (WBA), Quincy Taylor (WBC), Bernard Hopkins (IBF)
1998	William Joppy (WBA), Hassine Cherifi (WBC), Bernard Hopkins (IBF)
1999–2000	William Joppy (WBA), Keith Holmes (WBC), Bernard Hopkins (IBF)
2001	Felix Trinidad (WBA), Bernard Hopkins (WBC, IBF)
2002	William Joppy (WBA), Bernard Hopkins (WBC, IBF)
2003–04	Bernard Hopkins (WBA, WBC, IBF)
2005	Maselino Masoe (WBA), Jermain Taylor (WBC, IBF)

1. Retired. 2. Abandoned title. 3. Died. 4. National Boxing Association and New York Commission disagreed on champions. Those listed were accepted by one or the other until Zale gained world-wide recognition. 5. Ended retirement in 1954. 6. NBA withdrew recognition. 7. Recognized by New York, Massachusetts, and Europe.

Welterweight

1892–94	Mysterious Billy Smith
1894–96	Tommy Ryan
1896	Kid McCoy[1]
1896–	
1900	Mysterious Billy Smith
1900	Rube Ferns
1900–01	Matty Matthews
1901	Ruby Ferns
1901–04	Joe Walcott
1904	Dixie Kid[1]
1904–06	Joe Walcott
1906–07	Honey Mellody
1907	Mike (Twin) Sullivan[1]
1915–19	Ted Lewis
1919–22	Jack Britton
1922–26	Mickey Walker
1926–27	Pete Latzo
1927–29	Joe Dundee
1929–30	Jackie Fields
1930	Young Jack Thompson
1930–31	Tommy Freeman
1931	Young Jack Thompson
1931–32	Lou Brouillard
1932–33	Jackie Fields
1933	Young Corbett 3rd

1933–34	Jimmy McLarnin, Barney Ross
1934–35	Jimmy McLarnin
1935–38	Barney Ross
1938–40	Henry Armstrong
1940–41	Fritzie Zivic
1941–46	Freddie Cochrane
1946	Marty Servo[2]
1946–51	Ray Robinson[1]
1951	Johnny Bratton (NBA)
1951–54	Kid Gavilan
1954–55	Johnny Saxton
1955	Tony DeMarco
1955–56	Carmen Basilio
1956	Johnny Saxton
1956–57	Carmen Basilio[1]
1958	Virgil Akins
1959–60	Don Jordan
1960–61	Benny (Kid) Paret
1961	Emile Griffith
1961–62	Benny (Kid) Paret
1962–63	Emile Griffith, Luis Rodriguez
1963–66	Emile Griffith[1]
1966–69	Curtis Cokes
1969	Curtis Cokes, José Napoles
1970	José Napoles, Billy Backus
1971	Billy Backus, José Napoles
1972–74	José Napoles
1975	José Napoles (WBA, WBC),[3] Angel Espada (WBA), John Stracey (WBC)
1976	Angel Espada (WBA), José Cuevas (WBA), John Stracey (WBC), Carlos Palomino
1977–78	José Cuevas (WBA), Carlos Palomino (WBC)
1979	José Cuevas (WBA), Carlos Palomino (WBC), Wilfredo Benitez (WBC)
1980	José Cuevas (WBA), Ray Leonard (WBC), Roberto Duran (WBC), Thomas Hearns (WBA)
1981	Ray Leonard (WBC), Thomas Hearns (WBA), Ray Leonard (WBC, WBA)
1982	Ray Leonard
1983–85	Donald Curry (WBA), Milton McCrory (WBC)
1985–86	Donald Curry (undisputed)
1987	Mark Breland (WBA), Marlon Starling (WBA), Lloyd Honeyghan (IBF)
1988	Marlon Starling (WBA), Tomas Molinares (WBA), Lloyd Honeyghan (WBC), Simon Brown (IBF)
1989	Mark Breland (WBA), Marlon Starling (WBC), Simon Brown (IBF)
1990	Mark Breland (WBA), Aaron Davis (WBA), Simon Brown (IBF), Marlon Starling (WBC), Maurice Blocker (WBC)
1991	Meldrick Taylor (WBA), Simon Brown (IBF, WBC)
1992	Meldrick Taylor (WBA), James "Buddy" McGirt (WBC), Maurice Blocker (IBF)
1993	Cristianto Espana (WBA), Pernell Whitaker (WBC), Felix Trinidad (IBF)
1994	Ike Quartey (WBA), Pernell Whitaker (WBC), Felix Trinidad (IBF)
1995	Ike Quartey (WBA), Pernell Whitaker (WBC), Felix Trinidad (IBF)
1996–97	Ike Quartey (WBA), Pernell Whitaker (WBC), Felix Trinidad (IBF)
1998	Ike Quartey (WBA), Oscar De La Hoya (WBC), Felix Trinidad (IBF)
1999	James Page (WBA), Oscar De La Hoya (WBC), Felix Trinidad (IBF, WBC)
2000	James Page (WBA), Shane Mosley (WBC), Vacant (IBF)
2001	Andrew Lewis (WBA), Shane Mosley (WBC), Vernon Forrest (IBF)
2002	Ricardo Mayorga (WBA), Vernon Forrest (WBC), Michele Piccirillo (IBF)
2003	Ricardo Mayorga (WBA, WBC), Cory Spinks (IBF)
2004	Cory Spinks (WBC, WBA, IBF)
2005	Luis Collazo (WBA), Zab Judah (WBC, IBF)

1. Retired. 2. Abandoned title. 3. WBA withdrew recognition.

Lightweight

1869–99	Kid Lavigne
1899–	
1902	Frank Erne
1902–08	Joe Gans
1908–10	Battling Nelson
1910–12	Ad Wolgast
1912–14	Willie Ritchie
1914–17	Freddy Welsh
1917–25	Benny Leonard[1]
1925	Jimmy Goodrich
1925–26	Rocky Kansas
1926–30	Sammy Mandell
1930	Al Singer
1930–33	Tony Canzoneri
1933–35	Barney Ross[2]
1935–36	Tony Canzoneri
1936–38	Lou Ambers
1938–39	Henry Armstrong
1939–40	Lou Ambers
1940–41	Lew Jenkins
1941–42	Sammy Angott[1]
1943–47	Beau Jack (N.Y.), Bob Montgomery (N.Y.), Sammy Angott (NBA), Juan Zurita (NBA), Ike Williams (NBA)
1947–51	Ike Williams
1951–52	James Carter
1952	Lauro Salas
1952–54	James Carter
1954	Paddy DeMarco
1954–55	James Carter
1955–56	Wallace Smith
1956–62	Joe Brown
1962–65	Carlos Ortiz
1965	Ismael Laguna
1965–68	Carlos Ortiz
1968	Teo Cruz
1969	Teo Cruz, Mando Ramos
1970	Mando Ramos, Ismael Laguna, Ken Buchanan
1971	Ken Buchanan (WBA), Mando Ramos (WBC), Pedro Carrasco (WBC)
1972	Ken Buchanan (WBA), Roberto Duran (WBA), Pedro Carrasco (WBA), Mando Ramos (WBC), Chango Carmona (WBC), Rodolfo Gonzalez (WBC)
1973	Roberto Duran (WBA), Rodolfo Gonzalez (WBC)
1974	Roberto Duran (WBA), Rodolfo Gonzalez (WBC), Guts Ishimatsu (WBC)
1975	Roberto Duran (WBA), Guts Ishimatsu (WBC)
1976	Roberto Duran (WBA), Guts Ishimatsu (WBC), Esteban De Jesus (WBC)
1977	Roberto Duran (WBA), Esteban De Jesus (WBC)
1978	Roberto Duran (WBA, WBC)
1979	Roberto Duran,[2] Jim Watt (WBC), Ernesto Espana (WBA)
1980	Ernesto Espana (WBA), Hilmer Kenty (WBA), Jim Watt (WBC)
1981	Hilmer Kenty (WBA), Sean O'Grady (WBA), James Watt (WBC), Alexis Arguello (WBC), Arturo Frias (WBA)
1982	Arturo Frias (WBA), Ray Mancini (WBA), Alexis Arguello (WBC)
1983	Edwin Rosario (WBC), Ray Mancini (WBA)
1984	Edwin Rosario (WBC), Livingstone Bramble (WBA)
1985	Jose Luis Ramirez (WBC), Hector Camacho (WBC), Livingstone Bramble (WBA)
1986	Hector Camacho (WBC), Livingstone Bramble (WBA), Jim Paul (IBF)
1987	Edwin Rosario (WBA), Jose Luis Ramirez (WBC), Greg Haugen (IBF)
1988	Jose Luis Ramirez (WBC), Julio Cesar Chavez (WBA), Greg Haugen (IBF), Julio Cesar Chavez (WBC & WBA title unified)
1989	Pernell Whitaker (IBF, WBC), Edwin Rosario (WBA)
1990	Pernell Whitaker (IBF, WBC), Juan Nazario (WBA)
1991	Pernell Whitaker (IBF, WBA, WBC)
1992	Pernell Whitaker (IBF, WBA, WBC), Joey Gamache (WBA)
1993	Dingaan Thobela (WBA), Angel Gonzalez (WBC), Freddie Pendleton (IBF)
1994	Orzubek Nazarov (WBA), Angel Gonzalez (WBC), Rafael Ruelas (IBF)
1995	Orzubek Nazarov (WBA), Angel Gonzalez (WBC), Oscar De La Hoya (IBF)

1996	Gusshie Nazarov (WBA), Jean Baptiste Mendy (WBC), Phillip Holiday (IBF)
1997	Orzubek Nazarov (WBA), Jean Baptiste Mendy (WBC), Philip Holiday (IBF)
1998	Jean Baptiste Mendy (WBA), Cesar Bazan (WBC), Shane Mosley (IBF)
1999	Stefano Zoff (WBA), Stevie Johnston (WBC), Paul Spadafora (IBF)
2000	Takanori Hatakeyama (WBA), Jose Luis Castillo (WBC), Paul Spadafora (IBF)
2001	Julien Lorcy (WBA), Jose Luis Castillo (WBC), Paul Spadafora (IBF)
2002	Leonard Dorin (WBA), Floyd Mayweather (WBC), Paul Spadafora (IBF)
2003	Leonard Dorin (WBA), Floyd Mayweather (WBC), Vacant (IBF)
2004	Jose Luis Castillo (WBC), Juan Diaz (WBA, IBF)
2005	Juan Diaz (WBA), Diego Corrales (WBC), Leavander Johnson (IBF)

1. Retired. 2. Abandoned title. 3. Moved up in weight class, so resigned titles.

Featherweight

1889	Dal Hawkins[1]
1890	Billy Murphy
1892–	
1900	George Dixon
1900–01	Terry McGovern
1901	Young Corbett[1]
1901–12	Abe Attell
1912–23	Johnny Kilbane
1923	Eugene Criqui
1923–25	Johnny Dundee[1]
1925–27	Louis (Kid) Kaplan[1]
1927–28	Benny Bass
1928	Tony Canzoneri
1928–29	Andre Routis
1929–32	Battling Battalino[1]
1932	Tommy Paul (NBA), Kid Chocolate (N.Y.)
1933–36	Freddie Miller
1936–37	Petey Sarron
1937–38	Henry Armstrong[1]
1938–40	Joey Archibald
1940–41	Harry Jefra, Joey Archibald
1941–42	Chalky Wright
1942–48	Willie Pep
1948–49	Sandy Saddler[2]
1949–50	Willie Pep
1950–57	Sandy Saddler
1957–59	Kid Bassey
1959–63	Davey Moore
1963–64	Sugar Ramos
1964–67	Vicente Saldivar[2]
1968	Howard Winstone, José Legra,[3] Paul Rojas (WBA), Sho Saijo (WBA)
1969	Sho Saijo (WBA), Johnny Famechon[3]
1970	Sho Saijo (WBA), Johnny Famechon,[3] Vicente Salvidar,[3] Kuniaki Shibata[3]
1971	Sho Saijo (WBA), Antonio Gomez (WBA), Kuniaki Shibata (WBC)
1972	Antonio Gomez (WBA), Ernesto Marcel (WBA), Kuniaki Shibata (WBC), Clemente Sanchez (WBC), José Legra (WBC)
1973	Ernesto Marcel (WBA), José Legra (WBC), Eder Jofre (WBC)
1974	Ernesto Marcel (WBA),[2] Ruben Olivares (WBA), Alexis Arguello (WBA), Eder Jofre (WBC), Bobby Chacon (WBC)
1975	Alexis Arguello (WBA), Bobby Chacon (WBC), Ruben Olivares (WBC), David Kotey (WBC)
1976	Alexis Arguello (WBA),[2] David Kotey (WBC), Danny Lopez (WBC)
1977	Rafael Ortega (WBA), Danny Lopez (WBC)
1978	Rafael Ortega (WBA), Cecilio Lastra (WBA), Eusebio Pedroza (WBA), Danny Lopez (WBC)
1979	Eusebio Pedroza (WBA), Danny Lopez (WBC)
1980	Eusebio Pedroza (WBA), Danny Lopez (WBC), Salvador Sanchez (WBC)
1981	Eusebio Pedroza (WBA), Salvador Sanchez (WBC)
1982	Eusebio Pedroza (WBA), Salvador Sanchez (WBC)[4]
1983	Juan Laporte (WBC), Eusebio Pedroza (WBA)
1984	Wilfred Gomez (WBC), Eusebio Pedroza (WBA)
1985	Eusebio Pedroza (WBA), Barry McGuigan (WBA), Azumah Nelson (WBC)
1986	Barry McGuigan (WBA), Stevie Cruz (WBA), Azumah Nelson (WBC)
1987	Azumah Nelson (WBC), Antonio Esparragoza (WBA)
1988	Calvin Grove (IBF), Jorge Paez (IBF), Antonio Esparragoza (WBA), Jeff Fenech (WBC)
1989	Jorge Paez (IBF), Antonio Esparragoza (WBA), Jeff Fenech (WBC)
1990	Marcos Villasana (WBC), Antonio Esparragoza (WBA), Jorge Paez (IBF)
1991	Yung-Kyun Park (WBA), Troy Dorsey (IBF), Marcos Villagana (WBC)
1992	Paul Hodkinson (WBC), Manuel Medina (IBF), Yung-Kyun Park (WBA)
1993	Yung-Kyun Park (WBA), Goyo Vargas (WBC), Tom Johnson (IBF)
1994	Eloy Rojas (WBA), Kevin Kelley (WBC), Tom Johnson (IBF)
1995	Eloy Rojas (WBA), Alejandro Gonzalez (WBC), Tom Johnson (IBF)
1996	Wilfredo Vázquez (WBA), Luisto Espinoza (WBC), Tom Johnson (IBF)
1997	Elroy Rojas (WBA), Luisito Espinoza (WBC), Tom Johnson (IBF)
1998	vacant (WBA), Luisito Espinoza (WBC), Manuel Medina (IBF)
1999	Freddie Norwood (WBA), Cesar Soto (WBC), Manuel Medina (IBF)
2000	Freddie Norwood (WBA), Guty Espadas (WBC), Paul Ingle (IBF)
2001	Derrick Gainer (WBA), Erik Morales (WBC), Frankie Toledo (IBF)
2002	Derrick Gainer (WBA), vacant (WBC), Johnny Tapia (IBF)
2003	Derrick Gainer (WBA), Erik Morales (WBC), Manuel Marquez (IBF)
2004	In-Jin Chi (WBC), Juan Manuel Marquez (WBA, IBF)
2005	Chris John (WBA), In-Jin Chi (WBC), Juan Manuel Marquez (IBF)

1. Abandoned title. 2. Retired. 3. Recognized in Europe, Mexico, and Asia. 4. Killed in auto accident.

Bantamweight

1890–92	George Dixon[1]
1894–99	Jimmy Barry[2]
1899–	
1900	Terry McGovern[1]
1901	Harry Harris[1]
1902–03	Harry Forbes
1903–04	Frankie Neil
1904	Joe Bowker[1]
1905–07	Jimmy Walsh[1]
1910–14	Johnny Coulon
1914–17	Kid Williams
1917–20	Pete Herman
1920	Joe Lynch
1920–21	Joe Lynch, Pete Herman, Johnny Buff
1922	Johnny Buff, Joe Lynch
1923	Joe Lynch
1924	Joe Lynch, Abe Goldstein, Eddie "Cannonball" Martin
1925	Eddie "Cannonball" Martin, Charlie (Phil) Rosenberg[3]
1927–28	Bud Taylor (NBA)[1]
1929–34	Al Brown
1935	Al Brown, Baltazar Sangchili
1936	Baltazar Sangchili, Tony Marino, Sixto Escobar
1937	Sixto Escobar, Harry Jeffra
1938	Harry Jeffra, Sixto Escobar
1939–40	Sixto Escobar[2]
1940–42	Lou Salica
1942–46	Manuel Ortiz
1947	Manuel Ortiz, Harold Dade
1948–50	Manuel Ortiz
1950–52	Vic Toweel
1952–54	Jimmy Carruthers[2]
1954–55	Robert Cohen
1956	Robert Cohen, Mario D'Agata, Raul Macias (NBA)
1957	Mario D'Agata, Alphonse Halimi
1958–59	Alphonse Halimi

1959–60	Jose Becerra[2]	1980	Jorge Lujan (WBA),	1993	Jorge Julio (WBA),
1960–61	Alphonse Halimi[4]		Lupe Pintor (WBC),		Byun-Jong-il (WBC),
1961–62	Johnny Caldwell[4]		Julian Solis (WBA),		Orlando Canizales (IBF)
1961–65	Eder Jofre		Jeff Chandler (WBA)	1994	John Michael Johnson
1965–68	Masahika "Fighting"	1981	Lupe Pintor (WBC),		(WBA),
	Harada		Jeff Chandler (WBA)		Yasuei Yakushiji (WBC),
1968	Masahika "Fighting"	1982	Lupe Pintor (WBC),		Orlando Canizales (IBF)
	Harada,		Jeff Chandler (WBA)	1995	Daorun Chuwatang (WBA),
	Lionel Rose	1983	Jeff Chandler (WBA),		Yasuei Yakushiji (WBC),
1969	Lionel Rose,		Albert Dauila (WBC)		Mbulelo Botile (IBF)
	Ruben Olivares	1984	Richie Sandqual (WBA),	1996–97	Nana Konadu (WBA),
1970	Ruben Olivares,		Albert Dauila (WBC)		Wayne McCullough
	Chucho Castillo	1985	Richard Sandoval (WBA),		(WBC),
1971	Chucho Castillo,		Daniel Zaragoza (WBC),		Mbulelo Botile (IBF)
	Ruben Olivares		Miguel Lora (WBC)	1998	Nana Konadu (WBA),
1972	Ruben Olivares,	1986	Richard Sandoval (WBA),		Joichiro Tatsuyoshi (WBC),
	Rafael Herrera,		Bernardo Pinango (WBA),		Tim Austin (IBF)
	Enrique Pinder		Jeff Fenech (IBF)	1999–	Paulie Ayala (WBA),
1973	Enrique Pinder (WBA),	1987	Bernardo Pinango (WBA),	2001	Veeraphol Sahaprom
	Romeo Anaya (WBA),		Takuya Muguruma (WBA),		(WBC), Tim Austin (IBF)
	Arnold Taylor (WBA),		Miguel Lora (WBC)	2002	Johnny Bredahl (WBA),
	Rodolfo Martinez (WBC),	1988	Wilfredo Vásquez (WBA),		Veeraphol Sahaprom
	Rafael Herrera		Jibaro Perez (WBC),		(WBC),
1974	Arnold Taylor (WBA),		Moon Sung-gil (WBA),		Tim Austin (IBF)
	Soo Hwan Hong (WBA),		Orlando Canizales (IBF)	2003–04	Johnny Bredahl (WBA),
	Rafael Herrera (WBC),	1989	Jibaro Perez (WBC),		Veerapol Sahaprom
	Rodolfo Martinez (WBC)		Moon Sung-gil (WBA),		(WBC), Rafael Marquez
1975	Soo Hwan Hong (WBA),		Orlando Canizales (IBF),		(IBF)
	Alfonso Zamora (WBA),		Kaokor Galaxy (WBA),	2005	Wladimir Sidorenko
	Rodolfo Martinez (WBC)		Luis Espinosa (WBA)		(WBA), Hozumi Hasegawa
1976	Alfonso Zamora (WBA),	1990	Orlando Canizales (IBF),		(WBC), Rafael Marquez
	Rodolfo Martinez (WBC),		Jibaro Perez (WBC),		(IBF)
	Carlos Zarate (WBC)		Luis Espinosa (WBA)		
1977	Alfonso Zamora (WBA),	1991	Greg Richardson (WBC),		
	Jorge Lujan (WBA),		Orlando Canizales (IBF),		
	Carlos Zarate (WBC)		Luis Espinosa (WBA)		
1978	Jorge Lujan (WBA),	1992	Joichiro Tatsuyoshi (WBC),		
	Carlos Zarate (WBC)		Victor Manuel Rabanales		
1979	Jorge Lujan (WBA),		(WBC),		
	Carlos Zarate (WBC),		Eddie Cook (WBA),		
	Lupe Pintor (WBC)		Orlando Gonzales (IBF)		

1. Abandoned title. 2. Retired. 3. Deprived of title for failing to make weight. 4. Recognized in Europe.

Horse Racing

Ancient drawings on stone and bone prove that horse racing is at least 3,000 years old, but thoroughbred racing is a modern development. Practically every thoroughbred in training today traces its registered ancestry back to one or more of three sires that arrived in England about 1728 from the Near East and became known, from the names of their owners, as the Byerly Turk, the Darley Arabian, and the Godolphin Arabian. The Jockey Club (English) was founded at Newmarket in 1750 or 1751 and became the custodian of the Stud Book as well as the court of last resort in deciding turf affairs.

Horse racing took place in this country before the Revolution, but the great lift to the breeding industry came with the importation in 1798, by Col. John Hoomes of Virginia, of Diomed, winner of the Epsom Derby of 1780. Diomed's lineal descendants included such famous 19th-century stars of the American turf as American Eclipse, Sir Archy, and Lexington. From 1800 to the time of the Civil War there were race courses and breeding establishments plentifully scattered through Virginia, North Carolina, South Carolina, Tennessee, Kentucky, and Louisiana.

The oldest stake event in North America is the Queen's Plate, a Canadian fixture that was first run in the Province of Quebec in 1836. The oldest stake event in the United States is the Travers, which was first run at Saratoga in 1864. The gambling that goes with horse racing and trickery by jockeys, trainers, owners, and track officials caused attacks on the sport by reformers and a demand among horse racing enthusiasts for an honest and effective control of some kind, but nothing of lasting value to racing came of this until the formation in 1894 of the Jockey Club (American).

"TRIPLE CROWN" WINNERS IN THE UNITED STATES

(Kentucky Derby, Preakness, and Belmont Stakes)

Year	Horse	Owner	Year	Horse	Owner
1919	Sir Barton	J. K. L. Ross	1946	Assault	Robert J. Kleberg
1930	Gallant Fox	William Woodward	1948	Citation	Warren Wright
1935	Omaha	William Woodward	1973	Secretariat	Meadow Stable
1937	War Admiral	Samuel D. Riddle	1977	Seattle Slew	Karen Taylor
1941	Whirlaway	Warren Wright	1978	Affirmed	Louis Wolfson
1943	Count Fleet	Mrs. John Hertz			

KENTUCKY DERBY

Churchill Downs; 3-year-olds; 1¼ mi

Year	Winner	Jockey	Year	Winner	Jockey	Year	Winner	Jockey
1875	Aristides	O. Lewis	1921	Behave Yourself	C. Thompson	1965	Lucky Debonair	W. Shoemaker
1876	Vagrant	R. Swim	1922	Morvich	A. Johnson	1966	Kauai King	D. Brumfield
1877	Baden Baden	W. Walker	1923	Zev	E. Sande	1967	Proud Clarion	R. Ussery
1878	Day Star	J. Carter	1924	Black Gold	J. D. Mooney	1968	Forward Pass[1]	I. Valenzuela
1879	Lord Murphy	C. Shauer	1925	Flying Ebony	E. Sande	1969	Majestic Prince	W. Hartack
1880	Fonso	G. Lewis	1926	Bubbling Over	A. Johnson	1970	Dust Com-	
1881	Hindoo	J. McLaughlin	1927	Whiskery	L. McAtee		mander	M. Manganello
1882	Apollo	B. Hurd	1928	Reigh Count	C. Lang	1971	Canonero II	G. Avila
1883	Leonatus	W. Donohue	1929	Clyde Van		1972	Riva Ridge	R. Turcotte
1884	Buchanan	I. Murphy		Dusen	L. McAtee	1973	Secretariat	R. Turcotte
1885	Joe Cotton	B. Henderson	1930	Gallant Fox	E. Sande	1974	Cannonade	A. Cordero, Jr.
1886	Ben Ali	P. Duffy	1931	Twenty Grand	C. Kurtsinger	1975	Foolish Plea-	
1887	Montrose	I. Lewis	1932	Burgoo King	E. James		sure	J. Vasquez
1888	Macbeth II	G. Covington	1933	Brokers Tip	D. Meade	1976	Bold Forbes	A. Cordero, Jr.
1889	Spokane	T. Kiley	1934	Cavalcade	M. Garner	1977	Seattle Slew	J. Cruguet
1890	Riley	I. Murphy	1935	Omaha	W. Saunders	1978	Affirmed	S. Cauthen
1891	Kingman	I. Murphy	1936	Bold Venture	I. Hanford	1979	Spectacular Bid	R. Franklin
1892	Azra	L. Clayton	1937	War Admiral	C. Kurtsinger	1980	Genuine Risk	J. Vasquez
1893	Lookout	E. Kunze	1938	Lawrin	E. Arcaro	1981	Pleasant Colony	J. Velasquez
1894	Chant	F. Goodale	1939	Johnstown	J. Stout	1982	Gato del Sol	E. Delahoussaye
1895	Halma	S. Perkins	1940	Gallahadion	C. Bierman	1983	Sunny's Halo	E. Delahoussaye
1896	Ben Brush	W. Simms	1941	Whirlaway	E. Arcaro	1984	Swale	L. Pincay, Jr.
1897	Typhoon II	B. Garner	1942	Shut Out	W. D. Wright	1985	Spend a Buck	A. Cordero, Jr.
1898	Plaudit	W. Simms	1943	Count Fleet	J. Longden	1986	Ferdinand	W. Shoemaker
1899	Manuel	F. Taral	1944	Pensive	C. McCreary	1987	Alysheba	C. McCarron
1900	Lieut. Gibson	J. Boland	1945	Hoop Jr.	E. Arcaro	1988	Winning Colors	G. Stevens
1901	His Eminence	J. Winkfield	1946	Assault	W. Mehrtens	1989	Sunday Silence	P. Valenzuela
1902	Alan-a-Dale	J. Winkfield	1947	Jet Pilot	E. Guerin	1990	Unbridled	C. Perret
1903	Judge Himes	H. Booker	1948	Citation	E. Arcaro	1991	Strike the Gold	C. Antley
1904	Elwood	F. Prior	1949	Ponde	S. Brooks	1992	Lil E. Tee	P. Day
1905	Agile	J. Martin	1950	Middleground	W. Boland	1993	Sea Hero	J. Bailey
1906	Sir Huon	R. Troxler	1951	Count Turf	C. McCreary	1994	Go For Gin	C. McCarron
1907	Pink Star	A. Minder	1952	Hill Gail	E. Arcaro	1995	Thunder Gulch	G. Stevens
1908	Stone Street	A. Pickens	1953	Dark Star	H. Moreno	1996	Grindstone	J. Bailey
1909	Wintergreen	V. Powers	1954	Determine	R. York	1997	Silver Charm	G. Stevens
1910	Donau	F. Herbert	1955	Swaps	W. Shoemaker	1998	Real Quiet	K. Desormeaux
1911	Meridian	G. Archibald	1956	Needles	D. Erb	1999	Charismatic	C. Antley
1912	Worth	C. H. Shilling	1957	Iron Liege	W. Hartack	2000	Fusaichi	
1913	Donerail	R. Goose	1958	Tim Tam	I. Valenzuela		Pegasus	K. Desormeaux
1914	Old Rosebud	J. McCabe	1959	Tomy Lee	W. Shoemaker	2001	Monarchos	J. Chavez
1915	Regret	J. Notter	1960	Venetian Way	W. Hartack	2002	War Emblem	V. Espinoza
1916	George Smith	J. Loftus	1961	Carry Back	J. Sellers	2003	Funny Cide	J. Santos
1917	Omar Khayyam	C. Borel	1962	Decidedly	W. Hartack	2004	Smarty Jones	S. Elliott
1918	Exterminator	W. Knapp	1963	Chateaugay	B. Baeza	2005	Giacomo	M. Smith
1919	Sir Barton	J. Loftus	1964	Northern				
1920	Paul Jones	T. Rice		Dancer	W. Hartack			

1. Dancer's Image finished first but was disqualified after traces of drugs were found in his system.

PREAKNESS STAKES

Pimlico; 3-year-olds; 1³⁄₁₆ mi

Year	Winner	Jockey	Year	Winner	Jockey	Year	Winner	Jockey
1873	Survivor	G. Barbee	1884	Knight of Ellerslie	S. Fisher	1897	Paul Kauvar	T. Thorpe
1874	Culpepper	W. Donohue	1885	Tecumseh	J. McLaughlin	1898	Sly Fox	W. Simms
1875	Tom Ochiltree	L. Hughes	1886	The Bard	S. Fisher	1899	Half Time	R. Clawson
1876	Shirley	G. Barbee	1887	Dunboyne	W. Donohue	1900	Hindus	H. Spencer
1877	Cloverbrook	C. Holloway	1888	Refund	F. Littlefield	1901	The Parader	F. Landry
1878	Duke of Magenta	C. Holloway	1889	Buddhist	W. Anderson	1902	Old England	L. Jackson
1879	Harold	L. Hughes	1890	Montague	W. Martin	1903	Flocarline	W. Gannon
1880	Grenada	L. Hughes	1891-93	Not held		1904	Bryn Mawr	E. Hildebrand
1881	Saunterer	T. Costello	1894	Assignee	F. Taral	1905	Cairngorm	W. Davis
1882	Vanguard	T. Costello	1895	Belmar	F. Taral	1906	Whimsical	W. Miller
1883	Jacobus	G. Barbee	1896	Margrave	H. Griffin	1907	Don Enrique	G. Mountain

Year	Winner	Jockey	Year	Winner	Jockey	Year	Winner	Jockey
1908	Royal Tourist	E. Dugan	1941	Whirlaway	E. Arcaro	1975	Master Derby	D. McHargue
1909	Effendi	W. Doyle	1942	Alsab	B. James	1976	Elocutionist	J. Lively
1910	Layminster	R. Estep	1943	Count Fleet	J. Longden	1977	Seattle Slew	J. Cruguet
1911	Watervale	E. Dugan	1944	Pensive	C. McCreary	1978	Affirmed	S. Cauthen
1912	Colonel Holloway	C. Turner	1945	Polynesian	W.D. Wright	1979	Spectacular Bid	R. Franklin
1913	Buskin	J. Butwell	1946	Assault	W. Mehrtens	1980	Codex	A. Cordero
1914	Holiday	A. Schuttinger	1947	Faultless	D. Dodson	1981	Pleasant Colony	J. Velasquez
1915	Rhine Maiden	D. Hoffman	1948	Citation	E. Arcaro	1982	Aloma's Ruler	J. Kaenel
1916	Damrosch	L. McAtee	1949	Capot	T. Atkinson	1983	Deputed	
1917	Kalitan	E. Haynes	1950	Hill Prince	E. Arcaro		Testamony	D. Miller
1918	War Cloud	J. Loftus	1951	Bold	E. Arcaro	1984	Gate Dancer	A. Cordero
1918	Jack Hare Jr.	C. Peak	1952	Blue Man	C. McCreary	1985	Tank's Prospect	P. Day
1919	Sir Barton	J. Loftus	1953	Native Dancer	E. Guerin	1986	Snow Chief	A. Solis
1920	Man o' War	C. Kummer	1954	Hasty Road	J. Adams	1987	Alysheba	C. McCarron
1921	Broomspun	F. Coltiletti	1955	Nashua	E. Arcaro	1988	Risen Star	E. Delahoussaye
1922	Pillory	L. Morris	1956	Fabius	W. Hartack	1989	Sunday Silence	P. Valenzuela
1923	Vigil	B. Marinelli	1957	Bold Ruler	E. Arcaro	1990	Summer Squall	P. Day
1924	Nellie Morse	J. Merimee	1958	Tim Tam	I. Valenzuela	1991	Hansel	J. Bailey
1925	Coventry	C. Kummer	1959	Royal Orbit	W. Harmatz	1992	Pine Bluff	C. McCarron
1926	Display	J. Maiben	1960	Bally Ache	R. Ussery	1993	Prairie Bayou	M. Smith
1927	Bostonian	W. Abel	1961	Carry Back	J. Sellers	1994	Tabasco Cat	P. Day
1928	Victorian	S. Workman	1962	Greek Money	J. Rotz	1995	Timber Country	P. Day
1929	Dr. Freeland	L. Schaefer	1963	Candy Spots	W. Shoemaker	1996	Louis Quatorze	P. Day
1930	Gallant Fox	E. Sande	1964	Northern Dancer	W. Hartack	1997	Silver Charm	G. Stevens
1931	Mate	G. Ellis	1965	Tom Rolfe	R. Turcotte	1998	Real Quiet	K. Desormeaux
1932	Burgoo King	E. James	1966	Kauai King	D. Brumfield	1999	Charismatic	C. Antley
1933	Head Play	C. Kurtsinger	1967	Damascus	W. Shoemaker	2000	Red Bullet	J. Bailey
1934	High Quest	R. Jones	1968	Forward Pass	I. Valenzuela	2001	Point Given	G. Stevens
1935	Omaha	W. Saunders	1969	Majestic Prince	W. Hartack	2002	War Emblem	V. Espinoza
1936	Bold Venture	G. Woolf	1970	Personality	E. Belmonte	2003	Funny Cide	J. Santos
1937	War Admiral	C. Kurtsinger	1971	Canonero II	G. Avila	2004	Smarty Jones	S. Elliott
1938	Dauber	M. Peters	1972	Bee Bee Bee	E. Nelson	2005	Afleet Alex	J. Rose
1939	Challedon	G. Seabo	1973	Secretariat	R. Turcotte			
1940	Bimelech	F.A. Smith	1974	Little Current	M. Rivera			

BELMONT STAKES

Belmont Park; 3-year-olds; 1½ mi

Run at Jerome Park 1867 to 1890; at Morris Park 1890–94; at Belmont Park 1905–62; at Aqueduct 1963–67. Distance 1⅝ mi prior to 1874; reduced to 1½ mi, 1874; reduced to 1¼ mi, 1890; reduced to 1⅛ mi, 1893; increased to 1¼ mi, 1895; increased to 1⅜ mi, 1896; reduced to 1¼ mi in 1904; increased to 1½ mi, 1926.

Year	Winner	Jockey	Year	Winner	Jockey	Year	Winner	Jockey
1867	Ruthless	J. Gilpatrick	1885	Tyrant	P. Duffy	1902	Masterman	J. Bullman
1868	General Duke	B. Swim	1886	Inspector B	J. McLaughlin	1903	Africander	J. Bullman
1869	Fenian	C. Miller	1887	Hanover	J. McLaughlin	1904	Delhi	G. Odom
1870	Kingfisher	W. Dick	1888	Sir Dixon	J. McLaughlin	1905	Tanya	E. Hildebrand
1871	Harry Bassett	W. Miller	1889	Eric	W. Hayward	1906	Burgomaster	L. Lyne
1872	Joe Daniels	J. Roe	1890	Burlington	P. Barnes	1907	Peter Pan	G. Mountain
1873	Springbok	J. Roe	1891	Foxford	E. Garrison	1908	Colin	J. Notter
1874	Saxon	G. Barbee	1892	Patron	W. Hayward	1909	Joe Madden	E. Dugan
1875	Calvin	B. Swim	1893	Commanche	W. Simms	1910	Sweep	J. Butwell
1876	Algerine	B. Donohue	1894	Henry of Navarre	W. Simms	1911-12	Not held	
1877	Cloverbrook	C. Holloway		(11/2)		1913	Prince Eugene	R. Troxler
1878	Duke of Magenta	L. Hughes	1895	Belmar	F. Taral	1914	Luke McLuke	M. Buxton
1879	Spendthrift	G. Evans	1896	Hastings	H. Griffin	1915	The Finn	G. Byrne
1880	Grenada	L. Hughes	1897	Scottish Chieftain	J. Scherrer	1916	Friar Rock	E. Haynes
1881	Saunterer	T. Costello	1898	Bowling Brook	F. Littlefield	1917	Hourless	J. Butwell
1882	Forester	J. McLaughlin	1899	Jean Beraud	R. Clawson	1918	Johren	F. Robinson
1883	George Kinney	J. McLaughlin	1900	Ildrim	N. Turner	1919	Sir Barton	J. Loftus
1884	Panique	J. McLaughlin	1901	Commando	H. Spencer	1920	Man o' War	C. Kummer

Year	Winner	Jockey	Year	Winner	Jockey	Year	Winner	Jockey
1921	Grey Lag	E. Sande	1951	Counterpoint	D. Gorman	1980	Temperence Hill	E. Maple
1922	Pillory	C.H. Miller	1952	One Count	E. Arcaro	1981	Summing	G. Martens
1923	Zev	E. Sande	1953	Native Dancer	E. Guerin	1982	Conquistador Cielo	L. Pincay, Jr.
1924	Mad Play	E. Sande	1954	High Gun	E. Guerin			
1925	American Flag	A. Johnson	1955	Nashua	E. Arcaro	1983	Caveat	L. Pincay, Jr.
1926	Crusader	A. Johnson	1956	Needles	D. Erb	1984	Swale	L. Pincay, Jr.
1927	Chance Shot	E. Sande	1957	Gallant Man	W. Shoemaker	1985	Creme Fraiche	E. Maple
1928	Vito	C. Kummer	1958	Cavan	P. Anderson	1986	Danzig Connection	C. McCarron
1929	Blue Larkspur	M. Garner	1959	Sword Dancer	W. Shoemaker			
1930	Gallant Fox	E. Sande	1960	Celtic Ash	W. Hartack	1987	Bet Twice	C. Perret
1931	Twenty Grand	C. Kurtsinger	1961	Sherluck	B. Baeza	1988	Risen Star	E. Delahoussaye
1932	Faireno	T. Malley	1962	Jaipur	W. Shoemaker	1989	Easy Goer	P. Day
1933	Hurryoff	M. Garner	1963	Chateaugay	B. Baeza	1990	Go And Go	M. Kinane
1934	Peace Chance	W. D. Wright	1964	Quadrangle	M. Ycaza	1991	Hansel	J. Bailey
1935	Omaha	W. Saunders	1965	Hail to All	J. Sellers	1992	A.P. Indy	E. Delahoussaye
1936	Granville	J. Stout	1966	Amberoid	W. Boland	1993	Colonial Affair	J. Krone
1937	War Admiral	C. Kurtsinger	1967	Damascus	W. Shoemaker	1994	Tabasco Cat	P. Day
1938	Pasteurized	J. Stout	1968	Stage Door Johnny	H. Gustines	1995	Thunder Gulch	G.Stevens
1939	Johnstown	J. Stout				1996	Editor's Note	R. Douglas
1940	Bimelech	F.A. Smith	1969	Arts and Letters	B. Baeza	1997	Touch Gold	C. McCarron
1941	Whirlaway	E. Arcaro	1970	High Echelon	J. Rotz	1998	Victory Gallop	G. Stevens
1942	Shut Out	E. Arcaro	1971	Pass Catcher	R. Blum	1999	Lemon Drop Kid	J. Santos
1943	Count Fleet	J. Longden	1972	Riva Ridge	R. Turcotte	2000	Commendable	P. Day
1944	Bounding Home	G.L. Smith	1973	Secretariat	R. Turcotte	2001	Point Given	G. Stevens
1945	Pavot	E. Arcaro	1974	Little Current	M. Rivera	2002	Sarava	E. Prado
1946	Assault	W. Mehrtens	1975	Avatar	W. Shoemaker	2003	Empire Maker	J. Bailey
1947	Phalanx	R. Donoso	1976	Bold Forbes	A. Cordero, Jr.	2004	Birdstone	E. Prado
1948	Citation	E. Arcaro	1977	Seattle Slew	J. Cruguet	2005	Afleet Alex	J. Rose
1949	Capot	T. Atkinson	1978	Affirmed	S. Cauthen			
1950	Middleground	W. Boland	1979	Coastal	R. Hernandez			

TRIPLE CROWN RACES—2005

Kentucky Derby (Churchill Downs, Louisville, Ky., May 7, 2005.) Purse: $2,000,000. Distance: 1¼ mi. Order of finish: 1. Giacomo (Smith), mutuel returns: $102.60, $45.80, $19.80. 2. Closing Argument (Velasquez), $70.0, $24.80. 3. Afleet Alex (Rose), $4.60. 4. Don't Get Mad (Baze). 5. Buzzards Bay (Guidry). 6. Wilko (Nakatani). 7. Bellamy Road (Castellano). 8. Andromeda's Hero (Bejarano). 9. Flower Alley (Chavez). 10. High Fly (Bailey). 11. Greeley's Galaxy (Desormeaux). 12. Coin Silver (Valenzuela). 13. Greater Good (McKee). 14. Noble Causeway (Stevens). 15. Sun King (Prado). 16. Spanish Chestnut (Bravo). 17. Sort It Out (Blanc). 18. Going Wild (Valdivia, Jr.). 19. Bandini (Velazquez). 20. High Limit (Dominguez). Winner's purse: $1,639,600. Margin of victory: ½ length. Time of race: 2:02.75.

Preakness Stakes (Pimlico, Baltimore, Md., May 21, 2005.) Purse: $1,000,000. Distance: 1³⁄₁₆ mi. Order of finish: 1. Afleet Alex (Rose), mutuel returns: $8.60, $5.00, $3.20. 2. Scrappy T (Dominguez), $11.20, $5.80. 3. Giacomo (Smith), $4.80. 4. Sun King (Bejarano). 5. High Limit (Prado). 6. Greeley's Galaxy (Stevens). 7. Greeley's Galaxy (Flores). 8. Malibu Moonshine (Hamilton). 9. Closing Argument (Velasquez). 10. High Fly (Bailey). 11. Hal's Image (Santos). 12. Wilko (Nakatani). 13. Galloping Grocer (Bravo). 11. Going Wild (Albarado). Winner's purse: $650,000. Margin of victory: 4¾ lengths. Time of race: 1:55.04.

Belmont Stakes (Belmont Park, Elmont, N.Y., June 11, 2005.) Gross purse: $1,000,000. Distance: 1½ mi. Order of finish: 1. Afleet Alex (Rose), mutuel returns: $4.30, $3.60, $3.00. 2. Andromeda's Hero (Bejarano), $8.20, $5.80. 3. Nolan's Cat (Arroyo, Jr.), $7.20. 4. Indy Storm (Prado). 5. A. P. Arrow (Bailey). 6. Chekhov (Stevens). 7. Giacomo (Smith). 8. Southern Africa (Court). 9. Watchmon (Castellano). 10. Reverberate (Santos). 11. Pinpoint (Velazquez). Winner's purse: $600,000. Margin of victory: 7 lengths. Time of race: 2:28.75.

ECLIPSE AWARDS—2004

(Presented on Jan. 24, 2005)

Horse of the Year	Ghostzapper
2-year-old colt	Declan's Moon
2-year-old filly	Sweet Catomine
3-year-old colt	Smarty Jones
3-year-old filly	Ashado
Older male	Ghostzapper
Older female	Azeri
Sprinter	Speightstown
Male turf	Kitten's Joy
Female turf	Ouija Board
Steeplechase	Hirapour
Owner	Kenneth and Sarah Ramsey
Breeder	Adena Springs
Jockey	John Velazquez
Apprentice jockey	Brian Hernandez, Jr.
Trainer	Todd Pletcher

(Based on vote by the Thoroughbred Racing Associations, the *Daily Racing Form,* and the National Turf Writers Association.)

Track and Field

WORLD OUTDOOR RECORDS—MEN

(Through Aug. 30, 2005)

Recognized by the International Athletic Federation. The IAAF decided late in 1976 not to recognize records in yards except for the one-mile run. The IAAF also requires automatic timing for all records for races of 400 meters or less.

Event	Record	Holder	Home country	Where made	Date
Running					
100 m	0:09.77	Asafa Powell	Jamaica	Athens, Greece	June 14, 2005
200 m	0:19.32	Michael Johnson	United States	Atlanta, Ga.	Aug. 1, 1996
400 m	0:43.18	Michael Johnson	United States	Seville, Spain	Aug. 26, 1999
800 m	1:41.11	Wilson Kipketer	Denmark	Köln, Germany	Aug. 24, 1997
1,000 m	2:11.96	Noah Ngeny	Kenya	Rieti, Italy	Sept. 5, 1999
1,500 m	3:26.00	Hicham El Guerrouj	Morocco	Rome, Italy	July 14, 1998
1 mile	3:43.13	Hicham El Guerrouj	Morocco	Rome, Italy	July 7, 1999
2,000 m	4:44.79	Hicham El Guerrouj	Morocco	Berlin, Germany	Sept. 7, 1999
3,000 m	7:20.67	Daniel Komen	Kenya	Rieti, Italy	Sept. 1, 1996
3,000 m steeplechase	7:53.63	Saif Saaeed Shaheen	Qatar	Brussels, Belgium	Sept. 3, 2004
5,000 m	12:37.35	Kenenisa Bekele	Ethiopia	Hengelo, Netherlands	May 31, 2004
10,000 m	26:17.53[1]	Kenenisa Bekele	Ethiopia	Brussels, Belgium	Aug. 26, 2005
20,000 m	56:55.60	Arturo Barrios	Mexico	La Fléche, France	March 30, 1991
25,000 m	1:13:55.80	Toshihiko Seko	Japan	Christchurch, N.Z.	March 22, 1981
30,000 m	1:29:18.80	Toshihiko Seko	Japan	Christchurch, N.Z.	March 22, 1981
1 hour	21,101 m	Arturo Barrios	Mexico	La Fleche, France	March 30, 1991
Marathon[2]	2:04.55	Paul Tergat	Kenya	Berlin, Germany	Sept. 28, 2003
Walking					
20,000 m	1:17:25.60	Bernardo Segura	Mexico	Bergen, Norway	May 7, 1994
30,000 m	2:01:44.10	Maurizio Damilano	Italy	Cuneo, Italy	Oct. 3, 1992
50,000 m	3:40:57.90	Thierry Toutain	France	Héricourt, France	Sep[t. 29, 1996
2 hours	29,572 m	Maurizio Damilano	Italy	Cuneo, Italy	Oct. 3, 1992
Hurdles					
110 m	0:12.91	Colin Jackson	Great Britain	Stuttgart, Germany	Aug. 20, 1993
	0:12.91	Xiang Liu	China	Athens, Greece	Aug. 27, 2004
400 m	0:46.78	Kevin Young	United States	Barcelona, Spain	Aug. 6, 1992
Relay races					
400 m (4 × 100)	0:37.40	National Team	United States	Barcelona, Spain	Aug. 8, 1992
	0:37.40	National Team	United States	Stuttgart, Germany	Aug. 21, 1993
800 m (4 × 200)	1:18.68	Santa Monica T.C.	United States	Walnut, Calif.	April 17, 1994
1,600 m (4 × 400)	2:54.20	National Team	United States	New York, N.Y.	July 22, 1998
3,200 m (4 × 800)	7:03.89	National Team	Britain	London, England	Aug. 30, 1982
6,000 m	14:38.80	National Team	West Germany	Köln, W. Germany	Aug. 17, 1977
Field events					
High jump	2.45 m	Javier Sotomayor	Cuba	Salamanca, Spain	July 27, 1993
Long jump	8.95 m	Mike Powell	United States	Tokyo, Japan	Aug. 30, 1991
Triple jump	18.29 m	Jonathan Edwards	Great Britain	Goteborg, Sweden	Aug. 7, 1995
Pole vault	6.14 m	Sergey Bubka	Ukraine	Sestriere, Italy	July 31, 1994
Shot-put	23.12 m	Randy Barnes	United States	Los Angeles, Calif.	May 20, 1990
Discus throw	74.08 m	Jürgen Schult	East Germany	Neubrandenburg, E. Germany	June 6, 1986
Hammer throw	86.74 m	Yuriy Sedykh	USSR	Stuttgart, W. Germany	Aug. 30, 1986
Javelin throw	98.48 m	Jan Zelezny	Czech Republic	Jena, Germany	May 25, 1996
Decathlon	9,026 pts.	Roman Sebrle	Czech Republic	Götzis, Austria	May 27, 2001

1. Awaiting IAAF ratification. 2. Not recognized by IAAF as world record, but considered to be "world-best performance."
Source: IAAF.

WORLD OUTDOOR RECORDS—WOMEN

(Through Aug. 30, 2005)

Event	Record	Holder	Home country	Where made	Date
Running					
100 m	0:10.49	Florence Griffith-Joyner	United States	Indianapolis, Ind.	July 16, 1988
200 m	0:21.34	Florence Griffith-Joyner	United States	Seoul, South Korea	Sept. 29, 1988
400 m	0:47.60	Marita Koch	East Germany	Canberra, Australia	Oct. 6, 1985
800 m	1:53.28	Jarmila Kratochvílová	Czechoslovakia	Munich, W. Germany	July 26, 1983
1000 m	2:28.98	Svetlana Masterkova	Russia	Brussels, Belgium	Aug. 23, 1996
1,500 m	3:50.46	Qu Yunxia	China	Beijing, China	Sept. 11, 1993

Event	Record	Holder	Home country	Where made	Date
1 mile	4:12.56	Svetlana Masterkova	Russia	Zurich, Switzerland	Aug. 14, 1996
2,000 m	5:25.36	Sonia O'Sullivan	Ireland	Edinburgh, Scotland	July 8, 1994
3,000 m	8:06.11	Wang Junxia	China	Beijing, China	Sept. 13, 1993
5,000 m	14:24.68	Elvan Abeylegesse	Turkey	Bergen, Norway	June 11, 2004
10,000 m	29:31.78	Wang Junxia	China	Beijing, China	Sept. 8, 1993
20,000 m	1:05:26.60	Tegla Loroupe	Kenya	Borgholzhausen, Germany	Sept. 3, 2000
25,000 m	1:27:05.90	Tegla Loroupe	Kenya	Mengerskirchen, Germany	Sept. 21, 2002
30,000 m	1:45:50.00	Tegla Loroupe	Kenya	Warstein, Germany	June 6, 2003
1 hour	18,340 m	Tegla Loroupe	Kenya	Borgholzhausen, Germany	July 8, 1998
3,000 m steeplechase	9:01.59	Gulnara Samitova	Russia	Iráklio, Greece	July 4, 2004
Marathon[1]	2:15:25	Paula Radcliffe	Great Britain	London, England	April 13, 2003
Walking					
10,000 m	41:56.23	Nadezhda Ryashkina	Russia	Seattle, Wash.	July 24, 1990
20,000 m	1:26:52.30	Olimpiada Ivanova	Russia	Brisbane, Australia	Sept. 6, 2001
Hurdles					
100 m	0:12.21	Yordanka Donkova	Bulgaria	Stara Zagora, Bulgaria	Aug. 20, 1988
400 m	0:52.34	Yuliya Pechonkina	Russia	Tula, Russia	Aug. 8, 2003
Relay races					
400 m (4 × 100)	0:41.37	East Germany	E. Germany	Canberra, Australia	Oct. 6, 1985
800 m (4 × 200)	1:27.46	United States "Blue"	United States	Philadelphia, Pa.	April 29, 2000
1,600 m (4 × 400)	3:15.17	USSR	USSR	Seoul, South Korea	Oct. 1, 1988
3,200 m (4 × 800)	7:50.17	USSR	USSR	Moscow, USSR	Aug. 5, 1984
Field events					
High jump	2.09 m	Stefka Kostadinova	Bulgaria	Rome, Italy	Aug. 30, 1987
Pole vault	5.01 m[2]	Yelena Isinbayeva	Russia	Helsinki, Finland	Aug. 12, 2005
Long jump	7.52 m	Galina Chistyakova	USSR	Leningrad, Russia	June 11, 1988
Triple jump	15.50 m	Inessa Kravets	Ukraine	Göteborg, Sweden	Aug. 10, 1995
Shot-put	22.63 m	Natalya Lisovskaya	USSR	Moscow, Russia	June 7, 1987
Discus throw	76.80 m	Gabriele Reinsch	East Germany	Neubrandenburg, E. Ger.	July 9, 1988
Hammer throw	77.06 m[2]	Tatyana Lysenko	Russia	Moscow, Russia	July 15, 2005
Javelin throw	71.70 m[2]	Osleidys Menéndez	Cuba	Helsinki, Finland	Aug. 14, 2005
Heptathlon	7,291 pts	Jackie Joyner-Kersee	United States	Seoul, South Korea	Sept. 24, 1988
Decathlon	8,358 pts	Austra Skujyte	Lithuania	Columbia, Mo.	April 15, 2005

1. Not recognized by IAAF as world record, but considered to be "world-best performance." 2. Awaiting IAAF ratification.
Source: IAAF.

AMERICAN OUTDOOR RECORDS—MEN
(Through Aug. 30, 2005)

Event	Record	Holder	Where made	Date
Running				
100 m	0:09.78	Tim Montgomery	Paris, France	Sept. 14, 2002
200 m	0:19.32	Michael Johnson	Atlanta, Ga.	Aug. 1, 1996
400 m	0:43.18	Michael Johnson	Seville, Spain	Aug. 26, 1999
800 m	1:42.60	Johnny Gray	Koblenz, W. Germany	Aug. 28, 1985
1,000 m	2:13.90	Richard Wohlhuter	Oslo, Norway	July 20, 1974
1,500 m	3:29.30	Bernard Lagat	Rieti, Italy	Aug. 28, 2005
1 mile	3:47.69	Steve Scott	Oslo, Norway	July 7, 1982
2,000 m	4:52.44	Jim Spivey	Lausanne, Switzerland	Sept. 15, 1987
3,000 m	7:30.84	Bob Kennedy	Fontvieille, Monaco	Aug. 8, 1998
5,000 m	12:58.21	Bob Kennedy	Zurich, Switzerland	Aug. 14, 1996
10,000 m	27:13.98	Meb Keflezighi	Stanford, Calif.	May 4, 2001
3,000-m steeplechase	8:09.17	Henry Marsh	Koblenz, W. Germany	Aug. 29, 1985
Marathon	2:05:38	Khalid Khannouchi	London, England	April 14, 2002
Hurdles				
110 m	0:12.92	Roger Kingdom	Zurich, Switzerland	Aug. 16, 1989
		Allen Johnson	Atlanta, Ga.	June 23, 1996
400 m	0:46.78	Kevin Young	Barcelona	Aug. 6, 1992
Relay races				
400 m (4 × 100)	0:37.40	Olympic Team	Barcelona, Spain	Aug. 8, 1992
		USA National Team	Stuttgart, Germany	Aug. 21, 1993
800 m (4 × 200)	1:18.68	Santa Monica T.C.	Walnut, Calif.	April 17, 1994
1,600 m (4 × 400)	2:54.20	USA National Team	Uniondale, N.Y.	July 22, 1998
3,200 m (4 × 800)	7:06.50	Santa Monica T.C.	Walnut, Calif.	Apr. 26, 1986
6,000 m (4 × 1,500)	14:46.30	National Team	Bourges, France	June 24, 1979

Event	Record	Holder	Where made	Date
Field events				
High jump	2.40 m	Charles Austin	Zurich, Switzerland	Aug. 7, 1991
Long jump	8.95 m	Mike Powell	Tokyo, Japan	Aug. 30, 1991
Triple jump	18.09 m	Kenny Harrison	Atlanta, Ga.	July 27, 1996
Pole vault	6.03 m	Jeff Hartwig	Jonesboro, Ark.	June 14, 2000
Shot-put	23.12 m	Randy Barnes	Westwood, Calif.	May 20, 1990
Discus throw	72.34 m	Ben Plucknett	Stockholm, Sweden	July 7, 1981
Javelin throw	87.68 m	Breaux Greer	Fontvieille, Monaco	Sept. 19, 2004
Hammer throw	82.52 m	Lance Deal	Milan, Italy	Sept. 17, 1996
Decathlon	8,891 pts	Dan O'Brien	Talence, France	Sept. 4, 1992

AMERICAN OUTDOOR RECORDS—WOMEN
(Through Aug. 30, 2005)

Event	Record	Holder	Where made	Date
Running				
100 m	0:10.49	Florence Griffith Joyner	Indianapolis, Ind.	July 16, 1988
200 m	21.34	Florence Griffith Joyner	Seoul, South Korea	Sept. 29, 1988
400 m	0:48.83	Valerie Brisco-Hooks	Los Angeles, Calif.	Aug. 6, 1984
800 m	1:56.40	Jearl Miles-Clark	Zurich, Switzerland	Aug. 11, 1999
1,000 m	2:31.80	Regina Jacobs	Brunswick, Maine	July 2, 1999
1,500 m	3:57.12	Mary Slaney	Stockholm, Sweden	July 26, 1983
2,000 m	5:32.70	Mary Slaney	Eugene, Ore.	Aug. 3, 1984
1 mile	4:16.71	Mary Slaney	Zurich, Switzerland	Aug. 21, 1985
3,000 m	8:25.83	Mary Slaney	Rome, Italy	Sept. 7, 1985
5,000 m	14:45.35	Regina Jacobs	Sacramento, Calif.	July 21, 2000
10,000 m	30:52.32	Deena Drossin	Stanford, Calif.	May 3, 2002
3,000 m steeplechase	9:29.32	Brianna Shook	Heusden Zolder, Belgium	July 31, 2004
Marathon	2:21:16	Deena Drossin Kastor	London, England	April 13, 2003
Hurdles				
100 m	0:12.33	Gail Devers	Sacramento, Calif.	July 23, 2000
400 m	0:52.61	Kim Batten	Göteborg, Sweden	Aug. 11, 1995
Relay races				
400 m (4 × 100)	41.47	U.S.A. National Team	Athens, Greece	Aug. 8, 1997
800 m (4 × 200)	1:27.46	United States Blue Team	Philadelphia, Pa.	April 29, 2000
1,600 m (4 × 400)	3:15.51	U.S. Olympic Team	Seoul, South Korea	Oct. 1, 1988
3,200 m (4 × 800)	8:19.90	U.S.A. National Team	Bourges, France	June 24, 1979
Field events				
Pole vault	4.83 m	Stacy Dragila	Ostrava, Czech Republic	June 8, 2004
High jump	2.03 m	Louise Ritter	Austin, Tex.	July 8, 1988
Long jump	7.49 m	Jackie Joyner-Kersee	New York, N.Y.	May 22, 1994
Triple jump	14.45 m	Tiombé Hurd	Sacramento, Calif.	July 11, 2004
Shot-put	20.18 m	Ramona Pagel	San Diego, Calif.	June 25, 1988
Discus throw	66.10 m	Carol Cady	San Jose, Calif.	May 31, 1986
Hammer throw	72.12 m	Erin Gilreath	Tempe, Ariz.	April 10, 2004
Javelin throw (old)	69.32 m	Kate Schmidt	Fürth, W. Ger.	Sept. 10, 1977
Javelin throw (new)	60.86 m	Kim Kreiner	Santo Domingo, Dom. Rep.	Aug. 7, 2003
Heptathlon	7,291 pts	Jackie Joyner-Kersee	Seoul, South Korea	Sept. 23, 1988

HISTORY OF THE RECORD FOR THE MILE RUN
(Under 4 minutes)

Time	Athlete	Country	Year	Location
3:59.4	Roger Bannister	England	1954	Oxford, England
3:58.0	John Landy	Australia	1954	Turku, Finland
3:57.2	Derek Ibbotson	England	1957	London
3:54.5	Herb Elliott	Australia	1958	Dublin
3:54.4	Peter Snell	New Zealand	1962	Wanganui, N.Z.
3:54.1	Peter Snell	New Zealand	1964	Auckland, N.Z.
3:53.6	Michel Jazy	France	1965	Rennes, France
3:51.3	Jim Ryun	United States	1966	Berkeley, Calif.
3:51.1	Jim Ryun	United States	1967	Bakersfield, Calif.
3:51.0	Filbert Bayi	Tanzania	1975	Kingston, Jamaica
3:49.4	John Walker	New Zealand	1975	Goteborg, Sweden
3:49.0	Sebastian Coe	England	1979	Oslo
3:48.8	Steve Ovett	England	1980	Oslo
3:48.53	Sebastian Coe	England	1981	Zurich, Switzerland
3:48.40	Steve Ovett	England	1981	Koblenz, W. Ger.
3:47.33	Sebastian Coe	England	1981	Brussels
3:46.31	Steve Cram	England	1985	Oslo
3:44.39	Noureddine Morceli	Algeria	1993	Rieti, Italy
3:43.13	Hicham El Guerrouj	Morocco	1999	Rome, Italy

Source: USA Track & Field.

WORLD INDOOR RECORDS—MEN
(Through Aug. 30, 2005)

Event	Record	Holder	Home country	Where made	Date
Running					
50 m	0:05.56	Donovan Bailey	Canada	Reno, Nev.	Feb. 9, 1996
60 m	0:06.39	Maurice Greene	United States	Madrid, Spain	Feb. 3, 1998
	0:06.39	Maurice Greene	United States	Atlanta, Ga.	March 3, 2001
200 m	0:19.92	Frank Fredericks	Namibia	Liévin, France	Feb. 18, 1996
400 m	0:44.57	Kerron Clement	United States	Fayetteville, Ark.	March 12, 2005
800 m	1:42.67	Wilson Kipketer	Denmark	Paris, France	March 9, 1997
1,000 m	2:14.96	Wilson Kipketer	Denmark	Birmingham, England	Feb. 20, 2000
1,500 m	3:31.18	Hicham El Guerrouj	Morocco	Stuttgart, Germany	Feb. 2, 1997
1 mile	3:48.45	Hicham El Guerrouj	Morocco	Ghent, Belgium	Feb. 12, 1997
3,000 m	7:24.90	Daniel Komen	Kenya	Budapest, Hungary	Feb. 6, 1998
5,000 m	12:49.60	Kenenisa Bekele	Ethiopia	Birmingham, England	Feb. 20, 2004
5,000 m race walking	18:07.08	Mikhail Shchennikov	Russia	Moscow, Russia	Feb. 14, 1995
Hurdles					
50 m	0:06.25	Mark McKoy	Canada	Kobe, Japan	March 5, 1986
60 m	0:07.30	Colin Jackson	Great Britain	Sindelfingen, Germany	March 6, 1994
Relay races					
800 m (4 × 200)	1:22.11	Great Britain & Northern Ireland	Great Britain	Glasgow, Scotland	March 3, 1991
1,600 m (4 × 400)	3:02.83	National Team	United States	Maebashi, Japan	March 7, 1999
3,200 m (4 × 800)	7:13.94	Global Athletics & Marketing	United States	Boston, Mass.	Feb. 6, 2000
Field events					
High jump	2.43 m	Javier Sotomayor	Cuba	Budapest, Hungary	March 4, 1989
Pole vault	6.15 m	Sergey Bubka	Ukraine	Donetsk, Ukraine	Feb. 21, 1993
Long jump	8.79 m	Carl Lewis	United States	New York, N.Y.	Jan. 27, 1984
Triple jump	17.83 m	Aliecer Urrutia	Cuba	Sindelfingen, Germany	March 1, 1997
	17.83 m	Christian Olsson	Sweden	Budapest, Hungary	March 7, 2004
Shot-put	22.66 m	Randy Barnes	United States	Los Angeles, Calif.	Jan. 20, 1989
Heptathlon	6,476 pts	Dan O'Brien	United States	Toronto, Canada	March 14, 1993

Source: IAAF.

WORLD INDOOR RECORDS—WOMEN
(Through Aug. 30, 2005)

Event	Record	Holder	Home country	Where made	Date
Running					
50 m	0:05.96	Irina Privalova	Russia	Madrid, Spain	Feb. 9, 1995
60 m	0:06.92	Irina Privalova	Russia	Madrid, Spain	Feb. 11, 1993
	0:06.92	Irina Privalova	Russia	Madrid, Spain	Feb. 9, 1995
200 m	0:21.87	Merlene Ottey	Jamaica	Liévin, France	Feb. 13, 1993
400 m	0:49.59	Jarmila Kratochvílová	Czechoslovakia	Milan, Italy	March 7, 1982
800 m	1:55.82	Jolanda Ceplak	Slovak Republic	Vienna, Austria	March 3, 2002
1,000 m	2:30.94	Maria de Lurdes Mutola	Mozambique	Stockholm, Sweden	Feb. 25, 1999
1,500 m	3:59.98	Regina Jacobs	United States	Boston, Mass.	Feb. 1, 2003
1 mile	4:17.14	Doina Melinte	Romania	East Rutherford, N.J.	Feb. 9, 1990
3,000 m	8:29.15	Berhane Adere	Ethiopia	Stuttgart, Germany	Feb. 3, 2002
5,000 m	14:32.93	Tirunesh Dibaba	Ethiopia	Boston, Mass.	Jan. 29, 2005
3,000 m race walking	11:40.33	Claudia Stef	Romania	Bucharest, Romania	Jan. 30, 1999
Hurdles					
50 m	0:06.58	Cornelia Oschkenat	East Germany	Berlin, Germany	Feb. 20, 1988
60 m	0:07.69	Ludmila Engquist	Soviet Union	Chelyabinsk, Russia	Feb. 4, 1990
Relay races					
800 m (4 × 200)	1:32.41	National Team	Russia	Glasgow, Scotland	Jan. 29, 2005
1,600 m (4 × 400)	3:23.88	National Team	Russia	Budapest, Hungary	March 7, 2004
3,200 m (4 × 800)	8:18.71	National Team	Russia	Moscow, Russia	Feb. 4, 1994
Field events					
High jump	2.07 m	Heike Henkel	Germany	Karlsruhe, Germany	Feb. 8, 1992
Pole vault	4.90 m	Yelena Isinbayeva	Russia	Madrid, Spain	March 6, 2005
Long jump	7.37 m	Heike Drechsler	East Germany	Vienna, Austria	Feb. 13, 1988
Triple jump	15.36 m	Tatyana Lebedeva	Russia	Budapest, Hungary	March 6, 2004
Shot-put	22.50 m	Helena Fibingerová	Czechoslovakia	Jablonec, Czechoslovakia	Feb. 19, 1977
Pentathlon	4,991 pts.	Irina Belova	Unified Team	Berlin, Germany	Feb. 15, 1992

Source: IAAF.

Tennis

Lawn tennis is a comparatively modern modification of the ancient game of court tennis. Maj. Walter Clopton Wingfield thought that something like court tennis might be played outdoors on lawns, and in Dec. 1873, at Nantclwyd, Wales, he introduced his new game under the name of *Sphairistike* at a lawn party. The game was a success and spread rapidly, but the name was a total failure and almost immediately disappeared when all the players and spectators began to refer to the new game as *lawn tennis*. In the early part of 1874, a young lady named Mary Ewing Outerbridge returned from Bermuda to New York, bringing with her the implements and necessary equipment of the new game, which she had obtained from a British Army supply store in Bermuda. Miss Outerbridge and friends played the first game of lawn tennis in the United States on the grounds of the Staten Island Cricket and Baseball Club in the spring of 1874.

For a few years, the new game went along in haphazard fashion until about 1880, when standard measurements for the court and standard equipment within definite limits became the rule. In 1881, the U.S. Lawn Tennis Association (whose name was changed in 1975 to the U.S. Tennis Association) was formed and conducted the first national championship at Newport, R.I. The international matches for the Davis Cup began with a series between the British and U.S. players on the courts of the Longwood Cricket Club, Chestnut Hill, Mass., in 1900, with the home players winning.

Professional tennis, which got its start in 1926 when the French star Suzanne Lenglen was paid $50,000 for a tour, received full recognition in 1968. Staid old Wimbledon, the London home of what are considered the world championships, let the pros compete. This decision ended a long controversy over open tennis and changed the format of the competition. The U.S. championships were also opened to the pros and the site of the event, long held at Forest Hills, N.Y., was shifted to the National Tennis Center in Flushing Meadows, N.Y., in 1978. Pro tours for men and women became worldwide in play that continued throughout the year.

DAVIS CUP CHAMPIONSHIPS

No matches in 1901, 1910, 1915–1918, and 1940–1945

1900 United States 3, British Isles 0	1938 United States 3, Australia 2	1975 Sweden 3, Czechoslovakia 2
1902 United States 3, British Isles 2	1939 Australia 3, United States 2	1976 Italy 4, Chile 1
1903 British Isles 4, United States 1	1946 United States 5, Australia 0	1977 Australia 3, Italy 1
1904 British Isles 5, Belgium 0	1947 United States 4, Australia 1	1978 United States 4, Britain 1
1905 British Isles 5, United States 0	1948 United States 5, Australia 0	1979 United States 5, Italy 0
1906 British Isles 5, United States 0	1949 United States 4, Australia 1	1980 Czechoslovakia 3, Italy 2
1907 Australasia 3, British Isles 2	1950 Australia 4, United States 1	1981 United States 3, Argentina 1
1908 Australasia 3, United States 2	1951 Australia 3, United States 2	1982 United States 3, France 0
1909 Australasia 5, United States 0	1952 Australia 4, United States 1	1983 Australia 3, Sweden 2
1911 Australasia 5, United States 0	1953 Australia 3, United States 2	1984 Sweden 4, United States 1
1912 British Isles 3, Australasia 2	1954 United States 3, Australia 2	1985 Sweden 3, West Germany 2
1913 United States 3, British Isles 2	1955 Australia 5, United States 0	1986 Australia 3, Sweden 2
1914 Australasia 3, United States 2	1956 Australia 5, United States 0	1987 Sweden 5, India 0
1919 Australasia 4, British Isles 1	1957 Australia 3, United States 2	1988 West Germany 4, Sweden 1
1920 United States 5, Australasia 0	1958 United States 3, Australia 2	1989 West Germany 3, Sweden 2
1921 United States 5, Japan 0	1959 Australia 3, United States 2	1990 United States 3, Australia 2
1922 United States 4, Australasia 1	1960 Australia 4, Italy 1	1991 France 3, United States 1
1923 United States 4, Australasia 1	1961 Australia 5, Italy 0	1992 United States 3, Switzerland 1
1924 United States 5, Australasia 0	1962 Australia 5, Mexico 0	1993 Germany 4, Australia 1
1925 United States 5, France 0	1963 United States 3, Australia 2	1994 Sweden 4, Russia 1
1926 United States 4, France 1	1964 Australia 3, United States 2	1995 United States 3, Russia 1
1927 France 3, United States 2	1965 Australia 4, Spain 1	1996 France 3, Sweden 2
1928 France 4, United States 1	1966 Australia 4, India 1	1997 Sweden 5, United States 0
1929 France 3, United States 2	1967 Australia 4, Spain 1	1998 Sweden 4, Italy 1
1930 France 4, United States 1	1968 United States 4, Australia 1	1999 Australia 3, France 2
1931 France 3, Great Britain 2	1969 United States 5, Romania 0	2000 Spain 3, Australia 1
1932 France 3, United States 2	1970 United States 5, West	2001 France 3, Australia 2
1933 Great Britain 3, France 2	Germany 0	2002 Russia 3, France 2
1934 Great Britain 4, United States 1	1971 United States 3, Romania 2	2003 Australia 3, Spain 1
1935 Great Britain 5, United States 0	1972 United States 3, Romania 2	2004 Spain 3, United States 2
1936 Great Britain 3, Australia 2	1973 Australia 5, United States 0	
1937 United States 4, Great Britain 1	1974 South Africa (Default by India)	

FEDERATION CUP CHAMPIONSHIPS

World team competition for women conducted by International Lawn Tennis Federation

1963 United States 2, Australia 1	1969 United States 2, Australia 1	1975 Czechoslovakia 3, Australia 0
1964 Australia 2, United States 1	1970 Australia 3, West Germany 0	1976 United States 2, Australia 1
1965 Australia 2, United States 1	1971 Australia 3, Britain 0	1977 United States 2, Australia 1
1966 United States 3, West Germany 0	1972 South Africa 2, Britain 1	1978 United States 2, Australia 1
1967 United States 2, Britain 0	1973 Australia 3, South Africa 0	1979 United States 3, Australia 0
1968 Australia 3, Netherlands 0	1974 Australia 2, United States 1	1980 United States 3, Australia 0

1981 United States 3, Britain 0	1988 Czechoslovakia 2, Soviet Union 1	1998 Spain 3, Switzerland 2
1982 United States 3, West Germany 0	1989 United States 3, Spain 0	1999 United States 4, Russia 1
1983 Czechoslovakia 2, West Germany 1	1990 United States 2, Soviet Union 1	2000 United States 5, Spain 0
1984 Czechoslovakia 2, Australia 1	1991 Spain 2, United States 1	2001 Belgium 2, Russia 1
1985 Czechoslovakia 2, United States 1	1992 Germany 2, Spain 1	2002 Slovak Republic 3, Spain 1
1986 United States 3, Czechoslovakia 0	1993 Spain 3, Australia 0	2003 France 4, United States 1
1987 West Germany 2, United States 1	1994 Spain 3, United States 0	2004 Russia 3, France 2
	1995 Spain 3, United States 2	
	1996 United States 5, Spain 0	
	1997 France 4, Netherlands 1	

U.S. NATIONAL AND OPEN CHAMPIONS

SINGLES—MEN

NATIONAL					
1881–87	Richard D. Sears	1926–27	Jean Rene Lacoste	1957	Mal Anderson
1888–89	Henry Slocum, Jr.	1928	Henri Cochet	1958	Ashley Cooper
1890–92	Oliver S. Campbell	1929	Bill Tilden	1959–60	Neale Fraser
1893–94	Robert D. Wrenn	1930	John H. Doeg	1961	Roy Emerson
1895	Fred H. Hovey	1931–32	Ellsworth Vines	1962	Rod Laver
1896–97	Robert D. Wrenn	1933–34	Fred J. Perry	1963	Rafael Osuna
1898–		1935	Wilmer L. Allison	1964	Roy Emerson
1900	Malcolm Whitman	1936	Fred J. Perry	1965	Manuel Santana
1901–02	William A. Larned	1937–38	Don Budge	1966	Fred Stolle
1903	Hugh L. Doherty	1939	Robert L. Riggs	1967	John Newcombe
1904	Holcombe Ward	1940	Donald McNeill	1968	Arthur Ashe
1905	Beals C. Wright	1941	Robert L. Riggs	1969	Rod Laver
1906	William J. Clothier	1942	Fred Schroeder		
1907–11	William A. Larned	1943	Joseph Hunt	**OPEN**	
1912–13	Maurice McLoughlin[1]	1944–45	Frank Parker	1968	Arthur Ashe
1914	R. N. Williams II	1946–47	Jack Kramer	1969	Rod Laver
1915	William Johnston	1948–49	Richard Gonzales	1970	Ken Rosewall
1916	R. N. William II	1950	Arthur Larsen	1971	Stan Smith
1917–18	R. Lindley Murray[2]	1951–52	Frank Sedgman	1972	Ilie Nastase
1919	William Johnston	1953	Tony Trabert	1973	John Newcombe
1920–25	Bill Tilden	1954	Vic Seixas	1974	Jimmy Connors
		1955	Tony Trabert	1975	Manuel Orantes
		1956	Ken Rosewall	1976	Jimmy Connors

1977	Guillermo Vilas
1978	Jimmy Connors
1979–81	John McEnroe
1982–83	Jimmy Connors
1984	John McEnroe
1985–87	Ivan Lendl
1988	Mats Wilander
1989	Boris Becker
1990	Pete Sampras
1991–92	Stefan Edberg
1993	Pete Sampras
1994	Andre Agassi
1995–96	Pete Sampras
1997–98	Patrick Rafter
1999	Andre Agassi
2000	Marat Safin
2001	Lleyton Hewitt
2002	Pete Sampras
2003	Andy Roddick
2004–05	Roger Federer

1. Challenge Round abandoned in 1912. 2. Patriotic Tournament in 1917.

SINGLES—WOMEN

NATIONAL					
1887	Ellen F. Hansel	1915–18	Molla Bjurstedt	1954–55	Doris Hart
1888–89	Bertha Townsend	1919	Hazel Hotchkiss Wightman	1956	Shirley Fry
1890	Ellen C. Roosevelt	1920–22	Molla Bjurstedt Mallory	1957–58	Althea Gibson
1891–92	Mabel E. Cahill	1923–25	Helen N. Wills	1959	Maria Bueno
1893	Aline M. Terry	1926	Molla B. Mallory	1960–61	Darlene Hard
1894	Helen R. Helwig	1927–29	Helen N. Wills	1962	Margaret Smith
1895	Juliette P. Atkinson	1930	Betty Nuthall	1963–64	Maria Bueno
1896	Elisabeth H. Moore	1931	Helen Wills Moody	1965	Margaret Smith
1897–98	Juliette P. Atkinson	1932–35	Helen Jacobs	1966	Maria Bueno
1899	Marion Jones	1936	Alice Marble	1967	Billie Jean King
1900	Myrtle McAteer	1937	Anita Lizana	1968–69	Margaret Smith Court[1]
1901	Elisabeth H. Moore	1938–40	Alice Marble		
1902	Marion Jones	1941	Sarah Palfrey Cooke	**OPEN**	
1903	Elisabeth H. Moore	1942–44	Pauline Betz	1968	Virginia Wade
1904	May Sutton	1945	Sarah Cooke	1969–70	Margaret Court
1905	Elisabeth H. Moore	1946	Pauline Betz	1971–72	Billie Jean King
1906	Helen Homans	1947	Louise Brough	1973	Margaret Court
1907	Evelyn Sears	1948–50	Margaret Osborne duPont	1974	Billie Jean King
1908	Maud Bargar-Wallach	1951–53	Maureen Connolly	1975–78	Chris Evert
1909–11	Hazel V. Hotchkiss			1979	Tracy Austin
1912–14	Mary K. Browne			1980	Chris Evert-Lloyd
				1981	Tracy Austin

1982	Chris Evert-Lloyd
1983–84	Martina Navratilova
1985	Hana Mandlikova
1986–87	Martina Navratilova
1988–89	Steffi Graf
1990	Gabriela Sabatini
1991–92	Monica Seles
1993	Steffi Graf
1994	Arantxa Sanchez Vicario
1995–96	Steffi Graf
1997	Martina Hingis
1998	Lindsay Davenport
1999	Serena Williams
2000–01	Venus Williams
2002	Serena Williams
2003	Justine Henin-Hardenne
2004	Svetlana Kuznetsova
2005	Kim Clijsters

1. With the inaugural of the Open Tournament in 1968, the United States Lawn Tennis Association held a championship at Longwood, Chestnut Hill, Mass., which barred contract professionals in 1968 and 1969.

DOUBLES—MEN

NATIONAL

1920	Bill Johnston–C. J. Griffin
1921–22	Bill Tilden–Vincent Richards
1923	Bill Tilden–B. I. C. Norton
1924	H. O. Kinsey–R. G. Kinsey
1925–26	Vincent Richards–R. N. Williams II
1927	Bill Tilden–Frank Hunter
1928	G. M. Lott, Jr.–V. Hennessy
1929–30	G. M. Lott, Jr.–J. H. Doeg
1931	W. L. Allison–John Van Ryn
1932	E. H. Vines, Jr.–Keith Gledh
1933–34	G. M. Lott, Jr.–L. R. Stoefen
1935	W. L. Allison–John Van Ryn
1936	Don Budge–Gene Mako
1937	G. von Cramm–H. Henkel
1938	Don Budge–Gene Mako
1939	A. K. Quist–J. E. Bromwich
1940–41	Jack Kramer–F. R. Schroeder
1942	Gardnar Mulloy–Bill Talbert
1943	Jack Kramer–Frank Parker
1944	Don McNeill–Bob Falkenburg
1945–46	Gardnar Mulloy–Bill Talbert
1947	Jack Kramer–Fred Schroeder
1948	Gardnar Mulloy–Bill Talbert
1949	John Bromwich–William Sidwell
1950	John Bromwich–Frank Sedgman
1951	Frank Sedgman–Ken McGregor
1952	Vic Seixas–Mervyn Rose
1953	Mervyn Rose–Rex Hartwig
1954	Vic Seixas–Tony Trabert
1955	Kosei Kamo–Atsushi Miyagi
1956	Lewis Hoad–Ken Rosewall
1957	Ashley Cooper–Neale Fraser
1958	Ham Richardson–Alex Olmedo
1959–60	Neale Fraser–Roy Emerson
1961	Chuck McKinley–Dennis Ralston
1962	Rafael Osuna–Antonio Palafox
1963–64	Chuck McKinley–Dennis Ralston
1965–66	Fred Stolle–Roy Emerson
1967	John Newcombe–Tony Roche
1968	Stan Smith–Bob Lutz[1]
1969	Richard Crealy–Allan Stone[1]

OPEN

1968	Stan Smith–Bob Lutz
1969	Fred Stolle–Ken Rosewall
1970	Nikki Pilic–Fred Barthes
1971	John Newcombe–Roger Taylor
1972	Cliff Drysdale–Roger Taylor
1973	John Newcombe–Owen Davidson
1974	Bob Lutz–Stan Smith
1975	Jimmy Connors–Ilie Nastase
1976	Marty Riessen–Tom Okker
1977	Frew McMillan–Bob Hewitt
1978	Bob Lutz–Stan Smith
1979	John McEnroe–Peter Fleming
1980	Stan Smith–Bob Lutz
1981	John McEnroe–Peter Fleming
1982	Kevin Curren–Steve Denton
1983	John McEnroe–Peter Fleming
1984	John Fitzgerald–Tomas Smid
1985	Ken Flach–Robert Seguso
1986	Andres Gomez–Slobodan Zivojinovic
1987	Stefan Edberg–Anders Jarryd
1988	Sergio Casal–Emilio Sanchez
1989	John McEnroe–Mark Woodforde
1990	Pieter Aldrich–Danie Visser
1991	John Fitzgerald–Anders Jarryd
1992	Jim Grabb–Richey Reneberg
1993	Ken Flach–Rick Leach
1994	Jacco Hingh–Paul Haarhuis
1995–96	Todd Woodbridge–Mark Woodforde
1997	Yevgeny Kafelnikov–Daniel Vacek
1998	Sandon Stolle–Cyril Zuk
1999	Sebastien Lareau–Alex O'Brien
2000	Lleyton Hewitt–Max Mirnyi
2001	Wayne Black–Kevin Ullyett
2002	Mahesh Bhupathi–Max Mirnyi
2003	Jonas Bjorkman–Todd Woodbridge
2004	Mark Knowles–Daniel Nestor
2005	Bob Bryan–Mike Bryan

1. With the inaugural of the Open Tournament in 1968, the United States Lawn Tennis Association held a national championship at Longwood, Chestnut Hill, Mass., which barred contract professionals in 1968 and 1969.

DOUBLES—WOMEN

NATIONAL

1924	G. W. Wightman–Helen Wills
1925	Mary K. Browne–Helen Wills
1926	Elizabeth Ryan–Eleanor Goss
1927	L. A. Godfree–Ermyntrude Harvey
1928	Hazel Hotchkiss Wightman–Helen Wills
1929	Phoebe Watson–L. R. C. Michell
1930	Betty Nuthall–Sarah Palfrey
1931	Betty Nuthall–E. B. Wittingstall
1932	Helen Jacobs–Sarah Palfrey
1933	Betty Nuthall–Freda James
1934	Helen Jacobs–Sarah Palfrey
1935	Helen Jacobs–Sarah Palfrey Fabyan
1936	Marjorie G. Van Ryn–Carolin Babcock
1937–40	Sarah Palfrey Fabyan–Alice Marble
1941	Sarah Palfrey Cooke–Margaret Osborne
1942–47	A. Louise Brough–Margaret Osborne
1948–50	A. Louise Brough–Margaret O. duPont
1951–54	Doris Hart–Shirley Fry
1955–57	A. Louise Brough–Margaret O. duPont
1958–59	Darlene Hard–Jeanne Arth
1960	Darlene Hard–Maria Bueno
1961	Darlene Hard–Lesley Turner
1962	Darlene Hard–Maria Bueno
1963	Margaret Smith–Robyn Ebbern
1964	Karen Hantze Susman–Billie Jean Moffitt
1965	Nancy Richey–Carole Caldwell Graebner
1966	Nancy Richey–Maria Bueno
1967	Billie Jean King–Rosemary Casals
1968	Margaret Court–Maria Bueno[1]
1969	Margaret Court–Virginia Wade[1]

OPEN

1968	Maria Bueno–Margaret Court
1969	Darlene Hard–Francoise Durr
1970	Margaret Court–Judy Dalton
1971	Rosemary Casals–Judy Dalton
1972	Francoise Durr–Betty Stove
1973	Margaret Court–Virginia Wade
1974	Billie Jean King–Rosemary Casals
1975	Margaret Court–Virginia Wade
1976	Linky Boshoff–Ilana Kloss
1977	Martina Navratilova–Betty Stove
1978	Billie Jean King–Martina Navratilova
1979	Betty Stove–Wendy Turnbull
1980	Billie Jean King–Martina Navratilova
1981	Kathy Jordan–Anne Smith
1982	Rosemary Casals–Wendy Turnbull
1983–84	Martina Navratilova–Pam Shriver
1985	Claudia Khode-Kilsch–Helena Sukova
1986–87	Martina Navratilova–Pam Shriver
1988	Gigi Fernandez–Robin White
1989	Hana Mandlikova–Martina Navratilova
1990	Gigi Fernandez–Martina Navratilova
1991	Pam Shriver–Natalia Zvereva
1992	Gigi Fernandez–Natalia Zvereva
1993	Arantxa Sanchez Vicario–Helena Sukova
1994	Jana Novotna–Arantxa Sanchez Vicario
1995–96	Gigi Fernandez–Natasha Zvereva

1997	Lindsay Davenport–Jana Novotna	2000	Julie-Halard Decugis–Ai Sugiyama	2002–04	Virginia Ruano Pascual–Paola Suarez
1998	Martina Hingis–Jana Novotna	2001	Lisa Raymond–Renae Stubbs	2005	Lisa Raymond–Samantha Stosur
1999	Serena Williams–Venus Williams				

1. With the inaugural of the Open Tournament in 1968, the United States Lawn Tennis Association held a national championship at Longwood, Chestnut Hill, Mass., which barred contract professionals in 1968 and 1969.

U.S. OPEN, 2005
(Flushing Meadow, N.Y., Aug. 29–Sept. 11, 2005)

Men's singles—Roger Federer defeated Andre Agassi, 6–3, 2–6, 7–6 (7–1), 6–1.

Women's singles—Kim Clijsters defeated Mary Pierce, 6–3, 6–1.

Men's doubles—Bob Bryan and Mike Bryan defeated Jonas Bjorkman and Max Mirny, 6–1, 6–4.

Women's doubles—Lisa Raymond and Samantha Stosur defeated Elena Dementieva and Flavia Pennetta, 6–2, 5–7, 6–3.

Mixed doubles—Daniela Hantuchova and Mahesh Bhupathi defeated Katarina Srebotnik and Nenad Zimonjic, 6–4, 6–2.

BRITISH (WIMBLEDON) CHAMPIONS
(Amateur from inception in 1877 through 1967)
SINGLES—MEN

1908–09	Arthur Gore	1933	J. H. Crawford	1959	Alex Olmedo	1983–84	John McEnroe
1910–13	A. F. Wilding	1934–36	Fred Perry	1960	Neale Fraser	1985–86	Boris Becker
1914	N. E. Brookes	1937–38	Don Budge	1961–62	Rod Laver	1987	Pat Cash
1919	G. L. Patterson	1939	Robert L. Riggs	1963	Chuck McKinley	1988	Stefan Edberg
1920–21	Bill Tilden	1946	Yvon Petra	1964–65	Roy Emerson	1989	Boris Becker
1922	G. L. Patterson	1947	Jack Kramer	1966	Manuel Santana	1990	Stefan Edberg
1923	William Johnston	1948	R. Falkenburg	1967	John Newcombe	1991	Michael Stich
1924	Jean Borotra	1949	Fred Schroeder	1968–69	Rod Laver	1992	Andre Agassi
1925	Rene Lacoste	1950	Budge Patty	1970–71	John Newcombe	1993–95	Pete Sampras
1926	Jean Borotra	1951	Richard Savitt	1972	Stan Smith	1996	Richard Krajicek
1927	Henri Cochet	1952	Frank Sedgman	1973	Jan Kodes	1997–	
1928	Rene Lacoste	1953	Vic Siexas	1974	Jimmy Connors	2000	Pete Sampras
1929	Jean Cochet	1954	Jaroslav Drobny	1975	Arthur Ashe	2001	Goran Ivanisevic
1930	Bill Tilden	1955	Tony Trabert	1976–80	Bjorn Borg	2002	Lleyton Hewitt
1931	S. B. Wood	1956–57	Lewis Hoad	1981	John McEnroe	2003–05	Roger Federer
1932	Ellsworth Vines	1958	Ashley Cooper	1982	Jimmy Connors		

SINGLES—WOMEN

1919–23	Suzanne Lenglen	1946	Pauline M. Betz	1966–68	Billie Jean King	1988–89	Steffi Graf
1924	Kathleen McKane	1947	Margaret Osborne	1969	Ann Jones	1990	Martina Navratilova
1925	Suzanne Lenglen	1948–50	A. Louise Brough	1970	Margaret Court	1991–93	Steffi Graf
1926	Kathleen Godfree	1951	Doris Hart	1971	Evonne Goolagong	1994	Conchita Martinez
1927–29	Helen Wills	1952–54	Maureen Connolly	1972–73	Billie Jean King	1995–96	Steffi Graf
1930	Helen Wills Moody	1955	A. Louise Brough	1974	Chris Evert	1997	Martina Hingis
1931	Cilly Aussem	1956	Shirley Fry	1975	Billie Jean King	1998	Jana Novotna
1932–33	Helen Wills Moody	1957–58	Althea Gibson	1976	Chris Evert	1999	Lindsay Davenport
1934	D. E. Round	1959–60	Maria Bueno	1977	Virginia Wade	2000–01	Venus Williams
1935	Helen Wills Moody	1961	Angela Mortimer	1978–79	Martina Navratilova	2002–03	Serena Williams
1936	Helen Jacobs	1962	Karen Susman	1980	Evonne Goolagong Cawley	2004	Maria Sharapova
1937	D. E. Round	1963	Margaret Smith			2005	Venus Williams
1938	Helen Wills Moody	1964	Maria Bueno	1981	Chris Evert-Lloyd		
1939	Alice Marble	1965	Margaret Smith	1982–87	Martina Navratilova		

DOUBLES—MEN

1953	K. Rosewall–L. Hoad	1964	Fred Stolle–Bob Hewitt	1975	Vitas Gerulaitis–Sandy Mayer
1954	R. Hartwig–M. Rose	1965	John Newcombe–Tony Roche	1976	Brian Gottfried–Raul Ramirez
1955	R. Hartwig–L. Hoad				
1956	L. Hoad–K. Rosewall	1966	John Newcombe–Ken Fletcher	1977	Ross Case–Geoff Masters
1957	Gardnar Mulloy–Budge Patty	1967	Bob Hewitt–Frew McMillan	1978	Fred McMillan–Bob Hewitt
1958	Sven Davidson–Ulf Schmidt	1968–70	John Newcombe–Tony Roche	1979	Peter Fleming–John McEnroe
1959	Roy Emerson–Neale Fraser				
1960	Dennis Ralston–Rafael Osuna	1971	Rod Laver–Roy Emerson	1980	Peter McNamara–Paul McNamee
1961	Roy Emerson–Neale Fraser	1972	Bob Hewitt–Frew McMillan		
1962	Fred Stolle–Bob Hewitt	1973	Jimmy Connors–Ilie Nastase	1981	John McEnroe–Peter Fleming
1963	Rafael Osuna–Antonio Palafox	1974	John Newcombe–Tony Roche	1982	Paul McNamee–Peter McNamara

1983–84	John McEnroe–Peter Fleming	1990	Rick Leach–Jim Pugh	1999	Mahesh Bhupathi–Leander Paes	
1985	Heinz Gunthardt–Balazs Taroczy	1991	Anders Jarryd–John Fitzgerald	2000	Todd Woodbridge–Mark Woodforde	
1986	Joakim Nystrom–Mats Wilander	1992	John McEnroe–Michael Stich	2001	Donald Johnson–Jared Palmer	
1987–88	Ken Flach–Robert Seguso	1993–97	Todd Woodbridge–Mark Woodforde	2002–04	Todd Woodbridge–Jonas Bjorkman	
1989	John Fitzgerald–Anders Jarryd	1998	Jacco Eltingh–Paul Haarhuis	2005	Stephen Huss–Wesley Moodie	

DOUBLES—WOMEN

1956	Althea Gibson–Angela Buxton	1974	Evonne Goolagong–Peggy Michel	1989–90	Jana Novotna–Helena Sukova
1957	Althea Gibson–Darlene Hard	1975	Ann Kiyomura–Kazuko Sawamatsu	1991	Pam Shriver–Natalia Zvereva
1958	Althea Gibson–Maria Bueno			1992–94	Gigi Fernandez–Natalia Zvereva
1959	Darlene Hard–Jeanne Arth	1976	Chris Evert–Martina Navratilova	1995	Jana Novotna–Arantxa Sanchez Vicario
1960	Darlene Hard–Maria Bueno	1977	Helen Cawley–JoAnne Russell		
1961	Karen Hantze–Billie Jean Moffitt	1978	Wendy Turnbull–Kerry Reid	1996	Martina Hingis–Helena Sukova
1962	Karen Hantze Susman–Billie Jean Moffitt	1979	Billie Jean King–Martina Navratilova	1997	Gigi Fernandez–Natasha Zvereva
1963	Darlene Hard–Maria Bueno	1980	Kathy Jordan–Anne Smith	1998	Martina Hingis–Jana Novotna
1964	Margaret Smith–Les Turnerley	1981	Martina Navratilova–Pam Shriver	1999	Lindsay Davenport–Corina Morariu
1965	Billie Jean Moffitt–Maria Bueno	1982–84	Pam Shriver–Martina Navratilova	2000	Venus Williams–Serena Williams
1966	Nancy Richey–Maria Bueno	1985	Kathy Jordan–Elizabeth Smylie	2001	Lisa Raymond–Rennae Stubbs
1967–68	Billie Jean King–Rosemary Casals	1986	Pam Shriver–Martina Navratilova	2002	Serena Williams–Venus Williams
1969	Margaret Court–Judy Tegart	1987	Claudia Khode-Kilsch–Helena Sukova	2003	Kim Clijsters–Ai Sugiyama
1970–71	Billie Jean King–Rosemary Casals	1988	Steffi Graf–Gabriela Sabatini	2004	Cara Black–Rennae Stubbs
1972	Billie Jean King–Betty Stove			2005	Cara Black–Liezel Huber
1973	Billie Jean King–Rosemary Casals				

WIMBLEDON CHAMPIONS, 2005

(Wimbledon, England, June 20–July 3, 2005)

Men's singles—Roger Federer defeated Andy Roddick, 6–2, 7–6 (7–2), 6–4.

Women's singles—Venus Williams defeated Lindsay Davenport, 4–6, 7–6 (7–4), 9–7.

Men's doubles—Stephen Huss and Wesley Moodie defeated Bob Bryan and Mike Bryan, 7–6 (7–4), 6–3, 6–7 (2–7), 6–3.

Women's doubles—Cara Black and Liezel Huber defeated Svetlana Kuznetsova and Amelie Mauresmo, 6–2, 6–1.

Mixed doubles—Mary Pierce and Mahesh Bhupathi defeated Tatiana Perebiynis and Paul Hanley, 6–4, 6–2.

OTHER 2005 GRAND SLAM CHAMPIONS

French Open
(Paris, May 23–June 5, 2005)

Men's singles—Rafael Nadal defeated Mariano Puerta, 6–7 (6–8), 6–3, 6–1, 7–5.

Women's singles—Justine Henin-Hardenne defeated Mary Pierce, 6–1, 6–1.

Men's doubles—Jonas Björkman and Max Mirnyi defeated Bob Bryan and Mike Bryan, 2–6, 6–1, 6–4.

Women's doubles—Virginia Ruano Pascual and Paola Suárez defeated Cara Black and Liezel Huber, 4–6, 6–3, 6–3.

Mixed doubles—Daniela Hantuchová and Fabrice Santoro defeated Martina Navratilova and Leander Paes, 3–6, 6–3, 6–2.

Australian Open
(Melbourne, Australia, Jan. 16–29, 2005)

Men's singles—Marat Safin defeated Lleyton Hewitt, 1–6, 6–3, 6–4, 6–4.

Women's singles—Serena Williams defeated Lindsay Davenport, 2–6, 6–3, 6–0.

Men's doubles—Wayne Black and Keven Ullyett defeated Bob Bryan and Mike Bryan, 6–4, 6–4.

Women's doubles—Svetlana Kuznetsova and Alicia Molik defeated Lindsay Davenport and Corina Morariu, 6–3, 6–4.

Mixed doubles—Scott Draper and Samantha Stosur defeated Kevin Ullyett and Liezel Huber, 6–2, 2–6, 7–6 (10–6).

OTHER WTA TOURNAMENTS, 2005

Tournament	Singles champion
Medibank International, Sydney, Australia	Alicia Molik
Toray Pan Pacific Open, Tokyo, Japan	Maria Sharapova
Open Gaz de France, Paris, France	Dinara Safina
Proximus Diamond Games, Antwerp, Belgium	Amelie Mauresmo
Qatar Total Open, UAE	Maria Sharapova
Dubai Duty Free Women's Open, UAE	Lindsay Davenport
Pacific Life Open, Indian Wells, Calif.	Kim Clijsters
NASDAQ-100 Open, Miami, Fla.	Kim Clijsters
Bausch & Lomb Championships, Amelia Island, Fla.	Lindsay Davenport
Family Circle Cup, Charleston, S.C.	Justine Henin-Hardenne
J&S Cup, Warsaw, Poland	Justine Henin-Hardenne
Qatar Total German Open, Berlin, Germany	Justine Henin-Hardenne
Telecom Italia Masters, Rome, Italy	Amelie Mauresmo
Hastings Direct Int'l Championships, Eastbourne, England	Kim Clijsters
Bank of the West Classic, Stanford, Calif.	Kim Clijsters
Acura Classic, San Diego, Calif.	Mary Pierce
JP Morgan Chase Open, Los Angeles, Calif.	Kim Clijsters
Rogers Cup presented by American Express, Toronto, Canada	Kim Clijsters
Pilot Pen Tennis presented by Michelob Ultra, New Haven, Conn.	Lindsay Davenport

Source: www.wtatour.com.

OTHER ATP TOURNAMENTS, 2005

Tournament	Singles champion
ExxonMobil Open, Doha, Qatar	Roger Federer
ABN AMRO World Tennis, Rotterdam, Netherlands	Roger Federer
Dubai Duty Free, Dubai, UAE	Roger Federer
Abierto Mexicano TELCEL, Acapulco, Mexico	Rafael Nadal
Pacific Life Open, Indian Wells, Calif.	Roger Federer
NASDAQ-100 Open, Miami, Fla.	Roger Federer
Masters, Monte Carlo, Monaco	Rafael Nadal
Open Seat Godó 2005, Barcelona, Spain	Rafael Nadal
Estoril Open, Estoril, Portugal	Gaston Gaudio
Telecom Italia Masters, Rome, Italy	Rafael Nadal
Masters Series, Hamburg, Germany	Roger Federer
Stella Artois Championships, London, England	Andy Roddick
Gerry Weber Open, Halle, Germany	Roger Federer
Allianz Suisse Open, Gstaad, Switzerland	Gaston Gaudio
Mercedes Cup, Stuttgart, Germany	Rafael Nadal
RCA Championships, Indianapolis, Ind.	Robby Ginepri
Generali Open, Kitzbühel, Austria	Gaston Gaudio
Legg Mason Tennis Classic, Washington, DC	Andy Roddick
Rogers Masters, Montreal, Canada	Rafael Nadal
Pilot Pen Tennis, New Haven, Conn.	James Blake

Source: www.atptennis.com.

WOMEN'S TOP 5 MONEY WINNERS, 2005

1.	Kim Clijsters	$3,523,556
2.	Lindsay Davenport	1,921,990
3.	Mary Pierce	1,794,403
4.	Justine Henin-Hardenne	1,697,073
5.	Maria Sharapova	1,515,783

As of Sept. 11, 2005. *Source:* www.wtatour.com.

MEN'S TOP 5 MONEY WINNERS, 2005

1.	Roger Federer	$5,240,518
2.	Rafael Nadal	3,345,551
3.	Andy Roddick	1,541,385
4.	Lleyton Hewitt	1,443,887
5.	Andre Agassi	1,309,596

As of Sept. 11, 2005. *Source:* www.atptennis.com.

Harness Racing

Oliver Wendell Holmes, the famous Autocrat of the Breakfast Table, wrote that the running horse was a gambling toy but the trotting horse was useful and, furthermore, "horse-racing is not a republican institution; horse-trotting is." Oliver Wendell Holmes was a born-and-bred New Englander, and New England was the nursery of the harness racing sport in America. Pacers and trotters were matters of local pride and prejudice in colonial New England, and, shortly after the Revolution, the Messenger and Justin Morgan strains produced many winners in harness racing "matches" along the turnpikes of New York, Connecticut, Rhode Island, Massachusetts, Vermont, and New Hampshire.

There was English thoroughbred blood in Messenger and Justin Morgan, and, many years later, it was blended in Rysdyk's Hambletonian, foaled in 1849. Hambletonian was not particularly fast under harness but his descendants have had almost a monopoly of prizes, titles, and records in the harness racing game. Hambletonian was purchased as a foal with its dam for a total of $124 by William Rysdyk of Goshen, N.Y., and made a modest fortune for the purchaser.

Trotters and pacers often were raced under saddle in the old days, and, in fact, the custom still survives in some places in Europe. Dexter, the great trotter that lowered the mile record from 2:19¾ to 2:17¼ in 1867, was said to handle just as well under saddle as when pulling a sulky. But as sulkies were lightened in weight and improved in design, trotting under saddle became less common and finally faded out in the United States.

HISTORY OF TRADITIONAL HARNESS RACING STAKES

THE HAMBLETONIAN

Year	Winner	Driver	Best time	Total purse
1967	Speedy Streak	Del Cameron	2:00.0	$122,650
1968	Nevele Pride	Stanley Dancer	1:59.2	116,190
1969	Lindy's Pride	Howard Beissinger	1:57.3	124,910
1970	Timothy T.	John Simpson, Jr.	1:58.2[1]	143,630
1971	Speedy Crown	Howard Beissinger	1:57.2	129,770
1972	Super Bowl	Stanley Dancer	1:56.2	119,090
1973	Flirth	Ralph Baldwin	1:57.1	144,710
1974	Christopher T	Billy Haughton	1:58.3	160,150
1975	Bonefish	Stanley Dancer	1:59.0[2]	232,192
1976	Steve Lobell	Billy Haughton	1:56.2	263,524
1977	Green Speed	Billy Haughton	1:55.3	284,131
1978	Speedy Somolli	Howard Beissinger	1:55.0[3]	241,280
1979	Legend Hanover	George Sholty	1:56.1	300,000
1980	Burgomeister	Billy Haughton	1:56.3	293,570
1981	Shiaway St. Pat	Ray Remmen	2:01.1[4]	838,000
1982	Speed Bowl	Tommy Haughton	1:56.4	875,750
1983	Duenna	Stanley Dancer	1:57.2	1,000,000
1984	Historic Freight	Ben Webster	1:56.2[5]	1,219,000
1985	Prakas	Bill O'Donnell	1:54.3	1,272,000
1986	Nuclear Kosmos	Ulf Thoresen	1:55.2[6]	1,172,082
1987	Mack Lobell	John Campbell	1:53.3	1,046,300
1988	Armbro Goal	John Campbell	1:54.3	1,156,800
1989	Park Avenue Joe and Probe*	Ron Wayples Bill Fahy	1:54.3	1,131,000
1990	Harmonious	John Campbell	1:54.1	1,346,000
1991	Giant Victory	Jack Moiseyev	1:54.4	1,238,000
1992	Alf Palema	Mickey McNichol	1:56.2[7]	1,288,000
1993	American Winner	Ron Pierce	1:53.1	1,200,000
1994	Victory Dream	Mike Lachance	1:53.4	1,200,000
1995	Tagliabue	John Campbell	1:54.4	1,200,000
1996	Continentalvictory	Mike Lachance	1:52.1	1,200,000
1997	Malabar Man	Malvern Burroughs	1:53.4	1,000,000
1998	Muscles Yankee	John Campbell	1:52.2	1,000,000
1999	Self Possessed	Mike Lachance	1:51.3	1,000,000
2000	Yankee Paco	Travor Ritchie	1:53.2	1,000,000
2001	Scarlet Knight	Stefan Melander	1:53.4	1,000,000
2002	Chip Chip Hooray	Eric Ledford	1:53.3	1,000,000
2003	Amigo Hall	Mike Lachance	1:54.0	1,000,000
2004	Windsong's Legacy	Trond Smedshammer	1:54.1	1,000,000
2005	Vivid Photo	Roger Hammer	1:52.3[8]	1,500,000

Three-year-old trotters. One mile. Guy McKinney won first race at Syracuse in 1926; held at Goshen, N.Y., 1930–1942, 1944–1956; at Yonkers, N.Y., 1943; at Du Quoin, Ill., 1957–1980. Since 1981, the race has been held at The Meadowlands in East Rutherford, N.J. *Cowinners. Fastest heat won by: 1. By Formal Notice. 2. By Yankee Bambino. 3. By Speedy Somolli and Florida Pro. 4. By Super Juan. 5. Delvin G. Hanover. 6. Royal Prestige. 7. Baltic Sonata. 8. World record for 3-year-old trotting gelding. *Source:* www.hambletonian.org.

LITTLE BROWN JUG

Year	Winner	Driver	Best time	Total purse
1967	Best of All	Jim Hackett	1:59.0[1]	$84,778
1968	Rum Customer	Billy Haughton	1:59.3	104,226
1969	Laverne Hanover	Billy Haughton	2:00.2	109,731
1970	Most Happy Fella	Stanley Dancer	1:57.1	100,110
1971	Nansemond	Herve Filion	1:57.2	102,994
1972	Strike Out	Keith Waples	1:56.3	104,916
1973	Melvin's Woe	Joe O'Brien	1:57.3	120,000
1974	Ambro Omaha	Billy Haughton	1:57.0	132,630
1975	Seatrain	Ben Webster	1:57.0[2]	147,813
1976	Keystone Ore	Stanley Dancer	1:56.4[3]	153,799
1977	Governor Skipper	John Chapman	1:56.1	150,000
1978	Happy Escort	William Popfinger	1:55.2[4]	186,760
1979	Hot Hitter	Herve Filion	1:55.3	226,455
1980	Niatross	Clint Galbraith	1:54.4	207,361
1981	Fan Hanover	Glen Garnsey	1:56.0[5]	243,799
1982	Merger	John Campbell	1:56.3	328,900
1983	Ralph Hanover	Ron Waples	1:55.3	358,800
1984	Colt 46	Norman Boring	1:53.3	366,717
1985	Nihilator	Bill O'Donnell	1:52.1	350,730

Year	Winner	Driver	Best time	Total purse
1986	Barberry Spur	Bill O'Donnell	1:52.4	407,684
1987	Jaguar Spur	Richard Stillings	1:55.3	412,330
1988	B.J. Scoot	Mike Lachance	1:52.3	486,050
1989	Goalie Jeff	Mike Lachance	1:54.1	500,200
1990	Beach Towel	Ray Remmen	1:53.3	253,049
1991	Precious Bunny	Jack Moiseyev	1:54.1	575,150
1992	Fake Left	Ron Waples	1:54.2	556,210
1993	Life Sign	John Campbell	1:52.0	465,500
1994	Magical Mike	Mike Lachance	1:52.3	512,830
1995	Nick's Fantasy	John Campbell	1:51.2	543,670
1996	Armbro Operative	Jack Moiyesev	1:52.3	542,220
1997	Western Dreamer	Mike Lachance	1:51.1	605,210
1998	Shady Character	Ron Pierce	1:52.3	566,630
1999	Blissfull Hall	Ron Pierce	1:55.3	543,980
2000	Astreos	Chris Christoforou	1:55.3	547,972
2001	Bettor's Delight	Mike Lachance	1:51.4	646,050
2002	Million Dollar Cam	Luc Ouellette	1:50.2	618,625
2003	No Pan Intended	David Miller	1:50.0	605,050
2004	Timesareachanging	Ron Pierce	1:51.3	571,500

Three-year-old pacers. One Mile. Raced at Delaware County Fair Grounds, Delaware, Ohio. 1. By Nardin's Byrd. 2. By Albert's Star. 3. By Armbro Ranger. 4. By Falcon Almahurst. 5. By Seahawk Hanover.

HARNESS HORSE OF THE YEAR

1959	Bye Bye Byrd, Pacer	1977	Green Speed, Trotter	1992	Artsplace
1960–61	Adios Butler, Pacer	1978	Abercrombie, Pacer	1993	Staying Together
1962	Su Mac Lad, Trotter	1979–80	Niatross, Pacer	1994	Cam's Card Shark
1963	Speedy Scot, Trotter	1981	Fan Hanover, Pacer	1995	CR Kay Suzie
1964–66	Bret Hanover, Pacer	1982–83	Cam Fella, Pacer	1996	Continentalvictory
1967–69	Nevele Pride, Pacer	1984	Fancy Crown, Trotter	1997	Malabar Man
1970	Fresh Yankee, Trotter	1985	Nihilator, Trotter	1998–99	Moni Maker
1971–72	Albatross, Pacer	1986	Forrest Skipper	2000	Gallo Blue Chip
1973	Sir Dalrae, Pacer	1987–88	Mack Lobell	2001	Bunny Lake
1974	Delmonica Hanover, Trotter	1989	Matt's Scooter	2002	Real Desire
1975	Savoir, Trotter	1990	Beach Towell	2003	No Pan Intended
1976	Keystone Ore, Pacer	1991	Precious Bunny	2004	Rainbow Blue

Chosen in poll conducted by U.S. Trotting Association in conjunction with the U.S. Harness Writers Association.

Golf

It may be that golf originated in Holland—historians believe it did—but certainly Scotland fostered the game and is famous for it. In fact, in 1457 the Scottish Parliament, disturbed because football and golf had lured young Scots from the more soldierly exercise of archery, passed an ordinance that "futeball and golf be utterly cryit doun and nocht usit." James I and Charles I of the royal line of Stuarts were golf enthusiasts, whereby the game came to be known as "the royal and ancient game of golf."

The golf balls used in the early games were leather-covered and stuffed with feathers. Clubs of all kinds were fashioned by hand to suit individual players. The great step in spreading the game came with the change from the feather ball to the guttapercha ball about 1850. In 1860, formal competition began with the establishment of an annual tournament for the British Open championship, with Willie Park, Sr. winning the first tournament. There are records of "golf clubs" in the United States as far back as colonial days but no proof of actual play before John Reid and some friends laid out six holes on the Reid lawn in Yonkers, N.Y., in 1888 and played there with golf balls and clubs brought over from Scotland by Robert Lockhart. This group then formed the St. Andrews Golf Club of Yonkers, and golf was established in this country.

However, it remained a rather sedate and almost aristocratic pastime until a 20-year-old ex-caddy, Francis Ouimet of Boston, defeated two great British professionals, Harry Vardon and Ted Ray, in the United States Open championship at Brookline, Mass., in 1913. This feat put the game and Francis Ouimet on the front pages of the newspapers and stirred a wave of enthusiasm for the sport. The greatest feat so far in golf history is that of Robert Tyre Jones, Jr., of Atlanta, who won the British Open, the British Amateur, the U.S. Open, and the U.S. Amateur titles in one year, 1930.

THE MASTERS TOURNAMENT WINNERS

Augusta National Golf Club, Augusta, Ga.

Year	Winner	Score	Year	Winner	Score	Year	Winner	Score
1934	Horton Smith	284	1960	Arnold Palmer	282	1984	Ben Crenshaw	277
1935	Gene Sarazen[1]	282	1961	Gary Player	280	1985	Bernhard Langer	282
1936	Horton Smith	285	1962	Arnold Palmer[1]	280	1986	Jack Nicklaus	279
1937	Byron Nelson	283	1963	Jack Nicklaus	286	1987	Larry Mize[1]	285
1938	Henry Picard	285	1964	Arnold Palmer	276	1988	Sandy Lyle	281
1939	Ralph Guldahl	279	1965	Jack Nicklaus	271	1989	Nick Faldo[1]	283
1940	Jimmy Demaret	280	1966	Jack Nicklaus[1]	288	1990	Nick Faldo	278
1941	Craig Wood	280	1967	Gay Brewer, Jr.	280	1991	Ian Woosnam	277
1942	Byron Nelson[1]	280	1968	Bob Goalby	277	1992	Fred Couples	275
1943–45	No Tournaments		1969	George Archer	281	1993	Bernard Langer	277
1946	Herman Keiser	282	1970	Billy Casper[1]	279	1994	Jose Maria Olazabal	279
1947	Jimmy Demaret	281	1971	Charles Coody	279	1995	Ben Crenshaw	274
1948	Claude Harmon	279	1972	Jack Nicklaus	286	1996	Nick Faldo	276
1949	Sam Snead	282	1973	Tommy Aaron	283	1997	Tiger Woods	270
1950	Jimmy Demaret	283	1974	Gary Player	278	1998	Mark O'Meara	279
1951	Ben Hogan	280	1975	Jack Nicklaus	276	1999	Jose Maria Olazabal	280
1952	Sam Snead	286	1976	Ray Floyd	271	2000	Vijay Singh	278
1953	Ben Hogan	274	1977	Tom Watson	276	2001	Tiger Woods	272
1954	Sam Snead[1]	289	1978	Gary Player	277	2002	Tiger Woods	276
1955	Cary Middlecoff	279	1979	Fuzzy Zoeller[1]	280	2003	Mike Weir[1]	281
1956	Jack Burke	289	1980	Severiano Ballesteros	275	2004	Phil Mickelson	279
1957	Doug Ford	283	1981	Tom Watson	280	2005	Tiger Woods[1]	276
1958	Arnold Palmer	284	1982	Craig Stadler[1]	284			
1959	Art Wall, Jr.	284	1983	Severiano Ballesteros	280			

1. Winner in playoff.

U.S. OPEN CHAMPIONS

Year	Winner	Score	Where played	Year	Winner	Score	Where played
1895	Horace Rawlins	173	Newport	1936	Tony Manero	282	Baltusrol
1896	James Foulis	152	Shinnecock Hills	1937	Ralph Guldahl	281	Oakland Hills
1897	Joe Lloyd	162	Chicago	1938	Ralph Guldahl	284	Cherry Hills
1898[3]	Fred Herd	328	Myopia	1939	Byron Nelson[1]	284	Philadelphia
1899	Willie Smith	315	Baltimore	1940	Lawson Little[1]	287	Canterbury
1900	Harry Vardon	313	Chicago	1941	Craig Wood	284	Colonial
1901	Willie Anderson[1]	331	Myopia	1942–45	No tournaments[5]		
1902	Laurie Auchterlonie	307	Garden City	1946	Lloyd Mangrum[1]	284	Canterbury
1903	Willie Anderson[1]	307	Baltusrol	1947	Lew Worsham[1]	282	St. Louis
1904	Willie Anderson	303	Glen View	1948	Ben Hogan	276	Riviera
1905	Willie Anderson	314	Myopia	1949	Cary Middlecoff	286	Medinah
1906	Alex Smith	295	Onwentsia	1950	Ben Hogan[1]	287	Merion
1907	Alex Ross	302	Philadelphia	1951	Ben Hogan	287	Oakland Hills
1908	Fred McLeod[1]	322	Myopia	1952	Julius Boros	281	Northwood
1909	George Sargent	290	Englewood	1953	Ben Hogan	283	Oakmont
1910	Alex Smith[1]	298	Philadelphia	1954	Ed Furgol	284	Baltusrol
1911	John McDermott[1]	307	Chicago	1955	Jack Fleck[1]	287	Olympic
1912	John McDermott	294	Buffalo	1956	Cary Middlecoff	281	Oak Hill
1913	Francis Ouimet[1,2]	304	Brookline	1957	Dick Mayer[1]	298	Inverness
1914	Walter Hagen	290	Midlothian	1958	Tommy Bolt	283	Southern Hills
1915	Jerome D. Travers[2]	297	Baltusrol	1959	Bill Casper, Jr.	282	Winged Foot
1916	Charles Evans, Jr.[2]	286	Minikahda	1960	Arnold Palmer	280	Cherry Hills
1917–18	No tournaments[4]			1961	Gene Littler	281	Oakland Hills
1919	Walter Hagen[2]	301	Brae Burn	1962	Jack Nicklaus[1]	283	Oakmont
1920	Edward Ray	295	Inverness	1963	Julius Boros[1]	293	Country Club
1921	Jim Barnes	289	Columbia	1964	Ken Venturi	278	Congressional
1922	Gene Sarazen	288	Skokie	1965	Gary Player[1]	282	Bellerive
1923	R. T. Jones, Jr.[1,2]	296	Inwood	1966	Bill Casper[1]	278	Olympic
1924	Cyril Walker	297	Oakland Hills	1967	Jack Nicklaus	275	Baltusrol
1925	Willie Macfarlane[1]	291	Worcester	1968	Lee Trevino	275	Oak Hill
1926	R. T. Jones, Jr.[2]	293	Scioto	1969	Orville Moody	281	Champions G.C.
1927	Tommy Armour[1]	301	Oakmont	1970	Tony Jacklin	281	Hazeltine
1928	Johnny Farrell[1]	294	Olympia Fields	1971	Lee Trevino[1]	280	Merion
1929	R. T. Jones, Jr.[1,2]	294	Winged Foot	1972	Jack Nicklaus	290	Pebble Beach
1930	R. T. Jones, Jr.[2]	287	Interlachen	1973	Johnny Miller	279	Oakmont
1931	Billy Burke[1]	292	Inverness	1974	Hale Irwin	287	Winged Foot
1932	Gene Sarazen	286	Fresh Meadow	1975	Lou Graham[1]	287	Medinah
1933	John Goodman[2]	287	North Shore	1976	Jerry Pate	277	Atlanta A.C.
1934	Olin Dutra	293	Merion	1977	Hubert Green	278	Southern Hills
1935	Sam Parks, Jr.	299	Oakmont	1978	Andy North	285	Cherry Hills

Year	Winner	Score	Where played	Year	Winner	Score	Where played
1979	Hale Irwin	284	Inverness	1993	Lee Janzen	272	Baltusrol
1980	Jack Nicklaus	272	Baltusrol	1994	Ernie Els	279	Oakmont
1981	David Graham	273	Merion	1995	Corey Pavin	280	Shinnecock Hills
1982	Tom Watson	282	Pebble Beach	1996	Steve Jones	278	Oakland Hills
1983	Larry Nelson	280	Oakmont	1997	Ernie Els	276	Congressional C.C.
1984	Fuzzy Zoeller[1]	276	Winged Foot	1998	Lee Janzen	280	Olympic Country Club
1985	Andy North	279	Oakland Hills				
1986	Ray Floyd	279	Shinnecock Hills	1999	Payne Stewart	279	Pinehurst
1987	Scott Simpson	277	Olympic Golf Club	2000	Tiger Woods	272	Pebble Beach
1988	Curtis Strange[1]	278	The Country Club	2001	Retief Goosen	276	Southern Hills
1989	Curtis Strange	278	Oak Hill Country Club	2002	Tiger Woods	277	Bethpage Black
				2003	Jim Furyk	272	Olympia Fields
1990	Hale Irwin[1]	280	Medinah C.C.	2004	Retief Goosen	276	Shinnecock Hills
1991	Payne Stewart[1]	282	Hazeltine	2005	Michael Campbell	280	Pinehurst
1992	Tom Kite	285	Pebble Beach				

1. Winner in playoff. 2. Amateur. 3. In 1898, competition was extended to 72 holes. 4. In 1917, Jock Hutchison, with a 292, won an Open Patriotic Tournament for the benefit of the American Red Cross at Whitemarsh Valley Country Club. 5. In 1942, Ben Hogan, with a 271, won a Hale American National Open Tournament for the benefit of the Navy Relief Society and USO at Ridgemoor Country Club.

U.S. AMATEUR CHAMPIONS

1895	Charles B. Mac-donald	1926	George Von Elm	1957	Hillman Robbins	1981	Nathaniel Crosby
1896–97	H. J. Whigham	1927–28	R. T. Jones, Jr.	1958	Charles Coe	1982–83	Jay Sigel
1898	Findlay S. Douglas	1929	H. R. Johnston	1959	Jack Nicklaus	1984	Scott Verplank
1899	H. M. Harriman	1930	R. T. Jones, Jr.	1960	Deane Beman	1985	Sam Randolph
1900–01	Walter J. Travis	1931	Francis Ouimet	1961	Jack Nicklaus	1986	Buddy Alexander
1902	Louis N. James	1932	Ross Somerville	1962	Labron Harris, Jr.	1987	Bill Mayfair
1903	Walter J. Travis	1933	G. T. Dunlap, Jr.	1963	Deane Beman	1988	Eric Meeks
1904–05	H. Chandler Egan	1934–35	Lawson Little	1964	Bill Campbell	1989	Chris Patton
1906	Eben M. Byers	1936	John W. Fischer	1965[2]	Robert Murphy, Jr.	1990	Phil Mickelson
1907–08	Jerome D. Travers	1937	John Goodman	1966	Gary Cowan[1]	1991	Mitch Voges
1909	Robert A. Gardner	1938	Willie Turnesa	1967	Bob Dickson	1992	Justin Leonard
1910	W. C. Fownes, Jr.	1940	R. D. Chapman	1968	Bruce Fleisher	1993	John Harris
1911	Harold H. Hilton	1941	Marvin H. Ward	1969	Steven Melnyk	1994–96	Tiger Woods
1912–13	Jerome D. Travers	1946	Ted Bishop	1970	Lanny Wadkins	1997	Matthew Kuchar
1914	Francis Ouimet	1947	Robert Riegel	1971	Gary Cowan	1998	Hank Kuehne
1915	Robert A. Gardner	1948	Willie Turnesa	1972	Vinny Giles 3d	1999	David Gossett
1916	Charles Evans, Jr.	1949	Charles Coe	1973[3]	Craig Stadler	2000	Jeff Quinney
1919	S. D. Herron	1950	Sam Urzetta	1974	Jerry Pate	2001	Bubba Dickerson
1920	Charles Evans, Jr.	1951	Billy Maxwell	1975	Fred Ridley	2002	Ricky Barnes
1921	Jesse P. Guilford	1952	Jack Westland	1976	Bill Sander	2003	Nick Flanagan
1922	Jess W. Sweetser	1953	Gene Littler	1977	John Fought	2004	Ryan Moore
1923	Max R. Marston	1954	Arnold Palmer	1978	John Cook	2005	Edoardo Molinari
1924–25	R. T. Jones, Jr.	1955–56	Harvie Ward	1979	Mark O'Meara		
				1980	Hal Sutton		

1. Winner in playoff. 2. Tourney switched to medal play through 1972. 3. Return to match play.

U.S. PGA CHAMPIONS

1916	Jim Barnes	1946	Ben Hogan	1967	Don January[1]	1988	Jeff Sluman
1919	Jim Barnes	1947	Jim Ferrier	1968	Julius Boros	1989	Payne Stewart
1920	Jock Hutchison	1948	Ben Hogan	1969	Ray Floyd	1990	Wayne Grady
1921	Walter Hagen	1949	Sam Snead	1970	Dave Stockton	1991	John Daly
1922–23	Gene Sarazen	1950	Chandler Harper	1971	Jack Nicklaus	1992	Nick Price
1924–27	Walter Hagen	1951	Sam Snead	1972	Gary Player	1993	Paul Azinger[1]
1928–29	Leo Diegel	1952	Jim Turnesa	1973	Jack Nicklaus	1994	Nick Price
1930	Tommy Armour	1953	Walter Burkemo	1974	Lee Trevino	1995	Steve Elkington
1931	Tom Creavy	1954	Chick Harbert	1975	Jack Nicklaus	1996	Mark Brooks[1]
1932	Olin Dutra	1955	Doug Ford	1976	Dave Stockton	1997	Davis Love III
1933	Gene Sarazen	1956	Jack Burke, Jr.	1977	Lanny Wadkins[1]	1998	Vijay Singh
1934	Paul Runyan	1957	Lionel Hebert	1978	John Mahaffey	1999–	
1935	Johnny Revolta	1958[2]	Dow Finsterwald	1979	David Graham[1]	2000	Tiger Woods
1936–37	Denny Shute	1959	Bob Rosburg	1980	Jack Nicklaus	2001	David Toms
1938	Paul Runyan	1960	Jay Hebert	1981	Larry Nelson	2002	Rich Beem
1939	Henry Picard	1961	Jerry Barber[1]	1982	Ray Floyd	2003	Shaun Micheel
1940	Byron Nelson	1962	Gary Player	1983	Hal Sutton	2004	Vijay Singh
1941	Victor Ghezzi	1963	Jack Nicklaus	1984	Lee Trevino	2005	Phil Mickelson
1942	Sam Snead	1964	Bobby Nichols	1985	Hubert Green		
1944	Bob Hamilton	1965	Dave Marr	1986	Bob Tway		
1945	Byron Nelson	1966	Al Geiberger	1987	Larry Nelson		

1. Winner in playoff. 2. Switched to medal play.

U.S. WOMEN'S AMATEUR CHAMPIONS

Year	Winner	Year	Winner	Year	Winner	Year	Winner
1916	Alexa Stirling	1947	Louise Suggs	1967	Lou Dill	1989	Vicki Goetze
1919–20	Alexa Stirling	1948	Grace Lenczyk	1968	JoAnne G. Carner	1990	Pat Hurst
1921	Marion Hollins	1949	Mrs. D. G. Porter	1969	Catherine LaCoste	1991	Amy Fruhwirth
1922	Glenna Collett	1950	Beverly Hanson	1970	Martha Wilkinson	1992	Vicki Goetze
1923	Edith Cummings	1951	Dorothy Kirby	1971	Laura Baugh	1993	Jill McGill
1924	Dorothy Campbell Hurd	1952	Jacqueline Pung	1972	Mary Ann Budke	1994	Wendy Ward
1925	Glenna Collett	1953	Mary Lena Faulk	1973	Carol Semple	1995–96	Kelli Kuehne
1926	Helen Stetson	1954	Barbara Romack	1974	Cynthia Hill	1997	Silvia Cavalleri
1927	Mrs. M. B. Horn	1955	Patricia Lesser	1975	Beth Daniel	1998	Grace Park
1928–30	Glenna Collett	1956	Marlene Stewart	1976	Donna Horton	1999	Dorothy Delasin
1931	Helen Hicks	1957	JoAnne Gunderson	1977	Beth Daniel	2000	Marcy Newton
1932–34	Virginia Van Wie	1958	Anne Quast	1978	Cathy Sherk	2001	Meredith Duncan
1935	Glenna Collett Vare	1959	Barbara McIntire	1979	Carolyn Hill	2002	Becky Lucidi
1936	Pamela Barton	1960	JoAnne Gunderson	1980–82	Juli Inkster	2003	Virada Nirapathpongporn
1937	Mrs. J. A. Page, Jr.	1961	Anne Quast Decker	1983	Joanne Pacillo	2004	Jane Park
1938	Patty Berg	1962	JoAnne Gunderson	1984	Deb Richard	2005	Morgan Pressel
1939–40	Betty Jameson	1963	Anne Quast Welts	1985	Michiko Hattori		
1941	Mrs. Frank Newell	1964	Barbara McIntire	1986	Kay Cockerill		
1946	Mildred Zaharias	1965	Jean Ashley	1987	Kay Cockerill		
		1966	JoAnne Gunderson	1988	Pearl Sinn		

U.S. WOMEN'S OPEN CHAMPIONS

Year	Winner	Score	Year	Winner	Score	Year	Winner	Score
1946	Patty Berg (match play)	—	1966	Sandra Spuzich	297	1987	Laura Davies[1]	285
			1967	Catherine LaCoste[2]	294	1988	Liselotte Neumann	277
1947	Betty Jameson	295	1968	Susie Berning	289	1989	Betsy King	278
1948	Mildred D. Zaharias	300	1969	Donna Caponi	294	1990	Betsy King	284
1949	Louise Suggs	291	1970	Donna Caponi	287	1991	Meg Mallon	283
1950	Mildred D. Zaharias	291	1971	JoAnne Carner	288	1992	Patty Sheehan	280
1951	Betsy Rawls	293	1972	Susie Berning	299	1993	Lauri Merten	280
1952	Louise Suggs	284	1973	Susie Berning	290	1994	Patty Sheehan	277
1953	Betsy Rawls[1]	302	1974	Sandra Haynie	295	1995	Annika Sorenstam	278
1954	Mildred D. Zaharias	291	1975	Sandra Palmer	295	1996	Annika Sorenstam	272
1955	Fay Crocker	299	1976	JoAnne Carner[1]	292	1997	Alison Nicholas	274
1956	Katherine Cornelius[1]	302	1977	Hollis Stacy	292	1998	Se Ri Pak	290
1957	Betsy Rawls	299	1978	Hollis Stacy	289	1999	Juli Inkster	272
1958	Mickey Wright	290	1979	Jerilyn Britz	284	2000	Karrie Webb	282
1959	Mickey Wright	287	1980	Amy Alcott	280	2001	Karrie Webb	273
1960	Betsy Rawls	291	1981	Pat Bradley	279	2002	Juli Inkster	276
1961	Mickey Wright	293	1982	Janet Alex	283	2003	Hilary Lunke[1]	353
1962	Murle Lindstrom	301	1983	Jan Stephenson	290	2004	Meg Mallon	274
1963	Mary Mills	289	1984	Hollis Stacy	290	2005	Birdie Kim	287
1964	Mickey Wright[1]	290	1985	Kathy Baker	280			
1965	Carol Mann	290	1986	Jane Geddes[1]	287			

1. Winner in playoff. 2. Amateur.

BRITISH OPEN CHAMPIONS

Year	Winner	Score	Year	Winner	Score	Year	Winner	Score
1920	George Duncan	303	1947	Fred Daly	294	1968	Gary Player	289
1921	Jock Hutchison	296	1948	Henry Cotton	283	1969	Tony Jacklin	280
1922	Walter Hagen	300	1949	Bobby Locke	283	1970	Jack Nicklaus	283
1923	A. G. Havers	295	1950	Bobby Locke	279	1971	Lee Trevino	278
1924	Walter Hagen	301	1951	Max Faulkner	285	1972	Lee Trevino	278
1925	Jim Barnes	300	1952	Bobby Locke	287	1973	Tom Weiskopf	276
1926	R. T. Jones, Jr.	291	1953	Ben Hogan	282	1974	Gary Player	282
1927	R. T. Jones, Jr.	285	1954	Peter Thomson	283	1975	Tom Watson	279
1928	Walter Hagen	292	1955	Peter Thomson	281	1976	Johnny Miller	279
1929	Walter Hagen	292	1956	Peter Thomson	286	1977	Tom Watson	268
1930	R. T. Jones, Jr.	291	1957	Bobby Locke	279	1978	Jack Nicklaus	281
1931	Tommy Armour	296	1958	Peter Thomson	278	1979	Severiano Ballesteros	283
1932	Gene Sarazen	283	1959	Gary Player	284	1980	Tom Watson	271
1933	Denny Shute	292	1960	Kel Nagle	278	1981	Bill Rogers	276
1934	Henry Cotton	283	1961	Arnold Palmer	284	1982	Tom Watson	284
1935	A. Perry	283	1962	Arnold Palmer	276	1983	Tom Watson	275
1936	A. H. Padgham	287	1963	Bob Charles	277	1984	Severiano Ballesteros	276
1937	Henry Cotton	290	1964	Tony Lema	279	1985	Sandy Lyle	282
1938	R. A. Whitcombe	295	1965	Peter Thomson	285	1986	Greg Norman	280
1939	R. Burton	290	1966	Jack Nicklaus	282	1987	Nick Faldo	279
1940	Sam Snead	290	1967	Roberto de Vicenzo	278	1988	Seve Ballesteros	273

Year	Winner	Score	Year	Winner	Score	Year	Winner	Score
1989	Mark Calcavecchia	275	1995	John Daly	282	2001	David Duval	274
1990	Nick Faldo	270	1996	Tom Lehman	271	2002	Ernie Els	278
1991	Ian Baker-Finch	272	1997	Justin Leonard	272	2003	Ben Curtis	283
1992	Nick Faldo	272	1998	Mark O'Meara	280	2004	Todd Hamilton	274
1993	Greg Norman	267	1999	Paul Lawrie	290	2005	Tiger Woods	274
1994	Nick Price	268	2000	Tiger Woods	269			

OTHER 2005 PGA TOUR WINNERS

(Through Sept. 1, 2005)

Tournament—winner	Total purse
Mercedes Championship—Stuart Appleby	$5,300,000
Sony Open in Hawaii—Vijay Singh	4,800,000
Buick Invitational—Tiger Woods	4,800,000
Bob Hope Chrysler Classic—Justin Leonard	4,700,000
FBR Open—Phil Mickelson	5,200,000
AT&T Pebble Beach National Pro-Am—Phil Mickelson	5,300,000
Nissan Open—Adam Scott	4,800,000
WGC-Accenture Match Play Championship—David Toms	7,500,000
Ford Championship at Doral—Tiger Woods	5,500,000
The Honda Classic—Padraig Harrington	5,500,000
THE PLAYERS Championship—Fred Funk	8,000,000
BellSouth Classic—Phil Mickelson	5,000,000
MCI Heritage—Peter Lonard	5,200,000
Shell Houston Open—Vijay Singh	5,000,000
Zurich Classic of New Orleans—Tim Petrovic	5,500,000
Wachovia Championship—Vijay Singh	6,000,000
EDS Byron Nelson Championship—Ted Purdy	6,200,000
Bank of America Colonial—Kenny Perry	5,600,000
The Memorial—Bart Bryant	5,500,000
Barclays Classic—Padraig Harrington	5,750,000
The INTERNATIONAL—Retief Goosen	5,000,000
WGC-NEC Invitational—Tiger Woods	7,500,000

Source: www.pgatour.com.

OTHER 2005 LPGA TOUR WINNERS

(Through Sept. 1, 2005)

Tournament—winner	Total purse
MasterCard Classic—Annika Sorenstam	$1,200,000
Safeway International—Annika Sorenstam	1,400,000
Kraft Nabisco Championship—Annika Sorenstam	1,800,000
Takefuji Classic—Wendy Ward	1,100,000
Michelob ULTRA Open—Cristie Kerr	2,200,000
Chick-fil-A Charity Championship—Annika Sorenstam	1,600,000
Sybase Classic—Paula Creamer	1,250,000
Corning Classic—Jimin Kang	1,100,000
ShopRite LPGA Classic—Annika Sorenstam	1,400,000
McDonald's LPGA Championship—Annika Sorenstam	1,800,000
Wegman's Rochester LPGA—Lorena Ochoa	1,500,000
HSBC Women's World Match Play—Marisa Baena	2,000,000
Jamie Farr Owens Corning Classic—Heather Bowie	1,200,000
BMO Financial Group Canadian Women's Open—Meena Lee	1,300,000
Evian Masters—Paula Creamer	2,500,000
Weetabix Women's British Open—Jeong Jang	1,800,000
Safeway Classic—Soo-Yun Kang	1,400,000
Wendy's Championship for Children—Cristie Kerr	1,100,000
State Farm Classic—Pat Hurst	1,300,000

Source: Ladies Professional Golf Association.
Web: www.lpga.com.

Auto Racing

INDIANAPOLIS 500

Year	Winner	Car	Time	mph	Second place
1911	Ray Harroun	Marmon	6:42:08.000	74.590	Ralph Mulford
1912	Joe Dawson	National	6:21:06.000	78.720	Teddy Tetzloff
1913	Jules Goux	Peugeot	6:35:05.000	75.930	Spencer Wishart
1914	René Thomas	Delage	6:03:45.000	82.470	Arthur Duray
1915	Ralph DePalma	Mercedes	5:33:55.510	89.840	Dario Resta
1916[1]	Dario Resta	Peugeot	3:34:17.000	84.000	Wilbur D'Alene
1919	Howard Wilcox	Peugeot	5:40:42.870	88.050	Eddie Hearne
1920	Gaston Chevrolet	Monroe	5:38:32.000	88.620	René Thomas
1921	Tommy Milton	Frontenac	5:34:44.650	89.620	Roscoe Sarles
1922	Jimmy Murphy	Murphy Special	5:17:30.790	94.480	Harry Hartz
1923	Tommy Milton	H. C. S. Special	5:29.50.170	90.950	Harry Hartz
1924	L. L. Corum-Joe Boyer	Dusenberg Special	5:05:23.510	98.230	Earl Cooper
1925	Peter DePaolo	Dusenberg Special	4:56:39.450	101.130	Dave Lewis
1926[2]	Frank Lockhart	Miller Special	4:10:14.950	95.904	Harry Hartz
1927	George Souders	Dusenberg Special	5:07:33.080	97.540	Earl DeVore
1928	Louis Meyer	Miller Special	5:01:33.760	99.480	Lou Moore
1929	Ray Keech	Simplex Special	5:07:25.420	97.580	Louis Meyer
1930	Billy Arnold	Miller-Hartz Special	4:58:39.720	100.448	Shorty Cantlon
1931	Louis Schneider	Bowes Special	5:10:27.930	96.629	Fred Frame
1932	Fred Frame	Miller-Hartz Special	4:48:03.790	104.144	Howard Wilcox
1933	Louis Meyer	Tydol Special	4:48:00.750	104.162	Wilbur Shaw
1934	Bill Cummings	Boyle Products Special	4:46:05.200	104.863	Mauri Rose
1935	Kelly Petillo	Gilmore Special	4:42:22.710	106.240	Wilbur Shaw
1936	Louis Meyer	Ring Free Special	4:35:03.390	109.069	Ted Horn

Year	Winner	Car	Time	mph	Second place
1937	Wilbur Shaw	Shaw-Gilmore Special	4:24:07.800	113.580	Ralph Hepburn
1938	Floyd Roberts	Burd Piston Ring Special	4:15:58.400	117.200	Wilbur Shaw
1939	Wilbur Shaw	Boyle Special	4:20:47.390	115.035	Jimmy Snyder
1940	Wilbur Shaw	Boyle Special	4:22:31.170	114.277	Rex Mays
1941	Floyd Davis-Mauri Rose	Noc-Out Hose Clamp Special	4:20:36.240	115.117	Rex Mays
1946	George Robson	Thorne Engineering Special	4:21:26.710	114.820	Jimmy Jackson
1947	Mauri Rose	Blue Crown Special	4:17:52.170	116.338	Bill Holland
1948	Mauri Rose	Blue Crown Special	4:10:23.330	119.814	Bill Holland
1949	Bill Holland	Blue Crown Special	4:07:15.970	121.327	Johnny Parsons
1950[3]	Johnnie Parsons	Wynn's Friction Proof Special	2:46:55.970	124.002	Bill Holland
1951	Lee Wallard	Belanger Special	3:57:38.050	126.244	Mike Nazaruk
1952	Troy Ruttman	Agajanian Special	3:52:41.880	128.922	Jim Rathmann
1953	Bill Vukovich	Fuel Injection Special	3:53:01.690	128.740	Art Cross
1954	Bill Vukovich	Fuel Injection Special	3:49:17.270	130.840	Jim Bryan
1955	Bob Sweikert	John Zink Special	3:53:59.130	128.209	Tony Bettenhausen
1956	Pat Flaherty	John Zink Special	3:53:28.840	128.490	Sam Hanks
1957	Sam Hanks	Belond Exhaust Special	3:41:14.250	135.601	Jim Rathmann
1958	Jimmy Bryan	Belond A-P Special	3:44:13.800	133.791	George Amick
1959	Rodger Ward	Leader Card 500 Roadster	3:40:49.200	135.857	Jim Rathmann
1960	Jim Rathmann	Ken-Paul Special	3:36:11.360	138.767	Rodger Ward
1961	A. J. Foyt	Bowes Special	3:35:37.490	139.130	Eddie Sachs
1962	Rodger Ward	Leader Card Special	3:33:50.330	140.293	Len Sutton
1963	Parnelli Jones	Agajanian Special	3:29:35.400	143.137	Jim Clark
1964	A. J. Foyt	Sheraton-Thompson Spl.	3:23:35.830	147.350	Rodger Ward
1965	Jim Clark	Lotus-Ford	3:19:05.340	150.686	Parnelli Jones
1966	Graham Hill	Red Ball Lola-Ford	3:27:52.530	144.317	Jim Clark
1967[4]	A. J. Foyt	Sheraton-Thompson Coyote-Ford	3:18:24.220	151.207	Al Unser
1968	Bobby Unser	Rislone Eagle-Offenhauser	3:16:13.760	152.882	Dan Gurney
1969	Mario Andretti	STP Hawk-Ford	3:11:14.710	156.867	Dan Gurney
1970	Al Unser	Johnny Lightning P. J. Colt-Ford	3:12:37.040	155.749	Mark Donohue
1971	Al Unser	Johnny Lightning P. J. Colt-Ford	3:10:11.560	157.735	Peter Revson
1972	Mark Donohue	Sunoco McLaren-Offenhauser	3:04:05.540	162.962	Al Unser
1973[5]	Gordon Johncock	STP Eagle-Offenhauser	2:05:26.590	159.036	Bill Vukovich, Jr.
1974	Johnny Rutherford	McLaren-Offenhauser	3:09:10.060	158.589	Bobby Unser
1975[6]	Bobby Unser	Jorgensen Eagle-Offenhauser	2:54:55.080	149.213	Johnny Rutherford
1976[7]	Johnny Rutherford	Hy-gain McLaren-Offenhauser	1:42:52.000	148.725	A. J. Foyt
1977	A. J. Foyt	Gilmore Coyote-Foyt	3:05:57.160	161.331	Tom Sneva
1978	Al Unser	1st Nat'l City Lola-Cosworth	3:05:54.990	161.363	Tom Sneva
1979	Rick Mears	Gould Penske-Cosworth	3:08:47.970	158.899	A. J. Foyt
1980	Johnny Rutherford	Pennzoil Chaparral-Cosworth	3:29:59.560	142.862	Tom Sneva
1981[8]	Bobby Unser	Norton Penske-Cosworth	3:35:41.780	139.029	Mario Andretti
1982	Gordon Johncock	STP Wildcat-Cosworth	3:05:09.140	162.084	Rick Mears
1983	Tom Sneva	Texaco Star March-Cosworth	3:05:03.066	162.117	Al Unser
1984	Rick Mears	Pennzoil March-Cosworth	3:03:21.660	163.612	Roberto Guerrero
1985	Danny Sullivan	Miller March-Cosworth	3:16:06.069	152.982	Mario Andretti
1986	Bobby Rahal	Budweiser March-Cosworth	2:55:43.480	170.722	Kevin Cogan
1987	Al Unser, Sr.	Cummins March-Cosworth	3:04:59.147	162.175	Roberto Guerrero
1988	Rick Mears	Pennzoil Penske P.C.17-Chevrolet	3:27:10.204	144.809	Emerson Fittipaldi
1989	Emerson Fittipaldi	Marlboro Penske-Chevrolet	2:59:01.049	167.581	Al Unser, Jr.
1990	Arie Luyendyk	Domino's Pizza Lola-Cosworth	2:41:18.404	185.981	Bobby Rahal
1991	Rick Mears	Marlboro Penske-Chevrolet	2:50:00.791	176.457	Michael Andretti
1992	Al Unser, Jr.	Valvoline-Chevrolet	3:43.05.148	134.477	Scott Goodyear
1993	Emerson Fittipaldi	Penske-Chevrolet	3:10:49.860	157.207	Arie Luyendyk
1994	Al Unser, Jr.	Penske-Mercedes	3:06:29.006	160.872	Jacques Villeneuve
1995	Jacques Villeneuve	Reynard-Ford	3:15:17.561	153.616	Christian Fittipaldi
1996	Buddy Lazier	Reynard-Ford	3:22:45.753	147.956	Davy Jones
1997	Arie Luyendyk	G Force-Aurora	3:25:43.388	145.827	Scott Goodyear
1998	Eddie Cheever	Dallara-Aurora	3:26:40.524	145.155	Buddy Lazier
1999	Kenny Brack	Dallara-Aurora-Goodyear	3:15:51.182	153.176	Jeff Ward
2000	Juan Montoya	GForce-Aurora-Firestone	2:58:59.431	167.607	Buddy Lazier
2001	Helio Castroneves	Dallara-Aurora-Firestone	3:31:54.180	141.574	Gil de Ferran
2002	Helio Castroneves	Dallara-Chevrolet-Firestone	3:00:10.871	166.499	Paul Tracy
2003	Gil de Ferran	Panoz G Force-Toyota-Firestone	3:11:56.989	156.291	Helio Castroneves
2004[9]	Buddy Rice	Rahal-Letterman Argent/Pioneer	3:14:55.240	138.518	Tony Kanaan
2005	Dan Wheldon	Klein Tools/Jim Beam	3:10:21.077	157.603	Vitor Meira

1. 300 miles. 2. Race ended at 400 miles because of rain. 3. Race ended at 345 miles because of rain. 4. Race, postponed after 18 laps because of rain on May 30, was finished on May 31. 5. Race postponed May 28 and 29 was cut to 332.5 miles because of rain, May 30. 6. Race ended at 435 miles because of rain. 7. Race ended at 255 miles because of rain. 8. Andretti was awarded the victory the day after the race after Bobby Unser, whose car finished first, was penalized one lap and dropped from first place to second for passing other cars illegally under a yellow caution flag. Unser appealed the decision to the U.S. Auto Club but it was upheld. A panel ruled the penalty was too severe and instead fined Unser $40,000, but restored the victory to him. 9. Race ended with 20 laps to go because of rain.

2005 NASCAR NEXTEL CUP RACES

Date	Race	Raceway	Winner
Feb. 20	Daytona 500	Daytona International Speedway	Jeff Gordon
Feb. 27	Auto Club 500	California Speedway	Greg Biffle
March 13	UAW-DaimlerChrysler 400	Las Vegas Motor Speedway	Jimmie Johnson
March 20	Golden Corral 500	Atlanta Motor Speedway	Carl Edwards
April 3	Food City 500	Bristol Motor Speedway	Kevin Harvick
April 10	Advance Auto Parts 500	Martinsville Speedway	Jeff Gordon
April 17	Samsung/RadioShack 500	Texas Motor Speedway	Greg Biffle
April 23	Subway Fresh 500	Phoenix International Raceway	Kurt Busch
May 1	Aaron's 499	Talladega Superspeedway	Jeff Gordon
May 7	Dodge Charger 500	Darlington Raceway	Greg Biffle
May 14	Chevy American Revolution 400	Richmond International Raceway	Kasey Kahne
May 29	Coca-Cola 600	Lowe's Motor Speedway	Jimmie Johnson
June 5	MBNA RacePoints 400	Dover International Speedway	Greg Biffle
June 12	Pocono 500	Pocono Raceway	Carl Edwards
June 19	Batman Begins 400	Michigan International Speedway	Greg Biffle
June 26	Dodge/Save Mart 350	Infineon Raceway	Tony Stewart
July 2	Pepsi 400	Daytona International Speedway	Tony Stewart
July 10	USG Sheetrock 400	Chicagoland Speedway	Dale Earnhardt, Jr.
July 17	New England 300	New Hampshire International Speedway	Tony Stewart
July 24	Pennsylvania 500	Pocono Raceway	Kurt Busch
Aug. 7	Allstate 400 at the Brickyard	Indianapolis Motor Speedway	Tony Stewart
Aug. 14	Sirius Satellite Radio at The Glen	Watkins Glen International	Tony Stewart
Aug. 21	GFS Marketplace 400	Michigan International Speedway	Jeremy Mayfield
Aug. 27	Sharpie 500	Bristol Motor Speedway	Matt Kenseth
Sept. 4	Sony HD 500	California Speedway	Kyle Busch
Sept. 10	Chevy Rock & Roll 400	Richmond International Raceway	Kurt Busch

NASCAR NEXTEL CUP CHAMPIONS

1949	Red Byron	1962–63	Joe Weatherly	1979	Richard Petty	1993–94	Dale Earnhardt
1950	Bill Rexford	1964	Richard Petty	1980	Dale Earnhardt	1995	Jeff Gordon
1951	Herb Thomas	1965	Ned Jarrett	1981–82	Darrell Waltrip	1996	Terry Labonte
1952	Tim Flock	1966	David Pearson	1983	Bobby Allison	1997–98	Jeff Gordon
1953	Herb Thomas	1967	Richard Petty	1984	Terry Labonte	1999	Dale Jarrett
1954	Lee Petty	1968–69	David Pearson	1985	Darrell Waltrip	2000	Bobby Labonte
1955	Tim Flock	1970	Bobby Isaac	1986–87	Dale Earnhardt	2001	Jeff Gordon
1956–57	Buck Baker	1971–72	Richard Petty	1988	Bill Elliott	2002	Tony Stewart
1958–59	Lee Petty	1973	Benny Parsons	1989	Rusty Wallace	2003	Matt Kenseth
1960	Rex White	1974–75	Richard Petty	1990–91	Dale Earnhardt	2004	Kurt Busch
1961	Ned Jarrett	1976–78	Cale Yarborough	1992	Alan Kulwicki	2005	Tony Stewart[1]

1. Leader as of Sept. 10, 2005.

2005 NASCAR BUSCH SERIES RACES

Date	Race	Raceway	Winner
Feb. 19	Hershey's TAKE 5 300	Daytona International Speedway	Tony Stewart
Feb. 26	Stater Bros. 300	California Speedway	Mark Martin
March 6	Telcel MOTOROLA Mexico 200	Autodromo Hermanos Rodriguez	Martin Truex, Jr.
March 12	Sam's Town 300	Las Vegas Motor Speedway	Mark Martin
March 19	Aaron's 312	Atlanta Motor Speedway	Carl Edwards
March 26	Pepsi 300	Nashville Superspeedway	Reed Sorenson
April 4	Sharpie Professional 250	Bristol Motor Speedway	Kevin Harvick
April 16	O'Reilly 300	Texas Motor Speedway	Kasey Kahne
April 22	Bashas' Supermarkets 200	Phoenix International Raceway	Greg Biffle
April 30	Aaron's 312	Talladega Superspeedway	Martin Truex, Jr.
May 6	Diamond Hill Plywood 200	Darlington Raceway	Matt Kenseth
May 13	Funai 250	Richmond International Raceway	Carl Edwards
May 28	Carquest Auto Parts 300	Lowe's Motor Speedway	Kyle Busch
June 4	MBNA RacePoints 200	Dover International Speedway	Martin Truex, Jr.
June 12	Federated Auto Parts 300	Nashville Superspeedway	Clint Bowyer
June 18	Meijer 300	Kentucky Speedway	Carl Edwards
June 25	SBC 250	The Milwaukee Mile	Johnny Sauter
July 1	Winn-Dixie 250	Daytona International Speedway	Martin Truex, Jr.
July 9	USG Durock 300	Chicagoland Speedway	Kevin Harvick
July 16	New England 200	New Hampshire International Speedway	Martin Truex, Jr.
July 23	ITT Industries 250	Pikes Peak International Raceway	David Green
July 30	Wallace Family Tribute 250	Gateway International Raceway	Reed Sorenson
Aug. 6	Kroger 200	Indianapolis Raceway Park	Martin Truex, Jr.
Aug. 13	Zippo 200	Watkins Glen International	Ryan Newman
Aug. 20	Domino's Pizza 250	Michigan International Speedway	Ryan Newman
Aug. 26	Food City 250	Bristol Motor Speedway	Ryan Newman
Sept. 3	Ameriquest 300	California Speedway	Carl Edwards
Sept. 9	Emerson Radio 250	Richmond International Raceway	Kevin Harvick

INDYCAR/CART/CHAMP CAR CHAMPIONS

1910	Ray Harroun	1934	Bill Cummings	1965–66	Mario Andretti	1989	Emerson Fitti-
1911	Ralph Mulford	1935	Kelly Petillo	1967	A. J. Foyt		paldi
1912	Ralph DePalma	1936	Mauri Rose	1968	Bobby Unser	1990	Al Unser, Jr.
1913	Earl Cooper	1937	Wilbur Shaw	1969	Mario Andretti	1991	Michael Andretti
1914	Ralph DePalma	1938	Floyd Roberts	1970	Al Unser	1992	Bobby Rahal
1915	Earl Cooper	1939	Wilbur Shaw	1971–72	Joe Leonard	1993	Nigel Mansell
1916	Dario Resta	1940–41	Rex Mays	1973	Roger McCluskey	1994	Al Unser, Jr.
1917	Earl Cooper	1946–48	Ted Horn	1974	Bobby Unser	1995	Jacques Ville-
1918	Ralph Mulford	1949	Johnnie Parsons	1975	A. J. Foyt		neuve
1919	Howard Wilcox	1950	Henry Banks	1976	Gordon Johncock	1996	Jimmy Vasser
1920	Gaston Chevrolet	1951	Tony Betten-	1977–78	Tom Sneva	1997–98	Alessandro
1921	Tommy Milton		hausen	1979	Rick Mears		Zanardi
1922	James Murphy	1952	Chuck Stevenson		(CART), A. J.	1999	Juan Montoya
1923	Eddie Hearne	1953	Sam Hanks		Foyt (USAC)[1]	2000–01	Gil de Ferran
1924	James Murphy	1954	Jimmy Bryan	1980	Johnny Ruther-	2002	Cristiano da
1925	Peter DePaolo	1955	Bob Sweikert		ford		Matta
1926	Harry Hartz	1956–57	Jimmy Bryan	1981–82	Rick Mears	2003	Paul Tracy
1927	Peter DePaolo	1958	Tony Betten-	1983	Al Unser	2004	Sebastien Bour-
1928–29	Louis Meyer		hausen	1984	Mario Andretti		dais
1930	Billy Arnold	1959	Rodger Ward	1985	Al Unser	2005	Sebastien Bour-
1931	Louis Schneider	1960–61	A. J. Foyt	1986–87	Bobby Rahal		dais[2]
1932	Bob Carey	1962	Rodger Ward	1988	Danny Sullivan		
1933	Louis Meyer	1963–64	A. J. Foyt				

NOTE: Open Wheel Racing Series acquired CART in Dec. 2003. The Automobile Association of America (1909–1955), the U.S. Auto Club (1956–1979), and the Championship Auto Racing Team (CART), 1979–2003, were the previous sanctioning bodies for the series. 1. Two separate series were held in 1979. 2. Leader as of Sept. 10, 2005.

2005 INDY RACING LEAGUE RACES

Date	Race	Location	Winner
March 6	Toyota Indy 300	Homestead-Miami Speedway	Dan Wheldon
March 19	XM Satellite Radio Indy 200	Phoenix International Raceway	Sam Hornish, Jr.
April 3	Honda Grand Prix of St. Petersburg	Streets of St. Petersburg	Dan Wheldon
April 30	Indy Japan 300	Twin Ring Motegi	Dan Wheldon
June 11	Bombardier Learjet 500	Texas Motor Speedway	Tomas Scheckter
June 25	SunTrust Indy Challenge	Richmond International Raceway	Helio Castroneves
July 3	Argent Mortgage Indy 300	Kansas Speedway	Tony Kanaan
July 16	Firestone Indy 200	Nashville Superspeedway	Dario Franchitti
July 24	ABC Supply Co./A. J. Foyt 225	The Milwaukee Mile	Sam Hornish, Jr.
July 31	Firestone Indy 400	Michigan International Speedway	Bryan Herta
Aug. 14	AMBER Alert Portal Indy 300	Kentucky Speedway	Scott Sharp
Aug. 21	Honda Indy 225	Pikes Peak International Raceway	Dan Wheldon
Aug. 28	Argent Mortgage Indy Grand Prix	Infineon Raceway	Tony Kanaan

FORMULA 1/WORLD GRAND PRIX DRIVER CHAMPIONS

1950	Giuseppe Farina, Italy, Alfa Romeo	1976	James Hunt, Britain, McLaren-Ford
1951	Juan Fangio, Argentina, Alfa Romeo	1977	Niki Lauda, Austria, Ferrari
1952–53	Alberto Ascari, Italy, Ferrari	1978	Mario Andretti, United States, Lotus
1954	Juan Fangio, Argentina, Maserati, Mercedes-Benz	1979	Jody Scheckter, South Africa, Ferrari
1955	Juan Fangio, Argentina, Mercedes-Benz	1980	Alan Jones, Australia, Williams-Ford
1956	Juan Fangio, Argentina, Lancia-Ferrari	1981	Nelson Piquet, Brazil, Brabham-Ford
1957	Juan Fangio, Argentina, Masserati	1982	Keke Rosberg, Finland, Williams-Ford
1958	Mike Hawthorn, England, Ferrari	1983	Nelson Piquet, Brazil. Brabham-BMW
1959–60	Jack Brabham, Australia, Cooper	1984	Niki Lauda, Austria, McLaren-Porsche
1961	Phil Hill, United States, Ferrari	1985–86	Alain Prost, France, McLaren-Porsche
1962	Graham Hill, England, BRM	1987	Nelson Piquet, Brazil, Williams-Honda
1963	Jim Clark, Scotland, Lotus-Ford	1988	Aryton Senna, Brazil, McLaren-Honda
1964	John Surtees, England, Ferrari	1989	Alain Prost, France, McLaren-Honda
1965	Jim Clark, Scotland, Lotus-Ford	1990–91	Ayrton Senna, Brazil, McLaren-Honda
1966	Jack Brabham, Australia, Brabham-Repco	1992	Nigel Mansell, Britain, Williams-Renault
1967	Denis Hulme, New Zealand, Brabham-Repco	1993	Alain Prost, France, Williams-Renault
1968	Graham Hill, England, Lotus-Ford	1994–95	Michael Schumacher, Germany, Benetton
1969	Jackie Stewart, Scotland, Matra-Ford	1996	Damon Hill, Britain, Williams
1970	Jochen Rindt, Austria, Lotus-Ford	1997	Jacques Villeneuve, Canada, Williams-Renault
1971	Jackie Stewart, Scotland, Tyrrell-Ford	1998–99	Mika Hakkinen, Finland, McLaren-Mercedes
1972	Emerson Fittipaldi, Brazil, Lotus-Ford	2000–04	Michael Schumacher, Germany, Ferrari
1973	Jackie Stewart, Scotland, Tyrrell-Ford	2005	Fernando Alonso, Spain, Renault[1]
1974	Emerson Fittipaldi, Brazil, McLaren-Ford		
1975	Niki Lauda, Austria, Ferrari		1. Leader as of Sept. 10, 2005.

Bicycling

TOUR DE FRANCE–2005
(July 2–24, 2005)

		Team	Behind			Team	Behind
1.	Lance Armstrong, United States	Discovery Channel	(1)	6.	Levi Leipheimer, United States	Gerolsteiner	11:21
2.	Ivan Basso, Italy	Team CSC	04:40	7.	Mickael Rasmussen, Denmark	Rabobank	11:33
3.	Jan Ullrich, Germany	T-Mobile	06:21				
4.	Francisco Mancebo, Spain	Illes Balears-Casse d'Epargne	09:59	8.	Cadel Evans, Australia	Davitamon-Lotto	11:55
				9.	Floyd Landis, United States	Phonak Hearing Systems	12:44
5.	Alexandre Vinokourov, Kazakhstan	T-Mobile	11:01	10.	Oscar Pereiro Sio, Spain	Phonak Hearing Systems	16:14

1. Completed course in 86 hours, 15 minutes, 2 seconds.

Marathons

BOSTON MARATHON
(April 17, 2005)

Men	Time	Women	Time
Hailu Negussie, Ethiopia	2:11:45	Catherine Ndereba, Kenya	2:25:13
Wheelchair—Ernst Van Dyk, South Africa	1:24:11	Wheelchair—Cheri Blauwet, United States	1:47:45

OTHER 2005 MARATHONS

Los Angeles (March 6, 2005)

Men	Time
Mark Saina, Kenya	2:09:35
Wheelchair—Kurt Fearnley, Australia	1:30:11
Women	
Lyubov Denisova, Russia	2:26:11
Wheelchair—Cheri Blauwet, United States	1:51:45

Paris (April 10, 2005)

Men	Time
Salim Kipsang, Kenya	2:08:04
Wheelchair—Ernst Van Dyck, South Africa	1:32:17
Women	
Lydiya Grigoryeva, Russia	2:27:01

London (April 17, 2005)

Men	Time
Martin Lel, Kenya	2:07:26
Wheelchair—Saul Mendoza, Mexico	1:35:51
Women	
Paula Radcliffe, United Kingdom	2:17:42
Wheelchair—Francesca Porcellato, Italy	1:57:00

Stockholm (June 4, 2005)

Men	Time
Kasirai Sita, Zimbabwe	2:13:30
Wheelchair—Magnus Nilsson, Sweden	2:22:45
Women	
Tina Maria Ramos, Spain	2:41:32

Little League

LITTLE LEAGUE WORLD SERIES CHAMPIONS

Year	Champion	Runner-up	Score	Year	Champion	Runner-up	Score
1947	Williamsport, Pa.	Lock Haven, Pa.	16–7	1970	Wayne, N.J.	Campbell, Calif.	2–0
1948	Lock Haven, Pa.	St. Petersburg, Fla.	6–5	1971	Tainan, Taiwan	Gary, Ind.	12–3
1949	Hammonton, N.J.	Pensacola, Fla.	5–0	1972	Taipei, Taiwan	Hammond, Ind.	6–0
1950	Houston, Tex.	Bridgeport, Conn.	2–1	1973	Tainan City, Taiwan	Tucson, Ariz.	12–0
1951	Stamford, Conn.	Austin, Tex.	3–0	1974	Kao Hsiung, Taiwan	El Cajon, Calif.	7–2
1952	Norwalk, Conn.	Monongahela, Pa.	4–3	1975	Lakewood, N.J.	Tampa, Fla.	4–3
1953	Birmingham, Ala.	Schenectady, N.Y.	1–0	1976	Tokyo, Japan	Campbell, Calif.	10–3
1954	Schenectady, N.Y.	Colton, Calif.	7–5	1977	Kao Hsiung, Taiwan	El Cajon, Calif.	7–2
1955	Morrisville, Pa.	Merchantville, N.J.	4–3	1978	Pin-Tung, Taiwan	Danville, Calif.	11–1
1956	Roswell, N.M.	Merchantville, N.J.	3–1	1979	Hsien, Taiwan	Campbell, Calif.	2–1
1957	Monterrey, Mex.	LaMesa, Calif.	4–0	1980	Hua Lian, Taiwan	Tampa, Fla.	4–3
1958	Monterrey, Mex.	Kankakee, Ill.	10–1	1981	Tai-Chung, Taiwan	Tampa, Fla.	4–2
1959	Hamtramck, Mich.	Auburn, Calif.	12–0	1982	Kirkland, Wash.	Hsien, Taiwan	6–0
1960	Levittown, Pa.	Ft. Worth, Tex.	5–0	1983	Marietta, Ga.	Barahona, Dom. Rep.	3–1
1961	El Cajon, Calif.	El Campo, Tex.	4–2	1984	Seoul, S. Korea	Altamonte Springs, Fla.	6–2
1962	San Jose, Calif.	Kankakee, Ill.	3–0	1985	Seoul, S. Korea	Mexicali, Mex.	7–1
1963	Granada Hills, Calif.	Stratford, Conn.	2–1	1986	Tianan Park, Taiwan	Tucson, Ariz.	12–0
1964	Staten Island, N.Y.	Monterrey, Mex.	4–0	1987	Hua Lian, Taiwan	Irvine, Calif.	21–1
1965	Windsor Locks, Conn.	Stoney Creek, Can.	3–1	1988	Tai-Chung, Taiwan	Pearl City, Haw.	10–0
1966	Houston, Tex.	W. New York, N.J.	8–2	1989	Trumbull, Conn.	Kaohsiung, Taiwan	5–2
1967	West Tokyo, Japan	Chicago, Ill.	4–1	1990	Taipei, Taiwan	Shippensburg, Pa.	9–0
1968	Osaka, Japan	Richmond, Va.	1–0	1991	Tai-Chung, Taiwan	San Ramon Valley, Calif.	11–0
1969	Taipei, Taiwan	Santa Clara, Calif.	5–0				

Year	Champion	Runner-up	Score	Year	Champion	Runner-up	Score
1992	Long Beach, Calif.	Zamboanga, Phil.	6–0[1]	2000	Maracaibo, Venezuela	Bellaire, Tex.	3–2
1993	Long Beach, Calif.	David Chiriqui, Pan.	3–2	2001	Tokyo Kitasuna, Tokyo, Japan	Apopka, Fla.	2–1
1994	Maracaibo, Venezuela	Northridge, Calif.	4–3	2002	Louisville, Ky.	Sendai, Japan	1–0
1995	Tainan, Taiwan	Spring, Texas	17–3	2003	Musashi-Fuchu, Tokyo, Japan	East Boynton Beach, Fla.	10–1
1996	Kao-Hsuing City, Taipei	Cranston, R.I.	13–3	2004	Pabao Little League, Willemstad, Curaçao	Conejo Valley East, Thousand Oaks, Calif.	5–2
1997	Guadalupe, Mexico	South Mission Viejo, Calif.	5–4	2005	Ewa Beach, West Oahu, Hawaii	Pabao Little League, Willemstad, Curaçao	7–6[2]
1998	Toms River, N.J.	Kashima, Japan	12–9				
1999	Hirakata, Osaka, Japan	Phenix City, Ala.	5–0				

1. Long Beach declared a 6–0 winner after the international tournament committee determined that Zamboanga City had used players that were not within its city limits. 2. Game went to seven innings.

Baseball

The popular tradition that baseball was invented by Abner Doubleday at Cooperstown, N.Y., in 1839 has been enshrined in the Hall of Fame and National Museum of Baseball erected in that town, but research has proved that a game called "Base Ball" was played in this country and England before then. The first team baseball as we know it was played at the Elysian Fields, Hoboken, N.J., on June 19, 1846, between the Knickerbockers and the New York Nine. The next fifty years saw a gradual growth of baseball and an improvement of equipment and playing skill.

Historians have it that the first pitcher to throw a curve was William A. (Candy) Cummings in 1867. The Cincinnati Red Stockings were the first all-professional team, and in 1869 they played 64 games without a loss. The standard ball of the same size and weight, still the rule, was adopted in 1872. The first catcher's mask was worn in 1875. The National League was organized in 1876. The first chest protector was worn in 1885. The three-strike rule was put on the books in 1887, and the four-ball ticket to first base was instituted in 1889. The pitching distance was lengthened to 60 feet 6 inches in 1893, and the rules have been modified only slightly since that time.

The American League, under the vigorous leadership of B. B. Johnson, became a major league in 1901. Judge Kenesaw Mountain Landis, by action of the two major leagues, became Commissioner of Baseball in 1921.

In 2005, the Montreal Expos moved to Washington, DC and were renamed the Washington Nationals.

For 2005 season final statistics, *see* www.infoplease.com/2005baseball.

NATIONAL BASEBALL HALL OF FAME
Cooperstown, N.Y.

Fielders

Member	Active years	Member	Active years	Member	Active years
Aaron, Henry (Hank)	1954–1976	Cepeda, Orlando	1958–1974	Ewing, William	1880–1897
Anson, Adrian (Cap)	1876–1897	Chance, Frank	1898–1914	Evers, John	1902–1919
Aparicio, Luis	1956–1973	Charleston, Oscar[1]	1915–1954	Ferrell, Rick	1929–1947
Appling, Lucius (Luke)	1930–1950	Clarke, Fred	1894–1915	Fisk, Carlton	1969–1991
Ashburn, Richie	1948–1962	Clemente, Roberto	1955–1972	Flick, Elmer	1898–1910
Averill, H. Earl	1929–1941	Cobb, Tyrus	1905–1928	Fox, Nellie	1947–1965
Baker, J. Frank (Home Run)	1908–1922	Cochrane, Gordon (Mickey)	1925–1937	Foxx, James	1925–1945
Bancroft, David	1915–1930			Frisch, Frank	1919–1937
Banks, Ernest	1953–1971	Collins, Edward	1906–1930	Gehrig, H. Louis (Lou)	1923–1939
Beckley, Jacob	1888–1907	Collins, James	1895–1908	Gehringer, Charles	1924–1942
Bell, James (Cool Papa)[1]	1920–1947	Comiskey, Charles	1882–1894	Gibson, Josh[1]	1929–1946
Bench, John	1967–1983	Combs, Earle	1924–1935	Goslin, Leon (Goose)	1921–1938
Berra, Lawrence (Yogi)	1946–1965	Connor, Roger	1880–1897	Greenberg, Henry (Hank)	1933–1947
Boggs, Wade	1982–1999	Crawford, Samuel	1899–1917	Hafey, Charles (Chick)	1924–1937
Bottomley, James	1922–1937	Cronin, Joseph	1926–1945	Hamilton, William	1888–1901
Boudreau, Louis	1938–1952	Cuyler, Hazen (Kiki)	1921–1938	Hartnett, Charles (Gabby)	1922–1941
Bresnahan, Roger	1897–1915	Dandridge, Ray[1]	1933–1953	Heilmann, Harry	1914–1932
Brett, George	1973–1993	Davis, George	1890–1909	Herman, William	1931–1947
Brock, Lou	1961–1980	Delahanty, Edward	1888–1903	Hooper, Harry	1909–1925
Brouthers, Dennis	1879–1896	Dickey, William	1928–1946	Hornsby, Rogers	1915–1937
Burkett, Jesse	1890–1905	Dihigo, Martin[1]	1923–1945	Irvin, Monford (Monte)[1]	1939–1956
Campanella, Roy	1948–1957	DiMaggio, Joseph	1936–1951	Jackson, Reggie	1967–1987
Carew, Rod	1967–1985	Doby, Larry	1947–1959	Jackson, Travis	1922–1936
Carey, Max	1910–1929	Doerr, Bobby	1937–1951	Jennings, William	1891–1918
Carter, Gary	1974–1991	Duffy, Hugh	1888–1906	Johnson, William (Judy)[1]	1921–1937

Member	Active years	Member	Active years	Member	Active years
Kaline, Albert W.	1953–1974	Medwick, Joseph (Ducky)	1932–1948	Snider, Edwin D. (Duke)	1947–1964
Keeler, William (Wee Willie)	1892–1910	Mize, John (The Big Cat)	1936–1953	Speaker, Tristram	1907–1928
Kell, George	1943–1957	Molitor, Paul	1978–1998	Stargell, Willie	1962–1982
Kelley, Joseph	1891–1908	Morgan, Joe	1963–1984	Stearnes, Norman (Tur-key)	1921–1942
Kelly, George	1915–1932	Murray, Eddie	1977–1997		
Kelly, Michael (King)	1878–1893	Musial, Stanley	1941–1963	Terry, William	1923–1936
Killebrew, Harmon	1954–1975	O'Rourke, James	1876–1894	Thompson, Samuel	1885–1906
Kiner, Ralph	1946–1955	Ott, Melvin	1926–1947	Tinker, Joseph	1902–1916
Klein, Charles H. (Chuck)	1928–1944	Perez, Tony	1964–1983	Traynor, Harold (Pie)	1920–1937
Lajoie, Napoleon	1896–1916	Puckett, Kirby	1984–1995	Vaughan, Arky	1932–1948
Lazzeri, Tony	1926–1939	Reese, Harold (Pee Wee)	1940–1958	Wagner, John (Honus)	1897–1917
Leonard, Walter (Buck)[1]	1933–1955	Rice, Edgar (Sam)	1915–1934	Wallace, Roderick (Bobby)	1894–1918
Lindstrom, Frederick	1924–1936	Rizzuto, Phil	1941–1956	Waner, Lloyd	1927–1945
Lloyd, John Henry (Pop)[1]	1905–1931	Robinson, Brooks	1955–1977	Waner, Paul	1926–1945
Lombardi, Ernie	1932–1947	Robinson, Frank	1956–1976	Ward, John (Monte)	1878–1894
Mantle, Mickey	1951–1968	Robinson, Jack	1947–1956	Wells, Willie	1924–1949
Manush, Henry (Heinie)	1923–1939	Robinson, Wilbert	1886–1902	Wheat, Zachariah	1909–1927
Maranville, Walter (Rabbit)	1912–1935	Roush, Edd	1913–1931	Williams, Billy	1959–1976
Matthews, Edwin	1952–1968	Ruth, Babe	1914–1935	Williams, Theodore	1939–1960
Mays, Willie	1951–1973	Sandberg, Ryne	1981–1997	Wilson, Lewis R. (Hack)	1923–1934
Mazeroski, William Stanley (Maz)	1956–1972	Schalk, Raymond	1912–1929	Winfield, David Mark	1973–1995
		Schoendienst, Red	1945–1963	Yastrzemski, Carl	1961–1983
McCarthy, Thomas	1884–1896	Schmidt, Mike	1973–1989	Youngs, Ross (Pep)	1917–1926
McCovey, Willie	1959–1980	Sewell, Joseph	1920–1933	Yount, Robin	1974–1993
McGraw, John J.	1891–1906	Simmons, Al	1924–1944		
McPhee, John Alexander (Bid)	1882–1899	Sisler, George	1915–1930		
		Slaughter, Enos	1938–1959		
		Smith, Ozzie	1978–1996		

1. Negro League player selected by special committee.

Pitchers

Member	Active years	Member	Active years	Member	Active years
Alexander, Grover	1911–1930	Grove, Robert (Lefty)	1925–1941	Plank, Edward	1901–1917
Bender, Charles (Chief)	1903–1925	Haines, Jesse	1918–1937	Radbourn, Charles (Hoss)	1880–1891
Brown, Mordecai (3-Finger)	1903–1916	Hoyt, Waite	1918–1938	Rixey, Eppa	1912–1933
Bunning, Jim	1955–1971	Hubbell, Carl	1928–1943	Roberts, Robert (Robin)	1948–1966
Carlton, Steve	1965–1988	Hunter, Jim (Catfish)	1965–1979	Rogan, Wilber	1920–1938
Chesbro, John	1899–1909	Jenkins, Ferguson	1965–1983	Ruffing, Charles (Red)	1924–1947
Clarkson, John	1882–1894	Johnson, Walter	1907–1927	Rusie, Amos	1889–1901
Coveleski, Stanley	1912–1928	Joss, Adrian	1902–1910	Ryan, Nolan, Jr.	1966–1993
Day, Leon	1935–1955	Keefe, Timothy	1880–1893	Seaver, Tom	1967–1986
Dean, Jerome (Dizzy)	1930–1947	Koufax, Sanford (Sandy)	1955–1966	Smith, Hilton Lee	1932–1948
Drysdale, Don	1956–1969	Lemon, Robert	1946–1958	Spahn, Warren	1942–1965
Eckersley, Dennis	1975–1998	Lyons, Theodore	1923–1946	Sutton, Don	1966–1988
Faber, Urban (Red)	1914–1933	Marichal, Juan	1960–1975	Vance, Arthur (Dazzy)	1915–1935
Feller, Robert	1936–1956	Marquard, Richard (Rube)	1908–1924	Waddell, Rube	1897–1910
Fingers, Rollie	1968–1985	Mathewson, Christopher	1900–1916	Walsh, Edward	1904–1917
Ford, Edward (Whitey)	1950–1967	McGinnity, Joseph	1899–1908	Welch, Michael (Mickey)	1880–1892
Foster, Andrew (Rube)	1897–1926	Newhouser, Hal	1939–1955	Wilhelm, Hoyt	1952–1972
Foster, Bill	1923–1937	Nichols, Charles (Kid)	1890–1906	Williams, Joseph	1910–1932
Galvin, James (Pud)	1876–1892	Niekro, Phil	1959–1987	Willis, Vic	1898–1910
Gibson, Bob	1959–1975	Paige, Leroy (Satchel)[1]	1926–1965	Wynn, Early	1939–1963
Gomez, Vernon (Lefty)	1930–1943	Palmer, Jim	1965–1984	Young, Denton (Cy)	1890–1911
Griffith, Clark	1891–1914	Pennock, Herbert	1912–1934		
Grimes, Burleigh	1916–1934	Perry, Gaylord	1962–1983		

1. Negro League player selected by special committee.

Officials and Others

Alston, Walter[1]	Comiskey, Charles[1]	Hanlon, Ned[3]	Lasorda, Tommy[1]	Selee, Frank G.[1]
Anderson, Sparky[1]	Conlan, John[3]	Harridge, William[3]	Lopez, Alfonso R.[7]	Spalding, Albert G.[2]
Barlick, Al[2]	Connolly, Thomas[2]	Harris, Stanley R.[7]	Mack, Connie[1, 3]	Stengel, Charles D.[7]
Barrow, Edward[1, 3]	Cummings, William A.[6]	Hubbard, R. Calvin[2]	MacPhail, Lee, Jr.[3]	Veeck, Bill[3]
Bulkeley, Morgan G.[3]	Durocher, Leo[1]	Huggins, Miller J.[1]	MacPhail, Leland S.[3]	Weaver, Earl[1]
Cartwright, Alexander[3]	Evans, William G.[2, 3]	Hulbert, William[3]	McCarthy, Joseph V.[1]	Weiss, George M.[3]
Chadwick, Henry[4]	Foster, Rube[3]	Johnson, B. Bancroft[3]	McGowan, Bill[2]	Wright, George[6]
Chandler, A. B.[5]	Frick, Ford C.[3, 5]	Klem, William[2]	McKechnie, William B.[1]	Wright, Harry[1, 6]
Chylak, Nestor, Jr.[2]	Giles, Warren C.[3]	Landis, Kenesaw M.[5]	Rickey, W. Branch[1, 3]	Yawkey, Thomas[3]

1. Manager. 2. Umpire. 3. Executive. 4. Writer-statistician. 5. Commissioner. 6. Early player. 7. Player-manager.

MAJOR LEAGUE ALL-STAR GAME

Year	Date	Winning league (manager)	Runs	Losing league (manager)	Runs	Winning pitcher	Losing pitcher	Site	Paid attendance
1933	July 6	A.L. (Mack)	4	N.L. (McGraw)	2	Gomez	Hallahan	Chicago A.L.	47,595
1934	July 10	A.L. (Cronin)	9	N.L. (Terry)	7	Harder	Mungo	New York N.L.	48,363
1935	July 8	A.L. (Cochrane)	4	N.L. (Frisch)	1	Gomez	Walker	Cleveland A.L.	69,831
1936	July 7	N.L. (Grimm)	4	A.L. (McCarthy)	3	J. Dean	Grove	Boston N.L.	25,556
1937	July 7	A.L. (McCarthy)	8	N.L. (Terry)	3	Gomez	J. Dean	Washington A.L.	31,391
1938	July 6	N.L. (Terry)	4	A.L. (McCarthy)	1	Vander Meer	Gomez	Cincinnati N.L.	27,067
1939	July 11	A.L. (McCarthy)	3	N.L. (Hartnett)	1	Bridges	Lee	New York A.L.	62,892
1940	July 9	N.L. (McKechnie)	4	A.L. (Cronin)	0	Derringer	Ruffing	St. Louis N.L.	32,373
1941	July 8	A.L. (Baker)	7	N.L. (McKechnie)	5	E. Smith	Passeau	Detroit A.L.	54,674
1942	July 6	A.L. (McCarthy)	3	N.L. (Durocher)	1	Chandler	Cooper	New York N.L.	34,178
1943	July 13	A.L. (McCarthy)	5	N.L. (Southworth)	3	Leonard	Cooper	Philadelphia A.L.	31,938
1944	July 11	N.L. (Southworth)	7	A.L. (McCarthy)	1	Raffensberger	Hughson	Pittsburgh N.L.	29,589
1946	July 9	A.L. (O'Neill)	12	N.L. (Grimm)	0	Feller	Passeau	Boston A.L.	34,906
1947	July 8	A.L. (Cronin)	2	N.L. (Dyer)	1	Shea	Sain	Chicago N.L.	41,123
1948	July 13	A.L. (Harris)	5	N.L. (Durocher)	2	Raschi	Schmitz	St. Louis A.L.	34,009
1949	July 12	A.L. (Boudreau)	11	N.L. (Southworth)	7	Trucks	Newcombe	Brooklyn N.L.	32,577
1950	July 11	N.L. (Shotton)	4	A.L. (Stengel)	3[1]	Blackwell	Gray	Chicago A.L.	46,127
1951	July 10	N.L. (Sawyer)	8	A.L. (Stengel)	3	Maglie	Lopat	Detroit A.L.	52,075
1952	July 8	N.L. (Durocher)	3	A.L. (Stengel)	2[2]	Rush	Lemon	Philadelphia N.L.	32,785
1953	July 14	N.L. (Dressen)	5	A.L. (Stengel)	1	Spahn	Reynolds	Cincinnati N.L.	30,846
1954	July 13	A.L. (Stengel)	11	N.L. (Alston)	9	Stone	Conley	Cleveland A.L.	68,751
1955	July 12	N.L. (Durocher)	6	A.L. (Lopez)	5[3]	Conley	Sullivan	Milwaukee N.L.	45,643
1956	July 10	N.L. (Alston)	7	A.L. (Stengel)	3	Friend	Pierce	Washington A.L.	28,843
1957	July 9	A.L. (Stengel)	6	N.L. (Alston)	5	Bunning	Simmons	St. Louis N.L.	30,693
1958	July 8	A.L. (Stengel)	4	N.L. (Haney)	3	Wynn	Friend	Baltimore A.L.	48,829
1959[4]	July 7	N.L. (Haney)	5	A.L. (Stengel)	4	Antonelli	Ford	Pittsburgh N.L.	35,277
	Aug. 3	A.L. (Stengel)	5	N.L. (Haney)	3	Walker	Drysdale	Los Angeles N.L.	55,105
1960[4]	July 11	N.L. (Alston)	5	A.L. (Lopez)	3	Friend	Monbouquette	Kansas City A.L.	30,619
	July 13	N.L. (Alston)	6	A.L. (Lopez)	0	Law	Ford	New York A.L.	38,362
1961[4]	July 11	N.L. (Murtaugh)	5	A.L. (Richards)	4[5]	Miller	Wilhelm	San Francisco N.L.	44,115
	July 31	N.L. (Murtaugh)	1	A.L. (Richards)	1[6]	—	—	Boston A.L.	31,851
1962[4]	July 10	N.L. (Hutchinson)	3	A.L. (Houk)	1	Marichal	Pascual	Washington A.L.	45,480
	July 30	A.L. (Houk)	9	N.L. (Hutchinson)	4	Herbert	Mahaffey	Chicago A.L.	38,359
1963	July 9	N.L. (Dark)	5	A.L. (Houk)	3	Jackson	Bunning	Cleveland A.L.	44,160
1964	July 7	N.L. (Alston)	7	A.L. (Lopez)	4	Marichal	Radatz	New York N.L.	50,850
1965	July 13	N.L. (March)	6	A.L. (Lopez)	5	Koufax	McDowell	Minnesota A.L.	46,706
1966	July 12	N.L. (Alston)	2	A.L. (Mele)	1[5]	Perry	Rickert	St. Louis N.L.	49,926
1967	July 11	N.L. (Alston)	2	A.L. (Bauer)	1[7]	Drysdale	Hunter	Anaheim A.L.	46,309
1968	July 9	N.L. (Schoendienst)	1	A.L. (Williams)	0	Drysdale	Tiant	Houston N.L.	48,321
1969	July 23	N.L. (M. Smith)	9	A.L. (M. Smith)	3	Carlton	Stottlemyre	Washington N.L.	45,259
1970	July 14	N.L. (Hodges)	5	A.L. (Weaver)	4	Osteen	Wright	Cincinnati N.L.	51,838
1971	July 13	A.L. (Weaver)	6	N.L. (Anderson)	4	Blue	Ellis	Detroit A.L.	53,559
1972	July 25	N.L. (Murtaugh)	4	A.L. (Weaver)	3[5]	McGraw	McNally	Atlanta N.L.	53,107
1973	July 24	N.L. (Anderson)	7	A.L. (Williams)	1	Wise	Blyleven	Kansas City A.L.	40,849
1974	July 23	N.L. (Berra)	7	A.L. (Williams)	2	Brett	Tiant	Pittsburgh A.L.	50,706
1975	July 15	N.L. (Alston)	6	A.L. (Dark)	3	Matlack	Hunter	Milwaukee A.L.	51,540
1976	July 13	N.L. (Anderson)	7	A.L. (D. Johnson)	1	R. Jones	Fidrych	Philadelphia N.L.	63,974
1977	July 19	N.L. (Anderson)	7	A.L. (Martin)	5	Sutton	Palmer	New York A.L.	56,683
1978	July 11	N.L. (Lasorda)	7	A.L. (Martin)	3	Sutter	Gossage	San Diego N.L.	51,549
1979	July 17	N.L. (Lasorda)	7	A.L. (Lemon)	6	Sutter	Kern	Seattle A.L.	58,905
1980	July 8	N.L. (Tanner)	4	A.L. (Weaver)	2	Reuss	John	Los Angeles N.L.	56,088
1981[8]	Aug. 9	N.L. (Green)	5	A.L. (Frey)	4	Blue	Fingers	Cleveland A.L.	72,086
1982	July 13	N.L. (Lasorda)	4	A.L. (Martin)	1	Rogers	Eckersley	Montreal N.L.	59,057
1983	July 6	A.L. (Kuenn)	13	N.L. (Herzog)	3	Steib	Soto	Chicago A.L.	43,801
1984	July 11	N.L. (Owens)	3	A.L. (Altobelli)	1	Leg	Steib	San Francisco N.L.	57,756
1985	July 16	N.L. (Williams)	6	A.L. (Anderson)	1	Hoyt	Morris	Minneapolis A.L.	54,960
1986	July 15	A.L. (Howser)	3	N.L. (Herzog)	2	Clemens	Gooden	Houston N.L.	45,774
1987	July 14	N.L. (Johnson)	2	A.L. (McNamara)	0[9]	Smith	Howell	Oakland A.L.	49,671
1988	July 12	A.L. (Kelly)	2	N.L. (Herzog)	1	Viola	Gooden	Cincinnati, N.L	55,837
1989	July 11	A.L. (LaRussa)	5	N.L. (Lasorda)	3	Ryan	Smoltz	California A.L.	64,036
1990	July 10	A.L. (LaRussa)	2	N.L. (Craig)	0	Saberhagen	Brantley	Chicago N.L.	39,071
1991	July 9	A.L. (LaRussa)	4	N.L. (Piniella)	2	Key	Martinez	Toronto A.L.	52,383
1992	July 14	A.L. (Kelly)	13	N.L. (Cox)	6	Brown	Glavine	San Diego N.L.	59,372
1993	July 13	A.L. (Gaston)	9	N.L. (Cox)	3	McDowell	Burkett	Baltimore A.L.	48,147
1994	July 12	N.L. (Fregosi)	8	A.L. (Gaston)	7[5]	Jones	Bere	Pittsburgh N.L.	59,568
1995	July 11	N.L. (Alou)	3	A.L. (Showalter)	2	Slocumb	Rogers	Texas A.L.	50,920
1996	July 9	N.L. (Cox)	6	A.L. (Hargrove)	0	Smoltz	Nagy	Philadelphia N.L.	62,670
1997	July 8	A.L. (Torre)	3	N.L. (Cox)	1	Johnson	Maddux	Cleveland A.L.	44,916
1998	July 7	A.L. (Hargrove)	13	N.L. (Leyland)	3	Colon	Urbina	Denver N.L.	51,267
1999	July 13	A.L. (Torre)	4	N.L. (Bochy)	1	P. Martinez	Schilling	Boston A.L.	34,187

Year	Date	Winning league (manager)	Runs	Losing league (manager)	Runs	Winning pitcher	Losing pitcher	Site	Paid attendance
2000	July 11	A.L. (Torre)	6	N.L. (Cox)	3	Baldwin	Leiter	Atlanta N.L.	51,323
2001	July 10	A.L. (Torre)	4	N.L. (Valentine)	1	Garcia	Park	Seattle A.L.	47,364
2002	July 9	7–7 tie after 11 innings. Bob Brenley, N.L. manager, Joe Torre, A.L. manager						Milwaukee N.L.	41,871
2003	July 15	A.L. (Scioscia)	7	N.L. (Baker)	6	Donnelly	Gagne	Chicago A.L.	47,609
2004	July 13	A.L. (Torre)	9	N.L. (McKeon)	4	Mulder	Clemens	Houston, N.L.	41,866
2005	July 12	A.L. (Francona)	7	N.L. (La Russa)	5	Buehrle	Smoltz	Detroit, A.L.	41,617

1. Fourteen innings. 2. Five innings, rain. 3. Twelve innings. 4. Two games. 5. Ten innings. 6. Called because of rain after nine innings. 7. Fifteen innings. 8. Game was originally scheduled for July 14, but was put off because of players' strike. 9. Thirteen innings. NOTE: No game in 1945.

RECORD OF WORLD SERIES GAMES
(through 2004)

Figures in parentheses for winning pitchers (WP) and losing pitchers (LP) indicate the game number in the series.

1903—Boston A.L. 5 (Jimmy Collins); Pittsburgh N.L. 3 (Fred Clarke). WP—Boston: Dinneen (2, 6, 8), Young (5, 7); Pittsburgh: Phillippe (1, 3, 4). LP—Boston: Young (1), Hughes (3), Dinneen (4); Pittsburgh: Leever (2, 6), Kennedy (5), Phillippe (7, 8).

1904—No series.

1905—New York N.L. 4 (John J. McGraw); Philadelphia A.L. 1 (Connie Mack). WP—New York: Mathewson (1, 3, 5); McGinnity (4); Phila.: Bender (2). LP—New York: McGinnity (2); Phila.: Plank (1, 4), Coakley (5), Bender (5).

1906—Chicago A.L. 4 (Fielder Jones); Chicago N.L. 2 (Frank Chance). WP—Chicago: A.L.: Altrock (1), Walsh (3, 5), White (6); Chicago: N.L.: Reulbach (2), Brown (4). LP—Chicago A.L.: White (2), Altrock. (4); Chicago: N.L.: Brown (1, 6), Pfeister (3, 5).

1907—Chicago N.L. 4 (Frank Chance); Detroit A.L. 0 (Hugh Jennings). First game tied 3–3, 12 innings. WP—Pfeister (2), Reulbach (3), Overall (4), Brown (5). LP—Mullin (2, 5), Siever (3), Donovan (4).

1908—Chicago N.L. 4 (Frank Chance); Detroit A.L. 1 (Hugh Jennings). WP—Chicago: Brown (1, 4), Overall (2, 5); Det.: Mullin (3). LP—Chicago: Pfeister (2); Det.: Summers (1, 4), Donovan (2, 5).

1909—Pittsburgh N.L. 4 (Fred Clarke); Detroit A.L. 3 (Hugh Jennings). WP—Pittsburgh: Adams (1, 5, 7), Maddox (3); Det.: Donovan (2), Mullin (4, 6). LP—Pittsburgh: Camnitz (2), Leifield (4), Willis (6); Det.: Mullin (1), Summers (3, 5), Donovan (7).

1910—Philadelphia A.L. 4 (Connie Mack); Chicago N.L. 1 (Frank Chance). WP—Phila.: Bender (1), Coombs (2, 3, 5); Chicago: Brown (4). LP—Phila.: Bender (4); Chicago: Overall (1), Brown (2, 5), McIntyre (3).

1911—Philadelphia A.L. 4 (Connie Mack); New York N.L. 2 (John J. McGraw). WP—Phila.: Plank (2), Coombs (3), Bender (4, 6); New York: Mathewson (1), Crandall (5). LP—Phila.: Bender (1), Plank (5); New York: Marquard (2), Mathewson (3, 4), Ames (6).

1912—Boston A.L. 4 (J. Garland Stahl); New York N.L. 3 (John J. McGraw). Second game tied, 6–6, 11 innings. WP—Boston: Wood (1, 4, 8), Bedient (5); New York: Marquard (3, 6), Tesreau (7). LP—Boston: O'Brien (3, 6), Wood (7); New York: Tesreau (1, 4), Mathewson (5, 8).

1913—Philadelphia A.L. 4 (Connie Mack); New York N.L. 1 (John J. McGraw). WP—Phila.: Bender (1, 4), Bush (3), Plank (5); New York: Mathewson (2); LP—Phila.: Plank (2); New York: Marquard (1), Tesreau (3), Demaree (4), Mathewson (5).

1914—Boston N.L. 4 (George Stallings); Philadelphia A.L. 0 (Connie Mack). WP—Rudolph (1, 4), James (2, 3). LP—Bender (1), Plank (2), Bush (3), Shawkey (4).

1915—Boston A.L. 4 (Bill Carrigan); Philadelphia N.L. 1 (Pat Moran). WP—Boston: Foster (2, 5), Leonard (3), Shore (4); Phila.: Alexander (1). LP—Boston: Shore (1); Phila.: Mayer (2), Alexander (3), Chalmers (4), Rixey (5).

1916—Boston A.L. 4 (Bill Carrigan); Brooklyn N.L. 1 (Wilbert Robinson). WP—Boston: Shore (1, 5), Ruth (2), Leonard (4); Brooklyn: Coombs (3). LP—Boston: Mays (3); Brooklyn: Marquard (1, 4), Smith (2), Pfeffer (5).

1917—Chicago A.L. 4 (Clarence Rowland); New York N.L. 2 (John J. McGraw). WP—Chicago: Cicotte (1), Faber (2, 5, 6); New York: Benton (3), Schupp (4). LP—Chicago: Cicotte (3), Faber (4); New York: Sallee (1, 5), Anderson (3, 6).

1918—Boston A.L. 4 (Ed Barrow); Chicago N.L. 2 (Fred Mitchell). WP—Boston: Ruth (1, 4), Mays (3, 6); Chicago: Tyler (2), Vaughn (5). LP—Boston: Bush (2), Jones (5); Chicago: Vaughn (1, 3), Douglas (4), Tyler (6).

1919—Cincinnati N.L. 5 (Pat Moran); Chicago A.L. 3 (William Gleason). WP—Cincinnati: Ruether (1), Sallee (2), Ring (4), Eller (5, 8); Chicago: Kerr (3, 6), Cicotte (7). LP—Cincinnati: Fisher (3), Ring (6), Sallee (7); Chicago: Cicotte (1, 4), Williams (2, 5, 8).

1920—Cleveland A.L. 5 (Tris Speaker); Brooklyn N.L. 2 (Wilbert Robinson). WP—Cleve.: Coveleski (1, 4, 7), Bagby (5), Mails (6); Brooklyn: Grimes (2), Smith (3). LP—Cleve.: Bagby (2), Caldwell (3). Brooklyn: Marquard (1), Cadore (5), Grimes (5, 7), Smith (6).

1921—New York N.L. 5 (John J. McGraw); New York A.L. 3 (Miller Huggins). WP—New York N.L.: Barnes (3, 6), Douglas (4, 7), Nehf (8); New York A.L.: Mays (1), Hoyt (2, 5). LP—New York N.L.: Nehf (2, 5), Douglas (1). New York A.L.: Quinn (1), Mays (4, 7), Shawkey (6), Hoyt (8).

1922—New York N.L. 4 (John J. McGraw); New York A.L. 0 (Miller Huggins). Second game tied 3–3, 10 innings. WP—Ryan (1), Scott (3), McQuillan (4), Nehf (5); LP—Bush (1, 5), Hoyt (3), Mays (4).

1923—New York A.L. 4 (Miller Huggins); New York N.L. 2 (John J. McGraw). WP—New York A.L.: Pennock (2, 6), Shawkey (4), Bush (5); New York N.L.: Ryan (1), Nehf (3). LP—New York A.L.: Bush (1), Jones (3); New York N.L.: McQuillan (2), Scott (4), Bentley (5), Nehf (6).

1924—Washington A.L. 4 (Bucky Harris); New York N.L. 3 (John J. McGraw). WP—Washington: Zachary (2, 6), Mogridge (4), Johnson (7); New York: Nehf (1), McQuillan (3), Bentley (5). LP—Washington: Johnson (1, 5), Marberry (3); New York: Bentley (2, 7), Barnes (4), Nehf (6).

1925—Pittsburgh N.L. 4 (Bill McKechnie); Washington A.L. 3 (Bucky Harris). WP—Pittsburgh: Aldridge (2, 5), Kremer (6, 7); Washington: Johnson (1, 4), Ferguson (3). LP—Pittsburgh: Meadows (1), Kremer (5), Yde (4); Washington: Coveleski (2, 5), Ferguson (6), Johnson (7).

1926—St. Louis N.L. 4 (Rogers Hornsby); New York A.L. 3 (Miller Huggins). WP—St. Louis: Alexander (2, 6), Haines (3, 7); New York: Pennock (1, 5), Hoyt (4). LP—St. Louis: Sherdel (1, 5), Reinhart (4); New York: Shocker (2), Ruether (3), Shawkey (6), Hoyt (7).

1927—New York A.L. 4 (Miller Huggins); Pittsburgh N.L. 0 (Donie Bush). WP—Hoyt (1), Pipgras (2), Pennock (3), Moore (4). LP—Kremer (1), Aldridge (2), Meadows (3), Miljus (4).

1928—New York A.L. 4 (Miller Huggins); St. Louis N.L. 0 (Bill McKechnie). WP—Hoyt (1, 4), Pipgras (2), Zachary (3). LP—Sherdel (1, 4), Alexander (2), Haines (3).

1929—Philadelphia A.L. 4 (Connie Mack); Chicago N.L. 1 (Joe McCarthy). WP—Phila.: Ehmke (1), Earnshaw (2), Rommel (4), Walberg (5); Chicago: Bush (3). LP—Phila.: Earnshaw

(3) Chicago: Root (1), Malone (2, 5), Blake (4).

1930—Philadelphia A.L. 4 (Connie Mack); St. Louis N.L. 2 (Gabby Street). WP—Phila.: Grove (1, 5), Earnshaw (2, 6); St. Louis: Hallahan (3), Haines (4). LP—Phila.: Walberg (3), Grove (4); St. Louis: Grimes (1, 5), Rhem (2), Hallahan (6).

1931—St. Louis N.L. 4 (Gabby Street); Philadelphia A.L. 3 (Connie Mack). WP—St. Louis: Hallahan (2, 5), Grimes (3, 7); Phila.: Grove (1, 6), Earnshaw (4). LP—St. Louis: Derringer (1, 6), Johnson (4); Phila.: Earnshaw (2, 7), Grove (3), Hoyt (5).

1932—New York A.L. (Joe McCarthy); Chicago N.L. 0 (Charles Grimm). WP—Ruffing (1), Gomez (2), Pipgras (3), Moore (4). LP—Bush (1), Warneke (2), Root (3), May (4).

1933—New York N.L. 4 (Bill Terry); Washington A.L. 1 (Joe Cronin.). WP—New York: Hubbell (1, 4), Schumacher (2), Luque (3); Washington: Whitehill (3). LP—New York: Fitzsimmons (3); Washington: Stewart (1), Crowder (2), Weaver (4), Russell (5).

1934—St. Louis N.L. 4 (Frank Frisch); Detroit A.L. 3 (Mickey Cochrane). WP—St. Louis: J. Dean (1, 7), P. Dean (3, 6); Det.: Rowe (2), Auker (4), Bridges (5). LP—St. Louis: W. Walker (2, 4), J. Dean (5); Det.: Crowder (1), Bridges (3), Rowe (6), Auker (7).

1935—Detroit A.L. 4 (Mickey Cochrane); Chicago N.L. 2 (Charles Grimm). WP—Det.: Bridges (2, 6), Rowe (3), Crowder (4); Chicago: Warneke (1, 5); LP—Det.: Rowe (1, 5), Chicago: Root (2), French (3, 6), Carleton (4).

1936—New York A.L. 4 (Joe McCarthy); New York N.L. 2 (Bill Terry). WP—New York A.L.: Gomez (2, 6), Hadley (3), Pearson (4); New York N.L.: Hubbell (1), Schumacher (5); LP—New York A.L.: Ruffing (1), Malone (5); New York N.L.: Schumacher (2), Fitzsimmons (3, 6), Hubbell (4).

1937—New York A.L. 4 (Joe McCarthy); New York N.L. 1 (Bill Terry). WP—New York A.L.: Gomez (1, 5), Ruffing (2), Pearson (3); New York N.L.: Hubbell (4). LP—New York A.L.: Hadley (4); New York N.L.: Hubbell (1), Melton (2, 5), Schumacher (3).

1938—New York A.L. 4 (Joe McCarthy); Chicago N.L. 0 (Gabby Hartnett). WP—Ruffing (1, 4), Gomez (2), Pearson (3) LP—Lee (1, 4), Dean (2), Bryant (3).

1939—New York A.L. 4 (Joe McCarthy); Cincinnati N.L. 0 (Bill McKechnie). WP—Ruffing (1), Pearson (2), Hadley (3), Murphy (4). LP—Derringer (1), Walters (2, 4), Thompson (3).

1940—Cincinnati N.L. 4 (Bill McKechnie); Detroit A.L. 3 (Del Baker). WP—Cincinnati: Walters (2, 6), Derringer (4, 7); Det.: Newsom (1, 5), Bridges (3). LP—Cincinnati: Derringer (1), Turner (3), Thompson (5); Det.: Rowe (2, 6), Trout (4), Newsom (7).

1941—New York A.L. 4 (Joe McCarthy); Brooklyn N.L. 1 (Leo Durocher). WP—New York: Ruffing (1), Russo (3), Murphy (4), Bonham (5); Bklyn: Wyatt (2). LP—New York: Chandler (2); Bklyn: Davis (1), Casey (3, 4), Wyatt (5).

1942—St. Louis N.L. 4 (Billy Southworth); New York A.L. 1 (Joe McCarthy). WP—St. Louis: Beazley (2, 5), White (3), Lanier (4); New York: Ruffing (1). LP—St. Louis: Cooper (1); New York: Bonham (2), Chandler (3), Donald (4), Ruffing (5).

1943—New York A.L. 4 (Joe McCarthy); St. Louis N.L. 1 (Billy Southworth). WP—New York: Chandler (1, 5), Borowy (3), Russo (4); St. Louis: Cooper (2). LP—New York: Bonham (2); St. Louis: Lanier (1), Brazle (3), Brecheen (4), Cooper (5).

1944—St. Louis N.L. 4 (Billy Southworth); St. Louis A.L. 2 (Luke Sewell). WP—St. Louis N.L.: Donnelly (2), Brecheen (4), Cooper (5), Lanier (6); St. Louis A.L.: Galehouse (1), Kramer (3). LP—St. Louis N.L.: Cooper (1), Wilks (3); St. Louis A.L.: Muncrief (2), Jakucki (4), Galehouse (5), Potter (6).

1945—Detroit A.L. 4 (Steve O'Neill); Chicago N.L. 3 (Charles Grimm). WP—Det.: Trucks (2), Trout (4), Newhouser (5, 7); Chicago: Borowy (1, 6), Passeau (3). LP—Det.: Newhouser (1), Overmire (3), Trout (6); Chicago: Wyse (2), Prim (4), Borowy (5, 7).

1946—St. Louis N.L. 4 (Eddie Dyer); Boston A.L. 3 (Joe Cronin). WP—St. Louis: Brecheen (2, 6, 7), Munger (4); Boston: Johnson (1), Ferriss (3), Dobson (5). LP—St. Louis: Pollet (1), Dickson (3), Brazle (5); Boston: Harris (2, 6), Hughson (4), Klinger (7).

1947—New York A.L. 4 (Bucky Harris); Brooklyn N.L. 3 (Burt Shotton). WP—New York: Shea (1, 5), Reynolds (2), Page (7); Brooklyn: Casey (3, 4), Branca (6). LP—New York: Newsom (3), Bevens (4), Page (6); Brooklyn: Branca (1), Lombardi (2), Barney (5), Gregg (7).

1948—Cleveland A.L. 4 (Lou Boudreau); Boston N.L. 2 (Billy Southworth). WP—Cleve.: Lemon (2, 6), Bearden (3), Gromek (4); Boston: Sain (1), Spahn (5). LP—Cleve.: Feller (1, 5); Boston: Spahn (2), Bickford (3), Sain (4), Voiselle (6).

1949—New York A.L. 4 (Casey Stengel); Brooklyn N.L. 1 (Burt Shotton). WP—New York: Reynolds (1), Page (3), Lopat (4), Raschi (5); Brooklyn: Roe (2). LP—New York: Raschi (2); Brooklyn: Newcombe (1, 4), Branca (3), Barney (5).

1950—New York A.L. 4 (Casey Stengel); Philadelphia N.L. 0 (Eddie Sawyer). WP—Raschi (1), Reynolds (2), Ferrick (3), Ford (4). LP—Konstanty (1), Roberts (2), Meyer (3), Miller (4).

1951—New York A.L. 4 (Casey Stengel); New York N.L. 2 (Leo Durocher). WP—New York A.L.: Lopat (2, 5), Reynolds (4), Raschi (6); New York N.L.: Koslo (1), Hearn (3). LP—New York A.L.: Reynolds (1), Raschi (3); New York N.L.: Jansen (2, 5), Maglie (4), Koslo (6).

1952—New York A.L. 4 (Casey Stengel); Brooklyn N.L. 3 (Chuck Dressen). WP—New York: Raschi (2, 6), Reynolds (4, 7); Brooklyn: Black (1), Roe (3), Erskine (5). LP—New York: Reynolds (1), Lopat (2), Sain (3); Brooklyn: Erskine (2), Black (4, 7), Loes (6).

1953—New York A.L. 4 (Casey Stengel); Brooklyn N.L. 2 (Chuck Dressen). WP—New York: Sain (1), Lopat (2), McDonald (5), Reynolds (6); Brooklyn: Erskine (3), Loes (4). LP—New York: Raschi (3), Ford (4); Brooklyn: Labine (1, 6), Roe (2), Podres (5).

1954—New York N.L. 4 (Leo Durocher); Cleveland A.L. 0 (Al Lopez). WP—Grissom (1), Antonelli (2), Gomez (3), Liddle (4). LP—Lemon (1, 4), Wynn (2), Garcia (3).

1955—Brooklyn N.L. 4 (Walter Alston); New York A.L. 3 (Casey Stengel). WP—Brooklyn: Podres (3, 7), Labine (4), Craig (5); New York: Ford (1, 6), Byrne (5). LP—Brooklyn: Newcombe (1), Loes (2), Spooner (6); New York: Turley (3), Larsen (4), Grim (5), Byrne (7).

1956—New York A.L. 4 (Casey Stengel); Brooklyn N.L. 3 (Walter Alston). WP—New York: Ford (3), Sturdivant (4), Larsen (6), Kucks (7); Brooklyn: Maglie (1), Bessent (2), Labine (6). LP—New York: Ford (1), Morgan (2), Turley (6); Brooklyn: Craig (3), Erskine (4), Maglie (5), Newcombe (7).

1957—Milwaukee N.L. 4 (Fred Haney); New York A.L. 3 (Casey Stengel). WP—Milwaukee: Burdette (2, 5, 7), Spahn (4); New York: Ford (1), Larsen (3), Turley (6). LP—Milwaukee: Spahn (1), Buhl (3), Johnson (6); New York: Shantz (2), Grim (4), Ford (5), Larsen (7).

1958—New York A.L. 4 (Casey Stengel); Milwaukee N.L. 3 (Fred Haney). WP—New York: Larsen (3), Turley (5, 7), Duren (6); Milwaukee: Spahn (1, 4), Burdette (2). LP—New York: Duren (1), Turley (2), Ford (4); Milwaukee: Rush (3), Burdette (5, 7), Spahn (6).

1959—Los Angeles N.L. 4 (Walter Alston); Chicago A.L. 2 (Al Lopez). WP—Los Angeles: Podres (3), Drysdale (4), Sherry (4, 6); Chicago: Wynn (1), Shaw (5). LP—Los Angeles: Craig (1), Koufax (5); Chicago: Shaw (2), Donovan (3), Staley (4), Wynn (6).

1960—Pittsburgh N.L. 4 (Danny Murtaugh); New York A.L. 3 (Casey Stengel). WP—Pittsburgh: Law (1, 4), Haddix (5, 7); New York: Turley (2), Ford (3, 6). LP—Pittsburgh: Friend (2, 6), Mizell (3); New York: Ditmar (1, 5), Terry (4, 7).

1961—New York A.L. 4 (Ralph Houk); Cincinnati N.L. 1 (Fred Hutchinson). WP—New York: Ford (1, 4), Arroyo (3), Daley (5); Cincinnati: Jay (2). LP—New York: Terry (2); Cincinnati: O'Toole (1, 4), Purkey (3), Jay (5).

1962—New York A.L. 4 (Ralph Houk); San Francisco N.L. 3 (Al Dark). WP—New York: Ford (1), Stafford (3), Terry (5, 7); San Francisco Sanford (2), Larsen (4), Pierce (6). LP—New York: Terry (2), Coates (4), Ford (6); San Francisco: O'Dell (1),

Pierce (3), Sanford (5, 7).

1963—Los Angeles N.L. 4 (Walter Alston); New York A.L. 0 (Ralph Houk). WP—Koufax (1, 4), Podres (2), Drysdale (3). LP—Ford (1, 4), Downing (2), Bouton (3).

1964—St. Louis N.L. 4 (Johnny Keane); New York A.L. 3 (Yogi Berra). WP—St. Louis: Sadecki (1), Craig (4), Gibson (5, 7); New York: Stottlemyre (2), Bouton (3, 6). LP—St. Louis: Gibson (2), Schultz (3), Simmons (6); New York: Ford (1), Downing (4), Mikkelsen (5), Stottlemyre (7).

1965—Los Angeles N.L. 4 (Walter Alston); Minnesota A.L. 3 (Sam Mele). WP—Los Angeles: Osteen (3), Drysdale (4), Koufax (5, 7); Minnesota: Grant (1, 6), Kaat (2). LP—Los Angeles: Drysdale (1), Koufax (2), Osteen (6); Minnesota: Pascual (3), Grant (4), Kaat (5, 7).

1966—Baltimore A.L. 4 (Hank Bauer); Los Angeles N.L. 0 (Walter Alston). WP—Drabowsky (1), Palmer (2), Bunker (3), McNally (4). LP—Drysdale (1, 4), Koufax (2), Osteen (3).

1967—St. Louis N.L. 4 (Red Schoendienst); Boston A.L. 3 (Dick Williams). WP—St. Louis: Gibson (1, 4, 7), Briles (3); Boston: Lonborg (2, 5); Wyatt (6). LP—St. Louis: Hughes (2), Carlton (5), Lamabe (6). Boston: Santiago (1, 4), Bell (3), Lonborg (7).

1968—Detroit A.L. 4 (Mayo Smith); St. Louis N.L. 3 (Red Schoendienst). WP—Det.: Lolich (2, 5, 7), McLain (6); St. Louis: Gibson (1, 4), Washburn (3). LP—Det.: McLain (1, 4), Wilson (3); St. Louis: Briles (2), Hoerner (5), Washburn (6), Gibson (7).

1969—New York N.L. 4 (Gil Hodges); Baltimore A.L. 1 (Earl Weaver). WP—New York: Koosman (2, 5), Gentry (3), Seaver (4); Baltimore: Cuellar (1). LP—New York: Seaver (1); Baltimore: McNally (2), Palmer (3), Hall (4), Watt (5).

1970—Baltimore A.L. 4 (Earl Weaver); Cincinnati N.L. 1 (Sparky Anderson) 1. WP—Baltimore: Palmer (1), Phoebus (2), McNally (3), Cuellar (5); Cincinnati: Carroll (4). LP—Cincinnati: Nolan (1), Wilcox (2), Cloninger (3), Merritt (5); Baltimore: Watt (4).

1971—Pittsburgh N.L. 4 (Danny Murtaugh); Baltimore A.L. 3 (Earl Weaver). WP—Pittsburgh: Blass (3, 7), Kison (4), Briles (5); Baltimore: McNally (1, 6), Palmer (2). LP—Pittsburgh: Ellis (1), R. Johnson (2), Miller (6); Baltimore: Cuellar (3, 7), Watt (4) McNally (5).

1972—Oakland A.L. 4 (Dick Williams); Cincinnati N.L. (Sparky Anderson) 3. WP—Oakland: Holtzman (1), Hunter (2, 7), Fingers (4); Cincinnati: Billingham (3), Grimsley (5, 6). LP—Oakland: Odom (5), Fingers (6), Blue (6); Cincinnati: Nolan (1), Grimsley (2), Carroll (4), Borbon (7).

1973—Oakland A.L. 4 (Dick Williams); New York N.L. 3 (Yogi Berra). WP—Oakland: Holtzman (1, 7), Lindblad (3), Hunter (6). New York: McGraw (2), Matlack (4), Koosman (5). LP—Oakland: Fingers (2), Holtzman (4), Blue (5). New York: Matlack (1, 7) Parker (3), Seaver (2).

1974—Oakland A.L. 4 (Al Dark); Los Angeles N.L. 1 (Walter Alston). WP—Oakland: Fingers (1), Hunter (3), Holtzman (4), Odom (5). Los Angeles: Sutton (2). LP—Oakland: Blue (2), Los Angeles: Messersmith (1, 4), Downing (3), Marshall (5).

1975—Cincinnati N.L. 4 (Sparky Anderson); Boston A.L. 3 (Darrell Johnson). WP—Cincinnati: Eastwick (3), Gullett (5), Carroll (7); Boston: Tiant (1, 4), Wise (6). LP—Cincinnati: Gullett (1), Norman (4), Darcy (6); Boston: Drago (3), Willoughby (3), Cleveland (5), Burton (7).

1976—Cincinnati N.L. 4 (Sparky Anderson); New York A.L. 0 (Billy Martin). WP—Gullett (1), Billingham (2), Zachry (3), Nolan (4). LP—Alexander (1), Hunter (2), Ellis (3), Figueroa (4).

1977—New York A.L. 4 (Billy Martin); Los Angeles N.L. 2 (Tom Lasorda). WP—New York: Lyle (1), Torrez (3, 6), Guidry (4); Los Angeles: Hooton (2), Sutton (5). LP—New York: Hunter (2), Gullett (5); Los Angeles: Rhoden (3), John (3), Rau (4), Hooton (6).

1978—New York A.L. 4 (Bob Lemon), Los Angeles N.L. 2 (Tom Lasorda); WP—New York: Guidry (3), Gossage (4); Beattie (5), Hunter (6); Los Angeles: John (1), Hooton (2). LP—New York: Figueroa (1), Hunter (2); Los Angeles: Sutton (3, 6), Welch (4), Hooton (5).

1979—Pittsburgh N.L. 4 (Chuck Tanner), Baltimore A.L. 3 (Earl

Weaver); WP—Pittsburgh: D. Robinson (2), Blyleven (5), Candelaria (6), Jackson (7); Baltimore: Flanagan (1), McGregor (3), Stoddard (4). LP—Pittsburgh: Kison (1), Candelaria (3), Tekulve (4); Baltimore: Stanhouse (2), Flanagan (5), Palmer (6), McGregor (7).

1980—Philadelphia N.L. 4 (Dallas Green), Kansas City A.L. 2 (Jim Frey); WP—Philadelphia: Walk (1), Carlton (2), McGraw (5), Carlton (6); Kansas City: Quisenberry (3), Leonard (4). LP—Philadelphia: McGraw (3), Christenson (4); Kansas City: Leonard (1), Quisenberry (2), Quisenberry (5), Gale (6).

1981—Los Angeles N.L. 4 (Tom Lasorda), New York A.L. 2 (Bob Lemon); WP—Los Angeles: Valenzuela (3), Howe (4), Reuss (5), Hooton (6); New York: Guidry (1), John (2). LP—Los Angeles: Reuss (1), Hooton (2); New York: Frazier (3), Frazier (4), Guidry (5), Frazier (6).

1982—St. Louis N.L. 4 (Whitey Herzog), Milwaukee A.L. 3 (Harvey Kuenn); WP—St. Louis: Sutter (2), Andujar (3), Stuper (6), Andujar (7). Milwaukee: Caldwell (1), Slaton (4), Caldwell (5). LP—St. Louis: Forsch (1), Bair (4), Forsch (5). Milwaukee: McClure (2), Vuckovich (3), Sutton (6), McClure (7).

1983—Baltimore A.L. 4 (Joe Altobelli), Philadelphia N.L. 1 (Paul Owens); WP—Baltimore: Boddicker (2), Palmer (3), Davis (4), McGregor (5). Philadelphia: Denny (1).

1984—Detroit A.L. 4 (Sparky Anderson), San Diego N.L. 1 (Dick Williams); WP—Det.: Morris (1,4), Wilcox (3), Lopez (5), San Diego: Hawkins (2). LP—Det.: Petry (2), San Diego: Thurmond (3), Lollar (4), Show (4), Hawkins (5).

1985—Kansas City A.L. 4 (Dick Howser), St. Louis N.L. 3 (Whitey Herzog); WP—KC: Saberhagen (3,7) Quisenberry (6), Jackson (5). St. Louis: Tudor (1,4) Dayley (2). LP—KC: Jackson (1), Leibrandt (2), Black (4); St. Louis: Andujar (3), Forsch (5), Worrell (6), Tudor (7).

1986—New York N.L. 4 (Dave Johnson); Boston A.L. (John McNamara) 3 WP—New York—Ojeda (3), Darling (4), Aguilera (6), McDowell (7), Bos: Hurst (1), (5), Crawford (2). LP—New York Darling (1), Gooden (2, 5).

1987—Minnesota A.L. 4 (Tom Kelly); St. Louis N.L. (Whitey Herzog) 3. WP—Minnesota Viola (1, 7), Blyleven (2), Schatzeder (6), St. Louis: Tudor (3), Forsch (4), Cox (5). LP—Minnesota Berenguer (3), Viola (4), Blyleven (5); St. Louis: Magrane (1), Cox (2, 7), Tudor (6).

1988—Los Angeles N.L. 4 (Tommy Lasorda); Oakland A.L. (Tony LaRussa) 1. WP—Los Angeles: Hershiser (2, 5), Pena (1), Belcher (4); Oakland: Honeycutt (3). LP—Los Angeles: Howell (3); Oakland: Davis (2, 5), Eckersley (1), Stewart (4).

1989—Oakland A.L. 4 (Tony LaRussa); San Francisco N.L. 0 (Roger Craig). WP—Oakland: Dave Stewart (1, 3), Mike Moore (2, 4). LP—San Francisco: Scott Garrelts (1, 3), Don Robinson (4), Rick Reuschel (2).

1990—Cincinnati N.L. 4 (Lou Piniella); Oakland A.L. 0 (Tony LaRussa). WP—Cincinnati: Jose Rijo (1, 4), Rob Dibble (2), Tom Browning (3). LP—Oakland: Dave Stewart (1, 4), Dennis Eckersley (2), Mike Moore (3).

1991—Minnesota A.L. 4 (Tom Kelly); Atlanta N.L. 3 (Bobby Cox). WP—Minnesota: Morris (1,7), Tapani (2), Aguilera (6). Atlanta: Clancy (3), Stanton (4), Glavine (5). LP—Minnesota: Aguilera (3), Gurhtie (4), Tapani (5). Atlanta: Leibrandt (1, 6), Glavine (2), Pena (7).

1992—Toronto A.L. 4 (Cito Gaston); Atlanta N.L. 2 (Bobby Cox). WP—Toronto: Ward (2, 3), Key (4, 6). Atlanta: Glavine (1), Smoltz (5). LP—Toronto: Morris (1, 5). Atlanta: Leibrandt (6), Reardon (2), Avery (3), Glavine (4).

1993—Toronto A.L. 4 (Cito Gaston); Philadelphia N.L. 2 (Jim Fregosi). WP—Toronto: Leiter (1), Hentgen (3), Castillo (4), Ward (6). Philadelphia: Mullholland (2), Schilling (5). LP—Toronto: Stewart (2), Guzman (3). Philadelphia: Schilling (1), Jackson (3), Williams (4, 6).

1994—World Series cancelled due to players' strike.

1995—Atlanta N.L. 4 (Bobby Cox); Cleveland A.L. 2 (Mike Hargrove). WP—Atlanta: Maddux (1), Glavine (2,6), Avery (4). Cleveland: Mesa (3), Hershiser (5). LP—Atlanta: Pena (4), Maddux (5). Cleveland: Hershiser (1), Martinez (2), Hill (4), Poole (6).

1996—New York A.L. 4 (Joe Torre); Atlanta N.L. 2 (Bobby Cox). WP—New York: Cone (3), Lloyd (4), Pettitte (5), Key (6).

Atlanta: Smoltz (1), Maddux (2). LP—New York: Pettitte (1), Key (2). Atlanta: Glavine (3), Avery (4), Smoltz (5), Maddux (6).

1997—Florida N.L. 4 (Jim Leyland); Cleveland A.L. 3 (Mike Hargrove). WP—Florida: Hernandez (1, 5), Cook (3), Powell (7). Cleveland: Ogea (2, 6), Wright (4). LP—Florida: Brown (2, 6), Saunders (4). Cleveland: Hershiser (1, 5), Plunk (3), Nagy (7).

1998—New York A.L. 4 (Joe Torre); San Diego N.L. 0 (Bruce Bochy). WP—New York: Wells (1), Hernandez (2), Mendoza (3), Pettitte (4). LP—San Diego: Wall (1), Ashby (2), Hoffman (3), Brown (4).

1999—New York A.L. 4 (Joe Torre); Atlanta N.L. 0 (Bobby Cox). WP—New York: Hernandez (1), Cone (2), Rivera (3), Clemens (4). LP—Atlanta: Maddux (1), Millwood (2), Remlinger (3), Smoltz (4).

2000—New York Yankees A.L. 4 (Joe Torre); New York Mets N.L. 1 (Bobby Valentine). WP—Yankees: Stanton (1, 5), Clemens (2), Nelson (4). Mets: Franco (3). LP—Wendell (1), Hampton (2), Jones (4), Leiter (5). Yankees: Hernandez (3).

2001—Arizona Diamondbacks N.L. 4 (Bob Brenly); New York Yankees A.L. 3 (Joe Torre). WP—Arizona: Schilling (1), Johnson (2, 6, 7). New York: Clemens (3), Rivera (4), Hitchcock (5). LP—New York: Mussina (1), Pettitte (2, 6), Rivera (7). Arizona: Anderson (3), Kim (4), Lopez (5).

2002—Anaheim Angels A.L. 4 (Mike Scioscia); San Francisco Giants N.L. 3 (Dusty Baker). WP—Anaheim: Rodriguez (2), Ortiz (3), Donnelly (6), Lackey (7). San Francisco: Schmidt (1), Worrell (4), Zerbe (5). LP—Anaheim: Washburn (1, 5), Rodriguez (4). San Francisco: Rodriguez (2), Hernandez (3, 7), Worrell (6).

2003—Florida Marlins N.L. 4 (Jack McKeon); New York Yankees A.L. 2 (Joe Torre). WP—Florida: Penny (1, 5), Looper (4), Beckett (6). New York: Pettitte (2), Mussina (3), Wells (4). LP—Florida: Redman (2), Beckett (3). New York: Wells (1), Weaver (4), Contreras (5), Pettitte (6).

2004—Boston Red Sox A.L. 4 (Terry Francona); St. Louis Cardinals N.L. 0 (Tony La Russa). WP—Boston: Foulke (1), Schilling (2), Martinez (3), Lowe (4). LP—St. Louis: Tavarez (1), Morris (2), Suppan (3), Marquis (4).

WORLD SERIES CLUB STANDINGS
(through 2004)

	Series	Won	Lost	Pct.		Series	Won	Lost	Pct.
Toronto (A)	2	2	0	1.000	Baltimore (A)	6	3	3	.500
Florida (N)	2	2	0	1.000	Kansas City (A)	2	1	1	.500
Arizona (N)	1	1	0	1.000	Detroit (A)	9	4	5	.444
Anaheim (A)	1	1	0	1.000	Cleveland (A)	5	2	3	.400
Pittsburgh (N)	7	5	2	.714	New York (N-Giants)	14	5	9	.357
New York (A)	39	26	13	.667	Washington (A)	3	1	2	.333
Oakland (A)	6	4	2	.667	Atlanta (N)	5	1	4	.200
Minnesota (A)	3	2	1	.667	Philadelphia (N)	5	1	4	.200
Philadelphia (A)	8	5	3	.625	Chicago (N)	10	2	8	.200
Boston (A)	10	6	4	.600	Brooklyn (N)	9	1	8	.111
St. Louis (N)	16	9	7	.563	St. Louis (A)	1	0	1	.000
Los Angeles (N)	9	5	4	.556	San Francisco (N)	3	0	3	.000
Cincinnati (N)	9	5	4	.556	Milwaukee (A)	1	0	1	.000
New York (N-Mets)	4	2	2	.500	San Diego (N)	2	0	2	.000
Milwaukee (N)	2	1	1	.500	**Recapitulation**				**Won**
Boston (N)	2	1	1	.500	American League				58
Chicago (A)	4	2	2	.500	National League				40

WORLD SERIES SINGLE GAME AND SINGLE SERIES RECORDS
(through 2004)

Most hits game—5, Paul Molitor, Milwaukee A.L., first game vs. St. Louis N.L., 1982.

Most 4-hit games, series—2, Robin Yount, Milwaukee A.L., first and fifth games vs. St. Louis N.L., 1982.

Most hits inning—2, held by 17 players.

Most hits series—13 (7 games) Bobby Richardson, New York A.L., 1964; Lou Brock, St. Louis N.L., 1968; Marty Barrett, Boston A.L., 1986.

Most home runs, series—5 (6 games) Reggie Jackson, New York A.L., 1977; 4 (4 games) Lou Gehrig, New York A.L., 1928; 4 (6 games) Willie Aikens, Kansas City A.L., 1980; 4 (7 games) Babe Ruth, New York A.L., 1926; Duke Snider, Brooklyn N.L., 1952, 1955; Hank Bauer, New York A.L., 1958; Gene Tenace, Oakland A.L., 1972; 4 Barry Bonds, San Francisco N.L., 2002.

Most home runs, game—3, Babe Ruth, New York A.L., 1926 and 1928; Reggie Jackson, New York A.L., 1977.

Most strikeouts, series—12 (6 games) Willie Wilson, Kansas City A.L., 1980; 11 (7 games) Ed Mathews, Milwaukee N.L., 1958; Wayne Garrett, New York N.L., 1973; 9 (5 games) Carmelo Martinez, San Diego N.L., 1984; 7 (4 games) Bob Muesel, New York A.L., 1927; Ken Caminiti, San Diego N.L., 1998.

Most stolen bases, game—3, Honus Wagner, Pittsburgh N.L., 1909; Willie Davis, Los Angeles N.L., 1965; Lou Brock, St. Louis N.L., 1967 and 1968.

Most strikeouts by pitcher, game—17, Bob Gibson, St. Louis N.L. 1968.

Most strikeouts by pitcher in succession—6, Horace Eller, Cincinnati N.L., 1919; Moe Drabowsky, Baltimore A.L., 1966.

Most strikeouts by pitcher, series—35 (7 games) Bob Gibson, St. Louis N.L., 1968; 23 (4 games) Sandy Koufax, Los Angeles, 1963; 20 (6 games) Chief Bender, Philadelphia A.L., 1911; 18 (5 games) Christy Mathewson, New York N.L., 1905.

Most bases on balls, series—13 (7 games) Barry Bonds, San Francisco N.L., 2002; 11 (7 games) Babe Ruth, New York A.L., 1926; Gene Tenace, Oakland A.L., 1973; 9 (6 games) Willie Randolph, New York A.L., 1981; 7 (5 games) James Sheckard, Chicago N.L., 1910; Mickey Cochrane, Philadelphia A.L., 1929; Joe Gordon, New York A.L., 1941; 7 (4 games) Hank Thompson, New York N.L., 1954.

Most consecutive scoreless innings one series—27, Christy Mathewson, New York N.L., 1905.

LIFETIME WORLD SERIES RECORDS
(through 2004)

Most hits—71, Yogi Berra, New York A.L., 1947, 1949–53, 1955–58, 1960–63.

Most runs—42, Mickey Mantle, New York A.L., 1951–53, 1955–58, 1960–64.

Most runs batted in—40, Mickey Mantle, New York A.L., 1951–53, 1955–58, 1960–64.

Most home runs—18, Mickey Mantle, New York A.L., 1951–53, 1955–58, 1960–64.

Most bases on balls—43, Mickey Mantle, New York A.L., 1951–53, 1955–58, 1960–64.

Most strikeouts—54, Mickey Mantle, New York A.L., 1951–53, 1955–58, 1960–64.

Most stolen bases—14, Eddie Collins, Philadelphia A.L. 1910–11, 13–14; Chicago A.L., 1917, 1919. Lou Brock, St. Louis N.L., 1964, 67–68.

Most victories, pitcher—10, Whitey Ford, New York A.L., 1950, 1953, 1955–58, 1960–64.

Most times member of winning team—10, Yogi Berra, New York A.L., 1947, 1949–53, 1956, 1958, 1961–62.

Most victories, no defeats—6, Vernon Gomez, New York A.L., 1932, 1936(2), 1937(2), 1938.

Most shutouts—4, Christy Mathewson, New York N.L., 1905 (3), 1913.

Most innings pitched—146, Whitey Ford, New York A.L., 1950, 1953, 1955–58, 1960–1964

Most consecutive scoreless innings—33⅔, Whitey Ford, New York A.L., 1960 (18), 1961 (14), 1962 (1⅔).

Most strikeouts by pitcher—94, Whitey Ford, New York A.L., 1950, 1953, 1955–58, 1960–64.

BASEBALL'S PERFECTLY PITCHED GAMES[1]
(no opposing runner reached base)

Lee Richmond—Worcester vs. Cleveland (N.L.) June 12, 1880 (1–0)

John M. Ward—Providence vs. Buffalo (N.L.) June 17, 1880 (5–0)

Cy Young—Boston vs. Philadelphia (A.L.) May 5, 1904 (3–0)

Addie Joss—Cleveland vs. Chicago (A.L.) Oct. 2, 1908 (1–0)

Ernest Shore[2]—Boston vs. Washington (A.L.) June 23, 1917 (4–0)

Charles Robertson—Chicago vs. Detroit (A.L.) April 30, 1922 (2–0)

Don Larsen[3]—New York (A.L.) vs. Brooklyn (N.L.) Oct. 8, 1956 (2–0)

Jim Bunning—Philadelphia vs. New York (N.L.) June 21, 1964 (6–0)

Sandy Koufax—Los Angeles vs. Chicago (N.L.) Sept. 9, 1965 (1–0)

Jim Hunter—Oakland vs. Minnesota (A.L.) May 8, 1968 (4–0)

Len Barker—Cleveland vs. Toronto (A.L.) May 15, 1981 (3–0)

Mike Witt—California vs. Texas (A.L.) Sept. 30, 1984 (1–0)

Tom Browning—Cincinnati vs. Los Angeles (N.L.) Sept. 16, 1988 (1–0)

Dennis Martinez—Montreal vs. Los Angeles (N.L.) July 28, 1991 (2–0)

Kenny Rogers—Texas vs. California (A.L.) July 28, 1994 (4–0)

David Wells—New York vs. Minnesota (A.L.) May 17, 1998 (4–0)

David Cone[4]—New York (A.L.) vs. Montreal (N.L.) July 18, 1999 (6–0)

Randy Johnson—Arizona vs. Atlanta (N.L.) May 18, 2004 (2–0)

1. Harvey Haddix, of Pittsburgh, pitched 12 perfect innings against Milwaukee (N.L.), May 26, 1959, but lost game in 13th on error and hit. Montreal's Pedro Martinez pitched nine perfect innings against the San Diego Padres on June 3, 1995 before surrendering a leadoff double to Bip Roberts in the 10th. Mel Rojas finished the game, which Montreal won, 1–0. 2. Shore, relief pitcher for Babe Ruth who walked first batter before being ejected by umpire, retired 26 batters who faced him and base-runner was out stealing. 3. World Series. 4. Interleague game.

LIFETIME BATTING, PITCHING, AND BASE-RUNNING RECORDS
(Records through Sept. 6, 2005. Boldface indicates player active in 2005 season.)

Hits (3,000+)

Pete Rose	4,256
Ty Cobb	4,189
Hank Aaron	3,771
Stan Musial	3,630
Tris Speaker	3,514
Carl Yastrzemski	3,419
Cap Anson	3,418
Honus Wagner	3,415
Paul Molitor	3,319
Eddie Collins	3,315
Willie Mays	3,283
Eddie Murray	3,255
Nap Lajoie	3,242
Cal Ripken, Jr.	3,184
George Brett	3,154
Paul Waner	3,152
Robin Yount	3,142
Tony Gwynn	3,141
Dave Winfield	3,110
Rickey Henderson	3,055
Rod Carew	3,053
Lou Brock	3,023
Rafael Palmeiro	**3,020**
Wade Boggs	3,010
Al Kaline	3,007
Roberto Clemente	3,000

Earned Run Average (Minimum 1,500 innings pitched)

Ed Walsh	1.82
Addie Joss	1.89
Al Spalding	2.04
Mordecai Brown	2.06
John Ward	2.10
Christy Mathewson	2.13
Tommy Bond	2.14
Rube Waddell	2.16
Walter Johnson	2.17
Ed Reulbach	2.28
Will White	2.28
Ed Plank	2.35
Larry Corcoran	2.36
Ed Cicotte	2.38
Candy Cummings	2.39
Doc White	2.39
Nap Rucker	2.42
George Bradley	2.43
Jim McCormick	2.43

Runs Scored

Rickey Henderson	2,295
Ty Cobb	2,246
Hank Aaron	2,174
Babe Ruth	2,174
Pete Rose	2,165
Barry Bonds	**2,070**
Willie Mays	2,062
Cap Anson	1,996
Stan Musial	1,949
Lou Gehrig	1,888
Tris Speaker	1,882
Mel Ott	1,859
Frank Robinson	1,829
Eddie Collins	1,821
Carl Yastrzemski	1,816
Ted Williams	1,798
Paul Molitor	1,782
Charlie Gehringer	1,774
Jimmie Foxx	1,751
Honus Wagner	1,736
Jim O'Rourke	1,729
Jesse Burkett	1,720
Willie Keeler	1,719
Billy Hamilton	1,691
Craig Biggio	**1,682**
Bid McPhee	1,678
Mickey Mantle	1,677
Dave Winfield	1,669
Rafael Palmeiro	**1,663**
Joe Morgan	1,650

Strikeouts, Pitching

Nolan Ryan	5,714
Roger Clemens	**4,486**
Randy Johnson	**4,341**
Steve Carlton	4,136
Bert Blyleven	3,701
Tom Seaver	3,640
Don Sutton	3,574
Gaylord Perry	3,534
Walter Johnson	3,508
Phil Niekro	3,342
Ferguson Jenkins	3,192
Bob Gibson	3,117
Greg Maddux	**3,028**
Jim Bunning	2,855
Pedro Martinez	**2,841**
Mickey Lolich	2,832
Curt Schilling	**2,805**

Cy Young	2,803	Carl Yastrzemski	452	Nolan Ryan	61
Frank Tanana	2,773	**Jeff Bagwell**	**449**	Tom Seaver	61
David Cone	2,668	**Frank Thomas**	**448**	Bert Blyleven	60
Chuck Finley	2,610	**Gary Sheffield**	**443**	Don Sutton	58
Warren Spahn	2,583	Dave Kingman	442	Pud Galvin	57
Bob Feller	2,581	Andre Dawson	438	Ed Walsh	57
Tim Keefe	2,564	**Juan Gonzalez**	**434**	Bob Gibson	56
Jerry Koosman	2,556	Cal Ripken, Jr.	431	Mordecai Brown	55

Home Runs

		Jim Thome	**430**	Steve Carlton	55
Hank Aaron	755	Billy Williams	426	Jim Palmer	53
Babe Ruth	714	**Manny Ramirez**	**423**	Gaylord Perry	53
Barry Bonds	**703**	**Alex Rodriquez**	**421**		

Strikeouts, Batting

Walks

Willie Mays	660	Darrell Evans	414			**Barry Bonds**	**2,302**
Sammy Sosa	**588**	Duke Snider	407	Reggie Jackson	2,597	Rickey Henderson	2,190
Frank Robinson	586	Al Kaline	399	**Sammy Sosa**	**2,194**	Babe Ruth	2,062
Mark McGwire	583	Andres Galarraga	399	Andres Galarraga	2,003	Ted Williams	2,019
Harmon Killebrew	573	Dale Murphy	398	Jose Canseco	1,942	Joe Morgan	1,865
Rafael Palmeiro	**569**	Joe Carter	396	Willie Stargell	1,936	Carl Yastrzemski	1,845
Reggie Jackson	563	**Mike Piazza**	**392**	Mike Schmidt	1,883	Mickey Mantle	1,733
Mike Schmidt	548	Graig Nettles	390	**Fred McGriff**	**1,882**	Mel Ott	1,708
Mickey Mantle	536	Johnny Bench	389	Tony Perez	1,867	Eddie Yost	1,614
Ken Griffey, Jr.	**536**	Dwight Evans	385	Dave Kingman	1,816	Darrell Evans	1,605
Jimmie Foxx	534	Harold Baines	384	**Jim Thome**	**1,762**	Stan Musial	1,599
Willie McCovey	521	Frank Howard	382	Bobby Bonds	1,757	Pete Rose	1,566
Ted Williams	521	Jim Rice	382	Dale Murphy	1,748	Harmon Killebrew	1,559
Ernie Banks	512	Albert Belle	381	Lou Brock	1,730	Lou Gehrig	1,508
Eddie Mathews	512	Orlando Cepeda	379	Mickey Mantle	1,710	Mike Schmidt	1,507
Mel Ott	511	Tony Perez	379	Harmon Killebrew	1,699	Eddie Collins	1,499
Eddie Murray	504			Chili Davis	1,698	**Frank Thomas**	**1,466**

Shutouts

Lou Gehrig	493			Dwight Evans	1,697	Willie Mays	1,464
Fred McGriff	**493**	Walter Johnson	110	Rickey Henderson	1,694	Jimmie Foxx	1,452
Stan Musial	475	Grover Alexander	90	Dave Winfield	1,686	Eddie Mathews	1,444
Willie Stargell	475	Christy Mathewson	79	Gary Gaetti	1,602	Frank Robinson	1,420
Dave Winfield	465	Cy Young	76	Mark McGwire	1,596	Wade Boggs	1,412
Jose Canseco	462	Ed Plank	69	Lee May	1,570	Hank Aaron	1,402
		Warren Spahn	63	Dick Allen	1,556		

AMERICAN LEAGUE HOME RUN CHAMPIONS

Year	Player, team	No.	Year	Player, team	No.	Year	Player, team	No.
1901	Nap Lajoie, Philadelphia	13	1928	Babe Ruth, New York	54	1955	Mickey Mantle, New York	37
1902	Ralph Seybold, Philadelphia	16	1929	Babe Ruth, New York	46	1956	Mickey Mantle, New York	52
1903	Buck Freeman, Boston	13	1930	Babe Ruth, New York	49	1957	Roy Sievers, Washington	42
1904	Harry Davis, Philadelphia	10	1931	Lou Gehrig, New York; Babe	46	1958	Mickey Mantle, New York	42
1905	Harry Davis, Philadelphia	8		Ruth, New York		1959	Rocky Colavito, Cleveland;	42
1906	Harry Davis, Philadelphia	12	1932	Jimmie Foxx, Philadelphia	58		Harmon Killebrew,	
1907	Harry Davis, Philadelphia	8	1933	Jimmie Foxx, Philadelphia	48		Washington	
1908	Sam Crawford, Detroit	7	1934	Lou Gehrig, New York	49	1960	Mickey Mantle, New York	40
1909	Ty Cobb, Detroit	9	1935	Jimmie Foxx, Philadelphia;	36	1961	Roger Maris, New York	61
1910	J. Garland Stahl, Boston	10		Hank Greenberg, Detroit		1962	Harmon Killebrew,	48
1911	Franklin Baker, Philadelphia	9	1936	Lou Gehrig, New York	49		Minnesota	
1912	Franklin Baker, Philadelphia	10	1937	Joe DiMaggio, New York	46	1963	Harmon Killebrew,	45
1913	Franklin Baker, Philadelphia	12	1938	Hank Greenberg, Detroit	58		Minnesota	
1914	Franklin Baker, Philadelphia;	8	1939	Jimmie Foxx, Boston	35	1964	Harmon Killebrew,	49
	Sam Crawford, Detroit		1940	Hank Greenberg, Detroit	41		Minnesota	
1915	Robert Roth,	7	1941	Ted Williams, Boston	37	1965	Tony Conigliaro, Boston	32
	Chicago-Cleveland		1942	Ted Williams, Boston	36	1966	Frank Robinson, Baltimore	49
1916	Wally Pipp, New York	12	1943	Rudy York, Detroit	34	1967	Carl Yastrzemski, Boston;	44
1917	Wally Pipp, New York	9	1944	Nick Etten, New York	22		Harmon Killebrew,	
1918	Babe Ruth, Boston;	11	1945	Vern Stephens, St. Louis	24		Minnesota	
	Clarence Walker,		1946	Hank Greenberg, Detroit	44	1968	Frank Howard, Washington	44
	Philadelphia		1947	Ted Williams, Boston	32	1969	Harmon Killebrew,	49
1919	Babe Ruth, Boston	29	1948	Joe DiMaggio, New York	39		Minnesota	
1920	Babe Ruth, New York	54	1949	Ted Williams, Boston	43	1970	Frank Howard, Washington	44
1921	Babe Ruth, New York	59	1950	Al Rosen, Cleveland	37	1971	Bill Melton, Chicago	33
1922	Ken Williams, St. Louis	39	1951	Gus Zernial,	33	1972	Dick Allen, Chicago	37
1923	Babe Ruth, New York	41		Chicago-Philadelphia		1973	Reggie Jackson, Oakland	32
1924	Babe Ruth, New York	46	1952	Larry Doby, Cleveland	32	1974	Dick Allen, Chicago	32
1925	Bob Meusel, New York	33	1953	Al Rosen, Cleveland	43	1975	Reggie Jackson, Oakland;	36
1926	Babe Ruth, New York	47	1954	Larry Doby, Cleveland	32		George Scott, Milwaukee	
1927	Babe Ruth, New York	60				1976	Graig Nettles, New York	32

Year	Player, team	No.	Year	Player, team	No.	Year	Player, team	No.
1977	Jim Rice, Boston	39	1983	Jim Rice, Boston	39	1994[2]	Ken Griffey, Jr., Seattle	40
1978	Jim Rice, Boston	46	1984	Tony Armas, Boston	43	1995	Albert Belle, Cleveland	50
1979	Gorman Thomas, Milwaukee	45	1985	Darrell Evans, Detroit	40	1996	Mark McGwire, Oakland	52
1980	Reggie Jackson, New York;	41	1986	Jesse Barfield, Toronto	40	1997	Ken Griffey, Jr., Seattle	56
	Ben Oglivie, Milwaukee		1987	Mark McGwire, Oakland	49	1998	Ken Griffey, Jr., Seattle	56
1981[1]	Tony Armas, Oakland;	22	1988	Jose Canseco, Oakland	42	1999	Ken Griffey, Jr., Seattle	48
	Dwight Evans, Boston;		1989	Fred McGriff, Toronto	36	2000	Troy Glaus, Anaheim	47
	Bobby Grich, California;		1990	Cecil Fielder, Detroit	51	2001	Alex Rodriguez, Texas	52
	Eddie Murray, Baltimore (tie)		1991	Jose Canseco, Oakland;	44	2002	Alex Rodriguez, Texas	57
1982	Gorman Thomas,	39		Cecil Fielder, Detroit (tie)		2003	Alex Rodriguez, Texas	47
	Milwaukee; Reggie Jackson,		1992	Juan Gonzalez, Texas	43	2004	Manny Ramirez, Boston	43
	California		1993	Juan Gonzalez, Texas	46			

1. Split season because of players' strike. 2. Season ended on Aug. 12 because of players' strike.

AMERICAN LEAGUE BATTING CHAMPIONS

Year	Player, team	Avg.	Year	Player, team	Avg.	Year	Player, team	Avg.
1901	Nap Lajoie, Philadelphia	.422	1936	Luke Appling, Chicago	.388	1971	Tony Oliva, Minnesota	.337
1902	Ed Delahanty, Washington	.376	1937	Charley Gehringer, Detroit	.371	1972	Rod Carew, Minnesota	.318
1903	Nap Lajoie, Cleveland	.355	1938	Jimmie Foxx, Boston	.349	1973	Rod Carew, Minnesota	.350
1904	Nap Lajoie, Cleveland	.381	1939	Joe DiMaggio, New York	.381	1974	Rod Carew, Minnesota	.364
1905	Elmer Flick, Cleveland	.306	1940	Joe DiMaggio, New York	.352	1975	Rod Carew, Minnesota	.359
1906	George Stone, St. Louis	.358	1941	Ted Williams, Boston	.406	1976	George Brett, Kansas City	.333
1907	Ty Cobb, Detroit	.350	1942	Ted Williams, Boston	.356	1977	Rod Carew, Minnesota	.388
1908	Ty Cobb, Detroit	.324	1943	Luke Appling, Chicago	.328	1978	Rod Carew, Minnesota	.333
1909	Ty Cobb, Detroit	.377	1944	Lou Boudreau, Cleveland	.327	1979	Fred Lynn, Boston	.333
1910	Ty Cobb, Detroit	.385	1945	George Sternweiss, New	.309	1980	George Brett, Kansas City	.390
1911	Ty Cobb, Detroit	.420		York		1981[1]	Carney Lansford, Boston	.336
1912	Ty Cobb, Detroit	.410	1946	Mickey Vernon, Washington	.353	1982	Willie Wilson, Kansas City	.332
1913	Ty Cobb, Detroit	.390	1947	Ted Williams, Boston	.343	1983	Wade Boggs, Boston	.361
1914	Ty Cobb, Detroit	.368	1948	Ted Williams, Boston	.369	1984	Don Mattingly, New York	.343
1915	Ty Cobb, Detroit	.369	1949	George Kell, Detroit	.343	1985	Wade Boggs, Boston	.368
1916	Tris Speaker, Cleveland	.386	1950	Billy Goodman, Boston	.354	1986	Wade Boggs, Boston	.357
1917	Ty Cobb, Detroit	.383	1951	Ferris Fain, Philadelphia	.344	1987	Wade Boggs, Boston	.363
1918	Ty Cobb, Detroit	.382	1952	Ferris Fain, Philadelphia	.327	1988	Wade Boggs, Boston	.366
1919	Ty Cobb, Detroit	.384	1953	Mickey Vernon, Washington	.337	1989	Kirby Puckett, Minnesota	.339
1920	George Sisler, St. Louis	.407	1954	Bobby Avila, Cleveland	.341	1990	George Brett, Kansas City	.328
1921	Harry Heilmann, Detroit	.394	1955	Al Kaline, Detroit	.340	1991	Julio Franco, Texas	.341
1922	George Sisler, St. Louis	.420	1956	Mickey Mantle, New York	.353	1992	Edgar Martinez, Seattle	.343
1923	Harry Heilmann, Detroit	.403	1957	Ted Williams, Boston	.388	1993	John Olerud, Toronto	.363
1924	Babe Ruth, New York	.378	1958	Ted Williams, Boston	.328	1994[2]	Paul O'Neill, New York	.359
1925	Harry Heilmann, Detroit	.393	1959	Harvey Kuenn, Detroit	.353	1995	Edgar Martinez, Seattle	.356
1926	Heinie Manush, Detroit	.378	1960	Pete Runnels, Boston	.320	1996	Alex Rodriguez, Seattle	.358
1927	Harry Heilmann, Detroit	.398	1961	Norman Cash, Detroit	.361	1997	Frank Thomas, Chicago	.347
1928	Goose Goslin, Washington	.379	1962	Pete Runnels, Boston	.326	1998	Bernie Williams, New York	.339
1929	Lew Fonseca, Cleveland	.369	1963	Carl Yastrzemski, Boston	.321	1999	Nomar Garciaparra, Boston	.357
1930	Al Simmons, Philadelphia	.381	1964	Tony Oliva, Minnesota	.323	2000	Nomar Garciaparra, Boston	.372
1931	Al Simmons, Philadelphia	.390	1965	Tony Oliva, Minnesota	.321	2001	Ichiro Suzuki, Seattle	.350
1932	Dale Alexander,	.367	1966	Frank Robinson, Baltimore	.316	2002	Manny Ramirez, Boston	.349
	Detroit-Boston		1967	Carl Yastrzemski, Boston	.326	2003	Bill Mueller, Boston	.326
1933	Jimmie Foxx, Philadelphia	.356	1968	Carl Yastrzemski, Boston	.301	2004	Ichiro Suzuki, Seattle	.372
1934	Lou Gehrig, New York	.363	1969	Rod Carew, Minnesota	.332			
1935	Buddy Myer, Washington	.349	1970	Alex Johnson, California	.329			

1. Split season because of players' strike. 2. Season ended on Aug. 12 because of players' strike.

NATIONAL LEAGUE HOME RUN CHAMPIONS

Year	Player, team	No.	Year	Player, team	No.	Year	Player, team	No.
1876	George Hall, Philadelphia Athletics	5	1887	Roger Connor, New York; Wm. O'Brien, Washington	17	1895	Bill Joyce, Washington	17
1877	George Shaffer, Louisville	3	1888	Roger Connor, New York	14	1896	Ed Delahanty, Philadelphia; Sam Thompson, Philadelphia	13
1878	Paul Hines, Providence	4	1889	Sam Thompson, Philadelphia	20			
1879	Charles Jones, Boston	9				1897	Nap Lajoie, Philadelphia	10
1880	James O'Rourke, Boston; Harry Stovey, Worcester	6	1890	Tom Burns, Brooklyn; Mike Tiernan, New York	13	1898	James Colins, Boston	14
1881	Dan Brouthers, Buffalo	8	1891	Harry Stovey, Boston; Mike Tiernan, New York	16	1899	John Freeman, Washington	25
1882	George Wood, Detroit	7				1900	Herman Long, Boston	12
1883	William Ewing, New York	10	1892	Jim Holliday, Cincinnati	13	1901	Sam Crawford, Cincinnati	16
1884	Ed Williamson, Chicago	27	1893	Ed Delahanty, Philadelphia	19	1902	Tom Leach, Pittsburgh	6
1885	Abner Dalrymple, Chicago	11	1894	Hugh Duffy, Boston; Robert Lowe, Boston	18	1903	James Sheckard, Brooklyn	9
1886	Arthur Richardson, Detroit	11				1904	Harry Lumley, Brooklyn	9
						1905	Fred Odwell, Cincinnati	9

Year	Player, team	No.	Year	Player, team	No.	Year	Player, team	No.
1906	Tim Jordan, Brooklyn	12	1938	Mel Ott, New York	36	1970	Johnny Bench, Cincinnati	45
1907	David Brain, Boston	10	1939	John Mize, St. Louis	28	1971	Willie Stargell, Pittsburgh	48
1908	Tim Jordan, Brooklyn	12	1940	John Mize, St. Louis	43	1972	Johnny Bench, Cincinnati	40
1909	John Murray, New York	7	1941	Dolph Camilli, Brooklyn	34	1973	Willie Stargell, Pittsburgh	44
1910	Fred Beck, Boston; Frank Schulte, Chicago	10	1942	Mel Ott, New York	30	1974	Mike Schmidt, Philadelphia	36
			1943	Bill Nicholson, Chicago	29	1975	Mike Schmidt, Philadelphia	38
1911	Frank Schulte, Chicago	21	1944	Bill Nicholson, Chicago	33	1976	Mike Schmidt, Philadelphia	38
1912	Henry Zimmerman, Chicago	14	1945	Tommy Holmes, Boston	28	1977	George Foster, Cincinnati	52
1913	Cliff Cravath, Philadelphia	19	1946	Ralph Kiner, Pittsburgh	23	1978	George Foster, Cincinnati	40
1914	Cliff Cravath, Philadelphia	19	1947	Ralph Kiner, Pittsburgh; John Mize, New York	51	1979	Dave Kingman, Chicago	48
1915	Cliff Cravath, Philadelphia	24				1980	Mike Schmidt, Philadelphia	48
1916	Davis Robertson, New York; Fred Williams, Chicago	12	1948	Ralph Kiner, Pittsburgh; John Mize, New York	40	1981[1]	Mike Schmidt, Philadelphia	31
						1982	Dave Kingman, New York	37
1917	Davis Robertson, New York; Cliff Cravath, Philadelphia	12	1949	Ralph Kiner, Pittsburgh	54	1983	Mike Schmidt, Philadelphia	40
			1950	Ralph Kiner, Pittsburgh	47	1984	Mike Schmidt, Philadelphia; Dale Murphy, Atlanta	36
1918	Cliff Cravath, Philadelphia	8	1951	Ralph Kiner, Pittsburgh	42			
1919	Cliff Cravath, Philadelphia	12	1952	Ralph Kiner, Pittsburgh; Hank Sauer, Chicago	37	1985	Dale Murphy, Atlanta	37
1920	Cy Williams, Philadelphia	15				1986	Mike Schmidt, Philadelphia	37
1921	George Kelly, New York	23	1953	Ed Mathews, Milwaukee	47	1987	Andre Dawson, Chicago	49
1922	Rogers Hornsby, St. Louis	42	1954	Ted Kluszewski, Cincinnati	49	1988	Darryl Strawberry, New York	39
1923	Cy Williams, Philadelphia	41	1955	Willie Mays, New York	51	1989	Kevin Mitchell, San Francisco	47
1924	Jacques Fournier, Brooklyn	27	1956	Duke Snider, Brooklyn	43			
1925	Rogers Hornsby, St. Louis	39	1957	Hank Aaron, Milwaukee	44	1990	Ryne Sandberg, Chicago	40
1926	Hack Wilson, Chicago	21	1958	Ernie Banks, Chicago	47	1991	Howard Johnson, New York	38
1927	Hack Wilson, Chicago; Cy Williams, Philadelphia	30	1959	Ed Mathews, Milwaukee	46	1992	Fred McGriff, San Diego	35
			1960	Ernie Banks, Chicago	41	1993	Barry Bonds, San Francisco	46
1928	Hack Wilson, Chicago; Jim Bottomley, St. Louis	31	1961	Orlando Cepeda, San Francisco	46	1994[2]	Matt Williams, San Francisco	43
						1995	Dante Bichette, Colorado	40
1929	Chuck Klein, Philadelphia	43	1962	Willie Mays, San Francisco	49	1996	Andres Galarraga, Colorado	40
1930	Hack Wilson, Chicago	56	1963	Hank Aaron, Milwaukee; Willie McCovey, San Francisco	44	1997	Larry Walker, Colorado	49
1931	Chuck Klein, Philadelphia	31				1998	Mark McGwire, St. Louis	70
1932	Chuck Klein, Philadelphia; Mel Ott, New York	38	1964	Willie Mays, San Francisco	47	1999	Mark McGwire, St. Louis	65
1933	Chuck Klein, Philadelphia	28	1965	Willie Mays, San Francisco	52	2000	Sammy Sosa, Chicago	50
1934	Mel Ott, New York; Rip Collins, St. Louis	35	1966	Hank Aaron, Atlanta	44	2001	Barry Bonds, San Francisco	73
			1967	Hank Aaron, Atlanta	39	2002	Sammy Sosa, Chicago	49
1935	Wally Berger, Boston	34	1968	Willie McCovey, San Francisco	36	2003	Jim Thome, Philadelphia	47
1936	Mel Ott, New York	33	1969	Willie McCovey, San Francisco	45	2004	Adrian Beltre, Los Angeles	48
1937	Mel Ott, New York; Joe Medwick, St. Louis	31						

1. Split season because of players' strike. 2. Season ended on Aug. 12 because of players' strike.

NATIONAL LEAGUE BATTING CHAMPIONS

Year	Player, team	Avg.	Year	Player, team	Avg.	Year	Player, team	Avg.
1876	Roscoe Barnes, Chicago	.404	1901	Jesse Burkett, St. Louis	.382	1926	Gene Hargrave, Cincinnati	.353
1877	Jim White, Boston	.385	1902	Clarence Beaumont, Pittsburgh	.357	1927	Paul Waner; Pittsburgh	.380
1878	Abner Dalrymple, Milwaukee	.356				1928	Rogers Hornsby, Boston	.387
1879	Cap Anson, Chicago	.407	1903	Honus Wagner, Pittsburgh	.355	1929	Lefty O'Doul, Philadelphia	.398
1880	George Gore, Chicago	.365	1904	Honus Wagner, Pittsburgh	.349	1930	Bill Terry, New York	.401
1881	Cap Anson, Chicago	.399	1905	Cy Seymour, Cincinnati	.377	1931	Chick Hafey, St. Louis	.349
1882	Dan Brouthers, Buffalo	.367	1906	Honus Wagner, Pittsburgh	.339	1932	Lefty O'Doul, Brooklyn	.368
1883	Dan Brouthers, Buffalo	.371	1907	Honus Wagner, Pittsburgh	.350	1933	Chuck Klein, Philadelphia	.368
1884	James O'Rourke, Buffalo	.350	1908	Honus Wagner, Pittsburgh	.354	1934	Paul Waner, Pittsburgh	.362
1885	Roger Connor, New York	.371	1909	Honus Wagner, Pittsburgh	.339	1935	Arky Vaughan, Pittsburgh	.385
1886	King Kelly, Chicago	.388	1910	Sherwood Magee, Philadelphia	.331	1936	Paul Waner, Pittsburgh	.373
1887	Cap Anson, Chicago	.421				1937	Joe Medwick, St. Louis	.374
1888	Cap Anson, Chicago	.343	1911	Honus Wagner, Pittsburgh	.334	1938	Ernie Lombardi, Cincinnati	.342
1889	Dan Brouthers, Boston	.373	1912	Henry Zimmerman, Chicago	.372	1939	John Mize, St. Louis	.349
1890	John Glasscock, New York	.336	1913	Jake Daubert, Brooklyn	.350	1940	Debs Garms, Pittsburgh	.355
1891	William Hamilton, Philadelphia	.338	1914	Jake Daubert, Brooklyn	.329	1941	Pete Reiser, Brooklyn	.343
			1915	Larry Doyle, New York	.320	1942	Ernie Lombardi, Boston	.330
1892	Dan Brouthers, Brooklyn; Clarence Childs, Cleveland	.335	1916	Hal Chase, Cincinnati	.339	1943	Stan Musial, St. Louis	.357
			1917	Edd Roush, Cincinnati	.341	1944	Dixie Walker, Brooklyn	.357
1893	Hugh Duffy, Boston	.378	1918	Zack Wheat, Brooklyn	.335	1945	Phil Cavarretta, Chicago	.355
1894	Hugh Duffy, Boston	.438	1919	Edd Roush, Cincinnati	.321	1946	Stan Musial, St. Louis	.365
1895	Jesse Burkett, Cleveland	.423	1920	Rogers Hornsby, St. Louis	.370	1947	Harry Walker, St. Louis-Philadelphia	.363
1896	Jesse Burkett, Cleveland	.410	1921	Rogers Hornsby, St. Louis	.397			
1897	Willie Keeler, Baltimore	.432	1922	Rogers Hornsby, St. Louis	.401	1948	Stan Musial, St. Louis	.376
1898	Willie Keeler, Baltimore	.379	1923	Rogers Hornsby, St. Louis	.384	1949	Jackie Robinson, Brooklyn	.342
1899	Ed Delahanty, Philadelphia	.408	1924	Rogers Hornsby, St. Louis	.424	1950	Stan Musial, St. Louis	.346
1900	Honus Wagner, Pittsburgh	.381	1925	Rogers Hornsby, St. Louis	.403	1951	Stan Musial, St. Louis	.355

Year	Player, team	Avg.	Year	Player, team	Avg.	Year	Player, team	Avg.
1952	Stan Musial, St. Louis	.336	1970	Rico Carty, Atlanta	.366	1988	Tony Gwynn, San Diego	.313
1953	Carl Furillo, Brooklyn	.344	1971	Joe Torre, St. Louis	.363	1989	Tony Gwynn, San Diego	.336
1954	Willie Mays, New York	.345	1972	Billy Williams, Chicago	.333	1990	Willie McGee, St. Louis	.335
1955	Richie Ashburn, Philadelphia	.338	1973	Pete Rose, Cincinnati	.338	1991	Terry Pendleton, Atlanta	.319
1956	Hank Aaron, Milwaukee	.328	1974	Ralph Garr, Atlanta	.353	1992	Gary Sheffield, San Diego	.330
1957	Stan Musial, St. Louis	.351	1975	Bill Madlock, Chicago	.354	1993	Andres Galarraga, Colorado	.370
1958	Richie Ashburn, Philadelphia	.350	1976	Bill Madlock, Chicago	.339	1994²	Tony Gwynn, San Diego	.394
1959	Hank Aaron, Milwaukee	.355	1977	Dave Parker, Pittsburgh	.338	1995	Tony Gwynn, San Diego	.368
1960	Dick Groat, Pittsburgh	.325	1978	Dave Parker, Pittsburgh	.334	1996	Tony Gwynn, San Diego	.353
1961	Roberto Clemente, Pittsburgh	.351	1979	Keith Hernandez, St. Louis	.344	1997	Tony Gwynn, San Diego	.372
1962	Tommy Davis, Los Angeles	.346	1980	Bill Buckner, Chicago	.324	1998	Larry Walker, Colorado	.363
1963	Tommy Davis, Los Angeles	.326	1981¹	Bill Madlock, Pittsburgh	.341	1999	Larry Walker, Colorado	.379
1964	Roberto Clemente, Pittsburgh	.339	1982	Al Oliver, Montreal	.331	2000	Todd Helton, Colorado	.372
1965	Roberto Clemente, Pittsburgh	.329	1983	Bill Madlock, Pittsburgh	.323	2001	Larry Walker, Colorado	.350
1966	Matty Alou, Pittsburgh	.342	1984	Tony Gwynn, San Diego	.351	2002	Barry Bonds, San Francisco	.370
1967	Roberto Clemente, Pittsburgh	.357	1985	Willie McGee, St. Louis	.353	2003	Albert Pujols, St. Louis	.359
1968	Pete Rose, Cincinnati	.335	1986	Tim Raines, Montreal	.334	2004	Barry Bonds, San Francisco	.362
1969	Pete Rose, Cincinnati	.348	1987	Tony Gwynn, San Diego	.370			

1. Split season because of players' strike. 2. Season ended on Aug. 12 because of players' strike.

MOST VALUABLE PLAYERS
(Baseball Writers' Association selections)

American League

1931	Lefty Grove, Philadelphia
1932–33	Jimmie Foxx, Philadelphia
1934	Mickey Cochrane, Detroit
1935	Hank Greenberg, Detroit
1936	Lou Gehrig, New York
1937	Charlie Gehringer, Detroit
1938	Jimmie Foxx, Boston
1939	Joe DiMaggio, New York
1940	Hank Greenberg, Detroit
1941	Joe DiMaggio, New York
1942	Joe Gordon, New York
1943	Spurgeon Chandler, New York
1944–45	Hal Newhouser, Detroit
1946	Ted Williams, Boston
1947	Joe DiMaggio, New York
1948	Lou Boudreau, Cleveland
1949	Ted Williams, Boston
1950	Phil Rizzuto, New York
1951	Yogi Berra, New York
1952	Bobby Shantz, Philadelphia
1953	Al Rosen, Cleveland
1954–55	Yogi Berra, New York
1956–57	Mickey Mantle, New York
1958	Jackie Jensen, Boston
1959	Nellie Fox, Chicago
1960–61	Roger Maris, New York
1962	Mickey Mantle, New York
1963	Elston Howard, New York
1964	Brooks Robinson, Baltimore
1965	Zoilo Versalles, Minnesota
1966	Frank Robinson, Baltimore
1967	Carl Yastrzemski, Boston
1968	Dennis McLain, Detroit
1969	Harmon Killebrew, Minnesota
1970	John (Boog) Powell, Baltimore
1971	Vida Blue, Oakland
1972	Dick Allen, Chicago
1973	Reggie Jackson, Oakland
1974	Jeff Burroughs, Texas
1975	Fred Lynn, Boston
1976	Thurman Munson, New York
1977	Rod Carew, Minnesota
1978	Jim Rice, Boston
1979	Don Baylor, California
1980	George Brett, Kansas City
1981	Rollie Fingers, Milwaukee
1982	Robin Yount, Milwaukee
1983	Cal Ripken, Jr., Baltimore
1984	Willie Hernandez, Detroit
1985	Don Mattingly, New York
1986	Roger Clemens, Boston
1987	George Bell, Toronto
1988	Jose Canseco, Oakland
1989	Robin Yount, Milwaukee
1990	Rickey Henderson, Oakland
1991	Cal Ripken, Jr., Baltimore
1992	Dennis Eckersley, Oakland
1993–94	Frank Thomas, Chicago
1995	Mo Vaughn, Boston
1996	Juan Gonzalez, Texas
1997	Ken Griffey, Jr., Seattle
1998	Juan Gonzalez, Texas
1999	Ivan Rodriguez, Texas
2000	Jason Giambi, Oakland
2001	Ichiro Suzuki, Seattle
2002	Miguel Tejada, Oakland
2003	Alex Rodriguez, Texas
2004	Vladimir Guerrero, Anaheim

National League

1931	Frank Frisch, St. Louis
1932	Chuck Klein, Philadelphia
1933	Carl Hubbell, New York
1934	Dizzy Dean, St. Louis
1935	Gabby Hartnett, Chicago
1936	Carl Hubbell, New York
1937	Joe Medwick, St. Louis
1938	Ernie Lombardi, Cincinnati
1939	Bucky Walters, Cincinnati
1940	Frank McCormick, Cincinnati
1941	Dolph Camilli, Brooklyn
1942	Mort Cooper, St. Louis
1943	Stan Musial, St. Louis
1944	Marty Marion, St. Louis
1945	Phil Cavarretta, Chicago
1946	Stan Musial, St. Louis
1947	Bob Elliott, Boston
1948	Stan Musial, St. Louis
1949	Jackie Robinson, Brooklyn
1950	Jim Konstanty, Philadelphia
1951	Roy Campanella, Brooklyn
1952	Hank Sauer, Chicago
1953	Roy Campanella, Brooklyn
1954	Willie Mays, New York

1955	Roy Campanella, Brooklyn
1956	Don Newcombe, Brooklyn
1957	Hank Aaron, Milwaukee
1958–59	Ernie Banks, Chicago
1960	Dick Groat, Pittsburgh
1961	Frank Robinson, Cincinnati
1962	Maury Wills, Los Angeles
1963	Sandy Koufax, Los Angeles
1964	Ken Boyer, St. Louis
1965	Willie Mays, San Francisco
1966	Roberto Clemente, Pittsburgh
1967	Orlando Cepeda, St. Louis
1968	Bob Gibson, St. Louis
1969	Willie McCovey, San Francisco
1970	Johnny Bench, Cincinnati
1971	Joe Torre, St. Louis
1972	Johnny Bench, Cincinnati
1973	Pete Rose, Cincinnati
1974	Steve Garvey, Los Angeles
1975–76	Joe Morgan, Cincinnati
1977	George Foster, Cincinnati
1978	Dave Parker, Pittsburgh
1979	Willie Stargell, Pittsburgh
1979	Keith Hernandez, St. Louis
1980–81	Mike Schmidt, Philadelphia
1982–83	Dale Murphy, Atlanta
1984	Ryne Sandberg, Chicago
1985	Willie McGee, St. Louis
1986	Mike Schmidt, Philadelphia
1987	Andre Dawson, Chicago
1988	Kirk Gibson, Los Angeles
1989	Kevin Mitchell, San Francisco
1990	Barry Bonds, Pittsburgh
1991	Terry Pendleton, Atlanta
1992	Barry Bonds, Pittsburgh
1993	Barry Bonds, San Francisco
1994	Jeff Bagwell, Houston
1995	Barry Larkin, Cincinnati
1996	Ken Caminiti, San Diego
1997	Larry Walker, Colorado
1998	Sammy Sosa, Chicago
1999	Chipper Jones, Atlanta
2000	Jeff Kent, San Francisco
2001–04	Barry Bonds, San Francisco

MAJOR LEAGUE LIFETIME RECORDS

(through Sept. 6, 2005)

Pitching Wins
(Boldface indicates player active in 2005)

		W	L	ERA	G
1.	Cy Young	511	316	2.63	906
2.	Walter Johnson	417	279	2.17	802
3.	Grover Alexander	373	208	2.56	696
4.	Christy Mathewson	373	188	2.13	635
5.	Pud Galvin	365	310	2.85	705
6.	Warren Spahn	363	245	3.09	750
7.	Kid Nichols	361	208	2.95	620
8.	Tim Keefe	342	225	2.62	600
9.	**Roger Clemens**	**339**	**170**	**3.12**	**668**
10.	Steve Carlton	329	244	3.22	741
11.	John Clarkson	328	178	2.81	531
12.	Eddie Plank	326	194	2.35	623
13.	Nolan Ryan	324	292	3.19	807
14.	Don Sutton	324	256	3.26	774
15.	Phil Niekro	318	274	3.35	864
16.	**Greg Maddux**	**316**	**185**	**3.01**	**637**
17.	Gaylord Perry	314	265	3.11	777
18.	Tom Seaver	311	205	2.86	656
19.	Charley Radbourn	309	195	2.67	528
20.	Mickey Welch	307	210	2.71	565
21.	Lefty Grove	300	141	3.06	616
22.	Early Wynn	300	244	3.54	691
23.	Bobby Mathews	297	248	2.85	578
24.	Tommy John	288	231	3.34	760
25.	Bert Blyleven	287	250	3.31	692

Leading Batters, by Batting Average

		G	AB	H	Avg.
1.	Ty Cobb	3,035	11,429	4,191	.367
2.	Rogers Hornsby	2,259	8,173	2,930	.358
3.	Ed Delahanty	1,835	7,505	2,596	.346
4.	Tris Speaker	2,789	10,195	3,514	.345
5.	Billy Hamilton	1,591	6,269	2,159	.344
5.	Ted Williams	2,292	7,706	2,654	.344
7.	Dan Brouthers	1,673	6,711	2,296	.342
7.	Harry Heilmann	2,147	7,787	2,660	.342
7.	Babe Ruth	2,503	8,399	2,873	.342
10.	Willie Keeler	2,123	8,591	2,932	.341
10.	Bill Terry	1,721	6,428	2,193	.341
12.	Lou Gehrig	2,164	8,001	2,721	.340
13.	George Sisler	2,055	8,267	2,812	.340
14.	Jesse Burkett	2,066	8,421	2,850	.338
15.	Tony Gwynn	2,440	9,288	3,141	.338
16.	Nap Lajoie	2,480	9,589	3,242	.338
17.	Al Simmons	2,215	8,759	2,927	.334
18.	Cap Anson	2,523	10,278	3,418	.333
19.	Eddie Collins	2,826	9,949	3,315	.333
20.	Paul Waner	2,549	9,459	3,152	.333
21.	Stan Musial	3,026	10,972	3,630	.331
22.	Sam Thompson	1,407	5,984	1,979	.331
23.	Heinie Manush	2,008	7,654	2,524	.330
24.	Wade Boggs	2,440	9,180	3,010	.328
25.	Rod Carew	2,469	9,315	3,053	.328

Pitchers Active in 2005

		W	L	ERA	G
1.	Roger Clemens	339	170	3.12	668
2.	Greg Maddux	316	185	3.01	637
3.	Tom Glavine	272	183	3.46	598
4.	Randy Johnson	259	136	3.12	517
5.	David Wells	224	142	4.04	613
6.	Mike Mussina	223	127	3.64	441
7.	Kevin Brown	211	144	3.28	486
8.	Jamie Moyer	203	151	4.16	533
9.	Pedro Martinez	195	82	2.72	415
10.	Curt Schilling	189	130	3.40	509

Players Active in 2005 (3,000 at-bats minimum)

		G	AB	H	Avg.
1.	Todd Helton	1,254	4,475	1,501	.335
2.	Ichiro Suzuki	771	3,294	1,094	.332
3.	Vladimir Guerrero	1,278	4,816	1,560	.324
4.	Nomar Garciaparra	1,074	4,266	1,366	.320
5.	Derek Jeter	1,499	6,060	1,904	.314
6.	Manny Ramirez	1,661	6,032	1,891	.313
7.	Mike Piazza	1,687	6,156	1,920	.312
8.	Larry Walker	1,973	6,870	2,144	.312
9.	Magglio Ordonez	1,060	4,029	1,238	.307
10.	Alex Rodriguez	1,566	6,097	1,871	.307

MAJOR LEAGUE ALL-TIME PITCHING RECORDS

(through Sept. 6, 2005)

Most Games Won—511, Cy Young, Cleveland N.L., 1890–98, St. Louis N.L., 1899–1900, Boston A.L., 1901–08, Cleveland A.L., 1909–11, Boston N.L., 1911.

Most Games Won, Season—54, Al Spalding, Boston N.A., 1875. (Since 1900—41, Jack Chesbro, New York A.L., 1904.)

Most Consecutive Games Won—24, Carl Hubbell, New York N.L., 1936 (16) and 1937 (8).

Most Consecutive Games Won, Season—19, Tim Keefe, New York N.L., 1888; Rube Marquard, New York N.L., 1912.

Most Years Won 20 or More Games—16, Cy Young, Cleveland N.L., 1891–98, St. Louis N.L., 1899–1900, Boston A.L., 1901–04, 1907–08.

Most Shutouts—110, Walter Johnson, Washington A.L., 1907–27.

Most Shutouts, Season—16, Grover Alexander, Philadelphia N.L., 1916.

Most Consecutive Shutouts—6, Don Drysdale, Los Angeles N.L., 1968.

Most Consecutive Scoreless Innings—59, Orel Hershiser, Los Angeles Dodgers, 1988.

Most Strikeouts—5,714, Nolan Ryan, New York N.L., California A.L., Houston N.L., 1968–1988 Texas, 1989–93.

Most Strikeouts, Season—513, Matthew Kilroy, Baltimore A.A., 1886. (Since 1900—383, Nolan Ryan, California A.L., 1973.)

Most Strikeouts, Game—21, Tom Cheney, Washington A.L., 1962, 16 innings. 20, Roger Clemens, Boston A.L., 1986, nine innings; Kerry Wood, Chicago N.L., 1998, nine innings.

Most Consecutive Strikeouts—10, Tom Seaver, New York N.L. vs. San Diego, April 22, 1970.

Most Games, Season—106, Mike Marshall, Los Angeles N.L., 1974.

Most Complete Games, Season—75, William White, Cincinnati N.L., 1879. (Since 1900—48, Jack Chesbro, New York A.L., 1904.)

CY YOUNG AWARD

1956	Don Newcombe, Brooklyn N.L.
1957	Warren Spahn, Milwaukee N.L.
1958	Bob Turley, New York A.L.
1959	Early Wynn, Chicago A.L.
1960	Vernon Law, Pittsburgh N.L
1961	Whitey Ford, New York A.L.
1962	Don Drysdale, Los Angeles N.L.
1963	Sandy Koufax, Los Angeles N.L.
1964	Dean Chance, Los Angeles A.L.
1965	Sandy Koufax, Los Angeles N.L.
1966	Sandy Koufax, Los Angeles N.L.
1967	Jim Lonborg, Boston A.L.; Mike McCormick, San Francisco N.L.
1968	Dennis McLain, Detroit A.L.; Bob Gibson, St. Louis N.L.
1969	Mike Cuellar, Baltimore A.L. and Dennis McLain, Detroit A.L. (tied); Tom Seaver, New York N.L.
1970	Jim Perry, Minnesota A.L; Bob Gibson, St. Louis N.L.
1971	Vida Blue, Oakland A.L.; Ferguson Jenkins, Chicago N.L.
1972	Gaylord Perry, Cleveland A.L.; Steve Carlton, Philadelphia N.L.
1973	Jim Palmer, Baltimore A.L.; Tom Seaver, New York N.L.
1974	Catfish Hunter, Oakland A.L.; Mike Marshall, Los Angeles N.L.
1975	Jim Palmer, Baltimore A.L.; Tom Seaver, New York N.L.
1976	Jim Palmer, Baltimore A.L.; Randy Jones, San Diego N.L.
1977	Sparky Lyle, New York A.L.; Steve Carlton, Philadelphia N.L.
1978	Ron Guidry, New York A.L.; Gaylord Perry, San Diego N.L.
1979	Mike Flanagan, Baltimore A.L.; Bruce Sutter, Chicago N.L.
1980	Steve Stone, Baltimore A.L.; Steve Carlton, Philadelphia N.L.
1981	Rollie Fingers, Milwaukee A.L.; Fernando Valenzuela, Los Angeles N.L.
1982	Pete Vuckovich, Milwaukee A.L.; Steve Carlton, Philadelphia N.L.
1983	LaMarr Hoyt, Chicago A.L.; John Denny, Philadelphia N.L.
1984	Willie Hernandez, Detroit A.L.; Rick Sutcliffe, Chicago N.L.
1985	Bret Saberhagen, Kansas City A.L.; Dwight Gooden, New York N.L.
1986	Roger Clemens, Boston A.L.; Mike Scott, Houston N.L.
1987	Roger Clemens, Boston A.L.; Steve Bedrosian, Philadelphia N.L.
1988	Frank Viola, Minnesota A.L.; Orel Hershiser, Los Angeles, N.L.
1989	Bret Saberhagen, Kansas A.L.; Mark Davis, San Diego N.L.
1990	Bob Welch, Oakland A.L.; Doug Drabek, Pittsburgh N.L.
1991	Roger Clemens, Boston A.L.; Tom Glavine, Atlanta N.L.
1992	Dennis Eckersley, Oakland A.L.; Greg Maddux, Chicago N.L.
1993	Jack McDowell, Chicago A.L.; Greg Maddux, Atlanta N.L.
1994	David Cone, Kansas A.L.; Greg Maddux, Atlanta N.L.
1995	Randy Johnson, Seattle A.L.; Greg Maddux, Atlanta N.L.
1996	Pat Hentgen, Toronto A.L.; John Smoltz, Atlanta N.L.
1997	Roger Clemens, Toronto A.L.; Pedro Martinez, Montreal N.L.
1998	Roger Clemens, Toronto A.L.; Tom Glavine, Atlanta N.L.
1999	Pedro Martinez, Boston A.L.;
2000	Randy Johnson, Arizona N.L.
2001	Roger Clemens, New York A.L.; Randy Johnson, Arizona N.L.
2002	Barry Zito, Oakland A.L.; Randy Johnson, Arizona N.L.
2003	Roy Halladay, Toronto A.L. Eric Gagne, Los Angeles N.L.
2004	Johan Santana, Minnesota A.L. Roger Clemens, Houston N.L.

ROOKIE OF THE YEAR
(Baseball Writers' Association selections)

American League

1949	Roy Sievers, St. Louis
1950	Walt Dropo, Boston
1951	Gil McDougald, New York
1952	Harry Byrd, Philadelphia
1953	Harvey Kuenn, Detroit
1954	Bob Grim, New York
1955	Herb Score, Cleveland
1956	Luis Aparicio, Chicago
1957	Tony Kubek, New York
1958	Albie Pearson, Washington
1959	Bob Allison, Washington
1960	Ron Hansen, Baltimore
1961	Don Schwall, Boston
1962	Tom Tresh, New York
1963	Gary Peters, Chicago
1964	Tony Oliva, Minnesota
1965	Curt Blefary, Baltimore
1966	Tommy Agee, Chicago
1967	Rod Carew, Minnesota
1968	Stan Bahnsen, New York
1969	Lou Piniella, Kansas City
1970	Thurman Munson, New York
1971	Chris Chambliss, Cleveland
1972	Carlton Fisk, Boston
1973	Alonzo Bumbry, Baltimore
1974	Mike Hargrove, Texas
1975	Fred Lynn, Boston
1976	Mark Fidrych, Detroit
1977	Eddie Murray, Baltimore
1978	Lou Whitaker, Detroit
1979	Alfredo Griffin, Toronto
1979	John Castino, Minnesota
1980	Joe Charboneau, Cleveland
1981	Dave Righetti, New York
1982	Cal Ripken, Jr., Baltimore
1983	Ron Kittle, Chicago
1984	Alvin Davis, Seattle
1985	Ozzie Guillen, Chicago
1986	Jose Canseco, Oakland
1987	Mark McGwire, Oakland
1988	Walter Weiss, Oakland
1989	Gregg Olson, Baltimore
1990	Sandy Alomar Jr., Cleveland
1991	Chuck Knoblauch, Minnesota
1992	Pat Listach, Milwaukee
1993	Tim Salmon, California
1994	Bob Hamelin, Kansas City
1995	Marty Cordova, Minnesota
1996	Derek Jeter, New York
1997	Nomar Garciaparra, Boston
1998	Ben Grieve, Oakland
1999	Carlos Beltran, Kansas City
2000	Kazuhiro Sasaki, Seattle
2001	Ichiro Suzuki, Seattle
2002	Eric Hinske, Toronto
2003	Angel Berroa, Kansas City
2004	Bobby Crosby, Oakland

National League

1949	Don Newcombe, Brooklyn
1950	Sam Jethroe, Boston
1951	Willie Mays, New York
1952	Joe Black, Brooklyn
1953	Jim Gilliam, Brooklyn
1954	Wally Moon, St. Louis
1955	Bill Virdon, St. Louis
1956	Frank Robinson, Cincinnati
1957	Jack Sanford, Philadelphia
1958	Orlando Cepeda, San Francisco
1959	Willie McCovey, San Francisco
1960	Frank Howard, Los Angeles
1961	Billy Williams, Chicago
1962	Ken Hubbs, Chicago
1963	Pete Rose, Cincinnati
1964	Richie Allen, Philadelphia
1965	Jim Lefebvre, Los Angeles
1966	Tommy Helms, Cincinnati
1967	Tom Seaver, New York
1968	Johnny Bench, Cincinnati
1969	Ted Sizemore, Los Angeles
1970	Carl Morton, Montreal
1971	Earl Williams, Atlanta
1972	Jon Matlack, New York
1973	Gary Matthews, San Francisco
1974	Bake McBride, St. Louis
1975	John Montefusco, San Francisco
1976	Pat Zachry, Cincinnati
1976	Bruce Metzger, San Diego
1977	Andre Dawson, Montreal
1978	Bob Horner, Atlanta
1979	Rick Sutcliffe, Los Angeles
1980	Steve Howe, Los Angeles
1981	Fernando Valenzuela, Los Angeles
1982	Steve Sax, Los Angeles
1983	Darryl Strawberry, New York
1984	Dwight Gooden, New York
1985	Vince Coleman, St. Louis
1986	Todd Worrell, St. Louis
1987	Benito Santiago, San Diego
1988	Chris Sabo, Cincinnati
1989	Jerome Walton, Chicago
1990	Dave Justice, Atlanta
1991	Jeff Baguell, Houston
1992	Eric Karros, Los Angeles
1993	Mike Piazza, Los Angeles
1994	Raul Mondesi, Los Angeles
1995	Hideo Nomo, Los Angeles
1996	Todd Hollandsworth, Los Angeles
1997	Scott Rolen, Philadelphia
1998	Kerry Wood, Chicago
1999	Scott Williamson, Cincinnati
2000	Rafael Furcal, Atlanta
2001	Albert Pujols, St. Louis
2002	Jason Jennings, Colorado
2003	Dontrelle Willis, Florida
2004	Jason Bay, Pittsburgh

MAJOR LEAGUE INDIVIDUAL ALL-TIME HITTING RECORDS
(Through Sept. 6, 2005)

Highest Batting Average, Season—.440, Hugh Duffy, Boston N.L., 1894;.435, Tip O'Neill, St. Louis, A.A., 1887. (Since 1900—.426, Nap Lajoie, Phil. A.L., 1901); 424, Rogers Hornsby, St. Louis N.L., 1924.

Most Times at Bat—14,053, Pete Rose, Cincinnati N.L., 1963–78; Philadelphia N.L., 1979–83; Montreal N.L., 1984; Cincinnati N.L., 1984–86.

Most Hits—4,256, Pete Rose, Cincinnati 1963–79, Philadelphia 1980–83, Montreal 1984, Cincinnati 1984–86.

Most Hits, Season—262, Ichiro Suzuki, Seattle A.L., 2004.

Most Consecutive Games Batted Safely—56, Joe DiMaggio, New York A.L., 1941.

Most Runs—2,295, Rickey Henderson, Oakland A.L., 1979–84, 1989–93, 1994–95, 1998; New York A.L., 1985–89; Toronto A.L., 1993; San Diego N.L., 1996, 1997, 2001; Anaheim A.L., 1997; New York N.L., 1999–2000; Seattle A.L., 2000; Boston A.L., 2002; Los Angeles N.L., 2003.

Most Runs, Season—192, William Hamilton, Philadelphia N.L., 1894. (Since 1900—177, Babe Ruth, New York A.L., 1921.)

Most Runs Batted in—2,297, Hank Aaron, Milwaukee N.L., 1954–1965; Atlanta N.L., 1966–74; Milwaukee A.L., 1975–76.

Most Runs Batted in, Season—191, Hack Wilson, Chicago N.L., 1930.

Most Home Runs—755, Hank Aaron, Milwaukee N.L., 1954–1965; Atlanta N.L., 1966–74; Milwaukee A.L., 1975–76.

Most Home Runs, Season—162-game season: 73, Barry Bonds, San Francisco N.L., 2001; 70, Mark McGwire, St. Louis N.L., 1998; 66, Sammy Sosa, Chicago N.L., 1998; 65, Mark McGwire, St. Louis N.L., 1999; 64, Sammy Sosa, Chicago N.L., 2001; 63, Sammy Sosa, Chicago N.L., 1999; 61, Roger Maris, New York A.L., 1961. 154-game season: 60, Babe Ruth, New York A.L., 1927.

Most Home Runs with Bases Filled—23, Lou Gehrig, New York A.L., 1927–39.

Most 2-Base Hits—792, Tris Speaker, Boston A.L., 1907–15, Cleveland A.L., 1916–26, Washington A.L., 1927, Philadelphia A.L., 1928.

Most 2-Base Hits, Season—67, Earl Webb, Boston A.L., 1931.

Most 3-Base Hits—309, Sam Crawford, Cincinnati N.L., 1899–1902, Detroit A.L., 1903–17.

Most 3-Base Hits, Season—36, Owen Wilson, Pittsburgh N.L., 1912.

Most Games Played—3,562, Pete Rose, Cincinnati N.L., Philadelphia N.L., Montreal N.L., 1964–86.

Most Consecutive Games Played—2,632, Cal Ripken, Jr., Baltimore Orioles A.L., 1981–1998.

Most Bases on Balls—2,302, Barry Bonds, Pittsburgh N.L., 1986–92; San Francisco N.L., 1993–.

Most Bases on Balls, Season—232, Barry Bonds, San Francisco N.L., 2004.

Most Strikeouts, Season—195, Adam Dunn, Cincinnati N.L., 2004.

Most Stolen Bases, Lifetime—1,406, Rickey Henderson, Oakland A.L., 1979–84, 1989–93, 1994–95, 1998; New York A.L., 1985–89; Toronto A.L., 1993; San Diego N.L., 1996, 1997, 2001; Anaheim A.L., 1997; New York N.L., 1999–2000; Seattle A.L., 2000; Boston A.L., 2002; Los Angeles, 2003.

Most Stolen Bases, Season—138, Hugh Nicol, Cincinnati A.A., 1887. Since 1900: 130, Rickey Henderson, Oakland A.L., 1982; 118, Lou Brock, St. Louis N.L., 1974.

Most Stolen Bases, Game—7, George Gore, Chicago N.L. 1881; William Hamilton, Philadelphia N.L: 1894. (Since 1900—6, Eddie Collins, Philadelphia A.L., 1912.) and Otis Nixon, Atlanta N.L., 1991.

Most Times Stealing Home, Lifetime—50, Ty Cobb, Detroit-Phil. A.L., 1905–28.

MOST HOME RUNS IN ONE SEASON—45 OR MORE

HR	Player/Team	Year	HR	Player/Team	Year
73	Barry Bonds, San Francisco (N.L.)	2001	50	Brady Anderson, Baltimore (A.L.)	1996
70	Mark McGwire, St. Louis (N.L.)	1998	50	Sammy Sosa, Chicago (N.L.)	2000
66	Sammy Sosa, Chicago (N.L.)	1998	50	Greg Vaughn, San Diego (N.L.)	1998
65	Mark McGwire, St. Louis (N.L.)	1999	50	Andruw Jones, Atlanta (N.L.)	2005[1]
64	Sammy Sosa, Chicago (N.L.)	2001	49	Babe Ruth, New York (A.L.)	1930
63	Sammy Sosa, Chicago (N.L.)	1999	49	Lou Gehrig, New York (A.L.)	1934
61	Roger Maris, New York (A.L.)	1961	49	Lou Gehrig, New York (A.L.)	1936
60	Babe Ruth, New York (A.L.)	1927	49	Ted Kluszewski, Cincinnati (N.L.)	1954
59	Babe Ruth, New York (A.L.)	1921	49	Willie Mays, San Francisco (N.L.)	1962
58	Jimmie Foxx, Philadelphia (A.L.)	1932	49	Harmon Killebrew, Minnesota (A.L.)	1964
58	Hank Greenberg, Detroit (A.L.)	1938	49	Frank Robinson, Baltimore (A.L.)	1966
58	Mark McGwire, Oakland (A.L.), St. Louis (N.L.)	1997	49	Harmon Killebrew, Minnesota (A.L.)	1969
57	Luis Gonzalez. Arizona (N.L.)	2001	49	Mark McGwire, Oakland (A.L.)	1987
57	Alex Rodriguez, Texas (A.L.)	2002	49	Andre Dawson, Chicago (N.L.)	1987
56	Hack Wilson, Chicago (N.L.)	1930	49	Ken Griffey, Jr., Seattle (A.L.)	1996
56	Ken Griffey, Jr., Seattle (A.L.)	1997	49	Larry Walker, Colorado (N.L.)	1997
56	Ken Griffey, Jr., Seattle (A.L.)	1998	49	Albert Belle, Chicago (A.L.)	1998
54	Babe Ruth, New York (A.L.)	1920	49	Barry Bonds, San Francisco (N.L.)	2000
54	Babe Ruth, New York (A.L.)	1928	49	Shawn Green, Los Angeles (N.L.)	2001
54	Ralph Kiner, Pittsburgh (N.L.)	1949	49	Todd Helton, Colorado (N.L.)	2001
54	Mickey Mantle, New York (A.L.)	1961	49	Jim Thome, Cleveland (A.L.)	2001
52	Mickey Mantle, New York (A.L.)	1956	49	Sammy Sosa, Chicago (N.L.)	2002
52	Willie Mays, San Francisco (N.L.)	1965	48	Jimmie Foxx, Philadelphia (A.L.)	1933
52	George Foster, Cincinnati (N.L.)	1977	48	Harmon Killebrew, Minnesota (A.L.)	1962
52	Mark McGwire, Oakland (A.L.)	1996	48	Frank Howard, Washington (A.L.)	1969
52	Alex Rodriguez, Texas (A.L.)	2001	48	Willie Stargell, Pittsburgh (N.L.)	1971
52	Jim Thome, Cleveland (A.L.)	2002	48	Dave Kingman, Chicago (N.L.)	1979
51	Ralph Kiner, Pittsburgh (N.L.)	1947	48	Mike Schmidt, Philadelphia (N.L.)	1980
51	John Mize, New York (N.L.)	1947	48	Albert Belle, Cleveland (A.L.)	1996
51	Willie Mays, New York (N.L.)	1955	48	Ken Griffey, Jr., Seattle (A.L.)	1999
51	Cecil Fielder (A.L.)	1990	48	Adrian Beltre, Los Angeles (N.L.)	2004
50	Jimmie Foxx, Boston (A.L.)	1938	47	Babe Ruth, New York (A.L.)	1926
50	Albert Belle, Cleveland (A.L.)	1995	47	Ralph Kiner, Pittsburgh (N.L.)	1950

HR	Player/Team	Year
47	Ed Mathews, Milwaukee (N.L.)	1953
47	Ernie Banks, Chicago (N.L.)	1958
47	Willie Mays, San Francisco (N.L.)	1964
47	Hank Aaron, Atlanta (N.L.)	1971
47	Reggie Jackson, Oakland (A.L.)	1969
47	George Bell, Toronto (A.L.)	1987
47	Kevin Mitchell, San Francisco (N.L.)	1989
47	Andres Galarraga, Colorado (N.L.)	1996
47	Juan Gonzalez, Texas (A.L.)	1996
47	Rafael Palmeiro, Texas (A.L.)	1999
47	Jeff Bagwell, Houston (N.L.)	2000
47	Troy Glaus, Anaheim (A.L.)	2000
47	Rafael Palmeiro, Texas (A.L.)	2001
47	Alex Rodriguez, Texas (A.L.)	2003
47	Jim Thome, Philadelphia (N.L.)	2003
46	Babe Ruth, New York (A.L.)	1924
46	Babe Ruth, New York (A.L.)	1929
46	Babe Ruth, New York (A.L.)	1931
46	Lou Gehrig, New York (A.L.)	1931
46	Joe DiMaggio, New York (A.L.)	1937
46	Ed Mathews, Milwaukee (N.L.)	1959
46	Orlando Cepeda, San Francisco (N.L.)	1961
46	Jim Rice, Boston (A.L.)	1978
46	Juan Gonzalez, Texas (A.L.)	1993

HR	Player/Team	Year
46	Barry Bonds, San Francisco (N.L.)	1993
46	Jose Canseco, Toronto (A.L.)	1998
46	Vinnie Castilla, Colorado (N.L.)	1998
46	Barry Bonds, San Francisco (N.L.)	2002
46	Adam Dunn, Cincinnati (N.L.)	2004
46	Albert Pujols, St. Louis (N.L.)	2004
46	David Ortiz, Boston (A.L.)	2005[1]
45	Ernie Banks, Chicago (N.L.)	1959
45	Harmon Killebrew, Minnesota (A.L.)	1963
45	Willie McCovey, San Francisco (N.L.)	1969
45	Johnny Bench, Cincinnati (N.L.)	1970
45	Gorman Thomas, Milwaukee (A.L.)	1979
45	Hank Aaron, Milwaukee (N.L.)	1962
45	Ken Griffey, Jr., Seattle (A.L.)	1993
45	Juan Gonzalez, Texas (A.L.)	1998
45	Manny Ramirez, Cleveland (A.L.)	1998
45	Chipper Jones, Atlanta (N.L.)	1999
45	Greg Vaughn, Cincinnati (N.L.)	1999
45	Barry Bonds, San Francisco (N.L.)	2003
45	Richie Sexson, Milwaukee (N.L.)	2003
45	Barry Bonds, San Francisco (N.L.)	2004
45	Alex Rodriguez, New York (A.L.)	2005[1]

1. As of Sept. 21, 2005.

MAJOR LEAGUE BASEBALL—2005

(As of Sept. 21, 2005. Season ends Oct. 2. *See* www.infoplease.com/2005baseball for final statistics.)

AMERICAN LEAGUE STANDINGS

EASTERN DIVISION

Team	W	L	Pct	GB
Boston Red Sox	88	63	.583	—
New York Yankees	87	63	.580	0.5
Toronto Blue Jays[1]	74	76	.493	13.5
Baltimore Orioles[1]	70	80	.467	17.5
Tampa Bay Devil Rays[1]	63	89	.414	25.5

CENTRAL DIVISION

Team	W	L	Pct	GB
Chicago White Sox	91	59	.607	—
Cleveland Indians	88	63	.583	3.5
Minnesota Twins[1]	76	74	.507	15.0
Detroit Tigers[1]	67	84	.444	24.5
Kansas City Royals[1]	51	99	.340	40.0

WESTERN DIVISION

Team	W	L	Pct	GB
Los Angeles Angels	85	65	.567	—
Oakland Athletics	84	67	.556	1.5
Texas Rangers	75	76	.497	10.5
Seattle Mariners[1]	65	86	.430	20.5

1. Eliminated from winning the division.

AMERICAN LEAGUE LEADERS, 2005

Batting—M. Young, Texas	.329
Home runs—D. Ortiz, Boston	46
Runs batted in—D. Ortiz, Boston	140
Runs—D. Ortiz, Boston	114
Hits—M. Young, Texas	206
Stolen bases—S. Podsednik, Chicago	56
Doubles—M. Tejada, Baltimore	48
Triples—C. Crawford, Tampa Bay	15
Slugging percentage—D. Ortiz, Boston	.621

A.L. Pitching

Wins—B. Colon, Los Angeles	20
Earned run average—K. Millwood	2.97
Strikeouts—J. Santana, Minnesota	220
Innings pitched—M. Buehrle, Chicago	222.0
Complete games—R. Halladay, Toronto	5
Shutouts—J. Garland, Chicago	3
Saves—B. Wickman, Cleveland	44

NATIONAL LEAGUE STANDINGS

EASTERN DIVISION

Team	W	L	Pct	GB
Atlanta Braves	86	65	.570	—
Philadelphia Phillies	80	71	.530	6.0
Florida Marlins	79	72	.523	7.0
Washington Nationals	77	74	.510	9.0
New York Mets	74	76	.493	11.5

CENTRAL DIVISION

Team	W	L	Pct	GB
St. Louis Cardinals	95	57	.625	—
Houston Astros[1]	82	69	.543	12.5
Milwaukee Brewers[1]	74	76	.493	20.0
Chicago Cubs[1]	74	77	.490	20.5
Cincinnati Reds[1]	70	80	.467	24.0
Pittsburgh Pirates[1]	62	89	.411	32.5

WESTERN DIVISION

Team	W	L	Pct	GB
San Diego Padres	75	75	.500	—
San Francisco Giants	70	80	.467	5.0
Arizona Diamondbacks	68	83	.450	7.5
Los Angeles Dodgers	67	83	.447	8.0
Colorado Rockies[1]	62	88	.413	13.0

1. Eliminated from winning the division.

NATIONAL LEAGUE LEADERS, 2005

Batting—D. Lee, Chicago	.339
Home runs—A. Jones, Atlanta	50
Runs batted in—A. Jones, Atlanta	126
Runs—A. Pujols, St. Louis	120
Hits—D. Lee, Chicago	188
Stolen bases—J. Reyes, New York	55
Doubles—D. Lee, Chicago	47
Triples—J. Reyes, New York	16
Slugging percentage—D. Lee, Chicago	.672

N.L. Pitching

Wins—C. Carpenter, St. Louis and D. Willis, Florida	21
Earned run average—R. Clemens, Houston	1.89
Strikeouts—P. Martinez, New York and J. Peavy, San Diego	207
Innings pitched—L. Hernandez, Washington	231.1
Complete games—C. Carpenter, St. Louis and D. Willis, Florida	7
Shutouts—D. Willis, Florida	5
Saves—C. Cordero, Washington	46

AMERICAN LEAGUE STATISTICS, 2005

(As of Sept. 21, 2005. *See* www.infoplease.com/2005baseball for final statistics.)

Team Pitching

	W	L	ERA	SHO	H	R	SO
Oakland	84	67	3.63	12	1,218	607	1,000
Cleveland	88	63	3.65	8	1,271	605	976
Los Angeles	85	65	3.68	11	1,320	594	1,030
Minnesota	76	74	3.70	7	1,364	616	877
Chicago	91	59	3.70	10	1,294	613	951
Toronto	74	76	4.06	8	1,368	655	893
Seattle	65	86	4.47	7	1,389	700	819
New York	87	63	4.50	13	1,405	727	914
Baltimore	70	80	4.54	9	1,347	731	975
Detroit	67	84	4.56	2	1,411	746	864
Boston	88	63	4.77	8	1,448	758	892
Texas	75	76	5.00	6	1,484	805	878
Tampa Bay	63	89	5.42	3	1,484	887	898
Kansas City	51	99	5.49	5	1,520	861	851

Team Batting

	AB	R	H	HR	RBI	Avg.
Boston	5,258	853	1,483	185	809	.282
New York	5,210	818	1,438	209	782	.276
Tampa Bay	5,221	710	1,430	148	681	.274
Detroit	5,240	686	1,425	151	644	.272
Baltimore	5,143	671	1,396	172	644	.271
Cleveland	5,212	733	1,413	191	706	.271
Los Angeles	5,209	693	1,406	134	662	.270
Texas	5,333	817	1,435	252	786	.269
Toronto	5,172	713	1,372	126	677	.265
Oakland	5,256	732	1,387	145	699	.264
Chicago	5,113	698	1,343	188	671	.263
Kansas City	5,101	647	1,339	113	602	.262
Minnesota	5,178	640	1,350	127	599	.261
Seattle	5,150	668	1,328	127	628	.258

Individual Pitching (based on 10 decisions)

	W	L	ERA	IP	H	BB	SO
B. Colon, Los Angeles	20	7	3.34	212.2	200	40	149
J. Garland, Chicago	17	9	3.41	200.1	193	39	100
C. Lee, Cleveland	17	4	3.75	187.1	178	49	136
M. Buehrle, Chicago	15	8	3.28	222.0	233	37	137
T. Wakefield, Boston	15	11	4.07	205.2	193	66	138
J. Westbrook, Cleveland	15	14	4.60	195.2	202	54	109
J. Bonderman, Detroit	14	13	4.57	189.0	199	57	145
R. Johnson, New York	14	8	4.01	204.1	195	42	195
R. Lopez, Baltimore	14	10	4.86	192.2	214	55	112

Individual Batting (based on 300 at bats)

	AB	R	H	HR	RBI	Avg.
M. Young, Texas	627	107	206	22	83	.329
V. Guerrero, Los Angeles	491	91	157	31	103	.320
A. Rodriguez, New York	563	113	180	45	120	.320
J. Damon, Boston	582	107	185	9	72	.318
B. Roberts, Baltimore	561	92	176	18	73	.314
M. Tejada, Baltimore	605	82	187	25	92	.309
C. Crisp, Cleveland	547	81	168	15	65	.307
D. Jeter, New York	609	113	187	16	60	.307
T. Hafner, Cleveland	444	85	136	28	95	.306

NATIONAL LEAGUE STATISTICS, 2005

Team Pitching

	W	L	ERA	SHO	H	R	SO
St. Louis	95	57	3.40	13	1,307	583	901
Houston	82	69	3.52	11	1,244	570	1,088
New York	74	76	3.72	10	1,283	596	937
Washington	77	74	3.85	7	1,361	623	913
Atlanta	86	65	3.93	12	1,374	616	857
Milwaukee	74	76	3.93	5	1,285	638	1,065
Florida	79	72	4.10	15	1,349	673	1,039
Philadelphia	80	71	4.23	5	1,291	679	1,049
Chicago	74	77	4.24	9	1,268	671	1,168
San Diego	75	75	4.24	7	1,358	691	1,058
San Francisco	70	80	4.40	8	1,354	697	908
Pittsburgh	62	89	4.45	14	1,363	717	891
Los Angeles	67	83	4.47	9	1,347	712	929
Arizona	68	83	5.01	9	1,497	825	957
Cincinnati	70	80	5.09	1	1,518	811	893
Colorado	62	88	5.13	3	1,479	800	925

Team Batting

	AB	R	H	HR	RBI	Avg.
Chicago	5,217	666	1,419	186	640	.272
Florida	5,132	678	1,394	121	641	.272
St. Louis	5,192	748	1,395	159	701	.269
Colorado	5,124	687	1,366	141	652	.267
Philadelphia	5,144	730	1,375	149	686	.267
Atlanta	5,119	714	1,352	170	680	.264
Cincinnati	5,156	758	1,353	205	726	.262
San Francisco	5,050	614	1,325	120	583	.262
Pittsburgh	5,192	633	1,353	125	613	.261
New York	5,093	665	1,316	153	629	.258
San Diego	5,106	636	1,319	125	609	.258
Milwaukee	5,058	670	1,303	165	635	.258
Arizona	5,168	652	1,323	182	627	.256
Los Angeles	5,044	645	1,292	141	615	.256
Houston	5,092	641	1,301	146	608	.255
Washington	5,047	591	1,270	111	570	.252

Individual Pitching (based on 10 decisions)

	W	L	ERA	IP	H	BB	SO
C. Carpenter, St. Louis	21	4	2.42	230.1	183	47	203
D. Willis, Florida	21	9	2.48	217.1	190	48	148
C. Capuano, Milwaukee	17	10	3.64	202.2	191	79	164
R. Oswalt, Houston	17	12	2.87	222.2	217	46	165
A. Pettitte, Houston	17	9	2.45	209.1	181	41	161
M. Mulder, St. Louis	16	7	3.43	199.1	203	62	105
J. Beckett, Florida	15	8	3.51	171.2	148	56	160
L. Hernandez, Washington	15	8	3.93	231.1	252	81	135
J. Lieber, Philadelphia	15	12	4.40	196.1	203	35	127
P. Martinez, New York	15	7	2.80	212.0	153	45	207
J. Suppan, St. Louis	15	10	3.72	186.1	200	63	107

Individual Batting (based on 300 at bats)

	AB	R	H	HR	RBI	Avg.
D. Lee, Chicago	555	114	188	44	102	.339
A. Pujols, St. Louis	557	120	186	39	109	.334
M. Cabrera, Florida	582	103	187	32	111	.321
T. Helton, Colorado	469	80	148	17	69	.316
S. Casey, Cincinnati	529	75	165	9	58	.312
D. Wright, New York	532	89	165	21	89	.310
J. Bay, Pittsburgh	561	106	173	30	91	.308
M. Holliday, Colorado	430	61	132	17	77	.307
B. Clark, Milwaukee	554	86	169	11	44	.305
C. Delgado, Florida	490	79	149	32	109	.304
B. Giles, San Diego	507	86	153	15	78	.302
A. Ramirez, Chicago	463	72	140	31	92	.302
L. Castillo, Chicago	439	72	132	4	30	.301
K. Griffey, Cincinnati	491	85	148	35	92	.301
C. Tracy, Arizona	455	65	137	24	59	.301

AMERICAN LEAGUE PENNANT WINNERS

Year	Club	Manager	Won	Lost	Pct
1901	Chicago	Clark C. Griffith	83	53	.610
1902	Philadelphia	Connie Mack	83	53	.610
1903	Boston[1]	Jimmy Collins	91	47	.659
1904	Boston[2]	Jimmy Collins	95	59	.617
1905	Philadelphia	Connie Mack	92	56	.622
1906	Chicago[1]	Fielder A. Jones	93	58	.616
1907	Detroit	Hugh A. Jennings	92	58	.613
1908	Detroit	Hugh A. Jennings	90	63	.588
1909	Detroit	Hugh A. Jennings	98	54	.645
1910	Philadelphia[1]	Connie Mack	102	48	.680
1911	Philadelphia[1]	Connie Mack	101	50	.669
1912	Boston[1]	J. Garland Stahl	105	47	.691
1913	Philadelphia[1]	Connie Mack	96	57	.627
1914	Philadelphia	Connie Mack	99	53	.651
1915	Boston[1]	William F. Carrigan	101	50	.669
1916	Boston[1]	William F. Carrigan	91	63	.591
1917	Chicago[1]	Clarence H. Rowland	100	54	.649
1918	Boston[1]	Ed Barrow	75	51	.595
1919	Chicago	William Gleason	88	52	.629
1920	Cleveland[1]	Tris Speaker	98	56	.636
1921	New York	Miller J. Huggins	98	55	.641
1922	New York	Miller J. Huggins	94	60	.610
1923	New York[1]	Miller J. Huggins	98	54	.645
1924	Washington[1]	Stanley R. Harris	92	62	.597
1925	Washington	Stanley R. Harris	96	55	.636
1926	New York	Miller J. Huggins	91	63	.591
1927	New York[1]	Miller J. Huggins	110	44	.714
1928	New York[1]	Miller J. Huggins	101	53	.656
1929	Philadelphia[1]	Connie Mack	104	46	.693
1930	Philadelphia[1]	Connie Mack	102	52	.662
1931	Philadelphia	Connie Mack	107	45	.704
1932	New York[1]	Joseph V. McCarthy	107	47	.695
1933	Washington	Joseph E. Cronin	99	53	.651
1934	Detroit	Gordon Cochrane	101	53	.656
1935	Detroit[1]	Gordon Cochrane	93	58	.616
1936	New York[1]	Joseph V. McCarthy	102	51	.667
1937	New York[1]	Joseph V. McCarthy	102	52	.662
1938	New York[1]	Joseph V. McCarthy	99	53	.651
1939	New York[1]	Joseph V. McCarthy	106	45	.702
1940	Detroit	Delmar D. Baker	90	64	.584
1941	New York[1]	Joseph V. McCarthy	101	53	.656
1942	New York	Joseph V. McCarthy	103	51	.669
1943	New York[1]	Joseph V. McCarthy	98	56	.636
1944	St. Louis	Luke Sewell	89	65	.578
1945	Detroit[1]	Steve O'Neill	88	65	.575
1946	Boston	Joseph E. Cronin	104	50	.675
1947	New York[1]	Stanley R. Harris	97	57	.630
1948	Cleveland[1]	Lou Boudreau	97	58	.626
1949	New York[1]	Casey Stengel	97	57	.630
1950	New York[1]	Casey Stengel	98	56	.636
1951	New York[1]	Casey Stengel	98	56	.636
1952	New York[1]	Casey Stengel	95	59	.617
1953	New York[1]	Casey Stengel	99	52	.656
1954	Cleveland	Al Lopez	111	43	.721
1955	New York	Casey Stengel	96	58	.623
1956	New York[1]	Casey Stengel	97	57	.630
1957	New York	Casey Stengel	98	56	.636
1958	New York[1]	Casey Stengel	92	62	.597
1959	Chicago	Al Lopez	94	60	.610
1960	New York	Casey Stengel	97	57	.630
1961	New York[1]	Ralph Houk	109	53	.673
1962	New York[1]	Ralph Houk	96	66	.593
1963	New York	Ralph Houk	104	57	.646
1964	New York	Yogi Berra	99	63	.611
1965	Minnesota	Sam Mele	102	60	.630
1966	Baltimore[1]	Hank Bauer	97	53	.606
1967	Boston	Dick Williams	92	70	.568
1968	Detroit[1]	Mayo Smith	103	59	.636
1969	Baltimore[3]	Earl Weaver	109	53	.673
1970	Baltimore[1,3]	Earl Weaver	108	54	.667
1971	Baltimore[4]	Earl Weaver	101	57	.639
1972	Oakland[1,5]	Dick Williams	93	62	.600
1973	Oakland[1,6]	Dick Williams	94	68	.580
1974	Oakland[1,6]	Alvin Dark	90	72	.556
1975	Boston[4]	Darrell Johnson	95	65	.594
1976	New York[7]	Billy Martin	97	62	.610
1977	New York[1,7]	Billy Martin	100	62	.617
1978	New York[1,7]	Billy Martin and Bob Lemon	100	63	.613
1979	Baltimore[8]	Earl Weaver	102	57	.642
1980	Kansas City[9]	Jim Frey	97	65	.599
1981*	New York[4]	Gene Michael and Bob Lemon	59	48	.551
1982	Milwaukee[8]	Harvey Kuenn	95	67	.586
1983	Baltimore[1, 10]	Joe Altobelli	98	64	.605
1984	Detroit[1,7]	Sparky Anderson	104	58	.642
1985	Kansas City[1,11]		91	71	.562
1986	Boston[8]	John McNamara	95	66	.590
1987	Minnesota[5]	Tom Kelly	85	77	.525
1988	Oakland[12]	Tony LaRussa	104	58	.642
1989	Oakland[1,11]	Tony LaRussa	99	63	.611
1990	Oakland[12]	Tony LaRussa	103	59	.636
1991	Minnesota[1,11]	Tom Kelly	95	67	.586
1992	Toronto[1,4]	Cito Gaston	96	66	.593
1993	Toronto[1,10]	Cito Gaston	95	67	.586
1994	Strike ended season Aug. 11. No playoffs, no pennant winner.				
1995	Cleveland[13]	Mike Hargrove	100	44	.694
1996	New York[1,6]	Joe Torre	92	70	.568
1997	Cleveland[6]	Mike Hargrove	86	75	.534
1998	New York[1, 14]	Joe Torre	114	48	.704
1999	New York[1, 15]	Joe Torre	98	64	.605
2000	New York[1, 16]	Joe Torre	87	74	.540
2001	New York[15]	Joe Torre	95	65	.594
2002	Anaheim[17]	Mike Scioscia	99	63	.611
2003	New York[15]	Joe Torre	101	61	.623
2004	Boston[9]	Terry Francona	98	64	.605

*Split season because of players' strike. 1. World Series winner. 2. No World Series. 3. Defeated Minnesota, Western Division winner, in playoff. 4. Defeated Oakland, Western Division Leader, in playoff. 5. Defeated Detroit, Eastern Division winner, in playoff. 6. Defeated Baltimore, Eastern Division winner, in playoff. 7. Defeated Kansas City, Western Division winner, in playoff. 8. Defeated California, Western Division winner, in playoff. 9. Defeated New York, Eastern Division winner, in playoff. 10. Defeated Chicago, Western Division winner, in playoff. 11. Defeated Toronto, Eastern Division winner, in playoff. 12. Defeated Boston, Eastern division winner, in playoffs. 13. Defeated Seattle Mariners, Western Division winner, in playoff. 14. Defeated Cleveland Indians, Central Division winner, in playoff. 15. Defeated Boston Red Sox, Eastern Division wild-card team, in playoffs. 16. Defeated Seattle Mariners, Western Division wild-card team, in playoff. 17. Defeated Minnesota Twins, Central Division winner, in playoff.

NATIONAL LEAGUE PENNANT WINNERS

Year	Club	Manager	Won	Lost	Pct
1876	Chicago	Albert G. Spalding	52	14	.788
1877	Boston	Harry Wright	31	17	.646
1878	Boston	Harry Wright	41	19	.683
1879	Providence	George Wright	- 55	23	.705
1880	Chicago	Adrian C. Anson	67	17	.798
1881	Chicago	Adrian C. Anson	56	28	.667
1882	Chicago	Adrian C. Anson	55	29	.655
1883	Boston	John F. Morrill	63	35	.643
1884	Providence	Frank C. Bancroft	84	28	.750
1885	Chicago	Adrian C. Anson	87	25	.777
1886	Chicago	Adrian C. Anson	90	34	.726
1887	Detroit	W. H. Watkins	79	45	.637
1888	New York	James J. Mutrie	84	47	.641
1889	New York	James J. Mutrie	83	43	.659

Year	Club	Manager	Won	Lost	Pct	Year	Club	Manager	Won	Lost	Pct
1890	Brooklyn	Wm. H. McGunnigle	86	43	.667	1948	Boston	Wm. H. Southworth	91	62	.595
1891	Boston	Frank G. Selee	87	51	.630	1949	Brooklyn	Burton E. Shotton	97	57	.630
1892	Boston	Frank G. Selee	102	48	.680	1950	Philadelphia	Edwin M. Sawyer	91	63	.591
1893	Boston	Frank G. Selee	86	44	.662	1951	New York	Leo E. Durocher	98	59	.624
1894	Baltimore	Edward H. Hanlon	89	39	.695	1952	Brooklyn	Charles W. Dressen	96	57	.630
1895	Baltimore	Edward H. Hanlon	87	43	.669	1953	Brooklyn	Charles W. Dressen	105	49	.682
1896	Baltimore	Edward H. Hanlon	90	39	.698	1954	New York[2]	Leo E. Durocher	97	57	.630
1897	Boston	Frank G. Selee	93	39	.705	1955	Brooklyn[2]	Walter Alston	98	55	.641
1898	Boston	Frank G. Selee	102	47	.685	1956	Brooklyn	Walter Alston	93	61	.604
1899	Brooklyn	Edward H. Hanlon	88	42	.677	1957	Milwaukee[2]	Fred Haney	95	59	.617
1900	Brooklyn	Edward H. Hanlon	82	54	.603	1958	Milwaukee	Fred Haney	92	62	.597
1901	Pittsburgh	Fred C. Clarke	90	49	.647	1959	Los Angeles[2]	Walter Alston	88	68	.564
1902	Pittsburgh	Fred C. Clarke	103	36	.741	1960	Pittsburgh[2]	Danny Murtaugh	95	59	.617
1903	Pittsburgh	Fred C. Clarke	91	49	.650	1961	Cincinnati	Fred Hutchinson	93	61	.604
1904	New York[1]	John J. McGraw	106	47	.693	1962	San Francisco	Alvin Dark	103	62	.624
1905	New York[2]	John J. McGraw	105	48	.686	1963	Los Angeles[2]	Walter Alston	99	63	.611
1906	Chicago	Frank L. Chance	116	36	.763	1964	St. Louis[2]	Johnny Keane	93	69	.574
1907	Chicago[2]	Frank L. Chance	107	45	.704	1965	Los Angeles[2]	Walter Alston	97	65	.599
1908	Chicago[2]	Frank L. Chance	99	55	.643	1966	Los Angeles	Walter Alston	95	67	.586
1909	Pittsburgh[2]	Fred C. Clarke	110	42	.724	1967	St. Louis[2]	Red Schoendienst	101	60	.627
1910	Chicago	Frank L. Chance	104	50	.675	1968	St. Louis	Red Schoendienst	97	65	.599
1911	New York	John J. McGraw	99	54	.647	1969	New York[2,3]	Gil Hodges	100	62	.617
1912	New York	John J. McGraw	103	48	.682	1970	Cincinnati[4]	Sparky Anderson	102	60	.630
1913	New York	John J. McGraw	101	51	.664	1971	Pittsburgh[2,3]	Danny Murtaugh	97	65	.599
1914	Boston[2]	George T. Stallings	94	59	.614	1972	Cincinnati[4]	Sparky Anderson	95	59	.617
1915	Philadelphia	Patrick J. Moran	90	62	.592	1973	New York[6]	Yogi Berra	82	79	.509
1916	Brooklyn	Wilbert Robinson	94	60	.610	1974	Los Angeles[4]	Walter Alston	102	60	.630
1917	New York	John J. McGraw	98	56	.636	1975	Cincinnati[2,4]	Sparky Anderson	108	54	.667
1918	Chicago	Fred L. Mitchell	84	45	.651	1976	Cincinnati[2,7]	Sparky Anderson	102	60	.630
1919	Cincinnati[2]	Patrick J. Moran	96	44	.686	1977	Los Angeles[7]	Tom Lasorda	98	64	.605
1920	Brooklyn	Wilbert Robinson	93	61	.604	1978	Los Angeles[7]	Tom Lasorda	95	67	.586
1921	New York[2]	John J. McGraw	94	59	.614	1979	Pittsburgh[2,6]	Chuck Tanner	98	64	.605
1922	New York[2]	John J. McGraw	93	61	.604	1980	Philadelphia[2,8]	Dallas Green	91	71	.562
1923	New York	John J. McGraw	95	58	.621	1981	Los Angeles[2,9]	Tom Lasorda	63	47	.573
1924	New York	John J. McGraw	93	60	.608	1982	St. Louis[2,3]	Whitey Herzog	92	70	.568
1925	Pittsburgh[2]	Wm. B. McKechnie	95	58	.621	1983	Philadelphia[10]	Paul Owens	90	72	.556
1926	St. Louis[2]	Rogers Hornsby	89	65	.578	1984	San Diego[11]	Dick Williams	92	70	.568
1927	Pittsburgh	Donie Bush	94	60	.610	1985	St. Louis[11]	Whitey Herzog	101	61	.623
1928	St. Louis	Wm. B. McKechnie	95	59	.617	1986	New York[2,8]	Dave Johnson	108	54	.667
1929	Chicago	Joseph V. McCarthy	98	54	.645	1987	St. Louis[5]	Whitey Herzog	95	67	.586
1930	St. Louis	Gabby Street	92	62	.597	1988	Los Angeles[2,12]	Tom Lasorda	94	67	.584
1931	St. Louis[2]	Gabby Street	101	53	.656	1989	San Francisco[12]	Roger Craig	92	70	.568
1932	Chicago	Charles J. Grimm	90	64	.584	1990	Cincinnati[2,4]	Lou Piniella	91	71	.562
1933	New York[2]	William H. Terry	91	61	.599	1991	Atlanta[4]	Bobby Cox	94	68	.580
1934	St. Louis[2]	Frank F. Frisch	95	58	.621	1992	Atlanta[4]	Bobby Cox	98	64	.605
1935	Chicago	Charles J. Grimm	100	54	.649	1993	Philadelphia[3]	Jim Fregosi	97	65	.599
1936	New York	William H. Terry	92	62	.597	1994	Strike ended season Aug. 11. No playoffs, no pennant winner.				
1937	New York	William H. Terry	95	57	.625						
1938	Chicago	Gabby Hartnett	89	63	.586	1995	Atlanta[2,13]	Bobby Cox	90	54	.625
1939	Cincinnati	Wm. B. McKechnie	97	57	.630	1996	Atlanta[14]	Bobby Cox	96	66	.593
1940	Cincinnati[2]	Wm. B. McKechnie	100	53	.654	1997	Florida[2,15]	Jim Leyland	92	70	.568
1941	Brooklyn	Leo E. Durocher	100	54	.649	1998	San Diego[16]	Bruce Bochy	98	64	.605
1942	St. Louis[2]	Wm. H. Southworth	106	48	.688	1999	Atlanta[17]	Bobby Cox	103	59	.636
1943	St. Louis	Wm. H. Southworth	105	49	.682	2000	New York[18]	Bobby Valentine	94	68	.580
1944	St. Louis[2]	Wm. H. Southworth	105	49	.682	2001	Arizona[16]	Bob Brenly	92	70	.568
1945	Chicago	Charles J. Grimm	98	56	.636	2002	San Francisco[14]	Dusty Baker	95	66	.590
1946	St. Louis[2]	Edwin H. Dyer	98	58	.628	2003	Florida[19]	Jack McKeon	91	71	.562
1947	Brooklyn	Burton E. Shotton	94	60	.610	2004	St. Louis[20]	Tony La Russa	105	57	.648

*Split season because of players' strike. 1. No World Series. 2. World Series winner. 3. Defeated Atlanta, Western Division winner, in playoff. 4. Defeated Pittsburgh, Eastern Division winner, in playoff. 5. Defeated San Francisco, Western Division winner, in playoff. 6. Defeated Cincinnati, Western Division winner, in playoff. 7. Defeated Philadelphia, Eastern Division winner, in playoff. 8. Defeated Houston, Western Division winner, in playoff. 9. Defeated Montreal, Eastern Division winner, in playoff. 10. Defeated Los Angeles, Western Division winner, in playoff. 11. Defeated Chicago, Eastern Division champion, in playoff. 12. Defeated New York, Eastern Division winner, in playoff. 13. Defeated Cincinnati, Central Division winner, in playoff. 14. Defeated St. Louis, Central Division winner, in playoff. 15. Eastern Division wildcard Florida defeated Atlanta, Eastern Division winner, in playoff. 16. Defeated Atlanta, Eastern Division winner, in playoff. 17. Defeated New York, Eastern Division wild card team, in playoff. 18. Eastern Division wild card New York defeated Central Division winner St. Louis in playoff. 19. Defeated Chicago, Central Division champion, in playoff. 20. Defeated Houston, Central Division wild card team, in playoff.

2004 WORLD SERIES

Boston Red Sox defeated St. Louis Cardinals, 4 games to 0

Series MVP—Manny Ramirez

1st Game, at Boston, Oct. 23, 2004

					R	H	E
St. Louis	0 1 1	3 0 2	0 2 0	—	9	11	1
Boston	4 0 3	0 0 0	2 2 x	—	11	13	4

Pitchers—Boston: Wakefield, Arroyo, Timlin, Embree, Foulke. St. Louis: Williams, Haren, Calero, King, Eldred, Tavarez. Winner: Foulke. Loser: Tavarez.

2nd Game, at Boston, Oct. 24, 2004

					R	H	E
St. Louis	0 0 0	1 0 0	0 1 0	—	2	5	0
Boston	2 0 0	2 0 2	0 0 x	—	6	8	4

Pitchers—Boston: Schilling, Embree, Timlin, Foulke. St. Louis: Morris, Eldred, King, Marquis, Reyes. Winner: Schilling. Loser: Morris.

3rd Game, at St. Louis, Oct. 26, 2004

					R	H	E
Boston	1 0 0	1 2 0	0 0 0	—	4	9	0
St. Louis	0 0 0	0 0 0	0 0 1	—	1	4	0

Pitchers—Boston: Martinez, Timlin, Foulke. St. Louis: Suppan, Reyes, Calero, King, Tavarez. Winner: Martinez. Loser: Suppan.

4th Game, at St. Louis, Oct. 27, 2004

					R	H	E
Boston	1 0 2	0 0 0	0 0 0	—	3	9	0
St. Louis	0 0 0	0 0 0	0 0 0	—	0	4	0

Pitchers—Boston: Lowe, Arroyo, Embree, Foulke. St. Louis: Marquis, Haren, Isringhausen. Winner: Lowe. Loser: Marquis. Save: Foulke.

College World Series

Johnny Rosenblatt Stadium, Omaha Nebr., June 17–26, 2005

Bracket One

Florida 6, Tennessee 4

Nebraska 5, Arizona State 3

Arizona State 4, Tennessee 2

Florida 7, Nebraska 4

Arizona State 8, Nebraska 7

Arizona State 6, Florida 1

Florida 6, Arizona State 3

Bracket Two

Tulane 3, Oregon State 1

Texas 5, Baylor 1

Baylor 4, Oregon State 3

Texas 5, Tulane 0

Baylor 8, Tulane 7

Texas 4, Baylor 3

Championship Series—Texas wins series

Texas 4, Florida 2

Texas 6, Florida 1

Soccer

The early history of the sport is uncertain. A form of the game in which a leather ball was dribbled was played in China as early as the 4th century B.C. The Romans played a variation of soccer which eventually spread throughout Europe. British schools and universities played soccer (known as football) during the 1800s, however, each school used different sets of rules and the number of players varied. This difficulty was corrected on Oct. 26, 1863, when the Football Association (FA) was formed in London for the purpose of unifying the rules of the game.

The Federation of International Football Associations (FIFA) was created in 1913 as a world governing body to coordinate all of the national associations in the world. The FIFA held the first World Cup Championship tournament in 1930 in Montevideo, Uruguay. Today, soccer is the world's most popular sport. The first FIFA Women's World Cup was held in 1991 with the United States winning the title.

WORLD CUP

(W) indicates Women's World Cup

1930 Uruguay	1954 West Germany	1978 Argentina	1995 Norway (W)
1934 Italy	1958 Brazil	1982 Italy	1998 France
1938 Italy	1962 Brazil	1986 Argentina	1999 United States (W)
1942 No competition	1966 England	1990 West Germany	2002 Brazil
1946 No competition	1970 Brazil	1991 United States (W)	2003 Germany (W)
1950 Uruguay	1974 West Germany	1994 Brazil	

WOMEN'S WORLD CUP—2003

SEMIFINALS
Germany 3, United States 0
Sweden 2, Canada 1

THIRD PLACE
United States 3, Canada 1

CHAMPIONSHIP
Germany 2, Sweden 1

WORLD CUP—2002

QUARTERFINALS
Brazil 2, England 1
Germany 1, United States 0
South Korea 0, Spain 0 (South Korea won 5–3 in shootout)
Turkey 1, Senegal 0

SEMIFINALS
Germany 1, South Korea 0
Brazil 1, Turkey 0
THIRD PLACE
Turkey 3, South Korea 2

CHAMPIONSHIP
Brazil 2, Germany 0
Goals scored: Ronaldo 2 (67th min and 79th min)

WORLD CUP
All-Time Top Ten

	Country	App	Gm	Record (W–L–T)	Pts	GF	GA		Country	App	Gm	Record (W–L–T)	Pts	GF	GA
1.	Brazil	17	87	60–13–14	141	191	82	7.	France	11	44	21–16–7	49	86	61
2.	Germany	15	85	50–17–18	123	176	106	8.	Sweden	10	42	15–16–10	42	71	65
3.	Italy	15	70	39–14–17	96	110	67	9.	Russia	9	37	17–14–6	41	64	44
4.	Argentina	13	60	30–19–11	72	102	71	10.	Yugoslavia	9	37	16–13–8	40	60	46
5.	England	11	50	26–13–15	61	68	45		Uruguay	10	40	15–15–10	40	65	57
6.	Spain	11	45	20–15–10	54	71	53								

MAJOR LEAGUE SOCCER 2005 STANDINGS

(As of Sept. 14, 2005. *See* www.infoplease.com/2005soccer for updated statistics.)

The GF and GA columns refer to Goals For and Goals Against in regulation play.

EASTERN CONFERENCE

Team	GP	W	L	T	Pts	GF	GA
New England Revolution	26	15	5	6	51	46	27
D.C. United	27	13	9	5	44	46	31
Kansas City Wizards	27	11	7	9	42	45	35
Chicago Fire	26	13	10	3	42	43	42
MetroStars	26	9	7	10	37	41	37
Columbus Crew	25	9	13	3	30	25	35

WESTERN CONFERENCE

Team	GP	W	L	T	Pts	GF	GA
San Jose Earthquakes[1]	26	14	4	8	50	41	26
Los Angeles Galaxy	27	11	11	5	38	36	34
FC Dallas	25	10	9	6	36	40	36
Colorado Rapids	25	9	12	4	31	31	32
Real Salt Lake	25	5	16	4	19	24	51
Chivas USA	27	3	19	5	14	27	59

1. Clinched playoffs.

2005 REGULAR SEASON

(As of Sept. 14, 2005. *See* www.infoplease.com/2005soccer for updated statistics.)

GOAL SCORING LEADERS

	GP	Goals
Taylor Twellman, New England	20	14
Jaime Moreno, DC	24	12
Jeff Cunningham, Colorado	20	11
Landon Donovan, Los Angeles	18	11
Carlos Ruiz, Dallas	19	11
Christian Gomez, DC	27	9
Amado Guevara, MetroStars	21	9
Jason Kreis, Salt Lake	24	9
Scott Sealy, Kansas City	24	9
Clint Dempsey, New England	20	8
Pat Noonan, New England	17	8

SHOTS LEADERS

	GP	No
Ronnie O'Brien, Dallas	24	72
Chris Klein, Kansas City	26	70
Taylor Twellman, New England	20	66
Youri Djorkaeff, MetroStars	18	65
Jason Kreis, Salt Lake	24	65
Carlos Ruiz, Dallas	19	63
Jamie Moreno, DC	24	62
Davy Arnaud, Kansas City	27	56
Ante Razov, MetroStars	20	56
Christian Gomez, DC	27	55

ASSIST LEADERS

	GP	No
Dwayne De Rosario, San Jose	22	11
Clint Dempsey, New England	20	9
Ronnie O'Brien, Dallas	24	9
Josh Wolff, Kansas City	17	9
Ronald Cerritos, San Jose	26	8
Brad Davis, San Jose	17	8
Simon Elliott, Columbus	25	8
Christian Gomez, DC	27	8
Chris Klein, Kansas City	26	8
Justin Mapp, Chicago	23	8

LEADING GOALKEEPERS

	Gp	Shts	Svs	GA	GAA
Pat Onstad, San Jose	26	115	89	26	1.00
Jonny Walker, Columbus	11	48	37	11	1.00
Matt Reis, New England	25	125	100	25	1.00
Nick Rimando, DC	26	114	84	30	1.15
Zach Wells, MetroStars	17	90	69	21	1.24
Kevin Hartman, Los Angeles	27	117	83	34	1.26
Joe Cannon, Colorado	25	122	90	32	1.28
Bo Oshoniyi, Kansas City	27	123	88	35	1.30

Extreme Sports

2005 SUMMER EXTREME GAMES
(Los Angeles, Calif., Aug. 4–7, 2005)

Skateboard: Danny Way (men's big air), Pierre-Luc Gagnon (men's vert), Elissa Steamer (women's street), Cara-Beth Burnside (women's vert), Bob Burnquist (men's vert best trick)

BMX: Jamie Bestwick (vert), Dave Mirra (park), Corey Bohan (dirt), Jamie Bestwick (best trick)

Moto X: Jeremy Stenberg (best trick), Doug Henry (super moto), Tommy Clowers (step up), Travis Pastrana (freestyle)

Wakeboarding: Dallas Friday (women), Danny Harf (men)

Surfing: Team East

History of the Income Tax in the United States

Source: Tax Foundation.

The nation had few taxes in its early history. From 1791 to 1802, the United States government was supported by internal taxes on distilled spirits, carriages, refined sugar, tobacco and snuff, property sold at auction, corporate bonds, and slaves. The high cost of the War of 1812 brought about the nation's first sales taxes on gold, silverware, jewelry, and watches. In 1817, however, Congress did away with all internal taxes, relying on tariffs on imported goods to provide sufficient funds for running the government.

In 1862, in order to support the Civil War effort, Congress enacted the nation's first income tax law. It was a forerunner of our modern income tax in that it was based on the principles of graduated, or progressive, taxation and of withholding income at the source. During the Civil War, a person earning from $600 to $10,000 per year paid tax at the rate of 3%. Those with incomes of more than $10,000 paid taxes at a higher rate. Additional sales and excise taxes were added, and an "inheritance" tax also made its debut. In 1866, internal revenue collections reached their highest point in the nation's 90-year history—more than $310 million, an amount not reached again until 1911.

The Act of 1862 established the office of Commissioner of Internal Revenue. The Commissioner was given the power to assess, levy, and collect taxes, and the right to enforce the tax laws through seizure of property and income and through prosecution. The powers and authority remain very much the same today.

In 1868, Congress again focused its taxation efforts on tobacco and distilled spirits and eliminated the income tax in 1872. It had a short-lived revival in 1894 and 1895. In the latter year, the U.S. Supreme Court decided that the income tax was unconstitutional because it was not apportioned among the states in conformity with the Constitution.

In 1913, the 16th Amendment to the Constitution made the income tax a permanent fixture in the U.S. tax system. The amendment gave Congress legal authority to tax income and resulted in a revenue law that taxed incomes of both individuals and corporations. In fiscal year 1918, annual internal revenue collections for the first time passed the billion-dollar mark, rising to $5.4 billion by 1920. With the advent of World War II, employment increased, as did tax collections—to $7.3 billion. The withholding tax on wages was introduced in 1943 and was instrumental in increasing the number of taxpayers to 60 million and tax collections to $43 billion by 1945.

In 1981, Congress enacted the largest tax cut in U.S. history, approximately $750 billion over six years. The tax reduction, however, was partially offset by two tax acts, in 1982 and 1984, that attempted to raise approximately $265 billion.

On Oct. 22, 1986, President Reagan signed into law the Tax Reform Act of 1986, one of the most far-reaching reforms of the United States tax system since the adoption of the income tax. The top tax rate on individual income was lowered from 50% to 28%, the lowest it had been since 1916. Tax preferences were eliminated to make up most of the revenue. In an attempt to remain revenue neutral, the act called for a $120 billion increase in business taxation and a corresponding decrease in individual taxation over a five-year period.

On Aug. 10, 1993, President Clinton signed the Revenue Reconciliation Act of 1993 into law. The act's purpose was to reduce by approximately $496 billion the federal deficit that would otherwise accumulate in fiscal years 1994 through 1998. In 1997, Clinton signed another tax act. The act, which cut taxes by $152 billion, included a cut in capital-gains tax for individuals, a $500 per child tax credit, and tax incentives for education.

President George W. Bush signed tax cuts into law in 2001, 2002, 2003, and 2004. The largest was the first, the Economic Growth and Tax Relief Reconciliation Act of 2001. It was estimated to save taxpayers $1.3 trillion over ten years, making it the third largest tax cut since World War II, behind only the Kennedy tax cut signed by Johnson in 1964 and the Reagan tax cut in 1981. The Bush tax cut created a new lowest rate, 10% for the first several thousand dollars earned. It also established a slow schedule of incremental tax cuts that would eventually double the child tax credit from $500 to $1,000, adjust brackets so that middle-income couples owed the same tax as comparable singles, cut the top four tax rates (28% to 25%; 31% to 28%; 36% to 33%; and 39.6% to 35%).

The Job Creation and Workers Assistance Act of 2002 provided tax relief to businesses and included a 13-week extension on unemployment insurance and tax breaks for taxpayers affected by the Sept. 11, 2001, terrorist attacks. The Jobs and Growth Tax Relief and Reconciliation Act of 2003 accelerated the tax rate cuts that had been enacted in 2001, and temporarily reduced the tax rate on capital gains and dividends to 15%. In 2004, the U.S. was forced to eliminate a corporate tax provision that had been ruled illegal by the World Trade Organization. Along with that tax hike, Congress passed a cornucopia of tax breaks, which for individuals included an option to deduct the payment of whichever state taxes were higher, sales or income taxes.

Internal Revenue Service

The Internal Revenue Service (IRS), a bureau of the U.S. Treasury Department, is the federal agency charged with the administration of the tax laws passed by Congress.

Operations involving most taxpayers are carried out in district offices and service centers. District offices are organized into Resources Management, Examination, Collection, Taxpayer Service,

Internal Revenue Service

	2004	2000	1996	1995	1994	1970
U.S. population (in thousands)	294,721	283,212	270,581	267,456	264,301	204,878
Number of IRS employees	98,735	97,074	106,642	112,024	110,665	68,683
Cost to govt. of collecting $100 in taxes	$0.48	$0.39	$0.49	$0.54	$0.57	$0.45
Tax per capita	$6,848.87	$7,404.04	$5,493.90	$5,143.77	$4,829.59	$955.31
Collections by principal sources (in thousands of dollars)						
Total IRS collections	$2,018,502,103	$2,096,916,925	$1,486,546,674	$1,375,731,835	$1,276,466,776	$195,722,096
Income and profits taxes						
Individual	$990,248,760	$1,137,077,702	$745,313,276	$675,779,337	$619,819,153	$103,651,585
Corporation	$230,619,359	$235,654,894	$189,054,791	$174,422,173	$154,204,684	$35,036,983
Employment taxes	$717,247,296	$639,651,814	$492,365,178	$465,405,305	$443,831,352	$37,449,188
Estate and gift taxes	$25,579,462	$29,721,620	$17,591,817	$15,144,394	$15,606,793	$3,680,076
Alcohol taxes	(1)	(1)	(1)	(1)	(1)	$4,746,382
Tobacco taxes	(1)	(1)	(1)	(1)	(1)	$2,094,212
Excise taxes	$54,807,225	$54,810,895	$42,221,611	$44,980,627	$43,004,794	$2,380,609

NOTE: For fiscal year ending Sept. 30th. 1. Alcohol and tobacco tax collections are now collected and reported by the Bureau of Alcohol, Tobacco, and Firearms. *Source:* 2004 IRS Data Book.

Employee Plans and Exempt Organizations, and Criminal Investigation. All tax returns are filed with the service centers, where the IRS computer operations are located.

Prior to 1987, all tax return processing was performed by hand. In an attempt to improve the speed and efficiency of the manual processing procedure, the IRS began testing an electronic return filing system beginning with the filing of 1985 returns.

The two most significant results of the test were that refunds for the electronically filed returns were issued more quickly and the tax processing error rate was significantly lower when compared to paper returns. Electronic filing of individual income tax returns with refunds became an operational program in selected areas for the 1987 processing year.

Auditing Tax Returns

Most taxpayers' contacts with the IRS arise through the auditing of their tax returns. The service has been empowered by Congress to inquire about all persons who may be liable for any tax and to obtain for review the books and/or records pertinent to those taxpayers' returns.

In 2002 the IRS announced a new auditing policy that focuses less on wage earners—particularly those earning less than $100,000—and instead looks more closely at the very wealthy and business owners, as well as on complex business partnerships, tax shelters, and offshore accounts. A computer program helps to determine which returns have the potential for hidden or unreported income and thus merit an audit.

The Appeals Process

Taxpayers who, after audit of their tax returns, disagree with a proposed change in their tax liabilities are entitled to an independent review of their cases. Taxpayers are able to seek an immediate, informal appeal with the Appeals Office. If, however, the dispute arises from a field audit and the amount in question exceeds $10,000, a taxpayer must submit a written protest. Alternatively, the taxpayer can wait for the examiner's report and then request consideration by the Appeals Office and file a protest if necessary. Taxpayers may represent themselves or be represented by an attorney, accountant, or any other adviser authorized to practice before the IRS. Taxpayers can forgo their right to the above process and await receipt of a deficiency notice. At this juncture, taxpayers can either (1) not pay the deficiency and petition the Tax Court by a required deadline or (2) pay the deficiency and file a claim for refund with the District Director's office. If the claim is not allowed, a suit for refund may be brought either in the District Court or the Claims Court.

Percentages of Income Earned and Federal Individual Income Taxes Paid

Tax Share / Income Share

Income Group	Tax Share	Income Share
Top 1%	33.7%	16.1%
Top 5%	53.8%	30.6%
Top 10%	65.7%	41.8%
Top 25%	83.9%	64.4%
Top 50%	96.5%	85.8%
Bottom 50%	14.2%	3.5%

NOTE: Figures for fiscal year 2003. *Source:* Tax Foundation. Web: http://taxfoundation.org

Federal Individual Income Tax

Tax Brackets—2005 Taxable Income

Joint return	Single taxpayer	Rate
$0–$14,600	$0–$7,300	10.0%
14,601–59,400	7,301–29,700	15.0
59,401–119,950	29,701–71,950	25.0
119,951 –182,800	71,951–150,150	28.0
182,801–326,450	150,151–326,450	33.0
326,451 and up	326,451 and up	35.0

Source: Internal Revenue Service. Web: www.irs.gov.

The federal individual income tax is levied on the worldwide income of U.S. citizens and resident aliens and on certain types of U.S. source income of nonresidents. For a nonitemizer, "tax table income" is adjusted gross income less $3,000 for each personal exemption and the standard deduction. If a taxpayer itemizes, tax table income is adjusted gross income minus total itemized deductions and personal exemptions. In addition, individuals may also be subject to the alternative minimum tax.

Who Must File a Return[1]

If your filing status is:	Age at end of 2004	Gross income at least
Single	Under 65	$7,950
	65 or older	9,150
Married filing jointly	Under 65 (both spouses)	15,900
	65 or older (one spouse)	16,850
	65 or older (both spouses)	17,800
Married filing separately	Any age	3,100
Head of household	Under 65	10,250
	65 or older	11,450
Qualifying widow(er) with dependent child	Under 65	12,800
	65 or older	13,750

1. In 2004.

Adjusted Gross Income

Gross income consists of wages and salaries, unemployment compensation, tips and gratuities, interest, dividends, annuities, rents and royalties, up to 85% of Social Security benefits if the recipient's income exceeds a base amount, and certain other types of income. Among the items excluded from gross income, and thus not subject to tax, are public assistance benefits and interest on exempt securities (mostly state and local bonds).

Adjusted gross income is determined by subtracting from gross income: alimony paid, penalties on early withdrawal of savings, payments to an IRA (reduced proportionately based upon adjusted gross income levels if taxpayer is an active participant in an employer maintained retirement plan), payments to a Keogh retirement plan, and self-employed health insurance payments and moving expenses.

Itemized Deductions

Taxpayers may itemize deductions or take the standard deduction. The standard deduction amounts for 2004 were as follows: $4,850 for single persons, $7,150 for heads of household, $9,700 for married filing jointly or qualifying widower, and $4,850 for married filing separately. Taxpayers 65 and older or blind are entitled to an additional standard deduction of $950 to $1,200.

In itemizing deductions, the following are major items that may be deducted in 2004: state and local income and property taxes, charitable contributions, employee moving expenses, medical expenses (exceeding 7.5% of adjusted gross income), casualty losses (only the amount over the $100 floor which exceeds 10% of adjusted gross income), mortgage interest, and miscellaneous deductions (deductible only to the extent by which cumulatively they exceed 2% of adjusted gross income).

Personal Exemptions

Personal exemptions are available to the taxpayer for himself, his spouse, and his dependents. The 2004 amount was $3,100 for each individual. No exemption is allowed to a taxpayer who can be claimed as a dependent on another taxpayer's return.

Credits

Taxpayers can reduce their income tax liability by claiming the benefit of certain tax credits. Each dollar of tax credit offsets a dollar of tax liability. The following are a few of the available tax credits.

Certain low income households may claim an Earned Income Credit. The maximum Earned Income Credit for 2004 was $390 for taxpayers with no qualifying children, $2,604 for taxpayers with one qualifying child, $4,300 for taxpayers with two or more qualifying children. The maximum credit is reduced if earned income or adjusted gross income exceeds $13,750 for taxpayers with one or more children, or exceeds $6,250 for taxpayers with no children. For families filing jointly with no qualifying children, the credit is zero if earned income or adjusted gross income exceeds $12,490; for families with one qualifying child, the credit is zero if earned income or adjusted gross income exceeds $31,338; and for taxpayers with two or more qualifying children, the credit is zero if earned income or adjusted gross income exceeds $35,458. The earned income credit is a refundable credit.

A credit for Child and Dependent Care Expenses is available for amounts paid to care for a qualifying child or other dependent so that the taxpayer can work or look for work. The credit is up to 30% (depending on adjusted gross income) of up to $3,000 of employment-related expenses for one qualifying child or dependent and up to $6,000 of employment-related expenses for two qualifying individuals.

The elderly and those under 65 who are retired under total disability may be entitled to a credit of

Number of Individual Income Tax Returns Filed Electronically

Year	Number of returns (in thousands)	Percentage increase
1995	11,807	n.a.
1996	14,968	26.8%
1997	19,136	27.8
1998	24,580	28.4
1999	29,349	19.4
2000	35,394	20.6
2001	40,245	13.7
2002	46,890	16.5
2003	52,945	12.9
2004	61,507	16.2

Source: 2004 IRS Data Book.

State Taxes on Individuals

State	Sales/use tax (percent)[1]	Income tax (percent)[2]	State	Sales/use tax (percent)[1]	Income tax (percent)[2]
Alabama	4%	2.0%–5.0%	Nebraska	5.5%	2.56%–6.84%
Alaska	none	none	Nevada	6.5	none
Arizona	5.6	2.87–5.04	New Hampshire	none	(3)
Arkansas	6	1.0–7.0	New Jersey	6	1.4–8.97
California	6.25	1.0–9.3	New Mexico	5	1.7–6.0
Colorado	2.9	4.63	New York	4.25	4.0–7.70
Connecticut	6	3.0–5.0	North Carolina	4.5	6.0–8.25
Delaware	none	2.2–5.95	North Dakota	5	2.1–5.54
Florida	6	none	Ohio	6	0.743–7.5
Georgia	4	1.0–6.0	Oklahoma	4.5	0.5–6.65
Hawaii	4	1.4–8.25	Oregon	none	5.0–9.0
Idaho	6	1.6–7.8	Pennsylvania	6	3.07
Illinois	6.25	3.0	Rhode Island	7	25.0[4]
Indiana	6	3.4	South Carolina	5	2.5–7.0
Iowa	5	0.36–8.98	South Dakota	4	none
Kansas	5.3	3.5–6.45	Tennessee	7	(3)
Kentucky	6	2.0–6.0	Texas	6.25	none
Louisiana	4	2.0–6.0	Utah	4.75	2.3–7.0
Maine	5	2.0–8.5	Vermont	6	3.6–9.5
Maryland	5	2.0–4.75	Virginia	4	2.0–5.75
Massachusetts	5	5.3	Washington	6.5	none
Michigan	6	3.9	West Virginia	6	3.0–6.5
Minnesota	6.5	5.35–7.85	Wisconsin	5	4.6–6.75
Mississippi	7	3.0–5.0	Wyoming	4	none
Missouri	4.225	1.5–6.0	District of Columbia	5.75	5.0–9.0
Montana	none	2.0–6.9			

1. As of July 2004. Local and county taxes, if any, are additional. 2. As of January 1, 2005. Tax rate for individuals; unless otherwise noted, range denotes progressive structure: higher income pays higher rate. 3. State income tax is limited to dividends and interest. 4. Percentage of federal tax liability. *Source:* The Federation of Tax Administrators. Web: ewww.taxadmin.org.

up to $750 (if single) or $1,125 (if married and filing jointly). No credit is available if the taxpayer is single and has adjusted gross income of $17,500 or more. Similarly, the credit is unavailable to a married couple filing jointly if their adjusted gross income exceeds $25,000.

Effective for tax years beginning after Dec. 1, 1997, taxpayers who have qualifying children for whom the taxpayer may claim a dependency exemption and who are less than 17 years old as of the close of the tax year are entitled to the child tax credit. The amount of the credit for 2004 was $1,000. The child credit begins to phase out when AGI reaches $110,000 for joint filers and $75,000 for singles. Taxpayers who have three or more qualifying children may also be entitled to an additional credit.

Federal Estate and Gift Taxes

A Federal Estate Tax Return must generally be filed for the estate of every U.S. citizen or resident whose gross estate, taxable gifts, and specific exemptions exceed $1,500,000 for decedents dying in 2005, and according to the following table if dying in succeeding years:

Decedent dying in	Exclusion amount
2006, 2007, and 2008	$2,000,000
2009	3,500,000
2010	repealed
2011	1,000,000

The Economic Growth and Tax Relief Reconciliation Act of 2001 completely phases out the federal estate and gift tax by 2010. The tax rates are lowered and the exemption is raised between 2002 and 2009, and the tax is completely eliminated in 2010. However, the post-act law will bring the Estate and Gift Tax back into existence in 2011.

A unified credit of $202,050 is available to offset both estate and gift taxes. Any part of the credit used to offset gift taxes is not available to offset estate taxes. As a result, although they are still taxable as gifts, lifetime taxable transfers no longer cushion the impact of progressive estate tax rates. Lifetime transfers and transfers made at death are combined for estate tax rate purposes.

Gift taxes are computed by applying the uniform rate schedule to lifetime taxable transfers (after deducting the unified credit) and subtracting the taxes payable for prior taxable periods. In general, estate taxes are computed by applying the uniform rate schedule to cumulative transfers and subtracting the gift taxes paid. An appropriate adjustment is made for taxes on lifetime transfers—such as certain gifts within three years of death—in a decedent's estate.

For 2004, an annual gift tax exclusion is provided that permits tax-free gifts to each donee of $11,000 for each year. A husband and wife who agree to treat gifts to third persons as joint gifts can exclude up to $22,000 a year to each donee. An unlimited exclusion for medical expenses and school tuition both paid directly to the institution for the benefit of any donee is also available in addition to the annual gift tax exclusion.

Federal Corporation Taxes

Most large corporations are classified as C corporations and are required to file a federal corporate income tax return with the IRS every year. There are four basic rates—15%, 25%, 34%, and 35%—and two "bubble rates" of 39% and 38% which have the effect of taking away from high-income corporations the benefits of the lower rates.

If the corporation qualifies, it may elect to be an S corporation. These companies do not (with certain exceptions) pay corporate tax on income. Their income is instead passed through and taxed to shareholders. The reduction of individual income tax rates, passed in 2001 and accelerated in 2003, has greatly increased the number of firms that save taxes by organizing as S corporations.

In 2004, Congress enacted and the president signed the American Jobs Creation Act of 2004. It repealed the exclusion for extraterritorial income after that provision was ruled illegal by the World Trade Organization.

Corporate Tax Rates

Taxable income	Tax rate
First $50,000	15%
$50,001–$75,000	25%
$75,001–$100,000	34%
$100,001–$335,000	39%
$335,001–$10,000,000	34%
$10,000,001–$15,000,000	35%
$15,000,001–$18,333,333	38%
Over $18,333,333	35%

State Corporation Income and Franchise Taxes

Forty-five states impose a direct tax on corporations, measured at least partially by net income. Michigan, Nevada, South Dakota, Washington, and Wyoming are the exceptions, though Michigan imposes a value-added tax (VAT) and Washington a gross receipts tax. The states impose flat or progressive rates ranging from 2.3% to approximately 10.75%. Nearly all states follow the federal law in defining net income, but many provide for varying exclusions and adjustments.

A state is empowered to tax any net corporate income attributable to in-state activity no matter where the corporation is headquartered. Corporations must apportion their income among the states where they have a sufficient connection (the legal term is nexus) and pay tax in each of those states. Several states tax unincorporated businesses separately.

Federal Expenditures for Every Dollar of Taxes Sent to Washington

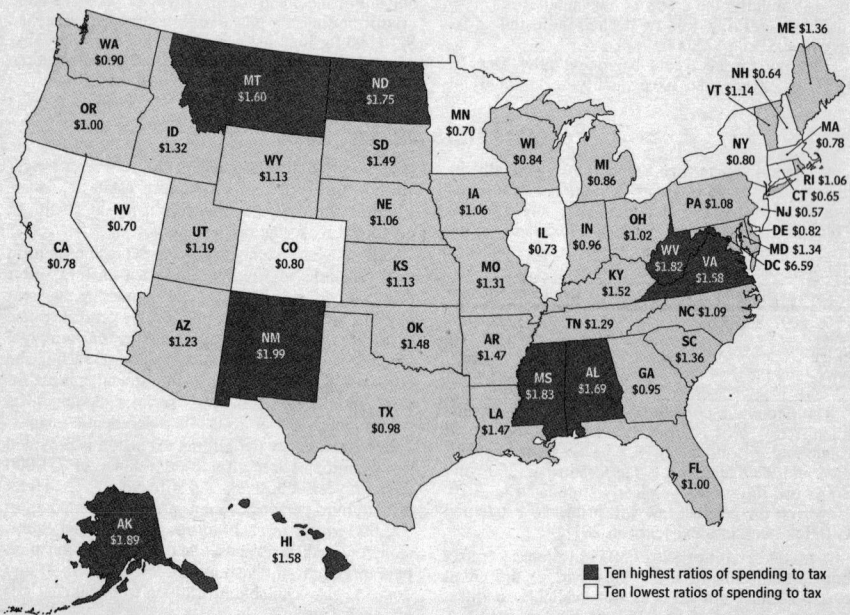

WA $0.90
OR $1.00
MT $1.60
ND $1.75
MN $0.70
ME $1.36
NH $0.64
VT $1.14
MA $0.78
ID $1.32
WY $1.13
SD $1.49
WI $0.84
MI $0.86
NY $0.80
RI $1.06
CT $0.65
NJ $0.57
NV $0.70
UT $1.19
CO $0.80
NE $1.06
IA $1.06
IL $0.73
IN $0.96
OH $1.02
PA $1.08
DE $0.82
MD $1.34
DC $6.59
CA $0.78
AZ $1.23
NM $1.99
KS $1.13
MO $1.31
KY $1.52
WV $1.82
VA $1.58
NC $1.09
OK $1.48
AR $1.47
TN $1.29
SC $1.36
TX $0.98
LA $1.47
MS $1.83
AL $1.69
GA $0.95
FL $1.00
AK $1.89
HI $1.58

■ Ten highest ratios of spending to tax
☐ Ten lowest ratios of spending to tax

NOTE: Figures for fiscal year 2003. *Source:* Tax Foundation. Web: http://taxfoundation.org

The Person of the Year

How "Lucky Lindy"—and a slow week for news—
gave birth to a memorable annual tradition

The founders of TIME Magazine, Henry Luce and Briton Haddon, were strong believers in the idea that history is shaped by the deeds of extraordinary men and women. This thesis, most memorably advanced by the British writer Thomas Carlyle, was well-suited to the American vision of the two Yale graduates, since it ran counter to the assertions of Karl Marx and others that history is made by impersonal economic and social forces.

TIME's insistence on the primacy of the individual finds its most memorable form in the magazine's annual designation of a Person of the Year—the individual whose actions most affected the course of the news within the last 12 months. But the magazine's signature annual tribute was not the result of high-level philosophizing: rather, it was driven by something far more important to journalists—a deadline.

The year was 1927; it was the last week in December. During the holiday season, the normal flow of public events had temporarily ebbed to a trickle. Looking to 1928, the editors at TIME were having trouble finding a newsworthy cover subject for the first issue of the new year. At the same time, they realized that they had passed up several opportunities during the year to put aviator Charles Lindbergh on its cover. Since his nonstop flight from New York to Paris in late May, the young pilot had been idolized—yet he had never appeared on the magazine's cover. So the editors came up with a new concept: instead of highlighting a personality of the week, it was decided that the cover for Jan. 2, 1928, would feature Lindbergh, and that beneath his likeness would be the words "Man of the Year."

A year later, the cover for TIME's first issue of 1929 revealed that its editors had named car magnate Walter P. Chrysler as Man of the Year for 1928—and it was obvious that an annual tradition had been born. Though TIME named a number of Women of the Year in the decades that followed, the editors eventually settled on the non-gender-specific term Person of the Year for the magazine's annual citation.

The term "Person of the Year"—redolent of countless Chamber of Commerce dinners—suggests to many people that it is awarded as an accolade. It is not. Rather, it designates the person who, in the editors' opinion, has most affected the course of history in the past twelve months—for good or for ill.

In 1938, for instance, Adolf Hitler completed his Anschluss of Austria and brokered the tragic agreement at Munich that put Czechoslovakia into his hands. However reluctantly, the editors concluded that Hitler's actions had most affected history's course, and he became the 1938 Man of the Year. Similarly, in 1979, Ayatullah Khomeini was named Man of the Year, even while he held Americans hostage in Teheran. TIME received more than 14,000 letters complaining about the choice.

After 75 years, the Person of the Year has become an institution: whereas in one sense it is a sort of intellectual parlor game, it also challenges TIME's editors and readers to reflect on the events of the past year critically, dispassionately, and rigorously. □

1927 Charles Lindbergh	1954 John Foster Dulles	1980 Ronald Reagan
1928 Walter P. Chrysler	1955 Harlow H. Curtice	1981 Lech Walesa
1929 Owen D. Young	1956 Hungarian Patriot	1982 The Personal Computer
1930 Mahatma Gandhi	1957 Nikita Khrushchev	1983 Ronald Reagan and
1931 Pierre Laval	1958 Charles DeGaulle	Yuri Andropov
1932 Franklin D. Roosevelt	1959 Dwight D. Eisenhower	1984 Peter Ueberroth
1933 Hugh S. Johnson	1960 U.S. Scientists	1985 Deng Xiaoping
1934 Franklin D. Roosevelt	1961 John F. Kennedy	1986 Corazon Aquino
1935 Haile Selassie	1962 Pope John XXIII	1987 Mikhail Gorbachev
1936 Wallis Warfield Simpson	1963 Rev. Martin Luther King, Jr.	1988 Endangered Earth
1937 Gen. and Mrs. Chiang	1964 Lyndon B. Johnson	1989 Mikhail Gorbachev
Kai-shek	1965 Gen. William Westmoreland	1990 George H. W. Bush
1938 Adolf Hitler	1966 Americans under 25	1991 Ted Turner
1939 Joseph Stalin	1967 Lyndon B. Johnson	1992 Bill Clinton
1940 Winston Churchill	1968 Astronauts Anders,	1993 The Peacemakers: Rabin,
1941 Franklin D. Roosevelt	Borman, Lovell	Arafat, Mandela, De Klerk
1942 Joseph Stalin	1969 The Middle Americans	1994 Pope John Paul II
1943 Gen. George C. Marshall	1970 Willy Brandt	1995 Newt Gingrich
1944 Gen. Dwight D. Eisenhower	1971 Richard M. Nixon	1996 Dr. David Ho
1945 Harry S. Truman	1972 Richard M. Nixon and	1997 Andrew Grove
1946 James F. Byrnes	Henry Kissinger	1998 Bill Clinton and
1947 Gen. George C. Marshall	1973 Judge John J. Sirica	Kenneth Starr
1948 Harry S. Truman	1974 King Faisal	1999 Jeff Bezos
1949 Winston Churchill	1975 American Women	2000 George W. Bush
1950 G.I. Joe	1976 Jimmy Carter	2001 Rudolph Giuliani
1951 Mohammed Mossadegh	1977 Anwar Sadat	2002 The Whistleblowers
1952 Queen Elizabeth II	1978 Deng Xiaoping	2003 The American Soldier
1953 Konrad Adenauer	1979 Ayatollah Khomeini	2004 George W. Bush

People in the News, 2005

Go to www.infoplease.com/2005newsmakers for additional entries.

Mahmoud Abbas (Abu Mazen), leader of the Palestine Liberation Organization, breezed to victory in January's election for president of the Palestinian Authority, winning 62% of the vote. Abbas succeeded former president Yasir Arafat, who died in Nov. 2004. At a summit meeting in Egypt in February, Abbas and Israeli prime minister Ariel Sharon agreed to a conditional cease-fire. International attention turned to Abbas in August, after Israel evacuated settlers from the Gaza Strip and parts of the West Bank, to see how he would handle the transition and control militant groups.

Jack Abramoff, high-powered Washington lobbyist, faced corruption investigations by two Senate committees and the FBI for allegedly defrauding Native American tribes—former clients—out of millions of dollars. Abramoff was also at the center of House majority leader Tom DeLay's ethics problems throughout 2005. News organizations reported that Abramoff gave expensive gifts to several DeLay aides and paid for trips taken by DeLay and other members of Congress in the late 1990s and early 2000s. House ethics rules prohibit lobbyists from financing congressional travel. In a separate scandal, Abramoff was indicted in August on charges that he defrauded lenders in the purchase of a $147.5 million casino cruise line in Florida in 2000.

Mahmoud Ahmadinejad, former mayor of Teheran and a hard-line conservative, was elected president of Iran in a runoff election in June. Ahmadinejad was highly popular among Iran's rural poor, who responded to his pledge to fight corruption among the country's elites. Unlike his predecessor, Mohammed Khatami, who frequently clashed with the country's supreme leader over reform, Ahmadinejad is a devout follower of Ayatollah Ali Khamenei. Ahmadinejad has announced plans to continue pursuing Iran's controversial nuclear program and has stated that "our nation . . . has no significant need for the United States."

Askar Akayev, former president of Kyrgyzstan, fled to Russia in March, after thousands of demonstrators took over the presidential palace in Bishkek to protest parliamentary elections that were widely considered flawed. He resigned in April and was succeeded by opposition leader Kurmanbek Bakiev. Once a popular leader, Akayev's standing diminished in recent years amid accusations of nepotism and corruption.

Kofi Annan, secretary general of the United Nations, in March proposed broad changes to the UN that included revamping the structure of the Security Council. Also in March, a committee investigating Iraq's oil-for-food program said Annan was not involved in the awarding of a $10 million contract to his son's employer, the Swiss company Cotecna Inspection. In its final report, released in September, the panel, headed by Paul Volcker, criticized Annan for not reining in corruption and management failures at the UN and for failing to investigate Kojo's potential conflicts of interest.

Lance Armstrong, American bicyclist, proved once again in July that he is indeed the King of the Mountains, as he breezed past his rivals to win a record-breaking seventh consecutive Tour de France race. He beat second-place finisher Ivan Basso by 4 min.

40 sec. Armstrong announced his retirement after the race. In 1996 Armstrong was diagnosed with cancer and given only a 50% chance to live.

Gloria Arroyo, president of the Philippines, faced a political crisis in the summer of 2005, after admitting to calling an election official during 2004's presidential race. A taped phone conversation between Arroyo and an election official suggested that she had tried to use her power to influence the outcome. In a televised address, Arroyo apologized for the "lapse of judgement." Several members of her cabinet quit over the scandal. Tens of thousands of protesters called for her resignation. The opposition filed an impeachment motion in July, which was rejected by Congress in September. In her state of the nation address, also in July, Arroyo proposed replacing the country's presidential system of government with a parliamentary one.

Buster Baxter, animated bunny and star of the PBS show *Postcards from Buster,* created a stir when he was criticized in January by Secretary of Education Margaret Spellings because an episode of the show included a lesbian couple. "Many parents would not want their young children exposed to the lifestyles portrayed in the episode," Spellings wrote to PBS. As a result of the controversy, PBS did not distribute the episode, primarily about maple sugaring in Vermont, to its stations.

Benedict XVI, formerly Cardinal Joseph Ratzinger, was named pope by the conclave of cardinals in April. He was born in Bavaria in 1927. Pope Benedict XVI is known as an accomplished scholar of theology and is considered an archconservative in his religious views. In the past few years he acted as Pope John Paul II's right-hand man and is expected to continue the policy of a "strong Rome," that is, keeping dioceses under tight control of Rome.

Tony Blair, prime minister of the United Kingdom, became the first Labour party leader to win a third term. Despite this victory, Blair's party was severely hurt in the May elections. The Labour party won just 36% of the national vote, the lowest percentage by a ruling party in British history. Blair acknowledged that the reason for the poor showing was Britain's involvement in the war in Iraq, which was widely unpopular. In July, London suffered a terrorist bombing that killed 52 and wounded 700. In response, the prime minister introduced tough new anti-terrorist legislation.

Robert Blake, actor, was acquitted by a California jury in March of the 2001 murder of his wife, Bonny Lee Bakley. He was also found not guilty of hiring two stuntmen to kill her. She was shot in the head in a car parked outside a California restaurant.

John Bolton, former state department official, was nominated by President Bush to become U.S. ambassador to the UN. His April confirmation hearings were rocky and contentious, with members of the Senate Foreign Relations Committee accusing Bolton of abusing his authority and berating subordinates who did not agree with his views on intelligence. Bolton has been an outspoken critic of the UN, once going as far as saying, "If the UN secretary building in New York lost 10 stories, it wouldn't make a bit of difference" and "there is no such thing as the United Nations." President Bush installed Bolton without Senate approval during August's congressional recess. Bolton immediately made waves at the

UN, proposing 800 changes to the millennium development goals, a document that outlines ambitious aid packages to the developing world.

Michael Brown, director of the Federal Emergency Management Agency (FEMA), faced scathing criticism in September for his handling of Hurricane Katrina and the devastation that followed in New Orleans when levees broke. Brown epitomized the agency's failure to grasp the scope of the crisis when he revealed on CNN that he had no idea that thousands of people had been stranded for days in putrid conditions in New Orleans's Convention Center without food or water. Brown resigned shortly after President Bush removed him from the relief effort. A lawyer, Brown worked for the International Arabian Horse Association before joining FEMA.

Jose Canseco, professional baseball player, put major league baseball in the spotlight with the February publication of *Juiced.* In the controversial tell-all memoir he unapologetically detailed his use of anabolic steroids and human growth hormones. He also alleged other players, including Mark McGwire and Sammy Sosa, abused these illegal drugs. In the best-selling book, Canseco, often called "the bad boy of baseball," claimed the league did nothing to discourage the use of steroids, and he attributed his success at the plate to the drugs. The book prompted congressional hearings on steroid use in professional baseball.

Prince Charles and Camilla Parker Bowles, British royalty, were married in a civil ceremony in April after a 25-year affair. Camilla's new title is Her Royal Highness the Duchess of Cornwall. Camilla had been regularly pilloried by the press as the "other woman," and as the source of the popular Princess Diana's failed marriage and unhappiness.

Christo and Jeanne-Claude, artists, stirred up heated debate over what constitutes art with the February debut of "The Gates," 7,500 billowing panels of saffron nylon suspended between 16-foot-tall painted steel posts that wound their way through 23 miles of footpaths in New York's Central Park. The self-funded project cost the couple a reported $20 million and was on display for only 16 days.

Philip Cooney, Bush administration official and former oil-industry lobbyist, resigned his post as chief of staff of the Council of Environmental Quality in June, two days after the *New York Times* reported that he had tampered with government documents on climate and global warming. The changes he made questioned the link between greenhouse gas emissions and the rise in temperatures. After resigning, he accepted a job with ExxonMobil.

Matthew Cooper, reporter for *TIME* magazine, narrowly avoided jail time in July, when a source, later revealed to be Karl Rove, relieved him of his promise of confidentiality. Rove's move allowed Cooper to testify before a grand jury about his reporting on the 2003 disclosure of the identity of CIA operative Valerie Plame Wilson. Judith Miller, of the *New York Times,* refused to testify and was jailed in Washington. The reporters insisted that confidentiality was essential to freedom of the press.

Curveball, Iraqi defector, was revealed to be the sole CIA source for U.S. claims that Iraq's Saddam Hussein was producing a fleet of mobile biological-weapons labs. Then–Secretary of State Colin Powell used the mobile labs to make the case for war before the UN Security Council. A presidential commission on intelligence, which released the results of its investigation in March, reported that CIA analysts who doubted Curveball's veracity were disregarded or were forced out of the division investigating the information.

Tom DeLay, House majority leader, faced increasing legal problems in early 2005 as investigations into his fund-raising and his connections to lobbyists intensified. While DeLay himself was not charged, two of his associates were indicted by a grand jury. DeLay drew fire in April when he lobbed a series of attacks—and what could be considered threats—on the judiciary, apparently out of anger over a federal court's refusal to order that Terri Schiavo's feeding tube be reinserted. "We will look at an arrogant, out of control, unaccountable judiciary that thumbed their nose at the Congress and president when given jurisdiction to hear this case anew and look at all the facts . . . The time will come for the men responsible for this to answer for their behavior, but not today," he said after the court decision. Several Democrats and a few Republicans have called on DeLay to step down as majority leader.

Bernard Ebbers, former chief executive of WorldCom, a telecommunications giant, was found guilty in March of conspiracy, securities fraud, and seven counts of filing false reports. He was sentenced to 25 years in prison in July. Ebbers's manipulation of the books to hide lagging sales amounted to a record fraud of $11 billion. WorldCom declared bankruptcy in 2002, the largest claim in U.S. history.

W. Mark Felt, former No. 2 official at the FBI, in May revealed himself to be "Deep Throat," the anonymous source who leaked information to *Washington Post* reporters Carl Bernstein and Bob Woodward about the FBI investigation into the 1972 Watergate break-in. Ironically, it was *Vanity Fair* magazine, not the *Post,* that broke the story. Only after the magazine released the story did Woodward and Bernstein confirm that Felt was their source. The disclosure ended more than three decades of speculation and conjecture over Deep Throat's true identity. Felt, who is 91 and in poor health, did not say why he leaked the information. Some people have said it was out of a sense of responsibility, while others said it was out of anger that he was not chosen to succeed J. Edgar Hoover as director of the FBI.

Carleton "Carly" Fiorina, business leader, was forced to resign as chief executive of Hewlett-Packard in February. HP's board of directors was unhappy with the company's profits and with her strategy, which failed to make the company competitive with rivals such as I.B.M. She took the helm in 1999, rising to become one of the most powerful women in business. Under her watch, the company's stock dropped by about 50%.

Steve Fossett, millionaire business executive and adventurer, completed a nonstop 23,000-mile journey around the world in March, making him the first person in the world to do so. He circumnavigated the globe in 67 hours. The plane, a GlobalFlyer, was built by Burt Rutan, who also built SpaceShipOne, the first private spaceship to leave Earth's atmosphere. Fossett had already set a world record for flying a balloon around the world and has many other flying and sailing records.

Maggie Gallagher and Armstrong Williams, syndicated columnists, were widely criticized in early 2005 for getting paid by the government to promote President Bush's agenda. Gallagher received $21,500 for writing favorable articles in 2002 and 2003 about Bush's "healthy marriage" initiative. Williams was paid $241,000 for promoting the No Child Left Behind Act on his cable TV and syndicated radio shows. Both apologized for not publicly acknowledging they were paid for their work, and the Bush administration announced it would end the practice.

Gang of 14, a bipartisan group of senators, hammered out a last-minute compromise in May, averting the enactment of the so-called "nuclear option" by Republican senators. The change in procedures would have prohibited the minority party in

Congress—in this case Democrats—from filibustering judicial nominees. In exchange, Democrats agreed to use the filibuster of judicial nominees only in "extraordinary" circumstances.

Alberto Gonzales, public official, became the country's first Hispanic attorney general in February. In a tighter vote than anticipated, the Senate approved his nomination 60–36. Gonzales, former counsel to President Bush, faced harsh questioning during his confirmation hearings from Democrats and Republicans alike about the abuse at the Abu Ghraib prison in Iraq. He has also been criticized for drafting policies that have drastically limited access to government information and allowed the Bush administration to circumscribe the Geneva Conventions.

Charles Graner, Jr., U.S. Army reservist, in January was found guilty by a military jury of abusing prisoners at the Abu Ghraib prison in Iraq. The jury sentenced him to serve ten years in a military prison. He was convicted of all charges, including assault, conspiracy, and maltreatment of detainees. He was described by the prosecution as the ringleader of the group of soldiers that physically and sexually abused and humiliated Iraqi prisoners.

Bunnatine Greenhouse, U.S. Army official who supervised contracts at the Army Corps of Engineers, was demoted in August. Long considered a stellar employee who earned high performance reviews, Greenhouse began receiving negative feedback in 2003, when she questioned why Kellogg Brown & Root, a subsidiary of Halliburton, won $7 billion in no-bid contracts and other preferential treatment for work in Iraq. Vice President Dick Cheney headed Halliburton before being elected vice president. Testifying before a congressional committee, Greenhouse said one of the contracts was "the most blatant and improper contract abuse I have witnessed during the course of my professional career."

James Guckert, journalist, attended several White House press briefings using the pseudonym Jeff Gannon. Although Guckert signed into the White House using his real name, Press Secretary Scott McClellan addressed him by the pseudonym. A writer for the conservative online Talon News, Guckert frequently asked McClellan softball questions that toed the administration's line. Guckert resigned in February, after bloggers discovered his real name and revealed that he had links to pornographic websites. Other members of the press corps had often challenged Guckert and questioned his motives.

King Gyanendra, leader of Nepal, fired the entire government and declared a state of emergency in February, saying the government had failed to make progress toward elections and to pursue negotiations with Maoist rebel groups. Many of the country's politicians were placed under house arrest, phone and Internet lines were cut, and the airports were closed. The state of emergency was lifted in April, but many of the restrictions have remained.

Ibrahim Jaafari, Iraqi politician, was named prime minister by Iraq's National Assembly in April, two months after the 275-seat Assembly was elected. In the 1970s Jaafari, a religious Shiite, took part in a movement against Saddam Hussein's government that was brutally suppressed. He went into exile in Iran and then the United Kingdom for 20 years. Jaafari served as vice president of Iraq under Iyad Allawi, the U.S.-appointed prime minister.

Michael Jackson, pop star, was acquitted by a California jury in June of ten felony charges, including molesting a child, conspiracy, and providing alcohol to minors. He was accused of molesting a child who was suffering from cancer at his Neverland Ranch in California in 2003. The verdict stunned many observers. After he was cleared, Jackson vowed he would never again share his bed—or bedroom—with a child. Jackson behaved erratically during the 2005

trial, falling ill and appearing late several times, earning the ire of and several warnings from Superior Court Judge Rodney S. Melville.

Islam Karimov, president of Uzbekistan, faced international criticism in May, after hundreds of antigovernment demonstrators in Andijan were killed in a military crackdown. The demonstration began after protesters stormed a prison and released about 2,000 prisoners to challenge what they saw as the rigged trial of 23 businessmen. The government claimed the men were Islamic terrorists; the protesters insisted they were antigovernment civic leaders.

Mikhail Khodorkovsky, founder of Russia's Yukos oil company and once the country's wealthiest man, was convicted by a Russian court in May and sentenced to nine years in prison. He was found guilty of fraud, embezzlement, tax evasion, and other charges. The conviction was widely considered retaliation for publicly challenging President Vladimir Putin and for his support of opposition figures.

Edgar Ray Killen, segregationist, was found guilty of manslaughter in June by a Mississippi jury in the 1964 murder of three young civil rights workers. The three victims had been working to register black voters in Mississippi during Freedom Summer and had gone to investigate the burning of a black church. They were arrested by the police on trumped-up charges, imprisoned for several hours, and then released after dark into the hands of the Ku Klux Klan, who beat and murdered them. It was later proven in court that a conspiracy existed between members of Neshoba County's law enforcement and the Ku Klux Klan to kill them. The jury reached its verdict on the 21st anniversary of the murders. Killen, 80, was sentenced to 60 years in jail.

L. Dennis Kozlowski, former chief executive of Tyco International, was found guilty in June by a New York jury of fraud, conspiracy, and grand larceny. Mark Swartz, the company's former chief financial officer, was also convicted. They bilked the company out of $600 million in a stock-fraud scheme and used the money for personal purposes.

Joan Humphrey Lefkow, federal judge, was the target of an assassination attempt by troubled electrician Bart Ross, who was outraged that she dismissed a malpractice suit he had filed. Lefkow was not at home when Ross entered her Chicago home in February to kill her, but her husband and elderly mother were. Ross shot and killed both. He committed suicide in March. In May, Lefkow criticized members of Congress who have spoken out against members of the judiciary, in particular ones they have labeled "activist judges." She called on the Senate Judiciary Committee to "publicly and persistently repudiate gratuitous attacks on the judiciary." She returned to the bench in July.

Ellen MacArthur, British sailor, finished a solo 27,000-mile circumnavigation in February, in 71 days, 14 hours, 18 minutes, and 33 seconds, breaking the world record for sailing around the world alone. She broke the previous record by 32 hours.

McCartney Sisters, five sisters from Northern Ireland, challenged the Irish Republican Army's code of secrecy and silence after their brother Robert was killed in a brutal bar brawl in Belfast in January. Several members of the IRA were suspected of being involved in and covering up the murder. The women's campaign to hold the IRA accountable reached an international audience and prompted many to question the legitimacy of the IRA, even in Catholic communities that had once been IRA strongholds. The IRA's subsequent offer to kill the men responsible generated further outrage. The sisters were invited to the White House for St. Patrick's Day.

Jean Charles de Menezes, 27-year-old Brazilian electrician, was shot and killed by London police who thought he was a suspect in the July 7 terrorist attacks on the city's transit system. Authorities later acknowledged that he was not involved in the bombings. In addition, a report leaked in August contradicted earlier reports that Menezes was wearing heavy clothing on a hot day and that he ran from police. The report also said he was shot while being restrained.

Judith Miller, *New York Times* reporter, was sent to jail in July after she refused to testify before a grand jury about confidential sources she interviewed while researching the illegal disclosure of the identity of CIA operative Valerie Plame Wilson. "If journalists cannot be trusted to guarantee confidentiality, then journalists cannot function and there cannot be a free press," Miller said. *TIME* reporter Matthew Cooper avoided a similar fate when he agreed to testify after receiving a waiver from his source, later revealed to be Karl Rove. Miller's incarceration followed the U.S. Supreme Court's refusal to hear the reporters' appeal of a 2004 decision that ordered them to comply. In 2003, columnist Robert Novak, citing two high-level members of the Bush administration, identified Valerie Plame as a CIA agent who specializes in weapons of mass destruction. Miller conducted interviews about the scandal but never wrote about it.

Zacarias Moussaoui, member of al-Qaeda, pleaded guilty in April to planning a terrorist attack against the United States. He was charged with conspiring in the Sept. 11 attacks, but in court he denied involvement in the tragedy and said he was involved in a separate plan to fly a plane into the White House. Moussaoui is the only person in the U.S. to be indicted on charges relating directly to the Sept. 11 attacks.

Mukhtar Mai, "Mukhtaran Bibi," Pakistani activist, made international headlines in June, when the Pakistani government banned her from traveling outside the country. After international protests, the government promised to return her passport. In 2002, a village council in Punjab Province ordered her to be gang raped as punishment for her brother's involvement with a woman from a rival tribe. She courageously went public with the crime. The government compensated Mukhtar, and she used the money to build schools in her village. In June, Pakistan's Supreme Court ordered the rearrest of 13 men who were involved in the crime. They had been acquitted by a lower court.

Ray Nagin, mayor of New Orleans, berated the Bush administration for its inadequate and slow response to Hurricane Katrina. In a radio interview, he announced that members of the federal government should "get off your asses and do something, and let's fix the biggest goddamn crisis in the history of this country." Nagin himself faced criticism for not having a finalized hurricane response plan in place for New Orleans.

John Negroponte, diplomat, was confirmed in April as the country's first national intelligence director. A career diplomat, Negroponte has held eight diplomatic posts and was Ronald Reagan's deputy assistant for national security affairs. Prior to his confirmation, Negroponte was the U.S. ambassador to Iraq. As national intelligence director, he will oversee all U.S. intelligence agencies, including the Central Intelligence Agency and the Federal Bureau of Investigation, and will have control over a budget of $40 billion.

Sandra Day O'Connor, associate justice of the U.S. Supreme Court, stunned the nation in July when she announced her retirement. O'Connor, who was the Court's first woman justice, was appointed by President Reagan in 1981 and served 24 terms. She was often a swing vote on such controversial issues as abortion, affirmative action, and the separation of church and state. O'Connor was widely considered the most powerful member of the Court, and her announcement sparked an intense partisan battle over the Court's future.

Rafael Palmeiro, Baltimore Orioles power hitter, was suspended for ten days in August after failing a drug test for steroids. During the previous off-season, Palmeiro was on the panel of players called before Congress to testify about steroid use in baseball. During testimony, he had adamantly denied ever taking steroids. The drug test he failed was administered only weeks after his congressional testimony.

Danica Patrick, race-car driver, placed fourth at May's Indianapolis 500 race, the best-ever performance by a woman. Patrick, 23, was in the lead with 10 laps to go but had to slow down to conserve fuel. She was passed by Briton Dan Wheldon and finished in fourth place.

Dennis Rader, suspected serial killer, was arrested in February in Kansas and charged with ten counts of first-degree murder. In letters to news outlets, Rader called himself BTK, for bind, torture, kill—the methods he typically used in the grisly murders, which date back to 1974. Rader's neighbors were shocked to learn that he had been arrested. By many accounts, he was active in his church and had been a scout leader and an attentive husband and father. He pleaded guilty to the murders in June and in August was sentenced to ten life terms in prison.

Dan Rather, broadcast journalist, signed off as anchor of CBS News in March, a year earlier than he originally planned. In Sept. 2004, CBS and Rather admitted that they could not definitively prove the authenticity of documents they used in a *60 Minutes* segment, which suggested President Bush received preferential treatment when he joined the National Guard and later when he served in it. A swirl of controversy followed, leading to Rather's resignation.

Condoleezza Rice, public official, was confirmed as secretary of state in January, despite Democratic criticism that she overlooked warnings of an al-Qaeda attack prior to Sept. 11 and for her role in the Iraq war. Rice, Bush's national security adviser during his first term, is the first black woman to hold the position. Rice and Bush are said to have the closest relationship since Nixon and Kissinger, and she has twice been named the world's most powerful woman by *Forbes*. She visited about 40 countries in 2005, setting the tone for U.S. diplomacy.

John Roberts, judge, was nominated by President Bush in July to replace Sandra Day O'Connor as an associate justice on the U.S. Supreme Court. By all accounts, the Harvard-educated, deeply religious lawyer, who has served on the U.S. Court of Appeals for the District of Columbia circuit since 2003, is extremely intelligent and a "regular guy" who is not seen as an ideologue. In September, President Bush nominated Roberts to succeed William Rehnquist as chief justice. Conservatives welcomed the nomination. Democrats, however, complained that Roberts was not sufficiently forthcoming in his answers to their questions during confirmation hearings.

Pat Robertson, evangelist, sparked international outrage in August when he suggested that the United States should assassinate Venezuelan president Hugo Chavez. "If he thinks we're trying to assassinate him, I think that we really ought to go ahead and do it," Robertson said on his television show, *The 700 Club.* "It's a whole lot cheaper than starting a war. And I don't think any oil shipments will stop." Venezuela has the largest oil reserves of any country excluding the Middle East. Robertson later retracted the statement.

Karl Rove, one of President Bush's closest advisers, was revealed to be the secret source used by *TIME* magazine reporter Matt Cooper for a story he wrote in 2003 about the disclosure of the identity of CIA operative Valerie Plame Wilson. "[I]t was, KR said,

Wilson's wife, who apparently works at the agency on wmd issues who authorized the trip," Cooper emailed to his bureau chief after speaking with Karl Rove. In a July 2003 op-ed piece in the *New York Times*, Wilson's husband, Joseph, a former ambassador, discredited President Bush's claim—and a justification for war in Iraq—that Saddam Hussein was pursuing a nuclear weapons program by seeking to obtain uranium from Niger. Days after Wilson's article was published, columnist Robert Novak identified Wilson's wife as a CIA agent who specializes in weapons of mass destruction. Rove reportedly also spoke to Novak about Plame Wilson.

Eric Robert Rudolph pleaded guilty in April to four bombings, including the Olympics in Atlanta in 1996, a gay club and a family-planning clinic in Atlanta in 1997, and an abortion clinic in Birmingham, Ala., in 1998. Two people died in the attacks and more than 150 were injured. He'll serve four consecutive life sentences rather than face the death penalty. He also agreed to disclose where he had hidden 250 pounds of dynamite. He was captured in May 2003 in North Carolina after spending five years in hiding.

Terri Schiavo, brain-damaged Florida woman, was at the center of a highly publicized and politically sensitive right-to-die case that started in state court and became a national issue after Congress—in a very unusual move—voted in March to send the case to a federal court. After a protracted legal battle, the feeding tube that had kept Schiavo alive for 15 years was removed. Her husband, Michael, said that Terri had indicated when she was well that she did not want to be kept alive by artificial means. Her parents, Robert and Mary Schindler, disagreed, and believed she could recover from the persistent vegetative state. President Bush signed emergency legislation allowing a federal court to decide if the tube should be reinserted, saying it conformed to his idea of a culture of life. The court refused to order that the feeding tube be reinserted. She died 13 days after the tube was removed. Schiavo's autopsy, released in June, found that her brain had deteriorated to half normal size and no treatment could have helped her.

Giuliana Sgrena, Italian journalist, was fired at by U.S. troops in March, shortly after she was released from captivity by Iraqi insurgents. Italian intelligence agent Nicola Calipari, who was traveling in a car with her, was shot and killed. The U.S. military said the driver of the car failed to respond to soldiers' repeated requests to stop. Italian government officials disputed this claim and demanded an investigation into the accident.

Cindy Sheehan, California mother whose son Casey died in Iraq in 2004, camped out a few miles away from President Bush's ranch in Crawford, Tex., while he was vacationing there in August. She demanded the president meet with her so she could explain to him why she thought U.S. troops should be withdrawn from Iraq. Extensive media coverage and poll numbers indicating waning U.S. support of the war helped to transform her vigil into an energized antiwar protest. Bush refused to meet with Sheehan, but he said in a statement that he shared her pain.

Dorothy Stang, American-born Roman Catholic nun, was shot and killed in Brazil's Amazon state of Pará in February. A naturalized Brazilian, Stang had been working with Brazil's rural poor since the 1970s, helping them farm and produce forest products and protecting them against illegal loggers who wanted to commandeer their land. The government sent 2,000 troops to Pará after the killing to calm the growing tension and banned logging in a large swath of the state.

Lawrence Summers, president of Harvard University, set off a storm of criticism in academia when he suggested at an economic conference in January that innate differences between men and women might explain why there are fewer women than men at the top levels in science and math. Summers apologized, saying the comment "did not serve our institution well." The controversy also ignited growing faculty discontent with Summers's autocratic management style. In March, the faculty of Arts and Sciences at Harvard voted that they "lacked confidence" in his leadership. In May, Summers announced that Harvard would spend $50 million over the next 10 years to recruit and promote more women scientists and minority faculty.

Kenneth Tomlinson, chairman of the Corporation for Public Broadcasting, drew criticism from Democrats in June for attempting to politicize the corporation, which annually contributes $400 million to public television and radio stations. In 2004, Tomlinson hired a conservative researcher—without informing CPB's board—to monitor the political leanings of guests and rate the discourse on the television show *Now*, which was then hosted by Bill Moyers. The corporation's inspector general is investigating Tomlinson for this move, for hiring two Republican lobbyists in 2004, and for other efforts to scrutinize content on public programs.

Antonio Villaraigosa, Los Angeles politician, was elected mayor of the city in May, defeating incumbent James Hahn, 59% to 41%. Villaraigosa, the city's first Hispanic mayor since 1872, faces the daunting task of stemming gang-related violence and improving a school system that graduates only 45% of its students. He lost the mayoral election to Hahn in 2001. He is a former city councilor and speaker of California's Assembly.

George Voinovich, politician, was the lone Republican senator to take a firm stand against John Bolton, President Bush's nominee to become U.S. ambassador to the UN. In May, Voinovich urged his colleagues to vote against Bolton's nomination. "In these dangerous times, we cannot afford to put at risk our nation's ability to successfully wage and win the war on terror with a controversial and ineffective ambassador to the United Nations," he wrote.

Jeff Weise, high school student, went on a shooting rampage in March on the Red Lake Indian Reservation in Minnesota, killing nine people before turning the gun on himself. His victims included his grandfather, his grandfather's companion, a security guard, a teacher, and five fellow students. He was known as a troubled teen interested in Nazi culture. Another student, 16-year-old Louis Jourdain, was later arrested in connection with the rampage.

Jennifer Wilbanks, reluctant bride, caused panic in Duluth, Ga., in late April when she disappeared days before her wedding. Local officials organized a massive search and questioned her fiancé, John Mason. She turned up in Albuquerque, N.M., initially telling police she had been kidnapped. After questioning, she admitted that she lied and had planned to run away, buying a bus ticket about a week in advance. She was indicted by a grand jury in May and charged with falsely reporting a crime and making a false statement to a government official.

Paul Wolfowitz, diplomat, in May became head of the World Bank, an international agency charged with overseeing development in third-world countries. Wolfowitz's many critics asserted that his failure to accurately predict the insurgency in Iraq and to prepare for postwar rebuilding undermined his credibility for assuming responsibility for the World Bank. Known for his sharp intelligence and his hawkish views, Wolfowitz had worked for every U.S. president since 1973 except President Clinton.

2005 Deaths

(through Sept. 15, 2005. Go to www.infoplease.com/2005deaths for additional entries.)

Eddie Albert, 99: comedic stage, screen, and television actor best known for his role as a city lawyer who moves to the country with his wife, played by Eva Gabor, in TV's *Green Acres.* His film credits include *Roman Holiday* and *I'll Cry Tomorrow.* May 26, 2005

Shana Alexander, 79: liberal journalist and commentator who frequently engaged in heated debates with conservative James Kilpatrick on *60 Minutes* during the 1970s. Their repartee was parodied on *Saturday Night Live.* Alexander, a former columnist for *Newsweek* and *Life* magazines, wrote several books. June 23, 2005

Victoria de los Angeles, 81: Spanish soprano who performed with the Metropolitan Opera from 1951 to 1961. Her best-known roles include Desdemona in *Otello* and Mimi in *La Bohème.* Jan. 15, 2005

Anne Bancroft, 73: Academy- and Tony Award–winning actress best known for her portrayal of Annie Sullivan, Helen Keller's teacher, in the stage and film versions of *The Miracle Worker.* She played Mrs. Robinson in the film *The Graduate.* Bancroft starred in dozens of films, including *The Turning Point* and *Agnes of God.* She was married to comedic actor and director Mel Brooks. June 6, 2005

Barbara Bel Geddes, 82: Emmy Award–winning actress who had a long career in film and on Broadway before landing the role that brought her wide fame: Miss Ellie, the Ewing matriarch on television's *Dallas.* Her film credits include *I Remember Mama* and *Vertigo.* She appeared in the original stage version of *Cat on a Hot Tin Roof.* Aug. 8, 2005

Saul Bellow, 89: novelist whose varied portrayals of Jewish American life among disillusioned modern city-dwellers won him the Nobel Prize for Literature in 1976. His novels, often set in Chicago and featuring larger-than-life characters and themes, include *Henderson the Rain King, Herzog,* and *The Adventures of Augie March.* April 5, 2005

Peter Benenson, 83: British lawyer who created human-rights organization Amnesty International in 1961 to assist "prisoners of conscience." He was moved to act after reading that two Portuguese students were sentenced to seven years in prison for drinking a toast to freedom. Amnesty International won the Nobel Peace Prize in 1977. Feb. 25, 2005

Obie Benson, 68: musician who was a founding member of the band the Four Tops. He wrote the popular antiwar song "What's Goin' On." July 1, 2005

Lazar Berman, 74: versatile Russian pianist whose repertoire ranged from Beethoven to Liszt to Rachmaninoff. Feb. 6, 2005

Hans Bethe, 98: physicist who was a leader in the development of the atom bomb for the U.S. government's Manhattan Project. During the 1980s and 1990s, Bethe championed the use of nuclear energy for peaceful purposes. He won a Nobel Prize in Physics in 1967 for his discovery of how the stars and the Sun continue to burn. He taught at Cornell University for more than 70 years. March 6, 2005

Oscar Brown, 78: singer, songwriter, and playwright whose often political work celebrated African American culture and denounced racism. He appeared in the television series *Brewster Place.* May 29, 2005

Lord James Callaghan, 92: British politician who served as prime minister from 1976 to 1979. His administration was plagued by a series of trade union strikes in the winter of 1978–1979, called the "Winter of Discontent." March 26, 2005

Johnny Carson, 79: legendary comedian who hosted NBC's *The Tonight Show* from 1962 to 1992, when he handed the microphone over to Jay Leno. Carson's quick wit, charm, monologues, and interviews made the show the highest-rated late-night program. He used his monologues to skewer the missteps of celebrities, politicians, and businesspeople. Carson began his career as a magician and went on to write comedy sketches for radio and to host daytime television quiz shows before taking over for Jack Paar in 1962. Jan. 23, 2005

Shirley Chisholm, 80: bold politician who was the first black woman elected to the U.S. House of Representatives and the first woman to run for the Democratic presidential nomination. In her seven terms in the House, Chisholm was a critic of the Vietnam War and an advocate for the urban poor. Jan. 1, 2005

Kenneth Clark, 90: educational psychologist and civil rights leader whose report on the detrimental effects of segregation and discrimination on children was cited by the U.S. Supreme Court in the 1954 ruling *Brown v. Board of Education,* which stated that "separate but equal" schools were unconstitutional. May 1, 2005

Johnnie Cochran, Jr., 67: media-savvy trial lawyer best known for defending O. J. Simpson in his 1995 murder trial. March 29, 2005

Larry Collins, 75: writer who, with coauthor Dominique Lapierre, meticulously chronicled Hitler's plan to burn Paris if the Allies captured it in the 1965 book *Is Paris Burning?* The two men also collaborated on *O Jerusalem!* June 20, 2005

Frank Conroy, 69: writer whose 1967 memoir *Stop-Time* about his troubled, lonely adolescence brought him celebrity and acclaim. He headed the prestigious Writers' Workshop at the University of Iowa for 18 years. April 6, 2005

Robin Cook, 59: British politician who served as foreign secretary in the Blair administration until he resigned in 2003 to protest Britain's participation in the war in Iraq. Aug. 6, 2005

Robert Creeley, 78: influential poet, essayist, short-story writer who was a leading member of the Black Mountain school of poetry. Known for his spare, compressed style, Creeley typically wrote emotional, intimate poems. In 1999, he won poetry's highest honor, the Bollingen Prize. March 30, 2005

Lloyd Cutler, 87: influential attorney and mediator who served as White House counsel to presidents Carter and Clinton. He also was a member of President Bush's commission that investigated pre–Sept. 11 intelligence lapses. His firm's clients included I.B.M., American Express, and major television networks, airlines, and pro sports teams. May 8, 2005

H. David Dalquist, 86: entrepreneur who in 1950 invented the Bundt pan. Jan. 2, 2005

Ossie Davis, 87: actor, playwright, director, and civil rights leader who appeared in several Spike Lee films, including *Do the Right Thing* and *Jungle Fever.* He wrote the Broadway play *Purlie Victorious.* He and his wife, Ruby Dee, frequently appeared in films and television movies together, and they worked for racial equality on and off the screen. Davis eulogized Malcolm X and Martin Luther King, Jr. Feb. 4, 2005

Sandra Dee, 62: spunky actress who played innocent tomboys in several teeny-bopper films in the late 1950s, including *Gidget* and *A Summer Place*. She was married to singer Bobby Darin from 1960 to 1967. Feb. 20, 2005

John DeLorean, 80: auto executive who left a high-level position at General Motors to start his own company in Northern Ireland. His flashy, stainless steel DeLorean sports car was featured in the *Back to the Future* movies. He was arrested for allegedly selling cocaine to support his near-bankrupt company. He was acquitted. March 19, 2005

Bob Denver, 70: actor who played Gilligan, the first mate of the S.S. *Minnow* on television's cult hit *Gilligan's Island*. He also played beatnik Maynard Krebs on *The Many Lives of Doby Gillis*. Sept. 2, 2005

Richard Doll, 92: British epidemiologist who was among the first scientists to link smoking with such diseases as lung cancer and emphysema. His work also showed that radiation and asbestos both cause cancer. July 24, 2005

James Doohan, 85: Canadian-born actor who played Scotty, the chief engineer of the USS *Enterprise* on *Star Trek*. July 20, 2005

Spencer Dryden, 66: musician who was a drummer for the rock band Jefferson Airplane. Jan. 10, 2005

Andrea Dworkin, 58: feminist writer whose often polemical works condemned pornography and violence against women. Her critics—some of them left-wing radicals like herself—accused her of condoning censorship in the interest of subverting pornography. Her books include *Pornography: Men Possessing Women* and *Heartbreak: The Political Memoir of a Feminist Militant*. April 9, 2005

Will Eisner, 87: pioneering comic-book artist who created the character Spirit, the superhero who lacked supernatural powers. Jan. 3, 2005

Dana Elcar, 77: actor who appeared in the television shows *MacGyver* and *Baa, Baa, Black Sheep*. June 6, 2004

Fahd ibn Abdul Aziz, 84: pro-Western king of Saudi Arabia whose reign was marked by the modernization of the staunchly conservative Islamic country. He courted the U.S., broadened women's rights, and expanded the economy. These acts, however, were accompanied by his support for Wahhabism, the country's influential religious establishment that has supported anti-Americanism and Islamic militancy. After a series of strokes in 1995, King Fahd passed authority to Crown Prince Abdullah, who assumed the throne upon Fahd's death. Aug. 1, 2005

Ibrahim Ferrer, 78: Cuban singer who gained fame late in his career with the 1997 release of the Grammy Award–winning album *Buena Vista Social Club*. Wim Wenders directed a film of the same name about the group. Aug. 6, 2005

John Fielder, 80: actor best known for providing the voice to Piglet in the Winnie-the-Pooh movies. He also appeared in Broadway's *A Raisin in the Sun* and the film *Twelve Angry Men*. June 25, 2005

Geraldine Fitzgerald, 91: outspoken Dublin-born actress whose frequent clashes with studio bosses limited her roles, which included *Dark Victory* and *Wuthering Heights*. She earned wide praise for her role in 1971's stage production of *Long Day's Journey into Night*. July 17, 2005

Dennis Flanagan, 85: editor who presided over *Scientific American* for 37 years. On his watch, the magazine's circulation increased from 40,000 to more than 600,000. Jan. 14, 2005

Arthur Fletcher, 80: civil rights activist known as the "father of affirmative action" who was an adviser to presidents Nixon, Ford, and Reagan and who led the U.S. Commission on Civil Rights during the George H. W. Bush administration. July 12, 2005

Shelby Foote, 88: historian whose reclusive lifestyle gave way to national fame when he provided elo-

quent commentary to Ken Burns's 1990 *Civil War* documentary on PBS. The author of six novels, Foote also wrote a three-volume history of the war. June 27, 2005

Tillie Fowler, 62: Republican politician who served four terms in Congress. Known as the "steel magnolia" for her sharp intelligence and grace, Fowler, once the highest-ranking woman in Congress, was a member of the House Armed Services Committee and the vice chairman of the House Republican Conference. March 2, 2005

Peter Foy, 79: innovator who used harnesses, wires, and pulleys to send theater actors aloft. His Broadway credits include *Peter Pan, Angels in America,* and *The Lion King*. Feb. 17, 2005

Christopher Fry, 97: British writer who was among the few 20th-century dramatists to write verse drama. His credits include *The Lady's Not for Burning* and *Venus Observed*. He also rewrote the script to *Ben-Hur*. June 30, 2005

Carlo Maria Giulini, 91: sophisticated Italian composer best known for his interpretations of works by Mozart and Verdi. June 14, 2005

Gnassingbé Eyadéma, 69: president of Togo who came to power in a coup in 1967. The longest-reigning leader in Africa, he was considered a repressive and dictatorial leader, despite some democratic reforms in the country in recent years. The day after his death, Parliament voted to change the constitution so that Gnassingbé's son Faure could assume the presidency. Feb. 5, 2005

Frank Gorshin, 72: versatile actor and impressionist who played the wisecracking, green-clad Riddler on television's *Batman*. He recently won praise for his impersonation of George Burns in Broadway's *Say Goodnight, Gracie*. May 17, 2005

L. Patrick Gray III, 88: acting director of the FBI during Watergate who testified during his 1973 Senate confirmation hearings that he had given the White House FBI files about its investigation into the break-in. Gray resigned in 1973, after admitting to burning forged papers from E. Howard Hunt's safe that were used to discredit members of the Kennedy family. July 6, 2005

Jimmy Griffin, 61: musician who was a founding member of the soft-rock band Bread. Jan. 11, 2005

Henry Grunwald, 82: Austrian-born journalist and diplomat who presided over *TIME* magazine as its managing editor from 1968 to 1979. He then became the editor in chief of TIME Inc. Under his tenure, the right-leaning magazine moved toward the center. He served as the U.S. ambassador to Austria under President Reagan. Feb. 26, 2005

Rafik Hariri, 60: independent-minded Lebanese politician and billionaire businessman who was responsible for Lebanon's economic rebirth in the last decade. He was assassinated by a car bomb, and many suspected Syrian involvement. Hariri, who frequently criticized Syria's continued domination of the country, served as prime minister for two terms and stepped down in Oct. 2004. Feb. 14, 2005

June Haver, 79: actress who appeared in several 1940s musicals, including *The Dolly Sisters* and *Look for the Silver Lining*. July 4, 2005

Edward Heath, 89: leader of Britain's Conservative Party who, as prime minister, guided the country's 1973 entry into Europe's Economic Community, now called the European Union. He confronted a sluggish economy further eroded by the oil crisis and intensifying violence in Northern Ireland. He lost his post as party leader in 1975 to Margaret Thatcher. July 17, 2005

Howard Heflin, 83: three-term Democratic senator from Alabama who supported civil rights legislation and voted against the nominations of Clarence Thomas and Robert Bork to the U.S. Supreme Court. He also served as the chief justice of Alabama's Supreme Court. March 29, 2005

Robert Heilbroner, 85: economist whose work simplified economic theory. Jan. 5, 2005

Al Held, 76: abstract artist known for his enormous works. He taught at Yale from 1960 to 1980. He started creating colorful pieces in the 1950s and shifted to black and white in the 1960s. He returned to color later in his career. July 26, 2005

George Herman, 85: journalist who worked for CBS for 43 years as a correspondent and the moderator of *Face the Nation*. Feb. 8, 2005

Hildegarde, 99: cabaret singer whose career spanned seven decades. She was known for performing in couture gowns, sparkling jewels, and white gloves. At the peak of her career, in the 1930s and '40s, she earned about $17,000 a week. July 29, 2005

Maurice Hilleman, 85: microbiologist who developed about 40 human and animal vaccines for diseases including mumps, measles, chickenpox, and meningitis, thus saving millions of lives. Hilleman created 8 of the 14 vaccines widely given to children. April 11, 2005

Bob Hunter, 63: Canadian journalist who in 1971 founded Greenpeace, an international environmental organization. May 2, 2005

Evan Hunter, 78: writer who created the police procedural genre. Using the pseudonym Ed McBain, he wrote the gritty 87th Precinct series of novels, beginning with 1956's *Cop Hater*, which paved the way for such TV series as *NYPD Blue*. July 6, 2005

Ruth Hussey, 93: actress who was nominated for an Academy Award for her role as a sassy reporter in *The Philadelphia Story*. Her other credits include *Northwest Passage*. April 19, 2005

Archbishop Iakovos, 93: primate of the Greek Orthodox Church in North and South America for 37 years who was the first Orthodox archbishop in more than 350 years to meet with a Roman Catholic pope. In 1965, Iakovos marched alongside Rev. Martin Luther King, Jr., in Selma, Ala. April 10, 2005

Elizabeth Janeway, 91: writer and critic who was an influential force in the women's movement. Her books about feminist issues include *Man's World, Woman's Place: A Study of Social Mythology*. She also wrote the best-selling novel *The Walsh Girls*. Jan. 15, 2005

Peter Jennings, 67: Canadian-born broadcast journalist who anchored ABC's *World News Tonight* from 1983 to April 2005, when he announced that he was battling lung cancer. By age 9, Jennings had his own radio show. In 1965, at age 26, he joined *ABC Evening News*, becoming America's youngest national network anchor. A high-school dropout, Jennings, known for his calm, measured delivery, covered every recent major war, from Vietnam to the war in Iraq, and reported from every state. Aug. 7, 2005

John Paul II (Karol Józef Wojtyła), 84: charismatic pope who was credited with hastening the fall of communism in Poland and in other Eastern bloc countries. He opposed war and the death penalty and spoke out against the war in Iraq. He was also a great champion of the poor and the underprivileged. On social issues, such as birth control, women's roles in the church, and homosexuality, he was staunchly conservative. John Paul II was the first Polish pope, and the first non-Italian pope since the Dutch pope Adrian VI, who served from 1522–1523. The third longest-reigning pope, having served the Catholic Church for 26 years, John Paul II spoke eight languages and traveled more than any pope in history. He visited 129 countries outside Italy. He canonized 482 saints and beatified 1,338 people, believed to be more than all his predecessors combined. John Paul II suffered from Parkinson's disease. April 2, 2005

John Johnson, 85: entrepreneur who built a publishing empire that now includes *Ebony* and *Jet* magazines and made him one of America's wealthiest people. The grandson of slaves, Johnson started his business in 1942 with a $500 loan. *Ebony* now has a circulation of 1.6 million. Aug. 8, 2005

Johnnie Johnson, 80: blues and rock pianist who played with Chuck Berry for more than 20 years. They collaborated on such hits as "Roll Over Beethoven," "Maybellene," and "Brown-Eyed Handsome Man." Berry wrote the song "Johnny B. Goode" in honor of Johnson. April 13, 2005

Philip Johnson, 98: well-known architect who introduced modern European glass-and-steel architecture to the United States. Johnson's designs, which evolved in style over time, include his glass-walled house in New Canaan, Conn., the Seagram Building and AT&T's headquarters in New York City, and Pennzoil Place in Houston, Tex. Jan. 26, 2005

Georgeanna Jones, 92: endocrinologist who, with her husband, Howard Jones, established the country's first in vitro fertilization program and created the first "test-tube baby," born in Dec. 1981. March 26, 2005

Charles Keeling, 77: pioneering scientist who in the 1950s became the first person to measure the amount of carbon dioxide in the atmosphere. His Keeling Curve illustrated that levels of the gas increased each year, setting the stage for concern over global warming. June 20, 2005

George Kennan, 101: influential diplomat and historian who, while working at the U.S. embassy in Moscow in 1946, devised the U.S. policy of containment to deal with the Soviet Union during the cold war. He believed that instead of declaring all-out war against communist countries and attempting to defeat them, the U.S. should keep the countries in their current state and prevent them from growing more powerful. Kennan also presciently stated that a drastic military solution was not necessary to defeat communism and would lead to unnecessary death and destruction. He left the foreign service in 1953 to head Princeton's Institute for Advanced Study. March 17, 2005

Rosemary Kennedy, 86: eldest sister of President John Kennedy who was born mildly retarded. In 1941, her father, Joseph Kennedy, had her lobotomized. The operation left Rosemary in an infantlike state, and she remained hospitalized for the remainder of her life. Jan. 7, 2005

Jack Kilby, 81: Nobel Prize–winning electrical engineer who designed and developed the integrated circuit, commonly called the microchip, which miniaturized many consumer electronic products. His invention helped to usher in the electronic age. June 20, 2005

Fred Korematsu, 86: welder who was arrested in 1942 when he refused to go to an internment camp for Japanese Americans. The U.S. Supreme Court upheld his conviction in 1944. In 1983 a federal court in San Francisco overturned the conviction, finding that the government's case had been based on false and racially biased information. In 1988 Congress passed legislation apologizing for the internments and awarded each survivor $20,000. Korematsu was awarded the Presidential Medal of Freedom in 1998. March 30, 2005

Frances Langford, 92: actress and singer who frequently performed with Bob Hope on his USO tours to entertain troops stationed overseas during World War II. July 11, 2005

Ernest Lehman, 89: esteemed screenwriter who penned the classic films *North by Northwest* and *Sweet Smell of Success*. He adapted the plays *Who's Afraid of Virginia Woolf?* and *The Sound of Music* for the big screen. July 2, 2005

Susan Gordon Lydon, 61: feminist and writer who was a founding editor of *Rolling Stone* magazine. Her essay, "The Politics of Orgasm," which appeared in *Ramparts* magazine, remains a must-read for women's studies students. July 15, 2005

Peter Malkin, 77: former Israeli intelligence agent who captured Adolf Eichmann, a leading architect of the Holocaust, in Argentina in 1960. March 1, 2005

Achille Maramotti, 78: Italian entrepreneur who founded the fashion house Max Mara. Jan. 12, 2005

Robert Matsui, 63: politician who served as a U.S. representative from California from 1978 until his death. During World War II, Matsui spent more than three years in internment camps for Japanese Americans. He was influential in the 1988 passage of an act that compensated victims. Jan. 1, 2005

Virginia Mayo, 84: film actress whose beauty prompted the sultan of Morocco to write that she was "tangible proof of the existence of God." She played the unfaithful wife of World War II veteran Dana Andrews in *The Best Years of Our Lives*. Jan. 17, 2005

Ernst Mayr, 100: top evolutionary biologist who developed the synthetic theory of evolution, which combined Darwin's theory of evolution with genetics. The theory, now widely accepted as true, states that when members of a species are separated—usually by geography—they slowly change genetically and can no longer interbreed. Feb. 3, 2005

Ismail Merchant, 68: Indian-born filmmaker who, with partner James Ivory, produced several visually stunning literary films, including *A Room with a View*—which won three Oscars—*Howards End*, and *Jefferson in Paris*. Merchant and Ivory teamed up in 1961 and frequently collaborated with screenwriter Ruth Prawer Jhabvala. May 25, 2005

Dale Messick, 98: cartoonist whose comic strip, *Brenda Starr, Reporter,* debuted in 1940 and appeared in 250 newspapers at its peak. Messick was perhaps the first—and most successful—woman in the profession. April 5, 2005

George Mikan, 80: professional basketball player who at 6'10" was the game's first "big man." He was a three-time All America player for DePaul and led the Minneapolis Lakers to five titles in six years. He was also the ABA's first commissioner. June 1, 2005

Arthur Miller, 89: one of the most respected and talented American playwrights. His work often focused on morality and the pressures faced by families striving to achieve the American dream. Miller's signature work, *Death of a Salesman*, won the Pulitzer Prize, the New York Drama Critics' Circle Award, and the Tony Award. His other important works include *The Crucible*, *A View from the Bridge*, and *All My Sons*. Feb. 10, 2005

Sir John Mills, 97: British film, television, and stage actor who appeared in more than 100 films over his 70-year career. He won an Oscar for his portrayal of a mentally impaired mute in *Ryan's Daughter*. His other films include *Great Expectations* and *In Which We Serve*. He also appeared in four films with his daughter, Hayley Mills. April 23, 2005

Robert Moog, 71: electronic music pioneer who in 1965 created the Moog synthesizer. Many experimental and rock bands, such as Tangerine Dream, used the synthesizer in the 1960s and '70s. Bands such as the Beastie Boys and Wilco have recently rediscovered the instrument. Aug. 21, 2005

Philip Morrison, 89: physicist who, as a member of the Manhattan Project, helped to assemble the first atom bomb—which was tested in July 1945, near Alamogordo, New Mexico—and the uranium bomb that was dropped on Hiroshima. After touring the devastated Hiroshima, Morrison spoke out against nuclear proliferation. He also hosted the PBS series *The Ring of Truth*. April 22, 2005

Marjorie "Mo" Mowlam, 55: charismatic British politician who, as secretary of state for Northern Ireland, was instrumental in negotiating 1998's landmark Good Friday Agreement. Mowlam was elected to the British Parliament in 1987. She was diagnosed with a brain tumor in 1997 and continued on in politics until she retired in 2001. Aug. 19, 2005

Hamilton Naki, 78: black South African self-taught surgeon who in 1967 assisted Dr. Christiaan Barnard in the first human heart transplant. Naki's role in the groundbreaking procedure was kept secret for nearly 30 years because of restrictions under apartheid. May 29, 2005

Gaylord Nelson, 89: pioneering environmentalist and three-term Democratic senator from Wisconsin who in 1970 created Earth Day, which is still celebrated each year on April 22. July 3, 2005

Jean O'Leary, 57: former nun and pioneer in the gay-rights movement who in 1977 organized the first meeting of gay leaders at the White House. She cofounded National Coming Out Day. June 4, 2005

John Ostrom, 77: influential paleontologist whose research strongly supported the theory that modern birds are related to dinosaurs. July 16, 2005

Frank Perdue, 84: chicken farmer whose folksy television commercials for his poultry company made him a household name—and face. When he began appearing in Perdue ads in 1970, annual sales were $56 million; by 1991 the figure reached $1.2 billion. March 31, 2005

Brock Peters, 78: actor and singer known for his explosive performances in movies and on the stage. He played Tom Robinson, the black man accused of rape in *To Kill a Mockingbird*. His other film credits include *Carmen Jones*. He appeared in the Broadway musical *Lost in the Stars*. Aug. 23, 2005

J. J. Pickle, 91: Democratic politician from Texas who, during his 15 terms in the U.S. House of Representatives, championed Social Security. A former aide to Lyndon Johnson, Pickle was elected to Johnson's seat in Congress in 1963. June 18, 2005

Rainier III, 81: Prince of Monaco who was Europe's longest-serving monarch, ruling for 56 years. Under Rainier, Monaco became a playground for the rich and famous, with its breathtaking beaches on the French Riviera and its lavish hotels and casinos. In 1956, he married American actress Grace Kelly, who died in a tragic car accident in 1982. April 6, 2005

John Raitt, 88: baritone who appeared in several Broadway hits, including *Carousel* and *The Pajama Game*. Later in his career he collaborated with his daughter, singer Bonnie Raitt. Feb. 20, 2005

William Rehnquist, 80: chief justice of the U.S. Supreme Court who was appointed to the Court in 1971 by President Nixon. He became chief justice in 1986. One of the more conservative members of the Court, Rehnquist successfully reversed the liberal trend of the Warren Court. He consistently voted to strengthen and expand states' rights. Rehnquist presided over *Gore v. Bush*, the controversial 5–4 decision that established the outcome of the 2000 presidential election. He also supervised the 1999 impeachment trial of President Clinton. Rehnquist was diagnosed with thyroid cancer in 2004. Sept. 3, 2005

Peter Rodino, 95: former Democratic congressman from New Jersey who as chairman of the House Judiciary Committee led the impeachment hearings of President Nixon. May 7, 2005

Joseph Rotblat, 96: Polish-born physicist who began working on the Manhattan Project in 1944. He left the program after nine months as his misgivings about the atomic bomb intensified. He was a founding member of the Pugwash Conferences on Science and World Affairs—a group of scientists, intellectuals, and political leaders who championed arms control and disarmament. Rotblat and the Pugwash Conferences won the Nobel Peace Prize in 1995. Aug. 31, 2005

Herb Sargent, 81: Emmy Award–winning comedy writer who worked on *Saturday Night Live* for more than 20 years, penning the news satire "Weekend Update." May 6, 2005

Maria Schell, 79: Austrian actress who appeared in dozens of European films before arriving in Hollywood in the 1950s. Her films include *The Brothers Karamazov* and *The Hanging Tree.* April 26, 2005

Max Schmeling, 99: German heavyweight-boxing champion who in 1936 gave Joe Louis his first-ever defeat. The 1938 rematch was filled with charged political overtones, and Louis's first-round knockout win was considered a symbolic victory against Nazi Germany. Feb. 2, 2005

Fritz Scholder, 67: expressionist painter and sculptor of San Luiseno descent who was a leader of what has been called the New Indian Art movement. Feb. 10, 2005

Bernard Schriever, 94: German-born general who led the development of the U.S. Air Force's space program, including the creation of intercontinental ballistic missiles. June 20, 2005

Jay Schulberg, 65: advertising executive responsible for such memorable ads as American Express's "Don't leave home without it" and the milk industry's campaign that featured celebrities sporting thick, white milk mustaches. Jan. 12, 2005

Bobby Short, 80: singer and pianist who performed popular standards at Manhattan's Carlyle Hotel for nearly 40 years. March 21, 2005

Claude Simon, 91: Nobel Prize–winning French novelist who was a leader of the *nouveau roman* (new novel) movement. His challenging books, which include *La Route de Flandres* (The Flanders Road), shunned convention, lacking plot and punctuation. July 6, 2005

Jimmy Smith, 76: jazz organist whose scintillating music, called "soul jazz," combined jazz, R&B, and bebop. He played on a Hammond B-3 electronic organ, an instrument not previously associated with jazz. In Jan. 2005, the National Endowment for the Arts designated Mr. Smith a Jazz Master, the nation's highest honor for jazz. Feb. 8, 2005

Leslie Smith, 87: British toymaker who cofounded Lesney Products, the manufacturer of Matchbox cars. The first car debuted in 1952, and by 1962, Lesney was producing more than 50 million cars a year. May 26, 2005

James Stockdale, 81: U.S. Navy vice admiral who won the Medal of Honor in 1976. He was captured by the North Vietnamese in 1965 and imprisoned for more than seven years, enduring repeated torture and four years of solitary confinement. He was H. Ross Perot's vice presidential running mate in 1992. July 5, 2005

Lorna Thayer, 85: actress whose role as a bitter waitress who refuses to serve Jack Nicholson toast with his omelet in the film *Five Easy Pieces* remains one of film's gems. June 4, 2005

Gerry Thomas, 83: inventor who introduced the TV dinner in 1954. More than 10 million of the meals were sold that year. July 18, 2005

Hunter S. Thompson, 67: cynical and subjective writer known for his drug-fueled yet wickedly perceptive coverage of the American political scene. In *Fear and Loathing: On the Campaign Trail '72,* he recounted his experiences covering the 1972 presidential race between George McGovern and Richard Nixon. Thompson was the most famous practitioner of the freewheeling, flamboyant style called "gonzo journalism." He committed suicide. Feb. 20, 2005

Luther Vandross, 54: Grammy Award–winning R&B singer who started his career singing backup vocals for stars such as David Bowie, Ringo Starr, and Barbra Streisand. In his trademark romantic, soulful style, he recorded 15 solo albums and topped the R&B charts with hits such as "Give Me the Reason" and "Here and Now." July 1, 2005

Simon Waronker, 90: record producer whose independent label, Liberty Records, released hits by Eddie Cochran, Julie London, and Alvin and the Chipmunks. June 7, 2005

Ruth Warrick, 88: actress who made her film debut in *Citizen Kane* but gained fame for her role as Phoebe Tyler Wallingford on the soap opera *All My Children.* Jan. 15, 2005

Dick Weber, 75: professional bowler who was one of the first—and best-known—stars of the sport. A three-time PBA Bowler of the Year, Weber won 30 Professional Bowlers Association titles in four decades. Feb. 14, 2005

Ezer Weizman, 80: Israeli politician who served as president from 1993 to 2000. He was a founder of the Israeli air force and commanded it from 1958 to 1966. In 1967, he led Israel's easy victory in the Arab-Israeli War. As a politician, Weizman went from hawk to dove, advocating for peace with the Palestinians and Egypt. His dialogue with Egyptian president Anwar Sadat helped secure the 1979 peace agreement between Israel and Egypt. April 24, 2005

William Westmoreland, 91: U.S. Army general who fought in North Africa and Europe during World War II, as well as in Korea. He commanded U.S. forces in Vietnam from 1964 to 1968, overseeing the buildup of troops from 16,000 to about 500,000. President Johnson replaced Westmoreland after the 1968 Tet offensive sparked wide protests against the war. July 18, 2005

Simon Wiesenthal, 96: Holocaust survivor who dedicated his life to tracking down fugitive Nazi war criminals. Calling himself the "bad conscience of the Nazis," Wiesenthal claimed he exposed more than 1,000 war criminals. He wrote a two-volume memoir about his work, *The Murderers Among Us* and *Justice, Not Vengeance.* His tenaciousness resulted in death threats against him and his family. Sept. 20, 2005

Paul Winchell, 82: ventriloquist and inventor who created the puppet Jerry Mahoney. He provided the voice for Tigger in the Winnie-the-Pooh movies. June 24, 2005

Herbert Warren Wind, 88: writer who eloquently covered golf for *Sports Illustrated* and *The New Yorker.* He also wrote more than a dozen books about the game. May 30, 2005

Robert Wise, 91: filmmaker who won Academy Awards for directing and producing *West Side Story* and *The Sound of Music.* He also directed *The Haunting* and *The Body Snatcher.* Sept. 14, 2005

Rose Mary Woods, 87: loyal secretary to President Nixon who took blame for a segment of the erasure of 18½ minutes of a taped conversation between the president and his chief of staff, H. R. Haldeman, days after the Watergate break-in. Jan. 22, 2005

Teresa Wright, 86: actress who was nominated for an Oscar in her first three films. She won for her role as Greer Garson's daughter-in-law in *Mrs. Miniver.* Her other credits include *The Pride of the Yankees* and *The Best Years of Our Lives.* March 6, 2005

Zhang Chunqiao, 88: radical Maoist who was the last surviving member of the Gang of Four, the group authorized by the Chinese Communist government to institute and uphold extreme measures of the Cultural Revolution. The group, which included Mao's wife Jiang Qing, was tried in 1980 and convicted of persecuting about 700,000 people. April 21, 2005

Zurab Zhvania, 41: prime minister of Georgia who was a reformist and an important ally to President Mikhail Saakashvili. He was accidentally killed by carbon monoxide poisoning. Feb. 3, 2005

PEOPLE IN THE
NEWS AND
DEATHS

SPORTS

WORLD STATISTICS
AND COUNTRIES

HEADLINE
HISTORY

CONSUMER
RESOURCES

BUSINESS
AND ECONOMY

ENVIRONMENT,
WEATHER
AND CLIMATE

COMPUTERS,
SCIENCE, AND
INVENTIONS

TIME HAPPINESS
SECTION

HEALTH

THE YEAR
IN PICTURES,
FLAGS, AND MAPS

infoplease®
All the knowledge you need.

Visit us online at
www.infoplease.com

If you value the information contained in this book, you'll
appreciate Infoplease.com. One of the leading reference
and research resources on the Web, infoplease.com
contains:

- Regular updates to the **TIME Almanac with
  Information Please**

- The **Columbia Encyclopedia,** a **dictionary,**
  and a **thesaurus**

- **An atlas** with maps and detailed profiles of every
  country and U.S. state

- Daily features such as **This Day in History,
  Biography of the Day, Today's Birthday,**
  and **Word Quiz**

- Timelines, quizzes, polls, and games

- Interactive features such as a **"convert anything"**
  tool and a **periodic table**

- A **Homework Center** for students

- A powerful **search tool** that provides relevant
  results instantly

See first page of book for additional tabs.